THE WORLD FACTBOOK

2005
(CIA's 2004 Edition)

Prepared by the Central Intelligence Agency

Potomac Books, Inc.
Washington, D.C.

Potomac Books's 2005 Edition (CIA's 2004 Edition)

In general, information available as of 1 January 2004 was used in the preparation of this edition.

The World Factbook is prepared by the Central Intelligence Agency for the use of US Government officials, and the style, format, coverage, and content are designed to meet their specific requirements. Information is provided by Antarctic Information Program (National Science Foundation), Bureau of the Census (Department of Commerce), Bureau of Labor Statistics (Department of Labor), Central Intelligence Agency, Council of Managers of National Antarctic Programs, Defense Intelligence Agency (Department of Defense), Department of State, Fish and Wildlife Service (Department of the Interior), Maritime Administration (Department of Transportation), National Geospatial-Intelligence Agency (Department of Defense), Naval Facilities Engineering Command (Department of Defense), Office of Insular Affairs (Department of the Interior), Office of Naval Intelligence (Department of Defense), US Board on Geographic Names (Department of the Interior), US Transportation Command (Department of Defense), and other public and private sources.

Potomac Books publishes a commercial version of *The World Factbook* in order to extend the limited audience reached by the CIA's publication. This annual is a valuable primary source of information, and Potomac Books seeks to make it more readily available to bookstores and libraries so that the taxpayers who fund the US government can directly benefit from this excellent effort. Potomac Books makes no claim to copyright to this publication. Potomac Books's edition differs in two minor aspects from the CIA publication. This current Potomac Books edition is identified by the year 2005, following the pattern Potomac Books uses in other annual publications. The CIA completes its volume late each year, and Potomac Books republishes it the following year. Also, as a commercial publisher, Potomac Books does not include the simple but expensive four-color maps contained in the CIA publication. The cost to the consumer would be prohibitive, and these maps are not unique and are readily available elsewhere.

ISBN 1-57488-942-7 (alk. paper)

Printed in the United States of America on acid-free paper that meets the American National Standards Institute Z39-48 Standard.

Potomac Books, Inc.
22841 Quicksilver Drive
Dulles, Virginia 20166

First Edition

10 9 8 7 6 5 4 3 2 1

Contents

Notes and Definitions

In addition to the updated information, *The World Factbook 2004* features seven new entries. In the **Economy** category, entries have been added for **Natural gas - production**, **Natural gas - consumption**, **Natural gas - exports**, and **Natural gas - imports**. In the **Communications** category, an **Internet hosts** entry replaces Internet Service Providers (ISPs). Lastly, in the **Transportation** category under **Merchant marine**, subfields have been added for **foreign-owned** vessels and those **registered in other countries**. Revision of some individual country maps, first introduced in the 2001 edition, is continued in this edition. The revised maps include elevation extremes and a partial geographic grid. Several regional maps have also been updated to reflect boundary changes and place name spelling changes.

Abbreviations: This information is included in **Appendix A: Abbreviations**, which includes all abbreviations and acronyms used in the *Factbook,* with their expansions.

Acronyms: An acronym is an abbreviation coined from the initial letter of each successive word in a term or phrase. In general, an acronym made up solely from the first letter of the major words in the expanded form is rendered in all capital letters (NATO from North Atlantic Treaty Organization; an exception would be ASEAN for Association of Southeast Asian Nations). In general, an acronym made up of more than the first letter of the major words in the expanded form is rendered with only an initial capital letter (Comsat from Communications Satellite Corporation; an exception would be NAM from Nonaligned Movement). Hybrid forms are sometimes used to distinguish between initially identical terms (WTO: WTrO for World Trade Organization and WToO for World Tourism Organization.)

Administrative divisions: This entry generally gives the numbers, designatory terms, and first-order administrative divisions as approved by the US Board on Geographic Names (BGN). Changes that have been reported but not yet acted on by BGN are noted.

Age structure: This entry provides the distribution of the population according to age. Information is included by sex and age group (*0-14 years*, *15-64 years*, *65 years and over*). The age structure of a population affects a nation's key socioeconomic issues. Countries with young populations (high percentage under age 15) need to invest more in schools, while countries with older populations (high percentage ages 65 and over) need to invest more in the health sector. The age structure can also be used to help predict potential political issues. For example, the rapid growth of a young adult population unable to find employment can lead to unrest.

Agriculture - products: This entry is an ordered listing of major crops and products starting with the most important.

Airports: This entry gives the total number of airports. The runway(s) may be paved (concrete or asphalt surfaces) or unpaved (grass, dirt, sand, or gravel surfaces), but must be usable. Not all airports have facilities for refueling, maintenance, or air traffic control.

Airports - with paved runways: This entry gives the total number of airports with paved runways (concrete or asphalt surfaces) by length. For airports with more than one runway, only the longest runway is included according to the following five groups - (1) *over 3,047 m*, (2) *2,438 to 3,047 m*, (3) *1,524 to 2,437 m*, (4) *914 to 1,523 m*, and (5) *under 914 m*. Only airports with usable runways are included in this listing. Not all airports have facilities for refueling, maintenance, or air traffic control.

Notes and Definitions *(continued)*

Airports - with unpaved runways: This entry gives the total number of airports with unpaved runways (grass, dirt, sand, or gravel surfaces) by length. For airports with more than one runway, only the longest runway is included according to the following five groups - (1) *over 3,047 m*, (2) *2,438 to 3,047 m*, (3) *1,524 to 2,437 m*, (4) *914 to 1,523 m*, and (5) *under 914 m*. Only airports with usable runways are included in this listing. Not all airports have facilities for refueling, maintenance, or air traffic control

Appendixes: This section includes *Factbook*-related material by topic.

Area: This entry includes three subfields. *Total* area is the sum of all land and water areas delimited by international boundaries and/or coastlines. *Land* area is the aggregate of all surfaces delimited by international boundaries and/or coastlines, excluding inland water bodies (lakes, reservoirs, rivers). *Water* area is the sum of all water surfaces delimited by international boundaries and/or coastlines, including inland water bodies (lakes, reservoirs, rivers).

Area - comparative: This entry provides an area comparison based on total area equivalents. Most entities are compared with the entire US or one of the 50 states based on area measurements (1990 revised) provided by the US Bureau of the Census. The smaller entities are compared with Washington, DC (178 sq km, 69 sq mi) or The Mall in Washington, DC (0.59 sq km, 0.23 sq mi, 146 acres).

Background: This entry usually highlights major historic events and current issues and may include a statement about one or two key future trends.

Birth rate: This entry gives the average annual number of births during a year per 1,000 persons in the population at midyear; also known as crude birth rate. The birth rate is usually the dominant factor in determining the rate of population growth. It depends on both the level of fertility and the age structure of the population.

Budget: This entry includes *revenues*, *total expenditures*, and capital expenditures. These figures are calculated on an exchange rate basis, i.e., <u>not</u> in purchasing power parity (PPP) terms

Capital: This entry gives the location of the seat of government.

Climate: This entry includes a brief description of typical weather regimes throughout the year.

Coastline: This entry gives the total length of the boundary between the land area (including islands) and the sea.

Communications: This category deals with the means of exchanging information and includes the telephone, radio, television, and Internet service provider entries.

Communications - note: This entry includes miscellaneous communications information of significance not included elsewhere.

Constitution: This entry includes the dates of adoption, revisions, and major amendments.

Country data codes: see **Data codes**

Country map: Most versions of the *Factbook* provide a country map in color. The maps were produced from the best information available at the time of preparation. Names and/or boundaries may have changed subsequently.

Country name: This entry includes all forms of the country's name approved by the US Board on Geographic Names (Italy is used as an example): *conventional long form* (Italian Republic), *conventional short form* (Italy), *local long form* (Repubblica Italiana), *local short form* (Italia), *former* (Kingdom of Italy), as well as the *abbreviation*. Also see the **Terminology** note.

Crude oil: See entry for oil.

Currency: This entry identifies the national medium of exchange and its basic subunit.

Currency code: This entry gives the International Organization for Standardization (ISO) 4217 alphabetic currency code for each country.

Data codes: This information is presented in **Appendix D: Cross-Reference List of Country Data Codes** and **Appendix E: Cross-Reference List of Hydrographic Data Codes**. This appendix includes the US Government approved Federal Information Processing Standards (FIPS) codes, the International Organization for Standardization (ISO) codes, and Internet codes for land entities. The appendix also includes the International Hydrographic Organization (IHO) codes, Aeronautical Chart and Information Center (ACIC; now a part of the National Geospatial-Intelligence Agency or NGA) codes, and Defense Intelligence Agency (DIA) codes for hydrographic entities. The US Government has not yet approved a standard for hydrographic data codes similar to the FIPS 10-4 standard for country data codes.

Date of information: In general, information available as of 1 January 2004, was used in the preparation of this edition.

Death rate: This entry gives the average annual number of deaths during a year per 1,000 population at midyear; also known as crude death rate. The death rate, while only a rough indicator of the mortality situation in a country, accurately indicates the current mortality impact on population growth. This indicator is significantly affected by age distribution, and most countries will eventually show a rise in the overall death rate, in spite of continued decline in mortality at all ages, as declining fertility results in an aging population.

Debt - external: This entry gives the total public and private debt owed to nonresidents repayable in foreign currency, goods, or services.

Dependency status: This entry describes the formal relationship between a particular nonindependent entity and an independent state.

Dependent areas: This entry contains an alphabetical listing of all nonindependent entities associated in some way with a particular independent state.

Diplomatic representation: The US Government has diplomatic relations with 186 independent states, including 185 of the 191 UN members (excluded UN members are Bhutan, Cuba, Iran, Iraq, North Korea, and the US itself). In addition, the US has diplomatic relations with 1 independent state that is not in the UN - Holy See.

Diplomatic representation in the US: This entry includes the *chief of mission, chancery, telephone, FAX, consulate general* locations, and *consulate* locations.

Diplomatic representation from the US: This entry includes the *chief of mission*, *embassy* address, *mailing address*, *telephone* number, *FAX* number, *branch office* locations, *consulate general* locations, and *consulate* locations.

Disputes - international: This entry includes a wide variety of situations that range from traditional bilateral boundary disputes to unilateral claims of one sort or another. Information regarding disputes over international terrestrial and maritime boundaries has been reviewed by the US Department of State. References to other situations involving borders or frontiers may also be included, such as resource disputes, geopolitical questions, or irredentist issues; however, inclusion does not necessarily constitute official acceptance or recognition by the US Government.

Distribution of family income - Gini index: This index measures the degree of inequality in the distribution of family income in a country. The index is calculated from the Lorenz curve, in which cumulative family income is plotted against the number of families arranged from the poorest to the richest. The index is the ratio of (a) the area between a country's Lorenz curve and the 45 degree helping line to (b) the entire triangular area under the 45 degree line. The more nearly equal a country's income distribution, the closer its Lorenz curve to the 45 degree line and the lower its Gini index, e.g., a Scandinavian country with an index of 25. The more unequal a country's income distribution, the farther its Lorenz curve from the 45 degree line and the higher its Gini index, e.g., a Sub-Saharan country with an index of 50. If income were distributed with perfect equality, the Lorenz curve would coincide with the 45 degree line and the index would be zero; if income were distributed with perfect inequality, the Lorenz curve would coincide with the horizontal axis and the right vertical axis and the index would be 100.

Economic aid - donor: This entry refers to net official development assistance (ODA) from Organization for Economic Cooperation and Development (OECD) nations to developing countries and multilateral organizations. ODA is defined as financial assistance that is concessional in character, has the main objective to promote economic development and welfare of the less developed countries (LDCs), and contains a grant element of at least 25%. The entry does not cover other official flows (OOF) or private flows.

Economic aid - recipient: This entry, which is subject to major problems of definition and statistical coverage, refers to the net inflow of Official Development Finance (ODF) to recipient countries. The figure includes assistance from the World Bank, the IMF, and other international organizations and from individual nation donors. Formal commitments of aid are included in the data. Omitted from the data are grants by private organizations. Aid comes in various forms including outright grants and loans. The entry thus is the difference between new inflows and repayments.

Economy: This category includes the entries dealing with the size, development, and management of productive resources, i.e., land, labor, and capital.

Economy - overview: This entry briefly describes the type of economy, including the degree of market orientation, the level of economic development, the most important natural resources, and the unique areas of specialization. It also characterizes major economic events and policy changes in the most recent 12 months and may include a statement about one or two key future macroeconomic trends.

Electricity - consumption: This entry consists of total electricity generated annually plus imports and minus exports, expressed in kilowatt-hours. The discrepancy between the amount of electricity generated and/or imported and the amount consumed and/or exported is accounted for as loss in transmission and distribution.

Electricity - exports: This entry is the total exported electricity in kilowatt-hours.

Electricity - imports: This entry is the total imported electricity in kilowatt-hours.

Electricity - production: This entry is the annual electricity generated expressed in kilowatt-hours. The discrepancy between the amount of electricity generated and/or imported and the amount consumed and/or exported is accounted for as loss in transmission and distribution.

Electricity - production by source: This entry states the percentage share of electricity generated from each energy source. These are *fossil fuel*, *hydro*, *nuclear*, and *other* (solar, geothermal, and wind).

Elevation extremes: This entry includes both the *highest point* and the *lowest point*.

Entities: Some of the independent states, dependencies, areas of special sovereignty, and governments included in this publication are not independent, and others are not officially recognized by the US Government. "Independent state" refers to a people politically organized into a sovereign state with a definite territory. "Dependencies" and "areas of special sovereignty" refer to a broad category of political entities that are associated in some way with an independent state. "Country" names used in the table of contents or for page headings are usually the short-form names as approved by the US Board on Geographic Names and may include independent states, dependencies, and areas of special sovereignty, or other geographic entities. There are a total of 268 separate geographic entities in *The World Factbook* that may be categorized as follows:

INDEPENDENT STATES

192   Afghanistan, Albania, Algeria, Andorra, Angola, Antigua and Barbuda, Argentina, Armenia, Australia, Austria, Azerbaijan, The Bahamas, Bahrain, Bangladesh, Barbados, Belarus, Belgium, Belize, Benin, Bhutan, Bolivia, Bosnia and Herzegovina, Botswana, Brazil, Brunei, Bulgaria, Burkina Faso, Burma, Burundi, Cambodia, Cameroon, Canada, Cape Verde, Central African Republic, Chad, Chile, China, Colombia, Comoros, Democratic Republic of the Congo, Republic of the Congo, Costa Rica, Cote d'Ivoire, Croatia, Cuba, Cyprus, Czech Republic, Denmark, Djibouti, Dominica, Dominican Republic, East Timor, Ecuador, Egypt, El Salvador, Equatorial Guinea, Eritrea, Estonia, Ethiopia, Fiji, Finland, France, Gabon, The Gambia, Georgia, Germany, Ghana, Greece, Grenada, Guatemala, Guinea, Guinea-Bissau, Guyana, Haiti, Holy See, Honduras, Hungary, Iceland, India, Indonesia, Iran, Iraq, Ireland, Israel, Italy, Jamaica, Japan, Jordan, Kazakhstan, Kenya, Kiribati, North Korea, South Korea, Kuwait, Kyrgyzstan, Laos, Latvia, Lebanon, Lesotho, Liberia, Libya, Liechtenstein, Lithuania, Luxembourg, The Former Yugoslav Republic of Macedonia, Madagascar, Malawi, Malaysia, Maldives, Mali, Malta, Marshall Islands, Mauritania, Mauritius, Mexico, Federated States of Micronesia, Moldova, Monaco, Mongolia, Morocco, Mozambique, Namibia, Nauru, Nepal, Netherlands, NZ, Nicaragua, Niger, Nigeria, Norway, Oman, Pakistan,

Palau, Panama, Papua New Guinea, Paraguay, Peru, Philippines, Poland, Portugal, Qatar, Romania, Russia, Rwanda, Saint Kitts and Nevis, Saint Lucia, Saint Vincent and the Grenadines, Samoa, San Marino, Sao Tome and Principe, Saudi Arabia, Senegal, Seychelles, Sierra Leone, Singapore, Slovakia, Slovenia, Solomon Islands, Somalia, South Africa, Spain, Sri Lanka, Sudan, Suriname, Swaziland, Sweden, Switzerland, Syria, Tajikistan, Tanzania, Thailand, Togo, Tonga, Trinidad and Tobago, Tunisia, Turkey, Turkmenistan, Tuvalu, Uganda, Ukraine, UAE, UK, US, Uruguay, Uzbekistan, Vanuatu, Venezuela, Vietnam, Yemen, Yugoslavia, Zambia, Zimbabwe

OTHER

1   Taiwan

DEPENDENCIES AND AREAS OF SPECIAL SOVEREIGNTY

6   Australia - Ashmore and Cartier Islands, Christmas Island, Cocos (Keeling) Islands, Coral Sea Islands, Heard Island and McDonald Islands, Norfolk Island

2   China - Hong Kong, Macau

2   Denmark - Faroe Islands, Greenland

16   France - Bassas da India, Clipperton Island, Europa Island, French Guiana, French Polynesia, French Southern and Antarctic Lands, Glorioso Islands, Guadeloupe, Juan de Nova Island, Martinique, Mayotte, New Caledonia, Reunion, Saint Pierre and Miquelon, Tromelin Island, Wallis and Futuna

2   Netherlands - Aruba, Netherlands Antilles

3   New Zealand - Cook Islands, Niue, Tokelau

3   Norway - Bouvet Island, Jan Mayen, Svalbard

15   UK - Anguilla, Bermuda, British Indian Ocean Territory, British Virgin Islands, Cayman Islands, Falkland Islands, Gibraltar, Guernsey, Jersey, Isle of Man, Montserrat, Pitcairn Islands, Saint Helena, South Georgia and the South Sandwich Islands, Turks and Caicos Islands

14   US - American Samoa, Baker Island, Guam, Howland Island, Jarvis Island, Johnston Atoll, Kingman Reef, Midway Islands, Navassa Island, Northern Mariana Islands, Palmyra Atoll, Puerto Rico, Virgin Islands, Wake Island

MISCELLANEOUS

6   Antarctica, Gaza Strip, Paracel Islands, Spratly Islands, West Bank, Western Sahara

OTHER ENTITIES

5   oceans - Arctic Ocean, Atlantic Ocean, Indian Ocean, Pacific Ocean, Southern Ocean

1   <u>World</u>

268   total

Environment - current issues: This entry lists the most pressing and important environmental problems. The following terms and abbreviations are used throughout the entry:

    acidification - the lowering of soil and water pH due to acid precipitation and deposition usually through precipitation; this process disrupts ecosystem nutrient flows and may kill freshwater fish and plants dependent on more neutral or alkaline conditions (see acid rain).

    acid rain - characterized as containing harmful levels of sulfur dioxide or nitrogen oxide; acid rain is damaging and potentially deadly to the earth's fragile ecosystems; acidity is measured using the pH scale where 7 is neutral, values greater than 7 are considered alkaline, and values below 5.6 are considered acid precipitation; note - a pH of 2.4 (the acidity of vinegar) has been measured in rainfall in New England.

aerosol - a collection of airborne particles dispersed in a gas, smoke, or fog.

afforestation - converting a bare or agricultural space by planting trees and plants; reforestation involves replanting trees on areas that have been cut or destroyed by fire.

asbestos - a naturally occurring soft fibrous mineral commonly used in fireproofing materials and considered to be highly carcinogenic in particulate form.

biodiversity - also biological diversity; the relative number of species, diverse in form and function, at the genetic, organism, community, and ecosystem level; loss of biodiversity reduces an ecosystem's ability to recover from natural or man-induced disruption.

bio-indicators - a plant or animal species whose presence, abundance, and health reveal the general condition of its habitat.

biomass - the total weight or volume of living matter in a given area or volume.

carbon cycle - the term used to describe the exchange of carbon (in various forms, e.g., as carbon dioxide) between the atmosphere, ocean, terrestrial biosphere, and geological deposits.

catchments - assemblages used to capture and retain rainwater and runoff; an important water management technique in areas with limited freshwater resources, such as Gibraltar.

DDT (dichloro-diphenyl-trichloro-ethane) - a colorless, odorless insecticide that has toxic effects on most animals; the use of DDT was banned in the US in 1972.

defoliants - chemicals which cause plants to lose their leaves artificially; often used in agricultural practices for weed control, and may have detrimental impacts on human and ecosystem health.

deforestation - the destruction of vast areas of forest (e.g., unsustainable forestry practices, agricultural and range land clearing, and the over exploitation of wood products for use as fuel) without planting new growth.

desertification - the spread of desert-like conditions in arid or semi-arid areas, due to overgrazing, loss of agriculturally productive soils, or climate change.

dredging - the practice of deepening an existing waterway; also, a technique used for collecting bottom-dwelling marine organisms (e.g., shellfish) or harvesting coral, often causing significant destruction of reef and ocean-floor ecosystems.

drift-net fishing - done with a net, miles in extent, that is generally anchored to a boat and left to float with the tide; often results in an over harvesting and waste of large populations of non-commercial marine species (by-catch) by its effect of "sweeping the ocean clean".

ecosystems - ecological units comprised of complex communities of organisms and their specific environments.

effluents - waste materials, such as smoke, sewage, or industrial waste which are released into the environment, subsequently polluting it.

endangered species - a species that is threatened with extinction either by direct hunting or habitat destruction.

freshwater - water with very low soluble mineral content; sources include lakes, streams, rivers, glaciers, and underground aquifers.

greenhouse gas - a gas that "traps" infrared radiation in the lower atmosphere causing surface warming; water vapor, carbon dioxide, nitrous oxide, methane, hydrofluorocarbons, and ozone are the primary greenhouse gases in the Earth's atmosphere.

groundwater - water sources found below the surface of the earth often in naturally occurring reservoirs in permeable rock strata; the source for wells and natural springs.

Highlands Water Project - a series of dams constructed jointly by Lesotho and South Africa to redirect Lesotho's abundant water supply into a rapidly growing area in South Africa; while it is the largest infrastructure project in southern Africa, it is also the most costly and controversial; objections to the project include claims that it forces people from their homes, submerges farmlands, and squanders economic resources.

Inuit Circumpolar Conference (ICC) - represents the 145,000 Inuits of Russia, Alaska, Canada, and Greenland in international environmental issues; a General Assembly convenes every three years to determine the focus of the ICC; the most current concerns are long-range transport of pollutants, sustainable development, and climate change.

metallurgical plants - industries which specialize in the science, technology, and processing of metals; these plants produce highly concentrated and toxic wastes which can contribute to pollution of ground water and air when not properly disposed.

noxious substances - injurious, very harmful to living beings.

overgrazing - the grazing of animals on plant material faster than it can naturally regrow leading to the permanent loss of plant cover, a common effect of too many animals grazing limited range land.

ozone shield - a layer of the atmosphere composed of ozone gas (O_3) that resides approximately 25 miles above the Earth's surface and absorbs solar ultraviolet radiation that can be harmful to living organisms.

poaching - the illegal killing of animals or fish, a great concern with respect to endangered or threatened species.

pollution - the contamination of a healthy environment by man-made waste.

potable water - water that is drinkable, safe to be consumed.

salination - the process through which fresh (drinkable) water becomes salt (undrinkable) water; hence, desalination is the reverse process; also involves the accumulation of salts in topsoil caused by evaporation of excessive irrigation water, a process that can eventually render soil incapable of supporting crops.

siltation - occurs when water channels and reservoirs become clotted with silt and mud, a side effect of deforestation and soil erosion.

slash-and-burn agriculture - a rotating cultivation technique in which trees are cut down and burned in order to clear land for temporary agriculture; the land is used until its productivity declines at which point a new plot is selected and the process repeats; this practice is sustainable while population levels are low and time is permitted for regrowth of natural vegetation; conversely, where these conditions do not exist, the practice can have disastrous consequences for the environment .

soil degradation - damage to the land's productive capacity because of poor agricultural practices such as the excessive use of pesticides or fertilizers, soil compaction from heavy equipment, or erosion of topsoil, eventually resulting in reduced ability to produce agricultural products.

soil erosion - the removal of soil by the action of water or wind, compounded by poor agricultural practices, deforestation, overgrazing, and desertification.

ultraviolet (UV) radiation - a portion of the electromagnetic energy emitted by the sun and naturally filtered in the upper atmosphere by the ozone layer; UV radiation can be harmful to living organisms and has been linked to increasing rates of skin cancer in humans.

water-born diseases - those in which the bacteria survive in, and is transmitted through, water; always a serious threat in areas with an untreated water supply.

Environment - international agreements: This entry separates country participation in international environmental agreements into two levels - *party to* and *signed but not ratified.* Agreements are listed in alphabetical order by the abbreviated form of the full name.

Environmental agreements: This information is presented in **Appendix C: Selected International Environmental Agreements**, which includes the name, abbreviation, date opened for signature, date entered into force, objective, and parties by category.

Ethnic groups: This entry provides an ordered listing of ethnic groups starting with the largest and normally includes the percent of total population.

Exchange rates: This entry provides the official value of a country's monetary unit at a given date or over a given period of time, as expressed in units of local currency per US dollar and as determined by international market forces or official fiat.

Executive branch: This entry includes several subfields. *Chief of state* includes the name and title of the titular leader of the country who represents the state at official and ceremonial functions but may not be involved with the day-to-day activities of the government. *Head of government* includes the name and title of the top administrative leader who is designated to manage the day-to-day activities of the government. For example, in the UK, the monarch is the chief of state, and the prime minister is the head of government. In the US, the president is both the chief of state and the head of government. *Cabinet* includes the official name for this body of high-ranking advisers and the method for selection of members. *Elections* includes the nature of election process or accession to power, date of the last election, and date of the next election. *Election results* includes the percent of vote for each candidate in the last election.

Exports: This entry provides the total US dollar amount of exports on an f.o.b. (free on board) basis.

Exports - commodities: This entry provides a rank ordering of exported products starting with the most important; it sometimes includes the percent of total dollar value.

Exports - partners: This entry provides a rank ordering of trading partners starting with the most important; it sometimes includes the percent of total dollar value.

Fiscal year: This entry identifies the beginning and ending months for a country's accounting period of 12 months, which often is the calendar year but which may begin in any month. All yearly references are for the calendar year (CY) unless indicated as a noncalendar fiscal year (FY).

Flag description: This entry provides a written flag description produced from actual flags or the best information available at the time the entry was written. The flags of independent states are used by their dependencies unless there is an officially recognized local flag. Some disputed and other areas do not have flags.

Flag graphic: Most versions of the *Factbook* include a color flag at the beginning of the country profile. The flag graphics were produced from actual flags or the best information available at the time of preparation. The flags of independent states are used by their dependencies unless there is an officially recognized local flag. Some disputed and other areas do not have flags.

GDP: This entry gives the gross domestic product (GDP) or value of all final goods and services produced within a nation in a given year. GDP dollar estimates in the *Factbook* are derived from purchasing power parity (PPP) calculations. See the note on **GDP methodology** for more information.

GDP methodology: In the **Economy** category, GDP dollar estimates for all countries are derived from purchasing power parity (PPP) calculations rather than from conversions at official currency exchange rates. The PPP method involves the use of standardized international dollar price weights, which are applied to the quantities of final goods and services produced in a given economy. The data derived from the PPP method provide the best available starting point for comparisons of economic strength and well-being between countries. The division of a GDP estimate in domestic currency by the corresponding PPP estimate in dollars gives the PPP conversion rate. Whereas PPP estimates for OECD countries are quite reliable, PPP estimates for developing countries are often rough approximations. Most of the GDP estimates are based on extrapolation of PPP numbers published by the UN International Comparison Program (UNICP) and by Professors Robert Summers and Alan Heston of the University of Pennsylvania and their colleagues. In contrast, the currency exchange rate method involves a variety of international and domestic financial forces that often have little relation to domestic output. In developing countries with weak currencies the exchange rate estimate of GDP in dollars is typically one-fourth to one-half the PPP estimate. Furthermore, exchange rates may suddenly go up or down by 10% or more because of market forces or official fiat whereas real output has remained unchanged. On 12 January 1994, for example, the 14 countries of the African Financial Community (whose currencies are tied to the French franc) devalued their currencies by 50%. This move, of course, did not cut the real output of these countries by half. One important caution: the proportion of, say, defense expenditures as a percentage of GDP in local currency accounts may differ substantially from the proportion when GDP accounts are expressed in PPP terms, as, for example, when an observer tries to estimate the dollar level of Russian or Japanese military expenditures. Note: the numbers for GDP and other economic data *cannot* be chained together from successive volumes of the *Factbook* because of changes in the US dollar measuring rod, revisions of data by statistical agencies, use of new or different sources of information, and changes in national statistical methods and practices.

GDP - composition by sector: This entry gives the percentage contribution of *agriculture*, *industry*, and *services* to total GDP.

GDP - per capita: This entry shows GDP on a purchasing power parity basis divided by population as of 1 July for the same year.

GDP - real growth rate: This entry gives GDP growth on an annual basis adjusted for inflation and expressed as a percent.

Geographic coordinates: This entry includes rounded latitude and longitude figures for the purpose of finding the approximate geographic center of an entity and is based on the *Gazetteer of Conventional Names*, Third Edition, August 1988, US Board on Geographic Names and on other sources.

Geographic names: This information is presented in **Appendix F: Cross-Reference List of Geographic Names**. It includes a listing of various alternate names, former names, local names, and regional names referenced to one or more related *Factbook* entries. Spellings are normally, but not always, those approved by the US Board on Geographic Names (BGN). Alternate names and additional information are included in parentheses.

Geography: This category includes the entries dealing with the natural environment and the effects of human activity.

Geography - note: This entry includes miscellaneous geographic information of significance not included elsewhere.

Gini index: See entry for **Distribution of family income - Gini index**

GNP: Gross national product (GNP) is the value of all final goods and services produced within a nation in a given year, plus income earned by its citizens abroad, minus income earned by foreigners from domestic production. The *Factbook*, following current practice, uses GDP rather than GNP to measure national production. However, the user must realize that in certain countries net remittances from citizens working abroad may be important to national well-being.

Government: This category includes the entries dealing with the system for the adoption and administration of public policy.

Government type: This entry gives the basic form of government. Definitions of the major governmental terms are as follows:

Anarchy - the condition of lawlessness or political disorder brought about by the absence of governmental authority.

Commonwealth - a nation, state, or other political entity founded on law and united by a compact of the people for the common good.

Communism - a system of government in which the state plans and controls the economy and a single - often authoritarian - party holds power. State controls are imposed with the elimination of private ownership of property or capital while claiming to make progress toward a higher social order in which all goods are equally shared by the people (i.e., a classless society).

Confederacy (Confederation) - a union by compact or treaty between states, provinces, or territories, that creates a central government with limited powers; the constituent entities retain supreme authority over all matters except those delegated to the central government.

Constitutional - a government by or operating under an authoritative document (constitution) that sets forth the system of fundamental laws and principles that determines the nature, functions, and limits of that government.

Constitutional Democracy - a form of government in which the sovereign power of the people is spelled out in a governing constitution.

Constitutional Monarchy - a system of government in which a monarch is guided by a constitution whereby his/her rights, duties, and responsibilities are spelled out in written law or by custom.

Democracy - a form of government in which the supreme power is retained by the people, but which is usually exercised indirectly through a system of representation and delegated authority periodically renewed.

Democratic Republic - a state in which the supreme power rests in the body of citizens entitled to vote for officers and representatives responsible to them.

Dictatorship - a form of government in which a ruler or small clique wield absolute power (not restricted by a constitution or laws).

Ecclesiastical - a government administrated by a church.

Federal (Federative) - a form of government in which sovereign power is formally divided - usually by means of a constitution - between a central authority and a number of constituent regions (states, colonies, or provinces) so that each region retains some management of its internal affairs. Differs from a confederacy in that the central government exerts influence directly upon both individuals as well as upon the regional units.

Federal Republic - a state in which the powers of the central government are restricted and in which the component parts (states, colonies, or provinces) retain a degree of self-government; ultimate sovereign power rests with the voters who chose their governmental representatives.

Maoism - the theory and practice of Marxism-Leninism developed in China by Mao Zedong (Mao Tse-tung), which states that a continuous revolution is necessary if the leaders of a communist state are to keep in touch with the people.

Marxism - the political, economic, and social principles espoused by 19th century economist Karl Marx. He viewed the struggle of workers as a progression of historical forces that would proceed from a class struggle of the proletariat (workers) exploited by capitalists (business owners), to a socialist "dictatorship of the proletariat," to, finally, a classless society - communism.

Marxism-Leninism - an expanded form of communism developed by Lenin from doctrines of Karl Marx. Lenin saw imperialism as the final stage of capitalism and shifted the focus of workers' struggle from developed to underdeveloped countries.

Monarchy - a government in which the supreme power is lodged in the hands of a monarch who reigns over a state or territory, usually for life and by hereditary right. The monarch may be either a sole absolute ruler or a sovereign - such as a king, queen, or prince - with constitutionally limited authority.

Oligarchy - a government in which control is exercised by a small group of individuals whose authority generally is based on wealth or power.

Parliamentary Democracy - a political system in which the legislature (parliament) selects the government - a prime minister, premier, or chancellor along with the cabinet ministers - according to party strength as expressed in elections. By this system, the government acquires a dual responsibility: to the people as well as to the parliament.

Parliamentary Government (Cabinet-Parliamentary Government) - a government in which members of an executive branch (the cabinet and its leader - a prime minister, premier, or chancellor) are nominated to their positions by a legislature or parliament, and are directly responsible to it. This type of government can be dissolved at will by the parliament (legislature) by means of a no confidence vote or the leader of the cabinet may dissolve the parliament if it can no longer function.

Parliamentary Monarchy - a state headed by a monarch who is not actively involved in policy formation or implementation (i.e., the exercise of sovereign powers by a monarch in a ceremonial capacity). True governmental leadership is carried out by a cabinet and its head - a prime minister, premier, or chancellor - who are drawn from a legislature (parliament).

Republic - a representative democracy in which the people's elected deputies (representatives), not the people themselves, vote on legislation.

Socialism - a government in which the means of planning, producing, and distributing goods is controlled by a central government that theoretically seeks a more just and equitable distribution of property and labor. In actuality, most socialist governments have ended up being no more than dictatorships over workers by a ruling elite.

Sultanate - similar to a monarchy, but a government in which the supreme power is in the hands of a sultan (the head of a Muslim state). The sultan may be an absolute ruler or a sovereign with constitutionally limited authority.

Theocracy - a form of government in which a Deity is recognized as the supreme civil ruler, but the Deity's laws are interpreted by ecclesiastical authorities (bishops, mullahs, etc.); a government subject to religious authority.

Totalitarian - a government that seeks to subordinate the individual to the state by controlling not only all political and economic matters, but also the attitudes, values, and beliefs of its population.

Government - note: This entry includes miscellaneous government information of significance not included elsewhere.

Gross domestic product: see **GDP**

Gross national product: see **GNP**

Gross world product: see **GWP**

GWP: This entry gives the gross world product (GWP) or aggregate value of all final goods and services produced worldwide in a given year.

Heliports: This entry gives the total number of established helicopter takeoff and landing sites (which may or may not have fuel or other services).

Highways: This entry states the *total* length of the highway system and the length of the *paved* and *unpaved* parts.

HIV/AIDS - adult prevalence rate: This entry gives an estimate of the percentage of adults (aged 15-49) living with HIV/AIDS. The adult prevalence rate is calculated by dividing the estimated number of adults living with HIV/AIDS at yearend by the total adult population at yearend.

HIV/AIDS - deaths: This entry gives an estimate of the number of adults and children who died of AIDS during a given calendar year.

HIV/AIDS - people living with HIV/AIDS: This entry gives an estimate of all people (adults and children) alive at yearend with HIV infection, whether or not they have developed symptoms of AIDS.

Household income or consumption by percentage share: Data on household income or consumption come from household surveys, the results adjusted for household size. Nations use different standards and procedures in collecting and adjusting the data. Surveys based on income will normally show a more unequal distribution than surveys based on consumption. The quality of surveys is improving with time, yet caution is still necessary in making inter-country comparisons.

Hydrographic data codes: see **Data codes**

Illicit drugs: This entry gives information on the five categories of illicit drugs - narcotics, stimulants, depressants (sedatives), hallucinogens, and cannabis. These categories include many drugs legally produced and prescribed by doctors as well as those illegally produced and sold outside of medical channels.
   Cannabis (Cannabis sativa) is the common hemp plant, which provides hallucinogens with some sedative properties, and includes marijuana (pot, Acapulco gold, grass, reefer), tetrahydrocannabinol (THC, Marinol), hashish (hash), and hashish oil (hash oil).
   Coca (mostly Erythroxylum coca) is a bush with leaves that contain the stimulant used to make cocaine. Coca is not to be confused with cocoa, which comes from cacao seeds and is used in making chocolate, cocoa, and cocoa butter.
   Cocaine is a stimulant derived from the leaves of the coca bush.
   Depressants (sedatives) are drugs that reduce tension and anxiety and include chloral hydrate, barbiturates (Amytal, Nembutal, Seconal, phenobarbital), benzodiazepines (Librium, Valium), methaqualone (Quaalude), glutethimide (Doriden), and others (Equanil, Placidyl, Valmid).
   Drugs are any chemical substances that effect a physical, mental, emotional, or behavioral change in an individual.
   Drug abuse is the use of any licit or illicit chemical substance that results in physical, mental, emotional, or behavioral impairment in an individual.

Hallucinogens are drugs that affect sensation, thinking, self-awareness, and emotion. Hallucinogens include LSD (acid, microdot), mescaline and peyote (mexc, buttons, cactus), amphetamine variants (PMA, STP, DOB), phencyclidine (PCP, angel dust, hog), phencyclidine analogues (PCE, PCPy, TCP), and others (psilocybin, psilocyn).

Hashish is the resinous exudate of the cannabis or hemp plant (Cannabis sativa).

Heroin is a semisynthetic derivative of morphine.

Mandrax is a trade name for methaqualone, a pharmaceutical depressant.

Marijuana is the dried leaf of the cannabis or hemp plant (Cannabis sativa).

Methaqualone is a pharmaceutical depressant, referred to as mandrax in Southwest Asia and Africa.

Narcotics are drugs that relieve pain, often induce sleep, and refer to opium, opium derivatives, and synthetic substitutes. Natural narcotics include opium (paregoric, parepectolin), morphine (MS-Contin, Roxanol), codeine (Tylenol with codeine, Empirin with codeine, Robitussan AC), and thebaine. Semisynthetic narcotics include heroin (horse, smack), and hydromorphone (Dilaudid). Synthetic narcotics include meperidine or Pethidine (Demerol, Mepergan), methadone (Dolophine, Methadose), and others (Darvon, Lomotil).

Opium is the brown, gummy exudate of the incised, unripe seedpod of the opium poppy.

Opium poppy (Papaver somniferum) is the source for the natural and semisynthetic narcotics.

Poppy straw is the entire cut and dried opium poppy-plant material, other than the seeds. Opium is extracted from poppy straw in commercial operations that produce the drug for medical use.

Qat (kat, khat) is a stimulant from the buds or leaves of Catha edulis that is chewed or drunk as tea.

Quaaludes is the North American slang term for methaqualone, a pharmaceutical depressant.

Stimulants are drugs that relieve mild depression, increase energy and activity, and include cocaine (coke, snow, crack), amphetamines (Desoxyn, Dexedrine), ephedrine, ecstasy (clarity, essence, doctor, Adam), phenmetrazine (Preludin), methylphenidate (Ritalin), and others (Cylert, Sanorex, Tenuate).

Imports: This entry provides the total US dollar amount of imports on a c.i.f. (cost, insurance, and freight) or f.o.b. (free on board) basis.

Imports - commodities: This entry provides a rank ordering of imported products starting with the most important; it sometimes includes the percent of total dollar value.

Imports - partners: This entry provides a rank ordering of trading partners starting with the most important; it sometimes includes the percent of total dollar value.

Independence: For most countries, this entry gives the date that sovereignty was achieved and from which nation, empire, or trusteeship. For the other countries, the date given may not represent "independence" in the strict sense, but rather some significant nationhood event such as the traditional founding date or the date of unification, federation, confederation, establishment, fundamental change in the form of government, or state succession. Dependent areas include the notation "none" followed by the nature of their dependency status. Also see the **Terminology** note.

Industrial production growth rate: This entry gives the annual percentage increase in industrial production (includes manufacturing, mining, and construction).

Industries: This entry provides a rank ordering of industries starting with the largest by value of annual output.

Notes and Definitions *(continued)*

Infant mortality rate: This entry gives the number of deaths of infants under one year old in a given year per 1,000 live births in the same year; included is the *total* death rate, and deaths by sex, *male* and *female*. This rate is often used as an indicator of the level of health in a country.

Inflation rate (consumer prices): This entry furnishes the annual percent change in consumer prices compared with the previous year's consumer prices.

Internet country code: This entry includes the two-letter codes maintained by the International Organization for Standardization (ISO) in the ISO 3166 Alpha-2 list and used by the Internet Assigned Numbers Authority (IANA) to establish country-coded top-level domains (ccTLDs).

Internet hosts: This entry lists the number of Internet hosts available within a country. An Internet host is a computer connected *directly* to the Internet; normally an Internet Service Provider's (ISP) computer is a host. Internet users may use either a hard-wired terminal, at an institution with a mainframe computer connected directly to the Internet, or may connect remotely by way of a modem via telephone line, cable, or satellite to the Internet Service Provider's host computer. The number of hosts is one indicator of the extent of Internet connectivity.

Internet users: This entry gives the number of users within a country that access the Internet. Statistics vary from country to country and may include users who access the Internet at least several times a week to those who access it only once within a period of several months.

International disputes: see **Disputes - international**

International organization participation: This entry lists in alphabetical order by abbreviation those international organizations in which the subject country is a member or participates in some other way.

International organizations: This information is presented in **Appendix B: International Organizations and Groups** which includes the name, abbreviation, date established, aim, and members by category.

Introduction: This category includes one entry, **Background**.

Irrigated land: This entry gives the number of square kilometers of land area that is artificially supplied with water.

Judicial branch: This entry contains the name(s) of the highest court(s) and a brief description of the selection process for members.

Labor force: This entry contains the total labor force figure.

Labor force - by occupation: This entry contains a rank ordering of component parts of the labor force by occupation.

Land boundaries: This entry contains the *total* length of all land boundaries and the individual lengths for each of the contiguous *border countries*.

Land use: This entry contains the percentage shares of total land area for three different types of land use: *arable land* - land cultivated for crops like wheat, maize, and rice that are replanted after each harvest; *permanent crops* - land cultivated for crops like citrus, coffee, and rubber that are not replanted after each harvest; includes land under flowering shrubs, fruit trees, nut trees, and vines, but excludes land under trees grown for wood or timber; *other* - any land not arable or under permanent crops; includes permanent meadows and pastures, forests and woodlands, built-on areas, roads, barren land, etc.

Languages: This entry provides a rank ordering of languages starting with the largest and sometimes includes the percent of total population speaking that language.

Legal system: This entry contains a brief description of the legal system's historical roots, role in government, and acceptance of International Court of Justice (ICJ) jurisdiction.

Legislative branch: This entry contains information on the structure (unicameral, bicameral, tricameral), formal name, number of seats, and term of office. *Elections* includes the nature of election process or accession to power, date of the last election, and date of the next election. *Election results* includes the percent of vote and/or number of seats held by each party in the last election.

Life expectancy at birth: This entry contains the average number of years to be lived by a group of people born in the same year, if mortality at each age remains constant in the future. The entry includes *total population* as well as the *male* and *female* components. Life expectancy at birth is also a measure of overall quality of life in a country and summarizes the mortality at all ages. It can also be thought of as indicating the potential return on investment in human capital and is necessary for the calculation of various actuarial measures.

Literacy: This entry includes a definition of literacy and Census Bureau percentages for the total population, males, and females. There are no universal definitions and standards of literacy. Unless otherwise specified, all rates are based on the most common definition - the ability to read and write at a specified age. Detailing the standards that individual countries use to assess the ability to read and write is beyond the scope of the *Factbook*. Information on literacy, while not a perfect measure of educational results, is probably the most easily available and valid for international comparisons. Low levels of literacy, and education in general, can impede the economic development of a country in the current rapidly changing, technology-driven world.

Location: This entry identifies the country's regional location, neighboring countries, and adjacent bodies of water.

Map references: This entry includes the name of the *Factbook* reference map on which a country may be found. The entry on **Geographic coordinates** may be helpful in finding some smaller countries.

Maritime claims: This entry includes the following claims, the definitions of which are excerpted from the United Nations Convention on the Law of the Sea (UNCLOS), which alone contains the full and definitive descriptions:
   territorial sea - the sovereignty of a coastal state extends beyond its land territory and internal waters to an adjacent belt of sea, described as the territorial sea in the UNCLOS (Part II); this sovereignty extends to the air space over the territorial sea as well as its underlying seabed and subsoil; every state has the right to establish the breadth of its territorial sea up to a limit not exceeding 12 nautical miles; the normal baseline for measuring the breadth of the territorial sea is the low-water line along the coast as marked on large-scale charts officially recognized by the coastal state; the UNCLOS describes specific rules for archipelagic states
   contiguous zone - according to the UNCLOS (Article 33), this is a zone contiguous to a coastal state's territorial sea, over which it may exercise the control necessary to: prevent infringement of its customs, fiscal, immigration, or sanitary laws and regulations within its territory or territorial sea; punish infringement of the above laws and regulations committed within its territory or territorial sea; the contiguous zone may not extend beyond 24 nautical miles from the baselines from which the breadth of the territorial sea is measured (e.g. the US has claimed a 12-nautical mile contiguous zone in addition to its 12-nautical mile territorial sea)

exclusive economic zone (EEZ) - the UNCLOS (Part V) defines the EEZ as a zone beyond and adjacent to the territorial sea in which a coastal state has: sovereign rights for the purpose of exploring and exploiting, conserving and managing the natural resources, whether living or non-living, of the waters superjacent to the seabed and of the seabed and its subsoil, and with regard to other activities for the economic exploitation and exploration of the zone, such as the production of energy from the water, currents, and winds; jurisdiction with regard to the establishment and use of artificial islands, installations, and structures; marine scientific research; the protection and preservation of the marine environment; the outer limit of the exclusive economic zone shall not exceed 200 nautical miles from the baselines from which the breadth of the territorial sea is measured

continental shelf - the UNCLOS (Article 76) defines the continental shelf of a coastal state as comprising the seabed and subsoil of the submarine areas that extend beyond its territorial sea throughout the natural prolongation of its land territory to the outer edge of the continental margin, or to a distance of 200 nautical miles from the baselines from which the breadth of the territorial sea is measured where the outer edge of the continental margin does not extend up to that distance; the continental margin comprises the submerged prolongation of the landmass of the coastal state, and consists of the seabed and subsoil of the shelf, the slope and the rise; wherever the continental margin extends beyond 200 nautical miles from the baseline, coastal states may extend their claim to a distance not to exceed 350 nautical miles from the baseline or 100 nautical miles from the 2500 meter isobath; it does not include the deep ocean floor with its oceanic ridges or the subsoil thereof

exclusive fishing zone - while this term is not used in the UNCLOS, some states (e.g. the United Kingdom) have chosen not to claim an EEZ, but rather to claim jurisdiction over the living resources off their coast; in such cases, the term exclusive fishing zone is often used; the breadth of this zone is normally the same as the EEZ or 200 nautical miles

Median age: This entry is the age that divides a population into two numerically equal groups; that is, half the people are younger than this age and half are older. It is a single index that summarizes the age distribution of a population. Currently, the median age ranges from a low of about 15 in Uganda and Gaza Strip to 40 or more in several European countries and Japan. See the entry for "Age structure" for the importance of a young versus an older age structure and, by implication, a low versus a higher median age.

Merchant marine: Merchant marine may be defined as all ships engaged in the carriage of goods; or all commercial vessels (as opposed to all nonmilitary ships), which excludes tugs, fishing vessels, offshore oil rigs, etc. This entry contains information in four fields - *total, ships by type, foreign-owned,* and *registered in other countries. Total* includes the number of ships (1,000 GRT or over), total DWT for those ships, and total GRT for those ships. DWT or dead weight tonnage is the total weight of cargo, plus bunkers, stores, etc., that a ship can carry when immersed to the appropriate load line. GRT or gross register tonnage is a figure obtained by measuring the entire sheltered volume of a ship available for cargo and passengers and converting it to tons on the basis of 100 cubic feet per ton; there is no stable relationship between GRT and DWT. *Ships by type* includes a listing of barge carriers, bulk cargo ships, cargo ships, chemical tankers, combination bulk carriers, combination ore/oil carriers, container ships, liquefied gas tankers, livestock carriers, multifunctional large-load carriers, petroleum tankers, passenger ships, passenger/cargo ships, railcar carriers, refrigerated cargo ships, roll-on/roll-off cargo ships, short-sea passenger ships, specialized tankers, and vehicle carriers. *Foreign-owned* are ships that fly the flag of one country but belong to owners in another. *Registered in other countries* are ships that belong to owners in one country but fly the flag of another.

Military: This category includes the entries dealing with a country's military structure, manpower, and expenditures.

Military branches: This entry lists the names of the ground, naval, air, marine, and other defense or security forces.

Military expenditures - dollar figure: This entry gives current military expenditures in US dollars; the figure is calculated by multiplying the estimated defense spending in percentage terms by the gross domestic product (GDP) calculated on an exchange rate basis, *not* purchasing power parity (PPP) terms. Dollar figures for military expenditures should be treated with caution because of different price patterns and accounting methods among nations, as well as wide variations in the strength of their currencies.

Military expenditures - percent of GDP: This entry gives current military expenditures as an estimated percent of gross domestic product (GDP).

Military manpower - availability: This entry gives the total numbers of males and females age 15-49 and assumes that every individual is fit to serve.

Military manpower - fit for military service: This entry gives the number of males and females age 15-49 fit for military service. This is a more refined measure of potential military manpower availability which tries to account for the health situation in the country and reduces the maximum potential number to a more realistic estimate of the actual number fit to serve.

Military manpower - military age: This entry gives the minimum age at which an individual may volunteer for military service or be subject to conscription.

Military manpower - reaching military age annually: This entry gives the number of draft-age males and females entering the military manpower pool in any given year and is a measure of the availability of draft-age young adults.

Military - note: This entry includes miscellaneous military information of significance not included elsewhere.

Money figures: All money figures are expressed in contemporaneous US dollars unless otherwise indicated.

National holiday: This entry gives the primary national day of celebration - usually independence day.

Nationality: This entry provides the identifying terms for citizens - *noun* and *adjective*.

Natural gas - production: This entry is the total natural gas produced in cubic meters (cu m). The discrepancy between the amount of natural gas produced and/or imported and the amount consumed and/or exported is due to the omission of stock changes and other complicating factors.

Natural gas - consumption: This entry is the total natural gas consumed in cubic meters (cu m). The discrepancy between the amount of natural gas produced and/or imported and the amount consumed and/or exported is due to the omission of stock changes and other complicating factors.

Natural gas - exports: This entry is the total natural gas exported in cubic meters (cu m).

Natural gas - imports: This entry is the total natural gas imported in cubic meters (cu m).

Natural gas - proved reserves: This entry is the stock of proved reserves of natural gas in cubic meters (cu m). Proved reserves are those quantities of natural gas, which, by analysis of geological and engineering data, can be estimated with a high degree of confidence to be commercially recoverable from a given date forward, from known reservoirs and under current economic conditions.

Natural hazards: This entry lists potential natural disasters.

Natural resources: This entry lists a country's mineral, petroleum, hydropower, and other resources of commercial importance.

Net migration rate: This entry includes the figure for the difference between the number of persons entering and leaving a country during the year per 1,000 persons (based on midyear population). An excess of persons entering the country is referred to as net immigration (e.g., 3.56 migrants/1,000 population); an excess of persons leaving the country as net emigration (e.g., -9.26 migrants/1,000 population). The net migration rate indicates the contribution of migration to the overall level of population change. High levels of migration can cause problems such as increasing unemployment and potential ethnic strife (if people are coming in) or a reduction in the labor force, perhaps in certain key sectors (if people are leaving).

Oil - production: This entry is the total oil produced in barrels per day (bbl/day). The discrepancy between the amount of oil produced and/or imported and the amount consumed and/or exported is due to the omission of stock changes, refinery gains, and other complicating factors.

Oil - consumption: This entry is the total oil consumed in barrels per day (bbl/day). The discrepancy between the amount of oil produced and/or imported and the amount consumed and/or exported is due to the omission of stock changes, refinery gains, and other complicating factors.

Oil - exports: This entry is the total oil exported in barrels per day (bbl/day), including both crude oil and oil products.

Oil - imports: This entry is the total oil imported in barrels per day (bbl/day), including both crude oil and oil products.

Oil - proved reserves: This entry is the stock of proved reserves of crude oil in barrels (bbl). Proved reserves are those quantities of petroleum which, by analysis of geological and engineering data, can be estimated with a high degree of confidence to be commercially recoverable from a given date forward, from known reservoirs and under current economic conditions.

People: This category includes the entries dealing with the characteristics of the people and their society.

People - note: This entry includes miscellaneous demographic information of significance not included elsewhere.

Personal Names - Capitalization: The *Factbook* capitalizes the surname or family name of individuals for the convenience of our users who are faced with a world of different cultures and naming conventions. The need for capitalization, bold type, underlining, italics, or some other indicator of the individual's surname is apparent in the following examples: MAO Zedong, Fidel CASTRO Ruz, George W. BUSH, and TUNKU SALAHUDDIN Abdul Aziz Shah ibni Al-Marhum Sultan Hisammuddin Alam Shah. By knowing the surname, a short form without all capital letters can be used with confidence as in President Castro, Chairman Mao,

President Bush, or Sultan Tunku Salahuddin. The same system of capitalization is extended to the names of leaders with surnames that are not commonly used such as Queen ELIZABETH II.

Personal Names - Spelling: The romanization of personal names in the *Factbook* normally follows the same transliteration system used by the US Board on Geographic Names for spelling place names. At times, however, a foreign leader expressly indicates a preference for, or the media or official documents regularly use, a romanized spelling that differs from the transliteration derived from the US Government standard. In such cases, the *Factbook* uses the alternative spelling.

Personal Names - Titles: The *Factbook* capitalizes any valid title (or short form of it) immediately preceding a person's name. A title standing alone is not capitalized. Examples: President PUTIN and President BUSH are chiefs of state. In Russia, the president is chief of state and the premier is the head of the government, while in the US, the president is both chief of state and head of government.

Petroleum: See entry for "oil."

Petroleum products: See entry for "oil."

Pipelines: This entry gives the lengths and types of pipelines for transporting products like natural gas, crude oil, or petroleum products.

Political parties and leaders: This entry includes a listing of significant political organizations and their leaders.

Political pressure groups and leaders: This entry includes a listing of organizations with leaders involved in politics, but not standing for legislative election.

Population: This entry gives an estimate from the US Bureau of the Census based on statistics from population censuses, vital statistics registration systems, or sample surveys pertaining to the recent past and on assumptions about future trends. The total population presents one overall measure of the potential impact of the country on the world and within its region. Note: starting with the 1993 *Factbook*, demographic estimates for some countries (mostly African) have explicitly taken into account the effects of the growing impact of the HIV/AIDS epidemic. These countries are currently: The Bahamas, Benin, Botswana, Brazil, Burkina Faso, Burma, Burundi, Cambodia, Cameroon, Central African Republic, Democratic Republic of the Congo, Republic of the Congo, Cote d'Ivoire, Ethiopia, Gabon, Ghana, Guyana, Haiti, Honduras, Kenya, Lesotho, Malawi, Mozambique, Namibia, Nigeria, Rwanda, South Africa, Swaziland, Tanzania, Thailand, Togo, Uganda, Zambia, and Zimbabwe.

Population below poverty line: National estimates of the percentage of the population falling below the poverty line are based on surveys of sub-groups, with the results weighted by the number of people in each group. Definitions of poverty vary considerably among nations. For example, rich nations generally employ more generous standards of poverty than poor nations.

Population growth rate: The average annual percent change in the population, resulting from a surplus (or deficit) of births over deaths and the balance of migrants entering and leaving a country. The rate may be positive or negative. The growth rate is a factor in determining how great a burden would be imposed on a country by the changing needs of its people for infrastructure (e.g., schools, hospitals, housing, roads), resources (e.g., food, water, electricity), and jobs. Rapid population growth can be seen as threatening by neighboring countries.

Notes and Definitions *(continued)*

Ports and harbors: This entry lists the major ports and harbors selected on the basis of overall importance to each country. This is determined by evaluating a number of factors (e.g., dollar value of goods handled, gross tonnage, facilities, military significance).

Radio broadcast stations: This entry includes the total number of AM, FM, and shortwave broadcast stations.

Railways: This entry states the *total* route length of the railway network and of its component parts by gauge: *broad*, *standard*, *narrow*, and *dual*. Other gauges are listed under *note*.

Reference maps: This section includes world and regional maps.

Religions: This entry is an ordered listing of religions by adherents starting with the largest group and sometimes includes the percent of total population.

Sex ratio: This entry includes the number of males for each female in five age groups - *at birth*, *under 15 years*, *15-64 years*, *65 years and over*, and for the *total population*. Sex ratio at birth has recently emerged as an indicator of certain kinds of sex discrimination in some countries. For instance, high sex ratios at birth in some Asian countries are now attributed to sex-selective abortion and infanticide due to a strong preference for sons. This will affect future marriage patterns and fertility patterns. Eventually it could cause unrest among young adult males who are unable to find partners.

Suffrage: This entry gives the age at enfranchisement and whether the right to vote is universal or restricted.

Telephone numbers: All telephone numbers in the *Factbook* consist of the country code in brackets, the city or area code (where required) in parentheses, and the local number. The one component that is not presented is the international access code, which varies from country to country. For example, an international direct dial telephone call placed from the US to Madrid, Spain, would be as follows:

011 [34] (1) 577-xxxx, where
011 is the international access code for station-to-station calls;
01 is for calls other
than station-to-station calls,
[34] is the country code for Spain,
(1) is the city code for Madrid,
577 is the local exchange, and
xxxx is the local telephone number.

An international direct dial telephone call placed from another country to the US would be as follows:

international access code + [1] (202) 939-xxxx, where
[1] is the country code for the US,
(202) is the area code for Washington, DC,
939 is the local exchange, and
xxxx is the local telephone number.

Notes and Definitions *(continued)*

Telephone system: This entry includes a brief *general assessment* of the system with details on the *domestic* and *international* components. The following terms and abbreviations are used throughout the entry:

Africa ONE - a fiber-optic submarine cable link encircling the continent of Africa.

Arabsat - Arab Satellite Communications Organization (Riyadh, Saudi Arabia).

Autodin - Automatic Digital Network (US Department of Defense).

CB - citizen's band mobile radio communications.

cellular telephone system - the telephones in this system are radio transceivers, with each instrument having its own private radio frequency and sufficient radiated power to reach the booster station in its area (cell), from which the telephone signal is fed to a telephone exchange.

Central American Microwave System - a trunk microwave radio relay system that links the countries of Central America and Mexico with each other.

coaxial cable - a multichannel communication cable consisting of a central conducting wire, surrounded by and insulated from a cylindrical conducting shell; a large number of telephone channels can be made available within the insulated space by the use of a large number of carrier frequencies.

Comsat - Communications Satellite Corporation (US).

DSN - Defense Switched Network (formerly Automatic Voice Network or Autovon); basic general-purpose, switched voice network of the Defense Communications System (US Department of Defense).

Eutelsat - European Telecommunications Satellite Organization (Paris).

fiber-optic cable - a multichannel communications cable using a thread of optical glass fibers as a transmission medium in which the signal (voice, video, etc.) is in the form of a coded pulse of light.

GSM - a global system for mobile (cellular) communications devised by the Groupe Special Mobile of the pan-European standardization organization, Conference Europeanne des Posts et Telecommunications (CEPT) in 1982.

HF - high frequency; any radio frequency in the 3,000- to 30,000-kHz range.

Inmarsat - International Maritime Satellite Organization (London); provider of global mobile satellite communications for commercial, distress, and safety applications at sea, in the air, and on land.

Intelsat - International Telecommunications Satellite Organization (Washington, DC).

Intersputnik - International Organization of Space Communications (Moscow); first established in the former Soviet Union and the East European countries, it is now marketing its services worldwide with earth stations in North America, Africa, and East Asia.

landline - communication wire or cable of any sort that is installed on poles or buried in the ground.

Marecs - Maritime European Communications Satellite used in the Inmarsat system on lease from the European Space Agency.

Marisat - satellites of the Comsat Corporation that participate in the Inmarsat system.

Medarabtel - the Middle East Telecommunications Project of the International Telecommunications Union (ITU) providing a modern telecommunications network, primarily by microwave radio relay, linking Algeria, Djibouti, Egypt, Jordan, Libya, Morocco, Saudi Arabia, Somalia, Sudan, Syria, Tunisia, and Yemen; it was initially started in Morocco in 1970 by the Arab Telecommunications Union (ATU) and was known at that time as the Middle East Mediterranean Telecommunications Network.

microwave radio relay - transmission of long distance telephone calls and television programs by highly directional radio microwaves that are received and sent on from one booster station to another on an optical path.

NMT - Nordic Mobile Telephone; an analog cellular telephone system that was developed jointly by the national telecommunications authorities of the Nordic countries (Denmark, Finland, Iceland, Norway, and Sweden).

Orbita - a Russian television service; also the trade name of a packet-switched digital telephone network.

radiotelephone communications - the two-way transmission and reception of sounds by broadcast radio on authorized frequencies using telephone handsets.

PanAmSat - PanAmSat Corporation (Greenwich, CT).

SAFE - South African Far East Cable

satellite communication system - a communication system consisting of two or more earth stations and at least one satellite that provide long distance transmission of voice, data, and television; the system usually serves as a trunk connection between telephone exchanges; if the earth stations are in the same country, it is a domestic system.

satellite earth station - a communications facility with a microwave radio transmitting and receiving antenna and required receiving and transmitting equipment for communicating with satellites.

satellite link - a radio connection between a satellite and an earth station permitting communication between them, either one-way (down link from satellite to earth station - television receive-only transmission) or two-way (telephone channels).

SHF - super high frequency; any radio frequency in the 3,000- to 30,000-MHz range.

shortwave - radio frequencies (from 1.605 to 30 MHz) that fall above the commercial broadcast band and are used for communication over long distances.

Solidaridad - geosynchronous satellites in Mexico's system of international telecommunications in the Western Hemisphere.

Statsionar - Russia's geostationary system for satellite telecommunications.

submarine cable - a cable designed for service under water.

TAT - Trans-Atlantic Telephone; any of a number of high-capacity submarine coaxial telephone cables linking Europe with North America.

telefax - facsimile service between subscriber stations via the public switched telephone network or the international Datel network.

telegraph - a telecommunications system designed for unmodulated electric impulse transmission.

telex - a communication service involving teletypewriters connected by wire through automatic exchanges.

tropospheric scatter - a form of microwave radio transmission in which the troposphere is used to scatter and reflect a fraction of the incident radio waves back to earth; powerful, highly directional antennas are used to transmit and receive the microwave signals; reliable over-the-horizon communications are realized for distances up to 600 miles in a single hop; additional hops can extend the range of this system for very long distances.

trunk network - a network of switching centers, connected by multichannel trunk lines.

UHF - ultra high frequency; any radio frequency in the 300- to 3,000-MHz range.

VHF - very high frequency; any radio frequency in the 30- to 300-MHz range.

Telephones - main lines in use: This entry gives the total number of main telephone lines in use.

Telephones - mobile cellular: This entry gives the total number of mobile cellular telephones in use.

Television - broadcast stations: This entry gives the total number of separate broadcast stations plus any repeater stations.

Terminology: Due to the highly structured nature of the *Factbook* database, some collective generic terms have to be used. For example, the word **Country** in the **Country name** entry refers to a wide variety of dependencies, areas of special sovereignty, uninhabited islands, and other entities in addition to the traditional countries or independent states. **Military** is also used as an umbrella term for various civil defense, security, and defense activities in many entries. The **Independence** entry includes the usual colonial independence dates and former ruling states as well as other significant nationhood dates such as the traditional founding date or the date of unification, federation, confederation, establishment, or state succession that are not strictly independence dates. Dependent areas have the nature of their dependency status noted in this same entry.

Terrain: This entry contains a brief description of the topography.

Total fertility rate: This entry gives a figure for the average number of children that would be born per woman if all women lived to the end of their childbearing years and bore children according to a given fertility rate at each age. The total fertility rate is a more direct measure of the level of fertility than the crude birth rate, since it refers to births per woman. This indicator shows the potential for population growth in the country. High rates will also place some limits on the labor force participation rates for women. Large numbers of children born to women indicate large family sizes that might limit the ability of the families to feed and educate their children.

Transnational Issues: This category includes only two entries at the present time - **Disputes - international** and **Illicit drugs** - that deal with current issues going beyond national boundaries.

Transportation: This category includes the entries dealing with the means for movement of people and goods.

Transportation - note: This entry includes miscellaneous transportation information of significance not included elsewhere.

Unemployment rate: This entry contains the percent of the labor force that is without jobs. Substantial underemployment might be noted.

Waterways: This entry gives the total length of navigable rivers, canals, and other inland bodies of water.

Years: All year references are for the calendar year (CY) unless indicated as fiscal year (FY). The calendar year is an accounting period of 12 months from 1 January to 31 December. The fiscal year is an accounting period of 12 months other than 1 January to 31 December.

Note: Information for the US and US dependencies was compiled from material in the public domain and does not represent Intelligence Community estimates.

Guide to Country Profiles (**Categories** , Fields, and *subfields*)

Introduction
Background

Geography
Location
Geographic coordinates
Map references
Area
total
land
water
Area - comparative
Land boundaries
total
border countries
Coastline
Maritime claims
territorial sea
contiguous zone
exclusive economic zone
continental shelf
exclusive fishing zone
Climate
Terrain
Elevation extremes
lowest point
highest point
Natural resources
Land use
arable land
permanent crops
other
Irrigated land
Natural hazards
Environment - current issues
Environment - international agreements
party to
signed, but not ratified
Geography - note

People
Population
Age structure
0-14 years
15-64 years
65 years and over
Median Age
total
male
female
Population growth rate
Birth rate
Death rate
Net migration rate
Sex ratio
at birth
under 15 years
15-64 years
65 years and over
total population
Infant mortality rate
total
male
female
Life expectancy at birth
total population
male
female

Total fertility rate
HIV/AIDS - adult prevalence rate
HIV/AIDS - people living with HIV/AIDS
HIV/AIDS - deaths
Nationality
noun
adjective
Ethnic groups
Religions
Languages
Literacy
definition
total population
male
female
People - note

Government
Country name
conventional long form
conventional short form
local long form
local short form
former
abbreviation
Dependency status
Government type
Capital
Administrative divisions
Dependent areas
Independence
National holiday
Constitution
Legal system
Suffrage
Executive branch
chief of state
head of government
cabinet
elections
election results
Legislative branch
elections
election results
Judicial branch
Political parties and leaders
Political pressure groups and leaders
International organization participation
Diplomatic representation in the US
chief of mission
chancery
telephone
FAX
consulate(s) general
consulate(s)
Diplomatic representation from the US
chief of mission
embassy
mailing address
telephone
FAX
consulate(s) general
consulate(s)
branch office(s)
Flag description
Government - note

Economy
Economy - overview
GDP
GDP - real growth rate
GDP - per capita
GDP - composition by sector
agriculture
industry
services
Population below poverty line
Household income or consumption by percentage share
lowest 10%
highest 10%
Distribution of family income - Gini index
Inflation rate (consumer prices)
Labor force
Labor force - by occupation
Unemployment rate
Budget
revenues
expenditures
Industries
Industrial production growth rate
Electricity - production
Electricity - production by source
fossil fuel
hydro
nuclear
other
Electricity - consumption
Electricity - exports
Electricity - imports
Oil - production
Oil - consumption
Oil - imports
Oil - exports
Oil - proved reserves
Natural gas - production
Natural gas - consumption
Natural gas - exports
Natural gas - imports
Natural gas - proved reserves
Agriculture - products
Exports
Exports - commodities
Exports - partners
Imports
Imports - commodities
Imports - partners
Debt - external
Economic aid - donor
Economic aid - recipient
Currency
Currency code
Exchange rates
Fiscal year

Communications
Telephones - main lines in use
Telephones - mobile cellular
Telephone system
general assessment
domestic
international
Radio broadcast stations
Television broadcast stations
Internet country code
Internet hosts
Internet users
Communications - note

Transportation
Railways
total
broad gauge
standard gauge
narrow gauge
dual gauge
Highways
total
paved
unpaved
Waterways
Pipelines
Ports and harbors
Merchant marine
total
ships by type
foreign owned
registered in other countries
Airports
Airports - with paved runways
total
over 3,047 m
2,438 to 3047 m
1,524 to 2,427 m
914 to 1,523 m
under 914 m
Airports - with unpaved runways
total
over 3,047 m
2,438 to 3,047 m
1,524 to 2,437 m
914 to 1,523 m
under 914 m
Heliports
Transportation - note

Military
Military branches
Military manpower - military age
Military manpower - availability
males age 15-49
females age 15-49
Military manpower - fit for military service
males age 15-49
females age 15-49
Military manpower - reaching military age annually
males
females
Military expenditures - dollar figure
Military expenditures - percent of GDP
Military - note

Transnational Issues
Disputes - international
Illicit drugs

Afghanistan

Background: Afghanistan's recent history is a story of war and civil unrest. The Soviet Union invaded in 1979, but was forced to withdraw 10 years later by anti-Communist mujahidin forces supplied and trained by the US, Saudi Arabia, Pakistan, and others. The Communist regime in Kabul fought on until collapsing in 1992. Fighting subsequently erupted among the various mujahidin factions, giving rise to a state of warlordism that eventually spawned the Taliban. Backed by foreign sponsors, the Taliban developed as a political force and ultimately seized power in 1996. The Taliban were able to capture most of the country, outside of Northern Alliance strongholds primarily in the northeast. Following the 11 September 2001 terrorist attacks, a US, Allied, and Northern Alliance military action toppled the Taliban. In late 2001, major leaders from the Afghan opposition groups and diaspora met in Bonn, Germany, and agreed on a plan for the formulation of a new government structure that resulted in the inauguration of Hamid KARZAI as Chairman of the Afghan Interim Authority (AIA) on 22 December 2001. The AIA held a nationwide Loya Jirga (Grand Assembly) in June 2002, and KARZAI was elected President by secret ballot of the Transitional Islamic State of Afghanistan (TISA). In December 2002, the TISA marked the one-year anniversary of the fall of the Taliban. The Transitional Authority convened a Constitutional Loya Jirga from 14 December 2003 until 4 January 2004 and ended with the approval of a new constitution. The constitution was signed on 16 January 2004 and highlights a strong executive branch, a moderate role for Islam, and basic protections for human rights. TISA's next task is to hold nationwide elections by June 2004, according to the Bonn Agreement timeline, but these may be delayed due to election preparations. National elections would formally dissolve the Transitional Authority and establish the Government of Afghanistan under the new constitution. In addition to occasionally violent political jockeying and ongoing military action to root out remaining terrorists and Taliban elements, the country suffers from enormous poverty, a lack of skilled and educated workers, a crumbling infrastructure, and widespread land mines.

Location: Southern Asia, north and west of Pakistan, east of Iran
Geographic coordinates: 33 00 N, 65 00 E
Map references: Asia
Area:
total: 647,500 sq km
land: 647,500 sq km
water: 0 sq km
Area - comparative: slightly smaller than Texas
Land boundaries:
total: 5,529 km
border countries: China 76 km, Iran 936 km, Pakistan 2,430 km, Tajikistan 1,206 km, Turkmenistan 744 km, Uzbekistan 137 km
Coastline: 0 km (landlocked)
Maritime claims: none (landlocked)
Climate: arid to semiarid; cold winters and hot summers
Terrain: mostly rugged mountains; plains in north and southwest
Elevation extremes:
lowest point: Amu Darya 258 m
highest point: Nowshak 7,485 m
Natural resources: natural gas, petroleum, coal, copper, chromite, talc, barites, sulfur, lead, zinc, iron ore, salt, precious and semiprecious stones
Land use:
arable land: 12.13%
permanent crops: 0.22%
other: 87.65% (1998 est.)
Irrigated land: 23,860 sq km (1998 est.)
Natural hazards: damaging earthquakes occur in Hindu Kush mountains; flooding; droughts
Environment - current issues: limited natural fresh water resources; inadequate supplies of potable water; soil degradation; overgrazing; deforestation (much of the remaining forests are being cut down for fuel and building materials); desertification; air and water pollution
Environment - international agreements:
party to: Biodiversity, Desertification, Endangered Species, Environmental Modification, Marine Dumping
signed, but not ratified: Climate Change, Hazardous Wastes, Law of the Sea, Marine Life Conservation
Geography - note: landlocked; the Hindu Kush mountains that run northeast to southwest divide the northern provinces from the rest of the country; the highest peaks are in the northern Vakhan (Wakhan Corridor)

Population: 28,513,677 (July 2004 est.)
Age structure:
0-14 years: 44.7% (male 6,525,929; female 6,222,497)
15-64 years: 52.9% (male 7,733,707; female 7,346,226)
65 years and over: 2.4% (male 334,427; female 350,891) (2004 est.)
Median age:
total: 17.5 years
male: 17.5 years
female: 17.6 years (2004 est.)
Population growth rate: 4.92%
note: this rate does not take into consideration the recent war and its continuing impact (2004 est.)
Birth rate: 47.27 births/1,000 population (2004 est.)
Death rate: 21.12 deaths/1,000 population (2004 est.)
Net migration rate: 23.06 migrant(s)/1,000 population (2004 est.)
Sex ratio:
at birth: 1.05 male(s)/female
under 15 years: 1.05 male(s)/female
15-64 years: 1.05 male(s)/female
65 years and over: 0.95 male(s)/female
total population: 1.05 male(s)/female (2004 est.)
Infant mortality rate:
total: 165.96 deaths/1,000 live births
male: 170.85 deaths/1,000 live births
female: 160.82 deaths/1,000 live births (2004 est.)
Life expectancy at birth:
total population: 42.46 years
male: 42.27 years
female: 42.66 years (2004 est.)
Total fertility rate: 6.78 children born/woman (2004 est.)
HIV/AIDS - adult prevalence rate: 0.01% (2001 est.)
HIV/AIDS - people living with HIV/AIDS: NA
HIV/AIDS - deaths: NA
Nationality:
noun: Afghan(s)
adjective: Afghan
Ethnic groups: Pashtun 42%, Tajik 27%, Hazara 9%, Uzbek 9%, Aimak 4%, Turkmen 3%, Baloch 2%, other 4%
Religions: Sunni Muslim 80%, Shi'a Muslim 19%, other 1%
Languages: Pashtu (official) 35%, Afghan Persian (Dari) 50%, Turkic languages (primarily Uzbek and Turkmen) 11%, 30 minor languages (primarily Balochi and Pashai) 4%, much bilingualism
Literacy:
definition: age 15 and over can read and write
total population: 36%
male: 51%
female: 21% (1999 est.)
People - note: of the estimated 4 million refugees in October 2001, 2.3 million have returned

Government

Country name:
conventional long form: Transitional Islamic State of Afghanistan
conventional short form: Afghanistan
local long form: Dowlat-e Eslami-ye Afghanestan
local short form: Afghanestan
former: Republic of Afghanistan
Government type: transitional
Capital: Kabul
Administrative divisions: 32 provinces (velayat, singular - velayat); Badakhshan, Badghis, Baghlan, Balkh, Bamian, Farah, Faryab, Ghazni, Ghowr, Helmand, Herat, Jowzjan, Kabol, Kandahar, Kapisa, Khowst, Konar, Kondoz, Laghman, Lowgar, Nangarhar, Nimruz, Nurestan, Oruzgan, Paktia, Paktika, Parvan, Samangan, Sar-e Pol, Takhar, Vardak, and Zabol
Independence: 19 August 1919 (from UK control over Afghan foreign affairs)
National holiday: Independence Day, 19 August (1919)
Constitution: new constitution drafted 14 December 2003 - 4 January 2004; signed 16 January 2004
Legal system: according to the new constitution, no law is contrary to Islam; the state is obliged to create a prosperous and progressive society based on social justice, protection of human dignity, protection of human rights, realization of democracy, and to ensure national unity and equality among all ethnic groups and tribes; the state shall abide by the UN charter, international treaties, international conventions that Afghanistan signed, and the Universal Declaration of Human Rights
Suffrage: 18 years of age; universal
Executive branch: note: on 10 June 2002, the structure of the second Transitional Authority (TA) was announced when an Emergency Loya Jirga (Grand Assembly) convened establishing the Transitional Islamic State of Afghanistan (TISA); subsequently, a Constitutional Loya Jirga was held and adopted a new constitution; under the new constitution the president is both the chief of state and head of government; the president and two vice presidents are elected by direct vote for a five-year term; if no candidate receives 50% or more of the vote in the first round of voting, the two candidates with the most votes will participate in a second round; a president can only be elected for two terms; former King ZAHIR Shah holds the honorific, "Father of the Country," and presides symbolically over certain occasions, but lacks any governing authority; the honorific is not hereditary
chief of state: President of the TISA, Hamid KARZAI (since 10 June 2002); note - the president is both chief of state and head of government
head of government: President of the TISA, Hamid KARZAI (since 10 June 2002); note - the president is both chief of state and head of government
cabinet: the 30-member TISA; note - under the new constitution, ministers are appointed by the president and approved by the National Assembly

elections: nationwide elections are to be held by June 2004, according to the Bonn Agreement
Legislative branch: nonfunctioning as of January 2004
note: under the new constitution, the bicameral National Assembly consists of the Wolesi Jirga or House of People (no more than 250 seats), directly elected for a five-year term, and the Meshrano Jirga or House of Elders (composed of one representative from each provincial council, one representative from each district council, and a number of presidential appointees; the presidential appointees will include two representatives of Kuchis and two representatives of the disabled; half of the presidential appointees will be women); the Bonn Agreement lays down a June 2004 deadline for elections for the first session of the National Assembly
note: on rare occasions the government may convene the Loya Jirga on issues of independence, national sovereignty, and territorial integrity; it can amend the provisions of the constitution and prosecute the president; it is made up of members of the National Assembly and chairpersons of the provincial and district councils
Judicial branch: the new constitution establishes a nine-member Stera Mahkama or Supreme Court (its nine justices are appointed for 10-year terms by the president with approval of the Wolesi Jirga) and subordinate High Courts and Appeals Courts; there is also a Minister of Justice; a separate Afghan Independent Human Rights Commission established by the Bonn Agreement is charged with investigating human rights abuses and war crimes
Political parties and leaders: NA; note - political parties in Afghanistan are in flux and many prominent players have plans to create new parties; the Transitional Islamic State of Afghanistan (TISA) is headed by President Hamid KARZAI; the TISA is a coalition government formed of leaders from across the Afghan political spectrum; there are also several political factions not holding positions in the Transitional government that are forming new groups and parties in the hopes of participating in the 2004 elections
Political pressure groups and leaders: Jamiat-e Islami (Society of Islam), [former President Burhanuddin RABBANIS]; Jombesh-e Milli (National Islamic Movement), [Abdul Rashjid DOSTUM]; Ittihad-e Islami (Islamic Union for the Liberation of Afghanistan), [Abdul Rasul SAYYAF]; there are also small monarchist, communist, and democratic groups
International organization participation: AsDB, CP, ECO, FAO, G-77, GUUAM, IAEA, IBRD, ICAO, ICCt, ICRM, IDA, IDB, IFAD, IFC, IFRCS, ILO, IMF, Interpol, IOC, IOM (observer), ITU, NAM, OIC, OPCW, OSCE, UN, UNCTAD, UNESCO, UNIDO, UPU, WFTU, WHO, WMO, WToO
Diplomatic representation in the US:
chief of mission: Ambassador Seyyed Tayeb JAWAD
chancery: 2341 Wyoming Avenue NW, Washington, DC 20008
telephone: 202-483-6410

FAX: 202-483-6487
consulate(s) general: New York
Diplomatic representation from the US:
chief of mission: Ambassador Zalmay KHALILZAD; note - embassy in Kabul reopened 16 December 2001, following closure in January 1989
embassy: Great Masood Road, Kabul
mailing address: 6180 Kabul Place, Dulles, VA 20189-6180
telephone: [93] (2) 290002, 290005, 290154
FAX: 00932290153
Flag description: three equal vertical bands of black (hoist), red, and green, with a gold emblem centered on the red band; the emblem features a temple-like structure encircled by a wreath on the left and right and by a bold Islamic inscription above

Economy

Economy - overview: Afghanistan's economic outlook has improved significantly over the past two years because of the infusion of over $2 billion in international assistance, dramatic improvements in agricultural production, and the end of a four-year drought in most of the country. However, Afghanistan remains extremely poor, landlocked, and highly dependent on foreign aid, farming, and trade with neighboring countries. It will probably take the remainder of the decade and continuing donor aid and attention to raise Afghanistan's living standards up from its current status among the lowest in the world. Much of the population continues to suffer from shortages of housing, clean water, electricity, medical care, and jobs, but the Afghan government and international donors remain committed to improving access to these basic necessities by prioritizing infrastructure development, education, housing development, jobs programs, and economic reform over the next year. Growing political stability and continued international commitment to Afghan reconstruction create an optimistic outlook for maintaining improvements to the Afghan economy in 2004. The replacement of the opium trade - which may account for one-third of GDP - is one of several potential spoilers for the economy over the long term.
GDP: purchasing power parity - $20 billion (2003 est.)
GDP - real growth rate: 29% (2003 est.)
note: this high growth rate reflects the extremely low levels of activity between 1999 and 2002, as well as the end of a four-year drought and the impact of donor assistance
GDP - per capita: purchasing power parity - $700 (2003 est.)
GDP - composition by sector:
agriculture: 60%
industry: 20%
services: 20% (1990 est.)
Population below poverty line: 23% (2002)
Household income or consumption by percentage share:
lowest 10%: NA%
highest 10%: NA%

Inflation rate (consumer prices): 5.2% (2003 est.)
Labor force: 11.8 million (2001 est.)
Labor force - by occupation: agriculture 80%, industry 10%, services 10% (1990 est.)
Unemployment rate: NA% (2003)
Budget:
revenues: $200 million
expenditures: $550 million, including capital expenditures of $NA (2003 plan est.)
Industries: small-scale production of textiles, soap, furniture, shoes, fertilizer, cement; handwoven carpets; natural gas, coal, copper
Industrial production growth rate: NA%
Electricity - production: 334.8 million kWh (2001)
Electricity - production by source:
fossil fuel: 36.3%
hydro: 63.7%
nuclear: 0%
other: 0% (2001)
Electricity - consumption: 511.4 million kWh (2001)
Electricity - exports: 0 kWh (2001)
Electricity - imports: 200 million kWh (2001)
Oil - production: 0 bbl/day (2001 est.)
Oil - consumption: 3,500 bbl/day (2001 est.)
Oil - exports: NA
Oil - imports: NA
Oil - proved reserves: 0 bbl (1 January 2002)
Natural gas - production: 220 million cu m (2001 est.)
Natural gas - consumption: 220 million cu m (2001 est.)
Natural gas - exports: 0 cu m (2001 est.)
Natural gas - imports: 0 cu m (2001 est.)
Natural gas - proved reserves: 49.98 billion cu m (1 January 2002)
Agriculture - products: opium, wheat, fruits, nuts, wool, mutton, sheepskins, lambskins
Exports: $98 million (not including illicit exports) (2002 est.)
Exports - commodities: opium, fruits and nuts, handwoven carpets, wool, cotton, hides and pelts, precious and semi-precious gems
Exports - partners: Pakistan 28.6%, India 27.6%, Finland 6.1%, Belgium 5.1%, Germany 5.1%, Russia 4.1%, US 4.1% (2002)
Imports: $1.007 billion (2002 est.)
Imports - commodities: capital goods, food, textiles, petroleum products
Imports - partners: Pakistan 24.3%, South Korea 14%, Japan 9.1%, US 8.7%, Germany 5.7%, Kenya 5.6% (2002)
Debt - external: $8 billion in bilateral debt, mostly to Russia; Afghanistan has $500 million in debt to Multilateral Development Banks (2004)
Economic aid - recipient: international pledges made by more than 60 countries and international financial institutions at the Tokyo Donors Conference for Afghan reconstruction in January 2002 reached $4.5 billion through 2006, with $1.8 billion allocated for 2002; another $1.7 billion was pledged for 2003.

Currency: afghani (AFA)
Currency code: AFA
Exchange rates: afghanis per US dollar - 50 (2003), 50 (2002), 3,000 (2001), 3,000 (2000), 3,000 (1999) note: in 2002, the afghani was revalued and the currency stabilized at about 50 afghanis to the dollar; before 2002, the market rate varied widely from the official rate
Fiscal year: 21 March - 20 March

Communications

Telephones - main lines in use: 33,100 (2002)
Telephones - mobile cellular: 12,000 (2002)
Telephone system:
general assessment: very limited telephone and telegraph service
domestic: telephone service is improving with the establishment of two mobile phone operators by 2003; telephone main lines remain weak with only .1 line per 10 people
international: country code - 93; satellite earth stations - 1 Intelsat (Indian Ocean) linked only to Iran and 1 Intersputnik (Atlantic Ocean region); commercial satellite telephone center in Ghazni
Radio broadcast stations: AM 7 (6 are inactive; the active station is in Kabul), FM 1, shortwave 1 (broadcasts in Pashtu, Afghan Persian (Dari), Urdu, and English) (1999)
Television broadcast stations: at least 10 (one government-run central television station in Kabul and regional stations in nine of the 32 provinces; the regional stations operate on a reduced schedule; also, in 1997, there was a station in Mazar-e Sharif reaching four northern Afghanistan provinces) (1998)
Internet country code: .af
Internet users: 1,000 (2002)
Communications - note: in March 2003 'af' was established as Afghanistan's domain name; Internet access is growing through Internet cafes as well as public "telekiosks" in Kabul that are part of a nationwide network proposed by the Transitional Authority for Internet access (2002)

Transportation

Railways:
total: 24.6 km
broad gauge: 9.6 km 1.524-m gauge from Gushgy (Turkmenistan) to Towraghondi; 15 km 1.524-m gauge from Termiz (Uzbekistan) to Kheyrabad transshipment point on south bank of Amu Darya (2001)
Highways:
total: 21,000 km
paved: 2,793 km
unpaved: 18,207 km (1999 est.)
Waterways: 1,200 km
note: chiefly Amu Darya, which handles vessels up to 500 DWT (2001)
Pipelines: gas 651 km (2003)
Ports and harbors: Kheyrabad, Shir Khan
Airports: 47 (2003 est.)

Airports - with paved runways:
total: 10
over 3,047 m: 3
2,438 to 3,047 m: 4
1,524 to 2,437 m: 2
under 914 m: 1 (2003 est.)
Airports - with unpaved runways:
total: 37
over 3,047 m: 1
2,438 to 3,047 m: 7
1,524 to 2,437 m: 14
914 to 1,523 m: 4
under 914 m: 11 (2003 est.)
Heliports: 5 (2003 est.)

Military

Military branches: Afghan National Army, currently being trained by the US with the assistance of the international community, is 7,000 strong; note - the December 2001 Bonn Agreement called for all militia forces to come under the authority of the central government, but regional leaders have continued to retain their militias and the formation of a national army remains a gradual process; Afghanistan's militia forces continue to be factionalized, largely along ethnic lines
Military manpower - military age: 22 years of age (2004 est.)
Military manpower - availability:
males age 15-49: 6,785,414 (2004 est.)
Military manpower - fit for military service:
males age 15-49: 3,642,659 (2004 est.)
Military manpower - reaching military age annually:
males: 263,406 (2004 est.)
Military expenditures - dollar figure: $61 million (2003)
Military expenditures - percent of GDP: 1% (2003)

Transnational Issues

Disputes - international: despite largely successful UN efforts at voluntary repatriation, thousands of Afghan refugees continue to reside in Iran and Pakistan; Pakistan has sent troops into remote tribal areas to control the border and stem organized terrorist and other illegal cross-border activites; regular meetings between Pakistani and coalition allies aim to resolve periodic claims of boundary encroachments; occasional conflicts over water-sharing arrangements with Amu Darya and Helmand River states
Illicit drugs: world's largest producer of opium; cultivation of opium poppy - used to make heroin - expanded to 30,750 hectares in 2002, despite eradication; potential opium production of 1,278 metric tons; source of hashish; many narcotics-processing labs throughout the country; drug trade source of instability and some government groups profit from the trade; 80-90% of the heroin consumed in Europe comes from Afghan opium; vulnerable to narcotics money laundering through informal financial networks

Albania

Introduction

Background: Between 1990 and 1992 Albania ended 46 years of xenophobic Communist rule and established a multiparty democracy. The transition has proven difficult as successive governments have tried to deal with high unemployment, widespread corruption, a dilapidated infrastructure, powerful organized crime networks with links to high government officials, and disruptive political opponents. International observers judged parliamentary elections in 2001 to be acceptable and a step toward democratic development, but identified serious deficiencies. Some of these were addressed through reforms in the Albanian electoral code prior to the nationwide municipal elections in 2003.

Geography

Location: Southeastern Europe, bordering the Adriatic Sea and Ionian Sea, between Greece and Serbia and Montenegro
Geographic coordinates: 41 00 N, 20 00 E
Map references: Europe
Area:
total: 28,748 sq km
land: 27,398 sq km
water: 1,350 sq km
Area - comparative: slightly smaller than Maryland
Land boundaries:
total: 720 km
border countries: Greece 282 km, The Former Yugoslav Republic of Macedonia 151 km, Serbia and Montenegro 287 km
Coastline: 362 km
Maritime claims:
territorial sea: 12 NM
continental shelf: 200-m depth or to the depth of exploitation
Climate: mild temperate; cool, cloudy, wet winters; hot, clear, dry summers; interior is cooler and wetter

Terrain: mostly mountains and hills; small plains along coast
Elevation extremes:
lowest point: Adriatic Sea 0 m
highest point: Maja e Korabit (Golem Korab) 2,753 m
Natural resources: petroleum, natural gas, coal, chromium, copper, timber, nickel, hydropower
Land use:
arable land: 21.09%
permanent crops: 4.45%
other: 74.46% (1998 est.)
Irrigated land: 3,400 sq km (1998 est.)
Natural hazards: destructive earthquakes; tsunamis occur along southwestern coast; floods; drought
Environment - current issues: deforestation; soil erosion; water pollution from industrial and domestic effluents
Environment - international agreements:
party to: Biodiversity, Climate Change, Desertification, Endangered Species, Hazardous Wastes, Law of the Sea, Ozone Layer Protection, Wetlands
signed, but not ratified: none of the selected agreements
Geography - note: strategic location along Strait of Otranto (links Adriatic Sea to Ionian Sea and Mediterranean Sea)

People

Population: 3,544,808 (July 2004 est.)
Age structure:
0-14 years: 26.4% (male 489,363; female 446,586)
15-64 years: 65.3% (male 1,184,670; female 1,130,065)
65 years and over: 8.3% (male 135,177; female 158,947) (2004 est.)
Median age:
total: 28.2 years
male: 27.6 years
female: 28.7 years (2004 est.)
Population growth rate: 0.51% (2004 est.)
Birth rate: 15.08 births/1,000 population (2004 est.)
Death rate: 5.02 deaths/1,000 population (2004 est.)
Net migration rate: -4.93 migrant(s)/1,000 population (2004 est.)
Sex ratio:
at birth: 1.1 male(s)/female
under 15 years: 1.1 male(s)/female
15-64 years: 1.05 male(s)/female
65 years and over: 0.85 male(s)/female
total population: 1.04 male(s)/female (2004 est.)
Infant mortality rate:
total: 22.31 deaths/1,000 live births
male: 23.01 deaths/1,000 live births
female: 21.54 deaths/1,000 live births (2004 est.)
Life expectancy at birth:
total population: 77.06 years
male: 74.37 years
female: 80.02 years (2004 est.)
Total fertility rate: 2.05 children born/woman (2004 est.)

HIV/AIDS - adult prevalence rate: NA
HIV/AIDS - people living with HIV/AIDS: NA
HIV/AIDS - deaths: NA
Nationality:
noun: Albanian(s)
adjective: Albanian
Ethnic groups: Albanian 95%, Greek 3%, other 2% (Vlach, Roma (Gypsy), Serb, and Macedonian or Bulgarian) (1989 est.)
note: in 1989, other estimates of the Greek population ranged from 1% (official Albanian statistics) to 12% (from a Greek organization)
Religions: Muslim 70%, Albanian Orthodox 20%, Roman Catholic 10%
note: percentages are estimates; there are no available current statistics on religious affiliation; all mosques and churches were closed in 1967 and religious observances prohibited; in November 1990, Albania began allowing private religious practice
Languages: Albanian (official - Tosk is the official dialect), Greek
Literacy:
definition: age 9 and over can read and write
total population: 86.5%
male: 93.3%
female: 79.5% (2003 est.)

Government

Country name:
conventional long form: Republic of Albania
conventional short form: Albania
local long form: Republika e Shqiperise
local short form: Shqiperia
former: People's Socialist Republic of Albania
Government type: emerging democracy
Capital: Tirana
Administrative divisions: 12 counties (qarqe, singular - qark); Qarku i Beratit, Qarku i Dibres, Qarku i Durresit, Qarku i Elbasanit, Qarku i Fierit, Qarku i Gjirokastres, Qarku i Korces, Qarku i Kukesit, Qarku i Lezhes, Qarku i Shkodres, Qarku i Tiranes, Qarku i Vlores
Independence: 28 November 1912 (from Ottoman Empire)
National holiday: Independence Day, 28 November (1912)
Constitution: a constitution was adopted by popular referendum on 28 November 1998
Legal system: has a civil law system; has not accepted compulsory ICJ jurisdiction; has accepted jurisdiction of the International Criminal Court for its citizens
Suffrage: 18 years of age; universal
Executive branch:
chief of state: President of the Republic Alfred MOISIU (since 24 July 2002)
head of government: Prime Minister Fatos NANO (since 31 July 2002)
cabinet: Council of Ministers proposed by the prime minister, nominated by the president, and approved by Parliament

Albania (continued)

elections: president elected by the People's Assembly for a five-year term; election last held 24 June 2002 (next to be held NA June 2007); prime minister appointed by the president

election results: Alfred MOISIU elected president; People's Assembly vote by number - total votes 116, for 97, against 19

Legislative branch: unicameral People's Assembly or Kuvendi Popullor (140 seats; 100 are elected by direct popular vote and 40 by proportional vote for four-year terms)

elections: last held 24 June 2001 with subsequent rounds on 8 July, 22 July, 29 July, 19 August 2001 (next to be held NA June 2005)

election results: percent of vote by party - PS 41.5%, PD and coalition allies 36.8%, NDP 5.2%, PSD 3.6%, PBDNJ 2.6%, PASH (now PAA) 2.6%, PAD 2.5%; seats by party - PS 73, PD and coalition allies 46, NDP 6, PSD 4, PBDNJ 3, PASH (now PAA) 3, PAD 3, independents 2

Judicial branch: Constitutional Court, Supreme Court (chairman is elected by the People's Assembly for a four-year term), and multiple appeals and district courts

Political parties and leaders: Environmentalist Agrarian Party or PAA [Lufter XHUVELI]; Christian Democratic Party or PDK [Nikolle LESI]; Communist Party of Albania or PKSH [Hysni MILLOSHI]; Democratic Alliance Party or PAD [Neritan CEKA]; Democratic Alliance Party II or PAD II [Arben IMAMI]; Democratic Party or PD [Sali BERISHA]; Legality Movement Party or PLL [Ekrem SPAHIU]; Liberal Democratic Union Party or PBLD [Teodor LACO]; National Front Party (Balli Kombetar) or PBK [Shpetim RROQI]; New Democratic Party or PDR [Genc POLLO]; Party of National Unity or PUK [Idajet BEQIRI]; Reformed Democratic Party or PDR [Dashamir SHEHI]; Republican Party or PR [Fatmir MEDIU]; Social Democracy Party or PDS [Paskal MILO]; Social Democratic Party or PSD [Skender GJINUSHI]; Socialist Party or PS (formerly the Albanian Party of Labor) [Fatos NANO]; Union for Human Rights Party or PBDNJ [Vangjel DULE]

note: the New (of Reformed) Democratic Party split into two groups - one led by Genc POLLO, the other by Dashamir SHEHI

Political pressure groups and leaders: Confederation of Trade Unions of Albania or KSSH [Kastriot MUCO]; Front for Albanian National Unification or FBKSH [Gafur ADILI]; Omonia [Jani JANI]; Union of Independent Trade Unions of Albania or BSPSH [Gezim KALAJA]

International organization participation: ACCT, BSEC, CE, CEI, EAPC, EBRD, FAO, IAEA, IBRD, ICAO, ICCt, ICFTU, ICRM, IDA, IDB, IFAD, IFC, IFRCS, ILO, IMF, IMO, Interpol, IOC, IOM, ISO (correspondent), ITU, OIC, OPCW, OSCE, PFP, UN, UNCTAD, UNESCO, UNIDO, UNOMIG, UPU, WCO, WFTU, WHO, WIPO, WMO, WToO, WTrO

Diplomatic representation in the US:
chief of mission: Ambassador Dr. Fatos TARIFA
chancery: 2100 S Street NW, Washington, DC 20008

telephone: [1] (202) 223-4942
FAX: [1] (202) 628-7342

Diplomatic representation from the US:
chief of mission: Ambassador James F. JEFFREY
embassy: Rruga Elbasanit, Labinoti #103, Tirana
mailing address: U. S. Department of State, 9510 Tirana Place, Dulles, VA 20189-9510
telephone: [355] (4) 247285
FAX: [355] (4) 232222

Flag description: red with a black two-headed eagle in the center

Economy

Economy - overview: Poor and backward by European standards, Albania is making the difficult transition to a more modern open-market economy. The government has taken measures to curb violent crime and to spur economic activity and trade. The economy is bolstered by remittances from abroad of $400-$600 million annually, mostly from Greece and Italy; this helps offset the sizable trade deficit. Agriculture, which accounts for one-half of GDP, is held back because of frequent drought and the need to modernize equipment and consolidate small plots of land. Severe energy shortages and antiquated and inadequate infrastructure make it difficult to attract and sustain foreign investment. The government plans to boost energy imports to relieve the shortages and is moving slowly to improve the poor national road and rail network, a long-standing barrier to sustained economic growth.

GDP: purchasing power parity - $16.13 billion (2003 est.)

GDP - real growth rate: 7% (2003 est.)

GDP - per capita: purchasing power parity - $4,500 (2003 est.)

GDP - composition by sector:
agriculture: 49%
industry: 27%
services: 24% (2002 est.)

Population below poverty line: 30% (2001 est.)

Household income or consumption by percentage share:
lowest 10%: NA%
highest 10%: NA%

Inflation rate (consumer prices): 3.3% (2003)

Labor force: 1.35 million (not including 352,000 emigrant workers) (2003 est.)

Labor force - by occupation: agriculture 57%, non-agricultural private sector 20%, public sector 23% (2003 est.)

Unemployment rate: 15.8% officially; may be as high as 30% (2003 est.)

Budget:
revenues: $1.65 billion
expenditures: $2 billion, including capital expenditures of $406 million (2004 est.)

Industries: food processing, textiles and clothing; lumber, oil, cement, chemicals, mining, basic metals, hydropower

Industrial production growth rate: 2.7% (2003 est.)

Electricity - production: 5.289 billion kWh (2001)

Electricity - production by source:
fossil fuel: 2.9%
hydro: 97.1%
nuclear: 0%
other: 0% (2001)

Electricity - consumption: 5.898 billion kWh (2001)

Electricity - exports: 221 million kWh (2001)

Electricity - imports: 1.2 billion kWh (2001)

Oil - production: 5,952 bbl/day (2001 est.)

Oil - consumption: 22,400 bbl/day (2001 est.)

Oil - exports: NA

Oil - imports: NA

Oil - proved reserves: 185.5 million bbl (1 January 2002)

Natural gas - production: 30 million cu m (2001 est.)

Natural gas - consumption: 30 million cu m (2001 est.)

Natural gas - exports: 0 cu m (2001 est.)

Natural gas - imports: 0 cu m (2001 est.)

Natural gas - proved reserves: 3.316 billion cu m (1 January 2002)

Agriculture - products: wheat, corn, potatoes, vegetables, fruits, sugar beets, grapes; meat, dairy products

Exports: $425 million f.o.b. (2003 est.)

Exports - commodities: textiles and footwear; asphalt, metals and metallic ores, crude oil; vegetables, fruits, tobacco

Exports - partners: Italy 71.5%, Greece 12.7%, Germany 5.5% (2002)

Imports: $1.76 billion f.o.b. (2003 est.)

Imports - commodities: machinery and equipment, foodstuffs, textiles, chemicals

Imports - partners: Italy 34.6%, Greece 21.7%, Turkey 6.1%, Germany 5.6% (2002)

Debt - external: $1.41 billion (2003)

Economic aid - recipient: ODA: $315 million (top donors were Italy, EU, Germany) (2000 est.)

Currency: lek (ALL)

Currency code: ALL

Exchange rates: leke per US dollar - 121.863 (2003), 140.155 (2002), 143.485 (2001), 143.709 (2000), 137.691 (1999)

Fiscal year: calendar year

Communications

Telephones - main lines in use: 240,000 (2003)

Telephones - mobile cellular: 851,000 (2002)

Telephone system:
general assessment: Despite new investment in fixed lines, the density of main lines remains the lowest in Europe with roughly 8 lines per 100 people. However, cellular telephone use is widespread and generally effective.
domestic: offsetting the shortage of fixed line capacity, mobile phone service has been available since 1996; by 2003 two companies were providing mobile services at a greater density than some of Albania's Balkan neighbors

international: country code - 355; inadequate fixed main lines; adequate cellular connections; international traffic carried by microwave radio relay from the Tirana exchange to Italy and Greece (2003)

Radio broadcast stations: AM 13, FM 4, shortwave 2 (2001)

Television broadcast stations: 3 (plus 58 repeaters) (2001)

Internet country code: .al

Internet hosts: 172 (2002)

Internet users: 17,000 (2003)

Transportation

Railways:

total: 447 km

standard gauge: 447 km 1.435-m gauge (2002)

Highways:

total: 18,000 km

paved: 5,400 km

unpaved: 12,600 km (2000)

Waterways: 43 km

note: includes Albanian sections of Lake Scutari, Lake Ohrid, and Lake Prespa (1990)

Pipelines: gas 339 km; oil 207 km (2003)

Ports and harbors: Durres, Sarande, Shengjin, Vlore

Merchant marine:

total: 22 ships (1,000 GRT or over) 40,878 GRT/ 62,676 DWT

by type: bulk 1, cargo 19, petroleum tanker 1, roll on/ roll off 1

foreign-owned: Denmark 1, Honduras 1, Netherlands 1

registered in other countries: 7 (2003 est.)

Airports: 11 (2003 est.)

Airports - with paved runways:

total: 3

2,438 to 3,047 m: 3 (2003 est.)

Airports - with unpaved runways:

total: 8

over 3,047 m: 1

1,524 to 2,437 m: 1

914 to 1,523 m: 2

under 914 m: 4 (2003 est.)

Heliports: 1 (2003 est.)

Military

Military branches: General Staff Headquarters, Land Forces Command (Army), Naval Forces Command, Air Forces Command, Doctrine and Exercises Command, Logistics Support Command

Military manpower - military age: 19 years of age (2004 est.)

Military manpower - availability:

males age 15-49: 956,107 (2004 est.)

Military manpower - fit for military service:

males age 15-49: 775,422 (2004 est.)

Military manpower - reaching military age annually:

males: 36,584 (2004 est.)

Military expenditures - dollar figure: $56.5 million (FY02)

Military expenditures - percent of GDP: 1.49% (FY02)

Transnational Issues

Disputes - international: the Albanian Government calls for the protection of the rights of ethnic Albanians in neighboring countries, and the peaceful resolution of interethnic disputes; some ethnic Albanian groups in neighboring countries advocate for a "greater Albania," but the idea has little appeal among Albanian nationals

Illicit drugs: increasingly active transshipment point for Southwest Asian opiates, hashish, and cannabis transiting the Balkan route and - to a far lesser extent - cocaine from South America destined for Western Europe; limited opium and growing cannabis production; ethnic Albanian narcotrafficking organizations active and rapidly expanding in Europe; vulnerable to money laundering associated with regional trafficking in narcotics, arms, contraband, and illegal aliens

Algeria

Introduction

Background: After a century of rule by France, and in the wake of 1948 elections rigged by French colonists to reverse the sweeping victory of a Muslim political party in 1947, Algerians fought through the 1950s to achieve independence in 1962. Algeria's primary political party, the National Liberation Front (FLN), has dominated politics ever since. Many Algerians in the subsequent generation were not satisfied, however, and moved to counter the FLN's centrality in Algerian politics. The surprising first round success of the fundamentalist Islamic Salvation Front (FIS) in the December 1991 balloting spurred the army to intervene and postpone the second round of elections to prevent an extremist-led government from assuming power. The Algerian army began a crack down on the FIS, that resulted in a continuous low-grade civil conflict between Islamic activists and the secular state apparatus. The government later allowed elections featuring pro-government and moderate religiously-based parties, but did not appease the activists who progressively widened their attacks. Operations by the activists and the army resulted in nearly 100,000 deaths during the decade-long conflict. The government gained the uppper hand by the mid-1990s and FIS's armed wing, the Islamic Salvation Army, disbanded in January 2000. Many armed militants of other groups surrendered under an amnesty program designed to promote national reconciliation, but small numbers of armed militants persist in confronting government forces and conducting ambushes and occasional attacks on villages. Issues facing the winner of the April 2004 presidential election include Berber unrest, large-scale unemployment, a shortage of housing, the presence of a group in the southern regions of the country that kidnapped European tourists in 2003, as well as the need to diversify Algeria's petroleum-based economy. Algeria assumed a two-year seat on the UN Security Council in January 2004.

Algeria *(continued)*

Geography

Location: Northern Africa, bordering the Mediterranean Sea, between Morocco and Tunisia

Geographic coordinates: 28 00 N, 3 00 E

Map references: Africa

Area:
total: 2,381,740 sq km
land: 2,381,740 sq km
water: 0 sq km

Area - comparative: slightly less than 3.5 times the size of Texas

Land boundaries:
total: 6,343 km
border countries: Libya 982 km, Mali 1,376 km, Mauritania 463 km, Morocco 1,559 km, Niger 956 km, Tunisia 965 km, Western Sahara 42 km

Coastline: 998 km

Maritime claims:
territorial sea: 12 NM
exclusive fishing zone: 32-52 NM

Climate: arid to semiarid; mild, wet winters with hot, dry summers along coast; drier with cold winters and hot summers on high plateau; sirocco is a hot, dust/sand-laden wind especially common in summer

Terrain: mostly high plateau and desert; some mountains; narrow, discontinuous coastal plain

Elevation extremes:
lowest point: Chott Melrhir -40 m
highest point: Tahat 3,003 m

Natural resources: petroleum, natural gas, iron ore, phosphates, uranium, lead, zinc

Land use:
arable land: 3.21%
permanent crops: 0.21%
other: 96.58% (1998 est.)

Irrigated land: 5,600 sq km (1998 est.)

Natural hazards: mountainous areas subject to severe earthquakes; mudslides and floods in rainy season

Environment - current issues: soil erosion from overgrazing and other poor farming practices; desertification; dumping of raw sewage, petroleum refining wastes, and other industrial effluents is leading to the pollution of rivers and coastal waters; Mediterranean Sea, in particular, becoming polluted from oil wastes, soil erosion, and fertilizer runoff; inadequate supplies of potable water

Environment - international agreements:
party to: Biodiversity, Climate Change, Desertification, Endangered Species, Environmental Modification, Hazardous Wastes, Law of the Sea, Ozone Layer Protection, Ship Pollution, Wetlands
signed, but not ratified: none of the selected agreements

Geography - note: second-largest country in Africa (after Sudan)

People

Population: 32,129,324 (July 2004 est.)

Age structure:
0-14 years: 29.9% (male 4,893,971; female 4,705,933)
15-64 years: 65.5% (male 10,593,840; female 10,443,300)
65 years and over: 4.6% (male 703,420; female 788,860) (2004 est.)

Median age:
total: 23.8 years
male: 23.7 years
female: 24 years (2004 est.)

Population growth rate: 1.28% (2004 est.)

Birth rate: 17.76 births/1,000 population (2004 est.)

Death rate: 4.61 deaths/1,000 population (2004 est.)

Net migration rate: -0.39 migrant(s)/1,000 population (2004 est.)

Sex ratio:
at birth: 1.05 male(s)/female
under 15 years: 1.04 male(s)/female
15-64 years: 1.01 male(s)/female
65 years and over: 0.89 male(s)/female
total population: 1.02 male(s)/female (2004 est.)

Infant mortality rate:
total: 32.16 deaths/1,000 live births
male: 36.06 deaths/1,000 live births
female: 28.06 deaths/1,000 live births (2004 est.)

Life expectancy at birth:
total population: 72.74 years
male: 71.22 years
female: 74.34 years (2004 est.)

Total fertility rate: 2.04 children born/woman (2004 est.)

HIV/AIDS - adult prevalence rate: 0.1% note - no country specific models provided (2001 est.)

HIV/AIDS - people living with HIV/AIDS: NA

HIV/AIDS - deaths: NA

Nationality:
noun: Algerian(s)
adjective: Algerian

Ethnic groups: Arab-Berber 99%, European less than 1%
note: almost all Algerians are Berber in origin, not Arab; the minority who identify themselves as Berber live mostly in the mountainous region of Kabylie east of Algeirs; the Berbers are also Muslim but identify with their Berber rather than Arab cultural heritage; Berbers have long agitated, sometimes violently, for autonomy; the government is unlikely to grant autonomy but has offered to begin sponsoring teaching Berber language in schools

Religions: Sunni Muslim (state religion) 99%, Christian and Jewish 1%

Languages: Arabic (official), French, Berber dialects

Literacy:
definition: age 15 and over can read and write
total population: 70%
male: 78.8%
female: 61% (2003 est.)

Government

Country name:
conventional long form: People's Democratic Republic of Algeria
conventional short form: Algeria
local long form: Al Jumhuriyah al Jaza'iriyah ad Dimuqratiyah ash Sha'biyah
local short form: Al Jaza'ir

Government type: republic

Capital: Algiers

Administrative divisions: 48 provinces (wilayas, singular - wilaya); Adrar, Ain Defla, Ain Temouchent, Alger, Annaba, Batna, Bechar, Bejaia, Biskra, Blida, Bordj Bou Arreridj, Bouira, Boumerdes, Chlef, Constantine, Djelfa, El Bayadh, El Oued, El Tarf, Ghardaia, Guelma, Illizi, Jijel, Khenchela, Laghouat, Mascara, Medea, Mila, Mostaganem, M'Sila, Naama, Oran, Ouargla, Oum el Bouaghi, Relizane, Saida, Setif, Sidi Bel Abbes, Skikda, Souk Ahras, Tamanghasset, Tebessa, Tiaret, Tindouf, Tipaza, Tissemsilt, Tizi Ouzou, Tlemcen

Independence: 5 July 1962 (from France)

National holiday: Revolution Day, 1 November (1954)

Constitution: 19 November 1976, effective 22 November 1976; revised 3 November 1988, 23 February 1989, and 28 November 1996

Legal system: socialist, based on French and Islamic law; judicial review of legislative acts in ad hoc Constitutional Council composed of various public officials, including several Supreme Court justices; has not accepted compulsory ICJ jurisdiction

Suffrage: 18 years of age; universal

Executive branch:
chief of state: President Abdelaziz BOUTEFLIKA (since 28 April 1999)
head of government: Prime Minister Ahmed OUYAHIA (since 9 May 2003)
cabinet: Cabinet of Ministers appointed by the president
elections: president elected by popular vote for a five-year term; election last held 15 April 1999 (next to be held NA April 2004); prime minister appointed by the president
election results: Abdelaziz BOUTEFLIKA elected president; percent of vote - Abdelaziz BOUTEFLIKA over 70%; note - his six opposing candidates withdrew on the eve of the election citing electoral fraud

Legislative branch: bicameral Parliament consists of the National People's Assembly or Al-Majlis Ech-Chaabi Al-Watani (389 seats - changed from 380 seats in the 2002 elections; members elected by popular vote to serve five-year terms) and the Council of Nations (Senate) (144 seats; one-third of the members appointed by the president, two-thirds elected by indirect vote; members serve six-year terms; the constitution requires half the council to be renewed every three years)
elections: National People's Assembly - last held 30 May 2002 (next to be held NA 2007); Council of Nations (Senate) - last held 30 December 2003 (next to be held NA 2009)

Algeria *(continued)*

election results: National People's Assembly - percent of vote by party - NA%; seats by party - FLN 199, RND 48, Islah 43, MSP 38, PT 21, FNA 8, EnNahda 1, PRA 1, MEN 1, independents 29; Council of Nations - percent of vote by party - NA%; seats by party NA%

Judicial branch: Supreme Court or Court Supreme

Political parties and leaders: Algerian National Front or FNA [Moussa TOUATI]; Democratic National Rally or RND [Ahmed OUYAHIA, chairman]; Islamic Salvation Front or FIS (outlawed April 1992) [Ali BELHADJ and Dr. Abassi MADANI, Rabeh KEBIR (self-exiled in Germany)]; Society of Peace Movement or MSP [Boujerra SOLTANI]; National Entente Movement or MEN [Ali BOUKHAZNA]; National Liberation Front or FLN [Ali BENFLIS, secretary general]; National Reform Movement or Islah (formerly MRN) [Abdellah DJABALLAH]; National Renewal Party or PRA [Yacine TERKMANE]; Progressive Republican Party [Khadir DRISS]; Rally for Culture and Democracy or RCD [Said SAADI, secretary general]; Renaissance Movement or EnNahda Movement [Fatah RABEI]; Social Liberal Party or PSL [Ahmed KHELIL]; Socialist Forces Front or FFS [Hocine Ait AHMED, secretary general (self-exiled in Switzerland)]; Workers Party or PT [Louisa HANOUN]

note: a law banning political parties based on religion was enacted in March 1997

Political pressure groups and leaders: NA

International organization participation: ABEDA, AfDB, AFESD, AMF, AMU, AU, BIS, FAO, G-15, G-24, G-77, IAEA, IBRD, ICAO, ICC, ICCt (signatory), ICFTU, ICRM, IDA, IDB, IFAD, IFC, IFRCS, IHO, ILO, IMF, IMO, Interpol, IOC, IOM, ISO, ITU, LAS, MONUC, NAM, OAPEC, OAS (observer), OIC, OPCW, OPEC, OSCE (partner), UN, UN Security Council (temporary), UNCTAD, UNESCO, UNHCR, UNIDO, UNMEE, UPU, WCO, WHO, WIPO, WMO, WToO, WTrO (observer)

Diplomatic representation in the US:
chief of mission: Ambassador Idriss JAZAIRY
chancery: 2137 Wyoming Ave NW, Washington, DC 20008
telephone: [1] (202) 265-2800
FAX: [1] (202) 667-2174

Diplomatic representation from the US:
chief of mission: Ambassador Richard W. ERDMAN (as of 10 July 2003)
embassy: 4 Chemin Cheikh Bachir El-Ibrahimi, Algiers
mailing address: B. P. Box 549, Alger-Gare, 16000 Algiers
telephone: [213] (21) 691-425/255/186
FAX: [213] (21) 69-39-79

Flag description: two equal vertical bands of green (hoist side) and white; a red, five-pointed star within a red crescent centered over the two-color boundary; the crescent, star, and color green are traditional symbols of Islam (the state religion)

Economy

Economy - overview: The hydrocarbons sector is the backbone of the economy, accounting for roughly 60% of budget revenues, 30% of GDP, and over 95% of export earnings. Algeria has the seventh-largest reserves of natural gas in the world and is the second-largest gas exporter; it ranks 14th in oil reserves. Economic policy reforms supported by the IMF and debt rescheduling from the Paris Club in the past decade have helped improve Algeria's financial and macroeconomic indicators. Because of sustained high oil prices in the past three years, Algeria's finances have further benefited from substantial trade surpluses and record foreign exchange reserves. Real GDP has risen due to higher oil output and increased government spending. The government's continued efforts to diversify the economy by attracting foreign and domestic investment outside the energy sector, however, has had little success in reducing high unemployment and improving living standards. Structural reform within the economy moves ahead slowly.

GDP: purchasing power parity - $194.3 billion (2003 est.)

GDP - real growth rate: 7.3% (2003 est.)

GDP - per capita: purchasing power parity - $5,900 (2003 est.)

GDP - composition by sector:
agriculture: 10.2%
industry: 56.6%
services: 33.2% (2003)

Population below poverty line: 23% (1999 est.)

Household income or consumption by percentage share:
lowest 10%: 2.8%
highest 10%: 26.8% (1995)

Distribution of family income - Gini index: 35.3 (1995)

Inflation rate (consumer prices): 3.1% (2003 est.)

Labor force: 9.5 million (2003)

Labor force - by occupation: government 32%, agriculture 14%, construction and public works 10%, industry 13.4%, trade 16%, other 14.6% (2002 est.)

Unemployment rate: 28.4% (2003 est.)

Budget:
revenues: $18.5 billion
expenditures: $22.7 billion, including capital expenditures of $5.8 billion (2003 est.)

Industries: petroleum, natural gas, light industries, mining, electrical, petrochemical, food processing

Industrial production growth rate: 8% (2003 est.)

Electricity - production: 24.69 billion kWh (2001)

Electricity - production by source:
fossil fuel: 99.7%
hydro: 0.3%
nuclear: 0%
other: 0% (2001)

Electricity - consumption: 22.9 billion kWh (2001)

Electricity - exports: 340 million kWh (2001)

Electricity - imports: 275 million kWh (2001)

Oil - production: 1.52 million bbl/day (2001 est.)

Oil - consumption: 209,000 bbl/day (2001 est.)

Oil - exports: NA

Oil - imports: NA

Oil - proved reserves: 13.1 billion bbl (1 January 2002)

Natural gas - production: 80.3 billion cu m (2001 est.)

Natural gas - consumption: 22.32 billion cu m (2001 est.)

Natural gas - exports: 57.98 billion cu m (2001 est.)

Natural gas - imports: 0 cu m (2001 est.)

Natural gas - proved reserves: 4.739 trillion cu m (1 January 2002)

Agriculture - products: wheat, barley, oats, grapes, olives, citrus, fruits; sheep, cattle

Exports: $24.96 billion f.o.b. (2003 est.)

Exports - commodities: petroleum, natural gas, and petroleum products 97%

Exports - partners: Italy 20.1%, US 14.2%, France 13.6%, Spain 12.1%, Netherlands 9%, Turkey 5.1%, Canada 5%, Brazil 4.8% (2002)

Imports: $12.42 billion f.o.b. (2003 est.)

Imports - commodities: capital goods, foodstuffs, consumer goods

Imports - partners: France 22.7%, US 9.8%, Italy 9.6%, Germany 7.2%, Spain 5.3% (2002)

Debt - external: $22 billion (2003 est.)

Economic aid - recipient: $182 million (2001 est.)

Currency: Algerian dinar (DZD)

Currency code: DZD

Exchange rates: Algerian dinars per US dollar - 77.395 (2003), 79.6819 (2002), 77.215 (2001), 75.2598 (2000), 66.5739 (1999)

Fiscal year: calendar year

Communications

Telephones - main lines in use: 2.2 million (2003)

Telephones - mobile cellular: 1,447,310 (2003)

Telephone system:
general assessment: telephone density in Algeria is very low, not exceeding five telephones per 100 persons; the number of fixed main lines increased in the last few years to a little more than 2,000,000, but only about two-thirds of these have subscribers; much of the infrastructure is outdated and inefficient
domestic: good service in north but sparse in south; domestic satellite system with 12 earth stations (20 additional domestic earth stations are planned)
international: country code - 213; 5 submarine cables; microwave radio relay to Italy, France, Spain, Morocco, and Tunisia; coaxial cable to Morocco and Tunisia; participant in Medarabtel; satellite earth stations - 2 Intelsat (1 Atlantic Ocean and 1 Indian Ocean), 1 Intersputnik, and 1 Arabsat (1998)

Radio broadcast stations: AM 25, FM 1, shortwave 8 (1999)

Television broadcast stations: 46 (plus 216 repeaters) (1995)

Algeria *(continued)*

Internet country code: .dz
Internet hosts: 821 (2002)
Internet users: 500,000 (2002)

Transportation

Railways:
total: 3,973 km
standard gauge: 2,888 km 1.435-m gauge (283 km electrified)
narrow gauge: 1,085 km 1.055-m gauge (2002)
Highways:
total: 104,000 km
paved: 71,656 km (including 640 km of expressways)
unpaved: 32,344 km (1999)
Waterways: none
Pipelines: condensate 1,344 km; gas 87,347 km; liquid petroleum gas 2,213 km; oil 6,496 km (2003)
Ports and harbors: Algiers, Annaba, Arzew, Bejaia, Beni Saf, Dellys, Djendjene, Ghazaouet, Jijel, Mostaganem, Oran, Skikda, Tenes
Merchant marine:
total: 59 ships (1,000 GRT or over) 837,676 GRT/ 929,847 DWT
by type: bulk 9, cargo 16, chemical tanker 6, liquefied gas 10, petroleum tanker 4, roll on/roll off 9, short-sea/ passenger 4, specialized tanker 1
foreign-owned: United Kingdom 4
registered in other countries: 4 (2003 est.)
Airports: 137 (2003 est.)
Airports - with paved runways:
total: 53
over 3,047 m: 10
2,438 to 3,047 m: 27
1,524 to 2,437 m: 10
914 to 1,523 m: 5
under 914 m: 1 (2003 est.)
Airports - with unpaved runways:
total: 84
2,438 to 3,047 m: 2
1,524 to 2,437 m: 25
914 to 1,523 m: 38
under 914 m: 19 (2003 est.)
Heliports: 1 (2003 est.)

Military

Military branches: People's National Army (ANP; includes Ground Forces), Algerian National Navy (ANN), Air Force (QJA), Territorial Air Defense
Military manpower - military age: 19 years of age (2004 est.)
Military manpower - availability:
males age 15-49: 9,311,747 (2004 est.)
Military manpower - fit for military service:
males age 15-49: 5,675,739 (2004 est.)
Military manpower - reaching military age annually:
males: 373,235 (2004 est.)
Military expenditures - dollar figure:
$2,196,600,000 (2003)
Military expenditures - percent of GDP: 3.5% (2003)

Transnational Issues

Disputes - international: Libya claims about 32,000 sq km in a dormant dispute still reflected on its maps in southeastern Algeria; Algeria remains concerned about armed bandits operating throughout the Sahel who destabilize southern Algerian towns; border with Morocco remains closed over mutual claims of harboring militants, arms smuggling; Algeria supports the exiled Sahrawi Polisario Front and rejects Moroccan administration of Western Sahara; Algerian FLN asserts claim to Chirac Pastures in southeastern Morocco

American Samoa
(territory of the US)

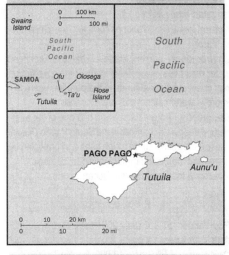

Introduction

Background: Settled as early as 1000 B.C., Samoa was "discovered" by European explorers in the 18th century. International rivalries in the latter half of the 19th century were settled by an 1899 treaty in which Germany and the US divided the Samoan archipelago. The US formally occupied its portion - a smaller group of eastern islands with the excellent harbor of Pago Pago - the following year.

Geography

Location: Oceania, group of islands in the South Pacific Ocean, about half way between Hawaii and New Zealand
Geographic coordinates: 14 20 S, 170 00 W
Map references: Oceania
Area:
total: 199 sq km
land: 199 sq km
water: 0 sq km
note: includes Rose Island and Swains Island
Area - comparative: slightly larger than Washington, DC
Land boundaries: 0 km
Coastline: 116 km
Maritime claims:
territorial sea: 12 NM
exclusive economic zone: 200 NM
Climate: tropical marine, moderated by southeast trade winds; annual rainfall averages about 3 m; rainy season from November to April, dry season from May to October; little seasonal temperature variation
Terrain: five volcanic islands with rugged peaks and limited coastal plains, two coral atolls (Rose Island, Swains Island)
Elevation extremes:
lowest point: Pacific Ocean 0 m
highest point: Lata 966 m
Natural resources: pumice, pumicite

Land use:
arable land: 5%
permanent crops: 10%
other: 85% (1998 est.)
Irrigated land: NA sq km
Natural hazards: typhoons common from December to March
Environment - current issues: limited natural fresh water resources; the water division of the government has spent substantial funds in the past few years to improve water catchments and pipelines
Geography - note: Pago Pago has one of the best natural deepwater harbors in the South Pacific Ocean, sheltered by shape from rough seas and protected by peripheral mountains from high winds; strategic location in the South Pacific Ocean

People

Population: 57,902 (July 2004 est.)
Age structure:
0-14 years: 36.6% (male 10,983; female 10,208)
15-64 years: 60.3% (male 18,010; female 16,933)
65 years and over: 3.1% (male 699; female 1,069) (2004 est.)
Median age:
total: 22.4 years
male: 22.1 years
female: 22.7 years (2004 est.)
Population growth rate: 0.04% (2004 est.)
Birth rate: 24.46 births/1,000 population (2004 est.)
Death rate: 3.39 deaths/1,000 population (2004 est.)
Net migration rate: -20.71 migrant(s)/1,000 population (2004 est.)
Sex ratio:
at birth: 1.06 male(s)/female
under 15 years: 1.08 male(s)/female
15-64 years: 1.06 male(s)/female
65 years and over: 0.65 male(s)/female
total population: 1.05 male(s)/female (2004 est.)
Infant mortality rate:
total: 9.48 deaths/1,000 live births
male: 10.06 deaths/1,000 live births
female: 8.86 deaths/1,000 live births (2004 est.)
Life expectancy at birth:
total population: 75.62 years
male: 72.05 years
female: 79.41 years (2004 est.)
Total fertility rate: 3.41 children born/woman (2004 est.)
HIV/AIDS - adult prevalence rate: NA%
HIV/AIDS - people living with HIV/AIDS: NA
HIV/AIDS - deaths: NA
Nationality:
noun: American Samoan(s)
adjective: American Samoan
Ethnic groups: Samoan (Polynesian) 89%, Caucasian 2%, Tongan 4%, other 5%
Religions: Christian Congregationalist 50%, Roman Catholic 20%, Protestant and other 30%
Languages: Samoan (closely related to Hawaiian and other Polynesian languages), English
note: most people are bilingual

Literacy:
definition: age 15 and over can read and write
total population: 97%
male: 98%
female: 97% (1980 est.)

Government

Country name:
conventional long form: Territory of American Samoa
conventional short form: American Samoa
abbreviation: AS
Dependency status: unincorporated and unorganized territory of the US; administered by the Office of Insular Affairs, US Department of the Interior
Government type: NA
Capital: Pago Pago
Administrative divisions: none (territory of the US); there are no first-order administrative divisions as defined by the US Government, but there are three districts and two islands* at the second order; Eastern, Manu'a, Rose Island*, Swains Island*, Western
Independence: none (territory of the US)
National holiday: Flag Day, 17 April (1900)
Constitution: ratified 1966, in effect 1967
Legal system: NA
Suffrage: 18 years of age; universal
Executive branch:
chief of state: President George W. BUSH of the US (since 20 January 2001) and Vice President Richard B. CHENEY (since 20 January 2001)
head of government: Governor Togiola TULAFONO (since 7 April 2003) following the death of Governor Tauese P. SUNIA on 26 March 2003; TULAFONO had been the Lieutenant Governor
cabinet: NA
elections: US president and vice president elected on the same ticket for four-year terms; governor and lieutenant governor elected on the same ticket by popular vote for four-year terms; election last held 7 November 2000 (next to be held 2 November 2004)
election results: Tauese P. SUNIA reelected governor; percent of vote - Tauese P. SUNIA (Democrat) 50.7%, Lealaifuaneva Peter REID (independent) 47.8%
note: Togiola TULAFONO became acting governor 26 March 2003 upon the death of Governor Tauese P. SUNIA
Legislative branch: bicameral Fono or Legislative Assembly consists of the House of Representatives (21 seats - 20 of which are elected by popular vote and 1 is an appointed, nonvoting delegate from Swains Island; members serve two-year terms) and the Senate (18 seats; members are elected from local chiefs and serve four-year terms)
elections: House of Representatives - last held 7 November 2002 (next to be held 2 November 2004); Senate - last held 7 November 2000 (next to be held 2 November 2004)
election results: House of Representatives - percent of vote by party - NA%; seats by party - NA; Senate - percent of vote by party - NA%; seats by party - independents 18

note: American Samoa elects one nonvoting representative to the US House of Representatives; election last held 7 November 2002 (next to be held 2 November 2004); results - Eni F. H. FALEOMAVAEGA (Democrat) reelected as delegate
Judicial branch: High Court (chief justice and associate justices are appointed by the US Secretary of the Interior)
Political parties and leaders: Democratic Party [leader NA]; Republican Party [leader NA]
Political pressure groups and leaders: NA
International organization participation: Interpol (subbureau), IOC
Diplomatic representation in the US: none (territory of the US)
Diplomatic representation from the US: none (territory of the US)
Flag description: blue, with a white triangle edged in red that is based on the outer side and extends to the hoist side; a brown and white American bald eagle flying toward the hoist side is carrying two traditional Samoan symbols of authority, a staff and a war club

Economy

Economy - overview: This is a traditional Polynesian economy in which more than 90% of the land is communally owned. Economic activity is strongly linked to the US, with which American Samoa conducts most of its foreign trade. Tuna fishing and tuna processing plants are the backbone of the private sector, with canned tuna the primary export. Transfers from the US Government add substantially to American Samoa's economic well-being. Attempts by the government to develop a larger and broader economy are restrained by Samoa's remote location, its limited transportation, and its devastating hurricanes. Tourism, a developing sector, has been held back by the recurring financial difficulties in East Asia.
GDP: purchasing power parity - $500 million (2000 est.)
GDP - real growth rate: NA%
GDP - per capita: purchasing power parity - $8,000 (2000 est.)
GDP - composition by sector:
agriculture: NA%
industry: NA%
services: NA%
Population below poverty line: NA%
Household income or consumption by percentage share:
lowest 10%: NA%
highest 10%: NA%
Inflation rate (consumer prices): NA% (2003 est.)
Labor force: 14,000 (1996)
Labor force - by occupation: government 33%, tuna canneries 34%, other 33% (1990)
Unemployment rate: 6% (2000)
Budget:
revenues: $121 million (37% in local revenue and 63% in US grants)
expenditures: $127 million, including capital expenditures of $NA (FY96/97)

Industries: tuna canneries (largely supplied by foreign fishing vessels), handicrafts
Industrial production growth rate: NA%
Electricity - production: 130 million kWh (2001)
Electricity - production by source:
fossil fuel: 100%
hydro: 0%
nuclear: 0%
other: 0% (2001)
Electricity - consumption: 120.9 million kWh (2001)
Electricity - exports: 0 kWh (2001)
Electricity - imports: 0 kWh (2001)
Oil - production: 0 bbl/day (2001 est.)
Oil - consumption: 3,800 bbl/day (2001 est.)
Oil - exports: NA
Oil - imports: NA
Agriculture - products: bananas, coconuts, vegetables, taro, breadfruit, yams, copra, pineapples, papayas; dairy products, livestock
Exports: $30 million (2002)
Exports - commodities: canned tuna 93%
Exports - partners: Indonesia 70%, Australia 6.7%, Japan 6.7%, Samoa 6.7% (2002)
Imports: $123 million (2002)
Imports - commodities: materials for canneries 56%, food 8%, petroleum products 7%, machinery and parts 6%
Imports - partners: Australia 36.6%, New Zealand 20.3%, South Korea 16.3%, Mauritius 4.9% (2002)
Debt - external: $NA (2002 est.)
Economic aid - recipient: important financial support from the US, more than $40 million in 1994
Currency: US dollar (USD)
Currency code: USD
Exchange rates: the US dollar is used
Fiscal year: 1 October - 30 September

Communications

Telephones - main lines in use: 15,000 (2001)
Telephones - mobile cellular: 2,377 (1999)
Telephone system:
general assessment: NA
domestic: good telex, telegraph, facsimile and cellular telephone services; domestic satellite system with 1 Comsat earth station
international: country code - 684; satellite earth station - 1 Intelsat (Pacific Ocean)
Radio broadcast stations: AM 1, FM 1, shortwave 0 (1998)
Television broadcast stations: 1 (1997)
Internet country code: .as
Internet users: NA

Transportation

Railways: 0 km
Highways:
total: 350 km
paved: 150 km
unpaved: 200 km

Waterways: none
Ports and harbors: Aunu'u (new construction), Auasi, Faleosao, Ofu, Pago Pago, Ta'u
Merchant marine: none
Airports: 3 (2003 est.)
Airports - with paved runways:
total: 2
2,438 to 3,047 m: 1
under 914 m: 1 (2003 est.)
Airports - with unpaved runways:
total: 1
under 914 m: 1 (2003 est.)

Military

Military - note: defense is the responsibility of the US

Transnational Issues

Disputes - international: none

Andorra

Introduction

Background: For 715 years, from 1278 to 1993, Andorrans lived under a unique co-principality, ruled by the French chief of state and the Spanish bishop of Urgel. In 1993, this feudal system was modified with the titular heads of state retained, but the government transformed into a parliamentary democracy. Long isolated and impoverished, mountainous Andorra achieved considerable prosperity since World War II through its tourist industry. Many immigrants (legal and illegal) are attracted to the thriving economy with its lack of income taxes.

Geography

Location: Southwestern Europe, between France and Spain
Geographic coordinates: 42 30 N, 1 30 E
Map references: Europe
Area:
total: 468 sq km
land: 468 sq km
water: 0 sq km
Area - comparative: 2.5 times the size of Washington, DC
Land boundaries:
total: 120.3 km
border countries: France 56.6 km, Spain 63.7 km
Coastline: 0 km (landlocked)
Maritime claims: none (landlocked)
Climate: temperate; snowy, cold winters and warm, dry summers
Terrain: rugged mountains dissected by narrow valleys
Elevation extremes:
lowest point: Riu Runer 840 m
highest point: Coma Pedrosa 2,946 m
Natural resources: hydropower, mineral water, timber, iron ore, lead

Andorra *(continued)*

Land use:
arable land: 2.22%
permanent crops: 0%
other: 97.78% (1998 est.)
Irrigated land: NA sq km
Natural hazards: avalanches
Environment - current issues: deforestation; overgrazing of mountain meadows contributes to soil erosion; air pollution; wastewater treatment and solid waste disposal
Environment - international agreements:
party to: Hazardous Wastes
signed, but not ratified: none of the selected agreements
Geography - note: landlocked; straddles a number of important crossroads in the Pyrenees

People

Population: 69,865 (July 2004 est.)
Age structure:
0-14 years: 15% (male 5,478; female 4,988)
15-64 years: 71.6% (male 26,268; female 23,766)
65 years and over: 13.4% (male 4,659; female 4,706) (2004 est.)
Median age:
total: 39.7 years
male: 40 years
female: 39.4 years (2004 est.)
Population growth rate: 1% (2004 est.)
Birth rate: 9.32 births/1,000 population (2004 est.)
Death rate: 5.9 deaths/1,000 population (2004 est.)
Net migration rate: 6.6 migrant(s)/1,000 population (2004 est.)
Sex ratio:
at birth: 1.07 male(s)/female
under 15 years: 1.1 male(s)/female
15-64 years: 1.11 male(s)/female
65 years and over: 0.99 male(s)/female
total population: 1.09 male(s)/female (2004 est.)
Infant mortality rate:
total: 4.05 deaths/1,000 live births
male: 4.39 deaths/1,000 live births
female: 3.7 deaths/1,000 live births (2004 est.)
Life expectancy at birth:
total population: 83.5 years
male: 80.59 years
female: 86.59 years (2004 est.)
Total fertility rate: 1.28 children born/woman (2004 est.)
HIV/AIDS - adult prevalence rate: NA%
HIV/AIDS - people living with HIV/AIDS: NA
HIV/AIDS - deaths: NA
Nationality:
noun: Andorran(s)
adjective: Andorran
Ethnic groups: Spanish 43%, Andorran 33%, Portuguese 11%, French 7%, other 6% (1998)
Religions: Roman Catholic (predominant)
Languages: Catalan (official), French, Castilian, Portuguese

Literacy:
definition: NA
total population: 100%
male: NA%
female: NA%

Government

Country name:
conventional long form: Principality of Andorra
conventional short form: Andorra
local long form: Principat d'Andorra
local short form: Andorra
Government type: parliamentary democracy (since March 1993) that retains as its chiefs of state a coprincipality; the two princes are the president of France and bishop of Seo de Urgel, Spain, who are represented locally by coprinces' representatives
Capital: Andorra la Vella
Administrative divisions: 7 parishes (parroquies, singular - parroquia); Andorra la Vella, Canillo, Encamp, La Massana, Escaldes-Engordany, Ordino, Sant Julia de Loria
Independence: 1278 (was formed under the joint suzerainty of the French count of Foix and the Spanish bishop of Urgel)
National holiday: Our Lady of Meritxell Day, 8 September (1278)
Constitution: Andorra's first written constitution was drafted in 1991; approved by referendum 14 March 1993; came into force 4 May 1993
Legal system: based on French and Spanish civil codes; no judicial review of legislative acts; has not accepted compulsory ICJ jurisdiction
Suffrage: 18 years of age; universal
Executive branch:
chief of state: French Coprince Jacques CHIRAC (since 17 May 1995), represented by Philippe MASSONI (since 26 July 2002); Spanish Coprince Bishop Joan Enric VIVES i SICILIA (since 12 May 2003), represented by Nemesi MARQUES i OSTE (since NA)
head of government: Executive Council President Marc FORNE MOLNE (since 21 December 1994)
cabinet: Executive Council or Govern designated by the Executive Council president
elections: Executive Council president elected by the General Council and formally appointed by the coprinces for a four-year term; election last held 4 March 2001 (next to be held NA 2005)
election results: Marc FORNE MOLNE elected executive council president; percent of General Council vote - NA%
Legislative branch: unicameral General Council of the Valleys or Consell General de las Valls (28 seats; members are elected by direct popular vote, 14 from a single national constituency and 14 to represent each of the 7 parishes; members serve four-year terms)
elections: last held 4 March 2001 (next to be held NA March 2005)

election results: percent of vote by party - PLA 46.1%, PSD 30%, PD 23.8%, other 0.1%; seats by party - PLA 15, PSD 6, PD 5, independents 2
Judicial branch: Tribunal of Judges or Tribunal de Batlles; Tribunal of the Courts or Tribunal de Corts; Supreme Court of Justice of Andorra or Tribunal Superior de Justicia d'Andorra; Supreme Council of Justice or Consell Superior de la Justicia; Fiscal Ministry or Ministeri Fiscal; Constitutional Tribunal or Tribunal Constitucional
Political parties and leaders: Democratic Party or PD (formerly part of National Democratic Group or AND) [Ladislau BARO SOLO]; Liberal Party of Andorra or PLA [Marc FORNE MOLNE] (used to be Liberal Union or UL); Liberal Union or UL [Francesc CERQUEDA]; National Democratic Group or AND [Ladislau BARO SOLO]; National Democratic Initiative or IDN [Vicenc MATEU ZAMORA]; New Democracy or ND [Jaume BARTOMEU CASSANY]; Social Democratic Party or PSD (formerly part of National Democratic Group of AND) [leader NA]; Union of the People of Ordino (Unio Parroquial d'Ordino) or UPO [Simo DURO COMA]
note: there are two other small parties
Political pressure groups and leaders: NA
International organization participation: CE, ICAO, ICCt, ICRM, IFRCS, Interpol, IOC, ITU, OPCW, OSCE, UN, UNESCO, WCO, WHO, WIPO, WToO, WTrO (observer)
Diplomatic representation in the US:
chief of mission: Ambassador (vacant); Charge d'Affaires Jelena V. PIA-COMELLA
chancery: 2 United Nations Plaza, 25th Floor, New York, NY 10017
telephone: [1] (212) 750-8064
FAX: [1] (212) 750-6630
Diplomatic representation from the US: the US does not have an embassy in Andorra; the US Ambassador to Spain is accredited to Andorra; US interests in Andorra are represented by the Consulate General's office in Barcelona (Spain); mailing address: Paseo Reina Elisenda, 23, 08034 Barcelona, Spain; telephone: (3493) 280-2227; FAX: (3493) 205-7705
Flag description: three equal vertical bands of blue (hoist side), yellow, and red with the national coat of arms centered in the yellow band; the coat of arms features a quartered shield; similar to the flags of Chad and Romania, which do not have a national coat of arms in the center, and the flag of Moldova, which does bear a national emblem

Economy

Economy - overview: Tourism, the mainstay of Andorra's tiny, well-to-do economy, accounts for roughly 80% of GDP. An estimated 9 million tourists visit annually, attracted by Andorra's duty-free status and by its summer and winter resorts. Andorra's comparative advantage has recently eroded as the economies of neighboring France and Spain have been opened up, providing broader availability of

Andorra *(continued)*

goods and lower tariffs. The banking sector, with its "tax haven" status, also contributes substantially to the economy. Agricultural production is limited - only 2% of the land is arable - and most food has to be imported. The principal livestock activity is sheep raising. Manufacturing output consists mainly of cigarettes, cigars, and furniture. Andorra is a member of the EU Customs Union and is treated as an EU member for trade in manufactured goods (no tariffs) and as a non-EU member for agricultural products.

GDP: purchasing power parity - $1.3 billion (2000 est.)

GDP - real growth rate: 3.8% (2000 est.)

GDP - per capita: purchasing power parity - $19,000 (2000 est.)

GDP - composition by sector:
agriculture: NA%
industry: NA%
services: NA%

Population below poverty line: NA%

Household income or consumption by percentage share:
lowest 10%: NA%
highest 10%: NA%

Inflation rate (consumer prices): 4.3% (2000)

Labor force: 33,000 (2001 est.)

Labor force - by occupation: agriculture 1%, industry 21%, services 78% (2000 est.)

Unemployment rate: 0% (1996 est.)

Budget:
revenues: $385 million
expenditures: $342 million, including capital expenditures of $NA (1997)

Industries: tourism (particularly skiing), cattle raising, timber, banking

Industrial production growth rate: NA%

Electricity - production: NA kWh

Electricity - production by source: NA

Electricity - consumption: NA kWh

Electricity - exports: 0 kWh (2002)

Electricity - imports: NA kWh; note - most electricity supplied by Spain and France; Andorra generates a small amount of hydropower

Agriculture - products: small quantities of rye, wheat, barley, oats, vegetables; sheep

Exports: $58 million f.o.b. (1998)

Exports - commodities: tobacco products, furniture

Exports - partners: Spain 58%, France 34% (2000)

Imports: $1.077 billion (1998)

Imports - commodities: consumer goods, food, electricity

Imports - partners: Spain 48%, France 35%, US 2.3% (2000)

Debt - external: $NA

Economic aid - recipient: none

Currency: euro (EUR)

Currency code: EUR

Exchange rates: euros per US dollar - 0.886 (2003), 1.0626 (2002), 1.12 (2001), 1.09 (2000), 0.94 (1999)

Fiscal year: calendar year

Telephones - main lines in use: 35,000 (2001)

Telephones - mobile cellular: 23,500 (2001)

Telephone system:
general assessment: NA
domestic: modern system with microwave radio relay connections between exchanges
international: country code - 376; landline circuits to France and Spain

Radio broadcast stations: AM 0, FM 15, shortwave 0 (1998)

Television broadcast stations: 0 (1997)

Internet country code: .ad

Internet hosts: 3,200 (2001)

Internet users: 24,500 (2001)

Transportation

Railways: 0 km

Highways:
total: 269 km
paved: 198 km
unpaved: 71 km (1994)

Waterways: none

Ports and harbors: none

Airports: none

Military

Military branches: no regular military forces, Police Service of Andorra

Military - note: defense is the responsibility of France and Spain

Transnational Issues

Disputes - international: none

Angola

Introduction

Background: Civil war has been the norm in Angola since independence from Portugal in 1975. A 1994 peace accord between the government and the National Union for the Total Independence of Angola (UNITA) provided for the integration of former UNITA insurgents into the government and armed forces. A national unity government was installed in April of 1997, but serious fighting resumed in late 1998, rendering hundreds of thousands of people homeless. Up to 1.5 million lives may have been lost in fighting over the past quarter century. The death of insurgent leader Jonas SAVIMBI in 2002 and a subsequent cease-fire with UNITA may bode well for the country.

Geography

Location: Southern Africa, bordering the South Atlantic Ocean, between Namibia and Democratic Republic of the Congo

Geographic coordinates: 12 30 S, 18 30 E

Map references: Africa

Area:
total: 1,246,700 sq km
land: 1,246,700 sq km
water: 0 sq km

Area - comparative: slightly less than twice the size of Texas

Land boundaries:
total: 5,198 km
border countries: Democratic Republic of the Congo 2,511 km (of which 225 km is the boundary of discontiguous Cabinda Province), Republic of the Congo 201 km, Namibia 1,376 km, Zambia 1,110 km

Coastline: 1,600 km

Maritime claims:
territorial sea: 12 NM
contiguous zone: 24 NM
exclusive economic zone: 200 NM

Angola *(continued)*

Climate: semiarid in south and along coast to Luanda; north has cool, dry season (May to October) and hot, rainy season (November to April)
Terrain: narrow coastal plain rises abruptly to vast interior plateau
Elevation extremes:
lowest point: Atlantic Ocean 0 m
highest point: Morro de Moco 2,620 m
Natural resources: petroleum, diamonds, iron ore, phosphates, copper, feldspar, gold, bauxite, uranium
Land use:
arable land: 2.41%
permanent crops: 0.4%
other: 97.19% (1998 est.)
Irrigated land: 750 sq km (1998 est.)
Natural hazards: locally heavy rainfall causes periodic flooding on the plateau
Environment - current issues: overuse of pastures and subsequent soil erosion attributable to population pressures; desertification; deforestation of tropical rain forest, in response to both international demand for tropical timber and to domestic use as fuel, resulting in loss of biodiversity; soil erosion contributing to water pollution and siltation of rivers and dams; inadequate supplies of potable water
Environment - international agreements:
party to: Biodiversity, Climate Change, Desertification, Law of the Sea, Ozone Layer Protection, Ship Pollution
signed, but not ratified: none of the selected agreements
Geography - note: the province of Cabinda is an exclave, separated from the rest of the country by the Democratic Republic of the Congo

People

Population: 10,978,552 (July 2004 est.)
Age structure:
0-14 years: 43.5% (male 2,410,326; female 2,363,368)
15-64 years: 53.7% (male 2,998,892; female 2,897,837)
65 years and over: 2.8% (male 137,340; female 170,789) (2004 est.)
Median age:
total: 18.1 years
male: 18.1 years
female: 18.1 years (2004 est.)
Population growth rate: 1.93% (2004 est.)
Birth rate: 45.14 births/1,000 population (2004 est.)
Death rate: 25.86 deaths/1,000 population (2004 est.)
Net migration rate: 0 migrant(s)/1,000 population (2004 est.)
Sex ratio:
at birth: 1.05 male(s)/female
under 15 years: 1.02 male(s)/female
15-64 years: 1.04 male(s)/female
65 years and over: 0.8 male(s)/female
total population: 1.02 male(s)/female (2004 est.)

Infant mortality rate:
total: 192.5 deaths/1,000 live births
male: 204.97 deaths/1,000 live births
female: 179.41 deaths/1,000 live births (2004 est.)
Life expectancy at birth:
total population: 36.79 years
male: 36.06 years
female: 37.55 years (2004 est.)
Total fertility rate: 6.33 children born/woman (2004 est.)
HIV/AIDS - adult prevalence rate: 5.5% (2001 est.)
HIV/AIDS - people living with HIV/AIDS: 350,000 (2001 est.)
HIV/AIDS - deaths: 24,000 (2001 est.)
Nationality:
noun: Angolan(s)
adjective: Angolan
Ethnic groups: Ovimbundu 37%, Kimbundu 25%, Bakongo 13%, mestico (mixed European and Native African) 2%, European 1%, other 22%
Religions: indigenous beliefs 47%, Roman Catholic 38%, Protestant 15% (1998 est.)
Languages: Portuguese (official), Bantu and other African languages
Literacy:
definition: age 15 and over can read and write
total population: 42%
male: 56%
female: 28% (1998 est.)

Government

Country name:
conventional long form: Republic of Angola
conventional short form: Angola
local long form: Republica de Angola
local short form: Angola
former: People's Republic of Angola
Government type: republic, nominally a multiparty democracy with a strong presidential system
Capital: Luanda
Administrative divisions: 18 provinces (provincias, singular - provincia); Bengo, Benguela, Bie, Cabinda, Cuando Cubango, Cuanza Norte, Cuanza Sul, Cunene, Huambo, Huila, Luanda, Lunda Norte, Lunda Sul, Malanje, Moxico, Namibe, Uige, Zaire
Independence: 11 November 1975 (from Portugal)
National holiday: Independence Day, 11 November (1975)
Constitution: 11 November 1975; revised 7 January 1978, 11 August 1980, 6 March 1991, and 26 August 1992; note - new constitution has not yet been approved
Legal system: based on Portuguese civil law system and customary law; recently modified to accommodate political pluralism and increased use of free markets
Suffrage: 18 years of age; universal
Executive branch:
chief of state: President Jose Eduardo DOS SANTOS (since 21 September 1979); note - the president is both chief of state and head of government

head of government: President Jose Eduardo DOS SANTOS (since 21 September 1979); note - the president is both chief of state and head of government; Fernando de Piedade Dias DOS SANTOS was appointed Prime Minister on 6 December 2002, but this is not a position of real power
cabinet: Council of Ministers appointed by the president
elections: president elected by universal ballot for a NA-year term; President DOS SANTOS originally elected (in 1979) without opposition under a one-party system and stood for reelection in Angola's first multiparty elections 29-30 September 1992 (next to be held NA)
election results: DOS SANTOS 49.6%, Jonas SAVIMBI 40.1%, making a run-off election necessary; the run-off was not held and SAVIMBI's National Union for the Total Independence of Angola (UNITA) repudiated the results of the first election; the civil war resumed
Legislative branch: unicameral National Assembly or Assembleia Nacional (220 seats; members elected by proportional vote to serve four-year terms)
elections: last held 29-30 September 1992 (next to be held NA)
election results: percent of vote by party - MPLA 54%, UNITA 34%, others 12%; seats by party - MPLA 129, UNITA 70, PRS 6, FNLA 5, PLD 3, others 7
Judicial branch: Supreme Court or Tribunal da Relacao (judges are appointed by the president)
Political parties and leaders: Liberal Democratic Party or PLD [Analia de Victoria PEREIRA]; National Front for the Liberation of Angola or FNLA [disputed leadership: Lucas NGONDA, Holden ROBERTO]; National Union for the Total Independence of Angola or UNITA [Isaias SAMAKUVA], largest opposition party has engaged in years of armed resistance; Popular Movement for the Liberation of Angola or MPLA [Jose Eduardo DOS SANTOS], ruling party in power since 1975; Social Renewal Party or PRS [disputed leadership: Eduardo KUANGANA, Antonio MUACHICUNGO]
note: about a dozen minor parties participated in the 1992 elections but only won a few seats and have little influence in the National Assembly
Political pressure groups and leaders: Front for the Liberation of the Enclave of Cabinda or FLEC [N'zita Henriques TIAGO; Antonio Bento BEMBE]
note: FLEC is waging a small-scale, highly factionalized, armed struggle for the independence of Cabinda Province
International organization participation: ACP, AfDB, AU, FAO, G-77, IAEA, IBRD, ICAO, ICCt (signatory), ICFTU, ICRM, IDA, IFAD, IFC, IFRCS, ILO, IMF, IMO, Interpol, IOC, IOM, ISO (correspondent), ITU, NAM, OAS (observer), SADC, UN, UN Security Council (temporary), UNCTAD, UNESCO, UNIDO, UPU, WCO, WFTU, WHO, WIPO, WMO, WToO, WTrO

Angola (continued)

Diplomatic representation in the US:
chief of mission: Ambassador Josefina Perpetua Pitra DIAKIDI
chancery: 2108 16th Street NW, Washington, DC 20009
telephone: [1] (202) 785-1156
FAX: [1] (202) 785-1258
consulate(s) general: Houston and New York
Diplomatic representation from the US:
chief of mission: Ambassador Christopher William DELL
embassy: number 32 Rua Houari Boumedienne (in the Miramar area of Luanda), Luanda
mailing address: international mail: Caixa Postal 6468, Luanda; pouch: American Embassy Luanda, Department of State, Washington, DC 20521-2550
telephone: [244] (2) 445-481, 447-028, 446-224
FAX: [244] (2) 446-924
Flag description: two equal horizontal bands of red (top) and black with a centered yellow emblem consisting of a five-pointed star within half a cogwheel crossed by a machete (in the style of a hammer and sickle)

Economy

Economy - overview: Angola has been an economy in disarray because of a quarter century of nearly continuous warfare. An apparently durable peace was established after the death of rebel leader Jonas SAVIMBI on February 22, 2002, but consequences from the conflict continue including the impact of wide-spread land mines. Subsistence agriculture provides the main livelihood for 85% of the population. Oil production and the supporting activities are vital to the economy, contributing about 45% to GDP and more than half of exports. Much of the country's food must still be imported. To fully take advantage of its rich natural resources - gold, diamonds, extensive forests, Atlantic fisheries, and large oil deposits - Angola will need to continue reforming government policies and to reduce corruption. While Angola made progress in bringing inflation down further, from 325% in 2000 to about 106% in 2002, the government has failed to make sufficient progress on reforms recommended by the IMF such as increasing foreign exchange reserves and promoting greater transparency in government spending. Increased oil production supported 7% GDP growth in 2003.
GDP: purchasing power parity - $20.59 billion (2003 est.)
GDP - real growth rate: 7.14% (2003 est.)
GDP - per capita: purchasing power parity - $1,900 (2003 est.)
GDP - composition by sector:
agriculture: 8%
industry: 67%
services: 25% (2001 est.)
Population below poverty line: 70% (2003 est.)
Household income or consumption by percentage share:
lowest 10%: NA%
highest 10%: NA%

Inflation rate (consumer prices): 106% (2002 est.)
Labor force: 6.23 million (2001 est.)
Labor force - by occupation: agriculture 85%, industry and services 15% (2003 est.)
Unemployment rate: extensive unemployment and underemployment affecting more than half the population (2003 est.)
Budget:
revenues: $928 million
expenditures: $2.5 billion, including capital expenditures of $963 million (1992 est.)
Industries: petroleum; diamonds, iron ore, phosphates, feldspar, bauxite, uranium, and gold; cement; basic metal products; fish processing; food processing; brewing; tobacco products; sugar; textiles
Industrial production growth rate: 1% (2000)
Electricity - production: 1.45 billion kWh (2001)
Electricity - production by source:
fossil fuel: 36.4%
hydro: 63.6%
nuclear: 0%
other: 0% (2001)
Electricity - consumption: 1.348 billion kWh (2001)
Electricity - exports: 0 kWh (2001)
Electricity - imports: 0 kWh (2001)
Oil - production: 742,400 bbl/day (2001 est.)
Oil - consumption: 31,000 bbl/day (2001 est.)
Oil - exports: NA
Oil - imports: NA
Oil - proved reserves: 5.691 billion bbl (1 January 2002)
Natural gas - production: 530 million cu m (2001 est.)
Natural gas - consumption: 530 million cu m (2001 est.)
Natural gas - exports: 0 cu m (2001 est.)
Natural gas - imports: 0 cu m (2001 est.)
Natural gas - proved reserves: 79.57 billion cu m (1 January 2002)
Agriculture - products: bananas, sugarcane, coffee, sisal, corn, cotton, manioc (tapioca), tobacco, vegetables, plantains; livestock; forest products; fish
Exports: $9.669 billion f.o.b. (2003 est.)
Exports - commodities: crude oil, diamonds, refined petroleum products, gas, coffee, sisal, fish and fish products, timber, cotton
Exports - partners: US 41%, China 13.6%, France 7.9%, Taiwan 7.5%, Belgium 6.2%, Japan 4.9%, Spain 4.3% (2002)
Imports: $4.08 billion f.o.b. (2003 est.)
Imports - commodities: machinery and electrical equipment, vehicles and spare parts; medicines, food, textiles, military goods
Imports - partners: Portugal 19.2%, South Africa 14.7%, US 13.2%, Brazil 7.1%, France 6.4%, Belgium 5% (2002)
Debt - external: $9.2 billion (2003 est.)
Economic aid - recipient: $383.5 million (1999)
Currency: kwanza (AOA)
Currency code: AOA

Exchange rates: kwanza per US dollar - 74.6063 (2003), 43.5302 (2002), 22.0579 (2001), 10.041 (2000), 2.791 (1999), 0.393 (1998); note - in December 1999 the kwanza was revalued with six zeroes dropped off the old value
Fiscal year: calendar year

Communications

Telephones - main lines in use: 85,000 (2002)
Telephones - mobile cellular: 130,000 (2002)
Telephone system:
general assessment: telephone service limited mostly to government and business use; HF radiotelephone used extensively for military links
domestic: limited system of wire, microwave radio relay, and tropospheric scatter
international: country code - 244; satellite earth stations - 2 Intelsat (Atlantic Ocean); fiber optic submarine cable (SAT-3/WASC) provides connectivity to Europe and Asia
Radio broadcast stations: AM 21, FM 6, shortwave 7 (2000)
Television broadcast stations: 6 (2000)
Internet country code: .ao
Internet hosts: 7 (2002)
Internet users: 41,000 (2002)

Transportation

Railways:
total: 2,761 km
narrow gauge: 2,638 km 1.067-m gauge; 123 km 0.600-m gauge (2002)
Highways:
total: 51,429 km
paved: 5,349 km
unpaved: 46,080 km (1999)
Waterways: 1,295 km
Pipelines: gas 214 km; liquid natural gas 14 km; liquid petroleum gas 30 km; oil 845 km; refined products 56 km (2003)
Ports and harbors: Ambriz, Cabinda, Lobito, Luanda, Malongo, Namibe (Mocamedes), Porto Amboim, Soyo
Merchant marine:
total: 7 ships (1,000 GRT or over) 26,123 GRT/42,879 DWT
by type: cargo 6, petroleum tanker 1
registered in other countries: 4 (2003 est.)
Airports: 244 (2003 est.)
Airports - with paved runways:
total: 32
over 3,047 m: 4
2,438 to 3,047 m: 8
1,524 to 2,437 m: 14
914 to 1,523 m: 5
under 914 m: 1 (2003 est.)
Airports - with unpaved runways:
total: 212
over 3,047 m: 2
2,438 to 3,047 m: 4

Angola (continued)

1,524 to 2,437 m: 30
914 to 1,523 m: 96
under 914 m: 80 (2003 est.)

Military

Military branches: Army, Navy (Marinha de Guerra, MdG), Air and Air Defense Forces (FANA)
Military manpower - military age: 18 years of age (2004 est.)
Military manpower - availability:
males age 15-49: 2,620,219 (2004 est.)
Military manpower - fit for military service:
males age 15-49: 1,317,328 (2004 est.)
Military manpower - reaching military age annually:
males: 113,103 (2004 est.)
Military expenditures - dollar figure: $265.1 million (2003)
Military expenditures - percent of GDP: 1.9% (2003)

Transnational Issues

Disputes - international: continues to give shelter to refugees from the Democratic Republic of the Congo while many Angolan refugees and Cabinda exclave secessionists reside in neighboring states
Illicit drugs: used as a transshipment point for cocaine destined for Western Europe and other African states

Anguilla
(overseas territory of the UK)

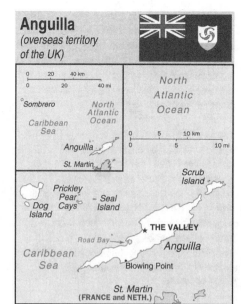

Introduction

Background: Colonized by English settlers from Saint Kitts in 1650, Anguilla was administered by Great Britain until the early 19th century, when the island - against the wishes of the inhabitants - was incorporated into a single British dependency, along with Saint Kitts and Nevis. Several attempts at separation failed. In 1971, two years after a revolt, Anguilla was finally allowed to secede; this arrangement was formally recognized in 1980, with Anguilla becoming a separate British dependency.

Geography

Location: Caribbean, islands between the Caribbean Sea and North Atlantic Ocean, east of Puerto Rico
Geographic coordinates: 18 15 N, 63 10 W
Map references: Central America and the Caribbean
Area:
total: 102 sq km
land: 102 sq km
water: 0 sq km
Area - comparative: about half the size of Washington, DC
Land boundaries: 0 km
Coastline: 61 km
Maritime claims:
territorial sea: 3 NM
exclusive fishing zone: 200 NM
Climate: tropical; moderated by northeast trade winds
Terrain: flat and low-lying island of coral and limestone
Elevation extremes:
lowest point: Caribbean Sea 0 m
highest point: Crocus Hill 65 m
Natural resources: salt, fish, lobster

Land use:
arable land: 0%
permanent crops: 0%
other: 100% (mostly rock with sparse scrub oak, few trees, some commercial salt ponds) (1998 est.)
Irrigated land: NA sq km
Natural hazards: frequent hurricanes and other tropical storms (July to October)
Environment - current issues: supplies of potable water sometimes cannot meet increasing demand largely because of poor distribution system
Geography - note: the most northerly of the Leeward Islands in the Lesser Antilles

People

Population: 13,008 (July 2004 est.)
Age structure:
0-14 years: 23.8% (male 1,569; female 1,523)
15-64 years: 69.4% (male 4,641; female 4,385)
65 years and over: 6.8% (male 396; female 494) (2004 est.)
Median age:
total: 30.4 years
male: 30.4 years
female: 30.3 years (2004 est.)
Population growth rate: 1.98% (2004 est.)
Birth rate: 14.45 births/1,000 population (2004 est.)
Death rate: 5.46 deaths/1,000 population (2004 est.)
Net migration rate: 10.76 migrant(s)/1,000 population (2004 est.)
Sex ratio:
at birth: 1.03 male(s)/female
under 15 years: 1.03 male(s)/female
15-64 years: 1.06 male(s)/female
65 years and over: 0.8 male(s)/female
total population: 1.03 male(s)/female (2004 est.)
Infant mortality rate:
total: 21.91 deaths/1,000 live births
male: 28.72 deaths/1,000 live births
female: 14.91 deaths/1,000 live births (2004 est.)
Life expectancy at birth:
total population: 76.9 years
male: 73.99 years
female: 79.91 years (2004 est.)
Total fertility rate: 1.74 children born/woman (2004 est.)
HIV/AIDS - adult prevalence rate: NA%
HIV/AIDS - people living with HIV/AIDS: NA
HIV/AIDS - deaths: NA
Nationality:
noun: Anguillan(s)
adjective: Anguillan
Ethnic groups: black (predominant), mulatto, white
Religions: Anglican 40%, Methodist 33%, Seventh-Day Adventist 7%, Baptist 5%, Roman Catholic 3%, other 12%
Languages: English (official)
Literacy:
definition: age 12 and over can read and write
total population: 95%
male: 95%
female: 95% (1984 est.)

Anguilla *(continued)*

Government

Country name:
conventional long form: none
conventional short form: Anguilla
Dependency status: overseas territory of the UK
Government type: NA
Capital: The Valley
Administrative divisions: none (overseas territory of the UK)
Independence: none (overseas territory of the UK)
National holiday: Anguilla Day, 30 May
Constitution: Anguilla Constitutional Order 1 April 1982; amended 1990
Legal system: based on English common law
Suffrage: 18 years of age; universal
Executive branch:
chief of state: Queen ELIZABETH II (since 6 February 1952); represented by Governor Peter JOHNSTONE (since NA February 2000); note - Alan HUCKLE will succeed in May 2004
head of government: Chief Minister Osbourne FLEMING (since 3 March 2000)
cabinet: Executive Council appointed by the governor from among the elected members of the House of Assembly
elections: none; the monarch is hereditary; governor appointed by the monarch; following legislative elections, the leader of the majority party or the leader of the majority coalition is usually appointed chief minister by the governor
Legislative branch: unicameral House of Assembly (11 seats total, 7 elected by direct popular vote, 2 ex officio members, and 2 appointed; members serve five-year terms)
elections: last held 3 March 2000 (next to be held NA June 2005)
election results: percent of vote by party - NA%; seats by party - ANA 3, AUM 2, ADP 1, independent 1
Judicial branch: High Court (judge provided by Eastern Caribbean Supreme Court)
Political parties and leaders: Anguilla United Movement or AUM [Hubert HUGHES]; The United Front or UF [Osbourne FLEMING, Victor BANKS], a coalition of the Anguilla Democratic Party or ADP and the Anguilla National Alliance or ANA; Anguilla Patriotic Movement or APM [Quincy GUMBS]; Movement for Grassroots Democracy or MFGD [Joyce KENTISH, John BENJAMIN]
Political pressure groups and leaders: NA
International organization participation: Caricom (associate), CDB, Interpol (subbureau), OECS (associate)
Diplomatic representation in the US: none (overseas territory of the UK)
Diplomatic representation from the US: none (overseas territory of the UK)
Flag description: blue, with the flag of the UK in the upper hoist-side quadrant and the Anguillan coat of arms centered in the outer half of the flag; the coat of arms depicts three orange dolphins in an interlocking circular design on a white background with blue wavy water below

Economy

Economy - overview: Anguilla has few natural resources, and the economy depends heavily on luxury tourism, offshore banking, lobster fishing, and remittances from emigrants. Increased activity in the tourism industry, which has spurred the growth of the construction sector, has contributed to economic growth. Anguillan officials have put substantial effort into developing the offshore financial sector, which is small, but growing. In the medium term, prospects for the economy will depend largely on the tourism sector and, therefore, on revived income growth in the industrialized nations as well as on favorable weather conditions.
GDP: purchasing power parity - $104 million (2001 est.)
GDP - real growth rate: 2.8% (2001 est.)
GDP - per capita: purchasing power parity - $8,600 (2001 est.)
GDP - composition by sector:
agriculture: 4%
industry: 18%
services: 78% (1997 est.)
Population below poverty line: NA%
Household income or consumption by percentage share:
lowest 10%: NA%
highest 10%: NA%
Inflation rate (consumer prices): 2.3%
Labor force: 6,049 (2001)
Labor force - by occupation: commerce 36%, services 29%, construction 18%, transportation and utilities 10%, manufacturing 3%, agriculture/fishing/forestry/mining 4% (2000 est)
Unemployment rate: 6.7% (2001)
Budget:
revenues: $22.8 million
expenditures: $22.5 million, including capital expenditures of $NA (2000 est.)
Industries: tourism, boat building, offshore financial services
Industrial production growth rate: 3.1% (1997 est.)
Electricity - production: NA
Electricity - production by source:
fossil fuel: NA%
hydro: NA%
nuclear: NA%
other: NA%
Electricity - consumption: 42.6 million kWh
Agriculture - products: small quantities of tobacco, vegetables; cattle raising
Exports: $2.6 million (1999)
Exports - commodities: lobster, fish, livestock, salt, concrete blocks, rum
Exports - partners: UK, US, Puerto Rico, Saint-Martin (2000)
Imports: $80.9 million (1999)
Imports - commodities: fuels, foodstuffs, manufactures, chemicals, trucks, textiles
Imports - partners: US, Puerto Rico, UK (2000)

Debt - external: $8.8 million (1998)
Economic aid - recipient: $3.5 million (1995)
Currency: East Caribbean dollar (XCD)
Currency code: XCD
Exchange rates: East Caribbean dollars per US dollar - 2.70 (fixed rate since 1976)
Fiscal year: 1 April - 31 March

Communications

Telephones - main lines in use: 6,200 (2002)
Telephones - mobile cellular: 1,800 (2002)
Telephone system:
general assessment: NA
domestic: modern internal telephone system
international: country code - 1-264; microwave radio relay to island of Saint Martin (Guadeloupe and Netherlands Antilles)
Radio broadcast stations: AM 5, FM 6, shortwave 1 (1998)
Television broadcast stations: 1 (1997)
Internet country code: .ai
Internet users: 3,000 (2002)

Transportation

Railways: 0 km
Highways:
total: 105 km
paved: 65 km
unpaved: 40 km (1997)
Waterways: none
Ports and harbors: Blowing Point, Road Bay
Merchant marine: none
Airports: 3 (2003 est.)
Airports - with paved runways:
total: 1
914 to 1,523 m: 1 (2003 est.)
Airports - with unpaved runways:
total: 2
under 914 m: 2 (2003 est.)

Military

Military - note: defense is the responsibility of the UK

Transnational Issues

Disputes - international: none
Illicit drugs: transshipment point for South American narcotics destined for the US and Europe

Antarctica

Introduction

Background: Speculation over the existence of a "southern land" was not confirmed until the early 1820s when British and American commercial operators and British and Russian national expeditions began exploring the Antarctic Peninsula region and other areas south of the Antarctic Circle. Not until 1840 was it established that Antarctica was indeed a continent and not just a group of islands. Several exploration "firsts" were achieved in the early 20th century. Following World War II, there was an upsurge in scientific research on the continent. A number of countries have set up year-round research stations on Antarctica. Seven have made territorial claims, but not all countries recognize these claims. In order to form a legal framework for the activities of nations on the continent, an Antarctic Treaty was negotiated that neither denies nor gives recognition to existing territorial claims; signed in 1959, it entered into force in 1961.

Geography

Location: continent mostly south of the Antarctic Circle
Geographic coordinates: 90 00 S, 0 00 E
Map references: Antarctic Region
Area:
total: 14 million sq km
land: 14 million sq km (280,000 sq km ice-free, 13.72 million sq km ice-covered) (est.)
note: fifth-largest continent, following Asia, Africa, North America, and South America, but larger than Australia and the subcontinent of Europe
Area - comparative: slightly less than 1.5 times the size of the US
Land boundaries: 0 km
note: see entry on Disputes - international
Coastline: 17,968 km

Maritime claims: Australia, Chile, and Argentina claim Exclusive Economic Zone (EEZ) rights or similar over 200 nm extensions seaward from their continental claims, but like the claims themselves, these zones are not accepted by other countries; 20 of 27 Antarctic consultative nations have made no claims to Antarctic territory (although Russia and the US have reserved the right to do so) and do not recognize the claims of the other nations; also see the Disputes - international entry
Climate: severe low temperatures vary with latitude, elevation, and distance from the ocean; East Antarctica is colder than West Antarctica because of its higher elevation; Antarctic Peninsula has the most moderate climate; higher temperatures occur in January along the coast and average slightly below freezing
Terrain: about 98% thick continental ice sheet and 2% barren rock, with average elevations between 2,000 and 4,000 meters; mountain ranges up to nearly 5,000 meters; ice-free coastal areas include parts of southern Victoria Land, Wilkes Land, the Antarctic Peninsula area, and parts of Ross Island on McMurdo Sound; glaciers form ice shelves along about half of the coastline, and floating ice shelves constitute 11% of the area of the continent
Elevation extremes:
lowest point: Bentley Subglacial Trench -2,555 m
highest point: Vinson Massif 4,897 m
note: the lowest known land point in Antarctica is hidden in the Bentley Subglacial Trench; at its surface is the deepest ice yet discovered and the world's lowest elevation not under seawater
Natural resources: iron ore, chromium, copper, gold, nickel, platinum and other minerals, and coal and hydrocarbons have been found in small uncommercial quantities; none presently exploited; krill, finfish, and crab have been taken by commercial fisheries
Land use:
arable land: 0%
permanent crops: 0%
other: 100% (ice 98%, barren rock 2%) (1998 est.)
Irrigated land: 0 sq km
Natural hazards: katabatic (gravity-driven) winds blow coastward from the high interior; frequent blizzards form near the foot of the plateau; cyclonic storms form over the ocean and move clockwise along the coast; volcanism on Deception Island and isolated areas of West Antarctica; other seismic activity rare and weak; large icebergs may calve from ice shelf
Environment - current issues: in 1998, NASA satellite data showed that the antarctic ozone hole was the largest on record, covering 27 million square kilometers; researchers in 1997 found that increased ultraviolet light coming through the hole damages the DNA of icefish, an antarctic fish lacking hemoglobin; ozone depletion earlier was shown to harm one-celled antarctic marine plants; in 2002, significant areas of ice shelves disintegrated in response to regional warming

Geography - note: the coldest, windiest, highest (on average), and driest continent; during summer, more solar radiation reaches the surface at the South Pole than is received at the Equator in an equivalent period; mostly uninhabitable

People

Population: no indigenous inhabitants, but there are both permanent and summer-only staffed research stations
note: 26 nations, all signatory to the Antarctic Treaty, operate seasonal (summer) and year-round research stations on the continent and in its surrounding oceans; the population of persons doing and supporting science on the continent and its nearby islands south of 60 degrees south latitude (the region covered by the Antarctic Treaty) varies from approximately 4,000 in summer to 1,000 in winter; in addition, approximately 1,000 personnel including ship's crew and scientists doing onboard research are present in the waters of the treaty region; summer (January) population - 3,687 total; Argentina 302, Australia 201, Belgium 13, Brazil 80, Bulgaria 16, Chile 352, China 70, Finland 11, France 100, Germany 51, India 60, Italy 106, Japan 136, South Korea 14, Netherlands 10, NZ 60, Norway 40, Peru 28, Poland 70, Russia 254, South Africa 80, Spain 43, Sweden 20, UK 192, US 1,378 (1998-99); winter (July) population - 964 total; Argentina 165, Australia 75, Brazil 12, Chile 129, China 33, France 33, Germany 9, India 25, Japan 40, South Korea 14, NZ 10, Poland 20, Russia 102, South Africa 10, UK 39, US 248 (1998-99); research stations operated within the Antarctic Treaty area (south of 60 degrees south) by members of the Council of Managers of National Antarctic Programs (COMNAP): year-round stations - 37 total; Argentina 6, Australia 3, Brazil 1, Chile 4, China 2, France 1, Germany 1, India 1, Japan 1, South Korea 1, NZ 1, Poland 1, Russia 6, South Africa 1, Ukraine 1, UK 2, US 3, Uruguay 1 (2004); summer-only stations - 36 total; Argentina 8, Australia 2, Bulgaria 1, Chile 5, Ecuador 1, Finland 1, Germany 1, India 1, Italy 1, Japan 3, Norway 2, Peru 1, Russia 2, South Africa 1, Spain 2, Sweden 2, UK 1, Italy and France jointly 1 (2003-2004); in addition, during the austral summer some nations have numerous occupied locations such as tent camps, summer-long temporary facilities, and mobile traverses in support of research

Government

Country name:
conventional long form: none
conventional short form: Antarctica
Government type: Antarctic Treaty Summary - the Antarctic Treaty, signed on 1 December 1959 and entered into force on 23 June 1961, establishes the legal framework for the management of Antarctica; the 26th Antarctic Treaty Consultative Meeting was held in Madrid, Spain in June 2003; at these periodic

meetings, decisions are made by consensus (not by vote) of all consultative member nations; at the end of 2003, there were 45 treaty member nations: 27 consultative and 18 non-consultative; consultative (decision-making) members include the seven nations that claim portions of Antarctica as national territory (some claims overlap) and 20 non-claimant nations; the US and Russia have reserved the right to make claims; the US does not recognize the claims of others; Antarctica is administered through meetings of the consultative member nations; decisions from these meetings are carried out by these member nations (with respect to their own nationals and operations) in accordance with their own national laws; the year in parentheses indicates when an acceding nation was accepted as a consultative member, while no date indicates the country was an original 1959 treaty signatory; claimant nations are - Argentina, Australia, Chile, France, New Zealand, Norway, and the UK. Nonclaimant consultative nations are - Belgium, Brazil (1983), Bulgaria (1998) China (1985), Ecuador (1990), Finland (1989), Germany (1981), India (1983), Italy (1987), Japan, South Korea (1989), Netherlands (1990), Peru (1989), Poland (1977), Russia, South Africa, Spain (1988), Sweden (1988), Uruguay (1985), and the US; non-consultative members, with year of accession in parentheses, are - Austria (1987), Canada (1988), Colombia (1989), Cuba (1984), Czech Republic (1993), Denmark (1965), Estonia (2001), Greece (1987), Guatemala (1991), Hungary (1984), North Korea (1987), Papua New Guinea (1981), Romania (1971), Slovakia (1993), Switzerland (1990), Turkey (1995), Ukraine (1992), and Venezuela (1999); Article 1 - area to be used for peaceful purposes only; military activity, such as weapons testing, is prohibited, but military personnel and equipment may be used for scientific research or any other peaceful purpose; Article 2 - freedom of scientific investigation and cooperation shall continue; Article 3 - free exchange of information and personnel, cooperation with the UN and other international agencies; Article 4 - does not recognize, dispute, or establish territorial claims and no new claims shall be asserted while the treaty is in force; Article 5 - prohibits nuclear explosions or disposal of radioactive wastes; Article 6 - includes under the treaty all land and ice shelves south of 60 degrees 00 minutes south and reserves high seas rights; Article 7 - treaty-state observers have free access, including aerial observation, to any area and may inspect all stations, installations, and equipment; advance notice of all expeditions and of the introduction of military personnel must be given; Article 8 - allows for jurisdiction over observers and scientists by their own states; Article 9 - frequent consultative meetings take place among member nations; Article 10 - treaty states will discourage activities by any country in Antarctica that are contrary to the treaty; Article 11 - disputes to be settled peacefully by the parties concerned or, ultimately, by the ICJ; Articles 12, 13, 14 - deal with upholding, interpreting, and amending the treaty among involved

nations; other agreements - some 200 recommendations adopted at treaty consultative meetings and ratified by governments include - Agreed Measures for Fauna and Flora (1964) which were later incorporated into the Environmental Protocol; Convention for the Conservation of Antarctic Seals (1972); Convention on the Conservation of Antarctic Marine Living Resources (1980); a mineral resources agreement was signed in 1988 but remains unratified; the Protocol on Environmental Protection to the Antarctic Treaty was signed 4 October 1991 and entered into force 14 January 1998; this agreement provides for the protection of the Antarctic environment through five specific annexes: 1) environmental impact assessment, 2) conservation of Antarctic fauna and flora, 3) waste disposal and waste management, 4) prevention of marine pollution, and 5) area protection and management; it prohibits all activities relating to mineral resources except scientific research

Legal system: Antarctica is administered through meetings of the consultative member nations; decisions from these meetings are carried out by these member nations (with respect to their own nationals and operations) in accordance with their own national laws; US law, including certain criminal offenses by or against US nationals, such as murder, may apply extra-territorially; some US laws directly apply to Antarctica; for example, the Antarctic Conservation Act, 16 U.S.C. section 2401 et seq., provides civil and criminal penalties for the following activities, unless authorized by regulation of statute: the taking of native mammals or birds; the introduction of nonindigenous plants and animals; entry into specially protected areas; the discharge or disposal of pollutants; and the importation into the US of certain items from Antarctica; violation of the Antarctic Conservation Act carries penalties of up to $10,000 in fines and one year in prison; the National Science Foundation and Department of Justice share enforcement responsibilities; Public Law 95-541, the US Antarctic Conservation Act of 1978, as amended in 1996, requires expeditions from the US to Antarctica to notify, in advance, the Office of Oceans, Room 5805, Department of State, Washington, DC 20520, which reports such plans to other nations as required by the Antarctic Treaty; for more information, contact Permit Office, Office of Polar Programs, National Science Foundation, Arlington, Virginia 22230; telephone: (703) 292-8030, or visit their website at www.nsf.gov

Economy

Economy - overview: Fishing off the coast and tourism, both based abroad, account for the limited economic activity. Antarctic fisheries in 2000-01 (1 July-30 June) reported landing 112,934 metric tons. Unregulated fishing, particularly of Patagonian toothfish, is a serious problem. The Convention on the Conservation of Antarctic Marine Living Resources determines the recommended catch limits for marine

species. A total of 13,571 tourists visited in the 2002-03 antarctic summer, up from the 11,588 who visited the previous year. Nearly all of them were passengers on commercial (nongovernmental) ships and several yachts that make trips during the summer. Most tourist trips last approximately two weeks.

Communications

Telephones - main lines in use: 0
note: information for US bases only (2001)
Telephones - mobile cellular: NA
Telephone system:
general assessment: local systems at some research stations
domestic: NA
international: country code - 672; via satellite (mobile Inmarsat and Iridium system) from some research stations
Radio broadcast stations: AM NA, FM 2, shortwave 1
note: information for US bases only (2002)
Television broadcast stations: 1 (cable system with six channels; American Forces Antarctic Network-McMurdo)
note: information for US bases only (2002)
Internet country code: .aq

Transportation

Ports and harbors: there are no developed ports and harbors in Antarctica; most coastal stations have offshore anchorages, and supplies are transferred from ship to shore by small boats, barges, and helicopters; a few stations have a basic wharf facility; US coastal stations include McMurdo (77 51 S, 166 40 E), Palmer (64 43 S, 64 03 W); government use only except by permit (see Permit Office under "Legal System"); all ships at port are subject to inspection in accordance with Article 7, Antarctic Treaty; offshore anchorage is sparse and intermittent

Airports: there are no developed public access airports or landing facilities; 30 stations, operated by 16 national governments party to the Antarctic Treaty, have restricted aircraft landing facilities for either helicopters and/or fixed-wing aircraft; commercial enterprises operate two additional aircraft landing facilities; helicopter pads are available at 27 stations; runways at 15 locations are gravel, sea-ice, blue-ice, or compacted snow suitable for landing wheeled, fixed-wing aircraft; of these, 1 is greater than 3 km in length, 6 are between 2 km and 3 km in length, 3 are between 1 km and 2 km in length, 3 are less than 1 km in length, and 2 are of unknown length; snow surface skiways, limited to use by ski-equipped, fixed-wing aircraft, are available at another 15 locations; of these, 4 are greater than 3 km in length, 3 are between 2 km and 3 km in length, 2 are between 1 km and 2 km in length, 2 are less than 1 km in length, and 4 are of unknown length; aircraft landing facilities generally subject to severe restrictions and limitations resulting from extreme seasonal and geographic conditions; aircraft landing facilities do not meet ICAO standards;

advance approval from the respective governmental or nongovernmental operating organization required for landing; landed aircraft are subject to inspection in accordance with Article 7, Antarctic Treaty (2003 est.)

Airports - with unpaved runways:
total: 20
over 3,047 m: 6
2,438 to 3,047 m: 3
1,524 to 2,437 m: 1
914 to 1,523 m: 4
under 914 m: 6 (2003 est.)

Heliports: 27 stations have restricted helicopter landing facilities (helipads) (2003 est.)

Military

Military - note: the Antarctic Treaty prohibits any measures of a military nature, such as the establishment of military bases and fortifications, the carrying out of military maneuvers, or the testing of any type of weapon; it permits the use of military personnel or equipment for scientific research or for any other peaceful purposes

Transnational Issues

Disputes - international: Antarctic Treaty freezes claims (see Antarctic Treaty Summary in Government type entry); sections (some overlapping) claimed by Argentina, Australia, Chile, France, NZ, Norway, and UK; the US and most other states do not recognize the territorial claims of other states and have made no claims themselves (the US and Russia reserve the right to do so); no claims have been made in the sector between 90 degrees west and 150 degrees west; several states with land claims in Antarctica have expressed their intention to submit data to the UN Commission on the Limits of the Continental Shelf to extend their continental shelf claims to adjoining undersea ridges

Antigua and Barbuda

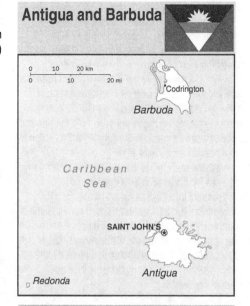

Introduction

Background: The Siboney were the first to inhabit the islands of Antigua and Barbuda in 2400 B.C., but Arawak and Carib Indians populated the islands when Columbus landed on his second voyage in 1493. Early settlements by the Spanish and French were succeeded by the English who formed a colony in 1667. Slavery, established to run the sugar plantations on Antigua, was abolished in 1834. The islands became an independent state within the British Commonwealth of Nations in 1981.

Geography

Location: Caribbean, islands between the Caribbean Sea and the North Atlantic Ocean, east-southeast of Puerto Rico

Geographic coordinates: 17 03 N, 61 48 W

Map references: Central America and the Caribbean

Area:
total: 443 sq km (Antigua 280 sq km; Barbuda 161 sq km)
land: 443 sq km
water: 0 sq km
note: includes Redonda, 1.6 sq km

Area - comparative: 2.5 times the size of Washington, DC

Land boundaries: 0 km

Coastline: 153 km

Maritime claims:
territorial sea: 12 NM
contiguous zone: 24 NM
exclusive economic zone: 200 NM
continental shelf: 200 NM or to the edge of the continental margin

Climate: tropical; little seasonal temperature variation

Terrain: mostly low-lying limestone and coral islands, with some higher volcanic areas

Elevation extremes:
lowest point: Caribbean Sea 0 m
highest point: Boggy Peak 402 m

Natural resources: NEGL; pleasant climate fosters tourism

Land use:
arable land: 18.18%
permanent crops: 0%
other: 81.82% (1998 est.)

Irrigated land: NA sq km

Natural hazards: hurricanes and tropical storms (July to October); periodic droughts

Environment - current issues: water management - a major concern because of limited natural fresh water resources - is further hampered by the clearing of trees to increase crop production, causing rainfall to run off quickly

Environment - international agreements:
party to: Biodiversity, Climate Change, Climate Change-Kyoto Protocol, Desertification, Endangered Species, Environmental Modification, Hazardous Wastes, Law of the Sea, Marine Dumping, Ozone Layer Protection, Ship Pollution, Whaling
signed, but not ratified: none of the selected agreements

Geography - note: Antigua has a deeply indented shoreline with many natural harbors and beaches; Barbuda has a very large western harbor

People

Population: 68,320 (July 2004 est.)

Age structure:
0-14 years: 28.1% (male 9,761; female 9,429)
15-64 years: 67.6% (male 23,179; female 23,023)
65 years and over: 4.3% (male 1,151; female 1,777) (2004 est.)

Median age:
total: 29.4 years
male: 28.9 years
female: 29.9 years (2004 est.)

Population growth rate: 0.6% (2004 est.)

Birth rate: 17.7 births/1,000 population (2004 est.)

Death rate: 5.55 deaths/1,000 population (2004 est.)

Net migration rate: -6.15 migrant(s)/1,000 population (2004 est.)

Sex ratio:
at birth: 1.05 male(s)/female
under 15 years: 1.04 male(s)/female
15-64 years: 1.01 male(s)/female
65 years and over: 0.65 male(s)/female
total population: 1 male(s)/female (2004 est.)

Infant mortality rate:
total: 20.18 deaths/1,000 live births
male: 24.29 deaths/1,000 live births
female: 15.87 deaths/1,000 live births (2004 est.)

Life expectancy at birth:
total population: 71.6 years
male: 69.26 years
female: 74.07 years (2004 est.)

Total fertility rate: 2.27 children born/woman (2004 est.)

Antigua and Barbuda *(continued)*

HIV/AIDS - adult prevalence rate: NA%
HIV/AIDS - people living with HIV/AIDS: NA
HIV/AIDS - deaths: NA
Nationality:
noun: Antiguan(s), Barbudan(s)
adjective: Antiguan, Barbudan
Ethnic groups: black, British, Portuguese, Lebanese, Syrian
Religions: Christian, (predominantly Anglican with other Protestant, and some Roman Catholic)
Languages: English (official), local dialects
Literacy:
definition: age 15 and over has completed five or more years of schooling
total population: 89%
male: 90%
female: 88% (1960 est.)

Government

Country name:
conventional long form: none
conventional short form: Antigua and Barbuda
Government type: constitutional monarchy with UK-style parliament
Capital: Saint John's (Antigua)
Administrative divisions: 6 parishes and 2 dependencies*; Barbuda*, Redonda*, Saint George, Saint John, Saint Mary, Saint Paul, Saint Peter, Saint Philip
Independence: 1 November 1981 (from UK)
National holiday: Independence Day (National Day), 1 November (1981)
Constitution: 1 November 1981
Legal system: based on English common law
Suffrage: 18 years of age; universal
Executive branch:
chief of state: Queen ELIZABETH II (since 6 February 1952), represented by Governor General James B. CARLISLE (since 10 June 1993)
head of government: Prime Minister Baldwin SPENCER (since 24 March 2004)
cabinet: Council of Ministers appointed by the governor general on the advice of the prime minister
elections: none; the monarch is hereditary; governor general chosen by the monarch on the advice of the prime minister; following legislative elections, the leader of the majority party or the leader of the majority coalition is usually appointed prime minister by the governor general
Legislative branch: bicameral Parliament consists of the Senate (17-member body appointed by the governor general) and the House of Representatives (17 seats; members are elected by proportional representation to serve five-year terms)
elections: House of Representatives - last held 23 March 2004 (next to be held NA 2009)
election results: percent of vote by party - NA; seats by party - ALP 4, UPP 12, contested 1; note - new election will decide the contested seat

Judicial branch: Eastern Caribbean Supreme Court (based in Saint Lucia; one judge of the Supreme Court is a resident of the islands and presides over the Court of Summary Jurisdiction)
Political parties and leaders: Antigua Labor Party or ALP [Lester Bryant BIRD]; Barbuda People's Movement or BPM [Thomas H. FRANK]; United Progressive Party or UPP [Baldwin SPENCER] (a coalition of three opposition parties - United National Democratic Party or UNDP, Antigua Caribbean Liberation Movement or ACLM, and Progressive Labor Movement or PLM)
Political pressure groups and leaders: Antigua Trades and Labor Union or ATLU [William ROBINSON]; People's Democratic Movement or PDM [Hugh MARSHALL]
International organization participation: ACP, C, Caricom, CDB, FAO, G-77, IBRD, ICAO, ICCt, ICFTU, ICRM, IFAD, IFC, IFRCS, ILO, IMF, IMO, Interpol, IOC, ISO (subscriber), ITU, OAS, OECS, OPANAL, UN, UNCTAD, UNESCO, UPU, WCL, WFTU, WHO, WIPO, WMO, WTrO
Diplomatic representation in the US:
chief of mission: Ambassador (vacant)
chancery: 3216 New Mexico Avenue NW, Washington, DC 20016
telephone: [1] (202) 362-5211
FAX: [1] (202) 362-5225
consulate(s) general: Miami
Diplomatic representation from the US: the US does not have an embassy in Antigua and Barbuda (embassy closed 30 June 1994); the US Ambassador to Barbados, Ambassador Mary E. KRAMER, is accredited to Antigua and Barbuda
Flag description: red, with an inverted isosceles triangle based on the top edge of the flag; the triangle contains three horizontal bands of black (top), light blue, and white, with a yellow rising sun in the black band

Economy

Economy - overview: Tourism continues to dominate the economy, accounting for more than half of GDP. Weak tourist arrival numbers since early 2000 have slowed the economy, however, and pressed the government into a tight fiscal corner. The dual-island nation's agricultural production is focused on the domestic market and constrained by a limited water supply and a labor shortage stemming from the lure of higher wages in tourism and construction. Manufacturing comprises enclave-type assembly for export with major products being bedding, handicrafts, and electronic components. Prospects for economic growth in the medium term will continue to depend on income growth in the industrialized world, especially in the US, which accounts for slightly more than one-third of tourist arrivals.
GDP: purchasing power parity - $750 million (2002 est.)
GDP - real growth rate: 3% (2002 est.)
GDP - per capita: purchasing power parity - $11,000 (2002 est.)

GDP - composition by sector:
agriculture: 3.9%
industry: 19.2%
services: 76.8% (2002)
Population below poverty line: NA%
Household income or consumption by percentage share:
lowest 10%: NA%
highest 10%: NA%
Inflation rate (consumer prices): 0.4% (2000 est.)
Labor force: 30,000
Labor force - by occupation: commerce and services 82%, agriculture 11%, industry 7% (1983)
Unemployment rate: 11% (2001 est.)
Budget:
revenues: $123.7 million
expenditures: $145.9 million, including capital expenditures of $NA (2000 est.)
Industries: tourism, construction, light manufacturing (clothing, alcohol, household appliances)
Industrial production growth rate: 6% (1997 est.)
Electricity - production: 105.3 million kWh (2001)
Electricity - production by source:
fossil fuel: 100%
hydro: 0%
nuclear: 0%
other: 0% (2001)
Electricity - consumption: 97.89 million kWh (2001)
Electricity - exports: 0 kWh (2001)
Electricity - imports: 0 kWh (2001)
Oil - production: 0 bbl/day (2001 est.)
Oil - consumption: 3,600 bbl/day (2001 est.)
Oil - exports: NA
OIl - Imports: NA
Agriculture - products: cotton, fruits, vegetables, bananas, coconuts, cucumbers, mangoes, sugarcane; livestock
Exports: $689 million (2002)
Exports - commodities: petroleum products 48%, manufactures 23%, machinery and transport equipment 17%, food and live animals 4%, other 8%
Exports - partners: France 68.7%, Germany 26.6%, Italy 1.2% (2002)
Imports: $692 million (2002 est.)
Imports - commodities: food and live animals, machinery and transport equipment, manufactures, chemicals, oil
Imports - partners: France 23%, Germany 14.9%, US 13%, South Korea 8.1%, Singapore 4.9%, Poland 4.6%, UK 4.3% (2002)
Debt - external: $231 million (1999)
Economic aid - recipient: $2.3 million (1995)
Currency: East Caribbean dollar (XCD)
Currency code: XCD
Exchange rates: East Caribbean dollars per US dollar - 2.7 (2003), 2.7 (2002), 2.7 (2001), 2.7 (2000), 2.7 (1999), 2.7 (1998) (fixed rate since 1976)
Fiscal year: 1 April - 31 March

Communications

Telephones - main lines in use: 38,000 (2002)
Telephones - mobile cellular: 38,200 (2002)
Telephone system:
general assessment: NA
domestic: good automatic telephone system
international: country code - 1-268; 1 coaxial submarine cable; satellite earth station - 1 Intelsat (Atlantic Ocean); tropospheric scatter to Saba (Netherlands Antilles) and Guadeloupe
Radio broadcast stations: AM 4, FM 2, shortwave 0 (1998)
Television broadcast stations: 2 (1997)
Internet country code: .ag
Internet hosts: 622 (2002)
Internet users: 10,000 (2002)

Transportation

Railways:
total: 77 km
narrow gauge: 64 km 0.760-m gauge; 13 km 0.610-m gauge (used almost exclusively for handling sugarcane) (2001 est.)
Highways:
total: 250 km (1999 est.)
Waterways: none
Ports and harbors: Saint John's
Merchant marine:
total: 867 ships (1,000 GRT or over) 5,873,626 GRT/ 7,683,143 DWT
by type: bulk 25, cargo 477, chemical tanker 13, container 284, liquefied gas 10, multi-functional large load carrier 15, refrigerated cargo 10, roll on/roll off 32, vehicle carrier 1
foreign-owned: Australia 1, Bahamas 1, Bangladesh 2, Belgium 3, Colombia 1, Cuba 1, Cyprus 1, Estonia 3, France 1, Germany 818, Greece 2, Iceland 5, Latvia 1, Lebanon 1, Lithuania 2, Malaysia 1, Netherlands 19, New Zealand 1, Norway 2, Portugal 1, Slovenia 5, Sweden 2, Switzerland 5, Turkey 3, United States 10
registered in other countries: 2 (2003 est.)
Airports: 3 (2003 est.)
Airports - with paved runways:
total: 2
2,438 to 3,047 m: 1
under 914 m: 1 (2003 est.)
Airports - with unpaved runways:
total: 1
under 914 m: 1 (2003 est.)

Military

Military branches: Royal Antigua and Barbuda Defense Force (including Coast Guard)
Military expenditures - dollar figure: NA
Military expenditures - percent of GDP: NA

Transnational Issues

Disputes - international: none
Illicit drugs: considered a minor transshipment point for narcotics bound for the US and Europe; more significant as an offshore financial center

Arctic Ocean

Introduction

Background: The Arctic Ocean is the smallest of the world's five oceans (after the Pacific Ocean, Atlantic Ocean, Indian Ocean, and the recently delimited Southern Ocean). The Northwest Passage (US and Canada) and Northern Sea Route (Norway and Russia) are two important seasonal waterways. A sparse network of air, ocean, river, and land routes circumscribes the Arctic Ocean.

Geography

Location: body of water between Europe, Asia, and North America, mostly north of the Arctic Circle
Geographic coordinates: 90 00 N, 0 00 E
Map references: Arctic Region
Area:
total: 14.056 million sq km
note: includes Baffin Bay, Barents Sea, Beaufort Sea, Chukchi Sea, East Siberian Sea, Greenland Sea, Hudson Bay, Hudson Strait, Kara Sea, Laptev Sea, Northwest Passage, and other tributary water bodies
Area - comparative: slightly less than 1.5 times the size of the US
Coastline: 45,389 km
Climate: polar climate characterized by persistent cold and relatively narrow annual temperature ranges; winters characterized by continuous darkness, cold and stable weather conditions, and clear skies; summers characterized by continuous daylight, damp and foggy weather, and weak cyclones with rain or snow
Terrain: central surface covered by a perennial drifting polar icepack that averages about 3 meters in thickness, although pressure ridges may be three times that size; clockwise drift pattern in the Beaufort Gyral Stream, but nearly straight-line movement from the New Siberian Islands (Russia) to Denmark Strait (between Greenland and Iceland); the icepack is surrounded by open seas during the summer, but more than doubles in size during the winter and

extends to the encircling landmasses; the ocean floor is about 50% continental shelf (highest percentage of any ocean) with the remainder a central basin interrupted by three submarine ridges (Alpha Cordillera, Nansen Cordillera, and Lomonosov Ridge)
Elevation extremes:
lowest point: Fram Basin -4,665 m
highest point: sea level 0 m
Natural resources: sand and gravel aggregates, placer deposits, polymetallic nodules, oil and gas fields, fish, marine mammals (seals and whales)
Natural hazards: ice islands occasionally break away from northern Ellesmere Island; icebergs calved from glaciers in western Greenland and extreme northeastern Canada; permafrost in islands; virtually ice locked from October to June; ships subject to superstructure icing from October to May
Environment - current issues: endangered marine species include walruses and whales; fragile ecosystem slow to change and slow to recover from disruptions or damage; thinning polar icepack
Geography - note: major chokepoint is the southern Chukchi Sea (northern access to the Pacific Ocean via the Bering Strait); strategic location between North America and Russia; shortest marine link between the extremes of eastern and western Russia; floating research stations operated by the US and Russia; maximum snow cover in March or April about 20 to 50 centimeters over the frozen ocean; snow cover lasts about 10 months

Economy

Economy - overview: Economic activity is limited to the exploitation of natural resources, including petroleum, natural gas, fish, and seals.

Transportation

Ports and harbors: Churchill (Canada), Murmansk (Russia), Prudhoe Bay (US)
Transportation - note: sparse network of air, ocean, river, and land routes; the Northwest Passage (North America) and Northern Sea Route (Eurasia) are important seasonal waterways

Transnational Issues

Disputes - international: some maritime disputes (see littoral states)

Argentina

Background: Following independence from Spain in 1816, Argentina experienced periods of internal political conflict between conservatives and liberals and between civilian and military factions. After World War II, a long period of Peronist authoritarian rule and interference in subsequent governments was followed by a military junta that took power in 1976. Democracy returned in 1983, and numerous elections since then have underscored Argentina's progress in democratic consolidation.

Geography

Location: Southern South America, bordering the South Atlantic Ocean, between Chile and Uruguay
Geographic coordinates: 34 00 S, 64 00 W
Map references: South America
Area:
total: 2,766,890 sq km
land: 2,736,690 sq km
water: 30,200 sq km

Area - comparative: slightly less than three-tenths the size of the US
Land boundaries:
total: 9,665 km
border countries: Bolivia 832 km, Brazil 1,224 km, Chile 5,150 km, Paraguay 1,880 km, Uruguay 579 km
Coastline: 4,989 km
Maritime claims:
territorial sea: 12 NM
contiguous zone: 24 NM
exclusive economic zone: 200 NM
continental shelf: 200 NM or to the edge of the continental margin
Climate: mostly temperate; arid in southeast; subantarctic in southwest
Terrain: rich plains of the Pampas in northern half, flat to rolling plateau of Patagonia in south, rugged Andes along western border
Elevation extremes:
lowest point: Laguna del Carbon -105 m (located between Puerto San Julian and Comandante Luis Piedra Buena in the province of Santa Cruz)
highest point: Cerro Aconcagua 6,960 m (located in the northwestern corner of the province of Mendoza)
Natural resources: fertile plains of the pampas, lead, zinc, tin, copper, iron ore, manganese, petroleum, uranium
Land use:
arable land: 9.14%
permanent crops: 0.8%
other: 90.06% (1998 est.)
Irrigated land: 15,610 sq km (1998 est.)
Natural hazards: San Miguel de Tucuman and Mendoza areas in the Andes subject to earthquakes; pamperos are violent windstorms that can strike the pampas and northeast; heavy flooding
Environment - current issues: environmental problems (urban and rural) typical of an industrializing economy such as deforestation, soil degradation, desertification, air pollution, and water pollution
note: Argentina is a world leader in setting voluntary greenhouse gas targets
Environment - international agreements:
party to: Antarctic-Environmental Protocol, Antarctic-Marine Living Resources, Antarctic Seals, Antarctic Treaty, Biodiversity, Climate Change, Climate Change-Kyoto Protocol, Desertification, Endangered Species, Environmental Modification, Hazardous Wastes, Law of the Sea, Marine Dumping, Ozone Layer Protection, Ship Pollution, Wetlands, Whaling
signed, but not ratified: Marine Life Conservation
Geography - note: second-largest country in South America (after Brazil); strategic location relative to sea lanes between the South Atlantic and the South Pacific Oceans (Strait of Magellan, Beagle Channel, Drake Passage); Cerro Aconcagua is South America's tallest mountain, while Laguna del Carbon is the lowest point in the Western Hemisphere

Population: 39,144,753 (July 2004 est.)
Age structure:
0-14 years: 25.9% (male 5,179,236; female 4,947,234)
15-64 years: 63.6% (male 12,452,566; female 12,457,451)
65 years and over: 10.5% (male 1,685,371; female 2,422,895) (2004 est.)
Median age:
total: 29.2 years
male: 28.3 years
female: 30.1 years (2004 est.)
Population growth rate: 1.02% (2004 est.)
Birth rate: 17.19 births/1,000 population (2004 est.)
Death rate: 7.57 deaths/1,000 population (2004 est.)
Net migration rate: 0.61 migrant(s)/1,000 population (2004 est.)
Sex ratio:
at birth: 1.05 male(s)/female
under 15 years: 1.05 male(s)/female
15-64 years: 1 male(s)/female
65 years and over: 0.7 male(s)/female
total population: 0.97 male(s)/female (2004 est.)
Infant mortality rate:
total: 15.66 deaths/1,000 live births
male: 17.6 deaths/1,000 live births
female: 13.63 deaths/1,000 live births (2004 est.)
Life expectancy at birth:
total population: 75.7 years
male: 71.95 years
female: 79.65 years (2004 est.)
Total fertility rate: 2.24 children born/woman (2004 est.)
HIV/AIDS - adult prevalence rate: 0.7% (2001 est.)
HIV/AIDS - people living with HIV/AIDS: 130,000 (2001 est.)
HIV/AIDS - deaths: 1,800 (2001 est.)
Nationality:
noun: Argentine(s)
adjective: Argentine
Ethnic groups: white (mostly Spanish and Italian) 97%, mestizo, Amerindian, or other nonwhite groups 3%
Religions: nominally Roman Catholic 92% (less than 20% practicing), Protestant 2%, Jewish 2%, other 4%
Languages: Spanish (official), English, Italian, German, French
Literacy:
definition: age 15 and over can read and write
total population: 97.1%
male: 97.1%
female: 97.1% (2003 est.)

Country name:
conventional long form: Argentine Republic
conventional short form: Argentina
local long form: Republica Argentina
local short form: Argentina

Argentina *(continued)*

Government type: republic
Capital: Buenos Aires
Administrative divisions: 23 provinces (provincias, singular - provincia), and 1 autonomous city* (distrito federal); Buenos Aires, Buenos Aires Capital Federal*, Catamarca, Chaco, Chubut, Cordoba, Corrientes, Entre Rios, Formosa, Jujuy, La Pampa, La Rioja, Mendoza, Misiones, Neuquen, Rio Negro, Salta, San Juan, San Luis, Santa Cruz, Santa Fe, Santiago del Estero, Tierra del Fuego - Antartida e Islas del Atlantico Sur, Tucuman
note: the US does not recognize any claims to Antarctica
Independence: 9 July 1816 (from Spain)
National holiday: Revolution Day, 25 May (1810)
Constitution: 1 May 1853; revised August 1994
Legal system: mixture of US and West European legal systems; has not accepted compulsory ICJ jurisdiction
Suffrage: 18 years of age; universal and mandatory
Executive branch:
chief of state: President Nestor KIRCHNER (since 25 May 2003); note - declared winner of a runoff election by default after Carlos Saul MENEM withdrew his candidacy on the eve of the election; Vice President Daniel SCIOLI (since 25 May 2003); note - the president is both the chief of state and head of government
head of government: President Nestor KIRCHNER (since 25 May 2003); note - declared winner of a runoff election by default after Carlos Saul MENEM withdrew his candidacy on the eve of the election; Vice President Daniel SCIOLI (since 25 May 2003); note - the president is both the chief of state and head of government
cabinet: Cabinet appointed by the president
elections: president and vice president elected on the same ticket by popular vote for four-year terms; the last election held was the presidential primary election of 27 April 2003 (next election to be held NA 2007); a runoff election slated for 25 May 2003 between the two candidates receiving the highest votes in the primary was awarded to KIRCHNER by default after MENEM withdrew his candidacy on the eve of the election
election results: results of the presidential primary of 27 April 2003: Carlos Saul MENEM 24.3%, Nestor KIRCHNER 22%, Ricardo Lopez MURPHY 16.4%, Adolfo Rodriguez SAA 14.4%, Elisa CARRIO 14.2%, other 8.7%; the subsequent runoff election slated for 25 May 2003 was awarded to KIRCHNER by default after MENEM withdrew his candidacy on the eve of the election
Legislative branch: bicameral National Congress or Congreso Nacional consists of the Senate (72 seats; members are elected by direct vote; presently one-third of the members elected every two years to a six-year term) and the Chamber of Deputies (257 seats; members are elected by direct vote; one-half of the members elected every two years to a four-year term)

elections: Senate - last held intermittently by province during the 2nd half of 2003 (next to be held NA 2005); Chamber of Deputies - last held intermittently by province during the 2nd half of 2003 (next to be held NA 2005)
election results: Senate - percent of vote by bloc or party - NA%; seats by bloc or party - PJ 41, UCR 16, provincial parties 15; Chamber of Deputies - percent of vote by bloc or party - NA%; seats by bloc or party - PJ 133, UCR 46, IF 23, ARI 11, Socialist 6, other/provincial parties 38
Judicial branch: Supreme Court or Corte Suprema (the nine Supreme Court judges are appointed by the president with approval by the Senate)
Political parties and leaders: Action for the Republic or AR [Domingo CAVALLO]; Alternative for a Republic of Equals or ARI [Elisa CARRIO]; Front for a Country in Solidarity or Frepaso (a four-party coalition) [Dario Pedro ALESSANDRO]; Interbloque Federal or IF (a broad coalition of approximately 12 parties including RECREAR) [leader NA]; Justicialist Party or PJ [leader NA] (Peronist umbrella political organization); Radical Civic Union or UCR [Angel ROZAS]; Federal Recreate Movement or RECREAR [Ricardo LOPEZ MURPHY]; Socialist Party or PS [Ruben GIUSTINIANI]; several provincial parties
Political pressure groups and leaders: Argentine Association of Pharmaceutical Labs (CILFA); Argentine Industrial Union (manufacturers' association); Argentine Rural Society (large landowners' association); business organizations; General Confederation of Labor or CGT (Peronist-leaning umbrella labor organization); Peronist-dominated labor movement; Roman Catholic Church; students
International organization participation: AfDB, Australia Group, BCIE, BIS, FAO, G-6, G-15, G-24, G-77, IADB, IAEA, IBRD, ICAO, ICC, ICCt, ICFTU, ICRM, IDA, IFAD, IFC, IFRCS, IHO, ILO, IMF, IMO, Interpol, IOC, IOM, ISO, ITU, LAES, LAIA, Mercosur, MICAH, MINURSO, NSG, OAS, OPANAL, OPCW, PCA, RG, UN, UNCTAD, UNESCO, UNFICYP, UNHCR, UNIDO, UNMIK, UNMOVIC, UNTSO, UPU, WCL, WCO, WFTU, WHO, WIPO, WMO, WToO, WTrO, ZC
Diplomatic representation in the US:
chief of mission: Ambassador Jose Octavio BORDON
chancery: 1600 New Hampshire Avenue NW, Washington, DC 20009
telephone: [1] (202) 238-6400
FAX: [1] (202) 332-3171
consulate(s) general: Atlanta, Chicago, Houston, Los Angeles, Miami, New York
Diplomatic representation from the US:
chief of mission: Ambassador Lino GUTIERREZ
embassy: Avenida Colombia 4300, C1425GMN Buenos Aires
mailing address: international mail: use street address; APO address: Unit 4334, APO AA 34034
telephone: [54] (11) 5777-4533
FAX: [54] (11) 5777-4240

Flag description: three equal horizontal bands of light blue (top), white, and light blue; centered in the white band is a radiant yellow sun with a human face known as the Sun of May

Economy

Economy - overview: Argentina benefits from rich natural resources, a highly literate population, an export-oriented agricultural sector, and a diversified industrial base. Over the past decade, however, the country has suffered recurring economic problems of inflation, external debt, capital flight, and budget deficits. Growth in 2000 was a negative 0.8%, as both domestic and foreign investors remained skeptical of the government's ability to pay debts and maintain the peso's fixed exchange rate with the US dollar. The economic situation worsened in 2001 with the widening of spreads on Argentine bonds, massive withdrawals from the banks, and a further decline in consumer and investor confidence. Government efforts to achieve a "zero deficit," to stabilize the banking system, and to restore economic growth proved inadequate in the face of the mounting economic problems. The peso's peg to the dollar was abandoned in January 2002, and the peso was floated in February; the exchange rate plunged and inflation picked up rapidly, but by mid-2002 the economy had stabilized, albeit at a lower level. Strong demand for the peso compelled the Central Bank to intervene in foreign exchange markets to curb its appreciation in 2003. Led by record exports, the economy began to recover with output up 8% in 2003, unemployment falling, and inflation reduced to under 4% at year-end.
GDP: purchasing power parity - $432.7 billion (2003 est.)
GDP - real growth rate: 8% (2003 est.)
GDP - per capita: purchasing power parity - $11,200 (2003 est.)
GDP - composition by sector:
agriculture: 5%
industry: 28%
services: 67% (2000 est.)
Population below poverty line: 51.7% (May 2003)
Household income or consumption by percentage share:
lowest 10%: NA%
highest 10%: NA%
Inflation rate (consumer prices): 3.7% (2003, yearend)
Labor force: 15 million (1999)
Labor force - by occupation: agriculture NA%, industry NA%, services NA%
Unemployment rate: 16.3% (September 2003)
Budget:
revenues: $44 billion
expenditures: $48 billion, including capital expenditures of $NA (2000 est.)
Industries: food processing, motor vehicles, consumer durables, textiles, chemicals and petrochemicals, printing, metallurgy, steel
Industrial production growth rate: 7% (2003 est.)

Argentina *(continued)*

Electricity - production: 97.17 billion kWh (2001)
Electricity - production by source:
fossil fuel: 52.2%
hydro: 40.8%
nuclear: 6.7%
other: 0.2% (2001)
Electricity - consumption: 92.12 billion kWh (2001)
Electricity - exports: 5.662 billion kWh (2001)
Electricity - imports: 7.417 billion kWh (2001)
Oil - production: 828,600 bbl/day (2001 est.)
Oil - consumption: 486,000 bbl/day (2001 est.)
Oil - exports: NA
Oil - imports: NA
Oil - proved reserves: 2.927 billion bbl (1 January 2002)
Natural gas - production: 37.15 billion cu m (2001 est.)
Natural gas - consumption: 31.1 billion cu m (2001 est.)
Natural gas - exports: 6.05 billion cu m (2001 est.)
Natural gas - imports: 0 cu m (2001 est.)
Natural gas - proved reserves: 768 billion cu m (1 January 2002)
Agriculture - products: sunflower seeds, lemons, soybeans, grapes, corn, tobacco, peanuts, tea, wheat; livestock
Exports: $29.57 billion f.o.b. (2003 est.)
Exports - commodities: edible oils, fuels and energy, cereals, feed, motor vehicles
Exports - partners: Brazil 18.8%, Chile 11.5%, US 11.5%, Spain 4.5%, China 4.2%, Netherlands 4.1% (2002)
Imports: $13.27 billion f.o.b. (2003 est.)
Imports - commodities: machinery and equipment, motor vehicles, chemicals, metal manufactures, plastics
Imports - partners: Brazil 28.1%, US 20.1%, Germany 6.2% (2002)
Debt - external: $142 billion (2002 est.)
Economic aid - recipient: $10 billion (2001 est.)
Currency: Argentine peso (ARS)
Currency code: ARS
Exchange rates: Argentine pesos per US dollar - 2.9003 (2003), 3.0633 (2002), 0.9995 (2001), 0.9995 (2000), 0.9995 (1999)
Fiscal year: calendar year

Communications

Telephones - main lines in use: 8,009,400 (2002)
Telephones - mobile cellular: 6.5 million (2002)
Telephone system:
general assessment: by opening the telecommunications market to competition and foreign investment with the "Telecommunications Liberalization Plan of 1998," Argentina encouraged the growth of modern telecommunication technology; fiber-optic cable trunk lines are being installed between all major cities; the major networks are entirely digital and the availability of telephone service is being improved; however, telephone density is presently minimal, and making telephone service universally available will take time
domestic: microwave radio relay, fiber-optic cable, and a domestic satellite system with 40 earth stations serve the trunk network; more than 110,000 pay telephones are installed and mobile telephone use is rapidly expanding
international: country code - 54; satellite earth stations - 8 Intelsat (Atlantic Ocean); Atlantis II and Unisur submarine cables; two international gateways near Buenos Aires (1999)
Radio broadcast stations: AM 260 (including 10 inactive stations), FM NA (probably more than 1,000, mostly unlicensed), shortwave 6 (1998)
Television broadcast stations: 42 (plus 444 repeaters) (1997)
Internet country code: .ar
Internet hosts: 495,920 (2002)
Internet users: 4.1 million (2002)

Transportation

Railways:
total: 34,463 km (168 km electrified)
broad gauge: 20,736 km 1.676-m gauge (142 km electrified)
standard gauge: 3,115 km 1.435-m gauge (26 km electrified)
narrow gauge: 10,375 km 1.000-m gauge; 237 km 0.750-m gauge (2002)
Highways:
total: 215,471 km
paved: 63,348 km (including 734 km of expressways)
unpaved: 152,123 km (1999)
Waterways: 10,950 km
Pipelines: gas 26,797 km; liquid petroleum gas 41 km; oil 3,668 km; refined products 2,945 km; unknown (oil/water) 13 km (2003)
Ports and harbors: Bahia Blanca, Buenos Aires, Comodoro Rivadavia, Concepcion del Uruguay, La Plata, Mar del Plata, Necochea, Rio Gallegos, Rosario, Santa Fe, Ushuaia
Merchant marine:
total: 45 ships (1,000 GRT or over) 149,007 GRT/212,620 DWT
by type: cargo 9, petroleum tanker 9, rail car carrier 1, refrigerated cargo 2, roll on/roll off 1, short-sea/passenger 1, specialized tanker 1
foreign-owned: Uruguay 1
registered in other countries: 26 (2003 est.)
Airports: 1,335 (2003 est.)
Airports - with paved runways:
total: 144
over 3,047 m: 4
2,438 to 3,047 m: 26
1,524 to 2,437 m: 62
914 to 1,523 m: 44
under 914 m: 8 (2003 est.)
Airports - with unpaved runways:
total: 1,191
over 3,047 m: 2
2,438 to 3,047 m: 2
1,524 to 2,437 m: 50
914 to 1,523 m: 570
under 914 m: 567 (2003 est.)

Military

Military branches: Argentine Army, Navy of the Argentine Republic (includes Naval Aviation and Marines), Argentine Air Force (Fuerza Aerea Argentina, FAA)
Military manpower - military age: 18 years of age (2004)
Military manpower - availability:
males age 15-49: 9,901,352 (2004 est.)
Military manpower - fit for military service:
males age 15-49: 8,042,304 (2004 est.)
Military manpower - reaching military age annually:
males: 327,738 (2004 est.)
Military expenditures - dollar figure: $4.3 billion (FY99)
Military expenditures - percent of GDP: 1.3% (FY00)

Transnational Issues

Disputes - international: UK continues to reject sovereignty talks requested by Argentina, whose constitution still claims UK-administered Falkland Islands (Islas Malvinas) and South Georgia and the South Sandwich Islands, but in 1995 ceded the right to settle the dispute by force; Beagle Channel islands dispute resolved through Papal mediation in 1984, but armed incidents persist since 1992 oil discovery; territorial claim in Antarctica partially overlaps UK and Chilean claims (see Antarctic disputes); unruly region at convergence of Argentina-Brazil-Paraguay borders is locus of money laundering, smuggling, arms and drug trafficking, and fundraising for extremist organizations; uncontested dispute between Brazil and Uruguay over Braziliera Island in the Quarai/Cuareim River leaves the tripoint with Argentina in question
Illicit drugs: used as a transshipment country for cocaine headed for Europe and the US; some money-laundering activity, especially in the Tri-Border Area; domestic consumption of drugs in urban centers is increasing

Armenia

Introduction

Background: Armenia prides itself on being the first nation to formally adopt Christianity (early 4th century). Despite periods of autonomy, over the centuries Armenia came under the sway of various empires including the Roman, Byzantine, Arab, Persian, and Ottoman. It was incorporated into Russia in 1828 and the USSR in 1920. Armenian leaders remain preoccupied by the long conflict with Muslim Azerbaijan over Nagorno-Karabakh, a primarily Armenian-populated region, assigned to Soviet Azerbaijan in the 1920s by Moscow. Armenia and Azerbaijan began fighting over the area in 1988; the struggle escalated after both countries attained independence from the Soviet Union in 1991. By May 1994, when a cease-fire took hold, Armenian forces held not only Nagorno-Karabakh but also a significant portion of Azerbaijan proper. The economies of both sides have been hurt by their inability to make substantial progress toward a peaceful resolution. Turkey imposed an economic blockade on Armenia and closed the common border because of the Armenian occupation of Nagorno-Karabakh and surrounding areas.

Geography

Location: Southwestern Asia, east of Turkey
Geographic coordinates: 40 00 N, 45 00 E
Map references: Asia
Area:
total: 29,800 sq km
land: 28,400 sq km
water: 1,400 sq km
Area - comparative: slightly smaller than Maryland
Land boundaries:
total: 1,254 km
border countries: Azerbaijan-proper 566 km, Azerbaijan-Naxcivan exclave 221 km, Georgia 164 km, Iran 35 km, Turkey 268 km
Coastline: 0 km (landlocked)

Maritime claims: none (landlocked)
Climate: highland continental, hot summers, cold winters
Terrain: Armenian Highland with mountains; little forest land; fast flowing rivers; good soil in Aras River valley
Elevation extremes:
lowest point: Debed River 400 m
highest point: Aragats Lerrnagagat' 4,090 m
Natural resources: small deposits of gold, copper, molybdenum, zinc, alumina
Land use:
arable land: 17.52%
permanent crops: 2.3%
other: 80.18% (1998 est.)
Irrigated land: 2,870 sq km (1998 est.)
Natural hazards: occasionally severe earthquakes; droughts
Environment - current issues: soil pollution from toxic chemicals such as DDT; the energy crisis of the 1990s led to deforestation when citizens scavenged for firewood; pollution of Hrazdan (Razdan) and Aras Rivers; the draining of Sevana Lich (Lake Sevan), a result of its use as a source for hydropower, threatens drinking water supplies; restart of Metsamor nuclear power plant in spite of its location in a seismically active zone
Environment - international agreements:
party to: Air Pollution, Biodiversity, Climate Change, Climate Change-Kyoto Protocol, Desertification, Hazardous Wastes, Law of the Sea, Ozone Layer Protection, Wetlands
signed, but not ratified: Air Pollution-Persistent Organic Pollutants
Geography - note: landlocked in the Lesser Caucasus Mountains; Sevana Lich (Lake Sevan) is the largest lake in this mountain range

People

Population: 2,991,360
note: Armenia's first census since independence was conducted in October 2001 (July 2004 est.)
Age structure:
0-14 years: 22.7% (male 357,094; female 323,396)
15-64 years: 66.7% (male 929,719; female 1,065,505)
65 years and over: 10.6% (male 128,027; female 187,619) (2004 est.)
Median age:
total: 29.7 years
male: 27.1 years
female: 32.4 years (2004 est.)
Population growth rate: -0.32% (2004 est.)
Birth rate: 11.43 births/1,000 population (2004 est.)
Death rate: 8.12 deaths/1,000 population (2004 est.)
Net migration rate: -6.47 migrant(s)/1,000 population (2004 est.)
Sex ratio:
at birth: 1.18 male(s)/female
under 15 years: 1.1 male(s)/female
15-64 years: 0.87 male(s)/female

65 years and over: 0.68 male(s)/female
total population: 0.9 male(s)/female (2004 est.)
Infant mortality rate:
total: 24.16 deaths/1,000 live births
male: 29.32 deaths/1,000 live births
female: 18.06 deaths/1,000 live births (2004 est.)
Life expectancy at birth:
total population: 71.23 years
male: 67.73 years
female: 75.36 years (2004 est.)
Total fertility rate: 1.31 children born/woman (2004 est.)
HIV/AIDS - adult prevalence rate: 0.2% (2001 est.)
HIV/AIDS - people living with HIV/AIDS: less than 2,400 (2001 est.)
HIV/AIDS - deaths: less than 100 (2001 est.)
Nationality:
noun: Armenian(s)
adjective: Armenian
Ethnic groups: Armenian 93%, Azeri 1%, Russian 2%, other (mostly Yezidi Kurds) 4% (2002)
note: as of the end of 1993, virtually all Azeris had emigrated from Armenia
Religions: Armenian Apostolic 94%, other Christian 4%, Yezidi (Zoroastrian/animist) 2%
Languages: Armenian 96%, Russian 2%, other 2%
Literacy:
definition: age 15 and over can read and write
total population: 98.6%
male: 99.4%
female: 98% (2003 est.)

Government

Country name:
conventional long form: Republic of Armenia
conventional short form: Armenia
local long form: Hayastani Hanrapetut'yun
local short form: Hayastan
former: Armenian Soviet Socialist Republic; Armenian Republic
Government type: republic
Capital: Yerevan
Administrative divisions: 11 provinces (marzer, singular - marz); Aragatsotn, Ararat, Armavir, Geghark'unik', Kotayk', Lorri, Shirak, Syunik', Tavush, Vayots' Dzor, Yerevan
Independence: 21 September 1991 (from Soviet Union)
National holiday: Independence Day, 21 September (1991)
Constitution: adopted by nationwide referendum 5 July 1995
Legal system: based on civil law system
Suffrage: 18 years of age; universal
Executive branch:
chief of state: President Robert KOCHARIAN (since 30 March 1998)
head of government: Prime Minister Andranik MARKARYAN (since 12 May 2000)
cabinet: Council of Ministers appointed by the prime minister

Armenia (continued)

elections: president elected by popular vote for a five-year term; election last held 19 February and 5 March 2003 (next to be held NA 2008); prime minister appointed by the president; the prime minister and Council of Ministers must resign if the National Assembly refuses to accept their program

election results: Robert KOCHARIAN reelected president; percent of vote - Robert KOCHARIAN 67.5%, Stepan DEMIRCHYAN 32.5%

Legislative branch: unicameral National Assembly (Parliament) or Azgayin Zhoghov (131 seats; members elected by popular vote to serve four-year terms; 75 members elected by party list, 56 by direct vote)

elections: last held 25 May 2003 (next to be held in the spring of 2007)

note: percent of vote by party - Republican Party 23.5%, Justice Bloc 13.6%, Rule of Law 12.3%, ARF (Dashnak) 11.4%, National Unity Party 8.8%, United Labor Party 5.7%; seats by party - Republican Party 23, Justice Bloc 14, Rule of Law 12, ARF (Dashnak) 11, National Unity 9, United Labor 6; note - seats by party change frequently as deputies switch parties or announce themselves independent

Judicial branch: Constitutional Court; Court of Cassation (Appeals Court)

Political parties and leaders: Agro-Industrial Party [Vladimir BADALIAN]; Armenia Party [Myasnik MALKHASYAN]; Armenian National Movement or ANM [Alex ARZUMANYAN, chairman]; Armenian Ramkavar Liberal Party or HRAK [Harutyun MIRZAKHANYAN, chairman]; Armenian Revolutionary Federation ("Dashnak" Party) or ARF [Vahan HOVHANISSIAN]; Democratic Party [Aram SARKISYAN]; Justice Bloc (comprised of the Democratic Party, National Democratic Party, National Democratic Union, and the People's Party); National Democratic Party [Shavarsh KOCHARIAN]; National Democratic Union or NDU [Vazgen MANUKIAN]; National Unity Party [Artashes GEGAMIAN, chairman]; People's Party of Armenia [Stepan DEMIRCHYAN]; Republic Party [Albert BAZEYAN and Aram SARKISYAN, chairmen]; Republican Party or RPA [Andranik MARKARYAN]; Rule of Law Party [Artur BAGDASARIAN, chairman]; Union of Constitutional Rights [Hrant KHACHATURYAN]; United Labor Party [Gurgen ARSENIAN]

Political pressure groups and leaders: Yerkrapah Union [Manvel GRIGORIAN]

International organization participation: BSEC, CE, CIS, EAPC, EBRD, FAO, IAEA, IBRD, ICAO, ICCt (signatory), ICRM, IDA, IFAD, IFC, IFRCS, ILO, IMF, Interpol, IOC, IOM, ISO, ITU, NAM (observer), OAS (observer), OPCW, OSCE, PFP, UN, UNCTAD, UNESCO, UNIDO, UPU, WCO, WFTU, WHO, WIPO, WMO, WToO, WTrO

Diplomatic representation in the US:
chief of mission: Ambassador Arman KIRAKOSSIAN
chancery: 2225 R Street NW, Washington, DC 20008
telephone: [1] (202) 319-1976
FAX: [1] (202) 319-2982
consulate(s) general: Los Angeles

Diplomatic representation from the US:
chief of mission: Ambassador John M. ORDWAY
embassy: 18 Baghramyan Ave., Yerevan 375019
mailing address: American Embassy Yerevan, Department of State, 7020 Yerevan Place, Washington, DC 20521-7020
telephone: [374](1) 521-611, 520-791, 542-177, 542-132, 524-661, 527-001, 524-840
FAX: [374](1) 520-800

Flag description: three equal horizontal bands of red (top), blue, and orange

Economy

Economy - overview: Under the old Soviet central planning system, Armenia had developed a modern industrial sector, supplying machine tools, textiles, and other manufactured goods to sister republics in exchange for raw materials and energy. Since the implosion of the USSR in December 1991, Armenia has switched to small-scale agriculture away from the large agroindustrial complexes of the Soviet era. The agricultural sector has long-term needs for more investment and updated technology. The privatization of industry has been at a slower pace, but has been given renewed emphasis by the current administration. Armenia is a food importer, and its mineral deposits (copper, gold, bauxite) are small. The ongoing conflict with Azerbaijan over the ethnic Armenian-dominated region of Nagorno-Karabakh and the breakup of the centrally directed economic system of the former Soviet Union contributed to a severe economic decline in the early 1990s. By 1994, however, the Armenian Government had launched an ambitious IMF-sponsored economic liberalization program that resulted in positive growth rates in 1995-2003. Armenia joined the WTrO in January 2003. Armenia also has managed to slash inflation, stabilize the local currency (the dram), and privatize most small- and medium-sized enterprises. The chronic energy shortages Armenia suffered in the early and mid-1990s have been offset by the energy supplied by one of its nuclear power plants at Metsamor. Armenia is now a net energy exporter, although it does not have sufficient generating capacity to replace Metsamor, which is under international pressure to close. The electricity distribution system was privatized in 2002. Armenia's severe trade imbalance has been offset somewhat by international aid and foreign direct investment. Economic ties with Russia remain close, especially in the energy sector.

GDP: purchasing power parity - $11.79 billion (2003 est.)

GDP - real growth rate: 9.9% (2003 est.)

GDP - per capita: purchasing power parity - $3,900 (2003 est.)

GDP - composition by sector:
agriculture: 23.1%
industry: 35.4%
services: 41.5% (2002 est.)

Population below poverty line: 50% (2002 est.)

Household income or consumption by percentage share:
lowest 10%: 2.3%
highest 10%: 46.2% (1999)

Distribution of family income - Gini index: 44.4 (1996)

Inflation rate (consumer prices): 4.3% (2003 est.)

Labor force: 1.4 million (2001)

Labor force - by occupation: agriculture 45%, services 30%, industry 25% (2002 est.)

Unemployment rate: 20% (2001 est.)

Budget:
revenues: $402 million
expenditures: $482 million, including capital expenditures of $NA (2003 est.)

Industries: diamond-processing, metal-cutting machine tools, forging-pressing machines, electric motors, tires, knitted wear, hosiery, shoes, silk fabric, chemicals, trucks, instruments, microelectronics, jewelry manufacturing, software development, food processing, brandy

Industrial production growth rate: 15% (2002 est.)

Electricity - production: 6.479 billion kWh (2001)

Electricity - production by source:
fossil fuel: 42.3%
hydro: 27%
nuclear: 30.7%
other: 0% (2001)

Electricity - consumption: 5.784 billion kWh (2001)

Electricity - exports: 704 million kWh; note - exports an unknown quantity to Georgia; includes exports to Nagorno-Karabakh region in Azerbaijan (2001)

Electricity - imports: 463 million kWh; note - imports an unknown quantity from Iran (2001)

Oil - production: 0 bbl/day (2001 est.)

Oil - consumption: 5,700 bbl/day (2001 est.)

Oil - exports: NA

Oil - imports: NA

Natural gas - production: 0 cu m (2001 est.)

Natural gas - consumption: 1.4 billion cu m (2001 est.)

Natural gas - exports: 0 cu m (2001 est.)

Natural gas - imports: 1.4 billion cu m (2001 est.)

Agriculture - products: fruit (especially grapes), vegetables; livestock

Exports: $735 million f.o.b. (2003 est.)

Exports - commodities: diamonds, mineral products, foodstuffs, energy

Exports - partners: Belgium 21.9%, Israel 16.4%, Russia 14.7%, Iran 11.2%, US 8.4%, Germany 6.6% (2002)

Imports: $1.18 billion f.o.b. (2003 est.)

Imports - commodities: natural gas, petroleum, tobacco products, foodstuffs, diamonds

Imports - partners: US 14.1%, Russia 11.9%, Belgium 11.3%, Israel 10%, Iran 9.5%, UAE 5.7%, Germany 5.1%, Italy 4.5%, Ukraine 4.2% (2002)

Debt - external: $905 million (June 2001)

Economic aid - recipient: ODA $170 million (2000)

Currency: dram (AMD)

Currency code: AMD

Armenia (continued)

Exchange rates: drams per US dollar - 578.763 (2002), 555.078 (2001), 539.526 (2000), 535.062 (1999)
Fiscal year: calendar year

Communications

Telephones - main lines in use: 542,800 (2002)
Telephones - mobile cellular: 71,900 (2002)
Telephone system:
general assessment: system inadequate; now 90% privately owned and undergoing modernization and expansion
domestic: the majority of subscribers and the most modern equipment are in Yerevan (this includes paging and mobile cellular service)
international: country code - 374; Yerevan is connected to the Trans-Asia-Europe fiber-optic cable through Iran; additional international service is available by microwave radio relay and landline connections to the other countries of the Commonwealth of Independent States and through the Moscow international switch and by satellite to the rest of the world; satellite earth stations - 1 Intelsat (2000)
Radio broadcast stations: AM 9, FM 6, shortwave 1 (1998)
Television broadcast stations: 3 (plus an unknown number of repeaters); (1998)
Internet country code: .am
Internet hosts: 2,850 (2002)
Internet users: 60,000 (2002)

Transportation

Railways:
total: 852 km in common carrier service; does not include industrial lines
broad gauge: 852 km 1.520-m gauge (779 km electrified) (2002)
Highways:
total: 15,918 km
paved: 15,329 km (includes 7,527 km of expressways)
unpaved: 589 km (2000)
Waterways: NA km
Pipelines: gas 2,031 km (2003)
Ports and harbors: none
Airports: 17 (2003 est.)
Airports - with paved runways:
total: 11
over 3,047 m: 2
2,438 to 3,047: 1
1,524 to 2,437 m: 5
914 to 1,523 m: 3 (2003 est.)
Airports - with unpaved runways:
total: 6
over 3,047 m: 1
1,524 to 2,437 m: 2
914 to 1,523 m: 2
under 914 m: 1 (2003 est.)

Military

Military branches: Army, Air Force and Air Defense Force
Military manpower - military age: 18 years of age (2004 est.)
Military manpower - availability:
males age 15-49: 812,140 (2004 est.)
Military manpower - fit for military service:
males age 15-49: 649,568 (2004 est.)
Military manpower - reaching military age annually:
males: 31,926 (2004 est.)
Military expenditures - dollar figure: $135 million (FY01)
Military expenditures - percent of GDP: 6.5% (FY01)

Transnational Issues

Disputes - international: Armenia supports ethnic Armenian secessionists in Nagorno-Karabakh and militarily occupies 16% of Azerbaijan - Organization for Security and Cooperation in Europe (OSCE) continues to mediate dispute; border with Turkey remains closed over Nagorno-Karabakh dispute; traditional demands regarding former Armenian lands in Turkey have subsided; ethnic Armenian groups in Javakheti region of Georgia seek greater autonomy from the new Georgian Government
Illicit drugs: illicit cultivation of small amount of cannabis for domestic consumption; used as a transit point for illicit drugs - mostly opium and hashish - moving from Southwest Asia to Russia and to a lesser extent the rest of Europe

Aruba
(part of the Kingdom of the Netherlands)

Introduction

Background: Discovered and claimed for Spain in 1499, Aruba was acquired by the Dutch in 1636. The island's economy has been dominated by three main industries. A 19th century gold rush was followed by prosperity brought on by the opening in 1924 of an oil refinery. The last decades of the 20th century saw a boom in the tourism industry. Aruba seceded from the Netherlands Antilles in 1986 and became a separate, autonomous member of the Kingdom of the Netherlands. Movement toward full independence was halted at Aruba's request in 1990.

Geography

Location: Caribbean, island in the Caribbean Sea, north of Venezuela
Geographic coordinates: 12 30 N, 69 58 W
Map references: Central America and the Caribbean
Area:
total: 193 sq km
land: 193 sq km
water: 0 sq km
Area - comparative: slightly larger than Washington, DC
Land boundaries: 0 km
Coastline: 68.5 km
Maritime claims:
territorial sea: 12 NM
Climate: tropical marine; little seasonal temperature variation
Terrain: flat with a few hills; scant vegetation
Elevation extremes:
lowest point: Caribbean Sea 0 m
highest point: Mount Jamanota 188 m
Natural resources: NEGL; white sandy beaches
Land use:
arable land: 10.53% (including aloe 0.01%)
permanent crops: 0%
other: 89.47% (1998 est.)

Aruba *(continued)*

Irrigated land: 0.01 sq km (1998 est.)
Natural hazards: lies outside the Caribbean hurricane belt
Environment - current issues: NA
Geography - note: a flat, riverless island renowned for its white sand beaches; its tropical climate is moderated by constant trade winds from the Atlantic Ocean; the temperature is almost constant at about 27 degrees Celsius (81 degrees Fahrenheit)

People

Population: 71,218 (July 2004 est.)
Age structure:
0-14 years: 20.3% (male 7,429; female 7,051)
15-64 years: 68.2% (male 23,587; female 25,007)
65 years and over: 11.4% (male 3,347; female 4,797) (2004 est.)
Median age:
total: 37.5 years
male: 35.7 years
female: 39.1 years (2004 est.)
Population growth rate: 0.51% (2004 est.)
Birth rate: 11.53 births/1,000 population (2004 est.)
Death rate: 6.47 deaths/1,000 population (2004 est.)
Net migration rate: 0 migrant(s)/1,000 population (2004 est.)
Sex ratio:
at birth: 1.05 male(s)/female
under 15 years: 1.05 male(s)/female
15-64 years: 0.94 male(s)/female
65 years and over: 0.7 male(s)/female
total population: 0.93 male(s)/female (2004 est.)
Infant mortality rate:
total: 6.02 deaths/1,000 live births
male: 6.85 deaths/1,000 live births
female: 5.14 deaths/1,000 live births (2004 est.)
Life expectancy at birth:
total population: 78.98 years
male: 75.64 years
female: 82.49 years (2004 est.)
Total fertility rate: 1.79 children born/woman (2004 est.)
HIV/AIDS - adult prevalence rate: NA%
HIV/AIDS - people living with HIV/AIDS: NA
HIV/AIDS - deaths: NA
Nationality:
noun: Aruban(s)
adjective: Aruban; Dutch
Ethnic groups: mixed white/Caribbean Amerindian 80%
Religions: Roman Catholic 82%, Protestant 8%, Hindu, Muslim, Confucian, Jewish
Languages: Dutch (official), Papiamento (a Spanish, Portuguese, Dutch, English dialect), English (widely spoken), Spanish
Literacy:
definition:
total population: 97%
male: NA%
female: NA%

Government

Country name:
conventional long form: none
conventional short form: Aruba
Dependency status: part of the Kingdom of the Netherlands; full autonomy in internal affairs obtained in 1986 upon separation from the Netherlands Antilles; Dutch Government responsible for defense and foreign affairs
Government type: parliamentary democracy
Capital: Oranjestad
Administrative divisions: none (part of the Kingdom of the Netherlands)
Independence: none (part of the Kingdom of the Netherlands)
National holiday: Flag Day, 18 March
Constitution: 1 January 1986
Legal system: based on Dutch civil law system, with some English common law influence
Suffrage: 18 years of age; universal
Executive branch:
chief of state: Queen BEATRIX of the Netherlands (since 30 April 1980), represented by Governor General Olindo KOOLMAN (since 1 January 1992)
head of government: Prime Minister Nelson O. ODUBER (since 30 October 2001); Deputy Prime Minister Fredis REFUNJOL
cabinet: Council of Ministers (elected by the Staten)
elections: the monarch is hereditary; governor general appointed for a six-year term by the monarch; prime minister and deputy prime minister elected by the Staten for four-year terms; election last held 28 September 2001 (next to be held by December 2005)
election results: Nelson O. ODUBER elected prime minister; percent of legislative vote - NA%
Legislative branch: unicameral Legislature or Staten (21 seats; members elected by direct, popular vote to serve four-year terms)
elections: last held 28 September 2001 (next to be held by NA 2005)
election results: percent of vote by party - MEP 52.4%, AVP 26.7%, PPA 9.6%, OLA 5.7%, Aliansa 3.5%, other 2.1%; seats by party - MEP 12, AVP 6, PPA 2, OLA 1
Judicial branch: Joint High Court of Justice (judges are appointed by the monarch)
Political parties and leaders: Aruba Solidarity Movement or MAS [leader NA]; Aruban Democratic Alliance or Aliansa [leader NA]; Aruban Democratic Party or PDA [Leo BERLINSKI]; Aruban Liberal Party or OLA [Glenbert CROES]; Aruban Patriotic Party or PPA [Benny NISBET]; Aruban People's Party or AVP [Jan (Henny) H. EMAN]; Concentration for the Liberation of Aruba or CLA [leader NA]; People's Electoral Movement Party or MEP [Nelson O. ODUBER]; For a Restructured Aruba Now or PARA [Urbana LOPEZ]; National Democratic Action or ADN [Pedro Charro KELLY]
Political pressure groups and leaders: NA
International organization participation: Interpol, IOC, UNESCO (associate), WCL, WToO (associate)

Diplomatic representation in the US: none (represented by the Kingdom of the Netherlands)
Diplomatic representation from the US: the US does not have an embassy in Aruba; the Consul General to Netherlands Antilles, Deborah A. BOLTON, is accredited to Aruba
Flag description: blue, with two narrow, horizontal, yellow stripes across the lower portion and a red, four-pointed star outlined in white in the upper hoist-side corner

Economy

Economy - overview: Tourism is the mainstay of the small, open Aruban economy, with offshore banking and oil refining and storage also important. The rapid growth of the tourism sector over the last decade has resulted in a substantial expansion of other activities. Construction has boomed, with hotel capacity five times the 1985 level. In addition, the reopening of the country's oil refinery in 1993, a major source of employment and foreign exchange earnings, has further spurred growth. Aruba's small labor force and low unemployment rate have led to a large number of unfilled job vacancies, despite sharp rises in wage rates in recent years. Tourist arrivals have declined in the aftermath of the 11 September 2001 terrorist attacks on the US. The government now must deal with a budget deficit and a negative trade balance.
GDP: purchasing power parity - $1.94 billion (2002 est.)
GDP - real growth rate: -1.5% (2002 est.)
GDP - per capita: purchasing power parity - $28,000 (2002 est.)
GDP - composition by sector:
agriculture: NA%
industry: NA%
services: NA%
Population below poverty line: NA%
Household income or consumption by percentage share:
lowest 10%: NA%
highest 10%: NA%
Inflation rate (consumer prices): 3.2% (2002 est.)
Labor force: 41,501 (1997 est.)
Labor force - by occupation: most employment is in wholesale and retail trade and repair, followed by hotels and restaurants; oil refining
Unemployment rate: 0.6% (2003 est.)
Budget:
revenues: $135.81 million
expenditures: $147 million, including capital expenditures of $NA (2000)
Industries: tourism, transshipment facilities, oil refining
Industrial production growth rate: NA (2002 est.)
Electricity - production: 531.9 million kWh (2001)
Electricity - production by source:
fossil fuel: 100%
hydro: 0%
nuclear: 0%
other: 0% (2001)

Aruba *(continued)*

Electricity - consumption: 494.7 million kWh (2001)
Electricity - exports: 0 kWh (2001)
Electricity - imports: 0 kWh (2001)
Oil - production: 0 bbl/day (2001 est.)
Oil - consumption: 6,500 bbl/day (2001 est.)
Oil - exports: NA
Oil - imports: NA
Agriculture - products: aloes; livestock; fish
Exports: $128 million f.o.b. (including oil reexports) (2002 est.)
Exports - commodities: live animals and animal products, art and collectibles, machinery and electrical equipment, transport equipment
Exports - partners: Netherlands 28.9%, Colombia 21.9%, Panama 17.2%, US 12.5%, Netherlands Antilles 8.6%, Venezuela 7.8% (2002)
Imports: $841 million f.o.b. (2002 est.)
Imports - commodities: machinery and electrical equipment, crude oil for refining and reexport, chemicals; foodstuffs
Imports - partners: US 54.6%, Netherlands 12.7%, UK 5.7% (2002)
Debt - external: $285 million (1996)
Economic aid - recipient: $26 million (1995); note - the Netherlands provided a $127 million aid package to Aruba and Suriname in 1996
Currency: Aruban guilder/florin (AWG)
Currency code: AWG
Exchange rates: Aruban guilders/florins per US dollar - 1.79 (2003), 1.79 (2002), 1.79 (2001), 1.79 (2000), 1.79 (1999)
Fiscal year: calendar year

Communications

Telephones - main lines in use: 37,100 (2002)
Telephones - mobile cellular: 53,000 (2001)
Telephone system:
general assessment: NA
domestic: more than adequate
international: country code - 297; 1 submarine cable to Sint Maarten (Netherlands Antilles); extensive interisland microwave radio relay links
Radio broadcast stations: AM 4, FM 6, shortwave 0 (1998)
Television broadcast stations: 1 (1997)
Internet country code: .aw
Internet hosts: 923 (2001)
Internet users: 24,000 (2002)

Transportation

Railways: 0 km
Highways:
total: 800 km
paved: 513 km
unpaved: 287 km
note: most coastal roads are paved, while unpaved roads serve large tracts of the interior (1995)
Waterways: none
Ports and harbors: Barcadera, Oranjestad, Sint Nicolaas

Merchant marine:
total: 3 ships (1,000 GRT or over) 5,772 GRT/7,068 DWT
by type: cargo 1, petroleum tanker 2
foreign-owned: Germany 1, Russia 1
registered in other countries: 1 (2003 est.)
Airports: 1 (2003 est.)
Airports - with paved runways:
total: 1
2,438 to 3,047 m: 1 (2003 est.)

Military

Military branches: no regular indigenous military forces; Royal Dutch Navy and Marines, Coast Guard
Military - note: defense is the responsibility of the Kingdom of the Netherlands

Transnational Issues

Disputes - international: none
Illicit drugs: transit point for US- and Europe-bound narcotics with some accompanying money-laundering activity

Ashmore and Cartier Islands
(territory of Australia)

Introduction

Background: These uninhabited islands came under Australian authority in 1931; formal administration began two years later. Ashmore Reef supports a rich and diverse avian and marine habitat; in 1983, it became a National Nature Reserve. Cartier Island, a former bombing range, is now a marine reserve.

Geography

Location: Southeastern Asia, islands in the Indian Ocean, midway between north-western Australia and Timor island
Geographic coordinates: 12 14 S, 123 05 E
Map references: Southeast Asia
Area:
total: 5 sq km
land: 5 sq km
water: 0 sq km
note: includes Ashmore Reef (West, Middle, and East Islets) and Cartier Island
Area - comparative: about eight times the size of The Mall in Washington, DC
Land boundaries: 0 km
Coastline: 74.1 km
Maritime claims:
territorial sea: 12 NM
contiguous zone: 12 NM
continental shelf: 200-m depth or to the depth of exploitation
exclusive fishing zone: 200 NM
Climate: tropical
Terrain: low with sand and coral
Elevation extremes:
lowest point: Indian Ocean 0 m
highest point: unnamed location 3 m
Natural resources: fish

Ashmore and Cartier Islands

(continued)

Land use:

arable land: 0%

permanent crops: 0%

other: 100% (all grass and sand) (1998 est.)

Irrigated land: 0 sq km (1998 est.)

Natural hazards: surrounded by shoals and reefs that can pose maritime hazards

Environment - current issues: NA

Geography - note: Ashmore Reef National Nature Reserve established in August 1983

People

Population: no indigenous inhabitants

note: Indonesian fishermen are allowed access to the lagoon and fresh water at Ashmore Reef's West Island (July 2004 est.)

People - note: the landing of illegal immigrants from Indonesia's Rote Island has become an ongoing problem

Government

Country name:

conventional long form: Territory of Ashmore and Cartier Islands

conventional short form: Ashmore and Cartier Islands

Dependency status: territory of Australia; administered by the Australian Department of Transport and Regional Services

Legal system: the laws of the Commonwealth of Australia and the laws of the Northern Territory of Australia, where applicable, apply

Diplomatic representation in the US: none (territory of Australia)

Diplomatic representation from the US: none (territory of Australia)

Flag description: the flag of Australia is used

Economy

Economy - overview: no economic activity

Transportation

Waterways: none

Ports and harbors: none; offshore anchorage only

Military

Military - note: defense is the responsibility of Australia; periodic visits by the Royal Australian Navy and Royal Australian Air Force

Transnational Issues

Disputes - international: Indonesian groups challenge Australia's claim to Ashmore Reef; Australia has closed the surrounding waters to Indonesian traditional fishing and has created a national park in the region while continuing to prospect for hydrocarbons in the vicinity

Atlantic Ocean

Introduction

Background: The Atlantic Ocean is the second largest of the world's five oceans (after the Pacific Ocean, but larger than the Indian Ocean, Southern Ocean, and Arctic Ocean). The Kiel Canal (Germany), Oresund (Denmark-Sweden), Bosporus (Turkey), Strait of Gibraltar (Morocco-Spain), and the Saint Lawrence Seaway (Canada-US) are important strategic access waterways. The decision by the International Hydrographic Organization in the spring of 2000 to delimit a fifth world ocean, the Southern Ocean, removed the portion of the Atlantic Ocean south of 60 degrees south.

Geography

Location: body of water between Africa, Europe, the Southern Ocean, and the Western Hemisphere

Geographic coordinates: 0 00 N, 25 00 W

Map references: Political Map of the World

Area:

total: 76.762 million sq km

note: includes Baltic Sea, Black Sea, Caribbean Sea, Davis Strait, Denmark Strait, part of the Drake Passage, Gulf of Mexico, Labrador Sea, Mediterranean Sea, North Sea, Norwegian Sea, almost all of the Scotia Sea, and other tributary water bodies

Area - comparative: slightly less than 6.5 times the size of the US

Coastline: 111,866 km

Climate: tropical cyclones (hurricanes) develop off the coast of Africa near Cape Verde and move westward into the Caribbean Sea; hurricanes can occur from May to December, but are most frequent from August to November

Terrain: surface usually covered with sea ice in Labrador Sea, Denmark Strait, and coastal portions of the Baltic Sea from October to June; clockwise warm-water gyre (broad, circular system of currents) in the northern Atlantic, counterclockwise warm-water gyre in the southern Atlantic; the ocean floor is dominated by the Mid-Atlantic Ridge, a rugged north-south centerline for the entire Atlantic basin

Elevation extremes:

lowest point: Milwaukee Deep in the Puerto Rico Trench -8,605 m

highest point: sea level 0 m

Natural resources: oil and gas fields, fish, marine mammals (seals and whales), sand and gravel aggregates, placer deposits, polymetallic nodules, precious stones

Natural hazards: icebergs common in Davis Strait, Denmark Strait, and the northwestern Atlantic Ocean from February to August and have been spotted as far south as Bermuda and the Madeira Islands; ships subject to superstructure icing in extreme northern Atlantic from October to May; persistent fog can be a maritime hazard from May to September; hurricanes (May to December)

Environment - current issues: endangered marine species include the manatee, seals, sea lions, turtles, and whales; drift net fishing is hastening the decline of fish stocks and contributing to international disputes; municipal sludge pollution off eastern US, southern Brazil, and eastern Argentina; oil pollution in Caribbean Sea, Gulf of Mexico, Lake Maracaibo, Mediterranean Sea, and North Sea; industrial waste and municipal sewage pollution in Baltic Sea, North Sea, and Mediterranean Sea

Geography - note: major chokepoints include the Dardanelles, Strait of Gibraltar, access to the Panama and Suez Canals; strategic straits include the Strait of Dover, Straits of Florida, Mona Passage, The Sound (Oresund), and Windward Passage; the Equator divides the Atlantic Ocean into the North Atlantic Ocean and South Atlantic Ocean

Economy

Economy - overview: The Atlantic Ocean provides some of the world's most heavily trafficked sea routes, between and within the Eastern and Western Hemispheres. Other economic activity includes the exploitation of natural resources, e.g., fishing, the dredging of aragonite sands (The Bahamas), and production of crude oil and natural gas (Caribbean Sea, Gulf of Mexico, and North Sea).

Transportation

Ports and harbors: Alexandria (Egypt), Algiers (Algeria), Antwerp (Belgium), Barcelona (Spain), Buenos Aires (Argentina), Casablanca (Morocco), Colon (Panama), Copenhagen (Denmark), Dakar (Senegal), Gdansk (Poland), Hamburg (Germany), Helsinki (Finland), Las Palmas (Canary Islands, Spain), Le Havre (France), Lisbon (Portugal), London (UK), Marseille (France), Montevideo (Uruguay), Montreal (Canada), Naples (Italy), New Orleans (US), New York (US), Oran (Algeria), Oslo (Norway), Peiraiefs or Piraeus (Greece), Rio de Janeiro (Brazil), Rotterdam (Netherlands), Saint Petersburg (Russia), Stockholm (Sweden)

Transportation - note: Kiel Canal and Saint Lawrence Seaway are two important waterways; significant domestic commercial and recreational use of Intracoastal Waterway on central and south Atlantic seaboard and Gulf of Mexico coast of US

Transnational Issues

Disputes - international: some maritime disputes (see littoral states)

Australia

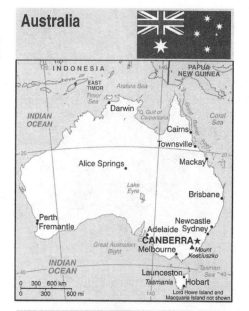

Introduction

Background: Aboriginal settlers arrived on the continent from Southeast Asia about 40,000 years before the first Europeans began exploration in the 17th century. No formal claims were made until 1770, when Capt. James COOK took possession in the name of Great Britain. Six colonies were created in the late 18th and 19th centuries; they federated and became the Commonwealth of Australia in 1901. The new country was able to take advantage of its natural resources in order to rapidly develop its agricultural and manufacturing industries and to make a major contribution to the British effort in World Wars I and II. Long-term concerns include pollution, particularly depletion of the ozone layer, and management and conservation of coastal areas, especially the Great Barrier Reef. A referendum to change Australia's status, from a commonwealth headed by the British monarch to a republic, was defeated in 1999.

Geography

Location: Oceania, continent between the Indian Ocean and the South Pacific Ocean
Geographic coordinates: 27 00 S, 133 00 E
Map references: Oceania
Area:
total: 7,686,850 sq km
land: 7,617,930 sq km
water: 68,920 sq km
note: includes Lord Howe Island and Macquarie Island
Area - comparative: slightly smaller than the US contiguous 48 states
Land boundaries: 0 km
Coastline: 25,760 km
Maritime claims:
territorial sea: 12 NM
contiguous zone: 24 NM

exclusive economic zone: 200 NM
continental shelf: 200 NM or to the edge of the continental margin
Climate: generally arid to semiarid; temperate in south and east; tropical in north
Terrain: mostly low plateau with deserts; fertile plain in southeast
Elevation extremes:
lowest point: Lake Eyre -15 m
highest point: Mount Kosciuszko 2,229 m
Natural resources: bauxite, coal, iron ore, copper, tin, gold, silver, uranium, nickel, tungsten, mineral sands, lead, zinc, diamonds, natural gas, petroleum
Land use:
arable land: 6.88%
permanent crops: 0.03%
other: 93.09% (1998 est.)
Irrigated land: 24,000 sq km (1998 est.)
Natural hazards: cyclones along the coast; severe droughts; forest fires
Environment - current issues: soil erosion from overgrazing, industrial development, urbanization, and poor farming practices; soil salinity rising due to the use of poor quality water; desertification; clearing for agricultural purposes threatens the natural habitat of many unique animal and plant species; the Great Barrier Reef off the northeast coast, the largest coral reef in the world, is threatened by increased shipping and its popularity as a tourist site; limited natural fresh water resources
Environment - international agreements:
party to: Antarctic-Environmental Protocol, Antarctic-Marine Living Resources, Antarctic Seals, Antarctic Treaty, Biodiversity, Climate Change, Desertification, Endangered Species, Environmental Modification, Hazardous Wastes, Law of the Sea, Marine Dumping, Marine Life Conservation, Ozone Layer Protection, Ship Pollution, Tropical Timber 83, Tropical Timber 94, Wetlands, Whaling
signed, but not ratified: Climate Change-Kyoto Protocol
Geography - note: world's smallest continent but sixth-largest country; population concentrated along the eastern and southeastern coasts; regular, tropical, invigorating, sea breeze known as "the Doctor" occurs along the west coast in the summer

People

Population: 19,913,144 (July 2004 est.)
Age structure:
0-14 years: 20.1% (male 2,044,449; female 1,948,574)
15-64 years: 67.2% (male 6,747,687; female 6,623,995)
65 years and over: 12.8% (male 1,121,522; female 1,426,917) (2004 est.)
Median age:
total: 36.3 years
male: 35.5 years
female: 37.1 years (2004 est.)

Population growth rate: 0.9% (2004 est.)
Birth rate: 12.4 births/1,000 population (2004 est.)
Death rate: 7.38 deaths/1,000 population (2004 est.)
Net migration rate: 3.98 migrant(s)/1,000 population (2004 est.)
Sex ratio:
at birth: 1.05 male(s)/female
under 15 years: 1.05 male(s)/female
15-64 years: 1.02 male(s)/female
65 years and over: 0.79 male(s)/female
total population: 0.99 male(s)/female (2004 est.)
Infant mortality rate:
total: 4.76 deaths/1,000 live births
male: 5.16 deaths/1,000 live births
female: 4.34 deaths/1,000 live births (2004 est.)
Life expectancy at birth:
total population: 80.26 years
male: 77.4 years
female: 83.27 years (2004 est.)
Total fertility rate: 1.76 children born/woman (2004 est.)
HIV/AIDS - adult prevalence rate: 0.1% (2001 est.)
HIV/AIDS - people living with HIV/AIDS: 12,000 (2001 est.)
HIV/AIDS - deaths: less than 100 (2001 est.)
Nationality:
noun: Australian(s)
adjective: Australian
Ethnic groups: Caucasian 92%, Asian 7%, aboriginal and other 1%
Religions: Anglican 26.1%, Roman Catholic 26%, other Christian 24.3%, non-Christian 11%, other 12.6%
Languages: English, native languages
Literacy:
definition: age 15 and over can read and write
total population: 100%
male: 100%
female: 100% (1980 est.)

Government

Country name:
conventional long form: Commonwealth of Australia
conventional short form: Australia
Government type: democratic, federal-state system recognizing the British monarch as sovereign
Capital: Canberra
Administrative divisions: 6 states and 2 territories*; Australian Capital Territory*, New South Wales, Northern Territory*, Queensland, South Australia, Tasmania, Victoria, Western Australia
Dependent areas: Ashmore and Cartier Islands, Christmas Island, Cocos (Keeling) Islands, Coral Sea Islands, Heard Island and McDonald Islands, Norfolk Island
Independence: 1 January 1901 (federation of UK colonies)
National holiday: Australia Day, 26 January (1788)
Constitution: 9 July 1900, effective 1 January 1901
Legal system: based on English common law; accepts compulsory ICJ jurisdiction, with reservations

Suffrage: 18 years of age; universal and compulsory
Executive branch:
chief of state: Queen of Australia ELIZABETH II (since 6 February 1952), represented by Governor General Maj. Gen. (Ret.) Michael JEFFREY (since 11 August 2003)
head of government: Prime Minister John Winston HOWARD (since 11 March 1996); Deputy Prime Minister John ANDERSON (since 20 July 1999)
cabinet: Parliament nominates and selects, from among its members, a list of candidates to serve as government ministers; from this list, the governor general swears in the final selections for the Cabinet
elections: none; the monarch is hereditary; governor general appointed by the monarch on the recommendation of the prime minister; following legislative elections, the leader of the majority party or leader of a majority coalition is sworn in as prime minister by the governor general
note: government coalition - Liberal Party and National Party
Legislative branch: bicameral Federal Parliament consists of the Senate (76 seats - 12 from each of the six states and two from each of the two mainland territories; one-half of the members elected every three years by popular vote to serve six-year terms) and the House of Representatives (150 seats - this is up from 148 seats in 2001 election; members elected by popular vote on the basis of preferential representation to serve three-year terms; no state can have fewer than five representatives)
elections: Senate - last held 10 November 2001 (next to be held by NA February 2005); House of Representatives - last held 10 November 2001 (next to be held by NA February 2005)
election results: Senate - percent of vote by party - NA%; seats by party - Liberal Party-National Party coalition 34, Australian Labor Party 28, Australian Democrats 7, Green Party 2, One Nation Party 1, Country Liberal Party 1, independent 3; House of Representatives - percent of vote by party - NA%; seats by party - Liberal Party-National Party coalition 81, Australian Labor Party 64, Green Party 1, Country Liberal Party 1, independent and other 3
Judicial branch: High Court (the chief justice and six other justices are appointed by the governor general)
Political parties and leaders: Australian Democrats [Andrew BARTLETT]; Australian Labor Party [Mark LATHAM]; Australian Progressive Alliance [Meg LEES]; Country Liberal Party [Paul BUNKER]; Australian Greens [Bob BROWN]; Liberal Party [John Winston HOWARD]; The Nationals [John ANDERSON]; One Nation Party [Len HARRIS]
Political pressure groups and leaders: Australian Monarchist League [leader NA]; Australian Republican Movement [leader NA]
International organization participation: ANZUS, APEC, ARF, AsDB, ASEAN (dialogue partner), Australia Group, BIS, C, CP, EBRD, FAO, IAEA, IBRD, ICAO, ICC, ICCt, ICFTU, ICRM, IDA, IEA, IFAD, IFC, IFRCS, IHO, ILO, IMF, IMO, Interpol, IOC, IOM, ISO, ITU, NAM (guest), NEA, NSG, OECD,

OPCW, Paris Club, PCA, PIF, Sparteca, UN, UNCTAD, UNESCO, UNHCR, UNMEE, UNMISET, UNTSO, UPU, WCO, WFTU, WHO, WIPO, WMO, WTrO, ZC
Diplomatic representation in the US:
chief of mission: Ambassador Michael J. THAWLEY
chancery: 1601 Massachusetts Avenue NW, Washington, DC 20036
telephone: [1] (202) 797-3000
FAX: [1] (202) 797-3168
consulate(s) general: Atlanta, Chicago, Honolulu, Los Angeles, New York, and San Francisco
Diplomatic representation from the US:
chief of mission: Ambassador J. Thomas SCHIEFFER
embassy: Moonah Place, Yarralumla, Canberra, Australian Capital Territory 2600
mailing address: APO AP 96549
telephone: [61] (02) 6214-5600
FAX: [61] (02) 6214-5970
consulate(s) general: Melbourne, Perth, Sydney
Flag description: blue with the flag of the UK in the upper hoist-side quadrant and a large seven-pointed star in the lower hoist-side quadrant known as the Commonwealth Star, representing the federation of the colonies of Australia in 1901; the star depicts one point for each of the six original states and one representing all of Australia's internal and external territories; the remaining half is a representation of the Southern Cross constellation in white with one small five-pointed star and four larger, seven-pointed stars

Economy

Economy - overview: Australia has a prosperous Western-style capitalist economy, with a per capita GDP on par with the four dominant West European economies. Rising output in the domestic economy has been offsetting the global slump, and business and consumer confidence remains robust. Australia's emphasis on reforms is another key factor behind the economy's strength. The impact of drought, weak foreign demand, and strong import demand pushed the trade deficit up to $14 billion in 2003 from $5 billion in 2002.
GDP: purchasing power parity - $570.3 billion (2003 est.)
GDP - real growth rate: 2.8% (2003 est.)
GDP - per capita: purchasing power parity - $28,900 (2003 est.)
GDP - composition by sector:
agriculture: 3%
industry: 25%
services: 72% (2003 est.)
Population below poverty line: NA%
Household income or consumption by percentage share:
lowest 10%: 2%
highest 10%: 25.4% (1994)
Distribution of family income - Gini index: 35.2 (1994)
Inflation rate (consumer prices): 2.7% (2003 est.)

Australia *(continued)*

Labor force: 9.2 million (December 2001)
Labor force - by occupation: services 73%, industry 22%, agriculture 5% (1997 est.)
Unemployment rate: 6.1% (2003)
Budget:
revenues: $86.8 billion
expenditures: $84.1 billion, including capital expenditures of $NA (FY00/01 est.)
Industries: mining, industrial and transportation equipment, food processing, chemicals, steel
Industrial production growth rate: 1.1% (2003 est.)
Electricity - production: 198.2 billion kWh (2001)
Electricity - production by source:
fossil fuel: 90.8%
hydro: 8.3%
nuclear: 0%
other: 0.9% (2001)
Electricity - consumption: 184.4 billion kWh (2001)
Electricity - exports: 0 kWh (2001)
Electricity - imports: 0 kWh (2001)
Oil - production: 731,000 bbl/day (2001 est.)
Oil - consumption: 796,500 bbl/day (2001 est.)
Oil - exports: 523,400 bbl/day (2001)
Oil - imports: 530,800 bbl/day (2001)
Oil - proved reserves: 3.664 billion bbl (1 January 2002)
Natural gas - production: 33.08 billion cu m (2001 est.)
Natural gas - consumption: 23.33 billion cu m (2001 est.)
Natural gas - exports: 9.744 billion cu m (2001 est.)
Natural gas - imports: 0 cu m (2001 est.)
Natural gas - proved reserves: 2.407 trillion cu m (1 January 2002)
Agriculture - products: wheat, barley, sugarcane, fruits; cattle, sheep, poultry
Exports: $68.67 billion (2003 est.)
Exports - commodities: coal, gold, meat, wool, alumina, iron ore, wheat, machinery and transport equipment
Exports - partners: Japan 18.5%, US 9.6%, South Korea 8.3%, China 6.9%, New Zealand 6.5%, UK 4.7%, Singapore 4.1%, Taiwan 4% (2002)
Imports: $82.91 billion (2003 est.)
Imports - commodities: machinery and transport equipment, computers and office machines, telecommunication equipment and parts; crude oil and petroleum products
Imports - partners: US 18.3%, Japan 12.3%, China 10.1%, Germany 5.7%, UK 4.6% (2002)
Debt - external: $193 billion (2003 est.)
Economic aid - donor: ODA, $894 million (FY99/00)
Currency: Australian dollar (AUD)
Currency code: AUD
Exchange rates: Australian dollars per US dollar - 1.5419 (2003), 1.8406 (2002), 1.9334 (2001), 1.7248 (2000), 1.55 (1999)
Fiscal year: 1 July - 30 June

Communications

Telephones - main lines in use: 10.59 million (2002)
Telephones - mobile cellular: 12.579 million (2002)
Telephone system:
general assessment: excellent domestic and international service
domestic: domestic satellite system; much use of radiotelephone in areas of low population density; rapid growth of mobile cellular telephones
international: country code - 61; submarine cables to New Zealand, Papua New Guinea, and Indonesia; satellite earth stations - 10 Intelsat (4 Indian Ocean and 6 Pacific Ocean), 2 Inmarsat (Indian and Pacific Ocean regions) (1998)
Radio broadcast stations: AM 262, FM 345, shortwave 1 (1998)
Television broadcast stations: 104 (1997)
Internet country code: .au
Internet hosts: 2,564,339 (2002)
Internet users: 9.472 million (2002)

Transportation

Railways:
total: 41,588 km (4,612 km electrified)
broad gauge: 2,193 km 1.600-m gauge
standard gauge: 23,648 km 1.435-m gauge
narrow gauge: 15,456 km 1.067-m gauge
dual gauge: 291 km dual gauge (2002)
Highways:
total: 811,603 km
paved: 314,090 km (including 18,619 km of expressways)
unpaved: 497,513 km (1999 est.)
Waterways: 8,368 km (mainly used by small, shallow-draft craft)
Pipelines: condensate 36 km; condensate/gas 243 km; gas 27,321 km; liquid petroleum gas 240 km; oil 4,779 km; oil/gas/water 104 km; water 40 km (2003)
Ports and harbors: Adelaide, Brisbane, Cairns, Darwin, Devonport (Tasmania), Fremantle, Geelong, Hobart (Tasmania), Launceston (Tasmania), Mackay, Melbourne, Sydney, Townsville
Merchant marine:
total: 52 ships (1,000 GRT or over) 1,531,461 GRT/1,999,409 DWT
by type: bulk 20, cargo 5, chemical tanker 3, combination bulk 2, container 3, liquefied gas 4, passenger 2, petroleum tanker 7, roll on/roll off 6
foreign-owned: United Kingdom 2, United States 12
registered in other countries: 60 (2003 est.)
Airports: 444 (2003 est.)
Airports - with paved runways:
total: 297
over 3,047 m: 10
2,438 to 3,047 m: 12
1,524 to 2,437 m: 129
914 to 1,523 m: 133
under 914 m: 13 (2003 est.)

Airports - with unpaved runways:
total: 147
1,524 to 2,437 m: 17
914 to 1,523 m: 116
under 914 m: 14 (2003 est.)

Military

Military branches: Australian Army, Royal Australian Navy, Royal Australian Air Force, new Special Operations Command (announced in December 2002)
Military manpower - military age: 17 years of age (2004 est.)
Military manpower - availability:
males age 15-49: 5,061,810 (2004 est.)
Military manpower - fit for military service:
males age 15-49: 4,356,671 (2004 est.)
Military manpower - reaching military age annually:
males: 140,182 (2004 est.)
Military expenditures - dollar figure: $14,120,100,000 (2003)
Military expenditures - percent of GDP: 2.8% (2003)

Transnational Issues

Disputes - international: the 1999 maritime delimitation established partial maritime boundaries with East Timor over part of the Timor Gap but temporary resource-sharing agreements over an unreconciled area grant Australia 90% share of exploited gas reserves and hamper creation of a southern maritime boundary with Indonesia (see Ashmore and Cartier Islands disputes); Australia asserts a territorial claim to Antarctica and to its continental shelf (see Antarctica)
Illicit drugs: Tasmania is one of the world's major suppliers of licit opiate products; government maintains strict controls over areas of opium poppy cultivation and output of poppy straw concentrate

Austria

Introduction

Background: Once the center of power for the large Austro-Hungarian Empire, Austria was reduced to a small republic after its defeat in World War I. Following annexation by Nazi Germany in 1938 and subsequent occupation by the victorious Allies in 1945, Austria's status remained unclear for a decade. A State Treaty signed in 1955 ended the occupation, recognized Austria's independence, and forbade unification with Germany. A constitutional law that same year declared the country's "perpetual neutrality" as a condition for Soviet military withdrawal. Following the Soviet Union's collapse in 1991 and Austria's entry into the European Union in 1995, some Austrian's have called into question this neutrality. A prosperous, democratic country, Austria entered the European Monetary Union in 1999.

Geography

Location: Central Europe, north of Italy and Slovenia
Geographic coordinates: 47 20 N, 13 20 E
Map references: Europe
Area:
total: 83,870 sq km
land: 82,444 sq km
water: 1,426 sq km
Area - comparative: slightly smaller than Maine
Land boundaries:
total: 2,562 km
border countries: Czech Republic 362 km, Germany 784 km, Hungary 366 km, Italy 430 km, Liechtenstein 35 km, Slovakia 91 km, Slovenia 330 km, Switzerland 164 km
Coastline: 0 km (landlocked)
Maritime claims: none (landlocked)
Climate: temperate; continental, cloudy; cold winters with frequent rain and some snow in lowlands and snow in mountains; moderate summers with occasional showers

Terrain: in the west and south mostly mountains (Alps); along the eastern and northern margins mostly flat or gently sloping
Elevation extremes:
lowest point: Neusiedler See 115 m
highest point: Grossglockner 3,798 m
Natural resources: iron ore, oil, timber, magnesite, lead, coal, lignite, copper, hydropower
Land use:
arable land: 16.89%
permanent crops: 0.99%
other: 82.12% (1998 est.)
Irrigated land: 457 sq km (2000 est.)
Natural hazards: landslides; avalanches; earthquakes
Environment - current issues: some forest degradation caused by air and soil pollution; soil pollution results from the use of agricultural chemicals; air pollution results from emissions by coal- and oil-fired power stations and industrial plants and from trucks transiting Austria between northern and southern Europe
Environment - international agreements:
party to: Air Pollution, Air Pollution-Nitrogen Oxides, Air Pollution-Sulfur 85, Air Pollution-Sulphur 94, Air Pollution-Volatile Organic Compounds, Antarctic Treaty, Biodiversity, Climate Change, Climate Change-Kyoto Protocol, Desertification, Endangered Species, Environmental Modification, Hazardous Wastes, Law of the Sea, Ozone Layer Protection, Ship Pollution, Tropical Timber 83, Tropical Timber 94, Wetlands, Whaling
signed, but not ratified: Air Pollution-Persistent Organic Pollutants
Geography - note: landlocked; strategic location at the crossroads of central Europe with many easily traversable Alpine passes and valleys; major river is the Danube; population is concentrated on eastern lowlands because of steep slopes, poor soils, and low temperatures elsewhere

People

Population: 8,174,762 (July 2004 est.)
Age structure:
0-14 years: 15.9% (male 665,680; female 633,560)
15-64 years: 68.1% (male 2,799,411; female 2,764,426)
65 years and over: 16% (male 518,748; female 792,937) (2004 est.)
Median age:
total: 40 years
male: 38.8 years
female: 41.2 years (2004 est.)
Population growth rate: 0.14% (2004 est.)
Birth rate: 8.9 births/1,000 population (2004 est.)
Death rate: 9.56 deaths/1,000 population (2004 est.)
Net migration rate: 2 migrant(s)/1,000 population (2004 est.)
Sex ratio:
at birth: 1.05 male(s)/female
under 15 years: 1.05 male(s)/female

15-64 years: 1.01 male(s)/female
65 years and over: 0.65 male(s)/female
total population: 0.95 male(s)/female (2004 est.)
Infant mortality rate:
total: 4.68 deaths/1,000 live births
male: 5.76 deaths/1,000 live births
female: 3.55 deaths/1,000 live births (2004 est.)
Life expectancy at birth:
total population: 78.87 years
male: 76 years
female: 81.89 years (2004 est.)
Total fertility rate: 1.35 children born/woman (2004 est.)
HIV/AIDS - adult prevalence rate: 0.2% (2001 est.)
HIV/AIDS - people living with HIV/AIDS: 9,000 (2003 est.)
HIV/AIDS - deaths: less than 100 (2001 est.)
Nationality:
noun: Austrian(s)
adjective: Austrian
Ethnic groups: German 88.5%, indigenous minorities 1.5% (includes Croatians, Slovenes, Hungarians, Czechs, Slovaks, Roma), recent immigrant groups 10% (includes Turks, Bosnians, Serbians, Croatians) (2001)
Religions: Roman Catholic 74%, Protestant 5%, Muslim 4%, other 17%
Languages: German
Literacy:
definition: age 15 and over can read and write
total population: 98%
male: NA%
female: NA%

Government

Country name:
conventional long form: Republic of Austria
conventional short form: Austria
local long form: Republik Oesterreich
local short form: Oesterreich
Government type: federal republic
Capital: Vienna
Administrative divisions: 9 states (Bundeslaender, singular - Bundesland); Burgenland, Kaernten, Niederoesterreich, Oberoesterreich, Salzburg, Steiermark, Tirol, Vorarlberg, Wien
Independence: 1156 (from Bavaria)
National holiday: National Day, 26 October (1955); note - commemorates the State Treaty restoring national sovereignty and the end of occupation and the passage of the law on permanent neutrality
Constitution: 1920; revised 1929 (reinstated 1 May 1945)
Legal system: civil law system with Roman law origin; judicial review of legislative acts by the Constitutional Court; separate administrative and civil/penal supreme courts; accepts compulsory ICJ jurisdiction
Suffrage: 18 years of age; universal; compulsory for presidential elections

Executive branch:

chief of state: President Thomas KLESTIL (since 8 July 1992) note - will remain in office until 8 July 2004

head of government: Chancellor Wolfgang SCHUESSEL (OeVP)(since 4 February 2000); Vice Chancellor Hubert GORBACH (since 21 October 2003)

cabinet: Council of Ministers chosen by the president on the advice of the chancellor

elections: president elected by direct popular vote for a six-year term; presidential election last held 19 April 1998 (next to be held 25 April 2004); chancellor traditionally chosen by the president from the plurality party in the National Council; vice chancellor chosen by the president on the advice of the chancellor

election results: Thomas KLESTIL reelected president; percent of vote - Thomas KLESTIL 63%, Gertraud KNOLL 14%, Heide SCHMIDT 11%, Richard LUGNER 10%, Karl NOWAK 2%

note: government coalition - OeVP and FPOe

Legislative branch: bicameral Federal Assembly or Bundesversammlung consists of Federal Council or Bundesrat (62 members; members represent each of the states on the basis of population, but with each state having at least three representatives; members serve a five- or six-year term) and the National Council or Nationalrat (183 seats; members elected by direct popular vote to serve four-year terms)

elections: National Council - last held 24 November 2002 (next to be held in the fall of 2006)

election results: National Council - percent of vote by party - OeVP 42.3%, SPOe 36.5%, FPOe 10.0%, Greens 9.5%; seats by party - OeVP 79, SPOe 69, FPOe 18, Greens 17

Judicial branch: Supreme Judicial Court or Oberster Gerichtshof; Administrative Court or Verwaltungsgerichtshof; Constitutional Court or Verfassungsgerichtshof

Political parties and leaders: Austrian People's Party or OeVP [Wolfgang SCHUESSEL]; Freedom Party of Austria (also known as the Liberal Party) or FPOe [Herbert HAUPT]; Social Democratic Party of Austria or SPOe [Alfred GUSENBAUER]; The Greens [Alexander VAN DER BELLEN]

Political pressure groups and leaders: Austrian Trade Union Federation (nominally independent but primarily Socialist) or OeGB; Federal Economic Chamber; OeVP-oriented League of Austrian Industrialists or VOel; Roman Catholic Church, including its chief lay organization, Catholic Action; three composite leagues of the Austrian People's Party or OeVP representing business, labor, and farmers and other non-government organizations in the areas of environment and human rights

International organization participation: AfDB, AsDB, Australia Group, BIS, BSEC (observer), CE, CEI, CERN, EAPC, EBRD, EIB, EMU, ESA, EU, FAO, G- 9, IADB, IAEA, IBRD, ICAO, ICC, ICCt, ICFTU, ICRM, IDA, IEA, IFAD, IFC, IFRCS, ILO, IMF, IMO, Interpol, IOC, IOM, ISO, ITU, MINURSO, NAM (guest), NEA, NSG, OAS (observer), OECD, OPCW, OSCE, Paris Club, PCA, PFP, UN, UNCTAD, UNDOF, UNESCO, UNFICYP, UNHCR, UNIDO, UNITAR, UNMEE, UNMIK, UNMISET, UNOMIG, UNTSO, UPU, WCL, WCO, WEU (observer), WFTU, WHO, WIPO, WMO, WToO, WTrO, ZC

Diplomatic representation in the US:

chief of mission: Ambassador Eva NOWOTNY

chancery: 3524 International Court NW, Washington, DC 20008-3035

telephone: [1] (202) 895-6700

FAX: [1] (202) 895-6750

consulate(s) general: Chicago, Los Angeles, and New York

Diplomatic representation from the US:

chief of mission: Ambassador William Lee LYONS BROWN, Jr.

embassy: Boltzmanngasse 16, A-1090, Vienna

mailing address: use embassy street address

telephone: [43] (1) 31339, 31375, 31335

FAX: [43] (1) 5125835

Flag description: three equal horizontal bands of red (top), white, and red

Economy

Economy - overview: Austria, with its well-developed market economy and high standard of living, is closely tied to other EU economies, especially Germany's. Membership in the EU has drawn an influx of foreign investors attracted by Austria's access to the single European market and proximity to EU aspirant economies. Slow growth in Germany and elsewhere in the world held the economy to 0.7% growth in 2001, 1.4% in 2002, and again less than 1% in 2003. However, recent data signal that the recovery has started. The government estimates economic growth in 2004 of 1.7-2.1% and of 2.5% in 2005. The government is planning a EURO 500 billion income tax cut in 2004, though some economists doubt it will have stimulative effects in 2004, because it will be offset by higher health insurance contributions and higher taxes on energy. For 2005, Austria plans a tax cut of EURO 2.5 billion and harmonization of the various pension schemes. To meet increased competition from both EU and Central European countries, particularly the new EU members, Austria will need to emphasize knowledge-based sectors of the economy, continue to deregulate the service sector, and lower its tax burden. A key issue is the encouragement of much greater participation in the labor market by its aging population.

GDP: purchasing power parity - $245.5 billion (2003 est.)

GDP - real growth rate: 0.8% (2003 est.)

GDP - per capita: purchasing power parity - $30,000 (2003 est.)

GDP - composition by sector:

agriculture: 2%

industry: 33%

services: 65% (2002 est.)

Population below poverty line: 3.9% (1999)

Household income or consumption by percentage share:

lowest 10%: 2.5%

highest 10%: 22.5% (1995)

Distribution of family income - Gini index: 31 (1995)

Inflation rate (consumer prices): 1.2% (2003 est.)

Labor force: 4.3 million (2001)

Labor force - by occupation: services 67%, industry and crafts 29%, agriculture and forestry 4% (2001 est.)

Unemployment rate: 4.3% (2003 est.)

Budget:

revenues: $67 billion

expenditures: $70 billion, including capital expenditures of $NA (2004 est.)

Industries: construction, machinery, vehicles and parts, food, chemicals, lumber and wood processing, paper and paperboard, communications equipment, tourism

Industrial production growth rate: 3.8% (2001 est.)

Electricity - production: 58.75 billion kWh (2001)

Electricity - production by source:

fossil fuel: 29.3%

hydro: 67.2%

nuclear: 0%

other: 3.5% (2001)

Electricity - consumption: 54.85 billion kWh (2001)

Electricity - exports: 14.25 billion kWh (2001)

Electricity - imports: 14.47 billion kWh (2001)

Oil - production: 20,670 bbl/day (2001 est.)

Oil - consumption: 262,400 bbl/day (2001 est.)

Oil - exports: 35,470 bbl/day (2001)

Oil - imports: 262,000 bbl/day (2001)

Oil - proved reserves: 85.69 million bbl (1 January 2002)

Natural gas - production: 1.731 billion cu m (2001 est.)

Natural gas - consumption: 7.81 billion cu m (2001 est.)

Natural gas - exports: 403 million cu m (2001 est.)

Natural gas - imports: 6.033 billion cu m (2001 est.)

Natural gas - proved reserves: 24.9 billion cu m (1 January 2002)

Agriculture - products: grains, potatoes, sugar beets, wine, fruit; dairy products, cattle, pigs, poultry; lumber

Exports: $83.45 billion f.o.b. (2003 est.)

Exports - commodities: machinery and equipment, motor vehicles and parts, paper and paperboard, metal goods, chemicals, iron and steel; textiles, foodstuffs

Exports - partners: Germany 31.5%, Italy 9.3%, Switzerland 5.4%, US 4.9%, UK 4.9%, France 4.7%, Hungary 4.3% (2002)

Imports: $81.59 billion f.o.b. (2003 est.)

Imports - commodities: machinery and equipment, motor vehicles, chemicals, metal goods, oil and oil products; foodstuffs

Imports - partners: Germany 42.6%, Italy 6.6%, Hungary 5.1%, Switzerland 4.8%, Netherlands 4.4% (2002)

Austria *(continued)*

Debt - external: $15.5 billion (2003 est.)
Economic aid - donor: ODA, $520 million (2002)
Currency: euro (EUR)
note: on 1 January 1999, the European Monetary Union introduced the euro as a common currency to be used by the financial institutions of member countries; as of 1 January 2002, the euro became the only legal tender in EMU member countries, including Austria
Currency code: EUR
Exchange rates: euros per US dollar - 0.886 (2003), 1.0626 (2002), 1.1175 (2001), 1.0854 (2000), 0.9386 (1999)
Fiscal year: calendar year

Communications

Telephones - main lines in use: 3.988 million (2003)
Telephones - mobile cellular: 6.415 million (2002)
Telephone system:
general assessment: highly developed and efficient
domestic: there are 48 main lines for every 100 persons; the fiber optic net is very extensive; all telephone applications and Internet services are available
international: country code - 43; satellite earth stations - 2 Intelsat (1 Atlantic Ocean and 1 Indian Ocean) and 1 Eutelsat; in addition, there are about 600 VSAT (very small aperture terminals) (2002)
Radio broadcast stations: AM 2, FM 65 (plus several hundred repeaters), shortwave 1 (2001)
Television broadcast stations: 10 (plus more than 1,000 repeaters) (2001)
Internet country code: .at
Internet hosts: 367,933 (2002)
Internet users: 3.34 million (2002)

Transportation

Railways:
total: 6,024 km (3,641 km electrified)
standard gauge: 5,566 km 1.435-m gauge (3,524 km electrified)
narrow gauge: 34 km 1.000-m gauge (28 km electrified); 424 km 0.760-m gauge (89 km electrified) (2002)
Highways:
total: 200,000 km
paved: 200,000 km (including 1,633 km of expressways)
unpaved: 0 km (2000)
Waterways: 358 km (1999)
Pipelines: gas 2,722 km; oil 687 km; refined products 149 km (2003)
Ports and harbors: Enns, Krems, Linz, Vienna
Merchant marine:
total: 6 ships (1,000 GRT or over) 29,624 GRT/37,425 DWT
by type: cargo 4, container 2
foreign-owned: Netherlands 1
registered in other countries: 34 (2003 est.)
Airports: 55 (2003 est.)

Airports - with paved runways:
total: 24
over 3,047 m: 1
2,438 to 3,047 m: 5
1,524 to 2,437 m: 1
914 to 1,523 m: 3
under 914 m: 14 (2003 est.)
Airports - with unpaved runways:
total: 31
1,524 to 2,437 m: 1
914 to 1,523 m: 3
under 914 m: 27 (2003 est.)
Heliports: 1 (2003 est.)

Military

Military branches: Land Forces (KdoLdSK), Air Forces (KdoLuSK)
Military manpower - military age: 19 years of age (2004 est.)
Military manpower - availability:
males age 15-49: 2,066,467 (2004 est.)
Military manpower - fit for military service:
males age 15-49: 1,699,384 (2004 est.)
Military manpower - reaching military age annually:
males: 48,981 (2004 est.)
Military expenditures - dollar figure: $1.497 billion (FY01/02)
Military expenditures - percent of GDP: 0.8% (FY01/02)

Transnational Issues

Disputes - international: minor disputes with the Czech Republic over the Temelin Nuclear Power Plant
Illicit drugs: transshipment point for Southwest Asian heroin and South American cocaine destined for Western Europe

Azerbaijan

Introduction

Background: Azerbaijan - a nation with a Turkic and majority-Muslim population - regained its independence after the collapse of the Soviet Union in 1991. Despite a 1994 cease-fire, Azerbaijan has yet to resolve its conflict with Armenia over the Azerbaijani Nagorno-Karabakh enclave (largely Armenian populated). Azerbaijan has lost 16% of its territory and must support some 800,000 refugees and internally displaced persons as a result of the conflict. Corruption is ubiquitous and the promise of widespread wealth from Azerbaijan's undeveloped petroleum resources remains largely unfulfilled.

Geography

Location: Southwestern Asia, bordering the Caspian Sea, between Iran and Russia, with a small European portion north of the Caucasus range
Geographic coordinates: 40 30 N, 47 30 E
Map references: Asia
Area:
total: 86,600 sq km
land: 86,100 sq km
water: 500 sq km
note: includes the exclave of Naxcivan Autonomous Republic and the Nagorno-Karabakh region; the region's autonomy was abolished by Azerbaijani Supreme Soviet on 26 November 1991
Area - comparative: slightly smaller than Maine
Land boundaries:
total: 2,013 km
border countries: Armenia (with Azerbaijan-proper) 566 km, Armenia (with Azerbaijan-Naxcivan exclave) 221 km, Georgia 322 km, Iran (with Azerbaijan-proper) 432 km, Iran (with Azerbaijan-Naxcivan exclave) 179 km, Russia 284 km, Turkey 9 km
Coastline: 0 km (landlocked); note - Azerbaijan borders the Caspian Sea (800 km, est.)
Climate: dry, semiarid steppe

Terrain: large, flat Kur-Araz Ovaligi (Kura-Araks Lowland) (much of it below sea level) with Great Caucasus Mountains to the north, Qarabag Yaylasi (Karabakh Upland) in west; Baku lies on Abseron Yasaqligi (Apsheron Peninsula) that juts into Caspian Sea

Elevation extremes:
lowest point: Caspian Sea -28 m
highest point: Bazarduzu Dagi 4,485 m

Natural resources: petroleum, natural gas, iron ore, nonferrous metals, alumina

Land use:
arable land: 19.31%
permanent crops: 3.04%
other: 77.65% (1998 est.)

Irrigated land: 14,550 sq km (1998 est.)

Natural hazards: droughts

Environment - current issues: local scientists consider the Abseron Yasaqligi (Apsheron Peninsula) (including Baku and Sumqayit) and the Caspian Sea to be the ecologically most devastated area in the world because of severe air, soil, and water pollution; soil pollution results from oil spills, from the use of DDT as a pesticide, and from toxic defoliants used in the production of cotton

Environment - international agreements:
party to: Air Pollution, Biodiversity, Climate Change, Climate Change-Kyoto Protocol, Desertification, Endangered Species, Hazardous Wastes, Marine Dumping, Ozone Layer Protection, Wetlands
signed, but not ratified: none of the selected agreements

Geography - note: both the main area of the country and the Naxcivan exclave are landlocked

People

Population: 7,868,385 (July 2004 est.)

Age structure:
0-14 years: 27% (male 1,081,579; female 1,046,270)
15-64 years: 65.2% (male 2,499,618; female 2,630,386)
65 years and over: 7.8% (male 242,253; female 368,279) (2004 est.)

Median age:
total: 27.3 years
male: 25.9 years
female: 28.8 years (2004 est.)

Population growth rate: 0.52% (2004 est.)

Birth rate: 19.81 births/1,000 population (2004 est.)

Death rate: 9.76 deaths/1,000 population (2004 est.)

Net migration rate: -4.9 migrant(s)/1,000 population (2004 est.)

Sex ratio:
at birth: 1.05 male(s)/female
under 15 years: 1.03 male(s)/female
15-64 years: 0.95 male(s)/female
65 years and over: 0.66 male(s)/female
total population: 0.95 male(s)/female (2004 est.)

Infant mortality rate:
total: 82.07 deaths/1,000 live births
male: 83.99 deaths/1,000 live births
female: 80.06 deaths/1,000 live births (2004 est.)

Life expectancy at birth:
total population: 63.25 years
male: 59.09 years
female: 67.62 years (2004 est.)

Total fertility rate: 2.39 children born/woman (2004 est.)

HIV/AIDS - adult prevalence rate: less than 0.1% (2001 est.)

HIV/AIDS - people living with HIV/AIDS: less than 1,400 (2001 est.)

HIV/AIDS - deaths: less than 100 (2001 est.)

Nationality:
noun: Azerbaijani(s)
adjective: Azerbaijani

Ethnic groups: Azeri 90%, Dagestani 3.2%, Russian 2.5%, Armenian 2%, other 2.3% (1998 est.)
note: almost all Armenians live in the separatist Nagorno-Karabakh region

Religions: Muslim 93.4%, Russian Orthodox 2.5%, Armenian Orthodox 2.3%, other 1.8% (1995 est.)
note: religious affiliation is still nominal in Azerbaijan; percentages for actual practicing adherents are much lower

Languages: Azerbaijani (Azeri) 89%, Russian 3%, Armenian 2%, other 6% (1995 est.)

Literacy:
definition: age 15 and over can read and write
total population: 97%
male: 99%
female: 96% (1989 est.)

Government

Country name:
conventional long form: Republic of Azerbaijan
conventional short form: Azerbaijan
local long form: Azarbaycan Respublikasi
local short form: none
former: Azerbaijan Soviet Socialist Republic

Government type: republic

Capital: Baku (Baki)

Administrative divisions: 59 rayons (rayonlar; rayon - singular), 11 cities* (saharlar; sahar - singular), 1 autonomous republic** (muxtar respublika); Abseron Rayonu, Agcabadi Rayonu, Agdam Rayonu, Agdas Rayonu, Agstafa Rayonu, Agsu Rayonu, Ali Bayramli Sahari*, Astara Rayonu, Baki Sahari*, Balakan Rayonu, Barda Rayonu, Beylaqan Rayonu, Bilasuvar Rayonu, Cabrayil Rayonu, Calilabad Rayonu, Daskasan Rayonu, Davaci Rayonu, Fuzuli Rayonu, Gadabay Rayonu, Ganca Sahari*, Goranboy Rayonu, Goycay Rayonu, Haciqabul Rayonu, Imisli Rayonu, Ismayilli Rayonu, Kalbacar Rayonu, Kurdamir Rayonu, Lacin Rayonu, Lankaran Rayonu, Lankaran Sahari*, Lerik Rayonu, Masalli Rayonu, Mingacevir Sahari*, Naftalan Sahari*, Naxcivan Muxtar Respublikasi**, Neftcala Rayonu, Oguz Rayonu, Qabala Rayonu, Qax Rayonu, Qazax Rayonu, Qobustan Rayonu, Quba Rayonu, Qubadli Rayonu, Qusar Rayonu, Saatli Rayonu, Sabirabad Rayonu, Saki Rayonu, Saki Sahari*, Salyan Rayonu, Samaxi Rayonu, Samkir Rayonu, Samux Rayonu, Siyazan Rayonu, Sumqayit Sahari*, Susa Rayonu, Susa Sahari*, Tartar Rayonu, Tovuz Rayonu, Ucar Rayonu, Xacmaz Rayonu, Xankandi Sahari*, Xanlar Rayonu, Xizi Rayonu, Xocali Rayonu, Xocavand Rayonu, Yardimli Rayonu, Yevlax Rayonu, Yevlax Sahari*, Zangilan Rayonu, Zaqatala Rayonu, Zardab Rayonu

Independence: 30 August 1991 (from Soviet Union)

National holiday: Founding of the Democratic Republic of Azerbaidzhan, 28 May (1918)

Constitution: adopted 12 November 1995

Legal system: based on civil law system

Suffrage: 18 years of age; universal

Executive branch:
chief of state: President Ilham ALIYEV (since 31 October 2003)
head of government: Prime Minister Artur RASIZADE (since 4 November 2003); First Deputy Prime Minister Abbas ABBASOV (since 10 November 2003)
cabinet: Council of Ministers appointed by the president and confirmed by the National Assembly
elections: president elected by popular vote to a five-year term; election last held 15 October 2003 (next to be held NA October 2008); prime minister and first deputy prime ministers appointed by the president and confirmed by the National Assembly
election results: Ilham ALIYEV elected president; percent of vote - Ilham ALIYEV 76.8%, Isa GAMBAR 14%

Legislative branch: unicameral National Assembly or Milli Mejlis (125 seats; members elected by popular vote to serve five-year terms)
elections: last held 4 November 2000 (next to be held NA November 2005)
note: 100 members of the current parliament were elected on the basis of single mandate constituencies, while 25 were elected based on proportional balloting; as a result of a 24 August 2002 national referendum on changes to the constitution, all 125 members of the next parliament will be elected from single mandate constituencies
election results: percent of vote by party - NA%; seats by party - NAP and allies 108, APF "Reform" 6, CSP 3, PNIA 2, Musavat Party 2, CPA 2, APF "Classic" 1, Compatriot Party 1
note: PNIA, Musavat, and APF "Classic" parties refused to take their seats

Judicial branch: Supreme Court

Political parties and leaders: Azerbaijan Popular Front or APF [Ali KARIMLI, leader of "Reform" faction; Mirmahmud MIRALI-OGLU, leader of "Classic" faction]; Civic Solidarity Party or CSP [Sabir RUSTAMKHANLY]; Civic Union Party [Ayaz MUTALIBOV]; Communist Party of Azerbaijan or CPA [Ramiz AHMADOV]; Compatriot Party [Mais SAFARLI]; Democratic Party for Azerbaijan or DPA [Rasul QULIYEV, chairman]; Justice Party [Ilyas ISMAILOV]; Liberal Party of Azerbaijan [Lala Shovkat HACIYEVA]; Musavat [Isa GAMBAR, chairman]; New Azerbaijan Party or NAP [vacant]; Party for National Independence of Azerbaijan or PNIA [Etibar MAMMADLI, chairman]; Social Democratic Party of Azerbaijan or SDP [Zardust ALIZADE] *note:* opposition parties regularly factionalize and form new parties

Political pressure groups and leaders: Sadval, Lezgin movement; self-proclaimed Armenian Nagorno-Karabakh Republic; Talysh independence movement; Union of Pro-Azerbaijani Forces (UPAF)

International organization participation: AsDB, BSEC, CE, CIS, EAPC, EBRD, ECO, FAO, GUUAM, IAEA, IBRD, ICAO, ICFTU, ICRM, IDA, IDB, IFAD, IFC, IFRCS, ILO, IMF, IMO, Interpol, IOC, IOM, ISO, ITU, OAS (observer), OIC, OPCW, OSCE, PFP, UN, UNCTAD, UNESCO, UNIDO, UPU, WCO, WFTU, WHO, WIPO, WMO, WToO, WTrO (observer)

Diplomatic representation in the US:
chief of mission: Ambassador Hafiz PASHAYEV
chancery: 2741 34th Street NW, Washington, DC 20008
telephone: [1] (202) 337-3500
FAX: [1] (202) 337-5911

Diplomatic representation from the US:
chief of mission: Ambassador Reno HARNISH
embassy: 83 Azadliq Prospekt, Baku 370007
mailing address: American Embassy Baku, Department of State, 7050 Baku Place, Washington, DC 20521-7050
telephone: [9] (9412) 98-03-35, 36, 37
FAX: [9] (9412) 90-66-71

Flag description: three equal horizontal bands of blue (top), red, and green; a crescent and eight-pointed star in white are centered in red band

Economy

Economy - overview: Azerbaijan's number one export is oil. Azerbaijan's oil production declined through 1997 but has registered an increase every year since. Negotiation of production-sharing arrangements (PSAs) with foreign firms, which have thus far committed $60 billion to long-term oilfield development, should generate the funds needed to spur future industrial development. Oil production under the first of these PSAs, with the Azerbaijan International Operating Company, began in November 1997. Azerbaijan shares all the formidable problems of the former Soviet republics in making the transition from a command to a market economy, but its considerable energy resources brighten its long-term prospects. Baku has only recently begun making progress on economic reform, and old economic ties and structures are slowly being replaced. One obstacle to economic progress is the need for stepped up foreign investment in the non-energy sector. A second obstacle is the continuing conflict with Armenia over the Nagorno-Karabakh region. Trade with Russia and the other former Soviet republics is declining in importance while trade is building with Turkey and the nations of Europe. Long-term prospects will depend on world oil prices, the location of new pipelines in the region, and Azerbaijan's ability to manage its oil wealth.

GDP: purchasing power parity - $26.34 billion (2003 est.)

GDP - real growth rate: 9.9% (2003 est.)

GDP - per capita: purchasing power parity - $3,400 (2003 est.)

GDP - composition by sector:
agriculture: 14.1%
industry: 45.7%
services: 40.2% (2002 est.)

Population below poverty line: 49% (2002 est.)

Household income or consumption by percentage share:
lowest 10%: 2.8%
highest 10%: 27.8% (1995)

Distribution of family income - Gini index: 36 (1995)

Inflation rate (consumer prices): 2.9% (2003 est.)

Labor force: 3.7 million (2001)

Labor force - by occupation: agriculture and forestry 41%, industry 7%, services 52% (2001)

Unemployment rate: 16% (official rate is 1.2%) (2003 est.)

Budget:
revenues: $786 million
expenditures: $807 million, including capital expenditures of $NA (2001)

Industries: petroleum and natural gas, petroleum products, oilfield equipment; steel, iron ore, cement; chemicals and petrochemicals; textiles

Industrial production growth rate: 5% (2003 est.)

Electricity - production: 18.23 billion kWh (2001)

Electricity - production by source:
fossil fuel: 89.7%
hydro: 10.3%
nuclear: 0%
other: 0% (2001)

Electricity - consumption: 16.65 billion kWh (2001)

Electricity - exports: 700 million kWh (2001)

Electricity - imports: 400 million kWh (2001)

Oil - production: 307,200 bbl/day (2001 est.)

Oil - consumption: 140,000 bbl/day (2001 est.)

Oil - exports: NA

Oil - imports: NA

Oil - proved reserves: 589 million bbl (1 January 2002)

Natural gas - production: 5.72 billion cu m (2001 est.)

Natural gas - consumption: 6.72 billion cu m (2001 est.)

Natural gas - exports: 0 cu m (2001 est.)

Natural gas - imports: 1 billion cu m (2001 est.)

Natural gas - proved reserves: 62.3 billion cu m (1 January 2002)

Agriculture - products: cotton, grain, rice, grapes, fruit, vegetables, tea, tobacco; cattle, pigs, sheep, goats

Exports: $2.605 billion f.o.b. (2003 est.)

Exports - commodities: oil and gas 90%, machinery, cotton, foodstuffs

Exports - partners: Italy 30.4%, Germany 15.6%, Czech Republic 9.9%, France 8.9%, Georgia 7.1%, Russia 4.9% (2002)

Imports: $2.498 billion f.o.b. (2003 est.)

Imports - commodities: machinery and equipment, oil products, foodstuffs, metals, chemicals

Imports - partners: Russia 16.8%, Turkey 13.5%, Germany 7.4%, Kazakhstan 6.8%, France 6.5%, Ukraine 6.3%, China 5.7%, UK 5.1%, US 4.2% (2002)

Debt - external: $1.5 billion (2003)

Economic aid - recipient: ODA, $140 million (2000 est.)

Currency: Azerbaijani manat (AZM)

Currency code: AZM

Exchange rates: Azerbaijani manats per US dollar - 4,910.73 (2003), 4,860.82 (2002), 4,656.58 (2001), 4,474.15 (2000), 4,120.17 (1999)

Fiscal year: calendar year

Communications

Telephones - main lines in use: 923,800 (2002)

Telephones - mobile cellular: 870,000 (2002)

Telephone system:
general assessment: inadequate; requires considerable expansion and modernization; teledensity of 10 main lines per 100 persons is low (2002)
domestic: the majority of telephones are in Baku and other industrial centers - about 700 villages still without public telephone service; satellite service connects Baku to a modern switch in its exclave of Naxcivan
international: country code - 994; the old Soviet system of cable and microwave is still serviceable; a satellite connection to Turkey enables Baku to reach about 200 additional countries, some of which are directly connected to Baku by satellite providers other than Turkey (1997)

Radio broadcast stations: AM 10, FM 17, shortwave 1 (1998)

Television broadcast stations: 2 (1997)

Internet country code: .az

Internet hosts: 1,139 (2002)

Internet users: 300,000 (2002)

Transportation

Railways:
total: 2,122 km
broad gauge: 2,122 km 1.520-m gauge (1,278 km electrified) (2002)

Highways:
total: 24,981 km
paved: 23,057 km
unpaved: 1,924 km (2000)

Waterways: none

Pipelines: gas 5,001 km; oil 1,631 km (2003)

Ports and harbors: Baku (Baki)

Merchant marine:
total: 56 ships (1,000 GRT or over) 253,004 GRT/ 318,922 DWT
by type: cargo 14, petroleum tanker 40, roll on/roll off 2
foreign-owned: Russia 1 (2003 est.)

Airports: 67 (2003 est.)

Azerbaijan (continued)

Airports - with paved runways:
total: 27
over 3,047 m: 2
2,438 to 3,047 m: 6
1,524 to 2,437 m: 15
914 to 1,523 m: 3
under 914 m: 1 (2003 est.)
Airports - with unpaved runways:
total: 40
2,438 to 3,047 m: 1
1,524 to 2,437 m: 1
914 to 1,523 m: 6
under 914 m: 32 (2003 est.)
Heliports: 2 (2003 est.)

Military

Military branches: Army, Navy, Air and Air Defense Forces
Military manpower - military age: 18 years of age (2004 est.)
Military manpower - availability:
males age 15-49: 2,187,847 (2004 est.)
Military manpower - fit for military service:
males age 15-49: 1,748,567 (2004 est.)
Military manpower - reaching military age annually:
males: 83,131 (2004 est.)
Military expenditures - dollar figure: $121 million (FY99)
Military expenditures - percent of GDP: 2.6% (FY99)

Transnational Issues

Disputes - international: Armenia supports ethnic Armenian secessionists in Nagorno-Karabakh and militarily occupies about one-sixth of Azerbaijan - Organization for Security and Cooperation in Europe (OSCE) continues to mediate dispute; Azerbaijan, Kazakhstan, and Russia ratify Caspian seabed delimitation treaties based on equidistance, while Iran continues to insist on an even one-fifth allocation and challenges Azerbaijan's hydrocarbon exploration in disputed waters; talks resume with Turkmenistan on dividing the seabed in 2004 as both sides await an ICJ decision on contested oilfields in the middle of the Caspian; Azerbaijan protests Georgian constructions at the Red Bridge crossing and several other small segments of boundary, which remain unresolved until delimitation
Illicit drugs: limited illicit cultivation of cannabis and opium poppy, mostly for CIS consumption; small government eradication program; transit point for Southwest Asian opiates bound for Russia and to a lesser extent the rest of Europe

Bahamas, The

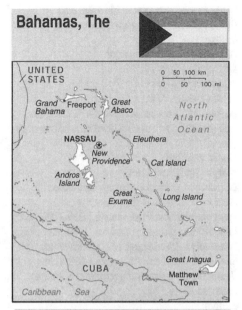

Introduction

Background: Arawak Indians inhabited the islands when Christopher Columbus first set foot in the New World on San Salvador in 1492. British settlement of the islands began in 1647; the islands became a colony in 1783. Since attaining independence from the UK in 1973, The Bahamas have prospered through tourism and international banking and investment management. Because of its geography, the country is a major transshipment point for illegal drugs, particularly shipments to the US, and its territory is used for smuggling illegal migrants into the US.

Geography

Location: Caribbean, chain of islands in the North Atlantic Ocean, southeast of Florida, northeast of Cuba
Geographic coordinates: 24 15 N, 76 00 W
Map references: Central America and the Caribbean
Area:
total: 13,940 sq km
land: 10,070 sq km
water: 3,870 sq km
Area - comparative: slightly smaller than Connecticut
Land boundaries: 0 km
Coastline: 3,542 km
Maritime claims:
territorial sea: 12 NM
exclusive economic zone: 200 NM
Climate: tropical marine; moderated by warm waters of Gulf Stream
Terrain: long, flat coral formations with some low rounded hills
Elevation extremes:
lowest point: Atlantic Ocean 0 m
highest point: Mount Alvernia, on Cat Island 63 m
Natural resources: salt, aragonite, timber, arable land

Land use:
arable land: 0.6%
permanent crops: 0.4%
other: 99% (1998 est.)
Irrigated land: NA sq km
Natural hazards: hurricanes and other tropical storms cause extensive flood and wind damage
Environment - current issues: coral reef decay; solid waste disposal
Environment - international agreements:
party to: Biodiversity, Climate Change, Climate Change-Kyoto Protocol, Desertification, Endangered Species, Hazardous Wastes, Law of the Sea, Ozone Layer Protection, Ship Pollution, Wetlands
signed, but not ratified: none of the selected agreements
Geography - note: strategic location adjacent to US and Cuba; extensive island chain of which 30 are inhabited

People

Population: 299,697
note: estimates for this country explicitly take into account the effects of excess mortality due to AIDS; this can result in lower life expectancy, higher infant mortality and death rates, lower population and growth rates, and changes in the distribution of population by age and sex than would otherwise be expected (July 2004 est.)
Age structure:
0-14 years: 28.3% (male 42,474; female 42,423)
15-64 years: 65.7% (male 96,825; female 99,985)
65 years and over: 6% (male 7,351; female 10,639) (2004 est.)
Median age:
total: 27.3 years
male: 26.5 years
female: 28 years (2004 est.)
Population growth rate: 0.72% (2004 est.)
Birth rate: 18.22 births/1,000 population (2004 est.)
Death rate: 8.82 deaths/1,000 population (2004 est.)
Net migration rate: -2.2 migrant(s)/1,000 population (2004 est.)
Sex ratio:
at birth: 1.02 male(s)/female
under 15 years: 1 male(s)/female
15-64 years: 0.97 male(s)/female
65 years and over: 0.69 male(s)/female
total population: 0.96 male(s)/female (2004 est.)
Infant mortality rate:
total: 25.7 deaths/1,000 live births
male: 31.73 deaths/1,000 live births
female: 19.55 deaths/1,000 live births (2004 est.)
Life expectancy at birth:
total population: 65.63 years
male: 62.21 years
female: 69.11 years (2004 est.)
Total fertility rate: 2.23 children born/woman (2004 est.)
HIV/AIDS - adult prevalence rate: 3.5% (2001 est.)
HIV/AIDS - people living with HIV/AIDS: 6,200 (2001 est.)

Bahamas, The *(continued)*

HIV/AIDS - deaths: 610 (2001 est.)
Nationality:
noun: Bahamian(s)
adjective: Bahamian
Ethnic groups: black 85%, white 12%, Asian and Hispanic 3%
Religions: Baptist 32%, Anglican 20%, Roman Catholic 19%, Methodist 6%, Church of God 6%, other Protestant 12%, none or unknown 3%, other 2%
Languages: English (official), Creole (among Haitian immigrants)
Literacy:
definition: age 15 and over can read and write
total population: 95.6%
male: 94.7%
female: 96.5% (2003 est.)

Government

Country name:
conventional long form: Commonwealth of The Bahamas
conventional short form: The Bahamas
Government type: constitutional parliamentary democracy
Capital: Nassau
Administrative divisions: 21 districts; Acklins and Crooked Islands, Bimini, Cat Island, Exuma, Freeport, Fresh Creek, Governor's Harbour, Green Turtle Cay, Harbour Island, High Rock, Inagua, Kemps Bay, Long Island, Marsh Harbour, Mayaguana, New Providence, Nichollstown and Berry Islands, Ragged Island, Rock Sound, Sandy Point, San Salvador and Rum Cay
Independence: 10 July 1973 (from UK)
National holiday: Independence Day, 10 July (1973)
Constitution: 10 July 1973
Legal system: based on English common law
Suffrage: 18 years of age; universal
Executive branch:
chief of state: Queen ELIZABETH II (since 6 February 1952), represented by Governor General Dame Ivy DUMONT (since NA May 2002)
head of government: Prime Minister Perry CHRISTIE (since 3 May 2002) and Deputy Prime Minister Cynthia PRATT (since 7 May 2002)
cabinet: Cabinet appointed by the governor general on the prime minister's recommendation
elections: none; the monarch is hereditary; governor general appointed by the monarch; following legislative elections, the leader of the majority party or the leader of the majority coalition is usually appointed prime minister by the governor general; the prime minister recommends the deputy prime minister
Legislative branch: bicameral Parliament consists of the Senate (16-member body appointed by the governor general upon the advice of the prime minister and the opposition leader for five-year terms) and the House of Assembly (40 seats; members elected by direct popular vote to serve five-year terms); the government may dissolve the parliament and call elections at any time

elections: last held 1 May 2002 (next to be held by May 2007)
election results: percent of vote by party - PLP 50.8%, FNM 41.1%, independents 5.2%; seats by party - PLP 29, FNM 7, independents 4
Judicial branch: Supreme Court; Court of Appeal; magistrates courts
Political parties and leaders: Free National Movement or FNM [Tommy TURNQUEST]; Progressive Liberal Party or PLP [Perry CHRISTIE]
Political pressure groups and leaders: NA
International organization participation: ACP, C, Caricom, CDB, FAO, G-77, IADB, IBRD, ICAO, ICCt (signatory), ICFTU, ICRM, IFC, IFRCS, ILO, IMF, IMO, Interpol, IOC, ITU, LAES, NAM, OAS, OPANAL, OPCW (signatory), UN, UNCTAD, UNESCO, UNIDO, UPU, WCO, WHO, WIPO, WMO, WTO (observer)
Diplomatic representation in the US:
chief of mission: Ambassador Joshua SEARS
chancery: 2220 Massachusetts Avenue NW, Washington, DC 20008
telephone: [1] (202) 319-2660
FAX: [1] (202) 319-2668
consulate(s) general: Miami and New York
Diplomatic representation from the US:
chief of mission: Ambassador (vacant); Charge d'Affaires Robert M. WITAJEWSKI
embassy: 42 Queen Street, Nassau
mailing address: local or express mail address: P. O. Box N-8197, Nassau; Department of State, 3370 Nassau Place, Washington, DC 20521-3370
telephone: [1] (242) 322-1181, 328-2206 (after hours)
FAX: [1] (242) 356-0222
Flag description: three equal horizontal bands of aquamarine (top), gold, and aquamarine, with a black equilateral triangle based on the hoist side

Economy

Economy - overview: The Bahamas is a stable, developing nation with an economy heavily dependent on tourism and offshore banking. Tourism alone accounts for more than 60% of GDP and directly or indirectly employs half of the archipelago's labor force. Steady growth in tourism receipts and a boom in construction of new hotels, resorts, and residences had led to solid GDP growth in recent years, but the slowdown in the US economy and the attacks of 11 September 2001 held back growth in these sectors in 2001-03. Financial services constitute the second-most important sector of the Bahamian economy, accounting for about 15% of GDP. However, since December 2000, when the government enacted new regulations on the financial sector, many international businesses have left The Bahamas. Manufacturing and agriculture together contribute approximately a tenth of GDP and show little growth, despite government incentives aimed at those sectors. Overall growth prospects in the short run rest heavily on the fortunes of the tourism sector, which depends on growth in the US, the source of

more than 80% of the visitors. In addition to tourism and banking, the government supports the development of a "third pillar," e-commerce.
GDP: purchasing power parity - $5.099 billion (2003 est.)
GDP - real growth rate: 1% (2003 est.)
GDP - per capita: purchasing power parity - $16,800 (2003 est.)
GDP - composition by sector:
agriculture: 3%
industry: 7%
services: 90% (2001 est.)
Population below poverty line: NA%
Household income or consumption by percentage share:
lowest 10%: NA%
highest 10%: NA%
Inflation rate (consumer prices): 1.7% (2002 est.)
Labor force: 156,000 (1999)
Labor force - by occupation: tourism 50%, other services 40%, industry 5%, agriculture 5% (1999 est.)
Unemployment rate: 6.9% (2001 est.)
Budget:
revenues: $918.5 million
expenditures: $956.5 million, including capital expenditures of $106.7 million (FY99/00)
Industries: tourism, banking, e-commerce, cement, oil refining and transshipment, salt, rum, aragonite, pharmaceuticals, spiral-welded steel pipe
Industrial production growth rate: NA% (2002 est.)
Electricity - production: 1.56 billion kWh (2001)
Electricity - production by source:
fossil fuel: 100%
hydro: 0%
nuclear: 0%
other: 0% (2001)
Electricity - consumption: 1.451 billion kWh (2001)
Electricity - exports: 0 kWh (2001)
Electricity - imports: 0 kWh (2001)
Oil - production: 0 bbl/day (2001 est.)
Oil - consumption: 23,000 bbl/day (2001 est.)
Oil - exports: NA
Oil - imports: NA
Agriculture - products: citrus, vegetables; poultry
Exports: $617 million (2002 est.)
Exports - commodities: fish and crawfish; rum, salt, chemicals; fruit and vegetables
Exports - partners: US 37.8%, Germany 11.8%, Spain 10.4%, Peru 8.6%, France 7.1%, Mexico 4.2% (2002)
Imports: $1.614 billion (2002 est.)
Imports - commodities: machinery and transport equipment, manufactures, chemicals, mineral fuels; food and live animals
Imports - partners: US 18.4%, South Korea 18.3%, Germany 10.5%, Norway 9.2%, Japan 9.1%, Italy 6.6%, Venezuela 4.1% (2002)
Debt - external: $308.5 million (2002)
Economic aid - recipient: $9.8 million (1995)
Currency: Bahamian dollar (BSD)
Currency code: BSD

Bahamas, The *(continued)*

Exchange rates: Bahamian dollars per US dollar - 1 (2003), 1 (2002), 1 (2001), 1 (2000), 1 (1999)
Fiscal year: 1 July - 30 June

Communications

Telephones - main lines in use: 126,600 (2002)
Telephones - mobile cellular: 121,800 (2002)
Telephone system:
general assessment: modern facilities
domestic: totally automatic system; highly developed
international: country code - 1-242; tropospheric scatter and submarine cable to Florida; 3 coaxial submarine cables; satellite earth station - 1 Intelsat (Atlantic Ocean) (1997)
Radio broadcast stations: AM 3, FM 4, shortwave 0 (1998)
Television broadcast stations: 1 (1997)
Internet country code: .bs
Internet hosts: 32 (2002)
Internet users: 60,000 (2002)

Transportation

Railways: 0 km
Highways:
total: 2,693 km
paved: 1,546 km
unpaved: 1,147 km (1999 est.)
Waterways: none
Ports and harbors: Freeport, Matthew Town, Nassau
Merchant marine:
total: 1,035 ships (1,000 GRT or over) 31,631,252 GRT/43,025,977 DWT
by type: bulk 165, cargo 188, chemical tanker 45, combination bulk 10, combination ore/oil 17, container 97, liquefied gas 27, livestock carrier 2, multi-functional large load carrier 4, passenger 108, passenger/cargo 1, petroleum tanker 163, refrigerated cargo 133, roll on/roll off 34, short-sea/ passenger 18, specialized tanker 3, vehicle carrier 20
foreign-owned: Algeria 1, Australia 7, Belgium 14, Bermuda 1, Canada 4, Chile 1, China 4, Croatia 1, Cuba 3, Cyprus 14, Denmark 49, Estonia 1, Faroe Islands 1, Finland 9, France 21, Germany 13, Gibraltar 1, Greece 163, Hong Kong 9, India 1, Indonesia 3, Ireland 1, Israel 3, Italy 7, Japan 35, Kenya 2, South Korea 1, Latvia 1, Liberia 1, Malaysia 11, Malta 1, Monaco 68, Netherlands 29, New Zealand 1, Norway 231, Panama 2, Philippines 3, Poland 14, Reunion 1, Russia 1, Saudi Arabia 9, Singapore 13, Slovenia 1, Spain 6, Sweden 9, Switzerland 1, Thailand 1, Trinidad and Tobago 2
registered in other countries: 11 (2003 est.)
Airports: 63 (2003 est.)
Airports - with paved runways:
total: 30
over 3,047 m: 2
2,438 to 3,047 m: 3
1,524 to 2,437 m: 13
914 to 1,523 m: 10
under 914 m: 2 (2003 est.)

Airports - with unpaved runways:
total: 33
1,524 to 2,437 m: 3
914 to 1,523 m: 9
under 914 m: 21 (2003 est.)
Heliports: 1 (2003 est.)

Military

Military branches: Royal Bahamas Defense Force (including Coast Guard)
Military expenditures - dollar figure: NA
Military expenditures - percent of GDP: NA

Transnational Issues

Disputes - international: have not been able to agree on a maritime boundary with the US; is concerned about refugees fleeing Haiti's deteriorated economic and political conditions
Illicit drugs: transshipment point for cocaine and marijuana bound for US and Europe; offshore financial center

Bahrain

Introduction

Background: Bahrain's small size and central location among Persian Gulf countries require it to play a delicate balancing act in foreign affairs among its larger neighbors. Facing declining oil reserves, Bahrain has turned to petroleum processing and refining and has transformed itself into an international banking center. The new amir, installed in 1999, has pushed economic and political reforms and has worked to improve relations with the Shi'a community. In February 2001, Bahraini voters approved a referendum on the National Action Charter - the centerpiece of the amir's political liberalization program. In February 2002, Amir HAMAD bin Isa Al Khalifa proclaimed himself king. In October 2002, Bahrainis elected members of the lower house of Bahrain's reconstituted bicameral legislature, the National Assembly.

Geography

Location: Middle East, archipelago in the Persian Gulf, east of Saudi Arabia
Geographic coordinates: 26 00 N, 50 33 E
Map references: Middle East
Area:
total: 665 sq km
land: 665 sq km
water: 0 sq km
Area - comparative: 3.5 times the size of Washington, DC
Land boundaries: 0 km
Coastline: 161 km
Maritime claims:
territorial sea: 12 NM
contiguous zone: 24 NM
continental shelf: extending to boundaries to be determined
Climate: arid; mild, pleasant winters; very hot, humid summers

Bahrain (continued)

Terrain: mostly low desert plain rising gently to low central escarpment

Elevation extremes:

lowest point: Persian Gulf 0 m

highest point: Jabal ad Dukhan 122 m

Natural resources: oil, associated and nonassociated natural gas, fish, pearls

Land use:

arable land: 4.35%

permanent crops: 4.35%

other: 91.3% (1998 est.)

Irrigated land: 50 sq km (1998 est.)

Natural hazards: periodic droughts; dust storms

Environment - current issues: desertification resulting from the degradation of limited arable land, periods of drought, and dust storms; coastal degradation (damage to coastlines, coral reefs, and sea vegetation) resulting from oil spills and other discharges from large tankers, oil refineries, and distribution stations; lack of freshwater resources, groundwater and seawater are the only sources for all water needs

Environment - international agreements:

party to: Biodiversity, Climate Change, Desertification, Hazardous Wastes, Law of the Sea, Ozone Layer Protection, Wetlands

signed, but not ratified: none of the selected agreements

Geography - note: close to primary Middle Eastern petroleum sources; strategic location in Persian Gulf, through which much of the Western world's petroleum must transit to reach open ocean

People

Population: 677,886

note: includes 235,108 non-nationals (July 2004 est.)

Age structure:

0-14 years: 28.4% (male 97,179; female 95,043)

15-64 years: 68.4% (male 271,015; female 192,342)

65 years and over: 3.3% (male 11,426; female 10,881) (2004 est.)

Median age:

total: 29 years

male: 31.9 years

female: 25.3 years (2004 est.)

Population growth rate: 1.56% (2004 est.)

Birth rate: 18.54 births/1,000 population (2004 est.)

Death rate: 4.03 deaths/1,000 population (2004 est.)

Net migration rate: 1.05 migrant(s)/1,000 population (2004 est.)

Sex ratio:

at birth: 1.03 male(s)/female

under 15 years: 1.02 male(s)/female

15-64 years: 1.41 male(s)/female

65 years and over: 1.05 male(s)/female

total population: 1.27 male(s)/female (2004 est.)

Infant mortality rate:

total: 17.91 deaths/1,000 live births

male: 20.93 deaths/1,000 live births

female: 14.8 deaths/1,000 live births (2004 est.)

Life expectancy at birth:

total population: 73.98 years

male: 71.52 years

female: 76.51 years (2004 est.)

Total fertility rate: 2.67 children born/woman (2004 est.)

HIV/AIDS - adult prevalence rate: 0.3% (2001 est.)

HIV/AIDS - people living with HIV/AIDS: less than 1,000

HIV/AIDS - deaths: NA

Nationality:

noun: Bahraini(s)

adjective: Bahraini

Ethnic groups: Bahraini 63%, Asian 19%, other Arab 10%, Iranian 8%

Religions: Shi'a Muslim 70%, Sunni Muslim 30%

Languages: Arabic, English, Farsi, Urdu

Literacy:

definition: age 15 and over can read and write

total population: 89.1%

male: 91.9%

female: 85% (2003 est.)

Government

Country name:

conventional long form: Kingdom of Bahrain

conventional short form: Bahrain

local long form: Mamlakat al Bahrayn

local short form: Al Bahrayn

former: Dilmun

Government type: constitutional hereditary monarchy

Capital: Manama

Administrative divisions: 12 municipalities (manatiq, singular - mintaqah); Al Hadd, Al Manamah, Al Mintaqah al Gharbiyah, Al Mintaqah al Wusta, Al Mintaqah ash Shamaliyah, Al Muharraq, Ar Rifa' wa al Mintaqah al Janubiyah, Jidd Hafs, Madinat Hamad, Madinat 'Isa, Juzur Hawar, Sitrah

note: all municipalities administered from Manama

Independence: 15 August 1971 (from UK)

National holiday: National Day, 16 December (1971); note - 15 August 1971 is the date of independence from the UK, 16 December 1971 is the date of independence from British protection

Constitution: adopted late December 2000; Bahrani voters approved on 13-14 February 2001 a referendum on legislative changes (revised constitution calls for a partially elected legislature, a constitutional monarchy, and an independent judiciary)

Legal system: based on Islamic law and English common law

Suffrage: 18 years of age; universal

Executive branch:

chief of state: King HAMAD bin Isa Al Khalifa (since 6 March 1999); Heir Apparent Crown Prince SALMAN bin Hamad (son of the monarch, born 21 October 1969)

head of government: Prime Minister KHALIFA bin Salman Al Khalifa (since NA 1971)

cabinet: Cabinet appointed by the monarch

elections: none; the monarchy is hereditary; prime minister appointed by the monarch

Legislative branch: bicameral Parliament consists of Shura Council (40 members appointed by the King) and House of Deputies (40 members directly elected to serve four-year terms)

elections: House of Deputies - last held 31 October 2002 (next election to be held NA 2006)

election results: House of Deputies - percent of vote by party - NA%; seats by party - independents 21, Sunni Islamists 9, other 10

note: first elections since 7 December 1973; unicameral National Assembly dissolved 26 August 1975; National Action Charter created bicameral legislature on 23 December 2000; approved by referendum 14 February 2001; first legislative session of Parliament held on 25 December 2002

Judicial branch: High Civil Appeals Court

Political parties and leaders: political parties prohibited but politically oriented societies are allowed

Political pressure groups and leaders: Shi'a activists fomented unrest sporadically in 1994-97, demanding the return of an elected National Assembly and an end to unemployment; several small, clandestine leftist and Islamic fundamentalist groups are active

International organization participation: ABEDA, AFESD, AMF, ESCWA, FAO, G-77, GCC, IBRD, ICAO, ICC, ICCt (signatory), ICRM, IDB, IFC, IFRCS, IHO, ILO, IMF, IMO, Interpol, IOC, ISO, ITU, LAS, NAM, OAPEC, OIC, OPCW, UN, UNCTAD, UNESCO, UNIDO, UPU, WCO, WFTU, WHO, WIPO, WMO, WToO, WTrO

Diplomatic representation in the US:

chief of mission: Ambassador Khalifa bin Ali bin Rashid AL KHALIFA

chancery: 3502 International Drive NW, Washington, DC 20008

telephone: [1] (202) 342-0741

FAX: [1] (202) 362-2192

consulate(s) general: New York

Diplomatic representation from the US:

chief of mission: Ambassador Ronald E. NEUMANN

embassy: Building #979, Road 3119 (next to Al-Ahli Sports Club), Block 321, Zinj District, Manama

mailing address: American Embassy Manama, PSC 451, FPO AE 09834-5100; international mail: American Embassy, Box 26431, Manama

telephone: [973] 273-300

FAX: [973] 272-594

Flag description: red with a white serrated band (five white points) on the hoist side; the five points represent the five pillars of Islam

Economy

Economy - overview: In well-to-do Bahrain, petroleum production and refining account for about 60% of export receipts, 60% of government revenues, and 30% of GDP. With its highly developed communication and transport facilities, Bahrain is home to numerous multinational firms with business in the Gulf. Bahrain is dependent on Saudi Arabia for oil granted as aid. A large share of exports consist of petroleum products made from refining imported crude. Construction proceeds on several major industrial projects. Unemployment, especially among the young, and the depletion of oil and underground water resources are major long-term economic problems.

GDP: purchasing power parity - $11.38 billion (2003 est.)

GDP - real growth rate: 3.6% (2003 est.)

GDP - per capita: purchasing power parity - $17,100 (2003 est.)

GDP - composition by sector:
agriculture: 1%
industry: 35%
services: 64% (2002 est.)

Population below poverty line: NA%

Household income or consumption by percentage share:
lowest 10%: NA%
highest 10%: NA%

Inflation rate (consumer prices): 0.4% (2003 est.)

Labor force: 295,000
note: 44% of the population in the 15-64 age group is non-national (1998 est.)

Labor force - by occupation: industry, commerce, and service 79%, government 20%, agriculture 1% (1997 est.)

Unemployment rate: 15% (1998 est.)

Budget:
revenues: $1.8 billion
expenditures: $2.2 billion, including capital expenditures of $700 million (2002 est.)

Industries: petroleum processing and refining, aluminum smelting, offshore banking, ship repairing; tourism

Industrial production growth rate: 2% (2000 est.)

Electricity - production: 6.257 billion kWh (2001)

Electricity - production by source:
fossil fuel: 100%
hydro: 0%
nuclear: 0%
other: 0% (2001)

Electricity - consumption: 5.819 billion kWh (2001)

Electricity - exports: 0 kWh (2001)

Electricity - imports: 0 kWh (2001)

Oil - production: 43,000 bbl/day (2001 est.)

Oil - consumption: 31,000 bbl/day (2001 est.)

Oil - exports: NA

Oil - imports: NA

Oil - proved reserves: 125 million bbl (1 January 2003)

Natural gas - production: 8.9 billion cu m (2001 est.)

Natural gas - consumption: 8.9 billion cu m (2001 est.)

Natural gas - exports: 0 cu m (2001 est.)

Natural gas - imports: 0 cu m (2001 est.)

Natural gas - proved reserves: 46 billion cu m (1 January 2003)

Agriculture - products: fruit, vegetables; poultry, dairy products; shrimp, fish

Exports: $6.492 billion (2003 est.)

Exports - commodities: petroleum and petroleum products, aluminum, textiles

Exports - partners: US 4.5%, India 3.2%, Saudi Arabia 2.1% (2002)

Imports: $5.126 billion (2003 est.)

Imports - commodities: crude oil, machinery, chemicals

Imports - partners: Saudi Arabia 29.5%, US 11.4%, Japan 7%, Germany 6.4%, UK 5.5% (2002)

Debt - external: $5.9 billion (2003)

Economic aid - recipient: $150 million; note - $50 million annually since 1992 from each of Saudi Arabia, UAE, and Kuwait (2002)

Currency: Bahraini dinar (BHD)

Currency code: BHD

Exchange rates: Bahraini dinars per US dollar - 0.376 (2003), 0.376 (2002), 0.376 (2001), 0.376 (2000), 0.376 (1999)

Fiscal year: calendar year

Communications

Telephones - main lines in use: 175,400 (2002)

Telephones - mobile cellular: 389,000 (2002)

Telephone system:
general assessment: modern system
domestic: modern fiber-optic integrated services; digital network with rapidly growing use of mobile cellular telephones
international: country code - 973; tropospheric scatter to Qatar and UAE; microwave radio relay to Saudi Arabia; submarine cable to Qatar, UAE, and Saudi Arabia; satellite earth stations - 2 Intelsat (1 Atlantic Ocean and 1 Indian Ocean) and 1 Arabsat (1997)

Radio broadcast stations: AM 2, FM 3, shortwave 0 (1998)

Television broadcast stations: 4 (1997)

Internet country code: .bh

Internet hosts: 1,339 (2002)

Internet users: 165,000 (2002)

Transportation

Railways: 0 km

Highways:
total: 3,261 km
paved: 2,531 km
unpaved: 730 km (2000)

Waterways: none

Pipelines: gas 20 km; oil 53 km (2003)

Ports and harbors: Manama, Mina' Salman, Sitrah

Merchant marine:
total: 6 ships (1,000 GRT or over) 219,083 GRT/ 312,638 DWT
by type: bulk 3, container 2, petroleum tanker 1
foreign-owned: Hong Kong 1, Kuwait 1
registered in other countries: 2 (2003 est.)

Airports: 4 (2003 est.)

Airports - with paved runways:
total: 3
over 3,047 m: 2
1524 to 2437 m: 1 (2003 est.)

Airports - with unpaved runways:
total: 1
1,524 to 2,437 m: 1 (2003 est.)

Heliports: 1 (2003 est.)

Military

Military branches: Bahrain Defense Forces (BDF): Ground Force (includes Air Defense), Navy, Air Force, National Guard

Military manpower - military age: 15 years of age (2004 est.)

Military manpower - availability:
males age 15-49: 221,661 (2004 est.)

Military manpower - fit for military service:
males age 15-49: 121,484 (2004 est.)

Military manpower - reaching military age annually:
males: 6,396 (2004 est.)

Military expenditures - dollar figure: $618.1 million (2003)

Military expenditures - percent of GDP: 7.5% (2003)

Transnational Issues

Disputes - international: none

Baker Island
(territory of the US)

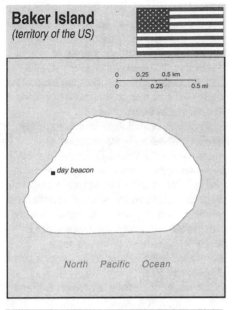

Introduction

Background: The US took possession of the island in 1857, and its guano deposits were mined by US and British companies during the second half of the 19th century. In 1935, a short-lived attempt at colonization was begun on this island - as well as on nearby Howland Island - but was disrupted by World War II and thereafter abandoned. Presently the island is a National Wildlife Refuge run by the US Department of the Interior; a day beacon is situated near the middle of the west coast.

Geography

Location: Oceania, atoll in the North Pacific Ocean, about half way between Hawaii and Australia
Geographic coordinates: 0 13 N, 176 31 W
Map references: Oceania
Area:
total: 1.4 sq km
land: 1.4 sq km
water: 0 sq km
Area - comparative: about 2.5 times the size of The Mall in Washington, DC
Land boundaries: 0 km
Coastline: 4.8 km
Maritime claims:
territorial sea: 12 NM
exclusive economic zone: 200 NM
Climate: equatorial; scant rainfall, constant wind, burning sun
Terrain: low, nearly level coral island surrounded by a narrow fringing reef
Elevation extremes:
lowest point: Pacific Ocean 0 m
highest point: unnamed location 8 m
Natural resources: guano (deposits worked until 1891), terrestrial and aquatic wildlife

Land use:
arable land: 0%
permanent crops: 0%
other: 100% (1998 est.)
Irrigated land: 0 sq km (1998 est.)
Natural hazards: the narrow fringing reef surrounding the island can be a maritime hazard
Environment - current issues: no natural fresh water resources
Geography - note: treeless, sparse, and scattered vegetation consisting of grasses, prostrate vines, and low growing shrubs; primarily a nesting, roosting, and foraging habitat for seabirds, shorebirds, and marine wildlife

People

Population: uninhabited
note: American civilians evacuated in 1942 after Japanese air and naval attacks during World War II; occupied by US military during World War II, but abandoned after the war; public entry is by special-use permit from US Fish and Wildlife Service only and generally restricted to scientists and educators; a cemetery and remnants of structures from early settlement are located near the middle of the west coast; visited annually by US Fish and Wildlife Service (2004 est.)

Government

Country name:
conventional long form: none
conventional short form: Baker Island
Dependency status: unincorporated territory of the US; administered from Washington, DC, by the Fish and Wildlife Service of the US Department of the Interior as part of the National Wildlife Refuge system
Legal system: the laws of the US, where applicable, apply
Flag description: the flag of the US is used

Economy

Economy - overview: no economic activity

Transportation

Waterways: none
Ports and harbors: none; offshore anchorage only; note - there is one small boat landing area along the middle of the west coast
Airports: 1 abandoned World War II runway of 1,665 m, completely covered with vegetation and unusable (2003 est.)
Transportation - note: there is a day beacon near the middle of the west coast

Military

Military - note: defense is the responsibility of the US; visited annually by the US Coast Guard

Transnational Issues

Disputes - international: none

Bangladesh

Introduction

Background: Bangladesh came into existence in 1971 when Bengali East Pakistan seceded from its union with West Pakistan. About a third of this extremely poor country floods annually during the monsoon rainy season, hampering economic development.

Geography

Location: Southern Asia, bordering the Bay of Bengal, between Burma and India
Geographic coordinates. 24 00 N, 90 00 E
Map references. Asia
Area.
total. 144,000 sq km
land. 133,910 sq km
water. 10,090 sq km
Area - comparative. slightly smaller than Iowa
Land boundaries.
total. 4,246 km
border countries. Burma 193 km, India 4,053 km
Coastline. 580 km
Maritime claims:
territorial sea. 12 NM
contiguous zone. 18 NM
exclusive economic zone. 200 NM
continental shelf. up to the outer limits of the continental margin
Climate. tropical; mild winter (October to March); hot, humid summer (March to June); humid, warm rainy monsoon (June to October)
Terrain. mostly flat alluvial plain; hilly in southeast
Elevation extremes.
lowest point. Indian Ocean 0 m
highest point. Keokradong 1,230 m
Natural resources. natural gas, arable land, timber, coal
Land use.
arable land. 60.7%
permanent crops. 2.61%
other. 36.69% (1998 est.)

Bangladesh (continued)

Irrigated land: 38,440 sq km (1998 est.)
Natural hazards: droughts, cyclones; much of the country routinely inundated during the summer monsoon season
Environment - current issues: many people are landless and forced to live on and cultivate flood-prone land; water-borne diseases prevalent in surface water; water pollution, especially of fishing areas, results from the use of commercial pesticides; ground water contaminated by naturally occurring arsenic; intermittent water shortages because of falling water tables in the northern and central parts of the country; soil degradation and erosion; deforestation; severe overpopulation
Environment - international agreements:
party to: Biodiversity, Climate Change, Climate Change-Kyoto Protocol, Desertification, Endangered Species, Environmental Modification, Hazardous Wastes, Law of the Sea, Ozone Layer Protection, Wetlands
signed, but not ratified: none of the selected agreements
Geography - note: most of the country is situated on deltas of large rivers flowing from the Himalayas: the Ganges unites with the Jamuna (main channel of the Brahmaputra) and later joins the Meghna to eventually empty into the Bay of Bengal

People

Population: 141,340,476 (July 2004 est.)
Age structure:
0-14 years: 33.5% (male 24,359,149; female 23,013,811)
15-64 years: 63.1% (male 45,557,963; female 43,626,950)
65 years and over: 3.4% (male 2,575,519; female 2,207,084) (2004 est.)
Median age:
total: 21.5 years
male: 21.5 years
female: 21.5 years (2004 est.)
Population growth rate: 2.08% (2004 est.)
Birth rate: 30.03 births/1,000 population (2004 est.)
Death rate: 8.52 deaths/1,000 population (2004 est.)
Net migration rate: -0.71 migrant(s)/1,000 population (2004 est.)
Sex ratio:
at birth: 1.06 male(s)/female
under 15 years: 1.06 male(s)/female
15-64 years: 1.04 male(s)/female
65 years and over: 1.17 male(s)/female
total population: 1.05 male(s)/female (2004 est.)
Infant mortality rate:
total: 64.32 deaths/1,000 live births
male: 65.41 deaths/1,000 live births
female: 63.16 deaths/1,000 live births (2004 est.)
Life expectancy at birth:
total population: 61.71 years
male: 61.8 years
female: 61.61 years (2004 est.)

Total fertility rate: 3.15 children born/woman (2004 est.)
HIV/AIDS - adult prevalence rate: less than 0.1% (2001 est.)
HIV/AIDS - people living with HIV/AIDS: 13,000 (2001 est.)
HIV/AIDS - deaths: 650 (2001 est.)
Nationality:
noun: Bangladeshi(s)
adjective: Bangladeshi
Ethnic groups: Bengali 98%, tribal groups, non-Bengali Muslims (1998)
Religions: Muslim 83%, Hindu 16%, other 1% (1998)
Languages: Bangla (official, also known as Bengali), English
Literacy:
definition: age 15 and over can read and write
total population: 43.1%
male: 53.9%
female: 31.8% (2003 est.)

Government

Country name:
conventional long form: People's Republic of Bangladesh
conventional short form: Bangladesh
former: East Pakistan
Government type: parliamentary democracy
Capital: Dhaka
Administrative divisions: 6 divisions; Barisal, Chittagong, Dhaka, Khulna, Rajshahi, and Sylhet
Independence: 16 December 1971 (from West Pakistan); note - 26 March 1971 is the date of independence from West Pakistan, 16 December 1971 is known as Victory Day and commemorates the official creation of the state of Bangladesh
National holiday: Independence Day, 26 March (1971); note - 26 March 1971 is the date of independence from West Pakistan, 16 December 1971 is Victory Day and commemorates the official creation of the state of Bangladesh
Constitution: 4 November 1972, effective 16 December 1972, suspended following coup of 24 March 1982, restored 10 November 1986, amended many times
Legal system: based on English common law
Suffrage: 18 years of age; universal
Executive branch:
chief of state: President Iajuddin AHMED (since 6 September 2002); note - the president's duties are normally ceremonial, but with the 13th amendment to the constitution ("Caretaker Government Amendment"), the president's role becomes significant at times when Parliament is dissolved and a caretaker government is installed - at presidential direction - to supervise the elections
head of government: Prime Minister Khaleda ZIA (since 10 October 2001)
cabinet: Cabinet selected by the prime minister and appointed by the president

elections: president elected by National Parliament for a five-year term; election scheduled for 16 September 2002 was not held since Iajuddin AHMED was the only presidential candidate; he was sworn in on 6 September 2002 (next election to be held by NA 2007); following legislative elections, the leader of the party that wins the most seats is usually appointed prime minister by the president
election results: Iajuddin AHMED declared by the Election Commission elected unopposed as president; percent of National Parliament vote - NA%
Legislative branch: unicameral National Parliament or Jatiya Sangsad; 300 seats elected by popular vote from single territorial constituencies (the constitutional amendment reserving 30 seats for women over and above the 300 regular parliament seats expired in May 2001); members serve five-year terms
elections: last held 1 October 2001 (next to be held before October 2006)
election results: percent of vote by party - BNP and alliance partners 46%, AL 42%; seats by party - BNP 191, AL 62, JI 18, JP (Ershad faction) 14, IOJ 2, JP (Naziur) 4, other 9; note - the election of October 2001 brought a majority BNP government aligned with three other smaller parties - Jamaat-i-Islami, Islami Oikya Jote, and Jatiya Party (Manzur)
Judicial branch: Supreme Court (the chief justices and other judges are appointed by the president)
Political parties and leaders: Awami League or AL [Sheikh HASINA]; Bangladesh Communist Party or BCP [Saifuddin Ahmed MANIK]; Bangladesh Nationalist Party or BNP [Khaleda ZIA, chairperson]; Islami Oikya Jote or IOJ [Mufti Fazlul Haq AMINI]; Jamaat-e-Islami or JI [Motiur Rahman NIZAMI]; Jatiya Party or JP (Ershad faction) [Hussain Mohammad ERSHAD]; Jatiya Party (Manzur faction) [Naziur Rahman MANZUR]
Political pressure groups and leaders: NA
International organization participation: AsDB, C, CP, FAO, G-77, IAEA, IBRD, ICAO, ICC, ICCt (signatory), ICFTU, ICRM, IDA, IDB, IFAD, IFC, IFRCS, IHO, ILO, IMF, IMO, Interpol, IOC, IOM, ISO, ITU, MINURSO, MONUC, NAM, OIC, OPCW, SAARC, UN, UNAMSIL, UNCTAD, UNESCO, UNHCR, UNIDO, UNMEE, UNMIK, UNMIL, UNMISET, UNOMIG, UPU, WCL, WCO, WFTU, WHO, WIPO, WMO, WToO, WTrO
Diplomatic representation in the US:
chief of mission: Ambassador Syed Hasan AHMAD
chancery: 3510 International Drive NW, Washington, DC 20008
telephone: [1] (202) 244-0183
FAX: [1] (202) 244-5366
consulate(s) general: Los Angeles and New York
Diplomatic representation from the US:
chief of mission: Ambassador Harry K. THOMAS, Jr.
embassy: Madani Avenue, Baridhara, Dhaka 1212
mailing address: G. P. O. Box 323, Dhaka 1000
telephone: [880] (2) 8824700 through 8824722
FAX: [880] (2) 8823744

Bangladesh (continued)

Flag description: green with a large red disk slightly to the hoist side of center; the red sun of freedom represents the blood shed to achieve independence; the green field symbolizes the lush countryside, and secondarily, the traditional color of Islam

Economy

Economy - overview: Despite sustained domestic and international efforts to improve economic and demographic prospects, Bangladesh remains a poor, overpopulated, and ill-governed nation. Although half of GDP is generated through the service sector, nearly two-thirds of Bangladeshis are employed in the agriculture sector, with rice as the single-most-important product. Major impediments to growth include frequent cyclones and floods, inefficient state-owned enterprises, inadequate port facilities, a rapidly growing labor force that cannot be absorbed by agriculture, delays in exploiting energy resources (natural gas), insufficient power supplies, and slow implementation of economic reforms. Economic reform is stalled in many instances by political infighting and corruption at all levels of government. Progress also has been blocked by opposition from the bureaucracy, public sector unions, and other vested interest groups. The BNP government, led by Prime Minister Khaleda ZIA, has the parliamentary strength to push through needed reforms, but the party's political will to do so has been lacking in key areas. One encouraging note: growth has been a steady 5% for the past several years.
GDP: purchasing power parity - $258.8 billion (2003 est.)
GDP - real growth rate: 5.3% (2003 est.)
GDP - per capita: purchasing power parity - $1,900 (2003 est.)
GDP - composition by sector:
agriculture: 24%
industry: 26.7%
services: 49.3% (2002 est.)
Population below poverty line: 35.6% (FY95/96 est.)
Household income or consumption by percentage share:
lowest 10%: 3.9%
highest 10%: 28.6% (1995-96 est.)
Distribution of family income - Gini index: 33.6 (FY95/96)
Inflation rate (consumer prices): 5.3% (2003 est.)
Labor force: 64.1 million
note: extensive export of labor to Saudi Arabia, Kuwait, UAE, Oman, Qatar, and Malaysia; workers' remittances estimated at $1.71 billion in 1998-99 (1998)
Labor force - by occupation: agriculture 63%, services 26%, industry 11% (FY95/96)
Unemployment rate: 40% (includes underemployment) (2002 est.)
Budget:
revenues: $4.9 billion
expenditures: $6.8 billion, including capital expenditures of $NA (FY99/00 est.)

Industries: cotton textiles, jute, garments, tea processing, paper newsprint, cement, chemical fertilizer, light engineering, sugar
Industrial production growth rate: 4% (2003 est.)
Electricity - production: 15.33 billion kWh (2001)
Electricity - production by source:
fossil fuel: 93.7%
hydro: 6.3%
nuclear: 0%
other: 0% (2001)
Electricity - consumption: 14.25 billion kWh (2001)
Electricity - exports: 0 kWh (2001)
Electricity - imports: 0 kWh (2001)
Oil - production: 3,581 bbl/day (2001 est.)
Oil - consumption: 71,000 bbl/day (2001 est.)
Oil - exports: NA
Oil - imports: NA
Oil - proved reserves: 28.45 million bbl (1 January 2002)
Natural gas - production: 9.9 billion cu m (2001 est.)
Natural gas - consumption: 9.9 billion cu m (2001 est.)
Natural gas - exports: 0 cu m (2001 est.)
Natural gas - imports: 0 cu m (2001 est.)
Natural gas - proved reserves: 150.3 billion cu m (1 January 2002)
Agriculture - products: rice, jute, tea, wheat, sugarcane, potatoes, tobacco, pulses, oilseeds, spices, fruit; beef, milk, poultry
Exports: $6.713 billion (2003 est.)
Exports - commodities: garments, jute and jute goods, leather, frozen fish and seafood (2001)
Exports - partners: US 27.6%, Germany 10.4%, UK 9.8%, France 5.7%, Italy 4% (2002)
Imports: $9.459 billion (2003 est.)
Imports - commodities: machinery and equipment, chemicals, iron and steel, textiles, foodstuffs, petroleum products, cement (2000)
Imports - partners: India 14.6%, China 11.6%, Singapore 11.5%, Japan 7.6%, Hong Kong 5.4%, South Korea 4.3% (2002)
Debt - external: $17.4 billion (2003)
Economic aid - recipient: $1.575 billion (2000 est.)
Currency: taka (BDT)
Currency code: BDT
Exchange rates: taka per US dollar - 58.15 (2003), 57.888 (2002), 55.8067 (2001), 52.1417 (2000), 49.0854 (1999)
Fiscal year: 1 July - 30 June

Communications

Telephones - main lines in use: 682,000 (2002)
Telephones - mobile cellular: 1.075 million (2002)
Telephone system:
general assessment: totally inadequate for a modern country
domestic: modernizing; introducing digital systems; trunk systems include VHF and UHF microwave radio relay links, and some fiber-optic cable in cities

international: country code - 880; satellite earth stations - 2 Intelsat (Indian Ocean); international radiotelephone communications and landline service to neighboring countries (2000)
Radio broadcast stations: AM 12, FM 12, shortwave 2 (1999)
Television broadcast stations: 15 (1999)
Internet country code: .bd
Internet hosts: 2 (2002)
Internet users: 204,000 (2002)

Transportation

Railways:
total: 2,706 km
broad gauge: 884 km 1.676-m gauge
narrow gauge: 1,822 km 1.000-m gauge (2002)
Highways:
total: 207,486 km
paved: 19,773 km
unpaved: 187,713 km (1999)
Waterways: up to 8,046 km depending on season
note: includes 3,058 km main cargo routes
Pipelines: gas 2,016 km (2003)
Ports and harbors: Chittagong, Dhaka, Mongla Port, Narayanganj
Merchant marine:
total: 40 ships (1,000 GRT or over) 319,897 GRT/440,575 DWT
by type: bulk 2, cargo 24, container 10, passenger 1, petroleum tanker 2, refrigerated cargo 1
foreign-owned: China 1, Singapore 9
registered in other countries: 10 (2003 est.)
Airports: 16 (2003 est.)
Airports - with paved runways:
total: 15
over 3,047 m: 1
2,438 to 3,047 m: 3
1,524 to 2,437 m: 4
914 to 1,523 m: 1
under 914 m: 6 (2003 est.)
Airports - with unpaved runways:
total: 1
1,524 to 2,437 m: 1 (2003 est.)

Military

Military branches: Army, Navy, Air Force
Military manpower - availability:
males age 15-49: 39,523,128 (2004 est.)
Military manpower - fit for military service:
males age 15-49: 23,441,482 (2004 est.)
Military expenditures - dollar figure: $606.8 million (2003)
Military expenditures - percent of GDP: 1.2% (2003)

Transnational Issues

Disputes - international: discussions with India remain stalled to delimit a small section of river boundary, exchange 162 miniscule enclaves in both countries, allocate divided villages, and stop illegal cross-border trade, migration, and violence;

Bangladesh *(continued)*

Bangladesh protests India's attempts to fence off high-traffic sections of the porous boundary; dispute with India over volcanic New Moore/South Talpatty/Purbasha Island in the Bay of Bengal deters maritime boundary delimitation; Burmese Muslim refugees strain Bangladesh's meager resources

Illicit drugs: transit country for illegal drugs produced in neighboring countries

Barbados

Introduction

Background: The island was uninhabited when first settled by the British in 1627. Slaves worked the sugar plantations established on the island until 1834 when slavery was abolished. The economy remained heavily dependent on sugar, rum, and molasses production through most of the 20th century. The gradual introduction of social and political reforms in the 1940s and 1950s led to complete independence from the UK in 1966. In the 1990s, tourism and manufacturing surpassed the sugar industry in economic importance.

Geography

Location: Caribbean, island in the North Atlantic Ocean, northeast of Venezuela
Geographic coordinates: 13 10 N, 59 32 W
Map references: Central America and the Caribbean
Area:
total: 431 sq km
land: 431 sq km
water: 0 sq km
Area - comparative: 2.5 times the size of Washington, DC
Land boundaries: 0 km
Coastline: 97 km
Maritime claims:
territorial sea: 12 NM
exclusive economic zone: 200 NM
Climate: tropical; rainy season (June to October)
Terrain: relatively flat; rises gently to central highland region
Elevation extremes:
lowest point: Atlantic Ocean 0 m
highest point: Mount Hillaby 336 m
Natural resources: petroleum, fish, natural gas

Land use:
arable land: 37.21%
permanent crops: 2.33%
other: 60.46% (1998 est.)
Irrigated land: 10 sq km (1998 est.)
Natural hazards: infrequent hurricanes; periodic landslides
Environment - current issues: pollution of coastal waters from waste disposal by ships; soil erosion; illegal solid waste disposal threatens contamination of aquifers
Environment - international agreements:
party to: Biodiversity, Climate Change, Climate Change-Kyoto Protocol, Desertification, Endangered Species, Hazardous Wastes, Law of the Sea, Marine Dumping, Ozone Layer Protection, Ship Pollution
signed, but not ratified: none of the selected agreements
Geography - note: easternmost Caribbean island

People

Population: 278,289 (July 2004 est.)
Age structure:
0-14 years: 21% (male 29,294; female 29,020)
15-64 years: 70.3% (male 95,675; female 99,864)
65 years and over: 8.8% (male 9,370; female 15,066) (2004 est.)
Median age:
total: 33.7 years
male: 32.6 years
female: 34.9 years (2004 est.)
Population growth rate: 0.36% (2004 est.)
Birth rate: 12.98 births/1,000 population (2004 est.)
Death rate: 9.08 deaths/1,000 population (2004 est.)
Net migration rate: -0.31 migrant(s)/1,000 population (2004 est.)
Sex ratio:
at birth: 1.01 male(s)/female
under 15 years: 1.01 male(s)/female
15-64 years: 0.96 male(s)/female
65 years and over: 0.62 male(s)/female
total population: 0.93 male(s)/female (2004 est.)
Infant mortality rate:
total: 12.61 deaths/1,000 live births
male: 14.26 deaths/1,000 live births
female: 10.94 deaths/1,000 live births (2004 est.)
Life expectancy at birth:
total population: 71.64 years
male: 69.51 years
female: 73.81 years (2004 est.)
Total fertility rate: 1.65 children born/woman (2004 est.)
HIV/AIDS - adult prevalence rate: 1.2% - note: no country specific models provided (2001 est.)
HIV/AIDS - people living with HIV/AIDS: 1,800 (2001 est.)
HIV/AIDS - deaths: 250 (2001 est.)
Nationality:
noun: Barbadian(s) or Bajan (colloquial)
adjective: Barbadian or Bajan (colloquial)

Barbados (continued)

Ethnic groups: black 90%, white 4%, Asian and mixed 6%

Religions: Protestant 67% (Anglican 40%, Pentecostal 8%, Methodist 7%, other 12%), Roman Catholic 4%, none 17%, other 12%

Languages: English

Literacy:

definition: age 15 and over has ever attended school

total population: 97.4%

male: 98%

female: 96.8% (1995 est.)

Government

Country name:

conventional long form: none

conventional short form: Barbados

Government type: parliamentary democracy; independent sovereign state within the Commonwealth

Capital: Bridgetown

Administrative divisions: 11 parishes; Christ Church, Saint Andrew, Saint George, Saint James, Saint John, Saint Joseph, Saint Lucy, Saint Michael, Saint Peter, Saint Philip, Saint Thomas; note - the city of Bridgetown may be given parish status

Independence: 30 November 1966 (from UK)

National holiday: Independence Day, 30 November (1966)

Constitution: 30 November 1966

Legal system: English common law; no judicial review of legislative acts

Suffrage: 18 years of age; universal

Executive branch:

chief of state: Queen ELIZABETH II (since 6 February 1952), represented by Governor General Sir Clifford Straughn HUSBANDS (since 1 June 1996)

head of government: Prime Minister Owen Seymour ARTHUR (since 6 September 1994); Deputy Prime Minister Mia MOTTLEY (since 26 May 2003)

cabinet: Cabinet appointed by the governor general on the advice of the prime minister

elections: none; the monarch is hereditary; governor general appointed by the monarch; following legislative elections, the leader of the majority party or the leader of the majority coalition is usually appointed prime minister by the governor general; the prime minister recommends the deputy prime minister

Legislative branch: bicameral Parliament consists of the Senate (21-member body appointed by the governor general) and the House of Assembly (30 seats; members are elected by direct popular vote to serve five-year terms)

elections: House of Assembly - last held 21 May 2003 (next to be held by May 2008)

election results: House of Assembly - percent of vote by party - NA%; seats by party - BLP 23, DLP 7

Judicial branch: Supreme Court of Judicature (judges are appointed by the Service Commissions for the Judicial and Legal Services)

Political parties and leaders: Barbados Labor Party or BLP [Owen ARTHUR]; Democratic Labor Party or DLP [Clyde Mascoll]

Political pressure groups and leaders: Barbados Workers Union [Leroy TROTMAN]; Clement Payne Labor Union [David COMMISSIONG]; People's Progressive Movement [Eric SEALY]; Worker's Party of Barbados [Dr. George BELLE]

International organization participation: ACP, C, Caricom, CDB, FAO, G-77, IADB, IBRD, ICAO, ICCt, ICFTU, ICRM, IDA, IFAD, IFC, IFRCS, ILO, IMF, IMO, Interpol, IOC, ISO, ITU, LAES, NAM, OAS, OPANAL, UN, UNCTAD, UNESCO, UNIDO, UPU, WCO, WFTU, WHO, WIPO, WMO, WTrO

Diplomatic representation in the US:

chief of mission: Ambassador Michael Ian KING

chancery: 2144 Wyoming Avenue NW, Washington, DC 20008

telephone: [1] (202) 339-9201

FAX: [1] (202) 332-7467

consulate(s) general: Miami and New York

consulate(s): Los Angeles

Diplomatic representation from the US:

chief of mission: Ambassador Mary E. KRAMER

embassy: Canadian Imperial Bank of Commerce Building, Broad Street, Bridgetown; (courier) ALICO Building-Cheapside, Bridgetown

mailing address: P. O. Box 302, Bridgetown; FPO AA 34055

telephone: [1] (246) 436-4950

FAX: [1] (246) 429-5246, 429-3379

Flag description: three equal vertical bands of blue (hoist side), gold, and blue with the head of a black trident centered on the gold band; the trident head represents independence and a break with the past (the colonial coat of arms contained a complete trident)

Economy

Economy - overview: Historically, the Barbadian economy had been dependent on sugarcane cultivation and related activities, but production in recent years has diversified into light industry and tourism. Offshore finance and information services are important foreign exchange earners. The government continues its efforts to reduce unemployment, to encourage direct foreign investment, and to privatize remaining state-owned enterprises. The economy contracted in 2002-03 mainly due to a decline in tourism. Growth should be positive in 2004, the precise level largely dependent on economic conditions in the US and Europe.

GDP: purchasing power parity - $4.496 billion (2003 est.)

GDP - real growth rate: -0.6% (2003 est.)

GDP - per capita: purchasing power parity - $16,200 (2003 est.)

GDP - composition by sector:

agriculture: 6%

industry: 16%

services: 78% (2000 est.)

Population below poverty line: NA%

Household income or consumption by percentage share:

lowest 10%: NA%

highest 10%: NA%

Inflation rate (consumer prices): -0.5% (2003 est.)

Labor force: 128,500 (2001 est.)

Labor force - by occupation: services 75%, industry 15%, agriculture 10% (1996 est.)

Unemployment rate: 10.7% (2003 est.)

Budget:

revenues: $847 million (including grants)

expenditures: $886 million, including capital expenditures of $NA (2000 est.)

Industries: tourism, sugar, light manufacturing, component assembly for export

Industrial production growth rate: -3.2% (2000 est.)

Electricity - production: 780 million kWh (2001)

Electricity - production by source:

fossil fuel: 100%

hydro: 0%

nuclear: 0%

other: 0% (2001)

Electricity - consumption: 725.4 million kWh (2001)

Electricity - exports: 0 kWh (2001)

Electricity - imports: 0 kWh (2001)

Oil - production: 1,271 bbl/day (2001 est.)

Oil - consumption: 10,900 bbl/day (2001 est.)

Oil - exports: NA

Oil - imports: NA

Oil - proved reserves: 1.254 million bbl (1 January 2002)

Natural gas - production: 29.17 million cu m (2001 est.)

Natural gas - consumption: 29.17 million cu m (2001 est.)

Natural gas - exports: 0 cu m (2001 est.)

Natural gas - imports: 0 cu m (2001 est.)

Natural gas - proved reserves: 70.79 million cu m (1 January 2002)

Agriculture - products: sugarcane, vegetables, cotton

Exports: $206 million (2002)

Exports - commodities: sugar and molasses, rum, other foods and beverages, chemicals, electrical components

Exports - partners: US 14.9%, Trinidad and Tobago 12%, UK 10.8%, Jamaica 6.2%, Saint Lucia 4.6% (2002)

Imports: $1.039 billion (2002)

Imports - commodities: consumer goods, machinery, foodstuffs, construction materials, chemicals, fuel, electrical components

Imports - partners: US 41.1%, Trinidad and Tobago 17%, UK 7.4%, Japan 4.2% (2002)

Debt - external: $668 million (2003)

Economic aid - recipient: $9.1 million (1995)

Currency: Barbadian dollar (BBD)

Currency code: BBD

Exchange rates: Barbadian dollars per US dollar - 2 (2003), 2 (2002), 2 (2001), 2 (2000), 2 (1999)

Fiscal year: 1 April - 31 March

Barbados (continued)

Communications

Telephones - main lines in use: 133,000 (2002)
Telephones - mobile cellular: 53,100 (2002)
Telephone system:
general assessment: NA
domestic: island-wide automatic telephone system
international: country code - 1-246; satellite earth stations - 4 Intelsat (Atlantic Ocean); tropospheric scatter to Trinidad and Saint Lucia
Radio broadcast stations: AM 2, FM 3, shortwave 0 (1998)
Television broadcast stations: 1 (plus two cable channels) (1997)
Internet country code: .bb
Internet hosts: 160 (2002)
Internet users: 30,000 (2002)

Transportation

Railways: 0 km
Highways:
total: 1,793 km
paved: 1,719 km
unpaved: 74 km (1999)
Waterways: none
Ports and harbors: Bridgetown, Speightstown (Port Charles Marina)
Merchant marine:
total: 42 ships (1,000 GRT or over) 427,465 GRT/668,195 DWT
by type: bulk 11, cargo 20, chemical tanker 1, combination bulk 3, petroleum tanker 6, roll on/roll off 1
foreign-owned: Australia 1, Bahamas 1, Bangladesh 1, Canada 5, Greece 7, Hong Kong 7, Italy 2, Lebanon 1, Norway 9, United Kingdom 10
registered in other countries: 3 (2003 est.)
Airports: 1 (2003 est.)
Airports - with paved runways:
total: 1
over 3,047 m: 1 (2003 est.)

Military

Military branches: Royal Barbados Defense Force (Troops Command and Coast Guard)
Military manpower - availability:
males age 15-49: 77,714 (2004 est.)
Military manpower - fit for military service:
males age 15-49: 53,127 (2004 est.)
Military expenditures - dollar figure: NA
Military expenditures - percent of GDP: NA

Transnational Issues

Disputes - international: Barbados intends to take its claim before UNCLOS arbitration that the northern limit of Trinidad and Tobago's maritime boundary with Venezuela extends into its waters; joins other Caribbean states to counter Venezuela's claim that Aves Island sustains human habitation, a criterion under UNCLOS, which permits Venezuela to extend its EEZ/continental shelf over a large portion of the Caribbean Sea

Illicit drugs: one of many Caribbean transshipment points for narcotics bound for Europe and the US; offshore financial center

Bassas da India
(possession of France)

Introduction

Background: This atoll is a volcanic rock surrounded by reefs and is awash at high tide. A French possession since 1897, it was placed under the administration of a commissioner residing in Reunion in 1968.

Geography

Location: Southern Africa, islands in the southern Mozambique Channel, about one-half of the way from Madagascar to Mozambique
Geographic coordinates: 21 30 S, 39 50 E
Map references: Africa
Area:
total: 0.2 sq km
land: 0.2 sq km
water: 0 sq km
Area - comparative: about one-third the size of The Mall in Washington, DC
Land boundaries: 0 km
Coastline: 35.2 km
Maritime claims:
territorial sea: 12 NM
exclusive economic zone: 200 NM
Climate: tropical
Terrain: volcanic rock
Elevation extremes:
lowest point: Indian Ocean 0 m
highest point: unnamed location 2.4 m
Natural resources: none
Land use:
arable land: 0%
permanent crops: 0%
other: 100% (all rock) (1998 est.)
Irrigated land: 0 sq km (1998 est.)
Natural hazards: maritime hazard since it is usually under water during high tide and surrounded by reefs; subject to periodic cyclones
Environment - current issues: NA

Bassas da India (continued)

Geography - note: the islands emerge from a circular reef that sits atop a long-extinct, submerged volcano

People

Population: uninhabited (July 2004 est.)

Government

Country name:
conventional long form: none
conventional short form: Bassas da India
Dependency status: possession of France; administered by a high commissioner of the Republic, resident in Reunion
Legal system: the laws of France, where applicable, apply
Flag description: the flag of France is used

Economy

Economy - overview: no economic activity

Transportation

Waterways: none
Ports and harbors: none; offshore anchorage only

Military

Military - note: defense is the responsibility of France

Transnational Issues

Disputes - international: claimed by Madagascar

Belarus

Introduction

Background: After seven decades as a constituent republic of the USSR, Belarus attained its independence in 1991. It has retained closer political and economic ties to Russia than any of the other former Soviet republics. Belarus and Russia signed a treaty on a two-state union on 8 December 1999 envisioning greater political and economic integration. Although Belarus agreed to a framework to carry out the accord, serious implementation has yet to take place.

Geography

Location: Eastern Europe, east of Poland
Geographic coordinates: 53 00 N, 28 00 E
Map references: Europe
Area:
total: 207,600 sq km
land: 207,600 sq km
water: 0 sq km
Area - comparative: slightly smaller than Kansas
Land boundaries:
total: 2,900 km
border countries: Latvia 141 km, Lithuania 502 km, Poland 407 km, Russia 959 km, Ukraine 891 km
Coastline: 0 km (landlocked)
Maritime claims: none (landlocked)
Climate: cold winters, cool and moist summers; transitional between continental and maritime
Terrain: generally flat and contains much marshland
Elevation extremes:
lowest point: Nyoman River 90 m
highest point: Dzyarzhynskaya Hara 346 m
Natural resources: forests, peat deposits, small quantities of oil and natural gas, granite, dolomitic limestone, marl, chalk, sand, gravel, clay
Land use:
arable land: 29.76%
permanent crops: 0.69%
other: 69.55% (1998 est.)

Irrigated land: 1,150 sq km (1998 est.)
Natural hazards: NA
Environment - current issues: soil pollution from pesticide use; southern part of the country contaminated with fallout from 1986 nuclear reactor accident at Chornobyl' in northern Ukraine
Environment - international agreements:
party to: Air Pollution, Air Pollution-Nitrogen Oxides, Air Pollution-Sulfur 85, Biodiversity, Climate Change, Desertification, Endangered Species, Environmental Modification, Hazardous Wastes, Marine Dumping, Ozone Layer Protection, Ship Pollution, Wetlands
signed, but not ratified: Law of the Sea
Geography - note: landlocked; glacial scouring accounts for the flatness of Belarusian terrain and for its 11,000 lakes; the country is geologically well endowed with extensive deposits of granite, dolomitic limestone, marl, chalk, sand, gravel, and clay

People

Population: 10,310,520 (July 2004 est.)
Age structure:
0-14 years: 16.3% (male 859,219; female 823,839)
15-64 years: 69.2% (male 3,469,926; female 3,662,203)
65 years and over: 14.5% (male 496,204; female 999,129) (2004 est.)
Median age:
total: 36.9 years
male: 34.2 years
female: 39.5 years (2004 est.)
Population growth rate: -0.11% (2004 est.)
Birth rate: 10.52 births/1,000 population (2004 est.)
Death rate: 14.1 deaths/1,000 population (2004 est.)
Net migration rate: 2.54 migrant(s)/1,000 population (2004 est.)
Sex ratio:
at birth: 1.05 male(s)/female
under 15 years: 1.04 male(s)/female
15-64 years: 0.95 male(s)/female
65 years and over: 0.5 male(s)/female
total population: 0.88 male(s)/female (2004 est.)
Infant mortality rate:
total: 13.62 deaths/1,000 live births
male: 14.71 deaths/1,000 live births
female: 12.47 deaths/1,000 live births (2004 est.)
Life expectancy at birth:
total population: 68.57 years
male: 62.79 years
female: 74.65 years (2004 est.)
Total fertility rate: 1.36 children born/woman (2004 est.)
HIV/AIDS - adult prevalence rate: 0.3% (2001 est.)
HIV/AIDS - people living with HIV/AIDS: 15,000 (2001 est.)
HIV/AIDS - deaths: 1,000 (2001 est.)
Nationality:
noun: Belarusian(s)
adjective: Belarusian
Ethnic groups: Belarusian 81.2%, Russian 11.4%, Polish, Ukrainian, and other 7.4%

Belarus *(continued)*

Religions: Eastern Orthodox 80%, other (including Roman Catholic, Protestant, Jewish, and Muslim) 20% (1997 est.)

Languages: Belarusian, Russian, other

Literacy:

definition: age 15 and over can read and write

total population: 99.6%

male: 99.8%

female: 99.5% (2003 est.)

Government

Country name:

conventional long form: Republic of Belarus

conventional short form: Belarus

local long form: Respublika Byelarus'

local short form: none

former: Belorussian (Byelorussian) Soviet Socialist Republic

Government type: republic

Capital: Minsk

Administrative divisions: 6 voblastsi (singular - voblasts') and one municipality* (harady, singular - horad); Brestskaya (Brest), Homyel'skaya (Homyel'), Horad Minsk*, Hrodzyenskaya (Hrodna), Mahilyowskaya (Mahilyow), Minskaya, Vitsyebskaya (Vitsyebsk); note - when using a place name with the adjectival ending 'skaya,' the word Voblasts' should be added to the place name

note: voblasti have the administrative center name following in parentheses

Independence: 25 August 1991 (from Soviet Union)

National holiday: Independence Day, 3 July (1944); note - 3 July 1944 was the date Minsk was liberated from German troops, 25 August 1991 was the date of independence from the Soviet Union

Constitution: 30 March 1994; revised by national referendum of 24 November 1996 giving the presidency greatly expanded powers and became effective 27 November 1996

Legal system: based on civil law system

Suffrage: 18 years of age; universal

Executive branch:

chief of state: President Aleksandr LUKASHENKO (since 20 July 1994)

head of government: Prime Minister Sergei SIDORSKY (since 19 December 2003); First Deputy Prime Minister Vladimir SEMASHKO (since December 2003); Deputy Prime Ministers Andrei KOBYAKOV (since December 2003), Vladimir DRAZHIN (since 24 September 2001), Roman VNUCHKO (since 10 July 2003), Anatoly TYUTYUNOV (since July 2002)

cabinet: Council of Ministers

elections: president elected by popular vote for a five-year term; first election took place 23 June and 10 July 1994; according to the 1994 constitution, the next election should have been held in 1999, however LUKASHENKO extended his term to 2001 via a November 1996 referendum; new election held 9 September 2001 (next election to be held by September 2006); prime minister and deputy prime ministers appointed by the president

election results: Aleksandr LUKASHENKO reelected president; percent of vote - Aleksandr LUKASHENKO 75.6%, Vladimir GONCHARIK 15.4%

Legislative branch: bicameral Parliament or Natsionalnoye Sobranie consists of the Council of the Republic or Soviet Respubliki (64 seats; 56 members elected by regional councils and 8 members appointed by the president, all for 4-year terms) and the Chamber of Representatives or Palata Pretsaviteley (110 seats; members elected by universal adult suffrage to serve 4-year terms)

elections: last held 15 and 29 October 2000 and 18 March and 1 April 2001 (next to be held Fall 2004)

election results: Soviet Respubliki - percent of vote by party - NA%; seats by party - NA; Palata Pretsaviteley - percent of vote by party - NA%; seats by party - KPB 6, AP 5, RPPS 2, LDPB 1, PPA 1, non-party 81, other 14

Judicial branch: Supreme Court (judges are appointed by the president); Constitutional Court (half of the judges appointed by the president and half appointed by the Chamber of Representatives)

Political parties and leaders: Agrarian Party or AP [Mikhail SHIMANSKY]; Belarusian Communist Party or KPB [Viktor CHIKIN, chairman]; Belarusian Ecological Green Party (merger of Belarusian Ecological Party and Green Party of Belarus) [leader NA]; Belarusian Patriotic Movement (Belarusian Patriotic Party) or BPR [Anatoliy BARANKEVICH, chairman]; Belarusian Popular Front or BNF [Vintsuk VYACHORKA]; Belarusian Social-Democrat Party or SDBP [Nikolay STATKEVICH, chairman]; Belarusian Social-Democratic Party or Hromada [Stanislav SHUSHKEVICH, chairman]; Belarusian Socialist Party [Vyacheslav KUZNETSOV]; Civic Accord Bloc (United Civic Party) or CAB [Anatol LEBEDKO]; Liberal Democratic Party or LDPB [Sergei GAYDUKEVICH, chairman]; Party of Communists Belarusian or PKB [Sergei KALYAKIN, chairman]; Republican Party of Labor and Justice or RPPS [Anatoliy NETYLKIN, chairman]; Social-Democrat Party of Popular Accord or PPA [Leanid SECHKA]; Women's Party or "Nadezhda" [Valentina POLEVIKOVA, chairperson]

Political pressure groups and leaders: NA

International organization participation: CEI, CIS, EAPC, EBRD, IAEA, IBRD, ICAO, ICFTU, ICRM, IFC, IFRCS, ILO, IMF, Interpol, IOC, IOM (observer), ISO, ITU, NAM, NSG, OPCW, OSCE, PCA, PFP, UN, UNCTAD, UNESCO, UNIDO, UPU, WCO, WFTU, WHO, WIPO, WMO, WTrO (observer)

Diplomatic representation in the US:

chief of mission: Ambassador Mikhail KHVOSTOV

chancery: 1619 New Hampshire Avenue NW, Washington, DC 20009

telephone: [1] (202) 986-1604

FAX: [1] (202) 986-1805

consulate(s) general: New York

Diplomatic representation from the US:

chief of mission: Ambassador George A. KROL

embassy: 46 Starovilenskaya St., Minsk 220002

mailing address: PSC 78, Box B Minsk, APO 09723

telephone: [375] (17) 210-12-83

FAX: [375] (17) 234-7853

Flag description: red horizontal band (top) and green horizontal band one-half the width of the red band; a white vertical stripe on the hoist side bears a Belarusian national ornament in red

Economy

Economy - overview: Belarus' economy in 2003 posted 6.1 percent growth and is likely to continue expanding through 2004, albeit at a slower growth rate. The Belarusian economy in 2004 is likely to be hampered by high inflation, persistent trade deficits, and ongoing rocky relations with Russia, Belarus' largest trading partner and energy supplier. Belarus has seen little structural reform since 1995, when President LUKASHENKO launched the country on the path of "market socialism." In keeping with this policy, LUKASHENKO reimposed administrative controls over prices and currency exchange rates and expanded the state's right to intervene in the management of private enterprises. In addition, businesses have been subject to pressure on the part of central and local governments, e.g., arbitrary changes in regulations, numerous rigorous inspections, retroactive application of new business regulations, and arrests of "disruptive" businessmen and factory owners. A wide range of redistributive policies has helped those at the bottom of the ladder. For the time being, Belarus remains self-isolated from the West and its open-market economies.

GDP: purchasing power parity - $61.91 billion (2003 est.)

GDP - real growth rate: 6.1% (2003 est.)

GDP - per capita: purchasing power parity - $6,000 (2003 est.)

GDP - composition by sector:

agriculture: 9%

industry: 31.5%

services: 59.5% (2002 est.)

Population below poverty line: 22% (1995 est.)

Household income or consumption by percentage share:

lowest 10%: 5.1%

highest 10%: 20% (1998)

Distribution of family income - Gini index: 21.7 (1998)

Inflation rate (consumer prices): 30% (2003 est.)

Labor force: 4.8 million (2000 est.)

Labor force - by occupation: NA%

Unemployment rate: 2.1% officially registered unemployed (December 2000); large number of underemployed workers (2003 est.)

Budget:

revenues: $4 billion

expenditures: $4.1 billion, including capital expenditures of $180 million (1997 est.)

Industries: metal-cutting machine tools, tractors, trucks, earthmovers, motorcycles, television sets, chemical fibers, fertilizer, textiles, radios, refrigerators

Belarus *(continued)*

Industrial production growth rate: 5% (2003 est.)
Electricity - production: 24.4 billion kWh (2001)
Electricity - production by source:
fossil fuel: 99.5%
hydro: 0.1%
nuclear: 0%
other: 0.4% (2001)
Electricity - consumption: 26.69 billion kWh (2001)
Electricity - exports: 300 million kWh (2001)
Electricity - imports: 4.3 billion kWh (2001)
Oil - production: 37,000 bbl/day (2001 est.)
Oil - consumption: 230,000 bbl/day (2001 est.)
Oil - exports: NA
Oil - imports: NA
Natural gas - production: 200 million cu m
(2001 est.)
Natural gas - consumption: 18 billion cu m
(2001 est.)
Natural gas - exports: 0 cu m (2001 est.)
Natural gas - imports: 17.8 billion cu m (2001 est.)
Agriculture - products: grain, potatoes, vegetables,
sugar beets, flax; beef, milk
Exports: $9.413 billion f.o.b. (2003 est.)
Exports - commodities: machinery and equipment,
mineral products, chemicals, metals; textiles,
foodstuffs
Exports - partners: Russia 59.9%, Germany 4.9%,
Ukraine 3.9% (2002)
Imports: $11.09 billion f.o.b. (2003 est.)
Imports - commodities: mineral products,
machinery and equipment, chemicals, foodstuffs,
metals
Imports - partners: Russia 68%, Germany 9.6%,
Poland 3% (2002)
Debt - external: $851 million (2001 est.)
Economic aid - recipient: $194.3 million (1995)
Currency: Belarusian ruble (BYB/BYR)
Currency code: BYB/BYR
Exchange rates: Belarusian rubles per US dollar -
1,790.92 (2003), 1,920 (2002), 1,390 (2001), 876.75
(2000), 248.795 (1999)
Fiscal year: calendar year

Communications

Telephones - main lines in use: 2,967,200 (2002)
Telephones - mobile cellular: 462,600 (2002)
Telephone system:
general assessment: the Ministry of
Telecommunications controls all telecommunications
through its carrier (a joint stock company) Beltelcom
which is a monopoly
domestic: local - Minsk has a digital metropolitan
network and a cellular NMT-450 network; waiting lists
for telephones are long; local service outside Minsk is
neglected and poor; intercity - Belarus has a partly
developed fiber-optic backbone system presently
serving at least 13 major cities (1998); Belarus' fiber
optics form synchronous digital hierarchy rings
through other countries' systems; an inadequate
analog system remains operational

international: country code - 375; Belarus is a member
of the Trans-European Line (TEL), Trans-Asia-Europe
(TAE) fiber-optic line, and has access to the
Trans-Siberia Line (TSL); three fiber-optic segments
provide connectivity to Latvia, Poland, Russia, and
Ukraine; worldwide service is available to Belarus
through this infrastructure; additional analog lines to
Russia; Intelsat, Eutelsat, and Intersputnik earth stations
Radio broadcast stations: AM 28, FM 37,
shortwave 11 (1998)
Television broadcast stations: 47 (plus 27
repeaters) (1995)
Internet country code: .by
Internet hosts: 4,025 (2002)
Internet users: 808,700 (2002)

Transportation

Railways:
total: 5,523 km
broad gauge: 5,523 km 1.520-m gauge (875 km
electrified) (2002)
Highways:
total: 74,385 km
paved: 66,203 km
unpaved: 8,182 km (2000)
Waterways: NA km; note - Belarus has extensive
and widely used canal and river systems
Pipelines: gas 4,519 km; oil 1,811 km; refined
products 1,686 km (2003)
Ports and harbors: Mazyr
Airports: 135 (2003 est.)
Airports - with paved runways:
total: 50
over 3,047 m: 2
2,438 to 3,047 m: 21
1,524 to 2,437 m: 6
under 914 m: 21 (2003 est.)
Airports - with unpaved runways:
total: 85
over 3,047 m: 3
2,438 to 3,047 m: 2
1,524 to 2,437 m: 5
914 to 1,523 m: 11
under 914 m: 64 (2003 est.)
Heliports: 1 (2003 est.)

Military

Military branches: Army, Air and Air Defense Force
Military manpower - military age: 18 years of age
(2004 est.)
Military manpower - availability:
males age 15-49: 2,764,856 (2004 est.)
Military manpower - fit for military service:
males age 15-49: 2,164,923 (2004 est.)
**Military manpower - reaching military age
annually:**
males: 86,716 (2004 est.)
Military expenditures - dollar figure: $176.1
million (FY02)
Military expenditures - percent of GDP: 1.4%
(FY02)

Transnational Issues

Disputes - international: 1997 boundary treaty with
Ukraine remains unratified over unresolved financial
claims, preventing demarcation and diminishing
border security; boundaries with Latvia and Lithuania
remain undemarcated despite European Union
financial support
Illicit drugs: limited cultivation of opium poppy and
cannabis, mostly for the domestic market;
transshipment point for illicit drugs to and via Russia,
and to the Baltics and Western Europe; a small and
lightly regulated financial center; new
anti-money-laundering legislation does not meet
international standards; few investigations or
prosecutions of money-laundering activities

Belgium

Introduction

Background: Belgium became independent from the Netherlands in 1830 and was occupied by Germany during World Wars I and II. It has prospered in the past half century as a modern, technologically advanced European state and member of NATO and the EU. Tensions between the Dutch-speaking Flemings of the north and the French-speaking Walloons of the south have led in recent years to constitutional amendments granting these regions formal recognition and autonomy.

Geography

Location: Western Europe, bordering the North Sea, between France and the Netherlands
Geographic coordinates: 50 50 N, 4 00 E
Map references: Europe
Area:
total: 30,510 sq km
land: 30,230 sq km
water: 280 sq km
Area - comparative: about the size of Maryland
Land boundaries:
total: 1,385 km
border countries: France 620 km, Germany 167 km, Luxembourg 148 km, Netherlands 450 km
Coastline: 66 km
Maritime claims:
territorial sea: 12 NM
exclusive economic zone: geographic coordinates define outer limit
continental shelf: median line with neighbors
Climate: temperate; mild winters, cool summers; rainy, humid, cloudy
Terrain: flat coastal plains in northwest, central rolling hills, rugged mountains of Ardennes Forest in southeast
Elevation extremes:
lowest point: North Sea 0 m
highest point: Signal de Botrange 694 m

Natural resources: coal, natural gas
Land use:
arable land: 25%
permanent crops: 0%
other: 75%
note: includes Luxembourg (1998 est.)
Irrigated land: 40 sq km (includes Luxembourg) (1998 est.)
Natural hazards: flooding is a threat in areas of reclaimed coastal land, protected from the sea by concrete dikes
Environment - current issues: the environment is exposed to intense pressures from human activities: urbanization, dense transportation network, industry, extensive animal breeding and crop cultivation; air and water pollution also have repercussions for neighboring countries; uncertainties regarding federal and regional responsibilities (now resolved) have slowed progress in tackling environmental challenges
Environment - international agreements:
party to: Air Pollution, Air Pollution-Nitrogen Oxides, Air Pollution-Sulfur 85, Air Pollution-Sulfur 94, Air Pollution-Volatile Organic Compounds, Antarctic-Environmental Protocol, Antarctic-Marine Living Resources, Antarctic Seals, Antarctic Treaty, Biodiversity, Climate Change, Climate Change-Kyoto Protocol, Desertification, Endangered Species, Environmental Modification, Hazardous Wastes, Law of the Sea, Marine Dumping, Marine Life Conservation, Ozone Layer Protection, Ship Pollution, Tropical Timber 83, Tropical Timber 94, Wetlands
signed, but not ratified: Air Pollution-Persistent Organic Pollutants
Geography - note: crossroads of Western Europe; majority of West European capitals within 1,000 km of Brussels, the seat of both the European Union and NATO

People

Population: 10,348,276 (July 2004 est.)
Age structure:
0-14 years: 17.1% (male 901,486; female 863,092)
15-64 years: 65.6% (male 3,424,438; female 3,364,057)
65 years and over: 17.3% (male 739,479; female 1,055,724) (2004 est.)
Median age:
total: 40.2 years
male: 38.9 years
female: 41.5 years (2004 est.)
Population growth rate: 0.16% (2004 est.)
Birth rate: 10.59 births/1,000 population (2004 est.)
Death rate: 10.2 deaths/1,000 population (2004 est.)
Net migration rate: 1.23 migrant(s)/1,000 population (2004 est.)
Sex ratio:
at birth: 1.05 male(s)/female
under 15 years: 1.04 male(s)/female
15-64 years: 1.02 male(s)/female
65 years and over: 0.7 male(s)/female
total population: 0.96 male(s)/female (2004 est.)

Infant mortality rate:
total: 4.76 deaths/1,000 live births
male: 5.36 deaths/1,000 live births
female: 4.12 deaths/1,000 live births (2004 est.)
Life expectancy at birth:
total population: 78.44 years
male: 75.26 years
female: 81.75 years (2004 est.)
Total fertility rate: 1.64 children born/woman (2004 est.)
HIV/AIDS - adult prevalence rate: 0.2% (2001 est.)
HIV/AIDS - people living with HIV/AIDS: 8,500 (2001 est.)
HIV/AIDS - deaths: less than 100 (2001 est.)
Nationality:
noun: Belgian(s)
adjective: Belgian
Ethnic groups: Fleming 58%, Walloon 31%, mixed or other 11%
Religions: Roman Catholic 75%, Protestant or other 25%
Languages: Dutch (official) 60%, French (official) 40%, German (official) less than 1%, legally bilingual (Dutch and French)
Literacy:
definition: age 15 and over can read and write
total population: 98%
male: NA%
female: NA%

Government

Country name:
conventional long form: Kingdom of Belgium
conventional short form: Belgium
local long form: Royaume de Belgique/Koninkrijk Belgie
local short form: Belgique/Belgie
Government type: federal parliamentary democracy under a constitutional monarch
Capital: Brussels
Administrative divisions: 10 provinces (French: provinces, singular - province; Dutch: provincies, singular - provincie) and 3 regions* (French: regions; Dutch: gewesten); Antwerpen, Brabant Wallon, Brussels* (Bruxelles), Flanders*, Hainaut, Liege, Limburg, Luxembourg, Namur, Oost-Vlaanderen, Vlaams-Brabant, Wallonia*, West-Vlaanderen
Independence: 4 October 1830 a provisional government declared independence from the Netherlands; 21 July 1831 the ascension of King Leopold I to the throne
National holiday: 21 July (1831) ascension to the Throne of King Leopold I
Constitution: 7 February 1831, last revised 14 July 1993; parliament approved a constitutional package creating a federal state
Legal system: civil law system influenced by English constitutional theory; judicial review of legislative acts; accepts compulsory ICJ jurisdiction, with reservations
Suffrage: 18 years of age; universal and compulsory

Belgium *(continued)*

Executive branch:
chief of state: King ALBERT II (since 9 August 1993); Heir Apparent Prince PHILIPPE, son of the monarch
head of government: Prime Minister Guy VERHOFSTADT (since 13 July 1999)
cabinet: Council of Ministers appointed by the monarch and approved by Parliament
elections: none; the monarchy is hereditary; following legislative elections, the leader of the majority party or the leader of the majority coalition is usually appointed prime minister by the monarch and then approved by Parliament
note: government coalition - VLD, MR, PS, and SP
Legislative branch: bicameral Parliament consists of a Senate or Senaat in Dutch, Senat in French (71 seats; 40 members are directly elected by popular vote, 31 are indirectly elected; members serve four-year terms) and a Chamber of Deputies or Kamer van Volksvertegenwoordigers in Dutch, Chambre des Representants in French (150 seats; members are directly elected by popular vote on the basis of proportional representation to serve four-year terms)
elections: Senate and Chamber of Deputies - last held 18 May 2003 (next to be held in NA May 2007)
election results: Senate - percent of vote by party - SP.A-Spirit 15.5%, VLD 15.4%, CD & V 12.7%, PS 12.8%, MR 12.1%, VB 9.4%, CDH 5.6%; seats by party - SP.A-Spirit 7, VLD 7, CD & V 6, PS 6, MR 5, VB 5, CDH 2, other 2 (note - there are also 31 indirectly elected senators); Chamber of Deputies - percent of vote by party - VLD 15.4%, SP.A-Spirit 14.9%, CD & V 13.3%, PS 13.0%, VB 11.6%, MR 11.4%, CDH 5.5%, Ecolo 3.1%; seats by party - VLD 25, SP.A-Spirit 23, CD & V 21, PS 25, VB 18, MR 24, CDH 8 Ecolo 4, other 2
note: as a result of the 1993 constitutional revision that furthered devolution into a federal state, there are now three levels of government (federal, regional, and linguistic community) with a complex division of responsibilities; this reality leaves six governments each with its own legislative assembly; for other acronyms of the listed parties see the Political parties and leaders entry
Judicial branch: Supreme Court of Justice or Hof van Cassatie (in Dutch) or Cour de Cassation (in French) (judges are appointed for life by the monarch, although selected by the Government)
Political parties and leaders: Ecolo (Francophone Greens) [Jean-Michel JAVAUK, Evelyne HUYTEBROECK, Claude BROUIR]; Flemish Liberal Democrats or VLD [Dirk STERCKX]; Francophone Humanist and Democratic Center of CDH (formerly Social Christian Party or PSC) [Joelle MILQUET]; Francophone Reformist Movement or MR (formerly Liberal Reformation Party or PRL) [Antoine DUQUESNE]; Francophone Socialist Party or PS [Elio DI RUPO]; GROEN! (formerly AGALEV, Flemish Greens) [Vera DUA]; National Front or FN [Daniel FERET]; New Flemish Alliance or NVA [Geert BOURGEOIS]; note - new party that emerged after the demise of the People's Union or VU; Social Progressive Alternative Party or SP.A [Steve

STEVAERT]; note - was Flemish Socialist Party or SP; Spirit [Els VAN WEERT]; note - new party that emerged after the demise of the People's Union or VU; Vlaams Blok or VB [Frank VANHECKE]; other minor parties
Political pressure groups and leaders: Christian and Socialist Trade Unions; Federation of Belgian Industries; numerous other associations representing bankers, manufacturers, middle-class artisans, and the legal and medical professions; various organizations represent the cultural interests of Flanders and Wallonia; various peace groups such as Pax Christi and groups representing immigrants
International organization participation: ACCT, AfDB, AsDB, Australia Group, Benelux, BIS, CE, CERN, EAPC, EBRD, EIB, EMU, ESA, EU, FAO, G- 9, G-10, IADB, IAEA, IBRD, ICAO, ICC, ICCt, ICFTU, ICRM, IDA, IEA, IFAD, IFC, IFRCS, IHO, ILO, IMF, IMO, Interpol, IOC, IOM, ISO, ITU, MONUC, NATO, NEA, NSG, OAS (observer), OECD, OPCW, OSCE, Paris Club, PCA, UN, UNCTAD, UNESCO, UNHCR, UNIDO, UNMIK, UNMOGIP, UNRWA, UNTSO, UPU, WADB (nonregional), WCL, WCO, WEU, WHO, WIPO, WMO, WTrO, ZC
Diplomatic representation in the US:
chief of mission: Ambassador Franciskus VAN DAELE
chancery: 3330 Garfield Street NW, Washington, DC 20008
telephone: [1] (202) 333-6900
FAX: [1] (202) 333-3079
consulate(s) general: Atlanta, Chicago, Los Angeles, and New York
Diplomatic representation from the US:
chief of mission: Ambassador Stephen Franklin BRAUER
embassy: Regentlaan 27 Boulevard du Regent, B-1000 Brussels
mailing address: PSC 82, Box 002, APO AE 09710
telephone: [32] (2) 508-2111
FAX: [32] (2) 511-2725
Flag description: three equal vertical bands of black (hoist side), yellow, and red; the design was based on the flag of France

Economy

Economy - overview: This modern private enterprise economy has capitalized on its central geographic location, highly developed transport network, and diversified industrial and commercial base. Industry is concentrated mainly in the populous Flemish area in the north. With few natural resources, Belgium must import substantial quantities of raw materials and export a large volume of manufactures, making its economy unusually dependent on the state of world markets. Roughly three-quarters of its trade is with other EU countries. Public debt is about 100% of GDP, and the government has succeeded in balancing its budget. Belgium, together with 11 of its EU partners, began circulating the euro currency in January 2002. Economic growth in 2001-03 dropped

sharply because of the global economic slowdown. Prospects for 2004 again depend largely on recovery in the EU and the US.
GDP: purchasing power parity - $298.2 billion (2003 est.)
GDP - real growth rate: 0.8% (2003 est.)
GDP - per capita: purchasing power parity - $29,000 (2003 est.)
GDP - composition by sector:
agriculture: 1.6%
industry: 26.8%
services: 71.6% (2002)
Population below poverty line: 4% (1989 est.)
Household income or consumption by percentage share:
lowest 10%: 3.2%
highest 10%: 23% (1996)
Distribution of family income - Gini index: 28.7 (1996)
Inflation rate (consumer prices): 1.4% (2003 est.)
Labor force: 4.44 million (2001)
Labor force - by occupation: services 73%, industry 25%, agriculture 2% (1999 est.)
Unemployment rate: 8.1% (2003 est.)
Budget:
revenues: $113.4 billion
expenditures: $106 billion, including capital expenditures of $7.17 billion (2000)
Industries: engineering and metal products, motor vehicle assembly, processed food and beverages, chemicals, basic metals, textiles, glass, petroleum, coal
Industrial production growth rate: 4.5% (2000 est.)
Electricity - production: 74.28 billion kWh (2001)
Electricity - production by source:
fossil fuel: 38.4%
hydro: 0.6%
nuclear: 59.3%
other: 1.8% (2001)
Electricity - consumption: 78.18 billion kWh (2001)
Electricity - exports: 6.712 billion kWh (2001)
Electricity - imports: 15.82 billion kWh (2001)
Oil - production: 0 bbl/day (2001 est.)
Oil - consumption: 595,100 bbl/day (2001 est.)
Oil - exports: 450,000 bbl/day (2001)
Oil - imports: 1.042 million bbl/day (2001)
Natural gas - production: 0 cu m (2001 est.)
Natural gas - consumption: 15.5 billion cu m (2001 est.)
Natural gas - exports: 0 cu m (2001 est.)
Natural gas - imports: 15.4 billion cu m (2001 est.)
Agriculture - products: sugar beets, fresh vegetables, fruits, grain, tobacco; beef, veal, pork, milk
Exports: $182.9 billion f.o.b. (2003 est.)
Exports - commodities: machinery and equipment, chemicals, diamonds, metals and metal products, foodstuffs
Exports - partners: Germany 18.6%, France 16.3%, Netherlands 11.6%, UK 9.6%, US 7.9%, Italy 5.4% (2002)

Belgium (continued)

Imports: $173 billion f.o.b. (2003 est.)
Imports - commodities: machinery and equipment, chemicals, metals and metal products, foodstuffs
Imports - partners: Germany 17.2%, Netherlands 15.6%, France 12.8%, UK 7.3%, Ireland 7%, US 6.4%, Italy 4% (2002)
Debt - external: $28.3 billion (1999 est.)
Economic aid - donor: ODA, $1.072 billion (2002)
Currency: euro (EUR)
note: on 1 January 1999, the European Monetary Union introduced the euro as a common currency to be used by financial institutions of member countries; on 1 January 2002, the euro became the sole currency for everyday transactions within the member countries
Currency code: EUR
Exchange rates: euros per US dollar - 0.886 (2003), 1.0626 (2002), 1.1175 (2001), 1.0854 (2000), 0.9386 (1999)
Fiscal year: calendar year

Communications

Telephones - main lines in use: 5,120,400 (2002)
Telephones - mobile cellular: 8,135,500 (2002)
Telephone system:
general assessment: highly developed, technologically advanced, and completely automated domestic and international telephone and telegraph facilities
domestic: nationwide cellular telephone system; extensive cable network; limited microwave radio relay network
international: country code - 32; 5 submarine cables; satellite earth stations - 2 Intelsat (Atlantic Ocean) and 1 Eutelsat
Radio broadcast stations: FM 79, AM 7, shortwave 1 (1998)
Television broadcast stations: 25 (plus 10 repeaters) (1997)
Internet country code: .be
Internet hosts: 336,604 (2002)
Internet users: 3.4 million (2002)

Transportation

Railways:
total: 3,471 km
standard gauge: 3,471 km 1.435-m gauge (2,631 km electrified) (2002)
Highways:
total: 148,216 km
paved: 116,687 km (including 1,727 km of expressways)
unpaved: 31,529 km (2000)
Waterways: 1,570 km (route length in regular commercial use) (2001)
Pipelines: gas 1,485 km; oil 158 km; refined products 535 km (2003)
Ports and harbors: Antwerp (one of the world's busiest ports), Brugge, Gent, Hasselt, Liege, Mons, Namur, Oostende, Zeebrugge

Merchant marine:
total: 50 ships (1,000 GRT or over) 1,146,301 GRT/ 1,588,184 DWT
by type: bulk 1, cargo 8, chemical tanker 11, container 6, liquefied gas 18, petroleum tanker 6
foreign-owned: Denmark 6, Finland 1, France 2, Netherlands 3
registered in other countries: 69 (2003 est.)
Airports: 42 (2003 est.)
Airports - with paved runways:
total: 25
over 3,047 m: 6
2,438 to 3,047 m: 8
1,524 to 2,437 m: 3
914 to 1,523 m: 1
under 914 m: 7 (2003 est.)
Airports - with unpaved runways:
total: 17
914 to 1,523 m: 2
under 914 m: 15 (2003 est.)
Heliports: 1 (2003 est.)

Military

Military branches: Army, Naval, and Air Operations Commands
Military manpower - military age: 19 years of age (2004 est.)
Military manpower - availability:
males age 15-49: 2,509,538 (2004 est.)
Military manpower - fit for military service:
males age 15-49: 2,068,221 (2004 est.)
Military manpower - reaching military age annually:
males: 61,270 (2004 est.)
Military expenditures - dollar figure: $3.999 billion (2003)
Military expenditures - percent of GDP: 1.3% (2003)

Transnational Issues

Disputes - international: none
Illicit drugs: growing producer of synthetic drugs; transit point for US-bound ecstasy; source of precursor chemicals for South American cocaine processors; transshipment point for cocaine, heroin, hashish, and marijuana entering Western Europe; despite a strengthening of legislation, the country remains vulnerable to money laundering related to narcotics, automobiles, alcohol and tobacco

Belize

Introduction

Background: Territorial disputes between the UK and Guatemala delayed the independence of Belize (formerly British Honduras) until 1981. Guatemala refused to recognize the new nation until 1992. Tourism has become the mainstay of the economy. The country remains plagued by high unemployment, growing involvement in the South American drug trade, and increased urban crime.

Geography

Location: Central America, bordering the Caribbean Sea, between Guatemala and Mexico
Geographic coordinates: 17 15 N, 88 45 W
Map references: Central America and the Caribbean
Area:
total: 22,966 sq km
land: 22,806 sq km
water: 160 sq km
Area - comparative: slightly smaller than Massachusetts
Land boundaries:
total: 516 km
border countries: Guatemala 266 km, Mexico 250 km
Coastline: 386 km
Maritime claims:
territorial sea: 12 NM in the north, 3 NM in the south; note - from the mouth of the Sarstoon River to Ranguana Cay, Belize's territorial sea is 3 NM; according to Belize's Maritime Areas Act, 1992, the purpose of this limitation is to provide a framework for the negotiation of a definitive agreement on territorial differences with Guatemala
exclusive economic zone: 200 NM
Climate: tropical; very hot and humid; rainy season (May to November); dry season (February to May)
Terrain: flat, swampy coastal plain; low mountains in south

Belize (continued)

Elevation extremes:
lowest point: Caribbean Sea 0 m
highest point: Victoria Peak 1,160 m
Natural resources: arable land potential, timber, fish, hydropower
Land use:
arable land: 2.81%
permanent crops: 1.1%
other: 96.09% (1998 est.)
Irrigated land: 30 sq km (1998 est.)
Natural hazards: frequent, devastating hurricanes (June to November) and coastal flooding (especially in south)
Environment - current issues: deforestation; water pollution from sewage, industrial effluents, agricultural runoff; solid and sewage waste disposal
Environment - international agreements:
party to: Biodiversity, Climate Change, Climate Change-Kyoto Protocol, Desertification, Endangered Species, Hazardous Wastes, Law of the Sea, Ozone Layer Protection, Ship Pollution, Wetlands
signed, but not ratified: none of the selected agreements
Geography - note: only country in Central America without a coastline on the North Pacific Ocean

People

Population: 272,945 (July 2004 est.)
Age structure:
0-14 years: 40.6% (male 56,530; female 54,322)
15-64 years: 55.8% (male 77,118; female 75,309)
65 years and over: 3.5% (male 4,674; female 4,992) (2004 est.)
Median age:
total: 19.1 years
male: 19 years
female: 19.3 years (2004 est.)
Population growth rate: 2.39% (2004 est.)
Birth rate: 29.89 births/1,000 population (2004 est.)
Death rate: 6.04 deaths/1,000 population (2004 est.)
Net migration rate: 0 migrant(s)/1,000 population (2004 est.)
Sex ratio:
at birth: 1.05 male(s)/female
under 15 years: 1.04 male(s)/female
15-64 years: 1.02 male(s)/female
65 years and over: 0.94 male(s)/female
total population: 1.03 male(s)/female (2004 est.)
Infant mortality rate:
total: 26.37 deaths/1,000 live births
male: 29.75 deaths/1,000 live births
female: 22.82 deaths/1,000 live births (2004 est.)
Life expectancy at birth:
total population: 67.43 years
male: 65.11 years
female: 69.86 years (2004 est.)
Total fertility rate: 3.77 children born/woman (2004 est.)
HIV/AIDS - adult prevalence rate: 2% (2001 est.)
HIV/AIDS - people living with HIV/AIDS: 2,500 (2001 est.)
HIV/AIDS - deaths: 300 (2001 est.)

Nationality:
noun: Belizean(s)
adjective: Belizean
Ethnic groups: mestizo 48.7%, Creole 24.9%, Maya 10.6%, Garifuna 6.1%, other 9.7%
Religions: Roman Catholic 49.6%, Protestant 27% (Anglican 5.3%, Methodist 3.5%, Mennonite 4.1%, Seventh-Day Adventist 5.2%, Pentecostal 7.4%, Jehovah's Witnesses 1.5%), none 9.4%, other 14% (2000)
Languages: English (official), Spanish, Mayan, Garifuna (Carib), Creole
Literacy:
definition: age 15 and over can read and write
total population: 94.1%
male: 94.1%
female: 94.1% (2003 est.)

Government

Country name:
conventional long form: none
conventional short form: Belize
former: British Honduras
Government type: parliamentary democracy
Capital: Belmopan
Administrative divisions: 6 districts; Belize, Cayo, Corozal, Orange Walk, Stann Creek, Toledo
Independence: 21 September 1981 (from UK)
National holiday: Independence Day, 21 September (1981)
Constitution: 21 September 1981
Legal system: English law
Suffrage: 18 years of age; universal
Executive branch:
chief of state: Queen ELIZABETH II (since 6 February 1952), represented by Governor General Sir Colville YOUNG, Sr. (since 17 November 1993)
head of government: Prime Minister Said Wilbert MUSA (since 28 August 1998); Deputy Prime Minister John BRICENO (since 1 September 1998)
cabinet: Cabinet appointed by the governor general on the advice of the prime minister
elections: none; the monarch is hereditary; governor general appointed by the monarch; following legislative elections, the leader of the majority party or the leader of the majority coalition is usually appointed prime minister by the governor general; prime minister recommends the deputy prime minister
Legislative branch: bicameral National Assembly consists of the Senate (12 members appointed by the governor general - six on the advice of the prime minister, three on the advice of the leader of the opposition, and one each on the advice of the Belize Council of Churches and Evangelical Association of Churches, the Belize Chamber of Commerce and Industry and the Belize Better Business Bureau, and the National Trade Union Congress and the Civil Society Steering Committee; members are appointed for five-year terms) and the House of Representatives (29 seats; members are elected by direct popular vote to serve five-year terms)

elections: House of Representatives - last held 5 March 2003 (next to be held NA March 2008)
election results: percent of vote by party - NA%; seats by party - PUP 21, UDP 8
Judicial branch: Supreme Court (the chief justice is appointed by the governor general on the advice of the prime minister)
Political parties and leaders: People's United Party or PUP [Said MUSA]; United Democratic Party or UDP [Dean BARROW, party leader; Douglas SINGH, party chairman]
Political pressure groups and leaders: Society for the Promotion of Education and Research or SPEAR [Adele CATZIM]
International organization participation: ACP, C, Caricom, CDB, FAO, G-77, IADB, IBRD, ICAO, ICCt, ICFTU, ICRM, IDA, IFAD, IFC, IFRCS, ILO, IMF, IMO, Interpol, IOC, IOM, ITU, LAES, NAM, OAS, OPANAL, OPCW, PCA, UN, UNCTAD, UNESCO, UNIDO, UPU, WCL, WHO, WIPO, WMO, WTrO
Diplomatic representation in the US:
chief of mission: Ambassador Lisa M. SHOMAN
chancery: 2535 Massachusetts Avenue NW, Washington, DC 20008
telephone: [1] (202) 332-9636
FAX: [1] (202) 332-6888
consulate(s) general: Los Angeles
Diplomatic representation from the US:
chief of mission: Ambassador Russell F. FREEMAN
embassy: 29 Gabourel Lane and Hutson Street, Belize City
mailing address: P. O. Box 286, Unit 7401, APO AA 34025
telephone: [501] 227-7161 through 7163
FAX: [501] 30802
Flag description: blue with a narrow red stripe along the top and the bottom edges; centered is a large white disk bearing the coat of arms; the coat of arms features a shield flanked by two workers in front of a mahogany tree with the related motto SUB UMBRA FLOREO (I Flourish in the Shade) on a scroll at the bottom, all encircled by a green garland

Economy

Economy - overview: In this small, essentially private enterprise economy the tourism industry is the number one foreign exchange earner followed by cane sugar, citrus, marine products, bananas, and garments. The government's expansionary monetary and fiscal policies, initiated in September 1998, led to GDP growth of 6.5% in 1999, 10.8% in 2000, 4.6% in 2001, and 3.7% in 2002. Major concerns continue to be the sizable trade deficit and foreign debt. A key short-term objective remains the reduction of poverty with the help of international donors.
GDP: purchasing power parity - $1.28 billion (2002 est.)
GDP - real growth rate: 3.7% (2002 est.)
GDP - per capita: purchasing power parity - $4,900 (2002 est.)

Belize (continued)

GDP - composition by sector:
agriculture: 18%
industry: 24%
services: 58% (2001 est.)
Population below poverty line: 33% (1999 est.)
Household income or consumption by percentage share:
lowest 10%: NA%
highest 10%: NA%
Inflation rate (consumer prices): 1.9% (2002 est.)
Labor force: 90,000
note: shortage of skilled labor and all types of technical personnel (2001 est.)
Labor force - by occupation: agriculture 27%, industry 18%, services 55% (2001 est.)
Unemployment rate: 9.1% (2002)
Budget:
revenues: $224 million
expenditures: $209 million, including capital expenditures of $70 million (2002 est.)
Industries: garment production, food processing, tourism, construction
Industrial production growth rate: 4.6% (1999)
Electricity - production: 199.5 million kWh (2001)
Electricity - production by source:
fossil fuel: 59.9%
hydro: 40.1%
nuclear: 0%
other: 0% (2001)
Electricity - consumption: 185.5 million kWh (2001)
Electricity - exports: 0 kWh (2001)
Electricity - imports: 0 kWh (2001)
Oil - production: 0 bbl/day (2001 est.)
Oil - consumption: 5,000 bbl/day (2001 est.)
Oil - exports: NA
Oil - imports: NA
Agriculture - products: bananas, coca, citrus, sugar; fish, cultured shrimp; lumber; garments
Exports: $207.8 million f.o.b. (2003 est.)
Exports - commodities: sugar, bananas, citrus, clothing, fish products, molasses, wood
Exports - partners: Mexico 68.3%, US 12.6%, UK 7.1% (2002)
Imports: $500.6 million f.o.b. (2003 est.)
Imports - commodities: machinery and transport equipment, manufactured goods; fuels, chemicals, pharmaceuticals; food, beverages, tobacco
Imports - partners: Mexico 69%, US 12%, Netherlands Antilles 2.3% (2002)
Debt - external: $475 million (2001 est.)
Economic aid - recipient: $NA
Currency: Belizean dollar (BZD)
Currency code: BZD
Exchange rates: Belizean dollars per US dollar - 2 (2003), 2 (2002), 2 (2001), 2 (2000), 2 (1999)
Fiscal year: 1 April - 31 March

Communications

Telephones - main lines in use: 31,300 (2002)
Telephones - mobile cellular: 51,700 (2002)
Telephone system:
general assessment: above-average system
domestic: trunk network depends primarily on microwave radio relay
international: country code - 501; satellite earth station - 1 Intelsat (Atlantic Ocean)
Radio broadcast stations: AM 1, FM 12, shortwave 0 (1998)
Television broadcast stations: 2 (1997)
Internet country code: .bz
Internet hosts: 1,498 (2002)
Internet users: 30,000 (2002)

Transportation

Railways: 0 km
Highways:
total: 2,872 km
paved: 488 km
unpaved: 2,384 km (1999 est.)
Waterways: 825 km (river network used by shallow-draft craft; seasonally navigable)
Ports and harbors: Belize City, Big Creek, Corozol, Punta Gorda
Merchant marine:
total: 336 ships (1,000 GRT or over) 1,015,270 GRT/1,336,890 DWT
by type: bulk 13, cargo 240, chemical tanker 11, combination bulk 4, combination ore/oil 1, container 10, multi-functional large load carrier 1, petroleum tanker 27, refrigerated cargo 18, roll on/roll off 8, short-sea/passenger 1, specialized tanker 2
foreign-owned: Bahamas 2, Belgium 1, British Virgin Islands 11, Cambodia 6, China 67, Cuba 2, Cyprus 1, Ecuador 1, Estonia 8, Germany 5, Greece 2, Grenada 1, Honduras 1, Hong Kong 27, Indonesia 4, Italy 2, Japan 5, Jordan 1, South Korea 13, Latvia 5, Liberia 2, Malaysia 4, Malta 1, Isle of Man 1, Marshall Islands 16, Mexico 1, Netherlands 1, Nigeria 2, Panama 15, Philippines 4, Portugal 1, Russia 9, Saint Vincent and the Grenadines 3, Singapore 9, Spain 6, Switzerland 2, Taiwan 1, Thailand 3, Tunisia 1, Turkey 2, Ukraine 3, United Kingdom 1, United States 3, Yemen 1
registered in other countries: 25 (2003 est.)
Airports: 43 (2003 est.)
Airports - with paved runways:
total: 5
1,524 to 2,437 m: 1
914 to 1,523 m: 2
under 914 m: 2 (2003 est.)
Airports - with unpaved runways:
total: 38
2,438 to 3,047 m: 1
914 to 1,523 m: 11
under 914 m: 26 (2003 est.)

Military

Military branches: Belize Defense Force (includes Army, Maritime Wing, Air Wing, and Volunteer Guard)
Military manpower - military age: 18 years of age (2004 est.)
Military manpower - availability:
males age 15-49: 68,518 (2004 est.)
Military manpower - fit for military service:
males age 15-49: 40,619 (2004 est.)
Military manpower - reaching military age annually:
males: 3,122 (2004 est.)
Military expenditures - dollar figure: $18 million (2003)
Military expenditures - percent of GDP: 2% (2003)

Transnational Issues

Disputes - international: Guatemalan squatters continue to settle along the border region; an OAS brokered Differendum in 2002 created a small adjustment to the land boundary, a large Guatemalan maritime corridor in Caribbean, a joint ecological park for disputed Sapodilla Cays, and a substantial US-UK financial package, but agreement was not brought to popular referendum leaving Guatemala to continue to claim the southern half of Belize
Illicit drugs: major transshipment point for cocaine; small-scale illicit producer of cannabis for the international drug trade; money-laundering activity related to narcotics trafficking and offshore sector

Benin

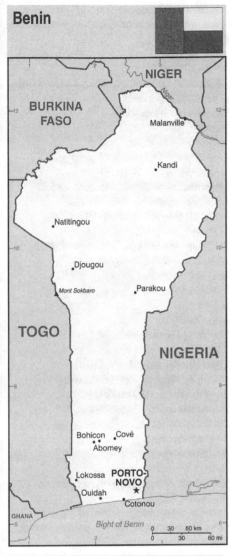

Introduction

Background: Present day Benin was the site of Dahomey, a prominent West African kingdom that rose in the 15th century. The territory became a French Colony in 1872 and achieved independence on 1 August 1960, as the Republic of Benin. A succession of military governments ended in 1972 with the rise to power of Mathieu KEREKOU and the establishment of a government based on Marxist-Leninist principles. A move to representative government began in 1989. Two years later, free elections ushered in former Prime Minister Nicephore SOGLO as president, marking the first successful transfer of power in Africa from a dictatorship to a democracy. KEREKOU was returned to power by elections held in 1996 and 2001, though some irregularities were alleged.

Geography

Location: Western Africa, bordering the Bight of Benin, between Nigeria and Togo
Geographic coordinates: 9 30 N, 2 15 E
Map references: Africa

Area:
total: 112,620 sq km
land: 110,620 sq km
water: 2,000 sq km
Area - comparative: slightly smaller than Pennsylvania
Land boundaries:
total: 1,989 km
border countries: Burkina Faso 306 km, Niger 266 km, Nigeria 773 km, Togo 644 km
Coastline: 121 km
Maritime claims:
territorial sea: 200 NM
Climate: tropical; hot, humid in south; semiarid in north
Terrain: mostly flat to undulating plain; some hills and low mountains
Elevation extremes:
lowest point: Atlantic Ocean 0 m
highest point: Mont Sokbaro 658 m
Natural resources: small offshore oil deposits, limestone, marble, timber
Land use:
arable land: 15.28%
permanent crops: 1.36%
other: 83.36% (1998 est.)
Irrigated land: 120 sq km (1998 est.)
Natural hazards: hot, dry, dusty harmattan wind may affect north from December to March
Environment - current issues: inadequate supplies of potable water; poaching threatens wildlife populations; deforestation; desertification
Environment - international agreements:
party to: Biodiversity, Climate Change, Climate Change-Kyoto Protocol, Desertification, Endangered Species, Environmental Modification, Hazardous Wastes, Law of the Sea, Ozone Layer Protection, Ship Pollution, Wetlands
signed, but not ratified: none of the selected agreements
Geography - note: sandbanks create difficult access to a coast with no natural harbors, river mouths, or islands

People

Population: 7,250,033
note: estimates for this country explicitly take into account the effects of excess mortality due to AIDS; this can result in lower life expectancy, higher infant mortality and death rates, lower population and growth rates, and changes in the distribution of population by age and sex than would otherwise be expected (July 2004 est.)
Age structure:
0-14 years: 46.8% (male 1,711,075; female 1,679,439)
15-64 years: 51% (male 1,802,990; female 1,890,915)
65 years and over: 2.3% (male 68,890; female 96,724) (2004 est.)

Median age:
total: 16.5 years
male: 16 years
female: 16.9 years (2004 est.)
Population growth rate: 2.89% (2004 est.)
Birth rate: 42.57 births/1,000 population (2004 est.)
Death rate: 13.69 deaths/1,000 population (2004 est.)
Net migration rate: 0 migrant(s)/1,000 population (2004 est.)
Sex ratio:
at birth: 1.03 male(s)/female
under 15 years: 1.02 male(s)/female
15-64 years: 0.95 male(s)/female
65 years and over: 0.71 male(s)/female
total population: 0.98 male(s)/female (2004 est.)
Infant mortality rate:
total: 85.88 deaths/1,000 live births
male: 90.89 deaths/1,000 live births
female: 80.71 deaths/1,000 live births (2004 est.)
Life expectancy at birth:
total population: 50.81 years
male: 50.25 years
female: 51.39 years (2004 est.)
Total fertility rate: 5.95 children born/woman (2004 est.)
HIV/AIDS - adult prevalence rate: 3.6% (2001 est.)
HIV/AIDS - people living with HIV/AIDS: 120,000 (2001 est.)
HIV/AIDS - deaths: 8,100 (2001 est.)
Nationality:
noun: Beninese (singular and plural)
adjective: Beninese
Ethnic groups: African 99% (42 ethnic groups, most important being Fon, Adja, Yoruba, Bariba), Europeans 5,500
Religions: indigenous beliefs 50%, Christian 30%, Muslim 20%
Languages: French (official), Fon and Yoruba (most common vernaculars in south), tribal languages (at least six major ones in north)
Literacy:
definition: age 15 and over can read and write
total population: 40.9%
male: 56.2%
female: 26.5% (2000)

Government

Country name:
conventional long form: Republic of Benin
conventional short form: Benin
local long form: Republique du Benin
local short form: Benin
former: Dahomey

Government type: republic under multiparty democratic rule; dropped Marxism-Leninism December 1989; democratic reforms adopted February 1990; transition to multiparty system completed 4 April 1991
Capital: Porto-Novo is the official capital; Cotonou is the seat of government

Benin *(continued)*

Administrative divisions: 12 departments; Alibori, Atakora, Atlantique, Borgou, Collines, Kouffo, Donga, Littoral, Mono, Oueme, Plateau, Zou
Independence: 1 August 1960 (from France)
National holiday: National Day, 1 August (1960)
Constitution: December 1990
Legal system: based on French civil law and customary law; has not accepted compulsory ICJ jurisdiction
Suffrage: 18 years of age; universal
Executive branch:
chief of state: President Mathieu KEREKOU (since 4 April 1996); note - the president is both the chief of state and head of government
head of government: President Mathieu KEREKOU (since 4 April 1996); note - the president is both the chief of state and head of government
cabinet: Council of Ministers appointed by the president
elections: president reelected by popular vote for a five-year term; runoff election held 22 March 2001 (next to be held NA March 2006)
election results: Mathieu KEREKOU reelected president; percent of vote - Mathieu KEREKOU 84.1%, Bruno AMOUSSOU 15.9%
note: the four top-ranking contenders following the first-round presidential elections were: Mathieu KEREKOU (incumbent) 45.4%, Nicephore SOGOLO (former president) 27.1%, Adrien HOUNGBEDJI (National Assembly Speaker) 12.6%, and Bruno AMOUSSOU (Minister of State) 8.6%; the second-round balloting, originally scheduled for 18 March 2001, was postponed four days because both SOGOLO and HOUNGBEDJI withdrew alleging electoral fraud; this left KEREKOU to run against his own Minister of State, AMOUSSOU, in what was termed a "friendly match"
Legislative branch: unicameral National Assembly or Assemblee Nationale (83 seats; members are elected by direct popular vote to serve four-year terms)
elections: last held 30 March 2003 (next to be held NA March 2007)
election results: percent of vote by party - NA%; seats by party - Presidential Movement 52, opposition (PRB, PRD, E'toile, and 5 other small parties) 31
Judicial branch: Constitutional Court or Cour Constitutionnelle; Supreme Court or Cour Supreme; High Court of Justice
Political parties and leaders: African Congress for Renewal or DUNYA [Saka SALEY]; African Movement for Democracy and Progress or MADEP [Sefou FAGBOHOUN]; Alliance of the Social Democratic Party or PSD [Bruno AMOUSSOU]; Coalition of Democratic Forces [Gatien HOUNGBEDJI]; Democratic Renewal Party or PRD [Adrien HOUNGBEDJI]; Front for Renewal and Development or FARD-ALAFIA [Jerome Sakia KINA]; Impulse for Progress and Democracy or IPD [Bertin BORNA]; Key Force or FC [leader NA]; Presidential Movement (UBF, MADEP, FC, IDP, and 4 other small parties); Renaissance Party du Benin or PRB [Nicephore SOGLO]; The Star Alliance (Alliance E'toile) [Sacca LAFIA]; Union of Tomorrow's Benin or UBF [Bruno AMOUSSOU]
note: approximately 20 additional minor parties
Political pressure groups and leaders: NA
International organization participation: ACCT, ACP, AfDB, AU, ECOWAS, Entente, FAO, FZ, G-77, IAEA, IBRD, ICAO, ICCt, ICFTU, ICRM, IDA, IDB, IFAD, IFC, IFRCS, ILO, IMF, IMO, Interpol, IOC, IOM, ISO (subscriber), ITU, MICAH, MONUC, NAM, OIC, OPCW, UN, UN Security Council (temporary), UNCTAD, UNESCO, UNIDO, UNMEE, UNMIL, UPU, WADB (regional), WAEMU, WCL, WCO, WFTU, WHO, WIPO, WMO, WToO, WTrO
Diplomatic representation in the US:
chief of mission: Ambassador Cyrille Segbe OGUIN
chancery: 2124 Kalorama Road NW, Washington, DC 20008
telephone: [1] (202) 232-6656
FAX: [1] (202) 265-1996
Diplomatic representation from the US:
chief of mission: Ambassador Wayne NEILL
embassy: Rue Caporal Bernard Anani, Cotonou
mailing address: 01 B. P. 2012, Cotonou
telephone: [229] 30-06-50
FAX: [229] 30-06-70
Flag description: two equal horizontal bands of yellow (top) and red with a vertical green band on the hoist side

Economy

Economy - overview: The economy of Benin remains underdeveloped and dependent on subsistence agriculture, cotton production, and regional trade. Growth in real output has averaged a stable 5% in the past six years, but rapid population rise has offset much of this increase. Inflation has subsided over the past several years. In order to raise growth still further, Benin plans to attract more foreign investment, place more emphasis on tourism, facilitate the development of new food processing systems and agricultural products, and encourage new information and communication technology. The 2001 privatization policy should continue in telecommunications, water, electricity, and agriculture in spite of initial government reluctance. The Paris Club and bilateral creditors have eased the external debt situation, while pressing for speeded-up structural reforms.
GDP: purchasing power parity - $7.742 billion (2003 est.)
GDP - real growth rate: 5.5% (2003 est.)
GDP - per capita: purchasing power parity - $1,100 (2003 est.)
GDP - composition by sector:
agriculture: 38%
industry: 15%
services: 47% (2002 est.)

Population below poverty line: 37% (2001 est.)
Household income or consumption by percentage share:
lowest 10%: NA%
highest 10%: NA%
Inflation rate (consumer prices): 3.3% (2002 est.)
Labor force: NA (1996)
Unemployment rate: NA%
Budget:
revenues: $377.4 million
expenditures: $561.8 million, including capital expenditures of $NA (2001)
Industries: textiles, food processing, chemical production, construction materials (2001)
Industrial production growth rate: 8.3% (2001 est.)
Electricity - production: 274.3 million kWh (2001)
Electricity - production by source:
fossil fuel: 14.2%
hydro: 85.8%
nuclear: 0%
other: 0% (2001)
Electricity - consumption: 631.1 million kWh (2001)
Electricity - exports: 0 kWh (2001)
Electricity - imports: 376 million kWh (2001)
Oil - production: 700 bbl/day (2001 est.)
Oil - consumption: 11,500 bbl/day (2001 est.)
Oil - exports: NA
Oil - imports: NA
Oil - proved reserves: 4.105 million bbl (1 January 2002)
Natural gas - proved reserves: 608.8 million cu m (1 January 2002)
Agriculture - products: cotton, corn, cassava (tapioca), yams, beans, palm oil, peanuts, livestock (2001)
Exports: $485 million f.o.b. (2003 est.)
Exports - commodities: cotton, crude oil, palm products, cocoa
Exports - partners: India 27.3%, Italy 12.1%, Indonesia 8.1%, China 7.6%, Thailand 7.1%, UK 5.1%, Niger 4.5% (2002)
Imports: $726 million f.o.b. (2003 est.)
Imports - commodities: foodstuffs, capital goods, petroleum products
Imports - partners: China 30%, France 15.3%, UK 4.7%, Italy 4.1% (2002)
Debt - external: $1.6 billion (2000)
Economic aid - recipient: $342.6 million (2000)
Currency: Communaute Financiere Africaine franc (XOF); note - responsible authority is the Central Bank of the West African States
Currency code: XOF
Exchange rates: Communaute Financiere Africaine francs (XOF) per US dollar - 581.2 (2003), 696.988 (2002), 733.039 (2001), 711.976 (2000), 615.699 (1999)
Fiscal year: calendar year

Benin *(continued)*

Communications

Telephones - main lines in use: 62,700 (2002)
Telephones - mobile cellular: 218,800 (2002)
Telephone system:
general assessment: NA
domestic: fair system of open-wire, microwave radio relay, and cellular connections
international: country code - 229; satellite earth station - 1 Intelsat (Atlantic Ocean); fiber optic submarine cable (SAT-3/WASC) provides connectivity to Europe and Asia
Radio broadcast stations: AM 2, FM 9, shortwave 4 (2000)
Television broadcast stations: 1 (2001)
Internet country code: .bj
Internet hosts: 574 (2002)
Internet users: 50,000 (2002)

Transportation

Railways:
total: 578 km
narrow gauge: 578 km 1.000-m gauge (2002)
Highways:
total: 6,787 km
paved: 1,357 km (including 10 km of expressways)
unpaved: 5,430 km (1999 est.)
Waterways: streams navigable along small sections, important only locally
Ports and harbors: Cotonou, Porto-Novo
Merchant marine: none
Airports: 5 (2003 est.)
Airports - with paved runways:
total: 1
1,524 to 2,437 m: 1 (2003 est.)
Airports - with unpaved runways:
total: 4
2,438 to 3,047 m: 1
1,524 to 2,437 m: 1
914 to 1,523 m: 2 (2003 est.)

Military

Military branches: Armed Forces: Army, Navy, Air Force
Military manpower - military age: 18 years of age (2004 est.)
Military manpower - availability:
males age 15-49: 1,638,010
females age 15-49: 1,647,850
note: both sexes are liable for military service (2004 est.)
Military manpower - fit for military service:
males age 15-49: 835,561
females age 15-49: 835,633 (2004 est.)
Military manpower - reaching military age annually:
males: 77,552
females: 81,841 (2004 est.)
Military expenditures - dollar figure: $98.3 million (2003)
Military expenditures - percent of GDP: 2.7% (2003)

Transnational Issues

Disputes - international: two villages remain in dispute along the border with Burkina Faso; accuses Burkina Faso of moving boundary pillars; much of Benin-Niger boundary, including tripoint with Nigeria, remains undemarcated, and ICJ ad hoc judges have been selected to rule on disputed Niger and Mekrou River islands; several villages along the Okpara River are in dispute with Nigeria; a joint boundary commission continues to resurvey the boundary with Togo to verify Benin's claim that Togo moved boundary stones
Illicit drugs: transshipment point for narcotics associated with Nigerian trafficking organizations and most commonly destined for Western Europe and the US; vulnerable to money laundering due to a poorly regulated financial infrastructure

Bermuda
(overseas territory of the UK)

Introduction

Background: Bermuda was first settled in 1609 by shipwrecked English colonists headed for Virginia. Tourism to the island to escape North American winters first developed in Victorian times. Tourism continues to be important to the island's economy, although international business has overtaken it in recent years. Bermuda has developed into a highly successful offshore financial center. A referendum on independence was soundly defeated in 1995.

Geography

Location: North America, group of islands in the North Atlantic Ocean, east of South Carolina (US)
Geographic coordinates: 32 20 N, 64 45 W
Map references: North America
Area:
total: 53.3 sq km
land: 53.3 sq km
water: 0 sq km
Area - comparative: about one-third the size of Washington, DC
Land boundaries: 0 km
Coastline: 103 km
Maritime claims:
territorial sea: 12 NM
exclusive fishing zone: 200 NM
Climate: subtropical; mild, humid; gales, strong winds common in winter
Terrain: low hills separated by fertile depressions
Elevation extremes:
lowest point: Atlantic Ocean 0 m
highest point: Town Hill 76 m
Natural resources: limestone, pleasant climate fostering tourism
Land use:
arable land: 6%
permanent crops: 0%

Bermuda (continued)

other: 94% (55% developed, 45% rural/open space)
(1998 est.)
Irrigated land: NA sq km
Natural hazards: hurricanes (June to November)
Environment - current issues: asbestos disposal;
water pollution; preservation of open space;
sustainable development
Geography - note: consists of about 138 coral
islands and islets with ample rainfall, but no rivers or
freshwater lakes; some land was leased by US
Government from 1941 to 1995

People

Population: 64,935 (July 2004 est.)
Age structure:
0-14 years: 19.1% (male 6,192; female 6,186)
15-64 years: 69.3% (male 22,268; female 22,703)
65 years and over: 11.7% (male 3,295; female 4,291)
(2004 est.)
Median age:
total: 39.2 years
male: 38.3 years
female: 40.1 years (2004 est.)
Population growth rate: 0.68% (2004 est.)
Birth rate: 11.83 births/1,000 population (2004 est.)
Death rate: 7.55 deaths/1,000 population (2004 est.)
Net migration rate: 2.49 migrant(s)/1,000
population (2004 est.)
Sex ratio:
at birth: 1.02 male(s)/female
under 15 years: 1 male(s)/female
15-64 years: 0.98 male(s)/female
65 years and over: 0.77 male(s)/female
total population: 0.96 male(s)/female (2004 est.)
Infant mortality rate:
total: 8.79 deaths/1,000 live births
male: 10.45 deaths/1,000 live births
female: 7.1 deaths/1,000 live births (2004 est.)
Life expectancy at birth:
total population: 77.6 years
male: 75.54 years
female: 79.7 years (2004 est.)
Total fertility rate: 1.9 children born/woman
(2004 est.)
HIV/AIDS - adult prevalence rate: NA%
HIV/AIDS - people living with HIV/AIDS: NA
HIV/AIDS - deaths: NA
Nationality:
noun: Bermudian(s)
adjective: Bermudian
Ethnic groups: black 58%, white 36%, other 6%
Religions: non-Anglican Protestant 39%, Anglican
27%, Roman Catholic 15%, other 19%
Languages: English (official), Portuguese
Literacy:
definition: age 15 and over can read and write
total population: 98%
male: 98%
female: 99% (1970 est.)

Government

Country name:
conventional long form: none
conventional short form: Bermuda
former: Somers Islands
Dependency status: overseas territory of the UK
Government type: parliamentary British overseas
territory with internal self-government
Capital: Hamilton
Administrative divisions: 9 parishes and 2
municipalities*; Devonshire, Hamilton, Hamilton*,
Paget, Pembroke, Saint George*, Saint George's,
Sandys, Smith's, Southampton, Warwick
Independence: none (overseas territory of the UK)
National holiday: Bermuda Day, 24 May
Constitution: 8 June 1968, amended 1989 and 2003
Legal system: English law
Suffrage: 18 years of age; universal
Executive branch:
chief of state: Queen ELIZABETH II (since 6 February
1952), represented by Governor Sir John VEREKER
(since NA April 2002)
head of government: Premier Alex SCOTT (since
24 July 2003); Deputy Premier Ewart BROWN
cabinet: Cabinet nominated by the premier, appointed
by the governor
elections: none; the monarch is hereditary; governor
appointed by the monarch; following legislative
elections, the leader of the majority party or the leader
of the majority coalition is usually appointed premier
by the governor
Legislative branch: bicameral Parliament consists
of the Senate (an 11-member body appointed by the
governor, the premier, and the opposition) and the
House of Assembly (36 seats; members are elected
by popular vote to serve up to five-year terms)
elections: last general election held 24 July 2003 (next
to be held NA July 2008)
election results: percent of vote by party - PLP 51.7%,
UBP 48%; seats by party - PLP 22, UBP 14
Judicial branch: Supreme Court; Court of Appeal;
Magistrate Courts
Political parties and leaders: Gombey Liberation
Party or GLP [Gavin Sundjata SMITH]; National
Liberal Party or NLP [Dessaline WALDRON];
Progressive Labor Party or PLP [William Alexander
SCOTT]; United Bermuda Party or UBP [Grant
GIBBONS];
Political pressure groups and leaders: Bermuda
Employer's Union [Eddie SAINTS]; Bermuda
Industrial Union or BIU [Derrick BURGESS]; Bermuda
Public Services Union or BPSU [Ed BALL]; Bermuda
Union of Teachers [Michael CHARLES]
International organization participation: Caricom
(associate), ICFTU, Interpol (subbureau), IOC, WCO,
Egmont Group, Caribbean Financial Action Task
Force
Diplomatic representation in the US: none
(overseas territory of the UK)

Diplomatic representation from the US:
chief of mission: Consul General Denis Patrick
COLEMAN, Jr.
consulate(s) general: Crown Hill, 16 Middle Road,
Devonshire DVO3
mailing address: P. O. Box HM325, Hamilton HMBX;
American Consulate General Hamilton, Department of
State, 5300 Hamilton Place, Washington, DC
20520-5300
telephone: [1] (441) 295-1342
FAX: [1] (441) 295-1592, [1] (441) 296-9233
Flag description: red, with the flag of the UK in the
upper hoist-side quadrant and the Bermudian coat of
arms (white and green shield with a red lion holding a
scrolled shield showing the sinking of the ship Sea
Venture off Bermuda in 1609) centered on the outer
half of the flag

Economy

Economy - overview: Bermuda enjoys one of the
highest per capita incomes in the world, equal to that
of the US. Its economy is primarily based on providing
financial services for international business and luxury
facilities for tourists. The effects of 11 September
2001 have had both positive and negative
ramifications for Bermuda. On the positive side, a
number of new reinsurance companies have located
on the island, contributing to the expansion of an
already robust international business sector. On the
negative side, Bermuda's tourism industry - which
derives over 80% of its visitors from the US - was
severely hit as American tourists chose not to travel.
Tourism rebounded somewhat in 2002-03. Most
capital equipment and food must be imported.
Bermuda's industrial sector is small, although
construction continues to be important; the average
cost of a house in June 2003 had risen to $976,000.
Agriculture is limited, only 6% of the land being arable.
GDP: purchasing power parity - $2.33 billion
(2003 est.)
GDP - real growth rate: 2% (2003 est.)
GDP - per capita: purchasing power parity - $36,000
(2003 est.)
GDP - composition by sector:
agriculture: 1%
industry: 10%
services: 89% (2002 est.)
Population below poverty line: 19% (2000)
**Household income or consumption by percentage
share:**
lowest 10%: NA%
highest 10%: NA%
Inflation rate (consumer prices): 3.3%
(mid-2003 est.)
Labor force: 37,472 (2000)
Labor force - by occupation: clerical 22%,
services 20%, laborers 17%, professional and
technical 17%, administrative and managerial 13%,
sales 8%, agriculture and fishing 3% (2000 est.)
Unemployment rate: 5% (2002 est.)

Bermuda (continued)

Budget:
revenues: $671.1 million
expenditures: $594.6 million, including capital expenditures of $55 million (FY03/04)
Industries: tourism, international business, light manufacturing
Industrial production growth rate: NA%
Electricity - production: 643.7 million kWh (2001)
Electricity - production by source:
fossil fuel: 100%
hydro: 0%
nuclear: 0%
other: 0% (2001)
Electricity - consumption: 598.6 million kWh (2001)
Electricity - exports: 0 kWh (2001)
Electricity - imports: 0 kWh (2001)
Oil - production: 0 bbl/day (2001 est.)
Oil - consumption: 4,000 bbl/day (2001 est.)
Oil - exports: NA
Oil - imports: NA
Agriculture - products: bananas, vegetables, citrus, flowers; dairy products
Exports: $879 million (2002)
Exports - commodities: reexports of pharmaceuticals
Exports - partners: France 77.6%, Peru 3.1%, UK 2.8% (2002)
Imports: $5.523 billion (2002)
Imports - commodities: machinery and transport equipment, construction materials, chemicals, food and live animals
Imports - partners: Kazakhstan 40.1%, France 21.1%, Italy 9%, US 8.3%, South Korea 7.2%, Mexico 4.1% (2002)
Debt - external: $160 million (FY99/00)
Economic aid - recipient: $NA
Currency: Bermudian dollar (BMD)
Currency code: BMD
Exchange rates: Bermudian dollar per US dollar - 1.0000 (fixed rate pegged to the US dollar)
Fiscal year: 1 April - 31 March

Communications

Telephones - main lines in use: 56,000 (2002)
Telephones - mobile cellular: 37,873 (2003)
Telephone system:
general assessment: good
domestic: modern, fully automatic telephone system
international: country code - 1-441; 3 submarine cables; satellite earth stations - 3 Intelsat (Atlantic Ocean)
Radio broadcast stations: AM 5, FM 3, shortwave 0 (1998)
Television broadcast stations: 4 (2003)
Internet country code: .bm
Internet hosts: 5,161 (2001)
Internet users: 34,500 (2003)

Transportation

Railways: 0 km
Highways:
total: 450 km
paved: 450 km
unpaved: 0 km
note: public roads - 209 km; private roads - 241 km (2002)
Waterways: none
Ports and harbors: Hamilton, Saint George's, Dockyard
Merchant marine:
total: 94 ships (1,000 GRT or over) 4,845,326 GRT/6,501,782 DWT
by type: bulk 25, cargo 4, container 17, liquefied gas 9, passenger 6, petroleum tanker 9, refrigerated cargo 11, roll on/roll off 10, short-sea/passenger 3
foreign-owned: Croatia 5, Germany 2, Greece 21, Hong Kong 9, Indonesia 1, Sweden 6, Switzerland 1, United Kingdom 33, United States 12
registered in other countries: 2 (2003 est.)
Airports: 1 (2003 est.)
Airports - with paved runways:
total: 1
2,438 to 3,047 m: 1 (2003 est.)

Military

Military branches: Bermuda Regiment
Military expenditures - dollar figure: $4.03 million (2001)
Military expenditures - percent of GDP: 0.11% (FY00/01)
Military - note: defense is the responsibility of the UK

Transnational Issues

Disputes - international: none

Bhutan

Introduction

Background: In 1865, Britain and Bhutan signed the Treaty of Sinchulu, under which Bhutan would receive an annual subsidy in exchange for ceding some border land. Under British influence, a monarchy was set up in 1907; three years later, a treaty was signed whereby the British agreed not to interfere in Bhutanese internal affairs and Bhutan allowed Britain to direct its foreign affairs. This role was assumed by independent India after 1947. Two years later, a formal Indo-Bhutanese accord returned the areas of Bhutan annexed by the British, formalized the annual subsidies the country received, and defined India's responsibilities in defense and foreign relations. A refugee issue of some 100,000 Bhutanese in Nepal remains unresolved; 90% of the refugees are housed in seven United Nations Office of the High Commissioner for Refugees (UNHCR) camps.

Geography

Location: Southern Asia, between China and India
Geographic coordinates: 27 30 N, 90 30 E
Map references: Asia
Area:
total: 47,000 sq km
land: 47,000 sq km
water: 0 sq km
Area - comparative: about half the size of Indiana
Land boundaries:
total: 1,075 km
border countries: China 470 km, India 605 km
Coastline: 0 km (landlocked)
Maritime claims: none (landlocked)
Climate: varies; tropical in southern plains; cool winters and hot summers in central valleys; severe winters and cool summers in Himalayas
Terrain: mostly mountainous with some fertile valleys and savanna

Bhutan (continued)

Elevation extremes:
lowest point: Drangme Chhu 97 m
highest point: Kula Kangri 7,553 m
Natural resources: timber, hydropower, gypsum, calcium carbide
Land use:
arable land: 2.98%
permanent crops: 0.43%
other: 96.59% (1998 est.)
Irrigated land: 400 sq km (1998 est.)
Natural hazards: violent storms from the Himalayas are the source of the country's name which translates as Land of the Thunder Dragon; frequent landslides during the rainy season
Environment - current issues: soil erosion; limited access to potable water
Environment - international agreements:
party to: Biodiversity, Climate Change, Climate Change-Kyoto Protocol, Endangered Species, Hazardous Wastes
signed, but not ratified: Law of the Sea
Geography - note: landlocked; strategic location between China and India; controls several key Himalayan mountain passes

People

Population: 2,185,569
note: other estimates range as low as 810,000 (July 2004 est.)
Age structure:
0-14 years: 39.3% (male 445,548; female 414,338)
15-64 years: 56.6% (male 637,637; female 600,253)
65 years and over: 4% (male 44,298; female 43,495) (2004 est.)
Median age:
total: 20.2 years
male: 20 years
female: 20.3 years (2004 est.)
Population growth rate: 2.12% (2004 est.)
Birth rate: 34.41 births/1,000 population (2004 est.)
Death rate: 13.2 deaths/1,000 population (2004 est.)
Net migration rate: 0 migrant(s)/1,000 population (2004 est.)
Sex ratio:
at birth: 1.05 male(s)/female
under 15 years: 1.08 male(s)/female
15-64 years: 1.06 male(s)/female
65 years and over: 1.02 male(s)/female
total population: 1.07 male(s)/female (2004 est.)
Infant mortality rate:
total: 102.56 deaths/1,000 live births
male: 100.35 deaths/1,000 live births
female: 104.89 deaths/1,000 live births (2004 est.)
Life expectancy at birth:
total population: 53.99 years
male: 54.27 years
female: 53.68 years (2004 est.)
Total fertility rate: 4.87 children born/woman (2004 est.)
HIV/AIDS - adult prevalence rate: less than 0.1% (2001 est.)

HIV/AIDS - people living with HIV/AIDS: less than 100 (1999 est.)
HIV/AIDS - deaths: NA
Nationality:
noun: Bhutanese (singular and plural)
adjective: Bhutanese
Ethnic groups: Bhote 50%, ethnic Nepalese 35% (includes Lhotsampas - one of several Nepalese ethnic groups), indigenous or migrant tribes 15%
Religions: Lamaistic Buddhist 75%, Indian- and Nepalese-influenced Hinduism 25%
Languages: Dzongkha (official), Bhotes speak various Tibetan dialects, Nepalese speak various Nepalese dialects
Literacy:
definition: age 15 and over can read and write
total population: 42.2%
male: 56.2%
female: 28.1% (1995 est.)

Government

Country name:
conventional long form: Kingdom of Bhutan
conventional short form: Bhutan
Government type: monarchy; special treaty relationship with India
Capital: Thimphu
Administrative divisions: 18 districts (dzongkhag, singular and plural); Bumthang, Chhukha, Chirang, Dagana, Geylegphug, Ha, Lhuntshi, Mongar, Paro, Pemagatsel, Punakha, Samchi, Samdrup Jongkhar, Shemgang, Tashigang, Thimphu, Tongsa, Wangdi Phodrang
note: there may be two new districts named Gasa and Yangtse
Independence: 8 August 1949 (from India)
National holiday: National Day (Ugyen WANGCHUCK became first hereditary king), 17 December (1907)
Constitution: no written constitution or bill of rights; note - in 2001 the King commissioned the drafting of a constitution, which is to become effective in 2005
Legal system: based on Indian law and English common law; has not accepted compulsory ICJ jurisdiction
Suffrage: each family has one vote in village-level elections; note - in late 2003 Bhutan's legislature passed a new election law, though no elections have been held
Executive branch:
chief of state: King Jigme Singye WANGCHUCK (since 24 July 1972)
head of government: Chairman of the Council of Ministers Lyonpo Jigme Y. THINLEY (since 30 August 2003)
cabinet: Council of Ministers (Lhengye Shungtsog) nominated by the monarch, approved by the National Assembly; members serve fixed, five-year terms; note - there is also a Royal Advisory Council (Lodoi Tsokde), members nominated by the monarch

elections: none; the monarch is hereditary, but democratic reforms in July 1998 grant the National Assembly authority to remove the monarch with two-thirds vote
Legislative branch: unicameral National Assembly or Tshogdu (150 seats; 105 elected from village constituencies, 10 represent religious bodies, and 35 are designated by the monarch to represent government and other secular interests; members serve three-year terms)
elections: local elections last held November 2002 (next to be held NA 2005)
election results: NA
Judicial branch: Supreme Court of Appeal (the monarch); High Court (judges appointed by the monarch)
Political parties and leaders: no legal parties
Political pressure groups and leaders: Buddhist clergy; ethnic Nepalese organizations leading militant antigovernment campaign; Indian merchant community; United Front for Democracy (exiled)
International organization participation: AsDB, CP, FAO, G-77, IBRD, ICAO, IDA, IFAD, IMF, IOC, IOM (observer), ITU, NAM, OPCW (signatory), SAARC, UN, UNCTAD, UNESCO, UNIDO, UPU, WCO, WHO, WIPO, WMO, WToO, WTrO (observer)
Diplomatic representation in the US: none; note - Bhutan has a Permanent Mission to the UN; address: 2 United Nations Plaza, 27th Floor, New York, NY 10017; telephone [1] (212) 826-1919; the Bhutanese mission to the UN has consular jurisdiction in the US
consulate(s) general: New York
Diplomatic representation from the US: the US and Bhutan have no formal diplomatic relations, although informal contact is maintained between the Bhutanese and US Embassy in New Delhi (India)
Flag description: divided diagonally from the lower hoist side corner; the upper triangle is yellow and the lower triangle is orange; centered along the dividing line is a large black and white dragon facing away from the hoist side

Economy

Economy - overview: The economy, one of the world's smallest and least developed, is based on agriculture and forestry, which provide the main livelihood for more than 90% of the population. Agriculture consists largely of subsistence farming and animal husbandry. Rugged mountains dominate the terrain and make the building of roads and other infrastructure difficult and expensive. The economy is closely aligned with India's through strong trade and monetary links and dependence on India's financial assistance. The industrial sector is technologically backward, with most production of the cottage industry type. Most development projects, such as road construction, rely on Indian migrant labor. Bhutan's hydropower potential and its attraction for tourists are key resources. Model education, social, and environment programs are underway with support from multilateral development organizations. Each

Bhutan (continued)

economic program takes into account the government's desire to protect the country's environment and cultural traditions. For example, the government in its cautious expansion of the tourist sector encourages the visits of upscale, environmentally conscientious visitors. Detailed controls and uncertain policies in areas like industrial licensing, trade, labor, and finance continue to hamper foreign investment.

GDP: purchasing power parity - $2.7 billion (2002 est.)

GDP - real growth rate: 7.7% (2002 est.)

GDP - per capita: purchasing power parity - $1,300 (2002 est.)

GDP - composition by sector:

agriculture: 45%

industry: 10%

services: 45% (2002 est.)

Population below poverty line: NA%

Household income or consumption by percentage share:

lowest 10%: NA%

highest 10%: NA%

Inflation rate (consumer prices): 3% (2002 est.)

Labor force: NA

note: massive lack of skilled labor (1997 est.)

Labor force - by occupation: agriculture 93%, services 5%, industry and commerce 2%

Unemployment rate: NA%

Budget:

revenues: $146 million

expenditures: $152 million, including capital expenditures of NA

note: the government of India finances nearly three-fifths of Bhutan's budget expenditures (FY95/96 est.)

Industries: cement, wood products, processed fruits, alcoholic beverages, calcium carbide

Industrial production growth rate: 9.3% (1996 est.)

Electricity - production: 1.896 billion kWh (2001)

Electricity - production by source:

fossil fuel: 0.1%

hydro: 99.9%

nuclear: 0%

other: 0% (2001)

Electricity - consumption: 379.5 million kWh (2001)

Electricity - exports: 1.4 billion kWh (2001)

Electricity - imports: 16 million kWh (2001)

Oil - production: 0 bbl/day (2001 est.)

Oil - consumption: 1,020 bbl/day (2001 est.)

Oil - exports: NA

Oil - imports: NA

Agriculture - products: rice, corn, root crops, citrus, foodgrains; dairy products, eggs

Exports: $154 million f.o.b. (2000 est.)

Exports - commodities: electricity (to India), cardamom, gypsum, timber, handicrafts, cement, fruit, precious stones, spices

Exports - partners: India 88.5%, US 2.7%, UK 2.7% (2002)

Imports: $196 million c.i.f. (2000 est.)

Imports - commodities: fuel and lubricants, grain, machinery and parts, vehicles, fabrics, rice

Imports - partners: India 62.7%, Japan 16.7%, Germany 4.5% (2002)

Debt - external: $245 million (2000)

Economic aid - recipient: substantial aid from India and other nations

Currency: ngultrum (BTN); Indian rupee (INR)

Currency code: BTN; INR

Exchange rates: ngultrum per US dollar - 46.5806 (2003), 48.6103 (2002), 47.1864 (2001), 44.9416 (2000), 43.0554 (1999)

Fiscal year: 1 July - 30 June

Communications

Telephones - main lines in use: 19,600 (2002)

Telephones - mobile cellular: NA

Telephone system:

general assessment: NA

domestic: domestic telephone service is very poor with few telephones in use

international: country code - 975; international telephone and telegraph service is by landline through India; a satellite earth station was planned (1990)

Radio broadcast stations: AM 0, FM 1, shortwave 1 (1998)

Television broadcast stations: 0 (1997)

Internet country code: .bt

Internet hosts: 1,242 (2002)

Internet users: 10,000 (2002)

Transportation

Railways: 0 km

Highways:

total: 3,690 km

paved: 2,240 km

unpaved: 1,450 km (1999 est.)

Waterways: none

Ports and harbors: none

Airports: 2 (2003 est.)

Airports - with paved runways:

total: 1

1,524 to 2,437 m: 1 (2003 est.)

Airports - with unpaved runways:

total: 1

914 to 1,523 m: 1 (2003 est.)

Military

Military branches: Royal Bhutan Army, Royal Bodyguard, National Militia

Military manpower - military age: 18 years of age (2004 est.)

Military manpower - availability:

males age 15-49: 544,560 (2004 est.)

Military manpower - fit for military service:

males age 15-49: 290,843 (2004 est.)

Military manpower - reaching military age annually:

males: 23,379 (2004 est.)

Military expenditures - dollar figure: $11.2 million (2003)

Military expenditures - percent of GDP: 1.9% (2003)

Transnational Issues

Disputes - international: approximately 100,000 Bhutanese refugees living in Nepal, 90% of whom reside in seven UN Office of the High Commissioner for Refugees camps, place decades-long strains on Nepal; India seeks cooperation from Bhutan to keep out Indian Nagaland insurgents

Bolivia

Introduction

Background: Bolivia, named after independence fighter Simon BOLIVAR, broke away from Spanish rule in 1825; much of its subsequent history has consisted of a series of nearly 200 coups and counter-coups. Comparatively democratic civilian rule was established in 1982, but leaders have faced difficult problems of deep-seated poverty, social unrest, and drug production. Current goals include attracting foreign investment, strengthening the educational system, resolving disputes with coca growers over Bolivia's counterdrug efforts, and waging an anticorruption campaign.

Geography

Location: Central South America, southwest of Brazil

Geographic coordinates: 17 00 S, 65 00 W

Map references: South America

Area:
total: 1,098,580 sq km
land: 1,084,390 sq km
water: 14,190 sq km

Area - comparative: slightly less than three times the size of Montana

Land boundaries:
total: 6,743 km
border countries: Argentina 832 km, Brazil 3,400 km, Chile 861 km, Paraguay 750 km, Peru 900 km

Coastline: 0 km (landlocked)

Maritime claims: none (landlocked)

Climate: varies with altitude; humid and tropical to cold and semiarid

Terrain: rugged Andes Mountains with a highland plateau (Altiplano), hills, lowland plains of the Amazon Basin

Elevation extremes:
lowest point: Rio Paraguay 90 m
highest point: Nevado Sajama 6,542 m

Natural resources: tin, natural gas, petroleum, zinc, tungsten, antimony, silver, iron, lead, gold, timber, hydropower

Land use:
arable land: 1.73%
permanent crops: 0.21%
other: 98.06% (1998 est.)

Irrigated land: 1,280 sq km (1998 est.)

Natural hazards: flooding in the northeast (March-April)

Environment - current issues: the clearing of land for agricultural purposes and the international demand for tropical timber are contributing to deforestation; soil erosion from overgrazing and poor cultivation methods (including slash-and-burn agriculture); desertification; loss of biodiversity; industrial pollution of water supplies used for drinking and irrigation

Environment - international agreements:
party to: Biodiversity, Climate Change, Climate Change-Kyoto Protocol, Desertification, Endangered Species, Hazardous Wastes, Law of the Sea, Marine Dumping, Ozone Layer Protection, Ship Pollution, Tropical Timber 83, Tropical Timber 94, Wetlands
signed, but not ratified: Environmental Modification, Marine Life Conservation, Ozone Layer Protection

Geography - note: landlocked; shares control of Lago Titicaca, world's highest navigable lake (elevation 3,805 m), with Peru

People

Population: 8,724,156 (July 2004 est.)

Age structure:
0-14 years: 36.4% (male 1,619,950; female 1,557,883)
15-64 years: 59.1% (male 2,522,086; female 2,631,944)
65 years and over: 4.5% (male 175,193; female 217,100) (2004 est.)

Median age:
total: 21.1 years
male: 20.4 years
female: 21.8 years (2004 est.)

Population growth rate: 1.56% (2004 est.)

Birth rate: 24.65 births/1,000 population (2004 est.)

Death rate: 7.77 deaths/1,000 population (2004 est.)

Net migration rate: -1.32 migrant(s)/1,000 population (2004 est.)

Sex ratio:
at birth: 1.05 male(s)/female
under 15 years: 1.04 male(s)/female
15-64 years: 0.96 male(s)/female
65 years and over: 0.81 male(s)/female
total population: 0.98 male(s)/female (2004 est.)

Infant mortality rate:
total: 54.58 deaths/1,000 live births
male: 58.23 deaths/1,000 live births
female: 50.75 deaths/1,000 live births (2004 est.)

Life expectancy at birth:
total population: 65.14 years
male: 62.54 years
female: 67.86 years (2004 est.)

Total fertility rate: 3.08 children born/woman (2004 est.)

HIV/AIDS - adult prevalence rate: 0.1% - note: no country specific models provided (2001 est.)

HIV/AIDS - people living with HIV/AIDS: 4,600 (2001 est.)

HIV/AIDS - deaths: 290 (2001 est.)

Nationality:
noun: Bolivian(s)
adjective: Bolivian

Ethnic groups: Quechua 30%, mestizo (mixed white and Amerindian ancestry) 30%, Aymara 25%, white 15%

Religions: Roman Catholic 95%, Protestant (Evangelical Methodist)

Languages: Spanish (official), Quechua (official), Aymara (official)

Literacy:
definition: age 15 and over can read and write
total population: 87.2%
male: 93.1%
female: 81.6% (2003 est.)

Government

Country name:
conventional long form: Republic of Bolivia
conventional short form: Bolivia
local long form: Republica de Bolivia
local short form: Bolivia

Government type: republic

Capital: La Paz (seat of government); Sucre (legal capital and seat of judiciary)

Administrative divisions: 9 departments (departamentos, singular - departamento); Chuquisaca, Cochabamba, Beni, La Paz, Oruro, Pando, Potosi, Santa Cruz, Tarija

Independence: 6 August 1825 (from Spain)

National holiday: Independence Day, 6 August (1825)

Constitution: 2 February 1967; revised in August 1994

Legal system: based on Spanish law and Napoleonic Code; has not accepted compulsory ICJ jurisdiction

Suffrage: 18 years of age, universal and compulsory (married); 21 years of age, universal and compulsory (single)

Executive branch:
chief of state: President Carlos Diego MESA Gisbert (since 17 October 2003); Vice President (vacant); note - the president is both the chief of state and head of government
head of government: President Carlos Diego MESA Gisbert (since 17 October 2003); Vice President (vacant); note - the president is both the chief of state and head of government
cabinet: Cabinet appointed by the president
elections: president and vice president elected on the same ticket by popular vote for five-year terms; election last held 30 June 2002 (next to be held NA June 2007)

Bolivia *(continued)*

election results: as a result of no candidate winning a majority in the 30 June 2002 election, Gonzalo SANCHEZ DE LOZADA Bustamante was chosen president by Congress; Congressional votes - Gonzalo SANCHEZ DE LOZADA Bustamante 84, Evo MORALES 43; note - following the resignation of the elected president on 17 October 2003, Vice President Carlos Diego MESA Gisbert assumed the presidency

Legislative branch: bicameral National Congress or Congreso Nacional consists of Chamber of Senators or Camara de Senadores (27 seats; members are elected by proportional representation from party lists to serve five-year terms) and Chamber of Deputies or Camara de Diputados (130 seats; 68 are directly elected from their districts and 62 are elected by proportional representation from party lists to serve five-year terms)

elections: Chamber of Senators and Chamber of Deputies - last held 30 June 2002 (next to be held NA June 2007)

election results: Chamber of Senators - percent of vote by party - NA%; seats by party - MNR 11, MAS 8, MIR 5, NFR 2, other 1; Chamber of Deputies - percent of vote by party - NA%; seats by party - MNR 36, MAS 27, MIR 26, NFR 25, others 16

Judicial branch: Supreme Court or Corte Suprema (judges appointed for 10-year terms by National Congress); District Courts (one in each department); provincial and local courts (to try minor cases)

Political parties and leaders: Bolivian Socialist Falange or FSB [Romel PANTOJA]; Civic Solidarity Union or UCS [Johnny FERNANDEZ]; Free Bolivia Movement or MBL [Franz BARRIOS]; Marshal of Ayacucho Institutional Vanguard or VIMA [Freddy ZABALA]; Movement of the Revolutionary Left or MIR [Jaime PAZ Zamora]; Movement Toward Socialism or MAS [Evo MORALES]; Movement Without Fear or MSM [Juan DEL GRANADO]; Nationalist Democratic Action or ADN [Jorge Fernando QUIROGA Ramirez]; Nationalist Revolutionary Movement or MNR [leader NA]; New Republican Force or NFR [Manfred REYES-VILLA]; Pachakuti Indigenous Movement or MIP [Felipe QUISPE]; Socialist Party or PS [Jeres JUSTINIANO]

Political pressure groups and leaders: Cocalero Groups; indigenous organizations; labor unions; Sole Confederation of Campesino Workers of Bolivia or CSUTCB [Roman LOAYZA]

International organization participation: CAN, FAO, G-77, IADB, IAEA, IBRD, ICAO, ICCt, ICRM, IDA, IFAD, IFC, IFRCS, ILO, IMF, IMO, Interpol, IOC, IOM, ISO (correspondent), ITU, LAES, LAIA, Mercosur (associate), MONUC, NAM, OAS, OPANAL, OPCW, PCA, RG, UN, UNAMSIL, UNCTAD, UNESCO, UNIDO, UNMIL, UNMISET, UPU, WCL, WCO, WFTU, WHO, WIPO, WMO, WToO, WTrO

Diplomatic representation in the US:
chief of mission: Ambassador Jaime APARICIO Otero

chancery: 3014 Massachusetts Avenue NW, Washington, DC 20008
telephone: [1] (202) 483-4410
FAX: [1] (202) 328-3712
consulate(s) general: Miami, New York, and San Francisco
consulate(s): Washington, DC

Diplomatic representation from the US:
chief of mission: Ambassador David N. GREENLEE
embassy: Avenida Arce 2780, San Jorge, La Paz
mailing address: P. O. Box 425, La Paz; APO AA 34032
telephone: [591] (2) 2430120, 2430251
FAX: [591] (2) 2433900

Flag description: three equal horizontal bands of red (top), yellow, and green with the coat of arms centered on the yellow band; similar to the flag of Ghana, which has a large black five-pointed star centered in the yellow band

Economy

Economy - overview: Bolivia, long one of the poorest and least developed Latin American countries, made considerable progress in the 1990s toward the development of a market-oriented economy. Successes under President SANCHEZ DE LOZADA (1993-97) included the signing of a free trade agreement with Mexico and becoming an associate member of the Southern Cone Common Market (Mercosur), as well as the privatization of the state airline, telephone company, railroad, electric power company, and oil company. Growth slowed in 1999, in part due to tight government budget policies, which limited needed appropriations for anti-poverty programs, and the fallout from the Asian financial crisis. In 2000, major civil disturbances held down growth to 2.5%. Bolivia's GDP failed to grow in 2001 due to the global slowdown and laggard domestic activity. Growth picked up slightly in 2002, but the first quarter of 2003 saw extensive civil riots and looting and loss of confidence in the government. Bolivia will remain highly dependent on foreign aid unless and until it can develop its substantial natural resources.

GDP: purchasing power parity - $20.88 billion (2003 est.)

GDP - real growth rate: 2.1% (2003 est.)

GDP - per capita: purchasing power parity - $2,400 (2003 est.)

GDP - composition by sector:
agriculture: 20%
industry: 20%
services: 60% (2002 est.)

Population below poverty line: 70% (1999 est.)

Household income or consumption by percentage share:
lowest 10%: 1.3%
highest 10%: 32% (1999)

Distribution of family income - Gini index: 58.9 (1997)

Inflation rate (consumer prices): 2% (2001 est.)

Labor force: 2.5 million (2001)

Labor force - by occupation: agriculture NA%, industry NA%, services NA%

Unemployment rate: 7.6%
note: widespread underemployment (2000)

Budget:
revenues: $4 billion
expenditures: $4 billion, including capital expenditures of $NA (2002 est.)

Industries: mining, smelting, petroleum, food and beverages, tobacco, handicrafts, clothing

Industrial production growth rate: 3.9% (1998)

Electricity - production: 3.901 billion kWh (2001)

Electricity - production by source:
fossil fuel: 44.4%
hydro: 54%
nuclear: 0%
other: 1.5% (2001)

Electricity - consumption: 3.634 billion kWh (2001)

Electricity - exports: 3 million kWh (2001)

Electricity - imports: 9 million kWh (2001)

Oil - production: 44,340 bbl/day (2001 est.)

Oil - consumption: 49,000 bbl/day (2001 est.)

Oil - exports: NA

Oil - imports: NA

Oil - proved reserves: 458.8 million bbl (1 January 2002)

Natural gas - production: 4.05 billion cu m (2001 est.)

Natural gas - consumption: 1.15 billion cu m (2001 est.)

Natural gas - exports: 2.9 billion cu m (2001 est.)

Natural gas - imports: 0 cu m (2001 est.)

Natural gas - proved reserves: 727.2 billion cu m (1 January 2002)

Agriculture - products: soybeans, coffee, coca, cotton, corn, sugarcane, rice, potatoes; timber

Exports: $1.495 billion f.o.b. (2003 est.)

Exports - commodities: soybeans, natural gas, zinc, gold, wood (2000)

Exports - partners: Brazil 24.3%, Switzerland 15.7%, US 14.1%, Venezuela 12.8%, Colombia 10.2%, Peru 5.4% (2002)

Imports: $1.505 billion f.o.b. (2003 est.)

Imports - commodities: capital goods, raw materials and semi-manufactures, chemicals, petroleum, food

Imports - partners: Brazil 22%, Argentina 17.4%, US 15.6%, Chile 6.9%, Japan 5.5%, Peru 5.4%, China 4.8% (2002)

Debt - external: $5.9 billion (2002 est.)

Economic aid - recipient: $588 million (1997)

Currency: boliviano (BOB)

Currency code: BOB

Exchange rates: bolivianos per US dollar - 7.6592 (2003), 7.17 (2002), 6.6069 (2001), 6.1835 (2000), 5.8124 (1999)

Fiscal year: calendar year

Bolivia *(continued)*

Communications

Telephones - main lines in use: 563,900 (2002)
Telephones - mobile cellular: 872,700 (2002)
Telephone system:
general assessment: new subscribers face bureaucratic difficulties; most telephones are concentrated in La Paz and other cities; mobile cellular telephone use expanding rapidly
domestic: primary trunk system, which is being expanded, employs digital microwave radio relay; some areas are served by fiber-optic cable; mobile cellular systems are being expanded
international: country code - 591; satellite earth station - 1 Intelsat (Atlantic Ocean)
Radio broadcast stations: AM 171, FM 73, shortwave 77 (1999)
Television broadcast stations: 48 (1997)
Internet country code: .bo
Internet hosts: 1,413 (2002)
Internet users: 270,000 (2002)

Transportation

Railways:
total: 3,519 km
narrow gauge: 3,519 km 1.000-m gauge (2002)
Highways:
total: 53,790 km
paved: 3,496 km (including 13 km of expressways)
unpaved: 50,294 km (2000 est.)
Waterways: 10,000 km (commercially navigable)
Pipelines: gas 4,860 km; liquid petroleum gas 47 km; oil 2,460 km; refined products 1,589 km; unknown (oil/water) 247 km (2003)
Ports and harbors: Puerto Aguirre (on the Paraguay/Parana waterway, at the Bolivia/Brazil border); also, Bolivia has free port privileges in maritime ports in Argentina, Brazil, Chile, and Paraguay
Merchant marine:
total: 56 ships (1,000 GRT or over) 413,407 GRT/699,901 DWT
by type: bulk 3, cargo 26, chemical tanker 4, container 3, livestock carrier 1, multi-functional large load carrier 1, petroleum tanker 10, refrigerated cargo 2, roll on/roll off 1, short-sea/passenger 3, specialized tanker 2
foreign-owned: Argentina 1, British Virgin Islands 1, Cambodia 1, China 1, Cyprus 1, Egypt 1, Eritrea 1, Germany 2, Greece 1, Hong Kong 1, Indonesia 1, Iran 1, Italy 2, Latvia 2, Panama 3, Romania 1, Russia 1, Saint Kitts and Nevis 1, Saint Vincent and the Grenadines 1, Saudi Arabia 2, Singapore 3, Syria 1, Turkey 1, United Kingdom 1, United States 3, Yemen 2
registered in other countries: 1 (2003 est.)
Airports: 1,067 (2003 est.)
Airports - with paved runways:
total: 13
over 3,047 m: 4
2,438 to 3,047 m: 2
1,524 to 2,437 m: 6
914 to 1,523 m: 3 (2003 est.)

Airports - with unpaved runways:
total: 1,052
over 3,047 m: 1
2,438 to 3,047 m: 3
1,524 to 2,437 m: 61
914 to 1,523 m: 210
under 914 m: 777 (2003 est.)

Military

Military branches: Army (Ejercito Boliviano), Navy (Fuerza Naval, includes Marines), Air Force (Fuerza Aerea Boliviana)
Military manpower - military age: 19 years of age (2004 est.)
Military manpower - availability:
males age 15-49: 2,175,384 (2004 est.)
Military manpower - fit for military service:
males age 15-49: 1,417,804 (2004 est.)
Military manpower - reaching military age annually:
males: 98,155 (2004 est.)
Military expenditures - dollar figure: $127 million (2003)
Military expenditures - percent of GDP: 1.6% (2003)

Transnational Issues

Disputes - international: has reactivated its claim to restore the Atacama corridor ceded to Chile in 1884 to secure sovereign maritime access for Bolivian natural gas
Illicit drugs: world's third-largest cultivator of coca (after Colombia and Peru) with an estimated 28,450 hectares under cultivation in June 2003, a 23% increase from June 2002; intermediate coca products and cocaine exported mostly to or through Brazil, Argentina, and Chile to European and US drug markets; eradication and alternative crop programs under the MESA administration have been unable to keep pace with farmers' attempts to increase cultivation; money-laundering activity related to narcotics trade, especially along the borders with Brazil and Paraguay

Bosnia and Herzegovina

Introduction

Background: Bosnia and Herzegovina's declaration of sovereignty in October 1991, was followed by a declaration of independence from the former Yugoslavia on 3 March 1992 after a referendum boycotted by ethnic Serbs. The Bosnian Serbs - supported by neighboring Serbia and Montenegro - responded with armed resistance aimed at partitioning the republic along ethnic lines and joining Serb-held areas to form a "greater Serbia." In March 1994, Bosniaks and Croats reduced the number of warring factions from three to two by signing an agreement creating a joint Bosniak/Croat Federation of Bosnia and Herzegovina. On 21 November 1995, in Dayton, Ohio, the warring parties initialed a peace agreement that brought to a halt three years of interethnic civil strife (the final agreement was signed in Paris on 14 December 1995). The Dayton Agreement retained Bosnia and Herzegovina's international boundaries and created a joint multi-ethnic and democratic government. This national government was charged with conducting foreign, diplomatic, and fiscal policy. Also recognized was a second tier of government comprised of two entities roughly equal in size: the Bosniak/Croat Federation of Bosnia and Herzegovina and the Bosnian Serb-led Republika Srpska (RS). The Federation and RS governments were charged with overseeing most government functions. The Office of the High Representative (OHR) was established to oversee the implementation of the civilian aspects of the agreement. In 1995-96, a NATO-led international peacekeeping force (IFOR) of 60,000 troops served in Bosnia to implement and monitor the military aspects of the agreement. IFOR was succeeded by a smaller, NATO-led Stabilization Force (SFOR) whose mission is to deter renewed hostilities. SFOR remains in place although troop levels are being reduced.

Bosnia and Herzegovina (continued)

Geography

Location: Southeastern Europe, bordering the Adriatic Sea and Croatia
Geographic coordinates: 44 00 N, 18 00 E
Map references: Europe
Area:
total: 51,129 sq km
land: 51,129 sq km
water: 0 sq km
Area - comparative: slightly smaller than West Virginia
Land boundaries:
total: 1,459 km
border countries: Croatia 932 km, Serbia and Montenegro 527 km
Coastline: 20 km
Maritime claims: No data available
Climate: hot summers and cold winters; areas of high elevation have short, cool summers and long, severe winters; mild, rainy winters along coast
Terrain: mountains and valleys
Elevation extremes:
lowest point: Adriatic Sea 0 m
highest point: Maglic 2,386 m
Natural resources: coal, iron, bauxite, manganese, forests, copper, chromium, lead, zinc, hydropower
Land use:
arable land: 9.8%
permanent crops: 2.94%
other: 87.26% (1998 est.)
Irrigated land: 20 sq km (1998 est.)
Natural hazards: destructive earthquakes
Environment - current issues: air pollution from metallurgical plants; sites for disposing of urban waste are limited; water shortages and destruction of infrastructure because of the 1992-95 civil strife; deforestation
Environment - international agreements:
party to: Air Pollution, Biodiversity, Climate Change, Hazardous Wastes, Law of the Sea, Marine Life Conservation, Ozone Layer Protection, Wetlands
signed, but not ratified: none of the selected agreements
Geography - note: within Bosnia and Herzegovina's recognized borders, the country is divided into a joint Bosniak/Croat Federation (about 51% of the territory) and the Bosnian Serb-led Republika Srpska or RS (about 49% of the territory); the region called Herzegovina is contiguous to Croatia and Serbia and Montenegro (Montenegro), and traditionally has been settled by an ethnic Croat majority in the west and an ethnic Serb majority in the east

People

Population: 4,007,608 (July 2004 est.)
Age structure:
0-14 years: 18.9% (male 389,062; female 368,721)
15-64 years: 70.6% (male 1,447,725; female 1,379,729)
65 years and over: 10.5% (male 180,801; female 241,570) (2004 est.)

Median age:
total: 35.9 years
male: 35.5 years
female: 36.2 years (2004 est.)
Population growth rate: 0.45% (2004 est.)
Birth rate: 12.56 births/1,000 population (2004 est.)
Death rate: 8.33 deaths/1,000 population (2004 est.)
Net migration rate: 0.31 migrant(s)/1,000 population (2004 est.)
Sex ratio:
at birth: 1.07 male(s)/female
under 15 years: 1.06 male(s)/female
15-64 years: 1.05 male(s)/female
65 years and over: 0.75 male(s)/female
total population: 1.01 male(s)/female (2004 est.)
Infant mortality rate:
total: 21.88 deaths/1,000 live births
male: 24.5 deaths/1,000 live births
female: 19.08 deaths/1,000 live births (2004 est.)
Life expectancy at birth:
total population: 72.57 years
male: 69.82 years
female: 75.51 years (2004 est.)
Total fertility rate: 1.71 children born/woman (2004 est.)
HIV/AIDS - adult prevalence rate: less than 0.1% (2001 est.)
HIV/AIDS - people living with HIV/AIDS: NA
HIV/AIDS - deaths: 100 (2001 est.)
Nationality:
noun: Bosnian(s), Herzegovinian(s)
adjective: Bosnian, Herzegovinian
Ethnic groups: Serb 37.1%, Bosniak 48%, Croat 14.3%, other 0.6% (2000)
note: Bosniak has replaced Muslim as an ethnic term in part to avoid confusion with the religious term Muslim - an adherent of Islam
Religions: Muslim 40%, Orthodox 31%, Roman Catholic 15%, other 14%
Languages: Bosnian, Croatian, Serbian
Literacy:
definition: NA
total population: NA%
male: NA%
female: NA%

Government

Country name:
conventional long form: none
conventional short form: Bosnia and Herzegovina
local long form: none
local short form: Bosna i Hercegovina
Government type: emerging federal democratic republic
Capital: Sarajevo
Administrative divisions: there are two first-order administrative divisions and one internationally supervised district* - Brcko district (Brcko Distrikt)*, the Bosniak/Croat Federation of Bosnia and Herzegovina (Federacija Bosna i Hercegovina) and the Bosnian Serb-led Republika Srpska; note - Brcko

district is in northeastern Bosnia and is an administrative unit under the sovereignty of Bosnia and Herzegovina; the district remains under international supervision
Independence: 1 March 1992 (from Yugoslavia; referendum for independence was completed 1 March 1992; independence was declared 3 March 1992)
National holiday: National Day, 25 November (1943)
Constitution: the Dayton Agreement, signed 14 December 1995, included a new constitution now in force; note - each of the entities also has its own constitution
Legal system: based on civil law system
Suffrage: 16 years of age, if employed; 18 years of age, universal
Executive branch:
chief of state: Chairman of the Presidency Sulejman TIHIC (chairman since 28 February 2004; presidency member since 5 October 2002 - Bosniak) other members of the three-member rotating (every eight months) presidency: Dragan COVIC (since 5 October 2002 - Croat) and Borislav PARAVAC (since 10 April 2003 - Serb); note - Mirko SAROVIC resigned 2 April 2003
head of government: Chairman of the Council of Ministers Adnan TERZIC (since 20 December 2002),
cabinet: Council of Ministers nominated by the council chairman; approved by the National House of Representatives
elections: the three members of the presidency (one Bosniak, one Croat, one Serb) are elected by popular vote for a four-year term; the member with the most votes becomes the chairman unless he or she was the incumbent chairman at the time of the election, but the chairmanship rotates every eight months; election last held 5 October 2002 (next to be held NA 2006); the chairman of the Council of Ministers is appointed by the presidency and confirmed by the National House of Representatives
election results: percent of vote - Mirko SAROVIC with 35.5% of the Serb vote was elected chairman of the collective presidency for the first eight months; Dragan COVIC received 61.5% of the Croat vote; Sulejman TIHIC received 37% of the Bosniak vote
note: President of the Federation of Bosnia and Herzegovina: Niko LOZANCIC (since 27 January 2003); Vice Presidents Sahbaz DZIHANOVIC (since NA 2003) and Desnica RADIVOJEVIC (since NA 2003); President of the Republika Srpska: Dragan CAVIC (since 28 November 2002)
Legislative branch: bicameral Parliamentary Assembly or Skupstina consists of the National House of Representatives or Predstavnicki Dom (42 seats - elected by proportional representation, 28 seats allocated from the Federation of Bosnia and Herzegovina and 14 seats from the Republika Srpska; members elected by popular vote to serve four-year terms) and the House of Peoples or Dom Naroda (15 seats - 5 Bosniak, 5 Croat, 5 Serb; members elected by the Bosniak/Croat Federation's House of Representatives and the Republika Srpska's National

Bosnia and Herzegovina *(continued)*

Assembly to serve four-year terms); note - Bosnia's election law specifies four-year terms for the state and first-order administrative division entity legislatures
elections: National House of Representatives - elections last held 5 October 2002 (next to be held in NA 2006); House of Peoples - last constituted NA January 2003 (next to be constituted in 2007)
election results: National House of Representatives - percent of vote by party/coalition - SDA 21.9%, SDS 14.0%, SBiH 10.5%, SDP 10.4%, SNSD 9.8%, HDZ 9.5%, PDP 4.6%, others 19.3%; seats by party/coalition - SDA 10, SDS 5, SBiH 6, SDP 4, SNSD 3, HDZ 5, PDP 2, others 7; House of Peoples - percent of vote by party/coalition - NA%; seats by party/coalition - NA
note: the Bosniak/Croat Federation has a bicameral legislature that consists of a House of Representatives (98 seats; members elected by popular vote to serve four-year terms); elections last held 5 October 2002 (next to be held NA October 2006); percent of vote by party - NA%; seats by party/coalition - SDA 32, HDZ-BiH 16, SDP 15, SBiH 15, other 20; and a House of Peoples (60 seats - 30 Bosniak, 30 Croat); last constituted December 2002; the Republika Srpska has a National Assembly (83 seats; members elected by popular vote to serve four-year terms); elections last held 5 October 2002 (next to be held in the fall of 2006); percent of vote by party - NA%; seats by party/coalition - SDS 26, SNSD 19, PDP 9, SDA 6, SRS 4, SPRS 3, DNZ 3, SBiH 4, SDP 3, others 6; as a result of the 2002 constitutional reform process, a 28-member Republika Srpska Council of Peoples (COP) was established in the Republika Srpska National Assembly; each constituent nation and "others" will have eight delegates
Judicial branch: BiH Constitutional Court (consists of nine members: four members are selected by the Bosniak/Croat Federation's House of Representatives, two members by the Republika Srpska's National Assembly, and three non-Bosnian members by the president of the European Court of Human Rights); BiH State Court (consists of nine judges and three divisions - Administrative, Appellate and Criminal - having jurisdiction over cases related to state-level law and appellate jurisdiction over cases initiated in the entities; note - a War Crimes Chamber may be added at a future date)
note: the entities each have a Supreme Court; each entity also has a number of lower courts; there are 10 cantonal courts in the Federation, plus a number of municipal courts; the Republika Srpska has five municipal courts
Political parties and leaders: Alliance of Independent Social Democrats or SNSD [Milorad DODIK]; Bosnian Party or BOSS [Mirnes AJANOVIC]; Civic Democratic Party or GDS [Ilija SIMIC]; Croatian Democratic Union of Bosnia and Herzegovina or HDZ [Barisa COLAK]; Croat Christian Democratic Union of Bosnia and Herzegovina or HKDU [Mijo IVANIC-LONIC]; Croat Party of Rights or HSP

[Zdravko HRISTIC]; Croat Peasants Party or HSS [Ilija SIMIC]; Democratic National Union or DNZ [Fikret ABDIC]; Liberal Democratic Party or LDS [Rasim KADIC]; New Croat Initiative or NHI [Kresimir ZUBAK]; Party for Bosnia and Herzegovina or SBiH [Safet HALILOVIC]; Party of Democratic Action or SDA [Sulejman TIHIC]; Party of Democratic Progress or PDP [Mladen IVANIC]; Pro-European People's Party or PROENS [Jadranko PRLIC]; Serb Democratic Party or SDS [Dragan KALINIC]; Serb Radical Party of the Republika Srpska or SRS-RS [Radislav KANJERIC]; Social Democratic Party of BIH or SDP [Zlatko LAGUMDZIJA]; Socialist Party of Republika Srpska or SPRS [Petar DJOKIC]
Political pressure groups and leaders: NA
International organization participation: BIS, CE, CEI, EBRD, FAO, G-77, IAEA, IBRD, ICAO, ICCt, IDA, IFAD, IFC, IFRCS, ILO, IMF, IMO, Interpol, IOC, IOM (observer), ISO, ITU, MONUC, NAM (guest), OAS (observer), OIC (observer), OPCW, OSCE, UN, UNCTAD, UNESCO, UNIDO, UNMEE, UPU, WHO, WIPO, WMO, WToO, WTrO (observer)
Diplomatic representation in the US:
chief of mission: Ambassador Igor DAVIDOVIC
chancery: 2109 E Street NW, Washington, DC 20037
telephone: [1] (202) 337-1500
FAX: [1] (202) 337-1502
consulate(s) general: New York
Diplomatic representation from the US:
chief of mission: Ambassador Clifford G. BOND
embassy: Alipasina 43, 71000 Sarajevo
mailing address: use street address
telephone: [387] (33) 445-700
FAX: [387] (33) 659-722
branch office(s): Banja Luka, Mostar
Flag description: a wide medium blue vertical band on the fly side with a yellow isosceles triangle abutting the band and the top of the flag; the remainder of the flag is medium blue with seven full five-pointed white stars and two half stars top and bottom along the hypotenuse of the triangle

Economy

Economy - overview: Bosnia and Herzegovina ranked next to The Former Yugoslav Republic of Macedonia as the poorest republic in the old Yugoslav federation. Although agriculture is almost all in private hands, farms are small and inefficient, and the republic traditionally is a net importer of food. Industry has been greatly overstaffed, one reflection of the socialist economic structure of Yugoslavia. TITO had pushed the development of military industries in the republic with the result that Bosnia hosted a number of Yugoslavia's defense plants. The interethnic warfare in Bosnia caused production to plummet by 80% from 1992 to 1995 and unemployment to soar. With an uneasy peace in place, output recovered in 1996-99 at high percentage rates from a low base; but output growth slowed in 2000-02. GDP remains far below the 1990 level. Economic data are of limited use because,

although both entities issue figures, national-level statistics are limited. Moreover, official data do not capture the large share of black market activity. The konvertibilna marka (convertible mark or BAM)- the national currency introduced in 1998 - is now pegged to the euro, and the Central Bank of Bosnia and Herzegovina has dramatically increased its reserve holdings. Implementation of privatization, however, has been slow, and local entities only reluctantly support national-level institutions. Banking reform accelerated in 2001 as all the Communist-era payments bureaus were shut down. The country receives substantial amounts of reconstruction assistance and humanitarian aid from the international community but will have to prepare for an era of declining assistance.
GDP: purchasing power parity - $24.39 billion (2003 est.)
GDP - real growth rate: 3.8% (2003 est.)
GDP - per capita: purchasing power parity - $6,100 (2003 est.)
GDP - composition by sector:
agriculture: 13%
industry: 40.9%
services: 46.1% (2001 est.)
Population below poverty line: NA%
Household income or consumption by percentage share:
lowest 10%: NA%
highest 10%: NA%
Inflation rate (consumer prices): 3.5% (2002 est.)
Labor force: 1.026 million (2001)
Labor force - by occupation: agriculture NA%, industry NA%, services NA%
Unemployment rate: 40% (2002 est.)
Budget:
revenues: $1.9 billion
expenditures: $2.2 billion, including capital expenditures of $NA (1999 est.)
Industries: steel, coal, iron ore, lead, zinc, manganese, bauxite, vehicle assembly, textiles, tobacco products, wooden furniture, tank and aircraft assembly, domestic appliances, oil refining (2001)
Industrial production growth rate: 5.5% (2003 est.)
Electricity - production: 9.979 billion kWh (2001)
Electricity - production by source:
fossil fuel: 53.5%
hydro: 46.5%
nuclear: 0%
other: 0% (2001)
Electricity - consumption: 8.116 billion kWh (2001)
Electricity - exports: 2.569 billion kWh (2001)
Electricity - imports: 1.405 billion kWh (2001)
Oil - production: 0 bbl/day (2001 est.)
Oil - consumption: 20,000 bbl/day (2001 est.)
Oil - exports: NA
Oil - imports: NA
Natural gas - production: 0 cu m (2001 est.)
Natural gas - consumption: 300 million cu m (2001 est.)

Bosnia and Herzegovina *(continued)*

Natural gas - exports: 0 cu m (2001 est.)
Natural gas - imports: 300 million cu m (2001 est.)
Agriculture - products: wheat, corn, fruits, vegetables; livestock
Exports: $1.28 billion f.o.b. (2003 est.)
Exports - commodities: metals, clothing, wood products
Exports - partners: Italy 31.6%, Croatia 17.9%, Germany 13.1%, Austria 10%, Slovenia 7.1%, Greece 4.2% (2002)
Imports: $4.7 billion f.o.b. (2003 est.)
Imports - commodities: machinery and equipment, chemicals, fuels, foodstuffs
Imports - partners: Croatia 22.8%, Slovenia 15.3%, Germany 13.7%, Italy 12.6%, Hungary 7.6%, Austria 7.4% (2002)
Debt - external: $2.8 billion (2001)
Economic aid - recipient: $650 million (2001 est.)
Currency: marka (BAM)
Currency code: BAM
Exchange rates: marka per US dollar - 1.7329 (2003), 1.7329 (2002), 2.1857 (2001), 2.1244 (2000), 1.8371 (1999)
Fiscal year: calendar year

Communications

Telephones - main lines in use: 902,800 (2002)
Telephones - mobile cellular: 748,800 (2002)
Telephone system:
general assessment: telephone and telegraph network needs modernization and expansion; many urban areas are below average as contrasted with services in other former Yugoslav republics
domestic: NA
international: country code - 387; no satellite earth stations
Radio broadcast stations: AM 8, FM 16, shortwave 1 (1998)
Television broadcast stations: 33 (plus 277 repeaters) (September 1995)
Internet country code: .ba
Internet hosts: 5,702 (2002)
Internet users: 100,000 (2002)

Transportation

Railways:
total: 1,021 km (795 km electrified)
standard gauge: 1,021 km 1.435-m gauge (2002)
Highways:
total: 21,846 km
paved: 11,424 km
unpaved: 10,422 km (1999 est.)
Waterways: NA km; large sections of the Sava blocked by downed bridges, silt, and debris
Pipelines: gas 170 km; oil 9 km (2003)
Ports and harbors: Bosanska Gradiska, Bosanski Brod, Bosanski Samac, and Brcko (all inland waterway ports on the Sava), Orasje
Merchant marine: none
Airports: 27 (2003 est.)

Airports - with paved runways:
total: 8
2,438 to 3,047 m: 4
1,524 to 2,437 m: 1
under 914 m: 3 (2003 est.)
Airports - with unpaved runways:
total: 19
1,524 to 2,437 m: 1
914 to 1,523 m: 7
under 914 m: 11 (2003 est.)
Heliports: 5 (2003 est.)

Military

Military branches: VF Army (the air and air defense forces are subordinate commands within the Army), VRS Army (the air and air defense forces are subordinate commands within the Army)
Military manpower - military age: 19 years of age (2004 est.)
Military manpower - availability:
males age 15-49: 1,133,847 (2004 est.)
Military manpower - fit for military service:
males age 15-49: 898,451 (2004 est.)
Military manpower - reaching military age annually:
males: 30,130 (2004 est.)
Military expenditures - dollar figure: $234.3 million (FY02)
Military expenditures - percent of GDP: 4.5% (FY02)

Transnational Issues

Disputes - international: Bosnia and Herzegovina and Serbia and Montenegro have delimited most of their boundary, but sections along the Drina River remain in dispute; discussions continue with Croatia on problem sections around Kostajnica on the Una River and villages at the base of Mount Pljesevica
Illicit drugs: minor transit point for marijuana and opiate trafficking routes to Western Europe; remains highly vulnerable to money laundering activity given a primarily cash-based and unregulated economy, weak law enforcement and instances of corruption

Botswana

Introduction

Background: Formerly the British protectorate of Bechuanaland, Botswana adopted its new name upon independence in 1966. Four decades of uninterrupted civilian leadership, progressive social policies, and significant capital investment have created one of the most dynamic economies in Africa. Mineral extraction, principally diamond mining, dominates economic activity, though tourism is a growing sector due to the country's conservation practices and extensive nature preserves. Botswana has the world's highest known rate of HIV/AIDS infection, but also one of Africa's most progressive and comprehensive programs for dealing with the disease.

Geography

Location: Southern Africa, north of South Africa
Geographic coordinates: 22 00 S, 24 00 E
Map references: Africa
Area:
total: 600,370 sq km
land: 585,370 sq km
water: 15,000 sq km
Area - comparative: slightly smaller than Texas
Land boundaries:
total: 4,013 km
border countries: Namibia 1,360 km, South Africa 1,840 km, Zimbabwe 813 km
Coastline: 0 km (landlocked)
Maritime claims: none (landlocked)
Climate: semiarid; warm winters and hot summers
Terrain: predominantly flat to gently rolling tableland; Kalahari Desert in southwest
Elevation extremes:
lowest point: junction of the Limpopo and Shashe Rivers 513 m
highest point: Tsodilo Hills 1,489 m
Natural resources: diamonds, copper, nickel, salt, soda ash, potash, coal, iron ore, silver

Botswana (continued)

Land use:
arable land: 0.61%
permanent crops: 0.01%
other: 99.38% (1998 est.)
Irrigated land: 10 sq km (1998 est.)
Natural hazards: periodic droughts; seasonal August winds blow from the west, carrying sand and dust across the country, which can obscure visibility
Environment - current issues: overgrazing; desertification; limited fresh water resources
Environment - international agreements:
party to: Biodiversity, Climate Change, Climate Change-Kyoto Protocol, Desertification, Endangered Species, Hazardous Wastes, Law of the Sea, Ozone Layer Protection, Wetlands
signed, but not ratified: none of the selected agreements
Geography - note: landlocked; population concentrated in eastern part of the country

People

Population: 1,561,973
note: estimates for this country explicitly take into account the effects of excess mortality due to AIDS; this can result in lower life expectancy, higher infant mortality and death rates, lower population and growth rates, and changes in the distribution of population by age and sex than would otherwise be expected (July 2004 est.)
Age structure:
0-14 years: 39.2% (male 310,282; female 302,452)
15-64 years: 56.2% (male 424,613; female 452,801)
65 years and over: 4.6% (male 30,896; female 40,929) (2004 est.)
Median age:
total: 19.2 years
male: 18.5 years
female: 19.9 years (2004 est.)
Population growth rate: -0.89% (2004 est.)
Birth rate: 24.71 births/1,000 population (2004 est.)
Death rate: 33.63 deaths/1,000 population (2004 est.)
Net migration rate: 0 migrant(s)/1,000 population (2004 est.)
Sex ratio:
at birth: 1.03 male(s)/female
under 15 years: 1.03 male(s)/female
15-64 years: 0.94 male(s)/female
65 years and over: 0.76 male(s)/female
total population: 0.96 male(s)/female (2004 est.)
Infant mortality rate:
total: 69.98 deaths/1,000 live births
male: 70.96 deaths/1,000 live births
female: 68.96 deaths/1,000 live births (2004 est.)
Life expectancy at birth:
total population: 30.76 years
male: 30.99 years
female: 30.53 years (2004 est.)
Total fertility rate: 3.17 children born/woman (2004 est.)
HIV/AIDS - adult prevalence rate: 38.8% (2001 est.)

HIV/AIDS - people living with HIV/AIDS: 330,000 (2001 est.)
HIV/AIDS - deaths: 26,000 (2001 est.)
Nationality:
noun: Motswana (singular), Batswana (plural)
adjective: Motswana (singular), Batswana (plural)
Ethnic groups: Tswana (or Setswana) 79%, Kalanga 11%, Basarwa 3%, other, including Kgalagadi and white 7%
Religions: indigenous beliefs 85%, Christian 15%
Languages: English (official), Setswana
Literacy:
definition: age 15 and over can read and write
total population: 79.8%
male: 76.9%
female: 82.4% (2003 est.)

Government

Country name:
conventional long form: Republic of Botswana
conventional short form: Botswana
former: Bechuanaland
Government type: parliamentary republic
Capital: Gaborone
Administrative divisions: 9 districts and four town councils*; Central, Francistown*, Gaborone*, Ghanzi, Kgalagadi, Kgatleng, Kweneng, Lobatse*, Northwest, Northeast, Selebi-Pikwe*, Southeast, Southern
Independence: 30 September 1966 (from UK)
National holiday: Independence Day (Botswana Day), 30 September (1966)
Constitution: March 1965, effective 30 September 1966
Legal system: based on Roman-Dutch law and local customary law; judicial review limited to matters of interpretation; has not accepted compulsory ICJ jurisdiction
Suffrage: 18 years of age; universal
Executive branch:
chief of state: President Festus MOGAE (since 1 April 1998) and Vice President Seretse Ian KHAMA (since 13 July 1998); note - the president is both the chief of state and head of government
head of government: President Festus MOGAE (since 1 April 1998) and Vice President Seretse Ian KHAMA (since 13 July 1998); note - the president is both the chief of state and head of government
cabinet: Cabinet appointed by the president
elections: president elected by the National Assembly for a five-year term; election last held 16 October 1999 (next to be held NA October 2004); vice president appointed by the president
election results: Festus MOGAE elected president; percent of National Assembly vote - 54.3%
Legislative branch: bicameral Parliament consists of the House of Chiefs (a largely advisory 15-member body consisting of the chiefs of the eight principal tribes, four elected subchiefs, and three members selected by the other 12 members) and the National Assembly (44 seats, 40 members are directly elected by popular vote and 4 are appointed by the majority party; members serve five-year terms)

elections: National Assembly elections last held 16 October 1999 (next to be held NA October 2004)
election results: percent of vote by party - BDP 54.3%, BNF 24.7%, other 21%; seats by party - BDP 33, BNF 6, other 1
Judicial branch: High Court; Court of Appeal; Magistrates' Courts (one in each district)
Political parties and leaders: Botswana Democratic Party or BDP [Seretse Ian KHAMA]; Botswana National Front or BNF [Otswoletse MOUPO]; Botswana Congress Party or BCP [Mokgweetsi KGOSIPULA]; Botswana Alliance Movement or BAM [Ephraim Lepetu SETSHWAELO]
note: a number of minor parties joined forces in 1999 to form the BAM but did not capture any parliamentary seats; the BAM parties are: the United Action Party [Ephraim Lepetu SETSHWAELO], the Independence Freedom Party or IFP [Motsamai MPHO], and the Botswana Progressive Union [D. K. KWELE]
Political pressure groups and leaders: NA
International organization participation: ACP, AfDB, AU, C, FAO, G-77, IAEA, IBRD, ICAO, ICCt, ICFTU, ICRM, IDA, IFAD, IFC, IFRCS, ILO, IMF, Interpol, IOC, ISO, ITU, NAM, OPCW, SACU, SADC, UN, UNCTAD, UNESCO, UNIDO, UPU, WCO, WFTU, WHO, WIPO, WMO, WToO, WTrO
Diplomatic representation in the US:
chief of mission: Ambassador Lapologang Caesar LEKOA
chancery: 1531-1533 New Hampshire Avenue NW, Washington, DC 20036
telephone: [1] (202) 244-4990
FAX: [1] (202) 244-4164
Diplomatic representation from the US:
chief of mission: Ambassador Joseph HUGGINS
embassy: address NA, Gaborone
mailing address: Embassy Enclave, P. O. Box 90, Gaborone
telephone: [267] 353982
FAX: [267] 312782
Flag description: light blue with a horizontal white-edged black stripe in the center

Economy

Economy - overview: Botswana has maintained one of the world's highest growth rates since independence in 1966. Through fiscal discipline and sound management, Botswana has transformed itself from one of the poorest countries in the world to a middle-income country with a per capita GDP of $8,800 in 2003. Two major investment services rank Botswana as the best credit risk in Africa. Diamond mining has fueled much of the expansion and currently accounts for more than one-third of GDP and for nine-tenths of export earnings. Tourism, subsistence farming, and cattle raising are other key sectors. On the downside, the government must deal with high rates of unemployment and poverty. Unemployment officially is 21%, but unofficial estimates place it closer to 40%. HIV/AIDS infection rates are the highest in the world and threaten

Botswana (continued)

Botswana's impressive economic gains. Long-term prospects are overshadowed by the expected leveling off in diamond mining production.

GDP: purchasing power parity - $13.9 billion (2003 est.)

GDP - real growth rate: 7.6% (2003 est.)

GDP - per capita: purchasing power parity - $8,800 (2003 est.)

GDP - composition by sector:
agriculture: 4%
industry: 44% (including 36% mining)
services: 52% (2001 est.)

Population below poverty line: 47% (2002 est.)

Household income or consumption by percentage share:
lowest 10%: NA%
highest 10%: NA%

Inflation rate (consumer prices): 8.1% (2002 est.)

Labor force: 264,000 formal sector employees (2000)

Labor force - by occupation: NA

Unemployment rate: 40% (official rate is 21%) (2001 est.)

Budget:
revenues: $2.3 billion
expenditures: $2.4 billion, including capital expenditures of $NA (FY01/02)

Industries: diamonds, copper, nickel, salt, soda ash, potash; livestock processing; textiles

Industrial production growth rate: 2.4% (2001 est.)

Electricity - production: 409.8 million kWh (2001)

Electricity - production by source:
fossil fuel: 100%
hydro: 0%
nuclear: 0%
other: 0% (2001)

Electricity - consumption: 1.564 billion kWh (2001)

Electricity - exports: 0 kWh (2001)

Electricity - imports: 1.183 billion kWh (2001)

Oil - production: 0 bbl/day (2001 est.)

Oil - consumption: 16,000 bbl/day (2001 est.)

Oil - exports: NA

Oil - imports: NA

Agriculture - products: livestock, sorghum, maize, millet, beans, sunflowers, groundnuts

Exports: $2.544 billion f.o.b. (2003 est.)

Exports - commodities: diamonds, copper, nickel, soda ash, meat, textiles

Exports - partners: European Free Trade Association (EFTA) 87%, Southern African Customs Union (SACU) 7%, Zimbabwe 4% (2000)

Imports: $1.753 billion f.o.b. (2003 est.)

Imports - commodities: foodstuffs, machinery, electrical goods, transport equipment, textiles, fuel and petroleum products, wood and paper products, metal and metal products

Imports - partners: Southern African Customs Union (SACU) 74%, EFTA 17%, Zimbabwe 4% (2000)

Debt - external: $360 million (2002)

Economic aid - recipient: $73 million (1995)

Currency: pula (BWP)

Currency code: BWP

Exchange rates: pulas per US dollar - 4.9499 (2003), 6.3278 (2002), 5.8412 (2001), 5.1018 (2000), 4.6244 (1999)

Fiscal year: 1 April - 31 March

Communications

Telephones - main lines in use: 150,000 (2002)

Telephones - mobile cellular: 415,000 (2002)

Telephone system:
general assessment: the system is expanding with the growth of mobile cellular service and participation in regional development
domestic: small system of open-wire lines, microwave radio relay links, and a few radiotelephone communication stations; mobile cellular service is growing fast
international: country code - 267; two international exchanges; digital microwave radio relay links to Namibia, Zambia, Zimbabwe, and South Africa; satellite earth station - 1 Intelsat (Indian Ocean)

Radio broadcast stations: AM 8, FM 13, shortwave 4 (2001)

Television broadcast stations: 1 (2001)

Internet country code: .bw

Internet hosts: 1,617 (2002)

Internet users: 50,000 (2002)

Transportation

Railways:
total: 888 km
narrow gauge: 888 km 1.067-m gauge (2002)

Highways:
total: 10,217 km
paved: 5,619 km
unpaved: 4,598 km (1999)

Waterways: none

Ports and harbors: none

Airports: 85 (2003 est.)

Airports - with paved runways:
total: 10
2,438 to 3,047 m: 2
1,524 to 2,437 m: 7
914 to 1,523 m: 1 (2003 est.)

Airports - with unpaved runways:
total: 75
1,524 to 2,437 m: 3
914 to 1,523 m: 54
under 914 m: 18 (2003 est.)

Military

Military branches: Botswana Defense Force (including an Air Wing)

Military manpower - military age: 18 years of age (2004 est.)

Military manpower - availability:
males age 15-49: 381,801 (2004 est.)

Military manpower - fit for military service:
males age 15-49: 202,176 (2004 est.)

Military manpower - reaching military age annually:
males: 20,651 (2004 est.)

Military expenditures - dollar figure: $298.9 million (2003)

Military expenditures - percent of GDP: 3.6% (2003)

Transnational Issues

Disputes - international: established a commission with Namibia to resolve small residual disputes along the Caprivi Strip, including the Situngu marshlands along the Linyanti River; downstream Botswana residents protest Namibia's planned construction of the Okavango hydroelectric dam at Popavalle (Popa Falls); Botswana, Namibia, Zambia, and Zimbabwe boundary convergence is not clearly defined or delimited

Bouvet Island

(territory of Norway)

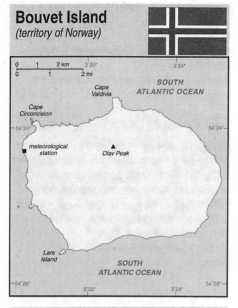

Introduction

Background: This uninhabited volcanic island is almost entirely covered by glaciers and is difficult to approach. It was discovered in 1739 by a French naval officer after whom the island was named. No claim was made until 1825, when the British flag was raised. In 1928, the UK waived its claim in favor of Norway, which had occupied the island the previous year. In 1971, Bouvet Island and the adjacent territorial waters were designated a nature reserve. Since 1977, Norway has run an automated meteorological station on the island.

Geography

Location: island in the South Atlantic Ocean, southwest of the Cape of Good Hope (South Africa)
Geographic coordinates: 54 26 S, 3 24 E
Map references: Antarctic Region
Area:
total: 58.5 sq km
land: 58.5 sq km
water: 0 sq km
Area - comparative: about 0.3 times the size of Washington, DC
Land boundaries: 0 km
Coastline: 29.6 km
Maritime claims:
territorial sea: 4 NM
Climate: antarctic
Terrain: volcanic; coast is mostly inaccessible
Elevation extremes:
lowest point: South Atlantic Ocean 0 m
highest point: Olav Peak 935 m
Natural resources: none
Land use:
arable land: 0%
permanent crops: 0%
other: 100% (93% ice) (1998 est.)
Irrigated land: 0 sq km (1998 est.)
Natural hazards: NA

Environment - current issues: NA
Geography - note: covered by glacial ice; declared a nature reserve

People

Population: uninhabited (July 2004 est.)

Government

Country name:
conventional long form: none
conventional short form: Bouvet Island
Dependency status: territory of Norway; administered by the Polar Department of the Ministry of Justice and Police from Oslo
Legal system: the laws of Norway, where applicable, apply
Flag description: the flag of Norway is used

Economy

Economy - overview: no economic activity; declared a nature reserve

Communications

Internet country code: .bv
Communications - note: automatic meteorological station

Transportation

Waterways: none
Ports and harbors: none; offshore anchorage only

Military

Military - note: defense is the responsibility of Norway

Transnational Issues

Disputes - international: none

Brazil

Introduction

Background: Following three centuries under the rule of Portugal, Brazil became an independent nation in 1822. By far the largest and most populous country in South America, Brazil has overcome more than half a century of military intervention in the governance of the country to pursue industrial and agricultural growth and development of the interior. Exploiting vast natural resources and a large labor pool, Brazil is today South America's leading economic power and a regional leader. Highly unequal income distribution remains a pressing problem.

Geography

Location: Eastern South America, bordering the Atlantic Ocean
Geographic coordinates: 10 00 S, 55 00 W
Map references: South America
Area:
total: 8,511,965 sq km
land: 8,456,510 sq km
water: 55,455 sq km
note: includes Arquipelago de Fernando de Noronha, Atol das Rocas, Ilha da Trindade, Ilhas Martin Vaz, and Penedos de Sao Pedro e Sao Paulo
Area - comparative: slightly smaller than the US
Land boundaries:
total: 14,691 km
border countries: Argentina 1,224 km, Bolivia 3,400 km, Colombia 1,643 km, French Guiana 673 km, Guyana 1,119 km, Paraguay 1,290 km, Peru 1,560 km, Suriname 597 km, Uruguay 985 km, Venezuela 2,200 km
Coastline: 7,491 km
Maritime claims:
territorial sea: 12 NM
contiguous zone: 24 NM
exclusive economic zone: 200 NM
continental shelf: 200 NM or to edge of the continental margin

Brazil *(continued)*

Climate: mostly tropical, but temperate in south
Terrain: mostly flat to rolling lowlands in north; some plains, hills, mountains, and narrow coastal belt
Elevation extremes:
lowest point: Atlantic Ocean 0 m
highest point: Pico da Neblina 3,014 m
Natural resources: bauxite, gold, iron ore, manganese, nickel, phosphates, platinum, tin, uranium, petroleum, hydropower, timber
Land use:
arable land: 6.3%
permanent crops: 1.42%
other: 92.28% (1998 est.)
Irrigated land: 26,560 sq km (1998 est.)
Natural hazards: recurring droughts in northeast; floods and occasional frost in south
Environment - current issues: deforestation in Amazon Basin destroys the habitat and endangers a multitude of plant and animal species indigenous to the area; there is a lucrative illegal wildlife trade; air and water pollution in Rio de Janeiro, Sao Paulo, and several other large cities; land degradation and water pollution caused by improper mining activities; wetland degradation; severe oil spills
Environment - international agreements:
party to: Antarctic-Environmental Protocol, Antarctic-Marine Living Resources, Antarctic Seals, Antarctic Treaty, Biodiversity, Climate Change, Climate Change-Kyoto Protocol, Desertification, Endangered Species, Environmental Modification, Hazardous Wastes, Law of the Sea, Marine Dumping, Ozone Layer Protection, Ship Pollution, Tropical Timber 83, Tropical Timber 94, Wetlands, Whaling
signed, but not ratified: none of the selected agreements
Geography - note: largest country in South America; shares common boundaries with every South American country except Chile and Ecuador

People

Population: 184,101,109
note: Brazil took a count in August 2000, which reported a population of 169,799,170; that figure was about 3.3% lower than projections by the US Census Bureau, and is close to the implied underenumeration of 4.6% for the 1991 census; estimates for this country explicitly take into account the effects of excess mortality due to AIDS; this can result in lower life expectancy, higher infant mortality and death rates, lower population and growth rates, and changes in the distribution of population by age and sex than would otherwise be expected (July 2004 est.)
Age structure:
0-14 years: 26.6% (male 24,915,902; female 23,966,713)
15-64 years: 67.6% (male 61,739,012; female 62,770,480)
65 years and over: 5.8% (male 4,389,659; female 6,319,343) (2004 est.)

Median age:
total: 27.4 years
male: 26.7 years
female: 28.2 years (2004 est.)
Population growth rate: 1.11% (2004 est.)
Birth rate: 17.25 births/1,000 population (2004 est.)
Death rate: 6.14 deaths/1,000 population (2004 est.)
Net migration rate: -0.03 migrant(s)/1,000 population (2004 est.)
Sex ratio:
at birth: 1.05 male(s)/female
under 15 years: 1.04 male(s)/female
15-64 years: 0.98 male(s)/female
65 years and over: 0.7 male(s)/female
total population: 0.98 male(s)/female (2004 est.)
Infant mortality rate:
total: 30.66 deaths/1,000 live births
male: 34.47 deaths/1,000 live births
female: 26.65 deaths/1,000 live births (2004 est.)
Life expectancy at birth:
total population: 71.41 years
male: 67.45 years
female: 75.57 years (2004 est.)
Total fertility rate: 1.97 children born/woman (2004 est.)
HIV/AIDS - adult prevalence rate: 0.7% (2001 est.)
HIV/AIDS - people living with HIV/AIDS: 610,000 (2001 est.)
HIV/AIDS - deaths: 8,400 (2001 est.)
Nationality:
noun: Brazilian(s)
adjective: Brazilian
Ethnic groups: white (includes Portuguese, German, Italian, Spanish, Polish) 55%, mixed white and black 38%, black 6%, other (includes Japanese, Arab, Amerindian) 1%
Religions: Roman Catholic (nominal) 80%
Languages: Portuguese (official), Spanish, English, French
Literacy:
definition: age 15 and over can read and write
total population: 86.4%
male: 86.1%
female: 86.6% (2003 est.)

Government

Country name:
conventional long form: Federative Republic of Brazil
conventional short form: Brazil
local long form: Republica Federativa do Brasil
local short form: Brasil
Government type: federative republic
Capital: Brasilia
Administrative divisions: 26 states (estados, singular - estado) and 1 federal district* (distrito federal); Acre, Alagoas, Amapa, Amazonas, Bahia, Ceara, Distrito Federal*, Espirito Santo, Goias, Maranhao, Mato Grosso, Mato Grosso do Sul, Minas Gerais, Para, Paraiba, Parana, Pernambuco, Piaui, Rio de Janeiro, Rio Grande do Norte, Rio Grande do Sul, Rondonia, Roraima, Santa Catarina, Sao Paulo, Sergipe, Tocantins

Independence: 7 September 1822 (from Portugal)
National holiday: Independence Day, 7 September (1822)
Constitution: 5 October 1988
Legal system: based on Roman codes; has not accepted compulsory ICJ jurisdiction
Suffrage: voluntary between 16 and 18 years of age and over 70; compulsory over 18 and under 70 years of age
Executive branch:
chief of state: President Luiz Inacio "Lula" DA SILVA (since 1 January 2003); Vice President Jose ALENCAR (since 1 January 2003); note - the president is both the chief of state and head of government
head of government: President Luiz Inacio "Lula" DA SILVA (since 1 January 2003); Vice President Jose ALENCAR (since 1 January 2003); note - the president is both the chief of state and head of government
cabinet: Cabinet appointed by the president
elections: president and vice president elected on the same ticket by popular vote for four-year terms; election last held 6 October 2002 (next to be held NA October 2006); runoff election held 27 October 2002
election results: in runoff election 27 October 2002, Luiz Inacio "Lula" DA SILVA (PT) was elected with 61.3% of the vote; Jose SERRA (PSDB) 38.7%
Legislative branch: bicameral National Congress or Congresso Nacional consists of the Federal Senate or Senado Federal (81 seats; three members from each state or federal district elected according to the principle of majority to serve eight-year terms; one-third elected after a four-year period, two-thirds elected after the next four-year period) and the Chamber of Deputies or Camara dos Deputados (513 seats; members are elected by proportional representation to serve four-year terms)
elections: Federal Senate - last held 6 October 2002 for two-thirds of the Senate (next to be held NA October 2006 for one-third of the Senate); Chamber of Deputies - last held 6 October 2002 (next to be held NA October 2006)
election results: Federal Senate - percent of vote by party - NA%; seats by party PMBD 19, PFL 19, PT 14, PSDB 11, PDT 5, PSB 4, PL 3, PTB 3, PPS 1, PSD 1, PP 1; Chamber of Deputies - percent of vote by party - NA%; seats by party - PT 91, PFL 84, PMDB 74, PSDB 71, PP 49, PL 26, PTB 26, PSB 22, PDT 21, PPS 15, PCdoB 12, PRONA 6, PV 5, other 11; note - many congressmen have changed party affiliation since the election
Judicial branch: Supreme Federal Tribunal (11 ministers are appointed by the president and confirmed by the Senate); Higher Tribunal of Justice; Regional Federal Tribunals (judges are appointed for life)
Political parties and leaders: Brazilian Democratic Movement Party or PMDB [Michel TEMER]; Brazilian Labor Party or PTB [Roberto JEFFERSON]; Brazilian Social Democracy Party or PSDB [Senator Jose

Brazil *(continued)*

SERRA]; Brazilian Socialist Party or PSB [Miguel ARRAES]; Brazilian Progressive Party or PP [Paulo Salim MALUF]; Communist Party of Brazil or PCdoB [Renato RABELO]; Democratic Labor Party or PDT [Leonel BRIZOLA]; Green Party or PV [Jose Luiz DE FRANCA Penna]; Liberal Front Party or PFL [Jorge BORNHAUSEN]; Liberal Party or PL [Deputy Valdemar COSTA Neto]; National Order Reconstruction Party or PRONA [Dr. Eneas CARNEIRO]; Popular Socialist Party or PPS [Senator Roberto FREIRE]; Social Democratic Party or PSD [leader NA]; Worker's Party or PT [Jose GENOINO]

Political pressure groups and leaders: left wing of the Catholic Church; Landless Worker's Movement; labor unions allied to leftist Workers' Party

International organization participation: AfDB, BIS, FAO, G-15, G-24, G-77, IADB, IAEA, IBRD, ICAO, ICC, ICCt, ICFTU, ICRM, IDA, IFAD, IFC, IFRCS, IHO, ILO, IMF, IMO, Interpol, IOC, IOM (observer), ISO, ITU, LAES, LAIA, Mercosur, NAM (observer), NSG, OAS, OPANAL, OPCW, PCA, RG, UN, UN Security Council (temporary), UNCTAD, UNESCO, UNHCR, UNIDO, UNITAR, UNMIL, UNMISET, UNMOVIC, UPU, WCL, WCO, WFTU, WHO, WIPO, WMO, WToO, WTrO

Diplomatic representation in the US:
chief of mission: Ambassador Roberto ABDENUR
chancery: 3006 Massachusetts Avenue NW, Washington, DC 20008
telephone: [1] (202) 238-2700
FAX: [1] (202) 238-2827
consulate(s) general: Boston, Chicago, Houston, Los Angeles, Miami, New York, and San Francisco

Diplomatic representation from the US:
chief of mission: Ambassador Donna J. HRINAK
embassy: Avenida das Nacoes, Quadra 801, Lote 3, Distrito Federal Cep 70403-900, Brasilia
mailing address: Unit 3500, APO AA 34030
telephone: [55] (61) 312-7000
FAX: [55] (61) 225-9136
consulate(s) general: Rio de Janeiro, Sao Paulo
consulate(s): Recife

Flag description: green with a large yellow diamond in the center bearing a blue celestial globe with 27 white five-pointed stars (one for each state and the Federal District) arranged in the same pattern as the night sky over Brazil; the globe has a white equatorial band with the motto ORDEM E PROGRESSO (Order and Progress)

Economy

Economy - overview: Possessing large and well-developed agricultural, mining, manufacturing, and service sectors, Brazil's economy outweighs that of all other South American countries and is expanding its presence in world markets. From 2001-03 real wages fell and Brazil's economy grew, on average, only 1.1% per year, as the country absorbed a series of domestic and international economic shocks. That Brazil absorbed these shocks without financial collapse is a tribute to the resiliency

of the Brazilian economy and the economic program put in place by former President CARDOSO and strengthened by President Lula DA SILVA. The three pillars of the economic program are a floating exchange rate, an inflation-targeting regime, and tight fiscal policy, which have been reinforced by a series of IMF programs. The currency depreciated sharply in 2001 and 2002, which contributed to a dramatic current account adjustment: in 2003, Brazil ran a record trade surplus and recorded the first current account surplus since 1992. While economic management has been good, there remain important economic vulnerabilities. The most significant are debt-related: the government's largely domestic debt increased steadily from 1994 to 2003, straining government finances, while Brazil's foreign debt (a mix of private and public debt) is large in relation to Brazil's modest (but growing) export base. Another challenge is maintaining economic growth over a period of time to generate employment and make the government debt burden more manageable.

GDP: purchasing power parity - $1.379 trillion (2003 est.)

GDP - real growth rate: 0.1% (2003 est.)

GDP - per capita: purchasing power parity - $7,600 (2003 est.)

GDP - composition by sector:
agriculture: 8.2%
industry: 37.8%
services: 53.9% (2002 est.)

Population below poverty line: 22% (1998 est.)

Household income or consumption by percentage share:
lowest 10%: 0.7%
highest 10%: 48% (1998)

Distribution of family income - Gini index: 60.7 (1998)

Inflation rate (consumer prices): 9.3% (2003)

Labor force: 79 million (1999 est.)

Labor force - by occupation: services 53%, agriculture 23%, industry 24%

Unemployment rate: 12.2% (2003 est.)

Budget:
revenues: $100.6 billion
expenditures: $91.6 billion, including capital expenditures of $NA (2000)

Industries: textiles, shoes, chemicals, cement, lumber, iron ore, tin, steel, aircraft, motor vehicles and parts, other machinery and equipment

Industrial production growth rate: 3.4% (2003 est.)

Electricity - production: 321.2 billion kWh (2001)

Electricity - production by source:
fossil fuel: 8.3%
hydro: 82.7%
nuclear: 4.4%
other: 4.6% (2001)

Electricity - consumption: 335.9 billion kWh (2001)

Electricity - exports: 0 kWh (2001)

Electricity - imports: 37.19 billion kWh; note - supplied by Paraguay (2001)

Oil - production: 1.561 million bbl/day (2001 est.)

Oil - consumption: 2.199 million bbl/day (2001 est.)

Oil - exports: NA

Oil - imports: NA

Oil - proved reserves: 8.507 billion bbl (1 January 2002)

Natural gas - production: 5.95 billion cu m (2001 est.)

Natural gas - consumption: 9.59 billion cu m (2001 est.)

Natural gas - exports: 0 cu m (2001 est.)

Natural gas - imports: 3.64 billion cu m (2001 est.)

Natural gas - proved reserves: 221.7 billion cu m (1 January 2002)

Agriculture - products: coffee, soybeans, wheat, rice, corn, sugarcane, cocoa, citrus; beef

Exports: $73.28 billion f.o.b. (2003 est.)

Exports - commodities: transport equipment, iron ore, soybeans, footwear, coffee, autos

Exports - partners: US 25.8%, Netherlands 5.3%, Germany 4.2%, China 4.2% (2002)

Imports: $48.25 billion f.o.b. (2003 est.)

Imports - commodities: machinery, electrical and transport equipment, chemical products, oil

Imports - partners: US 22.1%, Argentina 10.1%, Germany 9.3%, Japan 5% (2002)

Debt - external: $223.6 billion (2003)

Economic aid - recipient: $30 billion IMF disbursement (2002)

Currency: real (BRL)

Currency code: BRL

Exchange rates: reals per US dollar - 3.0771 (2003), 2.9208 (2002), 2.3577 (2001), 1.8301 (2000), 1.8147 (1999)

note: from October 1994 through 14 January 1999, the official rate was determined by a managed float; since 15 January 1999, the official rate floats independently with respect to the US dollar

Fiscal year: calendar year

Communications

Telephones - main lines in use: 38.81 million (2002)

Telephones - mobile cellular: 34.881 million (2002)

Telephone system:
general assessment: good working system
domestic: extensive microwave radio relay system and a domestic satellite system with 64 earth stations
international: country code - 55; 3 coaxial submarine cables; satellite earth stations - 3 Intelsat (Atlantic Ocean), 1 Inmarsat (Atlantic Ocean region east), connected by microwave relay system to Mercosur Brazilsat B3 satellite earth station

Radio broadcast stations: AM 1,365, FM 296, shortwave 161 (of which 91 are collocated with AM stations) (1999)

Television broadcast stations: 138 (1997)

Internet country code: .br

Internet hosts: 2,237,527 (2002)

Internet users: 14.3 million (2002)

Brazil (continued)

Transportation

Railways:
total: 31,543 km (1,981 km electrified)
broad gauge: 4,961 km 1.600-m gauge (692 km electrified)
standard gauge: 194 km 1.440-m gauge (630 km electrified)
narrow gauge: 25,992 km 1.000-m gauge (581 km electrified)
dual gauge: 396 km 1.000-m and 1.600-m gauges (three rails) (78 km electrified) (2002)

Highways:
total: 1,724,929 km
paved: 94,871 km
unpaved: 1,630,058 km (2000)

Waterways: 50,000 km

Pipelines: condensate/gas 243 km; gas 10,984 km; liquid petroleum gas 341 km; oil 5,113 km; refined products 4,800 km (2003)

Ports and harbors: Belem, Fortaleza, Ilheus, Imbituba, Manaus, Paranagua, Porto Alegre, Recife, Rio de Janeiro, Rio Grande, Salvador, Santos, Vitoria

Merchant marine:
total: 151 ships (1,000 GRT or over) 2,961,431 GRT/4,725,267 DWT
by type: bulk 29, cargo 22, chemical tanker 7, combination ore/oil 6, container 12, liquefied gas 12, multi-functional large load carrier 1, passenger/cargo 5, petroleum tanker 48, roll on/roll off 8, short-sea/passenger 1
foreign-owned: Chile 2, Germany 7, Monaco 9, Panama 1, Spain 7
registered in other countries: 11 (2003 est.)

Airports: 3,803 (2003 est.)

Airports - with paved runways:
total: 677
over 3,047 m: 7
2,438 to 3,047 m: 23
1,524 to 2,437 m: 157
914 to 1,523 m: 445
under 914 m: 45 (2003 est.)

Airports - with unpaved runways:
total: 3,126
1,524 to 2,437 m: 75
914 to 1,523 m: 1,434
under 914 m: 1,617 (2003 est.)

Heliports: 417 (2003 est.)

Military

Military branches: Brazilian Army, Brazilian Navy (including Naval Air and Marines), Brazilian Air Force (FAB)

Military manpower - military age: 18 years of age (2004 est.)

Military manpower - availability:
males age 15-49: 52,100,042 (2004 est.)

Military manpower - fit for military service:
males age 15-49: 34,799,098 (2004 est.)

Military manpower - reaching military age annually:
males: 1,788,495 (2004 est.)

Military expenditures - dollar figure:
$10,439,400,000 (2003)

Military expenditures - percent of GDP: 2.1% (2003)

Transnational Issues

Disputes - international: unruly region at convergence of Argentina-Brazil-Paraguay borders is locus of money laundering, smuggling, arms and drug trafficking, and fundraising for extremist organizations; uncontested dispute with Uruguay over certain islands in the Quarai/Cuareim and Invernada boundary streams and the resulting tripoint with Argentina

Illicit drugs: illicit producer of cannabis; minor coca cultivation in the Amazon region, used for domestic consumption; government has a large-scale eradication program to control cannabis; important transshipment country for Bolivian, Colombian and Peruvian cocaine headed for Europe and the US; also used by traffickers as a way station for narcotics air transshipments between Peru and Colombia; upsurge in drug-related violence and weapons smuggling; important market for Colombian, Bolivian, and Peruvian cocaine; illicit narcotics proceeds earned in Brazil are often laundered through the financial system; significant illicit financial activity in the Tri-Border Area

---

British Indian Ocean Territory
(overseas territory of the UK)

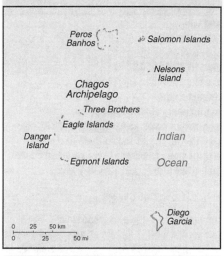

Introduction

Background: Established as a territory of the UK in 1965, a number of the British Indian Ocean Territory (BIOT) islands were transferred to the Seychelles when it attained independence in 1976. Subsequently, BIOT has consisted only of the six main island groups comprising the Chagos Archipelago. The largest and most southerly of the islands, Diego Garcia, contains a joint UK-US naval support facility. All of the remaining islands are uninhabited. Former agricultural workers, earlier residents in the islands, were relocated primarily to Mauritius but also to the Seychelles, between 1967 and 1973. In 2000, a British High Court ruling invalidated the local immigration order that had excluded them from the archipelago, but upheld the special military status of Diego Garcia.

Geography

Location: archipelago in the Indian Ocean, south of India, about one-half the way from Africa to Indonesia

Geographic coordinates: 6 00 S, 71 30 E

Map references: Political Map of the World

Area:
total: 60 sq km
land: 60 sq km
water: 0 sq km
note: includes the entire Chagos Archipelago

Area - comparative: about 0.3 times the size of Washington, DC

Land boundaries: 0 km

Coastline: 698 km

Maritime claims:
territorial sea: 3 NM
exclusive fishing zone: 200 NM

Climate: tropical marine; hot, humid, moderated by trade winds

British Indian Ocean Territory *(continued)*

Terrain: flat and low (most areas do not exceed four meters in elevation)
Elevation extremes:
lowest point: Indian Ocean 0 m
highest point: unnamed location on Diego Garcia 15 m
Natural resources: coconuts, fish, sugarcane
Land use:
arable land: NEGL
permanent crops: 0%
other: 100% (1998 est.)
Irrigated land: 0 sq km (1998 est.)
Natural hazards: NA
Environment - current issues: NA
Geography - note: archipelago of 2,300 islands; Diego Garcia, largest and southernmost island, occupies strategic location in central Indian Ocean; island is site of joint US-UK military facility

People

Population: no indigenous inhabitants
note: approximately 1,200 former agricultural workers resident in the Chagos Archipelago, often referred to as Chagossians or Ilois, were relocated to Mauritius and the Seychelles in the 1960s and 1970s, in November 2000 they were granted the right of return by a British High Court ruling, though no timetable has been set; in 2001, there were approximately 1,500 UK and US military personnel and 2,000 civilian contractors living on the island of Diego Garcia (July 2004 est.)

Government

Country name:
conventional long form: British Indian Ocean Territory
conventional short form: none
abbreviation: BIOT
Dependency status: overseas territory of the UK; administered by a commissioner, resident in the Foreign and Commonwealth Office in London
Legal system: the laws of the UK, where applicable, apply
Executive branch:
chief of state: Queen ELIZABETH II (since 6 February 1952)
head of government: Commissioner Tony CROMBIE (since January 2004); Administrator Charles A. HAMILTON (since 2002); note - both reside in the UK
cabinet: NA
elections: none; the monarch is hereditary; commissioner and administrator appointed by the monarch
Diplomatic representation in the US: none (overseas territory of the UK)
Diplomatic representation from the US: none (overseas territory of the UK)
Flag description: white with six blue wavy horizontal stripes; the flag of the UK is in the upper hoist-side quadrant; the striped section bears a palm tree and yellow crown centered on the outer half of the flag

Economy

Economy - overview: All economic activity is concentrated on the largest island of Diego Garcia, where joint UK-US defense facilities are located. Construction projects and various services needed to support the military installations are done by military and contract employees from the UK, Mauritius, the Philippines, and the US. There are no industrial or agricultural activities on the islands. When the Ilois return, they plan to reestablish sugarcane production and fishing.
Electricity - production: NA kWh; note - electricity supplied by the US military
Electricity - consumption: NA kWh

Communications

Telephones - main lines in use: NA
Telephone system:
general assessment: separate facilities for military and public needs are available
domestic: all commercial telephone services are available, including connection to the Internet
international: international telephone service is carried by satellite (2000)
Radio broadcast stations: AM 1, FM 2, shortwave 0 (1998)
Television broadcast stations: 1 (1997)
Internet country code: .io

Transportation

Highways:
total: NA km
paved: short section of paved road between port and airfield on Diego Garcia
unpaved: NA km
Waterways: none
Ports and harbors: Diego Garcia
Airports: 1 (2003 est.)
Airports - with paved runways:
total: 1
over 3,047 m: 1 (2003 est.)

Military

Military - note: defense is the responsibility of the UK; the US lease on Diego Garcia expires in 2016

Transnational Issues

Disputes - international: Mauritius and Seychelles claim the Chagos Archipelago and its former inhabitants, who reside chiefly in Mauritius, but in 2001 were granted UK citizenship and the right to repatriation since eviction in 1965; the UK resists the Chagossians' demand for an immediate return to the islands; repatriation is complicated by the exclusive US military lease of Diego Garcia that restricted access to the largest island in the chain

British Virgin Islands
(overseas territory of the UK)

Background: First settled by the Dutch in 1648, the islands were annexed in 1672 by the English. The economy is closely tied to the larger and more populous US Virgin Islands to the west; the US dollar is the legal currency.

Geography

Location: Caribbean, between the Caribbean Sea and the North Atlantic Ocean, east of Puerto Rico
Geographic coordinates: 18 30 N, 64 30 W
Map references: Central America and the Caribbean
Area:
total: 153 sq km
land: 153 sq km
water: 0 sq km
note: comprised of 16 inhabited and more than 20 uninhabited islands; includes the island of Anegada
Area - comparative: about 0.9 times the size of Washington, DC
Land boundaries: 0 km
Coastline: 80 km
Maritime claims:
territorial sea: 3 NM
exclusive fishing zone: 200 NM
Climate: subtropical; humid; temperatures moderated by trade winds
Terrain: coral islands relatively flat; volcanic islands steep, hilly
Elevation extremes:
lowest point: Caribbean Sea 0 m
highest point: Mount Sage 521 m
Natural resources: NEGL
Land use:
arable land: 20%
permanent crops: 6.67%
other: 73.33% (1998 est.)

British Virgin Islands *(continued)*

Irrigated land: NA sq km
Natural hazards: hurricanes and tropical storms (July to October)
Environment - current issues: limited natural fresh water resources (except for a few seasonal streams and springs on Tortola, most of the islands' water supply comes from wells and rainwater catchments)
Geography - note: strong ties to nearby US Virgin Islands and Puerto Rico

People

Population: 22,187 (July 2004 est.)
Age structure:
0-14 years: 21.5% (male 2,402; female 2,361)
15-64 years: 73.5% (male 8,395; female 7,911)
65 years and over: 5% (male 594; female 524) (2004 est.)
Median age:
total: 30.9 years
male: 31.1 years
female: 30.7 years (2004 est.)
Population growth rate: 2.06% (2004 est.)
Birth rate: 14.96 births/1,000 population (2004 est.)
Death rate: 4.42 deaths/1,000 population (2004 est.)
Net migration rate: 10.01 migrant(s)/1,000 population (2004 est.)
Sex ratio:
at birth: 1.05 male(s)/female
under 15 years: 1.02 male(s)/female
15-64 years: 1.06 male(s)/female
65 years and over: 1.13 male(s)/female
total population: 1.06 male(s)/female (2004 est.)
Infant mortality rate:
total: 18.05 deaths/1,000 live births
male: 21.02 deaths/1,000 live births
female: 14.95 deaths/1,000 live births (2004 est.)
Life expectancy at birth:
total population: 76.27 years
male: 75.24 years
female: 77.36 years (2004 est.)
Total fertility rate: 1.72 children born/woman (2004 est.)
HIV/AIDS - adult prevalence rate: NA%
HIV/AIDS - people living with HIV/AIDS: NA
HIV/AIDS - deaths: NA
Nationality:
noun: British Virgin Islander(s)
adjective: British Virgin Islander
Ethnic groups: black 83%, white, Indian, Asian and mixed
Religions: Protestant 86% (Methodist 33%, Anglican 17%, Church of God 9%, Seventh-Day Adventist 6%, Baptist 4%, Jehovah's Witnesses 2%, other 15%), Roman Catholic 10%, none 2%, other 2% (1991)
Languages: English (official)
Literacy:
definition: age 15 and over can read and write
total population: 97.8% (1991 est.)
male: NA%
female: NA%

Government

Country name:
conventional long form: none
conventional short form: British Virgin Islands
abbreviation: BVI
Dependency status: overseas territory of the UK; internal self-governing
Government type: NA
Capital: Road Town
Administrative divisions: none (overseas territory of the UK)
Independence: none (overseas territory of the UK)
National holiday: Territory Day, 1 July
Constitution: 1 June 1977
Legal system: English law
Suffrage: 18 years of age; universal
Executive branch:
chief of state: Queen ELIZABETH II (since 6 February 1952), represented by Governor Tom MACAN (since 14 October 2002)
head of government: Chief Minister Orlando D. SMITH (since 17 June 2003)
cabinet: Executive Council appointed by the governor from members of the Legislative Council
elections: none; the monarch is hereditary; governor appointed by the monarch; following legislative elections, the leader of the majority party or the leader of the majority coalition is usually appointed chief minister by the governor
Legislative branch: unicameral Legislative Council (13 seats; members are elected by direct popular vote, one member from each of 9 electoral districts, four at-large members; members serve four-year terms)
elections: last held 16 May 2003 (next to be held NA 2007)
election results: percent of vote by party - NA%; seats by party - NDP 8, VIP 5
Judicial branch: Eastern Caribbean Supreme Court, consisting of the High Court of Justice and the Court of Appeal (one judge of the Supreme Court is a resident of the islands and presides over the High Court); Magistrate's Court; Juvenile Court; Court of Summary Jurisdiction
Political parties and leaders: Concerned Citizens Movement or CCM [Ethlyn SMITH]; National Democratic Party or NDP [Orlando SMITH]; United Party or UP [Gregory MADURO]; Virgin Islands Party or VIP [Ralph T. O'NEAL]
Political pressure groups and leaders: NA
International organization participation: Caricom (associate), CDB, Interpol (subbureau), IOC, OECS (associate), UNESCO (associate)
Diplomatic representation in the US: none (overseas territory of the UK)
Diplomatic representation from the US: none (overseas territory of the UK)
Flag description: blue, with the flag of the UK in the upper hoist-side quadrant and the Virgin Islander coat of arms centered in the outer half of the flag; the coat of arms depicts a woman flanked on either side by a vertical column of six oil lamps above a scroll bearing the Latin word VIGILATE (Be Watchful)

Economy

Economy - overview: The economy, one of the most stable and prosperous in the Caribbean, is highly dependent on tourism, generating an estimated 45% of the national income. An estimated 350,000 tourists, mainly from the US, visited the islands in 1998. Tourism suffered in 2002 because of the lackluster US economy. In the mid-1980s, the government began offering offshore registration to companies wishing to incorporate in the islands, and incorporation fees now generate substantial revenues. Roughly 400,000 companies were on the offshore registry by yearend 2000. The adoption of a comprehensive insurance law in late 1994, which provides a blanket of confidentiality with regulated statutory gateways for investigation of criminal offenses, is expected to make the British Virgin Islands even more attractive to international business. Livestock raising is the most important agricultural activity; poor soils limit the islands' ability to meet domestic food requirements. Because of traditionally close links with the US Virgin Islands, the British Virgin Islands has used the dollar as its currency since 1959.
GDP: purchasing power parity - $320 million (2002 est.)
GDP - real growth rate: 1% (2002 est.)
GDP - per capita: purchasing power parity - $16,000 (2002 est.)
GDP - composition by sector:
agriculture: 1.8%
industry: 6.2%
services: 92% (1996 est.)
Population below poverty line: NA%
Household income or consumption by percentage share:
lowest 10%: NA%
highest 10%: NA%
Inflation rate (consumer prices): 2.5% (2002)
Labor force: 4,911 (1980)
Labor force - by occupation: agriculture NA%, industry NA%, services NA%
Unemployment rate: 3% (1995)
Budget:
revenues: $121.5 million
expenditures: $115.5 million, including capital expenditures of $NA (1997)
Industries: tourism, light industry, construction, rum, concrete block, offshore financial center
Industrial production growth rate: NA
Electricity - production: 38.1 million kWh (2001)
Electricity - production by source:
fossil fuel: 100%
hydro: 0%
nuclear: 0%
other: 0% (2001)
Electricity - consumption: 35.43 million kWh (2001)
Electricity - exports: 0 kWh (2001)
Electricity - imports: 0 kWh (2001)
Oil - production: 0 bbl/day (2001 est.)
Oil - consumption: 420 bbl/day (2001 est.)

British Virgin Islands (continued)

Oil - exports: NA
Oil - imports: NA
Agriculture - products: fruits, vegetables; livestock, poultry; fish
Exports: $25.3 million (2002)
Exports - commodities: rum, fresh fish, fruits, animals; gravel, sand
Exports - partners: Virgin Islands (US), Puerto Rico, US
Imports: $187 million (2002 est.)
Imports - commodities: building materials, automobiles, foodstuffs, machinery
Imports - partners: Virgin Islands (US), Puerto Rico, US
Debt - external: $36.1 million (1997)
Economic aid - recipient: NA%
Currency: US dollar (USD)
Currency code: USD
Exchange rates: the US dollar is used
Fiscal year: 1 April - 31 March

Communications

Telephones - main lines in use: 11,700 (2002)
Telephones - mobile cellular: 8,000 (2002)
Telephone system:
general assessment: worldwide telephone service
domestic: NA
international: country code - 1-284; submarine cable to Bermuda
Radio broadcast stations: AM 1, FM 4, shortwave 0 (1998)
Television broadcast stations: 1 (plus one cable company) (1997)
Internet country code: .vg
Internet users: NA

Transportation

Railways: 0 km
Highways:
total: 177 km
paved: 177 km
unpaved: 0 km (2000)
Waterways: none
Ports and harbors: Road Town
Merchant marine:
total: 3 ships (1,000 GRT or over) 83,825 GRT/ 155,909 DWT
by type: cargo 1, liquefied gas 1, petroleum tanker 1
foreign-owned: Norway 1
registered in other countries: 32 (2003 est.)
Airports: 3 (2003 est.)
Airports - with paved runways:
total: 2
914 to 1,523 m: 1
under 914 m: 1 (2003 est.)
Airports - with unpaved runways:
total: 1
914 to 1,523 m: 1 (2003 est.)

Military

Military - note: defense is the responsibility of the UK

Transnational Issues

Disputes - international: none
Illicit drugs: transshipment point for South American narcotics destined for the US and Europe; large offshore financial center makes it vulnerable to money laundering

Brunei

Introduction

Background: The Sultanate of Brunei's influence peaked between the 15th and 17th centuries when its control extended over coastal areas of northwest Borneo and the southern Philippines. Brunei subsequently entered a period of decline brought on by internal strife over royal succession, colonial expansion of European powers, and piracy. In 1888, Brunei became a British protectorate; independence was achieved in 1984. The same family has ruled Brunei for over six centuries. Brunei benefits from extensive petroleum and natural gas fields, the source of one of the highest per capita GDPs in the developing world.

Geography

Location: Southeastern Asia, bordering the South China Sea and Malaysia
Geographic coordinates: 4 30 N, 114 40 E
Map references: Southeast Asia
Area:
total: 5,770 sq km
land: 5,270 sq km
water: 500 sq km
Area - comparative: slightly smaller than Delaware
Land boundaries:
total: 381 km
border countries: Malaysia 381 km
Coastline: 161 km
Maritime claims:
territorial sea: 12 NM
exclusive economic zone: 200 NM or to median line
Climate: tropical; hot, humid, rainy
Terrain: flat coastal plain rises to mountains in east; hilly lowland in west
Elevation extremes:
lowest point: South China Sea 0 m
highest point: Bukit Pagon 1,850 m

Brunei *(continued)*

Natural resources: petroleum, natural gas, timber
Land use:
arable land: 0.57%
permanent crops: 0.76%
other: 98.67% (1998 est.)
Irrigated land: 10 sq km (1998 est.)
Natural hazards: typhoons, earthquakes, and severe flooding are rare
Environment - current issues: seasonal smoke/haze resulting from forest fires in Indonesia
Environment - international agreements:
party to: Endangered Species, Hazardous Wastes, Law of the Sea, Ozone Layer Protection, Ship Pollution
signed, but not ratified: none of the selected agreements
Geography - note: close to vital sea lanes through South China Sea linking Indian and Pacific Oceans; two parts physically separated by Malaysia; almost an enclave of Malaysia

People

Population: 365,251 (July 2004 est.)
Age structure:
0-14 years: 29.1% (male 54,243; female 52,013)
15-64 years: 68% (male 131,682; female 116,631)
65 years and over: 2.9% (male 5,035; female 5,647) (2004 est.)
Median age:
total: 26.7 years
male: 27.3 years
female: 26 years (2004 est.)
Population growth rate: 1.95% (2004 est.)
Birth rate: 19.33 births/1,000 population (2004 est.)
Death rate: 3.4 deaths/1,000 population (2004 est.)
Net migration rate: 3.59 migrant(s)/1,000 population (2004 est.)
Sex ratio:
at birth: 1.06 male(s)/female
under 15 years: 1.04 male(s)/female
15-64 years: 1.13 male(s)/female
65 years and over: 0.89 male(s)/female
total population: 1.1 male(s)/female (2004 est.)
Infant mortality rate:
total: 13.05 deaths/1,000 live births
male: 16.51 deaths/1,000 live births
female: 9.41 deaths/1,000 live births (2004 est.)
Life expectancy at birth:
total population: 74.54 years
male: 72.13 years
female: 77.09 years (2004 est.)
Total fertility rate: 2.33 children born/woman (2004 est.)
HIV/AIDS - adult prevalence rate: 0.2% (2001 est.)
HIV/AIDS - people living with HIV/AIDS: less than 100 (2001 est.)
HIV/AIDS - deaths: NA
Nationality:
noun: Bruneian(s)
adjective: Bruneian

Ethnic groups: Malay 67%, Chinese 15%, indigenous 6%, other 12%
Religions: Muslim (official) 67%, Buddhist 13%, Christian 10%, indigenous beliefs and other 10%
Languages: Malay (official), English, Chinese
Literacy:
definition: age 15 and over can read and write
total population: 91.8%
male: 94.8%
female: 88.5% (2003 est.)

Government

Country name:
conventional long form: Negara Brunei Darussalam
conventional short form: Brunei
Government type: constitutional sultanate
Capital: Bandar Seri Begawan
Administrative divisions: 4 districts (daerah-daerah, singular - daerah); Belait, Brunei and Muara, Temburong, Tutong
Independence: 1 January 1984 (from UK)
National holiday: National Day, 23 February (1984); note - 1 January 1984 was the date of independence from the UK, 23 February 1984 was the date of independence from British protection
Constitution: 29 September 1959 (some provisions suspended under a State of Emergency since December 1962, others since independence on 1 January 1984)
Legal system: based on English common law; for Muslims, Islamic Shari'a law supersedes civil law in a number of areas
Suffrage: none
Executive branch:
chief of state: Sultan and Prime Minister Sir HASSANAL Bolkiah (since 5 October 1967); note - the monarch is both the chief of state and head of government
head of government: Sultan and Prime Minister Sir HASSANAL Bolkiah (since 5 October 1967); note - the monarch is both the chief of state and head of government
cabinet: Council of Cabinet Ministers appointed and presided over by the monarch; deals with executive matters; note - there is also a Religious Council (members appointed by the monarch) that advises on religious matters, a Privy Council (members appointed by the monarch) that deals with constitutional matters, and the Council of Succession (members appointed by the monarch) that determines the succession to the throne if the need arises
elections: none; the monarch is hereditary
Legislative branch: Legislation falls under the Prime Minister's Office; there is a privy council that serves in a consultative capacity and other state councils whose members are appointed by the Sultan.
elections: last held in March 1962
Judicial branch: Supreme Court (chief justice and judges are sworn in by the monarch for three-year terms)

Political parties and leaders: other parties include Brunei People's Party or PRB (banned in 1962) and Brunei National Democratic Party (registered in May 1965, deregistered by the Brunei Government in 1988)
Political pressure groups and leaders: NA
International organization participation: APEC, ARF, ASEAN, C, G-77, IBRD, ICAO, ICRM, IDB, IFRCS, IMF, IMO, Interpol, IOC, ISO (correspondent), ITU, NAM, OIC, OPCW, UN, UNCTAD, UPU, WCO, WHO, WIPO, WMO, WTrO
Diplomatic representation in the US:
chief of mission: Ambassador Penigran Anak Dato PUTEH
chancery: 3520 International Court NW, Washington, DC 20008
telephone: [1] (202) 237-1838
FAX: [1] (202) 885-0560
Diplomatic representation from the US:
chief of mission: Ambassador Gene B. CHRISTY
embassy: Third Floor, Teck Guan Plaza, Jalan Sultan, Bandar Seri Begawan
mailing address: PSC 470 (BSB), FPO AP 96507
telephone: [673] (2) 229670
FAX: [673] (2) 225293
Flag description: yellow with two diagonal bands of white (top, almost double width) and black starting from the upper hoist side; the national emblem in red is superimposed at the center; the emblem includes a swallow-tailed flag on top of a winged column within an upturned crescent above a scroll and flanked by two upraised hands

Economy

Economy - overview: This small, wealthy economy encompasses a mixture of foreign and domestic entrepreneurship, government regulation, welfare measures, and village tradition. Crude oil and natural gas production account for nearly half of GDP. Per capita GDP is far above most other Third World countries, and substantial income from overseas investment supplements income from domestic production. The government provides for all medical services and subsidizes rice and housing. Brunei's leaders are concerned that steadily increased integration in the world economy will undermine internal social cohesion, although it became a more prominent player by serving as chairman for the 2000 APEC (Asian Pacific Economic Cooperation) forum. Plans for the future include upgrading the labor force, reducing unemployment, strengthening the banking and tourist sectors, and, in general, further widening the economic base beyond oil and gas.
GDP: purchasing power parity - $6.5 billion (2002 est.)
GDP - real growth rate: 3% (2002 est.)
GDP - per capita: purchasing power parity - $18,600 (2002 est.)
GDP - composition by sector:
agriculture: 5%
industry: 45%
services: 50% (2001 est.)

Brunei (continued)

Population below poverty line: NA%
Household income or consumption by percentage share:
lowest 10%: NA%
highest 10%: NA%
Inflation rate (consumer prices): -2% (2002 est.)
Labor force: 143,400
note: includes foreign workers and military personnel; temporary residents make up about 40% of labor force (1999 est.)
Labor force - by occupation: government 48%, production of oil, natural gas, services, and construction 42%, agriculture, forestry, and fishing 10% (1999 est.)
Unemployment rate: 10% (2001 est.)
Budget:
revenues: $2.5 billion
expenditures: $2.6 billion, including capital expenditures of $1.35 billion (1997 est.)
Industries: petroleum, petroleum refining, liquefied natural gas, construction
Industrial production growth rate: 5% (2002 est.)
Electricity - production: 2.497 billion kWh (2001)
Electricity - production by source:
fossil fuel: 100%
hydro: 0%
nuclear: 0%
other: 0% (2001)
Electricity - consumption: 2.322 billion kWh (2001)
Electricity - exports: 0 kWh (2001)
Electricity - imports: 0 kWh (2001)
Oil - production: 217,200 bbl/day (2001 est.)
Oil - consumption: 13,000 bbl/day (2001 est.)
Oil - exports: NA
Oil - imports: NA
Oil - proved reserves: 1.255 billion bbl (1 January 2002)
Natural gas - production: 10.35 billion cu m (2001 est.)
Natural gas - consumption: 1.35 billion cu m (2001 est.)
Natural gas - exports: 9 billion cu m (2001 est.)
Natural gas - imports: 0 cu m (2001 est.)
Natural gas - proved reserves: 315 billion cu m (1 January 2002)
Agriculture - products: rice, vegetables, fruits, chickens, water buffalo
Exports: $3.439 billion f.o.b. (2002 est.)
Exports - commodities: crude oil, natural gas, refined products
Exports - partners: Japan 40%, South Korea 12.2%, Thailand 12%, Australia 9.1%, US 8.1%, China 6.4%, Singapore 5.6% (2002)
Imports: $1.63 billion c.i.f. (2002 est.)
Imports - commodities: machinery and transport equipment, manufactured goods, food, chemicals
Imports - partners: Singapore 30.7%, Japan 21.5%, Malaysia 17.4%, UK 6.1% (2002)
Debt - external: $0
Economic aid - recipient: $4.3 million (1995)
Currency: Bruneian dollar (BND)
Currency code: BND

Exchange rates: Bruneian dollars per US dollar - 1.7422 (2003), 1.7906 (2002), 1.7917 (2001), 1.724 (2000), 1.695 (1999)
Fiscal year: calendar year

Communications

Telephones - main lines in use: 90,000 (2002)
Telephones - mobile cellular: 137,000 (2002)
Telephone system:
general assessment: service throughout the country is excellent; international service is good to East Asia, Europe, and the US
domestic: every service available
international: country code - 673; satellite earth stations - 2 Intelsat (1 Indian Ocean and 1 Pacific Ocean); digital submarine cable links to Malaysia, the Philippines, and Singapore (2001)
Radio broadcast stations: AM 3, FM 10, shortwave 0 (1998)
Television broadcast stations: 2 (1997)
Internet country code: .bn
Internet hosts: 8,668 (2002)
Internet users: 35,000 (2002)

Transportation

Railways:
total: 13 km (private line)
narrow gauge: 13 km 0.610-m gauge (2001 est.)
Highways:
total: 2,525 km
paved: 2,525 km
unpaved: 0 km (2000)
Waterways: 209 km; navigable by craft drawing less than 1.2 m
Pipelines: gas 665 km; oil 439 km (2003)
Ports and harbors: Bandar Seri Begawan, Kuala Belait, Muara, Seria, Tutong
Merchant marine:
total: 8 ships (1,000 GRT or over) 465,937 GRT/ 413,393 DWT
by type: liquefied gas 8
foreign-owned: United Kingdom 8 (2003 est.)
Airports: 2 (2003 est.)
Airports - with paved runways:
total: 1
over 3,047 m: 1 (2003 est.)
Airports - with unpaved runways:
total: 1
914 to 1,523 m: 1 (2003 est.)
Heliports: 3 (2003 est.)

Military

Military branches: Royal Brunei Land Forces, Royal Brunei Navy, Royal Brunei Air Force
Military manpower - military age: 18 years of age (2004 est.)
Military manpower - availability:
males age 15-49: 112,630 (2004 est.)
Military manpower - fit for military service:
males age 15-49: approx. 60,000 (2004 est.)

Military manpower - reaching military age annually:
males: 3,425 (2004 est.)
Military expenditures - dollar figure: $339.5 million (2003)
Military expenditures - percent of GDP: 5.9% (2003)

Transnational Issues

Disputes - international: in 2003 Brunei and Malaysia ceased gas and oil exploration in their offshore and deepwater seabeds until negotiations progress to an agreement over allocation of disputed areas; Malaysia's land boundary with Brunei around Limbang is in dispute; Brunei established an exclusive economic fishing zone encompassing Louisa Reef in southern Spratly Islands in 1984 but makes no public territorial claim to the offshore reefs; the 2002 "Declaration on the Conduct of Parties in the South China Sea" has eased tensions in the Spratly Islands but falls short of a legally binding "code of conduct" desired by several of the disputants
Illicit drugs: drug trafficking and illegally importing controlled substances are serious offenses in Brunei and carry a mandatory death penalty

Bulgaria

Introduction

Background: The Bulgars, a Central Asian Turkic tribe, merged with the local Slavic inhabitants in the late 7th century to form the first Bulgarian state. In succeeding centuries, Bulgaria struggled with the Byzantine Empire to assert its place in the Balkans, but by the end of the 14th century the country was overrun by the Ottoman Turks. Bulgaria regained its independence in 1878 but, having fought on the losing side in both World Wars, it fell within the Soviet sphere of influence and became a People's Republic in 1946. Communist domination ended in 1990, when Bulgaria held its first multiparty election since World War II and began the contentious process of moving toward political democracy and a market economy while combating inflation, unemployment, corruption, and crime. Today, reforms and democratization keep Bulgaria on a path toward eventual integration into NATO and the EU - with which it began accession negotiations in 2000.

Geography

Location: Southeastern Europe, bordering the Black Sea, between Romania and Turkey
Geographic coordinates: 43 00 N, 25 00 E
Map references: Europe
Area:
total: 110,910 sq km
land: 110,550 sq km
water: 360 sq km
Area - comparative: slightly larger than Tennessee
Land boundaries:
total: 1,808 km
border countries: Greece 494 km, The Former Yugoslav Republic of Macedonia 148 km, Romania 608 km, Serbia and Montenegro 318 km, Turkey 240 km
Coastline: 354 km

Maritime claims:
territorial sea: 12 NM
contiguous zone: 24 NM
exclusive economic zone: 200 NM
Climate: temperate; cold, damp winters; hot, dry summers
Terrain: mostly mountains with lowlands in north and southeast
Elevation extremes:
lowest point: Black Sea 0 m
highest point: Musala 2,925 m
Natural resources: bauxite, copper, lead, zinc, coal, timber, arable land
Land use:
arable land: 39%
permanent crops: 1.8%
other: 59.2% (1998 est.)
Irrigated land: 8,000 sq km (1998 est.)
Natural hazards: earthquakes, landslides
Environment - current issues: air pollution from industrial emissions; rivers polluted from raw sewage, heavy metals, detergents; deforestation; forest damage from air pollution and resulting acid rain; soil contamination from heavy metals from metallurgical plants and industrial wastes
Environment - international agreements:
party to: Air Pollution, Air Pollution-Nitrogen Oxides, Air Pollution-Persistent Organic Pollutants, Air Pollution-Sulfur 85, Air Pollution-Volatile Organic Compounds, Antarctic-Environmental Protocol, Antarctic-Marine Living Resources, Antarctic Treaty, Biodiversity, Climate Change, Climate Change-Kyoto Protocol, Desertification, Endangered Species, Environmental Modification, Hazardous Wastes, Law of the Sea, Ozone Layer Protection, Ship Pollution, Wetlands
signed, but not ratified: Air Pollution-Sulfur 94
Geography - note: strategic location near Turkish Straits; controls key land routes from Europe to Middle East and Asia

People

Population: 7,517,973 (July 2004 est.)
Age structure:
0-14 years: 14.4% (male 553,801; female 526,856)
15-64 years: 68.5% (male 2,533,784; female 2,615,968)
65 years and over: 17.1% (male 535,954; female 751,610) (2004 est.)
Median age:
total: 40.5 years
male: 38.4 years
female: 42.4 years (2004 est.)
Population growth rate: -0.92% (2004 est.)
Birth rate: 9.65 births/1,000 population (2004 est.)
Death rate: 14.25 deaths/1,000 population (2004 est.)
Net migration rate: -4.58 migrant(s)/1,000 population (2004 est.)

Sex ratio:
at birth: 1.06 male(s)/female
under 15 years: 1.05 male(s)/female
15-64 years: 0.97 male(s)/female
65 years and over: 0.71 male(s)/female
total population: 0.93 male(s)/female (2004 est.)
Infant mortality rate:
total: 21.31 deaths/1,000 live births
male: 25.15 deaths/1,000 live births
female: 17.23 deaths/1,000 live births (2004 est.)
Life expectancy at birth:
total population: 71.75 years
male: 68.14 years
female: 75.59 years (2004 est.)
Total fertility rate: 1.37 children born/woman (2004 est.)
HIV/AIDS - adult prevalence rate: less than 0.1% - note: no country specific models provided (2001 est.)
HIV/AIDS - people living with HIV/AIDS: 346 (2001 est.)
HIV/AIDS - deaths: 100 (2001 est.)
Nationality:
noun: Bulgarian(s)
adjective: Bulgarian
Ethnic groups: Bulgarian 83.9%, Turk 9.4%, Roma 4.7%, other 2% (including Macedonian, Armenian, Tatar, Circassian) (2001)
Religions: Bulgarian Orthodox 82.6%, Muslim 12.2%, Roman Catholic 1.7%, Jewish 0.1%, Protestant, Gregorian-Armenian, and other 3.4% (1998)
Languages: Bulgarian, secondary languages closely correspond to ethnic breakdown
Literacy:
definition: age 15 and over can read and write
total population: 98.6%
male: 99.1%
female: 98.2% (2003 est.)

Government

Country name:
conventional long form: Republic of Bulgaria
conventional short form: Bulgaria
Government type: parliamentary democracy
Capital: Sofia
Administrative divisions: 28 provinces (oblasti, singular - oblast); Blagoevgrad, Burgas, Dobrich, Gabrovo, Khaskovo, Kurdzhali, Kyustendil, Lovech, Montana, Pazardzhik, Pernik, Pleven, Plovdiv, Razgrad, Ruse, Shumen, Silistra, Sliven, Smolyan, Sofiya, Sofiya-Grad, Stara Zagora, Turgovishte, Varna, Veliko Turnovo, Vidin, Vratsa, Yambol
Independence: 3 March 1878 (from Ottoman Empire)
National holiday: Liberation Day, 3 March (1878)
Constitution: adopted 12 July 1991
Legal system: civil law and criminal law based on Roman law; accepts compulsory ICJ jurisdiction

Bulgaria (continued)

Suffrage: 18 years of age; universal

Executive branch:

chief of state: President Georgi PURVANOV (since 22 January 2002); Vice President Angel MARIN (since 22 January 2002)

head of government: Chairman of the Council of Ministers (Prime Minister) Simeon SAXE-COBURG-GOTHA (since 24 July 2001); Deputy Prime Ministers Nikolay VASILEV (since 24 July 2001), and Lidiya SHULEVA (since 24 July 2001), Plamen PANAYOTOV (since 17 July 2003)

cabinet: Council of Ministers elected by the National Assembly

elections: president and vice president elected on the same ticket by popular vote for five-year terms; election last held 11 November and 18 November 2001 (next to be held NA 2006); chairman of the Council of Ministers (prime minister) nominated by the president; deputy prime ministers nominated by the prime minister

election results: Georgi PURVANOV elected president; percent of vote - Georgi PURVANOV 54.13%, Petar STOYANOV 45.87%

Legislative branch: unicameral National Assembly or Narodno Sobranie (240 seats; members elected by popular vote to serve four-year terms)

elections: last held 17 June 2001 (next to be held NA June 2005)

election results: percent of vote by party - NMS2 42.74%, UtdDF 18.18%, CfB 17.15%, MRF 7.45%; seats by party - NMS2 120, UtdDF 51, CfB 48, MRF 21; note - seating as of January 2004 - NMS2 108, UtdDF 49, CfB 48, MRF 20, independents 15

Judicial branch: Supreme Administrative Court; Supreme Court of Cassation; Constitutional Court (12 justices appointed or elected for nine-year terms); Supreme Judicial Council (consists of the chairmen of the two Supreme Courts, the Chief Prosecutor, and 22 other members; responsible for appointing the justices, prosecutors, and investigating magistrates in the justice system; members of the Supreme Judicial Council elected for five-year terms, 11 elected by the National Assembly and 11 by bodies of the judiciary)

Political parties and leaders: Bulgarian Socialist Party or BSP [Sergei STANISHEV]; Coalition for Bulgaria or CfB (coalition of parties dominated by BSP) [Sergei STANISHEV]; Movement for Rights and Freedoms or MRF [Ahmed DOGAN]; National Movement for Simeon II or NMS2 [Simeon SAXE-COBURG-GOTHA]; Union of Democratic Forces or UDF [Nadezhda MIKHAYLOVA]; Union of Free Democrats or UFD [Stefan SOFIYANSKI]; United Democratic Forces or UtdDF (a coalition between the UDF and other center-right parties)

Political pressure groups and leaders: agrarian movement; Confederation of Independent Trade Unions of Bulgaria or CITUB; Podkrepa Labor Confederation; numerous regional, ethnic, and national interest groups with various agendas

International organization participation: ACCT, Australia Group, BIS, BSEC, CE, CEI, CERN, EAPC, EBRD, EU (applicant), FAO, G- 9, IAEA, IBRD, ICAO, ICCt, ICFTU, ICRM, IFC, IFRCS, IHO (pending member), ILO, IMF, IMO, Interpol, IOC, IOM, ISO, ITU, NAM (guest), NSG, OAS (observer), OPCW, OSCE, PCA, PFP, UN, UNCTAD, UNESCO, UNIDO, UNMEE, UNMIK, UPU, WCL, WCO, WEU (associate partner), WFTU, WHO, WIPO, WMO, WToO, WTrO, ZC

Diplomatic representation in the US:

chief of mission: Ambassador Elena B. POPTODOROVA

chancery: 1621 22nd Street NW, Washington, DC 20008

telephone: [1] (202) 387-0174

FAX: [1] (202) 234-7973

consulate(s): New York

Diplomatic representation from the US:

chief of mission: Ambassador James William PARDEW

embassy: 1 Suborna Street, Sofia 1000

mailing address: American Embassy Sofia, Department of State, 5740 Sofia Place, Washington, DC 20521-5740

telephone: [359] (2) 937-5100

FAX: [359] (2) 981-89-77

Flag description: three equal horizontal bands of white (top), green, and red; the national emblem formerly on the hoist side of the white stripe has been removed - it contained a rampant lion within a wreath of wheat ears below a red five-pointed star and above a ribbon bearing the dates 681 (first Bulgarian state established) and 1944 (liberation from Nazi control)

Economy

Economy - overview: Bulgaria, a former communist country striving to enter the European Union, has experienced macroeconomic stability and strong growth since a major economic downturn in 1996 led to the fall of the then socialist government. As a result, the government became committed to economic reform and responsible fiscal planning. A $300 million stand-by agreement negotiated with the IMF at the end of 2001 has supported government efforts to overcome high rates of poverty and unemployment.

GDP: purchasing power parity - $57.13 billion (2003 est.)

GDP - real growth rate: 4.4% (2003 est.)

GDP - per capita: purchasing power parity - $7,600 (2003 est.)

GDP - composition by sector:

agriculture: 12.5%

industry: 27.8%

services: 59.7% (2002)

Population below poverty line: 13.4% (2002 est.)

Household income or consumption by percentage share:

lowest 10%: 4.5%

highest 10%: 22.8% (1997)

Distribution of family income - Gini index: 26.4 (2001)

Inflation rate (consumer prices): 5.6% (2003 est.)

Labor force: 3.83 million (2000 est.)

Labor force - by occupation: agriculture 26%, industry 31%, services 43% (1998 est.)

Unemployment rate: 13.5% (2003)

Budget:

revenues: $6.68 billion

expenditures: $6.69 billion, including capital expenditures of $NA (2002 est.)

Industries: electricity, gas and water; food, beverages and tobacco; machinery and equipment, base metals, chemical products, coke, refined petroleum, nuclear fuel

Industrial production growth rate: 5% (2003 est.)

Electricity - production: 41.38 billion kWh (2001)

Electricity - production by source:

fossil fuel: 47.8%

hydro: 8.1%

nuclear: 44.1%

other: 0% (2001)

Electricity - consumption: 32.52 billion kWh (2001)

Electricity - exports: 6.79 billion kWh (2001)

Electricity - imports: 830 million kWh (2001)

Oil - production: 603 bbl/day (2001 est.)

Oil - consumption: 94,000 bbl/day (2001 est.)

Oil - exports: NA

Oil - imports: NA

Oil - proved reserves: 8.1 million bbl (1 January 2002)

Natural gas - production: 4 million cu m (2001 est.)

Natural gas - consumption: 5.804 billion cu m (2001 est.)

Natural gas - exports: 0 cu m (2001 est.)

Natural gas - imports: 5.8 billion cu m (2001 est.)

Natural gas - proved reserves: 3.724 billion cu m (1 January 2002)

Agriculture - products: vegetables, fruits, tobacco, livestock, wine, wheat, barley, sunflowers, sugar beets

Exports: $7.337 billion f.o.b. (2003 est.)

Exports - commodities: clothing, footwear, iron and steel, machinery and equipment, fuels

Exports - partners: Italy 15.5%, Germany 9.6%, Turkey 9.4%, Greece 9.2%, France 5.3%, US 4.8% (2002)

Imports: $9.723 billion f.o.b. (2003 est.)

Imports - commodities: fuels, minerals, and raw materials; machinery and equipment; metals and ores; chemicals and plastics; food, textiles

Imports - partners: Russia 14.6%, Germany 14.4%, Italy 11.4%, Greece 6.1%, France 5.7%, Turkey 5% (2002)

Debt - external: $12.6 billion (yearend 2003)

Economic aid - recipient: $300 million (2000 est.)

Currency: lev (BGL)

Currency code: BGN

Exchange rates: leva per US dollar - 1.7327 (2003), 2.077 (2002), 2.1847 (2001), 2.1233 (2000), 1.8364 (1999)

note: on 5 July 1999, the lev was redenominated; the post-5 July 1999 lev is equal to 1,000 of the pre-5 July 1999 lev

Fiscal year: calendar year

Bulgaria *(continued)*

Communications

Telephones - main lines in use: 2,868,200 (2002)
Telephones - mobile cellular: 2,597,500 (2002)
Telephone system:
general assessment: extensive but antiquated
domestic: more than two-thirds of the lines are residential; telephone service is available in most villages; a fairly modern digital cable trunk line now connects switching centers in most of the regions, the others are connected by digital microwave radio relay
international: country code - 359; direct dialing to 58 countries; satellite earth stations - 1 Intersputnik (Atlantic Ocean region); 2 Intelsat (Atlantic and Indian Ocean regions)
Radio broadcast stations: AM 31, FM 63, shortwave 2 (2001)
Television broadcast stations: 39 (plus 1,242 repeaters) (2001)
Internet country code: .bg
Internet hosts: 32,986 (2002)
Internet users: 630,000 (2002)

Transportation

Railways:
total: 4,294 km
standard gauge: 4,049 km 1.435-m gauge (2,710 km electrified)
narrow gauge: 245 km 0.760-m gauge (2002)
Highways:
total: 37,286 km
paved: 35,049 km (including 324 km of expressways)
unpaved: 2,237 km (2000)
Waterways: 470 km (1987)
Pipelines: gas 2,425 km; oil 339 km; refined products 156 km (2003)
Ports and harbors: Burgas, Lom, Nesebur, Ruse, Varna, Vidin
Merchant marine:
total: 60 ships (1,000 GRT or over) 757,972 GRT/1,115,238 DWT
by type: bulk 37, cargo 7, chemical tanker 4, container 2, petroleum tanker 3, rail car carrier 2, roll on/roll off 3, short-sea/passenger 1, specialized tanker 1
registered in other countries: 45 (2003 est.)
Airports: 212 (2003 est.)
Airports - with paved runways:
total: 127
over 3,047 m: 1
2,438 to 3,047 m: 19
1,524 to 2,437 m: 15
914 to 1,523 m: 1
under 914 m: 91 (2003 est.)
Airports - with unpaved runways:
total: 85
1,524 to 2,437 m: 2
914 to 1,523 m: 11
under 914 m: 72 (2003 est.)
Heliports: 1 (2003 est.)

Military

Military branches: Army, Navy, Air and Air Defense Forces
Military manpower - military age: 19 years of age (2004 est.)
Military manpower - availability:
males age 15-49: 1,829,203 (2004 est.)
Military manpower - fit for military service:
males age 15-49: 1,530,657 (2004 est.)
Military manpower - reaching military age annually:
males: 52,811 (2004 est.)
Military expenditures - dollar figure: $356 million (FY02)
Military expenditures - percent of GDP: 2.6% (2003)

Transnational Issues

Disputes - international: none
Illicit drugs: major European transshipment point for Southwest Asian heroin and, to a lesser degree, South American cocaine for the European market; limited producer of precursor chemicals; some money laundering of drug-related proceeds through financial institutions

Burkina Faso

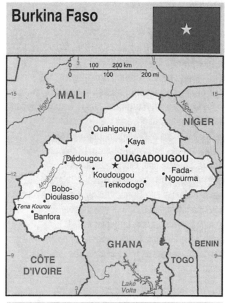

Introduction

Background: Burkina Faso (formerly Upper Volta) achieved independence from France in 1960. Repeated military coups during the 1970s and 1980s were followed by multiparty elections in the early 1990s. Burkina Faso's high population density and limited natural resources result in poor economic prospects for the majority of its citizens. Recent unrest in Cote d'Ivoire and northern Ghana has hindered the ability of several hundred thousand seasonal Burkinabe farm workers to find employment in neighboring countries.

Geography

Location: Western Africa, north of Ghana
Geographic coordinates: 13 00 N, 2 00 W
Map references: Africa
Area:
total: 274,200 sq km
land: 273,800 sq km
water: 400 sq km
Area - comparative: slightly larger than Colorado
Land boundaries:
total: 3,193 km
border countries: Benin 306 km, Cote d'Ivoire 584 km, Ghana 549 km, Mali 1,000 km, Niger 628 km, Togo 126 km
Coastline: 0 km (landlocked)
Maritime claims: none (landlocked)
Climate: tropical; warm, dry winters; hot, wet summers
Terrain: mostly flat to dissected, undulating plains; hills in west and southeast
Elevation extremes:
lowest point: Mouhoun (Black Volta) River 200 m
highest point: Tena Kourou 749 m
Natural resources: manganese, limestone, marble; small deposits of gold, antimony, copper, nickel, bauxite, lead, phosphates, zinc, silver

Burkina Faso *(continued)*

Land use:
arable land: 12.43%
permanent crops: 0.18%
other: 87.39% (1998 est.)
Irrigated land: 250 sq km (1998 est.)
Natural hazards: recurring droughts
Environment - current issues: recent droughts and desertification severely affecting agricultural activities, population distribution, and the economy; overgrazing; soil degradation; deforestation
Environment - international agreements:
party to: Biodiversity, Climate Change, Desertification, Endangered Species, Hazardous Wastes, Marine Life Conservation, Ozone Layer Protection, Wetlands
signed, but not ratified: Law of the Sea
Geography - note: landlocked savanna cut by the three principal rivers of the Black, Red, and White Voltas

People

Population: 13,574,820
note: estimates for this country explicitly take into account the effects of excess mortality due to AIDS; this can result in lower life expectancy, higher infant mortality and death rates, lower population and growth rates, and changes in the distribution of population by age and sex than would otherwise be expected (July 2004 est.)
Age structure:
0-14 years: 46% (male 3,135,098; female 3,114,354)
15-64 years: 51.1% (male 3,391,848; female 3,545,115)
65 years and over: 2.9% (male 163,137; female 225,268) (2004 est.)
Median age:
total: 16.8 years
male: 16.4 years
female: 17.2 years (2004 est.)
Population growth rate: 2.57% (2004 est.)
Birth rate: 44.46 births/1,000 population (2004 est.)
Death rate: 18.79 deaths/1,000 population (2004 est.)
Net migration rate: 0 migrant(s)/1,000 population (2004 est.)
Sex ratio:
at birth: 1.03 male(s)/female
under 15 years: 1.01 male(s)/female
15-64 years: 0.96 male(s)/female
65 years and over: 0.72 male(s)/female
total population: 0.97 male(s)/female (2004 est.)
Infant mortality rate:
total: 98.67 deaths/1,000 live births
male: 106.7 deaths/1,000 live births
female: 90.39 deaths/1,000 live births (2004 est.)
Life expectancy at birth:
total population: 44.2 years
male: 42.62 years
female: 45.83 years (2004 est.)
Total fertility rate: 6.28 children born/woman (2004 est.)

HIV/AIDS - adult prevalence rate: 6.5% (2001 est.)
HIV/AIDS - people living with HIV/AIDS: 440,000 (2001 est.)
HIV/AIDS - deaths: 44,000 (2001 est.)
Nationality:
noun: Burkinabe (singular and plural)
adjective: Burkinabe
Ethnic groups: Mossi over 40%, Gurunsi, Senufo, Lobi, Bobo, Mande, Fulani
Religions: indigenous beliefs 40%, Muslim 50%, Christian (mainly Roman Catholic) 10%
Languages: French (official), native African languages belonging to Sudanic family spoken by 90% of the population
Literacy:
definition: age 15 and over can read and write
total population: 26.6%
male: 36.9%
female: 16.6% (2003 est.)

Government

Country name:
conventional long form. none
conventional short form. Burkina Faso
former. Upper Volta, Republic of Upper Volta
Government type. parliamentary republic
Capital. Ouagadougou
Administrative divisions. 45 provinces; Bale, Bam, Banwa, Bazega, Bougouriba, Boulgou, Boulkiemde, Comoe, Ganzourgou, Gnagna, Gourma, Houet, Ioba, Kadiogo, Kenedougou, Komondjari, Kompienga, Kossi, Koulpelogo, Kouritenga, Kourweogo, Leraba, Loroum, Mouhoun, Namentenga, Nahouri, Nayala, Noumbiel, Oubritenga, Oudalan, Passore, Poni, Sanguie, Sanmatenga, Seno, Sissili, Soum, Sourou, Tapoa, Tuy, Yagha, Yatenga, Ziro, Zondoma, Zoundweogo
Independence. 5 August 1960 (from France)
National holiday. Republic Day, 11 December (1958)
Constitution. 2 June 1991 approved by referendum; 11 June 1991 formally adopted; ammended April 2000
Legal system. based on French civil law system and customary law
Suffrage. universal
Executive branch.
chief of state. President Blaise COMPAORE (since 15 October 1987)
head of government. Prime Minister Ernest Paramanga YONLI (since 6 November 2000)
cabinet. Council of Ministers appointed by the president on the recommendation of the prime minister
elections. president elected by popular vote for a five-year term; election last held 15 November 1998 (next to be held NA 2005); in April 2000, the constitution was amended reducing the presidential term from seven to five years, enforceable as of 2005, and allowing the president to be reelected only once;

it is unclear whether this amendment will be applied retroactively or not; prime minister appointed by the president with the consent of the legislature
election results: Blaise COMPAORE reelected president with 87.5% percent of the vote
Legislative branch: unicameral National Assembly or Assemblee Nationale (111 seats; members are elected by popular vote to serve five-year terms)
elections: National Assembly election last held 5 May 2002 (next to be held NA May 2007)
election results: percent of vote by party - NA%; seats by party - CDP 57, RDA-ADF 17, PDP/PS 10, CFD 5, PAI 5, others 17
Judicial branch: Supreme Court; Appeals Court
Political parties and leaders: African Democratic Rally-Alliance for Democracy and Federation or RDA-ADF [Herman YAMEOGO]; Confederation for Federation and Democracy or CFD [Amadou Diemdioda DICKO]; Congress for Democracy and Progress or CDP [Roch Marc-Christian KABORE]; Movement for Tolerance and Progress or MTP [Nayabtigungou Congo KABORE]; Party for African Independence or PAI [Philippe OUEDRAOGO]; Party for Democracy and Progress or PDP [Joseph KI-ZERBO]; Union of Greens for the Development of Burkina Faso or UVDB [Ram OVEDRAGO]
Political pressure groups and leaders: Burkinabe General Confederation of Labor or CGTB; Burkinabe Movement for Human Rights or MBDHP; Group of 14 February; National Confederation of Burkinabe Workers or CNTB; National Organization of Free Unions or ONSL; watchdog/political action groups throughout the country in both organizations and communities
International organization participation: ACCT, ACP, AfDB, AU, ECOWAS, Entente, FAO, FZ, G-77, IAEA, IBRD, ICAO, ICC, ICCt (signatory), ICFTU, ICRM, IDA, IDB, IFAD, IFC, IFRCS, ILO, IMF, Interpol, IOC, IOM, ITU, MONUC, NAM, OIC, OPCW, PCA, UN, UNCTAD, UNESCO, UNIDO, UPU, WADB (regional), WAEMU, WCL, WCO, WFTU, WHO, WIPO, WMO, WToO, WTrO
Diplomatic representation in the US:
chief of mission: Ambassador Tertius ZONGO
chancery: 2340 Massachusetts Avenue NW, Washington, DC 20008
telephone: [1] (202) 332-5577
FAX: [1] (202) 667-1882
Diplomatic representation from the US:
chief of mission: Ambassador Anthony HOLMES
embassy: 602 Avenue Raoul Follereau, Koulouba, Secteur 4
mailing address: 01 B. P. 35, Ouagadougou 01; pouch mail - U. S. Department of State, 2440 Ouagadougou Place, Washington, DC 20521-2440
telephone: [226] 306723
FAX: [226] 303890
Flag description: two equal horizontal bands of red (top) and green with a yellow five-pointed star in the center; uses the popular pan-African colors of Ethiopia

Burkina Faso (continued)

Economy

Economy - overview: One of the poorest countries in the world, landlocked Burkina Faso has few natural resources, a fragile soil, and a highly unequal distribution of income. About 90% of the population is engaged in (mainly subsistence) agriculture, which is vulnerable to variations in rainfall. Cotton is the key crop. Industry remains dominated by unprofitable government-controlled corporations. Following the African franc currency devaluation in January 1994 the government updated its development program in conjunction with international agencies, and exports and economic growth have increased. Maintenance of macroeconomic progress depends on continued low inflation, reduction in the trade deficit, and reforms designed to encourage private investment. The internal crisis in neighboring Cote d'Ivoire continues to hurt trade and industrial prospects and deepens the need for international assistance.

GDP: purchasing power parity - $14.33 billion (2003 est.)

GDP - real growth rate: 4.6% (2003 est.)

GDP - per capita: purchasing power parity - $1,100 (2003 est.)

GDP - composition by sector:

agriculture: 35%

industry: 17%

services: 48% (2001)

Population below poverty line: 45% (2003 est.)

Household income or consumption by percentage share:

lowest 10%: 2%

highest 10%: 46.8% (1994)

Distribution of family income - Gini index: 48.2 (1994)

Inflation rate (consumer prices): 4.5% (2003 est.)

Labor force: 5 million

note: a large part of the male labor force migrates annually to neighboring countries for seasonal employment (2003)

Labor force - by occupation: agriculture 90% (2003 est.)

Unemployment rate: NA%

Budget:

revenues: $316 million

expenditures: $NA, including capital expenditures of $NA (2001)

Industries: cotton lint, beverages, agricultural processing, soap, cigarettes, textiles, gold

Industrial production growth rate: 14% (2001 est.)

Electricity - production: 279.2 million kWh (2001)

Electricity - production by source:

fossil fuel: 69.9%

hydro: 30.1%

nuclear: 0%

other: 0% (2001)

Electricity - consumption: 259.6 million kWh (2001)

Electricity - exports: 0 kWh (2001)

Electricity - imports: 0 kWh (2001)

Oil - production: 0 bbl/day (2001 est.)

Oil - consumption: 8,000 bbl/day (2001 est.)

Oil - exports: NA

Oil - imports: NA

Agriculture - products: cotton, peanuts, shea nuts, sesame, sorghum, millet, corn, rice; livestock

Exports: $293 million f.o.b. (2003 est.)

Exports - commodities: cotton, livestock, gold

Exports - partners: Singapore 15.2%, Italy 11.7%, Colombia 8.8%, France 7.6%, India 7%, Ghana 6.4%, Japan 4.7%, Thailand 4.1% (2002)

Imports: $633.6 million f.o.b. (2003 est.)

Imports - commodities: capital goods, foodstuffs, petroleum

Imports - partners: France 27.4%, Cote d'Ivoire 22.6%, Togo 4.2% (2002)

Debt - external: $1.3 billion (2000)

Economic aid - recipient: $484.1 million (1995)

Currency: Communaute Financiere Africaine franc (XOF); note - responsible authority is the Central Bank of the West African States

Currency code: XOF

Exchange rates: Communaute Financiere Africaine francs (XOF) per US dollar - 581.2 (2003), 696.988 (2002), 733.039 (2001), 711.976 (2000), 615.699 (1999)

Fiscal year: calendar year

Communications

Telephones - main lines in use: 64,300 (2002)

Telephones - mobile cellular: 89,900 (2002)

Telephone system:

general assessment: all services only fair

domestic: microwave radio relay, open-wire, and radiotelephone communication stations

international: country code - 226; satellite earth station - 1 Intelsat (Atlantic Ocean)

Radio broadcast stations: AM 3, FM 17, shortwave 3 (2002)

Television broadcast stations: 1 (2002)

Internet country code: .bf

Internet hosts: 409 (2002)

Internet users: 25,000 (2002)

Transportation

Railways:

total: 622 km

narrow gauge: 622 km 1.000-m gauge

note: another 660 km of this railway extends into Cote D'Ivoire (2002)

Highways:

total: 12,506 km

paved: 2,001 km

unpaved: 10,505 km (1999)

Waterways: none

Ports and harbors: none

Airports: 33 (2003 est.)

Airports - with paved runways:

total: 2

over 3,047 m: 1

2,438 to 3,047 m: 1 (2003 est.)

Airports - with unpaved runways:

total: 31

1,524 to 2,437 m: 3

914 to 1,523 m: 11

under 914 m: 17 (2003 est.)

Military

Military branches: Army, Air Force

Military manpower - availability:

males age 15-49: 3,047,306 (2004 est.)

Military manpower - fit for military service:

males age 15-49: 1,552,212 (2004 est.)

Military expenditures - dollar figure: $52.7 million (2003)

Military expenditures - percent of GDP: 1.6% (2003)

Transnational Issues

Disputes - international: two villages are in dispute along the border with Benin; Benin accuses Burkina Faso of moving boundary pillars; Burkina Faso border regions have become a staging area for Liberia and Cote d'Ivoire rebels and an asylum for refugees caught in regional fighting; the Ivoirian Government accuses Burkina Faso of supporting Ivoirian rebels

Burma

Introduction

Background: Britain conquered Burma over a period of 62 years (1824-1886) and incorporated it into its Indian Empire. Burma was administered as a province of India until 1937 when it became a separate, self-governing colony; independence outside of the Commonwealth was attained in 1948. Gen. NE WIN dominated the government from 1962 to 1988, first as military ruler, then as president, and later as political kingmaker. Despite multiparty elections in 1990 that resulted in the main opposition party - the National League for Democracy (NLD) - winning a landslide victory, the ruling junta refused to hand over power. NLD leader and Nobel Peace Prize recipient AUNG SAN SUU KYI, who was under house arrest from 1989 to 1995 and 2000 to 2002, was arrested in May 2003 and is currently under house arrest. Her supporters are routinely harassed or jailed.

Geography

Location: Southeastern Asia, bordering the Andaman Sea and the Bay of Bengal, between Bangladesh and Thailand
Geographic coordinates: 22 00 N, 98 00 E

Map references: Southeast Asia
Area:
total: 678,500 sq km
land: 657,740 sq km
water: 20,760 sq km
Area - comparative: slightly smaller than Texas
Land boundaries:
total: 5,876 km
border countries: Bangladesh 193 km, China 2,185 km, India 1,463 km, Laos 235 km, Thailand 1,800 km
Coastline: 1,930 km
Maritime claims:
territorial sea: 12 NM
contiguous zone: 24 NM
exclusive economic zone: 200 NM
continental shelf: 200 NM or to the edge of the continental margin
Climate: tropical monsoon; cloudy, rainy, hot, humid summers (southwest monsoon, June to September); less cloudy, scant rainfall, mild temperatures, lower humidity during winter (northeast monsoon, December to April)
Terrain: central lowlands ringed by steep, rugged highlands
Elevation extremes:
lowest point: Andaman Sea 0 m
highest point: Hkakabo Razi 5,881 m
Natural resources: petroleum, timber, tin, antimony, zinc, copper, tungsten, lead, coal, some marble, limestone, precious stones, natural gas, hydropower
Land use:
arable land: 14.53%
permanent crops: 0.9%
other: 84.57% (1998 est.)
Irrigated land: 15,920 sq km (1998 est.)
Natural hazards: destructive earthquakes and cyclones; flooding and landslides common during rainy season (June to September); periodic droughts
Environment - current issues: deforestation; industrial pollution of air, soil, and water; inadequate sanitation and water treatment contribute to disease
Environment - international agreements:
party to: Biodiversity, Climate Change, Climate Change-Kyoto Protocol, Desertification, Endangered Species, Law of the Sea, Ozone Layer Protection, Ship Pollution, Tropical Timber 83, Tropical Timber 94
signed, but not ratified: none of the selected agreements
Geography - note: strategic location near major Indian Ocean shipping lanes

People

Population: 42,720,196
note: estimates for this country take into account the effects of excess mortality due to AIDS; this can result in lower life expectancy, higher infant mortality and death rates, lower population growth rates, and changes in the distribution of population by age and sex than would otherwise be expected (July 2004 est.)

Age structure:
0-14 years: 27.6% (male 6,023,874; female 5,774,055)
15-64 years: 67.5% (male 14,317,308; female 14,504,500)
65 years and over: 4.9% (male 927,570; female 1,172,889) (2004 est.)
Median age:
total: 25.7 years
male: 25.2 years
female: 26.3 years (2004 est.)
Population growth rate: 0.47% (2004 est.)
Birth rate: 18.64 births/1,000 population (2004 est.)
Death rate: 12.16 deaths/1,000 population (2004 est.)
Net migration rate: -1.8 migrant(s)/1,000 population (2004 est.)
Sex ratio:
at birth: 1.06 male(s)/female
under 15 years: 1.04 male(s)/female
15-64 years: 0.99 male(s)/female
65 years and over: 0.79 male(s)/female
total population: 0.99 male(s)/female (2004 est.)
Infant mortality rate:
total: 68.78 deaths/1,000 live births
male: 74.78 deaths/1,000 live births
female: 62.42 deaths/1,000 live births (2004 est.)
Life expectancy at birth:
total population: 56.01 years
male: 54.22 years
female: 57.9 years (2004 est.)
Total fertility rate: 2.08 children born/woman (2004 est.)
HIV/AIDS - adult prevalence rate: 1.99% (2001 est.)
HIV/AIDS - people living with HIV/AIDS: 530,000 (2001 est.)
HIV/AIDS - deaths: 65,000 (2001 est.)
Nationality:
noun: Burmese (singular and plural)
adjective: Burmese
Ethnic groups: Burman 68%, Shan 9%, Karen 7%, Rakhine 4%, Chinese 3%, Indian 2%, Mon 2%, other 5%
Religions: Buddhist 89%, Christian 4% (Baptist 3%, Roman Catholic 1%), Muslim 4%, animist 1%, other 2%
Languages: Burmese, minority ethnic groups have their own languages
Literacy:
definition: age 15 and over can read and write
total population: 83.1%
male: 88.7%
female: 77.7% (1995 est.)
note: these are official statistics; estimates of functional literacy are likely closer to 30% (1999 est.)

Government

Country name:
conventional long form: Union of Burma
conventional short form: Burma
local long form: Pyidaungzu Myanma Naingngandaw (translated by the US Government as Union of Myanma and by the Burmese as Union of Myanmar)

local short form: Myanma Naingngandaw

former: Socialist Republic of the Union of Burma

note: since 1989 the military authorities in Burma have promoted the name Myanmar as a conventional name for their state; this decision was not approved by any sitting legislature in Burma, and the US Government did not adopt the name, which is a derivative of the Burmese short-form name Myanma Naingngandaw

Government type: military regime

Capital: Rangoon (regime refers to the capital as Yangon)

Administrative divisions: 7 divisions* (taing-myar, singular - taing) and 7 states (pyi ne-myar, singular - pyi ne); Chin State, Ayeyarwady*, Bago*, Kachin State, Kayin State, Kayah State, Magway*, Mandalay*, Mon State, Rakhine State, Sagaing*, Shan State, Tanintharyi*, Yangon*

Independence: 4 January 1948 (from UK)

National holiday: Independence Day, 4 January (1948)

Constitution: 3 January 1974 (suspended since 18 September 1988); national convention started on 9 January 1993 to draft a new constitution; progress has since been stalled

Legal system: has not accepted compulsory ICJ jurisdiction

Suffrage: 18 years of age; universal

Executive branch:

chief of state: Chairman of the State Peace and Development Council Sr. Gen. THAN SHWE (since 23 April 1992)

head of government: Chairman of the State Peace and Development Council Sr. Gen. THAN SHWE (since 23 April 1992); note - the appointed Prime Minister, Gen. KNIN NYUNT (since 25 August 2003), is not the head of government

cabinet: State Peace and Development Council (SPDC); military junta, so named 15 November 1997, which initially assumed power 18 September 1988 under the name State Law and Order Restoration Council; the SPDC oversees the cabinet

elections: none

Legislative branch: unicameral People's Assembly or Pyithu Hluttaw (485 seats; members elected by popular vote to serve four-year terms)

elections: last held 27 May 1990, but Assembly never convened

election results: percent of vote by party - NA%; seats by party - NLD 392, SNLD 23, NUP 10, other 60

Judicial branch: remnants of the British-era legal system are in place, but there is no guarantee of a fair public trial; the judiciary is not independent of the executive

Political parties and leaders: National League for Democracy or NLD [AUNG SHWE, chairman, AUNG SAN SUU KYI, general secretary]; National Unity Party or NUP (progovernment) [THA KYAW]; Shan Nationalities League for Democracy or SNLD [KHUN HTUN OO]; and other smaller parties

Political pressure groups and leaders: All Burma Student Democratic Front or ABSDF; Kachin Independence Army or KIA; Karen National Union or KNU; National Coalition Government of the Union of Burma or NCGUB [Dr. SEIN WIN] consists of individuals legitimately elected to the People's Assembly but not recognized by the military regime (the group fled to a border area and joined with insurgents in December 1990 to form a parallel government); several Shan factions; United Wa State Army or UWSA; Union Solidarity and Development Association or USDA (progovernment, a social and political organization) [THAN AUNG, general secretary]

International organization participation: ARF, AsDB, ASEAN, CP, FAO, G-77, IAEA, IBRD, ICAO, ICRM, IDA, IFAD, IFC, IFRCS, IHO, ILO, IMF, IMO, Interpol, IOC, ITU, NAM, OPCW (signatory), UN, UNCTAD, UNESCO, UNIDO, UPU, WCO, WHO, WIPO, WMO, WTrO

Diplomatic representation in the US:

chief of mission: Ambassador LINN MYAING

chancery: 2300 S Street NW, Washington, DC 20008

telephone: [1] (202) 332-9044

FAX: [1] (202) 332-9046

consulate(s) general: New York

Diplomatic representation from the US:

chief of mission: Permanent Charge d'Affaires Carmen M. MARTINEZ

embassy: 581 Merchant Street, Rangoon (GPO 521)

mailing address: Box B, APO AP 96546

telephone: [95] (1) 379 880, 379 881

FAX: [95] (1) 256 018

Flag description: red with a blue rectangle in the upper hoist-side corner bearing, 14 white five-pointed stars encircling a cogwheel containing a stalk of rice; the 14 stars represent the 14 administrative divisions

Economy

Economy - overview: Burma is a resource-rich country that suffers from government controls and abject rural poverty. The military regime took steps in the early 1990s to liberalize the economy after decades of failure under the "Burmese Way to Socialism", but those efforts have since stalled. Burma has been unable to achieve monetary or fiscal stability, resulting in an economy that suffers from serious macroeconomic imbalances - including a steep inflation rate and an official exchange rate that overvalues the Burmese kyat by more than 100 times the market rate. In addition, most overseas development assistance ceased after the junta suppressed the democracy movement in 1988 and subsequently ignored the results of the 1990 election. A crisis in the private banking sector in early 2003 followed by economic moves against Burma by the United States, the European Union, and Japan - including a US ban on imports from Burma and a Japanese freeze on new bilateral economic aid - further weakened the Burmese economy. Burma is data poor, and official statistics are often dated and inaccurate. Published estimates of Burma's foreign trade are greatly understated because of the size of the black market and border trade - often estimated to be one to two times the official economy. Better relations with foreign countries and relaxed controls at home are needed to promote foreign investment, exports, and tourism. In February 2003, a major banking crisis hit the country's 20 private banks, shutting them down and disrupting the economy. In July and August 2003, the United States imposed a ban on all Burmese imports and a ban on provision of financial services, hampering Burma's ability to obtain foreign exchange. As of January 2004, the largest private banks remained moribund, leaving the private sector with little formal access to credit outside of government contracts.

GDP: purchasing power parity - $78.8 billion (2003 est.)

GDP - real growth rate: 5.2% (2003 est.)

GDP - per capita: purchasing power parity - $1,900 (2003 est.)

GDP - composition by sector:

agriculture: 60%

industry: 9%

services: 31% (2002 est.)

Population below poverty line: 25% (2000 est.)

Household income or consumption by percentage share:

lowest 10%: 2.8%

highest 10%: 32.4% (1998)

Inflation rate (consumer prices): 52.8% (2003 est.)

Labor force: 23.7 million (1999 est.)

Labor force - by occupation: agriculture 70%, industry 7%, services 23% (2001 est.)

Unemployment rate: 5.1% (2001 est.)

Budget:

revenues: $7.9 billion

expenditures: $12.2 billion, including capital expenditures of $5.7 billion (FY96/97)

Industries: agricultural processing; knit and woven apparel; wood and wood products; copper, tin, tungsten, iron; construction materials; pharmaceuticals; fertilizer; cement

Industrial production growth rate: NA%

Electricity - production: 6.139 billion kWh (2001)

Electricity - production by source:

fossil fuel: 44.5%

hydro: 43.4%

nuclear: 0%

other: 12.1% (2002)

Electricity - consumption: 5.709 billion kWh (2001)

Electricity - exports: 0 kWh (2001)

Electricity - imports: 0 kWh (2001)

Oil - production: 18,590 bbl/day (2002 est.)

Oil - consumption: 38,000 bbl/day (2001 est.)

Oil - exports: NA

Oil - imports: NA

Oil - proved reserves: 115 million bbl (1 January 2003)

Natural gas - production: 7.35 billion cu m (2001 est.)

Natural gas - consumption: 2.15 billion cu m (2001 est.)

Natural gas - exports: 5.2 billion cu m (2001 est.)

Burma *(continued)*

Natural gas - imports: 0 cu m (2001 est.)
Natural gas - proved reserves: 314.4 billion cu m (1 January 2003)
Agriculture - products: rice, pulses, beans, sesame, groundnuts, sugarcane; hardwood; fish and fish products
Exports: $2.434 billion f.o.b. (2003 est.)
Exports - commodities: Clothing, gas, wood products, pulses, beans, fish, rice
Exports - partners: Thailand 31.6%, US 13.1%, India 7.4%, China 4.7% (2002)
Imports: $2.071 billion f.o.b. (2003 est.)
Imports - commodities: Fabric, petroleum products, plastics, machinery, transport equipment, construction materials, crude oil; food products
Imports - partners: China 27%, Singapore 19.6%, Thailand 12.1%, Malaysia 8.9%, South Korea 5.4%, Taiwan 4.9%, Japan 4.3% (2002)
Debt - external: $6.2 billion (2002 est.)
Economic aid - recipient: $127 million (2001 est.)
Currency: kyat (MMK)
Currency code: MMK
Exchange rates: kyats per US dollar - 6.0764 (2003), 6.5734 (2002), 6.6841 (2001), 6.5167 (2000), 6.2858 (1999), Note: these are official exchange rates; unofficial exchange rates ranged in 2003 from 100 kyat/US dollar to nearly 1000 kyat/US dollar.
Fiscal year: 1 April - 31 March

Communications

Telephones - main lines in use: 342,300 (2002)
Telephones - mobile cellular: 48,000 (2002)
Telephone system:
general assessment: barely meets minimum requirements for local and intercity service for business and government; international service is fair
domestic: NA
international: country code - 95; satellite earth station - 1 Intelsat (Indian Ocean)
Radio broadcast stations: AM 2, FM 3, shortwave 3 (1998)
Television broadcast stations: 2 (2003)
Internet country code: .mm
Internet hosts: 2 (2002)
Internet users: 25,000 (2002)

Transportation

Railways:
total: 3,955 km
narrow gauge: 3,955 km 1.000-m gauge (2002)
Highways:
total: 28,200 km
paved: 3,440 km
unpaved: 24,760 km (1996 est.)
Waterways: 12,800 km
note: 3,200 km navigable by large commercial vessels
Pipelines: gas 2,056 km; oil 558 km (2003)
Ports and harbors: Bhamo, Chauk, Mandalay, Moulmein, Myitkyina, Pathein, Rangoon, Sittwe, Tavoy

Merchant marine:
total: 31 ships (1,000 GRT or over) 384,529 GRT/ 608,609 DWT
by type: bulk 8, cargo 18, container 1, passenger/ cargo 3, petroleum tanker 1
foreign-owned: Germany 6, Japan 4 (2003 est.)
Airports: 79 (2003 est.)
Airports - with paved runways:
total: 9
over 3,047 m: 2
2,438 to 3,047 m: 5
1,524 to 2,437 m: 2 (2003 est.)
Airports - with unpaved runways:
total: 70
over 3,047 m: 2
1,524 to 2,437 m: 16
914 to 1,523 m: 20
under 914 m: 32 (2003 est.)
Heliports: 1 (2003 est.)

Military

Military branches: Army, Navy, Air Force
Military manpower - military age: 18 years of age (2004 est.)
Military manpower - availability:
males age 15-49: 12,450,884
females age 15-49: 12,457,077
note: both sexes liable for military service (2004 est.)
Military manpower - fit for military service:
males age 15-49: 6,609,995
females age 15-49: 6,595,611 (2004 est.)
Military manpower - reaching military age annually:
males: 441,333
females: 440,914 (2004 est.)
Military expenditures - dollar figure: $39 million (FY97)
Military expenditures - percent of GDP: 2.1% (FY97)

Transnational Issues

Disputes - international: despite continuing border committee talks, significant differences remain with Thailand over boundary alignment and the handling of ethnic rebels, refugees, and illegal cross-border activities; groups in Burma and Thailand express concern over China's construction of 13 hydroelectric dams on the Salween River in Yunnan Province; India seeks cooperation from Burma to keep out Indian Nagaland insurgents
Illicit drugs: world's second largest producer of illicit opium (potential production in 2002 - 630 metric tons, down 27% due to drought and, to a lesser extent, eradication; cultivation in 2002 - 77,000 hectares, a 27% decline from 2001); surrender of drug warlord KHUN SA's Mong Tai Army in January 1996 was hailed by Rangoon as a major counternarcotics success, but lack of government will and ability to take on major narcotrafficking groups and lack of serious commitment against money laundering continues to hinder the overall antidrug effort; major source of methamphetamine and heroin for regional consumption; currently under Financial Action Task Force countermeasures due to continued failure to address its inadequate money-laundering controls

Burundi

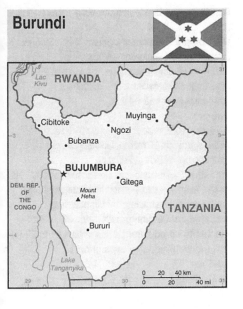

Introduction

Background: Burundi's first democratically elected president was assassinated in October 1993 after only four months in office. Since then, some 200,000 Burundians have perished in widespread, often intense ethnic violence between Hutu and Tutsi factions. Hundreds of thousands have been internally displaced or have become refugees in neighboring countries. Burundi troops, seeking to secure their borders, intervened in the conflict in the Democratic Republic of the Congo in 1998. More recently, many of these troops have been redeployed back to Burundi to deal with periodic upsurges in rebel activity. A new transitional government, inaugurated on 1 November 2001, was to be the first step toward holding national elections in three years. While the Government of Burundi signed a cease-fire agreement in December 2002 with three of Burundi's four Hutu rebel groups, implementation of the agreement has been problematic and one rebel group refuses to sign on, clouding prospects for a sustainable peace.

Geography

Location: Central Africa, east of Democratic Republic of the Congo
Geographic coordinates: 3 30 S, 30 00 E
Map references: Africa
Area:
total: 27,830 sq km
land: 25,650 sq km
water: 2,180 sq km
Area - comparative: slightly smaller than Maryland
Land boundaries:
total: 974 km
border countries: Democratic Republic of the Congo 233 km, Rwanda 290 km, Tanzania 451 km
Coastline: 0 km (landlocked)
Maritime claims: none (landlocked)

Climate: equatorial; high plateau with considerable altitude variation (772 m to 2,670 m above sea level); average annual temperature varies with altitude from 23 to 17 degrees centigrade but is generally moderate as the average altitude is about 1,700 m; average annual rainfall is about 150 cm; wet seasons from February to May and September to November, and dry seasons from June to August and December to January
Terrain: hilly and mountainous, dropping to a plateau in east, some plains
Elevation extremes:
lowest point: Lake Tanganyika 772 m
highest point: Mount Heha 2,670 m
Natural resources: nickel, uranium, rare earth oxides, peat, cobalt, copper, platinum (not yet exploited), vanadium, arable land, hydropower
Land use:
arable land: 29.98%
permanent crops: 12.85%
other: 57.17% (1998 est.)
Irrigated land: 740 sq km (1998 est.)
Natural hazards: flooding, landslides, drought
Environment - current issues: soil erosion as a result of overgrazing and the expansion of agriculture into marginal lands; deforestation (little forested land remains because of uncontrolled cutting of trees for fuel); habitat loss threatens wildlife populations
Environment - international agreements:
party to: Biodiversity, Climate Change, Climate Change-Kyoto Protocol, Desertification, Endangered Species, Hazardous Wastes, Ozone Layer Protection
signed, but not ratified: Law of the Sea
Geography - note: landlocked; straddles crest of the Nile-Congo watershed; the Kagera, which drains into Lake Victoria, is the most remote headstream of the White Nile

People

Population: 6,231,221
note: estimates for this country explicitly take into account the effects of excess mortality due to AIDS; this can result in lower life expectancy, higher infant mortality and death rates, lower population and growth rates, and changes in the distribution of population by age and sex than would otherwise be expected (July 2004 est.)
Age structure:
0-14 years: 46.4% (male 1,459,251; female 1,430,332)
15-64 years: 50.9% (male 1,566,274; female 1,607,705)
65 years and over: 2.7% (male 66,306; female 101,353) (2004 est.)
Median age:
total: 16.5 years
male: 16.1 years
female: 16.8 years (2004 est.)
Population growth rate: 2.2% (2004 est.)
Birth rate: 39.68 births/1,000 population (2004 est.)

Death rate: 17.61 deaths/1,000 population (2004 est.)
Net migration rate: -0.06 migrant(s)/1,000 population (2004 est.)
Sex ratio:
at birth: 1.03 male(s)/female
under 15 years: 1.02 male(s)/female
15-64 years: 0.97 male(s)/female
65 years and over: 0.65 male(s)/female
total population: 0.99 male(s)/female (2004 est.)
Infant mortality rate:
total: 70.4 deaths/1,000 live births
male: 77.15 deaths/1,000 live births
female: 63.45 deaths/1,000 live births (2004 est.)
Life expectancy at birth:
total population: 43.36 years
male: 42.73 years
female: 44 years (2004 est.)
Total fertility rate: 5.9 children born/woman (2004 est.)
HIV/AIDS - adult prevalence rate: 8.3% (2001 est.)
HIV/AIDS - people living with HIV/AIDS: 390,000 (2001 est.)
HIV/AIDS - deaths: 40,000 (2001 est.)
Nationality:
noun: Burundian(s)
adjective: Burundian
Ethnic groups: Hutu (Bantu) 85%, Tutsi (Hamitic) 14%, Twa (Pygmy) 1%, Europeans 3,000, South Asians 2,000
Religions: Christian 67% (Roman Catholic 62%, Protestant 5%), indigenous beliefs 23%, Muslim 10%
Languages: Kirundi (official), French (official), Swahili (along Lake Tanganyika and in the Bujumbura area)
Literacy:
definition: age 15 and over can read and write
total population: 51.6%
male: 58.5%
female: 45.2% (2003 est.)

Government

Country name:
conventional long form: Republic of Burundi
conventional short form: Burundi
local long form: Republika y'u Burundi
local short form: Burundi
former: Urundi
Government type: republic
Capital: Bujumbura
Administrative divisions: 16 provinces; Bubanza, Bujumbura, Bururi, Cankuzo, Cibitoke, Gitega, Karuzi, Kayanza, Kirundo, Makamba, Muramvya, Muyinga, Mwaro, Ngozi, Rutana, Ruyigi
Independence: 1 July 1962 (from UN trusteeship under Belgian administration)
National holiday: Independence Day, 1 July (1962)
Constitution: 13 March 1992; provided for establishment of a plural political system; supplanted on 6 June 1998 by a Transitional Constitution which enlarged the National Assembly and created two vice presidents

Legal system: based on German and Belgian civil codes and customary law; has not accepted compulsory ICJ jurisdiction

Suffrage: NA years of age; universal adult

Executive branch:

chief of state: President Domitien NDAYIZEYE (since 30 April 2003); note - NDAYIZEYE, a Hutu, was sworn in as president for the second half of the three-year transitional government inaugurated on 1 November 2001; Vice President Alphonse KADEGE (since 30 April 2003); note - KADEGE is from the Tutsi minority

head of government: President Domitien NDAYIZEYE (since 30 April 2003); note - NDAYIZEYE, a Hutu, was sworn in as president for the second half of the three-year transitional government inaugurated on 1 November 2001; Vice President Alphonse KADEGE (since 30 April 2003); note - KADEGE is from the Tutsi minority

cabinet: Council of Ministers appointed by president

elections: NA; current president assumed power on 30 April 2003 as part of the transitional government established by the 2000 Arusha Accord

Legislative branch: bicameral, consists of a National Assembly or Assemblee Nationale (expanded from 121 to approximately 140 seats under the transitional government inaugurated 1 November 2001; members are elected by popular vote to serve five-year terms) and a Senate (54 seats; term length is undefined, the current senators will likely serve out the three-year transition period)

elections: last held 29 June 1993 (next was scheduled to be held in 1998, but was suspended by presidential decree in 1996; elections are planned to follow the completion of the three-year transitional government)

election results: percent of vote by party - FRODEBU 71.04%, UPRONA 21.4%, other 7.56%; seats by party - FRODEBU 65, UPRONA 16, civilians 27, other parties 13

Judicial branch: Supreme Court or Cour Supreme; Constitutional Court; Courts of Appeal (there are three in separate locations); Tribunals of First Instance (17 at the province level and 123 small local tribunals)

Political parties and leaders: the two national, mainstream, governing parties are: Unity for National Progress or UPRONA [Alphonse KADEGE, president]; Burundi Democratic Front or FRODEBU [Jean MINANI, president]

note: a multiparty system was introduced after 1998, included are: Burundi African Alliance for the Salvation or ABASA [Terrence NSANZE]; Rally for Democracy and Economic and Social Development or RADDES [Joseph NZEYIMANA]; Party for National Redress or PARENA [Jean-Baptiste BAGAZA]; People's Reconciliation Party or PRP [Mathias HITIMANA]

Political pressure groups and leaders: loosely organized Hutu and Tutsi militias, often affiliated with Hutu and Tutsi extremist parties or subordinate to government security forces

International organization participation: ACCT, ACP, AfDB, AU, CEPGL, FAO, G-77, IBRD, ICAO, ICCt (signatory), ICFTU, ICRM, IDA, IFAD, IFC, IFRCS, ILO, IMF, Interpol, IOC, IOM (observer), ISO (subscriber), ITU, NAM, OPCW, UN, UNCTAD, UNESCO, UNIDO, UPU, WCO, WHO, WIPO, WMO, WToO, WTrO

Diplomatic representation in the US:

chief of mission: Ambassador Antoine NTAMOBWA

chancery: Suite 212, 2233 Wisconsin Avenue NW, Washington, DC 20007

telephone: [1] (202) 342-2574

FAX: [1] (202) 342-2578

Diplomatic representation from the US:

chief of mission: Ambassador James Howard YELLIN

embassy: Avenue des Etats-Unis, Bujumbura

mailing address: B. P. 1720, Bujumbura

telephone: [257] 223454

FAX: [257] 222926

Flag description: divided by a white diagonal cross into red panels (top and bottom) and green panels (hoist side and outer side) with a white disk superimposed at the center bearing three red six-pointed stars outlined in green arranged in a triangular design (one star above, two stars below)

Economy

Economy - overview: Burundi is a landlocked, resource-poor country with an underdeveloped manufacturing sector. The economy is predominantly agricultural with roughly 90% of the population dependent on subsistence agriculture. Economic growth depends on coffee and tea exports, which account for 90% of foreign exchange earnings. The ability to pay for imports, therefore, rests primarily on weather conditions and international coffee and tea prices. The Tutsi minority, 14% of the population, dominates the government and the coffee trade at the expense of the Hutu majority, 85% of the population. Since October 1993 an ethnic-based war has resulted in more than 200,000 deaths, forced 800,000 refugees into Tanzania, and displaced 525,000 others internally. Doubts about the prospects for sustainable peace continue to impede development. Only one in two children go to school, and approximately one in ten adults has HIV/AIDS. Food, medicine, and electricity remain in short supply.

GDP: purchasing power parity - $3.83 billion (2003 est.)

GDP - real growth rate: 0% (2003 est.)

GDP - per capita: purchasing power parity - $600 (2003 est.)

GDP - composition by sector:

agriculture: 40.5%

industry: 18.6%

services: 40.9% (2002 est.)

Population below poverty line: 68% (2002 est.)

Household income or consumption by percentage share:

lowest 10%: 1.8%

highest 10%: 32.9% (1998)

Distribution of family income - Gini index: 42.5 (1998)

Inflation rate (consumer prices): 11% (2003 est.)

Labor force: 2.99 million (2002)

Labor force - by occupation: agriculture 93.6%, industry 2.3%, services 4.1% (2002 est.)

Unemployment rate: NA%

Budget:

revenues: $125 million

expenditures: $176 million, including capital expenditures of $NA (2000 est.)

Industries: light consumer goods such as blankets, shoes, soap; assembly of imported components; public works construction; food processing

Industrial production growth rate: 18% (2001)

Electricity - production: 155.4 million kWh (2001)

Electricity - production by source:

fossil fuel: 0.6%

hydro: 99.4%

nuclear: 0%

other: 0% (2001)

Electricity - consumption: 177.5 million kWh (2001)

Electricity - exports: 0 kWh (2001)

Electricity - imports: 33 million kWh; note - supplied by the Democratic Republic of the Congo (2001)

Oil - production: 0 bbl/day (2001 est.)

Oil - consumption: 2,750 bbl/day (2001 est.)

Oil - exports: NA

Oil - imports: NA

Agriculture - products: coffee, cotton, tea, corn, sorghum, sweet potatoes, bananas, manioc (tapioca); beef, milk, hides

Exports: $40 million f.o.b. (2003 est.)

Exports - commodities: coffee, tea, sugar, cotton, hides

Exports - partners: Germany 25%, Belgium 14.3%, Kenya 10.7%, Netherlands 7.1%, Rwanda 7.1% (2002)

Imports: $128 million f.o.b. (2003 est.)

Imports - commodities: capital goods, petroleum products, foodstuffs

Imports - partners: Belgium 12%, Saudi Arabia 12%, France 7.5%, Kenya 7.5%, Tanzania 6%, Algeria 5.3%, India 4.5% (2002)

Debt - external: $1,132.5 million (2002)

Economic aid - recipient: $92.7 million (2000)

Currency: Burundi franc (BIF)

Currency code: BIF

Exchange rates: Burundi francs per US dollar - 1,082.62 (2003), 930.749 (2002), 830.353 (2001), 720.673 (2000), 563.562 (1999)

Fiscal year: calendar year

Communications

Telephones - main lines in use: 22,100 (2002)

Telephones - mobile cellular: 52,000 (2002)

Telephone system:

general assessment: primitive system

domestic: sparse system of open-wire, radiotelephone communications, and low-capacity microwave radio relay *international:* country code - 257; satellite earth station - 1 Intelsat (Indian Ocean)

Radio broadcast stations: AM 0, FM 4, shortwave 1 (2001)

Television broadcast stations: 1 (2001)

Internet country code: .bi

Internet hosts: 3 (2002)

Internet users: 8,400 (2002)

Transportation

Railways: 0 km

Highways:

total: 14,480 km

paved: 1,028 km

unpaved: 13,452 km (1999 est.)

Waterways: Lake Tanganyika

Ports and harbors: Bujumbura

Airports: 8 (2003 est.)

Airports - with paved runways:

total: 1

over 3,047 m: 1 (2003 est.)

Airports - with unpaved runways:

total: 7

914 to 1,523 m: 4

under 914 m: 3 (2003 est.)

Military

Military branches: Army (including Naval Detachment and Air Wing), National Gendarmerie

Military manpower - military age: 16 years of age (2004 est.)

Military manpower - availability:

males age 15-49: 1,419,755 (2004 est.)

Military manpower - fit for military service:

males age 15-49: 747,400 (2004 est.)

Military manpower - reaching military age annually:

males: 81,862 (2004 est.)

Military expenditures - dollar figure: $33.3 million (2003)

Military expenditures - percent of GDP: 6% (2003)

Transnational Issues

Disputes - international: Tutsi, Hutu, and other conflicting ethnic groups, associated political rebels, armed gangs, and various government forces continue fighting in the Great Lakes region, transcending the boundaries of Burundi, Democratic Republic of the Congo, Rwanda, and Uganda to gain control over populated and natural resource areas; government heads pledge to end conflict, but localized violence continues despite UN peacekeeping efforts

Cambodia

Introduction

Background: Following a five-year struggle, Communist Khmer Rouge forces captured Phnom Penh in April 1975 and ordered the evacuation of all cities and towns; over 1.5 million displaced people died from execution, enforced hardships, or starvation. A 1978 Vietnamese invasion drove the Khmer Rouge into the countryside and touched off almost 13 years of civil war. The 1991 Paris Peace Accords mandated democratic elections and a ceasefire, which was not fully respected by the Khmer Rouge. UN-sponsored elections in 1993 helped restore some semblance of normalcy and the final elements of the Khmer Rouge surrendered in early 1999. Factional fighting in 1997 ended the first coalition government, but a second round of national elections in 1998 led to the formation of another coalition government and renewed political stability. The July 2003 elections were relatively peaceful, but negotiations among contending political parties have yet to yield a new coalition government.

Geography

Location: Southeastern Asia, bordering the Gulf of Thailand, between Thailand, Vietnam, and Laos

Geographic coordinates: 13 00 N, 105 00 E

Map references: Southeast Asia

Area:

total: 181,040 sq km

land: 176,520 sq km

water: 4,520 sq km

Area - comparative: slightly smaller than Oklahoma

Land boundaries:

total: 2,572 km

border countries: Laos 541 km, Thailand 803 km, Vietnam 1,228 km

Coastline: 443 km

Maritime claims:

territorial sea: 12 NM

contiguous zone: 24 NM

exclusive economic zone: 200 NM

continental shelf: 200 NM

Climate: tropical; rainy, monsoon season (May to November); dry season (December to April); little seasonal temperature variation

Terrain: mostly low, flat plains; mountains in southwest and north

Elevation extremes:

lowest point: Gulf of Thailand 0 m

highest point: Phnum Aoral 1,810 m

Natural resources: oil and gas, timber, gemstones, some iron ore, manganese, phosphates, hydropower potential

Land use:

arable land: 20.96%

permanent crops: 0.61%

other: 78.43% (1998 est.)

Irrigated land: 2,700 sq km (1998 est.)

Natural hazards: monsoonal rains (June to November); flooding; occasional droughts

Environment - current issues: illegal logging activities throughout the country and strip mining for gems in the western region along the border with Thailand have resulted in habitat loss and declining biodiversity (in particular, destruction of mangrove swamps threatens natural fisheries); soil erosion; in rural areas, most of the population does not have access to potable water; declining fish stocks because of illegal fishing and overfishing

Environment - international agreements:

party to: Biodiversity, Climate Change, Climate Change-Kyoto Protocol, Desertification, Endangered Species, Hazardous Wastes, Marine Life Conservation, Ozone Layer Protection, Ship Pollution, Tropical Timber 94, Wetlands

signed, but not ratified: Law of the Sea

Geography - note: a land of paddies and forests dominated by the Mekong River and Tonle Sap

People

Population: 13,363,421

note. estimates for this country take into account the effects of excess mortality due to AIDS; this can result in lower life expectancy, higher infant mortality and death rates, lower population growth rates, and changes in the distribution of population by age and sex than would otherwise be expected (July 2004 est.)

Age structure.

0-14 years. 38.3% (male 2,583,606; female 2,534,460)

15-64 years. 58.6% (male 3,742,178; female 4,095,303)

65 years and over. 3.1% (male 149,466; female 258,408) (2004 est.)

Median age.

total. 19.5 years

male. 18.8 years

female. 20.4 years (2004 est.)

Cambodia *(continued)*

Population growth rate: 1.8% (2004 est.)
Birth rate: 27.13 births/1,000 population (2004 est.)
Death rate: 9.1 deaths/1,000 population (2004 est.)
Net migration rate: 0 migrant(s)/1,000 population (2004 est.)
Sex ratio:
at birth: 1.05 male(s)/female
under 15 years: 1.02 male(s)/female
15-64 years: 0.91 male(s)/female
65 years and over: 0.58 male(s)/female
total population: 0.94 male(s)/female (2004 est.)
Infant mortality rate:
total: 73.67 deaths/1,000 live births
male: 82.51 deaths/1,000 live births
female: 64.44 deaths/1,000 live births (2004 est.)
Life expectancy at birth:
total population: 58.41 years
male: 55.71 years
female: 61.23 years (2004 est.)
Total fertility rate: 3.51 children born/woman (2004 est.)
HIV/AIDS - adult prevalence rate: 2.7% (2001 est.)
HIV/AIDS - people living with HIV/AIDS: 170,000 (2001 est.)
HIV/AIDS - deaths: 12,000 (2001 est.)
Nationality:
noun: Cambodian(s)
adjective: Cambodian
Ethnic groups: Khmer 90%, Vietnamese 5%, Chinese 1%, other 4%
Religions: Theravada Buddhist 95%, other 5%
Languages: Khmer (official) 95%, French, English
Literacy:
definition: age 15 and over can read and write
total population: 69.9%
male: 80.5%
female: 60.3% (2003 est.)

Government

Country name:
conventional long form: Kingdom of Cambodia
conventional short form: Cambodia
local long form: Preahreacheanacha Kampuchea (phonetic pronunciation)
local short form: Kampuchea
former: Kingdom of Cambodia, Khmer Republic, Democratic Kampuchea, People's Republic of Kampuchea, State of Cambodia
Government type: multiparty democracy under a constitutional monarchy established in September 1993
Capital: Phnom Penh
Administrative divisions: 20 provinces (khaitt, singular and plural) and 4 municipalities* (krong, singular and plural); Banteay Mean Chey, Batdambang, Kampong Cham, Kampong Chhnang, Kampong Spoe, Kampong Thum, Kampot, Kandal, Koh Kong, Keb*, Kracheh, Mondol Kiri, Otdar Mean Chey, Pailin*, Phnom Penh*, Pouthisat, Preah Sihanouk (formerly Kompong Som)*, Preah Vihear, Prey Veng, Rotanakir, Siem Reab, Stoeng Treng, Svay Rieng, Takao

Independence: 9 November 1953 (from France)
National holiday: Independence Day, 9 November (1953)
Constitution: promulgated 21 September 1993
Legal system: primarily a civil law mixture of French-influenced codes from the United Nations Transitional Authority in Cambodia (UNTAC) period, royal decrees, and acts of the legislature, with influences of customary law and remnants of communist legal theory; increasing influence of common law in recent years
Suffrage: 18 years of age; universal
Executive branch:
chief of state: King NORODOM Sihanouk (reinstated 24 September 1993)
head of government: Prime Minister HUN Sen (since 30 November 1998) and Deputy Prime Ministers SAR Kheng (since 1993) and TOL Lah (since 1998)
cabinet: Council of Ministers in theory appointed by the monarch; in practice named by the prime minister
elections: none; the monarch is chosen by a Royal Throne Council; following legislative elections, a member of the majority party or majority coalition is named prime minister by the Chairman of the National Assembly and appointed by the king
Legislative branch: bicameral consists of the National Assembly (123 seats; members elected by popular vote to serve five-year terms) and the Senate (61 seats; two members appointed by the monarch, two elected by the National Assembly, and 57 elected by "functional constituencies"; members serve five-year terms)
elections: National Assembly - last held 27 July 2003 (next to be held in July 2008); Senate - last held 2 March 1999 (scheduled to be held in 2004 but delayed)
election results: National Assembly - percent of vote by party - CPP 47%, SRP 22%, FUNCINPEC 21%, other 10%; seats by party - CPP 73, FUNCINPEC 26, SRP 24; Senate - percent of vote by party - NA%; seats by party - CPP 31, FUNCINPEC 21, SRP 7, other 2 (July 2003)
Judicial branch: Supreme Council of the Magistracy (provided for in the constitution and formed in December 1997); Supreme Court (and lower courts) exercises judicial authority
Political parties and leaders: Cambodian Pracheachon Party (Cambodian People's Party) or CPP [CHEA Sim]; National United Front for an Independent, Neutral, Peaceful, and Cooperative Cambodia or FUNCINPEC [Prince NORODOM Ranariddh]; Sam Rangsi Party or SRP [SAM Rangsi]
Political pressure groups and leaders: NA
International organization participation: ACCT, ARF, AsDB, ASEAN, CP, FAO, G-77, IBRD, ICAO, ICCt, ICRM, IDA, IFAD, IFC, IFRCS, ILO, IMF, IMO, Interpol, IOC, IOM, ISO (subscriber), ITU, NAM, OPCW (signatory), PCA, UN, UNCTAD, UNESCO, UNIDO, UPU, WCO, WFTU, WHO, WIPO, WMO, WToO, WTrO (observer)

Diplomatic representation in the US:
chief of mission: Ambassador ROLAND Eng
chancery: 4530 16th Street NW, Washington, DC 20011
telephone: [1] (202) 726-7742
FAX: [1] (202) 726-8381
Diplomatic representation from the US:
chief of mission: Ambassador Charles Aaron RAY
embassy: 27 EO Street 240, Phnom Penh
mailing address: Box P, APO AP 96546
telephone: [855] (23) 216-436/438
FAX: [855] (23) 216-437/811
Flag description: three horizontal bands of blue (top), red (double width), and blue with a white three-towered temple representing Angkor Wat outlined in black in the center of the red band; only flag in the world to incorporate a building in its design

Economy

Economy - overview: Cambodia's economy slowed dramatically in 1997-1998 due to the regional economic crisis, civil violence, and political infighting. Foreign investment and tourism fell off. In 1999, the first full year of peace in 30 years, progress was made on economic reforms. Growth resumed and has remained about 5.0% during 2000-2003. Tourism was Cambodia's fastest growing industry, with arrivals up 34% in 2000 and up another 40% in 2001 before the 11 September 2001 terrorist attacks in the US. Cambodia expects 1 million foreign tourists in 2004. Economic growth has been largely driven by expansion in the clothing sector and tourism. Clothing exports were fostered by the U.S.-Cambodian Bilateral Textile Agreement signed in 1999. Even given Cambodia's recent growth, the long-term development of the economy after decades of war remains a daunting challenge. The population lacks education and productive skills, particularly in the poverty-ridden countryside, which suffers from an almost total lack of basic infrastructure. Fear of renewed political instability and a dysfunctional legal system coupled with government corruption discourage foreign investment. The Cambodian government continues to work with bilateral and multilateral donors to address the country's many pressing needs. The major economic challenge for Cambodia over the next decade will be fashioning an economic environment in which the private sector can create enough jobs to handle Cambodia's demographic imbalance. About 60% of the population is 20 years or younger; most of these citizens will seek to enter the workforce over the course of the next 10 years.
GDP: purchasing power parity - $22.76 billion (2003 est.)
GDP - real growth rate: 5.5% (2003 est.)
GDP - per capita: purchasing power parity - $1,700 (2003 est.)
GDP - composition by sector:
agriculture: 30%
industry: 40%
services: 30% (2003 est.)

Cambodia *(continued)*

Population below poverty line: 36% (1997 est.)

Household income or consumption by percentage share:

lowest 10%: 2.9%

highest 10%: 33.8% (1997)

Distribution of family income - Gini index: 40.4 (1997)

Inflation rate (consumer prices): 3% (2003 est.)

Labor force: 7 million (2003 est.)

Labor force - by occupation: agriculture 75% (2003 est.)

Unemployment rate: 2.5% (2000 est.)

Budget:

revenues: $438 million

expenditures: $630, including capital expenditures of $291 million of which 75% was financed by external assistance (2002 est.)

Industries: tourism, garments, rice milling, fishing, wood and wood products, rubber, cement, gem mining, textiles

Industrial production growth rate: 22% (2002 est.)

Electricity - production: 119 million kWh (2001)

Electricity - production by source:

fossil fuel: 65%

hydro: 35%

nuclear: 0%

other: 0% (2001)

Electricity - consumption: 110.6 million kWh (2001)

Electricity - exports: 0 kWh (2001)

Electricity - imports: 0 kWh (2001)

Oil - production: 0 bbl/day (2001 est.)

Oil - consumption: 3,600 bbl/day (2001 est.)

Oil - exports: NA

Oil - imports: NA

Agriculture - products: rice, rubber, corn, vegetables, cashews, tapioca

Exports: $1.616 billion f.o.b. (2003 est.)

Exports - commodities: Clothing, timber, rubber, rice, fish, tobacco, footwear

Exports - partners: US 59.9%, Germany 9.2%, UK 7%, Singapore 4.4% (2002)

Imports: $2.124 billion f.o.b. (2003 est.)

Imports - commodities: petroleum products, cigarettes, gold, construction materials, machinery, motor vehicles, pharmaceutical products

Imports - partners: Thailand 22.9%, Singapore 15.7%, Hong Kong 15.1%, China 11.2%, Taiwan 8.5%, South Korea 5.1%, Vietnam 4.8% (2002)

Debt - external: $2.4 billion (2002 est.)

Economic aid - recipient: $548 million pledged in grants and concessional loans for 2001 by international donors (actual disbursement in 2002 was about $500 million)

Currency: riel (KHR)

Currency code: KHR

Exchange rates: riels per US dollar - 3,973.33 (2003), 3,912.08 (2002), 3,916.33 (2001), 3,840.75 (2000), 3,807.83 (1999)

Fiscal year: calendar year

Communications

Telephones - main lines in use: 35,400 (2002)

Telephones - mobile cellular: 380,000 (2002)

Telephone system:

general assessment: adequate landline and/or cellular service in Phnom Penh and other provincial cities; mobile phone coverage is rapidly expanding in rural areas

domestic: NA

international: country code - 855; adequate but expensive landline and cellular service available to all countries from Phnom Penh and major provincial cities; satellite earth station - 1 Intersputnik (Indian Ocean region)

Radio broadcast stations: AM 2, FM 17, (2003)

Television broadcast stations: 7 (2003)

Internet country code: .kh

Internet hosts: 1,391 (2002)

Internet users: 30,000 (2002)

Transportation

Railways:

total: 602 km

narrow gauge: 602 km 1.000-m gauge (2002)

Highways:

total: 12,323 km

paved: 1,996 km

unpaved: 10,327 km (2000 est)

Waterways: 3,700 km

note: navigable all year to craft drawing 0.6 m or less; 282 km navigable to craft drawing as much as 1.8 m

Ports and harbors: Kampong Som (Sihanoukville), Kampot, Krong Kaoh Kong, Phnom Penh, Sre Ambol, Keo Phoh Port (privately owned) (2003)

Merchant marine:

total: 467 ships (1,000 GRT or over) 1,913,910 GRT/2,713,967 DWT

by type: bulk 42, cargo 360, chemical tanker 6, combination bulk 3, container 13, liquefied gas 1, livestock carrier 4, multi-functional large load carrier 1, passenger/cargo 1, petroleum tanker 16, refrigerated cargo 13, roll on/roll off 5, short-sea/passenger 2

foreign-owned: Algeria 2, Angola 1, Aruba 1, Bahamas 1, Belize 10, British Virgin Islands 7, Bulgaria 1, Canada 4, China 35, Cyprus 14, Egypt 8, Finland 1, France 1, Georgia 1, Germany 1, Gibraltar 1, Greece 9, Honduras 8, Hong Kong 12, Indonesia 2, Iran 1, Italy 2, Japan 1, Jordan 1, North Korea 2, South Korea 31, Lebanon 2, Liberia 7, Malaysia 1, Malta 2, Marshall Islands 11, Netherlands 2, Nigeria 2, Norway 1, Panama 8, Romania 1, Russia 81, Saint Kitts and Nevis 2, Saint Vincent and the Grenadines 5, Samoa 2, Singapore 7, Spain 1, Syria 19, Taiwan 1, Turkey 11

registered in other countries: 19 (2003 est.)

Airports: 20 (2003 est.)

Airports - with paved runways:

total: 5

2,438 to 3,047 m: 2

1,524 to 2,437 m: 2

914 to 1,523 m: 1 (2003 est.)

Airports - with unpaved runways:

total: 15

1,524 to 2,437 m: 2

914 to 1,523 m: 12

under 914 m: 1 (2003 est.)

Heliports: 2 (2003 est.)

Military

Military branches: Royal Cambodian Armed Forces: Army, Navy, Air Force

Military manpower - military age: 18 years of age (2004 est.)

Military manpower - availability:

males age 15-49: 3,402,703 (2004 est.)

Military manpower - fit for military service:

males age 15-49: 1,899,710 (2004 est.)

Military manpower - reaching military age annually:

males: 170,072 (2004 est.)

Military expenditures - dollar figure: $112 million (FY01 est.)

Military expenditures - percent of GDP: 3% (FY01 est.)

Transnational Issues

Disputes - international: land boundary disputes persist among Cambodian claims that Thailand and Vietnam moved or destroyed boundary markers; maritime boundary with Vietnam is hampered by dispute over offshore islands; Cambodia periodically accuses Thailand of obstructing access to Preah Vihear temple ruins awarded to Cambodia by ICJ decision in 1962; 2003 anti-Thai riots in Phnom Penh resulted in the destruction of the Thai Embassy, damage to 17 Thai-owned businesses, and disputes over full payment of compensation

Illicit drugs: narcotics-related corruption reportedly involving some in the government, military, and police; possible small-scale opium, heroin, and amphetamine production; large producer of cannabis for the international market; vulnerable to money laundering due to its cash-based economy and porous borders

Cameroon

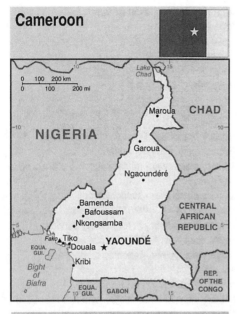

Introduction

Background: The former French Cameroon and part of British Cameroon merged in 1961 to form the present country. Cameroon has generally enjoyed stability, which has permitted the development of agriculture, roads, and railways, as well as a petroleum industry. Despite movement toward democratic reform, political power remains firmly in the hands of an ethnic oligarchy.

Geography

Location: Western Africa, bordering the Bight of Biafra, between Equatorial Guinea and Nigeria
Geographic coordinates: 6 00 N, 12 00 E
Map references: Africa
Area:
total: 475,440 sq km
land: 469,440 sq km
water: 6,000 sq km
Area - comparative: slightly larger than California
Land boundaries:
total: 4,591 km
border countries: Central African Republic 797 km, Chad 1,094 km, Republic of the Congo 523 km, Equatorial Guinea 189 km, Gabon 298 km, Nigeria 1,690 km
Coastline: 402 km
Maritime claims:
territorial sea: 50 NM
Climate: varies with terrain, from tropical along coast to semiarid and hot in north
Terrain: diverse, with coastal plain in southwest, dissected plateau in center, mountains in west, plains in north
Elevation extremes:
lowest point: Atlantic Ocean 0 m
highest point: Fako (on Mount Cameroon) 4,095 m
Natural resources: petroleum, bauxite, iron ore, timber, hydropower

Land use:
arable land: 12.81%
permanent crops: 2.58%
other: 84.61% (1998 est.)
Irrigated land: 330 sq km (1998 est.)
Natural hazards: volcanic activity with periodic releases of poisonous gases from Lake Nyos and Lake Monoun volcanoes
Environment - current issues: water-borne diseases are prevalent; deforestation; overgrazing; desertification; poaching; overfishing
Environment - international agreements:
party to: Biodiversity, Climate Change, Climate Change-Kyoto Protocol, Desertification, Endangered Species, Hazardous Wastes, Law of the Sea, Ozone Layer Protection, Tropical Timber 83, Tropical Timber 94
signed, but not ratified: none of the selected agreements
Geography - note: sometimes referred to as the hinge of Africa; throughout the country there are areas of thermal springs and indications of current or prior volcanic activity; Mount Cameroon, the highest mountain in Sub-Saharan west Africa, is an active volcano

People

Population: 16,063,678
note: estimates for this country explicitly take into account the effects of excess mortality due to AIDS; this can result in lower life expectancy, higher infant mortality and death rates, lower population and growth rates, and changes in the distribution of population by age and sex than would otherwise be expected (July 2004 est.)
Age structure:
0-14 years: 42% (male 3,416,086; female 3,334,904)
15-64 years: 54.8% (male 4,425,246; female 4,370,329)
65 years and over: 3.2% (male 233,506; female 283,607) (2004 est.)
Median age:
total: 18.5 years
male: 18.3 years
female: 18.6 years (2004 est.)
Population growth rate: 1.97% (2004 est.)
Birth rate: 35.08 births/1,000 population (2004 est.)
Death rate: 15.34 deaths/1,000 population (2004 est.)
Net migration rate: 0 migrant(s)/1,000 population (2004 est.)
Sex ratio:
at birth: 1.03 male(s)/female
under 15 years: 1.02 male(s)/female
15-64 years: 1.01 male(s)/female
65 years and over: 0.82 male(s)/female
total population: 1.01 male(s)/female (2004 est.)
Infant mortality rate:
total: 69.18 deaths/1,000 live births
male: 73.16 deaths/1,000 live births
female: 65.09 deaths/1,000 live births (2004 est.)

Life expectancy at birth:
total population: 47.95 years
male: 47.1 years
female: 48.83 years (2004 est.)
Total fertility rate: 4.55 children born/woman (2004 est.)
HIV/AIDS - adult prevalence rate: 11.8% (2001 est.)
HIV/AIDS - people living with HIV/AIDS: 920,000 (2001 est.)
HIV/AIDS - deaths: 53,000 (2001 est.)
Nationality:
noun: Cameroonian(s)
adjective: Cameroonian
Ethnic groups: Cameroon Highlanders 31%, Equatorial Bantu 19%, Kirdi 11%, Fulani 10%, Northwestern Bantu 8%, Eastern Nigritic 7%, other African 13%, non-African less than 1%
Religions: indigenous beliefs 40%, Christian 40%, Muslim 20%
Languages: 24 major African language groups, English (official), French (official)
Literacy:
definition: age 15 and over can read and write
total population: 79%
male: 84.7%
female: 73.4% (2003 est.)

Government

Country name:
conventional long form: Republic of Cameroon
conventional short form: Cameroon
former: French Cameroon
Government type: unitary republic; multiparty presidential regime (opposition parties legalized in 1990)
note: preponderance of power remains with the president
Capital: Yaounde
Administrative divisions: 10 provinces; Adamaoua, Centre, Est, Extreme-Nord, Littoral, Nord, Nord-Ouest, Ouest, Sud, Sud-Ouest
Independence: 1 January 1960 (from French-administered UN trusteeship)
National holiday: Republic Day (National Day), 20 May (1972)
Constitution: 20 May 1972 approved by referendum; 2 June 1972 formally adopted; revised January 1996
Legal system: based on French civil law system, with common law influence; has not accepted compulsory ICJ jurisdiction
Suffrage: 20 years of age; universal
Executive branch:
chief of state: President Paul BIYA (since 6 November 1982)
head of government: Prime Minister Peter Mafany MUSONGE (since 19 September 1996)
cabinet: Cabinet appointed by the president from proposals submitted by the prime minister

Cameroon (continued)

elections: president elected by popular vote for a seven-year term; election last held 12 October 1997 (next to be held NA October 2004); prime minister appointed by the president

election results: President Paul BIYA reelected; percent of vote - Paul BIYA 92.6%; note - supporters of the opposition candidates boycotted the elections, making a comparison of vote shares relatively meaningless

Legislative branch: unicameral National Assembly or Assemblee Nationale (180 seats; members are elected by direct popular vote to serve five-year terms; note - the president can either lengthen or shorten the term of the legislature)

elections: last held 23 June 2002 (next to be held NA 2007)

election results: percent of vote by party - NA%; seats by party - RDCP 133, SDF 21, UDC 5, other 21

note: the constitution calls for an upper chamber for the legislature, to be called a Senate, but it has yet to be established

Judicial branch: Supreme Court (judges are appointed by the president); High Court of Justice (consists of 9 judges and 6 substitute judges, elected by the National Assembly)

Political parties and leaders: Cameroonian Democratic Union or UDC [Adamou NDAM NJOYA]; Democratic Rally of the Cameroon People or RDCP [Paul BIYA]; Movement for the Defense of the Republic or MDR [Dakole DAISSALA]; Movement for the Liberation and Development of Cameroon or MLDC [leader Marcel YONDO]; Movement for the Youth of Cameroon or MYC [Dieudonne TINA]; National Union for Democracy and Progress or UNDP [Maigari BELLO BOUBA]; Social Democratic Front or SDF [John FRU NDI]; Union of Cameroonian Populations or UPC [Augustin Frederic KODOCK]

Political pressure groups and leaders: Southern Cameroon National Council [Ayamba Ette OTUN]; Human Rights Defense Group [Albert MUKONG, president]

International organization participation: ABEDA, ACCT, ACP, AfDB, AU, BDEAC, C, CEMAC, FAO, FZ, G-77, IAEA, IBRD, ICAO, ICC, ICCt (signatory), ICFTU, ICRM, IDA, IDB, IFAD, IFC, IFRCS, ILO, IMF, IMO, Interpol, IOC, ISO (correspondent), ITU, MONUC, NAM, OIC, OPCW, PCA, UN, UNCTAD, UNESCO, UNIDO, UNMIK, UPU, WCL, WCO, WFTU, WHO, WIPO, WMO, WToO, WTrO

Diplomatic representation in the US:

chief of mission: Ambassador Jerome MENDOUGA

chancery: 2349 Massachusetts Avenue NW, Washington, DC 20008

telephone: [1] (202) 265-8790

FAX: [1] (202) 387-3826

Diplomatic representation from the US:

chief of mission: Ambassador George McDade STAPLES

embassy: Rue Nachtigal, Yaounde

mailing address: P. O. Box 817, Yaounde; pouch: American Embassy, Department of State, Washington, DC 20521-2520

telephone: [237] 223-05-12, 222-25-89, 222-17-94, 223-40-14

FAX: [237] 223-07-53

branch office(s): Douala

Flag description: three equal vertical bands of green (hoist side), red, and yellow with a yellow five-pointed star centered in the red band; uses the popular pan-African colors of Ethiopia

Economy

Economy - overview: Because of its oil resources and favorable agricultural conditions, Cameroon has one of the best-endowed primary commodity economies in sub-Saharan Africa. Still, it faces many of the serious problems facing other underdeveloped countries, such as a top-heavy civil service and a generally unfavorable climate for business enterprise. Since 1990, the government has embarked on various IMF and World Bank programs designed to spur business investment, increase efficiency in agriculture, improve trade, and recapitalize the nation's banks. In June 2000, the government completed an IMF-sponsored, three-year structural adjustment program; however, the IMF is pressing for more reforms, including increased budget transparency, privatization, and poverty reduction programs. International oil and cocoa prices have considerable impact on the economy.

GDP: purchasing power parity - $27.59 billion (2003 est.)

GDP - real growth rate: 3.6% (2003 est.)

GDP - per capita: purchasing power parity - $1,800 (2003 est.)

GDP - composition by sector:

agriculture: 46%

industry: 21%

services: 33% (2001 est.)

Population below poverty line: 48% (2000 est.)

Household income or consumption by percentage share:

lowest 10%: 1.9%

highest 10%: 36.6% (1996)

Distribution of family income - Gini index: 47.7 (1996)

Inflation rate (consumer prices): 4.5% (2002 est.)

Labor force: NA (2000)

Labor force - by occupation: agriculture 70%, industry and commerce 13%, other 17%

Unemployment rate: 30% (2001 est.)

Budget:

revenues: $2.2 billion

expenditures: $2.1 billion, including capital expenditures of $NA (FY00/01 est.)

Industries: petroleum production and refining, food processing, light consumer goods, textiles, lumber

Industrial production growth rate: 4.2% (1999 est.)

Electricity - production: 3.613 billion kWh (2001)

Electricity - production by source:

fossil fuel: 2.7%

hydro: 97.3%

nuclear: 0%

other: 0% (2001)

Electricity - consumption: 3.36 billion kWh (2001)

Electricity - exports: 0 kWh (2001)

Electricity - imports: 0 kWh (2001)

Oil - production: 76,650 bbl/day (2001 est.)

Oil - consumption: 22,000 bbl/day (2001 est.)

Oil - exports: NA

Oil - imports: NA

Oil - proved reserves: 200 million bbl (1 January 2002)

Natural gas - production: 0 cu m (2001 est.)

Natural gas - consumption: 0 cu m (2001 est.)

Natural gas - exports: 0 cu m (2001 est.)

Natural gas - imports: 0 cu m (2001 est.)

Natural gas - proved reserves: 55.22 billion cu m (1 January 2002)

Agriculture - products: coffee, cocoa, cotton, rubber, bananas, oilseed, grains, root starches; livestock; timber

Exports: $1.873 billion f.o.b. (2003 est.)

Exports - commodities: crude oil and petroleum products, lumber, cocoa beans, aluminum, coffee, cotton

Exports - partners: Italy 17.4%, Spain 16.8%, France 13.4%, US 8.7%, Netherlands 8.6%, China 5.4%, UK 4.7%, Germany 4.1% (2002)

Imports: $1.959 billion f.o.b. (2003 est.)

Imports - commodities: machinery, electrical equipment, transport equipment, fuel, food

Imports - partners: France 28%, Nigeria 12.7%, US 7.9%, Belgium 5.7%, Germany 4.8%, Italy 4.3% (2002)

Debt - external: $8.6 billion (2002 est.)

Economic aid - recipient: on 23 January 2001, the Paris Club agreed to reduce Cameroon's debt of $1.3 billion by $900 million; debt relief now totals $1.26 billion

Currency: Communaute Financiere Africaine franc (XAF); note - responsible authority is the Bank of the Central African States

Currency code: XAF

Exchange rates: Communaute Financiere Africaine francs (XAF) per US dollar - 581.2 (2003), 696.988 (2002), 733.039 (2001), 711.976 (2000), 615.699 (1999)

Fiscal year: 1 July - 30 June

Communications

Telephones - main lines in use: 110,900 (2002)

Telephones - mobile cellular: 675,700 (2002)

Telephone system:

general assessment: available only to business and government

domestic: cable, microwave radio relay, and tropospheric scatter

international: country code - 237; satellite earth stations - 2 Intelsat (Atlantic Ocean); fiber optic submarine cable (SAT-3/WASC) provides connectivity to Europe and Asia

Cameroon *(continued)*

Radio broadcast stations: AM 2, FM 9, shortwave 3 (2002)
Television broadcast stations: 1 (2002)
Internet country code: .cm
Internet hosts: 439 (2002)
Internet users: 60,000 (2002)
note: Cameroon also had more than 100 cyber-cafes in 2001

Transportation

Railways:
total: 1,008 km
narrow gauge: 1,008 km 1.000-m gauge (2002)
Highways:
total: 34,300 km
paved: 4,288 km
unpaved: 30,012 km (1999 est.)
Waterways: 2,090 km (of decreasing importance) (2002)
Pipelines: gas 90 km; liquid petroleum gas 9 km; oil 1,124 km (2003)
Ports and harbors: Bonaberi, Douala, Garoua, Kribi, Tiko
Merchant marine:
total: 1 ships (1,000 GRT or over) 169,593 GRT/357,023 DWT
by type: petroleum tanker 1 (2003 est.)
Airports: 47 (2003 est.)
Airports - with paved runways:
total: 11
over 3,047 m: 2
2,438 to 3,047 m: 4
1,524 to 2,437 m: 3
914 to 1,523 m: 1
under 914 m: 1 (2003 est.)
Airports - with unpaved runways:
total: 36
1,524 to 2,437 m: 7
914 to 1,523 m: 20
under 914 m: 9 (2003 est.)

Military

Military branches: Army, Navy (includes Naval Infantry), Air Force
Military manpower - military age: 18 years of age (2004 est.)
Military manpower - availability:
males age 15-49: 3,898,944 (2004 est.)
Military manpower - fit for military service:
males age 15-49: 1,979,151 (2004 est.)
Military manpower - reaching military age annually:
males: 184,054 (2004 est.)
Military expenditures - dollar figure: $189.2 million (2003)
Military expenditures - percent of GDP: 1.4% (2003)

Transnational Issues

Disputes - international: ICJ ruled in 2002 on the entire Cameroon-Nigeria land and maritime boundary but the parties formed a Joint Border Commission to resolve differences bilaterally and have commenced with demarcation in less-contested sections of the boundary, starting in Lake Chad in the north; the ICF ruled on an equidistance settlement of Cameroon-Equatorial Guinea-Nigeria maritime boundary in the Gulf of Guinea, however, implementation of the decision is delayed due to imprecisely defined coordinates, the unresolved Bakasi allocation, and a sovereignty dispute between Equatorial Guinea and Cameroon over an island at the mouth of the Ntem River; Nigeria initially rejected cession of the Bakasi Peninsula; Lake Chad Commission continues to urge signatories Cameroon, Chad, Niger, and Nigeria to ratify delimitation treaty over the lake region, which remains the site of armed clashes among local populations and militias

Canada

Geography - note: second-largest country in world (after Russia); strategic location between Russia and US via north polar route; approximately 90% of the population is concentrated within 300 km of the US border

People

Population: 32,507,874 (July 2004 est.)
Age structure:
0-14 years: 18.2% (male 3,038,800; female 2,890,579)
15-64 years: 68.7% (male 11,225,686; female 11,111,941)
65 years and over: 13% (male 1,807,472; female 2,433,396) (2004 est.)
Median age:
total: 38.2 years
male: 37.2 years
female: 39.2 years (2004 est.)
Population growth rate: 0.92% (2004 est.)
Birth rate: 10.91 births/1,000 population (2004 est.)
Death rate: 7.67 deaths/1,000 population (2004 est.)
Net migration rate: 5.96 migrant(s)/1,000 population (2004 est.)
Sex ratio:
at birth: 1.05 male(s)/female
under 15 years: 1.05 male(s)/female
15-64 years: 1.01 male(s)/female
65 years and over: 0.74 male(s)/female
total population: 0.98 male(s)/female (2004 est.)
Infant mortality rate:
total: 4.82 deaths/1,000 live births
male: 5.28 deaths/1,000 live births
female: 4.33 deaths/1,000 live births (2004 est.)
Life expectancy at birth:
total population: 79.96 years
male: 76.59 years
female: 83.5 years (2004 est.)
Total fertility rate: 1.61 children born/woman (2004 est.)
HIV/AIDS - adult prevalence rate: 0.3% (2001 est.)
HIV/AIDS - people living with HIV/AIDS: 55,000 (2001 est.)
HIV/AIDS - deaths: less than 500 (2001 est.)
Nationality:
noun: Canadian(s)
adjective: Canadian
Ethnic groups: British Isles origin 28%, French origin 23%, other European 15%, Amerindian 2%, other, mostly Asian, African, Arab 6%, mixed background 26%
Religions: Roman Catholic 46%, Protestant 36%, other 18%
note: based on the 1991 census
Languages: English 59.3% (official), French 23.2% (official), other 17.5%
Literacy:
definition: age 15 and over can read and write
total population: 97% (1986 est.)
male: NA%
female: NA%

Introduction

Background: A land of vast distances and rich natural resources, Canada became a self-governing dominion in 1867 while retaining ties to the British crown. Economically and technologically the nation has developed in parallel with the US, its neighbor to the south across an unfortified border. Its paramount political problem continues to be the relationship of the province of Quebec, with its French-speaking residents and unique culture, to the remainder of the country.

Geography

Location: Northern North America, bordering the North Atlantic Ocean on the east, North Pacific Ocean on the west, and the Arctic Ocean on the north, north of the conterminous US
Geographic coordinates: 60 00 N, 95 00 W
Map references: North America
Area:
total: 9,984,670 sq km
land: 9,093,507 sq km
water: 891,163 sq km
Area - comparative: somewhat larger than the US
Land boundaries:
total: 8,893 km
border countries: US 8,893 km (includes 2,477 km with Alaska)
Coastline: 202,080 km
Maritime claims:
territorial sea: 12 NM
contiguous zone: 24 NM
exclusive economic zone: 200 NM
continental shelf: 200 NM or to the edge of the continental margin
Climate: varies from temperate in south to subarctic and arctic in north
Terrain: mostly plains with mountains in west and lowlands in southeast

Elevation extremes:
lowest point: Atlantic Ocean 0 m
highest point: Mount Logan 5,959 m
Natural resources: iron ore, nickel, zinc, copper, gold, lead, molybdenum, potash, diamonds, silver, fish, timber, wildlife, coal, petroleum, natural gas, hydropower
Land use:
arable land: 4.94%
permanent crops: 0.02%
other: 95.04% (1998 est.)
Irrigated land: 7,200 sq km (1998 est.)
Natural hazards: continuous permafrost in north is a serious obstacle to development; cyclonic storms form east of the Rocky Mountains, a result of the mixing of air masses from the Arctic, Pacific, and North American interior, and produce most of the country's rain and snow east of the mountains
Environment - current issues: air pollution and resulting acid rain severely affecting lakes and damaging forests; metal smelting, coal-burning utilities, and vehicle emissions impacting on agricultural and forest productivity; ocean waters becoming contaminated due to agricultural, industrial, mining, and forestry activities
Environment - international agreements:
party to: Air Pollution, Air Pollution-Nitrogen Oxides, Air Pollution-Persistent Organic Pollutants, Air Pollution-Sulfur 85, Air Pollution-Sulfur 94, Antarctic-Environmental Protocol, Antarctic-Marine Living Resources, Antarctic Seals, Antarctic Treaty, Biodiversity, Climate Change, Climate Change-Kyoto Protocol, Desertification, Endangered Species, Environmental Modification, Hazardous Wastes, Law of the Sea, Marine Dumping, Ozone Layer Protection, Ship Pollution, Tropical Timber 83, Tropical Timber 94, Wetlands
signed, but not ratified: Air Pollution-Volatile Organic Compounds, Marine Life Conservation

Canada *(continued)*

Country name:
conventional long form: none
conventional short form: Canada
Government type: confederation with parliamentary democracy
Capital: Ottawa
Administrative divisions: 10 provinces and 3 territories*; Alberta, British Columbia, Manitoba, New Brunswick, Newfoundland and Labrador, Northwest Territories*, Nova Scotia, Nunavut*, Ontario, Prince Edward Island, Quebec, Saskatchewan, Yukon Territory*
Independence: 1 July 1867 (from UK)
National holiday: Canada Day, 1 July (1867)
Constitution: 17 April 1982 (Constitution Act); originally, the machinery of the government was set up in the British North America Act of 1867; charter of rights and unwritten customs
Legal system: based on English common law, except in Quebec, where civil law system based on French law prevails; accepts compulsory ICJ jurisdiction, with reservations
Suffrage: 18 years of age; universal
Executive branch:
chief of state: Queen ELIZABETH II (since 6 February 1952), represented by Governor General Adrienne CLARKSON (since 7 October 1999)
head of government: Prime Minister Paul MARTIN (since 12 December 2003); Deputy Prime Minister Anne MCLELLAN (since 12 December 2003)
cabinet: Federal Ministry chosen by the prime minister from among the members of his own party sitting in Parliament
elections: none; the monarchy is hereditary; governor general appointed by the monarch on the advice of the prime minister for a five-year term; following legislative elections, the leader of the majority party or the leader of the majority coalition in the House of Commons is automatically designated prime minister by the governor general
Legislative branch: bicameral Parliament or Parlement consists of the Senate or Senat (members appointed by the governor general with the advice of the prime minister and serve until reaching 75 years of age; its normal limit is 105 senators) and the House of Commons or Chambre des Communes (301 seats; members elected by direct, popular vote to serve for up to five-year terms)
elections: House of Commons - last held 27 November 2000 (next to be held by NA 2005)
election results: House of Commons - percent of vote by party - Liberal Party 41%, Canadian Alliance 26%, Bloc Quebecois 11%, New Democratic Party 9%, Progressive Conservative Party 12%; seats by party - Liberal Party 172, Canadian Alliance 66, Bloc Quebecois 38, New Democratic Party 13, Progressive Conservative Party 12; note - seats by party as of December 2003 - Liberal Party 170, Canadian Alliance 59, Bloc Quebecois 33, New Democratic Party 14, Progressive Conservative Party 18, Independent 4, vacant seats 3

Judicial branch: Supreme Court of Canada (judges are appointed by the prime minister through the governor general); Federal Court of Canada; Federal Court of Appeal; Provincial Courts (these are named variously Court of Appeal, Court of Queens Bench, Superior Court, Supreme Court, and Court of Justice)
Political parties and leaders: Bloc Quebecois [Gilles DUCEPPE]; Conservative Party of Canada (a merger of the Canadian Alliance and the Progressive Conservative Party) [Stephen HARPER]; Liberal Party [Paul MARTIN]; New Democratic Party [Jack LAYTON]
Political pressure groups and leaders: NA
International organization participation: ACCT, AfDB, APEC, ARF, AsDB, ASEAN (dialogue partner), Australia Group, BIS, C, CDB, CE (observer), EAPC, EBRD, ESA (cooperating state), FAO, G-7, G-8, G-10, IADB, IAEA, IBRD, ICAO, ICC, ICCt, ICFTU, ICRM, IDA, IEA, IFAD, IFC, IFRCS, IHO, ILO, IMF, IMO, Interpol, IOC, IOM, ISO, ITU, MICAH, MONUC, NAM (guest), NATO, NEA, NSG, OAS, OECD, OPCW, OSCE, Paris Club, PCA, UN, UNAMSIL, UNCTAD, UNDOF, UNESCO, UNFICYP, UNHCR, UNMIK, UNMOVIC, UNTSO, UPU, WCL, WCO, WFTU, WHO, WIPO, WMO, WToO, WTrO, ZC
Diplomatic representation in the US:
chief of mission: Ambassador Michael F. KERGIN
chancery: 501 Pennsylvania Avenue NW, Washington, DC 20001
telephone: [1] (202) 682-1740
FAX: [1] (202) 682-7726
consulate(s) general: Atlanta, Boston, Buffalo, Chicago, Dallas, Detroit, Los Angeles, Miami, Minneapolis, New York, and Seattle
consulate(s): Houston, Princeton, Raleigh-Durham, San Diego, San Francisco, and San Jose
Diplomatic representation from the US:
chief of mission: Ambassador Paul CELLUCCI
embassy: 490 Sussex Drive, Ottawa, Ontario K1N 1G8
mailing address: P. O. Box 5000, Ogdensburgh, NY 13669-0430
telephone: [1] (613) 238-5335, 4470
FAX: [1] (613) 688-3097
consulate(s) general: Calgary, Halifax, Montreal, Quebec, Toronto, and Vancouver
Flag description: two vertical bands of red (hoist and fly side, half width), with white square between them; an 11-pointed red maple leaf is centered in the white square; the official colors of Canada are red and white

Economy - overview: As an affluent, high-tech industrial society, Canada today closely resembles the US in its market-oriented economic system, pattern of production, and high living standards. Since World War II, the impressive growth of the manufacturing, mining, and service sectors has transformed the nation from a largely rural economy into one primarily industrial and urban. The 1989 US-Canada Free Trade Agreement (FTA) and the

1994 North American Free Trade Agreement (NAFTA) (which includes Mexico) touched off a dramatic increase in trade and economic integration with the US. As a result of the close cross-border relationship, the economic sluggishness in the United States in 2001-02 had a negative impact on the Canadian economy. Real growth averaged nearly 3% during 1993-2000, but declined in 2001, with moderate recovery in 2002-03. Unemployment is up, with contraction in the manufacturing and natural resource sectors. Nevertheless, given its great natural resources, skilled labor force, and modern capital plant Canada enjoys solid economic prospects. Two shadows loom, the first being the continuing constitutional impasse between English- and French-speaking areas, which has been raising the specter of a split in the federation. Another long-term concern is the flow south to the US of professionals lured by higher pay, lower taxes, and the immense high-tech infrastructure. A key strength in the economy is the substantial trade surplus. Roughly 90% of the population lives within 160 kilometers of the US border.
GDP: purchasing power parity - $957.7 billion (2003 est.)
GDP - real growth rate: 1.6% (2003 est.)
GDP - per capita: purchasing power parity - $29,700 (2003 est.)
GDP - composition by sector:
agriculture: 2.2%
industry: 26%
services: 71.8% (2002 est.)
Population below poverty line: NA%
Household income or consumption by percentage share:
lowest 10%: 2.8%
highest 10%: 23.8% (1994)
Distribution of family income - Gini index: 31.5 (1994)
Inflation rate (consumer prices): 2.8% (2003 est.)
Labor force: 16.4 million (2001 est.)
Labor force - by occupation: services 74%, manufacturing 15%, construction 5%, agriculture 3%, other 3% (2000)
Unemployment rate: 7.7% (2003 est.)
Budget:
revenues: $178.6 billion
expenditures: $161.4 billion, including capital expenditures of $NA (FY00/01 est.)
Industries: transportation equipment, chemicals, processed and unprocessed minerals, food products; wood and paper products; fish products, petroleum and natural gas
Industrial production growth rate: 0% (2003 est.)
Electricity - production: 566.3 billion kWh (2001)
Electricity - production by source:
fossil fuel: 28%
hydro: 57.9%
nuclear: 12.9%
other: 1.3% (2001)
Electricity - consumption: 504.4 billion kWh (2001)
Electricity - exports: 38.4 billion kWh (2001)

Canada *(continued)*

Electricity - imports: 16.11 billion kWh (2001)
Oil - production: 2.738 million bbl/day (2001 est.)
Oil - consumption: 1.703 million bbl/day (2001 est.)
Oil - exports: 2.008 million bbl/day (2001)
Oil - imports: 1.145 million bbl/day (2001)
Oil - proved reserves: 5.112 billion bbl (1 January 2002)
Natural gas - production: 186.8 billion cu m (2001 est.)
Natural gas - consumption: 82.25 billion cu m (2001 est.)
Natural gas - exports: 109 billion cu m (2001 est.)
Natural gas - imports: 4.46 billion cu m (2001 est.)
Natural gas - proved reserves: 1.691 trillion cu m (1 January 2002)
Agriculture - products: wheat, barley, oilseed, tobacco, fruits, vegetables; dairy products; forest products; fish
Exports: $279.3 billion f.o.b. (2003 est.)
Exports - commodities: motor vehicles and parts, industrial machinery, aircraft, telecommunications equipment; chemicals, plastics, fertilizers; wood pulp, timber, crude petroleum, natural gas, electricity, aluminum
Exports - partners: US 87.7%, Japan 2%, UK 1.1% (2002)
Imports: $240.4 billion f.o.b. (2003 est.)
Imports - commodities: machinery and equipment, motor vehicles and parts, crude oil, chemicals, electricity, durable consumer goods
Imports - partners: US 62.6%, China 4.6%, Japan 4.4% (2002)
Debt - external: $1.9 billion (2000)
Economic aid - donor: ODA, $1.3 billion (1999)
Currency: Canadian dollar (CAD)
Currency code: CAD
Exchange rates: Canadian dollars per US dollar - 1.4011 (2003), 1.5693 (2002), 1.5488 (2001), 1.4851 (2000), 1.4857 (1999)
Fiscal year: 1 April - 31 March

Communications

Telephones - main lines in use: 19,962,100 (2002)
Telephones - mobile cellular: 11.849 million (2002)
Telephone system:
general assessment: excellent service provided by modern technology
domestic: domestic satellite system with about 300 earth stations
international: country code - 1; 5 coaxial submarine cables; satellite earth stations - 5 Intelsat (4 Atlantic Ocean and 1 Pacific Ocean) and 2 Intersputnik (Atlantic Ocean region)
Radio broadcast stations: AM 535, FM 53, shortwave 6 (1998)
Television broadcast stations: 80 (plus many repeaters) (1997)
Internet country code: .ca
Internet hosts: 2,993,982 (2002)
Internet users: 16.11 million (2002)

Transportation

Railways:
total: 73,301 km
standard gauge: 73,301 km 1.435-m gauge (129 km electrified) (2001)
Highways:
total: 1,408,800 km
paved: 497,306 km (including 16,900 km of expressways)
unpaved: 911,494 km (2002)
Waterways: 3,000 km (including Saint Lawrence Seaway)
Pipelines: crude and refined oil 23,564 km; natural gas 74,980 km
Ports and harbors: Becancour (Quebec), Churchill, Halifax, Hamilton, Montreal, New Westminster, Prince Rupert, Quebec, Saint John (New Brunswick), St. John's (Newfoundland), Sept Isles, Sydney, Trois-Rivieres, Thunder Bay, Toronto, Vancouver, Windsor
Merchant marine:
total: 119 ships (1,000 GRT or over) 1,784,229 GRT/2,657,499 DWT
by type: barge carrier 1, bulk 59, cargo 13, chemical tanker 6, combination bulk 2, combination ore/oil 1, passenger 2, passenger/cargo 1, petroleum tanker 18, rail car carrier 1, roll on/roll off 11, short-sea/passenger 3, specialized tanker 1
foreign-owned: Germany 3, Hong Kong 2, Monaco 18, United Kingdom 3, United States 2
registered in other countries: 43 (2003 est.)
Airports: 1,357 (2003 est.)
Airports - with paved runways:
total: 505
over 3,047 m: 18
2,438 to 3,047 m: 16
1,524 to 2,437 m: 150
914 to 1,523 m: 246
under 914 m: 75 (2003 est.)
Airports - with unpaved runways:
total: 852
1,524 to 2,437 m: 69
914 to 1,523 m: 359
under 914 m: 424 (2003 est.)
Heliports: 12 (2003 est.)

Military

Military branches: Canadian Armed Forces: Land Forces Command, Maritime Command, Air Command
Military manpower - military age: 17 years of age (2004 est.)
Military manpower - availability:
males age 15-49: 8,417,314 (2004 est.)
Military manpower - fit for military service:
males age 15-49: 7,176,642 (2004 est.)
Military manpower - reaching military age annually:
males: 214,623 (2004 est.)
Military expenditures - dollar figure:
$9,801,700,000 (2003)

Military expenditures - percent of GDP: 1.1% (2003)

Transnational Issues

Disputes - international: managed maritime boundary disputes with the US at Dixon Entrance, Beaufort Sea, Strait of Juan de Fuca, and around the disputed Machias Seal Island and North Rock; uncontested dispute with Denmark over Hans Island sovereignty in the Kennedy Channel between Ellesmere Island and Greenland
Illicit drugs: illicit producer of cannabis for the domestic drug market and export to US; use of hydroponics technology permits growers to plant large quantities of high-quality marijuana indoors; transit point for heroin and cocaine entering the US market; vulnerable to narcotics money laundering because of its mature financial services sector

Cape Verde

Introduction

Background: The uninhabited islands were discovered and colonized by the Portuguese in the 15th century; Cape Verde subsequently became a trading center for African slaves and later an important coaling and resupply stop for whaling and transatlantic shipping. Following independence in 1975, and a tentative interest in unification with Guinea-Bissau, a one-party system was established and maintained until multi-party elections were held in 1990. Cape Verde continues to exhibit one of Africa's most stable democratic governments. Repeated droughts during the second half of the 20th century caused significant hardship and prompted heavy emigration. As a result, Cape Verde's expatriate population is greater than its domestic one. Most Cape Verdeans have both African and Portuguese antecedents.

Geography

Location: Western Africa, group of islands in the North Atlantic Ocean, west of Senegal
Geographic coordinates: 16 00 N, 24 00 W
Map references: Political Map of the World
Area:
total: 4,033 sq km
land: 4,033 sq km
water: 0 sq km
Area - comparative: slightly larger than Rhode Island
Land boundaries: 0 km
Coastline: 965 km
Maritime claims: measured from claimed archipelagic baselines
territorial sea: 12 NM
contiguous zone: 24 NM
exclusive economic zone: 200 NM
Climate: temperate; warm, dry summer; precipitation meager and very erratic
Terrain: steep, rugged, rocky, volcanic

Elevation extremes:
lowest point: Atlantic Ocean 0 m
highest point: Mt. Fogo 2,829 m (a volcano on Fogo Island)
Natural resources: salt, basalt rock, limestone, kaolin, fish
Land use:
arable land: 9.68%
permanent crops: 0.5%
other: 89.82% (1998 est.)
Irrigated land: 30 sq km (1998 est.)
Natural hazards: prolonged droughts; seasonal harmattan wind produces obscuring dust; volcanically and seismically active
Environment - current issues: soil erosion; demand for wood used as fuel has resulted in deforestation; desertification; environmental damage has threatened several species of birds and reptiles; illegal beach sand extraction; overfishing
Environment - international agreements:
party to: Biodiversity, Climate Change, Desertification, Environmental Modification, Hazardous Wastes, Law of the Sea, Marine Dumping, Ozone Layer Protection
signed, but not ratified: none of the selected agreements
Geography - note: strategic location 500 km from west coast of Africa near major north-south sea routes; important communications station; important sea and air refueling site

People

Population: 415,294 (July 2004 est.)
Age structure:
0-14 years: 40% (male 83,835; female 82,318)
15-64 years: 53.3% (male 106,846; female 114,312)
65 years and over: 6.7% (male 10,580; female 17,403) (2004 est.)
Median age:
total: 19 years
male: 18.2 years
female: 19.9 years (2004 est.)
Population growth rate: 0.73% (2004 est.)
Birth rate: 26.13 births/1,000 population (2004 est.)
Death rate: 6.72 deaths/1,000 population (2004 est.)
Net migration rate: -12.07 migrant(s)/1,000 population (2004 est.)
Sex ratio:
at birth: 1.03 male(s)/female
under 15 years: 1.02 male(s)/female
15-64 years: 0.94 male(s)/female
65 years and over: 0.61 male(s)/female
total population: 0.94 male(s)/female (2004 est.)
Infant mortality rate:
total: 49.14 deaths/1,000 live births
male: 54.39 deaths/1,000 live births
female: 43.73 deaths/1,000 live births (2004 est.)
Life expectancy at birth:
total population: 70.14 years
male: 66.83 years
female: 73.54 years (2004 est.)

Total fertility rate: 3.62 children born/woman (2004 est.)
HIV/AIDS - adult prevalence rate: 0.04% (2001 est.)
HIV/AIDS - people living with HIV/AIDS: 775 (2001)
HIV/AIDS - deaths: 225 (as of 2001)
Nationality:
noun: Cape Verdean(s)
adjective: Cape Verdean
Ethnic groups: Creole (mulatto) 71%, African 28%, European 1%
Religions: Roman Catholic (infused with indigenous beliefs); Protestant (mostly Church of the Nazarene)
Languages: Portuguese, Crioulo (a blend of Portuguese and West African words)
Literacy:
definition: age 15 and over can read and write
total population: 76.6%
male: 85.8%
female: 69.2% (2003 est.)

Government

Country name:
conventional long form: Republic of Cape Verde
conventional short form: Cape Verde
local long form: Republica de Cabo Verde
local short form: Cabo Verde
Government type: republic
Capital: Praia
Administrative divisions: 17 municipalities (concelhos, singular - concelho); Boa Vista, Brava, Maio, Mosteiros, Paul, Praia, Porto Novo, Ribeira Grande, Sal, Santa Catarina, Santa Cruz, Sao Domingos, Sao Filipe, Sao Miguel, Sao Nicolau, Sao Vicente, Tarrafal
Independence: 5 July 1975 (from Portugal)
National holiday: Independence Day, 5 July (1975)
Constitution: new constitution came into force 25 September 1992; underwent a major revision on 23 November 1995, substantially increasing the powers of the president, and a further revision in 1999, to create the position of national ombudsman (Provedor de Justica)
Legal system: derived from the legal system of Portugal
Suffrage: 18 years of age; universal
Executive branch:
chief of state: President Pedro PIRES (since 22 March 2001)
head of government: Prime Minister Jose Maria Pereira NEVES (since 1 February 2001)
cabinet: Council of Ministers appointed by the president on the recommendation of the prime minister
elections: president elected by popular vote for a five-year term; election last held 11 and 25 February 2001 (next to be held NA February 2006); prime minister nominated by the National Assembly and appointed by the president

Cape Verde (continued)

election results: Pedro PIRES elected president; percent of vote - Pedro PIRES (PAICV) 49.43%, Carlos VIEGA (MPD) 49.42%; note - the election was won by only twelve votes

Legislative branch: unicameral National Assembly or Assembleia Nacional (72 seats; members are elected by popular vote to serve five-year terms)

elections: last held 14 January 2001 (next to be held NA December 2005)

election results: percent of vote by party - PAICV 47.3%, MPD 39.8%, ADM 6%, other 6.9%; seats by party - PAICV 40, MPD 30, ADM 2

Judicial branch: Supreme Tribunal of Justice or Supremo Tribunal de Justia

Political parties and leaders: African Party for Independence of Cape Verde or PAICV [Jose Maria Pereira NEVES, chairman]; Democratic Alliance for Change or ADM [Dr. Eurico MONTEIRO] (a coalition of PCD, PTS, and UCID); Democratic Christian Party or PDC [Manuel RODRIGUES, chairman]; Democratic Renovation Party or PRD [Jacinto SANTOS, president]; Movement for Democracy or MPD [Agostinho LOPES, president]; Party for Democratic Convergence or PCD [Dr. Eurico MONTEIRO, president]; Party of Work and Solidarity or PTS [Isaias RODRIGUES, president]; Social Democratic Party or PSD [Joao ALEM, president]

Political pressure groups and leaders: NA

International organization participation: ACCT, ACP, AfDB, AU, ECOWAS, FAO, G-77, IBRD, ICAO, ICCt (signatory), ICFTU, ICRM, IDA, IFAD, IFC, IFRCS, ILO, IMF, IMO, Interpol, IOC, IOM, ITU, NAM, OPCW, UN, UNCTAD, UNESCO, UNIDO, UPU, WCO, WHO, WIPO, WMO, WToO, WTrO (observer)

Diplomatic representation in the US:

chief of mission: Ambassador Jose BRITO

chancery: 3415 Massachusetts Avenue NW, Washington, DC 20007

telephone: [1] (202) 965-6820

FAX: [1] (202) 965-1207

consulate(s) general: Boston

Diplomatic representation from the US:

chief of mission: Ambassador Donald C. JOHNSON

embassy: Rua Abilio m. Macedo 81, Praia

mailing address: C. P. 201, Praia

telephone: [238] 61 56 16, 61 56 17

FAX: [238] 61 13 55

Flag description: three horizontal bands of light blue (top, double width), white (with a horizontal red stripe in the middle third), and light blue; a circle of 10 yellow five-pointed stars is centered on the hoist end of the red stripe and extends into the upper and lower blue bands

Economy

Economy - overview: This island economy suffers from a poor natural resource base, including serious water shortages exacerbated by cycles of long-term drought. The economy is service-oriented, with commerce, transport, tourism, and public services accounting for 72% of GDP. Although nearly 70% of the population lives in rural areas, the share of agriculture in GDP in 2001 was only 11%, of which fishing accounted for 1.5%. About 82% of food must be imported. The fishing potential, mostly lobster and tuna, is not fully exploited. Cape Verde annually runs a high trade deficit, financed by foreign aid and remittances from emigrants; remittances supplement GDP by more than 20%. Economic reforms are aimed at developing the private sector and attracting foreign investment to diversify the economy. Prospects for 2004 depend heavily on the maintenance of aid flows, tourism, remittances, and the momentum of the government's development program.

GDP: purchasing power parity - $600 million (2002 est.)

GDP - real growth rate: 4% (2002 est.)

GDP - per capita: purchasing power parity - $1,400 (2002 est.)

GDP - composition by sector:

agriculture: 11%

industry: 17%

services: 72% (2001)

Population below poverty line: 30% (2000)

Household income or consumption by percentage share:

lowest 10%: NA%

highest 10%: NA%

Inflation rate (consumer prices): 3% (2002)

Labor force: NA (1980)

Unemployment rate: 21% (2000 est.)

Budget:

revenues: $112 million

expenditures: $198 million, including capital expenditures of $NA (2000)

Industries: food and beverages, fish processing, shoes and garments, salt mining, ship repair

Industrial production growth rate: NA%

Electricity - production: 42.03 million kWh (2001)

Electricity - production by source:

fossil fuel: 100%

hydro: 0%

nuclear: 0%

other: 0% (2001)

Electricity - consumption: 39.08 million kWh (2001)

Electricity - exports: 0 kWh (2001)

Electricity - imports: 0 kWh (2001)

Oil - production: 0 bbl/day (2001 est.)

Oil - consumption: 2,000 bbl/day (2001 est.)

Oil - exports: NA

Oil - imports: NA

Agriculture - products: bananas, corn, beans, sweet potatoes, sugarcane, coffee, peanuts; fish

Exports: $50.68 million f.o.b. (2003 est.)

Exports - commodities: fuel, shoes, garments, fish, hides

Exports - partners: Portugal 38.1%, France 23.8%, UK 23.8%, US 9.5% (2002)

Imports: $315.5 million f.o.b. (2003 est.)

Imports - commodities: foodstuffs, industrial products, transport equipment, fuels

Imports - partners: Portugal 47.7%, Netherlands 7.1%, Germany 5.6% (2002)

Debt - external: $325 million (2002)

Economic aid - recipient: $136 million (1999)

Currency: Cape Verdean escudo (CVE)

Currency code: CVE

Exchange rates: Cape Verdean escudos (CVE) per US dollar - 97.703 (2003), 117.168 (2002), 123.228 (2001), 115.877 (2000), 102.7 (1999)

Fiscal year: calendar year

Communications

Telephones - main lines in use: 70,200 (2002)

Telephones - mobile cellular: 42,900 (2002)

Telephone system:

general assessment: effective system, being improved

domestic: interisland microwave radio relay system with both analog and digital exchanges; work is in progress on a submarine fiber-optic cable system which is scheduled for completion in 2003

international: country code - 238; 2 coaxial submarine cables; HF radiotelephone to Senegal and Guinea-Bissau; satellite earth station - 1 Intelsat (Atlantic Ocean)

Radio broadcast stations: AM 0, FM 15 (and 17 repeaters), shortwave 0 (2002)

Television broadcast stations: 1 (and 7 repeaters) (2002)

Internet country code: .cv

Internet hosts: 48 (2002)

Internet users: 16,000 (2002)

Transportation

Railways: 0 km

Highways:

total: 1,100 km

paved: 858 km

unpaved: 242 km (1999 est.)

Waterways: none

Ports and harbors: Mindelo, Praia, Tarrafal

Merchant marine:

total: 4 ships (1,000 GRT or over) 5,395 GRT/6,614 DWT

by type: cargo 2, chemical tanker 1, passenger/cargo 1

foreign-owned: United Kingdom 1 (2003 est.)

Airports: 7

note: 3 airports are reported to be nonoperational (2003 est.)

Airports - with paved runways:

total: 6

over 3,047 m: 1

914 to 1,523 m: 5 (2003 est.)

Airports - with unpaved runways:

total: 1

under 914 m: 1 (2003 est.)

Cape Verde (continued)

Military

Military branches: Army, Coast Guard
Military manpower - availability:
males age 15-49: 98,394 (2004 est.)
Military manpower - fit for military service:
males age 15-49: 55,477 (2004 est.)
Military expenditures - dollar figure: $12.3 million (2003)
Military expenditures - percent of GDP: 1.5% (2003)

Transnational Issues

Disputes - international: none
Illicit drugs: used as a transshipment point for illicit drugs moving from Latin America and Asia destined for Western Europe; the lack of a well-developed financial system limits the country's utility as a money-laundering center

Cayman Islands
(overseas territory of the UK)

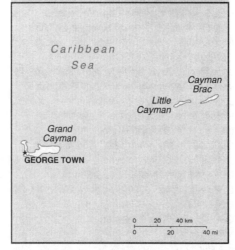

Introduction

Background: The Cayman Islands were colonized from Jamaica by the British during the 18th and 19th centuries. Administered by Jamaica since 1863, they remained a British dependency after 1962 when the former became independent.

Geography

Location: Caribbean, island group in Caribbean Sea, nearly one-half of the way from Cuba to Honduras
Geographic coordinates: 19 30 N, 80 30 W
Map references: Central America and the Caribbean
Area:
total: 262 sq km
land: 262 sq km
water: 0 sq km
Area - comparative: 1.5 times the size of Washington, DC
Land boundaries: 0 km
Coastline: 160 km
Maritime claims:
territorial sea: 12 NM
exclusive fishing zone: 200 NM
Climate: tropical marine; warm, rainy summers (May to October) and cool, relatively dry winters (November to April)
Terrain: low-lying limestone base surrounded by coral reefs
Elevation extremes:
lowest point: Caribbean Sea 0 m
highest point: The Bluff 43 m
Natural resources: fish, climate and beaches that foster tourism
Land use:
arable land: 0%
permanent crops: 0%
other: 100% (1998 est.)

Irrigated land: NA sq km
Natural hazards: hurricanes (July to November)
Environment - current issues: no natural fresh water resources; drinking water supplies must be met by rainwater catchments
Geography - note: important location between Cuba and Central America

People

Population: 43,103 (July 2004 est.)
Age structure:
0-14 years: 21.4% (male 4,608; female 4,616)
15-64 years: 70.6% (male 14,858; female 15,593)
65 years and over: 8% (male 1,607; female 1,821) (2004 est.)
Median age:
total: 36.5 years
male: 36.2 years
female: 36.8 years (2004 est.)
Population growth rate: 2.71% (2004 est.)
Birth rate: 13.11 births/1,000 population (2004 est.)
Death rate: 4.76 deaths/1,000 population (2004 est.)
Net migration rate: 18.75 migrant(s)/1,000 population
note: major destination for Cubans trying to migrate to the US (2004 est.)
Sex ratio:
at birth: 1.02 male(s)/female
under 15 years: 1 male(s)/female
15-64 years: 0.95 male(s)/female
65 years and over: 0.88 male(s)/female
total population: 0.96 male(s)/female (2004 est.)
Infant mortality rate:
total: 8.41 deaths/1,000 live births
male: 9.64 deaths/1,000 live births
female: 7.16 deaths/1,000 live births (2004 est.)
Life expectancy at birth:
total population: 79.81 years
male: 77.21 years
female: 82.45 years (2004 est.)
Total fertility rate: 1.9 children born/woman (2004 est.)
HIV/AIDS - adult prevalence rate: NA%
HIV/AIDS - people living with HIV/AIDS: NA
HIV/AIDS - deaths: NA
Nationality:
noun: Caymanian(s)
adjective: Caymanian
Ethnic groups: mixed 40%, white 20%, black 20%, expatriates of various ethnic groups 20%
Religions: United Church (Presbyterian and Congregational), Anglican, Baptist, Church of God, other Protestant, Roman Catholic
Languages: English
Literacy:
definition: age 15 and over has ever attended school
total population: 98%
male: 98%
female: 98% (1970 est.)

Cayman Islands *(continued)*

Government

Country name:
conventional long form: none
conventional short form: Cayman Islands
Dependency status: overseas territory of the UK
Government type: British crown colony
Capital: George Town
Administrative divisions: 8 districts; Creek, Eastern, Midland, South Town, Spot Bay, Stake Bay, West End, Western
Independence: none (overseas territory of the UK)
National holiday: Constitution Day, first Monday in July
Constitution: 1959, revised 1972 and 1992
Legal system: British common law and local statutes
Suffrage: 18 years of age; universal
Executive branch:
chief of state: Queen ELIZABETH II (since 6 February 1952); Governor Bruce DINWIDDY (since 29 May 2002)
head of government: Chief Secretary W. McKeeva BUSH (since NA December 2001)
cabinet: Executive Council (three members appointed by the governor, four members elected by the Legislative Assembly)
elections: none; the monarch is hereditary; the governor is appointed by the monarch; the chief secretary is appointed by the governor
Legislative branch: unicameral Legislative Assembly (18 seats, three appointed members from the Executive Council and 15 elected by popular vote; members serve four-year terms)
elections: last held 8 November 2000 (next to be held 17 November 2004)
election results: percent of vote - NA%; seats - NA
Judicial branch: Summary Court; Grand Court; Cayman Islands Court of Appeal
Political parties and leaders: no national teams (loose groupings of political organizations) were formed for the 2000 elections; United Democratic Party or UDP [leader McKeeva BUSH]; People's Progressive Movement or PPM [leader Kurt TIBBETTS]
Political pressure groups and leaders: NA
International organization participation: Caricom (associate), CDB, Interpol (subbureau), IOC, UNESCO (associate)
Diplomatic representation in the US: none (overseas territory of the UK)
Diplomatic representation from the US: none (overseas territory of the UK)
Flag description: blue, with the flag of the UK in the upper hoist-side quadrant and the Caymanian coat of arms centered on the outer half of the flag; the coat of arms includes a pineapple and turtle above a shield with three stars (representing the three islands) and a scroll at the bottom bearing the motto HE HATH FOUNDED IT UPON THE SEAS

Economy

Economy - overview: With no direct taxation, the islands are a thriving offshore financial center. More than 40,000 companies were registered in the Cayman Islands as of 1998, including almost 600 banks and trust companies; banking assets exceed $500 billion. A stock exchange was opened in 1997. Tourism is also a mainstay, accounting for about 70% of GDP and 75% of foreign currency earnings. The tourist industry is aimed at the luxury market and caters mainly to visitors from North America. Total tourist arrivals exceeded 1.2 million in 1997, with 600,000 from the US. About 90% of the islands' food and consumer goods must be imported. The Caymanians enjoy one of the highest outputs per capita and one of the highest standards of living in the world.
GDP: purchasing power parity - $1.27 billion (2002 est.)
GDP - real growth rate: 1.7% (2002 est.)
GDP - per capita: purchasing power parity - $35,000 (2002 est.)
GDP - composition by sector:
agriculture: 1.4%
industry: 3.2%
services: 95.4% (1994 est.)
Population below poverty line: NA% (2002 est.)
Household income or consumption by percentage share:
lowest 10%: NA%
highest 10%: NA%
Inflation rate (consumer prices): 2.8% (2002)
Labor force: 19,820 (1995)
Labor force - by occupation: agriculture 1.4%, industry 12.6%, services 86% (1995)
Unemployment rate: 4.1% (1997)
Budget:
revenues: $265.2 million
expenditures: $248.9 million, including capital expenditures of $NA (1997)
Industries: tourism, banking, insurance and finance, construction, construction materials, furniture
Industrial production growth rate: NA%
Electricity - production: 381.9 million kWh (2001)
Electricity - production by source:
fossil fuel: 100%
hydro: 0%
nuclear: 0%
other: 0% (2001)
Electricity - consumption: 355.2 million kWh (2001)
Electricity - exports: 0 kWh (2001)
Electricity - imports: 0 kWh (2001)
Oil - production: 0 bbl/day (2001 est.)
Oil - consumption: 2,400 bbl/day (2001 est.)
Oil - exports: NA
Oil - imports: NA
Agriculture - products: vegetables, fruit; livestock, turtle farming

Exports: $1.2 million (1999)
Exports - commodities: turtle products, manufactured consumer goods
Exports - partners: mostly US
Imports: $457.4 million (1999)
Imports - commodities: foodstuffs, manufactured goods
Imports - partners: US, Trinidad and Tobago, UK, Netherlands Antilles, Japan
Debt - external: $70 million (1996)
Economic aid - recipient: $NA (1999)
Currency: Caymanian dollar (KYD)
Currency code: KYD
Exchange rates: Caymanian dollars per US dollar - 0.82 (29 October 2001), 0.83 (3 November 1995), 0.85 (22 November 1993)
Fiscal year: 1 April - 31 March

Communications

Telephones - main lines in use: 38,000 (2002)
Telephones - mobile cellular: 17,000 (2002)
Telephone system:
general assessment: NA
domestic: NA
international: country code - 1-345; 1 submarine coaxial cable; satellite earth station - 1 Intelsat (Atlantic Ocean)
Radio broadcast stations: AM 1, FM 5, shortwave 0 (1998)
Television broadcast stations: 1 with cable system
Internet country code: .ky
Internet users: NA

Transportation

Railways: 0 km
Highways:
total: 785 km
paved: 785 km (2000)
Waterways: none
Ports and harbors: Cayman Brac, George Town
Merchant marine:
total: 137 ships (1,000 GRT or over) 2,827,837 GRT/4,555,974 DWT
by type: bulk 27, cargo 7, chemical tanker 36, container 2, liquefied gas 1, petroleum tanker 25, refrigerated cargo 33, roll on/roll off 4, short-sea/passenger 1, specialized tanker 1
foreign-owned: Germany 9, Greece 25, Hong Kong 3, Italy 14, Norway 4, Singapore 1, Spain 11, Sweden 13, Switzerland 1, United Kingdom 18, United States 43
registered in other countries: 2 (2003 est.)
Airports: 3 (2003 est.)
Airports - with paved runways:
total: 2
1,524 to 2,437 m: 2 (2003 est.)
Airports - with unpaved runways:
total: 1
914 to 1,523 m: 1 (2003 est.)

Cayman Islands *(continued)*

Military

Military branches: no regular military forces; Royal Cayman Islands Police Force
Military - note: defense is the responsibility of the UK

Transnational Issues

Disputes - international: none
Illicit drugs: offshore financial center; vulnerable to drug transshipment to the US and Europe

Central African Republic

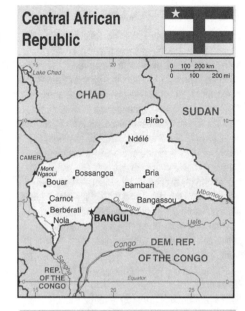

Introduction

Background: The former French colony of Ubangi-Shari became the Central African Republic upon independence in 1960. After three tumultuous decades of misrule - mostly by military governments - civilian rule was established in 1993 and lasted for one decade. In March 2003 a military coup led by General Francois BOZIZE deposed the civilian government of President Ange-Felix PATASSE and has since established a transitional government. Though the government has the tacit support of civil society groups and the main parties, this is likely to weaken in the run-up to municipal, legislative, and presidential elections scheduled for December 2004 or January 2005. The government still does not fully control the countryside, where pockets of lawlessness persist.

Geography

Location: Central Africa, north of Democratic Republic of the Congo
Geographic coordinates: 7 00 N, 21 00 E
Map references: Africa
Area:
total: 622,984 sq km
land: 622,984 sq km
water: 0 sq km
Area - comparative: slightly smaller than Texas
Land boundaries:
total: 5,203 km
border countries: Cameroon 797 km, Chad 1,197 km, Democratic Republic of the Congo 1,577 km, Republic of the Congo 467 km, Sudan 1,165 km
Coastline: 0 km (landlocked)
Maritime claims: none (landlocked)
Climate: tropical; hot, dry winters; mild to hot, wet summers
Terrain: vast, flat to rolling, monotonous plateau; scattered hills in northeast and southwest

Elevation extremes:
lowest point: Oubangui River 335 m
highest point: Mont Ngaoui 1,420 m
Natural resources: diamonds, uranium, timber, gold, oil, hydropower
Land use:
arable land: 3.1%
permanent crops: 0.14%
other: 96.76% (1998 est.)
Irrigated land: NA sq km
Natural hazards: hot, dry, dusty harmattan winds affect northern areas; floods are common
Environment - current issues: tap water is not potable; poaching has diminished the country's reputation as one of the last great wildlife refuges; desertification; deforestation
Environment - international agreements:
party to: Biodiversity, Climate Change, Desertification, Endangered Species, Ozone Layer Protection, Tropical Timber 94
signed, but not ratified: Law of the Sea
Geography - note: landlocked; almost the precise center of Africa

People

Population: 3,742,482
note: estimates for this country explicitly take into account the effects of excess mortality due to AIDS; this can result in lower life expectancy, higher infant mortality and death rates, lower population and growth rates, and changes in the distribution of population by age and sex than would otherwise be expected (July 2004 est.)
Age structure:
0-14 years: 42.8% (male 806,506; female 795,639)
15-64 years: 53.8% (male 990,522; female 1,021,491)
65 years and over: 3.4% (male 53,860; female 74,464) (2004 est.)
Median age:
total: 18 years
male: 17.7 years
female: 18.4 years (2004 est.)
Population growth rate: 1.56% (2004 est.)
Birth rate: 35.55 births/1,000 population (2004 est.)
Death rate: 19.99 deaths/1,000 population (2004 est.)
Net migration rate: 0 migrant(s)/1,000 population (2004 est.)
Sex ratio:
at birth: 1.03 male(s)/female
under 15 years: 1.01 male(s)/female
15-64 years: 0.97 male(s)/female
65 years and over: 0.72 male(s)/female
total population: 0.98 male(s)/female (2004 est.)
Infant mortality rate:
total: 92.15 deaths/1,000 live births
male: 99.09 deaths/1,000 live births
female: 84.99 deaths/1,000 live births (2004 est.)

Life expectancy at birth:
total population: 41.36 years
male: 39.7 years
female: 43.08 years (2004 est.)
Total fertility rate: 4.59 children born/woman
(2004 est.)
HIV/AIDS - adult prevalence rate: 12.9%
(2001 est.)
HIV/AIDS - people living with HIV/AIDS: 250,000
(2001 est.)
HIV/AIDS - deaths: 22,000 (2001 est.)
Nationality:
noun: Central African(s)
adjective: Central African
Ethnic groups: Baya 33%, Banda 27%,
Mandjia 13%, Sara 10%, Mboum 7%, M'Baka 4%,
Yakoma 4%, other 2%
Religions: indigenous beliefs 35%, Protestant 25%,
Roman Catholic 25%, Muslim 15%
note: animistic beliefs and practices strongly influence
the Christian majority
Languages: French (official), Sangho (lingua franca
and national language), tribal languages
Literacy:
definition: age 15 and over can read and write
total population: 51%
male: 63.3%
female: 39.9% (2003 est.)

Government

Country name:
conventional long form: Central African Republic
conventional short form: none
local long form: Republique Centrafricaine
local short form: none
former: Ubangi-Shari, Central African Empire
abbreviation: CAR
Government type: republic
Capital: Bangui
Administrative divisions: 14 prefectures
(prefectures, singular - prefecture), 2 economic
prefectures* (prefectures economiques, singular -
prefecture economique), and 1 commune**;
Bamingui-Bangoran, Bangui**, Basse-Kotto,
Haute-Kotto, Haut-Mbomou, Kemo, Lobaye,
Mambere-Kadei, Mbomou, Nana-Grebizi*,
Nana-Mambere, Ombella-Mpoko, Ouaka, Ouham,
Ouham-Pende, Sangha-Mbaere*, Vakaga
Independence: 13 August 1960 (from France)
National holiday: Republic Day, 1 December (1958)
Constitution: passed by referendum 29 December
1994; adopted 7 January 1995
Legal system: based on French law
Suffrage: 21 years of age; universal
Executive branch:
chief of state: President Francois BOZIZE (since
15 March 2003 coup) and Vice President Abel
GOUMA (since 12 December 2003)
head of government: Prime Minister Celestin
GAOMBALET (since 12 December 2003)
cabinet: Council of Ministers

elections: NA; municipal, legislative and presidential
elections scheduled for December 2004 or
January 2005; prime minister appointed by the
president
Legislative branch: unicameral National Assembly
or Assemblee Nationale (109 seats; members are
elected by popular vote to serve five-year terms;
note - there were 85 seats in the National Assembly
before the 1998 election)
elections: last held 22-23 November and
13 December 1998 (next to be held NA 2004)
election results: percent of vote by party - MLPC 43%,
RDC 18%, MDD 9%, FPP 6%, PSD 5%, ADP 4%,
PUN 3%, FODEM 2%, PLD 2%, UPR 1%, FC 1%,
independents 6%; seats by party - MLPC 47, RDC 20,
MDD 8, FPP 7, PSD 6, ADP 5, PUN 3, FODEM 2,
PLD 2, UPR 1, FC 1, independents 7
Judicial branch: Supreme Court or Cour Supreme;
Constitutional Court (3 judges appointed by the
president, 3 by the president of the National
Assembly, and 3 by fellow judges); Court of Appeal;
Criminal Courts; Inferior Courts
Political parties and leaders: Alliance for
Democracy and Progress or ADP [Jacques
MBOLIEDAS]; Central African Democratic Assembly
or RDC [Andre KOLINGBA]; Civic Forum or FC [Gen.
Timothee MALENDOMA]; Democratic Forum for
Modernity or FODEM [Charles MASSI]; Liberal
Democratic Party or PLD [Nestor
KOMBO-NAGUEMON]; Movement for Democracy
and Development or MDD [David DACKO]; Movement
for the Liberation of the Central African People or
MLPC [the party of deposed president, Ange-Felix
PATASSE]; Patriotic Front for Progress or FPP [Abel
GOUMBA]; People's Union for the Republic or UPR
[Pierre Sammy MAKFOY]; National Unity Party or
PUN [Jean-Paul NGOUPANDE]; Social Democratic
Party or PSD [Enoch LAKOUE]
Political pressure groups and leaders: NA
International organization participation: ACCT,
ACP, AfDB, AU, BDEAC, CEMAC, FAO, FZ, G-77,
IAEA, IBRD, ICAO, ICCt, ICFTU, ICRM, IDA, IFAD,
IFC, IFRCS, ILO, IMF, Interpol, IOC, ITU, NAM, OIC
(observer), OPCW (signatory), UN, UNCTAD,
UNESCO, UNIDO, UPU, WCL, WCO, WHO, WIPO,
WMO, WToO, WTrO
Diplomatic representation in the US:
chief of mission: Ambassador Emmanuel TOUABOY
chancery: 1618 22nd Street NW, Washington, DC
20008
telephone: [1] (202) 483-7800
FAX: [1] (202) 332-9893
Diplomatic representation from the US:
chief of mission: Ambassador (vacant)
embassy: Avenue David Dacko, Bangui
mailing address: B. P. 924, Bangui
telephone: [236] 61 02 00
FAX: [236] 61 44 94
note: The embassy is currently operating with a
minimal staff

Flag description: four equal horizontal bands of
blue (top), white, green, and yellow with a vertical red
band in center; there is a yellow five-pointed star on
the hoist side of the blue band

Economy

Economy - overview: Subsistence agriculture,
together with forestry, remains the backbone of the
economy of the Central African Republic (CAR), with
more than 70% of the population living in outlying
areas. The agricultural sector generates half of GDP.
Timber has accounted for about 16% of export
earnings and the diamond industry for 54%. Important
constraints to economic development include the
CAR's landlocked position, a poor transportation
system, a largely unskilled work force, and a legacy of
misdirected macroeconomic policies. Factional
fighting between the government and its opponents
remains a drag on economic revitalization, with GDP
likely to contract in 2004. Distribution of income is
extraordinarily unequal. Grants from France and the
international community can only partially meet
humanitarian needs.
GDP: purchasing power parity - $4.584 billion
(2003 est.)
GDP - real growth rate: 1% (2003 est.)
GDP - per capita: purchasing power parity - $1,200
(2003 est.)
GDP - composition by sector:
agriculture: 55%
industry: 20%
services: 25% (2001 est.)
Population below poverty line: NA% (1993)
**Household income or consumption by percentage
share:**
lowest 10%: 0.7%
highest 10%: 47.7% (1993)
Distribution of family income - Gini index: 61.3
(1993)
Inflation rate (consumer prices): 3.6% (2001 est.)
Labor force: NA (2000 est.)
Unemployment rate: 8% (23% for Bangui)
(2001 est.)
Budget:
revenues: $NA
expenditures: $NA, including capital expenditures of
$NA
Industries: diamond mining, logging, brewing,
textiles, footwear, assembly of bicycles and
motorcycles
Industrial production growth rate: 3% (2002)
Electricity - production: 106 million kWh (2001)
Electricity - production by source:
fossil fuel: 19.8%
hydro: 80.2%
nuclear: 0%
other: 0% (2001)
Electricity - consumption: 98.63 million kWh
(2001)
Electricity - exports: 0 kWh (2001)
Electricity - imports: 0 kWh (2001)

Oil - production: 0 bbl/day (2001 est.)
Oil - consumption: 2,400 bbl/day (2001 est.)
Oil - exports: NA
Oil - imports: NA
Agriculture - products: cotton, coffee, tobacco, manioc (tapioca), yams, millet, corn, bananas; timber
Exports: $172 million f.o.b. (2002 est.)
Exports - commodities: diamonds, timber, cotton, coffee, tobacco
Exports - partners: Belgium 70.3%, Spain 7%, Italy 4.1% (2002)
Imports: $136 million f.o.b. (2002 est.)
Imports - commodities: food, textiles, petroleum products, machinery, electrical equipment, motor vehicles, chemicals, pharmaceuticals
Imports - partners: France 30.9%, US 5.1%, Cameroon 4.4% (2002)
Debt - external: $881.4 million (2000 est.)
Economic aid - recipient: ODA $73 million; note - traditional budget subsidies from France (2000 est.)
Currency: Communaute Financiere Africaine franc (XAF); note - responsible authority is the Bank of the Central African States
Currency code: XAF
Exchange rates: Communaute Financiere Africaine francs (XAF) per US dollar - 581.2 (2003), 696.988 (2002), 733.039 (2001), 711.976 (2000), 615.699 (1999)
Fiscal year: calendar year

Communications

Telephones - main lines in use: 9,000 (2002)
Telephones - mobile cellular: 12,600 (2002)
Telephone system:
general assessment: fair system
domestic: network consists principally of microwave radio relay and low-capacity, low-powered radiotelephone communication
international: country code - 236; satellite earth station - 1 Intelsat (Atlantic Ocean)
Radio broadcast stations: AM 1, FM 5, shortwave 1 (2002)
Television broadcast stations: 1 (2001)
Internet country code: .cf
Internet hosts: 6 (2002)
Internet users: 5,000 (2002)

Transportation

Railways: 0 km
Highways:
total: 23,810 km
paved: 643 km
unpaved: 23,167 km (1999 est.)
Waterways: 900 km
note: traditional trade carried on by means of shallow-draft dugouts; Oubangui is the most important river, navigable all year to craft drawing 0.6 m or less; 282 km navigable to craft drawing as much as 1.8 m
Ports and harbors: Bangui, Nola, Salo, Nzinga
Airports: 50 (2003 est.)

Airports - with paved runways:
total: 3
2,438 to 3,047 m: 1
1,524 to 2,437 m: 2 (2003 est.)
Airports - with unpaved runways:
total: 47
2,438 to 3,047 m: 1
1,524 to 2,437 m: 10
914 to 1,523 m: 23
under 914 m: 13 (2003 est.)

Military

Military branches: Central African Armed Forces (FACA): Republican Guard, Ground Forces, Naval Forces, Air Force
Military manpower - availability:
males age 15-49: 878,980 (2004 est.)
Military manpower - fit for military service:
males age 15-49: 460,469 (2004 est.)
Military expenditures - dollar figure: $14.5 million (2003)
Military expenditures - percent of GDP: 1.1% (2003)

Transnational Issues

Disputes - international: internal political instabilities with fighting and violence overlap into Chad and CAR, leaving refugees and rebel groups in both countries; Sudan has pledged to work with CAR to stem violent skirmishes over water and grazing rights among related pastoral populations along the border

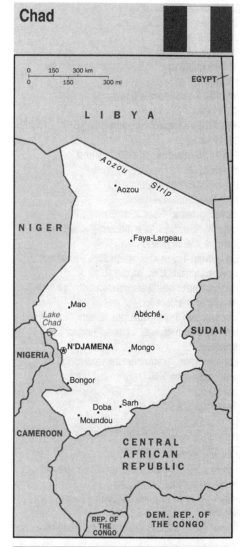

Chad

Introduction

Background: Chad, part of France's African holdings until 1960, endured three decades of ethnic warfare as well as invasions by Libya before a semblance of peace was finally restored in 1990. The government eventually suppressed or came to terms with most political-military groups, settled a territorial dispute with Libya on terms favorable to Chad, drafted a democratic constitution, and held multiparty presidential elections in 1996 and 1997. In 1998, a new rebellion broke out in northern Chad, which sporadically flares up despite two peace agreements signed in 2002 and 2003 between the government and the rebels. Despite movement toward democratic reform, power remains in the hands of a northern ethnic oligarchy.

Geography

Location: Central Africa, south of Libya
Geographic coordinates: 15 00 N, 19 00 E
Map references: Africa
Area:
total: 1.284 million sq km
land: 1,259,200 sq km
water: 24,800 sq km

Chad (continued)

Area - comparative: slightly more than three times the size of California

Land boundaries:

total: 5,968 km

border countries: Cameroon 1,094 km, Central African Republic 1,197 km, Libya 1,055 km, Niger 1,175 km, Nigeria 87 km, Sudan 1,360 km

Coastline: 0 km (landlocked)

Maritime claims: none (landlocked)

Climate: tropical in south, desert in north

Terrain: broad, arid plains in center, desert in north, mountains in northwest, lowlands in south

Elevation extremes:

lowest point: Djourab Depression 160 m

highest point: Emi Koussi 3,415 m

Natural resources: petroleum, uranium, natron, kaolin, fish (Lake Chad)

Land use:

arable land: 2.78%

permanent crops: 0.02%

other: 97.2% (1998 est.)

Irrigated land: 200 sq km (1998 est.)

Natural hazards: hot, dry, dusty harmattan winds occur in north; periodic droughts; locust plagues

Environment - current issues: inadequate supplies of potable water; improper waste disposal in rural areas contributes to soil and water pollution; desertification

Environment - international agreements:

party to: Biodiversity, Climate Change, Desertification, Endangered Species, Ozone Layer Protection, Wetlands

signed, but not ratified: Law of the Sea, Marine Dumping

Geography - note: landlocked; Lake Chad is the most significant water body in the Sahel

People

Population: 9,538,544 (July 2004 est.)

Age structure:

0-14 years: 47.9% (male 2,297,490; female 2,269,801)

15-64 years: 49.3% (male 2,245,586; female 2,459,796)

65 years and over: 2.8% (male 107,594; female 158,277) (2004 est.)

Median age:

total: 16 years

male: 15.3 years

female: 16.7 years (2004 est.)

Population growth rate: 3% (2004 est.)

Birth rate: 46.5 births/1,000 population (2004 est.)

Death rate: 16.38 deaths/1,000 population (2004 est.)

Net migration rate: -0.11 migrant(s)/1,000 population (2004 est.)

Sex ratio:

at birth: 1.04 male(s)/female

under 15 years: 1.01 male(s)/female

15-64 years: 0.91 male(s)/female

65 years and over: 0.68 male(s)/female

total population: 0.95 male(s)/female (2004 est.)

Infant mortality rate:

total: 94.78 deaths/1,000 live births

male: 104.01 deaths/1,000 live births

female: 85.17 deaths/1,000 live births (2004 est.)

Life expectancy at birth:

total population: 48.24 years

male: 46.91 years

female: 49.63 years (2004 est.)

Total fertility rate: 6.38 children born/woman (2004 est.)

HIV/AIDS - adult prevalence rate: 3.6% 5%-7% (2001 est.)

HIV/AIDS - people living with HIV/AIDS: 150,000 (2001 est.)

HIV/AIDS - deaths: 14,000 (confirmed AIDS cases, actual number far higher but difficult to estimate) (2001 est.)

Nationality:

noun: Chadian(s)

adjective: Chadian

Ethnic groups: 200 distinct groups; in the north and center: Arabs, Gorane (Toubou, Daza, Kreda), Zaghawa, Kanembou, Ouaddai, Baguirmi, Hadjerai, Fulbe, Kotoko, Hausa, Boulala, and Maba, most of whom are Muslim; in the south: Sara (Ngambaye, Mbaye, Goulaye), Moundang, Moussei, Massa, most of whom are Christian or animist; about 1,000 French citizens live in Chad

Religions: Muslim 51%, Christian 35%, animist 7%, other 7%

Languages: French (official), Arabic (official), Sara (in south), more than 120 different languages and dialects

Literacy:

definition: age 15 and over can read and write French or Arabic

total population: 47.5%

male: 56%

female: 39.3% (2003 est.)

Government

Country name:

conventional long form: Republic of Chad

conventional short form: Chad

local long form: Republique du Tchad

local short form: Tchad

Government type: republic

Capital: N'Djamena

Administrative divisions: 14 prefectures (prefectures, singular - prefecture); Batha, Biltine, Borkou-Ennedi-Tibesti, Chari-Baguirmi, Guera, Kanem, Lac, Logone Occidental, Logone Oriental, Mayo-Kebbi, Moyen-Chari, Ouaddai, Salamat, Tandjile

note: instead of 14 prefectures, there may be a new administrative structure of 28 departments (departments, singular - department), and 1 city*; Assongha, Baguirmi, Bahr El Gazal, Bahr Koh, Batha Oriental, Batha Occidental, Biltine, Borkou, Dababa,

Ennedi, Guera, Hadjer Lamis, Kabia, Kanem, Lac, Lac Iro, Logone Occidental, Logone Oriental, Mandoul, Mayo-Boneye, Mayo-Dallah, Monts de Lam, N'Djamena*, Ouaddai, Salamat, Sila, Tandjile Oriental, Tandjile Occidental, Tibesti

Independence: 11 August 1960 (from France)

National holiday: Independence Day, 11 August (1960)

Constitution: passed by referendum 31 March 1996

Legal system: based on French civil law system and Chadian customary law; has not accepted compulsory ICJ jurisdiction

Suffrage: 18 years of age; universal

Executive branch:

chief of state: President Lt. Gen. Idriss DEBY (since 4 December 1990)

head of government: Prime Minister Moussa Faki MAHAMAT (since NA July 2003)

cabinet: Council of State, members appointed by the president on the recommendation of the prime minister

elections: president elected by popular vote to serve five-year term; if no candidate receives at least 50% of the total vote, the two candidates receiving the most votes must stand for a second round of voting; last held 20 May 2001 (next to be held NA 2006); prime minister appointed by the president

election results: Lt. Gen. Idriss DEBY reelected president; percent of vote - Lt. Gen. Idriss DEBY 63%, Ngarlegy YORONGAR 16%, Saleh KEBZABO 7%

note: government coalition - MPS, UNDR, and URD

Legislative branch: bicameral according to constitution, consists of a National Assembly (155 seats; members elected by popular vote to serve four-year terms) and a Senate (not yet created and size unspecified, members to serve six-year terms, one-third of membership renewable every two years)

elections: National Assembly - last held 21 April 2002 (next to be held in NA April 2006)

election results: percent of vote by party - NA%; seats by party - MPS 110, RDP 12, FAR 9, RNDP 5, URD 5, UNDR 3, others 11

Judicial branch: Supreme Court; Court of Appeal; Criminal Courts; Magistrate Courts

Political parties and leaders: Federation Action for the Republic or FAR [Ngarlejy YORONGAR]; National Rally for Development and Progress or RNDP [Mamadou BISSO]; National Union for Democracy and Renewal or UNDR [Saleh KEBZABO]; Patriotic Salvation Movement or MPS [Mahamat Saleh AHMAT, chairman] (originally in opposition but now the party in power and the party of the president); Rally for Democracy and Progress or RPD [leader NA]; Union for Renewal and Democracy or URD [Gen. Wadal Abdelkader KAMOUGUE]; Viva Rally for Development and Progress or Viva RNDP [Delwa Kassire COUMAKOYE]

Political pressure groups and leaders: NA

International organization participation: ACCT, ACP, AfDB, AU, BDEAC, CEMAC, FAO, FZ, G-77, IBRD, ICAO, ICCt (signatory), ICFTU, ICRM, IDA, IDB, IFAD, IFC, IFRCS, ILO, IMF, Interpol, IOC, ITU,

Chad (continued)

NAM, OIC, OPCW (signatory), UN, UNCTAD, UNESCO, UNIDO, UPU, WCL, WHO, WIPO, WMO, WToO, WTrO

Diplomatic representation in the US:
chief of mission: Ambassador Hassaballah Abdelhadi Ahmat SOUBIANE
chancery: 2002 R Street NW, Washington, DC 20009
telephone: [1] (202) 462-4009
FAX: [1] (202) 265-1937

Diplomatic representation from the US:
chief of mission: Ambassador Christopher E. GOLDTHWAIT
embassy: Avenue Felix Eboue, N'Djamena
mailing address: B. P. 413, N'Djamena
telephone: [235] (51) 70-09
FAX: [235] (51) 56-54

Flag description: three equal vertical bands of blue (hoist side), yellow, and red; similar to the flag of Romania; also similar to the flags of Andorra and Moldova, both of which have a national coat of arms centered in the yellow band; design was based on the flag of France

Economy

Economy - overview: Chad's primarily agricultural economy will continue to be boosted by major oilfield and pipeline projects that began in 2000. Over 80% of Chad's population relies on subsistence farming and stock raising for its livelihood. Cotton, cattle, and gum arabic provide the bulk of Chad's export earnings, but Chad will begin to export oil in 2004. Chad's economy has long been handicapped by its landlocked position, high energy costs, and a history of instability. Chad relies on foreign assistance and foreign capital for most public and private sector investment projects. A consortium led by two US companies has been investing $3.7 billion to develop oil reserves estimated at 1 billion barrels in southern Chad. Oil production came on stream in late 2003.

GDP: purchasing power parity - $10.86 billion (2003 est.)

GDP - real growth rate: 15% (2003 est.)

GDP - per capita: purchasing power parity - $1,200 (2003 est.)

GDP - composition by sector:
agriculture: 38%
industry: 13%
services: 49% (2001 est.)

Population below poverty line: 80% (2001 est.)

Household income or consumption by percentage share:
lowest 10%: NA%
highest 10%: NA%

Inflation rate (consumer prices): 6% (2002 est.)

Labor force: NA (2002)

Labor force - by occupation: agriculture more than 80% (subsistence farming, herding, and fishing)

Unemployment rate: NA% (2000)

Budget:
revenues: $198 million
expenditures: $218 million, including capital expenditures of $146 million (1998 est.)

Industries: oil, cotton textiles, meatpacking, beer brewing, natron (sodium carbonate), soap, cigarettes, construction materials

Industrial production growth rate: 5% (1995)

Electricity - production: 94.04 million kWh (2001)

Electricity - production by source:
fossil fuel: 100%
hydro: 0%
nuclear: 0%
other: 0% (2001)

Electricity - consumption: 87.46 million kWh (2001)

Electricity - exports: 0 kWh (2001)

Electricity - imports: 0 kWh (2001)

Oil - production: 0 bbl/day (2001 est.)

Oil - consumption: 1,500 bbl/day (2001 est.)

Oil - exports: NA

Oil - imports: NA

Agriculture - products: cotton, sorghum, millet, peanuts, rice, potatoes, manioc (tapioca); cattle, sheep, goats, camels

Exports: $365 million f.o.b. (2003 est.)

Exports - commodities: cotton, cattle, gum arabic

Exports - partners: Portugal 30.3%, Germany 15.2%, US 9.1%, France 6.1%, Nigeria 6.1%, Spain 6.1%, Morocco 4.5%, Poland 4.5% (2002)

Imports: $760 million f.o.b. (2003 est.)

Imports - commodities: machinery and transportation equipment, industrial goods, petroleum products, foodstuffs, textiles

Imports - partners: France 31.5%, US 31.3%, Germany 5.6%, Nigeria 4.7% (2002)

Debt - external: $1.1 billion (2000 est.)

Economic aid - recipient: $238.3 million; note - $125 million committed by Taiwan (August 1997); $30 million committed by African Development Bank; ODA $150 million (2001 est.)

Currency: Communaute Financiere Africaine franc (XAF); note - responsible authority is the Bank of the Central African States

Currency code: XAF

Exchange rates: Communaute Financiere Africaine francs (XAF) per US dollar - 581.2 (2003), 696.988 (2002), 733.039 (2001), 711.976 (2000), 615.699 (1999)

Fiscal year: calendar year

Communications

Telephones - main lines in use: 11,800 (2002)

Telephones - mobile cellular: 34,200 (2002)

Telephone system:
general assessment: primitive system
domestic: fair system of radiotelephone communication stations
international: country code - 235; satellite earth station - 1 Intelsat (Atlantic Ocean)

Radio broadcast stations: AM 2, FM 4, shortwave 5 (2002)

Television broadcast stations: 1 (2002)

Internet country code: .td

Internet hosts: 11 (2002)

Internet users: 15,000 (2002)

Transportation

Railways: 0 km
Highways:
total: 33,400 km
paved: 267 km
unpaved: 33,133 km (1999 est.)
Waterways: 2,000 km
Pipelines: oil 205 km (2003)
Ports and harbors: none
Airports: 50 (2003 est.)
Airports - with paved runways:
total: 7
over 3,047 m: 2
2,438 to 3,047 m: 3
1,524 to 2,437 m: 1
under 914 m: 1 (2003 est.)
Airports - with unpaved runways:
total: 43
1,524 to 2,437 m: 13
914 to 1,523 m: 20
under 914 m: 10 (2003 est.)

Military

Military branches: Armed Forces: National Army (ANT), Air Force, and Republican Guard

Military manpower - military age: 20 years of age (2004 est.)

Military manpower - availability:
males age 15-49: 2,008,825 (2004 est.)

Military manpower - fit for military service:
males age 15-49: 1,051,802 (2004 est.)

Military manpower - reaching military age annually:
males: 91,231 (2004 est.)

Military expenditures - dollar figure: $55.4 million (2003)

Military expenditures - percent of GDP: 2.1% (2003)

Transnational Issues

Disputes - international: civil war in Sudan overlaps into Chad as both states step up border patrols, leaving refugees and rebel groups in both countries; Chad serves as an important mediator in the Sudanese civil conflict; Chadian Aozou rebels reside in southern Libya; Lake Chad Commission continues to urge signatories Cameroon, Chad, Niger, and Nigeria to ratify delimitation treaty over lake region; Chad rejects Nigerian request to redemarcate boundary, the site of periodic cross-border incidents

Chile

Easter Island and Isla Sala y Gomez are not shown.

Introduction

Background: A three-year-old Marxist government was overthrown in 1973 by a dictatorial military regime led by Augusto PINOCHET, who ruled until a freely elected president was installed in 1990. Sound economic policies, maintained consistently since the 1980s, have contributed to steady growth and have helped secure the country's commitment to democratic and representative government. Chile has increasingly assumed regional and international leadership roles befitting its status as a stable, democratic nation.

Geography

Location: Southern South America, bordering the South Pacific Ocean, between Argentina and Peru
Geographic coordinates: 30 00 S, 71 00 W
Map references: South America
Area:
total: 756,950 sq km
land: 748,800 sq km
water: 8,150 sq km
note: includes Easter Island (Isla de Pascua) and Isla Sala y Gomez

Area - comparative: slightly smaller than twice the size of Montana
Land boundaries:
total: 6,171 km
border countries: Argentina 5,150 km, Bolivia 861 km, Peru 160 km
Coastline: 6,435 km
Maritime claims:
territorial sea: 12 NM
contiguous zone: 24 NM
exclusive economic zone: 200 NM
continental shelf: 200/350 NM
Climate: temperate; desert in north; Mediterranean in central region; cool and damp in south
Terrain: low coastal mountains; fertile central valley; rugged Andes in east
Elevation extremes:
lowest point: Pacific Ocean 0 m
highest point: Nevado Ojos del Salado 6,880 m
Natural resources: copper, timber, iron ore, nitrates, precious metals, molybdenum, hydropower
Land use:
arable land: 2.65%
permanent crops: 0.42%
other: 96.93% (1998 est.)
Irrigated land: 18,000 sq km (1998 est.)
Natural hazards: severe earthquakes; active volcanism; tsunamis
Environment - current issues: widespread deforestation and mining threaten natural resources; air pollution from industrial and vehicle emissions; water pollution from raw sewage
Environment - international agreements:
party to: Antarctic-Environmental Protocol, Antarctic-Marine Living Resources, Antarctic Seals, Antarctic Treaty, Biodiversity, Climate Change, Climate Change-Kyoto Protocol, Desertification, Endangered Species, Environmental Modification, Hazardous Wastes, Law of the Sea, Marine Dumping, Ozone Layer Protection, Ship Pollution, Wetlands, Whaling
signed, but not ratified: none of the selected agreements
Geography - note: strategic location relative to sea lanes between Atlantic and Pacific Oceans (Strait of Magellan, Beagle Channel, Drake Passage); Atacama Desert is one of world's driest regions

People

Population: 15,823,957 (July 2004 est.)
Age structure:
0-14 years: 25.8% (male 2,090,165; female 1,996,972)
15-64 years: 66.3% (male 5,235,061; female 5,261,820)
65 years and over: 7.8% (male 515,698; female 724,241) (2004 est.)
Median age:
total: 29.8 years
male: 28.9 years
female: 30.7 years (2004 est.)

Population growth rate: 1.01% (2004 est.)
Birth rate: 15.77 births/1,000 population (2004 est.)
Death rate: 5.71 deaths/1,000 population (2004 est.)
Net migration rate: 0 migrant(s)/1,000 population (2004 est.)
Sex ratio:
at birth: 1.05 male(s)/female
under 15 years: 1.05 male(s)/female
15-64 years: 1 male(s)/female
65 years and over: 0.71 male(s)/female
total population: 0.98 male(s)/female (2004 est.)
Infant mortality rate:
total: 9.05 deaths/1,000 live births
male: 9.81 deaths/1,000 live births
female: 8.25 deaths/1,000 live births (2004 est.)
Life expectancy at birth:
total population: 76.38 years
male: 73.09 years
female: 79.82 years (2004 est.)
Total fertility rate: 2.06 children born/woman (2004 est.)
HIV/AIDS - adult prevalence rate: 0.3% (2001 est.)
HIV/AIDS - people living with HIV/AIDS: 20,000 (2001 est.)
HIV/AIDS - deaths: 220 (2001 est.)
Nationality:
noun: Chilean(s)
adjective: Chilean
Ethnic groups: white and white-Amerindian 95%, Amerindian 3%, other 2%
Religions: Roman Catholic 89%, Protestant 11%, Jewish NEGL%
Languages: Spanish
Literacy:
definition: age 15 and over can read and write
total population: 96.2%
male: 96.4%
female: 96.1% (2003 est.)

Government

Country name:
conventional long form: Republic of Chile
conventional short form: Chile
local long form: Republica de Chile
local short form: Chile
Government type: republic
Capital: Santiago
Administrative divisions: 13 regions (regiones, singular - region); Aisen del General Carlos Ibanez del Campo, Antofagasta, Araucania, Atacama, Bio-Bio, Coquimbo, Libertador General Bernardo O'Higgins, Los Lagos, Magallanes y de la Antartica Chilena, Maule, Region Metropolitana (Santiago), Tarapaca, Valparaiso
note: the US does not recognize claims to Antarctica
Independence: 18 September 1810 (from Spain)
National holiday: Independence Day, 18 September (1810)
Constitution: 11 September 1980, effective 11 March 1981, amended 30 July 1989, 1993, and 1997

Legal system: based on Code of 1857 derived from Spanish law and subsequent codes influenced by French and Austrian law; judicial review of legislative acts in the Supreme Court; has not accepted compulsory ICJ jurisdiction
note: Chile is in the process of completely overhauling its criminal justice system; a new, US-style adversarial system is being gradually implemented throughout the country with the final stage of implementation in the Santiago metropolitan region expected in June 2005
Suffrage: 18 years of age; universal and compulsory
Executive branch:
chief of state: President Ricardo LAGOS Escobar (since 11 March 2000); note - the president is both the chief of state and head of government
head of government: President Ricardo LAGOS Escobar (since 11 March 2000); note - the president is both the chief of state and head of government
cabinet: Cabinet appointed by the president
elections: president elected by popular vote for a six-year term; election last held 12 December 1999, with runoff election held 16 January 2000 (next to be held NA December 2005)
election results: Ricardo LAGOS Escobar elected president; percent of vote - Ricardo LAGOS Escobar 51.32%, Joaquin LAVIN 48.68%
Legislative branch: bicameral National Congress or Congreso Nacional consists of the Senate or Senado (48 seats, 38 elected by popular vote, 9 designated members, and 1 former president who has served a full six-year term and is senator for life); elected members serve eight-year terms (one-half elected every four years) and the Chamber of Deputies or Camara de Diputados (120 seats; members are elected by popular vote to serve four-year terms)
elections: Senate - last held 16 December 2001 (next to be held NA December 2005); Chamber of Deputies - last held 16 December 2001 (next to be held NA December 2005)
election results: Senate - percent of vote by party - NA%; seats by party - CPD 20 (PDC 12, PS 5, PPD 3), APC 16 (UDI 9, RN 7), independents 2; Chamber of Deputies - percent of vote by party - NA%; seats by party - CPD 62 (PDC 24, PPD 21, PS 11, PRSD 6), UDI 35, RN 22, independent 1
Judicial branch: Supreme Court or Corte Suprema (judges are appointed by the president and ratified by the Senate from lists of candidates provided by the court itself; the president of the Supreme Court is elected by the 21-member court); Constitutional Tribunal
Political parties and leaders: Alliance for Chile ("Alianza") or APC - including RN and UDI; Christian Democratic Party or PDC [Adolfo ZALDIVAR]; Coalition of Parties for Democracy ("Concertacion") or CPD - including PDC, PS, PPD, PRSD; Communist Party or PC [Gladys MARIN]; Independent Democratic Union or UDI [Pablo LONGUEIRA]; National Renewal or RN [Sebastian PINERA]; Party for Democracy or PPD [Victor BARRUETO]; Radical Social Democratic Party or PRSD [Orlando CANTUARIAS]; Socialist Party or PS [Gonzalo MARTNER]

Political pressure groups and leaders: revitalized university student federations at all major universities; Roman Catholic Church; United Labor Central or CUT includes trade unionists from the country's five largest labor confederations
International organization participation: APEC, BIS, FAO, G-15, G-77, IADB, IAEA, IBRD, ICAO, ICC, ICCt (signatory), ICFTU, ICRM, IDA, IFAD, IFC, IFRCS, IHO, ILO, IMF, IMO, Interpol, IOC, IOM, ISO, ITU, LAES, LAIA, Mercosur (associate), MONUC, NAM, OAS, OPANAL, OPCW, PCA, RG, UN, UN Security Council (temporary), UNCTAD, UNESCO, UNHCR, UNIDO, UNMOGIP, UNTSO, UPU, WCL, WCO, WFTU, WHO, WIPO, WMO, WToO, WTrO
Diplomatic representation in the US:
chief of mission: Ambassador Andres BIANCHI
chancery: 1732 Massachusetts Avenue NW, Washington, DC 20036
telephone: [1] (202) 785-1746
FAX: [1] (202) 887-5579
consulate(s) general: Chicago, Houston, Los Angeles, Miami, New York, Philadelphia, San Francisco, and San Juan (Puerto Rico)
Diplomatic representation from the US:
chief of mission: Ambassador William R. BROWNFIELD
embassy: Avenida Andres Bello 2800, Las Condes, Santiago
mailing address: APO AA 34033
telephone: [56] (2) 232-2600
FAX: [56] (2) 330-3710
Flag description: two equal horizontal bands of white (top) and red; there is a blue square the same height as the white band at the hoist-side end of the white band; the square bears a white five-pointed star in the center representing a guide to progress and honor; blue symbolizes the sky, white is for the snow-covered Andes, and red stands for the blood spilled to achieve independence; design was influenced by the US flag

Economy

Economy - overview: Chile has a market-oriented economy characterized by a high level of foreign trade. During the early 1990s, Chile's reputation as a role model for economic reform was strengthened when the democratic government of Patricio AYLWIN - which took over from the military in 1990 - deepened the economic reform initiated by the military government. Growth in real GDP averaged 8% during 1991-97, but fell to half that level in 1998 because of tight monetary policies implemented to keep the current account deficit in check and because of lower export earnings - the latter a product of the global financial crisis. A severe drought exacerbated the recession in 1999, reducing crop yields and causing hydroelectric shortfalls and electricity rationing, and Chile experienced negative economic growth for the first time in more than 15 years. Despite the effects of the recession, Chile maintained its reputation for strong financial institutions and sound policy that have

given it the strongest sovereign bond rating in South America. By the end of 1999, exports and economic activity had begun to recover, and growth rebounded to 4.2% in 2000. Growth fell back to 3.1% in 2001 and 2.1% in 2002, largely due to lackluster global growth and the devaluation of the Argentine peso, but recovered to 3.2% in 2003. Unemployment, although declining over the past year, remains stubbornly high, putting pressure on President LAGOS to improve living standards. One bright spot was the signing of a free trade agreement with the US, which took effect on 1 January 2004. In 2004, GDP growth is set to accelerate to more than 4% as copper prices rise, export earnings grow, and foreign direct investment picks up.
GDP: purchasing power parity - $154.6 billion (2003 est.)
GDP - real growth rate: 3.2% (2003 est.)
GDP - per capita: purchasing power parity - $9,900 (2003 est.)
GDP - composition by sector:
agriculture: 6.4%
industry: 38.8%
services: 54.8% (2003 est.)
Population below poverty line: 20.6% (2000 est.)
Household income or consumption by percentage share:
lowest 10%: 3.7%
highest 10%: 41% (2000)
Distribution of family income - Gini index: 56.7 (2000)
Inflation rate (consumer prices): 1.1% (2003 est.)
Labor force: 5.68 million (2000 est.)
Labor force - by occupation: agriculture 13.6%, industry 23.4%, services 63% (2003 est.)
Unemployment rate: 8.5% (2003 est.)
Budget:
revenues: $14.7 billion
expenditures: $15.6 billion, including capital expenditures of $NA (2003 est.)
Industries: copper, other minerals, foodstuffs, fish processing, iron and steel, wood and wood products, transport equipment, cement, textiles
Industrial production growth rate: 3.5% (2003 est.)
Electricity - production: 41.66 billion kWh (2001)
Electricity - production by source:
fossil fuel: 47%
hydro: 51.5%
nuclear: 0%
other: 1.4% (2001)
Electricity - consumption: 40.13 billion kWh (2001)
Electricity - exports: 0 kWh (2001)
Electricity - imports: 1.386 billion kWh (2001)
Oil - production: 13,640 bbl/day (2001 est.)
Oil - consumption: 241,000 bbl/day (2001 est.)
Oil - exports: NA
Oil - imports: NA
Oil - proved reserves: 81.05 million bbl (1 January 2002)
Natural gas - production: 1.2 billion cu m (2001 est.)

Chile (continued)

Natural gas - consumption: 6.47 billion cu m (2001 est.)

Natural gas - exports: 0 cu m (2001 est.)

Natural gas - imports: 5.27 billion cu m (2001 est.)

Natural gas - proved reserves: 67.78 billion cu m (1 January 2002)

Agriculture - products: grapes, apples, pears, onions, wheat, corn, oats, peaches, garlic, asparagus, beans, beef, poultry, wool; fish; timber

Exports: $20.44 billion f.o.b. (2003 est.)

Exports - commodities: copper, fish, fruits, paper and pulp, chemicals, wine

Exports - partners: US 19.1%, Japan 10.5%, China 6.7%, Mexico 5%, Italy 4.7%, UK 4.4% (2002)

Imports: $17.4 billion f.o.b. (2003 est.)

Imports - commodities: consumer goods, chemicals, motor vehicles, fuels, electrical machinery, heavy industrial machinery, food

Imports - partners: Argentina 18%, US 14.9%, Brazil 9.5%, China 6.5%, Germany 4.3% (2002)

Debt - external: $42.5 billion (2003)

Economic aid - recipient: ODA, $40 million (2001 est.)

Currency: Chilean peso (CLP)

Currency code: CLP

Exchange rates: Chilean pesos per US dollar - 691.433 (2003), 688.936 (2002), 634.938 (2001), 535.466 (2000), 508.777 (1999)

Fiscal year: calendar year

Communications

Telephones - main lines in use: 3.467 million (2002)

Telephones - mobile cellular: 6,445,700 (2002)

Telephone system:

general assessment: modern system based on extensive microwave radio relay facilities

domestic: extensive microwave radio relay links; domestic satellite system with 3 earth stations

international: country code - 56; satellite earth stations - 2 Intelsat (Atlantic Ocean)

Radio broadcast stations: AM 180 (eight inactive), FM 64, shortwave 17 (one inactive) (1998)

Television broadcast stations: 63 (plus 121 repeaters) (1997)

Internet country code: .cl

Internet hosts: 135,155 (2002)

Internet users: 3.575 million (2002)

Transportation

Railways:

total: 6,585 km

broad gauge: 2,831 km 1.676-m gauge (1,317 km electrified)

narrow gauge: 3,754 km 1.000-m gauge (2002)

Highways:

total: 79,814 km

paved: 15,484 km (including 294 km of expressways)

unpaved: 64,330 km (2000)

Waterways: 725 km

Pipelines: gas 2,267 km; gas/liquid petroleum gas 42 km; liquid petroleum gas 531 km; oil 983 km; refined products 545 km (2003)

Ports and harbors: Antofagasta, Arica, Chanaral, Coquimbo, Iquique, Puerto Montt, Punta Arenas, San Antonio, San Vicente, Talcahuano, Valparaiso

Merchant marine:

total: 47 ships (1,000 GRT or over) 725,216 GRT/ 954,519 DWT

by type: bulk 10, cargo 5, chemical tanker 9, container 3, liquefied gas 1, passenger 3, petroleum tanker 7, roll on/roll off 4, short-sea/passenger 1, vehicle carrier 4

foreign-owned: Argentina 1

registered in other countries: 28 (2003 est.)

Airports: 363 (2003 est.)

Airports - with paved runways:

total: 71

over 3,047 m: 6

2,438 to 3,047 m: 6

1,524 to 2,437 m: 21

914 to 1,523 m: 23

under 914 m: 15 (2003 est.)

Airports - with unpaved runways:

total: 292

over 3,047 m: 1

2,438 to 3,047 m: 4

1,524 to 2,437 m: 11

914 to 1,523 m: 60

under 914 m: 216 (2003 est.)

Military

Military branches: Army of the Nation, National Navy (including Naval Air, Coast Guard, and Marine Corps), Air Force of the Nation, Chilean Carabineros (National Police)

Military manpower - military age: 19 years of age (2004 est.)

Military manpower - availability:

males age 15-49: 4,207,066 (2004 est.)

Military manpower - fit for military service:

males age 15-49: 3,107,454 (2004 est.)

Military manpower - reaching military age annually:

males: 131,283 (2004 est.)

Military expenditures - dollar figure: $2,839,600,000 (2003)

Military expenditures - percent of GDP: 4% (2003)

Transnational Issues

Disputes - international: Bolivia has reactivated its claim to the Atacama corridor ceded to Chile in 1884 to secure sovereign maritime access for Bolivian natural gas; dispute with Peru over the economic zone delimited by the maritime boundary; Beagle Channel islands dispute resolved through Papal mediation in 1984, but armed incidents persist since 1992 oil discovery; territorial claim in Antarctica (Chilean Antarctic Territory) partially overlaps Argentine and British claims

Illicit drugs: important transshipment country for cocaine destined for Europe and the US; economic prosperity and increasing trade have made Chile more attractive to traffickers seeking to launder drug profits, especially through the Iquique Free Trade Zone, but a new anti-money-laundering law improves controls; imported precursors passed on to Bolivia; domestic cocaine consumption is rising

China
(also see separate Hong Kong, Macau, and Taiwan entries)

Introduction

Background: For centuries China stood as a leading civilization, outpacing the rest of the world in the arts and sciences. But in the 19th and early 20th centuries, China was beset by civil unrest, major famines, military defeats, and foreign occupation. After World War II, the Communists under MAO Zedong established a dictatorship that, while ensuring China's sovereignty, imposed strict controls over everyday life and cost the lives of tens of millions of people. After 1978, his successor DENG Xiaoping gradually introduced market-oriented reforms and decentralized economic decision making. Output quadrupled by 2000. Political controls remain tight while economic controls continue to be relaxed.

Geography

Location: Eastern Asia, bordering the East China Sea, Korea Bay, Yellow Sea, and South China Sea, between North Korea and Vietnam
Geographic coordinates: 35 00 N, 105 00 E
Map references: Asia
Area:
total: 9,596,960 sq km
land: 9,326,410 sq km
water: 270,550 sq km
Area - comparative: slightly smaller than the US
Land boundaries:
total: 22,117 km
border countries: Afghanistan 76 km, Bhutan 470 km, Burma 2,185 km, India 3,380 km, Kazakhstan 1,533 km, North Korea 1,416 km, Kyrgyzstan 858 km, Laos 423 km, Mongolia 4,677 km, Nepal 1,236 km, Pakistan 523 km, Russia (northeast) 3,605 km, Russia (northwest) 40 km, Tajikistan 414 km, Vietnam 1,281 km
Coastline: 14,500 km
Maritime claims:
territorial sea: 12 NM
contiguous zone: 24 NM
exclusive economic zone: 200 NM

continental shelf: 200 NM or to the edge of the continental margin
Climate: extremely diverse; tropical in south to subarctic in north
Terrain: mostly mountains, high plateaus, deserts in west; plains, deltas, and hills in east
Elevation extremes:
lowest point: Turpan Pendi -154 m
highest point: Mount Everest 8,850 m
Natural resources: coal, iron ore, petroleum, natural gas, mercury, tin, tungsten, antimony, manganese, molybdenum, vanadium, magnetite, aluminum, lead, zinc, uranium, hydropower potential (world's largest)
Land use:
arable land: 13.31%
permanent crops: 1.2%
other: 85.49% (1998 est.)
Irrigated land: 525,800 sq km (1998 est.)
Natural hazards: frequent typhoons (about five per year along southern and eastern coasts); damaging floods; tsunamis; earthquakes; droughts; land subsidence
Environment - current issues: air pollution (greenhouse gases, sulfur dioxide particulates) from reliance on coal produces acid rain; water shortages, particularly in the north; water pollution from untreated wastes; deforestation; estimated loss of one-fifth of agricultural land since 1949 to soil erosion and economic development; desertification; trade in endangered species
Environment - international agreements:
party to: Antarctic-Environmental Protocol, Antarctic Treaty, Biodiversity, Climate Change, Climate Change-Kyoto Protocol, Desertification, Endangered Species, Hazardous Wastes, Law of the Sea, Marine Dumping, Ozone Layer Protection, Ship Pollution, Tropical Timber 83, Tropical Timber 94, Wetlands, Whaling
signed, but not ratified: none of the selected agreements

Geography - note: world's fourth largest country (after Russia, Canada, and US); Mount Everest on the border with Nepal is the world's tallest peak;

People

Population: 1,298,847,624 (July 2004 est.)
Age structure:
0-14 years: 22.3% (male 153,401,051; female 135,812,993)
15-64 years: 70.3% (male 469,328,664; female 443,248,860)
65 years and over: 7.5% (male 46,308,923; female 50,747,133) (2004 est.)
Median age:
total: 31.8 years
male: 31.5 years
female: 32.2 years (2004 est.)
Population growth rate: 0.57% (2004 est.)
Birth rate: 12.98 births/1,000 population (2004 est.)
Death rate: 6.92 deaths/1,000 population (2004 est.)
Net migration rate: -0.4 migrant(s)/1,000 population (2004 est.)
Sex ratio:
at birth: 1.12 male(s)/female
under 15 years: 1.13 male(s)/female
15-64 years: 1.06 male(s)/female
65 years and over: 0.91 male(s)/female
total population: 1.06 male(s)/female (2004 est.)
Infant mortality rate:
total: 25.28 deaths/1,000 live births
male: 21.84 deaths/1,000 live births
female: 29.14 deaths/1,000 live births (2004 est.)
Life expectancy at birth:
total population: 71.96 years
male: 70.4 years
female: 73.72 years (2004 est.)
Total fertility rate: 1.69 children born/woman (2004 est.)
HIV/AIDS - adult prevalence rate: less than 0.1% (2001 est.)
HIV/AIDS - people living with HIV/AIDS: 850,000 (2001 est.)
HIV/AIDS - deaths: 30,000 (2001 est.)
Nationality:
noun: Chinese (singular and plural)
adjective: Chinese
Ethnic groups: Han Chinese 91.9%, Zhuang, Uygur, Hui, Yi, Tibetan, Miao, Manchu, Mongol, Buyi, Korean, and other nationalities 8.1%
Religions: Daoist (Taoist), Buddhist, Muslim 1%-2%, Christian 3%-4%
note: officially atheist (2002 est.)
Languages: Standard Chinese or Mandarin (Putonghua, based on the Beijing dialect), Yue (Cantonese), Wu (Shanghaiese), Minbei (Fuzhou), Minnan (Hokkien-Taiwanese), Xiang, Gan, Hakka dialects, minority languages (see Ethnic groups entry)
Literacy:
definition: age 15 and over can read and write
total population: 86%
male: 92.9%
female: 78.8% (2003 est.)

China (continued)

Government

Country name:
conventional long form: People's Republic of China
conventional short form: China
local long form: Zhonghua Renmin Gongheguo
local short form: Zhong Guo
abbreviation: PRC
Government type: Communist state
Capital: Beijing
Administrative divisions: 23 provinces (sheng, singular and plural), 5 autonomous regions* (zizhiqu, singular and plural), and 4 municipalities** (shi, singular and plural); Anhui, Beijing**, Chongqing**, Fujian, Gansu, Guangdong, Guangxi*, Guizhou, Hainan, Hebei, Heilongjiang, Henan, Hubei, Hunan, Jiangsu, Jiangxi, Jilin, Liaoning, Nei Mongol*, Ningxia*, Qinghai, Shaanxi, Shandong, Shanghai**, Shanxi, Sichuan, Tianjin**, Xinjiang*, Xizang* (Tibet), Yunnan, Zhejiang; note - China considers Taiwan its 23rd province; see separate entries for the special administrative regions of Hong Kong and Macau
Independence: 221 BC (unification under the Qin or Ch'in Dynasty 221 BC; Qing or Ch'ing Dynasty replaced by the Republic on 12 February 1912; People's Republic established 1 October 1949)
National holiday: Anniversary of the Founding of the People's Republic of China, 1 October (1949)
Constitution: most recent promulgation 4 December 1982
Legal system: a complex amalgam of custom and statute, largely criminal law; rudimentary civil code in effect since 1 January 1987; new legal codes in effect since 1 January 1980; continuing efforts are being made to improve civil, administrative, criminal, and commercial law
Suffrage: 18 years of age; universal
Executive branch:
chief of state: President HU Jintao (since 15 March 2003) and Vice President ZENG Qinghong (since 15 March 2003)
head of government: Premier WEN Jiabao (since 16 March 2003); Vice Premiers HUANG Ju (since 17 March 2003), WU Yi (17 March 2003), ZENG Peiyan (since 17 March 2003), and HUI Liangyu (since 17 March 2003)
cabinet: State Council appointed by the National People's Congress (NPC)
elections: president and vice president elected by the National People's Congress for five-year terms; elections last held 15-17 March 2003 (next to be held mid-March 2008); premier nominated by the president, confirmed by the National People's Congress
election results: HU Jintao elected president by the Tenth National People's Congress with a total of 2,937 votes (4 delegates voted against him, 4 abstained, and 38 did not vote); ZENG Qinghong elected vice president by the Tenth National People's Congress with a total of 2,578 votes (177 delegates voted against him, 190 abstained, and 38 did not vote); 2 seats were vacant

Legislative branch: unicameral National People's Congress or Quanguo Renmin Daibiao Dahui (2,985 seats; members elected by municipal, regional, and provincial people's congresses to serve five-year terms)
elections: last held December 2002-February 2003 (next to be held late 2007-February 2008)
election results: percent of vote - NA%; seats - NA
Judicial branch: Supreme People's Court (judges appointed by the National People's Congress); Local Peoples Courts (comprise higher, intermediate and local courts); Special Peoples Courts (primarily military, maritime, and railway transport courts)
Political parties and leaders: Chinese Communist Party or CCP [HU Jintao, General Secretary of the Central Committee]; eight registered small parties controlled by CCP
Political pressure groups and leaders: no substantial political opposition groups exist, although the government has identified the Falungong spiritual movement and the China Democracy Party as subversive groups
International organization participation: AfDB, APEC, ARF, AsDB, ASEAN (dialogue partner), BIS, CDB, FAO, G-77, IAEA, IBRD, ICAO, ICC, ICRM, IDA, IFAD, IFC, IFRCS, IHO, ILO, IMF, IMO, Interpol, IOC, IOM (observer), ISO, ITU, LAIA (observer), MINURSO, MONUC, NAM (observer), OPCW, PCA, SCO, UN, UN Security Council, UNAMSIL, UNCTAD, UNESCO, UNHCR, UNIDO, UNITAR, UNMEE, UNMIL, UNMOVIC, UNTSO, UPU, WCO, WHO, WIPO, WMO, WToO, WTrO, ZC
Diplomatic representation in the US:
chief of mission: Ambassador YANG Jiechi
chancery: 2300 Connecticut Avenue NW, Washington, DC 20008
telephone: [1] (202) 328-2500
FAX: [1] (202) 328-2582
consulate(s) general: Chicago, Houston, Los Angeles, New York, and San Francisco
Diplomatic representation from the US:
chief of mission: Ambassador Clark T. RANDT, Jr.
embassy: Xiu Shui Bei Jie 3, 100600 Beijing
mailing address: PSC 461, Box 50, FPO AP 96521-0002
telephone: [86] (10) 6532-3831
FAX: [86] (10) 6532-6929
consulate(s) general: Chengdu, Guangzhou, Hong Kong, Shanghai, Shenyang
Flag description: red with a large yellow five-pointed star and four smaller yellow five-pointed stars (arranged in a vertical arc toward the middle of the flag) in the upper hoist-side corner

Economy

Economy - overview: In late 1978 the Chinese leadership began moving the economy from a sluggish, inefficient, Soviet-style centrally planned economy to a more market-oriented system. Whereas the system operates within a political framework of strict Communist control, the economic influence of non-state organizations and individual citizens has been steadily increasing. The authorities switched to a system of household and village responsibility in agriculture in place of the old collectivization, increased the authority of local officials and plant managers in industry, permitted a wide variety of small-scale enterprises in services and light manufacturing, and opened the economy to increased foreign trade and investment. The result has been a quadrupling of GDP since 1978. Measured on a purchasing power parity (PPP) basis, China in 2003 stood as the second-largest economy in the world after the US, although in per capita terms the country is still poor. Agriculture and industry have posted major gains especially in coastal areas near Hong Kong, opposite Taiwan, and in Shanghai, where foreign investment has helped spur output of both domestic and export goods. The leadership, however, often has experienced - as a result of its hybrid system - the worst results of socialism (bureaucracy and lassitude) and of capitalism (growing income disparities and rising unemployment). China thus has periodically backtracked, retightening central controls at intervals. The government has struggled to (a) sustain adequate jobs growth for tens of millions of workers laid off from state-owned enterprises, migrants, and new entrants to the work force; (b) reduce corruption and other economic crimes; and (c) keep afloat the large state-owned enterprises, many of which had been shielded from competition by subsidies and had been losing the ability to pay full wages and pensions. From 80 to 120 million surplus rural workers are adrift between the villages and the cities, many subsisting through part-time, low-paying jobs. Popular resistance, changes in central policy, and loss of authority by rural cadres have weakened China's population control program, which is essential to maintaining long-term growth in living standards. Another long-term threat to growth is the deterioration in the environment, notably air pollution, soil erosion, and the steady fall of the water table especially in the north. China continues to lose arable land because of erosion and economic development. Beijing says it will intensify efforts to stimulate growth through spending on infrastructure - such as water supply and power grids - and poverty relief and through rural tax reform. Accession to the World Trade Organization helps strengthen its ability to maintain strong growth rates but at the same time puts additional pressure on the hybrid system of strong political controls and growing market influences. China has benefited from a huge expansion in computer internet use. Foreign investment remains a strong element in China's remarkable economic growth. Growing shortages of electric power and raw materials will hold back the expansion of industrial output in 2004.
GDP: purchasing power parity - $6.449 trillion (2003 est.)
GDP - real growth rate: 9.1% (official data) (2003 est.)
GDP - per capita: purchasing power parity - $5,000 (2003 est.)

China (continued)

GDP - composition by sector:
agriculture: 14.5%
industry and construction: 51.7%
services: 33.8% (2002)
Population below poverty line: 10% (2001 est.)
Household income or consumption by percentage share:
lowest 10%: 2.4%
highest 10%: 30.4% (1998)
Distribution of family income - Gini index: 40 (2001)
Inflation rate (consumer prices): 1.2% (2003 est.)
Labor force: 753.6 million (2002 est.)
Labor force - by occupation: agriculture 50%, industry 22%, services 28% (2001 est.)
Unemployment rate: urban unemployment roughly 10%; substantial unemployment and underemployment in rural areas (2003 est.)
Budget:
revenues: $228.4 billion
expenditures: $267.1 billion, including capital expenditures of $NA (2002 est.)
Industries: iron and steel, coal, machine building, armaments, textiles and apparel, petroleum, cement, chemical fertilizers, footwear, toys, food processing, automobiles, consumer electronics, telecommunications
Industrial production growth rate: 16.2% (2003 est.)
Electricity - production: 1.42 trillion kWh (2001)
Electricity - production by source:
fossil fuel: 80.2%
hydro: 18.5%
nuclear: 1.2%
other: 0.1% (2001)
Electricity - consumption: 1.312 trillion kWh (2001)
Electricity - exports: 10.3 billion kWh (2001)
Electricity - imports: 1.8 billion kWh (2001)
Oil - production: 3.3 million bbl/day (2001 est.)
Oil - consumption: 4.57 million bbl/day (2001 est.)
Oil - exports: 151,200 bbl/day (2001)
Oil - imports: 1.207 million bbl/day (2001)
Oil - proved reserves: 26.75 billion bbl (1 January 2002)
Natural gas - production: 30.3 billion cu m (2001 est.)
Natural gas - consumption: 27.4 billion cu m (2001 est.)
Natural gas - exports: 0 cu m (2001 est.)
Natural gas - imports: 0 cu m (2001 est.)
Natural gas - proved reserves: 1.29 trillion cu m (1 January 2002)
Agriculture - products: rice, wheat, potatoes, sorghum, peanuts, tea, millet, barley, cotton, oilseed, pork, fish
Exports: $436.1 billion f.o.b. (2003 est.)
Exports - commodities: machinery and equipment, textiles and clothing, footwear, toys and sporting goods, mineral fuels
Exports - partners: US 21.5%, Hong Kong 18%, Japan 14.9%, South Korea 4.8% (2002)

Imports: $397.4 billion f.o.b. (2003 est.)
Imports - commodities: machinery and equipment, mineral fuels, plastics, iron and steel, chemicals
Imports - partners: Japan 18.1%, Taiwan 12.8%, South Korea 9.7%, US 9.2%, Germany 5.6% (2002)
Debt - external: $184 billion (2003 est.)
Economic aid - recipient: NA
Currency: yuan (CNY)
note: also referred to as the Renminbi (RMB)
Currency code: CNY
Exchange rates: yuan per US dollar - 8.277 (2003), 8.277 (2002), 8.2771 (2001), 8.2785 (2000), 8.2783 (1999)
Fiscal year: calendar year

Communications

Telephones - main lines in use: 214.42 million (2002)
Telephones - mobile cellular: 206.62 million (2002)
Telephone system:
general assessment: domestic and international services are increasingly available for private use; unevenly distributed domestic system serves principal cities, industrial centers, and many towns
domestic: interprovincial fiber-optic trunk lines and cellular telephone systems have been installed; a domestic satellite system with 55 earth stations is in place
international: country code - 86; satellite earth stations - 5 Intelsat (4 Pacific Ocean and 1 Indian Ocean), 1 Intersputnik (Indian Ocean region) and 1 Inmarsat (Pacific and Indian Ocean regions); several international fiber-optic links to Japan, South Korea, Hong Kong, Russia, and Germany (2000)
Radio broadcast stations: AM 369, FM 259, shortwave 45 (1998)
Television broadcast stations: 3,240 (of which 209 are operated by China Central Television, 31 are provincial TV stations and nearly 3,000 are local city stations) (1997)
Internet country code: .cn
Internet hosts: 156,531 (2002)
Internet users: 59.1 million (2002)

Transportation

Railways:
total: 71,600 km
standard gauge: 68,000 km 1.435-m gauge (14,600 km electrified)
narrow gauge: 3,600 km 1.000-m and 0.750-m gauge local industrial lines (2002)
Highways:
total: 1,402,698 km
paved: 314,204 km (with at least 16,314 km of expressways)
unpaved: 1,088,494 km (2000)
Waterways: 110,000 km (1999)
Pipelines: gas 13,845 km; oil 15,143 km; refined products 3,280 km (2003)

Ports and harbors: Dalian, Fuzhou, Guangzhou, Haikou, Huangpu, Lianyungang, Nanjing, Nantong, Ningbo, Qingdao, Qinhuangdao, Shanghai, Shantou, Shenzhen, Tianjin, Wenzhou, Xiamen, Xingang, Yantai, Zhanjiang (2001)
Merchant marine:
total: 1,850 ships (1,000 GRT or over) 18,724,653 GRT/27,749,784 DWT
by type: barge carrier 2, bulk 355, cargo 822, chemical tanker 28, combination bulk 10, combination ore/oil 2, container 165, liquefied gas 28, multi-functional large load carrier 8, passenger 6, passenger/cargo 46, petroleum tanker 272, rail car carrier 1, refrigerated cargo 27, roll on/roll off 25, short-sea/passenger 39, specialized tanker 10, vehicle carrier 4
foreign-owned: Cambodia 1, Greece 2, Hong Kong 12, Japan 1, South Korea 2, Liberia 1, Malaysia 1, Panama 1, Taiwan 2, Tanzania 1
registered in other countries: 790 (2003 est.)
Airports: 507 (2003 est.)
Airports - with paved runways:
total: 332
over 3,047 m: 49
2,438 to 3,047 m: 97
1,524 to 2,437 m: 129
914 to 1,523 m: 22
under 914 m: 35 (2003 est.)
Airports - with unpaved runways:
total: 175
over 3,047 m: 23
2,438 to 3,047 m: 10
1,524 to 2,437 m: 36
914 to 1,523 m: 40
under 914 m: 66 (2003 est.)
Heliports: 15 (2003 est.)

Military

Military branches: People's Liberation Army (PLA): comprises ground forces, Navy (including naval infantry and naval aviation), Air Force, and II Artillery Corps (strategic missile force), People's Armed Police Force (internal security troops, nominally a state security body but included by the Chinese as part of the "armed forces" and considered to be an adjunct to the PLA), militia
Military manpower - military age: 18 years of age (2004 est.)
Military manpower - availability:
males age 15-49: 379,524,688 (2004 est.)
Military manpower - fit for military service:
males age 15-49: 208,143,352 (2004 est.)
Military manpower - reaching military age annually:
males: 12,494,201 (2004 est.)
Military expenditures - dollar figure: $60 billion (2003 est.)
Military expenditures - percent of GDP: 3.5-5.0% (FY03 est.)

China (continued)

Transnational Issues

Disputes - international: involved in complex dispute with Malaysia, Philippines, Taiwan, Vietnam, and possibly Brunei over the Spratly Islands; the 2002 "Declaration on the Conduct of Parties in the South China Sea" has eased tensions but falls short of a legally binding "code of conduct" desired by several of the disputants; most of the rugged, militarized boundary with India is in dispute, but the two sides are committed to begin resolution with discussions on the least disputed Middle Sector; Kashmir remains the world's largest and highly militarized territorial dispute with portions under the de facto administration of China (Aksai Chin), India (Jammu and Kashmir) and Pakistan (Azad Kashmir and Northern Areas), but recent discussion and confidence-building measures among parties are beginning to defuse tensions, India does not recognize Pakistan's ceding lands to China in a 1964 boundary agreement; in 2003 China together with Taiwan asserted their claims to the Japanese-administered Senkaku Islands (Diaoyu Tai) with increased media coverage and protest actions; China and Kazakhstan have resolved their border dispute and are working to demarcate their large open borders to control population migration, illegal activities, and trade; certain islands in Yalu and Tumen rivers are in an uncontested dispute with North Korea and a section of boundary around Mount Paektu is indefinite - China has been attempting to stem mass illegal migration of North Koreans escaping famine and oppression into northern China; China continues to seek a mutually acceptable solution to the disputed alluvial islands with Russia at the confluence of the Amur and Ussuri rivers and a small island on the Argun river as part of the 2001 Treaty of Good Neighborliness, Friendship, and Cooperation; boundary delimitation agreements signed in 2002 with Tajikistan cedes 1,000 sq km of Pamir Mountain range to China in return for China's relinquishing claims to 28,000 sq km, but demarcation has not commenced; demarcation of land boundary with Vietnam continues but maritime boundary and joint fishing zone agreement remains unratified; China occupies Paracel Islands also claimed by Vietnam and Taiwan; groups in Burma and Thailand express concern over China's construction of 13 hydroelectric dams on the Salween River in Yunnan Province

Illicit drugs: major transshipment point for heroin produced in the Golden Triangle; growing domestic drug abuse problem; source country for chemical precursors and methamphetamine

Christmas Island
(territory of Australia)

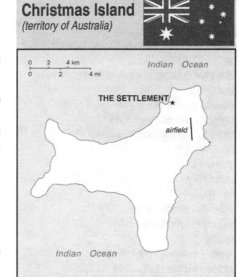

Introduction

Background: Named in 1643 for the day of its discovery, the island was annexed and settlement was begun by the UK in 1888. Phosphate mining began in the 1890s. The UK transferred sovereignty to Australia in 1958. Almost two-thirds of the island has been declared a national park.

Geography

Location: Southeastern Asia, island in the Indian Ocean, south of Indonesia
Geographic coordinates: 10 30 S, 105 40 E
Map references: Southeast Asia
Area:
total: 135 sq km
land: 135 sq km
water: 0 sq km
Area - comparative: about 0.7 times the size of Washington, DC
Land boundaries: 0 km
Coastline: 80 km
Maritime claims:
territorial sea: 12 NM
contiguous zone: 12 NM
exclusive fishing zone: 200 NM
Climate: tropical with a wet and dry season; heat and humidity moderated by trade winds; wet season December to April
Terrain: steep cliffs along coast rise abruptly to central plateau
Elevation extremes:
lowest point: Indian Ocean 0 m
highest point: Murray Hill 361 m
Natural resources: phosphate, beaches
Land use:
arable land: 0%
permanent crops: 0%
other: 100%

note: mainly tropical rainforest; 63% of the island is a national park (1998 est.)
Irrigated land: NA sq km
Natural hazards: the narrow fringing reef surrounding the island can be a maritime hazard
Environment - current issues: NA
Geography - note: located along major sea lanes of Indian Ocean

People

Population: 396 (July 2004 est.)
Age structure:
0-14 years: NA%
15-64 years: NA%
65 years and over: NA% (2004 est.)
Population growth rate: -9% (2004 est.)
Birth rate: NA births/1,000 population (2004 est.)
Death rate: NA deaths/1,000 population (2004 est.)
Net migration rate: NA migrant(s)/1,000 population (2004 est.)
Sex ratio: NA (2004 est.)
Infant mortality rate:
total: NA%
male: NA%
female: NA% (2004 est.)
Life expectancy at birth:
total population: NA years
male: NA years
female: NA years (2004 est.)
Total fertility rate: NA children born/woman (2004 est.)
HIV/AIDS - adult prevalence rate: NA%
HIV/AIDS - people living with HIV/AIDS: NA
HIV/AIDS - deaths: NA
Nationality:
noun: Christmas Islander(s)
adjective: Christmas Island
Ethnic groups: Chinese 70%, European 20%, Malay 10%
note: no indigenous population (2001)
Religions: Buddhist 36%, Muslim 25%, Christian 18%, other 21% (1997)
Languages: English (official), Chinese, Malay
Literacy: NA
People - note: The Australian Bureau of Statistics reports a population of 1508 as of the 2001 Census

Government

Country name:
conventional long form: Territory of Christmas Island
conventional short form: Christmas Island
Dependency status: territory of Australia; administered by the Australian Department of Transport and Regional Services
Government type: NA
Capital: The Settlement
Administrative divisions: none (territory of Australia)
Independence: none (territory of Australia)

Christmas Island (continued)

National holiday: Australia Day, 26 January (1788)
Constitution: NA
Legal system: under the authority of the governor general of Australia and Australian law
Executive branch:
chief of state: Queen ELIZABETH II (since 6 February 1952), represented by the Australian governor general
head of government: Administrator Evan WILLIAMS (since 1 November 2003)
elections: none; the monarch is hereditary; administrator appointed by the governor general of Australia and represents the monarch and Australia
Legislative branch: unicameral Christmas Island Shire Council (9 seats; members elected by popular vote to serve four-year terms)
elections: held every two years with half the members standing for election; last held 3 May 2003 (next to be held NA 2005)
election results: percent of vote - NA%; seats - independents 9
Judicial branch: Supreme Court; District Court; Magistrate's Court
Political parties and leaders: none
Political pressure groups and leaders: none
International organization participation: none
Diplomatic representation in the US: none (territory of Australia)
Diplomatic representation from the US: none (territory of Australia)
Flag description: the flag of Australia is used; note - in early 1986, the Christmas Island Assembly held a design competition for an island flag, however, the winning design has never been formally adopted as the official flag of the territory

Economy

Economy - overview: Phosphate mining had been the only significant economic activity, but in December 1987 the Australian Government closed the mine. In 1991, the mine was reopened. With the support of the government, a $34 million casino opened in 1993. The casino closed in 1998. The Australian Government in 2001 agreed to support the creation of a commercial space-launching site on the island, projected to begin operations in mid-2004
GDP: purchasing power parity - $NA
GDP - real growth rate: NA%
GDP - per capita: purchasing power parity - $NA
GDP - composition by sector:
agriculture: NA%
industry: NA%
services: NA%
Population below poverty line: NA%
Household income or consumption by percentage share:
lowest 10%: NA%
highest 10%: NA%
Inflation rate (consumer prices): NA%
Labor force: NA
Labor force - by occupation: NA

Unemployment rate: NA%
Budget:
revenues: $NA
expenditures: $NA, including capital expenditures of $NA
Industries: tourism, phosphate extraction (near depletion)
Industrial production growth rate: NA%
Electricity - production: NA kWh
Electricity - production by source:
fossil fuel: NA%
hydro: NA%
nuclear: NA%
other: NA%
Electricity - consumption: NA kWh
Agriculture - products: NA
Exports: $NA
Exports - commodities: phosphate
Exports - partners: Australia, NZ
Imports: $NA
Imports - commodities: consumer goods
Imports - partners: principally Australia
Debt - external: $NA
Economic aid - recipient: $NA
Currency: Australian dollar (AUD)
Currency code: AUD
Exchange rates: Australian dollars per US dollar - 1.5419 (2003), 1.9354 (2002), 1.9320 (2001), 1.7173(2000), 1.5497 (1999)
Fiscal year: 1 July - 30 June

Communications

Telephones - main lines in use: NA
Telephones - mobile cellular: NA
Telephone system:
general assessment: service provided by the Australian network
domestic: only analog mobile telephone service is available
international: country code - 61; satellite earth stations - one Intelsat earth station provides telephone and telex service (2000)
Radio broadcast stations: AM 1, FM 1, shortwave 0 (2004)
Television broadcast stations: NA
Internet country code: .cx
Internet users: NA

Transportation

Railways: 24 km to serve phosphate mines
Highways:
total: 240 km
paved: 30 km
unpaved: 210 km (2000)
Waterways: none
Ports and harbors: Flying Fish Cove
Merchant marine: none
Airports: 1 (2003 est.)
Airports - with paved runways:
total: 1
1,524 to 2,437 m: 1 (2003 est.)

Military

Military - note: defense is the responsibility of Australia

Transnational Issues

Disputes - international: none

Clipperton Island
(possession of France)

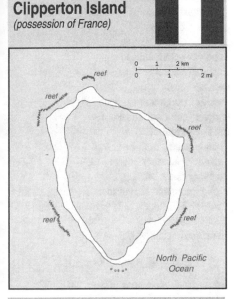

Introduction

Background: This isolated island was named for John CLIPPERTON, a pirate who made it his hideout early in the 18th century. Annexed by France in 1855, it was seized by Mexico in 1897. Arbitration eventually awarded the island to France, which took possession in 1935.

Geography

Location: Middle America, atoll in the North Pacific Ocean, 1,120 km southwest of Mexico
Geographic coordinates: 10 17 N, 109 13 W
Map references: Political Map of the World
Area:
total: 6 sq km
land: 6 sq km
water: 0 sq km
Area - comparative: about 12 times the size of The Mall in Washington, DC
Land boundaries: 0 km
Coastline: 11.1 km
Maritime claims:
territorial sea: 12 NM
exclusive economic zone: 200 NM
Climate: tropical; humid, average temperature 20-32 degrees C, rains May-October
Terrain: coral atoll
Elevation extremes:
lowest point: Pacific Ocean 0 m
highest point: Rocher Clipperton 29 m
Natural resources: fish
Land use:
arable land: 0%
permanent crops: 0%
other: 100% (all coral) (1998 est.)
Irrigated land: 0 sq km (1998 est.)
Natural hazards: NA
Environment - current issues: NA
Geography - note: reef 12 km in circumference

Population: uninhabited (July 2004 est.)

Government

Country name:
conventional long form: none
conventional short form: Clipperton Island
local long form: none
local short form: Ile Clipperton
former: sometimes called Ile de la Passion
Dependency status: possession of France; administered by France from French Polynesia by a high commissioner of the Republic
Legal system: the laws of France, where applicable, apply
Flag description: the flag of France is used

Economy

Economy - overview: Although 115 species of fish have been identified in the territorial waters of Clipperton Island, the only economic activity is tuna fishing.

Transportation

Waterways: none
Ports and harbors: none; offshore anchorage only

Military

Military - note: defense is the responsibility of France

Transnational Issues

Disputes - international: none

Cocos (Keeling) Islands
(territory of Australia)

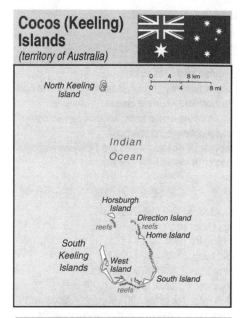

Introduction

Background: There are 27 coral islands in the group. Captain William KEELING discovered the islands in 1609, but they remained uninhabited until the 19th century. Annexed by the UK in 1857, they were transferred to the Australian Government in 1955. The population on the two inhabited islands generally is split between the ethnic Europeans on West Island and the ethnic Malays on Home Island.

Geography

Location: Southeastern Asia, group of islands in the Indian Ocean, southwest of Indonesia, about halfway from Australia to Sri Lanka
Geographic coordinates: 12 30 S, 96 50 E
Map references: Southeast Asia
Area:
total: 14 sq km
land: 14 sq km
water: 0 sq km
note: includes the two main islands of West Island and Home Island
Area - comparative: about 24 times the size of The Mall in Washington, DC
Land boundaries: 0 km
Coastline: 26 km
Maritime claims:
territorial sea: 12 NM
exclusive fishing zone: 200 NM
Climate: tropical with high humidity, moderated by the southeast trade winds for about nine months of the year
Terrain: flat, low-lying coral atolls
Elevation extremes:
lowest point: Indian Ocean 0 m
highest point: unnamed location 5 m
Natural resources: fish

Cocos (Keeling) Islands (continued)

Land use:
arable land: 0%
permanent crops: 0%
other: 100% (1998 est.)
Irrigated land: NA sq km
Natural hazards: cyclone season is October to April
Environment - current issues: fresh water resources are limited to rainwater accumulations in natural underground reservoirs
Geography - note: islands are thickly covered with coconut palms and other vegetation

People

Population: 629 (July 2004 est.)
Age structure:
0-14 years: NA%
15-64 years: NA%
65 years and over: NA% (2004 est.)
Population growth rate: 0% (2004 est.)
Birth rate: NA births/1,000 population (2004 est.)
Death rate: NA deaths/1,000 population (2004 est.)
Net migration rate: NA migrant(s)/1,000 population (2004 est.)
Infant mortality rate:
total: NA%
male: NA%
female: NA% (2004 est.)
Life expectancy at birth:
total population: NA years
male: NA years
female: NA years (2004 est.)
Total fertility rate: NA children born/woman (2004 est.)
HIV/AIDS - adult prevalence rate: NA%
HIV/AIDS - people living with HIV/AIDS: NA
HIV/AIDS - deaths: NA
Nationality:
noun: Cocos Islander(s)
adjective: Cocos Islander
Ethnic groups: Europeans, Cocos Malays
Religions: Sunni Muslim 80%, other 20% (2002 est.)
Languages: Malay (Cocos dialect), English

Government

Country name:
conventional long form: Territory of Cocos (Keeling) Islands
conventional short form: Cocos (Keeling) Islands
Dependency status: territory of Australia; administered from Canberra by the Australian Department of Transport and Regional Services
Government type: NA
Capital: West Island
Administrative divisions: none (territory of Australia)
Independence: none (territory of Australia)
National holiday: Australia Day, 26 January (1788)
Constitution: Cocos (Keeling) Islands Act of 1955
Legal system: based upon the laws of Australia and local laws
Suffrage: NA

Executive branch:
chief of state: Queen ELIZABETH II (since 6 February 1952), represented by the Australian governor general
head of government: Administrator (nonresident) Evan WILLIAMS (since 1 November 2003)
cabinet: NA
elections: none; the monarch is hereditary; administrator appointed by the governor general of Australia and represents the monarch and Australia
Legislative branch: unicameral Cocos (Keeling) Islands Shire Council (7 seats)
elections: held every two years with half the members standing for election; last held NA
Judicial branch: Supreme Court; Magistrate's Court
Political parties and leaders: none
Political pressure groups and leaders: none
International organization participation: none
Diplomatic representation in the US: none (territory of Australia)
Diplomatic representation from the US: none (territory of Australia)
Flag description: the flag of Australia is used

Economy

Economy - overview: Grown throughout the islands, coconuts are the sole cash crop. Small local gardens and fishing contribute to the food supply, but additional food and most other necessities must be imported from Australia. There is a small tourist industry.
GDP: purchasing power parity - $NA
GDP - real growth rate: NA%
GDP - per capita: purchasing power parity - $NA
GDP - composition by sector:
agriculture: NA%
industry: NA%
services: NA% (2001 est.)
Population below poverty line: NA%
Household income or consumption by percentage share:
lowest 10%: NA%
highest 10%: NA%
Inflation rate (consumer prices): NA%
Labor force: NA
Labor force - by occupation: the Cocos Islands Cooperative Society Ltd. employs construction workers, stevedores, and lighterage workers; tourism employs others
Unemployment rate: 60% (2000 est.)
Budget:
revenues: $NA
expenditures: $NA, including capital expenditures of $NA
Industries: copra products and tourism
Industrial production growth rate: NA%
Electricity - production: NA kWh
Electricity - production by source:
fossil fuel: NA%
hydro: NA%
nuclear: NA%
other: NA%

Electricity - consumption: NA kWh
Agriculture - products: vegetables, bananas, pawpaws, coconuts
Exports: $NA
Exports - commodities: copra
Exports - partners: Australia
Imports: $NA
Imports - commodities: foodstuffs
Imports - partners: Australia
Debt - external: $NA
Economic aid - recipient: $NA
Currency: Australian dollar (AUD)
Currency code: AUD
Exchange rates: Australian dollars per US dollar - 1.5419 (2003), 1.9354 (2002), 1.9320 (2001), 1.7173 (2000), 1.5497 (1999)
Fiscal year: 1 July - 30 June

Communications

Telephones - main lines in use: 287 (1992)
Telephones - mobile cellular: note - analog cellular service available
Telephone system:
general assessment: connected within Australia's telecommunication system
domestic: NA
international: country code - 61(08); telephone, telex, and facsimile communications with Australia and elsewhere via satellite; 1 satellite earth station of NA type (2002)
Radio broadcast stations: AM 1, FM 2, shortwave 0 (2004)
Television broadcast stations: NA
Internet country code: .cc
Internet users: NA

Transportation

Railways: 0 km
Highways:
total: 15 km
paved: NA km
unpaved: NA km (2003)
Waterways: none
Ports and harbors: none; lagoon anchorage only
Merchant marine: none
Airports: 1 (2003 est.)
Airports - with paved runways:
total: 1
1,524 to 2,437 m: 1 (2003 est.)

Military

Military - note: defense is the responsibility of Australia; the territory does have a five-person police force

Transnational Issues

Disputes - international: none

Colombia

Introduction

Background: Colombia was one of the three countries that emerged from the collapse of Gran Colombia in 1830 (the others being Ecuador and Venezuela). A 40-year insurgent campaign to overthrow the Colombian Government escalated during the 1990s, undergirded in part by funds from the drug trade. Although the violence is deadly and large swaths of the countryside are under guerrilla influence, the movement lacks the military strength or popular support necessary to overthrow the government. An anti-insurgent army of paramilitaries has grown to be several thousand strong in recent years, challenging the insurgents for control of territory and illicit industries such as the drug trade and the government's ability to exert its dominion over rural areas. While Bogota steps up efforts to reassert government control throughout the country, neighboring countries worry about the violence spilling over their borders.

Geography

Location: Northern South America, bordering the Caribbean Sea, between Panama and Venezuela, and bordering the North Pacific Ocean, between Ecuador and Panama

Geographic coordinates: 4 00 N, 72 00 W

Map references: South America

Area:
total: 1,138,910 sq km
land: 1,038,700 sq km
water: 100,210 sq km
note: includes Isla de Malpelo, Roncador Cay, Serrana Bank, and Serranilla Bank

Area - comparative: slightly less than three times the size of Montana

Land boundaries:
total: 6,004 km
border countries: Brazil 1,643 km, Ecuador 590 km, Panama 225 km, Peru 1,496 km (est.), Venezuela 2,050 km

Coastline: 3,208 km (Caribbean Sea 1,760 km, North Pacific Ocean 1,448 km)

Maritime claims:
territorial sea: 12 NM
exclusive economic zone: 200 NM
continental shelf: 200-m depth or to the depth of exploitation

Climate: tropical along coast and eastern plains; cooler in highlands

Terrain: flat coastal lowlands, central highlands, high Andes Mountains, eastern lowland plains

Elevation extremes:
lowest point: Pacific Ocean 0 m
highest point: Pico Cristobal Colon 5,775 m
note: nearby Pico Simon Bolivar also has the same elevation

Natural resources: petroleum, natural gas, coal, iron ore, nickel, gold, copper, emeralds, hydropower

Land use:
arable land: 1.9%
permanent crops: 1.96%
other: 96.14% (1998 est.)

Irrigated land: 8,500 sq km (1998 est.)

Natural hazards: highlands subject to volcanic eruptions; occasional earthquakes; periodic droughts

Environment - current issues: deforestation; soil and water quality damage from overuse of pesticides; air pollution, especially in Bogota, from vehicle emissions

Environment - international agreements:
party to: Antarctic Treaty, Biodiversity, Climate Change, Climate Change-Kyoto Protocol, Desertification, Endangered Species, Hazardous Wastes, Marine Life Conservation, Ozone Layer Protection, Ship Pollution, Tropical Timber 83, Tropical Timber 94, Wetlands
signed, but not ratified: Law of the Sea

Geography - note: only South American country with coastlines on both North Pacific Ocean and Caribbean Sea

People

Population: 42,310,775 (July 2004 est.)

Age structure:
0-14 years: 31% (male 6,644,080; female 6,489,677)
15-64 years: 63.9% (male 13,171,416; female 13,879,115)
65 years and over: 5% (male 940,762; female 1,185,725) (2004 est.)

Median age:
total: 25.8 years
male: 24.9 years
female: 26.7 years (2004 est.)

Population growth rate: 1.53% (2004 est.)

Birth rate: 21.19 births/1,000 population (2004 est.)

Death rate: 5.61 deaths/1,000 population (2004 est.)

Net migration rate: -0.31 migrant(s)/1,000 population (2004 est.)

Sex ratio:
at birth: 1.03 male(s)/female
under 15 years: 1.02 male(s)/female

15-64 years: 0.95 male(s)/female
65 years and over: 0.79 male(s)/female
total population: 0.96 male(s)/female (2004 est.)

Infant mortality rate:
total: 21.72 deaths/1,000 live births
male: 25.69 deaths/1,000 live births
female: 17.61 deaths/1,000 live births (2004 est.)

Life expectancy at birth:
total population: 71.43 years
male: 67.58 years
female: 75.41 years (2004 est.)

Total fertility rate: 2.59 children born/woman (2004 est.)

HIV/AIDS - adult prevalence rate: 0.4% (2001 est.)

HIV/AIDS - people living with HIV/AIDS: 140,000 (2001 est.)

HIV/AIDS - deaths: 5,600 (2001 est.)

Nationality:
noun: Colombian(s)
adjective: Colombian

Ethnic groups: mestizo 58%, white 20%, mulatto 14%, black 4%, mixed black-Amerindian 3%, Amerindian 1%

Religions: Roman Catholic 90%

Languages: Spanish

Literacy:
definition: age 15 and over can read and write
total population: 92.5%
male: 92.4%
female: 92.6% (2003 est.)

Government

Country name:
conventional long form: Republic of Colombia
conventional short form: Colombia
local long form: Republica de Colombia
local short form: Colombia

Government type: republic; executive branch dominates government structure

Capital: Bogota

Administrative divisions: 32 departments (departamentos, singular - departamento) and 1 capital district* (distrito capital); Amazonas, Antioquia, Arauca, Atlantico, Distrito Capital de Bogota*, Bolivar, Boyaca, Caldas, Caqueta, Casanare, Cauca, Cesar, Choco, Cordoba, Cundinamarca, Guainia, Guaviare, Huila, La Guajira, Magdalena, Meta, Narino, Norte de Santander, Putumayo, Quindio, Risaralda, San Andres y Providencia, Santander, Sucre, Tolima, Valle del Cauca, Vaupes, Vichada

Independence: 20 July 1810 (from Spain)

National holiday: Independence Day, 20 July (1810)

Constitution: 5 July 1991

Legal system: based on Spanish law; a new criminal code modeled after US procedures was enacted in 1992-93; judicial review of executive and legislative acts; accepts compulsory ICJ jurisdiction, with reservations

Suffrage: 18 years of age; universal

Colombia (continued)

Executive branch:
chief of state: President Alvaro URIBE Velez (since 7 August 2002); Vice President Francisco SANTOS (since 7 August 2002); note - the president is both the chief of state and head of government
head of government: President Alvaro URIBE Velez (since 7 August 2002); Vice President Francisco SANTOS (since 7 August 2002); note - the president is both the chief of state and head of government
cabinet: Cabinet consists of a coalition of the two dominant parties - the PL and PSC - and independents
elections: president and vice president elected by popular vote for a four-year term; election last held 26 May 2002 (next to be held NA May 2006)
election results: President Alvaro URIBE Velez received 53% of the vote; Vice President Francisco SANTOS was elected on the same ticket
Legislative branch: bicameral Congress or Congreso consists of the Senate or Senado (102 seats; members are elected by popular vote to serve four-year terms) and the House of Representatives or Camara de Representantes (166 seats; members are elected by popular vote to serve four-year terms)
elections: Senate - last held 10 March 2002 (next to be held NA March 2006); House of Representatives - last held 10 March 2002 (next to be held NA March 2006)
election results: Senate - percent of vote by party - NA%; seats by party - PL 28, PSC 13, independents and smaller parties (many aligned with conservatives) 61; House of Representatives - percent of vote by party - NA%; seats by party - PL 54, PSC 21, independents and other parties 91
Judicial branch: four coequal, supreme judicial organs; Supreme Court of Justice or Corte Suprema de Justical (highest court of criminal law; judges are selected from the nominees of the Higher Council of Justice for eight-year terms); Council of State (highest court of administrative law, judges are selected from the nominees of the Higher Council of Justice for eight-year terms); Constitutional Court (guards integrity and supremacy of the constitution, rules on constitutionality of laws, amendments to the constitution, and international treaties); Higher Council of Justice (administers and disciplines the civilian judiciary; members of the disciplinary chamber resolve jurisdictional conflicts arising between other courts; members are elected by three sister courts and Congress for eight-year terms)
Political parties and leaders: Conservative Party or PSC [Carlos HOLGUIN Sardi]; Liberal Party or PL [Camilo SANCHEZ]; Colombian Communist Party or PCC [Jaime CAICEDO]; Democratic Pole or PDI [Antonio NAVARRO Wolff]
note: Colombia has about 60 formally recognized political parties, most of which do not have a presence in either house of Congress
Political pressure groups and leaders: two largest insurgent groups active in Colombia - Revolutionary Armed Forces of Colombia or FARC and National Liberation Army or ELN; largest anti-insurgent paramilitary group is United Self-Defense Groups of Colombia or AUC

International organization participation: BCIE, CAN, Caricom (observer), CDB, FAO, G-3, G-24, G-77, IADB, IAEA, IBRD, ICAO, ICC, ICCt, ICFTU, ICRM, IDA, IFAD, IFC, IFRCS, IHO, ILO, IMF, IMO, Interpol, IOC, IOM, ISO, ITU, LAES, LAIA, NAM, OAS, OPANAL, OPCW, PCA, RG, UN, UNCTAD, UNESCO, UNHCR, UNIDO, UPU, WCL, WCO, WFTU, WHO, WIPO, WMO, WToO, WTrO
Diplomatic representation in the US:
chief of mission: Ambassador Luis Alberto MORENO Mejia
chancery: 2118 Leroy Place NW, Washington, DC 20008
telephone: [1] (202) 387-8338
FAX: [1] (202) 232-8643
consulate(s) general: Boston, Chicago, Houston, Los Angeles, Miami, New York, San Francisco, San Juan (Puerto Rico), and Washington, DC
consulate(s): Atlanta
Diplomatic representation from the US:
chief of mission: Ambassador William B. WOOD
embassy: Calle 22D-BIS, numbers 47-51, Apartado Aereo 3831
mailing address: Carrera 45 #22D-45, Bogota, D.C., APO AA 34038
telephone: [57] (1) 315-0811
FAX: [57] (1) 315-2197
Flag description: three horizontal bands of yellow (top, double-width), blue, and red; similar to the flag of Ecuador, which is longer and bears the Ecuadorian coat of arms superimposed in the center

Economy

Economy - overview: Colombia's economy suffers from weak domestic and foreign demand, austere government budgets, and serious internal armed conflict, but seems poised for recovery. Other economic problems facing President URIBE range from reforming the pension system to reducing high unemployment. Two of Colombia's leading exports, oil and coffee, face an uncertain future; new exploration is needed to offset declining oil production, while coffee harvests and prices are depressed. On the positive side, several international financial institutions have praised the economic reforms introduced by URIBE, which includes measures designed to reduce the public-sector deficit below 2.5% of GDP in 2004. The government's economic policy and democratic security strategy have engendered a growing sense of confidence in the economy, particularly within the business sector, and GDP growth in 2003 was among the highest in Latin America.
GDP: purchasing power parity - $262.5 billion (2003 est.)
GDP - real growth rate: 3.4% (2003 est.)
GDP - per capita: purchasing power parity - $6,300 (2003 est.)
GDP - composition by sector:
agriculture: 13.9%
industry: 30.3%
services: 55.8% (2003 est.)

Population below poverty line: 55% (2001)
Household income or consumption by percentage share:
lowest 10%: 1%
highest 10%: 44% (1999)
Distribution of family income - Gini index: 57.1 (1996)
Inflation rate (consumer prices): 7.2% (2003 est.)
Labor force: 18.3 million (1999 est.)
Labor force - by occupation: services 46%, agriculture 30%, industry 24% (1990)
Unemployment rate: 13.6% (2003 est.)
Budget:
revenues: $24 billion
expenditures: $25.6 billion, including capital expenditures of $NA (2001 est.)
Industries: textiles, food processing, oil, clothing and footwear, beverages, chemicals, cement; gold, coal, emeralds
Industrial production growth rate: 4% (2001 est.)
Electricity - production: 42.99 billion kWh (2001)
Electricity - production by source:
fossil fuel: 26%
hydro: 72.7%
nuclear: 0%
other: 1.3% (2001)
Electricity - consumption: 39.81 billion kWh (2001)
Electricity - exports: 210 million kWh (2001)
Electricity - imports: 40 million kWh (2001)
Oil - production: 614,400 bbl/day (2001 est.)
Oil - consumption: 252,000 bbl/day (2001 est.)
Oil - exports: NA
Oil - imports: NA
Oil - proved reserves: 1.8 billion bbl (1 January 2002)
Natural gas - production: 5.7 billion cu m (2001 est.)
Natural gas - consumption: 5.7 billion cu m (2001 est.)
Natural gas - exports: 0 cu m (2001 est.)
Natural gas - imports: 0 cu m (2001 est.)
Natural gas - proved reserves: 132 billion cu m (1 January 2002)
Agriculture - products: coffee, cut flowers, bananas, rice, tobacco, corn, sugarcane, cocoa beans, oilseed, vegetables; forest products; shrimp
Exports: $12.96 billion f.o.b. (2003 est.)
Exports - commodities: petroleum, coffee, coal, apparel, bananas, cut flowers
Exports - partners: US 44.8%, Venezuela 9.4%, Ecuador 6.8% (2002)
Imports: $13.06 billion f.o.b. (2003 est.)
Imports - commodities: industrial equipment, transportation equipment, consumer goods, chemicals, paper products, fuels, electricity
Imports - partners: US 32.7%, Venezuela 6.7%, Brazil 5.8%, Japan 5.3%, Mexico 5.1%, Germany 4.2% (2002)
Debt - external: $38 billion (2003 est.)
Economic aid - recipient: $NA
Currency: Colombian peso (COP)

Colombia *(continued)*

Currency code: COP
Exchange rates: Colombian pesos per US dollar - 2,877.65 (2003), 2,504.24 (2002), 2,299.63 (2001), 2,087.9 (2000), 1,756.23 (1999)
Fiscal year: calendar year

Communications

Telephones - main lines in use: 7.766 million (2002)
Telephones - mobile cellular: 4,596,600 (2002)
Telephone system:
general assessment: modern system in many respects
domestic: nationwide microwave radio relay system; domestic satellite system with 41 earth stations; fiber-optic network linking 50 cities
international: country code - 57; satellite earth stations - 6 Intelsat, 1 Inmarsat; 3 fully digitalized international switching centers; 8 submarine cables
Radio broadcast stations: AM 454, FM 34, shortwave 27 (1999)
Television broadcast stations: 60 (includes seven low-power stations) (1997)
Internet country code: .co
Internet hosts: 55,626 (2002)
Internet users: 2 million (2002)

Transportation

Railways:
total: 3,304 km
standard gauge: 150 km 1.435-m gauge
narrow gauge: 3,154 km 0.914-m gauge (2002)
Highways:
total: 110,000 km
paved: 26,000 km
unpaved: 84,000 km (2000)
Waterways: 18,140 km (navigable by river boats) (April 1996)
Pipelines: gas 4,360 km; oil 6,134 km; refined products 3,140 km (2003)
Ports and harbors: Bahia de Portete, Barranquilla, Buenaventura, Cartagena, Leticia, Puerto Bolivar, San Andres, Santa Marta, Tumaco, Turbo
Merchant marine:
total: 13 ships (1,000 GRT or over) 35,427 GRT/46,301 DWT
by type: bulk 4, cargo 5, container 1, liquefied gas 1, petroleum tanker 2
registered in other countries: 16 (2003 est.)
Airports: 980 (2003 est.)
Airports - with paved runways:
total: 100
over 3,047 m: 2
2,438 to 3,047 m: 9
1,524 to 2,437 m: 39
914 to 1,523 m: 38
under 914 m: 12 (2003 est.)
Airports - with unpaved runways:
total: 880
2,438 to 3,047 m: 1
1,524 to 2,437 m: 34

914 to 1,523 m: 272
under 914 m: 573 (2003 est.)
Heliports: 1 (2003 est.)

Military

Military branches: Army (Ejercito Nacional), Navy (Armada Nacional, including Naval Aviation, Marines, and Coast Guard), Air Force (Fuerza Aerea Colombiana)
Military manpower - military age: 18 years of age (2004 est.)
Military manpower - availability:
males age 15-49: 11,252,027 (2004 est.)
Military manpower - fit for military service:
males age 15-49: 7,495,462 (2004 est.)
Military manpower - reaching military age annually:
males: 392,656 (2004 est.)
Military expenditures - dollar figure: $3.3 billion (FY01)
Military expenditures - percent of GDP: 3.4% (FY01)

Transnational Issues

Disputes - international: Nicaragua filed a claim against Honduras in 1999 and against Colombia in 2001 at the ICJ over disputed maritime boundary involving 50,000 sq km in the Caribbean Sea, including the Archipelago de San Andres y Providencia and Quita Sueno Bank; maritime boundary dispute with Venezuela in the Gulf of Venezuela; Colombian drug activities penetrate Peruvian border area; the continuing civil disorder in Colombia has created a serious refugee crisis in neighboring states, especially Ecuador
Illicit drugs: illicit producer of coca, opium poppy, and cannabis; world's leading coca cultivator (cultivation of coca in 2002 was 144,450 hectares, a 15% decline since 2001); potential production of opium between 2001 and 2002 declined by 25% to 91 metric tons; potential production of heroin declined to 11.3 metric tons; the world's largest processor of coca derivatives into cocaine; supplier of about 90% of the cocaine to the US market and the great majority of cocaine to other international drug markets; important supplier of heroin to the US market; active aerial eradication program; a significant portion of non-US narcotics proceeds are either laundered or invested in Colombia through the black market peso exchange

Comoros

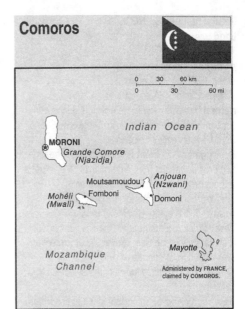

Introduction

Background: Unstable Comoros has endured 19 coups or attempted coups since gaining independence from France in 1975. In 1997, the islands of Anjouan and Moheli declared their independence from Comoros. In 1999, military chief Col. AZALI seized power. He pledged to resolve the secessionist crisis through a confederal arrangement named the 2000 Fomboni Accord. In December 2001, voters approved a new constitution and presidential elections took place in the spring of 2002. Each island in the archipelago elected its own president and a new union president was sworn in on 26 May 2002.

Geography

Location: Southern Africa, group of islands at the northern mouth of the Mozambique Channel, about two-thirds of the way between northern Madagascar and northern Mozambique
Geographic coordinates: 12 10 S, 44 15 E
Map references: Africa
Area:
total: 2,170 sq km
land: 2,170 sq km
water: 0 sq km
Area - comparative: slightly more than 12 times the size of Washington, DC
Land boundaries: 0 km
Coastline: 340 km
Maritime claims:
territorial sea: 12 NM
exclusive economic zone: 200 NM
Climate: tropical marine; rainy season (November to May)
Terrain: volcanic islands, interiors vary from steep mountains to low hills
Elevation extremes:
lowest point: Indian Ocean 0 m
highest point: Le Kartala 2,360 m

Comoros (continued)

Natural resources: NEGL
Land use:
arable land: 34.98%
permanent crops: 17.94%
other: 47.08% (1998 est.)
Irrigated land: NA sq km
Natural hazards: cyclones possible during rainy season (December to April); Le Kartala on Grand Comore is an active volcano
Environment - current issues: soil degradation and erosion results from crop cultivation on slopes without proper terracing; deforestation
Environment - international agreements:
party to: Biodiversity, Climate Change, Desertification, Endangered Species, Hazardous Wastes, Law of the Sea, Ozone Layer Protection, Ship Pollution, Wetlands
signed, but not ratified: none of the selected agreements
Geography - note: important location at northern end of Mozambique Channel

People

Population: 651,901 (July 2004 est.)
Age structure:
0-14 years: 42.8% (male 140,083; female 139,245)
15-64 years: 54.2% (male 174,216; female 179,050)
65 years and over: 3% (male 9,136; female 10,171) (2004 est.)
Median age:
total: 18.6 years
male: 18.3 years
female: 18.9 years (2004 est.)
Population growth rate: 2.94% (2004 est.)
Birth rate: 38 births/1,000 population (2004 est.)
Death rate: 8.63 deaths/1,000 population (2004 est.)
Net migration rate: 0 migrant(s)/1,000 population (2004 est.)
Sex ratio:
at birth: 1.03 male(s)/female
under 15 years: 1.01 male(s)/female
15-64 years: 0.97 male(s)/female
65 years and over: 0.9 male(s)/female
total population: 0.99 male(s)/female (2004 est.)
Infant mortality rate:
total: 77.22 deaths/1,000 live births
male: 85.9 deaths/1,000 live births
female: 68.28 deaths/1,000 live births (2004 est.)
Life expectancy at birth:
total population: 61.57 years
male: 59.29 years
female: 63.91 years (2004 est.)
Total fertility rate: 5.15 children born/woman (2004 est.)
HIV/AIDS - adult prevalence rate: 0.12% (2001 est.)
HIV/AIDS - people living with HIV/AIDS: NA
HIV/AIDS - deaths: NA
Nationality:
noun: Comoran(s)
adjective: Comoran

Ethnic groups: Antalote, Cafre, Makoa, Oimatsaha, Sakalava
Religions: Sunni Muslim 98%, Roman Catholic 2%
Languages: Arabic (official), French (official), Shikomoro (a blend of Swahili and Arabic)
Literacy:
definition: age 15 and over can read and write
total population: 56.5%
male: 63.6%
female: 49.3% (2003 est.)

Government

Country name:
conventional long form: Union of the Comoros
conventional short form: Comoros
local long form: Union des Comores
local short form: Comores
Government type: independent republic
Capital: Moroni
Administrative divisions: 3 islands; Grande Comore (Njazidja), Anjouan (Nzwani), and Moheli (Mwali); note - there are also four municipalities named Domoni, Fomboni, Moroni, and Moutsamoudou
Independence: 6 July 1975 (from France)
National holiday: Independence Day, 6 July (1975)
Constitution: 23 December 2001
note: a Transitional National Unity Government (GUNT) was formed on 20 January 2002 following the passing of the new constitution; the GUNT governed until the presidential elections on 14 April 2002
Legal system: French and Sharia (Islamic) law in a new consolidated code
Suffrage: 18 years of age; universal
Executive branch:
chief of state: President AZALI Assoumani (since 26 May 2002); note - following a 1999 coup AZALI was appointed president; in January 2002 he resigned his position to run in the 14 April 2002 presidential elections; Prime Minister Hamada Madi BOLERO was appointed interim president until replaced again by AZALI in May 2002 when BOLERO was appointed Minister of External Defense and Territorial Security; the president is both the chief of state and the head of government
head of government: President AZALI Assoumani (since 26 May 2002); note - following a 1999 coup AZALI was appointed president; in January 2002 he resigned his position to run in the 14 April 2002 presidential elections; Prime Minister Hamada Madi BOLERO was appointed interim president until replaced again by AZALI in May 2002 when BOLERO was appointed Minister of External Defense and Territorial Security; the president is both the chief of state and the head of government
cabinet: Council of Ministers appointed by the president
elections: as defined by the 2001 constitution, the presidency rotates every four years among the elected presidents from the three main islands in the Union; election last held 14 April 2002 (next to be held

NA April 2007); prime minister appointed by the president; note - AZALI has not appointed a Prime Minister since he was sworn into office in May 2002
election results: President AZALI Assoumani elected president with 75% of the vote
Legislative branch: unicameral Assembly of the Union (30 seats; half the deputies are selected by the individual islands' local assemblies and the other half by universal suffrage; deputies serve for five years); note - elections for the former legislature, the Federal Assembly (dissolved in 1999) were held on 1 and 8 December 1996; the next elections for the Assembly of the Union were scheduled to be held on 18 and 25 April 2004
Judicial branch: Supreme Court or Cour Supremes (two members appointed by the president, two members elected by the Federal Assembly, one elected by the Council of each island, and others are former presidents of the republic)
Political parties and leaders: Forces pour l'Action Republicaine or FAR [Col. Abdourazak ABDULHAMID]; Forum pour la Redressement National or FRN (alliance of 12 parties); Front Democratique or FD [Moustoifa Said CHEIKH]; Front National pour la Justice or FNJ (Islamic party in opposition) [Ahmed RACHID]; Movement des Citoyens pour la Republique or MCR [Mahamoud MRADABI]; Mouvement Populaire Anjouanais or MPA (Anjouan separatist movement) [leader NA]; Mouvement pour la Democratie et le Progress or MDP-NGDC [Abbas DJOUSSOUF]; Movement pour le Socialisme et la Democratie or MSD (splinter group of FD) [Abdou SOEFOU]; Parti Comorien pour la Democratie et le Progress or PCDP [Ali MROUDJAE]; Rassemblement National pour le Development or RND (party of the government) [Omar TAMOU, Abdoulhamid AFFRAITANE]
Political pressure groups and leaders: NA
International organization participation: ACCT, ACP, AfDB, AMF, AU, FAO, G-77, IBRD, ICAO, ICCt (signatory), ICRM, IDA, IDB, IFAD, IFC, IFRCS, ILO, IMF, IMO, InOC, Interpol, IOC, ITU, LAS, NAM, OIC, OPCW (signatory), UN, UNCTAD, UNESCO, UNIDO, UPU, WCO, WHO, WMO
Diplomatic representation in the US:
chief of mission: Ambassador Mahmoud M. ABOUD (ambassador to the US and Canada and permanent representative to the UN)
chancery: (temporary) care of the Permanent Mission of the Union of the Comoros to the United Nations, 420 East 50th Street, New York, NY 10022
telephone: [1] (212) 972-8010 and 223-2711
FAX: [1] (212) 983-4712 and 715-0699
Diplomatic representation from the US: the US does not have an embassy in Comoros; the ambassador to Mauritius is accredited to Comoros
Flag description: four equal horizontal bands of yellow (top), white, red, and blue with a green isosceles triangle based on the hoist; centered within the triangle is a white crescent with the convex side facing the hoist and four white, five-pointed stars placed vertically in a line between the points of the

crescent; the horizontal bands and the four stars represent the four main islands of the archipelago - Mwali, Njazidja, Nzwani, and Mayotte (a territorial collectivity of France, but claimed by Comoros); the crescent, stars, and color green are traditional symbols of Islam

Economy

Economy - overview: One of the world's poorest countries, Comoros is made up of three islands that have inadequate transportation links, a young and rapidly increasing population, and few natural resources. The low educational level of the labor force contributes to a subsistence level of economic activity, high unemployment, and a heavy dependence on foreign grants and technical assistance. Agriculture, including fishing, hunting, and forestry, contributes 40% to GDP, employs 80% of the labor force, and provides most of the exports. The country is not self-sufficient in food production; rice, the main staple, accounts for the bulk of imports. The government - which is hampered by internal political disputes - is struggling to upgrade education and technical training, to privatize commercial and industrial enterprises, to improve health services, to diversify exports, to promote tourism, and to reduce the high population growth rate. Increased foreign support is essential if the goal of 4% annual GDP growth is to be met. Remittances from 150,000 Comorans abroad help supplement GDP.

GDP: purchasing power parity - $441 million (2002 est.)

GDP - real growth rate: 2% (2002 est.)

GDP - per capita: purchasing power parity - $700 (2002 est.)

GDP - composition by sector:
agriculture: 40%
industry: 4%
services: 56% (2001 est.)

Population below poverty line: 60% (2002 est.)

Household income or consumption by percentage share:
lowest 10%: NA%
highest 10%: NA%

Inflation rate (consumer prices): 3.5% (2001 est.)

Labor force: 144,500 (1996 est.)

Labor force - by occupation: agriculture 80%

Unemployment rate: 20% (1996 est.)

Budget:
revenues: $27.6 million
expenditures: $NA, including capital expenditures of $NA (2001 est.)

Industries: tourism, perfume distillation

Industrial production growth rate: -2% (1999 est.)

Electricity - production: 21.27 million kWh (2001)

Electricity - production by source:
fossil fuel: 90.6%
hydro: 9.4%
nuclear: 0%
other: 0% (2001)

Electricity - consumption: 19.78 million kWh (2001)

Electricity - exports: 0 kWh (2001)

Electricity - imports: 0 kWh (2001)

Oil - production: 0 bbl/day (2001 est.)

Oil - consumption: 700 bbl/day (2001 est.)

Oil - exports: NA

Oil - imports: NA

Agriculture - products: vanilla, cloves, perfume essences, copra, coconuts, bananas, cassava (tapioca)

Exports: $28 million f.o.b. (2002 est.)

Exports - commodities: vanilla, ylang-ylang, cloves, perfume oil, copra

Exports - partners: France 32.1%, Germany 17.9%, US 17.9%, Singapore 10.7%, Netherlands 7.1% (2002)

Imports: $88 million f.o.b. (2002 est.)

Imports - commodities: rice and other foodstuffs, consumer goods; petroleum products, cement, transport equipment

Imports - partners: France 34.1%, South Africa 11.4%, Japan 5.7%, Kenya 5.7%, UAE 5.7%, Mauritius 4.5%, Thailand 4.5% (2002)

Debt - external: $232 million (2000 est.)

Economic aid - recipient: $10 million (2001 est.)

Currency: Comoran franc (KMF)

Currency code: KMF

Exchange rates: Comoran francs (KMF) per US dollar - 435.9 (2003), 522.741 (2002), 549.779 (2001), 533.982 (2000), 461.775 (1999)
note: prior to January 1999, the official rate was pegged to the French franc at 75 Comoran francs per French franc; since 1 January 1999, the Comoran franc is pegged to the euro at a rate of 491.9677 Comoran francs per euro

Fiscal year: calendar year

Communications

Telephones - main lines in use: 10,300 (2002)

Telephones - mobile cellular: NA

Telephone system:
general assessment: sparse system of microwave radio relay and HF radiotelephone communication stations
domestic: HF radiotelephone communications and microwave radio relay
international: country code - 269; HF radiotelephone communications to Madagascar and Reunion

Radio broadcast stations: AM 1, FM 4, shortwave 1 (2001)

Television broadcast stations: NA

Internet country code: .km

Internet hosts: 12 (2002)

Internet users: 3,200 (2002)

Transportation

Railways: 0 km

Highways:
total: 880 km
paved: 673 km
unpaved: 207 km (1999 est)

Waterways: none

Ports and harbors: Fomboni, Moroni, Moutsamoudou

Merchant marine:
total: 62 ships (1,000 GRT or over) 452,801 GRT/ 681,343 DWT
by type: bulk 9, cargo 31, chemical tanker 1, combination bulk 1, livestock carrier 1, passenger 4, petroleum tanker 5, refrigerated cargo 3, roll on/roll off 1, short-sea/passenger 2, specialized tanker 4
foreign-owned: Bahamas 1, Bulgaria 1, Cyprus 1, Greece 7, Honduras 1, India 1, Kenya 1, Lebanon 7, Liberia 1, Marshall Islands 3, Pakistan 4, Panama 2, Russia 1, Saint Vincent and the Grenadines 1, Saudi Arabia 2, Syria 4, Turkey 21, United Kingdom 1, United States 1, Yemen 2 (2003 est.)

Airports: 4 (2003 est.)

Airports - with paved runways:
total: 4
2,438 to 3,047 m: 1
914 to 1,523 m: 3 (2003 est.)

Military

Military branches: Comoran Security Force

Military manpower - availability:
males age 15-49: 154,843 (2004 est.)

Military manpower - fit for military service:
males age 15-49: 91,825 (2004 est.)

Military expenditures - dollar figure: $6 million (2003)

Military expenditures - percent of GDP: 3% (2003)

Transnational Issues

Disputes - international: claims French-administered Mayotte

Congo, Democratic Republic of the

Introduction

Background: Since 1997, the Democratic Republic of the Congo (DROC; formerly called Zaire) has been rent by ethnic strife and civil war, touched off by a massive inflow in 1994 of refugees from the fighting in Rwanda and Burundi. The government of former president MOBUTU Sese Seko was toppled by a rebellion led by Laurent KABILA in May 1997; his regime was subsequently challenged by a Rwanda- and Uganda-backed rebellion in August 1998. Troops from Zimbabwe, Angola, Namibia, Chad, and Sudan intervened to support the Kinshasa regime. A cease-fire was signed on 10 July 1999 by the DROC, Zimbabwe, Angola, Uganda, Namibia, Rwanda, and Congolese armed rebel groups, but sporadic fighting continued. KABILA was assassinated on 16 January 2001 and his son Joseph KABILA was named head of state ten days later. In October 2002, the new president was successful in getting occupying Rwandan forces to withdraw from eastern Congo; two months later, an agreement was signed by all remaining warring parties to end the fighting and set up a government of national unity.

Geography

Location: Central Africa, northeast of Angola
Geographic coordinates: 0 00 N, 25 00 E
Map references: Africa
Area:
total: 2,345,410 sq km
land: 2,267,600 sq km
water: 77,810 sq km
Area - comparative: slightly less than one-fourth the size of the US
Land boundaries:
total: 10,730 km
border countries: Angola 2,511 km (of which 225 km is the boundary of Angola's discontiguous Cabinda Province), Burundi 233 km, Central African Republic 1,577 km, Republic of the Congo 2,410 km, Rwanda 217 km, Sudan 628 km, Tanzania 459 km, Uganda 765 km, Zambia 1,930 km
Coastline: 37 km
Maritime claims:
territorial sea: 12 NM
exclusive economic zone: boundaries with neighbors
Climate: tropical; hot and humid in equatorial river basin; cooler and drier in southern highlands; cooler and wetter in eastern highlands; north of Equator - wet season April to October, dry season December to February; south of Equator - wet season November to March, dry season April to October
Terrain: vast central basin is a low-lying plateau; mountains in east
Elevation extremes:
lowest point: Atlantic Ocean 0 m
highest point: Pic Marguerite on Mont Ngaliema (Mount Stanley) 5,110 m
Natural resources: cobalt, copper, cadmium, petroleum, industrial and gem diamonds, gold, silver, zinc, manganese, tin, germanium, uranium, radium, bauxite, iron ore, coal, hydropower, timber
Land use:
arable land: 2.96%
permanent crops: 0.52%
other: 96.52% (1998 est.)
Irrigated land: 110 sq km (1998 est.)
Natural hazards: periodic droughts in south; Congo River floods (seasonal); in the east, in the Great Rift Valley, there are active volcanoes
Environment - current issues: poaching threatens wildlife populations; water pollution; deforestation; refugees responsible for significant deforestation, soil erosion, and wildlife poaching; mining of minerals (coltan - a mineral used in creating capacitors, diamonds, and gold) causing environmental damage
Environment - international agreements:
party to: Biodiversity, Climate Change, Desertification, Endangered Species, Hazardous Wastes, Law of the Sea, Marine Dumping, Ozone Layer Protection, Tropical Timber 83, Tropical Timber 94, Wetlands
signed, but not ratified: Environmental Modification
Geography - note: straddles equator; has very narrow strip of land that controls the lower Congo River and is only outlet to South Atlantic Ocean; dense tropical rain forest in central river basin and eastern highlands

People

Population: 58,317,930
note: estimates for this country explicitly take into account the effects of excess mortality due to AIDS; this can result in lower life expectancy, higher infant mortality and death rates, lower population and growth rates, and changes in the distribution of population by age and sex than would otherwise be expected (July 2004 est.)

Age structure:
0-14 years: 48.2% (male 14,122,237; female 14,008,654)
15-64 years: 49.3% (male 14,097,301; female 14,646,285)
65 years and over: 2.5% (male 590,262; female 853,191) (2004 est.)
Median age:
total: 15.8 years
male: 15.4 years
female: 16.2 years (2004 est.)
Population growth rate: 2.99% (2004 est.)
Birth rate: 44.73 births/1,000 population (2004 est.)
Death rate: 14.64 deaths/1,000 population (2004 est.)
Net migration rate: -0.17 migrant(s)/1,000 population
note: fighting between the Congolese Government and Uganda- and Rwanda-backed Congolese rebels spawned a regional war in DROC in August 1998, which left 1.8 million Congolese internally displaced and caused 300,000 Congolese refugees to flee to surrounding countries (2004 est.)
Sex ratio:
at birth: 1.03 male(s)/female
under 15 years: 1.01 male(s)/female
15-64 years: 0.96 male(s)/female
65 years and over: 0.69 male(s)/female
total population: 0.98 male(s)/female (2004 est.)
Infant mortality rate:
total: 94.69 deaths/1,000 live births
male: 103.18 deaths/1,000 live births
female: 85.95 deaths/1,000 live births (2004 est.)
Life expectancy at birth:
total population: 49.14 years
male: 47.06 years
female: 51.28 years (2004 est.)
Total fertility rate: 6.62 children born/woman (2004 est.)
HIV/AIDS - adult prevalence rate: 4.9% (2001 est.)
HIV/AIDS - people living with HIV/AIDS: 1.3 million (2001 est.)
HIV/AIDS - deaths: 120,000 (2001 est.)
Nationality:
noun: Congolese (singular and plural)
adjective: Congolese or Congo
Ethnic groups: over 200 African ethnic groups of which the majority are Bantu; the four largest tribes - Mongo, Luba, Kongo (all Bantu), and the Mangbetu-Azande (Hamitic) make up about 45% of the population
Religions: Roman Catholic 50%, Protestant 20%, Kimbanguist 10%, Muslim 10%, other syncretic sects and indigenous beliefs 10%
Languages: French (official), Lingala (a lingua franca trade language), Kingwana (a dialect of Kiswahili or Swahili), Kikongo, Tshiluba
Literacy:
definition: age 15 and over can read and write French, Lingala, Kingwana, or Tshiluba
total population: 65.5%
male: 76.2%
female: 55.1% (2003 est.)

Congo, Democratic Republic of the (continued)

Government

Country name:
conventional long form: Democratic Republic of the Congo
conventional short form: none
local long form: Republique Democratique du Congo
local short form: none
former: Congo Free State, Belgian Congo, Congo/Leopoldville, Congo/Kinshasa, Zaire
abbreviation: DROC

Government type: dictatorship; presumably undergoing a transition to representative government

Capital: Kinshasa

Administrative divisions: 10 provinces (provinces, singular - province) and one city* (ville); Bandundu, Bas-Congo, Equateur, Kasai-Occidental, Kasai-Oriental, Katanga, Kinshasa*, Maniema, Nord-Kivu, Orientale, Sud-Kivu

Independence: 30 June 1960 (from Belgium)

National holiday: Independence Day, 30 June (1960)

Constitution: 24 June 1967, amended August 1974, revised 15 February 1978, amended April 1990; transitional constitution promulgated in April 1994; in November 1998, a draft constitution was approved by former President Laurent KABILA but it was not ratified by a national referendum; one outcome of the ongoing inter-Congolese dialogue will be a new constitution

Legal system: based on Belgian civil law system and tribal law; has not accepted compulsory ICJ jurisdiction

Suffrage: 18 years of age; universal and compulsory

Executive branch:
chief of state: President Joseph KABILA (since 26 January 2001); note - following the assassination of his father, Laurent Desire KABILA, on 16 January 2001, Joseph KABILA succeeded to the presidency; the president is both the chief of state and head of government
head of government: President Joseph KABILA (since 26 January 2001); note - following the assassination of his father, Laurent Desire KABILA, on 16 January 2001, Joseph KABILA succeeded to the presidency; the president is both the chief of state and head of government
cabinet: National Executive Council, appointed by the president
elections: prior to the overthrow of MOBUTU Sese Seko, the president was elected by popular vote for a seven-year term; election last held 29 July 1984 (next was scheduled to be held in May 1997); formerly, there was also a prime minister who was elected by the High Council of the Republic; note - a Transitional Government is drafting a new constitution with free elections scheduled to be held in NA 2005
election results: results of the last election were: MOBUTU Sese Seko Kuku Ngbendu wa Za Banga reelected president in 1984 without opposition
note: Joseph KABILA succeeded his father, Laurent Desire KABILA, following the latter's assassination in January 2001, negotiations with rebel leaders led to

the establishment of a transitional government in July 2003 with free elections scheduled to be held in NA 2005

Legislative branch: a 300-member Transitional Constituent Assembly established in August 2000
elections: NA; members of the Transitional Constituent Assembly were appointed by former President Laurent Desire KABILA

Judicial branch: Supreme Court or Cour Supreme

Political parties and leaders: Democratic Social Christian Party or PDSC [Andre BO-BOLIKO]; Forces for Renovation for Union and Solidarity or FONUS [Joseph OLENGHANKOY]; National Congolese Lumumbist Movement or MNC [Francois LUMUMBA]; Popular Movement of the Revolution or MPR (three factions: MPR-Fait Prive [Catherine NZUZI wa Mbombo]; MPR/Vunduawe [Felix VUNDUAWE]; MPR/Mananga [MANANGA Dintoka Mpholo]); Unified Lumumbast Party or PALU [Antoine GIZENGA]; Union for Democracy and Social Progress or UDPS [Etienne TSHISEKEDI wa Mulumba]; Union of Federalists and Independent Republicans or UFERI (two factions: UFERI [Lokambo OMOKOKO]; UFERI/OR [Adolph Kishwe MAYA])

Political pressure groups and leaders: NA

International organization participation: ACCT, ACP, AfDB, AU, CEPGL, FAO, G-24, G-77, IAEA, IBRD, ICAO, ICCt, ICFTU, ICRM, IDA, IFAD, IFC, IFRCS, IHO, ILO, IMF, IMO, Interpol, IOC, IOM, ISO (correspondent), ITU, NAM, OPCW (signatory), PCA, SADC, UN, UNCTAD, UNESCO, UNHCR, UNIDO, UPU, WCL, WCO, WFTU, WHO, WIPO, WMO, WToO, WTrO

Diplomatic representation in the US:
chief of mission: Ambassador Faida MITIFU
chancery: 1800 New Hampshire Avenue NW, Washington, DC 20009
telephone: [1] (202) 234-7690, 7691
FAX: [1] (202) 234-2609

Diplomatic representation from the US:
chief of mission: Ambassador Aubrey HOOKS
embassy: 310 Avenue des Aviateurs, Kinshasa
mailing address: Unit 31550, APO AE 09828
telephone: [243] (88) 43608
FAX: [243] (88) 43467

Flag description: light blue with a large yellow five-pointed star in the center and a columnar arrangement of six small yellow five-pointed stars along the hoist side

Economy

Economy - overview: The economy of the Democratic Republic of the Congo - a nation endowed with vast potential wealth - has declined drastically since the mid-1980s. The war, which began in August 1998, has dramatically reduced national output and government revenue, has increased external debt, and has resulted in the deaths from war, famine, and disease of perhaps 3.5 million people. Foreign businesses have curtailed operations due to

uncertainty about the outcome of the conflict, lack of infrastructure, and the difficult operating environment. The war has intensified the impact of such basic problems as an uncertain legal framework, corruption, inflation, and lack of openness in government economic policy and financial operations. Conditions improved in late 2002 with the withdrawal of a large portion of the invading foreign troops. Several IMF and World Bank missions have met with the government to help it develop a coherent economic plan, and President KABILA has begun implementing reforms. Much economic activity lies outside the GDP data. Economic stability, aided by international donors, improved in 2003. New mining contracts have been approved, which - combined with high mineral and metal prices - could improve Kinshasa's fiscal position and GDP growth.

GDP: purchasing power parity - $35.62 billion (2003 est.)

GDP - real growth rate: 6% (2003 est.)

GDP - per capita: purchasing power parity - $600 (2003 est.)

GDP - composition by sector:
agriculture: 55%
industry: 11%
services: 34% (2000 est.)

Population below poverty line: NA%

Household income or consumption by percentage share:
lowest 10%: NA%
highest 10%: NA%

Inflation rate (consumer prices): 14% (2003 est.)

Labor force: 14.51 million (1993 est.)

Labor force - by occupation: NA

Unemployment rate: NA% (2003 est.)

Budget:
revenues: $269 million
expenditures: $244 million, including capital expenditures of $24 million (1996 est.)

Industries: mining (diamonds, copper, zinc), mineral processing, consumer products (including textiles, footwear, cigarettes, processed foods and beverages), cement

Industrial production growth rate: NA%

Electricity - production: 5.243 billion kWh (2001)

Electricity - production by source:
fossil fuel: 1.8%
hydro: 98.2%
nuclear: 0%
other: 0% (2001)

Electricity - consumption: 3.839 billion kWh (2001)

Electricity - exports: 1.097 billion kWh (2001)

Electricity - imports: 60 million kWh (2001)

Oil - production: 24,000 bbl/day (2001 est.)

Oil - consumption: 14,000 bbl/day (2001 est.)

Oil - exports: NA

Oil - imports: NA

Oil - proved reserves: 1.538 billion bbl (1 January 2002)

Natural gas - proved reserves: 104.8 billion cu m (1 January 2002)

Agriculture - products: coffee, sugar, palm oil, rubber, tea, quinine, cassava (tapioca), palm oil, bananas, root crops, corn, fruits; wood products
Exports: $1.417 billion f.o.b. (2002 est.)
Exports - commodities: diamonds, copper, crude oil, coffee, cobalt
Exports - partners: Belgium 64.3%, US 13.4%, Zimbabwe 6.7%, Finland 4.9% (2002)
Imports: $933 million f.o.b. (2002 est.)
Imports - commodities: foodstuffs, mining and other machinery, transport equipment, fuels
Imports - partners: South Africa 15.9%, Belgium 14.1%, Nigeria 10.1%, France 9.2%, Germany 7.4%, Netherlands 5.1%, Kenya 5% (2002)
Debt - external: $11.6 billion (2000 est.)
Economic aid - recipient: $195.3 million (1995)
Currency: Congolese franc (CDF)
Currency code: CDF
Exchange rates: Congolese francs per US dollar - NA (2003), 346.485 (2002), 206.617 (2001), 21.82 (2000), 4.02 (1999)
Fiscal year: calendar year

Communications

Telephones - main lines in use: 10,000 (2002)
Telephones - mobile cellular: 560,000 (2002)
Telephone system:
general assessment: poor
domestic: barely adequate wire and microwave radio relay service in and between urban areas; domestic satellite system with 14 earth stations
international: country code - 243; satellite earth station - 1 Intelsat (Atlantic Ocean)
Radio broadcast stations: AM 3, FM 11, shortwave 2 (2001)
Television broadcast stations: 4 (2001)
Internet country code: .cd
Internet hosts: 134 (2002)
Internet users: 50,000 (2002)

Transportation

Railways:
total: 4,772 km
narrow gauge: 3,621 km 1.067-m gauge (858 km electrified); 125 km 1.000-m gauge; 1,026 km 0.600-m gauge (2002)
Highways:
total: 157,000 km (including 30 km of expressways)
paved: NA km
unpaved: NA km (1999 est.)
Waterways: 15,000 km (including the Congo and its tributaries, and unconnected lakes)
Pipelines: gas 54 km; oil 71 km (2003)
Ports and harbors: Banana, Boma, Bukavu, Bumba, Goma, Kalemie, Kindu, Kinshasa, Kisangani, Matadi, Mbandaka
Merchant marine: none
Airports: 230 (2003 est.)
Airports - with paved runways:
total: 24
over 3,047 m: 4

2,438 to 3,047 m: 2
1,524 to 2,437 m: 16
914 to 1,523 m: 2 (2003 est.)
Airports - with unpaved runways:
total: 206
1,524 to 2,437 m: 17
914 to 1,523 m: 92
under 914 m: 97 (2003 est.)

Military

Military branches: Army, Navy, Air Force
Military manpower - availability:
males age 15-49: 12,706,971 (2004 est.)
Military manpower - fit for military service:
males age 15-49: 6,480,645 (2004 est.)
Military expenditures - dollar figure: $115.5 million (2003)
Military expenditures - percent of GDP: 1.4% (2003)

Transnational Issues

Disputes - international: Democratic Republic of the Congo is in the grip of a civil war, tribal conflict, and rebel gang fighting that has drawn in neighboring states of Burundi, Rwanda and Uganda; in the Great Lakes region and Sudan, heads of the Great Lakes states and UN pledge to end conflict, but unchecked localized violence continues unabated; the location of the boundary in the broad Congo River with the Republic of the Congo is indefinite except in the Pool Malebo/Stanley Pool area
Illicit drugs: illicit producer of cannabis, mostly for domestic consumption; while rampant corruption and inadequate supervision leaves the banking system vulnerable to money laundering, the lack of a well-developed financial system limits the country's utility as a money-laundering center

Congo, Republic of the

Introduction

Background: Upon independence in 1960, the former French region of Middle Congo became the Republic of the Congo. A quarter century of experimentation with Marxism was abandoned in 1990 and a democratically elected government installed in 1992. A brief civil war in 1997 restored former Marxist President SASSOU-NGUESSO, but ushered in a period of ethnic unrest. Southern-based rebel groups agreed to a final peace accord in March 2003. The Republic of Congo is one of Africa's largest petroleum producers with significant potential for offshore development.

Geography

Location: Western Africa, bordering the South Atlantic Ocean, between Angola and Gabon
Geographic coordinates: 1 00 S, 15 00 E
Map references: Africa
Area:
total: 342,000 sq km
land: 341,500 sq km
water: 500 sq km
Area - comparative: slightly smaller than Montana
Land boundaries:
total: 5,504 km
border countries: Angola 201 km, Cameroon 523 km, Central African Republic 467 km, Democratic Republic of the Congo 2,410 km, Gabon 1,903 km
Coastline: 169 km
Maritime claims:
territorial sea: 200 NM
Climate: tropical; rainy season (March to June); dry season (June to October); constantly high temperatures and humidity; particularly enervating climate astride the Equator
Terrain: coastal plain, southern basin, central plateau, northern basin

Elevation extremes:
lowest point: Atlantic Ocean 0 m
highest point: Mount Berongou 903 m
Natural resources: petroleum, timber, potash, lead, zinc, uranium, copper, phosphates, natural gas, hydropower
Land use:
arable land: 0.5%
permanent crops: 0.13%
other: 99.37% (1998 est.)
Irrigated land: 10 sq km (1998 est.)
Natural hazards: seasonal flooding
Environment - current issues: air pollution from vehicle emissions; water pollution from the dumping of raw sewage; tap water is not potable; deforestation
Environment - international agreements:
party to: Biodiversity, Climate Change, Desertification, Endangered Species, Ozone Layer Protection, Tropical Timber 83, Tropical Timber 94, Wetlands
signed, but not ratified: Law of the Sea
Geography - note: about 70% of the population lives in Brazzaville, Pointe-Noire, or along the railroad between them

People

Population: 2,998,040
note: estimates for this country explicitly take into account the effects of excess mortality due to AIDS; this can result in lower life expectancy, higher infant mortality and death rates, lower population and growth rates, and changes in the distribution of population by age and sex than would otherwise be expected (July 2004 est.)
Age structure:
0-14 years: 37.9% (male 571,224; female 563,723)
15-64 years: 58.5% (male 865,596; female 888,125)
65 years and over: 3.6% (male 45,093; female 64,279) (2004 est.)
Median age:
total: 20.4 years
male: 20 years
female: 20.9 years (2004 est.)
Population growth rate: 1.42% (2004 est.)
Birth rate: 28.66 births/1,000 population (2004 est.)
Death rate: 14.49 deaths/1,000 population (2004 est.)
Net migration rate: 0 migrant(s)/1,000 population (2004 est.)
Sex ratio:
at birth: 1.03 male(s)/female
under 15 years: 1.01 male(s)/female
15-64 years: 0.98 male(s)/female
65 years and over: 0.7 male(s)/female
total population: 0.98 male(s)/female (2004 est.)
Infant mortality rate:
total: 93.86 deaths/1,000 live births
male: 99.95 deaths/1,000 live births
female: 87.59 deaths/1,000 live births (2004 est.)
Life expectancy at birth:
total population: 49.51 years
male: 48.51 years
female: 50.55 years (2004 est.)

Total fertility rate: 3.54 children born/woman (2004 est.)
HIV/AIDS - adult prevalence rate: 7.2% (2001 est.)
HIV/AIDS - people living with HIV/AIDS: 110,000 (2001 est.)
HIV/AIDS - deaths: 11,000 (2001 est.)
Nationality:
noun: Congolese (singular and plural)
adjective: Congolese or Congo
Ethnic groups: Kongo 48%, Sangha 20%, M'Bochi 12%, Teke 17%, Europeans and other 3%
note: Europeans estimated at 8,500, mostly French, before the 1997 civil war; may be half that in 1998, following the widespread destruction of foreign businesses in 1997
Religions: Christian 50%, animist 48%, Muslim 2%
Languages: French (official), Lingala and Monokutuba (lingua franca trade languages), many local languages and dialects (of which Kikongo is the most widespread)
Literacy:
definition: age 15 and over can read and write
total population: 83.8%
male: 89.6%
female: 78.4% (2003 est.)

Government

Country name:
conventional long form: Republic of the Congo
conventional short form: Congo (Brazzaville)
local long form: Republique du Congo
local short form: none
former: Middle Congo, Congo/Brazzaville, Congo
Government type: republic
Capital: Brazzaville
Administrative divisions: 10 regions (regions, singular - region) and 1 commune*; Bouenza, Brazzaville*, Cuvette, Cuvette-Ouest, Kouilou, Lekoumou, Likouala, Niari, Plateaux, Pool, Sangha
Independence: 15 August 1960 (from France)
National holiday: Independence Day, 15 August (1960)
Constitution: constitution approved by referendum 20 January 2002
Legal system: based on French civil law system and customary law
Suffrage: 18 years of age; universal
Executive branch:
chief of state: President Denis SASSOU-NGUESSO (since 25 October 1997, following the civil war in which he toppled elected president Pascal LISSOUBA); note - the president is both the chief of state and head of government
head of government: President Denis SASSOU-NGUESSO (since 25 October 1997, following the civil war in which he toppled elected president Pascal LISSOUBA); note - the president is both the chief of state and head of government
cabinet: Council of Ministers appointed by the president

elections: president elected by popular vote for a seven-year term (eligible for a second seven-year term); election last held 10 March 2002 (next to be held NA 2009)
election results: Denis SASSOU-NGUESSO reelected president; percent of vote - Denis SASSOU-NGUESSO 89.4%, Joseph Kignoumbi Kia MBOUNGOU 2.7%
Legislative branch: bicameral Parliament consists of the Senate (66 seats; members are elected by popular vote to serve five-year terms) and the National Assembly (137 seats; members are elected by popular vote to serve five-year terms)
elections: Senate - last held 11 July 2002 (next to be held NA July 2007); National Assembly - last held 27 May and 26 June 2002 (next to be held by NA May 2007)
election results: Senate - percent of vote by party - NA%; seats by party - FDP 56, other 10; National Assembly - percent of vote by party - NA%; seats by party - FDP 83, UDR 6, UPADS 3, other 45
Judicial branch: Supreme Court or Cour Supreme
Political parties and leaders: the most important of the many parties are the Democratic and Patriotic Forces or FDP (an alliance of Convention for Alternative Democracy, Congolese Labor Party or PCT, Liberal Republican Party, National Union for Democracy and Progress, Patriotic Union for the National Reconstruction, and Union for the National Renewal) [Denis SASSOU-NGUESSO, president]; Congolese Movement for Democracy and Integral Development or MCDDI [Michel MAMPOUYA]; Pan-African Union for Social Development or UPADS [Martin MBERI]; Rally for Democracy and Social Progress or RDPS [Jean-Pierre Thystere TCHICAYA, president]; Rally for Democracy and the Republic or RDR [Raymond Damasge NGOLLO]; Union for Democracy and Republic or UDR [leader NA]; Union of Democratic Forces or UFD [Sebastian EBAO]
Political pressure groups and leaders: Congolese Trade Union Congress or CSC; General Union of Congolese Pupils and Students or UGEEC; Revolutionary Union of Congolese Women or URFC; Union of Congolese Socialist Youth or UJSC
International organization participation: ACCT, ACP, AfDB, AU, BDEAC, CEMAC, FAO, FZ, G-77, IBRD, ICAO, ICCt (signatory), ICFTU, ICRM, IDA, IFAD, IFC, IFRCS, ILO, IMF, IMO, Interpol, IOC, IOM, ITU, NAM, OPCW (signatory), UN, UNCTAD, UNESCO, UNIDO, UPU, WCL, WCO, WFTU, WHO, WIPO, WMO, WToO, WTrO
Diplomatic representation in the US:
chief of mission: Ambassador Serge MOMBOULI
chancery: 4891 Colorado Avenue NW, Washington, DC 20011
telephone: [1] (202) 726-5500
FAX: [1] (202) 726-1860
Diplomatic representation from the US:
chief of mission: Ambassador Robin R. SANDERS
embassy: NA
mailing address: NA
telephone: [243] (88) 43608

note: the embassy is temporarily collocated with the US Embassy in the Democratic Republic of the Congo (US Embassy Kinshasa, 310 Avenue des Aviateurs, Kinshasa)

Flag description: divided diagonally from the lower hoist side by a yellow band; the upper triangle (hoist side) is green and the lower triangle is red; uses the popular pan-African colors of Ethiopia

Economy

Economy - overview: The economy is a mixture of village agriculture and handicrafts, an industrial sector based largely on oil, support services, and a government characterized by budget problems and overstaffing. Oil has supplanted forestry as the mainstay of the economy, providing a major share of government revenues and exports. In the early 1980s, rapidly rising oil revenues enabled the government to finance large-scale development projects with GDP growth averaging 5% annually, one of the highest rates in Africa. The government has mortgaged a substantial portion of its oil earnings, contributing to a shortage of revenues. The 12 January 1994 devaluation of Franc Zone currencies by 50% resulted in inflation of 61% in 1994, but inflation has subsided since. Economic reform efforts continued with the support of international organizations, notably the World Bank and the IMF. The reform program came to a halt in June 1997 when civil war erupted. Denis SASSOU-NGUESSO, who returned to power when the war ended in October 1997, publicly expressed interest in moving forward on economic reforms and privatization and in renewing cooperation with international financial institutions. However, economic progress was badly hurt by slumping oil prices and the resumption of armed conflict in December 1998, which worsened the republic's budget deficit. The current administration presides over an uneasy internal peace and faces difficult economic problems of stimulating recovery and reducing poverty.

GDP: purchasing power parity - $2.186 billion (2003 est.)

GDP - real growth rate: 2% (2003 est.)

GDP - per capita: purchasing power parity - $700 (2003 est.)

GDP - composition by sector:
agriculture: 10%
industry: 48%
services: 42% (2001 est.)

Population below poverty line: NA%

Household income or consumption by percentage share:
lowest 10%: NA%
highest 10%: NA%

Inflation rate (consumer prices): 4% (2002 est.)

Labor force: NA (2000 est.)

Unemployment rate: NA% (2003)

Budget:
revenues: $870 million
expenditures: $970 million, including capital expenditures of $NA (1997 est.)

Industries: petroleum extraction, cement, lumber, brewing, sugar, palm oil, soap, flour, cigarettes

Industrial production growth rate: 0% (2002 est.)

Electricity - production: 358.1 million kWh (2001)

Electricity - production by source:
fossil fuel: 0.3%
hydro: 99.7%
nuclear: 0%
other: 0% (2001)

Electricity - consumption: 633 million kWh (2001)

Electricity - exports: 0 kWh (2001)

Electricity - imports: 300 million kWh (2001)

Oil - production: 275,000 bbl/day (2001 est.)

Oil - consumption: 5,000 bbl/day (2001 est.)

Oil - exports: NA

Oil - imports: NA

Oil - proved reserves: 93.5 million bbl (1 January 2002)

Natural gas - production: 0 cu m (2001 est.)

Natural gas - consumption: 0 cu m (2001 est.)

Natural gas - exports: 0 cu m (2001 est.)

Natural gas - imports: 0 cu m (2001 est.)

Natural gas - proved reserves: 495.5 million cu m (1 January 2002)

Agriculture - products: cassava (tapioca), sugar, rice, corn, peanuts, vegetables, coffee, cocoa; forest products

Exports: $2.293 billion f.o.b. (2003 est.)

Exports - commodities: petroleum, lumber, plywood, sugar, cocoa, coffee, diamonds

Exports - partners: South Korea 24.1%, Taiwan 16.3%, China 11%, US 10%, Germany 6.9%, France 6.1% (2002)

Imports: $666.9 million f.o.b. (2003 est.)

Imports - commodities: capital equipment, construction materials, foodstuffs

Imports - partners: France 21.9%, Italy 8.5%, Belgium 6%, US 5.2%, India 4.1% (2002)

Debt - external: $5 billion (2000 est.)

Economic aid - recipient: $159.1 million (1995)

Currency: Communaute Financiere Africaine franc (XAF); note - responsible authority is the Bank of the Central African States

Currency code: XAF

Exchange rates: Communaute Financiere Africaine francs (XAF) per US dollar - 581.2 (2003), 696.988 (2002), 733.039 (2001), 711.98 (2000), 615.7 (1999)

Fiscal year: calendar year

Communications

Telephones - main lines in use: 22,000 (2002)

Telephones - mobile cellular: 221,800 (2002)

Telephone system:
general assessment: services barely adequate for government use; key exchanges are in Brazzaville, Pointe-Noire, and Loubomo; intercity lines frequently out of order
domestic: primary network consists of microwave radio relay and coaxial cable
international: country code - 242; satellite earth station - 1 Intelsat (Atlantic Ocean)

Radio broadcast stations: AM 1, FM 5, shortwave 3 (2001)

Television broadcast stations: 1 (2002)

Internet country code: .cg

Internet hosts: 36 (2002)

Internet users: 5,000 (2002)

Transportation

Railways:
total: 894 km
narrow gauge: 894 km 1.067-m gauge (2002)

Highways:
total: 12,800 km
paved: 1,242 km
unpaved: 11,558 km (1999 est.)

Waterways: 1,120 km
note: the Congo and Ubangi (Oubangui) rivers provide 1,120 km of commercially navigable water transport; other rivers are used for local traffic only

Pipelines: gas 53 km; oil 673 km (2003)

Ports and harbors: Brazzaville, Impfondo, Ouesso, Oyo, Pointe-Noire

Airports: 32 (2003 est.)

Airports - with paved runways:
total: 4
over 3,047 m: 1
1,524 to 2,437 m: 3 (2003 est.)

Airports - with unpaved runways:
total: 28
1,524 to 2,437 m: 6
914 to 1,523 m: 11
under 914 m: 11 (2003 est.)

Military

Military branches: Congolese Armed Forces (FAC): Army, Air Force, Navy

Military manpower - military age: 20 years of age (2004 est.)

Military manpower - availability:
males age 15-49: 773,790 (2004 est.)

Military manpower - fit for military service:
males age 15-49: 390,884 (2004 est.)

Military manpower - reaching military age annually:
males: 31,964 (2004 est.)

Military expenditures - dollar figure: $68.6 million (2003)

Military expenditures - percent of GDP: 2.8% (2003)

Transnational Issues

Disputes - international: the location of the boundary in the broad Congo River with the Democratic Republic of the Congo is indefinite except in the Pool Malebo/Stanley Pool area

Cook Islands
(self-governing in free association with New Zealand)

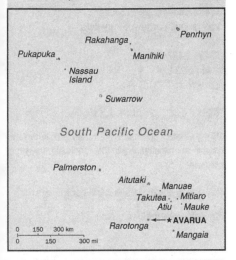

Introduction

Background: Named after Captain Cook, who sighted them in 1770, the islands became a British protectorate in 1888. By 1900, administrative control was transferred to New Zealand; in 1965 residents chose self-government in free association with New Zealand. The emigration of skilled workers to New Zealand and government deficits are continuing problems.

Geography

Location: Oceania, group of islands in the South Pacific Ocean, about one-half of the way from Hawaii to New Zealand
Geographic coordinates: 21 14 S, 159 46 W
Map references: Oceania
Area:
total: 240 sq km
land: 240 sq km
water: 0 sq km
Area - comparative: 1.3 times the size of Washington, DC
Land boundaries: 0 km
Coastline: 120 km
Maritime claims:
territorial sea: 12 NM
exclusive economic zone: 200 NM
continental shelf: 200 NM or to the edge of the continental margin
Climate: tropical; moderated by trade winds
Terrain: low coral atolls in north; volcanic, hilly islands in south
Elevation extremes:
lowest point: Pacific Ocean 0 m
highest point: Te Manga 652 m
Natural resources: NEGL

Land use:
arable land: 17.39%
permanent crops: 13.04%
other: 69.57% (1998 est.)
Irrigated land: NA sq km
Natural hazards: typhoons (November to March)
Environment - current issues: NA
Environment - international agreements:
party to: Biodiversity, Climate Change, Climate Change-Kyoto Protocol, Desertification, Law of the Sea
signed, but not ratified: none of the selected agreements
Geography - note: the northern Cook Islands are seven low-lying, sparsely populated, coral atolls; the southern Cook Islands consist of eight elevated, fertile, volcanic isles where most of the populace lives

People

Population: 21,200 (July 2004 est.)
Age structure:
0-14 years: NA%
15-64 years: NA%
65 years and over: NA% (2004 est.)
Population growth rate: NA% (2004 est.)
Birth rate: NA births/1,000 population (2004 est.)
Death rate: NA deaths/1,000 population (2004 est.)
Sex ratio: NA (2004 est.)
Infant mortality rate:
total: NA%
male: NA%
female: NA% (2004 est.)
Life expectancy at birth:
total population: NA years
male: NA years
female: NA years (2004 est.)
Total fertility rate: NA children born/woman (2004 est.)
HIV/AIDS - adult prevalence rate: NA%
HIV/AIDS - people living with HIV/AIDS: NA
HIV/AIDS - deaths: NA
Nationality:
noun: Cook Islander(s)
adjective: Cook Islander
Ethnic groups: Polynesian (full blood) 81.3%, Polynesian and European 7.7%, Polynesian and non-European 7.7%, European 2.4%, other 0.9%
Religions: Christian (majority of populace are members of the Cook Islands Christian Church)
Languages: English (official), Maori
Literacy:
definition: NA
total population: 95%
male: NA%
female: NA%

Government

Country name:
conventional long form: none
conventional short form: Cook Islands
former: Harvey Islands

Dependency status: self-governing in free association with New Zealand; Cook Islands is fully responsible for internal affairs; New Zealand retains responsibility for external affairs and defense, in consultation with the Cook Islands
Government type: self-governing parliamentary democracy
Capital: Avarua
Administrative divisions: none
Independence: none (became self-governing in free association with New Zealand on 4 August 1965 and has the right at any time to move to full independence by unilateral action)
National holiday: Constitution Day, first Monday in August (1965)
Constitution: 4 August 1965
Legal system: based on New Zealand law and English common law
Suffrage: NA years of age; universal adult
Executive branch:
chief of state: Queen ELIZABETH II (since 6 February 1952), represented by Frederick GOODWIN (since NA); New Zealand High Commissioner Kurt MEYER (since NA), representative of New Zealand
head of government: Prime Minister Dr. Robert WOONTON (since 12 February 2002); Deputy Prime Minister Ngamau MUNOKOA (since 5 November 2003)
cabinet: Cabinet chosen by the prime minister; collectively responsible to Parliament
elections: none; the monarch is hereditary; the UK representative is appointed by the monarch; the New Zealand high commissioner is appointed by the New Zealand Government; following legislative elections, the leader of the majority party or the leader of the majority coalition usually becomes prime minister
Legislative branch: unicameral Parliament (25 seats; members elected by popular vote to serve five-year terms)
elections: last held 16 June 1999 (next to be held by NA 2004)
election results: percent of vote by party - NA%; seats by party - CIP 12, DAP 12, NAP 1
note: the House of Ariki (chiefs) advises on traditional matters and maintains considerable influence, but has no legislative powers
Judicial branch: High Court
Political parties and leaders: Cook Islands People's Party or CIP [Geoffrey HENRY]; Democratic Alliance Party or DAP [Terepai MAOATE]; New Alliance Party or NAP [Norman GEORGE]; Cook Islands National Party or CIN [Teariki HEATHER]
Political pressure groups and leaders: NA
International organization participation: ACP, AsDB, FAO, ICAO, ICFTU, IFAD, IFRCS, IOC, OPCW, PIF, Sparteca, UNESCO, WHO, WMO
Diplomatic representation in the US: none (self-governing in free association with New Zealand)
Diplomatic representation from the US: none (self-governing in free association with New Zealand)

Cook Islands (continued)

Flag description: blue, with the flag of the UK in the upper hoist-side quadrant and a large circle of 15 white five-pointed stars (one for every island) centered in the outer half of the flag

Economy

Economy - overview: Like many other South Pacific island nations, the Cook Islands' economic development is hindered by the isolation of the country from foreign markets, the limited size of domestic markets, lack of natural resources, periodic devastation from natural disasters, and inadequate infrastructure. Agriculture provides the economic base with major exports made up of copra and citrus fruit. Manufacturing activities are limited to fruit processing, clothing, and handicrafts. Trade deficits are offset by remittances from emigrants and by foreign aid, overwhelmingly from New Zealand. In the 1980s and 1990s, the country lived beyond its means, maintaining a bloated public service and accumulating a large foreign debt. Subsequent reforms, including the sale of state assets, the strengthening of economic management, the encouragement of tourism, and a debt restructuring agreement, have rekindled investment and growth.

GDP: purchasing power parity - $105 million (2001 est.)

GDP - real growth rate: 7.1% (2001 est.)

GDP - per capita: purchasing power parity - $5,000 (2001 est.)

GDP - composition by sector:
agriculture: 17%
industry: 7.8%
services: 75.2% (2000 est.)

Population below poverty line: NA%

Household income or consumption by percentage share:
lowest 10%: NA%
highest 10%: NA%

Inflation rate (consumer prices): 3.2% (2000 est.)

Labor force: 8,000 (1996)

Labor force - by occupation: agriculture 29%, industry 15%, services 56%
note: shortage of skilled labor (1995)

Unemployment rate: 13% (1996)

Budget:
revenues: $28 million
expenditures: $27 million, including capital expenditures of $3.3 million (FY00/01 est.)

Industries: fruit processing, tourism, fishing, clothing, handicrafts

Industrial production growth rate: 1% (2002)

Electricity - production: 27.43 million kWh (2001)

Electricity - production by source:
fossil fuel: 100%
hydro: 0%
nuclear: 0%
other: 0% (2001)

Electricity - consumption: 25.51 million kWh (2001)

Electricity - exports: 0 kWh (2001)

Electricity - imports: 0 kWh (2001)

Oil - production: 0 bbl/day (2001 est.)

Oil - consumption: 450 bbl/day (2001 est.)

Oil - exports: NA

Oil - imports: NA

Agriculture - products: copra, citrus, pineapples, tomatoes, beans, pawpaws, bananas, yams, taro, coffee; pigs, poultry

Exports: $9.1 million (2000)

Exports - commodities: copra, papayas, fresh and canned citrus fruit, coffee; fish; pearls and pearl shells; clothing

Exports - partners: Australia 34%, Japan 27%, New Zealand 25%, US 8% (2000)

Imports: $50.7 million (2000)

Imports - commodities: foodstuffs, textiles, fuels, timber, capital goods

Imports - partners: NZ 61%, Fiji 19%, US 9%, Australia 6%, Japan 2% (2000)

Debt - external: $141 million (1996 est.)

Economic aid - recipient: $13.1 million; note - New Zealand continues to furnish the greater part (1995)

Currency: New Zealand dollar (NZD)

Currency code: NZD

Exchange rates: New Zealand dollars per US dollar - 1.7229 (2003), 2.1622 (2002), 2.3776 (2001), 2.1863 (2000), 1.8886 (1999)

Fiscal year: 1 April - 31 March

Communications

Telephones - main lines in use: 6,200 (2002)

Telephones - mobile cellular: 1,500 (2002)

Telephone system:
general assessment: NA
domestic: the individual islands are connected by a combination of satellite earth stations, microwave systems, and VHF and HF radiotelephone; within the islands, service is provided by small exchanges connected to subscribers by open-wire, cable, and fiber-optic cable
international: country code - 682; satellite earth station - 1 Intelsat (Pacific Ocean)

Radio broadcast stations: AM 1, FM 2, shortwave 0 (1998)

Television broadcast stations: 2 (plus eight low-power repeaters) (1997)

Internet country code: .ck

Internet users: 3,600 (2002)

Transportation

Railways: 0 km

Highways:
total: 320 km
paved: 33 km
unpaved: 287 km (2000)

Waterways: none

Ports and harbors: Avarua, Avatiu

Merchant marine:
total: 2 ships (1,000 GRT or over) 4,074 GRT/7,520 DWT
by type: cargo 1, petroleum tanker 1

foreign-owned: Australia 1, United Kingdom 1 (2003 est.)

Airports: 9 (2003 est.)

Airports - with paved runways:
total: 1
1,524 to 2,437 m: 1 (2003 est.)

Airports - with unpaved runways:
total: 8
1,524 to 2,437 m: 3
914 to 1,523 m: 4
under 914 m: 1 (2003 est.)

Military

Military - note: defense is the responsibility of New Zealand, in consultation with the Cook Islands and at its request

Transnational Issues

Disputes - international: none

Coral Sea Islands
(territory of Australia)

Introduction

Background: Scattered over some 1 million square kilometers of ocean, the Coral Sea Islands were declared a territory of Australia in 1969. They are uninhabited except for a small meteorological staff on the Willis Islets. Automated weather stations, beacons, and a lighthouse occupy many other islands and reefs.

Geography

Location: Oceania, islands in the Coral Sea, northeast of Australia
Geographic coordinates: 18 00 S, 152 00 E
Map references: Oceania
Area:
total: less than 3 sq km
land: less than 3 sq km
water: 0 sq km
note: includes numerous small islands and reefs scattered over a sea area of about 780,000 sq km, with the Willis Islets the most important
Area - comparative: NA
Land boundaries: 0 km
Coastline: 3,095 km
Maritime claims:
territorial sea: 3 NM
exclusive fishing zone: 200 NM
Climate: tropical
Terrain: sand and coral reefs and islands (or cays)
Elevation extremes:
lowest point: Pacific Ocean 0 m
highest point: unnamed location on Cato Island 6 m
Natural resources: NEGL
Land use:
arable land: 0%
permanent crops: 0%
other: 100% (mostly grass or scrub cover) (1998 est.)
Irrigated land: 0 sq km (1998 est.)
Natural hazards: occasional tropical cyclones

Environment - current issues: no permanent fresh water resources
Geography - note: important nesting area for birds and turtles

People

Population: no indigenous inhabitants
note: there is a staff of three to four at the meteorological station (2004 est.)

Government

Country name:
conventional long form: Coral Sea Islands Territory
conventional short form: Coral Sea Islands
Dependency status: territory of Australia; administered from Canberra by the Department of the Environment, Sport, and Territories
Legal system: the laws of Australia, where applicable, apply
Executive branch: administered from Canberra by the Department of the Environment, Sport, and Territories
Diplomatic representation in the US: none (territory of Australia)
Diplomatic representation from the US: none (territory of Australia)
Flag description: the flag of Australia is used

Economy

Economy - overview: no economic activity

Communications

Communications - note: there are automatic weather stations on many of the isles and reefs relaying data to the mainland

Transportation

Waterways: none
Ports and harbors: none; offshore anchorage only

Military

Military - note: defense is the responsibility of Australia; visited regularly by the Royal Australian Navy; Australia has control over the activities of visitors

Transnational Issues

Disputes - international: none

Costa Rica

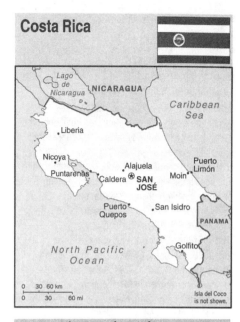

Introduction

Background: Costa Rica is a Central American success story: since the late 19th century, only two brief periods of violence have marred its democratic development. Although still a largely agricultural country, it has expanded its economy to include strong technology and tourism sectors. The standard of living is relatively high. Land ownership is widespread.

Geography

Location: Central America, bordering both the Caribbean Sea and the North Pacific Ocean, between Nicaragua and Panama
Geographic coordinates: 10 00 N, 84 00 W
Map references: Central America and the Caribbean
Area:
total: 51,100 sq km
land: 50,660 sq km
water: 440 sq km
note: includes Isla del Coco
Area - comparative: slightly smaller than West Virginia
Land boundaries:
total: 639 km
border countries: Nicaragua 309 km, Panama 330 km
Coastline: 1,290 km
Maritime claims:
territorial sea: 12 NM
exclusive economic zone: 200 NM
continental shelf: 200 NM
Climate: tropical and subtropical; dry season (December to April); rainy season (May to November); cooler in highlands
Terrain: coastal plains separated by rugged mountains including over 100 volcanic cones, of which several are major volcanoes
Elevation extremes:
lowest point: Pacific Ocean 0 m
highest point: Cerro Chirripo 3,810 m

Costa Rica *(continued)*

Natural resources: hydropower
Land use:
arable land: 4.41%
permanent crops: 5.48%
other: 90.11% (1998 est.)
Irrigated land: 1,260 sq km (1998 est.)
Natural hazards: occasional earthquakes, hurricanes along Atlantic coast; frequent flooding of lowlands at onset of rainy season and landslides; active volcanoes
Environment - current issues: deforestation and land use change, largely a result of the clearing of land for cattle ranching and agriculture; soil erosion; coastal marine pollution; fisheries protection; solid waste management; air pollution
Environment - international agreements:
party to: Biodiversity, Climate Change, Climate Change-Kyoto Protocol, Desertification, Endangered Species, Environmental Modification, Hazardous Wastes, Law of the Sea, Marine Dumping, Ozone Layer Protection, Wetlands, Whaling
signed, but not ratified: Marine Life Conservation
Geography - note: four volcanoes, two of them active, rise near the capital of San Jose in the center of the country; one of the volcanoes, Irazu, erupted destructively in 1963-65

People

Population: 3,956,507 (July 2004 est.)
Age structure:
0-14 years: 29.5% (male 597,332; female 570,008)
15-64 years: 65% (male 1,300,206; female 1,271,010)
65 years and over: 5.5% (male 101,270; female 116,681) (2004 est.)
Median age:
total: 25.7 years
male: 25.2 years
female: 26.2 years (2004 est.)
Population growth rate: 1.52% (2004 est.)
Birth rate: 18.99 births/1,000 population (2004 est.)
Death rate: 4.32 deaths/1,000 population (2004 est.)
Net migration rate: 0.51 migrant(s)/1,000 population (2004 est.)
Sex ratio:
at birth: 1.05 male(s)/female
under 15 years: 1.05 male(s)/female
15-64 years: 1.02 male(s)/female
65 years and over: 0.87 male(s)/female
total population: 1.02 male(s)/female (2004 est.)
Infant mortality rate:
total: 10.26 deaths/1,000 live births
male: 11.17 deaths/1,000 live births
female: 9.3 deaths/1,000 live births (2004 est.)
Life expectancy at birth:
total population: 76.63 years
male: 74.07 years
female: 79.33 years (2004 est.)
Total fertility rate: 2.33 children born/woman (2004 est.)
HIV/AIDS - adult prevalence rate: 0.6% (2001 est.)

HIV/AIDS - people living with HIV/AIDS: 11,000 (2001 est.)
HIV/AIDS - deaths: 890 (2001 est.)
Nationality:
noun: Costa Rican(s)
adjective: Costa Rican
Ethnic groups: white (including mestizo) 94%, black 3%, Amerindian 1%, Chinese 1%, other 1%
Religions: Roman Catholic 76.3%, Evangelical 13.7%, Jehovah's Witnesses 1.3%, other Protestant 0.7%, other 4.8%, none 3.2%
Languages: Spanish (official), English
Literacy:
definition: age 15 and over can read and write
total population: 96%
male: 95.9%
female: 96.1% (2003 est.)

Government

Country name:
conventional long form: Republic of Costa Rica
conventional short form: Costa Rica
local long form: Republica de Costa Rica
local short form: Costa Rica
Government type: democratic republic
Capital: San Jose
Administrative divisions: 7 provinces (provincias, singular - provincia); Alajuela, Cartago, Guanacaste, Heredia, Limon, Puntarenas, San Jose
Independence: 15 September 1821 (from Spain)
National holiday: Independence Day, 15 September (1821)
Constitution: 7 November 1949
Legal system: based on Spanish civil law system; judicial review of legislative acts in the Supreme Court; has accepted compulsory ICJ jurisdiction
Suffrage: 18 years of age; universal and compulsory
Executive branch:
chief of state: President Abel PACHECO (since 8 May 2002); First Vice President Lineth SABORIO (since NA May 2002); Second Vice President Luis FISHMAN (since NA May 2002); note - the president is both the chief of state and head of government
head of government: President Abel PACHECO (since 8 May 2002); First Vice President Lineth SABORIO (since NA May 2002); Second Vice President Luis FISHMAN (since NA May 2002); note - the president is both the chief of state and head of government
cabinet: Cabinet selected by the president
elections: president and vice presidents elected on the same ticket by popular vote for four-year terms; election last held 3 February 2002; run-off election held 7 April 2002 (next to be held NA February 2006)
election results: Abel PACHECO elected president; percent of vote - Abel PACHECO (PUSC) 58%; Rolando ARAYA (PLN) 42%
Legislative branch: unicameral Legislative Assembly or Asamblea Legislativa (57 seats; members are elected by direct, popular vote to serve four-year terms)

elections: last held 3 February 2002 (next to be held 3 February 2006)
election results: percent of vote by party - NA%; seats by party - PUSC 19, PLN 17, PAC 14, PML 6, PRC 1
Judicial branch: Supreme Court or Corte Suprema (22 justices are elected for eight-year terms by the Legislative Assembly)
Political parties and leaders: Agricultural Labor Action or PALA [Carlos Alberto SOLIS Blanco]; Citizen Action Party or PAC [Otton SOLIS]; Costa Rican Renovation Party or PRC [Justo OROZCO]; Democratic Force Party or PFD [Jose M. NUNEZ]; Libertarian Movement Party or PML [Otto GUEVARA Guth]; National Christian Alliance Party or ANC [Alejandro MADRIGAL]; National Independent Party or PNI [Jorge GONZALEZ Marten]; National Integration Party or PIN [Walter MUNOZ Cespedes]; National Liberation Party or PLN [Sonia PICADO]; Social Christian Unity Party or PUSC [Luis Manuel CHACON]
note: mainly a two-party system - PUSC and PLN - until the 3 February 2002 election in which the PAC captured a significant percentage, forcing a run-off in April 2002
Political pressure groups and leaders: Authentic Confederation of Democratic Workers or CATD (Communist Party affiliate); Chamber of Coffee Growers; Confederated Union of Workers or CUT (Communist Party affiliate); Costa Rican Confederation of Democratic Workers or CCTD (Liberation Party affiliate); Federation of Public Service Workers or FTSP; National Association for Economic Development or ANFE; National Association of Educators or ANDE; Rerum Novarum or CTRN (PLN affiliate) [Gilbert Brown]
International organization participation: BCIE, CACM, FAO, G-77, IADB, IAEA, IBRD, ICAO, ICC, ICCt, ICFTU, ICRM, IDA, IFAD, IFC, IFRCS, ILO, IMF, IMO, Interpol, IOC, IOM, ISO, ITU, LAES, LAIA (observer), NAM (observer), OAS, OPANAL, OPCW, PCA, RG, UN, UNCTAD, UNESCO, UNIDO, UPU, WCL, WCO, WFTU, WHO, WIPO, WMO, WToO, WTrO
Diplomatic representation in the US:
chief of mission: Ambassador Jaime DAREMBLUM Rosenstein
chancery: 2114 S Street NW, Washington, DC 20008
telephone: [1] (202) 234-2945
FAX: [1] (202) 265-4795
consulate(s) general: Atlanta, Chicago, Denver, Durham (North Carolina), Houston, Los Angeles, Miami, New Orleans, New York, Phoenix, San Antonio, San Francisco, St. Paul, and Tampa
consulate(s): Austin
Diplomatic representation from the US:
chief of mission: Ambassador John J. DANILOVICH
embassy: Calle 120 Avenida O, Pavas, San Jose
mailing address: APO AA 34020
telephone: [506] 220-3939
FAX: [506] 220-2305

Costa Rica *(continued)*

Flag description: five horizontal bands of blue (top), white, red (double width), white, and blue, with the coat of arms in a white elliptical disk on the hoist side of the red band; above the coat of arms a light blue ribbon contains the words, AMERICA CENTRAL, and just below it near the top of the coat of arms is a white ribbon with the words, REPUBLICA COSTA RICA

Economy

Economy - overview: Costa Rica's basically stable economy depends on tourism, agriculture, and electronics exports. Poverty has been substantially reduced over the past 15 years, and a strong social safety net has been put into place. Foreign investors remain attracted by the country's political stability and high education levels, and tourism continues to bring in foreign exchange. Low prices for coffee and bananas have hurt the agricultural sector. The government continues to grapple with its large deficit and massive internal debt. The reduction of inflation remains a difficult problem because of rises in the price of imports, labor market rigidities, and fiscal deficits. Costa Rica recently concluded negotiations to participate in the US - Central American Free Trade Agreement, which, if ratified by the Costa Rican Legislature, would result in economic reforms and an improved investment climate.

GDP: purchasing power parity - $35.16 billion (2003 est.)

GDP - real growth rate: 5.2% (2003 est.)

GDP - per capita: purchasing power parity - $9,000 (2003 est.)

GDP - composition by sector:
agriculture: 9%
industry: 30%
services: 61% (2002 est.)

Population below poverty line: 20.6% (2002 est.)

Household income or consumption by percentage share:
lowest 10%: 1.1%
highest 10%: 36.8% (2002)

Distribution of family income - Gini index: 45.9 (1997)

Inflation rate (consumer prices): 9.4% (2003 est.)

Labor force: 1.8 million (July 2003)

Labor force - by occupation: agriculture 20%, industry 22%, services 58% (1999 est.)

Unemployment rate: 6.7% (July 2003 est.)

Budget:
revenues: $2.17 billion
expenditures: $2.84 billion, including capital expenditures of $NA (2002 est.)

Industries: microprocessors, food processing, textiles and clothing, construction materials, fertilizer, plastic products

Industrial production growth rate: 8.6% (2003 est.)

Electricity - production: 6.839 billion kWh (2001)

Electricity - production by source:
fossil fuel: 1.5%
hydro: 81.9%
nuclear: 0%
other: 16.6% (2001)

Electricity - consumption: 6.109 billion kWh (2001)

Electricity - exports: 379 million kWh (2001)

Electricity - imports: 128 million kWh (2001)

Oil - production: 0 bbl/day (2001 est.)

Oil - consumption: 37,000 bbl/day (2001 est.)

Oil - exports: NA

Oil - imports: NA

Agriculture - products: coffee, pineapples, bananas, sugar, corn, rice, beans, potatoes; beef; timber

Exports: $6.176 billion (2003 est.)

Exports - commodities: coffee, bananas, sugar; pineapples; textiles, electronic components, medical equipment

Exports - partners: US 29.2%, Netherlands 8.2%, UK 4.2%, Mexico 4% (2002)

Imports: $7.057 billion (2003 est.)

Imports - commodities: raw materials, consumer goods, capital equipment, petroleum

Imports - partners: US 35.4%, Japan 4.3%, Mexico 3.9% (2002)

Debt - external: $3.654 billion (September 2003 est.)

Currency: Costa Rican colon (CRC)

Currency code: CRC

Exchange rates: Costa Rican colones per US dollar - 398.663 (2003), 359.817 (2002), 328.871 (2001), 308.187 (2000), 285.685 (1999)

Fiscal year: calendar year

Communications

Telephones - main lines in use: 1.132 million (2002)

Telephones - mobile cellular: 528,047 (2002)

Telephone system:
general assessment: good domestic telephone service in terms of breadth of coverage; restricted cellular telephone service
domestic: point-to-point and point-to-multi-point microwave, fiber-optic, and coaxial cable link rural areas; Internet service is available
international: country code - 506; connected to Central American Microwave System; satellite earth stations - 2 Intelsat (Atlantic Ocean); two submarine cables (1999)

Radio broadcast stations: AM 65, FM 51, shortwave 19 (2002)

Television broadcast stations: 20 (plus 43 repeaters) (2002)

Internet country code: .cr

Internet hosts: 7,725 (2002)

Internet users: 800,000 (2002)

Transportation

Railways:
total: 950 km
narrow gauge: 950 km 1.067-m gauge (260 km electrified) (2002)

Highways:
total: 35,892 km
paved: 7,896 km
unpaved: 27,996 km (2000)

Waterways: 730 km (seasonally navigable)

Pipelines: refined products 421 km (2003)

Ports and harbors: Caldera, Golfito, Moin, Puerto Limon, Puerto Quepos, Puntarenas

Merchant marine:
total: 1 ships (1,000 GRT or over) 1,716 GRT/ DWT
by type: passenger 1
registered in other countries: 1 (2003 est.)

Airports: 149 (2003 est.)

Airports - with paved runways:
total: 30
2,438 to 3,047 m: 2
1,524 to 2,437 m: 2
914 to 1,523 m: 18
under 914 m: 8 (2003 est.)

Airports - with unpaved runways:
total: 119
914 to 1,523 m: 24
under 914 m: 95 (2003 est.)

Military

Military branches: no regular military forces; Ministry of Public Security

Military manpower - military age: 18 years of age (2004 est.)

Military manpower - availability:
males age 15-49: 1,101,887 (2004 est.)

Military manpower - fit for military service:
males age 15-49: 736,007 (2004 est.)

Military manpower - reaching military age annually:
males: 41,709 (2004 est.)

Military expenditures - dollar figure: $64 million (2003)

Military expenditures - percent of GDP: 0.4% (2003)

Transnational Issues

Disputes - international: legal dispute over navigational rights of Rio San Juan on the border with Nicaragua remains unsolved

Illicit drugs: transshipment country for cocaine and heroin from South America; illicit production of cannabis on small, scattered plots; domestic cocaine consumption is rising, particularly crack cocaine

Cote d'Ivoire

Introduction

Background: Close ties to France since independence in 1960, the development of cocoa production for export, and foreign investment made Cote d'Ivoire one of the most prosperous of the tropical African states, but did not protect it from political turmoil. On 25 December 1999, a military coup - the first ever in Cote d'Ivoire's history - overthrew the government led by President Henri Konan BEDIE. Junta leader Robert GUEI held elections in late 2000, but excluded prominent opposition leader Alassane OUATTARA, blatantly rigged the polling results, and declared himself winner. Popular protest forced GUEI to step aside and brought runner-up Laurent GBAGBO into power. GBAGBO spent his first two years in office trying to consolidate power to strengthen his weak mandate, but he was unable to appease his opponents, who launched a failed coup attempt in September 2002. Rebel forces claimed the northern half of the country and in January 2003 were granted ministerial positions in a unity government under the auspices of the Linas-Marcoussis Peace Accord. President GBAGBO and rebel forces resumed implementation of the peace accord in December 2003 after a three-month stalemate, but ethnically-charged issues that sparked the civil war, such as land reform and grounds for nationality remain unresolved. The central government has yet to exert control over the northern regions and tensions remain high between GBAGBO and rebel leaders. Several thousand French and West African troops remain in Cote d'Ivoire to maintain peace and facilitate the disarmament, demobilization, and rehabilitation process.

Geography

Location: Western Africa, bordering the North Atlantic Ocean, between Ghana and Liberia
Geographic coordinates: 8 00 N, 5 00 W
Map references: Africa

Area:
total: 322,460 sq km
land: 318,000 sq km
water: 4,460 sq km
Area - comparative: slightly larger than New Mexico
Land boundaries:
total: 3,110 km
border countries: Burkina Faso 584 km, Ghana 668 km, Guinea 610 km, Liberia 716 km, Mali 532 km
Coastline: 515 km
Maritime claims:
territorial sea: 12 NM
exclusive economic zone: 200 NM
continental shelf: 200 NM
Climate: tropical along coast, semiarid in far north; three seasons - warm and dry (November to March), hot and dry (March to May), hot and wet (June to October)
Terrain: mostly flat to undulating plains; mountains in northwest
Elevation extremes:
lowest point: Gulf of Guinea 0 m
highest point: Mont Nimba 1,752 m
Natural resources: petroleum, natural gas, diamonds, manganese, iron ore, cobalt, bauxite, copper, hydropower
Land use:
arable land: 9.28%
permanent crops: 13.84%
other: 76.88% (1998 est.)
Irrigated land: 730 sq km (1998 est.)
Natural hazards: coast has heavy surf and no natural harbors; during the rainy season torrential flooding is possible
Environment - current issues: deforestation (most of the country's forests - once the largest in West Africa - have been heavily logged); water pollution from sewage and industrial and agricultural effluents
Environment - international agreements:
party to: Biodiversity, Climate Change, Desertification, Endangered Species, Hazardous Wastes, Law of the Sea, Marine Dumping, Ozone Layer Protection, Ship Pollution, Tropical Timber 83, Tropical Timber 94, Wetlands
signed, but not ratified: none of the selected agreements
Geography - note: most of the inhabitants live along the sandy coastal region; apart from the capital area, the forested interior is sparsely populated

People

Population: 17,327,724
note: estimates for this country explicitly take into account the effects of excess mortality due to AIDS; this can result in lower life expectancy, higher infant mortality and death rates, lower population and growth rates, and changes in the distribution of population by age and sex than would otherwise be expected (July 2004 est.)

Age structure:
0-14 years: 45.1% (male 3,856,130; female 3,965,930)
15-64 years: 52.6% (male 4,651,921; female 4,468,085)
65 years and over: 2.2% (male 182,995; female 202,663) (2004 est.)
Median age:
total: 17 years
male: 17.4 years
female: 16.7 years (2004 est.)
Population growth rate: 2.11% (2004 est.)
Birth rate: 39.64 births/1,000 population (2004 est.)
Death rate: 18.48 deaths/1,000 population (2004 est.)
Net migration rate: -0.07 migrant(s)/1,000 population (2004 est.)
Sex ratio:
at birth: 1.03 male(s)/female
under 15 years: 0.97 male(s)/female
15-64 years: 1.04 male(s)/female
65 years and over: 0.9 male(s)/female
total population: 1.01 male(s)/female (2004 est.)
Infant mortality rate:
total: 97.1 deaths/1,000 live births
male: 113.87 deaths/1,000 live births
female: 79.83 deaths/1,000 live births (2004 est.)
Life expectancy at birth:
total population: 42.48 years
male: 40.27 years
female: 44.76 years (2004 est.)
Total fertility rate: 5.42 children born/woman (2004 est.)
HIV/AIDS - adult prevalence rate: 9.7% (2001 est.)
HIV/AIDS - people living with HIV/AIDS: 770,000 (2001 est.)
HIV/AIDS - deaths: 75,000 (2001 est.)
Nationality:
noun: Ivoirian(s)
adjective: Ivoirian
Ethnic groups: Akan 42.1%, Voltaiques or Gur 17.6%, Northern Mandes 16.5%, Krous 11%, Southern Mandes 10%, other 2.8% (includes 130,000 Lebanese and 14,000 French) (1998)
Religions: Christian 20-30%, Muslim 35-40%, indigenous 25-40% (2001)
note: the majority of foreigners (migratory workers) are Muslim (70%) and Christian (20%)
Languages: French (official), 60 native dialects with Dioula the most widely spoken
Literacy:
definition: age 15 and over can read and write
total population: 50.9%
male: 57.9%
female: 43.6% (2003 est.)

Government

Country name:
conventional long form: Republic of Cote d'Ivoire
conventional short form: Cote d'Ivoire
local long form: Republique de Cote d'Ivoire
local short form: Cote d'Ivoire
former: Ivory Coast

Cote d'Ivoire *(continued)*

Government type: republic; multiparty presidential regime established 1960

Capital: Yamoussoukro; note - although Yamoussoukro has been the official capital since 1983, Abidjan remains the commercial and administrative center; the US, like other countries, maintains its Embassy in Abidjan

Administrative divisions: 19 regions; Agneby, Bafing, Bas-Sassandra, Denguele, Dix-Huit Montagnes, Fromager, Haut-Sassandra, Lacs, Lagunes, Marahoue, Moyen-Cavally, Moyen-Comoe, N'zi-Comoe, Savanes, Sud-Bandama, Sud-Comoe, Vallee du Bandama, Worodougou, Zanzan

Independence: 7 August 1960 (from France)

National holiday: Independence Day, 7 August (1960)

Constitution: 3 November 1960; has been amended numerous times, most recently 27 July 1998

Legal system: based on French civil law system and customary law; judicial review in the Constitutional Chamber of the Supreme Court; has not accepted compulsory ICJ jurisdiction

Suffrage: 18 years of age; universal

Executive branch:

chief of state: President Laurent GBAGBO (since 26 October 2000); note - seized power following a popular overthrow of the interim leader Gen. Robert GUEI who had claimed a dubious victory in presidential elections; Gen. GUEI himself had assumed power on 25 December 1999, following a military coup against the government of former President Henri Konan BEDIE

head of government: Prime Minister Seydou DIARRA (since 25 January 2003); note - appointed as transitional Prime Minister by President GBAGBO as part of a French brokered peace plan

cabinet: Council of Ministers appointed by the president

elections: president elected by popular vote for a five-year term; election last held 26 October 2000 (next to be held NA 2005); prime minister appointed by the president

election results: Laurent GBAGBO elected president; percent of vote - Laurent GBAGBO 59.4%, Robert GUEI 32.7%, Francis WODIE 5.7%, other 2.2%

Legislative branch: unicameral National Assembly or Assemblee Nationale (225 seats; members are elected in single- and multi-district elections by direct popular vote to serve five-year terms)

elections: elections last held 10 December 2000 with by-elections on 14 January 2001 (next to be held NA 2005)

election results: percent of vote by party - NA%; seats by party - FPI 96, PDCI-RDA 94, RDR 5, PIT 4, other 2, independents 22, vacant 2

note: a Senate is scheduled to be created in the next full election in 2005

Judicial branch: Supreme Court or Cour Supreme consists of four chambers: Judicial Chamber for criminal cases, Audit Chamber for financial cases, Constitutional Chamber for judicial review cases, and Administrative Chamber for civil cases; there is no legal limit to the number of members

Political parties and leaders: Democratic Party of Cote d'Ivoire-African Democratic Rally or PDCI-RDA [Aime Henri Konan BEDIE]; Ivorian Popular Front or FPI [Laurent GBAGBO]; Ivorian Worker's Party or PIT [Francis WODIE]; Rally of the Republicans or RDR [Alassane OUATTARA]; Union for Democracy and Peace or UDPCI [leader NA]; over 20 smaller parties

Political pressure groups and leaders: NA

International organization participation: ACCT, ACP, AfDB, AU, ECOWAS, Entente, FAO, FZ, G-24, G-77, IAEA, IBRD, ICAO, ICCt (signatory), ICFTU, ICRM, IDA, IDB, IFAD, IFC, IFRCS, ILO, IMF, IMO, Interpol, IOC, IOM, ISO, ITU, NAM, OIC, OPCW, UN, UNCTAD, UNESCO, UNHCR, UNIDO, UNMIK, UPU, WADB (regional), WAEMU, WCL, WCO, WFTU, WHO, WIPO, WMO, WToO, WTrO

Diplomatic representation in the US:

chief of mission: Ambassador Pascal Dago KOKORA

chancery: 3421 Massachusetts Avenue NW, Washington, DC 20007

telephone: [1] (202) 797-0300

FAX: [1] (202) 462-9444

Diplomatic representation from the US:

chief of mission: Ambassador Arlene RENDER

embassy: 5 Rue Jesse Owens, Abidjan

mailing address: B. P. 1712, Abidjan 01

telephone: [225] 20 21 09 79

FAX: [225] 20 22 32 59

Flag description: three equal vertical bands of orange (hoist side), white, and green; similar to the flag of Ireland, which is longer and has the colors reversed - green (hoist side), white, and orange; also similar to the flag of Italy, which is green (hoist side), white, and red; design was based on the flag of France

Economy

Economy - overview: Cote d'Ivoire is among the world's largest producers and exporters of coffee, cocoa beans, and palm oil. Consequently, the economy is highly sensitive to fluctuations in international prices for these products and to weather conditions. Despite government attempts to diversify the economy, it is still heavily dependent on agriculture and related activities, which engage roughly 68% of the population. After several years of lagging performance, the Ivorian economy began a comeback in 1994, due to the 50% devaluation of the CFA franc and improved prices for cocoa and coffee, growth in nontraditional primary exports such as pineapples and rubber, limited trade and banking liberalization, offshore oil and gas discoveries, and generous external financing and debt rescheduling by multilateral lenders and France. Moreover, government adherence to donor-mandated reforms led to a jump in growth to 5% annually during 1996-99. Growth was negative in 2000-03 because of the difficulty of meeting the conditions of international donors, continued low prices of key exports, and severe civil war. Political uncertainty will continue to cloud the economic outlook in 2004, but rising world prices for cocoa will help both the current account and the government balances.

GDP: purchasing power parity - $24.51 billion (2003 est.)

GDP - real growth rate: -1.9% (2003 est.)

GDP - per capita: purchasing power parity - $1,400 (2003 est.)

GDP - composition by sector:

agriculture: 29%

industry: 22%

services: 49% (2001 est.)

Population below poverty line: 37% (1995)

Household income or consumption by percentage share:

lowest 10%: 3.1%

highest 10%: 28.8% (1995)

Distribution of family income - Gini index: 36.7 (1995)

Inflation rate (consumer prices): 4.1% (2003 est.)

Labor force: 68% agricultural (1996 est.)

Unemployment rate: 13% in urban areas (1998)

Budget:

revenues: $1.72 billion

expenditures: $2.4 billion, including capital expenditures of $420 million (2001 est.)

Industries: foodstuffs, beverages; wood products, oil refining, truck and bus assembly, textiles, fertilizer, building materials, electricity

Industrial production growth rate: 15% (1998 est.)

Electricity - production: 4.605 billion kWh (2001)

Electricity - production by source:

fossil fuel: 61.9%

hydro: 38.1%

nuclear: 0%

other: 0% (2001)

Electricity - consumption: 2.983 billion kWh (2001)

Electricity - exports: 1.3 billion kWh (2001)

Electricity - imports: 0 kWh (2001)

Oil - production: 11,000 bbl/day (2001 est.)

Oil - consumption: 32,000 bbl/day (2001 est.)

Oil - exports: NA

Oil - imports: NA

Oil - proved reserves: 50 million bbl (1 January 2002)

Natural gas - production: 1.35 billion cu m (2001 est.)

Natural gas - consumption: 1.35 billion cu m (2001 est.)

Natural gas - exports: 0 cu m (2001 est.)

Natural gas - imports: 0 cu m (2001 est.)

Natural gas - proved reserves: 14.87 billion cu m (1 January 2002)

Agriculture - products: coffee, cocoa beans, bananas, palm kernels, corn, rice, manioc (tapioca), sweet potatoes, sugar, cotton, rubber; timber

Exports: $5.299 billion f.o.b. (2003 est.)

Exports - commodities: cocoa, coffee, timber, petroleum, cotton, bananas, pineapples, palm oil, fish

Exports - partners: France 13.7%, Netherlands 12.2%, US 7.2%, Germany 5.3%, Mali 4.4%, Belgium 4.2%, Spain 4.1% (2002)

Imports: $2.781 billion f.o.b. (2003 est.)

Imports - commodities: fuel, capital equipment, foodstuffs

Cote d'Ivoire *(continued)*

Imports - partners: France 22.4%, Nigeria 16.3%, China 7.8%, Italy 4.1% (2002)
Debt - external: $10.7 billion (2003 est.)
Economic aid - recipient: ODA, $1 billion (1996 est.)
Currency: Communaute Financiere Africaine franc (XOF); note - responsible authority is the Central Bank of the West African States
Currency code: XOF
Exchange rates: Communaute Financiere Africaine francs (XOF) per US dollar - 581.2 (2003), 696.988 (2002), 733.039 (2001), 711.976 (2000), 615.699 (1999)
Fiscal year: calendar year

Communications

Telephones - main lines in use: 336,100 (2002)
Telephones - mobile cellular: 1,027,100 (2002)
Telephone system:
general assessment: well developed by African standards but operating well below capacity
domestic: open-wire lines and microwave radio relay; 90% digitalized
international: country code - 225; satellite earth stations - 2 Intelsat (1 Atlantic Ocean and 1 Indian Ocean); 2 submarine cables (June 1999)
Radio broadcast stations: AM 2, FM 9, shortwave 3 (1998)
Television broadcast stations: 14 (1999)
Internet country code: .ci
Internet hosts: 4,397 (2002)
Internet users: 90,000 (2002)

Transportation

Railways:
total: 660 km
narrow gauge: 660 km 1.000-meter gauge
note: an additional 622 km of this railroad extends into Burkina Faso (2002)
Highways:
total: 50,400 km
paved: 4,889 km
unpaved: 45,511 km (1999 est.)
Waterways: 980 km (navigable rivers, canals, and numerous coastal lagoons)
Pipelines: condensate 107 km; gas 223 km; oil 104 km (2003)
Ports and harbors: Abidjan, Aboisso, Dabou, San-Pedro
Airports: 37 (2003 est.)
Airports - with paved runways:
total: 7
over 3,047 m: 1
2,438 to 3,047 m: 2
1,524 to 2,437 m: 4 (2003 est.)
Airports - with unpaved runways:
total: 30
1,524 to 2,437 m: 7
914 to 1,523 m: 15
under 914 m: 8 (2003 est.)

Military

Military branches: Army, Navy, Air Force, paramilitary Gendarmerie, Republican Guard (includes Presidential Guard)
Military manpower - military age: 18 years of age (2004 est.)
Military manpower - availability:
males age 15-49: 4,135,309 (2004 est.)
Military manpower - fit for military service:
males age 15-49: 2,164,014 (2004 est.)
Military manpower - reaching military age annually:
males: 204,434 (2004 est.)
Military expenditures - dollar figure: $173.6 million (2003)
Military expenditures - percent of GDP: 1.2% (2003)

Transnational Issues

Disputes - international: continuing rebel fighting extends to neighboring states and has kept out foreign workers from nearby countries; the Ivorian Government accuses Burkina Faso and Liberia of supporting Ivorian rebels
Illicit drugs: illicit producer of cannabis, mostly for local consumption; transshipment point for Southwest and Southeast Asian heroin to Europe and occasionally to the US, and for Latin American cocaine destined for Europe and South Africa; while rampant corruption and inadequate supervision leave the banking system vulnerable to money laundering, the lack of a developed financial system limits the country's utility as a major money-laundering center

Croatia

Introduction

Background: The lands that today comprise Croatia were part of the Austro-Hungarian Empire until the close of World War I. In 1918, the Croats, Serbs, and Slovenes formed a kingdom known after 1929 as Yugoslavia. Following World War II, Yugoslavia became a federal independent Communist state under the strong hand of Marshal TITO. Although Croatia declared its independence from Yugoslavia in 1991, it took four years of sporadic, but often bitter, fighting before occupying Serb armies were mostly cleared from Croatian lands. Under UN supervision, the last Serb-held enclave in eastern Slavonia was returned to Croatia in 1998.

Geography

Location: Southeastern Europe, bordering the Adriatic Sea, between Bosnia and Herzegovina and Slovenia
Geographic coordinates: 45 10 N, 15 30 E
Map references: Europe
Area:
total: 56,542 sq km
land: 56,414 sq km
water: 128 sq km
Area - comparative: slightly smaller than West Virginia
Land boundaries:
total: 2,197 km
border countries: Bosnia and Herzegovina 932 km, Hungary 329 km, Serbia and Montenegro (north) 241 km, Serbia and Montenegro (south) 25 km, Slovenia 670 km
Coastline: 5,835 km (mainland 1,777 km, islands 4,058 km)
Maritime claims:
territorial sea: 12 NM
continental shelf: 200-m depth or to the depth of exploitation

Croatia *(continued)*

Climate: Mediterranean and continental; continental climate predominant with hot summers and cold winters; mild winters, dry summers along coast
Terrain: geographically diverse; flat plains along Hungarian border, low mountains and highlands near Adriatic coastline and islands
Elevation extremes:
lowest point: Adriatic Sea 0 m
highest point: Dinara 1,830 m
Natural resources: oil, some coal, bauxite, low-grade iron ore, calcium, natural asphalt, silica, mica, clays, salt, hydropower
Land use:
arable land: 23.55%
permanent crops: 2.24%
other: 74.21% (1998 est.)
Irrigated land: 30 sq km (1998 est.)
Natural hazards: destructive earthquakes
Environment - current issues: air pollution (from metallurgical plants) and resulting acid rain is damaging the forests; coastal pollution from industrial and domestic waste; landmine removal and reconstruction of infrastructure consequent to 1992-95 civil strife
Environment - international agreements:
party to: Air Pollution, Air Pollution-Sulfur 94, Biodiversity, Climate Change, Desertification, Endangered Species, Hazardous Wastes, Law of the Sea, Marine Dumping, Ozone Layer Protection, Ship Pollution, Wetlands
signed, but not ratified: Air Pollution-Persistent Organic Pollutants, Climate Change-Kyoto Protocol
Geography - note: controls most land routes from Western Europe to Aegean Sea and Turkish Straits

People

Population: 4,496,869 (July 2004 est.)
Age structure:
0-14 years: 16.6% (male 383,729; female 364,287)
15-64 years: 67% (male 1,497,525; female 1,515,956)
65 years and over: 16.4% (male 277,616; female 457,756) (2004 est.)
Median age:
total: 39.7 years
male: 37.7 years
female: 41.5 years (2004 est.)
Population growth rate: -0.02% (2004 est.)
Birth rate: 9.51 births/1,000 population (2004 est.)
Death rate: 11.3 deaths/1,000 population (2004 est.)
Net migration rate: 1.58 migrant(s)/1,000 population (2004 est.)
Sex ratio:
at birth: 1.06 male(s)/female
under 15 years: 1.05 male(s)/female
15-64 years: 0.99 male(s)/female
65 years and over: 0.61 male(s)/female
total population: 0.92 male(s)/female (2004 est.)
Infant mortality rate:
total: 6.96 deaths/1,000 live births
male: 7.03 deaths/1,000 live births
female: 6.9 deaths/1,000 live births (2004 est.)

Life expectancy at birth:
total population: 74.14 years
male: 70.21 years
female: 78.29 years (2004 est.)
Total fertility rate: 1.39 children born/woman (2004 est.)
HIV/AIDS - adult prevalence rate: less than 0.1% (2001 est.)
HIV/AIDS - people living with HIV/AIDS: 200 (2001 est.)
HIV/AIDS - deaths: less than 10 (2001 est.)
Nationality:
noun: Croat(s), Croatian(s)
adjective: Croatian
Ethnic groups: Croat 89.6%, Serb 4.5%, Bosniak 0.5%, Hungarian 0.4%, Slovene 0.3%, Czech 0.2%, Roma 0.2%, Albanian 0.1%, Montenegrin 0.1%, others 4.1% (2001)
Religions: Roman Catholic 87.8%, Orthodox 4.4%, Muslim 1.3%, Protestant 0.3%, others and unknown 6.2% (2001)
Languages: Croatian 96%, other 4% (including Italian, Hungarian, Czech, Slovak, and German)
Literacy:
definition: age 15 and over can read and write
total population: 98.5%
male: 99.4%
female: 97.8% (2003 est.)

Government

Country name:
conventional long form: Republic of Croatia
conventional short form: Croatia
local long form: Republika Hrvatska
local short form: Hrvatska
Government type: presidential/parliamentary democracy
Capital: Zagreb
Administrative divisions: 20 counties (zupanije, zupanija - singular) and 1 city* (grad - singular); Bjelovarsko-Bilogorska Zupanija, Brodsko-Posavska Zupanija, Dubrovacko-Neretvanska Zupanija, Istarska Zupanija, Karlovacka Zupanija, Koprivnicko-Krizevacka Zupanija, Krapinsko-Zagorska Zupanija, Licko-Senjska Zupanija, Medimurska Zupanija, Osjecko-Baranjska Zupanija, Pozesko-Slavonska Zupanija, Primorsko-Goranska Zupanija, Sibensko-Kninska Zupanija, Sisacko-Moslavacka Zupanija, Splitsko-Dalmatinska Zupanija, Varazdinska Zupanija, Viroviticko-Podravska Zupanija, Vukovarsko-Srijemska Zupanija, Zadarska Zupanija, Zagreb*, Zagrebacka Zupanija
Independence: 25 June 1991 (from Yugoslavia)
National holiday: Statehood Day, 25 June (1991)
Constitution: adopted on 22 December 1990
Legal system: based on civil law system
Suffrage: 18 years of age; universal (16 years of age, if employed)
Executive branch:
chief of state: President Stjepan (Stipe) MESIC (since 18 February 2000)

head of government: Prime Minister Ivo SANADER (since 9 December 2003); Deputy Prime Ministers Jadranka KOSOR (since 23 December 2003) and Andrija HEBRANG (since 23 December 2003)
cabinet: Council of Ministers named by the prime minister and approved by the House of Representatives
elections: president elected by popular vote for a five-year term; election last held 7 February 2000 (next to be held NA 2005); prime minister nominated by the president in line with the balance of power in the Assembly
election results: Stjepan MESIC elected president; percent of vote - Stjepan MESIC (HNS) 56%, Drazen BUDISA (HSLS) 44%
note: minority government coalition - HDZ, DC, HSLS
Legislative branch: unicameral Assembly or Sabor (152 seats; note - one seat was added in the November 2003 parliamentary elections; members elected by popular vote to serve four-year terms); note - House of Counties was abolished in March 2001
elections: Assembly - last held 23 November 2003 (next to be held in 2007)
election results: Assembly - percent of vote by party - NA%; number of seats by party - HDZ 66, SDP 34, HSS 10, HNS 10, HSP 8, IDS 4, Libra 3, HSU 3, SDSS 3, other 11
Judicial branch: Supreme Court; Constitutional Court; judges for both courts appointed for eight-year terms by the Judicial Council of the Republic, which is elected by the Assembly
Political parties and leaders: Croatian Bloc or HB [Ivic PASALIC]; Croatian Christian Democratic Union or HKDU [Anto KOVACEVIC]; Croatian Democratic Union or HDZ [Ivo SANADER]; Croatian Party of Rights or HSP [Anto DJAPIC]; Croatian Peasant Party or HSS [Zlatko TOMCIC]; Croatian Pensioner Party or HSU [Vladimir JORDAN]; Croatian People's Party or HNS [Vesna PUSIC]; Croatian Social Liberal Party or HSLS [Drazen BUDISA]; Croatian True Revival Party or HIP [Miroslav TUDJMAN]; Democratic Centre or DC [Mate GRANIC]; Independent Democratic Serb Party or SDSS [Vojislav STRANIMIROVIC]; Istrian Democratic Assembly or IDS [Ivan JAKOVCIC]; Liberal Party or LS [Ivo BANAC]; Party of Liberal Democrats or Libra [Jozo RADOS]; Social Democratic Party of Croatia or SDP [Ivica RACAN]
Political pressure groups and leaders: NA
International organization participation: BIS, CE, CEI, EAPC, EBRD, FAO, IADB, IAEA, IBRD, ICAO, ICC, ICCt, ICFTU, ICRM, IDA, IFAD, IFC, IFRCS, IHO, ILO, IMF, IMO, Interpol, IOC, IOM, ISO, ITU, MINURSO, NAM (observer), OAS (observer), OPCW, OSCE, PCA, PFP, UN, UNAMSIL, UNCTAD, UNESCO, UNIDO, UNMEE, UNMIL, UNMISET, UNMOGIP, UPU, WCO, WHO, WIPO, WMO, WToO, WTrO
Diplomatic representation in the US:
chief of mission: Ambassador Ivan GRDESIC
chancery: 2343 Massachusetts Avenue NW, Washington, DC 20008

Croatia *(continued)*

telephone: [1] (202) 588-5899
FAX: [1] (202) 588-8936
consulate(s) general: Chicago, Los Angeles, New York
Diplomatic representation from the US:
chief of mission: Ambassador Ralph FRANK
embassy: Thomasa Jeffersona 2, 10010 Zagreb
mailing address: use street address
telephone: [385] (1) 661-2200
FAX: [385] (1) 661-2373
Flag description: red, white, and blue horizontal bands with Croatian coat of arms (red and white checkered)

Economy

Economy - overview: Before the dissolution of Yugoslavia, the Republic of Croatia, after Slovenia, was the most prosperous and industrialized area, with a per capita output perhaps one-third above the Yugoslav average. The economy emerged from its mild recession in 2000 with tourism the main factor, but massive structural unemployment remains a key negative element. The government's failure to press the economic reforms needed to spur growth is largely the result of coalition politics and public resistance, particularly from the trade unions. Opponents fear reforms would cut jobs, wages, and social benefits. The government has a heavy back log of civil cases, many involving tenure land. The country is likely to experience only moderate growth without disciplined fiscal and structural reform.
GDP: purchasing power parity - $47.14 billion (2003 est.)
GDP - real growth rate: 4.5% (2003 est.)
GDP - per capita: purchasing power parity - $10,700 (2003 est.)
GDP - composition by sector:
agriculture: 8.4%
industry: 29.8%
services: 61.8% (2002 est.)
Population below poverty line: NA%
Household income or consumption by percentage share:
lowest 10%: 3.7%
highest 10%: 23.3% (1998)
Distribution of family income - Gini index: 29 (1998)
Inflation rate (consumer prices): 1.5% (2003 est.)
Labor force: 1.79 million (2003)
Labor force - by occupation: agriculture 13.2%, industry 25.4%, services 46.4% (2002)
Unemployment rate: 18.9% (2003)
Budget:
revenues: $8.6 billion
expenditures: $9 billion, including capital expenditures of $NA (2001 est.)
Industries: chemicals and plastics, machine tools, fabricated metal, electronics, pig iron and rolled steel products, aluminum, paper, wood products, construction materials, textiles, shipbuilding, petroleum and petroleum refining, food and beverages; tourism

Industrial production growth rate: 5.6% (2003 est.)
Electricity - production: 12.12 billion kWh (2001)
Electricity - production by source:
fossil fuel: 33.6%
hydro: 66%
nuclear: 0%
other: 0.4% (2001)
Electricity - consumption: 14.27 billion kWh (2001)
Electricity - exports: 386 million kWh (2001)
Electricity - imports: 3.386 billion kWh (2001)
Oil - production: 29,000 bbl/day (2001 est.)
Oil - consumption: 89,000 bbl/day (2001 est.)
Oil - exports: NA
Oil - imports: NA
Oil - proved reserves: 93.6 million bbl (1 January 2002)
Natural gas - production: 1.76 billion cu m (2001 est.)
Natural gas - consumption: 2.84 billion cu m (2001 est.)
Natural gas - exports: 0 cu m (2001 est.)
Natural gas - imports: 1.08 billion cu m (2001 est.)
Natural gas - proved reserves: 34.36 billion cu m (1 January 2002)
Agriculture - products: wheat, corn, sugar beets, sunflower seed, barley, alfalfa, clover, olives, citrus, grapes, soybeans, potatoes; livestock, dairy products
Exports: $6.355 billion f.o.b. (2003 est.)
Exports - commodities: transport equipment, textiles, chemicals, foodstuffs, fuels
Exports - partners: Italy 22.4%, Bosnia and Herzegovina 14.4%, Germany 12.5%, Slovenia 8%, Austria 7.3% (2002)
Imports: $12.86 billion f.o.b. (2003 est.)
Imports - commodities: machinery, transport and electrical equipment, chemicals, fuels and lubricants, foodstuffs
Imports - partners: Italy 16.8%, Germany 16.4%, Slovenia 7.8%, Russia 6.8%, Austria 6.7%, France 5.2% (2002)
Debt - external: $19 billion (yearend 2003 est.)
Economic aid - recipient: ODA $66 million (2000)
Currency: kuna (HRK)
Currency code: HRK
Exchange rates: kuna per US dollar - 6.7035 (2003), 7.8687 (2002), 8.34 (2001), 8.2766 (2000), 7.1124 (1999)
Fiscal year: calendar year

Communications

Telephones - main lines in use: 1.825 million (2002)
Telephones - mobile cellular: 2.34 million (2002)
Telephone system:
general assessment: NA
domestic: reconstruction plan calls for replacement of all analog circuits with digital and enlarging the network; a backup will be included in the plan for the main trunk

international: country code - 385; digital international service is provided through the main switch in Zagreb; Croatia participates in the Trans-Asia-Europe (TEL) fiber-optic project, which consists of two fiber-optic trunk connections with Slovenia and a fiber-optic trunk line from Rijeka to Split and Dubrovnik; Croatia is also investing in ADRIA 1, a joint fiber-optic project with Germany, Albania, and Greece (2000)
Radio broadcast stations: AM 16, FM 98, shortwave 5 (1999)
Television broadcast stations: 36 (plus 321 repeaters) (September 1995)
Internet country code: .hr
Internet hosts: 29,644 (2002)
Internet users: 789,000 (2002)

Transportation

Railways:
total: 2,296 km
standard gauge: 2,296 km 1.435-m gauge (983 km electrified) (2002)
Highways:
total: 28,123 km
paved: 23,792 km (including 410 km of expressways)
unpaved: 4,331 km (2000)
Waterways: 785 km
note: (perennially navigable; large sections of Sava blocked by downed bridges, silt, and debris)
Pipelines: gas 1,374 km; oil 583 km (2003)
Ports and harbors: Dubrovnik, Dugi Rat, Omisalj, Ploce, Pula, Rijeka, Sibenik, Split, Vukovar (inland waterway port on Danube), Zadar
Merchant marine:
total: 51 ships (1,000 GRT or over) 750,579 GRT/1,178,786 DWT
by type: bulk 16, cargo 14, chemical tanker 4, combination bulk 5, multi-functional large load carrier 1, passenger 1, petroleum tanker 2, refrigerated cargo 1, roll on/roll off 4, short-sea/passenger 3
foreign-owned: Hong Kong 3, Russia 1
registered in other countries: 44 (2003 est.)
Airports: 68 (2003 est.)
Airports - with paved runways:
total: 23
over 3,047 m: 2
2,438 to 3,047 m: 6
1,524 to 2,437 m: 2
914 to 1,523 m: 4
under 914 m: 9 (2003 est.)
Airports - with unpaved runways:
total: 45
1,524 to 2,437 m: 1
914 to 1,523 m: 7
under 914 m: 37 (2003 est.)
Heliports: 1 (2003 est.)

Military

Military branches: Ground Forces (Hrvatska Vojska, HKoV), Naval Forces (Hrvatska Ratna Mornarica, HRM), Air and Air Defense Forces (Hrvatsko Ratno Zrakoplovstvo i Protuzrakoplovna Obrana, HRZiPZO)

Croatia (continued)

Military manpower - military age: 19 years of age (2004 est.)

Military manpower - availability:
males age 15-49: 1,100,132 (2004 est.)

Military manpower - fit for military service:
males age 15-49: 873,994 (2004 est.)

Military manpower - reaching military age annually:
males: 30,639 (2004 est.)

Military expenditures - dollar figure: $520 million (2002 est.)

Military expenditures - percent of GDP: 2.39% (2002 est.)

Transnational Issues

Disputes - international: discussions continue with Bosnia and Herzegovina over disputed territory around Kostajnica on the Una River and villages at the base of Mount Pljesevica; the Croatia-Slovenia land and maritime boundary agreement, which would have ceded most of Pirin Bay and maritime access to Slovenia and several villages to Croatia, remains controversial, has not been ratified, and has been complicated by Croatia's declaration of an ecological-fisheries zone in the Adriatic Sea

Illicit drugs: transit point along the Balkan route for Southwest Asian heroin to Western Europe; has been used as a transit point for maritime shipments of South American cocaine bound for Western Europe

Cuba

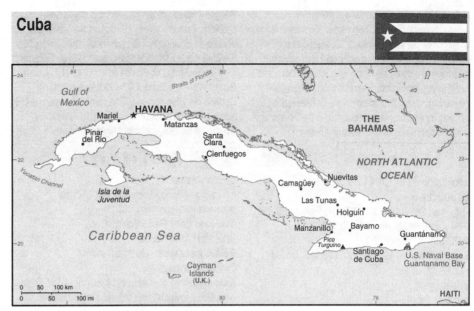

Introduction

Background: The native Amerindian population of Cuba began to decline after the European discovery of the island by Christopher COLUMBUS in 1492 and following its development as a Spanish colony during the next several centuries. Large numbers of African slaves were imported to work the coffee and sugar plantations and Havana became the launching point for the annual treasure fleets bound for Spain from Mexico and Peru. Spanish rule was severe and exploitative and occasional rebellions were harshly suppressed. It was US intervention during the Spanish-American War in 1898 that finally overthrew Spanish rule. The subsequent Treaty of Paris established Cuban independence, which was granted in 1902 after a three-year transition period. Fidel CASTRO led a rebel army to victory in 1959; his iron rule has held the regime together since then. Cuba's Communist revolution, with Soviet support, was exported throughout Latin America and Africa during the 1960s, 1970s, and 1980s. The country is now slowly recovering from a severe economic recession in 1990, following the withdrawal of former Soviet subsidies, worth $4 billion to $6 billion annually. Cuba portrays its difficulties as the result of the US embargo in place since 1961. Illicit migration to the US - using homemade rafts, alien smugglers, air flights, or via the southwest border - is a continuing problem. Some 2,500 Cubans attempted the crossing of the Straits of Florida in 2003; the US Coast Guard apprehended about 60% of the individuals.

Geography

Location: Caribbean, island between the Caribbean Sea and the North Atlantic Ocean, 150 km south of Key West, Florida

Geographic coordinates: 21 30 N, 80 00 W

Map references: Central America and the Caribbean

Area:
total: 110,860 sq km
land: 110,860 sq km
water: 0 sq km

Area - comparative: slightly smaller than Pennsylvania

Land boundaries:
total: 29 km
border countries: US Naval Base at Guantanamo Bay 29 km
note: Guantanamo Naval Base is leased by the US and thus remains part of Cuba

Coastline: 3,735 km

Maritime claims:
territorial sea: 12 NM
exclusive economic zone: 200 NM

Climate: tropical; moderated by trade winds; dry season (November to April); rainy season (May to October)

Terrain: mostly flat to rolling plains, with rugged hills and mountains in the southeast

Elevation extremes:
lowest point: Caribbean Sea 0 m
highest point: Pico Turquino 2,005 m

Natural resources: cobalt, nickel, iron ore, chromium, copper, salt, timber, silica, petroleum, arable land

Land use:
arable land: 33.04%
permanent crops: 7.61%
other: 59.35% (1998 est.)

Irrigated land: 870 sq km (1998 est.)

Natural hazards: the east coast is subject to hurricanes from August to November (in general, the country averages about one hurricane every other year); droughts are common

Environment - current issues: air and water pollution; biodiversity loss; deforestation

Cuba (continued)

Environment - international agreements:
party to: Antarctic Treaty, Biodiversity, Climate Change, Climate Change-Kyoto Protocol, Desertification, Endangered Species, Environmental Modification, Hazardous Wastes, Law of the Sea, Marine Dumping, Ozone Layer Protection, Ship Pollution, Wetlands
signed, but not ratified: Marine Life Conservation
Geography - note: largest country in Caribbean and westernmost island of the Greater Antilles

People

Population: 11,308,764 (July 2004 est.)
Age structure:
0-14 years: 20% (male 1,163,741; female 1,102,391)
15-64 years: 69.8% (male 3,949,197; female 3,948,196)
65 years and over: 10.1% (male 528,162; female 617,077) (2004 est.)
Median age:
total: 34.8 years
male: 34.2 years
female: 35.5 years (2004 est.)
Population growth rate: 0.34% (2004 est.)
Birth rate: 12.18 births/1,000 population (2004 est.)
Death rate: 7.17 deaths/1,000 population (2004 est.)
Net migration rate: -1.58 migrant(s)/1,000 population (2004 est.)
Sex ratio:
at birth: 1.06 male(s)/female
under 15 years: 1.06 male(s)/female
15-64 years: 1 male(s)/female
65 years and over: 0.86 male(s)/female
total population: 1 male(s)/female (2004 est.)
Infant mortality rate:
total: 6.45 deaths/1,000 live births
male: 7.25 deaths/1,000 live births
female: 5.6 deaths/1,000 live births (2004 est.)
Life expectancy at birth:
total population: 77.04 years
male: 74.77 years
female: 79.44 years (2004 est.)
Total fertility rate: 1.66 children born/woman (2004 est.)
HIV/AIDS - adult prevalence rate: less than 0.1% (2001 est.)
HIV/AIDS - people living with HIV/AIDS: 3,200 (2001 est.)
HIV/AIDS - deaths: 120 (2001 est.)
Nationality:
noun: Cuban(s)
adjective: Cuban
Ethnic groups: mulatto 51%, white 37%, black 11%, Chinese 1%
Religions: nominally 85% Roman Catholic prior to CASTRO assuming power; Protestants, Jehovah's Witnesses, Jews, and Santeria are also represented
Languages: Spanish
Literacy:
definition: age 15 and over can read and write
total population: 97%
male: 97.2%
female: 96.9% (2003 est.)

People - note: illicit migration is a continuing problem; Cubans attempt to depart the island and enter the US using homemade rafts, alien smugglers, direct flights, or falsified visas; some 2,500 Cubans took to the Straits of Florida in 2003; the US Coast Guard interdicted about 60% of these migrants; Cubans also use non-maritime routes to enter the US; some 1,500 Cubans arrived overland via the southwest border and direct flights to Miami in 2003

Government

Country name:
conventional long form: Republic of Cuba
conventional short form: Cuba
local long form: Republica de Cuba
local short form: Cuba
Government type: Communist state
Capital: Havana
Administrative divisions: 14 provinces (provincias, singular - provincia) and 1 special municipality* (municipio especial); Camaguey, Ciego de Avila, Cienfuegos, Ciudad de La Habana, Granma, Guantanamo, Holguin, Isla de la Juventud*, La Habana, Las Tunas, Matanzas, Pinar del Rio, Sancti Spiritus, Santiago de Cuba, Villa Clara
Independence: 20 May 1902 (from Spain 10 December 1898; administered by the US from 1898 to 1902)
National holiday: Independence Day, 10 December (1898); note - 10 December 1898 is the date of independence from Spain, 20 May 1902 is the date of independence from US administration; Rebellion Day, 26 July (1953)
Constitution: 24 February 1976, amended July 1992 and June 2002
Legal system: based on Spanish and American law, with large elements of Communist legal theory; has not accepted compulsory ICJ jurisdiction
Suffrage: 16 years of age; universal
Executive branch:
chief of state: President of the Council of State and President of the Council of Ministers Fidel CASTRO Ruz (prime minister from February 1959 until 24 February 1976 when office was abolished; president since 2 December 1976); First Vice President of the Council of State and First Vice President of the Council of Ministers Gen. Raul CASTRO Ruz (since 2 December 1976); note - the president is both the chief of state and head of government
head of government: President of the Council of State and President of the Council of Ministers Fidel CASTRO Ruz (prime minister from February 1959 until 24 February 1976 when office was abolished; president since 2 December 1976); First Vice President of the Council of State and First Vice President of the Council of Ministers Gen. Raul CASTRO Ruz (since 2 December 1976); note - the president is both the chief of state and head of government
cabinet: Council of Ministers proposed by the president of the Council of State and appointed by the National Assembly or the 31-member Council of State, elected by the Assembly to act on its behalf when it is not in session

elections: president and vice presidents elected by the National Assembly for a term of five years; election last held 6 March 2003 (next to be held in 2008)
election results: Fidel CASTRO Ruz reelected president; percent of legislative vote - 100%; Raul CASTRO Ruz elected vice president; percent of legislative vote - 100%
Legislative branch: unicameral National Assembly of People's Power or Asemblea Nacional del Poder Popular (609 seats, elected directly from slates approved by special candidacy commissions; members serve five-year terms)
elections: last held 19 January 2003 (next to be held in NA 2008)
election results: percent of vote - PCC 97.6%; seats - PCC 609
Judicial branch: People's Supreme Court or Tribunal Supremo Popular (president, vice president, and other judges are elected by the National Assembly)
Political parties and leaders: only party - Cuban Communist Party or PCC [Fidel CASTRO Ruz, first secretary]
Political pressure groups and leaders: NA
International organization participation: FAO, G-77, IAEA, ICAO, ICC, ICRM, IFAD, IFRCS, IHO, ILO, IMO, Interpol, IOC, IOM (observer), ISO, ITU, LAES, LAIA, NAM, OAS (excluded from formal participation since 1962), OPANAL, OPCW, PCA, UN, UNCTAD, UNESCO, UNIDO, UPU, WCL, WCO, WFTU, WHO, WIPO, WMO, WToO, WTrO
Diplomatic representation in the US: none; note - Cuba has an Interests Section in the Swiss Embassy, headed by Principal Officer Dagoberto RODRIGUEZ Barrera; address: Cuban Interests Section, Swiss Embassy, 2630 16th Street NW, Washington, DC 20009; telephone: [1] (202) 797-8518
Diplomatic representation from the US: none; note - the US has an Interests Section in the Swiss Embassy, headed by Principal Officer James C. CASON; address: USINT, Swiss Embassy, Calzada between L and M Streets, Vedado, Havana; telephone: [53] (7) 33-3551 through 3559 (operator assistance required); FAX: [53] (7) 33-3700; protecting power in Cuba is Switzerland
Flag description: five equal horizontal bands of blue (top and bottom) alternating with white; a red equilateral triangle based on the hoist side bears a white, five-pointed star in the center; design influenced by the US flag

Economy

Economy - overview: The government continues to balance the need for economic loosening against a desire for firm political control. It has undertaken limited reforms to increase enterprise efficiency and alleviate serious shortages of food, consumer goods, and services. A major feature of the economy is the dichotomy between relatively efficient export enclaves and inefficient domestic sectors. The average Cuban's standard of living remains at a lower level than before the depression of the 1990s, which was

Cuba *(continued)*

caused by the loss of Soviet aid and domestic inefficiencies. The government reluctantly allows a large dollar market sector, fueled by tourism and remittances from Cubans abroad.

GDP: purchasing power parity - $31.59 billion (2003 est.)
GDP - real growth rate: 1.3% (2003 est.)
GDP - per capita: purchasing power parity - $2,800 (2003 est.)
GDP - composition by sector:
agriculture: 7.6%
industry: 34.5%
services: 57.9% (2001 est.)
Population below poverty line: NA%
Household income or consumption by percentage share:
lowest 10%: NA%
highest 10%: NA%
Inflation rate (consumer prices): 5% (2003 est.)
Labor force: 4.3 million
note: state sector 78%, non-state sector 22% (2000 est.)
Labor force - by occupation: agriculture 24%, industry 25%, services 51% (1999)
Unemployment rate: 3.2% (2003 est.)
Budget:
revenues: $14.9 billion
expenditures: $15.6 billion, including capital expenditures of $NA (2000 est.)
Industries: sugar, petroleum, tobacco, construction, nickel, steel, cement, agricultural machinery, pharmaceuticals
Industrial production growth rate: 0.6% (2003 est.)
Electricity - production: 14.38 billion kWh (2001)
Electricity - production by source:
fossil fuel: 93.9%
hydro: 0.6%
nuclear: 0%
other: 5.4% (2001)
Electricity - consumption: 13.38 billion kWh (2001)
Electricity - exports: 0 kWh (2001)
Electricity - imports: 0 kWh (2001)
Oil - production: 50,000 bbl/day (2001 est.)
Oil - consumption: 163,000 bbl/day (2001 est.)
Oil - exports: NA
Oil - imports: NA
Oil - proved reserves: 532 million bbl (1 January 2002)
Natural gas - production: 600 million cu m (2001 est.)
Natural gas - consumption: 600 million cu m (2001 est.)
Natural gas - exports: 0 cu m (2001 est.)
Natural gas - imports: 0 cu m (2001 est.)
Natural gas - proved reserves: 42.62 billion cu m (1 January 2002)
Agriculture - products: sugar, tobacco, citrus, coffee, rice, potatoes, beans; livestock
Exports: $1.467 billion f.o.b. (2003 est.)
Exports - commodities: sugar, nickel, tobacco, fish, medical products, citrus, coffee

Exports - partners: Netherlands 18.5%, Russia 17.5%, Canada 13.8%, Spain 9.2%, China 7% (2002)
Imports: $4.531 billion f.o.b. (2003 est.)
Imports - commodities: petroleum, food, machinery and equipment, chemicals
Imports - partners: Spain 16.3%, China 11.3%, Venezuela 11.1%, Italy 8.6%, France 7.2%, Canada 5.9%, US 5.3%, Mexico 4.7% (2002)
Debt - external: $13.2 billion (convertible currency); another $15 billion -$20 billion owed to Russia (2003 est.)
Economic aid - recipient: $68.2 million (1997 est.)
Currency: Cuban peso (CUP)
Currency code: CUP
Exchange rates: Cuban pesos per US dollar - 1.0000 (nonconvertible, official rate, for international transactions, pegged to the US dollar); convertible peso sold for domestic use at a rate of 27 pesos per US dollar by the Government of Cuba (2002)
Fiscal year: calendar year

Communications

Telephones - main lines in use: 574,400 (2002)
Telephones - mobile cellular: 17,900 (2002)
Telephone system:
general assessment: greater investment beginning in 1994 and the establishment of a new Ministry of Information Technology and Communications in 2000 has resulted in improvements in the system; cellular service, initially restricted, was opened to public access in 2003
domestic: national fiber-optic system scheduled to be completed by end of 2003; 85% of switches digitized by end of 2002 with entire system by end 2003; telephone line density remains low; cellular service expanding
international: country code - 53; fiber-optic cable laid to but not linked to US network; satellite earth station - 1 Intersputnik (Atlantic Ocean region)
Radio broadcast stations: AM 169, FM 55, shortwave 1 (1998)
Television broadcast stations: 58 (1997)
Internet country code: .cu
Internet hosts: 1,133 (2002)
Internet users: 120,000 (2002)

Transportation

Railways:
total: 3,442 km
standard gauge: 3,442 km 1.435-m gauge (142 km electrified)
note: an additional 7,742 km of track is used by sugar plantations; about 65% of this track is standard gauge; the rest is narrow gauge (2002)
Highways:
total: 60,858 km
paved: 29,820 km (including 638 km of expressway)
unpaved: 31,038 km (1999 est.)
Waterways: 240 km

Pipelines: gas 49 km; oil 230 km (2003)
Ports and harbors: Cienfuegos, Havana, Manzanillo, Mariel, Matanzas, Nuevitas, Santiago de Cuba
Merchant marine:
total: 13 ships (1,000 GRT or over) 54,818 GRT/ 81,850 DWT
by type: bulk 3, cargo 4, liquefied gas 1, petroleum tanker 3, refrigerated cargo 2
registered in other countries: 35 (2003 est.)
Airports: 170 (2003 est.)
Airports - with paved runways:
total: 79
over 3,047 m: 7
2,438 to 3,047 m: 9
1,524 to 2,437 m: 20
914 to 1,523 m: 6
under 914 m: 37 (2003 est.)
Airports - with unpaved runways:
total: 91
914 to 1,523 m: 29
under 914 m: 62 (2003 est.)

Military

Military branches: Revolutionary Armed Forces (FAR): Revolutionary Army (ER), Revolutionary Navy (MGR), Air and Air Defense Force (DAAFAR), Territorial Militia Troops (MTT), Youth Labor Army (EJT)
Military manpower - military age: 17 years of age (2004 est.)
Military manpower - availability:
males age 15-49: 3,134,622
females age 15-49: 3,075,534
note: both sexes are liable for military service (2004 est.)
Military manpower - fit for military service:
males age 15-49: 1,929,370
females age 15-49: 1,888,498 (2004 est.)
Military manpower - reaching military age annually:
males: 83,992
females: 91,901 (2004 est.)
Military expenditures - dollar figure: $572.3 million (2003)
Military expenditures - percent of GDP: 1.8% (2003)
Military - note: Moscow, for decades the key military supporter and supplier of Cuba, cut off almost all military aid by 1993

Transnational Issues

Disputes - international: US Naval Base at Guantanamo Bay is leased to US and only mutual agreement or US abandonment of the area can terminate the lease
Illicit drugs: territorial waters and air space serve as transshipment zone for cocaine and heroin bound for the US and Europe; established the death penalty for certain drug-related crimes in 1999

Cyprus

Introduction

Background: Independence from the UK was approved in 1960, with constitutional guarantees by the Greek Cypriot majority to the Turkish Cypriot minority. In 1974, a Greek-sponsored attempt to seize the government was met by military intervention from Turkey, which soon controlled almost 40% of the island. In 1983, the Turkish-held area declared itself the "Turkish Republic of Northern Cyprus," but it is recognized only by Turkey. UN-led direct talks between the two sides to reach a comprehensive settlement to the division of the island began in January 2002 and will reach a culmination when a referendum of all Cypriots is held on 21 April 2004, just 10 days before the Greek part of Cyprus is scheduled to join the EU.

Geography

Location: Middle East, island in the Mediterranean Sea, south of Turkey
Geographic coordinates: 35 00 N, 33 00 E
Map references: Middle East
Area:
total: 9,250 sq km (of which 3,355 sq km are in the Turkish Cypriot area)
land: 9,240 sq km
water: 10 sq km
Area - comparative: about 0.6 times the size of Connecticut
Land boundaries: 0 km
Coastline: 648 km
Maritime claims:
territorial sea: 12 NM
continental shelf: 200-m depth or to the depth of exploitation
Climate: temperate; Mediterranean with hot, dry summers and cool winters
Terrain: central plain with mountains to north and south; scattered but significant plains along southern coast

Elevation extremes:
lowest point: Mediterranean Sea 0 m
highest point: Olympus 1,951 m
Natural resources: copper, pyrites, asbestos, gypsum, timber, salt, marble, clay earth pigment
Land use:
arable land: 14.4%
permanent crops: 4.5%
other: 81.1% (2001 est.)
Irrigated land: 382 sq km (2001 est.)
Natural hazards: moderate earthquake activity; droughts
Environment - current issues: water resource problems (no natural reservoir catchments, seasonal disparity in rainfall, sea water intrusion to island's largest aquifer, increased salination in the north); water pollution from sewage and industrial wastes; coastal degradation; loss of wildlife habitats from urbanization
Environment - international agreements:
party to: Air Pollution, Biodiversity, Climate Change, Climate Change-Kyoto Protocol, Desertification, Endangered Species, Environmental Modification, Hazardous Wastes, Law of the Sea, Marine Dumping, Ozone Layer Protection, Ship Pollution
signed, but not ratified: Air Pollution-Persistent Organic Pollutants
Geography - note: the third largest island in the Mediterranean Sea (after Sicily and Sardinia)

People

Population: 775,927 (July 2004 est.)
Age structure:
0-14 years: 21.4% (male 84,850; female 81,235)
15-64 years: 67.4% (male 264,441; female 258,150)
65 years and over: 11.2% (male 38,058; female 49,193) (2004 est.)
Median age:
total: 34.4 years
male: 33.4 years
female: 35.5 years (2004 est.)

Population growth rate: 0.55% (2004 est.)
Birth rate: 12.66 births/1,000 population (2004 est.)
Death rate: 7.63 deaths/1,000 population (2004 est.)
Net migration rate: 0.43 migrant(s)/1,000 population (2004 est.)
Sex ratio:
at birth: 1.05 male(s)/female
under 15 years: 1.05 male(s)/female
15-64 years: 1.02 male(s)/female
65 years and over: 0.77 male(s)/female
total population: 1 male(s)/female (2004 est.)
Infant mortality rate:
total: 7.36 deaths/1,000 live births
male: 9.19 deaths/1,000 live births
female: 5.44 deaths/1,000 live births (2004 est.)
Life expectancy at birth:
total population: 77.46 years
male: 75.11 years
female: 79.92 years (2004 est.)
Total fertility rate: 1.85 children born/woman (2004 est.)
HIV/AIDS - adult prevalence rate: 0.1% (2003 est.)
HIV/AIDS - people living with HIV/AIDS: less than 1,000 (1999 est.)
HIV/AIDS - deaths: NA
Nationality:
noun: Cypriot(s)
adjective: Cypriot
Ethnic groups: Greek 77%, Turkish 18%, other 5% (2001)
Religions: Greek Orthodox 78%, Muslim 18%, Maronite, Armenian Apostolic, and other 4%
Languages: Greek, Turkish, English
Literacy:
definition: age 15 and over can read and write
total population: 97.6%
male: 98.9%
female: 96.3% (2003 est.)

Government

Country name:
conventional long form: Republic of Cyprus
conventional short form: Cyprus
note: the Turkish Cypriot area refers to itself as the "Turkish Republic of Northern Cyprus" (TRNC)
Government type: republic
note: a disaggregation of the two ethnic communities inhabiting the island began following the outbreak of communal strife in 1963; this separation was further solidified after the Turkish intervention in July 1974 after a Greek junta-based coup attempt gave the Turkish Cypriots de facto control in the north; Greek Cypriots control the only internationally recognized government; on 15 November 1983 Turkish Cypriot "President" Rauf DENKTASH declared independence and the formation of a "Turkish Republic of Northern Cyprus" (TRNC), recognized only by Turkey; both sides publicly support a settlement based on a federation (Greek Cypriot position) or confederation (Turkish Cypriot position)
Capital: Nicosia

Cyprus (continued)

Administrative divisions: 6 districts; Famagusta, Kyrenia, Larnaca, Limassol, Nicosia, Paphos; note - Turkish Cypriot area's administrative divisions include Kyrenia, all but a small part of Famagusta, and small parts of Lefkosia (Nicosia) and Larnaca

Independence: 16 August 1960 (from UK); note - Turkish Cypriot area proclaimed self-rule on 13 February 1975

National holiday: Independence Day, 1 October (1960); note - Turkish Cypriot area celebrates 15 November (1983) as Independence Day

Constitution: 16 August 1960; negotiations to create the basis for a new or revised constitution to govern the island and to better relations between Greek and Turkish Cypriots have been held intermittently; in 1975 Turkish Cypriots created their own constitution and governing bodies within the "Turkish Federated State of Cyprus," which was renamed the "Turkish Republic of Northern Cyprus" in 1983; a new constitution for the Turkish Cypriot area passed by referendum on 5 May 1985

Legal system: based on common law, with civil law modifications

Suffrage: 18 years of age; universal

Executive branch:
chief of state: President Tassos PAPADOPOULOS (since 1 March 2003); note - the president is both the chief of state and head of government; post of vice president is currently vacant; under the 1960 constitution, the post is reserved for a Turkish Cypriot
head of government: President Tassos PAPADOPOULOS (since 1 March 2003); note - the president is both the chief of state and head of government; post of vice president is currently vacant; under the 1960 constitution, the post is reserved for a Turkish Cypriot
cabinet: Council of Ministers appointed jointly by the president and vice president
elections: president elected by popular vote for a five-year term; election last held 16 February 2003 (next to be held NA February 2008)
election results: Tassos PAPADOPOULOS elected president; percent of vote - Tassos PAPADOPOULOS 51.5%, Glafkos KLIRIDIS 38.8%, Alekos MARKIDIS 6.6%
note: Rauf R. DENKTASH has been "president" of the Turkish Cypriot area since 13 February 1975 ("president" elected by popular vote for a five-year term); elections last held 15 April 2000 (next to be held NA April 2005); results - Rauf R. DENKTASH reelected president after the other contender withdrew; Mehmet Ali TALAT has been "prime minister" of the Turkish Cypriot area since mid-January 2004; there is a Council of Ministers (cabinet) in the Turkish Cypriot area

Legislative branch: unicameral - Greek Cypriot area: House of Representatives or Vouli Antiprosopon (80 seats; 56 assigned to the Greek Cypriots, 24 to Turkish Cypriots; note - only those assigned to Greek Cypriots are filled; members are elected by popular vote to serve five-year terms); Turkish Cypriot area:

Assembly of the Republic or Cumhuriyet Meclisi (50 seats; members are elected by popular vote to serve five-year terms)
elections: Greek Cypriot area: last held 27 May 2001 (next to be held NA May 2006); Turkish Cypriot area: last held 14 December 2003 (next to be held NA December 2008)
election results: Greek Cypriot area: House of Representatives - percent of vote by party - AKEL 34.71%, DISY 34%, DIKO 14.84%, KISOS 6.51%, others 9.94%; seats by party - AKEL (Communist) 20, DISY 19, DIKO 9, KISOS 4, others 4; Turkish Cypriot area: Assembly of the Republic - percent of vote by party - CTP 35.8%, UBP 32.3%, Peace and Democratic Movement 13.4%, DP 12.3%; seats by party - CTP 19, UBP 18, Peace and Democratic Movement 6, DP 7

Judicial branch: Supreme Court (judges are appointed jointly by the president and vice president)
note: there is also a Supreme Court in the Turkish Cypriot area

Political parties and leaders: Greek Cypriot area: Democratic Party or DIKO [Tassos PAPADOPOULOS]; Democratic Rally or DISY [Nikos ANASTASIADHIS]; Fighting Democratic Movement or ADIK [Dinos MIKHAILIDIS]; Green Party of Cyprus [George PERDIKIS]; New Horizons [Nikolaus KOUTSOU]; Restorative Party of the Working People or AKEL (Communist Party) [Dimitrios CHRISTOFIAS]; Social Democrats Movement or KISOS (formerly United Democratic Union of Cyprus or EDEK) [Yiannakis OMIROU]; United Democrats Movement or EDE [George VASSILIOU]; Turkish Cypriot area: Democratic Party or DP [Serder DENKTASH]; National Birth Party or UDP [Enver EMIN]; National Unity Party or UBP [Dervis EROGLU]; Our Party or BP [Okyay SADIKOGLU]; Patriotic Unity Movement or YBH [Alpay DURDURAN]; Peace and Democratic Movement [Mustafa AKINCI]; Republican Turkish Party or CTP [Mehmet ALI TALAT]

Political pressure groups and leaders: Confederation of Cypriot Workers or SEK (pro-West); Confederation of Revolutionary Labor Unions or Dev-Is; Federation of Turkish Cypriot Labor Unions or Turk-Sen; Pan-Cyprian Labor Federation or PEO (Communist controlled)

International organization participation: Australia Group, C, CE, EBRD, EU (new member), FAO, G-77, IAEA, IBRD, ICAO, ICC, ICCt, ICFTU, IDA, IFAD, IFC, IHO, ILO, IMF, IMO, Interpol, IOC, IOM, ISO, ITU, NAM, NSG, OAS (observer), OPCW, OSCE, PCA, UN, UNCTAD, UNESCO, UNHCR, UNIDO, UPU, WCL, WCO, WFTU, WHO, WIPO, WMO, WToO, WTrO

Diplomatic representation in the US:
chief of mission: Ambassador Euripides L. EVRIVIADES
chancery: 2211 R Street NW, Washington, DC 20008
telephone: [1] (202) 462-5772
FAX: [1] (202) 483-6710

consulate(s) general: New York
consulate(s): New York
note: representative of the Turkish Cypriot area in the US is Ahmet ERDENGIZ; office at 1667 K Street NW, Washington, DC; telephone [1] (202) 887-6198

Diplomatic representation from the US:
chief of mission: Ambassador Michael KLOSSON
embassy: corner of Metochiou and Ploutarchou Streets, Engomi, 2407 Nicosia
mailing address: P. O. Box 24536, 1385 Nicosia
telephone: [357] (22) 776400
FAX: [357] (22) 780944

Flag description: white with a copper-colored silhouette of the island (the name Cyprus is derived from the Greek word for copper) above two green crossed olive branches in the center of the flag; the branches symbolize the hope for peace and reconciliation between the Greek and Turkish communities
note: the Turkish Cypriot flag has a horizontal red stripe at the top and bottom between which is a red crescent and red star on a white field

Economy

Economy - overview: The Greek Cypriot economy is prosperous but highly susceptible to external shocks. Erratic growth rates over the past decade reflect the economy's vulnerability to swings in tourist arrivals, caused by political instability in the region and fluctuations in economic conditions in Western Europe. Economic policy is focused on meeting the criteria for admission to the EU. EU-driven tax reforms in 2003 have introduced fiscal imbalances, which, coupled with a sluggish tourism sector, have resulted in growing fiscal deficits. As in the Turkish sector, water shortages are a perennial problem; a few desalination plants are now on-line. After 10 years of drought, the country received substantial rainfall from 2001-03, alleviating immediate concerns. The Turkish Cypriot economy has roughly one-third of the per capita GDP of the south. Because it is recognized only by Turkey, it has had much difficulty arranging foreign financing and investment. It remains heavily dependent on agriculture and government service, which together employ about half of the work force. To compensate for the economy's weakness, Turkey provides grants and loans to support economic development. Ankara provided $200 million in 2002 and pledged $450 million for the 2003-05 period. Future events throughout the island will be highly influenced by the outcome of negotiations on the UN-sponsored agreement to unite the Greek and Turkish areas.

GDP: Greek Cypriot area: purchasing power parity - $8.9 billion (2003 est.); Turkish Cypriot area: purchasing power parity - $1.217 billion (2003 est.)

GDP - real growth rate: Greek Cypriot area: 1.6% (2003 est.); Turkish Cypriot area: 2.6% (2003 est.)

GDP - per capita: Greek Cypriot area: purchasing power parity - $16,000 (2003 est.); Turkish Cypriot area: purchasing power parity - $5,600 (2003 est.)

Cyprus *(continued)*

GDP - composition by sector:
Greek Cypriot area: agriculture 4.9%; industry 19.9%; services 75.6%
Turkish Cypriot area: agriculture 10.6%; industry 20.5%; services 68.9% (2003)
Population below poverty line: NA%
Household income or consumption by percentage share:
lowest 10%: NA%
highest 10%: NA%
Inflation rate (consumer prices): Greek Cypriot area: 4% (2003 est.); Turkish Cypriot area: 12.6% (2003 est.)
Labor force: Greek Cypriot area: 306,000; Turkish Cypriot area: 95,025 (2000)
Labor force - by occupation: Greek Cypriot area: services 75.6%, industry 19.4%, agriculture 4.9% (2003); Turkish Cypriot area: services 68.9%, industry 20.5%, agriculture 10.6% (2003)
Unemployment rate: Greek Cypriot area: 3.4%; Turkish Cypriot area: 5.6% (2003 est.)
Budget:
revenues: Greek Cypriot area - $4.4 billion, Turkish Cypriot area - $231.3 million (2002 est.)
expenditures: $3.7 billion, Greek Cypriot area - $539 million, including capital expenditures of $539 million, Turkish Cypriot area - $432.8 million, including capital expenditures of NA (2003 est.)
Industries: food, beverages, textiles, chemicals, metal products, tourism, wood products
Industrial production growth rate: Greek Cypriot area: -1.4% (2002); Turkish Cypriot area: -0.3% (2002)
Electricity - production: 3.401 billion kWh; Turkish Cypriot area: NA kWh (2001)
Electricity - production by source:
fossil fuel: 100%
hydro: 0%
nuclear: 0%
other: 0% (2001)
Electricity - consumption: Greek Cypriot area: 3.163 billion kWh; Turkish Cypriot area: NA kWh (2001)
Electricity - exports: 0 kWh (2001)
Electricity - imports: 0 kWh (2001)
Oil - production: 0 bbl/day (2001 est.)
Oil - consumption: 49,000 bbl/day (2001 est.)
Oil - exports: NA
Oil - imports: NA
Agriculture - products: potatoes, citrus, vegetables, barley, grapes, olives, vegetables, poultry, pork, lamb, kids, dairy
Exports: Greek Cypriot area: $1.054 billion f.o.b. Turkish Cypriot area: $46 million f.o.b. (2003 est.)
Exports - commodities: Greek Cypriot area: citrus, potatoes, pharmaceuticals, cement, clothing and cigarettes; Turkish Cypriot area: citrus, potatoes, textiles
Exports - partners: UK 26.7%, Greece 6.6%, France 4.9%, Poland 4.3% (2002)

Imports: Greek Cypriot area: $4.637 billion f.o.b.; Turkish Cypriot area: $301 million f.o.b. (2003 est.)
Imports - commodities: Greek Cypriot area: consumer goods, petroleum and lubricants, intermediate goods, machinery, transport equipment; Turkish Cypriot area: food, minerals, chemicals, machinery
Imports - partners: Russia 17.1%, Greece 7.1%, Germany 6.6%, France 6.4%, UK 6.3%, Italy 6.3%, South Korea 5.4%, Japan 5.1% (2002)
Debt - external: Greek Cypriot area: $8 billion; Turkish Cypriot area: $NA (2002)
Economic aid - recipient: Greek Cypriot area - $17 million (1998); Turkish Cypriot area - $700 million from Turkey in grants and loans (1990-97), which are usually forgiven (1998)
Currency: Greek Cypriot area: Cypriot pound (CYP); Turkish Cypriot area: Turkish lira (TRL)
Currency code: CYP; TRL
Exchange rates: Cypriot pounds per US dollar - 0.5174 (2003), 0.6107 (2002), 0.6431 (2001), 0.6224 (2000), 0.5429 (1999), Turkish lira per US dollar 1.505 million (2003), 1.507 million (2002), 1,225,590 (2001), 625,218 (2000), 418,783 (1999)
Fiscal year: calendar year

Communications

Telephones - main lines in use: Greek Cypriot area: 405,000 (1998); Turkish Cypriot area: 83,162 (1998)
Telephones - mobile cellular: Greek Cypriot area: 68,000 (1998); Turkish Cypriot area: 70,000 (1999)
Telephone system:
general assessment: excellent in both the Greek Cypriot and Turkish Cypriot areas
domestic: open-wire, fiber-optic cable, and microwave radio relay
international: country code - 357; tropospheric scatter; 3 coaxial and 5 fiber-optic submarine cables; satellite earth stations - 3 Intelsat (1 Atlantic Ocean and 2 Indian Ocean), 2 Eutelsat, 2 Intersputnik, and 1 Arabsat
Radio broadcast stations: Greek Cypriot area: AM 7, FM 60, shortwave 1 (1998); Turkish Cypriot area: AM 3, FM 11, shortwave 1 (1998)
Television broadcast stations: Greek Cypriot area: 4 (plus 225 low-power repeaters) (September 1995);; Turkish Cypriot area: 4 (plus 5 repeaters) (September 1995)
Internet country code: .cy
Internet hosts: 2,692 (2002)
Internet users: 210,000 (2002)

Transportation

Railways: 0 km
Highways:
total: 13,491 km
note: Greek Cypriot area: 11,141 km; Turkish Cypriot area: 2,350 km

paved: Greek Cypriot area: 6,428 km; Turkish Cypriot area: 1,370 km
unpaved: Greek Cypriot area: 4,713 km; Turkish Cypriot area: 980 km (2000/1996)
Waterways: none
Ports and harbors: Famagusta, Kyrenia, Larnaca, Limassol, Paphos, Vasilikos
Merchant marine:
total: 1,066 ships (1,000 GRT or over) 22,016,374 GRT/35,760,004 DWT
by type: bulk 403, cargo 276, chemical tanker 28, combination bulk 21, combination ore/oil 2, container 145, liquefied gas 1, multi-functional large load carrier 2, passenger 8, passenger/cargo 1, petroleum tanker 109, refrigerated cargo 30, roll on/roll off 29, short-sea/passenger 5, specialized tanker 3, vehicle carrier 3
foreign-owned: Austria 11, Belgium 1, Bulgaria 1, Canada 6, China 13, Croatia 2, Cuba 8, Egypt 2, Estonia 2, Germany 210, Greece 499, Guam 1, Hong Kong 5, India 6, Iran 3, Ireland 1, Israel 3, Italy 2, Japan 20, South Korea 6, Latvia 11, Malta 1, Mexico 1, Monaco 3, Netherlands 18, Norway 7, Panama 1, Philippines 2, Poland 20, Portugal 2, Russia 51, Singapore 2, Slovenia 4, Spain 5, Sudan 2, Sweden 6, Switzerland 1, Ukraine 2, United Kingdom 16, United States 4, Vietnam 1
registered in other countries: 100 (2003 est.)
Airports: 17 (2003 est.)
Airports - with paved runways:
total: 13
2,438 to 3,047 m: 7
1,524 to 2,437 m: 2
914 to 1,523 m: 3
under 914 m: 1 (2003 est.)
Airports - with unpaved runways:
total: 4
914 to 1,523 m: 2
under 914 m: 2 (2003 est.)
Heliports: 10 (2003 est.)

Military

Military branches:
Greek Cypriot area: Greek Cypriot National Guard (GCNG; including air and naval elements), Greek Cypriot Police
Turkish Cypriot area: Turkish Cypriot Security Force (GKK)
Military manpower - military age: 18 years of age (2004 est.)
Military manpower - availability:
males age 15-49: 202,966 (2004 est.)
Military manpower - fit for military service:
males age 15-49: 139,255 (2004 est.)
Military manpower - reaching military age annually:
males: 6,614 (2004 est.)
Military expenditures - dollar figure: $384 million (FY02)
Military expenditures - percent of GDP: 3.8% (FY02)

Cyprus (continued)

Cyprus *(continued)*

Transnational Issues

Disputes - international: hostilities in 1974 divided the island into two de facto autonomous areas, a Greek Cypriot area controlled by the internationally recognized Cypriot Government and a Turkish-Cypriot area, separated by a UN buffer zone; March 2003 reunification talks failed, but Turkish-Cypriots later opened their borders to temporary visits by Greek Cypriots; a UN-brokered peace plan attempts to break the stalemate over final status before the Greek Cypriot area enters the EU in May 2004

Illicit drugs: minor transit point for heroin and hashish via air routes and container traffic to Europe, especially from Lebanon and Turkey; some cocaine transits as well; despite a strengthening of anti-money laundering legislation, remains highly vulnerable to money laundering; identification of benefiting owners and reporting of suspicious transactions by nonresident-controlled companies in offshore sector remains weak

Czech Republic

Introduction

Background: Following the First World War, the closely related Czechs and Slovaks of the former Austro-Hungarian Empire merged to form Czechoslovakia. During the interwar years, the new country's leaders were frequently preoccupied with meeting the demands of other ethnic minorities within the republic, most notably the Sudeten Germans and the Ruthenians (Ukrainians). After World War II, a truncated Czechoslovakia fell within the Soviet sphere of influence. In 1968, an invasion by Warsaw Pact troops ended the efforts of the country's leaders to liberalize Communist party rule and create "socialism with a human face." Anti-Soviet demonstrations the following year ushered in a period of harsh repression. With the collapse of Soviet authority in 1989, Czechoslovakia regained its freedom through a peaceful "Velvet Revolution." On 1 January 1993, the country underwent a "velvet divorce" into its two national components, the Czech Republic and Slovakia. Now a member of NATO, the Czech Republic has moved toward integration in world markets, a development that poses both opportunities and risks. In December 2002, the Czech Republic was invited to join the European Union (EU). It is expected that the Czech Republic will accede to the EU in 2004.

Geography

Location: Central Europe, southeast of Germany
Geographic coordinates: 49 45 N, 15 30 E
Map references: Europe
Area:
total: 78,866 sq km
land: 77,276 sq km
water: 1,590 sq km
Area - comparative: slightly smaller than South Carolina

Land boundaries:
total: 1,881 km
border countries: Austria 362 km, Germany 646 km, Poland 658 km, Slovakia 215 km
Coastline: 0 km (landlocked)
Maritime claims: none (landlocked)
Climate: temperate; cool summers; cold, cloudy, humid winters
Terrain: Bohemia in the west consists of rolling plains, hills, and plateaus surrounded by low mountains; Moravia in the east consists of very hilly country
Elevation extremes:
lowest point: Elbe River 115 m
highest point: Snezka 1,602 m
Natural resources: hard coal, soft coal, kaolin, clay, graphite, timber
Land use:
arable land: 40%
permanent crops: 3.04%
other: 56.96% (1998 est.)
Irrigated land: 240 sq km (1998 est.)
Natural hazards: flooding
Environment - current issues: air and water pollution in areas of northwest Bohemia and in northern Moravia around Ostrava present health risks; acid rain damaging forests; efforts to bring industry up to EU code should improve domestic pollution
Environment - international agreements:
party to: Air Pollution, Air Pollution-Nitrogen Oxides, Air Pollution-Sulfur 85, Air Pollution-Sulfur 94, Air Pollution-Volatile Organic Compounds, Antarctic Treaty, Biodiversity, Climate Change, Climate Change-Kyoto Protocol, Desertification, Endangered Species, Environmental Modification, Hazardous Wastes, Law of the Sea, Ozone Layer Protection, Ship Pollution, Wetlands
signed, but not ratified: Air Pollution-Persistent Organic Pollutants
Geography - note: landlocked; strategically located astride some of oldest and most significant land routes in Europe; Moravian Gate is a traditional military corridor between the North European Plain and the Danube in central Europe

People

Population: 10,246,178 (July 2004 est.)
Age structure:
0-14 years: 15% (male 789,987; female 748,476)
15-64 years: 70.9% (male 3,643,574; female 3,622,276)
65 years and over: 14.1% (male 557,496; female 884,369) (2004 est.)
Median age:
total: 38.6 years
male: 36.9 years
female: 40.5 years (2004 est.)
Population growth rate: -0.05% (2004 est.)
Birth rate: 9.1 births/1,000 population (2004 est.)

Czech Republic (continued)

Death rate: 10.54 deaths/1,000 population (2004 est.)
Net migration rate: 0.97 migrant(s)/1,000 population (2004 est.)
Sex ratio:
at birth: 1.06 male(s)/female
under 15 years: 1.06 male(s)/female
15-64 years: 1.01 male(s)/female
65 years and over: 0.63 male(s)/female
total population: 0.95 male(s)/female (2004 est.)
Infant mortality rate:
total: 3.97 deaths/1,000 live births
male: 4.32 deaths/1,000 live births
female: 3.59 deaths/1,000 live births (2004 est.)
Life expectancy at birth:
total population: 75.78 years
male: 72.52 years
female: 79.24 years (2004 est.)
Total fertility rate: 1.18 children born/woman (2004 est.)
HIV/AIDS - adult prevalence rate: less than 0.1% (2001 est.)
HIV/AIDS - people living with HIV/AIDS: 500 (2001 est.)
HIV/AIDS - deaths: less than 10 (2001 est.)
Nationality:
noun: Czech(s)
adjective: Czech
Ethnic groups: Czech 81.2%, Moravian 13.2%, Slovak 3.1%, Polish 0.6%, German 0.5%, Silesian 0.4%, Roma 0.3%, Hungarian 0.2%, other 0.5% (1991)
Religions: Roman Catholic 39.2%, Protestant 4.6%, Orthodox 3%, other 13.4%, atheist 39.8%
Languages: Czech
Literacy:
definition: NA
total population: 99.9% (1999 est.)
male: NA%
female: NA%

Government

Country name:
conventional long form: Czech Republic
conventional short form: Czech Republic
local long form: Ceska Republika
local short form: Ceska Republika
Government type: parliamentary democracy
Capital: Prague
Administrative divisions: 13 regions (kraje, singular - kraj) and 1 capital city* (hlavni mesto); Jihocesky Kraj, Jihomoravsky Kraj, Karlovarsky Kraj, Kralovehradecky Kraj, Liberecky Kraj, Moravskoslezsky Kraj, Olomoucky Kraj, Pardubicky Kraj, Plzensky Kraj, Praha*, Stredocesky Kraj, Ustecky Kraj, Vysocina, Zlinsky Kraj
Independence: 1 January 1993 (Czechoslovakia split into the Czech Republic and Slovakia)
National holiday: Czech Founding Day, 28 October (1918)
Constitution: ratified 16 December 1992; effective 1 January 1993

Legal system: civil law system based on Austro-Hungarian codes; has not accepted compulsory ICJ jurisdiction; legal code modified to bring it in line with Organization on Security and Cooperation in Europe (OSCE) obligations and to expunge Marxist-Leninist legal theory
Suffrage: 18 years of age; universal
Executive branch:
chief of state: President Vaclav KLAUS (since 7 March 2003)
note: the Czech Republic's first president Vaclav HAVEL stepped down from office on 2 February 2003 having served exactly 10 years; parliament finally elected a successor on 28 February 2003 after two inconclusive elections in January 2003
head of government: Prime Minister Vladimir SPIDLA (since 12 July 2002), Deputy Prime Ministers Bohuslav SOBOTKA (since 20 August 2003), Cyril SVOBODA (since July 2002), Stanislav GROSS (since July 2002), Petr MARES (since July 2002)
cabinet: Cabinet appointed by the president on the recommendation of the prime minister
elections: president elected by Parliament for a five-year term; last successful election held 28 February 2003 (after earlier elections held 15 and 24 January 2003 were inconclusive; next election to be held NA January 2008); prime minister appointed by the president
election results: Vaclav KLAUS elected president on 28 February 2003; Vaclav KLAUS 142 votes, Jan SOKOL 124 votes (third round; combined votes of both chambers of parliament)
Legislative branch: bicameral Parliament or Parlament consists of the Senate or Senat (81 seats; members are elected by popular vote to serve six-year terms; one-third elected every two years) and the Chamber of Deputies or Poslanecka Snemovna (200 seats; members are elected by popular vote to serve four-year terms)
elections: Senate - last held in two rounds 25-26 October and 1-2 November 2002 (next to be held NA November 2004); Chamber of Deputies - last held 14-15 June 2002 (next to be held by NA June 2006)
election results: Senate - percent of vote by party - NA%; seats by party - ODS 26, KDU-CSL 14, CSSD 11, US 9, KSCM 3, independents 18; Chamber of Deputies - percent of vote by party - CSSD 30.2%, ODS 24.5%, KSCM 18.5%, KDU-CSL & US-DEU coalition 14.3%, other minor 12.5%; seats by party - CSSD 70, ODS 58, KSCM 41, KDU-CSL 21, US-DEU 10
Judicial branch: Supreme Court; Constitutional Court; chairman and deputy chairmen are appointed by the president for a 10-year term
Political parties and leaders: Christian and Democratic Union-Czechoslovak People's Party or KDU-CSL [Miroslav KALOUSEK, chairman]; Civic Democratic Alliance or ODA [Michael ZANTOVSKY, chairman]; Civic Democratic Party or ODS [Mirek TOPOLANEK, chairman]; Communist Party of Bohemia and Moravia or KSCM [Miroslav

GREBENICEK, chairman]; Communist Party of Czechoslovakia or KSC [Miroslav STEPAN, chairman]; Czech National Social Party of CSNS [Jaroslav ROVNY, chairman]; Czech Social Democratic Party or CSSD [Vladimir SPIDLA, chairman]; Freedom Union-Democratic Union or US-DEU [Petr MARES, chairman]
Political pressure groups and leaders: Bohemian and Moravian Trade Union Confederation [Milan STECH]
International organization participation: ACCT (observer), Australia Group, BIS, CE, CEI, CERN, EAPC, EBRD, EU (new member), FAO, IAEA, IBRD, ICAO, ICC, ICCt (signatory), ICFTU, ICRM, IDA, IEA, IFC, IFRCS, ILO, IMF, IMO, Interpol, IOC, IOM, ISO, ITU, MONUC, NATO, NEA, NSG, OAS (observer), OECD, OPCW, OSCE, PCA, PFP, UN, UNAMSIL, UNCTAD, UNESCO, UNIDO, UNITAR, UNMEE, UNMIK, UNOMIG, UPU, WCL, WCO, WEU (associate), WFTU, WHO, WIPO, WMO, WToO, WTrO, ZC
Diplomatic representation in the US:
chief of mission: Ambassador Martin PALOUS
chancery: 3900 Spring of Freedom Street NW, Washington, DC 20008
telephone: [1] (202) 274-9100
FAX: [1] (202) 966-8540
consulate(s) general: Los Angeles and New York
Diplomatic representation from the US:
chief of mission: Ambassador William J. CABANISS
embassy: Trziste 15, 11801 Prague 1
mailing address: use embassy street address
telephone: [420] (2) 5753-0663
FAX: [420] (2) 5753-0583
Flag description: two equal horizontal bands of white (top) and red with a blue isosceles triangle based on the hoist side (identical to the flag of the former Czechoslovakia)

Economy

Economy - overview: One of the most stable and prosperous of the post-Communist states, the Czech Republic has been recovering from recession since mid-1999. Growth in 2000-03 was supported by exports to the EU, primarily to Germany, and a near doubling of foreign direct investment. Domestic demand is playing an ever more important role in underpinning growth as interest rates drop and the availability of credit cards and mortgages increases. High current account deficits - averaging around 5% of GDP in the last several years - could be a persistent problem. Inflation is under control. The EU put the Czech Republic just behind Poland and Hungary in preparations for accession, which will give further impetus and direction to structural reform. Moves to complete banking, telecommunications, and energy privatization will encourage additional foreign investment, while intensified restructuring among large enterprises and banks, and improvements in the financial sector, should strengthen output growth. Nonetheless, revival in the European economies remains essential to stepped-up growth.

Czech Republic (continued)

GDP: purchasing power parity - $160.5 billion (2003 est.)
GDP - real growth rate: 2.5% (2003 est.)
GDP - per capita: purchasing power parity - $15,700 (2003 est.)
GDP - composition by sector:
agriculture: 3.8%
industry: 41%
services: 55.2% (2001)
Population below poverty line: NA%
Household income or consumption by percentage share:
lowest 10%: 4.3%
highest 10%: 22.4% (1996)
Distribution of family income - Gini index: 25.4 (1996)
Inflation rate (consumer prices): 0% (2003 est.)
Labor force: 5.203 million (1999 est.)
Labor force - by occupation: agriculture 5%, industry 35%, services 60% (2001 est.)
Unemployment rate: 10.5% (2003)
Budget:
revenues: $16.7 billion
expenditures: $18 billion, including capital expenditures of $NA (2001 est.)
Industries: metallurgy, machinery and equipment, motor vehicles, glass, armaments
Industrial production growth rate: 5.7% (2003)
Electricity - production: 70.04 billion kWh (2001)
Electricity - production by source:
fossil fuel: 76.1%
hydro: 2.9%
nuclear: 20%
other: 1% (2001)
Electricity - consumption: 55.6 billion kWh (2001)
Electricity - exports: 18.92 billion kWh (2001)
Electricity - imports: 9.38 billion kWh (2001)
Oil - production: 7,419 bbl/day (2001 est.)
Oil - consumption: 175,700 bbl/day (2001 est.)
Oil - exports: 26,670 bbl/day (2001)
Oil - imports: 192,300 bbl/day (2001)
Oil - proved reserves: 17.25 million bbl (1 January 2002)
Natural gas - production: 160 million cu m (2001 est.)
Natural gas - consumption: 9.892 billion cu m (2001 est.)
Natural gas - exports: 1 million cu m (2001 est.)
Natural gas - imports: 9.521 billion cu m (2001 est.)
Natural gas - proved reserves: 3.057 billion cu m (1 January 2002)
Agriculture - products: wheat, potatoes, sugar beets, hops, fruit; pigs, poultry
Exports: $46.77 billion f.o.b. (2003 est.)
Exports - commodities: machinery and transport equipment 44%, intermediate manufactures 25%, chemicals 7%, raw materials and fuel 7% (2000)
Exports - partners: Germany 36.6%, Slovakia 7.7%, UK 5.8%, Austria 5.6%, Poland 4.7%, France 4.7%, Italy 4.1% (2002)
Imports: $50.4 billion f.o.b. (2003 est.)

Imports - commodities: machinery and transport equipment 40%, intermediate manufactures 21%, raw materials and fuels 13%, chemicals 11% (2000)
Imports - partners: Germany 32.9%, Italy 5.5%, Slovakia 5.3%, France 4.9%, China 4.7%, Russia 4.6%, Austria 4.4%, Poland 4.1% (2002)
Debt - external: $28.2 billion (2003)
Economic aid - recipient: $108 million; EU structural adjustment funds (2002)
Currency: Czech koruna (CZK)
Currency code: CZK
Exchange rates: koruny per US dollar - 28.209 (2003), 32.7385 (2002), 38.0353 (2001), 38.5984 (2000), 34.5692 (1999)
Fiscal year: calendar year

Communications

Telephones - main lines in use: 3,675,500 (2002)
Telephones - mobile cellular: 9.2 million (2003)
Telephone system:
general assessment: privatization and modernization of the Czech telecommunication system got a late start but is advancing steadily; growth in the use of mobile cellular telephones is particularly vigorous
domestic: 86% of exchanges now digital; existing copper subscriber systems now being enhanced with Asymmetric Digital Subscriber Line (ADSL) equipment to accommodate Internet and other digital signals; trunk systems include fiber-optic cable and microwave radio relay
international: country code - 420; satellite earth stations - 2 Intersputnik (Atlantic and Indian Ocean regions), 1 Intelsat, 1 Eutelsat, 1 Inmarsat, 1 Globalstar
Radio broadcast stations: AM 31, FM 304, shortwave 17 (2000)
Television broadcast stations: 150 (plus 1,434 repeaters) (2000)
Internet country code: .cz
Internet hosts: 226,429 (2002)
Internet users: 2.6 million (2002)

Transportation

Railways:
total: 9,462 km
standard gauge: 9,363 km 1.435-m gauge (1,745 km electrified)
narrow gauge: 99 km 0.760-m gauge (2002)
Highways:
total: 55,408 km
paved: 55,408 km (including 499 km of expressways)
unpaved: 0 km (2000)
Waterways: 303 km
note: the Labe (Elbe) is the principal river (2000)
Pipelines: gas 7,020 km; oil 547 km; refined products 94 km (2003)
Ports and harbors: Decin, Prague, Usti nad Labem
Airports: 120 (2003 est.)
Airports - with paved runways:
total: 44
over 3,047 m: 2

2,438 to 3,047 m: 9
1,524 to 2,437 m: 14
914 to 1,523 m: 2
under 914 m: 17 (2003 est.)
Airports - with unpaved runways:
total: 76
1,524 to 2,437 m: 1
914 to 1,523 m: 27
under 914 m: 48 (2003 est.)
Heliports: 2 (2003 est.)

Military

Military branches: Czech Army: Ground Forces, Air Forces, Special Forces
Military manpower - military age: 18 years of age (2004 est.)
Military manpower - availability:
males age 15-49: 2,623,386 (2004 est.)
Military manpower - fit for military service:
males age 15-49: 2,003,748 (2004 est.)
Military manpower - reaching military age annually:
males: 67,195 (2004 est.)
Military expenditures - dollar figure: $1,190.2 million (FY01)
Military expenditures - percent of GDP: 2.1% (FY01)

Transnational Issues

Disputes - international: Liechtenstein's royal family claims restitution for 1,600 sq km of land in the Czech Republic confiscated in 1918; individual Sudeten Germans seek restitution for property confiscated in connection with their expulsion after World War II; Austria has minor dispute with Czech Republic over the Temelin Nuclear Power Plant
Illicit drugs: transshipment point for Southwest Asian heroin and minor transit point for Latin American cocaine to Western Europe; producer of synthetic drugs for local and regional markets; susceptible to money laundering related to drug trafficking, organized crime

Denmark

Introduction

Background: Once the seat of Viking raiders and later a major north European power, Denmark has evolved into a modern, prosperous nation that is participating in the general political and economic integration of Europe. It joined NATO in 1949 and the EEC (now the EU) in 1973. However, the country has opted out of certain elements of the European Union's Maastricht Treaty, including the European Economic and Monetary Union (EMU) and issues concerning certain justice and home affairs.

Geography

Location: Northern Europe, bordering the Baltic Sea and the North Sea, on a peninsula north of Germany (Jutland); also includes two major islands (Sjaelland and Fyn)

Geographic coordinates: 56 00 N, 10 00 E

Map references: Europe

Area:
total: 43,094 sq km
land: 42,394 sq km
water: 700 sq km
note: includes the island of Bornholm in the Baltic Sea and the rest of metropolitan Denmark (the Jutland Peninsula, and the major islands of Sjaelland and Fyn), but excludes the Faroe Islands and Greenland

Area - comparative: slightly less than twice the size of Massachusetts

Land boundaries:
total: 68 km
border countries: Germany 68 km

Coastline: 7,314 km

Maritime claims:
territorial sea: 12 NM
exclusive economic zone: 200 NM
continental shelf: 200-m depth or to the depth of exploitation

Climate: temperate; humid and overcast; mild, windy winters and cool summers

Terrain: low and flat to gently rolling plains

Elevation extremes:
lowest point: Lammefjord -7 m
highest point: Yding Skovhoej 173 m

Natural resources: petroleum, natural gas, fish, salt, limestone, stone, gravel and sand

Land use:
arable land: 55.74%
permanent crops: 0.19%
other: 44.07% (1998 est.)

Irrigated land: 4,760 sq km (1998 est.)

Natural hazards: flooding is a threat in some areas of the country (e.g., parts of Jutland, along the southern coast of the island of Lolland) that are protected from the sea by a system of dikes

Environment - current issues: air pollution, principally from vehicle and power plant emissions; nitrogen and phosphorus pollution of the North Sea; drinking and surface water becoming polluted from animal wastes and pesticides

Environment - international agreements:
party to: Air Pollution, Air Pollution-Nitrogen Oxides, Air Pollution-Persistent Organic Pollutants, Air Pollution-Sulfur 85, Air Pollution-Sulfur 94, Air Pollution-Volatile Organic Compounds, Antarctic Treaty, Biodiversity, Climate Change, Climate Change-Kyoto Protocol, Desertification, Endangered Species, Environmental Modification, Hazardous Wastes, Marine Dumping, Marine Life Conservation, Ozone Layer Protection, Ship Pollution, Tropical Timber 83, Tropical Timber 94, Wetlands, Whaling
signed, but not ratified: Law of the Sea

Geography - note: controls Danish Straits (Skagerrak and Kattegat) linking Baltic and North Seas; about one-quarter of the population lives in greater Copenhagen

People

Population: 5,413,392 (July 2004 est.)

Age structure:
0-14 years: 18.9% (male 523,888; female 497,420)
15-64 years: 66.2% (male 1,808,376; female 1,774,388)
65 years and over: 15% (male 344,113; female 465,207) (2004 est.)

Median age:
total: 39.2 years
male: 38.3 years
female: 40.2 years (2004 est.)

Population growth rate: 0.35% (2004 est.)

Birth rate: 11.59 births/1,000 population (2004 est.)

Death rate: 10.53 deaths/1,000 population (2004 est.)

Net migration rate: 2.48 migrant(s)/1,000 population (2004 est.)

Sex ratio:
at birth: 1.06 male(s)/female
under 15 years: 1.05 male(s)/female
15-64 years: 1.02 male(s)/female
65 years and over: 0.74 male(s)/female
total population: 0.98 male(s)/female (2004 est.)

Infant mortality rate:
total: 4.63 deaths/1,000 live births
male: 4.65 deaths/1,000 live births
female: 4.6 deaths/1,000 live births (2004 est.)

Life expectancy at birth:
total population: 77.44 years
male: 75.17 years
female: 79.83 years (2004 est.)

Total fertility rate: 1.74 children born/woman (2004 est.)

HIV/AIDS - adult prevalence rate: 0.2% (2001 est.)

HIV/AIDS - people living with HIV/AIDS: 3,800 (2001 est.)

HIV/AIDS - deaths: less than 100 (2001 est.)

Nationality:
noun: Dane(s)
adjective: Danish

Ethnic groups: Scandinavian, Inuit, Faroese, German, Turkish, Iranian, Somali

Religions: Evangelical Lutheran 95%, other Protestant and Roman Catholic 3%, Muslim 2%

Languages: Danish, Faroese, Greenlandic (an Inuit dialect), German (small minority)
note: English is the predominant second language

Literacy:
definition: age 15 and over can read and write
total population: 100%
male: NA%
female: NA%

Government

Country name:
conventional long form: Kingdom of Denmark
conventional short form: Denmark
local long form: Kongeriget Danmark
local short form: Danmark

Government type: constitutional monarchy

Capital: Copenhagen

Administrative divisions: metropolitan Denmark - 14 counties (amter, singular - amt) and 2 boroughs* (amtskommuner, singular - amtskomunes); Arhus, Bornholm, Fredericksberg*, Frederiksborg, Fyn, Kobenhavn, Kobenhavns*, Nordjylland, Ribe, Ringkobing, Roskilde, Sonderjylland, Storstrom, Vejle, Vestsjalland, Viborg
note: see separate entries for the Faroe Islands and Greenland, which are part of the Kingdom of Denmark and are self-governing overseas administrative divisions

Independence: first organized as a unified state in 10th century; in 1849 became a constitutional monarchy

National holiday: none designated; Constitution Day, 5 June is generally viewed as the National Day

Constitution: 1849 was the original constitution; there was a major overhaul 5 June 1953, allowing for a unicameral legislature and a female chief of state

Legal system: civil law system; judicial review of legislative acts; accepts compulsory ICJ jurisdiction, with reservations

Suffrage: 18 years of age; universal

Denmark *(continued)*

Executive branch:
chief of state: Queen MARGRETHE II (since 14 January 1972); Heir Apparent Crown Prince FREDERIK, elder son of the monarch (born 26 May 1968)
head of government: Prime Minister Anders Fogh RASMUSSEN (since 27 November 2001)
cabinet: Cabinet appointed by the prime minister and approved by Parliament
elections: none; the monarch is hereditary; following legislative elections, the leader of the majority party or the leader of the majority coalition is usually appointed prime minister by the monarch
Legislative branch: unicameral Parliament or Folketing (179 seats, including 2 from Greenland and 2 from the Faroe Islands; members are elected by popular vote on the basis of proportional representation to serve four-year terms)
elections: last held 20 November 2001 (next to be held by November 2005)
election results: percent of vote by party - Liberal Party 31%, Social Democrats 29%, Danish People's Party 12%, Conservative Party 9%, Socialist People's Party 6%, Social Liberal Party 5%, Christian People's Party (now Christian Democrats) 2%, Unity List 2%; seats by party - Liberal Party 56, Social Democrats 52, Danish People's Party 22, Conservative Party 16, Socialist People's Party 12, Social Liberal Party 9, Christian People's Party (now Christian Democrats) 4, Unity List 4; note - does not include the 2 seats from Greenland and the 2 seats from the Faroe Islands
Judicial branch: Supreme Court (judges are appointed by the monarch for life)
Political parties and leaders: Center Democratic Party [Mimi JAKOBSEN]; Christian Democrats (was Christian People's Party) [Marianne KARLSMOSE]; Conservative Party (sometimes known as Conservative People's Party) [Bendt BENDTSEN]; Danish People's Party [Pia KJAERSGAARD]; Liberal Party [Anders Fogh RASMUSSEN]; Social Democratic Party [Mogens LYKKETOFT]; Social Liberal Party (sometimes called the Radical Left) [Marianne JELVED, leader; Johannes LEBECH, chairman]; Socialist People's Party [Holger K. NIELSEN]; Red-Green Unity List (bloc includes Left Socialist Party, Communist Party of Denmark, Socialist Workers' Party) [collective leadership]
Political pressure groups and leaders: NA
International organization participation: AfDB, AsDB, Australia Group, BIS, CBSS, CE, CERN, EAPC, EBRD, EIB, ESA, EU, FAO, G- 9, IADB, IAEA, IBRD, ICAO, ICC, ICCt, ICFTU, ICRM, IDA, IEA, IFAD, IFC, IFRCS, IHO, ILO, IMF, IMO, Interpol, IOC, IOM, ISO, ITU, MONUC, NATO, NC, NEA, NIB, NSG, OAS (observer), OECD, OPCW, OSCE, Paris Club, PCA, UN, UNAMSIL, UNCTAD, UNESCO, UNHCR, UNIDO, UNMEE, UNMIK, UNMIL, UNMISET, UNMOGIP, UNOMIG, UNTSO, UPU, WCO, WEU (observer), WHO, WIPO, WMO, WTrO, ZC
Diplomatic representation in the US:
chief of mission: Ambassador Ulrik Andreas FEDERSPIEL

chancery: 3200 Whitehaven Street NW, Washington, DC 20008
telephone: [1] (202) 234-4300
FAX: [1] (202) 328-1470
consulate(s) general: Chicago and New York
Diplomatic representation from the US:
chief of mission: Ambassador Stuart A. BERNSTEIN
embassy: Dag Hammarskjolds Alle 24, 2100 Copenhagen
mailing address: PSC 73, APO AE 09716
telephone: [45] 35 55 31 44
FAX: [45] 35 43 02 23
Flag description: red with a white cross that extends to the edges of the flag; the vertical part of the cross is shifted to the hoist side, and that design element of the Dannebrog (Danish flag) was subsequently adopted by the other Nordic countries of Finland, Iceland, Norway, and Sweden

Economy

Economy - overview: This thoroughly modern market economy features high-tech agriculture, up-to-date small-scale and corporate industry, extensive government welfare measures, comfortable living standards, a stable currency, and high dependence on foreign trade. Denmark is a net exporter of food and energy and enjoys a comfortable balance of payments surplus. Government objectives include streamlining the bureaucracy and further privatization of state assets. The government has been successful in meeting, and even exceeding, the economic convergence criteria for participating in the third phase (a common European currency) of the European Economic and Monetary Union (EMU), but Denmark has decided not to join 12 other EU members in the euro; even so, the Danish Krone remains pegged to the euro. Given the sluggish state of the European economy, growth in 2003 was a mere 0.3%.
GDP: purchasing power parity - $167.7 billion (2003 est.)
GDP - real growth rate: 0.3% (2003 est.)
GDP - per capita: purchasing power parity - $31,200 (2003 est.)
GDP - composition by sector:
agriculture: 3%
industry: 26%
services: 71% (2002 est.)
Population below poverty line: NA%
Household income or consumption by percentage share:
lowest 10%: 2%
highest 10%: 24% (2000 est.)
Distribution of family income - Gini index: 24.7 (1992)
Inflation rate (consumer prices): 2.1% (2003 est.)
Labor force: 2.856 million (2000 est.)
Labor force - by occupation: services 79%, industry 17%, agriculture 4% (2002 est.)

Unemployment rate: 6% (2003)
Budget:
revenues: $52.9 billion
expenditures: $51.3 billion, including capital expenditures of $500 million (2001 est.)
Industries: food processing, machinery and equipment, textiles and clothing, chemical products, electronics, construction, furniture and other wood products, shipbuilding, windmills
Industrial production growth rate: 1.4% (2002 est.)
Electricity - production: 35.47 billion kWh (2001)
Electricity - production by source:
fossil fuel: 82.7%
hydro: 0.1%
nuclear: 0%
other: 17.3% (2001)
Electricity - consumption: 32.41 billion kWh (2001)
Electricity - exports: 8.775 billion kWh (2001)
Electricity - imports: 8.199 billion kWh (2001)
Oil - production: 346,200 bbl/day (2001 est.)
Oil - consumption: 218,000 bbl/day (2001 est.)
Oil - exports: 332,100 bbl/day (2001)
Oil - imports: 195,000 bbl/day (2001)
Oil - proved reserves: 1.23 billion bbl (1 January 2002)
Natural gas - production: 8.38 billion cu m (2001 est.)
Natural gas - consumption: 5.28 billion cu m (2001 est.)
Natural gas - exports: 3.1 billion cu m (2001 est.)
Natural gas - imports: 0 cu m (2001 est.)
Natural gas - proved reserves: 81.98 billion cu m (1 January 2002)
Agriculture - products: barley, wheat, potatoes, sugar beets; pork, dairy products; fish
Exports: $64.16 billion f.o.b. (2003 est.)
Exports - commodities: machinery and instruments, meat and meat products, dairy products, fish, chemicals, furniture, ships, windmills
Exports - partners: Germany 19.4%, Sweden 11.8%, UK 9.8%, US 6.4%, Norway 6%, France 4.7%, Netherlands 4.5% (2002)
Imports: $54.47 billion f.o.b. (2003 est.)
Imports - commodities: machinery and equipment, raw materials and semimanufactures for industry, chemicals, grain and foodstuffs, consumer goods
Imports - partners: Germany 22.3%, Sweden 12.1%, UK 8.9%, Netherlands 6.8%, France 6%, Norway 4.7%, Italy 4.3% (2002)
Debt - external: $21.7 billion (2000)
Economic aid - donor: ODA, $1.63 billion (1999)
Currency: Danish krone (DKK)
Currency code: DKK
Exchange rates: Danish kroner per US dollar - 6.5877 (2003), 7.8947 (2002), 8.3228 (2001), 8.0831 (2000), 6.9762 (1999)
Fiscal year: calendar year

Denmark (continued)

Communications

Telephones - main lines in use: 3,700,900 (2002)
Telephones - mobile cellular: 4,477,800 (2002)
Telephone system:
general assessment: excellent telephone and telegraph services
domestic: buried and submarine cables and microwave radio relay form trunk network, 4 cellular mobile communications systems
international: country code - 45; 18 submarine fiber-optic cables linking Denmark with Canada, Faroe Islands, Germany, Iceland, Netherlands, Norway, Poland, Russia, Sweden, and UK; satellite earth stations - 6 Intelsat, 10 Eutelsat, 1 Orion, 1 Inmarsat (Blaavand-Atlantic-East); note - the Nordic countries (Denmark, Finland, Iceland, Norway, and Sweden) share the Danish earth station and the Eik, Norway, station for worldwide Inmarsat access (1997)
Radio broadcast stations: AM 2, FM 355, shortwave 0 (1998)
Television broadcast stations: 26 (plus 51 repeaters) (1998)
Internet country code: .dk
Internet hosts: 836,631 (2002)
Internet users: 2.756 million (2002)

Transportation

Railways:
total: 3,164 km
standard gauge: 2,324 km 1.435-m gauge (595 km electrified)
note: total includes 840 km of suburban track (2002)
Highways:
total: 71,591 km
paved: 71,591 km (including 880 km of expressways)
unpaved: 0 km (2000)
Waterways: 417 km
Pipelines: condensate 12 km; gas 3,892 km; oil 455 km; oil/gas/water 2 km; unknown (oil/water) 64 km (2003)
Ports and harbors: Aabenraa, Aalborg, Aarhus, Copenhagen, Esbjerg, Fredericia, Frederikshavn, Hirtshals, Kolding, Odense, Roenne (Bornholm), Vejle
Merchant marine:
total: 276 ships (1,000 GRT or over) 6,952,473 GRT/9,030,444 DWT
by type: bulk 4, cargo 77, chemical tanker 36, container 83, liquefied gas 15, livestock carrier 5, petroleum tanker 27, rail car carrier 1, refrigerated cargo 8, roll on/roll off 11, short-sea/passenger 5, specialized tanker 4
foreign-owned: Germany 1, Greece 1, Indonesia 2, Norway 5
registered in other countries: 284 (2003 est.)
Airports: 99 (2003 est.)
Airports - with paved runways:
total: 28
over 3,047 m: 2
2,438 to 3,047 m: 7
1,524 to 2,437 m: 4
914 to 1,523 m: 12
under 914 m: 3 (2003 est.)
Airports - with unpaved runways:
total: 71
914 to 1,523 m: 6
under 914 m: 65 (2003 est.)

Military

Military branches: Royal Danish Army, Royal Danish Navy, Royal Danish Air Force, Home Guard
Military manpower - military age: 18 years of age; note - conscripts serve an initial training period that varies from four to 12 months according to specialization; following their conscript service, reservists are assigned to mobilization units (2004 est.)
Military manpower - availability:
males age 15-49: 1,276,087 (2004 est.)
Military manpower - fit for military service:
males age 15-49: 1,088,751 (2004 est.)
Military manpower - reaching military age annually:
males: 30,333 (2004 est.)
Military expenditures - dollar figure: $3,271,600,000 (2003)
Military expenditures - percent of GDP: 1.6% (2003)

Transnational Issues

Disputes - international: Rockall continental shelf dispute involving Denmark, Iceland, and the UK (Ireland and the UK have signed a boundary agreement in the Rockall area) remains dormant; dispute with Iceland over the Faroe Islands' fisheries median line boundary within 200 NM; disputes with Iceland, the UK, and Ireland over the Faroe Islands continental shelf boundary outside 200 NM; Faroese continue to study proposals for full independence; uncontested dispute with Canada over Hans Island sovereignty in the Kennedy Channel between Ellesmere Island and Greenland

Djibouti

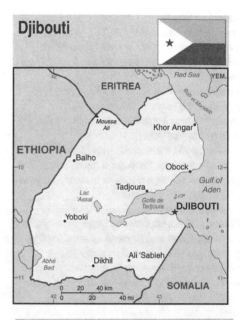

Introduction

Background: The French Territory of the Afars and the Issas became Djibouti in 1977. Hassan Gouled APTIDON installed an authoritarian one-party state and proceeded to serve three consecutive six-year terms as president. Unrest among the Afars minority during the 1990s led to multi-party elections resulting in President Ismail Omar GUELLEH attaining office in May 1999. A peace accord in 2001 ended the final phases of a ten-year uprising by Afar rebels. Djibouti occupies a very strategic geographic location at the mouth of the Red Sea and serves as an important transshipment location for goods entering and leaving the east African highlands. GUELLEH favors close ties to France, which maintains a significant military presence in the country.

Geography

Location: Eastern Africa, bordering the Gulf of Aden and the Red Sea, between Eritrea and Somalia
Geographic coordinates: 11 30 N, 43 00 E
Map references: Africa
Area:
total: 23,000 sq km
land: 22,980 sq km
water: 20 sq km
Area - comparative: slightly smaller than Massachusetts
Land boundaries:
total: 516 km
border countries: Eritrea 109 km, Ethiopia 349 km, Somalia 58 km
Coastline: 314 km
Maritime claims:
territorial sea: 12 NM
contiguous zone: 24 NM
exclusive economic zone: 200 NM
Climate: desert; torrid, dry
Terrain: coastal plain and plateau separated by central mountains

Djibouti (continued)

Elevation extremes:
lowest point: Lac Assal -155 m
highest point: Moussa Ali 2,028 m
Natural resources: geothermal areas
Land use:
arable land: 0%
permanent crops: 0%
other: 100% (1998 est.)
Irrigated land: 10 sq km (1998 est.)
Natural hazards: earthquakes; droughts; occasional cyclonic disturbances from the Indian Ocean bring heavy rains and flash floods
Environment - current issues: inadequate supplies of potable water; limited arable land; desertification; endangered species
Environment - international agreements:
party to: Biodiversity, Climate Change, Climate Change-Kyoto Protocol, Desertification, Endangered Species, Hazardous Wastes, Law of the Sea, Ozone Layer Protection, Ship Pollution
signed, but not ratified: none of the selected agreements
Geography - note: strategic location near world's busiest shipping lanes and close to Arabian oilfields; terminus of rail traffic into Ethiopia; mostly wasteland; Lac Assal (Lake Assal) is the lowest point in Africa

People

Population: 466,900 (July 2004 est.)
Age structure:
0-14 years: 43.2% (male 101,168; female 100,545)
15-64 years: 53.7% (male 131,320; female 119,387)
65 years and over: 3.1% (male 7,327; female 7,153) (2004 est.)
Median age:
total: 18.3 years
male: 18.8 years
female: 17.7 years (2004 est.)
Population growth rate: 2.1% (2004 est.)
Birth rate: 40.39 births/1,000 population (2004 est.)
Death rate: 19.42 deaths/1,000 population (2004 est.)
Net migration rate: 0 migrant(s)/1,000 population (2004 est.)
Sex ratio:
at birth: 1.03 male(s)/female
under 15 years: 1.01 male(s)/female
15-64 years: 1.1 male(s)/female
65 years and over: 1.02 male(s)/female
total population: 1.06 male(s)/female (2004 est.)
Infant mortality rate:
total: 105.54 deaths/1,000 live births
male: 113.3 deaths/1,000 live births
female: 97.54 deaths/1,000 live births (2004 est.)
Life expectancy at birth:
total population: 43.12 years
male: 41.83 years
female: 44.44 years (2004 est.)
Total fertility rate: 5.48 children born/woman (2004 est.)

HIV/AIDS - adult prevalence rate: 11.75% (2001 est.)
HIV/AIDS - people living with HIV/AIDS: 37,000 (2001 est.)
HIV/AIDS - deaths: 2,000 (2001 est.)
Nationality:
noun: Djiboutian(s)
adjective: Djiboutian
Ethnic groups: Somali 60%, Afar 35%, French, Arab, Ethiopian, and Italian 5%
Religions: Muslim 94%, Christian 6%
Languages: French (official), Arabic (official), Somali, Afar
Literacy:
definition: age 15 and over can read and write
total population: 67.9%
male: 78%
female: 58.4% (2003 est.)

Government

Country name:
conventional long form: Republic of Djibouti
conventional short form: Djibouti
former: French Territory of the Afars and Issas, French Somaliland
Government type: republic
Capital: Djibouti
Administrative divisions: 5 districts (cercles, singular - cercle); 'Ali Sabih, Dikhil, Djibouti, Obock, Tadjoura
Independence: 27 June 1977 (from France)
National holiday: Independence Day, 27 June (1977)
Constitution: multiparty constitution approved by referendum 4 September 1992
Legal system: based on French civil law system, traditional practices, and Islamic law
Suffrage: 18 years of age; universal adult
Executive branch:
chief of state: President Ismail Omar GUELLEH (since 8 May 1999)
head of government: Prime Minister DILEITA Mohamed Dileita (since 4 March 2001)
cabinet: Council of Ministers responsible to the president
elections: president elected by popular vote for a six-year term; election last held 9 April 1999 (next to be held NA 2005); prime minister appointed by the president
election results: Ismail Omar GUELLEH elected president; percent of vote - Ismail Omar GUELLEH 74.4%, IDRIS Moussa Ahmed 25.6%
Legislative branch: unicameral Chamber of Deputies or Chambre des Deputes (65 seats; members elected by popular vote for five-year terms)
elections: last held 10 January 2003 (next to be held NA January 2008)
election results: percent of vote - RPP 62.2%, FRUD 36.9%; seats - RPP 65, FRUD 0; note - RPP (the ruling party) dominated the election
Judicial branch: Supreme Court or Cour Supreme

Political parties and leaders: Democratic National Party or PND [ADEN Robleh Awaleh]; Democratic Renewal Party or PRD [Abdillahi HAMARITEH]; Djibouti Development Party or PDD [Mohamed Daoud CHEHEM]; Front pour la Restauration de l'Unite Democratique or FRUD [Ali Mohamed DAOUD]; People's Progress Assembly or RPP (governing party) [Ismail Omar GUELLEH]; Peoples Social Democratic Party or PPSD [Moumin Bahdon FARAH]; Republican Alliance for Democracy or ARD [Ahmed Dini AHMED]; Union for Democracy and Justice or UDJ [leader NA]
Political pressure groups and leaders: Union for Presidential Majority UMP (coalition includes RPP, FRUD, PPSD and PND); Union for Democratic Changeover or UAD (opposition coalition includes ARD, MRDD, UDJ, and PDD) [Ahmed Dini AHMED]
International organization participation: ACCT, ACP, AfDB, AFESD, AMF, AU, FAO, G-77, IBRD, ICAO, ICCt, ICFTU, ICRM, IDA, IDB, IFAD, IFC, IFRCS, IGAD, ILO, IMF, IMO, Interpol, IOC, ITU, LAS, NAM, OIC, OPCW (signatory), UN, UNCTAD, UNESCO, UNIDO, UPU, WFTU, WHO, WIPO, WMO, WToO, WTrO
Diplomatic representation in the US:
chief of mission: Ambassador ROBLE Olhaye
chancery: Suite 515, 1156 15th Street NW, Washington, DC 20005
telephone: [1] (202) 331-0270
FAX: [1] (202) 331-0302
Diplomatic representation from the US:
chief of mission: Ambassador Marguerita RAGSDALE
embassy: Plateau du Serpent, Boulevard Marechal Joffre, Djibouti
mailing address: B. P. 185, Djibouti
telephone: [253] 35 39 95
FAX: [253] 35 39 40
Flag description: two equal horizontal bands of light blue (top) and light green with a white isosceles triangle based on the hoist side bearing a red five-pointed star in the center

Economy

Economy - overview: The economy is based on service activities connected with the country's strategic location and status as a free trade zone in northeast Africa. Two-thirds of the inhabitants live in the capital city, the remainder being mostly nomadic herders. Scanty rainfall limits crop production to fruits and vegetables, and most food must be imported. Djibouti provides services as both a transit port for the region and an international transshipment and refueling center. It has few natural resources and little industry. The nation is, therefore, heavily dependent on foreign assistance to help support its balance of payments and to finance development projects. An unemployment rate of 50% continues to be a major problem. Inflation is not a concern, however, because of the fixed tie of the franc to the US dollar. Per capita

Djibouti *(continued)*

consumption dropped an estimated 35% over the last seven years because of recession, civil war, and a high population growth rate (including immigrants and refugees). Faced with a multitude of economic difficulties, the government has fallen in arrears on long-term external debt and has been struggling to meet the stipulations of foreign aid donors.

GDP: purchasing power parity - $619 million (2002 est.)

GDP - real growth rate: 3.5% (2002 est.)

GDP - per capita: purchasing power parity - $1,300 (2002 est.)

GDP - composition by sector:
agriculture: 3.5%
industry: 15.8%
services: 80.7% (2001 est.)

Population below poverty line: 50% (2001 est.)

Household income or consumption by percentage share:
lowest 10%: NA%
highest 10%: NA%

Inflation rate (consumer prices): 2% (2002 est.)

Labor force: 282,000 (2000)

Labor force - by occupation: NA%

Unemployment rate: 50% (2000 est.)

Budget:
revenues: $135 million
expenditures: $182 million, including capital expenditures of $NA (1999 est.)

Industries: construction, agricultural processing

Industrial production growth rate: 3% (1996 est.)

Electricity - production: 180 million kWh (2001)

Electricity - production by source:
fossil fuel: 100%
hydro: 0%
nuclear: 0%
other: 0% (2001)

Electricity - consumption: 167.4 million kWh (2001)

Electricity - exports: 0 kWh (2001)

Electricity - imports: 0 kWh (2001)

Oil - production: 0 bbl/day (2001 est.)

Oil - consumption: 11,300 bbl/day (2001 est.)

Oil - exports: NA

Oil - imports: NA

Agriculture - products: fruits, vegetables; goats, sheep, camels

Exports: $155 million f.o.b. (2002 est.)

Exports - commodities: reexports, hides and skins, coffee (in transit)

Exports - partners: Somalia 61.9%, Yemen 21.9%, Pakistan 5.2%, Ethiopia 4.5% (2002)

Imports: $665 million f.o.b. (2002 est.)

Imports - commodities: foods, beverages, transport equipment, chemicals, petroleum products

Imports - partners: Saudi Arabia 18.2%, Ethiopia 10.5%, US 9.3%, France 8.6%, China 8.3%, Netherlands 4.2% (2002)

Debt - external: $366 million (2002 est.)

Economic aid - recipient: $36 million (2001)

Currency: Djiboutian franc (DJF)

Currency code: DJF

Exchange rates: Djiboutian francs per US dollar - 177.721 (2003), 177.721 (2002), 177.721 (2001), 177.721 (2000), 177.721 (1999)

Fiscal year: calendar year

Communications

Telephones - main lines in use: 10,100 (2002)

Telephones - mobile cellular: 15,000 (2002)

Telephone system:
general assessment: telephone facilities in the city of Djibouti are adequate as are the microwave radio relay connections to outlying areas of the country
domestic: microwave radio relay network
international: country code - 253; submarine cable to Jiddah, Suez, Sicily, Marseilles, Colombo, and Singapore; satellite earth stations - 1 Intelsat (Indian Ocean) and 1 Arabsat; Medarabtel regional microwave radio relay telephone network

Radio broadcast stations: AM 1, FM 2, shortwave 0 (2001)

Television broadcast stations: 1 (2002)

Internet country code: .dj

Internet hosts: 498 (2002)

Internet users: 4,500 (2002)

Transportation

Railways:
total: 100 km (Djibouti segment of the Addis Ababa-Djibouti railway)
narrow gauge: 100 km 1.000-m gauge
note: railway under joint control of Djibouti and Ethiopia (2002)

Highways:
total: 2,890 km
paved: 364 km
unpaved: 2,526 km (1999 est.)

Waterways: none

Ports and harbors: Djibouti

Merchant marine:
total: 1 ships (1,000 GRT or over) 1,369 GRT/3,030 DWT
by type: cargo 1 (2003 est.)

Airports: 13 (2003 est.)

Airports - with paved runways:
total: 3
over 3,047 m: 1
2,438 to 3,047 m: 1
1524 to 2437 m: 1 (2003 est.)

Airports - with unpaved runways:
total: 10
1,524 to 2,437 m: 2
914 to 1,523 m: 5
under 914 m: 3 (2003 est.)

Military

Military branches: Djibouti National Army (including Navy and Air Force)

Military manpower - availability:
males age 15-49: 108,771 (2004 est.)

Military manpower - fit for military service:
males age 15-49: 64,540 (2004 est.)

Military expenditures - dollar figure: $26.5 million (2003)

Military expenditures - percent of GDP: 4.4% (2003)

Transnational Issues

Disputes - international: Djibouti maintains economic ties and border accords with "Somaliland" leadership while maintaining some political ties to various factions in Somalia including the Somali Transitional National Government in Mogadishu

Dominica

Introduction

Background: Dominica was the last of the Caribbean islands to be colonized by Europeans, due chiefly to the fierce resistance of the native Caribs. France ceded possession to Great Britain in 1763, which made the island a colony in 1805. In 1980, two years after independence, Dominica's fortunes improved when a corrupt and tyrannical administration was replaced by that of Mary Eugenia CHARLES, the first female prime minister in the Caribbean, who remained in office for 15 years. Some 3,000 Carib Indians still living on Dominica are the only pre-Columbian population remaining in the eastern Caribbean.

Geography

Location: Caribbean, island between the Caribbean Sea and the North Atlantic Ocean, about one-half of the way from Puerto Rico to Trinidad and Tobago
Geographic coordinates: 15 25 N, 61 20 W
Map references: Central America and the Caribbean
Area:
total: 754 sq km
land: 754 sq km
water: 0 sq km
Area - comparative: slightly more than four times the size of Washington, DC
Land boundaries: 0 km
Coastline: 148 km
Maritime claims:
territorial sea: 12 NM
contiguous zone: 24 NM
exclusive economic zone: 200 NM
Climate: tropical; moderated by northeast trade winds; heavy rainfall
Terrain: rugged mountains of volcanic origin

Elevation extremes:
lowest point: Caribbean Sea 0 m
highest point: Morne Diablatins 1,447 m
Natural resources: timber, hydropower, arable land
Land use:
arable land: 4%
permanent crops: 16%
other: 80% (1998 est.)
Irrigated land: NA sq km
Natural hazards: flash floods are a constant threat; destructive hurricanes can be expected during the late summer months
Environment - current issues: NA
Environment - international agreements:
party to: Biodiversity, Climate Change, Desertification, Endangered Species, Environmental Modification, Hazardous Wastes, Law of the Sea, Ozone Layer Protection, Ship Pollution, Whaling
signed, but not ratified: none of the selected agreements
Geography - note: known as "The Nature Island of the Caribbean" due to its spectacular, lush, and varied flora and fauna, which are protected by an extensive natural park system; the most mountainous of the Lesser Antilles, its volcanic peaks are cones of lava craters and include Boiling Lake, the second-largest, thermally active lake in the world

People

Population: 69,278 (July 2004 est.)
Age structure:
0-14 years: 27.3% (male 9,563; female 9,349)
15-64 years: 64.8% (male 23,097; female 21,804)
65 years and over: 7.9% (male 2,209; female 3,256) (2004 est.)
Median age:
total: 29 years
male: 28.7 years
female: 29.4 years (2004 est.)
Population growth rate: -0.45% (2004 est.)
Birth rate: 16.25 births/1,000 population (2004 est.)
Death rate: 6.9 deaths/1,000 population (2004 est.)
Net migration rate: -13.87 migrant(s)/1,000 population (2004 est.)
Sex ratio:
at birth: 1.05 male(s)/female
under 15 years: 1.02 male(s)/female
15-64 years: 1.06 male(s)/female
65 years and over: 0.68 male(s)/female
total population: 1.01 male(s)/female (2004 est.)
Infant mortality rate:
total: 14.75 deaths/1,000 live births
male: 19.49 deaths/1,000 live births
female: 9.77 deaths/1,000 live births (2004 est.)
Life expectancy at birth:
total population: 74.38 years
male: 71.48 years
female: 77.43 years (2004 est.)
Total fertility rate: 1.98 children born/woman (2004 est.)

HIV/AIDS - adult prevalence rate: NA%
HIV/AIDS - people living with HIV/AIDS: NA
HIV/AIDS - deaths: NA
Nationality:
noun: Dominican(s)
adjective: Dominican
Ethnic groups: black, mixed black and European, European, Syrian, Carib Amerindian
Religions: Roman Catholic 77%, Protestant 15% (Methodist 5%, Pentecostal 3%, Seventh-Day Adventist 3%, Baptist 2%, other 2%), none 2%, other 6%
Languages: English (official), French patois
Literacy:
definition: age 15 and over has ever attended school
total population: 94%
male: 94%
female: 94% (2003 est.)

Government

Country name:
conventional long form: Commonwealth of Dominica
conventional short form: Dominica
Government type: parliamentary democracy; republic within the Commonwealth
Capital: Roseau
Administrative divisions: 10 parishes; Saint Andrew, Saint David, Saint George, Saint John, Saint Joseph, Saint Luke, Saint Mark, Saint Patrick, Saint Paul, Saint Peter
Independence: 3 November 1978 (from UK)
National holiday: Independence Day, 3 November (1978)
Constitution: 3 November 1978
Legal system: based on English common law
Suffrage: 18 years of age; universal
Executive branch:
chief of state: President Nicholas J. O. LIVERPOOL (since October 2003)
head of government: Prime Minister Roosevelt SKERRIT (since 8 January 2004); note - assumed post after death of Prime Minister Pierre CHARLES
cabinet: Cabinet appointed by the president on the advice of the prime minister
elections: president elected by the House of Assembly for a five-year term; election last held 1 October 2003 (next to be held NA October 2008); prime minister appointed by the president
election results: Nicholas LIVERPOOL elected president; percent of legislative vote - NA%
Legislative branch: unicameral House of Assembly (30 seats, 9 appointed senators, 21 elected by popular vote; members serve five-year terms)
elections: last held 31 January 2000 (next to be held by 17 July 2005); note - tradition dictates that the election will be held within five years of the last election, but technically it is five years from the first seating of parliament (17 April 2000) plus a 90 day grace period
election results: percent of vote by party - NA%; seats by party - DLP 10, UWP 9, DFP 2

Dominica (continued)

Judicial branch: Eastern Caribbean Supreme Court, consisting of the Court of Appeal and the High Court (located in Saint Lucia; one of the six judges must reside in Dominica and preside over the Court of Summary Jurisdiction)

Political parties and leaders: Dominica Freedom Party or DFP [Charles SAVARIN]; Dominica Labor Party or DLP [Roosevelt SKERRIT]; United Workers Party or UWP [Edison JAMES]

Political pressure groups and leaders: Dominica Liberation Movement or DLM (a small leftist party)

International organization participation: ACCT, ACP, C, Caricom, CDB, FAO, G-77, IBRD, ICCt, ICFTU, ICRM, IDA, IFAD, IFC, IFRCS, ILO, IMF, IMO, Interpol, IOC, ISO (subscriber), ITU, NAM (observer), OAS, OECS, OPANAL, OPCW, UN, UNCTAD, UNESCO, UNIDO, UPU, WCL, WHO, WIPO, WMO, WTrO

Diplomatic representation in the US:
chief of mission: Ambassador Swinburne LESTRADE
chancery: 3216 New Mexico Avenue NW, Washington, DC 20016
telephone: [1] (202) 364-6781
FAX: [1] (202) 364-6791
consulate(s) general: New York

Diplomatic representation from the US: the US does not have an embassy in Dominica; the US Ambassador to Barbados, Ambassador Mary E. KRAMER, is accredited to Dominica

Flag description: green, with a centered cross of three equal bands - the vertical part is yellow (hoist side), black, and white and the horizontal part is yellow (top), black, and white; superimposed in the center of the cross is a red disk bearing a sisserou parrot encircled by 10 green, five-pointed stars edged in yellow; the 10 stars represent the 10 administrative divisions (parishes)

Economy

Economy - overview: The Dominican economy depends on agriculture, primarily bananas, and remains highly vulnerable to climatic conditions and international economic developments. Production of bananas dropped precipitously in 2003, a major reason for the 1% decline in GDP. Tourism increased in 2003 as the government sought to promote Dominica as an "ecotourism" destination. Development of the tourism industry remains difficult, however, because of the rugged coastline, lack of beaches, and the absence of an international airport. The government began a comprehensive restructuring of the economy in 2003 - including elimination of price controls, privatization of the state banana company, and tax increases - to address Dominica's economic crisis and to meet IMF targets. In order to diversify the island's production base the government is attempting to develop an offshore financial sector and is planning to construct an oil refinery on the eastern part of the island.

GDP: purchasing power parity - $380 million (2002 est.)

GDP - real growth rate: -1% (2003 est.)

GDP - per capita: purchasing power parity - $5,400 (2002 est.)

GDP - composition by sector:
agriculture: 18%
industry: 24%
services: 58% (2002 est.)

Population below poverty line: 30% (2002 est.)

Household income or consumption by percentage share:
lowest 10%: NA%
highest 10%: NA%

Inflation rate (consumer prices): 1% (2001 est.)

Labor force: 25,000 (1999 est.)

Labor force - by occupation: agriculture 40%, industry and commerce 32%, services 28%

Unemployment rate: 23% (2000 est.)

Budget:
revenues: $73.9 million
expenditures: $84.4 million, including capital expenditures of $NA (2001)

Industries: soap, coconut oil, tourism, copra, furniture, cement blocks, shoes

Industrial production growth rate: -10% (1997 est.)

Electricity - production: 72.41 million kWh (2001)

Electricity - production by source:
fossil fuel: 47.1%
hydro: 52.9%
nuclear: 0%
other: 0% (2001)

Electricity - consumption: 67.35 million kWh (2001)

Electricity - exports: 0 kWh (2001)

Electricity - imports: 0 kWh (2001)

Oil - production: 0 bbl/day (2001 est.)

Oil - consumption: 600 bbl/day (2001 est.)

Oil - exports: NA

Oil - imports: NA

Agriculture - products: bananas, citrus, mangoes, root crops, coconuts, cocoa; forest and fishery potential not exploited

Exports: $39 million f.o.b. (2003 est.)

Exports - commodities: bananas, soap, bay oil, vegetables, grapefruit, oranges

Exports - partners: UK 36.1%, Jamaica 16.4%, US 8.2%, Antigua and Barbuda 6.6%, Guyana 4.9%, Trinidad and Tobago 4.9% (2002)

Imports: $98.2 million f.o.b. (2003 est.)

Imports - commodities: manufactured goods, machinery and equipment, food, chemicals

Imports - partners: China 23.8%, US 23.8%, Trinidad and Tobago 11.9%, South Korea 7.6%, UK 7.1%, Japan 4.3% (2002)

Debt - external: $161.5 million (2001)

Economic aid - recipient: $22.8 million (2003 est.)

Currency: East Caribbean dollar (XCD)

Currency code: XCD

Exchange rates: East Caribbean dollars per US dollar - 2.7 (2003), 2.7 (2002), 2.7 (2001), 2.7 (2000), 2.7 (1999)

Fiscal year: 1 July - 30 June

Communications

Telephones - main lines in use: 23,700 (2002)
Telephones - mobile cellular: 9,400 (2002)
Telephone system:
general assessment: NA
domestic: fully automatic network
international: country code - 1-767; microwave radio relay and SHF radiotelephone links to Martinique and Guadeloupe; VHF and UHF radiotelephone links to Saint Lucia
Radio broadcast stations: AM 2, FM 4, shortwave 0 (2004)
Television broadcast stations: 1 (2004)
Internet country code: .dm
Internet hosts: 464 (2002)
Internet users: 12,500 (2002)

Transportation

Railways: 0 km
Highways:
total: 780 km
paved: 393 km
unpaved: 387 km (1999 est.)
Waterways: none
Ports and harbors: Portsmouth, Roseau
Merchant marine:
total: 6 ships (1,000 GRT or over) 13,771 GRT/19,736 DWT
by type: cargo 3, container 2, petroleum tanker 1
foreign-owned: Bahamas 1, Cyprus 1, Estonia 1, Greece 1, Panama 1, Singapore 1 (2003 est.)
Airports: 2 (2003 est.)
Airports - with paved runways:
total: 2
914 to 1,523 m: 2 (2003 est.)

Military

Military branches: no regular military forces; Commonwealth of Dominica Police Force (including Coast Guard)
Military expenditures - dollar figure: NA
Military expenditures - percent of GDP: NA

Transnational Issues

Disputes - international: joins other Caribbean states to counter Venezuela's claim that Aves Island sustains human habitation, a criterion under UNCLOS, which permits Venezuela to extend its EEZ/continental shelf over a large portion of the Caribbean Sea

Illicit drugs: transshipment point for narcotics bound for the US and Europe; minor cannabis producer; anti-money-laundering enforcement is weak, making the country particularly vulnerable to money laundering

Dominican Republic

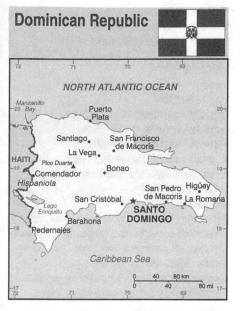

Introduction

Background: Explored and claimed by Columbus on his first voyage in 1492, the island of Hispaniola became a springboard for Spanish conquest of the Caribbean and the American mainland. In 1697, Spain recognized French dominion over the western third of the island, which in 1804 became Haiti. The remainder of the island, by then known as Santo Domingo, sought to gain its own independence in 1821, but was conquered and ruled by the Haitians for 22 years; it finally attained independence as the Dominican Republic in 1844. A legacy of unsettled, mostly non-representative, rule for much of its subsequent history was brought to an end in 1966 when Joaquin BALAGUER became president. He maintained a tight grip on power for most of the next 30 years when international reaction to flawed elections forced him to curtail his term in 1996. Since then, regular competitive elections have been held in which opposition candidates have won the presidency. The Dominican economy has had one of the fastest growth rates in the hemisphere over the past decade.

Geography

Location: Caribbean, eastern two-thirds of the island of Hispaniola, between the Caribbean Sea and the North Atlantic Ocean, east of Haiti
Geographic coordinates: 19 00 N, 70 40 W
Map references: Central America and the Caribbean
Area:
total: 48,730 sq km
land: 48,380 sq km
water: 350 sq km
Area - comparative: slightly more than twice the size of New Hampshire
Land boundaries:
total: 360 km
border countries: Haiti 360 km

Coastline: 1,288 km
Maritime claims:
territorial sea: 6 NM
contiguous zone: 24 NM
exclusive economic zone: 200 NM
continental shelf: 200 NM or to the edge of the continental margin
Climate: tropical maritime; little seasonal temperature variation; seasonal variation in rainfall
Terrain: rugged highlands and mountains with fertile valleys interspersed
Elevation extremes:
lowest point: Lago Enriquillo -46 m
highest point: Pico Duarte 3,175 m
Natural resources: nickel, bauxite, gold, silver
Land use:
arable land: 21.08%
permanent crops: 9.92%
other: 69% (1998 est.)
Irrigated land: 2,590 sq km (1998 est.)
Natural hazards: lies in the middle of the hurricane belt and subject to severe storms from June to October; occasional flooding; periodic droughts
Environment - current issues: water shortages; soil eroding into the sea damages coral reefs; deforestation
Environment - international agreements:
party to: Biodiversity, Climate Change, Climate Change-Kyoto Protocol, Desertification, Endangered Species, Hazardous Wastes, Marine Dumping, Marine Life Conservation, Ozone Layer Protection, Ship Pollution
signed, but not ratified: Law of the Sea
Geography - note: shares island of Hispaniola with Haiti

People

Population: 8,833,634 (July 2004 est.)
Age structure:
0-14 years: 33.3% (male 1,502,062; female 1,435,135)
15-64 years: 61.4% (male 2,767,880; female 2,658,861)
65 years and over: 5.3% (male 219,230; female 250,466) (2004 est.)
Median age:
total: 23.7 years
male: 23.5 years
female: 23.9 years (2004 est.)
Population growth rate: 1.33% (2004 est.)
Birth rate: 23.6 births/1,000 population (2004 est.)
Death rate: 7.1 deaths/1,000 population (2004 est.)
Net migration rate: -3.22 migrant(s)/1,000 population (2004 est.)
Sex ratio:
at birth: 1.05 male(s)/female
under 15 years: 1.05 male(s)/female
15-64 years: 1.04 male(s)/female
65 years and over: 0.88 male(s)/female
total population: 1.03 male(s)/female (2004 est.)

Infant mortality rate:
total: 33.28 deaths/1,000 live births
male: 35.75 deaths/1,000 live births
female: 30.68 deaths/1,000 live births (2004 est.)
Life expectancy at birth:
total population: 67.63 years
male: 65.98 years
female: 69.35 years (2004 est.)
Total fertility rate: 2.89 children born/woman (2004 est.)
HIV/AIDS - adult prevalence rate: 2.5% (2001 est.)
HIV/AIDS - people living with HIV/AIDS: 130,000 (2001 est.)
HIV/AIDS - deaths: 7,800 (2001 est.)
Nationality:
noun: Dominican(s)
adjective: Dominican
Ethnic groups: white 16%, black 11%, mixed 73%
Religions: Roman Catholic 95%
Languages: Spanish
Literacy:
definition: age 15 and over can read and write
total population: 84.7%
male: 84.6%
female: 84.8% (2003 est.)

Government

Country name:
conventional long form: Dominican Republic
conventional short form: none
local long form: Republica Dominicana
local short form: none
Government type: representative democracy
Capital: Santo Domingo
Administrative divisions: 31 provinces (provincias, singular - provincia) and 1 district* (distrito); Azua, Baoruco, Barahona, Dajabon, Distrito Nacional*, Duarte, Elias Pina, El Seibo, Espaillat, Hato Mayor, Independencia, La Altagracia, La Romana, La Vega, Maria Trinidad Sanchez, Monsenor Nouel, Monte Cristi, Monte Plata, Pedernales, Peravia, Puerto Plata, Salcedo, Samana, Sanchez Ramirez, San Cristobal, San Jose de Ocoa, San Juan, San Pedro de Macoris, Santiago, Santiago Rodriguez, Santo Domingo, Valverde
Independence: 27 February 1844 (from Haiti)
National holiday: Independence Day, 27 February (1844)
Constitution: 28 November 1966
Legal system: based on French civil codes; undergoing modification in 2004 towards an accusatory system
Suffrage: 18 years of age, universal and compulsory; married persons regardless of age
note: members of the armed forces and police cannot vote
Executive branch:
chief of state: President Rafael Hipolito MEJIA Dominguez (since 16 August 2000); Vice President Milagros ORTIZ-BOSCH (since 16 August 2000); note - the president is both the chief of state and head of government

Dominican Republic (continued)

head of government: President Rafael Hipolito MEJIA Dominguez (since 16 August 2000); Vice President Milagros ORTIZ-BOSCH (since 16 August 2000); note - the president is both the chief of state and head of government

cabinet: Cabinet nominated by the president

elections: president and vice president elected on the same ticket by popular vote for four-year terms; election last held 16 May 2000 (next to be held 16 May 2004)

election results: Raphael Hipolito MEJIA Dominguez elected president; percent of vote - Rafael Hipolito MEJIA Dominguez (PRD) 49.87%, Danilo MEDINA (PLD) 24.95%, Joaquin BALAGUER (PRSC) 24.6%

Legislative branch: bicameral National Congress or Congreso Nacional consists of the Senate or Senado (32 seats; members are elected by popular vote to serve four-year terms) and the Chamber of Deputies or Camara de Diputados (150 seats; members are elected by popular vote to serve four-year terms)

elections: Senate - last held 16 May 2002 (next to be held NA May 2006); Chamber of Deputies - last held 16 May 2002 (next to be held NA May 2006)

election results: Senate - percent of vote by party - NA%; seats by party - PRD 29, PLD 2, PRSC 1; Chamber of Deputies - percent of vote by party - NA%; seats by party - PRD 73, PLD 41, PRSC 36

Judicial branch: Supreme Court or Corte Suprema (judges are elected by a Council made up of members of the legislative and executive branches with the president presiding)

Political parties and leaders: Dominican Liberation Party or PLD [Leonel FERNANDEZ Reyna]; Dominican Revolutionary Party or PRD [Hatuey DE CAMPS]; Social Christian Reformist Party or PRSC [Eduardo ESTRELLA]

Political pressure groups and leaders: Collective of Popular Organizations or COP; Citizen Participation Group (Participacion Ciudadania)

International organization participation: ACP, Caricom (observer), FAO, G-77, IADB, IAEA, IBRD, ICAO, ICCt (signatory), ICFTU, ICRM, IDA, IFAD, IFC, IFRCS, IHO, ILO, IMF, IMO, Interpol, IOC, IOM, ISO (subscriber), ITU, LAES, LAIA (observer), NAM, OAS, OPANAL, OPCW (signatory), PCA, RG, UN, UNCTAD, UNESCO, UNIDO, UPU, WCL, WFTU, WHO, WIPO, WMO, WToO, WTrO

Diplomatic representation in the US:
chief of mission: Ambassador Hugo GUILIANI Cury
chancery: 1715 22nd Street NW, Washington, DC 20008
telephone: [1] (202) 332-6280
FAX: [1] (202) 265-8057
consulate(s) general: Boston, Chicago, Jacksonville, Mayaguez (Puerto Rico), Miami, New Orleans, New York, Philadelphia, San Francisco, and San Juan (Puerto Rico)
consulate(s): Mobile and Ponce (Puerto Rico)

Diplomatic representation from the US:
chief of mission: Ambassador Hans H. HERTELL
embassy: corner of Calle Cesar Nicolas Penson and Calle Leopoldo Navarro, Santo Domingo

mailing address: Unit 5500, APO AA 34041-5500
telephone: [1] (809) 221-2171
FAX: [1] (809) 686-7437

Flag description: a centered white cross that extends to the edges divides the flag into four rectangles - the top ones are blue (hoist side) and red, and the bottom ones are red (hoist side) and blue; a small coat of arms featuring a shield supported by an olive branch (left) and a palm branch (right) is at the center of the cross; above the shield a blue ribbon displays the motto, DIOS, PATRIA, LIBERTAD (God, Fatherland, Liberty), and below the shield, REPUBLICA DOMINICANA appears on a red ribbon

Economy

Economy - overview: The Dominican Republic is a Caribbean representative democracy which enjoyed GDP growth of more than 7% in 1998-2000. Growth subsequently plummeted as part of the global economic slowdown. Although the country has long been viewed primarily as an exporter of sugar, coffee, and tobacco, in recent years the service sector has overtaken agriculture as the economy's largest employer, due to growth in tourism and free trade zones. The country suffers from marked income inequality; the poorest half of the population receives less than one-fifth of GNP, while the richest 10% enjoys nearly 40% of national income. Growth turned negative in 2003 with reduced tourism, a major bank fraud, and limited growth in the US economy, the source of 87% of export revenues. Resumption of a badly needed IMF loan was slowed due to government repurchase of electrical power plants.

GDP: purchasing power parity - $52.16 billion (2003 est.)

GDP - real growth rate: -1.8% (2003 est.)

GDP - per capita: purchasing power parity - $6,000 (2003 est.)

GDP - composition by sector:
agriculture: 11%
industry: 34%
services: 55% (2001)

Population below poverty line: 25%

Household income or consumption by percentage share:
lowest 10%: 2.1%
highest 10%: 37.9% (1998)

Distribution of family income - Gini index: 47.4 (1998)

Inflation rate (consumer prices): 21.2% (2003 est.)

Labor force: 2.3 million - 2.6 million (2000 est.)

Labor force - by occupation: services and government 58.7%, industry 24.3%, agriculture 17% (1998 est.)

Unemployment rate: 15.5% (2003 est.)

Budget:
revenues: $2.9 billion
expenditures: $3.2 billion, including capital expenditures of $1.1 billion (2001 est.)

Industries: tourism, sugar processing, ferronickel and gold mining, textiles, cement, tobacco

Industrial production growth rate: 2% (2001 est.)

Electricity - production: 9.186 billion kWh (2001)

Electricity - production by source:
fossil fuel: 92%
hydro: 7.6%
nuclear: 0%
other: 0.4% (2001)

Electricity - consumption: 8.543 billion kWh (2001)

Electricity - exports: 0 kWh (2001)

Electricity - imports: 0 kWh (2001)

Oil - production: 0 bbl/day (2001 est.)

Oil - consumption: 129,000 bbl/day (2001 est.)

Oil - exports: NA

Oil - imports: NA

Agriculture - products: sugarcane, coffee, cotton, cocoa, tobacco, rice, beans, potatoes, corn, bananas; cattle, pigs, dairy products, beef, eggs

Exports: $5.524 billion f.o.b. (2003 est.)

Exports - commodities: ferronickel, sugar, gold, silver, coffee, cocoa, tobacco, meats, consumer goods

Exports - partners: US 85.3%, Canada 1.6%, UK 1.6% (2002)

Imports: $7.911 billion f.o.b. (2003 est.)

Imports - commodities: foodstuffs, petroleum, cotton and fabrics, chemicals and pharmaceuticals

Imports - partners: US 51.1%, Venezuela 9.1%, Mexico 4.8% (2002)

Debt - external: $6.5 billion (2003 est.)

Economic aid - recipient: $239.6 million (1995)

Currency: Dominican peso (DOP)

Currency code: DOP

Exchange rates: Dominican pesos per US dollar - 30.8307 (2003), 18.6098 (2002), 16.9516 (2001), 16.415 (2000), 16.0331 (1999)

Fiscal year: calendar year

Communications

Telephones - main lines in use: 909,000 (2002)

Telephones - mobile cellular: 1,700,600 (2002)

Telephone system:
general assessment: NA
domestic: relatively efficient system based on island-wide microwave radio relay network
international: country code - 1-809; 1 coaxial submarine cable; satellite earth station - 1 Intelsat (Atlantic Ocean)

Radio broadcast stations: AM 120, FM 56, shortwave 4 (1998)

Television broadcast stations: 25 (2003)

Internet country code: .do

Internet hosts: 45,508 (2002)

Internet users: 300,000 (2002)

Transportation

Railways:
total: 1,503 km
standard gauge: 375 km 1.435-m gauge
narrow gauge: 142 km 0.762-m gauge
note: additional 986 km operated by sugar companies in 1.076-m, 0.889-m, and 0.762-m gauges (2002)

Highways:
total: 12,600 km
paved: 6,224 km
unpaved: 6,376 km (1999)
Waterways: none
Pipelines: crude oil 96 km; petroleum products 8 km
Ports and harbors: Barahona, La Romana, Manzanillo, Puerto Plata, San Pedro de Macoris, Santo Domingo
Merchant marine:
total: 3 ships (1,000 GRT or over) 11,230 GRT/17,011 DWT
by type: cargo 1, petroleum tanker 2
foreign-owned: Pakistan 1, Singapore 1
registered in other countries: 1 (2003 est.)
Airports: 31 (2003 est.)
Airports - with paved runways:
total: 13
over 3,047 m: 3
2,438 to 3,047 m: 3
1,524 to 2,437 m: 3
914 to 1,523 m: 3
under 914 m: 1 (2003 est.)
Airports - with unpaved runways:
total: 18
1,524 to 2,437 m: 3
914 to 1,523 m: 5
under 914 m: 10 (2003 est.)

Military

Military branches: Army, Navy, Air Force
Military manpower - military age: 18 years of age (2004 est.)
Military manpower - availability:
males age 15-49: 2,354,800 (2004 est.)
Military manpower - fit for military service:
males age 15-49: 1,474,978 (2004 est.)
Military manpower - reaching military age annually:
males: 90,434 (2004 est.)
Military expenditures - dollar figure: $180 million (1998)
Military expenditures - percent of GDP: 1.1% (1998)

Transnational Issues

Disputes - international: despite efforts to control illegal migration, destitute Haitians fleeing poverty and violence continue to cross into the Dominican Republic; illegal migration of Dominicans and other nationals across the Mona Passage to Puerto Rico has increased in the last year
Illicit drugs: transshipment point for South American drugs destined for the US and Europe; has become a transshipment point for ecstasy from the Netherlands and Belgium destined for US and Canada; substantial money-laundering activity; Colombian narcotics traffickers favor the Dominican Republic for illicit financial transactions

East Timor

Introduction

Background: The Portuguese colony of Timor declared itself independent from Portugal on 28 November 1975 and was invaded and occupied by Indonesian forces nine days later. It was incorporated into Indonesia in July 1976 as the province of East Timor. A campaign of pacification followed over the next two decades, during which an estimated 100,000 to 250,000 individuals lost their lives. On 30 August 1999, in a UN-supervised popular referendum, the people of East Timor voted for independence from Indonesia. During 1999-2001, anti-independence militias - supported by Indonesia - conducted indiscriminate violence. On 20 May 2002, East Timor was internationally recognized as an independent state and the world's newest democracy.

Geography

Location: Southeastern Asia, northwest of Australia in the Lesser Sunda Islands at the eastern end of the Indonesian archipelago; note - East Timor includes the eastern half of the island of Timor, the Oecussi (Ambeno) region on the northwest portion of the island of Timor, and the islands of Pulau Atauro and Pulau Jaco
Geographic coordinates: 8 50 S, 125 55 E
Map references: Southeast Asia
Area:
total: 15,007 sq km
land: NA sq km
water: NA sq km
Area - comparative: slightly larger than Connecticut
Land boundaries:
total: 228 km
border countries: Indonesia 228 km
Coastline: 706 km
Maritime claims:
territorial sea: NA NM
exclusive economic zone: NA NM

continental shelf: NA NM
exclusive fishing zone: NA NM
extended fishing zone: NA NM
Climate: tropical; hot, humid; distinct rainy and dry seasons
Terrain: mountainous
Elevation extremes:
lowest point: Timor Sea, Savu Sea, and Banda Sea 0 m
highest point: Foho Tatamailau 2,963 m
Natural resources: gold, petroleum, natural gas, manganese, marble
Land use:
arable land: NA%
permanent crops: NA%
other: NA%
Irrigated land: 1,065 sq km (est.)
Natural hazards: floods and landslides are common; earthquakes, tsunamis, tropical cyclones
Environment - current issues: widespread use of slash and burn agriculture has led to deforestation and soil erosion
Environment - international agreements: NA
Geography - note: Timor comes from the Malay word for "East;" the island of Timor is part of the Malay Archipelago and is the largest and easternmost of the Lesser Sunda Islands

People

Population: 1,019,252
note: other estimates range as low as 800,000 (July 2004 est.)
Age structure:
0-14 years: 37.8% (male 196,007; female 189,584)
15-64 years: 59.2% (male 308,254; female 295,584)
65 years and over: 2.9% (male 14,663; female 15,160) (2004 est.)
Median age:
total: 20 years
male: 20.1 years
female: 19.9 years (2004 est.)
Population growth rate: 2.11% (2004 est.)
Birth rate: 27.46 births/1,000 population (2004 est.)
Death rate: 6.36 deaths/1,000 population (2004 est.)
Net migration rate: 0 migrant(s)/1,000 population (2004 est.)
Sex ratio:
at birth: 1.05 male(s)/female
under 15 years: 1.03 male(s)/female
15-64 years: 1.04 male(s)/female
65 years and over: 0.97 male(s)/female
total population: 1.04 male(s)/female (2004 est.)
Infant mortality rate:
total: 48.86 deaths/1,000 live births
male: 55.34 deaths/1,000 live births
female: 42.05 deaths/1,000 live births (2004 est.)
Life expectancy at birth:
total population: 65.56 years
male: 63.31 years
female: 67.92 years (2004 est.)
Total fertility rate: 3.7 children born/woman (2004 est.)

East Timor (continued)

HIV/AIDS - adult prevalence rate: NA%
HIV/AIDS - people living with HIV/AIDS: NA
HIV/AIDS - deaths: NA
Nationality:
noun: Timorese
adjective: Timorese
Ethnic groups: Austronesian (Malayo-Polynesian), Papuan, small Chinese minority
Religions: Roman Catholic 90%, Muslim 4%, Protestant 3%, Hindu 0.5%, Buddhist, Animist (1992 est.)
Languages: Tetum (official), Portuguese (official), Indonesian, English
note: there are about 16 indigenous languages; Tetum, Galole, Mambae, and Kemak are spoken by significant numbers of people
Literacy:
definition: age 15 and over can read and write
total population: 48% (2001)
male: NA%
female: NA%

Government

Country name:
conventional long form: Democratic Republic of Timor-Leste
conventional short form: East Timor
local long form: Republika Demokratika Timor Lorosa'e [Tetum]; Republica Democratica de Timor-Leste [Portuguese]
local short form: Timor Lorosa'e [Tetum]; Timor-Leste [Portuguese]
former: Portuguese Timor
Government type: republic
Capital: Dili
Administrative divisions: 13 administrative districts; Aileu, Ainaro, Baucau, Bobonaro (Maliana), Cova-Lima (Suai), Dili, Ermera, Lautem (Los Palos), Liquica, Manatuto, Manufahi (Same), Oecussi (Ambeno), Viqueque
Independence: 28 November 1975 (date of proclamation of independence from Portugal); note - 20 May 2002 is the official date of international recognition of East Timor's independence from Indonesia
National holiday: Independence Day, 28 November (1975)
Constitution: 22 March 2002 (based on the Portuguese model)
Legal system: UN-drafted legal system based on Indonesian law (2002)
Suffrage: 17 years of age; universal
Executive branch:
chief of state: President Kay Rala Xanana GUSMAO (since 20 May 2002); note - the president plays a largely symbolic role but is able to veto some legislation; he formally used the name Jose Alexander GUSMAO
head of government: Prime Minister Mari Bin Amude ALKATIRI (since 20 May 2002)
cabinet: Council of State

elections: president elected by popular vote for a five-year term; election last held 14 April 2002 (next to be held NA April 2007); after the first legislative elections, the leader of the majority party was appointed prime minister by the president, suggesting a precedent for the future
election results: Kay Rala Xanana GUSMAO elected president; percent of vote - Kay Rala Xanana GUSMAO 82.7%, Francisco Xavier do AMARAL 17.3%
Legislative branch: unicameral National Parliament (number of seats can vary, minimum requirement of 52 and a maximum of 65 seats; members elected by popular vote to serve five-year terms); note - for its first term of office, the National Parliament is comprised of 88 members on an exceptional basis
elections: (next to be held August 2006); direct elections for national parliament were never held; elected delegates to the national convention named themselves legislators instead of having elections; hence the exceptional numbers for this term of the national parliament.
election results: percent of vote by party - FRETILIN 57.37%, PD 8.72%, PSD 8.18%, ASDT 7.84%, UDT 2.36%, PNT 2.21%, KOTA 2.13%, PPT 2.01%, PDC 1.98%, PST 1.78%, independents/other 5.42%; seats by party - FRETILIN 55, PD 7, PSD 6, ASDT 6, PDC 2, UDT 2, KOTA 2, PNT 2, PPT 2, UDC/PDC 1, PST 1, PL 1, independent 1
Judicial branch: Supreme Court of Justice, one judge appointed by the National Parliament and the rest appointed by the Superior Council for the Judiciary
Political parties and leaders: Associacao Social-Democrata Timorense or ASDT [Francisco Xavier do AMARAL]; Christian Democratic Party of Timor or PDC [Antonio XIMENES]; Christian Democratic Union of Timor or UDC [Vicente da Silva GUTERRES]; Democratic Party or PD [Fernando de ARAUJO]; Liberal Party or PL [leader NA]; Maubere Democratic Party or PDM [leader NA]; People's Party of Timor or PPT [Jacob XAVIER]; Revolutionary Front of Independent East Timor or FRETILIN [Lu OLO]; Social Democrat Party of East Timor or PSD [Mario CARRASCALAO]; Socialist Party of Timor or PST [leader NA]; Sons of the Mountain Warriors (also known as Association of Timorese Heroes) or KOTA [Clementino dos Reis AMARAL]; Timor Democratic Union or UDT [Joao CARRASCALAO]; Timor Labor Party or PTT [Paulo Freitas DA SILVA]; Timorese Nationalist Party or PNT [Abilio ARAUJO]; Timorese Popular Democratic Association or APODETI [Frederico Almeida-Santos DA COSTA]
Political pressure groups and leaders: the Popular Council for the Defense of the Democratic Republic of East Timor or CPD-RDTL is the largest political pressure group; it rejects the current government and claims to be the rightful government; it is led by Cristiano DA COSTA, a.k.a. Aitahan MATAK; Kolimau 2000 is another opposition group; leader is Dr. BRUNO (NFI) according to Indonesian press

International organization participation: AsDB, IBRD, ICCt, IDA, IFAD, IFRCS, ILO, IMF, Interpol, IOC, OPCW, PIF (observer), UN, UNESCO, UNIDO, UPU, WCO, WHO
Diplomatic representation in the US:
chief of mission: Ambassador Jose Luis GUTERRES
chancery: 3415 Massachusetts Avenue, Washington, DC 20007
telephone: 202 965-1515
FAX: 202 965-1517
consulate(s) general: New York (the ambassador resides in New York) (2003)
Diplomatic representation from the US:
chief of mission: Ambassador Grover Joseph REES
embassy: Vila 10, Avenida de Portugal, Farol, Dili
mailing address: Department of State, 8250 Dili Place, Washington, DC 20521-8250
telephone: (670) 332-4684, 331-3205/3160/3472
FAX: (670) 331-3206
Flag description: red, with a black isosceles triangle (based on the hoist side) superimposed on a slightly longer yellow arrowhead that extends to the center of the flag; there is a white star in the center of the black triangle

Economy

Economy - overview: In late 1999, about 70% of the economic infrastructure of East Timor was laid waste by Indonesian troops and anti-independence militias, and 260,000 people fled westward. Over the next three years, however, a massive international program, manned by 5,000 peacekeepers (8,000 at peak) and 1,300 police officers, led to substantial reconstruction in both urban and rural areas. By mid-2002, all but about 50,000 of the refugees had returned. Growth was held back in 2003 by extensive drought and the gradual winding down of the international presence. The country faces great challenges in continuing the rebuilding of infrastructure, strengthening the infant civil administration, and generating jobs for young people entering the workforce. One promising long-term project is the planned development of oil and gas resources in nearby waters, but the government faces a substantial financing gap over the next several years before these revenues start flowing into state coffers.
GDP: purchasing power parity - $440 million (2001 est.)
GDP - real growth rate: -3% (2003 est.)
GDP - per capita: purchasing power parity - $500 (2001 est.)
GDP - composition by sector:
agriculture: 25.4%
industry: 17.2%
services: 57.4% (2001)
Population below poverty line: 42% (2003 est.)
Household income or consumption by percentage share:
lowest 10%: NA%
highest 10%: NA%
Distribution of family income - Gini index: 38 (2002 est.)

Inflation rate (consumer prices): 8% NA%
(2003 est.)
Labor force: NA
Labor force - by occupation: NA
Unemployment rate: 50% (including
underemployment) (1992 est.)
Budget:
revenues: $36 million
expenditures: $97 million, including capital
expenditures of $NA (2003 est.)
Industries: printing, soap manufacturing,
handicrafts, woven cloth
Industrial production growth rate: 8.5%
Electricity - production: NA kWh (2001)
Electricity - production by source:
fossil fuel: 100%
hydro: 0%
nuclear: 0%
other: 0% (2001)
Electricity - consumption: NA kWh (2001)
Electricity - exports: 0 kWh (2001)
Electricity - imports: 0 kWh (2001)
Agriculture - products: coffee, rice, maize,
cassava, sweet potatoes, soybeans, cabbage,
mangoes, bananas, vanilla
Exports: $8 million (2001 est.)
Exports - commodities: coffee, sandalwood,
marble; note - the potential for oil and vanilla exports
Exports - partners: NA
Imports: $237 million (2001 est.)
Imports - commodities: mainly food (2001)
Imports - partners: NA
Debt - external: $NA
Economic aid - recipient: $2.2 billion
(1999-2002 est.)
Currency: US dollar (USD)
Currency code: IDR
Exchange rates: the US dollar is the legal tender
Fiscal year: 1 July - 30 June

Communications

Telephones - main lines in use: NA
Telephones - mobile cellular: NA
Telephone system: NA
Radio broadcast stations: AM NA, FM NA,
shortwave NA
Television broadcast stations: NA
Internet country code: .tp
Internet users: NA

Transportation

Railways: 0 km
Highways:
total: 3,800 km
paved: 428 km
unpaved: 3,372 km (1995)
Waterways: NA
Pipelines: NA
Ports and harbors: NA
Merchant marine: none

Airports: 8 (2003 est.)
Airports - with paved runways:
total: 3
2,438 to 3,047 m: 1
1,524 to 2,427 m: 1
914 to 1,523 m: 1 (2003 est.)
Airports - with unpaved runways:
total: 5
914 to 1,523 m: 3
under 914 m: 2 (2003 est.)
Heliports: 1 (2003 est.)

Military

Military branches: East Timor Defense Force
(Forcas de Defesa de Timor-L'este, FDTL): Army,
Navy
Military manpower - military age: 18 years of age
(2004 est.)
Military manpower - availability: NA (2004 est.)
Military manpower - fit for military service: NA
(2004 est.)
**Military manpower - reaching military age
annually:** NA (2004 est.)
Military expenditures - dollar figure: $4.4 million
(FY03)
Military expenditures - percent of GDP: NA%

Transnational Issues

Disputes - international: East Timor-Indonesia
Boundary Committee continues to meet, survey, and
delimit the land boundary, but several sections of the
boundary especially around the Oekussi enclave
remain unresolved; Indonesia and East Timor contest
the sovereignty of the uninhabited coral island of
Palau Batek/Fatu Sinai, which may delay decision on
the northern maritime boundaries; numbers of East
Timor refugees in Indonesia refuse repatriation; the
1999 maritime delimitation established partial
maritime boundaries with Australia over part of the
Timor Gap but temporary resource-sharing
agreements over an unreconciled area grant Australia
a 90% share of exploited gas reserves and hamper
creation of a southern maritime boundary with
Indonesia
Illicit drugs: NA

Ecuador

Introduction

Background: The "Republic of the Equator" was one
of three countries that emerged from the collapse of
Gran Colombia in 1830 (the others being Colombia
and Venezuela). Between 1904 and 1942, Ecuador
lost territories in a series of conflicts with its neighbors.
A border war with Peru that flared in 1995 was
resolved in 1999.

Geography

Location: Western South America, bordering the
Pacific Ocean at the Equator, between Colombia and
Peru
Geographic coordinates: 2 00 S, 77 30 W
Map references: South America
Area:
total: 283,560 sq km
land: 276,840 sq km
water: 6,720 sq km
note: includes Galapagos Islands
Area - comparative: slightly smaller than Nevada
Land boundaries:
total: 2,010 km
border countries: Colombia 590 km, Peru 1,420 km
Coastline: 2,237 km
Maritime claims:
territorial sea: 200 NM
continental shelf: 100 NM from 2,500 meter isobath
Climate: tropical along coast, becoming cooler
inland at higher elevations; tropical in Amazonian
jungle lowlands
Terrain: coastal plain (costa), inter-Andean central
highlands (sierra), and flat to rolling eastern jungle
(oriente)
Elevation extremes:
lowest point: Pacific Ocean 0 m
highest point: Chimborazo 6,267 m
Natural resources: petroleum, fish, timber,
hydropower

Ecuador (continued)

Land use:
arable land: 5.69%
permanent crops: 5.15%
other: 89.16% (1998 est.)
Irrigated land: 8,650 sq km (1998 est.)
Natural hazards: frequent earthquakes, landslides, volcanic activity; floods; periodic droughts
Environment - current issues: deforestation; soil erosion; desertification; water pollution; pollution from oil production wastes in ecologically sensitive areas of the Amazon Basin and Galapagos Islands
Environment - international agreements:
party to: Antarctic-Environmental Protocol, Antarctic Treaty, Biodiversity, Climate Change, Climate Change-Kyoto Protocol, Desertification, Endangered Species, Hazardous Wastes, Ozone Layer Protection, Ship Pollution, Tropical Timber 83, Tropical Timber 94, Wetlands
signed, but not ratified: none of the selected agreements
Geography - note: Cotopaxi in Andes is highest active volcano in world

People

Population: 13,212,742 (July 2004 est.)
Age structure:
0-14 years: 33.9% (male 2,285,775; female 2,199,356)
15-64 years: 61.2% (male 4,020,873; female 4,062,672)
65 years and over: 4.9% (male 302,129; female 341,937) (2004 est.)
Median age:
total: 23 years
male: 22.5 years
female: 23.5 years (2004 est.)
Population growth rate: 1.03% (2004 est.)
Birth rate: 23.18 births/1,000 population (2004 est.)
Death rate: 4.26 deaths/1,000 population (2004 est.)
Net migration rate: -8.58 migrant(s)/1,000 population (2004 est.)
Sex ratio:
at birth: 1.05 male(s)/female
under 15 years: 1.04 male(s)/female
15-64 years: 0.99 male(s)/female
65 years and over: 0.88 male(s)/female
total population: 1 male(s)/female (2004 est.)
Infant mortality rate:
total: 24.49 deaths/1,000 live births
male: 29.34 deaths/1,000 live births
female: 19.4 deaths/1,000 live births (2004 est.)
Life expectancy at birth:
total population: 76.01 years
male: 73.15 years
female: 79 years (2004 est.)
Total fertility rate: 2.78 children born/woman (2004 est.)
HIV/AIDS - adult prevalence rate: 0.3% (2001 est.)
HIV/AIDS - people living with HIV/AIDS: 20,000 (2001 est.)
HIV/AIDS - deaths: 1,700 (2001 est.)

Nationality:
noun: Ecuadorian(s)
adjective: Ecuadorian
Ethnic groups: mestizo (mixed Amerindian and white) 65%, Amerindian 25%, Spanish and others 7%, black 3%
Religions: Roman Catholic 95%
Languages: Spanish (official), Amerindian languages (especially Quechua)
Literacy:
definition: age 15 and over can read and write
total population: 92.5%
male: 94%
female: 91% (2003 est.)

Government

Country name:
conventional long form: Republic of Ecuador
conventional short form: Ecuador
local long form: Republica del Ecuador
local short form: Ecuador
Government type: republic
Capital: Quito
Administrative divisions: 22 provinces (provincias, singular - provincia); Azuay, Bolivar, Canar, Carchi, Chimborazo, Cotopaxi, El Oro, Esmeraldas, Galapagos, Guayas, Imbabura, Loja, Los Rios, Manabi, Morona-Santiago, Napo, Orellana, Pastaza, Pichincha, Sucumbios, Tungurahua, Zamora-Chinchipe
Independence: 24 May 1822 (from Spain)
National holiday: Independence Day (independence of Quito), 10 August (1809)
Constitution: 10 August 1998
Legal system: based on civil law system; has not accepted compulsory ICJ jurisdiction
Suffrage: 18 years of age; universal, compulsory for literate persons ages 18-65, optional for other eligible voters
Executive branch:
chief of state: President Lucio GUTIERREZ (since 15 January 2003); Vice President Alfredo PALACIO (since 15 January 2003); note - the president is both the chief of state and head of government
head of government: President Lucio GUTIERREZ (since 15 January 2003); Vice President Alfredo PALACIO (since 15 January 2003); note - the president is both the chief of state and head of government
cabinet: Cabinet appointed by the president
elections: the president and vice president are elected on the same ticket by popular vote for four-year term (no reelection); election last held 20 October 2002; runoff election held 24 November 2002 (next to be held NA October 2006)
election results: results of the 24 November 2002 runoff election - Lucio GUTIERREZ elected president; percent of vote - Lucio GUTIERREZ 54.3%; Alvaro NOBOA 45.7%
Legislative branch: unicameral National Congress or Congreso Nacional (100 seats; members are popularly elected by province to serve four-year terms)
elections: last held 20 October 2002 (next to be held NA October 2006)

election results: percent of vote by party - NA%; seats by party - PSC 25, PRE 15, ID 16, PRIAN 10, PSP 9, Pachakutik Movement 6, MPD 5, DP 4, PS-FA 3, independents 7; note - defections by members of National Congress are commonplace, resulting in frequent changes in the numbers of seats held by the various parties
Judicial branch: Supreme Court or Corte Suprema (new justices are elected by the full Supreme Court)
Political parties and leaders: Concentration of Popular Forces or CFP [Averroes BUCARAM]; Democratic Left or ID [Rodrigo BORJA Cevallos]; National Action Institutional Renewal Party or PRIAN [Alvaro NOBOA]; Pachakutik Movement [Gilberto TALAHUA]; Patriotic Society Party or PSP [Lucio GUTIERREZ Borbua]; Popular Democracy or DP [Dr. Juan Manuel FUERTES]; Popular Democratic Movement or MPD [Gustavo TERAN Acosta]; Radical Alfarista Front or FRA [Fabian ALARCON, director]; Roldosist Party or PRE [Abdala BUCARAM Ortiz, director]; Social Christian Party or PSC [Pascual DEL CIOPPO]; Socialist Party - Broad Front or PS-FA [Victor GRANDA]
Political pressure groups and leaders: Confederation of Indigenous Nationalities of Ecuador or CONAIE [Leonidas IZA, president]; Coordinator of Social Movements or CMS [F. Napoleon SANTOS]; Federation of Indigenous Evangelists of Ecuador or FEINE [Marco MURILLO, president]; National Federation of Indigenous Afro-Ecuatorianos and Peasants or FENOCIN [Pedro DE LA CRUZ, president]; Popular Front or FP [Luis VILLACIS]
International organization participation: CAN, FAO, G-77, IADB, IAEA, IBRD, ICAO, ICC, ICCt, ICFTU, ICRM, IDA, IFAD, IFC, IFRCS, IHO, ILO, IMF, IMO, Interpol, IOC, IOM, ISO, ITU, LAES, LAIA, NAM, OAS, OPANAL, OPCW, PCA, RG, UN, UNCTAD, UNESCO, UNHCR, UNIDO, UNMIL, UPU, WCL, WCO, WFTU, WHO, WIPO, WMO, WToO, WTrO
Diplomatic representation in the US:
chief of mission: Ambassador Raul GANGOTENA Rivadeneira
chancery: 2535 15th Street NW, Washington, DC 20009
telephone: [1] (202) 234-7200
FAX: [1] (202) 667-3482
consulate(s) general: Chicago, Houston, Los Angeles, Miami, New Orleans, New York, Newark, Philadelphia, and San Francisco
Diplomatic representation from the US:
chief of mission: Ambassador Kristie Anne KENNEY
embassy: Avenida 12 de Octubre y Avenida Patria, Quito
mailing address: APO AA 34039
telephone: [593] (2) 256-2890
FAX: [593] (2) 250-2052
consulate(s) general: Guayaquil
Flag description: three horizontal bands of yellow (top, double width), blue, and red with the coat of arms superimposed at the center of the flag; similar to the flag of Colombia, which is shorter and does not bear a coat of arms

Ecuador *(continued)*

Economy

Economy - overview: Ecuador has substantial petroleum resources, which have accounted for 40% of the country's export earnings and one-fourth of public sector revenues in recent years. Consequently, fluctuations in world market prices can have a substantial domestic impact. In the late 1990s, Ecuador suffered its worst economic crisis, with natural disasters and sharp declines in world petroleum prices driving Ecuador's economy into free fall in 1999. Real GDP contracted by more than 6%, with poverty worsening significantly. The banking system also collapsed, and Ecuador defaulted on its external debt later that year. The currency depreciated by some 70% in 1999, and, on the brink of hyperinflation, the MAHAUD government announced it would dollarize the economy. A coup, however, ousted MAHAUD from office in January 2000, and after a short-lived junta failed to garner military support, Vice President Gustavo NOBOA took over the presidency. In March 2000, Congress approved a series of structural reforms that also provided the framework for the adoption of the US dollar as legal tender. Dollarization stabilized the economy, and growth returned to its pre-crisis levels in the years that followed. Under the administration of Lucio GUTIERREZ, who took office in January 2003, Ecuador benefited from higher world petroleum prices, but the government has made little progress on fiscal reforms and reforms of state-owned enterprises necessary to reduce Ecuador's vulnerability to petroleum price swings and financial crises. The government is using oil revenues to pay off Ecuador's massive foreign debt and has secured a new standby agreement with the IMF.

GDP: purchasing power parity - $45.46 billion (2003 est.)

GDP - real growth rate: 2.6% (2003 est.)

GDP - per capita: purchasing power parity - $3,300 (2003 est.)

GDP - composition by sector:
agriculture: 11%
industry: 33%
services: 56% (2001 est.)

Population below poverty line: 65% (2003 est.)

Household income or consumption by percentage share:
lowest 10%: 2.2%
highest 10%: 33.8% (1995)

Distribution of family income - Gini index: 43.7 (1995)

Inflation rate (consumer prices): 6.1% (yearend 2003 est.)

Labor force: 3.8 million (urban) (2002)

Labor force - by occupation: agriculture 30%, industry 25%, services 45% (2001 est.)

Unemployment rate: 9.8%; note - underemployment of 47% (2003 est.)

Budget:
revenues: $6.3 billion

expenditures: planned $5.3 billion, including capital expenditures of $1.6 billion (2002)

Industries: petroleum, food processing, textiles, wood products, chemicals

Industrial production growth rate: 5% (2001 est.)

Electricity - production: 75.23 billion kWh (2001)

Electricity - production by source:
fossil fuel: 81%
hydro: 19%
nuclear: 0%
other: 0% (2001)

Electricity - consumption: 69.96 billion kWh (2001)

Electricity - exports: 0 kWh (2001)

Electricity - imports: 0 kWh (2001)

Oil - production: 421,200 bbl/day (2001 est.)

Oil - consumption: 129,000 bbl/day (2001 est.)

Oil - exports: NA

Oil - imports: NA

Oil - proved reserves: 2.358 billion bbl (1 January 2002)

Natural gas - production: 160 million cu m (2001 est.)

Natural gas - consumption: 160 million cu m (2001 est.)

Natural gas - exports: 0 cu m (2001 est.)

Natural gas - imports: 0 cu m (2001 est.)

Natural gas - proved reserves: 106.5 billion cu m (1 January 2002)

Agriculture - products: bananas, coffee, cocoa, rice, potatoes, manioc (tapioca), plantains, sugarcane; cattle, sheep, pigs, beef, pork, dairy products; balsa wood; fish, shrimp

Exports: $6.073 billion (2003 est.)

Exports - commodities: petroleum, bananas, cut flowers, shrimp

Exports - partners: US 40.3%, Colombia 5.8%, Germany 5.4%, South Korea 5.3%, Italy 4.6% (2002)

Imports: $6.22 billion (2003 est.)

Imports - commodities: consumer goods, industrial raw materials, capital goods

Imports - partners: US 26.8%, Colombia 13.6%, Brazil 6.5%, Venezuela 5.7%, Japan 5.7%, Chile 4.2% (2002)

Debt - external: $14.4 billion (2002)

Economic aid - recipient: $120 million (2001)

Currency: US dollar (USD)

Currency code: USD

Exchange rates: Ecuador formally adopted the US dollar as legal tender in March 2000

Fiscal year: calendar year

Communications

Telephones - main lines in use: 1,426,200 (2002)

Telephones - mobile cellular: 1,560,900 (2002)

Telephone system:
general assessment: generally elementary but being expanded
domestic: facilities generally inadequate and unreliable
international: country code - 593; satellite earth station - 1 Intelsat (Atlantic Ocean)

Radio broadcast stations: AM 392, FM 35, shortwave 29 (2001)

Television broadcast stations: 7 (plus 14 repeaters) (2001)

Internet country code: .ec

Internet hosts: 2,648 (2002)

Internet users: 537,900 (2002)

Transportation

Railways:
total: 966 km
narrow gauge: 966 km 1.067-m gauge (2002)

Highways:
total: 43,197 km
paved: 8,164 km
unpaved: 35,033 km (2000)

Waterways: 1,500 km

Pipelines: gas 71 km; oil 1,575 km; refined products 1,185 km (2003)

Ports and harbors: Esmeraldas, Guayaquil, La Libertad, Manta, Puerto Bolivar, San Lorenzo

Merchant marine:
total: 34 ships (1,000 GRT or over) 241,403 GRT/ 391,898 DWT
by type: cargo 2, chemical tanker 4, liquefied gas 1, passenger 5, petroleum tanker 21, specialized tanker 1
foreign-owned: Greece 1, Paraguay 1, Peru 1
registered in other countries: 3 (2003 est.)

Airports: 205 (2003 est.)

Airports - with paved runways:
total: 61
over 3,047 m: 3
2,438 to 3,047 m: 4
1,524 to 2,437 m: 18
914 to 1,523 m: 18
under 914 m: 18 (2003 est.)

Airports - with unpaved runways:
total: 144
914 to 1,523 m: 31
under 914 m: 113 (2003 est.)

Heliports: 1 (2003 est.)

Military

Military branches: Army, Navy (including Marines), Air Force, National Police

Military manpower - military age: 20 years of age (2004 est.)

Military manpower - availability:
males age 15-49: 3,440,371 (2004 est.)

Military manpower - fit for military service:
males age 15-49: 2,315,808 (2004 est.)

Military manpower - reaching military age annually:
males: 132,476 (2004 est.)

Military expenditures - dollar figure: $650 million (2003)

Military expenditures - percent of GDP: 2.4% (2003)

Disputes - international: the continuing civil disorder in Colombia has created a serious refugee crisis in neighboring states, especially Ecuador

Illicit drugs: significant transit country for cocaine originating in Colombia and Peru; importer of precursor chemicals used in production of illicit narcotics; attractive location for cash-placement by drug traffickers laundering money because of dollarization and weak anti-money-laundering regime, especially vulnerable along the border with Colombia; increased activity on the northern frontier by trafficking groups and Colombian insurgents

Egypt

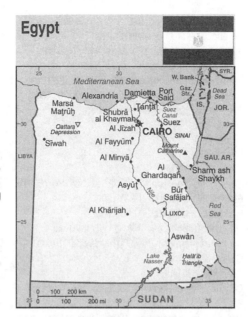

Introduction

Background: The regularity and richness of the annual Nile River flood, coupled with semi-isolation provided by deserts to the east and west, allowed for the development of one of the world's great civilizations. A unified kingdom arose circa 3200 B.C. and a series of dynasties ruled in Egypt for the next three millennia. The last native dynasty fell to the Persians in 341 B.C., who in turn were replaced by the Greeks, Romans, and Byzantines. It was the Arabs who introduced Islam and the Arabic language in the 7th century and who ruled for the next six centuries. A local military caste, the Mamluks took control about 1250 and continued to govern after the conquest of Egypt by the Ottoman Turks in 1517. Following the completion of the Suez Canal in 1869, Egypt became an important world transportation hub, but also fell heavily into debt. Ostensibly to protect its investments, Britain seized control of Egypt's government in 1882, but nominal allegiance to the Ottoman Empire continued until 1914. Partially independent from the UK in 1922, Egypt acquired full sovereignty following World War II. The completion of the Aswan High Dam in 1971 and the resultant Lake Nasser have altered the time-honored place of the Nile River in the agriculture and ecology of Egypt. A rapidly growing population (the largest in the Arab world), limited arable land, and dependence on the Nile all continue to overtax resources and stress society. The government has struggled to ready the economy for the new millennium through economic reform and massive investment in communications and physical infrastructure.

Geography

Location: Northern Africa, bordering the Mediterranean Sea, between Libya and the Gaza Strip, and the Red Sea north of Sudan, and includes the Asian Sinai Peninsula

Geographic coordinates: 27 00 N, 30 00 E

Map references: Africa

Area:
total: 1,001,450 sq km
land: 995,450 sq km
water: 6,000 sq km

Area - comparative: slightly more than three times the size of New Mexico

Land boundaries:
total: 2,665 km
border countries: Gaza Strip 11 km, Israel 266 km, Libya 1,115 km, Sudan 1,273 km

Coastline: 2,450 km

Maritime claims:
territorial sea: 12 NM
contiguous zone: 24 NM
exclusive economic zone: 200 NM
continental shelf: 200-m depth or to the depth of exploitation

Climate: desert; hot, dry summers with moderate winters

Terrain: vast desert plateau interrupted by Nile valley and delta

Elevation extremes:
lowest point: Qattara Depression -133 m
highest point: Mount Catherine 2,629 m

Natural resources: petroleum, natural gas, iron ore, phosphates, manganese, limestone, gypsum, talc, asbestos, lead, zinc

Land use:
arable land: 2.85%
permanent crops: 0.47%
other: 96.68% (1998 est.)

Irrigated land: 33,000 sq km (1998 est.)

Natural hazards: periodic droughts; frequent earthquakes, flash floods, landslides; hot, driving windstorm called khamsin occurs in spring; dust storms, sandstorms

Environment - current issues: agricultural land being lost to urbanization and windblown sands; increasing soil salination below Aswan High Dam; desertification; oil pollution threatening coral reefs, beaches, and marine habitats; other water pollution from agricultural pesticides, raw sewage, and industrial effluents; very limited natural fresh water resources away from the Nile which is the only perennial water source; rapid growth in population overstraining the Nile and natural resources

Environment - international agreements:
party to: Biodiversity, Climate Change, Desertification, Endangered Species, Environmental Modification, Hazardous Wastes, Law of the Sea, Marine Dumping, Ozone Layer Protection, Ship Pollution, Tropical Timber 83, Tropical Timber 94, Wetlands
signed, but not ratified: Climate Change-Kyoto Protocol

Geography - note: controls Sinai Peninsula, only land bridge between Africa and remainder of Eastern Hemisphere; controls Suez Canal, a sea link between Indian Ocean and Mediterranean Sea; size, and

Egypt (continued)

juxtaposition to Israel, establish its major role in Middle Eastern geopolitics; dependence on upstream neighbors; dominance of Nile basin issues; prone to influxes of refugees

People

Population: 76,117,421 (July 2004 est.)

Age structure:

0-14 years: 33.4% (male 13,038,369; female 12,418,254)

15-64 years: 62.2% (male 23,953,949; female 23,419,418)

65 years and over: 4.3% (male 1,407,248; female 1,880,183) (2004 est.)

Median age:

total: 23.4 years

male: 23 years

female: 23.8 years (2004 est.)

Population growth rate: 1.83% (2004 est.)

Birth rate: 23.84 births/1,000 population (2004 est.)

Death rate: 5.3 deaths/1,000 population (2004 est.)

Net migration rate: -0.22 migrant(s)/1,000 population (2004 est.)

Sex ratio:

at birth: 1.05 male(s)/female

under 15 years: 1.05 male(s)/female

15-64 years: 1.02 male(s)/female

65 years and over: 0.75 male(s)/female

total population: 1.02 male(s)/female (2004 est.)

Infant mortality rate:

total: 33.9 deaths/1,000 live births

male: 34.64 deaths/1,000 live births

female: 33.12 deaths/1,000 live births (2004 est.)

Life expectancy at birth:

total population: 70.71 years

male: 68.22 years

female: 73.31 years (2004 est.)

Total fertility rate: 2.95 children born/woman (2004 est.)

HIV/AIDS - adult prevalence rate: less than 0.1% (2001 est.)

HIV/AIDS - people living with HIV/AIDS: 8,000 (2001 est.)

HIV/AIDS - deaths: NA

Nationality:

noun: Egyptian(s)

adjective: Egyptian

Ethnic groups: Eastern Hamitic stock (Egyptians, Bedouins, and Berbers) 99%, Greek, Nubian, Armenian, other European (primarily Italian and French) 1%

Religions: Muslim (mostly Sunni) 94%, Coptic Christian and other 6%

Languages: Arabic (official), English and French widely understood by educated classes

Literacy:

definition: age 15 and over can read and write

total population: 57.7%

male: 68.3%

female: 46.9% (2003 est.)

Government

Country name:

conventional long form: Arab Republic of Egypt

conventional short form: Egypt

local long form: Jumhuriyat Misr al-Arabiyah

local short form: Misr

former: United Arab Republic (with Syria)

Government type: republic

Capital: Cairo

Administrative divisions: 26 governorates (muhafazat, singular - muhafazah); Ad Daqahliyah, Al Bahr al Ahmar, Al Buhayrah, Al Fayyum, Al Gharbiyah, Al Iskandariyah, Al Isma'iliyah, Al Jizah, Al Minufiyah, Al Minya, Al Qahirah, Al Qalyubiyah, Al Wadi al Jadid, Ash Sharqiyah, As Suways, Aswan, Asyut, Bani Suwayf, Bur Sa'id, Dumyat, Janub Sina', Kafr ash Shaykh, Matruh, Qina, Shamal Sina', Suhaj

Independence: 28 February 1922 (from UK)

National holiday: Revolution Day, 23 July (1952)

Constitution: 11 September 1971

Legal system: based on English common law, Islamic law, and Napoleonic codes; judicial review by Supreme Court and Council of State (oversees validity of administrative decisions); accepts compulsory ICJ jurisdiction, with reservations

Suffrage: 18 years of age; universal and compulsory

Executive branch:

chief of state: President Mohammed Hosni MUBARAK (since 14 October 1981)

head of government: Prime Minister Atef Mohammed ABEID (since 5 October 1999)

cabinet: Cabinet appointed by the president

elections: president nominated by the People's Assembly for a six-year term, the nomination must then be validated by a national, popular referendum; national referendum last held 26 September 1999 (next to be held NA October 2005); prime minister appointed by the president

election results: national referendum validated President MUBARAK's nomination by the People's Assembly to a fourth term

Legislative branch: bicameral system consists of the People's Assembly or Majlis al-Sha'b (454 seats; 444 elected by popular vote, 10 appointed by the president; members serve five-year terms) and the Advisory Council or Majlis al-Shura - which functions only in a consultative role (264 seats; 176 elected by popular vote, 88 appointed by the president; members serve six-year terms)

elections: People's Assembly - three-phase voting - last held 19 October, 29 October, 8 November 2000 (next to be held NA November 2005); Advisory Council - last held May-June 2001 (next to be held NA 2007)

election results: People's Assembly - percent of vote by party - NDP 88%, independents 8%, opposition 4%; seats by party - NDP 398, NWP 7, Tagammu 6, Nasserists 2, LSP 1, independents 38, undecided 2; Advisory Council - percent of vote by party - NDP 99%, independents 1%; seats by party - NA

Judicial branch: Supreme Constitutional Court

Political parties and leaders: Liberal Party or LSP [leader NA]; Nasserist Arab Democratic Party or Nasserists [Dia' al-din DAWUD]; National Democratic Party or NDP [President Mohammed Hosni MUBARAK] - governing party; National Progressive Unionist Grouping or Tagammu [Rlfaat EL-SAID]; New Wafd Party or NWP [No'man GOMA]; Socialist Liberal Party or Al-Ahrar [Hilmi SALIM]

note: formation of political parties must be approved by the government

Political pressure groups and leaders: despite a constitutional ban against religious-based parties, the technically illegal Muslim Brotherhood constitutes MUBARAK's potentially most significant political opposition; MUBARAK tolerated limited political activity by the Brotherhood for his first two terms, but moved more aggressively since then to block its influence; civic society groups are sanctioned, but constrained in practical terms; trade unions and professional associations are officially sanctioned

International organization participation: ABEDA, ACC, ACCT, AfDB, AFESD, AMF, AU, BSEC (observer), CAEU, EBRD, FAO, G-15, G-24, G-77, IAEA, IBRD, ICAO, ICC, ICCt (signatory), ICRM, IDA, IDB, IFAD, IFC, IFRCS, IHO, ILO, IMF, IMO, Interpol, IOC, IOM, ISO, ITU, LAS, MINURSO, MONUC, NAM, OAPEC, OAS (observer), OIC, OSCE (partner), PCA, UN, UNAMSIL, UNCTAD, UNESCO, UNIDO, UNITAR, UNMIK, UNOMIG, UNRWA, UPU, WCO, WFTU, WHO, WIPO, WMO, WToO, WTrO

Diplomatic representation in the US:

chief of mission: Ambassador M. Nabil FAHMY

chancery: 3521 International Court NW, Washington, DC 20008

telephone: [1] (202) 895-5400

FAX: [1] (202) 244-4319

consulate(s) general: Chicago, Houston, New York, and San Francisco

Diplomatic representation from the US:

chief of mission: Ambassador C. David WELCH

embassy: 5 Latin America St., Garden City, Cairo

mailing address: Unit 64900, Box 15, APO AE 09839-4900

telephone: [20] (2) 797-3300

FAX: [20] (2) 797-3200

Flag description: three equal horizontal bands of red (top), white, and black with the national emblem (a shield superimposed on a golden eagle facing the hoist side above a scroll bearing the name of the country in Arabic) centered in the white band; similar to the flag of Yemen, which has a plain white band; also similar to the flag of Syria, which has two green stars, and to the flag of Iraq, which has three green stars (plus an Arabic inscription) in a horizontal line centered in the white band

Economy

Economy - overview: Lack of substantial progress on economic reform since the mid 1990s has limited foreign direct investment in Egypt and kept annual GDP growth in the range of 2-3 percent in 2001-03.

Egypt (continued)

Egyptian officials in late 2003 and early 2004 proposed new privatization and customs reform measures, but the government is likely to pursue these initiatives cautiously and gradually to avoid a public backlash over potential inflation or layoffs associated with the reforms. Monetary pressures on an overvalued Egyptian pound led the government to float the currency in January 2003, leading to a sharp drop in its value and consequent inflationary pressure. The existence of a black market for hard currency is evidence that the government continues to influence the official exchange rate offered in banks. In September 2003, Egyptian officials increased subsidies on basic foodstuffs, helping to calm a frustrated public but widening an already deep budget deficit. Egypt's balance-of-payments position was not hurt by the war in Iraq in 2003, as tourism and Suez Canal revenues fared well. The development of an export market for natural gas is a bright spot for future growth prospects, but improvement in the capital-intensive hydrocarbons sector does little to reduce Egypt's persistent unemployment.

GDP: purchasing power parity - $294.3 billion (2003 est.)

GDP - real growth rate: 2.8% (2003 est.)

GDP - per capita: purchasing power parity - $3,900 (2003 est.)

GDP - composition by sector:
agriculture: 17%
industry: 33%
services: 50% (2003)

Population below poverty line: 16.7% (2000 est.)

Household income or consumption by percentage share:
lowest 10%: 3.7%
highest 10%: 29.5% (1999)

Distribution of family income - Gini index: 34.4 (1999)

Inflation rate (consumer prices): 4.5% (2003 est.)

Labor force: 20.1 million (2003 est.)

Labor force - by occupation: agriculture 32%, industry 17%, services 51% (2001 est.)

Unemployment rate: 9.9% (2003 est.)

Budget:
revenues: $14 billion
expenditures: $18.1 billion, including capital expenditures of $2.7 billion (2003 est.)

Industries: textiles, food processing, tourism, chemicals, hydrocarbons, construction, cement, metals

Industrial production growth rate: 1.5% (2003 est.)

Electricity - production: 75.23 billion kWh (2001)

Electricity - production by source:
fossil fuel: 81%
hydro: 19%
nuclear: 0%
other: 0% (2001)

Electricity - consumption: 69.96 billion kWh (2001)

Electricity - exports: 0 kWh (2001)

Electricity - imports: 0 kWh (2001)

Oil - production: 816,900 bbl/day (2001 est.)

Oil - consumption: 562,000 bbl/day (2001 est.)

Oil - exports: NA

Oil - imports: NA

Oil - proved reserves: 3.308 billion bbl (1 January 2002)

Natural gas - production: 21.2 billion cu m (2001 est.)

Natural gas - consumption: 21.2 billion cu m (2001 est.)

Natural gas - exports: 0 cu m (2001 est.)

Natural gas - imports: 0 cu m (2001 est.)

Natural gas - proved reserves: 1.264 trillion cu m (1 January 2002)

Agriculture - products: cotton, rice, corn, wheat, beans, fruits, vegetables; cattle, water buffalo, sheep, goats

Exports: $8.759 billion f.o.b. (2003 est.)

Exports - commodities: crude oil and petroleum products, cotton, textiles, metal products, chemicals

Exports - partners: US 18.5%, Italy 13.8%, UK 8.5%, France 4% (2002)

Imports: $14.75 billion f.o.b. (2003 est.)

Imports - commodities: machinery and equipment, foodstuffs, chemicals, wood products, fuels

Imports - partners: US 16.1%, Germany 7.5%, Italy 6.4%, France 6.2%, China 4.8% (2002)

Debt - external: $30 billion (2003 est.)

Economic aid - recipient: ODA, $1.2 billion (2001)

Currency: Egyptian pound (EGP)

Currency code: EGP

Exchange rates: Egyptian pounds per US dollar - 5.8509 (2003), 4.4997 (2002), 3.973 (2001), 3.4721 (2000), 3.3953 (1999)

Fiscal year: 1 July - 30 June

Communications

Telephones - main lines in use: 7.43 million (2002)

Telephones - mobile cellular: 4,494,700 (2002)

Telephone system:
general assessment: large system; underwent extensive upgrading during 1990s and is reasonably modern; Internet access and cellular service are available
domestic: principal centers at Alexandria, Cairo, Al Mansurah, Ismailia, Suez, and Tanta are connected by coaxial cable and microwave radio relay
international: country code - 20; satellite earth stations - 2 Intelsat (Atlantic Ocean and Indian Ocean), 1 Arabsat, and 1 Inmarsat; 5 coaxial submarine cables; tropospheric scatter to Sudan; microwave radio relay to Israel; a participant in Medarabtel and a signatory to Project Oxygen (a global submarine fiber-optic cable system)

Radio broadcast stations: AM 42 (plus 15 repeaters), FM 14, shortwave 3 (1999)

Television broadcast stations: 98 (September 1995)

Internet country code: .eg

Internet hosts: 3,061 (2002)

Internet users: 1.9 million (2002)

Transportation

Railways:
total: 5,105 km
standard gauge: 5,105 km 1.435-m gauge (42 km electrified) (2002)

Highways:
total: 64,000 km
paved: 49,984 km
unpaved: 14,016 km (1999 est.)

Waterways: 3,500 km
note: includes the Nile, Lake Nasser, Alexandria-Cairo Waterway, and numerous smaller canals in the delta; Suez Canal (193.5 km including approaches), used by oceangoing vessels drawing up to 16.1 m of water

Pipelines: condensate 327 km; condensate/gas 94 km; gas 6,145 km; liquid petroleum gas 382 km; oil 5,726 km; oil/gas/water 36 km; water 62 km (2003)

Ports and harbors: Alexandria, Al Ghardaqah, Aswan, Asyut, Bur Safajah, Damietta, Marsa Matruh, Port Said, Suez

Merchant marine:
total: 159 ships (1,000 GRT or over) 1,194,696 GRT/ 1,754,815 DWT
by type: bulk 18, cargo 41, container 5, passenger 64, petroleum tanker 14, roll on/roll off 13, short-sea/ passenger 4
foreign-owned: China 2, Cyprus 1, Denmark 1, Greece 6, Lebanon 2, Turkey 1
registered in other countries: 50 (2003 est.)

Airports: 89 (2003 est.)

Airports - with paved runways:
total: 72
over 3,047 m: 13
2,438 to 3,047 m: 38
1,524 to 2,437 m: 17
under 914 m: 4 (2003 est.)

Airports - with unpaved runways:
total: 17
2,438 to 3,047 m: 1
1,524 to 2,437 m: 2
914 to 1,523 m: 5
under 914 m: 9 (2003 est.)

Heliports: 2 (2003 est.)

Military

Military branches: Army, Navy, Air Force, Air Defense Command

Military manpower - military age: 20 years of age (2004 est.)

Military manpower - availability:
males age 15-49: 20,340,716 (2004 est.)

Military manpower - fit for military service:
males age 15-49: 13,148,944 (2004 est.)

Military manpower - reaching military age annually:
males: 756,233 (2004 est.)

Military expenditures - dollar figure: $2,443,200,000 (2003)

Military expenditures - percent of GDP: 3.6% (2003)

Disputes - international: Egypt and Sudan retain claims to administer the triangular areas that extend north and south of the 1899 Treaty boundary along the 22nd Parallel, but have withdrawn their military presence - Egypt is economically developing and effectively administers the "Hala'ib triangle" north of the Treaty line

Illicit drugs: transit point for Southwest Asian and Southeast Asian heroin and opium moving to Europe, Africa, and the US; transit stop for Nigerian couriers; concern as money-laundering site due to lax financial regulations and enforcement

El Salvador

Introduction

Background: El Salvador achieved independence from Spain in 1821 and from the Central American Federation in 1839. A 12-year civil war, which cost about 75,000 lives, was brought to a close in 1992 when the government and leftist rebels signed a treaty that provided for military and political reforms.

Geography

Location: Central America, bordering the North Pacific Ocean, between Guatemala and Honduras
Geographic coordinates: 13 50 N, 88 55 W
Map references: Central America and the Caribbean
Area:
total: 21,040 sq km
land: 20,720 sq km
water: 320 sq km
Area - comparative: slightly smaller than Massachusetts
Land boundaries:
total: 545 km
border countries: Guatemala 203 km, Honduras 342 km
Coastline: 307 km
Maritime claims:
territorial sea: 200 NM
Climate: tropical; rainy season (May to October); dry season (November to April); tropical on coast; temperate in uplands
Terrain: mostly mountains with narrow coastal belt and central plateau
Elevation extremes:
lowest point: Pacific Ocean 0 m
highest point: Cerro El Pital 2,730 m
Natural resources: hydropower, geothermal power, petroleum, arable land

Land use:
arable land: 27.27%
permanent crops: 12.11%
other: 60.62% (1998 est.)
Irrigated land: 360 sq km (1998 est.)
Natural hazards: known as the Land of Volcanoes; frequent and sometimes very destructive earthquakes and volcanic activity; extremely susceptible to hurricanes
Environment - current issues: deforestation; soil erosion; water pollution; contamination of soils from disposal of toxic wastes
Environment - international agreements:
party to: Biodiversity, Climate Change, Climate Change-Kyoto Protocol, Desertification, Endangered Species, Hazardous Wastes, Ozone Layer Protection, Wetlands
signed, but not ratified: Law of the Sea
Geography - note: smallest Central American country and only one without a coastline on Caribbean Sea

People

Population: 6,587,541 (July 2004 est.)
Age structure:
0-14 years: 36.8% (male 1,237,262; female 1,185,750)
15-64 years: 58.1% (male 1,819,035; female 2,009,032)
65 years and over: 5.1% (male 150,221; female 186,241) (2004 est.)
Median age:
total: 21.4 years
male: 20.2 years
female: 22.5 years (2004 est.)
Population growth rate: 1.78% (2004 est.)
Birth rate: 27.48 births/1,000 population (2004 est.)
Death rate: 5.93 deaths/1,000 population (2004 est.)
Net migration rate: -3.74 migrant(s)/1,000 population (2004 est.)

El Salvador (continued)

Sex ratio:
at birth: 1.05 male(s)/female
under 15 years: 1.04 male(s)/female
15-64 years: 0.91 male(s)/female
65 years and over: 0.81 male(s)/female
total population: 0.95 male(s)/female (2004 est.)

Infant mortality rate:
total: 25.93 deaths/1,000 live births
male: 28.79 deaths/1,000 live births
female: 22.92 deaths/1,000 live births (2004 est.)

Life expectancy at birth:
total population: 70.92 years
male: 67.31 years
female: 74.7 years (2004 est.)

Total fertility rate: 3.2 children born/woman (2004 est.)

HIV/AIDS - adult prevalence rate: 0.6% (2001 est.)

HIV/AIDS - people living with HIV/AIDS: 24,000 (2001 est.)

HIV/AIDS - deaths: 2,100 (2001 est.)

Nationality:
noun: Salvadoran(s)
adjective: Salvadoran

Ethnic groups: mestizo 90%, Amerindian 1%, white 9%

Religions: Roman Catholic 83%
note: there is extensive activity by Protestant groups throughout the country; by the end of 1992, there were an estimated 1 million Protestant evangelicals in El Salvador

Languages: Spanish, Nahua (among some Amerindians)

Literacy:
definition: age 10 and over can read and write
total population: 80.2%
male: 82.8%
female: 77.7% (2003 est.)

Government

Country name:
conventional long form: Republic of El Salvador
conventional short form: El Salvador
local long form: Republica de El Salvador
local short form: El Salvador

Government type: republic

Capital: San Salvador

Administrative divisions: 14 departments (departamentos, singular - departamento); Ahuachapan, Cabanas, Chalatenango, Cuscatlan, La Libertad, La Paz, La Union, Morazan, San Miguel, San Salvador, Santa Ana, San Vicente, Sonsonate, Usulutan

Independence: 15 September 1821 (from Spain)

National holiday: Independence Day, 15 September (1821)

Constitution: 23 December 1983

Legal system: based on civil and Roman law, with traces of common law; judicial review of legislative acts in the Supreme Court; accepts compulsory ICJ jurisdiction, with reservations

Suffrage: 18 years of age; universal

Executive branch:
chief of state: President Francisco FLORES Perez (since 1 June 1999); Vice President Carlos QUINTANILLA Schmidt (since 1 June 1999); note - the president is both the chief of state and head of government
head of government: President Francisco FLORES Perez (since 1 June 1999); Vice President Carlos QUINTANILLA Schmidt (since 1 June 1999); note - the president is both the chief of state and head of government
cabinet: Council of Ministers selected by the president
elections: president and vice president elected on the same ticket by popular vote for five-year terms; election last held 21 March 2004 (next to be held NA March 2009)
election results: Antonio SACA elected president; percent of vote - Antonio SACA (ARENA) 57.7%, Schafik HANDAL (FMLN) 35.6%, Hector SILVA (CDU-PDC) 3.9%, other 2.8%; note - Antonio SACA will assume the presidency on 1 June 2004

Legislative branch: unicameral Legislative Assembly or Asamblea Legislativa (84 seats; members are elected by direct, popular vote to serve three-year terms)
elections: last held 16 March 2003 (next to be held NA March 2006)
election results: percent of vote by party - NA%; seats by party - FMLN 31, ARENA 28, PCN 15, PDC 5, CD 5

Judicial branch: Supreme Court or Corte Suprema (judges are selected by the Legislative Assembly)

Political parties and leaders: Christian Democratic Party or PDC [Rodolfo PARKER]; United Democratic Center or CDU [Ruben ZAMORA, secretary general]; Democratic Party or PD [Jorge MELENDEZ]; Farabundo Marti National Liberation Front or FMLN [Fabio CASTILLO]; Liberal Democratic Party or PLD [Kirio Waldo SALGADO, president]; National Action Party or PAN [Gustavo Rogelio SALINAS, secretary general]; National Conciliation Party or PCN [Ciro CRUZ ZEPEDA, president]; National Republican Alliance or ARENA [Walter ARAUJO]; Social Christian Union or USC (formed by the merger of Christian Social Renewal Party or PRSC and Unity Movement or MU) [Abraham RODRIGUEZ, president]; Social Democratic Party or PSD [Juan MEDRANO]

Political pressure groups and leaders: labor organizations - Electrical Industry Union of El Salvador or SIES; Federation of the Construction Industry, Similar Transport and other activities, or FESINCONTRANS; National Confederation of Salvadoran Workers or CNTS; National Union of Salvadoran Workers or UNTS; Port Industry Union of El Salvador or SIPES; Salvadoran Union of Ex-Petrolleros and Peasant Workers or USEPOC; Salvadoran Workers Central or CTS; Workers Union of Electrical Corporation or STCEL; business organizations - National Association of Small Enterprise or ANEP; Salvadoran Assembly Industry Association or ASIC; Salvadoran Industrial Association or ASI

International organization participation: BCIE, CACM, FAO, G-77, IADB, IAEA, IBRD, ICAO, ICFTU, ICRM, IDA, IFAD, IFC, IFRCS, ILO, IMF, IMO, Interpol, IOC, IOM, ISO (correspondent), ITU, LAES, LAIA (observer), MINURSO, OAS, OPANAL, OPCW, PCA, RG, UN, UNCTAD, UNESCO, UNIDO, UPU, WCL, WFTU, WHO, WIPO, WMO, WToO, WTrO

Diplomatic representation in the US:
chief of mission: Ambassador Rene Antonio LEON Rodriguez
chancery: 2308 California Street NW, Washington, DC 20008
telephone: [1] (202) 265-9671
FAX: [1] (202) 234-3834
consulate(s) general: Boston, Chicago, Dallas, Houston, Los Angeles, Miami, New York, San Francisco, and Washington, DC

Diplomatic representation from the US:
chief of mission: Ambassador H. Douglas BARCLAY
embassy: Final Boulevard Santa Elena Sur, Antiguo Cuscatlan, La Libertad, San Salvador
mailing address: Unit 3116, APO AA 34023
telephone: [503] 278-4444
FAX: [503] 278-6011

Flag description: three equal horizontal bands of blue (top), white, and blue with the national coat of arms centered in the white band; the coat of arms features a round emblem encircled by the words REPUBLICA DE EL SALVADOR EN LA AMERICA CENTRAL; similar to the flag of Nicaragua, which has a different coat of arms centered in the white band - it features a triangle encircled by the words REPUBLICA DE NICARAGUA on top and AMERICA CENTRAL on the bottom; also similar to the flag of Honduras, which has five blue stars arranged in an X pattern centered in the white band

Economy

Economy - overview: With the adoption of the US dollar as its currency, El Salvador has lost control over monetary policy and must concentrate on maintaining a disciplined fiscal policy. GDP per capita is roughly only half that of Brazil, Argentina, and Chile, and the distribution of income is highly unequal. The trade deficit has been offset by annual remittances of almost $2 billion from Salvadorans living abroad and external aid. The government is striving to open new export markets, encourage foreign investment, modernize the tax and healthcare systems, and stimulate the sluggish economy.

GDP: purchasing power parity - $30.99 billion (2003 est.)

GDP - real growth rate: 1.4% (2003 est.)

GDP - per capita: purchasing power parity - $4,800 (2003 est.)

GDP - composition by sector:
agriculture: 10%
industry: 30%
services: 60% (2001)

Population below poverty line: 48% (1999 est.)

El Salvador (continued)

Household income or consumption by percentage share:
lowest 10%: 1.4%
highest 10%: 39.3% (2001)
Distribution of family income - Gini index: 52.2 (1998)
Inflation rate (consumer prices): 2.1% (2003 est.)
Labor force: 2.35 million (1999)
Labor force - by occupation: agriculture 30%, industry 15%, services 55% (1999 est.)
Unemployment rate: 6.5% - but the economy has much underemployment (2003 est.)
Budget:
revenues: $2.1 billion
expenditures: $2.5 billion, including capital expenditures of $NA (2001 est.)
Industries: food processing, beverages, petroleum, chemicals, fertilizer, textiles, furniture, light metals
Industrial production growth rate: 1.4% (2003 est.)
Electricity - production: 3.729 billion kWh (2001)
Electricity - production by source:
fossil fuel: 44%
hydro: 30.9%
nuclear: 0%
other: 25.1% (2001)
Electricity - consumption: 3.777 billion kWh (2001)
Electricity - exports: 44 million kWh (2001)
Electricity - imports: 353 million kWh (2001)
Oil - production: 0 bbl/day (2001 est.)
Oil - consumption: 39,000 bbl/day (2001 est.)
Oil - exports: NA
Oil - imports: NA
Agriculture - products: coffee, sugar, corn, rice, beans, oilseed, cotton, sorghum; shrimp; beef, dairy products
Exports: $3.162 billion (2003 est.)
Exports - commodities: offshore assembly exports, coffee, sugar, shrimp, textiles, chemicals, electricity
Exports - partners: US 62.9%, Guatemala 11.9%, Honduras 6.8%, Nicaragua 4.4% (2002)
Imports: $5.466 billion (2003 est.)
Imports - commodities: raw materials, consumer goods, capital goods, fuels, foodstuffs, petroleum, electricity
Imports - partners: US 38.2%, Guatemala 9.9%, Mexico 6.1% (2002)
Debt - external: $6.5 billion (2003 est.)
Economic aid - recipient: total $252 million; $57 million from US (1995)
Currency: US dollar (USD)
Currency code: USD
Exchange rates: the US dollar is the legal tender
Fiscal year: calendar year

Communications

Telephones - main lines in use: 667,700 (2002)
Telephones - mobile cellular: 888,800 (2002)
Telephone system:
general assessment: NA
domestic: nationwide microwave radio relay system

international: country code - 503; satellite earth station - 1 Intelsat (Atlantic Ocean); connected to Central American Microwave System
Radio broadcast stations: AM 61 (plus 24 repeaters), FM 30, shortwave 0 (1998)
Television broadcast stations: 5 (1997)
Internet country code: .sv
Internet hosts: 269 (2002)
Internet users: 300,000 (2002)

Transportation

Railways:
total: 283 km
narrow gauge: 283 km 0.914-m gauge
note: length of operational route reduced from 562 km to 283 km by disuse and lack of maintenance (2002)
Highways:
total: 10,029 km
paved: 1,986 km (including 327 km of expressways)
unpaved: 8,043 km (1999 est.)
Waterways: Rio Lempa partially navigable
Ports and harbors: Acajutla, Puerto Cutuco, La Libertad, La Union, Puerto El Triunfo
Merchant marine: none
Airports: 73 (2003 est.)
Airports - with paved runways:
total: 4
over 3,047 m: 1
1,524 to 2,437 m: 1
914 to 1,523 m: 2 (2003 est.)
Airports - with unpaved runways:
total: 69
914 to 1,523 m: 15
under 914 m: 54 (2003 est.)
Heliports: 1 (2003 est.)

Military

Military branches: Army, Navy (FNES), Air Force
Military manpower - military age: 18 years of age (2004 est.)
Military manpower - availability:
males age 15-49: 1,571,299 (2004 est.)
Military manpower - fit for military service:
males age 15-49: 995,672 (2004 est.)
Military manpower - reaching military age annually:
males: 69,993 (2004 est.)
Military expenditures - dollar figure: $157 million (2003)
Military expenditures - percent of GDP: 1.1% (2003)

Transnational Issues

Disputes - international: in 1992, the ICJ ruled on the delimitation of "bolsones" (disputed areas) along the El Salvador-Honduras boundary, and the OAS is assisting with a technical resolution of undemarcated bolsones; in 2003, the ICJ rejected El Salvador's request to revise its decision on one part of the bolsones; the 1992 ICJ ruling advised a tripartite

resolution to a maritime boundary in the Gulf of Fonseca with consideration of Honduran access to the Pacific; El Salvador continues to claim tiny Conejo Island, not mentioned by the ICJ, off Honduras in the Gulf de Fonseca
Illicit drugs: transshipment point for cocaine; small amounts of marijuana produced for local consumption; domestic cocaine abuse on the rise

Equatorial Guinea

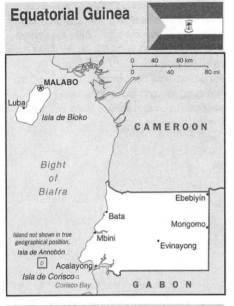

Introduction

Background: Equatorial Guinea gained independence in 1968 after 190 years of Spanish rule. This tiny country, composed of a mainland portion plus five inhabited islands, is one of the smallest on the African continent. President OBIANG NGUEM MBASOGO has ruled the country for over two decades since seizing power from his uncle, then President MACIAS, in a 1979 coup. Although nominally a constitutional democracy since 1991, the 1996 and 2002 presidential elections - as well as the 1999 legislative elections - were widely seen as being flawed. The president controls most opposition parties through the judicious use of patronage. Despite the country's economic windfall from oil production resulting in a massive increase in government revenue in recent years, there have been few improvements in the country's living standards.

Geography

Location: Western Africa, bordering the Bight of Biafra, between Cameroon and Gabon
Geographic coordinates: 2 00 N, 10 00 E
Map references: Africa
Area:
total: 28,051 sq km
land: 28,051 sq km
water: 0 sq km
Area - comparative: slightly smaller than Maryland
Land boundaries:
total: 539 km
border countries: Cameroon 189 km, Gabon 350 km
Coastline: 296 km
Maritime claims:
territorial sea: 12 NM
exclusive economic zone: 200 NM
Climate: tropical; always hot, humid
Terrain: coastal plains rise to interior hills; islands are volcanic

Elevation extremes:
lowest point: Atlantic Ocean 0 m
highest point: Pico Basile 3,008 m
Natural resources: oil, petroleum, timber, small unexploited deposits of gold, manganese, uranium, titanium, iron ore
Land use:
arable land: 4.63%
permanent crops: 3.57%
other: 91.8% (1998 est.)
Irrigated land: NA sq km
Natural hazards: violent windstorms, flash floods
Environment - current issues: tap water is not potable; deforestation
Environment - international agreements:
party to: Biodiversity, Climate Change, Climate Change-Kyoto Protocol, Desertification, Endangered Species, Hazardous Wastes, Law of the Sea, Ship Pollution
signed, but not ratified: none of the selected agreements
Geography - note: insular and continental regions rather widely separated

People

Population: 523,051 (July 2004 est.)
Age structure:
0-14 years: 42% (male 110,268; female 109,222)
15-64 years: 54.3% (male 136,370; female 147,431)
65 years and over: 3.8% (male 8,745; female 11,015) (2004 est.)
Median age:
total: 18.7 years
male: 18.1 years
female: 19.4 years (2004 est.)
Population growth rate: 2.43% (2004 est.)
Birth rate: 36.56 births/1,000 population (2004 est.)
Death rate: 12.27 deaths/1,000 population (2004 est.)
Net migration rate: 0 migrant(s)/1,000 population (2004 est.)
Sex ratio:
at birth: 1.03 male(s)/female
under 15 years: 1.01 male(s)/female
15-64 years: 0.93 male(s)/female
65 years and over: 0.79 male(s)/female
total population: 0.95 male(s)/female (2004 est.)
Infant mortality rate:
total: 87.08 deaths/1,000 live births
male: 93.27 deaths/1,000 live births
female: 80.71 deaths/1,000 live births (2004 est.)
Life expectancy at birth:
total population: 55.15 years
male: 53 years
female: 57.36 years (2004 est.)
Total fertility rate: 4.68 children born/woman (2004 est.)
HIV/AIDS - adult prevalence rate: 3.4% (2001 est.)
HIV/AIDS - people living with HIV/AIDS: 5,900 (2001 est.)
HIV/AIDS - deaths: 370 (2001 est.)

Nationality:
noun: Equatorial Guinean(s) or Equatoguinean(s)
adjective: Equatorial Guinean or Equatoguinean
Ethnic groups: Bioko (primarily Bubi, some Fernandinos), Rio Muni (primarily Fang), Europeans less than 1,000, mostly Spanish
Religions: nominally Christian and predominantly Roman Catholic, pagan practices
Languages: Spanish (official), French (official), pidgin English, Fang, Bubi, Ibo
Literacy:
definition: age 15 and over can read and write
total population: 85.7%
male: 93.3%
female: 78.4% (2003 est.)

Government

Country name:
conventional long form: Republic of Equatorial Guinea
conventional short form: Equatorial Guinea
local long form: Republica de Guinea Ecuatorial
local short form: Guinea Ecuatorial
former: Spanish Guinea
Government type: republic
Capital: Malabo
Administrative divisions: 7 provinces (provincias, singular - provincia); Annobon, Bioko Norte, Bioko Sur, Centro Sur, Kie-Ntem, Litoral, Wele-Nzas
Independence: 12 October 1968 (from Spain)
National holiday: Independence Day, 12 October (1968)
Constitution: approved by national referendum 17 November 1991; amended January 1995
Legal system: partly based on Spanish civil law and tribal custom
Suffrage: 18 years of age; universal adult
Executive branch:
chief of state: President Brig. Gen. (Ret.) Teodoro OBIANG NGUEMA MBASOGO (since 3 August 1979 when he seized power in a military coup)
head of government: Prime Minister Candido Muatetema RIVAS (since 26 February 2001); First Deputy Prime Minister Miguel OYONO NDONG (since NA January 1998); Deputy Prime Minister Demetrio Elo NDONG NZE FUMU (since NA January 1998)
cabinet: Council of Ministers appointed by the president
elections: president elected by popular vote for a seven-year term; election last held 15 December 2002 (next to be held NA December 2009); prime minister and deputy prime ministers appointed by the president
election results: Teodoro OBIANG NGUEMA MBASOGO reelected president; percent of vote - Teodoro OBIANG NGUEMA MBASOGO 97.1%, Celestino Bonifacio BACALE 2.2%; elections marred by widespread fraud
Legislative branch: unicameral House of People's Representatives or Camara de Representantes del Pueblo (80 seats; members directly elected by popular vote to serve five-year terms)

Equatorial Guinea (continued)

elections: last held 7 March 1999 (next to be held 24 April 2004)

election results: percent of vote by party - PDGE 80%, UP 6%, CPDS 5%; seats by party - PDGE 75, UP 4 and CPDS 1

note: Parliament has little power since the constitution vests all executive authority in the president

Judicial branch: Supreme Tribunal

Political parties and leaders: Convergence Party for Social Democracy or CPDS [Placido MIKO Abogo]; Democratic Party for Equatorial Guinea or PDGE (ruling party) [Teodoro OBIANG NGUEMA MBASOGO]; Party for Progress of Equatorial Guinea or PPGE [Severo MOTO]; Popular Action of Equatorial Guinea or APGE [Miguel Esono EMAN]; Popular Union or UP [Andres Moises Bda ADA]; Progressive Democratic Alliance or ADP [Victorino Bolekia BONAY]; Union of Independent Democrats of UDI [Daniel OYONO]

Political pressure groups and leaders: NA

International organization participation: ACCT, ACP, AfDB, AU, BDEAC, CEMAC, FAO, FZ, G-77, IBRD, ICAO, ICRM, IDA, IFAD, IFC, IFRCS, ILO, IMF, IMO, Interpol, IOC, ITU, NAM, OAS (observer), OPCW, UN, UNCTAD, UNESCO, UNIDO, UPU, WHO, WIPO, WToO, WTrO (observer)

Diplomatic representation in the US:

chief of mission: Ambassador Teodoro Biyogo NSUE

chancery: 2020 16th Street NW, Washington, DC 20009

telephone: [1] (202) 518-5700

FAX: [1] (202) 518-5252

Diplomatic representation from the US: the US does not have an embassy in Equatorial Guinea (embassy closed September 1995); the US ambassador to Cameroon is accredited to Equatorial Guinea; the US State Department is considering opening a Consulate Agency in Malabo

Flag description: three equal horizontal bands of green (top), white, and red with a blue isosceles triangle based on the hoist side and the coat of arms centered in the white band; the coat of arms has six yellow six-pointed stars (representing the mainland and five offshore islands) above a gray shield bearing a silk-cotton tree and below which is a scroll with the motto UNIDAD, PAZ, JUSTICIA (Unity, Peace, Justice)

Economy

Economy - overview: The discovery and exploitation of large oil reserves have contributed to dramatic economic growth in recent years. Forestry, farming, and fishing are also major components of GDP. Subsistence farming predominates. Although pre-independence Equatorial Guinea counted on cocoa production for hard currency earnings, the neglect of the rural economy under successive regimes has diminished potential for agriculture-led growth (the government has stated its intention to reinvest some oil revenue into agriculture). A number of aid programs sponsored by the World Bank and the IMF have been cut off since 1993 because of corruption and mismanagement. No longer eligible for concessional financing because of large oil revenues, the government has been unsuccessfully trying to agree on a "shadow" fiscal management program with the World Bank and IMF. Businesses, for the most part, are owned by government officials and their family members. Undeveloped natural resources include titanium, iron ore, manganese, uranium, and alluvial gold. Growth will remain strong in 2004, led by oil.

GDP: purchasing power parity - $1.27 billion (2002 est.)

GDP - real growth rate: 20% (2002 est.)

GDP - per capita: purchasing power parity - $2,700 (2002 est.)

GDP - composition by sector:

agriculture: 20%

industry: 60%

services: 20% (1999 est.)

Population below poverty line: NA%

Household income or consumption by percentage share:

lowest 10%: NA%

highest 10%: NA%

Inflation rate (consumer prices): 6% (2002 est.)

Labor force: NA (October 2000)

Unemployment rate: 30% (1998 est.)

Budget:

revenues: $200 million

expenditures: $158 million, including capital expenditures of $NA (2001 est.)

Industries: petroleum, fishing, sawmilling, natural gas

Industrial production growth rate: 30% (2002 est.)

Electricity - production: 23.56 million kWh (2001)

Electricity - production by source:

fossil fuel: 94.3%

hydro: 5.7%

nuclear: 0%

other: 0% (2001)

Electricity - consumption: 21.91 million kWh (2001)

Electricity - exports: 0 kWh (2001)

Electricity - imports: 0 kWh (2001)

Oil - production: 181,400 bbl/day (2001 est.)

Oil - consumption: 2,000 bbl/day (2001 est.)

Oil - exports: NA

Oil - imports: NA

Oil - proved reserves: 563.5 million bbl (1 January 2002)

Natural gas - production: 20 million cu m (2001 est.)

Natural gas - consumption: 20 million cu m (2001 est.)

Natural gas - exports: 0 cu m (2001 est.)

Natural gas - imports: 0 cu m (2001 est.)

Natural gas - proved reserves: 68.53 billion cu m (1 January 2002)

Agriculture - products: coffee, cocoa, rice, yams, cassava (tapioca), bananas, palm oil nuts; livestock; timber

Exports: $2.1 billion f.o.b. (2003 est.)

Exports - commodities: petroleum, methanol, timber, cocoa

Exports - partners: US 28.3%, Spain 25.3%, China 17.5%, Canada 10.6%, France 5% (2002)

Imports: $1.371 billion f.o.b. (2003 est.)

Imports - commodities: petroleum sector equipment, other equipment

Imports - partners: US 27.8%, Spain 15.1%, UK 14.2%, Norway 10.7%, France 10%, Netherlands 4.6%, Italy 4.4% (2002)

Debt - external: $248 million (2000 est.)

Economic aid - recipient: $33.8 million (1995)

Currency: Communaute Financiere Africaine franc (XAF); note - responsible authority is the Bank of the Central African States

Currency code: XAF

Exchange rates: Communaute Financiere Africaine francs (XAF) per US dollar - 581.2 (2003), 696.988 (2002), 733.039 (2001), 711.976 (2000), 615.699 (1999)

Fiscal year: 1 January - 31 December

Communications

Telephones - main lines in use: 8,800 (2002)

Telephones - mobile cellular: 32,000 (2002)

Telephone system:

general assessment: poor system with adequate government services

domestic: NA

international: country code - 240; international communications from Bata and Malabo to African and European countries; satellite earth station - 1 Intelsat (Indian Ocean)

Radio broadcast stations: AM 0, FM 3, shortwave 5 (2002)

Television broadcast stations: 1 (2002)

Internet country code: .gq

Internet hosts: 3 (2002)

Internet users: 1,800 (2002)

Transportation

Railways:

total: 0 km

Highways:

total: 2,880 km (1999 est.)

Waterways: none

Pipelines: condensate 37 km; gas 39 km; liquid natural gas 4 km; oil 24 km (2003)

Ports and harbors: Bata, Luba, Malabo

Merchant marine:

total: 3 ships (1,000 GRT or over) 6,556 GRT/9,704 DWT

by type: cargo 2, passenger/cargo 1

registered in other countries: 1 (2003 est.)

Airports: 3 (2003 est.)

Airports - with paved runways:

total: 2

2,438 to 3,047 m: 1

1,524 to 2,437 m: 1 (2003 est.)

Airports - with unpaved runways:

total: 1

under 914 m: 1 (2003 est.)

Military

Military

Military branches: Army, Navy, Air Force, Rapid Intervention Force
Military manpower - availability:
males age 15-49: 120,463 (2004 est.)
Military manpower - fit for military service:
males age 15-49: 61,084 (2004 est.)
Military expenditures - dollar figure: $75.1 million (2003)
Military expenditures - percent of GDP: 2.5% (2003)

Transnational Issues

Disputes - international: in 2002, ICJ ruled on an equidistance settlement of Cameroon-Equatorial Guinea-Nigeria maritime boundary in the Gulf of Guinea, but a dispute between Equatorial Guinea and Cameroon over an island at the mouth of the Ntem River, imprecisely defined coordinates in the ICJ decision, and the unresolved Bakasi allocation contribute to the delay in implementation; creation of a maritime boundary in hydrocarbon-rich Corisco Bay with Gabon is hampered by dispute over Mbane Island, administered and occupied by Gabon since the 1970s

Eritrea

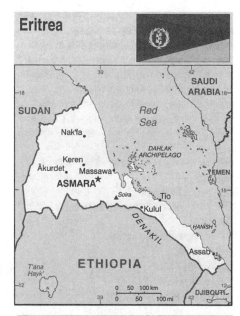

Introduction

Background: Eritrea was awarded to Ethiopia in 1952 as part of a federation. Ethiopia's annexation of Eritrea as a province 10 years later sparked a 30-year struggle for independence that ended in 1991 with Eritrean rebels defeating governmental forces; independence was overwhelmingly approved in a 1993 referendum. A two-and-a-half-year border war with Ethiopia that erupted in 1998 ended under UN auspices on 12 December 2000. Eritrea currently hosts a UN peacekeeping operation that is monitoring a 25 km-wide Temporary Security Zone on the border with Ethiopia. An international commission, organized to resolve the border dispute, posted its findings in 2002 but final demarcation is on hold due to Ethiopian objections.

Geography

Location: Eastern Africa, bordering the Red Sea, between Djibouti and Sudan
Geographic coordinates: 15 00 N, 39 00 E
Map references: Africa
Area:
total: 121,320 sq km
land: 121,320 sq km
water: 0 sq km
Area - comparative: slightly larger than Pennsylvania
Land boundaries:
total: 1,626 km
border countries: Djibouti 109 km, Ethiopia 912 km, Sudan 605 km
Coastline: 2,234 km total; mainland on Red Sea 1,151 km, islands in Red Sea 1,083 km
Maritime claims:
territorial sea: 12 NM
Climate: hot, dry desert strip along Red Sea coast; cooler and wetter in the central highlands (up to 61 cm of rainfall annually); semiarid in western hills and lowlands; rainfall heaviest during June-September except in coastal desert

Terrain: dominated by extension of Ethiopian north-south trending highlands, descending on the east to a coastal desert plain, on the northwest to hilly terrain and on the southwest to flat-to-rolling plains
Elevation extremes:
lowest point: near Kulul within the Denakil depression -75 m
highest point: Soira 3,018 m
Natural resources: gold, potash, zinc, copper, salt, possibly oil and natural gas, fish
Land use:
arable land: 3.87%
permanent crops: 0.02%
other: 96.11% (1998 est.)
Irrigated land: 220 sq km (1998 est.)
Natural hazards: frequent droughts; locust swarms
Environment - current issues: deforestation; desertification; soil erosion; overgrazing; loss of infrastructure from civil warfare
Environment - international agreements:
party to: Biodiversity, Climate Change, Desertification, Endangered Species
signed, but not ratified: none of the selected agreements
Geography - note: strategic geopolitical position along world's busiest shipping lanes; Eritrea retained the entire coastline of Ethiopia along the Red Sea upon de jure independence from Ethiopia on 24 May 1993

People

Population: 4,447,307 (July 2004 est.)
Age structure:
0-14 years: 44.8% (male 998,404; female 993,349)
15-64 years: 51.9% (male 1,140,892; female 1,166,481)
65 years and over: 3.3% (male 72,776; female 75,405) (2004 est.)
Median age:
total: 17.5 years
male: 17.3 years
female: 17.7 years (2004 est.)
Population growth rate: 2.57% (2004 est.)
Birth rate: 39.03 births/1,000 population (2004 est.)
Death rate: 13.36 deaths/1,000 population (2004 est.)
Net migration rate: 0 migrant(s)/1,000 population
note: UNHCR began repatriating about 150,000 Eritrean refugees from Sudan in 2001 following the restoration of diplomatic relations between the two countries in 2000 (2004 est.)
Sex ratio:
at birth: 1.03 male(s)/female
under 15 years: 1.01 male(s)/female
15-64 years: 0.98 male(s)/female
65 years and over: 0.97 male(s)/female
total population: 0.99 male(s)/female (2004 est.)
Infant mortality rate:
total: 75.59 deaths/1,000 live births
male: 83.03 deaths/1,000 live births
female: 67.94 deaths/1,000 live births (2004 est.)

Eritrea (continued)

Life expectancy at birth:
total population: 52.7 years
male: 51.32 years
female: 54.12 years (2004 est.)
Total fertility rate: 5.67 children born/woman
(2004 est.)
HIV/AIDS - adult prevalence rate: 2.8% (2001 est.)
HIV/AIDS - people living with HIV/AIDS: 55,000
(2001 est.)
HIV/AIDS - deaths: 350 (2001 est.)
Nationality:
noun: Eritrean(s)
adjective: Eritrean
Ethnic groups: ethnic Tigrinya 50%, Tigre and
Kunama 40%, Afar 4%, Saho (Red Sea coast
dwellers) 3%, other 3%
Religions: Muslim, Coptic Christian, Roman
Catholic, Protestant
Languages: Afar, Arabic, Tigre and Kunama,
Tigrinya, other Cushitic languages
Literacy:
definition: NA
total population: 58.6%
male: 69.9%
female: 47.6% (2003 est.)

Government

Country name:
conventional long form: State of Eritrea
conventional short form: Eritrea
local long form: Hagere Ertra
local short form: Ertra
former: Eritrea Autonomous Region in Ethiopia
Government type: transitional government
note: following a successful referendum on
independence for the Autonomous Region of Eritrea
on 23-25 April 1993, a National Assembly, composed
entirely of the People's Front for Democracy and
Justice or PFDJ, was established as a transitional
legislature; a Constitutional Commission was also
established to draft a constitution; ISAIAS Afworki was
elected president by the transitional legislature; the
constitution, ratified in May 1997, did not enter into
effect, pending parliamentary and presidential
elections; parliamentary elections had been
scheduled in December 2001, but were postponed
indefinitely; currently the sole legal party is the
People's Front for Democracy and Justice (PFDJ)
Capital: Asmara (formerly Asmera)
Administrative divisions: 6 regions (regions,
singular - region); Central, Anelba, Southern Red Sea,
Northern Red Sea, Southern, Gash-Barka
Independence: 24 May 1993 (from Ethiopia)
National holiday: Independence Day, 24 May (1993)
Constitution: the transitional constitution, decreed
on 19 May 1993, was replaced by a new constitution
adopted on 23 May 1997, but not yet implemented
Legal system: primary basis is the Ethiopian legal
code of 1957, with revisions; new civil, commercial,
and penal codes have not yet been promulgated; also
relies on customary and post-independence-enacted
laws and, for civil cases involving Muslims, Sharia law

Suffrage: 18 years of age; universal
Executive branch:
chief of state: President ISAIAS Afworki (since 8 June
1993); note - the president is both the chief of state
and head of government and is head of the State
Council and National Assembly
head of government: President ISAIAS Afworki (since
8 June 1993); note - the president is both the chief of
state and head of government and is head of the State
Council and National Assembly
cabinet: State Council is the collective executive
authority; members appointed by the president
elections: president elected by the National Assembly;
election last held 8 June 1993 (next election date
uncertain as the National Assembly did not hold a
presidential election in December 2001 as anticipated)
election results: ISAIAS Afworki elected president;
percent of National Assembly vote - ISAIAS
Afworki 95%
Legislative branch: unicameral National Assembly
(150 seats; term limits not established)
elections: in May 1997, following the adoption of the
new constitution, 75 members of the PFDJ Central
Committee (the old Central Committee of the EPLF),
60 members of the 527-member Constituent
Assembly, that had been established in 1997 to
discuss and ratify the new constitution, and 15
representatives of Eritreans living abroad were formed
into a Transitional National Assembly to serve as the
country's legislative body until countrywide elections
to a National Assembly were held; although only 75 of
150 members of the Transitional National Assembly
were elected, the constitution stipulates that once past
the transition stage, all members of the National
Assembly will be elected by secret ballot of all eligible
voters; National Assembly elections scheduled for
December 2001 were postponed indefinitely
Judicial branch: High Court - regional, subregional,
and village courts; also have military and special courts
Political parties and leaders: People's Front for
Democracy and Justice or PFDJ, the only party
recognized by the government [ISAIAS Afworki];
note - a National Assembly committee drafted a law
on political parties in January 2001, but the full
National Assembly has not yet debated or voted on it
Political pressure groups and leaders: Eritrean
Islamic Jihad or EIJ [leader NA] (also including
Eritrean Islamic Jihad Movement or EIJM (also known
as the Abu Sihel Movement) [leader NA]); Eritrean
Islamic Salvation or EIS (also known as the Arafa
Movement) [leader NA]; Eritrean Liberation Front or
ELF [ABDULLAH Muhammed]; Eritrean National
Alliance or ENA (a coalition including EIJ, EIS, ELF,
and a number of ELF factions) [HERUY Tedla Biru];
Eritrean Public Forum or EPF [ARADOM Iyob]
International organization participation: ACP,
AfDB, AU, FAO, G-77, IAEA, IBRD, ICAO, ICCt
(signatory), ICFTU, IDA, IFAD, IFC, IFRCS, IGAD,
ILO, IMF, IMO, Interpol, IOC, ISO (subscriber), ITU,
NAM, OPCW, PCA, UN, UNCTAD, UNESCO,
UNIDO, UPU, WCO, WFTU, WHO, WIPO, WMO,
WToO

Diplomatic representation in the US:
chief of mission: Ambassador GIRMA Asmerom
chancery: 1708 New Hampshire Avenue NW,
Washington, DC 20009
telephone: [1] (202) 319-1991
FAX: [1] (202) 319-1304
consulate(s) general: Oakland (California)
Diplomatic representation from the US:
chief of mission: Ambassador Donald J.
McCONNELL
embassy: Franklin D. Roosevelt Street, Asmara
mailing address: P. O. Box 211, Asmara
telephone: [291] (1) 120004
FAX: [291] (1) 127584
Flag description: red isosceles triangle (based on
the hoist side) dividing the flag into two right triangles;
the upper triangle is green, the lower one is blue; a
gold wreath encircling a gold olive branch is centered
on the hoist side of the red triangle

Economy

Economy - overview: Since independence from
Ethiopia on 24 May 1993, Eritrea has faced the
economic problems of a small, desperately poor
country. Like the economies of many African nations,
the economy is largely based on subsistence
agriculture, with 80% of the population involved in
farming and herding. The Ethiopian-Eritrea war in
1998-2000 severely hurt Eritrea's economy. GDP
growth fell to zero in 1999 and to -12.1% in 2000. The
May 2000 Ethiopian offensive into northern Eritrea
caused some $600 million in property damage and
loss, including losses of $225 million in livestock and
55,000 homes. The attack prevented planting of
crops in Eritrea's most productive region, causing
food production to drop by 62%. Even during the war,
Eritrea developed its transportation infrastructure,
asphalting new roads, improving its ports, and
repairing war damaged roads and bridges. Since the
war ended, the government has maintained a firm
grip on the economy, expanding the use of the
military and party-owned businesses to complete
Eritrea's development agenda. Erratic rainfall and the
delayed demobilization of agriculturalists from the
military kept cereal production well below normal,
holding down growth in 2002. Eritrea's economic
future depends upon its ability to master social
problems such as illiteracy, unemployment, and low
skills, and to open its economy to private enterprise
so the diaspora's money and expertise can foster
economic growth.
GDP: purchasing power parity - $3.3 billion
(2002 est.)
GDP - real growth rate: 2% (2002 est.)
GDP - per capita: purchasing power parity - $700
(2002 est.)
GDP - composition by sector:
agriculture: 17%
industry: 29%
services: 54% (2001 est.)
Population below poverty line: 53% (1993-94)

Eritrea (continued)

Household income or consumption by percentage share:
lowest 10%: NA%
highest 10%: NA%
Inflation rate (consumer prices): 15% (2001)
Labor force: NA (1999)
Labor force - by occupation: agriculture 80%, industry and services 20%
Unemployment rate: NA% (2003 est.)
Budget:
revenues: $206.4 million
expenditures: $615.7 million, including capital expenditures of $NA (2000 est.)
Industries: food processing, beverages, clothing and textiles
Industrial production growth rate: NA%
Electricity - production: 220.5 million kWh (2001)
Electricity - production by source:
fossil fuel: 100%
hydro: 0%
nuclear: 0%
other: 0% (2001)
Electricity - consumption: 205.1 million kWh (2001)
Electricity - exports: 0 kWh NA kWh (2001)
Electricity - imports: 0 kWh NA kWh (2001)
Oil - production: 0 bbl/day (2001 est.)
Oil - consumption: 6,000 bbl/day (2001 est.)
Oil - exports: NA
Oil - imports: NA
Agriculture - products: sorghum, lentils, vegetables, corn, cotton, tobacco, coffee, sisal; livestock, goats; fish
Exports: $56 million f.o.b. (2003 est.)
Exports - commodities: livestock, sorghum, textiles, food, small manufactures (2000)
Exports - partners: Malaysia 30.8%, Italy 25.2%, Germany 11.4%, France 7% (2002)
Imports: $600 million f.o.b. (2003 est.)
Imports - commodities: machinery, petroleum products, food, manufactured goods (2000)
Imports - partners: Italy 25.8%, US 14.9%, Germany 6.8%, Ukraine 5.5%, Turkey 5.2%, France 4.3% (2002)
Debt - external: $311 million (2000 est.)
Economic aid - recipient: $77 million (1999)
Currency: nakfa (ERN)
Currency code: ERN
Exchange rates: nakfa (ERN) per US dollar - NA (2003), 13.9582 (2002), 11.3095 (2001), 9.5 (2000), 7.6 (1999)
Fiscal year: calendar year

Communications

Telephones - main lines in use: 35,900 (2002)
Telephones - mobile cellular: NA
Telephone system:
general assessment: inadequate
domestic: very inadequate; most telephones are in Asmara; government is seeking international tenders to improve the system (2002)
international: country code - 291; note - international connections exist

Radio broadcast stations: AM 2, FM NA, shortwave 2 (2000)
Television broadcast stations: 1 (2000)
Internet country code: .er
Internet hosts: 859 (2002)
Internet users: 9,000 (2002)

Transportation

Railways:
total: 306 km
narrow gauge: 306 km 0.950-m gauge
note: railway is being rebuilt (2002)
Highways:
total: 4,010 km
paved: 874 km
unpaved: 3,136 km (1999 est.)
Waterways: none
Ports and harbors: Assab (Aseb), Massawa (Mits'iwa)
Merchant marine:
total: 5 ships (1,000 GRT or over) 16,069 GRT/19,549 DWT
by type: bulk 1, cargo 1, liquefied gas 1, petroleum tanker 1, roll on/roll off 1
registered in other countries: 1 (2003 est.)
Airports: 18 (2003 est.)
Airports - with paved runways:
total: 5
over 3,047 m: 3
2,438 to 3,047 m: 2 (2003 est.)
Airports - with unpaved runways:
total: 13
over 3,047 m: 1
2,438 to 3,047 m: 1
1,524 to 2,437 m: 5
914 to 1,523 m: 4
under 914 m: 2 (2003 est.)

Military

Military branches: Army, Navy, Air Force
Military expenditures - dollar figure: $77.9 million (2003)
Military expenditures - percent of GDP: 11.8% (2003)

Transnational Issues

Disputes - international: Eritrea and Ethiopia agreed to abide by 2002 Ethiopia-Eritrea Border Commission's (EEBC) delimitation decision, but demarcation has been delayed, despite intense international intervention, by Ethiopian insistence that the decision ignored "human geography," made technical errors in the delimitation, and incorrectly awarded Badme, the focus of the 1998-2000 war, and other areas to Eritrea and Eritrea's insistence on not deviating from the commission's decision; UN Peacekeeping Mission to Ethiopia and Eritrea (UNMEE) continues to monitor a 25km-wide Temporary Security Zone in Eritrea until the demarcation; Sudan accuses Eritrea of supporting Sudanese rebel groups; Eritrea protests Yemeni fishing around the Hanish Islands awarded to Eritrea by the ICJ in 1999

Estonia

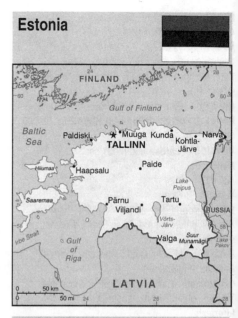

Introduction

Background: After centuries of Danish, Swedish, German, and Russian rule, Estonia attained independence in 1918. Forcibly incorporated into the USSR in 1940, it regained its freedom in 1991, with the collapse of the Soviet Union. Since the last Russian troops left in 1994, Estonia has been free to promote economic and political ties with Western Europe. It will accede to the EU in May 2004 and to NATO in the summer of 2004.

Geography

Location: Eastern Europe, bordering the Baltic Sea and Gulf of Finland, between Latvia and Russia
Geographic coordinates: 59 00 N, 26 00 E
Map references: Europe
Area:
total: 45,226 sq km
land: 43,211 sq km
water: 2,015 sq km
note: includes 1,520 islands in the Baltic Sea
Area - comparative: slightly smaller than New Hampshire and Vermont combined
Land boundaries:
total: 633 km
border countries: Latvia 339 km, Russia 294 km
Coastline: 3,794 km
Maritime claims:
territorial sea: 12 NM
exclusive economic zone: limits fixed in coordination with neighboring states
Climate: maritime, wet, moderate winters, cool summers
Terrain: marshy, lowlands; flat in the north, hilly in the south
Elevation extremes:
lowest point: Baltic Sea 0 m
highest point: Suur Munamagi 318 m

Estonia (continued)

Natural resources: oil shale, peat, phosphorite, clay, limestone, sand, dolomite, arable land, sea mud
Land use:
arable land: 26.5%
permanent crops: 0.35%
other: 73.15% (1998 est.)
Irrigated land: 40 sq km (1998 est.)
Natural hazards: sometimes flooding occurs in the spring
Environment - current issues: air polluted with sulfur dioxide from oil-shale burning power plants in northeast; however, the amount of pollutants emitted to the air have fallen steadily, the emissions of 2000 were 80% less than in 1980; the amount of unpurified wastewater discharged to water bodies in 2000 was one twentieth the level of 1980; in connection with the start-up of new water purification plants, the pollution load of wastewater decreased; Estonia has more than 1,400 natural and manmade lakes, the smaller of which in agricultural areas need to be monitored; coastal seawater is polluted in certain locations
Environment - international agreements:
party to: Air Pollution, Air Pollution-Nitrogen Oxides, Air Pollution-Sulfur 85, Air Pollution-Volatile Organic Compounds, Antarctic Treaty, Biodiversity, Climate Change, Climate Change-Kyoto Protocol, Endangered Species, Hazardous Wastes, Ship Pollution, Ozone Layer Protection, Wetlands
signed, but not ratified: none of the selected agreements
Geography - note: the mainland terrain is flat, boggy, and partly wooded; offshore lie more than 1,500 islands

People

Population: 1,341,664 (July 2004 est.)
Age structure:
0-14 years: 16% (male 110,452; female 104,363)
15-64 years: 67.5% (male 431,493; female 474,255)
65 years and over: 16.5% (male 72,819; female 148,282) (2004 est.)
Median age:
total: 38.8 years
male: 35.1 years
female: 42.1 years (2004 est.)
Population growth rate: -0.66% (2004 est.)
Birth rate: 9.79 births/1,000 population (2004 est.)
Death rate: 13.27 deaths/1,000 population (2004 est.)
Net migration rate: -3.16 migrant(s)/1,000 population (2004 est.)
Sex ratio:
at birth: 1.06 male(s)/female
under 15 years: 1.06 male(s)/female
15-64 years: 0.91 male(s)/female
65 years and over: 0.49 male(s)/female
total population: 0.85 male(s)/female (2004 est.)
Infant mortality rate:
total: 8.08 deaths/1,000 live births
male: 9.32 deaths/1,000 live births
female: 6.76 deaths/1,000 live births (2004 est.)

Life expectancy at birth:
total population: 71.38 years
male: 65.78 years
female: 77.33 years (2004 est.)
Total fertility rate: 1.39 children born/woman (2004 est.)
HIV/AIDS - adult prevalence rate: 1% (2001 est.)
HIV/AIDS - people living with HIV/AIDS: less than 7,700 (2001 est.)
HIV/AIDS - deaths: less than 100 (2001 est.)
Nationality:
noun: Estonian(s)
adjective: Estonian
Ethnic groups: Estonian 65.3%, Russian 28.1%, Ukrainian 2.5%, Belarusian 1.5%, Finn 1%, other 1.6% (1998)
Religions: Evangelical Lutheran, Russian Orthodox, Estonian Orthodox, Baptist, Methodist, Seventh-Day Adventist, Roman Catholic, Pentecostal, Word of Life, Jewish
Languages: Estonian (official), Russian, Ukrainian, Finnish, other
Literacy:
definition: age 15 and over can read and write
total population: 99.8%
male: 99.8%
female: 99.8% (2003 est.)

Government

Country name:
conventional long form: Republic of Estonia
conventional short form: Estonia
local long form: Eesti Vabariik
local short form: Eesti
former: Estonian Soviet Socialist Republic
Government type: parliamentary republic
Capital: Tallinn
Administrative divisions: 15 counties (maakonnad, singular - maakond): Harjumaa (Tallinn), Hiiumaa (Kardla), Ida-Virumaa (Johvi), Jarvamaa (Paide), Jogevamaa (Jogeva), Laanemaa (Haapsalu), Laane-Virumaa (Rakvere), Parnumaa (Parnu), Polvamaa (Polva), Raplamaa (Rapla), Saaremaa (Kuressaare), Tartumaa (Tartu), Valgamaa (Valga), Viljandimaa (Viljandi), Vorumaa (Voru)
note: counties have the administrative center name following in parentheses
Independence: regained on 20 August 1991 (from Soviet Union)
National holiday: Independence Day, 24 February (1918); note - 24 February 1918 is the date Estonia declared its independence from Soviet Russia; 20 August 1991 is the date it declared its independence from the Soviet Union
Constitution: adopted 28 June 1992
Legal system: based on civil law system; no judicial review of legislative acts
Suffrage: 18 years of age; universal for all Estonian citizens
Executive branch:
chief of state: President Arnold RUUTEL (since 8 October 2001)

head of government: Prime Minister Juhan PARTS (since 10 April 2003)
cabinet: Council of Ministers appointed by the prime minister, approved by Parliament
elections: president elected by Parliament for a five-year term; if he or she does not secure two-thirds of the votes after three rounds of balloting in the Parliament, then an electoral assembly (made up of Parliament plus members of local governments) elects the president, choosing between the two candidates with the largest percentage of votes; election last held 21 September 2001 (next to be held in the fall of 2006); prime minister nominated by the president and approved by Parliament
election results: Arnold RUUTEL elected president on 21 September 2001 by a 367-member electoral assembly that convened following Parliament's failure in August to elect then-President MERI's successor; on the second ballot of voting, RUUTEL received 188 votes to Parliament Speaker Toomas SAVI's 155; the remaining 24 ballots were either left blank or invalid
Legislative branch: unicameral Parliament or Riigikogu (101 seats; members are elected by popular vote to serve four-year terms)
elections: last held 2 March 2003 (next to be held NA March 2007)
election results: percent of vote by party - Center Party 25.4%, Res Publica 24.6%, Reform Party 17.7%, Estonian People's Union 13%, Pro Patria Union (Fatherland League) 7.3% People's Party Moodukad 7%; seats by party - Center Party 28, Res Publica 28, Reform Party 19, Estonian People's Union 13, Pro Patria Union 7, People's Party Moodukad 6
Judicial branch: National Court (chairman appointed by Parliament for life)
Political parties and leaders: Center Party of Estonia (Keskerakond) [Edgar SAVISAAR, chairman]; Estonian People's Union (Rahvaliit) [Villu REILJAN]; Estonian Reform Party (Reformierakond) [Siim KALLAS]; Estonian United Russian People's Party or EUVRP [Yevgeniy TOMBERG, chairman]; Pro Patria Union (Isamaaliit) [Tunne KELAM, chairman]; Res Publica [Juhan PARTS]; Russian Baltic Party [Sergei IVANOV]; Social Democratic Party (formerly People's Party Moodukad) [Ivari PADAR, chairman]
Political pressure groups and leaders: NA
International organization participation: BIS, CBSS, CE, EAPC, EBRD, EU (new member), FAO, IAEA, IBRD, ICAO, ICCt, ICFTU, ICRM, IFC, IFRCS, IHO, ILO, IMF, IMO, Interpol, IOC, IOM (observer), ISO (correspondent), ITU, OAS (observer), OPCW, OSCE, PCA, PFP, UN, UNCTAD, UNESCO, UNTSO, UPU, WCO, WEU (associate partner), WHO, WIPO, WMO, WTrO
Diplomatic representation in the US:
chief of mission: Ambassador Juri LUIK
chancery: 2131 Massachusetts Ave. NW, Washington, DC 20008
telephone: [1] (202) 588-0101
FAX: [1] (202) 588-0108
consulate(s) general: New York

Estonia *(continued)*

Diplomatic representation from the US:
chief of mission: Ambassador Joseph M. DeTHOMAS
embassy: Kentmanni 20, 15099 Tallinn
mailing address: use embassy street address
telephone: [372] 668-8100
FAX: [372] 668-8134
Flag description: pre-1940 flag restored by Supreme Soviet in May 1990 - three equal horizontal bands of blue (top), black, and white

Economy

Economy - overview: Estonia, as a new member of the World Trade Organization, is steadily moving toward a modern market economy with increasing ties to the West, including the pegging of its currency to the euro. The economy benefits from strong electronics and telecommunications sectors. Estonia has been invited to join the European Union and will do so in May 2004. The economy is greatly influenced by developments in Finland, Sweden, Russia, and Germany, four major trading partners. The high current account deficit remains a concern. However, the state budget enjoyed a surplus of $130 million in 2003.
GDP: purchasing power parity - $17.37 billion (2003 est.)
GDP - real growth rate: 4.8% (2003 est.)
GDP - per capita: purchasing power parity - $12,300 (2003 est.)
GDP - composition by sector:
agriculture: 5.2%
industry: 29.3%
services: 65.5% (2002)
Population below poverty line: NA% (2000)
Household income or consumption by percentage share:
lowest 10%: 3%
highest 10%: 29.8% (1998)
Distribution of family income - Gini index: 37 (1999)
Inflation rate (consumer prices): 1.5% (2003 est.)
Labor force: 608,600 (2001 est.)
Labor force - by occupation: industry 20%, agriculture 11%, services 69% (1999 est.)
Unemployment rate: 5.5% (June 2003)
Budget:
revenues: $3.13 billion
expenditures: $3 billion, including capital expenditures of $NA (2003 est.)
Industries: engineering, electronics, wood and wood products, textile; information technology, telecommunications
Industrial production growth rate: 5% (2000 est.)
Electricity - production: 7.937 billion kWh (2001)
Electricity - production by source:
fossil fuel: 99.8%
hydro: 0.1%
nuclear: 0%
other: 0.2% (2001)
Electricity - consumption: 6.192 billion kWh (2001)
Electricity - exports: 1.19 billion kWh (2001)

Electricity - imports: 0 kWh (2001)
Oil - production: 5,100 bbl/day (2001 est.)
Oil - consumption: 24,000 bbl/day (2001 est.)
Oil - exports: NA
Oil - imports: NA
Natural gas - production: 0 cu m (2001 est.)
Natural gas - consumption: 1.27 billion cu m (2001 est.)
Natural gas - exports: 0 cu m (2001 est.)
Natural gas - imports: 1.27 billion cu m (2001 est.)
Agriculture - products: potatoes, vegetables; livestock and dairy products; fish
Exports: $4.075 billion f.o.b. (2003 est.)
Exports - commodities: machinery and equipment 33%, wood and paper 15%, textiles 14%, food products 8%, furniture 7%, metals, chemical products (2001)
Exports - partners: Finland 20.4%, Sweden 12.4%, Russia 10%, Germany 8.3%, Latvia 7.7%, UK 4.2%, Lithuania 4.1% (2002)
Imports: $5.535 billion f.o.b. (2003 est.)
Imports - commodities: machinery and equipment 33.5%, chemical products 11.6%, textiles 10.3%, foodstuffs 9.4%, transportation equipment 8.9% (2001)
Imports - partners: Finland 15.6%, Russia 12%, Germany 11.1%, Sweden 8.4%, China 4.6%, Italy 4.1% (2002)
Debt - external: $5.8 billion (2003 est.)
Economic aid - recipient: $108 million (2000)
Currency: Estonian kroon (EEK)
Currency code: EEK
Exchange rates: krooni per US dollar - 13.8564 (2003), 16.6118 (2002), 17.4781 (2001), 16.9686 (2000), 14.6776 (1999)
Fiscal year: calendar year

Communications

Telephones - main lines in use: 475,000 (2002)
Telephones - mobile cellular: 881,000 (2002)
Telephone system:
general assessment: foreign investment in the form of joint business ventures greatly improved telephone service; substantial fiber-optic cable systems carry telephone, TV, and radio traffic in the digital mode; Internet services are available throughout most of the country - only about 11,000 subscriber requests were unfilled by September 2000
domestic: a wide range of high quality voice, data, and Internet services is available throughout the country
international: country code - 372; fiber-optic cables to Finland, Sweden, Latvia, and Russia provide worldwide packet-switched service; two international switches are located in Tallinn (2001)
Radio broadcast stations: AM 0, FM 98, shortwave 0 (2001)
Television broadcast stations: 3 (2001)
Internet country code: .ee
Internet hosts: 63,364 (2002)
Internet users: 444,000 (2002)

Transportation

Railways:
total: 968 km
broad gauge: 968 km 1.520-m/1.524-m gauge (132 km electrified)
note: gauge being increased from 1.520-m to 1.524-m to reduce wear on wheels and rail as lines are modernized (2002)
Highways:
total: 51,411 km
paved: 10,334 km (including 94 km of expressways)
unpaved: 41,077 km (2000)
Waterways: 320 km (perennially navigable) (2002)
Pipelines: gas 859 km (2003)
Ports and harbors: Haapsalu, Kunda, Muuga, Paldiski, Parnu, Tallinn
Merchant marine:
total: 32 ships (1,000 GRT or over) 212,998 GRT/ 177,488 DWT
by type: bulk 2, cargo 12, container 4, petroleum tanker 2, roll on/roll off 7, short-sea/passenger 5
foreign-owned: Netherlands 1
registered in other countries: 45 (2003 est.)
Airports: 29 (2003 est.)
Airports - with paved runways:
total: 14
over 3,047 m: 1
2,438 to 3,047 m: 8
1,524 to 2,437 m: 1
914 to 1,523 m: 3
under 914 m: 1 (2003 est.)
Airports - with unpaved runways:
total: 15
over 3,047 m: 1
2,438 to 3,047 m: 1
1,524 to 2,437 m: 3
914 to 1,523 m: 4
under 914 m: 6 (2003 est.)

Military

Military branches: Estonia Defense Forces (including Ground Forces, Navy, Air Force), Republic Security Forces (internal and border troops), Volunteer Defense League (Kaitseliit), Maritime Border Guard, Coast Guard
note: Border Guards and Ministry of Internal Affairs become part of the Estonian Defense Forces in wartime; the Coast Guard is subordinate to the Ministry of Defense in peacetime and the Estonian Navy in wartime
Military manpower - military age: 18 years of age (Estonia has committed to retaining conscription up to 2010) (2004 est.)
Military manpower - availability:
males age 15-49: 326,803 (2004 est.)
Military manpower - fit for military service:
males age 15-49: 257,386 (2004 est.)
Military manpower - reaching military age annually:
males: 10,884 (2004 est.)

Estonia (continued)

Military expenditures - dollar figure: $155 million (2002 est.)
Military expenditures - percent of GDP: 2% (2002 est.)

Disputes - international: Russia continues to reject signing and ratifying the joint December 1996 technical border agreement with Estonia
Illicit drugs: transshipment point for opiates and cannabis from Southwest Asia and the Caucasus via Russia, cocaine from Latin America to Western Europe and Scandinavia, and synthetic drugs from Western Europe to Scandinavia; increasing domestic drug abuse problem; possible precursor manufacturing and/or trafficking; potential money laundering related to organized crime and drug trafficking is a concern as is possible use of the gambling sector to launder funds

Ethiopia

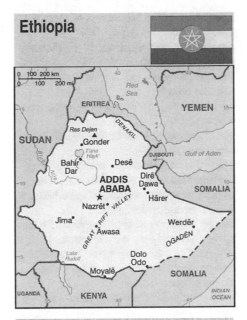

Introduction

Background: Unique among African countries, the ancient Ethiopian monarchy maintained its freedom from colonial rule, one exception being the Italian occupation of 1936-41. In 1974 a military junta, the Derg, deposed Emperor Haile SELASSIE (who had ruled since 1930) and established a socialist state. Torn by bloody coups, uprisings, wide-scale drought, and massive refugee problems, the regime was finally toppled by a coalition of rebel forces, the Ethiopian People's Revolutionary Democratic Front (EPRDF), in 1991. A constitution was adopted in 1994 and Ethiopia's first multiparty elections were held in 1995. A two and a half year border war with Eritrea ended with a peace treaty on 12 December 2000. Final demarcation of the boundary is currently on hold due to Ethiopian objections to an international commission's finding requiring it to surrender sensitive territory.

Geography

Location: Eastern Africa, west of Somalia
Geographic coordinates: 8 00 N, 38 00 E
Map references: Africa
Area:
total: 1,127,127 sq km
land: 1,119,683 sq km
water: 7,444 sq km
Area - comparative: slightly less than twice the size of Texas
Land boundaries:
total: 5,328 km
border countries: Djibouti 349 km, Eritrea 912 km, Kenya 861 km, Somalia 1,600 km, Sudan 1,606 km
Coastline: 0 km (landlocked)
Maritime claims: none (landlocked)
Climate: tropical monsoon with wide topographic-induced variation
Terrain: high plateau with central mountain range divided by Great Rift Valley

Elevation extremes:
lowest point: Denakil Depression -125 m
highest point: Ras Dejen 4,620 m
Natural resources: small reserves of gold, platinum, copper, potash, natural gas, hydropower
Land use:
arable land: 9.9%
permanent crops: 0.65%
other: 89.45% (1998 est.)
Irrigated land: 1,900 sq km (1998 est.)
Natural hazards: geologically active Great Rift Valley susceptible to earthquakes, volcanic eruptions; frequent droughts
Environment - current issues: deforestation; overgrazing; soil erosion; desertification; water shortages in some areas from water-intensive farming and poor management
Environment - international agreements:
party to: Biodiversity, Climate Change, Desertification, Endangered Species, Hazardous Wastes, Ozone Layer Protection
signed, but not ratified: Environmental Modification, Law of the Sea
Geography - note: landlocked - entire coastline along the Red Sea was lost with the de jure independence of Eritrea on 24 May 1993; the Blue Nile, the chief headstream of the Nile by water volume, rises in T'ana Hayk (Lake Tana) in northwest Ethiopia; three major crops are believed to have originated in Ethiopia: coffee, grain sorghum, and castor bean

People

Population: 67,851,281
note: estimates for this country explicitly take into account the effects of excess mortality due to AIDS; this can result in lower life expectancy, higher infant mortality and death rates, lower population and growth rates, and changes in the distribution of population by age and sex than would otherwise be expected (July 2004 est.)
Age structure:
0-14 years: 44.7% (male 15,189,921; female 15,109,870)
15-64 years: 52.5% (male 17,857,758; female 17,767,411)
65 years and over: 2.8% (male 855,103; female 1,071,218) (2004 est.)
Median age:
total: 17.4 years
male: 17.3 years
female: 17.4 years (2004 est.)
Population growth rate: 1.89% (2004 est.)
Birth rate: 39.23 births/1,000 population (2004 est.)
Death rate: 20.36 deaths/1,000 population (2004 est.)
Net migration rate: 0 migrant(s)/1,000 population
note: repatriation of Ethiopians who fled to Sudan for refuge from war and famine in earlier years is expected to continue for several years; some Sudanese and Somali refugees, who fled to Ethiopia from the fighting or famine in their own countries, continue to return to their homes (2004 est.)

Ethiopia (continued)

Sex ratio:
at birth: 1.03 male(s)/female
under 15 years: 1.01 male(s)/female
15-64 years: 1.01 male(s)/female
65 years and over: 0.8 male(s)/female
total population: 1 male(s)/female (2004 est.)
Infant mortality rate:
total: 102.12 deaths/1,000 live births
male: 112.22 deaths/1,000 live births
female: 91.72 deaths/1,000 live births (2004 est.)
Life expectancy at birth:
total population: 40.88 years
male: 40.03 years
female: 41.75 years (2004 est.)
Total fertility rate: 5.44 children born/woman
(2004 est.)
HIV/AIDS - adult prevalence rate: 6.4% (2001 est.)
HIV/AIDS - people living with HIV/AIDS: 2.1 million
(2001 est.)
HIV/AIDS - deaths: 160,000 (2001 est.)
Nationality:
noun: Ethiopian(s)
adjective: Ethiopian
Ethnic groups: Oromo 40%, Amhara and
Tigre 32%, Sidamo 9%, Shankella 6%, Somali 6%,
Afar 4%, Gurage 2%, other 1%
Religions: Muslim 45%-50%, Ethiopian Orthodox
35%-40%, animist 12%, other 3%-8%
Languages: Amharic, Tigrinya, Oromigna,
Guaragigna, Somali, Arabic, other local languages,
English (major foreign language taught in schools)
Literacy:
definition: age 15 and over can read and write
total population: 42.7%
male: 50.3%
female: 35.1% (2003 est.)

Government

Country name:
conventional long form: Federal Democratic Republic
of Ethiopia
conventional short form: Ethiopia
local long form: Ityop'iya Federalawi Demokrasiyawi
Ripeblik
local short form: Ityop'iya
former: Abyssinia, Italian East Africa
abbreviation: FDRE
Government type: federal republic
Capital: Addis Ababa
Administrative divisions: 9 ethnically-based states
(kililoch, singular - kilil) and 2 self-governing
administrations* (astedaderoch, singular - astedader);
Adis Abeba* (Addis Ababa), Afar, Amara (Amhara),
Binshangul Gumuz, Dire Dawa*, Gambela Hizboch
(Gambela Peoples), Hareri Hizb (Harari People),
Oromiya (Oromia), Sumale (Somali), Tigray, Ye
Debub Biheroch Bihereseboch na Hizboch (Southern
Nations, Nationalities and Peoples)
Independence: oldest independent country in Africa
and one of the oldest in the world - at least 2,000 years
National holiday: National Day (defeat of
MENGISTU regime), 28 May (1991)

Constitution: ratified December 1994; effective
22 August 1995
Legal system: currently transitional mix of national
and regional courts
Suffrage: 18 years of age; universal
Executive branch:
chief of state: President GIRMA Woldegiorgis (since
8 October 2001)
head of government: Prime Minister MELES Zenawi
(since NA August 1995)
cabinet: Council of Ministers as provided for in the
December 1994 constitution; ministers are selected
by the prime minister and approved by the House of
People's Representatives
elections: president elected by the House of People's
Representatives for a six-year term; election last held
8 October 2001 (next to be held NA October 2007);
prime minister designated by the party in power
following legislative elections
election results: GIRMA Woldegiorgis elected
president; percent of vote by the House of People's
Representatives - 100%
Legislative branch: bicameral Parliament consists
of the House of Federation or upper chamber (108
seats; members are chosen by state assemblies to
serve five-year terms) and the House of People's
Representatives or lower chamber (548 seats;
members are directly elected by popular vote from
single-member districts to serve five-year terms)
elections: last held 14 May 2000 (next to be held
NA May 2005)
election results: percent of vote - NA%; seats by party -
OPDO 177, ANDM 134, TPLF 38, WGGPDO 27,
EPRDF 19, SPDO 18, GNDM 15, KSPDO 10, ANDP 8,
GPRDF 7, SOPDM 7, BGPDUF 6, BMPDO 5, KAT 4,
other regional political groupings 22, independents 8;
note - 43 seats unconfirmed
note: irregularities and violence at some polling
stations necessitated the rescheduling of voting in
certain constituencies; voting postponed in Somali
regional state because of severe drought
Judicial branch: Federal Supreme Court (the
president and vice president of the Federal Supreme
Court are recommended by the prime minister and
appointed by the House of People's Representatives;
for other federal judges, the prime minister submits to
the House of People's Representatives for
appointment candidates selected by the Federal
Judicial Administrative Council)
Political parties and leaders: Afar National
Democratic Party or ANDP [leader NA]; Amhara
National Democratic Movement or ANDM [ADDISU
Legesse]; Bench Madji People's Democratic
Organization or BMPDO [leader NA]; Benishangul
Gumuz People's Democratic Unity Front or BGPDUF
[leader NA]; Ethiopian People's Revolutionary
Democratic Front or EPRDF [MELES Zenawi] (an
alliance of ANDM, OPDO, SEPDF, and TPLF);
Gedeyo People's Revolutionary Democratic Front or
GPRDF [leader NA]; Gurage Nationalities' Democratic
Movement or GNDM [leader NA]; Kafa Shaka
People's Democratic Organization or KSPDO [leader

NA]; Kembata, Alabaa and Tembaro or KAT [leader
NA]; Oromo People's Democratic Organization or
OPDO [JUNEDI Sado]; Sidamo People's Democratic
Organization or SPDO [leader NA]; South Omo
People's Democratic Movement or SOPDM [leader
NA]; Tigrayan People's Liberation Front or TPLF
[MELES Zenawi]; Walayta, Gamo, Gofa, Dawro, and
Konta People's Democratic Organization or
WGGPDO [leader NA]; dozens of small parties
Political pressure groups and leaders: Afar
Revolutionary Democratic Union Front or ARDUF
[leader NA]; Council of Alternative Forces for Peace
and Democracy in Ethiopia or CAFPDE [BEYANE
Petros]; Southern Ethiopia People's Democratic
Coalition or SEPDC [BEYANE Petros]
International organization participation: ACP,
AfDB, AU, FAO, G-24, G-77, IAEA, IBRD, ICAO,
ICRM, IDA, IFAD, IFC, IFRCS, IGAD, ILO, IMF, IMO,
Interpol, IOC, IOM (observer), ISO, ITU, NAM,
OPCW, PCA, UN, UNCTAD, UNESCO, UNHCR,
UNIDO, UNMIL, UPU, WCO, WFTU, WHO, WIPO,
WMO, WToO, WTrO (observer)
Diplomatic representation in the US:
chief of mission: Ambassador KASSAHUN Ayele
chancery: 3506 International Drive NW, Washington,
DC 20008
telephone: [1] (202) 364-1200
FAX: [1] (202) 686-9551
consulate(s) general: Los Angeles
consulate(s): New York
Diplomatic representation from the US:
chief of mission: Ambassador Aurelia A. BRAZEAL
embassy: Entoto Street, Addis Ababa
mailing address: P. O. Box 1014, Addis Ababa
telephone: [251] (1) 550666
FAX: [251] (1) 551328
Flag description: three equal horizontal bands of
green (top), yellow, and red with a yellow pentagram
and single yellow rays emanating from the angles
between the points on a light blue disk centered on the
three bands; Ethiopia is the oldest independent
country in Africa, and the three main colors of her flag
were so often adopted by other African countries upon
independence that they became known as the
pan-African colors

Economy

Economy - overview: Ethiopia's poverty-stricken
economy is based on agriculture, which accounts for
half of GDP, 60% of exports, and 80% of total
employment. The agricultural sector suffers from
frequent drought and poor cultivation practices.
Coffee is critical to the Ethiopian economy with
exports of some $156 million in 2002, but historically
low prices have seen many farmers switching to qat to
supplement income. The war with Eritrea in
1998-2000 and recurrent drought have buffeted the
economy, in particular coffee production. In
November 2001 Ethiopia qualified for debt relief from
the Highly Indebted Poor Countries (HIPC) initiative.
Under Ethiopia's land tenure system, the government
owns all land and provides long-term leases to the

tenants; the system continues to hamper growth in the industrial sector as entrepreneurs are unable to use land as collateral for loans. Drought struck again late in 2002, leading to a 2% decline in GDP in 2003. Return to normal weather patterns late in 2003 should help agricultural and GDP growth recover in 2004. The government estimates that annual growth of 7% is needed to reduce poverty.

GDP: purchasing power parity - $48.47 billion (2003 est.)

GDP - real growth rate: -2% (2003 est.)

GDP - per capita: purchasing power parity - $700 (2003 est.)

GDP - composition by sector:
agriculture: 52.3%
industry: 11.1%
services: 36.5% (2002 est.)

Population below poverty line: 50% (2003 est.)

Household income or consumption by percentage share:
lowest 10%: 3%
highest 10%: 33.7% (1995)

Distribution of family income - Gini index: 40 (1995)

Inflation rate (consumer prices): 12.6% (2003 est.)

Labor force: NA (2001 est.)

Labor force - by occupation: agriculture and animal husbandry 80%, government and services 12%, industry and construction 8% (1985)

Unemployment rate: NA% (2002)

Budget:
revenues: $1.4 billion
expenditures: $2.4 billion, including capital expenditures of $788 million (FY02/03 est.)

Industries: food processing, beverages, textiles, chemicals, metals processing, cement

Industrial production growth rate: 6.7% (2001 est.)

Electricity - production: 1.713 billion kWh (2001)

Electricity - production by source:
fossil fuel: 1.3%
hydro: 97.6%
nuclear: 0%
other: 1.2% (2001)

Electricity - consumption: 1.594 billion kWh (2001)

Electricity - exports: 0 kWh (2001)

Electricity - imports: 0 kWh (2001)

Oil - production: 0 bbl/day (2001 est.)

Oil - consumption: 23,000 bbl/day (2001 est.)

Oil - exports: NA

Oil - imports: NA

Oil - proved reserves: 214,000 bbl (1 January 2002)

Natural gas - proved reserves: 12.46 billion cu m (1 January 2002)

Agriculture - products: cereals, pulses, coffee, oilseed, sugarcane, potatoes, qat; hides, cattle, sheep, goats

Exports: $537 million f.o.b. (2003 est.)

Exports - commodities: coffee, qat, gold, leather products, live animals, oilseeds

Exports - partners: UK 16.5%, Djibouti 11.1%, Germany 7.5%, Italy 7.3%, Japan 6.8%, Saudi Arabia 6.6%, US 4.5% (2002)

Imports: $1.964 billion f.o.b. (2003 est.)

Imports - commodities: food and live animals, petroleum and petroleum products, chemicals, machinery, motor vehicles, cereals, textiles

Imports - partners: Saudi Arabia 27.9%, Switzerland 6.3%, China 5.9%, Italy 5.7%, India 4.6%, Germany 4% (2002)

Debt - external: $2.9 billion (2001 est.)

Economic aid - recipient: $308 million (FY00/01)

Currency: birr (ETB)

Currency code: ETB

Exchange rates: birr per US dollar - NA (2003), 8.5678 (2002), 8.4575 (2001), 8.2173 (2000), 7.9423 (1999)
note: since 24 October 2001 exchange rates are determined on a daily basis via interbank transactions regulated by the Central Bank

Fiscal year: 8 July - 7 July

Communications

Telephones - main lines in use: 353,800 (2002)

Telephones - mobile cellular: 50,400 (2002)

Telephone system:
general assessment: open-wire and microwave radio relay system; adequate for government use
domestic: open-wire; microwave radio relay; radio communication in the HF, VHF, and UHF frequencies; two domestic satellites provide the national trunk service
international: country code - 251; open-wire to Sudan and Djibouti; microwave radio relay to Kenya and Djibouti; satellite earth stations - 3 Intelsat (1 Atlantic Ocean and 2 Pacific Ocean)

Radio broadcast stations: AM 8, FM 0, shortwave 1 (2001)

Television broadcast stations: 1 plus 24 repeaters (2002)

Internet country code: .et

Internet hosts: 41 (2002)

Internet users: 50,000 (2002)

Transportation

Railways:
total: 681 km (Ethiopian segment of the Addis Ababa-Djibouti railroad)
narrow gauge: 681 km 1.000-m gauge
note: railway under joint control of Djibouti and Ethiopia (2002)

Highways:
total: 31,571 km
paved: 3,789 km
unpaved: 27,782 km (2000)

Waterways: none

Ports and harbors: none; Ethiopia is landlocked and was by agreement with Eritrea using the ports of Assab and Massawa; since the border dispute with Eritrea flared, Ethiopia has used the port of Djibouti for nearly all of its imports

Merchant marine:
total: 9 ships (1,000 GRT or over) 81,933 GRT/ 101,287 DWT
by type: cargo 5, container 1, petroleum tanker 1, roll on/roll off 2 (2003 est.)

Airports: 82 (2003 est.)

Airports - with paved runways:
total: 14
over 3,047 m: 3
2,438 to 3,047 m: 5
1,524 to 2,437 m: 5
914 to 1,523 m: 1 (2003 est.)

Airports - with unpaved runways:
total: 68
over 3,047 m: 3
2,438 to 3,047 m: 2
1,524 to 2,437 m: 13
914 to 1,523 m: 27
under 914 m: 23 (2003 est.)

Military

Military branches: Ethiopian National Defense Force: Ground Forces, Air Force, Mobilized Militia
note: Ethiopia is landlocked and has no navy; following the secession of Eritrea, Ethiopian naval facilities remained in Eritrean possession

Military manpower - military age: 18 years of age (2004 est.)

Military manpower - availability:
males age 15-49: 15,748,632 (2004 est.)

Military manpower - fit for military service:
males age 15-49: 8,234,442 (2004 est.)

Military manpower - reaching military age annually:
males: 760,868 (2004 est.)

Military expenditures - dollar figure: $345 million (2003)

Military expenditures - percent of GDP: 5.2% (2003)

Transnational Issues

Disputes - international: Eritrea and Ethiopia agreed to abide by the 2002 independent boundary commission's delimitation decision, but demarcation has been delayed, despite intense international intervention, by Ethiopian insistence that the decision ignored "human geography," made technical errors in the delimitation, and incorrectly awarded Badme - the focus of the 1998-2000 war - and other areas to Eritrea and Eritrea's insistence on not deviating from the commission's decision; Ethiopia maintains only an administrative line and no international border with the Oromo region of southern Somalia and maintains alliances with local clans in opposition to the Transitional National Government, which lost its mandate in August 2003, in Mogadishu; "Somaliland" secessionists provide port facilities and trade ties to landlocked Ethiopia; efforts to demarcate the porous boundary with Sudan have been delayed by civil war

Ethiopia *(continued)*

Illicit drugs: Transit hub for heroin originating in Southwest and Southeast Asia and destined for Europe and North America as well as cocaine destined for markets in southern Africa; cultivates qat (khat) for local use and regional export, principally to Djibouti and Somalia (legal in all three countries); the lack of a well-developed financial system limits the country's utility as a money-laundering center

Europa Island
(possession of France)

Introduction

Background: A French possession since 1897, the island is heavily wooded; it is the site of a small military garrison that staffs a weather station.

Geography

Location: Southern Africa, island in the Mozambique Channel, about one-half of the way from southern Madagascar to southern Mozambique
Geographic coordinates: 22 20 S, 40 22 E
Map references: Africa
Area:
total: 28 sq km
land: 28 sq km
water: 0 sq km
Area - comparative: about 0.16 times the size of Washington, DC
Land boundaries: 0 km
Coastline: 22.2 km
Maritime claims:
territorial sea: 12 NM
exclusive economic zone: 200 NM
Climate: tropical
Terrain: low and flat
Elevation extremes:
lowest point: Indian Ocean 0 m
highest point: unnamed location 24 m
Natural resources: NEGL
Land use:
arable land: 0%
permanent crops: 0%
other: 100% (mangrove forests and woodlands) (1998 est.)
Irrigated land: 0 sq km (1998 est.)
Natural hazards: NA
Environment - current issues: NA
Geography - note: wildlife sanctuary

People

Population: no indigenous inhabitants
note: there is a small French military garrison and a few meteorologists; visited by scientists (July 2004 est.)

Government

Country name:
conventional long form: none
conventional short form: Europa Island
local long form: none
local short form: Ile Europa
Dependency status: possession of France; administered by a high commissioner of the Republic, resident in Reunion
Legal system: the laws of France, where applicable, apply
Flag description: the flag of France is used

Economy

Economy - overview: no economic activity

Communications

Communications - note: 1 meteorological station

Transportation

Waterways: none
Ports and harbors: none; offshore anchorage only
Airports: 1 (2003 est.)
Airports - with unpaved runways:
total: 1
914 to 1,523 m: 1 (2003 est.)

Military

Military - note: defense is the responsibility of France

Transnational Issues

Disputes - international: claimed by Madagascar

Falkland Islands (Islas Malvinas)

(overseas territory of the UK; also claimed by Argentina)

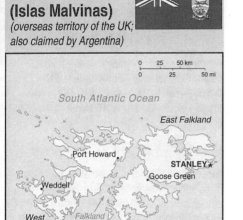

Administered by U.K., claimed by ARGENTINA.

Introduction

Background: Although first sighted by an English navigator in 1592, the first landing (English) did not occur until almost a century later in 1690, and the first settlement (French) was not established until 1764. The colony was turned over to Spain two years later and the islands have since been the subject of a territorial dispute, first between Britain and Spain, then between Britain and Argentina. The UK asserted its claim to the islands by establishing a naval garrison there in 1833. Argentina invaded the islands on 2 April 1982. The British responded with an expeditionary force that landed seven weeks later and after fierce fighting forced Argentine surrender on 14 June 1982.

Geography

Location: Southern South America, islands in the South Atlantic Ocean, east of southern Argentina
Geographic coordinates: 51 45 S, 59 00 W
Map references: South America
Area:
total: 12,173 sq km
land: 12,173 sq km
water: 0 sq km
note: includes the two main islands of East and West Falkland and about 200 small islands
Area - comparative: slightly smaller than Connecticut
Land boundaries: 0 km
Coastline: 1,288 km
Maritime claims:
territorial sea: 12 NM
continental shelf: 200 NM
exclusive fishing zone: 200 NM
Climate: cold marine; strong westerly winds, cloudy, humid; rain occurs on more than half of days in year; average annual rainfall is 24 inches in Stanley; occasional snow all year, except in January and February, but does not accumulate

Terrain: rocky, hilly, mountainous with some boggy, undulating plains
Elevation extremes:
lowest point: Atlantic Ocean 0 m
highest point: Mount Usborne 705 m
Natural resources: fish, squid, wildlife, calcified seaweed, sphagnum moss
Land use:
arable land: 0%
permanent crops: 0%
other: 100% (99% permanent pastures, 1% other) (1998 est.)
Irrigated land: NA sq km
Natural hazards: strong winds persist throughout the year
Environment - current issues: overfishing by unlicensed vessels is a problem; reindeer were introduced to the islands in 2001 for commercial reasons; this is the only commercial reindeer herd in the world unaffected by the Chornobyl disaster
Geography - note: deeply indented coast provides good natural harbors; short growing season

People

Population: 2,967 (July 2004 est.)
Age structure:
0-14 years: NA%
15-64 years: NA%
65 years and over: NA% (2004 est.)
Population growth rate: 2.44% (2004 est.)
Birth rate: NA births/1,000 population (2004 est.)
Death rate: NA deaths/1,000 population (2004 est.)
Net migration rate: NA migrant(s)/1,000 population (2004 est.)
Infant mortality rate:
total: NA%
male: NA%
female: NA% (2004 est.)
Life expectancy at birth:
total population: NA years
male: NA years
female: NA years (2004 est.)
Total fertility rate: NA children born/woman (2004 est.)
HIV/AIDS - adult prevalence rate: NA%
HIV/AIDS - people living with HIV/AIDS: NA
HIV/AIDS - deaths: NA
Nationality:
noun: Falkland Islander(s)
adjective: Falkland Island
Ethnic groups: British
Religions: primarily Anglican, Roman Catholic, United Free Church, Evangelist Church, Jehovah's Witnesses, Lutheran, Seventh-Day Adventist
Languages: English

Government

Country name:
conventional long form: none
conventional short form: Falkland Islands (Islas Malvinas)

Dependency status: overseas territory of the UK; also claimed by Argentina
Government type: NA
Capital: Stanley
Administrative divisions: none (overseas territory of the UK; also claimed by Argentina)
Independence: none (overseas territory of the UK; also claimed by Argentina)
National holiday: Liberation Day, 14 June (1982)
Constitution: 3 October 1985; amended 1997 and 1998
Legal system: English common law
Suffrage: 18 years of age; universal
Executive branch:
chief of state: Queen ELIZABETH II (since 6 February 1952)
head of government: Governor Howard PEARCE (since 3 December 2002); Chief Executive Chris SIMPKINS (since NA March 2003); Financial Secretary Derek F. HOWATT (since NA)
cabinet: Executive Council; three members elected by the Legislative Council, two ex officio members (chief executive and the financial secretary), and the governor
elections: none; the monarchy is hereditary; governor appointed by the monarch
Legislative branch: unicameral Legislative Council (10 seats - 2 ex officio, 8 elected by popular vote, members serve four-year terms); presided over by the governor
elections: last held 22 November 2001 (next to be held NA November 2005)
election results: percent of vote - NA%; seats - independents 8; note - 71% voter turnout
Judicial branch: Supreme Court (chief justice is a nonresident); Magistrates Court (senior magistrate presides over civil and criminal divisions); Court of Summary Jurisdiction
Political parties and leaders: none; all independents
Political pressure groups and leaders: none
International organization participation: ICFTU
Diplomatic representation in the US: none (overseas territory of the UK; also claimed by Argentina)
Diplomatic representation from the US: none (overseas territory of the UK; also claimed by Argentina)
Flag description: blue with the flag of the UK in the upper hoist-side quadrant and the Falkland Island coat of arms centered on the outer half of the flag; the coat of arms contains a white ram (sheep raising is the major economic activity) above the sailing ship Desire (whose crew discovered the islands) with a scroll at the bottom bearing the motto DESIRE THE RIGHT

Economy

Economy - overview: The economy was formerly based on agriculture, mainly sheep farming, but today fishing contributes the bulk of economic activity. In 1987 the government began selling fishing licenses to foreign trawlers operating within the Falklands exclusive fishing zone. These license fees total more than $40 million per year, which goes to support the

Falkland Islands (Islas Malvinas) *(continued)*

island's health, education, and welfare system. Squid accounts for 75% of the fish taken. Dairy farming supports domestic consumption; crops furnish winter fodder. Exports feature shipments of high-grade wool to the UK and the sale of postage stamps and coins. The islands are now self-financing except for defense. The British Geological Survey announced a 200-mile oil exploration zone around the islands in 1993, and early seismic surveys suggest substantial reserves capable of producing 500,000 barrels per day; to date no exploitable site has been identified. An agreement between Argentina and the UK in 1995 seeks to defuse licensing and sovereignty conflicts that would dampen foreign interest in exploiting potential oil reserves. Tourism, especially eco-tourism, is increasing rapidly, with about 30,000 visitors in 2001. Another large source of income is interest paid on money the government has in the bank. The British military presence also provides a sizeable economic boost.

GDP: purchasing power parity - $75 million (2002 est.)
GDP - real growth rate: NA%
GDP - per capita: purchasing power parity - $25,000 (2002 est.)
GDP - composition by sector:
agriculture: NA%
industry: NA%
services: NA%
Population below poverty line: NA%
Household income or consumption by percentage share:
lowest 10%: NA%
highest 10%: NA%
Inflation rate (consumer prices): 3.6% (1998)
Labor force: 1,100 (est.)
Labor force - by occupation: agriculture 95% (mostly sheepherding and fishing)
Unemployment rate: full employment; labor shortage (2001)
Budget:
revenues: $66.2 million
expenditures: $67.9 million, including capital expenditures of $23.2 million (FY98/99 est.)
Industries: fish and wool processing; tourism
Industrial production growth rate: NA%
Electricity - production: 16.33 million kWh (2001)
Electricity - production by source:
fossil fuel: 100%
hydro: 0%
nuclear: 0%
other: 0% (2001)
Electricity - consumption: 15.19 million kWh (2001)
Electricity - exports: 0 kWh (2001)
Electricity - imports: 0 kWh (2001)
Oil - production: 0 bbl/day (2001 est.)
Oil - consumption: 200 bbl/day (2001 est.)
Oil - exports: NA
Oil - imports: NA
Agriculture - products: fodder and vegetable crops; sheep, dairy products

Exports: $82 million (2002)
Exports - commodities: wool, hides, meat
Exports - partners: Spain 73.2%, UK 8.5%, US 7.3% (2002)
Imports: $53 million (2002)
Imports - commodities: fuel, food and drink, building materials, clothing
Imports - partners: UK 54.7%, Spain 18.9%, Italy 15.1%, Czech Republic 7.5% (2002)
Debt - external: $NA (1999 est.)
Economic aid - recipient: none (1997 est.)
Currency: Falkland pound (FKP)
Currency code: FKP
Exchange rates: Falkland pounds per US dollar - 0.6125 (2003), 0.6661 (2002), 0.6944 (2001), 0.6596 (2000), 0.618 (1999), 0.6037 (1998); note - the Falkland pound is at par with the British pound
Fiscal year: 1 April - 31 March

Communications

Telephones - main lines in use: 2,400 (2002)
Telephones - mobile cellular: 0 (2001)
Telephone system:
general assessment: NA
domestic: government-operated radiotelephone and private VHF/CB radiotelephone networks provide effective service to almost all points on both islands
international: country code - 500; satellite earth station - 1 Intelsat (Atlantic Ocean) with links through London to other countries
Radio broadcast stations: AM 1, FM 7, shortwave 0 (1998)
Television broadcast stations: 2 (operated by the British Forces Broadcasting Service)
note: cable television is available in Stanley (2002)
Internet country code: .fk
Internet users: NA; however one-half of all households are reported to have internet access (2002)

Transportation

Railways: 0 km
Highways:
total: 440 km
paved: 50 km
unpaved: 390 km (2002)
Waterways: none
Ports and harbors: Stanley
note: the primary port is located in Stanley Harbour and known locally as FIPASS (Falkland Interim Port and Storage System); the facility consists of seven permanently moored barges providing 300 meters of berthing space; it was installed by the military after 1982 and handed over to the Falkland Islands Government in 1988
Merchant marine: none
Airports: 5 (2003 est.)
Airports - with paved runways:
total: 2
2,438 to 3,047 m: 1
under 914 m: 1 (2003 est.)

Airports - with unpaved runways:
total: 3
under 914 m: 3 (2003 est.)

Military

Military branches: no regular military forces
Military expenditures - dollar figure: $NA
Military expenditures - percent of GDP: NA%
Military - note: defense is the responsibility of the UK

Transnational Issues

Disputes - international: claimed by Argentina whose forces briefly occupied it in 1982, but now declares it will no longer seek settlement by force; UK continues to reject Argentine requests for sovereignty talks

Faroe Islands
(part of the Kingdom of Denmark)

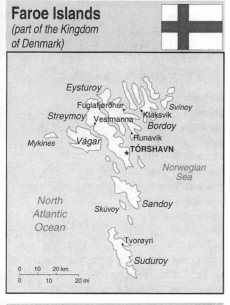

Background: The population of the Faroe Islands is largely descended from Viking settlers who arrived in the 9th century. The islands have been connected politically to Denmark since the 14th century. A high degree of self-government was attained in 1948.

Geography

Location: Northern Europe, island group between the Norwegian Sea and the North Atlantic Ocean, about one-half of the way from Iceland to Norway
Geographic coordinates: 62 00 N, 7 00 W
Map references: Europe
Area:
total: 1,399 sq km
land: 1,399 sq km
water: 0 sq km (some lakes and streams)
Area - comparative: eight times the size of Washington, DC
Land boundaries: 0 km
Coastline: 1,117 km
Maritime claims:
territorial sea: 3 NM
continental shelf: 200 NM or agreed boundaries or median line
exclusive fishing zone: 200 NM or agreed boundaries or median line
Climate: mild winters, cool summers; usually overcast; foggy, windy
Terrain: rugged, rocky, some low peaks; cliffs along most of coast
Elevation extremes:
lowest point: Atlantic Ocean 0 m
highest point: Slaettaratindur 882 m
Natural resources: fish, whales, hydropower
Land use:
arable land: 2.14%
permanent crops: 0%
other: 97.86% (1998 est.)

Irrigated land: 0 sq km (1998 est.)
Natural hazards: NA
Environment - current issues: NA
Geography - note: archipelago of 17 inhabited islands and one uninhabited island, and a few uninhabited islets; strategically located along important sea lanes in northeastern Atlantic; precipitous terrain limits habitation to small coastal lowlands

People

Population: 46,662 (July 2004 est.)
Age structure:
0-14 years: 21.6% (male 5,056; female 5,041)
15-64 years: 64.6% (male 15,975; female 14,187)
65 years and over: 13.7% (male 2,877; female 3,526) (2004 est.)
Median age:
total: 35.1 years
male: 34.6 years
female: 35.8 years (2004 est.)
Population growth rate: 0.66% (2004 est.)
Birth rate: 13.89 births/1,000 population (2004 est.)
Death rate: 8.68 deaths/1,000 population (2004 est.)
Net migration rate: 1.41 migrant(s)/1,000 population (2004 est.)
Sex ratio:
at birth: 1 male(s)/female
under 15 years: 1 male(s)/female
15-64 years: 1.13 male(s)/female
65 years and over: 0.82 male(s)/female
total population: 1.05 male(s)/female (2004 est.)
Infant mortality rate:
total: 6.38 deaths/1,000 live births
male: 7.72 deaths/1,000 live births
female: 5.03 deaths/1,000 live births (2004 est.)
Life expectancy at birth:
total population: 79.05 years
male: 75.6 years
female: 82.51 years (2004 est.)
Total fertility rate: 2.22 children born/woman (2004 est.)
HIV/AIDS - adult prevalence rate: NA%
HIV/AIDS - people living with HIV/AIDS: NA
HIV/AIDS - deaths: NA
Nationality:
noun: Faroese (singular and plural)
adjective: Faroese
Ethnic groups: Scandinavian
Religions: Evangelical Lutheran
Languages: Faroese (derived from Old Norse), Danish
Literacy:
definition: NA
total population: NA%
male: NA%
female: NA%
note: probably the same as Denmark proper

Government

Country name:
conventional long form: none
conventional short form: Faroe Islands
local long form: none
local short form: Foroyar
Dependency status: part of the Kingdom of Denmark; self-governing overseas administrative division of Denmark since 1948
Government type: NA
Capital: Torshavn
Administrative divisions: none (part of the Kingdom of Denmark; self-governing overseas administrative division of Denmark); there are no first-order administrative divisions as defined by the US Government, but there are 49 municipalities
Independence: none (part of the Kingdom of Denmark; self-governing overseas administrative division of Denmark)
National holiday: Olaifest, 29 July
Constitution: 5 June 1953 (Danish constitution)
Legal system: Danish
Suffrage: 18 years of age; universal
Executive branch:
chief of state: Queen MARGRETHE II of Denmark (since 14 January 1972), represented by High Commissioner Birgit KLEIS, chief administrative officer (since 1 November 2001)
head of government: Prime Minister Joannes EIDESGAARD (since 3 February 2004)
cabinet: Landsstyri appointed by the prime minister
elections: the monarch is hereditary; high commissioner appointed by the monarch; following legislative elections, the leader of the majority party or the leader of the majority coalition is usually elected prime minister by the Faroese Parliament; election last held 30 April 2002 (next to be held no later than April 2006)
election results: Anfinn KALLSBERG elected prime minister; percent of parliamentary vote - 52.8%
note: coalition of Social Democrats, Union Party, and People's Party
Legislative branch: unicameral Faroese Parliament or Logting (32 seats; members are elected by popular vote on a proportional basis from the seven constituencies to serve four-year terms)
elections: last held 20 January 2004 (next to be held no later than January 2008)
election results: percent of vote by party - Union Party 23.7%, Social Democrats 21.8%, Republican Party 21.7%, People's Party 20.6%, Center Party 5.2%, Independence Party 4.6%; seats by party - Union Party 7, Social Democrats 7, Republican Party 8, People's Party 7, Center Party 2, Independence Party 1
note: election of 2 seats to the Danish Parliament was last held on 20 November 2001 (next to be held no later than November 2005); results - percent of vote by party - NA; seats by party - Republican Party 1, Union Party 1

Faroe Islands *(continued)*

Judicial branch: none
Political parties and leaders: Center Party [Tordur NICLASEN]; Independence Party [Helena Dam a NEYSTABO]; People's Party [Oli BRECKMANN]; Republican Party [Finnabogi ISAKSON]; Social Democratic Party [Joannes EIDESGAARD]; Union Party [Edmund JOENSEN]
Political pressure groups and leaders: NA
International organization participation: IMO (associate), NC, NIB
Diplomatic representation in the US: none (self-governing overseas administrative division of Denmark)
Diplomatic representation from the US: none (self-governing overseas administrative division of Denmark)
Flag description: white with a red cross outlined in blue extending to the edges of the flag; the vertical part of the cross is shifted toward the hoist side in the style of the Dannebrog (Danish flag)

Economy

Economy - overview: The Faroese economy has had a strong performance since 1994, mostly as a result of increasing fish landings and high and stable export prices. Unemployment is falling and there are signs of labor shortages in several sectors. The positive economic development has helped the Faroese Home Rule Government produce increasing budget surpluses, which in turn help to reduce the large public debt, most of it owed to Denmark. However, the total dependence on fishing makes the Faroese economy extremely vulnerable, and the present fishing efforts appear in excess of what is a sustainable level of fishing in the long term. Oil finds close to the Faroese area give hope for deposits in the immediate Faroese area, which may eventually lay the basis for a more diversified economy and thus lessen dependence on Danish economic assistance. Aided by a substantial annual subsidy (15% of GDP) from Denmark, the Faroese have a standard of living not far below the Danes and other Scandinavians.
GDP: purchasing power parity - $1 billion (2001 est.)
GDP - real growth rate: 10% (2001 est.)
GDP - per capita: purchasing power parity - $22,000 (2001 est.)
GDP - composition by sector:
agriculture: 27%
industry: 11%
services: 62% (1999)
Population below poverty line: NA%
Household income or consumption by percentage share:
lowest 10%: NA%
highest 10%: NA%
Inflation rate (consumer prices): 5.1% (1999)
Labor force: 24,250 (October 2000)
Labor force - by occupation: fishing, fish processing, and manufacturing 33%, construction and private services 33%, public services 34%
Unemployment rate: 1% (October 2000)

Budget:
revenues: $488 million
expenditures: $484 million, including capital expenditures of $21 million (1999)
Industries: fishing, fish processing, shipbuilding, construction, handicrafts
Industrial production growth rate: 8% (1999 est.)
Electricity - production: 160.4 million kWh (2001)
Electricity - production by source:
fossil fuel: 62.4%
hydro: 37.6%
nuclear: 0%
other: 0% (2001)
Electricity - consumption: 149.1 million kWh (2001)
Electricity - exports: 0 kWh (2001)
Electricity - imports: 0 kWh (2001)
Oil - production: 0 bbl/day (2001 est.)
Oil - consumption: 4,500 bbl/day (2001 est.)
Oil - exports: NA
Oil - imports: NA
Agriculture - products: milk, potatoes, vegetables; sheep; salmon, other fish
Exports: $408 million f.o.b. (2002)
Exports - commodities: fish and fish products 94%, stamps, ships (1999)
Exports - partners: Denmark 37.7%, UK 33.8%, Norway 6.6%, Netherlands 6.4% (2002)
Imports: $466 million c.i.f. (2002)
Imports - commodities: machinery and transport equipment 29%, consumer goods 36%, raw materials and semi-manufactures 32%, fuels, fish and salt (1999)
Imports - partners: Denmark 57.7%, Norway 21%, Iceland 5.6% (2002)
Debt - external: $64 million (1999)
Economic aid - recipient: $135 million (annual subsidy from Denmark) (1998)
Currency: Danish krone (DKK)
Currency code: DKK
Exchange rates: Danish kroner per US dollar - 6.5877 (2003), 7.89 (2002), 8.323 (2001), 8.083 (2000), 6.976 (1999)
Fiscal year: calendar year

Communications

Telephones - main lines in use: 23,000 (2002)
Telephones - mobile cellular: 30,700 (2002)
Telephone system:
general assessment: good international communications; good domestic facilities
domestic: digitalization was completed in 1998; both NMT (analog) and GSM (digital) mobile telephone systems are installed
international: country code - 298; satellite earth stations - 1 Orion; 1 fiber-optic submarine cable to the Shetland Islands, linking the Faroe Islands with Denmark and Iceland; fiber-optic submarine cable connection to Canada-Europe cable
Radio broadcast stations: AM 1, FM 13, shortwave 0 (1998)

Television broadcast stations: 3 (plus 43 low-power repeaters) (September 1995)
Internet country code: .fo
Internet users: 25,000 (2002)

Transportation

Railways: 0 km
Highways:
total: 463 km
paved: 454 km
unpaved: 9 km (1999)
Waterways: none
Ports and harbors: Torshavn, Klaksvik, Tvoroyri, Runavik, Fuglafjordhur
Merchant marine:
total: 7 ships (1,000 GRT or over) 24,051 GRT/11,998 DWT
by type: cargo 3, container 1, petroleum tanker 1, roll on/roll off 1, short-sea/passenger 1
foreign-owned: Denmark 2, Norway 1, United Kingdom 1
registered in other countries: 1 (2003 est.)
Airports: 1 (2003 est.)
Airports - with paved runways:
total: 1
914 to 1,523 m: 1 (2003 est.)

Military

Military branches: no regular military forces
Military expenditures - dollar figure: NA
Military expenditures - percent of GDP: NA
Military - note: defense is the responsibility of Denmark

Transnational Issues

Disputes - international: Faroese are considering proposals for full independence; Denmark dispute with Iceland over the Faroe Islands fisheries median line boundary of 200 NM; Denmark disputes with Iceland, the UK, and Ireland the Faroe Islands claim extending its continental shelf boundary beyond 200 NM

Fiji

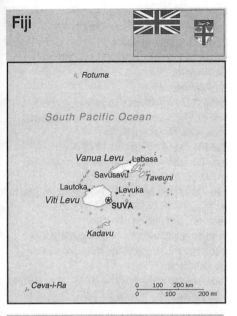

Introduction

Background: Fiji became independent in 1970, after nearly a century as a British colony. Democratic rule was interrupted by two military coups in 1987, caused by concern over a government perceived as dominated by the Indian community (descendants of contract laborers brought to the islands by the British in the 19th century). A 1990 constitution favored native Melanesian control of Fiji, but led to heavy Indian emigration; the population loss resulted in economic difficulties, but ensured that Melanesians became the majority. Amendments enacted in 1997 made the constitution more equitable. Free and peaceful elections in 1999 resulted in a government led by an Indo-Fijian, but a coup in May 2000 ushered in a prolonged period of political turmoil. Parliamentary elections held in August 2001 provided Fiji with a democratically elected government and gave a mandate to the government of Prime Minister Laisenia QARASE.

Geography

Location: Oceania, island group in the South Pacific Ocean, about two-thirds of the way from Hawaii to New Zealand
Geographic coordinates: 18 00 S, 175 00 E
Map references: Oceania
Area:
total: 18,270 sq km
land: 18,270 sq km
water: 0 sq km
Area - comparative: slightly smaller than New Jersey
Land boundaries: 0 km
Coastline: 1,129 km
Maritime claims: measured from claimed archipelagic straight baselines
territorial sea: 12 NM
exclusive economic zone: 200 NM
continental shelf: 200-m depth or to the depth of exploitation; rectilinear shelf claim added

Climate: tropical marine; only slight seasonal temperature variation
Terrain: mostly mountains of volcanic origin
Elevation extremes:
lowest point: Pacific Ocean 0 m
highest point: Tomanivi 1,324 m
Natural resources: timber, fish, gold, copper, offshore oil potential, hydropower
Land use:
arable land: 10.95%
permanent crops: 4.65%
other: 84.4% (1998 est.)
Irrigated land: 30 sq km (1998 est.)
Natural hazards: cyclonic storms can occur from November to January
Environment - current issues: deforestation; soil erosion
Environment - international agreements:
party to: Biodiversity, Climate Change, Climate Change-Kyoto Protocol, Desertification, Endangered Species, Law of the Sea, Marine Life Conservation, Ozone Layer Protection, Tropical Timber 83, Tropical Timber 94
signed, but not ratified: none of the selected agreements
Geography - note: includes 332 islands of which approximately 110 are inhabited

People

Population: 880,874 (July 2004 est.)
Age structure:
0-14 years: 31.7% (male 142,412; female 136,754)
15-64 years: 64.3% (male 283,690; female 283,027)
65 years and over: 4% (male 16,047; female 18,944) (2004 est.)
Median age:
total: 24 years
male: 23.6 years
female: 24.4 years (2004 est.)
Population growth rate: 1.41% (2004 est.)
Birth rate: 22.91 births/1,000 population (2004 est.)
Death rate: 5.68 deaths/1,000 population (2004 est.)
Net migration rate: -3.14 migrant(s)/1,000 population (2004 est.)
Sex ratio:
at birth: 1.05 male(s)/female
under 15 years: 1.04 male(s)/female
15-64 years: 1 male(s)/female
65 years and over: 0.85 male(s)/female
total population: 1.01 male(s)/female (2004 est.)
Infant mortality rate:
total: 12.99 deaths/1,000 live births
male: 14.36 deaths/1,000 live births
female: 11.54 deaths/1,000 live births (2004 est.)
Life expectancy at birth:
total population: 69.2 years
male: 66.74 years
female: 71.79 years (2004 est.)
Total fertility rate: 2.78 children born/woman (2004 est.)
HIV/AIDS - adult prevalence rate: 0.1% (2001 est.)

HIV/AIDS - people living with HIV/AIDS: 300 (2001 est.)
HIV/AIDS - deaths: NA
Nationality:
noun: Fijian(s)
adjective: Fijian
Ethnic groups: Fijian 51% (predominantly Melanesian with a Polynesian admixture), Indian 44%, European, other Pacific Islanders, overseas Chinese, and other 5% (1998 est.)
Religions: Christian 52% (Methodist 37%, Roman Catholic 9%), Hindu 38%, Muslim 8%, other 2%
note: Fijians are mainly Christian, Indians are Hindu, and there is a Muslim minority (1986)
Languages: English (official), Fijian, Hindustani
Literacy:
definition: age 15 and over can read and write
total population: 93.7%
male: 95.5%
female: 91.9% (2003 est.)

Government

Country name:
conventional long form: Republic of the Fiji Islands
conventional short form: Fiji
Government type: republic
note: military coup leader Maj. Gen. Sitiveni RABUKA formally declared Fiji a republic on 6 October 1987
Capital: Suva (Viti Levu)
Administrative divisions: 4 divisions and 1 dependency*; Central, Eastern, Northern, Rotuma*, Western
Independence: 10 October 1970 (from UK)
National holiday: Independence Day, second Monday of October (1970)
Constitution: promulgated on 25 July 1990 and amended on 25 July 1997 to allow nonethnic Fijians greater say in government and to make multiparty government mandatory; entered into force 28 July 1998; note - the May 1999 election was the first test of the amended constitution and introduced open voting - not racially prescribed - for the first time at the national level
Legal system: based on British system
Suffrage: 21 years of age; universal
Executive branch:
chief of state: President Ratu Josefa ILOILOVATU Uluivuda (since NA 2000); Vice President Jope SENILOLI (since NA 2000)
head of government: Prime Minister Laisenia QARASE (since 10 September 2000)
cabinet: Cabinet appointed by the prime minister from among the members of Parliament and is responsible to Parliament; note - there is also a Presidential Council that advises the president on matters of national importance and a Great Council of Chiefs, which consists of the highest ranking members of the traditional chief system
elections: president elected by the Great Council of Chiefs for a five-year term; prime minister appointed by the president

Fiji (continued)

election results: Ratu Josefa ILOILOVATU Uluivuda elected president by the Great Council of Chiefs; percent of vote - NA%

Legislative branch: bicameral Parliament consists of the Senate (34 seats; 24 appointed by the President on the advice of the Great Council of Chiefs, nine appointed by the president, and one appointed by the council of Rotuma) and the House of Representatives (71 seats; 23 reserved for ethnic Fijians, 19 reserved for ethnic Indians, three reserved for other ethnic groups, one reserved for the council of Rotuma constituency encompassing the whole of Fiji, and 25 open seats; members serve five-year terms)

elections: House of Representatives - last held 25 August through 1 September, 19 September 2001 (next to be held not later than September 2006)

election results: House of Representatives - percent of vote by party - FLP 26.5%, SDL 27.5%, NFP 1.2%, MV 4.2%, NLUP 1.3%, UGP .3%, independents 1.4%; seats by party - FLP 27, SDL 32, MV 6, NFP 1, NLUP 2, UGP 1, independents 2

Judicial branch: Supreme Court (judges are appointed by the president); Court of Appeal; High Court; Magistrates' Courts

Political parties and leaders: Bai Kei Viti Party or BKV [Ratu Tevita MOMOEDONU]; Conservative Alliance Party/Matanitu Vanua or MV [Ratu Rakuita VAKALALABURE]; Dodonu Ni Taukei Party or DNT [Fereti S. DEWA]; Fiji Democratic Party or FDP [Felipe BOLE] (a merger of the Christian Democrat Alliance or VLV [Poesci Waqalevu BUNE], Fijian Association Party or FAP [Adi Kuini SPEED], Fijian Political Party or SVT (primarily Fijian) [Felipe BOLE], and New Labor Unity Party or NLUP [Tupeni BABA]); Fiji Labor Party or FLP [Mahendra CHAUDRHRY]; General Voters Party or GVP [leader NA] (became part of United General Party); Girmit Heritage Party or GHP [leader NA]; Justice and Freedom Party or AIM [leader NA]; Lio 'On Famor Rotuma Party or LFR [leader NA]; National Federation Party or NFP (primarily Indian) [Pramond RAE]; Nationalist Vanua Takolavo Party or NVTLP [Saula TELAWA]; Party of National Unity or PANU [Meli BOGILEKA]; Party of the Truth or POTT [leader NA]; United Fiji Party/Sogosogo Duavata ni Lewenivanua or SDL [Laisenia QARASE]; United General Party or UGP [Millis Mick BEDDOES]

Political pressure groups and leaders: NA

International organization participation: ACP, AsDB, C, CP, FAO, G-77, IBRD, ICAO, ICCt, ICFTU, ICRM, IDA, IFAD, IFC, IFRCS, IHO, ILO, IMF, IMO, Interpol, IOC, ISO (subscriber), ITU, OPCW, PCA, PIF, Sparteca, UN, UNCTAD, UNESCO, UNIDO, UNMIK, UNMISET, UPU, WCO, WFTU, WHO, WIPO, WMO, WToO, WTrO

Diplomatic representation in the US:
chief of mission: Ambassador Anare JALE
chancery: 2233 Wisconsin Avenue NW, Suite 240, Washington, DC 20007
telephone: [1] (202) 337-8320
FAX: [1] (202) 337-1996

Diplomatic representation from the US:
chief of mission: Ambassador David L. LYON
embassy: 31 Loftus Street, Suva
mailing address: P. O. Box 218, Suva
telephone: [679] 331-4466
FAX: [679] 330-0081

Flag description: light blue with the flag of the UK in the upper hoist-side quadrant and the Fijian shield centered on the outer half of the flag; the shield depicts a yellow lion above a white field quartered by the cross of Saint George featuring stalks of sugarcane, a palm tree, bananas, and a white dove

Economy

Economy - overview: Fiji, endowed with forest, mineral, and fish resources, is one of the most developed of the Pacific island economies, though still with a large subsistence sector. Sugar exports and a growing tourist industry - with 300,000 to 400,000 tourists annually - are the major sources of foreign exchange. Sugar processing makes up one-third of industrial activity. Long-term problems include low investment, uncertain land ownership rights, and the government's ability to manage its budget. Yet short-run economic prospects are good, provided tensions do not again erupt between indigenous Fijians and Indo-Fijians.

GDP: purchasing power parity - $5.007 billion (2003 est.)

GDP - real growth rate: 4.8% (2003 est.)

GDP - per capita: purchasing power parity - $5,800 (2003 est.)

GDP - composition by sector:
agriculture: 16.6%
industry: 22.4%
services: 61% (2001 est.)

Population below poverty line: 25.5% (1990-91)

Household income or consumption by percentage share:
lowest 10%: NA%
highest 10%: NA%

Inflation rate (consumer prices): 1.6% (2002 est.)

Labor force: 137,000 (1999)

Labor force - by occupation: agriculture, including subsistence agriculture 70% (2001 est.)

Unemployment rate: 7.6% (1999)

Budget:
revenues: $427.9 million
expenditures: $531.4 million, including capital expenditures of $NA (2000 est.)

Industries: tourism, sugar, clothing, copra, gold, silver, lumber, small cottage industries

Industrial production growth rate: NA%

Electricity - production: 520.1 million kWh (2001)

Electricity - production by source:
fossil fuel: 18.5%
hydro: 81.5%
nuclear: 0%
other: 0% (2001)

Electricity - consumption: 483.7 million kWh (2001)

Electricity - exports: 0 kWh (2001)

Electricity - imports: 0 kWh (2001)

Oil - production: 0 bbl/day (2001 est.)

Oil - consumption: 5,700 bbl/day (2001 est.)

Oil - exports: NA

Oil - imports: NA

Agriculture - products: sugarcane, coconuts, cassava (tapioca), rice, sweet potatoes, bananas; cattle, pigs, horses, goats; fish

Exports: $609 million f.o.b. (2002)

Exports - commodities: sugar, garments, gold, timber, fish, molasses, coconut oil

Exports - partners: US 25.5%, Australia 19.7%, UK 10.7%, Japan 6.4%, Samoa 5.6% (2002)

Imports: $835 million c.i.f. (2002)

Imports - commodities: manufactured goods, machinery and transport equipment, petroleum products, food, chemicals

Imports - partners: Australia 37.5%, New Zealand 17.2%, Singapore 16%, Japan 4.2%, China 4.1% (2002)

Debt - external: $188.1 million (2001 est.)

Economic aid - recipient: $40.3 million (1995)

Currency: Fijian dollar (FJD)

Currency code: FJD

Exchange rates: Fijian dollars per US dollar - 1.8958 (2003), 2.1869 (2002), 2.2766 (2001), 2.1286 (2000), 1.9696 (1999)

Fiscal year: calendar year

Communications

Telephones - main lines in use: 97,500 (2002)

Telephones - mobile cellular: 89,900 (2002)

Telephone system:
general assessment: modern local, interisland, and international (wire/radio integrated) public and special-purpose telephone, telegraph, and teleprinter facilities; regional radio communications center
domestic: NA
international: country code - 679; access to important cable links between US and Canada as well as between NZ and Australia; satellite earth station - 1 Intelsat (Pacific Ocean)

Radio broadcast stations: AM 13, FM 40, shortwave 0 (1998)

Television broadcast stations: NA

Internet country code: .fj

Internet hosts: 785 (2002)

Internet users: 50,000 (2002)

Transportation

Railways:
total: 597 km
narrow gauge: 597 km 0.600-m gauge
note: belongs to the government-owned Fiji Sugar Corporation; used to haul sugarcane during harvest season (May to September) (2002)

Highways:
total: 3,440 km
paved: 1,692 km
unpaved: 1,748 km (1999 est.)

Waterways: 203 km
note: 122 km navigable by motorized craft and 200-metric-ton barges
Ports and harbors: Lambasa, Lautoka, Levuka, Malau, Savusavu, Suva, Vuda
Merchant marine:
total: 2 ships (1,000 GRT or over) 6,372 GRT/7,453 DWT
by type: chemical tanker 1, passenger 1
foreign-owned: Australia 1, Singapore 1 (2003 est.)
Airports: 28 (2003 est.)
Airports - with paved runways:
total: 3
over 3,047 m: 1
1,524 to 2,437 m: 1
914 to 1,523 m: 1 (2003 est.)
Airports - with unpaved runways:
total: 25
914 to 1,523 m: 6
under 914 m: 19 (2003 est.)

Military

Military branches: Republic of Fiji Military Forces (RFMF): Land Forces, Naval Division
Military manpower - military age: 18 years of age (2004 est.)
Military manpower - availability:
males age 15-49: 239,221 (2004 est.)
Military manpower - fit for military service:
males age 15-49: 131,349 (2004 est.)
Military manpower - reaching military age annually:
males: 9,302 (2004 est.)
Military expenditures - dollar figure: $34 million (2003)
Military expenditures - percent of GDP: 2.2% (FY02)

Transnational Issues

Disputes - international: none

Finland

Introduction

Background: Finland was a province and then a grand duchy under Sweden from the 12th to the 19th centuries and an autonomous grand duchy of Russia after 1809. It won its complete independence in 1917. During World War II, it was able to successfully defend its freedom and resist invasions by the Soviet Union - albeit with some loss of territory. In the subsequent half century, the Finns made a remarkable transformation from a farm/forest economy to a diversified modern industrial economy; per capita income is now on par with Western Europe. As a member of the European Union, Finland was the only Nordic state to join the euro system at its initiation in January 1999.

Geography

Location: Northern Europe, bordering the Baltic Sea, Gulf of Bothnia, and Gulf of Finland, between Sweden and Russia
Geographic coordinates: 64 00 N, 26 00 E
Map references: Europe

Area:
total: 337,030 sq km
land: 305,470 sq km
water: 31,560 sq km
Area - comparative: slightly smaller than Montana
Land boundaries:
total: 2,628 km
border countries: Norway 729 km, Sweden 586 km, Russia 1,313 km
Coastline: 1,126 km (excludes islands and coastal indentations)
Maritime claims:
territorial sea: 12 NM (in the Gulf of Finland - 3 NM)
continental shelf: 200-m depth or to the depth of exploitation
exclusive fishing zone: 12 NM; extends to continental shelf boundary with Sweden
Climate: cold temperate; potentially subarctic but comparatively mild because of moderating influence of the North Atlantic Current, Baltic Sea, and more than 60,000 lakes
Terrain: mostly low, flat to rolling plains interspersed with lakes and low hills
Elevation extremes:
lowest point: Baltic Sea 0 m
highest point: Halti 1,328 m
Natural resources: timber, copper, zinc, iron ore, silver
Land use:
arable land: 6.98%
permanent crops: 0.01%
other: 93.01% (1998 est.)
Irrigated land: 640 sq km (1998 est.)
Natural hazards: NA
Environment - current issues: air pollution from manufacturing and power plants contributing to acid rain; water pollution from industrial wastes, agricultural chemicals; habitat loss threatens wildlife populations
Environment - international agreements:
party to: Air Pollution, Air Pollution-Nitrogen Oxides, Air Pollution-Sulfur 85, Air Pollution-Sulfur 94, Air Pollution-Volatile Organic Compounds, Antarctic-Environmental Protocol, Antarctic-Marine Living Resources, Antarctic Treaty, Biodiversity, Climate Change, Climate Change-Kyoto Protocol, Desertification, Endangered Species, Environmental Modification, Hazardous Wastes, Law of the Sea, Marine Dumping, Marine Life Conservation, Ozone Layer Protection, Ship Pollution, Tropical Timber 83, Tropical Timber 94, Wetlands, Whaling
signed, but not ratified: Air Pollution-Persistent Organic Pollutants
Geography - note: long boundary with Russia; Helsinki is northernmost national capital on European continent; population concentrated on small southwestern coastal plain

Finland *(continued)*

People

Population: 5,214,512 (July 2004 est.)
Age structure:
0-14 years: 17.5% (male 466,036; female 448,339)
15-64 years: 66.7% (male 1,760,472; female 1,719,917)
65 years and over: 15.7% (male 323,082; female 496,666) (2004 est.)
Median age:
total: 40.7 years
male: 39.1 years
female: 42.2 years (2004 est.)
Population growth rate: 0.18% (2004 est.)
Birth rate: 10.56 births/1,000 population (2004 est.)
Death rate: 9.69 deaths/1,000 population (2004 est.)
Net migration rate: 0.95 migrant(s)/1,000 population (2004 est.)
Sex ratio:
at birth: 1.04 male(s)/female
under 15 years: 1.04 male(s)/female
15-64 years: 1.02 male(s)/female
65 years and over: 0.65 male(s)/female
total population: 0.96 male(s)/female (2004 est.)
Infant mortality rate:
total: 3.59 deaths/1,000 live births
male: 3.91 deaths/1,000 live births
female: 3.26 deaths/1,000 live births (2004 est.)
Life expectancy at birth:
total population: 78.24 years
male: 74.73 years
female: 81.89 years (2004 est.)
Total fertility rate: 1.73 children born/woman (2004 est.)
HIV/AIDS - adult prevalence rate: less than 0.1% (2001 est.)
HIV/AIDS - people living with HIV/AIDS: 1,200 (2001 est.)
HIV/AIDS - deaths: less than 100 (2001 est.)
Nationality:
noun: Finn(s)
adjective: Finnish
Ethnic groups: Finn 93%, Swede 6%, Sami 0.11%, Roma 0.12%, Tatar 0.02%
Religions: Evangelical Lutheran 89%, Russian Orthodox 1%, none 9%, other 1%
Languages: Finnish 93.4% (official), Swedish 5.9% (official), small Sami- and Russian-speaking minorities
Literacy:
definition: age 15 and over can read and write
total population: 100% (1980 est.)
male: NA%
female: NA%

Government

Country name:
conventional long form: Republic of Finland
conventional short form: Finland
local long form: Suomen Tasavalta
local short form: Suomi

Government type: republic
Capital: Helsinki
Administrative divisions: 6 provinces (laanit, singular - laani); Aland, Etela-Suomen Laani, Ita-Suomen Laani, Lansi-Suomen Laani, Lappi, Oulun Laani
Independence: 6 December 1917 (from Russia)
National holiday: Independence Day, 6 December (1917)
Constitution: 1 March 2000
Legal system: civil law system based on Swedish law; Supreme Court may request legislation interpreting or modifying laws; accepts compulsory ICJ jurisdiction, with reservations
Suffrage: 18 years of age; universal
Executive branch:
chief of state: President Tarja HALONEN (since 1 March 2000)
head of government: Prime Minister Matti VANHANEN (since 24 June 2003) and Deputy Prime Minister Antti KALLIOMAKI (since 17 April 2003); note - former Prime Minister Anneli JAATTEENMAKI resigned
cabinet: Council of State or Valtioneuvosto appointed by the president, responsible to Parliament
elections: president elected by popular vote for a six-year term; election last held 16 January 2000 and 6 February 2000 (next to be held NA February 2006); prime minister and deputy prime minister appointed from the majority party by the president after parliamentary elections
election results: Tarja HALONEN elected president; percent of vote - Tarja HALONEN (SDP) 51.6%, Esko AHO (Kesk) 48.4%
note: government coalition - KESK, SDP, and SFP
Legislative branch: unicameral Parliament or Eduskunta (200 seats; members are elected by popular vote on a proportional basis to serve four-year terms)
elections: last held 16 March 2003 (next to be held NA March 2007)
election results: percent of vote by party - Kesk 24.7%, SDP 24.5%, Kok 18.5%, VAS 9.9%, VIHR 8%, KD 5.3%, SFP 4.6%; seats by party - Kesk 55, SDP 53, Kok 40, VAS 19, VIHR 14, KD 7, SFP 8, others 4
Judicial branch: Supreme Court or Korkein Oikeus (judges appointed by the president)
Political parties and leaders: Center Party or Kesk [Matti VANHANEN]; Christian Democrats or KD [Bjarne KALLIS]; Green League or VIHR [Osmo SOININVAARA]; Left Alliance or VAS (Communist) composed of People's Democratic League and Democratic Alternative [Suvi-Anne SIIMES]; National Coalition (conservative) Party or Kok [Ville ITALA]; Social Democratic Party or SDP [Paavo LIPPONEN]; Swedish People's Party or SFP [Jan-Erik ENESTAM]
International organization participation: AfDB, AsDB, Australia Group, BIS, CBSS, CE, CERN, EAPC, EBRD, EIB, EMU, ESA, EU, FAO, G- 9, IADB, IAEA, IBRD, ICAO, ICC, ICCt, ICFTU, ICRM, IDA, IEA, IFAD, IFC, IFRCS, IHO, ILO, IMF, IMO, Interpol, IOC, IOM, ISO, ITU, NAM (guest), NC, NEA, NIB,

NSG, OAS (observer), OECD, OPCW, OSCE, Paris Club, PCA, PFP, UN, UNCTAD, UNESCO, UNFICYP, UNHCR, UNIDO, UNMEE, UNMIK, UNMIL, UNMOGIP, UNTSO, UPU, WCO, WEU (observer), WFTU, WHO, WIPO, WMO, WTrO, ZC
Diplomatic representation in the US:
chief of mission: Ambassador Jukka Robert VALTASAARI
chancery: 3301 Massachusetts Avenue NW, Washington, DC 20008
telephone: [1] (202) 298-5800
FAX: [1] (202) 298-6030
consulate(s) general: Los Angeles and New York
Diplomatic representation from the US:
chief of mission: Ambassador (vacant)
embassy: Itainen Puistotie 14A, FIN-00140, Helsinki
mailing address: APO AE 09723
telephone: [358] (9) 616250
FAX: [358] (9) 174681
Flag description: white with a blue cross extending to the edges of the flag; the vertical part of the cross is shifted to the hoist side in the style of the Dannebrog (Danish flag)

Economy

Economy - overview: Finland has a highly industrialized, largely free-market economy, with per capita output roughly that of the UK, France, Germany, and Italy. Its key economic sector is manufacturing - principally the wood, metals, engineering, telecommunications, and electronics industries. Trade is important, with exports equaling one-third of GDP. Except for timber and several minerals, Finland depends on imports of raw materials, energy, and some components for manufactured goods. Because of the climate, agricultural development is limited to maintaining self-sufficiency in basic products. Forestry, an important export earner, provides a secondary occupation for the rural population. Rapidly increasing integration with Western Europe - Finland was one of the 12 countries joining the European Economic and Monetary Union (EMU) - will dominate the economic picture over the next several years. Growth in 2003 was held back by the global slowdown but will pick up in 2004 provided the world economy suffers no further blows.
GDP: purchasing power parity - $141.7 billion (2003 est.)
GDP - real growth rate: 1.5% (2003 est.)
GDP - per capita: purchasing power parity - $27,300 (2003 est.)
GDP - composition by sector:
agriculture: 3.1%
industry: 29.4%
services: 67.5% (2003 est.)
Population below poverty line: NA%
Household income or consumption by percentage share:
lowest 10%: 4.2%
highest 10%: 21.6% (1991)

Finland *(continued)*

Distribution of family income - Gini index: 25.6 (1991)
Inflation rate (consumer prices): 1.1% (2003 est.)
Labor force: 2.6 million (2000 est.)
Labor force - by occupation: public services 32%, industry 22%, commerce 14%, finance, insurance, and business services 10%, agriculture and forestry 8%, transport and communications 8%, construction 6%
Unemployment rate: 9.2% (2003 est.)
Budget:
revenues: $36.1 billion
expenditures: $31 billion, including capital expenditures of $NA (2000 est.)
Industries: metal products, electronics, shipbuilding, pulp and paper, copper refining, foodstuffs, chemicals, textiles, clothing
Industrial production growth rate: 0.7% (2003 est.)
Electricity - production: 71.2 billion kWh (2001)
Electricity - production by source:
fossil fuel: 39%
hydro: 18.7%
nuclear: 30.4%
other: 11.8% (2001)
Electricity - consumption: 76.18 billion kWh (2001)
Electricity - exports: 1.81 billion kWh (2001)
Electricity - imports: 11.77 billion kWh (2001)
Oil - production: 0 bbl/day (2001 est.)
Oil - consumption: 211,400 bbl/day (2001 est.)
Oil - exports: 101,000 bbl/day (2001)
Oil - imports: 318,300 bbl/day (2001)
Natural gas - production: 0 cu m (2001 est.)
Natural gas - consumption: 4.557 billion cu m (2001 est.)
Natural gas - exports: 0 cu m (2001 est.)
Natural gas - imports: 4.567 billion cu m (2001 est.)
Agriculture - products: barley, wheat, sugar beets, potatoes; dairy cattle; fish
Exports: $54.28 billion f.o.b. (2003 est.)
Exports - commodities: machinery and equipment, chemicals, metals; timber, paper, pulp (1999)
Exports - partners: Germany 11.8%, UK 9.6%, US 9%, Sweden 8.5%, Russia 6.6%, Netherlands 4.6%, France 4.5% (2002)
Imports: $37.35 billion f.o.b. (2003 est.)
Imports - commodities: foodstuffs, petroleum and petroleum products, chemicals, transport equipment, iron and steel, machinery, textile yarn and fabrics, grains (1999)
Imports - partners: Germany 14.5%, Sweden 10.9%, Russia 9.9%, UK 5.7%, France 4.3%, Denmark 4.2% (2002)
Debt - external: $30 billion (December 1993)
Economic aid - donor: ODA, $379 million (2001)
Currency: euro (EUR)
note: on 1 January 1999, the European Monetary Union introduced the euro as a common currency to be used by financial institutions of member countries; on 1 January 2002, the euro became the sole currency for everyday transactions within the member countries

Currency code: EUR
Exchange rates: euros per US dollar - 0.886 (2003), 1.0626 (2002), 1.1175 (2001), 1.0854 (2000), 0.9386 (1999)
Fiscal year: calendar year

Communications

Telephones - main lines in use: 2,725,600 (2002)
Telephones - mobile cellular: 4,516,800 (2002)
Telephone system:
general assessment: modern system with excellent service
domestic: cable, microwave radio relay, and an extensive cellular net provide domestic needs
international: country code - 358; 1 submarine cable; satellite earth stations - access to Intelsat transmission service via a Swedish satellite earth station, 1 Inmarsat (Atlantic and Indian Ocean regions); note - Finland shares the Inmarsat earth station with the other Nordic countries (Denmark, Iceland, Norway, and Sweden)
Radio broadcast stations: AM 2, FM 186, shortwave 1 (1998)
Television broadcast stations: 120 (plus 431 repeaters) (1999)
Internet country code: .fi
Internet hosts: 1,220,062 (2002)
Internet users: 2.65 million (2002)

Transportation

Railways:
total: 5,850 km
broad gauge: 5,850 km 1.524-m gauge (2,400 km electrified) (2002)
Highways:
total: 77,943 km
paved: 50,305 km (including 750 km of expressways)
unpaved: 27,688 km (2001)
Waterways: 6,675 km
note: includes Saimaa Canal; 3,700 km suitable for large ships
Pipelines: gas 694 km (2003)
Ports and harbors: Hamina, Helsinki, Kokkola, Kotka, Loviisa, Oulu, Pori, Rauma, Turku, Uusikaupunki, Varkaus
Merchant marine:
total: 90 ships (1,000 GRT or over) 1,152,175 GRT/ 1,053,906 DWT
by type: bulk 9, cargo 26, chemical tanker 5, container 1, passenger 2, petroleum tanker 9, roll on/ roll off 28, short-sea/passenger 10
foreign-owned: Estonia 1
registered in other countries: 39 (2003 est.)
Airports: 148 (2003 est.)
Airports - with paved runways:
total: 75
over 3,047 m: 2
2,438 to 3,047 m: 27
1,524 to 2,437 m: 10
914 to 1,523 m: 23
under 914 m: 13 (2003 est.)

Airports - with unpaved runways:
total: 73
914 to 1,523 m: 4
under 914 m: 69 (2003 est.)

Military

Military branches: Army, Navy, Air Force
Military manpower - military age: 18 years of age (2004 est.)
Military manpower - availability:
males age 15-49: 1,226,890 (2004 est.)
Military manpower - fit for military service:
males age 15-49: 1,013,961 (2004 est.)
Military manpower - reaching military age annually:
males: 32,058 (2004 est.)
Military expenditures - dollar figure: $1.8 billion (FY98/99)
Military expenditures - percent of GDP: 2% (FY98/99)

Transnational Issues

Disputes - international: none

France

Background: Although ultimately a victor in World Wars I and II, France suffered extensive losses in its empire, wealth, manpower, and rank as a dominant nation-state. Nevertheless, France today is one of the most modern countries in the world and is a leader among European nations. Since 1958, it has constructed a presidential democracy resistant to the instabilities experienced in earlier parliamentary democracies. In recent years, its reconciliation and cooperation with Germany have proved central to the economic integration of Europe, including the introduction of a common exchange currency, the euro, in January 1999. At present, France is at the forefront of European states seeking to exploit the momentum of monetary union to advance the creation of a more unified and capable European defense and security apparatus.

Geography

Location: Western Europe, bordering the Bay of Biscay and English Channel, between Belgium and Spain, southeast of the UK; bordering the Mediterranean Sea, between Italy and Spain
Geographic coordinates: 46 00 N, 2 00 E
Map references: Europe
Area:
total: 547,030 sq km
land: 545,630 sq km
water: 1,400 sq km
note: includes only metropolitan France; excludes the overseas administrative divisions
Area - comparative: slightly less than twice the size of Colorado
Land boundaries:
total: 2,889 km
border countries: Andorra 56.6 km, Belgium 620 km, Germany 451 km, Italy 488 km, Luxembourg 73 km, Monaco 4.4 km, Spain 623 km, Switzerland 573 km
Coastline: 3,427 km

Maritime claims:
territorial sea: 12 NM
contiguous zone: 24 NM
exclusive economic zone: 200 NM (does not apply to the Mediterranean)
continental shelf: 200-m depth or to the depth of exploitation
Climate: generally cool winters and mild summers, but mild winters and hot summers along the Mediterranean; occasional strong, cold, dry, north-to-northwesterly wind known as mistral
Terrain: mostly flat plains or gently rolling hills in north and west; remainder is mountainous, especially Pyrenees in south, Alps in east
Elevation extremes:
lowest point: Rhone River delta -2 m
highest point: Mont Blanc 4,807 m
Natural resources: coal, iron ore, bauxite, zinc, potash, timber, fish
Land use:
arable land: 33.3%
permanent crops: 2.11%
other: 64.59% (1998 est.)
Irrigated land: 20,000 sq km (1998 est.)
Natural hazards: flooding; avalanches; midwinter windstorms; drought; forest fires in south near the Mediterranean
Environment - current issues: some forest damage from acid rain; air pollution from industrial and vehicle emissions; water pollution from urban wastes, agricultural runoff
Environment - international agreements:
party to: Air Pollution, Air Pollution-Nitrogen Oxides, Air Pollution-Sulfur 85, Air Pollution-Sulfur 94, Air Pollution-Volatile Organic Compounds, Antarctic-Environmental Protocol, Antarctic-Marine Living Resources, Antarctic Seals, Antarctic Treaty, Biodiversity, Climate Change, Climate Change-Kyoto Protocol, Desertification, Endangered Species, Hazardous Wastes, Law of the Sea, Marine Dumping, Marine Life Conservation, Ozone Layer Protection, Ship Pollution, Tropical Timber 83, Tropical Timber 94, Wetlands, Whaling
signed, but not ratified: Air Pollution-Persistent Organic Pollutants
Geography - note: largest West European nation

People

Population: 60,424,213 (July 2004 est.)
Age structure:
0-14 years: 18.5% (male 5,724,185; female 5,446,716)
15-64 years: 65.1% (male 19,698,497; female 19,663,776)
65 years and over: 16.4% (male 4,049,970; female 5,841,069) (2004 est.)
Median age:
total: 38.6 years
male: 37 years
female: 40.1 years (2004 est.)

Population growth rate: 0.39% (2004 est.)
Birth rate: 12.34 births/1,000 population (2004 est.)
Death rate: 9.06 deaths/1,000 population (2004 est.)
Net migration rate: 0.66 migrant(s)/1,000 population (2004 est.)
Sex ratio:
at birth: 1.05 male(s)/female
under 15 years: 1.05 male(s)/female
15-64 years: 1 male(s)/female
65 years and over: 0.69 male(s)/female
total population: 0.95 male(s)/female (2004 est.)
Infant mortality rate:
total: 4.31 deaths/1,000 live births
male: 4.83 deaths/1,000 live births
female: 3.78 deaths/1,000 live births (2004 est.)
Life expectancy at birth:
total population: 79.44 years
male: 75.8 years
female: 83.27 years (2004 est.)
Total fertility rate: 1.85 children born/woman (2004 est.)
HIV/AIDS - adult prevalence rate: 0.3% (2001 est.)
HIV/AIDS - people living with HIV/AIDS: 100,000 (2001 est.)
HIV/AIDS - deaths: 800 (2001 est.)
Nationality:
noun: Frenchman(men), Frenchwoman(women)
adjective: French
Ethnic groups: Celtic and Latin with Teutonic, Slavic, North African, Indochinese, Basque minorities
Religions: Roman Catholic 83%-88%, Protestant 2%, Jewish 1%, Muslim 5%-10%, unaffiliated 4%
Languages: French 100%, rapidly declining regional dialects and languages (Provencal, Breton, Alsatian, Corsican, Catalan, Basque, Flemish)
Literacy:
definition: age 15 and over can read and write
total population: 99%
male: 99%
female: 99% (1980 est.)

Government

Country name:
conventional long form: French Republic
conventional short form: France
local long form: Republique Francaise
local short form: France
Government type: republic
Capital: Paris
Administrative divisions: 22 regions (regions, singular - region); Alsace, Aquitaine, Auvergne, Basse-Normandie, Bourgogne, Bretagne, Centre, Champagne-Ardenne, Corse, Franche-Comte, Haute-Normandie, Ile-de-France, Languedoc-Roussillon, Limousin, Lorraine, Midi-Pyrenees, Nord-Pas-de-Calais, Pays de la Loire, Picardie, Poitou-Charentes, Provence-Alpes-Cote d'Azur, Rhone-Alpes
note: metropolitan France is divided into 22 regions (including the "territorial collectivity" of Corse or Corsica) and is subdivided into 96 departments; see

France (continued)

separate entries for the overseas departments (French Guiana, Guadeloupe, Martinique, Reunion) and the overseas territorial collectivities (Mayotte, Saint Pierre and Miquelon)

Dependent areas: Bassas da India, Clipperton Island, Europa Island, French Polynesia, French Southern and Antarctic Lands, Glorioso Islands, Juan de Nova Island, New Caledonia, Tromelin Island, Wallis and Futuna

note: the US does not recognize claims to Antarctica

Independence: 486 (unified by Clovis)

National holiday: Bastille Day, 14 July (1789)

Constitution: 28 September 1958, amended concerning election of president in 1962, amended to comply with provisions of 1992 EC Maastricht Treaty, 1996 Amsterdam Treaty, 2000 Treaty of Nice; amended to tighten immigration laws in 1993; amended to change the seven-year presidential term to a five-year term in 2000

Legal system: civil law system with indigenous concepts; review of administrative but not legislative acts

Suffrage: 18 years of age; universal

Executive branch:

chief of state: President Jacques CHIRAC (since 17 May 1995)

head of government: Prime Minister Jean-Pierre RAFFARIN (since 7 May 2002)

cabinet: Council of Ministers appointed by the president on the suggestion of the prime minister

elections: president elected by popular vote for a five-year term (changed from seven-year term in October 2000); election last held 21 April and 5 May 2002 (next to be held, first round NA April 2007, second round NA May 2007); prime minister nominated by the National Assembly majority and appointed by the president

election results: Jacques CHIRAC reelected president; percent of vote, second ballot - Jacques CHIRAC (RPR) 81.96%, Jean-Marie LE PEN (FN) 18.04%

Legislative branch: bicameral Parliament or Parlement consists of the Senate or Senat (321 seats - 296 for metropolitan France, 13 for overseas departments and territories, and 12 for French nationals abroad; members are indirectly elected by an electoral college to serve nine-year terms; elected by thirds every three years); note - between now and 2010, 25 new seats will be added to the Senate for a total of 346 seats - 326 for metropolitan France and overseas departments, 2 for New Caledonia, 2 for Mayotte, 1 for Saint-Pierre and Miquelon, 3 for overseas territories, and 12 for French nationals abroad; members will be indirectly elected by an electoral college to serve six-year terms, with one-half the seats being renewed every three years; and the National Assembly or Assemblee Nationale (577 seats; members are elected by popular vote under a single-member majoritarian system to serve five-year terms)

elections: Senate - last held 23 September 2001 (next to be held NA September 2004); National Assembly - last held 8-16 June 2002 (next to be held not later than June 2007)

election results: Senate - percent of vote by party - NA%; seats by party - RPR 83, PS 68, UDF 37, DL 35, RDES 16, PCF 16, other 66; National Assembly - percent of vote by party - NA%; seats by party - UMP 355, PS 140, UDF 29, PCF 21, Radical Party 7, Greens 3, other 22

Judicial branch: Supreme Court of Appeals or Cour de Cassation (judges are appointed by the president from nominations of the High Council of the Judiciary); Constitutional Council or Conseil Constitutionnel (three members appointed by the president, three appointed by the president of the National Assembly, and three appointed by the president of the Senate); Council of State or Conseil d'Etat

Political parties and leaders: Citizen and Republican Movement or MCR [Jean Pierre CHEVENEMENT]; Democratic and European Social Rally or RDSE (mainly RAD and PRG) [Jacques PELLETIER]; French Communist Party or PCF [Marie-George BUFFET]; Left Radical Party or PRG (previously Radical Socialist Party or PRS and the Left Radical Movement or MRG) [Jean-Michel BAYLET]; Movement for France or MPF [Philippe DE VILLIERS]; Rally for France or RPF [Charles PASQUA]; Socialist Party or PS [Francois HOLLANDE]; Greens [Gilles LEMAIRE, Francine BAVAY, Jean DESESSARD, Christophe PORQUIER, Maud LELIEVRE]; Union for French Democracy or UDF (formed when RPR and DL fused and dissolved) [Francois BAYROU]; Union for a Popular Movement or UMP (including RPR, DL, and a part of UDF) [Alain JUPPE]

Political pressure groups and leaders: historically-Communist labor union (Confederation Generale du Travail) or CGT, approximately 700,000 members (claimed); left-leaning labor union (Confederation Francaise Democratique du Travail) or CFDT, approximately 889,000 members (claimed); independent labor union (Confederation Generale du Travail - Force Ouvriere) or FO, 300,000 members (est.); independent white-collar union (Confederation Generale des Cadres) or CGC, 196,000 members (claimed); employers' union (Mouvement des Entreprises de France) or MEDEF, 750,000 companies as members (claimed)

International organization participation: ABEDA, ACCT, AfDB, AsDB, Australia Group, BDEAC, BIS, BSEC (observer), CE, CERN, EAPC, EBRD, EIB, EMU, ESA, EU, FAO, G-5, G-7, G-8, G-10, IADB, IAEA, IBRD, ICAO, ICC, ICCt, ICFTU, ICRM, IDA, IEA, IFAD, IFC, IFRCS, IHO, ILO, IMF, IMO, InOC, Interpol, IOC, IOM, ISO, ITU, MICAH, MINURSO, MONUC, NAM (guest), NATO, NEA, NSG, OAS (observer), OECD, OPCW, OSCE, Paris Club, PCA, UN, UN Security Council, UNCTAD, UNESCO, UNHCR, UNIDO, UNIFIL, UNITAR, UNMEE, UNMIK, UNMIL, UNMOVIC, UNOMIG, UNRWA, UNTSO, UPU, WADB (nonregional), WCL, WCO, WEU, WFTU, WHO, WIPO, WMO, WToO, WTrO, ZC

Diplomatic representation in the US:

chief of mission: Ambassador Jean-David LEVITTE

chancery: 4101 Reservoir Road NW, Washington, DC 20007

telephone: [1] (202) 944-6000

FAX: [1] (202) 944-6166

consulate(s) general: Atlanta, Boston, Chicago, Houston, Los Angeles, Miami, New Orleans, New York, and San Francisco

Diplomatic representation from the US:

chief of mission: Ambassador Howard H. LEACH

embassy: 2 Avenue Gabriel, 75382 Paris Cedex 08

mailing address: PSC 116, APO AE 09777

telephone: [33] (1) 43-12-22-22

FAX: [33] (1) 42 66 97 83

consulate(s) general: Marseille, Strasbourg

Flag description: three equal vertical bands of blue (hoist side), white, and red; known as the French Tricouleur (Tricolor); the design and/or colors are similar to a number of other flags, including those of Belgium, Chad, Ireland, Cote d'Ivoire, Luxembourg, and Netherlands; the official flag for all French dependent areas

Economy

Economy - overview: France is in the midst of transition, from a well-to-do modern economy that has featured extensive government ownership and intervention to one that relies more on market mechanisms. The Socialist-led government partially or fully privatized many large companies, banks, and insurers, but the government retains controlling stakes in several leading firms, including Air France, France Telecom, Renault, and Thales, and is dominant in some sectors, particularly power, public transport, and defense industries. The telecommunications sector is gradually being opened to competition. France's leaders remain committed to a capitalism in which they maintain social equity by means of laws, tax policies, and social spending that reduce income disparity and the impact of free markets on public health and welfare. The current government has lowered income taxes and introduced measures to boost employment. The government is focusing on the problems of the high cost of labor and labor market inflexibility resulting from the 35-hour workweek and restrictions on lay-offs. The government is also pushing for pension reforms and simplification of administrative procedures. The tax burden remains one of the highest in Europe (43.8% of GDP in 2003). The current economic slowdown and inflexible budget items have pushed the 2003 deficit to 4% of GDP, above the EU's 3% debt limit. Business investment remains listless because of low rates of capital utilization, sluggish demand, high debt, and the steep cost of capital.

GDP: purchasing power parity - $1.654 trillion (2003 est.)

GDP - real growth rate: 0.1% (2003 est.)

GDP - per capita: purchasing power parity - $27,500 (2003 est.)

GDP - composition by sector:

agriculture: 3%

industry: 26%

services: 71% (2002 est.)

France (continued)

Population below poverty line: 6.5% (2000)
Household income or consumption by percentage share:
lowest 10%: 2.8%
highest 10%: 25.1% (1995)
Distribution of family income - Gini index: 32.7 (1995)
Inflation rate (consumer prices): 2% (2003 est.)
Labor force: 27.1 million (2003 est.)
Labor force - by occupation: services 71.5%, industry 24.4%, agriculture 4.1% (1999)
Unemployment rate: 9.6% (2003 est.)
Budget:
revenues: $217 billion
expenditures: $274 billion, including capital expenditures of $23 billion (2003 est.)
Industries: machinery, chemicals, automobiles, metallurgy, aircraft, electronics; textiles, food processing; tourism
Industrial production growth rate: 1.1% (2003)
Electricity - production: 520.1 billion kWh (2001)
Electricity - production by source:
fossil fuel: 8.2%
hydro: 14%
nuclear: 77.1%
other: 0.7% (2001)
Electricity - consumption: 415.3 billion kWh (2001)
Electricity - exports: 72.6 billion kWh (2001)
Electricity - imports: 4.2 billion kWh (2001)
Oil - production: 34,920 bbl/day (2001 est.)
Oil - consumption: 2.026 million bbl/day (2001 est.)
Oil - exports: 409,600 bbl/day (2001)
Oil - imports: 2.281 million bbl/day (2001)
Oil - proved reserves: 144.3 million bbl (1 January 2002)
Natural gas - production: 1.898 billion cu m (2001 est.)
Natural gas - consumption: 42.01 billion cu m (2001 est.)
Natural gas - exports: 1.725 billion cu m (2001 est.)
Natural gas - imports: 40.26 billion cu m (2001 est.)
Natural gas - proved reserves: 12.86 billion cu m (1 January 2002)
Agriculture - products: wheat, cereals, sugar beets, potatoes, wine grapes; beef, dairy products; fish
Exports: $346.5 billion f.o.b. (2003 est.)
Exports - commodities: machinery and transportation equipment, aircraft, plastics, chemicals, pharmaceutical products, iron and steel, beverages
Exports - partners: Germany 15%, UK 9.8%, Spain 9%, Italy 9%, US 7.8%, Belgium 6.9% (2002)
Imports: $339.9 billion f.o.b. (2003 est.)
Imports - commodities: machinery and equipment, vehicles, crude oil, aircraft, plastics, chemicals
Imports - partners: Germany 19.4%, Belgium 9.2%, Italy 8.8%, UK 7.3%, Netherlands 7%, US 6.8%, Spain 6.7% (2002)
Debt - external: NA
Economic aid - donor: ODA, $5.4 billion (2002)
Currency: euro (EUR)

note: on 1 January 1999, the European Monetary Union introduced the euro as a common currency to be used by financial institutions of member countries; on 1 January 2002, the euro became the sole currency for everyday transactions within the member countries
Currency code: EUR
Exchange rates: euros per US dollar - 0.886 (2003), 1.0626 (2002), 1.1175 (2001), 1.0854 (2000), 0.9386 (1999)
Fiscal year: calendar year

Communications

Telephones - main lines in use: 33,928,700 (2002)
Telephones - mobile cellular: 38,585,300 (2002)
Telephone system:
general assessment: highly developed
domestic: extensive cable and microwave radio relay; extensive introduction of fiber-optic cable; domestic satellite system
international: country code - 33; satellite earth stations - 2 Intelsat (with total of 5 antennas - 2 for Indian Ocean and 3 for Atlantic Ocean), NA Eutelsat, 1 Inmarsat (Atlantic Ocean region); HF radiotelephone communications with more than 20 countries
Radio broadcast stations: AM 41, FM about 3,500 (this figure is an approximation and includes many repeaters), shortwave 2 (1998)
Television broadcast stations: 584 (plus 9,676 repeaters) (1995)
Internet country code: .fr
Internet hosts: 1,388,681 (2002)
Internet users: 18.716 million (2002)

Transportation

Railways:
total: 32,682 km
standard gauge: 32,515 km 1.435-m gauge (14,104 km electrified)
narrow gauge: 167 km 1.000-m gauge (2002)
Highways:
total: 894,000 km
paved: 894,000 km (including 11,500 km of expressways)
unpaved: 0 km (2000)
Waterways: 14,932 km (6,969 km heavily traveled)
Pipelines: gas 13,946 km; oil 3,024 km; refined products 4,889 km (2003)
Ports and harbors: Bordeaux, Boulogne, Cherbourg, Dijon, Dunkerque, La Pallice, Le Havre, Lyon, Marseille, Mulhouse, Nantes, Paris, Rouen, Saint Nazaire, Saint Malo, Strasbourg (2003)
Merchant marine:
total: 32 ships (1,000 GRT or over) 703,639 GRT/ 889,705 DWT
by type: cargo 3, chemical tanker 6, container 2, liquefied gas 4, passenger 1, petroleum tanker 10, roll on/roll off 2, short-sea/passenger 4
foreign-owned: Germany 1, Monaco 2, New Caledonia 1, Sweden 5
registered in other countries: 118 (2003 est.)

Airports: 477 (2003 est.)
Airports - with paved runways:
total: 281
over 3,047 m: 13
2,438 to 3,047 m: 28
1,524 to 2,437 m: 95
914 to 1,523 m: 82
under 914 m: 63 (2003 est.)
Airports - with unpaved runways:
total: 196
1,524 to 2,437 m: 3
914 to 1,523 m: 70
under 914 m: 123 (2003 est.)
Heliports: 3 (2003 est.)

Military

Military branches: Army (includes Marines, Foreign Legion, Army Light Aviation), Navy (including naval air), Air Force (including Air Defense), National Gendarmerie
Military manpower - military age: 18 years of age (2004 est.)
Military manpower - availability:
males age 15-49: 14,487,165 (2004 est.)
Military manpower - fit for military service:
males age 15-49: 12,044,827 (2004 est.)
Military manpower - reaching military age annually:
males: 394,413 (2004 est.)
Military expenditures - dollar figure: $45,238,100,000 (2003)
Military expenditures - percent of GDP: 2.6% (2003)

Transnational Issues

Disputes - international: Madagascar claims Bassas da India, Europa Island, Glorioso Islands, and Juan de Nova Island; Comoros claims Mayotte; Mauritius claims Tromelin Island; territorial dispute between Suriname and French Guiana; territorial claim in Antarctica (Adelie Land); Matthew and Hunter Islands, east of New Caledonia, claimed by France and Vanuatu
Illicit drugs: transshipment point for and consumer of South American cocaine, Southwest Asian heroin, and European synthetics

French Guiana
(overseas department of France)

Introduction

Background: First settled by the French in 1604, French Guiana was the site of notorious penal settlements until 1951. The European Space Agency launches its communication satellites from Kourou.

Geography

Location: Northern South America, bordering the North Atlantic Ocean, between Brazil and Suriname
Geographic coordinates: 4 00 N, 53 00 W
Map references: South America
Area:
total: 91,000 sq km
land: 89,150 sq km
water: 1,850 sq km
Area - comparative: slightly smaller than Indiana
Land boundaries:
total: 1,183 km
border countries: Brazil 673 km, Suriname 510 km
Coastline: 378 km
Maritime claims:
territorial sea: 12 NM
exclusive economic zone: 200 NM
Climate: tropical; hot, humid; little seasonal temperature variation
Terrain: low-lying coastal plains rising to hills and small mountains
Elevation extremes:
lowest point: Atlantic Ocean 0 m
highest point: Bellevue de l'Inini 851 m
Natural resources: bauxite, timber, gold (widely scattered), cinnabar, kaolin, fish
Land use:
arable land: 0.11% NEGL
permanent crops: 0.03%
other: 99.86% (90% forest, 10% other) (1998 est.)
Irrigated land: 20 sq km (1998 est.)
Natural hazards: high frequency of heavy showers and severe thunderstorms; flooding
Environment - current issues: NA

Geography - note: mostly an unsettled wilderness; the only non-independent portion of the South American continent

People

Population: 191,309 (July 2004 est.)
Age structure:
0-14 years: 29.6% (male 28,959; female 27,657)
15-64 years: 64.5% (male 66,388; female 57,020)
65 years and over: 5.9% (male 5,736; female 5,549) (2004 est.)
Median age:
total: 28.3 years
male: 29.4 years
female: 27.2 years (2004 est.)
Population growth rate: 2.25% (2004 est.)
Birth rate: 21 births/1,000 population (2004 est.)
Death rate: 4.82 deaths/1,000 population (2004 est.)
Net migration rate: 6.27 migrant(s)/1,000 population (2004 est.)
Sex ratio:
at birth: 1.05 male(s)/female
under 15 years: 1.05 male(s)/female
15-64 years: 1.16 male(s)/female
65 years and over: 1.03 male(s)/female
total population: 1.12 male(s)/female (2004 est.)
Infant mortality rate:
total: 12.46 deaths/1,000 live births
male: 13.3 deaths/1,000 live births
female: 11.58 deaths/1,000 live births (2004 est.)
Life expectancy at birth:
total population: 76.89 years
male: 73.57 years
female: 80.38 years (2004 est.)
Total fertility rate: 3.05 children born/woman (2004 est.)
HIV/AIDS - adult prevalence rate: NA%
HIV/AIDS - people living with HIV/AIDS: NA
HIV/AIDS - deaths: NA
Nationality:
noun: French Guianese (singular and plural)
adjective: French Guianese
Ethnic groups: black or mulatto 66%, white 12%, East Indian, Chinese, Amerindian 12%, other 10%
Religions: Roman Catholic
Languages: French
Literacy:
definition: age 15 and over can read and write
total population: 83%
male: 84%
female: 82% (1982 est.)

Government

Country name:
conventional long form: Department of Guiana
conventional short form: French Guiana
local long form: none
local short form: Guyane
Dependency status: overseas department of France
Government type: NA

Capital: Cayenne
Administrative divisions: none (overseas department of France)
Independence: none (overseas department of France)
National holiday: Bastille Day, 14 July (1789)
Constitution: 28 September 1958 (French Constitution)
Legal system: French legal system
Suffrage: 18 years of age; universal
Executive branch:
chief of state: President Jacques CHIRAC of France (since 17 May 1995), represented by Prefect Ange MANCINI (since 31 July 2002)
head of government: President of the General Council Joseph HO-TEN-YOU (since 26 March 2001); President of the Regional Council Antoine KARAM (since 22 March 1992)
cabinet: NA
elections: French president elected by popular vote for a five-year term; prefect appointed by the French president on the advice of the French Ministry of Interior; presidents of the General and Regional Councils are appointed by the members of those councils
Legislative branch: unicameral General Council or Conseil General (19 seats; members are elected by popular vote to serve six-year terms) and a unicameral Regional Council or Conseil Regional (31 seats; members are elected by popular vote to serve six-year terms)
elections: General Council - last held NA March 2000 (next to be held NA 2006); Regional Council - last held 15 March 1998 (next to be held NA 2004)
election results: General Council - percent of vote by party - NA%; seats by party - PSG 5, various left-wing parties 5, independents 7, other 2; Regional Council - percent of vote by party - PS 28.28%, various left parties 22.56%, RPR 15.91%, independents 8.6%, Walwari Committee 6%; seats by party - PS 11, various left parties 9, RPR 6, independents 3, Walwari Committee 2
note: one seat was elected to the French Senate on 27 September 1998 (next to be held NA September 2007); results - percent of vote by party - NA%; seats by party - NA; 2 seats were elected to the French National Assembly on 9 June-16 June 2002 (next to be held NA 2007); results - percent of vote by party - NA%; seats by party - UMP/RPR 1, Walwari Committee 1
Judicial branch: Court of Appeals or Cour d'Appel (highest local court based in Martinique with jurisdiction over Martinique, Guadeloupe, and French Guiana)
Political parties and leaders: Guyanese Democratic Action or ADG [Andre LECANTE]; Guyanese Socialist Party or PSG [Marie-Claude VERDAN]; Guyana Democratic Forces or FDG [Georges OTHILY]; Popular National Guyanese Party or PNPG [Jose DORCY]; Socialist Party or PS [Paul DEBRIETTE]; Union for a Popular Movement or UMP [Muriel ICARE]; Walwari Committee (aligned with the PRG in France) [Christine TAUBIRA-DELANON]
Political pressure groups and leaders: NA

French Guiana (continued)

International organization participation: WCL, WFTU
Diplomatic representation in the US: none (overseas department of France)
Diplomatic representation from the US: none (overseas department of France)
Flag description: the flag of France is used

Economy

Economy - overview: The economy is tied closely to the larger French economy through subsidies and imports. Besides the French space center at Kourou (which accounts for 25% of GDP), fishing and forestry are the most important economic activities. Forest and woodland cover 90% of the country. The large reserves of tropical hardwoods, not fully exploited, support an expanding sawmill industry that provides sawn logs for export. Cultivation of crops is limited to the coastal area, where the population is largely concentrated; rice and manioc are the major crops. French Guiana is heavily dependent on imports of food and energy. Unemployment is a serious problem, particularly among younger workers.
GDP: purchasing power parity - $1.551 billion (2003 est.)
GDP - real growth rate: NA%
GDP - per capita: purchasing power parity - $8,300 (2003 est.)
GDP - composition by sector:
agriculture: NA%
industry: NA%
services: NA% (2001 est.)
Population below poverty line: NA%
Household income or consumption by percentage share:
lowest 10%: NA%
highest 10%: NA%
Inflation rate (consumer prices): 1.5% (2002 est.)
Labor force: 58,800 (1997)
Labor force - by occupation: services, government, and commerce 60.6%, industry 21.2%, agriculture 18.2% (1980)
Unemployment rate: 22% (2001)
Budget:
revenues: $225 million
expenditures: $390 million, including capital expenditures of $105 million (1996)
Industries: construction, shrimp processing, forestry products, rum, gold mining
Industrial production growth rate: NA%
Electricity - production: 455 million kWh (2001)
Electricity - production by source:
fossil fuel: 100%
hydro: 0%
nuclear: 0%
other: 0% (2001)
Electricity - consumption: 423.2 million kWh (2001)
Electricity - exports: 0 kWh (2001)
Electricity - imports: 0 kWh (2001)
Oil - production: 0 bbl/day (2001 est.)

Oil - consumption: 6,500 bbl/day (2001 est.)
Oil - exports: NA
Oil - imports: NA
Agriculture - products: corn, rice, manioc (tapioca), sugar, cocoa, vegetables, bananas; cattle, pigs, poultry
Exports: $155 million f.o.b. (2002 est.)
Exports - commodities: shrimp, timber, gold, rum, rosewood essence, clothing
Exports - partners: France 62%, Switzerland 7%, US 2% (2001)
Imports: $625 million c.i.f. (2002 est.)
Imports - commodities: food (grains, processed meat), machinery and transport equipment, fuels and chemicals
Imports - partners: France 63%, US, Trinidad and Tobago, Italy (2002)
Debt - external: $1.2 billion (1988)
Economic aid - recipient: $NA (1995)
Currency: euro (EUR)
Currency code: EUR
Exchange rates: Euros per US dollar - 0.886 (2003), 1.0626 (2002), 1.1175 (2001), 1.0854 (2000), 0.9386 (1999)
Fiscal year: calendar year

Communications

Telephones - main lines in use: 51,000 (2001)
Telephones - mobile cellular: 138,200 (2002)
Telephone system:
general assessment: NA
domestic: fair open-wire and microwave radio relay system
international: country code - 594; satellite earth station - 1 Intelsat (Atlantic Ocean)
Radio broadcast stations: AM 2, FM 14 (including 6 repeaters), shortwave 6 (including 5 repeaters) (1998)
Television broadcast stations: 3 (plus eight low-power repeaters) (1997)
Internet country code: .gf
Internet users: 3,200 (2002)

Transportation

Railways: 0 km
Highways:
total: 722 km
paved: NA km
unpaved: NA km (1996)
Waterways: 3,300 km navigable by native craft
note: 460 km navigable by small oceangoing vessels and coastal and river steamers
Ports and harbors: Cayenne, Degrad des Cannes, Saint-Laurent du Maroni
Merchant marine: none
Airports: 11 (2003 est.)
Airports - with paved runways:
total: 4
over 3,047 m: 1
914 to 1,523 m: 2
under 914 m: 1 (2003 est.)

Airports - with unpaved runways:
total: 7
914 to 1,523 m: 2
under 914 m: 5 (2003 est.)

Military

Military branches: no regular military forces; Gendarmerie
Military manpower - availability:
males age 15-49: 52,294 (2004 est.)
Military manpower - fit for military service:
males age 15-49: 33,914 (2004 est.)
Military expenditures - dollar figure: NA
Military expenditures - percent of GDP: NA
Military - note: defense is the responsibility of France

Transnational Issues

Disputes - international: Suriname claims area between Riviere Litani and Riviere Marouini (both headwaters of the Lawa)
Illicit drugs: small amount of marijuana grown for local consumption; minor transshipment point to Europe

French Polynesia

(overseas territory of France)

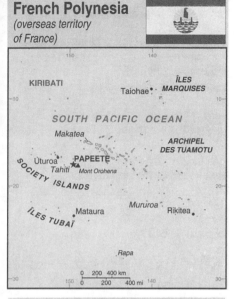

Introduction

Background: The French annexed various Polynesian island groups during the 19th century. In September 1995, France stirred up widespread protests by resuming nuclear testing on the Mururoa atoll after a three-year moratorium. The tests were suspended in January 1996.

Geography

Location: Oceania, archipelago in the South Pacific Ocean, about one-half of the way from South America to Australia

Geographic coordinates: 15 00 S, 140 00 W

Map references: Oceania

Area:
total: 4,167 sq km (118 islands and atolls)
land: 3,660 sq km
water: 507 sq km

Area - comparative: slightly less than one-third the size of Connecticut

Land boundaries: 0 km

Coastline: 2,525 km

Maritime claims:
territorial sea: 12 NM
exclusive economic zone: 200 NM

Climate: tropical, but moderate

Terrain: mixture of rugged high islands and low islands with reefs

Elevation extremes:
lowest point: Pacific Ocean 0 m
highest point: Mont Orohena 2,241 m

Natural resources: timber, fish, cobalt, hydropower

Land use:
arable land: 1.64%
permanent crops: 6.01%
other: 92.35% (1998 est.)

Irrigated land: NA sq km

Natural hazards: occasional cyclonic storms in January

Environment - current issues: NA

Geography - note: includes five archipelagoes (4 volcanic, 1 coral); Makatea in French Polynesia is one of the three great phosphate rock islands in the Pacific Ocean - the others are Banaba (Ocean Island) in Kiribati and Nauru

People

Population: 266,339 (July 2004 est.)

Age structure:
0-14 years: 27.5% (male 37,372; female 35,818)
15-64 years: 66.9% (male 92,594; female 85,455)
65 years and over: 5.7% (male 7,616; female 7,484) (2004 est.)

Median age:
total: 27.1 years
male: 27.4 years
female: 26.7 years (2004 est.)

Population growth rate: 1.57% (2004 est.)

Birth rate: 17.34 births/1,000 population (2004 est.)

Death rate: 4.58 deaths/1,000 population (2004 est.)

Net migration rate: 2.94 migrant(s)/1,000 population (2004 est.)

Sex ratio:
at birth: 1.05 male(s)/female
under 15 years: 1.04 male(s)/female
15-64 years: 1.08 male(s)/female
65 years and over: 1.02 male(s)/female
total population: 1.07 male(s)/female (2004 est.)

Infant mortality rate:
total: 8.61 deaths/1,000 live births
male: 9.92 deaths/1,000 live births
female: 7.24 deaths/1,000 live births (2004 est.)

Life expectancy at birth:
total population: 75.67 years
male: 73.29 years
female: 78.18 years (2004 est.)

Total fertility rate: 2.09 children born/woman (2004 est.)

HIV/AIDS - adult prevalence rate: NA%

HIV/AIDS - people living with HIV/AIDS: NA

HIV/AIDS - deaths: NA

Nationality:
noun: French Polynesian(s)
adjective: French Polynesian

Ethnic groups: Polynesian 78%, Chinese 12%, local French 6%, metropolitan French 4%

Religions: Protestant 54%, Roman Catholic 30%, other 10%, no religion 6%

Languages: French (official), Tahitian (official)

Literacy:
definition: age 14 and over can read and write
total population: 98%
male: 98%
female: 98% (1977 est.)

Government

Country name:
conventional long form: Territory of French Polynesia
conventional short form: French Polynesia
local long form: Territoire de la Polynesie Francaise
local short form: Polynesie Francaise

former: French Colony of Oceania

Dependency status: overseas territory of France since 1946

Government type: NA

Capital: Papeete

Administrative divisions: none (overseas territory of France); there are no first-order administrative divisions as defined by the US Government, but there are 5 archipelagic divisions named Archipel des Marquises, Archipel des Tuamotu, Archipel des Tubuai, Iles du Vent, and Iles Sous-le-Vent

note: Clipperton Island is administered by France from French Polynesia

Independence: none (overseas territory of France)

National holiday: Bastille Day, 14 July (1789)

Constitution: 28 September 1958 (French Constitution)

Legal system: based on French system

Suffrage: 18 years of age; universal

Executive branch:
chief of state: President Jacques CHIRAC of France (since 17 May 1995), represented by High Commissioner of the Republic Michel MATHIEU (since 24 October 2001)
head of government: President of the Territorial Government of French Polynesia Gaston FLOSSE (since 4 April 1991); President of the Territorial Assembly Lucette TAERO (since 17 May 2001)
cabinet: Council of Ministers; president submits a list of members of the Territorial Assembly for approval by them to serve as ministers
elections: French president elected by popular vote for a five-year term; high commissioner appointed by the French president on the advice of the French Ministry of Interior; president of the Territorial Government and the president of the Territorial Assembly are elected by the members of the assembly

Legislative branch: unicameral Territorial Assembly or Assemblee Territoriale (49 seats - changed from 41 seats for May 2001 election; members are elected by popular vote to serve five-year terms)
elections: last held 6 May 2001 (next to be held NA May 2006)
election results: percent of vote by party - NA%; seats by party - People's Rally for the Republic (Gaullist) 28, Independent Front for the Liberation of Polynesia 13, New Fatherland Party 7, other 1
note: one seat was elected to the French Senate on NA September 1998 (next to be held NA September 2007); results - percent of vote by party - NA%; seats by party - NA; two seats were elected to the French National Assembly on 9 June-16 June 2002 (next to be held NA 2007); results - percent of vote by party - NA%; seats by party - UMP/RPR 1, UMP 1

Judicial branch: Court of Appeal or Cour d'Appel; Court of the First Instance or Tribunal de Premiere Instance; Court of Administrative Law or Tribunal Administratif

Political parties and leaders: Independent Front for the Liberation of Polynesia (Tavini Huiraatira) [Oscar TEMARU]; New Fatherland Party (Ai'a Api)

French Polynesia (continued)

[Emile VERNAUDON]; People's Rally for the Republic of Polynesia or RPR (Tahoeraa Huiraatira) [Gaston FLOSSE]; The New Star (Te Fetia Api) [leader NA]
Political pressure groups and leaders: NA
International organization participation: FZ, ICFTU, WMO
Diplomatic representation in the US: none (overseas territory of France)
Diplomatic representation from the US: none (overseas territory of France)
Flag description: two narrow red horizontal bands encase a wide white band; centered on the white band is a disk with blue and white wave pattern on the lower half and gold and white ray pattern on the upper half; a stylized red, blue and white ship rides on the wave pattern; the French flag is used for official occasions

Economy

Economy - overview: Since 1962, when France stationed military personnel in the region, French Polynesia has changed from a subsistence agricultural economy to one in which a high proportion of the work force is either employed by the military or supports the tourist industry. With the halt of French nuclear testing in 1996, the military contribution to the economy fell sharply. Tourism accounts for about one-fourth of GDP and is a primary source of hard currency earnings. Other sources of income are pearl farming and deep-sea commercial fishing. The small manufacturing sector primarily processes agricultural products. The territory benefits substantially from development agreements with France aimed principally at creating new businesses and strengthening social services.
GDP: purchasing power parity - $4.58 billion (2001 est.)
GDP - real growth rate: 4% (2001 est.)
GDP - per capita: purchasing power parity - $17,500 (2001 est.)
GDP - composition by sector:
agriculture: 6%
industry: 18%
services: 76% (1997)
Population below poverty line: NA%
Household income or consumption by percentage share:
lowest 10%: NA%
highest 10%: NA%
Inflation rate (consumer prices): 1.5% (2002 est.)
Labor force: 70,000 (1996)
Labor force - by occupation: agriculture 13%, industry 19%, services 68% (1997)
Unemployment rate: 11.8% (1994)
Budget:
revenues: $1 billion
expenditures: $900 million, including capital expenditures of $185 million (1996)
Industries: tourism, pearls, agricultural processing, handicrafts, phosphates
Industrial production growth rate: NA%
Electricity - production: 428.3 million kWh (2001)

Electricity - production by source:
fossil fuel: 60.7%
hydro: 39.3%
nuclear: 0%
other: 0%;
Electricity - consumption: 398.3 million kWh (2001)
Electricity - exports: 0 kWh (2001)
Electricity - imports: 0 kWh (2001)
Oil - production: 0 bbl/day (2001 est.)
Oil - consumption: 4,750 bbl/day (2001 est.)
Oil - exports: NA
Oil - imports: NA
Agriculture - products: coconuts, vanilla, vegetables, fruits; poultry, beef, dairy products, coffee
Exports: $244 million f.o.b. (2002)
Exports - commodities: cultured pearls, coconut products, mother-of-pearl, vanilla, shark meat
Exports - partners: France 36.5%, Japan 34.4%, US 17.2% (2002)
Imports: $1.341 billion f.o.b. (2002)
Imports - commodities: fuels, foodstuffs, machinery and equipment
Imports - partners: France 57.4%, Australia 11.9%, New Zealand 6.8%, US 6.5% (2002)
Debt - external: $NA (2000 est.)
Economic aid - recipient: $367 million (1997)
Currency: Comptoirs Francais du Pacifique franc (XPF)
Currency code: XPF
Exchange rates: Comptoirs Francais du Pacifique francs (XPF) per US dollar - 105.73 (2003), 126.72 (2002), 133.26 (2001), 129.43 (2000), 111.93 (1999)
note: pegged at the rate of 119.25 XPF to the euro
Fiscal year: calendar year

Communications

Telephones - main lines in use: 52,500 (2002)
Telephones - mobile cellular: 90,000 (2002)
Telephone system:
general assessment: NA
domestic: NA
international: country code - 689; satellite earth station - 1 Intelsat (Pacific Ocean)
Radio broadcast stations: AM 2, FM 14, shortwave 2 (1998)
Television broadcast stations: 7 (plus 17 low-power repeaters) (1997)
Internet country code: .pf
Internet hosts: 3,661 (2002)
Internet users: 35,000 (2002)

Transportation

Railways: 0 km
Highways:
total: 2,590 km
paved: 1,735 km
unpaved: 855 km (1999)
Waterways: none
Ports and harbors: Mataura, Papeete, Rikitea, Uturoa

Merchant marine:
total: 10 ships (1,000 GRT or over) 17,537 GRT/ 15,150 DWT
by type: cargo 3, passenger 2, passenger/cargo 3, refrigerated cargo 1, roll on/roll off 1 (2003 est.)
Airports: 49 (2003 est.)
Airports - with paved runways:
total: 37
over 3,047 m: 2
1,524 to 2,437 m: 5
914 to 1,523 m: 23
under 914 m: 7 (2003 est.)
Airports - with unpaved runways:
total: 12
914 to 1,523 m: 5
under 914 m: 7 (2003 est.)
Heliports: 1 (2003 est.)

Military

Military branches: no regular military forces; Gendarmerie and National Police Force
Military - note: defense is the responsibility of France

Transnational Issues

Disputes - international: none

French Southern and Antarctic Lands

(overseas territory of France)

Indian Ocean

Île Amsterdam
Île Saint-Paul

Îles Crozet

Îles Kerguelen

| 0 | 400 | 800 km |
| 0 | 400 | 800 mi |

Introduction

Background: The Southern Lands consist of two archipelagos, Iles Crozet and Iles Kerguelen, and two volcanic islands, Ile Amsterdam and Ile Saint-Paul. They contain no permanent inhabitants and are visited only by researchers studying the native fauna. The Antarctic portion consists of "Adelie Land," a thin slice of the Antarctic continent discovered and claimed by the French in 1840.

Geography

Location: southeast of Africa, islands in the southern Indian Ocean, about equidistant between Africa, Antarctica, and Australia; note - French Southern and Antarctic Lands include Ile Amsterdam, Ile Saint-Paul, Iles Crozet, and Iles Kerguelen in the southern Indian Ocean, along with the French-claimed sector of Antarctica, "Adelie Land"; the US does not recognize the French claim to "Adelie Land"

Geographic coordinates: 43 00 S, 67 00 E

Map references: Antarctic Region

Area:

total: 7,829 sq km

land: 7,829 sq km

water: 0 sq km

note: includes Ile Amsterdam, Ile Saint-Paul, Iles Crozet and Iles Kerguelen; excludes "Adelie Land" claim of about 500,000 sq km in Antarctica that is not recognized by the US

Area - comparative: slightly less than 1.3 times the size of Delaware

Land boundaries: 0 km

Coastline: 1,232 km

Maritime claims:

territorial sea: 12 NM

exclusive economic zone: 200 NM from Iles Kerguelen (does not include the rest of French Southern and Antarctic Lands)

Climate: antarctic

Terrain: volcanic

Elevation extremes:

lowest point: Indian Ocean 0 m

highest point: Mont Ross on Iles Kerguelen 1,850 m

Natural resources: fish, crayfish

Land use:

arable land: 0%

permanent crops: 0%

other: 100% (1998 est.)

Irrigated land: 0 sq km (1998 est.)

Natural hazards: Ile Amsterdam and Ile Saint-Paul are extinct volcanoes

Environment - current issues: NA

Geography - note: islands component is widely scattered across remote locations in the southern Indian Ocean

People

Population: no indigenous inhabitants (July 2002 est.)

note: in 2002, there were 145 researchers whose numbers vary from winter (July) to summer (January) (July 2004 est.)

Government

Country name:

conventional long form: Territory of the French Southern and Antarctic Lands

conventional short form: French Southern and Antarctic Lands

local long form: Territoire des Terres Australes et Antarctiques Francaises

local short form: Terres Australes et Antarctiques Francaises

Dependency status: overseas territory of France since 1955; administered from Paris by Administrateur Superieur Francois GARDE (since 24 May 2000), assisted by Secretary General Jean-Yves HERMOSO (since NA)

Administrative divisions: none (overseas territory of France); there are no first-order administrative divisions as defined by the US Government, but there are 3 districts named Ile Crozet, Iles Kerguelen, and Iles Saint-Paul et Amsterdam; excludes "Adelie Land" claim in Antarctica that is not recognized by the US

Legal system: the laws of France, where applicable, apply

Diplomatic representation in the US: none (overseas territory of France)

Diplomatic representation from the US: none (overseas territory of France)

Flag description: the flag of France is used

Economy

Economy - overview: Economic activity is limited to servicing meteorological and geophysical research stations and French and other fishing fleets. The fish catches landed on Iles Kerguelen by foreign ships are exported to France and Reunion.

Communications

Internet country code: .tf

Transportation

Waterways: none

Ports and harbors: none; offshore anchorage only

Merchant marine:

total: 70 ships (1,000 GRT or over) 3,092,387 GRT/ 5,056,658 DWT

by type: bulk 4, cargo 2, chemical tanker 19, container 11, liquefied gas 7, petroleum tanker 14, roll on/roll off 11, vehicle carrier 2

foreign-owned: Denmark 2, France 49, Japan 4, Monaco 5, Norway 5, Sweden 5 (2003 est.)

Airports: none

Military

Military - note: defense is the responsibility of France

Transnational Issues

Disputes - international: French claim to "Adelie Land" in Antarctica is not recognized by the US

Gabon

Introduction

Background: Only two autocratic presidents have ruled Gabon since independence from France in 1960. Gabon's current President, El Hadj Omar BONGO - one of the longest-serving heads of state in the world - has dominated Gabon's political scene for almost four decades. President BONGO introduced a nominal multiparty system and a new constitution in the early 1990s. However, the low turnout and allegations of electoral fraud during the most recent local elections in 2002-03 have exposed the weaknesses of formal political structures in Gabon. In addition, recent strikes have underscored the popular disenchantment with the political system. Presidential elections scheduled for 2005 are unlikely to bring change since the opposition remains weak, divided, and financially dependent on the current regime. Despite political conditions, a small population, abundant natural resources, and considerable foreign support have helped make Gabon one of the more prosperous and stable African countries.

Geography

Location: Western Africa, bordering the Atlantic Ocean at the Equator, between Republic of the Congo and Equatorial Guinea
Geographic coordinates: 1 00 S, 11 45 E
Map references: Africa
Area:
total: 267,667 sq km
land: 257,667 sq km
water: 10,000 sq km
Area - comparative: slightly smaller than Colorado
Land boundaries:
total: 2,551 km
border countries: Cameroon 298 km, Republic of the Congo 1,903 km, Equatorial Guinea 350 km
Coastline: 885 km

Maritime claims:
territorial sea: 12 NM
contiguous zone: 24 NM
exclusive economic zone: 200 NM
Climate: tropical; always hot, humid
Terrain: narrow coastal plain; hilly interior; savanna in east and south
Elevation extremes:
lowest point: Atlantic Ocean 0 m
highest point: Mont Iboundji 1,575 m
Natural resources: petroleum, manganese, uranium, gold, timber, iron ore, hydropower
Land use:
arable land: 1.26%
permanent crops: 0.66%
other: 98.08% (1998 est.)
Irrigated land: 150 sq km (1998 est.)
Natural hazards: NA
Environment - current issues: deforestation; poaching
Environment - international agreements:
party to: Biodiversity, Climate Change, Desertification, Endangered Species, Law of the Sea, Marine Dumping, Ozone Layer Protection, Ship Pollution, Tropical Timber 83, Tropical Timber 94, Wetlands
signed, but not ratified: none of the selected agreements
Geography - note: a small population and oil and mineral reserves have helped Gabon become one of Africa's wealthier countries; in general, these circumstances have allowed the country to maintain and conserve its pristine rain forest and rich biodiversity

People

Population: 1,355,246
note: estimates for this country explicitly take into account the effects of excess mortality due to AIDS; this can result in lower life expectancy, higher infant mortality and death rates, lower population and growth rates, and changes in the distribution of population by age and sex than would otherwise be expected (July 2004 est.)
Age structure:
0-14 years: 42.2% (male 286,819; female 285,184)
15-64 years: 53.7% (male 362,311; female 365,132)
65 years and over: 4.1% (male 23,157; female 32,643) (2004 est.)
Median age:
total: 18.5 years
male: 18.3 years
female: 18.8 years (2004 est.)
Population growth rate: 2.5% (2004 est.)
Birth rate: 36.4 births/1,000 population (2004 est.)
Death rate: 11.43 deaths/1,000 population (2004 est.)
Net migration rate: 0 migrant(s)/1,000 population (2004 est.)

Sex ratio:
at birth: 1.03 male(s)/female
under 15 years: 1.01 male(s)/female
15-64 years: 0.99 male(s)/female
65 years and over: 0.71 male(s)/female
total population: 0.98 male(s)/female (2004 est.)
Infant mortality rate:
total: 54.34 deaths/1,000 live births
male: 64.15 deaths/1,000 live births
female: 44.23 deaths/1,000 live births (2004 est.)
Life expectancy at birth:
total population: 56.46 years
male: 54.85 years
female: 58.12 years (2004 est.)
Total fertility rate: 4.8 children born/woman (2004 est.)
HIV/AIDS - adult prevalence rate: 9% (2001 est.)
HIV/AIDS - people living with HIV/AIDS: 23,000 (1999 est.)
HIV/AIDS - deaths: 3,000 (2001 est.)
Nationality:
noun: Gabonese (singular and plural)
adjective: Gabonese
Ethnic groups: Bantu tribes including four major tribal groupings (Fang, Bapounou, Nzebi, Obamba), other Africans and Europeans 154,000, including 10,700 French and 11,000 persons of dual nationality
Religions: Christian 55%-75%, animist, Muslim less than 1%
Languages: French (official), Fang, Myene, Nzebi, Bapounou/Eschira, Bandjabi
Literacy:
definition: age 15 and over can read and write
total population: 63.2%
male: 73.7%
female: 53.3% (1995 est.)

Government

Country name:
conventional long form: Gabonese Republic
conventional short form: Gabon
local long form: Republique Gabonaise
local short form: Gabon
Government type: republic; multiparty presidential regime (opposition parties legalized in 1990)
Capital: Libreville
Administrative divisions: 9 provinces; Estuaire, Haut-Ogooue, Moyen-Ogooue, Ngounie, Nyanga, Ogooue-Ivindo, Ogooue-Lolo, Ogooue-Maritime, Woleu-Ntem
Independence: 17 August 1960 (from France)
National holiday: Founding of the Gabonese Democratic Party (PDG), 12 March (1968)
Constitution: adopted 14 March 1991
Legal system: based on French civil law system and customary law; judicial review of legislative acts in Constitutional Chamber of the Supreme Court; has not accepted compulsory ICJ jurisdiction
Suffrage: 21 years of age; universal

Gabon (continued)

Executive branch:

chief of state: President El Hadj Omar BONGO (since 2 December 1967)

head of government: Prime Minister Jean-Francois NTOUTOUME-EMANE (since 23 January 1999)

cabinet: Council of Ministers appointed by the prime minister in consultation with the president

elections: president elected by popular vote for a seven-year term; election last held 6 December 1998 (next to be held NA 2005); prime minister appointed by the president

election results: President El Hadj Omar BONGO reelected; percent of vote - El Hadj Omar BONGO 66.6%, Pierre MAMBOUNDOU 16.5%, Fr. Paul M'BA-ABESSOLE 13.4%

Legislative branch:
bicameral legislature consists of the Senate (91 seats; members elected by members of municipal councils and departmental assemblies) and the National Assembly or Assemblee Nationale (120 seats; members are elected by direct, popular vote to serve five-year terms)

elections: National Assembly - last held 9 and 23 December 2001 (next to be held NA December 2006); Senate - last held 26 January and 9 February 2003 (next to be held by January 2009)

election results: National Assembly - percent of vote by party - NA%; seats by party - PDG 86, RNB-RPG 8, PGP 3, ADERE 3, CLR 2, PUP 1, PSD 1, independents 13, others 3; Senate - percent of vote by party - NA%; seats by party - PDG 53, RNB 20, PGP 4, ADERE 3, RDP 1, CLR 1, independents 9

Judicial branch:
Supreme Court or Cour Supreme consisting of three chambers - Judicial, Administrative, and Accounts; Constitutional Court; Courts of Appeal; Court of State Security; County Courts

Political parties and leaders:
Circle of Liberal Reformers or CLR [General Jean Boniface ASSELE]; Democratic and Republican Alliance or ADERE [Divungui-di-Ndinge DIDJOB]; Gabonese Democratic Party or PDG, former sole party [Simplice Nguedet MANZELA]; Gabonese Party for Progress or PGP [Pierre-Louis AGONDJO-OKAWE,]; National Rally of Woodcutters-Rally for Gabon or RNB-RPG (Bucherons) [Fr. Paul M'BA-ABESSOLE]; People's Unity Party or PUP [Louis Gaston MAYILA]; Rally for Democracy and Progress or RDP [Pierre EMBONI]; Social Democratic Party or PSD [Pierre Claver MAGANGA-MOUSSAVOU]

Political pressure groups and leaders: NA

International organization participation:
ACCT, ACP, AfDB, AU, BDEAC, CEMAC, FAO, FZ, G-24, G-77, IAEA, IBRD, ICAO, ICCt, ICFTU, IDA, IDB, IFAD, IFC, IFRCS, ILO, IMF, IMO, Interpol, IOC, ITU, NAM, OIC, OPCW, UN, UNCTAD, UNESCO, UNIDO, UPU, WCL, WCO, WHO, WIPO, WMO, WToO, WTrO

Diplomatic representation in the US:

chief of mission: Ambassador Jules Marius OGOUEBANDJA

chancery: Suite 200, 2034 20th Street NW, Washington, DC 20009

telephone: [1] (202) 797-1000

FAX: [1] (202) 332-0668

consulate(s): New York

Diplomatic representation from the US:

chief of mission: Ambassador Kenneth P. MOOREFIELD

embassy: Boulevard de la Mer, Libreville

mailing address: Centre Ville, B. P. 4000, Libreville

telephone: [241] 76 20 03 through 76 20 04, after hours - 74 34 92

FAX: [241] 74 55 07

Flag description:
three equal horizontal bands of green (top), yellow, and blue

Economy

Economy - overview: Gabon enjoys a per capita income four times that of most nations of sub-Saharan Africa. This has supported a sharp decline in extreme poverty; yet because of high income inequality a large proportion of the population remains poor. Gabon depended on timber and manganese until oil was discovered offshore in the early 1970s. The oil sector now accounts for 50% of GDP. Gabon continues to face fluctuating prices for its oil, timber, and manganese exports. Despite the abundance of natural wealth, poor fiscal management hobbles the economy. Devaluation of its Francophone currency by 50% on 12 January 1994 sparked a one-time inflationary surge, to 35%; the rate dropped to 6% in 1996. The IMF provided a one-year standby arrangement in 1994-95, a three-year Enhanced Financing Facility (EFF) at near commercial rates beginning in late 1995, and stand-by credit of $119 million in October 2000. Those agreements mandate progress in privatization and fiscal discipline. France provided additional financial support in January 1997 after Gabon had met IMF targets for mid-1996. In 1997, an IMF mission to Gabon criticized the government for overspending on off-budget items, overborrowing from the central bank, and slipping on its schedule for privatization and administrative reform. The rebound of oil prices in 1999-2000 helped growth, but drops in production hampered Gabon from fully realizing potential gains. In December 2000, Gabon signed a new agreement with the Paris Club to reschedule its official debt. A follow-up bilateral repayment agreement with the US was signed in December 2001. Short-term progress depends on an upbeat world economy and fiscal and other adjustments in line with IMF policies.

GDP: purchasing power parity - $7.301 billion (2003 est.)

GDP - real growth rate: 1.2% (2003 est.)

GDP - per capita: purchasing power parity - $5,500 (2003 est.)

GDP - composition by sector:

agriculture: 15%

industry: 60%

services: 25% (2001 est.)

Population below poverty line: NA%

Household income or consumption by percentage share:

lowest 10%: NA%

highest 10%: NA%

Inflation rate (consumer prices): 2.3% (2002 est.)

Labor force: 600,000 (1999 est.)

Labor force - by occupation: agriculture 60%, services 25%, industry 15%

Unemployment rate: 21% (1997 est.)

Budget:

revenues: $1.8 billion

expenditures: $1.8 billion, including capital expenditures of $310 million (2002 est.)

Industries: petroleum extraction and refining; manganese, and gold mining; chemicals; ship repair; food and beverage; textile; lumbering and plywood; cement

Industrial production growth rate: 1.6% (2002 est.)

Electricity - production: 798.4 million kWh (2001)

Electricity - production by source:

fossil fuel: 34.5%

hydro: 65.5%

nuclear: 0%

other: 0% (2001)

Electricity - consumption: 742.5 million kWh (2001)

Electricity - exports: 0 kWh (2001)

Electricity - imports: 0 kWh (2001)

Oil - production: 301,300 bbl/day (2001 est.)

Oil - consumption: 13,000 bbl/day (2001 est.)

Oil - exports: NA

Oil - imports: NA

Oil - proved reserves: 2.45 billion bbl (1 January 2002)

Natural gas - production: 80 million cu m (2001 est.)

Natural gas - consumption: 80 million cu m (2001 est.)

Natural gas - exports: 0 cu m (2001 est.)

Natural gas - imports: 0 cu m (2001 est.)

Natural gas - proved reserves: 66.47 billion cu m (1 January 2002)

Agriculture - products: cocoa, coffee, sugar, palm oil, rubber; cattle; okoume (a tropical softwood); fish

Exports: $2.891 billion f.o.b. (2003 est.)

Exports - commodities: crude oil 77%, timber, manganese, uranium (2001)

Exports - partners: US 50.9%, France 12.7%, China 7.1% (2002)

Imports: $1.079 billion f.o.b. (2003 est.)

Imports - commodities: machinery and equipment, foodstuffs, chemicals, construction materials

Imports - partners: France 51%, US 6.3%, Netherlands 3.7% (2002)

Debt - external: $3.8 billion (2002 est.)

Economic aid - recipient: $331 million (1995)

Currency: Communaute Financiere Africaine franc (XAF); note - responsible authority is the Bank of the Central African States

Currency code: XAF

Gabon *(continued)*

Exchange rates: Communaute Financiere Africaine francs (XAF) per US dollar - 581.2 (2003), 696.988 (2002), 733.039 (2001), 711.976 (2000), 615.699 (1999)

Fiscal year: calendar year

Communications

Telephones - main lines in use: 32,100 (2002)
Telephones - mobile cellular: 279,300 (2002)
Telephone system:
general assessment: adequate service by African standards and improving with the help of the growing mobile cell system
domestic: adequate system of cable, microwave radio relay, tropospheric scatter, radiotelephone communication stations, and a domestic satellite system with 12 earth stations
international: country code - 241; satellite earth stations - 3 Intelsat (Atlantic Ocean); fiber optic submarine cable (SAT-3/WASC) provides connectivity to Europe and Asia
Radio broadcast stations: AM 6, FM 7 (and 11 repeaters), shortwave 4 (2001)
Television broadcast stations: 4 (plus four low-power repeaters) (2001)
Internet country code: .ga
Internet hosts: 79 (2002)
Internet users: 25,000 (2002)

Transportation

Railways:
total: 814 km
standard gauge: 814 km 1.435-m gauge (2002)
Highways:
total: 8,464 km
paved: 838 km
unpaved: 7,626 km (2000 est.)
Waterways: 1,600 km (perennially navigable)
Pipelines: gas 210 km; oil 1,426 km; water 3 km (2003)
Ports and harbors: Cap Lopez, Kango, Lambarene, Libreville, Mayumba, Owendo, Port-Gentil
Airports: 56 (2003 est.)
Airports - with paved runways:
total: 11
over 3,047 m: 1
2,438 to 3,047 m: 1
1,524 to 2,437 m: 8
914 to 1,523 m: 1 (2003 est.)
Airports - with unpaved runways:
total: 45
1,524 to 2,437 m: 7
914 to 1,523 m: 15
under 914 m: 23 (2003 est.)

Military

Military branches: Army, Navy, Air Force, National Gendarmerie, National Police
Military manpower - military age: 20 years of age (2004 est.)
Military manpower - availability:
males age 15-49: 314,434 (2004 est.)
Military manpower - fit for military service:
males age 15-49: 162,847 (2004 est.)
Military manpower - reaching military age annually:
males: 13,462 (2004 est.)
Military expenditures - dollar figure: $149.3 million (2003)
Military expenditures - percent of GDP: 2% (2003)

Transnational Issues

Disputes - international: creation of a maritime boundary in hydrocarbon-rich Corisco Bay with Equatorial Guinea is hampered by dispute over Mbane Island, administered and occupied by Gabon since the 1970s

Gambia, The

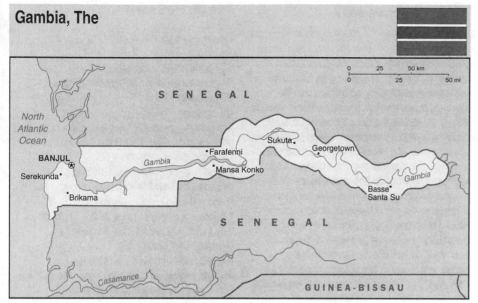

Introduction

Background: The Gambia gained its independence from the UK in 1965; it formed a short-lived federation of Senegambia with Senegal between 1982 and 1989. In 1991 the two nations signed a friendship and cooperation treaty. A military coup in 1994 overthrew the president and banned political activity, but a 1996 constitution and presidential elections, followed by parliamentary balloting in 1997, completed a nominal return to civilian rule. The country undertook another round of presidential and legislative elections in late 2001 and early 2002.

Geography

Location: Western Africa, bordering the North Atlantic Ocean and Senegal
Geographic coordinates: 13 28 N, 16 34 W
Map references: Africa
Area:
total: 11,300 sq km
land: 10,000 sq km
water: 1,300 sq km
Area - comparative: slightly less than twice the size of Delaware
Land boundaries:
total: 740 km
border countries: Senegal 740 km
Coastline: 80 km
Maritime claims:
territorial sea: 12 NM
contiguous zone: 18 NM
continental shelf: not specified
exclusive fishing zone: 200 NM
Climate: tropical; hot, rainy season (June to November); cooler, dry season (November to May)
Terrain: flood plain of the Gambia River flanked by some low hills

Elevation extremes:
lowest point: Atlantic Ocean 0 m
highest point: unnamed location 53 m
Natural resources: fish
Land use:
arable land: 19.5%
permanent crops: 0.5%
other: 80% (1998 est.)
Irrigated land: 20 sq km (1998 est.)
Natural hazards: drought (rainfall has dropped by 30% in the last 30 years)
Environment - current issues: deforestation; desertification; water-borne diseases prevalent
Environment - international agreements:
party to: Biodiversity, Climate Change, Climate Change-Kyoto Protocol, Desertification, Endangered Species, Hazardous Wastes, Law of the Sea, Ozone Layer Protection, Ship Pollution, Wetlands
signed, but not ratified: none of the selected agreements
Geography - note: almost an enclave of Senegal; smallest country on the continent of Africa

People

Population: 1,546,848 (July 2004 est.)
Age structure:
0-14 years: 44.7% (male 347,349; female 344,264)
15-64 years: 52.6% (male 403,297; female 410,382)
65 years and over: 2.7% (male 21,459; female 20,097) (2004 est.)
Median age:
total: 17.5 years
male: 17.4 years
female: 17.7 years (2004 est.)
Population growth rate: 2.98% (2004 est.)
Birth rate: 40.3 births/1,000 population (2004 est.)
Death rate: 12.08 deaths/1,000 population (2004 est.)
Net migration rate: 1.57 migrant(s)/1,000 population (2004 est.)

Sex ratio:
at birth: 1.03 male(s)/female
under 15 years: 1.01 male(s)/female
15-64 years: 0.98 male(s)/female
65 years and over: 1.07 male(s)/female
total population: 1 male(s)/female (2004 est.)
Infant mortality rate:
total: 73.48 deaths/1,000 live births
male: 80.14 deaths/1,000 live births
female: 66.62 deaths/1,000 live births (2004 est.)
Life expectancy at birth:
total population: 54.79 years
male: 52.76 years
female: 56.87 years (2004 est.)
Total fertility rate: 5.46 children born/woman (2004 est.)
HIV/AIDS - adult prevalence rate: 1.6% (2001 est.)
HIV/AIDS - people living with HIV/AIDS: 8,400 (2001 est.)
HIV/AIDS - deaths: 400 (2001 est.)
Nationality:
noun: Gambian(s)
adjective: Gambian
Ethnic groups: African 99% (Mandinka 42%, Fula 18%, Wolof 16%, Jola 10%, Serahuli 9%, other 4%), non-African 1%
Religions: Muslim 90%, Christian 9%, indigenous beliefs 1%
Languages: English (official), Mandinka, Wolof, Fula, other indigenous vernaculars
Literacy:
definition: age 15 and over can read and write
total population: 40.1%
male: 47.8%
female: 32.8% (2003 est.)

Government

Country name:
conventional long form: Republic of The Gambia
conventional short form: The Gambia
Government type: republic under multiparty democratic rule
Capital: Banjul
Administrative divisions: 5 divisions and 1 city*; Banjul*, Central River, Lower River, North Bank, Upper River, Western
Independence: 18 February 1965 (from UK)
National holiday: Independence Day, 18 February (1965)
Constitution: 24 April 1970; suspended July 1994; rewritten and approved by national referendum 8 August 1996; reestablished January 1997
Legal system: based on a composite of English common law, Koranic law, and customary law; accepts compulsory ICJ jurisdiction, with reservations
Suffrage: 18 years of age; universal
Executive branch:
chief of state: President Yahya A. J. J. JAMMEH (since 18 October 1996; note - from 1994 to 1996 he was Chairman of the Junta); Vice President Isatou Njie SAIDY (since 20 March 1997); note - the president is both the chief of state and head of government

head of government: President Yahya A. J. J. JAMMEH (since 18 October 1996; note - from 1994 to 1996 was he Chairman of the Junta); Vice President Isatou Njie SAIDY (since 20 March 1997); note - the president is both the chief of state and head of government

cabinet: Cabinet appointed by the president

elections: president elected by popular vote for a five-year term; the number of terms is not restricted; election last held 18 October 2001 (next to be held NA October 2006)

election results: Yahya A. J. J. JAMMEH reelected president; percent of vote - Yahya A. J. J. JAMMEH 52.9%, Ousainou DARBOE 32.7%

Legislative branch: unicameral National Assembly (53 seats; 48 elected by popular vote, five appointed by the president; members serve five-year terms)

elections: last held 17 January 2002 (next to be held NA January 2007)

election results: percent of vote by party - NA%; seats by party - APRC 45, PDOIS 2, NRP 1,

Judicial branch: Supreme Court

Political parties and leaders: Alliance for Patriotic Reorientation and Construction or APRC [Yahya A. J. J. JAMMEH]; Gambian People's Party-Progressive People's Party-United Democratic Party or GPP-PPP-UDP Coalition [Ousainou DARBOE]; National Convention Party or NCP [Sheriff DIBBA]; National Reconciliation Party or NRP [Hamat N. K. BAH]; People's Democratic Organization for Independence and Socialism or PDOIS [Sidia JATTA]

note: in August 2001, an independent electoral commission allowed the reregistration of the GPP, NCP, and PPP, three parties banned since 1996

Political pressure groups and leaders: NA

International organization participation: ACP, AfDB, AU, C, ECOWAS, FAO, G-77, IBRD, ICAO, ICCt, ICFTU, ICRM, IDA, IDB, IFAD, IFC, IFRCS, ILO, IMF, IMO, Interpol, IOC, IOM, ITU, NAM, OIC, OPCW, UN, UNAMSIL, UNCTAD, UNESCO, UNIDO, UNMEE, UNMIL, UPU, WCL, WCO, WFTU, WHO, WIPO, WMO, WToO, WTrO

Diplomatic representation in the US:

chief of mission: Ambassador (vacant); Charge d'Affaires Lena Manga Sagnia SECK

chancery: Suite 905, 1156 15th Street NW, Washington, DC 20005

telephone: [1] (202) 785-1379

FAX: [1] (202) 785-1430

Diplomatic representation from the US:

chief of mission: Ambassador Jackson McDONALD

embassy: Kairaba Avenue, Fajara, Banjul

mailing address: P. M. B. No. 19, Banjul

telephone: [220] 392856, 392858, 391971

FAX: [220] 392475

Flag description: three equal horizontal bands of red (top), blue with white edges, and green

Economy

Economy - overview: The Gambia has no important mineral or other natural resources and has a limited agricultural base. About 75% of the population depends on crops and livestock for its livelihood. Small-scale manufacturing activity features the processing of peanuts, fish, and hides. Reexport trade normally constitutes a major segment of economic activity, but a 1999 government-imposed preshipment inspection plan, and instability of the Gambian dalasi (currency) have drawn some of the reexport trade away from The Gambia. The government's 1998 seizure of the private peanut firm Alimenta eliminated the largest purchaser of Gambian groundnuts; the following two marketing seasons have seen substantially lower prices and sales. A decline in tourism in 2000 has also held back growth. Unemployment and underemployment rates are extremely high. Shortrun economic progress remains highly dependent on sustained bilateral and multilateral aid, on responsible government economic management as forwarded by IMF technical help and advice, and on expected growth in the construction sector.

GDP: purchasing power parity - $2.597 billion (2003 est.)

GDP - real growth rate: 0.5% (2003 est.)

GDP - per capita: purchasing power parity - $1,700 (2003 est.)

GDP - composition by sector:

agriculture: 33%

industry: 13%

services: 54% (1999 est.)

Population below poverty line: NA%

Household income or consumption by percentage share:

lowest 10%: NA%

highest 10%: NA%

Inflation rate (consumer prices): 5.5% (2002 est.)

Labor force: 400,000 (1996)

Labor force - by occupation: agriculture 75%, industry, commerce, and services 19%, government 6%

Unemployment rate: NA% (2002 est.)

Budget:

revenues: $90.5 million

expenditures: $80.9 million, including capital expenditures of $4.1 million (2001 est.)

Industries: processing peanuts, fish, and hides; tourism; beverages; agricultural machinery assembly, woodworking, metalworking; clothing

Industrial production growth rate: NA%

Electricity - production: 85.33 million kWh (2001)

Electricity - production by source:

fossil fuel: 100%

hydro: 0%

nuclear: 0%

other: 0% (2001)

Electricity - consumption: 79.36 million kWh (2001)

Electricity - exports: 0 kWh (2001)

Electricity - imports: 0 kWh (2001)

Oil - production: 0 bbl/day (2001 est.)

Oil - consumption: 1,900 bbl/day (2001 est.)

Oil - exports: NA

Oil - imports: NA

Agriculture - products: rice, millet, sorghum, peanuts, corn, sesame, cassava (tapioca), palm kernels; cattle, sheep, goats

Exports: $156 million f.o.b. (2003 est.)

Exports - commodities: peanut products, fish, cotton lint, palm kernels, re-exports

Exports - partners: France 22.2%, UK 18.5%, Italy 11.1%, Malaysia 11.1%, Belgium 7.4%, Germany 7.4% (2002)

Imports: $271 million f.o.b. (2003 est.)

Imports - commodities: foodstuffs, manufactures, fuel, machinery and transport equipment

Imports - partners: China 22.3%, Senegal 9.2%, UK 6.7%, Brazil 5.9%, Netherlands 5.4%, India 5%, Belgium 4.7%, Germany 4% (2002)

Debt - external: $476 million (2001 est.)

Economic aid - recipient: $45.4 million (1995)

Currency: dalasi (GMD)

Currency code: GMD

Exchange rates: dalasi per US dollar - NA (2003), 19.9182 (2002), 15.6872 (2001), 12.7876 (2000), 11.3951 (1999)

Fiscal year: calendar year

Communications

Telephones - main lines in use: 38,400 (2002)

Telephones - mobile cellular: 100,000 (2002)

Telephone system:

general assessment: adequate; a packet switched data network is available

domestic: adequate network of microwave radio relay and open-wire

international: country code - 220; microwave radio relay links to Senegal and Guinea-Bissau; satellite earth station - 1 Intelsat (Atlantic Ocean)

Radio broadcast stations: AM 3, FM 2, shortwave 0 (2001)

Television broadcast stations: 1 (government-owned) (1997)

Internet country code: .gm

Internet hosts: 568 (2002)

Internet users: 25,000 (2002)

Transportation

Railways: 0 km

Highways:

total: 2,700 km

paved: 956 km

unpaved: 1,744 km (1999)

Waterways: 400 km

Gambia, The *(continued)*

Ports and harbors: Banjul
Merchant marine: none
Airports: 1 (2003 est.)
Airports - with paved runways:
total: 1
over 3,047 m: 1 (2003 est.)

Military

Military branches: Gambian National Army (GNA) (including Naval Unit), Presidential Guard
Military manpower - availability:
males age 15-49: 350,256 (2004 est.)
Military manpower - fit for military service:
males age 15-49: 176,733 (2004 est.)
Military expenditures - dollar figure: $900,000 (2003)
Military expenditures - percent of GDP: 0.3% (2003)

Transnational Issues

Disputes - international: attempts to stem refugees, cross-border raids, arms smuggling, other illegal activities, and political instability from separatist movement in southern Senegal's Casamance region

Gaza Strip

Introduction

Background: The Israel-PLO Declaration of Principles on Interim Self-Government Arrangements (the DOP), signed in Washington on 13 September 1993, provided for a transitional period not exceeding five years of Palestinian interim self-government in the Gaza Strip and the West Bank. Under the DOP, Israel agreed to transfer certain powers and responsibilities to the Palestinian Authority, which includes the Palestinian Legislative Council elected in January 1996, as part of the interim self-governing arrangements in the West Bank and Gaza Strip. A transfer of powers and responsibilities for the Gaza Strip and Jericho took place pursuant to the Israel-PLO 4 May 1994 Cairo Agreement on the Gaza Strip and the Jericho Area and in additional areas of the West Bank pursuant to the Israel-PLO 28 September 1995 Interim Agreement, the Israel-PLO 15 January 1997 Protocol Concerning Redeployment in Hebron, the Israel-PLO 23 October 1998 Wye River Memorandum, and the 4 September 1999 Sharm el-Sheikh Agreement. The DOP provides that Israel will retain responsibility during the transitional period for external and internal security and for public order of settlements and Israeli citizens. Direct negotiations to determine the permanent status of Gaza and West Bank that began in September 1999 after a three-year hiatus, were derailed by a second intifadah that broke out in September 2000. The resulting widespread violence in the West Bank and Gaza Strip, Israel's military response, and instability within the Palestinian Authority continue to undermine progress toward a permanent agreement.

Geography

Location: Middle East, bordering the Mediterranean Sea, between Egypt and Israel
Geographic coordinates: 31 25 N, 34 20 E
Map references: Middle East

Area:
total: 360 sq km
land: 360 sq km
water: 0 sq km
Area - comparative: slightly more than twice the size of Washington, DC
Land boundaries:
total: 62 km
border countries: Egypt 11 km, Israel 51 km
Coastline: 40 km
Maritime claims: Israeli-occupied with current status subject to the Israeli-Palestinian Interim Agreement - permanent status to be determined through further negotiation
Climate: temperate, mild winters, dry and warm to hot summers
Terrain: flat to rolling, sand- and dune-covered coastal plain
Elevation extremes:
lowest point: Mediterranean Sea 0 m
highest point: Abu 'Awdah (Joz Abu 'Auda) 105 m
Natural resources: arable land, natural gas
Land use:
arable land: 26.32%
permanent crops: 39.47%
other: 34.21% (1998 est.)
Irrigated land: 120 sq km (1998 est.)
Natural hazards: droughts
Environment - current issues: desertification; salination of fresh water; sewage treatment; water-borne disease; soil degradation; depletion and contamination of underground water resources
Geography - note: there are 25 Israeli settlements and civilian land use sites in the Gaza Strip (February 2002 est.)

People

Population: 1,324,991
note: in addition, there are more than 5,000 Israeli settlers in the Gaza Strip (July 2004 est.)
Age structure:
0-14 years: 49% (male 332,582; female 316,606)
15-64 years: 48.3% (male 326,450; female 314,098)
65 years and over: 2.7% (male 14,847; female 20,408) (2004 est.)
Median age:
total: 15.5 years
male: 15.3 years
female: 15.6 years (2004 est.)
Population growth rate: 3.83% (2004 est.)
Birth rate: 40.62 births/1,000 population (2004 est.)
Death rate: 3.95 deaths/1,000 population (2004 est.)
Net migration rate: 1.6 migrant(s)/1,000 population (2004 est.)
Sex ratio:
at birth: 1.05 male(s)/female
under 15 years: 1.05 male(s)/female
15-64 years: 1.04 male(s)/female
65 years and over: 0.73 male(s)/female
total population: 1.04 male(s)/female (2004 est.)

Infant mortality rate:
total: 23.54 deaths/1,000 live births
male: 24.71 deaths/1,000 live births
female: 22.31 deaths/1,000 live births (2004 est.)
Life expectancy at birth:
total population: 71.59 years
male: 70.31 years
female: 72.94 years (2004 est.)
Total fertility rate: 6.04 children born/woman
(2004 est.)
HIV/AIDS - adult prevalence rate: NA%
HIV/AIDS - people living with HIV/AIDS: NA
HIV/AIDS - deaths: NA
Nationality:
noun: NA
adjective: NA
Ethnic groups: Palestinian Arab and other 99.4%,
Jewish 0.6%
Religions: Muslim (predominantly Sunni) 98.7%,
Christian 0.7%, Jewish 0.6%
Languages: Arabic, Hebrew (spoken by Israeli
settlers and many Palestinians), English (widely
understood)
Literacy:
definition: NA
total population: NA%
male: NA%
female: NA%

Government

Country name:
conventional long form: none
conventional short form: Gaza Strip
local long form: none
local short form: Qita Ghazzah

Economy

Economy - overview: Economic output in the Gaza
Strip - under the responsibility of the Palestinian
Authority since the Cairo Agreement of May 1994 -
declined by about one-third between 1992 and 1996.
The downturn was largely the result of Israeli closure
policies - the imposition of generalized border
closures in response to security incidents in Israel -
which disrupted previously established labor and
commodity market relationships between Israel and
the WBGS (West Bank and Gaza Strip). The most
serious negative social effect of this downturn was the
emergence of high unemployment; unemployment in
the WBGS during the 1980s was generally under 5%;
by 1995 it had risen to over 20%. Israel's use of
comprehensive closures decreased during the next
few years and, in 1998, Israel implemented new
policies to reduce the impact of closures and other
security procedures on the movement of Palestinian
goods and labor. These changes fueled an almost
three-year-long economic recovery in the West Bank
and Gaza Strip; real GDP grew by 5% in 1998 and 6%
in 1999. Recovery was upended in the last quarter of

2000 with the outbreak of violence, triggering tight
Israeli closures of Palestinian self-rule areas and a
severe disruption of trade and labor movements. In
2001, and even more severely in 2002, Israeli military
measures in Palestinian Authority areas resulted in
the destruction of capital plant and administrative
structure, widespread business closures, and a sharp
drop in GDP. Including West Bank, the UN estimates
that more than 100,000 Palestinians out of the
125,000 who used to work in Israel, in Israeli
settlements, or in joint industrial zones have lost their
jobs. In addition, about 80,000 Palestinian workers
inside the Territories are losing their jobs. International
aid of $2 billion in 2001-02 to the West Bank and Gaza
Strip prevented the complete collapse of the economy
and allowed Finance Minister Salam FAYYAD to
implement several financial and economic reforms.
Budgetary support, however, was not as forthcoming
in 2003.
GDP: purchasing power parity - $768 million
(2003 est.)
GDP - real growth rate: 4.5% (2003 est.)
GDP - per capita: purchasing power parity - $600
(2003 est.)
GDP - composition by sector:
agriculture: 9%
industry: 28%
services: 63% (includes West Bank) (2002 est.)
Population below poverty line: 60% (2003 est.)
**Household income or consumption by percentage
share:**
lowest 10%: NA%
highest 10%: NA%
Inflation rate (consumer prices): 2.2% (includes
West Bank) (2001 est.)
Labor force: NA (1997)
Labor force - by occupation: services 66%,
industry 21%, agriculture 13% (1996)
Unemployment rate: 50% (includes West Bank)
(2003 est.)
Budget:
revenues: $676.6 million
expenditures: $1.155 billion, including capital
expenditures of $NA (includes West Bank) (2003)
Industries: generally small family businesses that
produce textiles, soap, olive-wood carvings, and
mother-of-pearl souvenirs; the Israelis have
established some small-scale modern industries in an
industrial center
Industrial production growth rate: NA%
Electricity - production: NA kWh; note - electricity
supplied by Israel
Electricity - consumption: NA kWh
Electricity - exports: 0 kWh (2001)
Electricity - imports: NA kWh; note - electricity
supplied by Israel (2001)
Agriculture - products: olives, citrus, vegetables;
beef, dairy products
Exports: $603 million f.o.b., includes West Bank
Exports - commodities: citrus, flowers

Exports - partners: Israel, Egypt, West Bank
Imports: $1.9 billion c.i.f., includes West Bank
Imports - commodities: food, consumer goods,
construction materials
Imports - partners: Israel, Egypt, West Bank
Debt - external: $108 million (includes West Bank)
(1997 est.)
Economic aid - recipient: $2 billion (includes West
Bank) (2001-02 est.)
Currency: new Israeli shekel (ILS)
Currency code: ILS
Exchange rates: new Israeli shekels per US dollar -
4.55 (2003), 4.74 (2002), 4.21 (2001), 4.08 (2000), 4.14
(1999)
Fiscal year: calendar year

Communications

Telephones - main lines in use: 95,729 (total for
Gaza Strip and West Bank) (1997)
Telephones - mobile cellular: 320,000 (cellular
subscribers in both Gaza Strip and West Bank) (2002)
Telephone system:
general assessment: NA
domestic: rudimentary telephone services provided
by an open-wire system
international: NA
Radio broadcast stations: AM 0, FM 0,
shortwave 0 (1998)
Television broadcast stations: 2 (operated by the
Palestinian Broadcasting Corporation) (1997)
Internet users: 60,000 (includes West Bank) (2001)

Transportation

Railways:
total: NA km; note - one line, abandoned and in
disrepair, little trackage remains (2001 est.)
Highways:
total: NA km
paved: NA km
unpaved: NA km
note: small, poorly developed road network
Waterways: none
Ports and harbors: Gaza
Airports: 2 (2001)
note: includes Gaza International Airport (GIA),
inaugurated on 24 November 1998 as part of
agreements stipulated in the September 1995 Oslo II
Accord and the 23 October 1998 Wye River
Memorandum; GIA has been largely closed since
October 2000 by Israeli orders and its runway was
destroyed by the Israeli Defense Forces in
December 2001 (2003 est.)
Airports - with paved runways:
total: 1
over 3,047 m: 1 (2003 est.)
Airports - with unpaved runways:
total: 1
under 914 m: 1 (2003 est.)
Heliports: 1 (2003 est.)

Military

Military branches: in accordance with the peace agreement, the Palestinian Authority is not permitted conventional military forces; there are, however, a Public Security Force and a civil Police Force
Military expenditures - dollar figure: NA
Military expenditures - percent of GDP: NA

Transnational Issues

Disputes - international: West Bank and Gaza Strip are Israeli-occupied with current status subject to the Israeli-Palestinian Interim Agreement - permanent status to be determined through further negotiation

Georgia

Introduction

Background: Georgia was absorbed into the Russian Empire in the 19th century. Independent for three years (1918-1921) following the Russian revolution, it was forcibly incorporated into the USSR until the Soviet Union dissolved in 1991. Ethnic separation in Abkhazia and South Ossetia, poor governance, and Russian military bases deny the government effective control over the entirety of the state's internationally recognized territory. Despite myriad problems, some progress on market reforms and democratization has been made. An attempt by the government to manipulate legislative elections in November 2003 touched off widespread protests that led to the resignation of Eduard SHEVARDNADZE, president since 1995.

Geography

Location: Southwestern Asia, bordering the Black Sea, between Turkey and Russia
Geographic coordinates: 42 00 N, 43 30 E
Map references: Asia
Area:
total: 69,700 sq km
land: 69,700 sq km
water: 0 sq km
Area - comparative: slightly smaller than South Carolina
Land boundaries:
total: 1,461 km
border countries: Armenia 164 km, Azerbaijan 322 km, Russia 723 km, Turkey 252 km
Coastline: 310 km
Maritime claims: No data available
Climate: warm and pleasant; Mediterranean-like on Black Sea coast
Terrain: largely mountainous with Great Caucasus Mountains in the north and Lesser Caucasus Mountains in the south; Kolkhet'is Dablobi (Kolkhida

Lowland) opens to the Black Sea in the west; Mtkvari River Basin in the east; good soils in river valley flood plains, foothills of Kolkhida Lowland
Elevation extremes:
lowest point: Black Sea 0 m
highest point: Mt'a Shkhara 5,201 m
Natural resources: forests, hydropower, manganese deposits, iron ore, copper, minor coal and oil deposits; coastal climate and soils allow for important tea and citrus growth
Land use:
arable land: 11.21%
permanent crops: 4.09%
other: 84.7% (1998 est.)
Irrigated land: 4,700 sq km (1998 est.)
Natural hazards: earthquakes
Environment - current issues: air pollution, particularly in Rust'avi; heavy pollution of Mtkvari River and the Black Sea; inadequate supplies of potable water; soil pollution from toxic chemicals
Environment - international agreements:
party to: Air Pollution, Biodiversity, Climate Change, Climate Change-Kyoto Protocol, Desertification, Endangered Species, Hazardous Wastes, Law of the Sea, Ozone Layer Protection, Ship Pollution, Wetlands
signed, but not ratified: none of the selected agreements
Geography - note: strategically located east of the Black Sea; Georgia controls much of the Caucasus Mountains and the routes through them

People

Population: 4,693,892 (July 2004 est.)
Age structure:
0-14 years: 18.7% (male 461,967; female 416,898)
15-64 years: 65.8% (male 1,480,217; female 1,607,509)
65 years and over: 15.5% (male 290,534; female 436,767) (2004 est.)

Median age:

total: 37 years

male: 34.5 years

female: 39.2 years (2004 est.)

Population growth rate: -0.36% (2004 est.)

Birth rate: 10.1 births/1,000 population (2004 est.)

Death rate: 8.98 deaths/1,000 population (2004 est.)

Net migration rate: -4.7 migrant(s)/1,000 population (2004 est.)

Sex ratio:

at birth: 1.16 male(s)/female

under 15 years: 1.11 male(s)/female

15-64 years: 0.92 male(s)/female

65 years and over: 0.67 male(s)/female

total population: 0.91 male(s)/female (2004 est.)

Infant mortality rate:

total: 19.34 deaths/1,000 live births

male: 21.5 deaths/1,000 live births

female: 16.84 deaths/1,000 live births (2004 est.)

Life expectancy at birth:

total population: 75.62 years

male: 72.35 years

female: 79.44 years (2004 est.)

Total fertility rate: 1.4 children born/woman (2004 est.)

HIV/AIDS - adult prevalence rate: less than 0.1% (2001 est.)

HIV/AIDS - people living with HIV/AIDS: less than 900 (2001 est.)

HIV/AIDS - deaths: less than 100 (2001 est.)

Nationality:

noun: Georgian(s)

adjective: Georgian

Ethnic groups: Georgian 70.1%, Armenian 8.1%, Russian 6.3%, Azeri 5.7%, Ossetian 3%, Abkhaz 1.8%, other 5%

Religions: Georgian Orthodox 65%, Muslim 11%, Russian Orthodox 10%, Armenian Apostolic 8%, unknown 6%

Languages: Georgian 71% (official), Russian 9%, Armenian 7%, Azeri 6%, other 7%

note: Abkhaz is the official language in Abkhazia

Literacy:

definition: age 15 and over can read and write

total population: 99%

male: 100%

female: 98% (1999 est.)

Government

Country name:

conventional long form: none

conventional short form: Georgia

local long form: none

local short form: Sak'art'velo

former: Georgian Soviet Socialist Republic

Government type: republic

Capital: T'bilisi

Administrative divisions: 9 regions, (mkharebi, singular - mkhare), 9 cities* (k'alak'ebi, singular - k'alak'i), and 2 autonomous republics** (avtomnoy respubliki, singular - avtom respublika); Abkhazia or

Ap'khazet'is Avtonomiuri Respublika** (Sokhumi), Ajaria or Acharis Avtonomiuri Respublika** (Bat'umi), Chiat'ura*, Gori*, Guria, Imereti, Kakheti, K'ut'aisi*, Kvemo Kartli, Mtskheta-Mtianeti, P'ot'i*, Racha-Lechkhumi and Kvemo Svaneti, Rust'avi*, Samegrelo and Zemo Svaneti, Samtskhe-Javakheti, Shida Kartli, T'bilisi*, Tqibuli*, Tsqaltubo*, Zugdidi*

note: the administrative centers of the 2 autonomous republics are shown in parentheses

Independence: 9 April 1991 (from Soviet Union)

National holiday: Independence Day, 26 May (1918); note - 26 May 1918 is the date of independence from Soviet Russia, 9 April 1991 is the date of independence from the Soviet Union

Constitution: adopted 17 October 1995

Legal system: based on civil law system

Suffrage: 18 years of age; universal

Executive branch:

chief of state: President Mikheil SAAKASHVILI (since 25 January 2004); note - the president is both the chief of state and head of government for the power ministries: state security, interior, and defense

head of government: President Mikheil SAAKASHVILI (since 25 January 2004); Prime Minister Zurab ZHVANIA (since 9 February 2004); note - the president is the chief of state and head of government for the power ministries: state security, interior, and defense; the prime minister is head of the remaining ministries of government

cabinet: Cabinet of Ministers

elections: president elected by popular vote for a five-year term; election last held 4 January 2004 (next to be held NA 2009)

election results: Mikheil SAAKASHVILI elected president; percent of vote - Mikheil SAAKASHVILI 96.3%, Temur SHASHIASHVILI 1.9%

Legislative branch: unicameral Supreme Council (commonly referred to as Parliament) or Umaghlesi Sabcho (235 seats - 150 elected by party lists); members are elected by popular vote to serve four-year terms)

elections: last held 28 March 2004 (next to be held spring 2008)

election results: percent of vote by party - National Movement-Democrats 67.6%, Rightist Opposition 7.6%, all other parties received less than 7% each; seats by party - National Movement-Democrats 135, Rightist Opposition 15

Judicial branch: Supreme Court (judges elected by the Supreme Council on the president's recommendation); Constitutional Court

Political parties and leaders: Citizen's Union of Georgia or CUG [Avtandil JORBENADZE]; Georgian People's Front [Nodar NATADZE]; Georgian United Communist Party or UCPG [Panteleimon GIORGADZE]; Greens [Giorgi GACHECHILADZE]; Industry Will Save Georgia or IWSG [Georgi TOPADZE]; Labor Party [Shalva NATELASHVILI]; National Democratic Party or NDP [Irina SARISHVILI-CHANTURIA]; New National Movement [Mikheil SAAKASHVILI]; New Right [Levan GACHECHILADZE]; Republican Party [David

BERDZENISHVILI]; "Revival" Union Party or AGUR [Alsan ABASHIDZE]; Socialist Party or SPG [Irakli MINDELI]; Traditionalists [Akaki ASATIANI]

Political pressure groups and leaders: Georgian independent deputies from Abkhaz government in exile; separatists in the breakaway regions of Abkhazia and South Ossetia; supporters of the late ousted President Zviad GAMSAKHURDYA

International organization participation: BSEC, CE, CIS, EAPC, EBRD, FAO, GUUAM, IAEA, IBRD, ICAO, ICC, ICCt, ICFTU, IDA, IFAD, IFC, IFRCS, ILO, IMF, IMO, Interpol, IOC, IOM, ITU, OAS (observer), OPCW, OSCE, PFP, UN, UNCTAD, UNESCO, UNIDO, UPU, WCO, WHO, WIPO, WMO, WToO, WTrO

Diplomatic representation in the US:

chief of mission: Ambassador Levan MIKELADZE

chancery: Suite 300, 1615 New Hampshire Avenue NW, Washington, DC 20009

telephone: [1] (202) 387-2390

FAX: [1] (202) 393-6060

Diplomatic representation from the US:

chief of mission: Ambassador Richard M. MILES

embassy: #25 Atoneli Street, T'bilisi 380026

mailing address: 7060 Tbilisi Place, Washington, DC 20521-7060

telephone: [995] (32) 989-967/68

FAX: [995] (32) 933-759

Flag description: white rectangle, in its central portion a red cross connecting all four sides of the flag; in each of the four corners is a small red bolnur-katskhuri cross; the five-cross flag appears to date back to the 14th century

Economy

Economy - overview: Georgia's main economic activities include the cultivation of agricultural products such as citrus fruits, tea, hazelnuts, and grapes; mining of manganese and copper; and output of a small industrial sector producing alcoholic and nonalcoholic beverages, metals, machinery, and chemicals. The country imports the bulk of its energy needs, including natural gas and oil products. Its only sizable internal energy resource is hydropower. Despite the severe damage the economy has suffered due to civil strife, Georgia, with the help of the IMF and World Bank, has made substantial economic gains since 1995, achieving positive GDP growth and curtailing inflation. However, the Georgian Government suffers from limited resources due to a chronic failure to collect tax revenues. Georgia also suffers from energy shortages; it privatized the T'bilisi distribution network in 1998, but collection rates are low, making the venture unprofitable. The country is pinning its hopes for long-term growth on its role as a transit state for pipelines and trade. The start of construction on the Baku-T'bilisi-Ceyhan oil pipeline and the Baku-T'bilisi-Erzerum gas pipeline will bring much-needed investment and job opportunities.

GDP: purchasing power parity - $12.18 billion (2003 est.)

GDP - real growth rate: 5.5% (2003 est.)

Georgia *(continued)*

GDP - per capita: purchasing power parity - $2,500 (2003 est.)

GDP - composition by sector:
agriculture: 18.3%
industry: 19%
services: 62.7% (2002 est.)

Population below poverty line: 54% (2001 est.)

Household income or consumption by percentage share:
lowest 10%: 2.3%
highest 10%: 27.9% (1996)

Distribution of family income - Gini index: 37.1 (1996)

Inflation rate (consumer prices): 5% (2003 est.)

Labor force: 2.1 million (2001 est.)

Labor force - by occupation: industry 20%, agriculture 40%, services 40% (1999 est.)

Unemployment rate: 17% (2001 est.)

Budget:
revenues: $499 million
expenditures: $554 million, including capital expenditures of $NA (2001 est.)

Industries: steel, aircraft, machine tools, electrical appliances, mining (manganese and copper), chemicals, wood products, wine

Industrial production growth rate: 3% (2000)

Electricity - production: 7.27 billion kWh (2001)

Electricity - production by source:
fossil fuel: 19.7%
hydro: 80.3%
nuclear: 0%
other: 0% (2001)

Electricity - consumption: 7.611 billion kWh (2001)

Electricity - exports: 0 kWh (2001)

Electricity - imports: 850 million kWh (2001)

Oil - production: 2,000 bbl/day (2001 est.)

Oil - consumption: 31,500 bbl/day (2001 est.)

Oil - exports: NA

Oil - imports: NA

Natural gas - production: 60 million cu m (2001 est.)

Natural gas - consumption: 1.16 billion cu m (2001 est.)

Natural gas - exports: 0 cu m (2001 est.)

Natural gas - imports: 1.1 billion cu m (2001 est.)

Agriculture - products: citrus, grapes, tea, hazelnuts, vegetables; livestock

Exports: $615 million (2003 est.)

Exports - commodities: scrap metal, machinery, chemicals; fuel reexports; citrus fruits, tea, wine

Exports - partners: Turkey 21.7%, Italy 11.4%, Russia 10.7%, Greece 8.1%, Netherlands 7.1%, Spain 5.5%, Turkmenistan 4.5% (2002)

Imports: $1.25 billion (2003 est.)

Imports - commodities: fuels, machinery and parts, transport equipment, grain and other foods, pharmaceuticals

Imports - partners: Azerbaijan 11.7%, Turkey 10.6%, US 10.4%, Russia 9.5%, Germany 7.4%, Ukraine 6%, Italy 5.3%, Bulgaria 5.1%, France 4.4% (2002)

Debt - external: $1.8 billion (2002)

Economic aid - recipient: ODA $150 million (2000 est.)

Currency: lari (GEL)

Currency code: GEL

Exchange rates: lari per US dollar - 2.1457 (2003), 2.1957 (2002), 2.073 (2001), 1.9762 (2000), 2.0245 (1999)

Fiscal year: calendar year

Communications

Telephones - main lines in use: 648,500 (2002)

Telephones - mobile cellular: 503,600 (2002)

Telephone system:
general assessment: NA
domestic: local - T'bilisi and K'ut'aisi have cellular telephone networks; urban telephone density is about 20 per 100 people; rural telephone density is about 4 per 100 people; intercity facilities include a fiber-optic line between T'bilisi and K'ut'aisi; nationwide pager service is available
international: country code - 995; Georgia and Russia are working on a fiber-optic line between P'ot'i and Sochi (Russia); present international service is available by microwave, landline, and satellite through the Moscow switch; international electronic mail and telex service are available

Radio broadcast stations: AM 7, FM 12, shortwave 4 (1998)

Television broadcast stations: 12 (plus repeaters) (1998)

Internet country code: .ge

Internet hosts: 3,032 (2002)

Internet users: 73,500 (2002)

Transportation

Railways:
total: 1,612 km
broad gauge: 1,575 km 1.520-m gauge
narrow gauge: 37 km 0.912-m gauge (2002)

Highways:
total: 20,363 km
paved: 19,038 km
unpaved: 1,325 km (2000)

Waterways: none

Pipelines: gas 1,495 km; oil 1,029 km; refined products 232 km (2003)

Ports and harbors: Bat'umi, P'ot'i, Sokhumi

Merchant marine:
total: 144 ships (1,000 GRT or over) 855,908 GRT/ 1,288,812 DWT
by type: bulk 20, cargo 95, chemical tanker 1, container 11, liquefied gas 1, multi-functional large load carrier 1, passenger 1, petroleum tanker 9, refrigerated cargo 1, roll on/roll off 2, short-sea/ passenger 1, specialized tanker 1
foreign-owned: Albania 2, Belize 2, British Virgin Islands 2, Bulgaria 1, Cyprus 5, Ecuador 1, Egypt 3, Estonia 1, Germany 1, Gibraltar 1, Greece 13, Israel 1, Italy 1, Latvia 4, Lebanon 3, Liberia 2, Madagascar 1, Malta 1, Netherlands 2, Norway 1, Panama 8, Romania 6, Russia 10, Saint Kitts and Nevis 3, Saint Vincent and the Grenadines 4, Saudi Arabia 1, Syria 31, Turkey 10, Ukraine 16,

registered in other countries: 1 (2003 est.)

Airports: 31 (2003 est.)

Airports - with paved runways:
total: 17
over 3,047 m: 1
2,438 to 3,047 m: 7
1,524 to 2,437 m: 5
914 to 1,523 m: 2
under 914 m: 2 (2003 est.)

Airports - with unpaved runways:
total: 14
1,524 to 2,437 m: 4
914 to 1,523 m: 3
under 914 m: 7 (2003 est.)

Heliports: 2 (2003 est.)

Transportation - note: transportation network is in poor condition resulting from ethnic conflict, criminal activities, and fuel shortages; network lacks maintenance and repair

Military

Military branches: Ground Forces (including National Guard), Air and Air Defense Forces, Maritime Defense Force

Military manpower - military age: 18 years of age (2004 est.)

Military manpower - availability:
males age 15-49: 1,156,302 (2004 est.)

Military manpower - fit for military service:
males age 15-49: 906,400 (2004 est.)

Military manpower - reaching military age annually:
males: 39,570 (2004 est.)

Military expenditures - dollar figure: $23 million (FY00)

Military expenditures - percent of GDP: 0.59% (FY00)

Military - note: a CIS peacekeeping force of Russian troops is deployed in the Abkhazia region of Georgia together with a UN military observer group; a Russian peacekeeping battalion is deployed in South Ossetia

Transnational Issues

Disputes - international: about a third of the boundary with Russia remains undelimited, and none of it demarcated, with several small, strategic segments remaining in dispute; OSCE observers monitor volatile areas such as the Pankisi Gorge in the Akhmeti region and the Argun Gorge in Abkhazia; Meshkheti Turks scattered throughout the former Soviet Union seek to return to Georgia; boundary with Armenia remains undemarcated; ethnic Armenian groups in Javakheti region of Georgia seek greater autonomy from the Georgian government; Azerbaijan protests Georgian construction at the Red Bridge crossing and several other small segments of boundary, which remain unresolved until delimitation

Illicit drugs: limited cultivation of cannabis and opium poppy, mostly for domestic consumption; used as transshipment point for opiates via Central Asia to Western Europe and Russia

Germany

Introduction

Background: As Europe's largest economy and most populous nation, Germany remains a key member of the continent's economic, political, and defense organizations. European power struggles immersed Germany in two devastating World Wars in the first half of the 20th century and left the country occupied by the victorious Allied powers of the US, UK, France, and the Soviet Union in 1945. With the advent of the Cold War, two German states were formed in 1949: the western Federal Republic of Germany (FRG) and the eastern German Democratic Republic (GDR). The democratic FRG embedded itself in key Western economic and security organizations, the EC, which became the EU, and NATO, while the Communist GDR was on the front line of the Soviet-led Warsaw Pact. The decline of the USSR and the end of the Cold War allowed for German unification in 1990. Since then, Germany has expended considerable funds to bring Eastern productivity and wages up to Western standards. In January 1999, Germany and 10 other EU countries introduced a common European exchange currency, the euro.

Geography

Location: Central Europe, bordering the Baltic Sea and the North Sea, between the Netherlands and Poland, south of Denmark
Geographic coordinates: 51 00 N, 9 00 E
Map references: Europe
Area:
total: 357,021 sq km
land: 349,223 sq km
water: 7,798 sq km
Area - comparative: slightly smaller than Montana
Land boundaries:
total: 3,621 km
border countries: Austria 784 km, Belgium 167 km, Czech Republic 646 km, Denmark 68 km, France 451 km, Luxembourg 138 km, Netherlands 577 km, Poland 456 km, Switzerland 334 km

Coastline: 2,389 km
Maritime claims:
territorial sea: 12 NM
exclusive economic zone: 200 NM
continental shelf: 200-m depth or to the depth of exploitation
Climate: temperate and marine; cool, cloudy, wet winters and summers; occasional warm mountain (foehn) wind
Terrain: lowlands in north, uplands in center, Bavarian Alps in south
Elevation extremes:
lowest point: Neuendorf bei Wilster -3.54 m
highest point: Zugspitze 2,963 m
Natural resources: iron ore, coal, potash, timber, lignite, uranium, copper, natural gas, salt, nickel, arable land
Land use:
arable land: 33.88%
permanent crops: 0.65%
other: 65.47% (1998 est.)
Irrigated land: 4,850 sq km (1998 est.)
Natural hazards: flooding
Environment - current issues: emissions from coal-burning utilities and industries contribute to air pollution; acid rain, resulting from sulfur dioxide emissions, is damaging forests; pollution in the Baltic Sea from raw sewage and industrial effluents from rivers in eastern Germany; hazardous waste disposal; government established a mechanism for ending the use of nuclear power over the next 15 years; government working to meet EU commitment to identify nature preservation areas in line with the EU's Flora, Fauna, and Habitat directive
Environment - international agreements:
party to: Air Pollution, Air Pollution-Nitrogen Oxides, Air Pollution-Sulfur 85, Air Pollution-Sulfur 94, Air Pollution-Volatile Organic Compounds, Antarctic-Environmental Protocol, Antarctic-Marine Living Resources, Antarctic Seals, Antarctic Treaty, Biodiversity, Climate Change, Climate Change-Kyoto Protocol, Desertification, Endangered Species, Environmental Modification, Hazardous Wastes, Law of the Sea, Marine Dumping, Ozone Layer Protection, Ship Pollution, Tropical Timber 83, Tropical Timber 94, Wetlands, Whaling
signed, but not ratified: Air Pollution-Persistent Organic Pollutants
Geography - note: strategic location on North European Plain and along the entrance to the Baltic Sea

People

Population: 82,424,609 (July 2004 est.)
Age structure:
0-14 years: 14.7% (male 6,197,490; female 5,879,052)
15-64 years: 67% (male 28,119,536; female 27,132,713)
65 years and over: 18.3% (male 6,096,106; female 8,999,712) (2004 est.)

Median age:
total: 41.7 years
male: 40.4 years
female: 43.2 years (2004 est.)
Population growth rate: 0.02% (2004 est.)
Birth rate: 8.45 births/1,000 population (2004 est.)
Death rate: 10.44 deaths/1,000 population (2004 est.)
Net migration rate: 2.18 migrant(s)/1,000 population (2004 est.)
Sex ratio:
at birth: 1.06 male(s)/female
under 15 years: 1.05 male(s)/female
15-64 years: 1.04 male(s)/female
65 years and over: 0.68 male(s)/female
total population: 0.96 male(s)/female (2004 est.)
Infant mortality rate:
total: 4.2 deaths/1,000 live births
male: 4.64 deaths/1,000 live births
female: 3.73 deaths/1,000 live births (2004 est.)
Life expectancy at birth:
total population: 78.54 years
male: 75.56 years
female: 81.68 years (2004 est.)
Total fertility rate: 1.38 children born/woman (2004 est.)
HIV/AIDS - adult prevalence rate: 0.1% (2001 est.)
HIV/AIDS - people living with HIV/AIDS: 41,000 (2001 est.)
HIV/AIDS - deaths: 660 (2001 est.)
Nationality:
noun: German(s)
adjective: German
Ethnic groups: German 91.5%, Turkish 2.4%, other 6.1% (made up largely of Greek, Italian, Polish, Russian, Serbo-Croatian, Spanish)
Religions: Protestant 34%, Roman Catholic 34%, Muslim 3.7%, unaffiliated or other 28.3%
Languages: German
Literacy:
definition: age 15 and over can read and write
total population: 99% (1977 est.)
male: NA%
female: NA%

Government

Country name:
conventional long form: Federal Republic of Germany
conventional short form: Germany
local long form: Bundesrepublik Deutschland
local short form: Deutschland
former: German Empire, German Republic, German Reich
Government type: federal republic
Capital: Berlin
Administrative divisions: 16 states (Laender, singular - Land); Baden-Wuerttemberg, Bayern, Berlin, Brandenburg, Bremen, Hamburg, Hessen, Mecklenburg-Vorpommern, Niedersachsen, Nordrhein-Westfalen, Rheinland-Pfalz, Saarland, Sachsen, Sachsen-Anhalt, Schleswig-Holstein, Thueringen

Germany (continued)

Independence: 18 January 1871 (German Empire unification); divided into four zones of occupation (UK, US, USSR, and later, France) in 1945 following World War II; Federal Republic of Germany (FRG or West Germany) proclaimed 23 May 1949 and included the former UK, US, and French zones; German Democratic Republic (GDR or East Germany) proclaimed 7 October 1949 and included the former USSR zone; unification of West Germany and East Germany took place 3 October 1990; all four powers formally relinquished rights 15 March 1991

National holiday: Unity Day, 3 October (1990)

Constitution: 23 May 1949, known as Basic Law; became constitution of the united German people 3 October 1990

Legal system: civil law system with indigenous concepts; judicial review of legislative acts in the Federal Constitutional Court; has not accepted compulsory ICJ jurisdiction

Suffrage: 18 years of age; universal

Executive branch:
chief of state: President Johannes RAU (since 1 July 1999)
head of government: Chancellor Gerhard SCHROEDER (since 27 October 1998)
cabinet: Cabinet or Bundesminister (Federal Ministers) appointed by the president on the recommendation of the chancellor
elections: president elected for a five-year term by a Federal Convention including all members of the Federal Assembly and an equal number of delegates elected by the state parliaments; election last held 23 May 1999 (next to be held 23 May 2004); chancellor elected by an absolute majority of the Federal Assembly for a four-year term; election last held 22 September 2002 (next to be held NA September 2006)
election results: Johannes RAU elected president; percent of Federal Convention vote - 57.6%; Gerhard SCHROEDER elected chancellor; percent of Federal Assembly vote 50.7%

Legislative branch: bicameral Parliament or Parlament consists of the Federal Assembly or Bundestag (603 seats; elected by popular vote under a system combining direct and proportional representation; a party must win 5% of the national vote or three direct mandates to gain representation; members serve four-year terms) and the Federal Council or Bundesrat (69 votes; state governments are directly represented by votes; each has 3 to 6 votes depending on population and are required to vote as a block)
elections: Federal Assembly - last held 22 September 2002 (next to be held NA September 2006); note - there are no elections for the Bundesrat; composition is determined by the composition of the state-level governments; the composition of the Bundesrat has the potential to change any time one of the 16 states holds an election
election results: Federal Assembly - percent of vote by party - SPD 38.5%, CDU/CSU 38.5%, Alliance '90/ Greens 8.6%, FDP 7.4%, PDS 4%; seats by party -

SPD 251, CDU/CSU 248, Alliance '90/Greens 55, FDP 47, PDS 2; Federal Council - current composition - NA

Judicial branch: Federal Constitutional Court or Bundesverfassungsgericht (half the judges are elected by the Bundestag and half by the Bundesrat)

Political parties and leaders: Alliance '90/Greens [Angelika BEER and Reinhard BUETIKOFER]; Christian Democratic Union or CDU [Angela MERKEL]; Christian Social Union or CSU [Edmund STOIBER, chairman]; Free Democratic Party or FDP [Guido WESTERWELLE, chairman]; Party of Democratic Socialism or PDS [Lothar BISKY]; Social Democratic Party or SPD [Franz MUENTEFERING]

Political pressure groups and leaders: business associations, employers' organizations; expellee, refugee, trade unions, and veterans groups

International organization participation: AfDB, AsDB, Australia Group, BDEAC, BIS, BSEC (observer), CBSS, CDB, CE, CERN, EAPC, EBRD, EIB, EMU, ESA, EU, FAO, G-5, G-7, G-8, G-10, IADB, IAEA, IBRD, ICAO, ICC, ICCt, ICFTU, ICRM, IDA, IEA, IFAD, IFC, IFRCS, IHO, ILO, IMF, IMO, Interpol, IOC, IOM, ISO, ITU, NAM (guest), NATO, NEA, NSG, OAS (observer), OECD, OPCW, OSCE, Paris Club, PCA, UN, UN Security Council (temporary), UNAMSIL, UNCTAD, UNESCO, UNHCR, UNIDO, UNMIK, UNMOVIC, UNOMIG, UPU, WADB (nonregional), WCO, WEU, WHO, WIPO, WMO, WToO, WTrO, ZC

Diplomatic representation in the US:
chief of mission: Ambassador Wolfgang Friedrich ISCHINGER
chancery: 4645 Reservoir Road NW, Washington, DC 20007
telephone: [1] (202) 298-8140
FAX: [1] (202) 298-4249
consulate(s) general: Atlanta, Boston, Chicago, Detroit, Houston, Los Angeles, Miami, New York, San Francisco

Diplomatic representation from the US:
chief of mission: Ambassador Daniel R. COATS
embassy: Neustaedtische Kirchstrasse 4-5, 10117 Berlin; note - a new embassy will be built near the Brandenburg Gate in Berlin
mailing address: PSC 120, Box 1000, APO AE 09265
telephone: [49] (30) 238-5174
FAX: [49] (30) 238-6290
consulate(s) general: Duesseldorf, Frankfurt am Main, Hamburg, Leipzig, Munich

Flag description: three equal horizontal bands of black (top), red, and gold

Economy

Economy - overview: Germany's affluent and technologically powerful economy- the fifth largest national economy in the world - has become one of the slowest growing economies in the entire euro zone, and a quick turnaround is not in the offing in the foreseeable future. Growth in 2001-03 fell short of 1%. The modernization and integration of the eastern

German economy continues to be a costly long-term process, with annual transfers from west to east amounting to roughly $70 billion. Germany's ageing population, combined with high unemployment, has pushed social security outlays to a level exceeding contributions from workers. Structural rigidities in the labor market - including strict regulations on laying off workers and the setting of wages on a national basis - have made unemployment a chronic problem. Corporate restructuring and growing capital markets are setting the foundations that could allow Germany to meet the long-term challenges of European economic integration and globalization, particularly if labor market rigidities are further addressed. The government is also starting long-needed structural reforms designed to revitalize the country's economy. In the short run, however, the fall in government revenues and the rise in expenditures have raised the deficit above the EU's 3% debt limit.

GDP: purchasing power parity - $2.271 trillion (2003 est.)

GDP - real growth rate: -0.1% (2003 est.)

GDP - per capita: purchasing power parity - $27,600 (2003 est.)

GDP - composition by sector:
agriculture: 1%
industry: 31%
services: 68% (2002 est.)

Population below poverty line: NA%

Household income or consumption by percentage share:
lowest 10%: 3.6%
highest 10%: 25.1% (1997)

Distribution of family income - Gini index: 30 (1994)

Inflation rate (consumer prices): 0.9% (2003 est.)

Labor force: 41.9 million (2001)

Labor force - by occupation: industry 33.4%, agriculture 2.8%, services 63.8% (1999)

Unemployment rate: 10.7% (2003 est.)

Budget:
revenues: $802 billion
expenditures: $825 billion, including capital expenditures of $NA (2001 est.)

Industries: among the world's largest and most technologically advanced producers of iron, steel, coal, cement, chemicals, machinery, vehicles, machine tools, electronics, food and beverages; shipbuilding; textiles

Industrial production growth rate: 0.1% (2003 est.)

Electricity - production: 544.8 billion kWh (2001)

Electricity - production by source:
fossil fuel: 61.8%
hydro: 4.2%
nuclear: 29.9%
other: 4.1% (2001)

Electricity - consumption: 506.8 billion kWh (2001)

Electricity - exports: 43.9 billion kWh (2001)

Electricity - imports: 44 billion kWh (2001)

Oil - production: 85,860 bbl/day (2001 est.)

Oil - consumption: 2.813 million bbl/day (2001 est.)

Germany (continued)

Oil - exports: 404,300 bbl/day (2001)
Oil - imports: 3.081 million bbl/day (2001)
Oil - proved reserves: 327.3 million bbl (1 January 2002)
Natural gas - production: 22.16 billion cu m (2001 est.)
Natural gas - consumption: 94.34 billion cu m (2001 est.)
Natural gas - exports: 6.674 billion cu m (2001 est.)
Natural gas - imports: 78.73 billion cu m (2001 est.)
Natural gas - proved reserves: 298.3 billion cu m (1 January 2002)
Agriculture - products: potatoes, wheat, barley, sugar beets, fruit, cabbages; cattle, pigs, poultry
Exports: $696.9 billion f.o.b. (2003 est.)
Exports - commodities: machinery, vehicles, chemicals, metals and manufactures, foodstuffs, textiles
Exports - partners: France 10.7%, US 10.3%, UK 8.4%, Italy 7.3%, Netherlands 6.1%, Austria 5.1%, Belgium 4.8%, Spain 4.6%, Switzerland 4.2% (2002)
Imports: $585 billion f.o.b. (2003 est.)
Imports - commodities: machinery, vehicles, chemicals, foodstuffs, textiles, metals
Imports - partners: France 9.5%, Netherlands 8.2%, US 7.7%, UK 6.5%, Italy 6.4%, Belgium 5.2%, Austria 4%, China 4% (2002)
Debt - external: $NA (2000 est.)
Economic aid - donor: ODA, $5.6 billion (1998)
Currency: euro (EUR)
note: on 1 January 1999, the European Monetary Union introduced the euro as a common currency to be used by financial institutions of member countries; on 1 January 2002, the euro became the sole currency for everyday transactions within the member countries
Currency code: EUR
Exchange rates: euros per US dollar - 0.886 (2003), 1.0626 (2002), 1.1175 (2001), 1.0854 (2000), 0.9386 (1999)
Fiscal year: calendar year

Communications

Telephones - main lines in use: 53.72 million (2002)
Telephones - mobile cellular: 60.043 million (2002)
Telephone system:
general assessment: Germany has one of the world's most technologically advanced telecommunications systems; as a result of intensive capital expenditures since reunification, the formerly backward system of the eastern part of the country, dating back to World War II, has been modernized and integrated with that of the western part
domestic: Germany is served by an extensive system of automatic telephone exchanges connected by modern networks of fiber-optic cable, coaxial cable, microwave radio relay, and a domestic satellite system; cellular telephone service is widely available, expanding rapidly, and includes roaming service to many foreign countries
international: country code - 49; Germany's international service is excellent worldwide, consisting of extensive land and undersea cable facilities as well as earth stations in the INMARSAT, INTELSAT, EUTELSAT, and INTERSPUTNIK satellite systems (2001)
Radio broadcast stations: AM 51, FM 787, shortwave 4 (1998)
Television broadcast stations: 373 (plus 8,042 repeaters) (1995)
Internet country code: .de
Internet hosts: 2,594,323 (2002)
Internet users: 34 million (2002)

Transportation

Railways:
total: 45,514 km (21,000 km electrified)
standard gauge: 45,276 km 1.435-m gauge (20,084 km electrified)
narrow gauge: 214 km 1.000-m gauge (16 km electrified); 24 km 0.750-m gauge (2002)
Highways:
total: 230,735 km
paved: 230,735 km (including 11,515 km of expressways)
unpaved: 0 km (1999)
Waterways: 7,500 km
note: major rivers include the Rhine and Elbe; Kiel Canal is an important connection between the Baltic Sea and North Sea (1999)
Pipelines: condensate 325 km; gas 25,289 km; oil 3,743 km; refined products 3,827 km (2003)
Ports and harbors: Berlin, Bonn, Brake, Bremen, Bremerhaven, Cologne, Dresden, Duisburg, Emden, Hamburg, Karlsruhe, Kiel, Luebeck, Magdeburg, Mannheim, Rostock, Stuttgart
Merchant marine:
total: 278 ships (1,000 GRT or over) 5,721,495 GRT/6,810,631 DWT
by type: cargo 71, chemical tanker 14, container 169, liquefied gas 3, multi-functional large load carrier 1, passenger 3, petroleum tanker 5, rail car carrier 2, roll on/roll off 3, short-sea/passenger 7
foreign-owned: Finland 4, Iceland 1, Netherlands 3
registered in other countries: 2,295 (2003 est.)
Airports: 550 (2003 est.)
Airports - with paved runways:
total: 331
over 3,047 m: 13
2,438 to 3,047 m: 51
1,524 to 2,437 m: 62
914 to 1,523 m: 71
under 914 m: 134 (2003 est.)
Airports - with unpaved runways:
total: 219
2,438 to 3,047 m: 1
1,524 to 2,437 m: 2
914 to 1,523 m: 31
under 914 m: 185 (2003 est.)
Heliports: 34 (2003 est.)

Military

Military branches: Army (Bundeswehr), Navy (Deutsche Marine; including Naval Air arm), Air Force (Luftwaffe), Joint Support Service, Central Medical Service
Military manpower - military age: 18 years of age (conscripts serve a nine-month tour of compulsory military service) (2004 est.)
Military manpower - availability:
males age 15-49: 20,468,942 (2004 est.)
Military manpower - fit for military service:
males age 15-49: 17,338,435 (2004 est.)
Military manpower - reaching military age annually:
males: 484,837 (2004 est.)
Military expenditures - dollar figure: $35.063 billion (2003)
Military expenditures - percent of GDP: 1.5% (2003)

Transnational Issues

Disputes - international: none
Illicit drugs: source of precursor chemicals for South American cocaine processors; transshipment point for and consumer of Southwest Asian heroin, Latin American cocaine, and European-produced synthetic drugs; major financial center

Ghana

Introduction

Background: Formed from the merger of the British colony of the Gold Coast and the Togoland trust territory, Ghana in 1957 became the first country in colonial Africa to gain its independence. A long series of coups resulted in the suspension of the constitution in 1981 and the banning of political parties. A new constitution, restoring multiparty politics, was approved in 1992. Lt. Jerry RAWLINGS, head of state since 1981, won presidential elections in 1992 and 1996, but was constitutionally prevented from running for a third term in 2000. He was succeeded by John KUFUOR, who defeated former Vice President Atta MILLS in a free and fair election.

Geography

Location: Western Africa, bordering the Gulf of Guinea, between Cote d'Ivoire and Togo
Geographic coordinates: 8 00 N, 2 00 W
Map references: Africa
Area:
total: 239,460 sq km
land: 230,940 sq km
water: 8,520 sq km
Area - comparative: slightly smaller than Oregon
Land boundaries:
total: 2,094 km
border countries: Burkina Faso 549 km, Cote d'Ivoire 668 km, Togo 877 km
Coastline: 539 km
Maritime claims:
territorial sea: 12 NM
contiguous zone: 24 NM
exclusive economic zone: 200 NM
continental shelf: 200 NM
Climate: tropical; warm and comparatively dry along southeast coast; hot and humid in southwest; hot and dry in north

Terrain: mostly low plains with dissected plateau in south-central area
Elevation extremes:
lowest point: Atlantic Ocean 0 m
highest point: Mount Afadjato 880 m
Natural resources: gold, timber, industrial diamonds, bauxite, manganese, fish, rubber, hydropower
Land use:
arable land: 15.82%
permanent crops: 7.47%
other: 76.71% (1998 est.)
Irrigated land: 110 sq km (1998 est.)
Natural hazards: dry, dusty, northeastern harmattan winds occur from January to March; droughts
Environment - current issues: recurrent drought in north severely affects agricultural activities; deforestation; overgrazing; soil erosion; poaching and habitat destruction threatens wildlife populations; water pollution; inadequate supplies of potable water
Environment - international agreements:
party to: Biodiversity, Climate Change, Climate Change-Kyoto Protocol, Desertification, Endangered Species, Environmental Modification, Hazardous Wastes, Law of the Sea, Ozone Layer Protection, Ship Pollution, Tropical Timber 83, Tropical Timber 94, Wetlands
signed, but not ratified: Marine Life Conservation
Geography - note: Lake Volta is the world's largest artificial lake

People

Population: 20,757,032
note: estimates for this country explicitly take into account the effects of excess mortality due to AIDS; this can result in lower life expectancy, higher infant mortality and death rates, lower population and growth rates, and changes in the distribution of population by age and sex than would otherwise be expected (July 2004 est.)
Age structure:
0-14 years: 38% (male 3,988,800; female 3,904,989)
15-64 years: 58.3% (male 6,030,151; female 6,071,725)
65 years and over: 3.7% (male 359,042; female 402,325) (2004 est.)
Median age:
total: 20 years
male: 19.8 years
female: 20.3 years (2004 est.)
Population growth rate: 1.36% (2004 est.)
Birth rate: 24.9 births/1,000 population (2004 est.)
Death rate: 10.67 deaths/1,000 population (2004 est.)
Net migration rate: -0.64 migrant(s)/1,000 population (2004 est.)
Sex ratio:
at birth: 1.03 male(s)/female
under 15 years: 1.02 male(s)/female
15-64 years: 0.99 male(s)/female
65 years and over: 0.89 male(s)/female
total population: 1 male(s)/female (2004 est.)

Infant mortality rate:
total: 52.22 deaths/1,000 live births
male: 55.1 deaths/1,000 live births
female: 49.25 deaths/1,000 live births (2004 est.)
Life expectancy at birth:
total population: 56.27 years
male: 55.36 years
female: 57.22 years (2004 est.)
Total fertility rate: 3.17 children born/woman (2004 est.)
HIV/AIDS - adult prevalence rate: 3% (2001 est.)
HIV/AIDS - people living with HIV/AIDS: 360,000 (2001 est.)
HIV/AIDS - deaths: 28,000 (2001 est.)
Nationality:
noun: Ghanaian(s)
adjective: Ghanaian
Ethnic groups: black African 98.5% (major tribes - Akan 44%, Moshi-Dagomba 16%, Ewe 13%, Ga 8%, Gurma 3%, Yoruba 1%), European and other 1.5% (1998)
Religions: Christian 63%, Muslim 16%, indigenous beliefs 21%
Languages: English (official), African languages (including Akan, Moshi-Dagomba, Ewe, and Ga)
Literacy:
definition: age 15 and over can read and write
total population: 74.8%
male: 82.7%
female: 67.1% (2003 est.)
People - note: there are 9,500 Liberians, 2,000 Sierra Leoneans, and 1,000 Togolese refugees residing in Ghana (2002)

Government

Country name:
conventional long form: Republic of Ghana
conventional short form: Ghana
former: Gold Coast
Government type: constitutional democracy
Capital: Accra
Administrative divisions: 10 regions; Ashanti, Brong-Ahafo, Central, Eastern, Greater Accra, Northern, Upper East, Upper West, Volta, Western
Independence: 6 March 1957 (from UK)
National holiday: Independence Day, 6 March (1957)
Constitution: approved 28 April 1992
Legal system: based on English common law and customary law; has not accepted compulsory ICJ jurisdiction
Suffrage: 18 years of age; universal
Executive branch:
chief of state: President John Agyekum KUFUOR (since 7 January 2001); Vice President Alhaji Aliu MAHAMA (since 7 January 2001); note - the president is both the chief of state and head of government
head of government: President John Agyekum KUFUOR (since 7 January 2001); Vice President Alhaji Aliu MAHAMA (since 7 January 2001); note - the president is both the chief of state and head of government

Ghana (continued)

cabinet: Council of Ministers; president nominates members subject to approval by Parliament
elections: president and vice president elected on the same ticket by popular vote for four-year terms; election last held 7 and 28 December 2000 (next to be held NA December 2004)
election results: John Agyekum KUFUOR elected president in runoff election; percent of vote - John KUFUOR 56.4%, John Atta MILLS 43.6%
Legislative branch: unicameral Parliament (200 seats; members are elected by direct, popular vote to serve four-year terms)
elections: last held 7 December 2000 (next to be held NA December 2004)
election results: percent of vote by party - NA%; seats by party - NPP 100, NDC 92, PNC 3, CPP 1, independents 4
Judicial branch: Supreme Court
Political parties and leaders: Convention People's Party or CPP [Nii Noi DOWUONA, general secretary]; Every Ghanaian Living Everywhere or EGLE [Owuraku AMOFA, chairman]; Great Consolidated Popular Party or GCPP [Dan LARTY]; National Convention Party or NCP [Sarpong KUMA-KUMA]; National Democratic Congress or NDC [Dr. Huudu YAHAYA, general secretary]; New Patriotic Party or NPP [Samuel Arthur ODOI-SYKES]; People's Convention Party or PCP [P. K. DONKOH-AYIFI, acting chairman]; People's Heritage Party or PHP [Emmanuel Alexander ERSKINE]; People's National Convention or PNC [Edward MAHAMA]; Reform Party [Kyeretwie OPUKU, general secretary]
Political pressure groups and leaders: NA
International organization participation: ACP, AfDB, AU, C, ECOWAS, FAO, G-24, G-77, IAEA, IBRD, ICAO, ICC, ICCt, ICFTU, ICRM, IDA, IFAD, IFC, IFRCS, ILO, IMF, IMO, Interpol, IOC, IOM (observer), ISO, ITU, MINURSO, MONUC, NAM, OAS (observer), OPCW, UN, UNAMSIL, UNCTAD, UNESCO, UNIDO, UNIFIL, UNITAR, UNMEE, UNMIK, UNMIL, UPU, WCL, WCO, WFTU, WHO, WIPO, WMO, WToO, WTrO
Diplomatic representation in the US:
chief of mission: Ambassador Alan J. KYEREMATEN
chancery: 3512 International Drive NW, Washington, DC 20008
telephone: [1] (202) 686-4520
FAX: [1] (202) 686-4527
consulate(s) general: New York
Diplomatic representation from the US:
chief of mission: Ambassador Mary Carlin YATES
embassy: 6th and 10th Lanes, 798/1 Osu, Accra
mailing address: P. O. Box 194, Accra
telephone: [233] (21) 775-347, 775-348
FAX: [233] (21) 701-813
Flag description: three equal horizontal bands of red (top), yellow, and green with a large black five-pointed star centered in the yellow band; uses the popular pan-African colors of Ethiopia; similar to the flag of Bolivia, which has a coat of arms centered in the yellow band

Economy

Economy - overview: Well endowed with natural resources, Ghana has roughly twice the per capita output of the poorer countries in West Africa. Even so, Ghana remains heavily dependent on international financial and technical assistance. Gold, timber, and cocoa production are major sources of foreign exchange. The domestic economy continues to revolve around subsistence agriculture, which accounts for 35% of GDP and employs 60% of the work force, mainly small landholders. Ghana opted for debt relief under the Heavily Indebted Poor Country (HIPC) program in 2002. Policy priorities include tighter monetary and fiscal policies, accelerated privatization, and improvement of social services. Receipts from the gold sector should help sustain GDP growth in 2004. Inflation should ease, but remain a major internal problem.
GDP: purchasing power parity - $44.49 billion (2003 est.)
GDP - real growth rate: 4.8% (2003 est.)
GDP - per capita: purchasing power parity - $2,200 (2003 est.)
GDP - composition by sector:
agriculture: 35.2%
industry: 25.4%
services: 39.4% (2001 est.)
Population below poverty line: 31.4% (1992 est.)
Household income or consumption by percentage share:
lowest 10%: 2.2%
highest 10%: 30.1% (1999)
Distribution of family income - Gini index: 40.7 (1999)
Inflation rate (consumer prices): 26.4% (2003 est.)
Labor force: 9 million (2000 est.)
Labor force - by occupation: agriculture 60%, industry 15%, services 25% (1999 est.)
Unemployment rate: 20% (1997 est.)
Budget:
revenues: $1.603 billion
expenditures: $1.975 billion, including capital expenditures of $NA (2001 est.)
Industries: mining, lumbering, light manufacturing, aluminum smelting, food processing
Industrial production growth rate: 3.8% (2000 est.)
Electricity - production: 8.801 billion kWh (2001)
Electricity - production by source:
fossil fuel: 5%
hydro: 95%
nuclear: 0%
other: 0% (2001)
Electricity - consumption: 8.835 billion kWh (2001)
Electricity - exports: 300 million kWh (2001)
Electricity - imports: 950 million kWh (2001)
Oil - production: 7,000 bbl/day (2001 est.)
Oil - consumption: 38,000 bbl/day (2001 est.)
Oil - exports: NA
Oil - imports: NA

Oil - proved reserves: 8.255 million bbl (1 January 2002)
Natural gas - proved reserves: 11.89 billion cu m (1 January 2002)
Agriculture - products: cocoa, rice, coffee, cassava (tapioca), peanuts, corn, shea nuts, bananas; timber
Exports: $2.642 billion f.o.b. (2003 est.)
Exports - commodities: gold, cocoa, timber, tuna, bauxite, aluminum, manganese ore, diamonds
Exports - partners: Netherlands 14.6%, UK 9.7%, US 6.9%, Germany 6.4%, France 5.7%, Nigeria 4.7%, Belgium 4.4%, Italy 4.1% (2002)
Imports: $3.24 billion f.o.b. (2003 est.)
Imports - commodities: capital equipment, petroleum, foodstuffs
Imports - partners: Nigeria 20.8%, UK 7%, US 6.4%, China 6%, Cote d'Ivoire 6%, Italy 6%, Germany 4.6% (2002)
Debt - external: $7.4 billion (2003 est.)
Economic aid - recipient: $6.9 billion (1999)
Currency: cedi (GHC)
Currency code: GHC
Exchange rates: cedis per US dollar - NA (2003), 7,932.7 (2002), 7,170.76 (2001), 5,455.06 (2000), 2,669.3 (1999)
Fiscal year: calendar year

Communications

Telephones - main lines in use: 274,300 (2002)
Telephones - mobile cellular: 449,400 (2002)
Telephone system:
general assessment: poor to fair system; Internet accessible; many rural communities not yet connected; expansion of services is underway
domestic: primarily microwave radio relay; wireless local loop has been installed
international: country code - 233; satellite earth stations - 4 Intelsat (Atlantic Ocean); microwave radio relay link to Panaftel system connects Ghana to its neighbors; fiber optic submarine cable (SAT-3/WASC) provides connectivity to Europe and Asia
Radio broadcast stations: AM 0, FM 49, shortwave 3 (2001)
Television broadcast stations: 10 (2001)
Internet country code: .gh
Internet hosts: 313 (2002)
Internet users: 170,000 (2002)

Transportation

Railways:
total: 953 km
narrow gauge: 953 km 1.067-m gauge (2002)
Highways:
total: 39,409 km
paved: 11,665 km
unpaved: 27,744 km (1999 est.)
Waterways: 1,293 km
note: Volta, Ankobra, and Tano Rivers provide 168 km of perennial navigation for launches and lighters; Lake Volta provides 1,125 km of arterial and feeder waterways

Pipelines: refined products 74 km (2003)
Ports and harbors: Takoradi, Tema
Merchant marine:
total: 8 ships (1,000 GRT or over) 19,086 GRT/26,185 DWT
by type: petroleum tanker 3, refrigerated cargo 5
foreign-owned: Brazil 1, Saint Vincent and the Grenadines 1, Spain 1 (2003 est.)
Airports: 12 (2003 est.)
Airports - with paved runways:
total: 7
2,438 to 3,047 m: 1
1,524 to 2,437 m: 4
914 to 1,523 m: 2 (2003 est.)
Airports - with unpaved runways:
total: 5
914 to 1,523 m: 3
under 914 m: 2 (2003 est.)

Military

Military branches: Army, Navy, Air Force
Military manpower - military age: 18 years of age (2004 est.)
Military manpower - availability:
males age 15-49: 5,391,378 (2004 est.)
Military manpower - fit for military service:
males age 15-49: 2,994,600 (2004 est.)
Military manpower - reaching military age annually:
males: 244,809 (2004 est.)
Military expenditures - dollar figure: $44 million (2003)
Military expenditures - percent of GDP: 0.6% (2003)

Transnational Issues

Disputes - international: Ghana must still deal with refugees and returning nationals escaping rebel fighting in Cote d'Ivoire
Illicit drugs: illicit producer of cannabis for the international drug trade; major transit hub for Southwest and Southeast Asian heroin and, to a lesser extent, South American cocaine destined for Europe and the US; widespread crime and corruption have made money laundering a problem, but the lack of a well-developed financial infrastructure limits the country's utility as a money-laundering center

Gibraltar
(overseas territory of the UK)

Introduction

Background: Strategically important, Gibraltar was ceded to Great Britain by Spain in the 1713 Treaty of Utrecht; the British garrison was formally declared a colony in 1830. In referendums held in 1967 and 2002, Gibraltarians ignored Spanish pressure and voted overwhelmingly to remain a British dependency.

Geography

Location: Southwestern Europe, bordering the Strait of Gibraltar, which links the Mediterranean Sea and the North Atlantic Ocean, on the southern coast of Spain
Geographic coordinates: 36 8 N, 5 21 W
Map references: Europe
Area:
total: 6.5 sq km
land: 6.5 sq km
water: 0 sq km
Area - comparative: about 11 times the size of The Mall in Washington, DC
Land boundaries:
total: 1.2 km
border countries: Spain 1.2 km
Coastline: 12 km
Maritime claims:
territorial sea: 3 NM
Climate: Mediterranean with mild winters and warm summers
Terrain: a narrow coastal lowland borders the Rock of Gibraltar
Elevation extremes:
lowest point: Mediterranean Sea 0 m
highest point: Rock of Gibraltar 426 m
Natural resources: NEGL
Land use:
arable land: 0%
permanent crops: 0%
other: 100% (1998 est.)

Irrigated land: NA sq km
Natural hazards: NA
Environment - current issues: limited natural freshwater resources: large concrete or natural rock water catchments collect rainwater (no longer used for drinking water) and adequate desalination plant
Geography - note: strategic location on Strait of Gibraltar that links the North Atlantic Ocean and Mediterranean Sea

People

Population: 27,833 (July 2004 est.)
Age structure:
0-14 years: 18% (male 2,554; female 2,452)
15-64 years: 66.2% (male 9,460; female 8,965)
65 years and over: 15.8% (male 1,939; female 2,463) (2004 est.)
Median age:
total: 39 years
male: 38.8 years
female: 39.2 years (2004 est.)
Population growth rate: 0.19% (2004 est.)
Birth rate: 10.99 births/1,000 population (2004 est.)
Death rate: 9.05 deaths/1,000 population (2004 est.)
Net migration rate: 0 migrant(s)/1,000 population (2004 est.)
Sex ratio:
at birth: 1.05 male(s)/female
under 15 years: 1.04 male(s)/female
15-64 years: 1.06 male(s)/female
65 years and over: 0.79 male(s)/female
total population: 1.01 male(s)/female (2004 est.)
Infant mortality rate:
total: 5.22 deaths/1,000 live births
male: 5.81 deaths/1,000 live births
female: 4.59 deaths/1,000 live births (2004 est.)
Life expectancy at birth:
total population: 79.52 years
male: 76.65 years
female: 82.54 years (2004 est.)
Total fertility rate: 1.65 children born/woman (2004 est.)
HIV/AIDS - adult prevalence rate: NA%
HIV/AIDS - people living with HIV/AIDS: NA
HIV/AIDS - deaths: NA
Nationality:
noun: Gibraltarian(s)
adjective: Gibraltar
Ethnic groups: Spanish, Italian, English, Maltese, Portuguese
Religions: Roman Catholic 76.9%, Church of England 6.9%, Muslim 6.9%, Jewish 2.3%, none or other 7% (1991)
Languages: English (used in schools and for official purposes), Spanish, Italian, Portuguese
Literacy:
definition: NA
total population: above 80%
male: NA%
female: NA%

Gibraltar (continued)

Government

Country name:
conventional long form: none
conventional short form: Gibraltar
Dependency status: overseas territory of the UK
Government type: NA
Capital: Gibraltar
Administrative divisions: none (overseas territory of the UK)
Independence: none (overseas territory of the UK)
National holiday: National Day, 10 September (1967); note - day of the national referendum to decide whether to remain with the UK or go with Spain
Constitution: 30 May 1969
Legal system: English law
Suffrage: 18 years of age; universal, plus other UK subjects who have been residents six months or more
Executive branch:
chief of state: Queen ELIZABETH II (since 6 February 1952), represented by Governor and Commander-in-Chief Sir Francis RICHARDS (since 27 May 2003)
head of government: Chief Minister Peter CARUANA (since 17 May 1996)
cabinet: Council of Ministers appointed from among the 15 elected members of the House of Assembly by the governor in consultation with the chief minister
elections: none; the monarch is hereditary; governor appointed by the monarch; following legislative elections, the leader of the majority party or the leader of the majority coalition is usually appointed chief minister by the governor
Legislative branch: unicameral House of Assembly (18 seats - 15 elected by popular vote, one appointed for the Speaker, and two ex officio members; members serve four-year terms)
elections: last held 27 November 2003 (next to be held not later than NA 2007)
election results: percent of vote by party - GSD 58%, GSLP 41%; seats by party - GSD 8, GSLP 7
Judicial branch: Supreme Court; Court of Appeal
Political parties and leaders: Gibraltar Liberal Party [Joseph GARCIA]; Gibraltar Social Democrats or GSD [Peter CARUANA]; Gibraltar Socialist Labor Party or GSLP [Joseph John BOSSANO]
Political pressure groups and leaders: Chamber of Commerce; Gibraltar Representatives Organization; Women's Association
International organization participation: Interpol (subbureau)
Diplomatic representation in the US: none (overseas territory of the UK)
Diplomatic representation from the US: none (overseas territory of the UK)
Flag description: two horizontal bands of white (top, double width) and red with a three-towered red castle in the center of the white band; hanging from the castle gate is a gold key centered in the red band

Economy

Economy - overview: Gibraltar benefits from an extensive shipping trade, offshore banking, and its position as an international conference center. The British military presence has been sharply reduced and now contributes about 7% to the local economy, compared with 60% in 1984. The financial sector, tourism (almost 5 million visitors in 1998), shipping services fees, and duties on consumer goods also generate revenue. The financial sector, the shipping sector, and tourism each contribute 25%-30% of GDP. Telecommunications accounts for another 10%. In recent years, Gibraltar has seen major structural change from a public to a private sector economy, but changes in government spending still have a major impact on the level of employment.
GDP: purchasing power parity - $500 million (1997 est.)
GDP - real growth rate: NA%
GDP - per capita: purchasing power parity - $17,500 (1997 est.)
GDP - composition by sector:
agriculture: NA%
industry: NA%
services: NA% (2002 est.)
Population below poverty line: NA%
Household income or consumption by percentage share:
lowest 10%: NA%
highest 10%: NA%
Inflation rate (consumer prices): 1.5% (1998)
Labor force: 14,800 (including non-Gibraltar laborers) (1999)
Labor force - by occupation: services 60%, industry 40%, agriculture NEGL%
Unemployment rate: 2% (2001 est.)
Budget:
revenues: $307 million
expenditures: $284 million, including capital expenditures of $NA (FY00/01 est.)
Industries: tourism, banking and finance, ship repairing, tobacco
Industrial production growth rate: NA%
Electricity - production: 100 million kWh (2001)
Electricity - production by source:
fossil fuel: 100%
hydro: 0%
nuclear: 0%
other: 0% (2001)
Electricity - consumption: 93 million kWh (2001)
Electricity - exports: 0 kWh (2001)
Electricity - imports: 0 kWh (2001)
Oil - production: 0 bbl/day (2001 est.)
Oil - consumption: 42,000 bbl/day (2001 est.)
Oil - exports: NA
Oil - imports: NA
Agriculture - products: none
Exports: $136 million f.o.b. (2002)
Exports - commodities: (principally reexports) petroleum 51%, manufactured goods 41%, other 8%
Exports - partners: Switzerland 28.7%, UK 22.8%, Germany 9.6%, France 5.9%, Hong Kong 5.1%, Spain 5.1%, Turkmenistan 4.4% (2002)
Imports: $1.743 billion c.i.f. (2002)
Imports - commodities: fuels, manufactured goods, and foodstuffs
Imports - partners: Germany 27.5%, Spain 21.9%, UK 12.2%, Italy 8% (2002)
Debt - external: $NA (2000 est.)
Economic aid - recipient: $NA
Currency: Gibraltar pound (GIP)
Currency code: GIP
Exchange rates: Gibraltar pounds per US dollar - 0.6661 (2002), 0.6944 (2001), 0.6596 (2000), 0.6180 (1999), 0.6037 (1998); note - the Gibraltar pound is at par with the British pound
Fiscal year: 1 July - 30 June

Communications

Telephones - main lines in use: 24,512 (2002)
Telephones - mobile cellular: 9,797 (2002)
Telephone system:
general assessment: adequate, automatic domestic system and adequate international facilities
domestic: automatic exchange facilities
international: country code - 350; radiotelephone; microwave radio relay; satellite earth station - 1 Intelsat (Atlantic Ocean)
Radio broadcast stations: AM 1, FM 5, shortwave 0 (1998)
Television broadcast stations: 1 (plus three low-power repeaters) (1997)
Internet country code: .gi
Internet users: 6,200 (2002)

Transportation

Highways:
total: 29 km
paved: 29 km
unpaved: 0 km (2002)
Waterways: none
Pipelines: 0 km
Ports and harbors: Gibraltar
Merchant marine:
total: 133 ships (1,000 GRT or over) 980,636 GRT/ 1,254,661 DWT
by type: bulk 3, cargo 69, chemical tanker 14, container 27, multi-functional large load carrier 3, passenger 2, petroleum tanker 13, roll on/roll off 2
foreign-owned: Belgium 1, Cyprus 3, Denmark 1, Estonia 1, France 1, Germany 92, Greece 11, Hong Kong 2, Iceland 1, Monaco 4, Norway 6, Spain 1, United Kingdom 6, United States 2
registered in other countries: 4 (2003 est.)
Airports: 1 (2003 est.)
Airports - with paved runways:
total: 1
1,524 to 2,437 m: 1 (2003 est.)

Military

Military branches: Royal Gibraltar Regiment
Military - note: defense is the responsibility of the UK; the last British regular infantry forces left Gibraltar in 1992, replaced by the Royal Gibraltar Regiment

Transnational Issues

Disputes - international: since Gibraltar residents voted overwhelmingly by referendum in 2003 against a "total shared sovereignty" arrangement, talks between the UK and Spain over the fate of the 300-year-old UK colony have stalled; Spain disapproves of UK plans to grant Gibraltar greater autonomy

Glorioso Islands
(possession of France)

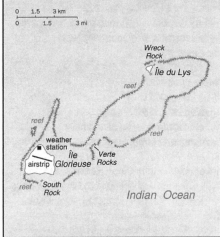

Introduction

Background: A French possession since 1892, the Glorioso Islands are composed of two lushly vegetated coral islands (Ile Glorieuse and Ile du Lys) and three rock islets. A military garrison operates a weather and radio station on Ile Glorieuse.

Geography

Location: Southern Africa, group of islands in the Indian Ocean, northwest of Madagascar
Geographic coordinates: 11 30 S, 47 20 E
Map references: Africa
Area:
total: 5 sq km
land: 5 sq km
water: 0 sq km
note: includes Ile Glorieuse, Ile du Lys, Verte Rocks, Wreck Rock, and South Rock
Area - comparative: about eight times the size of The Mall in Washington, DC
Land boundaries: 0 km
Coastline: 35.2 km
Maritime claims:
territorial sea: 12 NM
exclusive economic zone: 200 NM
Climate: tropical
Terrain: low and flat
Elevation extremes:
lowest point: Indian Ocean 0 m
highest point: unnamed location 12 m
Natural resources: guano, coconuts
Land use:
arable land: 0%
permanent crops: 0%
other: 100% (all lush vegetation and coconut palms) (1998 est.)
Irrigated land: 0 sq km (1998 est.)
Natural hazards: periodic cyclones

Environment - current issues: NA
Geography - note: the islands and rocks are surrounded by an extensive reef system

People

Population: no indigenous inhabitants
note: there is a small French military garrison along with a few meteorologists; visited by scientists (July 2004 est.)

Government

Country name:
conventional long form: none
conventional short form: Glorioso Islands
local long form: none
local short form: Iles Glorieuses
Dependency status: possession of France; administered by a high commissioner of the Republic, resident in Reunion
Legal system: the laws of France, where applicable, apply
Diplomatic representation in the US: none (possession of France)
Diplomatic representation from the US: none (possession of France)
Flag description: the flag of France is used

Economy

Economy - overview: no economic activity

Communications

Communications - note: 1 meteorological station

Transportation

Waterways: none
Ports and harbors: none; offshore anchorage only
Airports: 1 (2003 est.)
Airports - with unpaved runways:
total: 1
914 to 1,523 m: 1 (2003 est.)

Military

Military - note: defense is the responsibility of France

Transnational Issues

Disputes - international: claimed by Madagascar

Greece

Introduction

Background: Greece achieved its independence from the Ottoman Empire in 1829. During the second half of the 19th century and the first half of the 20th century, it gradually added neighboring islands and territories, most with Greek-speaking populations. Following the defeat of Communist rebels in 1949, Greece joined NATO in 1952. A military dictatorship, which in 1967 suspended many political liberties and forced the king to flee the country, lasted seven years. The 1974 democratic elections and a referendum created a parliamentary republic and abolished the monarchy; Greece joined the European Community or EC in 1981 (which became the EU in 1992).

Geography

Location: Southern Europe, bordering the Aegean Sea, Ionian Sea, and the Mediterranean Sea, between Albania and Turkey
Geographic coordinates: 39 00 N, 22 00 E
Map references: Europe
Area:
total: 131,940 sq km
land: 130,800 sq km
water: 1,140 sq km
Area - comparative: slightly smaller than Alabama
Land boundaries:
total: 1,228 km
border countries: Albania 282 km, Bulgaria 494 km, Turkey 206 km, The Former Yugoslav Republic of Macedonia 246 km
Coastline: 13,676 km
Maritime claims:
territorial sea: 12 NM
continental shelf: 200-m depth or to the depth of exploitation
Climate: temperate; mild, wet winters; hot, dry summers

Terrain: mostly mountains with ranges extending into the sea as peninsulas or chains of islands
Elevation extremes:
lowest point: Mediterranean Sea 0 m
highest point: Mount Olympus 2,917 m
Natural resources: bauxite, lignite, magnesite, petroleum, marble, hydropower potential
Land use:
arable land: 22%
permanent crops: 8%
other: 70% (2004 est.)
Irrigated land: 14,220 sq km (1998 est.)
Natural hazards: severe earthquakes
Environment - current issues: air pollution; water pollution
Environment - international agreements:
party to: Air Pollution, Air Pollution-Nitrogen Oxides, Air Pollution-Sulfur 94, Antarctic-Environmental Protocol, Antarctic-Marine Living Resources, Antarctic Treaty, Biodiversity, Climate Change, Climate Change-Kyoto Protocol, Desertification, Endangered Species, Environmental Modification, Hazardous Wastes, Law of the Sea, Marine Dumping, Ozone Layer Protection, Ship Pollution, Tropical Timber 83, Tropical Timber 94, Wetlands
signed, but not ratified: Air Pollution-Persistent Organic Pollutants, Air Pollution-Volatile Organic Compounds
Geography - note: strategic location dominating the Aegean Sea and southern approach to Turkish Straits; a peninsular country, possessing an archipelago of about 2,000 islands

People

Population: 10,647,529 (July 2004 est.)
Age structure:
0-14 years: 14.5% (male 792,938; female 746,119)
15-64 years: 67% (male 3,563,703; female 3,566,549)
65 years and over: 18.6% (male 873,540; female 1,104,680) (2004 est.)
Median age:
total: 40.2 years
male: 39.1 years
female: 41.3 years (2004 est.)
Population growth rate: 0.2% (2004 est.)
Birth rate: 9.73 births/1,000 population (2004 est.)
Death rate: 10.08 deaths/1,000 population (2004 est.)
Net migration rate: 2.35 migrant(s)/1,000 population (2004 est.)
Sex ratio:
at birth: 1.06 male(s)/female
under 15 years: 1.06 male(s)/female
15-64 years: 1 male(s)/female
65 years and over: 0.79 male(s)/female
total population: 0.97 male(s)/female (2004 est.)
Infant mortality rate:
total: 5.63 deaths/1,000 live births
male: 6.19 deaths/1,000 live births
female: 5.04 deaths/1,000 live births (2004 est.)

Life expectancy at birth:
total population: 78.94 years
male: 76.44 years
female: 81.59 years (2004 est.)
Total fertility rate: 1.32 children born/woman (2004 est.)
HIV/AIDS - adult prevalence rate: 0.2% (2001 est.)
HIV/AIDS - people living with HIV/AIDS: 8,800 (2001 est.)
HIV/AIDS - deaths: less than 100 (2001 est.)
Nationality:
noun: Greek(s)
adjective: Greek
Ethnic groups: Greek 98%, other 2%
note: the Greek Government states there are no ethnic divisions in Greece
Religions: Greek Orthodox 98%, Muslim 1.3%, other 0.7%
Languages: Greek 99% (official), English, French
Literacy:
definition: age 15 and over can read and write
total population: 97.5%
male: 98.6%
female: 96.5% (2003 est.)

Government

Country name:
conventional long form: Hellenic Republic
conventional short form: Greece
local long form: Elliniki Dhimokratia
local short form: Ellas or Ellada
former: Kingdom of Greece
Government type: parliamentary republic; monarchy rejected by referendum 8 December 1974
Capital: Athens
Administrative divisions: 51 prefectures (nomoi, singular - nomos) and 1 autonomous region*; Agion Oros* (Mt. Athos), Achaia, Aitolia kai Akarmania, Argolis, Arkadia, Arta, Attiki, Chalkidiki, Chanion, Chios, Dodekanisos, Drama, Evros, Evrytania, Evvoia, Florina, Fokidos, Fthiotis, Grevena, Ileia, Imathia, Ioannina, Irakleion, Karditsa, Kastoria, Kavala, Kefallinia, Kerkyra, Kilkis, Korinthia, Kozani, Kyklades, Lakonia, Larisa, Lasithi, Lefkas, Lesvos, Magnisia, Messinia, Pella, Pieria, Preveza, Rethynnis, Rodopi, Samos, Serrai, Thesprotia, Thessaloniki, Trikala, Voiotia, Xanthi, Zakynthos
Independence: 1829 (from the Ottoman Empire)
National holiday: Independence Day, 25 March (1821)
Constitution: 11 June 1975; amended March 1986 and April 2001
Legal system: based on codified Roman law; judiciary divided into civil, criminal, and administrative courts
Suffrage: 18 years of age; universal and compulsory
Executive branch:
chief of state: President Konstandinos (Kostis) STEPHANOPOULOS (since 10 March 1995)
head of government: Prime Minister Konstandinos KARAMANLIS (since NA March 2004)

Greece *(continued)*

cabinet: Cabinet appointed by the president on the recommendation of the prime minister

elections: president elected by Parliament for a five-year term; election last held 8 February 2000 (next to be held by NA February 2005); president appoints leader of the party securing plurality of vote in election

election results: Konstandinos STEPHANOPOULOS reelected president; percent of Parliament vote - 90%

Legislative branch: unicameral Parliament or Vouli ton Ellinon (300 seats; members are elected by direct popular vote to serve four-year terms)

elections: elections last held 7 March 2004 (next to be held by March 2008)

election results: percent of vote by party - ND 45.4%, PASOK 40.6%, KKE 5.9%, Synaspismos 3.3%; seats by party - ND 165, PASOK 117, KKE 12, Synaspismos 6

Judicial branch: Supreme Judicial Court; Special Supreme Tribunal; all judges appointed for life by the president after consultation with a judicial council

Political parties and leaders: Coalition of the Left and Progress (Synaspismos) [Nikolaos KONSTANTOPOULOS]; Communist Party of Greece or KKE [Aleka PAPARIGA]; New Democracy or ND (conservative) [Konstandinos KARAMANLIS]; Panhellenic Socialist Movement or PASOK [Yiorgos PAPANDREOU]

Political pressure groups and leaders: NA

International organization participation: Australia Group, BIS, BSEC, CE, CERN, EAPC, EBRD, EIB, EMU, EU, FAO, G- 6, IAEA, IBRD, ICAO, ICC, ICCt, ICFTU, ICRM, IDA, IEA, IFAD, IFC, IFRCS, IHO, ILO, IMF, IMO, Interpol, IOC, IOM, ISO, ITU, MINURSO, NAM (guest), NATO, NEA, NSG, OAS (observer), OECD, OPCW, OSCE, PCA, UN, UNCTAD, UNESCO, UNHCR, UNIDO, UNMEE, UNMIK, UNOMIG, UPU, WCO, WEU, WFTU, WHO, WIPO, WMO, WToO, WTrO, ZC

Diplomatic representation in the US:

chief of mission: Ambassador Yeoryios SAVVAIDIS

chancery: 2221 Massachusetts Avenue NW, Washington, DC 20008

telephone: [1] (202) 939-1300

FAX: [1] (202) 939-1324

consulate(s) general: Boston, Chicago, Los Angeles, New York, and San Francisco

consulate(s): Atlanta, Houston, and New Orleans

Diplomatic representation from the US:

chief of mission: Ambassador Thomas J. MILLER

embassy: 91 Vasilissis Sophias Avenue, 101 60 Athens

mailing address: PSC 108, APO AE 09842-0108

telephone: [30] (210) 721-2951

FAX: [30] (210) 645-6282

consulate(s) general: Thessaloniki

Flag description: nine equal horizontal stripes of blue alternating with white; there is a blue square in the upper hoist-side corner bearing a white cross; the cross symbolizes Greek Orthodoxy, the established religion of the country

Economy

Economy - overview: Greece has a mixed capitalist economy with the public sector accounting for half of GDP and with per capita GDP 70% of the leading euro-zone economies. Tourism provides 15% of GDP. Immigrants make up nearly one-fifth of the work force, mainly in menial jobs. Greece is a major beneficiary of EU aid, equal to about 3.3% of GDP. The Greek economy grew by 4.0% in 2003 and is expected to grow by 4.2% in 2004, the year that Athens will host the 2004 Olympic Games. Remaining challenges include the reduction of the public debt, inflation, and unemployment; and further restructuring of the economy, including privatizing several state enterprises, undertaking pension and other reforms, and minimizing bureaucratic inefficiencies.

GDP: purchasing power parity - $212.2 billion (2003 est.)

GDP - real growth rate: 4% (2003 est.)

GDP - per capita: purchasing power parity - $19,900 (2003 est.)

GDP - composition by sector:

agriculture: 8.1%

industry: 22.3%

services: 69.3% (2002 est.)

Population below poverty line: NA%

Household income or consumption by percentage share:

lowest 10%: 3%

highest 10%: 25.3% (1993 est.)

Distribution of family income - Gini index: 32.7 (1993)

Inflation rate (consumer prices): 3.3% (2003 est.)

Labor force: 4,406,700 (2nd quarter 2003 est.)

Labor force - by occupation: industry 20%, agriculture 20%, services 59% (2000 est.)

Unemployment rate: 9.8% (2003 est.)

Budget:

revenues: $45 billion

expenditures: $47.6 billion, including capital expenditures of $NA (1998 est.)

Industries: tourism; food and tobacco processing, textiles; chemicals, metal products; mining, petroleum

Industrial production growth rate: 7% (2000 est.)

Electricity - production: 49.79 billion kWh (2001)

Electricity - production by source:

fossil fuel: 94.5%

hydro: 3.8%

nuclear: 0%

other: 1.7% (2001)

Electricity - consumption: 48.8 billion kWh (2001)

Electricity - exports: 1.062 billion kWh (2001)

Electricity - imports: 3.562 billion kWh (2001)

Oil - production: 5,992 bbl/day (2001 est.)

Oil - consumption: 405,700 bbl/day (2001 est.)

Oil - exports: 84,720 bbl/day (2001)

Oil - imports: 468,300 bbl/day (2001)

Oil - proved reserves: 4.5 million bbl (1 January 2002)

Natural gas - production: 35 million cu m (2001 est.)

Natural gas - consumption: 2.021 billion cu m (2001 est.)

Natural gas - exports: 0 cu m (2001 est.)

Natural gas - imports: 2.018 billion cu m (2001 est.)

Natural gas - proved reserves: 254.9 million cu m (1 January 2002)

Agriculture - products: wheat, corn, barley, sugar beets, olives, tomatoes, wine, tobacco, potatoes; beef, dairy products

Exports: $5.899 billion f.o.b. (2003 est.)

Exports - commodities: food and beverages, manufactured goods, petroleum products, chemicals, textiles

Exports - partners: Germany 10.4%, Italy 8.5%, UK 6.3%, Bulgaria 5.4%, US 5.3%, Cyprus 4.7% (2002)

Imports: $33.27 billion f.o.b. (2003 est.)

Imports - commodities: machinery, transport equipment, fuels, chemicals

Imports - partners: Germany 12.2%, Italy 11.5%, Russia 7.4%, South Korea 6%, France 5.7%, Netherlands 5.6%, US 4.7%, Belgium 4.3%, UK 4.1% (2002)

Debt - external: $63.4 billion (2002 est.)

Economic aid - recipient: $5.4 billion from EU (1995)

Currency: euro (EUR)

note: on 1 January 1999, the European Monetary Union introduced the euro as a common currency to be used by financial institutions of member countries; on 1 January 2002, the euro became the sole currency for everyday transactions within the member countries

Currency code: EUR

Exchange rates: euros per US dollar - 0.886 (2003), 1.0626 (2002), 1.1175 (2001), 365.399 (2000), 305.647 (1999)

Fiscal year: calendar year

Communications

Telephones - main lines in use: 5,412,800 (2002)

Telephones - mobile cellular: 9,314,300 (2002)

Telephone system:

general assessment: adequate, modern networks reach all areas; good mobile telephone and international service

domestic: microwave radio relay trunk system; extensive open-wire connections; submarine cable to offshore islands

international: country code - 30; tropospheric scatter; 8 submarine cables; satellite earth stations - 2 Intelsat (1 Atlantic Ocean and 1 Indian Ocean), 1 Eutelsat, and 1 Inmarsat (Indian Ocean region)

Radio broadcast stations: AM 26, FM 88, shortwave 4 (1998)

Television broadcast stations: 36 (plus 1,341 low-power repeaters); also two stations in the US Armed Forces Radio and Television Service (1995)

Internet country code: .gr

Internet hosts: 160,829 (2002)

Internet users: 1,704,900 (2002)

Transportation

Railways:
total: 2,571 km (764 km electrified)
standard gauge: 1,565 km 1.435-m gauge
narrow gauge: 961 km 1.000-m gauge; 22 km
0.750-m gauge
dual gauge: 23 km combined 1.435-m and 1.000-m
gauges (three rail system) (2002)
Highways:
total: 117,000 km
paved: 107,406 km (including 470 km of
expressways)
unpaved: 9,594 km (1999 est.)
Waterways: 80 km
note: system consists of three coastal canals
including the Corinth Canal (6 km) which crosses the
Isthmus of Corinth connecting the Gulf of Corinth with
the Saronic Gulf and shortens the sea voyage from
the Adriatic to Peiraiefs (Piraeus) by 325 km; there are
also three unconnected rivers
Pipelines: gas 1,531 km; oil 108 km (2003)
Ports and harbors: Alexandroupolis, Elefsis,
Irakleion (Crete), Kavala, Kerkyra, Chalkis,
Igoumenitsa, Lavrion, Patrai, Peiraiefs (Piraeus),
Thessaloniki, Volos
Merchant marine:
total: 793 ships (1,000 GRT or over) 30,186,624 GRT/
52,943,968 DWT
by type: bulk 298, cargo 57, chemical tanker 38,
combination bulk 5, combination ore/oil 3, container 49,
liquefied gas 5, passenger 10, petroleum tanker 267,
refrigerated cargo 1, roll on/roll off 19, short-sea/
passenger 38, specialized tanker 3
foreign-owned: Belgium 1, Cyprus 1, Israel 1, Italy 1,
Liberia 3, Malta 1, Marshall Islands 1, Norway 2,
Panama 3, Singapore 1, Sweden 1, United Kingdom 2,
United States 5
registered in other countries: 2,443 (2003 est.)
Airports: 79 (note - new Athens airport at Spata
opened in March 2001) (2003 est.)
Airports - with paved runways:
total: 65
over 3,047 m: 6
2,438 to 3,047 m: 15
1,524 to 2,437 m: 20
914 to 1,523 m: 16
under 914 m: 8 (2003 est.)
Airports - with unpaved runways:
total: 14
914 to 1,523 m: 3
under 914 m: 11 (2003 est.)
Heliports: 7 (2003 est.)

Military

Military branches: Hellenic Army, Hellenic Navy,
Hellenic Air Force (EPA), National Guard
Military manpower - military age: 19 years of age
(2004 est.)
Military manpower - availability:
males age 15-49: 2,638,949 (2004 est.)
Military manpower - fit for military service:
males age 15-49: 2,004,343 (2004 est.)
**Military manpower - reaching military age
annually:**
males: 63,496 (2004 est.)
Military expenditures - dollar figure:
$7,288,900,000 (2003)
Military expenditures - percent of GDP: 4.3%
(2003)

Transnational Issues

Disputes - international: Greece and Turkey have
resumed discussions to resolve their complex
maritime, air, territorial, and boundary disputes in the
Aegean Sea; Cyprus question with Turkey; dispute
with The Former Yugoslav Republic of Macedonia
over its name
Illicit drugs: a gateway to Europe for traffickers
smuggling cannabis and heroin from the Middle East
and Southwest Asia to the West and precursor
chemicals to the East; some South American cocaine
transits or is consumed in Greece; money laundering
related to drug trafficking and organized crime

Greenland
(part of the Kingdom of Denmark)

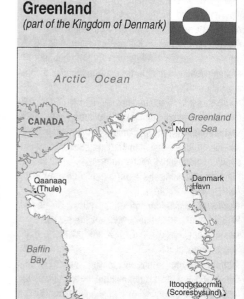

Introduction

Background: The world's largest non-continental
island, about 81% ice-capped, Greenland was
granted self-government in 1979 by the Danish
parliament. The law went into effect the following year.
Denmark continues to exercise control of Greenland's
foreign affairs.

Geography

Location: Northern North America, island between
the Arctic Ocean and the North Atlantic Ocean,
northeast of Canada
Geographic coordinates: 72 00 N, 40 00 W
Map references: Arctic Region
Area:
total: 2,166,086 sq km
land: 2,166,086 sq km (410,449 sq km ice-free,
1,755,637 sq km ice-covered) (2000 est.)
Area - comparative: slightly more than three times
the size of Texas
Land boundaries: 0 km
Coastline: 44,087 km

Greenland (continued)

Maritime claims:
territorial sea: 3 NM
continental shelf: 200 NM or agreed boundaries or median line
exclusive fishing zone: 200 NM or agreed boundaries or median line
Climate: arctic to subarctic; cool summers, cold winters
Terrain: flat to gradually sloping icecap covers all but a narrow, mountainous, barren, rocky coast
Elevation extremes:
lowest point: Atlantic Ocean 0 m
highest point: Gunnbjorn 3,700 m
Natural resources: zinc, lead, iron ore, coal, molybdenum, gold, platinum, uranium, fish, seals, whales, hydropower, possible oil and gas
Land use:
arable land: 0%
permanent crops: 0%
other: 100% (1998 est.)
Irrigated land: NA sq km
Natural hazards: continuous permafrost over northern two-thirds of the island
Environment - current issues: protection of the arctic environment; preservation of the Inuit traditional way of life, including whaling and seal hunting
Geography - note: dominates North Atlantic Ocean between North America and Europe; sparse population confined to small settlements along coast, but close to one-quarter of the population lives in the capital, Nuuk; world's second largest ice cap

People

Population: 56,384 (July 2004 est.)
Age structure:
0-14 years: 25.5% (male 7,344; female 7,029)
15-64 years: 68.5% (male 20,894; female 17,715)
65 years and over: 6% (male 1,585; female 1,817) (2004 est.)
Median age:
total: 33.5 years
male: 34.8 years
female: 31.9 years (2004 est.)
Population growth rate: -0.01% (2004 est.)
Birth rate: 15.96 births/1,000 population (2004 est.)
Death rate: 7.7 deaths/1,000 population (2004 est.)
Net migration rate: -8.37 migrant(s)/1,000 population (2004 est.)
Sex ratio:
at birth: 1.02 male(s)/female
under 15 years: 1.05 male(s)/female
15-64 years: 1.18 male(s)/female
65 years and over: 0.87 male(s)/female
total population: 1.12 male(s)/female (2004 est.)
Infant mortality rate:
total: 16.31 deaths/1,000 live births
male: 17.62 deaths/1,000 live births
female: 14.96 deaths/1,000 live births (2004 est.)

Life expectancy at birth:
total population: 69.32 years
male: 65.75 years
female: 72.98 years (2004 est.)
Total fertility rate: 2.42 children born/woman (2004 est.)
HIV/AIDS - adult prevalence rate: NA%
HIV/AIDS - people living with HIV/AIDS: 100 (1999)
HIV/AIDS - deaths: NA
Nationality:
noun: Greenlander(s)
adjective: Greenlandic
Ethnic groups: Greenlander 88% (Inuit and Greenland-born whites), Danish and others 12% (January 2000)
Religions: Evangelical Lutheran
Languages: Greenlandic (East Inuit), Danish, English
Literacy:
definition: NA
total population: NA%
male: NA%
female: NA%
note: similar to Denmark proper

Government

Country name:
conventional long form: none
conventional short form: Greenland
local long form: none
local short form: Kalaallit Nunaat
Dependency status: part of the Kingdom of Denmark; self-governing overseas administrative division of Denmark since 1979
Government type: parliamentary democracy within a constitutional monarchy
Capital: Nuuk (Godthab)
Administrative divisions: 3 districts (landsdele); Avannaa (Nordgronland), Tunu (Ostgronland), Kitaa (Vestgronland)
note: there are 18 municipalities in Greenland
Independence: none (part of the Kingdom of Denmark; self-governing overseas administrative division of Denmark since 1979)
note: foreign affairs is the responsibility of Denmark, but Greenland actively participates in international agreements relating to Greenland
National holiday: June 21 (longest day)
Constitution: 5 June 1953 (Danish constitution)
Legal system: Danish
Suffrage: 18 years of age; universal
Executive branch:
chief of state: Queen MARGRETHE II of Denmark (since 14 January 1972), represented by High Commissioner Gunnar MARTENS (since NA 1995)
head of government: Prime Minister Hans ENOKSEN (since 14 December 2002)
cabinet: Home Rule Government is elected by the Parliament (Landstinget) on the basis of the strength of parties

elections: the monarchy is hereditary; high commissioner appointed by the monarch; prime minister is elected by Parliament (usually the leader of the majority party); election last held 3 December 2002 (next to be held NA December 2006)
election results: Hans ENOKSEN elected prime minister
note: government coalition - Siumut and Inuit Ataqatigiit
Legislative branch: unicameral Parliament or Landstinget (31 seats; members are elected by popular vote on the basis of proportional representation to serve four-year terms)
elections: last held on 3 December 2002 (next to be held by NA December 2006)
election results: percent of vote by party - Siumut 28.7%, Inuit Ataqatigiit 25.5%, Atassut Party 20.4%, Demokratiit 15.6%, Katusseqatigiit 5.3%; seats by party - Siumut 10, Inuit Ataqatigiit 8, Atassut 7, Demokratiit 5, Katusseqatigiit 1
note: two representatives were elected to the Danish Parliament or Folketing on 20 November 2001 (next to be held no later than November 2005); percent of vote by party - NA%; seats by party - Siumut 1, Inuit Ataqatigiit 1
Judicial branch: High Court or Landsret (appeals can be made to the Ostre Landsret or Eastern Division of the High Court or Supreme Court in Copenhagen)
Political parties and leaders: Akulliit Party [Bjarne KREUTZMANN]; Atassut Party (Solidarity, a conservative party favoring continuing close relations with Denmark) [Augusta SALLING]; Demokratiit [Per BERTHELSEN]; Inuit Ataqatigiit or IA (Eskimo Brotherhood, a leftist party favoring complete independence from Denmark rather than home rule) [Josef MOTZFELDT]; Issituup (Polar Party) [Nicolai HEINRICH]; Kattusseqatigiit (Candidate List, an independent right-of-center party with no official platform [leader NA]; Siumut (Forward Party, a social democratic party advocating more distinct Greenlandic identity and greater autonomy from Denmark) [Hans ENOKSEN]
Political pressure groups and leaders: NA
International organization participation: NC, NIB
Diplomatic representation in the US: none (self-governing overseas administrative division of Denmark)
Diplomatic representation from the US: none (self-governing overseas administrative division of Denmark)
Flag description: two equal horizontal bands of white (top) and red with a large disk slightly to the hoist side of center - the top half of the disk is red, the bottom half is white

Economy

Economy - overview: The economy remains critically dependent on exports of fish and substantial support from the Danish Government, which supplies about half of government revenues. The public sector, including publicly-owned enterprises and the

Greenland (continued)

municipalities, plays the dominant role in the economy. Despite several interesting hydrocarbon and minerals exploration activities, it will take several years before production can materialize. Tourism is the only sector offering any near-term potential, and even this is limited due to a short season and high costs.

GDP: purchasing power parity - $1.1 billion (2001 est.)

GDP - real growth rate: 1.8% (2001 est.)

GDP - per capita: purchasing power parity - $20,000 (2001 est.)

GDP - composition by sector:
agriculture: NA%
industry: NA%
services: NA%

Population below poverty line: NA%

Household income or consumption by percentage share:
lowest 10%: NA%
highest 10%: NA%

Inflation rate (consumer prices): 1.6% (1999 est.)

Labor force: 24,500 (1999 est.)

Unemployment rate: 10% (2000 est.)

Budget:
revenues: $646 million
expenditures: $629 million, including capital expenditures of $85 million (1999)

Industries: fish processing (mainly shrimp and Greenland halibut), handicrafts, hides and skins, small shipyards, mining

Industrial production growth rate: NA%

Electricity - production: 245 million kWh (2001)

Electricity - production by source:
fossil fuel: 100%
hydro: 0%
nuclear: 0%
other: 0%
note: Greenland is shifting its electricity production from fossil fuel to hydropower production (2001)

Electricity - consumption: 227.9 million kWh (2001)

Electricity - exports: 0 kWh (2001)

Electricity - imports: 0 kWh (2001)

Oil - production: 0 bbl/day (2001 est.)

Oil - consumption: 3,700 bbl/day (2001 est.)

Oil - exports: NA

Oil - imports: NA

Agriculture - products: forage crops, garden and greenhouse vegetables; sheep, reindeer; fish

Exports: $388 million f.o.b. (2002)

Exports - commodities: fish and fish products 94% (prawns 63%)

Exports - partners: Denmark 63.7%, Japan 14.4%, US 5.4%, Thailand 4.6% (2002)

Imports: $445 million c.i.f. (2002)

Imports - commodities: machinery and transport equipment, manufactured goods, food, petroleum products

Imports - partners: Denmark 82.5%, Norway 8.5%, Russia 1.8% (2002)

Debt - external: $25 million (1999)

Economic aid - recipient: $380 million subsidy from Denmark (1997)

Currency: Danish krone (DKK)

Currency code: DKK

Exchange rates: Danish kroner per US dollar - 6.5877 (2003), 7.8947 (2002), 8.323 (2001), 8.083 (2000), 6.976 (1999)

Fiscal year: calendar year

Communications

Telephones - main lines in use: 26,000 (2001)

Telephones - mobile cellular: 16,747 (2001)

Telephone system:
general assessment: adequate domestic and international service provided by satellite, cables and microwave radio relay; totally digitalized in 1995
domestic: microwave radio relay and satellite
international: country code - 299; satellite earth stations - 12 Intelsat, 1 Eutelsat, 2 Americom GE-2 (all Atlantic Ocean)

Radio broadcast stations: AM 5, FM 12, shortwave 0 (1998)

Television broadcast stations: 1 publicly-owned station, some local low-power stations, and three AFRTS (US Air Force) stations (1997)

Internet country code: .gl

Internet hosts: 2,583 (2001)

Internet users: 20,000 (2002)

Transportation

Railways: 0 km

Highways:
total: NA (there are no roads between towns) (2003)

Waterways: none

Ports and harbors: Aasiaat (Egedesminde), Ilulissat (Jakobshavn), Kangerlussuaq, Nanortalik, Narsarsuaq, Nuuk (Godthab), Qaqortoq (Julianehab), Sisimiut (Holsteinsborg), Tasiilaq

Merchant marine:
total: 3 ships (1,000 GRT or over) 4,593 GRT/3,640 DWT
by type: cargo 2, passenger 1
foreign-owned: Denmark 1 (2003 est.)

Airports: 14 (2003 est.)

Airports - with paved runways:
total: 9
over 3,047 m: 1
2,438 to 3,047 m: 1
1,524 to 2,437 m: 1
914 to 1,523 m: 1
under 914 m: 5 (2003 est.)

Airports - with unpaved runways:
total: 5
1,524 to 2,437 m: 1
914 to 1,523 m: 2
under 914 m: 2 (2003 est.)

Military

Military - note: defense is the responsibility of Denmark

Transnational Issues

Disputes - international: uncontested dispute between Canada and Denmark over Hans Island in the Kennedy Channel between Canada's Ellesmere Island and Greenland

Grenada

Introduction

Background: One of the smallest independent countries in the western hemisphere, Grenada was seized by a Marxist military council on 19 October 1983. Six days later the island was invaded by US forces and those of six other Caribbean nations, which quickly captured the ringleaders and their hundreds of Cuban advisers. Free elections were reinstituted the following year.

Geography

Location: Caribbean, island between the Caribbean Sea and Atlantic Ocean, north of Trinidad and Tobago
Geographic coordinates: 12 07 N, 61 40 W
Map references: Central America and the Caribbean
Area:
total: 344 sq km
land: 344 sq km
water: 0 sq km
Area - comparative: twice the size of Washington, DC
Land boundaries: 0 km
Coastline: 121 km
Maritime claims:
territorial sea: 12 NM
exclusive economic zone: 200 NM
Climate: tropical; tempered by northeast trade winds
Terrain: volcanic in origin with central mountains
Elevation extremes:
lowest point: Caribbean Sea 0 m
highest point: Mount Saint Catherine 840 m
Natural resources: timber, tropical fruit, deepwater harbors
Land use:
arable land: 5.88%
permanent crops: 26.47%
other: 67.65% (1998 est.)
Irrigated land: NA sq km
Natural hazards: lies on edge of hurricane belt; hurricane season lasts from June to November

Environment - current issues: NA
Environment - international agreements:
party to: Biodiversity, Climate Change, Climate Change-Kyoto Protocol, Desertification, Endangered Species, Law of the Sea, Ozone Layer Protection, Whaling
signed, but not ratified: none of the selected agreements
Geography - note: the administration of the islands of the Grenadines group is divided between Saint Vincent and the Grenadines and Grenada

People

Population: 89,357 (July 2004 est.)
Age structure:
0-14 years: 34.5% (male 15,580; female 15,212)
15-64 years: 62% (male 29,321; female 26,104)
65 years and over: 3.5% (male 1,467; female 1,673) (2004 est.)
Median age:
total: 20.9 years
male: 21.4 years
female: 20.4 years (2004 est.)
Population growth rate: 0.14% (2004 est.)
Birth rate: 22.61 births/1,000 population (2004 est.)
Death rate: 7.31 deaths/1,000 population (2004 est.)
Net migration rate: -13.92 migrant(s)/1,000 population (2004 est.)
Sex ratio:
at birth: 1 male(s)/female
under 15 years: 1.02 male(s)/female
15-64 years: 1.12 male(s)/female
65 years and over: 0.88 male(s)/female
total population: 1.08 male(s)/female (2004 est.)
Infant mortality rate:
total: 14.62 deaths/1,000 live births
male: 14.18 deaths/1,000 live births
female: 15.07 deaths/1,000 live births (2004 est.)
Life expectancy at birth:
total population: 64.52 years
male: 62.74 years
female: 66.31 years (2004 est.)
Total fertility rate: 2.41 children born/woman (2004 est.)
HIV/AIDS - adult prevalence rate: NA%
HIV/AIDS - people living with HIV/AIDS: NA
HIV/AIDS - deaths: NA
Nationality:
noun: Grenadian(s)
adjective: Grenadian
Ethnic groups: black 82%, mixed black and European 13%, European and East Indian 5% , and trace of Arawak/Carib Amerindian
Religions: Roman Catholic 53%, Anglican 13.8%, other Protestant 33.2%
Languages: English (official), French patois
Literacy:
definition: age 15 and over can read and write
total population: 98%
male: 98%
female: 98% (1970 est.)

Government

Country name:
conventional long form: none
conventional short form: Grenada
Government type: constitutional monarchy with Westminster-style parliament
Capital: Saint George's
Administrative divisions: 6 parishes and 1 dependency*; Carriacou and Petit Martinique*, Saint Andrew, Saint David, Saint George, Saint John, Saint Mark, Saint Patrick
Independence: 7 February 1974 (from UK)
National holiday: Independence Day, 7 February (1974)
Constitution: 19 December 1973
Legal system: based on English common law
Suffrage: 18 years of age; universal
Executive branch:
chief of state: Queen ELIZABETH II (since 6 February 1952), represented by Governor General Daniel WILLIAMS (since 9 August 1996)
head of government: Prime Minister Keith MITCHELL (since 22 June 1995)
cabinet: Cabinet appointed by the governor general on the advice of the prime minister
elections: none; the monarch is hereditary; governor general appointed by the monarch; following legislative elections, the leader of the majority party or the leader of the majority coalition is usually appointed prime minister by the governor general
Legislative branch: bicameral Parliament consists of the Senate (a 13-member body, 10 appointed by the government and three by the leader of the opposition) and the House of Representatives (15 seats; members are elected by popular vote to serve five-year terms)
elections: last held on 27 November 2003 (next to be held by NA November 2008)
election results: House of Representatives - percent of vote by party - NA%; seats by party - NNP 8, NDC 7
Judicial branch: West Indies Associate States Supreme Court (an associate judge resides in Grenada)
Political parties and leaders: Grenada United Labor Party or GULP [Herbert PREUDHOMME]; National Democratic Congress or NDC [leader vacant]; New National Party or NNP [George McGUIRE]; People Labor Movement or PLM [leader NA]
Political pressure groups and leaders: NA
International organization participation: ACP, C, Caricom, CDB, FAO, G-77, IBRD, ICAO, ICFTU, ICRM, IDA, IFAD, IFC, IFRCS, ILO, IMF, IMO, Interpol, IOC, ISO (subscriber), ITU, LAES, NAM, OAS, OECS, OPANAL, OPCW (signatory), UN, UNCTAD, UNESCO, UNIDO, UPU, WHO, WIPO, WTrO
Diplomatic representation in the US:
chief of mission: Ambassador Denis G. ANTOINE
chancery: 1701 New Hampshire Avenue NW, Washington, DC 20009

Grenada *(continued)*

telephone: [1] (202) 265-2561
FAX: [1] (202) 265-2468
consulate(s) general: New York
Diplomatic representation from the US:
chief of mission: the US Ambassador to Barbados, Ambassador Mary E. KRAMER, is accredited to Grenada
embassy: Lance-aux-Epines Stretch, Saint George's
mailing address: P. O. Box 54, Saint George's, Grenada, West Indies
telephone: [1] (473) 444-1173 through 1176
FAX: [1] (473) 444-4820
Flag description: a rectangle divided diagonally into yellow triangles (top and bottom) and green triangles (hoist side and outer side), with a red border around the flag; there are seven yellow, five-pointed stars with three centered in the top red border, three centered in the bottom red border, and one on a red disk superimposed at the center of the flag; there is also a symbolic nutmeg pod on the hoist-side triangle (Grenada is the world's second-largest producer of nutmeg, after Indonesia); the seven stars represent the seven administrative divisions

Economy

Economy - overview: Grenada relies on tourism as its main source of foreign exchange, especially since the construction of an international airport in 1985. Strong performances in construction and manufacturing, together with the development of an offshore financial industry, have also contributed to growth in national output.
GDP: purchasing power parity - $440 million (2002 est.)
GDP - real growth rate: 2.5% (2002 est.)
GDP - per capita: purchasing power parity - $5,000 (2002 est.)
GDP - composition by sector:
agriculture: 7.7%
industry: 23.9%
services: 68.4% (2000)
Population below poverty line: 32% (2000)
Household income or consumption by percentage share:
lowest 10%: NA%
highest 10%: NA%
Inflation rate (consumer prices): 2.8% (2001 est.)
Labor force: 42,300 (1996)
Labor force - by occupation: services 62%, agriculture 24%, industry 14% (1999 est.)
Unemployment rate: 12.5% (2000)
Budget:
revenues: $85.8 million
expenditures: $102.1 million, including capital expenditures of $28 million (1997)
Industries: food and beverages, textiles, light assembly operations, tourism, construction
Industrial production growth rate: 0.7% (1997 est.)
Electricity - production: 138 million kWh (2001)
Electricity - production by source:
fossil fuel: 100%

hydro: 0%
nuclear: 0%
other: 0% (2001)
Electricity - consumption: 128.3 million kWh (2001)
Electricity - exports: 0 kWh (2001)
Electricity - imports: 0 kWh (2001)
Oil - production: 0 bbl/day (2001 est.)
Oil - consumption: 1,000 bbl/day (2001 est.)
Oil - exports: NA
Oil - imports: NA
Agriculture - products: bananas, cocoa, nutmeg, mace, citrus, avocados, root crops, sugarcane, corn, vegetables
Exports: $46 million (2002 est.)
Exports - commodities: bananas, cocoa, nutmeg, fruit and vegetables, clothing, mace
Exports - partners: US 15.2%, Germany 13%, Bangladesh 10.9%, Netherlands 8.7%, Saint Lucia 6.5%, Antigua and Barbuda 4.3%, Dominica 4.3%, France 4.3%, Saint Kitts and Nevis 4.3%, Trinidad and Tobago 4.3%, UK 4.3% (2002)
Imports: $208 million (2002 est.)
Imports - commodities: food, manufactured goods, machinery, chemicals, fuel
Imports - partners: US 29.8%, Trinidad and Tobago 26.9%, UK 4.3% (2002)
Debt - external: $196 million (2000)
Economic aid - recipient: $8.3 million (1995)
Currency: East Caribbean dollar (XCD)
Currency code: XCD
Exchange rates: East Caribbean dollars per US dollar - 2.7 (2003), 2.7 (2002), 2.7 (2001), 2.7 (2000), 2.7 (1999)
Fiscal year: calendar year

Communications

Telephones - main lines in use: 33,500 (2002)
Telephones - mobile cellular: 7,600 (2002)
Telephone system:
general assessment: automatic, islandwide telephone system
domestic: interisland VHF and UHF radiotelephone links
international: country code - 1-473; new SHF radiotelephone links to Trinidad and Tobago and Saint Vincent; VHF and UHF radio links to Trinidad
Radio broadcast stations: AM 2, FM 13, shortwave 0 (1998)
Television broadcast stations: 2 (1997)
Internet country code: .gd
Internet hosts: 14 (2002)
Internet users: 15,000 (2002)

Transportation

Railways: 0 km
Highways:
total: 1,040 km
paved: 638 km
unpaved: 402 km (1999 est.)
Waterways: none

Ports and harbors: Grenville, Saint George's
Merchant marine: none
Airports: 3 (2003 est.)
Airports - with paved runways:
total: 3
2,438 to 3,047 m: 1
1,524 to 2,437 m: 1
under 914 m: 1 (2003 est.)

Military

Military branches: no regular military forces; Royal Grenada Police Force
Military expenditures - dollar figure: NA
Military expenditures - percent of GDP: NA

Transnational Issues

Disputes - international: none
Illicit drugs: small-scale cannabis cultivation; lesser transshipment point for marijuana and cocaine to US

Guadeloupe
(overseas department of France)

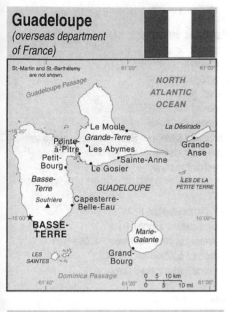

Introduction

Background: Guadeloupe has been a French possession since 1635. The island of Saint Martin is shared with the Netherlands; its southern portion is named Sint Maarten and is part of the Netherlands Antilles and its northern portion is named Saint-Martin and is part of Guadeloupe

Geography

Location: Caribbean, islands between the Caribbean Sea and the North Atlantic Ocean, southeast of Puerto Rico
Geographic coordinates: 16 15 N, 61 35 W
Map references: Central America and the Caribbean
Area:
total: 1,780 sq km
land: 1,706 sq km
water: 74 sq km
note: Guadeloupe is an archipelago of nine inhabited islands, including Basse-Terre, Grande-Terre, Marie-Galante, La Desirade, Iles des Saintes (2), Saint-Barthelemy, Iles de la Petite Terre, and Saint-Martin (French part of the island of Saint Martin)
Area - comparative: 10 times the size of Washington, DC
Land boundaries:
total: 10.2 km
border countries: Netherlands Antilles (Sint Maarten) 10.2 km
Coastline: 306 km
Maritime claims:
territorial sea: 12 NM
exclusive economic zone: 200 NM
Climate: subtropical tempered by trade winds; moderately high humidity
Terrain: Basse-Terre is volcanic in origin with interior mountains; Grande-Terre is low limestone formation; most of the seven other islands are volcanic in origin

Elevation extremes:
lowest point: Caribbean Sea 0 m
highest point: Soufriere 1,484 m
Natural resources: cultivable land, beaches and climate that foster tourism
Land use:
arable land: 10.65%
permanent crops: 4.14%
other: 85.21% (1998 est.)
Irrigated land: 20 sq km (1998 est.)
Natural hazards: hurricanes (June to October); Soufriere de Guadeloupe is an active volcano
Environment - current issues: NA
Geography - note: a narrow channel, the Riviere Salee, divides Guadeloupe proper into two islands: the larger, western Basse-Terre and the smaller, eastern Grande-Terre

People

Population: 444,515 (July 2004 est.)
Age structure:
0-14 years: 24.4% (male 55,386; female 52,977)
15-64 years: 66.6% (male 146,772; female 149,314)
65 years and over: 9% (male 16,730; female 23,336) (2004 est.)
Median age:
total: 31.4 years
male: 30.6 years
female: 32.3 years (2004 est.)
Population growth rate: 0.96% (2004 est.)
Birth rate: 15.79 births/1,000 population (2004 est.)
Death rate: 6.05 deaths/1,000 population (2004 est.)
Net migration rate: -0.15 migrant(s)/1,000 population (2004 est.)
Sex ratio:
at birth: 1.05 male(s)/female
under 15 years: 1.05 male(s)/female
15-64 years: 0.98 male(s)/female
65 years and over: 0.72 male(s)/female
total population: 0.97 male(s)/female (2004 est.)
Infant mortality rate:
total: 8.83 deaths/1,000 live births
male: 10.07 deaths/1,000 live births
female: 7.53 deaths/1,000 live births (2004 est.)
Life expectancy at birth:
total population: 77.71 years
male: 74.56 years
female: 81.03 years (2004 est.)
Total fertility rate: 1.91 children born/woman (2004 est.)
HIV/AIDS - adult prevalence rate: NA%
HIV/AIDS - people living with HIV/AIDS: NA
HIV/AIDS - deaths: NA
Nationality:
noun: Guadeloupian(s)
adjective: Guadeloupe
Ethnic groups: black or mulatto 90%, white 5%, East Indian, Lebanese, Chinese less than 5%
Religions: Roman Catholic 95%, Hindu and pagan African 4%, Protestant 1%
Languages: French (official) 99%, Creole patois

Literacy:
definition: age 15 and over can read and write
total population: 90%
male: 90%
female: 90% (1982 est.)

Government

Country name:
conventional long form: Department of Guadeloupe
conventional short form: Guadeloupe
local long form: Departement de la Guadeloupe
local short form: Guadeloupe
Dependency status: overseas department of France
Government type: NA
Capital: Basse-Terre
Administrative divisions: none (overseas department of France)
Independence: none (overseas department of France)
National holiday: Bastille Day, 14 July (1789)
Constitution: 28 September 1958 (French Constitution)
Legal system: French legal system
Suffrage: 18 years of age; universal
Executive branch:
chief of state: President Jacques CHIRAC of France (since 17 May 1995), represented by Prefect Dominique VIAN (since 6 August 2002)
head of government: President of the General Council Jacques GILLOT (since 26 March 2001); President of the Regional Council Lucette MICHAUX-CHEVRY (since 22 March 1992)
cabinet: NA
elections: French president elected by popular vote for a five-year term; prefect appointed by the French president on the advice of the French Ministry of Interior; the presidents of the General and Regional Councils are elected by the members of those councils
election results: NA
Legislative branch: unicameral General Council or Conseil General (42 seats; members are elected by popular vote to serve six-year terms) and the unicameral Regional Council or Conseil Regional (41 seats; members are elected by popular vote to serve six-year terms)
elections: General Council - last held 22 March 1998 (next to be held by NA 2004); Regional Council - last held 28 March 2004 (next to be held NA 2010)
election results: General Council - percent of vote by party - NA%; seats by party - left-wing candidates 11, PS 8, RPR 8, PPDG 6, right-wing candidates 5, PCG 3, UDF 1; Regional Council (second round) - percent of vote by party - PS 58.4%, UMP 41.6%; seats by party - PS 29, UMP 12
note: Guadeloupe elects two representatives to the French Senate; elections last held NA September 1995 (next to be held NA September 2004); percent of vote by party - NA%; seats by party - RPR 1, FGPS 1; Guadeloupe elects four representatives to the French

Guadeloupe (continued)

National Assembly; elections last held 9 June-16 June 2002 (next to be held NA 2007); percent of vote by party - NA%; seats by party - RPR 2, PS 1, different right parties 1

Judicial branch: Court of Appeal or Cour d'Appel with jurisdiction over Guadeloupe, French Guiana, and Martinique

Political parties and leaders: Communist Party of Guadeloupe or PCG [Mona CADOCE]; FGPS [Dominique LARIFLA]; Left Radical Party or PRG [Flavien FERRANT]; Progressive Democratic Party or PPDG [Henri BANGOU]; Socialist Party or PS [Marlene MELISSE and Favrot DAVRAIN]; Union for French Democracy or UDF [Marcel ESDRAS]; Union for a Popular Movement or UMP [Robert JOYEUX]

Political pressure groups and leaders: Christian Movement for the Liberation of Guadeloupe or KLPG; General Federation of Guadeloupe Workers or CGT-G; General Union of Guadeloupe Workers or UGTG; Movement for Independent Guadeloupe or MPGI; The Socialist Renewal Movement

International organization participation: WCL, WFTU

Diplomatic representation in the US: none (overseas department of France)

Diplomatic representation from the US: none (overseas department of France)

Flag description: the flag of France is used

Economy

Economy - overview: The Caribbean economy depends on agriculture, tourism, light industry, and services. It also depends on France for large subsidies and imports. Tourism is a key industry, with most tourists from the US; an increasingly large number of cruise ships visit the islands. The traditional sugarcane crop is slowly being replaced by other crops, such as bananas (which now supply about 50% of export earnings), eggplant, and flowers. Other vegetables and root crops are cultivated for local consumption, although Guadeloupe is still dependent on imported food, mainly from France. Light industry features sugar and rum production. Most manufactured goods and fuel are imported. Unemployment is especially high among the young. Hurricanes periodically devastate the economy.

GDP: purchasing power parity - $3.513 billion (2003 est.)

GDP - real growth rate: NA%

GDP - per capita: purchasing power parity - $8,000 (1997 est.)

GDP - composition by sector:
agriculture: 15%
industry: 17%
services: 68% (1997 est.)

Population below poverty line: NA%

Household income or consumption by percentage share:
lowest 10%: NA%
highest 10%: NA%

Inflation rate (consumer prices): NA% (2003 est.)

Labor force: 125,900 (1997)

Labor force - by occupation: NA

Unemployment rate: 27.8% (1998)

Budget:
revenues: $225 million
expenditures: $390 million, including capital expenditures of $105 million (1996)

Industries: construction, cement, rum, sugar, tourism

Industrial production growth rate: NA%

Electricity - production: 1.155 billion kWh (2001)

Electricity - production by source:
fossil fuel: 100%
hydro: 0%
nuclear: 0%
other: 0% (2001)

Electricity - consumption: 1.074 billion kWh (2001)

Electricity - exports: 0 kWh (2001)

Electricity - imports: 0 kWh (2001)

Oil - production: 0 bbl/day (2001 est.)

Oil - consumption: 13,000 bbl/day (2001 est.)

Oil - exports: NA

Oil - imports: NA

Agriculture - products: bananas, sugarcane, tropical fruits and vegetables; cattle, pigs, goats

Exports: $140 million f.o.b. (1997)

Exports - commodities: bananas, sugar, rum

Exports - partners: France 60%, Martinique 18%, US 4% (1999)

Imports: $1.7 billion c.i.f. (1997)

Imports - commodities: foodstuffs, fuels, vehicles, clothing and other consumer goods, construction materials

Imports - partners: France 63%, Germany 4%, US 3%, Japan 2%, Netherlands Antilles 2% (1999)

Debt - external: $NA (yearend 2003 est.)

Economic aid - recipient: $NA; note - substantial annual French subsidies (1995)

Currency: euro (EUR); French franc (FRF)

Currency code: EUR; FRF

Exchange rates: euros per US dollar - 0.886 (2003), 1.0626 (2002), 1.1175 (2001), 1.0854 (2000), 0.9386 (1999)

Fiscal year: calendar year

Communications

Telephones - main lines in use: 210,000 (2001)

Telephones - mobile cellular: 323,500 (2002)

Telephone system:
general assessment: domestic facilities inadequate
domestic: NA
international: country code - 590; satellite earth station - 1 Intelsat (Atlantic Ocean); microwave radio relay to Antigua and Barbuda, Dominica, and Martinique

Radio broadcast stations: AM 1, FM 17, shortwave 0 (1998)

Television broadcast stations: 5 (plus several low-power repeaters) (1997)

Internet country code: .gp

Internet users: 20,000 (2002)

Transportation

Railways: NA km; privately owned, narrow-gauge plantation lines

Highways:
total: 2,467 km
paved: NA km
unpaved: NA km (1998)

Waterways: none

Ports and harbors: Basse-Terre, Gustavia (on Saint Barthelemy), Marigot, Pointe-a-Pitre

Merchant marine:
total: 1 ships (1,000 GRT or over) 1,240 GRT/109 DWT
by type: passenger 1
foreign-owned: France 1
registered in other countries: 1 (2003 est.)

Airports: 9 (2003 est.)

Airports - with paved runways:
total: 8
over 3,047 m: 1
914 to 1,523 m: 2
under 914 m: 5 (2003 est.)

Airports - with unpaved runways:
total: 1
under 914 m: 1 (2003 est.)

Military

Military branches: no regular military forces

Military - note: defense is the responsibility of France

Transnational Issues

Disputes - international: none

Guam
(territory of the US)

Introduction

Background: Guam was ceded to the US by Spain in 1898. Captured by the Japanese in 1941, it was retaken by the US three years later. The military installation on the island is one of the most strategically important US bases in the Pacific.

Geography

Location: Oceania, island in the North Pacific Ocean, about three-quarters of the way from Hawaii to the Philippines

Geographic coordinates: 13 28 N, 144 47 E

Map references: Oceania

Area:
total: 549 sq km
land: 549 sq km
water: 0 sq km

Area - comparative: three times the size of Washington, DC

Land boundaries: 0 km

Coastline: 125.5 km

Maritime claims:
territorial sea: 12 NM
exclusive economic zone: 200 NM

Climate: tropical marine; generally warm and humid, moderated by northeast trade winds; dry season from January to June, rainy season from July to December; little seasonal temperature variation

Terrain: volcanic origin, surrounded by coral reefs; relatively flat coralline limestone plateau (source of most fresh water), with steep coastal cliffs and narrow coastal plains in north, low hills in center, mountains in south

Elevation extremes:
lowest point: Pacific Ocean 0 m
highest point: Mount Lamlam 406 m

Natural resources: fishing (largely undeveloped), tourism (especially from Japan)

Land use:
arable land: 10.91%

permanent crops: 10.91%
other: 78.18% (1998 est.)

Irrigated land: NA sq km

Natural hazards: frequent squalls during rainy season; relatively rare, but potentially very destructive typhoons (June - December)

Environment - current issues: extirpation of native bird population by the rapid proliferation of the brown tree snake, an exotic, invasive species

Geography - note: largest and southernmost island in the Mariana Islands archipelago; strategic location in western North Pacific Ocean

People

Population: 166,090 (July 2004 est.)

Age structure:
0-14 years: 29.8% (male 25,577; female 23,850)
15-64 years: 64% (male 54,220; female 52,026)
65 years and over: 6.3% (male 4,912; female 5,505) (2004 est.)

Median age:
total: 28.2 years
male: 28 years
female: 28.4 years (2004 est.)

Population growth rate: 1.5% (2004 est.)

Birth rate: 19.31 births/1,000 population (2004 est.)

Death rate: 4.35 deaths/1,000 population (2004 est.)

Net migration rate: 0 migrant(s)/1,000 population (2004 est.)

Sex ratio:
at birth: 1.06 male(s)/female
under 15 years: 1.07 male(s)/female
15-64 years: 1.04 male(s)/female
65 years and over: 0.89 male(s)/female
total population: 1.04 male(s)/female (2004 est.)

Infant mortality rate:
total: 7.15 deaths/1,000 live births
male: 7.8 deaths/1,000 live births
female: 6.46 deaths/1,000 live births (2004 est.)

Life expectancy at birth:
total population: 78.12 years
male: 75.08 years
female: 81.34 years (2004 est.)

Total fertility rate: 2.61 children born/woman (2004 est.)

HIV/AIDS - adult prevalence rate: NA%

HIV/AIDS - people living with HIV/AIDS: NA

HIV/AIDS - deaths: NA

Nationality:
noun: Guamanian(s)
adjective: Guamanian

Ethnic groups: Chamorro 37%, Filipino 26%, white 10%, Chinese, Japanese, Korean, and other 27%

Religions: Roman Catholic 85%, other 15% (1999 est.)

Languages: English, Chamorro, Japanese

Literacy:
definition: age 15 and over can read and write
total population: 99%
male: 99%
female: 99% (1990 est.)

Government

Country name:
conventional long form: Territory of Guam
conventional short form: Guam
local long form: Guahan

Dependency status: organized, unincorporated territory of the US with policy relations between Guam and the US under the jurisdiction of the Office of Insular Affairs, US Department of the Interior

Government type: NA

Capital: Hagatna (Agana)

Administrative divisions: none (territory of the US)

Independence: none (territory of the US)

National holiday: Discovery Day, first Monday in March (1521)

Constitution: Organic Act of 1 August 1950

Legal system: modeled on US; US federal laws apply

Suffrage: 18 years of age; universal; US citizens, but do not vote in US presidential elections

Executive branch:
chief of state: President George W. BUSH of the US (since 20 January 2001); Vice President Richard B. CHENEY (since 20 January 2001)
head of government: Governor Felix P. P. CAMACHO (since 6 January 2003) and Lieutenant Governor Kaleo MOYLAN (since 6 January 2003)
cabinet: executive departments; heads appointed by the governor with the consent of the Guam legislature
elections: US president and vice president elected on the same ticket for a four-year term; governor and lieutenant governor elected on the same ticket by popular vote for four-year term; election last held 5 November 2002 (next to be held NA November 2006)
election results: Felix P. P. CAMACHO elected governor; percent of vote - Felix P. P. CAMACHO (Republican Party) 55.4%, Robert A. UNDERWOOD (Democratic Party) 44.6%

Legislative branch: unicameral Legislature (15 seats; members are elected by popular vote to serve two-year terms)
elections: last held 5 November 2002 (next to be held 2 November 2004)
election results: percent of vote by party - NA%; seats by party - Democratic Party 9, Republican Party 6
note: Guam elects one nonvoting delegate to the US House of Representatives; election last held 5 November 2002 (next to be held 2 November 2004); results - Madeleine BORDALLO (Democratic Party) was elected as delegate; percent of vote by party - Democratic Party 64.6%, Republican Party 35.4%; seats by party - Democratic Party 1

Judicial branch: Federal District Court (judge is appointed by the president); Territorial Superior Court (judges appointed for eight-year terms by the governor)

Political parties and leaders: Democratic Party (controls the legislature) [speaker, Vicente (Ben) PANGELINAN]; Republican Party (party of Governor CAMACHO) [leader NA]

Guam *(continued)*

Political pressure groups and leaders: NA
International organization participation: Interpol (subbureau), IOC
Diplomatic representation in the US: none (territory of the US)
Diplomatic representation from the US: none (territory of the US)
Flag description: territorial flag is dark blue with a narrow red border on all four sides; centered is a red-bordered, pointed, vertical ellipse containing a beach scene, outrigger canoe with sail, and a palm tree with the word GUAM superimposed in bold red letters; US flag is the national flag

E c o n o m y

Economy - overview: The economy depends on US military spending, tourism, and the export of fish and handicrafts. Total US grants, wage payments, and procurement outlays amounted to $1 billion in 1998. Over the past 20 years, the tourist industry has grown rapidly, creating a construction boom for new hotels and the expansion of older ones. More than 1 million tourists visit Guam each year. The industry has recently suffered setbacks because of the continuing Japanese slowdown; the Japanese normally make up almost 90% of the tourists. Most food and industrial goods are imported. Guam faces the problem of building up the civilian economic sector to offset the impact of military downsizing.
GDP: purchasing power parity - $3.2 billion (2000 est.)
GDP - real growth rate: NA%
GDP - per capita: purchasing power parity - $21,000 (2000 est.)
GDP - composition by sector:
agriculture: 7%
industry: 15%
services: 78% (2002 est.)
Population below poverty line: 23% (2001 est.)
Household income or consumption by percentage share:
lowest 10%: NA%
highest 10%: NA%
Inflation rate (consumer prices): 0% (1999 est.)
Labor force: 60,000 (2000 est.)
Labor force - by occupation: federal and territorial government 26%, private 74% (trade 24%, other services 40%, industry 10%) (2000 est.)
Unemployment rate: 15% (2000 est.)
Budget:
revenues: $340 million
expenditures: $445 million, including capital expenditures of $NA (2000 est.)
Industries: US military, tourism, construction, transshipment services, concrete products, printing and publishing, food processing, textiles
Industrial production growth rate: NA%
Electricity - production: 830 million kWh (2001)
Electricity - production by source:
fossil fuel: 100%
hydro: 0%
nuclear: 0%
other: 0% (2001)

Electricity - consumption: 771.9 million kWh (2001)
Electricity - exports: 0 kWh (2001)
Electricity - imports: 0 kWh (2001)
Oil - production: 0 bbl/day (2001 est.)
Oil - consumption: 20,000 bbl/day (2001 est.)
Oil - exports: NA
Oil - imports: NA
Agriculture - products: fruits, copra, vegetables; eggs, pork, poultry, beef
Exports: $38 million f.o.b. (2002 est.)
Exports - commodities: mostly transshipments of refined petroleum products; construction materials, fish, food and beverage products
Exports - partners: Japan 81.6%, South Korea 5.3%, Canada 2.6% (2002)
Imports: $462 million f.o.b. (2002 est.)
Imports - commodities: petroleum and petroleum products, food, manufactured goods
Imports - partners: Singapore 39.2%, South Korea 21%, Japan 20.8%, Hong Kong 7.8% (2002)
Debt - external: $NA (2003 est.)
Economic aid - recipient: Guam receives large transfer payments from the US Federal Treasury ($143 million in 1997) into which Guamanians pay no income or excise taxes; under the provisions of a special law of Congress, the Guam Treasury, rather than the US Treasury, receives federal income taxes paid by military and civilian Federal employees stationed in Guam (2001 est.)
Currency: US dollar (USD)
Currency code: USD
Exchange rates: the US dollar is used
Fiscal year: 1 October - 30 September

C o m m u n i c a t i o n s

Telephones - main lines in use: 84,134 (2001)
Telephones - mobile cellular: 32,600 (2001)
Telephone system:
general assessment: modern system, integrated with US facilities for direct dialing, including free use of 800 numbers
domestic: modern digital system, including cellular mobile service and local access to the Internet
international: country code - 1-671; satellite earth stations - 2 Intelsat (Pacific Ocean); submarine cables to US and Japan (Guam is a trans-Pacific communications hub for MCI, Sprint, AT&T, IT&E, and GTE, linking the US and Asia)
Radio broadcast stations: AM 4, FM 7, shortwave 2 (2003)
Television broadcast stations: 5 (1997)
Internet country code: .gu
Internet users: 50,000 (2002)

T r a n s p o r t a t i o n

Railways: 0 km
Highways:
total: 885 km
paved: 675 km
unpaved: 210 km

note: there are also 685 km of roads classified non-public, including roads located on federal government installations
Waterways: none
Ports and harbors: Apra Harbor
Merchant marine: none
Airports: 5 (2003 est.)
Airports - with paved runways:
total: 4
over 3,047 m: 2
2,438 to 3,047 m: 1
914 to 1,523 m: 1 (2003 est.)
Airports - with unpaved runways:
total: 1
under 914 m: 1 (2003 est.)

M i l i t a r y

Military - note: defense is the responsibility of the US

T r a n s n a t i o n a l I s s u e s

Disputes - international: none

Guatemala

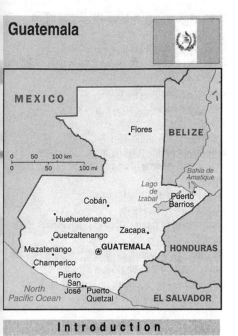

Introduction

Background: Guatemala was freed of Spanish colonial rule in 1821. During the second half of the 20th century, it experienced a variety of military and civilian governments as well as a 36-year guerrilla war. In 1996, the government signed a peace agreement formally ending the conflict, which had led to the death of more than 100,000 people and had created some 1 million refugees.

Geography

Location: Central America, bordering the North Pacific Ocean, between El Salvador and Mexico, and bordering the Gulf of Honduras (Caribbean Sea) between Honduras and Belize

Geographic coordinates: 15 30 N, 90 15 W

Map references: Central America and the Caribbean

Area:
total: 108,890 sq km
land: 108,430 sq km
water: 460 sq km

Area - comparative: slightly smaller than Tennessee

Land boundaries:
total: 1,687 km
border countries: Belize 266 km, El Salvador 203 km, Honduras 256 km, Mexico 962 km

Coastline: 400 km

Maritime claims:
territorial sea: 12 NM
exclusive economic zone: 200 NM
continental shelf: 200-m depth or to the depth of exploitation

Climate: tropical; hot, humid in lowlands; cooler in highlands

Terrain: mostly mountains with narrow coastal plains and rolling limestone plateau (Peten)

Elevation extremes:
lowest point: Pacific Ocean 0 m
highest point: Volcan Tajumulco 4,211 m

Natural resources: petroleum, nickel, rare woods, fish, chicle, hydropower

Land use:
arable land: 12.54%
permanent crops: 5.03%
other: 82.43% (1998 est.)

Irrigated land: 1,250 sq km (1998 est.)

Natural hazards: numerous volcanoes in mountains, with occasional violent earthquakes; Caribbean coast extremely susceptible to hurricanes and other tropical storms

Environment - current issues: deforestation in the Peten rainforest; soil erosion; water pollution

Environment - international agreements:
party to: Antarctic Treaty, Biodiversity, Climate Change, Climate Change-Kyoto Protocol, Desertification, Endangered Species, Environmental Modification, Hazardous Wastes, Law of the Sea, Marine Dumping, Ozone Layer Protection, Ship Pollution, Wetlands
signed, but not ratified: none of the selected agreements

Geography - note: no natural harbors on west coast

People

Population: 14,280,596 (July 2004 est.)

Age structure:
0-14 years: 42.6% (male 3,118,396; female 2,970,729)
15-64 years: 54% (male 3,898,939; female 3,817,435)
65 years and over: 3.3% (male 221,154; female 253,943) (2004 est.)

Median age:
total: 18.4 years
male: 18.1 years
female: 18.6 years (2004 est.)

Population growth rate: 2.61% (2004 est.)

Birth rate: 34.58 births/1,000 population (2004 est.)

Death rate: 6.79 deaths/1,000 population (2004 est.)

Net migration rate: -1.67 migrant(s)/1,000 population (2004 est.)

Sex ratio:
at birth: 1.05 male(s)/female
under 15 years: 1.05 male(s)/female
15-64 years: 1.02 male(s)/female
65 years and over: 0.87 male(s)/female
total population: 1.03 male(s)/female (2004 est.)

Infant mortality rate:
total: 36.91 deaths/1,000 live births
male: 37.71 deaths/1,000 live births
female: 36.07 deaths/1,000 live births (2004 est.)

Life expectancy at birth:
total population: 65.19 years
male: 64.3 years
female: 66.13 years (2004 est.)

Total fertility rate: 4.6 children born/woman (2004 est.)

HIV/AIDS - adult prevalence rate: 1% (2001 est.)

HIV/AIDS - people living with HIV/AIDS: 67,000 (2001 est.)

HIV/AIDS - deaths: 5,200 (2001 est.)

Nationality:
noun: Guatemalan(s)
adjective: Guatemalan

Ethnic groups: Mestizo (mixed Amerindian-Spanish or assimilated Amerindian - in local Spanish called Ladino), approximately 55%, Amerindian or predominantly Amerindian, approximately 43%, whites and others 2%

Religions: Roman Catholic, Protestant, indigenous Mayan beliefs

Languages: Spanish 60%, Amerindian languages 40% (23 officially recognized Amerindian languages, including Quiche, Cakchiquel, Kekchi, Mam, Garifuna, and Xinca)

Literacy:
definition: age 15 and over can read and write
total population: 70.6%
male: 78%
female: 63.3% (2003 est.)

Government

Country name:
conventional long form: Republic of Guatemala
conventional short form: Guatemala
local long form: Republica de Guatemala
local short form: Guatemala

Government type: constitutional democratic republic

Capital: Guatemala

Administrative divisions: 22 departments (departamentos, singular - departamento); Alta Verapaz, Baja Verapaz, Chimaltenango, Chiquimula, El Progreso, Escuintla, Guatemala, Huehuetenango, Izabal, Jalapa, Jutiapa, Peten, Quetzaltenango, Quiche, Retalhuleu, Sacatepequez, San Marcos, Santa Rosa, Solola, Suchitepequez, Totonicapan, Zacapa

Independence: 15 September 1821 (from Spain)

National holiday: Independence Day, 15 September (1821)

Constitution: 31 May 1985, effective 14 January 1986; note - suspended 25 May 1993 by former President SERRANO; reinstated 5 June 1993 following ouster of president; amended November 1993

Legal system: civil law system; judicial review of legislative acts; has not accepted compulsory ICJ jurisdiction

Suffrage: 18 years of age; universal (active duty members of the armed forces may not vote and are restricted to their barracks on election day)

Executive branch:
chief of state: President Oscar Jose Rafael BERGER Perdomo (since 14 January 2004); Vice President Eduardo STEIN Barillas (since 14 January 2004); note - the president is both the chief of state and head of government

Guatemala (continued)

head of government: President Oscar Jose Rafael BERGER Perdomo (since 14 January 2004); Vice President Eduardo STEIN Barillas (since 14 January 2004); note - the president is both the chief of state and head of government

cabinet: Council of Ministers appointed by the president

elections: president elected by popular vote for a four-year term; election last held 9 November 2003; runoff held 28 December 2003 (next to be held NA November 2007)

election results: Oscar BERGER Perdomo elected president; percent of vote - Oscar BERGER Perdomo (GANA) 54.1%, Alvaro COLOM (UNE) 45.9%

Legislative branch: unicameral Congress of the Republic or Congreso de la Republica (158 seats; members are elected by popular vote to serve four-year terms)

elections: last held 9 November 2003 (next to be held NA November 2007)

election results: percent of vote by party - NA%; seats by party - GANA 49, FRG 41, UNE 33, PAN 17, other 18

note: for the 9 November 2003 election, the number of congressional seats increased from 113 to 158

Judicial branch: Constitutional Court or Corte de Constitutcionalidad is Guatemala's highest court (five judges are elected for concurrent five-year terms by Congress, each serving one year as president of the Constitutional Court; one is elected by Congress, one elected by the Supreme Court of Justice, one appointed by the President, one elected by Superior Counsel of Universidad San Carlos de Guatemala, and one by Colegio de Abogados); Supreme Court of Justice or Corte Suprema de Justicia (thirteen members serve concurrent five-year terms and elect a president of the Court each year from among their number; the president of the Supreme Court of Justice also supervises trial judges around the country, who are named to five-year terms)

Political parties and leaders: Authentic Integral Development or DIA [Eduardo SUGER]; Democratic Union or UD [Rodolfo PAIZ Andrade]; Grand National Alliance or GANA [Oscar BERGER Perdomo]; Green Party or LOV [Rodolfo ROSALES Garcis-Salaz]; Guatemalan Christian Democracy or DCG [Vinicio CEREZO Arevalo]; Guatemalan National Revolutionary Unity or URNG [Alba ESTELA Maldonado, secretary general]; Guatemalan Republican Front or FRG [Efrain RIOS Montt]; Movement for Guatemalan Unity or MGU [Jacobo ARBENZ Villanueva]; Movement for Principals and Values or MPV [Francisco BIANCHI]; National Advancement Party or PAN [Leonel LOPEZ Rodas, secretary general]; National Unity for Hope or UNE [Alvarado COLOM Caballeros]; New Nation Alliance or ANN, formed by an alliance of DIA, URNG, and several splinter groups most of whom subsequently defected [led by three co-equal partners - Nineth Varenca MONTENEGRO Cottom, Rodolfo BAUER Paiz, and Jorge Antonio BALSELLS TUT]; Patriot Party or PP [retired General Otto PEREZ Molina];

Progressive Liberator Party or PLP [Acisclo VALLADARES Molina]; Reform Movement or MR [Alfredo SKINNER-KLEE, secretary general]; Unionista Party [leader NA]

Political pressure groups and leaders: Agrarian Owners Group or UNAGRO; Alliance Against Impunity or AAI; Committee for Campesino Unity or CUC; Coordinating Committee of Agricultural, Commercial, Industrial, and Financial Associations or CACIF; Mutual Support Group or GAM

International organization participation: BCIE, CACM, FAO, G-24, G-77, IADB, IAEA, IBRD, ICAO, ICFTU, ICRM, IDA, IFAD, IFC, IFRCS, IHO, ILO, IMF, IMO, Interpol, IOC, IOM, ISO (correspondent), ITU, LAES, LAIA (observer), NAM, OAS, OPANAL, OPCW, PCA, RG, UN, UNCTAD, UNESCO, UNIDO, UPU, WCL, WCO, WFTU, WHO, WIPO, WMO, WToO, WTrO

Diplomatic representation in the US:

chief of mission: Ambassador (vacant)

chancery: 2220 R Street NW, Washington, DC 20008

telephone: [1] (202) 745-4952

FAX: [1] (202) 745-1908

consulate(s) general: Chicago, Denver, Houston, Los Angeles, Miami, New York, and San Francisco

Diplomatic representation from the US:

chief of mission: Ambassador (vacant)

embassy: 7-01 Avenida Reforma, Zone 10, Guatemala City

mailing address: APO AA 34024

telephone: [502] 331-1541/55

FAX: [502] 334-8477

Flag description: three equal vertical bands of light blue (hoist side), white, and light blue with the coat of arms centered in the white band; the coat of arms includes a green and red quetzal (the national bird) and a scroll bearing the inscription LIBERTAD 15 DE SEPTIEMBRE DE 1821 (the original date of independence from Spain) all superimposed on a pair of crossed rifles and a pair of crossed swords and framed by a wreath

---

Economy

Economy - overview: Guatemala is the largest and most populous of the Central American countries with a GDP per capita roughly one-half that of Brazil, Argentina, and Chile. The agricultural sector accounts for about one-fourth of GDP, two-thirds of exports, and half of the labor force. Coffee, sugar, and bananas are the main products. The 1996 signing of peace accords, which ended 36 years of civil war, removed a major obstacle to foreign investment, but widespread political violence and corruption scandals continue to dampen investor confidence. The distribution of income remains highly unequal, with perhaps 75% of the population below the poverty line. Ongoing challenges include increasing government revenues, negotiating further assistance from international donors, upgrading both government and private financial operations, curtailing drug trafficking, and narrowing the trade deficit.

GDP: purchasing power parity - $56.53 billion (2003 est.)

GDP - real growth rate: 2.2% (2003 est.)

GDP - per capita: purchasing power parity - $4,100 (2003 est.)

GDP - composition by sector:

agriculture: 22.5%

industry: 15%

services: 62.5% (2002 est.)

Population below poverty line: 75% (2002 est.)

Household income or consumption by percentage share:

lowest 10%: 1.6%

highest 10%: 46% (1998)

Distribution of family income - Gini index: 55.8 (1998)

Inflation rate (consumer prices): 5.6% (2003 est.)

Labor force: 4.2 million (1999 est.)

Labor force - by occupation: agriculture 50%, industry 15%, services 35% (1999 est.)

Unemployment rate: 7.5% (2003 est.)

Budget:

revenues: $2.3 billion

expenditures: $2.7 billion, including capital expenditures of $750 million (2002 est.)

Industries: sugar, textiles and clothing, furniture, chemicals, petroleum, metals, rubber, tourism

Industrial production growth rate: 4.1% (1999)

Electricity - production: 6.237 billion kWh (2001)

Electricity - production by source:

fossil fuel: 51.9%

hydro: 35.2%

nuclear: 0%

other: 12.9% (2001)

Electricity - consumption: 5.559 billion kWh (2001)

Electricity - exports: 336 million kWh (2001)

Electricity - imports: 95 million kWh (2001)

Oil - production: 21,080 bbl/day (2001 est.)

Oil - consumption: 61,000 bbl/day (2001 est.)

Oil - exports: NA

Oil - imports: NA

Oil - proved reserves: 263 million bbl (1 January 2002)

Natural gas - proved reserves: 1.543 billion cu m (1 January 2002)

Agriculture - products: sugarcane, corn, bananas, coffee, beans, cardamom; cattle, sheep, pigs, chickens

Exports: $2.763 billion f.o.b. (2003 est.)

Exports - commodities: coffee, sugar, bananas, fruits and vegetables, cardamom, meat, apparel, petroleum, electricity

Exports - partners: US 59%, El Salvador 9.4%, Nicaragua 3.2% (2002)

Imports: $5.749 billion f.o.b. (2003 est.)

Imports - commodities: fuels, machinery and transport equipment, construction materials, grain, fertilizers, electricity

Imports - partners: US 34.3%, Mexico 8.6%, South Korea 8.4%, El Salvador 5.9%, China 4.1% (2002)

Debt - external: $5.6 billion (2003 est.)

Guatemala (continued)

Economic aid - recipient: $250 million (2000 est.)
Currency: quetzal (GTQ), US dollar (USD), others allowed
Currency code: GTQ; USD
Exchange rates: quetzales per US dollar - 7.9409 (2003), 7.8216 (2002), 7.8586 (2001), 7.7632 (2000), 7.3856 (1999)
Fiscal year: calendar year

Communications

Telephones - main lines in use: 846,000 (2002)
Telephones - mobile cellular: 1,577,100 (2002)
Telephone system:
general assessment: fairly modern network centered in the city of Guatemala
domestic: NA
international: country code - 502; connected to Central American Microwave System; satellite earth station - 1 Intelsat (Atlantic Ocean)
Radio broadcast stations: AM 130, FM 487, shortwave 15 (2000)
Television broadcast stations: 26 (plus 27 repeaters) (1997)
Internet country code: .gt
Internet hosts: 9,789 (2002)
Internet users: 400,000 (2002)

Transportation

Railways:
total: 886 km
narrow gauge: 886 km 0.914-m gauge (2002)
Highways:
total: 14,118 km
paved: 4,871 km (including 74 km of expressways)
unpaved: 9,247 km (1999)
Waterways: 990 km
note: 260 km navigable year round; additional 730 km navigable during high-water season
Pipelines: oil 480 km (2003)
Ports and harbors: Champerico, Puerto Barrios, Puerto Quetzal, San Jose, Santo Tomas de Castilla
Merchant marine: none
Airports: 452 (2003 est.)
Airports - with paved runways:
total: 11
2,438 to 3,047 m: 3
1,524 to 2,437 m: 2
914 to 1,523 m: 4
under 914 m: 2 (2003 est.)
Airports - with unpaved runways:
total: 441
2,438 to 3,047 m: 1
1,524 to 2,437 m: 8
914 to 1,523 m: 109
under 914 m: 323 (2003 est.)

Military

Military branches: Army, Navy (includes Marines), Air Force
Military manpower - military age: 18 years of age (2004 est.)

Military manpower - availability:
males age 15-49: 3,421,682 (2004 est.)
Military manpower - fit for military service:
males age 15-49: 2,233,562 (2004 est.)
Military manpower - reaching military age annually:
males: 156,865 (2004 est.)
Military expenditures - dollar figure: $202.6 million (2003)
Military expenditures - percent of GDP: 0.8% (2003)

Transnational Issues

Disputes - international: Guatemalan squatters continue to settle in Belize border region; OAS brokered Differendum in 2002 creating small adjustment to land boundary, large Guatemalan maritime corridor in Caribbean, joint ecological park for disputed Sapodilla Cays, and substantial US-UK financial package, but agreement was not brought to popular referendum leaving Guatemala to continue to claim the southern half of Belize intact; numbers of Guatemalans enter Mexico seeking work or transit to the US
Illicit drugs: major transit country for cocaine and heroin; minor producer of illicit opium poppy and cannabis for mostly domestic consumption; proximity to Mexico makes Guatemala a major staging area for drugs (particularly for cocaine); money laundering is a serious problem; corruption is a major problem; remains on Financial Action Task Force Non-Cooperative Countries and Territories List for continued failure to address deficiencies in money-laundering control regime

Guernsey
(British crown dependency)

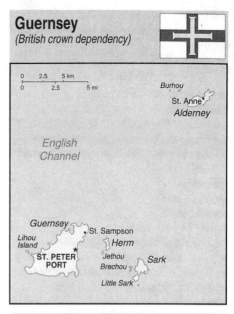

Introduction

Background: The island of Guernsey and the other Channel Islands represent the last remnants of the medieval Dukedom of Normandy, which held sway in both France and England. The islands were the only British soil occupied by German troops in World War II.

Geography

Location: Western Europe, islands in the English Channel, northwest of France
Geographic coordinates: 49 28 N, 2 35 W
Map references: Europe
Area:
total: 78 sq km
land: 78 sq km
water: 0 sq km
note: includes Alderney, Guernsey, Herm, Sark, and some other smaller islands
Area - comparative: about one-half the size of Washington, DC
Land boundaries: 0 km
Coastline: 50 km
Maritime claims:
territorial sea: 3 NM
exclusive fishing zone: 12 NM
Climate: temperate with mild winters and cool summers; about 50% of days are overcast
Terrain: mostly level with low hills in southwest
Elevation extremes:
lowest point: Atlantic Ocean 0 m
highest point: unnamed location on Sark 114 m
Natural resources: cropland
Land use:
arable land: NA%
permanent crops: NA%
other: NA%
Irrigated land: NA sq km
Natural hazards: NA

Guernsey (continued)

Environment - current issues: NA
Geography - note: large, deepwater harbor at Saint Peter Port

People

Population: 65,031 (July 2004 est.)
Age structure:
0-14 years: 15.6% (male 5,161; female 5,013)
15-64 years: 66.7% (male 21,497; female 21,897)
65 years and over: 17.6% (male 4,812; female 6,651)
(2004 est.)
Median age:
total: 40.6 years
male: 39.6 years
female: 41.5 years (2004 est.)
Population growth rate: 0.31% (2004 est.)
Birth rate: 9.16 births/1,000 population (2004 est.)
Death rate: 9.87 deaths/1,000 population (2004 est.)
Net migration rate: 3.84 migrant(s)/1,000 population (2004 est.)
Sex ratio:
at birth: 1.03 male(s)/female
under 15 years: 1.03 male(s)/female
15-64 years: 0.98 male(s)/female
65 years and over: 0.72 male(s)/female
total population: 0.94 male(s)/female (2004 est.)
Infant mortality rate:
total: 4.78 deaths/1,000 live births
male: 5.35 deaths/1,000 live births
female: 4.19 deaths/1,000 live births (2004 est.)
Life expectancy at birth:
total population: 80.17 years
male: 77.17 years
female: 83.27 years (2004 est.)
Total fertility rate: 1.38 children born/woman (2004 est.)
HIV/AIDS - adult prevalence rate: NA%
HIV/AIDS - people living with HIV/AIDS: NA
HIV/AIDS - deaths: NA
Nationality:
noun: Channel Islander(s)
adjective: Channel Islander
Ethnic groups: UK and Norman-French descent
Religions: Anglican, Roman Catholic, Presbyterian, Baptist, Congregational, Methodist
Languages: English, French, Norman-French dialect spoken in country districts
Literacy:
definition: NA
total population: NA%
male: NA%
female: NA%

Government

Country name:
conventional long form: Bailiwick of Guernsey
conventional short form: Guernsey
Dependency status: British crown dependency
Government type: NA
Capital: Saint Peter Port

Administrative divisions: none (British crown dependency); there are no first-order administrative divisions as defined by the US Government, but there are 10 parishes including Saint Peter Port, Saint Sampson, Vale, Castel, Saint Saviour, Saint Pierre du Bois, Torteval, Forest, Saint Martin, Saint Andrew
Independence: none (British crown dependency)
National holiday: Liberation Day, 9 May (1945)
Constitution: unwritten; partly statutes, partly common law and practice
Legal system: English law and local statute; justice is administered by the Royal Court
Suffrage: 18 years of age; universal
Executive branch:
chief of state: Queen ELIZABETH II (since 6 February 1952)
head of government: Lieutenant Governor and Commander-in-Chief Lt. Gen. Sir John FOLEY (since NA 2000) and Bailiff de Vic Graham CAREY (since NA 1999)
cabinet: Advisory and Finance Committee appointed by the Assembly of the States
elections: none; the monarch is hereditary; lieutenant governor appointed by the monarch; bailiff appointed by the monarch
Legislative branch: unicameral Assembly of the States; consists of the bailiff, 10 Douzaine (parish council) representatives, 45 people's deputies elected by popular vote, 2 representatives from Alderney, Her Majesty's Procureur (Attorney General), Her Majesty's Comptroller (Solicitor General) and Her Majesty's Greffier (Court Recorder and Registrar General); note - Alderney and Sark have their own parliaments
elections: last held 12 April 2000 (next to be held NA 2004)
election results: percent of vote - NA%; seats - all independents
Judicial branch: Royal Court
Political parties and leaders: none; all independents
Political pressure groups and leaders: none
International organization participation: none
Diplomatic representation in the US: none (British crown dependency)
Diplomatic representation from the US: none (British crown dependency)
Flag description: white with the red cross of Saint George (patron saint of England) extending to the edges of the flag and a yellow equal-armed cross of William the Conqueror superimposed on the Saint George cross

Economy

Economy - overview: Financial services - banking, fund management, insurance, etc. - account for about 55% of total income in this tiny Channel Island economy. Tourism, manufacturing, and horticulture, mainly tomatoes and cut flowers, have been declining. Light tax and death duties make Guernsey a popular tax haven. The evolving economic integration of the EU nations is changing the environment under which Guernsey operates.

GDP: purchasing power parity - $1.3 billion (1999 est.)
GDP - real growth rate: 5.7% (1999 est.)
GDP - per capita: purchasing power parity - $20,000 (1999 est.)
GDP - composition by sector:
agriculture: 3%
industry: 10%
services: 87% (2000)
Population below poverty line: NA%
Household income or consumption by percentage share:
lowest 10%: NA%
highest 10%: NA%
Inflation rate (consumer prices): 3.99% (2000 est.)
Labor force: 31,322 (2000)
Unemployment rate: 0.5% (1999 est.)
Budget:
revenues: $381.3 million
expenditures: $368.8 million, including capital expenditures of $NA (2000 est.)
Industries: tourism, banking
Industrial production growth rate: NA%
Electricity - production: NA kWh
Electricity - production by source:
fossil fuel: NA%
hydro: NA%
nuclear: NA%
other: NA%
Electricity - consumption: NA kWh
Electricity - exports: 0 kWh (2002)
Electricity - imports: 0 kWh (2002)
Agriculture - products: tomatoes, greenhouse flowers, sweet peppers, eggplant, fruit; Guernsey cattle
Exports: $NA
Exports - commodities: tomatoes, flowers and ferns, sweet peppers, eggplant, other vegetables
Exports - partners: UK (regarded as internal trade)
Imports: $NA
Imports - commodities: coal, gasoline, oil, machinery and equipment
Imports - partners: UK (regarded as internal trade)
Debt - external: $NA
Economic aid - recipient: $NA
Currency: British pound (GBP); note - there is also a Guernsey pound
Currency code: GBP
Exchange rates: Guernsey pounds per US dollar - 0.6661 (2002), 0.6944 (2001), 0.6596 (2000), 0.6180 (1999), 0.6037 (1998); note - the Guernsey pound is at par with the British pound
Fiscal year: calendar year

Communications

Telephones - main lines in use: 55,000 (2001)
Telephones - mobile cellular: 31,500 (2001)
Telephone system:
general assessment: NA
domestic: NA
international: 1 submarine cable

Guernsey *(continued)*

Radio broadcast stations: AM 1, FM 1, shortwave 0 (1998)
Television broadcast stations: 1 (1997)
Internet country code: .gg
Internet users: NA

Transportation

Railways: 5 km
Highways:
total: NA km
paved: NA km
unpaved: NA km
Waterways: none
Ports and harbors: Saint Peter Port, Saint Sampson
Merchant marine: none
Airports: 2 (2003 est.)
Airports - with paved runways:
total: 2
914 to 1,523 m: 1
under 914 m: 1 (2003 est.)

Military

Military - note: defense is the responsibility of the UK

Transnational Issues

Disputes - international: none

Guinea

Introduction

Background: Independent from France since 1958, Guinea did not hold democratic elections until 1993 when Gen. Lansana CONTE (head of the military government) was elected president of the civilian government. He was reelected in 1998 and again in 2003. Unrest in Sierra Leone and Liberia has spilled over into Guinea on several occasions over the past decade, threatening stability and creating humanitarian emergencies.

Geography

Location: Western Africa, bordering the North Atlantic Ocean, between Guinea-Bissau and Sierra Leone
Geographic coordinates: 11 00 N, 10 00 W
Map references: Africa
Area:
total: 245,857 sq km
land: 245,857 sq km
water: 0 sq km
Area - comparative: slightly smaller than Oregon
Land boundaries:
total: 3,399 km
border countries: Cote d'Ivoire 610 km, Guinea-Bissau 386 km, Liberia 563 km, Mali 858 km, Senegal 330 km, Sierra Leone 652 km
Coastline: 320 km
Maritime claims:
territorial sea: 12 NM
exclusive economic zone: 200 NM
Climate: generally hot and humid; monsoonal-type rainy season (June to November) with southwesterly winds; dry season (December to May) with northeasterly harmattan winds
Terrain: generally flat coastal plain, hilly to mountainous interior
Elevation extremes:
lowest point: Atlantic Ocean 0 m
highest point: Mont Nimba 1,752 m

Natural resources: bauxite, iron ore, diamonds, gold, uranium, hydropower, fish
Land use:
arable land: 3.6%
permanent crops: 2.44%
other: 93.96% (1998 est.)
Irrigated land: 950 sq km (1998 est.)
Natural hazards: hot, dry, dusty harmattan haze may reduce visibility during dry season
Environment - current issues: deforestation; inadequate supplies of potable water; desertification; soil contamination and erosion; overfishing, overpopulation in forest region; poor mining practices have led to environmental damage
Environment - international agreements:
party to: Biodiversity, Climate Change, Climate Change-Kyoto Protocol, Desertification, Endangered Species, Hazardous Wastes, Law of the Sea, Ozone Layer Protection, Wetlands, Whaling
signed, but not ratified: none of the selected agreements
Geography - note: the Niger and its important tributary the Milo have their sources in the Guinean highlands

People

Population: 9,246,462 (July 2004 est.)
Age structure:
0-14 years: 44.4% (male 2,075,652; female 2,032,936)
15-64 years: 52.4% (male 2,417,440; female 2,428,085)
65 years and over: 3.2% (male 127,654; female 164,695) (2004 est.)
Median age:
total: 17.7 years
male: 17.4 years
female: 17.9 years (2004 est.)
Population growth rate: 2.37% (2004 est.)
Birth rate: 42.26 births/1,000 population (2004 est.)
Death rate: 15.53 deaths/1,000 population (2004 est.)
Net migration rate: -3.06 migrant(s)/1,000 population
note: as a result of conflict in neighboring countries, Guinea is host to approximately 150,000 Liberian and Sierra Leonean refugees (2004 est.)
Sex ratio:
at birth: 1.03 male(s)/female
under 15 years: 1.02 male(s)/female
15-64 years: 1 male(s)/female
65 years and over: 0.78 male(s)/female
total population: 1 male(s)/female (2004 est.)
Infant mortality rate:
total: 91.82 deaths/1,000 live births
male: 97.3 deaths/1,000 live births
female: 86.18 deaths/1,000 live births (2004 est.)
Life expectancy at birth:
total population: 49.7 years
male: 48.45 years
female: 50.99 years (2004 est.)

Guinea (continued)

Total fertility rate: 5.87 children born/woman (2004 est.)
HIV/AIDS - adult prevalence rate: 1.54% (2001 est.)
HIV/AIDS - people living with HIV/AIDS: 55,000 (1999 est.)
HIV/AIDS - deaths: 9,000 (2001 est.)
Nationality:
noun: Guinean(s)
adjective: Guinean
Ethnic groups: Peuhl 40%, Malinke 30%, Soussou 20%, smaller ethnic groups 10%
Religions: Muslim 85%, Christian 8%, indigenous beliefs 7%
Languages: French (official), each ethnic group has its own language
Literacy:
definition: age 15 and over can read and write
total population: 35.9%
male: 49.9%
female: 21.9% (1995 est.)

Government

Country name:
conventional long form: Republic of Guinea
conventional short form: Guinea
local long form: Republique de Guinee
local short form: Guinee
former: French Guinea
Government type: republic
Capital: Conakry
Administrative divisions: 33 prefectures and 1 special zone (zone special)*; Beyla, Boffa, Boke, Conakry*, Coyah, Dabola, Dalaba, Dinguiraye, Dubreka, Faranah, Forecariah, Fria, Gaoual, Gueckedou, Kankan, Kerouane, Kindia, Kissidougou, Koubia, Koundara, Kouroussa, Labe, Lelouma, Lola, Macenta, Mali, Mamou, Mandiana, Nzerekore, Pita, Siguiri, Telimele, Tougue, Yomou
Independence: 2 October 1958 (from France)
National holiday: Independence Day, 2 October (1958)
Constitution: 23 December 1990 (Loi Fundamentale)
Legal system: based on French civil law system, customary law, and decree; legal codes currently being revised; has not accepted compulsory ICJ jurisdiction
Suffrage: 18 years of age; universal
Executive branch:
chief of state: President Lansana CONTE (head of military government since 5 April 1984, elected president 19 December 1993)
head of government: Prime Minister Francois Lonseny FALL (since 23 February 2004)
cabinet: Council of Ministers appointed by the president
elections: president elected by popular vote for a five-year term; candidate must receive a majority of the votes cast to be elected president; election last held 21 December 2003 (next to be held NA December 2008); the prime minister is appointed by the president

election results: Lansana CONTE reelected president; percent of vote - Lansana CONTE (PUP) 95.3%, Mamadou Boye BARRY (UPR) 4.6%
Legislative branch: unicameral People's National Assembly or Assemblee Nationale Populaire (114 seats; members are elected by direct, popular vote to serve five-year terms)
elections: last held 30 June 2002 (next to be held NA 2007)
election results: percent of vote by party - PUP 61.6%, UPR 26.6%, other 11.8%; seats by party - PUP 85, UPR 20, other 9
Judicial branch: Court of Appeal or Cour d'Appel
Political parties and leaders: Democratic Party of Guinea-African Democratic Rally or PDG-RDA [El Hadj Ismael Mohamed Gassim GUSHEIN]; National Union for Progress or UPN [Mamadou Bhoye BARRY]; Party for Unity and Progress or PUP [Lansana CONTE] - the governing party; People's Party of Guinea or PPG [Pascal TOLNO]; Rally for the Guinean People or RPG [Alpha CONDE]; Union for Progress and Renewal or UPR [Siradiou DIALLO]; Union for Progress of Guinea or UPG [Jean-Marie DORE, secretary-general]; Union of Republican Forces or UFR [Sidya TOURE]
Political pressure groups and leaders: NA
International organization participation: ACCT, ACP, AfDB, AU, ECOWAS, FAO, G-77, IBRD, ICAO, ICCt, ICFTU, ICRM, IDA, IDB, IFAD, IFC, IFRCS, ILO, IMF, IMO, Interpol, IOC, IOM, ITU, MINURSO, NAM, OIC, OPCW, UN, UNAMSIL, UNCTAD, UNESCO, UNHCR, UNIDO, UPU, WCL, WCO, WFTU, WHO, WIPO, WMO, WToO, WTrO
Diplomatic representation in the US:
chief of mission: Ambassador Rafiou Alpha Oumar BARRY
chancery: 2112 Leroy Place NW, Washington, DC 20008
telephone: [1] (202) 986-4300
FAX: [1] (202) 478-3010
Diplomatic representation from the US:
chief of mission: Ambassador Barrie R. WALKLEY
embassy: Rue Ka 038, Conakry
mailing address: B. P. 603, Conakry
telephone: [224] 41 15 20, 41 15 21, 41 15 23
FAX: [224] 41 15 22
Flag description: three equal vertical bands of red (hoist side), yellow, and green; uses the popular pan-African colors of Ethiopia

Economy

Economy - overview: Guinea possesses major mineral, hydropower, and agricultural resources, yet remains an underdeveloped nation. The country possesses over 30% of the world's bauxite reserves and is the second-largest bauxite producer. The mining sector accounted for about 75% of exports in 1999. Long-run improvements in government fiscal arrangements, literacy, and the legal framework are needed if the country is to move out of poverty. Fighting along the Sierra Leonean and Liberian borders, as well as refugee movements, have caused

major economic disruptions, including a loss in investor confidence. Foreign mining companies have reduced expatriate staff, while panic buying has created food shortages and inflation in local markets. Guinea is not receiving multilateral aid. The IMF and World Bank cut off most assistance in 2003. Growth should strengthen in 2004, however, because of a slowly improving security situation and increased investor confidence.
GDP: purchasing power parity - $18.87 billion (2003 est.)
GDP - real growth rate: 2.2% (2003 est.)
GDP - per capita: purchasing power parity - $2,100 (2003 est.)
GDP - composition by sector:
agriculture: 25%
industry: 37%
services: 38% (2001 est.)
Population below poverty line: 40% (2003 est.)
Household income or consumption by percentage share:
lowest 10%: 2.6%
highest 10%: 32% (1994)
Distribution of family income - Gini index: 40.3 (1994)
Inflation rate (consumer prices): 8% (2003 est.)
Labor force: 3 million (1999)
Labor force - by occupation: agriculture 80%, industry and services 20% (2000 est.)
Unemployment rate: NA% (2002 est.)
Budget:
revenues: $395.7 million
expenditures: $472.4 million, including capital expenditures of $NA million (2000 est.)
Industries: bauxite, gold, diamonds; alumina refining; light manufacturing and agricultural processing industries
Industrial production growth rate: 3.2% (1994)
Electricity - production: 790.6 million kWh (2001)
Electricity - production by source:
fossil fuel: 45.5%
hydro: 54.5%
nuclear: 0%
other: 0% (2001)
Electricity - consumption: 735.2 million kWh (2001)
Electricity - exports: 0 kWh (2001)
Electricity - imports: 0 kWh (2001)
Oil - production: 0 bbl/day (2001 est.)
Oil - consumption: 8,600 bbl/day (2001 est.)
Oil - exports: NA
Oil - imports: NA
Agriculture - products: rice, coffee, pineapples, palm kernels, cassava (tapioca), bananas, sweet potatoes; cattle, sheep, goats; timber
Exports: $726 million f.o.b. (2003 est.)
Exports - commodities: bauxite, alumina, gold, diamonds, coffee, fish, agricultural products
Exports - partners: South Korea 17%, Spain 9.7%, Cameroon 9.3%, Belgium 9.2%, US 8.9%, Ireland 8.2%, France 6.8%, Russia 6.4%, Ukraine 6.3%, Germany 4.8% (2002)

Guinea (continued)

Imports: $646 million f.o.b. (2003 est.)
Imports - commodities: petroleum products, metals, machinery, transport equipment, textiles, grain and other foodstuffs
Imports - partners: France 17.9%, Cote d'Ivoire 10.6%, Italy 8.5%, US 7.8%, Belgium 7.2%, China 5.4%, UK 5% (2002)
Debt - external: $3.25 billion (2001 est.)
Economic aid - recipient: $359.2 million (1998)
Currency: Guinean franc (GNF)
Currency code: GNF
Exchange rates: Guinean francs per US dollar - NA (2003), 1,975.84 (2002), 1,950.56 (2001), 1,746.87 (2000), 1,387.4 (1999)
Fiscal year: calendar year

Communications

Telephones - main lines in use: 26,000 (2002)
Telephones - mobile cellular: 90,800 (2002)
Telephone system:
general assessment: poor to fair system of open-wire lines, small radiotelephone communication stations, and new microwave radio relay system
domestic: microwave radio relay and radiotelephone communication
international: country code - 224; satellite earth station - 1 Intelsat (Atlantic Ocean)
Radio broadcast stations: AM 4 (one station is inactive), FM 1 (plus 7 repeaters), shortwave 3 (2001)
Television broadcast stations: 6 low-power stations (2001)
Internet country code: .gn
Internet hosts: 251 (2002)
Internet users: 35,000 (2002)

Transportation

Railways:
total: 1,115 km
standard gauge: 311 km 1.435-m gauge
narrow gauge: 804 km 1.000-m gauge (2002)
Highways:
total: 30,500 km
paved: 5,033 km
unpaved: 25,467 km (1999 est.)
Waterways: 1,295 km (navigable by shallow-draft native craft)
Ports and harbors: Boke, Conakry, Kamsar
Merchant marine:
total: 3 ships (1,000 GRT or over) 5,344 GRT/5,003 DWT
by type: cargo 1, petroleum tanker 1, roll on/roll off 1
foreign-owned: Iraq 1 (2003 est.)
Airports: 16 (2003 est.)
Airports - with paved runways:
total: 5
over 3,047 m: 1
2,438 to 3,047 m: 1
1,524 to 2,437 m: 3 (2003 est.)

Airports - with unpaved runways:
total: 11
1,524 to 2,437 m: 6
914 to 1,523 m: 3
under 914 m: 2 (2003 est.)

Military

Military branches: Army, Navy, Air Force, Republican Guard, Presidential Guard, National Gendarmerie, General Directorate of National Police
Military manpower - availability:
males age 15-49: 2,108,948 (2004 est.)
Military manpower - fit for military service:
males age 15-49: 1,064,965 (2004 est.)
Military expenditures - dollar figure: $58.5 million (2003)
Military expenditures - percent of GDP: 1.7% (2003)

Transnational Issues

Disputes - international: domestic fighting among disparate rebel groups in Guinea, domestic fighting among disparate rebel groups, warlords, and youth gangs in Guinea, Liberia, and Sierra Leone have created insurgencies, street violence, looting, arms trafficking, ethnic conflicts skirmishes, deaths, and refugees in border areas; in 2003, Guinea and Sierra Leone established a boundary commission to resolve a dispute over the town of Yenga

Guinea-Bissau

Introduction

Background: Since independence from Portugal in 1974, Guinea-Bissau has experienced considerable upheaval. The founding government consisted of a single party system and command economy. In 1980, a military coup established Joao VIEIRA as president and a path to a market economy and multiparty system was implemented. A number of coup attempts through the 1980s and early 1990s failed to unseat him and in 1994 he was elected president in the country's first free elections. A military coup attempt and civil war in 1998 eventually led to VIEIRA's ouster in 1999. In February 2000, an interim government turned over power when opposition leader Kumba YALA took office following two rounds of transparent presidential elections. YALA was ousted in a bloodless coup in September 2003, and Henrique ROSA was sworn in as President. Guinea-Bissau's transition back to democracy will be complicated by its crippled economy, devastated in the civil war.

Geography

Location: Western Africa, bordering the North Atlantic Ocean, between Guinea and Senegal
Geographic coordinates: 12 00 N, 15 00 W
Map references: Africa
Area:
total: 36,120 sq km
land: 28,000 sq km
water: 8,120 sq km
Area - comparative: slightly less than three times the size of Connecticut
Land boundaries:
total: 724 km
border countries: Guinea 386 km, Senegal 338 km
Coastline: 350 km
Maritime claims:
territorial sea: 12 NM
exclusive economic zone: 200 NM

Guinea-Bissau *(continued)*

Climate: tropical; generally hot and humid; monsoonal-type rainy season (June to November) with southwesterly winds; dry season (December to May) with northeasterly harmattan winds
Terrain: mostly low coastal plain rising to savanna in east
Elevation extremes:
lowest point: Atlantic Ocean 0 m
highest point: unnamed location in the northeast corner of the country 300 m
Natural resources: fish, timber, phosphates, bauxite, unexploited deposits of petroleum
Land use:
arable land: 10.67%
permanent crops: 1.78%
other: 87.55% (1998 est.)
Irrigated land: 170 sq km (1998 est.)
Natural hazards: hot, dry, dusty harmattan haze may reduce visibility during dry season; brush fires
Environment - current issues: deforestation; soil erosion; overgrazing; overfishing
Environment - international agreements:
party to: Biodiversity, Climate Change, Desertification, Endangered Species, Law of the Sea, Wetlands
signed, but not ratified: none of the selected agreements
Geography - note: this small country is swampy along its western coast and low-lying further inland

People

Population: 1,388,363 (July 2004 est.)
Age structure:
0-14 years: 41.7% (male 288,760; female 289,975)
15-64 years: 55.4% (male 367,728; female 400,996)
65 years and over: 2.9% (male 17,570; female 23,334) (2004 est.)
Median age:
total: 18.9 years
male: 18.3 years
female: 19.5 years (2004 est.)
Population growth rate: 1.99% (2004 est.)
Birth rate: 38.03 births/1,000 population (2004 est.)
Death rate: 16.57 deaths/1,000 population (2004 est.)
Net migration rate: -1.57 migrant(s)/1,000 population (2004 est.)
Sex ratio:
at birth: 1.03 male(s)/female
under 15 years: 1 male(s)/female
15-64 years: 0.92 male(s)/female
65 years and over: 0.75 male(s)/female
total population: 0.94 male(s)/female (2004 est.)
Infant mortality rate:
total: 108.72 deaths/1,000 live births
male: 119.37 deaths/1,000 live births
female: 97.74 deaths/1,000 live births (2004 est.)
Life expectancy at birth:
total population: 46.98 years
male: 45.09 years
female: 48.92 years (2004 est.)

Total fertility rate: 5 children born/woman (2004 est.)
HIV/AIDS - adult prevalence rate: 10% (2003 est.)
HIV/AIDS - people living with HIV/AIDS: 17,000 (2001 est.)
HIV/AIDS - deaths: 1,200 (2001 est.)
Nationality:
noun: Guinean(s)
adjective: Guinean
Ethnic groups: African 99% (Balanta 30%, Fula 20%, Manjaca 14%, Mandinga 13%, Papel 7%), European and mulatto less than 1%
Religions: indigenous beliefs 50%, Muslim 45%, Christian 5%
Languages: Portuguese (official), Crioulo, African languages
Literacy:
definition: age 15 and over can read and write
total population: 42.4%
male: 58.1%
female: 27.4% (2003 est.)

Government

Country name:
conventional long form: Republic of Guinea-Bissau
conventional short form: Guinea-Bissau
local long form: Republica da Guine-Bissau
local short form: Guine-Bissau
former: Portuguese Guinea
Government type: republic, multiparty since mid-1991
Capital: Bissau
Administrative divisions: 9 regions (regioes, singular - regiao); Bafata, Biombo, Bissau, Bolama, Cacheu, Gabu, Oio, Quinara, Tombali; note - Bolama may have been renamed Bolama/Bijagos
Independence: 24 September 1973 (unilaterally declared by Guinea-Bissau); 10 September 1974 (recognized by Portugal)
National holiday: Independence Day, 24 September (1973)
Constitution: 16 May 1984, amended 4 May 1991, 4 December 1991, 26 February 1993, 9 June 1993, and 1996
Legal system: NA
Suffrage: 18 years of age; universal
Executive branch:
chief of state: President Henrique ROSA (interim; since 28 September 2003); note - a September 2003 coup overthrew the elected government of Kumba YALA; General Verissimo Correia SEABRA served as interim president from 14 to 28 September 2003
head of government: Prime Minister Artur SANHA (since 28 September 2003)
cabinet: NA
elections: president elected by popular vote for a five-year term; election last held 28 November 1999 and 16 January 2000 (next to be held NA 2004); prime minister appointed by the president after consultation with party leaders in the legislature

election results: Kumba YALA elected president; percent of vote, second ballot - Kumba YALA (PRS) 72%, Malan Bacai SANHA (PAIGC) 28%
note: a bloodless coup led to the dissolution of the elected government of Kumba YALA in September 2003; General Verissimo Correia SEABRA served as interim president from 14 September 2003 until stepping aside on 28 September 2003 with the establishment of a caretaker government
Legislative branch: unicameral National People's Assembly or Assembleia Nacional Popular (100 seats; members are elected by popular vote to serve a maximum of four years); note - President YALA dissolved the National People's Assembly in November 2002, elections for a new legislature were scheduled to fall in February 2003 but were then postponed to April, then July, then September, and were last scheduled to occur in March 2004
elections: last held 28 March 2004 (next to be held NA 2009)
election results: percent of vote by party - PAIGC 31.5%, PRS 24.8%, PUSD 16.1%, UE 4.1%, APU 1.3%, 13 other parties 22.2% ; seats by party - PAIGC 45, PRS 35, PUSD 17, UE 2, APU 1
Judicial branch: Supreme Court or Supremo Tribunal da Justica (consists of nine justices who are appointed by the president and serve at his pleasure; final court of appeals in criminal and civil cases); Regional Courts (one in each of nine regions; first court of appeals for Sectoral Court decisions; hear all felony cases and civil cases valued at over $1,000); 24 Sectoral Courts (judges are not necessarily trained lawyers; they hear civil cases under $1,000 and misdemeanor criminal cases)
Political parties and leaders: African Party for the Independence of Guinea-Bissau and Cape Verde or PAIGC [Carlos GOMES Junior]; Front for the Liberation and Independence of Guinea or FLING [Francois MENDY]; Guinea-Bissau Resistance-Ba Fata Movement or RGB-MB [Helder Vaz LOPES]; Guinean Civic Forum or FCG [Antonieta Rosa GOMES]; International League for Ecological Protection or LIPE [Alhaje Bubacar DJALO, president]; National Union for Democracy and Progress or UNDP [Abubacer BALDE, secretary general]; Party for Democratic Convergence or PCD [Victor MANDINGA]; Social Renovation Party or PRS [Kumba YALA]; Union for Change or UM [Jorge MANDINGA, president, Dr. Anne SAAD, secretary general]; United Platform or UP [coalition formed by PCD, FDS, FLING, and RGB-MB]; United Social Democratic Party or PUSD [Francisco Jose FADUL]
Political pressure groups and leaders: NA
International organization participation: ACCT, ACP, AfDB, AU, ECOWAS, FAO, FZ, G-77, IBRD, ICAO, ICCt (signatory), ICFTU, ICRM, IDA, IDB, IFAD, IFC, IFRCS, ILO, IMF, IMO, Interpol, IOC, IOM, ITU, NAM, OIC, OPCW (signatory), UN, UNCTAD, UNESCO, UNIDO, UNMIL, UPU, WADB (regional), WAEMU, WFTU, WHO, WIPO, WMO, WToO, WTrO

Guinea-Bissau *(continued)*

Diplomatic representation in the US:
chief of mission: Ambassador (vacant); Charge d'Affaires Henrique Adriano DA SILVA
chancery: 1511 K Street NW, Suite 519, Washington, DC 20005
telephone: [1] (202) 347-3950
FAX: [1] (202) 347-3954
Diplomatic representation from the US: the US Embassy suspended operations on 14 June 1998 in the midst of violent conflict between forces loyal to then President VIEIRA and military-led junta; US embassy Dakar is responsible for covering Guinea-Bissau: telephone - [221] 823-4296; FAX - [221] 822-5903
Flag description: two equal horizontal bands of yellow (top) and green with a vertical red band on the hoist side; there is a black five-pointed star centered in the red band; uses the popular pan-African colors of Ethiopia

Economy

Economy - overview: One of the 10 poorest countries in the world, Guinea-Bissau depends mainly on farming and fishing. Cashew crops have increased remarkably in recent years, and the country now ranks sixth in cashew production. Guinea-Bissau exports fish and seafood along with small amounts of peanuts, palm kernels, and timber. Rice is the major crop and staple food. However, intermittent fighting between Senegalese-backed government troops and a military junta destroyed much of the country's infrastructure and caused widespread damage to the economy in 1998; the civil war led to a 28% drop in GDP that year, with partial recovery in 1999-2002. Before the war, trade reform and price liberalization were the most successful part of the country's structural adjustment program under IMF sponsorship. The tightening of monetary policy and the development of the private sector had also begun to reinvigorate the economy. Because of high costs, the development of petroleum, phosphate, and other mineral resources is not a near-term prospect. However, unexploited offshore oil reserves could provide much-needed revenue in the long run. The inequality of income distribution is one of the most extreme in the world. The government and international donors continue to work out plans to forward economic development from a lamentably low base. Government drift and indecision, however, have resulted in low growth in 2002-03 and dim prospects for 2004.
GDP: purchasing power parity - $1.164 billion (2003 est.)
GDP - real growth rate: 1.8% (2003 est.)
GDP - per capita: purchasing power parity - $900 (2003 est.)
GDP - composition by sector:
agriculture: 62%
industry: 12%
services: 26% (1999 est.)
Population below poverty line: NA%

Household income or consumption by percentage share:
lowest 10%: 0.5%
highest 10%: 42.4% (1991)
Inflation rate (consumer prices): 4% (2002 est.)
Labor force: 480,000 (1999)
Labor force - by occupation: agriculture 82% (2000 est.)
Unemployment rate: NA% (1998)
Budget:
revenues: $NA
expenditures: $NA, including capital expenditures of $NA
Industries: agricultural products processing, beer, soft drinks
Industrial production growth rate: 2.6% (1997 est.)
Electricity - production: 55 million kWh (2001)
Electricity - production by source:
fossil fuel: 100%
hydro: 0%
nuclear: 0%
other: 0% (2001)
Electricity - consumption: 51.15 million kWh (2001)
Electricity - exports: 0 kWh (2001)
Electricity - imports: 0 kWh (2001)
Oil - production: 0 bbl/day (2001 est.)
Oil - consumption: 2,500 bbl/day (2001 est.)
Oil - exports: NA
Oil - imports: NA
Agriculture - products: rice, corn, beans, cassava (tapioca), cashew nuts, peanuts, palm kernels, cotton; timber; fish
Exports: $54 million f.o.b. (2002 est.)
Exports - commodities: cashew nuts, shrimp, peanuts, palm kernels, sawn lumber
Exports - partners: India 50%, Thailand 19.2%, Uruguay 19.2% (2002)
Imports: $104 million f.o.b. (2002 est.)
Imports - commodities: foodstuffs, machinery and transport equipment, petroleum products
Imports - partners: Senegal 19.6%, Portugal 18.8%, India 15.2% (2002)
Debt - external: $941.5 million (2000 est.)
Economic aid - recipient: $115.4 million (1995)
Currency: Communaute Financiere Africaine franc (XOF); note - responsible authority is the Central Bank of the West African States; previously the Guinea-Bissau peso (GWP) was used
Currency code: XOF; GWP
Exchange rates: Communaute Financiere Africaine francs (XOF) per US dollar - 581.2 (2003), 696.988 (2002), 733.039 (2001), 711.976 (2000), 615.699 (1999)
note: as of 1 May 1997, Guinea-Bissau adopted the XOF franc as the national currency; since 1 January 1999, the XOF franc is pegged to the euro at a rate of 655.957 XOF francs per euro
Fiscal year: calendar year

Communications

Telephones - main lines in use: 11,200 (2002)
Telephones - mobile cellular: NA
Telephone system:
general assessment: small system
domestic: combination of microwave radio relay, open-wire lines, radiotelephone, and cellular communications
international: country code - 245
Radio broadcast stations: AM 1 (transmitter out of service), FM 4, shortwave 0 (2002)
Television broadcast stations: NA (1997)
Internet country code: .gw
Internet hosts: 20 (2002)
Internet users: 5,000 (2002)

Transportation

Railways: 0 km
Highways:
total: 4,400 km
paved: 453 km
unpaved: 3,947 km (1999 est.)
Waterways: several rivers are accessible to coastal shipping
Ports and harbors: Bissau, Buba, Cacheu, Farim
Merchant marine: none
Airports: 28 (2003 est.)
Airports - with paved runways:
total: 3
over 3,047 m: 1
1,524 to 2,437 m: 1
914 to 1,523 m: 1 (2003 est.)
Airports - with unpaved runways:
total: 25
1,524 to 2,437 m: 1
914 to 1,523 m: 4
under 914 m: 20 (2003 est.)

Military

Military branches: People's Revolutionary Armed Force (FARP; includes Army, Navy, and Air Force), paramilitary force
Military manpower - availability:
males age 15-49: 326,864 (2004 est.)
Military manpower - fit for military service:
males age 15-49: 185,801 (2004 est.)
Military expenditures - dollar figure: $8.4 million (2003)
Military expenditures - percent of GDP: 2.8% (2003)

Transnational Issues

Disputes - international: attempts to stem refugees and cross-border raids, arms smuggling, and political instability from a separatist movement in Senegal's Casamance region

Guyana

Introduction

Background: Originally a Dutch colony in the 17th century, by 1815 Guyana had become a British possession. The abolition of slavery led to black settlement of urban areas and the importation of indentured servants from India to work the sugar plantations. This ethnocultural divide has persisted and has led to turbulent politics. Guyana achieved independence from the UK in 1966, but until the early 1990s it was ruled mostly by socialist-oriented governments. In 1992, Cheddi JAGAN was elected president, in what is considered the country's first free and fair election since independence. Upon his death five years later, he was succeeded by his wife Janet, who resigned in 1999 due to poor health. Her successor, Bharrat JAGDEO, was reelected in 2001.

Geography

Location: Northern South America, bordering the North Atlantic Ocean, between Suriname and Venezuela
Geographic coordinates: 5 00 N, 59 00 W
Map references: South America

Area:
total: 214,970 sq km
land: 196,850 sq km
water: 18,120 sq km
Area - comparative: slightly smaller than Idaho
Land boundaries:
total: 2,462 km
border countries: Brazil 1,119 km, Suriname 600 km, Venezuela 743 km
Coastline: 459 km
Maritime claims:
territorial sea: 12 NM
exclusive economic zone: 200 NM
continental shelf: 200 NM or to the outer edge of the continental margin
Climate: tropical; hot, humid, moderated by northeast trade winds; two rainy seasons (May to mid-August, mid-November to mid-January)
Terrain: mostly rolling highlands; low coastal plain; savanna in south
Elevation extremes:
lowest point: Atlantic Ocean 0 m
highest point: Mount Roraima 2,835 m
Natural resources: bauxite, gold, diamonds, hardwood timber, shrimp, fish
Land use:
arable land: 2.44%
permanent crops: 0.08%
other: 97.48% (1998 est.)
Irrigated land: 1,500 sq km (1998 est.)
Natural hazards: flash floods are a constant threat during rainy seasons
Environment - current issues: water pollution from sewage and agricultural and industrial chemicals; deforestation
Environment - international agreements:
party to: Biodiversity, Climate Change, Climate Change-Kyoto Protocol, Desertification, Endangered Species, Hazardous Wastes, Law of the Sea, Ozone Layer Protection, Ship Pollution, Tropical Timber 83, Tropical Timber 94
signed, but not ratified: none of the selected agreements
Geography - note: the third-smallest country in South America after Suriname and Uruguay; substantial portions of its western and eastern territories are claimed by Venezuela and Suriname respectively

People

Population: 705,803
note: estimates for this country explicitly take into account the effects of excess mortality due to AIDS; this can result in lower life expectancy, higher infant mortality and death rates, lower population and growth rates, and changes in the distribution of population by age and sex than would otherwise be expected (July 2004 est.)
Age structure:
0-14 years: 26.5% (male 95,431; female 91,806)
15-64 years: 68.3% (male 243,224; female 239,047)

65 years and over: 5.1% (male 16,000; female 20,295) (2004 est.)
Median age:
total: 26.2 years
male: 25.6 years
female: 26.8 years (2004 est.)
Population growth rate: 0.61% (2004 est.)
Birth rate: 17.85 births/1,000 population (2004 est.)
Death rate: 9.71 deaths/1,000 population (2004 est.)
Net migration rate: -2.07 migrant(s)/1,000 population (2004 est.)
Sex ratio:
at birth: 1.05 male(s)/female
under 15 years: 1.04 male(s)/female
15-64 years: 1.02 male(s)/female
65 years and over: 0.79 male(s)/female
total population: 1.01 male(s)/female (2004 est.)
Infant mortality rate:
total: 37.22 deaths/1,000 live births
male: 41.28 deaths/1,000 live births
female: 32.95 deaths/1,000 live births (2004 est.)
Life expectancy at birth:
total population: 62.43 years
male: 60.12 years
female: 64.84 years (2004 est.)
Total fertility rate: 2.06 children born/woman (2004 est.)
HIV/AIDS - adult prevalence rate: 2.7% (2001 est.)
HIV/AIDS - people living with HIV/AIDS: 18,000 (2001 est.)
HIV/AIDS - deaths: 1,300 (2001 est.)
Nationality:
noun: Guyanese (singular and plural)
adjective: Guyanese
Ethnic groups: East Indian 50%, black 36%, Amerindian 7%, white, Chinese, and mixed 7%
Religions: Christian 50%, Hindu 35%, Muslim 10%, other 5%
Languages: English, Amerindian dialects, Creole, Hindi, Urdu
Literacy:
definition: age 15 and over has ever attended school
total population: 98.8%
male: 99.1%
female: 98.5% (2003 est.)

Government

Country name:
conventional long form: Co-operative Republic of Guyana
conventional short form: Guyana
former: British Guiana
Government type: republic within the Commonwealth
Capital: Georgetown
Administrative divisions: 10 regions; Barima-Waini, Cuyuni-Mazaruni, Demerara-Mahaica, East Berbice-Corentyne, Essequibo Islands-West Demerara, Mahaica-Berbice, Pomeroon-Supenaam, Potaro-Siparuni, Upper Demerara-Berbice, Upper Takutu-Upper Essequibo

Guyana (continued)

Independence: 26 May 1966 (from UK)
National holiday: Republic Day, 23 February (1970)
Constitution: 6 October 1980
Legal system: based on English common law with certain admixtures of Roman-Dutch law; has not accepted compulsory ICJ jurisdiction
Suffrage: 18 years of age; universal
Executive branch:
chief of state: President Bharrat JAGDEO (since 11 August 1999); note - assumed presidency after resignation of President Janet JAGAN
head of government: Prime Minister Samuel HINDS (since NA December 1997)
cabinet: Cabinet of Ministers appointed by the president, responsible to the legislature
elections: president elected by the majority party in the National Assembly following legislative elections, which must be held at least every five years; elections last held 19 March 2001 (next to be held by March 2006); prime minister appointed by the president
election results: President Bharrat JAGDEO reelected; percent of legislative vote - NA%
Legislative branch: unicameral National Assembly (68 seats, 65 elected by popular vote, 1 elected Speaker of the National Assembly, and 2 nonvoting members appointed by the president; members serve five-year terms)
elections: last held 19 March 2001 (next to be held NA March 2006)
election results: percent of vote by party - NA%; seats by party - PPP/C 34, PNC 27, GAP and WPA 2, ROAR 1, TUF 1
Judicial branch: Supreme Court of Judicature; Judicial Court of Appeal; High Court
Political parties and leaders: Alliance for Guyana or AFG (includes Guyana Labor Party or GLP and Working People's Alliance or WPA) [Rupert ROOPNARAINE]; Guyana Action Party or GAP [Paul HARDY]; Guyana Labor Party or GLP [leader NA]; People's National Congress or PNC/R [Robert Herman Orlando CORBIN]; People's Progressive Party/Civic or PPP/C [Bharrat JAGDEO]; Rise, Organize, and Rebuild or ROAR [Ravi DEV]; The United Force or TUF [Manzoor NADIR]; Working People's Alliance or WPA [Rupert ROOPNARAINE]
Political pressure groups and leaders: Civil Liberties Action Committee or CLAC; Guyana Council of Indian Organizations or GCIO; Trades Union Congress or TUC
note: the GCIO and the CLAC are small and active but not well organized
International organization participation: ACP, C, Caricom, CDB, FAO, G-77, IADB, IBRD, ICAO, ICCt (signatory), ICFTU, ICRM, IDA, IFAD, IFC, IFRCS, ILO, IMF, IMO, Interpol, IOC, ISO (subscriber), ITU, LAES, NAM, OAS, OIC, OPANAL, OPCW, PCA, RG, UN, UNCTAD, UNESCO, UNIDO, UPU, WCL, WCO, WFTU, WHO, WIPO, WMO, WTrO
Diplomatic representation in the US:
chief of mission: Ambassador Dr. Ali Odeen ISHMAEL

chancery: 2490 Tracy Place NW, Washington, DC 20008
telephone: [1] (202) 265-6900
FAX: [1] (202) 232-1297
consulate(s) general: New York
Diplomatic representation from the US:
chief of mission: Ambassador Ronald D. GODARD
embassy: 100 Young and Duke Streets, Kingston, Georgetown
mailing address: P. O. Box 10507, Georgetown
telephone: [592] 225-4900 through 4909
FAX: [592] 225-8497
Flag description: green, with a red isosceles triangle (based on the hoist side) superimposed on a long, yellow arrowhead; there is a narrow, black border between the red and yellow, and a narrow, white border between the yellow and the green

Economy

Economy - overview: The Guyanese economy exhibited moderate economic growth in 2001-02, based on expansion in the agricultural and mining sectors, a more favorable atmosphere for business initiatives, a more realistic exchange rate, fairly low inflation, and the continued support of international organizations. Growth then slowed in 2003. Chronic problems include a shortage of skilled labor and a deficient infrastructure. The government is juggling a sizable external debt against the urgent need for expanded public investment. The bauxite mining sector should benefit in the near term by restructuring and partial privatization.
GDP: purchasing power parity - $2.792 billion (2003 est.)
GDP - real growth rate: 0.3% (2003 est.)
GDP - per capita: purchasing power parity - $4,000 (2003 est.)
GDP - composition by sector:
agriculture: 35%
industry: 21%
services: 44% (2002 est.)
Population below poverty line: NA%
Household income or consumption by percentage share:
lowest 10%: NA%
highest 10%: NA%
Inflation rate (consumer prices): 4.7% (2002 est.)
Labor force: 418,000 (2001 est.)
Labor force - by occupation: agriculture NA%, industry NA%, services NA%
Unemployment rate: 9.1% (understated) (2000)
Budget:
revenues: $227 million
expenditures: $235.2 million, including capital expenditures of $93.4 million (2000)
Industries: bauxite, sugar, rice milling, timber, textiles, gold mining
Industrial production growth rate: 7.1% (1997 est.)
Electricity - production: 852 million kWh (2001)

Electricity - production by source:
fossil fuel: 99.4%
hydro: 0.6%
nuclear: 0%
other: 0% (2001)
Electricity - consumption: 792.4 million kWh (2001)
Electricity - exports: 0 kWh (2001)
Electricity - imports: 0 kWh (2001)
Oil - production: 0 bbl/day (2001 est.)
Oil - consumption: 11,000 bbl/day (2001 est.)
Oil - exports: NA
Oil - imports: NA
Agriculture - products: sugar, rice, wheat, vegetable oils; beef, pork, poultry, dairy products; fish (shrimp)
Exports: $512 million f.o.b. (2003 est.)
Exports - commodities: sugar, gold, bauxite/alumina, rice, shrimp, molasses, rum, timber
Exports - partners: Canada 26.3%, US 22.3%, UK 13%, Jamaica 5.1%, Portugal 5.1%, Belgium 4.2% (2002)
Imports: $612 million f.o.b. (2003 est.)
Imports - commodities: manufactures, machinery, petroleum, food
Imports - partners: US 25.1%, Trinidad and Tobago 16%, Netherlands Antilles 13.7%, Italy 6.6%, UK 5.5%, Cuba 4.4% (2002)
Debt - external: $1.2 billion (2002)
Economic aid - recipient: $84 million (1995), Heavily Indebted Poor Country Initiative (HIPC) $253 million (1997) (2000 est.)
Currency: Guyanese dollar (GYD)
Currency code: GYD
Exchange rates: Guyanese dollars per US dollar - NA (2003), 190.665 (2002), 187.321 (2001), 182.43 (2000), 177.995 (1999)
Fiscal year: calendar year

Communications

Telephones - main lines in use: 80,400 (2002)
Telephones - mobile cellular: 87,300 (2002)
Telephone system:
general assessment: fair system for long-distance calling
domestic: microwave radio relay network for trunk lines
international: country code - 592; tropospheric scatter to Trinidad; satellite earth station - 1 Intelsat (Atlantic Ocean)
Radio broadcast stations: AM 3, FM 3, shortwave 1 (1998)
Television broadcast stations: 3 (one public station; two private stations which relay US satellite services) (1997)
Internet country code: .gy
Internet hosts: 63 (2002)
Internet users: 125,000 (2002)

Guyana *(continued)*

Transportation

Railways:
total: 187 km
standard gauge: 139 km 1.435-m gauge
narrow gauge: 48 km 0.914-m gauge
note: all dedicated to ore transport (2001 est.)
Highways:
total: 7,970 km
paved: 590 km
unpaved: 7,380 km (1999 est.)
Waterways: 5,900 km (total length of navigable waterways)
note: Berbice, Demerara, and Essequibo rivers are navigable by oceangoing vessels for 150 km, 100 km, and 80 km, respectively
Ports and harbors: Bartica, Georgetown, Linden, New Amsterdam, Parika
Merchant marine:
total: 5 ships (1,000 GRT or over) 7,475 GRT/8,758 DWT
by type: cargo 3, container 1, refrigerated cargo 1
foreign-owned: Barbados 1, Panama 1
registered in other countries: 8 (2003 est.)
Airports: 49 (2003 est.)
Airports - with paved runways:
total: 8
1,524 to 2,437 m: 3
under 914 m: 5 (2003 est.)
Airports - with unpaved runways:
total: 41
1,524 to 2,437 m: 1
914 to 1,523 m: 8
under 914 m: 32 (2003 est.)

Military

Military branches: Guyana Defense Force: Ground Forces, Coast Guard, Air Corps; Guyana People's Militia
Military manpower - availability:
males age 15-49: 209,545 (2004 est.)
Military manpower - fit for military service:
males age 15-49: 157,264 (2004 est.)
Military expenditures - dollar figure: $6.5 million (2003)
Military expenditures - percent of GDP: 0.8% (2003)

Transnational Issues

Disputes - international: all of the area west of the Essequibo (river) is claimed by Venezuela preventing any discussion of a maritime boundary; Guyana has expressed its intention to join Barbados in asserting claims before UNCLOS that Trinidad and Tobago's maritime boundary with Venezuela extends into their waters; Suriname claims a triangle of land between the New and Kutari/Koetari rivers in a historic dispute over the headwaters of the Courantyne; Guyana seeks UNCLOS arbitration to resolve the long-standing dispute with Suriname over the axis of the territorial sea boundary in potentially oil-rich waters
Illicit drugs: transshipment point for narcotics from South America - primarily Venezuela - to Europe and the US; producer of cannabis

Haiti

Introduction

Background: The native Arawak Amerindians - who inhabited the island of Hispaniola when it was discovered by Columbus in 1492 - were virtually annihilated by Spanish settlers within 25 years. In the early 17th century, the French established a presence on Hispaniola, and in 1697, Spain ceded to the French the western third of the island - Haiti. The French colony, based on forestry and sugar-related industries, became one of the wealthiest in the Caribbean, but only through the heavy importation of African slaves and considerable environmental degradation. In the late 18th century, Haiti's nearly half million slaves revolted under Toussaint L'OUVERTURE and after a prolonged struggle, became the first black republic to declare its independence in 1804. Haiti has been plagued by political violence for most of its history. It is the poorest country in the Western Hemisphere.

Geography

Location: Caribbean, western one-third of the island of Hispaniola, between the Caribbean Sea and the North Atlantic Ocean, west of the Dominican Republic
Geographic coordinates: 19 00 N, 72 25 W
Map references: Central America and the Caribbean
Area:
total: 27,750 sq km
land: 27,560 sq km
water: 190 sq km
Area - comparative: slightly smaller than Maryland
Land boundaries:
total: 360 km
border countries: Dominican Republic 360 km
Coastline: 1,771 km
Maritime claims:
territorial sea: 12 NM
contiguous zone: 24 NM

exclusive economic zone: 200 NM
continental shelf: to depth of exploitation
Climate: tropical; semiarid where mountains in east cut off trade winds
Terrain: mostly rough and mountainous
Elevation extremes:
lowest point: Caribbean Sea 0 m
highest point: Chaine de la Selle 2,680 m
Natural resources: bauxite, copper, calcium carbonate, gold, marble, hydropower
Land use:
arable land: 20.3%
permanent crops: 12.7%
other: 67% (1998 est.)
Irrigated land: 750 sq km (1998 est.)
Natural hazards: lies in the middle of the hurricane belt and subject to severe storms from June to October; occasional flooding and earthquakes; periodic droughts
Environment - current issues: extensive deforestation (much of the remaining forested land is being cleared for agriculture and used as fuel); soil erosion; inadequate supplies of potable water
Environment - international agreements:
party to: Biodiversity, Climate Change, Desertification, Law of the Sea, Marine Dumping, Marine Life Conservation, Ozone Layer Protection
signed, but not ratified: Hazardous Wastes
Geography - note: shares island of Hispaniola with Dominican Republic (western one-third is Haiti, eastern two-thirds is the Dominican Republic)

People

Population: 7,656,166
note: estimates for this country explicitly take into account the effects of excess mortality due to AIDS; this can result in lower life expectancy, higher infant mortality and death rates, lower population and growth rates, and changes in the distribution of population by age and sex than would otherwise be expected (July 2004 est.)
Age structure:
0-14 years: 42.2% (male 1,646,216; female 1,583,294)
15-64 years: 54.1% (male 2,018,914; female 2,124,287)
65 years and over: 3.7% (male 133,241; female 150,214) (2004 est.)
Median age:
total: 18.1 years
male: 17.6 years
female: 18.7 years (2004 est.)
Population growth rate: 1.71% (2004 est.)
Birth rate: 33.76 births/1,000 population (2004 est.)
Death rate: 13.21 deaths/1,000 population (2004 est.)
Net migration rate: -3.4 migrant(s)/1,000 population (2004 est.)
Sex ratio:
at birth: 1.05 male(s)/female
under 15 years: 1.04 male(s)/female
15-64 years: 0.95 male(s)/female

Haiti *(continued)*

65 years and over: 0.89 male(s)/female
total population: 0.99 male(s)/female (2004 est.)
Infant mortality rate:
total: 74.38 deaths/1,000 live births
male: 79.83 deaths/1,000 live births
female: 68.65 deaths/1,000 live births (2004 est.)
Life expectancy at birth:
total population: 51.78 years
male: 50.52 years
female: 53.12 years (2004 est.)
Total fertility rate: 4.76 children born/woman
(2004 est.)
HIV/AIDS - adult prevalence rate: 6.1% (2001 est.)
HIV/AIDS - people living with HIV/AIDS: 250,000
(2001 est.)
HIV/AIDS - deaths: 30,000 (2001 est.)
Nationality:
noun: Haitian(s)
adjective: Haitian
Ethnic groups: black 95%, mulatto and white 5%
Religions: Roman Catholic 80%, Protestant 16%
(Baptist 10%, Pentecostal 4%, Adventist 1%,
other 1%), none 1%, other 3% (1982)
note: roughly half of the population practices Voodoo
Languages: French (official), Creole (official)
Literacy:
definition: age 15 and over can read and write
total population: 52.9%
male: 54.8%
female: 51.2% (2003 est.)

Government

Country name:
conventional long form: Republic of Haiti
conventional short form: Haiti
local long form: Republique d'Haiti
local short form: Haiti
Government type: elected government
Capital: Port-au-Prince
Administrative divisions: 9 departments
(departements, singular - departement); Artibonite,
Centre, Grand 'Anse, Nord, Nord-Est, Nord-Ouest,
Ouest, Sud, Sud-Est
Independence: 1 January 1804 (from France)
National holiday: Independence Day, 1 January
(1804)
Constitution: approved March 1987; suspended
June 1988 with most articles reinstated March 1989;
in October 1991 government claimed to be observing
the constitution; returned to constitutional rule in
October 1994
Legal system: based on Roman civil law system;
accepts compulsory ICJ jurisdiction
Suffrage: 18 years of age; universal
Executive branch:
chief of state: Interim President Boniface
ALEXANDER (since 29 February 2004)
note: Jean-Bertrand ARISTIDE resigned as president
on 29 February 2004
head of government: Prime Minister Gerald
LATORTUE (since 12 March 2004)

cabinet: Cabinet chosen by the prime minister in
consultation with the president
elections: president elected by popular vote for a
five-year term; election last held 26 November 2000
(next to be held in 2004); prime minister appointed by
the president, ratified by the National Assembly
election results: Jean-Bertrand ARISTIDE elected
president; percent of vote - Jean-Bertrand ARISTIDE
92%
Legislative branch: bicameral National Assembly or
Assemblee Nationale consists of the Senate (27
seats; members elected by popular vote to serve
six-year terms; one-third elected every two years) and
the Chamber of Deputies (83 seats; members are
elected by popular vote to serve four-year terms)
elections: Senate - last held for two-thirds of seats
21 May 2000 with runoffs on 9 July boycotted by the
opposition; seven seats still disputed; election for
remaining one-third held on 26 November 2000 (next
to be held in 2004); Chamber of Deputies - last held
21 May 2000 with runoffs on 30 July boycotted by the
opposition; one vacant seat rerun 26 November 2000
(next to be held in 2004)
election results: Senate - percent of vote by party -
NA%; seats by party - FL 26, independent 1; Chamber
of Deputies - percent of vote by party - NA%; seats by
party - FL 73, MOCHRENA 3, PLB 2, OPL 1, vacant 1,
other minor parties and independents 3
Judicial branch: Supreme Court or Cour de
Cassation
Political parties and leaders: Alliance for the
Liberation and Advancement of Haiti or ALAH
[Reynold GEORGES]; Assembly of Progressive
National Democrats or RDNP [Leslie MANIGAT];
Convention for Democratic Unity or KID [leader NA];
Convergence (opposition coalition composed of
ESPACE, OPL, and MOCHRENA) [Gerard
PIERRE-CHARLES, Evans PAUL, Luc MESADIEU,
Victor BENOIT]; Democratic Consultation Group
coalition or ESPACE [Evans PAUL, Victor BENOIT]
composed of the following parties: National Congress
of Democratic Movements or KONAKOM, National
Progressive Revolutionary Party or PANPRA,
Generation 2004, and Haiti Can; Haitian Christian
Democratic Party or PDCH [Marie-France CLAUDE];
Haitian Democratic Party or PADEM [Clark PARENT];
Lavalas Family or FL [Jean-Bertrand ARISTIDE];
Mobilization for National Development or MDN
[Hubert DE RONCERAY]; Movement for National
Reconstruction or MRN [Rene THEODORE];
Movement for the Installation of Democracy in Haiti or
MIDH [Marc BAZIN]; Movement for the Organization
of the Country or MOP [Gesner COMEAU and Jean
MOLIERE]; National Cooperative Action Movement or
MKN [Volrick Remy JOSEPH]; National Front for
Change and Democracy or FNCD [Evans PAUL and
Turneb DELPE]; New Christian Movement for a New
Haiti or MOCHRENA [Luc MESADIEU]; Open the
Gate or PLB [Renaud BERNARDIN]; Struggling
People's Organization or OPL [Gerard
PIERRE-CHARLES]

Political pressure groups and leaders:
Autonomous Haitian Workers or CATH;
Confederation of Haitian Workers or CTH; Federation
of Workers Trade Unions or FOS; National Popular
Assembly or APN; Papaye Peasants Movement or
MPP; Popular Organizations Gathering Power or
PROP; Roman Catholic Church
International organization participation: ACCT,
ACP, Caricom, FAO, G-77, IADB, IAEA, IBRD, ICAO,
ICCt (signatory), ICRM, IDA, IFAD, IFC, IFRCS, ILO,
IMF, IMO, Interpol, IOC, IOM, ITU, LAES, OAS,
OPANAL, OPCW (signatory), PCA, UN, UNCTAD,
UNESCO, UNIDO, UPU, WCL, WCO, WFTU, WHO,
WIPO, WMO, WToO, WTrO
Diplomatic representation in the US:
chief of mission: Ambassador Raymond VALCIN (as
of December 2003)
chancery: 2311 Massachusetts Avenue NW,
Washington, DC 20008
telephone: [1] (202) 332-4090
FAX: [1] (202) 745-7215
consulate(s) general: Boston, Chicago, Miami, New
York, and San Juan (Puerto Rico)
Diplomatic representation from the US:
chief of mission: Ambassador James B. FOLEY (as of
September 2003)
embassy: 5 Harry S Truman Boulevard,
Port-au-Prince
mailing address: P. O. Box 1761, Port-au-Prince
telephone: [509] 222-0354, 222-0368, 222-0200,
222-0612
FAX: [509] 223-1641
Flag description: two equal horizontal bands of blue
(top) and red with a centered white rectangle bearing
the coat of arms, which contains a palm tree flanked by
flags and two cannons above a scroll bearing the motto
L'UNION FAIT LA FORCE (Union Makes Strength)

Economy

Economy - overview: In this poorest country in the
Western Hemisphere, 80% of the population lives in
abject poverty. Two-thirds of all Haitians depend on
the agriculture sector, which consists mainly of
small-scale subsistence farming. Following legislative
elections in May 2000, fraught with irregularities,
international donors - including the US and EU -
suspended almost all aid to Haiti. The economy
shrank an estimated 1.2% in 2001 and an estimated
0.9% in 2002. Suspended aid and loan disbursements
totaled more than $500 million at the start of 2003.
Haiti also suffers from rampant inflation, a lack of
investment, and a severe trade deficit. The
resumption of aid flows from all donors will alleviate
but not end the nation's bitter economic problems.
Extensive civil strife in early 2004, marked by the flight
of President ARISTIDE, further impoverished Haiti.
GDP: purchasing power parity - $12.18 billion
(2003 est.)
GDP - real growth rate: -1% (2003 est.)
GDP - per capita: purchasing power parity - $1,600
(2003 est.)

Haiti (continued)

GDP - composition by sector:
agriculture: 30%
industry: 20%
services: 50% (2001 est.)
Population below poverty line: 80% (2003 est.)
Household income or consumption by percentage share:
lowest 10%: NA%
highest 10%: NA%
Inflation rate (consumer prices): 37.3% (2003 est.)
Labor force: 3.6 million
note: shortage of skilled labor, unskilled labor abundant (2003)
Labor force - by occupation: agriculture 66%, services 25%, industry 9%
Unemployment rate: widespread unemployment and underemployment; more than two-thirds of the labor force do not have formal jobs (2002 est.)
Budget:
revenues: $273 million
expenditures: $361 million, including capital expenditures of $NA (FY00/01 est.)
Industries: sugar refining, flour milling, textiles, cement, light assembly industries based on imported parts
Industrial production growth rate: NA
Electricity - production: 580 million kWh (2001)
Electricity - production by source:
fossil fuel: 60.3%
hydro: 39.7%
nuclear: 0%
other: 0% (2001)
Electricity - consumption: 539.4 million kWh (2001)
Electricity - exports: 0 kWh (2001)
Electricity - imports: 0 kWh (2001)
Oil - production: 0 bbl/day (2001 est.)
Oil - consumption: 11,000 bbl/day (2001 est.)
Oil - exports: NA
Oil - imports: NA
Agriculture - products: coffee, mangoes, sugarcane, rice, corn, sorghum, wood
Exports: $321 million f.o.b. (2003 est.)
Exports - commodities: manufactures, coffee, oils, cocoa
Exports - partners: US 84.5%, Dominican Republic 6.7%, Canada 2.5% (2002)
Imports: $1.028 billion f.o.b. (2003 est.)
Imports - commodities: food, manufactured goods, machinery and transport equipment, fuels, raw materials
Imports - partners: US 52.5%, Dominican Republic 5.2%, Colombia 3.4% (2002)
Debt - external: $1.2 billion (1999)
Economic aid - recipient: $120 million (FY02)
Currency: gourde (HTG)
Currency code: HTG
Exchange rates: gourdes per US dollar - 40.5 (2003), 29.2505 (2002), 24.4291 (2001), 21.1707 (2000), 16.9379 (1999)
Fiscal year: 1 October - 30 September

Communications

Telephones - main lines in use: 130,000 (2002)
Telephones - mobile cellular: 140,000 (2002)
Telephone system:
general assessment: domestic facilities barely adequate; international facilities slightly better
domestic: coaxial cable and microwave radio relay trunk service
international: country code - 509; satellite earth station - 1 Intelsat (Atlantic Ocean)
Radio broadcast stations: AM 41, FM 26, shortwave 0 (1999)
Television broadcast stations: 2 (plus a cable TV service) (1997)
Internet country code: .ht
Internet hosts: NA
Internet users: 80,000 (2002)

Transportation

Railways:
total: 40 km
narrow gauge: 40 km 0.760-m gauge; single-track
note: privately owned industrial line; closed in early 1990s (2001 est.)
Highways:
total: 4,160 km
paved: 1,011 km
unpaved: 3,149 km (1999 est.)
Waterways: less than 100 km navigable
Ports and harbors: Cap-Haitien, Gonaives, Jacmel, Jeremie, Les Cayes, Miragoane, Port-au-Prince, Port-de-Paix, Saint-Marc
Merchant marine: none
Airports: 12 (2003 est.)
Airports - with paved runways:
total: 3
2,438 to 3,047 m: 1
914 to 1,523 m: 2 (2003 est.)
Airports - with unpaved runways:
total: 9
914 to 1,523 m: 4
under 914 m: 5 (2003 est.)

Military

Military branches: Haitian National Police (HNP)
note: the regular Haitian Army, Navy, and Air Force have been demobilized but still exist on paper until or unless they are constitutionally abolished
Military manpower - military age: 18 years of age (2004 est.)
Military manpower - availability:
males age 15-49: 1,792,112 (2004 est.)
Military manpower - fit for military service:
males age 15-49: 975,341 (2004 est.)
Military manpower - reaching military age annually:
males: 97,429 (2004 est.)
Military expenditures - dollar figure: $25.8 million (2003)
Military expenditures - percent of GDP: 0.9% (2003)

Transnational Issues

Disputes - international: despite efforts to control illegal migration, Haitians fleeing economic privation and civil unrest continue to cross into Dominican Republic and to sail to neighboring countries; Haiti claims US-administered Navassa Island
Illicit drugs: major Caribbean transshipment point for cocaine en route to the US and Europe; substantial money-laundering activity; Colombian narcotics traffickers favor Haiti for illicit financial transactions; pervasive corruption

Heard Island and McDonald Islands

(territory of Australia)

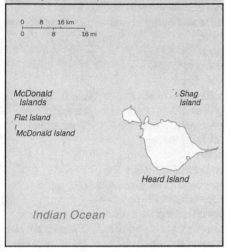

Introduction

Background: These uninhabited, barren, sub-Antarctic islands were transferred from the UK to Australia in 1947. Populated by large numbers of seal and bird species, the islands have been designated a nature preserve.

Geography

Location: islands in the Indian Ocean, about two-thirds of the way from Madagascar to Antarctica
Geographic coordinates: 53 06 S, 72 31 E
Map references: Antarctic Region
Area:
total: 412 sq km
land: 412 sq km
water: 0 sq km
Area - comparative: slightly more than two times the size of Washington, DC
Land boundaries: 0 km
Coastline: 101.9 km
Maritime claims:
territorial sea: 12 NM
exclusive fishing zone: 200 NM
Climate: antarctic
Terrain: Heard Island - 80% ice-covered, bleak and mountainous, dominated by a large massif (Big Ben) and an active volcano (Mawson Peak); McDonald Islands - small and rocky
Elevation extremes:
lowest point: Indian Ocean 0 m
highest point: Mawson Peak, on Big Ben 2,745 m
Natural resources: fish
Land use:
arable land: 0%
permanent crops: 0%
other: 100% (1998 est.)
Irrigated land: 0 sq km (1998 est.)

Natural hazards: Mawson Peak, an active volcano, is on Heard Island
Environment - current issues: NA

People

Population: uninhabited (July 2004 est.)

Government

Country name:
conventional long form: Territory of Heard Island and McDonald Islands
conventional short form: Heard Island and McDonald Islands
Dependency status: territory of Australia; administered from Canberra by the Australian Antarctic Division of the Department of the Environment and Heritage
Legal system: the laws of Australia, where applicable, apply
Diplomatic representation in the US: none (territory of Australia)
Diplomatic representation from the US: none (territory of Australia)
Flag description: the flag of Australia is used

Economy

Economy - overview: No indigenous economic activity, but the Australian Government allows limited fishing around the islands.

Communications

Internet country code: .hm

Transportation

Waterways: none
Ports and harbors: none; offshore anchorage only

Military

Military - note: defense is the responsibility of Australia; Australia conducts fisheries patrols

Transnational Issues

Disputes - international: none

Holy See
(Vatican City)

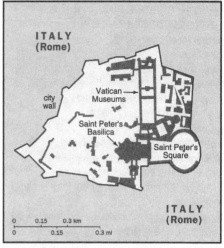

Introduction

Background: Popes in their secular role ruled portions of the Italian peninsula for more than a thousand years until the mid 19th century, when many of the Papal States were seized by the newly united Kingdom of Italy. In 1870, the pope's holdings were further circumscribed when Rome itself was annexed. Disputes between a series of "prisoner" popes and Italy were resolved in 1929 by three Lateran Treaties, which established the independent state of Vatican City and granted Roman Catholicism special status in Italy. In 1984, a concordat between the Holy See and Italy modified certain of the earlier treaty provisions, including the primacy of Roman Catholicism as the Italian state religion. Present concerns of the Holy See include religious freedom, international development, the Middle East, terrorism, the failing health of Pope JOHN PAUL II, interreligious dialogue and reconciliation, and the application of church doctrine in an era of rapid change and globalization. About 1 billion people worldwide profess the Catholic faith.

Geography

Location: Southern Europe, an enclave of Rome (Italy)
Geographic coordinates: 41 54 N, 12 27 E
Map references: Europe
Area:
total: 0.44 sq km
land: 0.44 sq km
water: 0 sq km
Area - comparative: about 0.7 times the size of The Mall in Washington, DC
Land boundaries:
total: 3.2 km
border countries: Italy 3.2 km
Coastline: 0 km (landlocked)
Maritime claims: none (landlocked)

Holy See (Vatican City) *(continued)*

Climate: temperate; mild, rainy winters (September to mid-May) with hot, dry summers (May to September)
Terrain: low hill
Elevation extremes:
lowest point: unnamed location 19 m
highest point: unnamed location 75 m
Natural resources: none
Land use:
arable land: 0%
permanent crops: 0%
other: 100% (urban area) (1998 est.)
Irrigated land: 0 sq km (1998 est.)
Natural hazards: NA
Environment - current issues: NA
Environment - international agreements:
party to: none of the selected agreements
signed, but not ratified: Air Pollution, Environmental Modification
Geography - note: urban; landlocked; enclave in Rome, Italy; world's smallest state; outside the Vatican City, 13 buildings in Rome and Castel Gandolfo (the pope's summer residence) enjoy extraterritorial rights

People

Population: 921 (July 2004 est.)
Population growth rate: 0.01% (2004 est.)
HIV/AIDS - adult prevalence rate: NA%
HIV/AIDS - people living with HIV/AIDS: NA
HIV/AIDS - deaths: NA
Nationality:
noun: none
adjective: none
Ethnic groups: Italians, Swiss, other
Religions: Roman Catholic
Languages: Italian, Latin, French, various other languages
Literacy:
definition: NA
total population: 100%
male: NA%
female: NA%

Government

Country name:
conventional long form: The Holy See (State of the Vatican City)
conventional short form: Holy See (Vatican City)
local long form: Santa Sede (Stato della Citta del Vaticano)
local short form: Santa Sede (Citta del Vaticano)
Government type: ecclesiastical
Capital: Vatican City
Administrative divisions: none
Independence: 11 February 1929 (from Italy)
note: on 11 February 1929, three treaties were signed with Italy which, among other things, acknowledged the full sovereignty of the Vatican and established its territorial extent; however, the origin of the Papal States, which over the years have varied considerably in extent, may be traced back to the 8th century

National holiday: Coronation Day of Pope JOHN PAUL II, 22 October (1978)
Constitution: Apostolic Constitution of 1967 (effective 1 March 1968)
Legal system: based on Code of Canon Law and revisions to it
Suffrage: limited to cardinals less than 80 years old
Executive branch:
chief of state: Pope JOHN PAUL II (since 16 October 1978)
head of government: Secretary of State Cardinal Angelo SODANO (since 2 December 1990)
cabinet: Pontifical Commission appointed by the pope
elections: pope elected for life by the College of Cardinals; election last held 16 October 1978 (next to be held after the death of the current pope); secretary of state appointed by the pope
election results: Karol WOJTYLA elected pope
Legislative branch: unicameral Pontifical Commission
Judicial branch: there are three tribunals responsible for civil and criminal matters within Vatican City; three other tribunals rule on issues pertaining to the Holy See
note: judicial duties were established by the Motu Proprio of Pius XII on 1 May 1946
Political parties and leaders: none
Political pressure groups and leaders: none (exclusive of influence exercised by church officers)
International organization participation: CE (observer), IAEA, ICFTU, IOM (observer), ITU, NAM (guest), OAS (observer), OPCW, OSCE, UN (observer), UNCTAD, UNHCR, UPU, WHO (observer), WIPO, WToO (observer), WTrO (observer)
Diplomatic representation in the US:
chief of mission: Apostolic Nuncio Archbishop Gabriel MONTALVO
chancery: 3339 Massachusetts Avenue NW, Washington, DC 20008
telephone: [1] (202) 333-7121
FAX: [1] (202) 337-4036
Diplomatic representation from the US:
chief of mission: Ambassador R. James "Jim" NICHOLSON
embassy: Villa Domiziana, Via delle Terme Deciane 26, 00153 Rome
mailing address: PSC 59, Box 66, APO AE 09624
telephone: [39] (06) 4674-3428
FAX: [39] (06) 5758346
Flag description: two vertical bands of yellow (hoist side) and white with the crossed keys of Saint Peter and the papal miter centered in the white band

Economy

Economy - overview: This unique, noncommercial economy is supported financially by an annual contribution from Roman Catholic dioceses throughout the world, as well as by special collections (known as Peter's Pence); the sale of postage stamps, coins, medals, and tourist mementos; fees for

admission to museums; and the sale of publications. Investments and real estate income also account for a sizable portion of revenue. The incomes and living standards of lay workers are comparable to those of counterparts who work in the city of Rome.
Population below poverty line: NA%
Household income or consumption by percentage share:
lowest 10%: NA%
highest 10%: NA%
Labor force: NA
Labor force - by occupation: essentially services with a small amount of industry; note - dignitaries, priests, nuns, guards, and 3,000 lay workers live outside the Vatican
Budget:
revenues: $245.2 million
expenditures: $260.4 million, including capital expenditures of $NA (2002)
Industries: printing; production of coins, medals, postage stamps, a small amount of mosaics and staff uniforms; worldwide banking and financial activities
Electricity - production: NA kWh
Electricity - consumption: NA kWh
Electricity - exports: 0 kWh
Electricity - imports: NA kWh; note - electricity supplied by Italy
Economic aid - recipient: none
Currency: euro (EUR)
Currency code: EUR
Exchange rates: euros per US dollar - 0.886 (2003),1.1324 (2002), 1.1175 (2001), 1.0854 (2000), 0.9386 (1999)
Fiscal year: calendar year

Communications

Telephones - main lines in use: NA
Telephones - mobile cellular: NA
Telephone system:
general assessment: automatic exchange
domestic: tied into Italian system
international: country code - 39; uses Italian system
Radio broadcast stations: AM 3, FM 4, shortwave 2 (1998)
Television broadcast stations: 1 (1996)
Internet country code: .va
Internet users: NA

Transportation

Railways:
total: 0.86 km
standard gauge: 0.86 km 1.435-m gauge
note: a spur of the Italian Railways system, serving Rome's Saint Peter's station (2001 est.)
Highways: none; all city streets
Waterways: none
Ports and harbors: none
Airports: none (2003 est.)

Holy See (Vatican City) *(continued)*

Military

Military branches: Swiss Guards Corps (Corpo della Guardia Svizzera)
Military - note: defense is the responsibility of Italy; Swiss Papal Guards are posted at entrances to the Vatican City to provide security and protect the Pope

Transnational Issues

Disputes - international: none

Honduras

Introduction

Background: Part of Spain's vast empire in the New World, Honduras became an independent nation in 1821. After two and one-half decades of mostly military rule, a freely elected civilian government came to power in 1982. During the 1980s, Honduras proved a haven for anti-Sandinista contras fighting the Marxist Nicaraguan Government and an ally to Salvadoran Government forces fighting against leftist guerrillas. The country was devastated by Hurricane Mitch in 1998, which killed about 5,600 people and caused approximately $2 billion in damage.

Geography

Location: Central America, bordering the Caribbean Sea, between Guatemala and Nicaragua and bordering the Gulf of Fonseca (North Pacific Ocean), between El Salvador and Nicaragua
Geographic coordinates: 15 00 N, 86 30 W
Map references: Central America and the Caribbean
Area:
total: 112,090 sq km
land: 111,890 sq km
water: 200 sq km
Area - comparative: slightly larger than Tennessee
Land boundaries:
total: 1,520 km
border countries: Guatemala 256 km, El Salvador 342 km, Nicaragua 922 km
Coastline: 820 km
Maritime claims:
territorial sea: 12 NM
contiguous zone: 24 NM
exclusive economic zone: 200 NM
continental shelf: natural extension of territory or to 200 NM
Climate: subtropical in lowlands, temperate in mountains

Terrain: mostly mountains in interior, narrow coastal plains
Elevation extremes:
lowest point: Caribbean Sea 0 m
highest point: Cerro Las Minas 2,870 m
Natural resources: timber, gold, silver, copper, lead, zinc, iron ore, antimony, coal, fish, hydropower
Land use:
arable land: 15.15%
permanent crops: 3.13%
other: 81.72% (1998 est.)
Irrigated land: 760 sq km (1998 est.)
Natural hazards: frequent, but generally mild, earthquakes; extremely susceptible to damaging hurricanes and floods along the Caribbean coast
Environment - current issues: urban population expanding; deforestation results from logging and the clearing of land for agricultural purposes; further land degradation and soil erosion hastened by uncontrolled development and improper land use practices such as farming of marginal lands; mining activities polluting Lago de Yojoa (the country's largest source of fresh water), as well as several rivers and streams, with heavy metals
Environment - international agreements:
party to: Biodiversity, Climate Change, Climate Change-Kyoto Protocol, Desertification, Endangered Species, Hazardous Wastes, Law of the Sea, Marine Dumping, Ozone Layer Protection, Ship Pollution, Tropical Timber 83, Tropical Timber 94, Wetlands
signed, but not ratified: none of the selected agreements
Geography - note: has only a short Pacific coast but a long Caribbean shoreline, including the virtually uninhabited eastern Mosquito Coast

People

Population: 6,823,568
note: estimates for this country explicitly take into account the effects of excess mortality due to AIDS; this can result in lower life expectancy, higher infant mortality and death rates, lower population and growth rates, and changes in the distribution of population by age and sex than would otherwise be expected (July 2004 est.)
Age structure:
0-14 years: 41.2% (male 1,434,555; female 1,376,216)
15-64 years: 55.1% (male 1,866,219; female 1,896,027)
65 years and over: 3.7% (male 118,404; female 132,147) (2004 est.)
Median age:
total: 19 years
male: 18.6 years
female: 19.4 years (2004 est.)
Population growth rate: 2.24% (2004 est.)
Birth rate: 31.04 births/1,000 population (2004 est.)
Death rate: 6.64 deaths/1,000 population (2004 est.)
Net migration rate: -1.99 migrant(s)/1,000 population (2004 est.)

Honduras (continued)

Sex ratio:
at birth: 1.05 male(s)/female
under 15 years: 1.04 male(s)/female
15-64 years: 0.98 male(s)/female
65 years and over: 0.9 male(s)/female
total population: 1 male(s)/female (2004 est.)
Infant mortality rate:
total: 29.64 deaths/1,000 live births
male: 33.22 deaths/1,000 live births
female: 25.89 deaths/1,000 live births (2004 est.)
Life expectancy at birth:
total population: 66.15 years
male: 64.99 years
female: 67.37 years (2004 est.)
Total fertility rate: 3.97 children born/woman
(2004 est.)
HIV/AIDS - adult prevalence rate: 1.6% (2001 est.)
HIV/AIDS - people living with HIV/AIDS: 57,000
(2001 est.)
HIV/AIDS - deaths: 3,300 (2001 est.)
Nationality:
noun: Honduran(s)
adjective: Honduran
Ethnic groups: mestizo (mixed Amerindian and
European) 90%, Amerindian 7%, black 2%, white 1%
Religions: Roman Catholic 97%, Protestant minority
Languages: Spanish, Amerindian dialects
Literacy:
definition: age 15 and over can read and write
total population: 76.2%
male: 76.1%
female: 76.3% (2003 est.)

Government

Country name:
conventional long form: Republic of Honduras
conventional short form: Honduras
local long form: Republica de Honduras
local short form: Honduras
Government type: democratic constitutional
republic
Capital: Tegucigalpa
Administrative divisions: 18 departments
(departamentos, singular - departamento); Atlantida,
Choluteca, Colon, Comayagua, Copan, Cortes, El
Paraiso, Francisco Morazan, Gracias a Dios, Intibuca,
Islas de la Bahia, La Paz, Lempira, Ocotepeque,
Olancho, Santa Barbara, Valle, Yoro
Independence: 15 September 1821 (from Spain)
National holiday: Independence Day,
15 September (1821)
Constitution: 11 January 1982, effective 20 January
1982; amended 1995
Legal system: rooted in Roman and Spanish civil
law with increasing influence of English common
law; recent judicial reforms include abandoning
Napoleonic legal codes in favor of the oral
adversarial system; accepts ICJ jurisdiction, with
reservations
Suffrage: 18 years of age; universal and compulsory

Executive branch:
chief of state: President Ricardo (Joest) MADURO
(since 27 January 2002); First Vice President Vicente
WILLIAMS Agasse (since 27 January 2002); Second
Vice President Armida Villela Maria DE LOPEZ
Contreras (since 27 January 2002); Third Vice
President Alberto DIAZ Lobo (since 27 January 2002);
note - the president is both the chief of state and head
of government
head of government: President Ricardo (Joest)
MADURO (since 27 January 2002); First Vice
President Vicente WILLIAMS Agasse (since
27 January 2002); Second Vice President Armida
Villela Maria DE LOPEZ Contreras (since 27 January
2002); Third Vice President Alberto DIAZ Lobo (since
27 January 2002); note - the president is both the chief
of state and head of government
cabinet: Cabinet appointed by president
elections: president elected by popular vote for a
four-year term; election last held 25 November 2001
(next to be held NA November 2005)
election results: Ricardo (Joest) MADURO (PN)
elected president - 52.2%, Raphael PINEDA Ponce
(PL) 44.3%, others 3.5%
Legislative branch: unicameral National Congress
or Congreso Nacional (128 seats; members are
elected proportionally to the number of votes their
party's presidential candidate receives to serve
four-year terms)
elections: last held 25 November 2001 (next to be
held NA November 2005)
election results: percent of vote by party - NA%; seats
by party - PN 61, PL 55, PUD 5, PDC 4, PINU-SD 3
Judicial branch: Supreme Court of Justice or Corte
Suprema de Justicia (judges are elected for
seven-year terms by the National Congress)
Political parties and leaders: Christian Democratic
Party or PDC [Juan Ramon VALAZQUEZ Nazzar];
Democratic Unification Party or PUD [Cesar David
Adolfo HAM Pena]; Liberal Party or PL [Roberto
MICHELETTI Bain]; National Innovation and Unity
Party-Social Democratic Party or PINU-SD [Olban F.
VALLADARES]; National Party of Honduras or PN
[Jose Celin DISCUA Elvir]
Political pressure groups and leaders:
Committee for the Defense of Human Rights in
Honduras or CODEH; Confederation of Honduran
Workers or CTH; Coordinating Committee of Popular
Organizations or CCOP; General Workers
Confederation or CGT; Honduran Council of Private
Enterprise or COHEP; National Association of
Honduran Campesinos or ANACH; National Union of
Campesinos or UNC; Popular Bloc or BP; United
Federation of Honduran Workers or FUTH
International organization participation: BCIE,
CACM, FAO, G-77, IADB, IAEA, IBRD, ICAO, ICCt,
ICFTU, ICRM, IDA, IFAD, IFC, IFRCS, ILO, IMF, IMO,
Interpol, IOC, IOM, ISO (subscriber), ITU, LAES, LAIA
(observer), MINURSO, NAM, OAS, OPANAL, OPCW
(signatory), PCA, RG, UN, UNCTAD, UNESCO,
UNIDO, UPU, WCL, WFTU, WHO, WIPO, WMO,
WToO, WTrO

Diplomatic representation in the US:
chief of mission: Ambassador Mario Miguel
CANAHUATI
chancery: Suite 4-M, 3007 Tilden Street NW,
Washington, DC 20008
telephone: [1] (202) 966-7702
FAX: [1] (202) 966-9751
consulate(s) general: Chicago, Houston, Los
Angeles, Miami, New Orleans, New York, Phoenix,
San Francisco
honorary consulate(s): Atlanta, Boston, Detroit,
Jacksonville
Diplomatic representation from the US:
chief of mission: Ambassador Larry Leon PALMER
embassy: Avenida La Paz, Apartado Postal No. 3453,
Tegucigalpa
mailing address: American Embassy, APO AA 34022,
Tegucigalpa
telephone: [504] 238-5114, 236-9320
FAX: [504] 236-9037
Flag description: three equal horizontal bands of
blue (top), white, and blue with five blue, five-pointed
stars arranged in an X pattern centered in the white
band; the stars represent the members of the former
Federal Republic of Central America - Costa Rica, El
Salvador, Guatemala, Honduras, and Nicaragua;
similar to the flag of El Salvador, which features a
round emblem encircled by the words REPUBLICA
DE EL SALVADOR EN LA AMERICA CENTRAL
centered in the white band; also similar to the flag of
Nicaragua, which features a triangle encircled by the
word REPUBLICA DE NICARAGUA on top and
AMERICA CENTRAL on the bottom, centered in the
white band

Economy

Economy - overview: Honduras, one of the
poorest countries in the Western Hemisphere with
an extraordinarily unequal distribution of income and
massive unemployment, is banking on expanded
trade privileges under the Enhanced Caribbean
Basin Initiative and on debt relief under the Heavily
Indebted Poor Countries (HIPC) initiative. While the
country has met most of its macroeconomic targets,
it has failed to meet the IMF's goals to liberalize its
energy and telecommunications sectors. Growth
remains dependent on the status of the US
economy, its major trading partner, on commodity
prices, particularly coffee, and on reduction of the
high crime rate.
GDP: purchasing power parity - $17.46 billion
(2003 est.)
GDP - real growth rate: 2.5% (2003 est.)
GDP - per capita: purchasing power parity - $2,600
(2003 est.)
GDP - composition by sector:
agriculture: 13.5%
industry: 30.7%
services: 55.8% (2002 est.)
Population below poverty line: 53% (1993 est.)

Honduras (continued)

Household income or consumption by percentage share:
lowest 10%: 0.6%
highest 10%: 42.7% (1998)
Distribution of family income - Gini index: 56.3 (1998)
Inflation rate (consumer prices): 7.7% (2003 est.)
Labor force: 2.3 million (1997 est.)
Labor force - by occupation: agriculture 34%, industry 21%, services 45% (2001 est.)
Unemployment rate: 27.5% (2003 est.)
Budget:
revenues: $607 million
expenditures: $411.9 million, including capital expenditures of $106 million (1999 est.)
Industries: sugar, coffee, textiles, clothing, wood products
Industrial production growth rate: 7.7% (2003 est.)
Electricity - production: 3.778 billion kWh (2001)
Electricity - production by source:
fossil fuel: 50.2%
hydro: 49.8%
nuclear: 0%
other: 0% (2001)
Electricity - consumption: 3.822 billion kWh (2001)
Electricity - exports: 0 kWh (2001)
Electricity - imports: 308 million kWh (2001)
Oil - production: 0 bbl/day (2001 est.)
Oil - consumption: 29,000 bbl/day (2001 est.)
Oil - exports: NA
Oil - imports: NA
Agriculture - products: bananas, coffee, citrus; beef; timber; shrimp
Exports: $1.37 billion f.o.b. (2003 est.)
Exports - commodities: coffee, bananas, shrimp, lobster, meat; zinc, lumber (2000)
Exports - partners: US 69%, El Salvador 3%, Guatemala 2% (2002)
Imports: $3.11 billion f.o.b. (2003 est.)
Imports - commodities: machinery and transport equipment, industrial raw materials, chemical products, fuels, foodstuffs (2000)
Imports - partners: US 53.3%, Mexico 4.3%, El Salvador 4.2% (2002)
Debt - external: $5.1 billion (2003)
Economic aid - recipient: $557.8 million (1999)
Currency: lempira (HNL)
Currency code: HNL
Exchange rates: lempiras per US dollar - 17.3453 (2003), 16.4334 (2002), 15.4737 (2001), 14.8392 (2000), 14.2132 (1999)
Fiscal year: calendar year

Communications

Telephones - main lines in use: 322,500 (2002)
Telephones - mobile cellular: 326,500 (2002)
Telephone system:
general assessment: inadequate system
domestic: NA
international: country code - 504; satellite earth stations - 2 Intelsat (Atlantic Ocean); connected to Central American Microwave System

Radio broadcast stations: AM 241, FM 53, shortwave 12 (1998)
Television broadcast stations: 11 (plus 17 repeaters) (1997)
Internet country code: .hn
Internet hosts: 160 (2002)
Internet users: 168,600 (2002)

Transportation

Railways:
total: 699 km
narrow gauge: 279 km 1.067-m gauge; 420 km 0.914-m gauge (2002)
Highways:
total: 13,603 km
paved: 2,775 km
unpaved: 10,828 km (1999 est.)
Waterways: 465 km (navigable by small craft)
Ports and harbors: La Ceiba, Puerto Castilla, Puerto Cortes, San Lorenzo, Tela, Puerto Lempira
Merchant marine:
total: 238 ships (1,000 GRT or over) 598,600 GRT/ 616,158 DWT
by type: bulk 12, cargo 139, chemical tanker 5, combination bulk 1, container 5, liquefied gas 1, livestock carrier 1, passenger 3, passenger/cargo 2, petroleum tanker 54, refrigerated cargo 8, roll on/roll off 4, short-sea/passenger 3
foreign-owned: Argentina 1, Bahrain 1, British Virgin Islands 1, Bulgaria 1, Cayman Islands 1, China 4, Costa Rica 1, Cyprus 1, Egypt 5, El Salvador 1, Greece 16, Hong Kong 3, Indonesia 2, Israel 1, Italy 1, Japan 2, Jordan 1, South Korea 9, Lebanon 4, Liberia 4, Maldives 2, Marshall Islands 3, Mexico 1, Nigeria 2, Panama 10, Philippines 1, Russia 1, Saint Kitts and Nevis 3, Saint Vincent and the Grenadines 1, Saudi Arabia 1, Singapore 22, Spain 1, Taiwan 2, Tanzania 1, Thailand 1, Turkey 2, Turks and Caicos Islands 1, United States 7, Vanuatu 1, Vietnam 1
registered in other countries: 16 (2003 est.)
Airports: 115 (2003 est.)
Airports - with paved runways:
total: 12
2,438 to 3,047 m: 3
1,524 to 2,437 m: 2
914 to 1,523 m: 3
under 914 m: 4 (2003 est.)
Airports - with unpaved runways:
total: 103
1,524 to 2,437 m: 2
914 to 1,523 m: 18
under 914 m: 83 (2003 est.)

Military

Military branches: Army, Navy (including Naval Infantry), Air Force
Military manpower - military age: 18 years of age (2004 est.)
Military manpower - availability:
males age 15-49: 1,642,029 (2004 est.)

Military manpower - fit for military service:
males age 15-49: 977,130 (2004 est.)
Military manpower - reaching military age annually:
males: 76,143 (2004 est.)
Military expenditures - dollar figure: $99.8 million (2003)
Military expenditures - percent of GDP: 1.5% (2003)

Transnational Issues

Disputes - international: in 1992, ICJ ruled on the delimitation of "bolsones" (disputed areas) along the El Salvador-Honduras border, and the OAS is assisting with a technical resolution of bolsones; in 2003, the ICJ rejected El Salvador's request to revise its decision on one bolsone; the 1992 ICJ ruling advised a tripartite resolution to a maritime boundary in the Gulf of Fonseca with consideration of Honduran access to the Pacific; El Salvador continues to claim tiny Conejo Island, not mentioned by the ICJ, off Honduras in the Gulf of Fonseca; Honduras claims Sapodilla Cays off the coast of Belize but agreed to creation of a joint ecological park and Guatemalan corridor in the Caribbean in the failed 2002 Belize-Guatemala Differendum; Nicaragua filed a claim against Honduras in 1999 and against Colombia in 2001 at the ICJ over a complex maritime dispute in the Caribbean Sea
Illicit drugs: transshipment point for drugs and narcotics; illicit producer of cannabis, cultivated on small plots and used principally for local consumption; corruption is a major problem; some money-laundering activity

Hong Kong
(special administrative region of China)

Introduction

Background: Occupied by the UK in 1841, Hong Kong was formally ceded by China the following year; various adjacent lands were added later in the 19th century. Pursuant to an agreement signed by China and the UK on 19 December 1984, Hong Kong became the Hong Kong Special Administrative Region (SAR) of China on 1 July 1997. In this agreement, China has promised that, under its "one country, two systems" formula, China's socialist economic system will not be imposed on Hong Kong and that Hong Kong will enjoy a high degree of autonomy in all matters except foreign and defense affairs for the next 50 years.

Geography

Location: Eastern Asia, bordering the South China Sea and China
Geographic coordinates: 22 15 N, 114 10 E
Map references: Southeast Asia
Area:
total: 1,092 sq km
land: 1,042 sq km
water: 50 sq km
Area - comparative: six times the size of Washington, DC
Land boundaries:
total: 30 km
regional border: China 30 km
Coastline: 733 km
Maritime claims:
territorial sea: 3 NM
Climate: tropical monsoon; cool and humid in winter, hot and rainy from spring through summer, warm and sunny in fall
Terrain: hilly to mountainous with steep slopes; lowlands in north
Elevation extremes:
lowest point: South China Sea 0 m

highest point: Tai Mo Shan 958 m
Natural resources: outstanding deepwater harbor, feldspar
Land use:
arable land: 5.05%
permanent crops: 1.01%
other: 93.94% (1998 est.)
Irrigated land: 20 sq km (1998 est.)
Natural hazards: occasional typhoons
Environment - current issues: air and water pollution from rapid urbanization
Environment - international agreements:
party to: Marine Dumping (associate member)
Geography - note: more than 200 islands

People

Population: 6,855,125 (July 2004 est.)
Age structure:
0-14 years: 14.2% (male 510,702; female 465,145)
15-64 years: 73.3% (male 2,461,914; female 2,560,382)
65 years and over: 12.5% (male 394,697; female 462,285) (2004 est.)
Median age:
total: 39.4 years
male: 39.3 years
female: 39.6 years (2004 est.)
Population growth rate: 0.65% (2004 est.)
Birth rate: 7.23 births/1,000 population (2004 est.)
Death rate: 5.98 deaths/1,000 population (2004 est.)
Net migration rate: 5.24 migrant(s)/1,000 population (2004 est.)
Sex ratio:
at birth: 1.09 male(s)/female
under 15 years: 1.1 male(s)/female
15-64 years: 0.96 male(s)/female
65 years and over: 0.85 male(s)/female
total population: 0.97 male(s)/female (2004 est.)
Infant mortality rate:
total: 2.97 deaths/1,000 live births
male: 3.16 deaths/1,000 live births
female: 2.77 deaths/1,000 live births (2004 est.)
Life expectancy at birth:
total population: 81.39 years
male: 78.72 years
female: 84.3 years (2004 est.)
Total fertility rate: 0.91 children born/woman (2004 est.)
HIV/AIDS - adult prevalence rate: 0.1% (2001 est.)
HIV/AIDS - people living with HIV/AIDS: 2,600 (2001 est.)
HIV/AIDS - deaths: less than 100 (2001 est.)
Nationality:
noun: Chinese/Hong Konger
adjective: Chinese/Hong Kong
Ethnic groups: Chinese 95%, other 5%
Religions: eclectic mixture of local religions 90%, Christian 10%
Languages: Chinese (Cantonese), English; both are official

Literacy:
definition: age 15 and over has ever attended school
total population: 94%
male: 97.1%
female: 90.5% (2003 est.)

Government

Country name:
conventional long form: Hong Kong Special Administrative Region
conventional short form: Hong Kong
local long form: Xianggang Tebie Xingzhengqu
local short form: Xianggang
abbreviation: HK
Dependency status: special administrative region of China
Government type: limited democracy
Administrative divisions: none (special administrative region of China)
Independence: none (special administrative region of China)
National holiday: National Day (Anniversary of the Founding of the People's Republic of China), 1 October (1949); note - 1 July 1997 is celebrated as Hong Kong Special Administrative Region Establishment Day
Constitution: Basic Law approved in March 1990 by China's National People's Congress is Hong Kong's "mini-constitution"
Legal system: based on English common law
Suffrage: direct election 18 years of age; universal for permanent residents living in the territory of Hong Kong for the past seven years; indirect election limited to about 100,000 members of functional constituencies and an 800-member election committee drawn from broad regional groupings, municipal organizations, and central government bodies
Executive branch:
chief of state: President of China HU Jintao (since 15 March 2003)
head of government: Chief Executive TUNG Chee-hwa (since 1 July 1997)
cabinet: Executive Council consists of three ex-officio members and 10 appointed members; ex-officio members are: Chief Secretary Donald TSANG Yam-kuen (since 1 May 2001), Financial Secretary Henry TANG (since 2 August 2003), and Secretary of Justice Elsie LEUNG (since 1 July 1997)
elections: TUNG Chee-hwa was elected to a second term in March 2002 by an 800-member election committee dominated by pro-Beijing forces; the next election is scheduled to be held in 2007
Legislative branch: unicameral Legislative Council or LEGCO (60 seats; in 2004 30 seats indirectly elected by functional constituencies, 30 elected by popular vote; members serve four-year terms)
elections: last held 10 September 2000 (next to be held in September 2004)
election results: percent of vote by party - NA%; seats by party - Democratic Party 12, Democratic Alliance for the Betterment of Hong Kong 10, Liberal Party 7,

Hong Kong *(continued)*

Frontier Party 5, Hong Kong Progressive Alliance 4, New Century Forum 2, Hong Kong Association for Democracy and People's Livelihood 1, independents 19

Judicial branch: Court of Final Appeal in the Hong Kong Special Administrative Region

Political parties and leaders: Association for Democracy and People's Livelihood [Frederick FUNG Kin-kee, chairman]; Citizens Party [Alex CHAN Kai-chung]; Democratic Alliance for the Betterment of Hong Kong [MA Lik, chairman]; Democratic Party [YEUNG Sum, chairman]; Frontier Party [Emily LAU Wai-hing, chairwoman]; Hong Kong Progressive Alliance [Ambrose LAU Hon-chuen]; Liberal Party [James TIEN Pei-chun, chairman]; New Century Forum [MA Fung-kwok, chairman]

note: political blocs include: pro-democracy - Association for Democracy and People's Livelihood, Citizens Party, Democratic Party, Frontier Party; pro-Beijing - Democratic Alliance for the Betterment of Hong Kong, Hong Kong Progressive Alliance, Liberal Party, New Century Forum

Political pressure groups and leaders: Chinese General Chamber of Commerce (pro-China); Chinese Manufacturers' Association of Hong Kong; Confederation of Trade Unions (pro-democracy) [LAU Chin-shek, president; LEE Cheuk-yan, general secretary]; Federation of Hong Kong Industries; Federation of Trade Unions (pro-China) [CHENG Yiu-tong, executive councilor]; Hong Kong Alliance in Support of the Patriotic Democratic Movement in China [Szeto WAH, chairman]; Hong Kong and Kowloon Trade Union Council (pro-Taiwan); Hong Kong General Chamber of Commerce; Hong Kong Professional Teachers' Union [CHEUNG Man-kwong, president]; Liberal Democratic Federation [HU Fa-kuang, chairman]

International organization participation: APEC, AsDB, BIS, ICC, ICFTU, IHO, IMO (associate), Interpol (subbureau), IOC, ISO (correspondent), WCL, WCO, WMO, WToO (associate), WTrO

Diplomatic representation in the US: none (special administrative region of China)

Diplomatic representation from the US:

chief of mission: Consul General James KEITH

consulate(s) general: 26 Garden Road, Hong Kong

mailing address: PSC 461, Box 1, FPO AP 96521-0006

telephone: [852] 2523-9011

FAX: [852] 2524-0860

Flag description: red with a stylized, white, five-petal bauhinia flower in the center

Economy

Economy - overview: Hong Kong has a free market economy highly dependent on international trade. Natural resources are limited, and food and raw materials must be imported. Imports and exports, including reexports, each exceed GDP in dollar value. Even before Hong Kong reverted to Chinese administration on 1 July 1997 it had extensive trade and investment ties with China. Hong Kong has been further integrating its economy with China because China's growing openness to the world economy has increased competitive pressure on Hong Kong's service industries, and Hong Kong's re-export business from China is a major driver of growth. Per capita GDP compares with the level in the four big economies of Western Europe. GDP growth averaged a strong 5% in 1989-1997, but Hong Kong suffered two recessions in the past 6 years because of the Asian financial crisis in 1998 and the global downturn of 2001-2002. The Severe Acute Respiratory Syndrome (SARS) outbreak also battered Hong Kong's economy, but a boom in tourism from the mainland because of China's easing of travel restrictions, a return of consumer confidence, and a solid rise in exports resulted in the resumption of strong growth in late 2003.

GDP: purchasing power parity - $212.2 billion (2003 est.)

GDP - real growth rate: 2.9% (2003 est.)

GDP - per capita: purchasing power parity - $28,700 (2003 est.)

GDP - composition by sector:

agriculture: 0.1%

industry: 12.9%

services: 87.1% (2002 est.)

Population below poverty line: NA%

Household income or consumption by percentage share:

lowest 10%: NA%

highest 10%: NA%

Inflation rate (consumer prices): -2.6% (2003 est.)

Labor force: 3.48 million (2002 est.)

Labor force - by occupation: wholesale and retail trade, restaurants, and hotels 43.5%, financing, insurance, and real estate 19.5%, community and social services 17.8%, manufacturing 8.2%, transport and communications 7.8%, construction 2.9% (Note: above data exclude public sector) (2002 est.)

Unemployment rate: 7.9% (2003)

Budget:

revenues: $22.8 billion

expenditures: $30.7 billion, including capital expenditures of $5 billion (FY02/03)

Industries: textiles, clothing, tourism, banking, shipping, electronics, plastics, toys, watches, clocks

Industrial production growth rate: 2.7% (2003 est.)

Electricity - production: 30.48 billion kWh (2001)

Electricity - production by source:

fossil fuel: 100%

hydro: 0%

nuclear: 0%

other: 0% (2001)

Electricity - consumption: 37.12 billion kWh (2001)

Electricity - exports: 1.581 billion kWh (2001)

Electricity - imports: 10.36 billion kWh (2001)

Oil - production: 0 bbl/day (2001 est.)

Oil - consumption: 257,000 bbl/day (2001 est.)

Oil - exports: NA

Oil - imports: NA

Natural gas - production: 0 cu m (2001 est.)

Natural gas - consumption: 680.9 million cu m (2001 est.)

Natural gas - exports: 0 cu m (2001 est.)

Natural gas - imports: 680.9 million cu m (2001 est.)

Agriculture - products: fresh vegetables, poultry, fish, pork

Exports: $225.9 billion f.o.b., including reexports (2003 est.)

Exports - commodities: electrical machinery and appliances, textiles, apparel, footwear, watches and clocks, toys, plastics, precious stones

Exports - partners: China 39.3%, US 21.4%, Japan 5.4% (2002)

Imports: $230.3 billion (2003 est.)

Imports - commodities: electrical machinery and appliances, textiles, foodstuffs, transport equipment, raw materials, semimanufactures, petroleum, plastics; a large share is reexported

Imports - partners: China 44.3%, Japan 11.3%, Taiwan 7.2%, US 5.7%, South Korea 4.7%, Singapore 4.7% (2002)

Debt - external: $61.2 billion (2003 est.)

Currency: Hong Kong dollar (HKD)

Currency code: HKD

Exchange rates: Hong Kong dollars per US dollar - 7.7868 (2003), 7.7989 (2002), 7.7988 (2001), 7.7912 (2000), 7.7575 (1999)

Fiscal year: 1 April - 31 March

Communications

Telephones - main lines in use: 3,831,800 (2002)

Telephones - mobile cellular: 6,395,700 (2002)

Telephone system:

general assessment: modern facilities provide excellent domestic and international services

domestic: microwave radio relay links and extensive fiber-optic network

international: country code - 852; satellite earth stations - 3 Intelsat (1 Pacific Ocean and 2 Indian Ocean); coaxial cable to Guangzhou, China; access to 5 international submarine cables providing connections to ASEAN member nations, Japan, Taiwan, Australia, Middle East, and Western Europe

Radio broadcast stations: AM 7, FM 13, shortwave 0 (1998)

Television broadcast stations: 4 (plus two repeaters) (1997)

Internet country code: .hk

Internet hosts: 398,151 (2002)

Internet users: 2,918,800 (2002)

Transportation

Railways:

total: 34 km

standard gauge: 34 km 1.435-m gauge (electrified and double-tracked)

note: connects to China railway system at Hong Kong-China border (2001)

Hong Kong (continued)

Highways:
total: 1,831 km
paved: 1,831 km
unpaved: 0 km (1999 est.)
Waterways: none
Ports and harbors: Hong Kong
Merchant marine:
total: 663 ships (1,000 GRT or over) 20,478,042 GRT/
34,554,455 DWT
by type: barge carrier 1, bulk 364, cargo 78, chemical
tanker 23, combination bulk 2, combination ore/oil 3,
container 97, liquefied gas 20, multi-functional large
load carrier 1, petroleum tanker 60, refrigerated
cargo 3, roll on/roll off 4, short-sea/passenger 1,
specialized tanker 2, vehicle carrier 4
foreign-owned: Australia 2, Belgium 1, British Virgin
Islands 1, China 178, Cyprus 1, Denmark 3, France 2,
Germany 14, Greece 4, India 9, Indonesia 2, Japan
22, South Korea 2, Malaysia 3, Monaco 9, Norway 16,
Panama 4, Philippines 17, Singapore 22, Taiwan 3,
Thailand 1, United Kingdom 22, United States 1
registered in other countries: 569 (2003 est.)
Airports: 4 (2003 est.)
Airports - with paved runways:
total: 4
over 3,047 m: 1
1,524 to 2,437 m: 1
914 to 1523 m: 1
under 914 m: 1 (2003 est.)
Heliports: 2 (2003 est.)

Military

Military branches: no regular indigenous military
forces; Hong Kong garrison of China's People's
Liberation Army (PLA) including elements of the PLA
Ground Forces, PLA Navy, and PLA Air Force; these
forces are under the direct leadership of the Central
Military Commission in Beijing and under
administrative control of the adjacent Guangzhou
Military Region
Military manpower - military age: 18 years of age
(2004 est.)
Military manpower - availability:
males age 15-49: 1,878,574 (2004 est.)
Military manpower - fit for military service:
males age 15-49: 1,404,705 (2004 est.)
**Military manpower - reaching military age
annually:**
males: 41,821 (2004 est.)
Military expenditures - percent of GDP: NA%
(FY02)
Military - note: defense is the responsibility of China

Transnational Issues

Disputes - international: none
Illicit drugs: Makes strenuous law enforcement
efforts, but faces difficult challenges in controlling
transit of heroin and methamphetamine to regional
and world markets; modern banking system provides
a conduit for money laundering; rising indigenous use
of synthetic drugs, especially among young people

Howland Island
(territory of the US)

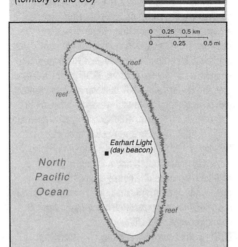

Introduction

Background: Discovered by the US early in the 19th
century, the island was officially claimed by the US in
1857. Both US and British companies mined for guano
until about 1890. Earhart Light is a day beacon near the
middle of the west coast that was partially destroyed
during World War II, but has since been rebuilt; it is
named in memory of the famed aviatrix Amelia
EARHART. The island is administered by the US
Department of the Interior as a National Wildlife Refuge.

Geography

Location: Oceania, island in the North Pacific
Ocean, about half way between Hawaii and Australia
Geographic coordinates: 0 48 N, 176 38 W
Map references: Oceania
Area:
total: 1.6 sq km
land: 1.6 sq km
water: 0 sq km
Area - comparative: about three times the size of
The Mall in Washington, DC
Land boundaries: 0 km
Coastline: 6.4 km
Maritime claims:
territorial sea: 12 NM
exclusive economic zone: 200 NM
Climate: equatorial; scant rainfall, constant wind,
burning sun
Terrain: low-lying, nearly level, sandy, coral island
surrounded by a narrow fringing reef; depressed
central area
Elevation extremes:
lowest point: Pacific Ocean 0 m
highest point: unnamed location 3 m
Natural resources: guano (deposits worked until
late 1800s), terrestrial and aquatic wildlife
Land use:
arable land: 0%
permanent crops: 0%

other: 100% (1998 est.)
Irrigated land: 0 sq km (1998 est.)
Natural hazards: the narrow fringing reef
surrounding the island can be a maritime hazard
Environment - current issues: no natural fresh
water resources
Geography - note: almost totally covered with
grasses, prostrate vines, and low-growing shrubs;
small area of trees in the center; primarily a nesting,
roosting, and foraging habitat for seabirds, shorebirds,
and marine wildlife

People

Population: uninhabited
note: American civilians evacuated in 1942 after
Japanese air and naval attacks during World War II;
occupied by US military during World War II, but
abandoned after the war; public entry is by
special-use permit from US Fish and Wildlife Service
only and generally restricted to scientists and
educators; visited annually by US Fish and Wildlife
Service (July 2004 est.)

Government

Country name:
conventional long form: none
conventional short form: Howland Island
Dependency status: unincorporated territory of the
US; administered from Washington, DC, by the Fish
and Wildlife Service of the US Department of the
Interior as part of the National Wildlife Refuge system
Legal system: the laws of the US, where applicable,
apply
Flag description: the flag of the US is used

Economy

Economy - overview: no economic activity

Transportation

Waterways: none
Ports and harbors: none; offshore anchorage only;
note - there is one small boat landing area along the
middle of the west coast
Airports: airstrip constructed in 1937 for scheduled
refueling stop on the round-the-world flight of Amelia
EARHART and Fred NOONAN - they left Lae, New
Guinea, for Howland Island, but were never seen
again; the airstrip is no longer serviceable (2003 est.)
Transportation - note: Earhart Light is a day
beacon near the middle of the west coast that was
partially destroyed during World War II, but has since
been rebuilt; named in memory of famed aviatrix
Amelia EARHART

Military

Military - note: defense is the responsibility of the
US; visited annually by the US Coast Guard

Transnational Issues

Disputes - international: none

Hungary

Introduction

Background: Hungary was part of the polyglot Austro-Hungarian Empire, which collapsed during World War I. The country fell under Communist rule following World War II. In 1956, a revolt and announced withdrawal from the Warsaw Pact were met with a massive military intervention by Moscow. Under the leadership of Janos KADAR in 1968, Hungary began liberalizing its economy, introducing so-called "goulash Communism." Hungary held its first multiparty elections in 1990 and initiated a free market economy. It joined NATO in 1999 and is scheduled to accede to the EU along with nine other states on 1 May 2004. In an April 2003 referendum, 84 percent voted in favor of joining the EU.

Geography

Location: Central Europe, northwest of Romania
Geographic coordinates: 47 00 N, 20 00 E
Map references: Europe
Area:
total: 93,030 sq km
land: 92,340 sq km
water: 690 sq km
Area - comparative: slightly smaller than Indiana
Land boundaries:
total: 2,171 km
border countries: Austria 366 km, Croatia 329 km, Romania 443 km, Serbia and Montenegro 151 km, Slovakia 677 km, Slovenia 102 km, Ukraine 103 km
Coastline: 0 km (landlocked)
Maritime claims: none (landlocked)
Climate: temperate; cold, cloudy, humid winters; warm summers
Terrain: mostly flat to rolling plains; hills and low mountains on the Slovakian border
Elevation extremes:
lowest point: Tisza River 78 m
highest point: Kekes 1,014 m

Natural resources: bauxite, coal, natural gas, fertile soils, arable land
Land use:
arable land: 52.2%
permanent crops: 2.46%
other: 45.34% (1998 est.)
Irrigated land: 2,100 sq km (1998 est.)
Environment - current issues: the upgrading of Hungary's standards in waste management, energy efficiency, and air, soil, and water pollution with environmental requirements for EU accession will require large investments
Environment - international agreements:
party to: Air Pollution, Air Pollution-Nitrogen Oxides, Air Pollution-Sulfur 85, Air Pollution-Volatile Organic Compounds, Antarctic Treaty, Biodiversity, Climate Change, Climate Change-Kyoto Protocol, Desertification, Endangered Species, Environmental Modification, Hazardous Wastes, Law of the Sea, Marine Dumping, Ozone Layer Protection, Ship Pollution, Wetlands
signed, but not ratified: Air Pollution-Persistent Organic Pollutants, Air Pollution-Sulfur 94
Geography - note: landlocked; strategic location astride main land routes between Western Europe and Balkan Peninsula as well as between Ukraine and Mediterranean basin; the north-south flowing Duna (Danube) and Tisza Rivers divide the country into three large regions

People

Population: 10,032,375 (July 2004 est.)
Age structure:
0-14 years: 16% (male 826,032; female 782,687)
15-64 years: 69% (male 3,407,931; female 3,517,450)
65 years and over: 15% (male 545,488; female 952,787) (2004 est.)
Median age:
total: 38.4 years
male: 35.9 years

female: 41.1 years (2004 est.)
Population growth rate: -0.25% (2004 est.)
Birth rate: 9.77 births/1,000 population (2004 est.)
Death rate: 13.16 deaths/1,000 population (2004 est.)
Net migration rate: 0.86 migrant(s)/1,000 population (2004 est.)
Sex ratio:
at birth: 1.06 male(s)/female
under 15 years: 1.06 male(s)/female
15-64 years: 0.97 male(s)/female
65 years and over: 0.57 male(s)/female
total population: 0.91 male(s)/female (2004 est.)
Infant mortality rate:
total: 8.68 deaths/1,000 live births
male: 9.34 deaths/1,000 live births
female: 7.98 deaths/1,000 live births (2004 est.)
Life expectancy at birth:
total population: 72.25 years
male: 68.07 years
female: 76.69 years (2004 est.)
Total fertility rate: 1.31 children born/woman (2004 est.)
HIV/AIDS - adult prevalence rate: 0.1% (2001 est.)
HIV/AIDS - people living with HIV/AIDS: 2,800 (2001 est.)
HIV/AIDS - deaths: less than 100 (2001 est.)
Nationality:
noun: Hungarian(s)
adjective: Hungarian
Ethnic groups: Hungarian 89.9%, Roma 4%, German 2.6%, Serb 2%, Slovak 0.8%, Romanian 0.7%
Religions: Roman Catholic 67.5%, Calvinist 20%, Lutheran 5%, atheist and other 7.5%
Languages: Hungarian 98.2%, other 1.8%
Literacy:
definition: age 15 and over can read and write
total population: 99.4%
male: 99.5%
female: 99.3% (2003 est.)

Government

Country name:
conventional long form: Republic of Hungary
conventional short form: Hungary
local long form: Magyar Koztarsasag
local short form: Magyarorszag
Government type: parliamentary democracy
Capital: Budapest
Administrative divisions: 19 counties (megyek, singular - megye), 20 urban counties* (singular - megyei varos), and 1 capital city** (fovaros); Bacs-Kiskun, Baranya, Bekes, Bekescsaba*, Borsod-Abauj-Zemplen, Budapest**, Csongrad, Debrecen*, Dunaujvaros*, Eger*, Fejer, Gyor*, Gyor-Moson-Sopron, Hajdu-Bihar, Heves, Hodmezovasarhely*, Jasz-Nagykun-Szolnok, Kaposvar*, Kecskemet*, Komarom-Esztergom, Miskolc*, Nagykanizsa*, Nograd, Nyiregyhaza*, Pecs*, Pest, Somogy, Sopron*,

Szabolcs-Szatmar-Bereg, Szeged*, Szekesfehervar*, Szolnok*, Szombathely*, Tatabanya*, Tolna, Vas, Veszprem, Veszprem*, Zala, Zalaegerszeg*

Independence: 1001 (unification by King Stephen I)

National holiday: Saint Stephen's Day, 20 August

Constitution: 18 August 1949, effective 20 August 1949, revised 19 April 1972; 18 October 1989 revision ensured legal rights for individuals and constitutional checks on the authority of the prime minister and also established the principle of parliamentary oversight; 1997 amendment streamlined the judicial system

Legal system: rule of law based on Western model

Suffrage: 18 years of age; universal

Executive branch:

chief of state: Ferenc MADL (since 4 August 2000)

head of government: Prime Minister Peter MEDGYESSY (since 27 May 2002)

cabinet: Council of Ministers elected by the National Assembly on the recommendation of the president

elections: president elected by the National Assembly for a five-year term; election last held 6 June 2000 (next to be held by June 2005); prime minister elected by the National Assembly on the recommendation of the president

election results: Ferenc MADL elected president; percent of legislative vote - NA% (but by a simple majority in the third round of voting); Peter MEDGYESSY elected prime minister; percent of legislative vote - NA%

note: to be elected, the president must win two-thirds of legislative vote in the first two rounds or a simple majority in the third round

Legislative branch: unicameral National Assembly or Orszaggyules (386 seats; members are elected by popular vote under a system of proportional and direct representation to serve four-year terms)

elections: last held 7 and 21 April 2002 (next to be held NA April 2006)

election results: percent of vote by party (5% or more of the vote required for parliamentary representation in the first round) - Fidesz/MDF 48.70%, MSzP 46.11%, SzDSz 4.92%, other 0.27%; seats by party - Fidesz 164, MSzP 178, MDF 24, SzDSz 20

Judicial branch: Constitutional Court (judges are elected by the National Assembly for nine-year terms)

Political parties and leaders: Alliance of Free Democrats or SzDSz [Gabor KUNCZE]; Hungarian Civic Alliance or Fidesz-MPP [Viktor ORBAN, chairman]; Hungarian Democratic Forum or MDF [Ibolya DAVID]; Hungarian Democratic People's Party or MDNP [Erzsebet PUSZTAI, chairman]; Hungarian Socialist Party or MSzP [Laszlo KOVACS, chairman]; Hungarian Workers' Party or MMP [Gyula THURMER, chairman]

Political pressure groups and leaders: NA

International organization participation: Australia Group, BIS, CE, CEI, CERN, EAPC, EBRD, ESA (cooperating state), EU (new member), FAO, G-9, IAEA, IBRD, ICAO, ICC, ICCt, ICFTU, ICRM, IDA, IEA, IFC, IFRCS, ILO, IMF, IMO, Interpol, IOC, IOM, ISO, ITU, MINURSO, NAM (guest), NATO, NEA, NSG, OAS (observer), OECD, OPCW, OSCE, PCA, PFP, UN,
UNCTAD, UNESCO, UNFICYP, UNHCR, UNIDO, UNMIK, UNOMIG, UPU, WCL, WCO, WEU (associate), WFTU, WHO, WIPO, WMO, WToO, WTrO, ZC

Diplomatic representation in the US:

chief of mission: Ambassador Andras SIMONYI

chancery: 3910 Shoemaker Street NW, Washington, DC 20008

telephone: [1] (202) 362-6730

FAX: [1] (202) 966-8135

consulate(s) general: Los Angeles and New York

Diplomatic representation from the US:

chief of mission: Ambassador George Herbert WALKER

embassy: 1054 Szabadsag ter 12, Budapest

mailing address: pouch: American Embassy Budapest, 5270 Budapest Place, Department of State, Washington, DC 20521-5270

telephone: [36] (1) 475-4400

FAX: [36] (1) 475-4764

Flag description: three equal horizontal bands of red (top), white, and green

Economy

Economy - overview: Hungary has made the transition from a centrally planned to a market economy, with a per capita income one-half that of the Big Four European nations. Hungary continues to demonstrate strong economic growth and to work toward accession to the European Union in May 2004. The private sector accounts for over 80% of GDP. Foreign ownership of and investment in Hungarian firms are widespread, with cumulative foreign direct investment totaling more than $23 billion since 1989. Hungarian sovereign debt was upgraded in 2000 to the second-highest rating among all the Central European transition economies. Inflation has declined substantially, from 14% in 1998 to 4.7% in 2003; unemployment has persisted around the 6% level. Germany is by far Hungary's largest economic partner. Short-term issues include the reduction of the public sector deficit to 3% in 2004 and avoiding unjustified increases in wages.

GDP: purchasing power parity - $139.7 billion (2003 est.)

GDP - real growth rate: 2.8% (2003 est.)

GDP - per capita: purchasing power parity - $13,900 (2003 est.)

GDP - composition by sector:

agriculture: 4.3%

industry: 28.4%

services: 67.3% (2001 est.)

Population below poverty line: 8.6% (1993 est.)

Household income or consumption by percentage share:

lowest 10%: 4.1%

highest 10%: 20.5% (1998)

Distribution of family income - Gini index: 24.4 (1998)

Inflation rate (consumer prices): 4.7% (2003 est.)

Labor force: 4.2 million (1997)

Labor force - by occupation: services 65%, industry 27%, agriculture 8% (1996)

Unemployment rate: 6.1% (2003 est.)

Budget:

revenues: $13 billion

expenditures: $14.4 billion, including capital expenditures of $NA (2000 est.)

Industries: mining, metallurgy, construction materials, processed foods, textiles, chemicals (especially pharmaceuticals), motor vehicles

Industrial production growth rate: 2.5% (2003 est.)

Electricity - production: 34.39 billion kWh (2001)

Electricity - production by source:

fossil fuel: 60.1%

hydro: 0.5%

nuclear: 39%

other: 0.3% (2001)

Electricity - consumption: 35.15 billion kWh (2001)

Electricity - exports: 7.261 billion kWh (2001)

Electricity - imports: 10.43 billion kWh (2001)

Oil - production: 41,190 bbl/day (2001 est.)

Oil - consumption: 140,700 bbl/day (2001 est.)

Oil - exports: 47,180 bbl/day (2001)

Oil - imports: 136,600 bbl/day (2001)

Oil - proved reserves: 110.7 million bbl (1 January 2002)

Natural gas - production: 3.231 billion cu m (2001 est.)

Natural gas - consumption: 13.37 billion cu m (2001 est.)

Natural gas - exports: 4 million cu m (2001 est.)

Natural gas - imports: 9.587 billion cu m (2001 est.)

Natural gas - proved reserves: 50.45 billion cu m (1 January 2002)

Agriculture - products: wheat, corn, sunflower seed, potatoes, sugar beets; pigs, cattle, poultry, dairy products

Exports: $42.03 billion f.o.b. (2003 est.)

Exports - commodities: machinery and equipment 57.6%, other manufactures 31.0%, food products 7.5%, raw materials 1.9%, fuels and electricity 1.9% (2001)

Exports - partners: Germany 35.5%, Austria 7.1%, Italy 5.7%, France 5.7%, UK 4.7%, Sweden 4.3%, Netherlands 4.2% (2002)

Imports: $46.19 billion f.o.b. (2003 est.)

Imports - commodities: machinery and equipment 51.6%, other manufactures 35.3%, fuels and electricity 8.2%, food products 2.9%, raw materials 2.0% (2001)

Imports - partners: Germany 24.2%, Italy 7.5%, Austria 6.9%, Russia 6.1%, China 5.6%, France 4.8%, Japan 4.2% (2002)

Debt - external: $41.3 billion (2003 est.)

Economic aid - recipient: ODA $250 million (2000)

Currency: forint (HUF)

Currency code: HUF

Exchange rates: forints per US dollar - 224.307 (2003), 257.887 (2002), 286.49 (2001), 282.179 (2000), 237.146 (1999)

Fiscal year: calendar year

Hungary (continued)

Communications

Telephones - main lines in use: 3,666,400 (2002)
Telephones - mobile cellular: 6,862,800 (2002)
Telephone system:
general assessment: the telephone system has been modernized and is capable of satisfying all requests for telecommunication service
domestic: the system is digitalized and highly automated; trunk services are carried by fiber-optic cable and digital microwave radio relay; a program for fiber-optic subscriber connections was initiated in 1996; heavy use is made of mobile cellular telephones
international: country code - 36; Hungary has fiber-optic cable connections with all neighboring countries; the international switch is in Budapest; satellite earth stations - 2 Intelsat (Atlantic Ocean and Indian Ocean regions), 1 Inmarsat, 1 very small aperture terminal (VSAT) system of ground terminals
Radio broadcast stations: AM 17, FM 57, shortwave 3 (1998)
Television broadcast stations: 35 (plus 161 low-power repeaters) (1995)
Internet country code: .hu
Internet hosts: 194,503 (2002)
Internet users: 1.6 million (2002)

Transportation

Railways:
total: 7,875 km
broad gauge: 36 km 1.524-m gauge
standard gauge: 7,620 km 1.435-m gauge (2,628 km electrified)
narrow gauge: 219 km 0.760-m gauge
note: Hungary and Austria jointly manage a cross-border, standard-gauge railway connecting Gyor, Sopron, and Ebenfurt (Gysev railroad) with a route length of 101 km in Hungary and 65 km in Austria; 156 km of this line is electrified (2002)
Highways:
total: 188,203 km
paved: 81,680 km (including 438 km of expressways)
unpaved: 106,523 km (1999)
Waterways: 1,373 km (permanently navigable) (1997)
Pipelines: gas 4,397 km; oil 990 km; refined products 335 km (2003)
Ports and harbors: Budapest, Dunaujvaros, Gyor-Gonyu, Csepel, Baja, Mohacs (2003)
Merchant marine:
total: 2 ships (1,000 GRT or over) 7,568 GRT/10,025 DWT
by type: cargo 2
registered in other countries: 8 (2003 est.)
Airports: 43 (2003 est.)
Airports - with paved runways:
total: 16
over 3,047 m: 2
2,438 to 3,047 m: 8
1,524 to 2,437 m: 4
914 to 1,523 m: 1
under 914 m: 1 (2003 est.)

Airports - with unpaved runways:
total: 27
2,438 to 3,047 m: 3
1,524 to 2,437 m: 4
914 to 1,523 m: 11
under 914 m: 9 (2003 est.)
Heliports: 5 (2003 est.)

Military

Military branches: Ground Forces, Air Forces
Military manpower - military age: 18 years of age (2004 est.)
Military manpower - availability:
males age 15-49: 2,519,052 (2004 est.)
Military manpower - fit for military service:
males age 15-49: 2,011,750 (2004 est.)
Military manpower - reaching military age annually:
males: 64,426 (2004 est.)
Military expenditures - dollar figure: $1.08 billion (2002 est.)
Military expenditures - percent of GDP: 1.75% (2002 est.)

Transnational Issues

Disputes - international: Hungary amended the status law extending special social and cultural benefits to ethnic Hungarians in neighboring states, who had objected to the law; Slovakia and Hungary have renewed discussions on ways to resolve differences over the Gabcikovo-Nagymaros hydroelectric dam on the Danube, with possible resort again to the ICJ for final resolution
Illicit drugs: transshipment point for Southwest Asian heroin and cannabis and for South American cocaine destined for Western Europe; limited producer of precursor chemicals, particularly for amphetamine and methamphetamine; improving, but remains vulnerable to money laundering related to organized crime and drug trafficking

Iceland

Introduction

Background: Settled by Norwegian and Celtic (Scottish and Irish) immigrants during the late 9th and 10th centuries A.D., Iceland boasts the world's oldest functioning legislative assembly, the Althing, established in 930. Independent for over 300 years, Iceland was subsequently ruled by Norway and Denmark. Fallout from the Askja volcano of 1875 devastated the Icelandic economy and caused widespread famine. Over the next quarter century, 20% of the island's population emigrated, mostly to Canada and the US. Limited home rule from Denmark was granted in 1874 and complete independence attained in 1944. Literacy, longevity, income, and social cohesion are first-rate by world standards.

Geography

Location: Northern Europe, island between the Greenland Sea and the North Atlantic Ocean, northwest of the UK
Geographic coordinates: 65 00 N, 18 00 W
Map references: Arctic Region
Area:
total: 103,000 sq km
land: 100,250 sq km
water: 2,750 sq km
Area - comparative: slightly smaller than Kentucky
Land boundaries: 0 km
Coastline: 4,988 km
Maritime claims:
territorial sea: 12 NM
exclusive economic zone: 200 NM
continental shelf: 200 NM or to the edge of the continental margin
Climate: temperate; moderated by North Atlantic Current; mild, windy winters; damp, cool summers
Terrain: mostly plateau interspersed with mountain peaks, icefields; coast deeply indented by bays and fiords

Iceland *(continued)*

Elevation extremes:
lowest point: Atlantic Ocean 0 m
highest point: Hvannadalshnukur 2,119 m (at Vatnajokull glacier)
Natural resources: fish, hydropower, geothermal power, diatomite
Land use:
arable land: 1%
permanent crops: 0%
permanent pastures: 28%
forest and woodlands: 1%
other: 70% (2001 est.)
Irrigated land: NA sq km
Natural hazards: earthquakes and volcanic activity
Environment - current issues: water pollution from fertilizer runoff; inadequate wastewater treatment
Environment - international agreements:
party to: Air Pollution, Biodiversity, Climate Change, Climate Change-Kyoto Protocol, Desertification, Endangered Species, Hazardous Wastes, Kyoto Protocol, Law of the Sea, Marine Dumping, Ozone Layer Protection, Ship Pollution, Transboundary Air Pollution, Wetlands
signed, but not ratified: Air Pollution-Persistent Organic Pollutants, Environmental Modification, Marine Life Conservation
Geography - note: strategic location between Greenland and Europe; westernmost European country; Reykjavik is the northernmost national capital in the world; more land covered by glaciers than in all of continental Europe

People

Population: 293,966 (July 2004 est.)
Age structure:
0-14 years: 22.5% (male 33,522; female 32,489)
15-64 years: 65.8% (male 98,091; female 95,450)
65 years and over: 11.7% (male 15,552; female 18,862) (2004 est.)
Median age:
total: 33.8 years
male: 33.3 years
female: 34.3 years (2004 est.)
Population growth rate: 0.97% (2004 est.)
Birth rate: 13.83 births/1,000 population (2004 est.)
Death rate: 6.57 deaths/1,000 population (2004 est.)
Net migration rate: 2.38 migrant(s)/1,000 population (2004 est.)
Sex ratio:
at birth: 1.04 male(s)/female
under 15 years: 1.03 male(s)/female
15-64 years: 1.03 male(s)/female
65 years and over: 0.83 male(s)/female
total population: 1 male(s)/female (2004 est.)
Infant mortality rate:
total: 3.31 deaths/1,000 live births
male: 3.44 deaths/1,000 live births
female: 3.17 deaths/1,000 live births (2004 est.)
Life expectancy at birth:
total population: 80.18 years
male: 78.18 years
female: 82.27 years (2004 est.)

Total fertility rate: 1.93 children born/woman (2004 est.)
HIV/AIDS - adult prevalence rate: 0.2% (2001 est.)
HIV/AIDS - people living with HIV/AIDS: 220 (2001 est.)
HIV/AIDS - deaths: less than 100 (2001 est.)
Nationality:
noun: Icelander(s)
adjective: Icelandic
Ethnic groups: homogeneous mixture of descendants of Norse and Celts 94%, population of foreign origin 6%
Religions: Evangelical Lutheran 87.1%, other Protestant 4.1%, Roman Catholic 1.7%, other 7.1% (2002)
Languages: Icelandic, English, Nordic languages, German widely spoken
Literacy:
definition: age 15 and over can read and write
total population: 99.9% (1997 est.)
male: NA%
female: NA%

Government

Country name:
conventional long form: Republic of Iceland
conventional short form: Iceland
local long form: Lydhveldidh Island
local short form: Island
Government type: constitutional republic
Capital: Reykjavik
Administrative divisions: 8 regions; Austurland, Hofudhborgarsvaedhi, Nordhurland Eystra, Nordhurland Vestra, Sudhurland, Sudhurnes, Vestfirdhir, Vesturland
Independence: 1 December 1918 (became a sovereign state under the Danish Crown); 17 June 1944 (from Denmark)
National holiday: Independence Day, 17 June (1944)
Constitution: 16 June 1944, effective 17 June 1944
Legal system: civil law system based on Danish law; has not accepted compulsory ICJ jurisdiction
Suffrage: 18 years of age; universal
Executive branch:
chief of state: President Olafur Ragnar GRIMSSON (since 1 August 1996)
head of government: Prime Minister David ODDSSON (since 30 April 1991)
cabinet: Cabinet appointed by the prime minister and approved by Parliament
elections: president, which is largely a ceremonial post, elected by popular vote for a four-year term; election last held 29 June 1996 (next to be held NA June 2004); President GRIMSSON ran unopposed in June 2000 so there were no elections; prime minister appointed by the president
election results: Olafur Ragnar GRIMSSON ran unopposed in 2000 and was reelected
Legislative branch: unicameral Parliament or Althing (63 seats; members are elected by popular vote to serve four-year terms)

elections: last held 10 May 2003 (next to be held by May 2007)
election results: percent of vote by party - Independence Party 33.7%, Social Democratic Alliance 31.0%, Progressive Party 17.7%, Left-Green Alliance 8.8%, Liberal Party 7.4%; seats by party - Independence Party 22, Social Democratic Alliance 20, Progressive Party 12, Left-Green Alliance 5, Liberal Party 4
Judicial branch: Supreme Court or Haestirettur (justices are appointed for life by the Minister of Justice); eight district courts (justices are appointed for life by the Minister of Justice)
Political parties and leaders: Independence Party or IP [David ODDSSON]; Left-Green Alliance or LGP [Steingrimur SIGFUSSON]; Liberal Party or LP [Gudjon KRISTJANSSON]; Progressive Party or PP [Halldor ASGRIMSSON]; Social Democratic Alliance (includes People's Alliance or PA, Social Democratic Party or SDP, Women's List)or SDA [Ossur SKARPHEDINSSON]; Social Democratic Party or SDP [Sighvatur BJORGVINSSON]; Women's List or WL [Kristin ASTGEIRSDOTTIR]
Political pressure groups and leaders: NA
International organization participation: Australia Group, BIS, CBSS, CE, EAPC, EBRD, EFTA, FAO, IAEA, IBRD, ICAO, ICC, ICCt, ICFTU, ICRM, IDA, IFAD, IFC, IFRCS, IHO, ILO, IMF, IMO, Interpol, IOC, ISO, ITU, NATO, NC, NEA, NIB, OECD, OPCW, OSCE, PCA, UN, UNCTAD, UNESCO, UNMIK, UPU, WCO, WEU (associate), WHO, WIPO, WMO, WTrO
Diplomatic representation in the US:
chief of mission: Ambassador Helgi AGUSTSSON
chancery: Suite 1200, 1156 15th Street NW, Washington, DC 20005-1704
telephone: [1] (202) 265-6653
FAX: [1] (202) 265-6656
consulate(s) general: New York
Diplomatic representation from the US:
chief of mission: Ambassador James I. GADSDEN
embassy: Laufasvegur 21, 101 Reykjavik
mailing address: US Embassy, PSC 1003, Box 40, FPO AE 09728-0340
telephone: [354] 5629100
FAX: [354] 5629118
Flag description: blue with a red cross outlined in white extending to the edges of the flag; the vertical part of the cross is shifted to the hoist side in the style of the Dannebrog (Danish flag)

Economy

Economy - overview: Iceland's Scandinavian-type economy is basically capitalistic, yet with an extensive welfare system (including generous housing subsidies), low unemployment, and remarkably even distribution of income. In the absence of other natural resources (except for abundant geothermal power), the economy depends heavily on the fishing industry, which provides 70% of export earnings and employs 12% of the work force. The economy remains sensitive to declining fish stocks as well as to fluctuations in world prices for its main exports: fish and fish products, aluminum, and ferrosilicon. Government policies include reducing the budget and current account deficits, limiting foreign borrowing, containing inflation, revising agricultural and fishing policies, diversifying the economy, and privatizing state-owned industries. The government remains opposed to EU membership, primarily because of Icelanders' concern about losing control over their fishing resources. Iceland's economy has been diversifying into manufacturing and service industries in the last decade, and new developments in software production, biotechnology, and financial services are taking place. The tourism sector is also expanding, with the recent trends in ecotourism and whale watching. Growth had been remarkably steady in 1996-2001 at 3%-5%, but could not be sustained in 2002 in an environment of global recession. Growth resumed in 2003, and inflation dropped back from 5% to 2%.

GDP: purchasing power parity - $8.678 billion (2003 est.)

GDP - real growth rate: 2.6% (2003 est.)

GDP - per capita: purchasing power parity - $30,900 (2003 est.)

GDP - composition by sector:
agriculture: 14% (includes fishing 12%)
industry: 20%
services: 66% (2002 est.)

Population below poverty line: NA%

Household income or consumption by percentage share:
lowest 10%: NA%
highest 10%: NA%

Inflation rate (consumer prices): 2% (2003 est.)

Labor force: 159,000 (2000)

Labor force - by occupation: agriculture 5.1%, fishing and fish processing 11.8%, manufacturing 12.9%, construction 10.7%, other services 59.5% (1999)

Unemployment rate: 3.5% (2003 est.)

Budget:
revenues: $3.5 billion
expenditures: $3.3 billion, including capital expenditures of $467 million (1999)

Industries: fish processing; aluminum smelting, ferrosilicon production, geothermal power; tourism

Industrial production growth rate: 5.7% (2003 est.)

Electricity - production: 7.894 billion kWh (2001)

Electricity - production by source:
fossil fuel: 0.1%
hydro: 82.5%
nuclear: 0%
other: 17.5% (geothermal) (2001)

Electricity - consumption: 7.341 billion kWh (2001)

Electricity - exports: 0 kWh (2001)

Electricity - imports: 0 kWh (2001)

Oil - production: 0 bbl/day (2001 est.)

Oil - consumption: 16,300 bbl/day (2001 est.)

Oil - exports: 0 bbl/day (2001)

Oil - imports: 15,470 bbl/day (2001)

Agriculture - products: potatoes, green vegetables, mutton, dairy products, fish

Exports: $2.379 billion f.o.b. (2003 est.)

Exports - commodities: fish and fish products 70%, animal products, aluminum, diatomite, ferrosilicon

Exports - partners: Germany 18.5%, UK 17.5%, Netherlands 11.4%, US 10.9%, Spain 5.2%, Denmark 4.6%, Portugal 4.3%, Norway 4.2% (2002)

Imports: $2.59 billion (2003 est.)

Imports - commodities: machinery and equipment, petroleum products; foodstuffs, textiles

Imports - partners: US 10.9%, Germany 10.7%, Denmark 8.5%, Norway 8%, UK 7.5%, Netherlands 6.1%, Sweden 5.9% (2002)

Debt - external: $2.6 billion (1999)

Economic aid - donor: $NA

Currency: Icelandic krona (ISK)

Currency code: ISK

Exchange rates: Icelandic kronur per US dollar - 76.709 (2003), 91.6617 (2002), 97.4246 (2001), 78.6159 (2000), 72.3353 (1999)

Fiscal year: calendar year

Communications

Telephones - main lines in use: 188,000 (2002)

Telephones - mobile cellular: 260,900 (2002)

Telephone system:
general assessment: extensive domestic service
domestic: the trunk network consists of coaxial and fiber-optic cables and microwave radio relay links
international: country code - 354; satellite earth stations - 2 Intelsat (Atlantic Ocean), 1 Inmarsat (Atlantic and Indian Ocean regions); note - Iceland shares the Inmarsat earth station with the other Nordic countries (Denmark, Finland, Norway, and Sweden)

Radio broadcast stations: AM 3, FM about 70 (including repeaters), shortwave 1 (1998)

Television broadcast stations: 14 (plus 156 low-power repeaters) (1997)

Internet country code: .is

Internet hosts: 68,261 (2002)

Internet users: 186,600 (2002)

Transportation

Railways: 0 km

Highways:
total: 12,955 km
paved/oiled gravel: 3,863 km
unpaved: 9,092 km (2003)

Waterways: none

Ports and harbors: Akureyri, Hornafjordhur, Isafjordhur, Keflavik, Raufarhofn, Reykjavik, Seydhisfjordhur, Straumsvik, Vesttmannaeyjar

Merchant marine:
total: 1 ships (1,000 GRT or over) 4,341 GRT/6,019 DWT
by type: petroleum tanker 1
registered in other countries: 26 (2003 est.)

Airports: 100 (2003 est.)

Airports - with paved runways:
total: 5

over 3,047 m: 1
1,524 to 2,437 m: 3
914 to 1,523 m: 1 (2003 est.)

Airports - with unpaved runways:
total: 95
1,524 to 2,437 m: 4
914 to 1,523 m: 29
under 914 m: 62 (2003 est.)

Military

Military branches: no regular armed forces; Police, Coast Guard

Military manpower - availability:
males age 15-49: 75,568 (2004 est.)

Military manpower - fit for military service:
males age 15-49: 66,503 (2004 est.)

Military expenditures - dollar figure: 0

Military - note: defense is provided by the US-manned Icelandic Defense Force (IDF) headquartered at Keflavik

Transnational Issues

Disputes - international: Rockall continental shelf dispute involving Denmark, Iceland, and the UK (Ireland and the UK have signed a boundary agreement in the Rockall area) remains dormant; dispute with Denmark over the Faroe Islands' fisheries median line boundary within 200 NM; disputes with Denmark, the UK, and Ireland over the Faroe Islands continental shelf boundary outside 200 NM

India

Introduction

Background: The Indus Valley civilization, one of the oldest in the world, dates back at least 5,000 years. Aryan tribes from the northwest invaded about 1500 B.C.; their merger with the earlier inhabitants created the classical Indian culture. Arab incursions starting in the 8th century and Turkish in the 12th were followed by European traders, beginning in the late 15th century. By the 19th century, Britain had assumed political control of virtually all Indian lands. Nonviolent resistance to British colonialism under Mohandas GANDHI and Jawaharlal NEHRU led to independence in 1947. The subcontinent was divided into the secular state of India and the smaller Muslim state of Pakistan. A third war between the two countries in 1971 resulted in East Pakistan becoming the separate nation of Bangladesh. Fundamental concerns in India include the ongoing dispute with Pakistan over Kashmir, massive overpopulation, environmental degradation, extensive poverty, and ethnic and religious strife, all this despite impressive gains in economic investment and output.

Geography

Location: Southern Asia, bordering the Arabian Sea and the Bay of Bengal, between Burma and Pakistan
Geographic coordinates: 20 00 N, 77 00 E
Map references: Asia
Area:
total: 3,287,590 sq km
land: 2,973,190 sq km
water: 314,400 sq km
Area - comparative: slightly more than one-third the size of the US
Land boundaries:
total: 14,103 km
border countries: Bangladesh 4,053 km, Bhutan 605 km, Burma 1,463 km, China 3,380 km, Nepal 1,690 km, Pakistan 2,912 km
Coastline: 7,000 km

Maritime claims:
territorial sea: 12 NM
contiguous zone: 24 NM
exclusive economic zone: 200 NM
continental shelf: 200 NM or to the edge of the continental margin
Climate: varies from tropical monsoon in south to temperate in north
Terrain: upland plain (Deccan Plateau) in south, flat to rolling plain along the Ganges, deserts in west, Himalayas in north
Elevation extremes:
lowest point: Indian Ocean 0 m
highest point: Kanchenjunga 8,598 m
Natural resources: coal (fourth-largest reserves in the world), iron ore, manganese, mica, bauxite, titanium ore, chromite, natural gas, diamonds, petroleum, limestone, arable land
Land use:
arable land: 54.35%
permanent crops: 2.66%
other: 42.99% (1998 est.)
Irrigated land: 590,000 sq km (1998 est.)
Natural hazards: droughts; flash floods, as well as widespread and destructive flooding from monsoonal rains; severe thunderstorms; earthquakes
Environment - current issues: deforestation; soil erosion; overgrazing; desertification; air pollution from industrial effluents and vehicle emissions; water pollution from raw sewage and runoff of agricultural pesticides; tap water is not potable throughout the country; huge and growing population is overstraining natural resources
Environment - international agreements:
party to: Antarctic-Environmental Protocol, Antarctic-Marine Living Resources, Antarctic Treaty, Biodiversity, Climate Change, Climate Change-Kyoto Protocol, Desertification, Endangered Species, Environmental Modification, Hazardous Wastes, Law of the Sea, Ozone Layer Protection, Ship Pollution, Tropical Timber 83, Tropical Timber 94, Wetlands, Whaling
signed, but not ratified: none of the selected agreements
Geography - note: dominates South Asian subcontinent; near important Indian Ocean trade routes

People

Population: 1,065,070,607 (July 2004 est.)
Age structure:
0-14 years: 31.7% (male 173,869,856; female 164,003,915)
15-64 years: 63.5% (male 349,785,804; female 326,289,402)
65 years and over: 4.8% (male 25,885,725; female 25,235,905) (2004 est.)
Median age:
total: 24.4 years
male: 24.4 years
female: 24.4 years (2004 est.)

Population growth rate: 1.44% (2004 est.)
Birth rate: 22.8 births/1,000 population (2004 est.)
Death rate: 8.38 deaths/1,000 population (2004 est.)
Net migration rate: -0.07 migrant(s)/1,000 population (2004 est.)
Sex ratio:
at birth: 1.05 male(s)/female
under 15 years: 1.06 male(s)/female
15-64 years: 1.07 male(s)/female
65 years and over: 1.03 male(s)/female
total population: 1.07 male(s)/female (2004 est.)
Infant mortality rate:
total: 57.92 deaths/1,000 live births
male: 58.52 deaths/1,000 live births
female: 57.29 deaths/1,000 live births (2004 est.)
Life expectancy at birth:
total population: 63.99 years
male: 63.25 years
female: 64.77 years (2004 est.)
Total fertility rate: 2.85 children born/woman (2004 est.)
HIV/AIDS - adult prevalence rate: 0.8% (2001 est.)
HIV/AIDS - people living with HIV/AIDS: 3.97 million (2001 est.)
HIV/AIDS - deaths: 310,000 (2001 est.)
Nationality:
noun: Indian(s)
adjective: Indian
Ethnic groups: Indo-Aryan 72%, Dravidian 25%, Mongoloid and other 3% (2000)
Religions: Hindu 81.3%, Muslim 12%, Christian 2.3%, Sikh 1.9%, other groups including Buddhist, Jain, Parsi 2.5% (2000)
Languages: English enjoys associate status but is the most important language for national, political, and commercial communication; Hindi is the national language and primary tongue of 30% of the people; there are 14 other official languages: Bengali, Telugu, Marathi, Tamil, Urdu, Gujarati, Malayalam, Kannada, Oriya, Punjabi, Assamese, Kashmiri, Sindhi, and Sanskrit; Hindustani is a popular variant of Hindi/Urdu spoken widely throughout northern India but is not an official language
Literacy:
definition: age 15 and over can read and write
total population: 59.5%
male: 70.2%
female: 48.3% (2003 est.)

Government

Country name:
conventional long form: Republic of India
conventional short form: India
Government type: federal republic
Capital: New Delhi
Administrative divisions: 28 states and 7 union territories*; Andaman and Nicobar Islands*, Andhra Pradesh, Arunachal Pradesh, Assam, Bihar, Chandigarh*, Chhattisgarh, Dadra and Nagar Haveli*, Daman and Diu*, Delhi*, Goa, Gujarat, Haryana, Himachal Pradesh, Jammu and Kashmir, Jharkhand, Karnataka, Kerala, Lakshadweep*, Madhya Pradesh,

India (continued)

Maharashtra, Manipur, Meghalaya, Mizoram, Nagaland, Orissa, Pondicherry*, Punjab, Rajasthan, Sikkim, Tamil Nadu, Tripura, Uttaranchal, Uttar Pradesh, West Bengal

Independence: 15 August 1947 (from UK)

National holiday: Republic Day, 26 January (1950)

Constitution: 26 January 1950

Legal system: based on English common law; limited judicial review of legislative acts; accepts compulsory ICJ jurisdiction, with reservations

Suffrage: 18 years of age; universal

Executive branch:

chief of state: President Abdul KALAM (since 26 July 2002); Vice President Bhairon Singh SHEKHAWAT (since 19 August 2002)

head of government: Prime Minister Atal Bihari VAJPAYEE (since 19 March 1998)

cabinet: Council of Ministers appointed by the president on the recommendation of the prime minister

elections: president elected by an electoral college consisting of elected members of both houses of Parliament and the legislatures of the states for a five-year term; election last held NA July 2002 (next to be held 18 July 2007); vice president elected by both houses of Parliament for a five-year term; election last held 12 August 2002 (next to be held NA August 2007); prime minister elected by parliamentary members of the majority party following legislative elections; election last held 3 October 1999 (next to be held NA October 2004)

election results: Abdul KALAM elected president; percent of electoral college vote - 89.6%; Bhairon Singh SHEKHAWAT elected vice president; percent of Parliament vote - 59.8%; Atal Bihari VAJPAYEE elected prime minister; percent of vote - NA%

Legislative branch: bicameral Parliament or Sansad consists of the Council of States or Rajya Sabha (a body consisting of not more than 250 members, up to 12 of which are appointed by the president, the remainder are chosen by the elected members of the state and territorial assemblies; members serve six-year terms) and the People's Assembly or Lok Sabha (545 seats; 543 elected by popular vote, 2 appointed by the president; members serve five-year terms)

elections: People's Assembly - last held 5 September through 3 October 1999 (next to be held NA 2004)

election results: People's Assembly - percent of vote by party - BJP alliance 40.8%, Congress (I) 33.8%, other 25.4%; seats by party - BJP alliance 304, Congress (I) 134, other 107

Judicial branch: Supreme Court (judges are appointed by the president and remain in office until they reach the age of 65)

Political parties and leaders: All India Anna Dravida Munnetra Kazhagam or AIADMK [C. Jayalalitha JAYARAM]; All India Forward Bloc or AIFB, [D. BISWAS, general secretary]; Asom Gana Parishad [Brindaban GOSWAMI]; Bahujan Samaj Party or BSP [MAYAWATI]; Bharatiya Janata Party or BJP [Venkaiah NAIDU]; Biju Janata Dal or BJD

[Naveen PATNAIK]; Communist Party of India or CPI [Ardhendu Bhushan BARDHAN]; Communist Party of India/Marxist-Leninist or CPI/ML [Dipankar BHATTACHARYA]; Congress (I) Party [Sonia GANDHI]; Dravida Munnetra Kazagham or DMK (a regional party in Tamil Nadu) [M. KARUNANIDHI]; Indian National League [Suliaman SAITH]; Janata Dal (Secular) [H. D. Deve GOWDA]; Janata Dal (United) or JDU [Sharad YADAV]; Kerala Congress (Mani faction) [K. M. MANI]; Marumalarchi Dravida Munnetra Kazhagam or MDMK [VAIKO]; Muslim League [G. M. BANATWALA]; Nationalist Congress Party or NCP [Sharad PAWAR]; Rashtriya Janata Dal or RJD [Laloo Prasad YADAV]; Revolutionary Socialist Party or RSP [Abani ROY]; Samajwadi Party or SP [Mulayam Singh YADAV]; Shiromani Akali Dal [G. S. TOHRA]; Shiv Sena [Bal THACKERAY]; Tamil Maanila Congress [G. K. VASAN]; Telugu Desam Party or TDP [Chandrababu NAIDU]; Trinamool Congress [Mamata BANERJEE]

Political pressure groups and leaders: numerous religious or militant/chauvinistic organizations, including Vishwa Hindu Parishad, Bajrang Dal, and Rashtriya Swayamsevak Sangh; various separatist groups seeking greater communal and/or regional autonomy, including the All Parties Hurriyat Conference

International organization participation: AfDB, ARF, AsDB, ASEAN (dialogue partner), BIS, C, CP, FAO, G- 6, G-15, G-19, G-24, G-77, IAEA, IBRD, ICAO, ICC, ICFTU, ICRM, IDA, IFAD, IFC, IFRCS, IHO, ILO, IMF, IMO, Interpol, IOC, IOM (observer), ISO, ITU, MICAH, MONUC, NAM, OAS (observer), OPCW, PCA, SAARC, UN, UNCTAD, UNESCO, UNHCR, UNIDO, UNIFIL, UNMEE, UNMIK, UNMOVIC, UPU, WCL, WCO, WFTU, WHO, WIPO, WMO, WToO, WTrO

Diplomatic representation in the US:

chief of mission: Ambassador Lalit MANSINGH

chancery: 2107 Massachusetts Avenue NW, Washington, DC 20008; note - Embassy located at 2536 Massachusetts Avenue NW, Washington, DC 20008

telephone: [1] (202) 939-7000

FAX: [1] (202) 483-3972

consulate(s) general: Chicago, Houston, New York, and San Francisco

Diplomatic representation from the US:

chief of mission: Ambassador David C. Mulford

embassy: Shantipath, Chanakyapuri, New Delhi 110021

mailing address: use embassy street address

telephone: [91] (11) 419-8000

FAX: [91] (11) 419-0017

consulate(s) general: Chennai (Madras), Kolkata (Calcutta), Mumbai (Bombay)

Flag description: three equal horizontal bands of saffron (subdued orange) (top), white, and green with a blue chakra (24-spoked wheel) centered in the white band; similar to the flag of Niger, which has a small orange disk centered in the white band

Economy - overview: India's economy encompasses traditional village farming, modern agriculture, handicrafts, a wide range of modern industries, and a multitude of support services. Government controls have been reduced on foreign trade and investment, and privatization of domestic output has proceeded slowly. The economy has posted an excellent average growth rate of 6% since 1990, reducing poverty by about 10 percentage points. India is capitalizing on its large numbers of well-educated people skilled in the English language to become a major exporter of software services and software workers. Despite strong growth, the World Bank and others worry about the continuing public-sector budget deficit, running at approximately 10% of GDP.

GDP: purchasing power parity - $3.022 trillion (2003 est.)

GDP - real growth rate: 7.6% (2003 est.)

GDP - per capita: purchasing power parity - $2,900 (2003 est.)

GDP - composition by sector:

agriculture: 23.6%

industry: 28.4%

services: 48% (2002 est.)

Population below poverty line: 25% (2002 est.)

Household income or consumption by percentage share:

lowest 10%: 3.5%

highest 10%: 33.5% (1997)

Distribution of family income - Gini index: 37.8 (1997)

Inflation rate (consumer prices): 4.6% (2003 est.)

Labor force: 406 million (1999)

Labor force - by occupation: agriculture 60%, services 23%, industry 17% (1999)

Unemployment rate: 9.1% (2003)

Budget:

revenues: $48.3 billion

expenditures: $78.2 billion, including capital expenditures of $13.5 (FY01/02 est.)

Industries: textiles, chemicals, food processing, steel, transportation equipment, cement, mining, petroleum, machinery, software

Industrial production growth rate: 6% (2003 est.)

Electricity - production: 533.3 billion kWh (2001)

Electricity - production by source:

fossil fuel: 81.7%

hydro: 14.5%

nuclear: 3.4%

other: 0.3% (2001)

Electricity - consumption: 497.2 billion kWh (2001)

Electricity - exports: 321 million kWh (2001)

Electricity - imports: 1.54 billion kWh (2001)

Oil - production: 732,400 bbl/day (2001 est.)

Oil - consumption: 2.13 million bbl/day (2001 est.)

Oil - exports: NA

Oil - imports: NA

Oil - proved reserves: 4.33 billion bbl (1 January 2002)

Natural gas - production: 22.75 billion cu m (2001 est.)

Natural gas - consumption: 22.75 billion cu m (2001 est.)

Natural gas - exports: 0 cu m (2001 est.)

Natural gas - imports: 0 cu m (2001 est.)

Natural gas - proved reserves: 542.4 billion cu m (1 January 2002)

Agriculture - products: rice, wheat, oilseed, cotton, jute, tea, sugarcane, potatoes; cattle, water buffalo, sheep, goats, poultry; fish

Exports: $57.24 billion f.o.b. (2003 est.)

Exports - commodities: textile goods, gems and jewelry, engineering goods, chemicals, leather manufactures

Exports - partners: US 22.4%, UK 5.1%, Hong Kong 4.5%, Germany 4.3%, China 4.1% (2002)

Imports: $74.15 billion f.o.b. (2003 est.)

Imports - commodities: crude oil, machinery, gems, fertilizer, chemicals

Imports - partners: US 6.9%, Belgium 6.4%, China 4.5%, Singapore 4.4%, UK 4.4% (2002)

Debt - external: $95.3 billion (2003 est.)

Economic aid - recipient: $2.9 billion (FY98/99)

Currency: Indian rupee (INR)

Currency code: INR

Exchange rates: Indian rupees per US dollar - 46.5806 (2003), 48.6103 (2002), 47.1864 (2001), 44.9416 (2000), 43.0554 (1999)

Fiscal year: 1 April - 31 March

Communications

Telephones - main lines in use: 41.42 million (2002)

Telephones - mobile cellular: 21,991,743 (2003)

Telephone system:

general assessment: mediocre service; local and long distance service provided throughout all regions of the country, with services primarily concentrated in the urban areas; major objective is to continue to expand and modernize long-distance network to keep pace with rapidly growing number of local subscriber lines; steady improvement is taking place with the recent admission of private and private-public investors, but, with telephone density at about two for each 100 persons and a waiting list of over 2 million, demand for main line telephone service will not be satisfied for a very long time

domestic: local service is provided by microwave radio relay and coaxial cable, with open wire and obsolete electromechanical and manual switchboard systems still in use in rural areas; starting in the 1980s, a substantial amount of digital switch gear has been introduced for local and long-distance service; long-distance traffic is carried mostly by coaxial cable and low-capacity microwave radio relay; since 1985, significant trunk capacity has been added in the form of fiber-optic cable and a domestic satellite system with 254 earth stations; mobile cellular service was introduced in 1994 and is organized nation-wide into four metropolitan cities and 19 telecom circles

international: country code - 91; satellite earth stations - 8 Intelsat (Indian Ocean) and 1 Inmarsat (Indian Ocean region); nine gateway exchanges operating from Mumbai (Bombay), New Delhi, Kolkata (Calcutta), Chennai (Madras), Jalandhar, Kanpur, Gandhinagar, Hyderabad, and Ernakulam; 4 submarine cables - LOCOM linking Chennai (Madras) to Penang; Indo-UAE-Gulf cable linking Mumbai (Bombay) to Al Fujayrah, UAE; India-SEA-ME-WE-3, SEA-ME-WE-2 with landing sites at Cochin and Mumbai (Bombay); Fiber-Optic Link Around the Globe (FLAG) with landing site at Mumbai (Bombay) (2000)

Radio broadcast stations: AM 153, FM 91, shortwave 68 (1998)

Television broadcast stations: 562 (of which 82 stations have 1 kW or greater power and 480 stations have less than 1 kW of power) (1997)

Internet country code: .in

Internet hosts: 78,595 (2002)

Internet users: 16.58 million (2002)

Transportation

Railways:

total: 63,518 km (15,009 km electrified)

broad gauge: 45,142 km 1.676-m gauge

narrow gauge: 15,013 km 1.000-m gauge; 3,363 km 0.762-m gauge and 0.610-m gauge (2002)

Highways:

total: 3,319,644 km

paved: 1,517,077 km

unpaved: 1,802,567 km (1999 est.)

Waterways: 16,180 km

note: 3,631 km navigable by large vessels

Pipelines: gas 5,798 km; liquid petroleum gas 1,195 km; oil 5,613 km; refined products 5,567 km (2003)

Ports and harbors: Chennai (Madras), Cochin, Jawaharal Nehru, Kandla, Kolkata (Calcutta), Mumbai (Bombay), Vishakhapatnam

Merchant marine:

total: 306 ships (1,000 GRT or over) 6,555,507 GRT/ 11,069,791 DWT

by type: bulk 90, cargo 77, chemical tanker 14, combination bulk 1, combination ore/oil 2, container 10, liquefied gas 10, passenger/cargo 5, petroleum tanker 93, roll on/roll off 1, short-sea/passenger 2, specialized tanker 1

foreign-owned: China 2, Portugal 1

registered in other countries: 63 (2003 est.)

Airports: 333 (2003 est.)

Airports - with paved runways:

total: 234

over 3,047 m: 14

2,438 to 3,047 m: 47

1,524 to 2,437 m: 78

914 to 1,523 m: 74

under 914 m: 21 (2003 est.)

Airports - with unpaved runways:

total: 99

2,438 to 3,047 m: 3

1,524 to 2,437 m: 9

914 to 1,523 m: 42

under 914 m: 45 (2003 est.)

Heliports: 20 (2003 est.)

Military

Military branches: Army, Navy (including naval air arm), Air Force, Coast Guard, various security or paramilitary forces (including Border Security Force, Assam Rifles, National Security Guards, Indo-Tibetan Border Police, Special Frontier Force, Central Reserve Police Force, Central Industrial Security Force, Railway Protection Force, and Defense Security Corps)

Military manpower - military age: 17 years of age (2004 est.)

Military manpower - availability:

males age 15-49: 293,677,117 (2004 est.)

Military manpower - fit for military service:

males age 15-49: 172,153,371 (2004 est.)

Military manpower - reaching military age annually:

males: 11,174,415 (2004 est.)

Military expenditures - dollar figure: $14,018,800,000 (2003)

Military expenditures - percent of GDP: 2.4% (2003)

Transnational Issues

Disputes - international: Kashmir remains the world's most highly militarized territorial dispute with portions under the de facto administration of China (Aksai Chin), India (Jammu and Kashmir), and Pakistan (Azad Kashmir and Northern Areas), but recent discussions and confidence-building measures among parties are beginning to defuse tensions; India does not recognize Pakistan's ceding lands to China in the 1965 boundary agreement; disputes with Pakistan over Indus River water sharing and the terminus of the Sir Creek Estuary at the mouth of the Rann of Kutch, which prevents maritime boundary delimitation; Pakistani maps continue to show Junagadh claim in Indian Gujarat State; most of the rugged, militarized boundary with China is in dispute, but sides have committed to begin resolution with discussions on the least disputed Middle Sector; Joint Border Committee with Nepal continues to work on resolution of minor disputed boundary sections; discussions with Bangladesh remain stalled to delimit a small section of river boundary, to exchange 162 miniscule enclaves in both countries, to allocate divided villages, and to stop illegal cross-border trade, migration, and violence; Bangladesh protests India's attempts to fence off high-traffic sections of the porous boundary; dispute with Bangladesh over volcanic New Moore/South Talpatty/Purbasha Island in the Bay of Bengal deters maritime boundary delimitation; India seeks cooperation from Bhutan and Burma to keep out Indian Nagaland insurgents; joint border commission continues to work on small disputed sections of boundary with Nepal; India has instituted a stricter border regime to restrict transit of Maoist insurgents and illegal cross-border activities from Nepal

India (continued)

Illicit drugs: world's largest producer of licit opium for the pharmaceutical trade, but an undetermined quantity of opium is diverted to illicit international drug markets; transit point for illicit narcotics produced in neighboring countries; illicit producer of methaqualone; vulnerable to narcotics money laundering through the hawala system

Indian Ocean

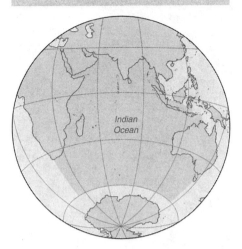

Indian Ocean

Introduction

Background: The Indian Ocean is the third largest of the world's five oceans (after the Pacific Ocean and Atlantic Ocean, but larger than the Southern Ocean and Arctic Ocean). Four critically important access waterways are the Suez Canal (Egypt), Bab el Mandeb (Djibouti-Yemen), Strait of Hormuz (Iran-Oman), and Strait of Malacca (Indonesia-Malaysia). The decision by the International Hydrographic Organization in the spring of 2000 to delimit a fifth ocean, the Southern Ocean, removed the portion of the Indian Ocean south of 60 degrees south.

Geography

Location: body of water between Africa, the Southern Ocean, Asia, and Australia
Geographic coordinates: 20 00 S, 80 00 E
Map references: Political Map of the World
Area:
total: 68.556 million sq km
note: includes Andaman Sea, Arabian Sea, Bay of Bengal, Flores Sea, Great Australian Bight, Gulf of Aden, Gulf of Oman, Java Sea, Mozambique Channel, Persian Gulf, Red Sea, Savu Sea, Strait of Malacca, Timor Sea, and other tributary water bodies
Area - comparative: about 5.5 times the size of the US
Coastline: 66,526 km
Climate: northeast monsoon (December to April), southwest monsoon (June to October); tropical cyclones occur during May/June and October/November in the northern Indian Ocean and January/February in the southern Indian Ocean
Terrain: surface dominated by counterclockwise gyre (broad, circular system of currents) in the southern Indian Ocean; unique reversal of surface currents in the northern Indian Ocean; low atmospheric pressure over southwest Asia from hot, rising, summer air results in the southwest monsoon and southwest-to-northeast winds and currents, while high pressure over northern Asia from cold, falling, winter air results in the northeast monsoon and northeast-to-southwest winds and currents; ocean floor is dominated by the Mid-Indian Ocean Ridge and subdivided by the Southeast Indian Ocean Ridge, Southwest Indian Ocean Ridge, and Ninetyeast Ridge
Elevation extremes:
lowest point: Java Trench -7,258 m
highest point: sea level 0 m
Natural resources: oil and gas fields, fish, shrimp, sand and gravel aggregates, placer deposits, polymetallic nodules
Natural hazards: occasional icebergs pose navigational hazard in southern reaches
Environment - current issues: endangered marine species include the dugong, seals, turtles, and whales; oil pollution in the Arabian Sea, Persian Gulf, and Red Sea
Geography - note: major chokepoints include Bab el Mandeb, Strait of Hormuz, Strait of Malacca, southern access to the Suez Canal, and the Lombok Strait

Economy

Economy - overview: The Indian Ocean provides major sea routes connecting the Middle East, Africa, and East Asia with Europe and the Americas. It carries a particularly heavy traffic of petroleum and petroleum products from the oilfields of the Persian Gulf and Indonesia. Its fish are of great and growing importance to the bordering countries for domestic consumption and export. Fishing fleets from Russia, Japan, South Korea, and Taiwan also exploit the Indian Ocean, mainly for shrimp and tuna. Large reserves of hydrocarbons are being tapped in the offshore areas of Saudi Arabia, Iran, India, and western Australia. An estimated 40% of the world's offshore oil production comes from the Indian Ocean. Beach sands rich in heavy minerals and offshore placer deposits are actively exploited by bordering countries, particularly India, South Africa, Indonesia, Sri Lanka, and Thailand.

Transportation

Ports and harbors: Chennai (Madras; India), Colombo (Sri Lanka), Durban (South Africa), Jakarta (Indonesia), Kolkata (Calcutta; India) Melbourne (Australia), Mumbai (Bombay; India), Richards Bay (South Africa)

Transnational Issues

Disputes - international: some maritime disputes (see littoral states)

Indonesia

Introduction

Background: Indonesia is the world's largest archipelago; it achieved independence from the Netherlands in 1949. Current issues include: alleviating widespread poverty, preventing terrorism, effecting a transition to a popularly-elected government after four decades of authoritarianism, implementing reforms of the banking sector, addressing charges of cronyism and corruption, holding the military and police accountable for human rights violations, and resolving separatist pressures in Aceh and Papua.

Geography

Location: Southeastern Asia, archipelago between the Indian Ocean and the Pacific Ocean
Geographic coordinates: 5 00 S, 120 00 E
Map references: Southeast Asia
Area:
total: 1,919,440 sq km
land: 1,826,440 sq km
water: 93,000 sq km
Area - comparative: slightly less than three times the size of Texas
Land boundaries:
total: 2,830 km
border countries: East Timor 228 km, Malaysia 1,782 km, Papua New Guinea 820 km
Coastline: 54,716 km
Maritime claims: measured from claimed archipelagic straight baselines
territorial sea: 12 NM
exclusive economic zone: 200 NM
Climate: tropical; hot, humid; more moderate in highlands
Terrain: mostly coastal lowlands; larger islands have interior mountains
Elevation extremes:
lowest point: Indian Ocean 0 m
highest point: Puncak Jaya 5,030 m

Natural resources: petroleum, tin, natural gas, nickel, timber, bauxite, copper, fertile soils, coal, gold, silver
Land use:
arable land: 9.9%
permanent crops: 7.2%
other: 82.9% (1998 est.)
Irrigated land: 48,150 sq km (1998 est.)
Natural hazards: occasional floods, severe droughts, tsunamis, earthquakes, volcanoes, forest fires
Environment - current issues: deforestation; water pollution from industrial wastes, sewage; air pollution in urban areas; smoke and haze from forest fires
Environment - international agreements:
party to: Biodiversity, Climate Change, Desertification, Endangered Species, Hazardous Wastes, Law of the Sea, Ozone Layer Protection, Ship Pollution, Tropical Timber 83, Tropical Timber 94, Wetlands
signed, but not ratified: Climate Change-Kyoto Protocol, Marine Life Conservation
Geography - note: archipelago of more than 17,000 islands (6,000 inhabited); straddles equator; strategic location astride or along major sea lanes from Indian Ocean to Pacific Ocean

People

Population: 238,452,952 (July 2004 est.)
Age structure:
0-14 years: 29.4% (male 35,635,790; female 34,416,854)
15-64 years: 65.5% (male 78,097,767; female 78,147,909)
65 years and over: 5.1% (male 5,308,986; female 6,845,646) (2004 est.)
Median age:
total: 26.1 years
male: 25.7 years
female: 26.6 years (2004 est.)
Population growth rate: 1.49% (2004 est.)

Birth rate: 21.11 births/1,000 population (2004 est.)
Death rate: 6.26 deaths/1,000 population (2004 est.)
Net migration rate: 0 migrant(s)/1,000 population (2004 est.)
Sex ratio:
at birth: 1.05 male(s)/female
under 15 years: 1.04 male(s)/female
15-64 years: 1 male(s)/female
65 years and over: 0.78 male(s)/female
total population: 1 male(s)/female (2004 est.)
Infant mortality rate:
total: 36.82 deaths/1,000 live births
male: 42.09 deaths/1,000 live births
female: 31.29 deaths/1,000 live births (2004 est.)
Life expectancy at birth:
total population: 69.26 years
male: 66.84 years
female: 71.8 years (2004 est.)
Total fertility rate: 2.47 children born/woman (2004 est.)
HIV/AIDS - adult prevalence rate: 0.1% (2001 est.)
HIV/AIDS - people living with HIV/AIDS: 120,000 (2001 est.)
HIV/AIDS - deaths: 4,600 (2001 est.)
Nationality:
noun: Indonesian(s)
adjective: Indonesian
Ethnic groups: Javanese 45%, Sundanese 14%, Madurese 7.5%, coastal Malays 7.5%, other 26%
Religions: Muslim 88%, Protestant 5%, Roman Catholic 3%, Hindu 2%, Buddhist 1%, other 1% (1998)
Languages: Bahasa Indonesia (official, modified form of Malay), English, Dutch, local dialects, the most widely spoken of which is Javanese
Literacy:
definition: age 15 and over can read and write
total population: 88.5%
male: 92.9%
female: 84.1% (2003 est.)

Government

Country name:
conventional long form: Republic of Indonesia
conventional short form: Indonesia
local long form: Republik Indonesia
local short form: Indonesia
former: Netherlands East Indies; Dutch East Indies
Government type: republic
Capital: Jakarta
Administrative divisions: 27 provinces (propinsi-propinsi, singular - propinsi), 2 special regions* (daerah-daerah istimewa, singular - daerah istimewa), and 1 special capital city district** (daerah khusus ibukota); Aceh*, Bali, Banten, Bengkulu, Gorontalo, Jakarta Raya**, Jambi, Jawa Barat, Jawa Tengah, Jawa Timur, Kalimantan Barat, Kalimantan Selatan, Kalimantan Tengah, Kalimantan Timur, Kepulauan Bangka Belitung, Lampung, Maluku, Maluku Utara, Nusa Tenggara Barat, Nusa Tenggara Timur, Papua, Riau, Sulawesi Selatan, Sulawesi Tengah, Sulawesi Tenggara, Sulawesi Utara, Sumatera Barat, Sumatera Selatan, Sumatera Utara,

Indonesia (continued)

Yogyakarta*; note - with the implementation of decentralization on 1 January 2001, the 357 districts (regencies) have become the key administrative units responsible for providing most government services

note: following the 30 August 1999 provincial referendum for independence that was overwhelmingly approved by the people of Timor Timur and the October 1999 concurrence of Indonesia's national legislature, the name Timor Leste (East Timor) was adopted as the name for the political entity formerly known as Propinsi Timor Timur; East Timor gained its formal independence on 20 May 2002

Independence: 17 August 1945 (proclaimed independence; on 27 December 1949, Indonesia became legally independent from the Netherlands)

National holiday: Independence Day, 17 August (1945)

Constitution: August 1945, abrogated by Federal Constitution of 1949 and Provisional Constitution of 1950, restored 5 July 1959

Legal system: based on Roman-Dutch law, substantially modified by indigenous concepts and by new criminal procedures and election codes; has not accepted compulsory ICJ jurisdiction

Suffrage: 17 years of age; universal and married persons regardless of age

Executive branch:

chief of state: President MEGAWATI Sukarnoputri (since 23 July 2001) and Vice President Hamzah HAZ (since 26 July 2001); note - the president is both the chief of state and head of government

head of government: President MEGAWATI Sukarnoputri (since 23 July 2001) and Vice President Hamzah HAZ (since 26 July 2001); note - the president is both the chief of state and head of government

cabinet: Cabinet appointed by the president

elections: president and vice president previously were elected separately by the People's Consultative Assembly or MPR for five-year terms; next election to be held 5 July 2004; in accordance with constitutional changes, the election of the president and vice president will be by direct vote of the citizenry

election results: MEGAWATI Sukarnoputri elected president, receiving 591 votes in favor (91 abstentions); Hamzah HAZ elected vice president, receiving 340 votes in favor (237 against)

note: the People's Consultative Assembly (Majelis Permusyawaratan Rakyat or MPR) includes the House of Representatives (Dewan Perwakilan Rakyat or DPR) plus 195 indirectly selected members; it meets every five years to approve broad outlines of national policy and also has yearly meetings to consider constitutional and legislative changes; constitutional amendments adopted in 2001 and 2002 provide for the MPR to be restructured in 2004 and to consist entirely of popularly-elected members who will be in the DPR and the new House of Regional Representatives (Dewan Perwakilan Daerah or DPD); the MPR will no longer formulate national policy

Legislative branch: unicameral House of Representatives or Dewan Perwakilan Rakyat (DPR) (495 seats; 457 elected by popular vote, 38 are appointed military representatives until 2004 election when military seats expire; members serve five-year terms)

elections: last held 7 June 1999 (next to be held 5 April 2004)

election results: percent of vote by party - PDI-P 37.4%, Golkar 20.9%, PKB 17.4%, PPP 10.7%, PAN 7.3%, PBB 1.8%, other 4.5%; seats by party - PDI-P 154, Golkar 120, PPP 58, PKB 51, PAN 35, PBB 14, other 30; note - subsequent to the election, there has been a change in the distribution of seats; the new distribution is: PDI-P 153, Golkar 120, PPP 58, PKB 51, PAN 35, PBB 13, other 32

Judicial branch: Supreme Court or Mahkamah Agung (justices appointed by the president from a list of candidates approved by the legislature); note - the Supreme Court is preparing to assume administrative responsibility for the lower court system, currently run by the Ministry of Justice and Human Rights; a separate Constitutional Court was invested by the president on 16 August 2003

Political parties and leaders: Crescent Moon and Star Party or PBB [Yusril Ihza MAHENDRA, chairman]; Functional Groups or Golkar [Akbar TANDJUNG, general chairman]; Indonesia Democratic Party-Struggle or PDI-P [MEGAWATI Sukarnoputri, chairperson]; National Awakening Party or PKB [Alwi SHIHAB, chairman]; National Mandate Party or PAN [Amien RAIS, chairman]; Prosperous Justice Party or PKS [Hidayat NUR WAHID, chairman]; United Development Party or PPP [Hamzah HAZ, chairman]

Political pressure groups and leaders: NA

International organization participation: APEC, ARF, AsDB, ASEAN, BIS, CP, FAO, G-15, G-77, IAEA, IBRD, ICAO, ICC, ICFTU, ICRM, IDA, IDB, IFAD, IFC, IFRCS, IHO, ILO, IMF, IMO, Interpol, IOC, IOM (observer), ISO, ITU, MONUC, NAM, OIC, OPCW, OPEC, UN, UNAMSIL, UNCTAD, UNESCO, UNIDO, UNMIL, UNOMIG, UPU, WCL, WCO, WFTU, WHO, WIPO, WMO, WToO, WTrO

Diplomatic representation in the US:

chief of mission: Ambassador SOEMADI Brotodiningrat

chancery: 2020 Massachusetts Avenue NW, Washington, DC 20036

telephone: [1] (202) 775-5200

FAX: [1] (202) 775-5365

consulate(s) general: Chicago, Houston, Los Angeles, New York, and San Francisco

Diplomatic representation from the US:

chief of mission: Ambassador Ralph L. BOYCE

embassy: Jalan 1 Medan Merdeka Selatan 3-5, Jakarta 10110

mailing address: Unit 8129, Box 1, FPO AP 96520

telephone: [62] (21) 3435-9000

FAX: [62] (21) 385-7189

consulate(s) general: Surabaya

Flag description: two equal horizontal bands of red (top) and white; similar to the flag of Monaco, which is shorter; also similar to the flag of Poland, which is white (top) and red

Economy

Economy - overview: Indonesia, a vast polyglot nation, faces economic development problems stemming from recent acts of terrorism, unequal resource distribution among regions, endemic corruption, the lack of reliable legal recourse in contract disputes, weaknesses in the banking system, and a generally poor climate for foreign investment. Indonesia withdrew from its IMF program at the end of 2003, but issued a "White Paper" that commits the government to maintaining fundamentally sound macroeconomic policies previously established under IMF guidelines. Investors, however, continued to face a host of on-the-ground microeconomic problems and an inadequate judicial system. Keys to future growth remain internal reform, building up the confidence of international and domestic investors, and strong global economic growth.

GDP: purchasing power parity - $758.1 billion (2003 est.)

GDP - real growth rate: 4% (2003 est.)

GDP - per capita: purchasing power parity - $3,200 (2003 est.)

GDP - composition by sector:

agriculture: 15.9%

industry: 42.1%

services: 42% (2002 est.)

Population below poverty line: 27% (1999)

Household income or consumption by percentage share:

lowest 10%: 4%

highest 10%: 26.7% (1999)

Distribution of family income - Gini index: 37 (2001)

Inflation rate (consumer prices): 6.9% (2003 est.)

Labor force: 100.5 million (2002)

Labor force - by occupation: agriculture 45%, industry 16%, services 39% (1999 est.)

Unemployment rate: 10.5% (2003 est.)

Budget:

revenues: $39 billion

expenditures: $43 billion, including capital expenditures of $NA (2003 est.)

Industries: petroleum and natural gas, textiles, apparel, footwear, mining, cement, chemical fertilizers, plywood, rubber, food, tourism

Industrial production growth rate: 3.6% (2003 est.)

Electricity - production: 95.78 billion kWh (2001)

Electricity - production by source:

fossil fuel: 86.9%

hydro: 10.5%

nuclear: 0%

other: 2.6% (2001)

Electricity - consumption: 89.08 billion kWh (2001)

Electricity - exports: 0 kWh (2001)

Indonesia *(continued)*

Electricity - imports: 0 kWh (2001)
Oil - production: 1.451 million bbl/day (2001 est.)
Oil - consumption: 1.045 million bbl/day (2001 est.)
Oil - exports: NA
Oil - imports: NA
Oil - proved reserves: 7.083 billion bbl (1 January 2002)
Natural gas - production: 69 billion cu m (2001 est.)
Natural gas - consumption: 36.2 billion cu m (2001 est.)
Natural gas - exports: 32.8 billion cu m (2001 est.)
Natural gas - imports: 0 cu m (2001 est.)
Natural gas - proved reserves: 2.549 trillion cu m (1 January 2002)
Agriculture - products: rice, cassava (tapioca), peanuts, rubber, cocoa, coffee, palm oil, copra, poultry, beef, pork, eggs
Exports: $63.89 billion f.o.b. (2003 est.)
Exports - commodities: oil and gas, electrical appliances, plywood, textiles, rubber
Exports - partners: Japan 21.1%, US 13.2%, Singapore 9.4%, South Korea 7.2%, China 5.1% (2002)
Imports: $40.22 billion f.o.b. (2003 est.)
Imports - commodities: machinery and equipment, chemicals, fuels, foodstuffs
Imports - partners: Japan 14.1%, Singapore 13.1%, US 8.5%, China 7.8%, South Korea 5.3%, Australia 5.1% (2002)
Debt - external: $132.9 billion (2003 est.)
Economic aid - recipient: $43 billion Indonesia finished its IMF program in December 2003 but still receives bilateral aid through the Consultative Group on Indonesia (CGI), which pledged $2.8 billion in grants and loans for 2004. (2003 est.)
Currency: Indonesian rupiah (IDR)
Currency code: IDR
Exchange rates: Indonesian rupiahs per US dollar - 8,577.13 (2003), 9,311.19 (2002), 10,260.8 (2001), 8,421.77 (2000), 7,855.15 (1999)
Fiscal year: calendar year; note - previously was 1 April - 31 March, but starting with 2001, has been changed to calendar year

Communications

Telephones - main lines in use: 7.75 million (2002)
Telephones - mobile cellular: 11.7 million (2002)
Telephone system:
general assessment: domestic service fair, international service good
domestic: interisland microwave system and HF radio police net; domestic satellite communications system
international: country code - 62; satellite earth stations - 2 Intelsat (1 Indian Ocean and 1 Pacific Ocean)
Radio broadcast stations: AM 678, FM 43, shortwave 82 (1998)
Television broadcast stations: 41 (1999)
Internet country code: .id
Internet hosts: 61,279 (2002)
Internet users: 8 million (2002)

Transportation

Railways:
total: 6,458 km
narrow gauge: 5,961 km 1.067-m gauge (125 km electrified); 497 km 0.750-m gauge (2002)
Highways:
total: 342,700 km
paved: 158,670 km
unpaved: 184,030 km (1999 est.)
Waterways: 21,579 km total
note: Sumatra 5,471 km, Java and Madura 820 km, Kalimantan 10,460 km, Sulawesi (Celebes) 241 km, Irian Jaya 4,587 km
Pipelines: condensate 672 km; condensate/gas 125 km; gas 8,183 km; oil 7,429 km; oil/gas/water 66 km; refined products 1,329 km; water 72 km (2003)
Ports and harbors: Cilacap, Cirebon, Jakarta, Kupang, Makassar, Palembang, Semarang, Surabaya
Merchant marine:
total: 718 ships (1,000 GRT or over) 3,192,847 GRT/ 4,319,739 DWT
by type: bulk 47, cargo 398, chemical tanker 13, container 57, liquefied gas 6, livestock carrier 1, passenger 10, passenger/cargo 13, petroleum tanker 128, refrigerated cargo 2, roll on/roll off 15, short-sea/ passenger 9, specialized tanker 12, vehicle carrier 7
foreign-owned: France 1, Germany 1, Greece 1, Honduras 1, Hong Kong 2, Japan 3, Malaysia 1, Monaco 2, Panama 1, Philippines 2, Singapore 12, Switzerland 1, United Kingdom 2, United States 1
registered in other countries: 109 (2003 est.)
Airports: 661 (2003 est.)
Airports - with paved runways:
total: 154
over 3,047 m: 4
2,438 to 3,047 m: 13
1,524 to 2,437 m: 44
914 to 1,523 m: 49
under 914 m: 44 (2003 est.)
Airports - with unpaved runways:
total: 507
2,438 to 3,047 m: 1
1,524 to 2,437 m: 5
914 to 1,523 m: 23
under 914 m: 478 (2003 est.)
Heliports: 22 (2003 est.)

Military

Military branches: Indonesia Armed Forces (TNI): Army (TNI-AD), Navy (TNI-AL, including Marines, Naval Air arm), Air Force (TNI-AU)
Military manpower - military age: 18 years of age (2004 est.)
Military manpower - availability:
males age 15-49: 66,458,805 (2004 est.)
Military manpower - fit for military service:
males age 15-49: 38,728,029 (2004 est.)
Military manpower - reaching military age annually:
males: 2,196,424 (2004 est.)

Military expenditures - dollar figure: $1 billion (FY98)
Military expenditures - percent of GDP: 1.3% (FY98)

Transnational Issues

Disputes - international: East Timor-Indonesia Boundary Committee continues to meet, survey and delimit land boundary, but several sections of the boundary remain unresolved; Indonesia and East Timor contest the sovereignty of the uninhabited coral island of Palau Batek/Fatu Sinai, which hinders a decision on a southern maritime boundary; numbers of East Timor refugees in Indonesia refuse repatriation; the Australia-East Timor 1999 maritime delimitation establishes partial maritime boundaries over part of the Timor Gap, but temporary resource-sharing agreements over an unreconciled area hamper creation of a shared maritime boundary with Indonesia; ICJ's award of Sipadan and Ligitan islands to Malaysia in 2002 prompted Indonesia to assert claims to and to establish a presence on its smaller outer islands; Indonesian secessionists, squatters and illegal migrants create repatriation problems for Papua New Guinea
Illicit drugs: illicit producer of cannabis largely for domestic use; possible growing role as transshipment point for Golden Triangle heroin

Iran

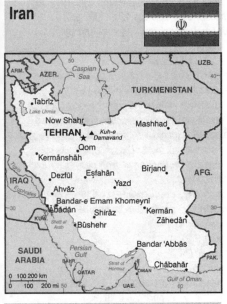

Introduction

Background: Known as Persia until 1935, Iran became an Islamic republic in 1979 after the ruling shah was forced into exile. Conservative clerical forces established a theocratic system of government with ultimate political authority vested in a learned religious scholar. A group of Iranian students seized the US Embassy in Tehran on 4 November 1979 and held it until 20 January 1981. During 1980-88, Iran fought a bloody, indecisive war with Iraq over disputed territory. Over the past decade, popular dissatisfaction with the government, driven by demographic changes, restrictive social policies, and poor economic conditions, has been pressuring for political reform.

Geography

Location: Middle East, bordering the Gulf of Oman, the Persian Gulf, and the Caspian Sea, between Iraq and Pakistan

Geographic coordinates: 32 00 N, 53 00 E

Map references: Middle East

Area:
total: 1.648 million sq km
land: 1.636 million sq km
water: 12,000 sq km

Area - comparative: slightly larger than Alaska

Land boundaries:
total: 5,440 km
border countries: Afghanistan 936 km, Armenia 35 km, Azerbaijan-proper 432 km, Azerbaijan-Naxcivan exclave 179 km, Iraq 1,458 km, Pakistan 909 km, Turkey 499 km, Turkmenistan 992 km

Coastline: 2,440 km; note - Iran also borders the Caspian Sea (740 km)

Maritime claims:
territorial sea: 12 NM
contiguous zone: 24 NM
exclusive economic zone: bilateral agreements or median lines in the Persian Gulf
continental shelf: natural prolongation

Climate: mostly arid or semiarid, subtropical along Caspian coast

Terrain: rugged, mountainous rim; high, central basin with deserts, mountains; small, discontinuous plains along both coasts

Elevation extremes:
lowest point: Caspian Sea -28 m
highest point: Kuh-e Damavand 5,671 m

Natural resources: petroleum, natural gas, coal, chromium, copper, iron ore, lead, manganese, zinc, sulfur

Land use:
arable land: 10.17%
permanent crops: 1.16%
other: 88.67% (1998 est.)

Irrigated land: 75,620 sq km (1998 est.)

Natural hazards: periodic droughts, floods; dust storms, sandstorms; earthquakes

Environment - current issues: air pollution, especially in urban areas, from vehicle emissions, refinery operations, and industrial effluents; deforestation; overgrazing; desertification; oil pollution in the Persian Gulf; wetland losses from drought; soil degradation (salination); inadequate supplies of potable water; water pollution from raw sewage and industrial waste; urbanization

Environment - international agreements:
party to: Biodiversity, Climate Change, Desertification, Endangered Species, Hazardous Wastes, Marine Dumping, Ozone Layer Protection, Wetlands
signed, but not ratified: Environmental Modification, Law of the Sea, Marine Life Conservation

Geography - note: strategic location on the Persian Gulf and Strait of Hormuz, which are vital maritime pathways for crude oil transport

People

Population: 69,018,924 (July 2004 est.)

Age structure:
0-14 years: 28% (male 9,935,527; female 9,411,647)
15-64 years: 67.2% (male 23,608,621; female 22,744,128)
65 years and over: 4.8% (male 1,645,246; female 1,673,755) (2004 est.)

Median age:
total: 23.5 years
male: 23.3 years
female: 23.7 years (2004 est.)

Population growth rate: 1.07% (2004 est.)

Birth rate: 17.1 births/1,000 population (2004 est.)

Death rate: 5.53 deaths/1,000 population (2004 est.)

Net migration rate: -0.84 migrant(s)/1,000 population (2004 est.)

Sex ratio:
at birth: 1.05 male(s)/female
under 15 years: 1.06 male(s)/female
15-64 years: 1.04 male(s)/female
65 years and over: 0.98 male(s)/female
total population: 1.04 male(s)/female (2004 est.)

Infant mortality rate:
total: 42.86 deaths/1,000 live births
male: 43.01 deaths/1,000 live births
female: 42.69 deaths/1,000 live births (2004 est.)

Life expectancy at birth:
total population: 69.66 years
male: 68.31 years
female: 71.07 years (2004 est.)

Total fertility rate: 1.93 children born/woman (2004 est.)

HIV/AIDS - adult prevalence rate: less than 0.1% (2001 est.)

HIV/AIDS - people living with HIV/AIDS: 20,000 (2001 est.)

HIV/AIDS - deaths: 290 (2001 est.)

Nationality:
noun: Iranian(s)
adjective: Iranian

Ethnic groups: Persian 51%, Azeri 24%, Gilaki and Mazandarani 8%, Kurd 7%, Arab 3%, Lur 2%, Baloch 2%, Turkmen 2%, other 1%

Religions: Shi'a Muslim 89%, Sunni Muslim 9%, Zoroastrian, Jewish, Christian, and Baha'i 2%

Languages: Persian and Persian dialects 58%, Turkic and Turkic dialects 26%, Kurdish 9%, Luri 2%, Balochi 1%, Arabic 1%, Turkish 1%, other 2%

Literacy:
definition: age 15 and over can read and write
total population: 79.4%
male: 85.6%
female: 73% (2003 est.)

Government

Country name:
conventional long form: Islamic Republic of Iran
conventional short form: Iran
local long form: Jomhuri-ye Eslami-ye Iran
local short form: Iran
former: Persia

Government type: theocratic republic

Capital: Tehran

Administrative divisions: 28 provinces (ostanha, singular - ostan); Ardabil, Azarbayjan-e Gharbi, Azarbayjan-e Sharqi, Bushehr, Chahar Mahall va Bakhtiari, Esfahan, Fars, Gilan, Golestan, Hamadan, Hormozgan, Ilam, Kerman, Kermanshah, Khorasan, Khuzestan, Kohgiluyeh va Buyer Ahmad, Kordestan, Lorestan, Markazi, Mazandaran, Qazvin, Qom, Semnan, Sistan va Baluchestan, Tehran, Yazd, Zanjan

Independence: 1 April 1979 (Islamic Republic of Iran proclaimed)

National holiday: Republic Day, 1 April (1979)
note: additional holidays celebrated widely in Iran include Revolution Day, 11 February (1979); Noruz (New Year's Day), 21 March; Constitutional Monarchy Day, 5 August (1925)

Constitution: 2-3 December 1979; revised 1989 to expand powers of the presidency and eliminate the prime ministership

Legal system: the Constitution codifies Islamic principles of government

Iran (continued)

Suffrage: 15 years of age; universal

Executive branch:

chief of state: Supreme Leader Ayatollah Ali Hoseini-KHAMENEI (since 4 June 1989)

head of government: President (Ali) Mohammad KHATAMI-Ardakani (since 3 August 1997); First Vice President Dr. Mohammad Reza AREF-Yazdi (since 26 August 2001)

cabinet: Council of Ministers selected by the president with legislative approval; the Supreme Leader has some control over appointments to the more sensitive ministries

elections: leader of the Islamic Revolution appointed for life by the Assembly of Experts; president elected by popular vote for a four-year term; election last held 8 June 2001 (next to be held June 2005)

election results: (Ali) Mohammad KHATAMI-Ardakani reelected president; percent of vote - (Ali) Mohammad KHATAMI-Ardakani 77%

Legislative branch: unicameral Islamic Consultative Assembly or Majles-e-Shura-ye-Eslami (290 seats, note - changed from 270 seats with the 18 February 2000 election; members elected by popular vote to serve four-year terms)

elections: last held 18 February 2000 with a runoff held 5 May 2000 (next to be held February 2004)

election results: percent of vote - NA%; seats by party - reformers 189, conservatives 54, independents 42, seats reserved for religious minorities 5

Judicial branch: Supreme Court

Political parties and leaders: formal political parties are a relatively new phenomenon in the Islamic Republic and most conservatives still prefer to work through political pressure groups rather than parties; a loose pro-reform coalition called the 2nd Khordad front, which includes political parties as well as less formal pressure groups and organizations, achieved considerable success at elections to the sixth Majles in early 2000; groups in the coalition include: Islamic Iran Participation Front (IIPF); Executives of Construction Party (Kargozaran); Solidarity Party; Islamic Labor Party; Mardom Salari; Mojahedin of the Islamic Revolution Organization (MIRO); and Militant Clerics Society (Ruhaniyun); the coalition is expected to participate in the seventh Majles elections in early 2004; a new apparently conservative group, the Builders of Islamic Iran, emerged at the local level in early 2003

Political pressure groups and leaders: political pressure groups conduct most of Iran's political activities; groups that generally support the Islamic Republic include Ansar-e Hizballah, Muslim Students Following the Line of the Imam, Tehran Militant Clergy Association (Ruhaniyat), Islamic Coalition Association (Motalefeh), and Islamic Engineers Society; active pro-reform student groups include the Organization for Strengthening Unity; opposition groups include Freedom Movement of Iran, the National Front, Marz-e Por Gohar, and various ethnic and Monarchist organizations; armed political groups that have been almost completely repressed by the government include Mojahedin-e Khalq Organization (MEK), People's Fedayeen, Democratic Party of Iranian Kurdistan, and Komala

International organization participation: CP, ECO, FAO, G-24, G-77, IAEA, IBRD, ICAO, ICC, ICCt (signatory), ICRM, IDA, IDB, IFAD, IFC, IFRCS, IHO, ILO, IMF, IMO, Interpol, IOC, IOM, ISO, ITU, NAM, OIC, OPCW, OPEC, PCA, UN, UNCTAD, UNESCO, UNHCR, UNIDO, UPU, WCL, WCO, WFTU, WHO, WIPO, WMO, WToO

Diplomatic representation in the US: none; note - Iran has an Interests Section in the Pakistani Embassy; address: Iranian Interests Section, Pakistani Embassy, 2209 Wisconsin Avenue NW, Washington, DC 20007; telephone: [1] (202) 965-4990

Diplomatic representation from the US: none; note - protecting power in Iran is Switzerland

Flag description: three equal horizontal bands of green (top), white, and red; the national emblem (a stylized representation of the word Allah in the shape of a tulip, a symbol of martyrdom) in red is centered in the white band; ALLAH AKBAR (God is Great) in white Arabic script is repeated 11 times along the bottom edge of the green band and 11 times along the top edge of the red band

Economy

Economy - overview: Iran's economy is marked by a bloated, inefficient state sector, over reliance on the oil sector, and statist policies that create major distortions throughout. Most economic activity is controlled by the state. Private sector activity is typically small-scale - workshops, farming, and services. President KHATAMI has continued to follow the market reform plans of former President RAFSANJANI, with limited progress. Relatively high oil prices in recent years have enabled Iran to amass some $22 billion in foreign exchange reserves, but have not eased economic hardships such as high unemployment and inflation. In December 2003 a major earthquake devastated the city of Bam in southeastern Iran, killing more than 30,000 people.

GDP: purchasing power parity - $477.8 billion (2003 est.)

GDP - real growth rate: 6% (2003 est.)

GDP - per capita: purchasing power parity - $7,000 (2003 est.)

GDP - composition by sector:

agriculture: 19%

industry: 26%

services: 55% (2002 est.)

Population below poverty line: 40% (2002 est.)

Household income or consumption by percentage share:

lowest 10%: NA%

highest 10%: NA%

Inflation rate (consumer prices): 18% (2003 est.)

Labor force: 20 million

note: shortage of skilled labor (2002 est.)

Labor force - by occupation: agriculture 30%, industry 25%, services 45% (2001 est.)

Unemployment rate: 15.7% (2002 est.)

Budget:

revenues: $41.2 billion

expenditures: $43.4 billion, including capital expenditures of $7.6 billion (2003 est.)

Industries: petroleum, petrochemicals, textiles, cement and other construction materials, food processing (particularly sugar refining and vegetable oil production), metal fabricating, armaments

Industrial production growth rate: 5.5% excluding oil (2001 est.)

Electricity - production: 124.6 billion kWh (2001)

Electricity - production by source:

fossil fuel: 97.1%

hydro: 2.9%

nuclear: 0%

other: 0% (2001)

Electricity - consumption: 115.9 billion kWh (2001)

Electricity - exports: 0 kWh (2001)

Electricity - imports: 0 kWh (2001)

Oil - production: 3.804 million bbl/day (2001 est.)

Oil - consumption: 1.277 million bbl/day (2001 est.)

Oil - exports: 2.2 million bbl/day (2003)

Oil - imports: NA

Oil - proved reserves: 94.39 billion bbl (1 January 2002)

Natural gas - production: 61.5 billion cu m (2001 est.)

Natural gas - consumption: 65.59 billion cu m (2001 est.)

Natural gas - exports: 110 million cu m (2001 est.)

Natural gas - imports: 4.2 billion cu m (2001 est.)

Natural gas - proved reserves: 24.8 trillion cu m (1 January 2002)

Agriculture - products: wheat, rice, other grains, sugar beets, fruits, nuts, cotton; dairy products, wool; caviar

Exports: $29.88 billion f.o.b. (2003 est.)

Exports - commodities: petroleum 80%, chemical and petrochemical products, fruits and nuts, carpets

Exports - partners: Japan 20.1%, China 9.9%, Italy 7.6%, South Korea 5.7% (2002)

Imports: $25.26 billion f.o.b. (2003 est.)

Imports - commodities: industrial raw materials and intermediate goods, capital goods, foodstuffs and other consumer goods, technical services, military supplies

Imports - partners: Germany 17.1%, Switzerland 9.3%, UAE 9.1%, France 5.9%, Italy 5.8%, South Korea 4.8%, China 4.7%, Russia 4.3% (2002)

Debt - external: $10.2 billion (2003 est.)

Economic aid - recipient: $408 million (2002 est.)

Currency: Iranian rial (IRR)

Currency code: IRR

Exchange rates: rials per US dollar - 8,193.89 (2003), 6,906.96 (2002), 1,753.56 (2001), 1,764.43 (2000), 1,752.93 (1999)

note: Iran has been using a managed floating exchange rate regime since unifying multiple exchange rates in March 2002.

Fiscal year: 21 March - 20 March

Iran *(continued)*

Communications

Telephones - main lines in use: 12,200,200 (2002)
Telephones - mobile cellular: 2.187 million (2002)
Telephone system:

general assessment: inadequate but currently being modernized and expanded with the goal of not only improving the efficiency and increasing the volume of the urban service but also bringing telephone service to several thousand villages, not presently connected

domestic: as a result of heavy investing in the telephone system since 1994, the number of long-distance channels in the microwave radio relay trunk has grown substantially; many villages have been brought into the net; the number of main lines in the urban systems has approximately doubled; and thousands of mobile cellular subscribers are being served; moreover, the technical level of the system has been raised by the installation of thousands of digital switches

international: country code - 98; HF radio and microwave radio relay to Turkey, Azerbaijan, Pakistan, Afghanistan, Turkmenistan, Syria, Kuwait, Tajikistan, and Uzbekistan; submarine fiber-optic cable to UAE with access to Fiber-Optic Link Around the Globe (FLAG); Trans-Asia-Europe (TAE) fiber-optic line runs from Azerbaijan through the northern portion of Iran to Turkmenistan with expansion to Georgia and Azerbaijan; satellite earth stations - 9 Intelsat and 4 Inmarsat
Radio broadcast stations: AM 72, FM 5, shortwave 5 (1998)
Television broadcast stations: 28 (plus 450 low-power repeaters) (1997)
Internet country code: .ir
Internet hosts: 3,491 (2002)
Internet users: 3.168 million (2002)

Transportation

Railways:
total: 7,201 km
broad gauge: 94 km 1.676-m gauge
standard gauge: 7,107 km 1.435-m gauge (146 km electrified) (2002)
Highways:
total: 167,157 km
paved: 94,109 km (including 890 km of expressways)
unpaved: 73,048 km (1998)
Waterways: 904 km
note: the Shatt al Arab is usually navigable by maritime traffic for about 130 km; channel has been dredged to 3 m and is in use
Pipelines: condensate/gas 212 km; gas 16,998 km; liquid petroleum gas 570 km; oil 8,256 km; refined products 7,808 km (2003)
Ports and harbors: Abadan (largely destroyed in fighting during 1980-88 war), Ahvaz, Bandar 'Abbas, Bandar-e Anzali, Bushehr, Bandar-e Emam Khomeyni, Bandar-e Lengeh, Bandar-e Mahshahr, Bandar-e Torkaman, Chabahar (Bandar Beheshti),

Jazireh-ye Khark, Jazireh-ye Lavan, Jazireh-ye Sirri, Khorramshahr (limited operation since November 1992), Now Shahr
Merchant marine:
total: 134 ships (1,000 GRT or over) 4,715,242 GRT/ 8,240,069 DWT
by type: bulk 40, cargo 36, chemical tanker 3, container 7, liquefied gas 1, multi-functional large load carrier 5, petroleum tanker 33, roll on/roll off 8, short-sea/passenger 1
registered in other countries: 10 (2003 est.)
Airports: 303 (2003 est.)
Airports - with paved runways:
total: 125
over 3,047 m: 39
2,438 to 3,047 m: 25
1,524 to 2,437 m: 26
914 to 1,523 m: 31
under 914 m: 4 (2003 est.)
Airports - with unpaved runways:
total: 178
over 3,047 m: 1
1,524 to 2,437 m: 9
914 to 1,523 m: 129
under 914 m: 39 (2003 est.)
Heliports: 13 (2003 est.)

Military

Military branches: Islamic Republic of Iran regular forces (includes Ground Forces, Navy, Air Force and Air Defense Command), Iranian Revolutionary Guards Corps (IRGC) (includes Ground Forces, Air Force, Navy, Qods Force [special operations], and Basij [Popular Mobilization Army]), Law Enforcement Forces
Military manpower - military age: 21 years of age (2004 est.)
Military manpower - availability:
males age 15-49: 20,937,348 (2004 est.)
Military manpower - fit for military service:
males age 15-49: 12,434,810 (2004 est.)
Military manpower - reaching military age annually:
males: 912,569 (2004 est.)
Military expenditures - dollar figure: $4.3 billion (2003 est.)
Military expenditures - percent of GDP: 3.3% (2003 est.)

Transnational Issues

Disputes - international: Iran protests Afghanistan's limiting flow of dammed waters on Helmand River tributaries in periods of drought; thousands of Afghan refugees still reside in Iran; creation of a maritime boundary with Iraq remains in hiatus until full sovereignty is restored in Iraq; Iran and UAE engage in direct talks and solicit Arab League support to resolve disputes over Iran's occupation of Tunb Islands and Abu Musa Island; Iran stands alone among littoral states in insisting upon a division of the Caspian Sea into five equal sectors

Illicit drugs: despite substantial interdiction efforts, Iran remains a key transshipment point for Southwest Asian heroin to Europe; domestic narcotics consumption remains a persistent problem and according to official Iranian statistics there are at least 2 million drug users in the country; lax anti-money-laundering regulations

Iraq

Introduction

Background: Formerly part of the Ottoman Empire, Iraq was occupied by Britain during the course of World War I; in 1920, it was declared a League of Nations mandate under UK administration. In stages over the next dozen years, Iraq attained its independence as a kingdom in 1932. A "republic" was proclaimed in 1958, but in actuality a series of military strongmen have ruled the country since then, the latest being SADDAM Husayn. Territorial disputes with Iran led to an inconclusive and costly eight-year war (1980-88). In August 1990, Iraq seized Kuwait, but was expelled by US-led, UN coalition forces during the Gulf War of January-February 1991. Following Kuwait's liberation, the UN Security Council (UNSC) required Iraq to scrap all weapons of mass destruction and long-range missiles and to allow UN verification inspections. Continued Iraqi noncompliance with UNSC resolutions over a period of 12 years resulted in the US-led invasion of Iraq in March 2003 and the ouster of the SADDAM Husayn regime. Coalition forces remain in Iraq, helping to restore degraded infrastructure and facilitating the establishment of a freely elected government. The Coalition plans to return sovereignty to the Iraqi people by July 2004.

Geography

Location: Middle East, bordering the Persian Gulf, between Iran and Kuwait
Geographic coordinates: 33 00 N, 44 00 E
Map references: Middle East
Area:
total: 437,072 sq km
land: 432,162 sq km
water: 4,910 sq km
Area - comparative: slightly more than twice the size of Idaho
Land boundaries:
total: 3,650 km

border countries: Iran 1,458 km, Jordan 181 km, Kuwait 240 km, Saudi Arabia 814 km, Syria 605 km, Turkey 352 km
Coastline: 58 km
Maritime claims:
territorial sea: 12 NM
continental shelf: not specified
Climate: mostly desert; mild to cool winters with dry, hot, cloudless summers; northern mountainous regions along Iranian and Turkish borders experience cold winters with occasionally heavy snows that melt in early spring, sometimes causing extensive flooding in central and southern Iraq
Terrain: mostly broad plains; reedy marshes along Iranian border in south with large flooded areas; mountains along borders with Iran and Turkey
Elevation extremes:
lowest point: Persian Gulf 0 m
highest point: unamed peak 3,611 m; note - this peak is not Gundah Zhur 3,607 m or Kuh-e Hajji-Ebrahim 3,595 m
Natural resources: petroleum, natural gas, phosphates, sulfur
Land use:
arable land: 11.89%
permanent crops: 0.78%
other: 87.33% (1998 est.)
Irrigated land: 35,250 sq km (1998 est.)
Natural hazards: dust storms, sandstorms, floods
Environment - current issues: government water control projects have drained most of the inhabited marsh areas east of An Nasiriyah by drying up or diverting the feeder streams and rivers; a once sizable population of Marsh Arabs, who inhabited these areas for thousands of years, has been displaced; furthermore, the destruction of the natural habitat poses serious threats to the area's wildlife populations; inadequate supplies of potable water; development of the Tigris and Euphrates rivers system contingent upon agreements with upstream riparian Turkey; air and water pollution; soil degradation (salination) and erosion; desertification
Environment - international agreements:
party to: Law of the Sea
signed, but not ratified: Environmental Modification
Geography - note: strategic location on Shatt al Arab waterway and at the head of the Persian Gulf

People

Population: 25,374,691 (July 2004 est.)
Age structure:
0-14 years: 40.3% (male 5,198,966; female 5,039,173)
15-64 years: 56.7% (male 7,280,167; female 7,094,688)
65 years and over: 3% (male 357,651; female 404,046) (2004 est.)
Median age:
total: 19.2 years
male: 19.1 years
female: 19.3 years (2004 est.)

Population growth rate: 2.74% (2004 est.)
Birth rate: 33.09 births/1,000 population (2004 est.)
Death rate: 5.66 deaths/1,000 population (2004 est.)
Net migration rate: 0 migrant(s)/1,000 population (2004 est.)
Sex ratio:
at birth: 1.05 male(s)/female
under 15 years: 1.03 male(s)/female
15-64 years: 1.03 male(s)/female
65 years and over: 0.89 male(s)/female
total population: 1.02 male(s)/female (2004 est.)
Infant mortality rate:
total: 52.71 deaths/1,000 live births
male: 58.58 deaths/1,000 live births
female: 46.55 deaths/1,000 live births (2004 est.)
Life expectancy at birth:
total population: 68.26 years
male: 67.09 years
female: 69.48 years (2004 est.)
Total fertility rate: 4.4 children born/woman (2004 est.)
HIV/AIDS - adult prevalence rate: less than 0.1% (2001 est.)
HIV/AIDS - people living with HIV/AIDS: less than 1,000
HIV/AIDS - deaths: NA
Nationality:
noun: Iraqi(s)
adjective: Iraqi
Ethnic groups: Arab 75%-80%, Kurdish 15%-20%, Turkoman, Assyrian or other 5%
Religions: Muslim 97% (Shi'a 60%-65%, Sunni 32%-37%), Christian or other 3%
Languages: Arabic, Kurdish (official in Kurdish regions), Assyrian, Armenian
Literacy:
definition: age 15 and over can read and write
total population: 40.4%
male: 55.9%
female: 24.4% (2003 est.)

Government

Country name:
conventional long form: Republic of Iraq
conventional short form: Iraq
local long form: Al Jumhuriyah al Iraqiyah
local short form: Al Iraq
Government type: in transition following April 2003 defeat of SADDAM Husayn regime by US-led coalition
Capital: Baghdad
Administrative divisions: 18 governorates (muhafazat, singular - muhafazah); Al Anbar, Al Basrah, Al Muthanna, Al Qadisiyah, An Najaf, Arbil, As Sulaymaniyah, At Ta'mim, Babil, Baghdad, Dahuk, Dhi Qar, Diyala, Karbala', Maysan, Ninawa, Salah ad Din, Wasit
Independence: 3 October 1932 (from League of Nations mandate under British administration)
National holiday: Revolution Day, 17 July (1968)
Constitution: in transition following April 2003 defeat of SADDAM Husayn regime by US-led coalition

Iraq *(continued)*

Legal system: in transition following April 2003 defeat of SADDAM Husayn regime by US-led coalition

Suffrage: formerly 18 years of age; universal; note - in transition following April 2003 defeat of SADDAM Husayn regime by US-led coalition

Executive branch:

chief of state: in transition following April 2003 defeat of SADDAM Husayn regime by US-led coalition

Legislative branch: in transition following April 2003 defeat of SADDAM Husayn regime by US-led coalition

Judicial branch: in transition following April 2003 defeat of SADDAM Husayn regime by US-led coalition

Political parties and leaders: in transition following April 2003 defeat of SADDAM Husayn regime by US-led coalition

Political pressure groups and leaders: in transition following April 2003 defeat of SADDAM Husayn regime by US-led coalition

International organization participation: ABEDA, ACC, AFESD, AMF, CAEU, FAO, G-77, IAEA, IBRD, ICAO, ICRM, IDA, IDB, IFAD, IFC, IFRCS, ILO, IMF, IMO, Interpol, IOC, ISO, ITU, LAS, NAM, OAPEC, OIC, OPEC, PCA, UN, UNCTAD, UNESCO, UNIDO, UPU, WCO, WFTU, WHO, WIPO, WMO, WToO

Diplomatic representation in the US: in transition following April 2003 defeat of SADDAM Husayn regime by US-led coalition

Diplomatic representation from the US: in transition following April 2003 defeat of SADDAM Husayn regime by US-led coalition

Flag description: three equal horizontal bands of red (top), white, and black with three green five-pointed stars in a horizontal line centered in the white band; the phrase ALLAHU AKBAR (God is Great) in green Arabic script - Allahu to the right of the middle star and Akbar to the left of the middle star - was added in January 1991 during the Persian Gulf crisis; similar to the flag of Syria which has two stars but no script and the flag of Yemen, which has a plain white band; also similar to the flag of Egypt which has a symbolic eagle centered in the white band

note: the current Iraqi Governing Council has formed a committee to design a new flag for Iraq that is broadly acceptable to all parties and ethnic/sectarian groups

Economy

Economy - overview: Iraq's economy is dominated by the oil sector, which has traditionally provided about 95% of foreign exchange earnings. In the 1980s financial problems caused by massive expenditures in the eight-year war with Iran and damage to oil export facilities by Iran led the government to implement austerity measures, borrow heavily, and later reschedule foreign debt payments; Iraq suffered economic losses from that war of at least $100 billion. After hostilities ended in 1988, oil exports gradually increased with the construction of new pipelines and restoration of damaged facilities. Iraq's seizure of Kuwait in August 1990, subsequent international economic sanctions, and damage from military action by an international coalition beginning in January 1991 drastically reduced economic activity. Although government policies supporting large military and internal security forces and allocating resources to key supporters of the regime have hurt the economy, implementation of the UN's oil-for-food program beginning in December 1996 helped improve conditions for the average Iraqi citizen. Iraq was allowed to export limited amounts of oil in exchange for food, medicine, and some infrastructure spare parts. In December 1999, the UN Security Council authorized Iraq to export under the program as much oil as required to meet humanitarian needs. The drop in GDP in 2001-02 was largely the result of the global economic slowdown and lower oil prices. Per capita food imports increased significantly, while medical supplies and health care services steadily improved. Per capita output and living standards were still well below the pre-1991 level, but any estimates have a wide range of error. The military victory of the US-led coalition in March-April 2003 resulted in the shutdown of much of the central economic administrative structure, but with the loss of a comparatively small amount of capital plant. The rebuilding of oil, electricity, and other production is proceeding steadily at the start of 2004 with foreign support and despite the continuation of severe internal strife. A joint UN and World Bank report released in the fall of 2003 estimated that Iraq's key reconstruction needs through 2007 would cost $55 billion. In October 2003, international donors pledged assistance worth more than $33 billion toward this rebuilding effort.

GDP: purchasing power parity - $38.79 billion (2003 est.)

GDP - real growth rate: -20% (2003 est.)

GDP - per capita: purchasing power parity - $1,600 (2003 est.)

GDP - composition by sector:

agriculture: 6%

industry: 13%

services: 81% (1993 est.)

Population below poverty line: NA

Household income or consumption by percentage share:

lowest 10%: NA%

highest 10%: NA%

Inflation rate (consumer prices): 27.5% (2003 est.)

Labor force: 7.8 million (2004 est.)

Labor force - by occupation: agriculture NA%, industry NA%, services NA%

Unemployment rate: NA% (2003 est.)

Budget:

revenues: $12.8 billion $NA

expenditures: $13.4 billion $NA, including capital expenditures of $NA (2004 budget)

Industries: petroleum, chemicals, textiles, construction materials, food processing

Industrial production growth rate: NA%

Electricity - production: 36.01 billion kWh (2001)

Electricity - production by source:

fossil fuel: 98.4%

hydro: 1.6%

nuclear: 0%

other: 0% (2001)

Electricity - consumption: 33.49 billion kWh (2001)

Electricity - exports: 0 kWh (2001)

Electricity - imports: 0 kWh (2001)

Oil - production: 2.2 million bbl/day; note - prewar production was 2.8 million bbl/day (January 2004 est.)

Oil - consumption: 460,000 bbl/day (2001 est.)

Oil - exports: 1.7 million bbl/day (January 2004)

Oil - imports: NA

Oil - proved reserves: 113.8 billion bbl (1 January 2002)

Natural gas - production: 2.76 billion cu m (2001 est.)

Natural gas - consumption: 2.76 billion cu m (2001 est.)

Natural gas - exports: 0 cu m (2001 est.)

Natural gas - imports: 0 cu m (2001 est.)

Natural gas - proved reserves: 3.149 trillion cu m (1 January 2002)

Agriculture - products: wheat, barley, rice, vegetables, dates, cotton; cattle, sheep

Exports: $7.542 billion f.o.b. (2003 est.)

Exports - commodities: crude oil

Exports - partners: US 37.4%, Taiwan 7.7%, Canada 7.5%, France 7.5%, Jordan 6.9%, Netherlands 5.8%, Italy 4.9%, Morocco 4.3%, Spain 4.1% (2002)

Imports: $6.521 billion f.o.b. (2003 est.)

Imports - commodities: food, medicine, manufactures

Imports - partners: Jordan 10.4%, France 8.4%, China 7.9%, Vietnam 7.9%, Germany 7.2%, Russia 6.9%, Australia 6.8%, Italy 6.1%, Japan 5.3% (2002)

Debt - external: $120 billion (2003 est.)

Economic aid - recipient: more than $33 billion in foreign aid pledged for 2004-07 (2004)

Currency: New Iraqi dinar (NID) as of 22 January 2004

Currency code: NID, IQD prior to 22 January 2004

Exchange rates: New Iraqi dinars per US dollar - 1,890 (second half, 2003)

Fiscal year: calendar year

Communications

Telephones - main lines in use: 675,000; note - an unknown number of telephone lines were damaged or destroyed during the March-April 2003 war (2003)

Telephones - mobile cellular: 20,000 (2002)

Telephone system:

general assessment: the 2003 war severely disrupted telecommunications throughout Iraq including international connections; USAID is overseeing the repair of switching capability and the contruction of mobile and satellite communications facilities

domestic: repairs to switches and lines destroyed in the recent fighting continue but sabotage remains a problem; cellular service is expected to be in place within two years

Iraq (continued)

international: country code - 964; satellite earth stations - 2 Intelsat (1 Atlantic Ocean and 1 Indian Ocean), 1 Intersputnik (Atlantic Ocean region), and 1 Arabsat (inoperative); coaxial cable and microwave radio relay to Jordan, Kuwait, Syria, and Turkey; Kuwait line is probably nonoperational

Radio broadcast stations: AM 19 (5 are inactive), FM 51, shortwave 4 (1998)

Television broadcast stations: 13 (1997); note - unknown number were destroyed during the March-April 2003 war

Internet country code: .iq

Internet users: 25,000 (2002)

Transportation

Railways:
total: 1,963 km
standard gauge: 1,963 km 1.435-m gauge (2003)

Highways:
total: 45,550 km
paved: 38,399 km
unpaved: 7,151 km (2000 est.)

Waterways: 1,015 km
note: Shatt al Arab is usually navigable by maritime traffic for about 130 km; channel has been dredged to 3 m and is in use; Tigris and Euphrates Rivers have navigable sections for shallow-draft boats; Shatt al Basrah canal was navigable by shallow-draft craft before closing in 1991 because of the Gulf war

Pipelines: gas 1,739 km; oil 5,418 km; refined products 1,343 km (2003)

Ports and harbors: Umm Qasr, Khawr az Zubayr, and Al Basrah have limited functionality

Merchant marine:
total: 13 ships (1,000 GRT or over) 83,221 GRT/ 125,255 DWT
by type: cargo 6, passenger/cargo 1, petroleum tanker 5, roll on/roll off 1
registered in other countries: 3 (2003 est.)

Airports: 111; note - unknown number were damaged during the March-April 2003 war (2003 est.)

Airports - with paved runways:
total: 79
over 3,047 m: 21
2,438 to 3,047 m: 36
1,524 to 2,437 m: 5
914 to 1,523 m: 7
under 914 m: 10 (2003 est.)

Airports - with unpaved runways:
total: 32
over 3,047 m: 2
2,438 to 3,047 m: 4
1,524 to 2,437 m: 5
914 to 1,523 m: 12
under 914 m: 9 (2003 est.)

Heliports: 6 (2003 est.)

Military

Military branches:
note: the US and UK Coalition Provisional Authority (CPA) dissolved the former Iraqi Armed Forces, together with the Ministry of Defense and other security institutions, and is implementing plans to create a new Iraqi Army with a purely defensive mission and capability; recruiting and training began in July 2003, with strength projected to be 3 divisions comprising approximately 36,000 personnel by July 2004; there are also plans to reconstitute an Iraqi Army Aviation Corps and Navy in the future but, as of early 2004, there are no plans to reconstitute an Iraqi Air Force (January 2004)

Military manpower - military age: 18 years of age; note - US-led coalition is planning to create a new Iraqi military force of men aged 18 to 40 to defend Iraqi territory from external threats (2004 est.)

Military manpower - availability:
males age 15-49: 6,547,762 (2004 est.)

Military manpower - fit for military service:
males age 15-49: 3,654,947 (2004 est.)

Military manpower - reaching military age annually:
males: 304,527 (2004 est.)

Military expenditures - dollar figure: $1.3 billion (FY00)

Military expenditures - percent of GDP: NA%

Transnational Issues

Disputes - international: coalition forces assist Iraqis in monitoring boundary security, but resolution of disputes and creation of maritime boundaries with neighboring states will remain in hiatus until full sovereignty is restored in Iraq; Turkey has expressed concern over the status of Kurds in Iraq

Ireland

Introduction

Background: Celtic tribes settled on the island in the 4th century B.C. Invasions by Norsemen that began in the late 8th century were finally ended when King Brian BORU defeated the Danes in 1014. English invasions began in the 12th century and set off more than seven centuries of Anglo-Irish struggle marked by fierce rebellions and harsh repressions. A failed 1916 Easter Monday Rebellion touched off several years of guerrilla warfare that in 1921 resulted in independence from the UK for 26 southern counties; six northern (Ulster) counties remained part of the United Kingdom. In 1948 Ireland withdrew from the British Commonwealth; it joined the European Community in 1973. Irish governments have sought the peaceful unification of Ireland and have cooperated with Britain against terrorist groups. A peace settlement for Northern Ireland, known as the Good Friday Agreement and approved in 1998, is being implemented with some difficulties.

Geography

Location: Western Europe, occupying five-sixths of the island of Ireland in the North Atlantic Ocean, west of Great Britain

Geographic coordinates: 53 00 N, 8 00 W

Map references: Europe

Area:
total: 70,280 sq km
land: 68,890 sq km
water: 1,390 sq km

Area - comparative: slightly larger than West Virginia

Land boundaries:
total: 360 km
border countries: UK 360 km

Coastline: 1,448 km

Maritime claims:
territorial sea: 12 NM
exclusive fishing zone: 200 NM

Ireland *(continued)*

Climate: temperate maritime; modified by North Atlantic Current; mild winters, cool summers; consistently humid; overcast about half the time
Terrain: mostly level to rolling interior plain surrounded by rugged hills and low mountains; sea cliffs on west coast
Elevation extremes:
lowest point: Atlantic Ocean 0 m
highest point: Carrauntoohil 1,041 m
Natural resources: zinc, lead, natural gas, barite, copper, gypsum, limestone, dolomite, peat, silver
Land use:
arable land: 19.49%
permanent crops: 0.04%
other: 80.47% (1998 est.)
Irrigated land: NA sq km
Natural hazards: NA
Environment - current issues: water pollution, especially of lakes, from agricultural runoff
Environment - international agreements:
party to: Air Pollution, Air Pollution-Nitrogen Oxides, Air Pollution-Sulfur 94, Biodiversity, Climate Change, Climate Change-Kyoto Protocol, Desertification, Endangered Species, Environmental Modification, Hazardous Wastes, Law of the Sea, Marine Dumping, Ozone Layer Protection, Ship Pollution, Tropical Timber 83, Tropical Timber 94, Wetlands, Whaling
signed, but not ratified: Air Pollution-Persistent Organic Pollutants, Marine Life Conservation
Geography - note: strategic location on major air and sea routes between North America and northern Europe; over 40% of the population resides within 97 km of Dublin

People

Population: 3,969,558 (July 2004 est.)
Age structure:
0-14 years: 21% (male 430,905; female 404,218)
15-64 years: 67.5% (male 1,342,233; female 1,337,580)
65 years and over: 11.5% (male 199,379; female 255,243) (2004 est.)
Median age:
total: 33.4 years
male: 32.6 years
female: 34.2 years (2004 est.)
Population growth rate: 1.16% (2004 est.)
Birth rate: 14.47 births/1,000 population (2004 est.)
Death rate: 7.91 deaths/1,000 population (2004 est.)
Net migration rate: 4.99 migrant(s)/1,000 population (2004 est.)
Sex ratio:
at birth: 1.07 male(s)/female
under 15 years: 1.07 male(s)/female
15-64 years: 1 male(s)/female
65 years and over: 0.78 male(s)/female
total population: 0.99 male(s)/female (2004 est.)
Infant mortality rate:
total: 5.5 deaths/1,000 live births
male: 6.04 deaths/1,000 live births
female: 4.92 deaths/1,000 live births (2004 est.)

Life expectancy at birth:
total population: 77.36 years
male: 74.74 years
female: 80.15 years (2004 est.)
Total fertility rate: 1.87 children born/woman (2004 est.)
HIV/AIDS - adult prevalence rate: 0.1% (2001 est.)
HIV/AIDS - people living with HIV/AIDS: 2,400 (2001 est.)
HIV/AIDS - deaths: less than 100 (2001 est.)
Nationality:
noun: Irishman(men), Irishwoman(women), Irish (collective plural)
adjective: Irish
Ethnic groups: Celtic, English
Religions: Roman Catholic 91.6%, Church of Ireland 2.5%, other 5.9% (1998)
Languages: English is the language generally used, Irish (Gaelic) spoken mainly in areas located along the western seaboard
Literacy:
definition: age 15 and over can read and write
total population: 98% (1981 est.)
male: NA
female: NA

Government

Country name:
conventional long form: none
conventional short form: Ireland
Government type: republic
Capital: Dublin
Administrative divisions: 26 counties; Carlow, Cavan, Clare, Cork, Donegal, Dublin, Galway, Kerry, Kildare, Kilkenny, Laois, Leitrim, Limerick, Longford, Louth, Mayo, Meath, Monaghan, Offaly, Roscommon, Sligo, Tipperary, Waterford, Westmeath, Wexford, Wicklow
note: Cavan, Donegal, and Monaghan are part of Ulster Province
Independence: 6 December 1921 (from UK by treaty)
National holiday: Saint Patrick's Day, 17 March
Constitution: 29 December 1937; adopted 1 July 1937 by plebiscite
Legal system: based on English common law, substantially modified by indigenous concepts; judicial review of legislative acts in Supreme Court; has not accepted compulsory ICJ jurisdiction
Suffrage: 18 years of age; universal
Executive branch:
chief of state: President Mary MCALEESE (since 11 November 1997)
head of government: Prime Minister Bertie AHERN (since 26 June 1997)
cabinet: Cabinet appointed by the president with previous nomination by the prime minister and approval of the House of Representatives
elections: president elected by popular vote for a seven-year term; election last held 31 October 1997 (next to be held NA November 2004); prime minister nominated by the House of Representatives and appointed by the president

election results: Mary MCALEESE elected president; percent of vote - Mary MCALEESE 44.8%, Mary BANOTTI 29.6%
note: government coalition - Fianna Fail and the Progressive Democrats
Legislative branch: bicameral Parliament or Oireachtas consists of the Senate or Seanad Eireann (60 seats - 49 elected by the universities and from candidates put forward by five vocational panels, 11 are nominated by the prime minister; members serve five-year terms) and the House of Representatives or Dail Eireann (166 seats; members are elected by popular vote on the basis of proportional representation to serve five-year terms)
elections: Senate - last held 16 and 17 July 2002 (next to be held by July 2007); House of Representatives - last held 17 May 2002 (next to be held by May 2007)
election results: Senate - percent of vote by party - NA%; seats by party - Fianna Fail 30, Fine Gael 15, Labor Party 5, Progressive Democrats 4, independents and others 6; House of Representatives - percent of vote by party - Fianna Fail 41.5%, Fine Gael 22.5%, Labor Party 10.8%, Sinn Fein 6.5%, Progressive Democrats 4.0%, Green Party 3.8%, others 10.9%; seats by party - Fianna Fail 81, Fine Gael 31, Labor Party 21, Progressive Democrats 8, Green Party 6, Sinn Fein 5, others 14
Judicial branch: Supreme Court (judges appointed by the president on the advice of the prime minister and cabinet)
Political parties and leaders: Fianna Fail [Bertie AHERN]; Fine Gael [Enda KENNY]; Green Party [Trevor SARGENT]; Labor Party [Pat RABBITTE]; Progressive Democrats [Mary HARNEY]; Sinn Fein [Gerry ADAMS]; Socialist Party [Joe HIGGINS]; The Workers' Party [Sean GARLAND]
Political pressure groups and leaders: NA
International organization participation: Australia Group, BIS, CE, EAPC, EBRD, EIB, EMU, ESA, EU, FAO, IAEA, IBRD, ICAO, ICC, ICCt, ICFTU, ICRM, IDA, IEA, IFAD, IFC, IFRCS, ILO, IMF, IMO, Interpol, IOC, IOM, ISO, ITU, MINURSO, MONUC, NAM (guest), NEA, NSG, OAS (observer), OECD, OPCW, OSCE, Paris Club, PCA, PFP, UN, UNCTAD, UNESCO, UNFICYP, UNHCR, UNIDO, UNIFIL, UNMIL, UNMISET, UNTSO, UPU, WCO, WEU (observer), WHO, WIPO, WMO, WTrO, ZC
Diplomatic representation in the US:
chief of mission: Ambassador Noel FAHEY
chancery: 2234 Massachusetts Avenue NW, Washington, DC 20008
telephone: [1] (202) 462-3939
FAX: [1] (202) 232-5993
consulate(s) general: Boston, Chicago, New York, and San Francisco
Diplomatic representation from the US:
chief of mission: Ambassador James C. KENNY
embassy: 42 Elgin Road, Ballsbridge, Dublin 4
mailing address: use embassy street address
telephone: [353] (1) 668-8777
FAX: [353] (1) 668-9946

Ireland *(continued)*

Flag description: three equal vertical bands of green (hoist side), white, and orange; similar to the flag of Cote d'Ivoire, which is shorter and has the colors reversed - orange (hoist side), white, and green; also similar to the flag of Italy, which is shorter and has colors of green (hoist side), white, and red

Economy

Economy - overview: Ireland is a small, modern, trade-dependent economy with growth averaging a robust 8% in 1995-2002. The global slowdown, especially in the information technology sector, pressed growth down to 2.1% in 2003. Agriculture, once the most important sector, is now dwarfed by industry and services. Industry accounts for 46% of GDP and about 80% of exports and employs 28% of the labor force. Although exports remain the primary engine for Ireland's growth, the economy has also benefited from a rise in consumer spending, construction, and business investment. Per capita GDP is 10% above that of the four big European economies. Over the past decade, the Irish Government has implemented a series of national economic programs designed to curb inflation, reduce government spending, increase labor force skills, and promote foreign investment. Ireland joined in launching the euro currency system in January 1999 along with 10 other EU nations.

GDP: purchasing power parity - $117 billion (2003 est.)

GDP - real growth rate: 2.1% (2003 est.)

GDP - per capita: purchasing power parity - $29,800 (2003 est.)

GDP - composition by sector:
agriculture: 5%
industry: 46%
services: 49% (2002 est.)

Population below poverty line: 10% (1997 est.)

Household income or consumption by percentage share:
lowest 10%: 2%
highest 10%: 27.3% (1997)

Distribution of family income - Gini index: 35.9 (1987)

Inflation rate (consumer prices): 3.7% (2003 est.)

Labor force: 1.8 million (2001)

Labor force - by occupation: agriculture 8%, industry 29%, services 64% (2002 est.)

Unemployment rate: 5% (2003 est.)

Budget:
revenues: $30.7 billion
expenditures: $30.5 billion, including capital expenditures of $5.5 billion (2002)

Industries: food products, brewing, textiles, clothing; chemicals, pharmaceuticals, machinery, transportation equipment, glass and crystal; software

Industrial production growth rate: 4% (2003 est.)

Electricity - production: 23.53 billion kWh (2001)

Electricity - production by source:
fossil fuel: 95.9%
hydro: 2.3%

nuclear: 0%
other: 1.7% (2001)

Electricity - consumption: 21.63 billion kWh (2001)

Electricity - exports: 285 million kWh (2001)

Electricity - imports: 38 million kWh (2001)

Oil - production: 0 bbl/day (2001 est.)

Oil - consumption: 174,400 bbl/day (2001 est.)

Oil - exports: 27,450 bbl/day (2001)

Oil - imports: 178,600 bbl/day (2001)

Oil - proved reserves: 0 bbl (1 January 2002)

Natural gas - production: 815 million cu m (2001 est.)

Natural gas - consumption: 4.199 billion cu m (2001 est.)

Natural gas - exports: 0 cu m (2001 est.)

Natural gas - imports: 3.384 billion cu m (2001 est.)

Natural gas - proved reserves: 9.911 billion cu m (1 January 2002)

Agriculture - products: turnips, barley, potatoes, sugar beets, wheat; beef, dairy products

Exports: $98.31 billion f.o.b. (2003 est.)

Exports - commodities: machinery and equipment, computers, chemicals, pharmaceuticals; live animals, animal products (1999)

Exports - partners: UK 23.3%, US 16.7%, Belgium 14.6%, Germany 7.3%, France 5% (2002)

Imports: $57.54 billion f.o.b. (2003 est.)

Imports - commodities: data processing equipment, other machinery and equipment, chemicals; petroleum and petroleum products, textiles, clothing

Imports - partners: UK 41.1%, US 15.3%, Germany 6.8% (2002)

Debt - external: $11 billion (1998)

Economic aid - donor: ODA, $283 million (2001)

Currency: euro (EUR)
note: on 1 January 1999, the European Monetary Union introduced the euro as a common currency to be used by financial institutions of member countries; on 1 January 2002, the euro became the sole currency for everyday transactions within the member countries

Currency code: EUR

Exchange rates: euros per US dollar - 0.886 (2003), 1.0626 (2002), 1.1175 (2001), 1.0854 (2000), 0.9386 (1999)

Fiscal year: calendar year

Communications

Telephones - main lines in use: 1.975 million (2002)

Telephones - mobile cellular: 3 million (2002)

Telephone system:
general assessment: modern digital system using cable and microwave radio relay
domestic: microwave radio relay
international: country code - 353; satellite earth station - 1 Intelsat (Atlantic Ocean)

Radio broadcast stations: AM 9, FM 106, shortwave 0 (1998)

Television broadcast stations: 4 (many low-power repeaters) (2001)

Internet country code: .ie

Internet hosts: 136,487 (2002)

Internet users: 1.065 million (2002)

Transportation

Railways:
total: 3,312 km
broad gauge: 1,947 km 1.600-m gauge (46 km electrified)
narrow gauge: 1,365 km 0.914-m gauge (operated by the Irish Peat Board to transport peat to power stations and briquetting plants) (2002)

Highways:
total: 92,500 km
paved: 87,043 km (including 115 km of expressways)
unpaved: 5,457 km (2000 est.)

Waterways: 700 km (limited facilities for commercial traffic) (1998)

Pipelines: gas 1,795 km (2003)

Ports and harbors: Arklow, Cork, Drogheda, Dublin, Foynes, Galway, Limerick, New Ross, Waterford

Merchant marine:
total: 35 ships (1,000 GRT or over) 288,401 GRT/ 383,628 DWT
by type: bulk 7, cargo 22, chemical tanker 1, container 3, roll on/roll off 1, short-sea/passenger 1
foreign-owned: Germany 3, Italy 7, Norway 2
registered in other countries: 18 (2003 est.)

Airports: 36 (2003 est.)

Airports - with paved runways:
total: 16
over 3,047 m: 1
2,438 to 3,047 m: 1
1,524 to 2,437 m: 4
914 to 1,523 m: 4
under 914 m: 6 (2003 est.)

Airports - with unpaved runways:
total: 20
914 to 1,523 m: 3
under 914 m: 17 (2003 est.)

Military

Military branches: Army (including Naval Service and Air Corps)

Military manpower - military age: 17 years of age (2004 est.)

Military manpower - availability:
males age 15-49: 1,029,525 (2004 est.)

Military manpower - fit for military service:
males age 15-49: 827,811 (2004 est.)

Military manpower - reaching military age annually:
males: 30,083 (2004 est.)

Military expenditures - dollar figure: $700 million (FY00/01)

Military expenditures - percent of GDP: 0.9% (FY00/01)

Ireland *(continued)*

Transnational Issues

Disputes - international: disputes with Iceland, Denmark, and the UK over the Faroe Islands continental shelf boundary outside 200 NM

Illicit drugs: transshipment point for and consumer of hashish from North Africa to the UK and Netherlands and of European-produced synthetic drugs; minor transshipment point for heroin and cocaine destined for Western Europe; despite recent legislation, narcotics-related money laundering using bureaux de change, trusts, shell companies involving the offshore financial community remains a concern

Israel
(also see separate Gaza Strip and West Bank entries)

Introduction

Background: Following World War II, the British withdrew from their mandate of Palestine, and the UN partitioned the area into Arab and Jewish states, an arrangement rejected by the Arabs. Subsequently, the Israelis defeated the Arabs in a series of wars without ending the deep tensions between the two sides. The territories occupied by Israel since the 1967 war are not included in the Israel country profile, unless otherwise noted. On 25 April 1982, Israel withdrew from the Sinai pursuant to the 1979 Israel-Egypt Peace Treaty. Outstanding territorial and other disputes with Jordan were resolved in the 26 October 1994 Israel-Jordan Treaty of Peace. In addition, on 25 May 2000, Israel withdrew unilaterally from southern Lebanon, which it had occupied since 1982. In keeping with the framework established at the Madrid Conference in October 1991, bilateral negotiations were conducted between Israel and Palestinian representatives (from the Israeli-occupied West Bank and Gaza Strip) and Syria to achieve a permanent settlement. On 24 June 2002, US President Bush laid out a "road map" for resolving the Israeli-Palestinian conflict, which envisions a

two-state solution. However, progress toward a permanent status agreement has been undermined by the outbreak of Palestinian-Israeli violence since September 2000.

Geography

Location: Middle East, bordering the Mediterranean Sea, between Egypt and Lebanon

Geographic coordinates: 31 30 N, 34 45 E

Map references: Middle East

Area:
total: 20,770 sq km
land: 20,330 sq km
water: 440 sq km

Area - comparative: slightly smaller than New Jersey

Land boundaries:
total: 1,017 km
border countries: Egypt 266 km, Gaza Strip 51 km, Jordan 238 km, Lebanon 79 km, Syria 76 km, West Bank 307 km

Coastline: 273 km

Maritime claims:
territorial sea: 12 NM
continental shelf: to depth of exploitation

Climate: temperate; hot and dry in southern and eastern desert areas

Terrain: Negev desert in the south; low coastal plain; central mountains; Jordan Rift Valley

Elevation extremes:
lowest point: Dead Sea -408 m
highest point: Har Meron 1,208 m

Natural resources: timber, potash, copper ore, natural gas, phosphate rock, magnesium bromide, clays, sand

Land use:
arable land: 17.02%
permanent crops: 4.17%
other: 78.81% (1998 est.)

Irrigated land: 1,990 sq km (1998 est.)

Natural hazards: sandstorms may occur during spring and summer; droughts; periodic earthquakes

Environment - current issues: limited arable land and natural fresh water resources pose serious constraints; desertification; air pollution from industrial and vehicle emissions; groundwater pollution from industrial and domestic waste, chemical fertilizers, and pesticides

Environment - international agreements:
party to: Biodiversity, Climate Change, Desertification, Endangered Species, Hazardous Wastes, Ozone Layer Protection, Ship Pollution, Wetlands
signed, but not ratified: Climate Change-Kyoto Protocol, Marine Life Conservation

Geography - note: there are 242 Israeli settlements and civilian land use sites in the West Bank, 42 in the Israeli-occupied Golan Heights, 25 in the Gaza Strip, and 29 in East Jerusalem (February 2002 est.); Sea of Galilee is an important freshwater source

Israel (continued)

People

Population: 6,199,008 (July 2002 est.)
note: includes about 187,000 Israeli settlers in the West Bank, about 20,000 in the Israeli-occupied Golan Heights, more than 5,000 in the Gaza Strip, and fewer than 177,000 in East Jerusalem (July 2004 est.)
Age structure:
0-14 years: 26.7% (male 847,591; female 808,399)
15-64 years: 63.4% (male 1,976,539; female 1,954,782)
65 years and over: 9.9% (male 262,781; female 348,916) (2004 est.)
Median age:
total: 29.2 years
male: 28.3 years
female: 30 years (2004 est.)
Population growth rate: 1.29% (2004 est.)
Birth rate: 18.45 births/1,000 population (2004 est.)
Death rate: 6.19 deaths/1,000 population (2004 est.)
Net migration rate: 0.68 migrant(s)/1,000 population (2004 est.)
Sex ratio:
at birth: 1.05 male(s)/female
under 15 years: 1.05 male(s)/female
15-64 years: 1.01 male(s)/female
65 years and over: 0.75 male(s)/female
total population: 0.99 male(s)/female (2004 est.)
Infant mortality rate:
total: 7.21 deaths/1,000 live births
male: 7.96 deaths/1,000 live births
female: 6.42 deaths/1,000 live births (2004 est.)
Life expectancy at birth:
total population: 79.17 years
male: 77.08 years
female: 81.37 years (2004 est.)
Total fertility rate: 2.47 children born/woman (2004 est.)
HIV/AIDS - adult prevalence rate: 0.1% (2001 est.)
HIV/AIDS - people living with HIV/AIDS: 2,400 (1999 est.)
HIV/AIDS - deaths: 100 (2001 est.)
Nationality:
noun: Israeli(s)
adjective: Israeli
Ethnic groups: Jewish 80.1% (Europe/America-born 32.1%, Israel-born 20.8%, Africa-born 14.6%, Asia-born 12.6%), non-Jewish 19.9% (mostly Arab) (1996 est.)
Religions: Jewish 80.1%, Muslim 14.6% (mostly Sunni Muslim), Christian 2.1%, other 3.2% (1996 est.)
Languages: Hebrew (official), Arabic used officially for Arab minority, English most commonly used foreign language
Literacy:
definition: age 15 and over can read and write
total population: 95.4%
male: 97.3%
female: 93.6% (2003 est.)

Government

Country name:
conventional long form: State of Israel
conventional short form: Israel
local long form: Medinat Yisra'el
local short form: Yisra'el
Government type: parliamentary democracy
Capital: Jerusalem; note - Israel proclaimed Jerusalem as its capital in 1950, but the US, like nearly all other countries, maintains its Embassy in Tel Aviv
Administrative divisions: 6 districts (mehozot, singular - mehoz); Central, Haifa, Jerusalem, Northern, Southern, Tel Aviv
Independence: 14 May 1948 (from League of Nations mandate under British administration)
National holiday: Independence Day, 14 May (1948); note - Israel declared independence on 14 May 1948, but the Jewish calendar is lunar and the holiday may occur in April or May
Constitution: no formal constitution; some of the functions of a constitution are filled by the Declaration of Establishment (1948), the Basic Laws of the parliament (Knesset), and the Israeli citizenship law
Legal system: mixture of English common law, British Mandate regulations, and, in personal matters, Jewish, Christian, and Muslim legal systems; in December 1985, Israel informed the UN Secretariat that it would no longer accept compulsory ICJ jurisdiction
Suffrage: 18 years of age; universal
Executive branch:
chief of state: President Moshe KATSAV (since 31 July 2000)
head of government: Prime Minister Ariel SHARON (since 7 March 2001)
cabinet: Cabinet selected by prime minister and approved by the Knesset
elections: president is largely a ceremonial role and is elected by the Knesset for a seven-year term; election last held 31 July 2000 (next to be held NA 2007); following legislative elections, the president assigns a Knesset member - traditionally the leader of the largest party - the task of forming a governing coalition; election last held 28 January 2003 (next to be held fall of 2007)
election results: Moshe KATSAV elected president by the 120-member Knesset with a total of 60 votes, other candidate, Shimon PERES, received 57 votes (there were three abstentions); Ariel SHARON continues as prime minister after Likud Party victory in January 2003 Knesset elections; Likud won 38 seats and then formed coalition government with Shinui, the National Religious Party, and the National Union
Legislative branch: unicameral Knesset or parliament (120 seats; members elected by popular vote to serve four-year terms)
elections: last held 28 January 2003 (next to be held fall of 2007)

election results: percent of vote by party - Likud Party 29.4%, Labor 14.5%, Shinui 12.3%, Shas 8.2%, National Union 5.5%, Meretz 5.2%, United Torah Judaism 4.3%, National Religious Party 4.2%, Democratic Front for Peace and Equality 3.0%, One Nation 2.8%, National Democratic Assembly 2.3%, Yisra'el Ba'Aliya (YBA) 2.2%, United Arab List 2.1%, Green Leaf Party 1.2%, Herut 1.2%, other 1.6%; seats by party - Likud 38, Labor 19, Shinui 15, Shas 11, National Union 7, Meretz 6, National Religious Party 6, United Torah Judaism 5, Democratic Front for Peace and Equality 3, One Nation 3, National Democratic Assembly 3, YBA 2, United Arab List 2
Judicial branch: Supreme Court (justices appointed for life by the president)
Political parties and leaders: Democratic Front for Peace and Equality (Hadash) [Muhammad BARAKA]; Green Leaf Party (no longer active) [Boaz WACHTEL and Shlomi SANDAK]; Herut (no longer active) [Michael KLEINER]; Labor Party [Shimon PEREZ]; Likud Party [Ariel SHARON]; Meretz (merged with YAHAD) [Zahava GALON]; National Democratic Assembly (Balad) [Azmi BISHARA]; National Religious Party [Efie EITAM]; National Union (Haichud Haleumi) [Avigdor LIBERMAN] (includes Tekuma Moledet and Yisra'el Beiteinu); One Nation [Amir PERETZ]; Shas [Eliyahu YISHAI]; Shinui [Tommy LAPID]; United Arab List [Abd al-Malik DAHAMSHAH]; United Torah Judaism [Yaakov LITZMAN]; YAHAD [Yossi BEILIN]; Yisra'el Ba'Aliya or YBA (merged with Likud) [Natian SHARANSKY]
Political pressure groups and leaders: Israeli nationalists advocating Jewish settlement on the West Bank and Gaza Strip; Peace Now supports territorial concessions in the West Bank and Gaza Strip; Yesha (settler) Council promotes settler interests and opposes territorial compromise; B'Tselem monitors human rights abuses
International organization participation: BIS, BSEC (observer), CE (observer), CERN (observer), EBRD, FAO, IADB, IAEA, IBRD, ICAO, ICC, ICCt (signatory), ICFTU, IDA, IFAD, IFC, IFRCS (observer), ILO, IMF, IMO, Interpol, IOC, IOM, ISO, ITU, OAS (observer), OPCW (signatory), OSCE (partner), PCA, UN, UNCTAD, UNESCO, UNHCR, UNIDO, UPU, WCO, WHO, WIPO, WMO, WToO, WTrO
Diplomatic representation in the US:
chief of mission: Ambassador Daniel AYALON
chancery: 3514 International Drive NW, Washington, DC 20008
telephone: [1] (202) 364-5500
FAX: [1] (202) 364-5607
consulate(s) general: Atlanta, Boston, Chicago, Houston, Los Angeles, Miami, New York, Philadelphia, and San Francisco
Diplomatic representation from the US:
chief of mission: Ambassador Daniel C. KURTZER
embassy: 71 Hayarkon Street, Tel Aviv
mailing address: PSC 98, Box 29, APO AE 09830

Israel (continued)

telephone: [972] (3) 519-7369/7453/7454/7457/7458/ 7551/7575

FAX: [972] (3) 516-4390

consulate(s) general: Jerusalem; note - an independent US mission, established in 1928, whose members are not accredited to a foreign government

Flag description: white with a blue hexagram (six-pointed linear star) known as the Magen David (Shield of David) centered between two equal horizontal blue bands near the top and bottom edges of the flag

Economy

Economy - overview: Israel has a technologically advanced market economy with substantial government participation. It depends on imports of crude oil, grains, raw materials, and military equipment. Despite limited natural resources, Israel has intensively developed its agricultural and industrial sectors over the past 20 years. Israel imports substantial quantities of grain but is largely self-sufficient in other agricultural products. Cut diamonds, high-technology equipment, and agricultural products (fruits and vegetables) are the leading exports. Israel usually posts sizable current account deficits, which are covered by large transfer payments from abroad and by foreign loans. Roughly half of the government's external debt is owed to the US, which is its major source of economic and military aid. The bitter Israeli-Palestinian conflict; difficulties in the high-technology, construction, and tourist sectors; and fiscal austerity in the face of growing inflation led to small declines in GDP in 2001 and 2002. The economy grew at 1% in 2003, with improvements in tourism and foreign direct investment. In 2004, rising business and consumer confidence - as well as higher demand for Israeli exports - are forecast to boost GDP by 2.5%.

GDP: purchasing power parity - $120.6 billion (2003 est.)

GDP - real growth rate: 1% (2003 est.)

GDP - per capita: purchasing power parity - $19,700 (2003 est.)

GDP - composition by sector:
agriculture: 2.6%
industry: 36.2%
services: 61.2% (2001 est.)

Population below poverty line: 18% (2001 est.)

Household income or consumption by percentage share:
lowest 10%: 2.4%
highest 10%: 28.3% (1997)

Distribution of family income - Gini index: 35.5 (2001)

Inflation rate (consumer prices): 1.1% (2003 est.)

Labor force: 2.6 million (2003 est.)

Labor force - by occupation: public services 31.2%, manufacturing 20.2%, finance and business 13.1%, commerce 12.8%, construction 7.5%, personal and other services 6.4%, transport, storage, and communications 6.2%, agriculture, forestry, and fishing 2.6% (1996)

Unemployment rate: 10.7% (2003 est.)

Budget:
revenues: $38.5 billion
expenditures: $45.1 billion, including capital expenditures of $NA (2002 est.)

Industries: high-technology projects (including aviation, communications, computer-aided design and manufactures, medical electronics), wood and paper products, potash and phosphates, food, beverages, and tobacco, caustic soda, cement, diamond cutting

Industrial production growth rate: 0.7% (2003 est.)

Electricity - production: 42.24 billion kWh (2001)

Electricity - production by source:
fossil fuel: 99.9%
hydro: 0.1%
nuclear: 0%
other: 0% (2001)

Electricity - consumption: 37.82 billion kWh (2001)

Electricity - exports: 1.457 billion kWh (2001)

Electricity - imports: 0 kWh (2001)

Oil - production: 80 bbl/day (2001 est.)

Oil - consumption: 260,000 bbl/day (2001 est.)

Oil - exports: NA

Oil - imports: NA

Oil - proved reserves: 1.92 million bbl (1 January 2002)

Natural gas - production: 10 million cu m (2001 est.)

Natural gas - consumption: 10 million cu m (2001 est.)

Natural gas - exports: 0 cu m (2001 est.)

Natural gas - imports: 0 cu m (2001 est.)

Natural gas - proved reserves: 20.81 billion cu m (1 January 2002)

Agriculture - products: citrus, vegetables, cotton; beef, poultry, dairy products

Exports: $29.32 billion f.o.b. (2003 est.)

Exports - commodities: machinery and equipment, software, cut diamonds, agricultural products, chemicals, textiles and apparel

Exports - partners: US 40.3%, Belgium 6.3%, Hong Kong 4.7%, UK 4% (2002)

Imports: $32.27 billion f.o.b. (2003 est.)

Imports - commodities: raw materials, military equipment, investment goods, rough diamonds, fuels, grain, consumer goods

Imports - partners: US 18.5%, Belgium 9.1%, Germany 7.1%, UK 6.7%, Switzerland 6.3%, Italy 4.6% (2002)

Debt - external: $68.9 billion (2003 est.)

Economic aid - recipient: $662 million from US (2003 est.)

Currency: new Israeli shekel (ILS); note - NIS is the currency abbreviation; ILS is the International Organization for Standarization (ISO) code for the NIS

Currency code: ILS

Exchange rates: new Israeli shekels per US dollar - 4.5541 (2003), 4.7378 (2002), 4.2057 (2001), 4.0773 (2000), 4.1397 (1999)

Fiscal year: calendar year

Communications

Telephones - main lines in use: 3.1 million (2002)

Telephones - mobile cellular: 6.334 million (2002)

Telephone system:
general assessment: most highly developed system in the Middle East although not the largest
domestic: good system of coaxial cable and microwave radio relay; all systems are digital
international: country code - 972; 3 submarine cables; satellite earth stations - 3 Intelsat (2 Atlantic Ocean and 1 Indian Ocean)

Radio broadcast stations: AM 23, FM 15, shortwave 2 (1998)

Television broadcast stations: 17 (plus 36 low-power repeaters) (1995)

Internet country code: .il

Internet hosts: 146,791 (2002)

Internet users: 2 million (2002)

Transportation

Railways:
total: 640 km
standard gauge: 640 km 1.435-m gauge (2002)

Highways:
total: 16,281 km
paved: 16,281 km (including 56 km of expressways)
unpaved: 0 km (2000)

Waterways: none

Pipelines: gas 100 km; oil 1,509 km (2003)

Ports and harbors: Ashdod, Ashqelon, Elat (Eilat), Hadera, Haifa, Tel Aviv-Yafo

Merchant marine:
total: 18 ships (1,000 GRT or over) 752,873 GRT/ 881,711 DWT
by type: container 18
registered in other countries: 40 (2003 est.)

Airports: 51 (2003 est.)

Airports - with paved runways:
total: 28
over 3,047 m: 2
2,438 to 3,047 m: 4
1,524 to 2,437 m: 8
914 to 1,523 m: 10
under 914 m: 4 (2003 est.)

Airports - with unpaved runways:
total: 23
1,524 to 2,437 m: 1
914 to 1,523 m: 2
under 914 m: 20 (2003 est.)

Heliports: 3 (2003 est.)

Military

Military branches: Israel Defense Forces (IDF): Ground Corps (including Pioneer Fighting Youth (Nahal)), Navy, Air Force(including Air Defense Forces); note - historically there have been no separate Israeli military services

Military manpower - military age: 18 years of age (2004 est.)

Military manpower - availability:
males age 15-49: 1,581,883

Israel *(continued)*

females age 15-49: 1,532,234
note: both sexes are liable for military service
(2004 est.)
Military manpower - fit for military service:
males age 15-49: 1,294,742
females age 15-49: 1,250,969 (2004 est.)
Military manpower - reaching military age annually:
males: 51,054
females: 53,515 (2004 est.)
Military expenditures - dollar figure: $9.11 billion (FY03)
Military expenditures - percent of GDP: 8.7% (FY02)

Transnational Issues

Disputes - international: West Bank and Gaza Strip are Israeli-occupied with current status subject to the Israeli-Palestinian Interim Agreement - permanent status to be determined through further negotiation; Golan Heights is Israeli-occupied (Lebanon claims the Shab'a Farms area of Golan Heights)
Illicit drugs: increasingly concerned about cocaine and heroin abuse; drugs arrive in country from Lebanon and, increasingly, from Jordan; money-laundering center

Italy

Introduction

Background: Italy became a nation-state in 1861 when the city-states of the peninsula, along with Sardinia and Sicily, were united under King Victor EMMANUEL II. An era of parliamentary government came to a close in the early 1920s when Benito MUSSOLINI established a Fascist dictatorship. His disastrous alliance with Nazi Germany led to Italy's defeat in World War II. A democratic republic replaced the monarchy in 1946 and economic revival followed. Italy was a charter member of NATO and the European Economic Community (EEC). It has been at the forefront of European economic and political unification, joining the European Monetary Union in 1999. Persistent problems include illegal immigration, organized crime, corruption, high unemployment, sluggish economic growth, and the low incomes and technical standards of southern Italy compared with the prosperous north.

Geography

Location: Southern Europe, a peninsula extending into the central Mediterranean Sea, northeast of Tunisia
Geographic coordinates: 42 50 N, 12 50 E
Map references: Europe
Area:
total: 301,230 sq km
land: 294,020 sq km
water: 7,210 sq km
note: includes Sardinia and Sicily
Area - comparative: slightly larger than Arizona
Land boundaries:
total: 1,932.2 km
border countries: Austria 430 km, France 488 km, Holy See (Vatican City) 3.2 km, San Marino 39 km, Slovenia 232 km, Switzerland 740 km
Coastline: 7,600 km

Maritime claims:
territorial sea: 12 NM
continental shelf: 200-m depth or to the depth of exploitation
Climate: predominantly Mediterranean; Alpine in far north; hot, dry in south
Terrain: mostly rugged and mountainous; some plains, coastal lowlands
Elevation extremes:
lowest point: Mediterranean Sea 0 m
highest point: Mont Blanc (Monte Bianco) de Courmayeur 4,748 m (a secondary peak of Mont Blanc)
Natural resources: mercury, potash, marble, sulfur, natural gas and crude oil reserves, fish, coal, arable land
Land use:
arable land: 28.07%
permanent crops: 9.25%
other: 62.68% (1998 est.)
Irrigated land: 26,980 sq km (1998 est.)
Natural hazards: regional risks include landslides, mudflows, avalanches, earthquakes, volcanic eruptions, flooding; land subsidence in Venice
Environment - current issues: air pollution from industrial emissions such as sulfur dioxide; coastal and inland rivers polluted from industrial and agricultural effluents; acid rain damaging lakes; inadequate industrial waste treatment and disposal facilities
Environment - international agreements:
party to: Air Pollution, Air Pollution-Nitrogen Oxides, Air Pollution-Sulfur 85, Air Pollution-Sulfur 94, Air Pollution-Volatile Organic Compounds, Antarctic-Environmental Protocol, Antarctic-Marine Living Resources, Antarctic Seals, Antarctic Treaty, Biodiversity, Climate Change, Climate Change-Kyoto Protocol, Desertification, Endangered Species, Environmental Modification, Hazardous Wastes, Law of the Sea, Marine Dumping, Ozone Layer Protection, Ship Pollution, Tropical Timber 83, Tropical Timber 94, Wetlands, Whaling
signed, but not ratified: Air Pollution-Persistent Organic Pollutants
Geography - note: strategic location dominating central Mediterranean as well as southern sea and air approaches to Western Europe

People

Population: 58,057,477 (July 2004 est.)
Age structure:
0-14 years: 14% (male 4,181,946; female 3,935,565)
15-64 years: 66.9% (male 19,590,497; female 19,256,747)
65 years and over: 19.1% (male 4,608,479; female 6,484,243) (2004 est.)
Median age:
total: 41.4 years
male: 39.8 years
female: 43 years (2004 est.)

Italy *(continued)*

Population growth rate: 0.09% (2004 est.)
Birth rate: 9.05 births/1,000 population (2004 est.)
Death rate: 10.21 deaths/1,000 population (2004 est.)
Net migration rate: 2.07 migrant(s)/1,000 population (2004 est.)
Sex ratio:
at birth: 1.07 male(s)/female
under 15 years: 1.06 male(s)/female
15-64 years: 1.02 male(s)/female
65 years and over: 0.71 male(s)/female
total population: 0.96 male(s)/female (2004 est.)
Infant mortality rate:
total: 6.07 deaths/1,000 live births
male: 6.68 deaths/1,000 live births
female: 5.41 deaths/1,000 live births (2004 est.)
Life expectancy at birth:
total population: 79.54 years
male: 76.61 years
female: 82.66 years (2004 est.)
Total fertility rate: 1.27 children born/woman (2004 est.)
HIV/AIDS - adult prevalence rate: 0.4% (2001 est.)
HIV/AIDS - people living with HIV/AIDS: 100,000 (2001 est.)
HIV/AIDS - deaths: 1,100 (2001 est.)
Nationality:
noun: Italian(s)
adjective: Italian
Ethnic groups: Italian (includes small clusters of German-, French-, and Slovene-Italians in the north and Albanian-Italians and Greek-Italians in the south)
Religions: predominately Roman Catholic with mature Protestant and Jewish communities and a growing Muslim immigrant community
Languages: Italian (official), German (parts of Trentino-Alto Adige region are predominantly German speaking), French (small French-speaking minority in Valle d'Aosta region), Slovene (Slovene-speaking minority in the Trieste-Gorizia area)
Literacy:
definition: age 15 and over can read and write
total population: 98.6%
male: 99%
female: 98.3% (2003 est.)

Government

Country name:
conventional long form: Italian Republic
conventional short form: Italy
local long form: Repubblica Italiana
local short form: Italia
former: Kingdom of Italy
Government type: republic
Capital: Rome
Administrative divisions: 20 regions (regioni, singular - regione); Abruzzi, Basilicata, Calabria, Campania, Emilia-Romagna, Friuli-Venezia Giulia, Lazio, Liguria, Lombardia, Marche, Molise, Piemonte, Puglia, Sardegna, Sicilia, Toscana, Trentino-Alto Adige, Umbria, Valle d'Aosta, Veneto

Independence: 17 March 1861 (Kingdom of Italy proclaimed; Italy was not finally unified until 1870)
National holiday: Republic Day, 2 June (1946)
Constitution: 1 January 1948
Legal system: based on civil law system; appeals treated as new trials; judicial review under certain conditions in Constitutional Court; has not accepted compulsory ICJ jurisdiction
Suffrage: 18 years of age; universal (except in senatorial elections, where minimum age is 25)
Executive branch:
chief of state: President Carlo Azeglio CIAMPI (since 13 May 1999)
head of government: Prime Minister (referred to in Italy as the president of the Council of Ministers) Silvio BERLUSCONI (since 10 June 2001)
cabinet: Council of Ministers nominated by the prime minister and approved by the president
elections: president elected by an electoral college consisting of both houses of Parliament and 58 regional representatives for a seven-year term; election last held 13 May 1999 (next to be held NA May 2006); prime minister appointed by the president and confirmed by Parliament
election results: Carlo Azeglio CIAMPI elected president; percent of electoral college vote - 70%
note: a five-party government coalition includes Forza Italia, National Alliance, Northern League, Democratic Christian Center, United Christian Democrats
Legislative branch: bicameral Parliament or Parlamento consists of the Senate or Senato della Repubblica (315 seats elected by popular vote of which 232 are directly elected and 83 are elected by regional proportional representation; in addition, there are a small number of senators-for-life including former presidents of the republic; members serve five-year terms) and the Chamber of Deputies or Camera dei Deputati (630 seats; 475 are directly elected, 155 by regional proportional representation; members serve five-year terms)
elections: Senate - last held 13 May 2001 (next to be held NA 2006); Chamber of Deputies - last held 13 May 2001 (next to be held NA 2006)
election results: Senate - percent of vote by party - NA%; seats by party - House of Liberties 177 (Forza Italia 82, National Alliance 46, CCD-CDU 29, Northern League 17, others 3), Olive Tree 128 (Democrats of the Left 62, Daisy Alliance 42, Sunflower Alliance 16, Italian Communist Party 3, independents 5), non-affiliated with either coalition 10, senators for life 9; Chamber of Deputies - percent of vote by party - NA%; seats by party - House of Liberties 367 (Forza Italia 189, National Alliance 96, CCD-CDU 40, Northern League 30, others 12), Olive Tree 248 (Democrats of the Left 138, Daisy Alliance 76, Sunflower Alliance 18, Italian Communist Party 9, independents 7), non-affiliated with either coalition 15
Judicial branch: Constitutional Court or Corte Costituzionale (composed of 15 judges: one-third appointed by the president, one-third elected by Parliament, one-third elected by the ordinary and administrative Supreme Courts)

Political parties and leaders: Center-Left Olive Tree Coalition [Francesco RUTELLI] - Democrats of the Left, Daisy Alliance (including Italian Popular Party, Italian Renewal, Union of Democrats for Europe, The Democrats), Sunflower Alliance (including Green Federation, Italian Democratic Socialists), Italian Communist Party; Center-Right Freedom House Coalition [Silvio BERLUSCONI] (formerly House of Liberties and Freedom Alliance) - Forza Italia, National Alliance, The Whiteflower Alliance (includes Christian Democratic Center, United Christian Democrats), Northern League; Christian Democratic Center or CCD [Marco FOLLINI]; Democrats of the Left or DS [Piero FASSINO]; Forza Italia or FI [Silvio BERLUSCONI]; Green Federation [Alfonso Pecoraro SCANIO]; Italian Communist Party or PdCI [Armando COSSUTTA]; Italian Popular Party or PPI [Pierluigi CASTAGNETTI]; Italian Renewal or RI [Lamberto DINI]; Italian Social Democrats or SDI [Enrico BOSELLI]; Socialist Movement-Tricolor Flame or MS-Fiamma [Luca ROMAGNOLI]; National Alliance or AN [Gianfranco FINI]; Northern League or NL [Umberto BOSSI]; Southern Tyrols People's Party or SVP (German speakers) [Siegfried BRUGGER]; Sunflower Alliance (includes Green Federation, Italian Social Democrats); The Daisy Alliance (includes Italian Popular Party, Italian Renewal, Union of Democrats for Europe, The Democrats); The Democrats [Arturo PARISI]; The Radicals (formerly Pannella Reformers and Autonomous List) [Marco PANNELLA]; The Whiteflower Alliance (includes Christian Democratic Center, United Christian Democrats); Union of Democrats for Europe or UDEUR [Clemente MASTELLA]; United Christian Democrats or CDU [Rocco BUTTIGLIONE]
Political pressure groups and leaders: Italian manufacturers and merchants associations (Confindustria, Confcommercio); organized farm groups (Confcoltivatori, Confagricoltura); Roman Catholic Church; three major trade union confederations (Confederazione Generale Italiana del Lavoro or CGIL [Guglielmo EPIFANI] which is left wing, Confederazione Italiana dei Sindacati Lavoratori or CISL [Savino PEZZOTTA], which is Roman Catholic centrist, and Unione Italiana del Lavoro or UIL [Luigi ANGELETTI] which is lay centrist)
International organization participation: AfDB, AsDB, Australia Group, BIS, BSEC (observer), CDB, CE, CEI, CERN, EAPC, EBRD, EIB, EMU, ESA, EU, FAO, G-7, G-8, G-10, IADB, IAEA, IBRD, ICAO, ICC, ICCt, ICFTU, ICRM, IDA, IEA, IFAD, IFC, IFRCS, IHO, ILO, IMF, IMO, Interpol, IOC, IOM, ISO, ITU, LAIA (observer), MINURSO, NAM (guest), NATO, NEA, NSG, OAS (observer), OECD, OPCW, OSCE, Paris Club, PCA, UN, UNCTAD, UNESCO, UNHCR, UNIDO, UNIFIL, UNMEE, UNMIK, UNMOGIP, UNTSO, UPU, WCL, WCO, WEU, WHO, WIPO, WMO, WToO, WTrO, ZC

Italy (continued)

Diplomatic representation in the US:
chief of mission: Ambassador Sergio VENTO
chancery: 3000 Whitehaven Street NW, Washington, DC 20008
telephone: [1] (202) 612-4400
FAX: [1] (202) 518-2151
consulate(s) general: Boston, Chicago, Houston, Miami, New York, Los Angeles, Philadelphia, and San Francisco
consulate(s): Detroit

Diplomatic representation from the US:
chief of mission: Ambassador Melvin F. SEMBLER
embassy: Via Vittorio Veneto 119/A, 00187-Rome
mailing address: PSC 59, Box 100, APO AE 09624
telephone: [39] (06) 46741
FAX: [39] (06) 488-2672, 4674-2356
consulate(s) general: Florence, Milan, Naples

Flag description: three equal vertical bands of green (hoist side), white, and red; similar to the flag of Ireland, which is longer and is green (hoist side), white, and orange; also similar to the flag of the Cote d'Ivoire, which has the colors reversed - orange (hoist side), white, and green
note: inspired by the French flag brought to Italy by Napoleon in 1797

Economy

Economy - overview: Italy has a diversified industrial economy with roughly the same total and per capita output as France and the UK. This capitalistic economy remains divided into a developed industrial north, dominated by private companies, and a less developed, welfare-dependent agricultural south, with 20% unemployment. Most raw materials needed by industry and more than 75% of energy requirements are imported. Over the past decade, Italy has pursued a tight fiscal policy in order to meet the requirements of the Economic and Monetary Unions and has benefited from lower interest and inflation rates. The current government has enacted numerous short-term reforms aimed at improving competitiveness and long-term growth. Italy has moved slowly, however, on implementing needed structural reforms, such as lightening the high tax burden and overhauling Italy's rigid labor market and over-generous pension system, because of the current economic slowdown and opposition from labor unions.
GDP: purchasing power parity - $1.552 trillion (2003 est.)
GDP - real growth rate: 0.5% (2003 est.)
GDP - per capita: purchasing power parity - $26,800 (2003 est.)
GDP - composition by sector:
agriculture: 2.4%
industry: 30%
services: 67.6% (2001 est.)
Population below poverty line: NA%
Household income or consumption by percentage share:
lowest 10%: 2.1%
highest 10%: 26.6% (2000)

Distribution of family income - Gini index: 27.3 (1995)
Inflation rate (consumer prices): 2.3% (2003 est.)
Labor force: 23.6 million (2001 est.)
Labor force - by occupation: services 63%, industry 32%, agriculture 5% (2001)
Unemployment rate: 9.2% (2003 est.)
Budget:
revenues: $504 billion
expenditures: $517 billion, including capital expenditures of $NA (2001 est.)
Industries: tourism, machinery, iron and steel, chemicals, food processing, textiles, motor vehicles, clothing, footwear, ceramics
Industrial production growth rate: -0.2% (2003)
Electricity - production: 258.8 billion kWh (2001)
Electricity - production by source:
fossil fuel: 78.6%
hydro: 18.4%
nuclear: 0%
other: 3% (2001)
Electricity - consumption: 289.1 billion kWh (2001)
Electricity - exports: 556 million kWh (2001)
Electricity - imports: 48.93 billion kWh (2001)
Oil - production: 79,460 bbl/day (2001 est.)
Oil - consumption: 1.866 million bbl/day (2001 est.)
Oil - exports: 456,600 bbl/day (2001)
Oil - imports: 2.158 million bbl/day (2001)
Oil - proved reserves: 586.6 million bbl (1 January 2002)
Natural gas - production: 15.49 billion cu m (2001 est.)
Natural gas - consumption: 71.18 billion cu m (2001 est.)
Natural gas - exports: 61 million cu m (2001 est.)
Natural gas - imports: 54.78 billion cu m (2001 est.)
Natural gas - proved reserves: 209.7 billion cu m (1 January 2002)
Agriculture - products: fruits, vegetables, grapes, potatoes, sugar beets, soybeans, grain, olives; beef, dairy products; fish
Exports: $278.1 billion f.o.b. (2003 est.)
Exports - commodities: engineering products, textiles and clothing, production machinery, motor vehicles, transport equipment, chemicals; food, beverages and tobacco; minerals and nonferrous metals
Exports - partners: Germany 13.7%, France 12.2%, US 9.8%, UK 6.9%, Spain 6.4% (2002)
Imports: $271.1 billion f.o.b. (2003 est.)
Imports - commodities: engineering products, chemicals, transport equipment, energy products, minerals and nonferrous metals, textiles and clothing; food, beverages and tobacco
Imports - partners: Germany 17.8%, France 11.3%, Netherlands 5.9%, UK 5%, US 4.9%, Spain 4.6%, Belgium 4.4% (2002)
Debt - external: NA
Economic aid - donor: ODA, $1 billion (2002 est.)
Currency: euro (EUR)

note: on 1 January 1999, the European Monetary Union introduced the euro as a common currency to be used by financial institutions of member countries on 1 January 2002, the euro became the sole currency for everyday transactions within the member countries
Currency code: EUR
Exchange rates: euros per US dollar - 0.886 (2003) 1.0626 (2002), 1.1175 (2001), 1.0854 (2000), 0.9386 (1999)
Fiscal year: calendar year

Communications

Telephones - main lines in use: 27.142 million (2002)
Telephones - mobile cellular: 53.003 million (2002)
Telephone system:
general assessment: modern, well developed, fast; fully automated telephone, telex, and data services
domestic: high-capacity cable and microwave radio relay trunks
international: country code - 39; satellite earth stations - 3 Intelsat (with a total of 5 antennas - 3 for Atlantic Ocean and 2 for Indian Ocean), 1 Inmarsat (Atlantic Ocean region), and NA Eutelsat; 21 submarine cables
Radio broadcast stations: AM about 100, FM about 4,600, shortwave 9 (1998)
Television broadcast stations: 358 (plus 4,728 repeaters) (1995)
Internet country code: .it
Internet hosts: 672,638 (2002)
Internet users: 19.9 million (2002)

Transportation

Railways:
total: 19,493 km
standard gauge: 18,090 km 1.435-m gauge (11,375 km electrified)
narrow gauge: 88 km 1.000-m gauge (88 km electrified); 1,315 km 0.950-m gauge (189 km electrified) (2002)
Highways:
total: 479,688 km
paved: 479,688 km (including 6,621 km of expressways)
unpaved: 0 km (1999)
Waterways: 2,400 km
note: serves various types of commercial traffic, although of limited overall value (2002)
Pipelines: gas 17,448 km; oil 1,245 km (2003)
Ports and harbors: Augusta (Sicily), Bagnoli, Bari, Brindisi, Gela, Genoa, La Spezia, Livorno, Milazzo, Naples, Porto Foxi, Porto Torres (Sardinia), Salerno, Savona, Taranto, Trieste, Venice (2001)
Merchant marine:
total: 475 ships (1,000 GRT or over) 8,970,017 GRT/ 10,354,685 DWT
by type: bulk 39, cargo 40, chemical tanker 106, combination ore/oil 2, container 23, liquefied gas 43, livestock carrier 2, multi-functional large load carrier 1

passenger 13, passenger/cargo 1, petroleum tanker 74, refrigerated cargo 4, roll on/roll off 62, short-sea/passenger 31, specialized tanker 11, vehicle carrier 23

foreign-owned: Denmark 4, France 3, Greece 5, Japan 1, Isle of Man 1, Monaco 22, Netherlands 4, Panama 2, Switzerland 2, Taiwan 10, United Kingdom 5, United States 13

registered in other countries: 144 (2003 est.)

Airports: 134 (2003 est.)

Airports - with paved runways:

total: 96
over 3,047 m: 6
2,438 to 3,047 m: 32
1,524 to 2,437 m: 16
914 to 1,523 m: 30
under 914 m: 12 (2003 est.)

Airports - with unpaved runways:

total: 38
1,524 to 2,437 m: 2
914 to 1,523 m: 18
under 914 m: 18 (2003 est.)

Heliports: 4 (2003 est.)

Military

Military branches: Army, Navy, Air Force (Aeronautica Militare Italiana, AMI), Carabinieri

Military manpower - military age: 18 years of age (2004 est.)

Military manpower - availability:
males age 15-49: 14,408,392 (2004 est.)

Military manpower - fit for military service:
males age 15-49: 12,279,516 (2004 est.)

Military manpower - reaching military age annually:
males: 285,601 (2004 est.)

Military expenditures - dollar figure:
$28,182,800,000 (2003)

Military expenditures - percent of GDP: 1.9% (2003)

Transnational Issues

Disputes - international: none

Illicit drugs: important gateway for and consumer of Latin American cocaine and Southwest Asian heroin entering the European market; money laundering by organized crime and from smuggling

Jamaica

Introduction

Background: Jamaica gained full independence within the British Commonwealth in 1962. Deteriorating economic conditions during the 1970s led to recurrent violence and a drop off in tourism. Elections in 1980 saw the democratic socialists voted out of office. Political violence marred elections during the 1990s.

Geography

Location: Caribbean, island in the Caribbean Sea, south of Cuba

Geographic coordinates: 18 15 N, 77 30 W

Map references: Central America and the Caribbean

Area:
total: 10,991 sq km
land: 10,831 sq km
water: 160 sq km

Area - comparative: slightly smaller than Connecticut

Land boundaries: 0 km

Coastline: 1,022 km

Maritime claims: measured from claimed archipelagic straight baselines
territorial sea: 12 NM
contiguous zone: 24 NM
exclusive economic zone: 200 NM
continental shelf: 200 NM or to edge of the continental margin

Climate: tropical; hot, humid; temperate interior

Terrain: mostly mountains, with narrow, discontinuous coastal plain

Elevation extremes:
lowest point: Caribbean Sea 0 m
highest point: Blue Mountain Peak 2,256 m

Natural resources: bauxite, gypsum, limestone

Land use:
arable land: 16.07%

permanent crops: 9.23%
other: 74.7% (1998 est.)

Irrigated land: 250 sq km (1998 est.)

Natural hazards: hurricanes (especially July to November)

Environment - current issues: heavy rates of deforestation; coastal waters polluted by industrial waste, sewage, and oil spills; damage to coral reefs; air pollution in Kingston results from vehicle emissions

Environment - international agreements:
party to: Biodiversity, Climate Change, Climate Change-Kyoto Protocol, Desertification, Endangered Species, Hazardous Wastes, Law of the Sea, Marine Dumping, Marine Life Conservation, Ozone Layer Protection, Ship Pollution, Wetlands
signed, but not ratified: none of the selected agreements

Geography - note: strategic location between Cayman Trench and Jamaica Channel, the main sea lanes for the Panama Canal

People

Population: 2,713,130 (July 2004 est.)

Age structure:
0-14 years: 28.2% (male 390,966; female 372,961)
15-64 years: 65% (male 883,053; female 880,296)
65 years and over: 6.9% (male 82,788; female 103,066) (2004 est.)

Median age:
total: 26.8 years
male: 26.2 years
female: 27.6 years (2004 est.)

Population growth rate: 0.66% (2004 est.)

Birth rate: 16.94 births/1,000 population (2004 est.)

Death rate: 5.4 deaths/1,000 population (2004 est.)

Net migration rate: -4.92 migrant(s)/1,000 population (2004 est.)

Sex ratio:
at birth: 1.05 male(s)/female
under 15 years: 1.05 male(s)/female
15-64 years: 1 male(s)/female

Jamaica (continued)

65 years and over: 0.8 male(s)/female
total population: 1 male(s)/female (2004 est.)
Infant mortality rate:
total: 12.81 deaths/1,000 live births
male: 13.82 deaths/1,000 live births
female: 11.75 deaths/1,000 live births (2004 est.)
Life expectancy at birth:
total population: 76.07 years
male: 74.04 years
female: 78.21 years (2004 est.)
Total fertility rate: 1.98 children born/woman
(2004 est.)
HIV/AIDS - adult prevalence rate: 1.2% (2001 est.)
HIV/AIDS - people living with HIV/AIDS: 20,000
(2001 est.)
HIV/AIDS - deaths: 980 (2001 est.)
Nationality:
noun: Jamaican(s)
adjective: Jamaican
Ethnic groups: black 90.9%, East Indian 1.3%,
white 0.2%, Chinese 0.2%, mixed 7.3%, other 0.1%
Religions: Protestant 61.3% (Church of God 21.2%,
Baptist 8.8%, Anglican 5.5%, Seventh-Day Adventist
9%, Pentecostal 7.6%, Methodist 2.7%, United
Church 2.7%, Brethren 1.1%, Jehovah's Witness
1.6%, Moravian 1.1%), Roman Catholic 4%, other
including some spiritual cults 34.7%
Languages: English, patois English
Literacy:
definition: age 15 and over has ever attended school
total population: 87.9%
male: 84.1%
female: 91.6% (2003 est.)

Government

Country name:
conventional long form: none
conventional short form: Jamaica
Government type: constitutional parliamentary
democracy
Capital: Kingston
Administrative divisions: 14 parishes; Clarendon,
Hanover, Kingston, Manchester, Portland, Saint
Andrew, Saint Ann, Saint Catherine, Saint Elizabeth,
Saint James, Saint Mary, Saint Thomas, Trelawny,
Westmoreland
note: for local government purposes, Kingston and
Saint Andrew were amalgamated in 1923 into the
present single corporate body known as the Kingston
and Saint Andrew Corporation
Independence: 6 August 1962 (from UK)
National holiday: Independence Day, first Monday
in August (1962)
Constitution: 6 August 1962
Legal system: based on English common law; has
not accepted compulsory ICJ jurisdiction
Suffrage: 18 years of age; universal
Executive branch:
chief of state: Queen ELIZABETH II (since 6 February
1952), represented by Governor General Sir Howard
Felix COOKE (since 1 August 1991)

head of government: Prime Minister Percival James
PATTERSON (since 30 March 1992)
cabinet: Cabinet appointed by the governor general
on the advice of the prime minister
elections: none; the monarch is hereditary; governor
general appointed by the monarch on the
recommendation of the prime minister; following
legislative elections, the leader of the majority party or
the leader of the majority coalition in the House of
Representatives is appointed prime minister by the
governor general; the deputy prime minister is
recommended by the prime minister
Legislative branch: bicameral Parliament consists
of the Senate (a 21-member body appointed by the
governor general on the recommendations of the
prime minister and the leader of the opposition; ruling
party is allocated 13 seats, and the opposition is
allocated eight seats) and the House of
Representatives (60 seats; members are elected by
popular vote to serve five-year terms)
elections: last held 16 October 2002 (next to be held
in October 2007)
election results: percent of vote by party - PNP 52%,
JLP 47.3%; seats by party - PNP 34, JLP 26
Judicial branch: Supreme Court (judges appointed
by the governor general on the advice of the prime
minister); Court of Appeal
Political parties and leaders: Jamaica Labor Party
or JLP [Edward SEAGA]; National Democratic
Movement or NDM [Hyacinth BENNETT]; People's
National Party or PNP [Percival James
PATTERSON]
Political pressure groups and leaders: New
Beginnings Movement or NBM; Rastafarians (black
religious/racial cultists, pan-Africanists)
International organization participation: ACP, C,
Caricom, CDB, FAO, G-15, G-77, IADB, IAEA, IBRD,
ICAO, ICCt (signatory), ICFTU, ICRM, IFAD, IFC,
IFRCS, IHO, ILO, IMF, IMO, Interpol, IOC, IOM
(observer), ISO, ITU, LAES, NAM, OAS, OPANAL,
OPCW, UN, UNCTAD, UNESCO, UNIDO, UPU,
WCO, WFTU, WHO, WIPO, WMO, WToO, WTrO
Diplomatic representation in the US:
chief of mission: Charge d'Affaires Courtenay
RATTAY
chancery: 1520 New Hampshire Avenue NW,
Washington, DC 20036
telephone: [1] (202) 452-0660
FAX: [1] (202) 452-0081
consulate(s) general: Miami and New York
Diplomatic representation from the US:
chief of mission: Ambassador Sue McCourt COBB
embassy: Jamaica Mutual Life Center, 2 Oxford
Road, 3rd floor, Kingston 5
mailing address: use embassy street address
telephone: [1] (876) 929-4850 through 4859
FAX: [1] (876) 935-6001
Flag description: diagonal yellow cross divides the
flag into four triangles - green (top and bottom) and
black (hoist side and outer side)

Economy

Economy - overview: The Jamaican economy is
heavily dependent on services, which now account for
70% of GDP. The country continues to derive most of
its foreign exchange from tourism, remittances, and
bauxite/alumina. The global economic slowdown,
particularly after the terrorist attacks in the US on
11 September 2002, stunted economic growth; the
economy rebounded moderately in 2003, with one of
the best tourist seasons on record. But the economy
faces serious long-term problems: high interest rates;
increased foreign competition; a pressured,
sometimes sliding, exchange rate; a sizable
merchandise trade deficit; large-scale unemployment;
and a growing internal debt, the result of government
bailouts to ailing sectors of the economy. The ratio of
debt to GDP is close to 150%. Inflation, previously a
bright spot, is expected to remain in the double digits.
Depressed economic conditions have led to increased
civil unrest, including gang violence fueled by the drug
trade. In 2004, the government faces the difficult
prospect of having to achieve fiscal discipline in order
to maintain debt payments while simultaneously
attacking a serious and growing crime problem that is
hampering economic growth.
GDP: purchasing power parity - $10.21 billion
(2003 est.)
GDP - real growth rate: 1.9% (2003 est.)
GDP - per capita: purchasing power parity - $3,800
(2003 est.)
GDP - composition by sector:
agriculture: 6%
industry: 24%
services: 70% (2003 est.)
Population below poverty line: 19.7% (2002 est.)
**Household income or consumption by percentage
share:**
lowest 10%: 2.7%
highest 10%: 30.3% (2000)
Distribution of family income - Gini index: 37.9
(2000)
Inflation rate (consumer prices): 14.1% (2003 est.)
Labor force: 1.12 million (1998)
Labor force - by occupation: services 60%,
agriculture 21%, industry 19% (1998)
Unemployment rate: 15.9% (2003 est.)
Budget:
revenues: $2.23 billion
expenditures: $2.56 billion, including capital
expenditures of $236 million (FY99/00 est.)
Industries: tourism, bauxite/alumina, textiles, agro
processing, wearing apparel, light manufactures, rum,
cement, metal, paper, chemical products,
telecommunications
Industrial production growth rate: -2% (2000 est.)
Electricity - production: 6.272 billion kWh (2001)
Electricity - production by source:
fossil fuel: 96.8%
hydro: 1.8%
nuclear: 0%
other: 1.4% (2001)

Jamaica (continued)

Electricity - consumption: 5.833 billion kWh (2001)
Electricity - exports: 0 kWh (2002)
Electricity - imports: 0 kWh (2002)
Oil - production: 0 bbl/day (2002 est.)
Oil - consumption: 66,000 bbl/day (2002 est.)
Oil - exports: NA
Oil - imports: NA (2001)
Agriculture - products: sugarcane, bananas, coffee, citrus, yams, vegetables, poultry, goats, milk, crustaceans, and mollusks
Exports: $1.355 billion f.o.b. (2003 est.)
Exports - commodities: alumina, bauxite, sugar, bananas, rum, coffee, yams, beverages, chemicals, wearing apparel, mineral fuels
Exports - partners: US 28.3%, Canada 14.1%, Netherlands 12.2%, UK 12.1%, Norway 8.4% (2002)
Imports: $3.265 billion f.o.b. (2003 est.)
Imports - commodities: food and other consumer goods, industrial supplies, fuel, parts and accessories of capital goods, machinery and transport equipment, construction materials
Imports - partners: US 44%, Trinidad and Tobago 9.1%, Japan 5.9%, Venezuela 4% (2002)
Debt - external: $4.3 billion (2003 est.)
Economic aid - recipient: $16 million (2003)
Currency: Jamaican dollar (JMD)
Currency code: JMD
Exchange rates: Jamaican dollars per US dollar - 57.7409 (2003), 48.4159 (2002), 45.9962 (2001), 42.7011 (2000), 39.0435 (1999)
Fiscal year: 1 April - 31 March

Communications

Telephones - main lines in use: 444,400 (2002)
Telephones - mobile cellular: 1.4 million (2002)
Telephone system:
general assessment: fully automatic domestic telephone network
domestic: NA
international: country code - 1-876; satellite earth stations - 2 Intelsat (Atlantic Ocean); 3 coaxial submarine cables
Radio broadcast stations: AM 10, FM 13, shortwave 0 (1998)
Television broadcast stations: 7 (1997)
Internet country code: .jm
Internet hosts: 1,276 (2002)
Internet users: 600,000 (2002)

Transportation

Railways:
total: 272 km
standard gauge: 272 km 1.435-m gauge
note: 207 km belonging to the Jamaica Railway Corporation were in common carrier service but are no longer operational; the remaining track is privately owned and used to transport bauxite (2002)
Highways:
total: 18,700 km
paved: 13,109 km
unpaved: 5,591 km (1999 est.)

Waterways: none
Pipelines: petroleum products 10 km
Ports and harbors: Alligator Pond, Discovery Bay, Kingston, Montego Bay, Ocho Rios, Port Antonio, Rocky Point, Port Esquivel (Longswharf)
Merchant marine:
total: 6 ships (1,000 GRT or over) 74,881 GRT/ 100,682 DWT
by type: bulk 2, petroleum tanker 1, refrigerated cargo 2, short-sea/passenger 1
foreign-owned: Greece 2, Iceland 1, Latvia 1, United States 2 (2003 est.)
Airports: 35 (2003 est.)
Airports - with paved runways:
total: 11
2,438 to 3,047 m: 2
914 to 1,523 m: 4
under 914 m: 5 (2003 est.)
Airports - with unpaved runways:
total: 24
914 to 1,523 m: 2
under 914 m: 22 (2003 est.)

Military

Military branches: Jamaica Defense Force: Ground Forces, Coast Guard, Air Wing
Military manpower - military age: 18 years of age (2004 est.)
Military manpower - availability:
males age 15-49: 764,266 (2004 est.)
Military manpower - fit for military service:
males age 15-49: 533,768 (2004 est.)
Military manpower - reaching military age annually:
males: 27,126 (2004 est.)
Military expenditures - dollar figure: $31 million (2003)
Military expenditures - percent of GDP: 0.4% (2003)

Transnational Issues

Disputes - international: none
Illicit drugs: major transshipment point for cocaine from South America to North America and Europe; illicit cultivation of cannabis; government has an active manual cannabis eradication program; corruption is a major concern; substantial money-laundering activity; Colombian narcotics traffickers favor Jamaica for illicit financial transactions

Jan Mayen
(territory of Norway)

Introduction

Background: This desolate, mountainous island was named after a Dutch whaling captain who indisputably discovered it in 1614 (earlier claims are inconclusive). Visited only occasionally by seal hunters and trappers over the following centuries, the island came under Norwegian sovereignty in 1929. The long dormant Haakon VII Toppen/Beerenberg volcano resumed activity in 1970; it is the northernmost active volcano on earth.

Geography

Location: Northern Europe, island between the Greenland Sea and the Norwegian Sea, northeast of Iceland
Geographic coordinates: 71 00 N, 8 00 W
Map references: Arctic Region
Area:
total: 373 sq km
land: 373 sq km
water: 0 sq km
Area - comparative: slightly more than twice the size of Washington, DC
Land boundaries: 0 km
Coastline: 124.1 km
Maritime claims:
territorial sea: 4 NM
contiguous zone: 10 NM
exclusive economic zone: 200 NM
continental shelf: 200-m depth or to the depth of exploitation
Climate: arctic maritime with frequent storms and persistent fog
Terrain: volcanic island, partly covered by glaciers
Elevation extremes:
lowest point: Norwegian Sea 0 m
highest point: Haakon VII Toppen/Beerenberg 2,277 m
Natural resources: none

Jan Mayen (continued)

Land use:
arable land: 0%
permanent crops: 0%
other: 100% (1998 est.)
Irrigated land: 0 sq km (1998 est.)
Natural hazards: dominated by the volcano Haakon VII Toppen/Beerenberg; volcanic activity resumed in 1970
Environment - current issues: NA
Geography - note: barren volcanic island with some moss and grass

People

Population: no indigenous inhabitants
note: personnel operate the Long Range Navigation (Loran-C) base and the weather and coastal services radio station (July 2004 est.)

Government

Country name:
conventional long form: none
conventional short form: Jan Mayen
Dependency status: territory of Norway; since August 1994, administered from Oslo through the county governor (fylkesmann) of Nordland; however, authority has been delegated to a station commander of the Norwegian Defense Communication Service
Legal system: the laws of Norway, where applicable, apply
Flag description: the flag of Norway is used

Economy

Economy - overview: Jan Mayen is a volcanic island with no exploitable natural resources. Economic activity is limited to providing services for employees of Norway's radio and meteorological stations on the island.

Communications

Radio broadcast stations: AM NA, FM NA, shortwave NA
note: there is one radio and meteorological station (1998)

Transportation

Waterways: none
Ports and harbors: none; offshore anchorage only
Airports: 1 (2003 est.)
Airports - with unpaved runways:
total: 1
1,524 to 2,437 m: 1 (2003 est.)

Military

Military - note: defense is the responsibility of Norway

Transnational Issues

Disputes - international: none

Japan

Introduction

Background: While retaining its time-honored culture, Japan rapidly absorbed Western technology during the late 19th and early 20th centuries. After its defeat in World War II, Japan recovered to become an economic power and a staunch ally of the US. While the emperor retains his throne as a symbol of national unity, actual power rests in networks of powerful politicians, bureaucrats, and business executives. The economy experienced a major slowdown starting in the 1990s following three decades of unprecedented growth.

Geography

Location: Eastern Asia, island chain between the North Pacific Ocean and the Sea of Japan, east of the Korean Peninsula
Geographic coordinates: 36 00 N, 138 00 E
Map references: Asia
Area:
total: 377,835 sq km
land: 374,744 sq km
water: 3,091 sq km
note: includes Bonin Islands (Ogasawara-gunto), Daito-shoto, Minami-jima, Okino-tori-shima, Ryukyu Islands (Nansei-shoto), and Volcano Islands (Kazan-retto)
Area - comparative: slightly smaller than California
Land boundaries: 0 km
Coastline: 29,751 km
Maritime claims:
territorial sea: 12 NM; between 3 NM and 12 NM in the international straits - La Perouse or Soya, Tsugaru, Osumi, and Eastern and Western Channels of the Korea or Tsushima Strait
contiguous zone: 24 NM
exclusive economic zone: 200 NM
Climate: varies from tropical in south to cool temperate in north

---

Terrain: mostly rugged and mountainous
Elevation extremes:
lowest point: Hachiro-gata -4 m
highest point: Mount Fuji 3,776 m
Natural resources: negligible mineral resources, fish
Land use:
arable land: 12.13%
permanent crops: 1.01%
other: 86.86% (1998 est.)
Irrigated land: 26,790 sq km (1998 est.)
Natural hazards: many dormant and some active volcanoes; about 1,500 seismic occurrences (mostly tremors) every year; tsunamis; typhoons
Environment - current issues: air pollution from power plant emissions results in acid rain; acidification of lakes and reservoirs degrading water quality and threatening aquatic life; Japan is one of the largest consumers of fish and tropical timber, contributing to the depletion of these resources in Asia and elsewhere
Environment - international agreements:
party to: Antarctic-Environmental Protocol, Antarctic-Marine Living Resources, Antarctic Seals, Antarctic Treaty, Biodiversity, Climate Change, Climate Change-Kyoto Protocol, Desertification, Endangered Species, Environmental Modification, Hazardous Wastes, Law of the Sea, Marine Dumping, Ozone Layer Protection, Ship Pollution, Tropical Timber 83, Tropical Timber 94, Wetlands, Whaling
Geography - note: strategic location in northeast Asia

People

Population: 127,333,002 (July 2004 est.)
Age structure:
0-14 years: 14.3% (male 9,337,867; female 8,876,996)
15-64 years: 66.7% (male 42,697,264; female 42,196,835)
65 years and over: 19% (male 10,169,190; female 14,054,850) (2004 est.)
Median age:
total: 42.3 years
male: 40.5 years
female: 44.1 years (2004 est.)
Population growth rate: 0.08% (2004 est.)
Birth rate: 9.56 births/1,000 population (2004 est.)
Death rate: 8.75 deaths/1,000 population (2004 est.)
Net migration rate: 0 migrant(s)/1,000 population (2004 est.)
Sex ratio:
at birth: 1.05 male(s)/female
under 15 years: 1.05 male(s)/female
15-64 years: 1.01 male(s)/female
65 years and over: 0.72 male(s)/female
total population: 0.96 male(s)/female (2004 est.)
Infant mortality rate:
total: 3.28 deaths/1,000 live births
male: 3.54 deaths/1,000 live births
female: 3 deaths/1,000 live births (2004 est.)

Japan (continued)

Life expectancy at birth:

total population: 81.04 years

male: 77.74 years

female: 84.51 years (2004 est.)

Total fertility rate: 1.38 children born/woman (2004 est.)

HIV/AIDS - adult prevalence rate: less than 0.1% (2001 est.)

HIV/AIDS - people living with HIV/AIDS: 12,000 (2001 est.)

HIV/AIDS - deaths: 430 (2001 est.)

Nationality:

noun: Japanese (singular and plural)

adjective: Japanese

Ethnic groups: Japanese 99%, others 1% (Korean 511,262, Chinese 244,241, Brazilian 182,232, Filipino 89,851, other 237,914)

note: up to 230,000 Brazilians of Japanese origin migrated to Japan in the 1990s to work in industries; some have returned to Brazil (2004)

Religions: observe both Shinto and Buddhist 84%, other 16% (including Christian 0.7%)

Languages: Japanese

Literacy:

definition: age 15 and over can read and write

total population: 99% (1995 est.)

male: NA%

female: NA%

Government

Country name:

conventional long form: none

conventional short form: Japan

Government type: constitutional monarchy with a parliamentary government

Capital: Tokyo

Administrative divisions: 47 prefectures; Aichi, Akita, Aomori, Chiba, Ehime, Fukui, Fukuoka, Fukushima, Gifu, Gumma, Hiroshima, Hokkaido, Hyogo, Ibaraki, Ishikawa, Iwate, Kagawa, Kagoshima, Kanagawa, Kochi, Kumamoto, Kyoto, Mie, Miyagi, Miyazaki, Nagano, Nagasaki, Nara, Niigata, Oita, Okayama, Okinawa, Osaka, Saga, Saitama, Shiga, Shimane, Shizuoka, Tochigi, Tokushima, Tokyo, Tottori, Toyama, Wakayama, Yamagata, Yamaguchi, Yamanashi

Independence: 660 BC (traditional founding by Emperor Jimmu)

National holiday: Birthday of Emperor AKIHITO, 23 December (1933)

Constitution: 3 May 1947

Legal system: modeled after European civil law system with English-American influence; judicial review of legislative acts in the Supreme Court; accepts compulsory ICJ jurisdiction with reservations

Suffrage: 20 years of age; universal

Executive branch:

chief of state: Emperor AKIHITO (since 7 January 1989)

head of government: Prime Minister Junichiro KOIZUMI (since 26 April 2001)

cabinet: Cabinet appointed by the prime minister

elections: none; the monarch is hereditary; the Diet designates the prime minister; the constitution requires that the prime minister must command a parliamentary majority; therefore, following legislative elections, the leader of the majority party or leader of a majority coalition in the House of Representatives usually becomes prime minister

note: following the resignation of Prime Minister Yoshiro MORI, Junichiro KOIZUMI was elected as the new president of the majority Liberal Democratic Party and soon thereafter designated by the Diet to become the next prime minister

Legislative branch: bicameral Diet or Kokkai consists of the House of Councillors or Sangi-in (247 seats - members elected for six-year terms; half reelected every three years; 149 members in multi-seat constituencies and 98 by proportional representation); House of Representatives or Shugi-in (480 seats - members elected for four-year terms; 300 in single-seat constituencies; 180 members by proportional representation in 11 regional blocs)

elections: House of Councillors - last held 29 July 2001 (next to be held in July 2004 - number of seats to be reduced by five to 242); House of Representatives - last held 9 November 2003 (next election by November 2007)

election results: House of Councillors - percent of vote by party - NA%; seats by party - LDP 110, DPJ 59, Komeito 23, JCP 20, SDP 8, Liberal Party 8, Conservative Party 5, independents 14; distribution of seats as of July 2001 was: LDP 115, DPJ 60, Komeito 24, JCP 20, SDP 8, Liberal Party 8 (merged with DPJ in 2003), independents 6, others 6; House of Representatives - percent of vote by party - LDP 49.38%, DPJ 36.88%, Komeito 7.09%, JCP 1.88%, SDP 1.25%, NCP .84%; seats by party - LDP 237, DPJ 177, Komeito 34, JCP 9, SDP 6, NCP 4, others 13; distribution of seats as of 13 November 2003 was: LDP 244, DPJ 177, Komeito 34, JCP 9, SDP 6, others 10

note: the Liberal Party merged with the Democratic Party of Japan in September 2003; the New Conservative Party merged with the Liberal Democratic Party following the election in November 2003

Judicial branch: Supreme Court (chief justice is appointed by the monarch after designation by the cabinet; all other justices are appointed by the cabinet)

Political parties and leaders: Democratic Party of Japan or DPJ [Naoto KAN, leader; Katsuya OKADA, secretary general]; Japan Communist Party or JCP [Kazuo SHII, chairman; Tadayoshi ICHIDA, secretary general]; Komeito [Takenori KANZAKI, president; Tetsuzo FUYUSHIBA, secretary general]; Liberal Democratic Party or LDP [Junichiro KOIZUMI, president; Shinzo ABE, secretary general]; Social Democratic Party or SDP [Mizuho FUKUSHIMA, chairperson; Seiji MATAICHI, secretary general]

Political pressure groups and leaders: NA

International organization participation: AfDB, APEC, ARF, AsDB, ASEAN (dialogue partner), Australia Group, BIS, CE (observer), CERN (observer), CP, EBRD, FAO, G-5, G-7, G-8, G-10, IADB, IAEA, IBRD, ICAO, ICC, ICFTU, ICRM, IDA, IEA, IFAD, IFC, IFRCS, IHO, ILO, IMF, IMO, Interpol, IOC, IOM, ISO, ITU, NAM (guest), NEA, NSG, OAS (observer), OECD, OPCW, OSCE (partner), Paris Club, PCA, UN, UNCTAD, UNDOF, UNESCO, UNHCR, UNIDO, UNITAR, UNMISET, UNMOVIC, UNRWA, UPU, WCL, WCO, WFTU, WHO, WIPO, WMO, WToO, WTrO, ZC

Diplomatic representation in the US:

chief of mission: Ambassador Ryozo KATO

chancery: 2520 Massachusetts Avenue NW, Washington, DC 20008

telephone: [1] (202) 238-6700

FAX: [1] (202) 328-2187

consulate(s) general: Anchorage, Atlanta, Boston, Chicago, Denver, Detroit, Hagatna (Guam), Honolulu, Houston, Kansas City (Missouri), Los Angeles, Miami, New Orleans, New York, Portland (Oregon), San Francisco, and Seattle

consulate(s): Saipan (Northern Mariana Islands)

Diplomatic representation from the US:

chief of mission: Ambassador Howard H. BAKER, Jr.

embassy: 10-5 Akasaka 1-chome, Minato-ku, Tokyo 107-8420

mailing address: Unit 45004, Box 258, APO AP 96337-5004

telephone: [81] (03) 3224-5000

FAX: [81] (03) 3505-1862

consulate(s) general: Naha (Okinawa), Osaka-Kobe, Sapporo

consulate(s): Fukuoka, Nagoya

Flag description: white with a large red disk (representing the sun without rays) in the center

Economy

Economy - overview: Government-industry cooperation, a strong work ethic, mastery of high technology, and a comparatively small defense allocation (1% of GDP) helped Japan advance with extraordinary rapidity to the rank of second most technologically-powerful economy in the world after the US and third-largest economy after the US and China. One notable characteristic of the economy is the working together of manufacturers, suppliers, and distributors in closely-knit groups called keiretsu. A second basic feature has been the guarantee of lifetime employment for a substantial portion of the urban labor force. Both features are now eroding. Industry, the most important sector of the economy, is heavily dependent on imported raw materials and fuels. The much smaller agricultural sector is highly subsidized and protected, with crop yields among the highest in the world. Usually self-sufficient in rice, Japan must import about 50% of its requirements of other grain and fodder crops. Japan maintains one of the world's largest fishing fleets and accounts for nearly 15% of the global catch. For three decades overall real economic growth had been spectacular: a 10% average in the 1960s, a 5% average in the 1970s, and a 4% average in the 1980s. Growth slowed markedly in the 1990s, averaging just 1.7%, largely because of the after effects of overinvestment during the late 1980s and contractionary domestic policies intended to wring speculative excesses from the stock and real estate markets. Government efforts to revive economic growth have met with little success and were further hampered in 2000-03 by the slowing of the US, European, and Asian economies. Japan's huge government debt, which is approaching 150% of GDP, and the ageing of the population are two major long-run problems. Robotics constitutes a key long-term economic strength with Japan possessing 410,000 of the world's 720,000 "working robots." Internal conflict over the proper way to reform the ailing banking system continues.

GDP: purchasing power parity - $3.567 trillion (2003 est.)

GDP - real growth rate: 2.3% (2003 est.)

GDP - per capita: purchasing power parity - $28,000 (2003 est.)

GDP - composition by sector:
agriculture: 1.4%
industry: 30.9%
services: 67.7% (2001 est.)

Population below poverty line: NA%

Household income or consumption by percentage share:
lowest 10%: 4.8%
highest 10%: 21.7% (1993)

Distribution of family income - Gini index: 24.9 (1993)

Inflation rate (consumer prices): -0.3% (2003 est.)

Labor force: 66.66 million (2003)

Labor force - by occupation: services 70%, industry 25%, agriculture 5% (2002 est.)

Unemployment rate: 5.3% (2003)

Budget:
revenues: $380 billion
expenditures: $746 billion, including capital expenditures (public works only) of about $71 billion (FY03/04 est.)

Industries: among world's largest and technologically advanced producers of motor vehicles, electronic equipment, machine tools, steel and nonferrous metals, ships, chemicals, textiles, processed foods

Industrial production growth rate: 1.9% (2003 est.)

Electricity - production: 1.037 trillion kWh (2001)

Electricity - production by source:
fossil fuel: 60%
hydro: 8.4%
nuclear: 29.8%
other: 1.8% (2001)

Electricity - consumption: 964.4 billion kWh (2001)

Electricity - exports: 0 kWh (2001)

Electricity - imports: 0 kWh (2001)

Oil - production: 17,330 bbl/day (2001 est.)

Oil - consumption: 5.29 million bbl/day (2001 est.)

Oil - exports: 93,360 bbl/day (2001)

Oil - imports: 5.449 million bbl/day (2001)

Oil - proved reserves: 29.29 million bbl (1 January 2002)

Natural gas - production: 2.519 billion cu m (2001 est.)

Natural gas - consumption: 80.42 billion cu m (2001 est.)

Natural gas - exports: 0 cu m (2001 est.)

Natural gas - imports: 77.73 billion cu m (2001 est.)

Natural gas - proved reserves: 20.02 billion cu m (1 January 2002)

Agriculture - products: rice, sugar beets, vegetables, fruit, pork, poultry, dairy products, eggs, fish

Exports: $447.1 billion f.o.b. (2003 est.)

Exports - commodities: motor vehicles, semiconductors, office machinery, chemicals

Exports - partners: US 28.8%, China 9.6%, South Korea 6.9%, Taiwan 6.3%, Hong Kong 6.1% (2002)

Imports: $346.6 billion f.o.b. (2003 est.)

Imports - commodities: machinery and equipment, fuels, foodstuffs, chemicals, textiles, raw materials (2001)

Imports - partners: China 18.3%, US 17.4%, South Korea 4.6%, Indonesia 4.2%, Australia 4.1% (2002)

Debt - external: $NA (2002 est.)

Economic aid - donor: ODA, $7 billion (FY03/04)

Currency: yen (JPY)

Currency code: JPY

Exchange rates: yen per US dollar - 115.933 (2003), 125.388 (2002), 121.529 (2001), 107.765 (2000), 113.907 (1999)

Fiscal year: 1 April - 31 March

Communications

Telephones - main lines in use: 71.149 million (2002)

Telephones - mobile cellular: 81,118,400 (2002)

Telephone system:
general assessment: excellent domestic and international service
domestic: high level of modern technology and excellent service of every kind
international: country code - 81; satellite earth stations - 5 Intelsat (4 Pacific Ocean and 1 Indian Ocean), 1 Intersputnik (Indian Ocean region), and 1 Inmarsat (Pacific and Indian Ocean regions); submarine cables to China, Philippines, Russia, and US (via Guam) (1999)

Radio broadcast stations: AM 215 plus 370 repeaters, FM 89 plus 485 repeaters, shortwave 21 (2001)

Television broadcast stations: 211 plus 7,341 repeaters
note: in addition, US Forces are served by 3 TV stations and 2 TV cable services (1999)

Internet country code: .jp

Internet hosts: 9,260,117 (2002)

Internet users: 57.2 million (2002)

Transportation

Railways:
total: 23,167 km (15,995 km electrified)
standard gauge: 3,204 km 1.435-m gauge (3,204 km electrified)
narrow gauge: 77 km 1.372-m gauge (77 km electrified); 19,855 km 1.067-m gauge (12,683 km electrified); 31 km 0.762-m gauge (31 km electrified) (2002)

Highways:
total: 1,161,894 km
paved: 534,471 km (including 6,455 km of expressways)
unpaved: 627,423 km (1999)

Waterways: 1,770 km approximately
note: seagoing craft ply all coastal inland seas

Pipelines: gas 2,719 km; oil 170 km; oil/gas/water 60 km (2003)

Ports and harbors: Akita, Amagasaki, Chiba, Hachinohe, Hakodate, Higashi-Harima, Himeji, Hiroshima, Kawasaki, Kinuura, Kobe, Kushiro, Mizushima, Moji, Nagoya, Osaka, Sakai, Sakaide, Shimizu, Tokyo, Tomakomai

Merchant marine:
total: 568 ships (1,000 GRT or over) 10,149,196 GRT/ 12,680,544 DWT
by type: bulk 113, cargo 39, chemical tanker 18, combination bulk 31, combination ore/oil 1, container 14, liquefied gas 53, passenger 8, passenger/cargo 1, petroleum tanker 170, refrigerated cargo 6, roll on/roll off 58, short-sea/passenger 7, vehicle carrier 49
foreign-owned: China 1, Panama 1, Philippines 1, Singapore 1
registered in other countries: 1,989 (2003 est.)

Airports: 174 (2003 est.)

Airports - with paved runways:
total: 143
over 3,047 m: 7
2,438 to 3,047 m: 37
1,524 to 2,437 m: 39
914 to 1,523 m: 28
under 914 m: 32 (2003 est.)

Airports - with unpaved runways:
total: 31
over 3047 m: 1
914 to 1,523 m: 4
under 914 m: 26 (2003 est.)

Heliports: 15 (2003 est.)

Military

Military branches: Ground Self-Defense Force (Army), Maritime Self-Defense Force (Navy), Air Self-Defense Force (Air Force), Coast Guard

Military manpower - military age: 18 years of age (2004 est.)

Military manpower - availability:
males age 15-49: 29,179,095 (2004 est.)

Military manpower - fit for military service:
males age 15-49: 25,189,438 (2004 est.)

Japan (continued)

Military manpower - reaching military age annually:
males: 700,931 (2004 est.)
Military expenditures - dollar figure:
$42,488,100,000 (2003)
Military expenditures - percent of GDP: 1% (2003)

Transnational Issues

Disputes - international: The sovereignty dispute over the islands of Etorofu, Kunashiri, and Shikotan, and the Habomai group, known in Japan as the "Northern Territories" and in Russia as the "Southern Kuril Islands", occupied by the Soviet Union in 1945, now administered by Rusia and claimed by Japan, remains the primary sticking point to signing a peace treaty formally ending World War II hostilities; intensified media coverage and protests highlight dispute over the fishing-rich Liancourt Rocks (Take-shima/Tok-do) also claimed by South Korea; China and Taiwan have intensified their claims to the Senkaku Islands (Diaoyu Tai) administered by Japan

Jarvis Island
(territory of the US)

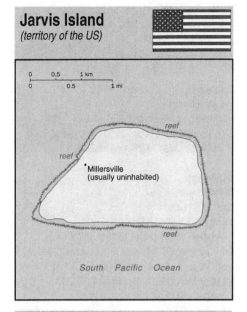

Introduction

Background: First discovered by the British in 1821, the uninhabited island was annexed by the US in 1858, but abandoned in 1879 after tons of guano had been removed. The UK annexed the island in 1889, but never carried out plans for further exploitation. The US occupied and reclaimed the island in 1935. Abandoned after World War II, the island is currently a National Wildlife Refuge administered by the US Department of the Interior; a day beacon is situated near the middle of the west coast.

Geography

Location: Oceania, island in the South Pacific Ocean, about half way between Hawaii and the Cook Islands
Geographic coordinates: 0 22 S, 160 03 W
Map references: Oceania
Area:
total: 4.5 sq km
land: 4.5 sq km
water: 0 sq km
Area - comparative: about eight times the size of The Mall in Washington, DC
Land boundaries: 0 km
Coastline: 8 km
Maritime claims:
territorial sea: 12 NM
exclusive economic zone: 200 NM
Climate: tropical; scant rainfall, constant wind, burning sun
Terrain: sandy, coral island surrounded by a narrow fringing reef
Elevation extremes:
lowest point: Pacific Ocean 0 m
highest point: unnamed location 7 m
Natural resources: guano (deposits worked until late 1800s), terrestrial and aquatic wildlife

Land use:
arable land: 0%
permanent crops: 0%
other: 100% (1998 est.)
Irrigated land: 0 sq km (1998 est.)
Natural hazards: the narrow fringing reef surrounding the island poses a maritime hazard
Environment - current issues: no natural fresh water resources
Geography - note: sparse bunch grass, prostrate vines, and low-growing shrubs; primarily a nesting, roosting, and foraging habitat for seabirds, shorebirds, and marine wildlife

People

Population: uninhabited
note: Millersville settlement on western side of island occasionally used as a weather station from 1935 until World War II, when it was abandoned; reoccupied in 1957 during the International Geophysical Year by scientists who left in 1958; public entry is by special-use permit from US Fish and Wildlife Service only and generally restricted to scientists and educators; visited annually by US Fish and Wildlife Service (July 2004 est.)

Government

Country name:
conventional long form: none
conventional short form: Jarvis Island
Dependency status: unincorporated territory of the US; administered from Washington, DC, by the Fish and Wildlife Service of the US Department of the Interior as part of the National Wildlife Refuge system
Legal system: the laws of the US, where applicable, apply
Flag description: the flag of the US is used

Economy

Economy - overview: no economic activity

Transportation

Waterways: none
Ports and harbors: none; offshore anchorage only; note - there is one small boat landing area in the middle of the west coast and another near the southwest corner of the island
Transportation - note: there is a day beacon near the middle of the west coast

Military

Military - note: defense is the responsibility of the US; visited annually by the US Coast Guard

Transnational Issues

Disputes - international: none

Jersey
(British crown dependency)

Introduction

Background: The island of Jersey and the other Channel Islands represent the last remnants of the medieval Dukedom of Normandy that held sway in both France and England. These islands were the only British soil occupied by German troops in World War II.

Geography

Location: Western Europe, island in the English Channel, northwest of France
Geographic coordinates: 49 15 N, 2 10 W
Map references: Europe
Area:
total: 116 sq km
land: 116 sq km
water: 0 sq km
Area - comparative: about 0.7 times the size of Washington, DC
Land boundaries: 0 km
Coastline: 70 km
Maritime claims:
territorial sea: 3 NM
exclusive fishing zone: 12 NM
Climate: temperate; mild winters and cool summers
Terrain: gently rolling plain with low, rugged hills along north coast
Elevation extremes:
lowest point: Atlantic Ocean 0 m
highest point: unnamed location 143 m
Natural resources: arable land
Land use:
arable land: NEGL%
permanent crops: 0%
other: 100% (1998 est.)
Irrigated land: NA sq km
Natural hazards: NA
Environment - current issues: NA

Geography - note: largest and southernmost of Channel Islands; about 30% of population concentrated in Saint Helier

People

Population: 90,502 (July 2004 est.)
Age structure:
0-14 years: 17.7% (male 8,268; female 7,716)
15-64 years: 67.1% (male 30,237; female 30,490)
65 years and over: 15.2% (male 6,016; female 7,775) (2004 est.)
Median age:
total: 40.3 years
male: 39.6 years
female: 41.1 years (2004 est.)
Population growth rate: 0.36% (2004 est.)
Birth rate: 10.04 births/1,000 population (2004 est.)
Death rate: 9.17 deaths/1,000 population (2004 est.)
Net migration rate: 2.76 migrant(s)/1,000 population (2004 est.)
Sex ratio:
at birth: 1.08 male(s)/female
under 15 years: 1.07 male(s)/female
15-64 years: 0.99 male(s)/female
65 years and over: 0.77 male(s)/female
total population: 0.97 male(s)/female (2004 est.)
Infant mortality rate:
total: 5.33 deaths/1,000 live births
male: 5.7 deaths/1,000 live births
female: 4.94 deaths/1,000 live births (2004 est.)
Life expectancy at birth:
total population: 79.09 years
male: 76.63 years
female: 81.74 years (2004 est.)
Total fertility rate: 1.57 children born/woman (2004 est.)
HIV/AIDS - adult prevalence rate: NA%
HIV/AIDS - people living with HIV/AIDS: NA
HIV/AIDS - deaths: NA
Nationality:
noun: Channel Islander(s)
adjective: Channel Islander
Ethnic groups: UK and Norman-French descent
Religions: Anglican, Roman Catholic, Baptist, Congregational New Church, Methodist, Presbyterian
Languages: English (official), French (official), Norman-French dialect spoken in country districts
Literacy:
definition: NA
total population: NA%
male: NA%
female: NA%

Government

Country name:
conventional long form: Bailiwick of Jersey
conventional short form: Jersey
Dependency status: British crown dependency
Government type: NA
Capital: Saint Helier

Administrative divisions: none (British crown dependency)
Independence: none (British crown dependency)
National holiday: Liberation Day, 9 May (1945)
Constitution: unwritten; partly statutes, partly common law and practice
Legal system: English law and local statute; justice is administered by the Royal Court
Suffrage: NA years of age; universal adult
Executive branch:
chief of state: Queen ELIZABETH II (since 6 February 1952)
head of government: Lieutenant Governor and Commander in Chief Air Chief Marshall Sir John CHESHIRE (since 24 January 2001) and Bailiff Philip Martin BAILHACHE (since NA February 1995)
cabinet: committees appointed by the Assembly of the States
elections: none; the monarch is hereditary; lieutenant governor and bailiff appointed by the monarch
Legislative branch: unicameral Assembly of the States (55 voting members - 12 senators (elected for 6-year terms), 12 constables or heads of parishes (elected for 3-year terms), 29 deputies (elected for 3-year terms); the bailiff and the deputy bailiff; and 3 non-voting members - the Dean of Jersey, the Attorney General, and the Solicitor General all appointed by the monarch)
elections: last held NA (next to be held NA)
election results: percent of vote - NA%; seats - independents 52
Judicial branch: Royal Court (judges elected by an electoral college and the bailiff)
Political parties and leaders: none; all independents
Political pressure groups and leaders: none
Diplomatic representation in the US: none (British crown dependency)
Diplomatic representation from the US: none (British crown dependency)
Flag description: white with a diagonal red cross extending to the corners of the flag and in the upper quadrant, surmounted by a yellow crown, a red shield holding the three lions of England in yellow

Economy

Economy - overview: The economy is based largely on international financial services, agriculture, and tourism. Potatoes, cauliflower, tomatoes, and especially flowers are important export crops, shipped mostly to the UK. The Jersey breed of dairy cattle is known worldwide and represents an important export income earner. Milk products go to the UK and other EU countries. In 1996 the finance sector accounted for about 60% of the island's output. Tourism, another mainstay of the economy, accounts for 24% of GDP. In recent years, the government has encouraged light industry to locate in Jersey, with the result that an electronics industry has developed alongside the traditional manufacturing of knitwear. All raw material and energy requirements are imported, as well as a large share of Jersey's food needs. Light taxes and death duties make the island a popular tax haven.

GDP: purchasing power parity - $2.2 billion (1999 est.)

GDP - real growth rate: NA%

GDP - per capita: purchasing power parity - $24,800 (1999 est.)

GDP - composition by sector:
agriculture: 5%
industry: 2%
services: 93% (1996)

Population below poverty line: NA%

Household income or consumption by percentage share:
lowest 10%: NA%
highest 10%: NA%

Inflation rate (consumer prices): 4.7% (1998)

Labor force: 57,050 (1996)

Unemployment rate: 0.7% (1998 est.)

Budget:
revenues: $601 million
expenditures: $588 million, including capital expenditures of $98 million (2000 est.)

Industries: tourism, banking and finance, dairy

Industrial production growth rate: NA%

Electricity - imports: NA kWh; note - electricity supplied by France

Agriculture - products: potatoes, cauliflower, tomatoes; beef, dairy products

Exports: $NA

Exports - commodities: light industrial and electrical goods, foodstuffs, textiles

Exports - partners: UK

Imports: $NA

Imports - commodities: machinery and transport equipment, manufactured goods, foodstuffs, mineral fuels, chemicals

Imports - partners: UK

Debt - external: none

Economic aid - recipient: none

Currency: British pound (GBP); note - there is also a Jersey pound

Currency code: GBP

Exchange rates: Jersey pounds per US dollar - 0.6661 (2002), 0.6944 (2001), 0.6596 (2000), 0.6180 (1999); the Jersey pound is at par with the British pound

Fiscal year: 1 April - 31 March

Communications

Telephones - main lines in use: 73,900 (2001)

Telephones - mobile cellular: 61,400 (2001)

Telephone system:
general assessment: NA
domestic: NA
international: 3 submarine cables

Radio broadcast stations: AM NA, FM 1, shortwave 0 (1998)

Television broadcast stations: 2 (1997)

Internet country code: .je

Internet users: NA

Transportation

Railways: 0 km

Highways:
total: 577 km
paved: NA km
unpaved: NA km

Waterways: none

Ports and harbors: Gorey, Saint Aubin, Saint Helier

Merchant marine: none

Airports: 1 (2003 est.)

Airports - with paved runways:
total: 1
1,524 to 2,437 m: 1 (2003 est.)

Military

Military - note: defense is the responsibility of the UK

Transnational Issues

Disputes - international: none

Johnston Atoll
(territory of the US)

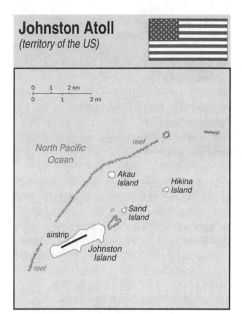

Introduction

Background: Both the US and the Kingdom of Hawaii annexed Johnston Atoll in 1858, but it was the US that mined the guano deposits until the late 1880s. Johnston and Sand Islands were designated wildlife refuges in 1926. The US Navy took over the atoll in 1934, and subsequently the US Air Force assumed control in 1948. The site was used for high-altitude nuclear tests in the 1950s and 1960s, and until late in 2000 the atoll was maintained as a storage and disposal site for chemical weapons. Munitions destruction is now complete. Cleanup and closure of the facility is progressing, with completion anticipated in 2004.

Geography

Location: Oceania, atoll in the North Pacific Ocean 717 NM (1328 km) southwest of Honolulu, Hawaii, about one-third of the way from Hawaii to the Marshall Islands

Geographic coordinates: 16 45 N, 169 31 W

Map references: Oceania

Area:
total: 2.8 sq km
land: 2.8 sq km
water: 0 sq km

Area - comparative: about 4.7 times the size of The Mall in Washington, DC

Land boundaries: 0 km

Coastline: 34 km

Maritime claims:
territorial sea: 12 NM
exclusive economic zone: 200 NM

Climate: tropical, but generally dry; consistent northeast trade winds with little seasonal temperature variation

Terrain: mostly flat

Elevation extremes:
lowest point: Pacific Ocean 0 m
highest point: Summit Peak 5 m

Johnston Atoll *(continued)*

Natural resources: guano deposits worked until depletion about 1890, terrestrial and aquatic wildlife
Land use:
arable land: 0%
permanent crops: 0%
other: 100% (1998 est.)
Irrigated land: 0 sq km (1998 est.)
Natural hazards: NA
Environment - current issues: no natural fresh water resources
Geography - note: strategic location in the North Pacific Ocean; Johnston Island and Sand Island are natural islands, which have been expanded by coral dredging; North Island (Akau) and East Island (Hikina) are manmade islands formed from coral dredging; the egg-shaped reef is 34 km in circumference; closed to the public; a former US nuclear weapons test site; site of now-closed Johnston Atoll Chemical Agent Disposal System (JACADS); most facilities dismantled and cleanup complete in 2004; some low-growing vegetation

People

Population: 396 no indigenous inhabitants
note: in previous years, there was an average of 1,100 US military and civilian contractor personnel present; as of September 2001, population had decreased significantly when US Army Chemical Activity Pacific (USACAP) departed; as of January 2004 the island population was just above 200 personnel, including US Air Force, US Fish and Wildlife Service, and civilian contractor personnel (July 2004 est.)

Government

Country name:
conventional long form: none
conventional short form: Johnston Atoll
Dependency status: unincorporated territory of the US; administered from Honolulu, HI, by Pacific Air Forces, Hickam Air Force Base, and the Fish and Wildlife Service of the US Department of the Interior as part of the National Wildlife Refuge system
Legal system: the laws of the US, where applicable, apply
Flag description: the flag of the US is used

Economy

Economy - overview: Economic activity is limited to providing services to US military personnel and contractors located on the island. All food and manufactured goods must be imported.

Communications

Telephone system:
general assessment: NA
domestic: 512 KB satellite link to Hawaii teleport; 20 (POTS) voice and data lines
international: NA (2002)

Transportation

Waterways: none
Ports and harbors: Johnston Island
Airports: 1 (2003 est.)
Airports - with paved runways:
total: 1
2,438 to 3,047 m: 1 (2003 est.)

Military

Military - note: defense is the responsibility of the US

Jordan

Introduction

Background: For most of its history since independence from British administration in 1946, Jordan was ruled by King HUSSEIN (1953-99). A pragmatic ruler, he successfully navigated competing pressures from the major powers (US, USSR, and UK), various Arab states, Israel, and a large internal Palestinian population, despite several wars and coup attempts. In 1989 he reinstituted parliamentary elections and gradually political liberalization; in 1994 he signed a formal peace treaty with Israel. King ABDALLAH II - the eldest son of King HUSSEIN and Princess MUNA - assumed the throne following his father's death in February 1999. Since then, he has consolidated his power and undertaken an aggressive economic reform program. Jordan acceded to the World Trade Organization in 2000, and began to participate in the European Free Trade Association in 2001. After a two-year delay, parliamentary and municipal elections took place in the summer of 2003. The prime minister and government appointed in October 2003 declared their commitment to accelerated economic and political reforms and the new cabinet includes an unprecedented three women as ministers.

Geography

Location: Middle East, northwest of Saudi Arabia
Geographic coordinates: 31 00 N, 36 00 E
Map references: Middle East
Area:
total: 92,300 sq km
land: 91,971 sq km
water: 329 sq km
Area - comparative: slightly smaller than Indiana
Land boundaries:
total: 1,635 km
border countries: Iraq 181 km, Israel 238 km, Saudi Arabia 744 km, Syria 375 km, West Bank 97 km
Coastline: 26 km

Jordan *(continued)*

Maritime claims:

territorial sea: 3 NM

Climate: mostly arid desert; rainy season in west (November to April)

Terrain: mostly desert plateau in east, highland area in west; Great Rift Valley separates East and West Banks of the Jordan River

Elevation extremes:

lowest point: Dead Sea -408 m

highest point: Jabal Ram 1,734 m

Natural resources: phosphates, potash, shale oil

Land use:

arable land: 2.87%

permanent crops: 1.52%

other: 95.61% (1998 est.)

Irrigated land: 750 sq km (1998 est.)

Natural hazards: droughts; periodic earthquakes

Environment - current issues: limited natural fresh water resources; deforestation; overgrazing; soil erosion; desertification

Environment - international agreements:

party to: Biodiversity, Climate Change, Climate Change-Kyoto Protocol, Desertification, Endangered Species, Hazardous Wastes, Law of the Sea, Marine Dumping, Ozone Layer Protection, Wetlands

signed, but not ratified: none of the selected agreements

Geography - note: strategic location at the head of the Gulf of Aqaba and as the Arab country that shares the longest border with Israel and the occupied West Bank

People

Population: 5,611,202 (July 2004 est.)

Age structure:

0-14 years: 35.2% (male 1,009,604; female 967,645)

15-64 years: 61.1% (male 1,829,984; female 1,598,141)

65 years and over: 3.7% (male 100,896; female 104,932) (2004 est.)

Median age:

total: 22.2 years

male: 22.8 years

female: 21.5 years (2004 est.)

Population growth rate: 2.67% (2004 est.)

Birth rate: 22.73 births/1,000 population (2004 est.)

Death rate: 2.62 deaths/1,000 population (2004 est.)

Net migration rate: 6.59 migrant(s)/1,000 population (2004 est.)

Sex ratio:

at birth: 1.06 male(s)/female

under 15 years: 1.04 male(s)/female

15-64 years: 1.15 male(s)/female

65 years and over: 0.96 male(s)/female

total population: 1.1 male(s)/female (2004 est.)

Infant mortality rate:

total: 18.11 deaths/1,000 live births

male: 21.63 deaths/1,000 live births

female: 14.37 deaths/1,000 live births (2004 est.)

Life expectancy at birth:

total population: 78.06 years

male: 75.59 years

female: 80.69 years (2004 est.)

Total fertility rate: 2.86 children born/woman (2004 est.)

HIV/AIDS - adult prevalence rate: less than 0.1% (2001 est.)

HIV/AIDS - people living with HIV/AIDS: less than 1,000

HIV/AIDS - deaths: NA

Nationality:

noun: Jordanian(s)

adjective: Jordanian

Ethnic groups: Arab 98%, Circassian 1%, Armenian 1%

Religions: Sunni Muslim 92%, Christian 6% (majority Greek Orthodox, but some Greek and Roman Catholics, Syrian Orthodox, Coptic Orthodox, Armenian Orthodox, and Protestant denominations), other 2% (several small Shi'a Muslim and Druze populations) (2001 est.)

Languages: Arabic (official), English widely understood among upper and middle classes

Literacy:

definition: age 15 and over can read and write

total population: 91.3%

male: 95.9%

female: 86.3% (2003 est.)

Government

Country name:

conventional long form: Hashemite Kingdom of Jordan

conventional short form: Jordan

local long form: Al Mamlakah al Urduniyah al Hashimiyah

local short form: Al Urdun

former: Transjordan

Government type: constitutional monarchy

Capital: 'Amman

Administrative divisions: 12 governorates (muhafazat, singular - muhafazah); Ajlun, Al 'Aqabah, Al Balqa', Al Karak, Al Mafraq, 'Amman, At Tafilah, Az Zarqa', Irbid, Jarash, Ma'an, Madaba

Independence: 25 May 1946 (from League of Nations mandate under British administration)

National holiday: Independence Day, 25 May (1946)

Constitution: 8 January 1952

Legal system: based on Islamic law and French codes; judicial review of legislative acts in a specially provided High Tribunal; has not accepted compulsory ICJ jurisdiction

Suffrage: 18 years of age; universal

Executive branch:

chief of state: King ABDALLAH II (since 7 February 1999); Crown Prince HAMZAH (half brother of the monarch, born 29 March 1980)

head of government: Prime Minister Faisal al-FAYEZ (since 25 October 2003)

cabinet: Cabinet appointed by the prime minister in consultation with the monarch

elections: none; the monarch is hereditary; prime minister appointed by the monarch

Legislative branch: bicameral National Assembly or Majlis al-'Umma consists of the Senate, also called the House of Notables (Majlis al-Ayan) (55 seats; members appointed by the monarch from designated categories of public figures; members serve four-year terms) and the House of Representatives, also called the House of Deputies (Majlis al-Nuwaab) (110 seats; members elected by popular vote on the basis of proportional representation to serve four-year terms; note - six seats are reserved for women and are allocated by a special electoral panel if no women are elected)

elections: House of Representatives - last held 17 June 2003 (next to be held NA 2007)

election results: House of Representatives - percent of vote by party - independents and others 89.6%, Islamic Action Front 10.4%; seats by party - independents and others 92, Islamic Action Front 18; note - one of the six quota seats was given to a female IAF candidate

note: the House of Representatives has been convened and dissolved by the monarch several times since 1974; in November 1989, the first parliamentary elections in 22 years were held; political parties were not legalized until 1992; King ABDALLAH delayed the 2001 elections until 2003

Judicial branch: Court of Cassation; Supreme Court (court of final appeal)

Political parties and leaders: Al-Umma (Nation) Party [Ahmad al-HANANDEH, secretary general]; Arab Land Party [Dr. Muhammad al-'ORAN, secretary general]; Communist Party [Munir HAMARINAH, secretary general]; Constitutional Front [Mahdi al-TALL, secretary general]; Jordanian Democratic Popular Unity Party [Sa'id DHIYAB, secretary general]; Jordanian Progressive Party [Fawwaz al-ZUBI, secretary general]; Jordanian People's Democratic (Hashd) Party [Salim al-NAHHAS, secretary general]; Islamic Action Front [Hazma MANSOUR, secretary general]; National Action (Haqq) Party [Muhammad al-ZUBI, secretary general]; National Constitutional Party [Abdul Hadi MAJALI, secretary general]; (Arab) Socialist Ba'th Party [Taysif al-HIMSI, secretary general]; Pan-Arab (Democratic) Movement [Mahmud al-NUWAYHI, secretary general]

Political pressure groups and leaders: Anti-Normalization Committee [Ali Abu SUKKAR, president vice chairman]; Jordanian Bar Association [Saleh ARMOUTI, president]; Jordanian Press Association [Sayf al-SHARIF, president]; Muslim Brotherhood [Abd-al-Majid DHUNAYBAT, secretary general]

International organization participation: ABEDA, ACC, AFESD, AMF, CAEU, FAO, G-77, IAEA, IBRD, ICAO, ICC, ICCt, ICFTU, ICRM, IDA, IDB, IFAD, IFC, IFRCS, ILO, IMF, IMO, Interpol, IOC, IOM, ISO, ITU, LAS, MONUC, NAM, OIC, OPCW, OSCE (partner), PCA, UN, UNAMSIL, UNCTAD, UNESCO, UNIDO, UNMEE, UNMIK, UNMIL, UNMISET, UNOMIG, UNRWA, UPU, WCO, WFTU, WHO, WIPO, WMO, WToO, WTrO

Jordan (continued)

Diplomatic representation in the US:
chief of mission: Ambassador Karim Tawfiq KAWAR
chancery: 3504 International Drive NW, Washington, DC 20008
telephone: [1] (202) 966-2664
FAX: [1] (202) 966-3110
Diplomatic representation from the US:
chief of mission: Ambassador Edward William GNEHM, Jr.
embassy: Abdoun, Amman
mailing address: P. O. Box 354, Amman 11118 Jordan; Unit 70200, Box 5, APO AE 09892-0200
telephone: [962] (6) 5906000
FAX: [962] (6) 5920121
Flag description: three equal horizontal bands of black (top, the Abbassid Caliphate of Islam), white (the Ummayyad Caliphate of Islam), and green (the Fatimid Caliphate of Islam) with a red isosceles triangle (representing the Great Arab Revolt of 1916) based on the hoist side bearing a small white seven-pointed star symbolizing the seven verses of the opening Sura (Al-Fatiha) of the Holy Koran; the seven points on the star represent faith in One God, humanity, national spirit, humility, social justice, virtue, and aspirations

Economy

Economy - overview: Jordan is a small Arab country with inadequate supplies of water and other natural resources such as oil. Debt, poverty, and unemployment are fundamental problems, but King ABDALLAH, since assuming the throne in 1999, has undertaken some broad economic reforms in a long-term effort to improve living standards. 'Amman in the past three years has worked closely with the IMF, practiced careful monetary policy, and made substantial headway with privatization. The government also has liberalized the trade regime sufficiently to secure Jordan's membership in the WTrO (2000), a free trade accord with the US (2000), and an association agreement with the EU (2001). These measures have helped improve productivity and have put Jordan on the foreign investment map. The US-led war in Iraq in 2003 dealt an economic blow to Jordan, which was dependent on Iraq for discounted oil (worth $300-$600 million a year). Several Gulf nations have provided temporary aid to compensate for the loss of this oil; when this foreign aid expires, the Jordanian government has pledged to raise retail petroleum product prices and the sales tax base. Other ongoing challenges include fiscal adjustment to reduce the budget deficit, broader investment incentives to promote job-creating ventures, and the encouragement of tourism.
GDP: purchasing power parity - $23.64 billion (2003 est.)
GDP - real growth rate: 3.1% (2003 est.)
GDP - per capita: purchasing power parity - $4,300 (2003 est.)
GDP - composition by sector:
agriculture: 3.7%

industry: 26%
services: 70.3% (2002 est.)
Population below poverty line: 30% (2001 est.)
Household income or consumption by percentage share:
lowest 10%: 3.3%
highest 10%: 29.8% (1997)
Distribution of family income - Gini index: 36.4 (1997)
Inflation rate (consumer prices): 3.5% (2003 est.)
Labor force: 1.36 million (2002)
Labor force - by occupation: services 82.5%, industry 12.5%, agriculture 5% (2001 est.)
Unemployment rate: 16% official rate; actual rate is 25%-30% (2001 est.)
Budget:
revenues: $3.3 billion
expenditures: $3.7 billion, including capital expenditures of $582 million (2003 est.)
Industries: phosphate mining, pharmaceuticals, petroleum refining, cement, potash, light manufacturing, pharmaceuticals, tourism
Industrial production growth rate: 7% (2003 est.)
Electricity - production: 7.091 billion kWh (2001)
Electricity - production by source:
fossil fuel: 99.4%
hydro: 0.6%
nuclear: 0%
other: 0% (2001)
Electricity - consumption: 6.86 billion kWh (2001)
Electricity - exports: 2 million kWh (2001)
Electricity - imports: 267 million kWh (2001)
Oil - production: 40 bbl/day (2001 est.)
Oil - consumption: 103,000 bbl/day (2001 est.)
Oil - exports: NA
Oil - imports: NA
Oil - proved reserves: 445,000 bbl (1 January 2002)
Natural gas - production: 290 million cu m (2001 est.)
Natural gas - consumption: 290 million cu m (2001 est.)
Natural gas - exports: 0 cu m (2001 est.)
Natural gas - imports: 0 cu m (2001 est.)
Natural gas - proved reserves: 3.256 billion cu m (1 January 2002)
Agriculture - products: wheat, barley, citrus, tomatoes, melons, olives; sheep, goats, poultry
Exports: $2.908 billion f.o.b. (2003 est.)
Exports - commodities: clothing, phosphates, fertilizers, potash, vegetables, manufactures, pharmaceuticals
Exports - partners: Iraq 20.6%, US 14.9%, India 8.3%, Saudi Arabia 5.5%, UAE 4% (2002)
Imports: $4.946 billion f.o.b. (2003 est.)
Imports - commodities: crude oil, textile fabrics, machinery, transport equipment, manufactured goods
Imports - partners: Iraq 13.3%, Germany 8.7%, US 7.9%, China 6%, France 4.2%, UK 4.1%, Italy 4% (2002)
Debt - external: $8.2 billion (2002 est.)

Economic aid - recipient: ODA, $553 million (2000 est.)
Currency: Jordanian dinar (JOD)
Currency code: JOD
Exchange rates: Jordanian dinars per US dollar - 0.709 (2003), 0.709 (2002), 0.709 (2001), 0.709 (2000), 0.709 (1999)
Fiscal year: calendar year

Communications

Telephones - main lines in use: 674,500 (2002)
Telephones - mobile cellular: 1,219,600 (2002)
Telephone system:
general assessment: service has improved recently with increased use of digital switching equipment, but better access to the telephone system is needed in the rural areas and easier access to pay telephones is needed by the urban public
domestic: microwave radio relay transmission and coaxial and fiber-optic cable are employed on trunk lines; considerable use of mobile cellular systems; Internet service is available
international: country code - 962; satellite earth stations - 3 Intelsat, 1 Arabsat, and 29 land and maritime Inmarsat terminals; fiber-optic cable to Saudi Arabia and microwave radio relay link with Egypt and Syria; connection to international submarine cable FLAG (Fiber-Optic Link Around the Globe); participant in MEDARABTEL; international links total about 4,000
Radio broadcast stations: AM 6, FM 5, shortwave 1 (1999)
Television broadcast stations: 20 (plus 96 repeaters) (1995)
Internet country code: .jo
Internet hosts: 4,116 (2002)
Internet users: 307,500 (2002)

Transportation

Railways:
total: 505 km
narrow gauge: 505 km 1.050-m gauge (2002)
Highways:
total: 7,245 km
paved: 7,245 km
unpaved: 0 km (2000)
Waterways: none
Pipelines: gas 10 km; oil 743 km (2003)
Ports and harbors: Al 'Aqabah
Merchant marine:
total: 9 ships (1,000 GRT or over) 78,814 GRT/92,695 DWT
by type: cargo 2, container 1, roll on/roll off 5, short-sea/passenger 1
foreign-owned: Greece 6
registered in other countries: 11 (2003 est.)
Airports: 17 (2003 est.)
Airports - with paved runways:
total: 15
over 3,047 m: 7
2,438 to 3,047 m: 6
914 to 1,523 m: 1
under 914 m: 1 (2003 est.)

Airports - with unpaved runways:
total: 2
under 914 m: 2 (2003 est.)
Heliports: 1 (2003 est.)

Military

Military branches: Jordanian Armed Forces (JAF) (Royal Jordanian Land Force, Royal Naval Force, Royal Jordanian Air Force, and Special Operations Command or SOCOM); note - Public Security Directorate normally falls under Ministry of Interior but comes under JAF in wartime or crisis situations
Military manpower - military age: 17 years of age (conscription at age 18 was suspended in 1999, although all males under age 37 are required to register; recruits are accepted from age 17) (2004 est.)
Military manpower - availability:
males age 15-49: 1,636,537 (2004 est.)
Military manpower - fit for military service:
males age 15-49: 1,153,385 (2004 est.)
Military manpower - reaching military age annually:
males: 59,471 (2004 est.)
Military expenditures - dollar figure:
$2,043,200,000 (2003)
Military expenditures - percent of GDP: 20.2% (2003)

Transnational Issues

Disputes - international: none

Juan de Nova Island
(possession of France)

Introduction

Background: Named after a famous 15th century Spanish navigator and explorer, the island has been a French possession since 1897. It has been exploited for its guano and phosphate. Presently a small military garrison oversees a meteorological station.

Geography

Location: Southern Africa, island in the Mozambique Channel, about one-third of the way between Madagascar and Mozambique
Geographic coordinates: 17 03 S, 42 45 E
Map references: Africa
Area:
total: 4.4 sq km
land: 4.4 sq km
water: 0 sq km
Area - comparative: about seven times the size of The Mall in Washington, DC
Land boundaries: 0 km
Coastline: 24.1 km
Maritime claims:
territorial sea: 12 NM
exclusive economic zone: 200 NM
continental shelf: 200-m depth or to the depth of exploitation
Climate: tropical
Terrain: low and flat
Elevation extremes:
lowest point: Indian Ocean 0 m
highest point: unnamed location 10 m
Natural resources: guano deposits and other fertilizers
Land use:
arable land: 0%
permanent crops: 0%
other: 100% (90% forest) (1998 est.)
Irrigated land: 0 sq km (1998 est.)

Natural hazards: periodic cyclones
Environment - current issues: NA
Geography - note: wildlife sanctuary

People

Population: no indigenous inhabitants
note: there is a small French military garrison along with a few meteorologists; occasionally visited by scientists (July 2004 est.)

Government

Country name:
conventional long form: none
conventional short form: Juan de Nova Island
local long form: none
local short form: Ile Juan de Nova
Dependency status: possession of France; administered by a high commissioner of the Republic, resident in Reunion
Legal system: the laws of France, where applicable, apply
Diplomatic representation in the US: none (possession of France)
Diplomatic representation from the US: none (possession of France)
Flag description: the flag of France is used

Economy

Economy - overview: Up to 12,000 tons of guano are mined per year.

Communications

Communications - note: 1 meteorological station

Transportation

Railways:
total: NA km; short line going to a jetty
Waterways: none
Ports and harbors: none; offshore anchorage only
Airports: 1 (2003 est.)
Airports - with unpaved runways:
total: 1
914 to 1,523 m: 1 (2003 est.)

Military

Military - note: defense is the responsibility of France

Transnational Issues

Disputes - international: claimed by Madagascar

Kazakhstan

Geography - note: landlocked; Russia leases approximately 6,000 sq km of territory enclosing the Baykonur Cosmodrome

Introduction

Background: Native Kazakhs, a mix of Turkic and Mongol nomadic tribes who migrated into the region in the 13th century, were rarely united as a single nation. The area was conquered by Russia in the 18th century and Kazakhstan became a Soviet Republic in 1936. During the 1950s and 1960s agricultural "Virgin Lands" program, Soviet citizens were encouraged to help cultivate Kazakhstan's northern pastures. This influx of immigrants (mostly Russians, but also some other deported nationalities) skewed the ethnic mixture and enabled non-Kazakhs to outnumber natives. Independence in 1991 caused many of these newcomers to emigrate. Current issues include: developing a cohesive national identity; expanding the development of the country's vast energy resources and exporting them to world markets; achieving a sustainable economic growth outside the oil, gas, and mining sectors; and strengthening relations with neighboring states and other foreign powers.

Geography

Location: Central Asia, northwest of China; a small portion west of the Ural River in eastern-most Europe
Geographic coordinates: 48 00 N, 68 00 E
Map references: Asia
Area:
total: 2,717,300 sq km
land: 2,669,800 sq km
water: 47,500 sq km
Area - comparative: slightly less than four times the size of Texas
Land boundaries:
total: 12,012 km
border countries: China 1,533 km, Kyrgyzstan 1,051 km, Russia 6,846 km, Turkmenistan 379 km, Uzbekistan 2,203 km
Coastline: 0 km (landlocked); note - Kazakhstan borders the Aral Sea, now split into two bodies of water (1,070 km), and the Caspian Sea (1,894 km)

Climate: continental, cold winters and hot summers, arid and semiarid
Terrain: extends from the Volga to the Altai Mountains and from the plains in western Siberia to oases and desert in Central Asia
Elevation extremes:
lowest point: Vpadina Kaundy -132 m
highest point: Khan Tangiri Shyngy (Pik Khan-Tengri) 6,995 m
Natural resources: major deposits of petroleum, natural gas, coal, iron ore, manganese, chrome ore, nickel, cobalt, copper, molybdenum, lead, zinc, bauxite, gold, uranium
Land use:
arable land: 11.23%
permanent crops: 0.05%
other: 88.72% (1998 est.)
Irrigated land: 23,320 sq km (1998 est.)
Natural hazards: earthquakes in the south, mudslides around Almaty
Environment - current issues: radioactive or toxic chemical sites associated with former defense industries and test ranges scattered throughout the country pose health risks for humans and animals; industrial pollution is severe in some cities; because the two main rivers which flowed into the Aral Sea have been diverted for irrigation, it is drying up and leaving behind a harmful layer of chemical pesticides and natural salts; these substances are then picked up by the wind and blown into noxious dust storms; pollution in the Caspian Sea; soil pollution from overuse of agricultural chemicals and salination from poor infrastructure and wasteful irrigation practices
Environment - international agreements:
party to: Air Pollution, Biodiversity, Climate Change, Desertification, Endangered Species, Hazardous Wastes, Ozone Layer Protection, Ship Pollution
signed, but not ratified: Climate Change-Kyoto Protocol

People

Population: 15,143,704 (July 2004 est.)
Age structure:
0-14 years: 24.4% (male 1,884,369; female 1,807,585)
15-64 years: 68% (male 5,028,455; female 5,268,726)
65 years and over: 7.6% (male 404,940; female 749,629) (2004 est.)
Median age:
total: 28.3 years
male: 26.6 years
female: 30 years (2004 est.)
Population growth rate: 0.26% (2004 est.)
Birth rate: 15.52 births/1,000 population (2004 est.)
Death rate: 9.59 deaths/1,000 population (2004 est.)
Net migration rate: -3.35 migrant(s)/1,000 population (2004 est.)
Sex ratio:
at birth: 1.06 male(s)/female
under 15 years: 1.04 male(s)/female
15-64 years: 0.95 male(s)/female
65 years and over: 0.54 male(s)/female
total population: 0.94 male(s)/female (2004 est.)
Infant mortality rate:
total: 30.54 deaths/1,000 live births
male: 35.24 deaths/1,000 live births
female: 25.57 deaths/1,000 live births (2004 est.)
Life expectancy at birth:
total population: 66.07 years
male: 60.72 years
female: 71.73 years (2004 est.)
Total fertility rate: 1.9 children born/woman (2004 est.)
HIV/AIDS - adult prevalence rate: 0.1% (2001 est.)
HIV/AIDS - people living with HIV/AIDS: 6,000 (2001 est.)
HIV/AIDS - deaths: less than 300 (2001 est.)
Nationality:
noun: Kazakhstani(s)
adjective: Kazakhstani
Ethnic groups: Kazakh (Qazaq) 53.4%, Russian 30%, Ukrainian 3.7%, Uzbek 2.5%, German 2.4%, Uighur 1.4%, other 6.6% (1999 census)
Religions: Muslim 47%, Russian Orthodox 44%, Protestant 2%, other 7%
Languages: Kazakh (Qazaq, state language) 64.4%, Russian (official, used in everyday business, designated the "language of interethnic communication") 95% (2001 est.)
Literacy:
definition: age 15 and over can read and write
total population: 98.4%
male: 99.1%
female: 97.7% (1999 est.)

Kazakhstan (continued)

Government

Country name:
conventional long form: Republic of Kazakhstan
conventional short form: Kazakhstan
local long form: Qazaqstan Respublikasy
local short form: none
former: Kazakh Soviet Socialist Republic
Government type: republic
Capital: Astana; note - the government moved from Almaty to Astana in December 1998
Administrative divisions: 14 provinces (oblystar, singular - oblys) and 3 cities* (qala, singular - qalasy); Almaty Oblysy, Almaty Qalasy*, Aqmola Oblysy (Astana), Aqtobe Oblysy, Astana Qalasy*, Atyrau Oblysy, Batys Qazaqstan Oblysy (Oral), Bayqongyr Qalasy*, Mangghystau Oblysy (Aqtau), Ongtustik Qazaqstan Oblysy (Shymkent), Pavlodar Oblysy, Qaraghandy Oblysy, Qostanay Oblysy, Qyzylorda Oblysy, Shyghys Qazaqstan Oblysy (Oskemen), Soltustik Qazaqstan Oblysy (Petropavlovsk), Zhambyl Oblysy (Taraz)
note: administrative divisions have the same names as their administrative centers (exceptions have the administrative center name following in parentheses); in 1995 the Governments of Kazakhstan and Russia entered into an agreement whereby Russia would lease for a period of 20 years an area of 6,000 sq km enclosing the Baykonur space launch facilities and the city of Bayqongyr (Baykonyr, formerly Leninsk)
Independence: 16 December 1991 (from the Soviet Union)
National holiday: Republic Day, 25 October (1990)
Constitution: adopted by national referendum 30 August 1995; first post-independence constitution was adopted 28 January 1993
Legal system: based on civil law system
Suffrage: 18 years of age; universal
Executive branch:
chief of state: President Nursultan A. NAZARBAYEV (chairman of the Supreme Soviet from 22 February 1990, elected president 1 December 1991)
head of government: Prime Minister Daniyal AKHMETOV (since 13 June 2003), First Deputy Prime Minister Grigoriy MARCHENKO (since 6 January 2004)
cabinet: Council of Ministers appointed by the president
elections: president elected by popular vote for a seven-year term; election last held 10 January 1999, a year before it was previously scheduled (next to be held NA 2006); note - President NAZARBAYEV's previous term was extended to 2000 by a nationwide referendum held 30 April 1995; prime minister and first deputy prime minister appointed by the president
election results: Nursultan A. NAZARBAYEV reelected president; percent of vote - Nursultan A. NAZARBAYEV 81.7%, Serikbolsyn ABDILDIN 12.1%, Gani KASYMOV 4.7%, Engels GABBASSOV 1.5%
note: President NAZARBAYEV expanded his presidential powers by decree: only he can initiate constitutional amendments, appoint and dismiss the government, dissolve Parliament, call referenda at his discretion, and appoint administrative heads of regions and cities
Legislative branch: bicameral Parliament consists of the Senate (39 seats; 7 senators are appointed by the president; other members are popularly elected, two from each of the 14 oblasts, the capital of Astana, and the city of Almaty, to serve six-year terms; note - formerly composed of 47 seats) and the Majilis (77 seats; 10 out of the 77 Majilis members are elected from the winning party's lists; members are popularly elected to serve five-year terms)
elections: Senate - (indirect) last held 17 September 1999 (next to be held NA December 2005); Majilis - last held 10 and 24 October and 26 December 1999 (next to be held NA October 2004)
election results: Senate - percent of vote by party - NA%; seats by party - NA; candidates nominated by local councils; Majilis - percent of vote by party - Otan 30.9%, Communist Party 17.8%, Agrarian Party 12.6%, Civic Party 11.2%; seats by party - Otan 23, Civic Party 13, Communist Party 3, Agrarian Party 3, People's Cooperative Party 1, independents 34; note - most independent candidates are affiliated with parastatal enterprises and other pro-government institutions
Judicial branch: Supreme Court (44 members); Constitutional Council (7 members)
Political parties and leaders: Agrarian Party [Romin MADINOV]; Ak Zhol Party "White Road" [Bulat ABILOV, Uraz ZHANDOSOV, Zhanat YERTLESOVA, Alikhan BAYMENOV, Altynbek SARSENBAYEV, co-chairs]; ASAR "All Together" [Dariga NAZARBAYEVA, chairwoman]; AUL "Village" [leader NA]; Civic Party [Azat PERUASHEV, first secretary]; Communist Party or KPK [Serikbolsyn ABDILDIN, first secretary]; Otan "Fatherland" [Gani YESIMOV, chairman]; Patriots' Party [Gani KASYMOV]
note: only eight parties in Kazakhstan have been registered under the new political party law passed in July 2002
Political pressure groups and leaders: Adil-Soz [Tamara KALEYEVA]; Alash [Sabet-Kazy AKATAY]; AZAMAT "Citizen" Movement [Petr SVOIK, Murat AUEZOV, and Galym ABILSEITOV, cochairmen]; Democratic Choice of Kazakhstan [Galymzhan ZHAKIYANOV, Nurzhan SUBKHANBERDIN, cochairmen]; Labor and Worker's Movement [Madel ISMAILOV, chairman]; Kazakhstan International Bureau on Human Rights [Yevgeniy ZHOVTIS, executive director]; Orleu "Development" Movement [Seidakhmet KUTTYKADAM]; Pensioners Movement or Pokoleniye [Irina SAVOSTINA, chairwoman]; People's Congress of Kazakhstan of NKK [Olzhas SULEIMENOV, chairman]; People's Cooperative Party of Kazakhstan [Umirzak SARSENOV]; Republican People's Party of Kazakhstan or RNPK [Akezhan KAZHEGELDIN]; Socialist Party [Petr SVOIK]
International organization participation: AsDB, CIS, EAPC, EBRD, ECO, FAO, IAEA, IBRD, ICAO, IDA, IDB, IFAD, IFC, IFRCS, ILO, IMF, IMO, Interpol, IOC, IOM, ISO, ITU, NAM (observer), NSG, OAS (observer), OIC, OPCW, OSCE, PFP, SCO, UN, UNCTAD, UNESCO, UNIDO, UPU, WCL, WCO, WFTU, WHO, WIPO, WMO, WToO, WTrO (observer)
Diplomatic representation in the US:
chief of mission: Ambassador Kanat B. SAUDABAYEV
chancery: 1401 16th Street NW, Washington, DC 20036
telephone: [1] (202) 232-5488
FAX: [1] (202) 232-5845
consulate(s): New York
Diplomatic representation from the US:
chief of mission: Ambassador Larry C. NAPPER
embassy: 99/97A Furmanova Street, Almaty, Republic of Kazakhstan 480091
mailing address: use embassy street address
telephone: [7] (3272) 63-39-21, 63-13-75, 50-76-23, 50-76-27 (emergency number)
FAX: [7] (3272) 63-38-83
Flag description: sky blue background representing the endless sky and a gold sun with 32 rays soaring above a golden steppe eagle in the center; on the hoist side is a "national ornamentation" in gold

Economy

Economy - overview: Kazakhstan, the largest of the former Soviet republics in territory, excluding Russia, possesses enormous fossil fuel reserves as well as plentiful supplies of other minerals and metals. It also is a large agricultural - livestock and grain - producer. Kazakhstan's industrial sector rests on the extraction and processing of these natural resources and also on a growing machine-building sector specializing in construction equipment, tractors, agricultural machinery, and some defense items. The breakup of the USSR in December 1991 and the collapse in demand for Kazakhstan's traditional heavy industry products resulted in a short-term contraction of the economy, with the steepest annual decline occurring in 1994. In 1995-97, the pace of the government program of economic reform and privatization quickened, resulting in a substantial shifting of assets into the private sector. Kazakhstan enjoyed double-digit growth in 2000-01 - and a solid 9.5% in 2002 - thanks largely to its booming energy sector, but also to economic reform, good harvests, and foreign investment. The opening of the Caspian Consortium pipeline in 2001, from western Kazakhstan's Tengiz oilfield to the Black Sea, substantially raised export capacity. The country has embarked upon an industrial policy designed to diversify the economy away from overdependence on the oil sector, by developing light industry. Additionally, the policy aims to reduce the influence of foreign investment and foreign personnel; the government has engaged in several disputes with foreign oil companies over the terms of production agreements, and tensions continue.
GDP: purchasing power parity - $105.3 billion (2003 est.)

GDP - real growth rate: 9% (2003 est.)
GDP - per capita: purchasing power parity - $7,000 (2003 est.)
GDP - composition by sector:
agriculture: 7.9%
industry: 35.4%
services: 56.7% (2002 est.)
Population below poverty line: 26% (2001 est.)
Household income or consumption by percentage share:
lowest 10%: 2.8%
highest 10%: 27.3% (2001)
Distribution of family income - Gini index: 35.4 (1996)
Inflation rate (consumer prices): 6.2% (2003 est.)
Labor force: 8.4 million (1999)
Labor force - by occupation: industry 30%, agriculture 20%, services 50% (2002 est.)
Unemployment rate: 8.6% (2003 est.)
Budget:
revenues: $4.2 billion
expenditures: $5.1 billion, including capital expenditures of $NA (2001 est.)
Industries: oil, coal, iron ore, manganese, chromite, lead, zinc, copper, titanium, bauxite, gold, silver, phosphates, sulfur, iron and steel; tractors and other agricultural machinery, electric motors, construction materials
Industrial production growth rate: 11.6% (2003 est.)
Electricity - production: 52.43 billion kWh (2001)
Electricity - production by source:
fossil fuel: 84.3%
hydro: 15.7%
nuclear: 0%
other: 0% (2001)
Electricity - consumption: 48.36 billion kWh (2001)
Electricity - exports: 3.6 billion kWh (2001)
Electricity - imports: 3.2 billion kWh (2001)
Oil - production: 798,200 bbl/day (2001 est.)
Oil - consumption: 195,000 bbl/day (2001 est.)
Oil - exports: NA
Oil - imports: NA
Oil - proved reserves: 2.709 billion bbl (1 January 2002)
Natural gas - production: 10.08 billion cu m (2001 est.)
Natural gas - consumption: 14.3 billion cu m (2001 est.)
Natural gas - exports: 4.1 billion cu m (2001 est.)
Natural gas - imports: 8.3 billion cu m (2001 est.)
Natural gas - proved reserves: 920.3 billion cu m (1 January 2002)
Agriculture - products: grain (mostly spring wheat), cotton; livestock
Exports: $12.72 billion f.o.b. (2003 est.)
Exports - commodities: oil and oil products 58%, ferrous metals 24%, chemicals 5%, machinery 3%, grain, wool, meat, coal (2001)
Exports - partners: Bermuda 20.8%, Russia 15.5%, China 10.6%, Italy 9.3%, Switzerland 8.2%, UAE 4.9% (2002)

Imports: $8.621 billion f.o.b. (2003 est.)
Imports - commodities: machinery and equipment 41%, metal products 28%, foodstuffs 8% (2001)
Imports - partners: Russia 38.7%, Germany 8.9%, US 7%, China 4.8% (2002)
Debt - external: $22 billion (2003 est.)
Economic aid - recipient: $610 million in US assistance programs, 1992-2000 (2000)
Currency: tenge (KZT)
Currency code: KZT
Exchange rates: tenge per US dollar - 149.576 (2003), 153.279 (2002), 146.736 (2001), 142.133 (2000), 119.523 (1999)
Fiscal year: calendar year

Communications

Telephones - main lines in use: 2,081,900 (2002)
Telephones - mobile cellular: 1.027 million (2002)
Telephone system:
general assessment: service is poor; equipment antiquated
domestic: intercity by landline and microwave radio relay; mobile cellular systems are available in most of Kazakhstan
international: country code - 7; international traffic with other former Soviet republics and China carried by landline and microwave radio relay and with other countries by satellite and by the Trans-Asia-Europe (TAE) fiber-optic cable; satellite earth stations - 2 Intelsat
Radio broadcast stations: AM 60, FM 17, shortwave 9 (1998)
Television broadcast stations: 12 (plus nine repeaters) (1998)
Internet country code: .kz
Internet hosts: 16,562 (2002)
Internet users: 250,000 (2002)

Transportation

Railways:
total: 13,601 km
broad gauge: 13,601 km 1.520-m gauge (3,661 km electrified) (2002)
Highways:
total: 81,331 km
paved: 77,020 km
unpaved: 4,311 km (2000)
Waterways: 3,900 km
note: on the Syr Darya (Syrdariya) and Ertis (Irtysh) rivers
Pipelines: condensate 640 km; gas 10,527 km; oil 9,771 km; refined products 1,187 km; water 1,465 km (2003)
Ports and harbors: Aqtau (Shevchenko), Atyrau (Gur'yev), Oskemen (Ust-Kamenogorsk), Pavlodar, Semey (Semipalatinsk)
Merchant marine:
total: 1 ships (1,000 GRT or over) 1,064 GRT/646 DWT
by type: roll on/roll off 1
foreign-owned: 26 Netherlands 1 (2003 est.)

Airports: 392 (2003 est.)
Airports - with paved runways:
total: 64
over 3,047 m: 9
2,438 to 3,047 m: 26
1,524 to 2,437 m: 16
914 to 1,523 m: 3
under 914 m: 10 (2003 est.)
Airports - with unpaved runways:
total: 328
over 3,047 m: 7
2,438 to 3,047 m: 11
1,524 to 2,437 m: 22
914 to 1,523 m: 71
under 914 m: 217 (2003 est.)
Heliports: 1 (2003 est.)

Military

Military branches: Ground Forces, Air and Air Defense Forces, Naval Force, Republican Guard
Military manpower - military age: 18 years of age (2004 est.)
Military manpower - availability:
males age 15-49: 4,233,623 (2004 est.)
Military manpower - fit for military service:
males age 15-49: 3,381,606 (2004 est.)
Military manpower - reaching military age annually:
males: 169,004 (2004 est.)
Military expenditures - dollar figure: $221.8 million (Ministry of Defense expenditures) (FY02)
Military expenditures - percent of GDP: 0.9% (Ministry of Defense expenditures) (FY02)

Transnational Issues

Disputes - international: Kazakhstan and China have resolved their border dispute and are working to demarcate their borders to control population migration, illegal activities, and trade; delimitation of boundary with Russia is almost complete - delimitations with Turkmenistan and Uzbekistan are complete with demarcations underway - delimitation with Kyrgyzstan is largely complete; creation of a seabed boundary with Turkmenistan in the Caspian Sea is under discussion; equidistant seabed treaties have been signed with Azerbaijan and Russia in the Caspian Sea, but no resolution has been made on dividing the water column among any of the littoral states
Illicit drugs: significant illicit cultivation of cannabis for CIS markets, as well as limited cultivation of opium poppy and ephedra (for the drug ephedrine); limited government eradication of illicit crops; transit point for Southwest Asian narcotics bound for Russia and the rest of Europe

Kenya

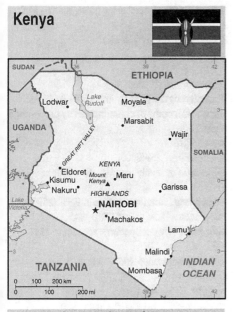

Introduction

Background: Founding president and liberation struggle icon Jomo KENYATTA led Kenya from independence until his death in 1978, when President Daniel Toroitich arap MOI took power in a constitutional succession. The country was a de facto one-party state from 1969 until 1982 when the ruling Kenya African National Union (KANU) made itself the sole legal party in Kenya. MOI acceded to internal and external pressure for political liberalization in late 1991. The ethnically fractured opposition failed to dislodge KANU from power in elections in 1992 and 1997, which were marred by violence and fraud, but are viewed as having generally reflected the will of the Kenyan people. President MOI stepped down in December of 2002 following fair and peaceful elections. Mwai KIBAKI, running as the candidate of the multiethnic, united opposition group, the National Rainbow Coalition, defeated KANU candidate Uhuru KENYATTA and assumed the presidency following a campaign centered on an anticorruption platform.

Geography

Location: Eastern Africa, bordering the Indian Ocean, between Somalia and Tanzania
Geographic coordinates: 1 00 N, 38 00 E
Map references: Africa
Area:
total: 582,650 sq km
land: 569,250 sq km
water: 13,400 sq km
Area - comparative: slightly more than twice the size of Nevada
Land boundaries:
total: 3,477 km
border countries: Ethiopia 861 km, Somalia 682 km, Sudan 232 km, Tanzania 769 km, Uganda 933 km
Coastline: 536 km

Maritime claims:
territorial sea: 12 NM
exclusive economic zone: 200 NM
continental shelf: 200-m depth or to the depth of exploitation
Climate: varies from tropical along coast to arid in interior
Terrain: low plains rise to central highlands bisected by Great Rift Valley; fertile plateau in west
Elevation extremes:
lowest point: Indian Ocean 0 m
highest point: Mount Kenya 5,199 m
Natural resources: gold, limestone, soda ash, salt, rubies, fluorspar, garnets, wildlife, hydropower
Land use:
arable land: 7.03%
permanent crops: 0.91%
other: 92.06% (1998 est.)
Irrigated land: 670 sq km (1998 est.)
Natural hazards: recurring drought; flooding during rainy seasons
Environment - current issues: water pollution from urban and industrial wastes; degradation of water quality from increased use of pesticides and fertilizers; water hyacinth infestation in Lake Victoria; deforestation; soil erosion; desertification; poaching
Environment - international agreements:
party to: Biodiversity, Climate Change, Desertification, Endangered Species, Hazardous Wastes, Law of the Sea, Marine Dumping, Marine Life Conservation, Ozone Layer Protection, Ship Pollution, Wetlands, Whaling
signed, but not ratified: none of the selected agreements
Geography - note: the Kenyan Highlands comprise one of the most successful agricultural production regions in Africa; glaciers are found on Mount Kenya, Africa's second highest peak; unique physiography supports abundant and varied wildlife of scientific and economic value

People

Population: 32,021,856
note: estimates for this country explicitly take into account the effects of excess mortality due to AIDS; this can result in lower life expectancy, higher infant mortality and death rates, lower population and growth rates, and changes in the distribution of population by age and sex than would otherwise be expected (July 2004 est.)
Age structure:
0-14 years: 40.6% (male 6,575,409; female 6,430,218)
15-64 years: 56.5% (male 9,126,847; female 8,962,905)
65 years and over: 2.9% (male 399,050; female 527,427) (2004 est.)
Median age:
total: 18.6 years
male: 18.5 years
female: 18.7 years (2004 est.)

Population growth rate: 1.14% (2004 est.)
Birth rate: 27.82 births/1,000 population (2004 est.)
Death rate: 16.31 deaths/1,000 population (2004 est.)
Net migration rate: -0.1 migrant(s)/1,000 population
note: according to UNHCR, by the end of 2001 Kenya was host to 220,000 refugees from neighboring countries, including: Somalia 145,000 and Sudan 68,000 (2004 est.)
Sex ratio:
at birth: 1.03 male(s)/female
under 15 years: 1.02 male(s)/female
15-64 years: 1.02 male(s)/female
65 years and over: 0.76 male(s)/female
total population: 1.01 male(s)/female (2004 est.)
Infant mortality rate:
total: 62.62 deaths/1,000 live births
male: 65.55 deaths/1,000 live births
female: 59.6 deaths/1,000 live births (2004 est.)
Life expectancy at birth:
total population: 44.94 years
male: 44.79 years
female: 45.1 years (2004 est.)
Total fertility rate: 3.31 children born/woman (2004 est.)
HIV/AIDS - adult prevalence rate: 15% (2001 est.)
HIV/AIDS - people living with HIV/AIDS: 2.5 million (2001 est.)
HIV/AIDS - deaths: 190,000 (2001 est.)
Nationality:
noun: Kenyan(s)
adjective: Kenyan
Ethnic groups: Kikuyu 22%, Luhya 14%, Luo 13%, Kalenjin 12%, Kamba 11%, Kisii 6%, Meru 6%, other African 15%, non-African (Asian, European, and Arab) 1%
Religions: Protestant 45%, Roman Catholic 33%, indigenous beliefs 10%, Muslim 10%, other 2%
note: a large majority of Kenyans are Christian, but estimates for the percentage of the population that adheres to Islam or indigenous beliefs vary widely
Languages: English (official), Kiswahili (official), numerous indigenous languages
Literacy:
definition: age 15 and over can read and write
total population: 85.1%
male: 90.6%
female: 79.7% (2003 est.)

Government

Country name:
conventional long form: Republic of Kenya
conventional short form: Kenya
former: British East Africa
Government type: republic
Capital: Nairobi
Administrative divisions: 7 provinces and 1 area*; Central, Coast, Eastern, Nairobi Area*, North Eastern, Nyanza, Rift Valley, Western
Independence: 12 December 1963 (from UK)
National holiday: Independence Day, 12 December (1963)

Kenya (continued)

Constitution: 12 December 1963, amended as a republic 1964; reissued with amendments 1979, 1983, 1986, 1988, 1991, 1992, 1997, and 2001

Legal system: based on Kenyan statutory law, Kenyan and English common law, tribal law, and Islamic law; judicial review in High Court; accepts compulsory ICJ jurisdiction, with reservations; constitutional amendment of 1982 making Kenya a de jure one-party state repealed in 1991

Suffrage: 18 years of age; universal

Executive branch:

chief of state: President Mwai KIBAKI (since 30 December 2002) and Vice President Moody AWORI (since 25 September 2003); note - the president is both the chief of state and head of government

head of government: President Mwai KIBAKI (since 30 December 2002) and Vice President Moody AWORI (since 25 September 2003); note - the president is both the chief of state and head of government

cabinet: Cabinet appointed by the president

elections: president elected by popular vote for a five-year term; in addition to receiving the largest number of votes in absolute terms, the presidential candidate must also win 25% or more of the vote in at least five of Kenya's seven provinces and one area to avoid a runoff; election last held 27 December 2002 (next to be held NA December 2007); vice president appointed by the president

election results: President Mwai KIBAKI elected; percent of vote - Mwai KIBAKI 63%, Uhuru KENYATTA 30%

Legislative branch: unicameral National Assembly or Bunge (224 seats; 210 members elected by popular vote to serve five-year terms, 12 so-called "nominated" members who are appointed by the president but selected by the parties in proportion to their parliamentary vote totals, 2 ex-officio members)

elections: last held 27 December 2002 (next to be held by early 2007)

election results: percent of vote by party - NA%; seats by party - NARC 125, KANU 64, FORD-P 14, other 7; ex-officio 2; seats appointed by the president - NARC 7, KANU 4, FORD-P 1

Judicial branch: Court of Appeal (chief justice is appointed by the president); High Court

Political parties and leaders: Forum for the Restoration of Democracy-People or FORD-People [Kimaniwa NYOIKE, chairman]; Kenya African National Union or KANU [Uhuru KENYATTA]; National Rainbow Coalition or NARC [Mwai KIBAKI] - the governing party

Political pressure groups and leaders: human rights groups; labor unions; Muslim organizations; National Convention Executive Council or NCEC, a proreform coalition of political parties and nongovernment organizations [Kivutha KIBWANA]; Protestant National Council of Churches of Kenya or NCCK [Mutava MUSYIMI]; Roman Catholic and other Christian churches; Supreme Council of Kenya Muslims or SUPKEM [Shaykh Abdul Gafur al-BUSAIDY]

International organization participation: ACP, AfDB, AU, C, EADB, FAO, G-15, G-77, IAEA, IBRD, ICAO, ICCt (signatory), ICFTU, ICRM, IDA, IFAD, IFC, IFRCS, IGAD, ILO, IMF, IMO, Interpol, IOC, IOM, ISO, ITU, MINURSO, MONUC, NAM, OPCW, UN, UNAMSIL, UNCTAD, UNESCO, UNHCR, UNIDO, UNMEE, UNMIK, UNMIL, UNMISET, UPU, WCO, WHO, WIPO, WMO, WToO, WTrO

Diplomatic representation in the US:

chief of mission: Ambassador Yusuf Abdulraham NZIBO

chancery: 2249 R Street NW, Washington, DC 20008

telephone: [1] (202) 387-6101

FAX: [1] (202) 462-3829

consulate(s) general: offices in Los Angeles and New York are closed; mission to the UN remains open

Diplomatic representation from the US:

chief of mission: Ambassador Johnnie CARSON

embassy: US Embassy, United Nations Ave., Gigiti; P. O. Box 606 Village Market Nairobi

mailing address: Box 21A, Unit 64100, APO AE 09831

telephone: [254] (2) 537-800

FAX: [254] (2) 537-810

Flag description: three equal horizontal bands of black (top), red, and green; the red band is edged in white; a large warrior's shield covering crossed spears is superimposed at the center

Economy

Economy - overview: The regional hub for trade and finance in East Africa, Kenya has been hampered by corruption, notably in the judicial system, and by reliance upon several primary goods whose prices have remained low. In 1997, the IMF suspended Kenya's Enhanced Structural Adjustment Program due to the government's failure to maintain reforms and curb corruption. A severe drought from 1999 to 2000 compounded Kenya's problems, causing water and energy rationing and reducing agricultural output. As a result, GDP contracted by 0.2% in 2000. The IMF, which had resumed loans in 2000 to help Kenya through the drought, again halted lending in 2001 when the government failed to institute several anticorruption measures. Despite the return of strong rains in 2001, weak commodity prices, endemic corruption, and low investment limited Kenya's economic growth to 1.2%. Growth lagged at 1.1% in 2002 because of erratic rains, low investor confidence, meager donor support, and political infighting up to the elections. In the key 27 December 2002 elections, Daniel Arap MOI's 24-year-old reign ended, and a new opposition government took on the formidable economic problems facing the nation. In 2003, progress was made in rooting out corruption, and encouraging donor support, with GDP growth edging up to 1.7%.

GDP: purchasing power parity - $33.09 billion (2003 est.)

GDP - real growth rate: 1.7% (2003 est.)

GDP - per capita: purchasing power parity - $1,000 (2003 est.)

GDP - composition by sector:

agriculture: 19.1%

industry: 18.3%

services: 62.6% (2002 est.)

Population below poverty line: 50% (2000 est.)

Household income or consumption by percentage share:

lowest 10%: 2%

highest 10%: 37.2% (2000)

Distribution of family income - Gini index: 44.9 (1997)

Inflation rate (consumer prices): 9.6% (2003 est.)

Labor force: 12.95 million (2001 est.)

Labor force - by occupation: agriculture 75% (2003 est.)

Unemployment rate: 40% (2001 est.)

Budget:

revenues: $2.91 billion

expenditures: $2.97 billion, including capital expenditures of $NA (2000 est.)

Industries: small-scale consumer goods (plastic, furniture, batteries, textiles, soap, cigarettes, flour), agricultural products processing; oil refining, cement; tourism

Industrial production growth rate: 1.8% (2003 est.)

Electricity - production: 4.033 billion kWh (2001)

Electricity - production by source:

fossil fuel: 17.7%

hydro: 71%

nuclear: 0%

other: 11.3% (2001)

Electricity - consumption: 3.981 billion kWh (2001)

Electricity - exports: 0 kWh (2001)

Electricity - imports: 230 million kWh (2001)

Oil - production: 0 bbl/day (2001 est.)

Oil - consumption: 57,000 bbl/day (2001 est.)

Oil - exports: NA

Oil - imports: NA

Agriculture - products: tea, coffee, corn, wheat, sugarcane, fruit, vegetables; dairy products, beef, pork, poultry, eggs

Exports: $2.514 billion f.o.b. (2003 est.)

Exports - commodities: tea, horticultural products, coffee, petroleum products, fish, cement

Exports - partners: Uganda 18.4%, UK 13%, US 8.1%, Netherlands 7.6%, Pakistan 5%, Egypt 4.1% (2002)

Imports: $3.705 billion f.o.b. (2003 est.)

Imports - commodities: machinery and transportation equipment, petroleum products, motor vehicles, iron and steel, resins and plastics

Imports - partners: UAE 12%, Saudi Arabia 8.7%, South Africa 8.1%, US 8.1%, UK 7.1%, France 5.8%, China 5.5%, Japan 5%, India 4.8% (2002)

Debt - external: $5.9 billion (2003 est.)

Economic aid - recipient: $453 million (1997)

Currency: Kenyan shilling (KES)

Currency code: KES

Kenya *(continued)*

Exchange rates: Kenyan shillings per US dollar - 75.9356 (2003), 78.7491 (2002), 78.5632 (2001), 76.1755 (2000), 70.3262 (1999)
Fiscal year: 1 July - 30 June

Communications

Telephones - main lines in use: 328,100 (2002)
Telephones - mobile cellular: 1,325,200 (2002)
Telephone system:
general assessment: unreliable; little attempt to modernize except for service to business
domestic: trunks are primarily microwave radio relay; business data commonly transferred by a very small aperture terminal (VSAT) system
international: country code - 254; satellite earth stations - 4 Intelsat
Radio broadcast stations: AM 24, FM 18, shortwave 6 (2001)
Television broadcast stations: 8 (2002)
Internet country code: .ke
Internet hosts: 2,963 (2002)
Internet users: 400,000 (2002)

Transportation

Railways:
total: 2,778 km
narrow gauge: 2,778 km 1.000-m gauge (2002)
Highways:
total: 63,942 km
paved: 7,737 km
unpaved: 56,205 km (2000)
Waterways: NA
note: part of the Lake Victoria system is within the boundaries of Kenya
Pipelines: refined products 752 km (2003)
Ports and harbors: Kisumu, Lamu, Mombasa
Merchant marine:
total: 3 ships (1,000 GRT or over) 6,049 GRT/7,082 DWT
by type: petroleum tanker 1, roll on/roll off 2
registered in other countries: 9 (2003 est.)
Airports: 221 (2003 est.)
Airports - with paved runways:
total: 15
over 3,047 m: 4
2,438 to 3,047 m: 1
1,524 to 2,437 m: 3
914 to 1,523 m: 6
under 914 m: 1 (2003 est.)
Airports - with unpaved runways:
total: 206
1,524 to 2,437 m: 12
914 to 1,523 m: 110
under 914 m: 84 (2003 est.)

Military

Military branches: Army, Navy, Air Force
Military manpower - availability:
males age 15-49: 8,313,051 (2004 est.)
Military manpower - fit for military service:
males age 15-49: 5,150,405 (2004 est.)

Military expenditures - dollar figure: $231 million (2003)
Military expenditures - percent of GDP: 1.8% (2003)

Transnational Issues

Disputes - international: Kenya's administrative boundary still extends into the Sudan, creating the "Ilemi triangle"; Kenya has acted as an important mediator in Sudan's north-south civil war; Kenya and Uganda are working together to stem cattle rustling and violence by Lord's Resistance Army along the border
Illicit drugs: widespread harvesting of small plots of marijuana; transit country for South Asian heroin destined for Europe and North America; Indian methaqualone also transits on way to South Africa; significant potential for money-laundering activity given the country's status as a regional financial center, massive corruption, and relatively high levels of narcotics-associated activities

Kingman Reef
(territory of the US)

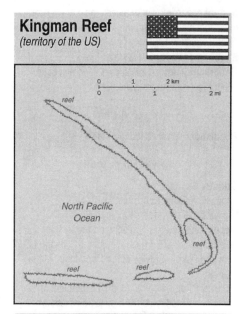

Introduction

Background: The US annexed the reef in 1922. Its sheltered lagoon served as a way station for flying boats on Hawaii-to-American Samoa flights during the late 1930s. There are no terrestrial plants on the reef, which is frequently awash, but it does support abundant and diverse marine fauna and flora. In 2001, the waters surrounding the reef out to 12 NM around the reef were designated a US National Wildlife Refuge.

Geography

Location: Oceania, reef in the North Pacific Ocean, about half way between Hawaii and American Samoa
Geographic coordinates: 6 24 N, 162 24 W
Map references: Oceania
Area:
total: 1 sq km
land: 1 sq km
water: 0 sq km
Area - comparative: about 1.7 times the size of The Mall in Washington, DC
Land boundaries: 0 km
Coastline: 3 km
Maritime claims:
territorial sea: 12 NM
exclusive economic zone: 200 NM
Climate: tropical; moderated by prevailing winds
Terrain: low and nearly level
Elevation extremes:
lowest point: Pacific Ocean 0 m
highest point: unnamed location 1 m
Natural resources: terrestrial and aquatic wildlife
Land use:
arable land: 0%
permanent crops: 0%
other: 100% (1998 est.)
Irrigated land: 0 sq km (1998 est.)

Kingman Reef (continued)

Natural hazards: wet or awash most of the time, maximum elevation of about 1 meter makes Kingman Reef a maritime hazard
Environment - current issues: none
Geography - note: barren coral atoll with deep interior lagoon; closed to the public

People

Population: uninhabited (July 2004 est.)

Government

Country name:
conventional long form: none
conventional short form: Kingman Reef
Dependency status: unincorporated territory of the US; administered from Washington, DC, by the US Fish and Wildlife Service of the Department of the Interior
note: on 1 September 2000, the Department of the Interior accepted restoration of its administrative jurisdiction over Kingman Reef from the Department of the Navy; Executive Order 3223 signed 18 January 2001 established Kingman Reef National Wildlife Refuge to be administered by the Director, US Fish and Wildlife Service; this refuge is managed to protect the terrestrial and aquatic wildlife of Kingman Reef out to the 12-nautical-mile territorial sea limit
Legal system: the laws of the US, where applicable, apply
Flag description: the flag of the US is used

Economy

Economy - overview: no economic activity

Transportation

Waterways: none
Ports and harbors: none; offshore anchorage only
Airports: lagoon was used as a halfway station between Hawaii and American Samoa by Pan American Airways for flying boats in 1937 and 1938 (2003 est.)

Military

Military - note: defense is the responsibility of the US

Transnational Issues

Disputes - international: none

Kiribati

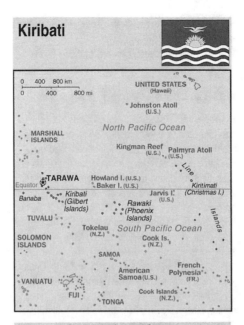

Introduction

Background: The Gilbert Islands were granted self-rule by the UK in 1971 and complete independence in 1979 under the new name of Kiribati. The US relinquished all claims to the sparsely inhabited Phoenix and Line Island groups in a 1979 treaty of friendship with Kiribati.

Geography

Location: Oceania, group of 33 coral atolls in the Pacific Ocean, straddling the equator; the capital Tarawa is about one-half of the way from Hawaii to Australia; note - on 1 January 1995, Kiribati proclaimed that all of its territory lies in the same time zone as its Gilbert Islands group (GMT +12) even though the Phoenix Islands and the Line Islands under its jurisdiction lie on the other side of the International Date Line
Geographic coordinates: 1 25 N, 173 00 E
Map references: Oceania
Area:
total: 811 sq km
land: 811 sq km
water: 0 sq km
note: includes three island groups - Gilbert Islands, Line Islands, Phoenix Islands
Area - comparative: four times the size of Washington, DC
Land boundaries: 0 km
Coastline: 1,143 km
Maritime claims:
territorial sea: 12 NM
exclusive economic zone: 200 NM
Climate: tropical; marine, hot and humid, moderated by trade winds
Terrain: mostly low-lying coral atolls surrounded by extensive reefs
Elevation extremes:
lowest point: Pacific Ocean 0 m
highest point: unnamed location on Banaba 81 m

Natural resources: phosphate (production discontinued in 1979)
Land use:
arable land: 0%
permanent crops: 50.68%
other: 49.32% (1998 est.)
Irrigated land: NA sq km
Natural hazards: typhoons can occur any time, but usually November to March; occasional tornadoes; low level of some of the islands make them very sensitive to changes in sea level
Environment - current issues: heavy pollution in lagoon of south Tarawa atoll due to heavy migration mixed with traditional practices such as lagoon latrines and open-pit dumping; ground water at risk
Environment - international agreements:
party to: Biodiversity, Climate Change, Climate Change-Kyoto Protocol, Desertification, Hazardous Wastes, Law of the Sea, Marine Dumping, Ozone Layer Protection
signed, but not ratified: none of the selected agreements
Geography - note: 21 of the 33 islands are inhabited; Banaba (Ocean Island) in Kiribati is one of the three great phosphate rock islands in the Pacific Ocean - the others are Makatea in French Polynesia, and Nauru

People

Population: 100,798 (July 2004 est.)
Age structure:
0-14 years: 39.3% (male 20,087; female 19,566)
15-64 years: 57.3% (male 28,523; female 29,280)
65 years and over: 3.3% (male 1,434; female 1,908) (2004 est.)
Median age:
total: 19.8 years
male: 19.4 years
female: 20.3 years (2004 est.)
Population growth rate: 2.25% (2004 est.)
Birth rate: 30.99 births/1,000 population (2004 est.)
Death rate: 8.49 deaths/1,000 population (2004 est.)
Net migration rate: 0 migrant(s)/1,000 population (2004 est.)
Sex ratio:
at birth: 1.05 male(s)/female
under 15 years: 1.03 male(s)/female
15-64 years: 0.97 male(s)/female
65 years and over: 0.75 male(s)/female
total population: 0.99 male(s)/female (2004 est.)
Infant mortality rate:
total: 49.9 deaths/1,000 live births
male: 55.04 deaths/1,000 live births
female: 44.49 deaths/1,000 live births (2004 est.)
Life expectancy at birth:
total population: 61.32 years
male: 58.34 years
female: 64.44 years (2004 est.)
Total fertility rate: 4.24 children born/woman (2004 est.)

Kiribati (continued)

HIV/AIDS - adult prevalence rate: NA%
HIV/AIDS - people living with HIV/AIDS: NA
HIV/AIDS - deaths: NA
Nationality:
noun: I-Kiribati (singular and plural)
adjective: I-Kiribati
Ethnic groups: predominantly Micronesian with some Polynesian
Religions: Roman Catholic 52%, Protestant (Congregational) 40%, some Seventh-Day Adventist, Muslim, Baha'i, Latter-day Saints, and Church of God (1999)
Languages: I-Kiribati, English (official)
Literacy:
definition: NA
total population: NA%
male: NA%
female: NA%

Government

Country name:
conventional long form: Republic of Kiribati
conventional short form: Kiribati
note: pronounced keer-ree-bahss
former: Gilbert Islands
Government type: republic
Capital: Tarawa
Administrative divisions: 3 units; Gilbert Islands, Line Islands, Phoenix Islands; note - in addition, there are 6 districts (Banaba, Central Gilberts, Line Islands, Northern Gilberts, Southern Gilberts, Tarawa) and 21 island councils - one for each of the inhabited islands (Abaiang, Abemama, Aranuka, Arorae, Banaba, Beru, Butaritari, Kanton, Kiritimati, Kuria, Maiana, Makin, Marakei, Nikunau, Nonouti, Onotoa, Tabiteuea, Tabuaeran, Tamana, Tarawa, Teraina)
Independence: 12 July 1979 (from UK)
National holiday: Independence Day, 12 July (1979)
Constitution: 12 July 1979
Legal system: NA
Suffrage: 18 years of age; universal
Executive branch:
chief of state: President Anote TONG (since 10 July 2003); Vice President Teima ONORIO; note - the president is both the chief of state and head of government
head of government: President Anote TONG (since 10 July 2003); Vice President Teima ONORIO; note - the president is both the chief of state and head of government
cabinet: 12-member Cabinet appointed by the president from among the members of the House of Parliament
elections: the House of Parliament chooses the presidential candidates from among their members and then those candidates compete in a general election; president is elected by popular vote for a four-year term; election last held 4 July 2003 (next to be held not later than July 2007); vice president appointed by the president

election results: Anote TONG 47.4%, Harry TONG 43.5%, Banuera BERINA 9.1%
Legislative branch: unicameral House of Parliament or Maneaba Ni Maungatabu (42 seats; 39 elected by popular vote, one ex officio member - the attorney general, one appointed to represent Banaba, and one other; members serve four-year terms)
elections: first round elections last held 29 November 2002; second round elections held 6 December 2002 (next to be held by November 2006)
election results: percent of vote by party - NA%; seats by party - BTK 17, MTM 16, independents 7, other 2 (includes attorney general)
note: new legislative elections were held in two rounds - the first round on 9 May 2003 and the second round on 14 May 2003
Judicial branch: Court of Appeal; High Court; 26 Magistrates' courts; judges at all levels are appointed by the president
Political parties and leaders: Boutokaan Te Koaua Party or BTK [Taberannang TIMEON]; Maneaban Te Mauri Party or MTM [Teburoro TITO]; Maurin Kiribati Pati or MKP [leader NA]; National Progressive Party or NPP [Dr. Harry TONG]
note: there is no tradition of formally organized political parties in Kiribati; they more closely resemble factions or interest groups because they have no party headquarters, formal platforms, or party structures
Political pressure groups and leaders: NA
International organization participation: ACP, AsDB, C, FAO, IBRD, ICAO, ICFTU, ICRM, IDA, IFC, IFRCS, ILO, IMF, IMO, IOC, ITU, OPCW, PIF, Sparteca, UN, UNESCO, UPU, WHO, WMO
Diplomatic representation in the US: Kiribati does not have an embassy in the US; there is an honorary consulate in Honolulu
Diplomatic representation from the US: the US does not have an embassy in Kiribati; the ambassador to the Marshall Islands is accredited to Kiribati
Flag description: the upper half is red with a yellow frigate bird flying over a yellow rising sun, and the lower half is blue with three horizontal wavy white stripes to represent the ocean

Economy

Economy - overview: A remote country of 33 scattered coral atolls, Kiribati has few natural resources. Commercially viable phosphate deposits were exhausted at the time of independence from the UK in 1979. Copra and fish now represent the bulk of production and exports. The economy has fluctuated widely in recent years. Economic development is constrained by a shortage of skilled workers, weak infrastructure, and remoteness from international markets. Tourism provides more than one-fifth of GDP. The financial sector is at an early stage of development as is the expansion of private sector initiatives. Foreign financial aid from UK, Japan, Australia, New Zealand, and China is a critical supplement to GDP, equal to 25%-50% of GDP in recent years. Remittances from workers abroad account for more than $5 million each year.

GDP: purchasing power parity - $79 million - supplemented by a nearly equal amount from external sources (2001 est.)
GDP - real growth rate: 1.5% (2001 est.)
GDP - per capita: purchasing power parity - $800 (2001 est.)
GDP - composition by sector:
agriculture: 30%
industry: 7%
services: 63% (1998 est.)
Population below poverty line: NA%
Household income or consumption by percentage share:
lowest 10%: NA%
highest 10%: NA%
Inflation rate (consumer prices): 2.5% (2001 est.)
Labor force: 7,870 economically active, not including subsistence farmers (2001 est.)
Unemployment rate: 2%; underemployment 70% (1992 est.)
Budget:
revenues: $28.4 million
expenditures: $37.2 million, including capital expenditures of $NA (2000 est.)
Industries: fishing, handicrafts
Industrial production growth rate: 0.7% (1991 est.)
Electricity - production: 7 million kWh (2001)
Electricity - production by source:
fossil fuel: 100%
hydro: 0%
nuclear: 0%
other: 0% (2001)
Electricity - consumption: 6.51 million kWh (2001)
Electricity - exports: 0 kWh (2001)
Electricity - imports: 0 kWh (2001)
Oil - production: 0 bbl/day (2001 est.)
Oil - consumption: 190 bbl/day (2001 est.)
Oil - exports: NA
Oil - imports: NA
Agriculture - products: copra, taro, breadfruit, sweet potatoes, vegetables; fish
Exports: $35 million f.o.b. (2002)
Exports - commodities: copra 62%, coconuts, seaweed, fish
Exports - partners: Japan 54.3%, South Korea 17.1%, Thailand 17.1% (2002)
Imports: $83 million c.i.f. (2002)
Imports - commodities: foodstuffs, machinery and equipment, miscellaneous manufactured goods, fuel
Imports - partners: France 30.1%, Australia 27.7%, Fiji 13.3%, Japan 9.6%, US 4.8% (2002)
Debt - external: $10 million (1999 est.)
Economic aid - recipient: $15.5 million largely from UK and Japan (2001 est.)
Currency: Australian dollar (AUD)
Currency code: AUD
Exchange rates: Australian dollars per US dollar - 1.5419 (2003), 1.8406 (2002), 1.9334 (2001), 1.7248 (2000), 1.55 (1999)
Fiscal year: NA

Kiribati *(continued)*

Communications

Telephones - main lines in use: 4,500 (2002)
Telephones - mobile cellular: 500 (2002)
Telephone system:
general assessment: NA
domestic: NA
international: satellite earth station - 1 Intelsat (Pacific Ocean)
note: country code - 686; Kiribati is being linked to the Pacific Ocean Cooperative Telecommunications Network, which should improve telephone service
Radio broadcast stations: AM 1, FM 2, shortwave 1
note: the shortwave station may be inactive (2002)
Television broadcast stations: 1 (not reported to be active) (2002)
Internet country code: .ki
Internet users: 2,000 (2002)

Transportation

Railways: 0 km
Highways:
total: 670 km
paved: NA km
unpaved: NA km (1999 est.)
Waterways: 5 km (small network of canals in Line Islands)
Ports and harbors: Banaba, Betio, English Harbour, Kanton
Merchant marine:
total: 1 ships (1,000 GRT or over) 1,291 GRT/1,295 DWT
by type: passenger 1 (2003 est.)
Airports: 20 (2003 est.)
Airports - with paved runways:
total: 3
1,524 to 2,437 m: 3 (2003 est.)
Airports - with unpaved runways:
total: 17
1,524 to 2,437 m: 1
914 to 1,523 m: 12
under 914 m: 4 (2003 est.)

Military

Military branches: no regular military forces; Police Force (carries out law enforcement functions and paramilitary duties; small police posts are on all islands)
Military expenditures - dollar figure: NA
Military expenditures - percent of GDP: NA
Military - note: Kiribati does not have military forces; defense assistance is provided by Australia and NZ

Transnational Issues

Disputes - international: none

Korea, North

Introduction

Background: Following World War II, Korea was split, with the northern half coming under Communist domination and the southern portion becoming Western-oriented. KIM Chong-il has ruled North Korea since his father and the country's founder, president KIM Il-song, died in 1994. After decades of mismanagement, the North relies heavily on international food aid to feed its population while continuing to expend resources to maintain an army of about 1 million. North Korea's long-range missile development and research into nuclear, chemical, and biological weapons and massive conventional armed forces are of major concern to the international community. In December 2002, North Korea repudiated a 1994 agreement that shut down its nuclear reactors and expelled UN monitors, further raising fears it would produce nuclear weapons.

Geography

Location: Eastern Asia, northern half of the Korean Peninsula bordering the Korea Bay and the Sea of Japan, between China and South Korea
Geographic coordinates: 40 00 N, 127 00 E
Map references: Asia
Area:
total: 120,540 sq km
land: 120,410 sq km
water: 130 sq km
Area - comparative: slightly smaller than Mississippi
Land boundaries:
total: 1,673 km
border countries: China 1,416 km, South Korea 238 km, Russia 19 km
Coastline: 2,495 km
Maritime claims:
territorial sea: 12 NM
exclusive economic zone: 200 NM

note: military boundary line 50 NM in the Sea of Japan and the exclusive economic zone limit in the Yellow Sea where all foreign vessels and aircraft without permission are banned
Climate: temperate with rainfall concentrated in summer
Terrain: mostly hills and mountains separated by deep, narrow valleys; coastal plains wide in west, discontinuous in east
Elevation extremes:
lowest point: Sea of Japan 0 m
highest point: Paektu-san 2,744 m
Natural resources: coal, lead, tungsten, zinc, graphite, magnesite, iron ore, copper, gold, pyrites, salt, fluorspar, hydropower
Land use:
arable land: 14.12%
permanent crops: 2.49%
other: 83.39% (1998 est.)
Irrigated land: 14,600 sq km (1998 est.)
Natural hazards: late spring droughts often followed by severe flooding; occasional typhoons during the early fall
Environment - current issues: water pollution; inadequate supplies of potable water; water-borne disease; deforestation; soil erosion and degradation
Environment - international agreements:
party to: Antarctic Treaty, Biodiversity, Climate Change, Environmental Modification, Ozone Layer Protection, Ship Pollution
signed, but not ratified: Law of the Sea
Geography - note: strategic location bordering China, South Korea, and Russia; mountainous interior is isolated and sparsely populated

People

Population: 22,697,553 (July 2004 est.)
Age structure:
0-14 years: 24.6% (male 2,836,991; female 2,755,127)
15-64 years: 67.8% (male 7,575,590; female 7,812,878)
65 years and over: 7.6% (male 583,463; female 1,133,504) (2004 est.)
Median age:
total: 31.4 years
male: 30.2 years
female: 32.6 years (2004 est.)
Population growth rate: 0.98% (2004 est.)
Birth rate: 16.77 births/1,000 population (2004 est.)
Death rate: 6.99 deaths/1,000 population (2004 est.)
Net migration rate: 0 migrant(s)/1,000 population (2004 est.)
Sex ratio:
at birth: 1.05 male(s)/female
under 15 years: 1.03 male(s)/female
15-64 years: 0.97 male(s)/female
65 years and over: 0.52 male(s)/female
total population: 0.94 male(s)/female (2004 est.)
Infant mortality rate:
total: 24.84 deaths/1,000 live births

male: 26.59 deaths/1,000 live births
female: 23 deaths/1,000 live births (2004 est.)
Life expectancy at birth:
total population: 71.08 years
male: 68.38 years
female: 73.92 years (2004 est.)
Total fertility rate: 2.2 children born/woman (2004 est.)
HIV/AIDS - adult prevalence rate: NA
HIV/AIDS - people living with HIV/AIDS: NA
HIV/AIDS - deaths: NA
Nationality:
noun: Korean(s)
adjective: Korean
Ethnic groups: racially homogeneous; there is a small Chinese community and a few ethnic Japanese
Religions: traditionally Buddhist and Confucianist, some Christian and syncretic Chondogyo (Religion of the Heavenly Way)
note: autonomous religious activities now almost nonexistent; government-sponsored religious groups exist to provide illusion of religious freedom
Languages: Korean
Literacy:
definition: age 15 and over can read and write Korean
total population: 99%
male: 99%
female: 99%

Government

Country name:
conventional long form: Democratic People's Republic of Korea
conventional short form: North Korea
local long form: Choson-minjujuui-inmin-konghwaguk
local short form: none
note: the North Koreans generally use the term "Choson" to refer to their country
abbreviation: DPRK
Government type: Communist state one-man dictatorship
Capital: Pyongyang
Administrative divisions: 9 provinces (do, singular and plural) and 4 special cities* (si, singular and plural); Chagang-do (Chagang Province), Hamgyong-bukto (North Hamgyong Province), Hamgyong-namdo (South Hamgyong Province), Hwanghae-bukto (North Hwanghae Province), Hwanghae-namdo (South Hwanghae Province), Kaesong-si* (Kaesong City), Kangwon-do (Kangwon Province), Najin Sonbong-si*, Namp'o-si* (Namp'o City), P'yongan-bukto (North P'yongan Province), P'yongan-namdo (South P'yongan Province), P'yongyang-si* (Pyongyang City), Yanggang-do (Yanggang Province)
Independence: 15 August 1945 (from Japan)
National holiday: Founding of the Democratic People's Republic of Korea (DPRK), 9 September (1948)
Constitution: adopted 1948, completely revised 27 December 1972, revised again in April 1992 and September 1998

Legal system: based on German civil law system with Japanese influences and Communist legal theory; no judicial review of legislative acts; has not accepted compulsory ICJ jurisdiction
Suffrage: 17 years of age; universal
Executive branch:
chief of state: KIM Chong-il (since NA July 1994); note - on 3 September 2003, KIM Chong-il was reelected Chairman of the National Defense Commission, a position accorded the nation's "highest administrative authority"; KIM Yong-nam was reelected President of the Supreme People's Assembly Presidium and given the responsibility of representing the state and receiving diplomatic credentials
head of government: Premier PAK Pong-chu (since 3 September 2003); Vice Premiers KWAK Pom-ki (since 5 September 1998), CHON Sung-hun (since 3 September 2003), NO Tu-chol (since 3 September 2003)
cabinet: Cabinet (Naegak), members, except for the Minister of People's Armed Forces, are appointed by the Supreme People's Assembly
elections: premier elected by the Supreme People's Assembly; election last held NA September 1998 (next to be held NA)
election results: PAK Pong-chu elected premier; percent of Supreme People's Assembly vote - NA%
Legislative branch: unicameral Supreme People's Assembly or Ch'oego Inmin Hoeui (687 seats; members elected by popular vote to serve five-year terms)
elections: last held 3 August 2003 (next to be held in August 2008)
election results: percent of vote by party - NA; seats by party - NA; the KWP approves a list of candidates who are elected without opposition; some seats are held by minor parties
Judicial branch: Central Court (judges are elected by the Supreme People's Assembly)
Political parties and leaders: Chondoist Chongu Party [YU Mi-yong, chairwoman]; Social Democratic Party [KIM Yong-tae, chairman]; major party - Korean Workers' Party or KWP [KIM Chong-il, general secretary]
Political pressure groups and leaders: NA
International organization participation: ARF, FAO, G-77, ICAO, ICRM, IFAD, IFRCS, IHO, IMO, IOC, ISO, ITU, NAM, UN, UNCTAD, UNESCO, UNIDO, UPU, WFTU, WHO, WIPO, WMO, WToO
Diplomatic representation in the US: none; note - North Korea has a Permanent Mission to the UN in New York
Diplomatic representation from the US: none (Swedish Embassy in P'yongyang represents the US as consular protecting power)
Flag description: three horizontal bands of blue (top), red (triple width), and blue; the red band is edged in white; on the hoist side of the red band is a white disk with a red five-pointed star

Economy

Economy - overview: North Korea, one of the world's most centrally planned and isolated economies, faces desperate economic conditions. Industrial capital stock is nearly beyond repair as a result of years of underinvestment and spare parts shortages. Industrial and power output have declined in parallel. The nation has suffered its tenth year of food shortages because of a lack of arable land, collective farming, weather-related problems, and chronic shortages of fertilizer and fuel. Massive international food aid deliveries have allowed the regime to escape mass starvation since 1995-96, but the population remains the victim of prolonged malnutrition and deteriorating living conditions. Large-scale military spending eats up resources needed for investment and civilian consumption. In 2003, heightened political tensions with key donor countries and general donor fatigue threatened the flow of desperately needed food aid and fuel aid as well. Black market prices continued to rise following the increase in official prices and wages in the summer of 2002, leaving some vulnerable groups, such as the elderly and unemployed, less able to buy goods. The regime, however, relaxed restrictions on farmers' market activities in spring 2003, leading to an expansion of market activity.
GDP: purchasing power parity - $22.85 billion (2003 est.)
GDP - real growth rate: 1% (2003 est.)
GDP - per capita: purchasing power parity - $1,000 (2003 est.)
GDP - composition by sector:
agriculture: 30.2%
industry: 33.8%
services: 36% (2002 est.)
Population below poverty line: NA%
Household income or consumption by percentage share:
lowest 10%: NA%
highest 10%: NA%
Inflation rate (consumer prices): NA% (2003 est.)
Labor force: 9.6 million
Labor force - by occupation: agricultural 36%, nonagricultural 64%
Unemployment rate: NA% (2003)
Budget:
revenues: $NA
expenditures: $NA, including capital expenditures of $NA
Industries: military products; machine building, electric power, chemicals; mining (coal, iron ore, magnesite, graphite, copper, zinc, lead, and precious metals), metallurgy; textiles, food processing; tourism
Industrial production growth rate: NA%
Electricity - production: 30.01 billion kWh (2001)
Electricity - production by source:
fossil fuel: 29%
hydro: 71%
nuclear: 0%
other: 0% (2001)

Electricity - consumption: 27.91 billion kWh (2001)
Electricity - exports: 0 kWh (2001)
Electricity - imports: 0 kWh (2001)
Oil - production: 0 bbl/day (2001 est.)
Oil - consumption: 85,000 bbl/day (2001 est.)
Oil - exports: NA
Oil - imports: NA
Agriculture - products: rice, corn, potatoes, soybeans, pulses; cattle, pigs, pork, eggs
Exports: $1.044 billion f.o.b. (2002 est.)
Exports - commodities: minerals, metallurgical products, manufactures (including armaments); textiles and fishery products
Exports - partners: South Korea 28.5%, China 28.4%, Japan 24.7% (2002)
Imports: $2.042 billion c.i.f. (2002 est.)
Imports - commodities: petroleum, coking coal, machinery and equipment; textiles, grain
Imports - partners: China 39.7%, Thailand 14.6%, Japan 11.2%, Germany 7.6%, South Korea 6.2% (2002)
Debt - external: $12 billion (1996 est.)
Economic aid - recipient: $NA; note - over $133 million in food aid through the World Food Program in 2003 plus additional aid from bilateral donors and non-governmental organizations
Currency: North Korean won (KPW)
Currency code: KPW
Exchange rates: official: North Korean won per US dollar - 150 (December 2002), 2.15 (December 2001), 2.15 (May 1994), 2.13 (May 1992), 2.14 (September 1991), 2.1 (January 1990); market: North Korean won per US dollar - 300-600 (December 2002), 200 (December 2001)
Fiscal year: calendar year

Communications

Telephones - main lines in use: 1.1 million (2001)
Telephones - mobile cellular: NA
Telephone system:
general assessment: NA
domestic: NA
international: country code - 850; satellite earth stations - 1 Intelsat (Indian Ocean) and 1 Russian (Indian Ocean region); other international connections through Moscow and Beijing
Radio broadcast stations: AM 16, FM 14, shortwave 12 (1999)
Television broadcast stations: 38 (1999)
Internet country code: .kp
Internet users: NA

Transportation

Railways:
total: 5,214 km
standard gauge: 4,549 km 1.435-m gauge (3,500 km electrified)
narrow gauge: 665 km 0.762-m gauge (2002)
Highways:
total: 31,200 km
paved: 1,997 km
unpaved: 29,203 km (1999 est.)

Waterways: 2,253 km
note: mostly navigable by small craft only
Pipelines: oil 136 km (2003)
Ports and harbors: Ch'ongjin, Haeju, Hungnam (Hamhung), Kimch'aek, Kosong, Najin, Namp'o, Sinuiju, Songnim, Sonbong (formerly Unggi), Ungsang, Wonsan
Merchant marine:
total: 203 ships (1,000 GRT or over) 921,577 GRT/ 1,339,929 DWT
by type: bulk 6, cargo 166, combination bulk 2, container 3, liquefied gas 1, livestock carrier 3, multi-functional large load carrier 1, passenger/cargo 1, petroleum tanker 11, refrigerated cargo 6, roll on/roll off 2, short-sea/passenger 1
foreign-owned: Albania 1, Belize 1, Bolivia 1, Cambodia 3, Cyprus 1, Egypt 3, Germany 1, Greece 4, Italy 1, Lebanon 2, Marshall Islands 1, Pakistan 1, Portugal 1, Romania 8, Saint Kitts and Nevis 1, Syria 9, Tanzania 1, Tunisia 1, Turkey 5, Ukraine 2, United States 3
registered in other countries: 4 (2003 est.)
Airports: 78 (2003 est.)
Airports - with paved runways:
total: 35
over 3,047 m: 3
2,438 to 3,047 m: 23
1,524 to 2,437 m: 5
914 to 1,523 m: 1
under 914 m: 3 (2003 est.)
Airports - with unpaved runways:
total: 43
2,438 to 3,047 m: 1
1,524 to 2,437 m: 20
914 to 1,523 m: 14
under 914 m: 8 (2003 est.)
Heliports: 19 (2003 est.)

Military

Military branches: Korean People's Army (includes Army, Navy, Air Force), Civil Security Forces
Military manpower - military age: 17 years of age (2004 est.)
Military manpower - availability:
males age 15-49: 6,181,038 (2004 est.)
Military manpower - fit for military service:
males age 15-49: 3,694,855 (2004 est.)
Military manpower - reaching military age annually:
males: 189,014 (2004 est.)
Military expenditures - dollar figure: $5,217.4 million (FY02)
Military expenditures - percent of GDP: 33.9% (FY02)

Transnational Issues

Disputes - international: with China, certain islands in Yalu and Tumen rivers are in uncontested dispute; a section of boundary around Paektu-san (mountain) is indefinite; China has been attempting to stop mass illegal migration of North Koreans escaping famine, economic privation, and oppression into northern China; Military Demarcation Line within the 4-km wide Demilitarized Zone has separated North from South Korea since 1953; periodic maritime disputes with South Korea
Illicit drugs: for years from the 1970's into the 1990's, citizens of the Democratic People's Republic of (North) Korea (DPRK), many of them diplomatic employees of the government, were apprehended abroad while trafficking in narcotics. In recent years, police investigations in Taiwan and Japan have linked North Korea to large illicit shipments of heroin and methamphetamine, with the attempt by the North Korean merchant ship Pong Su to deliver 125 kg of heroin to Australia in April 2003 the most recent example of Pyongyang's involvement in the drug trade; all indications point to North Korea emerging as an important regional source of illicit drugs targeting markets in Japan, Taiwan, the Russian Far East, and China.

Korea, South

Introduction

Background: After World War II, a republic was set up in the southern half of the Korean Peninsula while a Communist-style government was installed in the north. During the Korean War (1950-1953), US and other UN forces intervened to defend South Korea from North Korean attacks supported by the Chinese. An armistice was signed in 1953, splitting the peninsula along a demilitarized zone at about the 38th parallel. Thereafter, South Korea achieved rapid economic growth with per capita income rising to roughly 18 times the level of North Korea. South Korea has maintained its commitment to democratize its political processes. In June 2000, a historic first North-South summit took place between the South's President KIM Dae-jung and the North's leader KIM Chong-il.

Geography

Location: Eastern Asia, southern half of the Korean Peninsula bordering the Sea of Japan and the Yellow Sea

Geographic coordinates: 37 00 N, 127 30 E

Map references: Asia

Area:
total: 98,480 sq km
land: 98,190 sq km
water: 290 sq km

Area - comparative: slightly larger than Indiana

Land boundaries:
total: 238 km
border countries: North Korea 238 km

Coastline: 2,413 km

Maritime claims:
territorial sea: 12 NM; between 3 NM and 12 NM in the Korea Strait
contiguous zone: 24 NM
exclusive economic zone: 200 NM
continental shelf: not specified

Climate: temperate, with rainfall heavier in summer than winter

Terrain: mostly hills and mountains; wide coastal plains in west and south

Elevation extremes:
lowest point: Sea of Japan 0 m
highest point: Halla-san 1,950 m

Natural resources: coal, tungsten, graphite, molybdenum, lead, hydropower potential

Land use:
arable land: 17.44%
permanent crops: 2.05%
other: 80.51% (1998 est.)

Irrigated land: 11,590 sq km (1998 est.)

Natural hazards: occasional typhoons bring high winds and floods; low-level seismic activity common in southwest

Environment - current issues: air pollution in large cities; acid rain; water pollution from the discharge of sewage and industrial effluents; drift net fishing

Environment - international agreements:
party to: Antarctic-Environmental Protocol, Antarctic-Marine Living Resources, Antarctic Treaty, Biodiversity, Climate Change, Climate Change-Kyoto Protocol, Desertification, Endangered Species, Environmental Modification, Hazardous Wastes, Law of the Sea, Marine Dumping, Ozone Layer Protection, Ship Pollution, Tropical Timber 83, Tropical Timber 94, Wetlands, Whaling
signed, but not ratified: none of the selected agreements

Geography - note: strategic location on Korea Strait

People

Population: 48,598,175 (July 2004 est.)

Age structure:
0-14 years: 20.4% (male 5,223,344; female 4,681,594)
15-64 years: 71.4% (male 17,625,302; female 17,072,029)
65 years and over: 8.2% (male 1,597,085; female 2,398,821) (2004 est.)

Median age:
total: 33.7 years
male: 32.8 years
female: 34.7 years (2004 est.)

Population growth rate: 0.62% (2004 est.)

Birth rate: 12.33 births/1,000 population (2004 est.)

Death rate: 6.13 deaths/1,000 population (2004 est.)

Net migration rate: 0 migrant(s)/1,000 population (2004 est.)

Sex ratio:
at birth: 1.09 male(s)/female
under 15 years: 1.12 male(s)/female
15-64 years: 1.03 male(s)/female
65 years and over: 0.67 male(s)/female
total population: 1.01 male(s)/female (2004 est.)

Infant mortality rate:
total: 7.18 deaths/1,000 live births
male: 7.64 deaths/1,000 live births
female: 6.68 deaths/1,000 live births (2004 est.)

Life expectancy at birth:
total population: 75.58 years
male: 71.96 years
female: 79.54 years (2004 est.)

Total fertility rate: 1.56 children born/woman (2004 est.)

HIV/AIDS - adult prevalence rate: less than 0.1% (2001 est.)

HIV/AIDS - people living with HIV/AIDS: 4,000 (2001 est.)

HIV/AIDS - deaths: 220 (2001 est.)

Nationality:
noun: Korean(s)
adjective: Korean

Ethnic groups: homogeneous (except for about 20,000 Chinese)

Religions: no affiliation 46%, Christian 26%, Buddhist 26%, Confucianist 1%, other 1%

Languages: Korean, English widely taught in junior high and high school

Literacy:
definition: age 15 and over can read and write
total population: 98.1%
male: 99.3%
female: 97% (2003 est.)

Government

Country name:
conventional long form: Republic of Korea
conventional short form: South Korea
local long form: Taehan-min'guk
local short form: none
note: the South Koreans generally use the term "Han'guk" to refer to their country
abbreviation: ROK

Government type: republic

Capital: Seoul

Administrative divisions: 9 provinces (do, singular and plural) and 7 metropolitan cities* (gwangyoksi, singular and plural); Cheju-do, Cholla-bukto, Cholla-namdo, Ch'ungch'ong-bukto, Ch'ungch'ong-namdo, Inch'on-gwangyoksi*, Kangwon-do, Kwangju-gwangyoksi*, Kyonggi-do, Kyongsang-bukto, Kyongsang-namdo, Pusan-gwangyoksi*, Soul-t'ukpyolsi*, Taegu-gwangyoksi*, Taejon-gwangyoksi*, Ulsan-gwangyoksi*

Independence: 15 August 1945 (from Japan)

National holiday: Liberation Day, 15 August (1945)

Constitution: 17 July 1948

Legal system: combines elements of continental European civil law systems, Anglo-American law, and Chinese classical thought

Suffrage: 20 years of age; universal

Executive branch:
chief of state: President NO Mu-hyun (ROH Moo-hyun) (since 25 February 2003)
note: President NO was impeached on 12 March 2004; KO Kun is the acting president

Korea, South (continued)

head of government: Prime Minister KO Kun (KOH Kun) (since 27 February 2003); Deputy Prime Ministers YI Hon-chae (LEE Hun-jai) (since 10 February 2004) and AN Pyong-yong (AHN Byung-young) (since 23 December 2003)
cabinet: State Council appointed by the president on the prime minister's recommendation
elections: president elected by popular vote for a single five-year term; election last held 19 December 2002 (next to be held in December 2007); prime minister appointed by the president; deputy prime ministers appointed by the president on the prime minister's recommendation
election results: results of the 19 December 2002 election - NO Mu-hyun elected president; percent of vote - NO Mu-hyun (MDP) 48.9%; YI Hoe-ch'ang (GNP) 46.6%; other 4.5%
Legislative branch: unicameral National Assembly or Kukhoe (273 seats total - 227 elected by direct, popular vote; members serve four-year terms); note - beginning in 2004, all members will be directly elected; possible redistricting before 2004 may affect the number of seats in the National Assembly
elections: last held 13 April 2000 (next to be held 15 April 2004)
election results: percent of vote by party - NA%; seats by party - GNP 133, MDP 115, ULD 17, other 8; note - the distribution of seats as of April 2003 was: GNP 153, MDP 101, ULD 11, DPP 1, PPR 1, independents 5; one seat vacant
Judicial branch: Supreme Court (justices are appointed by the president with the consent of the National Assembly)
Political parties and leaders: Democratic People's Party or DPP [leader NA]; Grand National Party or GNP [PAK Kun-hye, chairman]; Millennium Democratic Party or MDP [CHO Sun-hyong, chairman]; United Liberal Democrats or ULD [KIM Chong-p'il, president]; Uri Party [CHONG Tong-yong, chairman]
Political pressure groups and leaders: Federation of Korean Industries; Federation of Korean Trade Unions; Korean Confederation of Trade Unions; Korean National Council of Churches; Korean Traders Association; Korean Veterans' Association; National Council of Labor Unions; National Democratic Alliance of Korea; National Federation of Farmers' Associations; National Federation of Student Associations
International organization participation: AfDB, APEC, ARF, AsDB, ASEAN (dialogue partner), Australia Group, BIS, CP, EBRD, FAO, IAEA, IBRD, ICAO, ICC, ICCt, ICFTU, ICRM, IDA, IEA, IFAD, IFC, IFRCS, IHO, ILO, IMF, IMO, Interpol, IOC, IOM, ISO, ITU, MINURSO, NAM (guest), NEA, NSG, OAS (observer), OECD, OPCW, OSCE (partner), PCA, UN, UNCTAD, UNESCO, UNFICYP, UNIDO, UNMIL, UNMISET, UNMOGIP, UNOMIG, UPU, WCL, WCO, WHO, WIPO, WMO, WToO, WTrO, ZC
Diplomatic representation in the US:
chief of mission: Ambassador HAN Sung-chu (HAN Sung-joo)

chancery: 2450 Massachusetts Avenue NW, Washington, DC 20008
telephone: [1] (202) 939-5600
FAX: [1] (202) 387-0205
consulate(s) general: Atlanta, Boston, Chicago, Honolulu, Houston, Los Angeles, New York, San Francisco, and Seattle
consulate(s): New York, Tamuning (Guam)
Diplomatic representation from the US:
chief of mission: Ambassador Thomas C. HUBBARD
embassy: 82 Sejong-no, Jongno-gu, Seoul 110-710
mailing address: American Embassy, Unit 15550, APO AP 96205-5550
telephone: [82] (2) 397-4114
FAX: [82] (2) 738-8845
Flag description: white with a red (top) and blue yin-yang symbol in the center; there is a different black trigram from the ancient I Ching (Book of Changes) in each corner of the white field

Economy

Economy - overview: Since the early 1960s, South Korea has achieved an incredible record of growth and integration into the high-tech modern world economy. Four decades ago GDP per capita was comparable with levels in the poorer countries of Africa and Asia. Today its GDP per capita is 18 times North Korea's and equal to the lesser economies of the European Union. This success through the late 1980s was achieved by a system of close government/business ties, including directed credit, import restrictions, sponsorship of specific industries, and a strong labor effort. The government promoted the import of raw materials and technology at the expense of consumer goods and encouraged savings and investment over consumption. The Asian financial crisis of 1997-99 exposed longstanding weaknesses in South Korea's development model, including high debt/equity ratios, massive foreign borrowing, and an undisciplined financial sector. Growth plunged to a negative 6.6% in 1998, then strongly recovered to 10.8% in 1999 and 9.2% in 2000. Growth fell back to 3.3% in 2001 because of the slowing global economy, falling exports, and the perception that much-needed corporate and financial reforms had stalled. Led by consumer spending and exports, growth in 2002 was an impressive 6.2%, despite anemic global growth, followed by moderate 2.8% growth in 2003. In 2003 the National Assembly approved legislation reducing the six-day work week to five days.
GDP: purchasing power parity - $855.3 billion (2003 est.)
GDP - real growth rate: 2.8% (2003 est.)
GDP - per capita: purchasing power parity - $17,700 (2003 est.)
GDP - composition by sector:
agriculture: 4.4%
industry: 37.6%
services: 58% (2002 est.)
Population below poverty line: 4% (2001 est.)

Household income or consumption by percentage share:
lowest 10%: 2.9%
highest 10%: 22.5% (1999 est.)
Distribution of family income - Gini index: 31.6 (1993)
Inflation rate (consumer prices): 3.5% (2003 est.)
Labor force: 23 million (2003)
Labor force - by occupation: services 69%, industry 21.5%, agriculture 9.5% (2001)
Unemployment rate: 3.4% (2003 est.)
Budget:
revenues: $127 billion
expenditures: $108 billion, including capital expenditures of $23.5 billion (2002)
Industries: electronics, telecommunications, automobile production, chemicals, shipbuilding, steel
Industrial production growth rate: 3% (2003 est.)
Electricity - production: 290.7 billion kWh (2001)
Electricity - production by source:
fossil fuel: 62.4%
hydro: 0.8%
nuclear: 36.6%
other: 0.2% (2001)
Electricity - consumption: 270.3 billion kWh (2001)
Electricity - exports: 0 kWh (2001)
Electricity - imports: 0 kWh (2001)
Oil - production: 0 bbl/day (2001 est.)
Oil - consumption: 2.14 million bbl/day (2001 est.)
Oil - exports: 804,700 bbl/day (2001)
Oil - imports: 2.965 million bbl/day (2001)
Natural gas - production: 0 cu m (2001 est.)
Natural gas - consumption: 20.92 billion cu m (2001 est.)
Natural gas - exports: 0 cu m (2001 est.)
Natural gas - imports: 21.11 billion cu m (2001 est.)
Agriculture - products: rice, root crops, barley, vegetables, fruit; cattle, pigs, chickens, milk, eggs; fish
Exports: $201.3 billion f.o.b. (2003 est.)
Exports - commodities: Semiconductors, wireless telecommunications equipment, motor vehicles, computers, steel, ships, petrochemicals
Exports - partners: US 20.4%, China 14.7%, Japan 9.4%, Hong Kong 6.3%, Taiwan 4.1% (2002)
Imports: $175.6 billion f.o.b. (2003 est.)
Imports - commodities: machinery, electronics and electronic equipment, oil, steel, transport equipment, organic chemicals, plastics
Imports - partners: Japan 19.6%, US 15.2%, China 11.4%, Saudi Arabia 5% (2002)
Debt - external: $134.9 billion (yearend 2003 est.)
Economic aid - donor: ODA $200 million
Currency: South Korean won (KRW)
Currency code: KRW
Exchange rates: South Korean won per US dollar - 1,191.61 (2003), 1,251.09 (2002), 1,290.99 (2001), 1,130.96 (2000), 1,188.82 (1999)
Fiscal year: calendar year

Communications

Telephones - main lines in use: 23.257 million (2002)

Telephones - mobile cellular: 32.342 million (2002)

Telephone system:

general assessment: excellent domestic and international services

domestic: NA

international: country code - 82; fiber-optic submarine cable to China; the Russia-Korea-Japan submarine cable; satellite earth stations - 3 Intelsat (2 Pacific Ocean and 1 Indian Ocean) and 1 Inmarsat (Pacific Ocean region)

Radio broadcast stations: AM 104, FM 136, shortwave 5 (2001)

Television broadcast stations: 121 (plus 850 repeater stations and the eight-channel American Forces Korea Network) (1999)

Internet country code: .kr

Internet hosts: 407,318 (2002)

Internet users: 26.27 million (2002)

Transportation

Railways:

total: 3,125 km

standard gauge: 3,125 km 1.435-m gauge (661 km electrified) (2002)

Highways:

total: 86,990 km

paved: 64,808 km (including 1,996 km of expressways)

unpaved: 22,182 km (1999 est.)

Waterways: 1,609 km

note: restricted to small native craft

Pipelines: gas 1,433 km; refined products 827 km (2003)

Ports and harbors: Chinhae, Inch'on, Kunsan, Masan, Mokp'o, P'ohang, Pusan, Tonghae-hang, Ulsan, Yosu

Merchant marine:

total: 535 ships (1,000 GRT or over) 5,978,949 GRT/ 9,761,699 DWT

by type: bulk 97, cargo 174, chemical tanker 61, combination bulk 10, container 60, liquefied gas 19, passenger 3, petroleum tanker 73, refrigerated cargo 20, roll on/roll off 7, short-sea/passenger 2, specialized tanker 6, vehicle carrier 3

foreign-owned: Bahrain 1, China 1, Gibraltar 1, Honduras 1, Indonesia 1, Japan 3, Malaysia 1, Panama 1, Philippines 1, Saint Vincent and the Grenadines 1, United Kingdom 1, United States 1

registered in other countries: 442 (2003 est.)

Airports: 102 (2003 est.)

Airports - with paved runways:

total: 69

over 3,047 m: 3

2,438 to 3,047 m: 20

1,524 to 2,437 m: 14

914 to 1,523 m: 11

under 914 m: 21 (2003 est.)

Airports - with unpaved runways:

total: 33

914 to 1,523 m: 3

under 914 m: 30 (2003 est.)

Heliports: 206 (2003 est.)

Military

Military branches: Army, Navy, Air Force, Marine Corps, National Maritime Police (Coast Guard)

Military manpower - military age: 18 years of age (24-28 months mandatory service required, depending on the military baranch involved) (2004 est.)

Military manpower - availability:

males age 15-49: 14,233,895 (2004 est.)

Military manpower - fit for military service:

males age 15-49: 8,966,241 (2004 est.)

Military manpower - reaching military age annually:

males: 341,697 (2004 est.)

Military expenditures - dollar figure: $14.522 billion (FY03)

Military expenditures - percent of GDP: 2.7% (FY03)

Transnational Issues

Disputes - international: Military Demarcation Line within the 4-km wide Demilitarized Zone has separated North from South Korea since 1953; periodic maritime disputes with North Korea; intensified media coverage and protests highlight dispute over Liancourt Rocks (Take-shima/Tok-do) in rich fishing grounds also claimed by Japan

Kuwait

Introduction

Background: Britain oversaw foreign relations and defense for the ruling Kuwaiti AL-SABAH dynasty from 1899 until independence in 1961. Kuwait was attacked and overrun by Iraq on 2 August 1990. Following several weeks of aerial bombardment, a US-led, UN coalition began a ground assault on 23 February 1991 that liberated Kuwait in four days. Kuwait spent more than $5 billion to repair oil infrastructure damaged during 1990-91.

Geography

Location: Middle East, bordering the Persian Gulf, between Iraq and Saudi Arabia

Geographic coordinates: 29 30 N, 45 45 E

Map references: Middle East

Area:

total: 17,820 sq km

land: 17,820 sq km

water: 0 sq km

Area - comparative: slightly smaller than New Jersey

Land boundaries:

total: 462 km

border countries: Iraq 240 km, Saudi Arabia 222 km

Coastline: 499 km

Maritime claims:

territorial sea: 12 NM

Climate: dry desert; intensely hot summers; short, cool winters

Terrain: flat to slightly undulating desert plain

Elevation extremes:

lowest point: Persian Gulf 0 m

highest point: unnamed location 306 m

Natural resources: petroleum, fish, shrimp, natural gas

Land use:

arable land: 0.34%

permanent crops: 0.06%

other: 99.6% (1998 est.)

Kuwait (continued)

Irrigated land: 60 sq km (1998 est.)
Natural hazards: sudden cloudbursts are common from October to April and bring heavy rain, which can damage roads and houses; sandstorms and dust storms occur throughout the year, but are most common between March and August
Environment - current issues: limited natural fresh water resources; some of world's largest and most sophisticated desalination facilities provide much of the water; air and water pollution; desertification
Environment - international agreements:
party to: Biodiversity, Climate Change, Desertification, Endangered Species, Environmental Modification, Hazardous Wastes, Law of the Sea, Ozone Layer Protection
signed, but not ratified: Marine Dumping
Geography - note: strategic location at head of Persian Gulf

People

Population: 2,257,549
note: includes 1,291,354 non-nationals (July 2004 est.)
Age structure:
0-14 years: 27.5% (male 316,237; female 304,671)
15-64 years: 69.8% (male 1,007,298; female 569,128)
65 years and over: 2.7% (male 38,408; female 21,807) (2004 est.)
Median age:
total: 25.9 years
male: 28.2 years
female: 22 years (2004 est.)
Population growth rate: 3.36%
note: this rate reflects a return to pre-Gulf crisis immigration of expatriates (2004 est.)
Birth rate: 21.85 births/1,000 population (2004 est.)
Death rate: 2.44 deaths/1,000 population (2004 est.)
Net migration rate: 14.18 migrant(s)/1,000 population (2004 est.)
Sex ratio:
at birth: 1.04 male(s)/female
under 15 years: 1.04 male(s)/female
15-64 years: 1.77 male(s)/female
65 years and over: 1.76 male(s)/female
total population: 1.52 male(s)/female (2004 est.)
Infant mortality rate:
total: 10.26 deaths/1,000 live births
male: 11.27 deaths/1,000 live births
female: 9.22 deaths/1,000 live births (2004 est.)
Life expectancy at birth:
total population: 76.84 years
male: 75.86 years
female: 77.86 years (2004 est.)
Total fertility rate: 3.03 children born/woman (2004 est.)
HIV/AIDS - adult prevalence rate: 0.12% (2001 est.)
HIV/AIDS - people living with HIV/AIDS: NA
HIV/AIDS - deaths: NA
Nationality:
noun: Kuwaiti(s)
adjective: Kuwaiti

Ethnic groups: Kuwaiti 45%, other Arab 35%, South Asian 9%, Iranian 4%, other 7%
Religions: Muslim 85% (Sunni 70%, Shi'a 30%), Christian, Hindu, Parsi, and other 15%
Languages: Arabic (official), English widely spoken
Literacy:
definition: age 15 and over can read and write
total population: 83.5%
male: 85.1%
female: 81.7% (2003 est.)

Government

Country name:
conventional long form: State of Kuwait
conventional short form: Kuwait
local long form: Dawlat al Kuwayt
local short form: Al Kuwayt
Government type: nominal constitutional monarchy
Capital: Kuwait
Administrative divisions: 5 governorates (muhafazat, singular - muhafazah); Al Ahmadi, Al Farwaniyah, Al 'Asimah, Al Jahra', Hawalli
Independence: 19 June 1961 (from UK)
National holiday: National Day, 25 February (1950)
Constitution: approved and promulgated 11 November 1962
Legal system: civil law system with Islamic law significant in personal matters; has not accepted compulsory ICJ jurisdiction
Suffrage: adult males who have been naturalized for 30 years or more or have resided in Kuwait since before 1920 and their male descendants at age 21
note: only 10% of all citizens are eligible to vote; in 1996, naturalized citizens who do not meet the pre-1920 qualification but have been naturalized for 30 years were eligible to vote for the first time
Executive branch:
chief of state: Amir JABIR al-Ahmad al-Jabir Al Sabah (since 31 December 1977)
head of government: Prime Minister SABAH al-Ahmad al-Jabir Al Sabah (since 13 July 2003); First Deputy Prime Minister NAWWAF al-Ahmad Al Sabah (since 2003); Deputy Prime Ministers JABIR MUBARAK al-Hamad Al Sabah (since 2001) and Muhammad Dayfallah al-SHARAR (since 2003)
cabinet: Council of Ministers appointed by the prime minister and approved by the monarch
elections: none; the monarch is hereditary; prime minister and deputy prime ministers appointed by the monarch
Legislative branch: unicameral National Assembly or Majlis al-Umma (50 seats; members elected by popular vote to serve four-year terms)
elections: last held 6 July 2003 (next to be held NA 2007)
election results: percent of vote - NA%; seats - Islamists 21, government supporters 14, liberals 3, and independents 12; note - all cabinet ministers are also ex officio members of the National Assembly
Judicial branch: High Court of Appeal
Political parties and leaders: none; formation of political parties is illegal

Political pressure groups and leaders: several political groups act as de facto parties: Bedouins, merchants, Sunni and Shi'a activists, and secular leftists and nationalists
International organization participation: ABEDA, AfDB, AFESD, AMF, BDEAC, CAEU, FAO, G-77, GCC, IAEA, IBRD, ICAO, ICC, ICCt (signatory), ICRM, IDA, IDB, IFAD, IFC, IFRCS, IHO, ILO, IMF, IMO, Interpol, IOC, ISO, ITU, LAS, NAM, OAPEC, OIC, OPCW, OPEC, PCA, UN, UNCTAD, UNESCO, UNIDO, UNITAR, UPU, WCO, WFTU, WHO, WIPO, WMO, WToO, WTrO
Diplomatic representation in the US:
chief of mission: Ambassador Sheikh SALIM al-Abdallah Jabir Al Sabah
chancery: 2940 Tilden Street NW, Washington, DC 20008
telephone: [1] (202) 966-0702
FAX: [1] (202) 966-0517
Diplomatic representation from the US:
chief of mission: Ambassador Richard H. JONES
embassy: Bayan, Area 14, Al-Masjed Al-Aqsa Street (near the Bayan palace), Kuwait City
mailing address: P. O. Box 77 Safat, 13001 Safat, Kuwait Unit 69000, APO AE 09880-9000
telephone: [965] 539-5307, ext. 2240
FAX: [965] 538-0282
Flag description: three equal horizontal bands of green (top), white, and red with a black trapezoid based on the hoist side

Economy

Economy - overview: Kuwait is a small, rich, relatively open economy with proved crude oil reserves of about 98 billion barrels - 10% of world reserves. Petroleum accounts for nearly half of GDP, 95% of export revenues, and 80% of government income. Kuwait's climate limits agricultural development. Consequently, with the exception of fish, it depends almost wholly on food imports. About 75% of potable water must be distilled or imported. Kuwait continues its discussions with foreign oil companies to develop fields in the northern part of the country.
GDP: purchasing power parity - $39.54 billion (2003 est.)
GDP - real growth rate: 4.4% (2003 est.)
GDP - per capita: purchasing power parity - $18,100 (2003 est.)
GDP - composition by sector:
agriculture: 0.5%
industry: 63.3%
services: 36.2% (2001)
Population below poverty line: NA%
Household income or consumption by percentage share:
lowest 10%: NA%
highest 10%: NA%
Inflation rate (consumer prices): 1.2% (2003 est.)
Labor force: 1.3 million
note: non-Kuwaitis represent about 80% of the labor force. (1998 est.)

Kuwait *(continued)*

Labor force - by occupation: agriculture NA%, industries NA%, services NA%
Unemployment rate: 7% (2002 est.)
Budget:
revenues: $11 billion
expenditures: $19.5 billion, including capital expenditures of $NA (FY03/04)
Industries: petroleum, petrochemicals, desalination, food processing, construction materials
Industrial production growth rate: -5% (2002 est.)
Electricity - production: 31.49 billion kWh (2001)
Electricity - production by source:
fossil fuel: 100%
hydro: 0%
nuclear: 0%
other: 0% (2001)
Electricity - consumption: 29.29 billion kWh (2001)
Electricity - exports: 0 kWh (2001)
Electricity - imports: 0 kWh (2001)
Oil - production: 2.27 million bbl/day (2003 est.)
Oil - consumption: 293,000 bbl/day (2003 est.)
Oil - exports: 1.97 million bbl/day (2003)
Oil - imports: NA
Oil - proved reserves: 97.68 billion bbl (1 January 2002)
Natural gas - production: 8.7 billion cu m (2002 est.)
Natural gas - consumption: 8.7 billion cu m (2002 est.)
Natural gas - exports: 0 cu m (2002 est.)
Natural gas - imports: 0 cu m (2002 est.)
Natural gas - proved reserves: 1.548 trillion cu m (1 January 2002)
Agriculture - products: practically no crops; fish
Exports: $22.29 billion f.o.b. (2003 est.)
Exports - commodities: oil and refined products, fertilizers
Exports - partners: Japan 24.1%, South Korea 12.8%, US 11.8%, Singapore 10%, Taiwan 7.4%, Netherlands 4.4%, Pakistan 4.3% (2002)
Imports: $9.606 billion f.o.b. (2003 est.)
Imports - commodities: food, construction materials, vehicles and parts, clothing
Imports - partners: US 12.8%, Japan 10.9%, Germany 9.7%, Saudi Arabia 6.4%, UK 5.9%, Italy 5.3%, France 5.1% (2002)
Debt - external: $11.2 billion (2003 est.)
Economic aid - recipient: $NA (2001)
Currency: Kuwaiti dinar (KD)
Currency code: KWD
Exchange rates: Kuwaiti dinars per US dollar - 0.298 (2003), 0.3039 (2002), 0.3067 (2001), 0.3068 (2000), 0.3044 (1999)
Fiscal year: 1 April - 31 March

Communications

Telephones - main lines in use: 481,900 (2002)
Telephones - mobile cellular: 1.227 million (2002)
Telephone system:
general assessment: the quality of service is excellent
domestic: new telephone exchanges provide a large capacity for new subscribers; trunk traffic is carried by microwave radio relay, coaxial cable, and open-wire and fiber-optic cable; a cellular telephone system operates throughout Kuwait, and the country is well supplied with pay telephones
international: country code - 965; coaxial cable and microwave radio relay to Saudi Arabia; linked to Bahrain, Qatar, UAE via the Fiber-Optic Gulf (FOG) cable; satellite earth stations - 3 Intelsat (1 Atlantic Ocean, 2 Indian Ocean), 1 Inmarsat (Atlantic Ocean), and 2 Arabsat
Radio broadcast stations: AM 6, FM 11, shortwave 1 (1998)
Television broadcast stations: 13 (plus several satellite channels) (1997)
Internet country code: .kw
Internet hosts: 3,261 (2002)
Internet users: 250,000 (2002)

Transportation

Railways: 0 km
Highways:
total: 4,450 km
paved: 3,587 km
unpaved: 863 km (1999 est.)
Waterways: none
Pipelines: gas 169 km; oil 540 km; refined products 57 km (2003)
Ports and harbors: Ash Shu'aybah, Ash Shuwaykh, Kuwait, Mina' 'Abd Allah, Mina' al Ahmadi, Mina' Su'ud
Merchant marine:
total: 38 ships (1,000 GRT or over) 2,319,082 GRT/ 3,768,828 DWT
by type: bulk 1, container 6, liquefied gas 5, livestock carrier 4, petroleum tanker 21, roll on/roll off 1
foreign-owned: India 1, Saudi Arabia 1
registered in other countries: 5 (2003 est.)
Airports: 7 (2003 est.)
Airports - with paved runways:
total: 4
over 3,047 m: 1
2,438 to 3,047 m: 2
1,524 to 2,437 m: 1 (2003 est.)
Airports - with unpaved runways:
total: 3
1,524 to 2,437 m: 1
under 914 m: 2 (2003 est.)
Heliports: 3 (2003 est.)

Military

Military branches: Land Forces, Navy, Air Force (including Air Defense Force), National Guard
Military manpower - military age: 18 years of age (2004 est.)
Military manpower - availability:
males age 15-49: 880,461 (2004 est.)
Military manpower - fit for military service:
males age 15-49: 531,556 (2004 est.)
Military manpower - reaching military age annually:
males: 18,849 (2004 est.)
Military expenditures - dollar figure: $2,500,400,000 (2003)
Military expenditures - percent of GDP: 5.8% (2003)

Transnational Issues

Disputes - international: Kuwait and Saudi Arabia continue negotiating a joint maritime boundary with Iran; no maritime boundary exists with Iraq in the Persian Gulf

Kyrgyzstan

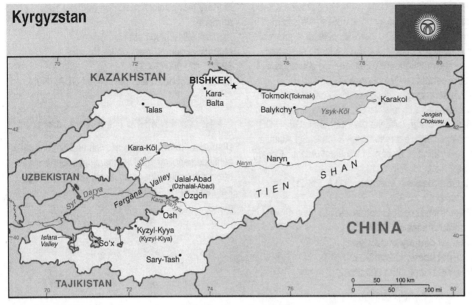

Introduction

Background: A Central Asian country of incredible natural beauty and proud nomadic traditions, Kyrgyzstan was annexed by Russia in 1864; it achieved independence from the Soviet Union in 1991. Current concerns include: privatization of state-owned enterprises, expansion of democracy and political freedoms, interethnic relations, and combating terrorism.

Geography

Location: Central Asia, west of China
Geographic coordinates: 41 00 N, 75 00 E
Map references: Asia
Area:
total: 198,500 sq km
land: 191,300 sq km
water: 7,200 sq km
Area - comparative: slightly smaller than South Dakota
Land boundaries:
total: 3,878 km
border countries: China 858 km, Kazakhstan 1,051 km, Tajikistan 870 km, Uzbekistan 1,099 km
Coastline: 0 km (landlocked)
Maritime claims: none (landlocked)
Climate: dry continental to polar in high Tien Shan; subtropical in southwest (Fergana Valley); temperate in northern foothill zone
Terrain: peaks of Tien Shan and associated valleys and basins encompass entire nation
Elevation extremes:
lowest point: Kara-Daryya (Karadar'ya) 132 m
highest point: Jengish Chokusu (Pik Pobedy) 7,439 m
Natural resources: abundant hydropower; significant deposits of gold and rare earth metals; locally exploitable coal, oil, and natural gas; other deposits of nepheline, mercury, bismuth, lead, and zinc

Land use:
arable land: 7.04%
permanent crops: 0.39%
other: 92.57%
note: Kyrgyzstan has the world's largest natural growth walnut forest (1998 est.)
Irrigated land: 10,740 sq km (1998 est.)
Natural hazards: NA
Environment - current issues: water pollution; many people get their water directly from contaminated streams and wells; as a result, water-borne diseases are prevalent; increasing soil salinity from faulty irrigation practices
Environment - international agreements:
party to: Air Pollution, Biodiversity, Climate Change, Climate Change-Kyoto Protocol, Desertification, Hazardous Wastes, Ozone Layer Protection
signed, but not ratified: none of the selected agreements
Geography - note: landlocked; entirely mountainous, dominated by the Tien Shan range; many tall peaks, glaciers, and high-altitude lakes

People

Population: 5,081,429 (July 2004 est.)
Age structure:
0-14 years: 32.3% (male 835,599; female 804,384)
15-64 years: 61.6% (male 1,535,447; female 1,594,972)
65 years and over: 6.1% (male 120,555; female 190,472) (2004 est.)
Median age:
total: 23.1 years
male: 22.2 years
female: 24 years (2004 est.)
Population growth rate: 1.25% (2004 est.)
Birth rate: 22.13 births/1,000 population (2004 est.)
Death rate: 7.19 deaths/1,000 population (2004 est.)
Net migration rate: -2.45 migrant(s)/1,000 population (2004 est.)

Sex ratio:
at birth: 1.05 male(s)/female
under 15 years: 1.04 male(s)/female
15-64 years: 0.96 male(s)/female
65 years and over: 0.63 male(s)/female
total population: 0.96 male(s)/female (2004 est.)
Infant mortality rate:
total: 36.81 deaths/1,000 live births
male: 42.23 deaths/1,000 live births
female: 31.11 deaths/1,000 live births (2004 est.)
Life expectancy at birth:
total population: 67.84 years
male: 63.84 years
female: 72.05 years (2004 est.)
Total fertility rate: 2.71 children born/woman (2004 est.)
HIV/AIDS - adult prevalence rate: less than 0.1% (2001 est.)
HIV/AIDS - people living with HIV/AIDS: over 500 (2001 est.)
HIV/AIDS - deaths: less than 100 (2001 est.)
Nationality:
noun: Kyrgyzstani(s)
adjective: Kyrgyzstani
Ethnic groups: Kyrgyz 52.4%, Russian 18%, Uzbek 12.9%, Ukrainian 2.5%, German 2.4%, other 11.8%
Religions: Muslim 75%, Russian Orthodox 20%, other 5%
Languages: Kyrgyz - official language, Russian - official language
note: in December 2001, the Kyrgyzstani legislature made Russian an official language, equal in status to Kyrgyz
Literacy:
definition: age 15 and over can read and write
total population: 97%
male: 99%
female: 96% (1989 est.)

Government

Country name:
conventional long form: Kyrgyz Republic
conventional short form: Kyrgyzstan
local long form: Kyrgyz Respublikasy
local short form: none
former: Kirghiz Soviet Socialist Republic
Government type: republic
Capital: Bishkek
Administrative divisions: 7 provinces (oblastlar, singular - oblasty) and 1 city* (shaar); Batken Oblasty, Bishkek Shaary*, Chuy Oblasty (Bishkek), Jalal-Abad Oblasty, Naryn Oblasty, Osh Oblasty, Talas Oblasty, Ysyk-Kol Oblasty (Karakol)
note: administrative divisions have the same names as their administrative centers (exceptions have the administrative center name following in parentheses)
Independence: 31 August 1991 (from Soviet Union)
National holiday: Independence Day, 31 August (1991)

Kyrgyzstan (continued)

Constitution: adopted 5 May 1993; note - amendment proposed by President AKAYEV and passed in a national referendum on 2 February 2003 significantly expands the powers of the president at the expense of the legislature

Legal system: based on civil law system

Suffrage: 18 years of age; universal

Executive branch:

chief of state: President Askar AKAYEV (since 28 October 1990)

head of government: Prime Minister Nikolay TANAYEV (since 22 May 2002); note - Prime Minister Kurmanbek BAKIYEV resigned on 22 May 2002 when five demonstrators were killed in a clash with police in March of 2002; First Deputy Prime Minister Kubanychbek JUMALIYEV (since 19 March 2004)

cabinet: Cabinet of Ministers appointed by the president on the recommendation of the prime minister

elections: president reelected by popular vote for a five-year term; elections last held 29 October 2000 (next to be held November or December 2005); prime minister appointed by the president; note - President AKAYEV has publicly stated that he will not seek reelection when his current term expires in 2005

election results: Askar AKAYEV reelected president; percent of vote - Askar AKAYEV 74%, Omurbek TEKEBAYEV 14%, other candidates 12%; note - election marred by serious irregularities

Legislative branch: bicameral Supreme Council or Zhogorku Kenesh consists of the Assembly of People's Representatives (70 seats; members are elected by popular vote to serve five-year terms) and the Legislative Assembly (35 seats; members are elected by popular vote to serve five-year terms); note - in accordance with a 2003 referendum, the Parliament is slated to become unicameral with 75 deputies after the 2005 elections

elections: Assembly of People's Representatives - last held 20 February and 12 March 2000 (next to be held NA February 2005); Legislative Assembly - last held 20 February and 12 March 2000 (next to be held NA February 2005)

election results: Assembly of People's Representatives - percent of vote by party - NA%; seats by party - NA; and Legislative Assembly - percent of vote by party - NA%; seats by party - NA; note - total seats by party in the Supreme Council were as follows: Union of Democratic Forces 12, Communists 6, My Country Party of Action 4, independents 73, other 10

note: the legislature became bicameral for the 5 February 1995 elections; the 2000 election results include both the Assembly of People's Representatives and the Legislative Assembly

Judicial branch: Supreme Court (judges are appointed for 10-year terms by the Supreme Council on the recommendation of the president); Constitutional Court; Higher Court of Arbitration

Political parties and leaders: Agrarian Labor Party of Kyrgyzstan [Uson S. SYDYKOV]; Agrarian Party of Kyrgyzstan [Arkin ALIYEV]; ar-Namys (Honor) Party [Feliks KULOV]; Ata-Meken or Fatherland [Omurbek TEKEBAYEV]; Banner National Revival Party or ASABA [Azimbek BEKNAZAROV]; Communist Party of Kyrgyzstan [Klara ADZHIBEKOVA]; Democratic Movement of Kyrgyzstan or DDK [Jypar JEKSHEYEV]; Democratic Women's Party of Kyrgyzstan [Tokon SHAILIYEVA]; El Muras (People's Heritage) [Toktokan BOROMBAYEVA]; Erkin Kyrgyzstan Progressive and Democratic Party [B. ASANOV]; Erkindik (Freedom) Party [Topchubek TURGUNALIYEV]; Justice Party [Chingiz AYTMATOV]; Movement for the People's Salvation [Jumgalbek AMAMBAYEV]; Mutual Help Movement or Ashar [Jumagazy USUPOV]; My Country Party of Action [Almazbek ISMANKULOV]; National Unity Democratic Movement or DDNE [Yury RAZGULYAYEV]; Novoe Vremya [leader NA]; Party of Communists of Kyrgyzstan or KCP [Absamat M. MASALIYEV]; Party of Justice and Progress [Muratbek IMANALIEV]; Party of the Veterans of the War in Afghanistan [leader NA]; Peasant Party [leader NA]; People's Party [Melis ESHIMKANOV]; Republican Popular Party of Kyrgyzstan [J. SHARSHENALIYEV]; Social Democratic Party or PSD [J. IBRAMOV]; Union of Democratic Forces (composed of Social Democratic Party of Kyrgyzstan or PSD [J. IBRAMOV], Economic Revival Party, and Birimdik Party)

Political pressure groups and leaders: Council of Free Trade Unions; Kyrgyz Committee on Human Rights [Ramazan DYRYLDAYEV]; National Unity Democratic Movement; Union of Entrepreneurs

International organization participation: AsDB, CIS, EAPC, EBRD, ECO, FAO, IAEA, IBRD, ICAO, ICCt (signatory), ICRM, IDA, IDB, IFAD, IFC, IFRCS, ILO, IMF, Interpol, IOC, IOM, ISO (correspondent), ITU, NAM (observer), OIC, OPCW, OSCE, PCA, PFP, SCO, UN, UNAMSIL, UNCTAD, UNESCO, UNIDO, UNMIK, UPU, WCO, WFTU, WHO, WIPO, WMO, WToO, WTrO

Diplomatic representation in the US:

chief of mission: Ambassador Bakyt ABDRISAYEV

chancery: 1732 Wisconsin Avenue NW, Washington, DC 20007

telephone: [1] (202) 338-5141

FAX: [1] (202) 338-5139

consulate(s): New York

Diplomatic representation from the US:

chief of mission: Ambassador Stephen M. YOUNG

embassy: 171 Prospect Mira, 720016 Bishkek

mailing address: use embassy street address

telephone: [996] (312) 551-241, (517) 777-217

FAX: [996] (312) 551-264

Flag description: red field with a yellow sun in the center having 40 rays representing the 40 Kyrgyz tribes; on the obverse side the rays run counterclockwise, on the reverse, clockwise; in the center of the sun is a red ring crossed by two sets of three lines, a stylized representation of the roof of the traditional Kyrgyz yurt

Economy - overview: Kyrgyzstan is a poor, mountainous country with a predominantly agricultural economy. Cotton, tobacco, wool, and meat are the main agricultural products, although only tobacco and cotton are exported in any quantity. Industrial exports include gold, mercury, uranium, and natural gas and electricity. Kyrgyzstan has been fairly progressive in carrying out market reforms, such as an improved regulatory system and land reform. Kyrgyzstan was the first CIS country to be accepted into the World Trade Organization. With fits and starts, inflation has been lowered to an estimated 7% in 2001, 2.1% in 2002, and 4.0% in 2003. Much of the government's stock in enterprises has been sold. Drops in production had been severe after the breakup of the Soviet Union in December 1991, but by mid-1995 production began to recover and exports began to increase. Kyrgyzstan has distinguished itself by adopting relatively liberal economic policies. The drop in output at the Kumtor gold mine sparked a 0.5% decline in GDP in 2002, but GDP growth bounced back to 6% in 2003. The government has made steady strides in controlling its substantial fiscal deficit and aims to reduce the deficit to 4.4 percent of GDP in 2004. The government and the international financial institutions have been engaged in a comprehensive medium-term poverty reduction and economic growth strategy. Further restructuring of domestic industry and success in attracting foreign investment are keys to future growth.

GDP: purchasing power parity - $7.725 billion (2003 est.)

GDP - real growth rate: 6% (2003 est.)

GDP - per capita: purchasing power parity - $1,600 (2003 est.)

GDP - composition by sector:

agriculture: 35%

industry: 25%

services: 40% (2002 est.)

Population below poverty line: 50% (2003 est.)

Household income or consumption by percentage share:

lowest 10%: 3.2%

highest 10%: 27.7% (1999)

Distribution of family income - Gini index: 34.6 (1999)

Inflation rate (consumer prices): 4% (2003 est.)

Labor force: 2.7 million (2000)

Labor force - by occupation: agriculture 55%, industry 15%, services 30% (2000 est.)

Unemployment rate: 7.2% (1999 est.)

Budget:

revenues: $207.4 million

expenditures: $238.7 million, including capital expenditures of $NA (1999 est.)

Industries: small machinery, textiles, food processing, cement, shoes, sawn logs, refrigerators, furniture, electric motors, gold, rare earth metals

Industrial production growth rate: 6% (2000 est.)

Electricity - production: 13.45 billion kWh (2001)

Kyrgyzstan (continued)

Electricity - production by source:
fossil fuel: 7.6%
hydro: 92.4%
nuclear: 0%
other: 0% (2001)
Electricity - consumption: 10.46 billion kWh (2001)
Electricity - exports: 2.25 billion kWh (2001)
Electricity - imports: 200 million kWh (2001)
Oil - production: 2,000 bbl/day (2001 est.)
Oil - consumption: 20,000 bbl/day (2001 est.)
Oil - exports: NA
Oil - imports: NA
Natural gas - production: 16 million cu m
(2001 est.)
Natural gas - consumption: 2.016 billion cu m
(2001 est.)
Natural gas - exports: 0 cu m (2001 est.)
Natural gas - imports: 2 billion cu m (2001 est.)
Agriculture - products: tobacco, cotton, potatoes,
vegetables, grapes, fruits and berries; sheep, goats,
cattle, wool
Exports: $548 million f.o.b. (2003 est.)
Exports - commodities: cotton, wool, meat,
tobacco; gold, mercury, uranium, natural gas,
hydropower; machinery; shoes
Exports - partners: Switzerland 19.8%, Russia
16.5%, UAE 14.2%, China 8.4%, Kazakhstan 7.6%,
US 7.4%, Uzbekistan 5.8% (2002)
Imports: $601 million f.o.b. (2003 est.)
Imports - commodities: oil and gas, machinery and
equipment, chemicals, foodstuffs
Imports - partners: Kazakhstan 21.1%, Russia
19.9%, Uzbekistan 10.2%, China 10.1%, US 8%,
Germany 5.3% (2002)
Debt - external: $1.5 billion (2002 est.)
Economic aid - recipient: $50 million from the US
(2001)
Currency: Kyrgyzstani som (KGS)
Currency code: KGS
Exchange rates: soms per US dollar - 43.6484
(2003), 46.9371 (2002), 48.378 (2001), 47.7038
(2000), 39.0077 (1999)
Fiscal year: calendar year

Communications

Telephones - main lines in use: 394,800 (2002)
Telephones - mobile cellular: 53,100 (2002)
Telephone system:
general assessment: poorly developed; about
100,000 unsatisfied applications for household
telephones
domestic: principally microwave radio relay; one
cellular provider, probably limited to Bishkek region
international: country code - 996; connections with
other CIS countries by landline or microwave radio
relay and with other countries by leased connections
with Moscow international gateway switch and by
satellite; satellite earth stations - 1 Intersputnik and 1
Intelsat; connected internationally by the
Trans-Asia-Europe (TAE) fiber-optic line

Radio broadcast stations: AM 12 (plus 10 repeater
stations), FM 14, shortwave 2 (1998)
Television broadcast stations: NA (repeater
stations throughout the country relay programs from
Russia, Uzbekistan, Kazakhstan, and Turkey) (1997)
Internet country code: .kg
Internet hosts: 5,930 (2002)
Internet users: 152,000 (2002)

Transportation

Railways:
total: 420 km
broad gauge: 420 km 1.520-m gauge (2002)
Highways:
total: 18,500 km
paved: 16,854 km (including 140 km of expressways)
unpaved: 1,646 km (1999 est.)
Waterways: 600 km
Pipelines: gas 367 km; oil 13 km (2003)
Ports and harbors: Balykchy (Ysyk-Kol or
Rybach'ye)
Airports: 61 (2003 est.)
Airports - with paved runways:
total: 17
over 3,047 m: 1
2,438 to 3,047 m: 3
1,524 to 2,437 m: 11
under 914 m: 2 (2003 est.)
Airports - with unpaved runways:
total: 44
1,524 to 2,437 m: 3
914 to 1,523 m: 4
under 914 m: 37 (2003 est.)

Military

Military branches: Army, Air and Air Defense,
Security Forces, Border Troops
Military manpower - military age: 18 years of age
(2004 est.)
Military manpower - availability:
males age 15-49: 1,347,312 (2004 est.)
Military manpower - fit for military service:
males age 15-49: 1,091,548 (2004 est.)
**Military manpower - reaching military age
annually:**
males: 59,759 (2004 est.)
Military expenditures - dollar figure: $19.2 million
(FY01)
Military expenditures - percent of GDP: 1.4% (FY01)

Transnational Issues

Disputes - international: boundary with China is
fully demarcated; delimitation with Kazakhstan is
largely complete with only minor disputed areas;
disputes in Isfara Valley delay completion of
delimitation with Tajikistan; delimitation is underway
with Uzbekistan but serious disputes around enclaves
and elsewhere continue to mar progress for some
130 km of border

Illicit drugs: limited illicit cultivation of cannabis and
opium poppy for CIS markets; limited government
eradication of illicit crops; transit point for Southwest
Asian narcotics bound for Russia and the rest of
Europe

Laos

Introduction

Background: In 1975, the Communist Pathet Lao took control of the government, ending a six-century-old monarchy. Initial closer ties to Vietnam and socialization were replaced with a gradual return to private enterprise, a liberalization of foreign investment laws, and the admission into ASEAN in 1997.

Geography

Location: Southeastern Asia, northeast of Thailand, west of Vietnam
Geographic coordinates: 18 00 N, 105 00 E
Map references: Southeast Asia
Area:
total: 236,800 sq km
land: 230,800 sq km
water: 6,000 sq km
Area - comparative: slightly larger than Utah
Land boundaries:
total: 5,083 km
border countries: Burma 235 km, Cambodia 541 km, China 423 km, Thailand 1,754 km, Vietnam 2,130 km
Coastline: 0 km (landlocked)
Maritime claims: none (landlocked)
Climate: tropical monsoon; rainy season (May to November); dry season (December to April)
Terrain: mostly rugged mountains; some plains and plateaus
Elevation extremes:
lowest point: Mekong River 70 m
highest point: Phou Bia 2,817 m
Natural resources: timber, hydropower, gypsum, tin, gold, gemstones
Land use:
arable land: 3.47%
permanent crops: 0.23%
other: 96.3% (1998 est.)

Irrigated land: 1,640 sq km
note: rainy season irrigation - 2,169 sq km; dry season irrigation - 750 sq km (1998 est.)
Natural hazards: floods, droughts
Environment - current issues: unexploded ordnance; deforestation; soil erosion; most of the population does not have access to potable water
Environment - international agreements:
party to: Biodiversity, Climate Change, Climate Change-Kyoto Protocol, Desertification, Endangered Species, Environmental Modification, Law of the Sea, Ozone Layer Protection
signed, but not ratified: none of the selected agreements
Geography - note: landlocked; most of the country is mountainous and thickly forested; the Mekong River forms a large part of the western boundary with Thailand

People

Population: 6,068,117 (July 2004 est.)
Age structure:
0-14 years: 41.9% (male 1,277,152; female 1,265,761)
15-64 years: 54.9% (male 1,642,895; female 1,688,175)
65 years and over: 3.2% (male 87,995; female 106,139) (2004 est.)
Median age:
total: 18.6 years
male: 18.3 years
female: 19 years (2004 est.)
Population growth rate: 2.44% (2004 est.)
Birth rate: 36.47 births/1,000 population (2004 est.)
Death rate: 12.1 deaths/1,000 population (2004 est.)
Net migration rate: 0 migrant(s)/1,000 population (2004 est.)
Sex ratio:
at birth: 1.04 male(s)/female
under 15 years: 1.01 male(s)/female
15-64 years: 0.97 male(s)/female
65 years and over: 0.83 male(s)/female
total population: 0.98 male(s)/female (2004 est.)
Infant mortality rate:
total: 87.06 deaths/1,000 live births
male: 97.05 deaths/1,000 live births
female: 76.69 deaths/1,000 live births (2004 est.)
Life expectancy at birth:
total population: 54.69 years
male: 52.71 years
female: 56.75 years (2004 est.)
Total fertility rate: 4.86 children born/woman (2004 est.)
HIV/AIDS - adult prevalence rate: less than 0.1% (2001 est.)
HIV/AIDS - people living with HIV/AIDS: 1,400 (2001 est.)
HIV/AIDS - deaths: less than 150 (2001 est.)
Nationality:
noun: Lao(s) or Laotian(s)
adjective: Lao or Laotian

Ethnic groups: Lao Loum (lowland) 68%, Lao Theung (upland) 22%, Lao Soung (highland) including the Hmong and the Yao 9%, ethnic Vietnamese/Chinese 1%
Religions: Buddhist 60%, animist and other 40% (including various Christian denominations 1.5%)
Languages: Lao (official), French, English, and various ethnic languages
Literacy:
definition: age 15 and over can read and write
total population: 52.8%
male: 67.5%
female: 38.1% (2003 est.)

Government

Country name:
conventional long form: Lao People's Democratic Republic
conventional short form: Laos
local long form: Sathalanalat Paxathipatai Paxaxon Lao
local short form: none
Government type: Communist state
Capital: Vientiane
Administrative divisions: 16 provinces (khoueng, singular and plural), 1 municipality* (kampheng nakhon, singular and plural), and 1 special zone** (khetphiset, singular and plural); Attapu, Bokeo, Bolikhamxai, Champasak, Houaphan, Khammouan, Louangnamtha, Louangphrabang, Oudomxai, Phongsali, Salavan, Savannakhet, Viangchan*, Viangchan, Xaignabouli, Xaisomboun**, Xekong, Xiangkhoang
Independence: 19 July 1949 (from France)
National holiday: Republic Day, 2 December (1975)
Constitution: promulgated 14 August 1991
Legal system: based on traditional customs, French legal norms and procedures, and socialist practice
Suffrage: 18 years of age; universal
Executive branch:
chief of state: President Gen. KHAMTAI Siphandon (since 26 February 1998) and Vice President Lt. Gen. CHOUMMALI Saignason (since 27 March 2001)
head of government: Prime Minister BOUNGNANG Volachit (since 27 March 2001); First Deputy Prime Minister Maj. Gen. ASANG Laoli (since May 2002), Deputy Prime Minister THONGLOUN Sisolit (since 27 March 2001), and Deputy Prime Minister SOMSAVAT Lengsavat (since 26 February 1998)
cabinet: Council of Ministers appointed by the president, approved by the National Assembly
elections: president elected by the National Assembly for a five-year term; election last held 24 February 2002 (next to be held in 2007); prime minister appointed by the president with the approval of the National Assembly for a five-year term
election results: KHAMTAI Siphandon elected president; percent of National Assembly vote - NA%
Legislative branch: unicameral National Assembly (109 seats; members elected by popular vote to serve five-year terms; note - total number of seats increased from 99 to 109 for the 2002 election)

Laos (continued)

elections: last held 24 February 2002 (next to be held in 2007)
election results: percent of vote by party - NA%; seats by party - LPRP or LPRP-approved (independent, non-party members) 109
Judicial branch: People's Supreme Court (the president of the People's Supreme Court is elected by the National Assembly on the recommendation of the National Assembly Standing Committee; the vice president of the People's Supreme Court and the judges are appointed by the National Assembly Standing Committee)
Political parties and leaders: Lao People's Revolutionary Party or LPRP [KHAMTAI Siphandon, party president]; other parties proscribed
Political pressure groups and leaders: noncommunist political groups proscribed; most opposition leaders fled the country in 1975
International organization participation: ACCT, ARF, AsDB, ASEAN, CP, FAO, G-77, IBRD, ICAO, ICRM, IDA, IFAD, IFC, IFRCS, ILO, IMF, Interpol, IOC, ITU, NAM, OPCW, PCA, UN, UNCTAD, UNESCO, UNIDO, UPU, WFTU, WHO, WIPO, WMO, WToO, WTrO (observer)
Diplomatic representation in the US:
chief of mission: Ambassador PHANTHONG Phommahaxay
chancery: 2222 S Street NW, Washington, DC 20008
telephone: [1] (202) 332-6416
FAX: [1] (202) 332-4923
Diplomatic representation from the US:
chief of mission: Ambassador Douglas A. HARTWICK
embassy: 19 Rue Bartholonie, B. P. 114, Vientiane
mailing address: American Embassy, Box V, APO AP 96546
telephone: [856] (21) 212581, 212582, 212585
FAX: [856] (21) 212584
Flag description: three horizontal bands of red (top), blue (double width), and red with a large white disk centered in the blue band

Economy

Economy - overview: The government of Laos - one of the few remaining official Communist states - began decentralizing control and encouraging private enterprise in 1986. The results, starting from an extremely low base, were striking - growth averaged 7% in 1988-2001 except during the short-lived drop caused by the Asian financial crisis beginning in 1997. Despite this high growth rate, Laos remains a country with a primitive infrastructure; it has no railroads, a rudimentary road system, and limited external and internal telecommunications. Electricity is available in only a few urban areas. Subsistence agriculture accounts for half of GDP and provides 80% of total employment. The economy will continue to benefit from aid from the IMF and other international sources and from new foreign investment in food processing and mining.
GDP: purchasing power parity - $10.34 billion (2003 est.)

GDP - real growth rate: 5.7% (2003 est.)
GDP - per capita: purchasing power parity - $1,700 (2003 est.)
GDP - composition by sector:
agriculture: 53%
industry: 23%
services: 24% (2001 est.)
Population below poverty line: 40% (2002 est.)
Household income or consumption by percentage share:
lowest 10%: 3.2%
highest 10%: 30.6% (1997)
Distribution of family income - Gini index: 37 (1997)
Inflation rate (consumer prices): 7.8% (2001 est.)
Labor force: 2.6 million (2001 est.)
Labor force - by occupation: agriculture 80% (1997 est.)
Unemployment rate: 5.7% (1997 est.)
Budget:
revenues: $211 million
expenditures: $462 million, including capital expenditures of $NA (FY98/99 est.)
Industries: tin and gypsum mining, timber, electric power, agricultural processing, construction, garments, tourism
Industrial production growth rate: 9.7% (2001 est.)
Electricity - production: 1.317 billion kWh (2001)
Electricity - production by source:
fossil fuel: 1.4%
hydro: 98.6%
nuclear: 0%
other: 0% (2001)
Electricity - consumption: 824.8 million kWh (2001)
Electricity - exports: 400 million kWh (2001)
Electricity - imports: 0 kWh (2001)
Oil - production: 0 bbl/day (2001 est.)
Oil - consumption: 2,750 bbl/day (2001 est.)
Oil - exports: NA
Oil - imports: NA
Agriculture - products: sweet potatoes, vegetables, corn, coffee, sugarcane, tobacco, cotton, tea, peanuts, rice, water buffalo, pigs, cattle, poultry
Exports: $332 million (2003 est.)
Exports - commodities: garments, wood products, coffee, electricity, tin
Exports - partners: Thailand 21.5%, Vietnam 16.9%, France 8.6%, Germany 5.6% (2002)
Imports: $492 million f.o.b. (2003 est.)
Imports - commodities: machinery and equipment, vehicles, fuel, consumer goods
Imports - partners: Thailand 60.7%, Vietnam 10.5%, China 8.2%, Singapore 4% (2002)
Debt - external: $2.49 billion (2001)
Economic aid - recipient: $243 million (2001 est.)
Currency: kip (LAK)
Currency code: LAK
Exchange rates: kips per US dollar - 10,443 (2003), 10,056.3 (2002), 8,954.58 (2001), 7,887.64 (2000), 7,102.02 (1999)
Fiscal year: 1 October - 30 September

Communications

Telephones - main lines in use: 61,900 (2002)
Telephones - mobile cellular: 55,200 (2002)
Telephone system:
general assessment: service to general public is poor but improving with over 20,000 telephones currently in service and an additional 48,000 expected by 2001; the government relies on a radiotelephone network to communicate with remote areas
domestic: radiotelephone communications
international: country code - 856; satellite earth station - 1 Intersputnik (Indian Ocean region)
Radio broadcast stations: AM 12, FM 1, shortwave 4 (1998)
Television broadcast stations: 4 (1999)
Internet country code: .la
Internet hosts: 281 (2002)
Internet users: 15,000 (2002)

Transportation

Railways: 0 km
Highways:
total: 21,716 km
paved: 9,664 km
unpaved: 12,052 km (1999 est.)
Waterways: 4,587 km approximately
note: primarily Mekong and tributaries; 2,897 additional km are intermittently navigable by craft drawing less than 0.5 m
Pipelines: refined products 540 km (2003)
Ports and harbors: none
Merchant marine:
total: 1 ships (1,000 GRT or over) 2,370 GRT/3,110 DWT
by type: cargo 1 (2003 est.)
Airports: 46 (2003 est.)
Airports - with paved runways:
total: 9
2,438 to 3,047 m: 1
1,524 to 2,437 m: 5
914 to 1,523 m: 3 (2003 est.)
Airports - with unpaved runways:
total: 37
1,524 to 2,437 m: 1
914 to 1,523 m: 13
under 914 m: 23 (2003 est.)

Military

Military branches: Lao People's Army (LPA; including Riverine Force), Air Force
Military manpower - military age: 18 years of age (2004 est.)
Military manpower - availability:
males age 15-49: 1,456,500 (2004 est.)
Military manpower - fit for military service:
males age 15-49: 783,800 (2004 est.)
Military manpower - reaching military age annually:
males: 68,563 (2004 est.)

Laos *(continued)*

Military expenditures - dollar figure: $10.9 million (2003)
Military expenditures - percent of GDP: 0.5% (2003)

Transnational Issues

Disputes - international: demarcation of boundaries with Cambodia, Thailand, and Vietnam is largely complete, but with Thailand several areas including Mekong River islets remain in dispute; ongoing disputes with Thailand and Vietnam over squatters

Illicit drugs: world's third-largest illicit opium producer (estimated cultivation in 2002 - 23,200 hectares, a 5% increase over 2001; estimated potential production in 2002 - 180 metric tons, a 10% decrease from 2001); potential heroin producer; transshipment point for heroin and methamphetamine produced in Burma; illicit producer of cannabis; growing methamphetamine abuse problem

Latvia

Introduction

Background: After a brief period of independence between the two World Wars, Latvia was annexed by the USSR in 1940. It reestablished its independence in 1991 following the breakup of the Soviet Union. Although the last Russian troops left in 1994, the status of the Russian minority (some 30% of the population) remains of concern to Moscow. Latvia will join the EU in May of 2004 and NATO in the summer of 2004.

Geography

Location: Eastern Europe, bordering the Baltic Sea, between Estonia and Lithuania
Geographic coordinates: 57 00 N, 25 00 E
Map references: Europe
Area:
total: 64,589 sq km
land: 63,589 sq km
water: 1,000 sq km
Area - comparative: slightly larger than West Virginia
Land boundaries:
total: 1,150 km
border countries: Belarus 141 km, Estonia 339 km, Lithuania 453 km, Russia 217 km
Coastline: 531 km
Maritime claims:
territorial sea: 12 NM
exclusive economic zone: 200 NM
continental shelf: 200-m depth or to the depth of exploitation
Climate: maritime; wet, moderate winters
Terrain: low plain
Elevation extremes:
lowest point: Baltic Sea 0 m
highest point: Gaizinkalns 312 m
Natural resources: peat, limestone, dolomite, amber, hydropower, wood, arable land

Land use:
arable land: 29.01%
permanent crops: 0.48%
other: 70.51% (1998 est.)
Irrigated land: 200 sq km
note: land in Latvia is often too wet, and in need of drainage, not irrigation; approximately 16,000 sq km or 85% of agricultural land has been improved by drainage (1998 est.)
Natural hazards: NA
Environment - current issues: Latvia's environment has benefited from a shift to service industries after the country regained independence; the main environmental priorities are improvement of drinking water quality and sewage system, household and hazardous waste management, and reduction of air pollution; in 2001, Latvia closed the EU accession negotiation chapter on environment committing to full enforcement of EU environmental directives by 2010
Environment - international agreements:
party to: Air Pollution, Biodiversity, Climate Change, Climate Change-Kyoto Protocol, Endangered Species, Hazardous Wastes, Ozone Layer Protection, Ship Pollution, Wetlands
signed, but not ratified: Air Pollution-Persistent Organic Pollutants
Geography - note: most of the country is composed of fertile, low-lying plains, with some hills in the east

People

Population: 2,306,306 (July 2004 est.)
Age structure:
0-14 years: 15% (male 177,223; female 169,241)
15-64 years: 69.2% (male 772,496; female 823,410)
65 years and over: 15.8% (male 118,035; female 245,901) (2004 est.)
Median age:
total: 38.8 years
male: 35.6 years
female: 41.9 years (2004 est.)
Population growth rate: -0.71% (2004 est.)

Latvia (continued)

Birth rate: 8.87 births/1,000 population (2004 est.)
Death rate: 13.73 deaths/1,000 population (2004 est.)
Net migration rate: -2.23 migrant(s)/1,000 population (2004 est.)
Sex ratio:
at birth: 1.05 male(s)/female
under 15 years: 1.05 male(s)/female
15-64 years: 0.94 male(s)/female
65 years and over: 0.48 male(s)/female
total population: 0.86 male(s)/female (2004 est.)
Infant mortality rate:
total: 9.67 deaths/1,000 live births
male: 11.45 deaths/1,000 live births
female: 7.8 deaths/1,000 live births (2004 est.)
Life expectancy at birth:
total population: 70.86 years
male: 65.91 years
female: 76.09 years (2004 est.)
Total fertility rate: 1.25 children born/woman (2004 est.)
HIV/AIDS - adult prevalence rate: 0.4% (2001 est.)
HIV/AIDS - people living with HIV/AIDS: 5,000 (2001 est.)
HIV/AIDS - deaths: less than 100 (2001 est.)
Nationality:
noun: Latvian(s)
adjective: Latvian
Ethnic groups: Latvian 57.7%, Russian 29.6%, Belarusian 4.1%, Ukrainian 2.7%, Polish 2.5%, Lithuanian 1.4%, other 2% (2002)
Religions: Lutheran, Roman Catholic, Russian Orthodox
Languages: Latvian (official), Lithuanian, Russian, other
Literacy:
definition: age 15 and over can read and write
total population: 99.8%
male: 99.8%
female: 99.8% (2003 est.)

Government

Country name:
conventional long form: Republic of Latvia
conventional short form: Latvia
local long form: Latvijas Republika
local short form: Latvija
former: Latvian Soviet Socialist Republic
Government type: parliamentary democracy
Capital: Riga
Administrative divisions: 26 counties (singular - rajons) and 7 municipalities*: Aizkraukles Rajons, Aluksnes Rajons, Balvu Rajons, Bauskas Rajons, Cesu Rajons, Daugavpils*, Daugavpils Rajons, Dobeles Rajons, Gulbenes Rajons, Jekabpils Rajons, Jelgava*, Jelgavas Rajons, Jurmala*, Kraslavas Rajons, Kuldigas Rajons, Liepaja*, Liepajas Rajons, Limbazu Rajons, Ludzas Rajons, Madonas Rajons, Ogres Rajons, Preilu Rajons, Rezekne*, Rezeknes Rajons, Riga*, Rigas Rajons, Saldus Rajons, Talsu Rajons, Tukuma Rajons, Valkas Rajons, Valmieras Rajons, Ventspils*, Ventspils Rajons
Independence: 21 August 1991 (from Soviet Union)

National holiday: Independence Day, 18 November (1918); note - 18 November 1918 is the date Latvia declared itself independent from Soviet Russia; 4 May 1990 is when it declared the renewal of independence; 21 August 1991 is the date of de facto independence from the Soviet Union
Constitution: the 1991 Constitutional Law, which supplements the 1922 constitution, provides for basic rights and freedoms
Legal system: based on civil law system
Suffrage: 18 years of age; universal for Latvian citizens
Executive branch:
chief of state: President Vaira VIKE-FREIBERGA (since 8 July 1999)
head of government: Prime Minister Indulis EMSIS (since 9 March 2004)
cabinet: Council of Ministers nominated by the prime minister and appointed by the Parliament
elections: president reelected by Parliament for a four-year term; election last held 20 June 2003 (next to be held by June 2007); prime minister appointed by the president
election results: Vaira VIKE-FREIBERGA reelected president; parliamentary vote - Vaira VIKE-FREIBERGA 88 of 94 votes cast
Legislative branch: unicameral Parliament or Saeima (100 seats; members are elected by direct, popular vote to serve four-year terms)
elections: last held 5 October 2002 (next to be held NA October 2006)
election results: percent of vote by party - New Era 23.9%, PCTVL 18.9%, People's Party 16.7%, ZZS 9.5%, First Party 7.6%, LNNK 5.4%; seats by party - New Era 26, PCTVL 24, People's Party 21, ZZS 12, First Party 10, LNNK 7
Judicial branch: Supreme Court (judges' appointments are confirmed by Parliament)
Political parties and leaders: Alliance of the Greens and Farmers Union or ZZS [Augusts BRIGMANIS (Farmer's Union); Indulis EMSIS (Green Party)]; CENTER Political Alliance [Juris CELMINS]; First Party of Latvia [Eriks JEKABSONS]; For Fatherland and Freedom or LNNK [Maris GRINBLATS]; For Human Rights in a United Latvia or PCTVL [Janis JURKANS], a coalition of the People's Harmony Party or TSP, the Latvian Socialist Party or LSP, and the Equal Rights Movement; Freedom Party [Ziedonis CEVERS]; Land of Mara [Irena SAPROVSKA]; Latvian Rebirth Party [Andris RUBINS]; Latvian Social-Democratic Workers Party (Social Democrats) or LSDSP [Juris BOJARS]; Latvia's Way Union or LC [Janis NAGLIS]; Light of Latgale or LG [Rihards EIGIMS]; New Era Party [Einars REPSE]; Our Land Party [Ilmars ANCANS]; Party of Latvians [Aivars GARDA]; People's Party [Andris SKELE]; Progressive Center Party [Inta STAMGUTE]; Russian Party [Mihails GAVRILOVS]; Social Democratic Union or SDS [Egils BALDZENS]; Social Democratic Welfare Party or SLP [Juris ZURAVLOVS]; United Republican Party of Latvia or LARP [Eriks Andrejs SAULUNS, Janis PUKIS, Sarmite JEGERE]

Political pressure groups and leaders: NA
International organization participation: BIS, CBSS, CE, EAPC, EBRD, EU (new member), FAO, IAEA, IBRD, ICAO, ICCt, ICFTU, ICRM, IDA, IFC, IFRCS, ILO, IMF, IMO, Interpol, IOC, IOM, ISO (correspondent), ITU, NSG, OAS (observer), OPCW, OSCE, PCA, PFP, UN, UNCTAD, UNESCO, UPU, WCO, WEU (associate partner), WHO, WIPO, WMO, WTrO
Diplomatic representation in the US:
chief of mission: Ambassador Aivis RONIS
chancery: 4325 17th Street NW, Washington, DC 20011
telephone: [1] (202) 726-8213, 8214
FAX: [1] (202) 726-6785
Diplomatic representation from the US:
chief of mission: Ambassador Brian E. CARLSON
embassy: 7 Raina Boulevard, Riga LV-1510
mailing address: American Embassy Riga, PSC 78, Box Riga, APO AE 09723
telephone: [371] 703-6200
FAX: [371] 781-0047
Flag description: three horizontal bands of maroon (top), white (half-width), and maroon

Economy

Economy - overview: Latvia's transitional economy recovered from the 1998 Russian financial crisis, largely due to the SKELE government's budget stringency and a gradual reorientation of exports toward EU countries, lessening Latvia's trade dependency on Russia. The majority of companies, banks, and real estate have been privatized, although the state still holds sizable stakes in a few large enterprises. Latvia officially joined the World Trade Organization in February 1999. Preparing for EU membership continues as a top foreign policy goal. The current account and internal government deficits remain major concerns, but the government's efforts to increase efficiency in revenue collection may lessen the budget deficit.
GDP: purchasing power parity - $23.77 billion (2003 est.)
GDP - real growth rate: 6.8% (2003 est.)
GDP - per capita: purchasing power parity - $10,100 (2003 est.)
GDP - composition by sector:
agriculture: 4.5%
industry: 20.9%
services: 74.6% (2002)
Population below poverty line: NA%
Household income or consumption by percentage share:
lowest 10%: 2.9%
highest 10%: 25.9% (1998)
Distribution of family income - Gini index: 32 (1999)
Inflation rate (consumer prices): 2.8% (2003 est.)
Labor force: 1.1 million (2001 est.)
Labor force - by occupation: agriculture 15%, industry 25%, services 60% (2000 est.)
Unemployment rate: 8.7% (2003 est.)

Latvia (continued)

Budget:
revenues: $2.4 billion
expenditures: $2.6 billion, including capital expenditures of $NA (2002 est.)
Industries: buses, vans, street and railroad cars, synthetic fibers, agricultural machinery, fertilizers, washing machines, radios, electronics, pharmaceuticals, processed foods, textiles; note - dependent on imports for energy and raw materials
Industrial production growth rate: 5.7% (2002 est.)
Electricity - production: 4.365 billion kWh (2001)
Electricity - production by source:
fossil fuel: 29.1%
hydro: 70.9%
nuclear: 0%
other: 0% (2001)
Electricity - consumption: 6.046 billion kWh (2001)
Electricity - exports: 703 million kWh (2001)
Electricity - imports: 2.69 billion kWh (2001)
Oil - production: 0 bbl/day (2001 est.)
Oil - consumption: 44,000 bbl/day (2001 est.)
Oil - exports: NA
Oil - imports: NA
Natural gas - production: 0 cu m (2001 est.)
Natural gas - consumption: 1.7 billion cu m (2001 est.)
Natural gas - exports: 0 cu m (2001 est.)
Natural gas - imports: 1.7 billion cu m (2001 est.)
Agriculture - products: grain, sugar beets, potatoes, vegetables; beef, pork, milk, eggs; fish
Exports: $3 billion f.o.b. (2003 est.)
Exports - commodities: wood and wood products, machinery and equipment, metals, textiles, foodstuffs
Exports - partners: Germany 15.3%, UK 14.4%, Sweden 10.4%, Lithuania 8.2%, Estonia 5.9%, Russia 5.8%, Denmark 5.6%, US 4.3% (2002)
Imports: $4.921 billion f.o.b. (2003 est.)
Imports - commodities: machinery and equipment, chemicals, fuels, vehicles
Imports - partners: Germany 17.2%, Lithuania 9.8%, Russia 8.8%, Finland 8%, Sweden 6.4%, Estonia 6.2%, Poland 5%, Italy 4.2% (2002)
Debt - external: $6.6 billion (2003 est.)
Economic aid - recipient: $96.2 million (1995)
Currency: Latvian lat (LVL)
Currency code: LVL
Exchange rates: lati per US dollar - 0.5715 (2003), 0.6182 (2002), 0.6279 (2001), 0.6065 (2000), 0.5852 (1999)
Fiscal year: calendar year

Communications

Telephones - main lines in use: 701,200 (2002)
Telephones - mobile cellular: 917,200 (2002)
Telephone system:
general assessment: inadequate, but is being modernized to provide an international capability independent of the Moscow international switch; more facilities are being installed for individual use
domestic: expansion underway in intercity trunk line connections, rural exchanges, and mobile systems; still many unsatisfied subscriber applications
international: country code - 371; international connections are now available via cable and a satellite earth station at Riga, enabling direct connections for most calls (1998)
Radio broadcast stations: AM 8, FM 56, shortwave 1 (1998)
Television broadcast stations: 44 (plus 31 repeaters) (1995)
Internet country code: .lv
Internet hosts: 35,492 (2002)
Internet users: 312,000 (2002)

Transportation

Railways:
total: 2,347 km
broad gauge: 2,314 km 1.520-m gauge (270 km electrified)
narrow gauge: 33 km 0.750-m gauge (2002)
Highways:
total: 73,202 km
paved: 28,256 km
unpaved: 44,946 km (2000)
Waterways: 300 km (perennially navigable)
Pipelines: gas 1,097 km; oil 412 km; refined products 421 km (2003)
Ports and harbors: Liepaja, Riga, Ventspils
Merchant marine:
total: 11 ships (1,000 GRT or over) 53,153 GRT/ 37,414 DWT
by type: cargo 6, petroleum tanker 1, refrigerated cargo 2, roll on/roll off 1, short-sea/passenger 1
foreign-owned: Germany 1, Greece 1, Ukraine 1
registered in other countries: 96 (2003 est.)
Airports: 51 (2003 est.)
Airports - with paved runways:
total: 27
2,438 to 3,047 m: 7
1,524 to 2,437 m: 2
914 to 1,523 m: 2
under 914 m: 16 (2003 est.)
Airports - with unpaved runways:
total: 24
2,438 to 3,047 m: 1
1,524 to 2,437 m: 2
914 to 1,523 m: 1
under 914 m: 20 (2003 est.)

Military

Military branches: Ground Forces, Navy, Air Force, Border Guard, Home Guard (Zemessardze)
Military manpower - military age: 18 years of age (2004 est.)
Military manpower - availability:
males age 15-49: 594,596 (2004 est.)
Military manpower - fit for military service:
males age 15-49: 466,659 (2004 est.)
Military manpower - reaching military age annually:
males: 19,209 (2004 est.)
Military expenditures - dollar figure: $87 million (FY01)
Military expenditures - percent of GDP: 1.2% (FY01)

Transnational Issues

Disputes - international: the Russian Duma refuses to ratify boundary delimitation treaty with Latvia; the Latvian Parliament has not ratified its 1998 maritime boundary treaty with Lithuania, primarily due to concerns over oil exploration rights
Illicit drugs: transshipment point for opiates and cannabis from Central and Southwest Asia to Western Europe and Scandinavia and Latin American cocaine and some synthetics from Western Europe to CIS; vulnerable to money laundering despite improved legislation due to nascent enforcement capabilities and comparatively weak regulation of offshore companies, exchange firms, and the gaming industry; organized crime (including counterfeiting, corruption, extortion, stolen cars, and prostitution) accounts for most laundered proceeds

Lebanon

Introduction

Background: Lebanon has made progress toward rebuilding its political institutions since 1991 and the end of the devastating 16-year civil war. Under the Ta'if Accord - the blueprint for national reconciliation - the Lebanese have established a more equitable political system, particularly by giving Muslims a greater say in the political process while institutionalizing sectarian divisions in the government. Since the end of the war, the Lebanese have conducted several successful elections, most of the militias have been weakened or disbanded, and the Lebanese Armed Forces (LAF) have extended central government authority over about two-thirds of the country. Hizballah, the radical Shi'a party, retains its weapons. Syria maintains about 16,000 troops in Lebanon, based mainly east of Beirut and in the Bekaa Valley. Syria's troop deployment was legitimized by the Arab League during Lebanon's civil war and in the Ta'if Accord. Damascus justifies its continued military presence in Lebanon by citing Beirut's requests and the failure of the Lebanese Government to implement all of the constitutional reforms in the Ta'if Accord. Israel's withdrawal from its security zone in southern Lebanon in May 2000, however, has emboldened some Lebanese Christians and Druze to demand that Syria withdraw its forces as well.

Geography

Location: Middle East, bordering the Mediterranean Sea, between Israel and Syria
Geographic coordinates: 33 50 N, 35 50 E
Map references: Middle East
Area:
total: 10,400 sq km
land: 10,230 sq km
water: 170 sq km
Area - comparative: about 0.7 times the size of Connecticut

Land boundaries:
total: 454 km
border countries: Israel 79 km, Syria 375 km
Coastline: 225 km
Maritime claims:
territorial sea: 12 NM
Climate: Mediterranean; mild to cool, wet winters with hot, dry summers; Lebanon mountains experience heavy winter snows
Terrain: narrow coastal plain; El Beqaa (Bekaa Valley) separates Lebanon and Anti-Lebanon Mountains
Elevation extremes:
lowest point: Mediterranean Sea 0 m
highest point: Qurnat as Sawda' 3,088 m
Natural resources: limestone, iron ore, salt, water-surplus state in a water-deficit region, arable land
Land use:
arable land: 17.6%
permanent crops: 12.51%
other: 69.89% (1998 est.)
Irrigated land: 1,200 sq km (1998 est.)
Natural hazards: dust storms, sandstorms
Environment - current issues: deforestation; soil erosion; desertification; air pollution in Beirut from vehicular traffic and the burning of industrial wastes; pollution of coastal waters from raw sewage and oil spills
Environment - international agreements:
party to: Biodiversity, Climate Change, Desertification, Hazardous Wastes, Law of the Sea, Ozone Layer Protection, Ship Pollution, Wetlands
signed, but not ratified: Environmental Modification, Marine Life Conservation
Geography - note: Nahr el Litani only major river in Near East not crossing an international boundary; rugged terrain historically helped isolate, protect, and develop numerous factional groups based on religion, clan, and ethnicity

People

Population: 3,777,218 (July 2004 est.)
Age structure:
0-14 years: 26.9% (male 517,356; female 496,888)
15-64 years: 66.3% (male 1,197,430; female 1,305,339)
65 years and over: 6.9% (male 117,930; female 142,275) (2004 est.)
Median age:
total: 26.9 years
male: 25.9 years
female: 27.9 years (2004 est.)
Population growth rate: 1.3% (2004 est.)
Birth rate: 19.31 births/1,000 population (2004 est.)
Death rate: 6.28 deaths/1,000 population (2004 est.)
Net migration rate: 0 migrant(s)/1,000 population (2004 est.)
Sex ratio:
at birth: 1.05 male(s)/female
under 15 years: 1.04 male(s)/female
15-64 years: 0.92 male(s)/female

65 years and over: 0.83 male(s)/female
total population: 0.94 male(s)/female (2004 est.)
Infant mortality rate:
total: 25.48 deaths/1,000 live births
male: 28.21 deaths/1,000 live births
female: 22.61 deaths/1,000 live births (2004 est.)
Life expectancy at birth:
total population: 72.35 years
male: 69.91 years
female: 74.91 years (2004 est.)
Total fertility rate: 1.95 children born/woman (2004 est.)
HIV/AIDS - adult prevalence rate: 0.09% (2001 est.)
HIV/AIDS - people living with HIV/AIDS: NA
HIV/AIDS - deaths: NA
Nationality:
noun: Lebanese (singular and plural)
adjective: Lebanese
Ethnic groups: Arab 95%, Armenian 4%, other 1%
Religions: Muslim 70% (including Shi'a, Sunni, Druze, Isma'ilite, Alawite or Nusayri), Christian 30% (including Orthodox Christian, Catholic, Protestant), Jewish NEGL%
Languages: Arabic (official), French, English, Armenian
Literacy:
definition: age 15 and over can read and write
total population: 87.4%
male: 93.1%
female: 82.2% (2003 est.)

Government

Country name:
conventional long form: Lebanese Republic
conventional short form: Lebanon
local long form: Al Jumhuriyah al Lubnaniyah
local short form: Lubnan
Government type: republic
Capital: Beirut
Administrative divisions: 6 governorates (mohafazat, singular - mohafazah); Beyrouth, Beqaa, Liban-Nord, Liban-Sud, Mont-Liban, Nabatiye
Independence: 22 November 1943 (from League of Nations mandate under French administration)
National holiday: Independence Day, 22 November (1943)
Constitution: 23 May 1926, amended a number of times, most recently Charter of Lebanese National Reconciliation (Ta'if Accord) of October 1989
Legal system: mixture of Ottoman law, canon law, Napoleonic code, and civil law; no judicial review of legislative acts; has not accepted compulsory ICJ jurisdiction
Suffrage: 21 years of age; compulsory for all males; authorized for women at age 21 with elementary education
Executive branch:
chief of state: President Emile LAHUD (since 24 November 1998)

Lebanon (continued)

head of government: Prime Minister Rafiq HARIRI (since 23 October 2000); Deputy Prime Minister Issam FARES (since 23 October 2000); note - HARIRI resigned on 15 April 2003, but was reappointed the next day
cabinet: Cabinet chosen by the prime minister in consultation with the president and members of the National Assembly
elections: president elected by the National Assembly for a six-year term; election last held 15 October 1998 (next to be held NA 2004); prime minister and deputy prime minister appointed by the president in consultation with the National Assembly; by custom, the president is a Maronite Christian, the prime minister is a Sunni Muslim, and the speaker of the legislature is a Shi'a Muslim
election results: Emile LAHUD elected president; National Assembly vote - 118 votes in favor, 0 against, 10 abstentions

Legislative branch: unicameral National Assembly or Majlis Alnuwab (Arabic) or Assemblee Nationale (French) (128 seats; members elected by popular vote on the basis of sectarian proportional representation to serve four-year terms)
elections: last held 27 August and 3 September 2000 (next to be held NA 2004)
election results: percent of vote by party - Muslim 57% (of which Sunni 25%, Sh'ite 25%, Druze 6%, Alawite less than 1%), Christian 43% (of which Maronite 23%); seats by party - Muslim 64 (of which Sunni 27, Sh'ite 27, Druze 8, Alawite 2), Christian 64 (of which Maronite 34)

Judicial branch: four Courts of Cassation (three courts for civil and commercial cases and one court for criminal cases); Constitutional Council (called for in Ta'if Accord - rules on constitutionality of laws); Supreme Council (hears charges against the president and prime minister as needed)

Political parties and leaders: political party activity is organized along largely sectarian lines; numerous political groupings exist, consisting of individual political figures and followers motivated by religious, clan, and economic considerations

Political pressure groups and leaders: NA

International organization participation: ABEDA, ACCT, AFESD, AMF, FAO, G-24, G-77, IAEA, IBRD, ICAO, ICC, ICFTU, ICRM, IDA, IDB, IFAD, IFC, IFRCS, ILO, IMF, IMO, Interpol, IOC, ISO (correspondent), ITU, LAS, NAM, OAS (observer), OIC, PCA, UN, UNCTAD, UNESCO, UNHCR, UNIDO, UNRWA, UPU, WCO, WFTU, WHO, WIPO, WMO, WToO, WTrO (observer)

Diplomatic representation in the US:
chief of mission: Ambassador Dr. Farid ABBOUD
chancery: 2560 28th Street NW, Washington, DC 20008
telephone: [1] (202) 939-6320
FAX: [1] (202) 939-6324
consulate(s) general: Detroit, New York, and Los Angeles

Diplomatic representation from the US:
chief of mission: Ambassador Vincent Martin BATTLE
embassy: Awkar, Lebanon
mailing address: P. O. Box 70840, Awkar, Lebanon; PSC 815, Box 2, FPO AE 09836-0002
telephone: 011-961-4-543-600/542-600
FAX: 011-961-4-544-136

Flag description: three horizontal bands of red (top), white (double width), and red with a green cedar tree centered in the white band

Economy

Economy - overview: The 1975-91 civil war seriously damaged Lebanon's economic infrastructure, cut national output by half, and all but ended Lebanon's position as a Middle Eastern entrepot and banking hub. Peace enabled the central government to restore control in Beirut, begin collecting taxes, and regain access to key port and government facilities. Economic recovery was helped by a financially sound banking system and resilient small- and medium-scale manufacturers. Family remittances, banking services, manufactured and farm exports, and international aid provided the main sources of foreign exchange. Lebanon's economy made impressive gains since the launch in 1993 of "Horizon 2000," the government's $20 billion reconstruction program. Real GDP grew 8% in 1994, 7% in 1995, 4% in 1996 and in 1997, but slowed to 1.2% in 1998, -1.6% in 1999, -0.6% in 2000, 0.8% in 2001, 1.5% in 2002, and 3% in 2003. During the 1990s, annual inflation fell to almost 0% from more than 100%. Lebanon has rebuilt much of its war-torn physical and financial infrastructure. The government nonetheless faces serious challenges in the economic arena. It has funded reconstruction by borrowing heavily - mostly from domestic banks. In order to reduce the ballooning national debt, the re-installed HARIRI government began an economic austerity program to rein in government expenditures, increase revenue collection, and privatize state enterprises. The HARIRI government met with international donors at the Paris II conference in November 2002 to seek bilateral assistance restructuring its domestic debt at lower rates of interest. While privatization of state-owned enterprises had not occurred by the end of 2003, massive receipts from donor nations stabilized government finances throughout 2002 and 2003.

GDP: purchasing power parity - $17.82 billion (2003 est.)
GDP - real growth rate: 3% (2003 est.)
GDP - per capita: purchasing power parity - $4,800 (2003 est.)
GDP - composition by sector:
agriculture: 12%
industry: 21%
services: 67% (2000)
Population below poverty line: 28% (1999 est.)

Household income or consumption by percentage share:
lowest 10%: NA%
highest 10%: NA%
Inflation rate (consumer prices): 2.5% (2003 est.)
Labor force: 1.5 million
note: in addition, there are as many as 1 million foreign workers (2001 est.)
Labor force - by occupation: services NA%, industry NA%, agriculture NA%
Unemployment rate: 18% (1997 est.)
Budget:
revenues: $4.5 billion
expenditures: $7.1 billion, including capital expenditures of $NA (2003 est.)
Industries: banking; food processing; jewelry; cement; textiles; mineral and chemical products; wood and furniture products; oil refining; metal fabricating
Industrial production growth rate: NA%
Electricity - production: 6.728 billion kWh (2001)
Electricity - production by source:
fossil fuel: 97.2%
hydro: 2.8%
nuclear: 0%
other: 0% (2001)
Electricity - consumption: 7.44 billion kWh (2001)
Electricity - exports: 0 kWh (2001)
Electricity - imports: 1.183 billion kWh (2001)
Oil - production: 0 bbl/day (2001 est.)
Oil - consumption: 107,000 bbl/day (2001 est.)
Oil - exports: NA
Oil - imports: NA
Agriculture - products: citrus, grapes, tomatoes, apples, vegetables, potatoes, olives, tobacco; sheep, goats
Exports: $1.359 billion f.o.b. (2003 est.)
Exports - commodities: authentic jewelry, inorganic chemicals, miscellaneous consumer goods, fruit, tobacco, construction minerals, electric power machinery and switchgear, textile fibers, paper
Exports - partners: UAE 11%, Switzerland 9.1%, Saudi Arabia 8.2%, US 6.2%, Jordan 4.2% (2002)
Imports: $6.073 billion f.o.b. (2003 est.)
Imports - commodities: petroleum products, cars, medicinal products, clothing, meat and live animals, consumer goods, paper, textile fabrics, tobacco
Imports - partners: Italy 11.3%, France 10.7%, Germany 8.3%, US 5.6%, Syria 5.4%, China 4.8%, Belgium 4.5%, UK 4.2% (2002)
Debt - external: $16.3 billion (2003 est.)
Economic aid - recipient: $3.5 billion (pledges 1997-2001); $4.2 billion in soft loan pledges November 2002 Paris II Aid Conference (2002)
Currency: Lebanese pound (LBP)
Currency code: LBP
Exchange rates: Lebanese pounds per US dollar - 1,507.5 (2003), 1,507.5 (2002), 1,507.5 (2001), 1,507.5 (2000), 1,507.84 (1999)
Fiscal year: calendar year

Lebanon (continued)

Communications

Telephones - main lines in use: 678,800 (2002)
Telephones - mobile cellular: 775,100 (2002)
Telephone system:
general assessment: telecommunications system severely damaged by civil war; rebuilding well underway
domestic: primarily microwave radio relay and cable
international: country code - 961; satellite earth stations - 2 Intelsat (1 Indian Ocean and 1 Atlantic Ocean) (erratic operations); coaxial cable to Syria; microwave radio relay to Syria but inoperable beyond Syria to Jordan; 3 submarine coaxial cables
Radio broadcast stations: AM 20, FM 22, shortwave 4 (1998)
Television broadcast stations: 15 (plus 5 repeaters) (1995)
Internet country code: .lb
Internet hosts: 7,199 (2002)
Internet users: 400,000 (2002)

Transportation

Railways:
total: 401 km
standard gauge: 319 km 1.435-m
narrow gauge: 82 km 1.050-m
note: rail system is unusable because of damage in civil war (2002)
Highways:
total: 7,300 km
paved: 6,198 km
unpaved: 1,102 km (1999 est.)
Waterways: none
Pipelines: oil 209 km (2003)
Ports and harbors: Antilyas, Batroun, Beirut, Chekka, El Mina, Ez Zahrani, Jbail, Jounie, Naqoura, Sidon, Tripoli, Tyre
Merchant marine:
total: 49 ships (1,000 GRT or over) 198,602 GRT/ 248,313 DWT
by type: bulk 5, cargo 23, chemical tanker 1, combination bulk 1, container 2, liquefied gas 1, livestock carrier 8, refrigerated cargo 1, roll on/roll off 4, vehicle carrier 3
foreign-owned: Greece 7, India 1, Netherlands 4, Saint Vincent and the Grenadines 1, Spain 1, Syria 2
registered in other countries: 52 (2003 est.)
Airports: 8 (2003 est.)
Airports - with paved runways:
total: 5
over 3,047 m: 1
2,438 to 3,047 m: 2
1,524 to 2,437 m: 1
under 914 m: 1 (2003 est.)
Airports - with unpaved runways:
total: 3
914 to 1,523 m: 2
under 914 m: 1 (2003 est.)

Military

Military branches: Lebanese Armed Forces (LAF; includes Army, Navy, and Air Force)
Military manpower - military age: 18 years of age (2004 est.)
Military manpower - availability:
males age 15-49: 1,049,097 (2004 est.)
Military manpower - fit for military service:
males age 15-49: 643,050 (2004 est.)
Military expenditures - dollar figure: $541 million (2002)
Military expenditures - percent of GDP: 4.8% (FY99)

Transnational Issues

Disputes - international: Syrian troops in central and eastern Lebanon since October 1976; Lebanese Government claims Shab'a Farms area of Israeli-occupied Golan Heights
Illicit drugs: cannabis cultivation dramatically reduced to 2,500 hectares in 2002; opium poppy cultivation minimal; small amounts of Latin American cocaine and Southwest Asian heroin transit country on way to European markets and for Middle Eastern consumption

Lesotho

Introduction

Background: Basutoland was renamed the Kingdom of Lesotho upon independence from the UK in 1966. King MOSHOESHOE was exiled in 1990. Constitutional government was restored in 1993 after 23 years of military rule. In 1998, violent protests and a military mutiny following a contentious election prompted a brief but bloody South African military intervention. Constitutional reforms have since restored political stability; peaceful parliamentary elections were held in 2002.

Geography

Location: Southern Africa, an enclave of South Africa
Geographic coordinates: 29 30 S, 28 30 E
Map references: Africa
Area:
total: 30,355 sq km
land: 30,355 sq km
water: 0 sq km
Area - comparative: slightly smaller than Maryland
Land boundaries:
total: 909 km
border countries: South Africa 909 km
Coastline: 0 km (landlocked)
Maritime claims: none (landlocked)
Climate: temperate; cool to cold, dry winters; hot, wet summers
Terrain: mostly highland with plateaus, hills, and mountains
Elevation extremes:
lowest point: junction of the Orange and Makhaleng Rivers 1,400 m
highest point: Thabana Ntlenyana 3,482 m
Natural resources: water, agricultural and grazing land, some diamonds and other minerals

Lesotho (continued)

Land use:

arable land: 10.71%
permanent crops: 0%
other: 89.29% (1998 est.)
Irrigated land: 10 sq km (1998 est.)
Natural hazards: periodic droughts
Environment - current issues: population pressure forcing settlement in marginal areas results in overgrazing, severe soil erosion, and soil exhaustion; desertification; Highlands Water Project controls, stores, and redirects water to South Africa
Environment - international agreements:
party to: Biodiversity, Climate Change, Climate Change-Kyoto Protocol, Desertification, Endangered Species, Hazardous Wastes, Marine Life Conservation, Ozone Layer Protection
signed, but not ratified: Law of the Sea
Geography - note: landlocked, completely surrounded by South Africa; mountainous, more than 80% of the country is 1,800 meters above sea level

People

Population: 1,865,040
note: estimates for this country explicitly take into account the effects of excess mortality due to AIDS; this can result in lower life expectancy, higher infant mortality and death rates, lower population and growth rates, and changes in the distribution of population by age and sex than would otherwise be expected (July 2004 est.)
Age structure:
0-14 years: 37.3% (male 350,288; female 345,815)
15-64 years: 57.2% (male 521,434; female 545,183)
65 years and over: 5.5% (male 41,903; female 60,417) (2004 est.)
Median age:
total: 20 years
male: 19.5 years
female: 20.6 years (2004 est.)
Population growth rate: 0.14% (2004 est.)
Birth rate: 26.91 births/1,000 population (2004 est.)
Death rate: 24.79 deaths/1,000 population (2004 est.)
Net migration rate: -0.74 migrant(s)/1,000 population (2004 est.)
Sex ratio:
at birth: 1.03 male(s)/female
under 15 years: 1.01 male(s)/female
15-64 years: 0.96 male(s)/female
65 years and over: 0.69 male(s)/female
total population: 0.96 male(s)/female (2004 est.)
Infant mortality rate:
total: 85.22 deaths/1,000 live births
male: 90.19 deaths/1,000 live births
female: 80.1 deaths/1,000 live births (2004 est.)
Life expectancy at birth:
total population: 36.81 years
male: 36.81 years
female: 36.81 years (2004 est.)
Total fertility rate: 3.44 children born/woman (2004 est.)
HIV/AIDS - adult prevalence rate: 31% (2001 est.)

HIV/AIDS - people living with HIV/AIDS: 360,000 (2001 est.)
HIV/AIDS - deaths: 25,000 (2001 est.)
Nationality:
noun: Mosotho (singular), Basotho (plural)
adjective: Basotho
Ethnic groups: Sotho 99.7%, Europeans, Asians, and other 0.3%,
Religions: Christian 80%, indigenous beliefs 20%
Languages: Sesotho (southern Sotho), English (official), Zulu, Xhosa
Literacy:
definition: age 15 and over can read and write
total population: 84.8%
male: 74.5%
female: 94.5% (2003 est.)

Government

Country name:
conventional long form: Kingdom of Lesotho
conventional short form: Lesotho
former: Basutoland
Government type: parliamentary constitutional monarchy
Capital: Maseru
Administrative divisions: 10 districts; Berea, Butha-Buthe, Leribe, Mafeteng, Maseru, Mohale's Hoek, Mokhotlong, Qacha's Nek, Quthing, Thaba-Tseka
Independence: 4 October 1966 (from UK)
National holiday: Independence Day, 4 October (1966)
Constitution: 2 April 1993
Legal system: based on English common law and Roman-Dutch law; judicial review of legislative acts in High Court and Court of Appeal; has not accepted compulsory ICJ jurisdiction
Suffrage: 18 years of age; universal
Executive branch:
chief of state: King LETSIE III (since 7 February 1996); note - King LETSIE III formerly occupied the throne from November 1990 to February 1995, while his father was in exile
head of government: Prime Minister Pakalitha MOSISILI (since 23 May 1998)
cabinet: Cabinet
elections: none; according to the constitution, the leader of the majority party in the Assembly automatically becomes prime minister; the monarch is hereditary, but, under the terms of the constitution, which came into effect after the March 1993 election, the monarch is a "living symbol of national unity" with no executive or legislative powers; under traditional law the college of chiefs has the power to determine who is next in the line of succession, who shall serve as regent in the event that the successor is not of mature age, and may even depose the monarch
Legislative branch: bicameral Parliament consists of the Senate (33 members - 22 principal chiefs and 11 other members appointed by the ruling party) and the Assembly (120 seats, 80 by direct popular vote and 40 by proportional vote; members elected by

popular vote for five-year terms); note - number of seats in the Assembly rose from 80 to 120 in the May 2002 election
elections: last held 25 May 2002 (next to be held NA May 2007)
election results: percent of vote by party - LCD 54%, BNP 21%, LPC 7%, other 18%; seats by party - LCD 76, BNP 21, LPC 5, other 18
Judicial branch: High Court (chief justice appointed by the monarch); Court of Appeal; Magistrate's Court; customary or traditional court
Political parties and leaders: Basotho Congress Party or BCP [Tseliso MAKHAKHE]; Basotho National Party or BNP [Maj. Gen. Justine Metsing LEKHANYA]; Lesotho Congress for Democracy or LCD [Phebe MOTEBANO, chairwoman; Pakalitha MOSISILI, leader] - the governing party; Lesotho People's Congress or LPC [Kelebone MAOPE]; United Democratic Party or UDP [Charles MOFELI]; Marematlou Freedom Party or MFP and Setlamo Alliance [Vincent MALEBO]; Progressive National Party or PNP [Chief Peete Nkoebe PEETE]; Sefate Democratic Party or SDP [Bofihla NKUEBE]
Political pressure groups and leaders: NA
International organization participation: ACP, AfDB, AU, C, FAO, G-77, IBRD, ICAO, ICCt, ICRM, IDA, IFAD, IFC, IFRCS, ILO, IMF, Interpol, IOC, ISO (subscriber), ITU, NAM, OPCW, SACU, SADC, UN, UNCTAD, UNESCO, UNHCR, UNIDO, UPU, WCO, WFTU, WHO, WIPO, WMO, WToO, WTrO
Diplomatic representation in the US:
chief of mission: Ambassador Molelekeng E. RAPOLAKI
chancery: 2511 Massachusetts Avenue NW, Washington, DC 20008
telephone: [1] (202) 797-5533 through 5536
FAX: [1] (202) 234-6815
Diplomatic representation from the US:
chief of mission: Ambassador Robert G. LOFTIS
embassy: 254 Kingsway, Maseru West (Consular Section)
mailing address: P. O. Box 333, Maseru 100, Lesotho
telephone: [266] 312666
FAX: [266] 310116
Flag description: divided diagonally from the lower hoist side corner; the upper half is white, bearing the brown silhouette of a large shield with crossed spear and club; the lower half is a diagonal blue band with a green triangle in the corner

Economy

Economy - overview: Small, landlocked, and mountainous, Lesotho relies on remittances from miners employed in South Africa and customs duties from the Southern Africa Customs Union for the majority of government revenue, but the government has strengthened its tax system to reduce dependency on customs duties. Completion of a major hydropower facility in January 1998 now permits the sale of water to South Africa, also generating royalties for Lesotho. As the number of mineworkers has declined steadily over the past

Lesotho *(continued)*

several years, a small manufacturing base has developed based on farm products that support the milling, canning, leather, and jute industries and a rapidly growing apparel-assembly sector. The economy is still primarily based on subsistence agriculture, especially livestock, although drought has decreased agricultural activity. The extreme inequality in the distribution of income remains a major drawback. Lesotho has signed an Interim Poverty Reduction and Growth Facility with the IMF.

GDP: purchasing power parity - $5.594 billion (2003 est.)

GDP - real growth rate: 4.2% (2003 est.)

GDP - per capita: purchasing power parity - $3,000 (2003 est.)

GDP - composition by sector:
agriculture: 20%
industry: 46%
services: 34% (2001)

Population below poverty line: 49% (1999)

Household income or consumption by percentage share:
lowest 10%: 0.9%
highest 10%: 43.4%

Distribution of family income - Gini index: 56 (1986-87)

Inflation rate (consumer prices): 10% (2002 est.)

Labor force: 838,000 (2000)

Labor force - by occupation: 86% of resident population engaged in subsistence agriculture; roughly 35% of the active male wage earners work in South Africa

Unemployment rate: 45% (2002)

Budget:
revenues: $76 million
expenditures: $80 million, including capital expenditures of $15 million (FY99/00 est.)

Industries: food, beverages, textiles, apparel assembly, handicrafts; construction; tourism

Industrial production growth rate: 15.5% (1999)

Electricity - production: 0 kWh NA kWh; note - electricity supplied by South Africa (2001)

Electricity - consumption: 40 million kWh (2001)

Electricity - exports: 0 kWh (2001)

Electricity - imports: 40 million kWh; note - electricity supplied by South Africa (2001)

Oil - production: 0 bbl/day (2001 est.)

Oil - consumption: 1,500 bbl/day (2001)

Oil - exports: NA

Oil - imports: NA

Agriculture - products: corn, wheat, pulses, sorghum, barley; livestock

Exports: $450 million f.o.b. (2003 est.)

Exports - commodities: manufactures 75% (clothing, footwear, road vehicles), wool and mohair, food and live animals (2000)

Exports - partners: US 97.5%, Canada 0.9%, France 0.6% (2002)

Imports: $661 million f.o.b. (2003 est.)

Imports - commodities: food; building materials, vehicles, machinery, medicines, petroleum products (2000)

Imports - partners: Hong Kong 48.3%, China 23.2%, Singapore 3.7% (2002)

Debt - external: $735 million (2002)

Economic aid - donor: ODA $4.4 million

Economic aid - recipient: $41.5 million (2000)

Currency: loti (LSL); South African rand (ZAR)

Currency code: LSL; ZAR

Exchange rates: maloti per US dollar - 7.5648 (2003), 10.5407 (2002), 8.6092 (2001), 6.9398 (2000), 6.1095 (1999)

Fiscal year: 1 April - 31 March

Communications

Telephones - main lines in use: 28,600 (2002)

Telephones - mobile cellular: 92,000 (2002)

Telephone system:
general assessment: rudimentary system
domestic: consists of a few landlines, a small microwave radio relay system, and a minor radiotelephone communication system; a cellular mobile telephone system is growing
international: country code - 266; satellite earth station - 1 Intelsat (Atlantic Ocean)

Radio broadcast stations: AM 1, FM 2, shortwave 1 (1998)

Television broadcast stations: 1 (2000)

Internet country code: .ls

Internet hosts: 45 (2002)

Internet users: 21,000 (2002)

Transportation

Railways:
total: 2.6 km; note - owned by, operated by, and included in the statistics of South Africa
narrow gauge: 2.6 km 1.067-m gauge (1995)

Highways:
total: 5,940 km
paved: 1,087 km
unpaved: 4,853 km (1999)

Waterways: none

Ports and harbors: none

Airports: 28 (2003 est.)

Airports - with paved runways:
total: 4
over 3,047 m: 1
914 to 1,523 m: 1
under 914 m: 2 (2003 est.)

Airports - with unpaved runways:
total: 24
914 to 1,523 m: 4
under 914 m: 20 (2003 est.)

Military

Military branches: Lesotho Defense Force (LDF; with Army and Air Wing)

Military manpower - availability:
males age 15-49: 465,827 (2004 est.)

Military manpower - fit for military service:
males age 15-49: 253,974 (2004 est.)

Military expenditures - dollar figure: $32.5 million (2003)

Military expenditures - percent of GDP: 2.6% (2003)

Military - note: the Lesotho Government in 1999 began an open debate on the future structure, size, and role of the armed forces, especially considering the Lesotho Defense Force's (LDF) history of intervening in political affairs

Transnational Issues

Disputes - international: none

Liberia

Introduction

Background: Years of fighting, coupled with the flight of most businesses, have disrupted formal economic activity. A still unsettled domestic security situation has slowed the process of rebuilding the social and economic structure of this war-torn country. President TAYLOR, who won the 1997 presidential elections after an eight-year-long civil war, was never able to fully eliminate rebel groups that sought to oust him by force. Rebel attacks on Monrovia, coupled with two years of UN-imposed sanctions for TAYLOR'S meddling in Sierra Leone's civil war, finally prompted TAYLOR'S abdication from power in August 2003. A transitional government - composed of rebel, government, and civil society groups - assumed control in October 2003. Chairman Gyude BRYANT, who has a two-year mandate to oversee efforts to rebuild Liberia, heads the new government.

Geography

Location: Western Africa, bordering the North Atlantic Ocean, between Cote d'Ivoire and Sierra Leone
Geographic coordinates: 6 30 N, 9 30 W
Map references: Africa
Area:
total: 111,370 sq km
land: 96,320 sq km
water: 15,050 sq km
Area - comparative: slightly larger than Tennessee
Land boundaries:
total: 1,585 km
border countries: Guinea 563 km, Cote d'Ivoire 716 km, Sierra Leone 306 km
Coastline: 579 km
Maritime claims:
territorial sea: 200 NM
Climate: tropical; hot, humid; dry winters with hot days and cool to cold nights; wet, cloudy summers with frequent heavy showers

Terrain: mostly flat to rolling coastal plains rising to rolling plateau and low mountains in northeast
Elevation extremes:
lowest point: Atlantic Ocean 0 m
highest point: Mount Wuteve 1,380 m
Natural resources: iron ore, timber, diamonds, gold, hydropower
Land use:
arable land: 1.97%
permanent crops: 2.08%
other: 95.95% (1998 est.)
Irrigated land: 30 sq km (1998 est.)
Natural hazards: dust-laden harmattan winds blow from the Sahara (December to March)
Environment - current issues: tropical rain forest deforestation; soil erosion; loss of biodiversity; pollution of coastal waters from oil residue and raw sewage
Environment - international agreements:
party to: Biodiversity, Climate Change-Kyoto Protocol, Desertification, Endangered Species, Ozone Layer Protection, Ship Pollution, Tropical Timber 83, Tropical Timber 94
signed, but not ratified: Climate Change, Environmental Modification, Law of the Sea, Marine Life Conservation
Geography - note: facing the Atlantic Ocean, the coastline is characterized by lagoons, mangrove swamps, and river-deposited sandbars; the inland grassy plateau supports limited agriculture

People

Population: 3,390,635 (July 2004 est.)
Age structure:
0-14 years: 43.4% (male 742,508; female 730,677)
15-64 years: 52.9% (male 875,951; female 918,570)
65 years and over: 3.6% (male 61,867; female 61,062) (2004 est.)
Median age:
total: 18.1 years
male: 17.7 years
female: 18.4 years (2004 est.)
Population growth rate: 2.7% (2004 est.)
Birth rate: 44.81 births/1,000 population (2004 est.)
Death rate: 17.86 deaths/1,000 population (2004 est.)
Net migration rate: 0 migrant(s)/1,000 population
note: at least 200,000 Liberian refugees are in surrounding countries; the uncertain security situation has hindered their ability to return (2004 est.)
Sex ratio:
at birth: 1.03 male(s)/female
under 15 years: 1.02 male(s)/female
15-64 years: 0.95 male(s)/female
65 years and over: 1.01 male(s)/female
total population: 0.98 male(s)/female (2004 est.)
Infant mortality rate:
total: 130.51 deaths/1,000 live births
male: 137.32 deaths/1,000 live births
female: 123.5 deaths/1,000 live births (2004 est.)

Life expectancy at birth:
total population: 47.93 years
male: 46.9 years
female: 48.99 years (2004 est.)
Total fertility rate: 6.16 children born/woman (2004 est.)
HIV/AIDS - adult prevalence rate: 9% (2001 est.)
HIV/AIDS - people living with HIV/AIDS: 125,000 (2001 est.)
HIV/AIDS - deaths: 5,000 (2001 est.)
Nationality:
noun: Liberian(s)
adjective: Liberian
Ethnic groups: indigenous African tribes 95% (including Kpelle, Bassa, Gio, Kru, Grebo, Mano, Krahn, Gola, Gbandi, Loma, Kissi, Vai, Dei, Bella, Mandingo, and Mende), Americo-Liberians 2.5% (descendants of immigrants from the US who had been slaves), Congo People 2.5% (descendants of immigrants from the Caribbean who had been slaves)
Religions: indigenous beliefs 40%, Christian 40%, Muslim 20%
Languages: English 20% (official), some 20 ethnic group languages, of which a few can be written and are used in correspondence
Literacy:
definition: age 15 and over can read and write
total population: 57.5%
male: 73.3%
female: 41.6%
note: (2003 est.)

Government

Country name:
conventional long form: Republic of Liberia
conventional short form: Liberia
Government type: republic
Capital: Monrovia
Administrative divisions: 15 counties; Bomi, Bong, Gbarpolu, Grand Bassa, Grand Cape Mount, Grand Gedeh, Grand Kru, Lofa, Margibi, Maryland, Montserrado, Nimba, River Cess, River Gee, Sinoe
Independence: 26 July 1847
National holiday: Independence Day, 26 July (1847)
Constitution: 6 January 1986
Legal system: dual system of statutory law based on Anglo-American common law for the modern sector and customary law based on unwritten tribal practices for indigenous sector
Suffrage: 18 years of age; universal
Executive branch:
chief of state: Chairman Gyude BRYANT (since 14 October 2003); note - this is an interim position until presidential elections in 2005; the chairman is both the chief of state and head of government
head of government: Chairman Gyude BRYANT (since 14 October 2003); note - this is an interim position until presidential elections in 2005; the chairman is both the chief of state and head of government

Liberia *(continued)*

cabinet: Cabinet appointed by the president and confirmed by the Senate; note - current cabinet positions are divided among groups participating in the Liberian peace process

elections: president elected by popular vote for a six-year term (renewable); election last held 19 July 1997 (next to be held NA October 2005)

election results: Charles Ghankay TAYLOR elected president; percent of vote - Charles Ghankay TAYLOR (NPP) 75.3%, Ellen Johnson SIRLEAF (UP) 9.6%, Alhaji KROMAH (ALCOP) 4%, other 11.1%; note - Taylor stepped down in August 2003

note: a UN-brokered cease-fire among warring factions and the Liberian government resulted in the August 2003 resignation of former president Charles TAYLOR; a jointly agreed upon replacement, Chairman Gyude BRYANT, assumed office as head of the National Transitional Government on 14 October 2003

Legislative branch: bicameral National Assembly consists of the Senate (26 seats; members elected by popular vote to serve nine-year terms) and the House of Representatives (64 seats; members elected by popular vote to serve six-year terms)

elections: Senate - last held 19 July 1997 (next to be held NA 2006); House of Representatives - last held 19 July 1997 (next to be held NA October 2005)

election results: Senate - percent of vote by party - NA%; seats by party - NPP 21, UP 3, ALCOP 2; House of Representatives - percent of vote by party - NA%; seats by party - NPP 49, UP 7, ALCOP 3, Alliance of Political Parties 2, UPP 2, LPP 1

Judicial branch: Supreme Court

Political parties and leaders: Alliance of Political Parties (a coalition of LAP and LUP) [leader NA]; All Liberia Coalition Party or ALCOP [Peter KERBAY]; Liberian Action Party or LAP [C. Gyude BRYANT]; Liberian People's Party or LPP [Koffa NAGBE]; Liberia Unification Party or LUP [leader NA]; National Patriotic Party or NPP [Cyril ALLEN] - governing party; United People's Party or UPP [Wesley JOHNSON]; Unity Party or UP [Charles CLARKE]

Political pressure groups and leaders: NA

International organization participation: ACP, AfDB, AU, ECOWAS, FAO, G-77, IAEA, IBRD, ICAO, ICCt (signatory), ICFTU, ICRM, IDA, IFAD, IFC, IFRCS, ILO, IMF, IMO, Interpol, IOC, IOM, ITU, NAM, OPCW (signatory), UN, UNCTAD, UNESCO, UNIDO, UPU, WCL, WCO, WFTU, WHO, WIPO, WMO

Diplomatic representation in the US:

chief of mission: Ambassador (vacant); Charge d'Affaires Aaron B. KOLLIE

chancery: 5201 16th Street NW, Washington, DC 20011

telephone: [1] (202) 723-0437

FAX: [1] (202) 723-0436

consulate(s) general: New York

Diplomatic representation from the US:

chief of mission: Ambassador John William BLANEY III

embassy: 111 United Nations Drive, P. O. Box 10-0098, Mamba Point, 1000 Monrovia, 10 Liberia

mailing address: use embassy street address

telephone: [231] 226-370 through 226-380

FAX: [231] 226-148

Flag description: 11 equal horizontal stripes of red (top and bottom) alternating with white; there is a white five-pointed star on a blue square in the upper hoist-side corner; the design was based on the US flag

Economy

Economy - overview: Civil war and misgovernment have destroyed much of Liberia's economy, especially the infrastructure in and around Monrovia. Many businessmen have fled the country, taking capital and expertise with them. Some have returned, many will not. Richly endowed with water, mineral resources, forests, and a climate favorable to agriculture, Liberia had been a producer and exporter of basic products - primarily raw timber and rubber. Local manufacturing, mainly foreign owned, had been small in scope. The departure of the former president, Charles TAYLOR, to Nigeria in August 2003, the establishment of the all-inclusive National Transition Government of Liberia (NTGL), and the arrival of a UN mission are all encouraging signs that the political crisis is coming to an end. The restoration of infrastructure and the raising of incomes in this ravaged economy depend on the implementation of sound macro- and micro-economic policies, including the encouragement of foreign investment, and generous support from donor countries.

GDP: purchasing power parity - $3.261 billion (2003 est.)

GDP - real growth rate: 3% (2003 est.)

GDP - per capita: purchasing power parity - $1,000 (2003 est.)

GDP - composition by sector:

agriculture: 76.9%

industry: 5.4%

services: 17.7% (2002 est.)

Population below poverty line: 80%

Household income or consumption by percentage share:

lowest 10%: NA%

highest 10%: NA%

Inflation rate (consumer prices): 15% (2003 est.)

Labor force - by occupation: agriculture 70%, industry 8%, services 22% (2000 est.)

Unemployment rate: 85% (2003 est.)

Budget:

revenues: $85.4 million

expenditures: $90.5 million, including capital expenditures of $NA (2000 est.)

Industries: rubber processing, palm oil processing, timber, diamonds

Industrial production growth rate: NA%

Electricity - production: 468.8 million kWh (2001)

Electricity - production by source:

fossil fuel: 100%

hydro: 0%

nuclear: 0%

other: 0% (2001)

Electricity - consumption: 435.9 million kWh (2001)

Electricity - exports: 0 kWh (2001)

Electricity - imports: 0 kWh (2001)

Oil - production: 0 bbl/day (2001 est.)

Oil - consumption: 3,100 bbl/day (2001 est.)

Oil - imports: NA

Agriculture - products: rubber, coffee, cocoa, rice, cassava (tapioca), palm oil, sugarcane, bananas; sheep, goats; timber

Exports: $1.079 billion f.o.b. (2002 est.)

Exports - commodities: rubber, timber, iron, diamonds, cocoa, coffee

Exports - partners: Germany 52.7%, France 8.2%, Poland 6.8%, Denmark 5.3%, China 4.7%, Italy 4.4%, US 4% (2002)

Imports: $5.051 billion f.o.b. (2002 est.)

Imports - commodities: fuels, chemicals, machinery, transportation equipment, manufactured goods; foodstuffs

Imports - partners: South Korea 31.1%, Japan 19.5%, Germany 16%, France 9.3%, Singapore 8.1% (2002)

Debt - external: $2.1 billion (2000 est.)

Economic aid - recipient: $94 million (1999)

Currency: Liberian dollar (LRD)

Currency code: LRD

Exchange rates: Liberian dollars per US dollar - NA (2003), 61.7542 (2002), 48.5833 (2001), 40.9525 (2000), 41.9025 (1999)

Fiscal year: calendar year

Communications

Telephones - main lines in use: 7,000 (2001)

Telephones - mobile cellular: 2,000 (2001)

Telephone system:

general assessment: telephone and telegraph service via microwave radio relay network; main center is Monrovia

domestic: NA

international: country code - 231; satellite earth station - 1 Intelsat (Atlantic Ocean)

Radio broadcast stations: AM 0, FM 7, shortwave 2 (2001)

Television broadcast stations: 1 (plus four low-power repeaters) (2001)

Internet country code: .lr

Internet users: 1,000 (2002)

Transportation

Railways:

total: 490 km

standard gauge: 345 km 1.435-m gauge

narrow gauge: 145 km 1.067-m gauge

note: none of the railways are in operation (2002)

Highways:

total: 10,600 km

paved: 657 km

unpaved: 9,943 km (1999 est.)

Waterways: none

Liberia (continued)

Ports and harbors: Buchanan, Greenville, Harper, Monrovia, Robertsport

Merchant marine:

total: 1,449 ships (1,000 GRT or over) 50,555,752 GRT/79,125,329 DWT

by type: bulk 278, cargo 67, chemical tanker 161, combination bulk 10, combination ore/oil 20, container 388, liquefied gas 77, multi-functional large load carrier 3, passenger 3, petroleum tanker 317, refrigerated cargo 62, roll on/roll off 14, short-sea/passenger 3, specialized tanker 13, vehicle carrier 33

foreign-owned: Argentina 9, Australia 3, Austria 16, Belgium 8, Bermuda 1, Brazil 5, Chile 7, China 40, Croatia 11, Cyprus 4, Denmark 4, Estonia 1, France 3, Germany 510, Greece 142, Hong Kong 56, Iceland 1, India 3, Indonesia 1, Israel 4, Italy 8, Japan 81, South Korea 7, Latvia 22, Isle of Man 5, Mexico 1, Monaco 59, Netherlands 11, Nigeria 2, Norway 54, Panama 1, Poland 2, Portugal 6, Russia 68, Saudi Arabia 23, Singapore 43, Slovenia 1, Spain 1, Sri Lanka 1, Sweden 9, Switzerland 7, Taiwan 36, Turkey 3, Ukraine 3, United Kingdom 36, United States 95, Uruguay 3

registered in other countries: 35 (2003 est.)

Airports: 53 (2003 est.)

Airports - with paved runways:

total: 2

over 3,047 m: 1

1,524 to 2,437 m: 1 (2003 est.)

Airports - with unpaved runways:

total: 51

1,524 to 2,437 m: 5

914 to 1,523 m: 8

under 914 m: 38 (2003 est.)

Military

Military branches: Armed Forces of Liberia (AFL): Army, Navy, Air Force

Military manpower - availability:

males age 15-49: 752,943 (2004 est.)

Military manpower - fit for military service:

males age 15-49: 406,293 (2004 est.)

Military expenditures - dollar figure: $10 million (2003)

Military expenditures - percent of GDP: 1.3% (2003)

Transnational Issues

Disputes - international: domestic fighting among disparate rebel groups, warlords, and youth gangs in Guinea, Liberia, and Sierra Leone have created insurgencies, street violence, looting, arms trafficking, and ethnic conflicts and refugees in border areas; the Cote d'Ivoire Government accuses Liberia of supporting Ivorian rebels

Illicit drugs: transshipment point for Southeast and Southwest Asian heroin and South American cocaine for the European and US markets; corruption, criminal activity, arms-dealing, and diamond trade provide significant potential for money laundering, but the lack of well-developed financial system limits the country's utility as a major money-laundering center

Libya

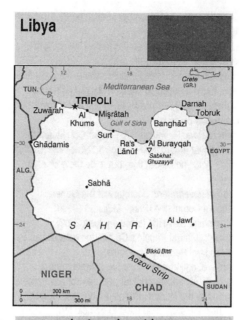

Introduction

Background: From the earliest days of his rule following his 1969 military coup, Col. Muammar Abu Minyar al-QADHAFI has espoused his own political system, the Third Universal Theory. The system is a combination of socialism and Islam derived in part from tribal practices and is supposed to be implemented by the Libyan people themselves in a unique form of "direct democracy." QADHAFI has always seen himself as a revolutionary and visionary leader. He used oil funds during the 1970s and 1980s to promote his ideology outside Libya, supporting subversives and terrorists abroad to hasten the end of Marxism and capitalism. In addition, beginning in 1973, he engaged in military operations in northern Chad's Aozou Strip to gain access to minerals and to use as a base of influence in Chadian politics. Chadian forces were able to force the Libyans to retreat from the Aozou Strip in 1987. UN sanctions in the 1990s isolated QADHAFI politically following the downing of Pan AM Flight 103 over Lockerbie, Scotland. Later, when QADHAFI found that he could not easily break free of the sanctions and when he realized that Arab nations were lukewarm to his many unusual political initiatives, he turned his attention to Africa where he achieved mixed success at influence-building. Libyan support for terrorism appears to have decreased after UN sanctions were imposed in 1992. During the 1990s QADHAFI also began to rebuild his relationships with Europe. UN sanctions were suspended in April 1999 and finally lifted in September 2003 after Libya resolved the Lockerbie case. In December 2003, Libya announced that it had agreed to reveal and end its programs to develop weapons of mass destruction.

Geography

Location: Northern Africa, bordering the Mediterranean Sea, between Egypt and Tunisia

Geographic coordinates: 25 00 N, 17 00 E

Map references: Africa

Area:

total: 1,759,540 sq km

land: 1,759,540 sq km

water: 0 sq km

Area - comparative: slightly larger than Alaska

Land boundaries:

total: 4,348 km

border countries: Algeria 982 km, Chad 1,055 km, Egypt 1,115 km, Niger 354 km, Sudan 383 km, Tunisia 459 km

Coastline: 1,770 km

Maritime claims:

territorial sea: 12 NM

note: Gulf of Sidra closing line - 32 degrees, 30 minutes north

Climate: Mediterranean along coast; dry, extreme desert interior

Terrain: mostly barren, flat to undulating plains, plateaus, depressions

Elevation extremes:

lowest point: Sabkhat Ghuzayyil -47 m

highest point: Bikku Bitti 2,267 m

Natural resources: petroleum, natural gas, gypsum

Land use:

arable land: 1.03%

permanent crops: 0.17%

other: 98.8% (1998 est.)

Irrigated land: 4,700 sq km (1998 est.)

Natural hazards: hot, dry, dust-laden ghibli is a southern wind lasting one to four days in spring and fall; dust storms, sandstorms

Environment - current issues: desertification; very limited natural fresh water resources; the Great Manmade River Project, the largest water development scheme in the world, is being built to bring water from large aquifers under the Sahara to coastal cities

Environment - international agreements:

party to: Biodiversity, Climate Change, Desertification, Endangered Species, Hazardous Wastes, Marine Dumping, Ozone Layer Protection

signed, but not ratified: Law of the Sea

Geography - note: more than 90% of the country is desert or semidesert

People

Population: 5,631,585

note: includes 166,510 non-nationals (July 2004 est.)

Age structure:

0-14 years: 34.2% (male 983,050; female 941,603)

15-64 years: 61.7% (male 1,794,396; female 1,679,828)

65 years and over: 4.1% (male 113,391; female 119,317) (2004 est.)

Median age:

total: 22.4 years

male: 22.5 years

female: 22.2 years (2004 est.)

Population growth rate: 2.37% (2004 est.)

Birth rate: 27.17 births/1,000 population (2004 est.)

Death rate: 3.48 deaths/1,000 population (2004 est.)

Net migration rate: 0 migrant(s)/1,000 population (2004 est.)

Sex ratio:

at birth: 1.05 male(s)/female

under 15 years: 1.04 male(s)/female

15-64 years: 1.07 male(s)/female

65 years and over: 0.95 male(s)/female

total population: 1.06 male(s)/female (2004 est.)

Infant mortality rate:

total: 25.7 deaths/1,000 live births

male: 28.04 deaths/1,000 live births

female: 23.26 deaths/1,000 live births (2004 est.)

Life expectancy at birth:

total population: 76.28 years

male: 74.1 years

female: 78.58 years (2004 est.)

Total fertility rate: 3.42 children born/woman (2004 est.)

HIV/AIDS - adult prevalence rate: 0.2% (2001 est.)

HIV/AIDS - people living with HIV/AIDS: 7,000 (2001 est.)

HIV/AIDS - deaths: NA

Nationality:

noun: Libyan(s)

adjective: Libyan

Ethnic groups: Berber and Arab 97%, Greeks, Maltese, Italians, Egyptians, Pakistanis, Turks, Indians, Tunisians

Religions: Sunni Muslim 97%

Languages: Arabic, Italian, English, all are widely understood in the major cities

Literacy:

definition: age 15 and over can read and write

total population: 82.6%

male: 92.4%

female: 72% (2003 est.)

Government

Country name:

conventional long form: Great Socialist People's Libyan Arab Jamahiriya

conventional short form: Libya

local long form: Al Jumahiriyah al Arabiyah al Libiyah ash Shabiyah al Ishtirakiyah al Uzma

local short form: none

Government type: Jamahiriya (a state of the masses) in theory, governed by the populace through local councils; in fact, a military dictatorship

Capital: Tripoli

Administrative divisions: 25 municipalities (baladiyat, singular - baladiyah); Ajdabiya, Al 'Aziziyah, Al Fatih, Al Jabal al Akhdar, Al Jufrah, Al Khums, Al Kufrah, An Nuqat al Khams, Ash Shati', Awbari, Az Zawiyah, Banghazi, Darnah, Ghadamis, Gharyan, Misratah, Murzuq, Sabha, Sawfajjin, Surt, Tarabulus, Tarhunah, Tubruq, Yafran, Zlitan; note - the 25 municipalities may have been replaced by 13 regions

Independence: 24 December 1951 (from Italy)

National holiday: Revolution Day, 1 September (1969)

Constitution: 11 December 1969, amended 2 March 1977

Legal system: based on Italian civil law system and Islamic law; separate religious courts; no constitutional provision for judicial review of legislative acts; has not accepted compulsory ICJ jurisdiction

Suffrage: 18 years of age; universal and compulsory

Executive branch:

chief of state: Revolutionary Leader Col. Muammar Abu Minyar al-QADHAFI (since 1 September 1969); note - holds no official title, but is de facto chief of state

head of government: Secretary of the General People's Committee (Prime Minister) Shukri Muhammad GHANIM (since 14 June 2003)

cabinet: General People's Committee established by the General People's Congress

elections: national elections are indirect through a hierarchy of people's committees; head of government elected by the General People's Congress; election last held 2 March 2000 (next to be held NA)

election results: NA

Legislative branch: unicameral General People's Congress (NA seats; members elected indirectly through a hierarchy of people's committees)

Judicial branch: Supreme Court

Political parties and leaders: none

Political pressure groups and leaders: various Arab nationalist movements with almost negligible memberships may be functioning clandestinely, as well as some Islamic elements

International organization participation: ABEDA, AfDB, AFESD, AMF, AMU, AU, CAEU, FAO, G-77, IAEA, IBRD, ICAO, ICRM, IDA, IDB, IFAD, IFC, IFRCS, ILO, IMF, IMO, Interpol, IOC, IOM (observer), ISO, ITU, LAS, NAM, OAPEC, OIC, OPCW, OPEC, PCA, UN, UNCTAD, UNESCO, UNIDO, UPU, WCO, WFTU, WHO, WIPO, WMO, WToO

Diplomatic representation in the US: Libya does not have an embassy in the US but maintains an interest section under the protective power of the Unites Arab Emirates Embassy in the US

Diplomatic representation from the US: the US suspended all embassy activities in Tripoli on 2 May 1980, and then resumed embassy activities in February 2004 under the protective power of the US interests section of the Belgian Embassy

Flag description: plain green; green is the traditional color of Islam (the state religion)

Economy

Economy - overview: The Libyan economy depends primarily upon revenues from the oil sector, which contribute practically all export earnings and about one-quarter of GDP. These oil revenues and a small population give Libya one of the highest per capita GDPs in Africa, but little of this income flows down to the lower orders of society. Libyan officials in the past three years have made progress on economic reforms as part of a broader campaign to reintegrate the country into the international fold. This effort picked up steam after UN sanctions were lifted in September 2003 and as Libya announced in December 2003 that it would abandon programs to build weapons of mass destruction. Libya faces a long road ahead in liberalizing the socialist-oriented economy, but initial steps - including applying for WTO membership, reducing some subsidies, and announcing plans for privatization - are laying the groundwork for a transition to a more market-based economy. The non-oil manufacturing and construction sectors, which account for about 20% of GDP, have expanded from processing mostly agricultural products to include the production of petrochemicals, iron, steel, and aluminum. Climatic conditions and poor soils severely limit agricultural output, and Libya imports about 75% of its food.

GDP: purchasing power parity - $35 billion (2003 est.)

GDP - real growth rate: 3.2% (2003 est.)

GDP - per capita: purchasing power parity - $6,400 (2003 est.)

GDP - composition by sector:

agriculture: 9%

industry: 45%

services: 46% (2001 est.)

Population below poverty line: NA%

Household income or consumption by percentage share:

lowest 10%: NA%

highest 10%: NA%

Inflation rate (consumer prices): 2.8% (2003 est.)

Labor force: 1.6 million (2001 est.)

Labor force - by occupation: services 54%, industry 29%, agriculture 17% (1997 est.)

Unemployment rate: 30% (2001)

Budget:

revenues: $10.2 billion

expenditures: $7.8 billion, including capital expenditures of $NA (2003 est.)

Industries: petroleum, food processing, textiles, handicrafts, cement

Industrial production growth rate: NA%

Electricity - production: 20.18 billion kWh (2001)

Electricity - production by source:

fossil fuel: 100%

hydro: 0%

nuclear: 0%

other: 0% (2001)

Electricity - consumption: 18.77 billion kWh (2001)

Electricity - exports: 0 kWh (2001)

Electricity - imports: 0 kWh (2001)

Oil - production: 1.429 million bbl/day (2001 est.)

Oil - consumption: 216,000 bbl/day (2001 est.)

Oil - exports: NA

Oil - imports: NA

Oil - proved reserves: 29.75 billion bbl (1 January 2002)

Natural gas - production: 6.18 billion cu m (2001 est.)

Natural gas - consumption: 5.41 billion cu m (2001 est.)

Libya *(continued)*

Natural gas - exports: 770 million cu m (2001 est.)
Natural gas - imports: 0 cu m (2001 est.)
Natural gas - proved reserves: 1.321 trillion cu m (1 January 2002)
Agriculture - products: wheat, barley, olives, dates, citrus, vegetables, peanuts, soybeans; cattle
Exports: $14.32 billion f.o.b. (2003 est.)
Exports - commodities: crude oil, refined petroleum products (1999)
Exports - partners: Italy 42.8%, Germany 14.1%, Spain 13.6%, Turkey 6.9% (2002)
Imports: $6.282 billion f.o.b. (2003 est.)
Imports - commodities: machinery, transport equipment, food, manufactured goods (1999)
Imports - partners: Italy 25.4%, Germany 9.9%, South Korea 6.5%, UK 6.5%, Tunisia 6.4%, Japan 6.3%, France 5.7% (2002)
Debt - external: $4.2 billion (2003 est.)
Economic aid - recipient: $15 million (2000)
Currency: Libyan dinar (LYD)
Currency code: LYD
Exchange rates: Libyan dinars per US dollar - 1.2929 (2003), 1.2707 (2002), 0.6051 (2001), 0.4994 (2000), 0.3936 (1999)
Fiscal year: calendar year

Communications

Telephones - main lines in use: 660,000 (2002)
Telephones - mobile cellular: 70,000 (2002)
Telephone system:
general assessment: telecommunications system is being modernized; mobile cellular telephone system became operational in 1996
domestic: microwave radio relay, coaxial cable, cellular, tropospheric scatter, and a domestic satellite system with 14 earth stations
international: country code - 218; satellite earth stations - 4 Intelsat, NA Arabsat, and NA Intersputnik; submarine cables to France and Italy; microwave radio relay to Tunisia and Egypt; tropospheric scatter to Greece; participant in Medarabtel (1999)
Radio broadcast stations: AM 16, FM 3, shortwave 3 (2002)
Television broadcast stations: 12 (plus one low-power repeater) (1999)
Internet country code: .ly
Internet hosts: 83 (2002)
Internet users: 125,000 (2002)

Transportation

Railways: 0 km
Highways:
total: 83,200 km
paved: 47,590 km
unpaved: 35,610 km (1999 est.)
Waterways: none
Pipelines: condensate 225 km; gas 3,196 km; oil 6,872 km (2003)
Ports and harbors: Al Khums, Banghazi, Darnah, Marsa al Burayqah, Misratah, Ra's Lanuf, Tobruk, Tripoli, Zuwarah

Merchant marine:
total: 20 ships (1,000 GRT or over) 129,627 GRT/ 105,110 DWT
by type: cargo 8, liquefied gas 3, petroleum tanker 1, roll on/roll off 4, short-sea/passenger 4
foreign-owned: Algeria 1, Kuwait 1 (2003 est.)
Airports: 140 (2003 est.)
Airports - with paved runways:
total: 60
over 3,047 m: 23
2,438 to 3,047 m: 6
1,524 to 2,437 m: 23
914 to 1,523 m: 5
under 914 m: 3 (2003 est.)
Airports - with unpaved runways:
total: 80
over 3,047 m: 5
2,438 to 3,047 m: 2
1,524 to 2,437 m: 14
914 to 1,523 m: 41
under 914 m: 18 (2003 est.)
Heliports: 1 (2003 est.)

Military

Military branches: Armed Peoples on Duty (Army), Navy, Air Force, Air Defense Command
Military manpower - military age: 17 years of age (2004 est.)
Military manpower - availability:
males age 15-49: 1,588,533 (2004 est.)
Military manpower - fit for military service:
males age 15-49: 938,196 (2004 est.)
Military manpower - reaching military age annually:
males: 61,828 (2004 est.)
Military expenditures - dollar figure: $1.3 billion (FY99)
Military expenditures - percent of GDP: 3.9% (FY99)

Transnational Issues

Disputes - international: Libya has claimed more than 32,000 sq km in southeastern Algeria and about 25,000 sq km in Niger in currently dormant disputes; various Chadian rebels from the Aozou region reside in southern Libya

Liechtenstein

Introduction

Background: The Principality of Liechtenstein was established within the Holy Roman Empire in 1719; it became a sovereign state in 1806. Until the end of World War I, it was closely tied to Austria, but the economic devastation caused by that conflict forced Liechtenstein to enter into a customs and monetary union with Switzerland. Since World War II (in which Liechtenstein remained neutral), the country's low taxes have spurred outstanding economic growth. Shortcomings in banking regulatory oversight have resulted in concerns about the use of the financial institutions for money laundering. Liechtenstein has, however, implemented new anti-money-laundering legislation and recently concluded a Mutual Legal Assistance Treaty with the US.

Geography

Location: Central Europe, between Austria and Switzerland
Geographic coordinates: 47 16 N, 9 32 E
Map references: Europe
Area:
total: 160 sq km
land: 160 sq km
water: 0 sq km
Area - comparative: about 0.9 times the size of Washington, DC
Land boundaries:
total: 76 km
border countries: Austria 34.9 km, Switzerland 41.1 km
Coastline: 0 km (doubly landlocked)
Maritime claims: none (landlocked)
Climate: continental; cold, cloudy winters with frequent snow or rain; cool to moderately warm, cloudy, humid summers
Terrain: mostly mountainous (Alps) with Rhine Valley in western third

Liechtenstein (continued)

Elevation extremes:
lowest point: Ruggeller Riet 430 m
highest point: Grauspitz 2,599 m
Natural resources: hydroelectric potential, arable land
Land use:
arable land: 25%
permanent crops: 0%
other: 75% (1998 est.)
Irrigated land: NA sq km
Natural hazards: NA
Environment - current issues: NA
Environment - international agreements:
party to: Air Pollution, Air Pollution-Nitrogen Oxides, Air Pollution-Sulfur 85, Air Pollution-Sulfur 94, Air Pollution-Volatile Organic Compounds, Biodiversity, Climate Change, Desertification, Endangered Species, Hazardous Wastes, Ozone Layer Protection, Wetlands
signed, but not ratified: Air Pollution-Persistent Organic Pollutants, Climate Change-Kyoto Protocol, Law of the Sea
Geography - note: along with Uzbekistan, one of only two doubly landlocked countries in the world; variety of microclimatic variations based on elevation

People

Population: 33,436 (July 2004 est.)
Age structure:
0-14 years: 17.8% (male 2,950; female 3,014)
15-64 years: 70.5% (male 11,745; female 11,837)
65 years and over: 11.6% (male 1,598; female 2,292) (2004 est.)
Median age:
total: 38.8 years
male: 38.3 years
female: 39.3 years (2004 est.)
Population growth rate: 0.86% (2004 est.)
Birth rate: 10.65 births/1,000 population (2004 est.)
Death rate: 6.94 deaths/1,000 population (2004 est.)
Net migration rate: 4.85 migrant(s)/1,000 population (2004 est.)
Sex ratio:
at birth: 1 male(s)/female
under 15 years: 0.98 male(s)/female
15-64 years: 0.99 male(s)/female
65 years and over: 0.7 male(s)/female
total population: 0.95 male(s)/female (2004 est.)
Infant mortality rate:
total: 4.77 deaths/1,000 live births
male: 6.47 deaths/1,000 live births
female: 3.07 deaths/1,000 live births (2004 est.)
Life expectancy at birth:
total population: 79.4 years
male: 75.8 years
female: 83.02 years (2004 est.)
Total fertility rate: 1.51 children born/woman (2004 est.)
HIV/AIDS - adult prevalence rate: NA%
HIV/AIDS - people living with HIV/AIDS: NA
HIV/AIDS - deaths: NA

Nationality:
noun: Liechtensteiner(s)
adjective: Liechtenstein
Ethnic groups: Alemannic 86%, Italian, Turkish, and other 14%
Religions: Roman Catholic 76.2%, Protestant 7%, unknown 10.6%, other 6.2% (June 2002)
Languages: German (official), Alemannic dialect
Literacy:
definition: age 10 and over can read and write
total population: 100%
male: 100%
female: 100%

Government

Country name:
conventional long form: Principality of Liechtenstein
conventional short form: Liechtenstein
local long form: Fuerstentum Liechtenstein
local short form: Liechtenstein
Government type: hereditary constitutional monarchy on a democratic and parliamentary basis
Capital: Vaduz
Administrative divisions: 11 communes (Gemeinden, singular - Gemeinde); Balzers, Eschen, Gamprin, Mauren, Planken, Ruggell, Schaan, Schellenberg, Triesen, Triesenberg, Vaduz
Independence: 23 January 1719 Imperial Principality of Liechtenstein established; 12 July 1806 established independence from the Holy Roman Empire
National holiday: Assumption Day, 15 August
Constitution: 5 October 1921
Legal system: local civil and penal codes; accepts compulsory ICJ jurisdiction, with reservations
Suffrage: 18 years of age; universal
Executive branch:
chief of state: Prince HANS ADAM II (since 13 November 1989, assumed executive powers 26 August 1984); Heir Apparent Prince ALOIS, son of the monarch (born 11 June 1968)
head of government: Head of Government Otmar HASLER (since 5 April 2001) and Deputy Head of Government Rita KIEBER-BECK (since 5 April 2001)
cabinet: Cabinet elected by the Parliament, confirmed by the monarch
elections: none; the monarch is hereditary; following legislative elections, the leader of the majority party in the Diet is usually appointed the head of government by the monarch and the leader of the largest minority party in the Diet is usually appointed the deputy head of government by the monarch
Legislative branch: unicameral Parliament or Landtag (25 seats; members are elected by direct, popular vote under proportional representation to serve four-year terms)
elections: last held 11 February 2001 (next to be held by NA 2005)
election results: percent of vote by party - FBP 49.90%, VU 41.35%, FL 8.71%; seats by party - FBP 13, VU 11, FL 1

Judicial branch: Supreme Court or Oberster Gerichtshof; Court of Appeal or Obergericht
Political parties and leaders: Patriotic Union (was Fatherland Union) or VU [Heinz FROMMELT]; Progressive Citizens' Party or FBP [Matt JOHANNES]; The Free List or FL [Dr. Pepo FRICK, Elisabeth TELLENBACH-FRICK, Adolf RITTER]
Political pressure groups and leaders: NA
International organization participation: CE, EBRD, EFTA, IAEA, ICCt, ICRM, IFRCS, Interpol, IOC, ITU, OPCW, OSCE, PCA, UN, UNCTAD, UPU, WCL, WHO (observer), WIPO, WTrO
Diplomatic representation in the US:
chief of mission: Ambassador Claudia FRITSCHE
chancery: 1300 Eye Street NW, Suite 550W, Washington, DC 20005
telephone: [1] (202) 216-0460
FAX: [1] (202) 216-0459
Diplomatic representation from the US: the US does not have an embassy in Liechtenstein, but the US Ambassador to Switzerland is also accredited to Liechtenstein
Flag description: two equal horizontal bands of blue (top) and red with a gold crown on the hoist side of the blue band

Economy

Economy - overview: Despite its small size and limited natural resources, Liechtenstein has developed into a prosperous, highly industrialized, free-enterprise economy with a vital financial service sector and living standards on a par with its large European neighbors. The Liechtenstein economy is widely diversified with a large number of small businesses. Low business taxes - the maximum tax rate is 20% - and easy incorporation rules have induced many holding or so-called letter box companies to establish nominal offices in Liechtenstein, providing 30% of state revenues. The country participates in a customs union with Switzerland and uses the Swiss franc as its national currency. It imports more than 90% of its energy requirements. Liechtenstein has been a member of the European Economic Area (an organization serving as a bridge between the European Free Trade Association (EFTA) and the EU) since May 1995. The government is working to harmonize its economic policies with those of an integrated Europe.
GDP: purchasing power parity - $825 million (1999 est.)
GDP - real growth rate: 11% (1999 est.)
GDP - per capita: purchasing power parity - $25,000 (1999 est.)
GDP - composition by sector:
agriculture: NA%
industry: 40%
services: NA% (1999)
Population below poverty line: NA%
Household income or consumption by percentage share:
lowest 10%: NA%
highest 10%: NA%

Liechtenstein *(continued)*

Inflation rate (consumer prices): 1% (2001)
Labor force: 29,000 of whom 19,000 are foreigners; 13,000 commute from Austria, Switzerland, and Germany to work each day (31 December 2001)
Labor force - by occupation: industry 47.4%, services 51.3%, agriculture 1.3% (31 December 2001 est.)
Unemployment rate: 1.3% (September 2002)
Budget:
revenues: $424.2 million
expenditures: $414.1 million, including capital expenditures of $NA (1998 est.)
Industries: electronics, metal manufacturing, dental products, ceramics, pharmaceuticals, food products, precision instruments, tourism, optical instruments
Industrial production growth rate: NA%
Agriculture - products: wheat, barley, corn, potatoes; livestock, dairy products
Exports: $2.47 billion (1996)
Exports - commodities: small specialty machinery, connectors for audio and video, parts for motor vehicles, dental products, hardware, prepared foodstuffs, electronic equipment, optical products
Exports - partners: EU 62.6% (Germany 24.3%, Austria 9.5%, France 8.9%, Italy 6.6%, UK 4.6%), US 18.9%, Switzerland 15.7%
Imports: $917.3 million (1996)
Imports - commodities: agricultural products, raw materials, machinery, metal goods, textiles, foodstuffs, motor vehicles
Imports - partners: EU, Switzerland
Debt - external: $0 (2001)
Economic aid - recipient: none
Currency: Swiss franc (CHF)
Currency code: CHF
Exchange rates: Swiss francs per US dollar - 1.3467 (2003), 1.5586 (2002), 1.6876 (2001), 1.6888 (2000), 1.5022 (1999)
Fiscal year: calendar year

Communications

Telephones - main lines in use: 19,900 (2002)
Telephones - mobile cellular: 11,400 (2002)
Telephone system:
general assessment: automatic telephone system
domestic: NA
international: country code - 423; linked to Swiss networks by cable and microwave radio relay
Radio broadcast stations: AM 0, FM 4, shortwave 0 (1998)
Television broadcast stations: NA (linked to Swiss networks) (1997)
Internet country code: .li
Internet users: 20,000 (2002)

Transportation

Railways:
total: 18.5 km
standard gauge: 18.5 km 1.435-m gauge (electrified)
note: owned, operated, and included in statistics of Austrian Federal Railways (2002)

Highways:
total: 250 km
paved: 250 km
unpaved: 0 km
Waterways: none
Pipelines: gas 20 km (2003)
Ports and harbors: none
Airports: none (2003 est.)

Military

Military - note: defense is the responsibility of Switzerland

Transnational Issues

Disputes - international: Liechtenstein's royal family claims restitution for 1,600 sq km of land in the Czech Republic confiscated in 1918
Illicit drugs: has strengthened money-laundering controls, but money laundering remains a concern due to Liechtenstein sophisticated offshore financial services sector

Lithuania

Introduction

Background: Independent between the two World Wars, Lithuania was annexed by the USSR in 1940. On 11 March 1990, Lithuania became the first of the Soviet republics to declare its independence, but Moscow did not recognize this proclamation until September of 1991 (following the abortive coup in Moscow). The last Russian troops withdrew in 1993. Lithuania subsequently has restructured its economy for eventual integration into Western European institutions. It will accede to the EU in May 2004 and to NATO in the summer of 2004.

Geography

Location: Eastern Europe, bordering the Baltic Sea, between Latvia and Russia
Geographic coordinates: 56 00 N, 24 00 E
Map references: Europe
Area:
total: 65,200 sq km
land: NA sq km
water: NA sq km
Area - comparative: slightly larger than West Virginia
Land boundaries:
total: 1,273 km
border countries: Belarus 502 km, Latvia 453 km, Poland 91 km, Russia (Kaliningrad) 227 km
Coastline: 99 km
Maritime claims:
territorial sea: 12 NM
Climate: transitional, between maritime and continental; wet, moderate winters and summers
Terrain: lowland, many scattered small lakes, fertile soil
Elevation extremes:
lowest point: Baltic Sea 0 m
highest point: Juozapines/Kalnas 292 m
Natural resources: peat, arable land

Lithuania (continued)

Land use:
arable land: 45.46%
permanent crops: 0.93%
other: 53.61% (1998 est.)
Irrigated land: 90 sq km (1998 est.)
Natural hazards: NA
Environment - current issues: contamination of soil and groundwater with petroleum products and chemicals at military bases
Environment - international agreements:
party to: Air Pollution, Biodiversity, Climate Change, Climate Change-Kyoto Protocol, Endangered Species, Hazardous Wastes, Law of the Sea, Ozone Layer Protection, Ship Pollution, Wetlands
signed, but not ratified: Air Pollution-Persistent Organic Pollutants
Geography - note: fertile central plains are separated by hilly uplands that are ancient glacial deposits

People

Population: 3,607,899 (July 2004 est.)
Age structure:
0-14 years: 16.7% (male 309,736; female 294,129)
15-64 years: 68.4% (male 1,202,603; female 1,262,784)
65 years and over: 14.9% (male 184,145; female 354,502) (2004 est.)
Median age:
total: 37.4 years
male: 34.8 years
female: 40.1 years (2004 est.)
Population growth rate: -0.33% (2004 est.)
Birth rate: 8.49 births/1,000 population (2004 est.)
Death rate: 11.03 deaths/1,000 population (2004 est.)
Net migration rate: -0.71 migrant(s)/1,000 population (2004 est.)
Sex ratio:
at birth: 1.06 male(s)/female
under 15 years: 1.05 male(s)/female
15-64 years: 0.95 male(s)/female
65 years and over: 0.52 male(s)/female
total population: 0.89 male(s)/female (2004 est.)
Infant mortality rate:
total: 7.13 deaths/1,000 live births
male: 8.61 deaths/1,000 live births
female: 5.57 deaths/1,000 live births (2004 est.)
Life expectancy at birth:
total population: 73.46 years
male: 68.22 years
female: 79 years (2004 est.)
Total fertility rate: 1.17 children born/woman (2004 est.)
HIV/AIDS - adult prevalence rate: 0.1% (2001 est.)
HIV/AIDS - people living with HIV/AIDS: less than 1,300 (2001 est.)
HIV/AIDS - deaths: less than 100 (2001 est.)
Nationality:
noun: Lithuanian(s)
adjective: Lithuanian

Ethnic groups: Lithuanian 80.6%, Russian 8.7%, Polish 7%, Belarusian 1.6%, other 2.1%
Religions: Roman Catholic (primarily), Lutheran, Russian Orthodox, Protestant, Evangelical Christian Baptist, Muslim, Jewish
Languages: Lithuanian (official), Polish, Russian
Literacy:
definition: age 15 and over can read and write
total population: 99.6%
male: 99.7%
female: 99.6% (2003 est.)

Government

Country name:
conventional long form: Republic of Lithuania
conventional short form: Lithuania
local long form: Lietuvos Respublika
local short form: Lietuva
former: Lithuanian Soviet Socialist Republic
Government type: parliamentary democracy
Capital: Vilnius
Administrative divisions: 10 counties (apskritys, singular - apskritis); Alytaus, Kauno, Klaipedos, Marijampoles, Panevezio, Siauliu, Taurages, Telsiu, Utenos, Vilniaus
Independence: 11 March 1990 (independence declared from Soviet Union); 6 September 1991 (Soviet Union recognizes Lithuania's independence)
National holiday: Independence Day, 16 February (1918); note - 16 February 1918 is the date Lithuania declared its independence from Soviet Russia and established its statehood; 11 March 1990 is the date it declared its independence from the Soviet Union
Constitution: adopted 25 October 1992
Legal system: based on civil law system; legislative acts can be appealed to the constitutional court
Suffrage: 18 years of age; universal
Executive branch:
chief of state: President Arturas PAULAUSKAS (acting since 6 April 2004); note - Rolandas PAKSAS, president since 26 February 2003, was ousted on 6 April 2004 on charges of abuse of office
head of government: Premier Algirdas Mykolas BRAZAUSKAS (since 3 July 2001)
cabinet: Council of Ministers appointed by the president on the nomination of the premier
elections: president elected by popular vote for a five-year term; election last held 22 December 2002 and 5 January 2003 (next normally would be held in late 2007, but a new election must be held in 60 days following the removal of President Rolandas PASKAS on 6 April 2004); premier appointed by the president on the approval of the Parliament
election results: Rolandas PAKSAS elected president; percent of vote - Rolandas PAKSAS 54.9%, Valdas ADAMKUS 45.1%
Legislative branch: unicameral Parliament or Seimas (141 seats, 71 members are directly elected by popular vote, 70 are elected by proportional representation; members serve four-year terms)
elections: last held 8 October 2000 (next to be held NA October 2004)

election results: percent of vote by party - Social Democratic Coalition 31.1%, New Union-Social Liberals 19.6%, Liberal Union 17.2%, TS 8.6%, remaining parties all less than 5%; seats by faction - Social Democratic Coalition 51, New Union-Social Liberals 25, United Political Group-Group of Liberals 24, Liberal Democrats 13, Conservatives 9, Farmers and New Democracy Parties 8, Mixed Group 6, independent 1 (four seats unfilled as of 1 June 2003)
note: the voting results from the 2000 elections do not correspond to the make up of the Seimas, which has evolved into a number of factions, each made up of members of several parties
Judicial branch: Constitutional Court; Supreme Court; Court of Appeal; judges for all courts appointed by the President
Political parties and leaders: Electoral Action of Lithuanian Poles [Valdemar TOMASZEVSKI, chairman]; Homeland Union/Conservative Party or TS [Andrius KUBILIUS, chairman]; Lithuanian Center Union or LCS [Kestutis GLAVECKAS, chairman]; Lithuanian Christian Democrats or LKD [Kazys BOBELIS]; Lithuanian Farmer's Party or LUP [Ramunas KARBAUSKIS, chairman]; Lithuanian Green Party [Rimantas BRAZIULIS]; Lithuanian Liberal Youth [Neringa MOROZAITE]; Lithuanian National Democratic Party [Vygintas GONTIS]; Lithuanian Social Democratic Coalition [Algirdas BRAZAUSKAS, chairman] consists of the Lithuanian Democratic Labor Party or LDDP, the Lithuanian Social Democratic Party or LSDP, and New Democracy; Moderate Conservative Union [Gediminas VAGNORIUS]; Modern Christian Democratic Union [Vytautas BOGUSIS, chairman]; New Democracy and Farmer's Union [Kazimiera PRUNSKIENE, chairman]; New Union-Social Liberals [Arturas PAULAUSKAS, chairman]; Young Lithuania [Arnoldas PLATELIS]
Political pressure groups and leaders: NA
International organization participation: ACCT (observer), BIS, CBSS, CE, EAPC, EBRD, EU (new member), FAO, IAEA, IBRD, ICAO, ICC, ICCt, ICFTU, ICRM, IFC, IFRCS, ILO, IMF, IMO, Interpol, IOC, IOM, ISO (correspondent), ITU, OPCW, OSCE, PFP, UN, UNCTAD, UNESCO, UNIDO, UNMIK, UPU, WCL, WCO, WEU (associate partner), WHO, WIPO, WMO, WToO, WTrO
Diplomatic representation in the US:
chief of mission: Ambassador Vygaudas USACKAS
chancery: 2622 16th Street NW, Washington, DC 20009
telephone: [1] (202) 234-5860
FAX: [1] (202) 328-0466
consulate(s) general: Chicago and New York
Diplomatic representation from the US:
chief of mission: Ambassador Stephen D. MULL
embassy: Akmenu 6, 2600 Vilnius
mailing address: American Embassy, Vilnius, PSC 78, Box V, APO AE 09723
telephone: [370] (5) 266 5500
FAX: [370] (5) 266 5510
Flag description: three equal horizontal bands of yellow (top), green, and red

Lithuania (continued)

Economy

Economy - overview: Lithuania, the Baltic state that has conducted the most trade with Russia, has slowly rebounded from the 1998 Russian financial crisis. Unemployment remains high, still 10.7% in 2003, but is improving. Growing domestic consumption and increased investment have furthered recovery. Trade has been increasingly oriented toward the West. Lithuania has gained membership in the World Trade Organization and has moved ahead with plans to join the EU. Privatization of the large, state-owned utilities, particularly in the energy sector, is nearing completion. Overall, more than 80% of enterprises have been privatized. Foreign government and business support have helped in the transition from the old command economy to a market economy.

GDP: purchasing power parity - $40.17 billion (2003 est.)

GDP - real growth rate: 7.1% (2003 est.)

GDP - per capita: purchasing power parity - $11,200 (2003 est.)

GDP - composition by sector:
agriculture: 7.1%
industry: 26.6%
services: 66.3% (2002 est.)

Population below poverty line: NA%

Household income or consumption by percentage share:
lowest 10%: 3.1%
highest 10%: 25.6% (1996)

Distribution of family income - Gini index: 34 (1999)

Inflation rate (consumer prices): -1% (2003 est.)

Labor force: 1.5 million (2001 est.)

Labor force - by occupation: industry 30%, agriculture 20%, services 50% (1997 est.)

Unemployment rate: 10.7% (2003 est.)

Budget:
revenues: $1.59 billion
expenditures: $1.77 billion, including capital expenditures of $NA (2001 est.)

Industries: metal-cutting machine tools, electric motors, television sets, refrigerators and freezers, petroleum refining, shipbuilding (small ships), furniture making, textiles, food processing, fertilizers, agricultural machinery, optical equipment, electronic components, computers, amber

Industrial production growth rate: 5% (2003 est.)

Electricity - production: 14.62 billion kWh (2001)

Electricity - production by source:
fossil fuel: 16.5%
hydro: 5.7%
nuclear: 77.7%
other: 0% (2001)

Electricity - consumption: 8.683 billion kWh (2001)

Electricity - exports: 6.3 billion kWh (2001)

Electricity - imports: 1.389 billion kWh (2001)

Oil - production: 4,594 bbl/day (2001 est.)

Oil - consumption: 72,000 bbl/day (2001 est.)

Oil - exports: NA

Oil - imports: NA

Natural gas - production: 0 cu m (2001 est.)

Natural gas - consumption: 2.76 billion cu m (2001 est.)

Natural gas - exports: 0 cu m (2001 est.)

Natural gas - imports: 2.76 billion cu m (2001 est.)

Agriculture - products: grain, potatoes, sugar beets, flax, vegetables; beef, milk, eggs; fish

Exports: $7.89 billion f.o.b. (2003 est.)

Exports - commodities: mineral products 23%, textiles and clothing 16%, machinery and equipment 11%, chemicals 6%, wood and wood products 5%, foodstuffs 5% (2001)

Exports - partners: UK 13.4%, Russia 12.1%, Germany 10.4%, Latvia 9.7%, Denmark 5.1%, Sweden 4.2%, France 4.1% (2002)

Imports: $9.2 billion f.o.b. (2003 est.)

Imports - commodities: mineral products 21%, machinery and equipment 17%, transport equipment 11%, chemicals 9%, textiles and clothing 9%, metals 5% (2001)

Imports - partners: Russia 22.2%, Germany 17.8%, Italy 5.1%, Poland 5% (2002)

Debt - external: $6.5 billion (2003 est.)

Economic aid - recipient: $228.5 million (1995)

Currency: litas (LTL)

Currency code: LTL

Exchange rates: litai per US dollar - 3.0609 (2003), 3.677 (2002), 4 (2001), 4 (2000), 4 (1999)

Fiscal year: calendar year

Communications

Telephones - main lines in use: 935,900 (2002)

Telephones - mobile cellular: 1,645,600 (2002)

Telephone system:
general assessment: inadequate, but is being modernized to provide an improved international capability and better residential access
domestic: a national, fiber-optic cable, interurban, trunk system is nearing completion; rural exchanges are being improved and expanded; mobile cellular systems are being installed; access to the Internet is available; still many unsatisfied telephone subscriber applications
international: country code - 370; landline connections to Latvia and Poland; major international connections to Denmark, Sweden, and Norway by submarine cable for further transmission by satellite

Radio broadcast stations: AM 29, FM 142, shortwave 1 (2001)

Television broadcast stations: 27
note: Lithuania has approximately 27 broadcasting stations, but may have as many as 100 transmitters, including repeater stations (2001)

Internet country code: .lt

Internet hosts: 54,605 (2002)

Internet users: 500,000 (2002)

Transportation

Railways:
total: 1,998 km
broad gauge: 1,807 km 1.524-m gauge (122 km electrified)
standard gauge: 22 km 1.435-m gauge
narrow gauge: 169 km 0.750-m gauge (all service suspended) (2002)

Highways:
total: 75,243 km
paved: 68,697 km (including 417 km of expressways)
unpaved: 6,546 km (2000)

Waterways: 600 km (perennially navigable)

Pipelines: gas 1,698 km; oil 331 km; refined products 109 km (2003)

Ports and harbors: Butinge, Kaunas, Klaipeda

Merchant marine:
total: 49 ships (1,000 GRT or over) 296,856 GRT/ 317,731 DWT
by type: cargo 20, chemical tanker 1, combination bulk 8, petroleum tanker 2, refrigerated cargo 12, roll on/roll off 2, short-sea/passenger 4
foreign-owned: Denmark 12, Netherlands 1
registered in other countries: 11 (2003 est.)

Airports: 102 (2003 est.)

Airports - with paved runways:
total: 28
over 3,047 m: 4
2,438 to 3,047 m: 1
1,524 to 2,437 m: 7
914 to 1,523 m: 2
under 914 m: 14 (2003 est.)

Airports - with unpaved runways:
total: 74
1,524 to 2,437 m: 2
914 to 1,523 m: 5
under 914 m: 67 (2003 est.)

Military

Military branches: National Defense Volunteer Forces (SKAT), Ground Forces, Navy, Air Force

Military manpower - military age: 16 years of age (2004 est.)

Military manpower - availability:
males age 15-49: 943,063 (2004 est.)

Military manpower - fit for military service:
males age 15-49: 738,602 (2004 est.)

Military manpower - reaching military age annually:
males: 28,300 (2004 est.)

Military expenditures - dollar figure: $230.8 million (FY01)

Military expenditures - percent of GDP: 1.9% (FY01)

Transnational Issues

Disputes - international: in May 2003, the Russian Parliament ratified the 1997 land and maritime boundary treaty with Lithuania, which ratified the treaty in 1999, legalizing limits of former Soviet republic borders; both states also implement a simplified transit regime for Russian nationals transiting Lithuania to and from the Russian Kaliningrad coastal enclave; the Latvian Parliament has not ratified its 1998 maritime boundary treaty with Lithuania, primarily due to concerns over oil exploration rights

Illicit drugs: transshipment point for opiates and other illicit drugs from Southwest Asia, Latin America, and Western Europe to Western Europe and Scandinavia; limited production of methamphetamine and ecstasy; susceptible to money laundering despite changes to banking legislation

Luxembourg

Introduction

Background: Founded in 963, Luxembourg became a grand duchy in 1815 and an independent state under the Netherlands. It lost more than half of its territory to Belgium in 1839, but gained a larger measure of autonomy. Full independence was attained in 1867. Overrun by Germany in both World Wars, it ended its neutrality in 1948 when it entered into the Benelux Customs Union and when it joined NATO the following year. In 1957, Luxembourg became one of the six founding countries of the European Economic Community (later the European Union), and in 1999 it joined the euro currency area.

Geography

Location: Western Europe, between France and Germany
Geographic coordinates: 49 45 N, 6 10 E
Map references: Europe
Area:
total: 2,586 sq km
land: 2,586 sq km
water: 0 sq km
Area - comparative: slightly smaller than Rhode Island
Land boundaries:
total: 359 km
border countries: Belgium 148 km, France 73 km, Germany 138 km
Coastline: 0 km (landlocked)
Maritime claims: none (landlocked)
Climate: modified continental with mild winters, cool summers
Terrain: mostly gently rolling uplands with broad, shallow valleys; uplands to slightly mountainous in the north; steep slope down to Moselle flood plain in the southeast
Elevation extremes:
lowest point: Moselle River 133 m
highest point: Buurgplaatz 559 m

Natural resources: iron ore (no longer exploited), arable land
Land use:
arable land: 25%
permanent crops: 0%
other: 75% (includes Belgium) (1998 est.)
Irrigated land: 40 sq km (includes Belgium) (1998 est.)
Natural hazards: NA
Environment - current issues: air and water pollution in urban areas, soil pollution of farmland
Environment - international agreements:
party to: Air Pollution, Air Pollution-Nitrogen Oxides, Air Pollution-Persistent Organic Pollutants, Air Pollution-Sulfur 85, Air Pollution-Sulfur 94, Air Pollution-Volatile Organic Compounds, Biodiversity, Climate Change, Climate Change-Kyoto Protocol, Desertification, Endangered Species, Hazardous Wastes, Law of the Sea, Marine Dumping, Ozone Layer Protection, Ship Pollution, Tropical Timber 83, Tropical Timber 94, Wetlands
signed, but not ratified: Environmental Modification
Geography - note: landlocked; the only Grand Duchy in the world

People

Population: 462,690 (July 2004 est.)
Age structure:
0-14 years: 19% (male 45,422; female 42,638)
15-64 years: 66.4% (male 155,519; female 151,891)
65 years and over: 14.5% (male 26,981; female 40,239) (2004 est.)
Median age:
total: 38.3 years
male: 37.4 years
female: 39.3 years (2004 est.)
Population growth rate: 1.28% (2004 est.)
Birth rate: 12.21 births/1,000 population (2004 est.)
Death rate: 8.42 deaths/1,000 population (2004 est.)
Net migration rate: 8.97 migrant(s)/1,000 population (2004 est.)
Sex ratio:
at birth: 1.07 male(s)/female
under 15 years: 1.07 male(s)/female
15-64 years: 1.02 male(s)/female
65 years and over: 0.67 male(s)/female
total population: 0.97 male(s)/female (2004 est.)
Infant mortality rate:
total: 4.88 deaths/1,000 live births
male: 4.84 deaths/1,000 live births
female: 4.92 deaths/1,000 live births (2004 est.)
Life expectancy at birth:
total population: 78.58 years
male: 75.31 years
female: 82.07 years (2004 est.)
Total fertility rate: 1.79 children born/woman (2004 est.)
HIV/AIDS - adult prevalence rate: 0.2% (2001 est.)
HIV/AIDS - people living with HIV/AIDS: NA
HIV/AIDS - deaths: less than 100 (2001 est.)

Luxembourg (continued)

Nationality:

noun: Luxembourger(s)

adjective: Luxembourg

Ethnic groups: Celtic base (with French and German blend), Portuguese, Italian, Slavs (from Montenegro, Albania, and Kosovo) and European (guest and resident workers)

Religions: 87% Roman Catholic, 13% Protestants, Jews, and Muslims (2000)

Languages: Luxembourgish (national language), German (administrative language), French (administrative language)

Literacy:

definition: age 15 and over can read and write

total population: 100%

male: 100%

female: 100% (2000 est.)

Government

Country name:

conventional long form: Grand Duchy of Luxembourg

conventional short form: Luxembourg

local long form: Grand Duche de Luxembourg

local short form: Luxembourg

Government type: constitutional monarchy

Capital: Luxembourg

Administrative divisions: 3 districts; Diekirch, Grevenmacher, Luxembourg

Independence: 1839 (from the Netherlands)

National holiday: National Day (Birthday of Grand Duchess Charlotte) 23 June

Constitution: 17 October 1868, occasional revisions

Legal system: based on civil law system; accepts compulsory ICJ jurisdiction

Suffrage: 18 years of age; universal and compulsory

Executive branch:

chief of state: Grand Duke HENRI (since 7 October 2000); Heir Apparent Prince GUILLAUME (son of the monarch, born 11 November 1981)

head of government: Prime Minister Jean-Claude JUNCKER (since 1 January 1995) and Vice Prime Minister Lydie POLFER (since 7 August 1999)

cabinet: Council of Ministers recommended by the prime minister and appointed by the monarch

elections: none; the monarch is hereditary; following popular elections to the Chamber of Deputies, the leader of the majority party or the leader of the majority coalition is usually appointed prime minister by the monarch; the deputy prime minister is appointed by the monarch; they are responsible to the Chamber of Deputies

note: government coalition - CSV and DP

Legislative branch: unicameral Chamber of Deputies or Chambre des Deputes (60 seats; members are elected by direct, popular vote to serve five-year terms)

elections: last held 13 June 1999 (next to be held by June 2004)

election results: percent of vote by party - CSV 29.79%, DP 21.58%, LSAP 23.75%, ADR 10.36%, Green Party 9.09%, the Left 3.77%; seats by party - CSV 19, DP 15, LSAP 13, ADR 6, Green Party 5, the Left 2

note: there is also a Council of State that serves as an advisory body to the Chamber of Deputies; the Council of State has 21 members appointed by the Grand Duke on the advice of the prime minister

Judicial branch: judicial courts and tribunals (3 Justices of the Peace, 2 district courts, and 1 Supreme Court of Appeals); administrative courts and tribunals (State Prosecutor's Office, administrative courts and tribunals, and the Constitutional Court); judges for all courts are appointed for life by the monarch

Political parties and leaders: Action Committee for Democracy and Justice or ADR [Robert MEHLEN]; Christian Social People's Party or CSV (known also as Christian Social Party or PCS) [Erna HENNICOT-SCHOEPGES]; Democratic Party or DP [Lydie POLFER]; Green Party [Abbes JACOBY and Felix BRAS]; Luxembourg Socialist Workers' Party or LSAP [Jean ASSELBORN]; Marxist and Reformed Communist Party DEI LENK (the Left) [no formal leadership]; other minor parties

Political pressure groups and leaders: ABBL (bankers' association); ALEBA (financial sector trade union); Centrale Paysanne (federation of agricultural producers); CEP (professional sector chamber); CGFP (trade union representing civil service); Chambre de Commerce (Chamber of Commerce); Chambre des Metiers (Chamber of Artisans); FEDIL (federation of industrialists); LCGP (center-right trade union); OGBL (center-left trade union)

International organization participation: ACCT, AsDB, Australia Group, Benelux, CE, EAPC, EBRD, EIB, EMU, EU, FAO, IAEA, IBRD, ICAO, ICC, ICCt, ICFTU, ICRM, IDA, IEA, IFAD, IFC, IFRCS, ILO, IMF, IMO, Interpol, IOC, IOM, ISO, ITU, NATO, NEA, NSG, OECD, OPCW, OSCE, PCA, UN, UNCTAD, UNESCO, UNIDO, UPU, WCL, WCO, WEU, WHO, WIPO, WMO, WTrO, ZC

Diplomatic representation in the US:

chief of mission: Ambassador Arlette CONZEMIUS-PACCOURD

chancery: 2200 Massachusetts Avenue NW, Washington, DC 20008

telephone: [1] (202) 265-4171

FAX: [1] (202) 328-8270

consulate(s) general: New York and San Francisco

Diplomatic representation from the US:

chief of mission: Ambassador Peter TERPELUK, Jr.

embassy: 22 Boulevard Emmanuel-Servais, L-2535 Luxembourg City

mailing address: American Embassy Luxembourg, Unit 1410, APO AE 09126-1410 (official mail); American Embassy Luxembourg, PSC 9, Box 9500, APO AE 09123 (personal mail)

telephone: [352] 46 01 23

FAX: [352] 46 14 01

Flag description: three equal horizontal bands of red (top), white, and light blue; similar to the flag of the Netherlands, which uses a darker blue and is shorter; design was based on the flag of France

Economy

Economy - overview: This stable, high-income economy features solid growth, low inflation, and low unemployment. The industrial sector, initially dominated by steel, has become increasingly diversified to include chemicals, rubber, and other products. Growth in the financial sector, which now accounts for about 22% of GDP, has more than compensated for the decline in steel. Most banks are foreign-owned and have extensive foreign dealings. Agriculture is based on small family-owned farms. The economy depends on foreign and trans-border workers for more than 30% of its labor force. Although Luxembourg, like all EU members, has suffered from the global economic slump, the country has maintained a fairly strong growth rate and enjoys an extraordinarily high standard of living.

GDP: purchasing power parity - $25.01 billion (2003 est.)

GDP - real growth rate: 1.2% (2003 est.)

GDP - per capita: purchasing power parity - $55,100 (2003 est.)

GDP - composition by sector:

agriculture: 0.5%

industry: 16.6%

services: 82.9% (2002 est.)

Population below poverty line: NA%

Household income or consumption by percentage share:

lowest 10%: NA%

highest 10%: NA%

Inflation rate (consumer prices): 2% (2003 est.)

Labor force: 262,300 (of whom 87,400 are foreign cross-border workers primarily from France, Belgium, and Germany) (2000)

Labor force - by occupation: services 90.1%, industry 8%, agriculture 1.9% (1999 est.)

Unemployment rate: 3% (2003 est.)

Budget:

revenues: $5.5 billion

expenditures: $5.5 billion, including capital expenditures of $760 million (2002 est.)

Industries: banking, iron and steel, food processing, chemicals, metal products, engineering, tires, glass, aluminum

Industrial production growth rate: 1.5% (2003 est.)

Electricity - production: 457 million kWh (2001)

Electricity - production by source:

fossil fuel: 57.3%

hydro: 25.2%

nuclear: 0%

other: 17.5% (2001)

Electricity - consumption: 6.07 billion kWh (2001)

Electricity - exports: 744 million kWh (2001)

Electricity - imports: 6.389 billion kWh (2001)

Oil - production: 0 bbl/day (2001 est.)

Oil - consumption: 50,650 bbl/day (2001 est.)

Oil - exports: 634 bbl/day (2001)

Oil - imports: 50,700 bbl/day (2001)

Luxembourg (continued)

Natural gas - production: 0 cu m (2001 est.)
Natural gas - consumption: 865 million cu m (2001 est.)
Natural gas - exports: 0 cu m (2001 est.)
Natural gas - imports: 867 million cu m (2001 est.)
Agriculture - products: barley, oats, potatoes, wheat, fruits, wine grapes; livestock products
Exports: $8.571 billion f.o.b. (2002)
Exports - commodities: machinery and equipment, steel products, chemicals, rubber products, glass
Exports - partners: Germany 23.9%, France 20.1%, Belgium 10.5%, UK 8.7%, Italy 6.1%, Spain 4.5%, Netherlands 4.4% (2002)
Imports: $11.61 billion c.i.f. (2002)
Imports - commodities: minerals, metals, foodstuffs, quality consumer goods
Imports - partners: Belgium 29.7%, Germany 23%, France 13.2%, Taiwan 7.3%, Netherlands 4.6% (2002)
Debt - external: $NA
Economic aid - donor: ODA, $147 million (2002)
Currency: euro (EUR)
note: on 1 January 1999, the European Monetary Union introduced the euro as a common currency to be used by financial institutions of member countries; on 1 January 2002, the euro became the sole currency for everyday transactions within the member countries
Currency code: EUR
Exchange rates: euros per US dollar - 0.886 (2003), 1.0626 (2002), 1.1175 (2001), 1.0854 (2000), 0.9386 (1999)
Fiscal year: calendar year

Communications

Telephones - main lines in use: 355,400 (2002)
Telephones - mobile cellular: 473,000 (2002)
Telephone system:
general assessment: highly developed, completely automated and efficient system, mainly buried cables
domestic: nationwide cellular telephone system; buried cable
international: country code - 352; 3 channels leased on TAT-6 coaxial submarine cable (Europe to North America)
Radio broadcast stations: AM 2, FM 9, shortwave 2 (1999)
Television broadcast stations: 5 (1999)
Internet country code: .lu
Internet hosts: 17,260 (2002)
Internet users: 165,000 (2002)

Transportation

Railways:
total: 274 km
standard gauge: 274 km 1.435-m gauge (242 km electrified) (2002)
Highways:
total: 5,189 km
paved: 5,189 km (including 114 km of expressways)
unpaved: 0 km (2000)

Waterways: 37 km (on the Moselle)
Pipelines: gas 155 km (2003)
Ports and harbors: Mertert
Merchant marine:
total: 40 ships (1,000 GRT or over) 652,454 GRT/ 805,101 DWT
by type: chemical tanker 11, container 8, liquefied gas 4, passenger 4, petroleum tanker 6, roll on/roll off 7
foreign-owned: Belgium 7, Denmark 1, Finland 3, France 3, Germany 10, Monaco 1, Netherlands 5, Switzerland 1, United Kingdom 7, United States 3
registered in other countries: 1 (2003 est.)
Airports: 2 (2003 est.)
Airports - with paved runways:
total: 1
over 3,047 m: 1 (2003 est.)
Airports - with unpaved runways:
total: 1
under 914 m: 1 (2003 est.)
Heliports: 1 (2003 est.)

Military

Military branches: Army
Military manpower - military age: 19 years of age (2004 est.)
Military manpower - availability:
males age 15-49: 115,721 (2004 est.)
Military manpower - fit for military service:
males age 15-49: 95,107 (2004 est.)
Military manpower - reaching military age annually:
males: 2,601 (2004 est.)
Military expenditures - dollar figure: $231.6 million (2003)
Military expenditures - percent of GDP: 0.9% (2003)

Transnational Issues

Disputes - international: none

Macau
(special administrative region of China)

Introduction

Background: Colonized by the Portuguese in the 16th century, Macau was the first European settlement in the Far East. Pursuant to an agreement signed by China and Portugal on 13 April 1987, Macau became the Macau Special Administrative Region (SAR) of China on 20 December 1999. China has promised that, under its "one country, two systems" formula, China's socialist economic system will not be practiced in Macau, and that Macau will enjoy a high degree of autonomy in all matters except foreign and defense affairs for the next 50 years.

Geography

Location: Eastern Asia, bordering the South China Sea and China
Geographic coordinates: 22 10 N, 113 33 E
Map references: Southeast Asia
Area:
total: 25.4 sq km
land: 25.4 sq km
water: 0 sq km
Area - comparative: about 0.1 times the size of Washington, DC

Macau (continued)

Land boundaries:

total: 0.34 km

regional border: China 0.34 km

Coastline: 41 km

Maritime claims: not specified

Climate: subtropical; marine with cool winters, warm summers

Terrain: generally flat

Elevation extremes:

lowest point: South China Sea 0 m

highest point: Coloane Alto 172.4 m

Natural resources: NEGL

Land use:

arable land: 0%

permanent crops: 0%

other: 100%

note: "green areas" represent 22.4% (1998 est.)

Irrigated land: NA sq km

Natural hazards: typhoons

Environment - current issues: NA

Geography - note: essentially urban; one causeway and two bridges connect the two islands of Coloane and Taipa to the peninsula on mainland

People

Population: 445,286 (July 2004 est.)

Age structure:

0-14 years: 18% (male 41,460; female 38,595)

15-64 years: 74.2% (male 157,629; female 172,810)

65 years and over: 7.8% (male 14,380; female 20,412) (2004 est.)

Median age:

total: 35.2 years

male: 34.9 years

female: 35.4 years (2004 est.)

Population growth rate: 0.87% (2004 est.)

Birth rate: 8.04 births/1,000 population (2004 est.)

Death rate: 4.23 deaths/1,000 population (2004 est.)

Net migration rate: 4.86 migrant(s)/1,000 population (2004 est.)

Sex ratio:

at birth: 1.05 male(s)/female

under 15 years: 1.07 male(s)/female

15-64 years: 0.91 male(s)/female

65 years and over: 0.7 male(s)/female

total population: 0.92 male(s)/female (2004 est.)

Infant mortality rate:

total: 4.39 deaths/1,000 live births

male: 4.59 deaths/1,000 live births

female: 4.19 deaths/1,000 live births (2004 est.)

Life expectancy at birth:

total population: 82.03 years

male: 79.2 years

female: 84.99 years (2004 est.)

Total fertility rate: 0.93 children born/woman (2004 est.)

HIV/AIDS - adult prevalence rate: NA%

HIV/AIDS - people living with HIV/AIDS: NA

HIV/AIDS - deaths: NA

Nationality:

noun: Chinese

adjective: Chinese

Ethnic groups: Chinese 95%, Macanese (mixed Portuguese and Asian ancestry), Portuguese, other

Religions: Buddhist 50%, Roman Catholic 15%, none and other 35% (1997 est.)

Languages: Portuguese, Chinese (Cantonese)

Literacy:

definition: age 15 and over can read and write

total population: 94.5%

male: 97.2%

female: 92% (2003 est.)

Government

Country name:

conventional long form: Macau Special Administrative Region

conventional short form: Macau

local long form: Aomen Tebie Xingzhengqu (Chinese); Regiao Administrativa Especial de Macau (Portuguese)

local short form: Aomen (Chinese); Macau (Portuguese)

Dependency status: special administrative region of China

Government type: limited democracy

Administrative divisions: none (special administrative region of China)

Independence: none (special administrative region of China)

National holiday: National Day (Anniversary of the Founding of the People's Republic of China), 1 October (1949); note - 20 December 1999 is celebrated as Macau Special Administrative Region Establishment Day

Constitution: Basic Law, approved in March 1993 by China's National People's Congress, is Macau's "mini-constitution"

Legal system: based on Portuguese civil law system

Suffrage: direct election 18 years of age, universal for permanent residents living in Macau for the past seven years; indirect election limited to organizations registered as "corporate voters" (257 are currently registered) and a 300-member Election Committee drawn from broad regional groupings, municipal organizations, and central government bodies

Executive branch:

chief of state: President of China HU Jintao (since 15 March 2003)

head of government: Chief Executive Edmund HO Hau-wah (since 20 December 1999)

cabinet: Executive Council consists of all five government secretaries, three legislators, and two businessmen

elections: chief executive chosen by a 200-member selection committee for up to two five-year terms

Legislative branch: unicameral Legislative Council or LEGCO (27 seats; 10 elected by popular vote, 10 by indirect vote, and 7 appointed by the chief executive; members serve four-year terms)

elections: last held 23 September 2001 (next to be held 2005)

election results: percent of vote - NA%; seats by political bloc - Entertainment Industry 3, pro-democracy 2, pro-Beijing Labor Union 2, pro-Beijing Neighborhood Association 2, pro-business 1

Judicial branch: The Court of Final Appeal in the Macau Special Administrative Region

Political parties and leaders: there are no formal political parties, however, there are civic associations that, for purposes of legislative voting, join together to form political blocs

Political pressure groups and leaders: Catholic Church [Domingos LAM, bishop]; Macau Society of Tourism and Entertainment or STDM [Stanley HO, managing director]; Union for Democracy Development [Antonio NG Kuok-cheong, leader]

International organization participation: IMO (associate), Interpol (sub-bureau), ISO (correspondent), UNESCO (associate), WCO, WMO, WToO (associate), WTrO

Diplomatic representation in the US: none (special administrative region of China)

Diplomatic representation from the US: the US has no offices in Macau; US interests are monitored by the US Consulate General in Hong Kong

Flag description: light green with a lotus flower above a stylized bridge and water in white, beneath an arc of five gold, five-pointed stars: one large in center of arc and four smaller

Economy

Economy - overview: Macau's well-to-do economy has remained one of the most open in the world since its reversion to China in 1999. The territory's net exports of goods and services account for roughly 41% of GDP with tourism and apparel exports as the mainstays. Although the territory was hit hard by the 1998 Asian financial crisis and the global downturn in 2001, its economy grew 9.5% in 2002. A rapid rise in the number of mainland visitors because of China's easing of restrictions on travel drove the recovery. The budget also returned to surplus in 2002 because of the surge in visitors from China and a hike in taxes on gambling profits, which generated about 70% of government revenue. The liberalization of Macao's gambling monopoly contributes to GDP growth, as the three companies awarded gambling licenses have pledged to invest $2.2 billion in the territory. Much of Macau's textile industry may move to the mainland as the Multi-Fiber Agreement is phased out. The territory may have to rely more on gambling and trade-related services to generate growth. The government estimated GDP growth at 4% in 2003 with the drop in large measure due to concerns over the Severe Acute Respiratory Syndrome (SARS), but private sector analysts think the figure may have been higher because of the continuing boom in tourism.

GDP: purchasing power parity - $9.1 billion (2003 est.)

Macau *(continued)*

GDP - real growth rate: 4% (2003 est.)
GDP - per capita: purchasing power parity - $19,400 (2003 est.)
GDP - composition by sector:
agriculture: 1%
industry: 12%
services: 87% (2002 est.)
Population below poverty line: NA%
Household income or consumption by percentage share:
lowest 10%: NA%
highest 10%: NA%
Inflation rate (consumer prices): -2.6% (2003 est.)
Labor force: 214,000 (2002)
Labor force - by occupation: restaurants and hotels 12%, manufacturing 20%, wholesale and retail trade 15%, public sector 8%, construction 7%, transport and communications 6%, gambling 7%, other services and agriculture 25% (2002 est.)
Unemployment rate: 6.3% (2003)
Budget:
revenues: $1.9 billion
expenditures: $1.68 billion, including capital expenditures of $194 million (2002)
Industries: tourism, gambling, clothing, textiles, electronics, footwear, toys
Industrial production growth rate: NA%
Electricity - production: 1.611 billion kWh (2002)
Electricity - production by source:
fossil fuel: 100%
hydro: 0%
nuclear: 0%
other: 0% (2001)
Electricity - consumption: 1.688 billion kWh (2002)
Electricity - exports: 1 million kWh (2001)
Electricity - imports: 193 million kWh (2002)
Oil - production: 0 bbl/day (2001 est.)
Oil - consumption: 11,190 bbl/day (2001 est.)
Oil - exports: NA
Oil - imports: NA
Agriculture - products: vegetables, livestock
Exports: $2.356 billion f.o.b. (2002)
Exports - commodities: clothing, textiles, footwear, cement, machines, and parts
Exports - partners: US 48.5%, China 15.5%, Germany 7.4%, Hong Kong 5.8%, UK 5.4% (2002)
Imports: $2.53 billion c.i.f. (2002)
Imports - commodities: clothing, textiles, yarn, foodstuffs, fuel, automobiles, capital goods
Imports - partners: China 41.7%, Hong Kong 14.5%, Japan 6.8%, Taiwan 6.6%, South Korea 5%, France 4.3%, US 4.2% (2002)
Debt - external: $121 million (2001 est.)
Economic aid - recipient: $NA (1997)
Currency: pataca (MOP)
Currency code: MOP
Exchange rates: patacas per US dollar - 8.0212 (2003), 8.0334 (2002), 8.0335 (2001), 8.0259 (2000), 7.9919 (1999)
Fiscal year: calendar year

Telephones - main lines in use: 176,100 (2002)
Telephones - mobile cellular: 276,100 (2002)
Telephone system:
general assessment: fairly modern communication facilities maintained for domestic and international services
domestic: NA
international: country code - 853; HF radiotelephone communication facility; access to international communications carriers provided via Hong Kong and China; satellite earth station - 1 Intelsat (Indian Ocean)
Radio broadcast stations: AM 0, FM 2, shortwave 0 (1998)
Television broadcast stations: 1 (2003)
Internet country code: .mo
Internet hosts: 150 (2002)
Internet users: 115,000 (2002)

Transportation

Railways: 0 km
Highways:
total: 271 km
paved: 271 km
unpaved: 0 km (2000)
Waterways: none
Ports and harbors: Macau
Merchant marine: none
Airports: 1 (2003 est.)
Airports - with paved runways:
total: 1
over 3,047 m: 1 (2003 est.)

Military

Military branches: responsibility for defense reverted to China on 20 December 1999; there are local police forces
Military manpower - availability:
males age 15-49: 125,060 (2004 est.)
Military manpower - fit for military service:
males age 15-49: 68,913 (2004 est.)

Transnational Issues

Disputes - international: none

Macedonia, The Former Yugoslav Republic of

Introduction

Background: International recognition of The Former Yugoslav Republic of Macedonia's (F.Y.R.O.M.) independence from Yugoslavia in 1991 was delayed by Greece's objection to the new state's use of what it considered a Hellenic name and symbols. Greece finally lifted its trade blockade in 1995, and the two countries agreed to normalize relations, despite continued disagreement over F.Y.R.O.M.'s use of "Macedonia." F.Y.R.O.M.'s large Albanian minority, an ethnic Albanian armed insurgency in F.Y.R.O.M. in 2001, and the status of neighboring Kosovo continue to be sources of ethnic tension.

Geography

Location: Southeastern Europe, north of Greece
Geographic coordinates: 41 50 N, 22 00 E
Map references: Europe
Area:
total: 25,333 sq km
land: 24,856 sq km
water: 477 sq km
Area - comparative: slightly larger than Vermont
Land boundaries:
total: 766 km
border countries: Albania 151 km, Bulgaria 148 km, Greece 246 km, Serbia and Montenegro 221 km
Coastline: 0 km (landlocked)
Maritime claims: none (landlocked)
Climate: warm, dry summers and autumns and relatively cold winters with heavy snowfall
Terrain: mountainous territory covered with deep basins and valleys; three large lakes, each divided by a frontier line; country bisected by the Vardar River
Elevation extremes:
lowest point: Vardar River 50 m
highest point: Golem Korab (Maja e Korabit) 2,753 m

Natural resources: chromium, lead, zinc, manganese, tungsten, nickel, low-grade iron ore, asbestos, sulfur, timber, arable land

Land use:

arable land: 23.59%

permanent crops: 1.85%

other: 74.56% (1998 est.)

Irrigated land: 550 sq km (1998 est.)

Natural hazards: high seismic risks

Environment - current issues: air pollution from metallurgical plants

Environment - international agreements:

party to: Air Pollution, Biodiversity, Climate Change, Endangered Species, Hazardous Wastes, Law of the Sea, Ozone Layer Protection, Wetlands

signed, but not ratified: none of the selected agreements

Geography - note: landlocked; major transportation corridor from Western and Central Europe to Aegean Sea and Southern Europe to Western Europe

People

Population: 2,071,210 (July 2004 est.)

Age structure:

0-14 years: 21.5% (male 231,078; female 213,906)

15-64 years: 67.8% (male 707,298; female 696,830)

65 years and over: 10.7% (male 97,437; female 124,661) (2004 est.)

Median age:

total: 32.8 years

male: 31.7 years

female: 33.9 years (2004 est.)

Population growth rate: 0.39% (2004 est.)

Birth rate: 13.14 births/1,000 population (2004 est.)

Death rate: 7.83 deaths/1,000 population (2004 est.)

Net migration rate: -1.45 migrant(s)/1,000 population (2004 est.)

Sex ratio:

at birth: 1.08 male(s)/female

under 15 years: 1.08 male(s)/female

15-64 years: 1.02 male(s)/female

65 years and over: 0.78 male(s)/female

total population: 1 male(s)/female (2004 est.)

Infant mortality rate:

total: 11.74 deaths/1,000 live births

male: 12.67 deaths/1,000 live births

female: 10.73 deaths/1,000 live births (2004 est.)

Life expectancy at birth:

total population: 74.73 years

male: 72.45 years

female: 77.2 years (2004 est.)

Total fertility rate: 1.74 children born/woman (2004 est.)

HIV/AIDS - adult prevalence rate: less than 0.1% (2001 est.)

HIV/AIDS - people living with HIV/AIDS: less than 100 (1999 est.)

HIV/AIDS - deaths: less than 100 (2001 est.)

Nationality:

noun: Macedonian(s)

adjective: Macedonian

Ethnic groups: Macedonian 64.2%, Albanian 25.2%, Turkish 3.8%, Roma 2.7%, Serb 1.8%, other 2.3% (2002)

Religions: Macedonian Orthodox 70%, Muslim 29%, other 1%

Languages: Macedonian 68%, Albanian 25%, Turkish 3%, Serbo-Croatian 2%, other 2%

Literacy:

definition: NA

total population: NA%

male: NA%

female: NA%

Government

Country name:

conventional long form: The Former Yugoslav Republic of Macedonia

conventional short form: none

local long form: Republika Makedonija

local short form: Makedonija

abbreviation: F.Y.R.O.M.

Government type: parliamentary democracy

Capital: Skopje

Administrative divisions: 123 municipalities (opstini, singular - opstina); Aracinovo, Bac, Belcista, Berovo, Bistrica, Bitola, Blatec, Bogdanci, Bogomila, Bogovinje, Bosilovo, Brvenica, Cair (Skopje), Capari, Caska, Cegrane, Centar (Skopje), Centar Zupa, Cesinovo, Cucer-Sandevo, Debar, Delcevo, Delogozdi, Demir Hisar, Demir Kapija, Dobrusevo, Dolna Banjica, Dolneni, Dorce Petrov (Skopje), Drugovo, Dzepciste, Gazi Baba (Skopje), Gevgelija, Gostivar, Gradsko, Ilinden, Izvor, Jegunovce, Kamenjane, Karbinci, Karpos (Skopje), Kavadarci, Kicevo, Kisela Voda (Skopje), Klecevce, Kocani, Konce, Kondovo, Konopiste, Kosel, Kratovo, Kriva Palanka, Krivogastani, Krusevo, Kuklis, Kukurecani, Kumanovo, Labunista, Lipkovo, Lozovo, Lukovo, Makedonska Kamenica, Makedonski Brod, Mavrovi Anovi, Meseista, Miravci, Mogila, Murtino, Negotino, Negotino-Polosko, Novaci, Novo Selo, Oblesevo, Ohrid, Orasac, Orizari, Oslomej, Pehcevo, Petrovec, Plasnica, Podares, Prilep, Probistip, Radovis, Rankovce, Resen, Rosoman, Rostusa, Samokov, Saraj, Sipkovica, Sopiste, Sopotnica, Srbinovo, Star Dojran, Staravina, Staro Nagoricane, Stip, Struga, Strumica, Studenicani, Suto Orizari (Skopje), Sveti Nikole, Tearce, Tetovo, Topolcani, Valandovo, Vasilevo, Velesta, Veles, Vevcani, Vinica, Vitoliste, Vranestica, Vrapciste, Vratnica, Vrutok, Zajas, Zelenikovo, Zeleno, Zitose, Zletovo, Zrnovci

note: the seven municipalities followed by Skopje in parentheses collectively constitute "greater Skopje"

Independence: 8 September 1991 referendum by registered voters endorsing independence (from Yugoslavia)

National holiday: Uprising Day, 2 August (1903); note - also known as Saint Elijah's Day and Ilinden

Constitution: adopted 17 November 1991, effective 20 November 1991

note: in November of 2001, the Macedonian Assembly approved a series of new constitutional amendments strengthening minority rights

Legal system: based on civil law system; judicial review of legislative acts

Suffrage: 18 years of age; universal

Executive branch:

chief of state: Acting President Ljupco JORDANOVSKI (since 26 February 2004); note - Boris TRAJKOVSKI was killed in a plane crash 26 February 2004; Parliament Speaker Ljupco JORDANOVSKI is acting president

head of government: Prime Minister Branko CRVENKOVSKI (since 1 November 2002)

cabinet: Council of Ministers elected by the majority vote of all the deputies in the Assembly; note - current cabinet formed by the government coalition parties SDSM, LDP, and DUI (or BDI)

elections: president elected by popular vote for a five-year term; election last held 14 November 1999 (next to be held NA October 2004); prime minister elected by the Assembly; election last held 1 November 2002 (next to be held NA 2006)

election results: Boris TRAJKOVSKI elected president on second-round ballot; percent of vote - Boris TRAJKOVSKI 52.4%, Tito PETKOVSKI 46.2%; Branko CRVENKOVSKI elected prime minister by the Assembly with 72% of the vote

Legislative branch: unicameral Assembly or Sobranie (120 seats - 85 members are elected by popular vote, 35 members come from lists of candidates submitted by parties based on the percentage that a party gains from the overall vote; all serve four-year terms)

elections: last held 15 September 2002 (next to be held NA 2006)

election results: percent of vote by party - NA%; seats by party - Together for Macedonia coalition (SDSM and LDP) 60, VMRO-DPMNE 33, Democratic Union for Integration 16, Democratic Party of Albanians 7, Party for Democratic Prosperity 2, National Democratic Party 1, Socialist Party of Macedonia 1

Judicial branch: Supreme Court - the Assembly appoints the judges; Constitutional Court - the Assembly appoints the judges; Republican Judicial Council - the Assembly appoints the judges

Political parties and leaders: Democratic Alternative or DA [Vasil TUPURKOVSKI, president]; Democratic Union for Integration or DUI (also BDI) [Ali AHMETI]; Democratic Party of Albanians or PDSH [Arben XHAFERI, president]; Internal Macedonian Revolutionary Organization-Democratic Party for Macedonian National Unity or VMRO-DPMNE [Nikola GRUEVSKI]; Internal Macedonian Revolutionary Organization-True Macedonian Reform Option or VMRO-VMRO [Boris ZMEJKOVSKI]; Internal Macedonian Revolutionary Organization-Macedonian [Boris STOJMENOV]; Liberal Democratic Party or LDP [Risto PENOV]; Liberal Party [Stojan ANDOV]; National Democratic Party or PDK [Basri HALITI]; Party for Democratic Prosperity or PPD [Abdulmenaf BEXHETI]; Social Democratic Alliance of Macedonia or SDSM [Branko CRVENKOVSKI, president]; Socialist Party of Macedonia or SP [Ljubisav IVANOV, president]; Together for Macedonia coalition (including the SDSM and LDP) [Branko CRVENKOVSKI]; Union of Romanies of Macedonia or SRM [leader NA]

Political pressure groups and leaders: NA

International organization participation: ACCT, BIS, CE, CEI, EAPC, EBRD, FAO, IAEA, IBRD, ICAO, ICCt, ICRM, IDA, IFAD, IFC, IFRCS, ILO, IMF, IMO, Interpol, IOC, IOM (observer), ISO, ITU, OPCW, OSCE, PCA, PFP, UN, UNCTAD, UNESCO, UNIDO, UPU, WCL, WCO, WHO, WIPO, WMO, WToO, WTrO

Diplomatic representation in the US:
chief of mission: Ambassador Nikola DIMITROV
chancery: Suite 302, 1101 30th Street NW, Washington, DC 20007
telephone: [1] (202) 337-3063
FAX: [1] (202) 337-3093
consulate(s) general: New York

Diplomatic representation from the US:
chief of mission: Ambassador Lawrence Edward BUTLER
embassy: Bul. Ilinden bb, 91000 Skopje
mailing address: American Embassy Skopje, Department of State, 7120 Skopje Place, Washington, DC 20521-7120 (pouch)
telephone: [389] 2 311-6180
FAX: [389] 2 311-7103

Flag description: a yellow sun with eight broadening rays extending to the edges of the red field

Economy

Economy - overview: At independence in September 1991, Macedonia was the least developed of the Yugoslav republics, producing a mere 5% of the total federal output of goods and services. The collapse of Yugoslavia ended transfer payments from the center and eliminated advantages from inclusion in a de facto free trade area. An absence of infrastructure, UN sanctions on Yugoslavia, one of its largest markets, and a Greek economic embargo over a dispute about the country's constitutional name and flag hindered economic growth until 1996. GDP subsequently rose each year through 2000. However, the leadership's commitment to economic reform, free trade, and regional integration was undermined by the ethnic Albanian insurgency of 2001. The economy shrank 4.5% because of decreased trade, intermittent border closures, increased deficit spending on security needs, and investor uncertainty. Growth barely recovered in 2002 to 0.9%, then rose to 2.8% in 2003. Unemployment at one-third of the workforce remains the most critical economic problem. The gray economy is estimated at around 40% of GDP. Politically, the country is more stable than in 2002.

GDP: purchasing power parity - $13.81 billion (2003 est.)

GDP - real growth rate: 2.8% (2003 est.)

GDP - per capita: purchasing power parity - $6,700 (2003 est.)

GDP - composition by sector:
agriculture: 9.9%
industry: 25.3%
services: 64.8% (2003 est.)

Population below poverty line: 30.2% (2002 est.)

Household income or consumption by percentage share:
lowest 10%: NA%
highest 10%: NA%

Inflation rate (consumer prices): 1.2% (2003 est.)

Labor force: 860,000 (2003 est.)

Labor force - by occupation: agriculture NA%, industry NA%, services NA%

Unemployment rate: 36.7% (2003 est.)

Budget:
revenues: $1.03 billion
expenditures: $1.05 billion, including capital expenditures of $80 million $NA (2003 est.)

Industries: coal, metallic chromium, lead, zinc, ferronickel, textiles, wood products, tobacco, food processing, buses, steel

Industrial production growth rate: 3% (2003 est.)

Electricity - production: 6.465 billion kWh (2001)

Electricity - production by source:
fossil fuel: 83.7%
hydro: 16.3%
nuclear: 0%
other: 0% (2001)

Electricity - consumption: 6.112 billion kWh (2001)

Electricity - exports: 0 kWh (2001)

Electricity - imports: 100 million kWh (2001)

Oil - production: 0 bbl/day (2001 est.)

Oil - consumption: 20,000 bbl/day (2001 est.)

Oil - exports: NA

Oil - imports: NA

Agriculture - products: rice, tobacco, wheat, corn, millet, cotton, sesame, mulberry leaves, citrus, vegetables; beef, pork, poultry, mutton

Exports: $1.346 billion f.o.b. (2003 est.)

Exports - commodities: food, beverages, tobacco; miscellaneous manufactures, iron and steel

Exports - partners: Germany 19.7%, Italy 9.5%, US 6.9%, Croatia 5.7%, Greece 4.7%, Netherlands 4.1% (2002)

Imports: $2.184 billion f.o.b. (2003 est.)

Imports - commodities: machinery and equipment, chemicals, fuels; food products

Imports - partners: Greece 18.2%, Germany 13.6%, Yugoslavia 8.6%, Slovenia 8.4%, Bulgaria 7%, Italy 6.4%, Turkey 5.6% (2002)

Debt - external: $1.7 billion (2003 est.)

Economic aid - recipient: $250 million (2003 est.)

Currency: Macedonian denar (MKD)

Currency code: MKD

Exchange rates: Macedonian denars per US dollar - NA (2003), 64.3498 (2002), 68.0371 (2001), 65.9039 (2000), 56.9018 (1999)

Fiscal year: calendar year

Communications

Telephones - main lines in use: 560,000 (2002)

Telephones - mobile cellular: 365,300 (2002)

Telephone system:
general assessment: NA
domestic: NA
international: country code - 389

Radio broadcast stations: AM 29, FM 20, shortwave 0 (1998)

Television broadcast stations: 31 (plus 166 repeaters) (1995)

Internet country code: .mk

Internet hosts: 3,167 (2002)

Internet users: 100,000 (2002)

Transportation

Railways:
total: 699 km
standard gauge: 699 km 1.435-m gauge (233 km electrified) (2002)

Highways:
total: 8,684 km
paved: 5,540 km (including 133 km of expressways)
unpaved: 3,144 km (1999 est.)

Waterways:
note: lake transport only, on the Greek and Albanian borders

Pipelines: gas 268 km; oil 120 km (2003)

Ports and harbors: none

Airports: 17 (2003 est.)

Airports - with paved runways:
total: 10
2,438 to 3,047 m: 2
under 914 m: 8 (2003 est.)

Airports - with unpaved runways:
total: 7
914 to 1,523 m: 3
under 914 m: 4 (2003 est.)

Military

Military branches: Army of the Republic of Macedonia (ARM; including Air and Air Defense Command)

Military manpower - military age: 19 years of age (2004 est.)

Military manpower - availability:
males age 15-49: 555,611 (2004 est.)

Military manpower - fit for military service:
males age 15-49: 448,095 (2004 est.)

Military manpower - reaching military age annually:
males: 17,595 (2004 est.)

Military expenditures - dollar figure: $200 million (FY01/02 est.)

Military expenditures - percent of GDP: 6% (FY01/02 est.)

Macedonia, The Former Yugoslav Republic of *(continued)*

Transnational Issues

Disputes - international: the Albanian government calls for the protection of the rights of ethnic Albanians in F.Y.R.O.M. while continuing to seek regional cooperation; ethnic Albanians in Kosovo resist demarcation of the F.Y.R.O.M.-Serbia and Montenegro boundary in accordance with the 2000 delimitation treaty, which transfered a small amount of land to F.Y.R.O.M.; dispute with Greece over country's name persists

Illicit drugs: major transshipment point for Southwest Asian heroin and hashish; minor transit point for South American cocaine destined for Europe; although most criminal activity is thought to be domestic and not a financial center, money laundering is a problem due to a mostly cash-based economy and weak enforcement (no arrests or prosecutions for money laundering to date)

Madagascar

Introduction

Background: Formerly an independent kingdom, Madagascar became a French colony in 1896, but regained its independence in 1960. During 1992-93, free presidential and National Assembly elections were held, ending 17 years of single-party rule. In 1997, in the second presidential race, Didier RATSIRAKA, the leader during the 1970s and 1980s, was returned to the presidency. The 2001 presidential election was contested between the followers of Didier RATSIRAKA and Marc RAVALOMANANA, nearly causing secession of half of the country. In April 2002, the High Constitutional Court announced RAVALOMANANA the winner.

Geography

Location: Southern Africa, island in the Indian Ocean, east of Mozambique
Geographic coordinates: 20 00 S, 47 00 E
Map references: Africa
Area:
total: 587,040 sq km
land: 581,540 sq km
water: 5,500 sq km

Area - comparative: slightly less than twice the size of Arizona
Land boundaries: 0 km
Coastline: 4,828 km
Maritime claims:
territorial sea: 12 NM
contiguous zone: 24 NM
exclusive economic zone: 200 NM
continental shelf: 200 NM or 100 NM from the 2,500-m deep isobath
Climate: tropical along coast, temperate inland, arid in south
Terrain: narrow coastal plain, high plateau and mountains in center
Elevation extremes:
lowest point: Indian Ocean 0 m
highest point: Maromokotro 2,876 m
Natural resources: graphite, chromite, coal, bauxite, salt, quartz, tar sands, semiprecious stones, mica, fish, hydropower
Land use:
arable land: 4.99%
permanent crops: 1.03%
other: 93.98% (2000 est.)
Irrigated land: 10,900 sq km (2000 est.)
Natural hazards: periodic cyclones, drought, and locust infestation
Environment - current issues: soil erosion results from deforestation and overgrazing; desertification; surface water contaminated with raw sewage and other organic wastes; several species of flora and fauna unique to the island are endangered
Environment - international agreements:
party to: Biodiversity, Climate Change, Climate Change-Kyoto Protocol, Desertification, Endangered Species, Hazardous Wastes, Law of the Sea, Marine Life Conservation, Ozone Layer Protection, Wetlands
signed, but not ratified: none of the selected agreements
Geography - note: world's fourth-largest island; strategic location along Mozambique Channel

People

Population: 17,501,871 (July 2004 est.)
Age structure:
0-14 years: 44.9% (male 3,935,523; female 3,922,077)
15-64 years: 52% (male 4,509,877; female 4,596,662)
65 years and over: 3.1% (male 245,168; female 292,564) (2004 est.)
Median age:
total: 17.4 years
male: 17.2 years
female: 17.7 years (2004 est.)
Population growth rate: 3.03% (2004 est.)
Birth rate: 41.91 births/1,000 population (2004 est.)
Death rate: 11.62 deaths/1,000 population (2004 est.)
Net migration rate: 0 migrant(s)/1,000 population (2004 est.)

Sex ratio:
at birth: 1.03 male(s)/female
under 15 years: 1 male(s)/female
15-64 years: 0.98 male(s)/female
65 years and over: 0.84 male(s)/female
total population: 0.99 male(s)/female (2004 est.)

Infant mortality rate:
total: 78.52 deaths/1,000 live births
male: 86.84 deaths/1,000 live births
female: 69.95 deaths/1,000 live births (2004 est.)

Life expectancy at birth:
total population: 56.54 years
male: 54.19 years
female: 58.96 years (2004 est.)

Total fertility rate: 5.7 children born/woman (2004 est.)

HIV/AIDS - adult prevalence rate: 0.3% (2001 est.)

HIV/AIDS - people living with HIV/AIDS: 22,000 (2001 est.)

HIV/AIDS - deaths: 870 (2001 est.)

Nationality:
noun: Malagasy (singular and plural)
adjective: Malagasy

Ethnic groups: Malayo-Indonesian (Merina and related Betsileo), Cotiers (mixed African, Malayo-Indonesian, and Arab ancestry - Betsimisaraka, Tsimihety, Antaisaka, Sakalava), French, Indian, Creole, Comoran

Religions: indigenous beliefs 52%, Christian 41%, Muslim 7%

Languages: French (official), Malagasy (official)

Literacy:
definition: age 15 and over can read and write
total population: 68.9%
male: 75.5%
female: 62.5% (2003 est.)

Government

Country name:
conventional long form: Republic of Madagascar
conventional short form: Madagascar
local long form: Republique de Madagascar
local short form: Madagascar
former: Malagasy Republic

Government type: republic

Capital: Antananarivo

Administrative divisions: 6 provinces (faritany); Antananarivo, Antsiranana, Fianarantsoa, Mahajanga, Toamasina, Toliara

Independence: 26 June 1960 (from France)

National holiday: Independence Day, 26 June (1960)

Constitution: 19 August 1992 by national referendum

Legal system: based on French civil law system and traditional Malagasy law; has not accepted compulsory ICJ jurisdiction

Suffrage: 18 years of age; universal

Executive branch:
chief of state: President Marc RAVALOMANANA (since 6 May 2002)

head of government: Prime Minister Jacques SYLLA (27 May 2002)
cabinet: Council of Ministers appointed by the prime minister
elections: president elected by popular vote for a five-year term; election last held 16 December 2001 (next to be held NA November 2006); prime minister appointed by the president
election results: percent of vote - Didier RATSIRAKA (AREMA) 37.7%, Marc RAVALOMANANA (TIM) 50.5%

Legislative branch: bicameral National Assembly or Assemblee Nationale (160 seats; members are directly elected by popular vote to serve four-year terms); Senate (100 seats; two-thirds of the seats filled by regional assemblies whose members will be elected by popular vote; the remaining one-third of the seats appointed by the president; all members will serve four-year terms)
elections: National Assembly - last held 15 December 2002 (next to be held NA 2006)
election results: National Assembly - percent of vote by party - NA%; seats by party - TIM 103, FP 22, AREMA 3, LEADER/Fanilo 2, RPSD 5, others 3, independents 22

Judicial branch: Supreme Court or Cour Supreme; High Constitutional Court or Haute Cour Constitutionnelle

Political parties and leaders: Association for the Rebirth of Madagascar or AREMA [Pierrot RAJAONARIVO]; Economic Liberalism and Democratic Action for National Recovery or LEADER/Fanilo [Herizo RAZAFIMAHALEO]; Fihaonana Party or FP [Guy-Willy RAZANAMASY]; I Love Madagascar or TIM [Marc RAVALOMANANA]; Renewal of the Social Democratic Party or RPSD [Evariste MARSON]

Political pressure groups and leaders: Committee for the Defense of Truth and Justice or KMMR; Committee for National Reconciliation or CRN [Albert Zafy]; National Council of Christian Churches or FFKM

International organization participation: ACCT, ACP, AfDB, AU, FAO, G-77, IAEA, IBRD, ICAO, ICCt (signatory), ICFTU, ICRM, IDA, IFAD, IFC, IFRCS, ILO, IMF, IMO, InOC, Interpol, IOC, IOM, ISO (correspondent), ITU, NAM, UN, UNCTAD, UNESCO, UNHCR, UNIDO, UPU, WCL, WCO, WFTU, WHO, WIPO, WMO, WToO, WTrO

Diplomatic representation in the US:
chief of mission: Ambassador Rajaonarivony NARISOA
chancery: 2374 Massachusetts Avenue NW, Washington, DC 20008
telephone: [1] (202) 265-5525, 5526
FAX: [1] (202) 483-7603
consulate(s) general: New York

Diplomatic representation from the US:
chief of mission: Ambassador Wanda L. NESBITT
embassy: 14-16 Rue Rainitovo, Antsahavola, Antananarivo 101
mailing address: B. P. 620, Antsahavola, Antananarivo

telephone: [261] (20) 22-212-57, 22-212-73, 22-209-56
FAX: [261] (20) 22-345-39

Flag description: two equal horizontal bands of red (top) and green with a vertical white band of the same width on hoist side

Economy

Economy - overview: Having discarded past socialist economic policies, Madagascar has since the mid 1990s followed a World Bank and IMF led policy of privatization and liberalization. This strategy has placed the country on a slow and steady growth path from an extremely low level. Agriculture, including fishing and forestry, is a mainstay of the economy, accounting for more than one-fourth of GDP and employing four-fifths of the population. Exports of apparel have boomed in recent years primarily due to duty-free access to the United States. Deforestation and erosion, aggravated by the use of firewood as the primary source of fuel are serious concerns. President RAVALOMANANA has worked aggressively to revive the economy following the 2002 political crisis, which triggered a 12% drop in GDP that year. Poverty reduction and combating corruption will be the centerpieces of economic policy for the next few years.

GDP: purchasing power parity - $13.02 billion (2003 est.)

GDP - real growth rate: 6% (2003 est.)

GDP - per capita: purchasing power parity - $800 (2003 est.)

GDP - composition by sector:
agriculture: 27.4%
industry: 12.8%
services: 59.8% (2002 est.)

Population below poverty line: 71% (1999 est.)

Household income or consumption by percentage share:
lowest 10%: 3%
highest 10%: 29% (1999)

Distribution of family income - Gini index: 38.1 (1999)

Inflation rate (consumer prices): 3.5% (2003 est.)

Labor force: 7.3 million (2000)

Unemployment rate: 5.9% (1998)

Budget:
revenues: $459.8 million
expenditures: $798.9 million, including capital expenditures of $331 million (2001)

Industries: meat processing, soap, breweries, tanneries, sugar, textiles, glassware, cement, automobile assembly plant, paper, petroleum, tourism

Industrial production growth rate: 3% (2000 est.)

Electricity - production: 830.2 million kWh (2001)

Electricity - production by source:
fossil fuel: 36.1%
hydro: 63.9%
nuclear: 0%
other: 0% (2001)

Electricity - consumption: 772.1 million kWh (2001)

Madagascar (continued)

Electricity - exports: 0 kWh (2001)
Electricity - imports: 0 kWh (2001)
Oil - production: 0 bbl/day (2001 est.)
Oil - consumption: 13,000 bbl/day (2001 est.)
Oil - exports: NA
Oil - imports: NA
Oil - proved reserves: 0 bbl (1 January 2002)
Natural gas - proved reserves: 0 cu m (1 January 2002)
Agriculture - products: coffee, vanilla, sugarcane, cloves, cocoa, rice, cassava (tapioca), beans, bananas, peanuts; livestock products
Exports: $700 million f.o.b. (2003 est.)
Exports - commodities: coffee, vanilla, shellfish, sugar; cotton cloth, chromite, petroleum products
Exports - partners: France 39.2%, US 19.8%, Germany 5.5%, Japan 4.8%, Singapore 4.2% (2002)
Imports: $920 million f.o.b. (2003 est.)
Imports - commodities: capital goods, petroleum, consumer goods, food
Imports - partners: France 16.6%, Bahrain 11.3%, UAE 6.9%, China 6.3%, South Africa 5.1%, India 4.2% (2002)
Debt - external: $4.6 billion (2002)
Economic aid - recipient: $354 million (2001)
Currency: Malagasy franc (MGF)
Currency code: MGF
Exchange rates: Malagasy francs per US dollar - 6,210 (2003), 6,831.96 (2002), 6,588.49 (2001), 6,767.48 (2000), 6,283.77 (1999)
Fiscal year: calendar year

Communications

Telephones - main lines in use: 59,500 (2002)
Telephones - mobile cellular: 163,000 (2002)
Telephone system:
general assessment: system is above average for the region
domestic: open-wire lines, coaxial cables, microwave radio relay, and tropospheric scatter links connect regions
international: country code - 261; submarine cable to Bahrain; satellite earth stations - 1 Intelsat (Indian Ocean) and 1 Intersputnik (Atlantic Ocean region)
Radio broadcast stations: AM 2 (plus a number of repeater stations), FM 9, shortwave 6 (2001)
Television broadcast stations: 1 (plus 36 repeaters) (2001)
Internet country code: .mg
Internet hosts: 509 (2002)
Internet users: 55,000 (2002)

Transportation

Railways:
total: 732 km
narrow gauge: 732 km 1.000-m gauge (2002)
Highways:
total: 49,827 km
paved: 5,780 km
unpaved: 44,047 km (1999 est.)
Waterways: of local importance only

Ports and harbors: Antsiranana, Antsohimbondrona, Mahajanga, Toamasina, Toliara
Merchant marine:
total: 11 ships (1,000 GRT or over) 14,865 GRT/ 17,936 DWT
by type: cargo 8, chemical tanker 1, roll on/roll off 2
registered in other countries: 2 (2003 est.)
Airports: 116 (2003 est.)
Airports - with paved runways:
total: 29
over 3,047 m: 1
2,438 to 3,047 m: 2
1,524 to 2,437 m: 4
914 to 1,523 m: 20
under 914 m: 2 (2003 est.)
Airports - with unpaved runways:
total: 87
1,524 to 2,437 m: 2
914 to 1,523 m: 42
under 914 m: 43 (2003 est.)

Military

Military branches: People's Armed Forces: comprising Intervention Force, Development Force, and Aeronaval - Navy and Air - Force; National Gendarmerie
Military manpower - military age: 20 years of age (2004 est.)
Military manpower - availability:
males age 15-49: 4,004,242 (2004 est.)
Military manpower - fit for military service:
males age 15-49: 2,373,342 (2004 est.)
Military manpower - reaching military age annually:
males: 169,186 (2004 est.)
Military expenditures - dollar figure: $69.8 million (2003)
Military expenditures - percent of GDP: 1.2% (2003)

Transnational Issues

Disputes - international: claims Bassas da India, Europa Island, Glorioso Islands, and Juan de Nova Island (all administered by France)
Illicit drugs: illicit producer of cannabis (cultivated and wild varieties) used mostly for domestic consumption; transshipment point for heroin

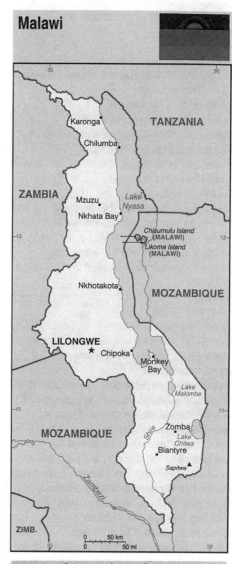

Malawi

Introduction

Background: Established in 1891, the British protectorate of Nyasaland became the independent nation of Malawi in 1964. After three decades of one-party rule under President Hastings Kamuzu BANDA the country held multiparty elections in 1994, under a provisional constitution, which came into full effect the following year. Current President Bakili MULUZI came to power in the 1994 elections and was reelected to office in 1999. His attempts to amend the constitution to allow for a third term have been unsuccessful. Increasing corruption, population growth, increasing pressure on agricultural lands, and HIV/AIDS pose major problems for the country.

Geography

Location: Southern Africa, east of Zambia
Geographic coordinates: 13 30 S, 34 00 E
Map references: Africa
Area:
total: 118,480 sq km
land: 94,080 sq km
water: 24,400 sq km

Area - comparative: slightly smaller than Pennsylvania

Land boundaries:

total: 2,881 km

border countries: Mozambique 1,569 km, Tanzania 475 km, Zambia 837 km

Coastline: 0 km (landlocked)

Maritime claims: none (landlocked)

Climate: sub-tropical; rainy season (November to May); dry season (May to November)

Terrain: narrow elongated plateau with rolling plains, rounded hills, some mountains

Elevation extremes:

lowest point: junction of the Shire River and international boundary with Mozambique 37 m

highest point: Sapitwa (Mount Mlanje) 3,002 m

Natural resources: limestone, arable land, hydropower, unexploited deposits of uranium, coal, and bauxite

Land use:

arable land: 19.93%

permanent crops: 1.33%

other: 78.74% (1998 est.)

Irrigated land: 280 sq km (1998 est.)

Natural hazards: NA

Environment - current issues: deforestation; land degradation; water pollution from agricultural runoff, sewage, industrial wastes; siltation of spawning grounds endangers fish populations

Environment - international agreements:

party to: Biodiversity, Climate Change, Climate Change-Kyoto Protocol, Desertification, Endangered Species, Environmental Modification, Hazardous Wastes, Marine Life Conservation, Ozone Layer Protection, Ship Pollution, Wetlands

signed, but not ratified: Law of the Sea

Geography - note: landlocked; Lake Nyasa, some 580 km long, is the country's most prominent physical feature

People

Population: 11,906,855

note: estimates for this country explicitly take into account the effects of excess mortality due to AIDS; this can result in lower life expectancy, higher infant mortality and death rates, lower population and growth rates, and changes in the distribution of population by age and sex than would otherwise be expected (July 2004 est.)

Age structure:

0-14 years: 46.8% (male 2,811,751; female 2,759,515)

15-64 years: 50.5% (male 2,978,406; female 3,029,735)

65 years and over: 2.8% (male 130,600; female 196,848) (2004 est.)

Median age:

total: 16.4 years

male: 16.1 years

female: 16.7 years (2004 est.)

Population growth rate: 2.14% (2004 est.)

Birth rate: 44.35 births/1,000 population (2004 est.)

Death rate: 23.01 deaths/1,000 population (2004 est.)

Net migration rate: 0 migrant(s)/1,000 population (2004 est.)

Sex ratio:

at birth: 1.03 male(s)/female

under 15 years: 1.02 male(s)/female

15-64 years: 0.98 male(s)/female

65 years and over: 0.66 male(s)/female

total population: 0.99 male(s)/female (2004 est.)

Infant mortality rate:

total: 104.23 deaths/1,000 live births

male: 108.4 deaths/1,000 live births

female: 99.93 deaths/1,000 live births (2004 est.)

Life expectancy at birth:

total population: 37.48 years

male: 37.08 years

female: 37.88 years (2004 est.)

Total fertility rate: 6.04 children born/woman (2004 est.)

HIV/AIDS - adult prevalence rate: 15% (2001 est.)

HIV/AIDS - people living with HIV/AIDS: 850,000 (2001 est.)

HIV/AIDS - deaths: 80,000 (2001 est.)

Nationality:

noun: Malawian(s)

adjective: Malawian

Ethnic groups: Chewa, Nyanja, Tumbuka, Yao, Lomwe, Sena, Tonga, Ngoni, Ngonde, Asian, European

Religions: Protestant 55%, Roman Catholic 20%, Muslim 20%, indigenous beliefs 3%, other 2%

Languages: English (official), Chichewa (official), other languages important regionally

Literacy:

definition: age 15 and over can read and write

total population: 62.7%

male: 76.1%

female: 49.8% (2003 est.)

Government

Country name:

conventional long form: Republic of Malawi

conventional short form: Malawi

former: British Central African Protectorate, Nyasaland Protectorate, Nyasaland

Government type: multiparty democracy

Capital: Lilongwe

Administrative divisions: 27 districts; Balaka, Blantyre, Chikwawa, Chiradzulu, Chitipa, Dedza, Dowa, Karonga, Kasungu, Likoma, Lilongwe, Machinga (Kasupe), Mangochi, Mchinji, Mulanje, Mwanza, Mzimba, Ntcheu, Nkhata Bay, Nkhotakota, Nsanje, Ntchisi, Phalombe, Rumphi, Salima, Thyolo, Zomba

Independence: 6 July 1964 (from UK)

National holiday: Independence Day (Republic Day), 6 July (1964)

Constitution: 18 May 1994

Legal system: based on English common law and customary law; judicial review of legislative acts in the Supreme Court of Appeal; has not accepted compulsory ICJ jurisdiction

Suffrage: 18 years of age; universal

Executive branch:

chief of state: President Bakili MULUZI (since 21 May 1994); note - the president is both the chief of state and head of government

head of government: President Bakili MULUZI (since 21 May 1994); note - the president is both the chief of state and head of government

cabinet: 46-member Cabinet named by the president

elections: president elected by popular vote for a five-year term; election last held 15 June 1999 (next to be held 18 May 2004)

election results: Bakili MULUZI reelected president; percent of vote - Bakili MULUZI (UDF) 51.4%, Gwandaguluwe CHAKUAMBA (MCP-AFORD) 44.3%

Legislative branch: unicameral National Assembly (193 seats; members elected by popular vote to serve five-year terms)

elections: last held 15 June 1999 (next to be held 18 May 2004)

election results: percent of vote by party - UDF 48%, MCP 34%, AFORD 15%, others 3%; seats by party - UDF 96, MCP 61, AFORD 30, others 6

Judicial branch: Supreme Court of Appeal; High Court (chief justice appointed by the president, puisne judges appointed on the advice of the Judicial Service Commission); magistrate's courts

Political parties and leaders: Alliance for Democracy or AFORD [Chakufwa CHIHANA]; Malawi Congress Party or MCP [John TEMBO]; Malawi Democratic Party or MDP [Kampelo KALUA]; Movement for Genuine Democratic Change or MGODE [Du MHANGO]; National Democratic Alliance or NDA [Brown MPINGANJIRA]; People's Progressive Movement or PPM [Aleke BANDA]; United Democratic Front or UDF [Bakili MULUZI] - governing party

Political pressure groups and leaders: NA

International organization participation: ACP, AfDB, AU, C, FAO, G-77, IBRD, ICAO, ICCt, ICFTU, ICRM, IDA, IFAD, IFC, IFRCS, ILO, IMF, IMO, Interpol, IOC, ISO (correspondent), ITU, MONUC, NAM, OPCW, SADC, UN, UNCTAD, UNESCO, UNIDO, UNMIK, UNMIL, UPU, WCL, WCO, WFTU, WHO, WIPO, WMO, WToO, WTrO

Diplomatic representation in the US:

chief of mission: Ambassador Paul Tony Steven KANDIERO

chancery: 2408 Massachusetts Avenue NW, Washington, DC 20008

telephone: [1] (202) 797-1007

FAX: [1] (202) 265-0976

Diplomatic representation from the US:

chief of mission: Ambassador Stephen BROWNING

embassy: Area 40, Plot 24, Kenyatta Road

mailing address: P. O. Box 30016, Lilongwe 3, Malawi

telephone: [265] (1) 773 166

FAX: [265] (1) 770 471

Malawi (continued)

Flag description: three equal horizontal bands of black (top), red, and green with a radiant, rising, red sun centered in the black band
Government - note: the executive exerts considerable influence over the legislature

Economy

Economy - overview: Landlocked Malawi ranks among the world's least developed countries. The economy is predominately agricultural, with about 90% of the population living in rural areas. Agriculture accounted for nearly 40% of GDP and 88% of export revenues in 2001. The economy depends on substantial inflows of economic assistance from the IMF, the World Bank, and individual donor nations. In late 2000, Malawi was approved for relief under the Heavily Indebted Poor Countries (HIPC) program. In November 2002 the World Bank approved a $50 million drought recovery package, which is to be used for famine relief. The government faces strong challenges, e.g., to fully develop a market economy, to improve educational facilities, to face up to environmental problems, to deal with the rapidly growing problem of HIV/AIDS, and to satisfy foreign donors that fiscal discipline is being tightened. The performance of the tobacco sector is key to short-term growth as tobacco accounts for over 50% of exports.
GDP: purchasing power parity - $6.845 billion (2003 est.)
GDP - real growth rate: 1.7% (2003 est.)
GDP - per capita: purchasing power parity - $600 (2003 est.)
GDP - composition by sector:
agriculture: 40%
industry: 20%
services: 40% (2002 est.)
Population below poverty line: 55% (2003 est.)
Household income or consumption by percentage share:
lowest 10%: NA%
highest 10%: NA%
Inflation rate (consumer prices): 27.4% (2001 est.)
Labor force: 4.5 million (2001 est.)
Labor force - by occupation: agriculture 90% (2003 est.)
Unemployment rate: NA% (2003 est.)
Budget:
revenues: $490 million
expenditures: $523 million, including capital expenditures of $NA (FY99/00 est.)
Industries: tobacco, tea, sugar, sawmill products, cement, consumer goods
Industrial production growth rate: -0.8% (2002 est.)
Electricity - production: 769.2 million kWh (2001)
Electricity - production by source:
fossil fuel: 3.3%
hydro: 96.7%
nuclear: 0%
other: 0% (2001)

Electricity - consumption: 715.3 million kWh (2001)
Electricity - exports: 0 kWh (2001)
Electricity - imports: 0 kWh (2001)
Oil - production: 0 bbl/day (2001 est.)
Oil - consumption: 5,400 bbl/day (2001 est.)
Oil - exports: NA
Oil - imports: NA
Agriculture - products: tobacco, sugarcane, cotton, tea, corn, potatoes, cassava (tapioca), sorghum, pulses; groundnuts, Macadamia nuts; cattle, goats
Exports: $455 million f.o.b. (2003 est.)
Exports - commodities: tobacco 60%, tea, sugar, cotton, coffee, peanuts, wood products, apparel
Exports - partners: South Africa 22%, US 14.7%, Germany 12.2%, Egypt 5.3%, Japan 5.1%, Netherlands 4.7%, Russia 4.1% (2002)
Imports: $505 million f.o.b. (2003 est.)
Imports - commodities: food, petroleum products, semimanufactures, consumer goods, transportation equipment
Imports - partners: South Africa 45.1%, Zambia 12.3%, US 5.4%, India 4.1% (2002)
Debt - external: $3 billion (2003)
Economic aid - recipient: $540 million (1999)
Currency: Malawian kwacha (MWK)
Currency code: MWK
Exchange rates: Malawian kwachas per US dollar - NA (2003), 76.6866 (2002), 72.1973 (2001), 59.5438 (2000), 44.0881 (1999)
Fiscal year: 1 July - 30 June

Communications

Telephones - main lines in use: 73,100 (2002)
Telephones - mobile cellular: 86,000 (2002)
Telephone system:
general assessment: NA
domestic: system employs open-wire lines, microwave radio relay links, and radiotelephone communications stations
international: country code - 265; satellite earth stations - 2 Intelsat (1 Indian Ocean and 1 Atlantic Ocean)
Radio broadcast stations: AM 9, FM 5 (plus 15 repeater stations), shortwave 2 (plus a third station held in standby status) (2001)
Television broadcast stations: 1 (2001)
Internet country code: .mw
Internet hosts: 17 (2002)
Internet users: 27,000 (2002)

Transportation

Railways:
total: 797 km
narrow gauge: 797 km 1.067-m gauge (2002)
Highways:
total: 28,400 km
paved: 5,254 km
unpaved: 23,146 km (1999 est.)
Waterways: 144 km
note: on Lake Nyasa (Lake Malawi) and Shire Riverall

Ports and harbors: Chipoka, Monkey Bay, Nkhata Bay, Nkhotakota, Chilumba
Airports: 42 (2003 est.)
Airports - with paved runways:
total: 6
over 3,047 m: 1
1,524 to 2,437 m: 1
914 to 1,523 m: 4 (2003 est.)
Airports - with unpaved runways:
total: 38
1,524 to 2,437 m: 1
914 to 1,523 m: 15
under 914 m: 20 (2003 est.)

Military

Military branches: Army (including Air Wing and Naval Detachment), Police (including Mobile Force Unit)
Military manpower - availability:
males age 15-49: 2,691,881 (2004 est.)
Military manpower - fit for military service:
males age 15-49: 1,381,607 (2004 est.)
Military expenditures - dollar figure: $11.5 million (2003)
Military expenditures - percent of GDP: 0.7% (2003)

Transnational Issues

Disputes - international: dispute with Tanzania over the boundary in Lake Nyasa (Lake Malawi) and the meandering Songwe River remain dormant

Malaysia

Introduction

Background: Malaysia was formed in 1963 through a federation of the former British colonies of Malaya and Singapore including the East Malaysian states of Sabah and Sarawak on the northern coast of Borneo. The first several years of the country's history were marred by Indonesian efforts to control Malaysia, Philippine claims to Sabah, and Singapore's secession from the federation in 1965.

Geography

Location: Southeastern Asia, peninsula bordering Thailand and northern one-third of the island of Borneo, bordering Indonesia, Brunei, and the South China Sea, south of Vietnam

Geographic coordinates: 2 30 N, 112 30 E

Map references: Southeast Asia

Area:
total: 329,750 sq km
land: 328,550 sq km
water: 1,200 sq km

Area - comparative: slightly larger than New Mexico

Land boundaries:
total: 2,669 km
border countries: Brunei 381 km, Indonesia 1,782 km, Thailand 506 km

Coastline: 4,675 km (Peninsular Malaysia 2,068 km, East Malaysia 2,607 km)

Maritime claims:
territorial sea: 12 NM
exclusive economic zone: 200 NM
continental shelf: 200-m depth or to the depth of exploitation; specified boundary in the South China Sea

Climate: tropical; annual southwest (April to October) and northeast (October to February) monsoons

Terrain: coastal plains rising to hills and mountains

Elevation extremes:
lowest point: Indian Ocean 0 m
highest point: Gunung Kinabalu 4,100 m

Natural resources: tin, petroleum, timber, copper, iron ore, natural gas, bauxite

Land use:
arable land: 5.54%
permanent crops: 17.61%
other: 76.85% (1998 est.)

Irrigated land: 3,650 sq km (1998 est.)

Natural hazards: flooding, landslides, forest fires

Environment - current issues: air pollution from industrial and vehicular emissions; water pollution from raw sewage; deforestation; smoke/haze from Indonesian forest fires

Environment - international agreements:
party to: Biodiversity, Climate Change, Climate Change-Kyoto Protocol, Desertification, Endangered Species, Hazardous Wastes, Law of the Sea, Marine Life Conservation, Ozone Layer Protection, Ship Pollution, Tropical Timber 83, Tropical Timber 94, Wetlands

Geography - note: strategic location along Strait of Malacca and southern South China Sea

People

Population: 23,522,482 (July 2004 est.)

Age structure:
0-14 years: 33.3% (male 4,033,037; female 3,806,451)
15-64 years: 62.1% (male 7,326,068; female 7,289,783)
65 years and over: 4.5% (male 469,499; female 597,644) (2004 est.)

Median age:
total: 23.8 years
male: 23.2 years
female: 24.4 years (2004 est.)

Population growth rate: 1.83% (2004 est.)

Birth rate: 23.37 births/1,000 population (2004 est.)

Death rate: 5.08 deaths/1,000 population (2004 est.)

Net migration rate: 0 migrant(s)/1,000 population
note: does not reflect net flow of an unknown number of illegal immigrants from other countries in the region (2004 est.)

Sex ratio:
at birth: 1.07 male(s)/female
under 15 years: 1.06 male(s)/female
15-64 years: 1.01 male(s)/female
65 years and over: 0.79 male(s)/female
total population: 1.01 male(s)/female (2004 est.)

Infant mortality rate:
total: 18.35 deaths/1,000 live births
male: 21.23 deaths/1,000 live births
female: 15.27 deaths/1,000 live births (2004 est.)

Life expectancy at birth:
total population: 71.95 years
male: 69.29 years
female: 74.81 years (2004 est.)

Total fertility rate: 3.1 children born/woman (2004 est.)

HIV/AIDS - adult prevalence rate: 0.4% (2001 est.)

HIV/AIDS - people living with HIV/AIDS: 42,000 (2001 est.)

HIV/AIDS - deaths: 2,500 (2001 est.)

Nationality:
noun: Malaysian(s)
adjective: Malaysian

Ethnic groups: Malay and other indigenous 58%, Chinese 24%, Indian 8%, others 10% (2000)

Religions: Muslim, Buddhist, Daoist, Hindu, Christian, Sikh; note - in addition, Shamanism is practiced in East Malaysia

Languages: Bahasa Melayu (official), English, Chinese dialects (Cantonese, Mandarin, Hokkien, Hakka, Hainan, Foochow), Tamil, Telugu, Malayalam, Panjabi, Thai; note - in addition, in East Malaysia several indigenous languages are spoken, the largest are Iban and Kadazan

Literacy:
definition: age 15 and over can read and write
total population: 88.9%
male: 92.4%
female: 85.4% (2003 est.)

Government

Country name:
conventional long form: none
conventional short form: Malaysia
former: Federation of Malaysia

Government type: constitutional monarchy
note: Malaya (what is now Peninsular Malaysia) formed 31 August 1957; Federation of Malaysia (Malaya, Sabah, Sarawak, and Singapore) formed 9 July 1963 (Singapore left the Federation on 9 August 1965); nominally headed by the paramount ruler and a bicameral Parliament consisting of a nonelected upper house and an elected lower house; all of the Peninsular Malaysian states have hereditary rulers except Melaka and Penang; Sabah and Sarawak in East Malaysia have governors appointed

Malaysia *(continued)*

by the Malaysian Government; powers of state governments are limited by the federal constitution; under the terms of federation, Sabah and Sarawak retain certain constitutional prerogatives (e.g., the right to maintain their own immigration controls); Sabah - currently holds 20 seats in House of Representatives and will hold 25 seats after the next election; Sarawak holds 28 seats in House of Representatives
Capital: Kuala Lumpur
note: Putrajaya is referred to as the administrative capital
Administrative divisions: 13 states (negeri-negeri, singular - negeri) and 3 federal territories* (wilayah-wilayah persekutuan, singular - wilayah persekutuan); Johor, Kedah, Kelantan, Labuan*, Melaka, Negeri Sembilan, Pahang, Perak, Perlis, Pulau Pinang, Putrajaya*, Sabah, Sarawak, Selangor, Terengganu, Wilayah Persekutuan*
note: the city of Kuala Lumpur is within the federal territory of Wilayah Persekutuan; the terms therefore are not interchangeable;
Independence: 31 August 1957 (from UK)
National holiday: Independence Day/Malaysia Day, 31 August (1957)
Constitution: 31 August 1957, amended 16 September 1963
Legal system: based on English common law; judicial review of legislative acts in the Supreme Court at request of supreme head of the federation; has not accepted compulsory ICJ jurisdiction
Suffrage: 21 years of age; universal
Executive branch:
chief of state: Paramount Ruler Tuanku SYED SIRAJUDDIN ibni Almarhum Tuanku Syed Putra Jamalullail, the Raja of Perlis (since 12 December 2001)
head of government: Prime Minister ABDULLAH bin Ahmad Badawi (since 31 October 2003); Deputy Prime Minister NAJIB Tun Razak (since 7 January 2004)
cabinet: Cabinet appointed by the prime minister from among the members of Parliament with consent of the paramount ruler
elections: paramount ruler elected by and from the hereditary rulers of nine of the states for five-year terms; election last held 12 December 2001 (next to be held NA 2006); prime minister designated from among the members of the House of Representatives; following legislative elections, the leader of the party that wins a plurality of seats in the House of Representatives becomes prime minister
election results: Tuanku SYED SIRAJUDDIN ibni Almarhum Tuanku Syed Putra Jamalullail elected paramount ruler
Legislative branch: bicameral Parliament or Parlimen consists of the Senate or Dewan Negara (69 seats; 43 appointed by the paramount ruler, 26 appointed by the state legislatures) and the House of Representatives or Dewan Rakyat (193 seats to be increased to 219 seats after the 2004 elections; members elected by popular vote to serve five-year terms)

elections: House of Representatives - last held 21 March 2004 (next must be held by 2009)
election results: House of Representatives - percent of vote by party - BN 64%, PAS 16%, DAP 10%, other 10%; seats by party - BN 198, DAP 12, PAS 7, Keadilan 1, independent 1
Judicial branch: Federal Court (judges appointed by the paramount ruler on the advice of the prime minister)
Political parties and leaders: ruling-coalition National Front (Barisan Nasional) or BN, consisting of the following parties: Gerakan Rakyat Malaysia Party or PGRM [LIM Kheng Yaik]; Liberal Democratic Party (Parti Liberal Demokratik - Sabah) or LDP [CHONG Kah Kiat]; Malaysian Chinese Association (Persatuan China Malaysia) or MCA [ONG Ka Ting]; Malaysian Indian Congress (Kongresi India Malaysia) or MIC [S. Samy VELLU]; Parti Bangsa Dayak Sarawak or PBDS [leadership in dispute]; Parti Bersatu Sabah or PBS [Joseph PAIRIN Kitingan]; Parti Pesaka Bumiputra Bersatu or PBB [Patinggi Haji Abdul TAIB Mahmud]; Sabah Progressive Party (Parti Progresif Sabah) or SAPP [YONG Teck Lee]; Sarawak United People's Party (Parti Bersatu Rakyat Sarawak) or SUPP [George CHAN Hong Nam]; United Malays National Organization or UMNO [ABDULLAH Ahmad Badawi]; United Pasokmomogun Kadazandusun Murut Organization (Pertubuhan Pasko Momogun Kadazan Dusun Bersatu) or UPKO [Bernard DOMPOK]; People's Progressive Party (Parti Progresif Penduduk Malaysia) or PPP [M.Keyveas]; Sarawak National Party or SNAP [leader NA]; Sarawak Progressive Democratic Party or SPDP [William MAWANI]; opposition parties: Democratic Action Party (Parti Tindakan Demokratik) or DAP [KERK Kim Hock]; Islamic Party of Malaysia (Parti Islam se Malaysia) or PAS [Abdul HADI Awang]; Malaysian People's Party (Parti Rakyat Malaysia) or PKM [Syed HUSIN Ali]; National Justice Party (Parti Keadilan Nasional) or Keadilan [WAN AZIZAH Wan Ismael]; opposition coalition Alternative Front (Barisan Alternatif) or BA consists of PAS, PKM, and Keadilan
Political pressure groups and leaders: NA
International organization participation: APEC, ARF, AsDB, ASEAN, BIS, C, CP, FAO, G-15, G-77, IAEA, IBRD, ICAO, ICFTU, ICRM, IDA, IDB, IFAD, IFC, IFRCS, IHO, ILO, IMF, IMO, Interpol, IOC, ISO, ITU, MINURSO, MONUC, NAM, OIC, OPCW, PCA, UN, UNAMSIL, UNCTAD, UNESCO, UNIDO, UNMEE, UNMIK, UNMISET, UPU, WCL, WCO, WFTU, WHO, WIPO, WMO, WToO, WTrO
Diplomatic representation in the US:
chief of mission: Ambassador GHAZZALI bin Sheikh Abdul Khalid
chancery: 3516 International Court NW, Washington, DC 20008
telephone: [1] (202) 572-9700
FAX: [1] (202) 572-9882
consulate(s) general: Los Angeles and New York

Diplomatic representation from the US:
chief of mission: Ambassador Marie T. HUHTALA
embassy: 376 Jalan Tun Razak, 50400 Kuala Lumpur
mailing address: P. O. Box No. 10035, 50700 Kuala Lumpur; American Embassy Kuala Lumpur, APO AP 96535-8152
telephone: [60] (3) 2168-5000
FAX: [60] (3) 2142-2207
Flag description: 14 equal horizontal stripes of red (top) alternating with white (bottom); there is a blue rectangle in the upper hoist-side corner bearing a yellow crescent and a yellow 14-pointed star; the crescent and the star are traditional symbols of Islam; the design was based on the flag of the US

Economy

Economy - overview: Malaysia, a middle-income country, transformed itself from 1971 through the late 1990s from a producer of raw materials into an emerging multi-sector economy. Growth was almost exclusively driven by exports - particularly of electronics. As a result Malaysia was hard hit by the global economic downturn and the slump in the information technology (IT) sector in 2001 and 2002. GDP in 2001 grew only 0.5% due to an estimated 11% contraction in exports, but a substantial fiscal stimulus package equal to US $1.9 billion mitigated the worst of the recession and the economy rebounded in 2002 with a 4.1% increase. The economy grew 4.9% in 2003, notwithstanding a difficult first half, when external pressures from SARS and the Iraq War led to caution in the business community. Healthy foreign exchange reserves and a relatively small external debt make it unlikely that Malaysia will experience a crisis similar to the one in 1997, but the economy remains vulnerable to a more protracted slowdown in Japan and the US, top export destinations and key sources of foreign investment. The Malaysian ringgit is pegged to the dollar, and the Japanese central bank continues to intervene and prop up the yen against the dollar.
GDP: purchasing power parity - $207.2 billion (2003 est.)
GDP - real growth rate: 4.9% (2003 est.)
GDP - per capita: purchasing power parity - $9,000 (2003 est.)
GDP - composition by sector:
agriculture: 8.4%
industry: 45.3%
services: 46.3% (2002 est.)
Population below poverty line: 8% (1998 est.)
Household income or consumption by percentage share:
lowest 10%: 1.4%
highest 10%: 39.2% (2003 est.)
Distribution of family income - Gini index: 49.2 (1997)
Inflation rate (consumer prices): 1.2% (2003 est.)
Labor force: 10.4 million (2003 est.)
Labor force - by occupation: agriculture 14.5%, industry 36%, services 49.5% (2000 est.)

Unemployment rate: 3.4% (2003 est.)

Budget:

revenues: $25.2 billion

expenditures: $28.9 billion, including capital expenditures of $9.4 billion (2004 est.)

Industries: Peninsular Malaysia - rubber and oil palm processing and manufacturing, light manufacturing industry, electronics, tin mining and smelting, logging and processing timber; Sabah - logging, petroleum production; Sarawak - agriculture processing, petroleum production and refining, logging

Industrial production growth rate: 8.5% (2003 est.)

Electricity - production: 75.33 billion kWh (2002)

Electricity - production by source:

fossil fuel: 89.5%

hydro: 10.5%

nuclear: 0%

other: 0% (2001)

Electricity - consumption: 68.4 billion kWh (2002)

Electricity - exports: 0 kWh (2002)

Electricity - imports: 0 kWh (2002)

Oil - production: 690,000 bbl/day (2003 est.)

Oil - consumption: 460,000 bbl/day (2003 est.)

Oil - exports: 230,200 bbl/day (2003)

Oil - imports: NA

Oil - proved reserves: 3.729 billion bbl (1 January 2002)

Natural gas - production: 53.66 billion cu m (2001 est.)

Natural gas - consumption: 31.25 billion cu m (2001 est.)

Natural gas - exports: 22.41 billion cu m (2001 est.)

Natural gas - imports: 0 cu m (2001 est.)

Natural gas - proved reserves: 2.23 trillion cu m (1 January 2002)

Agriculture - products: Peninsular Malaysia - rubber, palm oil, cocoa, rice; Sabah - subsistence crops, rubber, timber, coconuts, rice; Sarawak - rubber, pepper; timber

Exports: $98.4 billion f.o.b. (2003 est.)

Exports - commodities: electronic equipment, petroleum and liquefied natural gas, wood and wood products, palm oil, rubber, textiles, chemicals

Exports - partners: US 20.2%, Singapore 17.1%, Japan 11.3%, Hong Kong 5.7%, China 5.6%, Thailand 4.3% (2002)

Imports: $74.4 billion f.o.b. (2003 est.)

Imports - commodities: electronics, machinery, petroleum products, plastics, vehicles, iron and steel products, chemicals

Imports - partners: Japan 17.8%, US 16.5%, Singapore 12%, China 7.7%, Taiwan 5.6%, South Korea 5.3%, Thailand 4% (2002)

Debt - external: $39.94 billion (2003 est.)

Currency: ringgit (MYR)

Currency code: MYR

Exchange rates: ringgits per US dollar - 3.8 (2003), 3.8 (2002), 3.8 (2001), 3.8 (2000), 3.8 (1999)

Fiscal year: calendar year

Communications

Telephones - main lines in use: 4,669,900 (2002)

Telephones - mobile cellular: 9,241,400 (2002)

Telephone system:

general assessment: modern system; international service excellent

domestic: good intercity service provided on Peninsular Malaysia mainly by microwave radio relay; adequate intercity microwave radio relay network between Sabah and Sarawak via Brunei; domestic satellite system with 2 earth stations

international: country code - 60; submarine cables to India, Hong Kong, and Singapore; satellite earth stations - 2 Intelsat (1 Indian Ocean and 1 Pacific Ocean) (2001)

Radio broadcast stations: AM 35, FM 391, shortwave 15 (2001)

Television broadcast stations: 1 (plus 15 high-power repeaters) (2001)

Internet country code: .my

Internet hosts: 86,285 (2002)

Internet users: 7.841 million (2002)

Transportation

Railways:

total: 2,418 km

standard gauge: 57 km 1.435-m gauge

narrow gauge: 2,361 km 1.000-m gauge (150 km electrified) (2002)

Highways:

total: 65,877 km

paved: 49,935 km (including 1,192 km of expressways)

unpaved: 15,942 km (1999)

Waterways: 7,296 km

note: Peninsular Malaysia 3,209 km, Sabah 1,569 km, Sarawak 2,518 km

Pipelines: condensate 279 km; gas 5,047 km; oil 1,841 km; refined products 114 km (2003)

Ports and harbors: Bintulu, Kota Kinabalu, Kuantan, Kuching, Kudat, Labuan, Lahad Datu, Lumut, Miri, Pasir Gudang, George Town (Penang), Port Dickson, Port Kelang, Sandakan, Sibu, Tanjung Berhala, Tanjung Kidurong, Tawau

Merchant marine:

total: 360 ships (1,000 GRT or over) 5,389,397 GRT/ 7,539,178 DWT

by type: bulk 59, cargo 100, chemical tanker 38, container 66, liquefied gas 25, livestock carrier 1, passenger 2, petroleum tanker 56, roll on/roll off 5, vehicle carrier 8

foreign-owned: China 1, Germany 2, Hong Kong 8, Indonesia 2, Japan 2, South Korea 1, Liberia 1, Monaco 1, Norway 1, Philippines 2, Singapore 81, Vietnam 1

registered in other countries: 75 (2003 est.)

Airports: 117 (2003 est.)

Airports - with paved runways:

total: 37

over 3,047 m: 5

2,438 to 3,047 m: 7

1,524 to 2,437 m: 10

914 to 1,523 m: 8

under 914 m: 7 (2003 est.)

Airports - with unpaved runways:

total: 80

1,524 to 2,437 m: 1

914 to 1,523 m: 7

under 914 m: 72 (2003 est.)

Heliports: 1 (2003 est.)

Military

Military branches: Malaysian Army, Royal Malaysian Navy, Royal Malaysian Air Force, Royal Malaysian Marine Police, Sarawak Border Scouts

Military manpower - military age: 21 years of age (2004 est.)

Military manpower - availability:

males age 15-49: 6,193,587 (2004 est.)

Military manpower - fit for military service:

males age 15-49: 3,746,960 (2004 est.)

Military manpower - reaching military age annually:

males: 223,466 (2004 est.)

Military expenditures - dollar figure: $1.69 billion (FY00 est.)

Military expenditures - percent of GDP: 2.03% (FY00)

Transnational Issues

Disputes - international: involved in complex dispute with China, Philippines, Taiwan, Vietnam and possibly Brunei over the Spratly Islands; the 2002 "Declaration on the Conduct of Parties in the South China Sea" has eased tensions but falls short of a legally binding "code of conduct" desired by several of the disputants; disputes over deliveries of fresh water to Singapore, Singapore's land reclamation, bridge construction, maritime boundaries, and Pedra Branca Island/Pulau Batu Putih persist - parties agree to ICJ arbitration on island dispute within three years; ICJ awarded Ligitan and Sipadan islands off the coast of Sabah, also claimed by Indonesia and Philippines, to Malaysia; a 1 kilometer segment at the mouth of the Golok River remains in dispute with Thailand; Philippines retains a now dormant claim to Malaysia's Sabah State in northern Borneo based on the Sultanate of Sulu's granting the Philippines Government power of attorney to pursue the Sultanate's sovereignty claim; in 2003 Brunei and Malaysia ceased gas and oil exploration in their offshore and deepwater seabeds until negotiations progress to an agreement over allocation of disputed areas; Malaysia's land boundary with Brunei around Limbang is in dispute

Illicit drugs: transit point for some illicit drugs; drug trafficking prosecuted vigorously and carries severe penalties

Maldives

Introduction

Background: The Maldives were long a sultanate, first under Dutch and then under British protection. They became a republic in 1968, three years after independence. Tourism and fishing are being developed on the archipelago.

Geography

Location: Southern Asia, group of atolls in the Indian Ocean, south-southwest of India
Geographic coordinates: 3 15 N, 73 00 E
Map references: Asia
Area:
total: 300 sq km
land: 300 sq km
water: 0 sq km
Area - comparative: about 1.7 times the size of Washington, DC
Land boundaries: 0 km
Coastline: 644 km
Maritime claims: measured from claimed archipelagic straight baselines
territorial sea: 12 NM
contiguous zone: 24 NM
exclusive economic zone: 200 NM
Climate: tropical; hot, humid; dry, northeast monsoon (November to March); rainy, southwest monsoon (June to August)
Terrain: flat, with white sandy beaches
Elevation extremes:
lowest point: Indian Ocean 0 m
highest point: unnamed location on Wilingili island in the Addu Atoll 2.4 m
Natural resources: fish
Land use:
arable land: 3.33%
permanent crops: 6.67%
other: 90% (1998 est.)
Irrigated land: NA sq km

Natural hazards: low level of islands makes them very sensitive to sea level rise
Environment - current issues: depletion of freshwater aquifers threatens water supplies; global warming and sea level rise; coral reef bleaching
Environment - international agreements:
party to: Biodiversity, Climate Change, Climate Change-Kyoto Protocol, Hazardous Wastes, Law of the Sea, Ozone Layer Protection
signed, but not ratified: none of the selected agreements
Geography - note: 1,190 coral islands grouped into 26 atolls (200 inhabited islands, plus 80 islands with tourist resorts); archipelago with strategic location astride and along major sea lanes in Indian Ocean

People

Population: 339,330 (July 2004 est.)
Age structure:
0-14 years: 44.4% (male 77,424; female 73,191)
15-64 years: 52.6% (male 91,045; female 87,331)
65 years and over: 3% (male 5,207; female 5,132) (2004 est.)
Median age:
total: 17.5 years
male: 17.4 years
female: 17.6 years (2004 est.)
Population growth rate: 2.86% (2004 est.)
Birth rate: 36.06 births/1,000 population (2004 est.)
Death rate: 7.44 deaths/1,000 population (2004 est.)
Net migration rate: 0 migrant(s)/1,000 population (2004 est.)
Sex ratio:
at birth: 1.05 male(s)/female
under 15 years: 1.06 male(s)/female
15-64 years: 1.04 male(s)/female
65 years and over: 1.02 male(s)/female
total population: 1.05 male(s)/female (2004 est.)
Infant mortality rate:
total: 58.32 deaths/1,000 live births
male: 57.43 deaths/1,000 live births
female: 59.26 deaths/1,000 live births (2004 est.)
Life expectancy at birth:
total population: 63.68 years
male: 62.41 years
female: 65.01 years (2004 est.)
Total fertility rate: 5.14 children born/woman (2004 est.)
HIV/AIDS - adult prevalence rate: 0.1% (2001 est.)
HIV/AIDS - people living with HIV/AIDS: less than 100 (2001 est.)
HIV/AIDS - deaths: NA
Nationality:
noun: Maldivian(s)
adjective: Maldivian
Ethnic groups: South Indians, Sinhalese, Arabs
Religions: Sunni Muslim
Languages: Maldivian Dhivehi (dialect of Sinhala, script derived from Arabic), English spoken by most government officials

Literacy:
definition: age 15 and over can read and write
total population: 97.2%
male: 97.1%
female: 97.3% (2003 est.)

Government

Country name:
conventional long form: Republic of Maldives
conventional short form: Maldives
local long form: Dhivehi Raajjeyge Jumhooriyyaa
local short form: Dhivehi Raajje
Government type: republic
Capital: Male
Administrative divisions: 19 atolls (atholhu, singular and plural) and 1 other first-order administrative division*; Alifu, Baa, Dhaalu, Faafu, Gaafu Alifu, Gaafu Dhaalu, Gnaviyani, Haa Alifu, Haa Dhaalu, Kaafu, Laamu, Lhaviyani, Maale*, Meemu, Noonu, Raa, Seenu, Shaviyani, Thaa, Vaavu
Independence: 26 July 1965 (from UK)
National holiday: Independence Day, 26 July (1965)
Constitution: adopted January 1998
Legal system: based on Islamic law with admixtures of English common law primarily in commercial matters; has not accepted compulsory ICJ jurisdiction
Suffrage: 21 years of age; universal
Executive branch:
chief of state: President Maumoon Abdul GAYOOM (since 11 November 1978); note - the president is both the chief of state and head of government
head of government: President Maumoon Abdul GAYOOM (since 11 November 1978); note - the president is both the chief of state and head of government
cabinet: Cabinet of Ministers appointed by the president
elections: president nominated by the Majlis and then the nomination must be ratified by a national referendum (at least a 51% approval margin is required); president elected for a five-year term; election last held 17 October 2003 (next to be held NA 2008)
election results: President Maumoon Abdul GAYOOM reelected in referendum held 17 October 2003; percent of popular vote - Maumoon Abdul GAYOOM 90.3%
Legislative branch: unicameral People's Council or Majlis (50 seats; 42 elected by popular vote, 8 appointed by the president; members serve five-year terms)
elections: last held 20 November 1999 (next to be held NA November 2004)
election results: percent of vote - NA%; seats - independents 42
Judicial branch: High Court
Political parties and leaders: although political parties are not banned, none exist
Political pressure groups and leaders: none

Maldives *(continued)*

International organization participation: AsDB, C, CP, FAO, G-77, IBRD, ICAO, IDA, IDB, IFAD, IFC, IMF, IMO, Interpol, IOC, ITU, NAM, OIC, OPCW, SAARC, UN, UNCTAD, UNESCO, UNIDO, UPU, WCO, WHO, WMO, WToO, WTrO

Diplomatic representation in the US: Maldives does not have an embassy in the US, but does have a Permanent Mission to the UN in New York; permanent representative is Dr. Mohamed LATHEEF

Diplomatic representation from the US: the US does not have an embassy in Maldives; the US Ambassador to Sri Lanka is accredited to Maldives and makes periodic visits there

Flag description: red with a large green rectangle in the center bearing a vertical white crescent; the closed side of the crescent is on the hoist side of the flag

Economy

Economy - overview: Tourism, Maldives' largest industry, accounts for 20% of GDP and more than 60% of the Maldives' foreign exchange receipts. Over 90% of government tax revenue comes from import duties and tourism-related taxes. Fishing is a second leading sector. The Maldivian Government began an economic reform program in 1989 initially by lifting import quotas and opening some exports to the private sector. Subsequently, it has liberalized regulations to allow more foreign investment. Agriculture and manufacturing continue to play a lesser role in the economy, constrained by the limited availability of cultivable land and the shortage of domestic labor. Most staple foods must be imported. Industry, which consists mainly of garment production, boat building, and handicrafts, accounts for about 18% of GDP. Maldivian authorities worry about the impact of erosion and possible global warming on their low-lying country; 80% of the area is one meter or less above sea level.

GDP: purchasing power parity - $1.25 billion (2002 est.)

GDP - real growth rate: 2.3% (2002 est.)

GDP - per capita: purchasing power parity - $3,900 (2002 est.)

GDP - composition by sector:
agriculture: 20%
industry: 18%
services: 62% (2000 est.)

Population below poverty line: NA%

Household income or consumption by percentage share:
lowest 10%: NA%
highest 10%: NA%

Inflation rate (consumer prices): 1% (2002 est.)

Labor force: 88,000 (2000)

Labor force - by occupation: agriculture 22%, industry 18%, services 60% (1995)

Unemployment rate: NEGL% (2003 est.)

Budget:
revenues: $224 million (excluding foreign grants)
expenditures: $282 million, including capital expenditures of $80 million (2002 est.)

Industries: fish processing, tourism, shipping, boat building, coconut processing, garments, woven mats, rope, handicrafts, coral and sand mining

Industrial production growth rate: 4.4% (1996 est.)

Electricity - production: 117 million kWh (2001)

Electricity - production by source:
fossil fuel: 100%
hydro: 0%
nuclear: 0%
other: 0% (2001)

Electricity - consumption: 108.8 million kWh (2001)

Electricity - exports: 0 kWh (2001)

Electricity - imports: 0 kWh (2001)

Oil - production: 0 bbl/day (2001 est.)

Oil - consumption: 3,200 bbl/day (2001 est.)

Oil - exports: NA

Oil - imports: NA

Agriculture - products: coconuts, corn, sweet potatoes; fish

Exports: $90 million f.o.b. (2002 est.)

Exports - commodities: fish, clothing

Exports - partners: US 52.6%, Sri Lanka 13.3%, Thailand 9.5%, Japan 7.6%, UK 4.7% (2002)

Imports: $392 million f.o.b. (2002 est.)

Imports - commodities: consumer goods, intermediate and capital goods, petroleum products

Imports - partners: Singapore 26.6%, UAE 15%, Sri Lanka 13.2%, India 7%, Malaysia 5.7%, Thailand 4.1% (2002)

Debt - external: $281 million (2003 est.)

Economic aid - recipient: $NA (1995)

Currency: rufiyaa (MVR)

Currency code: MVR

Exchange rates: rufiyaa per US dollar - 12.8 (2003), 12.8 (2002), 12.2421 (2001), 11.77 (2000), 11.77 (1999)

Fiscal year: calendar year

Communications

Telephones - main lines in use: 28,700 (2002)

Telephones - mobile cellular: 41,900 (2002)

Telephone system:
general assessment: minimal domestic and international facilities
domestic: interatoll communication through microwave links; all inhabited islands are connected with telephone and fax service
international: country code - 960; satellite earth station - 3 Intelsat (Indian Ocean)

Radio broadcast stations: AM 1, FM 1, shortwave 1 (1998)

Television broadcast stations: 1 (1997)

Internet country code: .mv

Internet hosts: NA

Internet users: 15,000 (2002)

Transportation

Railways: 0 km

Highways:
total: NA km
paved: NA km
unpaved: NA km

Waterways: none

Ports and harbors: Gan, Male

Merchant marine:
total: 16 ships (1,000 GRT or over) 54,164 GRT/ 68,973 DWT
by type: cargo 13, petroleum tanker 1, refrigerated cargo 1, short-sea/passenger 1
foreign-owned: North Korea 1
registered in other countries: 2 (2003 est.)

Airports: 5 (2003 est.)

Airports - with paved runways:
total: 2
over 3,047 m: 1
2,438 to 3,047 m: 1 (2003 est.)

Airports - with unpaved runways:
total: 3
914 to 1,523 m: 3 (2003 est.)

Military

Military branches: National Security Service: comprising Security Branch (ground forces), Air Element; Coast Guard

Military manpower - availability:
males age 15-49: 81,221 (2004 est.)

Military manpower - fit for military service:
males age 15-49: 45,142 (2004 est.)

Military expenditures - dollar figure: $43.1 million (2003)

Military expenditures - percent of GDP: 8.6% (2003)

Transnational Issues

Disputes - international: none

Mali

Introduction

Background: The Sudanese Republic and Senegal became independent of France in 1960 as the Mali Federation. When Senegal withdrew after only a few months, what formerly made up the Sudanese Republic was renamed Mali. Rule by dictatorship was brought to a close in 1991 with a transitional government and in 1992 when Mali's first democratic presidential election was held. After his reelection in 1997, President Alpha KONARE continued to push through political and economic reforms and to fight corruption. In keeping with Mali's two-term constitutional limit, he stepped down in 2002 and was succeeded by Amadou TOURE.

Geography

Location: Western Africa, southwest of Algeria
Geographic coordinates: 17 00 N, 4 00 W
Map references: Africa
Area:
total: 1.24 million sq km
land: 1.22 million sq km
water: 20,000 sq km
Area - comparative: slightly less than twice the size of Texas
Land boundaries:
total: 7,243 km
border countries: Algeria 1,376 km, Burkina Faso 1,000 km, Guinea 858 km, Cote d'Ivoire 532 km, Mauritania 2,237 km, Niger 821 km, Senegal 419 km
Coastline: 0 km (landlocked)
Maritime claims: none (landlocked)
Climate: subtropical to arid; hot and dry February to June; rainy, humid, and mild June to November; cool and dry November to February
Terrain: mostly flat to rolling northern plains covered by sand; savanna in south, rugged hills in northeast

Elevation extremes:
lowest point: Senegal River 23 m
highest point: Hombori Tondo 1,155 m
Natural resources: gold, phosphates, kaolin, salt, limestone, uranium, hydropower
note: bauxite, iron ore, manganese, tin, and copper deposits are known but not exploited
Land use:
arable land: 3.77%
permanent crops: 0.04%
other: 96.19% (1998 est.)
Irrigated land: 1,380 sq km (1998 est.)
Natural hazards: hot, dust-laden harmattan haze common during dry seasons; recurring droughts; occasional Niger River flooding
Environment - current issues: deforestation; soil erosion; desertification; inadequate supplies of potable water; poaching
Environment - international agreements:
party to: Biodiversity, Climate Change, Climate Change-Kyoto Protocol, Desertification, Endangered Species, Hazardous Wastes, Law of the Sea, Ozone Layer Protection, Wetlands
signed, but not ratified: none of the selected agreements
Geography - note: landlocked; divided into three natural zones: the southern, cultivated Sudanese; the central, semiarid Sahelian; and the northern, arid Saharan

People

Population: 11,956,788 (July 2004 est.)
Age structure.
0-14 years. 47.1% (male 2,835,378; female 2,801,578)
15-64 years. 49.9% (male 2,862,075; female 3,101,009)
65 years and over. 3% (male 163,927; female 192,821) (2004 est.)
Median age.
total. 16.3 years
male. 15.7 years
female. 16.9 years (2004 est.)
Population growth rate. 2.78% (2004 est.)
Birth rate. 47.29 births/1,000 population (2004 est.)
Death rate. 19.12 deaths/1,000 population (2004 est.)
Net migration rate. -0.33 migrant(s)/1,000 population (2004 est.)
Sex ratio.
at birth. 1.03 male(s)/female
under 15 years. 1.01 male(s)/female
15-64 years. 0.92 male(s)/female
65 years and over. 0.85 male(s)/female
total population. 0.96 male(s)/female (2004 est.)
Infant mortality rate.
total. 117.99 deaths/1,000 live births
male. 124.51 deaths/1,000 live births
female. 111.27 deaths/1,000 live births (2004 est.)

Life expectancy at birth:
total population: 45.28 years
male: 44.7 years
female: 45.87 years (2004 est.)
Total fertility rate: 6.58 children born/woman (2004 est.)
HIV/AIDS - adult prevalence rate: 1.7% (2001 est.)
HIV/AIDS - people living with HIV/AIDS: 110,000 (2001 est.)
HIV/AIDS - deaths: 11,000 (2001 est.)
Nationality:
noun: Malian(s)
adjective: Malian
Ethnic groups: Mande 50% (Bambara, Malinke, Soninke), Peul 17%, Voltaic 12%, Songhai 6%, Tuareg and Moor 10%, other 5%
Religions: Muslim 90%, indigenous beliefs 9%, Christian 1%
Languages: French (official), Bambara 80%, numerous African languages
Literacy:
definition: age 15 and over can read and write
total population: 46.4%
male: 53.5%
female: 39.6% (2003 est.)

Government

Country name:
conventional long form. Republic of Mali
conventional short form. Mali
local long form. Republique de Mali
local short form. Mali
former. French Sudan and Sudanese Republic
Government type. republic
Capital. Bamako
Administrative divisions. 8 regions (regions, singular - region); Gao, Kayes, Kidal, Koulikoro, Mopti, Segou, Sikasso, Tombouctou
Independence. 22 September 1960 (from France)
National holiday. Independence Day, 22 September (1960)
Constitution. adopted 12 January 1992
Legal system. based on French civil law system and customary law; judicial review of legislative acts in Constitutional Court (which was formally established on 9 March 1994); has not accepted compulsory ICJ jurisdiction
Suffrage. 18 years of age; universal
Executive branch.
chief of state. President Amadou Toumani TOURE (since 8 June 2002)
head of government. Prime Minister Ahmed Mohamed Ag HAMANI (since 9 June 2002)
cabinet. Council of Ministers appointed by the prime minister
elections. president elected by popular vote for a five-year term (two-term limit); election last held 12 May 2002 (next to be held NA May 2007); prime minister appointed by the president

Mali (continued)

election results: Amadou Toumani TOURE elected president; percent of vote - Amadou Toumani TOURE 64.4%, Soumaila CISSE 35.6%

Legislative branch: unicameral National Assembly or Assemblee Nationale (147 seats; members are elected by popular vote to serve five-year terms)

elections: last held 14 July and 28 July 2002 (next to be held NA July 2007)

election results: percent of vote by party - NA%; seats by party - Hope 2002 coalition 66, ADEMA 51, other 30

Judicial branch: Supreme Court or Cour Supreme

Political parties and leaders: Alliance for Democracy or ADEMA [Diounconda Traore KEITA, party chairman]; Block of Alternative for the Renewal of Africa or BARA [Yoro DIAKITE]; Democratic and Social Convention or CDS [Mamadou Bakary SANGARE, chairman]; Hope 2002 [leader NA]; Movement for the Independence, Renaissance and Integration of Africa or MIRIA [Mohamed Lamine TRAORE, Mouhamedou DICKO]; National Congress for Democratic Initiative or CNID [Mountaga TALL, chairman]; Party for Democracy and Progress or PDP [Me Idrissa TRAORE]; Party for National Renewal or PARENA [Yoro DIAKITE, chairman; Tiebile DRAME, secretary general]; Rally for Democracy and Labor or RDT [Ali GNANGADO]; Rally for Democracy and Progress or RDP [Almamy SYLLA, chairman]; Rally for Mali or RPM [Ibrahim Bonbasor KEITA, chairman]; Sudanese Union/African Democratic Rally or US/RDA [Mamadou Bamou TOURE, secretary general]; Union of Democratic Forces for Progress or UFDP [Youssouf TOURE, secretary general]; Union for Democracy and Development or UDD [Moussa Balla COULIBALY]

Political pressure groups and leaders: Patriotic Movement of the Ghanda Koye or MPGK; United Movement and Fronts of Azawad or MFUA

International organization participation: ACCT, ACP, AfDB, AU, ECOWAS, FAO, FZ, G-77, IAEA, IBRD, ICAO, ICCt, ICFTU, ICRM, IDA, IDB, IFAD, IFC, IFRCS, ILO, IMF, Interpol, IOC, IOM, ISO (subscriber), ITU, MICAH, MONUC, NAM, OIC, OPCW, UN, UNAMSIL, UNCTAD, UNESCO, UNIDO, UNMIL, UPU, WADB (regional), WAEMU, WCO, WFTU, WHO, WIPO, WMO, WToO, WTrO

Diplomatic representation in the US:

chief of mission: Ambassador Abdoulaye DIOP

chancery: 2130 R Street NW, Washington, DC 20008

telephone: [1] (202) 332-2249, 939-8950

FAX: [1] (202) 332-6603

Diplomatic representation from the US:

chief of mission: Ambassador Vicki HUDDLESTONE

embassy: Rue Rochester NY and Rue Mohamed V, Bamako

mailing address: B. P. 34, Bamako

telephone: [223] (2) 223-833

FAX: [223] (2) 223-712

Flag description: three equal vertical bands of green (hoist side), yellow, and red; uses the popular pan-African colors of Ethiopia

Economy

Economy - overview: Mali is among the poorest countries in the world, with 65% of its land area desert or semidesert and with a highly unequal distribution of income. Economic activity is largely confined to the riverine area irrigated by the Niger. About 10% of the population is nomadic and some 80% of the labor force is engaged in farming and fishing. Industrial activity is concentrated on processing farm commodities. Mali is heavily dependent on foreign aid and vulnerable to fluctuations in world prices for cotton, its main export, along with gold. The government has continued its successful implementation of an IMF-recommended structural adjustment program that is helping the economy grow, diversify, and attract foreign investment. Mali's adherence to economic reform and the 50% devaluation of the African franc in January 1994 have pushed up economic growth to a sturdy 5% average in 1996-2002. Worker remittances and external trade routes have been jeopardized by continued unrest in neighboring Cote d'Ivoire.

GDP: purchasing power parity - $10.53 billion (2003 est.)

GDP - real growth rate: 0.5% (2003 est.)

GDP - per capita: purchasing power parity - $900 (2003 est.)

GDP - composition by sector:

agriculture: 45%

industry: 17%

services: 38% (2001 est.)

Population below poverty line: 64% average; 30% of the total population living in urban areas; 70% of the total population living in rural areas) (2001 est.)

Household income or consumption by percentage share:

lowest 10%: 1.8%

highest 10%: 40.4% (1994)

Distribution of family income - Gini index: 50.5 (1994)

Inflation rate (consumer prices): 4.5% (2002 est.)

Labor force: 3.93 million (2001 est.)

Labor force - by occupation: agriculture and fishing 80% (2001 est.)

Unemployment rate: 14.6% urban areas; 5.3% rural areas (2001 est.)

Budget:

revenues: $764 million

expenditures: $828 million, including capital expenditures of $NA (2002 est.)

Industries: food processing; construction; phosphate and gold mining

Industrial production growth rate: NA% (FY 96/97)

Electricity - production: 480.2 million kWh (2001)

Electricity - production by source:

fossil fuel: 41.7%

hydro: 58.3%

nuclear: 0%

other: 0% (2001)

Electricity - consumption: 446.6 million kWh (2001)

Electricity - exports: 0 kWh; note - recent hydropower developments may be providing electricity to Senegal and Mauritania (2001)

Electricity - imports: 0 kWh (2001)

Oil - production: 0 bbl/day (2001 est.)

Oil - consumption: 4,000 bbl/day (2001 est.)

Oil - exports: NA

Oil - imports: NA

Agriculture - products: cotton, millet, rice, corn, vegetables, peanuts; cattle, sheep, goats

Exports: $915 million f.o.b. (2002 est.)

Exports - commodities: cotton, gold, livestock

Exports - partners: Thailand 14.4%, Italy 10.2%, India 7.8%, Germany 4.8%, Spain 4.8%, Mauritius 4.2%, Portugal 4.2% (2002)

Imports: $927 million f.o.b. (2002 est.)

Imports - commodities: petroleum, machinery and equipment, construction materials, foodstuffs, textiles

Imports - partners: Cote d'Ivoire 16.9%, France 13.4%, Senegal 6.4% (2002)

Debt - external: $3.3 billion (2000)

Economic aid - recipient: $596.4 million (2001)

Currency: Communaute Financiere Africaine franc (XOF); note - responsible authority is the Central Bank of the West African States

Currency code: XOF

Exchange rates: Communaute Financiere Africaine francs (XOF) per US dollar - 581.2 (2003), 696.988 (2002), 733.039 (2001), 711.976 (2000), 615.699 (1999)

Fiscal year: calendar year

Communications

Telephones - main lines in use: 56,600 (2002)

Telephones - mobile cellular: 52,600 (2002)

Telephone system:

general assessment: domestic system unreliable but improving; provides only minimal service

domestic: network consists of microwave radio relay, open-wire, and radiotelephone communications stations; expansion of microwave radio relay in progress

international: country code - 223; satellite earth stations - 2 Intelsat (1 Atlantic Ocean and 1 Indian Ocean)

Radio broadcast stations: AM 1, FM 28, shortwave 1

note: the shortwave station in Bamako has seven frequencies and five transmitters and relays broadcasts for China Radio International (2001)

Television broadcast stations: 1 (plus repeaters) (2001)

Internet country code: .ml

Internet hosts: 158 (2002)

Internet users: 25,000 (2002)

Transportation

Railways:

total: 729 km

narrow gauge: 729 km 1.000-m gauge (2002)

Highways:

total: 15,100 km

paved: 1,827 km

unpaved: 13,273 km (1999 est.)

Mali *(continued)*

Waterways: 1,815 km
Ports and harbors: Koulikoro
Airports: 27 (2003 est.)
Airports - with paved runways:
total: 8
2,438 to 3,047 m: 4
1,524 to 2,437 m: 3
914 to 1,523 m: 1 (2003 est.)
Airports - with unpaved runways:
total: 19
2,438 to 3,047 m: 1
1,524 to 2,437 m: 5
914 to 1,523 m: 5
under 914 m: 8 (2003 est.)

Military

Military branches: Army, Air Force, National Guard
Military manpower - military age: 18 years of age (2004 est.)
Military manpower - availability:
males age 15-49: 2,529,147 (2004 est.)
Military manpower - fit for military service:
males age 15-49: 1,450,795 (2004 est.)
Military expenditures - dollar figure: $51.1 million (2003)
Military expenditures - percent of GDP: 1.3% (2003)

Transnational Issues

Disputes - international: none

Malta

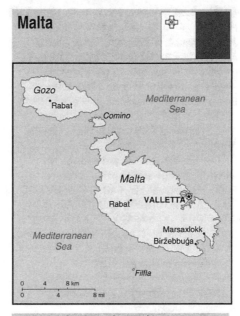

Introduction

Background: Great Britain formally acquired possession of Malta in 1814. The island staunchly supported the UK through both World Wars and remained in the Commonwealth when it became independent in 1964. A decade later Malta became a republic. Since about the mid-1980s, the island has become a freight transshipment point, financial center, and tourist destination. Malta is scheduled to become an EU member in May 2004.

Geography

Location: Southern Europe, islands in the Mediterranean Sea, south of Sicily (Italy)
Geographic coordinates: 35 50 N, 14 35 E
Map references: Europe
Area:
total: 316 sq km
land: 316 sq km
water: 0 sq km
Area - comparative: slightly less than twice the size of Washington, DC
Land boundaries: 0 km
Coastline: 196.8 km (does not include 56.01 km for the island of Gozo)
Maritime claims:
territorial sea: 12 NM
contiguous zone: 24 NM
continental shelf: 200-m depth or to the depth of exploitation
exclusive fishing zone: 25 NM
Climate: Mediterranean with mild, rainy winters and hot, dry summers
Terrain: mostly low, rocky, flat to dissected plains; many coastal cliffs
Elevation extremes:
lowest point: Mediterranean Sea 0 m
highest point: Ta'Dmejrek 253 m (near Dingli)
Natural resources: limestone, salt, arable land

Land use:
arable land: 31.25%
permanent crops: 3.13%
other: 65.62% (1998 est.)
Irrigated land: 20 sq km (1998 est.)
Natural hazards: NA
Environment - current issues: very limited natural fresh water resources; increasing reliance on desalination
Environment - international agreements:
party to: Air Pollution, Biodiversity, Climate Change, Climate Change-Kyoto Protocol, Desertification, Endangered Species, Hazardous Wastes, Law of the Sea, Marine Dumping, Ozone Layer Protection, Ship Pollution, Wetlands
signed, but not ratified: none of the selected agreements
Geography - note: the country comprises an archipelago, with only the three largest islands (Malta, Ghawdex or Gozo, and Kemmuna or Comino) being inhabited; numerous bays provide good harbors; Malta and Tunisia are discussing the commercial exploitation of the continental shelf between their countries, particularly for oil exploration

People

Population: 396,851 (July 2004 est.)
Age structure:
0-14 years: 18.1% (male 36,891; female 34,912)
15-64 years: 68.5% (male 137,259; female 134,611)
65 years and over: 13.4% (male 22,691; female 30,487) (2004 est.)
Median age:
total: 38 years
male: 36.6 years
female: 39.5 years (2004 est.)
Population growth rate: 0.42% (2004 est.)
Birth rate: 10.09 births/1,000 population (2004 est.)
Death rate: 7.93 deaths/1,000 population (2004 est.)
Net migration rate: 2.07 migrant(s)/1,000 population (2004 est.)
Sex ratio:
at birth: 1.06 male(s)/female
under 15 years: 1.06 male(s)/female
15-64 years: 1.02 male(s)/female
65 years and over: 0.74 male(s)/female
total population: 0.98 male(s)/female (2004 est.)
Infant mortality rate:
total: 3.94 deaths/1,000 live births
male: 4.45 deaths/1,000 live births
female: 3.4 deaths/1,000 live births (2004 est.)
Life expectancy at birth:
total population: 78.68 years
male: 76.51 years
female: 80.98 years (2004 est.)
Total fertility rate: 1.49 children born/woman (2004 est.)
HIV/AIDS - adult prevalence rate: 0.1% (2001 est.)
HIV/AIDS - people living with HIV/AIDS: NA
HIV/AIDS - deaths: less than 100 (2001 est.)

Malta *(continued)*

Nationality:
noun: Maltese (singular and plural)
adjective: Maltese
Ethnic groups: Maltese (descendants of ancient Carthaginians and Phoenicians, with strong elements of Italian and other Mediterranean stock)
Religions: Roman Catholic 98%
Languages: Maltese (official), English (official)
Literacy:
definition: age 10 and over can read and write
total population: 92.8%
male: 92%
female: 93.6% (2003 est.)

Government

Country name:
conventional long form: Republic of Malta
conventional short form: Malta
local long form: Repubblika ta' Malta
local short form: Malta
Government type: republic
Capital: Valletta
Administrative divisions: none (administered directly from Valletta); note - Local Councils carry out administrative orders
Independence: 21 September 1964 (from UK)
National holiday: Independence Day, 21 September (1964)
Constitution: 1964 constitution substantially amended on 13 December 1974 and again in 1987
Legal system: based on English common law and Roman civil law; accepts compulsory ICJ jurisdiction, with reservations
Suffrage: 18 years of age; universal
Executive branch:
chief of state: President Eddie FENECH ADAMI (since 4 April 2004)
head of government: Prime Minister Lawrence GONZI
cabinet: Cabinet appointed by the president on the advice of the prime minister
elections: president elected by the House of Representatives for a five-year term; election last held 29 March 2004 (next to be held by April 2009); following legislative elections, the leader of the majority party or leader of a majority coalition is usually appointed prime minister by the president for a five-year term; the deputy prime minister is appointed by the president on the advice of the prime minister
election results: Eddie FENECH ADAMI elected president; percent of House of Representatives vote - 33 out of 65 votes
Legislative branch: unicameral House of Representatives (usually 65 seats; note - additional seats are given to the party with the largest popular vote to ensure a legislative majority; members are elected by popular vote on the basis of proportional representation to serve five-year terms)
elections: last held 12 April 2003 (next to be held by April 2008)

election results: percent of vote by party - PN 51.7%, MLP 47.6%, AD 0.7%; seats by party - PN 34, MLP 31
Judicial branch: Constitutional Court; Court of Appeal; judges for both courts are appointed by the president on the advice of the prime minister
Political parties and leaders: Alternativa Demokratika/Alliance for Social Justice or AD [Harry VASSALLO]; Malta Labor Party or MLP [Alfred SANT]; Nationalist Party or PN [Edward FENECH ADAMI]
Political pressure groups and leaders: NA
International organization participation: C, CE, EBRD, EU (new member), FAO, G-77, IAEA, IBRD, ICAO, ICCt, ICFTU, ICRM, IFAD, IFRCS, ILO, IMF, IMO, Interpol, IOC, IOM, ISO, ITU, NAM, OPCW, OSCE, PCA, UN, UNCTAD, UNESCO, UNIDO, UPU, WCL, WCO, WHO, WIPO, WMO, WToO, WTrO
Diplomatic representation in the US:
chief of mission: Ambassador John LOWELL
chancery: 2017 Connecticut Avenue NW, Washington, DC 20008
telephone: [1] (202) 462-3611, 3612
FAX: [1] (202) 387-5470
consulate(s): New York
Diplomatic representation from the US:
chief of mission: Ambassador Anthony H. GIOIA
embassy: 3rd Floor, Development House, Saint Anne Street, Floriana, Malta VLT 01
mailing address: P. O. Box 535, Valletta, Malta
telephone: [356] 21-235-960
FAX: [356] 2124-3229
Flag description: two equal vertical bands of white (hoist side) and red; in the upper hoist-side corner is a representation of the George Cross, edged in red

Economy

Economy - overview: Major resources are limestone, a favorable geographic location, and a productive labor force. Malta produces only about 20% of its food needs, has limited fresh water supplies, and has no domestic energy sources. The economy is dependent on foreign trade, manufacturing (especially electronics and textiles), and tourism. Malta is privatizing state-controlled firms and liberalizing markets in order to prepare for membership in the European Union. The island remains divided politically, however, over the question of joining the EU. Continued sluggishness in the global economy is holding back exports, tourism, and overall growth.
GDP: purchasing power parity - $7.082 billion (2003 est.)
GDP - real growth rate: 0.8% (2003 est.)
GDP - per capita: purchasing power parity - $17,700 (2003 est.)
GDP - composition by sector:
agriculture: 3%
industry: 23%
services: 74% (2002 est.)
Population below poverty line: NA%

Household income or consumption by percentage share:
lowest 10%: NA%
highest 10%: NA%
Inflation rate (consumer prices): 0.8% (2003 est.)
Labor force: 160,000 (2002 est.)
Labor force - by occupation: industry 24%, services 71%, agriculture 5% (1999 est.)
Unemployment rate: 7% (2003 est.)
Budget:
revenues: $1.5 billion
expenditures: $1.6 billion, including capital expenditures of $NA (2000)
Industries: tourism; electronics, ship building and repair, construction; food and beverages, textiles, footwear, clothing, tobacco
Industrial production growth rate: NA%
Electricity - production: 1.768 billion kWh (2001)
Electricity - production by source:
fossil fuel: 100%
hydro: 0%
nuclear: 0%
other: 0% (2001)
Electricity - consumption: 1.644 billion kWh (2001)
Electricity - exports: 0 kWh (2001)
Electricity - imports: 0 kWh (2001)
Oil - production: 0 bbl/day (2001 est.)
Oil - consumption: 20,000 bbl/day (2001 est.)
Oil - exports: NA
Oil - imports: NA
Agriculture - products: potatoes, cauliflower, grapes, wheat, barley, tomatoes, citrus, cut flowers, green peppers; pork, milk, poultry, eggs
Exports: $2.175 billion f.o.b. (2003 est.)
Exports - commodities: machinery and transport equipment, manufactures
Exports - partners: Singapore 17.3%, US 11.4%, UK 9.4%, Germany 9.2%, France 7.3%, China 6.5%, Italy 6% (2002)
Imports: $2.761 billion f.o.b. (2003 est.)
Imports - commodities: machinery and transport equipment, manufactured and semi-manufactured goods; food, drink, and tobacco
Imports - partners: Italy 18.2%, France 12%, South Korea 11.3%, UK 7.5%, Germany 5.3%, Singapore 5.3%, Japan 4.9%, US 4.6%, Spain 4.2% (2002)
Debt - external: $130 million (1997)
Economic aid - recipient: $NA
Currency: Maltese lira (MTL)
Currency code: MTL
Exchange rates: Maltese liri per US dollar - 0.3772 (2003), 0.4336 (2002), 0.4501 (2001), 0.4382 (2000), 0.3989 (1999)
Fiscal year: 1 April - 31 March

Communications

Telephones - main lines in use: 207,300 (2002)
Telephones - mobile cellular: 276,900 (2002)
Telephone system:
general assessment: automatic system satisfies normal requirements

Malta *(continued)*

domestic: submarine cable and microwave radio relay between islands
international: country code - 356; 2 submarine cables; satellite earth station - 1 Intelsat (Atlantic Ocean)
Radio broadcast stations: AM 1, FM 18, shortwave 6 (1999)
Television broadcast stations: 6 (2000)
Internet country code: .mt
Internet hosts: 7,355 (2002)
Internet users: 82,900 (2002)

Transportation

Railways: 0 km
Highways:
total: 2,254 km
paved: 1,972 km
unpaved: 282 km (2000)
Waterways: none
Ports and harbors: Marsaxlokk, Valletta
Merchant marine:
total: 1,176 ships (1,000 GRT or over) 25,102,401 GRT/41,176,791 DWT
by type: bulk 468, cargo 251, chemical tanker 46, combination bulk 8, combination ore/oil 8, container 74, liquefied gas 4, livestock carrier 2, multi-functional large load carrier 1, passenger 7, passenger/cargo 1, petroleum tanker 210, refrigerated cargo 40, roll on/roll off 35, short-sea/passenger 6, vehicle carrier 15
foreign-owned: Australia 4, Austria 6, Bangladesh 3, Belgium 13, Bulgaria 19, Canada 8, China 14, Croatia 9, Cyprus 6, Denmark 4, Estonia 1, Finland 1, France 1, Germany 52, Greece 603, Hong Kong 3, Iceland 5, India 4, Indonesia 2, Iran 4, Israel 20, Italy 24, Japan 3, South Korea 2, Latvia 25, Lebanon 6, Madagascar 1, Monaco 14, Netherlands 5, Nigeria 1, Norway 32, Pakistan 1, Poland 30, Portugal 3, Romania 8, Russia 69, Saudi Arabia 1, Singapore 2, Slovenia 3, Switzerland 30, Syria 4, Taiwan 1, Turkey 108, Ukraine 22, United Kingdom 2, United States 8
registered in other countries: 18 (2003 est.)
Airports: 1 (2003 est.)
Airports - with paved runways:
total: 1
over 3,047 m: 1 (2003 est.)

Military

Military branches: Armed Forces: Land Forces (including Air Squadron and Maritime Squadron), Revenue Security Corps
Military manpower - availability:
males age 15-49: 99,324 (2004 est.)
Military manpower - fit for military service:
males age 15-49: 79,128 (2004 est.)
Military expenditures - dollar figure: $33.3 million (2003)
Military expenditures - percent of GDP: 0.7% (2003)

Transnational Issues

Disputes - international: none
Illicit drugs: minor transshipment point for hashish from North Africa to Western Europe

Man, Isle of
(British crown dependency)

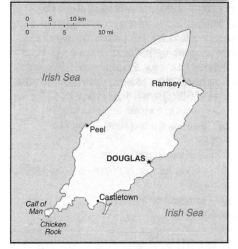

Introduction

Background: Part of the Norwegian Kingdom of the Hebrides until the 13th century when it was ceded to Scotland, the isle came under the British crown in 1765. Current concerns include reviving the almost extinct Manx Gaelic language.

Geography

Location: Western Europe, island in the Irish Sea, between Great Britain and Ireland
Geographic coordinates: 54 15 N, 4 30 W
Map references: Europe
Area:
total: 572 sq km
land: 572 sq km
water: 0 sq km
Area - comparative: slightly more than three times the size of Washington, DC
Land boundaries: 0 km
Coastline: 160 km
Maritime claims:
territorial sea: 12 NM
exclusive fishing zone: 12 NM
Climate: temperate; cool summers and mild winters; overcast about one-third of the time
Terrain: hills in north and south bisected by central valley
Elevation extremes:
lowest point: Irish Sea 0 m
highest point: Snaefell 621 m
Natural resources: none
Land use:
arable land: 0%
permanent crops: 0%
other: 100% (permanent pastures, forests, mountain, and heathland) (1998 est.)
Irrigated land: 0 sq km (1998 est.)
Natural hazards: NA

Environment - current issues: waste disposal (both household and industrial); transboundary air pollution
Geography - note: one small islet, the Calf of Man, lies to the southwest, and is a bird sanctuary

People

Population: 74,655 (July 2004 est.)
Age structure:
0-14 years: 17.4% (male 6,669; female 6,357)
15-64 years: 65.4% (male 24,527; female 24,302)
65 years and over: 17.1% (male 5,128; female 7,672) (2004 est.)
Median age:
total: 39.3 years
male: 38 years
female: 40.8 years (2004 est.)
Population growth rate: 0.53% (2004 est.)
Birth rate: 11.28 births/1,000 population (2004 est.)
Death rate: 11.35 deaths/1,000 population (2004 est.)
Net migration rate: 5.36 migrant(s)/1,000 population (2004 est.)
Sex ratio:
at birth: 1.05 male(s)/female
under 15 years: 1.05 male(s)/female
15-64 years: 1.01 male(s)/female
65 years and over: 0.67 male(s)/female
total population: 0.95 male(s)/female (2004 est.)
Infant mortality rate:
total: 6.05 deaths/1,000 live births
male: 7.08 deaths/1,000 live births
female: 4.96 deaths/1,000 live births (2004 est.)
Life expectancy at birth:
total population: 78.16 years
male: 74.8 years
female: 81.7 years (2004 est.)
Total fertility rate: 1.65 children born/woman (2004 est.)
HIV/AIDS - adult prevalence rate: NA%
HIV/AIDS - people living with HIV/AIDS: NA
HIV/AIDS - deaths: NA
Nationality:
noun: Manxman (men), Manxwoman (women)
adjective: Manx
Ethnic groups: Manx (Norse-Celtic descent), Briton
Religions: Anglican, Roman Catholic, Methodist, Baptist, Presbyterian, Society of Friends
Languages: English, Manx Gaelic
Literacy:
definition: NA
total population: NA%
male: NA%
female: NA%

Government

Country name:
conventional long form: none
conventional short form: Isle of Man
Dependency status: British crown dependency
Government type: parliamentary democracy

Man, Isle of (continued)

Capital: Douglas

Administrative divisions: there are no first-order administrative divisions as defined by the US Government, but there are 24 local authorities each with its own elections

Independence: none (British crown dependency)

National holiday: Tynwald Day, 5 July

Constitution: unwritten; note - The Isle of Man Constitution Act, 1961, does not embody the unwritten Manx Constitution

Legal system: English common law and Manx statute

Suffrage: 18 years of age; universal

Executive branch:

chief of state: Lord of Mann Queen ELIZABETH II (since 6 February 1952), represented by Lieutenant Governor Ian MACFADYEN (since 26 October 2002)

head of government: Chief Minister Richard CORKILL (since 6 December 2001)

cabinet: Council of Ministers

elections: the monarch is hereditary; lieutenant governor appointed by the monarch for a five-year term; the Chief Minister is elected by the Tynwald; election last held 6 December 2001 (next to be held NA December 2006)

election results: Richard CORKILL elected chief minister by the Tynwald

Legislative branch: bicameral Tynwald consists of the Legislative Council (an 11-member body composed of the President of Tynwald, the Lord Bishop of Sodor and Man, a nonvoting attorney general, and 8 others named by the House of Keys) and the House of Keys (24 seats; members are elected by popular vote to serve five-year terms)

elections: House of Keys - last held 22 November 2001 (next to be held NA November 2006)

election results: House of Keys - percent of vote by party - Man Labor Party 17.3%, Alliance for Progressive Government 14.6%; seats by party - Man Labor Party 2, Alliance for Progressive Government 3, independents 19

Judicial branch: High Court of Justice (justices are appointed by the Lord Chancellor of England on the nomination of the lieutenant governor)

Political parties and leaders: Man Labor Party [leader NA]; Alliance for Progressive Government [leader NA]; Man Nationalist Party [leader NA]

note: most members sit as independents

Political pressure groups and leaders: none

International organization participation: none

Diplomatic representation in the US: none (British crown dependency)

Diplomatic representation from the US: none (British crown dependency)

Flag description: red with the Three Legs of Man emblem (Trinacria), in the center; the three legs are joined at the thigh and bent at the knee; in order to have the toes pointing clockwise on both sides of the flag, a two-sided emblem is used

Economy

Economy - overview: Offshore banking, manufacturing, and tourism are key sectors of the economy. The government's policy of offering incentives to high-technology companies and financial institutions to locate on the island has paid off in expanding employment opportunities in high-income industries. As a result, agriculture and fishing, once the mainstays of the economy, have declined in their shares of GDP. Trade is mostly with the UK. The Isle of Man enjoys free access to EU markets.

GDP: purchasing power parity - $1.6 billion (2001 est.)

GDP - real growth rate: 13.5%

GDP - per capita: purchasing power parity - $21,000 (2001 est.)

GDP - composition by sector:

agriculture: 1%

industry: 13%

services: 86% (2000 est.)

Population below poverty line: NA%

Household income or consumption by percentage share:

lowest 10%: NA%

highest 10%: NA%

Inflation rate (consumer prices): 3.6% (March 2003 est.)

Labor force: 36,610 (1998)

Labor force - by occupation: agriculture, forestry and fishing 3%, manufacturing 11%, construction 10%, transport and communication 8%, wholesale and retail distribution 11%, professional and scientific services 18%, public administration 6%, banking and finance 18%, tourism 2%, entertainment and catering 3%, miscellaneous services 10%

Unemployment rate: 0.7% (March 2003)

Budget:

revenues: $485 million

expenditures: $463 million, including capital expenditures of $NA (FY00/01 est.)

Industries: financial services, light manufacturing, tourism

Industrial production growth rate: 3.2% (FY96/97)

Agriculture - products: cereals, vegetables; cattle, sheep, pigs, poultry

Exports: $NA

Exports - commodities: tweeds, herring, processed shellfish, beef, lamb

Exports - partners: UK (2000 est.)

Imports: $NA

Imports - commodities: timber, fertilizers, fish

Imports - partners: UK (2000)

Debt - external: $NA

Economic aid - recipient: $NA

Currency: British pound (GBP); note - there is also a Manx pound

Currency code: GBP

Exchange rates: Manx pounds per US dollar - 0.6125 (2003), 0.6661 (2002), 0.6944 (2001), 0.6596 (2000), 0.6180 (1999); the Manx pound is at par with the British pound

Fiscal year: 1 April - 31 March

Communications

Telephones - main lines in use: 51,000 (1999)

Telephones - mobile cellular: NA

Telephone system:

general assessment: NA

domestic: landline, telefax, mobile cellular telephone system

international: fiber-optic cable, microwave radio relay, satellite earth station, submarine cable

Radio broadcast stations: AM 1, FM 1, shortwave 0 (1998)

Television broadcast stations: 0 (receives broadcasts from the UK and satellite) (1999)

Internet country code: .im

Internet users: NA

Transportation

Railways:

total: 60 km (35 km electrified) (2002)

Highways:

total: 800 km

paved: 800 km

unpaved: 0 km (1999)

Waterways: none

Ports and harbors: Castletown, Douglas, Peel, Ramsey

Merchant marine:

total: 226 ships (1,000 GRT or over) 6,055,436 GRT/ 9,972,459 DWT

by type: bulk 25, cargo 40, chemical tanker 25, combination bulk 2, container 19, liquefied gas 31, multi-functional large load carrier 1, petroleum tanker 59, refrigerated cargo 1, roll on/roll off 17, specialized tanker 1, vehicle carrier 5

foreign-owned: Australia 3, Cyprus 4, Denmark 30, Estonia 3, France 1, Germany 57, Greece 8, Hong Kong 11, Iceland 1, Italy 6, Monaco 4, Netherlands 2, New Zealand 1, Norway 10, Singapore 2, Sweden 3, United Kingdom 80, United States 1

registered in other countries: 9 (2003 est.)

Airports: 1 (2003 est.)

Airports - with paved runways:

total: 1

1,524 to 2,437 m: 1 (2003 est.)

Military

Military - note: defense is the responsibility of the UK

Transnational Issues

Disputes - international: none

Marshall Islands

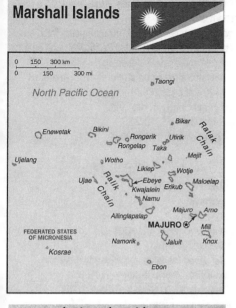

North Pacific Ocean

Taongi

Enewetak *Bikini* *Rongerik* *Utirik* *Bikar* Ratak Chain

Rongelap *Taka* *Mejit*

Ujelang *Wotho* *Likiep* *Wotje*

Ujae *Ebeye* *Maloelap*

Kwajalein *Erikub* Ralik Chain

Namu

Majuro *Arno*

Ailinglapalap **MAJURO** *Mill*

FEDERATED STATES OF MICRONESIA *Namorik* *Jaluit* *Knox*

Kosrae *Ebon*

Introduction

Background: After almost four decades under US administration as the easternmost part of the UN Trust Territory of the Pacific Islands, the Marshall Islands attained independence in 1986 under a Compact of Free Association. Compensation claims continue as a result of US nuclear testing on some of the atolls between 1947 and 1962. The Marshall Islands have been home to the US Army Base Kwajalein (USAKA) since 1964.

Geography

Location: Oceania, group of atolls and reefs in the North Pacific Ocean, about one-half of the way from Hawaii to Australia

Geographic coordinates: 9 00 N, 168 00 E

Map references: Oceania

Area:
total: 181.3 sq km
land: 181.3 sq km
water: 0 sq km
note: includes the atolls of Bikini, Enewetak, Kwajalein, Majuro, Rongelap, and Utirik

Area - comparative: about the size of Washington, DC

Land boundaries: 0 km

Coastline: 370.4 km

Maritime claims:
territorial sea: 12 NM
contiguous zone: 24 NM
exclusive economic zone: 200 NM

Climate: tropical; hot and humid; wet season from May to November; islands border typhoon belt

Terrain: low coral limestone and sand islands

Elevation extremes:
lowest point: Pacific Ocean 0 m
highest point: unnamed location on Likiep 10 m

Natural resources: coconut products, marine products, deep seabed minerals

Land use:
arable land: 16.67%
permanent crops: 0%
other: 83.33% (1998 est.)

Irrigated land: 0 sq km

Natural hazards: infrequent typhoons

Environment - current issues: inadequate supplies of potable water; pollution of Majuro lagoon from household waste and discharges from fishing vessels

Environment - international agreements:
party to: Biodiversity, Climate Change, Climate Change-Kyoto Protocol, Desertification, Hazardous Wastes, Law of the Sea, Ozone Layer Protection, Ship Pollution
signed, but not ratified: none of the selected agreements

Geography - note: two archipelagic island chains of 30 atolls and 1,152 islands; Bikini and Enewetak are former US nuclear test sites; Kwajalein, the famous World War II battleground, is now used as a US missile test range

People

Population: 57,738 (July 2004 est.)

Age structure:
0-14 years: 38.6% (male 11,347; female 10,934)
15-64 years: 58.7% (male 17,380; female 16,520)
65 years and over: 2.7% (male 748; female 809) (2004 est.)

Median age:
total: 19.6 years
male: 19.6 years
female: 19.6 years (2004 est.)

Population growth rate: 2.29% (2004 est.)

Birth rate: 33.88 births/1,000 population (2004 est.)

Death rate: 4.94 deaths/1,000 population (2004 est.)

Net migration rate: -6.04 migrant(s)/1,000 population (2004 est.)

Sex ratio:
at birth: 1.05 male(s)/female
under 15 years: 1.04 male(s)/female
15-64 years: 1.05 male(s)/female
65 years and over: 0.93 male(s)/female
total population: 1.04 male(s)/female (2004 est.)

Infant mortality rate:
total: 30.5 deaths/1,000 live births
male: 34.19 deaths/1,000 live births
female: 26.61 deaths/1,000 live births (2004 est.)

Life expectancy at birth:
total population: 69.7 years
male: 67.77 years
female: 71.73 years (2004 est.)

Total fertility rate: 4.02 children born/woman (2004 est.)

HIV/AIDS - adult prevalence rate: NA%

HIV/AIDS - people living with HIV/AIDS: NA

HIV/AIDS - deaths: NA

Nationality:
noun: Marshallese (singular and plural)
adjective: Marshallese

Ethnic groups: Micronesian

Religions: Christian (mostly Protestant)

Languages: English (widely spoken as a second language, both English and Marshallese are official languages), two major Marshallese dialects from the Malayo-Polynesian family, Japanese

Literacy:
definition: age 15 and over can read and write
total population: 93.7%
male: 93.6%
female: 93.7% (1999)

Government

Country name:
conventional long form: Republic of the Marshall Islands
conventional short form: Marshall Islands
former: Marshall Islands District (Trust Territory of the Pacific Islands)

Government type: constitutional government in free association with the US; the Compact of Free Association entered into force 21 October 1986

Capital: Majuro

Administrative divisions: 33 municipalities; Ailinginae, Ailinglaplap, Ailuk, Arno, Aur, Bikar, Bikini, Bokak, Ebon, Enewetak, Erikub, Jabat, Jaluit, Jemo, Kili, Kwajalein, Lae, Lib, Likiep, Majuro, Maloelap, Mejit, Mili, Namorik, Namu, Rongelap, Rongrik, Toke, Ujae, Ujelang, Utirik, Wotho, Wotje

Independence: 21 October 1986 (from the US-administered UN trusteeship)

National holiday: Constitution Day, 1 May (1979)

Constitution: 1 May 1979

Legal system: based on adapted Trust Territory laws, acts of the legislature, municipal, common, and customary laws

Suffrage: 18 years of age; universal

Executive branch:
chief of state: President Kessai Hesa NOTE (since 5 January 2004); note - the president is both the chief of state and head of government
head of government: President Kessai Hesa NOTE (since 5 January 2004); note - the president is both the chief of state and head of government
cabinet: Cabinet selected by the president from among the members of Parliament
elections: president elected by Parliament from among its own members for a four-year term; election last held 17 November 2003 (next to be held NA November 2007)
election results: Kessai Hesa NOTE elected president; percent of Parliament vote - 100%

Legislative branch: unicameral Parliament or Nitijela (33 seats; members elected by popular vote to serve four-year terms)
elections: last held 17 November 2003 (next to be held not later than November 2007)
election results: percent of vote by party - NA%; seats by party - NA
note: the Council of Chiefs is a 12-member body that advises on matters affecting customary law and practice

Judicial branch: Supreme Court; High Court

Political parties and leaders: traditionally there have been no formally organized political parties; what has existed more closely resembles factions or interest groups because they do not have party headquarters, formal platforms, or party structures; the following two "groupings" have competed in legislative balloting in recent years - Kabua Party [Imata KABUA] and United Democratic Party or UDP [Litokwa TOMEING]

Political pressure groups and leaders: NA

International organization participation: ACP, AsDB, FAO, G-77, IAEA, IBRD, ICAO, ICCt, IDA, IFC, IMF, IMO, Interpol, ITU, OPCW (signatory), PIF, Sparteca, UN, UNCTAD, UNESCO, WHO

Diplomatic representation in the US:
chief of mission: Ambassador Banny DE BRUM
chancery: 2433 Massachusetts Avenue NW, Washington, DC 20008
telephone: [1] (202) 234-5414
FAX: [1] (202) 232-3236
consulate(s) general: Honolulu

Diplomatic representation from the US:
chief of mission: Ambassador Michael J. SENKO
embassy: Oceanside, Mejen Weto, Long Island, Majuro
mailing address: P. O. Box 1379, Majuro, Republic of the Marshall Islands 96960-1379
telephone: [692] 247-4011
FAX: [692] 247-4012

Flag description: blue with two stripes radiating from the lower hoist-side corner - orange (top) and white; there is a white star with four large rays and 20 small rays on the hoist side above the two stripes

Economy

Economy - overview: US Government assistance is the mainstay of this tiny island economy. Agricultural production is primarily subsistence and is concentrated on small farms; the most important commercial crops are coconuts and breadfruit. Small-scale industry is limited to handicrafts, tuna processing, and copra. The tourist industry, now a small source of foreign exchange employing less than 10% of the labor force, remains the best hope for future added income. The islands have few natural resources, and imports far exceed exports. Under the terms of the Compact of Free Association, the US has provided more than $1 billion in aid since 1986. Negotiations have continued for an extended agreement. Government downsizing, drought, a drop in construction, the decline in tourism and foreign investment due to the Asian financial difficulties, and less income from the renewal of fishing vessel licenses have held GDP growth to an average of 1% over the past decade.

GDP: purchasing power parity - $115 million (2001 est.)

GDP - real growth rate: 1% (2001 est.)

GDP - per capita: purchasing power parity - $1,600 (2001 est.)

GDP - composition by sector:
agriculture: 14%
industry: 16%
services: 70% (2000 est.)

Population below poverty line: NA%

Household income or consumption by percentage share:
lowest 10%: NA%
highest 10%: NA%

Inflation rate (consumer prices): 2% (2001 est.)

Labor force: 28,698 (1996 est.)

Labor force - by occupation: agriculture 21.4%, industry 20.9%, services 57.7%

Unemployment rate: 30.9% (1999 est.)

Budget:
revenues: $42 million
expenditures: $40 million, including capital expenditures of $NA (1999)

Industries: copra, fish, tourism, craft items from shell, wood, and pearls

Industrial production growth rate: NA%

Electricity - production by source:
fossil fuel: 99%
hydro: 0%
nuclear: 0%
other: 1% (solar)

Agriculture - products: coconuts, tomatoes, melons, taro, breadfruit, fruits; pigs, chickens

Exports: $9 million f.o.b. (2000)

Exports - commodities: copra cake, coconut oil, handicrafts, fish

Exports - partners: US, Japan, Australia, China (2000)

Imports: $54 million f.o.b. (2000)

Imports - commodities: foodstuffs, machinery and equipment, fuels, beverages and tobacco

Imports - partners: US, Japan, Australia, NZ, Singapore, Fiji, China, Philippines (2000)

Debt - external: $86.5 million (FY99/00 est.)

Economic aid - recipient: more than $1 billion from the US, 1986-2002

Currency: US dollar (USD)

Currency code: USD

Exchange rates: the US dollar is the legal tender

Fiscal year: 1 October - 30 September

Communications

Telephones - main lines in use: 4,400 (2002)

Telephones - mobile cellular: 600 (2002)

Telephone system:
general assessment: digital switching equipment; modern services include telex, cellular, internet, international calling, caller ID, and leased data circuits
domestic: Majuro Atoll and Ebeye and Kwajalein islands have regular, seven-digit, direct-dial telephones; other islands interconnected by shortwave radiotelephone (used mostly for government purposes)
international: country code - 692; satellite earth stations - 2 Intelsat (Pacific Ocean); US Government satellite communications system on Kwajalein (2001)

Radio broadcast stations: AM 2, FM 1, shortwave 0
note: additionally, the US Armed Forces Radio and Television Services (Central Pacific Network) operate one FM and one AM station on Kwajalein (2002)

Television broadcast stations: 2 (both are US military stations) (2002)

Internet country code: .mh

Internet hosts: 5 (2002)

Internet users: 1,300 (2002)

Transportation

Railways: 0 km

Highways:
total: NA km
paved: 64.5 km
unpaved: NA km
note: paved roads on major islands (Majuro, Kwajalein), otherwise stone-, coral-, or laterite-surfaced roads and tracks (2002)

Waterways: none

Ports and harbors: Majuro

Merchant marine:
total: 420 ships (1,000 GRT or over) 16,954,092 GRT/ 28,176,762 DWT
by type: barge carrier 1, bulk 81, cargo 25, chemical tanker 41, combination bulk 4, combination ore/oil 7, container 77, liquefied gas 9, multi-functional large load carrier 5, passenger 6, petroleum tanker 149, refrigerated cargo 4, roll on/roll off 7, vehicle carrier 4
foreign-owned: Australia 2, Chile 3, Croatia 2, Cyprus 10, Denmark 2, Germany 119, Greece 82, Hong Kong 12, India 2, Japan 16, Monaco 18, Netherlands 6, New Zealand 1, Norway 5, Poland 11, Singapore 1, Slovenia 1, Switzerland 4, Thailand 2, Turkey 8, United Kingdom 10, United States 92
registered in other countries: 50 (2003 est.)

Airports: 15 (2003 est.)

Airports - with paved runways:
total: 4
1,524 to 2,437 m: 3
914 to 1,523 m: 1 (2003 est.)

Airports - with unpaved runways:
total: 11
914 to 1,523 m: 10
under 914 m: 1 (2003 est.)

Military

Military branches: no regular military forces; Marshall Islands Police

Military expenditures - dollar figure: NA

Military expenditures - percent of GDP: NA

Military - note: defense is the responsibility of the US

Transnational Issues

Disputes - international: claims US territory of Wake Island

Martinique

(overseas department of France)

Introduction

Background: Colonized by France in 1635, the island has subsequently remained a French possession except for three brief periods of foreign occupation.

Geography

Location: Caribbean, island between the Caribbean Sea and North Atlantic Ocean, north of Trinidad and Tobago
Geographic coordinates: 14 40 N, 61 00 W
Map references: Central America and the Caribbean
Area:
total: 1,100 sq km
land: 1,060 sq km
water: 40 sq km
Area - comparative: slightly more than six times the size of Washington, DC
Land boundaries: 0 km
Coastline: 350 km
Maritime claims:
territorial sea: 12 NM
exclusive economic zone: 200 NM
Climate: tropical; moderated by trade winds; rainy season (June to October); vulnerable to devastating cyclones (hurricanes) every eight years on average; average temperature 17.3 degrees C; humid
Terrain: mountainous with indented coastline; dormant volcano
Elevation extremes:
lowest point: Caribbean Sea 0 m
highest point: Montagne Pelee 1,397 m
Natural resources: coastal scenery and beaches, cultivable land
Land use:
arable land: 9.43%
permanent crops: 11.32%
other: 79.25% (1998 est.)

Irrigated land: 30 sq km (1998 est.)
Natural hazards: hurricanes, flooding, and volcanic activity (an average of one major natural disaster every five years)
Environment - current issues: NA
Geography - note: the island is dominated by Mount Pelee, which on 8 May 1902 erupted and completely destroyed the city of Saint Pierre, killing 30,000 inhabitants

People

Population: 429,510 (July 2004 est.)
Age structure:
0-14 years: 22.6% (male 49,245; female 47,845)
15-64 years: 67% (male 143,893; female 143,963)
65 years and over: 10.4% (male 20,043; female 24,521) (2004 est.)
Median age:
total: 33.1 years
male: 32.5 years
female: 33.8 years (2004 est.)
Population growth rate: 0.81% (2004 est.)
Birth rate: 14.56 births/1,000 population (2004 est.)
Death rate: 6.43 deaths/1,000 population (2004 est.)
Net migration rate: -0.05 migrant(s)/1,000 population (2004 est.)
Sex ratio:
at birth: 1.02 male(s)/female
under 15 years: 1.03 male(s)/female
15-64 years: 1 male(s)/female
65 years and over: 0.82 male(s)/female
total population: 0.99 male(s)/female (2004 est.)
Infant mortality rate:
total: 7.27 deaths/1,000 live births
male: 4.79 deaths/1,000 live births
female: 9.8 deaths/1,000 live births (2004 est.)
Life expectancy at birth:
total population: 78.88 years
male: 79.35 years
female: 78.4 years (2004 est.)
Total fertility rate: 1.79 children born/woman (2004 est.)
HIV/AIDS - adult prevalence rate: NA%
HIV/AIDS - people living with HIV/AIDS: NA
HIV/AIDS - deaths: NA
Nationality:
noun: Martiniquais (singular and plural)
adjective: Martiniquais
Ethnic groups: African and African-white-Indian mixture 90%, white 5%, East Indian, Chinese less than 5%
Religions: Roman Catholic 85%, Protestant 10.5%, Muslim 0.5%, Hindu 0.5%, other 3.5% (1997)
Languages: French, Creole patois
Literacy:
definition: age 15 and over can read and write
total population: 97.7%
male: 97.4%
female: 98.1% (2003 est.)

Government

Country name:
conventional long form: Department of Martinique
conventional short form: Martinique
local long form: Departement de la Martinique
local short form: Martinique
Dependency status: overseas department of France
Government type: NA
Capital: Fort-de-France
Administrative divisions: none (overseas department of France)
Independence: none (overseas department of France)
National holiday: Bastille Day, 14 July (1789)
Constitution: 28 September 1958 (French Constitution)
Legal system: French legal system
Suffrage: 18 years of age; universal
Executive branch:
chief of state: President Jacques CHIRAC of France (since 17 May 1995); Prefect Yves DASSONVILLE (since 14 January 2004); note - took office 8 February 2004
head of government: President of the General Council Claude LISE (since 22 March 1992); President of the Regional Council Alfred MARIE-JEANNE (since NA March 1998)
cabinet: NA
elections: French president elected by popular vote for a five-year term; prefect appointed by the French president on the advice of the French Ministry of Interior; the presidents of the General and Regional Councils are elected by the members of those councils
Legislative branch: unicameral General Council or Conseil General (45 seats; members are elected by popular vote to serve six-year terms) and a unicameral Regional Assembly or Conseil Regional (41 seats; members are elected by popular vote to serve six-year terms)
elections: General Council - last held NA March 2000 (next to be held NA 2006); Regional Assembly - last held on 28 March 2004 (next to be held by March 2010)
election results: General Council - percent of vote by party - NA%; seats by party - left-wing candidates 13, PPM 11, RPR 6, right-wing candidates 5, PCM 3, UDF 3, PMS 2, independents 2; note - the PPM won a plurality; Regional Assembly (second round) - percent of vote by party - MIM 53.8%, PPM 30.6%; seats by party - MIM 28, PPM 9, other 4
note: Martinique elects 2 seats to the French Senate; elections last held NA September 2001 (next to be held September 2004); results - percent of vote by party - NA%; seats by party - PPM 2; Martinique also elects 4 seats to the French National Assembly; elections last held, first round - 9 June 2002, second round - 16 June 2002 (next to be held not later than June 2007); results - percent of vote by party - NA%; seats by party - UMP-RPR 1, PS 1, MIM 1, left-wing

Martinique *(continued)*

candidate 1 (candidacy of the left-wing candidate was found invalid by the Constitutional Council; new elections will be called)

Judicial branch: Court of Appeal or Cour d'Appel

Political parties and leaders: Martinique Communist Party or PCM [Georges ERICHOT]; Martinique Independence Movement or MIM [Alfred MARIE-JEANNE]; Martinique Progressive Party or PPM [Pierre SUEDILE]; Martinique Socialist Party or PMS [Ernest WAN-AJOUHU]; Movement of Democrats and Ecologists for a Sovereign Martinique or Modemas [Garcin MALSA]; Rally for the Republic or RPR [Michel CHARLONE]; Socialist Revolution Group or GRS [Philippe PIERRE-CHARLES]; Union for French Democracy or UDF [Jean MAREN]

Political pressure groups and leaders: Caribbean Revolutionary Alliance or ARC; Central Union for Martinique Workers or CSTM [Marc PULVAR]; Frantz Fanon Circle; League of Workers and Peasants; Proletarian Action Group or GAP

International organization participation: WCL, WFTU

Diplomatic representation in the US: none (overseas department of France)

Diplomatic representation from the US: none (overseas department of France)

Flag description: a light blue background is divided into four quadrants by a white cross; in the center of each rectangle is a white snake; the flag of France is used for official occasions

Economy

Economy - overview: The economy is based on sugarcane, bananas, tourism, and light industry. Agriculture accounts for about 6% of GDP and the small industrial sector for 11%. Sugar production has declined, with most of the sugarcane now used for the production of rum. Banana exports are increasing, going mostly to France. The bulk of meat, vegetable, and grain requirements must be imported, contributing to a chronic trade deficit that requires large annual transfers of aid from France. Tourism, which employs more than 11,000 people, has become more important than agricultural exports as a source of foreign exchange.

GDP: purchasing power parity - $6.117 billion (2003 est.)

GDP - real growth rate: NA%

GDP - per capita: purchasing power parity - $14,400 (2001 est.)

GDP - composition by sector:
agriculture: 6%
industry: 11%
services: 83% (1997 est.)

Population below poverty line: NA%

Household income or consumption by percentage share:
lowest 10%: NA%
highest 10%: NA%

Inflation rate (consumer prices): 3.9% (1990)

Labor force: 165,900 (1998)

Labor force - by occupation: agriculture 10%, industry 17%, services 73% (1997)

Unemployment rate: 27.2% (1998)

Budget:
revenues: $900 million
expenditures: $2.5 billion, including capital expenditures of $140 million (1996)

Industries: construction, rum, cement, oil refining, sugar, tourism

Industrial production growth rate: NA%

Electricity - production: 1.151 billion kWh (2001)

Electricity - production by source:
fossil fuel: 100%
hydro: 0%
nuclear: 0%
other: 0% (2001)

Electricity - consumption: 1.07 billion kWh (2001)

Electricity - exports: 0 kWh (2001)

Electricity - imports: 0 kWh (2001)

Oil - production: 0 bbl/day (2001 est.)

Oil - consumption: 13,500 bbl/day (2001 est.)

Oil - exports: NA

Oil - imports: NA

Agriculture - products: pineapples, avocados, bananas, flowers, vegetables, sugarcane

Exports: $250 million f.o.b. (1997)

Exports - commodities: refined petroleum products, bananas, rum, pineapples (2001 est.)

Exports - partners: France 45%, Guadeloupe 28% (2000)

Imports: $2 billion c.i.f. (1997)

Imports - commodities: petroleum products, crude oil, foodstuffs, construction materials, vehicles, clothing and other consumer goods

Imports - partners: France 62%, Venezuela 6%, Germany 4%, Italy 4%, US 3% (2000)

Debt - external: $180 million (1994)

Economic aid - recipient: $NA; note - substantial annual aid from France (1998)

Currency: euro (EUR)

Currency code: EUR

Exchange rates: euros per US dollar - 0.8860 (2003), 1.0626 (2002), 1.1175 (2001), 1.0854 (2000), 0.9386 (1999); French francs per US dollar - 5.8995 (1998)

Fiscal year: calendar year

Communications

Telephones - main lines in use: 172,000 est (2001)

Telephones - mobile cellular: 319,900 (2002)

Telephone system:
general assessment: domestic facilities are adequate
domestic: NA
international: country code - 596; microwave radio relay to Guadeloupe, Dominica, and Saint Lucia; satellite earth stations - 2 Intelsat (Atlantic Ocean)

Radio broadcast stations: AM 0, FM 14, shortwave 0 (1998)

Television broadcast stations: 11 (plus nine repeaters) (1997)

Internet country code: .mq

Internet users: 40,000 (2002)

Transportation

Railways: 0 km

Highways:
total: 2,105 km
paved: NA km
unpaved: NA km (2000)

Waterways: none

Ports and harbors: Fort-de-France, La Trinite

Merchant marine: none

Airports: 2 (2003 est.)

Airports - with paved runways:
total: 1
over 3,047 m: 1 (2003 est.)

Airports - with unpaved runways:
total: 1
under 914 m: 1 (2003 est.)

Military

Military branches: no regular military forces; Gendarmerie

Military - note: defense is the responsibility of France

Transnational Issues

Disputes - international: none

Illicit drugs: transshipment point for cocaine and marijuana bound for the US and Europe

Mauritania

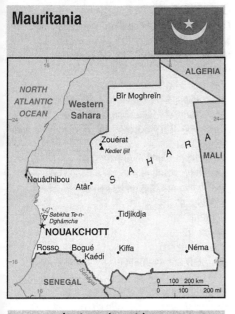

Introduction

Background: Independent from France in 1960, Mauritania annexed the southern third of the former Spanish Sahara (now Western Sahara) in 1976, but relinquished it after three years of raids by the Polisario guerrilla front seeking independence for the territory. Opposition parties were legalized and a new constitution approved in 1991. Two multiparty presidential elections since then were widely seen as flawed, but October 2001 legislative and municipal elections were generally free and open. Mauritania remains, in reality, a one-party state. The country continues to experience ethnic tensions between its black minority population and the dominant Maur (Arab-Berber) populace.

Geography

Location: Northern Africa, bordering the North Atlantic Ocean, between Senegal and Western Sahara

Geographic coordinates: 20 00 N, 12 00 W

Map references: Africa

Area:
total: 1,030,700 sq km
land: 1,030,400 sq km
water: 300 sq km

Area - comparative: slightly larger than three times the size of New Mexico

Land boundaries:
total: 5,074 km
border countries: Algeria 463 km, Mali 2,237 km, Senegal 813 km, Western Sahara 1,561 km

Coastline: 754 km

Maritime claims:
territorial sea: 12 NM
contiguous zone: 24 NM
exclusive economic zone: 200 NM
continental shelf: 200 NM or to the edge of the continental margin

Climate: desert; constantly hot, dry, dusty

Terrain: mostly barren, flat plains of the Sahara; some central hills

Elevation extremes:
lowest point: Sebkhet Te-n-Dghamcha -5 m
highest point: Kediet Ijill 915 m

Natural resources: iron ore, gypsum, copper, phosphate, diamonds, gold, oil, fish

Land use:
arable land: 0.48%
permanent crops: 0.01%
other: 99.51% (1998 est.)

Irrigated land: 490 sq km (1998 est.)

Natural hazards: hot, dry, dust/sand-laden sirocco wind blows primarily in March and April; periodic droughts

Environment - current issues: overgrazing, deforestation, and soil erosion aggravated by drought are contributing to desertification; very limited natural fresh water resources away from the Senegal, which is the only perennial river

Environment - international agreements:
party to: Biodiversity, Climate Change, Desertification, Endangered Species, Hazardous Wastes, Law of the Sea, Ozone Layer Protection, Ship Pollution, Wetlands
signed, but not ratified: none of the selected agreements

Geography - note: most of the population concentrated in the cities of Nouakchott and Nouadhibou and along the Senegal River in the southern part of the country

People

Population: 2,998,563 (July 2004 est.)

Age structure:
0-14 years: 45.9% (male 689,371; female 686,486)
15-64 years: 51.9% (male 767,551; female 788,520)
65 years and over: 2.2% (male 27,106; female 39,529) (2004 est.)

Median age:
total: 16.9 years
male: 16.7 years
female: 17.2 years (2004 est.)

Population growth rate: 2.91% (2004 est.)

Birth rate: 41.79 births/1,000 population (2004 est.)

Death rate: 12.74 deaths/1,000 population (2004 est.)

Net migration rate: 0 migrant(s)/1,000 population (2004 est.)

Sex ratio:
at birth: 1.03 male(s)/female
under 15 years: 1 male(s)/female
15-64 years: 0.97 male(s)/female
65 years and over: 0.69 male(s)/female
total population: 0.98 male(s)/female (2004 est.)

Infant mortality rate:
total: 72.35 deaths/1,000 live births
male: 75.22 deaths/1,000 live births
female: 69.39 deaths/1,000 live births (2004 est.)

Life expectancy at birth:
total population: 52.32 years
male: 50.15 years
female: 54.56 years (2004 est.)

Total fertility rate: 6.01 children born/woman (2004 est.)

HIV/AIDS - adult prevalence rate: 1.8% (2001 est.)

HIV/AIDS - people living with HIV/AIDS: 6,600 (1999 est.)

HIV/AIDS - deaths: 610 (2001 est.)

Nationality:
noun: Mauritanian(s)
adjective: Mauritanian

Ethnic groups: mixed Maur/black 40%, Maur 30%, black 30%

Religions: Muslim 100%

Languages: Hassaniya Arabic (official), Pulaar, Soninke, Wolof (official), French

Literacy:
definition: age 15 and over can read and write
total population: 41.7%
male: 51.8%
female: 31.9% (2003 est.)

Government

Country name:
conventional long form: Islamic Republic of Mauritania
conventional short form: Mauritania
local long form: Al Jumhuriyah al Islamiyah al Muritaniyah
local short form: Muritaniyah

Government type: republic

Capital: Nouakchott

Administrative divisions: 12 regions (regions, singular - region) and 1 capital district*; Adrar, Assaba, Brakna, Dakhlet Nouadhibou, Gorgol, Guidimaka, Hodh Ech Chargui, Hodh El Gharbi, Inchiri, Nouakchott*, Tagant, Tiris Zemmour, Trarza

Independence: 28 November 1960 (from France)

National holiday: Independence Day, 28 November (1960)

Constitution: 12 July 1991

Legal system: a combination of Shari'a (Islamic law) and French civil law

Suffrage: 18 years of age; universal

Executive branch:
chief of state: President Maaouya Ould Sid Ahmed TAYA (since 12 December 1984)
head of government: Prime Minister Sghair Ould M'BARECK (since 6 July 2003)
cabinet: Council of Ministers
elections: president elected by popular vote for a six-year term; election last held 7 November 2003 (next to be held NA 2009); prime minister appointed by the president
election results: President Maaouya Ould Sid Ahmed TAYA reelected for a third term with 60.8% of the vote

Legislative branch: bicameral legislature consists of the Senate or Majlis al-Shuyukh (56 seats, a part of the seats up for election every two years; members elected by municipal leaders to serve six-year terms) and the National Assembly or Majlis al-Watani (81 seats; members elected by popular vote to serve five-year terms)

elections: Senate - last held 12 April 2002 (next to be held NA April 2004); National Assembly - last held 19 and 26 October 2001 (next to be held NA 2006)

election results: Senate - percent of vote by party - NA%; seats by party - PRDS 54, RFD 1, UNDD 1; National Assembly - percent of vote by party - PRDS 79%, RDU 3.5%, UDP 3.5%, AC 5%, UFP 3.5%, FP 1.5%; seats by party - PRDS 64, UDP 3, RDU 3, AC 4, RFD 3, UFP 3, and FP 1

Judicial branch: Supreme Court or Cour Supreme; Court of Appeals; lower courts

Political parties and leaders: Action for Change or AC [Messoud Ould BOULKHEIR]; Alliance for Justice and Democracy or AJD [Kebe ABDOULAYE]; Democratic and Social Republican Party or PRDS (ruling party) [President Maaouya Ould Sid Ahmed TAYA]; Mauritanian Party for Renewal and Concorde or PMRC [Molaye El Hassen Ould JIYID]; National Union for Democracy and Development or UNDD [Tidjane KOITA]; Party for Liberty, Equality and Justice or PLEJ [Daouda M'BAGNIGA]; Popular Front or FP [Ch'bih Ould CHEIKH MALAININE]; Popular Progress Alliance or APP [Mohamed El Hafed Ould ISMAEL]; Popular Social and Democratic Union or UPSD [Mohamed Mahmoud Ould MAH]; Progress Force Union or UFP [Mohamed Ould MAOULOUD]; Rally of Democratic Forces or RFD [Ahmed Ould DADDAH]; Rally for Democracy and Unity or RDU [Ahmed Ould SIDI BABA]; Union for Democracy and Progress or UDP [Naha Mint MOUKNASS]

note: the Action for Change party was banned in January 2002; parties legalized by constitution ratified 12 July 1991, however, politics continue to be tribally based

Political pressure groups and leaders: Arab nationalists; Ba'athists; General Confederation of Mauritanian Workers or CGTM [Abdallahi Ould MOHAMED, secretary general]; Independent Confederation of Mauritanian Workers or CLTM [Samory Ould BEYE]; Islamists; Mauritanian Workers Union or UTM [Mohamed Ely Ould BRAHIM, secretary general]

International organization participation: ABEDA, ACCT, ACP, AfDB, AFESD, AMF, AMU, AU, CAEU, ECOWAS, FAO, G-77, IBRD, ICAO, ICFTU, ICRM, IDA, IDB, IFAD, IFC, IFRCS, IHO (pending member), ILO, IMF, IMO, Interpol, IOC, IOM, ITU, LAS, NAM, OIC, OPCW, UN, UNCTAD, UNESCO, UNIDO, UPU, WCL, WCO, WHO, WIPO, WMO, WToO, WTrO

Diplomatic representation in the US:

chief of mission: Ambassador Mohamedou Ould MICHEL

chancery: 2129 Leroy Place NW, Washington, DC 20008

telephone: [1] (202) 232-5700

FAX: [1] (202) 319-2623

Diplomatic representation from the US:

chief of mission: Ambassador Joseph E. LEBARON

embassy: Rue Abdallaye (between Presidency building and Spanish Embassy), Nouakchott

mailing address: BP 222, Nouakchott

telephone: [222] 25-26-60, 25-26-63, 25-11-41, 25-11-45

FAX: [222] 25-25-92

Flag description: green with a yellow five-pointed star above a yellow, horizontal crescent; the closed side of the crescent is down; the crescent, star, and color green are traditional symbols of Islam

Economy

Economy - overview: Half the population still depends on agriculture and livestock for a livelihood, even though many of the nomads and subsistence farmers were forced into the cities by recurrent droughts in the 1970s and 1980s. Mauritania has extensive deposits of iron ore, which account for nearly 40% of total exports. The decline in world demand for this ore, however, has led to cutbacks in production. The nation's coastal waters are among the richest fishing areas in the world, but overexploitation by foreigners threatens this key source of revenue. The country's first deepwater port opened near Nouakchott in 1986. In the past, drought and economic mismanagement resulted in a buildup of foreign debt. In February 2000, Mauritania qualified for debt relief under the Heavily Indebted Poor Countries (HIPC) initiative and in December 2001 received strong support from donor and lending countries at a triennial Consultative Group review. In 2001, exploratory oil wells in tracts 80 km offshore indicated potential extraction at current world oil prices. A new investment code approved in December 2001 improved the opportunities for direct foreign investment. Ongoing negotiations with the IMF involve problems of economic reforms and fiscal discipline. Substantial oil production and exports probably will not begin until 2005. Meantime the government emphasizes reduction of poverty, improvement of health and education, and promoting privatization of the economy.

GDP: purchasing power parity - $5.195 billion (2003 est.)

GDP - real growth rate: 4.5% (2003 est.)

GDP - per capita: purchasing power parity - $1,800 (2003 est.)

GDP - composition by sector:

agriculture: 25%

industry: 29%

services: 46% (2001 est.)

Population below poverty line: 50% (2001 est.)

Household income or consumption by percentage share:

lowest 10%: 2.5%

highest 10%: 30.2% (2000)

Distribution of family income - Gini index: 37.3 (1995)

Inflation rate (consumer prices): 7% (2003 est.)

Labor force: 786,000 (2001)

Labor force - by occupation: agriculture 50%, services 40%, industry 10% (2001 est.)

Unemployment rate: 21% (1999 est.)

Budget:

revenues: $421 million

expenditures: $378 million, including capital expenditures of $154 million (2002 est.)

Industries: fish processing, mining of iron ore and gypsum

Industrial production growth rate: 2% (2000 est.)

Electricity - production: 157.4 million kWh (2001)

Electricity - production by source:

fossil fuel: 85.9%

hydro: 14.1%

nuclear: 0%

other: 0% (2001)

Electricity - consumption: 146.3 million kWh (2001)

Electricity - exports: 0 kWh (2001)

Electricity - imports: 0 kWh (2001)

Oil - production: 0 bbl/day (2001 est.)

Oil - consumption: 24,000 bbl/day (2001 est.)

Oil - exports: NA

Oil - imports: NA

Agriculture - products: dates, millet, sorghum, rice, corn, dates; cattle, sheep

Exports: $541 million f.o.b. (2002)

Exports - commodities: iron ore, fish and fish products, gold

Exports - partners: Italy 14.2%, France 13.9%, Spain 11.6%, Germany 10.7%, Belgium 9.8%, Japan 7% (2002)

Imports: $860 million f.o.b. (2002)

Imports - commodities: machinery and equipment, petroleum products, capital goods, foodstuffs, consumer goods

Imports - partners: France 17.6%, Belgium 7.4%, China 6.6%, Spain 5.7%, Germany 5% (2002)

Debt - external: $2.5 billion (2000)

Economic aid - recipient: $220 million (2000)

Currency: ouguiya (MRO)

Currency code: MRO

Exchange rates: ouguiyas per US dollar - NA (2003), 271.739 (2002), 255.629 (2001)

Fiscal year: calendar year

Communications

Telephones - main lines in use: 31,500 (2002)

Telephones - mobile cellular: 247,200 (2002)

Telephone system:

general assessment: limited system of cable and open-wire lines, minor microwave radio relay links, and radiotelephone communications stations (improvements being made)

domestic: mostly cable and open-wire lines; a recently completed domestic satellite telecommunications system links Nouakchott with regional capitals

international: country code - 222; satellite earth stations - 1 Intelsat (Atlantic Ocean) and 2 Arabsat

Mauritania *(continued)*

Radio broadcast stations: AM 1, FM 14, shortwave 1 (2001)
Television broadcast stations: 1 (2002)
Internet country code: .mr
Internet hosts: 79 (2002)
Internet users: 10,000 (2002)

Transportation

Railways: 717 km
standard gauge: 717 km 1.435-m gauge (2002)
Highways:
total: 7,720 km
paved: 830 km
unpaved: 6,890 km (2000)
Waterways:
note: ferry traffic on the Senegal River
Ports and harbors: Bogue, Kaedi, Nouadhibou, Nouakchott, Rosso
Merchant marine: none
Airports: 24 (2003 est.)
Airports - with paved runways:
total: 8
2,438 to 3,047 m: 3
1,524 to 2,437 m: 5 (2003 est.)
Airports - with unpaved runways:
total: 16
1,524 to 2,437 m: 9
914 to 1,523 m: 6
under 914 m: 1 (2003 est.)

Military

Military branches: Army, Navy (including Naval Infantry), Air Force, National Gendarmerie, National Guard, National Police, Presidential Guard (BSSP)
Military manpower - availability:
males age 15-49: 686,629 (2004 est.)
Military manpower - fit for military service:
males age 15-49: 332,633 (2004 est.)
Military expenditures - dollar figure: $40.8 million (2003)
Military expenditures - percent of GDP: 3.7% (2003)

Transnational Issues

Disputes - international: Mauritanian claims to Western Sahara have been dormant in recent years

Mauritius

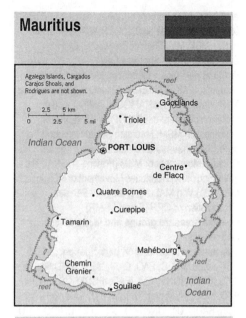

Agalega Islands, Cargados Carajos Shoals, and Rodrigues are not shown.

Indian Ocean

Introduction

Background: Discovered by the Portuguese in 1505, Mauritius was subsequently held by the Dutch, French, and British before independence was attained in 1968. A stable democracy with regular free elections and a positive human rights record, the country has attracted considerable foreign investment and has earned one of Africa's highest per capita incomes. Recent poor weather and declining sugar prices have slowed economic growth, leading to some protests over standards of living in the Creole community.

Geography

Location: Southern Africa, island in the Indian Ocean, east of Madagascar
Geographic coordinates: 20 17 S, 57 33 E
Map references: Political Map of the World
Area:
total: 2,040 sq km
land: 2,030 sq km
water: 10 sq km
note: includes Agalega Islands, Cargados Carajos Shoals (Saint Brandon), and Rodrigues
Area - comparative: almost 11 times the size of Washington, DC
Land boundaries: 0 km
Coastline: 177 km
Maritime claims:
territorial sea: 12 NM
exclusive economic zone: 200 NM
continental shelf: 200 NM or to the edge of the continental margin
Climate: tropical, modified by southeast trade winds; warm, dry winter (May to November); hot, wet, humid summer (November to May)
Terrain: small coastal plain rising to discontinuous mountains encircling central plateau

Elevation extremes:
lowest point: Indian Ocean 0 m
highest point: Mont Piton 828 m
Natural resources: arable land, fish
Land use:
arable land: 49.26%
permanent crops: 2.96%
other: 47.78% (2000 est.)
Irrigated land: 200 sq km (2000 est.)
Natural hazards: cyclones (November to April); almost completely surrounded by reefs that may pose maritime hazards
Environment - current issues: water pollution, degradation of coral reefs
Environment - international agreements:
party to: Biodiversity, Climate Change, Climate Change-Kyoto Protocol, Desertification, Endangered Species, Environmental Modification, Hazardous Wastes, Law of the Sea, Marine Life Conservation, Ozone Layer Protection, Ship Pollution, Wetlands
signed, but not ratified: none of the selected agreements
Geography - note: the main island, from which the country derives its name, is of volcanic origin and is almost entirely surrounded by coral reefs

People

Population: 1,220,481 (July 2004 est.)
Age structure:
0-14 years: 24.8% (male 152,424; female 149,908)
15-64 years: 68.8% (male 418,836; female 420,411)
65 years and over: 6.5% (male 31,104; female 47,798) (2004 est.)
Median age:
total: 30.1 years
male: 29.3 years
female: 31.1 years (2004 est.)
Population growth rate: 0.81% (2004 est.)
Birth rate: 15.85 births/1,000 population (2004 est.)
Death rate: 6.82 deaths/1,000 population (2004 est.)
Net migration rate: -0.9 migrant(s)/1,000 population (2004 est.)
Sex ratio:
at birth: 1.02 male(s)/female
under 15 years: 1.02 male(s)/female
15-64 years: 1 male(s)/female
65 years and over: 0.65 male(s)/female
total population: 0.98 male(s)/female (2004 est.)
Infant mortality rate:
total: 15.57 deaths/1,000 live births
male: 18.36 deaths/1,000 live births
female: 12.73 deaths/1,000 live births (2004 est.)
Life expectancy at birth:
total population: 72.09 years
male: 68.11 years
female: 76.13 years (2004 est.)
Total fertility rate: 1.97 children born/woman (2004 est.)
HIV/AIDS - adult prevalence rate: 0.1% (2001 est.)
HIV/AIDS - people living with HIV/AIDS: 700 (2001 est.)

Mauritius *(continued)*

HIV/AIDS - deaths: less than 100 (2001 est.)
Nationality:
noun: Mauritian(s)
adjective: Mauritian
Ethnic groups: Indo-Mauritian 68%, Creole 27%, Sino-Mauritian 3%, Franco-Mauritian 2%
Religions: Hindu 52%, Christian 28.3% (Roman Catholic 26%, Protestant 2.3%), Muslim 16.6%, other 3.1%
Languages: English (official), Creole, French (official), Hindi, Urdu, Hakka, Bhojpuri
Literacy:
definition: age 15 and over can read and write
total population: 85.6%
male: 88.6%
female: 82.7% (2003 est.)

Government

Country name:
conventional long form: Republic of Mauritius
conventional short form: Mauritius
Government type: parliamentary democracy
Capital: Port Louis
Administrative divisions: 9 districts and 3 dependencies*; Agalega Islands*, Black River, Cargados Carajos Shoals*, Flacq, Grand Port, Moka, Pamplemousses, Plaines Wilhems, Port Louis, Riviere du Rempart, Rodrigues*, Savanne
Independence: 12 March 1968 (from UK)
National holiday: Independence Day, 12 March (1968)
Constitution: 12 March 1968; amended 12 March 1992
Legal system: based on French civil law system with elements of English common law in certain areas
Suffrage: 18 years of age; universal
Executive branch:
chief of state: President Sir Anerood JUGNAUTH (since 7 October 2003) and Vice President Abdool Raouf BUNDHUN (since 25 February 2002)
head of government: Prime Minister Paul BERENGER (since 30 September 2003)
cabinet: Council of Ministers appointed by the president on the recommendation of the prime minister
elections: president and vice president elected by the National Assembly for five-year terms; election last held 25 February 2002 (next to be held NA 2007); prime minister and deputy prime minister appointed by the president, responsible to the National Assembly
election results: Karl OFFMANN elected president and Raouf BUNDHUN elected vice president; percent of vote by the National Assembly - NA%; note - Karl OFFMANN stepped down on 30 September 2003
Legislative branch: unicameral National Assembly (66 seats; 62 elected by popular vote, 4 appointed by the election commission from the losing political parties to give representation to various ethnic minorities; members serve five-year terms)
elections: last held on 11 September 2000 (next to be held NA September 2004)

election results: percent of vote by party - MSM/MMM 52.3%, MLP/PMSD 36.9%, OPR 10.8%; seats by party - MSM/MMM 54, MLP/PMSD 6, OPR 2
Judicial branch: Supreme Court
Political parties and leaders: Hizbullah [Cehl Mohamed FAKEEMEEAH]; Mauritian Labor Party or MLP [Navinchandra RAMGOOLAM]; Mauritian Militant Movement or MMM [Paul BERENGER] - in coalition with MSM; Mauritian Social Democrat Party or PMSD [Charles Xavier-Luc DUVAL]; Militant Socialist Movement or MSM [Pravind JUGNAUTH] - governing party; Rodrigues Movement or MR [Joseph (Nicholas) Von MALLY]; Rodrigues Peoples Organization or OPR [Serge CLAIR]
Political pressure groups and leaders: various labor unions
International organization participation: ACCT, ACP, AfDB, AU, C, FAO, G-77, IAEA, IBRD, ICAO, ICCt, ICFTU, ICRM, IDA, IFAD, IFC, IFRCS, ILO, IMF, IMO, InOC, Interpol, IOC, ISO, ITU, NAM, OPCW, PCA, SADC, UN, UNCTAD, UNESCO, UNIDO, UPU, WCL, WCO, WFTU, WHO, WIPO, WMO, WToO, WTrO
Diplomatic representation in the US:
chief of mission: Ambassador Usha JEETAH
chancery: 4301 Connecticut Avenue NW, Suite 441, Washington, DC 20008
telephone: [1] (202) 244-1491, 1492
FAX: [1] (202) 966-0983
Diplomatic representation from the US:
chief of mission: Ambassador John PRICE
embassy: 4th Floor, Rogers House, John Kennedy Street, Port Louis
mailing address: international mail: P. O. Box 544, Port Louis; US mail: American Embassy, Port Louis, Department of State, Washington, DC 20521-2450
telephone: [230] 202-4400
FAX: [230] 208-9534
Flag description: four equal horizontal bands of red (top), blue, yellow, and green

Economy

Economy - overview: Since independence in 1968, Mauritius has developed from a low-income, agriculturally based economy to a middle-income diversified economy with growing industrial, financial, and tourist sectors. For most of the period, annual growth has been in the order of 5% to 6%. This remarkable achievement has been reflected in more equitable income distribution, increased life expectancy, lowered infant mortality, and a much-improved infrastructure. Sugarcane is grown on about 90% of the cultivated land area and accounts for 25% of export earnings. The government's development strategy centers on expanding local financial institutions and building a domestic information telecommunications industry. Mauritius has attracted more than 9,000 offshore entities, many aimed at commerce in India and South Africa, and investment in the banking sector alone has reached over $1 billion. Mauritius, with its strong textile sector

and responsible fiscal management, has been well poised to take advantage of the Africa Growth and Opportunity Act (AGOA).
GDP: purchasing power parity - $13.85 billion (2003 est.)
GDP - real growth rate: 4.1% (2003 est.)
GDP - per capita: purchasing power parity - $11,400 (2003 est.)
GDP - composition by sector:
agriculture: 6%
industry: 33%
services: 61% (1999 est.)
Population below poverty line: 10% (2001 est.)
Household income or consumption by percentage share:
lowest 10%: NA%
highest 10%: NA%
Distribution of family income - Gini index: 37 (1987 est.)
Inflation rate (consumer prices): 6.4% (2002 est.)
Labor force: 514,000 (1995)
Labor force - by occupation: construction and industry 36%, services 24%, agriculture and fishing 14%, trade, restaurants, hotels 16%, transportation and communication 7%, finance 3% (1995)
Unemployment rate: 8.8% (2002 est.)
Budget:
revenues: $1.1 billion
expenditures: $1.2 billion, including capital expenditures of $NA (1999 est.)
Industries: food processing (largely sugar milling), textiles, clothing; chemicals, metal products, transport equipment, nonelectrical machinery; tourism
Industrial production growth rate: 8% (2000 est.)
Electricity - production: 1.311 billion kWh (2001)
Electricity - production by source:
fossil fuel: 90.8%
hydro: 9.2%
nuclear: 0%
other: 0% (2001)
Electricity - consumption: 1.219 billion kWh (2001)
Electricity - exports: 0 kWh (2001)
Electricity - imports: 0 kWh (2001)
Oil - production: 0 bbl/day (2001 est.)
Oil - consumption: 21,000 bbl/day (2001 est.)
Oil - exports: NA
Oil - imports: NA
Agriculture - products: sugarcane, tea, corn, potatoes, bananas, pulses; cattle, goats; fish
Exports: $1.965 billion f.o.b. (2003 est.)
Exports - commodities: clothing and textiles, sugar, cut flowers, molasses
Exports - partners: UK 30.5%, France 20.3%, US 20.2%, Madagascar 4% (2002)
Imports: $2.136 billion f.o.b. (2003 est.)
Imports - commodities: manufactured goods, capital equipment, foodstuffs, petroleum products, chemicals
Imports - partners: South Africa 12.6%, France 11%, China 8.5%, India 7.3%, Australia 4% (2002)
Debt - external: $2.4 billion (2002 est.)

Mauritius (continued)

Economic aid - recipient: $42 million (1997)
Currency: Mauritian rupee (MUR)
Currency code: MUR
Exchange rates: Mauritian rupees per US dollar -
27.9015 (2003), 29.962 (2002), 29.1293 (2001),
26.2496 (2000), 25.1858 (1999)
Fiscal year: 1 July - 30 June

Communications

Telephones - main lines in use: 327,200 (2002)
Telephones - mobile cellular: 350,000 (2002)
Telephone system:
general assessment: small system with good service
domestic: primarily microwave radio relay trunk
system
international: country code - 230; satellite earth
station - 1 Intelsat (Indian Ocean); new microwave link
to Reunion; HF radiotelephone links to several
countries; fiber optic submarine cable (SAT-3/WASC/
SAFE) provides connectivity to Europe and Asia
Radio broadcast stations: AM 4, FM 9,
shortwave 0 (2002)
Television broadcast stations: 2 (plus several
repeaters) (1997)
Internet country code: .mu
Internet hosts: 3,462 (2002)
Internet users: 120,000 (2002)

Transportation

Railways: 0 km
Highways:
total: 1,926 km
paved: 1,868 km (including 44 km of expressways)
unpaved: 58 km (2000)
Waterways: none
Ports and harbors: Port Louis
Merchant marine:
total: 8 ships (1,000 GRT or over) 22,946 GRT/27,102
DWT
by type: cargo 1, combination bulk 4, passenger/
cargo 1, refrigerated cargo 2
foreign-owned: Belgium 1, India 4, Switzerland 2
(2003 est.)
Airports: 5 (2003 est.)
Airports - with paved runways:
total: 2
over 3,047 m: 1
914 to 1,523 m: 1 (2003 est.)
Airports - with unpaved runways:
total: 3
914 to 1,523 m: 2
under 914 m: 1 (2003 est.)

Military

Military branches: National Police Force (includes
the paramilitary Special Mobile Force or SMF and
National Coast Guard)
Military manpower - availability:
males age 15-49: 342,482 (2004 est.)
Military manpower - fit for military service:
males age 15-49: 172,157 (2004 est.)

Military expenditures - dollar figure: $11.2 million
(2003)
Military expenditures - percent of GDP: 0.2%
(2003)

Transnational Issues

Disputes - international: Mauritius claims the
Chagos Archipelago (UK-administered British Indian
Ocean Territory), and its former inhabitants, who
reside chiefly in Mauritius, were granted UK
citizenship and the right to repatriation in 2001; claims
French-administered Tromelin Island
Illicit drugs: minor consumer and transshipment
point for heroin from South Asia; small amounts of
cannabis produced and consumed locally; significant
offshore financial industry creates potential for money
laundering, but corruption levels are relatively low and
the government appears generally to be committed to
regulating its banking industry

Mayotte
*(territorial collectivity
of France)*

Administered by FRANCE,
claimed by COMOROS.

Introduction

Background: Mayotte was ceded to France along
with the other islands of the Comoros group in 1843. It
was the only island in the archipelago that voted in
1974 to retain its link with France and forego
independence.

Geography

Location: Southern Africa, island in the Mozambique
Channel, about one-half of the way from northern
Madagascar to northern Mozambique
Geographic coordinates: 12 50 S, 45 10 E
Map references: Africa
Area:
total: 374 sq km
land: 374 sq km
water: 0 sq km
Area - comparative: slightly more than twice the
size of Washington, DC
Land boundaries: 0 km
Coastline: 185.2 km
Maritime claims:
territorial sea: 12 NM
exclusive economic zone: 200 NM
Climate: tropical; marine; hot, humid, rainy season
during northeastern monsoon (November to May); dry
season is cooler (May to November)
Terrain: generally undulating, with deep ravines and
ancient volcanic peaks
Elevation extremes:
lowest point: Indian Ocean 0 m
highest point: Benara 660 m
Natural resources: NEGL
Land use:
arable land: NA%
permanent crops: NA%
other: NA% (1998 est.)
Irrigated land: NA sq km
Natural hazards: cyclones during rainy season

Mayotte *(continued)*

Environment - current issues: NA
Geography - note: part of Comoro Archipelago; 18 islands

People

Population: 186,026 (July 2004 est.)
Age structure:
0-14 years: 46.4% (male 43,301; female 42,934)
15-64 years: 51.9% (male 52,534; female 44,100)
65 years and over: 1.7% (male 1,579; female 1,578)
(2004 est.)
Median age:
total: 16.9 years
male: 18.1 years
female: 15.8 years (2004 est.)
Population growth rate: 4.09% (2004 est.)
Birth rate: 42.19 births/1,000 population (2004 est.)
Death rate: 8.11 deaths/1,000 population (2004 est.)
Net migration rate: 6.78 migrant(s)/1,000 population (2004 est.)
Sex ratio:
at birth: 1.03 male(s)/female
under 15 years: 1.01 male(s)/female
15-64 years: 1.19 male(s)/female
65 years and over: 1 male(s)/female
total population: 1.1 male(s)/female (2004 est.)
Infant mortality rate:
total: 64.19 deaths/1,000 live births
male: 70.42 deaths/1,000 live births
female: 57.78 deaths/1,000 live births (2004 est.)
Life expectancy at birth:
total population: 60.99 years
male: 58.85 years
female: 63.2 years (2004 est.)
Total fertility rate: 5.98 children born/woman (2004 est.)
HIV/AIDS - adult prevalence rate: NA%
HIV/AIDS - people living with HIV/AIDS: NA
HIV/AIDS - deaths: NA
Nationality:
noun: Mahorais (singular and plural)
adjective: Mahoran
Ethnic groups: NA
Religions: Muslim 97%, Christian (mostly Roman Catholic)
Languages: Mahorian (a Swahili dialect), French (official language) spoken by 35% of the population
Literacy:
definition: NA
total population: NA%
male: NA%
female: NA%

Government

Country name:
conventional long form: Territorial Collectivity of Mayotte
conventional short form: Mayotte
Dependency status: territorial collectivity of France

Government type: NA
Capital: Mamoutzou
Administrative divisions: none (territorial collectivity of France)
Independence: none (territorial collectivity of France)
National holiday: Bastille Day, 14 July (1789)
Constitution: 28 September 1958 (French Constitution)
Legal system: French law
Suffrage: 18 years of age; universal
Executive branch:
chief of state: President Jacques CHIRAC of France (since 17 May 1995), represented by Prefect Jean-Jacques BROT (since 3 July 2002)
head of government: President of the General Council Younoussa BAMANA (since NA 1977)
cabinet: NA
elections: French president elected by popular vote for a five-year term; prefect appointed by the French president on the advice of the French Ministry of the Interior; president of the General Council elected by the members of the General Council for a six-year term
Legislative branch: unicameral General Council or Conseil General (19 seats; members are elected by popular vote to serve three-year terms)
elections: last held 7 October 2000 (next to be held NA 2003)
election results: percent of vote by party - NA%; seats by party - NA
note: Mayotte elects one member of the French Senate; elections last held 24 September 2001 (next to be held NA September 2007); results - percent of vote by party - NA%; seats by party - NA; Mayotte also elects one member to the French National Assembly; elections last held 16 June 2002 (next to be held as a special election on NA June 2005); results - percent of vote by party - UMP-RPR 55.08%, UDF 44.92%; seats by party - UMP-RPR 1
Judicial branch: Supreme Court or Tribunal Superieur d'Appel
Political parties and leaders: Democratic Front or FD [Youssouf MOUSSA]; Mahoran Popular Movement or MPM [Ahmed MADI]; Federation of Mahorans or RPR [Mansour KAMARDINE]; Movement for Department Status Mayotte or MDM [Mouhoutar SALIM]; Socialist Party or PS (local branch of French Parti Socialiste) [Ibrahim ABUBACAR]; Union for French Democracy or UDF [Henri JEAN-BAPTISTE]
Political pressure groups and leaders: NA
International organization participation: none
Diplomatic representation in the US: none (territorial collectivity of France)
Diplomatic representation from the US: none (territorial collectivity of France)
Flag description: the flag of France is used

Economy

Economy - overview: Economic activity is based primarily on the agricultural sector, including fishing and livestock raising. Mayotte is not self-sufficient and must import a large portion of its food requirements, mainly from France. The economy and future development of the island are heavily dependent on French financial assistance, an important supplement to GDP. Mayotte's remote location is an obstacle to the development of tourism.
GDP: purchasing power parity - $85 million (1998 est.)
GDP - real growth rate: NA%
GDP - per capita: purchasing power parity - $2,600 (1998 est.)
GDP - composition by sector:
agriculture: NA%
industry: NA%
services: NA% (2001 est.)
Population below poverty line: NA%
Household income or consumption by percentage share:
lowest 10%: NA%
highest 10%: NA%
Inflation rate (consumer prices): NA%
Labor force: 48,800 (2000)
Unemployment rate: 38% (1999)
Budget:
revenues: $NA
expenditures: $73 million, including capital expenditures of $NA (1991 est.)
Industries: newly created lobster and shrimp industry, construction
Industrial production growth rate: NA%
Electricity - production: NA kWh
Electricity - production by source:
fossil fuel: 0%
hydro: 0%
nuclear: 0%
other: 0%
Electricity - consumption: NA kWh
Agriculture - products: vanilla, ylang-ylang (perfume essence), coffee, copra
Exports: $3.44 million f.o.b. (1997)
Exports - commodities: ylang-ylang (perfume essence), vanilla, copra, coconuts, coffee, cinnamon
Exports - partners: France 80%, Comoros 15%, Reunion (2000)
Imports: $141.3 million f.o.b. (1997)
Imports - commodities: food, machinery and equipment, transportation equipment, metals, chemicals
Imports - partners: France 66%, Africa 14%, Southeast Asia 11% (2000 est.)
Debt - external: $NA
Economic aid - recipient: $107.7 million; note - extensive French financial assistance (1995)
Currency: euro (EUR)
Currency code: EUR

Mayotte *(continued)*

Exchange rates: euros per US dollar - 0.8860 (2003), 1.0626 (2002), 1.1175 (2001), 1.0854 (2000), 0.9386 (1999)
Fiscal year: calendar year

Communications

Telephones - main lines in use: 10,000 (2001)
Telephones - mobile cellular: 21,700 (2002)
Telephone system:
general assessment: small system administered by French Department of Posts and Telecommunications
domestic: NA
international: country code - 269; microwave radio relay and HF radiotelephone communications to Comoros (2001)
Radio broadcast stations: AM 1, FM 5, shortwave 0 (2001)
Television broadcast stations: 3 (2001)
Internet country code: .yt
Internet users: NA

Transportation

Railways: 0 km
Highways:
total: 93 km
paved: 72 km
unpaved: 21 km
Waterways: none
Ports and harbors: Dzaoudzi
Merchant marine: none
Airports: 1 (2003 est.)
Airports - with paved runways:
total: 1
1,524 to 2,437 m: 1 (2003 est.)

Military

Military - note: defense is the responsibility of France; small contingent of French forces stationed on the island

Transnational Issues

Disputes - international: claimed by Comoros

Mexico

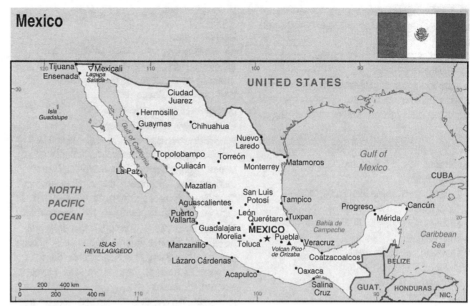

Introduction

Background: The site of advanced Amerindian civilizations, Mexico came under Spanish rule for three centuries before achieving independence early in the 19th century. A devaluation of the peso in late 1994 threw Mexico into economic turmoil, triggering the worst recession in over half a century. The nation continues to make an impressive recovery. Ongoing economic and social concerns include low real wages, underemployment for a large segment of the population, inequitable income distribution, and few advancement opportunities for the largely Amerindian population in the impoverished southern states. Elections held in July 2000 marked the first time since the 1910 Mexican Revolution that the opposition defeated the party in government, the Institutional Revolutionary Party (PRI). Vicente FOX of the National Action Party (PAN) was sworn in on 1 December 2000 as the first chief executive elected in free and fair elections.

Geography

Location: Middle America, bordering the Caribbean Sea and the Gulf of Mexico, between Belize and the US and bordering the North Pacific Ocean, between Guatemala and the US
Geographic coordinates: 23 00 N, 102 00 W
Map references: North America
Area:
total: 1,972,550 sq km
land: 1,923,040 sq km
water: 49,510 sq km
Area - comparative: slightly less than three times the size of Texas
Land boundaries:
total: 4,353 km
border countries: Belize 250 km, Guatemala 962 km, US 3,141 km
Coastline: 9,330 km

Maritime claims:
territorial sea: 12 NM
contiguous zone: 24 NM
exclusive economic zone: 200 NM
continental shelf: 200 NM or to the edge of the continental margin
Climate: varies from tropical to desert
Terrain: high, rugged mountains; low coastal plains; high plateaus; desert
Elevation extremes:
lowest point: Laguna Salada -10 m
highest point: Volcan Pico de Orizaba 5,700 m
Natural resources: petroleum, silver, copper, gold, lead, zinc, natural gas, timber
Land use:
arable land: 13.2%
permanent crops: 1.1%
other: 85.7% (1998 est.)
Irrigated land: 65,000 sq km (1998 est.)
Natural hazards: tsunamis along the Pacific coast, volcanoes and destructive earthquakes in the center and south, and hurricanes on the Pacific, Gulf of Mexico, and Caribbean coasts
Environment - current issues: scarcity of hazardous waste disposal facilities; rural to urban migration; natural fresh water resources scarce and polluted in north, inaccessible and poor quality in center and extreme southeast; raw sewage and industrial effluents polluting rivers in urban areas; deforestation; widespread erosion; desertification; deteriorating agricultural lands; serious air and water pollution in the national capital and urban centers along US-Mexico border; land subsidence in Valley of Mexico caused by groundwater depletion
note: the government considers the lack of clean water and deforestation national security issues
Environment - international agreements:
party to: Biodiversity, Climate Change, Climate Change-Kyoto Protocol, Desertification, Endangered Species, Hazardous Wastes, Law of the

Mexico (continued)

Sea, Marine Dumping, Marine Life Conservation, Ozone Layer Protection, Ship Pollution, Wetlands, Whaling

signed, but not ratified: none of the selected agreements

Geography - note: strategic location on southern border of US; corn (maize), one of the world's major grain crops, is thought to have originated in Mexico

People

Population: 104,959,594 (July 2004 est.)

Age structure:

0-14 years: 31.6% (male 16,913,290; female 16,228,552)

15-64 years: 62.9% (male 31,975,391; female 34,090,440)

65 years and over: 5.5% (male 2,618,713; female 3,133,208) (2004 est.)

Median age:

total: 24.6 years

male: 23.7 years

female: 25.5 years (2004 est.)

Population growth rate: 1.18% (2004 est.)

Birth rate: 21.44 births/1,000 population (2004 est.)

Death rate: 4.73 deaths/1,000 population (2004 est.)

Net migration rate: -4.87 migrant(s)/1,000 population (2004 est.)

Sex ratio:

at birth: 1.05 male(s)/female

under 15 years: 1.04 male(s)/female

15-64 years: 0.94 male(s)/female

65 years and over: 0.84 male(s)/female

total population: 0.96 male(s)/female (2004 est.)

Infant mortality rate:

total: 21.69 deaths/1,000 live births

male: 23.63 deaths/1,000 live births

female: 19.65 deaths/1,000 live births (2004 est.)

Life expectancy at birth:

total population: 74.94 years

male: 72.18 years

female: 77.83 years (2004 est.)

Total fertility rate: 2.49 children born/woman (2004 est.)

HIV/AIDS - adult prevalence rate: 0.3% (2001 est.)

HIV/AIDS - people living with HIV/AIDS: 150,000 (2001 est.)

HIV/AIDS - deaths: 4,200 (2001 est.)

Nationality:

noun: Mexican(s)

adjective: Mexican

Ethnic groups: mestizo (Amerindian-Spanish) 60%, Amerindian or predominantly Amerindian 30%, white 9%, other 1%

Religions: nominally Roman Catholic 89%, Protestant 6%, other 5%

Languages: Spanish, various Mayan, Nahuatl, and other regional indigenous languages

Literacy:

definition: age 15 and over can read and write

total population: 92.2%

male: 94%

female: 90.5% (2003 est.)

Government

Country name:

conventional long form: United Mexican States

conventional short form: Mexico

local long form: Estados Unidos Mexicanos

local short form: Mexico

Government type: federal republic

Capital: Mexico (Distrito Federal)

Administrative divisions: 31 states (estados, singular - estado) and 1 federal district* (distrito federal); Aguascalientes, Baja California, Baja California Sur, Campeche, Chiapas, Chihuahua, Coahuila de Zaragoza, Colima, Distrito Federal*, Durango, Guanajuato, Guerrero, Hidalgo, Jalisco, Mexico, Michoacan de Ocampo, Morelos, Nayarit, Nuevo Leon, Oaxaca, Puebla, Queretaro de Arteaga, Quintana Roo, San Luis Potosi, Sinaloa, Sonora, Tabasco, Tamaulipas, Tlaxcala, Veracruz-Llave, Yucatan, Zacatecas

Independence: 16 September 1810 (from Spain)

National holiday: Independence Day, 16 September (1810)

Constitution: 5 February 1917

Legal system: mixture of US constitutional theory and civil law system; judicial review of legislative acts; accepts compulsory ICJ jurisdiction, with reservations

Suffrage: 18 years of age; universal and compulsory (but not enforced)

Executive branch:

chief of state: President Vicente FOX Quesada (since 1 December 2000); note - the president is both the chief of state and head of government

head of government: President Vicente FOX Quesada (since 1 December 2000); note - the president is both the chief of state and head of government

cabinet: Cabinet appointed by the president; note - appointment of attorney general requires consent of the Senate

elections: president elected by popular vote for a six-year term; election last held 2 July 2000 (next to be held NA July 2006)

election results: Vicente FOX Quesada elected president; percent of vote - Vicente FOX Quesada (PAN) 42.52%, Francisco LABASTIDA Ochoa (PRI) 36.1%, Cuauhtemoc CARDENAS Solorzano (PRD) 16.64%, other 4.74%

Legislative branch: bicameral National Congress or Congreso de la Union consists of the Senate or Camara de Senadores (128 seats; 96 are elected by popular vote to serve six-year terms, and 32 are allocated on the basis of each party's popular vote) and the Federal Chamber of Deputies or Camara Federal de Diputados (500 seats; 300 members are directly elected by popular vote to serve three-year terms; remaining 200 members are allocated on the basis of each party's popular vote, also for three-year terms)

elections: Senate - last held 2 July 2000 for all of the seats (next to be held NA 2006); Chamber of Deputies - last held 6 July 2003 (next to be held NA 2006)

election results: Senate - percent of vote by party - NA%; seats by party - PRI 60, PAN 46, PRD 16, PVEM 5, unassigned 1; Chamber of Deputies - percent of vote by party - NA%; seats by party - PRI 222, PAN 151, PRD 95, PVEM 17, PT 6, CD 5, unassigned 4; note - special elections were held in December 2003; the PRI and the PRD each won one seat and were each assigned one additional proportional representation seat

Judicial branch: Supreme Court of Justice or Corte Suprema de Justicia (judges are appointed by the president with consent of the Senate)

Political parties and leaders: Convergence for Democracy or CD [Dante DELGADO Ranauro]; Institutional Revolutionary Party or PRI [Roberto MADRAZO Pintado]; Mexican Green Ecological Party or PVEM [Jorge Emilio GONZALEZ Martinez]; National Action Party or PAN [Luis Felipe BRAVO Mena]; Party of the Democratic Revolution or PRD [Leonel GODOY]; Workers Party or PT [Alberto ANAYA Gutierrez]

Political pressure groups and leaders: Confederation of Employers of the Mexican Republic or COPARMEX; Confederation of Industrial Chambers or CONCAMIN; Confederation of Mexican Workers or CTM; Confederation of National Chambers of Commerce or CONCANACO; Coordinator for Foreign Trade Business Organizations or COECE; Federation of Unions Providing Goods and Services or FESEBES; National Chamber of Transformation Industries or CANACINTRA; National Peasant Confederation or CNC; National Union of Workers or UNT; Regional Confederation of Mexican Workers or CROM; Revolutionary Confederation of Workers and Peasants or CROC; Roman Catholic Church

International organization participation: APEC, BCIE, BIS, Caricom (observer), CDB, CE (observer), EBRD, FAO, G-3, G-6, G-15, G-19, G-24, IADB, IAEA, IBRD, ICAO, ICC, ICCt (signatory), ICFTU, ICRM, IDA, IFAD, IFC, IFRCS, IHO, ILO, IMF, IMO, Interpol, IOC, IOM, ISO, ITU, LAES, LAIA, NAM (observer), NEA, OAS, OECD, OPANAL, OPCW, PCA, RG, UN, UNCTAD, UNESCO, UNHCR, UNIDO, UNITAR, UNMOVIC, UPU, WCL, WCO, WFTU, WHO, WIPO, WMO, WToO, WTrO

Diplomatic representation in the US:

chief of mission: Ambassador-designate Carlos Alberto de ICAZA Gonzalez

chancery: 1911 Pennsylvania Avenue NW, Washington, DC 20006

telephone: [1] (202) 728-1600

FAX: [1] (202) 728-1698

consulate(s) general: Atlanta, Austin, Boston, Chicago, Dallas, Denver, El Paso, Houston, Laredo (Texas), Los Angeles, Miami, New Orleans, New York, Nogales (Arizona), Phoenix, Sacramento, San Antonio, San Diego, San Francisco, San Jose, San Juan (Puerto Rico)

consulate(s): Albuquerque, Brownsville (Texas), Calexico (California), Del Rio (Texas), Detroit, Douglas (Arizona), Eagle Pass (Texas), Fresno

Mexico *(continued)*

(California), Indianapolis (Indiana), Kansas City (Missouri), Las Vegas, McAllen (Texas), Omaha, Orlando, Oxnard (California), Philadelphia, Portland (Oregon), Presidio (Texas), Raleigh, Salt Lake City, San Bernardino, Santa Ana (California), Seattle, Tucson, Yuma (Arizona)

Diplomatic representation from the US:
chief of mission: Ambassador Antonio O. GARZA
embassy: Paseo de la Reforma 305, Colonia Cuauhtemoc, 06500 Mexico, Distrito Federal
mailing address: P. O. Box 9000, Brownsville, TX 78520-0900
telephone: [52] (55) 5080-2000
FAX: [52] (55) 5080-2005, 5080-2834
consulate(s) general: Ciudad Juarez, Guadalajara, Monterrey, Tijuana
consulate(s): Hermosillo, Matamoros, Merida, Nuevo Laredo, Nogales

Flag description: three equal vertical bands of green (hoist side), white, and red; the coat of arms (an eagle perched on a cactus with a snake in its beak) is centered in the white band

Economy

Economy - overview: Mexico has a free market economy with a mixture of modern and outmoded industry and agriculture, increasingly dominated by the private sector. Recent administrations have expanded competition in seaports, railroads, telecommunications, electricity generation, natural gas distribution, and airports. Per capita income is one-fourth that of the US; income distribution remains highly unequal. Trade with the US and Canada has tripled since the implementation of NAFTA in 1994. Real GDP growth was a weak -0.3% in 2001, 0.9% in 2002, and 1.2% in 2003, with the US slowdown the principal cause. Mexico implemented free trade agreements with Guatemala, Honduras, El Salvador, and the European Free Trade Area in 2001, putting more than 90% of trade under free trade agreements. The government is cognizant of the need to upgrade infrastructure, modernize the tax system and labor laws, and provide incentives to invest in the energy sector, but progress is slow.

GDP: purchasing power parity - $942.2 billion (2003 est.)
GDP - real growth rate: 1.2% (2003 est.)
GDP - per capita: purchasing power parity - $9,000 (2003 est.)
GDP - composition by sector:
agriculture: 4%
industry: 26.3%
services: 69.7% (2003 est.)
Population below poverty line: 40% (2003 est.)
Household income or consumption by percentage share:
lowest 10%: 1.6%
highest 10%: 35.6% (2002)
Distribution of family income - Gini index: 53.1 (1998)
Inflation rate (consumer prices): 4% (2003 est.)

Labor force: 41.5 million (2003)
Labor force - by occupation: agriculture 18%, industry 24%, services 58% (2003)
Unemployment rate: 3.3% plus underemployment of perhaps 25% (2003)
Budget:
revenues: $174 billion
expenditures: $176 billion, including capital expenditures of $NA (2004 est.)
Industries: food and beverages, tobacco, chemicals, iron and steel, petroleum, mining, textiles, clothing, motor vehicles, consumer durables, tourism
Industrial production growth rate: 2.5% (2003 est.)
Electricity - production: 198.6 billion kWh (2001)
Electricity - production by source:
fossil fuel: 78.7%
hydro: 14.2%
nuclear: 4.2%
other: 2.9% (2001)
Electricity - consumption: 186.7 billion kWh (2001)
Electricity - exports: 77 million kWh (2001)
Electricity - imports: 2.068 billion kWh (2001)
Oil - production: 3.59 million bbl/day (2001 est.)
Oil - consumption: 1.507 million bbl/day (2001 est.)
Oil - exports: 1.881 million bbl/day (2001)
Oil - imports: 374,700 bbl/day (2001)
Oil - proved reserves: 15.11 billion bbl (1 January 2003)
Natural gas - production: 36.87 billion cu m (2001 est.)
Natural gas - consumption: 38.84 billion cu m (2001 est.)
Natural gas - exports: 254 million cu m (2001 est.)
Natural gas - imports: 2.967 billion cu m (2001 est.)
Natural gas - proved reserves: 969.2 billion cu m (1 January 2003)
Agriculture - products: corn, wheat, soybeans, rice, beans, cotton, coffee, fruit, tomatoes; beef, poultry, dairy products; wood products
Exports: $164.8 billion f.o.b. (2003 est.)
Exports - commodities: manufactured goods, oil and oil products, silver, fruits, vegetables, coffee, cotton
Exports - partners: US 89%, Canada 1.7%, Spain 0.9% (2002)
Imports: $168.9 billion f.o.b. (2003 est.)
Imports - commodities: metalworking machines, steel mill products, agricultural machinery, electrical equipment, car parts for assembly, repair parts for motor vehicles, aircraft, and aircraft parts
Imports - partners: US 63.2%, Japan 5.5%, China 3.7% (2002)
Debt - external: $159.3 billion (2003 est.)
Economic aid - recipient: $1.166 billion (1995)
Currency: Mexican peso (MXN)
Currency code: MXN
Exchange rates: Mexican pesos per US dollar - 10.789 (2003), 9.656 (2002), 9.3423 (2001), 9.4556 (2000), 9.5604 (1999)
Fiscal year: calendar year

Communications

Telephones - main lines in use: 15,958,700 (2003)
Telephones - mobile cellular: 28.125 million (2003)
Telephone system:
general assessment: low telephone density with about 15.2 main lines per 100 persons; privatized in December 1990; the opening to competition in January 1997 improved prospects for development, but Telemex remains dominant
domestic: adequate telephone service for business and government, but the population is poorly served; mobile subscribers far outnumber fixed-line subscribers; domestic satellite system with 120 earth stations; extensive microwave radio relay network; considerable use of fiber-optic cable and coaxial cable
international: country code - 52; satellite earth stations - 32 Intelsat, 2 Solidaridad (giving Mexico improved access to South America, Central America, and much of the US as well as enhancing domestic communications), numerous Inmarsat mobile earth stations; linked to Central American Microwave System of trunk connections; high capacity Columbus-2 fiber-optic submarine cable with access to the US, Virgin Islands, Canary Islands, Morocco, Spain, and Italy (1997)
Radio broadcast stations: AM 850, FM 545, shortwave 15 (2003)
Television broadcast stations: 236 (plus repeaters) (1997)
Internet country code: .mx
Internet hosts: 1,107,795 (2002)
Internet users: 10.033 million (2002)

Transportation

Railways:
total: 19,510 km
standard gauge: 19,510 km 1.435-m gauge (2002)
Highways:
total: 329,532 km
paved: 108,087 km (including 6,429 km of expressways)
unpaved: 221,445 km (1999 est.)
Waterways: 2,900 km
note: navigable rivers and coastal canals
Pipelines: crude oil 28,200 km; petroleum products 10,150 km; natural gas 13,254 km; petrochemical 1,400 km
Ports and harbors: Acapulco, Altamira, Bahias de Huatulco, Cabo San Lucas, Coatzacoalcos, Dos Bocas, Ensenada, Guaymas, Lazaro Cardenas, Manzanillo, Mazatlan, Puerto Progreso, Puerto Madero, Puerto Vallarta, Salina Cruz, Tampico, Topolobampo, Tuxpan, Veracruz (2003)
Merchant marine:
total: 50 ships (1,000 GRT or over) 649,389 GRT/ 942,766 DWT
by type: bulk 1, cargo 3, chemical tanker 3, combination ore/oil 1, liquefied gas 5, petroleum tanker 25, roll on/roll off 9, short-sea/passenger 3
foreign-owned: Denmark 1, Germany 1, Greece 1, Marshall Islands 1, Netherlands 2

registered in other countries: 13 (2003 est.)

Airports: 1,827 (2003 est.)

Airports - with paved runways:

total: 231

over 3,047 m: 12

2,438 to 3,047 m: 28

1,524 to 2,437 m: 84

914 to 1,523 m: 80

under 914 m: 27 (2003 est.)

Airports - with unpaved runways:

total: 1,596

over 3,047 m: 1

2,438 to 3,047 m: 1

1,524 to 2,437 m: 69

914 to 1,523 m: 454

under 914 m: 1,071 (2003 est.)

Heliports: 2 (2003 est.)

Military

Military branches: National Defense Secretariat (Sedena) (including Army and Air Force), Navy Secretariat (including Naval Air and Marines)

Military manpower - military age: 18 years of age (no conscription; all-volunteer force)

note: starting in 2000, females were allowed to volunteer for military service (2004 est.)

Military manpower - availability:

males age 15-49: 27,374,153 (2004 est.)

Military manpower - fit for military service:

males age 15-49: 19,755,614 (2004 est.)

Military manpower - reaching military age annually:

males: 1,055,368 (2004 est.)

Military expenditures - dollar figure: $5,168,300,000 (2003)

Military expenditures - percent of GDP: 0.9% (2003)

Transnational Issues

Disputes - international: prolonged drought, population growth, and outmoded practices and infrastructure in the border region have strained water-sharing arrangements with the US; nationals from Central America slip into Mexico seeking work or transit into the US; undocumented Mexican nationals continue to enter the United States

Illicit drugs: illicit cultivation of opium poppy (cultivation in 2001 - 4,400 hectares; potential heroin production - 7 metric tons) and of cannabis (in 2001 - 4,100 hectares); government eradication efforts have been key in keeping illicit crop levels low; major supplier of heroin and largest foreign supplier of marijuana and methamphetamine to the US market; continues as the primary transshipment country for US-bound cocaine from South America, accounting for about 70 percent of estimated annual cocaine movement to the US; major drug syndicates control majority of drug trafficking throughout the country; producer and distributor of ecstasy; significant money-laundering center

Micronesia, Federated States of

Introduction

Background: In 1979 the Federated States of Micronesia, a UN Trust Territory under US administration, adopted a constitution. In 1986 independence was attained under a Compact of Free Association with the US. Present concerns include large-scale unemployment, overfishing, and overdependence on US aid.

Geography

Location: Oceania, island group in the North Pacific Ocean, about three-quarters of the way from Hawaii to Indonesia

Geographic coordinates: 6 55 N, 158 15 E

Map references: Oceania

Area:

total: 702 sq km

land: 702 sq km

water: 0 sq km (fresh water only)

note: includes Pohnpei (Ponape), Chuuk (Truk) Islands, Yap Islands, and Kosrae (Kosaie)

Area - comparative: four times the size of Washington, DC (land area only)

Land boundaries: 0 km

Coastline: 6,112 km

Maritime claims:

territorial sea: 12 NM

exclusive economic zone: 200 NM

Climate: tropical; heavy year-round rainfall, especially in the eastern islands; located on southern edge of the typhoon belt with occasionally severe damage

Terrain: islands vary geologically from high mountainous islands to low, coral atolls; volcanic outcroppings on Pohnpei, Kosrae, and Chuuk

Elevation extremes:

lowest point: Pacific Ocean 0 m

highest point: Dolohmwar (Totolom) 791 m

Natural resources: forests, marine products, deep-seabed minerals

Land use:

arable land: 5.71%

permanent crops: 45.71%

other: 48.58% (1998 est.)

Irrigated land: NA sq km

Natural hazards: typhoons (June to December)

Environment - current issues: overfishing, climate change, pollution

Environment - international agreements:

party to: Biodiversity, Climate Change, Climate Change-Kyoto Protocol, Desertification, Hazardous Wastes, Law of the Sea, Ozone Layer Protection

signed, but not ratified: none of the selected agreements

Geography - note: four major island groups totaling 607 islands

People

Population: 108,155 (July 2004 est.)

Age structure:

0-14 years: 37.7% (male 20,830; female 19,993)

15-64 years: 59.2% (male 32,055; female 31,927)

65 years and over: 3.1% (male 1,505; female 1,845) (2004 est.)

Population growth rate: -0.02% (2004 est.)

Birth rate: 25.8 births/1,000 population (2004 est.)

Death rate: 4.97 deaths/1,000 population (2004 est.)

Net migration rate: -20.99 migrant(s)/1,000 population (2004 est.)

Sex ratio: 1.05 male(s)/female (2004 est.)

Infant mortality rate:

total: 31.28 deaths/1,000 live births

male: 34.45 deaths/1,000 live births

female: 27.95 deaths/1,000 live births (2004 est.)

Life expectancy at birth:

total population: 69.44 years

male: 67.68 years

female: 71.29 years (2004 est.)

Total fertility rate: 3.37 children born/woman (2004 est.)

HIV/AIDS - adult prevalence rate: NA%

HIV/AIDS - people living with HIV/AIDS: NA

HIV/AIDS - deaths: NA

Nationality:

noun: Micronesian(s)

adjective: Micronesian; Chuukese, Kosraen(s), Pohnpeian(s), Yapese

Ethnic groups: nine ethnic Micronesian and Polynesian groups

Religions: Roman Catholic 50%, Protestant 47%

Languages: English (official and common language), Trukese, Pohnpeian, Yapese, Kosrean, Ulithian, Woleaian, Nukuoro, Kapingamarangi

Literacy:

definition: age 15 and over can read and write

total population: 89%

male: 91%

female: 88% (1980 est.)

Micronesia, Federated States of *(continued)*

Government

Country name:
conventional long form: Federated States of Micronesia
conventional short form: none
former: Ponape, Truk, and Yap Districts (Trust Territory of the Pacific Islands)
abbreviation: FSM
Government type: constitutional government in free association with the US; the Compact of Free Association entered into force 3 November 1986; economic provisions of the Compact are being renegotiated
Capital: Palikir
Administrative divisions: 4 states; Chuuk (Truk), Kosrae (Kosaie), Pohnpei (Ponape), Yap
Independence: 3 November 1986 (from the US-administered UN Trusteeship)
National holiday: Constitution Day, 10 May (1979)
Constitution: 10 May 1979
Legal system: based on adapted Trust Territory laws, acts of the legislature, municipal, common, and customary laws
Suffrage: 18 years of age; universal
Executive branch:
chief of state: President Joseph J. URUSEMAL (since 11 May 2003); Vice President Redley KILLION (11 May 2003); note - the president is both the chief of state and head of government
head of government: President Joseph J. URUSEMAL (since 11 May 2003); Vice President Redley KILLION (11 May 2003); note - the president is both the chief of state and head of government
cabinet: Cabinet
elections: president and vice president elected by Congress from among the four senators at large for four-year terms; election last held 11 May 2003 (next to be held NA May 2007); note - a proposed constitutional amendment to establish popular elections for president and vice president failed
election results: Joseph J. URUSEMAL elected president; percent of Congress vote - NA%; Redley KILLION elected vice president; percent of Congress vote - NA%
Legislative branch: unicameral Congress (14 seats; four - one elected from each state to serve four-year terms and 10 - elected from single-member districts delineated by population to serve two-year terms; members elected by popular vote)
elections: elections for four-year term seats last held 4 March 2003 (next to be held NA March 2007); elections for two-year term seats last held 4 March 2003 (next to be held NA March 2005)
election results: percent of vote - NA%; seats - independents 14
Judicial branch: Supreme Court
Political parties and leaders: no formal parties
International organization participation: ACP, AsDB, G-77, IBRD, ICAO, IDA, IFC, IFRCS, IMF, IOC, ITU, OPCW, PIF, Sparteca, UN, UNCTAD, UNESCO, WHO, WMO

Diplomatic representation in the US:
chief of mission: Ambassador Jesse Bibiano MAREHALAU
chancery: 1725 N Street NW, Washington, DC 20036
telephone: [1] (202) 223-4383
FAX: [1] (202) 223-4391
consulate(s) general: Honolulu and Tamuning (Guam)
Diplomatic representation from the US:
chief of mission: Ambassador Larry M. DINGER
embassy: address NA, Kolonia
mailing address: P. O. Box 1286, Kolonia, Pohnpei, Federated States of Micronesia 96941
telephone: [691] 320-2187
FAX: [691] 320-2186
Flag description: light blue with four white five-pointed stars centered; the stars are arranged in a diamond pattern

Economy

Economy - overview: Economic activity consists primarily of subsistence farming and fishing. The islands have few mineral deposits worth exploiting, except for high-grade phosphate. The potential for a tourist industry exists, but the remote location, a lack of adequate facilities, and limited air connections hinder development. In November 2002, the country experienced a further reduction in future revenues from the Compact of Free Association - the agreement with the US in which Micronesia received $1.3 billion in financial and technical assistance over a 15-year period until 2001. The country's medium-term economic outlook appears fragile due not only to the reduction in US assistance but also to the slow growth of the private sector. Geographical isolation and a poorly developed infrastructure remain major impediments to long-term growth.
GDP: purchasing power parity - $277 million
note: GDP is supplemented by grant aid, averaging perhaps $100 million annually (2002 est.)
GDP - real growth rate: 1% (2002 est.)
GDP - per capita: purchasing power parity - $2,000 (2002 est.)
GDP - composition by sector:
agriculture: 50%
industry: 4%
services: 46% (2000 est.)
Population below poverty line: 26.7%
Household income or consumption by percentage share:
lowest 10%: NA%
highest 10%: NA%
Inflation rate (consumer prices): 1% (2002 est.)
Labor force: NA (2000 est.)
Labor force - by occupation: two-thirds are government employees
Unemployment rate: 16% (1999 est.)
Budget:
revenues: $161 million ($69 million less grants)
expenditures: $160 million, including capital expenditures of $NA (1998 est.)

Industries: tourism, construction, fish processing, specialized aquaculture, craft items from shell, wood, and pearls
Industrial production growth rate: NA%
Electricity - production: NA kWh
Electricity - production by source: NA
Electricity - consumption: NA kWh
Agriculture - products: black pepper, tropical fruits and vegetables, coconuts, cassava (tapioca), betel nuts, sweet potatoes; pigs, chickens
Exports: $22 million (f.o.b.) (FY99/00 est.)
Exports - commodities: fish, garments, bananas, black pepper
Exports - partners: Japan, US, Guam (2000)
Imports: $149 million f.o.b. (FY99/00 est.)
Imports - commodities: food, manufactured goods, machinery and equipment, beverages
Imports - partners: US, Australia, Japan (2000)
Debt - external: $53.1 million (FY02/03 est.)
Economic aid - recipient: under terms of the Compact of Free Association, the US pledged $1.3 billion in grant aid during the period 1986-2001
Currency: US dollar (USD)
Currency code: USD
Exchange rates: the US dollar is used
Fiscal year: 1 October - 30 September

Communications

Telephones - main lines in use: 10,100 (2001)
Telephones - mobile cellular: 1,800 (2002)
Telephone system:
general assessment: adequate system
domestic: islands interconnected by shortwave radiotelephone (used mostly for government purposes), satellite (Intelsat) ground stations, and some coaxial and fiber-optic cable; cellular service available on Kosrae, Pohnpei, and Yap
international: country code - 691; satellite earth stations - 5 Intelsat (Pacific Ocean) (2002)
Radio broadcast stations: AM 5, FM 1, shortwave 0 (2004)
Television broadcast stations: 3; note - cable TV also available (2004)
Internet country code: .fm
Internet users: 6,000 (2002)

Transportation

Railways: 0 km
Highways:
total: 240 km
paved: 42 km
unpaved: 198 km (1999 est.)
Waterways: none
Ports and harbors: Colonia (Yap), Kolonia (Pohnpei), Lele, Moen
Merchant marine: none
Airports: 6 (2003 est.)
Airports - with paved runways:
total: 6
1,524 to 2,437 m: 4
914 to 1,523 m: 2 (2003 est.)

Micronesia, Federated States of
(continued)

Military

Military - note: Federated States of Micronesia (FSM) is a sovereign, self-governing state in free association with the US; FSM is totally dependent on the US for its defense

Transnational Issues

Disputes - international: none

Midway Islands
(territory of the US)

Introduction

Background: The US took formal possession of the islands in 1867. The laying of the trans-Pacific cable, which passed through the islands, brought the first residents in 1903. Between 1935 and 1947, Midway was used as a refueling stop for trans-Pacific flights. The US naval victory over a Japanese fleet off Midway in 1942 was one of the turning points of World War II. The islands continued to serve as a naval station until closed in 1993. Today the islands are a national wildlife refuge. From 1996 to 2001 the refuge was open to the public. It is now temporarily closed.

Geography

Location: Oceania, atoll in the North Pacific Ocean, about one-third of the way from Honolulu to Tokyo
Geographic coordinates: 28 13 N, 177 22 W
Map references: Oceania
Area:
total: 6.2 sq km
land: 6.2 sq km
water: 0 sq km
note: includes Eastern Island, Sand Island, and Spit Island
Area - comparative: about nine times the size of The Mall in Washington, DC
Land boundaries: 0 km
Coastline: 15 km
Maritime claims:
territorial sea: 12 NM
exclusive economic zone: 200 NM
Climate: subtropical; moderated by prevailing easterly winds
Terrain: low, nearly level
Elevation extremes:
lowest point: Pacific Ocean 0 m
highest point: unnamed location 13 m
Natural resources: wildlife, terrestrial and aquatic

Land use:
arable land: 0%
permanent crops: 0%
other: 100% (1998 est.)
Irrigated land: 0 sq km (1998 est.)
Natural hazards: NA
Environment - current issues: NA
Geography - note: a coral atoll managed as a national wildlife refuge and open to the public for wildlife-related recreation in the form of wildlife observation and photography, sport fishing, snorkeling, and scuba diving; the refuge is temporarily closed for reorganization at present (2004)

People

Population: no indigenous inhabitants; approximately 40 people make up the staff of US Fish and Wildlife Service and their services contractor living at the atoll (July 2004 est.)

Government

Country name:
conventional long form: none
conventional short form: Midway Islands
Dependency status: unincorporated territory of the US; formerly administered from Washington, DC, by the US Navy, under Naval Facilities Engineering Command, Pacific Division; this facility has been operationally closed since 10 September 1993; on 31 October 1996, through a presidential executive order, the jurisdiction and control of the atoll was transferred to the Fish and Wildlife Service of the US Department of the Interior as part of the National Wildlife Refuge system
Legal system: the laws of the US, where applicable, apply
Flag description: the flag of the US is used

Economy

Economy - overview: The economy is based on providing support services for the national wildlife refuge activities located on the islands. All food and manufactured goods must be imported.

Transportation

Highways:
total: NA km
paved: NA km
unpaved: NA km
Waterways: none
Pipelines: 7.8 km
Ports and harbors: Sand Island
Airports: 3 (2003 est.)
Airports - with paved runways:
total: 2
1,524 to 2,437 m: 2 (2003 est.)
Airports - with unpaved runways:
total: 1
914 to 1,523 m: 1 (2003 est.)

Transportation - note: airfield serves as an emergency landing site for commercial aircraft crossing the Pacific Ocean

Military

Military - note: defense is the responsibility of the US

Transnational Issues

Disputes - international: none

Moldova

Introduction

Background: Formerly ruled by Romania, Moldova became part of the Soviet Union at the close of World War II. Although independent from the USSR since 1991, Russian forces have remained on Moldovan territory east of the Dniester River supporting the Slavic majority population, mostly Ukrainians and Russians, who have proclaimed a "Transnistria" republic. The poorest nation in Europe, Moldova became the first former Soviet state to elect a Communist as its president in 2001.

Geography

Location: Eastern Europe, northeast of Romania
Geographic coordinates: 47 00 N, 29 00 E
Map references: Europe
Area:
total: 33,843 sq km
land: 33,371 sq km
water: 472 sq km
Area - comparative: slightly larger than Maryland
Land boundaries:
total: 1,389 km
border countries: Romania 450 km, Ukraine 939 km

Coastline: 0 km (landlocked)
Maritime claims: none (landlocked)
Climate: moderate winters, warm summers
Terrain: rolling steppe, gradual slope south to Black Sea
Elevation extremes:
lowest point: Dniester River 2 m
highest point: Dealul Balanesti 430 m
Natural resources: lignite, phosphorites, gypsum, arable land, limestone
Land use:
arable land: 54.08%
permanent crops: 12.1%
other: 33.82% (1998 est.)
Irrigated land: 3,070 sq km (1998 est.)
Natural hazards: landslides (57 cases in 1998)
Environment - current issues: heavy use of agricultural chemicals, including banned pesticides such as DDT, has contaminated soil and groundwater; extensive soil erosion from poor farming methods
Environment - international agreements:
party to: Air Pollution, Biodiversity, Climate Change, Climate Change-Kyoto Protocol, Desertification, Endangered Species, Hazardous Wastes, Ozone Layer Protection
signed, but not ratified: Air Pollution-Persistent Organic Pollutants
Geography - note: landlocked; well endowed with various sedimentary rocks and minerals including sand, gravel, gypsum, and limestone

People

Population: 4,446,455 (July 2004 est.)
Age structure:
0-14 years: 20.6% (male 466,485; female 449,645)
15-64 years: 69.1% (male 1,478,220; female 1,595,695)
65 years and over: 10.3% (male 169,026; female 287,384) (2004 est.)
Median age:
total: 32.1 years
male: 29.9 years
female: 34.3 years (2004 est.)
Population growth rate: 0.18% (2004 est.)
Birth rate: 14.81 births/1,000 population (2004 est.)
Death rate: 12.76 deaths/1,000 population (2004 est.)
Net migration rate: -0.26 migrant(s)/1,000 population (2004 est.)
Sex ratio:
at birth: 1.05 male(s)/female
under 15 years: 1.04 male(s)/female
15-64 years: 0.93 male(s)/female
65 years and over: 0.59 male(s)/female
total population: 0.91 male(s)/female (2004 est.)
Infant mortality rate:
total: 41 deaths/1,000 live births
male: 43.96 deaths/1,000 live births
female: 37.89 deaths/1,000 live births (2004 est.)

Life expectancy at birth:
total population: 65.03 years
male: 60.88 years
female: 69.39 years (2004 est.)
Total fertility rate: 1.78 children born/woman (2004 est.)
HIV/AIDS - adult prevalence rate: 0.2% (2001 est.)
HIV/AIDS - people living with HIV/AIDS: 5,500 (2001 est.)
HIV/AIDS - deaths: less than 300 (2001 est.)
Nationality:
noun: Moldovan(s)
adjective: Moldovan
Ethnic groups: Moldovan/Romanian 64.5%, Ukrainian 13.8%, Russian 13%, Jewish 1.5%, Bulgarian 2%, Gagauz and other 5.2% (1989 est.)
note: internal disputes with ethnic Slavs in the Transnistrian region
Religions: Eastern Orthodox 98%, Jewish 1.5%, Baptist and other 0.5% (2000)
Languages: Moldovan (official, virtually the same as the Romanian language), Russian, Gagauz (a Turkish dialect)
Literacy:
definition: age 15 and over can read and write
total population: 99.1%
male: 99.6%
female: 98.7% (2003 est.)

Government

Country name:
conventional long form: Republic of Moldova
conventional short form: Moldova
local long form: Republica Moldova
local short form: none
former: Soviet Socialist Republic of Moldova; Moldavia
Government type: republic
Capital: Chisinau
Administrative divisions: 9 counties (judetele, singular - judetul), 1 municipality* (municipiul), 1 autonomous territorial unit** (unitate teritoriala autonoma), and 1 territorial unit*** (unitate teritoriala); Balti, Cahul, Chisinau, Chisinau*, Edinet, Gagauzia**, Lapusna, Orhei, Soroca, Stinga Nistrului***, Tighina, Ungheni
Independence: 27 August 1991 (from Soviet Union)
National holiday: Independence Day, 27 August (1991)
Constitution: new constitution adopted 28 July 1994; replaces old Soviet constitution of 1979
Legal system: based on civil law system; Constitutional Court reviews legality of legislative acts and governmental decisions of resolution; it is unclear if Moldova accepts compulsory ICJ jurisdiction but accepts many UN and Organization for Security and Cooperation in Europe (OSCE) documents
Suffrage: 18 years of age; universal
Executive branch:
chief of state: President Vladimir VORONIN (since 4 April 2001)

head of government: Prime Minister Vasile TARLEV (since 15 April 2001), First Deputy Prime Minister Vasile IOVV (since 29 January 2002); Deputy Prime Minister Dmitry TODOROGLO (since 19 April 2001)
cabinet: selected by president, subject to approval of Parliament
elections: president elected by Parliament for a four-year term; election last held 4 April 2001 (next to be held NA 2005); note - presidential elections were scheduled for December 2000, but in July 2000, Parliament canceled direct, popular elections; Parliament's failure to choose a new president in December 2000 led to early parliamentary elections in February 2001; prime minister designated by the president, upon consultation with Parliament; note - within 15 days from designation, the prime minister-designate must request a vote of confidence from the Parliament regarding his/her work program and entire cabinet; prime minister designated 15 April 2001, cabinet received a vote of confidence 19 April 2001
election results: Vladimir VORONIN elected president; parliamentary votes - Vladimir VORONIN 71, Dumitru BRAGHIS 15, Valerian CRISTEA 3; Vasile TARLEV designated prime minister; parliamentary votes of confidence - 75 of 101
Legislative branch: unicameral Parliament or Parlamentul (101 seats; parties and electoral blocs elected by popular vote to serve four-year terms)
elections: last held 25 February 2001 (next to be held NA 2005)
election results: percent of vote by party - PCM 50.1%, Braghis Alliance (now Our Moldova Alliance) 13.4%, PPCD 8.2%, other parties 28.3%; seats by party - PCM 71, Braghis Alliance (now Our Moldova Alliance) 19, PPCD 11
Judicial branch: Supreme Court; Constitutional Court (the sole authority for constitutional judicature)
Political parties and leaders: Democratic Party [Dumitru DIACOV]; Communist Party of Moldova or PCM [Vladimir VORONIN, first chairman]; Our Moldova Alliance [Dumitru BRAGHIS, Serafim URECHEANU]; Popular Christian Democratic Party or PPCD [Iurie ROSCA]; Social Liberal Party [Oleg SEREBRIAN]
Political pressure groups and leaders: NA
International organization participation: ACCT, BSEC, CE, CEI, CIS, EAPC, EBRD, FAO, GUUAM, IAEA, IBRD, ICAO, ICCt (signatory), ICFTU, IDA, IFAD, IFC, IFRCS, ILO, IMF, IMO, Interpol, IOC, IOM, ISO (correspondent), ITU, OPCW, OSCE, PFP, UN, UNCTAD, UNESCO, UNIDO, UNMIL, UPU, WCO, WHO, WIPO, WMO, WToO, WTrO
Diplomatic representation in the US:
chief of mission: Ambassador Mihail MANOLI
chancery: 2101 S Street NW, Washington, DC 20008
telephone: [1] (202) 667-1130
FAX: [1] (202) 667-1204
Diplomatic representation from the US:
chief of mission: Ambassador Heather M. HODGES
embassy: 103 Alexei Mateevici Street, Chisinau MD-2009

mailing address: use embassy street address
telephone: [373] (22) 23-37-72
FAX: [373] (22) 23-30-44
Flag description: same color scheme as Romania - three equal vertical bands of blue (hoist side), yellow, and red; emblem in center of flag is of a Roman eagle of gold outlined in black with a red beak and talons carrying a yellow cross in its beak and a green olive branch in its right talons and a yellow scepter in its left talons; on its breast is a shield divided horizontally red over blue with a stylized ox head, star, rose, and crescent all in black-outlined yellow

Economy

Economy - overview: Moldova remains the poorest country in Europe despite recent progress from its small economic base. It enjoys a favorable climate and good farmland but has no major mineral deposits. As a result, the economy depends heavily on agriculture, featuring fruits, vegetables, wine, and tobacco. Moldova must import almost all of its energy supplies from Russia. Energy shortages contributed to sharp production declines after the breakup of the Soviet Union in 1991. As part of an ambitious reform effort, Moldova introduced a convertible currency, freed prices, stopped issuing preferential credits to state enterprises, backed steady land privatization, removed export controls, and freed interest rates. The government entered into agreements with the World Bank and the IMF to promote growth and reduce poverty. The economy returned to positive growth, of 2.1% in 2000, 6.1% in 2001, 7.2% in 2002, and 6.3% in 2003. Further reforms will come slowly because of strong political forces backing government controls. The economy remains vulnerable to higher fuel prices, poor agricultural weather, and the skepticism of foreign investors.
GDP: purchasing power parity - $7.792 billion (2003 est.)
GDP - real growth rate: 6.3% (2003 est.)
GDP - per capita: purchasing power parity - $1,800 (2003 est.)
GDP - composition by sector:
agriculture: 28%
industry: 23%
services: 49% (2000)
Population below poverty line: 80% (2001 est.)
Household income or consumption by percentage share:
lowest 10%: 2.2%
highest 10%: 30.7% (1997)
Distribution of family income - Gini index: 40.6 (1997)
Inflation rate (consumer prices): 11.7% (2003 est.)
Labor force: 1.7 million (1998)
Labor force - by occupation: agriculture 40%, industry 14%, services 46% (1998)
Unemployment rate: 8% (roughly 25% of working age Moldovans are employed abroad) (2002 est.)

Moldova (continued)

Budget:

revenues: $536 million

expenditures: $594 million, including capital expenditures of $NA (1998 est.)

Industries: food processing, agricultural machinery, foundry equipment, refrigerators and freezers, washing machines, hosiery, sugar, vegetable oil, shoes, textiles

Industrial production growth rate: 17% (2003 est.)

Electricity - production: 3.394 billion kWh (2001)

Electricity - production by source:

fossil fuel: 90.6%

hydro: 9.4%

nuclear: 0%

other: 0% (2001)

Electricity - consumption: 3.216 billion kWh (2001)

Electricity - exports: 0 kWh (2001)

Electricity - imports: 60 million kWh (2001)

Oil - production: 0 bbl/day (2001 est.)

Oil - consumption: 24,000 bbl/day (2001 est.)

Oil - exports: NA

Oil - imports: NA

Natural gas - production: 0 cu m (2001 est.)

Natural gas - consumption: 2.05 billion cu m (2001 est.)

Natural gas - exports: 0 cu m (2001 est.)

Natural gas - imports: 2.05 billion cu m (2001 est.)

Agriculture - products: vegetables, fruits, wine, grain, sugar beets, sunflower seed, tobacco; beef, milk

Exports: $790 million f.o.b. (2003 est.)

Exports - commodities: foodstuffs, textiles, machinery

Exports - partners: Russia 34.6%, Italy 11.5%, Germany 9.1%, Ukraine 6.9%, Romania 6.2%, US 5.2%, Belarus 4.5%, Spain 4.1% (2002)

Imports: $1.34 billion f.o.b. (2003 est.)

Imports - commodities: mineral products and fuel 32%, machinery and equipment, chemicals, textiles (2000)

Imports - partners: Ukraine 22.6%, Russia 20.2%, Germany 10.7%, Romania 8.3%, Italy 7% (2002)

Debt - external: $1.3 billion (2002)

Economic aid - recipient: $100 million (2000)

Currency: Moldovan leu (MDL)

Currency code: MDL

Exchange rates: lei per US dollar - 13.9449 (2003), 13.5705 (2002), 12.8651 (2001), 12.4342 (2000), 10.5158 (1999)

Fiscal year: calendar year

Communications

Telephones - main lines in use: 706,900 (2002)

Telephones - mobile cellular: 338,200 (2002)

Telephone system:

general assessment: inadequate, outmoded, poor service outside Chisinau; some effort to modernize is under way

domestic: new subscribers face long wait for service; mobile cellular telephone service being introduced

international: country code - 373; service through Romania and Russia via landline; satellite earth stations - Intelsat, Eutelsat, and Intersputnik

Radio broadcast stations: AM 7, FM 50, shortwave 3 (1998)

Television broadcast stations: 1 (plus 30 repeaters) (1995)

Internet country code: .md

Internet hosts: 2,189 (2002)

Internet users: 150,000 (2002)

Transportation

Railways:

total: 1,300 km

broad gauge: 1,300 km 1.520-m gauge (2002)

Highways:

total: 12,657 km

paved: 11,012 km

unpaved: 1,645 km (1999)

Waterways: 424 km (1994)

Pipelines: gas 606 km (2003)

Ports and harbors: none

Airports: 24 (2003 est.)

Airports - with paved runways:

total: 6

over 3,047 m: 1

2,438 to 3,047 m: 2

1,524 to 2,437 m: 2

under 914 m: 1 (2003 est.)

Airports - with unpaved runways:

total: 18

2,438 to 3,047 m: 2

1,524 to 2,437 m: 1

914 to 1,523 m: 4

under 914 m: 11 (2003 est.)

Military

Military branches: National Army: Ground Forces, Air Force

Military manpower - military age: 18 years of age (12 months of national service required) (2004 est.)

Military manpower - availability:

males age 15-49: 1,186,818 (2004 est.)

Military manpower - fit for military service:

males age 15-49: 942,071 (2004 est.)

Military manpower - reaching military age annually:

males: 44,466 (2004 est.)

Military expenditures - dollar figure: $6.4 million (FY02)

Military expenditures - percent of GDP: 0.4% (FY02)

Transnational Issues

Disputes - international: difficulties with the Transnistria region complicate controlling border crossing and customs regimes with Ukraine, despite concordance on 2003 delimitation and customs protocols and OSCE assistance

Illicit drugs: limited cultivation of opium poppy and cannabis, mostly for CIS consumption; transshipment point for illicit drugs from Southwest Asia via Central Asia to Russia, Western Europe, and possibly the US; widespread crime and underground economic activity

Monaco

Introduction

Background: Economic development was spurred in the late 19th century with a railroad linkup to France and the opening of a casino. Since then, the principality's mild climate, splendid scenery, and gambling facilities have made Monaco world famous as a tourist and recreation center.

Geography

Location: Western Europe, bordering the Mediterranean Sea on the southern coast of France, near the border with Italy

Geographic coordinates: 43 44 N, 7 24 E

Map references: Europe

Area:

total: 1.95 sq km

land: 1.95 sq km

water: 0 sq km

Area - comparative: about three times the size of The Mall in Washington, DC

Land boundaries:

total: 4.4 km

border countries: France 4.4 km

Coastline: 4.1 km

Maritime claims:

territorial sea: 12 NM

Climate: Mediterranean with mild, wet winters and hot, dry summers

Terrain: hilly, rugged, rocky

Elevation extremes:

lowest point: Mediterranean Sea 0 m

highest point: Mont Agel 140 m

Natural resources: none

Land use:

arable land: 0%

permanent crops: 0%

other: 100% (urban area) (1998 est.)

Irrigated land: NA sq km

Natural hazards: NA

Environment - current issues: NA

Monaco (continued)

Environment - international agreements:
party to: Air Pollution, Air Pollution-Volatile Organic Compounds, Biodiversity, Climate Change, Desertification, Endangered Species, Hazardous Wastes, Law of the Sea, Marine Dumping, Ozone Layer Protection, Ship Pollution, Wetlands, Whaling
signed, but not ratified: Climate Change-Kyoto Protocol
Geography - note: second-smallest independent state in the world (after Holy See); almost entirely urban

People

Population: 32,270 (July 2004 est.)
Age structure:
0-14 years: 15.5% (male 2,554; female 2,453)
15-64 years: 62.1% (male 9,860; female 10,165)
65 years and over: 22.4% (male 2,959; female 4,279) (2004 est.)
Median age:
total: 45.1 years
male: 43.1 years
female: 47.1 years (2004 est.)
Population growth rate: 0.44% (2004 est.)
Birth rate: 9.36 births/1,000 population (2004 est.)
Death rate: 12.74 deaths/1,000 population (2004 est.)
Net migration rate: 7.75 migrant(s)/1,000 population (2004 est.)
Sex ratio:
at birth: 1.05 male(s)/female
under 15 years: 1.04 male(s)/female
15-64 years: 0.97 male(s)/female
65 years and over: 0.69 male(s)/female
total population: 0.91 male(s)/female (2004 est.)
Infant mortality rate:
total: 5.53 deaths/1,000 live births
male: 6.4 deaths/1,000 live births
female: 4.61 deaths/1,000 live births (2004 est.)
Life expectancy at birth:
total population: 79.42 years
male: 75.53 years
female: 83.5 years (2004 est.)
Total fertility rate: 1.76 children born/woman (2004 est.)
HIV/AIDS - adult prevalence rate: NA%
HIV/AIDS - people living with HIV/AIDS: NA
HIV/AIDS - deaths: NA
Nationality:
noun: Monegasque(s) or Monacan(s)
adjective: Monegasque or Monacan
Ethnic groups: French 47%, Monegasque 16%, Italian 16%, other 21%
Religions: Roman Catholic 90%
Languages: French (official), English, Italian, Monegasque
Literacy:
definition: NA
total population: 99%
male: NA%
female: NA%

Government

Country name:
conventional long form: Principality of Monaco
conventional short form: Monaco
local long form: Principaute de Monaco
local short form: Monaco
Government type: constitutional monarchy
Capital: Monaco
Administrative divisions: none; there are no first-order administrative divisions as defined by the US Government, but there are four quarters (quartiers, singular - quartier); Fontvieille, La Condamine, Monaco-Ville, Monte-Carlo
Independence: 1419 (beginning of the rule by the House of Grimaldi)
National holiday: National Day (Prince of Monaco Holiday), 19 November
Constitution: 17 December 1962
Legal system: based on French law; has not accepted compulsory ICJ jurisdiction
Suffrage: 21 years of age; universal
Executive branch:
chief of state: Prince RAINIER III (since 9 May 1949); Heir Apparent Prince ALBERT Alexandre Louis Pierre, son of the monarch (born 14 March 1958)
head of government: Minister of State Patrick LECLERCQ (since 5 January 2000)
cabinet: Council of Government is under the authority of the monarch
elections: none; the monarchy is hereditary; minister of state appointed by the monarch from a list of three French national candidates presented by the French Government
Legislative branch: unicameral National Council or Conseil National (24 seats; 16 members elected by list majority system, 8 by proportional representation; to serve five-year terms)
elections: last held 9 February 2003 (next to be held NA February 2008)
election results: percent of vote by party - NA%; seats by party - UNAM 21, UND 3
Judicial branch: Supreme Court or Tribunal Supreme (judges appointed by the monarch on the basis of nominations by the National Council)
Political parties and leaders: National and Democratic Union or UND [Jean-Louis CAMPORA]; Union for Monaco or UPM (including National Union for the Future of Monaco or UNAM [leader NA]
Political pressure groups and leaders: NA
International organization participation: ACCT, FAO, IAEA, ICAO, ICC, ICCt (signatory), ICRM, IFRCS, IHO, IMO, Interpol, IOC, ITU, OPCW, OSCE, UN, UNCTAD, UNESCO, UNIDO, UNITAR, UPU, WHO, WIPO, WMO, WToO
Diplomatic representation in the US: Monaco does not have an embassy in the US
consulate(s) general: New York
Diplomatic representation from the US: the US does not have an embassy in Monaco; the US Consul General in Marseille (France) is accredited to Monaco

Flag description: two equal horizontal bands of red (top) and white; similar to the flag of Indonesia which is longer and the flag of Poland which is white (top) and red

Economy

Economy - overview: Monaco, bordering France on the Mediterranean coast, is a popular resort, attracting tourists to its casino and pleasant climate. In 2001, a major construction project extended the pier used by cruise ships in the main harbor. The principality has successfully sought to diversify into services and small, high-value-added, nonpolluting industries. The state has no income tax and low business taxes and thrives as a tax haven both for individuals who have established residence and for foreign companies that have set up businesses and offices. The state retains monopolies in a number of sectors, including tobacco, the telephone network, and the postal service. Living standards are high, roughly comparable to those in prosperous French metropolitan areas. Monaco does not publish national income figures; the estimates below are extremely rough.
GDP: purchasing power parity - $870 million (1999 est.)
GDP - real growth rate: NA%
GDP - per capita: purchasing power parity - $27,000 (1999 est.)
GDP - composition by sector:
agriculture: NA%
industry: NA%
services: NA% (2001 est.)
Population below poverty line: NA%
Household income or consumption by percentage share:
lowest 10%: NA%
highest 10%: NA%
Inflation rate (consumer prices): NA%
Labor force: 30,540 (January 1994)
Unemployment rate: 3.1% (1998)
Budget:
revenues: $518 million
expenditures: $531 million, including capital expenditures of $NA (1995)
Industries: tourism, construction, small-scale industrial and consumer products
Industrial production growth rate: NA%
Electricity - consumption: NA kWh
Electricity - imports: NA kWh
note: electricity supplied by France
Agriculture - products: none
Exports: $NA; full customs integration with France, which collects and rebates Monegasque trade duties; also participates in EU market system through customs union with France
Imports: $NA; full customs integration with France, which collects and rebates Monegasque trade duties; also participates in EU market system through customs union with France
Debt - external: $NA
Economic aid - recipient: $NA

Currency: euro (EUR)
Currency code: EUR
Exchange rates: euros per US dollar - 0.8860 (2003), 1.0626 (2002), 1.1175 (2001), 1.0854 (2000), 0.9386 (1999)
Fiscal year: calendar year

Communications

Telephones - main lines in use: 33,700 (2002)
Telephones - mobile cellular: 19,300 (2002)
Telephone system:
general assessment: modern automatic telephone system
domestic: NA
international: country code - 377; no satellite earth stations; connected by cable into the French communications system
Radio broadcast stations: AM 1, FM NA, shortwave 8 (1998)
Television broadcast stations: 5 (1998)
Internet country code: .mc
Internet users: 16,000 (2002)

Transportation

Railways:
total: 1.7 km
standard gauge: 1.7 km 1.435-m gauge (2002)
Highways:
total: 50 km
paved: 50 km
unpaved: 0 km (1999 est.)
Waterways: none
Ports and harbors: Monaco
Merchant marine: none
Airports: none; linked to the airport at Nice, France by helicopter service (2003) (2003 est.)
Heliports: 1 (shuttle service between the international airport at Nice, France, and Monaco's heliport at Fontvieille) (2003 est.)

Military

Military - note: defense is the responsibility of France

Transnational Issues

Disputes - international: none

Mongolia

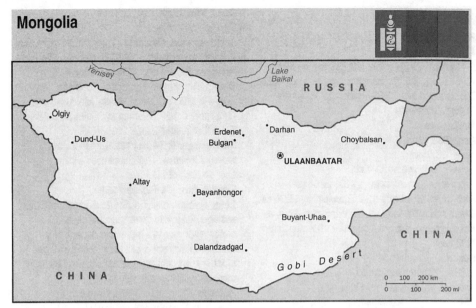

Introduction

Background: The Mongols gained fame in the 13th century when under Genghis KHAN they conquered a huge Eurasian empire. After his death the empire was divided into several powerful Mongol states, but these broke apart in the 14th century. The Mongols eventually retired to their original steppe homelands and came under Chinese rule. Mongolia won its independence in 1921 with Soviet backing. A Communist regime was installed in 1924. During the early 1990s, the ex-Communist Mongolian People's Revolutionary Party (MPRP) gradually yielded its monopoly on power to the Democratic Union Coalition (DUC), which defeated the MPRP in a national election in 1996. Over the next four years, the DUC put forward a number of key reforms to modernize the economy and to democratize the political system. The former Communists were a strong opposition that stalled additional restructuring and made implementation difficult. In 2000, the MPRP won an overwhelming victory in the legislature - with 72 of the 76 seats - and completely reshuffled the government. While it continues many of the reform policies, the MPRP has focused on social welfare and public order priorities.

Geography

Location: Northern Asia, between China and Russia
Geographic coordinates: 46 00 N, 105 00 E
Map references: Asia
Area:
total: 1.565 million sq km
land: 1,555,400 sq km
water: 9,600 sq km
Area - comparative: slightly smaller than Alaska
Land boundaries:
total: 8,162 km
border countries: China 4,677 km, Russia 3,485 km
Coastline: 0 km (landlocked)
Maritime claims: none (landlocked)

Climate: desert; continental (large daily and seasonal temperature ranges)
Terrain: vast semidesert and desert plains, grassy steppe, mountains in west and southwest; Gobi Desert in south-central
Elevation extremes:
lowest point: Hoh Nuur 518 m
highest point: Nayramadlin Orgil (Huyten Orgil) 4,374 m
Natural resources: oil, coal, copper, molybdenum, tungsten, phosphates, tin, nickel, zinc, wolfram, fluorspar, gold, silver, iron, phosphate
Land use:
arable land: 0.84%
permanent crops: 0%
other: 99.16% (1998 est.)
Irrigated land: 840 sq km (1998 est.)
Natural hazards: dust storms, grassland and forest fires, drought, and "zud," which is harsh winter conditions
Environment - current issues: limited natural fresh water resources in some areas; the policies of former Communist regimes promoted rapid urbanization and industrial growth that had negative effects on the environment; the burning of soft coal in power plants and the lack of enforcement of environmental laws severely polluted the air in Ulaanbaatar; deforestation, overgrazing, and the converting of virgin land to agricultural production increased soil erosion from wind and rain; desertification and mining activities had a deleterious effect on the environment
Environment - international agreements:
party to: Biodiversity, Climate Change, Climate Change-Kyoto Protocol, Desertification, Endangered Species, Environmental Modification, Hazardous Wastes, Law of the Sea, Ozone Layer Protection, Wetlands
signed, but not ratified: none of the selected agreements
Geography - note: landlocked; strategic location between China and Russia

Mongolia *(continued)*

People

Population: 2,751,314 (July 2004 est.)
Age structure:
0-14 years: 29.7% (male 415,735; female 400,560)
15-64 years: 66.7% (male 916,445; female 918,235)
65 years and over: 3.6% (male 43,205; female 57,134) (2004 est.)
Median age:
total: 23.9 years
male: 23.6 years
female: 24.3 years (2004 est.)
Population growth rate: 1.43% (2004 est.)
Birth rate: 21.44 births/1,000 population (2004 est.)
Death rate: 7.1 deaths/1,000 population (2004 est.)
Net migration rate: 0 migrant(s)/1,000 population (2004 est.)
Sex ratio:
at birth: 1.05 male(s)/female
under 15 years: 1.04 male(s)/female
15-64 years: 1 male(s)/female
65 years and over: 0.76 male(s)/female
total population: 1 male(s)/female (2004 est.)
Infant mortality rate:
total: 55.45 deaths/1,000 live births
male: 58.97 deaths/1,000 live births
female: 51.75 deaths/1,000 live births (2004 est.)
Life expectancy at birth:
total population: 64.17 years
male: 61.97 years
female: 66.48 years (2004 est.)
Total fertility rate: 2.27 children born/woman (2004 est.)
HIV/AIDS - adult prevalence rate: less than 0.1% (2001 est.)
HIV/AIDS - people living with HIV/AIDS: less than 100 (1999 est.)
HIV/AIDS - deaths: NA
Nationality:
noun: Mongolian(s)
adjective: Mongolian
Ethnic groups: Mongol (predominantly Khalkha) 85%, Turkic (of which Kazakh is the largest group) 7%, Tungusic 4.6%, other (including Chinese and Russian) 3.4% (1998)
Religions: Tibetan Buddhist Lamaism 96%, Muslim (primarily in the southwest), Shamanism, and Christian 4% (1998)
Languages: Khalkha Mongol 90%, Turkic, Russian (1999)
Literacy:
definition: age 15 and over can read and write
total population: 99.1%
male: 99.2%
female: 99% (2003 est.)

Government

Country name:
conventional long form: none
conventional short form: Mongolia
local long form: none
local short form: Mongol Uls
former: Outer Mongolia

Government type: parliamentary
Capital: Ulaanbaatar
Administrative divisions: 21 provinces (aymguud, singular - aymag) and 1 municipality* (singular - hot); Arhangay, Bayanhongor, Bayan-Olgiy, Bulgan, Darhan Uul, Dornod, Dornogovi, Dundgovi, Dzavhan, Govi-Altay, Govi-Sumber, Hentiy, Hovd, Hovsgol, Omnogovi, Orhon, Ovorhangay, Selenge, Suhbaatar, Tov, Ulaanbaatar*, Uvs
Independence: 11 July 1921 (from China)
National holiday: Independence Day/Revolution Day, 11 July (1921)
Constitution: 12 February 1992
Legal system: blend of Soviet, German, and US systems of law that combines aspects of a parliamentary system with some aspects of a presidential system; constitution ambiguous on judicial review of legislative acts; has not accepted compulsory ICJ jurisdiction
Suffrage: 18 years of age; universal
Executive branch:
chief of state: President Natsagiyn BAGABANDI (since 20 June 1997)
head of government: Prime Minister Nambaryn ENKHBAYAR (since 26 July 2000)
cabinet: Cabinet appointed by the State Great Hural in consultation with the president
elections: president nominated by parties in the State Great Hural and elected by popular vote for a four-year term; election last held 20 May 2001 (next to be held in May 2005); following legislative elections, the leader of the majority party or majority coalition is usually elected prime minister by the State Great Hural; election last held 2 July 2000 (next to be held in June 2004)
election results: Natsagiyn BAGABANDI reelected president; percent of vote - Natsagiyn BAGABANDI (MPRP) 58.13%, Radnaasumbereliyn GONCHIGDORJ (DP) 36.58%, Luvsandamba DASHNYAM (CWP) 3.54%, other 1.75%; Nambaryn ENKHBAYAR elected prime minister by a vote in the State Great Hural of 68 to 3
Legislative branch: unicameral State Great Hural (76 seats; members elected by popular vote to serve four-year terms)
elections: last held 2 July 2000 (next to be held June 2004)
election results: percent of vote by party - NA%; seats by party - MPRP 72, other 4
Judicial branch: Supreme Court (serves as appeals court for people's and provincial courts but rarely overturns verdicts of lower courts; judges are nominated by the General Council of Courts for approval by the president)
Political parties and leaders: Citizens' Will Party or CWP (also called Civil Will Party or Civil Courage Party) [Sanjaasurengyn OYUN]; Democratic Party or DP [M. ENKHSAIKHAN]; Mongolian People's Revolutionary Party or MPRP [Nambaryn ENKHBAYAR]; Mongolian New Socialist Democratic Party or MNSDP [B. ERDENEBAT]; Mongolian Republican Party or MRP [B. JARGALSAIHAN]

note: the MPRP is the ruling party
Political pressure groups and leaders: NA
International organization participation: ARF, AsDB, CP, EBRD, FAO, G-77, IAEA, IBRD, ICAO, ICC, ICCt, ICFTU, ICRM, IDA, IFAD, IFC, IFRCS, ILO, IMF, IMO, Interpol, IOC, ISO, ITU, MINURSO, MONUC, NAM, OPCW, UN, UNCTAD, UNESCO, UNIDO, UPU, WCO, WHO, WIPO, WMO, WToO, WTrO
Diplomatic representation in the US:
chief of mission: Ambassador Ravdangiyn BOLD
chancery: 2833 M Street NW, Washington, DC 20007
telephone: [1] (202) 333-7117
FAX: [1] (202) 298-9227
consulate(s) general: New York
Diplomatic representation from the US:
chief of mission: Ambassador Pamela J. SLUTZ
embassy: Micro Region 11, Big Ring Road, C.P.O. 1021, Ulaanbaatar 13
mailing address: PSC 461, Box 300, FPO AP 96521-0002
telephone: [976] (11) 329095
FAX: [976] (11) 320776
Flag description: three equal, vertical bands of red (hoist side), blue, and red; centered on the hoist-side red band in yellow is the national emblem ("soyombo" - a columnar arrangement of abstract and geometric representation for fire, sun, moon, earth, water, and the yin-yang symbol)

Economy

Economy - overview: Economic activity traditionally has been based on agriculture and breeding of livestock. Mongolia also has extensive mineral deposits; copper, coal, molybdenum, tin, tungsten, and gold account for a large part of industrial production. Soviet assistance, at its height one-third of GDP, disappeared almost overnight in 1990-91 at the time of the dismantlement of the USSR. Mongolia was driven into deep recession, prolonged by the Mongolian People's Revolutionary Party's (MPRP) reluctance to undertake serious economic reform. The Democratic Union Coalition (DUC) government embraced free-market economics, eased price controls, liberalized domestic and international trade, and attempted to restructure the banking system and the energy sector. Major domestic privatization programs were undertaken, as well as the fostering of foreign investment through international tender of the oil distribution company, a leading cashmere company, and banks. Reform was held back by the ex-Communist MPRP opposition and by the political instability brought about through four successive governments under the DC. Economic growth picked up in 1997-99 after stalling in 1996 due to a series of natural disasters and declines in world prices of copper and cashmere. In August and September 1999, the economy suffered from a temporary Russian ban on exports of oil and oil products, and Mongolia remains vulnerable in this sector. Mongolia joined the World Trade Organization (WTrO) in 1997. The international donor community pledged over $300 million per year at the Consultative Group Meeting, held in Ulaanbaatar in June 1999. The MPRP government, elected in July 2000, was anxious to improve the investment climate; it also had to deal with a heavy burden of external debt. Falling prices for Mongolia's mainly primary sector exports, widespread opposition to privatization, and adverse effects of weather on agriculture in early 2000 and 2001 restrained real GDP growth. Despite drought problems in 2002, GDP rose 4.0%, followed by a solid 5.0% increase in 2003. The first applications under the land privatization law have been marked by a number of disputes over particular sites. Russia claims Mongolia owes it $11 billion from the Soviet period; any settlement could substantially increase Mongolia's foreign debt burden.

GDP: purchasing power parity - $4.877 billion (2003 est.)

GDP - real growth rate: 5% (2003 est.)

GDP - per capita: purchasing power parity - $1,800 (2003 est.)

GDP - composition by sector:
agriculture: 20.6%
industry: 21.4%
services: 58% (2002 est.)

Population below poverty line: 36% (2001 est.)

Household income or consumption by percentage share:
lowest 10%: 2.1%
highest 10%: 37% (1995)

Distribution of family income - Gini index: 44 (1998)

Inflation rate (consumer prices): 1.5% (2002 est.)

Labor force: 1.4 million (2001)

Labor force - by occupation: herding/agriculture 46%, manufacturing 6%, trade 10.3%, public sector 4.7%, other/unemployed 33% (2001)

Unemployment rate: 4.6% (2001)

Budget:
revenues: $387 million
expenditures: $428 million, including capital expenditures of $NA (2001 est.)

Industries: construction materials; mining (coal, copper, molybdenum, fluorspar, and gold); oil; food and beverages; processing of animal products

Industrial production growth rate: 4.1% (2002 est.)

Electricity - production: 2.225 billion kWh (2001)

Electricity - production by source:
fossil fuel: 100%
hydro: 0%
nuclear: 0%
other: 0% (2001)

Electricity - consumption: 2.194 billion kWh (2001)

Electricity - exports: 25 million kWh (2001)

Electricity - imports: 196 million kWh (2001)

Oil - production: 0 bbl/day (2001 est.)

Oil - consumption: 8,750 bbl/day (2001 est.)

Oil - exports: NA

Oil - imports: NA

Agriculture - products: wheat, barley, potatoes, forage crops, sheep, goats, cattle, camels, horses

Exports: $524 million f.o.b. (2002 est.)

Exports - commodities: copper, livestock, animal products, cashmere, wool, hides, fluorspar, other nonferrous metals

Exports - partners: China 41.4%, US 31.7%, Russia 9.2%, South Korea 4.2% (2002)

Imports: $691 million c.i.f. (2002 est.)

Imports - commodities: machinery and equipment, fuels, food products, industrial consumer goods, chemicals, building materials, sugar, tea

Imports - partners: Russia 34.4%, China 20.1%, South Korea 12.4%, Japan 6.2%, Germany 4.3%, Hong Kong 4.1% (2002)

Debt - external: $885 million (2001 est.)

Economic aid - recipient: $211.3 million (2000 est.)

Currency: togrog/tugrik (MNT)

Currency code: MNT

Exchange rates: togrogs/tugriks per US dollar - 1,171 (2003), 1,110.31 (2002), 1,097.7 (2001), 1,076.67 (2000), 1,021.87 (1999)

Fiscal year: calendar year

Communications

Telephones - main lines in use: 128,000 (2002)

Telephones - mobile cellular: 216,000 (2002)

Telephone system:
general assessment: very low density: about 3.5 telephones for each thousand persons
domestic: NA
international: country code - 976; satellite earth station - 1 Intersputnik (Indian Ocean Region)

Radio broadcast stations: AM 7, FM 9, shortwave 4 (2001)

Television broadcast stations: 9 (plus 18 provincial repeaters and many low power repeaters) (2004)

Internet country code: .mn

Internet hosts: 127 (2002)

Internet users: 50,000 (2002)

Transportation

Railways: 1,815 km
broad gauge: 1,815 km 1.524-m gauge (2002)

Highways:
total: 49,250 km
paved: 1,724 km
unpaved: 47,526 km (2000)

Waterways: 400 km (1999)

Ports and harbors: none

Merchant marine:
total: 65 ships (1,000 GRT or over) 339,423 GRT/ 533,853 DWT
by type: bulk 4, cargo 53, chemical tanker 1, container 2, liquefied gas 2, passenger/cargo 1, petroleum tanker 1, specialized tanker 1
foreign-owned: Belize 1, Cambodia 1, China 4, Cuba 1, Hong Kong 2, Indonesia 1, Japan 1, North Korea 1, Lebanon 1, Malaysia 1, Malta 1, Marshall Islands 5, Moldova 1, Panama 3, Romania 1, Russia 14, Singapore 13, Syria 4, Thailand 1, Turkey 1, Ukraine 1, United States 3, Vietnam 4 (2003 est.)

Airports: 36 (2003 est.)

Airports - with paved runways:
total: 11
over 3,047 m: 1
2,438 to 3,047 m: 10 (2003 est.)

Airports - with unpaved runways:
total: 25
over 3,047 m: 2
2,438 to 3,047 m: 5
1,524 to 2,437 m: 11
914 to 1,523 m: 2
under 914 m: 5 (2003 est.)

Heliports: 2 (2003 est.)

Military

Military branches: Mongolian People's Army (comprising Ground Forces, Air Defense Forces), Border Guards, Internal Security Forces, Construction Corps Forces, Civil Defense Authority

Military manpower - military age: 18 years of age (2004 est.)

Military manpower - availability:
males age 15-49: 818,977 (2004 est.)

Military manpower - fit for military service:
males age 15-49: 530,594 (2004 est.)

Military manpower - reaching military age annually:
males: 33,718 (2004 est.)

Military expenditures - dollar figure: $23.1 million (FY02)

Military expenditures - percent of GDP: 2.2% (FY02)

Transnational Issues

Disputes - international: none

Montserrat

(overseas territory of the UK)

Introduction

Background: Much of this island was devastated and two-thirds of the population fled abroad because of the eruption of the Soufriere Hills Volcano that began on 18 July 1995.

Geography

Location: Caribbean, island in the Caribbean Sea, southeast of Puerto Rico
Geographic coordinates: 16 45 N, 62 12 W
Map references: Central America and the Caribbean
Area:
total: 102 sq km
land: 102 sq km
water: 0 sq km
Area - comparative: about 0.6 times the size of Washington, DC
Land boundaries: 0 km
Coastline: 40 km
Maritime claims:
territorial sea: 3 NM
exclusive fishing zone: 200 NM
Climate: tropical; little daily or seasonal temperature variation
Terrain: volcanic island, mostly mountainous, with small coastal lowland
Elevation extremes:
lowest point: Caribbean Sea 0 m
highest point: Chances Peak (in the Soufriere Hills volcanic complex) 914 m
Natural resources: negligible
Land use:
arable land: 20%
permanent crops: 0%
other: 80% (1998 est.)
Irrigated land: NA sq km
Natural hazards: severe hurricanes (June to November); volcanic eruptions (Soufriere Hills volcano has erupted continuously since 1995)

Environment - current issues: land erosion occurs on slopes that have been cleared for cultivation
Geography - note: the island is entirely volcanic in origin and contains seven active volcanoes

People

Population: 9,245
note: an estimated 8,000 refugees left the island following the resumption of volcanic activity in July 1995; some have returned (July 2004 est.)
Age structure:
0-14 years: 23.3% (male 1,092; female 1,062)
15-64 years: 65.5% (male 2,889; female 3,162)
65 years and over: 11.2% (male 543; female 497) (2004 est.)
Median age:
total: 28.2 years
male: 28 years
female: 28.4 years (2004 est.)
Population growth rate: 1.03% (2004 est.)
Birth rate: 17.63 births/1,000 population (2004 est.)
Death rate: 7.36 deaths/1,000 population (2004 est.)
Net migration rate: 0 migrant(s)/1,000 population (2004 est.)
Sex ratio:
at birth: 1.05 male(s)/female
under 15 years: 1.03 male(s)/female
15-64 years: 0.91 male(s)/female
65 years and over: 1.09 male(s)/female
total population: 0.96 male(s)/female (2004 est.)
Infant mortality rate:
total: 7.56 deaths/1,000 live births
male: 8.8 deaths/1,000 live births
female: 6.26 deaths/1,000 live births (2004 est.)
Life expectancy at birth:
total population: 78.53 years
male: 76.39 years
female: 80.78 years (2004 est.)
Total fertility rate: 1.79 children born/woman (2004 est.)
HIV/AIDS - adult prevalence rate: NA%
HIV/AIDS - people living with HIV/AIDS: NA
HIV/AIDS - deaths: NA
Nationality:
noun: Montserratian(s)
adjective: Montserratian
Ethnic groups: black, white
Religions: Anglican, Methodist, Roman Catholic, Pentecostal, Seventh-Day Adventist, other Christian denominations
Languages: English
Literacy:
definition: age 15 and over has ever attended school
total population: 97%
male: 97%
female: 97% (1970 est.)

Government

Country name:
conventional long form: none
conventional short form: Montserrat
Dependency status: overseas territory of the UK

Government type: NA
Capital: Plymouth (abandoned in 1997 due to volcanic activity; interim government buildings have been built at Brades Estate, in the Carr's Bay/Little Bay vicinity at the northwest end of Montserrat)
Administrative divisions: 3 parishes; Saint Anthony, Saint Georges, Saint Peter
Independence: none (overseas territory of the UK)
National holiday: Birthday of Queen ELIZABETH II, second Saturday in June (1926)
Constitution: present constitution came into force 19 December 1989
Legal system: English common law and statutory law
Suffrage: 18 years of age; universal
Executive branch:
chief of state: Queen ELIZABETH II (since 6 February 1952), represented by Governor Anthony LONGRIGG (since May 2001)
head of government: Chief Minister John OSBORNE (since 5 April 2001)
cabinet: Executive Council consists of the governor, the chief minister, three other ministers, the attorney general, and the finance secretary
elections: the monarch is hereditary; governor appointed by the monarch; following legislative elections, the leader of the majority party usually becomes chief minister
Legislative branch: unicameral Legislative Council (11 seats, 9 popularly elected; members serve five-year terms)
note: expanded in 2001 from 7 to 9 elected members with attorney general and financial secretary sitting as ex-officio members
elections: last held April 2001 (next to be held by November 2006)
election results: percent of vote by party - NA%; seats by party - NPLM 7, NPP 2
note: in 2001, the Elections Commission instituted a single constituency/voter-at-large system whereby all eligible voters cast ballots for all nine seats of the Legislative Council
Judicial branch: Eastern Caribbean Supreme Court (based in Saint Lucia, one judge of the Supreme Court is a resident of the islands and presides over the High Court)
Political parties and leaders: National Progressive Party or NPP [Reuben T. MEADE]; New People's Liberation Movement or NPLM [John A. OSBORNE]
Political pressure groups and leaders: NA
International organization participation: Caricom, CDB, ICFTU, Interpol (subbureau), OECS
Diplomatic representation in the US: none (overseas territory of the UK)
Diplomatic representation from the US: none (overseas territory of the UK)
Flag description: blue, with the flag of the UK in the upper hoist-side quadrant and the Montserratian coat of arms centered in the outer half of the flag; the coat of arms features a woman standing beside a yellow harp with her arm around a black cross

Montserrat (continued)

Economy

Economy - overview: Severe volcanic activity, which began in July 1995, has put a damper on this small, open economy. A catastrophic eruption in June 1997 closed the airports and seaports, causing further economic and social dislocation. Two-thirds of the 12,000 inhabitants fled the island. Some began to return in 1998, but lack of housing limited the number. The agriculture sector continued to be affected by the lack of suitable land for farming and the destruction of crops. Prospects for the economy depend largely on developments in relation to the volcano and on public sector construction activity. The UK has launched a three-year $122.8 million aid program to help reconstruct the economy. Half of the island is expected to remain uninhabitable for another decade.
GDP: purchasing power parity - $29 million (2002 est.)
GDP - real growth rate: -1% (2002 est.)
GDP - per capita: purchasing power parity - $3,400 (2002 est.)
GDP - composition by sector:
agriculture: 5.4%
industry: 13.6%
services: 81% (1996 est.)
Population below poverty line: NA%
Household income or consumption by percentage share:
lowest 10%: NA%
highest 10%: NA%
Inflation rate (consumer prices): 2.6% (2002 est.)
Labor force: 4,521 ; note - lowered by flight of people from volcanic activity (2000 est.)
Labor force - by occupation: agriculture NA%, industry NA%, services NA%
Unemployment rate: 6% (1998 est.)
Budget:
revenues: $31.4 million
expenditures: $31.6 million, including capital expenditures of $8.4 million (1997 est.)
Industries: tourism, rum, textiles, electronic appliances
Industrial production growth rate: NA%
Electricity - production: 2.5 million kWh (2001)
Electricity - production by source:
fossil fuel: 100%
hydro: 0%
nuclear: 0%
other: 0% (2001)
Electricity - consumption: 2.325 million kWh (2001)
Electricity - exports: 0 kWh (2001)
Electricity - imports: 0 kWh (2001)
Oil - production: 0 bbl/day (2001 est.)
Oil - consumption: 400 bbl/day (2001 est.)
Oil - exports: NA
Oil - imports: NA
Agriculture - products: cabbages, carrots, cucumbers, tomatoes, onions, peppers, livestock products
Exports: $700,000 (2001)

Exports - commodities: electronic components, plastic bags, apparel, hot peppers, live plants, cattle
Exports - partners: US, Antigua and Barbuda
Imports: $17 million (2001)
Imports - commodities: machinery and transportation equipment, foodstuffs, manufactured goods, fuels, lubricants, and related materials
Imports - partners: US, UK, Trinidad and Tobago, Japan, Canada
Debt - external: $8.9 million (1997)
Economic aid - recipient: Country Policy Plan (2001) is a three-year program for spending $122.8 million in British budgetary assistance (2002 est.)
Currency: East Caribbean dollar (XCD)
Currency code: XCD
Exchange rates: East Caribbean dollars per US dollar - 2.7000 (fixed rate since 1976)
Fiscal year: 1 April - 31 March

Communications

Telephones - main lines in use: NA
Telephones - mobile cellular: 70 (1994)
Telephone system:
general assessment: NA
domestic: NA
international: country code - 1-664
Radio broadcast stations: AM 1, FM 2, shortwave 0 (1998)
Television broadcast stations: 1 (1997)
Internet country code: .ms
Internet users: NA

Transportation

Railways: 0 km
Highways:
total: 227 km
paved: NA km
unpaved: NA km
note: volcanic eruptions beginning in 1995 destroyed most of the road system (2003)
Waterways: none
Ports and harbors: Plymouth (abandoned), Little Bay (anchorages and ferry landing), Carr's Bay
Merchant marine: none
Airports: 1 (2003 est.)
Airports - with paved runways:
total: 1
under 914 m: 1 (2003 est.)

Military

Military branches: no regular indigenous military forces; Police Force
Military - note: defense is the responsibility of the UK

Transnational Issues

Disputes - international: none
Illicit drugs: transshipment point for South American narcotics destined for the US and Europe

Morocco

Introduction

Background: Morocco's long struggle for independence from France ended in 1956. The internationalized city of Tangier was turned over to the new country that same year. Morocco virtually annexed Western Sahara during the late 1970s, but final resolution on the status of the territory remains unresolved. Gradual political reforms in the 1990s resulted in the establishment of a bicameral legislature in 1997. Parliamentary elections were held for the second time in September 2002 and municipal elections were held in September 2003.

Geography

Location: Northern Africa, bordering the North Atlantic Ocean and the Mediterranean Sea, between Algeria and Western Sahara
Geographic coordinates: 32 00 N, 5 00 W
Map references: Africa
Area:
total: 446,550 sq km
land: 446,300 sq km
water: 250 sq km
Area - comparative: slightly larger than California
Land boundaries:
total: 2,017.9 km
border countries: Algeria 1,559 km, Western Sahara 443 km, Spain (Ceuta) 6.3 km, Spain (Melilla) 9.6 km
Coastline: 1,835 km
Maritime claims:
territorial sea: 12 NM
contiguous zone: 24 NM
exclusive economic zone: 200 NM
continental shelf: 200-m depth or to the depth of exploitation
Climate: Mediterranean, becoming more extreme in the interior
Terrain: northern coast and interior are mountainous with large areas of bordering plateaus, intermontane valleys, and rich coastal plains

Morocco (continued)

Elevation extremes:
lowest point: Sebkha Tah -55 m
highest point: Jbel Toubkal 4,165 m
Natural resources: phosphates, iron ore, manganese, lead, zinc, fish, salt
Land use:
arable land: 20.12%
permanent crops: 2.05%
other: 77.83% (1998 est.)
Irrigated land: 12,910 sq km (1998 est.)
Natural hazards: northern mountains geologically unstable and subject to earthquakes; periodic droughts
Environment - current issues: land degradation/desertification (soil erosion resulting from farming of marginal areas, overgrazing, destruction of vegetation); water supplies contaminated by raw sewage; siltation of reservoirs; oil pollution of coastal waters
Environment - international agreements:
party to: Biodiversity, Climate Change, Climate Change-Kyoto Protocol, Desertification, Endangered Species, Hazardous Wastes, Marine Dumping, Ozone Layer Protection, Ship Pollution, Wetlands, Whaling
signed, but not ratified: Environmental Modification, Law of the Sea
Geography - note: strategic location along Strait of Gibraltar

People

Population: 32,209,101 (July 2004 est.)
Age structure:
0-14 years: 32.6% (male 5,355,388; female 5,156,762)
15-64 years: 62.5% (male 10,013,466; female 10,112,060)
65 years and over: 4.9% (male 692,465; female 878,960) (2004 est.)
Median age:
total: 23.3 years
male: 22.8 years
female: 23.8 years (2004 est.)
Population growth rate: 1.61% (2004 est.)
Birth rate: 22.79 births/1,000 population (2004 est.)
Death rate: 5.71 deaths/1,000 population (2004 est.)
Net migration rate: -0.98 migrant(s)/1,000 population (2004 est.)
Sex ratio:
at birth: 1.05 male(s)/female
under 15 years: 1.04 male(s)/female
15-64 years: 0.99 male(s)/female
65 years and over: 0.79 male(s)/female
total population: 1 male(s)/female (2004 est.)
Infant mortality rate:
total: 43.25 deaths/1,000 live births
male: 47.09 deaths/1,000 live births
female: 39.21 deaths/1,000 live births (2004 est.)
Life expectancy at birth:
total population: 70.35 years
male: 68.06 years
female: 72.74 years (2004 est.)

Total fertility rate: 2.81 children born/woman (2004 est.)
HIV/AIDS - adult prevalence rate: 0.1% (2001 est.)
HIV/AIDS - people living with HIV/AIDS: 13,000 (2001 est.)
HIV/AIDS - deaths: NA
Nationality:
noun: Moroccan(s)
adjective: Moroccan
Ethnic groups: Arab-Berber 99.1%, other 0.7%, Jewish 0.2%
Religions: Muslim 98.7%, Christian 1.1%, Jewish 0.2%
Languages: Arabic (official), Berber dialects, French often the language of business, government, and diplomacy
Literacy:
definition: age 15 and over can read and write
total population: 51.7%
male: 64.1%
female: 39.4% (2003 est.)

Government

Country name:
conventional long form: Kingdom of Morocco
conventional short form: Morocco
local long form: Al Mamlakah al Maghribiyah
local short form: Al Maghrib
Government type: constitutional monarchy
Capital: Rabat
Administrative divisions: 37 provinces and 2 wilayas*; Agadir, Al Hoceima, Azilal, Beni Mellal, Ben Slimane, Boulemane, Casablanca*, Chaouen, El Jadida, El Kelaa des Sraghna, Er Rachidia, Essaouira, Fes, Figuig, Guelmim, Ifrane, Kenitra, Khemisset, Khenifra, Khouribga, Laayoune, Larache, Marrakech, Meknes, Nador, Ouarzazate, Oujda, Rabat-Sale*, Safi, Settat, Sidi Kacem, Tanger, Tan-Tan, Taounate, Taroudannt, Tata, Taza, Tetouan, Tiznit; three additional provinces of Ad Dakhla (Oued Eddahab), Boujdour, and Es Smara as well as parts of Tan-Tan and Laayoune fall within Moroccan-claimed Western Sahara
note: as part of a 1997 decentralization/regionalization law passed by the legislature 16 new regions (provided below) were created although full details and scope of the reorganization are limited: Casablanca, Chaouia-Ourdigha, Doukkala-Abda, Fes-Boulmane, Gharb-Chrarda-Beni Hssen, Guelmim-Es Smara, Laayoune-Boujdour-Sakia El Hamra, Marrakech-Tensift-El Haouz, Meknes-Tafilalet, Oriental, Oued Eddahab-Lagouira, Rabat-Sale-Zemmour-Zaer, Souss-Massa-Draa, Tadla-Azilal, Tangier-Tetouan, Taza-Al Hoceima-Taounate
Independence: 2 March 1956 (from France)
National holiday: Throne Day (accession of King MOHAMED VI to the throne), 30 July (1999)
Constitution: 10 March 1972, revised 4 September 1992, amended (to create bicameral legislature) September 1996

Legal system: based on Islamic law and French and Spanish civil law system; judicial review of legislative acts in Constitutional Chamber of Supreme Court
Suffrage: 18 years of age; universal (as of January 2003)
Executive branch:
chief of state: King MOHAMED VI (since 30 July 1999)
head of government: Prime Minister Driss JETTOU (since 9 October 2002)
cabinet: Council of Ministers appointed by the monarch
elections: none; the monarch is hereditary; prime minister appointed by the monarch following legislative elections
Legislative branch: bicameral Parliament consists of an upper house or Chamber of Counselors (270 seats; members elected indirectly by local councils, professional organizations, and labor syndicates for nine-year terms; one-third of the members are renewed every three years) and a lower house or Chamber of Representatives (325 seats; 295 by multi-seat constituencies and 30 from national lists of women; members elected by popular vote for five-year terms)
elections: Chamber of Counselors - last held 6 October 2003 (next to be held NA 2006); Chamber of Representatives - last held 27 September 2002 (next to be held NA 2007)
election results: Chamber of Counselors - percent of vote by party - NA%; seats by party - RNI 42, MDS 33, UC 28, MP 27, PND 21, PI 21, USFP 16, MNP 15, PA 13, FFD 12, other 42; Chamber of Representatives - percent of vote by party - NA%; seats by party - USFP 50, PI 48, PJD 42, RNI 41, MP 27, MNP 18, UC 16, PND 12, PPS 11, UD 10, other 50
Judicial branch: Supreme Court (judges are appointed on the recommendation of the Supreme Council of the Judiciary, presided over by the monarch)
Political parties and leaders: Action Party or PA [Muhammad EL IDRISSI]; Alliance of Liberties or ADL [Ali BELHAJ]; Annahj Addimocrati or Annahj [Abdellah EL HARIF]; Avant Garde Social Democratic Party or PADS [Ahmed BENJELLOUN]; Citizen Forces or FC [Abderrahman LAHJOUJI]; Citizen's Initiatives for Development [Mohamed BENHAMOU]; Constitutional Union or UC [Mohamed ABIED (interim)]; Democratic and Independence Party or PDI [Abdelwahed MAACH]; Democratic and Social Movement or MDS [Mahmoud ARCHANE]; Democratic Socialist Party or PSD [Aissa OUARDIGHI]; Democratic Union or UD [Bouazza IKKEN]; Environment and Development Party or PED [Ahmed EL ALAMI]; Front of Democratic Forces or FFD [Thami EL KHYARI]; Istiqlal Party (Independence Party) or PI [Abbas El FASSI]; Justice and Development Party (formerly the Constitutional and Democratic Popular Movement) or PJD [Abdelkrim EL KHATIB]; Moroccan Liberal Party or PML [Mohamed ZIANE]; National Democratic Party or PND [Abdallah KADIRI]; National Ittihadi Congress Party or CNI

[Abdelmajid BOUZOUBAA]; National Popular Movement or MNP [Mahjoubi AHERDANE]; National Rally of Independents or RNI [Ahmed OSMAN]; National Union of Popular Forces or UNFP [Abdellah IBRAHIM]; Parti Al Ahd or Al Ahd [Najib EL OUAZZANI, chairman]; Party of Progress and Socialism or PPS [Ismail ALAOUI]; Party of Renewal and Equity or PRE [Chakir ACHABAR]; Party of the Unified Socialist Left or GSU [Mohamed Ben Said AIT IDDER]; Popular Movement or MP [Mohamed LAENSER]; Reform and Development Party or PRD [Abderrahmane EL KOUHEN]; Social Center Party or PSC [Lahcen MADIH]; Socialist Union of Popular Forces or USFP [Mohammed El-YAZGHI]

Political pressure groups and leaders: Democratic Confederation of Labor or CDT [Noubir AMAOUI]; General Union of Moroccan Workers or UGTM [Abderrazzak AFILAL]; Moroccan Employers Association or CGEM [Hassan CHAMI]; National Labor Union of Morocco or UNMT [Abdelslam MAATI]; Union of Moroccan Workers or UMT [Mahjoub BENSEDDIK]

International organization participation: ABEDA, ACCT, AfDB, AFESD, AMF, AMU, EBRD, FAO, G-77, IAEA, IBRD, ICAO, ICC, ICCt (signatory), ICFTU, ICRM, IDA, IDB, IFAD, IFC, IFRCS, IHO, ILO, IMF, IMO, Interpol, IOC, IOM, ISO, ITU, LAS, MONUC, NAM, OAS (observer), OIC, OPCW, OSCE (partner), PCA, UN, UNCTAD, UNESCO, UNHCR, UNIDO, UNITAR, UPU, WCL, WCO, WHO, WIPO, WMO, WToO, WTrO

Diplomatic representation in the US:
chief of mission: Ambassador Aziz MEKOUAR
chancery: 1601 21st Street NW, Washington, DC 20009
telephone: [1] (202) 462-7979 through 7982
FAX: [1] (202) 265-0161
consulate(s) general: New York

Diplomatic representation from the US:
chief of mission: Ambassador Mr. Thomas T. RILEY
embassy: 2 Avenue de Mohamed El Fassi, Rabat
mailing address: PSC 74, Box 021, APO AE 09718
telephone: [212] (37) 76 22 65
FAX: [212] (37) 76 56 61
consulate(s) general: Casablanca

Flag description: red with a green pentacle (five-pointed, linear star) known as Solomon's seal in the center of the flag; green is the traditional color of Islam

Economy

Economy - overview: Morocco faces the problems typical of developing countries - restraining government spending, reducing constraints on private activity and foreign trade, and achieving sustainable economic growth. Despite structural adjustment programs supported by the IMF, World Bank, and the Paris Club, the dirham is only fully convertible for current account transactions. Reforms of the financial sector are being contemplated. Droughts depressed activity in the key agricultural sector and contributed to a stagnant economy in 2002. Morocco reported large

foreign exchange inflows from the sale of a mobile telephone license, and partial privatization of the state-owned telecommunications company and the state tobacco company. Favorable rainfall in 2003 led to a growth of 6%. Formidable long-term challenges include: preparing the economy for freer trade with the EU and US, improving education, and attracting foreign investment to boost living standards and job prospects for Morocco's youth.
GDP: purchasing power parity - $128.3 billion (2003 est.)
GDP - real growth rate: 6% (2003 est.)
GDP - per capita: purchasing power parity - $4,000 (2003 est.)
GDP - composition by sector:
agriculture: 15%
industry: 33%
services: 52% (2000 est.)
Population below poverty line: 19% (1999 est.)
Household income or consumption by percentage share:
lowest 10%: 2.6%
highest 10%: 30.9% (1998-99)
Distribution of family income - Gini index: 39.5 (1998-99)
Inflation rate (consumer prices): 3.6% (2002 est.)
Labor force: 11 million (1999)
Labor force - by occupation: agriculture 40%, services 45%, industry 15% (2003 est.)
Unemployment rate: 19% (2003 est.)
Budget:
revenues: $13.8 billion
expenditures: $14 billion, including capital expenditures of $2.1 billion (2004 est.)
Industries: phosphate rock mining and processing, food processing, leather goods, textiles, construction, tourism
Industrial production growth rate: NA
Electricity - production: 13.35 billion kWh (2001)
Electricity - production by source:
fossil fuel: 95.4%
hydro: 4.6%
nuclear: 0%
other: 0% (2001)
Electricity - consumption: 14.61 billion kWh (2001)
Electricity - exports: 0 kWh (2001)
Electricity - imports: 2.2 billion kWh (2001)
Oil - production: 400 bbl/day (2001 est.)
Oil - consumption: 167,000 bbl/day (2001 est.)
Oil - exports: NA
Oil - imports: NA
Oil - proved reserves: 900,000 bbl (1 January 2002)
Natural gas - production: 50 million cu m (2001 est.)
Natural gas - consumption: 50 million cu m (2001 est.)
Natural gas - exports: 0 cu m (2001 est.)
Natural gas - imports: 0 cu m (2001 est.)
Natural gas - proved reserves: 665.4 million cu m (1 January 2002)

Agriculture - products: barley, wheat, citrus, wine, vegetables, olives; livestock
Exports: $8.466 billion f.o.b. (2003 est.)
Exports - commodities: clothing, fish, inorganic chemicals, transistors, crude minerals, fertilizers (including phosphates), petroleum products, fruits, vegetables
Exports - partners: France 25.9%, Spain 14%, UK 7.8%, Germany 5.7%, Italy 5.5%, US 4.7% (2002)
Imports: $12.75 billion f.o.b. (2003 est.)
Imports - commodities: crude petroleum, textile fabric, telecommunications equipment, wheat, gas and electricity, transistors, plastics
Imports - partners: France 21.1%, Spain 12.7%, Italy 6.4%, Germany 5.6%, US 4.6%, UK 4.1%, Saudi Arabia 4.1% (2002)
Debt - external: $17.1 billion (2003 est.)
Economic aid - recipient: $565.6 million (1995)
Currency: Moroccan dirham (MAD)
Currency code: MAD
Exchange rates: Moroccan dirhams per US dollar - 9.5744 (2003), 11.0206 (2002), 11.303 (2001), 10.6256 (2000), 9.8044 (1999)
Fiscal year: calendar year

Communications

Telephones - main lines in use: 1,127,400 (2002)
Telephones - mobile cellular: 6,198,700 (2002)
Telephone system:
general assessment: modern system with all important capabilities; however, density is low with only 4.6 main lines available for each 100 persons
domestic: good system composed of open-wire lines, cables, and microwave radio relay links; Internet available but expensive; principal switching centers are Casablanca and Rabat; national network nearly 100% digital using fiber-optic links; improved rural service employs microwave radio relay
international: country code - 212; 7 submarine cables; satellite earth stations - 2 Intelsat (Atlantic Ocean) and 1 Arabsat; microwave radio relay to Gibraltar, Spain, and Western Sahara; coaxial cable and microwave radio relay to Algeria; participant in Medarabtel; fiber-optic cable link from Agadir to Algeria and Tunisia (1998)
Radio broadcast stations: AM 27, FM 25, shortwave 6 (1998)
Television broadcast stations: 35 (plus 66 repeaters) (1995)
Internet country code: .ma
Internet hosts: 2,680 (2002)
Internet users: 700,000 (2002)

Transportation

Railways:
total: 1,907 km
standard gauge: 1,907 km 1.435-m gauge (1,003 km electrified) (2002)
Highways:
total: 57,707 km
paved: 32,547 km (including 481 km of expressways)
unpaved: 25,160 km (2000)

Morocco (continued)

Waterways: none
Pipelines: gas 695 km; oil 285 km (2003)
Ports and harbors: Agadir, El Jadida, Casablanca, El Jorf Lasfar, Kenitra, Mohammedia, Nador, Rabat, Safi, Tangier; also Spanish-controlled Ceuta and Melilla
Merchant marine:
total: 35 ships (1,000 GRT or over) 236,131 GRT/ 252,367 DWT
by type: cargo 8, chemical tanker 7, container 7, petroleum tanker 1, refrigerated cargo 5, roll on/roll off 5, short-sea/passenger 2
foreign-owned: France 1, Germany 2, Greece 1, Hong Kong 1, Netherlands 2, Norway 2, United Kingdom 1 (2003 est.)
Airports: 64 (2003 est.)
Airports - with paved runways:
total: 25
over 3,047 m: 11
2,438 to 3,047 m: 4
1,524 to 2,437 m: 8
914 to 1,523 m: 1
under 914 m: 1 (2003 est.)
Airports - with unpaved runways:
total: 39
2,438 to 3,047 m: 2
1,524 to 2,437 m: 11
914 to 1,523 m: 15
under 914 m: 11 (2003 est.)
Heliports: 1 (2003 est.)

Military

Military branches: Royal Armed Forces: Army, Navy, Air Force
Military manpower - military age: 18 years of age (2004 est.)
Military manpower - availability:
males age 15-49: 8,788,971 (2004 est.)
Military manpower - fit for military service:
males age 15-49: 5,529,267 (2004 est.)
Military manpower - reaching military age annually:
males: 352,711 (2004 est.)
Military expenditures - dollar figure: $2,297,200,000 (2003)
Military expenditures - percent of GDP: 4.8% (2003)

Transnational Issues

Disputes - international: claims and administers Western Sahara whose sovereignty remains unresolved - UN-administered cease-fire has remained in effect since September 1991, but attempts to hold a referendum have failed and parties thus far have rejected all brokered proposals; Polisario, Algeria, and European supporters agree to the latest US-brokered UN proposals for limited temporary autonomy for 4-5 years followed by a referendum on independence, but Morocco's final response is pending; Morocco protests Spain's control over the coastal enclaves of Ceuta, Melilla, and Penon

de Velez de la Gomera, the islands of Penon de Alhucemas and Islas Chafarinas, and surrounding waters; Morocco also rejected Spain's unilateral designation of a median line from the Canary Islands in 2002 to set limits to undersea resource exploration and refugee interdiction, but agreed in 2003 to discuss a comprehensive maritime delimitation; Morocco serves as the primary launching area of illegal migration into Spain from North Africa
Illicit drugs: illicit producer of hashish; trafficking increasing for both domestic and international drug markets; shipments of hashish mostly directed to Western Europe; transit point for cocaine from South America destined for Western Europe

Mozambique

Introduction

Background: Almost five centuries as a Portuguese colony came to a close with independence in 1975. Large-scale emigration by whites, economic dependence on South Africa, a severe drought, and a prolonged civil war hindered the country's development. The ruling party formally abandoned Marxism in 1989, and a new constitution the following year provided for multiparty elections and a free market economy. A UN-negotiated peace agreement with rebel forces ended the fighting in 1992. Heavy flooding in both 1999 and 2000 severely hurt the economy. Political stability and sound economic policies have encouraged recent foreign investment.

Geography

Location: South-eastern Africa, bordering the Mozambique Channel, between South Africa and Tanzania
Geographic coordinates: 18 15 S, 35 00 E
Map references: Africa
Area:
total: 801,590 sq km
land: 784,090 sq km

Mozambique (continued)

water: 17,500 sq km

Area - comparative: slightly less than twice the size of California

Land boundaries:

total: 4,571 km

border countries: Malawi 1,569 km, South Africa 491 km, Swaziland 105 km, Tanzania 756 km, Zambia 419 km, Zimbabwe 1,231 km

Coastline: 2,470 km

Maritime claims:

territorial sea: 12 NM

exclusive economic zone: 200 NM

Climate: tropical to subtropical

Terrain: mostly coastal lowlands, uplands in center, high plateaus in northwest, mountains in west

Elevation extremes:

lowest point: Indian Ocean 0 m

highest point: Monte Binga 2,436 m

Natural resources: coal, titanium, natural gas, hydropower, tantalum, graphite

Land use:

arable land: 3.98%

permanent crops: 0.29%

other: 95.73% (1998 est.)

Irrigated land: 1,070 sq km (1998 est.)

Natural hazards: severe droughts; devastating cyclones and floods occur in central and southern provinces

Environment - current issues: a long civil war and recurrent drought in the hinterlands have resulted in increased migration of the population to urban and coastal areas with adverse environmental consequences; desertification; pollution of surface and coastal waters; elephant poaching for ivory is a problem

Environment - international agreements:

party to: Biodiversity, Climate Change, Desertification, Endangered Species, Hazardous Wastes, Law of the Sea, Ozone Layer Protection

signed, but not ratified: none of the selected agreements

Geography - note: the Zambezi flows through the north-central and most fertile part of the country

People

Population: 18,811,731

note: estimates for this country explicitly take into account the effects of excess mortality due to AIDS; this can result in lower life expectancy, higher infant mortality and death rates, lower population and growth rates, and changes in the distribution of population by age and sex than would otherwise be expected; the 1997 Mozambican census reported a population of 16,099,246 (July 2004 est.)

Age structure:

0-14 years: 43.6% (male 4,126,178; female 4,074,759)

15-64 years: 53.6% (male 4,944,416; female 5,145,167)

65 years and over: 2.8% (male 215,418; female 305,793) (2004 est.)

Median age:

total: 18.2 years

male: 17.8 years

female: 18.6 years (2004 est.)

Population growth rate: 1.22% (2004 est.)

Birth rate: 36.06 births/1,000 population (2004 est.)

Death rate: 23.86 deaths/1,000 population (2004 est.)

Net migration rate: 0 migrant(s)/1,000 population (2004 est.)

Sex ratio:

at birth: 1.03 male(s)/female

under 15 years: 1.01 male(s)/female

15-64 years: 0.96 male(s)/female

65 years and over: 0.7 male(s)/female

total population: 0.98 male(s)/female (2004 est.)

Infant mortality rate:

total: 137.08 deaths/1,000 live births

male: 142.67 deaths/1,000 live births

female: 131.32 deaths/1,000 live births (2004 est.)

Life expectancy at birth:

total population: 37.1 years

male: 37.83 years

female: 36.34 years (2004 est.)

Total fertility rate: 4.78 children born/woman (2004 est.)

HIV/AIDS - adult prevalence rate: 13% (2001 est.)

HIV/AIDS - people living with HIV/AIDS: 1.1 million (2001 est.)

HIV/AIDS - deaths: 60,000 (2001 est.)

Nationality:

noun: Mozambican(s)

adjective: Mozambican

Ethnic groups: indigenous tribal groups 99.66% (Shangaan, Chokwe, Manyika, Sena, Makua, and others), Europeans 0.06%, Euro-Africans 0.2%, Indians 0.08%

Religions: indigenous beliefs 50%, Christian 30%, Muslim 20%

Languages: Portuguese (official), indigenous dialects

Literacy:

definition: age 15 and over can read and write

total population: 47.8%

male: 63.5%

female: 32.7% (2003 est.)

Government

Country name:

conventional long form: Republic of Mozambique

conventional short form: Mozambique

local long form: Republica de Mocambique

local short form: Mocambique

former: Portuguese East Africa

Government type: republic

Capital: Maputo

Administrative divisions: 10 provinces (provincias, singular - provincia), 1 city (cidade)*; Cabo Delgado, Gaza, Inhambane, Manica, Maputo, Cidade de Maputo*, Nampula, Niassa, Sofala, Tete, Zambezia

Independence: 25 June 1975 (from Portugal)

National holiday: Independence Day, 25 June (1975)

Constitution: 30 November 1990

Legal system: based on Portuguese civil law system and customary law

Suffrage: 18 years of age; universal

Executive branch:

chief of state: President Joaquim Alberto CHISSANO (since 6 November 1986); note - before being popularly elected, CHISSANO was elected president by Frelimo's Central Committee on 4 November 1986 (reelected by the Committee 30 July 1989)

head of government: Prime Minister Luisa DIOGO (since 17 February 2004)

cabinet: Cabinet

elections: president elected by popular vote for a five-year term; election last held 3-5 December 1999 (next to be held NA December 2004); prime minister appointed by the president

election results: Joaquim Alberto CHISSANO reelected president; percent of vote - Joaquim Alberto CHISSANO 52.3%, Afonso DHLAKAMA 47.7%

Legislative branch: unicameral Assembly of the Republic or Assembleia da Republica (250 seats; members are directly elected by popular vote on a secret ballot to serve five-year terms)

elections: last held 3-5 December 1999 (next to be held NA December 2004)

election results: percent of vote by party - Frelimo 48.54%, Renamo-UE 38.81%; seats by party - Frelimo 133, Renamo-UE 117

note: Renamo-UE ran as a multiparty coalition; none of the other opposition parties received the 5% required to win parliamentary seats; in September 2000, Renamo-UE member Raul DOMINGOS was expelled from the party; he continues to hold his parliamentary seat as an independent

Judicial branch: Supreme Court (the court of final appeal; some of its professional judges are appointed by the president and some are elected by the Assembly); other courts include an Administrative Court, customs courts, maritime courts, courts marshal, labor courts

note: although the constitution provides for the creation of a separate Constitutional Court, one has never been established; in its absence the Supreme Court reviews constitutional cases

Political parties and leaders: Front for the Liberation of Mozambique (Frente de Liberatacao de Mocambique) or Frelimo [Joaquim Alberto CHISSANO, president]; Mozambique National Resistance-Electoral Union (Resistencia Nacional Mocambicana-Uniao Eleitoral) or Renamo-UE [Afonso DHLAKAMA, president]

Political pressure groups and leaders: Institute for Peace and Democracy (Instituto para Paz e Democracia) or IPADE [Raul DOMINGOS, president]; Etica [Abdul CARIMO Issa, chairman]; Movement for Peace and Citizenship (Movimento para Paz e Cidadania); Mozambican League of Human Rights (Liga Mocambicana dos Direitos Humanos) or LDH

Mozambique (continued)

[Alice MABOTE, president]; Human Rights and Development (Direitos Humanos e Desenvolvimento) or DHD [Artemisia FRANCO, secretary general]
International organization participation: ACP, AfDB, AU, C, FAO, G-77, IBRD, ICAO, ICCt (signatory), ICFTU, ICRM, IDA, IDB, IFAD, IFC, IFRCS, IHO, ILO, IMF, IMO, Interpol, IOC, IOM (observer), ISO (correspondent), ITU, MONUC, NAM, OIC, OPCW, SADC, UN, UNCTAD, UNESCO, UNHCR, UNIDO, UNMISET, UPU, WCO, WFTU, WHO, WIPO, WMO, WToO, WTrO
Diplomatic representation in the US:
chief of mission: Ambassador Armando PANGUENE
chancery: 1990 M Street NW, Suite 570, Washington, DC 20036
telephone: [1] (202) 293-7146
FAX: [1] (202) 835-0245
Diplomatic representation from the US:
chief of mission: Ambassador Sharon P. WILKINSON
embassy: Avenida Kenneth Kuanda 193, Maputo
mailing address: P. O. Box 783, Maputo
telephone: [258] (1) 492797
FAX: [258] (1) 490448
Flag description: three equal horizontal bands of green (top), black, and yellow with a red isosceles triangle based on the hoist side; the black band is edged in white; centered in the triangle is a yellow five-pointed star bearing a crossed rifle and hoe in black superimposed on an open white book

Economy

Economy - overview: At independence in 1975, Mozambique was one of the world's poorest countries. Socialist mismanagement and a brutal civil war from 1977-92 exacerbated the situation. In 1987, the government embarked on a series of macroeconomic reforms designed to stabilize the economy. These steps, combined with donor assistance and with political stability since the multi-party elections in 1994, have led to dramatic improvements in the country's growth rate. Inflation was reduced to single digits during the late 1990s although it returned to double digits in 2000-03. Fiscal reforms, including the introduction of a value-added tax and reform of the customs service, have improved the government's revenue collection abilities. In spite of these gains, Mozambique remains dependent upon foreign assistance for much of its annual budget, and the majority of the population remains below the poverty line. Subsistence agriculture continues to employ the vast majority of the country's workforce. A substantial trade imbalance persists although the opening of the MOZAL aluminum smelter, the country's largest foreign investment project to date has increased export earnings. Additional investment projects in titanium extraction and processing and garment manufacturing should further close the import/export gap. Mozambique's once substantial foreign debt has been reduced through forgiveness and rescheduling under the IMF's Heavily Indebted Poor Countries (HIPC) and Enhanced HIPC initiatives, and is now at a manageable level.

GDP: purchasing power parity - $21.23 billion (2003 est.)
GDP - real growth rate: 7% (2003 est.)
GDP - per capita: purchasing power parity - $1,200 (2003 est.)
GDP - composition by sector:
agriculture: 22%
industry: 23%
services: 55% (2001 est.)
Population below poverty line: 70% (2001 est.)
Household income or consumption by percentage share:
lowest 10%: 2.5%
highest 10%: 31.7% (1997)
Distribution of family income - Gini index: 39.6 (1996-97)
Inflation rate (consumer prices): 15.2% (2002 est.)
Labor force: 9.2 million (2000 est.)
Labor force - by occupation: agriculture 81%, industry 6%, services 13% (1997 est.)
Unemployment rate: 21% (1997 est.)
Budget:
revenues: $393.1 million
expenditures: $1.025 billion, including capital expenditures of $479.4 million (2001 est.)
Industries: food, beverages, chemicals (fertilizer, soap, paints), aluminum, petroleum products, textiles, cement, glass, asbestos, tobacco
Industrial production growth rate: 3.4% (2000)
Electricity - production: 7.193 billion kWh (2001)
Electricity - production by source:
fossil fuel: 2.9%
hydro: 97.1%
nuclear: 0%
other: 0% (2001)
Electricity - consumption: 1.39 billion kWh (2001)
Electricity - exports: 5.8 billion kWh (2001)
Electricity - imports: 500 million kWh (2001)
Oil - production: 0 bbl/day (2001 est.)
Oil - consumption: 8,500 bbl/day (2001 est.)
Oil - exports: NA
Oil - imports: NA
Oil - proved reserves: 0 bbl (1 January 2002)
Natural gas - production: 60 million cu m (2001 est.)
Natural gas - consumption: 60 million cu m (2001 est.)
Natural gas - exports: 0 cu m (2001 est.)
Natural gas - imports: 0 cu m (2001 est.)
Natural gas - proved reserves: 63.71 billion cu m (1 January 2002)
Agriculture - products: cotton, cashew nuts, sugarcane, tea, cassava (tapioca), corn, coconuts, sisal, citrus and tropical fruits, potatoes, sunflowers; beef, poultry
Exports: $795 million f.o.b. (2003 est.)
Exports - commodities: aluminum, prawns, cashews, cotton, sugar, citrus, timber; bulk electricity
Exports - partners: Belgium 42.4%, South Africa 17.6%, Zimbabwe 5.7%, Spain 5.4%, Portugal 4.4% (2002)

Imports: $1.142 billion f.o.b. (2003 est.)
Imports - commodities: machinery and equipment, vehicles, fuel, chemicals, metal products, foodstuffs, textiles
Imports - partners: South Africa 30.4%, Portugal 6.1%, US 5.2%, India 4.2%, Australia 4.1% (2002)
Debt - external: $966 million (2002 est.)
Economic aid - recipient: $632.8 million (2001)
Currency: metical (MZM)
Currency code: MZM
Exchange rates: meticais per US dollar - 23,782.3 (2003), 23,678 (2002), 20,703.6 (2001), 15,447.1 (2000), 13,028.6 (1999)
note: effective October 2000, the exchange rate is determined as the weighted average of buying and selling exchange rates of all transactions of commercial banks and stock exchanges with the public
Fiscal year: calendar year

Communications

Telephones - main lines in use: 83,700 (2002)
Telephones - mobile cellular: 254,800 (2002)
Telephone system:
general assessment: fair system but not available generally (telephone density is only 16 telephones for each 1,000 persons)
domestic: the system consists of open-wire lines and trunk connection by microwave radio relay and tropospheric scatter
international: country code - 258; satellite earth stations - 5 Intelsat (2 Atlantic Ocean and 3 Indian Ocean)
Radio broadcast stations: AM 13, FM 17, shortwave 11 (2001)
Television broadcast stations: 1 (2001)
Internet country code: .mz
Internet hosts: 1,925 (2002)
Internet users: 30,000 (2002)

Transportation

Railways:
total: 3,123 km
narrow gauge: 2,983 km 1.067-m gauge; 140 km 0.762-m gauge (2002)
Highways:
total: 30,400 km
paved: 5,685 km
unpaved: 24,715 km (1999 est.)
Waterways: 3,750 km (navigable routes)
Pipelines: gas 189 km; refined products 292 km (2003)
Ports and harbors: Beira, Inhambane, Maputo, Nacala, Pemba, Quelimane
Merchant marine:
total: 3 ships (1,000 GRT or over) 4,125 GRT/7,024 DWT
by type: cargo 3
foreign-owned: Belgium 2 (2003 est.)
Airports: 158 (2003 est.)

Airports - with paved runways:
total: 22
over 3,047 m: 1
2,438 to 3,047 m: 3
1,524 to 2,437 m: 10
914 to 1,523 m: 3
under 914 m: 5 (2003 est.)
Airports - with unpaved runways:
total: 136
2,438 to 3,047 m: 1
1,524 to 2,437 m: 14
914 to 1,523 m: 34
under 914 m: 87 (2003 est.)

Military

Military branches: Army, Navy, Air and Air Defense Forces, Special Forces
Military manpower - availability:
males age 15-49: 4,335,294 (2004 est.)
Military manpower - fit for military service:
males age 15-49: 2,485,197 (2004 est.)
Military expenditures - dollar figure: $101.3 million (2003)
Military expenditures - percent of GDP: 2.2% (2003)

Transnational Issues

Disputes - international: none
Illicit drugs: Southern African transit point for South Asian hashish, South Asian heroin, and South American cocaine probably destined for the European and South African markets; producer of cannabis (for local consumption) and methaqualone (for export to South Africa); corruption and poor regulatory capability makes the banking system vulnerable to money laundering, but the lack of a well-developed financial infrastructure limits the country's utility as a money-laundering center

Namibia

Introduction

Background: South Africa occupied the German colony of South-West Africa during World War I and administered it as a mandate until after World War II, when it annexed the territory. In 1966 the Marxist South-West Africa People's Organization (SWAPO) guerrilla group launched a war of independence for the area that was soon named Namibia, but it was not until 1988 that South Africa agreed to end its administration in accordance with a UN peace plan for the entire region. Independence came in 1990 following multi-party elections and the establishment of a constitution. President NUJOMA is currently serving his third term as president.

Geography

Location: Southern Africa, bordering the South Atlantic Ocean, between Angola and South Africa
Geographic coordinates: 22 00 S, 17 00 E
Map references: Africa
Area:
total: 825,418 sq km
land: 825,418 sq km
water: 0 sq km
Area - comparative: slightly more than half the size of Alaska
Land boundaries:
total: 3,936 km
border countries: Angola 1,376 km, Botswana 1,360 km, South Africa 967 km, Zambia 233 km
Coastline: 1,572 km
Maritime claims:
territorial sea: 12 NM
contiguous zone: 24 NM
exclusive economic zone: 200 NM
Climate: desert; hot, dry; rainfall sparse and erratic
Terrain: mostly high plateau; Namib Desert along coast; Kalahari Desert in east

Elevation extremes:
lowest point: Atlantic Ocean 0 m
highest point: Konigstein 2,606 m
Natural resources: diamonds, copper, uranium, gold, lead, tin, lithium, cadmium, zinc, salt, vanadium, natural gas, hydropower, fish
note: suspected deposits of oil, coal, and iron ore
Land use:
arable land: 0.99%
permanent crops: 0%
other: 99.01% (1998 est.)
Irrigated land: 70 sq km (1998 est.)
Natural hazards: prolonged periods of drought
Environment - current issues: very limited natural fresh water resources; desertification; wildlife poaching; land degradation has led to few conservation areas
Environment - international agreements:
party to: Antarctic-Marine Living Resources, Biodiversity, Climate Change, Climate Change-Kyoto Protocol, Desertification, Endangered Species, Hazardous Wastes, Law of the Sea, Ozone Layer Protection, Wetlands
signed, but not ratified: none of the selected agreements
Geography - note: first country in the world to incorporate the protection of the environment into its constitution; some 14% of the land is protected, including virtually the entire Namib Desert coastal strip

People

Population: 1,954,033
note: estimates for this country explicitly take into account the effects of excess mortality due to AIDS; this can result in lower life expectancy, higher infant mortality and death rates, lower population and growth rates, and changes in the distribution of population by age and sex than would otherwise be expected (July 2004 est.)
Age structure:
0-14 years: 42.4% (male 419,700; female 409,156)
15-64 years: 54% (male 527,553; female 528,386)
65 years and over: 3.5% (male 30,427; female 38,811) (2004 est.)
Median age:
total: 18.3 years
male: 18 years
female: 18.6 years (2004 est.)
Population growth rate: 1.25% (2004 est.)
Birth rate: 33.51 births/1,000 population (2004 est.)
Death rate: 21.02 deaths/1,000 population (2004 est.)
Net migration rate: 0 migrant(s)/1,000 population (2004 est.)
Sex ratio:
at birth: 1.03 male(s)/female
under 15 years: 1.03 male(s)/female
15-64 years: 1 male(s)/female
65 years and over: 0.78 male(s)/female
total population: 1 male(s)/female (2004 est.)

Namibia (continued)

Infant mortality rate:
total: 69.58 deaths/1,000 live births
male: 72.65 deaths/1,000 live births
female: 66.43 deaths/1,000 live births (2004 est.)
Life expectancy at birth:
total population: 40.53 years
male: 42.36 years
female: 38.64 years (2004 est.)
Total fertility rate: 4.65 children born/woman
(2004 est.)
HIV/AIDS - adult prevalence rate: 22.5%
(2001 est.)
HIV/AIDS - people living with HIV/AIDS: 230,000
(2001 est.)
HIV/AIDS - deaths: 13,000 (2001 est.)
Nationality:
noun: Namibian(s)
adjective: Namibian
Ethnic groups: black 87.5%, white 6%, mixed 6.5%
note: about 50% of the population belong to the
Ovambo tribe and 9% to the Kavangos tribe; other
ethnic groups are: Herero 7%, Damara 7%, Nama 5%,
Caprivian 4%, Bushmen 3%, Baster 2%,
Tswana 0.5%
Religions: Christian 80% to 90% (Lutheran 50% at
least), indigenous beliefs 10% to 20%
Languages: English 7% (official), Afrikaans common
language of most of the population and about 60% of
the white population, German 32%, indigenous
languages: Oshivambo, Herero, Nama
Literacy:
definition: age 15 and over can read and write
total population: 84%
male: 84.4%
female: 83.7% (2003 est.)

Government

Country name:
conventional long form: Republic of Namibia
conventional short form: Namibia
former: German Southwest Africa, South-West Africa
Government type: republic
Capital: Windhoek
Administrative divisions: 13 regions; Caprivi,
Erongo, Hardap, Karas, Khomas, Kunene,
Ohangwena, Okavango, Omaheke, Omusati,
Oshana, Oshikoto, Otjozondjupa
Independence: 21 March 1990 (from South African
mandate)
National holiday: Independence Day, 21 March
(1990)
Constitution: ratified 9 February 1990; effective
12 March 1990
Legal system: based on Roman-Dutch law and
1990 constitution
Suffrage: 18 years of age; universal
Executive branch:
chief of state: President Sam Shafishuna NUJOMA
(since 21 March 1990)
head of government: Prime Minister Theo-Ben
GURIRAB (since 28 August 2002)

cabinet: Cabinet appointed by the president from
among the members of the National Assembly
elections: president elected by popular vote for a
five-year term; election last held 30 November-
1 December 1999 (next to be held NA November
2004)
election results: Sam Shafishuna NUJOMA elected
president; percent of vote - Sam Shafishuna NUJOMA
77%
Legislative branch: bicameral legislature consists
of the National Council (26 seats; two members are
chosen from each regional council to serve six-year
terms) and the National Assembly (72 seats;
members are elected by popular vote to serve
five-year terms)
elections: National Council - elections for regional
councils, to determine members of the National
Council, held 30 November-1 December 1998 (next to
be held NA November 2004); National Assembly - last
held 30 November-1 December 1999 (next to be held
NA November 2004)
election results: National Council - percent of vote by
party - NA%; seats by party - SWAPO 21, DTA 4,
UDF 1; National Assembly - percent of vote by party -
SWAPO 76%, COD 10%, DTA 9%, UDF 3%,
MAG 1%, other 1%; seats by party - SWAPO 55,
COD 7, DTA 7, UDF 2, MAG 1
note: the National Council is primarily an advisory
body
Judicial branch: Supreme Court (judges appointed
by the president on the recommendation of the
Judicial Service Commission)
Political parties and leaders: Congress of
Democrats or COD [Ben ULENGA]; Democratic
Turnhalle Alliance of Namibia or DTA [Katuutire
KAURA, president]; Monitor Action Group or MAG
[Kosie PRETORIUS]; South West Africa People's
Organization or SWAPO [Sam Shafishuna NUJOMA];
United Democratic Front or UDF [Justus GAROEB]
Political pressure groups and leaders: NA
International organization participation: ACP,
AfDB, AU, C, FAO, G-77, IAEA, IBRD, ICAO, ICCt,
ICFTU, ICRM, IFAD, IFC, IFRCS, ILO, IMF, IMO,
Interpol, IOC, IOM (observer), ISO (correspondent),
ITU, NAM, OPCW, SACU, SADC, UN, UNCTAD,
UNESCO, UNHCR, UNIDO, UNMEE, UNMIL, UPU,
WCL, WCO, WHO, WIPO, WMO, WToO, WTrO
Diplomatic representation in the US:
chief of mission: Ambassador Leonard Nangolo
IIPUMBU
chancery: 1605 New Hampshire Avenue NW,
Washington, DC 20009
telephone: [1] (202) 986-0540
FAX: [1] (202) 986-0443
Diplomatic representation from the US:
chief of mission: Ambassador Kevin J. McGUIRE
embassy: Ausplan Building, 14 Lossen Street,
Windhoek
mailing address: Private Bag 12029 Ausspannplatz,
Windhoek
telephone: [264] (61) 221601
FAX: [264] (61) 229792

Flag description: a large blue triangle with a yellow
sunburst fills the upper left section and an equal green
triangle (solid) fills the lower right section; the triangles
are separated by a red stripe that is contrasted by two
narrow white-edge borders

Economy

Economy - overview: The economy is heavily
dependent on the extraction and processing of
minerals for export. Mining accounts for 20% of GDP.
Rich alluvial diamond deposits make Namibia a
primary source for gem-quality diamonds. Namibia is
the fourth-largest exporter of nonfuel minerals in
Africa, the world's fifth-largest producer of uranium,
and the producer of large quantities of lead, zinc, tin,
silver, and tungsten. The mining sector employs only
about 3% of the population while about half of the
population depends on subsistence agriculture for its
livelihood. Namibia normally imports about 50% of its
cereal requirements; in drought years food shortages
are a major problem in rural areas. A high per capita
GDP, relative to the region, hides the great inequality
of income distribution; nearly one-third of Namibians
had annual incomes of less than $1,400 in constant
1994 dollars, according to a 1993 study. The
Namibian economy is closely linked to South Africa
with the Namibian dollar pegged to the South African
rand. Privatization of several enterprises in coming
years may stimulate long-run foreign investment.
Mining of zinc, copper, and silver and increased fish
production led growth in 2003.
GDP: purchasing power parity - $13.72 billion
(2003 est.)
GDP - real growth rate: 3.3% (2003 est.)
GDP - per capita: purchasing power parity - $7,100
(2003 est.)
GDP - composition by sector:
agriculture: 11%
industry: 26%
services: 63% (2002 est.)
Population below poverty line: 50% (2002 est.)
**Household income or consumption by percentage
share:**
lowest 10%: NA%
highest 10%: NA%
Inflation rate (consumer prices): 8% (2003)
Labor force: 725,000 (2000)
Labor force - by occupation: agriculture 47%,
industry 20%, services 33% (1999 est.)
Unemployment rate: 35% (1998)
Budget:
revenues: $883 million
expenditures: $950 million, including capital
expenditures of $NA (1998)
Industries: meatpacking, fish processing, dairy
products; mining (diamond, lead, zinc, tin, silver,
tungsten, uranium, copper)
Industrial production growth rate: NA%
Electricity - production: 26.95 million kWh (2001)
Electricity - production by source: NA
Electricity - consumption: 603.1 million kWh
(2001)

Namibia (continued)

Electricity - exports: 0 kWh (2001)
Electricity - imports: 578 million kWh; note - electricity supplied by South Africa (2001)
Oil - production: 0 bbl/day (2001 est.)
Oil - consumption: 13,000 bbl/day (2001 est.)
Oil - exports: NA
Oil - imports: NA
Oil - proved reserves: 0 bbl (1 January 2002)
Natural gas - proved reserves: 31.15 billion cu m (1 January 2002)
Agriculture - products: millet, sorghum, peanuts; livestock; fish
Exports: $1.09 billion f.o.b. (2003 est.)
Exports - commodities: diamonds, copper, gold, zinc, lead, uranium; cattle, processed fish, karakul skins
Exports - partners: EU 79%, US 4% (2001)
Imports: $1.371 billion f.o.b. (2003 est.)
Imports - commodities: foodstuffs; petroleum products and fuel, machinery and equipment, chemicals
Imports - partners: US 50%, EU 31% (2001)
Debt - external: $664 million (2003 est.)
Economic aid - recipient: ODA $160 million (2000 est.)
Currency: Namibian dollar (NAD); South African rand (ZAR)
Currency code: NAD; ZAR
Exchange rates: Namibian dollars per US dollar - 7.5648 (2003), 10.5407 (2002), 8.6092 (2001), 6.9398 (2000), 6.1095 (1999)
Fiscal year: 1 April - 31 March

Communications

Telephones - main lines in use: 121,400 (2002)
Telephones - mobile cellular: 150,000 (2002)
Telephone system:
general assessment: good system; about 6 telephones for each 100 persons
domestic: good urban services; fair rural service; microwave radio relay links major towns; connections to other populated places are by open wire; 100% digital
international: country code - 264; fiber-optic cable to South Africa, microwave radio relay link to Botswana, direct links to other neighboring countries; connected to Africa ONE and South African Far East (SAFE) submarine cables through South Africa; satellite earth stations - 4 Intelsat (2002)
Radio broadcast stations: AM 2, FM 39, shortwave 4 (2001)
Television broadcast stations: 8 (plus about 20 low-power repeaters) (1997)
Internet country code: .na
Internet hosts: 3,709 (2002)
Internet users: 50,000 (2002)

Transportation

Railways:
total: 2,382 km
narrow gauge: 2,382 km 1.067-m gauge (2002)

Highways:
total: 66,467 km
paved: 9,172 km
unpaved: 57,285 km (2000)
Waterways: none
Ports and harbors: Luderitz, Walvis Bay
Merchant marine: none
Airports: 136 (2003 est.)
Airports - with paved runways:
total: 21
over 3,047 m: 2
2,438 to 3,047 m: 2
1,524 to 2,437 m: 13
914 to 1,523 m: 4 (2003 est.)
Airports - with unpaved runways:
total: 115
2,438 to 3,047 m: 2
1,524 to 2,437 m: 22
914 to 1,523 m: 71
under 914 m: 20 (2003 est.)

Military

Military branches: Namibian Defense Force: Army (including Naval Wing, Air Wing), Police
Military manpower - availability:
males age 15-49: 468,934 (2004 est.)
Military manpower - fit for military service:
males age 15-49: 279,755 (2004 est.)
Military expenditures - dollar figure: $111.6 million (2003)
Military expenditures - percent of GDP: 2.5% (2003)

Transnational Issues

Disputes - international: commission established with Botswana to resolve small residual disputes along the Caprivi Strip, including the Situngu marshlands along the Linyanti River; Botswana residents protest Namibia's planned construction of the Okavango hydroelectric dam on Popa Falls; managed dispute with South Africa over the location of the boundary in the Orange River; Botswana, Namibia, Zambia, and Zimbabwe boundary convergence is not clearly defined or delimited; Angolan rebels and refugees still reside in Namibia

Nauru

Introduction

Background: Nauru's phosphate deposits began to be mined early in the 20th century by a German-British consortium; the island was occupied by Australian forces in World War I. Nauru achieved independence in 1968 and joined the UN in 1999. Nauru is the world's smallest independent republic.

Geography

Location: Oceania, island in the South Pacific Ocean, south of the Marshall Islands
Geographic coordinates: 0 32 S, 166 55 E
Map references: Oceania
Area:
total: 21 sq km
land: 21 sq km
water: 0 sq km
Area - comparative: about 0.1 times the size of Washington, DC
Land boundaries: 0 km
Coastline: 30 km
Maritime claims:
territorial sea: 12 NM
contiguous zone: 24 NM
exclusive economic zone: 200 NM
Climate: tropical with a monsoonal pattern; rainy season (November to February)
Terrain: sandy beach rises to fertile ring around raised coral reefs with phosphate plateau in center
Elevation extremes:
lowest point: Pacific Ocean 0 m
highest point: unnamed location along plateau rim 61 m
Natural resources: phosphates, fish
Land use:
arable land: 0%
permanent crops: 0%
other: 100% (1998 est.)
Irrigated land: NA sq km

Nauru *(continued)*

Natural hazards: periodic droughts

Environment - current issues: limited natural fresh water resources, roof storage tanks collect rainwater, but mostly dependent on a single, aging desalination plant; intensive phosphate mining during the past 90 years - mainly by a UK, Australia, and NZ consortium - has left the central 90% of Nauru a wasteland and threatens limited remaining land resources

Environment - international agreements:

party to: Biodiversity, Climate Change, Climate Change-Kyoto Protocol, Desertification, Hazardous Wastes, Law of the Sea, Marine Dumping, Ozone Layer Protection

signed, but not ratified: none of the selected agreements

Geography - note: Nauru is one of the three great phosphate rock islands in the Pacific Ocean - the others are Banaba (Ocean Island) in Kiribati and Makatea in French Polynesia; only 53 km south of Equator

People

Population: 12,809 (July 2004 est.)

Age structure:

0-14 years: 38.2% (male 2,516; female 2,372)

15-64 years: 60% (male 3,782; female 3,898)

65 years and over: 1.9% (male 128; female 113) (2004 est.)

Median age:

total: 19.9 years

male: 19.5 years

female: 20.4 years (2004 est.)

Population growth rate: 1.87% (2004 est.)

Birth rate: 25.61 births/1,000 population (2004 est.)

Death rate: 6.95 deaths/1,000 population (2004 est.)

Net migration rate: 0 migrant(s)/1,000 population (2004 est.)

Sex ratio:

at birth: 1.05 male(s)/female

under 15 years: 1.06 male(s)/female

15-64 years: 0.97 male(s)/female

65 years and over: 1.13 male(s)/female

total population: 1.01 male(s)/female (2004 est.)

Infant mortality rate:

total: 10.14 deaths/1,000 live births

male: 12.76 deaths/1,000 live births

female: 7.39 deaths/1,000 live births (2004 est.)

Life expectancy at birth:

total population: 62.33 years

male: 58.78 years

female: 66.06 years (2004 est.)

Total fertility rate: 3.29 children born/woman (2004 est.)

HIV/AIDS - adult prevalence rate: NA%

HIV/AIDS - people living with HIV/AIDS: NA

HIV/AIDS - deaths: NA

Nationality:

noun: Nauruan(s)

adjective: Nauruan

Ethnic groups: Nauruan 58%, other Pacific Islander 26%, Chinese 8%, European 8%

Religions: Christian (two-thirds Protestant, one-third Roman Catholic)

Languages: Nauruan (official, a distinct Pacific Island language), English widely understood, spoken, and used for most government and commercial purposes

Literacy:

definition: NA

total population: NA%

male: NA%

female: NA%

Government

Country name:

conventional long form: Republic of Nauru

conventional short form: Nauru

former: Pleasant Island

Government type: republic

Capital: no official capital; government offices in Yaren District

Administrative divisions: 14 districts; Aiwo, Anabar, Anetan, Anibare, Baiti, Boe, Buada, Denigomodu, Ewa, Ijuw, Meneng, Nibok, Uaboe, Yaren

Independence: 31 January 1968 (from the Australia-, NZ-, and UK-administered UN trusteeship)

National holiday: Independence Day, 31 January (1968)

Constitution: 29 January 1968

Legal system: acts of the Nauru Parliament and British common law

Suffrage: 20 years of age; universal and compulsory

Executive branch:

chief of state: President Rene R. HARRIS (since 8 August 2003) note - the president is both the chief of state and head of government

head of government: President Rene R. HARRIS (since 8 August 2003) note - the president is both the chief of state and head of government

cabinet: Cabinet appointed by the president from among the members of Parliament

elections: president elected by Parliament for a three-year term; election last held 8 August 2003 (next to be held NA 2006)

election results: Ludwig SCOTTY was removed from the presidency in a 9 to 8 no-confidence vote 8 August 2003; Rene HARRIS became president

Legislative branch: unicameral Parliament (18 seats; members elected by popular vote to serve three-year terms)

elections: last held 3 May 2003 (next to be held not later than May 2006)

election results: percent of vote - NA%; seats - Nauru First Party 3, independents 15

Judicial branch: Supreme Court

Political parties and leaders: loose multiparty system; Democratic Party [Kennan ADEANG]; Nauru Party (informal) [leader NA]; Naoero Amo (Nauru First) Party [leader NA]

Political pressure groups and leaders: NA

International organization participation: ACP, AsDB, C, FAO, ICAO, ICCt, Interpol, IOC, ITU, OPCW, PIF, Sparteca, SPC, UN, UNCTAD, UNESCO, UPU, WHO

Diplomatic representation in the US: Nauru does not have an embassy in the US, but does have a UN office at 800 2nd Avenue, Suite 400 D, New York, New York 10017; telephone: (212) 937-0074

consulate(s): Hagatna (Guam)

Diplomatic representation from the US: the US does not have an embassy in Nauru; the US Ambassador to Fiji is accredited to Nauru

Flag description: blue with a narrow, horizontal, yellow stripe across the center and a large white 12-pointed star below the stripe on the hoist side; the star indicates the country's location in relation to the Equator (the yellow stripe) and the 12 points symbolize the 12 original tribes of Nauru

Economy

Economy - overview: Revenues of this tiny island have come from exports of phosphates, but reserves are expected to be exhausted within a few years. Phosphate production has declined since 1989, as demand has fallen in traditional markets and as the marginal cost of extracting the remaining phosphate increases, making it less internationally competitive. While phosphates have given Nauruans one of the highest per capita incomes in the Third World, few other resources exist with most necessities being imported, including fresh water from Australia. The rehabilitation of mined land and the replacement of income from phosphates are serious long-term problems. In anticipation of the exhaustion of Nauru's phosphate deposits, substantial amounts of phosphate income have been invested in trust funds to help cushion the transition and provide for Nauru's economic future. The government has been borrowing heavily from the trusts to finance fiscal deficits. To cut costs the government has called for a freeze on wages, a reduction of over-staffed public service departments, privatization of numerous government agencies, and closure of some overseas consulates. In recent years Nauru has encouraged the registration of offshore banks and corporations. Tens of billions of dollars have been channeled through their accounts. Few comprehensive statistics on the Nauru economy exist, with estimates of Nauru's GDP varying widely.

GDP: purchasing power parity - $60 million (2001 est.)

GDP - real growth rate: NA%

GDP - per capita: purchasing power parity - $5,000 (2001 est.)

GDP - composition by sector:

agriculture: NA%

industry: NA%

services: NA%

Population below poverty line: NA%

Household income or consumption by percentage share:

lowest 10%: NA%

highest 10%: NA%

Nauru (continued)

Inflation rate (consumer prices): -3.6% (1993)
Labor force - by occupation: employed in mining phosphates, public administration, education, and transportation
Unemployment rate: 0% (2002 est.)
Budget:
revenues: $23.4 million
expenditures: $64.8 million, including capital expenditures of $NA (FY95/96)
Industries: phosphate mining, offshore banking, coconut products
Industrial production growth rate: NA%
Electricity - production: 30 million kWh (2001)
Electricity - production by source:
fossil fuel: 100%
hydro: 0%
nuclear: 0%
other: 0% (2001)
Electricity - consumption: 27.9 million kWh (2001)
Electricity - exports: 0 kWh (2001)
Electricity - imports: 0 kWh (2001)
Oil - production: 0 bbl/day (2001 est.)
Oil - consumption: 1,000 bbl/day (2001 est.)
Oil - exports: NA
Oil - imports: NA
Agriculture - products: coconuts
Exports: $18 million f.o.b. (2002)
Exports - commodities: phosphates
Exports - partners: India 44.4%, South Korea 16.7%, Australia 11.1%, Netherlands 5.6%, New Zealand 5.6%, US 5.6% (2002)
Imports: $31 million c.i.f. (2002)
Imports - commodities: food, fuel, manufactures, building materials, machinery
Imports - partners: Australia 61.3%, US 9.7%, Ireland 6.5%, Malaysia 6.5% (2002)
Debt - external: $33.3 million (2002)
Economic aid - recipient: $2.25 million from Australia (FY96/97 est.) (2000 est.)
Currency: Australian dollar (AUD)
Currency code: AUD
Exchange rates: Australian dollars per US dollar - 1.5419 (2003), 1.2641 (2002) 1.9320 (2001), 1.7173 (2000), 1.5497 (1999)
Fiscal year: 1 July - 30 June

Communications

Telephones - main lines in use: 1,900 (2002)
Telephones - mobile cellular: 1,500 (2002)
Telephone system:
general assessment: adequate local and international radiotelephone communication provided via Australian facilities
domestic: NA
international: country code - 674; satellite earth station - 1 Intelsat (Pacific Ocean)
Radio broadcast stations: AM 1, FM 0, shortwave 0 (1998)
Television broadcast stations: 1 (1997)
Internet country code: .nr
Internet users: 300 (2002)

Transportation

Railways:
total: 5 km
note: gauge unknown; used to haul phosphates from the center of the island to processing facilities on the southwest coast (2001)
Highways:
total: 30 km
paved: 24 km
unpaved: 6 km (1999 est.)
Waterways: none
Ports and harbors: Nauru
Merchant marine: none
Airports: 1 (2003 est.)
Airports - with paved runways:
total: 1
1,524 to 2,437 m: 1 (2003 est.)

Military

Military branches: no regular military forces; Nauru Police Force
Military manpower - availability:
males age 15-49: 3,275 (2004 est.)
Military manpower - fit for military service:
males age 15-49: 1,810 (2004 est.)
Military expenditures - dollar figure: NA
Military expenditures - percent of GDP: NA
Military - note: Nauru maintains no defense forces; under an informal agreement, defense is the responsibility of Australia

Transnational Issues

Disputes - international: none
Illicit drugs: offshore banking recently stopped, remains on Financial Action Task Force Non-Cooperative Countries and Territories List for continued failure to address deficiencies in money-laundering control regime

Navassa Island
(territory of the US)

Introduction

Background: This uninhabited island was claimed by the US in 1857 for its guano. Mining took place between 1865 and 1898. The lighthouse, built in 1917, was shut down in 1996 and administration of Navassa Island transferred from the Coast Guard to the Department of the Interior. A 1998 scientific expedition to the island described it as a unique preserve of Caribbean biodiversity; the following year it became a National Wildlife Refuge.

Geography

Location: Caribbean, island in the Caribbean Sea, about one-fourth of the way from Haiti to Jamaica
Geographic coordinates: 18 25 N, 75 02 W
Map references: Central America and the Caribbean
Area:
total: 5.2 sq km
land: 5.2 sq km
water: 0 sq km
Area - comparative: about nine times the size of The Mall in Washington, DC
Land boundaries: 0 km
Coastline: 8 km
Maritime claims:
territorial sea: 12 NM
exclusive economic zone: 200 NM
Climate: marine, tropical
Terrain: raised coral and limestone plateau, flat to undulating; ringed by vertical white cliffs (9 to 15 m high)
Elevation extremes:
lowest point: Caribbean Sea 0 m
highest point: unnamed location on southwest side 77 m
Natural resources: guano
Land use:
arable land: 0%

Navassa Island (continued)

permanent crops: 0%
other: 100% (1998 est.)
Irrigated land: 0 sq km (1998 est.)
Natural hazards: NA
Environment - current issues: NA
Geography - note: strategic location 160 km south of the US Naval Base at Guantanamo Bay, Cuba; mostly exposed rock but with enough grassland to support goat herds; dense stands of fig-like trees, scattered cactus

People

Population: uninhabited
note: transient Haitian fishermen and others camp on the island (July 2004 est.)

Government

Country name:
conventional long form: none
conventional short form: Navassa Island
Dependency status: unincorporated territory of the US; administered from Washington, DC, by the Fish and Wildlife Service, US Department of the Interior; in September 1996, the Coast Guard ceased operations and maintenance of Navassa Island Light, a 46-meter-tall lighthouse on the southern side of the island; there has also been a private claim advanced against the island
Legal system: the laws of the US, where applicable, apply
Flag description: the flag of the US is used

Economy

Economy - overview: no economic activity

Transportation

Waterways: none
Ports and harbors: none; offshore anchorage only

Military

Military - note: defense is the responsibility of the US

Transnational Issues

Disputes - international: claimed by Haiti

Nepal

Introduction

Background: In 1951, the Nepalese monarch ended the century-old system of rule by hereditary premiers and instituted a cabinet system of government. Reforms in 1990 established a multiparty democracy within the framework of a constitutional monarchy. A Maoist insurgency, launched in 1996, has gained traction and is threatening to bring down the regime. In 2001, the Crown Prince massacred ten members of the royal family, including the king and queen, and then took his own life. In October 2002, the new king dismissed the prime minister and his cabinet for "incompetence" after they dissolved the parliament and were subsequently unable to hold elections because of the ongoing insurgency. The country is now governed by the king and his appointed cabinet, which has negotiated a cease-fire with the Maoist insurgents until elections can be held at some unspecified future date.

Geography

Location: Southern Asia, between China and India
Geographic coordinates: 28 00 N, 84 00 E
Map references: Asia
Area:
total: 140,800 sq km
land: 136,800 sq km
water: 4,000 sq km
Area - comparative: slightly larger than Arkansas
Land boundaries:
total: 2,926 km
border countries: China 1,236 km, India 1,690 km
Coastline: 0 km (landlocked)
Maritime claims: none (landlocked)
Climate: varies from cool summers and severe winters in north to subtropical summers and mild winters in south
Terrain: Terai or flat river plain of the Ganges in south, central hill region, rugged Himalayas in north

Elevation extremes:
lowest point: Kanchan Kalan 70 m
highest point: Mount Everest 8,850 m (1999)
Natural resources: quartz, water, timber, hydropower, scenic beauty, small deposits of lignite, copper, cobalt, iron ore
Land use:
arable land: 20.27%
permanent crops: 0.49%
other: 79.24% (1998 est.)
Irrigated land: 11,350 sq km (1998 est.)
Natural hazards: severe thunderstorms, flooding, landslides, drought, and famine depending on the timing, intensity, and duration of the summer monsoons
Environment - current issues: deforestation (overuse of wood for fuel and lack of alternatives); contaminated water (with human and animal wastes, agricultural runoff, and industrial effluents); wildlife conservation; vehicular emissions
Environment - international agreements:
party to: Biodiversity, Climate Change, Desertification, Endangered Species, Hazardous Wastes, Law of the Sea, Ozone Layer Protection, Tropical Timber 83, Tropical Timber 94, Wetlands
signed, but not ratified: Marine Life Conservation
Geography - note: landlocked; strategic location between China and India; contains eight of world's 10 highest peaks, including Mount Everest - the world's tallest - on the border with China

People

Population: 27,070,666 (July 2004 est.)
Age structure:
0-14 years: 39.4% (male 5,500,698; female 5,151,705)
15-64 years: 57% (male 7,912,553; female 7,518,430)
65 years and over: 3.6% (male 483,998; female 503,282) (2004 est.)

Nepal (continued)

Median age:
total: 19.9 years
male: 19.7 years
female: 20 years (2004 est.)
Population growth rate: 2.23% (2004 est.)
Birth rate: 31.96 births/1,000 population (2004 est.)
Death rate: 9.66 deaths/1,000 population (2004 est.)
Net migration rate: 0 migrant(s)/1,000 population (2004 est.)
Sex ratio:
at birth: 1.05 male(s)/female
under 15 years: 1.07 male(s)/female
15-64 years: 1.05 male(s)/female
65 years and over: 0.96 male(s)/female
total population: 1.06 male(s)/female (2004 est.)
Infant mortality rate:
total: 68.77 deaths/1,000 live births
male: 67.1 deaths/1,000 live births
female: 70.53 deaths/1,000 live births (2004 est.)
Life expectancy at birth:
total population: 59.4 years
male: 59.73 years
female: 59.06 years (2004 est.)
Total fertility rate: 4.29 children born/woman (2004 est.)
HIV/AIDS - adult prevalence rate: 0.5% (2001 est.)
HIV/AIDS - people living with HIV/AIDS: 58,000 (2001 est.)
HIV/AIDS - deaths: 2,400 (2001 est.)
Nationality:
noun: Nepalese (singular and plural)
adjective: Nepalese
Ethnic groups: Brahman, Chetri, Newar, Gurung, Magar, Tamang, Rai, Limbu, Sherpa, Tharu, and others (1995)
Religions: Hinduism 86.2%, Buddhism 7.8%, Islam 3.8%, other 2.2%
note: only official Hindu state in the world (1995)
Languages: Nepali (official; spoken by 90% of the population), about a dozen other languages and about 30 major dialects; note - many in government and business also speak English (1995)
Literacy:
definition: age 15 and over can read and write
total population: 45.2%
male: 62.7%
female: 27.6% (2003 est.)

Government

Country name:
conventional long form: Kingdom of Nepal
conventional short form: Nepal
Government type: parliamentary democracy and constitutional monarchy
Capital: Kathmandu
Administrative divisions: 14 zones (anchal, singular and plural); Bagmati, Bheri, Dhawalagiri, Gandaki, Janakpur, Karnali, Kosi, Lumbini, Mahakali, Mechi, Narayani, Rapti, Sagarmatha, Seti
Independence: 1768 (unified by Prithvi Narayan Shah)

National holiday: Birthday of King GYANENDRA, 7 July (1946)
Constitution: 9 November 1990
Legal system: based on Hindu legal concepts and English common law; has not accepted compulsory ICJ jurisdiction
Suffrage: 18 years of age; universal
Executive branch:
chief of state: King GYANENDRA Bir Bikram Shah (succeeded to the throne 4 June 2001 following the death of his nephew, King DIPENDRA Bir Bikram Shah)
head of government: Prime Minister Surya Bahadur THAPA (since 4 June 2003); note - Prime Minister CHAND resigned 30 May 2003
cabinet: Cabinet appointed by the monarch on the recommendation of the prime minister
elections: none; the monarch is hereditary; following legislative elections, the leader of the majority party or leader of a majority coalition is usually appointed prime minister by the monarch
note: King BIRENDRA Bir Bikram Shah Dev died in a bloody shooting at the royal palace on 1 June 2001 that also claimed the lives of most of the royal family; King BIRENDRA's son, Crown Price DIPENDRA, is believed to have been responsible for the shootings before fatally wounding himself; immediately following the shootings and while still clinging to life, DIPENDRA was crowned king; he died three days later and was succeeded by his uncle
Legislative branch:
bicameral Parliament consists of the National Council (60 seats; 35 appointed by the House of Representatives, 10 by the king, and 15 elected by an electoral college; one-third of the members elected every two years to serve six-year terms) and the House of Representatives (205 seats; members elected by popular vote to serve five-year terms)
elections: House of Representatives - last held 3 and 17 May 1999 (next election NA 2004)
note: Nepal's Parliament was dissolved on 22 May 2002
election results: House of Representatives - percent of vote by party - NC 37.3%, CPN/UML 31.6%, NDP 10.4%, NSP 3.2%, Rastriya Jana Morcha 1.4%, Samyukta Janmorcha Nepal 0.8%, NWPP 0.5%, others 14.8%; seats by party - NC 113, CPN/UML 69, NDP 11, NSP 5, Rastriya Jana Morcha 5, Samyukta Janmorcha Nepal 1, NWPP 1
Judicial branch: Supreme Court or Sarbochha Adalat (chief justice is appointed by the monarch on recommendation of the Constitutional Council; the other judges are appointed by the monarch on recommendation of the Judicial Council)
Political parties and leaders: Communist Party of Nepal/United Marxist-Leninist or CPN/UML [Madhav Kumar NEPAL, general secretary]; National Democratic Party or NDP (also called Rastriya Prajantra Party or RPP) [Surya Bahadur THAPA, chairman]; National People's Front (Rastriya Jana Morcha) [Chitra BAHADUR, chairman]; Nepal Sadbhavana (Goodwill) Party or NSP [Bhadri Prasad

MANDAL, acting party president]; Nepal Workers and Peasants Party or NWPP [Narayan Man BIJUKCHHE, party chairman]; Nepali Congress or NC [Girija Prasad KOIRALA, party president; Sushil KOIRALA, general secretary]; Samyukta Janmorcha Nepal [Lila Mani POKHAREL, general secretary]
Political pressure groups and leaders: Maoist guerrilla-based insurgency [Pushpa Kamal DAHAL, also known as PRAHANDA, chairman; Dr. Baburam BHATTARAI, from Communist Party of Nepal/Maoist, chief negotiator]; numerous small, left-leaning student groups in the capital; several small, radical Nepalese antimonarchist groups
International organization participation: AsDB, CP, FAO, G-77, IBRD, ICAO, ICC, ICFTU, ICRM, IDA, IFAD, IFC, IFRCS, ILO, IMF, IMO, Interpol, IOC, IOM (observer), ISO (correspondent), ITU, MONUC, NAM, OPCW, SAARC, UN, UNAMSIL, UNCTAD, UNESCO, UNIDO, UNMEE, UNMIK, UNMIL, UNMISET, UNTSO, UPU, WCO, WFTU, WHO, WIPO, WMO, WToO, WTrO (observer)
Diplomatic representation in the US:
chief of mission: Ambassador (vacant)
chancery: 2131 Leroy Place NW, Washington, DC 20008
telephone: [1] (202) 667-4550
FAX: [1] (202) 667-5534
consulate(s) general: New York
Diplomatic representation from the US:
chief of mission: Ambassador Michael E. MALINOWSKI
embassy: Panipokhari, Kathmandu
mailing address: use embassy street address
telephone: [977] (1) 411179
FAX: [977] (1) 419963
Flag description: red with a blue border around the unique shape of two overlapping right triangles; the smaller, upper triangle bears a white stylized moon and the larger, lower triangle bears a white 12-pointed sun

Economy

Economy - overview: Nepal is among the poorest and least developed countries in the world with 42% of its population living below the poverty line. Agriculture is the mainstay of the economy, providing a livelihood for over 80% of the population and accounting for 40% of GDP. Industrial activity mainly involves the processing of agricultural produce including jute, sugarcane, tobacco, and grain. Security concerns in the wake of the Maoist conflict and the 11 September 2001 terrorist attacks in the US have led to a decrease in tourism, a key source of foreign exchange. Nepal has considerable scope for exploiting its potential in hydropower and tourism, areas of recent foreign investment interest. Prospects for foreign trade or investment in other sectors will remain poor, however, because of the small size of the economy, its technological backwardness, its remoteness, its landlocked geographic location, its civil strife, and its susceptibility to natural disaster. The international

Nepal *(continued)*

community's role of funding more than 60% of Nepal's development budget and more than 28% of total budgetary expenditures will likely continue as a major ingredient of growth.

GDP: purchasing power parity - $38.07 billion (2003 est.)

GDP - real growth rate: 2.4% (2003 est.)

GDP - per capita: purchasing power parity - $1,400 (2003 est.)

GDP - composition by sector:
agriculture: 40%
industry: 20%
services: 40% (2002 est.)

Population below poverty line: 42% (1995-96)

Household income or consumption by percentage share:
lowest 10%: 3.2%
highest 10%: 29.8% (1995-96)

Distribution of family income - Gini index: 36.7 (FY95/96)

Inflation rate (consumer prices): 2.9% (2002 est.)

Labor force: 10 million
note: severe lack of skilled labor (1996 est.)

Labor force - by occupation: agriculture 81%, services 16%, industry 3%

Unemployment rate: 47% (2001 est.)

Budget:
revenues: $665 million
expenditures: $1.1 billion, including capital expenditures of $NA (FY99/00 est.)

Industries: tourism, carpet, textile; small rice, jute, sugar, and oilseed mills; cigarette; cement and brick production

Industrial production growth rate: 8.7% (FY99/00)

Electricity - production: 1.755 billion kWh (2001)

Electricity - production by source:
fossil fuel: 8.5%
hydro: 91.5%
nuclear: 0%
other: 0% (2001)

Electricity - consumption: 1.764 billion kWh (2001)

Electricity - exports: 95 million kWh (2001)

Electricity - imports: 227 million kWh (2001)

Oil - production: 0 bbl/day (2001 est.)

Oil - consumption: 16,000 bbl/day (2001 est.)

Oil - exports: NA

Oil - imports: NA

Agriculture - products: rice, corn, wheat, sugarcane, root crops; milk, water buffalo meat

Exports: $568 million f.o.b., but does not include unrecorded border trade with India (2002 est.)

Exports - commodities: carpets, clothing, leather goods, jute goods, grain

Exports - partners: India 47.9%, US 27.8%, Germany 7.6% (2002)

Imports: $1.419 billion f.o.b. (2002 est.)

Imports - commodities: gold, machinery and equipment, petroleum products, fertilizer

Imports - partners: India 21.5%, China 13.3%, UAE 11.3%, Singapore 8.7%, Saudi Arabia 4.9%, Hong Kong 4.6%, Kuwait 4.2% (2002)

Debt - external: $2.7 billion (2001)

Economic aid - recipient: $424 million (FY00/01)

Currency: Nepalese rupee (NPR)

Currency code: NPR

Exchange rates: Nepalese rupees per US dollar - 76.1414 (2003), 77.8766 (2002), 74.9492 (2001), 71.0938 (2000), 68.2394 (1999)

Fiscal year: 16 July - 15 July

Communications

Telephones - main lines in use: 327,700 (2002)

Telephones - mobile cellular: 21,900 (2002)

Telephone system:
general assessment: poor telephone and telegraph service; fair radiotelephone communication service and mobile cellular telephone network
domestic: NA
international: country code - 977; radiotelephone communications; microwave landline to India; satellite earth station - 1 Intelsat (Indian Ocean)

Radio broadcast stations: AM 6, FM 5, shortwave 1 (January 2000)

Television broadcast stations: 1 (plus 9 repeaters) (1998)

Internet country code: .np

Internet hosts: 1,206 (2002)

Internet users: 80,000 (2002)

Transportation

Railways:
total: 59 km
narrow gauge: 59 km 0.762-m gauge (2002)

Highways:
total: 13,223 km
paved: 4,073 km
unpaved: 9,150 km (1999 est.)

Waterways: none

Ports and harbors: none

Airports: 46 (2003 est.)

Airports - with paved runways:
total: 9
over 3,047 m: 1
1,524 to 2,437 m: 1
914 to 1,523 m: 7 (2003 est.)

Airports - with unpaved runways:
total: 37
1,524 to 2,437 m: 1
914 to 1,523 m: 7
under 914 m: 29 (2003 est.)

Military

Military branches: Royal Nepalese Army (includes Royal Nepalese Army Air Service), Nepalese Police Force

Military manpower - military age: 17 years of age (2004 est.)

Military manpower - availability:
males age 15-49: 6,865,849 (2004 est.)

Military manpower - fit for military service:
males age 15-49: 3,566,576 (2004 est.)

Military manpower - reaching military age annually:
males: 308,776 (2004 est.)

Military expenditures - dollar figure: $295 million (FY03)

Military expenditures - percent of GDP: 1.6% (2003)

Transnational Issues

Disputes - international: joint border commission continues to work on small disputed sections of boundary with India; India has instituted a stricter border regime to restrict transit of Maoist insurgents and illegal cross-border activities

Illicit drugs: illicit producer of cannabis for the domestic and international drug markets; transit point for opiates from Southeast Asia to the West

Netherlands

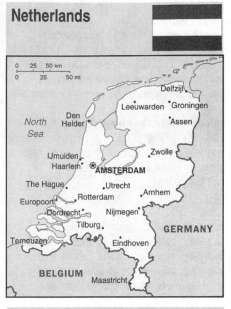

Introduction

Background: The Kingdom of the Netherlands was formed in 1815. In 1830 Belgium seceded and formed a separate kingdom. The Netherlands remained neutral in World War I, but suffered invasion and occupation by Germany in World War II. A modern, industrialized nation, the Netherlands is also a large exporter of agricultural products. The country was a founding member of NATO and the EC (now the EU), and participated in the introduction of the Economic and Monetary Union (EMU) in 1999.

Geography

Location: Western Europe, bordering the North Sea, between Belgium and Germany
Geographic coordinates: 52 30 N, 5 45 E
Map references: Europe
Area:
total: 41,526 sq km
land: 33,883 sq km
water: 7,643 sq km
Area - comparative: slightly less than twice the size of New Jersey
Land boundaries:
total: 1,027 km
border countries: Belgium 450 km, Germany 577 km
Coastline: 451 km
Maritime claims:
territorial sea: 12 NM
exclusive fishing zone: 200 NM
Climate: temperate; marine; cool summers and mild winters
Terrain: mostly coastal lowland and reclaimed land (polders); some hills in southeast
Elevation extremes:
lowest point: Zuidplaspolder -7 m
highest point: Vaalserberg 322 m
Natural resources: natural gas, petroleum, arable land

Land use:
arable land: 26.53%
permanent crops: 1.03%
other: 72.44% (1998 est.)
Irrigated land: 5,650 sq km (1998 est.)
Natural hazards: flooding
Environment - current issues: water pollution in the form of heavy metals, organic compounds, and nutrients such as nitrates and phosphates; air pollution from vehicles and refining activities; acid rain
Environment - international agreements:
party to: Air Pollution, Air Pollution-Nitrogen Oxides, Air Pollution-Persistent Organic Pollutants, Air Pollution-Sulfur 85, Air Pollution-Sulfur 94, Air Pollution-Volatile Organic Compounds, Antarctic-Environmental Protocol, Antarctic-Marine Living Resources, Antarctic Treaty, Biodiversity, Climate Change, Climate Change-Kyoto Protocol, Desertification, Endangered Species, Environmental Modification, Hazardous Wastes, Kyoto Protocol, Law of the Sea, Marine Dumping, Marine Life Conservation, Ozone Layer Protection, Ship Pollution, Tropical Timber 83, Tropical Timber 94, Wetlands, Whaling
Geography - note: located at mouths of three major European rivers (Rhine, Maas or Meuse, and Schelde)

People

Population: 16,318,199 (July 2004 est.)
Age structure:
0-14 years: 18.3% (male 1,527,316; female 1,457,192)
15-64 years: 67.8% (male 5,598,706; female 5,459,936)
65 years and over: 13.9% (male 953,370; female 1,321,679) (2004 est.)
Median age:
total: 38.7 years
male: 37.9 years
female: 39.6 years (2004 est.)
Population growth rate: 0.57% (2004 est.)
Birth rate: 11.41 births/1,000 population (2004 est.)
Death rate: 8.67 deaths/1,000 population (2004 est.)
Net migration rate: 2.91 migrant(s)/1,000 population (2004 est.)
Sex ratio:
at birth: 1.05 male(s)/female
under 15 years: 1.05 male(s)/female
15-64 years: 1.03 male(s)/female
65 years and over: 0.72 male(s)/female
total population: 0.98 male(s)/female (2004 est.)
Infant mortality rate:
total: 5.11 deaths/1,000 live births
male: 5.68 deaths/1,000 live births
female: 4.51 deaths/1,000 live births (2004 est.)
Life expectancy at birth:
total population: 78.68 years
male: 76.15 years
female: 81.34 years (2004 est.)

Total fertility rate: 1.66 children born/woman (2004 est.)
HIV/AIDS - adult prevalence rate: 0.2% (2001 est.)
HIV/AIDS - people living with HIV/AIDS: 17,000 (2001 est.)
HIV/AIDS - deaths: 110 (2001 est.)
Nationality:
noun: Dutchman(men), Dutchwoman(women)
adjective: Dutch
Ethnic groups: Dutch 83%, other 17% (of which 9% are non-Western origin mainly Turks, Moroccans, Antilleans, Surinamese and Indonesians) (1999 est.)
Religions: Roman Catholic 31%, Protestant 21%, Muslim 4.4%, other 3.6%, unaffiliated 40% (1998)
Languages: Dutch (official language), Frisian (official language)
Literacy:
definition: age 15 and over can read and write
total population: 99% (2000 est.)
male: NA%
female: NA%

Government

Country name:
conventional long form: Kingdom of the Netherlands
conventional short form: Netherlands
local long form: Koninkrijk der Nederlanden
local short form: Nederland
Government type: constitutional monarchy
Capital: Amsterdam; The Hague is the seat of government
Administrative divisions: 12 provinces (provincies, singular - provincie); Drenthe, Flevoland, Friesland, Gelderland, Groningen, Limburg, Noord-Brabant, Noord-Holland, Overijssel, Utrecht, Zeeland, Zuid-Holland
Dependent areas: Aruba, Netherlands Antilles
Independence: 1579 (from Spain); note - the northern provinces of the Low Country concluded the Union of Utrecht, but it was not until 1648 that Spain recognized their independence
National holiday: Queen's Day (Birthday of Queen-Mother JULIANA in 1909 and accession to the throne of her oldest daughter BEATRIX in 1980), 30 April
Constitution: adopted 1814; amended many times, last time 17 February 1983
Legal system: civil law system incorporating French penal theory; constitution does not permit judicial review of acts of the States General; accepts compulsory ICJ jurisdiction, with reservations
Suffrage: 18 years of age; universal
Executive branch:
chief of state: Queen BEATRIX (since 30 April 1980); Heir Apparent WILLEM-ALEXANDER (born 27 April 1967), son of the monarch
head of government: Prime Minister Jan Peter BALKENENDE (since 22 July 2002) and Deputy Prime Ministers Gerrit ZALM (since 27 May 2003) and Thom DE GRAAF (since 27 May 2003)
cabinet: Council of Ministers appointed by the monarch

elections: none; the monarchy is hereditary; following Second Chamber elections, the leader of the majority party or leader of a majority coalition is usually appointed prime minister by the monarch; vice prime ministers appointed by the monarch

note: there is also a Council of State composed of the monarch, heir apparent, and councilors that provides consultations to the prime minister on legislative and administrative policy

Legislative branch: bicameral States General or Staten Generaal consists of the First Chamber or Eerste Kamer (75 seats; members indirectly elected by the country's 12 provincial councils for four-year terms) and the Second Chamber or Tweede Kamer (150 seats; members directly elected by popular vote to serve four-year terms)

elections: First Chamber - last held 25 May 2003 (next to be held NA May 2007); Second Chamber - last held 22 January 2003 (next to be held NA January 2007)

election results: First Chamber - percent of vote by party - NA%; seats by party - CDA 23, PvdA 19, VVD 15, Green Party 5, Socialist Party 4, D66 3, other 6; Second Chamber - percent of vote by party - CDA 28.6%, PvdA 27.3%, VVD 12.9%, Socialist Party 6.3%, List Pim Fortuyn 5.7%, Green Party 5.1%, D66 4.1%; seats by party - CDA 44, PvdA 42, VVD 28, Socialist Party 9, List Pim Fortuyn 8, Green Party 8, D66 6, other 5

Judicial branch: Supreme Court or Hoge Raad (justices are nominated for life by the monarch)

Political parties and leaders: Christian Democratic Appeal or CDA [Maxime Jacques Marcel VERHAGEN]; Christian Union Party [Andre ROUVOET]; Democrats 66 or D66 [Boris DITTRICH]; Green Party [Femke HALSEMA]; Labor Party or PvdA [Wouter BOS]; List Pim Fortuyn [Mat HERBEN]; People's Party for Freedom and Democracy (Liberal) or VVD [Gerrit ZALM]; Socialist Party [Jan MARIJNISSEN]; a host of minor parties

Political pressure groups and leaders: Federation of Netherlands Trade Union Movement (comprising Socialist and Catholic trade unions) and a Protestant trade union; Federation of Catholic and Protestant Employers Associations; Interchurch Peace Council or IKV; large multinational firms; the nondenominational Federation of Netherlands Enterprises

International organization participation: AfDB, AsDB, Australia Group, Benelux, BIS, CE, CERN, EAPC, EBRD, EIB, EMU, ESA, EU, FAO, G-10, IADB, IAEA, IBRD, ICAO, ICC, ICCt, ICFTU, ICRM, IDA, IEA, IFAD, IFC, IFRCS, IHO, ILO, IMF, IMO, Interpol, IOC, IOM, ISO, ITU, NAM (guest), NATO, NEA, NSG, OAS (observer), OECD, OPCW, OSCE, Paris Club, PCA, UN, UNCTAD, UNESCO, UNHCR, UNIDO, UNITAR, UNMIL, UNTSO, UPU, WCL, WCO, WEU, WHO, WIPO, WMO, WToO, WTrO, ZC

Diplomatic representation in the US:
chief of mission: Ambassador Boudewijn J. VAN EENENNAAM
chancery: 4200 Linnean Avenue NW, Washington, DC 20008

telephone: [1] (202) 244-5300
FAX: [1] (202) 362-3430
consulate(s) general: Chicago, Houston, Los Angeles, Miami, New York
consulate(s): Boston

Diplomatic representation from the US:
chief of mission: Ambassador Clifford M. SOBEL
embassy: Lange Voorhout 102, 2514 EJ, The Hague
mailing address: PSC 71, Box 1000, APO AE 09715
telephone: [31] (70) 310-9209
FAX: [31] (70) 361-4688
consulate(s) general: Amsterdam

Flag description: three equal horizontal bands of red (top), white, and blue; similar to the flag of Luxembourg, which uses a lighter blue and is longer; one of the oldest flags in constant use, originating with William I, Prince of Orange, in the latter half of the 16th century

Economy

Economy - overview: The Netherlands has a prosperous and open economy, which depends heavily on foreign trade. The economy is noted for stable industrial relations, moderate unemployment and inflation, a sizable current account surplus, and an important role as a European transportation hub. Industrial activity is predominantly in food processing, chemicals, petroleum refining, and electrical machinery. A highly mechanized agricultural sector employs no more than 4% of the labor force but provides large surpluses for the food-processing industry and for exports. The Netherlands, along with 11 of its EU partners, began circulating the euro currency on 1 January 2002. The country continues to be one of the leading European nations for attracting foreign direct investment. Economic growth slowed considerably in 2001-03, as part of the global economic slowdown, but for the four years before that, annual growth averaged nearly 4%, well above the EU average. The government is wrestling with a deteriorating budget position, and is moving toward the EU 3% of GDP budget deficit limit.

GDP: purchasing power parity - $461.4 billion (2003 est.)

GDP - real growth rate: -0.7% (2003 est.)

GDP - per capita: purchasing power parity - $28,600 (2003 est.)

GDP - composition by sector:
agriculture: 2.6%
industry: 25%
services: 72.4% (2002 est.)

Population below poverty line: NA%

Household income or consumption by percentage share:
lowest 10%: 2.8%
highest 10%: 25.1% (1994)

Distribution of family income - Gini index: 32.6 (1994)

Inflation rate (consumer prices): 2% (2003 est.)

Labor force: 7.2 million (2000)

Labor force - by occupation: services 73%, industry 23%, agriculture 4% (1998 est.)

Unemployment rate: 4.2% (2003 est.)

Budget:
revenues: $134 billion
expenditures: $134 billion, including capital expenditures of $NA (2001 est.)

Industries: agroindustries, metal and engineering products, electrical machinery and equipment, chemicals, petroleum, construction, microelectronics, fishing

Industrial production growth rate: -1.9% (2003 est.)

Electricity - production: 88.32 billion kWh (2001)

Electricity - production by source:
fossil fuel: 89.9%
hydro: 0.1%
nuclear: 4.3%
other: 5.7% (2001)

Electricity - consumption: 99.42 billion kWh (2001)

Electricity - exports: 4.209 billion kWh (2001)

Electricity - imports: 21.49 billion kWh (2001)

Oil - production: 46,200 bbl/day (2001 est.)

Oil - consumption: 895,300 bbl/day (2001 est.)

Oil - exports: 1.418 million bbl/day (2001)

Oil - imports: 2.284 million bbl/day (2001)

Oil - proved reserves: 88.06 million bbl (1 January 2002)

Natural gas - production: 77.75 billion cu m (2001 est.)

Natural gas - consumption: 49.72 billion cu m (2001 est.)

Natural gas - exports: 49.28 billion cu m (2001 est.)

Natural gas - imports: 20.78 billion cu m (2001 est.)

Natural gas - proved reserves: 1.693 trillion cu m (1 January 2002)

Agriculture - products: grains, potatoes, sugar beets, fruits, vegetables; livestock

Exports: $253.2 billion f.o.b. (2003 est.)

Exports - commodities: machinery and equipment, chemicals, fuels; foodstuffs

Exports - partners: Germany 25.1%, Belgium 12.7%, UK 10.7%, France 10.2%, Italy 6%, US 4.6% (2002)

Imports: $217.7 billion f.o.b. (2003 est.)

Imports - commodities: machinery and transport equipment, chemicals, fuels; foodstuffs, clothing

Imports - partners: Germany 17.9%, Belgium 9.7%, US 9.1%, UK 6.9%, France 5.5%, China 5.1%, Japan 4% (2002)

Economic aid - donor: ODA, $3.3 billion (2002 est.)

Currency: euro (EUR)

note: on 1 January 1999, the European Monetary Union introduced the euro as a common currency to be used by financial institutions of member countries; on 1 January 2002, the euro became the sole currency for everyday transactions within the member countries

Currency code: EUR

Exchange rates: euros per US dollar - 0.886 (2003), 1.0626 (2002), 1.1175 (2001), 1.0854 (2000), 0.9386 (1999)

Fiscal year: calendar year

Netherlands *(continued)*

Communications

Telephones - main lines in use: 10.004 million (2002)

Telephones - mobile cellular: 12.06 million (2002)

Telephone system:

general assessment: highly developed and well maintained

domestic: extensive fixed-line fiber-optic network; cellular telephone system is one of the largest in Europe with five major network operators utilizing the third generation of the Global System for Mobile Communications (GSM)

international: country code - 31; 9 submarine cables; satellite earth stations - 3 Intelsat (1 Indian Ocean and 2 Atlantic Ocean), 1 Eutelsat, and 1 Inmarsat (Atlantic and Indian Ocean regions) (2004)

Radio broadcast stations: AM 4, FM 246, shortwave 3 (2004)

Television broadcast stations: 21 (plus 26 repeaters) (1995)

Internet country code: .nl

Internet hosts: 3,137,203 (2002)

Internet users: 8.2 million (2002)

Transportation

Railways:

total: 2,808 km

standard gauge: 2,808 km 1.435-m gauge (2,061 km electrified) (2002)

Highways:

total: 116,500 km

paved: 104,850 km (including 2,235 km of expressways)

unpaved: 11,650 km (1999)

Waterways: 5,046 km (of which 3,745 km are canals)

note: 47% of total route length is usable by craft of 1,000-metric-ton capacity or larger

Pipelines: condensate 325 km; gas 6,998 km; oil 590 km; refined products 716 km (2003)

Ports and harbors: Amsterdam, Delfzijl, Dordrecht, Eemshaven, Groningen, Haarlem, IJmuiden, Maastricht, Rotterdam, Terneuzen, Utrecht, Vlissingen

Merchant marine:

total: 635 ships (1,000 GRT or over) 4,796,460 GRT/ 5,212,557 DWT

by type: bulk 1, cargo 375, chemical tanker 59, combination bulk 1, container 71, liquefied gas 13, multi-functional large load carrier 15, passenger 12, petroleum tanker 28, refrigerated cargo 37, roll on/roll off 14, short-sea/passenger 2, specialized tanker 7

foreign-owned: Belgium 2, Denmark 4, Finland 9, Germany 54, Ireland 14, Norway 9, Singapore 1, Sweden 19, Thailand 1, United Kingdom 31, United States 16

registered in other countries: 241 (2003 est.)

Airports: 27 (2003 est.)

Airports - with paved runways:

total: 20

over 3,047 m: 2

2,438 to 3,047 m: 8

1,524 to 2,437 m: 4

914 to 1,523 m: 4

under 914 m: 2 (2003 est.)

Airports - with unpaved runways:

total: 7

914 to 1,523 m: 2

under 914 m: 5 (2003 est.)

Heliports: 1 (2003 est.)

Military

Military branches: Royal Netherlands Army, Royal Netherlands Navy (including Naval Air Service and Marine Corps), Royal Netherlands Air Force, Royal Constabulary, Defense Interservice Command

Military manpower - military age: 20 years of age (2004 est.)

Military manpower - availability:

males age 15-49: 4,070,043 (2004 est.)

Military manpower - fit for military service:

males age 15-49: 3,534,392 (2004 est.)

Military manpower - reaching military age annually:

males: 97,624

note: Netherlands has an all-volunteer, 74,100 force in 2001 (2004 est.)

Military expenditures - dollar figure: $8,044,400,000 (2003)

Military expenditures - percent of GDP: 1.6% (2003)

Transnational Issues

Disputes - international: none

Illicit drugs: major European producer of ecstasy, illicit amphetamines, and other synthetic drugs; important gateway for cocaine, heroin, and hashish entering Europe; major source of US-bound ecstasy; large financial sector vulnerable to money laundering

Netherlands Antilles

(part of the Kingdom of the Netherlands)

Introduction

Background: Once the center of the Caribbean slave trade, the island of Curacao was hard hit by the abolition of slavery in 1863. Its prosperity (and that of neighboring Aruba) was restored in the early 20th century with the construction of oil refineries to service the newly discovered Venezuelan oil fields. The island of Saint Martin is shared with France; its southern portion is named Sint Maarten and is part of the Netherlands Antilles; its northern portion is called Saint-Martin and is part of Guadeloupe.

Geography

Location: Caribbean, two island groups in the Caribbean Sea - one includes Curacao and Bonaire north of Venezuela; the other is east of the Virgin Islands

Geographic coordinates: 12 15 N, 68 45 W

Map references: Central America and the Caribbean

Area:

total: 960 sq km

land: 960 sq km

water: 0 sq km

note: includes Bonaire, Curacao, Saba, Sint Eustatius, and Sint Maarten (Dutch part of the island of Saint Martin)

Area - comparative: more than five times the size of Washington, DC

Land boundaries:

total: 10.2 km

border countries: Guadeloupe (Saint Martin) 10.2 km

Coastline: 364 km

Maritime claims:

territorial sea: 12 NM

exclusive fishing zone: 12 NM

Climate: tropical; ameliorated by northeast trade winds

Terrain: generally hilly, volcanic interiors

Netherlands Antilles (continued)

Elevation extremes:
lowest point: Caribbean Sea 0 m
highest point: Mount Scenery 862 m
Natural resources: phosphates (Curacao only), salt (Bonaire only)
Land use:
arable land: 10%
permanent crops: 0%
other: 90% (1998 est.)
Irrigated land: NA sq km
Natural hazards: Curacao and Bonaire are south of Caribbean hurricane belt and are rarely threatened; Sint Maarten, Saba, and Sint Eustatius are subject to hurricanes from July to October
Environment - current issues: NA
Geography - note: the five islands of the Netherlands Antilles are divided geographically into the Leeward Islands (northern) group (Saba, Sint Eustatius, and Sint Maarten) and the Windward Islands (southern) group (Bonaire and Curacao)

People

Population: 218,126 (July 2004 est.)
Age structure:
0-14 years: 24.5% (male 27,387; female 26,094)
15-64 years: 67.2% (male 70,024; female 76,552)
65 years and over: 8.3% (male 7,443; female 10,626) (2004 est.)
Median age:
total: 32.1 years
male: 30.6 years
female: 33.6 years (2004 est.)
Population growth rate: 0.86% (2004 est.)
Birth rate: 15.36 births/1,000 population (2004 est.)
Death rate: 6.4 deaths/1,000 population (2004 est.)
Net migration rate: -0.41 migrant(s)/1,000 population (2004 est.)
Sex ratio:
at birth: 1.05 male(s)/female
under 15 years: 1.05 male(s)/female
15-64 years: 0.92 male(s)/female
65 years and over: 0.7 male(s)/female
total population: 0.93 male(s)/female (2004 est.)
Infant mortality rate:
total: 10.37 deaths/1,000 live births
male: 11.18 deaths/1,000 live births
female: 9.52 deaths/1,000 live births (2004 est.)
Life expectancy at birth:
total population: 75.6 years
male: 73.37 years
female: 77.95 years (2004 est.)
Total fertility rate: 2.02 children born/woman (2004 est.)
HIV/AIDS - adult prevalence rate: NA%
HIV/AIDS - people living with HIV/AIDS: NA
HIV/AIDS - deaths: NA
Nationality:
noun: Dutch Antillean(s)
adjective: Dutch Antillean

Ethnic groups: mixed black 85%, Carib Amerindian, white, East Asian
Religions: Roman Catholic, Protestant, Jewish, Seventh-Day Adventist
Languages: Dutch (official), Papiamento (a Spanish-Portuguese-Dutch-English dialect) predominates, English widely spoken, Spanish
Literacy:
definition: age 15 and over can read and write
total population: 96.7%
male: 96.7%
female: 96.8% (2003 est.)

Government

Country name:
conventional long form: none
conventional short form: Netherlands Antilles
local long form: none
local short form: Nederlandse Antillen
former: Curacao and Dependencies
Dependency status: part of the Kingdom of the Netherlands; full autonomy in internal affairs granted in 1954; Dutch Government responsible for defense and foreign affairs
Government type: parliamentary
Capital: Willemstad
Administrative divisions: none (part of the Kingdom of the Netherlands)
note: each island has its own government
Independence: none (part of the Kingdom of the Netherlands)
National holiday: Queen's Day (Birthday of Queen-Mother JULIANA in 1909 and accession to the throne of her oldest daughter BEATRIX in 1980), 30 April
Constitution: 29 December 1954, Statute of the Realm of the Netherlands, as amended
Legal system: based on Dutch civil law system with some English common law influence
Suffrage: 18 years of age; universal
Executive branch:
chief of state: Queen BEATRIX of the Netherlands (since 30 April 1980), represented by Governor General Frits GOEDGEDRAG (since 1 July 2002)
head of government: Prime Minister Mirna LOUISA-GODETT (since 11 August 2003)
cabinet: Council of Ministers elected by the Staten (legislature)
elections: the monarch is hereditary; governor general appointed by the monarch for a six-year term; following legislative elections, the leader of the majority party is usually elected prime minister by the Staten; election last held 18 January 2002 (next to be held by NA 2006)
note: government coalition - PDB, DP-St. M, FOL, PLKP, PNP
Legislative branch: unicameral States or Staten (22 seats; members are elected by popular vote to serve four-year terms)

elections: last held 18 January 2002 (next to be held in 2006)
election results: percent of vote by party - NA%; seats by party - FOL 5, PAR 4, PNP 3, PLKP 2, DP-St.M 2, UPB 2, DP 1, MAN 1, PDB 1, WIPM 1; seats by party - PAR 4, PNP 3, FOL 2, MAN 2, UPB 2, DP-St. M 2, PDB 1, SEA 1, WIPM 1, other 4
note: the government of Prime Minister Mirna LOUISA-GODETT is a coalition of several parties;
Judicial branch: Joint High Court of Justice (judges appointed by the monarch)
Political parties and leaders: Antillean Restructuring Party or PAR [Miguel POURIER]; C 93 [Stanley BROWN]; Democratic Party of Bonaire or PDB [Jopi ABRAHAM]; Democratic Party of Curacao or DP [Errol HERNANDEZ]; Democratic Party of Sint Eustatius or DP-St. E [Julian WOODLEY]; Democratic Party of Sint Maarten or DP-St. M [Sarah WESCOTT-WILLIAMS]; Foundation Energetic Management Anti-Narcotics or FAME [Eric LODEWIJKS]; Labor Party People's Crusade or PLKP [Errol COVA]; National People's Party or PNP [Susanne F. C. CAMELIA-ROMER]; New Antilles Movement or MAN [Kenneth GIJSBERTHA]; Patriotic Union of Bonaire or UPB [Ramon BOOI]; Patriotic Movement of Sint Maarten or SPA [Vance JAMES, Jr.]; People's Party or PAPU [Richard Hodi]; Pro Curacao Party or PPK [Winston LOURENS]; Saba Democratic Labor Movement [Steve HASSELL]; Saba Unity Party [Carmen SIMMONDS]; St. Eustatius Alliance or SEA [Kenneth VAN PUTTEN]; Serious Alternative People's Party or Sapp [Julian ROLLOCKS]; Social Action Cause or KAS [Benny DEMEI]; Windward Islands People's Movement or WIPM [Will JOHNSTON]; Workers' Liberation Front or FOL [Anthony GODETT, Rignald LAK, Editha WRIGHT]
note: political parties are indigenous to each island
Political pressure groups and leaders: NA
International organization participation: Caricom (observer), Interpol, IOC, UNESCO (associate), WCL, WCO, WMO, WToO (associate)
Diplomatic representation in the US: none (represented by the Kingdom of the Netherlands)
Diplomatic representation from the US:
chief of mission: Consul General Deborah A. BOLTON
consulate(s) general: J. B. Gorsiraweg #1, Willemstad AN, Curacao
mailing address: P. O. Box 158, Willemstad, Curacao
telephone: [599] (9) 4613066
FAX: [599] (9) 4616489
Flag description: white, with a horizontal blue stripe in the center superimposed on a vertical red band, also centered; five white, five-pointed stars are arranged in an oval pattern in the center of the blue band; the five stars represent the five main islands of Bonaire, Curacao, Saba, Sint Eustatius, and Sint Maarten

Netherlands Antilles (continued)

Economy

Economy - overview: Tourism, petroleum refining, and offshore finance are the mainstays of this small economy, which is closely tied to the outside world. Although GDP has declined or grown slightly in each of the past seven years, the islands enjoy a high per capita income and a well-developed infrastructure compared with other countries in the region. Almost all consumer and capital goods are imported, the US and Mexico being the major suppliers. Poor soils and inadequate water supplies hamper the development of agriculture. Budgetary problems hamper reform of the health and pension systems of an aging population.

GDP: purchasing power parity - $2.45 billion (2003 est.)

GDP - real growth rate: 0.5% (2003 est.)

GDP - per capita: purchasing power parity - $11,400 (2003 est.)

GDP - composition by sector:
agriculture: 1%
industry: 15%
services: 84% (2000 est.)

Population below poverty line: NA%

Household income or consumption by percentage share:
lowest 10%: NA%
highest 10%: NA%

Inflation rate (consumer prices): 2.1% (2003 est.)

Labor force: 89,000 (2000)

Labor force - by occupation: agriculture 1%, industry 13%, services 86% (2000 est.)

Unemployment rate: 15.6% (2002 est.)

Budget:
revenues: $710.8 million
expenditures: $741.6 million, including capital expenditures of $NA (1997 est.)

Industries: tourism (Curacao, Sint Maarten, and Bonaire), petroleum refining (Curacao), petroleum transshipment facilities (Curacao and Bonaire), light manufacturing (Curacao)

Industrial production growth rate: NA%

Electricity - production: 1.061 billion kWh (2001)

Electricity - production by source:
fossil fuel: 100%
hydro: 0%
nuclear: 0%
other: 0% (2001)

Electricity - consumption: 986.8 million kWh (2001)

Electricity - exports: 0 kWh (2001)

Electricity - imports: 0 kWh (2001)

Oil - production: 0 bbl/day (2001 est.)

Oil - consumption: 72,000 bbl/day (2001 est.)

Oil - exports: NA

Oil - imports: NA

Agriculture - products: aloes, sorghum, peanuts, vegetables, tropical fruit

Exports: $1.579 billion f.o.b. (2002)

Exports - commodities: petroleum products

Exports - partners: US 23.6%, Venezuela 10.5%, Bahamas, The 8.2%, El Salvador 5.1%, Honduras 4.7%, Guyana 4.4%, Canada 4.4%, Panama 4.3%, Guatemala 4.2%, Netherlands 4.2% (2002)

Imports: $2.233 billion f.o.b. (2002)

Imports - commodities: crude petroleum, food, manufactures

Imports - partners: Venezuela 61.3%, US 13%, Netherlands 7.7%, Iraq 6.8% (2002)

Debt - external: $1.35 billion (1996)

Economic aid - recipient: IMF provided $61 million in 2000, and the Netherlands continued its support with $40 million (2000)

Currency: Netherlands Antillean guilder (ANG)

Currency code: ANG

Exchange rates: Netherlands Antillean guilders per US dollar - 1.79 (2003), 1.79 (2002), 1.79 (2001), 1.79 (2000), 1.79 (1999)

Fiscal year: calendar year

Communications

Telephones - main lines in use: 81,000 (2001)

Telephones - mobile cellular: 81,000 (2001)

Telephone system:
general assessment: generally adequate facilities
domestic: extensive interisland microwave radio relay links
international: country code - 599; submarine cables - 2; satellite earth stations - 2 Intelsat (Atlantic Ocean)

Radio broadcast stations: AM 8, FM 19, shortwave 0 (2004)

Television broadcast stations: 3 (there is also a cable service, which supplies programs received from various US satellite networks and two Venezuelan channels) (2004)

Internet country code: .an

Internet hosts: 119 (2001)

Internet users: 2,000 (2000)

Transportation

Railways: 0 km

Highways:
total: 600 km
paved: 300 km
unpaved: 300 km

Waterways: none

Ports and harbors: Kralendijk, Philipsburg, Willemstad

Merchant marine:
total: 162 ships (1,000 GRT or over) 1,317,007 GRT/ 1,668,499 DWT
by type: bulk 4, cargo 59, chemical tanker 1, combination bulk 1, combination ore/oil 3, container 28, liquefied gas 6, multi-functional large load carrier 22, passenger 1, petroleum tanker 1, refrigerated cargo 28, roll on/roll off 7, specialized tanker 1
foreign-owned: Belgium 3, Denmark 1, Germany 57, Monaco 4, Netherlands 70, New Zealand 1, Norway 5, Peru 1, Spain 1, Sweden 5, Turkey 2, United Kingdom 6
registered in other countries: 1 (2003 est.)

Airports: 5 (2003 est.)

Airports - with paved runways:
total: 5
over 3,047 m: 1
2038 to 3047 m: 1
1,524 to 2,437 m: 1
914 to 1,523 m: 1
under 914 m: 1 (2003 est.)

Military

Military branches: National Guard, Police Force

Military manpower - military age: 20 years of age (2004 est.)

Military manpower - availability:
males age 15-49: 55,536 (2004 est.)

Military manpower - fit for military service:
males age 15-49: 31,025 (2004 est.)

Military manpower - reaching military age annually:
males: 1,660 (2004 est.)

Military - note: defense is the responsibility of the Kingdom of the Netherlands

Transnational Issues

Disputes - international: none

Illicit drugs: transshipment point for South American drugs bound for the US and Europe; money-laundering center

New Caledonia
(overseas territory of France)

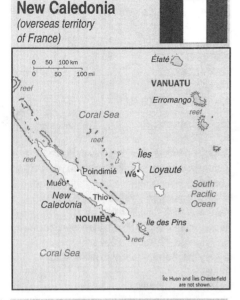

Introduction

Background: Settled by both Britain and France during the first half of the 19th century, the island was made a French possession in 1853. It served as a penal colony for four decades after 1864. Agitation for independence during the 1980s and early 1990s has dissipated.

Geography

Location: Oceania, islands in the South Pacific Ocean, east of Australia
Geographic coordinates: 21 30 S, 165 30 E
Map references: Oceania
Area:
total: 19,060 sq km
land: 18,575 sq km
water: 485 sq km
Area - comparative: slightly smaller than New Jersey
Land boundaries: 0 km
Coastline: 2,254 km
Maritime claims:
territorial sea: 12 NM
exclusive economic zone: 200 NM
Climate: tropical; modified by southeast trade winds; hot, humid
Terrain: coastal plains with interior mountains
Elevation extremes:
lowest point: Pacific Ocean 0 m
highest point: Mont Panie 1,628 m
Natural resources: nickel, chrome, iron, cobalt, manganese, silver, gold, lead, copper
Land use:
arable land: 0.38%
permanent crops: 0.33%
other: 99.29% (1998 est.)
Irrigated land: 160 sq km (1991)

Natural hazards: cyclones, most frequent from November to March
Environment - current issues: erosion caused by mining exploitation and forest fires
Geography - note: consists of the main island of New Caledonia (one of the largest in the Pacific Ocean), the archipelago of Iles Loyaute, and numerous small, sparsely populated islands and atolls

People

Population: 213,679 (July 2004 est.)
Age structure:
0-14 years: 29.4% (male 32,076; female 30,772)
15-64 years: 64.3% (male 69,150; female 68,310)
65 years and over: 6.3% (male 6,259; female 7,112) (2004 est.)
Median age:
total: 27.2 years
male: 26.9 years
female: 27.5 years (2004 est.)
Population growth rate: 1.33% (2004 est.)
Birth rate: 18.98 births/1,000 population (2004 est.)
Death rate: 5.64 deaths/1,000 population (2004 est.)
Net migration rate: 0 migrant(s)/1,000 population (2004 est.)
Sex ratio:
at birth: 1.05 male(s)/female
under 15 years: 1.04 male(s)/female
15-64 years: 1.01 male(s)/female
65 years and over: 0.88 male(s)/female
total population: 1.01 male(s)/female (2004 est.)
Infant mortality rate:
total: 7.89 deaths/1,000 live births
male: 8.59 deaths/1,000 live births
female: 7.14 deaths/1,000 live births (2004 est.)
Life expectancy at birth:
total population: 73.78 years
male: 70.82 years
female: 76.89 years (2004 est.)
Total fertility rate: 2.35 children born/woman (2004 est.)
HIV/AIDS - adult prevalence rate: NA%
HIV/AIDS - people living with HIV/AIDS: NA
HIV/AIDS - deaths: NA
Nationality:
noun: New Caledonian(s)
adjective: New Caledonian
Ethnic groups: Melanesian 42.5%, European 37.1%, Wallisian 8.4%, Polynesian 3.8%, Indonesian 3.6%, Vietnamese 1.6%, other 3%
Religions: Roman Catholic 60%, Protestant 30%, other 10%
Languages: French (official), 33 Melanesian-Polynesian dialects
Literacy:
definition: age 15 and over can read and write
total population: 91%
male: 92%
female: 90% (1976 est.)

Government

Country name:
conventional long form: Territory of New Caledonia and Dependencies
conventional short form: New Caledonia
local long form: Territoire des Nouvelle-Caledonie et Dependances
local short form: Nouvelle-Caledonie
Dependency status: overseas territory of France since 1956
Government type: NA
Capital: Noumea
Administrative divisions: none (overseas territory of France); there are no first-order administrative divisions as defined by the US Government, but there are 3 provinces named Iles Loyaute, Nord, and Sud
Independence: none (overseas territory of France); note - a referendum on independence was held in 1998 but did not pass; a new referendum is scheduled for 2014
National holiday: Bastille Day, 14 July (1789)
Constitution: 28 September 1958 (French Constitution)
Legal system: the 1988 Matignon Accords grant substantial autonomy to the islands; formerly under French law
Suffrage: 18 years of age; universal
Executive branch:
chief of state: President of France Jacques CHIRAC (since 17 May 1995), represented by High Commissioner Daniel CONSTANTIN (since 3 July 2002)
head of government: President of the Government Pierre FROGIER (since 5 April 2001)
cabinet: Consultative Committee
elections: French president elected by popular vote for a five-year term; high commissioner appointed by the French president on the advice of the French Ministry of Interior; president of the government elected by the members of the Territorial Congress; note - last election held 28 November 2002 when Pierre FROGIER was reelected
Legislative branch: unicameral Territorial Congress or Congres Territorial (54 seats; members are members of the three Provincial Assemblies or Assemblees Provinciales elected by popular vote to serve five-year terms)
elections: last held 9 May 1999 (next to be held NA 2004)
election results: percent of vote by party - NA%; seats by party - RPCR 24, FLNKS 12, UNI 6, FCCI 4, FN 4, Alliance pour la Caledonie 3, LKS 1
note: New Caledonia currently holds 1 seat in the French Senate; elections last held 24 September 2001 (next to be held not later than September 2007; between now and 2010 New Caledonia will gain a second seat in the French Senate); results - percent of vote by party - NA%; seats by party - NA; New Caledonia also elects 2 seats to the French National

New Caledonia *(continued)*

Assembly; elections last held 9 and 16 June 2002 (next to be held by June 2007); results - percent of vote by party - NA%; seats by party - UMP 2

Judicial branch: Court of Appeal or Cour d'Appel; County Courts; Joint Commerce Tribunal Court; Children's Court

Political parties and leaders: Alliance pour la Caledonie or APLC [Didier LE ROUX]; Federation des Comites de Coordination des Independantistes or FCCI [Francois BURCK]; Front National or FN [Guy GEORGE]; Front Uni de Liberation Kanak or FULK [Ernest UNE]; Kanak Socialist Front for National Liberation or FLNKS [leader NA] (includes PALIKA, UNI, UC, and UPM); Parti de Liberation Kanak or PALIKA [Paul NEAOUTYINE and Elie POIGOUNE]; Rally for Caledonia in the Republic (anti independent) or RPCR [Jacques LAFLEUR]; Union Nationale pour l'Independance or UNI [Paul NEAOUTYINE]; note - may no longer exist, but Paul NEAOUTYINE has since become a president of Parti de Liberation Kanak or PALIKA; Union Progressiste Melanesienne or UPM [Victor TUTUGORO]

Political pressure groups and leaders: NA
International organization participation: FZ, ICFTU, PIF (observer), WFTU, WMO
Diplomatic representation in the US: none (overseas territory of France)
Diplomatic representation from the US: none (overseas territory of France)
Flag description: the flag of France is used

Economy

Economy - overview: New Caledonia has about 25% of the world's known nickel resources. Only a small amount of the land is suitable for cultivation, and food accounts for about 20% of imports. In addition to nickel, substantial financial support from France - equal to more than one-fourth of GDP - and tourism are keys to the health of the economy. Substantial new investment in the nickel industry, combined with the recovery of global nickel prices, brightens the economic outlook for the next several years.
GDP: purchasing power parity - $3.158 billion (2003 est.)
GDP - real growth rate: NA
GDP - per capita: purchasing power parity - $15,000 (2002 est.)
GDP - composition by sector:
agriculture: 5%
industry: 30%
services: 65% (1997 est.)
Population below poverty line: NA%
Household income or consumption by percentage share:
lowest 10%: NA%
highest 10%: NA%
Inflation rate (consumer prices): -0.6% (2000 est.)
Labor force: 79,395 (including 15,018 unemployed, 1996)

Labor force - by occupation: agriculture 7%, industry 23%, services 70% (1999 est.)
Unemployment rate: 19% (1996)
Budget:
revenues: $861.3 million
expenditures: $735.3 million, including capital expenditures of $52 million (1996 est.)
Industries: nickel mining and smelting
Industrial production growth rate: -0.6% (1996)
Electricity - production: 1.613 billion kWh (2001)
Electricity - production by source:
fossil fuel: 76.3%
hydro: 23.7%
nuclear: 0%
other: 0% (2001)
Electricity - consumption: 1.5 billion kWh (2001)
Electricity - exports: 0 kWh (2001)
Electricity - imports: 0 kWh (2001)
Oil - production: 0 bbl/day (2001 est.)
Oil - consumption: 8,750 bbl/day (2001 est.)
Oil - exports: NA
Oil - imports: NA
Agriculture - products: vegetables; beef, deer, other livestock products
Exports: $448 million f.o.b. (2002)
Exports - commodities: ferronickels, nickel ore, fish
Exports - partners: France 22.8%, Japan 21.2%, Spain 8.7%, Australia 7.6%, South Korea 6.3%, Italy 5.6% (2002)
Imports: $1.007 billion f.o.b. (2002)
Imports - commodities: machinery and equipment, fuels, chemicals, foodstuffs
Imports - partners: France 39.6%, Australia 12.8%, Singapore 9.9%, New Zealand 5.1%, US 4.4% (2002)
Debt - external: $79 million (1998 est.)
Economic aid - recipient: $880 million annual subsidy from France (1998)
Currency: Comptoirs Francais du Pacifique franc (XPF); note - may adopt the euro in 2003
Currency code: XPF
Exchange rates: Comptoirs Francais du Pacifique francs (XPF) per US dollar - 105.73 (2003), 126.72 (2002), 133.26 (2001), 129.44 (2000), 111.93 (1999)
Fiscal year: calendar year

Communications

Telephones - main lines in use: 52,000 (2002)
Telephones - mobile cellular: 80,000 (2002)
Telephone system:
general assessment: NA
domestic: NA
international: country code - 687; satellite earth station - 1 Intelsat (Pacific Ocean)
Radio broadcast stations: AM 1, FM 5, shortwave 0 (1998)
Television broadcast stations: 6 (plus 25 low-power repeaters) (1997)
Internet country code: .nc
Internet hosts: 5,915 (2002)
Internet users: 30,000 (2002)

Transportation

Railways: 0 km
Highways:
total: 4,825 km
paved: 2,287 km
unpaved: 2,538 km (1999)
Waterways: none
Ports and harbors: Mueo, Noumea, Thio
Merchant marine:
total: 1 ships (1,000 GRT or over) 1,261 GRT/1,600 DWT
by type: cargo 1
foreign-owned: Malaysia 1
registered in other countries: 1 (2003 est.)
Airports: 25 (2003 est.)
Airports - with paved runways:
total: 11
over 3,047 m: 1
914 to 1,523 m: 8
under 914 m: 2 (2003 est.)
Airports - with unpaved runways:
total: 14
914 to 1,523 m: 8
under 914 m: 6 (2003 est.)
Heliports: 6 (2003 est.)

Military

Military branches: no regular indigenous military forces; French Armed Forces (including Army, Navy, Air Force, Gendarmerie); Police Force
Military expenditures - dollar figure: $192.3 million (FY96)
Military expenditures - percent of GDP: 5.3% (FY96)
Military - note: defense is the responsibility of France

Transnational Issues

Disputes - international: Matthew and Hunter Islands east of New Caledonia claimed by France and Vanuatu

New Zealand

Antipodes Islands, Auckland Islands, Bounty Islands, Campbell Island, Chatham Islands, and Kermadec Islands are not shown.

Introduction

Background: The Polynesian Maori reached New Zealand in about A.D. 800. In 1840, their chieftains entered into a compact with Britain, the Treaty of Waitangi, in which they ceded sovereignty to Queen Victoria while retaining territorial rights. In that same year, the British began the first organized colonial settlement. A series of land wars between 1843 and 1872 ended with the defeat of the native peoples. The British colony of New Zealand became an independent dominion in 1907 and supported the UK militarily in both World Wars. New Zealand's full participation in a number of defense alliances lapsed by the 1980s. In recent years, the government has sought to address longstanding Maori grievances.

Geography

Location: Oceania, islands in the South Pacific Ocean, southeast of Australia
Geographic coordinates: 41 00 S, 174 00 E
Map references: Oceania
Area:
total: 268,680 sq km
land: NA sq km

water: NA sq km
note: includes Antipodes Islands, Auckland Islands, Bounty Islands, Campbell Island, Chatham Islands, and Kermadec Islands
Area - comparative: about the size of Colorado
Land boundaries: 0 km
Coastline: 15,134 km
Maritime claims:
territorial sea: 12 NM
exclusive economic zone: 200 NM
continental shelf: 200 NM or to the edge of the continental margin
Climate: temperate with sharp regional contrasts
Terrain: predominately mountainous with some large coastal plains
Elevation extremes:
lowest point: Pacific Ocean 0 m
highest point: Aoraki-Mount Cook 3,754 m
Natural resources: natural gas, iron ore, sand, coal, timber, hydropower, gold, limestone
Land use:
arable land: 5.8%
permanent crops: 6.44%
other: 87.76% (1998 est.)
Irrigated land: 2,850 sq km (1998 est.)
Natural hazards: earthquakes are common, though usually not severe; volcanic activity
Environment - current issues: deforestation; soil erosion; native flora and fauna hard-hit by species introduced from outside
Environment - international agreements:
party to: Antarctic-Environmental Protocol, Antarctic-Marine Living Resources, Antarctic Treaty, Biodiversity, Climate Change, Climate Change-Kyoto Protocol, Desertification, Endangered Species, Environmental Modification, Hazardous Wastes, Law of the Sea, Marine Dumping, Ozone Layer Protection, Ship Pollution, Tropical Timber 83, Tropical Timber 94, Wetlands, Whaling
signed, but not ratified: Antarctic Seals, Marine Life Conservation
Geography - note: about 80% of the population lives in cities; Wellington is the southernmost national capital in the world

People

Population: 3,993,817 (July 2004 est.)
Age structure:
0-14 years: 21.7% (male 443,211; female 422,507)
15-64 years: 66.7% (male 1,337,383; female 1,325,683)
65 years and over: 11.6% (male 203,084; female 261,949) (2004 est.)
Median age:
total: 33.4 years
male: 32.6 years
female: 34.1 years (2004 est.)
Population growth rate: 1.05% (2004 est.)
Birth rate: 14.04 births/1,000 population (2004 est.)
Death rate: 7.54 deaths/1,000 population (2004 est.)
Net migration rate: 4.05 migrant(s)/1,000 population (2004 est.)

Sex ratio:
at birth: 1.04 male(s)/female
under 15 years: 1.05 male(s)/female
15-64 years: 1.01 male(s)/female
65 years and over: 0.78 male(s)/female
total population: 0.99 male(s)/female (2004 est.)
Infant mortality rate:
total: 5.96 deaths/1,000 live births
male: 6.83 deaths/1,000 live births
female: 5.05 deaths/1,000 live births (2004 est.)
Life expectancy at birth:
total population: 78.49 years
male: 75.5 years
female: 81.61 years (2004 est.)
Total fertility rate: 1.79 children born/woman (2004 est.)
HIV/AIDS - adult prevalence rate: 0.1% (2001 est.)
HIV/AIDS - people living with HIV/AIDS: 1,200 (2001 est.)
HIV/AIDS - deaths: less than 100 (2001 est.)
Nationality:
noun: New Zealander(s)
adjective: New Zealand
Ethnic groups: New Zealand European 74.5%, Maori 9.7%, other European 4.6%, Pacific Islander 3.8%, Asian and others 7.4%
Religions: Anglican 24%, Presbyterian 18%, Roman Catholic 15%, Methodist 5%, Baptist 2%, other Protestant 3%, unspecified or none 33% (1986)
Languages: English (official), Maori (official)
Literacy:
definition: age 15 and over can read and write
total population: 99% (1980 est.)
male: NA%
female: NA%

Government

Country name:
conventional long form: none
conventional short form: New Zealand
abbreviation: NZ
Government type: parliamentary democracy
Capital: Wellington
Administrative divisions: 16 regions; Auckland, Bay of Plenty, Canterbury, Gisborne, Hawke's Bay, Marlborough, Nelson, Northland, Otago, Southland, Taranaki, Tasman, Waikato, Manawatu-Wanganui, Wellington, West Coast
Dependent areas: Cook Islands, Niue, Tokelau
Independence: 26 September 1907 (from UK)
National holiday: Waitangi Day (Treaty of Waitangi established British sovereignty over New Zealand), 6 February (1840)
Constitution: consists of a series of legal documents, including certain acts of the UK and New Zealand Parliaments and The Constitution Act 1986 which is the principal formal charter
Legal system: based on English law, with special land legislation and land courts for the Maori; accepts compulsory ICJ jurisdiction, with reservations
Suffrage: 18 years of age; universal

New Zealand (continued)

Executive branch:

chief of state: Queen ELIZABETH II (since 6 February 1952), represented by Governor General Dame Silvia CARTWRIGHT (since 4 April 2001)

head of government: Prime Minister Helen CLARK (since 10 December 1999) and Deputy Prime Minister Michael CULLEN (since NA July 2002)

cabinet: Executive Council appointed by the governor general on the recommendation of the prime minister

elections: none; the monarch is hereditary; governor general appointed by the monarch; following legislative elections, the leader of the majority party or the leader of a majority coalition is usually appointed prime minister by the governor general; deputy prime minister appointed by the governor general

Legislative branch: unicameral House of Representatives - commonly called Parliament (120 seats; 69 members elected by popular vote in single-member constituencies including 7 Maori constituencies, and 51 proportional seats chosen from party lists, all to serve three-year terms)

elections: last held 27 July 2002 (next to be held NA 2005)

election results: percent of vote by party - NA%; seats by party - NZLP 52, NP 27, NZFP 13, ACT New Zealand 9, Green Party 9, UF 8, other 2

Judicial branch: High Court; Court of Appeal

Political parties and leaders: ACT New Zealand [Richard PREBBLE]; Green Party [Jeanette FITZSIMONS and Rod DONALD]; National Party or NP [Don BRASH]; New Zealand First Party or NZFP [Winston PETERS]; New Zealand Labor Party or NZLP [Helen CLARK]; Progressive Coalition [James (Jim) ANDERTON]; United Future or UF [Peter DUNNE]

Political pressure groups and leaders: NA

International organization participation: ANZUS (US suspended security obligations to NZ on 11 August 1986), APEC, ARF, AsDB, ASEAN (dialogue partner), Australia Group, BIS, C, CP, EBRD, FAO, IAEA, IBRD, ICAO, ICC, ICCt, ICFTU, ICRM, IDA, IEA, IFAD, IFC, IFRCS, IHO, ILO, IMF, IMO, Interpol, IOC, IOM, ISO, ITU, NAM (guest), NSG, OECD, OPCW, PCA, PIF, Sparteca, SPC, UN, UNAMSIL, UNCTAD, UNESCO, UNHCR, UNIDO, UNMISET, UNTSO, UPU, WCO, WFTU, WHO, WIPO, WMO, WTrO

Diplomatic representation in the US:

chief of mission: Ambassador L. John WOOD

chancery: 37 Observatory Circle NW, Washington, DC 20008

telephone: [1] (202) 328-4800

FAX: [1] (202) 667-5227

consulate(s) general: Los Angeles, New York

Diplomatic representation from the US:

chief of mission: Ambassador Charles J. SWINDELLS

embassy: 29 Fitzherbert Terrace, Thorndon, Wellington

mailing address: P. O. Box 1190, Wellington; PSC 467, Box 1, APO AP 96531-1034

telephone: [64] (4) 462-6000

FAX: [64] (4) 472-3478

consulate(s) general: Auckland

Flag description: blue with the flag of the UK in the upper hoist-side quadrant with four red five-pointed stars edged in white centered in the outer half of the flag; the stars represent the Southern Cross constellation

Economy

Economy - overview: Over the past 20 years the government has transformed New Zealand from an agrarian economy dependent on concessionary British market access to a more industrialized, free market economy that can compete globally. This dynamic growth has boosted real incomes (but left behind many at the bottom of the ladder), broadened and deepened the technological capabilities of the industrial sector, and contained inflationary pressures. Per capita income has been rising and is now 80% of the level of the four largest EU economies. New Zealand is heavily dependent on trade - particularly in agricultural products - to drive growth, and it has been affected by the global economic slowdown and the slump in commodity prices. Thus far the economy has been resilient, and growth should continue at the same level in 2004. Expenditures on health, education, and pensions will increase proportionately.

GDP: purchasing power parity - $85.26 billion (2003 est.)

GDP - real growth rate: 3.4% (2003 est.)

GDP - per capita: purchasing power parity - $21,600 (2003 est.)

GDP - composition by sector:

agriculture: 8%

industry: 25%

services: 67% (2002 est.)

Population below poverty line: NA%

Household income or consumption by percentage share:

lowest 10%: 0.3%

highest 10%: 29.8% (1991 est.)

Inflation rate (consumer prices): 1.8% (2003 est.)

Labor force: 1.92 million (2001 est.)

Labor force - by occupation: services 65%, industry 25%, agriculture 10% (1995)

Unemployment rate: 5.1% (2003 est.)

Budget:

revenues: $29.2 billion

expenditures: $31.2 billion, including capital expenditures of $NA (2002)

Industries: food processing, wood and paper products, textiles, machinery, transportation equipment, banking and insurance, tourism, mining

Industrial production growth rate: 3% (2001 est.)

Electricity - production: 37.51 billion kWh (2001)

Electricity - production by source:

fossil fuel: 31.6%

hydro: 57.8%

nuclear: 0%

other: 10.7% (2001)

Electricity - consumption: 34.88 billion kWh (2001)

Electricity - exports: 0 kWh (2001)

Electricity - imports: 0 kWh (2001)

Oil - production: 42,160 bbl/day (2001 est.)

Oil - consumption: 132,700 bbl/day (2001 est.)

Oil - exports: 30,220 bbl/day (2001)

Oil - imports: 119,700 bbl/day (2001)

Oil - proved reserves: 89.62 million bbl (1 January 2002)

Natural gas - production: 6.504 billion cu m (2001 est.)

Natural gas - consumption: 6.504 billion cu m (2001 est.)

Natural gas - exports: 0 cu m (2001 est.)

Natural gas - imports: 0 cu m (2001 est.)

Natural gas - proved reserves: 58.94 billion cu m (1 January 2002)

Agriculture - products: wheat, barley, potatoes, pulses, fruits, vegetables; wool, beef, dairy products; fish

Exports: $15.86 billion (2003 est.)

Exports - commodities: dairy products, meat, wood and wood products, fish, machinery

Exports - partners: Australia 20.3%, US 15.5%, Japan 11.5%, UK 4.8%, China 4.6%, South Korea 4.4% (2002)

Imports: $16.06 billion (2003 est.)

Imports - commodities: machinery and equipment, vehicles and aircraft, petroleum, electronics, textiles, plastics

Imports - partners: Australia 22.1%, US 13.7%, Japan 12%, China 8%, Germany 5.2% (2002)

Debt - external: $38.1 billion (2003 est.)

Economic aid - donor: ODA, $99.7 million

Currency: New Zealand dollar (NZD)

Currency code: NZD

Exchange rates: New Zealand dollars per US dollar - 1.7229 (2003), 2.1622 (2002), 2.3788 (2001), 2.2012 (2000), 1.8896 (1999)

Fiscal year: 1 July - 30 June

Communications

Telephones - main lines in use: 1.765 million (2002)

Telephones - mobile cellular: 2.449 million (2002)

Telephone system:

general assessment: excellent domestic and international systems

domestic: NA

international: country code - 64; submarine cables to Australia and Fiji; satellite earth stations - 2 Intelsat (Pacific Ocean)

Radio broadcast stations: AM 124, FM 290, shortwave 4 (1998)

Television broadcast stations: 41 (plus 52 medium-power repeaters and over 650 low-power repeaters) (1997)

Internet country code: .nz

Internet hosts: 432,957 (2002)

Internet users: 1.908 million (2002)

Transportation

Railways:
total: 3,898 km
narrow gauge: 3,898 km 1.067-m gauge (506 km electrified) (2002)
Highways:
total: 92,053 km
paved: 57,809 km (including at least 190 km of expressways)
unpaved: 34,244 km (2000)
Waterways: 1,609 km
note: of little importance in satisfying total transportation requirements
Pipelines: gas 2,213 km; liquid petroleum gas 79 km; oil 160 km; refined products 304 km (2003)
Ports and harbors: Auckland, Christchurch, Dunedin, Tauranga, Wellington
Merchant marine:
total: 10 ships (1,000 GRT or over) 77,523 GRT/ 108,352 DWT
by type: bulk 3, cargo 2, container 1, petroleum tanker 2, roll on/roll off 2
foreign-owned: Australia 1, Isle of Man 1
registered in other countries: 8 (2003 est.)
Airports: 113 (2003 est.)
Airports - with paved runways:
total: 46
over 3,047 m: 2
2,438 to 3,047 m: 1
1,524 to 2,437 m: 11
914 to 1,523 m: 27
under 914 m: 5 (2003 est.)
Airports - with unpaved runways:
total: 67
1,524 to 2,437 m: 2
914 to 1,523 m: 28
under 914 m: 37 (2003 est.)

Military

Military branches: New Zealand Army, Royal New Zealand Navy, Royal New Zealand Air Force
Military manpower - military age: 20 years of age (2004 est.)
Military manpower - availability:
males age 15-49: 1,033,464 (2004 est.)
Military manpower - fit for military service:
males age 15-49: 868,984 (2004 est.)
Military manpower - reaching military age annually:
males: 27,157 (2004 est.)
Military expenditures - dollar figure: $1.147 billion (FY03/04)
Military expenditures - percent of GDP: 1% (FY02)

Transnational Issues

Disputes - international: territorial claim in Antarctica (Ross Dependency)

Nicaragua

Introduction

Background: The Pacific Coast of Nicaragua was settled as a Spanish colony from Panama in the early 16th century. Independence from Spain was declared in 1821 and the country became an independent republic in 1838. Britain occupied the Caribbean Coast in the first half of the 19th century, but gradually ceded control of the region in subsequent decades. Violent opposition to governmental manipulation and corruption spread to all classes by 1978 and resulted in a short-lived civil war that brought the Marxist Sandinista guerrillas to power in 1979. Nicaraguan aid to leftist rebels in El Salvador caused the US to sponsor anti-Sandinista contra guerrillas through much of the 1980s. Free elections in 1990, 1996, and again in 2001 saw the Sandinistas defeated. The country has slowly rebuilt its economy during the 1990s, but was hard hit by Hurricane Mitch in 1998.

Geography

Location: Central America, bordering both the Caribbean Sea and the North Pacific Ocean, between Costa Rica and Honduras
Geographic coordinates: 13 00 N, 85 00 W
Map references: Central America and the Caribbean
Area:
total: 129,494 sq km
land: 120,254 sq km
water: 9,240 sq km
Area - comparative: slightly smaller than the state of New York
Land boundaries:
total: 1,231 km
border countries: Costa Rica 309 km, Honduras 922 km
Coastline: 910 km
Maritime claims:
territorial sea: 200 NM
continental shelf: natural prolongation

Climate: tropical in lowlands, cooler in highlands
Terrain: extensive Atlantic coastal plains rising to central interior mountains; narrow Pacific coastal plain interrupted by volcanoes
Elevation extremes:
lowest point: Pacific Ocean 0 m
highest point: Mogoton 2,438 m
Natural resources: gold, silver, copper, tungsten, lead, zinc, timber, fish
Land use:
arable land: 20.24%
permanent crops: 2.38%
other: 77.38% (1998 est.)
Irrigated land: 880 sq km (1998 est.)
Natural hazards: destructive earthquakes, volcanoes, landslides; extremely susceptible to hurricanes
Environment - current issues: deforestation; soil erosion; water pollution
Environment - international agreements:
party to: Biodiversity, Climate Change, Climate Change-Kyoto Protocol, Desertification, Endangered Species, Hazardous Wastes, Law of the Sea, Ozone Layer Protection, Ship Pollution, Wetlands
signed, but not ratified: Environmental Modification
Geography - note: largest country in Central America; contains the largest freshwater body in Central America, Lago de Nicaragua

People

Population: 5,359,759 (July 2004 est.)
Age structure:
0-14 years: 38.1% (male 1,038,887; female 1,001,518)
15-64 years: 58.9% (male 1,570,494; female 1,586,706)
65 years and over: 3% (male 71,125; female 91,029) (2004 est.)
Median age:
total: 20.2 years
male: 19.8 years
female: 20.6 years (2004 est.)
Population growth rate: 1.97% (2004 est.)
Birth rate: 25.5 births/1,000 population (2004 est.)
Death rate: 4.54 deaths/1,000 population (2004 est.)
Net migration rate: -1.22 migrant(s)/1,000 population (2004 est.)
Sex ratio:
at birth: 1.05 male(s)/female
under 15 years: 1.04 male(s)/female
15-64 years: 0.99 male(s)/female
65 years and over: 0.78 male(s)/female
total population: 1 male(s)/female (2004 est.)
Infant mortality rate:
total: 30.15 deaths/1,000 live births
male: 33.73 deaths/1,000 live births
female: 26.38 deaths/1,000 live births (2004 est.)
Life expectancy at birth:
total population: 70.02 years
male: 67.99 years
female: 72.16 years (2004 est.)

Nicaragua *(continued)*

Total fertility rate: 2.89 children born/woman (2004 est.)
HIV/AIDS - adult prevalence rate: 0.2% (2001 est.)
HIV/AIDS - people living with HIV/AIDS: 5,800 (2001 est.)
HIV/AIDS - deaths: 400 (2001 est.)
Nationality:
noun: Nicaraguan(s)
adjective: Nicaraguan
Ethnic groups: mestizo (mixed Amerindian and white) 69%, white 17%, black 9%, Amerindian 5%
Religions: Roman Catholic 85%, Protestant
Languages: Spanish (official)
note: English and indigenous languages on Atlantic coast
Literacy:
definition: age 15 and over can read and write
total population: 67.5%
male: 67.2%
female: 67.8% (2003 est.)

Government

Country name:
conventional long form: Republic of Nicaragua
conventional short form: Nicaragua
local long form: Republica de Nicaragua
local short form: Nicaragua
Government type: republic
Capital: Managua
Administrative divisions: 15 departments (departamentos, singular - departamento) and 2 autonomous regions* (regiones autonomistas, singular - region autonomista); Atlantico Norte*, Atlantico Sur*, Boaco, Carazo, Chinandega, Chontales, Esteli, Granada, Jinotega, Leon, Madriz, Managua, Masaya, Matagalpa, Nueva Segovia, Rio San Juan, Rivas
Independence: 15 September 1821 (from Spain)
National holiday: Independence Day, 15 September (1821)
Constitution: 9 January 1987, with reforms in 1995 and 2000
Legal system: civil law system; Supreme Court may review administrative acts
Suffrage: 16 years of age; universal
Executive branch:
chief of state: President Enrique BOLANOS Geyer (since 10 January 2002); Vice President Jose RIZO Castellon (since 10 January 2002); note - the president is both chief of state and head of government
head of government: President Enrique BOLANOS Geyer (since 10 January 2002); Vice President Jose RIZO Castellon (since 10 January 2002); note - the president is both chief of state and head of government
cabinet: Council of Ministers appointed by the president
elections: president and vice president elected on the same ticket by popular vote for a five-year term; election last held 4 November 2001 (next to be held by November 2006)

election results: Enrique BOLANOS Geyer (PLC) elected president - 56.3%, Daniel ORTEGA Saavedra (FSLN) 42.3%, Alberto SABORIO (PCN) 1.4%; Jose RIZO Castellon elected vice president
Legislative branch: unicameral National Assembly or Asamblea Nacional (92 seats; members are elected by proportional representation and party lists to serve five-year terms; one seat for previous President, one seat for runner-up in previous Presidential election
elections: last held 4 November 2001 (next to be held by November 2006)
election results: percent of vote by party - Liberal Alliance (ruling party - includes PCCN, PLC, PALI, PLIUN, and PUCA) 46.03%, FSLN 36.55%, PCN 2.12%; seats by party - Liberal Alliance 53, FSLN 38, PCN 1
Judicial branch: Supreme Court or Corte Suprema (16 judges elected for five-year terms by the National Assembly)
Political parties and leaders: Conservative Party of Nicaragua or PCN [Mario RAPPACCIOLI]; Independent Liberal Party or PLI [Virgilio GODOY]; Liberal Alliance (ruling alliance including Liberal Constitutional Party or PLC, New Liberal Party or PALI, Independent Liberal Party for National Unity or PLIUN, and Central American Unionist Party or PUCA) [leader NA]; Nicaraguan Party of the Christian Path or PCCN [Guillermo OSORNO, Roberto RODRIGUEZ]; Nicaraguan Resistance Party or PRN [Salvador TALAVERA]; Sandinista National Liberation Front or FSLN [Daniel ORTEGA Saavedra]; Sandinista Renovation Movement or MRS [leader NA]; Unity Alliance or AU [leader NA]
Political pressure groups and leaders: National Workers Front or FNT is a Sandinista umbrella group of eight labor unions including - Farm Workers Association or ATC, Health Workers Federation or FETASALUD, Heroes and Martyrs Confederation of Professional Associations or CONAPRO, National Association of Educators of Nicaragua or ANDEN, National Union of Employees or UNE, National Union of Farmers and Ranchers or UNAG, Sandinista Workers Central or CST, and Union of Journalists of Nicaragua or UPN; Permanent Congress of Workers or CPT is an umbrella group of four non-Sandinista labor unions including - Autonomous Nicaraguan Workers Central or CTN-A, Confederation of Labor Unification or CUS, Independent General Confederation of Labor or CGT-I, and Labor Action and Unity Central or CAUS; Nicaraguan Workers' Central or CTN is an independent labor union; Superior Council of Private Enterprise or COSEP is a confederation of business groups
International organization participation: BCIE, CACM, FAO, G-77, IADB, IAEA, IBRD, ICAO, ICFTU, ICRM, IDA, IFAD, IFC, IFRCS, ILO, IMF, IMO, Interpol, IOC, IOM, ISO (correspondent), ITU, LAES, LAIA (observer), NAM, OAS, OPANAL, OPCW, PCA, RG, UN, UNCTAD, UNESCO, UNHCR, UNIDO, UPU, WCL, WCO, WHO, WIPO, WMO, WToO, WTrO

Diplomatic representation in the US:
chief of mission: Ambassador Salvador STADTHAGEN (since 5 December 2003)
chancery: 1627 New Hampshire Avenue NW, Washington, DC 20009
telephone: [1] (202) 939-6570
FAX: [1] (202) 939-6542
consulate(s) general: Houston, Los Angeles, Miami, New Orleans, New York
Diplomatic representation from the US:
chief of mission: Ambassador Barbara Calandra MOORE
embassy: Apartado Postal 327, Kilometer 4.5 Carretera Sur, Managua
mailing address: APO AA 34021
telephone: [505] 266-6010, 266-2298, 266-6013
FAX: [505] 266-9074
Flag description: three equal horizontal bands of blue (top), white, and blue with the national coat of arms centered in the white band; the coat of arms features a triangle encircled by the words REPUBLICA DE NICARAGUA on the top and AMERICA CENTRAL on the bottom; similar to the flag of El Salvador, which features a round emblem encircled by the words REPUBLICA DE EL SALVADOR EN LA AMERICA CENTRAL centered in the white band; also similar to the flag of Honduras, which has five blue stars arranged in an X pattern centered in the white band

Economy

Economy - overview: Nicaragua, one of the hemisphere's poorest countries, faces low per capita income, massive unemployment, and huge external debt. Distribution of income is one of the most unequal on the globe. While the country has made progress toward macroeconomic stability over the past few years, GDP annual growth of 1.5% - 2.5% has been far too low to meet the country's need. Nicaragua will continue to be dependent on international aid and debt relief under the Heavily Indebted Poor Countries (HIPC) initiative. Nicaragua has undertaken significant economic reforms that are expected to help the country qualify for more than $4 billion in debt relief under HIPC in early 2004. Donors have made aid conditional on the openness of government financial operation, poverty alleviation, and human rights. A three-year poverty reduction and growth plan, agreed to with the IMF in December 2002, guides economic policy.
GDP: purchasing power parity - $11.49 billion (2003 est.)
GDP - real growth rate: 1.4% (2003 est.)
GDP - per capita: purchasing power parity - $2,200 (2003 est.)
GDP - composition by sector:
agriculture: 30.5%
industry: 22.5%
services: 47% (2002 est.)
Population below poverty line: 50% (2001 est.)

Nicaragua (continued)

Household income or consumption by percentage share:
lowest 10%: 0.7%
highest 10%: 48.8% (1998)
Distribution of family income - Gini index: 60.3 (1998)
Inflation rate (consumer prices): 5.3% (2003 est.)
Labor force: 1.7 million (1999)
Labor force - by occupation: services 43%, agriculture 42%, industry 15% (1999 est.)
Unemployment rate: 22% plus considerable underemployment (2003 est.)
Budget:
revenues: $726 million
expenditures: $908 million, including capital expenditures of $NA (2000 est.)
Industries: food processing, chemicals, machinery and metal products, textiles, clothing, petroleum refining and distribution, beverages, footwear, wood
Industrial production growth rate: 4.4% (2000 est.)
Electricity - production: 2.549 billion kWh (2001)
Electricity - production by source:
fossil fuel: 83.9%
hydro: 7.7%
nuclear: 0%
other: 8.4% (2001)
Electricity - consumption: 2.388 billion kWh (2001)
Electricity - exports: 0 kWh (2001)
Electricity - imports: 17 million kWh (2001)
Oil - production: 0 bbl/day (2001 est.)
Oil - consumption: 24,500 bbl/day (2001 est.)
Oil - exports: NA
Oil - imports: NA
Agriculture - products: coffee, bananas, sugarcane, cotton, rice, corn, tobacco, sesame, soya, beans; beef, veal, pork, poultry, dairy products
Exports: $632 million f.o.b. (2003 est.)
Exports - commodities: coffee, shrimp and lobster, cotton, tobacco, bananas, beef, sugar, gold
Exports - partners: US 59.4%, El Salvador 7.5%, Honduras 4.8% (2002)
Imports: $1.658 billion f.o.b. (2003 est.)
Imports - commodities: machinery and equipment, raw materials, petroleum products, consumer goods
Imports - partners: US 23.6%, Costa Rica 10.2%, Guatemala 7.8%, Venezuela 7.1%, El Salvador 6%, Mexico 4.9%, South Korea 4.6% (2002)
Debt - external: $5.8 billion (2003 est.)
Economic aid - recipient: Substantial foreign support (2001)
Currency: gold cordoba (NIO)
Currency code: NIO
Exchange rates: gold cordobas per US dollar - 14.2513 (2003), 14.2513 (2002), 13.3719 (2001), 12.6844 (2000), 11.8092 (1999)
Fiscal year: calendar year

Communications

Telephones - main lines in use: 171,600 (2002)
Telephones - mobile cellular: 202,800 (2002)
Telephone system:
general assessment: inadequate system being upgraded by foreign investment
domestic: low-capacity microwave radio relay and wire system being expanded; connected to Central American Microwave System
international: country code - 505; satellite earth stations - 1 Intersputnik (Atlantic Ocean region) and 1 Intelsat (Atlantic Ocean)
Radio broadcast stations: AM 63, FM 32, shortwave 1 (1998)
Television broadcast stations: 3 (plus seven low-power repeaters) (1997)
Internet country code: .ni
Internet hosts: 3,370 (2002)
Internet users: 90,000 (2002)

Transportation

Railways:
total: 6 km
narrow gauge: 6 km 1.067-m gauge (2002)
Highways:
total: 19,032 km
paved: 2,094 km
unpaved: 16,938 km (2000)
Waterways: 2,220 km (including 2 large lakes)
Pipelines: oil 54 km (2003)
Ports and harbors: Bluefields, Corinto, El Bluff, Puerto Cabezas, Puerto Sandino, Rama, San Juan del Sur
Merchant marine: none
Airports: 176 (2003 est.)
Airports - with paved runways:
total: 11
2,438 to 3,047 m: 3
1,524 to 2,437 m: 2
914 to 1,523 m: 3
under 914 m: 3 (2003 est.)
Airports - with unpaved runways:
total: 165
1,524 to 2,437 m: 1
914 to 1,523 m: 23
under 914 m: 141 (2003 est.)

Military

Military branches: Army (includes Navy), Navy
Military manpower - military age: 18 years of age (2004 est.)
Military manpower - availability:
males age 15-49: 1,399,356 (2004 est.)
Military manpower - fit for military service:
males age 15-49: 858,022 (2004 est.)
Military manpower - reaching military age annually:
males: 61,869 (2004 est.)

Military expenditures - dollar figure: $30.8 million (2003)
Military expenditures - percent of GDP: 1.2% (2003)

Transnational Issues

Disputes - international: territorial disputes with Colombia over the Archipelago de San Andres y Providencia and Quita Sueno Bank region; the 1992 ICJ ruling for El Salvador and Honduras advised a tripartite resolution to establish a maritime boundary in the Gulf of Fonseca, which considers Honduran access to the Pacific; legal dispute over navigational rights of San Juan River on border with Costa Rica
Illicit drugs: transshipment point for cocaine destined for the US and transshipment point for arms-for-drugs dealing

Niger

Introduction

Background: Not until 1993, 33 years after independence from France, did Niger hold its first free and open elections. A 1995 peace accord ended a five-year Tuareg insurgency in the north. Coups in 1996 and 1999 were followed by the creation of a National Reconciliation Council that effected a transition to civilian rule by December 1999. Niger is one of the poorest countries in the world with minimal government services and insufficient funds to develop its resource base. The largely agrarian and subsistence-based economy is frequently disrupted by extended droughts common to the Sahel region of Africa.

Geography

Location: Western Africa, southeast of Algeria
Geographic coordinates: 16 00 N, 8 00 E
Map references: Africa
Area:
total: 1.267 million sq km
land: 1,266,700 sq km
water: 300 sq km
Area - comparative: slightly less than twice the size of Texas
Land boundaries:
total: 5,697 km
border countries: Algeria 956 km, Benin 266 km, Burkina Faso 628 km, Chad 1,175 km, Libya 354 km, Mali 821 km, Nigeria 1,497 km
Coastline: 0 km (landlocked)
Maritime claims: none (landlocked)
Climate: desert; mostly hot, dry, dusty; tropical in extreme south
Terrain: predominately desert plains and sand dunes; flat to rolling plains in south; hills in north
Elevation extremes:
lowest point: Niger River 200 m
highest point: Mont Bagzane 2,022 m

Natural resources: uranium, coal, iron ore, tin, phosphates, gold, petroleum
Land use:
arable land: 3.94%
permanent crops: 0%
other: 96.06% (1998 est.)
Irrigated land: 660 sq km (1998 est.)
Natural hazards: recurring droughts
Environment - current issues: overgrazing; soil erosion; deforestation; desertification; wildlife populations (such as elephant, hippopotamus, giraffe, and lion) threatened because of poaching and habitat destruction
Environment - international agreements:
party to: Biodiversity, Climate Change, Desertification, Endangered Species, Environmental Modification, Hazardous Wastes, Ozone Layer Protection, Wetlands
signed, but not ratified: Climate Change-Kyoto Protocol, Law of the Sea
Geography - note: landlocked; one of the hottest countries in the world: northern four-fifths is desert, southern one-fifth is savanna, suitable for livestock and limited agriculture

People

Population: 11,360,538 (July 2004 est.)
Age structure:
0-14 years: 47.5% (male 2,749,039; female 2,643,479)
15-64 years: 50.4% (male 2,799,125; female 2,925,133)
65 years and over: 2.1% (male 128,101; female 115,661) (2004 est.)
Median age:
total: 16.2 years
male: 15.7 years
female: 16.7 years (2004 est.)
Population growth rate: 2.67% (2004 est.)
Birth rate: 48.91 births/1,000 population (2004 est.)
Death rate: 21.51 deaths/1,000 population (2004 est.)
Net migration rate: -0.67 migrant(s)/1,000 population (2004 est.)
Sex ratio:
at birth: 1.03 male(s)/female
under 15 years: 1.04 male(s)/female
15-64 years: 0.96 male(s)/female
65 years and over: 1.11 male(s)/female
total population: 1 male(s)/female (2004 est.)
Infant mortality rate:
total: 122.66 deaths/1,000 live births
male: 126.96 deaths/1,000 live births
female: 118.24 deaths/1,000 live births (2004 est.)
Life expectancy at birth:
total population: 42.18 years
male: 42.38 years
female: 41.97 years (2004 est.)
Total fertility rate: 6.83 children born/woman (2004 est.)
HIV/AIDS - adult prevalence rate: 4% (2001 est.)

HIV/AIDS - people living with HIV/AIDS: NA
HIV/AIDS - deaths: 6,000 (2001 est.)
Nationality:
noun: Nigerien(s)
adjective: Nigerien
Ethnic groups: Hausa 56%, Djerma 22%, Fula 8.5%, Tuareg 8%, Beri Beri (Kanouri) 4.3%, Arab, Toubou, and Gourmantche 1.2%, about 1,200 French expatriates
Religions: Muslim 80%, remainder indigenous beliefs and Christian
Languages: French (official), Hausa, Djerma
Literacy:
definition: age 15 and over can read and write
total population: 17.6%
male: 25.8%
female: 9.7% (2003 est.)

Government

Country name:
conventional long form: Republic of Niger
conventional short form: Niger
local long form: Republique du Niger
local short form: Niger
Government type: republic
Capital: Niamey
Administrative divisions: 7 departments (departements, singular - departement) and 1 capital district* (capitale district); Agadez, Diffa, Dosso, Maradi, Niamey*, Tahoua, Tillaberi, Zinder
Independence: 3 August 1960 (from France)
National holiday: Republic Day, 18 December (1958)
Constitution: the constitution of January 1993 was revised by national referendum on 12 May 1996 and again by referendum on 18 July 1999
Legal system: based on French civil law system and customary law; has not accepted compulsory ICJ jurisdiction
Suffrage: 18 years of age; universal
Executive branch:
chief of state: President TANDJA Mamadou (since 22 December 1999); note - the president is both chief of state and head of government
head of government: President TANDJA Mamadou (since 22 December 1999); note - the president is both chief of state and head of government; Prime Minister Hama AMADOU (since 31 December 1999) was appointed by the president and shares some executive responsibilities with the president
cabinet: 23-member Cabinet appointed by the president
elections: president elected by popular vote for a five-year term; last held 24 November 1999 (next to be held NA 2004); prime minister appointed by the president
election results: TANDJA Mamadou elected president; percent of vote - TANDJA Mamadou 59.9%, Mahamadou ISSOUFOU 40.1%
Legislative branch: unicameral National Assembly (83 seats, members elected by popular vote for five-year terms)

elections: last held 24 November 1999 (next to be held NA October 2004)

election results: percent of vote by party - NA%; seats by party - MNSD-Nassara 38, CDS-Rahama 17, PNDS-Tarayya 16, RDP-Jama'a 8, ANDPS-Zaman Lahiya 4

Judicial branch: State Court or Cour d'Etat; Court of Appeal or Cour d'Appel

Political parties and leaders: Democratic Rally of the People-Jama'a or RDP-Jama'a [Hamid ALGABID]; Democratic and Social Convention-Rahama or CDS-Rahama [Mahamane OUSMANE]; National Movement for a Developing Society-Nassara or MNSD-Nassara [Mamadou TANDJA, chairman]; Nigerien Alliance for Democracy and Social Progress-Zaman Lahiya or ANDPS-Zaman Lahiya [Moumouni Adamou DJERMAKOYE]; Nigerien Party for Democracy and Socialism-Tarayya or PNDS-Tarayya [Mahamadou ISSOUFOU]; Union of Democratic Patriots and Progressives-Chamoua or UPDP-Chamoua [Professor Andre' SALIFOU, chairman]

Political pressure groups and leaders: NA

International organization participation: ACCT, ACP, AfDB, AU, ECOWAS, Entente, FAO, FZ, G-77, IAEA, IBRD, ICAO, ICCt, ICFTU, ICRM, IDA, IDB, IFAD, IFC, IFRCS, ILO, IMF, Interpol, IOC, ISO (subscriber), ITU, MICAH, MONUC, NAM, OIC, OPCW, UN, UNCTAD, UNESCO, UNIDO, UNMIL, UPU, WADB (regional), WAEMU, WCL, WCO, WFTU, WHO, WIPO, WMO, WToO, WTrO

Diplomatic representation in the US:

chief of mission: Ambassador Joseph DIATTA

chancery: 2204 R Street NW, Washington, DC 20008

telephone: [1] (202) 483-4224 through 4227

FAX: [1] (202)483-3169

Diplomatic representation from the US:

chief of mission: Ambassador Gail Dennise Thomas MATHIEU

embassy: Rue Des Ambassades, Niamey

mailing address: B. P. 11201, Niamey

telephone: [227] 72 26 61 through 72 26 64

FAX: [227] 73 31 67, 72-31-46

Flag description: three equal horizontal bands of orange (top), white, and green with a small orange disk (representing the sun) centered in the white band; similar to the flag of India, which has a blue spoked wheel centered in the white band

Economy

Economy - overview: Niger is a poor, landlocked Sub-Saharan nation, whose economy centers on subsistence agriculture, animal husbandry, and reexport trade, and increasingly less on uranium, because of declining world demand. The 50% devaluation of the West African franc in January 1994 boosted exports of livestock, cowpeas, onions, and the products of Niger's small cotton industry. The government relies on bilateral and multilateral aid - which was suspended following the April 1999 coup d'etat - for operating expenses and public investment.

In 2000-01, the World Bank approved a structural adjustment loan of $105 million to help support fiscal reforms. However, reforms could prove difficult given the government's bleak financial situation. The IMF approved a $73 million poverty reduction and growth facility for Niger in 2000 and announced $115 million in debt relief under the Heavily Indebted Poor Countries (HIPC) initiative. Further disbursements of aid occurred in 2002. Future growth may be sustained by exploitation of oil, gold, coal, and other mineral resources.

GDP: purchasing power parity - $9.062 billion (2003 est.)

GDP - real growth rate: 3.8% (2003 est.)

GDP - per capita: purchasing power parity - $800 (2003 est.)

GDP - composition by sector:

agriculture: 39%

industry: 17%

services: 44% (2001)

Population below poverty line: 63% (1993 est.)

Household income or consumption by percentage share:

lowest 10%: 0.8%

highest 10%: 35.4% (1995)

Distribution of family income - Gini index: 50.5 (1995)

Inflation rate (consumer prices): 3% (2002 est.)

Labor force: 70,000 receive regular wages or salaries (2002 est.)

Labor force - by occupation: agriculture 90%, industry and commerce 6%, government 4%

Unemployment rate: NA% (2002 est.)

Budget:

revenues: $320 million - including $134 million from foreign sources

expenditures: $320 million, including capital expenditures of $178 million (2002 est.)

Industries: uranium mining, cement, brick, textiles, food processing, chemicals, slaughterhouses

Industrial production growth rate: NA% (2001 est.)

Electricity - production: 242 million kWh (2001)

Electricity - production by source:

fossil fuel: 100%

hydro: 0%

nuclear: 0%

other: 0% (2001)

Electricity - consumption: 325.1 million kWh (2001)

Electricity - exports: 0 kWh (2001)

Electricity - imports: 100 million kWh (2001)

Oil - production: 0 bbl/day (2001 est.)

Oil - consumption: 5,000 bbl/day (2001 est.)

Oil - exports: NA

Oil - imports: NA

Agriculture - products: cowpeas, cotton, peanuts, millet, sorghum, cassava (tapioca), rice; cattle, sheep, goats, camels, donkeys, horses, poultry

Exports: $280 million f.o.b. (2002 est.)

Exports - commodities: uranium ore, livestock, cowpeas, onions

Exports - partners: France 39.1%, Nigeria 33.3%, Japan 17.3% (2002)

Imports: $400 million f.o.b. (2002 est.)

Imports - commodities: foodstuffs, machinery, vehicles and parts, petroleum, cereals

Imports - partners: France 17%, Cote d'Ivoire 14.9%, China 9.9%, Nigeria 7.3%, US 5.3%, Japan 4.6%, India 4.3% (2002)

Debt - external: $1.6 billion (1999 est.)

Economic aid - recipient: $341 million (1997)

Currency: Communaute Financiere Africaine franc (XOF); note - responsible authority is the Central Bank of the West African States

Currency code: XOF

Exchange rates: Communaute Financiere Africaine francs (XOF) per US dollar - 581.2 (2003), 696.988 (2002), 733.039 (2001), 711.976 (2000), 615.699 (1999)

Fiscal year: calendar year

Communications

Telephones - main lines in use: 22,400 (2002)

Telephones - mobile cellular: 16,600 (2002)

Telephone system:

general assessment: small system of wire, radio telephone communications, and microwave radio relay links concentrated in the southwestern area of Niger

domestic: wire, radiotelephone communications, and microwave radio relay; domestic satellite system with 3 earth stations and 1 planned

international: country code - 227; satellite earth stations - 2 Intelsat (1 Atlantic Ocean and 1 Indian Ocean)

Radio broadcast stations: AM 5, FM 6, shortwave 4 (2001)

Television broadcast stations: 3 (plus seven low-power repeaters) (2002)

Internet country code: .ne

Internet hosts: 119 (2002)

Internet users: 15,000 (2002)

Transportation

Railways: 0 km

Highways:

total: 10,100 km

paved: 798 km

unpaved: 9,302 km (1999 est.)

Waterways: 300 km

note: the Niger River is navigable from Niamey to Gaya on the Benin frontier from mid-December through March

Ports and harbors: none

Airports: 27 (2003 est.)

Airports - with paved runways:

total: 9

2,438 to 3,047 m: 2

1,524 to 2,437 m: 6

under 914 m: 1 (2003 est.)

Airports - with unpaved runways:
total: 18
1,524 to 2,437 m: 2
914 to 1,523 m: 14
under 914 m: 2 (2003 est.)

Military

Military branches: Army, Air Force, National Intervention and Security Force
Military manpower - military age: 18 years of age (2004 est.)
Military manpower - availability:
males age 15-49: 2,460,637 (2004 est.)
Military manpower - fit for military service:
males age 15-49: 1,333,027 (2004 est.)
Military manpower - reaching military age annually:
males: 122,363 (2004 est.)
Military expenditures - dollar figure: $21.7 million (2003)
Military expenditures - percent of GDP: 1.1% (2003)

Transnational Issues

Disputes - international: Libya claims about 25,000 sq km in a currently dormant dispute; much of Benin-Niger boundary, including tripoint with Nigeria, remains undemarcated, and ICJ ad hoc judges have been selected to rule on disputed Niger and Mekrou River islands; Lake Chad Commission continues to urge signatories Cameroon, Chad, Niger, and Nigeria to ratify delimitation treaty over the lake region, which remains the site of armed clashes among local populations and militias

Nigeria

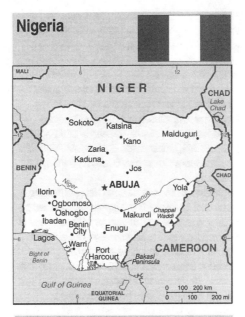

Introduction

Background: Following nearly 16 years of military rule, a new constitution was adopted in 1999, and a peaceful transition to civilian government was completed. The president faces the daunting task of rebuilding a petroleum-based economy, whose revenues have been squandered through corruption and mismanagement, and institutionalizing democracy. In addition, the OBASANJO administration must defuse longstanding ethnic and religious tensions, if it is to build a sound foundation for economic growth and political stability. Despite some irregularities, the April 2003 elections marked the first civilian transfer of power in Nigeria's history.

Geography

Location: Western Africa, bordering the Gulf of Guinea, between Benin and Cameroon
Geographic coordinates: 10 00 N, 8 00 E
Map references: Africa
Area:
total: 923,768 sq km
land: 910,768 sq km
water: 13,000 sq km
Area - comparative: slightly more than twice the size of California
Land boundaries:
total: 4,047 km
border countries: Benin 773 km, Cameroon 1,690 km, Chad 87 km, Niger 1,497 km
Coastline: 853 km
Maritime claims:
territorial sea: 12 NM
exclusive economic zone: 200 NM
continental shelf: 200-m depth or to the depth of exploitation
Climate: varies; equatorial in south, tropical in center, arid in north

Terrain: southern lowlands merge into central hills and plateaus; mountains in southeast, plains in north
Elevation extremes:
lowest point: Atlantic Ocean 0 m
highest point: Chappal Waddi 2,419 m
Natural resources: natural gas, petroleum, tin, columbite, iron ore, coal, limestone, lead, zinc, arable land
Land use:
arable land: 30.96%
permanent crops: 2.79%
other: 66.25% (1998 est.)
Irrigated land: 2,330 sq km (1998 est.)
Natural hazards: periodic droughts; flooding
Environment - current issues: soil degradation; rapid deforestation; urban air and water pollution; desertification; oil pollution - water, air, and soil; has suffered serious damage from oil spills; loss of arable land; rapid urbanization
Environment - international agreements:
party to: Biodiversity, Climate Change, Desertification, Endangered Species, Hazardous Wastes, Law of the Sea, Marine Dumping, Marine Life Conservation, Ozone Layer Protection, Wetlands
signed, but not ratified: none of the selected agreements
Geography - note: the Niger enters the country in the northwest and flows southward through tropical rain forests and swamps to its delta in the Gulf of Guinea

People

Population: 137,253,133
note: estimates for this country explicitly take into account the effects of excess mortality due to AIDS; this can result in lower life expectancy, higher infant mortality and death rates, lower population and growth rates, and changes in the distribution of population by age and sex than would otherwise be expected (July 2004 est.)
Age structure:
0-14 years: 43.4% (male 29,985,427; female 29,637,684)
15-64 years: 53.7% (male 37,502,756; female 36,205,442)
65 years and over: 2.9% (male 1,944,260; female 1,977,564) (2004 est.)
Median age:
total: 18.1 years
male: 18.2 years
female: 17.9 years (2004 est.)
Population growth rate: 2.45% (2004 est.)
Birth rate: 38.24 births/1,000 population (2004 est.)
Death rate: 13.99 deaths/1,000 population (2004 est.)
Net migration rate: 0.26 migrant(s)/1,000 population (2004 est.)
Sex ratio:
at birth: 1.03 male(s)/female
under 15 years: 1.01 male(s)/female
15-64 years: 1.04 male(s)/female
65 years and over: 0.98 male(s)/female
total population: 1.02 male(s)/female (2004 est.)

Nigeria (continued)

Infant mortality rate:
total: 70.49 deaths/1,000 live births
male: 73.55 deaths/1,000 live births
female: 67.34 deaths/1,000 live births (2004 est.)
Life expectancy at birth:
total population: 50.49 years
male: 50.35 years
female: 50.63 years (2004 est.)
Total fertility rate: 5.32 children born/woman
(2004 est.)
HIV/AIDS - adult prevalence rate: 5.8% (2001 est.)
HIV/AIDS - people living with HIV/AIDS: 3.5 million
(2001 est.)
HIV/AIDS - deaths: 170,000 (2001 est.)
Nationality:
noun: Nigerian(s)
adjective: Nigerian
Ethnic groups: Nigeria, which is Africa's most
populous country, is composed of more than 250
ethnic groups; the following are the most populous
and politically influential: Hausa and Fulani 29%,
Yoruba 21%, Igbo (Ibo) 18%, Ijaw 10%, Kanuri 4%,
Ibibio 3.5%, Tiv 2.5%
Religions: Muslim 50%, Christian 40%, indigenous
beliefs 10%
Languages: English (official), Hausa, Yoruba, Igbo
(Ibo), Fulani
Literacy:
definition: age 15 and over can read and write
total population: 68%
male: 75.7%
female: 60.6% (2003 est.)

Government

Country name:
conventional long form: Federal Republic of Nigeria
conventional short form: Nigeria
Government type: republic transitioning from
military to civilian rule
Capital: Abuja; note - on 12 December 1991 the
capital was officially transferred from Lagos to Abuja;
most federal government offices have now made the
move to Abuja
Administrative divisions: 36 states and 1 territory*;
Abia, Adamawa, Akwa Ibom, Anambra, Bauchi,
Bayelsa, Benue, Borno, Cross River, Delta, Ebonyi,
Edo, Ekiti, Enugu, Federal Capital Territory*, Gombe,
Imo, Jigawa, Kaduna, Kano, Katsina, Kebbi, Kogi,
Kwara, Lagos, Nassarawa, Niger, Ogun, Ondo, Osun,
Oyo, Plateau, Rivers, Sokoto, Taraba, Yobe, Zamfara
Independence: 1 October 1960 (from UK)
National holiday: Independence Day (National
Day), 1 October (1960)
Constitution: new constitution adopted May 1999
Legal system: based on English common law,
Islamic Shariah law (only in some northern states),
and traditional law
Suffrage: 18 years of age; universal
Executive branch:
chief of state: President Olusegun OBASANJO (since
29 May 1999); note - the president is both the chief of
state and head of government

head of government: President Olusegun
OBASANJO (since 29 May 1999); note - the president
is both the chief of state and head of government
cabinet: Federal Executive Council
elections: president is elected by popular vote for no
more than two four-year terms; election last held
19 April 2003 (next to be held NA 2007)
election results: Olusegun OBASANJO elected
president; percent of vote - Olusegun OBASANJO
(PDP) 61.9%, Muhammadu BUHARI (ANPP) 31.2%,
Chukwuemeka Odumegwu OJUKWU (APGA) 3.3%,
other 3.6%
Legislative branch: bicameral National Assembly
consists of Senate (107 seats, members elected by
popular vote to serve four-year terms) and House of
Representatives (346 seats, members elected by
popular vote to serve four-year terms)
elections: Senate - last held 12 April 2003 (next to be
held NA 2007); House of Representatives - last held
12 April 2003 (next to be held NA 2007)
election results: Senate - percent of vote by party -
PDP 53.6%, ANPP 27.9%, AD 9.7%; seats by party -
PDP 73, ANPP 28, AD 6; House of Representatives -
percent of vote by party - PDP 54.5%, ANPP 27.4%,
AD 9.3%, other 8.8%; seats by party - PDP 213, ANPP
95, AD 31, other 7; note - two constituencies are not
reported
Judicial branch: Supreme Court (judges appointed
by the President); Federal Court of Appeal (judges are
appointed by the federal government on the advice of
the Advisory Judicial Committee)
Political parties and leaders: Alliance for
Democracy or AD [Alhaji Adamu ABDULKADIR]; All
Nigeria Peoples' Party or ANPP [Don ETIEBET]; All
Progressives Grand Alliance or APGA [Chekwas
OKORIE]; National Democratic Party or NDP [Aliyu
Habu FARI]; Peoples Democratic Party or PDP [Audu
OGBEH]; Peoples Redemption Party or PRP
[Abdulkadir Balarabe MUSA]; Peoples Salvation Party
or PSP [Lawal MAITURARE]; United Nigeria Peoples
Party or UNPP [Saleh JAMBO]
Political pressure groups and leaders: Nigerian
Labor Congress or NLC [Adams OSHIOMOLE]
International organization participation: ACP,
AfDB, AU, C, ECOWAS, FAO, G-15, G-24, G-77,
IAEA, IBRD, ICAO, ICC, ICCt, ICFTU, ICRM, IDA,
IFAD, IFC, IFRCS, IHO, ILO, IMF, IMO, Interpol, IOC,
IOM, ISO, ITU, MINURSO, MONUC, NAM, OIC,
OPCW, OPEC, PCA, UN, UNAMSIL, UNCTAD,
UNESCO, UNHCR, UNIDO, UNITAR, UNMEE,
UNMIK, UNMIL, UNMOVIC, UPU, WCO, WFTU,
WHO, WIPO, WMO, WToO, WTrO
Diplomatic representation in the US:
chief of mission: Ambassador Jibril Muhammad
AMINU
chancery: 3519 International Court NW, Washington,
DC 20008
telephone: [1] (202) 986-8400
FAX: [1] (202) 775-1385
consulate(s) general: Atlanta and New York

Diplomatic representation from the US:
chief of mission: Ambassador Howard Franklin
JETER
embassy: 7 Mambilla Drive, Abuja
mailing address: P. O. Box 554, Lagos
telephone: [234] (9) 523-0916/0906/5857/2235/2205
FAX: [234] (9) 523-0353
Flag description: three equal vertical bands of
green (hoist side), white, and green

Economy

Economy - overview: Oil-rich Nigeria, long hobbled
by political instability, corruption, inadequate
infrastructure, and poor macroeconomic
management, is undertaking some reforms under the
new civilian administration. Nigeria's former military
rulers failed to diversify the economy away from
overdependence on the capital-intensive oil sector,
which provides 20% of GDP, 95% of foreign exchange
earnings, and about 65% of budgetary revenues. The
largely subsistence agricultural sector has failed to
keep up with rapid population growth - Nigeria is
Africa's most populous country - and the country, once
a large net exporter of food, now must import food.
Following the signing of an IMF stand-by agreement in
August 2000, Nigeria received a debt-restructuring
deal from the Paris Club and a $1 billion credit from
the IMF, both contingent on economic reforms.
Nigeria pulled out of its IMF program in April 2002,
after failing to meet spending and exchange rate
targets, making it ineligible for additional debt
forgiveness from the Paris Club. The government has
lacked the political will to implement the
market-oriented reforms urged by the IMF, such as to
modernize the banking system, to curb inflation by
blocking excessive wage demands, and to resolve
regional disputes over the distribution of earnings from
the oil industry. During 2003, however, the
government deregulated fuel prices and announced
the privatization of the country's four oil refineries.
GDP growth probably will rise marginally in 2004, led
by oil and natural gas exports.
GDP: purchasing power parity - $110.8 billion
(2003 est.)
GDP - real growth rate: 3.4% (2003 est.)
GDP - per capita: purchasing power parity - $800
(2003 est.)
GDP - composition by sector:
agriculture: 41.2%
industry: 15.7%
services: 43.1% (2002 est.)
Population below poverty line: 60% (2000 est.)
**Household income or consumption by percentage
share:**
lowest 10%: 1.6%
highest 10%: 40.8% (1996-97)
Distribution of family income - Gini index: 50.6
(1996-97)
Inflation rate (consumer prices): 11.7%
(2002 est.)
Labor force: 66 million (1999 est.)

Nigeria *(continued)*

Labor force - by occupation: agriculture 70%, industry 10%, services 20% (1999 est.)
Unemployment rate: 28% (1992 est.)
Budget:
revenues: $3.4 billion
expenditures: $3.6 billion, including capital expenditures of $NA (2000 est.)
Industries: crude oil, coal, tin, columbite, palm oil, peanuts, cotton, rubber, wood, hides and skins, textiles, cement and other construction materials, food products, footwear, chemicals, fertilizer, printing, ceramics, steel
Industrial production growth rate: 1.2% (2003 est.)
Electricity - production: 15.67 billion kWh (2001)
Electricity - production by source:
fossil fuel: 61.9%
hydro: 38.1%
nuclear: 0%
other: 0% (2001)
Electricity - consumption: 14.55 billion kWh (2001)
Electricity - exports: 20 million kWh (2001)
Electricity - imports: 0 kWh (2001)
Oil - production: 2.256 million bbl/day (2001 est.)
Oil - consumption: 275,000 bbl/day (2001 est.)
Oil - exports: NA
Oil - imports: NA
Oil - proved reserves: 27 billion bbl (1 January 2002)
Natural gas - production: 15.68 billion cu m (2001 est.)
Natural gas - consumption: 7.85 billion cu m (2001 est.)
Natural gas - exports: 7.83 billion cu m (2001 est.)
Natural gas - imports: 0 cu m (2001 est.)
Natural gas - proved reserves: 4.007 trillion cu m (1 January 2002)
Agriculture - products: cocoa, peanuts, palm oil, corn, rice, sorghum, millet, cassava (tapioca), yams, rubber; cattle, sheep, goats, pigs; timber; fish
Exports: $21.8 billion f.o.b. (2003 est.)
Exports - commodities: petroleum and petroleum products 95%, cocoa, rubber
Exports - partners: US 33.2%, Spain 7.4%, Brazil 6.4%, Indonesia 6%, France 5.7%, India 4.8%, Japan 4% (2002)
Imports: $14.54 billion f.o.b. (2003 est.)
Imports - commodities: machinery, chemicals, transport equipment, manufactured goods, food and live animals
Imports - partners: UK 9.5%, US 9.4%, China 9.3%, France 8.7%, Germany 6.5%, South Korea 6.1%, Netherlands 5.2%, Italy 4.7%, Brazil 4.5% (2002)
Debt - external: $30.9 billion (2003 est.)
Economic aid - recipient: IMF $1 billion (2000)
Currency: naira (NGN)
Currency code: NGN
Exchange rates: nairas per US dollar - 129.222 (2003), 120.578 (2002), 111.231 (2001), 101.697 (2000), 92.3381 (1999)
Fiscal year: calendar year

Communications

Telephones - main lines in use: 702,000 (2002)
Telephones - mobile cellular: 1,607,900 (2002)
Telephone system:
general assessment: an inadequate system, further limited by poor maintenance; major expansion is required and a start has been made
domestic: intercity traffic is carried by coaxial cable, microwave radio relay, a domestic communications satellite system with 19 earth stations, and a coastal submarine cable; mobile cellular facilities and the Internet are available
international: country code - 234; satellite earth stations - 3 Intelsat (2 Atlantic Ocean and 1 Indian Ocean); fiber optic submarine cable (SAT-3/WASC) provides connectivity to Europe and Asia
Radio broadcast stations: AM 83, FM 36, shortwave 11 (2001)
Television broadcast stations: 3 (the government controls 2 of the broadcasting stations and 15 repeater stations) (2002)
Internet country code: .ng
Internet hosts: 1,030 (2002)
Internet users: 420,000 (2002)

Transportation

Railways:
total: 3,557 km
narrow gauge: 3,505 km 1.067-m gauge
standard gauge: 52 km 1.435-m gauge (2002)
Highways:
total: 194,394 km
paved: 60,068 km (including 1,194 km of expressways)
unpaved: 134,326 km (1999 est.)
Waterways: 8,575 km
note: consisting of the Niger and Benue rivers and smaller rivers and creeks
Pipelines: condensate 105 km; gas 1,660 km; oil 3,634 km (2003)
Ports and harbors: Calabar, Lagos, Onne, Port Harcourt, Sapele, Warri
Merchant marine:
total: 45 ships (1,000 GRT or over) 327,808 GRT/608,076 DWT
by type: cargo 7, chemical tanker 5, petroleum tanker 30, refrigerated cargo 1, roll on/roll off 1, specialized tanker 1
foreign-owned: Norway 2, Pakistan 1, Togo 1, United States 1
registered in other countries: 26 (2003 est.)
Airports: 70 (2003 est.)
Airports - with paved runways:
total: 36
over 3,047 m: 7
2,438 to 3,047 m: 11
1,524 to 2,437 m: 9
914 to 1,523 m: 6
under 914 m: 3 (2003 est.)

Airports - with unpaved runways:
total: 34
1,524 to 2,437 m: 3
914 to 1,523 m: 13
under 914 m: 18 (2003 est.)
Heliports: 1 (2003 est.)

Military

Military branches: Army, Navy, Air Force
Military manpower - military age: 18 years of age (2004 est.)
Military manpower - availability:
males age 15-49: 32,665,407 (2004 est.)
Military manpower - fit for military service:
males age 15-49: 18,763,229 (2004 est.)
Military manpower - reaching military age annually:
males: 1,452,231 (2004 est.)
Military expenditures - dollar figure: $469.8 million (2003)
Military expenditures - percent of GDP: 0.9% (2003)

Transnational Issues

Disputes - international: ICJ ruled in 2002 on the entire Cameroon-Nigeria land and maritime boundary but the parties formed a Joint Border Commission to resolve differences bilaterally and have commenced with demarcation in less-contested sections of the boundary, starting in Lake Chad in the north; Nigeria initially rejected cession of the Bakasi Peninsula; the ICJ ruled on an equidistance settlement of Cameroon-Equatorial Guinea-Nigeria maritime boundary in the Gulf of Guinea, but imprecisely defined coordinates in the ICJ decision, the unresolved Bakasi allocation, and a sovereignty dispute between Equatorial Guinea and Cameroon over an island at the mouth of the Ntem River all contribute to the delay in implementation; several villages along the Okpara River are in dispute with Benin; Lake Chad Commission continues to urge signatories Cameroon, Chad, Niger, and Nigeria to ratify delimitation treaty over lake region, which remains the site of armed clashes among local populations and militias
Illicit drugs: a transit point for heroin and cocaine intended for European, East Asian, and North American markets; safehaven for Nigerian narcotraffickers operating worldwide; major money-laundering center; massive corruption and criminal activity, remains on Financial Action Task Force Non-Cooperative Countries and Territories List for continued failure to address deficiencies in money-laundering control regime

Niue

(self-governing in free association with New Zealand)

Introduction

Background: Niue's remoteness, as well as cultural and linguistic differences between its Polynesian inhabitants and those of the rest of the Cook Islands, have caused it to be separately administered. The population of the island continues to drop (from a peak of 5,200 in 1966 to about 2,100 in 2004), with substantial emigration to New Zealand, 2,400 km to the southwest.

Geography

Location: Oceania, island in the South Pacific Ocean, east of Tonga
Geographic coordinates: 19 02 S, 169 52 W
Map references: Oceania
Area:
total: 260 sq km
land: 260 sq km
water: 0 sq km
Area - comparative: 1.5 times the size of Washington, DC
Land boundaries: 0 km
Coastline: 64 km
Maritime claims:
territorial sea: 12 NM
exclusive economic zone: 200 NM
Climate: tropical; modified by southeast trade winds
Terrain: steep limestone cliffs along coast, central plateau
Elevation extremes:
lowest point: Pacific Ocean 0 m
highest point: unnamed location near Mutalau settlement 68 m
Natural resources: fish, arable land
Land use:
arable land: 19.23%
permanent crops: 7.69%
other: 73.08% (1998 est.)
Irrigated land: NA sq km

Natural hazards: typhoons
Environment - current issues: increasing attention to conservationist practices to counter loss of soil fertility from traditional slash and burn agriculture
Environment - international agreements:
party to: Biodiversity, Climate Change, Climate Change-Kyoto Protocol, Desertification
signed, but not ratified: Law of the Sea
Geography - note: one of world's largest coral islands

People

Population: 2,156 (July 2004 est.)
Age structure:
0-14 years: NA%
15-64 years: NA%
65 years and over: NA% (2004 est.)
Population growth rate: 0.01% (2004 est.)
Birth rate: NA births/1,000 population (2004 est.)
Death rate: NA deaths/1,000 population (2004 est.)
Net migration rate: NA migrant(s)/1,000 population (2004 est.)
Sex ratio: NA (2004 est.)
Infant mortality rate:
total: NA%
male: NA%
female: NA% (2004 est.)
Life expectancy at birth:
total population: NA years
male: NA years
female: NA years (2004 est.)
Total fertility rate: NA children born/woman (2004 est.)
HIV/AIDS - adult prevalence rate: NA%
HIV/AIDS - people living with HIV/AIDS: NA
HIV/AIDS - deaths: NA
Nationality:
noun: Niuean(s)
adjective: Niuean
Ethnic groups: Polynesian (with some 200 Europeans, Samoans, and Tongans)
Religions: Ekalesia Niue (Niuean Church - a Protestant church closely related to the London Missionary Society) 75%, Latter-Day Saints 10%, other 15% (mostly Roman Catholic, Jehovah's Witnesses, Seventh-Day Adventist)
Languages: Niuean, a Polynesian language closely related to Tongan and Samoan; English
Literacy:
definition: NA
total population: 95%
male: NA%
female: NA%

Government

Country name:
conventional long form: none
conventional short form: Niue
former: Savage Island
Dependency status: self-governing in free association with New Zealand since 1974; Niue fully responsible for internal affairs; New Zealand retains

responsibility for external affairs and defense; however, these responsibilities confer no rights of control and are only exercised at the request of the Government of Niue
Government type: self-governing parliamentary democracy
Capital: Alofi
Administrative divisions: none; note - there are no first-order administrative divisions as defined by the US Government, but there are 14 villages at the second order
Independence: on 19 October 1974, Niue became a self-governing parliamentary government in free association with New Zealand
National holiday: Waitangi Day (Treaty of Waitangi established British sovereignty over New Zealand), 6 February (1840)
Constitution: 19 October 1974 (Niue Constitution Act)
Legal system: English common law
note: Niue is self-governing, with the power to make its own laws
Suffrage: 18 years of age; universal
Executive branch:
chief of state: Queen ELIZABETH II (since 6 February 1952); the UK and New Zealand are represented by New Zealand High Commissioner John BRYAN (since NA May 2000)
head of government: Premier Young VIVIAN (since 1 May 2002)
cabinet: Cabinet consists of the premier and three ministers
elections: the monarch is hereditary; premier elected by the Legislative Assembly for a three-year term; election last held 1 May 2002 (next to be held NA May 2005)
election results: Young VIVIAN elected premier; percent of Legislative Assembly vote - Young VIVIAN (NPP) 70%, Hunukitama HUNUKI (AI) 30%
Legislative branch: unicameral Legislative Assembly (20 seats; members elected by popular vote to serve three-year terms; six elected from a common roll and 14 are village representatives)
elections: last held 21 March 2002 (next to be held NA March 2005)
election results: percent of vote by party - NA%; seats by party - NPP 9, independents 11; note - all 20 seats were reelected
Judicial branch: Supreme Court of New Zealand; High Court of Niue
Political parties and leaders: Niue People's Action Party or NPP [Young VIVIAN]; Alliance of Independents or AI [leader NA]
Political pressure groups and leaders: NA
International organization participation: ACP, FAO, PIF, Sparteca, UNESCO, WHO, WMO
Diplomatic representation in the US: none (self-governing territory in free association with New Zealand)
Diplomatic representation from the US: none (self-governing territory in free association with New Zealand)

Niue (continued)

Flag description: yellow with the flag of the UK in the upper hoist-side quadrant; the flag of the UK bears five yellow five-pointed stars - a large one on a blue disk in the center and a smaller one on each arm of the bold red cross

Economy

Economy - overview: The economy suffers from the typical Pacific island problems of geographic isolation, few resources, and a small population. Government expenditures regularly exceed revenues, and the shortfall is made up by critically needed grants from New Zealand that are used to pay wages to public employees. Niue has cut government expenditures by reducing the public service by almost half. The agricultural sector consists mainly of subsistence gardening, although some cash crops are grown for export. Industry consists primarily of small factories to process passion fruit, lime oil, honey, and coconut cream. The sale of postage stamps to foreign collectors is an important source of revenue. The island in recent years has suffered a serious loss of population because of migration of Niueans to New Zealand. Efforts to increase GDP include the promotion of tourism and a financial services industry, although Premier LAKATANI announced in February 2002 that Niue will shut down the offshore banking industry. Economic aid from New Zealand in 2002 was about $2.6 million.

GDP: purchasing power parity - $7.6 million (2000 est.)

GDP - real growth rate: -0.3% (2000 est.)

GDP - per capita: purchasing power parity - $3,600 (2000 est.)

GDP - composition by sector:
agriculture: NA%
industry: NA%
services: 55%

Population below poverty line: NA%

Household income or consumption by percentage share:
lowest 10%: NA%
highest 10%: NA%

Inflation rate (consumer prices): 1% (1995)

Labor force: NA (1998 est.)

Labor force - by occupation: most work on family plantations; paid work exists only in government service, small industry, and the Niue Development Board

Unemployment rate: NA% (March 1999)

Budget:
revenues: $NA
expenditures: $NA, including capital expenditures of $NA

Industries: tourism, handicrafts, food processing

Industrial production growth rate: NA%

Electricity - production: 3 million kWh (2001)

Electricity - production by source:
fossil fuel: 100%
hydro: 0%
nuclear: 0%
other: 0% (2001)

Electricity - consumption: 2.79 million kWh (2001)

Electricity - exports: 0 kWh (2001)

Electricity - imports: 0 kWh (2001)

Oil - production: 0 bbl/day (2001 est.)

Oil - consumption: 20 bbl/day (2001 est.)

Oil - exports: NA

Oil - imports: NA

Agriculture - products: coconuts, passion fruit, honey, limes, taro, yams, cassava (tapioca), sweet potatoes; pigs, poultry, beef cattle

Exports: $137,200 (1999)

Exports - commodities: canned coconut cream, copra, honey, vanilla, passion fruit products, pawpaws, root crops, limes, footballs, stamps, handicrafts

Exports - partners: NZ mainly, Fiji, Cook Islands, Australia (2000)

Imports: $2.38 million (1999)

Imports - commodities: food, live animals, manufactured goods, machinery, fuels, lubricants, chemicals, drugs

Imports - partners: NZ mainly, Fiji, Japan, Samoa, Australia, US (2000)

Debt - external: $418,000 (2002 est.)

Economic aid - recipient: $2.6 million from New Zealand (2002)

Currency: New Zealand dollar (NZD)

Currency code: NZD

Exchange rates: New Zealand dollars per US dollar - 1.7229 (2003), 2.1620 (2002), 2.3776 (2001), 2.1863 (2000), 1.8886 (1999)

Fiscal year: 1 April - 31 March

Communications

Telephones - main lines in use: 1,100 est (2002)

Telephones - mobile cellular: 400 (2002)

Telephone system:
domestic: single-line telephone system connects all villages on island
international: country code - 683

Radio broadcast stations: AM 1, FM 1, shortwave 0 (1998)

Television broadcast stations: 1 (1997)

Internet country code: .nu

Internet users: NA

Transportation

Railways: 0 km

Highways:
total: 234 km
paved: 86 km
unpaved: 148 km (2001)

Waterways: none

Ports and harbors: none; offshore anchorage only

Merchant marine: none

Airports: 1 (2003 est.)

Airports - with paved runways:
total: 1
1,524 to 2,437 m: 1 (2003 est.)

Military

Military branches: no regular indigenous military forces; Police Force

Military - note: defense is the responsibility of New Zealand

Transnational Issues

Disputes - international: none

Norfolk Island
(territory of Australia)

Introduction

Background: Two British attempts at establishing the island as a penal colony (1788-1814 and 1825-55) were ultimately abandoned. In 1856, the island was resettled by Pitcairn Islanders, descendants of the Bounty mutineers and their Tahitian companions.

Geography

Location: Oceania, island in the South Pacific Ocean, east of Australia
Geographic coordinates: 29 02 S, 167 57 E
Map references: Oceania
Area:
total: 34.6 sq km
land: 34.6 sq km
water: 0 sq km
Area - comparative: about 0.2 times the size of Washington, DC
Land boundaries: 0 km
Coastline: 32 km
Maritime claims:
territorial sea: 12 NM
exclusive fishing zone: 200 NM
Climate: subtropical; mild, little seasonal temperature variation
Terrain: volcanic formation with mostly rolling plains
Elevation extremes:
lowest point: Pacific Ocean 0 m
highest point: Mount Bates 319 m
Natural resources: fish
Land use:
arable land: 0%
permanent crops: 0%
other: 100% (1998 est.)
Irrigated land: NA sq km
Natural hazards: typhoons (especially May to July)
Environment - current issues: NA

Geography - note: most of the 32-km coastline consists of almost inaccessible cliffs, but the land slopes down to the sea in one small southern area on Sydney Bay, where the capital of Kingston is situated

People

Population: 1,841 (July 2004 est.)
Age structure:
0-14 years: 20.2%
15-64 years: 63.9%
65 years and over: 15.9% (2004 est.)
Population growth rate: -0.01% (2004 est.)
Birth rate: NA births/1,000 population (2004 est.)
Death rate: NA deaths/1,000 population (2004 est.)
Net migration rate: NA migrant(s)/1,000 population
Sex ratio: NA
Infant mortality rate:
total: NA%
male: NA%
female: NA%
Life expectancy at birth:
total population: NA years
male: NA years
female: NA years
Total fertility rate: NA children born/woman (2004 est.)
HIV/AIDS - adult prevalence rate: NA%
HIV/AIDS - people living with HIV/AIDS: NA
HIV/AIDS - deaths: NA
Nationality:
noun: Norfolk Islander(s)
adjective: Norfolk Islander(s)
Ethnic groups: descendants of the Bounty mutineers, Australian, New Zealander, Polynesians
Religions: Anglican 37.4%, Uniting Church in Australia 14.5%, Roman Catholic 11.5%, Seventh-Day Adventist 3.1%, none 12.2%, unknown 17.4%, other 3.9% (1996)
Languages: English (official), Norfolk a mixture of 18th century English and ancient Tahitian
Literacy: NA

Government

Country name:
conventional long form: Territory of Norfolk Island
conventional short form: Norfolk Island
Dependency status: territory of Australia; Canberra administers Commonwealth responsibilities on Norfolk Island through the Department of Environment, Sport, and Territories
Government type: NA
Capital: Kingston
Administrative divisions: none (territory of Australia)
Independence: none (territory of Australia)
National holiday: Pitcairners Arrival Day, 8 June (1856)
Constitution: Norfolk Island Act of 1979

Legal system: based on the laws of Australia, local ordinances and acts; English common law applies in matters not covered by either Australian or Norfolk Island law
Suffrage: 18 years of age; universal
Executive branch:
chief of state: Queen ELIZABETH II (since 6 February 1952); the UK and Australia are represented by Administrator Grant TAMBLING (since 1 November 2003)
head of government: Assembly President and Chief Minister Geoffrey Robert GARDNER (since 5 December 2001)
cabinet: Executive Council is made up of four of the nine members of the Legislative Assembly; the council devises government policy and acts as an advisor to the administrator
elections: the monarch is hereditary; administrator appointed by the governor general of Australia; chief minister elected by the Legislative Assembly for a term of not more than three years; election last held 29 November 2001 (next to be held by December 2004)
election results: Geoffrey Robert GARDNER elected chief minister; percent of Legislative Assembly vote - NA%
Legislative branch: unicameral Legislative Assembly (9 seats; members elected by electors who have nine equal votes each but only four votes can be given to any one candidate; members serve three-year terms)
elections: last held 29 November 2001 (next to be held by December 2004)
election results: percent of vote - NA%; seats - independents 9
Judicial branch: Supreme Court; Court of Petty Sessions
Political parties and leaders: none
Political pressure groups and leaders: none
International organization participation: none
Diplomatic representation in the US: none (territory of Australia)
Diplomatic representation from the US: none (territory of Australia)
Flag description: three vertical bands of green (hoist side), white, and green with a large green Norfolk Island pine tree centered in the slightly wider white band

Economy

Economy - overview: Tourism, the primary economic activity, has steadily increased over the years and has brought a level of prosperity unusual among inhabitants of the Pacific islands. The agricultural sector has become self-sufficient in the production of beef, poultry, and eggs.
GDP: purchasing power parity - $NA
GDP - real growth rate: NA%
GDP - per capita: purchasing power parity - $NA

Norfolk Island *(continued)*

GDP - composition by sector:
agriculture: NA%
industry: NA%
services: NA%
Population below poverty line: NA%
Household income or consumption by percentage share:
lowest 10%: NA%
highest 10%: NA%
Inflation rate (consumer prices): NA%
Labor force: NA
Labor force - by occupation: tourism NA%, subsistence agriculture NA%
Unemployment rate: NA%
Budget:
revenues: $4.6 million
expenditures: $4.8 million, including capital expenditures of $NA (FY92/93)
Industries: tourism
Industrial production growth rate: NA%
Electricity - production: NA kWh
Electricity - production by source:
fossil fuel: 0%
hydro: 0%
nuclear: 0%
other: 0% (2002)
Electricity - consumption: NA kWh
Agriculture - products: Norfolk Island pine seed, Kentia palm seed, cereals, vegetables, fruit; cattle, poultry
Exports: $1.5 million f.o.b. (FY91/92)
Exports - commodities: postage stamps, seeds of the Norfolk Island pine and Kentia palm, small quantities of avocados
Exports - partners: Australia, other Pacific island countries, NZ, Asia, Europe
Imports: $17.9 million c.i.f. (FY91/92)
Imports - commodities: NA
Imports - partners: Australia, other Pacific island countries, NZ, Asia, Europe
Debt - external: $NA
Economic aid - recipient: $NA
Currency: Australian dollar (AUD)
Currency code: AUD
Exchange rates: Australian dollars per US dollar - 1.5419 (2003), 1.8406 (2002), 1.9320 (2001), 1.7173 (2000), 1.5497 (1999)
Fiscal year: 1 July - 30 June

Communications

Telephones - main lines in use: 2,532; note: a mix of analog (2500) and digital (32) circuits (2004)
Telephones - mobile cellular: 0 (1983)
Telephone system:
general assessment: adequate
domestic: NA
international: country code - 672; undersea coaxial cable links with Australia, New Zealand, and Canada; satellite service planned for near future
Radio broadcast stations: AM 0, FM 3, shortwave 0 (1998)

Television broadcast stations: 1 (local programming station plus two repeaters that bring in Australian programs by satellite) (1998)
Internet country code: .nf
Internet users: NA

Transportation

Railways: 0 km
Highways:
total: 80 km
paved: 53 km
unpaved: 27 km (2001)
Waterways: none
Ports and harbors: none; loading jetties at Kingston and Cascade
Merchant marine: none
Airports: 1 (2003 est.)
Airports - with paved runways:
total: 1
1,524 to 2,437 m: 1 (2003 est.)

Military

Military - note: defense is the responsibility of Australia

Transnational Issues

Disputes - international: none

Northern Mariana Islands
(commonwealth in political union with the US)

Introduction

Background: Under US administration as part of the UN Trust Territory of the Pacific, the people of the Northern Mariana Islands decided in the 1970s not to seek independence but instead to forge closer links with the US. Negotiations for territorial status began in 1972. A covenant to establish a commonwealth in political union with the US was approved in 1975. A new government and constitution went into effect in 1978.

Geography

Location: Oceania, islands in the North Pacific Ocean, about three-quarters of the way from Hawaii to the Philippines
Geographic coordinates: 15 12 N, 145 45 E
Map references: Oceania
Area:
total: 477 sq km
land: 477 sq km
water: 0 sq km
note: includes 14 islands including Saipan, Rota, and Tinian
Area - comparative: 2.5 times the size of Washington, DC
Land boundaries: 0 km
Coastline: 1,482 km
Maritime claims:
territorial sea: 12 NM
exclusive economic zone: 200 NM
Climate: tropical marine; moderated by northeast trade winds, little seasonal temperature variation; dry season December to June, rainy season July to October
Terrain: southern islands are limestone with level terraces and fringing coral reefs; northern islands are volcanic

Northern Mariana Islands (continued)

Elevation extremes:
lowest point: Pacific Ocean 0 m
highest point: unnamed location on Agrihan 965 m
Natural resources: arable land, fish
Land use:
arable land: 15.22%
permanent crops: 6.52%
other: 78.26% (1998 est.)
Irrigated land: NA sq km
Natural hazards: active volcanoes on Pagan and Agrihan; typhoons (especially August to November)
Environment - current issues: contamination of groundwater on Saipan may contribute to disease; clean-up of landfill; protection of endangered species conflicts with development
Geography - note: strategic location in the North Pacific Ocean

People

Population: 78,252 (July 2004 est.)
Age structure:
0-14 years: 20.3% (male 8,286; female 7,625)
15-64 years: 78.1% (male 25,579; female 35,534)
65 years and over: 1.6% (male 603; female 625) (2004 est.)
Median age:
total: 29.2 years
male: 31.4 years
female: 28.2 years (2004 est.)
Population growth rate: 2.71% (2004 est.)
Birth rate: 19.77 births/1,000 population (2004 est.)
Death rate: 2.3 deaths/1,000 population (2004 est.)
Net migration rate: 9.61 migrant(s)/1,000 population (2004 est.)
Sex ratio:
at birth: 1.06 male(s)/female
under 15 years: 1.09 male(s)/female
15-64 years: 0.72 male(s)/female
65 years and over: 0.97 male(s)/female
total population: 0.79 male(s)/female (2004 est.)
Infant mortality rate:
total: 7.25 deaths/1,000 live births
male: 7.18 deaths/1,000 live births
female: 7.32 deaths/1,000 live births (2004 est.)
Life expectancy at birth:
total population: 75.67 years
male: 73.11 years
female: 78.38 years (2004 est.)
Total fertility rate: 1.33 children born/woman (2004 est.)
HIV/AIDS - adult prevalence rate: NA%
HIV/AIDS - people living with HIV/AIDS: NA
HIV/AIDS - deaths: NA
Nationality:
noun: NA
adjective: NA
Ethnic groups: Chamorro, Carolinians and other Micronesians, Caucasian, Japanese, Chinese, Filipino, Korean

Religions: Christian (Roman Catholic majority, although traditional beliefs and taboos may still be found)
Languages: English, Chamorro, Carolinian
note: 86% of population speaks a language other than English at home
Literacy:
definition: age 15 and over can read and write
total population: 97%
male: 97%
female: 96% (1980 est.)

Government

Country name:
conventional long form: Commonwealth of the Northern Mariana Islands
conventional short form: Northern Mariana Islands
former: Mariana Islands District (Trust Territory of the Pacific Islands)
Dependency status: commonwealth in political union with the US; federal funds to the Commonwealth administered by the US Department of the Interior, Office of Insular Affairs
Government type: commonwealth; self-governing with locally elected governor, lieutenant governor, and legislature
Capital: Saipan
Administrative divisions: none (commonwealth in political union with the US); there are no first-order administrative divisions as defined by the US Government, but there are four municipalities at the second order; Northern Islands, Rota, Saipan, Tinian
Independence: none (commonwealth in political union with the US)
National holiday: Commonwealth Day, 8 January (1978)
Constitution: Covenant Agreement effective 4 November 1986 and the Constitution of the Commonwealth of the Northern Mariana Islands effective 1 January 1978
Legal system: based on US system, except for customs, wages, immigration laws, and taxation
Suffrage: 18 years of age; universal; indigenous inhabitants are US citizens but do not vote in US presidential elections
Executive branch:
chief of state: President George W. BUSH of the US (since 20 January 2001); Vice President Richard B. CHENEY (since 20 January 2001)
head of government: Governor Juan N. BABAUTA (since NA January 2002); Lieutenant Governor Diego T. BENEVENTE (since NA January 2002)
cabinet: NA
elections: US president and vice president elected on the same ticket for four-year terms; governor and lieutenant governor elected on the same ticket by popular vote for four-year terms; election last held NA November 2001 (next to be held NA November 2005)

election results: Juan N. BABAUTA elected governor in a four-way race; percent of vote - Juan N. BABAUTA (Republican Party) 49%
Legislative branch: bicameral Legislature consists of the Senate (9 seats; members are elected by popular vote to serve four-year staggered terms) and the House of Representatives (18 seats; members are elected by popular vote to serve two-year terms)
elections: Senate - last held 1 November 2003 (next to be held 5 November 2005); House of Representatives - last held 1 November 2003 (next to be held 5 November 2005)
election results: Senate - percent of vote by party - NA%; seats by party - NA; House of Representatives - percent of vote by party - NA%; seats by party - Covenant Party 9, Republican Party 7, Democratic Party 1, independent 1
note: the Northern Mariana Islands does not have a nonvoting delegate in the US Congress; instead, it has an elected official or "resident representative" located in Washington, DC; seats by party - Republican Party 1 (Pedro A. TENORIO)
Judicial branch: Commonwealth Supreme Court; Superior Court; Federal District Court
Political parties and leaders: Democratic Party [Dr. Carlos S. CAMACHO]; Republican Party [NA]; Covenant Party [Benigno R. FITIAL]
Political pressure groups and leaders: NA
International organization participation: Interpol (subbureau)
Flag description: blue, with a white, five-pointed star superimposed on the gray silhouette of a latte stone (a traditional foundation stone used in building) in the center, surrounded by a wreath

Economy

Economy - overview: The economy benefits substantially from financial assistance from the US. The rate of funding has declined as locally generated government revenues have grown. The key tourist industry employs about 50% of the work force and accounts for roughly one-fourth of GDP. Japanese tourists predominate. Annual tourist entries have exceeded one-half million in recent years, but financial difficulties in Japan have caused a temporary slowdown. The agricultural sector is made up of cattle ranches and small farms producing coconuts, breadfruit, tomatoes, and melons. Garment production is by far the most important industry with employment of 17,500 mostly Chinese workers and sizable shipments to the US under duty and quota exemptions.
GDP: purchasing power parity - $900 million
note: GDP estimate includes US subsidy (2000 est.)
GDP - real growth rate: NA%
GDP - per capita: purchasing power parity - $12,500 (2000 est.)
GDP - composition by sector:
agriculture: NA%
industry: NA%
services: NA%

Northern Mariana Islands *(continued)*

Population below poverty line: NA%
Household income or consumption by percentage share:
lowest 10%: NA%
highest 10%: NA%
Inflation rate (consumer prices): 1.2% (1997 est.)
Labor force: 6,006 total indigenous labor force; 2,699 unemployed; 28,717 foreign workers (June 1995)
Labor force - by occupation: NA
Unemployment rate: NA%
Budget:
revenues: $193 million
expenditures: $223 million, including capital expenditures of NA (FY01/02 est.)
Industries: tourism, construction, garments, handicrafts
Industrial production growth rate: NA%
Electricity - production: NA kWh
Electricity - consumption: NA kWh
Electricity - exports: 0 kWh
Electricity - imports: 0 kWh
Agriculture - products: coconuts, fruits, vegetables; cattle
Exports: $NA
Exports - commodities: garments
Exports - partners: US (2000)
Imports: $NA
Imports - commodities: food, construction equipment and materials, petroleum products
Imports - partners: US, Japan (2000)
Debt - external: $NA
Economic aid - recipient: extensive funding from US
Currency: US dollar (USD)
Currency code: USD
Exchange rates: the US dollar is used
Fiscal year: 1 October - 30 September

Communications

Telephones - main lines in use: 21,000 (2000)
Telephones - mobile cellular: 3,000 (2000)
Telephone system:
general assessment: NA
domestic: NA
international: country code - 1-670; satellite earth stations - 2 Intelsat (Pacific Ocean)
Radio broadcast stations: AM 2, FM 3, shortwave 1 (1998)
Television broadcast stations: 1 (on Saipan and one station planned for Rota; in addition, two cable services on Saipan provide varied programming from satellite networks) (1997)
Internet country code: .mp
Internet users: NA

Transportation

Railways: 0 km
Highways:
total: 362 km
paved: NA km
unpaved: NA km (1991)

Waterways: none
Ports and harbors: Saipan, Tinian
Merchant marine: none
Airports: 6 (2003 est.)
Airports - with paved runways:
total: 3
2,438 to 3,047 m: 2
1,524 to 2,437 m: 1 (2003 est.)
Airports - with unpaved runways:
total: 3
2,438 to 3,047 m: 1
under 914 m: 2 (2003 est.)
Heliports: 1 (2003 est.)

Military

Military - note: defense is the responsibility of the US

Transnational Issues

Disputes - international: none

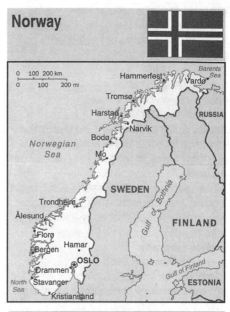

Norway

Introduction

Background: Two centuries of Viking raids into Europe tapered off following the adoption of Christianity by King Olav TRYGGVASON in 994. Conversion of the Norwegian kingdom occurred over the next several decades. In 1397, Norway was absorbed into a union with Denmark that was to last for more than four centuries. In 1814, Norwegians resisted the cession of their country to Sweden and adopted a new constitution. Sweden then invaded Norway but agreed to let Norway keep its constitution in return for accepting the union under a Swedish king. Rising nationalism throughout the 19th century led to a 1905 referendum granting Norway independence. Norway remained neutral in World War I and proclaimed its neutrality at the outset of World War II. Nevertheless, it was not able to avoid a five-year occupation by Nazi Germany (1940-45). In 1949, neutrality was abandoned and Norway became a member of NATO. Discovery of oil and gas in adjacent waters in the late 1960s boosted Norway's economic fortunes. The current focus is on containing spending on the extensive welfare system and planning for the time when petroleum reserves are depleted. In referenda held in 1972 and 1994, Norway rejected joining the EU.

Geography

Location: Northern Europe, bordering the North Sea and the North Atlantic Ocean, west of Sweden
Geographic coordinates. 62 00 N, 10 00 E
Map references. Europe
Area.
total. 324,220 sq km
land. 307,860 sq km
water. 16,360 sq km
Area - comparative. slightly larger than New Mexico
Land boundaries.
total. 2,544 km
border countries. Finland 729 km, Sweden 1,619 km, Russia 196 km

Norway (continued)

Coastline: 21,925 km (includes mainland 3,419 km, large islands 2,413 km, long fjords, numerous small islands, and minor indentations 16,093 km)

Maritime claims:

territorial sea: 12 NM

contiguous zone: 10 NM

exclusive economic zone: 200 NM

continental shelf: 200 NM

Climate: temperate along coast, modified by North Atlantic Current; colder interior with increased precipitation and colder summers; rainy year-round on west coast

Terrain: glaciated; mostly high plateaus and rugged mountains broken by fertile valleys; small, scattered plains; coastline deeply indented by fjords; arctic tundra in north

Elevation extremes:

lowest point: Norwegian Sea 0 m

highest point: Galdhopiggen 2,469 m

Natural resources: petroleum, copper, natural gas, pyrites, nickel, iron ore, zinc, lead, fish, timber, hydropower

Land use:

arable land: 2.94%

permanent crops: 0%

other: 97.06% (1998 est.)

Irrigated land: 1,270 sq km (1998 est.)

Natural hazards: rockslides, avalanches

Environment - current issues: water pollution; acid rain damaging forests and adversely affecting lakes, threatening fish stocks; air pollution from vehicle emissions

Environment - international agreements:

party to: Air Pollution, Air Pollution-Nitrogen Oxides, Air Pollution-Persistent Organic Pollutants, Air Pollution-Sulfur 85, Air Pollution-Sulfur 94, Air Pollution-Volatile Organic Compounds, Antarctic-Environmental Protocol, Antarctic-Marine Living Resources, Antarctic Seals, Antarctic Treaty, Biodiversity, Climate Change, Climate Change-Kyoto Protocol, Desertification, Endangered Species, Environmental Modification, Hazardous Wastes, Law of the Sea, Marine Dumping, Ozone Layer Protection, Ship Pollution, Tropical Timber 83, Tropical Timber 94, Wetlands, Whaling

signed, but not ratified: none of the selected agreements

Geography - note: about two-thirds mountains; some 50,000 islands off its much indented coastline; strategic location adjacent to sea lanes and air routes in North Atlantic; one of most rugged and longest coastlines in world

People

Population: 4,574,560 (July 2004 est.)

Age structure:

0-14 years: 19.8% (male 462,899; female 440,725)

15-64 years: 65.4% (male 1,520,481; female 1,473,101)

65 years and over: 14.8% (male 284,170; female 393,184) (2004 est.)

Median age:

total: 37.9 years

male: 37 years

female: 38.8 years (2004 est.)

Population growth rate: 0.41% (2004 est.)

Birth rate: 11.89 births/1,000 population (2004 est.)

Death rate: 9.51 deaths/1,000 population (2004 est.)

Net migration rate: 1.74 migrant(s)/1,000 population (2004 est.)

Sex ratio:

at birth: 1.05 male(s)/female

under 15 years: 1.05 male(s)/female

15-64 years: 1.03 male(s)/female

65 years and over: 0.72 male(s)/female

total population: 0.98 male(s)/female (2004 est.)

Infant mortality rate:

total: 3.73 deaths/1,000 live births

male: 4.11 deaths/1,000 live births

female: 3.34 deaths/1,000 live births (2004 est.)

Life expectancy at birth:

total population: 79.25 years

male: 76.64 years

female: 82.01 years (2004 est.)

Total fertility rate: 1.78 children born/woman (2004 est.)

HIV/AIDS - adult prevalence rate: 0.1% (2001 est.)

HIV/AIDS - people living with HIV/AIDS: 1,800 (2001 est.)

HIV/AIDS - deaths: less than 100 (2001 est.)

Nationality:

noun: Norwegian(s)

adjective: Norwegian

Ethnic groups: Norwegian, Sami 20,000

Religions: Evangelical Lutheran 86% (state church), other Protestant and Roman Catholic 3%, other 1%, none and unknown 10% (1997)

Languages: Norwegian (official)

note: small Sami- and Finnish-speaking minorities

Literacy:

definition: age 15 and over can read and write

total population: 100%

male: NA%

female: NA%

Government

Country name:

conventional long form: Kingdom of Norway

conventional short form: Norway

local long form: Kongeriket Norge

local short form: Norge

Government type: constitutional monarchy

Capital: Oslo

Administrative divisions: 19 counties (fylker, singular - fylke); Akershus, Aust-Agder, Buskerud, Finnmark, Hedmark, Hordaland, More og Romsdal, Nordland, Nord-Trondelag, Oppland, Oslo, Ostfold, Rogaland, Sogn og Fjordane, Sor-Trondelag, Telemark, Troms, Vest-Agder, Vestfold

Dependent areas: Bouvet Island, Jan Mayen, Svalbard

Independence: 7 June 1905 Norway declared the union with Sweden dissolved; 26 October 1905 Sweden agreed to the repeal of the union

National holiday: Constitution Day, 17 May (1814)

Constitution: 17 May 1814, modified in 1884

Legal system: mixture of customary law, civil law system, and common law traditions; Supreme Court renders advisory opinions to legislature when asked; accepts compulsory ICJ jurisdiction, with reservations

Suffrage: 18 years of age; universal

Executive branch:

chief of state: King HARALD V (since 17 January 1991); Heir Apparent Crown Prince HAAKON MAGNUS, son of the monarch (born 20 July 1973)

head of government: Prime Minister Kjell Magne BONDEVIK (since 19 October 2001)

cabinet: State Council appointed by the monarch with the approval of Parliament

elections: none; the monarch is hereditary; following parliamentary elections, the leader of the majority party or the leader of the majority coalition is usually appointed prime minister by the monarch with the approval of the Parliament

Legislative branch: modified unicameral Parliament or Storting (165 seats; members are elected by popular vote by proportional representation to serve four-year terms)

elections: last held 10 September 2001 (next to be held NA September 2005)

election results: percent of vote by party - Labor Party 24.3%, Conservative Party 21.2%, Progress Party 14.6%, Socialist Left Party 12.5%, Christian People's Party 12.4%, Center Party 5.6%, Liberal Party 3.9%, Coastal Party 1.7%, other 3.8%; seats by party - Labor Party 43, Conservative Party 38, Progress Party 26, Socialist Left Party 23, Christian People's Party 22, Center Party 10, Liberal Party 2, Coastal Party 1

note: for certain purposes, the Parliament divides itself into two chambers and elects one-fourth of its membership to an upper house or Lagting

Judicial branch: Supreme Court or Hoyesterett (justices appointed by the monarch)

Political parties and leaders: Center Party [Aslaug Marie HAGA]; Christian People's Party [Dagfinn HOYBRATEN]; Coastal Party [Steinar BASTESEN]; Conservative Party [Jan PETERSEN]; Labor Party [Jens STOLTENBERG]; Liberal Party [Lars SPONHEIM]; Progress Party [Carl I. HAGEN]; Socialist Left Party [Kristin HALVORSEN]

Political pressure groups and leaders: NA

International organization participation: AfDB, AsDB, Australia Group, BIS, CBSS, CE, CERN, EAPC, EBRD, EFTA, ESA, FAO, IADB, IAEA, IBRD, ICAO, ICC, ICCt, ICFTU, ICRM, IDA, IEA, IFAD, IFC, IFRCS, IHO, ILO, IMF, IMO, Interpol, IOC, IOM, ISO, ITU, MONUC, NAM (guest), NATO, NC, NEA, NIB, NSG, OAS (observer), OECD, OPCW, OSCE, Paris Club, PCA, UN, UNCTAD, UNESCO, UNHCR, UNIDO, UNMEE, UNMIK, UNMIL, UNTSO, UPU, WCO, WEU (associate), WHO, WIPO, WMO, WTrO, ZC

Norway *(continued)*

Diplomatic representation in the US:

chief of mission: Ambassador Knut VOLLEBAEK

chancery: 2720 34th Street NW, Washington, DC 20008

telephone: [1] (202) 333-6000

FAX: [1] (202) 337-0870

consulate(s) general: Houston, Miami, Minneapolis, New York, and San Francisco

Diplomatic representation from the US:

chief of mission: Ambassador John D. ONG

embassy: Drammensveien 18, 0244 Oslo

mailing address: PSC 69, Box 1000, APO AE 09707

telephone: [47] (22) 44 85 50

FAX: [47] (22) 44 33 63

Flag description: red with a blue cross outlined in white that extends to the edges of the flag; the vertical part of the cross is shifted to the hoist side in the style of the Dannebrog (Danish flag)

Economy

Economy - overview: The Norwegian economy is a prosperous bastion of welfare capitalism, featuring a combination of free market activity and government intervention. The government controls key areas, such as the vital petroleum sector (through large-scale state enterprises). The country is richly endowed with natural resources - petroleum, hydropower, fish, forests, and minerals - and is highly dependent on its oil production and international oil prices, with oil and gas accounting for one-third of exports. Only Saudi Arabia and Russia export more oil than Norway. Norway opted to stay out of the EU during a referendum in November 1994. The government has moved ahead with privatization. With arguably the highest quality of life worldwide, Norwegians still worry about that time in the next two decades when the oil and gas begin to run out. Accordingly, Norway has been saving its oil-boosted budget surpluses in a Government Petroleum Fund, which is invested abroad and now is valued at more than $43 billion. GDP growth was a lackluster 1% in 2002 and 0.5% in 2003 against the background of a faltering European economy.

GDP: purchasing power parity - $171.6 billion (2003 est.)

GDP - real growth rate: 0.5% (2003 est.)

GDP - per capita: purchasing power parity - $37,700 (2003 est.)

GDP - composition by sector:

agriculture: 1.7%

industry: 34%

services: 64.3% (2002)

Population below poverty line: NA%

Household income or consumption by percentage share:

lowest 10%: 4.1%

highest 10%: 21.8% (1995)

Distribution of family income - Gini index: 25.8 (1995)

Inflation rate (consumer prices): 2.6% (2003 est.)

Labor force: 2.4 million (2000 est.)

Labor force - by occupation: services 74%, industry 22%, agriculture, forestry, and fishing 4% (1995)

Unemployment rate: 4.5% (2003 est.)

Budget:

revenues: $71.7 billion

expenditures: $57.6 billion, including capital expenditures of $NA (2000 est.)

Industries: petroleum and gas, food processing, shipbuilding, pulp and paper products, metals, chemicals, timber, mining, textiles, fishing

Industrial production growth rate: -1% (2003 est.)

Electricity - production: 120.1 billion kWh (2001)

Electricity - production by source:

fossil fuel: 0.4%

hydro: 99.3%

nuclear: 0%

other: 0.4% (2001)

Electricity - consumption: 115.3 billion kWh (2001)

Electricity - exports: 7.162 billion kWh (2001)

Electricity - imports: 10.76 billion kWh (2001)

Oil - production: 3.408 million bbl/day (2001 est.)

Oil - consumption: 171,100 bbl/day (2001 est.)

Oil - exports: 3.466 million bbl/day (2001)

Oil - imports: 88,870 bbl/day (2001)

Oil - proved reserves: 9.859 billion bbl (1 January 2002)

Natural gas - production: 54.6 billion cu m (2001 est.)

Natural gas - consumption: 4.1 billion cu m (2001 est.)

Natural gas - exports: 50.5 billion cu m (2001 est.)

Natural gas - imports: 0 cu m (2001 est.)

Natural gas - proved reserves: 1.716 trillion cu m (1 January 2002)

Agriculture - products: barley, wheat, potatoes; pork, beef, veal, milk; fish

Exports: $67.27 billion f.o.b. (2003 est.)

Exports - commodities: petroleum and petroleum products, machinery and equipment, metals, chemicals, ships, fish

Exports - partners: UK 19.4%, Germany 12.4%, France 11.5%, Netherlands 9.3%, US 8.6%, Sweden 7.3% (2002)

Imports: $40.19 billion f.o.b. (2003 est.)

Imports - commodities: machinery and equipment, chemicals, metals, foodstuffs

Imports - partners: Sweden 15.7%, Germany 13.4%, Denmark 8.1%, UK 7.4%, US 6.2%, France 4.8%, Netherlands 4.8% (2002)

Debt - external: $0 (Norway is a net external creditor) (2003 est.)

Economic aid - donor: ODA, $1.4 billion (1998)

Currency: Norwegian krone (NOK)

Currency code: NOK

Exchange rates: Norwegian kroner per US dollar - 7.0802 (2003), 7.9838 (2002), 8.9917 (2001), 8.8018 (2000), 7.7992 (1999)

Fiscal year: calendar year

Communications

Telephones - main lines in use: 3.343 million (2002)

Telephones - mobile cellular: 3,840,400 (2002)

Telephone system:

general assessment: modern in all respects; one of the most advanced telecommunications networks in Europe

domestic: Norway has a domestic satellite system; moreover, the prevalence of rural areas encourages the wide use of cellular mobile systems instead of fixed-wire systems

international: country code - 47; 2 buried coaxial cable systems; 4 coaxial submarine cables; satellite earth stations - NA Eutelsat, NA Intelsat (Atlantic Ocean), and 1 Inmarsat (Atlantic and Indian Ocean regions); note - Norway shares the Inmarsat earth station with the other Nordic countries (Denmark, Finland, Iceland, and Sweden) (1999)

Radio broadcast stations: AM 5, FM at least 650, shortwave 1 (1998)

Television broadcast stations: 360 (plus 2,729 repeaters) (1995)

Internet country code: .no

Internet hosts: 255,742 (2002)

Internet users: 2.288 million (2002)

Transportation

Railways:

total: 4,178 km

standard gauge: 4,178 km 1.435-m gauge (2,518 km electrified) (2002)

Highways:

total: 91,454 km

paved: 69,505 km (including 143 km of expressways)

unpaved: 21,949 km (2000)

Waterways: 1,577 km (along west coast)

note: navigable by 2.4 m maximum draft vessels

Pipelines: condensate 411 km; gas 6,199 km; oil 2,213 km; oil/gas/water 746 km; unknown (oil/water) 38 km; water 96 km (2003)

Ports and harbors: Bergen, Drammen, Floro, Hammerfest, Harstad, Haugesund, Kristiansand, Larvik, Narvik, Oslo, Porsgrunn, Stavanger, Tromso, Trondheim

Merchant marine:

total: 693 ships (1,000 GRT or over) 18,820,495 GRT/ 27,449,456 DWT

by type: bulk 62, cargo 128, chemical tanker 124, combination bulk 7, combination ore/oil 32, container 15, liquefied gas 84, multi-functional large load carrier 1, passenger 6, petroleum tanker 113, refrigerated cargo 5, roll on/roll off 48, short-sea/passenger 22, specialized tanker 3, vehicle carrier 43

foreign-owned: Cyprus 3, Denmark 23, Estonia 2, Germany 12, Greece 15, Hong Kong 1, Iceland 2, Japan 10, Lithuania 1, Malta 1, Marshall Islands 1, Monaco 33, Poland 1, Saudi Arabia 3, Singapore 12, Sweden 31, United Kingdom 4, United States 5

registered in other countries: 695 (2003 est.)

Airports: 101 (2003 est.)
Airports - with paved runways:
total: 65
2,438 to 3,047 m: 13
1,524 to 2,437 m: 12
914 to 1,523 m: 14
under 914 m: 26 (2003 est.)
Airports - with unpaved runways:
total: 36
914 to 1,523 m: 7
under 914 m: 29 (2003 est.)
Heliports: 1 (2003 est.)

Military

Military branches: Norwegian Army, Royal Norwegian Navy (including Coast Artillery and Coast Guard), Royal Norwegian Air Force (Kongelige Norske Luftforsvaret, RNoAF), Home Guard
Military manpower - military age: 20 years of age (2004 est.)
Military manpower - availability:
males age 15-49: 1,106,484 (2004 est.)
Military manpower - fit for military service:
males age 15-49: 916,155 (2004 est.)
Military manpower - reaching military age annually:
males: 27,252 (2004 est.)
Military expenditures - dollar figure:
$4,033,500,000 (2003)
Military expenditures - percent of GDP: 1.9% (2003)

Transnational Issues

Disputes - international: Norway asserts a territorial claim in Antarctica (Queen Maud Land and its continental shelf); despite recent discussions, Russia and Norway continue to dispute their maritime limits in the Barents Sea and Russia's fishing rights beyond Svalbard's territorial limits within the Svalbard Treaty zone

Oman

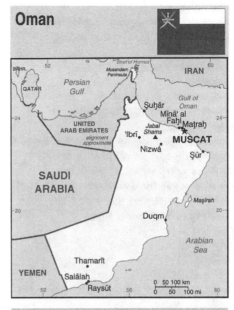

Introduction

Background: In 1970, QABOOS bin Said Al Said ousted his father and has ruled as sultan ever since. His extensive modernization program has opened the country to the outside world and has preserved a long-standing political and military relationship with the UK. Oman's moderate, independent foreign policy has sought to maintain good relations with all Middle Eastern countries.

Geography

Location: Middle East, bordering the Arabian Sea, Gulf of Oman, and Persian Gulf, between Yemen and UAE
Geographic coordinates: 21 00 N, 57 00 E
Map references: Middle East
Area:
total: 212,460 sq km
land: 212,460 sq km
water: 0 sq km
Area - comparative: slightly smaller than Kansas
Land boundaries:
total: 1,374 km
border countries: Saudi Arabia 676 km, UAE 410 km, Yemen 288 km
Coastline: 2,092 km
Maritime claims:
territorial sea: 12 NM
contiguous zone: 24 NM
exclusive economic zone: 200 NM
Climate: dry desert; hot, humid along coast; hot, dry interior; strong southwest summer monsoon (May to September) in far south
Terrain: central desert plain, rugged mountains in north and south
Elevation extremes:
lowest point: Arabian Sea 0 m
highest point: Jabal Shams 2,980 m

Natural resources: petroleum, copper, asbestos, some marble, limestone, chromium, gypsum, natural gas
Land use:
arable land: 0.08%
permanent crops: 0.22%
other: 99.7% (1998 est.)
Irrigated land: 620 sq km (1998 est.)
Natural hazards: summer winds often raise large sandstorms and dust storms in interior; periodic droughts
Environment - current issues: rising soil salinity; beach pollution from oil spills; very limited natural fresh water resources
Environment - international agreements:
party to: Biodiversity, Climate Change, Desertification, Hazardous Wastes, Law of the Sea, Marine Dumping, Ozone Layer Protection, Ship Pollution, Whaling
signed, but not ratified: none of the selected agreements
Geography - note: strategic location on Musandam Peninsula adjacent to Strait of Hormuz, a vital transit point for world crude oil

People

Population: 2,903,165
note: includes 577,293 non-nationals (July 2004 est.)
Age structure:
0-14 years: 42.4% (male 628,078; female 603,829)
15-64 years: 55.1% (male 955,765; female 643,687)
65 years and over: 2.5% (male 38,761; female 33,045) (2004 est.)
Median age:
total: 19.3 years
male: 22.1 years
female: 16.4 years (2004 est.)
Population growth rate: 3.35% (2004 est.)
Birth rate: 37.12 births/1,000 population (2004 est.)
Death rate: 3.91 deaths/1,000 population (2004 est.)
Net migration rate: 0.28 migrant(s)/1,000 population (2004 est.)
Sex ratio:
at birth: 1.05 male(s)/female
under 15 years: 1.04 male(s)/female
15-64 years: 1.49 male(s)/female
65 years and over: 1.17 male(s)/female
total population: 1.27 male(s)/female (2004 est.)
Infant mortality rate:
total: 20.26 deaths/1,000 live births
male: 23.18 deaths/1,000 live births
female: 17.19 deaths/1,000 live births (2004 est.)
Life expectancy at birth:
total population: 72.85 years
male: 70.66 years
female: 75.16 years (2004 est.)
Total fertility rate: 5.9 children born/woman (2004 est.)
HIV/AIDS - adult prevalence rate: 0.1% (2001 est.)
HIV/AIDS - people living with HIV/AIDS: 1,300 (2001 est.)

Oman (continued)

HIV/AIDS - deaths: NA

Nationality:

noun: Omani(s)

adjective: Omani

Ethnic groups: Arab, Baluchi, South Asian (Indian, Pakistani, Sri Lankan, Bangladeshi), African

Religions: Ibadhi Muslim 75%, Sunni Muslim, Shi'a Muslim, Hindu

Languages: Arabic (official), English, Baluchi, Urdu, Indian dialects

Literacy:

definition: NA

total population: 75.8%

male: 83.1%

female: 67.2% (2003 est.)

Government

Country name:

conventional long form: Sultanate of Oman

conventional short form: Oman

local long form: Saltanat Uman

local short form: Uman

former: Muscat and Oman

Government type: monarchy

Capital: Muscat

Administrative divisions: 6 regions (mintaqat, singular - mintaqah) and 2 governorates* (muhafazat, singular - muhafazah) Ad Dakhiliyah, Al Batinah, Al Wusta, Ash Sharqiyah, Az Zahirah, Masqat, Musandam*, Zufar*; note - the US Embassy in Oman reports that Masqat is a governorate, but this has not been confirmed by the US Board on Geographic Names (BGN)

Independence: 1650 (expulsion of the Portuguese)

National holiday: Birthday of Sultan QABOOS, 18 November (1940)

Constitution: none; note - on 6 November 1996, Sultan QABOOS issued a royal decree promulgating a new basic law which, among other things, clarifies the royal succession, provides for a prime minister, bars ministers from holding interests in companies doing business with the government, establishes a bicameral legislature, and guarantees basic civil liberties for Omani citizens

Legal system: based on English common law and Islamic law; ultimate appeal to the monarch; has not accepted compulsory ICJ jurisdiction

Suffrage: in Oman's most recent elections in 2000, limited to approximately 175,000 Omanis chosen by the government to vote in elections for the Majlis al-Shura

Executive branch:

chief of state: Sultan and Prime Minister QABOOS bin Said Al Said (since 23 July 1970); note - the monarch is both the chief of state and head of government

head of government: Sultan and Prime Minister QABOOS bin Said Al Said (since 23 July 1970); note - the monarch is both the chief of state and head of government

cabinet: Cabinet appointed by the monarch

elections: none; the monarch is hereditary

Legislative branch: bicameral Majlis Oman consists of an upper chamber or Majlis al-Dawla (48 seats; members appointed by the monarch; has advisory powers only) and a lower chamber or Majlis al-Shura (83 seats; members elected by limited suffrage for three-year term, however, the monarch makes final selections and can negate election results; body has some limited power to propose legislation, but otherwise has only advisory powers)

elections: last held 4 October 2003 (next to be held NA 2006)

election results: NA

Judicial branch: Supreme Court

note: the nascent civil court system, administered by region, has non-Islamic judges as well as traditional Islamic judges

Political parties and leaders: none

Political pressure groups and leaders: none

International organization participation: ABEDA, AFESD, AMF, FAO, G-77, GCC, IBRD, ICAO, ICCt (signatory), IDA, IDB, IFAD, IFC, IHO, ILO, IMF, IMO, Interpol, IOC, ISO, ITU, LAS, NAM, OIC, OPCW, UN, UNCTAD, UNESCO, UNIDO, UPU, WCO, WFTU, WHO, WIPO, WMO, WTrO

Diplomatic representation in the US:

chief of mission: Ambassador Muhammad bin Ali bin Thani AL-KHUSSAIBY

chancery: 2535 Belmont Road, NW, Washington, DC 20008

telephone: [1] (202) 387-1980 through 1981, 1988

FAX: [1] (202) 745-4933

Diplomatic representation from the US:

chief of mission: Ambassador Richard Lewis BALTIMORE III

embassy: Jameat A'Duwal Al Arabiya Street, Al Khuwair area, Muscat

mailing address: P. O. Box 202, P.C. 115, Madinat Al-Sultan Qaboos, Muscat

telephone: [968] 698989, extension 203

FAX: [968] 699771

Flag description: three horizontal bands of white, red, and green of equal width with a broad, vertical, red band on the hoist side; the national emblem (a khanjar dagger in its sheath superimposed on two crossed swords in scabbards) in white is centered near the top of the vertical band

Economy

Economy - overview: Oman is a well-off middle Eastern economy with large oil and gas resources, a substantial trade surplus, and low inflation. The government is moving ahead with privatization of its utilities, the development of a body of commercial law to facilitate foreign investment, and increased budgetary outlays. Oman continues to liberalize its markets and joined the World Trade Organization (WTrO) in November 2000. In order to reduce unemployment, the government is trying to replace expatriate workers with local workers. Other economic objectives are diversification of the economy and further privatization.

GDP: purchasing power parity - $37.5 billion (2003 est.)

GDP - real growth rate: 3.3% (2003 est.)

GDP - per capita: purchasing power parity - $13,400 (2003 est.)

GDP - composition by sector:

agriculture: 2.1%

industry: 53.4%

services: 44.5% (2002 est.)

Population below poverty line: NA%

Household income or consumption by percentage share:

lowest 10%: NA%

highest 10%: NA%

Inflation rate (consumer prices): 0.3% (2003 est.)

Labor force: 920,000 (2002 est.)

Labor force - by occupation: agriculture NA%, industry NA%, services NA%

Unemployment rate: NA%

Budget:

revenues: $9.2 billion

expenditures: $6.9 billion, including capital expenditures of $NA (2000 est.)

Industries: crude oil production and refining, natural gas production, construction, cement, copper

Industrial production growth rate: 4% (2000 est.)

Electricity - production: 9.274 billion kWh (2001)

Electricity - production by source:

fossil fuel: 100%

hydro: 0%

nuclear: 0%

other: 0% (2001)

Electricity - consumption: 8.625 billion kWh (2001)

Electricity - exports: 0 kWh (2001)

Electricity - imports: 0 kWh (2001)

Oil - production: 963,800 bbl/day (2001 est.)

Oil - consumption: 53,000 bbl/day (2001 est.)

Oil - exports: NA

Oil - imports: NA

Oil - proved reserves: 5.703 billion bbl (1 January 2002)

Natural gas - production: 13.77 billion cu m (2001 est.)

Natural gas - consumption: 6.34 billion cu m (2001 est.)

Natural gas - exports: 7.43 billion cu m (2001 est.)

Natural gas - imports: 0 cu m (2001 est.)

Natural gas - proved reserves: 846.4 billion cu m (1 January 2002)

Agriculture - products: dates, limes, bananas, alfalfa, vegetables; camels, cattle; fish

Exports: $11.7 billion f.o.b. (2003 est.)

Exports - commodities: petroleum, reexports, fish, metals, textiles

Exports - partners: Japan 22.1%, South Korea 19.9%, China 15.2%, Thailand 12.6%, Taiwan 5.5%, Singapore 4.7%, US 4.4% (2002)

Imports: $5.659 billion f.o.b. (2003 est.)

Imports - commodities: machinery and transport equipment, manufactured goods, food, livestock, lubricants

Oman (continued)

Imports - partners: UAE 27.6%, Japan 16.7%, UK 7.4%, US 6.9%, Germany 5% (2002)
Debt - external: $5.8 billion (2003 est.)
Economic aid - recipient: $76.4 million (1995)
Currency: Omani rial (OMR)
Currency code: OMR
Exchange rates: Omani rials per US dollar - 0.3845 (2003), 0.3845 (2002), 0.3845 (2001), 0.3845 (2000), 0.3845 (1999)
Fiscal year: calendar year

Communications

Telephones - main lines in use: 227,600 (2002)
Telephones - mobile cellular: 464,900 (2002)
Telephone system:
general assessment: modern system consisting of open-wire, microwave, and radiotelephone communication stations; limited coaxial cable
domestic: open-wire, microwave, radiotelephone communications, and a domestic satellite system with 8 earth stations
international: country code - 968; satellite earth stations - 2 Intelsat (Indian Ocean) and 1 Arabsat
Radio broadcast stations: AM 3, FM 9, shortwave 2 (1999)
Television broadcast stations: 13 (plus 25 low-power repeaters) (1999)
Internet country code: .om
Internet hosts: 676 (2002)
Internet users: 180,000 (2002)

Transportation

Railways: 0 km
Highways:
total: 34,965 km
paved: 9,673 km (including 550 km of expressways)
unpaved: 25,292 km (2001)
Waterways: none
Pipelines: gas 3,599 km; oil 3,187 km (2003)
Ports and harbors: Matrah, Mina' al Fahl, Mina' Raysut
Merchant marine:
total: 2 ships (1,000 GRT or over) 15,430 GRT/6,360 DWT
by type: passenger 2
registered in other countries: 1 (2003 est.)
Airports: 135 (2003 est.)
Airports - with paved runways:
total: 6
over 3,047 m: 4
2,438 to 3,047 m: 1
914 to 1,523 m: 1 (2003 est.)
Airports - with unpaved runways:
total: 129
over 3,047 m: 2
2,438 to 3,047 m: 6
1,524 to 2,437 m: 52
914 to 1,523 m: 34
under 914 m: 35 (2003 est.)
Heliports: 1 (2003 est.)

Military

Military branches: Royal Omani Armed Forces: Army, Navy, Air Force
Military manpower - military age: 14 years of age (2004 est.)
Military manpower - availability:
males age 15-49: 796,792 (2004 est.)
Military manpower - fit for military service:
males age 15-49: 443,006 (2004 est.)
Military manpower - reaching military age annually:
males: 31,274 (2004 est.)
Military expenditures - dollar figure: $242.07 million (2003)
Military expenditures - percent of GDP: 11.4% (2003)

Transnational Issues

Disputes - international: boundary agreement signed and ratified with UAE in 2003 for entire border, including Oman's Musandam Peninsula and Al Madhah enclaves

Pacific Ocean

Introduction

Background: The Pacific Ocean is the largest of the world's five oceans (followed by the Atlantic Ocean, Indian Ocean, Southern Ocean, and Arctic Ocean). Strategically important access waterways include the La Perouse, Tsugaru, Tsushima, Taiwan, Singapore, and Torres Straits. The decision by the International Hydrographic Organization in the spring of 2000 to delimit a fifth ocean, the Southern Ocean, removed the portion of the Pacific Ocean south of 60 degrees south.

Geography

Location: body of water between the Southern Ocean, Asia, Australia, and the Western Hemisphere
Geographic coordinates: 0 00 N, 160 00 W
Map references: Political Map of the World
Area:
total: 155.557 million sq km
note: includes Bali Sea, Bering Sea, Bering Strait, Coral Sea, East China Sea, Gulf of Alaska, Gulf of Tonkin, Philippine Sea, Sea of Japan, Sea of Okhotsk, South China Sea, Tasman Sea, and other tributary water bodies
Area - comparative: about 15 times the size of the US; covers about 28% of the global surface; larger than the total land area of the world
Coastline: 135,663 km
Climate: planetary air pressure systems and resultant wind patterns exhibit remarkable uniformity in the south and east; trade winds and westerly winds are well-developed patterns, modified by seasonal fluctuations; tropical cyclones (hurricanes) may form south of Mexico from June to October and affect Mexico and Central America; continental influences cause climatic uniformity to be much less pronounced in the eastern and western regions at the same latitude in the North Pacific Ocean; the western Pacific is monsoonal - a rainy season occurs during the summer months, when moisture-laden winds blow

Pacific Ocean *(continued)*

from the ocean over the land, and a dry season during the winter months, when dry winds blow from the Asian landmass back to the ocean; tropical cyclones (typhoons) may strike southeast and east Asia from May to December

Terrain: surface currents in the northern Pacific are dominated by a clockwise, warm-water gyre (broad circular system of currents) and in the southern Pacific by a counterclockwise, cool-water gyre; in the northern Pacific, sea ice forms in the Bering Sea and Sea of Okhotsk in winter; in the southern Pacific, sea ice from Antarctica reaches its northernmost extent in October; the ocean floor in the eastern Pacific is dominated by the East Pacific Rise, while the western Pacific is dissected by deep trenches, including the Mariana Trench, which is the world's deepest

Elevation extremes:
lowest point: Challenger Deep in the Mariana Trench -10,924 m
highest point: sea level 0 m

Natural resources: oil and gas fields, polymetallic nodules, sand and gravel aggregates, placer deposits, fish

Natural hazards: surrounded by a zone of violent volcanic and earthquake activity sometimes referred to as the "Pacific Ring of Fire"; subject to tropical cyclones (typhoons) in southeast and east Asia from May to December (most frequent from July to October); tropical cyclones (hurricanes) may form south of Mexico and strike Central America and Mexico from June to October (most common in August and September); cyclical El Nino/La Nina phenomenon occurs in the equatorial Pacific, influencing weather in the Western Hemisphere and the western Pacific; ships subject to superstructure icing in extreme north from October to May; persistent fog in the northern Pacific can be a maritime hazard from June to December

Environment - current issues: endangered marine species include the dugong, sea lion, sea otter, seals, turtles, and whales; oil pollution in Philippine Sea and South China Sea

Geography - note: the major chokepoints are the Bering Strait, Panama Canal, Luzon Strait, and the Singapore Strait; the Equator divides the Pacific Ocean into the North Pacific Ocean and the South Pacific Ocean; dotted with low coral islands and rugged volcanic islands in the southwestern Pacific Ocean

Economy

Economy - overview: The Pacific Ocean is a major contributor to the world economy and particularly to those nations its waters directly touch. It provides low-cost sea transportation between East and West, extensive fishing grounds, offshore oil and gas fields, minerals, and sand and gravel for the construction industry. In 1996, over 60% of the world's fish catch came from the Pacific Ocean. Exploitation of offshore oil and gas reserves is playing an ever-increasing role in the energy supplies of the US, Australia, NZ, China,

and Peru. The high cost of recovering offshore oil and gas, combined with the wide swings in world prices for oil since 1985, has led to fluctuations in new drillings.

Transportation

Ports and harbors: Bangkok (Thailand), Hong Kong, Kao-hsiung (Taiwan), Los Angeles (US), Manila (Philippines), Pusan (South Korea), San Francisco (US), Seattle (US), Shanghai (China), Singapore, Sydney (Australia), Vladivostok (Russia), Wellington (NZ), Yokohama (Japan)

Transportation - note: Inside Passage offers protected waters from southeast Alaska to Puget Sound (Washington state)

Transnational Issues

Disputes - international: some maritime disputes (see littoral states)

Pakistan

Introduction

Background: The separation in 1947 of British India into the Muslim state of Pakistan (with two sections West and East) and largely Hindu India was never satisfactorily resolved. A third war between these countries in 1971 resulted in East Pakistan seceding and becoming the separate nation of Bangladesh. In response to Indian nuclear weapons testing, Pakistan conducted its own tests in 1998. The dispute over the state of Kashmir is ongoing, but recent discussions and confidence-building measures may be a start toward lessened tensions.

Geography

Location: Southern Asia, bordering the Arabian Sea, between India on the east and Iran and Afghanistan on the west and China in the north

Geographic coordinates: 30 00 N, 70 00 E

Map references: Asia

Area:
total: 803,940 sq km
land: 778,720 sq km
water: 25,220 sq km

Area - comparative: slightly less than twice the size of California

Land boundaries:
total: 6,774 km
border countries: Afghanistan 2,430 km, China 523 km, India 2,912 km, Iran 909 km

Coastline: 1,046 km

Maritime claims:
territorial sea: 12 NM
contiguous zone: 24 NM
exclusive economic zone: 200 NM
continental shelf: 200 NM or to the edge of the continental margin

Climate: mostly hot, dry desert; temperate in northwest; arctic in north

Pakistan (continued)

Terrain: flat Indus plain in east; mountains in north and northwest; Balochistan plateau in west

Elevation extremes:
lowest point: Indian Ocean 0 m
highest point: K2 (Mt. Godwin-Austen) 8,611 m

Natural resources: land, extensive natural gas reserves, limited petroleum, poor quality coal, iron ore, copper, salt, limestone

Land use:
arable land: 27.81%
permanent crops: 0.79%
other: 71.4% (1998 est.)

Irrigated land: 180,000 sq km (1998 est.)

Natural hazards: frequent earthquakes, occasionally severe especially in north and west; flooding along the Indus after heavy rains (July and August)

Environment - current issues: water pollution from raw sewage, industrial wastes, and agricultural runoff; limited natural fresh water resources; a majority of the population does not have access to potable water; deforestation; soil erosion; desertification

Environment - international agreements:
party to: Biodiversity, Climate Change, Desertification, Endangered Species, Environmental Modification, Hazardous Wastes, Law of the Sea, Marine Dumping, Ozone Layer Protection, Ship Pollution, Wetlands
signed, but not ratified: Marine Life Conservation

Geography - note: controls Khyber Pass and Bolan Pass, traditional invasion routes between Central Asia and the Indian Subcontinent

People

Population: 159,196,336 (July 2004 est.)

Age structure:
0-14 years: 40.2% (male 32,919,441; female 31,058,929)
15-64 years: 55.8% (male 45,381,469; female 43,377,613)
65 years and over: 4.1% (male 3,123,594; female 3,335,290) (2004 est.)

Median age:
total: 19.4 years
male: 19.2 years
female: 19.5 years (2004 est.)

Population growth rate: 1.98% (2004 est.)

Birth rate: 31.22 births/1,000 population (2004 est.)

Death rate: 8.67 deaths/1,000 population (2004 est.)

Net migration rate: -2.77 migrant(s)/1,000 population (2004 est.)

Sex ratio:
at birth: 1.05 male(s)/female
under 15 years: 1.06 male(s)/female
15-64 years: 1.05 male(s)/female
65 years and over: 0.94 male(s)/female
total population: 1.05 male(s)/female (2004 est.)

Infant mortality rate:
total: 74.43 deaths/1,000 live births
male: 74.84 deaths/1,000 live births
female: 74 deaths/1,000 live births (2004 est.)

Life expectancy at birth:
total population: 62.61 years
male: 61.69 years
female: 63.58 years (2004 est.)

Total fertility rate: 4.29 children born/woman (2004 est.)

HIV/AIDS - adult prevalence rate: 0.1% (2001 est.)

HIV/AIDS - people living with HIV/AIDS: 78,000 (2001 est.)

HIV/AIDS - deaths: 4,500 (2001 est.)

Nationality:
noun: Pakistani(s)
adjective: Pakistani

Ethnic groups: Punjabi, Sindhi, Pashtun (Pathan), Baloch, Muhajir (immigrants from India at the time of partition and their descendants)

Religions: Muslim 97% (Sunni 77%, Shi'a 20%), Christian, Hindu, and other 3%

Languages: Punjabi 48%, Sindhi 12%, Siraiki (a Punjabi variant) 10%, Pashtu 8%, Urdu (official) 8%, Balochi 3%, Hindko 2%, Brahui 1%, English (official and lingua franca of Pakistani elite and most government ministries), Burushaski, and other 8%

Literacy:
definition: age 15 and over can read and write
total population: 45.7%
male: 59.8%
female: 30.6% (2003 est.)

Government

Country name:
conventional long form: Islamic Republic of Pakistan
conventional short form: Pakistan
former: West Pakistan

Government type: federal republic

Capital: Islamabad

Administrative divisions: 4 provinces, 1 territory*, and 1 capital territory**; Balochistan, Federally Administered Tribal Areas*, Islamabad Capital Territory**, North-West Frontier Province, Punjab, Sindh
note: the Pakistani-administered portion of the disputed Jammu and Kashmir region includes Azad Kashmir and the Northern Areas

Independence: 14 August 1947 (from UK)

National holiday: Republic Day, 23 March (1956)

Constitution: 10 April 1973, suspended 5 July 1977, restored with amendments 30 December 1985; suspended 15 October 1999, restored 31 December 2002

Legal system: based on English common law with provisions to accommodate Pakistan's status as an Islamic state; accepts compulsory ICJ jurisdiction, with reservations

Suffrage: 18 years of age; universal; joint electorates and reserved parliamentary seats for women and non-Muslims

Executive branch:
note: following a military takeover on 12 October 1999, Chief of Army Staff and Chairman of the Joint Chiefs of Staff Committee, General Pervez MUSHARRAF, suspended Pakistan's constitution and assumed the additional title of Chief Executive; on 12 May 2000, Pakistan's Supreme Court unanimously validated the October 1999 coup and granted MUSHARRAF executive and legislative authority for three years from the coup date; on 20 June 2001, MUSHARRAF named himself as president and was sworn in, replacing Mohammad Rafiq TARAR; in a referendum held on 30 April 2002, MUSHARRAF's presidency was extended by five more years; on 1 January 2004, MUSHARRAF won a vote of confidence in the Senate, National Assembly, and four provincial assemblies
chief of state: President Pervez MUSHARRAF (since 20 June 2001)
head of government: Prime Minister Mir Zafarullah Khan JAMALI (since 23 November 2002)
cabinet: Cabinet appointed by the Prime Minister
elections: the president is elected by Parliament for a five-year term; note - in a referendum held on 30 April 2002, MUSHARRAF's presidency was extended by five more years (next to be held NA 2007); the prime minister is selected by the National Assembly for a five-year term (next to be held NA 2007)
election results: results are for the 10 October 2002 election for prime minister - Mir Zafarullah Khan JAMALI elected prime minister

Legislative branch: bicameral Parliament or Majlis-e-Shoora consists of the Senate (100 seats - formerly 87; members indirectly elected by provincial assemblies to serve four-year terms; and the National Assembly (342 seats - formerly 217; 60 seats represent women; 10 seats represent minorities; members elected by popular vote to serve four-year terms)
elections: Senate - last held 24 and 27 February 2003 (next to be held by February 2007); National Assembly - last held 10 October 2002 (next to be held by October 2006)
election results: Senate results - percent of vote by party - NA%; seats by party - PML/Q 40, PPPP 11, MMA 21, MQM/A 6, PML/N 4, NA 3, PML/F 1, PkMAP 2, ANP 2, PPP/S 2, JWP 1, BNP-Awami 1, BNP-Mengal 1, BNM/H 1, independents 4; National Assembly results - percent of votes by party - NA%; seats by party - PML/Q 126, PPPP 81, MMA 63, PML/N 19, MQM/A 17, NA 16, PML/F 5, PML/J 3, PPP/S 2, BNP 1, JWP 1, PAT 1, PML/Z 1, PTI 1, MQM/H 1, PkMAP 1, independents 3

Judicial branch: Supreme Court (justices appointed by the president); Federal Islamic or Shari'a Court

Political parties and leaders: Awami National Party or ANP [Wali KHAN]; Balochistan National Movement/Hayee Group or BNM/H [Dr. Hayee BALUCH]; Baluch National Party or BNP [Sardar Akhtar MENGAL]; Baluch National Party/Awami or BNP/Awami [Moheem Khan BALOCH]; Jamhoori Watan Party or JWP [Akbar Khan BUGTI]; Jamiat-al-Hadith or JAH [Sajid MIR]; Jamiat Ulema-i-Islam, Fazlur Rehman faction or JUI/F [Fazlur REHMAN]; Jamiat Ulema-i-Islam, Sami ul-HAQ faction or JUI/S [Sami ul-HAQ]; Jamiat-i-Islami or JI [Qazi Hussain AHMED]; Jamiat Ulema-i-Pakistan, Noorani faction or JUP/NO

Pakistan *(continued)*

leader NA]; Millat Party or MP [Farooq LEGHARI]; Muttahida Qaumi Movement, Altaf faction or MQM/A [Altaf HUSSAIN]; Muhajir Quami Movement, Haqiqi faction or MQM/H [Afaq AHMAD]; Muttahida Majlis-e-Amal Pakistan or MMA [leader NA]; National Alliance or NA [Farooq Ahmad Khan LEGHARI]; National People's Party or NPP [Ghulam Mustapha JATOI]; Pakhtun Khwa Milli Awami Party or PkMAP [Mahmood Khan ACHAKZAI]; Pakhtun Quami Party or PQP [Mohammed Afzal KHAN]; Pakistan Awami Tehrik or PAT [Tahir ul QADRI]; Pakistan Democratic Party or PDP [Mehbooba Mufti SAYEED]; Pakistan Muslim League, Functional Group or PML/F [Pir PAGARO]; Pakistan Muslim League, Junejo faction or PML/J [Hamid Nasir CHATTHA]; Pakistan Muslim League, Nawaz Sharif faction or PML/N [Nawaz SHARIF]; Pakistan Muslim League, Quaid-I-Azam faction or PML/Q [Chaudhry Shujjat HUSSAIN]; Pakistan Muslim League, Zia-ul-HAQ or PML/Z [Ejaz ul-Haq]; Pakistan National Party or PNP [Hasil BIZENJO]; Pakistan People's Party or PPP [Benazir BHUTTO]; Pakistan People's Party/Sherpao or PPP/S [Aftab Ahmed Khan SHERPAO]; Pakistan People's Party/Shaheed Bhutto or PPP/SB [Ghinva BHUTTO]; Pakistan People's Party Parliamentarians or PPPP [Amin FAHIM]; Pakistan Tehrik-e-Insaaf or PTI [Imran KHAN]; Tehrik-i-Islami [Allama Sajid NAQVI]
note: political alliances in Pakistan can shift frequently

Political pressure groups and leaders: military remains most important political force; ulema (clergy), landowners, industrialists, and small merchants also influential

International organization participation: AsDB, C (suspended), CP, ECO, FAO, G-24, G-77, IAEA, IBRD, ICAO, ICC, ICFTU, ICRM, IDA, IDB, IFAD, IFC, IFRCS, IHO, ILO, IMF, IMO, Interpol, IOC, IOM, ISO, ITU, MINURSO, MONUC, NAM, OAS (observer), OIC, OPCW, PCA, SAARC, UN, UN Security Council (temporary), UNAMSIL, UNCTAD, UNESCO, UNHCR, UNIDO, UNITAR, UNMIK, UNMIL, UNMISET, UNOMIG, UPU, WCL, WCO, WFTU, WHO, WIPO, WMO, WToO, WTrO

Diplomatic representation in the US:
chief of mission: Ambassador Ashraf Jehangir QAZI
chancery: 3517 International Court, Washington, DC 20008
telephone: [1] (202) 243-3277
FAX: [1] (202) 686-1534
consulate(s) general: Los Angeles, New York, and Boston

Diplomatic representation from the US:
chief of mission: Ambassador Nancy J. POWELL
embassy: Diplomatic Enclave, Ramna 5, Islamabad
mailing address: P. O. Box 1048, Unit 62200, APO AE 09812-2200
telephone: [92] (51) 2080-0000
FAX: [92] (51) 2276427
consulate(s): Karachi, Lahore, Peshawar

Flag description: green with a vertical white band (symbolizing the role of religious minorities) on the hoist side; a large white crescent and star are centered in the green field; the crescent, star, and color green are traditional symbols of Islam

Economy

Economy - overview: Pakistan, an impoverished and underdeveloped country, has suffered from decades of internal political disputes, low levels of foreign investment, and a costly, ongoing confrontation with neighboring India. However, IMF-approved government policies, bolstered by generous foreign assistance and renewed access to global markets since late 2001, have generated solid macroeconomic recovery the last two years. The government has made substantial inroads in macroeconomic reform since 2000, although progress on more politically sensitive reforms has slowed. For example, in the third and final year of its $1.3 billion IMF Poverty Reduction and Growth Facility, Islamabad has continued to require waivers for energy sector reforms. While long-term prospects remain uncertain, given Pakistan's low level of development, medium-term prospects for job creation and poverty reduction are the best in nearly a decade. Islamabad has raised development spending from about 2% of GDP in the 1990s to 4% in 2003, a necessary step towards reversing the broad underdevelopment of its social sector. GDP growth is heavily dependent on rain-fed crops, and last year's end to a four-year drought should support moderate agricultural growth for the next few years. Foreign exchange reserves continued to reach new levels in 2003, supported by robust export growth and steady worker remittances.
GDP: purchasing power parity - $317.7 billion (2003 est.)
GDP - real growth rate: 5.4% (2003 est.)
GDP - per capita: purchasing power parity - $2,100 (2003 est.)
GDP - composition by sector:
agriculture: 23.6%
industry: 25.1%
services: 51.3% (2003 est.)
Population below poverty line: 35% (2001 est.)
Household income or consumption by percentage share:
lowest 10%: 4.1%
highest 10%: 27.6% (FY96/97)
Distribution of family income - Gini index: 41 (FY98/99)
Inflation rate (consumer prices): 3.1% (FY02/03 est.)
Labor force: 40.4 million
note: extensive export of labor, mostly to the Middle East, and use of child labor (2000)
Labor force - by occupation: agriculture 44%, industry 17%, services 39% (1999 est.)
Unemployment rate: 7.7% plus substantial underemployment (2003 est.)
Budget:
revenues: $12.2 billion
expenditures: $12.3 billion, including capital expenditures of $NA (FY02/03 est.)
Industries: textiles and apparel, food processing, pharmaceuticals, construction materials, paper products, fertilizer, shrimp

Industrial production growth rate: 5.4% (FY02/03 est.)
Electricity - production: 66.96 billion kWh (2001)
Electricity - production by source:
fossil fuel: 68.8%
hydro: 28.2%
nuclear: 3%
other: 0% (2001)
Electricity - consumption: 62.27 billion kWh (2001)
Electricity - exports: 0 kWh (2001)
Electricity - imports: 0 kWh (2001)
Oil - production: 62,870 bbl/day (2001 est.)
Oil - consumption: 365,000 bbl/day (2001 est.)
Oil - exports: NA
Oil - imports: NA
Oil - proved reserves: 297.1 million bbl (1 January 2002)
Natural gas - production: 23.4 billion cu m (2001 est.)
Natural gas - consumption: 23.4 billion cu m (2001 est.)
Natural gas - exports: 0 cu m NA (2001 est.)
Natural gas - imports: 0 cu m (2001 est.)
Natural gas - proved reserves: 695.6 billion cu m (1 January 2002)
Agriculture - products: cotton, wheat, rice, sugarcane, fruits, vegetables; milk, beef, mutton, eggs
Exports: $11.7 billion f.o.b. (2003 est.)
Exports - commodities: textiles (garments, bed linen, cotton cloth, and yarn), rice, leather goods, sports goods, chemicals, manufactures, carpets and rugs
Exports - partners: US 24.5%, UAE 8.5%, UK 7.2%, Germany 4.9%, Hong Kong 4.8% (2002)
Imports: $12.51 billion f.o.b. (2003 est.)
Imports - commodities: petroleum, petroleum products, machinery, plastics, transportation equipment, edible oils, paper and paperboard, iron and steel, tea
Imports - partners: UAE 11.7%, Saudi Arabia 11.7%, Kuwait 6.7%, US 6.4%, China 6.2%, Japan 6%, Malaysia 4.5%, Germany 4.4% (2002)
Debt - external: $33.2 billion (2003 est.)
Economic aid - recipient: $2.4 billion (FY01/02)
Currency: Pakistani rupee (PKR)
Currency code: PKR
Exchange rates: Pakistani rupees per US dollar - 57.752 (2003), 59.7238 (2002), 61.9272 (2001), 53.6482 (2000), 49.1183 (1999)
Fiscal year: 1 July - 30 June

Communications

Telephones - main lines in use: 3.655 million (2002)
Telephones - mobile cellular: 1,238,600 (2002)
Telephone system:
general assessment: the domestic system is mediocre, but improving; service is adequate for government and business use, in part because major businesses have established their own private systems; since 1988, the government has promoted investment in the national telecommunications system

on a priority basis, significantly increasing network capacity; despite major improvements in trunk and urban systems, telecommunication services are still not readily available to the majority of the rural population
domestic: microwave radio relay, coaxial cable, fiber-optic cable, cellular, and satellite networks
international: country code - 92; satellite earth stations - 3 Intelsat (1 Atlantic Ocean and 2 Indian Ocean); 3 operational international gateway exchanges (1 at Karachi and 2 at Islamabad); microwave radio relay to neighboring countries (1999)
Radio broadcast stations: AM 27, FM 1, shortwave 21 (1998)
Television broadcast stations: 22 (plus seven low-power repeaters) (1997)
Internet country code: .pk
Internet hosts: 12,707 (2002)
Internet users: 1.5 million (2002)

Transportation

Railways:
total: 8,163 km
broad gauge: 7,718 km 1.676-m gauge (293 km electrified)
narrow gauge: 445 km 1.000-m gauge (2002)
Highways:
total: 254,410 km
paved: 109,396 km (including 339 km of expressways)
unpaved: 145,014 km (1999)
Waterways: none
Pipelines: gas 9,945 km; oil 1,821 km (2003)
Ports and harbors: Karachi, Port Muhammad bin Qasim
Merchant marine:
total: 17 ships (1,000 GRT or over) 329,486 GRT/ 512,506 DWT
by type: cargo 11, container 2, petroleum tanker 4
registered in other countries: 16 (2003 est.)
Airports: 129 (2003 est.)
Airports - with paved runways:
total: 91
over 3,047 m: 14
2,438 to 3,047 m: 22
1,524 to 2,437 m: 33
914 to 1,523 m: 18
under 914 m: 4 (2003 est.)
Airports - with unpaved runways:
total: 38
over 3,047 m: 1
1,524 to 2,437 m: 8
914 to 1,523 m: 10
under 914 m: 19 (2003 est.)
Heliports: 15 (2003 est.)

Military

Military branches: Army, Navy, Air Force
Military manpower - military age: 17 years of age (2004 est.)
Military manpower - availability:
males age 15-49: 39,793,586 (2004 est.)

Military manpower - fit for military service:
males age 15-49: 24,355,985 (2004 est.)
Military manpower - reaching military age annually:
males: 1,891,101 (2004 est.)
Military expenditures - dollar figure: $2.7 billion (FY02/03)
Military expenditures - percent of GDP: 3.9% (FY02/03)

Transnational Issues

Disputes - international: Kashmir remains the world's largest and most highly militarized territorial dispute with portions under the de facto administration of China (Aksai Chin), India (Jammu and Kashmir), and Pakistan (Azad Kashmir, and Northern Areas), but recent discussions and confidence-building measures among the parties are beginning to defuse tensions; India does not recognize Pakistan's ceding lands to China in 1965 boundary agreement; disputes with Pakistan over Indus River water sharing and the terminus of the Sir Creek Estuary at the mouth of the Rann of Kutch, which prevents maritime boundary delimitation; Pakistani maps continue to show Junagadh claim in India's Gujarat State; despite largely successful UN efforts at voluntary repatriation, thousands of Afghan refugees continue to reside in Pakistan; Pakistan has sent troops into remote tribal areas to control the border with Afghanistan to stem organized terrorist and other illegal cross-border activities; regular meetings with Afghan and coalition allies aim to resolve periodic claims of boundary encroachments
Illicit drugs: opium poppy cultivation practically eliminated; key transit point for Southwest Asian heroin bound for Western markets; Afghan narcotics continue to transit Federally Administered Tribal Areas, Balochistan Province, and Karachi; financial crimes related to drug trafficking, terrorism, corruption, and smuggling remain problems

Palau

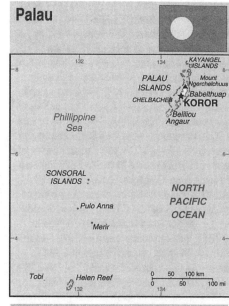

Introduction

Background: After three decades as part of the UN Trust Territory of the Pacific under US administration, this westernmost cluster of the Caroline Islands opted for independence in 1978 rather than join the Federated States of Micronesia. A Compact of Free Association with the US was approved in 1986, but not ratified until 1993. It entered into force the following year, when the islands gained independence.

Geography

Location: Oceania, group of islands in the North Pacific Ocean, southeast of the Philippines
Geographic coordinates: 7 30 N, 134 30 E
Map references: Oceania
Area:
total: 458 sq km
land: 458 sq km
water: 0 sq km
Area - comparative: slightly more than 2.5 times the size of Washington, DC
Land boundaries: 0 km
Coastline: 1,519 km
Maritime claims:
territorial sea: 3 NM
exclusive fishing zone: 12 NM
extended fishing zone: 200 NM
Climate: Tropical; hot and humid; wet season May to November
Terrain: varying geologically from the high, mountainous main island of Babelthuap to low, coral islands usually fringed by large barrier reefs
Elevation extremes:
lowest point: Pacific Ocean 0 m
highest point: Mount Ngerchelchuus 242 m
Natural resources: forests, minerals (especially gold), marine products, deep-seabed minerals
Land use:
arable land: 21.74%

Palau *(continued)*

permanent crops: 0%
other: 78.26% (1998 est.)
Irrigated land: NA sq km
Natural hazards: typhoons (June to December)
Environment - current issues: inadequate facilities for disposal of solid waste; threats to the marine ecosystem from sand and coral dredging, illegal fishing practices, and overfishing
Environment - international agreements:
party to: Biodiversity, Climate Change, Climate Change-Kyoto Protocol, Desertification, Law of the Sea, Ozone Layer Protection
signed, but not ratified: none of the selected agreements
Geography - note: westernmost archipelago in the Caroline chain, consists of six island groups totaling more than 300 islands; includes World War II battleground of Beliliou (Peleliu) and world-famous rock islands

People

Population: 20,016 (July 2004 est.)
Age structure:
0-14 years: 26.6% (male 2,746; female 2,578)
15-64 years: 68.8% (male 7,456; female 6,319)
65 years and over: 4.6% (male 437; female 480) (2004 est.)
Median age:
total: 31.1 years
male: 32.1 years
female: 30 years (2004 est.)
Population growth rate: 1.46% (2004 est.)
Birth rate: 18.69 births/1,000 population (2004 est.)
Death rate: 6.89 deaths/1,000 population (2004 est.)
Net migration rate: 2.85 migrant(s)/1,000 population (2004 est.)
Sex ratio:
at birth: 1.06 male(s)/female
under 15 years: 1.07 male(s)/female
15-64 years: 1.18 male(s)/female
65 years and over: 0.91 male(s)/female
total population: 1.14 male(s)/female (2004 est.)
Infant mortality rate:
total: 15.3 deaths/1,000 live births
male: 17.07 deaths/1,000 live births
female: 13.42 deaths/1,000 live births (2004 est.)
Life expectancy at birth:
total population: 69.82 years
male: 66.67 years
female: 73.15 years (2004 est.)
Total fertility rate: 2.46 children born/woman (2004 est.)
HIV/AIDS - adult prevalence rate: NA%
HIV/AIDS - people living with HIV/AIDS: NA
HIV/AIDS - deaths: NA
Nationality:
noun: Palauan(s)
adjective: Palauan
Ethnic groups: Palauan (Micronesian with Malayan and Melanesian admixtures) 70%, Asian (mainly Filipinos, followed by Chinese, Taiwanese, and Vietnamese) 28%, white 2% (2000 est.)

Religions: Christian (Roman Catholics 49%, Seventh-Day Adventists, Jehovah's Witnesses, the Assembly of God, the Liebenzell Mission, and Latter-Day Saints), Modekngei religion (one-third of the population observes this religion, which is indigenous to Palau)
Languages: English and Palauan official in all states except Sonsoral (Sonsoralese and English are official), Tobi (Tobi and English are official), and Angaur (Angaur, Japanese, and English are official)
Literacy:
definition: age 15 and over can read and write
total population: 92%
male: 93%
female: 90% (1980 est.)

Government

Country name:
conventional long form: Republic of Palau
conventional short form: Palau
local long form: Beluu er a Belau
local short form: Belau
former: Palau District (Trust Territory of the Pacific Islands)
Government type: constitutional government in free association with the US; the Compact of Free Association entered into force 1 October 1994
Capital: Koror; note - a new capital is being built about 20 km northeast of Koror
Administrative divisions: 16 states; Aimeliik, Airai, Angaur, Hatobohei, Kayangel, Koror, Melekeok, Ngaraard, Ngarchelong, Ngardmau, Ngatpang, Ngchesar, Ngeremlengui, Ngiwal, Peleliu, Sonsoral
Independence: 1 October 1994 (from the US-administered UN Trusteeship)
National holiday: Constitution Day, 9 July (1979)
Constitution: 1 January 1981
Legal system: based on Trust Territory laws, acts of the legislature, municipal, common, and customary laws
Suffrage: 18 years of age; universal
Executive branch:
chief of state: President Tommy Esang REMENGESAU, Jr. (since 19 January 2001) and Vice President Sandra PIERANTOZZI (since 19 January 2001); note - the president is both the chief of state and head of government
head of government: President Tommy Esang REMENGESAU, Jr. (since 19 January 2001) and Vice President Sandra PIERANTOZZI (since 19 January 2001); note - the president is both the chief of state and head of government
cabinet: Cabinet
elections: president and vice president elected on separate tickets by popular vote for four-year terms; election last held 7 November 2000 (next to be held NA November 2004)
election results: Tommy Esang REMENGESAU, Jr. elected president; percent of vote - Tommy Esang REMENGESAU, Jr. 53%, Peter SUGIYAMA 46%; Sandra PIERANTOZZI elected vice president; percent of vote - Sandra PIERANTOZZI 52%, Alan SEID 45%

Legislative branch: bicameral Parliament or Olbiil Era Kelulau (OEK) consists of the Senate (9 seats; members elected by popular vote on a population basis to serve four-year terms) and the House of Delegates (16 seats; members elected by popular vote to serve four-year terms)
elections: Senate - last held 7 November 2000 (next to be held NA November 2004); House of Delegates - last held 7 November 2000 (next to be held NA November 2004)
election results: Senate - percent of vote - NA%; seats - independents 9; House of Delegates - percent of vote - NA%; seats - independents 16
Judicial branch: Supreme Court; National Court; Court of Common Pleas
Political parties and leaders: none
Political pressure groups and leaders: NA
International organization participation: ACP, FAO, G-77, IBRD, ICAO, ICRM, IDA, IFC, IFRCS, IMF, IOC, OPCW, PIF, UN, UNCTAD, UNESCO, WHO
Diplomatic representation in the US:
chief of mission: Ambassador Hersey KYOTA
chancery: 1800 K Street NW, Suite 714, Washington, DC 20006
telephone: [1] (202) 452-6814
FAX: [1] (202) 452-6281
consulate(s): Saipan (Northern Mariana Islands)
Diplomatic representation from the US:
chief of mission: the Ambassador to the Philippines is accredited to Palau
embassy: address NA, Koror
mailing address: P. O. Box 6028, Republic of Palau 96940
telephone: [680] 488-2920, 2990
FAX: [680] 488-2911
Flag description: light blue with a large yellow disk (representing the moon) shifted slightly to the hoist side

Economy

Economy - overview: The economy consists primarily of tourism, subsistence agriculture and fishing. The government is the major employer of the work force, relying heavily on financial assistance from the US. Business and tourist arrivals numbered 50,000 in FY00/01. The population enjoys a per capita income twice that of the Philippines and much of Micronesia. Long-run prospects for the key tourist sector have been greatly bolstered by the expansion of air travel in the Pacific, the rising prosperity of leading East Asian countries, and the willingness of foreigners to finance infrastructure development.
GDP: purchasing power parity - $174 million
note: $174 million GDP estimate includes US subsidy (2001 est.)
GDP - real growth rate: 1% (2001 est.)
GDP - per capita: purchasing power parity - $9,000 (2001 est.)
GDP - composition by sector:
agriculture: NA%
industry: NA%
services: NA%

Palau *(continued)*

Population below poverty line: NA%
Household income or consumption by percentage share:
lowest 10%: NA%
highest 10%: NA%
Inflation rate (consumer prices): 3.4% (2000 est.)
Labor force: 9,845 (2000)
Labor force - by occupation: agriculture 20%, industry NA%, services NA% (1990)
Unemployment rate: 2.3% (2000 est.)
Budget:
revenues: $57.7 million
expenditures: $80.8 million, including capital expenditures of $17.1 million (FY 98/99 est.)
Industries: tourism, craft items (from shell, wood, pearls), construction, garment making
Industrial production growth rate: NA%
Electricity - production by source: NA
Agriculture - products: coconuts, copra, cassava (tapioca), sweet potatoes
Exports: $18 million f.o.b. (2001 est.)
Exports - commodities: shellfish, tuna, copra, garments
Exports - partners: US, Japan, Singapore (2000)
Imports: $99 million f.o.b. (2001 est.)
Imports - commodities: machinery and equipment, fuels, metals; foodstuffs
Imports - partners: US, Guam, Japan, Singapore, Korea (2000)
Debt - external: $0 (FY99/00)
Economic aid - recipient: $155.8 million ; note - the Compact of Free Association with the US, entered into after the end of the UN trusteeship on 1 October 1994, provides Palau with up to $700 million in US aid over 15 years in return for furnishing military facilities
Currency: US dollar (USD)
Currency code: USD
Exchange rates: the US dollar is used
Fiscal year: 1 October - 30 September

Communications

Telephones - main lines in use: 6,700 (2002)
Telephones - mobile cellular: 1,000 (2002)
Telephone system:
general assessment: NA
domestic: NA
international: country code - 680; satellite earth station - 1 Intelsat (Pacific Ocean)
Radio broadcast stations: AM 1, FM 4, shortwave 1 (2002)
Television broadcast stations: 1 (1997)
Internet country code: .pw

Transportation

Railways: 0 km
Highways:
total: 61 km
paved: 36 km
unpaved: 25 km
Waterways: none
Ports and harbors: Koror

Merchant marine: none
Airports: 3 (2003 est.)
Airports - with paved runways:
total: 1
1,524 to 2,437 m: 1 (2003 est.)
Airports - with unpaved runways:
total: 2
1,524 to 2,437 m: 2 (2003 est.)

Military

Military branches: no regular military forces; Police Force
Military expenditures - dollar figure: $NA
Military expenditures - percent of GDP: NA%
Military - note: defense is the responsibility of the US; under a Compact of Free Association between Palau and the US, the US military is granted access to the islands for 50 years

Transnational Issues

Disputes - international: none

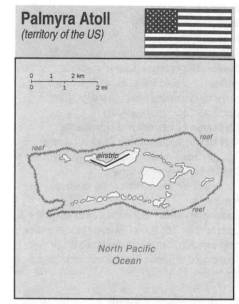

Palmyra Atoll
(territory of the US)

Introduction

Background: The Kingdom of Hawaii claimed the atoll in 1862, and the US included it among the Hawaiian Islands when it annexed the archipelago in 1898. The Hawaii Statehood Act of 1959 did not include Palmyra Atoll, which is now privately owned by the Nature Conservancy. This organization is managing the atoll as a nature preserve. The lagoons and surrounding waters within the 12 nautical mile US territorial seas were transferred to the US Fish and Wildlife Service and were designated a National Wildlife Refuge in January 2001.

Geography

Location: Oceania, atoll in the North Pacific Ocean, about half way between Hawaii and American Samoa
Geographic coordinates: 5 52 N, 162 06 W
Map references: Oceania
Area:
total: 11.9 sq km
land: 11.9 sq km
water: 0 sq km
Area - comparative: about 20 times the size of The Mall in Washington, DC
Land boundaries: 0 km
Coastline: 14.5 km
Maritime claims:
territorial sea: 12 NM
exclusive economic zone: 200 NM
Climate: equatorial, hot, and very rainy
Terrain: very low
Elevation extremes:
lowest point: Pacific Ocean 0 m
highest point: unnamed location 2 m
Natural resources: terrestrial and aquatic wildlife
Land use:
arable land: 0%
permanent crops: 0%
other: 100% (forests and woodlands) (1998 est.)
Irrigated land: 0 sq km (1998 est.)

Palmyra Atoll *(continued)*

Natural hazards: NA
Environment - current issues: NA
Geography - note: about 50 islets covered with dense vegetation, coconut trees, and balsa-like trees up to 30 meters tall

People

Population: no indigenous inhabitants; 4 to 20 Nature Conservancy staff, US Fish and Wildlife staff (July 2004 est.)

Government

Country name:
conventional long form: none
conventional short form: Palmyra Atoll
Dependency status: incorporated territory of the US; privately owned, but administered from Washington, DC, by the Fish and Wildlife Service of the US Department of the Interior; the Office of Insular Affairs of the US Department of the Interior continues to administer nine excluded areas comprising certain tidal and submerged lands within the 12 NM territorial sea or within the lagoon
Legal system: the laws of the US, where applicable, apply
Flag description: the flag of the US is used

Economy

Economy - overview: no economic activity

Transportation

Highways: most of the roads and many causeways built during World War II are unserviceable and overgrown (2001)
Waterways: none
Ports and harbors: West Lagoon
Airports: 1 (2003 est.)
Airports - with unpaved runways:
total: 1
1,524 to 2,437 m: 1 (2003 est.)

Military

Military - note: defense is the responsibility of the US

Transnational Issues

Disputes - international: none

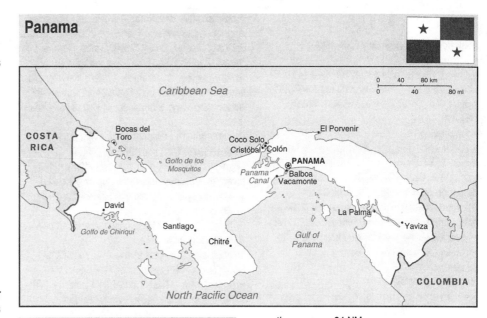

Panama

Introduction

Background: With US backing, Panama seceded from Colombia in 1903 and promptly signed a treaty with the US allowing for the construction of a canal and US sovereignty over a strip of land on either side of the structure (the Panama Canal Zone). The Panama Canal was built by the US Army Corps of Engineers between 1904 and 1914. On 7 September 1977, an agreement was signed for the complete transfer of the Canal from the US to Panama by the end of 1999. Certain portions of the Zone and increasing responsibility over the Canal were turned over in the intervening years. With US help, dictator Manuel NORIEGA was deposed in 1989. The entire Panama Canal, the area supporting the Canal, and remaining US military bases were turned over to Panama by or on 31 December 1999.

Geography

Location: Central America, bordering both the Caribbean Sea and the North Pacific Ocean, between Colombia and Costa Rica
Geographic coordinates: 9 00 N, 80 00 W
Map references: Central America and the Caribbean
Area:
total: 78,200 sq km
land: 75,990 sq km
water: 2,210 sq km
Area - comparative: slightly smaller than South Carolina
Land boundaries:
total: 555 km
border countries: Colombia 225 km, Costa Rica 330 km
Coastline: 2,490 km
Maritime claims:
territorial sea: 12 NM

contiguous zone: 24 NM
exclusive economic zone: 200 NM
Climate: tropical maritime; hot, humid, cloudy; prolonged rainy season (May to January), short dry season (January to May)
Terrain: interior mostly steep, rugged mountains and dissected, upland plains; coastal areas largely plains and rolling hills
Elevation extremes:
lowest point: Pacific Ocean 0 m
highest point: Volcan de Chiriqui 3,475 m
Natural resources: copper, mahogany forests, shrimp, hydropower
Land use:
arable land: 6.72%
permanent crops: 2.08%
other: 91.2% (1998 est.)
Irrigated land: 320 sq km (1998 est.)
Natural hazards: occasional severe storms and forest fires in the Darien area
Environment - current issues: water pollution from agricultural runoff threatens fishery resources; deforestation of tropical rain forest; land degradation and soil erosion threatens siltation of Panama Canal; air pollution in urban areas; mining threatens natural resources
Environment - international agreements:
party to: Biodiversity, Climate Change, Climate Change-Kyoto Protocol, Desertification, Endangered Species, Hazardous Wastes, Law of the Sea, Marine Dumping, Ozone Layer Protection, Ship Pollution, Tropical Timber 83, Tropical Timber 94, Wetlands, Whaling
signed, but not ratified: Marine Life Conservation
Geography - note: strategic location on eastern end of isthmus forming land bridge connecting North and South America; controls Panama Canal that links North Atlantic Ocean via Caribbean Sea with North Pacific Ocean

Panama (continued)

People

Population: 3,000,463 (July 2004 est.)
Age structure:
0-14 years: 30.2% (male 461,427; female 443,932)
15-64 years: 63.6% (male 967,490; female 940,344)
65 years and over: 6.2% (male 88,611; female 98,659) (2004 est.)
Median age:
total: 25.9 years
male: 25.6 years
female: 26.2 years (2004 est.)
Population growth rate: 1.31% (2004 est.)
Birth rate: 20.36 births/1,000 population (2004 est.)
Death rate: 6.39 deaths/1,000 population (2004 est.)
Net migration rate: -0.91 migrant(s)/1,000 population (2004 est.)
Sex ratio:
at birth: 1.05 male(s)/female
under 15 years: 1.04 male(s)/female
15-64 years: 1.03 male(s)/female
65 years and over: 0.9 male(s)/female
total population: 1.02 male(s)/female (2004 est.)
Infant mortality rate:
total: 20.95 deaths/1,000 live births
male: 23.08 deaths/1,000 live births
female: 18.72 deaths/1,000 live births (2004 est.)
Life expectancy at birth:
total population: 72.14 years
male: 69.82 years
female: 74.56 years (2004 est.)
Total fertility rate: 2.49 children born/woman (2004 est.)
HIV/AIDS - adult prevalence rate: 1.5% (2001 est.)
HIV/AIDS - people living with HIV/AIDS: 25,000 (2001 est.)
HIV/AIDS - deaths: 1,900 (2001 est.)
Nationality:
noun: Panamanian(s)
adjective: Panamanian
Ethnic groups: mestizo (mixed Amerindian and white) 70%, Amerindian and mixed (West Indian) 14%, white 10%, Amerindian 6%
Religions: Roman Catholic 85%, Protestant 15%
Languages: Spanish (official), English 14%
note: many Panamanians bilingual
Literacy:
definition: age 15 and over can read and write
total population: 92.6%
male: 93.2%
female: 91.9% (2003 est.)

Government

Country name:
conventional long form: Republic of Panama
conventional short form: Panama
local long form: Republica de Panama
local short form: Panama
Government type: constitutional democracy
Capital: Panama

Administrative divisions: 9 provinces (provincias, singular - provincia) and 1 territory* (comarca); Bocas del Toro, Chiriqui, Cocle, Colon, Darien, Herrera, Los Santos, Panama, San Blas*, and Veraguas
Independence: 3 November 1903 (from Colombia; became independent from Spain 28 November 1821)
National holiday: Independence Day, 3 November (1903)
Constitution: 11 October 1972; major reforms adopted 1978, 1983 and 1994
Legal system: based on civil law system; judicial review of legislative acts in the Supreme Court of Justice; accepts compulsory ICJ jurisdiction, with reservations
Suffrage: 18 years of age; universal and compulsory
Executive branch:
chief of state: President Mireya Elisa MOSCOSO Rodriguez (since 1 September 1999); First Vice President Arturo Ulises VALLARINO (since 1 September 1999); Second Vice President Dominador "Kaiser" Baldonero BAZAN Jimenez (since 1 September 1999); note - the president is both the chief of state and head of government
head of government: President Mireya Elisa MOSCOSO Rodriguez (since 1 September 1999); First Vice President Arturo Ulises VALLARINO (since 1 September 1999); Second Vice President Dominador "Kaiser" Baldonero BAZAN Jimenez (since 1 September 1999); note - the president is both the chief of state and head of government
cabinet: Cabinet appointed by the president
elections: president and vice presidents elected on the same ticket by popular vote for five-year terms; election last held 2 May 1999 (next to be held NA May 2004)
election results: Mireya Elisa MOSCOSO Rodriguez elected president; percent of vote - Mireya Elisa MOSCOSO Rodriguez (PA) 44%, Martin TORRIJOS (PRD) 37%
note: government coalition - PA, MOLIRENA, Democratic Change, MORENA, PLN, PS
Legislative branch: unicameral Legislative Assembly or Asamblea Legislativa (71 seats; members are elected by popular vote to serve five-year terms)
elections: last held 2 May 1999 (next to be held 2 May 2004)
election results: percent of vote by party - NA%; seats by party - PRD 34, PA 18, PDC 5, PS 4, MOLIRENA 3, PLN 3, Democratic Change 2, PRC 1, MORENA 1
note: legislators from outlying rural districts are chosen on a plurality basis while districts located in more populous towns and cities elect multiple legislators by means of a proportion-based formula
Judicial branch: Supreme Court of Justice or Corte Suprema de Justicia (nine judges appointed for 10-year terms); five superior courts; three courts of appeal
Political parties and leaders: Arnulfista Party or PA [Mireya Elisa MOSCOSO Rodriguez]; Civic Renewal Party or PRC [Serguei DE LA ROSA]; Democratic Change [Ricardo MARTINELLI]; Democratic

Revolutionary Party or PRD [Martin TORRIJOS]; National Liberal Party or PLN [Raul ARANGO Gasteazopo]; National Renovation Movement or MORENA [Pedro VALLARINO Cox]; Nationalist Republican Liberal Movement or MOLIRENA [Ramon MORALES]; Popular Party or PP (formerly Christian Democratic Party or PDC) [Ruben AROSEMENA]; Solidarity Party or PS [Samuel LEWIS Galindo]
Political pressure groups and leaders: Chamber of Commerce; National Civic Crusade; National Council of Organized Workers or CONATO; National Union of Construction and Similar Workers (SUNTRACS); National Council of Private Enterprise or CONEP; Panamanian Association of Business Executives or APEDE; Panamanian Industrialists Society or SIP; Workers Confederation of the Republic of Panama or CTRP
International organization participation: FAO, G-77, IADB, IAEA, IBRD, ICAO, ICCt, ICFTU, ICRM, IDA, IFAD, IFC, IFRCS, ILO, IMF, IMO, Interpol, IOC, IOM, ISO, ITU, LAES, LAIA (observer), NAM, OAS, OPANAL, OPCW, PCA, RG, UN, UNCTAD, UNESCO, UNIDO, UPU, WCL, WCO, WFTU, WHO, WIPO, WMO, WToO, WTrO
Diplomatic representation in the US:
chief of mission: Ambassador Roberto ALFARO Estripeaut
chancery: 2862 McGill Terrace NW, Washington, DC 20008
telephone: [1] (202) 483-1407
FAX: [1] (202) 483-8416
consulate(s) general: Atlanta, Houston, Miami, New Orleans, New York, Philadelphia, San Francisco, San Juan (Puerto Rico), Tampa
Diplomatic representation from the US:
chief of mission: Ambassador Linda Ellen WATT
embassy: Avenida Balboa and Calle 37, Apartado Postal 0816-02561, Zona 5, Panama City 5
mailing address: American Embassy Panama, Unit 0945, APO AA 34002
telephone: [507] 207-7000
FAX: [507] 227-1964
Flag description: divided into four, equal rectangles; the top quadrants are white (hoist side) with a blue five-pointed star in the center and plain red; the bottom quadrants are plain blue (hoist side) and white with a red five-pointed star in the center

Economy

Economy - overview: Panama's dollarised economy rests primarily on a well-developed services sector that accounts for three-fourths of GDP. Services include operating the Panama Canal, banking, the Colon Free Zone, insurance, container ports, flagship registry, and tourism. A slump in Colon Free Zone and agricultural exports, the global slowdown, and the withdrawal of US military forces held back economic growth in 2000-03. The government has been backing public works programs, tax reforms, new regional trade agreements, and development of tourism in order to stimulate growth. Unemployment remains at an unacceptably high level.

Panama *(continued)*

GDP: purchasing power parity - $18.62 billion (2003 est.)
GDP - real growth rate: 3.2% (2003 est.)
GDP - per capita: purchasing power parity - $6,300 (2003 est.)
GDP - composition by sector:
agriculture: 7%
industry: 17%
services: 76% (2001 est.)
Population below poverty line: 37% (1999 est.)
Household income or consumption by percentage share:
lowest 10%: 1.2%
highest 10%: 35.7% (1997)
Distribution of family income - Gini index: 48.5 (1997)
Inflation rate (consumer prices): 1.3% (2003 est.)
Labor force: 1.1 million
note: shortage of skilled labor, but an oversupply of unskilled labor (2000 est.)
Labor force - by occupation: agriculture 20.8%, industry 18%, services 61.2% (1995 est.)
Unemployment rate: 14.5% (2003 est.)
Budget:
revenues: $1.9 billion
expenditures: $2 billion, including capital expenditures of $471 million (2000 est.)
Industries: construction, petroleum refining, brewing, cement and other construction materials, sugar milling
Industrial production growth rate: 1% (2003 est.)
Electricity - production: 4.039 billion kWh (2001)
Electricity - production by source:
fossil fuel: 37%
hydro: 61.3%
nuclear: 0%
other: 1.7% (2001)
Electricity - consumption: 3.681 billion kWh (2001)
Electricity - exports: 118 million kWh (2001)
Electricity - imports: 43 million kWh (2001)
Oil - production: 0 bbl/day (2001 est.)
Oil - consumption: 52,000 bbl/day (2001 est.)
Oil - exports: NA
Oil - imports: NA
Agriculture - products: bananas, rice, corn, coffee, sugarcane, vegetables; livestock; shrimp
Exports: $5.237 billion f.o.b. (2003 est.)
Exports - commodities: bananas, shrimp, sugar, coffee, clothing (1999)
Exports - partners: US 47.8%, Sweden 5.8%, Costa Rica 4.8%, Honduras 4.5% (2002)
Imports: $6.622 billion f.o.b. (2003 est.)
Imports - commodities: capital goods, crude oil, foodstuffs, consumer goods, chemicals (1999)
Imports - partners: US 34.4%, Colombia 5.9%, Japan 5.4%, Costa Rica 4.2%, Venezuela 4.2% (2002)
Debt - external: $8.9 billion (2003 est.)
Economic aid - recipient: $197.1 million (1995)
Currency: balboa (PAB); US dollar (USD)
Currency code: PAB; USD

Exchange rates: balboas per US dollar - 1 (2003), 1 (2002), 1 (2001), 1 (2000), 1 (1999)
Fiscal year: calendar year

Communications

Telephones - main lines in use: 366,700 (2002)
Telephones - mobile cellular: 569,600 (2002)
Telephone system:
general assessment: domestic and international facilities well developed
domestic: NA
international: country code - 507; 1 coaxial submarine cable; satellite earth stations - 2 Intelsat (Atlantic Ocean); connected to the Central American Microwave System
Radio broadcast stations: AM 101, FM 134, shortwave 0 (1998)
Television broadcast stations: 38 (including repeaters) (1998)
Internet country code: .pa
Internet hosts: 7,393 (2002)
Internet users: 120,000 (2002)

Transportation

Railways:
total: 355 km
broad gauge: 76 km 1.524-m gauge
narrow gauge: 279 km 0.914-m gauge (2002)
Highways:
total: 11,400 km
paved: 3,944 km (including 30 km of expressways)
unpaved: 7,456 km (1999)
Waterways: 882 km
note: 800 km navigable by shallow draft vessels; 82 km Panama Canal
Pipelines: crude oil 130 km (2001)
Ports and harbors: Balboa, Cristobal, Coco Solo, Manzanillo (part of Colon area), Vacamonte
Merchant marine:
total: 4,833 ships (1,000 GRT or over) 122,960,929 GRT/183,615,337 DWT
by type: barge carrier 3, bulk 1,434, cargo 819, chemical tanker 388, combination bulk 73, combination ore/oil 18, container 613, liquefied gas 190, livestock carrier 3, multi-functional large load carrier 15, passenger 36, passenger/cargo 5, petroleum tanker 514, rail car carrier 1, refrigerated cargo 281, roll on/roll off 125, short-sea/passenger 37, specialized tanker 36, vehicle carrier 242
foreign-owned: Albania 2, Angola 1, Antigua and Barbuda 2, Argentina 7, Australia 11, Austria 1, Bahamas 3, Bangladesh 1, Belgium 5, Belize 4, Brazil 4, British Virgin Islands 8, Cambodia 2, Canada 6, Cayman Islands 1, Chile 13, China 286, Colombia 14, Croatia 3, Cuba 17, Cyprus 6, Denmark 4, Dominican Republic 1, Ecuador 1, Egypt 16, Equatorial Guinea 1, France 7, Germany 89, Greece 549, Haiti 1, Honduras 2, Hong Kong 288, India 22, Indonesia 44, Iran 1, Ireland 2, Israel 4, Italy 7, Japan 1630, Jordan 8, Kenya 1, South Korea 349, Kuwait 1, Latvia 11, Liberia 3, Lithuania 2, Luxembourg 1, Malaysia 12, Malta 1, Marshall Islands 3, Mexico 7, Monaco 29, Netherlands 14, Netherlands Antilles 1, New Zealand 1, Nigeria 6, Norway 86, Oman 1, Pakistan 1, Peru 17, Philippines 41, Poland 12, Portugal 6, Puerto Rico 3, Romania 9, Russia 8, Saint Kitts and Nevis 3, Saint Vincent and the Grenadines 6, Saudi Arabia 6, Singapore 105, South Africa 3, Spain 52, Sri Lanka 3, Sudan 1, Sweden 4, Switzerland 93, Syria 1, Taiwan 348, Thailand 14, Trinidad and Tobago 1, Turkey 12, Ukraine 2, United Kingdom 51, United States 99, Venezuela 4
registered in other countries: 85 (2003 est.)
Airports: 103 (2003 est.)
Airports - with paved runways:
total: 42
over 3,047 m: 1
2,438 to 3,047 m: 1
1,524 to 2,437 m: 5
914 to 1,523 m: 13
under 914 m: 22 (2003 est.)
Airports - with unpaved runways:
total: 61
914 to 1,523 m: 12
under 914 m: 49 (2003 est.)

Military

Military branches: an amendment to the Constitution abolished the armed forces, but there are security forces (Panamanian Public Forces or PPF includes the Panamanian National Police, National Maritime Service, and National Air Service)
Military manpower - availability:
males age 15-49: 810,341 (2004 est.)
Military manpower - fit for military service:
males age 15-49: 553,422 (2004 est.)
Military expenditures - dollar figure: $145 million (2003)
Military expenditures - percent of GDP: 1.2% (2003)
Military - note: on 10 February 1990, the government of then President ENDARA abolished Panama's military and reformed the security apparatus by creating the Panamanian Public Forces; in October 1994, Panama's Legislative Assembly approved a constitutional amendment prohibiting the creation of a standing military force, but allowing the temporary establishment of special police units to counter acts of "external aggression"

Transnational Issues

Disputes - international: none
Illicit drugs: major cocaine transshipment point and primary money-laundering center for narcotics revenue; money-laundering activity is especially heavy in the Colon Free Zone; offshore financial center; negligible signs of coca cultivation; monitoring of financial transactions is improving; official corruption remains a major problem

Papua New Guinea

Introduction

Background: The eastern half of the island of New Guinea - second largest in the world - was divided between Germany (north) and the UK (south) in 1885. The latter area was transferred to Australia in 1902, which occupied the northern portion during World War I and continued to administer the combined areas until independence in 1975. A nine-year secessionist revolt on the island of Bougainville ended in 1997 after claiming some 20,000 lives.

Geography

Location: Oceania, group of islands including the eastern half of the island of New Guinea between the Coral Sea and the South Pacific Ocean, east of Indonesia

Geographic coordinates: 6 00 S, 147 00 E

Map references: Oceania

Area:
total: 462,840 sq km
land: 452,860 sq km
water: 9,980 sq km

Area - comparative: slightly larger than California

Land boundaries:
total: 820 km
border countries: Indonesia 820 km

Coastline: 5,152 km

Maritime claims: measured from claimed archipelagic baselines
territorial sea: 12 NM
continental shelf: 200-m depth or to the depth of exploitation
exclusive fishing zone: 200 NM

Climate: tropical; northwest monsoon (December to March), southeast monsoon (May to October); slight seasonal temperature variation

Terrain: mostly mountains with coastal lowlands and rolling foothills

Elevation extremes:
lowest point: Pacific Ocean 0 m
highest point: Mount Wilhelm 4,509 m

Natural resources: gold, copper, silver, natural gas, timber, oil, fisheries

Land use:
arable land: 0.13%
permanent crops: 1.35%
other: 98.52% (1998 est.)

Irrigated land: NA sq km

Natural hazards: active volcanism; situated along the Pacific "Ring of Fire"; the country is subject to frequent and sometimes severe earthquakes; mud slides; tsunamis

Environment - current issues: rain forest subject to deforestation as a result of growing commercial demand for tropical timber; pollution from mining projects; severe drought

Environment - international agreements:
party to: Antarctic Treaty, Biodiversity, Climate Change, Climate Change-Kyoto Protocol, Desertification, Endangered Species, Environmental Modification, Hazardous Wastes, Law of the Sea, Marine Dumping, Ozone Layer Protection, Ship Pollution, Tropical Timber 83, Tropical Timber 94, Wetlands
signed, but not ratified: none of the selected agreements

Geography - note: shares island of New Guinea with Indonesia; one of world's largest swamps along southwest coast

People

Population: 5,420,280 (July 2004 est.)

Age structure:
0-14 years: 38.3% (male 1,053,940; female 1,019,492)
15-64 years: 58% (male 1,622,124; female 1,519,104)
65 years and over: 3.8% (male 96,638; female 108,982) (2004 est.)

Median age:
total: 21 years
male: 21.1 years
female: 20.8 years (2004 est.)

Population growth rate: 2.3% (2004 est.)

Birth rate: 30.52 births/1,000 population (2004 est.)

Death rate: 7.5 deaths/1,000 population (2004 est.)

Net migration rate: 0 migrant(s)/1,000 population (2004 est.)

Sex ratio:
at birth: 1.05 male(s)/female
under 15 years: 1.03 male(s)/female
15-64 years: 1.07 male(s)/female
65 years and over: 0.89 male(s)/female
total population: 1.05 male(s)/female (2004 est.)

Infant mortality rate:
total: 53.15 deaths/1,000 live births
male: 57.39 deaths/1,000 live births
female: 48.7 deaths/1,000 live births (2004 est.)

Life expectancy at birth:
total population: 64.56 years
male: 62.41 years
female: 66.81 years (2004 est.)

Total fertility rate: 4.04 children born/woman (2004 est.)

HIV/AIDS - adult prevalence rate: 0.7% (2001 est.)

HIV/AIDS - people living with HIV/AIDS: 17,000 (2001 est.)

HIV/AIDS - deaths: 880 (2001 est.)

Nationality:
noun: Papua New Guinean(s)
adjective: Papua New Guinean

Ethnic groups: Melanesian, Papuan, Negrito, Micronesian, Polynesian

Religions: Roman Catholic 22%, Lutheran 16%, Presbyterian/Methodist/London Missionary Society 8%, Anglican 5%, Evangelical Alliance 4%, Seventh-Day Adventist 1%, other Protestant 10%, indigenous beliefs 34%

Languages: Melanesian Pidgin serves as the lingua franca, English spoken by 1%-2%, Motu spoken in Papua region
note: 715 indigenous languages -- many unrelated

Literacy:
definition: age 15 and over can read and write
total population: 66%
male: 72.3%
female: 59.3% (2003 est.)

Government

Country name:
conventional long form: Independent State of Papua New Guinea
conventional short form: Papua New Guinea
former: Territory of Papua and New Guinea
abbreviation: PNG

Government type: constitutional monarchy with parliamentary democracy

Capital: Port Moresby

Administrative divisions: 20 provinces; Bougainville, Central, Chimbu, Eastern Highlands, East New Britain, East Sepik, Enga, Gulf, Madang, Manus, Milne Bay, Morobe, National Capital, New Ireland, Northern, Sandaun, Southern Highlands, Western, Western Highlands, West New Britain

Independence: 16 September 1975 (from the Australian-administered UN trusteeship)

National holiday: Independence Day, 16 September (1975)

Constitution: 16 September 1975

Legal system: based on English common law

Suffrage: 18 years of age; universal

Executive branch:
chief of state: Queen ELIZABETH II (since 6 February 1952), represented by Governor General Sir Albert KIPALAN (since 13 November 2003)
note: Sir Pato KAKRAYA was elected Governor General on 4 December 2003; he was scheduled to be sworn in on 20 January 2004 but the election was challenged; Bill SKATE was acting Governor General

Papua New Guinea (continued)

head of government: Prime Minister Sir Michael SOMARE (since 2 August 2002); Deputy Prime Minister Moses MALADINA (since 1 December 2003)
cabinet: National Executive Council appointed by the governor general on the recommendation of the prime minister
elections: none; the monarch is hereditary; governor general appointed by the National Executive Council; following legislative elections, the leader of the majority party or the leader of the majority coalition usually is appointed prime minister by the governor general
Legislative branch: unicameral National Parliament - sometimes referred to as the House of Assembly (109 seats, 89 elected from open electorates and 20 from provincial electorates; members elected by popular vote to serve five-year terms)
elections: last held 15-29 June 2002 and April and May 2003; completed in May 2003 (voting in the Southern Highlands was not completed during the June 2002 election period); next to be held not later than June 2007
election results: percent of vote by party - National Alliance 18%, URP 13%, PDM 12%, PPP 8%, Pangu 6%, PAP 5%, PLP 4%, others 34%; seats by party - National Alliance 19, UPR 14, PDM 13, PPP 8, Pangu 6, PAP 5, PLP 4, others 40; note - association with political parties is fluid (2003)
Judicial branch: Supreme Court (the chief justice is appointed by the governor general on the proposal of the National Executive Council after consultation with the minister responsible for justice; other judges are appointed by the Judicial and Legal Services Commission)
Political parties and leaders: Christian Democratic Party [Muki TARANUPI, party leader]; Melanesian Alliance Party or MAP [Bernard NAROKOBI, party leader]; National Alliance Party or NA [Michael SOMARE, party leader; George MANOA, party president]; National Party [John MUNNULL, party leader]; Papua and Niugini Union Party or PANGU [Rabbie NAMALU, party leader]; Papua New Guinea National Party [Robert LAK, party leader]; People's Action Party or PAP [Moses MALADINA, party leader]; People's Democratic Movement or PDM [Sir Mekere MORAUTA, party leader]; People's Labor Party or PLP [Peter YAMA, party leader]; People's National Congress or PNC [Bill SKATE, party leader]; People's Progressive Party or PPP [Andrew BAING, party leader]; Pipol's First Party [Luther WENGE, party leader]; Rural People's Party [Peter NAMUS, party leader]; United Resources Party or URP [Tim NEVILLE, party leader] (2003)
Political pressure groups and leaders: NA
International organization participation: ACP, APEC, ARF, AsDB, C, CP, FAO, G-77, IBRD, ICAO, ICFTU, ICRM, IDA, IFAD, IFC, IFRCS, IHO, ILO, IMF, IMO, Interpol, IOC, IOM (observer), ISO (correspondent), ITU, NAM, OPCW, PIF, Sparteca, UN, UNCTAD, UNESCO, UNIDO, UPU, WCO, WFTU, WHO, WIPO, WMO, WTrO

Diplomatic representation in the US:
chief of mission: Ambassador Evan Jeremy PAKI
chancery: 1779 Massachusetts Avenue NW, Suite 805, Washington, DC 20036
telephone: [1] (202) 745-3680
FAX: [1] (202) 745-3679
Diplomatic representation from the US:
chief of mission: Ambassador Robert W. FITTS
embassy: Douglas Street, Port Moresby
mailing address: 4240 Port Moresby PI, US Department of State, Washington DC 20521-4240
telephone: [675] 321-1455
FAX: [675] 321-3423
Flag description: divided diagonally from upper hoist-side corner; the upper triangle is red with a soaring yellow bird of paradise centered; the lower triangle is black with five, white, five-pointed stars of the Southern Cross constellation centered

Economy

Economy - overview: Papua New Guinea is richly endowed with natural resources, but exploitation has been hampered by rugged terrain and the high cost of developing infrastructure. Agriculture provides a subsistence livelihood for 85% of the population. Mineral deposits, including oil, copper, and gold, account for 72% of export earnings. The economy has faltered over the past four years. Former Prime Minister Mekere MORAUTA had tried to restore integrity to state institutions, to stabilize the kina, restore stability to the national budget, to privatize public enterprises where appropriate, and to ensure ongoing peace on Bougainville. The government has had considerable success in attracting international support, specifically gaining the backing of the IMF and the World Bank in securing development assistance loans. Challenges face Prime Minister Michael SOMARE, including curbing inflation, gaining further investor confidence, continuing efforts to privatize government assets, maintaining the support of members of Parliament, and balancing relations with Australia, the former colonial ruler.
GDP: purchasing power parity - $11.4 billion (2003 est.)
GDP - real growth rate: 0.7% (2003 est.)
GDP - per capita: purchasing power parity - $2,200 (2003 est.)
GDP - composition by sector:
agriculture: 32.1%
industry: 35.8%
services: 32.1% (2001 est.)
Population below poverty line: 37% (2002 est.)
Household income or consumption by percentage share:
lowest 10%: 1.7%
highest 10%: 40.5% (1996)
Distribution of family income - Gini index: 50.9 (1996)
Inflation rate (consumer prices): 17.2% (2003 est.)

Labor force: 2.3 million (1999)
Labor force - by occupation: agriculture 85%, industry NA%, services NA%
Unemployment rate: NA%
Budget:
revenues: $894 million
expenditures: $1.1 billion, including capital expenditures of $344 million (2000 est.)
Industries: copra crushing, palm oil processing, plywood production, wood chip production; mining of gold, silver, and copper; crude oil production; construction, tourism
Industrial production growth rate: NA (FY01/02 est.)
Electricity - production: 1.496 billion kWh (2001)
Electricity - production by source:
fossil fuel: 54.1%
hydro: 45.9%
nuclear: 0%
other: 0% (2001)
Electricity - consumption: 1.391 billion kWh (2001)
Electricity - exports: 0 kWh (2001)
Electricity - imports: 0 kWh (2001)
Oil - production: 67,500 bbl/day (2001 est.)
Oil - consumption: 15,000 bbl/day (2001 est.)
Oil - exports: NA
Oil - imports: NA
Oil - proved reserves: 345.2 million bbl (1 January 2002)
Natural gas - production: 110 million cu m (2001 est.)
Natural gas - consumption: 110 million cu m (2001 est.)
Natural gas - exports: 0 cu m (2001 est.)
Natural gas - imports: 0 cu m (2001 est.)
Natural gas - proved reserves: 385.5 billion cu m (1 January 2002)
Agriculture - products: coffee, cocoa, coconuts, palm kernels, tea, rubber, sweet potatoes, fruit, vegetables, poultry, pork
Exports: $1.938 billion f.o.b. (2003 est.)
Exports - commodities: oil, gold, copper ore, logs, palm oil, coffee, cocoa, crayfish, prawns
Exports - partners: Australia 24.2%, Japan 9.4%, China 5.4% (2002)
Imports: $967 million f.o.b. (2003 est.)
Imports - commodities: machinery and transport equipment, manufactured goods, food, fuels, chemicals
Imports - partners: Australia 49.2%, Singapore 18.8%, New Zealand 4.4%, Japan 4.3% (2002)
Debt - external: $2.7 billion (2003 est.)
Economic aid - recipient: $400 million (1999 est.)
Currency: kina (PGK)
Currency code: PGK
Exchange rates: kina per US dollar - 3.5635 (2003), 3.8952 (2002), 3.3887 (2001), 2.7822 (2000), 2.5708 (1999)
Fiscal year: calendar year

Papua New Guinea *(continued)*

Communications

Telephones - main lines in use: 64,000 (2002)
Telephones - mobile cellular: 15,000 (2002)
Telephone system:
general assessment: services are adequate and being improved; facilities provide radiotelephone and telegraph, coastal radio, aeronautical radio, and international radio communication services
domestic: mostly radiotelephone
international: country code - 675; submarine cables to Australia and Guam; satellite earth station - 1 Intelsat (Pacific Ocean); international radio communication service
Radio broadcast stations: AM 8, FM 19, shortwave 28 (1998)
Television broadcast stations: 3 (all in the Port Moresby area)
note: additional stations at Mt. Hagen, Goroka, Lae, and Rabaul are planned (2004)
Internet country code: .pg
Internet hosts: 517 (2002)
Internet users: 75,000 (2002)

Transportation

Railways: 0 km
Highways:
total: 19,600 km
paved: 686 km
unpaved: 18,914 km (1999 est.)
Waterways: 10,940 km
Pipelines: oil 264 km (2003)
Ports and harbors: Kieta, Lae, Madang, Port Moresby, Rabaul
Merchant marine:
total: 23 ships (1,000 GRT or over) 47,586 GRT/ 60,934 DWT
by type: bulk 1, cargo 12, chemical tanker 1, combination ore/oil 2, container 1, petroleum tanker 4, roll on/roll off 2
foreign-owned: Singapore 2, United Kingdom 6
registered in other countries: 1 (2003 est.)
Airports: 559 (2003 est.)
Airports - with paved runways:
total: 21
2,438 to 3,047 m: 2
1,524 to 2,437 m: 14
914 to 1,523 m: 4
under 914 m: 1 (2003 est.)
Airports - with unpaved runways:
total: 538
1,524 to 2,437 m: 10
914 to 1,523 m: 62
under 914 m: 466 (2003 est.)
Heliports: 2 (2003 est.)

Military

Military branches: Papua New Guinea Defense Force: Ground Force, Maritime Operations Element, and Air Operations Element
Military manpower - availability:
males age 15-49: 1,403,467 (2004 est.)
Military manpower - fit for military service:
males age 15-49: 775,064 (2004 est.)
Military expenditures - dollar figure: $16.9 million (2003)
Military expenditures - percent of GDP: 1.4% (FY02)

Transnational Issues

Disputes - international: seeks assistance from Australia to control illegal cross-border activities from primarily Indonesia, including smuggling, drug trafficking, and Indonesian squatters and secessionists

Paracel Islands

Introduction

Background: The Paracel Islands are surrounded by productive fishing grounds and by potential oil and gas reserves. In 1932, French Indochina annexed the islands and set up a weather station on Pattle Island; maintenance was continued by its successor, Vietnam. China has occupied the Paracel Islands since 1974, when its troops seized a South Vietnamese garrison occupying the western islands. The islands are claimed by Taiwan and Vietnam.

Geography

Location: Southeastern Asia, group of small islands and reefs in the South China Sea, about one-third of the way from central Vietnam to the northern Philippines
Geographic coordinates: 16 30 N, 112 00 E
Map references: Southeast Asia
Area:
total: NA sq km
land: NA sq km
water: 0 sq km
Area - comparative: NA
Land boundaries: 0 km
Coastline: 518 km
Maritime claims: NA
Climate: tropical
Terrain: mostly low and flat
Elevation extremes:
lowest point: South China Sea 0 m
highest point: unnamed location on Rocky Island 14 m
Natural resources: none
Land use:
arable land: 0%
permanent crops: 0%
other: 100% (1998 est.)
Irrigated land: 0 sq km (1998 est.)
Natural hazards: typhoons
Environment - current issues: NA

Geography - note: composed of 130 small coral islands and reefs divided into the northeast Amphitrite Group and the western Crescent Group

People

Population: no indigenous inhabitants
note: there are scattered Chinese garrisons (July 2004 est.)

Government

Country name:
conventional long form: none
conventional short form: Paracel Islands

Economy

Economy - overview: China announced plans in 1997 to open the islands for tourism.

Transportation

Waterways: none
Ports and harbors: small Chinese port facilities on Woody Island and Duncan Island being expanded
Airports: 1 (2003 est.)
Airports - with paved runways:
total: 1
1,524 to 2,437 m: 1 (2003 est.)

Military

Military - note: occupied by China

Transnational Issues

Disputes - international: occupied by China, but claimed by Taiwan and Vietnam

---

Paraguay

Introduction

Background: In the disastrous War of the Triple Alliance (1865-70), Paraguay lost two-thirds of all adult males and much of its territory. It stagnated economically for the next half century. In the Chaco War of 1932-35, large, economically important areas were won from Bolivia. The 35-year military dictatorship of Alfredo STROESSNER was overthrown in 1989, and, despite a marked increase in political infighting in recent years, relatively free and regular presidential elections have been held since then.

Geography

Location: Central South America, northeast of Argentina
Geographic coordinates: 23 00 S, 58 00 W
Map references: South America
Area:
total: 406,750 sq km
land: 397,300 sq km
water: 9,450 sq km
Area - comparative: slightly smaller than California
Land boundaries:
total: 3,920 km
border countries: Argentina 1,880 km, Bolivia 750 km, Brazil 1,290 km
Coastline: 0 km (landlocked)
Maritime claims: none (landlocked)
Climate: subtropical to temperate; substantial rainfall in the eastern portions, becoming semiarid in the far west
Terrain: grassy plains and wooded hills east of Rio Paraguay; Gran Chaco region west of Rio Paraguay mostly low, marshy plain near the river, and dry forest and thorny scrub elsewhere
Elevation extremes:
lowest point: junction of Rio Paraguay and Rio Parana 46 m
highest point: Cerro Pero (Cerro Tres Kandu) 842 m

Natural resources: hydropower, timber, iron ore, manganese, limestone
Land use:
arable land: 5.54%
permanent crops: 0.21%
other: 94.25% (1998 est.)
Irrigated land: 670 sq km (1998 est.)
Natural hazards: local flooding in southeast (early September to June); poorly drained plains may become boggy (early October to June)
Environment - current issues: deforestation; water pollution; inadequate means for waste disposal present health risks for many urban residents; loss of wetlands
Environment - international agreements:
party to: Biodiversity, Climate Change, Climate Change-Kyoto Protocol, Desertification, Endangered Species, Hazardous Wastes, Law of the Sea, Ozone Layer Protection, Wetlands
signed, but not ratified: none of the selected agreements
Geography - note: landlocked; lies between Argentina, Bolivia, and Brazil; population concentrated in southern part of country

People

Population: 6,191,368 (July 2004 est.)
Age structure:
0-14 years: 38.2% (male 1,201,459; female 1,162,954)
15-64 years: 57% (male 1,773,151; female 1,758,323)
65 years and over: 4.8% (male 136,376; female 159,105) (2004 est.)
Median age:
total: 21.1 years
male: 20.8 years
female: 21.3 years (2004 est.)
Population growth rate: 2.51% (2004 est.)
Birth rate: 29.78 births/1,000 population (2004 est.)
Death rate: 4.58 deaths/1,000 population (2004 est.)
Net migration rate: -0.08 migrant(s)/1,000 population (2004 est.)
Sex ratio:
at birth: 1.05 male(s)/female
under 15 years: 1.03 male(s)/female
15-64 years: 1.01 male(s)/female
65 years and over: 0.86 male(s)/female
total population: 1.01 male(s)/female (2004 est.)
Infant mortality rate:
total: 26.67 deaths/1,000 live births
male: 31.5 deaths/1,000 live births
female: 21.6 deaths/1,000 live births (2004 est.)
Life expectancy at birth:
total population: 74.64 years
male: 72.12 years
female: 77.29 years (2004 est.)
Total fertility rate: 3.98 children born/woman (2004 est.)
HIV/AIDS - adult prevalence rate: 0.11% (2001 est.)

Paraguay (continued)

HIV/AIDS - people living with HIV/AIDS: 3,000 (1999 est.)
HIV/AIDS - deaths: 220 (2001 est.)
Nationality:
noun: Paraguayan(s)
adjective: Paraguayan
Ethnic groups: mestizo (mixed Spanish and Amerindian) 95%
Religions: Roman Catholic 90%, Mennonite, and other Protestant
Languages: Spanish (official), Guarani (official)
Literacy:
definition: age 15 and over can read and write
total population: 94%
male: 94.9%
female: 93% (2003 est.)

Government

Country name:
conventional long form: Republic of Paraguay
conventional short form: Paraguay
local long form: Republica del Paraguay
local short form: Paraguay
Government type: constitutional republic
Capital: Asuncion
Administrative divisions: 17 departments (departamentos, singular - departamento) and 1 capital city*; Alto Paraguay, Alto Parana, Amambay, Asuncion*, Boqueron, Caaguazu, Caazapa, Canindeyu, Central, Concepcion, Cordillera, Guaira, Itapua, Misiones, Neembucu, Paraguari, Presidente Hayes, San Pedro
Independence: 14 May 1811 (from Spain)
National holiday: Independence Day, 14 May (1811) (observed 15 May annually)
Constitution: promulgated 20 June 1992
Legal system: based on Argentine codes, Roman law, and French codes; judicial review of legislative acts in Supreme Court of Justice
Suffrage: 18 years of age; universal and compulsory up to age 75
Executive branch:
chief of state: President Nicanor DUARTE Frutos (since 15 August 2003); Vice President Luis CASTIGLIONI Joria (since 15 August 2003); note - the president is both the chief of state and head of government
head of government: President Nicanor DUARTE Frutos (since 15 August 2003); Vice President Luis CASTIGLIONI Joria (since 15 August 2003); note - the president is both the chief of state and head of government
cabinet: Council of Ministers nominated by the president
elections: president and vice president elected on the same ticket by popular vote for five-year terms; election last held 27 April 2003 (next to be held NA April 2008)
election results: Nicanor DUARTE Frutos elected president; percent of vote - Nicanor DUARTE Frutos 37.1%, Julio Cesar Ramon FRANCO Gomez 23.9%, Pedro Nicolas Maraa FADUL Niella 21.3%, Guillermo SANCHEZ Guffanti 13.5%, other 4.2%

Legislative branch: bicameral Congress or Congreso consists of the Chamber of Senators or Camara de Senadores (45 seats; members are elected by popular vote to serve five-year terms) and the Chamber of Deputies or Camara de Diputados (80 seats; members are elected by popular vote to serve five-year terms)
elections: Chamber of Senators - last held 27 April 2003 (next to be held NA April 2008); Chamber of Deputies - last held 27 April 2003 (next to be held NA April 2008)
election results: Chamber of Senators - percent of vote by party - NA%; seats by party - Colorado Party 16, PLRA 12, UNACE 7, MPQ 7, PPS 2, PEN 1; Chamber of Deputies - percent of vote by party - NA%; seats by party - Colorado Party 37, PLRA 21, UNACE 10, MPQ 10, PPS 2
Judicial branch: Supreme Court of Justice or Corte Suprema de Justicia (judges appointed on the proposal of the Counsel of Magistrates or Consejo de la Magistratura)
Political parties and leaders: Asociacion Nacional Republicana - Colorado Party or ANR [leader NA]; Movimiento Patria Querida or MPQ [Pedro Nicolas Maraa FADUL Niella]; Movimiento Union Nacional de Colorados Eticos or UNACE [Lino Cesar OVIEDO Silva]; Partido Encuentro Nacional or PEN [Diego ABENTE Brun]; Partido Liberal Radical Autentico or PLRA [Julio Cesar FRANCO]; Partido Pais Solidario or PPS [Carlos Alberto FILIZZOLA Pallares]; note - Nicanor DUARTE Frutos on leave as party leader of the Colorado Party or ANR while serving as President of Paraguay
Political pressure groups and leaders: Ahorristas Estafados or AE; Coordinating Table of National Campesino Organizations or MCNOC; National Federation of Campesinos or FNC; National Workers Central or CNT; Paraguayan Workers Confederation or CPT; Roman Catholic Church; Unitary Workers Central or CUT;;
International organization participation: FAO, G-77, IADB, IAEA, IBRD, ICAO, ICCt, ICFTU, ICRM, IDA, IFAD, IFC, IFRCS, ILO, IMF, IMO, Interpol, IOC, IOM, ISO (correspondent), ITU, LAES, LAIA, Mercosur, MONUC, NAM (observer), OAS, OPANAL, OPCW, PCA, RG, UN, UNCTAD, UNESCO, UNIDO, UNMEE, UNMIL, UPU, WCL, WCO, WHO, WIPO, WMO, WToO, WTrO
Diplomatic representation in the US:
chief of mission: Ambassador James SPALDING Hellmers
chancery: 2400 Massachusetts Avenue NW, Washington, DC 20008
telephone: [1] (202) 483-6960 through 6962
FAX: [1] (202) 234-4508
consulate(s) general: Kansas City, Los Angeles, Miami, New Orleans, New York
Diplomatic representation from the US:
chief of mission: Ambassador John F. KEANE
embassy: 1776 Avenida Mariscal Lopez, Casilla Postal 402, Asuncion
mailing address: Unit 4711, APO AA 34036-0001

telephone: [595] (21) 213-715
FAX: [595] (21) 213-728
Flag description: three equal, horizontal bands of red (top), white, and blue with an emblem centered in the white band; unusual flag in that the emblem is different on each side; the obverse (hoist side at the left) bears the national coat of arms (a yellow five-pointed star within a green wreath capped by the words REPUBLICA DEL PARAGUAY, all within two circles); the reverse (hoist side at the right) bears the seal of the treasury (a yellow lion below a red Cap of Liberty and the words Paz y Justicia (Peace and Justice) capped by the words REPUBLICA DEL PARAGUAY, all within two circles)

Economy

Economy - overview: Paraguay has a market economy marked by a large informal sector. The informal sector features both reexport of imported consumer goods to neighboring countries as well as the activities of thousands of microenterprises and urban street vendors. Because of the importance of the informal sector, accurate economic measures are difficult to obtain. A large percentage of the population derives their living from agricultural activity, often on a subsistence basis. The formal economy grew by an average of about 3% annually in 1995-97; but GDP declined slightly in 1998, 1999, and 2000, rose slightly in 2001, only to fall again in 2002. On a per capita basis, real income has stagnated at 1980 levels. Most observers attribute Paraguay's poor economic performance to political uncertainty, corruption, lack of progress on structural reform, substantial internal and external debt, and deficient infrastructure.
GDP: purchasing power parity - $28.03 billion (2003 est.)
GDP - real growth rate: 1.3% (2003 est.)
GDP - per capita: purchasing power parity - $4,600 (2003 est.)
GDP - composition by sector:
agriculture: 27%
industry: 27%
services: 46% (2001 est.)
Population below poverty line: 36% (2001 est.)
Household income or consumption by percentage share:
lowest 10%: 0.5%
highest 10%: 43.8% (1998)
Distribution of family income - Gini index: 57.7 (1998)
Inflation rate (consumer prices): 10.5% (2002 est.)
Labor force: 2.5 million (2002 est.)
Labor force - by occupation: agriculture 45%
Unemployment rate: 16.4% (2002 est.)
Budget:
revenues: $1.3 billion
expenditures: $2 billion, including capital expenditures of $700 million (1999 est.)
Industries: sugar, cement, textiles, beverages, wood products, steel, metallurgic, electric power
Industrial production growth rate: 0% (2000 est.)

Paraguay (continued)

Electricity - production: 44.89 billion kWh (2001)
Electricity - production by source:
fossil fuel: 0%
hydro: 99.9%
nuclear: 0%
other: 0.1% (2001)
Electricity - consumption: 2.637 billion kWh (2001)
Electricity - exports: 39.11 billion kWh (2001)
Electricity - imports: 0 kWh (2001)
Oil - production: 0 bbl/day (2001 est.)
Oil - consumption: 25,000 bbl/day (2001 est.)
Oil - exports: NA
Oil - imports: NA
Agriculture - products: cotton, sugarcane, soybeans, corn, wheat, tobacco, cassava (tapioca), fruits, vegetables; beef, pork, eggs, milk; timber
Exports: $2.727 billion f.o.b. (2003 est.)
Exports - commodities: soybeans, feed, cotton, meat, edible oils, electricity, wood, leather
Exports - partners: Brazil 29.8%, Argentina 18%, Chile 5.5%, Bermuda 4% (2002)
Imports: $2.77 billion f.o.b. (2003 est.)
Imports - commodities: road vehicles, consumer goods, tobacco, petroleum products, electrical machinery
Imports - partners: Brazil 28.9%, US 22.5%, Argentina 17.7%, Uruguay 4.7%, Hong Kong 4.3%, China 4.1% (2002)
Debt - external: $3.2 billion (2002 est.)
Economic aid - recipient: $NA (2001)
Currency: guarani (PYG)
Currency code: PYG
Exchange rates: guarani per US dollar - 6,424.34 (2003), 5,716.26 (2002), 4,105.92 (2001), 3,486.35 (2000), 3,119.07 (1999)
Fiscal year: calendar year

Communications

Telephones - main lines in use: 273,200 (2002)
Telephones - mobile cellular: 1.667 million (2002)
Telephone system:
general assessment: meager telephone service; principal switching center is Asuncion
domestic: fair microwave radio relay network
international: country code - 595; satellite earth station - 1 Intelsat (Atlantic Ocean)
Radio broadcast stations: AM 46, FM 27, shortwave 6 (three inactive) (1998)
Television broadcast stations: 5 (2003)
Internet country code: .py
Internet hosts: 4,351 (2002)
Internet users: 100,000 (2002)

Transportation

Railways:
total: 441 km
standard gauge: 441 km 1.435-m gauge (2002)
Highways:
total: 29,500 km
paved: 14,986 km
unpaved: 14,514 km (1999 est)

Waterways: 3,100 km
Ports and harbors: Asuncion, Villeta, San Antonio, Encarnacion
Merchant marine:
total: 21 ships (1,000 GRT or over) 31,667 GRT/ 30,826 DWT
by type: cargo 14, livestock carrier 1, petroleum tanker 3, roll on/roll off 3
foreign-owned: Argentina 2, Japan 1
registered in other countries: 1 (2003 est.)
Airports: 880 (2003 est.)
Airports - with paved runways:
total: 11
over 3,047 m: 3
1,524 to 2,437 m: 4
914 to 1,523 m: 4 (2003 est.)
Airports - with unpaved runways:
total: 869
1,524 to 2,437 m: 27
914 to 1,523 m: 324
under 914 m: 518 (2003 est.)

Military

Military branches: Army, Navy (includes Naval Air and Marines), Air Force
Military manpower - military age: 18 years of age (2004 est.)
Military manpower - availability:
males age 15-49: 1,504,407 (2004 est.)
Military manpower - fit for military service:
males age 15-49: 1,084,087 (2004 est.)
Military manpower - reaching military age annually:
males: 63,386 (2004 est.)
Military expenditures - dollar figure: $52.7 million (2003)
Military expenditures - percent of GDP: 0.9% (2003)

Transnational Issues

Disputes - international: unruly region at convergence of Argentina-Brazil-Paraguay borders is locus of money laundering, smuggling, arms and drug trafficking, and fundraising for extremist organizations
Illicit drugs: major illicit producer of cannabis, most or all of which is consumed in Brazil, Argentina, and Chile; transshipment country for Andean cocaine headed for Brazil, other Southern Cone markets, Europe, and US; corruption and some money-laundering activity, especially in the Tri-Border Area

Peru

Introduction

Background: Ancient Peru was the seat of several prominent Andean civilizations, most notably that of the Incas whose empire was captured by the Spanish conquistadores in 1533. Peruvian independence was declared in 1821, and remaining Spanish forces defeated in 1824. After a dozen years of military rule, Peru returned to democratic leadership in 1980, but experienced economic problems and the growth of a violent insurgency. President Alberto FUJIMORI's election in 1990 ushered in a decade that saw a dramatic turnaround in the economy and significant progress in curtailing guerrilla activity. Nevertheless, the president's increasing reliance on authoritarian measures and an economic slump in the late 1990s generated mounting dissatisfaction with his regime. FUJIMORI won reelection to a third term in the spring of 2000, but international pressure and corruption scandals led to his ouster by Congress in November of that year. A caretaker government oversaw new elections in the spring of 2001, which ushered in Alejandro TOLEDO as the new head of government.

Geography

Location: Western South America, bordering the South Pacific Ocean, between Chile and Ecuador
Geographic coordinates: 10 00 S, 76 00 W
Map references: South America
Area:
total: 1,285,220 sq km
land: 1.28 million sq km
water: 5,220 sq km
Area - comparative: slightly smaller than Alaska
Land boundaries:
total: 5,536 km
border countries: Bolivia 900 km, Brazil 1,560 km, Chile 160 km, Colombia 1,496 km (est.), Ecuador 1,420 km
Coastline: 2,414 km

Peru (continued)

Maritime claims:
territorial sea: 200 NM
continental shelf: 200 NM

Climate: varies from tropical in east to dry desert in west; temperate to frigid in Andes

Terrain: western coastal plain (costa), high and rugged Andes in center (sierra), eastern lowland jungle of Amazon Basin (selva)

Elevation extremes:
lowest point: Pacific Ocean 0 m
highest point: Nevado Huascaran 6,768 m

Natural resources: copper, silver, gold, petroleum, timber, fish, iron ore, coal, phosphate, potash, hydropower, natural gas

Land use:
arable land: 2.85%
permanent crops: 0.38%
other: 96.77% (1998 est.)

Irrigated land: 11,950 sq km (1998 est.)

Natural hazards: earthquakes, tsunamis, flooding, landslides, mild volcanic activity

Environment - current issues: deforestation (some the result of illegal logging); overgrazing of the slopes of the costa and sierra leading to soil erosion; desertification; air pollution in Lima; pollution of rivers and coastal waters from municipal and mining wastes

Environment - international agreements:
party to: Antarctic-Environmental Protocol, Antarctic-Marine Living Resources, Antarctic Treaty, Biodiversity, Climate Change, Climate Change-Kyoto Protocol, Desertification, Endangered Species, Hazardous Wastes, Marine Dumping, Ozone Layer Protection, Ship Pollution, Tropical Timber 83, Tropical Timber 94, Wetlands, Whaling
signed, but not ratified: none of the selected agreements

Geography - note: shares control of Lago Titicaca, world's highest navigable lake, with Bolivia; a remote slope of Nevado Mismi, a 5,316 m peak, is the ultimate source of the Amazon River

People

Population: 27,544,305 (July 2004 est.)

Age structure:
0-14 years: 32.1% (male 4,496,146; female 4,340,580)
15-64 years: 62.8% (male 8,709,098; female 8,594,351)
65 years and over: 5.1% (male 660,734; female 743,396) (2004 est.)

Median age:
total: 24.6 years
male: 24.4 years
female: 24.9 years (2004 est.)

Population growth rate: 1.39% (2004 est.)

Birth rate: 21.27 births/1,000 population (2004 est.)

Death rate: 6.29 deaths/1,000 population (2004 est.)

Net migration rate: -1.05 migrant(s)/1,000 population (2004 est.)

Sex ratio:
at birth: 1.05 male(s)/female
under 15 years: 1.04 male(s)/female

15-64 years: 1.01 male(s)/female
65 years and over: 0.89 male(s)/female
total population: 1.01 male(s)/female (2004 est.)

Infant mortality rate:
total: 32.95 deaths/1,000 live births
male: 35.57 deaths/1,000 live births
female: 30.21 deaths/1,000 live births (2004 est.)

Life expectancy at birth:
total population: 69.22 years
male: 67.48 years
female: 71.03 years (2004 est.)

Total fertility rate: 2.61 children born/woman (2004 est.)

HIV/AIDS - adult prevalence rate: 0.4% (2001 est.)

HIV/AIDS - people living with HIV/AIDS: 53,000 (2001 est.)

HIV/AIDS - deaths: 3,900 (2001 est.)

Nationality:
noun: Peruvian(s)
adjective: Peruvian

Ethnic groups: Amerindian 45%, mestizo (mixed Amerindian and white) 37%, white 15%, black, Japanese, Chinese, and other 3%

Religions: Roman Catholic 90%

Languages: Spanish (official), Quechua (official), Aymara, and a large number of minor Amazonian languages

Literacy:
definition: age 15 and over can read and write
total population: 90.9%
male: 95.2%
female: 86.8% (2003 est.)

Government

Country name:
conventional long form: Republic of Peru
conventional short form: Peru
local long form: Republica del Peru
local short form: Peru

Government type: constitutional republic

Capital: Lima

Administrative divisions: 24 departments (departamentos, singular - departamento) and 1 constitutional province* (provincia constitucional); Amazonas, Ancash, Apurimac, Arequipa, Ayacucho, Cajamarca, Callao*, Cusco, Huancavelica, Huanuco, Ica, Junin, La Libertad, Lambayeque, Lima, Loreto, Madre de Dios, Moquegua, Pasco, Piura, Puno, San Martin, Tacna, Tumbes, Ucayali
note: some reports indicate that the 24 departments and 1 constitutional province are now being referred to as regions; Peru is implementing a decentralization program whereby these 25 administrative divisions will begin to exercise greater governmental authority over their territories; in November 2002, voters chose their new regional presidents and other regional leaders; the authority that the regional government will exercise has not yet been clearly defined, but it will be devolved to the regions over the course of several years

Independence: 28 July 1821 (from Spain)

National holiday: Independence Day, 28 July (1821)

Constitution: 31 December 1993

Legal system: based on civil law system; has not accepted compulsory ICJ jurisdiction

Suffrage: 18 years of age; universal and compulsory until the age of 70; note - members of the military may not vote

Executive branch:
chief of state: President Alejandro TOLEDO Manrique (since 28 July 2001); note - the president is both the chief of state and head of government; additionally two vice presidents are provided for by the constitution, First Vice President (vacant) and Second Vice President David WAISMAN (since 28 July 2001); note - Raul DIEZ Canseco resigned as First Vice President on 30 January 2004
head of government: President Alejandro TOLEDO Manrique (since 28 July 2001); note - the president is both the chief of state and head of government; additionally two vice presidents are provided for by the constitution, First Vice President (vacant) and Second Vice President David WAISMAN (since 28 July 2001); note - Raul DIEZ Canseco resigned as First Vice President on 30 January 2004
note: Prime Minister Carlos FERRERO Costa (since 15 December 2003) does not exercise executive power; this power is in the hands of the president; note - Beatriz MERINO was asked to resign on 12 December 2003 and was replaced by Carlos FERRERO Costa three days later
cabinet: Council of Ministers appointed by the president
elections: president elected by popular vote for a five-year term; special presidential and congressional elections held 8 April 2001, with runoff election held 3 June 2001; next to be held 9 April 2006
election results: President Alejandro TOLEDO Manrique elected president in runoff election; percent of vote - Alejandro TOLEDO Manrique 53.1%, Alan GARCIA 46.9%

Legislative branch: unicameral Congress of the Republic of Peru or Congreso de la Republica del Peru (120 seats; members are elected by popular vote to serve five-year terms)
elections: last held 8 April 2001 (next to be held 9 April 2006)
election results: percent of vote by party - Peru Posible 26.3%, APRA 19.7%, Unidad Nacional 13.8%, FIM 11.0%, others 29.2%; seats by party - Peru Posible 47, APRA 28, Unidad Nacional 17, FIM 11, others 17

Judicial branch: Supreme Court of Justice or Corte Suprema de Justicia (judges are appointed by the National Council of the Judiciary)

Political parties and leaders: Peruvian Aprista Party or PAP (also referred to by its original name Alianza Popular Revolucionaria Americana or APRA) [Alan GARCIA]; Independent Moralizing Front or FIM [Fernando OLIVERA Vega]; National Unity (Unidad Nacional) or UN [Lourdes FLORES Nano]; Peru Posible or PP [Luis SOLARI]; Popular Action or AP [Javier DIAZ Orihuela]; Solucion Popular [Carlos BOLANA]; Somos Peru or SP [Alberto ANDRADE]; Union for Peru or UPP [Roger GUERRA Garcia]

Political pressure groups and leaders: leftist guerrilla groups include Shining Path [Abimael GUZMAN Reynoso (imprisoned), Gabriel MACARIO (top leader at-large)]; Tupac Amaru Revolutionary Movement or MRTA [Victor POLAY (imprisoned), Hugo AVALLENEDA Valdez (top leader at-large)]
International organization participation: APEC, CAN, FAO, G-15, G-24, G-77, IADB, IAEA, IBRD, ICAO, ICC, ICCt, ICFTU, ICRM, IDA, IFAD, IFC, IFRCS, IHO, ILO, IMF, IMO, Interpol, IOC, IOM, ISO (correspondent), ITU, LAES, LAIA, MONUC, NAM, OAS, OPANAL, OPCW, PCA, RG, UN, UNCTAD, UNESCO, UNIDO, UNMEE, UNMIL, UPU, WCL, WCO, WFTU, WHO, WIPO, WMO, WToO, WTrO
Diplomatic representation in the US:
chief of mission: Ambassador Eduardo FERRERO Costa
chancery: 1700 Massachusetts Avenue NW, Washington, DC 20036
telephone: [1] (202) 833-9860 through 9869
FAX: [1] (202) 659-8124
consulate(s) general: Boston, Chicago, Denver, Houston, Los Angeles, Miami, New York, Paterson (New Jersey), San Francisco, Washington (DC)
Diplomatic representation from the US:
chief of mission: Ambassador J. Curtis STRUBLE
embassy: Avenida La Encalada, Cuadra 17s/n, Surco, Lima 33
mailing address: P. O. Box 1995, Lima 1; American Embassy (Lima), APO AA 34031-5000
telephone: [51] (1) 434-3000
FAX: [51] (1) 434-3037
Flag description: three equal, vertical bands of red (hoist side), white, and red with the coat of arms centered in the white band; the coat of arms features a shield bearing a vicuna, cinchona tree (the source of quinine), and a yellow cornucopia spilling out gold coins, all framed by a green wreath

Economy

Economy - overview: Peru's economy reflects its varied geography - an arid coastal region, the Andes further inland, and tropical lands bordering Colombia and Brazil. Abundant mineral resources are found in the mountainous areas, and Peru's coastal waters provide excellent fishing grounds. However, overdependence on minerals and metals subjects the economy to fluctuations in world prices, and a lack of infrastructure deters trade and investment. After several years of inconsistent economic performance, the Peruvian economy was one of the fastest growing in Latin America in 2002 and 2003, growing by 5% and 4%, respectively, with the exchange rate stable and an annual inflation lower than 2%. Foreign direct investment also was strong, thanks to the ongoing Camisea natural gas pipeline project (scheduled to begin operations in 2004) and investments in gold mining. Risk premiums on Peruvian bonds on secondary markets reached historically low levels in late 2003, reflecting investor optimism and the government's fiscal restraint. Despite the strong macroeconomic performance, political intrigue and allegations of corruption continued to swirl in 2003, with the TOLEDO administration growing increasingly unpopular, and local and foreign concern rising that the political turmoil could place the country's hard-won fiscal and financial stability at risk. Moreover, as of late 2003, unemployment had yet to respond to the strong growth in economic activity, owing in part to rigid labor market regulations that act as an impediment to hiring.
GDP: purchasing power parity - $146.9 billion (2003 est.)
GDP - real growth rate: 4% (2003 est.)
GDP - per capita: purchasing power parity - $5,200 (2003 est.)
GDP - composition by sector:
agriculture: 9.6%
industry: 26%
services: 64.4% (2001 est.)
Population below poverty line: 54% (2003 est.)
Household income or consumption by percentage share:
lowest 10%: 1.6%
highest 10%: 35.4% (1996)
Distribution of family income - Gini index: 46.2 (1996)
Inflation rate (consumer prices): 2.2% (2003 est.)
Labor force: 7.5 million (2000 est.)
Labor force - by occupation: agriculture, mining and quarrying, manufacturing, construction, transport, services
Unemployment rate: 13.4%; widespread underemployment (2003 est.)
Budget:
revenues: $10.4 billion
expenditures: $10.4 billion, including capital expenditures of $NA (2002 est.)
Industries: mining of metals, petroleum, fishing, textiles, clothing, food processing, cement, auto assembly, steel, shipbuilding, metal fabrication
Industrial production growth rate: 6.5% (2002 est.)
Electricity - production: 20.59 billion kWh (2001)
Electricity - production by source:
fossil fuel: 14.5%
hydro: 84.7%
nuclear: 0%
other: 0.8% (2001)
Electricity - consumption: 19.15 billion kWh (2001)
Electricity - exports: 0 kWh (2001)
Electricity - imports: 0 kWh (2001)
Oil - production: 95,100 bbl/day (2001 est.)
Oil - consumption: 161,000 bbl/day (2001 est.)
Oil - exports: NA
Oil - imports: NA
Oil - proved reserves: 614.7 million bbl (1 January 2002)
Natural gas - production: 370 million cu m (2001 est.)
Natural gas - consumption: 370 million cu m (2001 est.)
Natural gas - exports: 0 cu m (2001 est.)
Natural gas - imports: 0 cu m (2001 est.)
Natural gas - proved reserves: 245.1 billion cu m (1 January 2002)
Agriculture - products: coffee, cotton, sugarcane, rice, wheat, potatoes, corn, plantains, coca; poultry, beef, dairy products, wool; fish
Exports: $8.954 billion f.o.b. (2003 est.)
Exports - commodities: fish and fish products, gold, copper, zinc, crude petroleum and byproducts, lead, coffee, sugar, cotton
Exports - partners: US 26.1%, UK 11.6%, China 7.9%, Switzerland 7.5%, Japan 4.9% (2002)
Imports: $8.244 billion f.o.b. (2003 est.)
Imports - commodities: machinery, transport equipment, foodstuffs, petroleum, iron and steel, chemicals, pharmaceuticals
Imports - partners: US 27.5%, Spain 8.3%, Chile 7.9%, Brazil 4.7%, Colombia 4.6% (2002)
Debt - external: $29.2 billion (2002 est.)
Economic aid - recipient: $895.1 million (1995)
Currency: nuevo sol (PEN)
Currency code: PEN
Exchange rates: nuevo sol per US dollar - 3.4785 (2003), 3.5165 (2002), 3.5068 (2001), 3.49 (2000), 3.3833 (1999)
Fiscal year: calendar year

Communications

Telephones - main lines in use: 1,766,100 (2002)
Telephones - mobile cellular: 2,306,900 (2002)
Telephone system:
general assessment: adequate for most requirements
domestic: nationwide microwave radio relay system and a domestic satellite system with 12 earth stations
international: country code - 51; satellite earth stations - 2 Intelsat (Atlantic Ocean); Pan American submarine cable
Radio broadcast stations: AM 472, FM 198, shortwave 189 (1999)
Television broadcast stations: 13 (plus 112 repeaters) (1997)
Internet country code: .pe
Internet hosts: 19,447 (2002)
Internet users: 2.5 million (2002)

Transportation

Railways:
total: 1,829 km
standard gauge: 1,515 km 1.435-m gauge
narrow gauge: 314 km 0.914-m gauge (2002)
Highways:
total: 72,900 km
paved: 9,331 km
unpaved: 63,569 km (1999 est.)
Waterways: 8,808 km
note: 8,600 km of navigable tributaries of Amazon system and 208 km of Lago Titicaca
Pipelines: gas 388 km; oil 1,557 km; refined products 13 km (2003)

Ports and harbors: Callao, Chimbote, Ilo, Matarani, Paita, Puerto Maldonado, Salaverry, San Martin, Talara, Iquitos, Pucallpa, Yurimaguas
note: Iquitos, Pucallpa, and Yurimaguas are all on the upper reaches of the Amazon and its tributaries
Merchant marine:
total: 3 ships (1,000 GRT or over) 13,666 GRT/17,611 DWT
by type: cargo 2, petroleum tanker 1
foreign-owned: United States 1
registered in other countries: 19 (2003 est.)
Airports: 233 (2003 est.)
Airports - with paved runways:
total: 52
over 3,047 m: 5
2,438 to 3,047 m: 20
1,524 to 2,437 m: 16
914 to 1,523 m: 9
under 914 m: 2 (2003 est.)
Airports - with unpaved runways:
total: 181
1,524 to 2,437 m: 21
914 to 1,523 m: 62
under 914 m: 98 (2003 est.)
Heliports: 1 (2003 est.)

Military

Military branches: Army (Ejercito Peruano), Navy (Marina de Guerra del Peru; includes Naval Air, Naval Infantry, and Coast Guard), Air Force (Fuerza Aerea del Peru; FAP)
Military manpower - military age: 17 years of age (2004 est.)
Military manpower - availability:
males age 15-49: 7,374,187 (2004 est.)
Military manpower - fit for military service:
males age 15-49: 4,938,512 (2004 est.)
Military manpower - reaching military age annually:
males: 277,931 (2004 est.)
Military expenditures - dollar figure: $829.4 million (2003)
Military expenditures - percent of GDP: 1.3% (2003)

Transnational Issues

Disputes - international: Bolivia has reanimated its claim to restore the Atacama corridor ceded to Chile and adjoining Peru in 1884 to secure sovereign maritime assess for Bolivian natural gas
Illicit drugs: until 1996 the world's largest coca leaf producer; emerging opium producer; cultivation of coca in Peru fell 15 percent to 31,150 hectares between 2002 and the end of 2003; much of the cocaine base is shipped to neighboring Colombia for processing into cocaine, while finished cocaine is shipped out from Pacific ports to the international drug market; increasing amounts of base and finished cocaine, however, are being moved to Brazil and Bolivia for use in the Southern Cone or transshipped to Europe and Africa

Philippines

Introduction

Background: The Philippines were ceded by Spain to the US in 1898 following the Spanish-American War. They attained independence in 1946 after Japanese occupation in World War II. The 21-year rule of Ferdinand MARCOS ended in 1986, when a widespread popular rebellion forced him into exile. In 1992, the US closed its last military bases on the islands. The Philippines has had two electoral presidential transitions since the removal of MARCOS. In January 2001, the Supreme Court declared Joseph ESTRADA unable to rule in view of mass resignations from his government and administered the oath of office to Vice President Gloria MACAPAGAL-ARROYO as his constitutional successor. The government continues to struggle with Muslim insurgencies in the south.

Geography

Location: Southeastern Asia, archipelago between the Philippine Sea and the South China Sea, east of Vietnam
Geographic coordinates: 13 00 N, 122 00 E

Map references: Southeast Asia
Area:
total: 300,000 sq km
land: 298,170 sq km
water: 1,830 sq km
Area - comparative: slightly larger than Arizona
Land boundaries: 0 km
Coastline: 36,289 km
Maritime claims:
territorial sea: irregular polygon extending up to 100 NM from coastline as defined by 1898 treaty; since late 1970s has also claimed polygonal-shaped area in South China Sea up to 285 NM in breadth
exclusive economic zone: 200 NM
continental shelf: to depth of exploitation
Climate: tropical marine; northeast monsoon (November to April); southwest monsoon (May to October)
Terrain: mostly mountains with narrow to extensive coastal lowlands
Elevation extremes:
lowest point: Philippine Sea 0 m
highest point: Mount Apo 2,954 m
Natural resources: timber, petroleum, nickel, cobalt, silver, gold, salt, copper
Land use:
arable land: 18.45%
permanent crops: 14.76%
other: 66.79% (1998 est.)
Irrigated land: 15,500 sq km (1998 est.)
Natural hazards: astride typhoon belt, usually affected by 15 and struck by five to six cyclonic storms per year; landslides; active volcanoes; destructive earthquakes; tsunamis
Environment - current issues: uncontrolled deforestation especially in watershed areas; soil erosion; air and water pollution in major urban centers; coral reef degradation; increasing pollution of coastal mangrove swamps that are important fish breeding grounds
Environment - international agreements:
party to: Biodiversity, Climate Change, Climate Change-Kyoto Protocol, Desertification, Endangered Species, Hazardous Wastes, Law of the Sea, Marine Dumping, Ozone Layer Protection, Ship Pollution, Tropical Timber 83, Tropical Timber 94, Wetlands, Whaling
signed, but not ratified: Air Pollution-Persistent Organic Pollutants
Geography - note: favorably located in relation to many of Southeast Asia's main water bodies: the South China Sea, Philippine Sea, Sulu Sea, Celebes Sea, and Luzon Strait

People

Population: 86,241,697 (July 2004 est.)
Age structure:
0-14 years: 35.8% (male 15,758,255; female 15,152,291)
15-64 years: 60.2% (male 25,847,345; female 26,096,211)

Philippines (continued)

65 years and over: 3.9% (male 1,473,873; female 1,913,722) (2004 est.)

Median age:
total: 22.1 years
male: 21.6 years
female: 22.6 years (2004 est.)

Population growth rate: 1.88% (2004 est.)
Birth rate: 25.8 births/1,000 population (2004 est.)
Death rate: 5.53 deaths/1,000 population (2004 est.)
Net migration rate: -1.5 migrant(s)/1,000 population (2004 est.)

Sex ratio:
at birth: 1.05 male(s)/female
under 15 years: 1.04 male(s)/female
15-64 years: 0.99 male(s)/female
65 years and over: 0.77 male(s)/female
total population: 1 male(s)/female (2004 est.)

Infant mortality rate:
total: 24.24 deaths/1,000 live births
male: 27.11 deaths/1,000 live births
female: 21.22 deaths/1,000 live births (2004 est.)

Life expectancy at birth:
total population: 69.6 years
male: 66.74 years
female: 72.61 years (2004 est.)

Total fertility rate: 3.22 children born/woman (2004 est.)

HIV/AIDS - adult prevalence rate: less than 0.1% (2001 est.)

HIV/AIDS - people living with HIV/AIDS: 9,400 (2001 est.)

HIV/AIDS - deaths: 720 (2001 est.)

Nationality:
noun: Filipino(s)
adjective: Philippine

Ethnic groups: Christian Malay 91.5%, Muslim Malay 4%, Chinese 1.5%, other 3%

Religions: Roman Catholic 83%, Protestant 9%, Muslim 5%, Buddhist and other 3%

Languages: two official languages - Filipino (based on Tagalog) and English; eight major dialects - Tagalog, Cebuano, Ilocan, Hiligaynon or Ilonggo, Bicol, Waray, Pampango, and Pangasinense

Literacy:
definition: age 15 and over can read and write
total population: 95.9%
male: 96%
female: 95.8% (2003 est.)

Government

Country name:
conventional long form: Republic of the Philippines
conventional short form: Philippines
local long form: Republika ng Pilipinas
local short form: Pilipinas
Government type: republic
Capital: Manila
Administrative divisions: 79 provinces and 115 chartered cities*; Abra, Agusan del Norte, Agusan del Sur, Aklan, Albay, Angeles*, Antique, Apayao, Aurora, Bacolod*, Bago*, Baguio*, Bais*, Basilan, Basilan City*, Bataan, Batanes, Batangas, Batangas City*,

Biliran, Benguet, Bohol, Bukidnon, Bulacan, Butuan*, Cabanatuan*, Cadiz*, Cagayan, Cagayan de Oro*, Calbayog*, Caloocan*, Camarines Norte, Camarines Sur, Camiguin, Canlaon*, Capiz, Catanduanes, Cavite, Cavite City*, Cebu, Cebu City*, Compostela, Cotabato*, Dagupan*, Danao*, Dapitan*, Davao City*, Davao del Norte, Davao del Sur, Davao Oriental, Dipolog*, Dumaguete*, Eastern Samar, General Santos*, Gingoog*, Guimaras, Ifugao, Iligan*, Ilocos Norte, Ilocos Sur, Iloilo, Iloilo City*, Iriga*, Isabela, Kalinga, La Carlota*, Laguna, Lanao del Norte, Lanao del Sur, Laoag*, Lapu-Lapu*, La Union, Legaspi*, Leyte, Lipa*, Lucena*, Maguindanao, Mandaue*, Manila*, Marawi*, Marinduque, Masbate, Mindoro Occidental, Mindoro Oriental, Misamis Occidental, Misamis Oriental, Mountain, Naga*, Negros Occidental, Negros Oriental, North Cotabato, Northern Samar, Nueva Ecija, Nueva Vizcaya, Olongapo*, Ormoc*, Oroquieta*, Ozamis*, Pagadian*, Palawan, Palayan*, Pampanga, Pangasinan, Pasay*, Puerto Princesa*, Quezon, Quezon City*, Quirino, Rizal, Romblon, Roxas*, Samar, San Carlos* (in Negros Occidental), San Carlos* (in Pangasinan), San Jose*, San Pablo*, Sarangani, Silay*, Siquijor, Sorsogon, South Cotabato, Southern Leyte, Sultan Kudarat, Sulu, Surigao*, Surigao del Norte, Surigao del Sur, Tacloban*, Tagaytay*, Tagbilaran*, Tangub*, Tarlac, Tawi-Tawi, Toledo*, Trece Martires*, Zambales, Zamboanga*, Zamboanga del Norte, Zamboanga del Sur, Zamboanga Sibugay

Independence: 12 June 1898 (from Spain)
National holiday: Independence Day, 12 June (1898)
note: 12 June 1898 was the date of independence from Spain; 4 July 1946 was the date of independence from the US
Constitution: 2 February 1987, effective 11 February 1987
Legal system: based on Spanish and Anglo-American law; accepts compulsory ICJ jurisdiction, with reservations
Suffrage: 18 years of age; universal
Executive branch:
chief of state: President Gloria MACAPAGAL-ARROYO (since 20 January 2001) and Vice President Teofisto GUINGONA (since 20 January 2001); note - the president is both the chief of state and head of government
head of government: President Gloria MACAPAGAL-ARROYO (since 20 January 2001) and Vice President Teofisto GUINGONA (since 20 January 2001); note - the president is both the chief of state and head of government
cabinet: Cabinet appointed by the president with the consent of the Commission of Appointments
elections: president and vice president elected on separate tickets by popular vote for six-year terms; election last held 11 May 1998 (next to be held 10 May 2004)
election results: results of the last presidential election - Joseph Ejercito ESTRADA elected president; percent of vote - approximately 40%; Gloria

MACAPAGAL-ARROYO elected vice president; percent of vote - 49.56%; note - on 20 January 2001, Vice President Gloria MACAPAGAL-ARROYO was sworn in as the constitutional successor to President Joseph ESTRADA after the Supreme Court declared that ESTRADA was unable to rule in view of the mass resignations from his government; according to the Constitution, only in cases of death, permanent disability, removal from office, or resignation of the president, can the vice president serve for the unexpired term

Legislative branch: bicameral Congress or Kongreso consists of the Senate or Senado (24 seats - one-half elected every three years; members elected by popular vote to serve six-year terms) and the House of Representatives or Kapulungan Ng Mga Kinatawan (206 members representing districts plus 20 sectora party-list members; members elected by popular vote to serve three-year terms; note - additional members may be appointed by the president but the Constitution prohibits the House of Representatives from having more than 250 members)

elections: Senate - last held 14 May 2001 (next to be held 10 May 2004); House of Representatives - elections last held 14 May 2001 (next to be held 10 May 2004)

election results: Senate - percent of vote by party - NA%; seats by party - Lakas 13, PDP-Laban/LDP 11; House of Representatives - percent of vote by party - NA%; seats by party - Lakas 86, NPC 51, LDP 21, LP 20, independents 10, other 26 (May 2001)

Judicial branch: Supreme Court (15 justices are appointed by the president on the recommendation of the Judicial and Bar Council and serve until 70 years of age)

Political parties and leaders: Laban Ng Demokratikong Pilipino (Struggle of Filipino Democrats) or LDP [Edgardo ANGARA, president]; Lakas Ng Edsa (National Union of Christian Democrats) or Lakas [Jose DE VENECIA, president]; Liberal Party or LP [Florencio ABAD, president; Franklin DRILON, chairman]; National People's Coalition or NPC [Eduardo COJUANGCO, chairman emeritus; Frisco SAN JUAN, president; Faustino DY, chairman]; PDP-Laban [Aquilino PIMENTEL, chairman; Jejomar BINAY, president]; Pwersa ng Masang Pilipino (Party of the Philippine Masses) or PMP [Horacio MORALES, president]; Aksyon Demokratiko Party [Raul ROCO, president]; Reporma [Renato DE VILLA, chairman]; PROMDI [Emilio OSMENA, president]

Political pressure groups and leaders: Bayan Muna [Reps. Satur OCAMPO, Liza MAZA, and Crispin BELTRAN]; Bagong Alyasang Makabayan or BAYAN [Nathaniel SANTIAGO and Teddy CASINO]; League of Filipino Students [Noel COLINA]; AKBAYAN [Rep. Loretta ROSALES]; SANLAKAS [Renato CONSTANTINO]; Confederation for Unity, Reform and Advancement for Government Employees or COURAGE [Ferdinand GAITE] (2003)

Philippines *(continued)*

International organization participation: APEC, ARF, AsDB, ASEAN, BIS, CP, FAO, G-24, G-77, IAEA, IBRD, ICAO, ICC, ICCt (signatory), ICFTU, ICRM, IDA, IFAD, IFC, IFRCS, IHO, ILO, IMF, IMO, Interpol, IOC, IOM, ISO, ITU, NAM, OAS (observer), OPCW, UN, UN Security Council (temporary), UNCTAD, UNESCO, UNHCR, UNIDO, UNMIK, UNMIL, UNMISET, UPU, WCL, WCO, WFTU, WHO, WIPO, WMO, WToO, WTrO

Diplomatic representation in the US:
chief of mission: Ambassador Albert DEL ROSARIO
chancery: 1600 Massachusetts Avenue NW, Washington, DC 20036
telephone: [1] (202) 467-9300
FAX: [1] (202) 328-7614
consulate(s) general: Chicago, Honolulu, Los Angeles, New York, San Francisco, San Jose (Northern Mariana Islands), Tamuning (Guam)
consulate(s): San Diego

Diplomatic representation from the US:
chief of mission: Ambassador Francis J. RICCIARDONE
embassy: 1201 Roxas Boulevard, Manila
mailing address: PSC 500, FPO AP 96515-1000
telephone: [63] (2) 523-6300
FAX: [63] (2) 522-4361

Flag description: two equal horizontal bands of blue (top) and red with a white equilateral triangle based on the hoist side; in the center of the triangle is a yellow sun with eight primary rays (each containing three individual rays) and in each corner of the triangle is a small yellow five-pointed star

Economy

Economy - overview: The Philippines was less severely affected by the Asian financial crisis of 1998 than its neighbors, aided in part by annual remittances of $6-7 billion from overseas workers. From a 0.6% decline in 1998, GDP expanded by 2.4% in 1999, and 4.4% in 2000, but slowed to 3.2% in 2001 in the context of a global economic slowdown, an export slump, and political and security concerns. GDP growth accelerated to 4.4% in 2002 and 4.2% in 2003, reflecting the continued resilience of the service sector, gains in industrial output, and improved exports. Nonetheless, it will take a higher, sustained growth path to make appreciable progress in poverty alleviation given the Philippines' high annual population growth rate and unequal distribution of income. The MACAPAGAL-ARROYO Administration has promised to continue economic reforms to help the Philippines match the pace of development in the newly industrialized countries of East Asia. The strategy includes improving the infrastructure, strengthening tax collection to bolster government revenues, furthering deregulation and privatization of the economy, enhancing the viability of the financial system, and increasing trade integration with the region. Prospects for 2004 will depend on the economic performance of two major trading partners, the US and Japan, and on increased confidence on the part of the international investment community.

GDP: purchasing power parity - $390.7 billion (2003 est.)
GDP - real growth rate: 4.5% (2003 est.)
GDP - per capita: purchasing power parity - $4,600 (2003 est.)
GDP - composition by sector:
agriculture: 15%
industry: 35%
services: 50% (2003 est.)
Population below poverty line: 40% (2001 est.)
Household income or consumption by percentage share:
lowest 10%: 1.7%
highest 10%: 38.4% (2000)
Distribution of family income - Gini index: 48.1 (2000)
Inflation rate (consumer prices): 3.1% (2003 est.)
Labor force: 34.6 million (2003)
Labor force - by occupation: agriculture 45%, industry 15%, services 40% (2003 est.)
Unemployment rate: 11.4% (2003)
Budget:
revenues: $10.9 billion
expenditures: $15.1 billion, including capital expenditures of $2.4 million $NA (2002)
Industries: electronics assembly, textiles, pharmaceuticals, chemicals, wood products, food processing, petroleum refining, fishing
Industrial production growth rate: 3.7% (2002 est.)
Electricity - production: 45.21 billion kWh (2001)
Electricity - production by source:
fossil fuel: 55.6%
hydro: 17.5%
nuclear: 0%
other: 26.9% (2001)
Electricity - consumption: 42.04 billion kWh (2001)
Electricity - exports: 0 kWh (2001)
Electricity - imports: 0 kWh (2001)
Oil - production: 8,460 bbl/day (2001 est.)
Oil - consumption: 343,000 bbl/day (2001 est.)
Oil - exports: NA
Oil - imports: NA
Oil - proved reserves: 164 million bbl (1 January 2002)
Natural gas - production: 10 million cu m (2001 est.)
Natural gas - consumption: 10 million cu m (2001 est.)
Natural gas - exports: 0 cu m (2001 est.)
Natural gas - imports: 0 cu m (2001 est.)
Natural gas - proved reserves: 104.6 billion cu m (1 January 2002)
Agriculture - products: rice, coconuts, corn, sugarcane, bananas, pineapples, mangoes, pork, eggs, beef, fish
Exports: $34.56 billion f.o.b. (2003 est.)
Exports - commodities: electronic equipment, machinery and transport equipment, garments, coconut products, chemicals

Exports - partners: US 24.7%, Japan 15%, Netherlands 8.7%, Taiwan 7.1%, Singapore 7%, Hong Kong 6.7%, Malaysia 4.7% (2002)
Imports: $35.97 billion f.o.b. (2003 est.)
Imports - commodities: raw materials, machinery and equipment, fuels, chemicals
Imports - partners: US 20.6%, Japan 20.4%, South Korea 7.8%, Singapore 6.5%, Taiwan 5%, Hong Kong 4.5% (2002)
Debt - external: $56.7 billion (2003)
Economic aid - recipient: ODA commitments, $1.2 billion (2002)
Currency: Philippine peso (PHP)
Currency code: PHP
Exchange rates: Philippine pesos per US dollar - 54.2033 (2003), 51.6036 (2002), 50.9926 (2001), 44.1922 (2000), 39.089 (1999)
Fiscal year: calendar year

Communications

Telephones - main lines in use: 3,310,900 (2002)
Telephones - mobile cellular: 15.201 million (2002)
Telephone system:
general assessment: good international radiotelephone and submarine cable services; domestic and inter-island service adequate
domestic: domestic satellite system with 11 earth stations
international: country code - 63; 9 international gateways; satellite earth stations - 3 Intelsat (1 Indian Ocean and 2 Pacific Ocean); submarine cables to Hong Kong, Guam, Singapore, Taiwan, and Japan
Radio broadcast stations: AM 369, FM 583, shortwave 5
note: each shortwave station operates on multiple frequencies in the language of the target audience (2004)
Television broadcast stations: 225; note - 1373 CATV networks (2004)
Internet country code: .ph
Internet hosts: 38,440 (2002)
Internet users: 3.5 million (2002)

Transportation

Railways:
total: 897 km
narrow gauge: 897 km 1.067-m gauge (405 km are not in operation) (2002)
Highways:
total: 201,994 km
paved: 42,419 km
unpaved: 159,575 km (2000)
Waterways: 3,219 km
note: limited to vessels with a draft of less than 1.5 m
Pipelines: gas 565 km; oil 135 km; refined products 100 km (2003)
Ports and harbors: Batangas, Cagayan de Oro, Cebu, Davao, Guimaras Island, Iligan, Iloilo, Jolo, Legaspi, Manila, Masao, Puerto Princesa, San Fernando, Subic Bay, Zamboanga

Philippines (continued)

Merchant marine:

total: 385 ships (1,000 GRT or over) 4,524,259 GRT/
6,437,171 DWT

by type: bulk 99, cargo 103, chemical tanker 7,
combination bulk 7, container 8, liquefied gas 9,
livestock carrier 10, passenger 4, passenger/cargo
10, petroleum tanker 45, refrigerated cargo 21, roll on/
roll off 16, short-sea/passenger 26, specialized
tanker 1, vehicle carrier 19

foreign-owned: Australia 2, Canada 1, Germany 2,
Greece 11, Hong Kong 15, Japan 50, Malaysia 5,
Netherlands 15, Norway 6, Panama 1, United
Kingdom 2, United States 4

registered in other countries: 87 (2003 est.)

Airports: 253 (2003 est.)

Airports - with paved runways:

total: 82
over 3,047 m: 4
2,438 to 3,047 m: 6
1,524 to 2,437 m: 26
914 to 1,523 m: 35
under 914 m: 11 (2003 est.)

Airports - with unpaved runways:

total: 171
1,524 to 2,437 m: 5
914 to 1,523 m: 68
under 914 m: 98 (2003 est.)

Heliports: 2 (2003 est.)

Military

Military branches: Armed Forces of the Philippines
(AFP): Army, Navy (includes Coast Guard and Marine
Corps), Air Force

Military manpower - military age: 20 years of age
(2004 est.)

Military manpower - availability:
males age 15-49: 22,435,982 (2004 est.)

Military manpower - fit for military service:
males age 15-49: 15,780,602 (2004 est.)

**Military manpower - reaching military age
annually:**
males: 851,009 (2004 est.)

Military expenditures - dollar figure: $995 million
(FY98)

Military expenditures - percent of GDP: 1.5%
(FY98)

Transnational Issues

Disputes - international: involved in complex
dispute with China, Malaysia, Taiwan, Vietnam and
possibly Brunei over the Spratly Islands, known locally
as the Kalayaan (Freedom) Islands, the 2002
"Declaration on the Conduct of Parties in the South
China Sea," has eased tensions but falls short of a
legally binding "code of conduct" desired by several of
the disputants; Philippines retains a claim to
Malaysia's Sabah State in northern Borneo based on
the Sultanate of Sulu's granting the Philippines
Government power of attorney to pursue a
sovereignty claim

Illicit drugs: exports locally-produced marijuana and
hashish to East Asia, the US, and other Western
markets; serves as a transit point for heroin and
crystal methamphetamine; domestic
methamphetamine production is a growing problem;
remains on Financial Action Task Force
Non-Cooperative Countries and Territories List for
continued failure to address deficiencies in
money-laundering control regime

Pitcairn Islands
*(overseas territory
of the UK)*

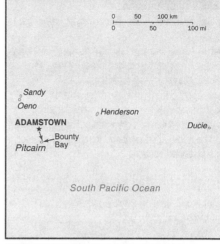

Introduction

Background: Pitcairn Island was discovered in 1767
by the British and settled in 1790 by the Bounty
mutineers and their Tahitian companions. Pitcairn was
the first Pacific island to become a British colony (in
1838) and today remains the last vestige of that
empire in the South Pacific. Outmigration, primarily to
New Zealand, has thinned the population from a peak
of 233 in 1937 to less than 50 today.

Geography

Location: Oceania, islands in the South Pacific
Ocean, about midway between Peru and New
Zealand

Geographic coordinates: 25 04 S, 130 06 W

Map references: Oceania

Area:
total: 47 sq km
land: 47 sq km
water: 0 sq km

Area - comparative: about 0.3 times the size of
Washington, DC

Land boundaries: 0 km

Coastline: 51 km

Maritime claims:
territorial sea: 3 NM
exclusive economic zone: 200 NM

Climate: tropical; hot and humid; modified by
southeast trade winds; rainy season (November to
March)

Terrain: rugged volcanic formation; rocky coastline
with cliffs

Elevation extremes:
lowest point: Pacific Ocean 0 m
highest point: Pawala Valley Ridge 347 m

Natural resources: miro trees (used for
handicrafts), fish

note: manganese, iron, copper, gold, silver, and zinc
have been discovered offshore

Pitcairn Islands *(continued)*

Land use:
arable land: NA%
permanent crops: NA%
other: NA%
Irrigated land: NA sq km
Natural hazards: typhoons (especially November to March)
Environment - current issues: deforestation (only a small portion of the original forest remains because of burning and clearing for settlement)
Geography - note: Britain's most isolated dependency; only the larger island of Pitcairn is inhabited but it has no port or natural harbor; supplies must be transported by rowed longboat from larger ships stationed offshore

People

Population: 46 (July 2004 est.)
Age structure:
0-14 years: NA%
15-64 years: NA%
65 years and over: NA%
Population growth rate: -0.01% (2004 est.)
Birth rate: NA births/1,000 population
Death rate: NA deaths/1,000 population
Net migration rate: NA migrant(s)/1,000 population
Sex ratio: NA
Infant mortality rate:
total: NA%
male: NA%
female: NA%
Life expectancy at birth:
total population: NA years
male: NA years
female: NA years
Total fertility rate: NA children born/woman
HIV/AIDS - adult prevalence rate: NA%
HIV/AIDS - people living with HIV/AIDS: NA
HIV/AIDS - deaths: NA
Nationality:
noun: Pitcairn Islander(s)
adjective: Pitcairn Islander
Ethnic groups: descendants of the Bounty mutineers and their Tahitian wives
Religions: Seventh-Day Adventist 100%
Languages: English (official), Pitcairnese (mixture of an 18th century English dialect and a Tahitian dialect)
Literacy: NA

Government

Country name:
conventional long form: Pitcairn, Henderson, Ducie, and Oeno Islands
conventional short form: Pitcairn Islands
Dependency status: overseas territory of the UK
Government type: NA
Capital: Adamstown
Administrative divisions: none (overseas territory of the UK)
Independence: none (overseas territory of the UK)

National holiday: Birthday of Queen ELIZABETH II, second Saturday in June (1926)
Constitution: 1838; reformed 1904 with additional reforms in 1940; further refined by the Local Government Ordinance of 1964
Legal system: local island by-laws
Suffrage: 18 years of age; universal with three years residency
Executive branch:
chief of state: Queen ELIZABETH II (since 6 February 1952), represented by UK High Commissioner to New Zealand and Governor (nonresident) of the Pitcairn Islands Richard FELL (since NA December 2001); Commissioner (nonresident) Leslie JACQUES (since November 2003); serves as liaison between the governor and the Island Council
head of government: Mayor and Chairman of the Island Council Steve CHRISTIAN (since 7 December 1999)
cabinet: NA
elections: the monarchy is hereditary; high commissioner and commissioner appointed by the monarch; island mayor elected by popular vote for a three-year term; election last held NA December 2002 (next to be held NA December 2005)
election results: Steve CHRISTIAN elected mayor; percent of vote - NA%
Legislative branch: unicameral Island Council (10 seats - 5 elected by popular vote, 1 nominated by the 5 elected members, 2 appointed by the governor including 1 seat for the Island Secretary, the Island Mayor, and a commissioner liaising between the governor and council; elected members serve one-year terms)
elections: last held 24 December 2003 (next to be held 24 December 2004)
election results: percent of vote - NA%; seats - all independents
Judicial branch: Island Court (island magistrate, appointed by the governor, presides over the court)
Political parties and leaders: none
Political pressure groups and leaders: none
International organization participation: none
Diplomatic representation in the US: none (overseas territory of the UK)
Diplomatic representation from the US: none (overseas territory of the UK)
Flag description: blue with the flag of the UK in the upper hoist-side quadrant and the Pitcairn Islander coat of arms centered on the outer half of the flag; the coat of arms is yellow, green, and light blue with a shield featuring a yellow anchor

Economy

Economy - overview: The inhabitants of this tiny isolated economy exist on fishing, subsistence farming, handicrafts, and postage stamps. The fertile soil of the valleys produces a wide variety of fruits and vegetables, including citrus, sugarcane, watermelons, bananas, yams, and beans. Bartering is an important

part of the economy. The major sources of revenue are the sale of postage stamps to collectors and the sale of handicrafts to passing ships.
GDP: purchasing power parity - $NA
GDP - real growth rate: NA%
GDP - per capita: purchasing power parity - $NA
GDP - composition by sector:
agriculture: NA%
industry: NA%
services: NA%
Population below poverty line: NA%
Household income or consumption by percentage share:
lowest 10%: NA%
highest 10%: NA%
Inflation rate (consumer prices): NA%
Labor force: 12 able-bodied men (1997)
Labor force - by occupation: no business community in the usual sense; some public works; subsistence farming and fishing
Unemployment rate: NA%
Budget:
revenues: $729,884
expenditures: $878,119, including capital expenditures of $NA (FY94/95 est.)
Industries: postage stamps, handicrafts
Industrial production growth rate: NA%
Electricity - production: NA kWh; note - electric power is provided by a small diesel-powered generator
Electricity - consumption: NA kWh
Agriculture - products: wide variety of fruits and vegetables, goats, chickens
Exports: $NA
Exports - commodities: fruits, vegetables, curios, stamps
Exports - partners: NA (2000)
Imports: $NA
Imports - commodities: fuel oil, machinery, building materials, flour, sugar, other foodstuffs
Imports - partners: NA (2000)
Debt - external: $NA
Economic aid - recipient: $NA
Currency: New Zealand dollar (NZD)
Currency code: NZD
Exchange rates: New Zealand dollars per US dollar - 1.7229 (2003), 2.162 (2002), 2.3776 (2001), 2.1863 (2000), 1.8886 (1999)
Fiscal year: 1 April - 31 March

Communications

Telephones - main lines in use: 1 (there are 17 telephones on one party line); (2004)
Telephone system:
general assessment: only party line telephone service is available for this small, closely related community
domestic: party line service only
international: country code - 672; satellite earth station (Inmarsat)
Radio broadcast stations: AM 1, FM 0, shortwave 0 (1998)

Pitcairn Islands *(continued)*

Television broadcast stations: 0 (1997)
Internet country code: .pn
Internet users: NA

Transportation

Railways: 0 km
Highways:
total: 6.4 km
paved: 0 km
unpaved: 6.4 km
Waterways: none
Ports and harbors: Adamstown (on Bounty Bay)
Merchant marine:
total: 1 ships (1,000 GRT or over) 3,313 GRT/5,651 DWT
by type: cargo 1 (2003 est.)
Airports: none (2003 est.)

Military

Military - note: defense is the responsibility of the UK

Transnational Issues

Disputes - international: none

Poland

Introduction

Background: Poland is an ancient nation that was conceived around the middle of the 10th century. Its golden age occurred in the 16th century. During the following century, the strengthening of the gentry and internal disorders weakened the nation. In a series of agreements between 1772 and 1795, Russia, Prussia, and Austria partitioned Poland amongst themselves. Poland regained its independence in 1918 only to be overrun by Germany and the Soviet Union in World War II. It became a Soviet satellite state following the war, but its government was comparatively tolerant and progressive. Labor turmoil in 1980 led to the formation of the independent trade union "Solidarity" that over time became a political force and by 1990 had swept parliamentary elections and the presidency. A "shock therapy" program during the early 1990s enabled the country to transform its economy into one of the most robust in Central Europe, but Poland currently suffers low GDP growth and high unemployment. Solidarity suffered a major defeat in the 2001 parliamentary elections when it failed to elect a single deputy to the lower house of Parliament, and the new leaders of the Solidarity Trade Union subsequently pledged to reduce the Trade Union's political role. Poland joined NATO in 1999 and is scheduled to accede to the European Union along with nine other states on 1 May 2004.

Geography

Location: Central Europe, east of Germany
Geographic coordinates: 52 00 N, 20 00 E
Map references: Europe
Area:
total: 312,685 sq km
land: 304,465 sq km
water: 8,220 sq km
Area - comparative: slightly smaller than New Mexico

Land boundaries:
total: 2,788 km
border countries: Belarus 407 km, Czech Republic 658 km, Germany 456 km, Lithuania 91 km, Russia (Kaliningrad Oblast) 206 km, Slovakia 444 km, Ukraine 526 km
Coastline: 491 km
Maritime claims:
territorial sea: 12 NM
exclusive economic zone: defined by international treaties
Climate: temperate with cold, cloudy, moderately severe winters with frequent precipitation; mild summers with frequent showers and thundershowers
Terrain: mostly flat plain; mountains along southern border
Elevation extremes:
lowest point: near Raczki Elblaskie -2 m
highest point: Rysy 2,499 m
Natural resources: coal, sulfur, copper, natural gas, silver, lead, salt, amber, arable land
Land use:
arable land: 45.81%
permanent crops: 1.23%
other: 52.96% (1998 est.)
Irrigated land: 1,000 sq km (1998 est.)
Natural hazards: flooding
Environment - current issues: situation has improved since 1989 due to decline in heavy industry and increased environmental concern by post-Communist governments; air pollution nonetheless remains serious because of sulfur dioxide emissions from coal-fired power plants, and the resulting acid rain has caused forest damage; water pollution from industrial and municipal sources is also a problem, as is disposal of hazardous wastes; pollution levels should continue to decrease as industrial establishments bring their facilities up to European Union code, but at substantial cost to business and the government
Environment - international agreements:
party to: Air Pollution, Antarctic-Environmental Protocol, Antarctic-Marine Living Resources, Antarctic Seals, Antarctic Treaty, Biodiversity, Climate Change, Climate Change-Kyoto Protocol, Desertification, Endangered Species, Environmental Modification, Hazardous Wastes, Kyoto Protocol, Law of the Sea, Marine Dumping, Ozone Layer Protection, Ship Pollution, Wetlands
signed, but not ratified: Air Pollution-Nitrogen Oxides, Air Pollution-Persistent Organic Pollutants, Air Pollution-Sulfur 94
Geography - note: historically, an area of conflict because of flat terrain and the lack of natural barriers on the North European Plain

People

Population: 38,626,349 (July 2004 est.)
Age structure:
0-14 years: 17.1% (male 3,388,247; female 3,216,085)

Poland (continued)

15-64 years: 70% (male 13,454,820; female 13,591,814)
65 years and over: 12.9% (male 1,896,940; female 3,078,443) (2004 est.)
Median age:
total: 36.2 years
male: 34.3 years
female: 38.2 years (2004 est.)
Population growth rate: 0.02% (2004 est.)
Birth rate: 10.64 births/1,000 population (2004 est.)
Death rate: 9.97 deaths/1,000 population (2004 est.)
Net migration rate: -0.49 migrant(s)/1,000 population (2004 est.)
Sex ratio:
at birth: 1.06 male(s)/female
under 15 years: 1.05 male(s)/female
15-64 years: 0.99 male(s)/female
65 years and over: 0.62 male(s)/female
total population: 0.94 male(s)/female (2004 est.)
Infant mortality rate:
total: 8.73 deaths/1,000 live births
male: 9.82 deaths/1,000 live births
female: 7.59 deaths/1,000 live births (2004 est.)
Life expectancy at birth:
total population: 74.16 years
male: 70.04 years
female: 78.52 years (2004 est.)
Total fertility rate: 1.38 children born/woman (2004 est.)
HIV/AIDS - adult prevalence rate: 0.1% - note: no country specific models provided (2001 est.)
HIV/AIDS - people living with HIV/AIDS: NA
HIV/AIDS - deaths: 100 (2001 est.)
Nationality:
noun: Pole(s)
adjective: Polish
Ethnic groups: Polish 96.7%, German 0.4%, Belarusian 0.1%, Ukrainian 0.1%, other 2.7% (2002)
Religions: Roman Catholic 95% (about 75% practicing), Eastern Orthodox, Protestant, and other 5%
Languages: Polish
Literacy:
definition: age 15 and over can read and write
total population: 99.8%
male: 99.8%
female: 99.7% (2003 est.)

Government

Country name:
conventional long form: Republic of Poland
conventional short form: Poland
local long form: Rzeczpospolita Polska
local short form: Polska
Government type: republic
Capital: Warsaw
Administrative divisions: 16 provinces (wojewodztwa, singular - wojewodztwo); Dolnoslaskie, Kujawsko-Pomorskie, Lodzkie, Lubelskie, Lubuskie, Malopolskie, Mazowieckie, Opolskie, Podkarpackie, Podlaskie, Pomorskie, Slaskie, Swietokrzyskie, Warminsko-Mazurskie, Wielkopolskie, Zachodniopomorskie
Independence: 11 November 1918 (independent republic proclaimed)
National holiday: Constitution Day, 3 May (1791)
Constitution: 16 October 1997; adopted by the National Assembly 2 April 1997; passed by national referendum 23 May 1997
Legal system: mixture of Continental (Napoleonic) civil law and holdover Communist legal theory; changes being gradually introduced as part of broader democratization process; limited judicial review of legislative acts, but rulings of the Constitutional Tribunal are final; court decisions can be appealed to the European Court of Justice in Strasbourg
Suffrage: 18 years of age; universal
Executive branch:
chief of state: President Aleksander KWASNIEWSKI (since 23 December 1995)
head of government: Prime Minister Leszek MILLER (SLD) (since 19 October 2001), Deputy Prime Ministers Marek POL (since 19 October 2001), Jerzy HAUSNER (since 11 June 2003), Jozef OLEKSY (since 19 January 2004)
cabinet: Council of Ministers responsible to the prime minister and the Sejm; the prime minister proposes, the president appoints, and the Sejm approves the Council of Ministers
elections: president elected by popular vote for a five-year term; election last held 8 October 2000 (next to be held NA October 2005); prime minister and deputy prime ministers appointed by the president and confirmed by the Sejm
election results: Aleksander KWASNIEWSKI reelected president; percent of popular vote - Aleksander KWASNIEWSKI 53.9%, Andrzej OLECHOWSKI 17.3%, Marian KRZAKLEWSKI 15.6%, Lech WALESA 1%
Legislative branch: bicameral National Assembly or Zgromadzenie Narodowe consists of the Sejm (460 seats; members are elected under a complex system of proportional representation to serve four-year terms) and the Senate or Senat (100 seats; members are elected by a majority vote on a provincial basis to serve four-year terms)
elections: Sejm elections last held 23 September 2001 (next to be held by September 2005); Senate - last held 23 September 2001 (next to be held by September 2005)
election results: Sejm - percent of vote by party - SLD-UP 41%, PO 12.7%, Samoobrona 10.2%, PiS 9.5%, PSL 9%, LPR 7.9%, AWSP 5.6% UW 3.1%, other 1%; seats by party (as of 16 January 2004) - SLD 190, PO 56, PiS 43, PSL 37, SO 31, LPR 29, UP 16, PLD 10, SKL 8, PBL 6, PRS 5, RKN 5, PP 3, ROP 3, German minorities 2, independents 16; Senate - percent of vote by party - NA%; seats by party (as of 16 January 2004)- SLD-UP 74, Block Senate 2001 10, PSL and unaffiliated 5, UW 4, SO 2, LPR 2, independents 2, PiS 1
note: two seats are assigned to ethnic minority parties
Judicial branch: Supreme Court (judges are appointed by the president on the recommendation of the National Council of the Judiciary for an indefinite period); Constitutional Tribunal (judges are chosen by the Sejm for nine-year terms)
Political parties and leaders: Catholic-National Movement or RKN [Antoni MACIEREWICZ]; Citizens Platform or PO [Donald TUSK]; Coalition Electoral Action Solidarity of the Right or AWSP; Conservative Peasants Party or SKL-RNP [Artur BALAZS]; Democratic Left Alliance or SLD [Leszek MILLER]; Freedom Union or UW [Wladyslaw FRASYNIUK]; German Minority of Lower Silesia or MNSO [Henryk KROLL]; Law and Justice or PiS [Jaroslaw KACZYNSKI]; League of Polish Families or LPR [Marek KOTLINOWSKI]; Movement for the Reconstruction of Poland or ROP [Jan OLSZEWSKI]; Peasant-Democratic Party or PLD [Roman JAGIELINSKI]; Polish Accord or PP [Jan LOPUSZANSKI]; Polish Peasant Bloc or PBL [Wojciech MOJZESOWICZ]; Polish Peasant Party or PSL [Jaroslaw KALINOWSKI]; Polish Raison d'Etat or PRS [Zbigniew Witaszek]; Samoobrona or SO [Andrzej LEPPER]; Social Movement or RS [Krzysztof PIESIEWICZ]; Union of Labor or UP [Marek POL]
Political pressure groups and leaders: All Poland Trade Union Alliance or OPZZ (trade union) [Maciej MANICKI]; Roman Catholic Church [Cardinal Jozef GLEMP]; Solidarity Trade Union [Janusz SNIADEK]
International organization participation: ACCT (observer), Australia Group, BIS, BSEC (observer), CBSS, CE, CEI, CERN, EAPC, EBRD, EU (new member), FAO, IAEA, IBRD, ICAO, ICC, ICCt, ICFTU, ICRM, IDA, IFC, IFRCS, IHO, ILO, IMF, IMO, Interpol, IOC, IOM, ISO, ITU, MINURSO, MONUC, NAM (guest), NATO, NSG, OAS (observer), OECD, OPCW, OSCE, PCA, PFP, UN, UNCTAD, UNDOF, UNESCO, UNHCR, UNIDO, UNIFIL, UNMEE, UNMIK, UNMIL, UNOMIG, UPU, WCL, WCO, WEU (associate), WFTU, WHO, WIPO, WMO, WToO, WTrO, ZC
Diplomatic representation in the US:
chief of mission: Ambassador Przemyslaw GRUDZINSKI
chancery: 2640 16th Street NW, Washington, DC 20009
telephone: [1] (202) 234-3800 through 3802
FAX: [1] (202) 328-6270
consulate(s) general: Chicago, Los Angeles, and New York
Diplomatic representation from the US:
chief of mission: Ambassador Christopher R. HILL
embassy: Aleje Ujazdowskie 29/31 00-540 Warsaw P1
mailing address: American Embassy Warsaw, US Department of State, 5010 Warsaw Place, Washington, DC 20521-5010 (pouch)
telephone: [48] (22) 504-2000
FAX: [48] (22) 504-2951
consulate(s) general: Krakow

Poland (continued)

Flag description: two equal horizontal bands of white (top) and red; similar to the flags of Indonesia and Monaco which are red (top) and white

Economy

Economy - overview: Poland has steadfastly pursued a policy of economic liberalization throughout the 1990s and today stands out as a success story among transition economies. Even so, much remains to be done. The privatization of small and medium state-owned companies and a liberal law on establishing new firms has encouraged the development of the private business sector, but legal and bureaucratic obstacles alongside persistent corruption are hampering its further development. Poland's agricultural sector remains handicapped by structural problems, surplus labor, inefficient small farms, and lack of investment. Restructuring and privatization of "sensitive sectors" (e.g., coal, steel, railroads, and energy), while recently initiated, have stalled. Reforms in health care, education, the pension system, and state administration have resulted in larger than expected fiscal pressures. Further progress in public finance depends mainly on privatization of Poland's remaining state sector, the reduction of state employment, and an overhaul of the tax code to incorporate the growing gray economy and farmers, most of whom pay no tax. The government's determination to enter the EU has shaped most aspects of its economic policy and new legislation; in a nationwide referendum in November 2003, 77% of the voters voted in favor of Poland's EU accession, now scheduled for May 2004. Improving Poland's export competitiveness and containing the internal budget deficit are top priorities. Due to political uncertainty, the zloty has recently depreciated in relation to the euro, while currencies of the other euro-zone aspirants have been appreciating. GDP per capita equals that of the three Baltic states.

GDP: purchasing power parity - $426.7 billion (2003 est.)

GDP - real growth rate: 3.6% (2003 est.)

GDP - per capita: purchasing power parity - $11,000 (2003 est.)

GDP - composition by sector:
agriculture: 3.1%
industry: 30.4%
services: 66.5% (2003 est.)

Population below poverty line: 18.4% (2000 est.)

Household income or consumption by percentage share:
lowest 10%: 3.2%
highest 10%: 24.7% (1998)

Distribution of family income - Gini index: 31.6 (1998)

Inflation rate (consumer prices): 0.7% (2003 est.)

Labor force: 17.6 million (2000 est.)

Labor force - by occupation: industry 22.1%, agriculture 27.5%, services 50.4% (1999)

Unemployment rate: 18% (2003)

Budget:
revenues: $49.6 billion
expenditures: $52.3 billion, including capital expenditures of $NA (1999)

Industries: machine building, iron and steel, coal mining, chemicals, shipbuilding, food processing, glass, beverages, textiles

Industrial production growth rate: 3% (2003)

Electricity - production: 135 billion kWh (2001)

Electricity - production by source:
fossil fuel: 98.1%
hydro: 1.5%
nuclear: 0%
other: 0.4% (2001)

Electricity - consumption: 118.8 billion kWh (2001)

Electricity - exports: 11.04 billion kWh (2001)

Electricity - imports: 4.306 billion kWh (2001)

Oil - production: 17,180 bbl/day (2001 est.)

Oil - consumption: 424,100 bbl/day (2001 est.)

Oil - exports: 53,000 bbl/day (2001)

Oil - imports: 413,700 bbl/day (2001)

Oil - proved reserves: 116.4 million bbl (1 January 2002)

Natural gas - production: 5.471 billion cu m (2001 est.)

Natural gas - consumption: 13.85 billion cu m (2001 est.)

Natural gas - exports: 41 million cu m (2001 est.)

Natural gas - imports: 8.782 billion cu m (2001 est.)

Natural gas - proved reserves: 154.4 billion cu m (1 January 2002)

Agriculture - products: potatoes, fruits, vegetables, wheat; poultry, eggs, pork

Exports: $57.6 billion f.o.b. (2003 est.)

Exports - commodities: machinery and transport equipment 30.2%, intermediate manufactured goods 25.5%, miscellaneous manufactured goods 20.9%, food and live animals 8.5% (1999)

Exports - partners: Germany 32.3%, France 6%, Italy 5.5%, UK 5.2%, Netherlands 4.5%, Czech Republic 4% (2002)

Imports: $63.65 billion f.o.b. (2003 est.)

Imports - commodities: machinery and transport equipment 38.2%, intermediate manufactured goods 20.8%, chemicals 14.3%, miscellaneous manufactured goods 9.5% (1999)

Imports - partners: Germany 24.3%, Italy 8.4%, Russia 8%, France 7% (2002)

Debt - external: $79.7 billion (2003)

Economic aid - recipient: EU structural adjustment funds (2000)

Currency: zloty (PLN)

Currency code: PLN

Exchange rates: zlotych per US dollar - 3.8891 (2003), 4.08 (2002), 4.0939 (2001), 4.3461 (2000), 3.9671 (1999)
note: zlotych is the plural form of zloty

Fiscal year: calendar year

Communications

Telephones - main lines in use: 11.4 million (2002)
Telephones - mobile cellular: 14 million (2002)
Telephone system:
general assessment: underdeveloped and outmoded system in the process of being overhauled; partial privatization of the state-owned telephone monopoly is underway; the long waiting list for main line telephone service has resulted in a boom in mobile cellular telephone use
domestic: cable, open-wire, and microwave radio relay; 3 cellular networks; local exchanges 56.6% digital
international: country code - 48; satellite earth stations - 2 Intelsat, NA Eutelsat, 2 Inmarsat (Atlantic and Indian Ocean regions), and 1 Intersputnik (Atlantic Ocean region)

Radio broadcast stations: AM 14, FM 777, shortwave 1 (1998)

Television broadcast stations: 179 (plus 256 repeaters) (September 1995)

Internet country code: .pl

Internet hosts: 657,495 (2002)

Internet users: 8.88 million (2002)

Transportation

Railways:
total: 23,420 km
broad gauge: 646 km 1.524-m gauge
standard gauge: 21,639 km 1.435-m gauge (11,626 km electrified)
narrow gauge: 1,135 km various gauges including 1.000-m, 0.785-m, 0.750-m, and 0.600-m (2002)

Highways:
total: 364,656 km
paved: 249,060 km (including 358 km of expressways)
unpaved: 115,596 km (2000)

Waterways: 3,812 km (navigable rivers and canals) (1996)

Pipelines: gas 12,901 km; oil 737 km (2003)

Ports and harbors: Gdansk, Gdynia, Gliwice, Kolobrzeg, Szczecin, Swinoujscie, Ustka, Warsaw, Wroclaw

Merchant marine:
total: 14 ships (1,000 GRT or over) 154,710 GRT/ 228,132 DWT
by type: bulk 7, cargo 3, chemical tanker 3, roll on/roll off 1
registered in other countries: 100 (2003 est.)

Airports: 122 (2003 est.)

Airports - with paved runways:
total: 83
over 3,047 m: 3
2,438 to 3,047 m: 30
1,524 to 2,437 m: 40
914 to 1,523 m: 8
under 914 m: 2 (2003 est.)

Poland (continued)

(continued)

Airports - with unpaved runways:
total: 39
2,438 to 3,047 m: 1
1,524 to 2,437 m: 4
914 to 1,523 m: 13
under 914 m: 21 (2003 est.)
Heliports: 3 (2003 est.)

Military

Military branches: Land Forces, Navy, Air Force
Military manpower - military age: 19 years of age (2004 est.)
Military manpower - availability:
males age 15-49: 10,291,628 (2004 est.)
Military manpower - fit for military service:
males age 15-49: 8,034,577 (2004 est.)
Military manpower - reaching military age annually:
males: 329,743 (2004 est.)
Military expenditures - dollar figure: $3.5 billion (2002)
Military expenditures - percent of GDP: 1.71% (2002)

Transnational Issues

Disputes - international: none
Illicit drugs: major illicit producer of synthetic drugs for the international market; minor transshipment point for Asian and Latin American illicit drugs to Western Europe

Portugal

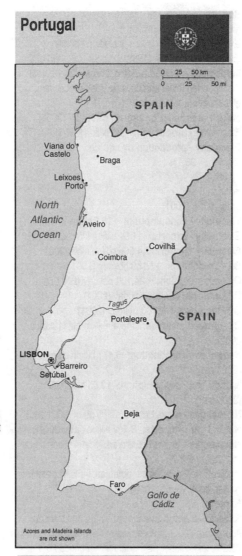

Azores and Madeira Islands are not shown

Introduction

Background: Following its heyday as a world power during the 15th and 16th centuries, Portugal lost much of its wealth and status with the destruction of Lisbon in a 1755 earthquake, occupation during the Napoleonic Wars, and the independence in 1822 of Brazil as a colony. A 1910 revolution deposed the monarchy; for most of the next six decades, repressive governments ran the country. In 1974, a left-wing military coup installed broad democratic reforms. The following year, Portugal granted independence to all of its African colonies. Portugal is a founding member of NATO and entered the EC (now the EU) in 1986.

Geography

Location: Southwestern Europe, bordering the North Atlantic Ocean, west of Spain
Geographic coordinates: 39 30 N, 8 00 W
Map references: Europe
Area:
total: 92,391 sq km
land: 91,951 sq km

water: 440 sq km
note: includes Azores and Madeira Islands
Area - comparative: slightly smaller than Indiana
Land boundaries:
total: 1,214 km
border countries: Spain 1,214 km
Coastline: 1,793 km
Maritime claims:
territorial sea: 12 NM
contiguous zone: 24 NM
exclusive economic zone: 200 NM
continental shelf: 200-m depth or to the depth of exploitation
Climate: maritime temperate; cool and rainy in north, warmer and drier in south
Terrain: mountainous north of the Tagus River, rolling plains in south
Elevation extremes:
lowest point: Atlantic Ocean 0 m
highest point: Ponta do Pico (Pico or Pico Alto) on Ilha do Pico in the Azores 2,351 m
Natural resources: fish, forests (cork), tungsten, iron ore, uranium ore, marble, arable land, hydropower
Land use:
arable land: 20.57%
permanent crops: 7.74%
other: 71.69% (1999 est.)
Irrigated land: 6,320 sq km (1998 est.)
Natural hazards: Azores subject to severe earthquakes
Environment - current issues: soil erosion; air pollution caused by industrial and vehicle emissions; water pollution, especially in coastal areas
Environment - international agreements:
party to: Air Pollution, Biodiversity, Climate Change, Climate Change-Kyoto Protocol, Desertification, Endangered Species, Hazardous Wastes, Law of the Sea, Marine Dumping, Marine Life Conservation, Ozone Layer Protection, Ship Pollution, Tropical Timber 83, Tropical Timber 94, Wetlands
signed, but not ratified: Air Pollution-Persistent Organic Pollutants, Air Pollution-Volatile Organic Compounds, Environmental Modification
Geography - note: Azores and Madeira Islands occupy strategic locations along western sea approaches to Strait of Gibraltar

People

Population: 10,524,145 (July 2004 est.)
Age structure:
0-14 years: 16.7% (male 916,106; female 840,574)
15-64 years: 66.4% (male 3,454,970; female 3,535,108)
65 years and over: 16.9% (male 735,407; female 1,041,980) (2004 est.)
Median age:
total: 37.9 years
male: 35.8 years
female: 40 years (2004 est.)

Portugal (continued)

Population growth rate: 0.41% (2004 est.)
Birth rate: 10.9 births/1,000 population (2004 est.)
Death rate: 10.37 deaths/1,000 population (2004 est.)
Net migration rate: 3.57 migrant(s)/1,000 population (2004 est.)
Sex ratio:
at birth: 1.07 male(s)/female
under 15 years: 1.09 male(s)/female
15-64 years: 0.98 male(s)/female
65 years and over: 0.71 male(s)/female
total population: 0.94 male(s)/female (2004 est.)
Infant mortality rate:
total: 5.13 deaths/1,000 live births
male: 5.6 deaths/1,000 live births
female: 4.62 deaths/1,000 live births (2004 est.)
Life expectancy at birth:
total population: 77.35 years
male: 74.06 years
female: 80.85 years (2004 est.)
Total fertility rate: 1.46 children born/woman (2004 est.)
HIV/AIDS - adult prevalence rate: 0.5% (2001 est.)
HIV/AIDS - people living with HIV/AIDS: 27,000 (2001 est.)
HIV/AIDS - deaths: 1,000 (2001 est.)
Nationality:
noun: Portuguese (singular and plural)
adjective: Portuguese
Ethnic groups: homogeneous Mediterranean stock; citizens of black African descent who immigrated to mainland during decolonization number less than 100,000; since 1990 East Europeans have entered Portugal
Religions: Roman Catholic 94%, Protestant (1995)
Languages: Portuguese (official), Mirandese (official - but locally used)
Literacy:
definition: age 15 and over can read and write
total population: 93.3%
male: 95.5%
female: 91.3% (2003 est.)

Government

Country name:
conventional long form: Portuguese Republic
conventional short form: Portugal
local long form: Republica Portuguesa
local short form: Portugal
Government type: parliamentary democracy
Capital: Lisbon
Administrative divisions: 18 districts (distritos, singular - distrito) and 2 autonomous regions* (regioes autonomas, singular - regiao autonoma); Aveiro, Acores (Azores)*, Beja, Braga, Braganca, Castelo Branco, Coimbra, Evora, Faro, Guarda, Leiria, Lisboa, Madeira*, Portalegre, Porto, Santarem, Setubal, Viana do Castelo, Vila Real, Viseu
Independence: 1143 (independent republic proclaimed 5 October 1910)
National holiday: Portugal Day, 10 June (1580)

Constitution: 25 April 1976, revised 30 October 1982, 1 June 1989, 5 November 1992, and 3 September 1997
Legal system: civil law system; the Constitutional Tribunal reviews the constitutionality of legislation; accepts compulsory ICJ jurisdiction, with reservations
Suffrage: 18 years of age; universal
Executive branch:
chief of state: President Jorge SAMPAIO (since 9 March 1996)
head of government: Prime Minister Jose Manuel DURAO BARROSO (since 6 April 2002)
cabinet: Council of Ministers appointed by the president on the recommendation of the prime minister
note: there is also a Council of State that acts as a consultative body to the president
elections: president elected by popular vote for a five-year term; election last held 14 January 2001 (next to be held NA January 2006); following legislative elections, the leader of the majority party or leader of a majority coalition is usually appointed prime minister by the president
election results: Jorge SAMPAIO reelected president; percent of vote - Jorge SAMPAIO (Socialist) 55.8%, Joaquim FERREIRA Do Amaral (Social Democrat) 34.5%, Antonio ABREU (Communist) 5.1%
Legislative branch: unicameral Assembly of the Republic or Assembleia da Republica (230 seats; members are elected by popular vote to serve four-year terms)
elections: last held 17 March 2002 (next to be held NA 2006)
election results: percent of vote by party - PSD 40.1%, PS 37.8%, PP 8.7%, PCP/PEV 6.9%, The Left Bloc 2.7%; seats by party - PSD 105, PS 96, PP 14, PCP/PEV 12, The Left Bloc 3
Judicial branch: Supreme Court or Supremo Tribunal de Justica (judges appointed for life by the Conselho Superior da Magistratura)
Political parties and leaders: The Greens or PEV [no leader]; Popular Party or PP [Paulo PORTAS]; Portuguese Communist Party/The Greens or PCP/PEV [Carlos CARVALHAS]; Portuguese Socialist Party or PS [Eduardo FERRO RODRIGUES]; Social Democratic Party or PSD [Jose Manuel DURAO BARROSO]; United Democratic Coalition or CDU [Carlos CARVALHAS]; The Left Bloc [Franciso Anacleto LOUCA]
Political pressure groups and leaders: NA
International organization participation: AfDB, AsDB, Australia Group, BIS, CE, CERN, EAPC, EBRD, EIB, EMU, ESA, EU, FAO, IADB, IAEA, IBRD, ICAO, ICC, ICCt, ICFTU, ICRM, IDA, IEA, IFAD, IFC, IFRCS, IHO, ILO, IMF, IMO, Interpol, IOC, IOM, ISO, ITU, LAIA (observer), NAM (guest), NATO, NEA, NSG, OAS (observer), OECD, OPCW, OSCE, PCA, UN, UNCTAD, UNESCO, UNIDO, UNMIK, UNMISET, UPU, WCL, WCO, WEU, WFTU, WHO, WIPO, WMO, WToO, WTrO, ZC

Diplomatic representation in the US:
chief of mission: Ambassador Pedro Manuel Dos Reis Alves CATARINO
chancery: 2125 Kalorama Road NW, Washington, DC 20008
telephone: [1] (202) 328-8610
FAX: [1] (202) 462-3726
consulate(s) general: Boston, New York, Newark (New Jersey), and San Francisco
consulate(s): Los Angeles, New Bedford (Massachusetts), Providence (Rhode Island)
Diplomatic representation from the US:
chief of mission: Ambassador John N. PALMER
embassy: Avenida das Forcas Armadas, 1600-081 Lisbon
mailing address: PSC 83, APO AE 09726
telephone: [351] (21) 727-3300
FAX: [351] (21) 726-9109
consulate(s): Ponta Delgada (Azores)
Flag description: two vertical bands of green (hoist side, two-fifths) and red (three-fifths) with the Portuguese coat of arms centered on the dividing line

Economy

Economy - overview: Portugal has become a diversified and increasingly service-based economy since joining the European Community in 1986. Over the past decade, successive governments have privatized many state-controlled firms and liberalized key areas of the economy, including the financial and telecommunications sectors. The country qualified for the European Monetary Union (EMU) in 1998 and began circulating the euro on 1 January 2002 along with 11 other EU member economies. Economic growth has been above the EU average for much of the past decade, but fell back in 2001-03. GDP per capita stands at 70% of that of the leading EU economies. A poor educational system, in particular, has been an obstacle to greater productivity and growth. Portugal has been increasingly overshadowed by lower-cost producers in Central Europe and Asia as a target for foreign direct investment. The coalition government faces tough choices in its attempts to boost Portugal's economic competitiveness and to keep the budget deficit within the 3% EU ceiling.
GDP: purchasing power parity - $182.3 billion (2003 est.)
GDP - real growth rate: -1% (2003 est.)
GDP - per capita: purchasing power parity - $18,000 (2003 est.)
GDP - composition by sector:
agriculture: 3.7%
industry: 29.3%
services: 67% (2002)
Population below poverty line: NA%
Household income or consumption by percentage share:
lowest 10%: 3.1%
highest 10%: 28.4% (1995 est.)
Distribution of family income - Gini index: 35.6 (1994-95)

Portugal (continued)

Inflation rate (consumer prices): 3.1% (2003 est.)
Labor force: 5.1 million (2000)
Labor force - by occupation: services 60%, industry 30%, agriculture 10% (1999 est.)
Unemployment rate: 6% (2003 est.)
Budget:
revenues: $45 billion
expenditures: $48 billion, including capital expenditures of $NA (2001 est.)
Industries: textiles and footwear; wood pulp, paper, and cork; metalworking; oil refining; chemicals; fish canning; wine; tourism
Industrial production growth rate: -2.2% (2003 est.)
Electricity - production: 44.32 billion kWh (2001)
Electricity - production by source:
fossil fuel: 64.5%
hydro: 31.3%
nuclear: 0%
other: 4.1% (2001)
Electricity - consumption: 41.48 billion kWh (2001)
Electricity - exports: 3.479 billion kWh (2001)
Electricity - imports: 3.743 billion kWh (2001)
Oil - production: 0 bbl/day (2001 est.)
Oil - consumption: 339,800 bbl/day (2001 est.)
Oil - exports: 28,830 bbl/day (2001)
Oil - imports: 357,300 bbl/day (2001)
Natural gas - production: 0 cu m (2001 est.)
Natural gas - consumption: 2.542 billion cu m (2001 est.)
Natural gas - exports: 0 cu m (2001 est.)
Natural gas - imports: 2.553 billion cu m (2001 est.)
Agriculture - products: grain, potatoes, olives, grapes; sheep, cattle, goats, poultry, beef, dairy products
Exports: $31.13 billion f.o.b. (2003 est.)
Exports - commodities: clothing and footwear, machinery, chemicals, cork and paper products, hides
Exports - partners: Spain 20.3%, Germany 18.4%, France 12.6%, UK 10.5%, US 5.8%, Italy 4.8%, Belgium 4.5% (2002)
Imports: $43.73 billion f.o.b. (2003 est.)
Imports - commodities: machinery and transport equipment, chemicals, petroleum, textiles, agricultural products
Imports - partners: Spain 28.1%, Germany 15%, France 10.2%, Italy 6.5%, UK 5.2%, Netherlands 4.5% (2002)
Debt - external: $211.7 billion (2003 est.)
Economic aid - donor: ODA, $271 million (1995)
Currency: euro (EUR)
note: on 1 January 1999, the European Monetary Union introduced the euro as a common currency to be used by financial institutions of member countries; on 1 January 2002, the euro became the sole currency for everyday transactions within the member countries
Currency code: EUR
Exchange rates: euros per US dollar - 0.886 (2003), 1.0626 (2002), 1.1175 (2001), 1.0854 (2000), 0.9386 (1999)
Fiscal year: calendar year

Telephones - main lines in use: 4,354,600 (2002)
Telephones - mobile cellular: 8,528,900 (2002)
Telephone system:
general assessment: Portugal's telephone system has achieved a state-of-the-art network with broadband, high-speed capabilities and a main line telephone density of 53%
domestic: integrated network of coaxial cables, open-wire, microwave radio relay, and domestic satellite earth stations
international: country code - 351; 6 submarine cables; satellite earth stations - 3 Intelsat (2 Atlantic Ocean and 1 Indian Ocean), NA Eutelsat; tropospheric scatter to Azores; note - an earth station for Inmarsat (Atlantic Ocean region) is planned
Radio broadcast stations: AM 47, FM 172 (many are repeaters), shortwave 2 (1998)
Television broadcast stations: 62 (plus 166 repeaters)
note: includes Azores and Madeira Islands (1995)
Internet country code: .pt
Internet hosts: 164,711 (2002)
Internet users: 3.6 million (2002)

Transportation

Railways:
total: 2,850 km
broad gauge: 2,576 km 1.668-m gauge (623 km electrified)
narrow gauge: 274 km 1.000-m gauge (2002)
Highways:
total: 68,732 km
paved: 59,110 km (including 1441 km of expressways)
unpaved: 9,622 km (2000)
Waterways: 820 km
note: relatively unimportant to national economy, used by shallow-draft craft limited to 300 metric-ton or less cargo capacity
Pipelines: gas 482 km (2003)
Ports and harbors: Aveiro, Funchal (Madeira Islands), Horta (Azores), Leixoes, Lisbon, Porto, Ponta Delgada (Azores), Praia da Vitoria (Azores), Setubal, Viana do Castelo
Merchant marine:
total: 122 ships (1,000 GRT or over) 872,557 GRT/ 1,236,025 DWT
by type: bulk 12, cargo 49, chemical tanker 19, container 8, liquefied gas 7, multi-functional large load carrier 1, passenger 6, petroleum tanker 7, refrigerated cargo 1, roll on/roll off 5, short-sea/ passenger 5, vehicle carrier 2
foreign-owned: Australia 1, Belgium 1, Cyprus 1, Denmark 7, Germany 21, Greece 2, Guadeloupe 1, Iceland 1, Italy 16, Japan 1, Malta 1, Norway 7, Panama 1, Spain 18, Switzerland 7, Ukraine 1, United Kingdom 1
registered in other countries: 24 (2003 est.)
Airports: 66 (2003 est.)

Airports - with paved runways:
total: 40
over 3,047 m: 5
2,438 to 3,047 m: 9
1,524 to 2,437 m: 4
914 to 1,523 m: 15
under 914 m: 7 (2003 est.)
Airports - with unpaved runways:
total: 26
914 to 1,523 m: 1
under 914 m: 25 (2003 est.)

Military branches: Army, Navy (PON; including Marines), Air Force (FAP), Republican Guard (including Fiscal Guard)
Military manpower - military age: 20 years of age (2004 est.)
Military manpower - availability:
males age 15-49: 2,628,892 (2004 est.)
Military manpower - fit for military service:
males age 15-49: 2,107,502 (2004 est.)
Military manpower - reaching military age annually:
males: 72,821 (2004 est.)
Military expenditures - dollar figure: $3,497,800,000 (2003)
Military expenditures - percent of GDP: 2.3% (2003)

Disputes - international: some Portuguese groups assert dormant claims to territories ceded to Spain around the town of Olivenza
Illicit drugs: gateway country for Latin American cocaine and Southwest Asian heroin entering the European market (especially from Brazil); transshipment point for hashish from North Africa to Europe; consumer of Southwest Asian heroin

Puerto Rico
(commonwealth associated with the US)

Introduction

Background: Populated for centuries by aboriginal peoples, the island was claimed by the Spanish Crown in 1493 following Columbus' second voyage to the Americas. In 1898, after 400 years of colonial rule that saw the indigenous population nearly exterminated and African slave labor introduced, Puerto Rico was ceded to the US as a result of the Spanish-American War. Puerto Ricans were granted US citizenship in 1917. Popularly-elected governors have served since 1948. In 1952, a constitution was enacted providing for internal self government. In plebiscites held in 1967, 1993, and 1998, voters chose to retain commonwealth status.

Geography

Location: Caribbean, island between the Caribbean Sea and the North Atlantic Ocean, east of the Dominican Republic

Geographic coordinates: 18 15 N, 66 30 W

Map references: Central America and the Caribbean

Area:
total: 9,104 sq km
land: 8,959 sq km
water: 145 sq km

Area - comparative: slightly less than three times the size of Rhode Island

Land boundaries: 0 km

Coastline: 501 km

Maritime claims:
territorial sea: 12 NM
exclusive economic zone: 200 NM

Climate: tropical marine, mild; little seasonal temperature variation

Terrain: mostly mountains with coastal plain belt in north; mountains precipitous to sea on west coast; sandy beaches along most coastal areas

Elevation extremes:
lowest point: Caribbean Sea 0 m
highest point: Cerro de Punta 1,338 m

Natural resources: some copper and nickel; potential for onshore and offshore oil

Land use:
arable land: 3.7%
permanent crops: 5.1%
other: 91.2% (1998 est.)

Irrigated land: 400 sq km (1998 est.)

Natural hazards: periodic droughts; hurricanes

Environment - current issues: erosion; occasional drought causing water shortages

Geography - note: important location along the Mona Passage - a key shipping lane to the Panama Canal; San Juan is one of the biggest and best natural harbors in the Caribbean; many small rivers and high central mountains ensure land is well watered; south coast relatively dry; fertile coastal plain belt in north

People

Population: 3,897,960 (July 2004 est.)

Age structure:
0-14 years: 22.4% (male 446,474; female 426,585)
15-64 years: 65.4% (male 1,220,721; female 1,329,936)
65 years and over: 12.2% (male 205,933; female 268,311) (2004 est.)

Median age:
total: 33.8 years
male: 32.1 years
female: 35.4 years (2004 est.)

Population growth rate: 0.49% (2004 est.)

Birth rate: 14.1 births/1,000 population (2004 est.)

Death rate: 7.77 deaths/1,000 population (2004 est.)

Net migration rate: -1.46 migrant(s)/1,000 population (2004 est.)

Sex ratio:
at birth: 1.05 male(s)/female
under 15 years: 1.05 male(s)/female
15-64 years: 0.92 male(s)/female
65 years and over: 0.77 male(s)/female
total population: 0.93 male(s)/female (2004 est.)

Infant mortality rate:
total: 8.37 deaths/1,000 live births
male: 9.7 deaths/1,000 live births
female: 6.98 deaths/1,000 live births (2004 est.)

Life expectancy at birth:
total population: 77.49 years
male: 73.49 years
female: 81.68 years (2004 est.)

Total fertility rate: 1.91 children born/woman (2004 est.)

HIV/AIDS - adult prevalence rate: NA%

HIV/AIDS - people living with HIV/AIDS: 7,397 (1997)

HIV/AIDS - deaths: NA

Nationality:
noun: Puerto Rican(s) (US citizens)
adjective: Puerto Rican

Ethnic groups: white (mostly Spanish origin) 80.5%, black 8%, Amerindian 0.4%, Asian 0.2%, mixed and other 10.9%

Religions: Roman Catholic 85%, Protestant and other 15%

Languages: Spanish, English

Literacy:
definition: age 15 and over can read and write
total population: 94.1%
male: 93.7%
female: 94.4% (2002)

Government

Country name:
conventional long form: Commonwealth of Puerto Rico
conventional short form: Puerto Rico

Dependency status: commonwealth associated with the US

Government type: commonwealth

Capital: San Juan

Administrative divisions: none (commonwealth associated with the US); there are no first-order administrative divisions as defined by the US Government, but there are 78 municipalities (municipios, singular - municipio) at the second order; Adjuntas, Aguada, Aguadilla, Aguas Buenas, Aibonito, Anasco, Arecibo, Arroyo, Barceloneta, Barranquitas, Bayamon, Cabo Rojo, Caguas, Camuy, Canovanas, Carolina, Catano, Cayey, Ceiba, Ciales, Cidra, Coamo, Comerio, Corozal, Culebra, Dorado, Fajardo, Florida, Guanica, Guayama, Guayanilla, Guaynabo, Gurabo, Hatillo, Hormigueros, Humacao, Isabela, Jayuya, Juana Diaz, Juncos, Lajas, Lares, Las Marias, Las Piedras, Loiza, Luquillo, Manati, Maricao, Maunabo, Mayaguez, Moca, Morovis, Naguabo, Naranjito, Orocovis, Patillas, Penuelas, Ponce, Quebradillas, Rincon, Rio Grande, Sabana Grande, Salinas, San German, San Juan, San Lorenzo, San Sebastian, Santa Isabel, Toa Alta, Toa Baja, Trujillo Alto, Utuado, Vega Alta, Vega Baja, Vieques, Villalba, Yabucoa, Yauco

Independence: none (commonwealth associated with the US)
National holiday: US Independence Day, 4 July (1776); Puerto Rico Constitution Day, 25 July (1952)
Constitution: ratified 3 March 1952; approved by US Congress 3 July 1952; effective 25 July 1952
Legal system: based on Spanish civil code and within the US Federal system of justice
Suffrage: 18 years of age; universal; island residents are US citizens but do not vote in US presidential elections
Executive branch:
chief of state: President George W. BUSH of the US (since 20 January 2001)
head of government: Governor Sila M. CALDERON (since 2 January 2001)
cabinet: Cabinet appointed by the governor with the consent of the legislature
elections: US president and vice president elected on the same ticket for four-year terms; governor elected by popular vote for a four-year term; election last held 7 November 2000 (next to be held 2 November 2004)
election results: Sila M. CALDERON (PPD) elected governor; percent of vote - 48.6%
Legislative branch: bicameral Legislative Assembly consists of the Senate (at least 27 seats - currently 29; members are directly elected by popular vote to serve four-year terms) and the House of Representatives (51 seats; members are directly elected by popular vote to serve four-year terms)
elections: Senate - last held 7 November 2000 (next to be held 2 November 2004); House of Representatives - last held 7 November 2000 (next to be held 2 November 2004)
election results: Senate - percent of vote by party - NA%; seats by party - PPD 20, PNP 8, PIP 1; House of Representatives - percent of vote by party - NA%; seats by party - PPD 30, PNP 20, PIP 1
note: Puerto Rico elects, by popular vote, a resident commissioner to serve a four-year term as a nonvoting representative in the US House of Representatives; aside from not voting on the House floor, he enjoys all the rights of a member of Congress; elections last held 7 November 2000 (next to be held 2 November 2004); results - percent of vote by party - PPD 49.3%; seats by party - PPD 1; Anibal ACEVEDO-VILA elected resident commissioner
Judicial branch: Supreme Court; Appellate Court; Court of First Instance composed of two sections: a Superior Court and a Municipal Court (justices for all these courts appointed by the governor with the consent of the Senate)
Political parties and leaders: National Democratic Party [Celeste BENITEZ]; National Republican Party of Puerto Rico [Luis FERRE]; New Progressive Party or PNP (pro-US statehood) [Pedro ROSSELLO]; Popular Democratic Party or PPD (pro-commonwealth) [Anibal ACEVEDO-VILA]; Puerto Rican Independence Party or PIP (pro-independence) [Ruben BERRIOS Martinez]

Political pressure groups and leaders: Armed Forces for National Liberation or FALN; Armed Forces of Popular Resistance; Boricua Popular Army (also known as the Macheteros); Volunteers of the Puerto Rican Revolution
International organization participation: Caricom (observer), ICFTU, Interpol (subbureau), IOC, WCL, WFTU, WHO (associate), WToO (associate)
Diplomatic representation in the US: none (commonwealth associated with the US)
Diplomatic representation from the US: none (commonwealth associated with the US)
Flag description: five equal horizontal bands of red (top and bottom) alternating with white; a blue isosceles triangle based on the hoist side bears a large, white, five-pointed star in the center; design initially influenced by the US flag, but similar to the Cuban flag, with the colors of the bands and triangle reversed

Economy

Economy - overview: Puerto Rico has one of the most dynamic economies in the Caribbean region. A diverse industrial sector has far surpassed agriculture as the primary locus of economic activity and income. Encouraged by duty-free access to the US and by tax incentives, US firms have invested heavily in Puerto Rico since the 1950s. US minimum wage laws apply. Sugar production has lost out to dairy production and other livestock products as the main source of income in the agricultural sector. Tourism has traditionally been an important source of income, with estimated arrivals of nearly 5 million tourists in 1999. Growth fell off in 2001-03, largely due to the slowdown in the US economy.
GDP: purchasing power parity - $65.28 billion (2003 est.)
GDP - real growth rate: 1.6% (2003 est.)
GDP - per capita: purchasing power parity - $16,800 (2003 est.)
GDP - composition by sector:
agriculture: 1%
industry: 42%
services: 57% (2002 est.)
Population below poverty line: NA%
Household income or consumption by percentage share:
lowest 10%: NA%
highest 10%: NA%
Inflation rate (consumer prices): 6.5% (2003 est.)
Labor force: 1.3 million (2002)
Labor force - by occupation: agriculture 3%, industry 20%, services 77% (2000 est.)
Unemployment rate: 12% (2002)
Budget:
revenues: $6.7 billion
expenditures: $9.6 billion, including capital expenditures of $NA (FY99/00)
Industries: pharmaceuticals, electronics, apparel, food products, tourism

Industrial production growth rate: NA%
Electricity - production: 20.9 billion kWh (2001)
Electricity - production by source:
fossil fuel: 99.2%
hydro: 0.8%
nuclear: 0%
other: 0% (2001)
Electricity - consumption: 19.44 billion kWh (2001)
Electricity - exports: 0 kWh (2001)
Electricity - imports: 0 kWh (2001)
Oil - production: 0 bbl/day (2001 est.)
Oil - consumption: 190,000 bbl/day (2001 est.)
Oil - exports: NA
Oil - imports: NA
Natural gas - production: 0 cu m (2001 est.)
Natural gas - consumption: 630 million cu m (2001 est.)
Natural gas - exports: 0 cu m (2001 est.)
Natural gas - imports: 630 million cu m (2001 est.)
Agriculture - products: sugarcane, coffee, pineapples, plantains, bananas, livestock products, chickens
Exports: $46.22 billion f.o.b. (2002)
Exports - commodities: chemicals, electronics, apparel, canned tuna, rum, beverage concentrates, medical equipment
Exports - partners: US 90.3%, UK 1.6%, Netherlands 1.4%, Dominican Republic 1.4% (2002)
Imports: $26.46 billion c.i.f. (2002)
Imports - commodities: chemicals, machinery and equipment, clothing, food, fish, petroleum products
Imports - partners: US 55.0%, Ireland 23.7%, Japan 5.4% (2002)
Debt - external: $NA
Economic aid - recipient: $NA (2001)
Currency: US dollar (USD)
Currency code: USD
Exchange rates: the US dollar is used
Fiscal year: 1 July - 30 June

Communications

Telephones - main lines in use: 1,329,500 (2002)
Telephones - mobile cellular: 1,211,111 (2001)
Telephone system:
general assessment: modern system integrated with that of the US by high-capacity submarine cable and Intelsat with high-speed data capability
domestic: digital telephone system; cellular telephone service
international: country code - 1-787; satellite earth station - 1 Intelsat; submarine cable to US
Radio broadcast stations: AM 72, FM 17, shortwave 0 (1998)
Television broadcast stations: 6 (19 relay stations) (2004)
Internet country code: .pr
Internet users: 600,000 (2002)

Transportation

Railways:
total: 96 km
narrow gauge: 96 km 1.000-m gauge (2002)
Highways:
total: 14,400 km
paved: 14,400 km
unpaved: 0 km (1999 est.)
Waterways: none
Ports and harbors: Aguadilla, Arecibo, Fajardo, Guanica, Guayanilla, Guayama, Mayaguez, Playa de Ponce, San Juan
Merchant marine:
total: 2 ships (1,000 GRT or over) 36,728 GRT/37,048 DWT
by type: container 1, roll on/roll off 1
foreign-owned: United States 2
registered in other countries: 5 (2003 est.)
Airports: 30 (2003 est.)
Airports - with paved runways:
total: 17
over 3,047 m: 3
1,524 to 2,437 m: 2
914 to 1,523 m: 7
under 914 m: 5 (2003 est.)
Airports - with unpaved runways:
total: 13
1,524 to 2, 437 m: 1
914 to 1,523 m: 2
under 914 m: 10 (2003 est.)

Military

Military branches: no regular indigenous military forces; paramilitary National Guard, Police Force
Military - note: defense is the responsibility of the US

Transnational Issues

Disputes - international: none

Qatar

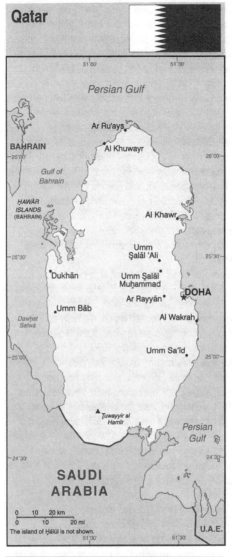

Introduction

Background: Ruled by the Al Thani family since the mid-1800s, Qatar transformed itself from a poor British protectorate noted mainly for pearling into an independent state with significant oil and natural gas revenues. During the late 1980s and early 1990s, the Qatari economy was crippled by a continuous siphoning off of petroleum revenues by the amir, who had ruled the country since 1972. He was overthrown by his son, the current Amir HAMAD bin Khalifa Al Thani, in a bloodless coup in 1995. In 2001, Qatar resolved its longstanding border disputes with both Bahrain and Saudi Arabia. Oil and natural gas revenues enable Qatar to have a per capita income not far below the leading industrial countries of Western Europe.

Geography

Location: Middle East, peninsula bordering the Persian Gulf and Saudi Arabia
Geographic coordinates: 25 30 N, 51 15 E
Map references: Middle East
Area:
total: 11,437 sq km
land: 11,437 sq km
water: 0 sq km
Area - comparative: slightly smaller than Connecticut
Land boundaries:
total: 60 km
border countries: Saudi Arabia 60 km
Coastline: 563 km
Maritime claims:
territorial sea: 12 NM
contiguous zone: 24 NM
exclusive economic zone: as determined by bilateral agreements or the median line
Climate: arid; mild, pleasant winters; very hot, humid summers
Terrain: mostly flat and barren desert covered with loose sand and gravel
Elevation extremes:
lowest point: Persian Gulf 0 m
highest point: Qurayn Abu al Bawl 103 m
Natural resources: petroleum, natural gas, fish
Land use:
arable land: 1.27%
permanent crops: 0.27%
other: 98.46% (1998 est.)
Irrigated land: 130 sq km (1998 est.)
Natural hazards: haze, dust storms, sandstorms common
Environment - current issues: limited natural fresh water resources are increasing dependence on large-scale desalination facilities
Environment - international agreements:
party to: Biodiversity, Climate Change, Desertification, Endangered Species, Hazardous Wastes, Law of the Sea, Ozone Layer Protection
signed, but not ratified: none of the selected agreements
Geography - note: strategic location in central Persian Gulf near major petroleum deposits

People

Population: 840,290 (July 2004 est.)
Age structure:
0-14 years: 24.2% (male 103,660; female 99,597)
15-64 years: 72.7% (male 426,559; female 184,067)
65 years and over: 3.1% (male 19,306; female 7,101) (2004 est.)
Median age:
total: 31.4 years
male: 36.7 years
female: 22 years (2004 est.)
Population growth rate: 2.74% (2004 est.)
Birth rate: 15.6 births/1,000 population (2004 est.)
Death rate: 4.52 deaths/1,000 population (2004 est.)
Net migration rate: 16.29 migrant(s)/1,000 population (2004 est.)
Sex ratio:
at birth: 1.05 male(s)/female
under 15 years: 1.04 male(s)/female
15-64 years: 2.32 male(s)/female

65 years and over: 2.72 male(s)/female

total population: 1.89 male(s)/female (2004 est.)

Infant mortality rate:

total: 19.32 deaths/1,000 live births

male: 22.77 deaths/1,000 live births

female: 15.7 deaths/1,000 live births (2004 est.)

Life expectancy at birth:

total population: 73.4 years

male: 70.9 years

female: 76.04 years (2004 est.)

Total fertility rate: 2.95 children born/woman (2004 est.)

HIV/AIDS - adult prevalence rate: 0.09% (2001 est.)

HIV/AIDS - people living with HIV/AIDS: NA

HIV/AIDS - deaths: NA

Nationality:

noun: Qatari(s)

adjective: Qatari

Ethnic groups: Arab 40%, Pakistani 18%, Indian 18%, Iranian 10%, other 14%

Religions: Muslim 95%

Languages: Arabic (official), English commonly used as a second language

Literacy:

definition: age 15 and over can read and write

total population: 82.5%

male: 81.4%

female: 85% (2003 est.)

Government

Country name:

conventional long form: State of Qatar

conventional short form: Qatar

local long form: Dawlat Qatar

local short form: Qatar

note: closest approximation of the native pronunciation falls between cutter and gutter, but not like guitar

Government type: traditional monarchy

Capital: Doha

Administrative divisions: 10 municipalities (baladiyat, singular - baladiyah); Ad Dawhah, Al Ghuwayriyah, Al Jumayliyah, Al Khawr, Al Wakrah, Ar Rayyan, Jarayan al Batinah, Madinat ash Shamal, Umm Sa'id, Umm Salal

Independence: 3 September 1971 (from UK)

National holiday: Independence Day, 3 September (1971)

Constitution: provisional constitution enacted 19 April 1972; in July 1999 Amir HAMAD issued a decree forming a committee to draft a permanent constitution; in the 29 April 2003 referendum, 96.6% of Qatari voters approved the new constitution

Legal system: discretionary system of law controlled by the amir, although civil codes are being implemented; Islamic law dominates family and personal matters

Suffrage: 18 years of age; universal

Executive branch:

chief of state: Amir HAMAD bin Khalifa Al Thani (since 27 June 1995 when, as crown prince, he ousted his father, Amir KHALIFA bin Hamad Al Thani, in a bloodless coup); Crown Prince TAMIM bin Hamad bin Khalifa Al Thani, third son of the monarch (selected crown prince by the monarch 5 August 2003); note - Amir HAMAD also holds the positions of Minister of Defense and Commander-in-chief of the Armed Forces

head of government: Prime Minister ABDALLAH bin Khalifa Al Thani, brother of the monarch (since 30 October 1996) Deputy Prime Minister MUHAMMAD bin Khalifa Al Thani, brother of the monarch (since 20 January 1998); First Deputy Prime Minister HAMAD bin JASIM bin JABIR Al Thani (since 16 September 2003; also Foreign Minister since 1992); Second Deputy Prime Minister Abdallah bin Hamad al-ATTIYAH (since 16 September 2003; also Energy Minister since NA 1992)

cabinet: Council of Ministers appointed by the monarch

elections: none; the monarch is hereditary

note: in April 2003, Qatar held nationwide elections for a 29-member Central Municipal Council (CMC), which has consultative powers aimed at improving the provision of municipal services; the first election for the CMC was held in March 1999

Legislative branch: unicameral Advisory Council or Majlis al-Shura (35 seats; members appointed)

note: no legislative elections have been held since 1970 when there were partial elections to the body; Council members have had their terms extended every four years since; the new constitution provides for a 45-member Consultative Council, or Majlis al-Shura; the public would elect two-thirds of the Majlis al-Shura; the Amir would appoint the remaining members

Judicial branch: Court of Appeal

Political parties and leaders: none

Political pressure groups and leaders: none

International organization participation: ABEDA, AFESD, AMF, FAO, G-77, GCC, IAEA, IBRD, ICAO, ICC, ICRM, IDB, IFAD, IFRCS, IHO (pending member), ILO, IMF, IMO, Interpol, IOC, ISO (correspondent), ITU, LAS, NAM, OAPEC, OAS (observer), OIC, OPCW, OPEC, UN, UNCTAD, UNESCO, UNIDO, UPU, WCO, WHO, WIPO, WMO, WToO, WTrO

Diplomatic representation in the US:

chief of mission: Ambassador Badr Umar al-DAFA

chancery: 4200 Wisconsin Avenue NW, Washington, DC 20016

telephone: [1] (202) 274-1600

FAX: [1] (202) 237-0061

consulate(s) general: Houston

Diplomatic representation from the US:

chief of mission: Ambassador Maureen E. QUINN

embassy: Al-Luqta District, 22 February Road, Doha

mailing address: P. O. Box 2399, Doha

telephone: [974] 488 4101

FAX: [974] 488 4298

Flag description: maroon with a broad white serrated band (nine white points) on the hoist side

Economy

Economy - overview: Oil and gas account for more than 55% of GDP, roughly 85% of export earnings, and 70% of government revenues. Oil and gas have given Qatar a per capita GDP about 80% of that of the leading West European industrial countries. Proved oil reserves of 14.5 billion barrels should ensure continued output at current levels for 23 years. Qatar's proved reserves of natural gas exceed 17.9 trillion cubic meters, more than 5% of the world total and third largest in the world. Long-term goals feature the development of offshore natural gas reserves to offset the ultimate decline in oil production. Since 2000, Qatar has consistently posted trade surpluses largely because of high oil prices and increased natural gas exports.

GDP: purchasing power parity - $17.54 billion (2003 est.)

GDP - real growth rate: 8.5% (2003 est.)

GDP - per capita: purchasing power parity - $21,500 (2003 est.)

GDP - composition by sector:

agriculture: 0.4%

industry: 64.7%

services: 34.9% (2002 est.)

Population below poverty line: NA%

Household income or consumption by percentage share:

lowest 10%: NA%

highest 10%: NA%

Inflation rate (consumer prices): 2% (2003)

Labor force: 280,122 (1997 est.)

Unemployment rate: 2.7% (2001)

Budget:

revenues: $5 billion

expenditures: $5.5 billion, including capital expenditures of $2.2 billion (FY02/03 est.)

Industries: crude oil production and refining, fertilizers, petrochemicals, steel reinforcing bars, cement

Industrial production growth rate: 10% (2003 est.)

Electricity - production: 9.264 billion kWh (2001)

Electricity - production by source:

fossil fuel: 100%

hydro: 0%

nuclear: 0%

other: 0% (2001)

Electricity - consumption: 8.616 billion kWh (2001)

Electricity - exports: 0 kWh (2001)

Electricity - imports: 0 kWh (2001)

Oil - production: 864,200 bbl/day (2001 est.)

Oil - consumption: 29,000 bbl/day (2001 est.)

Oil - exports: NA

Oil - imports: NA

Oil - proved reserves: 14.51 billion bbl (1 January 2002)

Natural gas - production: 32.4 billion cu m (2001 est.)

Natural gas - consumption: 15.86 billion cu m (2001 est.)

Natural gas - exports: 16.54 billion cu m (2001 est.)

Natural gas - imports: 0 cu m (2001 est.)

Qatar *(continued)*

Natural gas - proved reserves: 17.93 trillion cu m (1 January 2002)
Agriculture - products: fruits, vegetables; poultry, dairy products, beef; fish
Exports: $12.36 billion f.o.b. (2003 est.)
Exports - commodities: petroleum products, fertilizers, steel
Exports - partners: Japan 41.2%, South Korea 17.1%, Singapore 8.4%, US 4.2% (2002)
Imports: $5.711 billion f.o.b. (2003 est.)
Imports - commodities: machinery and transport equipment, food, chemicals
Imports - partners: France 17.8%, Japan 10.1%, US 8.5%, UK 8.3%, Germany 8.2%, Italy 6.7%, UAE 5.1%, Saudi Arabia 4.2%, South Korea 4% (2002)
Debt - external: $16.2 billion (2003 est.)
Economic aid - recipient: $NA
Currency: Qatari rial (QAR)
Currency code: QAR
Exchange rates: Qatari rials per US dollar - 3.64 (2003), 3.64 (2002), 3.64 (2001), 3.64 (2000), 3.64 (1999)
Fiscal year: 1 April - 31 March

Communications

Telephones - main lines in use: 176,500 (2002)
Telephones - mobile cellular: 267,200 (2002)
Telephone system:
general assessment: modern system centered in Doha
domestic: NA
international: country code - 974; tropospheric scatter to Bahrain; microwave radio relay to Saudi Arabia and UAE; submarine cable to Bahrain and UAE; satellite earth stations - 2 Intelsat (1 Atlantic Ocean and 1 Indian Ocean) and 1 Arabsat
Radio broadcast stations: AM 6, FM 5, shortwave 1 (1998)
Television broadcast stations: 1 (plus three repeaters) (2001)
Internet country code: .qa
Internet hosts: 171 (2002)
Internet users: 70,000 (2002)

Transportation

Railways: 0 km
Highways:
total: 1,230 km
paved: 1,107 km
unpaved: 123 km (1999 est.)
Waterways: none
Pipelines: condensate 90 km; condensate/gas 209 km; gas 902 km; liquid petroleum gas 87 km; oil 722 km; oil/gas/water 41 km (2003)
Ports and harbors: Doha, Halul Island, Umm Sa'id (Musay'id)
Merchant marine:
total: 22 ships (1,000 GRT or over) 525,051 GRT/ 772,635 DWT
by type: cargo 4, chemical tanker 4, container 8, petroleum tanker 5, roll on/roll off 1

foreign-owned: Cambodia 1, Kuwait 1 (2003 est.)
Airports: 4 (2003 est.)
Airports - with paved runways:
total: 2
over 3,047 m: 2 (2003 est.)
Airports - with unpaved runways:
total: 2
914 to 1,523 m: 1
under 914 m: 1 (2003 est.)
Heliports: 1 (2003 est.)

Military

Military branches: Land Force, Qatari Amiri Navy (QAN), Amiri Air Force
Military manpower - military age: 18 years of age (2004 est.)
Military manpower - availability:
males age 15-49: 324,001
note: includes non-nationals (2004 est.)
Military manpower - fit for military service:
males age 15-49: 170,266 (2004 est.)
Military manpower - reaching military age annually:
males: 7,496 (2004 est.)
Military expenditures - dollar figure: $723 million (FY00)
Military expenditures - percent of GDP: 10% (FY00)

Transnational Issues

Disputes - international: none

Reunion
(overseas department of France)

Introduction

Background: The Portuguese discovered the uninhabited island in 1513. From the 17th to the 19th centuries, French immigration, supplemented by influxes of Africans, Chinese, Malays, and Malabar Indians, gave the island its ethnic mix. The opening of the Suez Canal in 1869 cost the island its importance as a stopover on the East Indies trade route.

Geography

Location: Southern Africa, island in the Indian Ocean, east of Madagascar
Geographic coordinates: 21 06 S, 55 36 E
Map references: World
Area:
total: 2,517 sq km
land: 2,507 sq km
water: 10 sq km
Area - comparative: slightly smaller than Rhode Island
Land boundaries: 0 km
Coastline: 207 km
Maritime claims:
territorial sea: 12 NM
exclusive economic zone: 200 NM
Climate: tropical, but temperature moderates with elevation; cool and dry from May to November, hot and rainy from November to April
Terrain: mostly rugged and mountainous; fertile lowlands along coast
Elevation extremes:
lowest point: Indian Ocean 0 m
highest point: Piton des Neiges 3,069 m
Natural resources: fish, arable land, hydropower
Land use:
arable land: 13.2%
permanent crops: 2%
other: 84.8% (1998 est.)

Reunion (continued)

Irrigated land: 120 sq km (1998 est.)
Natural hazards: periodic, devastating cyclones (December to April); Piton de la Fournaise on the southeastern coast is an active volcano
Environment - current issues: NA
Geography - note: this mountainous, volcanic island has an active volcano, Piton de la Fournaise; there is a tropical cyclone center at Saint-Denis, which is the monitoring station for the whole of the Indian Ocean

People

Population: 766,153 (July 2004 est.)
Age structure:
0-14 years: 30.9% (male 121,050; female 115,440)
15-64 years: 63.1% (male 238,553; female 245,236)
65 years and over: 6% (male 18,626; female 27,248) (2004 est.)
Median age:
total: 26.5 years
male: 25.4 years
female: 27.7 years (2004 est.)
Population growth rate: 1.42% (2004 est.)
Birth rate: 19.69 births/1,000 population (2004 est.)
Death rate: 5.48 deaths/1,000 population (2004 est.)
Net migration rate: 0 migrant(s)/1,000 population (2004 est.)
Sex ratio:
at birth: 1.05 male(s)/female
under 15 years: 1.05 male(s)/female
15-64 years: 0.97 male(s)/female
65 years and over: 0.68 male(s)/female
total population: 0.98 male(s)/female (2004 est.)
Infant mortality rate:
total: 7.95 deaths/1,000 live births
male: 8.71 deaths/1,000 live births
female: 7.17 deaths/1,000 live births (2004 est.)
Life expectancy at birth:
total population: 73.69 years
male: 70.29 years
female: 77.26 years (2004 est.)
Total fertility rate: 2.5 children born/woman (2004 est.)
HIV/AIDS - adult prevalence rate: NA%
HIV/AIDS - people living with HIV/AIDS: NA
HIV/AIDS - deaths: NA
Nationality:
noun: Reunionese (singular and plural)
adjective: Reunionese
Ethnic groups: French, African, Malagasy, Chinese, Pakistani, Indian
Religions: Roman Catholic 86%, Hindu, Muslim, Buddhist (1995)
Languages: French (official), Creole widely used
Literacy:
definition: age 15 and over can read and write
total population: 88.9%
male: 87%
female: 90.8% (2003 est.)

Government

Country name:
conventional long form: Department of Reunion
conventional short form: Reunion
local long form: none
local short form: Ile de la Reunion
former: Bourbon Island
Dependency status: overseas department of France
Government type: NA
Capital: Saint-Denis
Administrative divisions: none (overseas department of France); there are no first-order administrative divisions as defined by the US Government, but there are 4 arrondissements, 24 communes, and 47 cantons
Independence: none (overseas department of France)
National holiday: Bastille Day, 14 July (1789)
Constitution: 28 September 1958 (French Constitution)
Legal system: French law
Suffrage: 18 years of age; universal
Executive branch:
chief of state: President Jacques CHIRAC of France (since 17 May 1995), represented by Prefect Gonthier FRIEDERICI (since NA)
head of government: President of the General Council Jean-Luc POUDROUX (since NA March 1998) and President of the Regional Council Paul VERGES (since NA March 1993)
cabinet: NA
elections: French president elected by popular vote for a five-year term; prefect appointed by the French president on the advice of the French Ministry of the Interior; the presidents of the General and Regional Councils are elected by the members of those councils
Legislative branch: unicameral General Council (49 seats; members are elected by direct, popular vote to serve six-year terms) and a unicameral Regional Council (45 seats; members are elected by direct, popular vote to serve six-year terms)
elections: General Council - last held 15 and 22 March 1998 (next to be held NA 2004); Regional Council - last held 28 March 2004 (next to be held NA 2010)
election results: General Council - percent of vote by party - NA%; seats by party - various right-wing candidates 13, PCR 10, PS 10, UDF 8, RPR 6, other left-wing candidates 2; Regional Council (second round) - percent of vote by party - PCR 44.9%, UMP 32.8%, PS-Greens 22.3%; seats by party - PCR 27, UMP 11, PS-Greens 7
note: Reunion elects three representatives to the French Senate; elections last held NA 2001 (next to be held NA 2006); results - percent of vote by party - NA%; seats by party - NA; Reunion also elects five deputies to the French National Assembly; elections last held 9 June-16 June 2002 (next to be held NA 2007); results - percent of vote by party - NA%; seats by party - UMP-RPR 1, UMP 1, PCR 1

Judicial branch: Court of Appeals or Cour d'Appel
Political parties and leaders: Communist Party of Reunion or PCR [Paul VERGES]; Rally for the Republic or RPR [Andre Maurice PIHOUEE]; Socialist Party or PS [Jean-Claude FRUTEAU]; Union for French Democracy or UDF [Gilbert GERARD]; Union for a Popular Movement or UMP [leader NA]
Political pressure groups and leaders: NA
International organization participation: InOC, WFTU
Diplomatic representation in the US: none (overseas department of France)
Diplomatic representation from the US: none (overseas department of France)
Flag description: the flag of France is used

Economy

Economy - overview: The economy has traditionally been based on agriculture, but services now dominate. Sugarcane has been the primary crop for more than a century, and in some years it accounts for 85% of exports. The government has been pushing the development of a tourist industry to relieve high unemployment, which amounts to one-third of the labor force. The gap in Reunion between the well-off and the poor is extraordinary and accounts for the persistent social tensions. The white and Indian communities are substantially better off than other segments of the population, often approaching European standards, whereas minority groups suffer the poverty and unemployment typical of the poorer nations of the African continent. The outbreak of severe rioting in February 1991 illustrates the seriousness of socioeconomic tensions. The economic well-being of Reunion depends heavily on continued financial assistance from France.
GDP: purchasing power parity - $9.387 billion (2003 est.)
GDP - real growth rate: 2.5% (2003 est.)
GDP - per capita: purchasing power parity - $12,400 (2003 est.)
GDP - composition by sector:
agriculture: 8%
industry: 19%
services: 73% (2000 est.)
Population below poverty line: NA%
Household income or consumption by percentage share:
lowest 10%: NA%
highest 10%: NA%
Inflation rate (consumer prices): NA%
Labor force: 309,900 (2000)
Labor force - by occupation: agriculture 13%, industry 12%, services 75% (2000)
Unemployment rate: 36% (1999 est.)
Budget:
revenues: $1.26 billion
expenditures: $2.62 billion, including capital expenditures of $NA (1998)
Industries: sugar, rum, cigarettes, handicraft items, flower oil extraction

Industrial production growth rate: NA%
Electricity - production: 1.08 billion kWh (2001)
Electricity - production by source:
fossil fuel: 55.5%
hydro: 44.5%
nuclear: 0%
other: 0% (2001)
Electricity - consumption: 1.005 billion kWh (2001)
Electricity - exports: 0 kWh (2001)
Electricity - imports: 0 kWh (2001)
Oil - production: 0 bbl/day (2001 est.)
Oil - consumption: 18,000 bbl/day (2001 est.)
Oil - exports: NA
Oil - imports: NA
Agriculture - products: sugarcane, vanilla, tobacco, tropical fruits, vegetables, corn
Exports: $214 million f.o.b. (1997)
Exports - commodities: sugar 63%, rum and molasses 4%, perfume essences 2%, lobster 3%, (1993)
Exports - partners: France 74%, Japan 6%, Comoros 4% (2000)
Imports: $2.5 billion c.i.f. (1997)
Imports - commodities: manufactured goods, food, beverages, tobacco, machinery and transportation equipment, raw materials, and petroleum products
Imports - partners: France 64%, Bahrain 3%, Germany 3%, Italy 3% (2000)
Debt - external: $NA
Economic aid - recipient: $NA; note - substantial annual subsidies from France (2001 est.)
Currency: euro (EUR)
Currency code: EUR
Exchange rates: euros per US dollar - 0.886 (2003), 1.0626 (2002), 1.1175 (2001), 1.0854 (2000), 0.9386 (1999)
Fiscal year: calendar year

Communications

Telephones - main lines in use: 300,000 est (2001)
Telephones - mobile cellular: 489,800 (2002)
Telephone system:
general assessment: adequate system; principal center is Saint-Denis
domestic: modern open-wire and microwave radio relay network
international: country code - 262; radiotelephone communication to Comoros, France, Madagascar; new microwave route to Mauritius; satellite earth station - 1 Intelsat (Indian Ocean); fiber optic submarine cable (SAT-3/WASC/SAFE) provides connectivity to Europe and Asia
Radio broadcast stations: AM 2, FM 55, shortwave 0 (2001)
Television broadcast stations: 35 (plus 18 low-power repeaters) (2001)
Internet country code: .re
Internet users: 150,000 (2002)

Transportation

Railways: 0 km
Highways:
total: 2,724 km
paved: 1,300 km (including 73 km of four-lane road)
unpaved: 1,424 km (1994)
Waterways: none
Ports and harbors: Le Port, Pointe des Galets
Airports: 2 (2003 est.)
Airports - with paved runways:
total: 2
2,438 to 3,047 m: 1
914 to 1,523 m: 1 (2003 est.)

Military

Military branches: no regular indigenous military forces; French forces (including Army, Navy, Air Force, and Gendarmerie)
Military manpower - military age: 18 years of age (2004 est.)
Military manpower - availability:
males age 15-49: 202,385 (2004 est.)
Military manpower - fit for military service:
males age 15-49: 103,073 (2004 est.)
Military manpower - reaching military age annually:
males: 7,070 (2004 est.)
Military - note: defense is the responsibility of France

Transnational Issues

Disputes - international: none

Romania

Introduction

Background: The principalities of Wallachia and Moldavia - for centuries under the suzerainty of the Turkish Ottoman Empire - secured their autonomy in 1856; they united in 1859 under the new name of Romania. The country gained full independence in 1878. It joined the Allied Powers in World War I and acquired new territories following the conflict. In 1940, it allied with the Axis powers and participated in the 1941 German invasion of the USSR. Three years later, overrun by the Soviets, Romania signed an armistice. The post-war Soviet occupation led to the formation of a Communist "people's republic" in 1947 and the abdication of the king. The decades-long rule of dictator Nicolae CEAUSESCU, who took power in 1965, and his Securitate police state became increasingly oppressive and draconian through the 1980s. CEAUSESCU was overthrown and executed in late 1989. Former Communists dominated the government until 1996, when they were swept from power by a fractious coalition of centrist parties. Currently, the Social Democratic Party forms a nominally minority government, which governs with the support of the opposition Democratic Union of Hungarians in Romania. Bucharest must address rampant corruption, while invigorating lagging economic and democratic reforms, before Romania can achieve its hope of joining the European Union.

Geography

Location: Southeastern Europe, bordering the Black Sea, between Bulgaria and Ukraine
Geographic coordinates: 46 00 N, 25 00 E
Map references: Europe
Area:
total: 237,500 sq km
land: 230,340 sq km
water: 7,160 sq km
Area - comparative: slightly smaller than Oregon

Romania (continued)

Land boundaries:
total: 2,508 km
border countries: Bulgaria 608 km, Hungary 443 km, Moldova 450 km, Serbia and Montenegro 476 km, Ukraine (north) 362 km, Ukraine (east) 169 km
Coastline: 225 km
Maritime claims:
territorial sea: 12 NM
contiguous zone: 24 NM
exclusive economic zone: 200 NM
continental shelf: 200-m depth or to the depth of exploitation
Climate: temperate; cold, cloudy winters with frequent snow and fog; sunny summers with frequent showers and thunderstorms
Terrain: central Transylvanian Basin is separated from the Plain of Moldavia on the east by the Carpathian Mountains and separated from the Walachian Plain on the south by the Transylvanian Alps
Elevation extremes:
lowest point: Black Sea 0 m
highest point: Moldoveanu 2,544 m
Natural resources: petroleum (reserves declining), timber, natural gas, coal, iron ore, salt, arable land, hydropower
Land use:
arable land: 40.57%
permanent crops: 2.4%
other: 57.03% (1998 est.)
Irrigated land: 28,800 sq km (1998 est.)
Natural hazards: earthquakes, most severe in south and southwest; geologic structure and climate promote landslides
Environment - current issues: soil erosion and degradation; water pollution; air pollution in south from industrial effluents; contamination of Danube delta wetlands
Environment - international agreements:
party to: Air Pollution, Antarctic Treaty, Biodiversity, Climate Change, Climate Change-Kyoto Protocol, Desertification, Endangered Species, Environmental Modification, Hazardous Wastes, Law of the Sea, Ozone Layer Protection, Ship Pollution, Wetlands
signed, but not ratified: Air Pollution-Persistent Organic Pollutants
Geography - note: controls most easily traversable land route between the Balkans, Moldova, and Ukraine

People

Population: 22,355,551 (July 2004 est.)
Age structure:
0-14 years: 16.2% (male 1,861,801; female 1,770,746)
15-64 years: 69.4% (male 7,712,612; female 7,791,900)
65 years and over: 14.4% (male 1,330,994; female 1,887,498) (2004 est.)

Median age:
total: 36.1 years
male: 34.7 years
female: 37.5 years (2004 est.)
Population growth rate: -0.11% (2004 est.)
Birth rate: 10.69 births/1,000 population (2004 est.)
Death rate: 11.69 deaths/1,000 population (2004 est.)
Net migration rate: -0.13 migrant(s)/1,000 population (2004 est.)
Sex ratio:
at birth: 1.06 male(s)/female
under 15 years: 1.05 male(s)/female
15-64 years: 0.99 male(s)/female
65 years and over: 0.71 male(s)/female
total population: 0.95 male(s)/female (2004 est.)
Infant mortality rate:
total: 27.24 deaths/1,000 live births
male: 30.41 deaths/1,000 live births
female: 23.86 deaths/1,000 live births (2004 est.)
Life expectancy at birth:
total population: 71.12 years
male: 67.63 years
female: 74.82 years (2004 est.)
Total fertility rate: 1.35 children born/woman (2004 est.)
HIV/AIDS - adult prevalence rate: less than 0.1% (2001 est.)
HIV/AIDS - people living with HIV/AIDS: 6,500 (2001 est.)
HIV/AIDS - deaths: 350 (2001 est.)
Nationality:
noun: Romanian(s)
adjective: Romanian
Ethnic groups: Romanian 89.5%, Hungarian 6.6%, Roma 2.5%, Ukrainian 0.3%, German 0.3%, Russian 0.2%, Turkish 0.2%, other 0.4% (2002)
Religions: Eastern Orthodox (including all sub-denominations) 87%, Protestant 6.8%, Catholic 5.6%, other (mostly Muslim) 0.4%, unaffiliated 0.2% (2002)
Languages: Romanian (official), Hungarian, German
Literacy:
definition: age 15 and over can read and write
total population: 98.4%
male: 99.1%
female: 97.7% (2003 est.)

Government

Country name:
conventional long form: none
conventional short form: Romania
local long form: none
local short form: Romania
Government type: republic
Capital: Bucharest
Administrative divisions: 41 counties (judete, singular - judet) and 1 municipality* (municipiu); Alba, Arad, Arges, Bacau, Bihor, Bistrita-Nasaud, Botosani, Braila, Brasov, Bucuresti*, Buzau, Calarasi,

Caras-Severin, Cluj, Constanta, Covasna, Dimbovita, Dolj, Galati, Gorj, Giurgiu, Harghita, Hunedoara, Ialomita, Iasi, Ilfov, Maramures, Mehedinti, Mures, Neamt, Olt, Prahova, Salaj, Satu Mare, Sibiu, Suceava, Teleorman, Timis, Tulcea, Vaslui, Vilcea, Vrancea
Independence: 9 May 1877 (independence proclaimed from Turkey; independence recognized 13 July 1878 by the Treaty of Berlin; kingdom proclaimed 26 March 1881; republic proclaimed 30 December 1947)
National holiday: Unification Day (of Romania and Transylvania), 1 December (1918)
Constitution: 8 December 1991
Legal system: former mixture of civil law system and communist legal theory; is now based on the constitution of France's Fifth Republic
Suffrage: 18 years of age; universal
Executive branch:
chief of state: President Ion ILIESCU (since 20 December 2000)
head of government: Prime Minister Adrian NASTASE (since 29 December 2000)
cabinet: Council of Ministers appointed by the prime minister
elections: president elected by popular vote for a four-year term; election last held 26 November 2000, with runoff between the top two candidates held 10 December 2000 (next to be held 28 November 2004 [first round] and 12 December 2004 [second round]); prime minister appointed by the president
election results: percent of vote - Ion ILIESCU 66.84%, Corneliu Vadim TUDOR 33.16%
Legislative branch: bicameral Parliament or Parlament consists of the Senate or Senat (140 seats; members are elected by direct, popular vote on a proportional representation basis to serve four-year terms) and the Chamber of Deputies or Adunarea Deputatilor (345 seats; members are elected by direct, popular vote on a proportional representation basis to serve four-year terms)
elections: Senate - last held 26 November 2000 (next to be held 28 November 2004); Chamber of Deputies - last held 26 November 2000 (next to be held 28 November 2004)
election results: Senate - percent of vote by party - PDSR (now PSD) 37.1%, PRM 21.0%, PD 7.6%, PNL 7.5%, UDMR 6.9%; seats by party - PSD 65, PRM 36, PNL 13, UDMR 12, PD 9, independents 5; Chamber of Deputies - percent of vote by party - PDSR (now PSD) 36.6%, PRM 19.5%, PD 7.0%, PNL 6.9%, UDMR 6.8%; seats by party - PSD 171, PRM 69, PD 29, PNL 27, UDMR 27, ethnic minorities 18, independents 4
Judicial branch: Supreme Court of Justice (judges are appointed by the president on the recommendation of the Superior Council of Magistrates)
Political parties and leaders: Democratic Party or PD [Traian BASESCU]; Democratic Union of Hungarians in Romania or UDMR [Bela MARKO]; National Liberal Party or PNL [Theodor STOLOJAN];

Romania (continued)

Romania Mare Party (Greater Romanian Party) or PRM [Corneliu Vadim TUDOR]; Social Democratic Party or PSD [Adrian NASTASE], formerly known as the Party of Social Democracy in Romania or PDSR
Political pressure groups and leaders: various human rights and professional associations
International organization participation: ACCT, Australia Group, BIS, BSEC, CE, CEI, EAPC, EBRD, EU (applicant), FAO, G- 9, G-77, IAEA, IBRD, ICAO, ICC, ICCt, ICFTU, ICRM, IFAD, IFC, IFRCS, ILO, IMF, IMO, Interpol, IOC, IOM, ISO, ITU, LAIA (observer), MONUC, NAM (guest), NSG, OAS (observer), OPCW, OSCE, PCA, PFP, UN, UN Security Council (temporary), UNCTAD, UNESCO, UNIDO, UNMEE, UNMIK, UNMIL, UPU, WCL, WCO, WEU (associate partner), WFTU, WHO, WIPO, WMO, WToO, WTrO, ZC
Diplomatic representation in the US:
chief of mission: Ambassador Sorin Dumitru DUCARU
chancery: 1607 23rd Street NW, Washington, DC 20008
telephone: [1] (202) 332-4846, 4848, 4851
FAX: [1] (202) 232-4748
consulate(s) general: Chicago, Los Angeles, and New York
Diplomatic representation from the US:
chief of mission: Ambassador Michael E. GUEST
embassy: Strada Tudor Arghezi 7-9, Bucharest
mailing address: American Embassy Bucharest, Department of State, 5260 Bucharest Place, Washington, DC 20521-5260 (pouch)
telephone: [40] (21) 210-4042
FAX: [40] (21) 210-0395
branch office(s): Cluj-Napoca
Flag description: three equal vertical bands of blue (hoist side), yellow, and red; the national coat of arms that used to be centered in the yellow band has been removed; now similar to the flag of Chad, also resembles the flags of Andorra and Moldova

Economy

Economy - overview: Romania began the transition from Communism in 1989 with a largely obsolete industrial base and a pattern of output unsuited to the country's needs. The country emerged in 2000 from a punishing three-year recession thanks to strong demand in EU export markets. Despite the global slowdown in 2001-02, strong domestic activity in construction, agriculture, and consumption have kept growth above 4%. An IMF Standby Agreement, signed in 2001, has been accompanied by slow but palpable gains in privatization, deficit reduction, and the curbing of inflation. The IMF Board approved Romania's completion of the standby agreement in October 2003, the first time Romania has successfully concluded an IMF agreement since the 1989 revolution. Nonetheless, recent macroeconomic gains have done little to address Romania's widespread poverty, while corruption and red tape hinder foreign investment.

GDP: purchasing power parity - $154.4 billion (2003 est.)
GDP - real growth rate: 4.5% (2003 est.)
GDP - per capita: purchasing power parity - $6,900 (2003 est.)
GDP - composition by sector:
agriculture: 15%
industry: 35%
services: 50% (2001)
Population below poverty line: 44.5% (2000)
Household income or consumption by percentage share:
lowest 10%: 3.2%
highest 10%: 25% (1998)
Distribution of family income - Gini index: 31.1 (1998)
Inflation rate (consumer prices): 14.3% (2003)
Labor force: 9.9 million (1999 est.)
Labor force - by occupation: agriculture 41.4%, industry 27.3%, services 31.3% (2000)
Unemployment rate: 7.3% (2003)
Budget:
revenues: $8.2 billion
expenditures: $9.6 billion, including capital expenditures of $NA (2002 est.)
Industries: textiles and footwear, light machinery and auto assembly, mining, timber, construction materials, metallurgy, chemicals, food processing, petroleum refining
Industrial production growth rate: 4.5% (2003)
Electricity - production: 50.86 billion kWh (2001)
Electricity - production by source:
fossil fuel: 62.5%
hydro: 27.6%
nuclear: 9.9%
other: 0% (2001)
Electricity - consumption: 46.1 billion kWh (2001)
Electricity - exports: 1.6 billion kWh (2001)
Electricity - imports: 400 million kWh (2001)
Oil - production: 127,500 bbl/day (2001 est.)
Oil - consumption: 215,000 bbl/day (2001 est.)
Oil - exports: NA
Oil - imports: NA
Oil - proved reserves: 1.055 billion bbl (1 January 2002)
Natural gas - production: 14.3 billion cu m (2001 est.)
Natural gas - consumption: 19.7 billion cu m (2001 est.)
Natural gas - exports: 0 cu m (2001 est.)
Natural gas - imports: 5.4 billion cu m (2001 est.)
Natural gas - proved reserves: 111.1 billion cu m (1 January 2002)
Agriculture - products: wheat, corn, barley, sugar beets, sunflower seed, potatoes, grapes; eggs, sheep
Exports: $17.63 billion f.o.b. (2003 est.)
Exports - commodities: textiles and footwear, metals and metal products, machinery and equipment, minerals and fuels, chemicals, agricultural products
Exports - partners: Italy 25.2%, Germany 15.6%, France 7.6%, UK 5.8%, US 4.3%, Turkey 4.1% (2002)

Imports: $22.17 billion f.o.b. (2003 est.)
Imports - commodities: machinery and equipment, fuels and minerals, chemicals, textile and products, basic metals, agricultural products
Imports - partners: Italy 20.8%, Germany 14.9%, Russia 7.2%, France 6.4% (2002)
Debt - external: $19.1 billion (2003 est.)
Currency: leu (ROL)
Currency code: ROL
Exchange rates: lei per US dollar - 33,200.1 (2003), 33,055.4 (2002), 29,060.8 (2001), 21,708.7 (2000), 15,332.8 (1999)
Fiscal year: calendar year

Communications

Telephones - main lines in use: 4,215,200 (2002)
Telephones - mobile cellular: 5,110,600 (2002)
Telephone system:
general assessment: poor domestic service, but improving
domestic: 90% of telephone network is automatic; trunk network is mostly microwave radio relay, with some fiber-optic cable; about one-third of exchange capacity is digital; roughly 3,300 villages have no service
international: country code - 40; satellite earth station - 1 Intelsat; new digital, international, direct-dial exchanges operate in Bucharest; note - Romania is an active participant in several international telecommunication network projects (1999)
Radio broadcast stations: AM 40, FM 202, shortwave 3 (1998)
Television broadcast stations: 48 (plus 392 repeaters) (1995)
Internet country code: .ro
Internet hosts: 40,971 (2002)
Internet users: 1.8 million (2002)

Transportation

Railways:
total: 11,385 km (3,888 km electrified)
standard gauge: 10,898 km 1.435-m gauge
broad gage: 60 km 1.524-m gauge
narrow gauge: 427 km 0.760-m gauge (2002)
Highways:
total: 198,603 km
paved: 98,308 km (including 113 km of expressways)
unpaved: 100,295 km (2000)
Waterways: 1,724 km (1984)
Pipelines: gas 3,508 km; oil 2,427 km (2003)
Ports and harbors: Braila, Constanta, Galati, Mangalia, Sulina, Tulcea
Merchant marine:
total: 45 ships (1,000 GRT or over) 395,350 GRT/ 510,232 DWT
by type: bulk 7, cargo 26, container 1, passenger 1, petroleum tanker 4, rail car carrier 2, roll on/roll off 4
foreign-owned: Greece 1, Italy 2
registered in other countries: 39 (2003 est.)

Airports: 62 (2003 est.)
Airports - with paved runways:
total: 25
over 3,047 m: 4
2,438 to 3,047 m: 9
1,524 to 2,437 m: 12 (2003 est.)
Airports - with unpaved runways:
total: 37
1,524 to 2,437 m: 2
914 to 1,523 m: 12
under 914 m: 23 (2003 est.)
Heliports: 1 (2003 est.)

Military

Military branches: Ground Forces, Naval Forces,
Air and Air Defense Forces (AMR), Civil Defense
Military manpower - military age: 20 years of age
(2004 est.)
Military manpower - availability:
males age 15-49: 5,952,834 (2004 est.)
Military manpower - fit for military service:
males age 15-49: 5,007,375 (2004 est.)
**Military manpower - reaching military age
annually:**
males: 163,577 (2004 est.)
Military expenditures - dollar figure: $985 million
(2002)
Military expenditures - percent of GDP: 2.47%
(2002)

Transnational Issues

Disputes - international: has not resolved claims to
Ukrainian-administered Zmyinyy (Snake) Island and
Black Sea maritime boundary despite ongoing talks
based on 1997 friendship treaty to find a solution in
two years; Hungary amended status law extending
special social and cultural benefits to ethnic
Hungarians in Romania, who had objected to the law
Illicit drugs: major transshipment point for
Southwest Asian heroin transiting the Balkan route
and small amounts of Latin American cocaine bound
for Western Europe; although not a significant
financial center, role as a narcotics conduit leaves it
vulnerable to laundering which occurs via the banking
system, currency exchange houses, and casinos

Russia

Introduction

Background: Repeated devastating defeats of the
Russian army in World War I led to widespread rioting
in the major cities of the Russian Empire and to the
overthrow in 1917 of the 300-year old Romanov
Dynasty. The Communists under Vladimir LENIN
seized power soon after and formed the USSR. The
brutal rule of Josef STALIN (1928-53) strengthened
Russian dominance of the Soviet Union at a cost of
tens of millions of lives. The Soviet economy and
society stagnated in the following decades until
General Secretary Mikhail GORBACHEV (1985-91)
introduced glasnost (openness) and perestroika
(restructuring) in an attempt to modernize
Communism, but his initiatives inadvertently released
forces that by December 1991 splintered the USSR
into 15 independent republics. Since then, Russia has
struggled in its efforts to build a democratic political
system and market economy to replace the strict
social, political, and economic controls of the
Communist period. While some progress has been
made on the economic front, recent years have seen
a recentralization of power under Vladimir PUTIN and
an erosion in nascent democratic institutions. A
determined guerrilla conflict still plagues Russia in
Chechnya.

Geography

Location: Northern Asia (that part west of the
Urals is included with Europe), bordering the
Arctic Ocean, between Europe and the North Pacific
Ocean
Geographic coordinates: 60 00 N, 100 00 E
Map references: Asia
Area:
total: 17,075,200 sq km
land: 16,995,800 sq km
water: 79,400 sq km
Area - comparative: approximately 1.8 times the
size of the US

Land boundaries:
total: 19,990 km
border countries: Azerbaijan 284 km, Belarus 959 km,
China (southeast) 3,605 km, China (south) 40 km,
Estonia 294 km, Finland 1,313 km, Georgia 723 km,
Kazakhstan 6,846 km, North Korea 19 km, Latvia
217 km, Lithuania (Kaliningrad Oblast) 227 km,
Mongolia 3,485 km, Norway 196 km, Poland
(Kaliningrad Oblast) 206 km, Ukraine 1,576 km
Coastline: 37,653 km
Maritime claims:
territorial sea: 12 NM
exclusive economic zone: 200 NM
continental shelf: 200-m depth or to the depth of
exploitation
Climate: ranges from steppes in the south through
humid continental in much of European Russia;
subarctic in Siberia to tundra climate in the polar north;
winters vary from cool along Black Sea coast to frigid
in Siberia; summers vary from warm in the steppes to
cool along Arctic coast
Terrain: broad plain with low hills west of Urals; vast
coniferous forest and tundra in Siberia; uplands and
mountains along southern border regions
Elevation extremes:
lowest point: Caspian Sea -28 m
highest point: Gora El'brus 5,633 m
Natural resources: wide natural resource base
including major deposits of oil, natural gas, coal, and
many strategic minerals, timber
note: formidable obstacles of climate, terrain, and
distance hinder exploitation of natural resources
Land use:
arable land: 7.46%
permanent crops: 0.11%
other: 92.43% (1998 est.)
Irrigated land: 46,630 sq km (1998 est.)
Natural hazards: permafrost over much of Siberia is
a major impediment to development; volcanic activity
in the Kuril Islands; volcanoes and earthquakes on the

Russia (continued)

Kamchatka Peninsula; spring floods and summer/autumn forest fires throughout Siberia and parts of European Russia

Environment - current issues: air pollution from heavy industry, emissions of coal-fired electric plants, and transportation in major cities; industrial, municipal, and agricultural pollution of inland waterways and seacoasts; deforestation; soil erosion; soil contamination from improper application of agricultural chemicals; scattered areas of sometimes intense radioactive contamination; groundwater contamination from toxic waste; urban solid waste management; abandoned stocks of obsolete pesticides

Environment - international agreements:
party to: Air Pollution, Air Pollution-Nitrogen Oxides, Air Pollution-Sulfur 85, Antarctic-Environmental Protocol, Antarctic-Marine Living Resources, Antarctic Seals, Antarctic Treaty, Biodiversity, Climate Change, Endangered Species, Environmental Modification, Hazardous Wastes, Law of the Sea, Marine Dumping, Ozone Layer Protection, Ship Pollution, Tropical Timber 83, Wetlands, Whaling
signed, but not ratified: Air Pollution-Sulfur 94, Climate Change-Kyoto Protocol

Geography - note: largest country in the world in terms of area but unfavorably located in relation to major sea lanes of the world; despite its size, much of the country lacks proper soils and climates (either too cold or too dry) for agriculture; Mount El'brus is Europe's tallest peak

People

Population: 143,782,338 (July 2004 est.)
Age structure:
0-14 years: 15% (male 11,064,109; female 10,518,595)
15-64 years: 71.3% (male 49,534,076; female 52,958,107)
65 years and over: 13.7% (male 6,177,580; female 13,529,871) (2004 est.)
Median age:
total: 37.9 years
male: 34.7 years
female: 40.7 years (2004 est.)
Population growth rate: -0.45% (2004 est.)
Birth rate: 9.63 births/1,000 population (2004 est.)
Death rate: 15.17 deaths/1,000 population (2004 est.)
Net migration rate: 1.02 migrant(s)/1,000 population (2004 est.)
Sex ratio:
at birth: 1.06 male(s)/female
under 15 years: 1.05 male(s)/female
15-64 years: 0.94 male(s)/female
65 years and over: 0.46 male(s)/female
total population: 0.87 male(s)/female (2004 est.)
Infant mortality rate:
total: 16.96 deaths/1,000 live births
male: 19.58 deaths/1,000 live births
female: 14.18 deaths/1,000 live births (2004 est.)

Life expectancy at birth:
total population: 66.39 years
male: 59.91 years
female: 73.27 years (2004 est.)
Total fertility rate: 1.26 children born/woman (2004 est.)
HIV/AIDS - adult prevalence rate: 0.9% (2001 est.)
HIV/AIDS - people living with HIV/AIDS: 700,000 (2001 est.)
HIV/AIDS - deaths: 9,000 (2001 est.)
Nationality:
noun: Russian(s)
adjective: Russian
Ethnic groups: Russian 81.5%, Tatar 3.8%, Ukrainian 3%, Chuvash 1.2%, Bashkir 0.9%, Belarusian 0.8%, Moldavian 0.7%, other 8.1% (1989)
Religions: Russian Orthodox, Muslim, other
Languages: Russian, other
Literacy:
definition: age 15 and over can read and write
total population: 99.6%
male: 99.7%
female: 99.5% (2003 est.)

Government

Country name:
conventional long form: Russian Federation
conventional short form: Russia
local long form: Rossiyskaya Federatsiya
local short form: Rossiya
former: Russian Empire, Russian Soviet Federative Socialist Republic
Government type: federation
Capital: Moscow
Administrative divisions: 49 oblasts (oblastey, singular - oblast), 21 republics* (respublik, singular - respublika), 10 autonomous okrugs**(avtonomnykh okrugov, singular - avtonomnyy okrug), 6 krays*** (krayev, singular - kray), 2 federal cities (singular - gorod)****, and 1 autonomous oblast*****(avtonomnaya oblast'); Adygeya (Maykop)*, Aginskiy Buryatskiy (Aginskoye)**, Altay (Gorno-Altaysk)*, Altayskiy (Barnaul)***, Amurskaya (Blagoveshchensk), Arkhangel'skaya, Astrakhanskaya, Bashkortostan (Ufa)*, Belgorodskaya, Bryanskaya, Buryatiya (Ulan-Ude)*, Chechnya (Groznyy)*, Chelyabinskaya, Chitinskaya, Chukotskiy (Anadyr')**, Chuvashiya (Cheboksary)*, Dagestan (Makhachkala)*, Evenkiyskiy (Tura)**, Ingushetiya (Nazran')*, Irkutskaya, Ivanovskaya, Kabardino-Balkariya (Nal'chik)*, Kaliningradskaya, Kalmykiya (Elista)*, Kaluzhskaya, Kamchatskaya (Petropavlovsk-Kamchatskiy), Karachayevo-Cherkesiya (Cherkessk)*, Kareliya (Petrozavodsk)*, Kemerovskaya, Khabarovskiy***, Khakasiya (Abakan)*, Khanty-Mansiyskiy (Khanty-Mansiysk)**, Kirovskaya, Komi (Syktyvkar)*, Koryakskiy (Palana)**, Kostromskaya, Krasnodarskiy***, Krasnoyarskiy***, Kurganskaya, Kurskaya, Leningradskaya, Lipetskaya, Magadanskaya, Mariy-El (Yoshkar-Ola)*, Mordoviya

(Saransk)*, Moskovskaya, Moskva (Moscow)****, Murmanskaya, Nenetskiy (Nar'yan-Mar)**, Nizhegorodskaya, Novgorodskaya, Novosibirskaya, Omskaya, Orenburgskaya, Orlovskaya (Orel), Penzenskaya, Permskaya, Komi-Permyatskiy (Kudymkar)**, Primorskiy (Vladivostok)***, Pskovskaya, Rostovskaya, Ryazanskaya, Sakha (Yakutiya)*, Sakhalinskaya (Yuzhno-Sakhalinsk), Samarskaya, Sankt-Peterburg (Saint Petersburg)****, Saratovskaya, Severnaya Osetiya-Alaniya [North Ossetia] (Vladikavkaz)*, Smolenskaya, Stavropol'skiy***, Sverdlovskaya (Yekaterinburg), Tambovskaya, Tatarstan (Kazan')*, Taymyrskiy (Dudinka)**, Tomskaya, Tul'skaya, Tverskaya, Tyumenskaya, Tyva (Kyzyl)*, Udmurtiya (Izhevsk)*, Ul'yanovskaya, Ust'-Ordynskiy Buryatskiy (Ust'-Ordynskiy)**, Vladimirskaya, Volgogradskaya, Vologodskaya, Voronezhskaya, Yamalo-Nenetskiy (Salekhard)**, Yaroslavskaya, Yevreyskaya*****; note - when using a place name with an adjectival ending 'skaya' or 'skiy,' the word Oblast' or Avonomnyy Okrug or Kray should be added to the place name
note: administrative divisions have the same names as their administrative centers (exceptions have the administrative center name following in parentheses)
Independence: 24 August 1991 (from Soviet Union)
National holiday: Russia Day, 12 June (1990)
Constitution: adopted 12 December 1993
Legal system: based on civil law system; judicial review of legislative acts
Suffrage: 18 years of age; universal
Executive branch:
chief of state: President Vladimir Vladimirovich PUTIN (acting president since 31 December 1999, president since 7 May 2000)
head of government: Premier Mikhail Yefimovich FRADKOV (since 5 March 2004); Deputy Premier Aleksandr Dmitriyevich ZHUKOV (since 9 March 2004)
cabinet: Ministries of the Government or "Government" composed of the premier and his deputy, ministers, and selected other individuals; all are appointed by the president
note: there is also a Presidential Administration (PA) that provides staff and policy support to the president, drafts presidential decrees, and coordinates policy among government agencies; a Security Council also reports directly to the president
elections: president elected by popular vote for a four-year term; election last held 14 March 2004 (next to be held NA March 2008); note - no vice president; if the president dies in office, cannot exercise his powers because of ill health, is impeached, or resigns, the premier succeeds him; the premier serves as acting president until a new presidential election is held, which must be within three months; premier appointed by the president with the approval of the Duma
election results: Vladimir Vladimirovich PUTIN reelected president; percent of vote - Vladimir Vladimirovich PUTIN 71.2%, Nikolay KHARITONOV 13.7%, other (no candidate above 5%) 15.1%

Legislative branch: bicameral Federal Assembly or Federalnoye Sobraniye consists of the Federation Council or Sovet Federatsii (178 seats; as of July 2000, members appointed by the top executive and legislative officials in each of the 89 federal administrative units - oblasts, krays, republics, autonomous okrugs and oblasts, and the federal cities of Moscow and Saint Petersburg; members serve four-year terms) and the State Duma or Gosudarstvennaya Duma (450 seats; 225 seats elected by proportional representation from party lists winning at least 5% of the vote, and 225 seats from single-member constituencies; members are elected by direct, popular vote to serve four-year terms)

elections: State Duma - last held 7 December 2003 (next to be held NA December 2007)

election results: State Duma - percent of vote received by parties clearing the 5% threshold entitling them to a proportional share of the 225 party list seats - United Russia 37.1%, CPRF 12.7%, LDPR 11.6%, Motherland 9.1%; seats by party - United Russia 222, CPRF 53, LDPR 38, Motherland 37, People's Party 19, Yabloko 4, Union of Rightist Forces 2, other 7, independents 65, repeat election required 3

Judicial branch: Constitutional Court; Supreme Court; Superior Court of Arbitration; judges for all courts are appointed for life by the Federation Council on the recommendation of the president

Political parties and leaders: Communist Party of the Russian Federation or CPRF [Gennadiy Andreyevich ZYUGANOV]; Liberal Democratic Party of Russia or LDPR [Vladimir Volfovich ZHIRINOVSKIY]; Motherland Bloc (Rodina) [Sergey GLAZYEV and Dmitriy ROGOZIN]; People's Party [Gennadiy RAYKOV]; Union of Rightist Forces or SPS [Anatoliy Borisovich CHUBAYS, Yegor Timurovich GAYDAR, Irina Mutsuovna KHAKAMADA, Boris Yefimovich NEMTSOV]; United Russia [Boris Vyacheslavovich GRYZLOV]; Yabloko Party [Grigoriy Alekseyevich YAVLINSKIY]

Political pressure groups and leaders: NA

International organization participation: APEC, ARF, ASEAN (dialogue partner), BIS, BSEC, CBSS, CE, CERN (observer), CIS, EAPC, EBRD, G-8, IAEA, IBRD, ICAO, ICC, ICCt (signatory), ICFTU, ICRM, IDA, IFC, IFRCS, IHO, ILO, IMF, IMO, Interpol, IOC, IOM (observer), ISO, ITU, LAIA (observer), MINURSO, MONUC, NAM (guest), NSG, OAS (observer), OPCW, OSCE, Paris Club, PCA, PFP, SCO, UN, UN Security Council, UNAMSIL, UNCTAD, UNHCR, UNIDO, UNITAR, UNMEE, UNMIK, UNMISET, UNMOVIC, UNOMIG, UNTSO, UPU, WCO, WFTU, WHO, WIPO, WMO, WToO, WTrO (observer), ZC

Diplomatic representation in the US:

chief of mission: Ambassador Yuriy Viktorovich USHAKOV

chancery: 2650 Wisconsin Avenue NW, Washington, DC 20007

telephone: [1] (202) 298-5700, 5701, 5704, 5708

FAX: [1] (202) 298-5735

consulate(s) general: New York, San Francisco, and Seattle

Diplomatic representation from the US:

chief of mission: Ambassador Alexander VERSHBOW

embassy: Bolshoy Devyatinskiy Pereulok No. 8, 121099 Moscow

mailing address: PSC-77, APO AE 09721

telephone: [7] (095) 728-5000

FAX: [7] (095) 728-5090

consulate(s) general: Saint Petersburg, Vladivostok, Yekaterinburg

Flag description: three equal horizontal bands of white (top), blue, and red

Economy

Economy - overview: Russia ended 2003 with its fifth straight year of growth, averaging 6.5% annually since the financial crisis of 1998. Although high oil prices and a relatively cheap ruble are important drivers of this economic rebound, since 2000 investment and consumer-driven demand have played a noticeably increasing role. Real fixed capital investments have averaged gains greater than 10% over the last four years and real personal incomes have averaged increases over 12%. Russia has also improved its international financial position since the 1998 financial crisis, with its foreign debt declining from 90% of GDP to around 28%. Strong oil export earnings have allowed Russia to increase its foreign reserves from only $12 billion to some $80 billion. These achievements, along with a renewed government effort to advance structural reforms, have raised business and investor confidence in Russia's economic prospects. Nevertheless, serious problems persist. Oil, natural gas, metals, and timber account for more than 80% of exports, leaving the country vulnerable to swings in world prices. Russia's manufacturing base is dilapidated and must be replaced or modernized if the country is to achieve broad-based economic growth. Other problems include a weak banking system, a poor business climate that discourages both domestic and foreign investors, corruption, local and regional government intervention in the courts, and widespread lack of trust in institutions. In addition, a string of investigations launched against a major Russian oil company, culminating with the arrest of its CEO in the fall of 2003, have raised concerns by some observers that President PUTIN is granting more influence to forces within his government that desire to reassert state control over the economy.

GDP: purchasing power parity - $1.287 trillion (2003 est.)

GDP - real growth rate: 7.3% (2003 est.)

GDP - per capita: purchasing power parity - $8,900 (2003 est.)

GDP - composition by sector:

agriculture: 5.2%

industry: 35%

services: 59.8% (2003 est.)

Population below poverty line: 25% (January 2003 est.)

Household income or consumption by percentage share:

lowest 10%: 5.9%

highest 10%: 47% (2001)

Distribution of family income - Gini index: 39.9 (2001)

Inflation rate (consumer prices): 12% (2003 est.)

Labor force: 71.5 million (2003 est.)

Labor force - by occupation: agriculture 12.3%, industry 22.7%, services 65% (2002 est.)

Unemployment rate: 8.4% plus considerable underemployment (December 2003 est.)

Budget:

revenues: $70 billion

expenditures: $62 billion, including capital expenditures of $NA (2002 est.)

Industries: complete range of mining and extractive industries producing coal, oil, gas, chemicals, and metals; all forms of machine building from rolling mills to high-performance aircraft and space vehicles; shipbuilding; road and rail transportation equipment; communications equipment; agricultural machinery, tractors, and construction equipment; electric power generating and transmitting equipment; medical and scientific instruments; consumer durables, textiles, foodstuffs, handicrafts

Industrial production growth rate: 7% (2003 est.)

Electricity - production: 915 billion kWh (2003)

Electricity - production by source:

fossil fuel: 66.3%

hydro: 17.2%

nuclear: 16.4%

other: 0.1% (2003)

Electricity - consumption: 773 billion kWh (2001)

Electricity - exports: 21.16 billion kWh (2001)

Electricity - imports: 7 billion kWh (2001)

Oil - production: 7.286 million bbl/day (2001 est.)

Oil - consumption: 2.595 million bbl/day (2001 est.)

Oil - exports: NA

Oil - imports: NA

Oil - proved reserves: 51.22 billion bbl (1 January 2002)

Natural gas - production: 580.8 billion cu m (2001 est.)

Natural gas - consumption: 408.1 billion cu m (2001 est.)

Natural gas - exports: 205.4 billion cu m (2001 est.)

Natural gas - imports: 32.7 billion cu m (2001 est.)

Natural gas - proved reserves: 47.86 trillion cu m (1 January 2002)

Agriculture - products: grain, sugar beets, sunflower seed, vegetables, fruits; beef, milk

Exports: $134.4 billion (2003 est.)

Exports - commodities: petroleum and petroleum products, natural gas, wood and wood products, metals, chemicals, and a wide variety of civilian and military manufactures

Russia (continued)

Exports - partners: Germany 7.5%, Italy 6.9%, Netherlands 6.7%, China 6.3%, US 6.1%, Ukraine 5.5%, Belarus 5.4%, Switzerland 5% (2002)
Imports: $74.8 billion (2003 est.)
Imports - commodities: machinery and equipment, consumer goods, medicines, meat, sugar, semifinished metal products
Imports - partners: Germany 14.3%, Belarus 8.9%, Ukraine 7.1%, US 6.4%, China 5.2%, Italy 4.8%, Kazakhstan 4.3%, France 4.1% (2002)
Debt - external: $165.4 billion (September 2003)
Economic aid - recipient: in FY01 from US, $979 million (including $750 million in non-proliferation subsidies); in 2001 from EU, $200 million (2000 est.)
Currency: Russian ruble (RUR)
Currency code: RUR
Exchange rates: Russian rubles per US dollar - 30.692 (2003), 31.3485 (2002), 29.1685 (2001), 28.1292 (2000), 24.6199 (1999)
note: the post-1 January 1998 ruble is equal to 1,000 of the pre-1 January 1998 rubles
Fiscal year: calendar year

Communications

Telephones - main lines in use: 35.5 million (2002)
Telephones - mobile cellular: 17,608,800 (2002)
Telephone system:
general assessment: the telephone system underwent significant changes in the 1990s; there are more than 1,000 companies licensed to offer communication services; access to digital lines has improved, particularly in urban centers; Internet and e-mail services are improving; Russia has made progress toward building the telecommunications infrastructure necessary for a market economy; however, a large demand for main line service remains unsatisfied
domestic: cross-country digital trunk lines run from Saint Petersburg to Khabarovsk, and from Moscow to Novorossiysk; the telephone systems in 60 regional capitals have modern digital infrastructures; cellular services, both analog and digital, are available in many areas; in rural areas, the telephone services are still outdated, inadequate, and low density
international: country code - 7; Russia is connected internationally by three undersea fiber-optic cables; digital switches in several cities provide more than 50,000 lines for international calls; satellite earth stations provide access to Intelsat, Intersputnik, Eutelsat, Inmarsat, and Orbita systems
Radio broadcast stations: AM 420, FM 447, shortwave 56 (1998)
Television broadcast stations: 7,306 (1998)
Internet country code: .ru; Russia also has responsibility for a legacy domain ".su" that was allocated to the Soviet Union, and whose legal status and ownership are contested by the Russian Government, ICANN, and several Russian commercial entities
Internet hosts: 409,229 (2002)
Internet users: 6 million (2002)

Transportation

Railways:
total: 87,157 km
broad gauge: 86,200 km 1.520-m gauge (40,300 km electrified)
narrow gauge: 957 km 1.067-m gauge (on Sakhalin Island)
note: an additional 30,000 km of non-common carrier lines serve industries (2002)
Highways:
total: 532,393 km
paved: 358,833 km
unpaved: 173,560 km (2000)
Waterways: 95,900 km (total routes in general use)
note: routes with navigation guides serving the Russian River Fleet - 95,900 km; routes with night navigational aids - 60,400 km; man-made navigable routes - 16,900 km (January 1994)
Pipelines: gas 135,771 km; oil 70,833 km; refined products 11,536 km; water 23 km (2003)
Ports and harbors: Aleksandrovsk-Sakhalinskiy, Arkhangel'sk, Astrakhan', De-Kastri, Indigirskiy, Kaliningrad, Kandalaksha, Kazan', Khabarovsk, Kholmsk, Krasnoyarsk, Lazarev, Mago, Mezen', Moscow, Murmansk, Nakhodka, Nevel'sk, Novorossiysk, Onega, Petropavlovsk-Kamchatskiy, Rostov, Shakhtersk, Saint Petersburg, Sochi, Taganrog, Tuapse, Uglegorsk, Vanino, Vladivostok, Volgograd, Vostochnyy, Vyborg
Merchant marine:
total: 958 ships (1,000 GRT or over) 4,521,472 GRT/ 5,505,118 DWT
by type: barge carrier 1, bulk 20, cargo 562, chemical tanker 13, combination bulk 21, combination ore/oil 36, container 28, multi-functional large load carrier 2, passenger 35, passenger/cargo 4, petroleum tanker 179, rail car carrier 1, refrigerated cargo 27, roll on/roll off 21, short-sea/passenger 6, specialized tanker 2
foreign-owned: Belize 2, Cambodia 2, Cyprus 9, Denmark 1, Estonia 3, Germany 1, Greece 3, Hong Kong 1, South Korea 1, Latvia 2, Lithuania 3, Malta 2, Moldova 3, Netherlands 2, Panama 2, Switzerland 4, Turkey 18, Turkmenistan 2, Ukraine 7, United Kingdom 3, United States 4
registered in other countries: 350 (2003 est.)
Airports: 2,609 (2003 est.)
Airports - with paved runways:
total: 585
over 3,047 m: 56
2,438 to 3,047 m: 201
1,524 to 2,437 m: 122
914 to 1,523 m: 100
under 914 m: 106 (2003 est.)
Airports - with unpaved runways:
total: 2,024
over 3,047 m: 19
2,438 to 3,047 m: 34
1,524 to 2,437 m: 120
914 to 1,523 m: 261
under 914 m: 1,590 (2003 est.)
Heliports: 36 (2003 est.)

Military

Military branches: Ground Forces, Navy, Air Forces; Airborne troops, Strategic Rocket Forces, and Military Space Forces are classified as independent combat arms, not subordinate to any of the three branches
Military manpower - military age: 18 years of age (2004 est.)
Military manpower - availability:
males age 15-49: 39,127,169 (2004 est.)
Military manpower - fit for military service:
males age 15-49: 30,600,088 (2004 est.)
Military manpower - reaching military age annually:
males: 1,262,339 (2004 est.)
Military expenditures - dollar figure: $NA
Military expenditures - percent of GDP: NA%

Transnational Issues

Disputes - international: China continues to seek a mutually acceptable solution to the disputed alluvial islands at the confluence of the Amur and Ussuri Rivers and a small island on the Argun River as part of the 2001 Treaty of Good Neighborliness, Friendship, and Cooperation; the sovereignty dispute over the islands of Etorofu, Kunashiri, Shikotan, and the Habomai group known in Japan as the "Northern Territories" and in Russia as the "Southern Kurils," occupied by the Soviet Union in 1945, now administered by Russia, and claimed by Japan, remains the primary sticking point to signing a peace treaty formally ending World War II hostilities; about a third of the boundary with Georgia remains undelimited and none of it demarcated with several small, strategic segments remaining in dispute; OSCE observers monitor volatile areas such as the Pankisi Gorge in the Akhmeti region and the Argun Gorge in Abkhazia; equidistant seabed treaties have been signed with Azerbaijan and Kazakhstan in the Caspian Sea but no consensus on dividing the water column among the littoral states; Russia and Norway dispute their maritime limits in the Barents Sea and Russia's fishing rights beyond Svalbard's territorial limits within the Svalbard Treaty zone; Russia continues to reject signing and ratifying the joint 1996 technical border agreement with Estonia; the Russian Parliament refuses to consider ratification of the boundary treaties with Estonia and Latvia, but in May 2003, ratified land and maritime boundary treaty with Lithuania, which ratified the 1997 treaty in 1999, legalizing limits of former Soviet republic borders; a simplified transit regime was adopted in July 2003 for residents of the Kaliningrad coastal exclave to travel through Lithuania to Russia; delimitation of land boundary with Ukraine is complete, but boundary through the Sea of Azov and Kerch Strait remains unresolved despite a December 2003 framework agreement and on-going expert-level discussions; Ukraine protests Russia's construction of a causeway in the direction of Ukrainian-administered Tuzla Island in the Kerch Strait; Kazakhstan and Russia will complete delimitation of their interstate border in 2004 and demarcation is underway; Russian Duma has not yet ratified 1990 Maritime Boundary Agreement with the US in the Bering Sea

Illicit drugs: limited cultivation of illicit cannabis and opium poppy and producer of methamphetamine, mostly for domestic consumption; government has active illicit crop eradication program; used as transshipment point for Asian opiates, cannabis, and Latin American cocaine bound for growing domestic markets, to a lesser extent Western and Central Europe, and occasionally to the US; major source of heroin precursor chemicals; corruption and organized crime are key concerns; heroin increasingly popular in domestic market

Rwanda

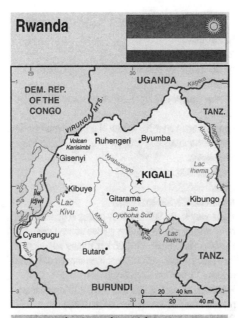

Introduction

Background: In 1959, three years before independence from Belgium, the majority ethnic group, the Hutus, overthrew the ruling Tutsi king. Over the next several years, thousands of Tutsis were killed, and some 150,000 driven into exile in neighboring countries. The children of these exiles later formed a rebel group, the Rwandan Patriotic Front, and began a civil war in 1990. The war, along with several political and economic upheavals, exacerbated ethnic tensions, culminating in April 1994 in the genocide of roughly 800,000 Tutsis and moderate Hutus. The Tutsi rebels defeated the Hutu regime and ended the killing in July 1994, but approximately 2 million Hutu refugees - many fearing Tutsi retribution - fled to neighboring Burundi, Tanzania, Uganda, and Zaire. Since then, most of the refugees have returned to Rwanda. Despite substantial international assistance and political reforms - including Rwanda's first local elections in March 1999 and its first post-genocide presidential and legislative elections in August and September 2003, respectively - the country continues to struggle to boost investment and agricultural output and to foster reconciliation. A series of massive population displacements, a nagging Hutu extremist insurgency, and Rwandan involvement in two wars over the past four years in the neighboring Democratic Republic of the Congo continue to hinder Rwanda's efforts.

Geography

Location: Central Africa, east of Democratic Republic of the Congo
Geographic coordinates: 2 00 S, 30 00 E
Map references: Africa
Area:
total: 26,338 sq km
land: 24,948 sq km
water: 1,390 sq km

Area - comparative: slightly smaller than Maryland
Land boundaries:
total: 893 km
border countries: Burundi 290 km, Democratic Republic of the Congo 217 km, Tanzania 217 km, Uganda 169 km
Coastline: 0 km (landlocked)
Maritime claims: none (landlocked)
Climate: temperate; two rainy seasons (February to April, November to January); mild in mountains with frost and snow possible
Terrain: mostly grassy uplands and hills; relief is mountainous with altitude declining from west to east
Elevation extremes:
lowest point: Rusizi River 950 m
highest point: Volcan Karisimbi 4,519 m
Natural resources: gold, cassiterite (tin ore), wolframite (tungsten ore), methane, hydropower, arable land
Land use:
arable land: 32.43%
permanent crops: 10.13%
other: 57.44% (1998 est.)
Irrigated land: 40 sq km (1998 est.)
Natural hazards: periodic droughts; the volcanic Virunga mountains are in the northwest along the border with Democratic Republic of the Congo
Environment - current issues: deforestation results from uncontrolled cutting of trees for fuel; overgrazing; soil exhaustion; soil erosion; widespread poaching
Environment - international agreements:
party to: Biodiversity, Climate Change, Desertification, Endangered Species, Hazardous Wastes, Ozone Layer Protection
signed, but not ratified: Law of the Sea
Geography - note: landlocked; most of the country is savanna grassland with the population predominantly rural

People

Population: 7,954,013
note: estimates for this country explicitly take into account the effects of excess mortality due to AIDS; this can result in lower life expectancy, higher infant mortality and death rates, lower population and growth rates, and changes in the distribution of population by age and sex than would otherwise be expected (July 2004 est.)
Age structure:
0-14 years: 42.3% (male 1,690,122; female 1,674,147)
15-64 years: 55% (male 2,178,956; female 2,194,526)
65 years and over: 2.7% (male 85,472; female 130,790) (2004 est.)
Median age:
total: 18.2 years
male: 18 years
female: 18.4 years (2004 est.)

Rwanda *(continued)*

Population growth rate: 1.82% (2004 est.)
Birth rate: 40.01 births/1,000 population (2004 est.)
Death rate: 21.86 deaths/1,000 population (2004 est.)
Net migration rate: 0 migrant(s)/1,000 population (2004 est.)
Sex ratio:
at birth: 1.03 male(s)/female
under 15 years: 1.01 male(s)/female
15-64 years: 0.99 male(s)/female
65 years and over: 0.65 male(s)/female
total population: 0.99 male(s)/female (2004 est.)
Infant mortality rate:
total: 101.68 deaths/1,000 live births
male: 106.68 deaths/1,000 live births
female: 96.53 deaths/1,000 live births (2004 est.)
Life expectancy at birth:
total population: 39.18 years
male: 38.43 years
female: 39.96 years (2004 est.)
Total fertility rate: 5.55 children born/woman (2004 est.)
HIV/AIDS - adult prevalence rate: 8.9% (2001 est.)
HIV/AIDS - people living with HIV/AIDS: 500,000 (2001 est.)
HIV/AIDS - deaths: 49,000 (2001 est.)
Nationality:
noun: Rwandan(s)
adjective: Rwandan
Ethnic groups: Hutu 84%, Tutsi 15%, Twa (Pygmoid) 1%
Religions: Roman Catholic 56.5%, Protestant 26%, Adventist 11.1%, Muslim 4.6%, indigenous beliefs 0.1%, none 1.7% (2001)
Languages: Kinyarwanda (official) universal Bantu vernacular, French (official), English (official), Kiswahili (Swahili) used in commercial centers
Literacy:
definition: age 15 and over can read and write
total population: 70.4%
male: 76.3%
female: 64.7% (2003 est.)
People - note: Rwanda is the most densely populated country in Africa

Government

Country name:
conventional long form: Rwandese Republic
conventional short form: Rwanda
local long form: Republika y'u Rwanda
local short form: Rwanda
former: Ruanda
Government type: republic; presidential, multiparty system
Capital: Kigali
Administrative divisions: 12 prefectures (in French - prefectures, singular - prefecture; in Kinyarwanda - plural - NA, singular - prefegitura); Butare, Byumba, Cyangugu, Gikongoro, Gisenyi, Gitarama, Kibungo, Kibuye, Kigali Rurale, Kigali-ville, Umutara, Ruhengeri

Independence: 1 July 1962 (from Belgium-administered UN trusteeship)
National holiday: Independence Day, 1 July (1962)
Constitution: on 5 May 1995, the Transitional National Assembly adopted as Fundamental Law the constitution of 18 June 1991, provisions of the 1993 Arusha peace accord, the July 1994 Declaration by the Rwanda Patriotic Front, and the November 1994 multiparty protocol of understanding
Legal system: based on German and Belgian civil law systems and customary law; judicial review of legislative acts in the Supreme Court; has not accepted compulsory ICJ jurisdiction
Suffrage: 18 years of age; universal adult
Executive branch:
chief of state: President Paul KAGAME (since 22 April 2000)
head of government: Prime Minister Bernard MAKUZA (since 8 March 2000)
cabinet: Council of Ministers appointed by the president
elections: last held 25 August 2003 (next to be held NA 2008)
election results: Paul KAGAME elected president in first direct popular vote; Paul KAGAME 95.05%, Faustin TWAGIRAMUNGU 3.62%, Jean-Nepomuscene NAYINZIRA 1.33%
Legislative branch: unicameral National Assembly or Assemblee Nationale (53 seats; members elected by direct vote)
elections: last held 29 September 2003 (next to be held NA)
election results: seats by party under the Arusha peace accord - RPF 40, PSD 7, PL 6
Judicial branch: Supreme Court; communal courts; appeals courts
Political parties and leaders: Centrist Democratic Party or PDC [Alfred MUKEZAMFURA]; Social Democratic Party or PSD [Vincent BIRUTA]; Democratic Popular Union of Rwanda or UDPR [Adrien RANGIRA]; Democratic Republican Movement or MDR (officially banned) [Celestin KABANDA]; Islamic Democratic Party or PDI [Andre BUMAYA]; Liberal Party or PL [Prosper HIGIRO]; Party for Democratic Renewal (officially banned) [Pasteur BIZIMUNGU and Charles NTAKARUTINKA]; Rwanda Patriotic Front or RPF [Paul KAGAME]
Political pressure groups and leaders: IBUKA - association of genocide survivors
International organization participation: ACCT, ACP, AfDB, AU, CEPGL, FAO, G-77, IBRD, ICAO, ICFTU, ICRM, IDA, IFAD, IFC, IFRCS, ILO, IMF, Interpol, IOC, IOM, ISO (correspondent), ITU, NAM, OPCW (signatory), UN, UNCTAD, UNESCO, UNIDO, UPU, WCL, WCO, WHO, WIPO, WMO, WToO, WTrO
Diplomatic representation in the US:
chief of mission: Ambassador Zac NSENGA
chancery: 1714 New Hampshire Ave. NW, Washington, DC 20009
telephone: [1] (202) 232-2882
FAX: [1] (202) 232-4544

Diplomatic representation from the US:
chief of mission: Ambassador Margaret K. McMILLION
embassy: #337 Boulevard de la Revolution, Kigali
mailing address: B. P. 28, Kigali
telephone: [250] 50 56 01 through 03
FAX: [250] 57 2128
Flag description: three horizontal bands of sky blue (top, double width), yellow, and green, with a golden sun with 24 rays near the fly end of the blue band

Economy

Economy - overview: Rwanda is a poor rural country with about 90% of the population engaged in (mainly subsistence) agriculture. It is the most densely populated country in Africa; landlocked with few natural resources and minimal industry. Primary foreign exchange earners are coffee and tea. The 1994 genocide decimated Rwanda's fragile economic base, severely impoverished the population, particularly women, and eroded the country's ability to attract private and external investment. However, Rwanda has made substantial progress in stabilizing and rehabilitating its economy to pre-1994 levels, although poverty levels are higher now. GDP has rebounded, and inflation has been curbed. Export earnings, however, have been hindered by low beverage prices, depriving the country of much needed hard currency. Attempts to diversify into non-traditional agriculture exports such as flowers and vegetables have been stymied by a lack of adequate transportation infrastructure. Despite Rwanda's fertile ecosystem, food production often does not keep pace with population growth, requiring food to be imported. Rwanda continues to receive substantial aid money and was approved for IMF-World Bank Heavily Indebted Poor Country (HIPC) initiative debt relief in late 2000. But Kigali's high defense expenditures cause tension between the government and international donors and lending agencies.
GDP: purchasing power parity - $10.11 billion (2003 est.)
GDP - real growth rate: 3.5% (2003 est.)
GDP - per capita: purchasing power parity - $1,300 (2003 est.)
GDP - composition by sector:
agriculture: 45%
industry: 20%
services: 35% (2002 est.)
Population below poverty line: 60% (2001 est.)
Household income or consumption by percentage share:
lowest 10%: 4.2%
highest 10%: 24.2% (1985)
Distribution of family income - Gini index: 28.9 (1985)
Inflation rate (consumer prices): 5.5% (2002 est.)
Labor force: 4.6 million (2000)
Labor force - by occupation: agriculture 90%
Unemployment rate: NA%

Rwanda *(continued)*

Budget:
revenues: $199.3 million
expenditures: $445 million, including capital expenditures of $NA (2001 est.)
Industries: cement, agricultural products, small-scale beverages, soap, furniture, shoes, plastic goods, textiles, cigarettes
Industrial production growth rate: 7% (2001 est.)
Electricity - production: 96.78 million kWh (2001)
Electricity - production by source:
fossil fuel: 2.3%
hydro: 97.7%
nuclear: 0%
other: 0% (2001)
Electricity - consumption: 140 million kWh (2001)
Electricity - exports: 0 kWh (2001)
Electricity - imports: 50 million kWh (2001)
Oil - production: 0 bbl/day (2001 est.)
Oil - consumption: 5,300 bbl/day (2001 est.)
Oil - exports: NA
Oil - imports: NA
Oil - proved reserves: 0 bbl (1 January 2002)
Natural gas - proved reserves: 28.32 billion cu m (1 January 2002)
Agriculture - products: coffee, tea, pyrethrum (insecticide made from chrysanthemums), bananas, beans, sorghum, potatoes; livestock
Exports: $73.33 million f.o.b. (2003 est.)
Exports - commodities: coffee, tea, hides, tin ore
Exports - partners: Indonesia 37.5%, Hong Kong 6.9%, China 3.5% (2002)
Imports: $245.8 million f.o.b. (2003 est.)
Imports - commodities: foodstuffs, machinery and equipment, steel, petroleum products, cement and construction material
Imports - partners: Kenya 23.2%, Belgium 8.3%, Germany 6.6% (2002)
Debt - external: $1.3 billion (2000 est.)
Economic aid - recipient: $372.9 million (1999)
Currency: Rwandan franc (RWF)
Currency code: RWF
Exchange rates: Rwandan francs per US dollar - 537.658 (2003), 476.327 (2002), 442.801 (2001), 389.696 (2000), 333.942 (1999)
Fiscal year: calendar year

Communications

Telephones - main lines in use: 23,200 (2002)
Telephones - mobile cellular: 110,800
note: Rwanda has mobile cellular service between Kigali and several prefecture capitals (2002)
Telephone system:
general assessment: telephone system primarily serves business and government
domestic: the capital, Kigali, is connected to the centers of the prefectures by microwave radio relay and, recently, by cellular telephone service; much of the network depends on wire and HF radiotelephone
international: country code - 250; international connections employ microwave radio relay to neighboring countries and satellite communications to more distant countries; satellite earth stations - 1 Intelsat (Indian Ocean) in Kigali (includes telex and telefax service)
Radio broadcast stations: AM 0, FM 3 (two main FM programs are broadcast through a system of repeaters and the third FM program is a 24 hour BBC program), shortwave 1 (2002)
Television broadcast stations: NA
Internet country code: .rw
Internet hosts: 1,233 (2002)
Internet users: 25,000 (2002)

Transportation

Railways: 0 km
Highways:
total: 12,000 km
paved: 996 km
unpaved: 11,004 km (1999 est.)
Waterways:
note: Lac Kivu navigable by shallow-draft barges and native craft
Ports and harbors: Cyangugu, Gisenyi, Kibuye
Airports: 9 (2003 est.)
Airports - with paved runways:
total: 4
over 3,047 m: 1
914 to 1,523 m: 2
under 914 m: 1 (2003 est.)
Airports - with unpaved runways:
total: 5
914 to 1,523 m: 2
under 914 m: 3 (2003 est.)

Military

Military branches: Rwandan Defense Forces (Army, Air Forces)
Military manpower - availability:
males age 15-49: 1,973,713 (2004 est.)
Military manpower - fit for military service:
males age 15-49: 1,004,296 (2004 est.)
Military expenditures - dollar figure: $47.7 million (2003)
Military expenditures - percent of GDP: 2.9% (2003)

Transnational Issues

Disputes - international: Tutsi, Hutu, Hema, Lendu, and other conflicting ethnic groups, associated political rebels, armed gangs, and various government forces continue fighting in Great Lakes region, transcending the boundaries of Burundi, Democratic Republic of the Congo, Rwanda, and Uganda to gain control over populated areas and natural resources - government heads pledge to end conflicts, but localized violence continues despite UN peacekeeping efforts

---

Saint Helena
(overseas territory of the UK)

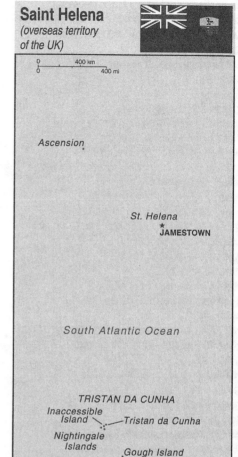

Introduction

Background: Uninhabited when first discovered by the Portuguese in 1502, Saint Helena was garrisoned by the British during the 17th century. It acquired fame as the place of Napoleon BONAPARTE's exile, from 1815 until his death in 1821, but its importance as a port of call declined after the opening of the Suez Canal in 1869. Ascension Island is the site of a US Air Force auxiliary airfield; Gough Island has a meteorological station.

Geography

Location: islands in the South Atlantic Ocean, about midway between South America and Africa
Geographic coordinates: 15 56 S, 5 42 W
Map references: Africa
Area:
total: 410 sq km
land: 410 sq km
water: 0 sq km
note: includes Saint Helena Island, Ascension, and the island group of Tristan da Cunha, which consists of Tristan da Cunha Island, Gough Island, Inaccessible Island, and the three Nightingale Islands

Saint Helena *(continued)*

Area - comparative: slightly more than twice the size of Washington, DC
Land boundaries: 0 km
Coastline: 60 km
Maritime claims:
territorial sea: 12 NM
exclusive fishing zone: 200 NM
Climate: Saint Helena - tropical; marine; mild, tempered by trade winds; Tristan da Cunha - temperate; marine, mild, tempered by trade winds (tends to be cooler than Saint Helena)
Terrain: Saint Helena - rugged, volcanic; small scattered plateaus and plains
note: the other islands of the group have a volcanic origin
Elevation extremes:
lowest point: Atlantic Ocean 0 m
highest point: Queen Mary's Peak on Tristan da Cunha 2,060 m
Natural resources: fish
Land use:
arable land: 12.9%
permanent crops: 0%
other: 87.1% (1998 est.)
Irrigated land: NA sq km
Natural hazards: active volcanism on Tristan da Cunha
Environment - current issues: NA
Geography - note: harbors at least 40 species of plants unknown anywhere else in the world; Ascension is a breeding ground for sea turtles and sooty terns

People

Population: 7,415 (July 2004 est.)
Age structure:
0-14 years: 18.9% (male 710; female 689)
15-64 years: 71.4% (male 2,739; female 2,559)
65 years and over: 9.7% (male 319; female 399) (2004 est.)
Median age:
total: 34.7 years
male: 34.9 years
female: 34.5 years (2004 est.)
Population growth rate: 0.62% (2004 est.)
Birth rate: 12.68 births/1,000 population (2004 est.)
Death rate: 6.47 deaths/1,000 population (2004 est.)
Net migration rate: 0 migrant(s)/1,000 population (2004 est.)
Sex ratio:
at birth: 1.04 male(s)/female
under 15 years: 1.03 male(s)/female
15-64 years: 1.07 male(s)/female
65 years and over: 0.8 male(s)/female
total population: 1.03 male(s)/female (2004 est.)
Infant mortality rate:
total: 19.85 deaths/1,000 live births
male: 23.7 deaths/1,000 live births
female: 15.81 deaths/1,000 live births (2004 est.)

Life expectancy at birth:
total population: 77.57 years
male: 74.67 years
female: 80.61 years (2004 est.)
Total fertility rate: 1.54 children born/woman (2004 est.)
HIV/AIDS - adult prevalence rate: NA%
HIV/AIDS - people living with HIV/AIDS: NA
HIV/AIDS - deaths: NA
Nationality:
noun: Saint Helenian(s)
adjective: Saint Helenian
Ethnic groups: African descent 50%, white 25%, Chinese 25%
Religions: Anglican (majority), Baptist, Seventh-Day Adventist, Roman Catholic
Languages: English
Literacy:
definition: age 20 and over can read and write
total population: 97%
male: 97%
female: 98% (1987 est.)

Government

Country name:
conventional long form: none
conventional short form: Saint Helena
Dependency status: overseas territory of the UK
Government type: NA
Capital: Jamestown
Administrative divisions: 1 administrative area and 2 dependencies*; Ascension*, Saint Helena, Tristan da Cunha*
Independence: none (overseas territory of the UK)
National holiday: Birthday of Queen ELIZABETH II, second Saturday in June (1926)
Constitution: 1 January 1989
Legal system: NA
Suffrage: NA years of age
Executive branch:
chief of state: Queen ELIZABETH II (since 6 February 1952)
head of government: Governor and Commander in Chief David HOLLAMBY (since 1999); Michael CLANCY (taking office in October 2004)
cabinet: Executive Council consists of the governor, two ex officio officers, and six elected members of the Legislative Council
elections: none; the monarch is hereditary; governor is appointed by the monarch
Legislative branch: unicameral Legislative Council (16 seats, including the speaker, 3 ex officio and 12 elected members; members are elected by popular vote to serve four-year terms)
elections: last held 27 June 2001 (next to be held NA June 2005)
election results: percent of vote - NA%; seats - independents 15
Judicial branch: Supreme Court; Magistrate's Court; Small Debts Court; Juvenile Court

Political parties and leaders: none
Political pressure groups and leaders: none
International organization participation: ICFTU
Diplomatic representation in the US: none (overseas territory of the UK)
Diplomatic representation from the US: none (overseas territory of the UK)
Flag description: blue with the flag of the UK in the upper hoist-side quadrant and the Saint Helenian shield centered on the outer half of the flag; the shield features a rocky coastline and three-masted sailing ship

Economy

Economy - overview: The economy depends largely on financial assistance from the UK, which amounted to about $5 million in 1997 or almost one-half of annual budgetary revenues. The local population earns income from fishing, the raising of livestock, and sales of handicrafts. Because there are few jobs, 25% of the work force has left to seek employment on Ascension Island, on the Falklands, and in the UK.
GDP: purchasing power parity - $18 million (1998 est.)
GDP - real growth rate: NA%
GDP - per capita: purchasing power parity - $2,500 (1998 est.)
GDP - composition by sector:
agriculture: NA%
industry: NA%
services: NA%
Population below poverty line: NA%
Household income or consumption by percentage share:
lowest 10%: NA%
highest 10%: NA%
Inflation rate (consumer prices): 3.2% (1997 est.)
Labor force: 3,500
note: 1,200 work offshore (1998 est.)
Labor force - by occupation: agriculture and fishing 6%, industry (mainly construction) 48%, services 46% (1987 est.)
Unemployment rate: 14% (1998 est.)
Budget:
revenues: $11.2 million
expenditures: $11 million, including capital expenditures of $NA (FY92/93)
Industries: construction, crafts (furniture, lacework, fancy woodwork), fishing
Industrial production growth rate: NA%
Electricity - production: 5 million kWh (2001)
Electricity - production by source:
fossil fuel: 100%
hydro: 0%
nuclear: 0%
other: 0% (2001)
Electricity - consumption: 4.65 million kWh (2001)
Electricity - exports: 0 kWh (2001)
Electricity - imports: 0 kWh (2001)

Saint Helena *(continued)*

Oil - production: 0 bbl/day (2001 est.)
Oil - consumption: 200 bbl/day (2001 est.)
Oil - exports: NA
Oil - imports: NA
Agriculture - products: corn, potatoes, vegetables; timber; fish, crawfish (on Tristan da Cunha)
Exports: $17 million f.o.b. (2002)
Exports - commodities: fish (frozen, canned, and salt-dried skipjack, tuna), coffee, handicrafts
Exports - partners: US 23.5%, Japan 17.6%, Tanzania 17.6%, Netherlands 11.8%, Indonesia 5.9%, Philippines 5.9%, Spain 5.9%, UK 5.9% (2002)
Imports: $42 million c.i.f. (2002)
Imports - commodities: food, beverages, tobacco, fuel oils, animal feed, building materials, motor vehicles and parts, machinery and parts
Imports - partners: UK 50%, South Africa 19%, Italy 11.9%, Tanzania 7.1%, US 4.8% (2002)
Debt - external: $NA (1996)
Economic aid - recipient: $12.6 million (1995); note - $5.3 million from UK (1997)
Currency: Saint Helenian pound (SHP)
Currency code: SHP
Exchange rates: Saint Helenian pounds per US dollar - 0.6661 (2002), 0.6944 (2001), 0.6596 (2000), 0.6180 (1999), 0.6037 (1998),
Fiscal year: 1 April - 31 March

Communications

Telephones - main lines in use: 2,200 (2002)
Telephones - mobile cellular: 0 (1997)
Telephone system:
general assessment: can communicate worldwide
domestic: automatic network
international: country code - 290; HF radiotelephone from Saint Helena to Ascension Island, which is a major coaxial submarine cable relay point between South Africa, Portugal, and UK; satellite earth stations - 2 Intelsat (Atlantic Ocean)
Radio broadcast stations: AM 1, FM 0, shortwave 0 (1998)
Television broadcast stations: 0
note: television programs are received in Saint Helena via satellite and distributed by cable (2002)
Internet country code: .sh
Internet users: 500 (2002)
Communications - note: Gough Island has a meteorological station

Transportation

Railways: 0 km
Highways:
total: 198 km (Saint Helena 138 km, Ascension 40 km, Tristan da Cunha 20 km)
paved: 168 km (Saint Helena 118km, Ascension 40 km, Tristan da Cunha 10 km)
unpaved: 30 km (Saint Helena 20 km, Ascension 0 km, Tristan da Cunha 10 km) (2000)
Waterways: none
Ports and harbors: Georgetown (on Ascension), Jamestown

Merchant marine: none
Airports: 1 (2003 est.)
Airports - with paved runways:
total: 1
over 3,047 m: 1 (2003 est.)

Military

Military - note: defense is the responsibility of the UK

Transnational Issues

Disputes - international: none

Saint Kitts and Nevis

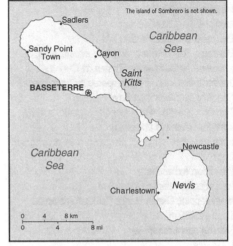

The island of Sombrero is not shown.

Introduction

Background: First settled by the British in 1623, the islands became an associated state with full internal autonomy in 1967. The island of Anguilla rebelled and was allowed to secede in 1971. Saint Kitts and Nevis achieved independence in 1983. In 1998, a vote in Nevis on a referendum to separate from Saint Kitts fell short of the two-thirds majority needed. Nevis is once more trying to separate from the Saint Kitts.

Geography

Location: Caribbean, islands in the Caribbean Sea, about one-third of the way from Puerto Rico to Trinidad and Tobago
Geographic coordinates: 17 20 N, 62 45 W
Map references: Central America and the Caribbean
Area:
total: 261 sq km (Saint Kitts 168 sq km; Nevis 93 sq km)
land: 261 sq km
water: 0 sq km
Area - comparative: 1.5 times the size of Washington, DC
Land boundaries: 0 km
Coastline: 135 km
Maritime claims:
territorial sea: 12 NM
contiguous zone: 24 NM
exclusive economic zone: 200 NM
continental shelf: 200 NM or to the edge of the continental margin
Climate: tropical tempered by constant sea breezes; little seasonal temperature variation; rainy season (May to November)
Terrain: volcanic with mountainous interiors
Elevation extremes:
lowest point: Caribbean Sea 0 m
highest point: Mount Liamuiga 1,156 m
Natural resources: arable land

Saint Kitts and Nevis *(continued)*

Land use:
arable land: 16.67%
permanent crops: 2.78%
other: 80.55% (1998 est.)
Irrigated land: NA sq km
Natural hazards: hurricanes (July to October)
Environment - current issues: NA
Environment - international agreements:
party to: Biodiversity, Climate Change,
Desertification, Endangered Species, Hazardous
Wastes, Law of the Sea, Ozone Layer Protection,
Ship Pollution, Whaling
signed, but not ratified: none of the selected
agreements
Geography - note: with coastlines in the shape of a
baseball bat and ball, the two volcanic islands are
separated by a three-km-wide channel called The
Narrows; on the southern tip of long, baseball
bat-shaped Saint Kitts lies the Great Salt Pond; Nevis
Peak sits in the center of its almost circular namesake
island and its ball shape complements that of its sister
island

People

Population: 38,836 (July 2004 est.)
Age structure:
0-14 years: 28.6% (male 5,675; female 5,422)
15-64 years: 63% (male 12,242; female 12,236)
65 years and over: 8.4% (male 1,349; female 1,912)
(2004 est.)
Median age:
total: 27.3 years
male: 26.5 years
female: 28.1 years (2004 est.)
Population growth rate: 0.25% (2004 est.)
Birth rate: 18.26 births/1,000 population (2004 est.)
Death rate: 8.65 deaths/1,000 population (2004 est.)
Net migration rate: -7.11 migrant(s)/1,000
population (2004 est.)
Sex ratio:
at birth: 1.06 male(s)/female
under 15 years: 1.05 male(s)/female
15-64 years: 1 male(s)/female
65 years and over: 0.71 male(s)/female
total population: 0.98 male(s)/female (2004 est.)
Infant mortality rate:
total: 14.94 deaths/1,000 live births
male: 16.72 deaths/1,000 live births
female: 13.05 deaths/1,000 live births (2004 est.)
Life expectancy at birth:
total population: 71.86 years
male: 69.03 years
female: 74.86 years (2004 est.)
Total fertility rate: 2.35 children born/woman
(2004 est.)
HIV/AIDS - adult prevalence rate: NA%
HIV/AIDS - people living with HIV/AIDS: NA
HIV/AIDS - deaths: NA
Nationality:
noun: Kittitian(s), Nevisian(s)
adjective: Kittitian, Nevisian

Ethnic groups: predominantly black; some British,
Portuguese, and Lebanese
Religions: Anglican, other Protestant, Roman
Catholic
Languages: English
Literacy:
definition: age 15 and over has ever attended school
total population: 97%
male: 97%
female: 98% (1980 est.)

Government

Country name:
conventional long form: Federation of Saint Kitts and
Nevis
conventional short form: Saint Kitts and Nevis
former: Federation of Saint Christopher and Nevis
Government type: constitutional monarchy with
Westminster-style parliament
Capital: Basseterre
Administrative divisions: 14 parishes; Christ
Church Nichola Town, Saint Anne Sandy Point, Saint
George Basseterre, Saint George Gingerland, Saint
James Windward, Saint John Capesterre, Saint John
Figtree, Saint Mary Cayon, Saint Paul Capesterre,
Saint Paul Charlestown, Saint Peter Basseterre, Saint
Thomas Lowland, Saint Thomas Middle Island, Trinity
Palmetto Point
Independence: 19 September 1983 (from UK)
National holiday: Independence Day,
19 September (1983)
Constitution: 19 September 1983
Legal system: based on English common law
Suffrage: 18 years of age; universal
Executive branch:
chief of state: Queen ELIZABETH II (since 6 February
1952), represented by Governor General Cuthbert
Montraville SEBASTIAN (since 1 January 1996)
head of government: Prime Minister Dr. Denzil
DOUGLAS (since 6 July 1995) and Deputy Prime
Minister Sam CONDOR (since 6 July 1995)
cabinet: Cabinet appointed by the governor general in
consultation with the prime minister
elections: none; the monarch is hereditary; the
governor general is appointed by the monarch;
following legislative elections, the leader of the
majority party or leader of a majority coalition is
usually appointed prime minister by the governor
general; deputy prime minister appointed by the
governor general
Legislative branch: unicameral National Assembly
(14 seats, 3 appointed and 11 popularly elected from
single-member constituencies; members serve
five-year terms)
elections: last held 6 March 2000 (next to be held by
July 2005)
election results: percent of vote by party - NA%; seats
by party - SKNLP 8, CCM 2, NRP 1
Judicial branch: Eastern Caribbean Supreme Court
(based on Saint Lucia; one judge of the Supreme
Court resides in Saint Kitts and Nevis)

Political parties and leaders: Concerned Citizens
Movement or CCM [Vance AMORY]; Nevis
Reformation Party or NRP [Joseph PARRY]; People's
Action Movement or PAM [Lindsey GRANT]; Saint
Kitts and Nevis Labor Party or SKNLP [Dr. Denzil
DOUGLAS]
Political pressure groups and leaders: NA
International organization participation: ACP, C,
Caricom, CDB, FAO, G-77, IBRD, ICAO, ICFTU,
ICRM, IDA, IFAD, IFC, IFRCS, ILO, IMF, IMO,
Interpol, IOC, OAS, OECS, OPANAL, OPCW
(signatory), UN, UNCTAD, UNESCO, UNIDO, UPU,
WHO, WIPO, WTrO
Diplomatic representation in the US:
chief of mission: Ambassador Dr. Izben Cordinal
WILLIAMS
chancery: 3216 New Mexico Avenue NW,
Washington, DC 20016
telephone: [1] (202) 686-2636
FAX: [1] (202) 686-5740
consulate(s) general: New York
Diplomatic representation from the US: the US
does not have an embassy in Saint Kitts and Nevis;
the US Ambassador to Barbados, Ambassador Mary
E. KRAMER, is accredited to Saint Kitts and Nevis
Flag description: divided diagonally from the lower
hoist side by a broad black band bearing two white,
five-pointed stars; the black band is edged in yellow;
the upper triangle is green, the lower triangle is red

Economy

Economy - overview: Sugar was the traditional
mainstay of the Saint Kitts economy until the 1970s.
Although the crop still dominates the agricultural
sector, activities such as tourism, export-oriented
manufacturing, and offshore banking have assumed
larger roles in the economy. As tourism revenues are
now the chief source of the islands' foreign exchange,
a decline in stopover tourist arrivals following the
11 September 2001 terrorist attacks has eroded
government finances. The opening of a 1,000+ bed
Marriott hotel in February 2003 was expected to bring
in much-needed revenue.
GDP: purchasing power parity - $339 million
(2002 est.)
GDP - real growth rate: -1.9% (2002 est.)
GDP - per capita: purchasing power parity - $8,800
(2002 est.)
GDP - composition by sector:
agriculture: 3.5%
industry: 25.8%
services: 70.7% (2001)
Population below poverty line: NA%
**Household income or consumption by percentage
share:**
lowest 10%: NA%
highest 10%: NA%
Inflation rate (consumer prices): 1.7% (2001 est.)
Labor force: 18,172 (June 1995)
Labor force - by occupation: NA
Unemployment rate: 4.5% (1997)

Budget:

revenues: $89.7 million

expenditures: $128.2 million, including capital expenditures of $19.5 million (2003 est.)

Industries: sugar processing, tourism, cotton, salt, copra, clothing, footwear, beverages

Industrial production growth rate: NA%

Electricity - production: 100.3 million kWh (2001)

Electricity - production by source:

fossil fuel: 100%

hydro: 0%

nuclear: 0%

other: 0% (2001)

Electricity - consumption: 93.26 million kWh (2001)

Electricity - exports: 0 kWh (2001)

Electricity - imports: 0 kWh (2001)

Oil - production: 0 bbl/day (2001 est.)

Oil - consumption: 710 bbl/day (2001 est.)

Oil - exports: NA

Oil - imports: NA

Agriculture - products: sugarcane, rice, yams, vegetables, bananas; fish

Exports: $70 million (2002 est.)

Exports - commodities: machinery, food, electronics, beverages, tobacco

Exports - partners: US 65.7%, Canada 7.1%, UK 7.1%, Portugal 5.7% (2002)

Imports: $195 million (2002 est.)

Imports - commodities: machinery, manufactures, food, fuels

Imports - partners: US 39%, Trinidad and Tobago 15.4%, Canada 9.2%, UK 6.7%, Denmark 6.2% (2002)

Debt - external: $171 million (2001)

Economic aid - recipient: $8 million (2001)

Currency: East Caribbean dollar (XCD)

Currency code: XCD

Exchange rates: East Caribbean dollars per US dollar - 2.7 (2003), 2.7 (2002), 2.7 (2001), 2.7 (2000), 2.7 (1999)

Fiscal year: calendar year

Communications

Telephones - main lines in use: 23,500 (2002)

Telephones - mobile cellular: 5,000 (2002)

Telephone system:

general assessment: good interisland and international connections

domestic: inter-island links to Antigua and Barbuda and Saint Martin (Guadeloupe and Netherlands Antilles) are handled by VHF/UHF/SHF radiotelephone

international: country code - 1-869; international calls are carried by radiotelephone to Antigua and Barbuda and switched there to submarine cable or to Intelsat; or carried to Saint Martin (Guadeloupe and Netherlands Antilles) by radiotelephone and switched to Intelsat

Radio broadcast stations: AM 3, FM 3, shortwave 0 (2004)

Television broadcast stations: 1 (plus three repeaters) (2004)

Internet country code: .kn

Internet hosts: 2 (2002)

Internet users: 10,000 (2002)

Transportation

Railways:

total: 50 km

narrow gauge: 50 km 0.762-m gauge on Saint Kitts to serve sugarcane plantations during harvest season (2002)

Highways:

total: 320 km

paved: 136 km

unpaved: 184 km (1999 est)

Waterways: none

Ports and harbors: Basseterre, Charlestown

Merchant marine: none

Airports: 2 (2003 est.)

Airports - with paved runways:

total: 2

1,524 to 2,437 m: 1

914 to 1,523 m: 1 (2003 est.)

Military

Military branches: Saint Kitts and Nevis Defense Force (including Coast Guard), Royal Saint Kitts and Nevis Police Force (including Special Service Unit)

Military expenditures - dollar figure: NA

Military expenditures - percent of GDP: NA

Transnational Issues

Disputes - international: joins other Caribbean states to counter Venezuela's claim that Aves Island sustains human habitation, a criterion under UNCLOS, which permits Venezuela to extend its EEZ/continental shelf over a large portion of the Caribbean Sea

Illicit drugs: transshipment point for South American drugs destined for the US and Europe; some money-laundering activity

Saint Lucia

Introduction

Background: The island, with its fine natural harbor at Castries, was contested between England and France throughout the 17th and early 18th centuries (changing possession 14 times); it was finally ceded to the UK in 1814. Self-government was granted in 1967 and independence in 1979.

Geography

Location: Caribbean, island between the Caribbean Sea and North Atlantic Ocean, north of Trinidad and Tobago

Geographic coordinates: 13 53 N, 60 68 W

Map references: Central America and the Caribbean

Area:

total: 616 sq km

land: 606 sq km

water: 10 sq km

Area - comparative: 3.5 times the size of Washington, DC

Land boundaries: 0 km

Coastline: 158 km

Maritime claims:

territorial sea: 12 NM

contiguous zone: 24 NM

exclusive economic zone: 200 NM

continental shelf: 200 NM or to the edge of the continental margin

Climate: tropical, moderated by northeast trade winds; dry season from January to April, rainy season from May to August

Terrain: volcanic and mountainous with some broad, fertile valleys

Elevation extremes:

lowest point: Caribbean Sea 0 m

highest point: Mount Gimie 950 m

Natural resources: forests, sandy beaches, minerals (pumice), mineral springs, geothermal potential

Saint Lucia (continued)

Land use:
arable land: 4.9%
permanent crops: 23%
other: 72.1% (1998 est.)
Irrigated land: 30 sq km (1998 est.)
Natural hazards: hurricanes and volcanic activity
Environment - current issues: deforestation; soil erosion, particularly in the northern region
Environment - international agreements:
party to: Biodiversity, Climate Change, Climate Change-Kyoto Protocol, Desertification, Endangered Species, Environmental Modification, Hazardous Wastes, Law of the Sea, Marine Dumping, Ozone Layer Protection, Ship Pollution, Whaling
signed, but not ratified: none of the selected agreements
Geography - note: the twin Pitons (Gros Piton and Petit Piton), striking cone-shaped peaks south of Soufriere, are one of the scenic natural highlights of the Caribbean

People

Population: 164,213 (July 2004 est.)
Age structure:
0-14 years: 30.7% (male 25,913; female 24,467)
15-64 years: 64.1% (male 51,750; female 53,530)
65 years and over: 5.2% (male 3,159; female 5,394) (2004 est.)
Median age:
total: 24.5 years
male: 23.7 years
female: 25.3 years (2004 est.)
Population growth rate: 1.27% (2004 est.)
Birth rate: 20.5 births/1,000 population (2004 est.)
Death rate: 5.18 deaths/1,000 population (2004 est.)
Net migration rate: -2.67 migrant(s)/1,000 population (2004 est.)
Sex ratio:
at birth: 1.07 male(s)/female
under 15 years: 1.06 male(s)/female
15-64 years: 0.97 male(s)/female
65 years and over: 0.59 male(s)/female
total population: 0.97 male(s)/female (2004 est.)
Infant mortality rate:
total: 13.95 deaths/1,000 live births
male: 15.09 deaths/1,000 live births
female: 12.73 deaths/1,000 live births (2004 est.)
Life expectancy at birth:
total population: 73.34 years
male: 69.78 years
female: 77.16 years (2004 est.)
Total fertility rate: 2.25 children born/woman (2004 est.)
HIV/AIDS - adult prevalence rate: NA%
HIV/AIDS - people living with HIV/AIDS: NA
HIV/AIDS - deaths: NA
Nationality:
noun: Saint Lucian(s)
adjective: Saint Lucian
Ethnic groups: black 90%, mixed 6%, East Indian 3%, white 1%

Religions: Roman Catholic 90%, Anglican 3%, other Protestant 7%
Languages: English (official), French patois
Literacy:
definition: age 15 and over has ever attended school
total population: 67%
male: 65%
female: 69% (1980 est.)

Government

Country name:
conventional long form: none
conventional short form: Saint Lucia
Government type: Westminster-style parliamentary democracy
Capital: Castries
Administrative divisions: 11 quarters; Anse-la-Raye, Castries, Choiseul, Dauphin, Dennery, Gros-Islet, Laborie, Micoud, Praslin, Soufriere, Vieux-Fort
Independence: 22 February 1979 (from UK)
National holiday: Independence Day, 22 February (1979)
Constitution: 22 February 1979
Legal system: based on English common law
Suffrage: 18 years of age; universal
Executive branch:
chief of state: Queen ELIZABETH II (since 6 February 1952), represented by Governor General Dr. Perlette LOUISY (since September 1997)
head of government: Prime Minister Kenneth Davis ANTHONY (since 24 May 1997) and Deputy Prime Minister Mario MICHEL (since 24 May 1997)
cabinet: Cabinet appointed by the governor general on the advice of the prime minister
elections: none; the monarch is hereditary; the governor general is appointed by the monarch; following legislative elections, the leader of the majority party or the leader of a majority coalition is usually appointed prime minister by the governor general; deputy prime minister appointed by the governor general
Legislative branch: bicameral Parliament consists of the Senate (11 seats; six members appointed on the advice of the prime minister, three on the advice of the leader of the opposition, and two after consultation with religious, economic, and social groups) and the House of Assembly (17 seats; members are elected by popular vote from single-member constituencies to serve five-year terms)
elections: House of Assembly - last held 3 December 2001 (next to be held in December 2006)
election results: House of Assembly - percent of vote by party - SLP 55%, UWP 37%, NA 3.5%; seats by party - SLP 14, UWP 3
Judicial branch: Eastern Caribbean Supreme Court (jurisdiction extends to Anguilla, Antigua and Barbuda, the British Virgin Islands, Dominica, Grenada, Montserrat, Saint Kitts and Nevis, Saint Lucia, and Saint Vincent and the Grenadines)

Political parties and leaders: National Alliance or NA [George ODLUM]; Saint Lucia Freedom Party or SFP [Martinus FRANCOIS]; Saint Lucia Labor Party or SLP [Kenneth ANTHONY]; Sou Tout Apwe Fete Fini or STAFF [Christopher HUNTE]; United Workers Party or UWP [Dr. Morella JOSEPH]
Political pressure groups and leaders: NA
International organization participation: ACCT, ACP, C, Caricom, CDB, FAO, G-77, IBRD, ICAO, ICCt (signatory), ICFTU, ICRM, IDA, IFAD, IFC, IFRCS, ILO, IMF, IMO, Interpol, IOC, ISO (correspondent), ITU, NAM, OAS, OECS, OPANAL, OPCW, UN, UNCTAD, UNESCO, UNIDO, UPU, WCL, WFTU, WHO, WIPO, WMO, WTrO
Diplomatic representation in the US:
chief of mission: Ambassador Sonia Merlyn JOHNNY
chancery: 3216 New Mexico Avenue NW, Washington, DC 20016
telephone: [1] (202) 364-6792 through 6795
FAX: [1] (202) 364-6723
consulate(s) general: Miami and New York
Diplomatic representation from the US: the US does not have an embassy in Saint Lucia; the US Ambassador to Barbados, Ambassador Mary E. KRAMER, is accredited to Saint Lucia
Flag description: blue, with a gold isosceles triangle below a black arrowhead; the upper edges of the arrowhead have a white border

Economy

Economy - overview: Changes in the EU import preference regime and the increased competition from Latin American bananas have made economic diversification increasingly important in Saint Lucia. The island nation has been able to attract foreign business and investment, especially in its offshore banking and tourism industries. The manufacturing sector is the most diverse in the Eastern Caribbean area, and the government is trying to revitalize the banana industry. Economic fundamentals remain solid.
GDP: purchasing power parity - $866 million (2002 est.)
GDP - real growth rate: 3.3% (2002 est.)
GDP - per capita: purchasing power parity - $5,400 (2002 est.)
GDP - composition by sector:
agriculture: 7%
industry: 20%
services: 73% (2002 est.)
Population below poverty line: NA%
Household income or consumption by percentage share:
lowest 10%: NA%
highest 10%: NA%
Inflation rate (consumer prices): 3% (2001 est.)
Labor force: 43,800 (2001 est.)
Labor force - by occupation: agriculture 21.7%, services 53.6%, industry, commerce, and manufacturing 24.7% (2002 est.)
Unemployment rate: 16.5% (1997 est.)

Saint Lucia (continued)

Budget:
revenues: $141.2 million
expenditures: $146.7 million, including capital expenditures of $25.1 million (2000 est.)
Industries: clothing, assembly of electronic components, beverages, corrugated cardboard boxes, tourism, lime processing, coconut processing
Industrial production growth rate: -8.9% (1997 est.)
Electricity - production: 120.2 million kWh (2001)
Electricity - production by source:
fossil fuel: 100%
hydro: 0%
nuclear: 0%
other: 0% (2001)
Electricity - consumption: 111.8 million kWh (2001)
Electricity - exports: 0 kWh (2001)
Electricity - imports: 0 kWh (2001)
Oil - production: 0 bbl/day (2001 est.)
Oil - consumption: 2,400 bbl/day (2001 est.)
Oil - exports: NA
Oil - imports: NA
Agriculture - products: bananas, coconuts, vegetables, citrus, root crops, cocoa
Exports: $66 million (2002 est.)
Exports - commodities: bananas 41%, clothing, cocoa, vegetables, fruits, coconut oil
Exports - partners: UK 48.5%, US 27.3%, Barbados 7.6% (2002)
Imports: $267 million (2002 est.)
Imports - commodities: food 23%, manufactured goods 21%, machinery and transportation equipment 19%, chemicals, fuels
Imports - partners: Brazil 46.1%, US 18.6%, Trinidad and Tobago 10.3% (2002)
Debt - external: $214 million (2000)
Economic aid - recipient: $51.8 million (1995)
Currency: East Caribbean dollar (XCD)
Currency code: XCD
Exchange rates: East Caribbean dollars per US dollar - 2.7 (2003), 2.7 (2002), 2.7 (2001), 2.7 (2000), 2.7 (1999)
Fiscal year: 1 April - 31 March

Communications

Telephones - main lines in use: 51,100 (2002)
Telephones - mobile cellular: 14,300 (2002)
Telephone system:
general assessment: adequate system
domestic: system is automatically switched
international: country code - 1-758; direct microwave radio relay link with Martinique and Saint Vincent and the Grenadines; tropospheric scatter to Barbados; international calls beyond these countries are carried by Intelsat from Martinique
Radio broadcast stations: AM 2, FM 7, shortwave 0 (2004)
Television broadcast stations: 2 (of which one is a commercial broadcast station and one is a community antenna television or CATV channel) (2004)

Internet country code: .lc
Internet hosts: 29 (2002)
Internet users: 13,000 (2002)

Transportation

Railways: 0 km
Highways:
total: 1,210 km
paved: 63 km
unpaved: 1,147 km (1999 est.)
Waterways: none
Ports and harbors: Castries, Vieux Fort
Merchant marine: none
Airports: 2 (2003 est.)
Airports - with paved runways:
total: 2
2,438 to 3,047 m: 1
1,524 to 2,437 m: 1 (2003 est.)

Military

Military branches: Royal Saint Lucia Police Force (including Special Service Unit, Coast Guard)
Military expenditures - dollar figure: NA
Military expenditures - percent of GDP: NA

Transnational Issues

Disputes - international: joins other Caribbean states to counter Venezuela's claim that Aves Island sustains human habitation, a criterion under UNCLOS, which permits Venezuela to extend its EEZ/ continental shelf over a large portion of the Caribbean Sea
Illicit drugs: transit point for South American drugs destined for the US and Europe

---

Saint Pierre and Miquelon
(territorial collectivity of France)

Introduction

Background: First settled by the French in the early 17th century, the islands represent the sole remaining vestige of France's once vast North American possessions.

Geography

Location: Northern North America, islands in the North Atlantic Ocean, south of Newfoundland (Canada)
Geographic coordinates: 46 50 N, 56 20 W
Map references: North America
Area:
total: 242 sq km
land: 242 sq km
water: 0 sq km
note: includes eight small islands in the Saint Pierre and the Miquelon groups
Area - comparative: 1.5 times the size of Washington, DC
Land boundaries: 0 km
Coastline: 120 km
Maritime claims:
territorial sea: 12 NM
exclusive economic zone: 200 NM
Climate: cold and wet, with much mist and fog; spring and autumn are windy
Terrain: mostly barren rock
Elevation extremes:
lowest point: Atlantic Ocean 0 m
highest point: Morne de la Grande Montagne 240 m
Natural resources: fish, deepwater ports
Land use:
arable land: 13.04%
permanent crops: 0%
other: 86.96% (1998 est.)
Irrigated land: NA sq km
Natural hazards: persistent fog throughout the year can be a maritime hazard
Environment - current issues: recent test drilling for oil in waters around Saint Pierre and Miquelon may bring future development that would impact the environment

Saint Pierre and Miquelon *(continued)*

Geography - note: vegetation scanty

People

Population: 6,995 (July 2004 est.)
Age structure:
0-14 years: 24.6% (male 878; female 840)
15-64 years: 64.9% (male 2,316; female 2,227)
65 years and over: 10.5% (male 323; female 411)
(2004 est.)
Median age:
total: 33.3 years
male: 33 years
female: 33.6 years (2004 est.)
Population growth rate: 0.26% (2004 est.)
Birth rate: 14.15 births/1,000 population (2004 est.)
Death rate: 6.72 deaths/1,000 population (2004 est.)
Net migration rate: -4.86 migrant(s)/1,000
population (2004 est.)
Sex ratio:
at birth: 1.06 male(s)/female
under 15 years: 1.05 male(s)/female
15-64 years: 1.04 male(s)/female
65 years and over: 0.79 male(s)/female
total population: 1.01 male(s)/female (2004 est.)
Infant mortality rate:
total: 7.76 deaths/1,000 live births
male: 8.91 deaths/1,000 live births
female: 6.55 deaths/1,000 live births (2004 est.)
Life expectancy at birth:
total population: 78.28 years
male: 75.97 years
female: 80.7 years (2004 est.)
Total fertility rate: 2.05 children born/woman
(2004 est.)
HIV/AIDS - adult prevalence rate: NA%
HIV/AIDS - people living with HIV/AIDS: NA
HIV/AIDS - deaths: NA
Nationality:
noun: Frenchman(men), Frenchwoman(women)
adjective: French
Ethnic groups: Basques and Bretons (French
fishermen)
Religions: Roman Catholic 99%
Languages: French (official)
Literacy:
definition: age 15 and over can read and write
total population: 99%
male: 99%
female: 99% (1982 est.)

Government

Country name:
conventional long form: Territorial Collectivity of
Saint Pierre and Miquelon
conventional short form: Saint Pierre and Miquelon
local long form: Departement de Saint-Pierre et
Miquelon
local short form: Saint-Pierre et Miquelon
Dependency status: self-governing territorial
collectivity of France
Government type: NA
Capital: Saint-Pierre

Administrative divisions: none (territorial
collectivity of France); note - there are no first-order
administrative divisions as defined by the US
Government, but there are two communes - Saint
Pierre, Miquelon at the second order
Independence: none (territorial collectivity of
France; has been under French control since 1763)
National holiday: Bastille Day, 14 July (1789)
Constitution: 28 September 1958 (French
Constitution)
Legal system: French law with special adaptations
for local conditions, such as housing and taxation
Suffrage: 18 years of age; universal
Executive branch:
chief of state: President Jacques CHIRAC of France
(since 17 May 1995), represented by Prefect Claude
VALLEIX (since 9 October 2002)
head of government: President of the General
Council Marc PLANTAGENEST (since NA)
cabinet: NA
elections: French president elected by popular vote
for a five-year term; election last held, first round -
21 April 2002, second round - 5 May 2002 (next to be
held NA 2007); prefect appointed by the French
president on the advice of the French Ministry of
Interior; president of the General Council is elected by
the members of the council
Legislative branch: unicameral General Council or
Conseil General (19 seats - 15 from Saint Pierre and
4 from Miquelon; members are elected by popular
vote to serve six-year terms)
elections: elections last held 19 and 26 March 2000
(next to be held NA April 2006)
election results: percent of vote by party - NA%;
seats by party - PS 12, PRG 2, UDF-RPR 5
note: Saint Pierre and Miquelon elect 1 seat to the
French Senate; elections last held NA September
1995 (next to be held NA September 2004); results -
percent of vote by party - NA%; seats by party - RPR 1;
Saint Pierre and Miquelon also elects 1 seat to the
French National Assembly; elections last held, first
round - 9 June 2002, second round - 16 June 2002
(next to be held NA 2007); results - percent of vote by
party - NA%; seats by party - UDF 1
Judicial branch: Superior Tribunal of Appeals or
Tribunal Superieur d'Appel
Political parties and leaders: PRG [leader NA];
Rassemblement pour la Republique or RPR (now
UMP) [leader NA]; Socialist Party or PS [leader NA];
Union pour la Democratie Francaise or UDF [leader NA]
Political pressure groups and leaders: NA
International organization participation: WFTU
Diplomatic representation in the US: none
(territorial collectivity of France)
Diplomatic representation from the US: none
(territorial collectivity of France)
Flag description: a yellow sailing ship facing the
hoist side rides on a dark blue background with yellow
wavy lines under the ship; on the hoist side, a vertical
band is divided into three parts: the top part (called
ikkurina) is red with a green diagonal cross extending
to the corners overlaid by a white cross dividing the
rectangle into four sections; the middle part has a

white background with an ermine pattern; the third part
has a red background with two stylized yellow lions
outlined in black, one above the other; these three
heraldic arms represent settlement by colonists from
the Basque Country (top), Brittany, and Normandy;
the flag of France is used for official occasions

Economy

Economy - overview: The inhabitants have
traditionally earned their livelihood by fishing and by
servicing fishing fleets operating off the coast of
Newfoundland. The economy has been declining,
however, because of disputes with Canada over
fishing quotas and a steady decline in the number of
ships stopping at Saint Pierre. In 1992, an arbitration
panel awarded the islands an exclusive economic
zone of 12,348 sq km to settle a longstanding
territorial dispute with Canada, although it represents
only 25% of what France had sought. The islands are
heavily subsidized by France to the great betterment
of living standards. The government hopes an
expansion of tourism will boost economic prospects.
Recent test drilling for oil may pave the way for
development of the energy sector.
GDP. purchasing power parity - $48.3 million -
supplemented by annual payments from France of
about $60 million (2003 est.)
GDP - real growth rate. NA%
GDP - per capita. purchasing power parity - $6,900
(2001 est.)
GDP - composition by sector.
agriculture. NA%
industry. NA%
services. NA%
Population below poverty line. NA%
**Household income or consumption by percentage
share.**
lowest 10%. NA%
highest 10%. NA%
Inflation rate (consumer prices). 2.1% (1991-96
average)
Labor force. 3,261 (1999)
Labor force - by occupation. fishing 18%, industry
(mainly fish-processing) 41%, services 41% (1996 est.)
Unemployment rate. 9.8% (1997)
Budget.
revenues. $70 million
expenditures. $60 million, including capital
expenditures of $24 million (1996 est.)
Industries. fish processing and supply base for
fishing fleets; tourism
Industrial production growth rate. NA%
Electricity - production. 42.03 million kWh (2001)
Electricity - production by source.
fossil fuel. 100%
hydro. 0%
nuclear. 0%
other. 0% (2001)
Electricity - consumption. 39.08 million kWh (2001)
Electricity - exports. 0 kWh (2001)
Electricity - imports. 0 kWh (2001)
Oil - production. 0 bbl/day (2001 est.)
Oil - consumption. 600 bbl/day (2001 est.)

Oil - exports. NA
Oil - imports. NA
Agriculture - products. vegetables; poultry, cattle, sheep, pigs; fish
Exports. $10 million f.o.b. (2002)
Exports - commodities. fish and fish products, soybeans, animal feed, mollusks and crustaceans, fox and mink pelts
Exports - partners. US 30%, Zambia 30%, Ecuador 20%, France 10% (2002)
Imports. $106 million f.o.b. (2002)
Imports - commodities. meat, clothing, fuel, electrical equipment, machinery, building materials
Imports - partners. Zambia 62.3%, France 21.7%, Canada 13.2% (2002)
Debt - external. $NA (2003 est.)
Economic aid - recipient. approximately $60 million in annual grants from France
Currency. euro (EUR)
Currency code. EUR
Exchange rates. euros per US dollar - 0.886 (2003), 1.0626 (2002), 1.0626 (2001), 1.08540 (2000), 0.93863 (1999)
Fiscal year. calendar year

Communications

Telephones - main lines in use: 4,800 (2002)
Telephones - mobile cellular: 0 (1994)
Telephone system:
general assessment: adequate
domestic: NA
international: country code - 508; radiotelephone communication with most countries in the world; 1 earth station in French domestic satellite system
Radio broadcast stations: AM 1, FM 4, shortwave 0 (1998)
Television broadcast stations: 0 (there are, however, two repeaters which rebroadcast programs from France, Canada, and the US) (1997)
Internet country code: .pm
Internet users: NA

Transportation

Railways: 0 km
Highways:
total: 114 km
paved: 69 km
unpaved: 45 km
Waterways: none
Ports and harbors: Saint Pierre
Merchant marine: none
Airports: 2 (2003 est.)
Airports - with paved runways:
total: 2
1,524 to 2,437 m: 1
914 to 1,523 m: 1 (2003 est.)

Military

Military - note: defense is the responsibility of France

Transnational Issues

Disputes - international: none

Saint Vincent and the Grenadines

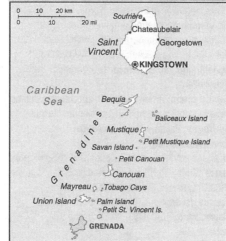

Introduction

Background: Disputed between France and the United Kingdom in the 18th century, Saint Vincent was ceded to the latter in 1783. Autonomy was granted in 1969 and independence in 1979.

Geography

Location: Caribbean, islands between the Caribbean Sea and North Atlantic Ocean, north of Trinidad and Tobago
Geographic coordinates: 13 15 N, 61 12 W
Map references: Central America and the Caribbean
Area:
total: 389 sq km (Saint Vincent 344 sq km)
land: 389 sq km
water: 0 sq km
Area - comparative: twice the size of Washington, DC
Land boundaries: 0 km
Coastline: 84 km
Maritime claims:
territorial sea: 12 NM
contiguous zone: 24 NM
exclusive economic zone: 200 NM
continental shelf: 200 NM
Climate: tropical; little seasonal temperature variation; rainy season (May to November)
Terrain: volcanic, mountainous
Elevation extremes:
lowest point: Caribbean Sea 0 m
highest point: Soufriere 1,234 m
Natural resources: hydropower, cropland
Land use:
arable land: 10.3%
permanent crops: 17.9%
other: 71.8% (1998 est.)
Irrigated land: 10 sq km (1998 est.)
Natural hazards: hurricanes; Soufriere volcano on the island of Saint Vincent is a constant threat

Environment - current issues: pollution of coastal waters and shorelines from discharges by pleasure yachts and other effluents; in some areas, pollution is severe enough to make swimming prohibitive
Environment - international agreements:
party to: Biodiversity, Climate Change, Desertification, Endangered Species, Environmental Modification, Hazardous Wastes, Law of the Sea, Marine Dumping, Ozone Layer Protection, Ship Pollution, Whaling
signed, but not ratified: Climate Change-Kyoto Protocol
Geography - note: the administration of the islands of the Grenadines group is divided between Saint Vincent and the Grenadines and Grenada; Saint Vincent and the Grenadines is comprised of 32 islands and cays

People

Population: 117,193 (July 2004 est.)
Age structure:
0-14 years: 27.6% (male 16,463; female 15,872)
15-64 years: 66% (male 39,827; female 37,547)
65 years and over: 6.4% (male 3,247; female 4,237) (2004 est.)
Median age:
total: 25.8 years
male: 25.7 years
female: 26 years (2004 est.)
Population growth rate: 0.31% (2004 est.)
Birth rate: 16.77 births/1,000 population (2004 est.)
Death rate: 6.04 deaths/1,000 population (2004 est.)
Net migration rate: -7.64 migrant(s)/1,000 population (2004 est.)
Sex ratio:
at birth: 1.03 male(s)/female
under 15 years: 1.04 male(s)/female
15-64 years: 1.06 male(s)/female
65 years and over: 0.77 male(s)/female
total population: 1.03 male(s)/female (2004 est.)
Infant mortality rate:
total: 15.24 deaths/1,000 live births
male: 16.58 deaths/1,000 live births
female: 13.86 deaths/1,000 live births (2004 est.)
Life expectancy at birth:
total population: 73.35 years
male: 71.54 years
female: 75.21 years (2004 est.)
Total fertility rate: 1.9 children born/woman (2004 est.)
HIV/AIDS - adult prevalence rate: NA%
HIV/AIDS - people living with HIV/AIDS: NA
HIV/AIDS - deaths: NA
Nationality:
noun: Saint Vincentian(s) or Vincentian(s)
adjective: Saint Vincentian or Vincentian
Ethnic groups: black 66%, mixed 19%, East Indian 6%, Carib Amerindian 2%, other 7%
Religions: Anglican 47%, Methodist 28%, Roman Catholic 13%, Hindu Seventh-Day Adventist, other Protestant
Languages: English, French patois

Saint Vincent and the Grenadines *(continued)*

Literacy:
definition: age 15 and over has ever attended school
total population: 96%
male: 96%
female: 96% (1970 est.)

Government

Country name:
conventional long form: none
conventional short form: Saint Vincent and the Grenadines
Government type: parliamentary democracy; independent sovereign state within the Commonwealth
Capital: Kingstown
Administrative divisions: 6 parishes; Charlotte, Grenadines, Saint Andrew, Saint David, Saint George, Saint Patrick
Independence: 27 October 1979 (from UK)
National holiday: Independence Day, 27 October (1979)
Constitution: 27 October 1979
Legal system: based on English common law
Suffrage: 18 years of age; universal
Executive branch:
chief of state: Queen ELIZABETH II (since 6 February 1952), represented by Governor General Sir Fredrick Nathaniel BALLANTYNE (since 2 September 2002)
head of government: Prime Minister Ralph E. GONSALVES (since 29 March 2001)
cabinet: Cabinet appointed by the governor general on the advice of the prime minister
elections: none; the monarch is hereditary; the governor general is appointed by the monarch; following legislative elections, the leader of the majority party is usually appointed prime minister by the governor general; deputy prime minister appointed by the governor general on the advice of the prime minister
Legislative branch: unicameral House of Assembly (21 seats, 15 elected representatives and 6 appointed senators; representatives are elected by popular vote from single-member constituencies to serve five-year terms)
elections: last held 28 March 2001 (next to be held by July 2006)
election results: percent of vote by party - NA%; seats by party - ULP 12, NDP 3
Judicial branch: Eastern Caribbean Supreme Court (based on Saint Lucia; one judge of the Supreme Court resides in Saint Vincent and the Grenadines)
Political parties and leaders: National Reform Party or NRP [Joel MIGUEL]; New Democratic Party or NDP [Arnhim EUSTACE]; People's Progressive Movement or PPM [Ken BOYEA]; Progressive Labor Party or PLP [leader NA]; United People's Movement or UPM [Adrian SAUNDERS]; Unity Labor Party or ULP [Ralph GONSALVES] (formed by the coalition of Saint Vincent Labor Party or SVLP and the Movement for National Unity or MNU)
Political pressure groups and leaders: NA

International organization participation: ACP, C, Caricom, CDB, FAO, G-77, IBRD, ICAO, ICCt, ICFTU, ICRM, IDA, IFAD, IFRCS, ILO, IMF, IMO, Interpol, IOC, ITU, OAS, OECS, OPANAL, OPCW, UN, UNCTAD, UNESCO, UNIDO, UPU, WCL, WFTU, WHO, WIPO, WTrO
Diplomatic representation in the US:
chief of mission: Ambassador Ellsworth I. A. JOHN
chancery: 3216 New Mexico Avenue NW, Washington, DC 20016
telephone: [1] (202) 364-6730
FAX: [1] (202) 364-6736
consulate(s) general: New York
Diplomatic representation from the US: the US does not have an embassy in Saint Vincent and the Grenadines; the US Ambassador to Barbados, Ambassador Mary E. KRAMER, is accredited to Saint Vincent and the Grenadines
Flag description: three vertical bands of blue (hoist side), gold (double width), and green; the gold band bears three green diamonds arranged in a V pattern

Economy

Economy - overview: Economic growth in this lower-middle-income country hinges upon seasonal variations in the agricultural and tourism sectors. Tropical storms wiped out substantial portions of crops in 1994, 1995, and 2002, and tourism in the Eastern Caribbean has suffered low arrivals following 11 September 2001. Saint Vincent is home to a small offshore banking sector and has moved to adopt international regulatory standards. Saint Vincent is also a large producer of marijuana and is being used as a transshipment point for illegal narcotics from South America.
GDP: purchasing power parity - $339 million (2002 est.)
GDP - real growth rate: -0.5% (2002 est.)
GDP - per capita: purchasing power parity - $2,900 (2002 est.)
GDP - composition by sector:
agriculture: 10%
industry: 26%
services: 64% (2001 est.)
Population below poverty line: NA%
Household income or consumption by percentage share:
lowest 10%: NA%
highest 10%: NA%
Inflation rate (consumer prices): -0.4% (2001 est.)
Labor force: 67,000 (1984 est.)
Labor force - by occupation: agriculture 26%, industry 17%, services 57% (1980 est.)
Unemployment rate: 22% (1997 est.)
Budget:
revenues: $94.6 million
expenditures: $85.8 million, including capital expenditures of $NA (2000 est.)
Industries: food processing, cement, furniture, clothing, starch
Industrial production growth rate: -0.9% (1997 est.)

Electricity - production: 92.48 million kWh (2001)
Electricity - production by source:
fossil fuel: 69.3%
hydro: 30.7%
nuclear: 0%
other: 0% (2001)
Electricity - consumption: 86 million kWh (2001)
Electricity - exports: 0 kWh (2001)
Electricity - imports: 0 kWh (2001)
Oil - production: 0 bbl/day (2001 est.)
Oil - consumption: 1,250 bbl/day (2001 est.)
Oil - exports: NA
Oil - imports: NA
Agriculture - products: bananas, coconuts, sweet potatoes, spices, small numbers of cattle, sheep, pigs, goats, fish
Exports: $38 million (2002 est.)
Exports - commodities: bananas 39%, eddoes and dasheen (taro), arrowroot starch, tennis racquets
Exports - partners: France 25.4%, Greece 19.2%, Spain 16.4%, UK 9.4%, US 7% (2002)
Imports: $174 million (2002 est.)
Imports - commodities: foodstuffs, machinery and equipment, chemicals and fertilizers, minerals and fuels
Imports - partners: France 32.6%, US 11.2%, Trinidad and Tobago 10.4%, Singapore 10.2%, Spain 7.9%, Greece 4.3% (2002)
Debt - external: $167.2 million (2000)
Economic aid - recipient: $47.5 million (1995); note - EU $34.5 million (1998)
Currency: East Caribbean dollar (XCD)
Currency code: XCD
Exchange rates: East Caribbean dollars per US dollar - 2.7 (2003), 2.7 (2002), 2.7 (2001), 2.7 (2000), 2.7 (1999)
Fiscal year: calendar year

Communications

Telephones - main lines in use: 27,300 (2002)
Telephones - mobile cellular: 10,000 (2002)
Telephone system:
general assessment: adequate system
domestic: islandwide, fully automatic telephone system; VHF/UHF radiotelephone from Saint Vincent to the other islands of the Grenadines
international: country code - 1-784; VHF/UHF radiotelephone from Saint Vincent to Barbados; new SHF radiotelephone to Grenada and to Saint Lucia; access to Intelsat earth station in Martinique through Saint Lucia
Radio broadcast stations: AM 1, FM 6, shortwave 0 (2004)
Television broadcast stations: 1 (plus three repeaters) (2004)
Internet country code: .vc
Internet hosts: NA
Internet users: 7,000 (2002)

Saint Vincent and the Grenadines

(continued)

Transportation

Railways: 0 km
Highways:
total: 1,040 km
paved: 320 km
unpaved: 720 km (1999 est.)
Waterways: none
Ports and harbors: Kingstown
Merchant marine:
total: 704 ships (1,000 GRT or over) 5,967,418 GRT/ 9,041,023 DWT
by type: bulk 120, cargo 346, chemical tanker 19, combination bulk 10, combination ore/oil 1, container 51, liquefied gas 5, livestock carrier 4, multi-functional large load carrier 4, passenger 8, petroleum tanker 31, refrigerated cargo 45, roll on/roll off 42, short-sea/ passenger 9, specialized tanker 8, vehicle carrier 1
foreign-owned: Albania 1, Angola 2, Argentina 1, Australia 3, Bangladesh 3, Barbados 2, Belgium 3, Bulgaria 16, China 114, Colombia 1, Croatia 7, Cyprus 2, Denmark 13, Egypt 5, Estonia 13, France 17, Germany 10, Greece 134, Guyana 8, Hong Kong 15, Iceland 7, India 5, Indonesia 1, Israel 3, Italy 21, Kenya 5, South Korea 4, Latvia 7, Lebanon 9, Liberia 5, Lithuania 3, Malta 4, Isle of Man 1, Marshall Islands 3, Mexico 2, Monaco 6, Netherlands 9, Nigeria 8, Norway 32, Pakistan 6, Panama 3, Poland 3, Portugal 1, Puerto Rico 2, Romania 2, Russia 21, Saint Kitts and Nevis 1, Saint Lucia 1, Saudi Arabia 3, Singapore 5, Slovenia 7, Spain 1, Sweden 9, Switzerland 8, Syria 6, Taiwan 1, Thailand 1, Trinidad and Tobago 1, Turkey 23, Ukraine 8, United Kingdom 11, United States 8
registered in other countries: 25 (2003 est.)
Airports: 6 (2003 est.)
Airports - with paved runways:
total: 5
914 to 1,523 m: 4
under 914 m: 1 (2003 est.)
Airports - with unpaved runways:
total: 1
under 914 m: 1 (2003 est.)

Military

Military branches: Royal Saint Vincent and the Grenadines Police Force (includes Special Service Unit), Coast Guard
Military expenditures - dollar figure: NA
Military expenditures - percent of GDP: NA

Transnational Issues

Disputes - international: joins other Caribbean states to counter Venezuela's claim that Aves Island sustains human habitation, a criterion under UNCLOS, which permits Venezuela to extend its EEZ/ continental shelf over a large portion of the Caribbean Sea
Illicit drugs: transshipment point for South American drugs destined for the US and Europe; small-scale cannabis cultivation

Samoa

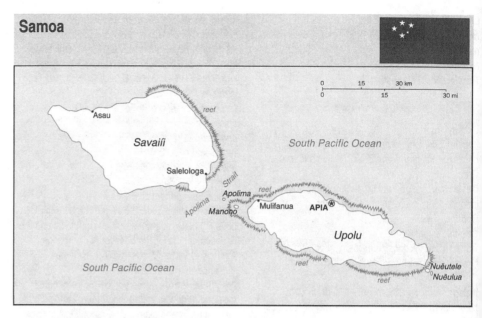

Introduction

Background: New Zealand occupied the German protectorate of Western Samoa at the outbreak of World War I in 1914. It continued to administer the islands as a mandate and then as a trust territory until 1962, when the islands became the first Polynesian nation to reestablish independence in the 20th century. The country dropped the "Western" from its name in 1997.

Geography

Location: Oceania, group of islands in the South Pacific Ocean, about one-half of the way from Hawaii to New Zealand
Geographic coordinates: 13 35 S, 172 20 W
Map references: Oceania
Area:
total: 2,944 sq km
land: 2,934 sq km
water: 10 sq km
Area - comparative: slightly smaller than Rhode Island
Land boundaries: 0 km
Coastline: 403 km
Maritime claims:
territorial sea: 12 NM
exclusive economic zone: 200 NM
Climate: tropical; rainy season (November to April), dry season (May to October)
Terrain: two main islands (Savaii, Upolu) and several smaller islands and uninhabited islets; narrow coastal plain with volcanic, rocky, rugged mountains in interior
Elevation extremes:
lowest point: Pacific Ocean 0 m
highest point: Mauga Silisili (Savaii) 1,857 m
Natural resources: hardwood forests, fish, hydropower
Land use:
arable land: 19.43%
permanent crops: 23.67%
other: 56.9% (1998 est.)

Irrigated land: NA sq km
Natural hazards: occasional typhoons; active volcanism
Environment - current issues: soil erosion, deforestation, invasive species, overfishing
Environment - international agreements:
party to: Biodiversity, Climate Change, Climate Change-Kyoto Protocol, Desertification, Hazardous Wastes, Law of the Sea, Ozone Layer Protection
signed, but not ratified: none of the selected agreements
Geography - note: occupies an almost central position within Polynesia

People

Population: 177,714 (July 2004 est.)
Age structure:
0-14 years: 28.3% (male 25,548; female 24,668)
15-64 years: 65.5% (male 72,820; female 43,563)
65 years and over: 6.3% (male 5,096; female 6,019) (2004 est.)
Median age:
total: 24.2 years
male: 26.8 years
female: 20.8 years (2004 est.)
Population growth rate: -0.25% (2004 est.)
Birth rate: 15.69 births/1,000 population (2004 est.)
Death rate: 6.47 deaths/1,000 population (2004 est.)
Net migration rate: -11.7 migrant(s)/1,000 population (2004 est.)
Sex ratio:
at birth: 1.05 male(s)/female
under 15 years: 1.04 male(s)/female
15-64 years: 1.67 male(s)/female
65 years and over: 0.85 male(s)/female
total population: 1.39 male(s)/female (2004 est.)
Infant mortality rate:
total: 28.72 deaths/1,000 live births
male: 33.83 deaths/1,000 live births
female: 23.35 deaths/1,000 live births (2004 est.)

Samoa (continued)

Life expectancy at birth:

total population: 70.41 years

male: 67.64 years

female: 73.33 years (2004 est.)

Total fertility rate: 3.11 children born/woman (2004 est.)

HIV/AIDS - adult prevalence rate: NA%

HIV/AIDS - people living with HIV/AIDS: 12

HIV/AIDS - deaths: 3

Nationality:

noun: Samoan(s)

adjective: Samoan

Ethnic groups: Samoan 92.6%, Euronesians 7% (persons of European and Polynesian blood), Europeans 0.4%

Religions: Christian 99.7% (about one-half of population associated with the London Missionary Society; includes Congregational, Roman Catholic, Methodist, Latter-Day Saints, Seventh-Day Adventist)

Languages: Samoan (Polynesian), English

Literacy:

definition: age 15 and over can read and write

total population: 99.7%

male: 99.6%

female: 99.7% (2003 est.)

Government

Country name:

conventional long form: Independent State of Samoa

conventional short form: Samoa

former: Western Samoa

Government type: constitutional monarchy under native chief

Capital: Apia

Administrative divisions: 11 districts; A'ana, Aiga-i-le-Tai, Atua, Fa'asaleleaga, Gaga'emauga, Gagaifomauga, Palauli, Satupa'itea, Tuamasaga, Va'a-o-Fonoti, Vaisigano

Independence: 1 January 1962 (from New Zealand-administered UN trusteeship)

National holiday: Independence Day Celebration, 1 June (1962); note - 1 January 1962 is the date of independence from the New Zealand-administered UN trusteeship, 1 June 1962 is the date that independence is celebrated

Constitution: 1 January 1962

Legal system: based on English common law and local customs; judicial review of legislative acts with respect to fundamental rights of the citizen; has not accepted compulsory ICJ jurisdiction

Suffrage: 21 years of age; universal

Executive branch:

chief of state: Chief Tanumafili II MALIETOA (cochief of state from 1 January 1962 until becoming sole chief of state 5 April 1963)

head of government: Prime Minister Sailele Malielegaoi TUILA'EPA (since 1996); note - TUILA'EPA served as deputy prime minister from 1992 until he assumed the prime ministership in 1996,

when former Prime Minister TOFILAU Eti Alesana resigned in poor health; TUILA'EPA was confirmed as prime minister (November 1998) after TOFILAU died; the post of deputy prime minister is currently vacant

cabinet: Cabinet consists of 12 members, appointed by the chief of state with the prime minister's advice

elections: upon the death of Chief Tanumafili II MALIETOA, a new chief of state will be elected by the Legislative Assembly to serve a five-year term; following legislative elections, the leader of the majority party is usually appointed prime minister by the chief of state with the approval of the Legislative Assembly

Legislative branch: unicameral Legislative Assembly or Fono (49 seats - 47 elected by voters affiliated with traditional village-based electoral districts, 2 elected by independent, mostly Eurasian, voters who cannot, (or choose not to) establish a village affiliation; only chiefs (matai) may stand for election to the Fono; members serve five-year terms)

elections: election last held 3 March 2001 (next election to be held not later than March 2006)

election results: percent of vote by party - NA%; seats by party - HRPP 30, SNDP 13, independents 6

Judicial branch: Supreme Court; Court of Appeal; Land and Titles Court

Political parties and leaders: Christian Democratic Party [leader NA]; Human Rights Protection Party or HRPP [Sailele Malielegaoi TUILA'EPA, chairman]; Samoa All People's Party or SAPP [Matatumua MAIMOANA]; Samoan National Development Party or SNDP [LE MAMEA Ropati, chairman] (opposition); Samoa National Party [FETU Tiatia, party secretary]; Samoan Progressive Conservative Party [LEOTA Ituau Ale]; Samoan United Independents Party or SUIP [Dr. Saleimoa VAAI]

Political pressure groups and leaders: NA

International organization participation: ACP, AsDB, C, FAO, G-77, IBRD, ICAO, ICCt, ICFTU, ICRM, IDA, IFAD, IFC, IFRCS, IMF, IMO, IOC, ITU, OPCW, PIF, Sparteca, UN, UNCTAD, UNESCO, UPU, WCO, WHO, WIPO, WMO, WTrO (observer)

Diplomatic representation in the US:

chief of mission: Ambassador Feturi ELISAIA

chancery: 800 Second Avenue, Suite 400D, New York, NY 10017

telephone: [1] (212) 599-6196, 6197

FAX: [1] (212) 599-0797

Diplomatic representation from the US:

chief of mission: the Ambassador to New Zealand, Ambassador Charles J. SWINDELLS, is accredited to Samoa

embassy: Vailima

mailing address: P. O. Box 3430, Apia

telephone: [685] 21631/22696

FAX: [685] 22030

Flag description: red with a blue rectangle in the upper hoist-side quadrant bearing five white five-pointed stars representing the Southern Cross constellation

Economy

Economy - overview: The economy of Samoa has traditionally been dependent on development aid, family remittances from overseas, and agriculture and fishing. The country is vulnerable to devastating storms. Agriculture employs two-thirds of the labor force, and furnishes 90% of exports, featuring coconut cream, coconut oil, and copra. The manufacturing sector mainly processes agricultural products. The decline of fish stocks in the area is a continuing problem. Tourism is an expanding sector, accounting for 25% of GDP; about 88,000 tourists visited the islands in 2001. The Samoan Government has called for deregulation of the financial sector, encouragement of investment, and continued fiscal discipline, meantime protecting the environment. Observers point to the flexibility of the labor market as a basic strength for future economic advances. Foreign reserves are in a relatively healthy state, the external debt is stable, and inflation is low.

GDP: purchasing power parity - $1 billion (2002 est.)

GDP - real growth rate: 5% (2002 est.)

GDP - per capita: purchasing power parity - $5,600 (2002 est.)

GDP - composition by sector:

agriculture: 14%

industry: 23%

services: 63% (2001 est.)

Population below poverty line: NA%

Household income or consumption by percentage share:

lowest 10%: NA%

highest 10%: NA%

Inflation rate (consumer prices): 4% (2001 est.)

Labor force: 90,000 (2000 est.)

Labor force - by occupation: NA

Unemployment rate: NA%; note - substantial underemployment

Budget:

revenues: $105 million

expenditures: $119 million, including capital expenditures of $NA (2001-02)

Industries: food processing, building materials, auto parts

Industrial production growth rate: 2.8% (2000)

Electricity - production: 105.1 million kWh (2001)

Electricity - production by source:

fossil fuel: 58%

hydro: 42%

nuclear: 0%

other: 0% (2001)

Electricity - consumption: 97.74 million kWh (2001)

Electricity - exports: 0 kWh (2001)

Electricity - imports: 0 kWh (2001)

Oil - production: 0 bbl/day (2001 est.)

Oil - consumption: 1,000 bbl/day (2001 est.)

Oil - exports: NA

Oil - imports: NA

Samoa *(continued)*

Agriculture - products: coconuts, bananas, taro, yams, coffee, cocoa
Exports: $14 million f.o.b. (2002)
Exports - commodities: fish, coconut oil and cream, copra, taro, automotive parts, garments, beer
Exports - partners: Australia 61%, Hong Kong 10.4%, US 9.1% (2002)
Imports: $113 million f.o.b. (2002)
Imports - commodities: machinery and equipment, industrial supplies, foodstuffs
Imports - partners: New Zealand 23.7%, Fiji 20.9%, Australia 16.4%, Japan 13.6%, US 4.5% (2002)
Debt - external: $197 million (2000)
Economic aid - recipient: $42.9 million (1995)
Currency: tala (SAT)
Currency code: SAT (former WST code is still in wide use)
Exchange rates: tala per US dollar - 2.9732 (2003), 3.3763 (2002), 3.478 (2001), 3.2864 (2000), 3.0132 (1999)
Fiscal year: June 1 - May 31

Communications

Telephones - main lines in use: 10,300 (2002)
Telephones - mobile cellular: 2,700 (2002)
Telephone system:
general assessment: adequate
domestic: NA
international: country code - 685; satellite earth station - 1 Intelsat (Pacific Ocean)
Radio broadcast stations: AM 1, FM 3, shortwave 0 (1998)
Television broadcast stations: 2 (2002)
Internet country code: .ws
Internet hosts: 5,705 (2002)
Internet users: 4,000 (2002)

Transportation

Railways: 0 km
Highways:
total: 790 km
paved: 332 km
unpaved: 458 km (1999 est.)
Waterways: none
Ports and harbors: Apia, Asau, Mulifanua, Salelologa
Merchant marine:
total: 1 ships (1,000 GRT or over) 7,091 GRT/8,127 DWT
by type: cargo 1
foreign-owned: Germany 1
registered in other countries: 2 (2003 est.)
Airports: 4 (2003 est.)
Airports - with paved runways:
total: 3
2,438 to 3,047 m: 1
under 914 m: 2 (2003 est.)
Airports - with unpaved runways:
total: 1
under 914 m: 1 (2003 est.)

Military

Military branches: no regular armed services; Samoa Police Force
Military expenditures - dollar figure: NA
Military expenditures - percent of GDP: NA
Military - note: Samoa has no formal defense structure or regular armed forces; informal defense ties exist with NZ, which is required to consider any Samoan request for assistance under the 1962 Treaty of Friendship

San Marino

Introduction

Background: The third smallest state in Europe (after the Holy See and Monaco) also claims to be the world's oldest republic. According to tradition, it was founded by a Christian stonemason named Marinus in 301 A.D. San Marino's foreign policy is aligned with that of Italy. Social and political trends in the republic also track closely with those of its larger neighbor.

Geography

Location: Southern Europe, an enclave in central Italy
Geographic coordinates: 43 46 N, 12 25 E
Map references: Europe
Area:
total: 61.2 sq km
land: 61.2 sq km
water: 0 sq km
Area - comparative: about 0.3 times the size of Washington, DC
Land boundaries:
total: 39 km
border countries: Italy 39 km
Coastline: 0 km (landlocked)
Maritime claims: none (landlocked)
Climate: Mediterranean; mild to cool winters; warm, sunny summers
Terrain: rugged mountains
Elevation extremes:
lowest point: Torrente Ausa 55 m
highest point: Monte Titano 755 m
Natural resources: building stone
Land use:
arable land: 16.67%
permanent crops: 0%
other: 83.33% (1998 est.)
Irrigated land: NA sq km
Natural hazards: NA
Environment - current issues: NA

San Marino (continued)

Environment - international agreements:
party to: Biodiversity, Climate Change, Desertification
signed, but not ratified: Air Pollution
Geography - note: landlocked; smallest independent state in Europe after the Holy See and Monaco; dominated by the Apennines

People

Population: 28,503 (July 2004 est.)
Age structure:
0-14 years: 16.5% (male 2,425; female 2,277)
15-64 years: 66.8% (male 9,200; female 9,834)
65 years and over: 16.7% (male 2,059; female 2,708) (2004 est.)
Median age:
total: 40 years
male: 39.6 years
female: 40.3 years (2004 est.)
Population growth rate: 1.33% (2004 est.)
Birth rate: 10.31 births/1,000 population (2004 est.)
Death rate: 7.96 deaths/1,000 population (2004 est.)
Net migration rate: 10.98 migrant(s)/1,000 population (2004 est.)
Sex ratio:
at birth: 1.09 male(s)/female
under 15 years: 1.07 male(s)/female
15-64 years: 0.94 male(s)/female
65 years and over: 0.76 male(s)/female
total population: 0.92 male(s)/female (2004 est.)
Infant mortality rate:
total: 5.85 deaths/1,000 live births
male: 6.28 deaths/1,000 live births
female: 5.38 deaths/1,000 live births (2004 est.)
Life expectancy at birth:
total population: 81.53 years
male: 78.02 years
female: 85.34 years (2004 est.)
Total fertility rate: 1.32 children born/woman (2004 est.)
HIV/AIDS - adult prevalence rate: NA%
HIV/AIDS - people living with HIV/AIDS: NA
HIV/AIDS - deaths: NA
Nationality:
noun: Sammarinese (singular and plural)
adjective: Sammarinese
Ethnic groups: Sammarinese, Italian
Religions: Roman Catholic
Languages: Italian
Literacy:
definition: age 10 and over can read and write
total population: 96%
male: 97%
female: 95% (1976 est.)

Government

Country name:
conventional long form: Republic of San Marino
conventional short form: San Marino
local long form: Repubblica di San Marino
local short form: San Marino
Government type: independent republic

Capital: San Marino
Administrative divisions: 9 municipalities (castelli, singular - castello); Acquaviva, Borgo Maggiore, Chiesanuova, Domagnano, Faetano, Fiorentino, Monte Giardino, San Marino, Serravalle
Independence: 3 September 301
National holiday: Founding of the Republic, 3 September (301)
Constitution: 8 October 1600; electoral law of 1926 serves some of the functions of a constitution
Legal system: based on civil law system with Italian law influences; has not accepted compulsory ICJ jurisdiction
Suffrage: 18 years of age; universal
Executive branch:
chief of state: cochiefs of state Captain Regent Paolo BOLLINI and Captain Regent Marino RICCARDI (for the period 1 April-30 September 2004)
head of government: Secretary of State for Foreign and Political Affairs Fiorenzo STOLFI (since 17 December 2002)
cabinet: Congress of State elected by the Great and General Council for a five-year term
elections: cochiefs of state (captains regent) elected by the Great and General Council for a six-month term; election last held NA March 2004 (next to be held NA September 2004); secretary of state for foreign and political affairs elected by the Great and General Council for a five-year term; election last held 17 December 2002 (next to be held NA June 2007)
election results: Paolo BOLLINI and Marino RICCARDI elected captains regent; percent of legislative vote - NA%; Fiorenzo STOLFI elected secretary of state for foreign and political affairs; percent of legislative vote - 40%
note: the popularly elected parliament (Grand and General Council) selects two of its members to serve as the Captains Regent (cochiefs of state) for a six-month period; they preside over meetings of the Grand and General Council and its cabinet (Congress of State), which has 10 other members, all selected by the Grand and General Council; assisting the captains regent are 10 secretaries of state; the secretary of state for Foreign Affairs has assumed some of the prerogatives of a prime minister
Legislative branch: unicameral Grand and General Council or Consiglio Grande e Generale (60 seats; members are elected by direct, popular vote to serve five-year terms)
elections: last held 10 June 2001 (next to be held by June 2006)
election results: percent of vote by party - PDCS 41.4%, PSS 24.2%, PD 20.8%, APDS 8.2%, RC 3.4%, AN 1.9%; seats by party - PDCS 25, PSS 15, PD 12, APDS 5, RC 2, AN 1
Judicial branch: Council of Twelve or Consiglio dei XII
Political parties and leaders: Communist Refoundation or RC [Ivan FOSHI]; Ideas in Movement or IM [Alessandro ROSSI]; National Alliance or AN [leader NA]; Party of Democrats or PD [Claudio FELICI]; San Marino Christian Democratic Party or

PDCS [Giovanni LONFERNINI]; San Marino Popular Alliance of Democrats or APDS [Roberto GIORGETTI]; San Marino Socialist Party or PSS [Alberto CECCHETTI]; Socialists for Reform or SR [Renzo GIARDI]
Political pressure groups and leaders: NA
International organization participation: CE, FAO, IBRD, ICAO, ICCt, ICFTU, ICRM, IFRCS, ILO, IMF, IMO, IOC, IOM (observer), ITU, OPCW, OSCE, UN, UNCTAD, UNESCO, UPU, WHO, WIPO, WToO
Diplomatic representation in the US: San Marino does not have an embassy in the US
honorary consulate(s) general: Washington, DC and New York
honorary consulate(s): Detroit and Honolulu
Diplomatic representation from the US: the US does not have an embassy in San Marino; the US Consul General in Florence (Italy) is accredited to San Marino
Flag description: two equal horizontal bands of white (top) and light blue with the national coat of arms superimposed in the center; the coat of arms has a shield (featuring three towers on three peaks) flanked by a wreath, below a crown and above a scroll bearing the word LIBERTAS (Liberty)

Economy

Economy - overview: The tourist sector contributes over 50% of GDP. In 2000 more than 3 million tourists visited San Marino. The key industries are banking, wearing apparel, electronics, and ceramics. Main agricultural products are wine and cheeses. The per capita level of output and standard of living are comparable to those of the most prosperous regions of Italy, which supplies much of its food.
GDP: purchasing power parity - $940 million (2001 est.)
GDP - real growth rate: 7.5% (2001 est.)
GDP - per capita: purchasing power parity - $34,600 (2001 est.)
GDP - composition by sector:
agriculture: NA%
industry: NA%
services: NA%
Population below poverty line: NA%
Household income or consumption by percentage share:
lowest 10%: NA%
highest 10%: NA%
Inflation rate (consumer prices): 3.3% (2001)
Labor force: 18,500 (1999)
Labor force - by occupation: services 57%, industry 42%, agriculture 1% (2000 est.)
Unemployment rate: 2.6% (2001)
Budget:
revenues: $400 million
expenditures: $400 million, including capital expenditures of $NA (2000 est.)
Industries: tourism, banking, textiles, electronics, ceramics, cement, wine
Industrial production growth rate: 6% (1997 est.)

Agriculture - products: wheat, grapes, corn, olives; cattle, pigs, horses, beef, cheese, hides
Exports: trade data are included with the statistics for Italy
Exports - commodities: building stone, lime, wood, chestnuts, wheat, wine, baked goods, hides, ceramics
Imports: trade data are included with the statistics for Italy
Imports - commodities: wide variety of consumer manufactures, food
Debt - external: $NA
Economic aid - recipient: $NA
Currency: euro (EUR)
Currency code: EUR
Exchange rates: euros per US dollar - 0.886 (2003), 1.0626 (2002), 1.1175 (2001), 1.0854 (2000), 0.9386 (1999)
Fiscal year: calendar year

Communications

Telephones - main lines in use: 20,600 (2002)
Telephones - mobile cellular: 16,800 (2002)
Telephone system:
general assessment: adequate connections
domestic: automatic telephone system completely integrated into Italian system
international: country code - 378; connected to Italian international network
Radio broadcast stations: AM 0, FM 3, shortwave 0 (1998)
Television broadcast stations: 1 (San Marino residents also receive broadcasts from Italy) (1997)
Internet country code: .sm
Internet users: 14,300 (2002)

Transportation

Railways: 0 km; note - there is a 1.5-km cable railway connecting the city of San Marino to Borgo Maggiore
Highways:
total: 220 km
paved: 220 km
unpaved: 0 km (2001)
Waterways: none
Ports and harbors: none
Airports: none (2003 est.)

Military

Military branches: Voluntary Military Force (Corpi Militari Voluntar); note - the Voluntary Military Force performs ceremonial duties and limited police assistance
Military expenditures - dollar figure: $700,000 (FY00/01)
Military expenditures - percent of GDP: NA%

Transnational Issues

Disputes - international: none

Sao Tome and Principe

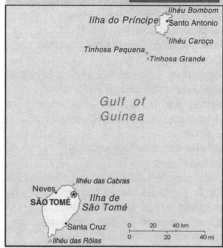

Introduction

Background: Discovered and claimed by Portugal in the late 15th century, the islands' sugar-based economy gave way to coffee and cocoa in the 19th century - all grown with plantation slave labor, a form of which lingered into the 20th century. Although independence was achieved in 1975, democratic reforms were not instituted until the late 1980s. Though the first free elections were held in 1991, the political environment has been one of continued instability with frequent changes in leadership and coup attempts in 1995 and 2003. The recent discovery of oil in the Gulf of Guinea is likely to have a significant impact on the country's economy.

Geography

Location: Western Africa, islands in the Gulf of Guinea, straddling the Equator, west of Gabon
Geographic coordinates: 1 00 N, 7 00 E
Map references: Africa
Area:
total: 1,001 sq km
land: 1,001 sq km
water: 0 sq km
Area - comparative: more than five times the size of Washington, DC
Land boundaries: 0 km
Coastline: 209 km
Maritime claims: measured from claimed archipelagic baselines
territorial sea: 12 NM
exclusive economic zone: 200 NM
Climate: tropical; hot, humid; one rainy season (October to May)
Terrain: volcanic, mountainous
Elevation extremes:
lowest point: Atlantic Ocean 0 m
highest point: Pico de Sao Tome 2,024 m
Natural resources: fish, hydropower

Land use:
arable land: 2%
permanent crops: 41%
other: 57% (1998 est.)
Irrigated land: 100 sq km (1998 est.)
Natural hazards: NA
Environment - current issues: deforestation; soil erosion and exhaustion
Environment - international agreements:
party to: Biodiversity, Climate Change, Desertification, Endangered Species, Environmental Modification, Law of the Sea, Ozone Layer Protection, Ship Pollution
signed, but not ratified: none of the selected agreements
Geography - note: the smallest country in Africa; the two main islands form part of a chain of extinct volcanoes and both are fairly mountainous

People

Population: 181,565 (July 2004 est.)
Age structure:
0-14 years: 47.7% (male 43,810; female 42,708)
15-64 years: 48.4% (male 42,469; female 45,456)
65 years and over: 3.9% (male 3,275; female 3,847) (2004 est.)
Median age:
total: 16.1 years
male: 15.5 years
female: 16.7 years (2004 est.)
Population growth rate: 3.18% (2004 est.)
Birth rate: 41.36 births/1,000 population (2004 est.)
Death rate: 6.89 deaths/1,000 population (2004 est.)
Net migration rate: -2.72 migrant(s)/1,000 population (2004 est.)
Sex ratio:
at birth: 1.03 male(s)/female
under 15 years: 1.03 male(s)/female
15-64 years: 0.93 male(s)/female
65 years and over: 0.85 male(s)/female
total population: 0.97 male(s)/female (2004 est.)
Infant mortality rate:
total: 44.58 deaths/1,000 live births
male: 46.57 deaths/1,000 live births
female: 42.53 deaths/1,000 live births (2004 est.)
Life expectancy at birth:
total population: 66.63 years
male: 65.11 years
female: 68.21 years (2004 est.)
Total fertility rate: 5.8 children born/woman (2004 est.)
HIV/AIDS - adult prevalence rate: NA%
HIV/AIDS - people living with HIV/AIDS: NA
HIV/AIDS - deaths: NA
Nationality:
noun: Sao Tomean(s)
adjective: Sao Tomean
Ethnic groups: mestico, angolares (descendants of Angolan slaves), forros (descendants of freed slaves), servicais (contract laborers from Angola,

Sao Tome and Principe *(continued)*

Mozambique, and Cape Verde), tongas (children of servicais born on the islands), Europeans (primarily Portuguese)

Religions: Christian 80% (Roman Catholic, Evangelical Protestant, Seventh-Day Adventist)

Languages: Portuguese (official)

Literacy:

definition: age 15 and over can read and write

total population: 79.3%

male: 85%

female: 62% (1991 est.)

Government

Country name:

conventional long form: Democratic Republic of Sao Tome and Principe

conventional short form: Sao Tome and Principe

local long form: Republica Democratica de Sao Tome e Principe

local short form: Sao Tome e Principe

Government type: republic

Capital: Sao Tome

Administrative divisions: 2 provinces; Principe, Sao Tome

note: Principe has had self-government since 29 April 1995

Independence: 12 July 1975 (from Portugal)

National holiday: Independence Day, 12 July (1975)

Constitution: approved March 1990; effective 10 September 1990

Legal system: based on Portuguese legal system and customary law; has not accepted compulsory ICJ jurisdiction

Suffrage: 18 years of age; universal

Executive branch:

chief of state: President Fradique DE MENEZES (since 3 September 2001)

head of government: Prime Minister Maria das NEVES (since 7 October 2002)

cabinet: Council of Ministers appointed by the president on the proposal of the prime minister

elections: president elected by popular vote for a five-year term; election last held 29 July 2001 (next to be held NA July 2006); prime minister chosen by the National Assembly and approved by the president

election results: Fradique DE MENEZES elected president in Sao Tome's third multiparty presidential election; percent of vote - NA%

Legislative branch: unicameral National Assembly or Assembleia Nacional (55 seats; members are elected by direct, popular vote to serve four-year terms)

elections: last held 3 March 2002 (next to be held NA March 2006)

election results: percent of vote by party - MLSTP 39.6%, Force for Change Democratic Movement 39.4%, Ue-Kedadji coalition 16.2%; seats by party - MLSTP 24, Force for Change Democratic Movement 23, Ue-Kedadji coalition 8

Judicial branch: Supreme Court (judges are appointed by the National Assembly)

Political parties and leaders: Democratic Renovation Party [Armindo GRACA]; Force for Change Democratic Movement [leader NA]; Independent Democratic Action or ADI [Carlos NEVES]; Movement for the Liberation of Sao Tome and Principe-Social Democratic Party or MLSTP-PSD [Manuel Pinto Da COSTA]; Party for Democratic Convergence or PCD [Aldo BANDEIRA]; Ue-Kedadji coalition [leader NA]; other small parties

Political pressure groups and leaders: NA

International organization participation: ACCT, ACP, AfDB, AU, FAO, G-77, IBRD, ICAO, ICCt (signatory), ICFTU, ICRM, IDA, IFAD, IFRCS, ILO, IMF, IMO, Interpol, IOC, IOM (observer), ITU, NAM, OPCW, UN, UNCTAD, UNESCO, UNIDO, UPU, WCL, WHO, WIPO, WMO, WToO, WTrO (observer)

Diplomatic representation in the US: Sao Tome and Principe does not have an embassy in the US, but does have a Permanent Mission to the UN, headed by First Secretary Domingos Augusto FERREIRA, located at 400 Park Avenue, 7th Floor, New York, NY 10022, telephone [1] (212) 317-0580

Diplomatic representation from the US: the US does not have an embassy in Sao Tome and Principe; the Ambassador to Gabon is accredited to Sao Tome and Principe on a nonresident basis and makes periodic visits to the islands

Flag description: three horizontal bands of green (top), yellow (double width), and green with two black five-pointed stars placed side by side in the center of the yellow band and a red isosceles triangle based on the hoist side; uses the popular pan-African colors of Ethiopia

Economy

Economy - overview: This small poor island economy has become increasingly dependent on cocoa since independence 29 years ago. Cocoa production has substantially declined in recent years because of drought and mismanagement, but strengthening prices helped boost export earnings in 2003. Sao Tome has to import all fuels, most manufactured goods, consumer goods, and a substantial amount of food. Over the years, it has been unable to service its external debt and has had to depend on concessional aid and debt rescheduling. Sao Tome benefited from $200 million in debt relief in December 2000 under the Highly Indebted Poor Countries (HIPC) program. Sao Tome's success in implementing structural reforms has been rewarded by international donors, who pledged increased assistance in 2001. Considerable potential exists for development of a tourist industry, and the government has taken steps to expand facilities in recent years. The government also has attempted to reduce price controls and subsidies. Sao Tome is optimistic that substantial petroleum discoveries are forthcoming in its territorial waters in the oil-rich waters of the Gulf of Guinea; production could begin as early as 2004.

GDP: purchasing power parity - $200 million (2002 est.)

GDP - real growth rate: 4% (2002 est.)

GDP - per capita: purchasing power parity - $1,200 (2002 est.)

GDP - composition by sector:

agriculture: 25%

industry: 10%

services: 65% (1999 est.)

Population below poverty line: NA%

Household income or consumption by percentage share:

lowest 10%: NA%

highest 10%: NA%

Inflation rate (consumer prices): 9% (2002 est.)

Labor force: NA

Labor force - by occupation: population mainly engaged in subsistence agriculture and fishing

note: shortages of skilled workers

Unemployment rate: NA%

Budget:

revenues: $58 million

expenditures: $114 million, including capital expenditures of $54 million (1993 est.)

Industries: light construction, textiles, soap, beer; fish processing; timber

Industrial production growth rate: NA%

Electricity - production: 17 million kWh (2001)

Electricity - production by source:

fossil fuel: 41.2%

hydro: 58.8%

nuclear: 0%

other: 0% (2001)

Electricity - consumption: 15.81 million kWh (2001)

Electricity - exports: 0 kWh (2001)

Electricity - imports: 0 kWh (2001)

Oil - production: 0 bbl/day (2001 est.)

Oil - consumption: 700 bbl/day (2001 est.)

Oil - exports: NA

Oil - imports: NA

Agriculture - products: cocoa, coconuts, palm kernels, copra, cinnamon, pepper, coffee, bananas, papayas, beans; poultry; fish

Exports: $6.479 million f.o.b. (2003 est.)

Exports - commodities: cocoa 80%, copra, coffee, palm oil

Exports - partners: Netherlands 37.5%, Belgium 12.5%, Canada 12.5%, Germany 12.5%, Spain 12.5% (2002)

Imports: $30.03 million f.o.b. (2003 est.)

Imports - commodities: machinery and electrical equipment, food products, petroleum products

Imports - partners: Portugal 50.8%, Germany 10.2%, UK 8.5%, Belgium 6.8% (2002)

Debt - external: $253.8 million (2000)

Economic aid - recipient: $200 million in December 2000 under the HIPC program

Currency: dobra (STD)

Currency code: STD

Sao Tome and Principe *(continued)*

Exchange rates: dobras per US dollar - 9,347.58 (2003), 9,088.32 (2002), 8,842.11 (2001), 7,978.17 (2000), 7,118.96 (1999)
Fiscal year: calendar year

Communications

Telephones - main lines in use: 6,200 (2002)
Telephones - mobile cellular: 2,000 (2002)
Telephone system:
general assessment: adequate facilities
domestic: minimal system
international: country code - 239; satellite earth station - 1 Intelsat (Atlantic Ocean)
Radio broadcast stations: AM 1, FM 5, shortwave 1 (2002)
Television broadcast stations: 2 (2002)
Internet country code: .st
Internet hosts: 1,069 (2002)
Internet users: 11,000 (2002)

Transportation

Railways: 0 km
Highways:
total: 320 km
paved: 218 km
unpaved: 102 km (1999 est.)
Waterways: none
Ports and harbors: Santo Antonio, Sao Tome
Merchant marine:
total: 24 ships (1,000 GRT or over) 79,490 GRT/ 97,077 DWT
by type: bulk 2, cargo 14, chemical tanker 2, livestock carrier 1, petroleum tanker 1, refrigerated cargo 1, roll on/roll off 3
foreign-owned: British Virgin Islands 1, Egypt 1, Greece 1, Lebanon 1, Portugal 1, Ukraine 2 (2003 est.)
Airports: 2 (2003 est.)
Airports - with paved runways:
total: 2
1,524 to 2,437 m: 1
914 to 1,523 m: 1 (2003 est.)

Military

Military branches: Army, Coast Guard, Presidential Guard, National Guard
Military manpower - availability:
males age 15-49: 38,347 (2004 est.)
Military manpower - fit for military service:
males age 15-49: 20,188 (2004 est.)
Military expenditures - dollar figure: $500,000 (2003)
Military expenditures - percent of GDP: 0.8% (2003)

Transnational Issues

Disputes - international: none

Saudi Arabia

Introduction

Background: In 1902, ABD AL-AZIZ bin Abd al-Rahman Al Saud captured Riyadh and set out on a 30-year campaign to unify the Arabian Peninsula. Today, the monarchy is ruled by a son of ABD AL-AZIZ, and the country's Basic Law stipulates that the throne shall remain in the hands of the aging sons and grandsons of the kingdom's founder. Following Iraq's invasion of Kuwait in 1990, Saudi Arabia accepted the Kuwaiti royal family and 400,000 refugees while allowing Western and Arab troops to deploy on its soil for the liberation of Kuwait the following year. The continuing presence of foreign troops on Saudi soil after Operation Desert Storm remained a source of tension between the royal family and the public until the US military's near-complete withdrawal to neighboring Qatar in 2003. The first major terrorist attacks in Saudi Arabia in several years, which occurred in May and November 2003, prompted renewed efforts on the part of the Saudi government to counter domestic terrorism and extremism, which also coincided with a slight upsurge in media freedom and announcement of government plans to phase in partial political representation. A burgeoning population, aquifer depletion, and an economy largely dependent on petroleum output and prices are all ongoing governmental concerns.

Geography

Location: Middle East, bordering the Persian Gulf and the Red Sea, north of Yemen
Geographic coordinates: 25 00 N, 45 00 E
Map references: Middle East
Area:
total: 1,960,582 sq km
land: 1,960,582 sq km
water: 0 sq km
Area - comparative: slightly more than one-fifth the size of the US

Land boundaries:
total: 4,431 km
border countries: Iraq 814 km, Jordan 744 km, Kuwait 222 km, Oman 676 km, Qatar 60 km, UAE 457 km, Yemen 1,458 km
Coastline: 2,640 km
Maritime claims:
territorial sea: 12 NM
contiguous zone: 18 NM
continental shelf: not specified
Climate: harsh, dry desert with great temperature extremes
Terrain: mostly uninhabited, sandy desert
Elevation extremes:
lowest point: Persian Gulf 0 m
highest point: Jabal Sawda' 3,133 m
Natural resources: petroleum, natural gas, iron ore, gold, copper
Land use:
arable land: 1.72%
permanent crops: 0.06%
other: 98.22% (1998 est.)
Irrigated land: 16,200 sq km (1998 est.)
Natural hazards: frequent sand and dust storms
Environment - current issues: desertification; depletion of underground water resources; the lack of perennial rivers or permanent water bodies has prompted the development of extensive seawater desalination facilities; coastal pollution from oil spills
Environment - international agreements:
party to: Biodiversity, Climate Change, Desertification, Endangered Species, Hazardous Wastes, Law of the Sea, Ozone Layer Protection
signed, but not ratified: none of the selected agreements
Geography - note: extensive coastlines on Persian Gulf and Red Sea provide great leverage on shipping (especially crude oil) through Persian Gulf and Suez Canal

People

Population: 25,795,938
note: includes 5,576,076 non-nationals (July 2004 est.)
Age structure:
0-14 years: 38.3% (male 5,039,578; female 4,845,937)
15-64 years: 59.3% (male 8,810,705; female 6,494,770)
65 years and over: 2.3% (male 327,047; female 277,901) (2004 est.)
Median age:
total: 21.2 years
male: 22.8 years
female: 19.1 years (2004 est.)
Population growth rate: 2.44% (2004 est.)
Birth rate: 29.74 births/1,000 population (2004 est.)
Death rate: 2.66 deaths/1,000 population (2004 est.)
Net migration rate: -2.71 migrant(s)/1,000 population (2004 est.)

Saudi Arabia (continued)

Sex ratio:

at birth: 1.05 male(s)/female

under 15 years: 1.04 male(s)/female

15-64 years: 1.36 male(s)/female

65 years and over: 1.18 male(s)/female

total population: 1.22 male(s)/female (2004 est.)

Infant mortality rate:

total: 13.7 deaths/1,000 live births

male: 15.72 deaths/1,000 live births

female: 11.58 deaths/1,000 live births (2004 est.)

Life expectancy at birth:

total population: 75.23 years

male: 73.26 years

female: 77.3 years (2004 est.)

Total fertility rate: 4.11 children born/woman (2004 est.)

HIV/AIDS - adult prevalence rate: 0.01% (2001 est.)

HIV/AIDS - people living with HIV/AIDS: NA

HIV/AIDS - deaths: NA

Nationality:

noun: Saudi(s)

adjective: Saudi or Saudi Arabian

Ethnic groups: Arab 90%, Afro-Asian 10%

Religions: Muslim 100%

Languages: Arabic

Literacy:

definition: age 15 and over can read and write

total population: 78.8%

male: 84.7%

female: 70.8% (2003 est.)

Government

Country name:

conventional long form: Kingdom of Saudi Arabia

conventional short form: Saudi Arabia

local long form: Al Mamlakah al Arabiyah as Suudiyah

local short form: Al Arabiyah as Suudiyah

Government type: monarchy

Capital: Riyadh

Administrative divisions: 13 provinces (mintaqat, singular - mintaqah); Al Bahah, Al Hudud ash Shamaliyah, Al Jawf, Al Madinah, Al Qasim, Ar Riyad, Ash Sharqiyah (Eastern Province), 'Asir, Ha'il, Jizan, Makkah, Najran, Tabuk

Independence: 23 September 1932 (Unification of the Kingdom)

National holiday: Unification of the Kingdom, 23 September (1932)

Constitution: governed according to Shari'a (Islamic law); the Basic Law that articulates the government's rights and responsibilities was introduced in 1993

Legal system: based on Islamic law, several secular codes have been introduced; commercial disputes handled by special committees; has not accepted compulsory ICJ jurisdiction

Suffrage: none

note: in October 2003, Council of Ministers announced its intent to introduce elections for half of the members of local and provincial assemblies and a third of the members of the national Consultative Council or Majlis al-Shura, incrementally over a period of four to five years

Executive branch:

chief of state: King and Prime Minister FAHD bin Abd al-Aziz Al Saud (since 13 June 1982, but largely incapacitated since late 1995); Crown Prince and First Deputy Prime Minister ABDALLAH bin Abd al-Aziz Al Saud since 13 June 1982, also Saudi Arabian National Guard Commander since 1963 and de facto ruler since early 1996; note - the monarch is both the chief of state and head of government

head of government: King and Prime Minister FAHD bin Abd al-Aziz Al Saud (since 13 June 1982, but largely incapacitated since late 1995); Crown Prince and First Deputy Prime Minister ABDALLAH bin Abd al-Aziz Al Saud since 13 June 1982, also Saudi Arabian National Guard Commander since 1963 and de facto ruler since early 1996; note - the monarch is both the chief of state and head of government

cabinet: Council of Ministers is appointed by the monarch and includes many royal family members

elections: none; the monarch is hereditary

Legislative branch: Consultative Council or Majlis al-Shura (120 members and a chairman appointed by the monarch for four-year terms)

Judicial branch: Supreme Council of Justice

Political parties and leaders: none

Political pressure groups and leaders: none

International organization participation: ABEDA, AfDB, AFESD, AMF, BIS, FAO, G-77, GCC, IAEA, IBRD, ICAO, ICC, ICRM, IDA, IDB, IFAD, IFC, IFRCS, ILO, IMF, IMO, Interpol, IOC, ISO, ITU, LAS, NAM, OAPEC, OAS (observer), OIC, OPCW, OPEC, PCA, UN, UNCTAD, UNESCO, UNIDO, UPU, WCO, WFTU, WHO, WIPO, WMO, WToO, WTrO (observer)

Diplomatic representation in the US:

chief of mission: Ambassador BANDAR bin Sultan bin Abd al-Aziz Al Saud

chancery: 601 New Hampshire Avenue NW, Washington, DC 20037

telephone: [1] (202) 342-3800

consulate(s) general: Houston, Los Angeles, and New York

Diplomatic representation from the US:

chief of mission: Ambassador James Curtis OBERWETTER (since 8 January 2004)

embassy: Collector Road M, Diplomatic Quarter, Riyadh

mailing address: American Embassy Riyadh, Unit 61307, APO AE 09803-1307; International Mail: P. O. Box 94309, Riyadh 11693

telephone: [966] (1) 488-3800

FAX: [966] (1) 488-7360

consulate(s) general: Dhahran, Jiddah (Jeddah)

Flag description: green with large white Arabic script (that may be translated as There is no God but God; Muhammad is the Messenger of God) above a white horizontal saber (the tip points to the hoist side); green is the traditional color of Islam

Economy

Economy - overview: This is an oil-based economy with strong government controls over major economic activities. Saudi Arabia has the largest reserves of petroleum in the world (25% of the proved reserves), ranks as the largest exporter of petroleum, and plays a leading role in OPEC. The petroleum sector accounts for roughly 75% of budget revenues, 45% of GDP, and 90% of export earnings. About 40% of GDP comes from the private sector. Roughly five and a half million foreign workers play an important role in the Saudi economy, for example, in the oil and service sectors. The government in 1999 announced plans to begin privatizing the electricity companies, which follows the ongoing privatization of the telecommunications company. The government is encouraging private sector growth to lessen the kingdom's dependence on oil and increase employment opportunities for the swelling Saudi population. Priorities for government spending in the short term include additional funds for education and for the water and sewage systems. Economic reforms proceed cautiously because of deep-rooted political and social conservatism.

GDP: purchasing power parity - $286.2 billion (2003 est.)

GDP - real growth rate: 4.7% (2003 est.)

GDP - per capita: purchasing power parity - $11,800 (2003 est.)

GDP - composition by sector:

agriculture: 5.2%

industry: 50.4%

services: 44.4% (2002 est.)

Population below poverty line: NA%

Household income or consumption by percentage share:

lowest 10%: NA%

highest 10%: NA%

Inflation rate (consumer prices): 1% (2003 est.)

Labor force: 7 million

note: more than 35% of the population in the 15-64 age group is non-national (1999)

Labor force - by occupation: agriculture 12%, industry 25%, services 63% (1999 est.)

Unemployment rate: 25% (2003)

Budget:

revenues: $78.7 billion

expenditures: $66.7 billion, including capital expenditures of $NA (2003 est.)

Industries: crude oil production, petroleum refining, basic petrochemicals, cement, construction, fertilizer, plastics

Industrial production growth rate: 1% (1997 est.)

Electricity - production: 122.4 billion kWh (2001)

Electricity - production by source:

fossil fuel: 100%

hydro: 0%

nuclear: 0%

other: 0% (2001)

Electricity - consumption: 113.8 billion kWh (2001)

Electricity - exports: 0 kWh (2001)

Saudi Arabia *(continued)*

Electricity - imports: 0 kWh (2001)
Oil - production: 8.711 million bbl/day (2001 est.)
Oil - consumption: 1.452 million bbl/day (2001 est.)
Oil - exports: 7.92 million bbl/day (2001)
Oil - imports: NA
Oil - proved reserves: 261.7 billion bbl (1 January 2002)
Natural gas - production: 53.69 billion cu m (2001 est.)
Natural gas - consumption: 53.69 billion cu m (2001 est.)
Natural gas - exports: 0 cu m (2001 est.)
Natural gas - imports: 0 cu m (2001 est.)
Natural gas - proved reserves: 6.339 trillion cu m (1 January 2002)
Agriculture - products: wheat, barley, tomatoes, melons, dates, citrus; mutton, chickens, eggs, milk
Exports: $86.53 billion f.o.b. (2003 est.)
Exports - commodities: petroleum and petroleum products 90%
Exports - partners: US 18.9%, Japan 15.9%, South Korea 10.3%, Singapore 5.2%, China 4.7% (2002)
Imports: $30.38 billion f.o.b. (2003 est.)
Imports - commodities: machinery and equipment, foodstuffs, chemicals, motor vehicles, textiles
Imports - partners: US 11.1%, Japan 8.7%, Germany 7.5%, UK 4.9%, France 4.8%, Italy 4% (2002)
Debt - external: $24.2 billion (2003)
Economic aid - donor: pledged $100 million in 1993 to fund reconstruction of Lebanon; since 2000, Saudi Arabia has committed $307 million for assistance to the Palestinians; pledged $240 million to development in Afghanistan; pledged $1 billion in export guarantees and soft loans to Iraq
Currency: Saudi riyal (SAR)
Currency code: SAR
Exchange rates: Saudi riyals per US dollar - 3.745 (2003), 3.745 (2002), 3.745 (2001), 3.745 (2000), 3.745 (1999)
Fiscal year: calendar year

Communications

Telephones - main lines in use: 3,317,500 (2002)
Telephones - mobile cellular: 5.008 million (2002)
Telephone system:
general assessment: modern system
domestic: extensive microwave radio relay, coaxial cable, and fiber-optic cable systems
international: country code - 966; microwave radio relay to Bahrain, Jordan, Kuwait, Qatar, UAE, Yemen, and Sudan; coaxial cable to Kuwait and Jordan; submarine cable to Djibouti, Egypt and Bahrain; satellite earth stations - 5 Intelsat (3 Atlantic Ocean and 2 Indian Ocean), 1 Arabsat, and 1 Inmarsat (Indian Ocean region)
Radio broadcast stations: AM 43, FM 31, shortwave 2 (1998)
Television broadcast stations: 117 (1997)
Internet country code: .sa
Internet hosts: 14,788 (2002)
Internet users: 1,418,900 (2002)

Transportation

Railways:
total: 1,392 km
standard gauge: 1,392 km 1.435-m gauge (with branch lines and sidings) (2002)
Highways:
total: 151,470 km
paved: 45,592 km
unpaved: 105,878 km (1999)
Waterways: none
Pipelines: condensate 212 km; gas 837 km; liquid petroleum gas 1,187 km; oil 5,062 km; refined products 69 km (2003)
Ports and harbors: Ad Dammam, Al Jubayl, Duba, Jiddah, Jizan, Rabigh, Ra's al Khafji, Mishab, Ras Tanura, Yanbu' al Bahr, Madinat Yanbu' al Sinaiyah
Merchant marine:
total: 66 ships (1,000 GRT or over) 1,306,706 GRT/1,963,191 DWT
by type: cargo 5, chemical tanker 11, container 4, livestock carrier 2, passenger 1, petroleum tanker 23, refrigerated cargo 4, roll on/roll off 10, short-sea/passenger 6
foreign-owned: Egypt 3, Greece 4, Norway 2, Sudan 1, United Kingdom 3
registered in other countries: 54 (2003 est.)
Airports: 204 (2003 est.)
Airports - with paved runways:
total: 71
over 3,047 m: 32
2,438 to 3,047 m: 12
1,524 to 2,437 m: 23
914 to 1,523 m: 2
under 914 m: 2 (2003 est.)
Airports - with unpaved runways:
total: 133
over 3047 m: 1
2,438 to 3,047 m: 5
1,524 to 2,437 m: 75
914 to 1,523 m: 38
under 914 m: 14 (2003 est.)
Heliports: 5 (2003 est.)

Military

Military branches: Land Force (Army), Navy, Air Force, Air Defense Force, National Guard, Ministry of Interior Forces (paramilitary)
Military manpower - military age: 17 years of age (2004 est.)
Military manpower - availability:
males age 15-49: 8,240,714 (2004 est.)
Military manpower - fit for military service:
males age 15-49: 4,725,514 (2004 est.)
Military manpower - reaching military age annually:
males: 246,343 (2004 est.)
Military expenditures - dollar figure: $18 billion (2002)
Military expenditures - percent of GDP: 10% (2002)

Transnational Issues

Disputes - international: nomadic groups on border region with Yemen resist demarcation of boundary; Yemen protests Saudi erection of a concrete-filled pipe as a security barrier in 2004 to stem illegal cross-border activities in sections of the boundary; Kuwait and Saudi Arabia continue discussions on a maritime boundary with Iran; because the treaties have not been made public, the exact alignment of the boundary with the UAE is still unknown and labeled approximate
Illicit drugs: death penalty for traffickers; increasing consumption of heroin, cocaine, and hashish; not a major money-laundering center, improving anti-money-laundering legislation

Senegal

Introduction

Background: Independent from France in 1960, Senegal joined with The Gambia to form the nominal confederation of Senegambia in 1982. However, the envisaged integration of the two countries was never carried out, and the union was dissolved in 1989. Despite peace talks, a southern separatist group sporadically has clashed with government forces since 1982. Senegal has a long history of participating in international peacekeeping.

Geography

Location: Western Africa, bordering the North Atlantic Ocean, between Guinea-Bissau and Mauritania
Geographic coordinates: 14 00 N, 14 00 W
Map references: Africa
Area:
total: 196,190 sq km
land: 192,000 sq km
water: 4,190 sq km
Area - comparative: slightly smaller than South Dakota
Land boundaries:
total: 2,640 km
border countries: The Gambia 740 km, Guinea 330 km, Guinea-Bissau 338 km, Mali 419 km, Mauritania 813 km
Coastline: 531 km
Maritime claims:
territorial sea: 12 NM
contiguous zone: 24 NM
exclusive economic zone: 200 NM
continental shelf: 200 NM or to the edge of the continental margin
Climate: tropical; hot, humid; rainy season (May to November) has strong southeast winds; dry season (December to April) dominated by hot, dry, harmattan wind

Terrain: generally low, rolling, plains rising to foothills in southeast
Elevation extremes:
lowest point: Atlantic Ocean 0 m
highest point: unnamed feature near Nepen Diakha 581 m
Natural resources: fish, phosphates, iron ore
Land use:
arable land: 11.58%
permanent crops: 0.19%
other: 88.23% (1998 est.)
Irrigated land: 710 sq km (1998 est.)
Natural hazards: lowlands seasonally flooded; periodic droughts
Environment - current issues: wildlife populations threatened by poaching; deforestation; overgrazing; soil erosion; desertification; overfishing
Environment - international agreements:
party to: Biodiversity, Climate Change, Climate Change-Kyoto Protocol, Desertification, Endangered Species, Hazardous Wastes, Law of the Sea, Marine Life Conservation, Ozone Layer Protection, Ship Pollution, Wetlands, Whaling
Geography - note: westernmost country on the African continent; The Gambia is almost an enclave within Senegal

People

Population: 10,852,147 (July 2004 est.)
Age structure:
0-14 years: 43.2% (male 2,368,011; female 2,325,298)
15-64 years: 53.7% (male 2,803,192; female 3,025,304)
65 years and over: 3% (male 158,881; female 171,461) (2004 est.)
Median age:
total: 18 years
male: 17.4 years
female: 18.5 years (2004 est.)
Population growth rate: 2.52% (2004 est.)
Birth rate: 35.72 births/1,000 population (2004 est.)
Death rate: 10.74 deaths/1,000 population (2004 est.)
Net migration rate: 0.2 migrant(s)/1,000 population (2004 est.)
Sex ratio:
at birth: 1.03 male(s)/female
under 15 years: 1.02 male(s)/female
15-64 years: 0.93 male(s)/female
65 years and over: 0.93 male(s)/female
total population: 0.97 male(s)/female (2004 est.)
Infant mortality rate:
total: 56.53 deaths/1,000 live births
male: 60.25 deaths/1,000 live births
female: 52.71 deaths/1,000 live births (2004 est.)
Life expectancy at birth:
total population: 56.56 years
male: 54.94 years
female: 58.23 years (2004 est.)
Total fertility rate: 4.84 children born/woman (2004 est.)

HIV/AIDS - adult prevalence rate: 0.5% (2001 est.)
HIV/AIDS - people living with HIV/AIDS: 27,000 (2001 est.)
HIV/AIDS - deaths: 2,500 (2001 est.)
Nationality:
noun: Senegalese (singular and plural)
adjective: Senegalese
Ethnic groups: Wolof 43.3%, Pular 23.8%, Serer 14.7%, Jola 3.7%, Mandinka 3%, Soninke 1.1%, European and Lebanese 1%, other 9.4%
Religions: Muslim 94%, indigenous beliefs 1%, Christian 5% (mostly Roman Catholic)
Languages: French (official), Wolof, Pulaar, Jola, Mandinka
Literacy:
definition: age 15 and over can read and write
total population: 40.2%
male: 50%
female: 30.7% (2003 est.)

Government

Country name:
conventional long form: Republic of Senegal
conventional short form: Senegal
local long form: Republique du Senegal
local short form: Senegal
Government type: republic under multiparty democratic rule
Capital: Dakar
Administrative divisions: 11 regions (regions, singular - region); Dakar, Diourbel, Fatick, Kaolack, Kolda, Louga, Matam, Saint-Louis, Tambacounda, Thies, Ziguinchor
Independence: 4 April 1960 (from France); complete independence was achieved upon dissolution of federation with Mali on 20 August 1960
National holiday: Independence Day, 4 April (1960)
Constitution: a new constitution was adopted 7 January 2001
Legal system: based on French civil law system; judicial review of legislative acts in Constitutional Court; the Council of State audits the government's accounting office; has not accepted compulsory ICJ jurisdiction
Suffrage: 18 years of age; universal
Executive branch:
chief of state: President Abdoulaye WADE (since 1 April 2000)
head of government: Prime Minister Idrissa SECK (since 4 November 2002)
cabinet: Council of Ministers appointed by the prime minister in consultation with the president
elections: president elected by popular vote for a five-year term under new constitution; election last held 27 February and 19 March 2000 (next to be held 27 February 2005); prime minister appointed by the president
election results: Abdoulaye WADE elected president; percent of vote in the second round of voting - Abdoulaye WADE (PDS) 58.49%, Abdou DIOUF (PS) 41.51%

Senegal (continued)

Legislative branch: unicameral National Assembly or Assemblee Nationale (120 seats; members are elected by direct, popular vote to serve five-year terms)

note: the former National Assembly, dissolved in the spring of 2001, had 140 seats

elections: last held 29 April 2001 (next to be held NA 2006)

election results: percent of vote by party - NA%; seats by party - SOPI Coalition 89, AFP 11, PS 10, other 10

Judicial branch: Constitutional Court; Council of State; Court of Final Appeals or Cour de Cassation; Court of Appeals; note - the judicial system was reformed in 1992

Political parties and leaders: African Party for Democracy and Socialism or And Jef (also known as PADS/AJ) [Landing SAVANE, secretary general]; African Party of Independence [Majhemout DIOP]; Alliance of Forces of Progress or AFP [Moustapha NIASSE]; Democratic and Patriotic Convention or CDP (also known as Garab-Gi) [Dr. Iba Der THIAM]; Democratic League-Labor Party Movement or LD-MPT [Dr. Abdoulaye BATHILY]; Front for Socialism and Democracy or FSD [Cheikh Abdoulaye DIEYE]; Gainde Centrist Bloc or BGC [Jean-Paul DIAS]; Independence and Labor Party or PIT [Amath DANSOKHO]; National Democratic Rally or RND [Madier DIOUF]; Senegalese Democratic Party or PDS [Abdoulaye WADE]; Socialist Party or PS [Ousmane Tanor DIENG]; SOPI Coalition (a coalition led by the PDS) [Abdoulaye WADE]; Union for Democratic Renewal or URD [Djibo Leyti KA]; other small parties

Political pressure groups and leaders: labor; Muslim brotherhoods; students; teachers

International organization participation: ACCT, ACP, AfDB, AU, ECOWAS, FAO, FZ, G-15, G-77, IAEA, IBRD, ICAO, ICC, ICCt, ICFTU, ICRM, IDA, IDB, IFAD, IFC, IFRCS, ILO, IMF, IMO, Interpol, IOC, IOM, ISO (correspondent), ITU, MICAH, MONUC, NAM, OIC, OPCW, PCA, UN, UNCTAD, UNESCO, UNIDO, UNMIK, UNMIL, UNMOVIC, UPU, WADB (regional), WAEMU, WCL, WCO, WFTU, WHO, WIPO, WMO, WToO, WTrO

Diplomatic representation in the US:

chief of mission: Ambassador Amadou Lamine BA

chancery: 2112 Wyoming Avenue NW, Washington, DC 20008

telephone: [1] (202) 234-0540

FAX: [1] (202) 332-6315

consulate(s) general: New York

Diplomatic representation from the US:

chief of mission: Ambassador Harriet L. ELAM-THOMAS

embassy: Avenue Jean XXIII at the corner of Rue Kleber, Dakar

mailing address: B. P. 49, Dakar

telephone: [221] 823-4296

FAX: [221] 822-2991

Flag description: three equal vertical bands of green (hoist side), yellow, and red with a small green five-pointed star centered in the yellow band; uses the popular pan-African colors of Ethiopia

Economy

Economy - overview: In January 1994, Senegal undertook a bold and ambitious economic reform program with the support of the international donor community. This reform began with a 50% devaluation of Senegal's currency, the CFA franc, which was linked at a fixed rate to the French franc. Government price controls and subsidies have been steadily dismantled. After seeing its economy contract by 2.1% in 1993, Senegal made an important turnaround, thanks to the reform program, with real growth in GDP averaging 5% annually during 1995-2003. Annual inflation had been pushed down to the low single digits. As a member of the West African Economic and Monetary Union (WAEMU), Senegal is working toward greater regional integration with a unified external tariff. Senegal also realized full Internet connectivity in 1996, creating a miniboom in information technology-based services. Private activity now accounts for 82% of GDP. On the negative side, Senegal faces deep-seated urban problems of chronic unemployment, trade union militancy, juvenile delinquency, and drug addiction.

GDP: purchasing power parity - $16.93 billion (2003 est.)

GDP - real growth rate: 4.5% (2003 est.)

GDP - per capita: purchasing power parity - $1,600 (2003 est.)

GDP - composition by sector:

agriculture: 18%

industry: 27%

services: 55% (2001 est.)

Population below poverty line: 54% (2001 est.)

Household income or consumption by percentage share:

lowest 10%: 2.6%

highest 10%: 33.5% (1995)

Distribution of family income - Gini index: 41.3 (1995)

Inflation rate (consumer prices): 3% (2002 est.)

Labor force: NA (2001 est.)

Labor force - by occupation: agriculture 70%

Unemployment rate: 48% (urban youth 40%) (2001 est.)

Budget:

revenues: $1.373 billion

expenditures: $1.373 billion, including capital expenditures of $357 million (2002 est.)

Industries: agricultural and fish processing, phosphate mining, fertilizer production, petroleum refining, construction materials

Industrial production growth rate: 8.1% (2002 est.)

Electricity - production: 1.518 billion kWh (2001)

Electricity - production by source:

fossil fuel: 100%

hydro: 0%

nuclear: 0%

other: 0% (2001)

Electricity - consumption: 1.412 billion kWh (2001)

Electricity - exports: 0 kWh (2001)

Electricity - imports: 0 kWh (2001)

Oil - production: 0 bbl/day (2001 est.)

Oil - consumption: 31,000 bbl/day (2001 est.)

Oil - exports: NA

Oil - imports: NA

Natural gas - production: 50 million cu m (2001 est.)

Natural gas - consumption: 50 million cu m (2001 est.)

Natural gas - exports: 0 cu m (2001 est.)

Natural gas - imports: 0 cu m (2001 est.)

Agriculture - products: peanuts, millet, corn, sorghum, rice, cotton, tomatoes, green vegetables; cattle, poultry, pigs; fish

Exports: $1.23 billion f.o.b. (2003 est.)

Exports - commodities: fish, groundnuts (peanuts), petroleum products, phosphates, cotton

Exports - partners: India 20.8%, France 13%, Mali 8.9%, Greece 7.7%, Italy 4.4% (2002)

Imports: $1.753 billion f.o.b. (2003 est.)

Imports - commodities: foods and beverages, capital goods, fuels

Imports - partners: France 25.5%, Nigeria 8.7%, Thailand 7.2%, US 5.4%, Germany 5.4%, Italy 4.5%, Spain 4% (2002)

Debt - external: $3 billion (2003 est.)

Economic aid - recipient: $362.6 million (2002 est.)

Currency: Communaute Financiere Africaine franc (XOF); note - responsible authority is the Central Bank of the West African States

Currency code: XOF

Exchange rates: Communaute Financiere Africaine francs (XOF) per US dollar - 581.2 (2003), 696.988 (2002), 733.039 (2001), 711.976 (2000), 615.699 (1999)

Fiscal year: calendar year

Communications

Telephones - main lines in use: 224,600 (2002)

Telephones - mobile cellular: 553,400 (2002)

Telephone system:

general assessment: good system

domestic: above-average urban system; microwave radio relay, coaxial cable and fiber-optic cable in trunk system

international: country code - 221; 4 submarine cables; satellite earth station - 1 Intelsat (Atlantic Ocean)

Radio broadcast stations: AM 8, FM 20, shortwave 1 (2001)

Television broadcast stations: 1 (1997)

Internet country code: .sn

Internet hosts: 761 (2002)

Internet users: 105,000 (2002)

Transportation

Railways:

total: 906 km

narrow gauge: 906 km 1.000-meter gauge (2002)

Highways:

total: 14,576 km

paved: 4,271 km including 7 km of expressways

unpaved: 10,305 km (2000)

Senegal (continued)

Waterways: 897 km
note: 785 km on the Senegal river, and 112 km on the Saloum river
Pipelines: gas 564 km (2003)
Ports and harbors: Dakar, Kaolack, Matam, Podor, Richard Toll, Saint-Louis, Ziguinchor
Airports: 20 (2003 est.)
Airports - with paved runways:
total: 9
over 3,047 m: 1
1,524 to 2,437 m: 6
914 to 1,523 m: 2 (2003 est.)
Airports - with unpaved runways:
total: 11
1,524 to 2,437 m: 6
914 to 1,523 m: 4
under 914 m: 1 (2003 est.)

Military

Military branches: Army, Navy, Air Force, National Gendarmerie, National Police (Surete Nationale)
Military manpower - military age: 18 years of age (2004 est.)
Military manpower - availability:
males age 15-49: 2,490,290 (2004 est.)
Military manpower - fit for military service:
males age 15-49: 1,301,761 (2004 est.)
Military manpower - reaching military age annually:
males: 119,833 (2004 est.)
Military expenditures - dollar figure: $95.8 million (2003)
Military expenditures - percent of GDP: 1.5% (2003)

Transnational Issues

Disputes - international: The Gambia and Guinea-Bissau attempt to stem refugees, cross border raids, arms smuggling, and political instability from a separatist movement in Senegal's Casamance region
Illicit drugs: transshipment point for Southwest and Southeast Asian heroin moving to Europe and North America; illicit cultivator of cannabis

Serbia and Montenegro

Introduction

Background: The Kingdom of Serbs, Croats, and Slovenes was formed in 1918; its name was changed to Yugoslavia in 1929. Occupation by Nazi Germany in 1941 was resisted by various paramilitary bands that fought each other as well as the invaders. The group headed by Marshal TITO took full control upon German expulsion in 1945. Although Communist, his new government and its successors (he died in 1980) managed to steer their own path between the Warsaw Pact nations and the West for the next four and a half decades. In the early 1990s, post-TITO Yugoslavia began to unravel along ethnic lines: Slovenia, Croatia, The Former Yugoslav Republic of Macedonia, and Bosnia and Herzegovina were recognized as independent states in 1992. The remaining republics of Serbia and Montenegro declared a new "Federal Republic of Yugoslavia" (FRY) in April 1992 and, under President Slobodan MILOSEVIC, Serbia led various military intervention efforts to unite ethnic Serbs in neighboring republics into a "Greater Serbia." All of these efforts were ultimately unsuccessful. In 1999, massive expulsions by FRY forces and Serb paramilitaries of ethnic Albanians living in Kosovo provoked an international response, including the NATO bombing of Serbia and the stationing of NATO, Russian, and other peacekeepers in Kosovo. Federal elections in the fall of 2000, brought about the ouster of MILOSEVIC and installed Vojislav KOSTUNICA as president. The arrest of MILOSEVIC in 2001 allowed for his subsequent transfer to the International Criminal Tribunal for the Former Yugoslavia in The Hague to be tried for crimes against humanity. In 2001, the country's suspension was lifted, and it was once more accepted into UN organizations under the name of Yugoslavia. Kosovo has been governed by the UN Interim Administration Mission in Kosovo (UNMIK) since June 1999, under the authority of UN Security Council Resolution 1244. In 2002, the Serbian and Montenegrin components of Yugoslavia began negotiations to forge a looser relationship.

These talks became a reality in February 2003 when lawmakers restructured the country into a loose federation of two republics called Serbia and Montenegro. An agreement was also reached to permit a referendum in each republic in three years on full independence.

Geography

Location: Southeastern Europe, bordering the Adriatic Sea, between Albania and Bosnia and Herzegovina
Geographic coordinates: 44 00 N, 21 00 E
Map references: Europe
Area:
total: 102,350 sq km
land: 102,136 sq km
water: 214 sq km
Area - comparative: slightly smaller than Kentucky
Land boundaries:
total: 2,246 km
border countries: Albania 287 km, Bosnia and Herzegovina 527 km, Bulgaria 318 km, Croatia (north) 241 km, Croatia (south) 25 km, Hungary 151 km, The Former Yugoslav Republic of Macedonia 221 km, Romania 476 km
Coastline: 199 km
Maritime claims: NA
Climate: in the north, continental climate (cold winters and hot, humid summers with well distributed rainfall); central portion, continental and Mediterranean climate; to the south, Adriatic climate along the coast, hot, dry summers and autumns and relatively cold winters with heavy snowfall inland
Terrain: extremely varied; to the north, rich fertile plains; to the east, limestone ranges and basins; to the southeast, ancient mountains and hills; to the southwest, extremely high shoreline with no islands off the coast
Elevation extremes:
lowest point: Adriatic Sea 0 m
highest point: Daravica 2,656 m
Natural resources: oil, gas, coal, antimony, copper, lead, zinc, nickel, gold, pyrite, chrome, hydropower, arable land
Land use:
arable land: 36.34%
permanent crops: 3.44%
other: 60.22% (1998 est.)
Irrigated land: 570 sq km
Natural hazards: destructive earthquakes
Environment - current issues: pollution of coastal waters from sewage outlets, especially in tourist-related areas such as Kotor; air pollution around Belgrade and other industrial cities; water pollution from industrial wastes dumped into the Sava which flows into the Danube
Environment - international agreements:
party to: Air Pollution, Biodiversity, Climate Change, Endangered Species, Hazardous Wastes, Law of the Sea, Marine Dumping, Marine Life Conservation, Ozone Layer Protection, Ship Pollution, Wetlands

Serbia and Montenegro (continued)

signed, but not ratified: none of the selected agreements

Geography - note: controls one of the major land routes from Western Europe to Turkey and the Near East; strategic location along the Adriatic coast

People

Population: 10,825,900 (July 2004 est.)
Age structure:
0-14 years: 18.3% (male 1,027,479; female 956,681)
15-64 years: 66.8% (male 3,602,959; female 3,627,616)
65 years and over: 14.9% (male 693,929; female 917,236) (2004 est.)
Median age:
total: 36.6 years
male: 35.1 years
female: 38.1 years (2004 est.)
Population growth rate: 0.03% (2004 est.)
Birth rate: 12.13 births/1,000 population (2004 est.)
Death rate: 10.53 deaths/1,000 population (2004 est.)
Net migration rate: -1.33 migrant(s)/1,000 population (2004 est.)
Sex ratio:
at birth: 1.08 male(s)/female
under 15 years: 1.07 male(s)/female
15-64 years: 0.99 male(s)/female
65 years and over: 0.76 male(s)/female
total population: 0.97 male(s)/female (2004 est.)
Infant mortality rate:
total: 13.43 deaths/1,000 live births
male: 15.04 deaths/1,000 live births
female: 11.68 deaths/1,000 live births (2004 est.)
Life expectancy at birth:
total population: 74.4 years
male: 71.9 years
female: 77.12 years (2004 est.)
Total fertility rate: 1.67 children born/woman (2004 est.)
HIV/AIDS - adult prevalence rate: 0.2% (2001 est.)
HIV/AIDS - people living with HIV/AIDS: 10,000 (2001 est.)
HIV/AIDS - deaths: less than 100 (2001 est.)
Nationality:
noun: Serb(s); Montenegrin(s)
adjective: Serbian; Montenegrin
Ethnic groups: Serb 62.6%, Albanian 16.5%, Montenegrin 5%, Hungarian 3.3%, other 12.6% (1991)
Religions: Orthodox 65%, Muslim 19%, Roman Catholic 4%, Protestant 1%, other 11%
Languages: Serbian 95%, Albanian 5%
Literacy:
definition: age 15 and over can read and write
total population: 93%
male: 97.2%
female: 88.9% (1991)

Government

Country name:
conventional long form: Serbia and Montenegro
conventional short form: none
local long form: Srbija i Crna Gora
local short form: none
abbreviation: SCG
Government type: republic
Capital: Belgrade
Administrative divisions: 2 republics (republike, singular - republika); and 2 nominally autonomous provinces* (autonomn pokrajine, singular - autonomna pokrajina); Kosovo*, Montenegro, Serbia, Vojvodina*
Independence: 27 April 1992 (Federal Republic of Yugoslavia or FRY - now Serbia and Montenegro - formed as self-proclaimed successor to the Socialist Federal Republic of Yugoslavia or SFRY)
National holiday: National Day, 27 April
Constitution: 4 February 2003
Legal system: based on civil law system
Suffrage: 16 years of age, if employed; 18 years of age, universal
Executive branch:
chief of state: President Svetozar MAROVIC (since 7 March 2003); note - the president is both the chief of state and head of government
head of government: President Svetozar MAROVIC (since 7 March 2003); note - the president is both the chief of state and head of government
cabinet: Federal Ministries act as Cabinet
elections: president elected by the Parliament for a four-year term; election last held 7 March 2003 (next to be held NA 2007); prime minister appointed by the president
election results: Svetozar MAROVIC elected president by the Parliament; vote was Svetozar MAROVIC 65, other 47
Legislative branch: unicameral Parliament (126 seats - 91 Serbian, 35 Montenegrin - filled by nominees of the two state parliaments for the first two years, after which the president will call for public elections
elections: last held 25 February 2003 (next to be held NA 2005)
election results: percent of vote by party - NA%; seats by party - DOS 37, DLECG 19, DSS 17, ZP 14, SPS 12, SRS 8, SDP 5, SSJ 5, other 9
Judicial branch: Federal Court or Savezni Sud; Constitutional Court; judges for both courts are elected by the Federal Assembly for nine-year terms
note: since the promulgation of the 2003 Constitution, the Federal Court has constitutional and administrative functions; it has an equal number of judges from each republic
Political parties and leaders: Democratic Opposition of Serbia or DOS (a coalition of many small parties including DSS; it disbanded in November 2003) [leader NA]; Alliance of Vojvodina Hungarians or SVM [Jozsef KASZA]; Democratic League of Kosovo or LDK [Dr. Ibrahim RUGOVA,

president]; Democratic List for European Montenegro or DLECG [Milo DJUKANOVIC, Ranko KRIVOKAPIC]; Democratic Party or DS [collective interim leadership led by Cedomir JOVANOVIC]; Democratic Party of Serbia or DSS [Vojislav KOSTUNICA]; Democratic Party of Socialists of Montenegro or DPS [Milo DJUKANOVIC]; G17+ [Miroljub LABUS]; Party of Serb Unity or SSJ [Borislav PELEVIC]; Serbian Radical Party or SRS [Tomislav NIKOLIC]; Serbian Socialist Party or SPS (former Communist Party and party of Slobodan MILOSEVIC) [Zoran ANDJELKOVIC, general secretary]; Social Democratic Party or SDP [Rasim LJAJIC]
Political pressure groups and leaders: Otpor Student Resistance Movement [leader NA]; Political Council for Presevo, Meveda and Bujanovac or PCPMB [leader NA]
International organization participation: CE, CEI, EBRD, FAO, G- 9, G-77, IAEA, IBRD, ICAO, ICC, ICCt, ICFTU, ICRM, IDA, IFAD, IFC, IFRCS, IHO, ILO, IMF, IMO, Interpol, IOC, IOM, ISO, ITU, MONUC, NAM, OAS (observer), OPCW, OSCE, PCA, UN, UNCTAD, UNESCO, UNHCR, UNIDO, UNMISET, UPU, WCL, WCO, WHO, WIPO, WMO, WToO, WTrO (observer)
Diplomatic representation in the US:
chief of mission: Ambassador Ivan VUJACIC
chancery: 2134 Kalorama Road NW, Washington, DC 20008
telephone: [1] (202) 332-0333
FAX: [1] (202) 332-3933
consulate(s) general: Chicago
Diplomatic representation from the US:
chief of mission: Ambassador (vacant); Charge d'Affaires Roderick W. MOORE; note - Michael C. POLT to become ambassador
embassy: Kneza Milosa 50, 11000 Belgrade
mailing address: 5070 Belgrade Place, Washington, DC 20521-5070
telephone: [381] (11) 361-9344
FAX: [381] (11) 361-8230
consulate(s): Podgornica
Flag description: three equal horizontal bands of blue (top), white, and red

Economy

Economy - overview: MILOSEVIC-era mismanagement of the economy, an extended period of economic sanctions, and the damage to Yugoslavia's infrastructure and industry during the NATO airstrikes in 1999 have left the economy only half the size it was in 1990. After the ousting of former Federal Yugoslav President MILOSEVIC in October 2000, the Democratic Opposition of Serbia (DOS) coalition government implemented stabilization measures and embarked on an aggressive market reform program. After renewing its membership in the IMF in December 2000, Yugoslavia continued to reintegrate into the international community by rejoining the World Bank (IBRD) and the European Bank for Reconstruction and Development (EBRD). A

Serbia and Montenegro *(continued)*

World Bank-European Commission sponsored Donors' Conference held in June 2001 raised $1.3 billion for economic restructuring. An agreement rescheduling the country's $4.5 billion Paris Club government debts was concluded in November 2001; it wrote off 66% of the debt. The smaller republic of Montenegro severed its economy from federal control and from Serbia during the MILOSEVIC era and continues to maintain its own central bank, uses the euro instead of the Yugoslav dinar as official currency, collects customs tariffs, and manages its own budget. Kosovo, while technically still part of the Federal Republic of Yugoslavia (now Serbia and Montenegro) according to United Nations Security Council Resolution 1244, is largely autonomous under United Nations Interim Administration Mission in Kosovo (UNMIK) and is greatly dependent on the international community and the diaspora for financial and technical assistance. The euro and the Yugoslav dinar are official currencies, and UNMIK collects taxes and manages the budget. The complexity of Serbia and Montenegro political relationships, slow progress in privatization, legal uncertainty over property rights, and scarcity of foreign-investment are holding back Serbia and Montenegro's economy. Arrangements with the IMF, especially requirements for fiscal discipline, are an important element in policy formation. Severe unemployment remains a key political economic problem.

GDP: purchasing power parity - $24.01 billion (2003 est.)

GDP - real growth rate: 2% (2003 est.)

GDP - per capita: purchasing power parity - $2,300 (2003 est.)

GDP - composition by sector:
agriculture: 26%
industry: 36%
services: 38% (2001 est.)

Population below poverty line: 30% (1999 est.)

Household income or consumption by percentage share:
lowest 10%: NA%
highest 10%: NA%

Inflation rate (consumer prices): 11.6% (2003 est.)

Labor force: 3 million (2001 est.)

Labor force - by occupation: agriculture NA%, industry NA%, services NA%

Unemployment rate: 34.5% (2003 est.)

Budget:
revenues: $3.9 billion
expenditures: $4.3 billion, including capital expenditures of $NA (2001 est.)

Industries: machine building (aircraft, trucks, and automobiles; tanks and weapons; electrical equipment; agricultural machinery); metallurgy (steel, aluminum, copper, lead, zinc, chromium, antimony, bismuth, cadmium); mining (coal, bauxite, nonferrous ore, iron ore, limestone); consumer goods (textiles, footwear, foodstuffs, appliances); electronics, petroleum products, chemicals, and pharmaceuticals

Industrial production growth rate: 1.7% (2002 est.)

Electricity - production: 31.71 billion kWh (2001)

Electricity - production by source:
fossil fuel: 62.9%
hydro: 37.1%
nuclear: 0%
other: 0% (2001)

Electricity - consumption: 32.37 billion kWh (2001)

Electricity - exports: 446 million kWh (2001)

Electricity - imports: 3.33 billion kWh (2001)

Oil - production: 15,000 bbl/day (2001 est.)

Oil - consumption: 64,000 bbl/day (2001 est.)

Oil - exports: NA

Oil - imports: NA

Oil - proved reserves: 38.75 million bbl (1 January 2002)

Natural gas - production: 602 million cu m (2001 est.)

Natural gas - consumption: 602 million cu m (2001 est.)

Natural gas - exports: 0 cu m (2001 est.)

Natural gas - imports: 0 cu m (2001 est.)

Natural gas - proved reserves: 24.07 billion cu m (1 January 2002)

Agriculture - products: cereals, fruits, vegetables, tobacco, olives; cattle, sheep, goats

Exports: $2.667 billion f.o.b. (2003 est.)

Exports - commodities: manufactured goods, food and live animals, raw materials

Exports - partners: Italy 32.5%, Germany 20.5%, Greece 7.1%, Austria 6.2%, France 4.7% (2002)

Imports: $7.144 billion f.o.b. (2003 est.)

Imports - commodities: machinery and transport equipment, fuels and lubricants, manufactured goods, chemicals, food and live animals, raw materials

Imports - partners: Germany 19.8%, Italy 17.8%, Austria 8.4%, Slovenia 7.9%, Greece 4.3%, France 4.3%, Bulgaria 4.1% (2002)

Debt - external: $12.8 billion (2003 est.)

Economic aid - recipient: $2 billion pledged in 2001 (disbursements to follow for several years)

Currency: new Yugoslav dinar (YUM); note - in Montenegro the euro is legal tender; in Kosovo both the euro and the Yugoslav dinar are legal (2002)

Currency code: YUM

Exchange rates: new Yugoslav dinars per US dollar - official rate: 65 (2002)

Fiscal year: calendar year

Communications

Telephones - main lines in use: 2.493 million (2002)

Telephones - mobile cellular: 2,750,400 (2002)

Telephone system:
general assessment: NA
domestic: NA
international: country code - 381; satellite earth station - 1 Intelsat (Atlantic Ocean)

Radio broadcast stations: AM 113, FM 194, shortwave 2 (1998)

Television broadcast stations: more than 771 (including 86 strong stations and 685 low-power stations, plus 20 repeaters in the principal networks; also numerous local or private stations in Serbia and Vojvodina) (1997)

Internet country code: .yu

Internet hosts: 16,972 (2002)

Internet users: 640,000 (2002)

Transportation

Railways:
total: 4,059 km
standard gauge: 4,059 km 1.435-m gauge (1,364 km electrified) (2002)

Highways:
total: 49,805 km
paved: 31,029 km (including 560 km of expressways)
unpaved: 18,776 km (2000)

Waterways: 587 km
note: the Danube River, central Europe's connection to the Black Sea, runs through Serbia; since early 2000, a pontoon bridge, replacing a destroyed conventional bridge, has obstructed river traffic at Novi Sad; the obstruction is bypassed by a canal system, but the inadequate lock size limits the size of vessels which may pass; the pontoon bridge can be opened for large ships but has slowed river traffic (2001)

Pipelines: gas 3,177 km; oil 393 km (2003)

Ports and harbors: Bar, Belgrade, Kotor, Novi Sad, Pancevo, Tivat, Zelenika

Airports: 45 (2003 est.)

Airports - with paved runways:
total: 19
over 3,047 m: 2
2,438 to 3,047 m: 5
1,524 to 2,437 m: 6
914 to 1,523 m: 2
under 914 m: 4 (2003 est.)

Airports - with unpaved runways:
total: 26
1,524 to 2,437 m: 2
914 to 1,523 m: 12
under 914 m: 12 (2003 est.)

Heliports: 4 (2003 est.)

Military

Military branches: Army (VJ) (including ground forces with border troops, naval forces, air and air defense forces)

Military manpower - military age: 19 years of age (nine months compulsory service) (2004)

Military manpower - availability:
males age 15-49: 2,718,234 (2004 est.)

Military manpower - fit for military service:
males age 15-49: 2,184,937 (2004 est.)

Military manpower - reaching military age annually:
males: 81,245 (2004 est.)

Military expenditures - dollar figure: $654 million (2002)

Military expenditures - percent of GDP: NA

Serbia and Montenegro (continued)

Transnational Issues

Disputes - international: the future status of Kosovo remains an unresolved issue in South Central Europe with Kosovo Albanians overwhelmingly supporting and Serbian officials opposing Kosovo independence; the international community has agreed to begin a process to determine final status only after significant progress has been made in solidifying multi-ethnic democracy in Kosovo as outlined in the policy of "standards before status"; the Contact group (including the US, UK, France, Germany, Italy, and Russia) will review progress on the UNMIK standard around mid-2005; ethnic Albanians in Kosovo resist demarcation of the F.Y.R.O.M. boundary in accordance with the 2000 delimitation treaty, which transfers on net a small amount of land to F.Y.R.O.M.; Serbia and Montenegro have delimited about half of the boundary with Bosnia and Herzegovina, but sections along the Drina River remain in dispute

Illicit drugs: transshipment point for Southwest Asian heroin moving to Western Europe on the Balkan route; economy vulnerable to money laundering

Seychelles

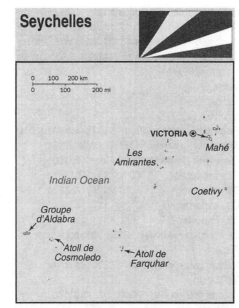

Introduction

Background: A lengthy struggle between France and Great Britain for the islands ended in 1814, when they were ceded to the latter. Independence came in 1976. Socialist rule was brought to a close with a new constitution and free elections in 1993. The most recent presidential elections were held 31 August-2 September 2001. President RENE, who has served since 1977, was re-elected.

Geography

Location: Eastern Africa, group of islands in the Indian Ocean, northeast of Madagascar
Geographic coordinates: 4 35 S, 55 40 E
Map references: Africa
Area:
total: 455 sq km
land: 455 sq km
water: 0 sq km
Area - comparative: 2.5 times the size of Washington, DC
Land boundaries: 0 km
Coastline: 491 km
Maritime claims:
territorial sea: 12 NM
contiguous zone: 24 NM
exclusive economic zone: 200 NM
continental shelf: 200 NM or to the edge of the continental margin
Climate: tropical marine; humid; cooler season during southeast monsoon (late May to September); warmer season during northwest monsoon (March to May)
Terrain: Mahe Group is granitic, narrow coastal strip, rocky, hilly; others are coral, flat, elevated reefs
Elevation extremes:
lowest point: Indian Ocean 0 m
highest point: Morne Seychellois 905 m
Natural resources: fish, copra, cinnamon trees

Land use:
arable land: 2.22%
permanent crops: 13.33%
other: 84.45% (1998 est.)
Irrigated land: NA sq km
Natural hazards: lies outside the cyclone belt, so severe storms are rare; short droughts possible
Environment - current issues: water supply depends on catchments to collect rainwater
Environment - international agreements:
party to: Biodiversity, Climate Change, Climate Change-Kyoto Protocol, Desertification, Endangered Species, Hazardous Wastes, Law of the Sea, Marine Dumping, Ozone Layer Protection, Ship Pollution
signed, but not ratified: none of the selected agreements
Geography - note: 40 granitic and about 50 coralline islands

People

Population: 80,832 (July 2004 est.)
Age structure:
0-14 years: 26.9% (male 10,987; female 10,717)
15-64 years: 66.9% (male 26,380; female 27,731)
65 years and over: 6.2% (male 1,638; female 3,379) (2004 est.)
Median age:
total: 27.3 years
male: 26.2 years
female: 28.4 years (2004 est.)
Population growth rate: 0.45% (2004 est.)
Birth rate: 16.55 births/1,000 population (2004 est.)
Death rate: 6.41 deaths/1,000 population (2004 est.)
Net migration rate: -5.69 migrant(s)/1,000 population (2004 est.)
Sex ratio:
at birth: 1.03 male(s)/female
under 15 years: 1.03 male(s)/female
15-64 years: 0.95 male(s)/female
65 years and over: 0.49 male(s)/female
total population: 0.93 male(s)/female (2004 est.)
Infant mortality rate:
total: 15.97 deaths/1,000 live births
male: 20.2 deaths/1,000 live births
female: 11.61 deaths/1,000 live births (2004 est.)
Life expectancy at birth:
total population: 71.53 years
male: 66.1 years
female: 77.14 years (2004 est.)
Total fertility rate: 1.77 children born/woman (2004 est.)
HIV/AIDS - adult prevalence rate: NA%
HIV/AIDS - people living with HIV/AIDS: NA
HIV/AIDS - deaths: NA
Nationality:
noun: Seychellois (singular and plural)
adjective: Seychellois
Ethnic groups: mixed French, African, Indian, Chinese, and Arab
Religions: Roman Catholic 86.6%, Anglican 6.8%, other Christian 2.5%, other 4.1%

Seychelles (continued)

Languages: English (official), French (official), Creole

Literacy:

definition: age 15 and over can read and write

total population: 58%

male: 56%

female: 60% (1971 est.)

Government

Country name:

conventional long form: Republic of Seychelles

conventional short form: Seychelles

Government type: republic

Capital: Victoria

Administrative divisions: 23 administrative districts; Anse aux Pins, Anse Boileau, Anse Etoile, Anse Louis, Anse Royale, Baie Lazare, Baie Sainte Anne, Beau Vallon, Bel Air, Bel Ombre, Cascade, Glacis, Grand' Anse (on Mahe), Grand' Anse (on Praslin), La Digue, La Riviere Anglaise, Mont Buxton, Mont Fleuri, Plaisance, Pointe La Rue, Port Glaud, Saint Louis, Takamaka

Independence: 29 June 1976 (from UK)

National holiday: Constitution Day (National Day), 18 June (1993)

Constitution: 18 June 1993

Legal system: based on English common law, French civil law, and customary law

Suffrage: 17 years of age; universal

Executive branch:

chief of state: President France Albert RENE (since 5 June 1977); note - the president is both the chief of state and head of government

head of government: President France Albert RENE (since 5 June 1977); note - the president is both the chief of state and head of government

cabinet: Council of Ministers appointed by the president

elections: president elected by popular vote for a five-year term; election last held 31 August-2 September 2001 (next to be held NA 2006)

election results: France Albert RENE re-elected president; percent of vote - France Albert RENE (SPPF) 54.19%, Wavel RAMKALAWAN (UO) 44.95%, Philippe BOULLE 0.86%; note - the first time that presidential elections have been held separately from legislative elections

Legislative branch: unicameral National Assembly or Assemblee Nationale (34 seats - 25 elected by popular vote, 9 allocated on a proportional basis to parties winning at least 10% of the vote; members serve five-year terms)

elections: last held 4-6 December 2002 (next held by 2007)

election results: percent of vote by party - SPPF 54.3%, SNP 42.6%, DP 3.1%; seats by party - SPPF 23, SNP 11

note: the 9 awarded seats are apportioned according to the percentage that each party won of the total vote

Judicial branch: Court of Appeal; Supreme Court; judges for both courts are appointed by the president

Political parties and leaders: Democratic Party or DP [James MANCHAM, Daniel BELLE]; Mouvement Seychellois pour la Democratie [Jacques HODOUL]; Seychelles National Party or SNP (formerly the United Opposition or UO) [Wavel RAMKALAWAN]; Seychelles People's Progressive Front or SPPF [France Albert RENE, James MICHEL] - the governing party

Political pressure groups and leaders: Roman Catholic Church; trade unions

International organization participation: ACCT, ACP, AfDB, AU, C, FAO, G-77, IAEA, IBRD, ICAO, ICCt (signatory), ICFTU, ICRM, IFAD, IFC, IFRCS, ILO, IMF, IMO, InOC, Interpol, IOC, ISO (correspondent), ITU, NAM, OPCW, SADC, UN, UNCTAD, UNESCO, UNIDO, UPU, WCO, WHO, WIPO, WMO, WToO, WTrO (observer)

Diplomatic representation in the US:

chief of mission: Ambassador Claude Sylvestre MOREL

chancery: 800 Second Avenue, Suite 400C, New York, NY 10017

telephone: [1] (212) 972-1785

FAX: [1] (212) 972-1786

Diplomatic representation from the US: the US does not have an embassy in Seychelles; the ambassador to Mauritius is accredited to the Seychelles

Flag description: five oblique bands of blue (hoist side), yellow, red, white, and green (bottom) radiating from the bottom of the hoist side

Economy

Economy - overview: Since independence in 1976, per capita output in this Indian Ocean archipelago has expanded to roughly seven times the old near-subsistence level. Growth has been led by the tourist sector, which employs about 30% of the labor force and provides more than 70% of hard currency earnings, and by tuna fishing. In recent years the government has encouraged foreign investment in order to upgrade hotels and other services. At the same time, the government has moved to reduce the dependence on tourism by promoting the development of farming, fishing, and small-scale manufacturing. A sharp drop illustrated the vulnerability of the tourist sector in 1991-92 due largely to the Gulf war, and once again following the 11 September 2001 terrorist attacks on the US. Other issues facing the government are the curbing of the budget deficit, including the containment of social welfare costs, and further privatization of public enterprises. Growth slowed in 1998-2002, due to sluggish tourist and tuna sectors. Also, tight controls on exchange rates and the scarcity of foreign exchange have impaired short-term economic prospects. The black market value of the Seychelles rupee is half the official exchange rate; without a devaluation of the currency the tourist sector should remain sluggish as vacationers seek cheaper destinations such as Comoros, Mauritius, and Madagascar.

GDP: purchasing power parity - $626 million (2002 est.)

GDP - real growth rate: 1.5% (2002 est.)

GDP - per capita: purchasing power parity - $7,800 (2002 est.)

GDP - composition by sector:

agriculture: 2.4%

industry: 24.4%

services: 73.2% (2000)

Population below poverty line: NA%

Household income or consumption by percentage share:

lowest 10%: NA%

highest 10%: NA%

Inflation rate (consumer prices): 0.5% (2002 est.)

Labor force: 30,900 (1996)

Labor force - by occupation: industry 19%, services 71%, agriculture 10% (1989)

Unemployment rate: NA%

Budget:

revenues: $249 million

expenditures: $262 million, including capital expenditures of $NA (1998 est.)

Industries: fishing; tourism; processing of coconuts and vanilla, coir (coconut fiber) rope, boat building, printing, furniture; beverages

Industrial production growth rate: NA%

Electricity - production: 160 million kWh (2001)

Electricity - production by source:

fossil fuel: 100%

hydro: 0%

nuclear: 0%

other: 0% (2001)

Electricity - consumption: 148.8 million kWh (2001)

Electricity - exports: 0 kWh (2001)

Electricity - imports: 0 kWh (2001)

Oil - production: 0 bbl/day (2001 est.)

Oil - consumption: 4,000 bbl/day (2001 est.)

Oil - exports: NA

Oil - imports: NA

Agriculture - products: coconuts, cinnamon, vanilla, sweet potatoes, cassava (tapioca), bananas; broiler chickens; tuna fish

Exports: $250 million f.o.b. (2003 est.)

Exports - commodities: canned tuna, frozen fish, cinnamon bark, copra, petroleum products (reexports)

Exports - partners: UK 24.4%, France 17%, Mauritius 8.6%, Italy 7.5%, US 7.2%, Germany 6.6%, Japan 5.7%, Netherlands 5.7%, Spain 5.7%, Thailand 5.5% (2002)

Imports: $383.7 million f.o.b. (2003 est.)

Imports - commodities: machinery and equipment, foodstuffs, petroleum products, chemicals

Imports - partners: Saudi Arabia 14.8%, France 12.2%, South Africa 10.9%, Spain 9.4%, Italy 9.1%, Singapore 6.8%, UK 5.7% (2002)

Debt - external: $170 million (2002 est.)

Economic aid - recipient: $16.4 million (1995)

Currency: Seychelles rupee (SCR)

Currency code: SCR

Seychelles *(continued)*

Exchange rates: Seychelles rupees per US dollar - 5.4007 (2003), 5.48 (2002), 5.8575 (2001), 5.7138 (2000), 5.3426 (1999)
Fiscal year: calendar year

Telephones - main lines in use: 21,700 (2002)
Telephones - mobile cellular: 44,700 (2002)
Telephone system:
general assessment: effective system
domestic: radiotelephone communications between islands in the archipelago
international: country code - 248; direct radiotelephone communications with adjacent island countries and African coastal countries; satellite earth station - 1 Intelsat (Indian Ocean)
Radio broadcast stations: AM 1, FM 1, shortwave 2 (1998)
Television broadcast stations: 2 (plus 9 repeaters) (1997)
Internet country code: .sc
Internet hosts: 266 (2002)
Internet users: 11,700 (2002)

Transportation

Railways: 0 km
Highways:
total: 373 km
paved: 315 km
unpaved: 58 km (1997 est.)
Waterways: none
Ports and harbors: Victoria
Merchant marine:
total: 8 ships (1,000 GRT or over) 42,223 GRT/63,538 DWT
by type: cargo 4, chemical tanker 3, container 1
foreign-owned: Bulgaria 1, Cyprus 1, Nigeria 1, South Africa 2 (2003 est.)
Airports: 15 (2003 est.)
Airports - with paved runways:
total: 8
2,438 to 3,047 m: 1
914 to 1,523 m: 4
under 914 m: 3 (2003 est.)
Airports - with unpaved runways:
total: 7
914 to 1,523 m: 3
under 914 m: 4 (2003 est.)

Military

Military branches: Army, Coast Guard (including Navy Wing, Air Wing), National Guard, Presidential Protection Unit (includes Presidential Guard), Seychelles National Police (includes Police Mobile Unit)
Military manpower - availability:
males age 15-49: 23,661 (2004 est.)
Military manpower - fit for military service:
males age 15-49: 11,712 (2004 est.)
Military expenditures - dollar figure: $11.6 million (2003)

Military expenditures - percent of GDP: 1.8% (2003)

Transnational Issues

Disputes - international: together with Mauritius, Seychelles claims the Chagos Archipelago (UK-administered British Indian Ocean Territory)

Sierra Leone

Introduction

Background: The 1991 to 2002 civil war between the government and the Revolutionary United Front (RUF) resulted in tens of thousands of deaths and the displacement of more than 2 million people (well over one-third of the population), many of whom are now refugees in neighboring countries. With the support of the UN peacekeeping force and contributions from the World Bank and international community, demobilization and disarmament of the RUF and Civil Defense Forces (CDF) combatants has been completed. National elections were held in May 2002 and the government continues to slowly reestablish its authority. However, the gradual withdrawal of most UN Mission in Sierra Leone (UNAMSIL) peacekeepers in 2004 and the tenuous security situation in neighboring Liberia may present challenges to the continuation of Sierra Leone's stability.

Geography

Location: Western Africa, bordering the North Atlantic Ocean, between Guinea and Liberia
Geographic coordinates: 8 30 N, 11 30 W
Map references: Africa
Area:
total: 71,740 sq km
land: 71,620 sq km
water: 120 sq km
Area - comparative: slightly smaller than South Carolina
Land boundaries:
total: 958 km
border countries: Guinea 652 km, Liberia 306 km
Coastline: 402 km
Maritime claims:
territorial sea: 12 NM
contiguous zone: 24 NM
exclusive economic zone: 200 NM
continental shelf: 200 NM

Sierra Leone (continued)

Climate, Geography & Environment

Climate: tropical; hot, humid; summer rainy season (May to December); winter dry season (December to April)

Terrain: coastal belt of mangrove swamps, wooded hill country, upland plateau, mountains in east

Elevation extremes:
lowest point: Atlantic Ocean 0 m
highest point: Loma Mansa (Bintimani) 1,948 m

Natural resources: diamonds, titanium ore, bauxite, iron ore, gold, chromite

Land use:
arable land: 6.76%
permanent crops: 0.78%
other: 92.46% (1998 est.)

Irrigated land: 290 sq km (1998 est.)

Natural hazards: dry, sand-laden harmattan winds blow from the Sahara (December to February); sandstorms, dust storms

Environment - current issues: rapid population growth pressuring the environment; overharvesting of timber, expansion of cattle grazing, and slash-and-burn agriculture have resulted in deforestation and soil exhaustion; civil war depleting natural resources; overfishing

Environment - international agreements:
party to: Biodiversity, Climate Change, Desertification, Endangered Species, Law of the Sea, Marine Life Conservation, Ozone Layer Protection, Ship Pollution, Wetlands
signed, but not ratified: Environmental Modification

Geography - note: rainfall along the coast can reach 495 cm (195 inches) a year, making it one of the wettest places along coastal, western Africa

People

Population: 5,883,889 (July 2004 est.)

Age structure:
0-14 years: 44.8% (male 1,291,621; female 1,343,827)
15-64 years: 52% (male 1,458,610; female 1,599,109)
65 years and over: 3.2% (male 91,232; female 99,490) (2004 est.)

Median age:
total: 17.5 years
male: 17.2 years
female: 17.8 years (2004 est.)

Population growth rate: 2.27% (2004 est.)

Birth rate: 43.34 births/1,000 population (2004 est.)

Death rate: 20.62 deaths/1,000 population (2004 est.)

Net migration rate: 0 migrant(s)/1,000 population
note: refugees currently in surrounding countries are slowly returning (2004 est.)

Sex ratio:
at birth: 1.03 male(s)/female
under 15 years: 0.96 male(s)/female
15-64 years: 0.91 male(s)/female
65 years and over: 0.92 male(s)/female
total population: 0.93 male(s)/female (2004 est.)

Infant mortality rate:
total: 145.24 deaths/1,000 live births
male: 162.64 deaths/1,000 live births
female: 127.32 deaths/1,000 live births (2004 est.)

Life expectancy at birth:
total population: 42.69 years
male: 40.23 years
female: 45.21 years (2004 est.)

Total fertility rate: 5.79 children born/woman (2004 est.)

HIV/AIDS - adult prevalence rate: 7% (2001 est.)

HIV/AIDS - people living with HIV/AIDS: 170,000 (2001 est.)

HIV/AIDS - deaths: 11,000 (2001 est.)

Nationality:
noun: Sierra Leonean(s)
adjective: Sierra Leonean

Ethnic groups: 20 native African tribes 90% (Temne 30%, Mende 30%, other 30%), Creole (Krio) 10% (descendants of freed Jamaican slaves who were settled in the Freetown area in the late-18th century), refugees from Liberia's recent civil war, small numbers of Europeans, Lebanese, Pakistanis, and Indians

Religions: Muslim 60%, indigenous beliefs 30%, Christian 10%

Languages: English (official, regular use limited to literate minority), Mende (principal vernacular in the south), Temne (principal vernacular in the north), Krio (English-based Creole, spoken by the descendants of freed Jamaican slaves who were settled in the Freetown area, a lingua franca and a first language for 10% of the population but understood by 95%)

Literacy:
definition: age 15 and over can read and write English, Mende, Temne, or Arabic
total population: 31.4%
male: 45.4%
female: 18.2% (1995 est.)

Government

Country name:
conventional long form: Republic of Sierra Leone
conventional short form: Sierra Leone

Government type: constitutional democracy

Capital: Freetown

Administrative divisions: 3 provinces and 1 area*; Eastern, Northern, Southern, Western*

Independence: 27 April 1961 (from UK)

National holiday: Independence Day, 27 April (1961)

Constitution: 1 October 1991; subsequently amended several times

Legal system: based on English law and customary laws indigenous to local tribes; has not accepted compulsory ICJ jurisdiction

Suffrage: 18 years of age; universal

Executive branch:
chief of state: President Ahmad Tejan KABBAH (since 29 March 1996, reinstated 10 March 1998); note - the president is both the chief of state and head of government
head of government: President Ahmad Tejan KABBAH (since 29 March 1996, reinstated 10 March 1998); note - the president is both the chief of state and head of government
cabinet: Ministers of State appointed by the president with the approval of the House of Representatives; the cabinet is responsible to the president
elections: president elected by popular vote for a five-year term; election last held 14 May 2002 (next to be held NA May 2007); note - president's tenure of office is limited to two five-year terms
election results: Ahmad Tejan KABBAH reelected president; percent of vote - Ahmad Tejan KABBAH (SLPP) 70.6%, Ernest KOROMA (APC) 22.4%

Legislative branch: unicameral Parliament (124 seats - 112 elected by popular vote, 12 filled by paramount chiefs elected in separate elections; members serve five-year terms)
elections: last held 14 May 2002 (next to be held NA May 2007)
election results: percent of vote by party - SLPP 70.06%, APC 22.35%, PLP 3%, others 4.59%; seats by party - SLPP 83, APC 27, PLP 2

Judicial branch: Supreme Court; Appeals Court; High Court

Political parties and leaders: All People's Congress or APC [Ben KANU]; Peace and Liberation Party or PLP [Darlington MORRISON, interim chairman]; Sierra Leone People's Party or SLPP [Sama BANYA]; numerous others

Political pressure groups and leaders: Trade Unions and Student Unions

International organization participation: ACP, AfDB, AU, C, ECOWAS, FAO, G-77, IAEA, IBRD, ICAO, ICCt, ICFTU, ICRM, IDA, IDB, IFAD, IFC, IFRCS, ILO, IMF, IMO, Interpol, IOC, IOM, ITU, NAM, OIC, OPCW (signatory), UN, UNCTAD, UNESCO, UNIDO, UPU, WCL, WCO, WFTU, WHO, WIPO, WMO, WToO, WTrO

Diplomatic representation in the US:
chief of mission: Ambassador Ibrahim M. KAMARA
chancery: 1701 19th Street NW, Washington, DC 20009
telephone: [1] (202) 939-9261 through 9263
FAX: [1] (202) 483-1793

Diplomatic representation from the US:
chief of mission: Ambassador Peter Russell CHAVEAS
embassy: Corner of Walpole and Siaka Stevens Streets, Freetown
mailing address: use embassy street address
telephone: [232] (22) 226481 through 226485
FAX: [232] (22) 225471

Flag description: three equal horizontal bands of light green (top), white, and light blue

Economy

Economy - overview: Sierra Leone is an extremely poor African nation with tremendous inequality in income distribution. It does have substantial mineral, agricultural, and fishery resources. However, the economic and social infrastructure is not well developed, and serious social disorders continue to hamper economic development, following a 11-year civil war. About two-thirds of the working-age population engages in subsistence agriculture.

Sierra Leone (continued)

Manufacturing consists mainly of the processing of raw materials and of light manufacturing for the domestic market. Plans continue to reopen bauxite and rutile mines shut down during the conflict. The major source of hard currency consists of the mining of diamonds. The fate of the economy depends upon the maintenance of domestic peace and the continued receipt of substantial aid from abroad, which is essential to offset the severe trade imbalance and to supplement government revenues.

GDP: purchasing power parity - $3.057 billion (2003 est.)

GDP - real growth rate: 6.5% (2003 est.)

GDP - per capita: purchasing power parity - $500 (2003 est.)

GDP - composition by sector:
agriculture: 49%
industry: 31%
services: 21% (2001 est.)

Population below poverty line: 68% (1989 est.)

Household income or consumption by percentage share:
lowest 10%: 0.5%
highest 10%: 43.6% (1989)

Distribution of family income - Gini index: 62.9 (1989)

Inflation rate (consumer prices): 1% (2002 est.)

Labor force: 1.369 million (1981 est.)

Labor force - by occupation: agriculture NA%, industry NA%, services NA%

Unemployment rate: NA%

Budget:
revenues: $96 million
expenditures: $351 million, including capital expenditures of $NA (2000 est.)

Industries: mining (diamonds); small-scale manufacturing (beverages, textiles, cigarettes, footwear); petroleum refining

Industrial production growth rate: NA%

Electricity - production: 250.1 million kWh (2001)

Electricity - production by source:
fossil fuel: 100%
hydro: 0%
nuclear: 0%
other: 0% (2001)

Electricity - consumption: 232.6 million kWh (2001)

Electricity - exports: 0 kWh (2001)

Electricity - imports: 0 kWh (2001)

Oil - production: 0 bbl/day (2001 est.)

Oil - consumption: 6,500 bbl/day (2001 est.)

Oil - exports: NA

Oil - imports: NA

Agriculture - products: rice, coffee, cocoa, palm kernels, palm oil, peanuts; poultry, cattle, sheep, pigs; fish

Exports: $49 million f.o.b. (2002 est.)

Exports - commodities: diamonds, rutile, cocoa, coffee, fish (1999)

Exports - partners: Belgium 41.6%, Germany 31.7%, UK 4%, US 4% (2002)

Imports: $264 million f.o.b. (2002 est.)

Imports - commodities: foodstuffs, machinery and equipment, fuels and lubricants, chemicals (1995)

Imports - partners: Germany 26.1%, UK 10.7%, Netherlands 7.5%, US 5.7%, Cote d'Ivoire 4.9%, Italy 4.3% (2002)

Debt - external: $1.5 billion (2002 est.)

Economic aid - recipient: $103 million (2001 est.)

Currency: leone (SLL)

Currency code: SLL

Exchange rates: leones per US dollar - 2,347.94 (2003), 2,099.03 (2002), 1,986.15 (2001), 2,092.12 (2000), 1,804.19 (1999)

Fiscal year: calendar year

Communications

Telephones - main lines in use: 24,000 (2002)

Telephones - mobile cellular: 66,300 (2002)

Telephone system:
general assessment: marginal telephone and telegraph service
domestic: the national microwave radio relay trunk system connects Freetown to Bo and Kenema
international: country code - 232; satellite earth station - 1 Intelsat (Atlantic Ocean)

Radio broadcast stations: AM 1, FM 9, shortwave 1 (1999)

Television broadcast stations: 2 (1999)

Internet country code: .sl

Internet hosts: 277 (2002)

Internet users: 8,000 (2002)

Transportation

Railways:
total: 84 km
narrow gauge: 84 km 1.067-m gauge
note: Sierra Leone has no common carrier railroads; the existing railroad is private and used on a limited basis while the mine at Marampa is closed (2001)

Highways:
total: 11,330 km
paved: 895 km
unpaved: 10,435 km (1999)

Waterways: 800 km (of which 600 km is navigable year round)

Ports and harbors: Bonthe, Freetown, Pepel

Merchant marine:
total: 2 ships (1,000 GRT or over) 7,435 GRT/8,750 DWT
by type: cargo 2 (2003 est.)

Airports: 10 (2003 est.)

Airports - with paved runways:
total: 1
over 3,047 m: 1 (2003 est.)

Airports - with unpaved runways:
total: 9
914 to 1,523 m: 7
under 914 m: 2 (2003 est.)

Heliports: 2 (2003 est.)

Military

Military branches: Army (RSLAF)

Military manpower - availability:
males age 15-49: 1,265,140 (2004 est.)

Military manpower - fit for military service:
males age 15-49: 614,338 (2004 est.)

Military expenditures - dollar figure: $11.7 million (2003)

Military expenditures - percent of GDP: 1.5% (2003)

Transnational Issues

Disputes - international: domestic fighting among disparate rebel groups, warlords, and youth gangs in Guinea, Liberia, and Sierra Leone have created insurgencies, street violence, looting, arms trafficking, ethnic conflicts, and refugees in border areas; in 2003, Guinea and Sierra Leone established a boundary commission to resolve a dispute over the town of Yenga

Singapore

Introduction

Background: Singapore was founded as a British trading colony in 1819. It joined the Malaysian Federation in 1963 but separated two years later and became independent. It subsequently became one of the world's most prosperous countries with strong international trading links (its port is the world's busiest in terms of tonnage handled) and with per capita GDP equal to that of the leading nations of Western Europe.

Geography

Location: Southeastern Asia, islands between Malaysia and Indonesia
Geographic coordinates: 1 22 N, 103 48 E
Map references: Southeast Asia
Area:
total: 692.7 sq km
land: 682.7 sq km
water: 10 sq km
Area - comparative: slightly more than 3.5 times the size of Washington, DC
Land boundaries: 0 km
Coastline: 193 km
Maritime claims:
territorial sea: 3 NM
exclusive fishing zone: within and beyond territorial sea, as defined in treaties and practice
Climate: tropical; hot, humid, rainy; two distinct monsoon seasons - Northeastern monsoon from December to March and Southwestern monsoon from June to September; inter-monsoon - frequent afternoon and early evening thunderstorms
Terrain: lowland; gently undulating central plateau contains water catchment area and nature preserve
Elevation extremes:
lowest point: Singapore Strait 0 m
highest point: Bukit Timah 166 m
Natural resources: fish, deepwater ports

Land use:
arable land: 1.64%
permanent crops: 0%
other: 98.36% (1998 est.)
Irrigated land: NA sq km
Natural hazards: NA
Environment - current issues: industrial pollution; limited natural fresh water resources; limited land availability presents waste disposal problems; seasonal smoke/haze resulting from forest fires in Indonesia
Environment - international agreements:
party to: Biodiversity, Climate Change, Desertification, Endangered Species, Hazardous Wastes, Law of the Sea, Ozone Layer Protection, Ship Pollution
signed, but not ratified: none of the selected agreements
Geography - note: focal point for Southeast Asian sea routes

People

Population: 4,353,893 (July 2004 est.)
Age structure:
0-14 years: 16.5% (male 370,660; female 345,713)
15-64 years: 75.8% (male 1,611,502; female 1,687,048)
65 years and over: 7.8% (male 149,452; female 189,518) (2004 est.)
Median age:
total: 36.2 years
male: 35.9 years
female: 36.6 years (2004 est.)
Population growth rate: 1.71% (2004 est.)
Birth rate: 9.63 births/1,000 population (2004 est.)
Death rate: 4.05 deaths/1,000 population (2004 est.)
Net migration rate: 11.53 migrant(s)/1,000 population (2004 est.)
Sex ratio:
at birth: 1.08 male(s)/female
under 15 years: 1.07 male(s)/female
15-64 years: 0.96 male(s)/female
65 years and over: 0.79 male(s)/female
total population: 0.96 male(s)/female (2004 est.)
Infant mortality rate:
total: 2.28 deaths/1,000 live births
male: 2.49 deaths/1,000 live births
female: 2.05 deaths/1,000 live births (2004 est.)
Life expectancy at birth:
total population: 81.53 years
male: 78.96 years
female: 84.29 years (2004 est.)
Total fertility rate: 1.04 children born/woman (2004 est.)
HIV/AIDS - adult prevalence rate: 0.2% (2001 est.)
HIV/AIDS - people living with HIV/AIDS: 3,400 (2001 est.)
HIV/AIDS - deaths: 140 (2001 est.)
Nationality:
noun: Singaporean(s)
adjective: Singapore
Ethnic groups: Chinese 76.7%, Malay 14%, Indian 7.9%, other 1.4%

Religions: Buddhist (Chinese), Muslim (Malays), Christian, Hindu, Sikh, Taoist, Confucianist
Languages: Chinese (official), Malay (official and national), Tamil (official), English (official)
Literacy:
definition: age 15 and over can read and write
total population: 93.2%
male: 96.7%
female: 89.7% (2003 est.)

Government

Country name:
conventional long form: Republic of Singapore
conventional short form: Singapore
Government type: parliamentary republic
Capital: Singapore
Administrative divisions: none
Independence: 9 August 1965 (from Malaysian Federation)
National holiday: Independence Day, 9 August (1965)
Constitution: 3 June 1959, amended 1965 (based on preindependence State of Singapore Constitution)
Legal system: based on English common law; has not accepted compulsory ICJ jurisdiction
Suffrage: 21 years of age; universal and compulsory
Executive branch:
chief of state: President Sellapan Rama (S. R.) NATHAN (since 1 September 1999)
head of government: Prime Minister GOH Chok Tong (since 28 November 1990) and Deputy Prime Ministers Brig. Gen. (Ret.) LEE Hsien Loong (since 28 November 1990) and Tony TAN Keng Yam (since 1 August 1995)
cabinet: Cabinet appointed by the president, responsible to Parliament
elections: president elected by popular vote for a six-year term; election last held 28 August 1999 (next to be held by August 2005); following legislative elections, the leader of the majority party or the leader of a majority coalition is usually appointed prime minister by the president; deputy prime ministers appointed by the president
election results: Sellapan Rama (S. R.) NATHAN elected president unopposed
Legislative branch: unicameral Parliament (84 seats; members elected by popular vote to serve five-year terms); note - in addition, there are up to nine nominated members; the losing opposition candidate who came closest to winning a seat may be appointed as a "nonconstituency" member
elections: last held 3 November 2001 (next to be held not later than 25 June 2007)
election results: percent of vote by party - PAP 75.3% (in contested constituencies), other 24.7%; seats by party - PAP 82, WP 1, SDA 1
Judicial branch: Supreme Court (chief justice is appointed by the president with the advice of the prime minister, other judges are appointed by the president with the advice of the chief justice); Court of Appeals

Singapore (continued)

Political parties and leaders: governing party: People's Action Party or PAP [GOH Chok Tong]; opposition parties: Democratic Progressive Party or DPP [LING How Dong]; National Solidarity Party or NSP [vacant] (SDA group); Singapore Democratic Alliance or SDA [CHIAM See Tong] (includes SPP, PKMS, NSP, SJP); Singapore Democratic Party or SDP [CHEE Soon Juan]; Singapore Justice Party or SJP [Desmond LIM] (SDA group); Singapore National Malay Organization or PKMS [Muhammad ALI Aman] (SDA group); Singapore People's Party or SPP [CHIAM See Tong] (SDA group); Workers' Party or WP [LOW Thia Kiang]

Political pressure groups and leaders: NA

International organization participation: APEC, ARF, AsDB, ASEAN, BIS, C, CP, G-77, IAEA, IBRD, ICAO, ICC, ICFTU, ICRM, IDA, IFC, IFRCS, IHO, ILO, IMF, IMO, Interpol, IOC, ISO, ITU, NAM, OPCW, PCA, UN, UNCTAD, UNMISET, UPU, WCL, WCO, WHO, WIPO, WMO, WTrO

Diplomatic representation in the US:

chief of mission: Ambassador CHAN Heng Chee

chancery: 3501 International Place NW, Washington, DC 20008

telephone: [1] (202) 537-3100

FAX: [1] (202) 537-0876

consulate(s) general: San Francisco

consulate(s): New York

Diplomatic representation from the US:

chief of mission: Ambassador Franklin L. LAVIN

embassy: 27 Napier Road, Singapore 258508

mailing address: FPO AP 96507-0001

telephone: [65] 6476-9100

FAX: [65] 6476-9340

Flag description: two equal horizontal bands of red (top) and white; near the hoist side of the red band, there is a vertical, white crescent (closed portion is toward the hoist side) partially enclosing five white five-pointed stars arranged in a circle

Economy

Economy - overview: Singapore, a highly developed and successful free market economy, enjoys a remarkably open and corruption-free environment, stable prices, and a high per capita GDP. The economy depends heavily on exports, particularly in electronics and manufacturing. It was hard hit in 2001-03 by the global recession and the slump in the technology sector. The government hopes to establish a new growth path that will be less vulnerable to the external business cycle but is unlikely to abandon efforts to establish Singapore as Southeast Asia's financial and high-tech hub. Fiscal stimulus, low interest rates, and global economic recovery should lead to much improved growth in 2004.

GDP: purchasing power parity - $109.1 billion (2003 est.)

GDP - real growth rate: 0.8% (2003 est.)

GDP - per capita: purchasing power parity - $23,700 (2003 est.)

GDP - composition by sector:

agriculture: negligible

industry: 30%

services: 70% (2001 est.)

Population below poverty line: NA%

Household income or consumption by percentage share:

lowest 10%: NA%

highest 10%: NA%

Inflation rate (consumer prices): 0.7% (2003 est.)

Labor force: 2 million (June 2003)

Labor force - by occupation: financial, business, and other services 49%, manufacturing 18%, construction 6%, transportation and communication 11%, other 16% (2003)

Unemployment rate: 5% (2003 est.)

Budget:

revenues: $17.4 billion

expenditures: $17.6 billion, including capital expenditures of $5.6 billion (FY03/04 est.)

Industries: electronics, chemicals, financial services, oil drilling equipment, petroleum refining, rubber processing and rubber products, processed food and beverages, ship repair, offshore platform construction, life sciences, entrepot trade

Industrial production growth rate: 7.5% (2003 est.)

Electricity - production: 30.48 billion kWh (2001)

Electricity - production by source:

fossil fuel: 100%

hydro: 0%

nuclear: 0%

other: 0% (2001)

Electricity - consumption: 28.35 billion kWh (2001)

Electricity - exports: 0 kWh (2001)

Electricity - imports: 0 kWh (2001)

Oil - production: 0 bbl/day (2001 est.)

Oil - consumption: 700,000 bbl/day (2001 est.)

Oil - exports: NA

Oil - imports: NA

Natural gas - production: 0 cu m (2001 est.)

Natural gas - consumption: 2.5 billion cu m (2001 est.)

Natural gas - exports: 0 cu m (2001 est.)

Natural gas - imports: 2.5 billion cu m

Note: from Indonesia and Malaysia (2001 est.)

Agriculture - products: rubber, copra, fruit, orchids, vegetables, poultry, eggs, fish, ornamental fish

Exports: $142.4 billion f.o.b. (2003 est.)

Exports - commodities: machinery and equipment (including electronics), consumer goods, chemicals, mineral fuels

Exports - partners: Malaysia 17.4%, US 15.3%, Hong Kong 9.2%, Japan 7.1%, China 5.5%, Taiwan 4.9%, Thailand 4.6%, South Korea 4.2% (2002)

Imports: $121.6 billion (2003 est.)

Imports - commodities: machinery and equipment, mineral fuels, chemicals, foodstuffs

Imports - partners: Malaysia 18.2%, US 14.3%, Japan 12.5%, China 7.6%, Thailand 4.6%, Taiwan 4.6% (2002)

Debt - external: $9.1 billion (2003 est.)

Economic aid - recipient: $NA

Currency: Singapore dollar (SGD)

Currency code: SGD

Exchange rates: Singapore dollars per US dollar - 1.7422 (2003), 1.7906 (2002), 1.7917 (2001), 1.724 (2000), 1.695 (1999)

Fiscal year: 1 April - 31 March

Communications

Telephones - main lines in use: 1,896,100 (2004)

Telephones - mobile cellular: 3,521,800 (2004)

Telephone system:

general assessment: excellent service

domestic: excellent domestic facilities

international: country code - 65; submarine cables to Malaysia (Sabah and Peninsular Malaysia), Indonesia, and the Philippines; satellite earth stations - 2 Intelsat (1 Indian Ocean and 1 Pacific Ocean), and 1 Inmarsat (Pacific Ocean region)

Radio broadcast stations: AM 0, FM 17, shortwave 2 (2003)

Television broadcast stations: 7 (2003)

Internet country code: .sg

Internet hosts: 338,349 (2002)

Internet users: 2.31 million (2002)

Transportation

Railways:

total: 38.6 km

narrow gauge: 38.6 km 1.000-m gauge

note: there is also an 83 km mass transit system with 48 stations

Highways:

total: 3,066 km

paved: 3,066 km (including 150 km of expressways)

unpaved: 0 km (1999)

Waterways: none

Pipelines: gas 139 km (2003)

Ports and harbors: Singapore

Merchant marine:

total: 900 ships (1,000 GRT or over) 23,065,290 GRT/ 36,393,317 DWT

by type: bulk 136, cargo 84, chemical tanker 96, combination bulk 4, combination ore/oil 8, container 186, liquefied gas 41, livestock carrier 3, multi-functional large load carrier 2, petroleum tanker 290, refrigerated cargo 2, roll on/roll off 5, short-sea/ passenger 1, specialized tanker 10, vehicle carrier 32

foreign-owned: Australia 6, China 15, Denmark 32, Germany 18, Greece 12, Hong Kong 31, India 3, Indonesia 33, Japan 58, South Korea 13, Malaysia 31, Monaco 19, Norway 53, Papua New Guinea 1, Philippines 9, Russia 2, Slovenia 1, Sweden 12, Switzerland 5, Taiwan 44, Tanzania 1, Thailand 16, United Kingdom 15, United States 1

registered in other countries: 383 (2003 est.)

Airports: 9 (2003 est.)

Airports - with paved runways:

total: 9

over 3,047 m: 2

Singapore (continued)

2,438 to 3,047 m: 1
1,524 to 2,437 m: 4
914 to 1,523 m: 1
under 914 m: 1 (2003 est.)

Military

Military branches: Army, Navy, Air Force, People's Defense Force
Military manpower - availability:
males age 15-49: 1,292,471 (2004 est.)
Military manpower - fit for military service:
males age 15-49: 934,317 (2004 est.)
Military expenditures - dollar figure: $4.47 billion (FY01 est.)
Military expenditures - percent of GDP: 4.9% (FY01)

Transnational Issues

Disputes - international: disputes with Malaysia over deliveries of fresh water to Singapore, Singapore's land reclamation works, bridge construction, maritime boundaries, and Pedra Branca Island/Pulau Batu Putih persist - parties agree to ICJ arbitration on island dispute within three years
Illicit drugs: as a transportation and financial services hub, Singapore is vulnerable, despite strict laws and enforcement, to be used as a transit point for Golden Triangle heroin and as a venue for money laundering

Slovakia

Introduction

Background: In 1918 the Slovaks joined the closely related Czechs to form Czechoslovakia. Following the chaos of World War II, Czechoslovakia became a Communist nation within Soviet-ruled Eastern Europe. Soviet influence collapsed in 1989 and Czechoslovakia once more became free. The Slovaks and the Czechs agreed to separate peacefully on 1 January 1993. Slovakia was invited to join NATO and the EU in 2002.

Geography

Location: Central Europe, south of Poland
Geographic coordinates: 48 40 N, 19 30 E
Map references: Europe
Area:
total: 48,845 sq km
land: 48,800 sq km
water: 45 sq km
Area - comparative: about twice the size of New Hampshire
Land boundaries:
total: 1,524 km
border countries: Austria 91 km, Czech Republic 215 km, Hungary 677 km, Poland 444 km, Ukraine 97 km
Coastline: 0 km (landlocked)
Maritime claims: none (landlocked)
Climate: temperate; cool summers; cold, cloudy, humid winters
Terrain: rugged mountains in the central and northern part and lowlands in the south
Elevation extremes:
lowest point: Bodrok River 94 m
highest point: Gerlachovsky Stit 2,655 m
Natural resources: brown coal and lignite; small amounts of iron ore, copper and manganese ore; salt; arable land

Land use:
arable land: 30.74%
permanent crops: 2.64%
other: 66.62% (1998 est.)
Irrigated land: 1,740 sq km (1998 est.)
Natural hazards: NA
Environment - current issues: air pollution from metallurgical plants presents human health risks; acid rain damaging forests
Environment - international agreements:
party to: Air Pollution, Air Pollution-Nitrogen Oxides, Air Pollution-Sulfur 85, Air Pollution-Sulfur 94, Air Pollution-Volatile Organic Compounds, Antarctic Treaty, Biodiversity, Climate Change, Climate Change-Kyoto Protocol, Desertification, Endangered Species, Environmental Modification, Hazardous Wastes, Law of the Sea, Ozone Layer Protection, Ship Pollution, Wetlands
signed, but not ratified: Air Pollution-Persistent Organic Pollutants
Geography - note: landlocked; most of the country is rugged and mountainous; the Tatra Mountains in the north are interspersed with many scenic lakes and valleys

People

Population: 5,423,567 (July 2004 est.)
Age structure:
0-14 years: 17.5% (male 485,523; female 463,173)
15-64 years: 70.8% (male 1,908,425; female 1,929,861)
65 years and over: 11.7% (male 239,081; female 397,504) (2004 est.)
Median age:
total: 35.1 years
male: 33.5 years
female: 36.9 years (2004 est.)
Population growth rate: 0.14% (2004 est.)
Birth rate: 10.57 births/1,000 population (2004 est.)
Death rate: 9.48 deaths/1,000 population (2004 est.)

Slovakia (continued)

Net migration rate: 0.3 migrant(s)/1,000 population (2004 est.)

Sex ratio:

at birth: 1.05 male(s)/female

under 15 years: 1.05 male(s)/female

15-64 years: 0.99 male(s)/female

65 years and over: 0.6 male(s)/female

total population: 0.94 male(s)/female (2004 est.)

Infant mortality rate:

total: 7.62 deaths/1,000 live births

male: 8.88 deaths/1,000 live births

female: 6.28 deaths/1,000 live births (2004 est.)

Life expectancy at birth:

total population: 74.19 years

male: 70.21 years

female: 78.37 years (2004 est.)

Total fertility rate: 1.31 children born/woman (2004 est.)

HIV/AIDS - adult prevalence rate: less than 0.1% (2001 est.)

HIV/AIDS - people living with HIV/AIDS: less than 100 (1999 est.)

HIV/AIDS - deaths: less than 100 (2001 est.)

Nationality:

noun: Slovak(s)

adjective: Slovak

Ethnic groups: Slovak 85.7%, Hungarian 10.6%, Roma 1.6% (the 1992 census figures underreport the Gypsy/Romany community, which is about 500,000), Czech, Moravian, Silesian 1.1%, Ruthenian and Ukrainian 0.6%, German 0.1%, Polish 0.1%, other 0.2% (1996)

Religions: Roman Catholic 60.3%, atheist 9.7%, Protestant 8.4%, Orthodox 4.1%, other 17.5%

Languages: Slovak (official), Hungarian

Literacy:

definition: NA

total population: NA%

male: NA%

female: NA%

Government

Country name:

conventional long form: Slovak Republic

conventional short form: Slovakia

local long form: Slovenska Republika

local short form: Slovensko

Government type: parliamentary democracy

Capital: Bratislava

Administrative divisions: 8 regions (kraje, singular - kraj); Banskobystricky, Bratislavsky, Kosicky, Nitriansky, Presovsky, Trenciansky, Trnavsky, Zilinsky

Independence: 1 January 1993 (Czechoslovakia split into the Czech Republic and Slovakia)

National holiday: Constitution Day, 1 September (1992)

Constitution: ratified 1 September 1992, fully effective 1 January 1993; changed in September 1998 to allow direct election of the president; amended February 2001 to allow Slovakia to apply for NATO and EU membership

Legal system: civil law system based on Austro-Hungarian codes; has not accepted compulsory ICJ jurisdiction; legal code modified to comply with the obligations of Organization on Security and Cooperation in Europe (OSCE) and to expunge Marxist-Leninist legal theory

Suffrage: 18 years of age; universal

Executive branch:

chief of state: President Rudolf SCHUSTER (since 15 June 1999)

head of government: Prime Minister Mikulas DZURINDA (since 30 October 1998)

cabinet: Cabinet appointed by the president on the recommendation of the prime minister

elections: president elected by direct, popular vote for a five-year term; election last held 29 May 1999 (next to be held 3 April 2004); following National Council elections, the leader of the majority party or the leader of a majority coalition is usually appointed prime minister by the president

election results: Rudolf SCHUSTER elected president in the first direct, popular election; percent of vote - Rudolf SCHUSTER 57%; Mikulas DZURINDA reelected prime minister October 2002

note: government coalition - SDKU, SMK, KDH, ANO

Legislative branch: unicameral National Council of the Slovak Republic or Narodna Rada Slovenskej Republiky (150 seats; members are elected on the basis of proportional representation to serve four-year terms)

elections: last held 20-21 September 2002 (next to be held NA September 2006)

election results: percent of vote by party - HZDS-LS 19.5%, SDKU 15.1%, SMER 13.5%, SMK 11.2%, KDH 8.3%, ANO 8%, KSS 6.3%; seats by party - governing coalition 67 (SDKU 21, SMK 20, KDH 15, ANO 11), opposition 83 (HZDS 26, Smer 25, KSS 10, People's Union 8, Free Forum 7, and independents 7)

Judicial branch: Supreme Court (judges are elected by the National Council); Constitutional Court (judges appointed by president from group of nominees approved by the National Council)

Political parties and leaders: Christian Democratic Movement or KDH [Pavol HRUSOVSKY]; Direction (Smer) [Robert FICO]; Free Forum [Ivan SIMKO]; Movement for a Democratic Slovakia-People's Party or HZDS-LS [Vladimir MECIAR]; New Citizens Alliance or ANO [Pavol RUSKO]; Party of the Hungarian Coalition or SMK [Bela BUGAR]; People's Union or LU [Vojtech TKAC]; Slovak Communist Party or KSS [Jozef SEVC]; Slovak Democratic and Christian Union or SDKU [Mikulas DZURINDA]; Slovak National Party or SNS [Peter SULOVSKY]

Political pressure groups and leaders: Association of Employers of Slovakia; Association of Towns and Villages or ZMOS; Confederation of Trade Unions or KOZ; Metal Workers Unions or KOVO and METALURG

International organization participation: Australia Group, BIS, BSEC (observer), CE, CEI, CERN, EAPC, EBRD, EU (new member), FAO, IAEA, IBRD, ICAO, ICC, ICCt, ICFTU, ICRM, IDA, IFC, IFRCS, ILO, IMF, IMO, Interpol, IOC, IOM, ISO, ITU, NAM

(guest), NEA, NSG, OAS (observer), OECD, OPCW, OSCE, PCA, PFP, UN, UNAMSIL, UNCTAD, UNDOF, UNESCO, UNFICYP, UNIDO, UNMEE, UNMISET, UNTSO, UPU, WCL, WCO, WEU (associate partner), WFTU, WHO, WIPO, WMO, WToO, WTrO, ZC

Diplomatic representation in the US:

chief of mission: Ambassador Rastislav KACER

chancery: 3523 International Court NW, Washington, DC 20008

telephone: [1] (202) 237-1054

FAX: [1] (202) 237-6438

Diplomatic representation from the US:

chief of mission: Ambassador Ronald WEISER

embassy: Hviezdoslavovo Namestie 4, 81102 Bratislava

mailing address: use embassy street address

telephone: [421] (2) 5443-3338

FAX: [421] (2) 5441-5148

Flag description: three equal horizontal bands of white (top), blue, and red superimposed with the Slovak cross in a shield centered on the hoist side; the cross is white centered on a background of red and blue

Economy

Economy - overview: Slovakia has mastered much of the difficult transition from a centrally planned economy to a modern market economy. The DZURINDA government made excellent progress during 2001-03 in macroeconomic stabilization and structural reform. Major privatizations are nearly complete, the banking sector is almost completely in foreign hands, and foreign investment has picked up. Slovakia's economy exceeded expectations in 2001-03, despite the general European slowdown. Unemployment, at an unacceptable 15% in 2003, remains the economy's Achilles heel. The government faces other strong challenges in 2004, especially cutting the budget deficit, containing inflation, and strengthening the health care system.

GDP: purchasing power parity - $72.29 billion (2003 est.)

GDP - real growth rate: 3.9% (2003 est.)

GDP - per capita: purchasing power parity - $13,300 (2003 est.)

GDP - composition by sector:

agriculture: 4.5%

industry: 34.1%

services: 61.4% (2000)

Population below poverty line: NA%

Household income or consumption by percentage share:

lowest 10%: 5.1%

highest 10%: 18.2% (1992)

Distribution of family income - Gini index: 26.3 (1996)

Inflation rate (consumer prices): 8.6% (2003 est.)

Labor force: 3 million (1999)

Labor force - by occupation: industry 29.3%, agriculture 8.9%, construction 8%, transport and communication 8.2%, services 45.6% (1994)

Slovakia (continued)

Unemployment rate: 15% (2003 est.)
Budget:
revenues: $5.2 billion
expenditures: $5.6 billion, including capital expenditures of $NA (1999)
Industries: metal and metal products; food and beverages; electricity, gas, coke, oil, nuclear fuel; chemicals and manmade fibers; machinery; paper and printing; earthenware and ceramics; transport vehicles; textiles; electrical and optical apparatus; rubber products
Industrial production growth rate: 7.2% (2003 est.)
Electricity - production: 30.29 billion kWh (2001)
Electricity - production by source:
fossil fuel: 30.3%
hydro: 16%
nuclear: 53.6%
other: 0% (2001)
Electricity - consumption: 24.41 billion kWh (2001)
Electricity - exports: 5.141 billion kWh (2001)
Electricity - imports: 1.381 billion kWh (2001)
Oil - production: 1,000 bbl/day (2001 est.)
Oil - consumption: 82,000 bbl/day (2001 est.)
Oil - exports: NA
Oil - imports: NA
Oil - proved reserves: 4.5 million bbl (1 January 2002)
Natural gas - production: 292 million cu m (2001 est.)
Natural gas - consumption: 7.932 billion cu m (2001 est.)
Natural gas - exports: 0 cu m (2001 est.)
Natural gas - imports: 7.205 billion cu m (2001 est.)
Natural gas - proved reserves: 7.504 billion cu m (1 January 2002)
Agriculture - products: grains, potatoes, sugar beets, hops, fruit; pigs, cattle, poultry; forest products
Exports: $21.25 billion f.o.b. (2003 est.)
Exports - commodities: machinery and transport equipment 39.4%, intermediate manufactured goods 27.5%, miscellaneous manufactured goods 13%, chemicals 8% (1999)
Exports - partners: Germany 26%, Czech Republic 15.2%, Italy 10.8%, Austria 7.7%, Hungary 5.5%, Poland 5.3%, France 4.2% (2002)
Imports: $21.9 billion f.o.b. (2003 est.)
Imports - commodities: machinery and transport equipment 37.7%, intermediate manufactured goods 18%, fuels 13%, chemicals 11%, miscellaneous manufactured goods 9.5% (1999)
Imports - partners: Germany 22.6%, Czech Republic 15.1%, Russia 12.5%, Italy 6.9%, France 4.4%, Austria 4.2% (2002)
Debt - external: $14.4 billion (2003 est.)
Economic aid - recipient: ODA $113 million (2000),; $92 million EU structural adjustment funds (2000)
Currency: Slovak koruna (SKK)
Currency code: SKK

Exchange rates: koruny per US dollar - 36.7729 (2003), 45.3267 (2002), 48.3548 (2001), 46.0352 (2000), 41.3628 (1999)
Fiscal year: calendar year

Communications

Telephones - main lines in use: 1,442,600 (2002)
Telephones - mobile cellular: 2,923,400 (2002)
Telephone system:
general assessment: a modernization and privatization program is increasing accessibility to telephone service, reducing the waiting time for new subscribers, and generally improving service quality
domestic: predominantly an analog system that is now receiving digital equipment and is being enlarged with fiber-optic cable, especially in the larger cities; mobile cellular capability has been added
international: country code - 421; three international exchanges (one in Bratislava and two in Banska Bystrica) are available; Slovakia is participating in several international telecommunications projects that will increase the availability of external services
Radio broadcast stations: AM 15, FM 78, shortwave 2 (1998)
Television broadcast stations: 38 (plus 864 repeaters) (1995)
Internet country code: .sk
Internet hosts: 85,998 (2002)
Internet users: 862,800 (2002)

Transportation

Railways:
total: 3,668 km
broad gauge: 106 km 1.520-m gauge
standard gauge: 3,511 km 1.435-m gauge (1,567 km electrified)
narrow gauge: 51 km (46 km 1,000-m gauge; 5 km 0.750-m gauge) (2002)
Highways:
total: 42,717 km
paved: 37,036 km (including 296 km of expressways)
unpaved: 5,681 km (2000)
Waterways: 172 km (all on the Danube)
Pipelines: gas 6,769 km; oil 449 km (2003)
Ports and harbors: Bratislava, Komarno
Merchant marine:
total: 8 ships (1,000 GRT or over) 41,891 GRT/63,185 DWT
by type: bulk 4, cargo 4
foreign-owned: Bulgaria 3, Estonia 1, Greece 1, India 1, Liberia 1, Panama 1 (2003 est.)
Airports: 34 (2003 est.)
Airports - with paved runways:
total: 17
over 3,047 m: 2
2,438 to 3,047 m: 2
1,524 to 2,437 m: 3
914 to 1,523 m: 3
under 914 m: 7 (2003 est.)

Airports - with unpaved runways:
total: 17
2,438 to 3,047 m: 1
914 to 1,523 m: 9
under 914 m: 7 (2003 est.)
Heliports: 1 (2003 est.)

Military

Military branches: Army (Ground Forces), Air and Air Defense Forces, Home Guard (Territorial Defense Forces)
Military manpower - military age: 18 years of age (conscripts serve nine months of basic military service; term of service will be reduced to six months effective 2004) (2004 est.)
Military manpower - availability:
males age 15-49: 1,477,017 (2004 est.)
Military manpower - fit for military service:
males age 15-49: 1,129,935 (2004 est.)
Military manpower - reaching military age annually:
males: 43,029 (2004 est.)
Military expenditures - dollar figure: $406 million (2002)
Military expenditures - percent of GDP: 1.89% (2002)

Transnational Issues

Disputes - international: Hungary amended its status law extending special social and cultural benefits to ethnic Hungarians in Slovakia, many of whom had protested the law; Slovakia and Hungary have renewed discussions on ways to resolve differences over the Gabcikovo-Nagymaros hydroelectric dam on the Danube, with possible resort again to the ICJ for final resolution
Illicit drugs: transshipment point for Southwest Asian heroin bound for Western Europe; producer of synthetic drugs for regional market

Slovenia

Introduction

Background: The Slovene lands were part of the Holy Roman Empire and Austria until 1918 when the Slovenes joined the Serbs and Croats in forming a new multinational state, renamed Yugoslavia in 1929. After World War II, Slovenia became a republic of the renewed Yugoslavia, which though Communist, distanced itself from Moscow's rule. Dissatisfied with the exercise of power of the majority Serbs, the Slovenes succeeded in establishing their independence in 1991 after a short 10-day war. Historical ties to Western Europe, a strong economy, and a stable democracy have assisted in Slovenia's transformation to a modern state. In a March 2003 referendum on NATO and EU membership, Slovenes voted 90% in favor of joining the EU and 66% in favor of joining NATO. Slovenia is scheduled to accede to both organizations in the early months of 2004.

Geography

Location: Central Europe, eastern Alps bordering the Adriatic Sea, between Austria and Croatia
Geographic coordinates: 46 07 N, 14 49 E
Map references: Europe
Area:
total: 20,273 sq km
land: 20,151 sq km
water: 122 sq km
Area - comparative: slightly smaller than New Jersey
Land boundaries:
total: 1,334 km
border countries: Austria 330 km, Croatia 670 km, Italy 232 km, Hungary 102 km
Coastline: 46.6 km
Maritime claims: NA
Climate: Mediterranean climate on the coast, continental climate with mild to hot summers and cold winters in the plateaus and valleys to the east

Terrain: a short coastal strip on the Adriatic, an alpine mountain region adjacent to Italy and Austria, mixed mountains and valleys with numerous rivers to the east
Elevation extremes:
lowest point: Adriatic Sea 0 m
highest point: Triglav 2,864 m
Natural resources: lignite coal, lead, zinc, mercury, uranium, silver, hydropower, forests
Land use:
arable land: 11.48%
permanent crops: 2.68%
other: 85.84% (1998 est.)
Irrigated land: 20 sq km (1998 est.)
Natural hazards: flooding and earthquakes
Environment - current issues: Sava River polluted with domestic and industrial waste; pollution of coastal waters with heavy metals and toxic chemicals; forest damage near Koper from air pollution (originating at metallurgical and chemical plants) and resulting acid rain
Environment - international agreements:
party to: Air Pollution, Air Pollution-Sulfur 94, Biodiversity, Climate Change, Climate Change-Kyoto Protocol, Desertification, Endangered Species, Hazardous Wastes, Law of the Sea, Marine Dumping, Ozone Layer Protection, Ship Pollution, Wetlands
signed, but not ratified: Air Pollution-Persistent Organic Pollutants
Geography - note: despite its small size, this eastern Alpine country controls some of Europe's major transit routes

People

Population: 2,011,473 (July 2004 est.)
Age structure:
0-14 years: 14.3% (male 147,506; female 139,435)
15-64 years: 70.6% (male 716,057; female 704,734)
65 years and over: 15.1% (male 115,391; female 188,350) (2004 est.)

Median age:
total: 39.8 years
male: 38.3 years
female: 41.3 years (2004 est.)
Population growth rate: -0.01% (2004 est.)
Birth rate: 8.9 births/1,000 population (2004 est.)
Death rate: 10.15 deaths/1,000 population (2004 est.)
Net migration rate: 1.12 migrant(s)/1,000 population (2004 est.)
Sex ratio:
at birth: 1.07 male(s)/female
under 15 years: 1.06 male(s)/female
15-64 years: 1.02 male(s)/female
65 years and over: 0.61 male(s)/female
total population: 0.95 male(s)/female (2004 est.)
Infant mortality rate:
total: 4.5 deaths/1,000 live births
male: 5.11 deaths/1,000 live births
female: 3.84 deaths/1,000 live births (2004 est.)
Life expectancy at birth:
total population: 75.93 years
male: 72.18 years
female: 79.92 years (2004 est.)
Total fertility rate: 1.23 children born/woman (2004 est.)
HIV/AIDS - adult prevalence rate: less than 0.1% (2001 est.)
HIV/AIDS - people living with HIV/AIDS: 280 (2001 est.)
HIV/AIDS - deaths: less than 100 (2001 est.)
Nationality:
noun: Slovene(s)
adjective: Slovenian
Ethnic groups: Slovene 92%, Croat 1%, Serb 0.5%, Hungarian 0.4%, Bosniak 0.3%, other 5.8% (1991)
Religions: Roman Catholic (Uniate 2%) 70.8%, Lutheran 1%, Muslim 1%, atheist 4.3%, other 22.9%
Languages: Slovenian 92%, Serbo-Croatian 6.2%, other 1.8%
Literacy:
definition: NA
total population: 99.7%
male: 99.7%
female: 99.6% (2003 est.)

Government

Country name:
conventional long form: Republic of Slovenia
conventional short form: Slovenia
local long form: Republika Slovenija
local short form: Slovenija
Government type: parliamentary democratic republic
Capital: Ljubljana
Administrative divisions: 182 municipalities (obcine, singular - obcina) and 11 urban municipalities* (mestne obcine , singular - mestna obcina) Ajdovscina, Beltinci, Benedikt, Bistrica ob Sotli, Bled, Bloke, Bohinj, Borovnica, Bovec, Braslovce, Brda, Brezice, Brezovica, Cankova, Celje*,

Slovenia (continued)

Cerklje na Gorenjskem, Cerknica, Cerkno, Cerkvenjak, Crensovci, Crna na Koroskem, Crnomelj, Destrnik, Divaca, Dobje, Dobrepolje, Dobrna, Dobrova-Horjul-Polhov Gradec, Dobrovnik-Dobronak, Dolenjske Toplice, Dol pri Ljubljani, Domzale, Dornava, Dravograd, Duplek, Gorenja Vas-Poljane, Gorisnica, Gornja Radgona, Gornji Grad, Gornji Petrovci, Grad, Grosuplje, Hajdina, Hoce-Slivnica, Hodos-Hodos, Horjul, Hrastnik, Hrpelje-Kozina, Idrija, Ig, Ilirska Bistrica, Ivancna Gorica, Izola-Isola, Jesenice, Jezersko, Jursinci, Kamnik, Kanal, Kidricevo, Kobarid, Kobilje, Kocevje, Komen, Komenda, Koper-Capodistria*, Kostel, Kozje, Kranj*, Kranjska Gora, Krizevci, Krsko, Kungota, Kuzma, Lasko, Lenart, Lendava-Lendva, Litija, Ljubljana*, Ljubno, Ljutomer, Logatec, Loska Dolina, Loski Potok, Lovrenc na Pohorju, Luce, Lukovica, Majsperk, Maribor*, Markovci, Medvode, Menges, Metlika, Mezica, Miklavz na Dravskem Polju, Miren-Kostanjevica, Mirna Pec, Mislinja, Moravce, Moravske Toplice, Mozirje, Murska Sobota*, Muta, Naklo, Nazarje, Nova Gorica*, Novo Mesto*, Odranci, Oplotnica, Ormoz, Osilnica, Pesnica, Piran-Pirano, Pivka, Podcetrtek, Podlehnik, Podvelka, Polzela, Postojna, Prebold, Preddvor, Prevalje, Ptuj*, Puconci, Race-Fram, Radece, Radenci, Radlje ob Dravi, Radovljica, Ravne na Koroskem, Razkrizje, Ribnica, Ribnica na Pohorju, Rogasovci, Rogaska Slatina, Rogatec, Ruse, Salovci, Selnica ob Dravi, Semic, Sempeter-Vrtojba, Sencur, Sentilj, Sentjernej, Sentjur pri Celju, Sevnica, Sezana, Skocjan, Skofja Loka, Skofljica, Slovenj Gradec*, Slovenska Bistrica, Slovenske Konjice, Smarje pri Jelsah, Smartno ob Paki, Smartno pri Litiji, Sodrazica, Solcava, Sostanj, Starse, Store, Sveta Ana, Sveti Andraz v Slovenskih Goricah, Sveti Jurij, Tabor, Tisina, Tolmin, Trbovlje, Trebnje, Trnovska Vas, Trzic, Trzin, Turnisce, Velenje*, Velika Polana, Velike Lasce, Verzej, Videm, Vipava, Vitanje, Vodice, Vojnik, Vransko, Vrhnika, Vuzenica, Zagorje ob Savi, Zalec, Zavrc, Zelezniki, Zetale, Ziri, Zirovnica, Zuzemberk, Zrece

note: there may be 45 more municipalities

Independence: 25 June 1991 (from Yugoslavia)

National holiday: Independence Day/Statehood Day, 25 June (1991)

Constitution: adopted 23 December 1991, effective 23 December 1991

Legal system: based on civil law system

Suffrage: 18 years of age; universal (16 years of age, if employed)

Executive branch:

chief of state: President Janez DRNOVSEK (since 22 December 2002)

head of government: Prime Minister Anton ROP (since 11 December 2002)

cabinet: Council of Ministers nominated by the prime minister and elected by the National Assembly

elections: president elected by popular vote for a five-year term; election last held 10 November and 1 December 2002 (next to be held in the fall of 2007); following National Assembly elections, the leader of the majority party or the leader of a majority coalition

is usually nominated to become prime minister by the president and elected by the National Assembly; election last held 6 December 2002 (next National Assembly elections to be held NA October 2004)

election results: Janez DRNOVSEK elected president; percent of vote - Janez DRNOVSEK 56.5%, Barbara BREZIGAR 43.5%; Anton ROP elected prime minister; National Assembly vote - 63 to 24

Legislative branch: bicameral Parliament consisting of a National Assembly or Drzavni Zbor (90 seats; 40 are directly elected and 50 are selected on a proportional basis; note - the numbers of directly elected and proportionally elected seats varies with each election; members are elected by popular vote to serve four-year terms) and the National Council or Drzavni Svet (this is primarily an advisory body organized on corporatist principles with limited legislative powers; it may propose laws, ask to review any National Assembly decisions, and call national referenda; in the election of 2002, 40 members were selected to represent local, professional, and socioeconomic interests; members are indirectly elected to five-year terms by an electoral college)

elections: National Assembly - last held 15 October 2000 (next to be held NA October 2004)

election results: percent of vote by party - LDS 36%, SDS 16%, ZLSD 12%, SLS/SKD 10%, NSi 9%, SMS 4%, SNS 4%, DeSUS 5%, other 4%; seats by party - LDS 34, SDS 13, ZLSD 11, SLS 10, NSi 8, SMS 4, SNS 4, DeSUS 4, Hungarian and Italian minorities 1 each

Judicial branch: Supreme Court (judges are elected by the National Assembly on the recommendation of the Judicial Council); Constitutional Court (judges elected for nine-year terms by the National Assembly and nominated by the president)

Political parties and leaders: Democratic Party of Retired (Persons) of Slovenia or DeSUS [Anton ROUS]; Liberal Democratic or LDS [Anton ROP]; New Slovenia or NSi [Andrej BAJUK]; Slovene National Party or SNS [Zmago JELINCIC]; Slovene People's Party or SLS [Franc BUT]; Slovene Youth Party or SMS [Dominic CERNJAK]; Social Democratic Party of Slovenia or SDS [Janez JANSA]; United List of Social Democrats or ZLSD [Borut PAHOR]

Political pressure groups and leaders: NA

International organization participation: ACCT (observer), BIS, CE, CEI, EAPC, EBRD, EU (new member), FAO, IADB, IAEA, IBRD, ICAO, ICC, ICCt, ICRM, IDA, IFC, IFRCS, IHO, ILO, IMF, IMO, Interpol, IOC, IOM, ISO, ITU, NAM (guest), NSG, OPCW, OSCE, PCA, PFP, UN, UNCTAD, UNESCO, UNIDO, UNMIK, UNTSO, UPU, WCO, WEU (associate partner), WHO, WIPO, WMO, WToO, WTrO, ZC

Diplomatic representation in the US:

chief of mission: Ambassador Davorin KRACUN

chancery: 1525 New Hampshire Avenue NW, Washington, DC 20036

telephone: [1] (202) 667-5363

FAX: [1] (202) 667-4563

consulate(s) general: New York and Cleveland

Diplomatic representation from the US:

chief of mission: Ambassador Johnny YOUNG

embassy: Presernova 31, 1000 Ljubljana

mailing address: American Embassy Ljubljana, Department of State, 7140 Ljubljana Place, Washington, DC 20521-7140

telephone: [386] (1) 200-5500

FAX: [386] (1) 200-5555

Flag description: three equal horizontal bands of white (top), blue, and red, with the Slovenian seal (a shield with the image of Triglav, Slovenia's highest peak, in white against a blue background at the center; beneath it are two wavy blue lines depicting seas and rivers, and above it are three six-pointed stars arranged in an inverted triangle, which are taken from the coat of arms of the Counts of Celje, the great Slovene dynastic house of the late 14th and early 15th centuries); the seal is located in the upper hoist side of the flag centered in the white and blue bands

Economy

Economy - overview: Slovenia, with its historical ties to Western Europe, enjoys a GDP per capita substantially higher than that of the other transitioning economies of Central Europe. In March 2004, Slovenia became the first transition country to graduate from borrower status to donor partner at the World Bank. Privatization of the economy proceeded at an accelerated pace in 2002-03, and the budget deficit dropped from 3.0% of GDP in 2002 to 1.6% in 2003. Despite the economic slowdown in Europe in 2001-03, Slovenia maintained 3% growth. Structural reforms to improve the business environment allow for greater foreign participation in Slovenia's economy and help to lower unemployment. Further measures to curb inflation are also needed. Corruption and the high degree of coordination between government, business, and central bank policy are issues of concern in the run-up to Slovenia's scheduled 1 May 2004 accession to the European Union.

GDP: purchasing power parity - $36.89 billion (2003 est.)

GDP - real growth rate: 2.5% (2003 est.)

GDP - per capita: purchasing power parity - $18,300 (2003 est.)

GDP - composition by sector:

agriculture: 3.1%

industry: 32.7%

services: 64.2% (2002 est.)

Population below poverty line: NA%

Household income or consumption by percentage share:

lowest 10%: 3.9%

highest 10%: 23% (1998)

Distribution of family income - Gini index: 28.4 (1998)

Inflation rate (consumer prices): 5.6% (2003 est.)

Labor force: 876,100 (2003)

Labor force - by occupation: agriculture NA%, industry NA%, services NA%

Unemployment rate: 11.2% (2003 est.)

Slovenia (continued)

Budget:
revenues: $9.9 billion
expenditures: $10.5 billion, including capital expenditures of $NA (2003 est.)
Industries: ferrous metallurgy and aluminum products, lead and zinc smelting, electronics (including military electronics), trucks, electric power equipment, wood products, textiles, chemicals, machine tools
Industrial production growth rate: 0.2% (2003)
Electricity - production: 13.69 billion kWh (2001)
Electricity - production by source:
fossil fuel: 35.2%
hydro: 27.3%
nuclear: 36.8%
other: 0.7% (2001)
Electricity - consumption: 13.83 billion kWh (2001)
Electricity - exports: 3 billion kWh (2001)
Electricity - imports: 4.1 billion kWh (2001)
Oil - production: 20 bbl/day NA bbl/day (2001 est.)
Oil - consumption: 53,300 bbl/day (2001 est.)
Oil - exports: NA
Oil - imports: NA
Natural gas - production: 0 cu m (2001 est.)
Natural gas - consumption: 1.04 billion cu m (2001 est.)
Natural gas - exports: 0 cu m (2001 est.)
Natural gas - imports: 1.04 billion cu m (2001 est.)
Agriculture - products: potatoes, hops, wheat, sugar beets, corn, grapes; cattle, sheep, poultry
Exports: $11.98 billion f.o.b. (2003 est.)
Exports - commodities: manufactured goods, machinery and transport equipment, chemicals, food
Exports - partners: Germany 24.7%, Italy 12.1%, Croatia 8.7%, Austria 7.1%, France 6.7%, Bosnia and Herzegovina 4.5% (2002)
Imports: $12.63 billion f.o.b. (2003 est.)
Imports - commodities: machinery and transport equipment, manufactured goods, chemicals, fuels and lubricants, food
Imports - partners: Germany 19.2%, Italy 17.9%, France 10.2%, Austria 8.3% (2002)
Debt - external: $12.8 billion (2003)
Economic aid - recipient: ODA, $62 million (2000 est.)
Currency: tolar (SIT)
Currency code: SIT
Exchange rates: tolars per US dollar - 207.099 (2003), 240.248 (2002), 242.749 (2001), 222.656 (2000), 181.769 (1999)
Fiscal year: calendar year

Communications

Telephones - main lines in use: 1,010,200 (2002)
Telephones - mobile cellular: 1,667,200 (2002)
Telephone system:
general assessment: NA
domestic: 100% digital (2000)
international: country code - 386
Radio broadcast stations: AM 17, FM 160, shortwave 0 (1998)

Television broadcast stations: 48 (2001)
Internet country code: .si
Internet hosts: 35,791 (2002)
Internet users: 750,000 (2002)

Transportation

Railways:
total: 1,201 km
standard gauge: 1,201 km 1.435-m gauge (499 km electrified) (2002)
Highways:
total: 20,177 km
paved: 20,157 km (including 427 km of expressways)
unpaved: 20 km (2000)
Waterways: NA
Pipelines: gas 2,526 km; oil 11 km (2003)
Ports and harbors: Izola, Koper, Piran
Airports: 14 (2003 est.)
Airports - with paved runways:
total: 6
over 3,047 m: 1
2,438 to 3,047 m: 1
1,524 to 2,437 m: 1
914 to 1,523 m: 2
under 914 m: 1 (2003 est.)
Airports - with unpaved runways:
total: 8
1,524 to 2,437 m: 2
914 to 1,523 m: 2
under 914 m: 4 (2003 est.)

Military

Military branches: Slovenian Army (includes Air and Naval Forces)
Military manpower - military age: 19 years of age (2004 est.)
Military manpower - availability:
males age 15-49: 525,983 (2004 est.)
Military manpower - fit for military service:
males age 15-49: 417,875 (2004 est.)
Military manpower - reaching military age annually:
males: 13,315 (2004 est.)
Military expenditures - dollar figure: $370 million (FY00)
Military expenditures - percent of GDP: 1.7% (FY00)

Transnational Issues

Disputes - international: the Croatia-Slovenia land and maritime boundary agreement, which would have ceded most of Piran Bay and maritime access to Slovenia and several villages to Croatia, remains controversial, has not been ratified, and has been complicated by Croatia's declaration of an ecological-fisheries zone in the Adriatic Sea
Illicit drugs: minor transit point for cocaine and Southwest Asian heroin bound for Western Europe, and for precursor chemicals

Solomon Islands

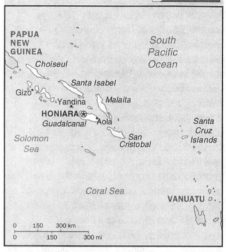

Introduction

Background: The UK established a protectorate over the Solomon Islands in the 1890s. Some of the bitterest fighting of World War II occurred on these islands. Self-government was achieved in 1976 and independence two years later. Ethnic violence, government malfeasance, and endemic crime have undermined stability and civil society. In June 2003, Prime Minister Sir Allen KEMAKEZA sought the assistance of Australia in reestablishing law and order; the following month, an Australian-led multinational force arrived to restore peace and disarm ethnic militias.

Geography

Location: Oceania, group of islands in the South Pacific Ocean, east of Papua New Guinea
Geographic coordinates: 8 00 S, 159 00 E
Map references: Oceania
Area:
total: 28,450 sq km
land: 27,540 sq km
water: 910 sq km
Area - comparative: slightly smaller than Maryland
Land boundaries: 0 km
Coastline: 5,313 km
Maritime claims: measured from claimed archipelagic baselines
territorial sea: 12 NM
exclusive economic zone: 200 NM
continental shelf: 200 NM
Climate: tropical monsoon; few extremes of temperature and weather
Terrain: mostly rugged mountains with some low coral atolls
Elevation extremes:
lowest point: Pacific Ocean 0 m
highest point: Mount Makarakomburu 2,447 m

Solomon Islands (continued)

Natural resources: fish, forests, gold, bauxite, phosphates, lead, zinc, nickel

Land use:

arable land: 1.5%

permanent crops: 0.64%

other: 97.86% (1998 est.)

Irrigated land: NA sq km

Natural hazards: typhoons, but rarely destructive; geologically active region with frequent earth tremors; volcanic activity

Environment - current issues: deforestation; soil erosion; many of the surrounding coral reefs are dead or dying

Environment - international agreements:

party to: Biodiversity, Climate Change, Climate Change-Kyoto Protocol, Desertification, Environmental Modification, Law of the Sea, Marine Dumping, Marine Life Conservation, Ozone Layer Protection, Whaling

signed, but not ratified: none of the selected agreements

Geography - note: strategic location on sea routes between the South Pacific Ocean, the Solomon Sea, and the Coral Sea

People

Population: 523,617 (July 2004 est.)

Age structure:

0-14 years: 42.4% (male 113,183; female 108,816)

15-64 years: 54.4% (male 144,157; female 140,769)

65 years and over: 3.2% (male 8,058; female 8,634) (2004 est.)

Median age:

total: 18.4 years

male: 18.3 years

female: 18.5 years (2004 est.)

Population growth rate: 2.76% (2004 est.)

Birth rate: 31.6 births/1,000 population (2004 est.)

Death rate: 4.04 deaths/1,000 population (2004 est.)

Net migration rate: 0 migrant(s)/1,000 population (2004 est.)

Sex ratio:

at birth: 1.05 male(s)/female

under 15 years: 1.04 male(s)/female

15-64 years: 1.02 male(s)/female

65 years and over: 0.93 male(s)/female

total population: 1.03 male(s)/female (2004 est.)

Infant mortality rate:

total: 22.09 deaths/1,000 live births

male: 25.15 deaths/1,000 live births

female: 18.87 deaths/1,000 live births (2004 est.)

Life expectancy at birth:

total population: 72.38 years

male: 69.9 years

female: 74.98 years (2004 est.)

Total fertility rate: 4.19 children born/woman (2004 est.)

HIV/AIDS - adult prevalence rate: NA%

HIV/AIDS - people living with HIV/AIDS: NA

HIV/AIDS - deaths: NA

Nationality:

noun: Solomon Islander(s)

adjective: Solomon Islander

Ethnic groups: Melanesian 93%, Polynesian 4%, Micronesian 1.5%, European 0.8%, Chinese 0.3%, other 0.4%

Religions: Anglican 45%, Roman Catholic 18%, United (Methodist/Presbyterian) 12%, Baptist 9%, Seventh-Day Adventist 7%, other Protestant 5%, indigenous beliefs 4%

Languages: Melanesian pidgin in much of the country is lingua franca; English is official but spoken by only 1%-2% of the population

note: 120 indigenous languages

Literacy:

definition: NA

total population: NA%

male: NA%

female: NA%

Government

Country name:

conventional long form: none

conventional short form: Solomon Islands

former: British Solomon Islands

Government type: parliamentary democracy tending toward anarchy

Capital: Honiara

Administrative divisions: 9 provinces and 1 capital territory*; Central, Choiseul, Guadalcanal, Honiara*, Isabel, Makira, Malaita, Rennell and Bellona, Temotu, Western

Independence: 7 July 1978 (from UK)

National holiday: Independence Day, 7 July (1978)

Constitution: 7 July 1978

Legal system: English common law, which is widely disregarded

Suffrage: 21 years of age; universal

Executive branch:

chief of state: Queen ELIZABETH II (since 6 February 1952), represented by Governor General Sir John LAPLI (since NA 1999)

head of government: Prime Minister Sir Allan KEMAKEZA (since 17 December 2001); Deputy Prime Minister Snyder RINI (since 17 December 2001)

cabinet: Cabinet consists of 20 members appointed by the governor general on the advice of the prime minister from among the members of Parliament

elections: none; the monarch is hereditary; governor general appointed by the monarch on the advice of Parliament for up to five years; following legislative elections, the leader of the majority party or the leader of a majority coalition is usually elected prime minister by Parliament; deputy prime minister appointed by the governor general on the advice of the prime minister from among the members of Parliament

Legislative branch: unicameral National Parliament (50 seats; members elected from single-member constituencies by popular vote to serve four-year terms)

elections: last held 5 December 2001 (next to be held not later than December 2005)

election results: percent of vote by party - PAP 40%, SIACC 40%, PPP 20%; seats by party - PAP 16, SIACC 13, PPP 2, SILP 1, independents 18

Judicial branch: Court of Appeal

Political parties and leaders: Association of Independents [Snyder RINI]; People's Alliance Party or PAP [Allan KEMAKEZA]; People's Progressive Party or PPP [Mannaseh Damukana SOGAVARE]; Solomon Islands Alliance for Change Coalition or SIACC [Bartholomew ULUFA'ALU]; Solomon Islands Labor Party or SILP [Joses TUHANUKU]

note: in general, Solomon Islands politics is characterized by fluid coalitions

Political pressure groups and leaders: NA

International organization participation: ACP, AsDB, C, ESCAP, FAO, G-77, IBRD, ICAO, ICCt (signatory), ICRM, IDA, IFAD, IFC, IFRCS, ILO, IMF, IMO, IOC, ITU, PIF, Sparteca, UN, UNCTAD, UNESCO, UPU, WFTU, WHO, WMO, WTrO

Diplomatic representation in the US:

chief of mission: Ambassador (vacant); Charge d'Affaires Colin BECK

chancery: 800 Second Avenue, Suite 400L, New York, NY 10017

telephone: [1] (212) 599-6192, 6193

FAX: [1] (212) 661-8925

Diplomatic representation from the US: the US does not have an embassy in Solomon Islands (embassy closed July 1993); the ambassador to Papua New Guinea, Ambassador Robert W. FITTS, is accredited to the Solomon Islands

Flag description: divided diagonally by a thin yellow stripe from the lower hoist-side corner; the upper triangle (hoist side) is blue with five white five-pointed stars arranged in an X pattern; the lower triangle is green

Government - note: June 2003 Prime Minister Sir Allen KEMAKEZA sought the intervention of Australia to aid in restoring order; parliament approved the request for intervention in July 2003; troops from Australia, New Zealand, Fiji, Papua New Guinea, and Tonga arrived 24 July 2003

Economy

Economy - overview: The bulk of the population depends on agriculture, fishing, and forestry for at least part of their livelihood. Most manufactured goods and petroleum products must be imported. The islands are rich in undeveloped mineral resources such as lead, zinc, nickel, and gold. However, severe ethnic violence, the closing of key business enterprises, and an empty government treasury have led to serious economic disarray, indeed near collapse. Tanker deliveries of crucial fuel supplies (including those for electrical generation) have become sporadic due to the government's inability to pay and attacks against ships. Telecommunications are threatened by the nonpayment of bills and by the lack of technical and maintenance staff many of whom

Solomon Islands (continued)

have left the country. The disintegration of law and order left the economy in tatters by mid-2003, and on 24 July 2003 more than 2000 Australian soldiers entered the Solomon Islands to restore order and to facilitate the restoration of basic services.

GDP: purchasing power parity - $800 million (2001 est.)

GDP - real growth rate: -10% (2001 est.)

GDP - per capita: purchasing power parity - $1,700 (2001 est.)

GDP - composition by sector:
agriculture: 42%
industry: 11%
services: 47% (2000 est.)

Population below poverty line: NA%

Household income or consumption by percentage share:
lowest 10%: NA%
highest 10%: NA%

Inflation rate (consumer prices): 9% (2002 est.)

Labor force: 26,842 (1999)

Labor force - by occupation: agriculture 75%, industry 5%, services 20% (2000 est.)

Unemployment rate: NA%

Budget:
revenues: $38 million
expenditures: $NA, including capital expenditures of $NA (2001)

Industries: fish (tuna), mining, timber

Industrial production growth rate: NA%

Electricity - production: 32 million kWh (2001)

Electricity - production by source:
fossil fuel: 100%
hydro: 0%
nuclear: 0%
other: 0% (2001)

Electricity - consumption: 29.76 million kWh (2001)

Electricity - exports: 0 kWh (2001)

Electricity - imports: 0 kWh (2001)

Oil - production: 0 bbl/day (2001 est.)

Oil - consumption: 1,250 bbl/day (2001 est.)

Oil - exports: NA

Oil - imports: NA

Agriculture - products: cocoa beans, coconuts, palm kernels, rice, potatoes, vegetables, fruit; cattle, pigs; timber; fish

Exports: $90 million f.o.b. (2002 est.)

Exports - commodities: timber, fish, copra, palm oil, cocoa

Exports - partners: Japan 21.1%, China 18.9%, South Korea 15.6%, Philippines 10%, Thailand 7.8%, Singapore 4.4% (2002)

Imports: $100 million f.o.b. (2002 est.)

Imports - commodities: food, plant and equipment, manufactured goods, fuels, chemicals

Imports - partners: Australia 32%, Singapore 20%, Fiji 5%, New Zealand 5%, Papua New Guinea 4% (2002)

Debt - external: $162.5 million (2001 est.)

Economic aid - recipient: $23 million annually, mainly from Australia (2000-03 est.)

Currency: Solomon Islands dollar (SBD)

Currency code: SBD

Exchange rates: Solomon Islands dollars per US dollar - NA (2003), 6.7488 (2002), 5.278 (2001), 5.0889 (2000), 4.8381 (1999)

Fiscal year: calendar year

Communications

Telephones - main lines in use: 6,600 (2002)

Telephones - mobile cellular: 1,000 (2002)

Telephone system:
general assessment: NA
domestic: NA
international: country code - 677; satellite earth station - 1 Intelsat (Pacific Ocean)

Radio broadcast stations: AM 3, FM 0, shortwave 0 (1998)

Television broadcast stations: 0 (1997)

Internet country code: .sb

Internet hosts: 470 (2002)

Internet users: 2,200 (2002)

Transportation

Railways: 0 km

Highways:
total: 1,360 km
paved: 34 km
unpaved: 1,326 km (1999 est.)

Waterways: none

Ports and harbors: Aola Bay, Honiara, Lofung, Noro, Viru Harbor, Yandina

Merchant marine: none

Airports: 33 (2003 est.)

Airports - with paved runways:
total: 2
1,524 to 2,437 m: 1
914 to 1,523 m: 1 (2003 est.)

Airports - with unpaved runways:
total: 31
1,524 to 2,437 m: 1
914 to 1,523 m: 9
under 914 m: 21 (2003 est.)

Military

Military branches: no regular military forces; Solomon Islands National Reconnaissance and Surveillance Force; Royal Solomon Islands Police (RSIP)

Military expenditures - dollar figure: NA

Military expenditures - percent of GDP: NA

Transnational Issues

Disputes - international: Australian defense personnel are dispatched at the invitation of the Solomon Islands' Government to restore law and order on the islands and reinforce regional security

Somalia

Introduction

Background: The SIAD BARRE regime was ousted in January 1991; turmoil, factional fighting, and anarchy have followed for thirteen years. In May of 1991, northern clans declared an independent Republic of Somaliland that now includes the administrative regions of Awdal, Woqooyi Galbeed, Togdheer, Sanaag, and Sool. Although not recognized by any government, this entity has maintained a stable existence, aided by the overwhelming dominance of a ruling clan and economic infrastructure left behind by British, Russian, and American military assistance programs. The regions of Bari and Nugaal and northern Mudug comprise a neighboring self-declared autonomous state of Puntland, which has been self-governing since 1998, but does not aim at independence; it has also made strides towards reconstructing a legitimate, representative government, but has suffered civil strife in 2002. Puntland disputes its border with Somaliland as it also claims portions of eastern Sool and Sanaag. Beginning in 1993, a two-year UN humanitarian effort (primarily in the south) was able to alleviate famine conditions, but when the UN withdrew in 1995, having suffered significant casualties, order still had not been restored. The mandate of the Transitional National Government (TNG), created in August 2000 in Arta, Djibouti, expired in August 2003. Discussions regarding the establishment of a new government are ongoing in Kenya. Numerous warlords and factions are still fighting for control of Mogadishu and the other southern regions. Suspicion of Somali links with global terrorism further complicates the picture.

Geography

Location: Eastern Africa, bordering the Gulf of Aden and the Indian Ocean, east of Ethiopia

Geographic coordinates: 10 00 N, 49 00 E

Map references: Africa

Somalia (continued)

Area:

total: 637,657 sq km
land: 627,337 sq km
water: 10,320 sq km

Area - comparative: slightly smaller than Texas

Land boundaries:

total: 2,340 km
border countries: Djibouti 58 km, Ethiopia 1,600 km, Kenya 682 km

Coastline: 3,025 km

Maritime claims:

territorial sea: 200 NM

Climate: principally desert; December to February - northeast monsoon, moderate temperatures in north and very hot in south; May to October - southwest monsoon, torrid in the north and hot in the south, irregular rainfall, hot and humid periods (tangambili) between monsoons

Terrain: mostly flat to undulating plateau rising to hills in north

Elevation extremes:

lowest point: Indian Ocean 0 m
highest point: Shimbiris 2,416 m

Natural resources: uranium and largely unexploited reserves of iron ore, tin, gypsum, bauxite, copper, salt, natural gas, likely oil reserves

Land use:

arable land: 1.66%
permanent crops: 0.04%
other: 98.3% (1998 est.)

Irrigated land: 2,000 sq km (1998 est.)

Natural hazards: recurring droughts; frequent dust storms over eastern plains in summer; floods during rainy season

Environment - current issues: famine; use of contaminated water contributes to human health problems; deforestation; overgrazing; soil erosion; desertification

Environment - international agreements:

party to: Endangered Species, Law of the Sea, Ozone Layer Protection

Geography - note: strategic location on Horn of Africa along southern approaches to Bab el Mandeb and route through Red Sea and Suez Canal

People

Population: 8,304,601

note: this estimate was derived from an official census taken in 1975 by the Somali Government; population counting in Somalia is complicated by the large number of nomads and by refugee movements in response to famine and clan warfare (July 2004 est.)

Age structure:

0-14 years: 44.7% (male 1,860,451; female 1,849,484)
15-64 years: 52.7% (male 2,197,572; female 2,176,762)
65 years and over: 2.7% (male 94,905; female 125,427) (2004 est.)

Median age:

total: 17.6 years

male: 17.5 years
female: 17.6 years (2004 est.)

Population growth rate: 3.41% (2004 est.)
Birth rate: 46.04 births/1,000 population (2004 est.)
Death rate: 17.3 deaths/1,000 population (2004 est.)
Net migration rate: 5.37 migrant(s)/1,000 population (2004 est.)

Sex ratio:

at birth: 1.03 male(s)/female
under 15 years: 1.01 male(s)/female
15-64 years: 1.01 male(s)/female
65 years and over: 0.76 male(s)/female
total population: 1 male(s)/female (2004 est.)

Infant mortality rate:

total: 118.52 deaths/1,000 live births
male: 127.95 deaths/1,000 live births
female: 108.81 deaths/1,000 live births (2004 est.)

Life expectancy at birth:

total population: 47.71 years
male: 46.02 years
female: 49.46 years (2004 est.)

Total fertility rate: 6.91 children born/woman (2004 est.)

HIV/AIDS - adult prevalence rate: 1% (2001 est.)

HIV/AIDS - people living with HIV/AIDS: 43,000 (2001 est.)

HIV/AIDS - deaths: NA

Nationality:

noun: Somali(s)
adjective: Somali

Ethnic groups: Somali 85%, Bantu and other non-Somali 15% (including Arabs 30,000)

Religions: Sunni Muslim

Languages: Somali (official), Arabic, Italian, English

Literacy:

definition: age 15 and over can read and write
total population: 37.8%
male: 49.7%
female: 25.8% (2001 est.)

Government

Country name:

conventional long form: none
conventional short form: Somalia
former: Somali Republic, Somali Democratic Republic

Government type: no permanent national government; transitional, parliamentary national government

Capital: Mogadishu

Administrative divisions: 18 regions (plural - NA, singular - gobolka); Awdal, Bakool, Banaadir, Bari, Bay, Galguduud, Gedo, Hiiraan, Jubbada Dhexe, Jubbada Hoose, Mudug, Nugaal, Sanaag, Shabeellaha Dhexe, Shabeellaha Hoose, Sool, Togdheer, Woqooyi Galbeed

Independence: 1 July 1960 (from a merger of British Somaliland, which became independent from the UK on 26 June 1960, and Italian Somaliland, which became independent from the Italian-administered UN trusteeship on 1 July 1960, to form the Somali Republic)

National holiday: Foundation of the Somali Republic, 1 July (1960); note - 26 June (1960) in Somaliland

Constitution: 25 August 1979, presidential approval 23 September 1979

note: the Transitional National Government formed in August 2000 had a three-year mandate to create a new constitution and hold elections, this goal was not achieved but the process is ongoing

Legal system: no national system; Shari'a and secular courts are in some localities

Suffrage: 18 years of age; universal

Executive branch:

chief of state: ABDIKASSIM Salad Hassan (since 26 August 2000); note - as of December 2002, there was no executive branch in southern Somalia; Interim President ABDIKASSIM was chosen for a three-year term by a 245-member National Assembly serving as a transitional government but has little power; the political situation, particularly in the south, with interclan fighting and random banditry, remains fluid
head of government: Prime Minister Muhammad Abdi YUSUF (since 8 December 2003)
cabinet: Cabinet appointed by the prime minister and sworn in on 20 October 2000; as of 1 January 2002, the Cabinet was in caretaker status following a no-confidence vote in October 2001 that ousted HASSAN's predecessor
election results: ABDIKASSIM Salad Hassan was elected president of an interim government at the Djibouti-sponsored Arta Peace Conference on 26 August 2000 by a broad representation of Somali clans that comprised a transitional National Assembly

Legislative branch: unicameral National Assembly

note: fledgling parliament; a transitional 245-member National Assembly began to meet on 13 August 2000 in the town of Arta, Djibouti and is now based in Mogadishu

Judicial branch: following the breakdown of national government, most regions have reverted to either Islamic (Shari'a) law with a provision for appeal of all sentences, or traditional clan-based arbitration

Political parties and leaders: none

Political pressure groups and leaders: numerous clan and subclan factions are currently vying for power

International organization participation: ACP, AfDB, AFESD, AMF, AU, CAEU, FAO, G-77, IBRD, ICAO, ICRM, IDA, IDB, IFAD, IFC, IFRCS, IGAD, ILO, IMF, IMO, Interpol, IOC, IOM (observer), ITU, LAS, NAM, OIC, UN, UNCTAD, UNESCO, UNHCR, UNIDO, UPU, WFTU, WHO, WIPO, WMO

Diplomatic representation in the US: Somalia does not have an embassy in the US (ceased operations on 8 May 1991); note - the TNG and other factions have representatives in Washington and at the United Nations

Diplomatic representation from the US: the US does not have an embassy in Somalia; US interests are represented by the US Embassy in Nairobi, Kenya at Mombasa Road; mailing address: P. O. Box 30137, Unit 64100, Nairobi; APO AE 09831; telephone: [254] (2) 537800; FAX [254] (2) 537810

Somalia (continued)

Flag description: light blue with a large white five-pointed star in the center; blue field influenced by the flag of the UN

Government - note: although an interim government was created in 2000 other governing bodies continue to exist and control various cities and regions of the country, including Somaliland, Puntland, and traditional clan and faction strongholds

Economy

Economy - overview: Somalia's economic fortunes are being driven by its deep political divisions. The northern area has declared its independence as "Somaliland"; the central area, Puntland, is a self-declared autonomous state; and the remaining southern portion is riddled with the struggles of rival factions. Economic life continues, in part because much activity is local and relatively easily protected. Agriculture is the most important sector, with livestock normally accounting for about 40% of GDP and about 65% of export earnings, but Saudi Arabia's recent ban on Somali livestock, because of Rift Valley Fever concerns, has severely hampered the sector. Nomads and semi-nomads, who are dependent upon livestock for their livelihood, make up a large portion of the population. Livestock, hides, fish, charcoal, and bananas are Somalia's principal exports, while sugar, sorghum, corn, qat, and machined goods are the principal imports. Somalia's small industrial sector, based on the processing of agricultural products, has largely been looted and sold as scrap metal. Despite the seeming anarchy, Somalia's service sector has managed to survive and grow. Telecommunication firms provide wireless services in most major cities and offer the lowest international call rates on the continent. In the absence of a formal banking sector, money exchange services have sprouted throughout the country, handling between $200 million and $500 million in remittances annually. Mogadishu's main market offers a variety of goods from food to the newest electronic gadgets. Hotels continue to operate, and militias provide security. The ongoing civil disturbances and clan rivalries, however, have interfered with any broad-based economic development and international aid arrangements. In 2002 Somalia's overdue financial obligations to the IMF continued to grow. Statistics on Somalia's GDP, growth, per capita income, and inflation should be viewed skeptically.

GDP: purchasing power parity - $4.361 billion (2003 est.)

GDP - real growth rate: 2.1% (2003 est.)

GDP - per capita: purchasing power parity - $500 (2003 est.)

GDP - composition by sector:
agriculture: 65%
industry: 10%
services: 25% (2000 est.)

Population below poverty line: NA%

Household income or consumption by percentage share:
lowest 10%: NA%
highest 10%: NA%

Inflation rate (consumer prices): note - businesses print their own money, so inflation rates cannot be sensibly determined (2003 est.)

Labor force: 3.7 million (very few are skilled laborers)

Labor force - by occupation: agriculture (mostly pastoral nomadism) 71%, industry and services 29%

Unemployment rate: NA%

Budget:
revenues: $NA
expenditures: $NA, including capital expenditures of $NA

Industries: a few light industries, including sugar refining, textiles, petroleum refining (mostly shut down), wireless communication

Industrial production growth rate: NA%

Electricity - production: 245.1 million kWh (2001)

Electricity - production by source:
fossil fuel: 100%
hydro: 0%
nuclear: 0%
other: 0% (2001)

Electricity - consumption: 227.9 million kWh (2001)

Electricity - exports: 0 kWh (2001)

Electricity - imports: 0 kWh (2001)

Oil - production: 0 bbl/day (2001 est.)

Oil - consumption: 4,000 bbl/day (2001 est.)

Oil - exports: NA

Oil - imports: NA

Oil - proved reserves: 0 bbl (1 January 2002)

Natural gas - proved reserves: 2.832 billion cu m (1 January 2002)

Agriculture - products: cattle, sheep, goats; bananas, sorghum, corn, coconuts, rice, sugarcane, mangoes, sesame seeds, beans; fish

Exports: $79 million f.o.b. (2002 est.)

Exports - commodities: livestock, bananas, hides, fish, charcoal, scrap metal

Exports - partners: UAE 41.8%, Yemen 22.8%, Oman 11.4% (2002)

Imports: $344 million f.o.b. (2002 est.)

Imports - commodities: manufactures, petroleum products, foodstuffs, construction materials, qat

Imports - partners: Djibouti 30.2%, Kenya 14%, Brazil 8.7%, Thailand 4.9%, UK 4.7%, UAE 4.4% (2002)

Debt - external: $2.6 billion (2000 est.)

Economic aid - recipient: $60 million (1999 est.)

Currency: Somali shilling (SOS)

Currency code: SOS

Exchange rates: Somali shillings per US dollar - 11,000 (November 2000), 2,620 (January 1999), 7,500 (November 1997 est.), 7,000 (January 1996 est.), 5,000 (1 January 1995)
note: the Republic of Somaliland, a self-declared independent country not recognized by any foreign government, issues its own currency, the Somaliland shilling

Fiscal year: NA

Communications

Telephones - main lines in use: 100,000 est (2002)

Telephones - mobile cellular: 35,000 (2002)

Telephone system:
general assessment: the public telecommunications system was almost completely destroyed or dismantled by the civil war factions; private wireless companies offer service in most major cities and charge the lowest international rates on the continent
domestic: local cellular telephone systems have been established in Mogadishu and in several other population centers
international: country code - 252; international connections are available from Mogadishu by satellite

Radio broadcast stations: AM 0, FM 11, shortwave 1 in Mogadishu; 1 FM in Puntland, 1 FM in Somaliland (2001)

Television broadcast stations: 4
note: two in Mogadishu; two in Hargeisa (2001)

Internet country code: .so

Internet users: 89,000 (2002)

Transportation

Railways: 0 km

Highways:
total: 22,100 km
paved: 2,608 km
unpaved: 19,492 km (1999 est.)

Waterways: none

Pipelines: crude oil 15 km

Ports and harbors: Boosaaso, Berbera, Chisimayu (Kismaayo), Merca, Mogadishu

Merchant marine: none

Airports: 60 (2003 est.)

Airports - with paved runways:
total: 6
over 3,047 m: 4
2438 to 3047 m: 1
1,524 to 2,437 m: 1 (2003 est.)

Airports - with unpaved runways:
total: 54
2,438 to 3,047 m: 4
1,524 to 2,437 m: 19
914 to 1,523 m: 29
under 914 m: 2 (2003 est.)

Military

Military branches: A Somali National Army was attempted under the interim government; numerous factions and clans maintain independent militias, and the Somaliland and Puntland regional governments maintain their own security and police forces

Military manpower - availability:
males age 15-49: 2,010,152 (2004 est.)

Military manpower - fit for military service:
males age 15-49: 1,109,405 (2004 est.)

Military expenditures - dollar figure: $18.9 million (2003)

Military expenditures - percent of GDP: 0.9% (2003)

Somalia (continued)

Disputes - international: "Somaliland" secessionists provide port facilities to land-locked Ethiopia and establish commercial ties with regional states; "Puntland" secessionists clash with "Somaliland" secessionists to establish territorial limits and clan loyalties, each seeking support from neighboring states; Ethiopia maintains only an administrative line with the Oromo region of southern Somalia and maintains alliances with local Somali clans opposed to the unrecognized Transitional National Government in Mogadishu

South Africa

Introduction

Background: After the British seized the Cape of Good Hope area in 1806, many of the Dutch settlers (the Boers) trekked north to found their own republics. The discovery of diamonds (1867) and gold (1886) spurred wealth and immigration and intensified the subjugation of the native inhabitants. The Boers resisted British encroachments, but were defeated in the Boer War (1899-1902). The resulting Union of South Africa operated under a policy of apartheid - the separate development of the races. The 1990s brought an end to apartheid politically and ushered in black majority rule.

Geography

Location: Southern Africa, at the southern tip of the continent of Africa
Geographic coordinates: 29 00 S, 24 00 E
Map references: Africa
Area:
total: 1,219,912 sq km
land: 1,219,912 sq km
water: 0 sq km
note: includes Prince Edward Islands (Marion Island and Prince Edward Island)
Area - comparative: slightly less than twice the size of Texas
Land boundaries:
total: 4,862 km
border countries: Botswana 1,840 km, Lesotho 909 km, Mozambique 491 km, Namibia 967 km, Swaziland 430 km, Zimbabwe 225 km
Coastline: 2,798 km
Maritime claims:
territorial sea: 12 NM
contiguous zone: 24 NM
exclusive economic zone: 200 NM
continental shelf: 200 NM or to edge of the continental margin

Climate: mostly semiarid; subtropical along east coast; sunny days, cool nights
Terrain: vast interior plateau rimmed by rugged hills and narrow coastal plain
Elevation extremes:
lowest point: Atlantic Ocean 0 m
highest point: Njesuthi 3,408 m
Natural resources: gold, chromium, antimony, coal, iron ore, manganese, nickel, phosphates, tin, uranium, gem diamonds, platinum, copper, vanadium, salt, natural gas
Land use:
arable land: 12.13%
permanent crops: 0.77%
other: 87.1% (1998 est.)
Irrigated land: 13,500 sq km (1998 est.)
Natural hazards: prolonged droughts
Environment - current issues: lack of important arterial rivers or lakes requires extensive water conservation and control measures; growth in water usage outpacing supply; pollution of rivers from agricultural runoff and urban discharge; air pollution resulting in acid rain; soil erosion; desertification
Environment - international agreements:
party to: Antarctic-Environmental Protocol, Antarctic-Marine Living Resources, Antarctic Seals, Antarctic Treaty, Biodiversity, Climate Change, Climate Change-Kyoto Protocol, Desertification, Endangered Species, Hazardous Wastes, Law of the Sea, Marine Dumping, Marine Life Conservation, Ozone Layer Protection, Ship Pollution, Wetlands, Whaling
signed, but not ratified: none of the selected agreements
Geography - note: South Africa completely surrounds Lesotho and almost completely surrounds Swaziland

People

Population: 42,718,530
note: South Africa took a census October 1996 that showed a population of 40,583,611 (after an official adjustment for a 6.8% underenumeration based on a postenumeration survey); estimates for this country explicitly take into account the effects of excess mortality due to AIDS; this can result in lower life expectancy, higher infant mortality and death rates, lower population and growth rates, and changes in the distribution of population by age and sex than would otherwise be expected (July 2004 est.)
Age structure:
0-14 years: 29.5% (male 6,337,468; female 6,254,925)
15-64 years: 65.3% (male 13,898,269; female 14,017,559)
65 years and over: 5.2% (male 886,801; female 1,323,508) (2004 est.)
Median age:
total: 24.7 years
male: 24.2 years
female: 25.3 years (2004 est.)

Population growth rate: -0.25% (2004 est.)
Birth rate: 18.38 births/1,000 population (2004 est.)
Death rate: 20.54 deaths/1,000 population (2004 est.)
Net migration rate: -0.29 migrant(s)/1,000 population (2004 est.)
Sex ratio:
at birth: 1.02 male(s)/female
under 15 years: 1.01 male(s)/female
15-64 years: 0.99 male(s)/female
65 years and over: 0.67 male(s)/female
total population: 0.98 male(s)/female (2004 est.)
Infant mortality rate:
total: 62.18 deaths/1,000 live births
male: 65.87 deaths/1,000 live births
female: 58.4 deaths/1,000 live births (2004 est.)
Life expectancy at birth:
total population: 44.19 years
male: 44.39 years
female: 43.98 years (2004 est.)
Total fertility rate: 2.18 children born/woman (2004 est.)
HIV/AIDS - adult prevalence rate: 20.1% (2001 est.)
HIV/AIDS - people living with HIV/AIDS: 5 million (2001 est.)
HIV/AIDS - deaths: 360,000 (2001 est.)
Nationality:
noun: South African(s)
adjective: South African
Ethnic groups: black 75.2%, white 13.6%, Colored 8.6%, Indian 2.6%
Religions: Christian 68% (includes most whites and Coloreds, about 60% of blacks and about 40% of Indians), Muslim 2%, Hindu 1.5% (60% of Indians), indigenous beliefs and animist 28.5%
Languages: 11 official languages, including Afrikaans, English, Ndebele, Pedi, Sotho, Swazi, Tsonga, Tswana, Venda, Xhosa, Zulu
Literacy:
definition: age 15 and over can read and write
total population: 86.4%
male: 87%
female: 85.7% (2003 est.)

Government

Country name:
conventional long form: Republic of South Africa
conventional short form: South Africa
former: Union of South Africa
abbreviation: RSA
Government type: republic
Capital: Pretoria; note - Cape Town is the legislative center and Bloemfontein the judicial center
Administrative divisions: 9 provinces; Eastern Cape, Free State, Gauteng, KwaZulu-Natal, Limpopo, Mpumalanga, North-West, Northern Cape, Western Cape
Independence: 31 May 1910 (from UK); note - South Africa became a republic in 1961 following an October 1960 referendum

National holiday: Freedom Day, 27 April (1994)
Constitution: 10 December 1996; this new constitution was certified by the Constitutional Court on 4 December 1996, was signed by then President MANDELA on 10 December 1996, and entered into effect on 3 February 1997; it is being implemented in phases
Legal system: based on Roman-Dutch law and English common law; accepts compulsory ICJ jurisdiction, with reservations
Suffrage: 18 years of age; universal
Executive branch:
chief of state: President Thabo MBEKI (since 16 June 1999); Executive Deputy President Jacob ZUMA (since 17 June 1999); note - the president is both the chief of state and head of government
head of government: President Thabo MBEKI (since 16 June 1999); Executive Deputy President Jacob ZUMA (since 17 June 1999); note - the president is both the chief of state and head of government
cabinet: Cabinet appointed by the president
elections: president elected by the National Assembly for a five-year term; election last held 2 June 1999 (next to be held 24 April 2004)
election results: Thabo MBEKI elected president; percent of National Assembly vote - 100% (by acclamation)
note: ANC-IFP is the governing coalition
Legislative branch: bicameral Parliament consisting of the National Assembly (400 seats; members are elected by popular vote under a system of proportional representation to serve five-year terms) and the National Council of Provinces (90 seats, 10 members elected by each of the nine provincial legislatures for five-year terms; has special powers to protect regional interests, including the safeguarding of cultural and linguistic traditions among ethnic minorities); note - following the implementation of the new constitution on 3 February 1997 the former Senate was disbanded and replaced by the National Council of Provinces with essentially no change in membership and party affiliations, although the new institution's responsibilities have been changed somewhat by the new constitution
elections: National Assembly and National Council of Provinces - last held 2 June 1999 (next to be held 14 April 2004)
election results: National Assembly - percent of vote by party - ANC 66.4%, DP 9.6%, IFP 8.6%, NNP 6.9%, UDM 3.4%, ACDP 1.4%, FF 0.8%, other 2.9%; seats by party - ANC 266, DP 38, IFP 34, NNP 28, UDM 14, ACDP 6, FF 3, other 11; National Council of Provinces - percent of vote by party - NA%; seats by party - ANC 61, NNP 17, FF 4, IFP 5, DP 3
Judicial branch: Constitutional Court; Supreme Court of Appeals; High Courts; Magistrate Courts
Political parties and leaders: African Christian Democratic Party or ACDP [Kenneth MESHOE, president]; African National Congress or ANC [Thabo MBEKI, president]; Democratic Alliance (formed from the merger of the Democratic Party or DP and the New National Party or NNP; note - NNP split from DP in

2001) [Anthony LEON]; Freedom Front or FF [Dr. Pieter MULDER, president]; Inkatha Freedom Party or IFP [Mangosuthu BUTHELEZI, president]; New National Party or NNP [Marthinus VAN SCHALKWYK]; Pan-Africanist Congress or PAC [Stanley MOGOBA, president]; United Democratic Movement or UDM [Bantu HOLOMISA]
Political pressure groups and leaders: Congress of South African Trade Unions or COSATU [Zwelinzima VAVI, general secretary]; South African Communist Party or SACP [Blade NZIMANDE, general secretary]; South African National Civics Organization or SANCO [Mlungisi HLONGWANE, national president]; note - COSATU and SACP are in a formal alliance with the ANC
International organization participation: ACP, AfDB, AU, BIS, C, FAO, G-24, G-77, IAEA, IBRD, ICAO, ICC, ICCt, ICFTU, ICRM, IDA, IFAD, IFC, IFRCS, IHO, ILO, IMF, IMO, Interpol, IOC, IOM, ISO, ITU, MONUC, NAM, NSG, OPCW, PCA, SACU, SADC, UN, UNCTAD, UNESCO, UNHCR, UNIDO, UNITAR, UNMEE, UNMIL, UPU, WCL, WCO, WFTU, WHO, WIPO, WMO, WToO, WTrO, ZC
Diplomatic representation in the US:
chief of mission: Ambassador Barbara Joyce Mosima MASEKELA
chancery: 3051 Massachusetts Avenue NW, Washington, DC 20008
telephone: [1] (202) 232-4400
FAX: [1] (202) 265-1607
consulate(s) general: Chicago, Los Angeles, and New York
Diplomatic representation from the US:
chief of mission: Ambassador Cameron H. HUME
embassy: 877 Pretorius Street, Pretoria
mailing address: P. O. Box 9536, Pretoria 0001
telephone: [27] (12) 342-1048
FAX: [27] (12) 342-2244
consulate(s) general: Cape Town, Durban, Johannesburg
Flag description: two equal width horizontal bands of red (top) and blue separated by a central green band which splits into a horizontal Y, the arms of which end at the corners of the hoist side; the Y embraces a black isosceles triangle from which the arms are separated by narrow yellow bands; the red and blue bands are separated from the green band and its arms by narrow white stripes

Economy

Economy - overview: South Africa is a middle-income, emerging market with an abundant supply of natural resources; well-developed financial, legal, communications, energy, and transport sectors; a stock exchange that ranks among the 10 largest in the world; and a modern infrastructure supporting an efficient distribution of goods to major urban centers throughout the region. However, growth has not been strong enough to lower South Africa's high unemployment rate; and daunting economic problems remain from the apartheid era, especially poverty and lack of economic empowerment among the disadvantaged groups. High crime and HIV/AIDS infection rates also deter investment. South African economic policy is fiscally conservative, but pragmatic, focusing on targeting inflation and liberalizing trade as means to increase job growth and household income.

GDP: purchasing power parity - $456.7 billion (2003 est.)

GDP - real growth rate: 1.9% (2003 est.)

GDP - per capita: purchasing power parity - $10,700 (2003 est.)

GDP - composition by sector:
agriculture: 4.4%
industry: 28.9%
services: 66.7% (2001)

Population below poverty line: 50% (2000 est.)

Household income or consumption by percentage share:
lowest 10%: 1.1%
highest 10%: 45.9% (1994)

Distribution of family income - Gini index: 59.3 (1993-94)

Inflation rate (consumer prices): 9.9% (2002 est.)

Labor force: 17 million economically active (1998 est.)

Labor force - by occupation: agriculture 30%, industry 25%, services 45% (1999 est.)

Unemployment rate: 37% (includes workers no longer looking for employment) (2001 est.)

Budget:
revenues: $22.6 billion
expenditures: $24.7 billion, including capital expenditures of $NA billion (FY02/03)

Industries: mining (world's largest producer of platinum, gold, chromium), automobile assembly, metalworking, machinery, textile, iron and steel, chemicals, fertilizer, foodstuffs

Industrial production growth rate: 3% (2002 est.)

Electricity - production: 195.6 billion kWh (2001)

Electricity - production by source:
fossil fuel: 93.5%
hydro: 1.1%
nuclear: 5.5%
other: 0% (2001)

Electricity - consumption: 181.2 billion kWh (2001)

Electricity - exports: 6.91 billion kWh (2001)

Electricity - imports: 6.2 billion kWh (2001)

Oil - production: 196,200 bbl/day (2001 est.)

Oil - consumption: 460,000 bbl/day (2001 est.)

Oil - exports: NA

Oil - imports: NA

Oil - proved reserves: 7.84 million bbl (1 January 2002)

Natural gas - production: 1.8 billion cu m (2001 est.)

Natural gas - consumption: 1.8 billion cu m (2001 est.)

Natural gas - exports: 0 cu m (2001 est.)

Natural gas - imports: 0 cu m (2001 est.)

Natural gas - proved reserves: 14.16 million cu m (1 January 2002)

Agriculture - products: corn, wheat, sugarcane, fruits, vegetables; beef, poultry, mutton, wool, dairy products

Exports: $36.77 billion f.o.b. (2003 est.)

Exports - commodities: gold, diamonds, platinum, other metals and minerals, machinery and equipment (1998 est.)

Exports - partners: UK 12.8%, US 12.7%, Germany 9.3%, Japan 8.9%, Italy 5.8% (2002)

Imports: $33.89 billion f.o.b. (2003 est.)

Imports - commodities: machinery and equipment, chemicals, petroleum products, scientific instruments, foodstuffs (2000 est.)

Imports - partners: Germany 15.5%, US 9.5%, UK 9.1%, Japan 5.8%, Saudi Arabia 5.3%, France 5%, China 4.9% (2002)

Debt - external: $24.7 billion (2002 est.)

Economic aid - recipient: $487.5 million (2000)

Currency: rand (ZAR)

Currency code: ZAR

Exchange rates: rand per US dollar - 7.5648 (2003), 10.5407 (2002), 8.6092 (2001), 6.9398 (2000), 6.1095 (1999)

Fiscal year: 1 April - 31 March

Communications

Telephones - main lines in use: 4.844 million (2002)

Telephones - mobile cellular: 13.814 million (2002)

Telephone system:
general assessment: the system is the best developed and most modern in Africa
domestic: consists of carrier-equipped open-wire lines, coaxial cables, microwave radio relay links, fiber-optic cable, radiotelephone communication stations, and wireless local loops; key centers are Bloemfontein, Cape Town, Durban, Johannesburg, Port Elizabeth, and Pretoria
international: country code - 27; 2 submarine cables; satellite earth stations - 3 Intelsat (1 Indian Ocean and 2 Atlantic Ocean)

Radio broadcast stations: AM 14, FM 347 (plus 243 repeaters), shortwave 1 (1998)

Television broadcast stations: 556 (plus 144 network repeaters) (1997)

Internet country code: .za

Internet hosts: 198,853 (2002)

Internet users: 3.1 million (2002)

Transportation

Railways:
total: 22,298 km
narrow gauge: 21,984 km 1.065-m gauge (10,436 km electrified); 314 km 0.610-m gauge
note: includes a 2,228 km commuter rail system (2002)

Highways:
total: 362,099 km
paved: 73,506 km (including 2,032 km of expressways)
unpaved: 288,593 km (2000)

Waterways: NA

Pipelines: condensate 100 km; gas 741 km; oil 847 km; refined products 1,354 km (2003)

Ports and harbors: Cape Town, Durban, East London, Mossel Bay, Port Elizabeth, Richards Bay, Saldanha

Merchant marine:
total: 4 ships (1,000 GRT or over) 31,505 GRT/37,091 DWT
by type: container 1, liquefied gas 1, petroleum tanker 2
foreign-owned: Denmark 1, Netherlands 1
registered in other countries: 7 (2003 est.)

Airports: 728 (2003 est.)

Airports - with paved runways:
total: 145
over 3,047 m: 10
2,438 to 3,047 m: 5
1,524 to 2,437 m: 51
914 to 1,523 m: 68
under 914 m: 11 (2003 est.)

Airports - with unpaved runways:
total: 583
1,524 to 2,437 m: 34
914 to 1,523 m: 299
under 914 m: 250 (2003 est.)

Military

Military branches: South African National Defense Force: Army, Navy, Air Force, and Medical Services

Military manpower - military age: 18 years of age (2004 est.)

Military manpower - availability:
males age 15-49: 11,924,500 (2004 est.)

Military manpower - fit for military service:
males age 15-49: 7,247,696 (2004 est.)

Military manpower - reaching military age annually:
males: 471,221 (2004 est.)

Military expenditures - dollar figure: $2,653,400,000 (2003)

Military expenditures - percent of GDP: 1.7% (2003)

Military - note: with the end of apartheid and the establishment of majority rule, former military, black homelands forces, and ex-opposition forces were integrated into the South African National Defense Force (SANDF); as of 2003 the integration process was considered complete

Transnational Issues

Disputes - international: managed dispute with Namibia over the location of the boundary in the Orange River

Illicit drugs: transshipment center for heroin, hashish, marijuana, and cocaine; cocaine consumption on the rise; world's largest market for illicit methaqualone, usually imported illegally from India through various east African countries; illicit cultivation of marijuana; attractive venue for money launderers given the increasing level of organized criminal and narcotics activity in the region

South Georgia and the South Sandwich Islands

(overseas territory of the UK, also claimed by Argentina)

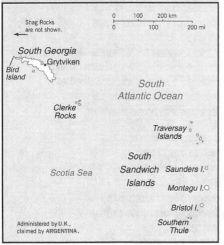

Shag Rocks are not shown.

South Georgia — Grytviken
Bird Island

South Atlantic Ocean

Clerke Rocks

Traversay Islands

Scotia Sea

South Sandwich Islands — Saunders I.
Montagu I.
Bristol I.
Southern Thule

Administered by U.K., claimed by ARGENTINA.

Introduction

Background: The islands lie approximately 1,000 km east of the Falkland Islands and have been under British administration since 1908, except for a brief period in 1982 when Argentina occupied them. Grytviken, on South Georgia, was a 19th and early 20th century whaling station. Famed explorer Ernest SHACKLETON stopped there in 1914 en route to his ill-fated attempt to cross Antarctica on foot. He returned some 20 months later with a few companions in a small boat and arranged a successful rescue for the rest of his crew, stranded off the Antarctic Peninsula. He died in 1922 on a subsequent expedition and is buried in Grytviken. Today, the station houses scientists from the British Antarctic Survey. The islands have large bird and seal populations, and, recognizing the importance of preserving the marine stocks in adjacent waters, the UK, in 1993, extended the exclusive fishing zone from 12 NM to 200 NM around each island.

Geography

Location: Southern South America, islands in the South Atlantic Ocean, east of the tip of South America
Geographic coordinates: 54 30 S, 37 00 W
Map references: Antarctic Region
Area:
total: 3,903 sq km
land: 3,903 sq km
water: 0 sq km
note: includes Shag Rocks, Black Rock, Clerke Rocks, South Georgia Island, Bird Island, and the South Sandwich Islands, which consist of some nine islands
Area - comparative: slightly larger than Rhode Island
Land boundaries: 0 km
Coastline: NA km

Maritime claims:
territorial sea: 12 NM
exclusive fishing zone: 200 NM
Climate: variable, with mostly westerly winds throughout the year interspersed with periods of calm; nearly all precipitation falls as snow
Terrain: most of the islands, rising steeply from the sea, are rugged and mountainous; South Georgia is largely barren and has steep, glacier-covered mountains; the South Sandwich Islands are of volcanic origin with some active volcanoes
Elevation extremes:
lowest point: Atlantic Ocean 0 m
highest point: Mount Paget (South Georgia) 2,934 m
Natural resources: fish
Land use:
arable land: 0%
permanent crops: 0%
other: 100% (largely covered by permanent ice and snow with some sparse vegetation consisting of grass, moss, and lichen) (1998 est.)
Irrigated land: 0 sq km (1998 est.)
Natural hazards: the South Sandwich Islands have prevailing weather conditions that generally make them difficult to approach by ship; they are also subject to active volcanism
Environment - current issues: NA
Geography - note: the north coast of South Georgia has several large bays, which provide good anchorage; reindeer, introduced early in the 20th century, live on South Georgia

People

Population: no indigenous inhabitants
note: the small military garrison on South Georgia withdrew in March 2001, to be replaced by a permanent group of scientists of the British Antarctic Survey, which also has a biological station on Bird Island; the South Sandwich Islands are uninhabited (July 2004 est.)

Government

Country name:
conventional long form: South Georgia and the South Sandwich Islands
conventional short form: none
Dependency status: overseas territory of the UK, also claimed by Argentina; administered from the Falkland Islands by a commissioner, who is concurrently governor of the Falkland Islands, representing Queen ELIZABETH II; Grytviken, formerly a whaling station on South Georgia, is a scientific base
National holiday: Liberation Day, 14 June (1982)
Constitution: adopted 3 October 1985
Legal system: the laws of the UK, where applicable, apply; the senior magistrate from the Falkland Islands presides over the Magistrates Court
Diplomatic representation in the US: none (overseas territory of the UK, also claimed by Argentina)

Diplomatic representation from the US: none (overseas territory of the UK, also claimed by Argentina)
Flag description: blue, with the flag of the UK in the upper hoist-side quadrant and the South Georgia and the South Sandwich Islands coat of arms centered on the outer half of the flag; the coat of arms features a shield with a golden lion centered; the shield is supported by a fur seal on the left and a penguin on the right; a reindeer appears above the shield, and below it on a scroll is the motto LEO TERRAM PROPRIAM PROTEGAT (Let the Lion Protect its Own Land)

Economy

Economy - overview: Some fishing takes place in adjacent waters. There is a potential source of income from harvesting finfish and krill. The islands receive income from postage stamps produced in the UK, sale of fishing licenses, and harbor and landing fees from tourist vessels. Tourism from specialized cruise ships is increasing rapidly.

Communications

Telephone system:
general assessment: NA
domestic: NA
international: coastal radiotelephone station at Grytviken
Radio broadcast stations: 0 (2003)
Television broadcast stations: 0 (2003)
Internet country code: .gs

Transportation

Waterways: none
Ports and harbors: Grytviken
Airports: none (2003 est.)

Military

Military - note: defense is the responsibility of the UK

Transnational Issues

Disputes - international: briefly occupied by military force in 1982 - claimed by Argentina in constitution but declares it will no longer seek settlement by force

Southern Ocean

Southern Ocean

Southern Ocean

Background: A decision by the International Hydrographic Organization in the spring of 2000 delimited a fifth world ocean - the Southern Ocean - from the southern portions of the Atlantic Ocean, Indian Ocean, and Pacific Ocean. The Southern Ocean extends from the coast of Antarctica north to 60 degrees south latitude, which coincides with the Antarctic Treaty Limit. The Southern Ocean is now the fourth largest of the world's five oceans (after the Pacific Ocean, Atlantic Ocean, and Indian Ocean, but larger than the Arctic Ocean).

Geography

Location: body of water between 60 degrees south latitude and Antarctica

Geographic coordinates: 65 00 S, 0 00 E (nominally), but the Southern Ocean has the unique distinction of being a large circumpolar body of water totally encircling the continent of Antarctica; this ring of water lies between 60 degrees south latitude and the coast of Antarctica and encompasses 360 degrees of longitude

Map references: Antarctic Region

Area:

total: 20.327 million sq km

note: includes Amundsen Sea, Bellingshausen Sea, part of the Drake Passage, Ross Sea, a small part of the Scotia Sea, Weddell Sea, and other tributary water bodies

Area - comparative: slightly more than twice the size of the US

Coastline: 17,968 km

Climate: sea temperatures vary from about 10 degrees Celsius to -2 degrees Celsius; cyclonic storms travel eastward around the continent and frequently are intense because of the temperature contrast between ice and open ocean; the ocean area from about latitude 40 south to the Antarctic Circle has

the strongest average winds found anywhere on Earth; in winter the ocean freezes outward to 65 degrees south latitude in the Pacific sector and 55 degrees south latitude in the Atlantic sector, lowering surface temperatures well below 0 degrees Celsius; at some coastal points intense persistent drainage winds from the interior keep the shoreline ice-free throughout the winter

Terrain: the Southern Ocean is deep, 4,000 to 5,000 meters over most of its extent with only limited areas of shallow water; the Antarctic continental shelf is generally narrow and unusually deep, its edge lying at depths of 400 to 800 meters (the global mean is 133 meters); the Antarctic icepack grows from an average minimum of 2.6 million square kilometers in March to about 18.8 million square kilometers in September, better than a sixfold increase in area; the Antarctic Circumpolar Current (21,000 km in length) moves perpetually eastward; it is the world's largest ocean current, transporting 130 million cubic meters of water per second - 100 times the flow of all the world's rivers

Elevation extremes:

lowest point: -7,235 m at the southern end of the South Sandwich Trench

highest point: sea level 0 m

Natural resources: probable large and possible giant oil and gas fields on the continental margin, manganese nodules, possible placer deposits, sand and gravel, fresh water as icebergs; squid, whales, and seals - none exploited; krill, fishes

Natural hazards: huge icebergs with drafts up to several hundred meters; smaller bergs and iceberg fragments; sea ice (generally 0.5 to 1 meter thick) with sometimes dynamic short-term variations and with large annual and interannual variations; deep continental shelf floored by glacial deposits varying widely over short distances; high winds and large waves much of the year; ship icing, especially May-October; most of region is remote from sources of search and rescue

Environment - current issues: increased solar ultraviolet radiation resulting from the Antarctic ozone hole in recent years, reducing marine primary productivity (phytoplankton) by as much as 15% and damaging the DNA of some fish; illegal, unreported, and unregulated fishing in recent years, especially the landing of an estimated five to six times more Patagonian toothfish than the regulated fishery, which is likely to affect the sustainability of the stock; large amount of incidental mortality of seabirds resulting from long-line fishing for toothfish

note: the now-protected fur seal population is making a strong comeback after severe overexploitation in the 18th and 19th centuries

Environment - international agreements: the Southern Ocean is subject to all international agreements regarding the world's oceans; in addition, it is subject to these agreements specific to the Antarctic region: International Whaling Commission (prohibits commercial whaling south of 40 degrees south [south of 60 degrees south between 50 degrees

and 130 degrees west]); Convention on the Conservation of Antarctic Seals (limits sealing); Convention on the Conservation of Antarctic Marine Living Resources (regulates fishing)

note: many nations (including the US) prohibit mineral resource exploration and exploitation south of the fluctuating Polar Front (Antarctic Convergence) which is in the middle of the Antarctic Circumpolar Current and serves as the dividing line between the very cold polar surface waters to the south and the warmer waters to the north

Geography - note: the major chokepoint is the Drake Passage between South America and Antarctica; the Polar Front (Antarctic Convergence) is the best natural definition of the northern extent of the Southern Ocean; it is a distinct region at the middle of the Antarctic Circumpolar Current that separates the very cold polar surface waters to the south from the warmer waters to the north; the Front and the Current extend entirely around Antarctica, reaching south of 60 degrees south near New Zealand and near 48 degrees south in the far South Atlantic coinciding with the path of the maximum westerly winds

Economy

Economy - overview: Fisheries in 2000-01 (1 July to 30 June) landed 112,934 metric tons, of which 87% was krill and 11% Patagonian toothfish. International agreements were adopted in late 1999 to reduce illegal, unreported, and unregulated fishing, which in the 2000-01 season landed, by one estimate, 8,376 metric tons of Patagonian and antarctic toothfish. In the 2000-01 antarctic summer 12,248 tourists, most of them seaborne, visited the Southern Ocean and Antarctica, compared to 14,762 the previous year.

Transportation

Ports and harbors: McMurdo, Palmer, and offshore anchorages in Antarctica

note: few ports or harbors exist on the southern side of the Southern Ocean; ice conditions limit use of most of them to short periods in midsummer; even then some cannot be entered without icebreaker escort; most antarctic ports are operated by government research stations and, except in an emergency, are not open to commercial or private vessels; vessels in any port south of 60 degrees south are subject to inspection by Antarctic Treaty observers (see Article 7)

Transportation - note: Drake Passage offers alternative to transit through the Panama Canal

Transnational Issues

Disputes - international: Antarctic Treaty defers claims (see Antarctica entry), but Argentina, Australia, Chile, France, NZ, Norway, and UK assert claims (some overlapping), including the continental shelf in the Southern Ocean; several states have expressed an interest in extending those continental shelf claims under the United Nations Convention on the Law of the Sea (UNCLOS) to include undersea ridges; the US and most other states do not recognize the land or maritime claims of other states and have made no claims themselves (the US and Russia have reserved the right to do so); no formal claims have been made in the sector between 90 degrees west and 150 degrees west

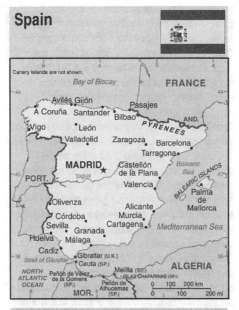

Spain

Canary Islands are not shown.

Introduction

Background: Spain's powerful world empire of the 16th and 17th centuries ultimately yielded command of the seas to England. Subsequent failure to embrace the mercantile and industrial revolutions caused the country to fall behind Britain, France, and Germany in economic and political power. Spain remained neutral in World Wars I and II, but suffered through a devastating civil war (1936-39). In the second half of the 20th century, Spain has played a catch-up role in the western international community; it joined the EU in 1986. Continuing challenges include Basque Fatherland and Liberty (ETA) terrorism and further reductions in unemployment.

Geography

Location: Southwestern Europe, bordering the Bay of Biscay, Mediterranean Sea, North Atlantic Ocean, and Pyrenees Mountains, southwest of France
Geographic coordinates: 40 00 N, 4 00 W
Map references: Europe
Area:
total: 504,782 sq km
land: 499,542 sq km
water: 5,240 sq km
note: there are 19 autonomous communities including Balearic Islands and Canary Islands, and three small Spanish possessions off the coast of Morocco - Islas Chafarinas, Penon de Alhucemas, and Penon de Velez de la Gomera
Area - comparative: slightly more than twice the size of Oregon
Land boundaries:
total: 1,917.8 km
border countries: Andorra 63.7 km, France 623 km, Gibraltar 1.2 km, Portugal 1,214 km, Morocco (Ceuta) 6.3 km, Morocco (Melilla) 9.6 km
Coastline: 4,964 km

Maritime claims:
territorial sea: 12 NM
contiguous zone: 24 NM
exclusive economic zone: 200 NM (applies only to the Atlantic Ocean)
Climate: temperate; clear, hot summers in interior, more moderate and cloudy along coast; cloudy, cold winters in interior, partly cloudy and cool along coast
Terrain: large, flat to dissected plateau surrounded by rugged hills; Pyrenees in north
Elevation extremes:
lowest point: Atlantic Ocean 0 m
highest point: Pico de Teide (Tenerife) on Canary Islands 3,718 m
Natural resources: coal, lignite, iron ore, uranium, mercury, pyrites, fluorspar, gypsum, zinc, lead, tungsten, copper, kaolin, potash, hydropower, arable land
Land use:
arable land: 28.6%
permanent crops: 9.56%
other: 61.84% (1998 est.)
Irrigated land: 36,400 sq km (1998 est.)
Natural hazards: periodic droughts
Environment - current issues: pollution of the Mediterranean Sea from raw sewage and effluents from the offshore production of oil and gas; water quality and quantity nationwide; air pollution; deforestation; desertification
Environment - international agreements:
party to: Air Pollution, Air Pollution-Nitrogen Oxides, Air Pollution-Sulfur 94, Air Pollution-Volatile Organic Compounds, Antarctic-Environmental Protocol, Antarctic-Marine Living Resources, Antarctic Treaty, Biodiversity, Climate Change, Climate Change-Kyoto Protocol, Desertification, Endangered Species, Environmental Modification, Hazardous Wastes, Law of the Sea, Marine Dumping, Marine Life Conservation, Ozone Layer Protection, Ship Pollution, Tropical Timber 83, Tropical Timber 94, Wetlands, Whaling
signed, but not ratified: Air Pollution-Persistent Organic Pollutants
Geography - note: strategic location along approaches to Strait of Gibraltar

People

Population: 40,280,780 (July 2004 est.)
Age structure:
0-14 years: 14.4% (male 2,989,053; female 2,811,350)
15-64 years: 68% (male 13,748,998; female 13,652,852)
65 years and over: 17.6% (male 2,958,387; female 4,120,140) (2004 est.)
Median age:
total: 39.1 years
male: 37.8 years
female: 40.5 years (2004 est.)
Population growth rate: 0.16% (2004 est.)

Spain (continued)

Birth rate: 10.11 births/1,000 population (2004 est.)
Death rate: 9.55 deaths/1,000 population (2004 est.)
Net migration rate: 0.99 migrant(s)/1,000 population (2004 est.)
Sex ratio:
at birth: 1.07 male(s)/female
under 15 years: 1.06 male(s)/female
15-64 years: 1.01 male(s)/female
65 years and over: 0.72 male(s)/female
total population: 0.96 male(s)/female (2004 est.)
Infant mortality rate:
total: 4.48 deaths/1,000 live births
male: 4.88 deaths/1,000 live births
female: 4.06 deaths/1,000 live births (2004 est.)
Life expectancy at birth:
total population: 79.37 years
male: 76.03 years
female: 82.94 years (2004 est.)
Total fertility rate: 1.27 children born/woman (2004 est.)
HIV/AIDS - adult prevalence rate: 0.5% (2001 est.)
HIV/AIDS - people living with HIV/AIDS: 130,000 (2001 est.)
HIV/AIDS - deaths: 2,300 (2001 est.)
Nationality:
noun: Spaniard(s)
adjective: Spanish
Ethnic groups: composite of Mediterranean and Nordic types
Religions: Roman Catholic 94%, other 6%
Languages: Castilian Spanish 74%, Catalan 17%, Galician 7%, Basque 2%
note: Castilian is the official language nationwide; the other languages are official regionally
Literacy:
definition: age 15 and over can read and write
total population: 97.9%
male: 98.7%
female: 97.2% (2003 est.)

Government

Country name:
conventional long form: Kingdom of Spain
conventional short form: Spain
local short form: Espana
Government type: parliamentary monarchy
Capital: Madrid
Administrative divisions: 19 autonomous communities (comunidades autonomas, singular - comunidad autonoma); Andalucia, Aragon, Asturias, Baleares (Balearic Islands), Ceuta, Canarias (Canary Islands), Cantabria, Castilla-La Mancha, Castilla y Leon, Cataluna, Communidad Valenciana, Extremadura, Galicia, La Rioja, Madrid, Melilla, Murcia, Navarra, Pais Vasco (Basque Country)
note: three small Spanish possessions are located off the coast of Morocco: Islas Chafarinas, Penon de Alhucemas, and Penon de Velez de la Gomera; Ceuta and Melilla on the coast of North Africa gained limited autonomous status in 1994

Independence: the Iberian peninsula was characterized by a variety of independent kingdoms prior to the Moslem occupation that began in the early 8th Century A. D. and lasted nearly seven centuries; the small Christian redoubts of the north began the reconquest almost immediately, culminating in the seizure of Granada in 1492; this event completed the unification of several kingdoms and is traditionally considered the forging of present-day Spain
National holiday: Hispanic Day, 12 October
Constitution: 6 December 1978, effective 29 December 1978
Legal system: civil law system, with regional applications; has not accepted compulsory ICJ jurisdiction
Suffrage: 18 years of age; universal
Executive branch:
chief of state: King JUAN CARLOS I (since 22 November 1975); Heir Apparent Prince FELIPE, son of the monarch, born 30 January 1968
head of government: President of the Government Jose Maria AZNAR Lopez (since 5 May 1996); First Vice President (and Minister of Economy) Rodrigo RATO Figaredo (since 4 September 2003) and Second Vice President (and Minister of the Presidency) Javier ARENAS (since 4 September 2003); note - incoming President of the Government Jose Luis RODRIGUEZ ZAPATERO will take office mid- to late April 2004
cabinet: Council of Ministers designated by the president
note: there is also a Council of State that is the supreme consultative organ of the government
elections: the monarch is hereditary; following legislative elections, the leader of the majority party or the leader of the majority coalition is usually proposed president by the monarch and elected by the National Assembly; election last held 12 March 2000 (next to be held 14 March 2004); vice presidents appointed by the monarch on the proposal of the president
election results: Jose Maria AZNAR Lopez (PP) elected president; percent of National Assembly vote - 44.54%; note - the Popular Party (PP) obtained an absolute majority of seats in both the Congress of Deputies and the Senate as a result of the March 2000 elections
Legislative branch: bicameral; General Courts or National Assembly or Las Cortes Generales consists of the Senate or Senado (259 seats - 208 members directly elected by popular vote and the other 51 appointed by the regional legislatures to serve four-year terms) and the Congress of Deputies or Congreso de los Diputados (350 seats; members are elected by popular vote on block lists by proportional representation to serve four-year terms)
elections: Senate - last held 14 March 2004 (next to be held NA March 2008); Congress of Deputies - last held 14 March 2004 (next to be held NA March 2008)
election results: Senate - percent of vote by party - NA%; seats by party - PP 102, PSOE 81, Entesa Catalona de Progress 12, CiU 4, PNV 4, CC 3, other 2;

Congress of Deputies - percent of vote by party - PSOE 42.6%, PP 37.6%, CiU 3.2%, ERC 2.5%, PNV 1.6%, IU 5.0%, CC 0.9%; seats by party - PSOE 164, PP 148, CiU 10, ERC 8 PNV 7, IU 5, CC 3, other 5
Judicial branch: Supreme Court or Tribunal Supremo
Political parties and leaders: Basque Nationalist Party or PNV [Josu Jon IMAZ]; Canarian Coalition or CC (a coalition of five parties) [Paulino RIVERO Baute]; Convergence and Union or CiU [Artur MAS i Gavarro] (a coalition of the Democratic Convergence of Catalonia or CDC [Artur MAS i Gavarro] and the Democratic Union of Catalonia or UDC [Josep Antoni DURAN y LLEIDA]); Entesa Catalonia de Progress [leader NA]; Galician Nationalist Bloc or BNG [Xose Manuel BEIRAS]; Party of Independents from Lanzarote or PIL [Dimas MARTIN Martin]; Popular Party or PP [Mariano RAJOY]; Republican Left of Catalonia [leader NA]; Spanish Socialist Workers Party or PSOE [Jose Luis RODRIGUEZ ZAPATERO]; United Left or IU (a coalition of parties including the PCE and other small parties) [Gaspar LLAMAZARES]
Political pressure groups and leaders: business and landowning interests; Catholic Church; free labor unions (authorized in April 1977); Socialist General Union of Workers or UGT and the smaller independent Workers Syndical Union or USO; university students; Workers Confederation or CC.OO; Nunca Mais (Galician for "Never Again"; formed in response to the oil tanker Prestige oil spill)
International organization participation: AfDB, AsDB, Australia Group, BIS, CE, EAPC, EBRD, EIB, EMU, ESA, EU, FAO, IADB, IAEA, IBRD, ICAO, ICC, ICCt, ICFTU, ICRM, IDA, IEA, IFAD, IFC, IFRCS, IHO, ILO, IMF, IMO, Interpol, IOC, IOM (observer), ISO, ITU, LAIA (observer), MONUC, NATO, NEA, NSG, OAS (observer), OECD, OPCW, OSCE, Paris Club, PCA, UN, UN Security Council (temporary), UNCTAD, UNESCO, UNHCR, UNIDO, UNMEE, UNMIK, UPU, WCL, WCO, WEU, WHO, WIPO, WMO, WToO, WTrO, ZC
Diplomatic representation in the US:
chief of mission: Ambassador Francisco Javier RUPEREZ Rubio
chancery: 2375 Pennsylvania Avenue NW, Washington, DC 20037
telephone: [1] (202) 452-0100, 728-2340
FAX: [1] (202) 833-5670
consulate(s) general: Boston, Chicago, Houston, Los Angeles, Miami, New Orleans, New York, San Francisco, and San Juan (Puerto Rico)
Diplomatic representation from the US:
chief of mission: Ambassador George L. ARGYROS
embassy: Serrano 75, 28006 Madrid
mailing address: PSC 61, APO AE 09642
telephone: [34] (91) 587-2200
FAX: [34] (91) 587-2303
consulate(s) general: Barcelona
Flag description: three horizontal bands of red (top), yellow (double width), and red with the national coat of arms on the hoist side of the yellow band; the

Spain (continued)

coat of arms includes the royal seal framed by the Pillars of Hercules, which are the two promontories (Gibraltar and Ceuta) on either side of the eastern end of the Strait of Gibraltar

Economy

Economy - overview: Spain's mixed capitalist economy supports a GDP that on a per capita basis is 80% that of the four leading West European economies. The center-right government of former President AZNAR successfully worked to gain admission to the first group of countries launching the European single currency (the euro) on 1 January 1999. The AZNAR administration continued to advocate liberalization, privatization, and deregulation of the economy and introduced some tax reforms to that end. Unemployment fell steadily under the AZNAR administration but remains high at 11.7%. Growth of 2.4% in 2003 was satisfactory given the background of a faltering European economy. Incoming President RODRIGUEZ ZAPATERO, whose party won the election three days after the Madrid train bombings in March, plans to reduce government intervention in business, combat tax fraud, and support innovation, research and development, but also intends to reintroduce labor market regulations that had been scraped by the AZNAR government. Adjusting to the monetary and other economic policies of an integrated Europe - and reducing unemployment - will pose challenges to Spain over the next few years.

GDP: purchasing power parity - $885.5 billion (2003 est.)

GDP - real growth rate: 2.4% (2003 est.)

GDP - per capita: purchasing power parity - $22,000 (2003 est.)

GDP - composition by sector:
agriculture: 3.4%
industry: 30.1%
services: 66.5% (2002 est.)

Population below poverty line: NA%

Household income or consumption by percentage share:
lowest 10%: 2.8%
highest 10%: 25.2% (1990)

Distribution of family income - Gini index: 32.5 (1990)

Inflation rate (consumer prices): 2.6% (2003 est.)

Labor force: 17.1 million (2001)

Labor force - by occupation: services 64%, manufacturing, mining, and construction 29%, agriculture 7% (2001 est.)

Unemployment rate: 11.7% (2003 est.)

Budget:
revenues: $105 billion
expenditures: $109 billion, including capital expenditures of $12.8 billion (2000 est.)

Industries: textiles and apparel (including footwear), food and beverages, metals and metal manufactures, chemicals, shipbuilding, automobiles, machine tools, tourism

Industrial production growth rate: 0.6% (2003 est.)

Electricity - production: 222.5 billion kWh (2001)

Electricity - production by source:
fossil fuel: 50.4%
hydro: 18.2%
nuclear: 27.2%
other: 4.1% (2001)

Electricity - consumption: 210.4 billion kWh (2001)

Electricity - exports: 4.138 billion kWh (2001)

Electricity - imports: 7.588 billion kWh (2001)

Oil - production: 7,099 bbl/day (2001 est.)

Oil - consumption: 1.497 million bbl/day (2001 est.)

Oil - exports: 135,100 bbl/day (2001)

Oil - imports: 1.582 million bbl/day (2001)

Oil - proved reserves: 10.5 million bbl (1 January 2002)

Natural gas - production: 516 million cu m (2001 est.)

Natural gas - consumption: 17.96 billion cu m (2001 est.)

Natural gas - exports: 0 cu m (2001 est.)

Natural gas - imports: 17.26 billion cu m (2001 est.)

Natural gas - proved reserves: 254.9 million cu m (1 January 2002)

Agriculture - products: grain, vegetables, olives, wine grapes, sugar beets, citrus; beef, pork, poultry, dairy products; fish

Exports: $159.4 billion f.o.b. (2003 est.)

Exports - commodities: machinery, motor vehicles; foodstuffs, other consumer goods

Exports - partners: France 19%, Germany 11.4%, UK 9.6%, Portugal 9.5%, Italy 9.3%, US 4.6% (2002)

Imports: $197.1 billion f.o.b. (2003 est.)

Imports - commodities: machinery and equipment, fuels, chemicals, semifinished goods; foodstuffs, consumer goods

Imports - partners: France 17%, Germany 16.5%, Italy 8.6%, UK 6.4%, Netherlands 4.8% (2002)

Debt - external: $90 billion (1993 est.)

Economic aid - donor: ODA, $1.33 billion (1999)

Currency: euro (EUR)

note: on 1 January 1999, the European Monetary Union introduced the euro as a common currency to be used by the financial institutions of member countries; on 1 January 2002, the euro became the sole currency for everyday transactions with the member countries

Currency code: EUR

Exchange rates: euros per US dollar - 0.886 (2003), 1.0626 (2002), 1.1175 (2001), 1.0854 (2000), 0.9386 (1999)

Fiscal year: calendar year

Communications

Telephones - main lines in use: 20,595,300 (2002)

Telephones - mobile cellular: 33.531 million (2002)

Telephone system:
general assessment: generally adequate, modern facilities; teledensity is 44 main lines for each 100 persons

domestic: NA

international: country code - 34; 22 coaxial submarine cables; satellite earth stations - 2 Intelsat (1 Atlantic Ocean and 1 Indian Ocean), NA Eutelsat; tropospheric scatter to adjacent countries

Radio broadcast stations: AM 208, FM 715, shortwave 1 (1998)

Television broadcast stations: 224 (plus 2,105 repeaters)

note: these figures include 11 television broadcast stations and 88 repeaters in the Canary Islands (1995)

Internet country code: .es

Internet hosts: 589,979 (2002)

Internet users: 7.388 million (2001)

Transportation

Railways:
total: 14,189 km
broad gauge: 11,804 km 1.668-m gauge (6,409 km electrified)
standard gauge: 455 km 1.435-m gauge (455 km electrified)
narrow gauge: 1,902 km 1.000-m gauge (781 km electrified); 28 km 0.914-m gauge (28 km electrified) (2002)

Highways:
total: 663,795 km
paved: 657,157 km (including 10,317 km of expressways)
unpaved: 6,638 km (1999)

Waterways: 1,045 km (of minor economic importance)

Pipelines: gas 7,290 km; oil 730 km; refined products 3,110 km; unknown (oil/water) 397 km (2003)

Ports and harbors: Aviles, Barcelona, Bilbao, Cadiz, Cartagena, Castellon de la Plana, Ceuta, Huelva, A Coruna, Las Palmas (Canary Islands), Malaga, Melilla, Pasajes, Gijon, Santa Cruz de Tenerife (Canary Islands), Santander, Tarragona, Valencia, Vigo

Merchant marine:
total: 149 ships (1,000 GRT or over) 1,740,974 GRT/ 2,157,551 DWT
by type: bulk 9, cargo 29, chemical tanker 13, container 17, liquefied gas 6, livestock carrier 1, passenger 1, petroleum tanker 21, refrigerated cargo 5, roll on/roll off 32, short-sea/passenger 7, specialized tanker 1, vehicle carrier 7
foreign-owned: Chile 1, Cuba 1, Denmark 1, Germany 9, Italy 2, Netherlands 1, Norway 6, Sweden 1, Uruguay 1
registered in other countries: 115 (2003 est.)

Airports: 156 (2003 est.)

Airports - with paved runways:
total: 94
over 3,047 m: 15
2,438 to 3,047 m: 10
1,524 to 2,437 m: 19
914 to 1,523 m: 23
under 914 m: 27 (2003 est.)

Spain (continued)

Airports - with unpaved runways:
total: 62
1,524 to 2,437 m: 2
914 to 1,523 m: 15
under 914 m: 45 (2003 est.)
Heliports: 8 (2003 est.)

Military

Military branches: Army, Navy, Air Force (Ejercito del Aire, EdA), Marines
Military manpower - military age: 20 years of age (2004 est.)
Military manpower - availability:
males age 15-49: 10,482,753 (2004 est.)
Military manpower - fit for military service:
males age 15-49: 8,336,273 (2004 est.)
Military manpower - reaching military age annually:
males: 245,007 (2004 est.)
Military expenditures - dollar figure:
$9,906,500,000 (2003)
Military expenditures - percent of GDP: 1.2% (2003)

Transnational Issues

Disputes - international: since Gibraltar residents voted overwhelmingly by referendum in 2003 against a "total shared sovereignty" arrangement, talks between the UK and Spain over the fate of the 300-year old UK colony have stalled; Spain disapproves of UK plans to grant Gibraltar greater autonomy; Morocco protests Spain's control over the coastal enclaves of Ceuta, Melilla, and the islands of Penon de Velez de la Gomera, Penon de Alhucemas and Islas Chafarinas, and surrounding waters; Morocco serves as the primary launching area of illegal migration into Spain from North Africa; Morocco rejected Spain's unilateral designation of a median line from the Canary Islands in 2002 to set limits to undersea resource exploration and refugee interdiction, but agreed in 2003 to discuss a comprehensive maritime delimitation; some Portuguese groups assert dormant claims to territories ceded to Spain around the town of Olivenza
Illicit drugs: key European gateway country and consumer for Latin American cocaine and North African hashish entering the European market; destination and minor transshipment point for Southwest Asian heroin; money laundering site for European earnings of Colombian narcotics trafficking organizations

Spratly Islands

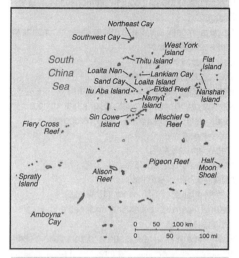

Introduction

Background: The Spratly Islands consist of more than 100 small islands or reefs. They are surrounded by rich fishing grounds and potentially by gas and oil deposits. They are claimed in their entirety by China, Taiwan, and Vietnam, while portions are claimed by Malaysia and the Philippines. About 50 islands are occupied by China (about 450 soldiers), Malaysia (70-90), the Philippines (about 100), and Vietnam (about 1,500). Brunei is a claimant but has no outposts.

Geography

Location: Southeastern Asia, group of reefs and islands in the South China Sea, about two-thirds of the way from southern Vietnam to the southern Philippines
Geographic coordinates: 8 38 N, 111 55 E
Map references: Southeast Asia
Area:
total: less than 5 sq km
land: less than 5 sq km
water: 0 sq km
note: includes 100 or so islets, coral reefs, and sea mounts scattered over an area of nearly 410,000 sq km of the central South China Sea
Area - comparative: NA
Land boundaries: 0 km
Coastline: 926 km
Maritime claims: NA
Climate: tropical
Terrain: flat
Elevation extremes:
lowest point: South China Sea 0 m
highest point: unnamed location on Southwest Cay 4 m
Natural resources: fish, guano, undetermined oil and natural gas potential
Land use:
arable land: 0%

permanent crops: 0%
other: 100% (1998 est.)
Irrigated land: 0 sq km (1998 est.)
Natural hazards: typhoons; serious maritime hazard because of numerous reefs and shoals
Environment - current issues: NA
Geography - note: strategically located near several primary shipping lanes in the central South China Sea; includes numerous small islands, atolls, shoals, and coral reefs

People

Population: no indigenous inhabitants
note: there are scattered garrisons occupied by personnel of several claimant states (July 2004 est.)

Government

Country name:
conventional long form: none
conventional short form: Spratly Islands

Economy

Economy - overview: Economic activity is limited to commercial fishing. The proximity to nearby oil- and gas-producing sedimentary basins suggests the potential for oil and gas deposits, but the region is largely unexplored; there are no reliable estimates of potential reserves; commercial exploitation has yet to be developed.

Transportation

Waterways: none
Ports and harbors: none; offshore anchorage only
Airports: 3 (2003 est.)
Airports - with paved runways:
total: 1
914 to 1,523 m: 1 (2003 est.)
Airports - with unpaved runways:
total: 2
914 to 1,523 m: 1
under 914 m: 1 (2003 est.)

Military

Military - note: Spratly Islands consist of more than 100 small islands or reefs, of which about 45 are claimed and occupied by China, Malaysia, the Philippines, Taiwan, and Vietnam

Transnational Issues

Disputes - international: all of the Spratly Islands are claimed by China, Taiwan, and Vietnam; parts of them are claimed by Malaysia and the Philippines; in 1984, Brunei established an exclusive fishing zone that encompasses Louisa Reef in the southern Spratly Islands but has not publicly claimed the reef; claimants in November 2002 signed the "Declaration on the Conduct of Parties in the South China Sea," which has eased tensions but falls short of a legally binding "code of conduct"

Sri Lanka

Introduction

Background: The Sinhalese arrived in Sri Lanka late in the 6th century B.C., probably from northern India. Buddhism was introduced beginning in about the mid-third century B.C., and a great civilization developed at the cities of Anuradhapura (kingdom from circa 200 B.C. to circa 1000 A.D.) and Polonnaruwa (from about 1070 to 1200). In the 14th century, a south Indian dynasty seized power in the north and established a Tamil kingdom. Occupied by the Portuguese in the 16th century and by the Dutch in the 17th century, the island was ceded to the British in 1796, became a crown colony in 1802, and was united under British rule by 1815. As Ceylon, it became independent in 1948; its name was changed to Sri Lanka in 1972. Tensions between the Sinhalese majority and Tamil separatists erupted in violence in the mid-1980s. Tens of thousands have died in an ethnic war that continues to fester. After two decades of fighting, the government and Liberation Tigers of Tamil Eelam began a ceasefire in December 2001, with Norway brokering peace negotiations.

Geography

Location: Southern Asia, island in the Indian Ocean, south of India
Geographic coordinates: 7 00 N, 81 00 E
Map references: Asia
Area:
total: 65,610 sq km
land: 64,740 sq km
water: 870 sq km
Area - comparative: slightly larger than West Virginia
Land boundaries: 0 km
Coastline: 1,340 km
Maritime claims:
territorial sea: 12 NM
contiguous zone: 24 NM
exclusive economic zone: 200 NM

continental shelf: 200 NM or to the edge of the continental margin
Climate: tropical monsoon; northeast monsoon (December to March); southwest monsoon (June to October)
Terrain: mostly low, flat to rolling plain; mountains in south-central interior
Elevation extremes:
lowest point: Indian Ocean 0 m
highest point: Pidurutalagala 2,524 m
Natural resources: limestone, graphite, mineral sands, gems, phosphates, clay, hydropower
Land use:
arable land: 13.43%
permanent crops: 15.78%
other: 70.79% (1998 est.)
Irrigated land: 6,510 sq km (1998 est.)
Natural hazards: occasional cyclones and tornadoes
Environment - current issues: deforestation; soil erosion; wildlife populations threatened by poaching and urbanization; coastal degradation from mining activities and increased pollution; freshwater resources being polluted by industrial wastes and sewage runoff; waste disposal; air pollution in Colombo
Environment - international agreements:
party to: Biodiversity, Climate Change, Climate Change-Kyoto Protocol, Desertification, Endangered Species, Environmental Modification, Hazardous Wastes, Law of the Sea, Ozone Layer Protection, Ship Pollution, Wetlands
signed, but not ratified: Marine Life Conservation
Geography - note: strategic location near major Indian Ocean sea lanes

People

Population: 19,905,165 (2003 est.)
note: since the outbreak of hostilities between the government and armed Tamil separatists in the mid-1980s, several hundred thousand Tamil civilians have fled the island; as of yearend 2000, approximately 65,000 were housed in 131 refugee camps in south India, another 40,000 lived outside the Indian camps, and more than 200,000 Tamils have sought refuge in the West (July 2004 est.)
Age structure:
0-14 years: 24.8% (male 2,526,143; female 2,414,876)
15-64 years: 68.2% (male 6,589,438; female 6,976,487)
65 years and over: 7% (male 655,636; female 742,585) (2004 est.)
Median age:
total: 29.1 years
male: 28 years
female: 30.1 years (2004 est.)
Population growth rate: 0.81% (2004 est.)
Birth rate: 15.88 births/1,000 population (2004 est.)
Death rate: 6.47 deaths/1,000 population (2004 est.)
Net migration rate: -1.31 migrant(s)/1,000 population (2004 est.)

Sex ratio:
at birth: 1.05 male(s)/female
under 15 years: 1.05 male(s)/female
15-64 years: 0.95 male(s)/female
65 years and over: 0.88 male(s)/female
total population: 0.96 male(s)/female (2004 est.)
Infant mortality rate:
total: 14.78 deaths/1,000 live births
male: 16.01 deaths/1,000 live births
female: 13.5 deaths/1,000 live births (2004 est.)
Life expectancy at birth:
total population: 72.89 years
male: 70.34 years
female: 75.57 years (2004 est.)
Total fertility rate: 1.88 children born/woman (2004 est.)
HIV/AIDS - adult prevalence rate: less than 0.1% (2001 est.)
HIV/AIDS - people living with HIV/AIDS: 4,800 (2001 est.)
HIV/AIDS - deaths: 250 (2001 est.)
Nationality:
noun: Sri Lankan(s)
adjective: Sri Lankan
Ethnic groups: Sinhalese 74%, Tamil 18%, Moor 7%, Burgher, Malay, and Vedda 1%
Religions: Buddhist 70%, Hindu 15%, Christian 8%, Muslim 7% (1999)
Languages: Sinhala (official and national language) 74%, Tamil (national language) 18%, other 8%
note: English is commonly used in government and is spoken competently by about 10% of the population
Literacy:
definition: age 15 and over can read and write
total population: 92.3%
male: 94.8%
female: 90% (2003 est.)

Government

Country name:
conventional long form: Democratic Socialist Republic of Sri Lanka
conventional short form: Sri Lanka
former: Serendib, Ceylon
Government type: republic
Capital: Colombo; note - Sri Jayewardenepura Kotte is the legislative capital
Administrative divisions: 8 provinces; Central, North Central, North Eastern, North Western, Sabaragamuwa, Southern, Uva, Western; note - North Eastern province may have been divided in two - Northern and Eastern
Independence: 4 February 1948 (from UK)
National holiday: Independence Day, 4 February (1948)
Constitution: adopted 16 August 1978
Legal system: a highly complex mixture of English common law, Roman-Dutch, Muslim, Sinhalese, and customary law; has not accepted compulsory ICJ jurisdiction
Suffrage: 18 years of age; universal

Sri Lanka (continued)

Executive branch:

chief of state: President Chandrika Bandaranaike KUMARATUNGA (since 12 November 1994); note - Mahinda RAJAPAKSE (since 6 April 2004)i s the prime minister; the president is considered both the chief of state and head of government

head of government: President Chandrika Bandaranaike KUMARATUNGA (since 12 November 1994); note - Mahinda RAJAPAKSE (since 6 April 2004) is the prime minister; the president is considered both the chief of state and head of government

cabinet: Cabinet appointed by the president in consultation with the prime minister

elections: president elected by popular vote for a six-year term; election last held 21 December 1999 (next to be held NA December 2005)

election results: Chandrika Bandaranaike KUMARATUNGA reelected president; percent of vote - Chandrika Bandaranaike KUMARATUNGA 51%, Ranil WICKREMASINGHE 42%, other 7%

Legislative branch: unicameral Parliament (225 seats; members elected by popular vote on the basis of a modified proportional representation system by district to serve six-year terms)

elections: last held 2 April 2004 (next to be held by 2010)

election results: percent of vote by party or electoral alliance - SLFP and JVP 45.6%, UNP 37.83%, TNA 6.84%, JHU 5.97%, SLMC 2.02%, UPF 0.54%, EPDP 0.27%, others 0.93%; seats by party or electoral alliance - SLFP and JVP 105, UNP 82, TNA 22, JHU 9, SLMC 5, UPF 1, EPDP 1

Judicial branch: Supreme Court; Court of Appeals; judges for both courts are appointed by the president

Political parties and leaders: All Ceylon Tamil Congress or ACTC [KUMARGURUPARAM]; Ceylon Workers Congress or CWC [Arumugam THONDAMAN]; Communist Party or CP [D. GUNASEKERA]; Democratic United National (Lalith) Front or DUNLF [Shrimani ATULATHMUDALI]; Eelam People's Democratic Party or EPDP [Douglas DEVANANDA]; Eelam People's Revolutionary Liberation Front or EPRLF [Suresh PREMACHANDRAN]; Janatha Vimukthi Perumuna or JVP [Tilvan SILVA]; National Unity Alliance or NUA [Ferial ASHRAFF]; National Heritage Party or JHU [Uduwe DHAMMALOKA]; People's Liberation Organization of Tamil Eelam or PLOTE [leader NA]; Sihala Urumaya or SU [Tilak KARUNARATNE]; Sri Lanka Freedom Party or SLFP [Chandrika Bandaranaike KUMARATUNGA]; Sri Lanka Muslim Congress or SLMC [Rauff HAKEEM]; Sri Lanka Progressive Front or SLPF [P. Nelson PERERA]; Tamil Eelam Liberation Organization or TELO [SABARATNAM]; Tamil National Alliance or TNA [Nadarajah RAVIRAJ]; Tamil United Liberation Front or TULF [R. SAMPATHAN]; United National Party or UNP [Ranil WICKREMASINGHE]; Up-country People's Front or UPF [P. CHANDRASEKARAN]; several ethnic Tamil and Muslim parties, represented in either Parliament or provincial councils

Political pressure groups and leaders: Buddhist clergy; labor unions; Liberation Tigers of Tamil Eelam or LTTE [Velupillai PRABHAKARAN](insurgent group fighting for a separate state); radical chauvinist Sinhalese groups such as the National Movement Against Terrorism; Sinhalese Buddhist lay groups

International organization participation: AsDB, C, CP, FAO, G-15, G-24, G-77, IAEA, IBRD, ICAO, ICC, ICFTU, ICRM, IDA, IFAD, IFC, IFRCS, IHO, ILO, IMF, IMO, Interpol, IOC, IOM, ISO, ITU, MINURSO, MONUC, NAM, OAS (observer), OPCW, PCA, SAARC, UN, UNCTAD, UNESCO, UNIDO, UPU, WCL, WCO, WFTU, WHO, WIPO, WMO, WToO, WTrO

Diplomatic representation in the US:

chief of mission: Ambassador Devinda R. SUBASINGHE

chancery: 2148 Wyoming Avenue NW, Washington, DC 20008

telephone: [1] (202) 483-4025 (through 4028)

FAX: [1] (202) 232-7181

consulate(s) general: Los Angeles

consulate(s): New York

Diplomatic representation from the US:

chief of mission: Ambassador Jeffrey J. LUNSTEAD

embassy: 210 Galle Road, Colombo 3

mailing address: P. O. Box 106, Colombo

telephone: [94] (1) 448007

FAX: [94] (1) 437345

Flag description: yellow with two panels; the smaller hoist-side panel has two equal vertical bands of green (hoist side) and orange; the other panel is a large dark red rectangle with a yellow lion holding a sword, and there is a yellow bo leaf in each corner; the yellow field appears as a border around the entire flag and extends between the two panels

Economy

Economy - overview: In 1977, Colombo abandoned statist economic policies and its import substitution trade policy for market-oriented policies and export-oriented trade. Sri Lanka's most dynamic sectors now are food processing, textiles and apparel, food and beverages, telecommunications, and insurance and banking. In 2003, plantation crops made up only 15% of exports (compared with 93% in 1970), while textiles and garments accounted for 63%. GDP grew at an average annual rate of 5.5% in the early 1990s until a drought and a deteriorating security situation lowered growth to 3.8% in 1996. The economy rebounded in 1997-2000 with average growth of 5.3%, but 2001 saw the first contraction in the country's history, -1.4%, due to a combination of power shortages, severe budgetary problems, the global slowdown, and continuing civil strife. Growth recovered to 4.0% in 2002 and 5.2% in 2003. About 800,000 Sri Lankans work abroad, 90% in the Middle East. They send home about $1 billion a year. The struggle by the Tamil Tigers of the north and east for a largely independent homeland continues to cast a shadow over the economy.

GDP: purchasing power parity - $73.49 billion (2003 est.)

GDP - real growth rate: 5.2% (2003 est.)

GDP - per capita: purchasing power parity - $3,700 (2003 est.)

GDP - composition by sector:

agriculture: 19.2%

industry: 25.3%

services: 55.5% (2002)

Population below poverty line: 22% (1997 est.)

Household income or consumption by percentage share:

lowest 10%: 3.5%

highest 10%: 28% (1995)

Distribution of family income - Gini index: 34.4 (1995)

Inflation rate (consumer prices): 9% (2003 est.)

Labor force: 6.6 million (1998)

Labor force - by occupation: services 45%, agriculture 38%, industry 17% (1998 est.)

Unemployment rate: 8% (2003)

Budget:

revenues: $2.8 billion

expenditures: $4.1 billion, including capital expenditures of $NA (2001 est.)

Industries: rubber processing, tea, coconuts, and other agricultural commodities; clothing, cement, petroleum refining, textiles, tobacco

Industrial production growth rate: 7.6% (2003)

Electricity - production: 6.36 billion kWh (2001)

Electricity - production by source:

fossil fuel: 51.7%

hydro: 48.3%

nuclear: 0%

other: 0% (2001)

Electricity - consumption: 5.915 billion kWh (2001)

Electricity - exports: 0 kWh (2001)

Electricity - imports: 0 kWh (2001)

Oil - production: 0 bbl/day (2001 est.)

Oil - consumption: 75,000 bbl/day (2001 est.)

Oil - exports: NA

Oil - imports: NA

Agriculture - products: rice, sugarcane, grains, pulses, oilseed, spices, tea, rubber, coconuts; milk, eggs, hides, beef

Exports: $5.269 billion f.o.b. (2003 est.)

Exports - commodities: textiles and apparel, tea, diamonds, coconut products, petroleum products

Exports - partners: US 37.7%, UK 12.6%, Germany 4.3% (2002)

Imports: $6.626 billion f.o.b. (2003 est.)

Imports - commodities: textiles, mineral products, petroleum, foodstuffs, machinery and equipment

Imports - partners: India 13.8%, Hong Kong 8.1%, Singapore 7.2%, Japan 5.9%, South Korea 5%, Taiwan 4.8%, UAE 4.5%, UK 4.3%, China 4.3% (2002)

Debt - external: $10.1 billion (2003)

Economic aid - recipient: $577 million (1998)

Currency: Sri Lankan rupee (LKR)

Currency code: LKR

Sri Lanka *(continued)*

Exchange rates: Sri Lankan rupees per US dollar - 96.521 (2003), 95.6621 (2002), 89.383 (2001), 77.0051 (2000), 70.6354 (1999)
Fiscal year: calendar year

Communications

Telephones - main lines in use: 883,100 (2002)
Telephones - mobile cellular: 931,600 (2002)
Telephone system:
general assessment: very inadequate domestic service, particularly in rural areas; likely improvement with privatization of national telephone company and encouragement to private investment; good international service (1999)
domestic: national trunk network consists mostly of digital microwave radio relay; fiber-optic links now in use in Colombo area and two fixed wireless local loops have been installed; competition is strong in mobile cellular systems; telephone density remains low at 2.6 main lines per 100 persons (1999)
international: country code - 94; submarine cables to Indonesia and Djibouti; satellite earth stations - 2 Intelsat (Indian Ocean) (1999)
Radio broadcast stations: AM 26, FM 45, shortwave 1 (1998)
Television broadcast stations: 21 (1997)
Internet country code: .lk
Internet hosts: 2,335 (2002)
Internet users: 200,000 (2002)

Transportation

Railways:
total: 1,508 km
broad gauge: 1,449 km 1.676-m gauge
narrow gauge: 59 km 0.762-m gauge (2002)
Highways:
total: 96,695 km
paved: 91,860 km
unpaved: 4,835 km (1999)
Waterways: 430 km (navigable by shallow-draft craft)
Pipelines: crude oil and petroleum products 62 km (1987)
Ports and harbors: Colombo, Galle, Jaffna, Trincomalee
Merchant marine:
total: 18 ships (1,000 GRT or over) 120,924 GRT/ 173,604 DWT
by type: cargo 14, container 2, petroleum tanker 2
foreign-owned: Germany 8, Singapore 1
registered in other countries: 4 (2003 est.)
Airports: 14 (2003 est.)
Airports - with paved runways:
total: 13
over 3,047 m: 1
1,524 to 2,437 m: 6
914 to 1,523 m: 6 (2003 est.)
Airports - with unpaved runways:
total: 1
under 914 m: 1 (2003 est.)

Military

Military branches: Army, Navy, Air Force, Police Force
Military manpower - military age: 18 years of age (2004 est.)
Military manpower - availability:
males age 15-49: 5,418,496 (2004 est.)
Military manpower - fit for military service:
males age 15-49: 4,195,736 (2004 est.)
Military manpower - reaching military age annually:
males: 179,869 (2004 est.)
Military expenditures - dollar figure: $518 million (2003)
Military expenditures - percent of GDP: 3.2% (2003)

Transnational Issues

Disputes - international: none

Sudan

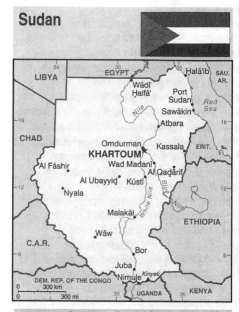

Introduction

Background: Military regimes favoring Islamic-oriented governments have dominated national politics since independence from the UK in 1956. Sudan has been embroiled in a civil war for all but 10 years of this period (1972-82). The wars are rooted in northern economic, political, and social domination of non-Muslim, non-Arab southern Sudanese. Since 1983, the war and war- and famine-related effects have led to more than 2 million deaths and over 4 million people displaced. The ruling regime is a mixture of military elite and an Islamist party that came to power in a 1989 coup. Some northern opposition parties have made common cause with the southern rebels and entered the war as a part of an anti-government alliance. Peace talks gained momentum in 2002-03 with the signing of several accords, including a cease-fire agreement.

Geography

Location: Northern Africa, bordering the Red Sea, between Egypt and Eritrea
Geographic coordinates: 15 00 N, 30 00 E
Map references: Africa
Area:
total: 2,505,810 sq km
land: 2.376 million sq km
water: 129,810 sq km
Area - comparative: slightly more than one-quarter the size of the US
Land boundaries:
total: 7,687 km
border countries: Central African Republic 1,165 km, Chad 1,360 km, Democratic Republic of the Congo 628 km, Egypt 1,273 km, Eritrea 605 km, Ethiopia 1,606 km, Kenya 232 km, Libya 383 km, Uganda 435 km
Coastline: 853 km

Sudan (continued)

Maritime claims:

territorial sea: 12 NM

contiguous zone: 18 NM

continental shelf: 200-m depth or to the depth of exploitation

Climate: tropical in south; arid desert in north; rainy season varies by region (April to November)

Terrain: generally flat, featureless plain; mountains in far south, northeast and west; desert dominates the north

Elevation extremes:

lowest point: Red Sea 0 m

highest point: Kinyeti 3,187 m

Natural resources: petroleum; small reserves of iron ore, copper, chromium ore, zinc, tungsten, mica, silver, gold, hydropower

Land use:

arable land: 7.03%

permanent crops: 0.08%

other: 92.89% (1998 est.)

Irrigated land: 19,500 sq km (1998 est.)

Natural hazards: dust storms and periodic persistent droughts

Environment - current issues: inadequate supplies of potable water; wildlife populations threatened by excessive hunting; soil erosion; desertification; periodic drought

Environment - international agreements:

party to: Biodiversity, Climate Change, Desertification, Endangered Species, Law of the Sea, Ozone Layer Protection

signed, but not ratified: none of the selected agreements

Geography - note: largest country in Africa; dominated by the Nile and its tributaries

People

Population: 39,148,162 (July 2004 est.)

Age structure:

0-14 years: 43.7% (male 8,730,609; female 8,358,569)

15-64 years: 54.1% (male 10,588,634; female 10,571,199)

65 years and over: 2.3% (male 490,869; female 408,282) (2004 est.)

Median age:

total: 17.9 years

male: 17.7 years

female: 18.1 years (2004 est.)

Population growth rate: 2.64% (2004 est.)

Birth rate: 35.79 births/1,000 population (2004 est.)

Death rate: 9.37 deaths/1,000 population (2004 est.)

Net migration rate: -0.02 migrant(s)/1,000 population (2004 est.)

Sex ratio:

at birth: 1.05 male(s)/female

under 15 years: 1.05 male(s)/female

15-64 years: 1 male(s)/female

65 years and over: 1.2 male(s)/female

total population: 1.02 male(s)/female (2004 est.)

Infant mortality rate:

total: 64.05 deaths/1,000 live births

male: 64.8 deaths/1,000 live births

female: 63.26 deaths/1,000 live births (2004 est.)

Life expectancy at birth:

total population: 58.13 years

male: 56.96 years

female: 59.36 years (2004 est.)

Total fertility rate: 4.97 children born/woman (2004 est.)

HIV/AIDS - adult prevalence rate: 2.6% (2001 est.)

HIV/AIDS - people living with HIV/AIDS: 450,000 (2001 est.)

HIV/AIDS - deaths: 23,000 (2001 est.)

Nationality:

noun: Sudanese (singular and plural)

adjective: Sudanese

Ethnic groups: black 52%, Arab 39%, Beja 6%, foreigners 2%, other 1%

Religions: Sunni Muslim 70% (in north), indigenous beliefs 25%, Christian 5% (mostly in south and Khartoum)

Languages: Arabic (official), Nubian, Ta Bedawie, diverse dialects of Nilotic, Nilo-Hamitic, Sudanic languages, English

note: program of "Arabization" in process

Literacy:

definition: age 15 and over can read and write

total population: 61.1%

male: 71.8%

female: 50.5% (2003 est.)

Government

Country name:

conventional long form: Republic of the Sudan

conventional short form: Sudan

local long form: Jumhuriyat as-Sudan

local short form: As-Sudan

former: Anglo-Egyptian Sudan

Government type: authoritarian regime - ruling military junta took power in 1989; government is run by an alliance of the military and the National Congress Party (NCP), formerly the National Islamic Front (NIF), which espouses an Islamist platform

Capital: Khartoum

Administrative divisions: 26 states (wilayat, singular - wilayah); A'ali an Nil, Al Bahr al Ahmar, Al Buhayrat, Al Jazirah, Al Khartum, Al Qadarif, Al Wahdah, An Nil al Abyad, An Nil al Azraq, Ash Shamaliyah, Bahr al Jabal, Gharb al Istiwa'iyah, Gharb Bahr al Ghazal, Gharb Darfur, Gharb Kurdufan, Janub Darfur, Janub Kurdufan, Junqali, Kassala, Nahr an Nil, Shamal Bahr al Ghazal, Shamal Darfur, Shamal Kurdufan, Sharq al Istiwa'iyah, Sinnar, Warab

Independence: 1 January 1956 (from Egypt and UK)

National holiday: Independence Day, 1 January (1956)

Constitution: 12 April 1973, suspended following coup of 6 April 1985; interim constitution of 10 October 1985 suspended following coup of 30 June 1989; new constitution implemented on 30 June 1998 partially suspended 12 December 1999 by President BASHIR

Legal system: based on English common law and Islamic law; as of 20 January 1991, the now defunct Revolutionary Command Council imposed Islamic law in the northern states; Islamic law applies to all residents of the northern states regardless of their religion; some separate religious courts; accepts compulsory ICJ jurisdiction, with reservations

Suffrage: 17 years of age; universal, but noncompulsory

Executive branch:

chief of state: President Lt. Gen. Umar Hassan Ahmad al-BASHIR (since 16 October 1993); First Vice President Ali Uthman Muhammad TAHA (since 17 February 1998), Second Vice President Moses MACHAR (since 12 February 2001); note - the president is both the chief of state and head of government

head of government: President Lt. Gen. Umar Hasan Ahmad al-BASHIR (since 16 October 1993); First Vice President Ali Uthman Muhammad TAHA (since 17 February 1998), Second Vice President Moses MACHAR (since 12 February 2001); note - the president is both the chief of state and head of government

cabinet: Council of Ministers appointed by the president; note - the National Congress Party or NCP (formerly the National Islamic Front or NIF) dominates al-BASHIR's cabinet

elections: president elected by popular vote for a five-year term; election last held 13-23 December 2000 (next to be held NA)

election results: Lt. Gen. Umar Hasan Ahmad al-BASHIR reelected president; percent of vote - Umar Hasan Ahmad al-BASHIR 86.5%, Ja'afar Muhammed NUMAYRI 9.6%, three other candidates received a combined vote of 3.9%; election widely viewed as rigged; all popular opposition parties boycotted elections because of a lack of guarantees for a free and fair election

note: Lt. Gen. al-BASHIR assumed supreme executive power in 1989 and retained it through several transitional governments in the early and mid-1990s before being popularly elected for the first time in March 1996

Legislative branch: unicameral National Assembly (360 seats; 270 popularly elected, 90 elected by supra assembly of interest groups known as National Congress; members serve four-year terms)

elections: last held 13-22 December 2000 (next to be held NA December 2004)

election results: NCP 355, others 5

Judicial branch: Supreme Court; Special Revolutionary Courts

Political parties and leaders: the government allows political "associations" under a 1998 law revised in 2000; to obtain government approval parties must accept the constitution and refrain from advocating or using violence against the regime; approved parties include the National Congress Party or NCP [Ibrahim Ahmed UMAR], Popular National Congress or PNC [Hassan al-TURABI], and over 20 minor, pro-government parties

Sudan (continued)

Political pressure groups and leaders:
Democratic Unionist Party [Muhammed Uthman
AL-MIRGHANI]; National Congress Party [Ibrahim
Ahmed UMAR]; National Democratic Alliance
[Muhammed Uthman AL-MIRGHANI, chairman];
Sudan People's Liberation Movement/Army [Dr. John
GARANG]; Umma Party [Sadiq al-MAHDI]
International organization participation: ABEDA,
ACP, AfDB, AFESD, AMF, AU, CAEU, FAO, G-77,
IAEA, IBRD, ICAO, ICCt (signatory), ICRM, IDA, IDB,
IFAD, IFC, IFRCS, IGAD, ILO, IMF, IMO, Interpol,
IOC, IOM, ISO (correspondent), ITU, LAS, NAM, OIC,
OPCW, PCA, UN, UNCTAD, UNESCO, UNHCR,
UNIDO, UPU, WCO, WFTU, WHO, WIPO, WMO,
WToO, WTrO (observer)
Diplomatic representation in the US:
chief of mission: Ambassador (vacant); Charge
d'Affaires, Ad Interim Khidir Haroun AHMED (since
April 2001)
chancery: 2210 Massachusetts Avenue NW,
Washington, DC 20008
telephone: [1] (202) 338-8565
FAX: [1] (202) 667-2406
Diplomatic representation from the US:
chief of mission: Ambassador (vacant); Charge
d'Affaires Gerard M. GALLUCCI
embassy: Sharia Abdul Latif Avenue, Khartoum
mailing address: P. O. Box 699, Khartoum; APO AE
09829
telephone: [249] (11) 774611 or 774700
FAX: [249] (11) 774137
Flag description: three equal horizontal bands of
red (top), white, and black with a green isosceles
triangle based on the hoist side

Economy

Economy - overview: Sudan has turned around a
struggling economy with sound economic policies and
infrastructure investments, but it still faces formidable
economic problems, starting from its low level of per
capita output. From 1997 to date, Sudan has been
implementing IMF macroeconomic reforms. In 1999,
Sudan began exporting crude oil and in the last
quarter of 1999 recorded its first trade surplus, which,
along with monetary policy, has stabilized the
exchange rate. Increased oil production, revived light
industry, and expanded export processing zones
helped sustain GDP growth at 6.1% in 2003.
Agriculture production remains Sudan's most
important sector, employing 80% of the work force
and contributing 39% of GDP, but most farms remain
rain-fed and susceptible to drought. Chronic
instability - including the long-standing civil war
between the Muslim north and the Christian/pagan
south, adverse weather, and weak world agricultural
prices - ensure that much of the population will remain
at or below the poverty line for years.
GDP: purchasing power parity - $70.75 billion
(2003 est.)
GDP - real growth rate: 6.1% (2003 est.)
GDP - per capita: purchasing power parity - $1,900
(2003 est.)

GDP - composition by sector:
agriculture: 39%
industry: 18%
services: 43% (2002 est.)
Population below poverty line: NA%
**Household income or consumption by percentage
share:**
lowest 10%: NA%
highest 10%: NA%
Inflation rate (consumer prices): 8.8% (2003 est.)
Labor force: 11 million (1996 est.)
Labor force - by occupation: agriculture 80%,
industry and commerce 7%, government 13%
(1998 est.)
Unemployment rate: 18.7% (2002 est.)
Budget:
revenues: $1.4 billion
expenditures: $1.6 billion, including capital
expenditures of $304 million (2001 est.)
Industries: oil, cotton ginning, textiles, cement,
edible oils, sugar, soap distilling, shoes, petroleum
refining, pharmaceuticals, armaments, automobile/
light truck assembly
Industrial production growth rate: 8.5%
(1999 est.)
Electricity - production: 2.389 billion kWh (2001)
Electricity - production by source:
fossil fuel: 52.1%
hydro: 47.9%
nuclear: 0%
other: 0% (2001)
Electricity - consumption: 2.222 billion kWh (2001)
Electricity - exports: 0 kWh (2001)
Electricity - imports: 0 kWh (2001)
Oil - production: 209,100 bbl/day (2001 est.)
Oil - consumption: 50,000 bbl/day (2001 est.)
Oil - exports: NA
Oil - imports: NA
Oil - proved reserves: 631.5 million bbl (1 January
2002)
Natural gas - proved reserves: 99.11 billion cu m
(1 January 2002)
Agriculture - products: cotton, groundnuts
(peanuts), sorghum, millet, wheat, gum arabic,
sugarcane, cassava (tapioca), mangos, papaya,
bananas, sweet potatoes, sesame; sheep, livestock
Exports: $2.45 billion f.o.b. (2003 est.)
Exports - commodities: oil and petroleum products;
cotton, sesame, livestock, groundnuts, gum arabic,
sugar
Exports - partners: China 53.3%, Japan 13.4%,
South Africa 4.9%, Saudi Arabia 4.7% (2002)
Imports: $2.383 billion f.o.b. (2003 est.)
Imports - commodities: foodstuffs, manufactured
goods, refinery and transport equipment, medicines
and chemicals, textiles, wheat
Imports - partners: China 20.1%, Saudi Arabia
7.5%, India 5.6%, UK 5.4%, Germany 5.4%,
Indonesia 4.7%, Australia 4% (2002)
Debt - external: $20.9 billion (yearend 2003 est.)
Economic aid - recipient: $172 million (2001)

Currency: Sudanese dinar (SDD)
Currency code: SDD
Exchange rates: Sudanese dinars per US dollar -
260.983 (2003), 263.306 (2002), 258.702 (2001),
257.122 (2000), 252.55 (1999)
Fiscal year: calendar year

Communications

Telephones - main lines in use: 671,800 (2002)
Telephones - mobile cellular: 190,800 (2002)
Telephone system:
general assessment: large, well-equipped system by
regional standards and being upgraded; cellular
communications started in 1996 and have expanded
substantially
domestic: consists of microwave radio relay, cable,
radiotelephone communications, tropospheric scatter,
and a domestic satellite system with 14 earth stations
international: country code - 249; satellite earth
stations - 1 Intelsat (Atlantic Ocean) and 1 Arabsat
(2000)
Radio broadcast stations: AM 12, FM 1,
shortwave 1 (1998)
Television broadcast stations: 3 (1997)
Internet country code: .sd
Internet hosts: NA
Internet users: 84,000 (2002)

Transportation

Railways:
total: 5,978 km
narrow gauge: 4,578 km 1.067-m gauge; 1,400 km
0.600-m gauge plantation line (2002)
Highways:
total: 11,900 km
paved: 4,320 km
unpaved: 7,580 km (1999 est.)
Waterways: 5,310 km
Pipelines: gas 156 km; oil 2,297 km; refined
products 810 km (2003)
Ports and harbors: Juba, Khartoum, Kusti, Malakal,
Nimule, Port Sudan, Sawakin
Merchant marine:
total: 3 ships (1,000 GRT or over) 20,466 GRT/26,973
DWT
by type: livestock carrier 1, roll on/roll off 2
registered in other countries: 4 (2003 est.)
Airports: 63 (2003 est.)
Airports - with paved runways:
total: 12
over 3,047 m: 1
2,438 to 3,047 m: 8
1,524 to 2,437 m: 3 (2003 est.)
Airports - with unpaved runways:
total: 51
over 3,047 m: 1
2,438 to 3,047 m: 1
1,524 to 2,437 m: 16
914 to 1,523 m: 23
under 914 m: 10 (2003 est.)
Heliports: 2 (2003 est.)

Sudan *(continued)*

Military

Military branches: Sudanese People's Armed Forces (SPAF), Navy, Air Force, Popular Defense Forces

Military manpower - military age: 18 years of age (2004 est.)

Military manpower - availability:
males age 15-49: 9,339,775 (2004 est.)

Military manpower - fit for military service:
males age 15-49: 5,743,783 (2004 est.)

Military manpower - reaching military age annually:
males: 442,242 (2004 est.)

Military expenditures - dollar figure: $581 million (2001 est.)

Military expenditures - percent of GDP: 2.5% (1999)

Transnational Issues

Disputes - international: the north-south civil war has affected Sudan's neighbors by drawing them into the fighting and by forcing them to provide shelter to refugees, to contend with infiltration by rebel groups, and to serve as mediators; Sudan has provided shelter to Ugandan refugees and cover to Lord's Resistance Army soldiers; Sudan accuses Eritrea of supporting Sudanese rebel groups; efforts to demarcate the porous boundary with Ethiopia have been delayed by fighting in Sudan; Kenya's administrative boundary still extends into the Sudan, creating the "Ilemi triangle"; Egypt and Sudan retain claims to administer the triangular areas that extend north and south of the 1899 Treaty boundary along the 22nd Parallel, but have withdrawn their military presence; Egypt is economically developing and currently effectively administers the "Hala'ib triangle" north of the Treaty Line; Sudan has pledged to work with the Central African Republic to stem violent skirmishes over water and grazing among related pastoral populations along the border

Suriname

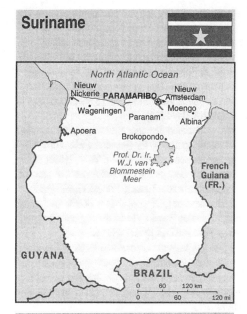

Introduction

Background: Independence from the Netherlands was granted in 1975. Five years later the civilian government was replaced by a military regime that soon declared a socialist republic. It continued to rule through a succession of nominally civilian administrations until 1987, when international pressure finally forced a democratic election. In 1989, the military overthrew the civilian government, but a democratically-elected government returned to power in 1991.

Geography

Location: Northern South America, bordering the North Atlantic Ocean, between French Guiana and Guyana

Geographic coordinates: 4 00 N, 56 00 W

Map references: South America

Area:
total: 163,270 sq km
land: 161,470 sq km
water: 1,800 sq km

Area - comparative: slightly larger than Georgia

Land boundaries:
total: 1,707 km
border countries: Brazil 597 km, French Guiana 510 km, Guyana 600 km

Coastline: 386 km

Maritime claims:
territorial sea: 12 NM
exclusive economic zone: 200 NM

Climate: tropical; moderated by trade winds

Terrain: mostly rolling hills; narrow coastal plain with swamps

Elevation extremes:
lowest point: unnamed location in the coastal plain -2 m
highest point: Juliana Top 1,230 m

Natural resources: timber, hydropower, fish, kaolin, shrimp, bauxite, gold, and small amounts of nickel, copper, platinum, iron ore

Land use:
arable land: 0.37%
permanent crops: 0.06%
other: 99.57%
note: there are 95,000 hectares of arable land, 7,000 hectares of permanent crops, and 15,000 hectares of permanent pastures (1998 est.)

Irrigated land: 490 sq km (1998 est.)

Natural hazards: NA

Environment - current issues: deforestation as timber is cut for export; pollution of inland waterways by small-scale mining activities

Environment - international agreements:
party to: Biodiversity, Climate Change, Desertification, Endangered Species, Law of the Sea, Marine Dumping, Ozone Layer Protection, Ship Pollution, Tropical Timber 94, Wetlands
signed, but not ratified: none of the selected agreements

Geography - note: smallest independent country on South American continent; mostly tropical rain forest; great diversity of flora and fauna that, for the most part, is increasingly threatened by new development; relatively small population, mostly along the coast

People

Population: 436,935 (July 2004 est.)

Age structure:
0-14 years: 30.2% (male 67,588; female 64,223)
15-64 years: 63.7% (male 142,656; female 135,819)
65 years and over: 6.1% (male 11,914; female 14,735) (2004 est.)

Median age:
total: 25.8 years
male: 25.4 years
female: 26.3 years (2004 est.)

Population growth rate: 0.31% (2004 est.)

Birth rate: 18.87 births/1,000 population (2004 est.)

Death rate: 6.99 deaths/1,000 population (2004 est.)

Net migration rate: -8.81 migrant(s)/1,000 population (2004 est.)

Sex ratio:
at birth: 1.05 male(s)/female
under 15 years: 1.05 male(s)/female
15-64 years: 1.05 male(s)/female
65 years and over: 0.81 male(s)/female
total population: 1.03 male(s)/female (2004 est.)

Infant mortality rate:
total: 24.15 deaths/1,000 live births
male: 28.24 deaths/1,000 live births
female: 19.85 deaths/1,000 live births (2004 est.)

Life expectancy at birth:
total population: 69.1 years
male: 66.77 years
female: 71.55 years (2004 est.)

Total fertility rate: 2.37 children born/woman (2004 est.)

HIV/AIDS - adult prevalence rate: 1.2% (2001 est.)

Suriname (continued)

HIV/AIDS - people living with HIV/AIDS: 3,700 (2001 est.)

HIV/AIDS - deaths: 330 (2001 est.)

Nationality:

noun: Surinamer(s)

adjective: Surinamese

Ethnic groups: Hindustani (also known locally as "East Indians"; their ancestors emigrated from northern India in the latter part of the 19th century) 37%, Creole (mixed white and black) 31%, Javanese 15%, "Maroons" (their African ancestors were brought to the country in the 17th and 18th centuries as slaves and escaped to the interior) 10%, Amerindian 2%, Chinese 2%, white 1%, other 2%

Religions: Hindu 27.4%, Muslim 19.6%, Roman Catholic 22.8%, Protestant 25.2% (predominantly Moravian), indigenous beliefs 5%

Languages: Dutch (official), English (widely spoken), Sranang Tongo (Surinamese, sometimes called Taki-Taki, is native language of Creoles and much of the younger population and is lingua franca among others), Hindustani (a dialect of Hindi), Javanese

Literacy:

definition: age 15 and over can read and write

total population: 93%

male: 95%

female: 91% (1995 est.)

Government

Country name:

conventional long form: Republic of Suriname

conventional short form: Suriname

local long form: Republiek Suriname

local short form: Suriname

former: Netherlands Guiana, Dutch Guiana

Government type: constitutional democracy

Capital: Paramaribo

Administrative divisions: 10 districts (distrikten, singular - distrikt); Brokopondo, Commewijne, Coronie, Marowijne, Nickerie, Para, Paramaribo, Saramacca, Sipaliwini, Wanica

Independence: 25 November 1975 (from Netherlands)

National holiday: Independence Day, 25 November (1975)

Constitution: ratified 30 September 1987

Legal system: based on Dutch legal system incorporating French penal theory

Suffrage: 18 years of age; universal

Executive branch:

chief of state: President Runaldo Ronald VENETIAAN (since 12 August 2000); Vice President Jules Rattankoemar AJODHIA (since 12 August 2000); note - the president is both the chief of state and head of government

head of government: President Runaldo Ronald VENETIAAN (since 12 August 2000); Vice President Jules Rattankoemar AJODHIA (since 12 August 2000); note - the president is both the chief of state and head of government

cabinet: Cabinet of Ministers appointed by the president from among the members of the National Assembly

elections: president and vice president elected by the National Assembly or, if no presidential or vice presidential candidate receives a constitutional majority in the National Assembly after two votes, by the larger People's Assembly (869 representatives from the national, local, and regional councils), for five-year terms; election last held 6 May 2000 (next to be held NA May 2005)

note: widespread demonstrations during the summer of 1999 led to the call for elections a year early

election results: Runaldo Ronald VENETIAAN elected president by the National Assembly; percent of legislative vote - Runaldo Ronald VENETIAAN 72.5%; Rashied DOEKHIE (NDP) 19.6%; total votes cast - Runaldo Ronald VENETIAAN (New Front) 37 votes, Rashied DOEKHIE (NDP) 10 votes

Legislative branch: unicameral National Assembly or Nationale Assemblee (51 seats; members are elected by popular vote to serve five-year terms)

elections: last held 5 May 2000 (next to be held NA May 2005)

election results: percent of vote by party - NA%; seats by party - NF 33, MC 10, DNP 2000 3, DA '91 2, PVF 2, PALU 1

note: widespread demonstrations during the summer of 1999 led to the call for elections a year early

Judicial branch: Court of Justice (justices are nominated for life)

Political parties and leaders: Democratic Alternative '91 or DA '91 (a coalition of the Alternative Forum or AF and Party for Brotherhood and Unity in Politics or BEP, formed in January 1991) [Winston JESSURUN]; Democratic National Platform 2000 or DNP 2000 (coalition of two parties, Democratic Party and Democrats of the 21st Century) [Jules WIJDENBOSCH]; Independent Progressive Democratic Alternative or OPDA [Joginder RAMKHILAWAN]; Millennium Combination or MC (a coalition of three parties, Democratic Alternative, Party for National Unity and Solidarity, and National Democratic Party) [leader NA]; National Democratic Party or NDP [Desire BOUTERSE]; Naya Kadam or NK [leader NA]; Party for Renewal and Democracy or BVD [Tjan GOBARDHAN]; Party of National Unity and Solidarity or KTPI [Willy SOEMITA]; Pertjaja Luhur [Paul SOMOHARDJO]; Progressive Workers' and Farm Laborers' Union or PALU [Ir Iwan KROLIS]; The New Front or NF (a coalition of four parties Suriname National Party or NPS, Progressive Reform Party or VHP, Suriname Labor Party or SPA, and Pertjaja Luhur) [Runaldo Ronald VENETIAAN]; The Progressive Development Alliance (a combination of three parties, Renewed Progressive Party or HPP, Party of the Federation of Land Workers or PVF, and Suriname Progressive People's Party or PSV) [Harry KISOENSINGH]

Political pressure groups and leaders: General Liberation and Development Party or ABOP [Ronnie BRUNSWIJK]; Mandela Bushnegro Liberation Movement [Leendert ADAMS]; Tucayana Amazonica [Alex JUBITANA, Thomas SABAJO]; Union for Liberation and Democracy [Kofi AFONGPONG]

International organization participation: ACP, Caricom, FAO, G-77, IADB, IBRD, ICAO, ICFTU, ICRM, IDB, IFAD, IFRCS, IHO, ILO, IMF, IMO, Interpol, IOC, ITU, LAES, NAM, OAS, OIC, OPANAL, OPCW, PCA, UN, UNCTAD, UNESCO, UNIDO, UPU, WCL, WHO, WIPO, WMO, WTrO

Diplomatic representation in the US:

chief of mission: Ambassador Henry Lothar ILLES

chancery: Suite 460, 4301 Connecticut Avenue NW, Washington, DC 20008

telephone: [1] (202) 244-7488

FAX: [1] (202) 244-5878

consulate(s) general: Miami

Diplomatic representation from the US:

chief of mission: Ambassador Marsha E. BARNES

embassy: Dr. Sophie Redmondstraat 129, Paramaribo

mailing address: Department of State, 3390 Paramaribo Place, Washington, DC, 20521-3390

telephone: [597] 472900

FAX: [597] 420800

Flag description: five horizontal bands of green (top, double width), white, red (quadruple width), white, and green (double width); there is a large, yellow, five-pointed star centered in the red band

Economy

Economy - overview: The economy is dominated by the bauxite industry, which accounts for more than 15% of GDP and 70% of export earnings. Suriname's economic prospects for the medium term will depend on renewed commitment to responsible monetary and fiscal policies and to the introduction of structural reforms to liberalize markets and promote competition. The government of Ronald VENETIAAN has begun an austerity program, raised taxes, and attempted to control spending. However, in 2002, President VENETIAAN agreed to a large pay raise for civil servants, which threatens his earlier gains in stabilizing the economy. The Dutch Government has agreed to restart the aid flow, which will allow Suriname to access international development financing. The short-term economic outlook depends on the government's ability to control inflation and on the development of projects in the bauxite and gold mining sectors.

GDP: purchasing power parity - $1.533 billion (2003 est.)

GDP - real growth rate: 1.5% (2003 est.)

GDP - per capita: purchasing power parity - $3,500 (2003 est.)

GDP - composition by sector:

agriculture: 13%

industry: 22%

services: 65% (2001 est.)

Population below poverty line: 70% (2002 est.)

Household income or consumption by percentage share:

lowest 10%: NA%

highest 10%: NA%

Inflation rate (consumer prices): 17% (2002 est.)

Suriname *(continued)*

Labor force: 100,000
Labor force - by occupation: agriculture NA%, industry NA%, services NA%
Unemployment rate: 17% (2000)
Budget:
revenues: $393 million
expenditures: $403 million, including capital expenditures of $34 million (1997 est.)
Industries: bauxite and gold mining, alumina production, oil, lumbering, food processing, fishing
Industrial production growth rate: 6.5% (1994 est.)
Electricity - production: 1.959 billion kWh (2001)
Electricity - production by source:
fossil fuel: 25.2%
hydro: 74.8%
nuclear: 0%
other: 0% (2001)
Electricity - consumption: 1.822 billion kWh (2001)
Electricity - exports: 0 kWh (2001)
Electricity - imports: 0 kWh (2001)
Oil - production: 10,000 bbl/day (2001 est.)
Oil - consumption: 10,000 bbl/day (2001 est.)
Oil - exports: NA
Oil - imports: NA
Oil - proved reserves: 37 million bbl (1 January 2002)
Natural gas - proved reserves: 0 cu m (1 January 2002)
Agriculture - products: paddy rice, bananas, palm kernels, coconuts, plantains, peanuts; beef, chickens; forest products; shrimp
Exports: $495 million f.o.b. (2002)
Exports - commodities: alumina, crude oil, lumber, shrimp and fish, rice, bananas
Exports - partners: US 25.7%, Norway 20.4%, France 8.3%, Trinidad and Tobago 6.5%, Canada 6.1%, Iceland 6.1%, Netherlands 5.7% (2002)
Imports: $604 million f.o.b. (2002)
Imports - commodities: capital equipment, petroleum, foodstuffs, cotton, consumer goods
Imports - partners: US 22.7%, Netherlands 16.1%, China 12.3%, Trinidad and Tobago 11.4%, France 7.6%, Japan 6%, Netherlands Antilles 4.5% (2002)
Debt - external: $321 million (2002 est.)
Economic aid - recipient: Netherlands provided $37 million for project and program assistance, European Development Fund $4 million, Belgium $2 million (1998)
Currency: Surinamese guilder (SRG)
Currency code: SRG
Exchange rates: Surinamese guilders per US dollar - NA (2003), 2,346.75 (2002), 2,178.5 (2001), 1,322.47 (2000), 859.437 (1999)
note: during 1998, the exchange rate splintered into four distinct rates; in January 1999 the government floated the guilder, but subsequently fixed it when the black-market rate plunged; the government currently allows trading within a band of SRG 500 around the official rate
Fiscal year: calendar year

Communications

Telephones - main lines in use: 78,700 (2002)
Telephones - mobile cellular: 108,400 (2002)
Telephone system:
general assessment: international facilities are good
domestic: microwave radio relay network
international: country code - 597; satellite earth stations - 2 Intelsat (Atlantic Ocean)
Radio broadcast stations: AM 4, FM 13, shortwave 1 (1998)
Television broadcast stations: 3 (plus seven repeaters) (2000)
Internet country code: .sr
Internet hosts: 24 (2002)
Internet users: 20,000 (2002)

Transportation

Railways:
total: 166 km (single-track)
standard gauge: 80 km 1.435-m gauge
narrow gauge: 86 km 1.000-m gauge
note: Suriname railroads are not in operation (2001)
Highways:
total: 4,492 km
paved: 1,168 km
unpaved: 3,324 km (2000)
Waterways: 1,200 km
note: most important means of transport; oceangoing vessels with drafts ranging up to 7 m can navigate many of the principal waterways
Pipelines: oil 51 km (2003)
Ports and harbors: Albina, Moengo, New Nickerie, Paramaribo, Paranam, Wageningen
Merchant marine:
total: 2 ships (1,000 GRT or over) 2,421 GRT/2,990 DWT
by type: cargo 1, container 1 (2003 est.)
Airports: 46 (2003 est.)
Airports - with paved runways:
total: 5
over 3,047 m: 1
under 914 m: 4 (2003 est.)
Airports - with unpaved runways:
total: 41
1,524 to 2,437 m: 1
914 to 1,523 m: 5
under 914 m: 35 (2003 est.)

Military

Military branches: National Army (includes small Navy and Air Force elements)
Military manpower - availability:
males age 15-49: 124,260 (2004 est.)
Military manpower - fit for military service:
males age 15-49: 72,576 (2004 est.)
Military expenditures - dollar figure: $7.5 million (2003)
Military expenditures - percent of GDP: 0.7% (2003)

Transnational Issues

Disputes - international: area claimed by French Guiana between Riviere Litani and Riviere Marouini (both headwaters of the Lawa); Suriname claims a triangle of land between the New and Kutari/Koetari Rivers in a historic dispute over the headwaters of the Courantyne; Guyana seeks UNCLOS arbitration to resolve the long-standing dispute with Suriname over the axis of the territorial sea boundary in potentially oil-rich waters
Illicit drugs: growing transshipment point for South American drugs destined for Europe and Brazil; transshipment point for arms-for-drugs dealing

Svalbard
(territory of Norway)

Introduction

Background: First discovered by the Norwegians in the 12th century, the islands served as an international whaling base during the 17th and 18th centuries. Norway's sovereignty was recognized in 1920; five years later it officially took over the territory.

Geography

Location: Northern Europe, islands between the Arctic Ocean, Barents Sea, Greenland Sea, and Norwegian Sea, north of Norway
Geographic coordinates: 78 00 N, 20 00 E
Map references: Arctic Region
Area:
total: 62,049 sq km
land: 62,049 sq km
water: 0 sq km
note: includes Spitsbergen and Bjornoya (Bear Island)
Area - comparative: slightly smaller than West Virginia
Land boundaries: 0 km
Coastline: 3,587 km
Maritime claims:
territorial sea: 4 NM
exclusive fishing zone: 200 NM unilaterally claimed by Norway but not recognized by Russia
Climate: arctic, tempered by warm North Atlantic Current; cool summers, cold winters; North Atlantic Current flows along west and north coasts of Spitsbergen, keeping water open and navigable most of the year
Terrain: wild, rugged mountains; much of high land ice covered; west coast clear of ice about one-half of the year; fjords along west and north coasts
Elevation extremes:
lowest point: Arctic Ocean 0 m
highest point: Newtontoppen 1,717 m
Natural resources: coal, copper, iron ore, phosphate, zinc, wildlife, fish

Land use:
arable land: 0%
permanent crops: 0%
other: 100% (no trees, and the only bushes are crowberry and cloudberry) (1998 est.)
Irrigated land: NA sq km
Natural hazards: ice floes often block the entrance to Bellsund (a transit point for coal export) on the west coast and occasionally make parts of the northeastern coast inaccessible to maritime traffic
Environment - current issues: NA
Geography - note: northernmost part of the Kingdom of Norway; consists of nine main islands; glaciers and snowfields cover 60% of the total area

People

Population: 2,756 (July 2004 est.)
Age structure:
0-14 years: NA%
15-64 years: NA%
65 years and over: NA%
Population growth rate: -0.02% (2004 est.)
Birth rate: NA births/1,000 population
Death rate: NA deaths/1,000 population
Net migration rate: NA migrant(s)/1,000 population
Sex ratio: NA
Infant mortality rate:
total: NA%
male: NA%
female: NA%
Life expectancy at birth:
total population: NA years
male: NA years
female: NA years
Total fertility rate: NA children born/woman
HIV/AIDS - adult prevalence rate: 0% (2001)
HIV/AIDS - people living with HIV/AIDS: 0 (2001)
HIV/AIDS - deaths: 0 (2001)
Ethnic groups: Norwegian 55.4%, Russian and Ukrainian 44.3%, other 0.3% (1998)
Languages: Norwegian, Russian
Literacy: NA

Government

Country name:
conventional long form: none
conventional short form: Svalbard (sometimes referred to as Spitzbergen)
Dependency status: territory of Norway; administered by the Polar Department of the Ministry of Justice, through a governor (sysselmann) residing in Longyearbyen, Spitsbergen; by treaty (9 February 1920) sovereignty was awarded to Norway
Government type: NA
Capital: Longyearbyen
Independence: none (territory of Norway)
National holiday: NA
Legal system: NA
Executive branch:
chief of state: King HARALD V of Norway (since 17 January 1991)

head of government: Governor Morten RUUD (since NA November 1998) and Assistant Governor Odd Redar HUMLEGAARD (since NA)
elections: none; the monarch is hereditary; governor and assistant governor responsible to the Polar Department of the Ministry of Justice
International organization participation: none
Flag description: the flag of Norway is used

Economy

Economy - overview: Coal mining is the major economic activity on Svalbard. The treaty of 9 February 1920 gives the 41 signatories equal rights to exploit mineral deposits, subject to Norwegian regulation. Although US, UK, Dutch, and Swedish coal companies have mined in the past, the only companies still mining are Norwegian and Russian. The settlements on Svalbard are essentially company towns. The Norwegian state-owned coal company employs nearly 60% of the Norwegian population on the island, runs many of the local services, and provides most of the local infrastructure. There is also some trapping of seal, polar bear, fox, and walrus.
GDP: purchasing power parity - $NA
GDP - real growth rate: NA%
GDP - per capita: purchasing power parity - $NA
Population below poverty line: NA%
Household income or consumption by percentage share:
lowest 10%: NA%
highest 10%: NA%
Inflation rate (consumer prices): NA%
Labor force: NA
Budget:
revenues: $11.5 million
expenditures: $11.5 million, including capital expenditures of $NA (1998 est.)
Industrial production growth rate: NA%
Electricity - production: NA kWh
Electricity - production by source:
fossil fuel: 58%
hydro: 42%
nuclear: 0%
other: 0%
Electricity - consumption: NA kWh
Exports: $NA
Imports: $NA
Economic aid - recipient: $8.2 million from Norway (1998)
Currency: Norwegian krone (NOK)
Currency code: NOK
Exchange rates: Norwegian kroner per US dollar - 7.0802 (2003), 7.9838 (2002), 8.9917 (2001), 8.8018 (2000), 7.7992 (1999)

Communications

Telephones - main lines in use: NA
Telephones - mobile cellular: NA
Telephone system:
general assessment: probably adequate
domestic: local telephone service

international: country code - 47-790; satellite earth station - 1 of unknown type (for communication with Norwegian mainland only)
Radio broadcast stations: AM 1, FM 1 (plus 2 repeaters), shortwave 0 (1998)
Television broadcast stations: NA
Internet country code: .sj
Internet users: NA

Transportation

Railways: 0 km
Highways:
total: NA km
paved: NA km
unpaved: NA km
Waterways: none
Ports and harbors: Barentsburg, Longyearbyen, Ny-Alesund, Pyramiden
Merchant marine: none
Airports: 4 (2003 est.)
Airports - with paved runways:
total: 2
1,524 to 2,437 m: 1
914 to 1523 m: 1 (2003 est.)
Airports - with unpaved runways:
total: 2
under 914 m: 2 (2003 est.)

Military

Military - note: demilitarized by treaty (9 February 1920)

Transnational Issues

Disputes - international: despite recent discussions, Russia and Norway dispute their maritime limits in the Barents Sea and Russia's fishing rights beyond Svalbard's territorial limits within the Svalbard Treaty zone

Swaziland

Introduction

Background: Autonomy for the Swazis of southern Africa was guaranteed by the British in the late 19th century; independence was granted in 1968. Student and labor unrest during the 1990s have pressured the monarchy (one of the oldest on the continent) to grudgingly allow political reform and greater democracy.

Geography

Location: Southern Africa, between Mozambique and South Africa
Geographic coordinates: 26 30 S, 31 30 E
Map references: Africa
Area:
total: 17,363 sq km
land: 17,203 sq km
water: 160 sq km
Area - comparative: slightly smaller than New Jersey
Land boundaries:
total: 535 km
border countries: Mozambique 105 km, South Africa 430 km
Coastline: 0 km (landlocked)
Maritime claims: none (landlocked)
Climate: varies from tropical to near temperate
Terrain: mostly mountains and hills; some moderately sloping plains
Elevation extremes:
lowest point: Great Usutu River 21 m
highest point: Emlembe 1,862 m
Natural resources: asbestos, coal, clay, cassiterite, hydropower, forests, small gold and diamond deposits, quarry stone, and talc
Land use:
arable land: 9.77%
permanent crops: 0.7%
other: 89.53% (1998 est.)
Irrigated land: 690 sq km (1998 est.)

Natural hazards: drought
Environment - current issues: limited supplies of potable water; wildlife populations being depleted because of excessive hunting; overgrazing; soil degradation; soil erosion
Environment - international agreements:
party to: Biodiversity, Climate Change, Desertification, Endangered Species, Ozone Layer Protection
signed, but not ratified: Law of the Sea
Geography - note: landlocked; almost completely surrounded by South Africa

People

Population: 1,169,241
note: estimates for this country explicitly take into account the effects of excess mortality due to AIDS; this can result in lower life expectancy, higher infant mortality and death rates, lower population and growth rates, and changes in the distribution of population by age and sex than would otherwise be expected (July 2004 est.)
Age structure:
0-14 years: 41% (male 242,090; female 237,395)
15-64 years: 55.3% (male 323,004; female 324,029)
65 years and over: 3.7% (male 18,685; female 24,038) (2004 est.)
Median age:
total: 18.6 years
male: 18.4 years
female: 18.8 years (2004 est.)
Population growth rate: 0.55% (2004 est.)
Birth rate: 28.55 births/1,000 population (2004 est.)
Death rate: 23.06 deaths/1,000 population (2004 est.)
Net migration rate: 0 migrant(s)/1,000 population (2004 est.)
Sex ratio:
at birth: 1.03 male(s)/female
under 15 years: 1.02 male(s)/female
15-64 years: 1 male(s)/female
65 years and over: 0.78 male(s)/female
total population: 1 male(s)/female (2004 est.)
Infant mortality rate:
total: 68.35 deaths/1,000 live births
male: 71.64 deaths/1,000 live births
female: 64.96 deaths/1,000 live births (2004 est.)
Life expectancy at birth:
total population: 37.54 years
male: 39.1 years
female: 35.94 years (2004 est.)
Total fertility rate: 3.81 children born/woman (2004 est.)
HIV/AIDS - adult prevalence rate: 33.4% (2001 est.)
HIV/AIDS - people living with HIV/AIDS: 170,000 (2001 est.)
HIV/AIDS - deaths: 12,000 (2001 est.)
Nationality:
noun: Swazi(s)
adjective: Swazi

Swaziland (continued)

Ethnic groups: African 97%, European 3%

Religions: Zionist (a blend of Christianity and indigenous ancestral worship) 40%, Roman Catholic 20%, Muslim 10%, Anglican, Bahai, Methodist, Mormon, Jewish and other 30%

Languages: English (official, government business conducted in English), siSwati (official)

Literacy:

definition: age 15 and over can read and write

total population: 81.6%

male: 82.6%

female: 80.8% (2003 est.)

Government

Country name:

conventional long form: Kingdom of Swaziland

conventional short form: Swaziland

Government type: monarchy; independent member of Commonwealth

Capital: Mbabane; note - Lobamba is the royal and legislative capital

Administrative divisions: 4 districts; Hhohho, Lubombo, Manzini, Shiselweni

Independence: 6 September 1968 (from UK)

National holiday: Independence Day, 6 September (1968)

Constitution: none; constitution of 6 September 1968 was suspended 12 April 1973; a new constitution was promulgated 13 October 1978, but was not formally presented to the people; since then a few more outlines for a constitution have been compiled under the Constitutional Review Commission (CRC), but so far none have been accepted

Legal system: based on South African Roman-Dutch law in statutory courts and Swazi traditional law and custom in traditional courts; has not accepted compulsory ICJ jurisdiction

Suffrage: 18 years of age

Executive branch:

chief of state: King MSWATI III (since 25 April 1986)

head of government: Prime Minister Absolom Themba DLAMINI (since 14 November 2003)

cabinet: Cabinet recommended by the prime minister and confirmed by the monarch

elections: none; the monarch is hereditary; prime minister appointed by the monarch

Legislative branch: bicameral Parliament or Libandla, an advisory body, consists of the Senate (30 seats - 10 appointed by the House of Assembly and 20 appointed by the monarch; members serve five-year terms) and the House of Assembly (65 seats - 10 appointed by the monarch and 55 elected by popular vote; members serve five-year terms)

elections: House of Assembly - last held 18 October 2003 (next to be held NA October 2008)

election results: House of Assembly - balloting is done on a nonparty basis; candidates for election are nominated by the local council of each constituency and for each constituency the three candidates with the most votes in the first round of voting are narrowed to a single winner by a second round

Judicial branch: High Court; Court of Appeal; judges for both courts are appointed by the monarch

Political parties and leaders: political parties are banned by the constitution - the following are considered political associations; Imbokodvo National Movement or INM [leader NA]; Ngwane National Liberatory Congress or NNLC [Obed DLAMINI, president]; People's United Democratic Movement or PUDEMO [Mario MASUKU, president]; Swaziland National Front or SWANAFRO [Elmond SHONGWE, president]

Political pressure groups and leaders: NA

International organization participation: ACP, AfDB, AU, C, FAO, G-77, IBRD, ICAO, ICFTU, ICRM, IDA, IFAD, IFC, IFRCS, ILO, IMF, Interpol, IOC, ISO (correspondent), ITU, NAM, OPCW, PCA, SACU, SADC, UN, UNCTAD, UNESCO, UNIDO, UPU, WCO, WHO, WIPO, WMO, WToO, WTrO

Diplomatic representation in the US:

chief of mission: Ambassador Mary Madzandza KANYA

chancery: 3400 International Drive NW, Washington, DC 20008

telephone: [1] (202) 362-6683

FAX: [1] (202) 244-8059

Diplomatic representation from the US:

chief of mission: Ambassador James D. McGEE

embassy: Central Bank Building, Warner Street, Mbabane

mailing address: P. O. Box 199, Mbabane

telephone: [268] 404-6441 through 404-6445

FAX: [268] 404-5959

Flag description: three horizontal bands of blue (top), red (triple width), and blue; the red band is edged in yellow; centered in the red band is a large black and white shield covering two spears and a staff decorated with feather tassels, all placed horizontally

Economy

Economy - overview: In this small, landlocked economy, subsistence agriculture occupies more than 80% of the population. The manufacturing sector has diversified since the mid-1980s. Sugar and wood pulp remain important foreign exchange earners. Mining has declined in importance in recent years with only coal and quarry stone mines remaining active. Surrounded by South Africa, except for a short border with Mozambique, Swaziland is heavily dependent on South Africa from which it receives about nine-tenths of its imports and to which it sends nearly three-quarters of its exports. Customs duties from the Southern African Customs Union and worker remittances from South Africa substantially supplement domestically earned income. The government is trying to improve the atmosphere for foreign investment. Overgrazing, soil depletion, drought, and sometimes floods persist as problems for the future. More than one-fourth of the population needed emergency food aid in 2002 because of drought, and more than one-third of the adult population was infected with HIV/AIDS.

GDP: purchasing power parity - $5.702 billion (2003 est.)

GDP - real growth rate: 2.2% (2003 est.)

GDP - per capita: purchasing power parity - $4,900 (2003 est.)

GDP - composition by sector:

agriculture: 17%

industry: 44%

services: 39% (2001 est.)

Population below poverty line: 40% (1995)

Household income or consumption by percentage share:

lowest 10%: 1%

highest 10%: 50.2% (1995)

Inflation rate (consumer prices): 11.8% (2002 est.)

Labor force: 383,200 (2000)

Labor force - by occupation: NA

Unemployment rate: 34% (2000 est.)

Budget:

revenues: $448 million

expenditures: $506.9 million, including capital expenditures of $147 million (FY01/02)

Industries: mining (coal), wood pulp, sugar, soft drink concentrates, textile and apparel

Industrial production growth rate: 3.7% (FY95/96)

Electricity - production: 348.3 million kWh (2001)

Electricity - production by source:

fossil fuel: 58%

hydro: 42%

nuclear: 0%

other: 0% (2001)

Electricity - consumption: 962.9 million kWh (2001)

Electricity - exports: 0 kWh (2001)

Electricity - imports: 639 million kWh; note - electricity supplied by South Africa (2001)

Oil - production: 0 bbl/day (2001 est.)

Oil - consumption: 3,500 bbl/day (2001 est.)

Oil - exports: NA

Oil - imports: NA

Agriculture - products: sugarcane, cotton, corn, tobacco, rice, citrus, pineapples, sorghum, peanuts; cattle, goats, sheep

Exports: $905.6 million f.o.b. (2003 est.)

Exports - commodities: soft drink concentrates, sugar, wood pulp, cotton yarn, refrigerators, citrus and canned fruit

Exports - partners: South Africa 72%, EU 14.2%, Mozambique 3.7%, US 3.5% (1999)

Imports: $1.088 billion f.o.b. (2003 est.)

Imports - commodities: motor vehicles, machinery, transport equipment, foodstuffs, petroleum products, chemicals

Imports - partners: South Africa 88.8%, EU 5.6%, Japan 0.6%, Singapore 0.4% (1999)

Debt - external: $320 million (2002 est.)

Economic aid - recipient: $104 million (2001)

Currency: lilangeni (SZL)

Currency code: SZL

Exchange rates: emalangeni per US dollar - 7.5648 (2003), 10.5407 (2002), 8.6092 (2001), 6.9398 (2000), 6.1095 (1999)

Fiscal year: 1 April - 31 March

Communications

Telephones - main lines in use: 40,000 (2004)
Telephones - mobile cellular: 70,000 (2004)
Telephone system:
general assessment: a somewhat modern but not an advanced system
domestic: system consists of carrier-equipped, open-wire lines and low-capacity, microwave radio relay
international: country code - 268; satellite earth station - 1 Intelsat (Atlantic Ocean)
Radio broadcast stations: AM 3, FM 2 plus 4 repeaters, shortwave 3 (2001)
Television broadcast stations: 5 plus 7 relay stations (2001)
Internet country code: .sz
Internet hosts: 1,329 (2002)
Internet users: 20,000 (2002)

Transportation

Railways:
total: 301 km
narrow gauge: 301 km 1.067-m gauge (2002)
Highways:
total: 3,247 km
paved: NA
unpaved: NA (1998)
Waterways: none
Ports and harbors: none
Airports: 18 (2003 est.)
Airports - with paved runways:
total: 1
2,438 to 3,047 m: 1 (2003 est.)
Airports - with unpaved runways:
total: 17
914 to 1,523 m: 7
under 914 m: 10 (2003 est.)

Military

Military branches: Umbutfo Swaziland Defense Force (Army, including Air Wing)
Military manpower - availability:
males age 15-49: 289,985 (2004 est.)
Military manpower - fit for military service:
males age 15-49: 168,257 (2004 est.)
Military expenditures - dollar figure: $29 million (2003)
Military expenditures - percent of GDP: 1.8% (2003)

Transnational Issues

Disputes - international: none

Sweden

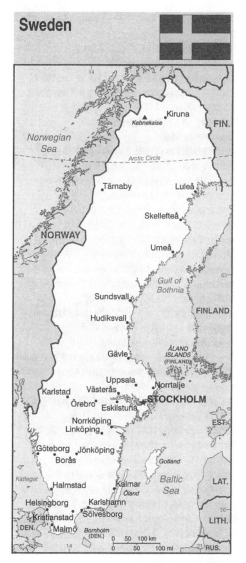

Introduction

Background: A military power during the 17th century, Sweden has not participated in any war in almost two centuries. An armed neutrality was preserved in both World Wars. Sweden's long-successful economic formula of a capitalist system interlarded with substantial welfare elements was challenged in the 1990s by high unemployment and in 2000-02 by the global economic downturn, but fiscal discipline over the past several years has allowed the country to weather economic vagaries. Indecision over the country's role in the political and economic integration of Europe delayed Sweden's entry into the EU until 1995, and waived the introduction of the euro in 1999.

Geography

Location: Northern Europe, bordering the Baltic Sea, Gulf of Bothnia, Kattegat, and Skagerrak, between Finland and Norway
Geographic coordinates: 62 00 N, 15 00 E
Map references: Europe
Area:
total: 449,964 sq km
land: 410,934 sq km
water: 39,030 sq km
Area - comparative: slightly larger than California
Land boundaries:
total: 2,205 km
border countries: Finland 586 km, Norway 1,619 km
Coastline: 3,218 km
Maritime claims:
territorial sea: 12 NM (adjustments made to return a portion of straits to high seas)
exclusive economic zone: agreed boundaries or midlines
continental shelf: 200-m depth or to the depth of exploitation
Climate: temperate in south with cold, cloudy winters and cool, partly cloudy summers; subarctic in north
Terrain: mostly flat or gently rolling lowlands; mountains in west
Elevation extremes:
lowest point: reclaimed bay of Lake Hammarsjon, near Kristianstad -2.41 m
highest point: Kebnekaise 2,111 m
Natural resources: zinc, iron ore, lead, copper, silver, timber, uranium, hydropower
Land use:
arable land: 6.8%
permanent crops: 0%
other: 93.2% (1998 est.)
Irrigated land: 1,150 sq km (1998 est.)
Natural hazards: ice floes in the surrounding waters, especially in the Gulf of Bothnia, can interfere with maritime traffic
Environment - current issues: acid rain damage to soils and lakes; pollution of the North Sea and the Baltic Sea
Environment - international agreements:
party to: Air Pollution, Air Pollution-Nitrogen Oxides, Air Pollution-Persistent Organic Pollutants, Air Pollution-Sulfur 85, Air Pollution-Sulfur 94, Air Pollution-Volatile Organic Compounds, Antarctic-Environmental Protocol, Antarctic-Marine Living Resources, Antarctic Treaty, Biodiversity, Climate Change, Climate Change-Kyoto Protocol, Desertification, Endangered Species, Environmental Modification, Hazardous Wastes, Law of the Sea, Marine Dumping, Ozone Layer Protection, Ship Pollution, Tropical Timber 83, Tropical Timber 94, Wetlands, Whaling
signed, but not ratified: none of the selected agreements
Geography - note: strategic location along Danish Straits linking Baltic and North Seas

People

Population: 8,986,400 (July 2004 est.)
Age structure:
0-14 years: 17.5% (male 807,193; female 762,882)
15-64 years: 65.2% (male 2,974,107; female 2,886,840)
65 years and over: 17.3% (male 668,719; female 886,659) (2004 est.)

Sweden (continued)

Median age:
total: 40.3 years
male: 39.2 years
female: 41.5 years (2004 est.)
Population growth rate: 0.18% (2004 est.)
Birth rate: 10.46 births/1,000 population (2004 est.)
Death rate: 10.38 deaths/1,000 population (2004 est.)
Net migration rate: 1.67 migrant(s)/1,000 population (2004 est.)
Sex ratio:
at birth: 1.06 male(s)/female
under 15 years: 1.06 male(s)/female
15-64 years: 1.03 male(s)/female
65 years and over: 0.75 male(s)/female
total population: 0.98 male(s)/female (2004 est.)
Infant mortality rate:
total: 2.77 deaths/1,000 live births
male: 2.93 deaths/1,000 live births
female: 2.6 deaths/1,000 live births (2004 est.)
Life expectancy at birth:
total population: 80.3 years
male: 78.12 years
female: 82.62 years (2004 est.)
Total fertility rate: 1.66 children born/woman (2004 est.)
HIV/AIDS - adult prevalence rate: 0.1% (2001 est.)
HIV/AIDS - people living with HIV/AIDS: 3,300 (2001 est.)
HIV/AIDS - deaths: less than 100 (2001 est.)
Nationality:
noun: Swede(s)
adjective: Swedish
Ethnic groups: indigenous population: Swedes and Finnish and Sami minorities; foreign-born or first-generation immigrants: Finns, Yugoslavs, Danes, Norwegians, Greeks, Turks
Religions: Lutheran 87%, Roman Catholic, Orthodox, Baptist, Muslim, Jewish, Buddhist
Languages: Swedish
note: small Sami- and Finnish-speaking minorities
Literacy:
definition: age 15 and over can read and write
total population: 99% (1979 est.)
male: NA%
female: NA%

Government

Country name:
conventional long form: Kingdom of Sweden
conventional short form: Sweden
local long form: Konungariket Sverige
local short form: Sverige
Government type: constitutional monarchy
Capital: Stockholm
Administrative divisions: 21 counties (lan, singular and plural); Blekinge, Dalarnas, Gavleborgs, Gotlands, Hallands, Jamtlands, Jonkopings, Kalmar, Kronobergs, Norrbottens, Orebro, Ostergotlands, Skane, Sodermanlands, Stockholms, Uppsala, Varmlands, Vasterbottens, Vasternorrlands, Vastmanlands, Vastra Gotalands

Independence: 6 June 1523 (Gustav VASA elected king)
National holiday: Flag Day, 6 June
Constitution: 1 January 1975
Legal system: civil law system influenced by customary law; accepts compulsory ICJ jurisdiction, with reservations
Suffrage: 18 years of age; universal
Executive branch:
chief of state: King CARL XVI GUSTAF (since 19 September 1973); Heir Apparent Princess VICTORIA Ingrid Alice Desiree, daughter of the monarch (born 14 July 1977)
head of government: Prime Minister Goran PERSSON (since 21 March 1996)
cabinet: Cabinet appointed by the prime minister
elections: the monarchy is hereditary; following legislative elections, the prime minister is elected by the Parliament; election last held 15 September 2002 (next to be held NA September 2006)
election results: Goran PERSSON reelected prime minister with 131 out of 349 votes
Legislative branch: unicameral Parliament or Riksdag (349 seats; members are elected by popular vote on a proportional representation basis to serve four-year terms)
elections: last held 15 September 2002 (next to be held NA September 2006)
election results: percent of vote by party - Social Democrats 39.8%, Moderates 15.2%, Liberal Party 13.3%, Christian Democrats 9.1%, Left Party 8.3%, Center Party 6.1%, Greens 4.6%; seats by party - Social Democrats 144, Moderates 55, Liberal Party 48, Christian Democrats 33, Left Party 30, Center Party 22, Greens 17
Judicial branch: Supreme Court or Hogsta Domstolen (judges are appointed by the prime minister and the cabinet)
Political parties and leaders: Center Party [Maud OLOFSSON]; Christian Democratic Party [Alf SVENSSON]; Green Party [no formal leader but party spokespersons are Maria WETTERSTRAND and Peter ERIKSSON]; Left Party or VP (formerly Communist) [Ulla HOFFMAN (acting)]; Liberal People's Party [Lars LEIJONBORG]; Moderate Party (conservative) [Fredrik REINFELDT]; Social Democratic Party [Goran PERSSON]
Political pressure groups and leaders: NA
International organization participation: AfDB, AsDB, Australia Group, BIS, CBSS, CE, CERN, EAPC, EBRD, EIB, ESA, EU, FAO, G- 6, G- 9, G-10, IADB, IAEA, IBRD, ICAO, ICC, ICCt, ICFTU, ICRM, IDA, IEA, IFAD, IFC, IFRCS, IHO, ILO, IMF, IMO, Interpol, IOC, IOM, ISO, ITU, MONUC, NAM (guest), NC, NEA, NIB, NSG, OAS (observer), OECD, OPCW, OSCE, Paris Club, PCA, PFP, UN, UNAMSIL, UNCTAD, UNDOF, UNESCO, UNHCR, UNIDO, UNITAR, UNMEE, UNMIK, UNMIL, UNMISET, UNMOGIP, UNOMIG, UNTSO, UPU, WCO, WEU (observer), WFTU, WHO, WIPO, WMO, WTrO, ZC

Diplomatic representation in the US:
chief of mission: Ambassador Jan ELIASSON
chancery: 1501 M Street NW, Washington, DC 20005-1702
telephone: [1] (202) 467-2600
FAX: [1] (202) 467-2699
consulate(s) general: Los Angeles and New York
Diplomatic representation from the US:
chief of mission: Ambassador Charles A. HEIMBOLD, Jr.
embassy: Dag Hammarskjolds VAG 31, SE-11589 Stockholm
mailing address: American Embassy Stockholm, Department of State, 5750 Stockholm Place, Washington, DC 20521-5750 (pouch)
telephone: [46] (08) 783 53 00
FAX: [46] (08) 661 19 64
Flag description: blue with a golden yellow cross extending to the edges of the flag; the vertical part of the cross is shifted to the hoist side in the style of the Dannebrog (Danish flag)

Economy

Economy - overview: Aided by peace and neutrality for the whole 20th century, Sweden has achieved an enviable standard of living under a mixed system of high-tech capitalism and extensive welfare benefits. It has a modern distribution system, excellent internal and external communications, and a skilled labor force. Timber, hydropower, and iron ore constitute the resource base of an economy heavily oriented toward foreign trade. Privately owned firms account for about 90% of industrial output, of which the engineering sector accounts for 50% of output and exports. Agriculture accounts for only 2% of GDP and 2% of the jobs. The government's commitment to fiscal discipline resulted in a substantial budgetary surplus in 2001, which was cut by more than half in 2002, due to the global economic slowdown, declining revenue, and increased spending. The Swedish central bank (the Riksbank) is focusing on price stability with its inflation target of 2%. Growth remained sluggish in 2003. On September 14, 2003, Swedish voters turned down entry into the euro system, concerned about the impact on democracy and sovereignty.
GDP: purchasing power parity - $238.1 billion (2003 est.)
GDP - real growth rate: 1.6% (2003 est.)
GDP - per capita: purchasing power parity - $26,800 (2003 est.)
GDP - composition by sector:
agriculture: 2%
industry: 29%
services: 69% (2001)
Population below poverty line: NA%
Household income or consumption by percentage share:
lowest 10%: 3.7%
highest 10%: 20.1% (1992)
Distribution of family income - Gini index: 25 (1992)

Sweden *(continued)*

Inflation rate (consumer prices): 2.3% (2003 est.)
Labor force: 4.4 million (2000 est.)
Labor force - by occupation: agriculture 2%, industry 24%, services 74% (2000 est.)
Unemployment rate: 4.6% (2003 est.)
Budget:
revenues: $119 billion
expenditures: $110 billion, including capital expenditures of $NA (2001 est.)
Industries: iron and steel, precision equipment (bearings, radio and telephone parts, armaments), wood pulp and paper products, processed foods, motor vehicles
Industrial production growth rate: 1.5% (2003 est.)
Electricity - production: 152.9 billion kWh (2001)
Electricity - production by source:
fossil fuel: 4%
hydro: 50.8%
nuclear: 43%
other: 2.3% (2001)
Electricity - consumption: 134.9 billion kWh (2001)
Electricity - exports: 18.45 billion kWh (2001)
Electricity - imports: 11.14 billion kWh (2001)
Oil - production: 0 bbl/day (2001 est.)
Oil - consumption: 328,600 bbl/day (2001 est.)
Oil - exports: 203,700 bbl/day (2001)
Oil - imports: 553,100 bbl/day (2001)
Natural gas - production: 0 cu m (2001 est.)
Natural gas - consumption: 949 million cu m (2001 est.)
Natural gas - exports: 0 cu m (2001 est.)
Natural gas - imports: 968 million cu m (2001 est.)
Agriculture - products: barley, wheat, sugar beets; meat, milk
Exports: $102.8 billion f.o.b. (2003 est.)
Exports - commodities: machinery 35%, motor vehicles, paper products, pulp and wood, iron and steel products, chemicals
Exports - partners: US 11.6%, Germany 10.1%, Norway 9%, UK 8.2%, Denmark 5.9%, Finland 5.5%, Netherlands 5.3%, France 5.1%, Belgium 4.7% (2002)
Imports: $83.27 billion f.o.b. (2003 est.)
Imports - commodities: machinery, petroleum and petroleum products, chemicals, motor vehicles, iron and steel; foodstuffs, clothing
Imports - partners: Germany 18.5%, Denmark 8.8%, UK 8.6%, Norway 8.2%, Netherlands 6.7%, France 5.4%, Finland 5.2%, US 5% (2002)
Debt - external: $66.5 billion (1994)
Economic aid - donor: ODA, $1.7 billion (1997)
Currency: Swedish krona (SEK)
Currency code: SEK
Exchange rates: Swedish kronor per US dollar - 8.0853 (2003), 9.7371 (2002), 10.3291 (2001), 9.1622 (2000), 8.2624 (1999)
Fiscal year: calendar year

Communications

Telephones - main lines in use: 6,579,200 (2002)
Telephones - mobile cellular: 7.949 million (2002)
Telephone system:
general assessment: excellent domestic and international facilities; automatic system
domestic: coaxial and multiconductor cables carry most of the voice traffic; parallel microwave radio relay systems carry some additional telephone channels
international: country code - 46; 5 submarine coaxial cables; satellite earth stations - 1 Intelsat (Atlantic Ocean), 1 Eutelsat, and 1 Inmarsat (Atlantic and Indian Ocean regions); note - Sweden shares the Inmarsat earth station with the other Nordic countries (Denmark, Finland, Iceland, and Norway)
Radio broadcast stations: AM 1, FM 265, shortwave 1 (1998)
Television broadcast stations: 169 (plus 1,299 repeaters) (1995)
Internet country code: .se
Internet hosts: 849,174 (2002)
Internet users: 5.125 million (2002)

Transportation

Railways:
total: 11,481 km
standard gauge: 11,481 km 1.435-m gauge (7,527 km electrified) (2002)
Highways:
total: 212,402 km
paved: 166,523 km (including 1,499 km of expressways)
unpaved: 45,879 km (2000)
Waterways: 2,052 km
note: navigable to small steamers and barges
Pipelines: gas 798 km (2003)
Ports and harbors: Gavle, Goteborg, Halmstad, Helsingborg, Hudiksvall, Kalmar, Karlshamn, Lulea, Malmo, Solvesborg, Stockholm, Sundsvall
Merchant marine:
total: 178 ships (1,000 GRT or over) 2,702,763 GRT/1,884,570 DWT
by type: bulk 7, cargo 36, chemical tanker 31, combination bulk 1, combination ore/oil 1, petroleum tanker 25, roll on/roll off 39, short-sea/passenger 8, specialized tanker 7, vehicle carrier 23
foreign-owned: Denmark 12, Finland 10, Germany 3, Italy 7, Japan 2, Netherlands 1, Norway 12, Russia 1
registered in other countries: 154 (2003 est.)
Airports: 255 (2003 est.)
Airports - with paved runways:
total: 155
over 3,047 m: 3
2,438 to 3,047 m: 11
1,524 to 2,437 m: 82
914 to 1,523 m: 23
under 914 m: 36 (2003 est.)
Airports - with unpaved runways:
total: 100

914 to 1,523 m: 10
under 914 m: 90 (2003 est.)
Heliports: 2 (2003 est.)

Military

Military branches: Army, Royal Navy, Air Force (Flygvapnet)
Military manpower - military age: 19 years of age; conscripts serve seven to 15 months depending on their role; after completing their initial service, soldiers have a reserve commitment until the age of 47 (2004 est.)
Military manpower - availability:
males age 15-49: 2,082,776 (2004 est.)
Military manpower - fit for military service:
males age 15-49: 1,821,394 (2004 est.)
Military manpower - reaching military age annually:
males: 56,859 (2004 est.)
Military expenditures - dollar figure: $4.395 billion (FY01)
Military expenditures - percent of GDP: 2.1% (FY01)

Transnational Issues

Disputes - international: none

Switzerland

Introduction

Background: Switzerland's independence and neutrality have long been honored by the major European powers, and Switzerland was not involved in either of the two World Wars. The political and economic integration of Europe over the past half century, as well as Switzerland's role in many UN and international organizations, has strengthened Switzerland's ties with its neighbors. However, the country did not officially become a UN member until 2002. Switzerland remains active in many UN and international organizations, but retains a strong commitment to neutrality.

Geography

Location: Central Europe, east of France, north of Italy
Geographic coordinates: 47 00 N, 8 00 E
Map references: Europe
Area:
total: 41,290 sq km
land: 39,770 sq km
water: 1,520 sq km
Area - comparative: slightly less than twice the size of New Jersey
Land boundaries:
total: 1,852 km
border countries: Austria 164 km, France 573 km, Italy 740 km, Liechtenstein 41 km, Germany 334 km
Coastline: 0 km (landlocked)
Maritime claims: none (landlocked)
Climate: temperate, but varies with altitude; cold, cloudy, rainy/snowy winters; cool to warm, cloudy, humid summers with occasional showers
Terrain: mostly mountains (Alps in south, Jura in northwest) with a central plateau of rolling hills, plains, and large lakes
Elevation extremes:
lowest point: Lake Maggiore 195 m
highest point: Dufourspitze 4,634 m

Natural resources: hydropower potential, timber, salt
Land use:
arable land: 10.57%
permanent crops: 0.61%
other: 88.82% (1998 est.)
Irrigated land: 250 sq km (1998 est.)
Natural hazards: avalanches, landslides, flash floods
Environment - current issues: air pollution from vehicle emissions and open-air burning; acid rain; water pollution from increased use of agricultural fertilizers; loss of biodiversity
Environment - international agreements:
party to: Air Pollution, Air Pollution-Nitrogen Oxides, Air Pollution-Persistent Organic Pollutants, Air Pollution-Sulfur 85, Air Pollution-Sulfur 94, Air Pollution-Volatile Organic Compounds, Antarctic Treaty, Biodiversity, Climate Change, Climate Change-Kyoto Protocol, Desertification, Endangered Species, Environmental Modification, Hazardous Wastes, Marine Dumping, Marine Life Conservation, Ozone Layer Protection, Ship Pollution, Tropical Timber 83, Tropical Timber 94, Wetlands, Whaling
signed, but not ratified: Law of the Sea
Geography - note: landlocked; crossroads of northern and southern Europe; along with southeastern France, northern Italy, and southwestern Austria, has the highest elevations in the Alps

People

Population: 7,450,867 (July 2004 est.)
Age structure:
0-14 years: 16.8% (male 647,362; female 602,333)
15-64 years: 67.9% (male 2,555,089; female 2,503,331)
65 years and over: 15.3% (male 466,615; female 676,137) (2004 est.)
Median age:
total: 39.5 years
male: 38.5 years
female: 40.5 years (2004 est.)
Population growth rate: 0.54% (2004 est.)

Birth rate: 9.83 births/1,000 population (2004 est.)
Death rate: 8.44 deaths/1,000 population (2004 est.)
Net migration rate: 4.05 migrant(s)/1,000 population (2004 est.)
Sex ratio:
at birth: 1.05 male(s)/female
under 15 years: 1.08 male(s)/female
15-64 years: 1.02 male(s)/female
65 years and over: 0.69 male(s)/female
total population: 0.97 male(s)/female (2004 est.)
Infant mortality rate:
total: 4.43 deaths/1,000 live births
male: 4.94 deaths/1,000 live births
female: 3.89 deaths/1,000 live births (2004 est.)
Life expectancy at birth:
total population: 80.31 years
male: 77.51 years
female: 83.27 years (2004 est.)
Total fertility rate: 1.42 children born/woman (2004 est.)
HIV/AIDS - adult prevalence rate: 0.5% (2001 est.)
HIV/AIDS - people living with HIV/AIDS: 19,000 (2001 est.)
HIV/AIDS - deaths: less than 100 (2001 est.)
Nationality:
noun: Swiss (singular and plural)
adjective: Swiss
Ethnic groups: German 65%, French 18%, Italian 10%, Romansch 1%, other 6%
Religions: Roman Catholic 46.1%, Protestant 40%, other 5%, none 8.9% (1990)
Languages: German (official) 63.7%, French (official) 19.2%, Italian (official) 7.6%, Romansch (official) 0.6%, other 8.9%
Literacy:
definition: age 15 and over can read and write
total population: 99% (1980 est.)
male:
female:

Government

Country name:
conventional long form: Swiss Confederation
conventional short form: Switzerland
local long form: Schweizerische Eidgenossenschaft (German), Confederation Suisse (French), Confederazione Svizzera (Italian)
local short form: Schweiz (German), Suisse (French), Svizzera (Italian)
Government type: federal republic
Capital: Bern
Administrative divisions: 26 cantons (cantons, singular - canton in French; cantoni, singular - cantone in Italian; kantone, singular - kanton in German); Aargau, Appenzell Ausser-Rhoden, Appenzell Inner-Rhoden, Basel-Landschaft, Basel-Stadt, Bern, Fribourg, Geneve, Glarus, Graubunden, Jura, Luzern, Neuchatel, Nidwalden, Obwalden, Sankt Gallen, Schaffhausen, Schwyz, Solothurn, Thurgau, Ticino, Uri, Valais, Vaud, Zug, Zurich
Independence: 1 August 1291 (Founding of the Swiss Confederation)

Switzerland (continued)

National holiday: Founding of the Swiss Confederation, 1 August (1291)

Constitution: revision of Constitution of 1874 approved by the Federal Parliament 18 December 1998; adopted by referendum 18 April 1999; officially entered into force 1 January 2000

Legal system: civil law system influenced by customary law; judicial review of legislative acts, except with respect to federal decrees of general obligatory character; accepts compulsory ICJ jurisdiction, with reservations

Suffrage: 18 years of age; universal

Executive branch:

chief of state: President Joseph DEISS (since 1 January 2004); Vice President Samuel SCHMID (since 1 January 2004); note - the president is both the chief of state and head of government

head of government: President Joseph DEISS (since 1 January 2004); Vice President Samuel SCHMID (since 1 January 2004); note - the president is both the chief of state and head of government

cabinet: Federal Council or Bundesrat (in German), Conseil Federal (in French), Consiglio Federale (in Italian) elected by the Federal Assembly usually from among its own members for a four-year term

elections: president and vice president elected by the Federal Assembly from among the members of the Federal Council for one-year terms that run concurrently; election last held NA December 2003 (next to be held NA December 2004)

election results: Joseph DEISS elected president; percent of Federal Assembly vote - 70.7%; Samuel SCHMID elected vice president; percent of legislative vote - 58.1%

Legislative branch: bicameral Federal Assembly or Bundesversammlung (in German), Assemblee Federale (in French), Assemblea Federale (in Italian) consists of the Council of States or Standerat (in German), Conseil des Etats (in French), Consiglio degli Stati (in Italian) (46 seats - members serve four-year terms) and the National Council or Nationalrat (in German), Conseil National (in French), Consiglio Nazionale (in Italian) (200 seats - members are elected by popular vote on the basis of proportional representation to serve four-year terms)

elections: Council of States - last held in most cantons 19 October 2003 (each canton determines when the next election will be held); National Council - last held 19 October 2003 (next to be held NA October 2007)

election results: Council of States - percent of vote by party - NA%; seats by party - CVP 15, FDP 14, SVP 8, SPS 6, other 3; National Council - percent of vote by party - SVP 26.6%, SPS 23.3%, FDP 17.3%, CVP 14.4%, Greens 7.4%, other small parties all under 5%; seats by party - SVP 55, SPS 54, FDP 36, CVP 28, Green Party 13, other small parties 14

Judicial branch: Federal Supreme Court (judges elected for six-year terms by the Federal Assembly)

Political parties and leaders: Green Party (Grune Partei der Schweiz or Grune, Parti Ecologiste Suisse or Les Verts, Partito Ecologista Svizzero or I Verdi, Partida Ecologica Svizra or La Verda) [Ruth GENNER]; Christian Democratic People's Party (Christichdemokratische Volkspartei der Schweiz or CVP, Parti Democrate-Chretien Suisse or PDC, Partito Democratico-Cristiano Popolare Svizzero or PDC, Partida Cristiandemocratica dalla Svizra or PCD) [Philipp STAEHELIN, president]; Radical Free Democratic Party (Freisinnig-Demokratische Partei der Schweiz or FDP, Parti Radical-Democratique Suisse or PRD, Partitio Liberal-Radicale Svizzero or PLR) [Christiane LANGENBERGER, president]; Social Democratic Party (Sozialdemokratische Partei der Schweiz or SPS, Parti Socialist Suisse or PSS, Partito Socialista Svizzero or PSS, Partida Socialdemocratica de la Svizra or PSS) [Christiane BRUNNER, president]; Swiss People's Party (Schweizerische Volkspartei or SVP, Union Democratique du Centre or UDC, Unione Democratica de Centro or UDC, Uniun Democratica dal Center or UDC) [Ueli MAURER, president]; and other minor parties

Political pressure groups and leaders: NA

International organization participation: ACCT, AfDB, AsDB, Australia Group, BIS, CE, CERN, EAPC, EBRD, EFTA, ESA, FAO, G-10, IADB, IAEA, IBRD, ICAO, ICC, ICCt, ICFTU, ICRM, IDA, IEA, IFAD, IFC, IFRCS, ILO, IMF, IMO, Interpol, IOC, IOM, ISO, ITU, LAIA (observer), MONUC, NAM (guest), NEA, NSG, OAS (observer), OECD, OPCW, OSCE, Paris Club, PCA, PFP, UN, UNCTAD, UNESCO, UNHCR, UNIDO, UNITAR, UNMEE, UNMIK, UNOMIG, UNTSO, UPU, WCL, WCO, WHO, WIPO, WMO, WToO, WTrO, ZC

Diplomatic representation in the US:

chief of mission: Ambassador Christian BLICKENSTORFER

chancery: 2900 Cathedral Avenue NW, Washington, DC 20008

telephone: [1] (202) 745-7900

FAX: [1] (202) 387-2564

consulate(s) general: Atlanta, Chicago, Houston, Los Angeles, New York, and San Francisco

consulate(s): Boston

Diplomatic representation from the US:

chief of mission: Ambassador Pamela WILLEFORD

embassy: Jubilaeumsstrasse 93, 3005 Bern

mailing address: use embassy street address

telephone: [41] (031) 357 70 11

FAX: [41] (031) 357 73 44

Flag description: red square with a bold, equilateral white cross in the center that does not extend to the edges of the flag

Economy

Economy - overview: Switzerland is a prosperous and stable modern market economy with low unemployment, a highly skilled labor force, and a per capita GDP larger than that of the big Western European economies. The Swiss in recent years have brought their economic practices largely into conformity with the EU's to enhance their international competitiveness. Switzerland remains a safe haven for investors, because it has maintained a degree of bank secrecy and has kept up the franc's long-term external value. Reflecting the anemic economic conditions of Europe, GDP growth dropped in 2001 to about 0.8%, to 0.2% in 2002, and to -0.3% in 2003.

GDP: purchasing power parity - $239.8 billion (2003 est.)

GDP - real growth rate: -0.3% (2003 est.)

GDP - per capita: purchasing power parity - $32,800 (2003 est.)

GDP - composition by sector:

agriculture: 1.5%

industry: 34%

services: 64.5% (2003 est.)

Population below poverty line: NA%

Household income or consumption by percentage share:

lowest 10%: 2.6%

highest 10%: 25.2% (1992)

Distribution of family income - Gini index: 33.1 (1992)

Inflation rate (consumer prices): 0.5% (2003 est.)

Labor force: 4 million (2001)

Labor force - by occupation: services 69.1%, industry 26.3%, agriculture 4.6% (1998)

Unemployment rate: 3.9% (2003 est.)

Budget:

revenues: $30 billion

expenditures: $30 billion, including capital expenditures of $NA (2001 est.)

Industries: machinery, chemicals, watches, textiles, precision instruments

Industrial production growth rate: 3.2% (2001)

Electricity - production: 68.68 billion kWh (2001)

Electricity - production by source:

fossil fuel: 1.3%

hydro: 59.5%

nuclear: 37.1%

other: 2% (2001)

Electricity - consumption: 53.43 billion kWh (2001)

Electricity - exports: 34.54 billion kWh (2001)

Electricity - imports: 24.1 billion kWh (2001)

Oil - production: 0 bbl/day (2001 est.)

Oil - consumption: 290,400 bbl/day (2001 est.)

Oil - exports: 10,420 bbl/day (2001)

Oil - imports: 289,500 bbl/day (2001)

Natural gas - production: 0 cu m (2001 est.)

Natural gas - consumption: 3.093 billion cu m (2001 est.)

Natural gas - exports: 0 cu m (2001 est.)

Natural gas - imports: 3.093 billion cu m (2001 est.)

Agriculture - products: grains, fruits, vegetables; meat, eggs

Exports: $110 billion f.o.b. (2003 est.)

Exports - commodities: machinery, chemicals, metals, watches, agricultural products

Exports - partners: Germany 20.4%, US 11.9%, France 9.1%, Italy 8.2%, UK 5.1% (2002)

Imports: $102.2 billion f.o.b. (2003 est.)

Imports - commodities: machinery, chemicals, vehicles, metals; agricultural products, textiles

Switzerland (continued)

Imports - partners: Germany 31.4%, Italy 10.3%, France 10%, US 6.6%, Netherlands 5.1%, UK 4.9%, Austria 4.1% (2002)
Debt - external: $NA (2000)
Economic aid - donor: ODA, $1.1 billion (1995)
Currency: Swiss franc (CHF)
Currency code: CHF
Exchange rates: Swiss francs per US dollar - 1.3467 (2003), 1.5586 (2002), 1.6876 (2001), 1.6888 (2000), 1.5022 (1999)
Fiscal year: calendar year

Communications

Telephones - main lines in use: 5.419 million (2002)
Telephones - mobile cellular: 5.747 million (2002)
Telephone system:
general assessment: excellent domestic and international services
domestic: extensive cable and microwave radio relay networks
international: country code - 41; satellite earth stations - 2 Intelsat (Atlantic Ocean and Indian Ocean)
Radio broadcast stations: AM 4, FM 113 (plus many low power stations), shortwave 2 (1998)
Television broadcast stations: 115 (plus 1,919 repeaters) (1995)
Internet country code: .ch
Internet hosts: 560,902 (2002)
Internet users: 2.556 million (2002)

Transportation

Railways:
total: 4,511 km
standard gauge: 3,483 km 1.435-m gauge (3,472 km electrified)
narrow gauge: 982 km 1.000-m gauge (975 km electrified); 46 km 0.800-m gauge (46 km electrified) (2002)
Highways:
total: 71,011 km
paved: 71,011 km (including 1,638 of expressways)
unpaved: 0 km (2000)
Waterways: 65 km
note: The Rhine carries heavy traffic on the Basel-Rheinfelden and Schaffhausen-Bodensee stretches; there are also 12 navigable lakes
Pipelines: gas 1,831 km; oil 212 km; refined products 7 km (2003)
Ports and harbors: Basel
Merchant marine:
total: 30 ships (1,000 GRT or over) 604,843 GRT/ 1,050,914 DWT
by type: bulk 15, cargo 6, chemical tanker 3, container 3, petroleum tanker 2, specialized tanker 1
foreign-owned: Belgium 1, Netherlands 1, United Kingdom 6, United States 1
registered in other countries: 182 (2003 est.)
Airports: 65 (2003 est.)

Airports - with paved runways:
total: 42
over 3,047 m: 3
2,438 to 3,047 m: 5
1,524 to 2,437 m: 10
914 to 1,523 m: 8
under 914 m: 16 (2003 est.)
Airports - with unpaved runways:
total: 23
under 914 m: 23 (2003 est.)
Heliports: 2 (2003 est.)

Military

Military branches: Land Forces, Air Force
Military manpower - military age: 20 years of age (2004 est.)
Military manpower - availability:
males age 15-49: 1,890,091 (2004 est.)
Military manpower - fit for military service:
males age 15-49: 1,606,391 (2004 est.)
Military manpower - reaching military age annually:
males: 45,654 (2004 est.)
Military expenditures - dollar figure: $2.548 billion (FY01)
Military expenditures - percent of GDP: 1% (FY01)

Transnational Issues

Disputes - international: none
Illicit drugs: a major international financial center vulnerable to the layering and integration stages of money laundering; despite significant legislation and reporting requirements, secrecy rules persist and nonresidents are permitted to conduct business through offshore entities and various intermediaries; transit country for and consumer of South American cocaine and Southwest Asian heroin

Syria

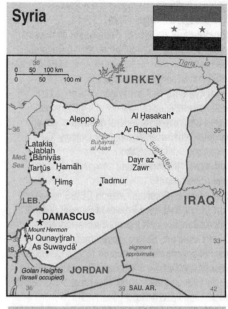

Introduction

Background: Following the breakup of the Ottoman Empire during World War I, Syria was administered by the French until independence in 1946. In the 1967 Arab-Israeli War, Syria lost the Golan Heights to Israel. Since 1976, Syrian troops have been stationed in Lebanon, ostensibly in a peacekeeping capacity. In recent years, Syria and Israel have held occasional peace talks over the return of the Golan Heights.

Geography

Location: Middle East, bordering the Mediterranean Sea, between Lebanon and Turkey
Geographic coordinates: 35 00 N, 38 00 E
Map references: Middle East
Area:
total: 185,180 sq km
land: 184,050 sq km
water: 1,130 sq km
note: includes 1,295 sq km of Israeli-occupied territory
Area - comparative: slightly larger than North Dakota
Land boundaries:
total: 2,253 km
border countries: Iraq 605 km, Israel 76 km, Jordan 375 km, Lebanon 375 km, Turkey 822 km
Coastline: 193 km
Maritime claims:
territorial sea: 12 NM
contiguous zone: 41 NM
Climate: mostly desert; hot, dry, sunny summers (June to August) and mild, rainy winters (December to February) along coast; cold weather with snow or sleet periodically in Damascus
Terrain: primarily semiarid and desert plateau; narrow coastal plain; mountains in west
Elevation extremes:
lowest point: unnamed location near Lake Tiberias -200 m
highest point: Mount Hermon 2,814 m

Syria (continued)

Natural resources: petroleum, phosphates, chrome and manganese ores, asphalt, iron ore, rock salt, marble, gypsum, hydropower

Land use:
arable land: 25.96%
permanent crops: 4.08%
other: 69.96% (1998 est.)

Irrigated land: 12,130 sq km (1998 est.)

Natural hazards: dust storms, sandstorms

Environment - current issues: deforestation; overgrazing; soil erosion; desertification; water pollution from raw sewage and petroleum refining wastes; inadequate potable water

Environment - international agreements:
party to: Biodiversity, Climate Change, Desertification, Endangered Species, Hazardous Wastes, Ozone Layer Protection, Ship Pollution, Wetlands
signed, but not ratified: Environmental Modification

Geography - note: there are 42 Israeli settlements and civilian land use sites in the Israeli-occupied Golan Heights (February 2002 est.)

People

Population: 18,016,874 (July 2002 est.)
note: in addition, about 40,000 people live in the Israeli-occupied Golan Heights - 20,000 Arabs (18,000 Druze and 2,000 Alawites) and about 20,000 Israeli settlers (February 2003 est.) (July 2004 est.)

Age structure:
0-14 years: 38% (male 3,524,406; female 3,319,323)
15-64 years: 58.7% (male 5,421,133; female 5,163,669)
65 years and over: 3.3% (male 281,795; female 306,548) (2004 est.)

Median age:
total: 20 years
male: 19.9 years
female: 20.2 years (2004 est.)

Population growth rate: 2.4% (2004 est.)

Birth rate: 28.93 births/1,000 population (2004 est.)

Death rate: 4.96 deaths/1,000 population (2004 est.)

Net migration rate: 0 migrant(s)/1,000 population (2004 est.)

Sex ratio:
at birth: 1.06 male(s)/female
under 15 years: 1.06 male(s)/female
15-64 years: 1.05 male(s)/female
65 years and over: 0.92 male(s)/female
total population: 1.05 male(s)/female (2004 est.)

Infant mortality rate:
total: 30.6 deaths/1,000 live births
male: 30.82 deaths/1,000 live births
female: 30.35 deaths/1,000 live births (2004 est.)

Life expectancy at birth:
total population: 69.71 years
male: 68.47 years
female: 71.02 years (2004 est.)

Total fertility rate: 3.61 children born/woman (2004 est.)

HIV/AIDS - adult prevalence rate: 0.01% (2001 est.)

HIV/AIDS - people living with HIV/AIDS: NA

HIV/AIDS - deaths: NA

Nationality:
noun: Syrian(s)
adjective: Syrian

Ethnic groups: Arab 90.3%, Kurds, Armenians, and other 9.7%

Religions: Sunni Muslim 74%, Alawite, Druze, and other Muslim sects 16%, Christian (various sects) 10%, Jewish (tiny communities in Damascus, Al Qamishli, and Aleppo)

Languages: Arabic (official); Kurdish, Armenian, Aramaic, Circassian widely understood; French, English somewhat understood

Literacy:
definition: age 15 and over can read and write
total population: 76.9%
male: 89.7%
female: 64% (2003 est.)

Government

Country name:
conventional long form: Syrian Arab Republic
conventional short form: Syria
local long form: Al Jumhuriyah al Arabiyah as Suriyah
local short form: Suriyah
former: United Arab Republic (with Egypt)

Government type: republic under military regime since March 1963

Capital: Damascus

Administrative divisions: 14 provinces (muhafazat, singular - muhafazah); Al Hasakah, Al Ladhiqiyah, Al Qunaytirah, Ar Raqqah, As Suwayda', Dar'a, Dayr az Zawr, Dimashq, Halab, Hamah, Hims, Idlib, Rif Dimashq, Tartus

Independence: 17 April 1946 (from League of Nations mandate under French administration)

National holiday: Independence Day, 17 April (1946)

Constitution: 13 March 1973

Legal system: based on Islamic law and civil law system; special religious courts; has not accepted compulsory ICJ jurisdiction

Suffrage: 18 years of age; universal

Executive branch:
chief of state: President Bashar al-ASAD (since 17 July 2000); Vice Presidents Abd al-Halim ibn Said KHADDAM (since 11 March 1984) and Muhammad Zuhayr MASHARIQA (since 11 March 1984)
head of government: Prime Minister Muhammad Naji al-UTRI (since 10 September 2003), Deputy Prime Ministers Lt. Gen. Mustafa TALAS (since 11 March 1984), Farouk al-SHARA (since 13 December 2001), Dr. Muhammad al-HUSAYN (since 13 December 2001)
cabinet: Council of Ministers appointed by the president
elections: president elected by popular vote for a seven-year term; referendum/election last held 10 July 2000 - after the death of President Hafiz al-ASAD, father of Bashar al-ASAD - (next to be held NA 2007); vice presidents appointed by the president; prime minister and deputy prime ministers appointed by the president

election results: Bashar al-ASAD elected president; percent of vote - Bashar al-ASAD 97.29%
note: Hafiz al-ASAD died on 10 June 2000; on 20 June 2000, the Ba'th Party nominated Bashar al-ASAD for president and presented his name to the People's Council on 25 June 2000

Legislative branch: unicameral People's Council or Majlis al-shaab (250 seats; members elected by popular vote to serve four-year terms)
elections: last held 2-3 March 2003 (next to be held NA 2007)
election results: percent of vote by party - NPF 67%, independents 33%; seats by party - NPF 167, independents 83; note - the constitution guarantees that the Ba'th Party (part of the NPF alliance) receives one-half of the seats

Judicial branch: Supreme Constitutional Court (justices are appointed for four-year terms by the president); High Judicial Council; Court of Cassation; State Security Courts

Political parties and leaders: National Progressive Front or NPF (includes Arab Socialist Renaissance (Ba'th) Party (governing party) [President Bashar al-ASAD, secretary general], Socialist Unionist Democratic Party [Ahmad al ASAD], Syrian Communist Party [leader NA], Unionist Socialist Party [leader NA], Arab Socialist Party [Abd al-Ghani QANNUT], and Arab Socialist Unionist Movement [Sami SUFAN]) [President Bashar al-ASAD, chairman]; Syrian Arab Socialist Party or ASP [Safwan QUDSI]; Syrian Communist Party or SCP [Yusuf FAYSAL]; Syrian Social National Party [Jubran URAYJI]

Political pressure groups and leaders: conservative religious leaders; Muslim Brotherhood (operates in exile in Jordan and Yemen); non-Ba'th parties have little effective political influence

International organization participation: ABEDA, AFESD, AMF, CAEU, FAO, G-24, G-77, IAEA, IBRD, ICAO, ICC, ICCt (signatory), ICRM, IDA, IDB, IFAD, IFC, IFRCS, IHO, ILO, IMF, IMO, Interpol, IOC, ISO, ITU, LAS, NAM, OAPEC, OIC, UN, UNCTAD, UNESCO, UNIDO, UNRWA, UPU, WCO, WFTU, WHO, WMO, WToO

Diplomatic representation in the US:
chief of mission: Ambassador Imad MUSTAFA
chancery: 2215 Wyoming Avenue NW, Washington, DC 20008
telephone: [1] (202) 232-6313
FAX: [1] (202) 234-9548

Diplomatic representation from the US:
chief of mission: Ambassador Margaret SCOBEY
embassy: Abou Roumaneh, Al-Mansur Street, No. 2, Damascus
mailing address: P. O. Box 29, Damascus
telephone: [963] (11) 333-1342
FAX: [963] (11) 331-9678

Flag description: three equal horizontal bands of red (top), white, and black, with two small green five-pointed stars in a horizontal line centered in the white band; similar to the flag of Yemen, which has a plain white band, and of Iraq, which has three green stars (plus an

Syria *(continued)*

Arabic inscription) in a horizontal line centered in the white band; also similar to the flag of Egypt, which has a heraldic eagle centered in the white band

Economy

Economy - overview: Syria's predominantly statist economy has been growing, on average, more slowly than its 2.4% annual population growth rate, causing a persistent decline in per capita GDP. Recent legislation allows private banks to operate in Syria, although a private banking sector will take years and further government cooperation to develop. Factors including the war between the US-led coalition and Iraq probably drove real annual GDP growth levels back below 1% in 2003 following growth of 3.5% in 2001 and 4.5% in 2002. A long-run economic constraint is the pressure on water supplies caused by rapid population growth, industrial expansion, and increased water pollution.

GDP: purchasing power parity - $58.01 billion (2003 est.)

GDP - real growth rate: 0.9% (2003 est.)

GDP - per capita: purchasing power parity - $3,300 (2003 est.)

GDP - composition by sector:
agriculture: 25.9%
industry: 27%
services: 47.1% (2001 est.)

Population below poverty line: 20% (2003 est.)

Household income or consumption by percentage share:
lowest 10%: NA%
highest 10%: NA%

Inflation rate (consumer prices): 1.5% (2003 est.)

Labor force: 5.2 million (2000 est.)

Labor force - by occupation: agriculture, industry, services NA

Unemployment rate: 20% (2002 est.)

Budget:
revenues: $4.3 billion
expenditures: $8.6 billion, including capital expenditures of $3.6 billion (2004 est.)

Industries: petroleum, textiles, food processing, beverages, tobacco, phosphate rock mining

Industrial production growth rate: NA%

Electricity - production: 23.26 billion kWh (2001)

Electricity - production by source:
fossil fuel: 57.6%
hydro: 42.4%
nuclear: 0%
other: 0% (2001)

Electricity - consumption: 21.63 billion kWh (2001)

Electricity - exports: 0 kWh (2001)

Electricity - imports: 0 kWh (2001)

Oil - production: 522,700 bbl/day (2001 est.)

Oil - consumption: 265,000 bbl/day (2001 est.)

Oil - exports: NA

Oil - imports: NA

Oil - proved reserves: 2.4 billion bbl (1 January 2002)

Natural gas - production: 5.84 billion cu m (2001 est.)

Natural gas - consumption: 5.84 billion cu m (2001 est.)

Natural gas - exports: 0 cu m (2001 est.)

Natural gas - imports: 0 cu m (2001 est.)

Natural gas - proved reserves: 240.7 billion cu m (1 January 2002)

Agriculture - products: wheat, barley, cotton, lentils, chickpeas, olives, sugar beets; beef, mutton, eggs, poultry, milk

Exports: $5.143 billion f.o.b. (2003 est.)

Exports - commodities: crude oil, petroleum products, fruits and vegetables, cotton fiber, clothing, meat and live animals, wheat

Exports - partners: Germany 17.5%, Italy 15.9%, Turkey 7.1%, France 6.8%, UAE 6.6%, Lebanon 4.8% (2002)

Imports: $4.845 billion f.o.b. (2003 est.)

Imports - commodities: machinery and transport equipment, electric power machinery, food and livestock, metal and metal products, chemicals and chemical products, plastics, yarn, paper

Imports - partners: Italy 8.1%, Germany 7.4%, China 5.6%, South Korea 4.6%, France 4.4%, US 4.3%, Turkey 4% (2002)

Debt - external: $21.5 billion (2003 est.)

Economic aid - recipient: $199 million (1997 est.)

Currency: Syrian pound (SYP)

Currency code: SYP

Exchange rates: Syrian pounds per US dollar - (Official rate): 11.225 (2003), 11.225 (2002), 11.225 (2001), 11.225 (2000), 11.225 (1999), (Free market rate): 49.65 (2001), 49.4 (2000), 51.7 (1999)

Fiscal year: calendar year

Communications

Telephones - main lines in use: 2,099,300 (2002)

Telephones - mobile cellular: 400,000 (2002)

Telephone system:
general assessment: fair system currently undergoing significant improvement and digital upgrades, including fiber-optic technology
domestic: coaxial cable and microwave radio relay network
international: country code - 963; satellite earth stations - 1 Intelsat (Indian Ocean) and 1 Intersputnik (Atlantic Ocean region); 1 submarine cable; coaxial cable and microwave radio relay to Iraq, Jordan, Lebanon, and Turkey; participant in Medarabtel

Radio broadcast stations: AM 14, FM 2, shortwave 1 (1998)

Television broadcast stations: 44 (plus 17 repeaters) (1995)

Internet country code: .sy

Internet hosts: 11 (2002)

Internet users: 220,000 (2002)

Transportation

Railways:
total: 2,743 km
standard gauge: 2,425 km 1.435-m gauge
narrow gauge: 318 km 1.050-m gauge (2002)

Highways:
total: 43,381 km
paved: 10,021 km (including 877 km of expressways)
unpaved: 33,360 km (1999)

Waterways: 870 km (minimal economic importance)

Pipelines: gas 2,300 km; oil 2,183 km (2003)

Ports and harbors: Baniyas, Jablah, Latakia, Tartus

Merchant marine:
total: 122 ships (1,000 GRT or over) 446,981 GRT/ 636,620 DWT
by type: bulk 12, cargo 101, container 2, livestock carrier 4, petroleum tanker 1, refrigerated cargo 1, roll on/roll off 1
foreign-owned: Egypt 1, Germany 1, Greece 1, Italy 1, Lebanon 10, Romania 1
registered in other countries: 83 (2003 est.)

Airports: 93 (2003 est.)

Airports - with paved runways:
total: 26
over 3,047 m: 5
2,438 to 3,047 m: 16
914 to 1,523 m: 3
under 914 m: 2 (2003 est.)

Airports - with unpaved runways:
total: 67
1,524 to 2,437 m: 2
914 to 1,523 m: 10
under 914 m: 55 (2003 est.)

Heliports: 7 (2003 est.)

Military

Military branches: Syrian Arab Army, Syrian Arab Navy, Syrian Arab Air Force (including Air Defense Command), Police and Security Force

Military manpower - military age: 19 years of age (2004 est.)

Military manpower - availability:
males age 15-49: 4,876,040 (2004 est.)

Military manpower - fit for military service:
males age 15-49: 2,716,054 (2004 est.)

Military manpower - reaching military age annually:
males: 216,077 (2004 est.)

Military expenditures - dollar figure: $858 million (FY00 est.); note - based on official budget data that may understate actual spending

Military expenditures - percent of GDP: 5.9% (FY00)

Transnational Issues

Disputes - international: Golan Heights is Israeli-occupied; Lebanon claims Shaba'a farms in Golan Heights; Syrian troops have been stationed in Lebanon since October 1976; Syria protests Turkish hydrological projects regulating upper Euphrates waters

Illicit drugs: a transit point for opiates and hashish bound for regional and Western markets; weak anti-money-laundering controls, bank privatization may leave it vulnerable to money-laundering

Tajikistan

Introduction

Background: Tajikistan has completed its transition from the civil war that plagued the country from 1992 to 1997. There have been no major security incidents in more than two years, although the country remains the poorest in the region. Attention by the international community in the wake of the war in Afghanistan has brought increased economic development assistance, which could create jobs and increase stability in the long term. Tajikistan is in the early stages of seeking World Trade Organization membership and has joined NATO's Partnership for Peace.

Geography

Location: Central Asia, west of China
Geographic coordinates: 39 00 N, 71 00 E
Map references: Asia
Area:
total: 143,100 sq km
land: 142,700 sq km
water: 400 sq km
Area - comparative: slightly smaller than Wisconsin
Land boundaries:
total: 3,651 km
border countries: Afghanistan 1,206 km, China 414 km, Kyrgyzstan 870 km, Uzbekistan 1,161 km
Coastline: 0 km (landlocked)
Maritime claims: none (landlocked)
Climate: midlatitude continental, hot summers, mild winters; semiarid to polar in Pamir Mountains
Terrain: Pamir and Alay Mountains dominate landscape; western Fergana Valley in north, Kofarnihon and Vakhsh Valleys in southwest
Elevation extremes:
lowest point: Syr Darya (Sirdaryo) 300 m
highest point: Qullai Ismoili Somoni 7,495 m
Natural resources: hydropower, some petroleum, uranium, mercury, brown coal, lead, zinc, antimony, tungsten, silver, gold

Land use:
arable land: 5.4%
permanent crops: 0.9%
other: 93.7% (1998 est.)
Irrigated land: 7,200 sq km (1998 est.)
Natural hazards: earthquakes and floods
Environment - current issues: inadequate sanitation facilities; increasing levels of soil salinity; industrial pollution; excessive pesticides
Environment - international agreements:
party to: Biodiversity, Climate Change, Desertification, Environmental Modification, Ozone Layer Protection, Wetlands
signed, but not ratified: none of the selected agreements
Geography - note: landlocked; mountainous region dominated by the Trans-Alay Range in the north and the Pamirs in the southeast; highest point, Qullai Ismoili Somoni (formerly Communism Peak), was the tallest mountain in the former USSR

People

Population: 7,011,556 (July 2004 est.)
Age structure:
0-14 years: 39.2% (male 1,384,035; female 1,361,137)
15-64 years: 56.1% (male 1,957,712; female 1,976,488)
65 years and over: 4.7% (male 145,717; female 186,467) (2004 est.)
Median age:
total: 19.5 years
male: 19.2 years
female: 19.8 years (2004 est.)
Population growth rate: 2.14% (2004 est.)
Birth rate: 32.63 births/1,000 population (2004 est.)
Death rate: 8.42 deaths/1,000 population (2004 est.)
Net migration rate: -2.86 migrant(s)/1,000 population (2004 est.)

Sex ratio:

at birth: 1.05 male(s)/female

under 15 years: 1.02 male(s)/female

15-64 years: 0.99 male(s)/female

65 years and over: 0.78 male(s)/female

total population: 0.99 male(s)/female (2004 est.)

Infant mortality rate:

total: 112.1 deaths/1,000 live births

male: 124.47 deaths/1,000 live births

female: 99.11 deaths/1,000 live births (2004 est.)

Life expectancy at birth:

total population: 64.47 years

male: 61.53 years

female: 67.55 years (2004 est.)

Total fertility rate: 4.11 children born/woman (2004 est.)

HIV/AIDS - adult prevalence rate: less than 0.1% (2001 est.)

HIV/AIDS - people living with HIV/AIDS: less than 200 (2001 est.)

HIV/AIDS - deaths: less than 100 (2001 est.)

Nationality:

noun: Tajikistani(s)

adjective: Tajikistani

Ethnic groups: Tajik 64.9%, Uzbek 25%, Russian 3.5% (declining because of emigration), other 6.6%

Religions: Sunni Muslim 85%, Shi'a Muslim 5%, other 10% (2003 est.)

Languages: Tajik (official), Russian widely used in government and business

Literacy:

definition: age 15 and over can read and write

total population: 99.4%

male: 99.6%

female: 99.1% (2003 est.)

Government

Country name:

conventional long form: Republic of Tajikistan

conventional short form: Tajikistan

local long form: Jumhurii Tojikiston

local short form: Tojikiston

former: Tajik Soviet Socialist Republic

Government type: republic

Capital: Dushanbe

Administrative divisions: 2 provinces (viloyatho, singular - viloyat) and 1 autonomous province* (viloyati mukhtor); Viloyati Mukhtori Kuhistoni Badakhshon* [Gorno-Badakhshan] (Khorugh), Viloyati Khatlon (Qurghonteppa), Viloyati Sughd (Khujand)

note: the administrative center name follows in parentheses

Independence: 9 September 1991 (from Soviet Union)

National holiday: Independence Day (or National Day), 9 September (1991)

Constitution: 6 November 1994

Legal system: based on civil law system; no judicial review of legislative acts

Suffrage: 18 years of age; universal

Executive branch:

chief of state: President Emomali RAHMONOV (since 6 November 1994; head of state and Supreme Assembly chairman since 19 November 1992)

head of government: Prime Minister Oqil OQILOV (since 20 January 1999)

cabinet: Council of Ministers appointed by the president, approved by the Supreme Assembly

elections: president elected by popular vote for a seven-year term; election last held 6 November 1999 (next to be held NA 2006); prime minister appointed by the president; Tajikistan held a constitutional referendum on 22 June 2003 that, among other things, set a term limit of two seven-year terms for the president

election results: Emomali RAHMONOV elected president; percent of vote - Emomali RAHMONOV 97%, Davlat USMON 2%

Legislative branch: bicameral Supreme Assembly or Majlisi Oli consists of the Assembly of Representatives (lower chamber) or Majlisi Namoyandagon (63 seats; members are elected by popular vote to serve five-year terms) and the National Assembly (upper chamber) or Majlisi Milliy (33 seats; members are indirectly elected, 25 selected by local deputies, 8 appointed by the president; all serve five-year terms)

elections: last held 27 February and 12 March 2000 for the Assembly of Representatives (next to be held NA 2005) and 23 March 2000 for the National Assembly (next to be held NA 2005)

election results: Assembly of Representatives - percent of vote by party - PDPT 65%, Communist Party 20%, Islamic Revival Party 7.5%, other 7.5%; seats by party - NA; National Assembly - percent of vote by party - NA%; seats by party - NA

Judicial branch: Supreme Court (judges are appointed by the president)

Political parties and leaders: Democratic Party or DPT [Mahmadruzi ISKANDAROV, chairman]; Islamic Revival Party [Said Abdullo NURI, chairman]; People's Democratic Party of Tajikistan or PDPT [Emomali RAHMONOV]; Social Democratic Party or SDPT [Rahmatullo ZOIROV]; Socialist Party or SPT [Mirhuseyn NAZRIYEV]; Tajik Communist Party or CPT [Shodi SHABDOLOV]

Political pressure groups and leaders: there are two unregistered political parties with 1,000 or more members: Progressive Party [Suton QUVVATOV]; Unity Party [Hikmatuko SAIDOV]

International organization participation: AsDB, CIS, EAPC, EBRD, ECO, FAO, IAEA, IBRD, ICAO, ICCt, ICRM, IDA, IDB, IFAD, IFC, IFRCS, ILO, IMF, IOC, IOM, ITU, OIC, OPCW, OSCE, PFP, SCO, UN, UNCTAD, UNESCO, UNIDO, UPU, WCO, WFTU, WHO, WIPO, WMO, WTrO (observer)

Diplomatic representation in the US:

chief of mission: Ambassador Hamrohon ZARIPOV

chancery: 1725 K Street NW, Suite 409, Washington, DC 20006

telephone: [1] (202) 223-6090

FAX: [1] (202) 223-6091

Diplomatic representation from the US:

chief of mission: Ambassador Richard E. HOAGLAND

embassy: 10 Pavlova Street, Dushanbe, Tajikistan 734003; note - the embassy in Dushanbe is not yet fully operational; most business is still handled in Almaty at: 531 Sayfullin Street, Almaty, Kazakhstan, telephone 7-3272-58-79-61, FAX 7-3272-58-79-68

mailing address: use embassy street address

telephone: [992] (372) 21-03-48 (Dushanbe)

FAX: [992] (372) 21-03-62

Flag description: three horizontal stripes of red (top), a wider stripe of white, and green; a gold crown surmounted by seven gold, five-pointed stars is located in the center of the white stripe

Economy

Economy - overview: Tajikistan has the lowest per capita GDP among the 15 former Soviet republics. Only 5% to 6% of the land area is arable. Cotton is the most important crop. Mineral resources, varied but limited in amount, include silver, gold, uranium, and tungsten. Industry consists only of a large aluminum plant, hydropower facilities, and small obsolete factories mostly in light industry and food processing. The civil war (1992-97) severely damaged the already weak economic infrastructure and caused a sharp decline in industrial and agricultural production. Even though 60% of its people continue to live in abject poverty, Tajikistan has experienced steady economic growth since 1997. Continued privatization of medium and large state-owned enterprises will further increase productivity. Tajikistan's economic situation, however, remains fragile due to uneven implementation of structural reforms, weak governance, widespread unemployment, and the external debt burden. A debt restructuring agreement was reached with Russia in December 2002, including an interest rate of 4%, a 3-year grace period, and a US $49.8 million credit to the Central Bank of Tajikistan.

GDP: purchasing power parity - $6.996 billion (2003 est.)

GDP - real growth rate: 9.9% (2003 est.)

GDP - per capita: purchasing power parity - $1,000 (2003 est.)

GDP - composition by sector:

agriculture: 19%

industry: 26%

services: 55% (2002 est.)

Population below poverty line: 60% (2003 est.)

Household income or consumption by percentage share:

lowest 10%: 3.2%

highest 10%: 25.2% (1998)

Distribution of family income - Gini index: 34.7 (1998)

Inflation rate (consumer prices): 16% (2003 est.)

Labor force: 3.187 million (2000)

Tajikistan *(continued)*

Labor force - by occupation: agriculture 67.2%, industry 7.5%, services 25.3% (2000 est.)
Unemployment rate: 40% (2002 est.)
Budget:
revenues: $502 million
expenditures: $520 million, including capital expenditures of $86 million (2002 est.)
Industries: aluminum, zinc, lead, chemicals and fertilizers, cement, vegetable oil, metal-cutting machine tools, refrigerators and freezers
Industrial production growth rate: 10.3% (2000 est.)
Electricity - production: 14.18 billion kWh (2001)
Electricity - production by source:
fossil fuel: 1.9%
hydro: 98.1%
nuclear: 0%
other: 0% (2001)
Electricity - consumption: 14.52 billion kWh (2001)
Electricity - exports: 3.909 billion kWh (2001)
Electricity - imports: 5.242 billion kWh (2001)
Oil - production: 250 bbl/day (2001 est.)
Oil - consumption: 20,000 bbl/day (2001 est.)
Oil - exports: NA
Oil - imports: NA
Natural gas - production: 50 million cu m (2001 est.)
Natural gas - consumption: 1.3 billion cu m (2001 est.)
Natural gas - exports: 0 cu m (2001 est.)
Natural gas - imports: 1.25 billion cu m (2001 est.)
Agriculture - products: cotton, grain, fruits, grapes, vegetables; cattle, sheep, goats
Exports: $750 million f.o.b. (2003 est.)
Exports - commodities: aluminum, electricity, cotton, fruits, vegetable oil, textiles
Exports - partners: Netherlands 29.4%, Turkey 16.1%, Russia 11.9%, Uzbekistan 9.9%, Switzerland 9.4%, Hungary 5.4%, Latvia 4.2% (2002)
Imports: $890 million f.o.b. (2003 est.)
Imports - commodities: electricity, petroleum products, aluminum oxide, machinery and equipment, foodstuffs
Imports - partners: Russia 23.1%, Uzbekistan 18.6%, Ukraine 11.4%, Kazakhstan 10.1%, Turkmenistan 6.6%, Azerbaijan 5.8%, India 4.5% (2002)
Debt - external: $1 billion (2002 est.)
Economic aid - recipient: $60.7 million from US (2001)
Currency: somoni
Currency code: TJS
Exchange rates: Tajikistani somoni per US dollar - 3.0614 (2003), 2.7641 (2002), 2.3722 (2001), 2.0763 (2000), 1.2378 (1999)
note: the new unit of exchange was introduced on 30 October 2000, with one somoni equal to 1,000 of the old Tajikistani rubles
Fiscal year: calendar year

Communications

Telephones - main lines in use: 237,600 (2002)
Telephones - mobile cellular: 13,200 (2002)
Telephone system:
general assessment: poorly developed and not well maintained; many towns are not reached by the national network
domestic: cable and microwave radio relay
international: country code - 992; linked by cable and microwave radio relay to other CIS republics and by leased connections to the Moscow international gateway switch; Dushanbe linked by Intelsat to international gateway switch in Ankara (Turkey); satellite earth stations - 1 Orbita and 2 Intelsat
Radio broadcast stations: AM 8, FM 10, shortwave 2 (2002)
Television broadcast stations: 13 (2001)
Internet country code: .tj
Internet hosts: 302 (2002)
Internet users: 3,500 (2002)

Transportation

Railways:
total: 482 km
broad gauge: 482 km 1.520-m gauge (2002)
Highways:
total: 27,767 km
paved: NA
unpaved: NA (2000)
Waterways: none
Pipelines: gas 540 km; oil 38 km (2003)
Ports and harbors: none
Airports: 66 (2003 est.)
Airports - with paved runways:
total: 15
over 3,047 m: 2
2,438 to 3,047 m: 4
1,524 to 2,437 m: 5
914 to 1,523 m: 2
under 914 m: 2 (2003 est.)
Airports - with unpaved runways:
total: 51
1,524 to 2,437 m: 1
914 to 1,523 m: 10
under 914 m: 40 (2003 est.)

Military

Military branches: Army, Air Force, Air Defense Force, Presidential National Guard
Military manpower - military age: 18 years of age (2004 est.)
Military manpower - availability:
males age 15-49: 1,762,730 (2004 est.)
Military manpower - fit for military service:
males age 15-49: 1,444,325 (2004 est.)
Military manpower - reaching military age annually:
males: 86,761 (2004 est.)

Military expenditures - dollar figure: $35.4 million (FY01)
Military expenditures - percent of GDP: 3.9% (FY01)

Transnational Issues

Disputes - international: prolonged regional drought creates water-sharing difficulties for Amu Darya river states; boundary agreements signed in 2002 cede 1,000 sq km of Pamir Mountain range to China in return for China relinquishing claims to 28,000 sq km of Tajikistani lands but demarcation has not yet commenced; talks continue with Uzbekistan to delimit border and remove minefields; disputes in Isfara Valley delay delimitation with Kyrgyzstan
Illicit drugs: major transit country for Afghan narcotics bound for Russian and, to a lesser extent, Western European markets; limited illicit cultivation of opium poppy for domestic consumption; Tajikistan seizes roughly 80 percent of all drugs captured in Central Asia and stands third world-wide in seizures of opiates (heroin and raw opium)

Tanzania

Introduction

Background: Shortly after independence, Tanganyika and Zanzibar merged to form the nation of Tanzania in 1964. One-party rule came to an end in 1995 with the first democratic elections held in the country since the 1970s. Zanzibar's semi-autonomous status and popular opposition have led to two contentious elections since 1995, which the ruling party won despite international observers' claims of voting irregularities.

Geography

Location: Eastern Africa, bordering the Indian Ocean, between Kenya and Mozambique
Geographic coordinates: 6 00 S, 35 00 E
Map references: Africa
Area:
total: 945,087 sq km
land: 886,037 sq km
water: 59,050 sq km
note: includes the islands of Mafia, Pemba, and Zanzibar
Area - comparative: slightly larger than twice the size of California
Land boundaries:
total: 3,861 km
border countries: Burundi 451 km, Democratic Republic of the Congo 459 km, Kenya 769 km, Malawi 475 km, Mozambique 756 km, Rwanda 217 km, Uganda 396 km, Zambia 338 km
Coastline: 1,424 km
Maritime claims:
territorial sea: 12 NM
exclusive economic zone: 200 NM
Climate: varies from tropical along coast to temperate in highlands
Terrain: plains along coast; central plateau; highlands in north, south

Elevation extremes:
lowest point: Indian Ocean 0 m
highest point: Kilimanjaro 5,895 m
Natural resources: hydropower, tin, phosphates, iron ore, coal, diamonds, gemstones, gold, natural gas, nickel
Land use:
arable land: 4.24%
permanent crops: 1.02%
other: 94.74% (1998 est.)
Irrigated land: 1,550 sq km (1998 est.)
Natural hazards: flooding on the central plateau during the rainy season; drought
Environment - current issues: soil degradation; deforestation; desertification; destruction of coral reefs threatens marine habitats; recent droughts affected marginal agriculture; wildlife threatened by illegal hunting and trade, especially for ivory
Environment - international agreements:
party to: Biodiversity, Climate Change, Climate Change-Kyoto Protocol, Desertification, Endangered Species, Hazardous Wastes, Law of the Sea, Ozone Layer Protection, Wetlands
signed, but not ratified: none of the selected agreements
Geography - note: Kilimanjaro is highest point in Africa; bordered by three of the largest lakes on the continent: Lake Victoria (the world's second-largest freshwater lake) in the north, Lake Tanganyika (the world's second deepest) in the west, and Lake Nyasa in the southwest

People

Population: 36,588,225
note: estimates for this country explicitly take into account the effects of excess mortality due to AIDS; this can result in lower life expectancy, higher infant mortality and death rates, lower population and growth rates, and changes in the distribution of population by age and sex than would otherwise be expected (July 2004 est.)
Age structure:
0-14 years: 44.2% (male 8,102,692; female 8,055,370)
15-64 years: 53.2% (male 9,646,342; female 9,834,925)
65 years and over: 2.6% (male 410,477; female 538,419) (2004 est.)
Median age:
total: 17.6 years
male: 17.3 years
female: 17.8 years (2004 est.)
Population growth rate: 1.95% (2004 est.)
Birth rate: 39 births/1,000 population (2004 est.)
Death rate: 17.45 deaths/1,000 population (2004 est.)
Net migration rate: -2.06 migrant(s)/1,000 population (2004 est.)
Sex ratio:
at birth: 1.03 male(s)/female
under 15 years: 1.01 male(s)/female

15-64 years: 0.98 male(s)/female
65 years and over: 0.76 male(s)/female
total population: 0.99 male(s)/female (2004 est.)
Infant mortality rate:
total: 102.13 deaths/1,000 live births
male: 111.62 deaths/1,000 live births
female: 92.35 deaths/1,000 live births (2004 est.)
Life expectancy at birth:
total population: 44.39 years
male: 43.2 years
female: 45.61 years (2004 est.)
Total fertility rate: 5.15 children born/woman (2004 est.)
HIV/AIDS - adult prevalence rate: 7.8% (2001 est.)
HIV/AIDS - people living with HIV/AIDS: 1.5 million (2001 est.)
HIV/AIDS - deaths: 140,000 (2001 est.)
Nationality:
noun: Tanzanian(s)
adjective: Tanzanian
Ethnic groups: mainland - native African 99% (of which 95% are Bantu consisting of more than 130 tribes), other 1% (consisting of Asian, European, and Arab); Zanzibar - Arab, native African, mixed Arab and native African
Religions: mainland - Christian 30%, Muslim 35%, indigenous beliefs 35%; Zanzibar - more than 99% Muslim
Languages: Kiswahili or Swahili (official), Kiunguju (name for Swahili in Zanzibar), English (official, primary language of commerce, administration, and higher education), Arabic (widely spoken in Zanzibar), many local languages
note: Kiswahili (Swahili) is the mother tongue of the Bantu people living in Zanzibar and nearby coastal Tanzania; although Kiswahili is Bantu in structure and origin, its vocabulary draws on a variety of sources, including Arabic and English, and it has become the lingua franca of central and eastern Africa; the first language of most people is one of the local languages
Literacy:
definition: age 15 and over can read and write Kiswahili (Swahili), English, or Arabic
total population: 78.2%
male: 85.9%
female: 70.7% (2003 est.)

Government

Country name:
conventional long form: United Republic of Tanzania
conventional short form: Tanzania
former: United Republic of Tanganyika and Zanzibar
Government type: republic
Capital: Dar es Salaam; note - legislative offices have been transferred to Dodoma, which is planned as the new national capital; the National Assembly now meets there on regular basis
Administrative divisions: 26 regions; Arusha, Dar es Salaam, Dodoma, Iringa, Kagera, Kigoma, Kilimanjaro, Lindi, Manyara, Mara, Mbeya, Morogoro, Mtwara, Mwanza, Pemba North, Pemba South,

Pwani, Rukwa, Ruvuma, Shinyanga, Singida, Tabora, Tanga, Zanzibar Central/South, Zanzibar North, Zanzibar Urban/West

Independence: 26 April 1964; Tanganyika became independent 9 December 1961 (from UK-administered UN trusteeship); Zanzibar became independent 19 December 1963 (from UK); Tanganyika united with Zanzibar 26 April 1964 to form the United Republic of Tanganyika and Zanzibar; renamed United Republic of Tanzania 29 October 1964

National holiday: Union Day (Tanganyika and Zanzibar), 26 April (1964)

Constitution: 25 April 1977; major revisions October 1984

Legal system: based on English common law; judicial review of legislative acts limited to matters of interpretation; has not accepted compulsory ICJ jurisdiction

Suffrage: 18 years of age; universal

Executive branch:

chief of state: President Benjamin William MKAPA (since 23 November 1995); Vice President Dr. Ali Mohammed SHEIN (since 5 July 2001); note - the president is both chief of state and head of government

head of government: President Benjamin William MKAPA (since 23 November 1995); Vice President Dr. Ali Mohammed SHEIN (since 5 July 2001); note - the president is both chief of state and head of government

note: Zanzibar elects a president who is head of government for matters internal to Zanzibar; Amani Abeid KARUME was elected to that office on 29 October 2000

cabinet: Cabinet ministers, including the prime minister, are appointed by the president from among the members of the National Assembly

elections: president and vice president elected on the same ballot by popular vote for five-year terms; election last held 29 October 2000 (next to be held NA October 2005); prime minister appointed by the president

election results: Benjamin William MKAPA reelected president; percent of vote - Benjamin William MKAPA 71.7%, Ibrahim Haruna LIPUMBA 16.3%, Augustine Lyatonga MREME 7.8%, John Momose CHEYO 4.2%

Legislative branch: unicameral National Assembly or Bunge (274 seats - 232 elected by popular vote, 37 allocated to women nominated by the president, five to members of the Zanzibar House of Representatives; members serve five-year terms); note - in addition to enacting laws that apply to the entire United Republic of Tanzania, the Assembly enacts laws that apply only to the mainland; Zanzibar has its own House of Representatives to make laws especially for Zanzibar (the Zanzibar House of Representatives has 50 seats, directly elected by universal suffrage to serve five-year terms)

elections: last held 29 October 2000 (next to be held NA October 2005)

election results: National Assembly - percent of vote by party - NA%; seats by party - CCM 244, CUF 16, CHADEMA 4, TLP 3, UDP 2, Zanzibar representatives 5; Zanzibar House of Representatives - percent of vote by party - NA%; seats by party - CCM 34, CUF 16

Judicial branch: Permanent Commission of Enquiry (official ombudsman); Court of Appeal (consists of a chief justice and four judges); High Court (consists of a Jaji Kiongozi and 29 judges appointed by the president; holds regular sessions in all regions); District Courts; Primary Courts (limited jurisdiction and appeals can be made to the higher courts)

Political parties and leaders: Chama Cha Demokrasia na Maendeleo (Party of Democracy and Development) or CHADEMA [Bob MAKANI]; Chama Cha Mapinduzi or CCM (Revolutionary Party) [Benjamin William MKAPA]; Civic United Front or CUF [Ibrahim LIPUMBA]; Democratic Party (unregistered) [Christopher MTIKLA]; Tanzania Labor Party or TLP [Augustine Lyatonga MREMA]; United Democratic Party or UDP [John CHEYO]

Political pressure groups and leaders: NA

International organization participation: ACP, AfDB, AU, C, EADB, FAO, G- 6, G-77, IAEA, IBRD, ICAO, ICC, ICCt, ICFTU, ICRM, IDA, IFAD, IFC, IFRCS, ILO, IMF, IMO, Interpol, IOC, IOM, ISO, ITU, NAM, OPCW, SADC, UN, UNAMSIL, UNCTAD, UNESCO, UNHCR, UNIDO, UNMEE, UPU, WCO, WFTU, WHO, WIPO, WMO, WToO, WTrO

Diplomatic representation in the US:

chief of mission: Ambassador Andrew Mhando DARAJA

chancery: 2139 R Street NW, Washington, DC 20008

telephone: [1] (202) 939-6125

FAX: [1] (202) 797-7408

Diplomatic representation from the US:

chief of mission: Ambassador Robert V. ROYALL

embassy: 140 Msese Road, Kinondoni District, Dar es Salaam

mailing address: P. O. Box 9123, Dar es Salaam

telephone: [255] (22) 2666-010 through 2666-015

FAX: [255] (22) 2666-701, 2668-501

Flag description: divided diagonally by a yellow-edged black band from the lower hoist-side corner; the upper triangle (hoist side) is green and the lower triangle is blue

Economy

Economy - overview: Tanzania is one of the poorest countries in the world. The economy depends heavily on agriculture, which accounts for about half of GDP, provides 85% of exports, and employs 80% of the work force. Topography and climatic conditions, however, limit cultivated crops to only 4% of the land area. Industry traditionally featured the processing of agricultural products and light consumer goods. The World Bank, the International Monetary Fund, and bilateral donors have provided funds to rehabilitate Tanzania's out-of-date economic infrastructure and to alleviate poverty. Growth in 1991-2002 featured a pickup in industrial production and a substantial increase in output of minerals, led by gold. Oil and gas exploration and development played an important role in this growth. Recent banking reforms have helped increase private sector growth and investment. Continued donor assistance and solid macroeconomic policies supported real GDP growth of more than 5.2% in 2004.

GDP: purchasing power parity - $21.58 billion (2003 est.)

GDP - real growth rate: 5.2% (2003 est.)

GDP - per capita: purchasing power parity - $600 (2003 est.)

GDP - composition by sector:

agriculture: 44.7%

industry: 16%

services: 39.4% (2001 est.)

Population below poverty line: 36% (2002 est.)

Household income or consumption by percentage share:

lowest 10%: 2.8%

highest 10%: 30.1% (1993)

Distribution of family income - Gini index: 38.2 (1993)

Inflation rate (consumer prices): 4.6% (2003 est.)

Labor force: 13.495 million

Labor force - by occupation: agriculture 80%, industry and services 20% (2002 est.)

Unemployment rate: NA%

Budget:

revenues: $1.2 billion

expenditures: $2 billion, including capital expenditures of $NA (FY02/03 est.)

Industries: agricultural processing (sugar, beer, cigarettes, sisal twine), diamond and gold mining, oil refining, shoes, cement, textiles, wood products, fertilizer, salt

Industrial production growth rate: 8.4% (1999 est.)

Electricity - production: 2.906 billion kWh (2001)

Electricity - production by source:

fossil fuel: 18.9%

hydro: 81.1%

nuclear: 0%

other: 0% (2001)

Electricity - consumption: 2.752 billion kWh (2001)

Electricity - exports: 0 kWh (2001)

Electricity - imports: 50 million kWh (2001)

Oil - production: 0 bbl/day (2001 est.)

Oil - consumption: 17,000 bbl/day (2001 est.)

Oil - exports: NA

Oil - imports: NA

Oil - proved reserves: 0 bbl (1 January 2002)

Natural gas - proved reserves: 11.33 billion cu m (1 January 2002)

Agriculture - products: coffee, sisal, tea, cotton, pyrethrum (insecticide made from chrysanthemums), cashew nuts, tobacco, cloves, corn, wheat, cassava (tapioca), bananas, fruits, vegetables; cattle, sheep, goats

Exports: $978 million f.o.b. (2003 est.)

Exports - commodities: gold, coffee, cashew nuts, manufactures, cotton

Tanzania (continued)

Exports - partners: UK 17.1%, France 16.2%, Japan 10.1%, India 6.7%, Netherlands 5.7% (2002)
Imports: $1.674 billion f.o.b. (2003 est.)
Imports - commodities: consumer goods, machinery and transportation equipment, industrial raw materials, crude oil
Imports - partners: South Africa 10.8%, Japan 7.9%, India 6.1%, UAE 5.5%, Kenya 5.4%, UK 5.4%, US 5.2%, China 4.5%, Australia 4.1%, Bahrain 4% (2002)
Debt - external: $6.8 billion (2002 est.)
Economic aid - recipient: $1.2 billion (2001)
Currency: Tanzanian shilling (TZS)
Currency code: TZS
Exchange rates: Tanzanian shillings per US dollar - NA (2003), 966.583 (2002), 876.412 (2001), 800.409 (2000), 744.759 (1999)
Fiscal year: 1 July - 30 June

Communications

Telephones - main lines in use: 161,600 (2002)
Telephones - mobile cellular: 670,000 (2002)
Telephone system:
general assessment: fair system operating below capacity and being modernized for better service; VSAT (very small aperture terminal) system under construction
domestic: trunk service provided by open-wire, microwave radio relay, tropospheric scatter, and fiber-optic cable; some links being made digital
international: country code - 255; satellite earth stations - 2 Intelsat (1 Indian Ocean and 1 Atlantic Ocean)
Radio broadcast stations: AM 12, FM 11, shortwave 2 (1998)
Television broadcast stations: 3 (1999)
Internet country code: .tz
Internet hosts: 1,731 (2002)
Internet users: 80,000 (2002)

Transportation

Railways:
total: 3,690 km
narrow gauge: 2,721 km 1.000-m gauge; 969 km 1.067-m gauge (2002)
Highways:
total: 88,200 km
paved: 3,704 km
unpaved: 84,496 km (1999 est.)
Waterways:
note: Lake Tanganyika, Lake Victoria, and Lake Nyasa are principal avenues of commerce between Tanzania and its neighbors on those lakes
Pipelines: gas 5 km; oil 866 km (2003)
Ports and harbors: Bukoba, Dar es Salaam, Kigoma, Kilwa Masoko, Lindi, Mtwara, Mwanza, Pangani, Tanga, Wete, Zanzibar
Merchant marine:
total: 10 ships (1,000 GRT or over) 25,481 GRT/ 31,011 DWT

by type: cargo 3, passenger/cargo 2, petroleum tanker 3, roll on/roll off 1, short-sea/passenger 1
registered in other countries: 5 (2003 est.)
Airports: 123 (2003 est.)
Airports - with paved runways:
total: 11
over 3,047 m: 2
2,438 to 3,047 m: 2
1,524 to 2,437 m: 5
914 to 1,523 m: 1
under 914 m: 1 (2003 est.)
Airports - with unpaved runways:
total: 112
1,524 to 2,437 m: 19
914 to 1,523 m: 60
under 914 m: 33 (2003 est.)

Military

Military branches: Tanzanian People's Defense Force: Army, Naval Wing, and Air Defense Command; National Service
Military manpower - availability:
males age 15-49: 8,687,477 (2004 est.)
Military manpower - fit for military service:
males age 15-49: 5,031,621 (2004 est.)
Military expenditures - dollar figure: $20.3 million (2003)
Military expenditures - percent of GDP: 0.2% (2003)

Transnational Issues

Disputes - international: disputes with Malawi over the boundary in Lake Nyasa (Lake Malawi) and the meandering Songwe River remain dormant
Illicit drugs: growing role in transshipment of Southwest and Southeast Asian heroin and South American cocaine destined for South African, European, and US markets and of South Asian methaqualone bound for Southern Africa; money laundering remains a problem

Thailand

Introduction

Background: A unified Thai kingdom was established in the mid-14th century. Known as Siam until 1939, Thailand is the only Southeast Asian country never to have been taken over by a European power. A bloodless revolution in 1932 led to a constitutional monarchy. In alliance with Japan during World War II, Thailand became a US ally following the conflict.

Geography

Location: Southeastern Asia, bordering the Andaman Sea and the Gulf of Thailand, southeast of Burma
Geographic coordinates: 15 00 N, 100 00 E
Map references: Southeast Asia
Area:
total: 514,000 sq km
land: 511,770 sq km
water: 2,230 sq km
Area - comparative: slightly more than twice the size of Wyoming

Thailand (continued)

Land boundaries:

total: 4,863 km

border countries: Burma 1,800 km, Cambodia 803 km, Laos 1,754 km, Malaysia 506 km

Coastline: 3,219 km

Maritime claims:

territorial sea: 12 NM

exclusive economic zone: 200 NM

continental shelf: 200-m depth or to the depth of exploitation

Climate: tropical; rainy, warm, cloudy southwest monsoon (mid-May to September); dry, cool northeast monsoon (November to mid-March); southern isthmus always hot and humid

Terrain: central plain; Khorat Plateau in the east; mountains elsewhere

Elevation extremes:

lowest point: Gulf of Thailand 0 m

highest point: Doi Inthanon 2,576 m

Natural resources: tin, rubber, natural gas, tungsten, tantalum, timber, lead, fish, gypsum, lignite, fluorite, arable land

Land use:

arable land: 32.88%

permanent crops: 7%

other: 60.12% (1998 est.)

Irrigated land: 47,490 sq km (1998 est.)

Natural hazards: land subsidence in Bangkok area resulting from the depletion of the water table; droughts

Environment - current issues: air pollution from vehicle emissions; water pollution from organic and factory wastes; deforestation; soil erosion; wildlife populations threatened by illegal hunting

Environment - international agreements:

party to: Biodiversity, Climate Change, Climate Change-Kyoto Protocol, Desertification, Endangered Species, Hazardous Wastes, Marine Life Conservation, Ozone Layer Protection, Tropical Timber 83, Tropical Timber 94, Wetlands

signed, but not ratified: Law of the Sea

Geography - note: controls only land route from Asia to Malaysia and Singapore

People

Population: 64,865,523

note: estimates for this country explicitly take into account the effects of excess mortality due to AIDS; this can result in lower life expectancy, higher infant mortality and death rates, lower population and growth rates, and changes in the distribution of population by age and sex than would otherwise be expected (July 2004 est.)

Age structure:

0-14 years: 24.1% (male 7,985,724; female 7,631,337)

15-64 years: 68.7% (male 21,998,552; female 22,538,765)

65 years and over: 7.3% (male 2,167,421; female 2,543,724) (2004 est.)

Median age:

total: 30.5 years

male: 29.7 years

female: 31.2 years (2004 est.)

Population growth rate: 0.91% (2004 est.)

Birth rate: 16.04 births/1,000 population (2004 est.)

Death rate: 6.94 deaths/1,000 population (2004 est.)

Net migration rate: 0 migrant(s)/1,000 population (2004 est.)

Sex ratio:

at birth: 1.05 male(s)/female

under 15 years: 1.05 male(s)/female

15-64 years: 0.98 male(s)/female

65 years and over: 0.85 male(s)/female

total population: 0.98 male(s)/female (2004 est.)

Infant mortality rate:

total: 21.14 deaths/1,000 live births

male: 22.49 deaths/1,000 live births

female: 19.73 deaths/1,000 live births (2004 est.)

Life expectancy at birth:

total population: 71.41 years

male: 69.23 years

female: 73.71 years (2004 est.)

Total fertility rate: 1.89 children born/woman (2004 est.)

HIV/AIDS - adult prevalence rate: 1.8% (2001 est.)

HIV/AIDS - people living with HIV/AIDS: 670,000 (2001 est.)

HIV/AIDS - deaths: 55,000 (2001 est.)

Nationality:

noun: Thai (singular and plural)

adjective: Thai

Ethnic groups: Thai 75%, Chinese 14%, other 11%

Religions: Buddhism 95%, Muslim 3.8%, Christianity 0.5%, Hinduism 0.1%, other 0.6% (1991)

Languages: Thai, English (secondary language of the elite), ethnic and regional dialects

Literacy:

definition: age 15 and over can read and write

total population: 96%

male: 97.5%

female: 94.6% (2003 est.)

Government

Country name:

conventional long form: Kingdom of Thailand

conventional short form: Thailand

former: Siam

Government type: constitutional monarchy

Capital: Bangkok

Administrative divisions: 76 provinces (changwat, singular and plural); Amnat Charoen, Ang Thong, Buriram, Chachoengsao, Chai Nat, Chaiyaphum, Chanthaburi, Chiang Mai, Chiang Rai, Chon Buri, Chumphon, Kalasin, Kamphaeng Phet, Kanchanaburi, Khon Kaen, Krabi, Krung Thep Mahanakhon (Bangkok), Lampang, Lamphun, Loei, Lop Buri, Mae Hong Son, Maha Sarakham, Mukdahan, Nakhon Nayok, Nakhon Pathom, Nakhon Phanom, Nakhon Ratchasima, Nakhon Sawan, Nakhon Si Thammarat, Nan, Narathiwat, Nong Bua Lamphu, Nong Khai, Nonthaburi, Pathum Thani, Pattani, Phangnga, Phatthalung, Phayao, Phetchabun, Phetchaburi, Phichit, Phitsanulok, Phra Nakhon Si Ayutthaya, Phrae, Phuket, Prachin Buri, Prachuap Khiri Khan, Ranong, Ratchaburi, Rayong, Roi Et, Sa Kaeo, Sakon Nakhon, Samut Prakan, Samut Sakhon, Samut Songkhram, Sara Buri, Satun, Sing Buri, Sisaket, Songkhla, Sukhothai, Suphan Buri, Surat Thani, Surin, Tak, Trang, Trat, Ubon Ratchathani, Udon Thani, Uthai Thani, Uttaradit, Yala, Yasothon

Independence: 1238 (traditional founding date; never colonized)

National holiday: Birthday of King PHUMIPHON, 5 December (1927)

Constitution: new constitution signed by King PHUMIPHON on 11 October 1997

Legal system: based on civil law system, with influences of common law; has not accepted compulsory ICJ jurisdiction

Suffrage: 18 years of age; universal and compulsory

Executive branch:

chief of state: King PHUMIPHON Adunyadet (since 9 June 1946)

head of government: Prime Minister THAKSIN Chinnawat (since 9 February 2001) and Deputy Prime Ministers CHAWALIT Yongchaiyut, Gen. (Ret.); PHOKIN Phalakun; SUWIT Khunkitti; CHATURON Chaisaeng; VISHANU Krua-ngam; PURACHAI Piamsombun; SOMKHIT Chatusiphithak (since 8 November 2003)

cabinet: Council of Ministers

note: there is also a Privy Council

elections: none; the monarch is hereditary; prime minister is designated from among the members of the House of Representatives; following national elections for the House of Representatives, the leader of the party that can organize a majority coalition usually is appointed prime minister by the king

Legislative branch: bicameral National Assembly or Rathasapha consists of the Senate or Wuthisapha (200 seats; members elected by popular vote to serve six-year terms) and the House of Representatives or Sapha Phuthaen Ratsadon (500 seats; members elected by popular vote to serve four-year terms)

elections: Senate - last held 4 March, 29 April, 4 June, 9 July, and 22 July 2000 (next to be held by March 2006); House of Representatives - last held 6 January 2001 (next to be held January 2005)

election results: Senate - percent of vote by party - NA%; seats by party - NA; House of Representatives - percent of vote by party - NA%; seats by party - TRT 248, DP 128, TNP 41, NDP 29, other 54

Judicial branch: Supreme Court or Sandika (judges appointed by the monarch)

Political parties and leaders: Democratic Party or DP (Prachathipat Party) [BANTADTAN Banyat]; National Development Party or NDP (Chat Phattana) [SUWAT Lipataphanlop]; Thai Nation Party or TNP (Chat Thai Party) [BANHAN Sinlapa-acha]; Thai Rak Thai Party or TRT [THAKSIN Chinnawat]

Political pressure groups and leaders: NA

Thailand *(continued)*

International organization participation: APEC, ARF, AsDB, ASEAN, BIS, CP, FAO, G-77, IAEA, IBRD, ICAO, ICC, ICCt (signatory), ICFTU, ICRM, IDA, IFAD, IFC, IFRCS, IHO, ILO, IMF, IMO, Interpol, IOC, IOM, ISO, ITU, NAM, OAS (observer), OIC (observer), OPCW, OSCE (partner), PCA, UN, UNAMSIL, UNCTAD, UNESCO, UNHCR, UNIDO, UNMISET, UPU, WCL, WCO, WFTU, WHO, WIPO, WMO, WToO, WTrO

Diplomatic representation in the US:
chief of mission: Ambassador SAKTHIP Krairiksh
chancery: 1024 Wisconsin Avenue NW, Washington, DC 20007
telephone: [1] (202) 944-3600
FAX: [1] (202) 944-3611
consulate(s) general: Chicago, Los Angeles, and New York

Diplomatic representation from the US:
chief of mission: Ambassador Darryl N. JOHNSON
embassy: 120/22 Wireless Road, Bangkok
mailing address: APO AP 96546
telephone: [66] (2) 205-4000
FAX: [66] (2) 254-2990, 205-4131
consulate(s) general: Chiang Mai

Flag description: five horizontal bands of red (top), white, blue (double width), white, and red

Economy

Economy - overview: Thailand has a free-enterprise economy and welcomes foreign investment. Exports feature textiles and footwear, fishery products, rice, rubber, jewelry, automobiles, computers and electrical appliances. Thailand has recovered from the 1997-98 Asian Financial Crisis and was one of East Asia's best performers in 2002. Increased consumption and investment spending and strong export growth pushed GDP growth up to 6.3% in 2003 despite a sluggish global economy. The highly popular government has pushed an expansionist policy, including major support of village economic development.

GDP: purchasing power parity - $475.7 billion (2003 est.)

GDP - real growth rate: 6.3% (2003 est.)

GDP - per capita: purchasing power parity - $7,400 (2003 est.)

GDP - composition by sector:
agriculture: 9%
industry: 42%
services: 49% (2002)

Population below poverty line: 10.4% (2002 est.)

Household income or consumption by percentage share:
lowest 10%: 2.8%
highest 10%: 32.4% (1998)

Distribution of family income - Gini index: 41.4 (1998)

Inflation rate (consumer prices): 1.8% (2003 est.)

Labor force: 33.4 million (2001 est.)

Labor force - by occupation: agriculture 49%, industry 14%, services 37% (2000 est.)

Unemployment rate: 2.2% (2003 est.)

Budget:
revenues: $21 billion
expenditures: $22 billion, including capital expenditures of $5 billion (2000 est.)

Industries: tourism, textiles and garments, agricultural processing, beverages, tobacco, cement, light manufacturing such as jewelry, electric appliances and components, computers and parts, integrated circuits, furniture, plastics, world's second-largest tungsten producer, and third-largest tin producer

Industrial production growth rate: 3% (2000 est.)

Electricity - production: 97.6 billion kWh (2001)

Electricity - production by source:
fossil fuel: 91.3%
hydro: 6.4%
nuclear: 0%
other: 2.4% (2001)

Electricity - consumption: 90.91 billion kWh (2001)

Electricity - exports: 200 million kWh (2001)

Electricity - imports: 350 million kWh (2001)

Oil - production: 173,800 bbl/day (2001 est.)

Oil - consumption: 785,000 bbl/day (2001 est.)

Oil - exports: NA

Oil - imports: NA

Oil - proved reserves: 600 million bbl (1 January 2003)

Natural gas - production: 18.73 billion cu m (2001 est.)

Natural gas - consumption: 23.93 billion cu m (2001 est.)

Natural gas - exports: 0 cu m (2001 est.)

Natural gas - imports: 5.2 billion cu m (2001 est.)

Natural gas - proved reserves: 368.2 billion cu m (1 January 2003)

Agriculture - products: rice, cassava (tapioca), rubber, corn, sugarcane, coconuts, soybeans

Exports: $75.99 billion f.o.b. (2003 est.)

Exports - commodities: computers, office machine parts, transistors, rubber, vehicles (cars and trucks), plastic, seafood (2002)

Exports - partners: US 19.6%, Japan 14.5%, Singapore 8.1%, Hong Kong 5.4%, China 5.2%, Malaysia 4.1% (2002)

Imports: $65.3 billion f.o.b. (2003 est.)

Imports - commodities: capital goods, intermediate goods and raw materials, consumer goods, fuels (2000)

Imports - partners: Japan 23%, US 9.6%, China 7.6%, Malaysia 5.6%, Singapore 4.5%, Taiwan 4.4% (2002)

Debt - external: $62.5 billion (2002 est.)

Economic aid - recipient: $131.5 million (1998 est.)

Currency: baht (THB)

Currency code: THB

Exchange rates: baht per US dollar - 41.4846 (2003), 42.9601 (2002), 44.4319 (2001), 40.1118 (2000), 37.8137 (1999)

Fiscal year: 1 October - 30 September

Communications

Telephones - main lines in use: 6,499,800 (2002)

Telephones - mobile cellular: 16.117 million (2002)

Telephone system:
general assessment: service to general public adequate, but investment in technological upgrades reduced by recession; bulk of service to government activities provided by multichannel cable and microwave radio relay network
domestic: microwave radio relay and multichannel cable; domestic satellite system being developed
international: country code - 66; satellite earth stations - 2 Intelsat (1 Indian Ocean and 1 Pacific Ocean)

Radio broadcast stations: AM 204, FM 334, shortwave 6 (1999)

Television broadcast stations: 5 (all in Bangkok; plus 131 repeaters) (1997)

Internet country code: .th

Internet hosts: 100,132 (2002)

Internet users: 4.8 million (2002)

Transportation

Railways:
total: 4,071 km
narrow gauge: 4,071 km 1.000-m gauge (2002)

Highways:
total: 64,600 km
paved: 62,985 km
unpaved: 1,615 km (1999 est.)

Waterways: 4,000 km
note: 3,701 km are navigable throughout the year by boats with drafts up to 0.9 meters; numerous minor waterways serve shallow-draft native craft

Pipelines: gas 3,066 km; refined products 265 km (2003)

Ports and harbors: Bangkok, Laem Chabang, Pattani, Phuket, Sattahip, Si Racha, Songkhla

Merchant marine:
total: 339 ships (1,000 GRT or over) 2,038,597 GRT/3,104,712 DWT
by type: bulk 40, cargo 135, chemical tanker 5, combination bulk 2, combination ore/oil 1, container 19, liquefied gas 22, multi-functional large load carrier 2, passenger 1, petroleum tanker 79, refrigerated cargo 22, roll on/roll off 2, short-sea/passenger 2, specialized tanker 6, vehicle carrier 1
foreign-owned: Egypt 1, Germany 3, Indonesia 1, Japan 4, Norway 38, Panama 2, Singapore 3
registered in other countries: 43 (2003 est.)

Airports: 109 (2003 est.)

Airports - with paved runways:
total: 65
over 3,047 m: 7
2,438 to 3,047 m: 10
1,524 to 2,437 m: 23
914 to 1,523 m: 19
under 914 m: 6 (2003 est.)

Airports - with unpaved runways:
total: 44
1,524 to 2,437 m: 1

Thailand (continued)

914 to 1,523 m: 15
under 914 m: 28 (2003 est.)
Heliports: 3 (2003 est.)

Military

Military branches: Royal Thai Army, Royal Thai Navy (including Royal Thai Marine Corps), Royal Thai Air Force
Military manpower - military age: 20 years of age; males are registered at 18 years of age (2004 est.)
Military manpower - availability:
males age 15-49: 17,944,151 (2004 est.)
Military manpower - fit for military service:
males age 15-49: 10,735,354 (2004 est.)
Military manpower - reaching military age annually:
males: 531,511 (2004 est.)
Military expenditures - dollar figure: $1.775 billion (FY00)
Military expenditures - percent of GDP: 1.8% (2003)

Transnational Issues

Disputes - international: a 1 kilometer segment at the mouth of the Golok River remains in dispute with Malaysia; demarcation with Laos complete except for certain Mekong River islets and complaints of Thai squatters; despite continuing border committee talks, significant differences remain with Burma over boundary alignment and the handling of ethnic rebels, refugees, and illegal cross-border activities; Cambodia accuses Thailand of moving boundary markers and obstructing access to Preah Vihear temple ruins awarded to Cambodia by ICJ decision in 1962; 2003 anti-Thai riots in Phnom Penh resulted in the destruction of the Thai Embassy and damage to 17 Thai-owned businesses and disputes over payments of full compensation persist; groups in Burma and Thailand express concern over China's construction of 13 hydroelectric dams on the Salween River in Yunnan Province
Illicit drugs: a minor producer of opium, heroin, and marijuana; illicit transit point for heroin en route to the international drug market from Burma and Laos; eradication efforts have reduced the area of cannabis cultivation and shifted some production to neighboring countries; opium poppy cultivation has been reduced by eradication efforts; also a drug money-laundering center; minor role in amphetamine production for regional consumption; increasing indigenous abuse of methamphetamine

Togo

Introduction

Background: French Togoland became Togo in 1960. Gen. Gnassingbe EYADEMA, installed as military ruler in 1967, is Africa's longest-serving head of state. Despite the facade of multiparty elections instituted in the early 1990s, the government continues to be dominated by President EYADEMA, whose Rally of the Togolese People (RPT) party has maintained power almost continually since 1967. In addition, Togo has come under fire from international organizations for human rights abuses and is plagued by political unrest. Most bilateral and multilateral aid to Togo remains frozen.

Geography

Location: Western Africa, bordering the Bight of Benin, between Benin and Ghana
Geographic coordinates: 8 00 N, 1 10 E
Map references: Africa
Area:
total: 56,785 sq km
land: 54,385 sq km
water: 2,400 sq km

Area - comparative: slightly smaller than West Virginia
Land boundaries:
total: 1,647 km
border countries: Benin 644 km, Burkina Faso 126 km, Ghana 877 km
Coastline: 56 km
Maritime claims:
territorial sea: 30 NM
exclusive economic zone: 200 NM
Climate: tropical; hot, humid in south; semiarid in north
Terrain: gently rolling savanna in north; central hills; southern plateau; low coastal plain with extensive lagoons and marshes
Elevation extremes:
lowest point: Atlantic Ocean 0 m
highest point: Mont Agou 986 m
Natural resources: phosphates, limestone, marble, arable land
Land use:
arable land: 41.37%
permanent crops: 1.84%
other: 56.79% (1998 est.)
Irrigated land: 70 sq km (1998 est.)
Natural hazards: hot, dry harmattan wind can reduce visibility in north during winter; periodic droughts
Environment - current issues: deforestation attributable to slash-and-burn agriculture and the use of wood for fuel; water pollution presents health hazards and hinders the fishing industry; air pollution increasing in urban areas
Environment - international agreements:
party to: Biodiversity, Climate Change, Desertification, Endangered Species, Law of the Sea, Ozone Layer Protection, Ship Pollution, Tropical Timber 83, Tropical Timber 94, Wetlands
signed, but not ratified: none of the selected agreements
Geography - note: the country's length allows it to stretch through six distinct geographic regions; climate varies from tropical to savanna

People

Population: 5,556,812
note: estimates for this country explicitly take into account the effects of excess mortality due to AIDS; this can result in lower life expectancy, higher infant mortality and death rates, lower population and growth rates, and changes in the distribution of population by age and sex than would otherwise be expected (July 2004 est.)
Age structure:
0-14 years: 43.9% (male 1,222,622; female 1,214,443)
15-64 years: 53.6% (male 1,455,373; female 1,522,456)
65 years and over: 2.6% (male 59,165; female 82,753) (2004 est.)

Togo (continued)

Median age:
total: 17.6 years
male: 17.2 years
female: 17.9 years (2004 est.)
Population growth rate: 2.27% (2004 est.)
Birth rate: 34.36 births/1,000 population (2004 est.)
Death rate: 11.64 deaths/1,000 population (2004 est.)
Net migration rate: 0 migrant(s)/1,000 population (2004 est.)
Sex ratio:
at birth: 1.03 male(s)/female
under 15 years: 1.01 male(s)/female
15-64 years: 0.96 male(s)/female
65 years and over: 0.72 male(s)/female
total population: 0.97 male(s)/female (2004 est.)
Infant mortality rate:
total: 67.66 deaths/1,000 live births
male: 75.4 deaths/1,000 live births
female: 59.69 deaths/1,000 live births (2004 est.)
Life expectancy at birth:
total population: 53.05 years
male: 51.07 years
female: 55.09 years (2004 est.)
Total fertility rate: 4.79 children born/woman (2004 est.)
HIV/AIDS - adult prevalence rate: 6% (2001 est.)
HIV/AIDS - people living with HIV/AIDS: 150,000 (2001 est.)
HIV/AIDS - deaths: 12,000 (2001 est.)
Nationality:
noun: Togolese (singular and plural)
adjective: Togolese
Ethnic groups: native African (37 tribes; largest and most important are Ewe, Mina, and Kabre) 99%, European and Syrian-Lebanese less than 1%
Religions: indigenous beliefs 51%, Christian 29%, Muslim 20%
Languages: French (official and the language of commerce), Ewe and Mina (the two major African languages in the south), Kabye (sometimes spelled Kabiye) and Dagomba (the two major African languages in the north)
Literacy:
definition: age 15 and over can read and write
total population: 60.9%
male: 75.4%
female: 46.9% (2003 est.)

Government

Country name:
conventional long form: Togolese Republic
conventional short form: Togo
local long form: Republique Togolaise
local short form: none
former: French Togoland
Government type: republic under transition to multiparty democratic rule
Capital: Lome
Administrative divisions: 5 regions (regions, singular - region); Kara, Plateaux, Savanes, Centrale, Maritime

Independence: 27 April 1960 (from French-administered UN trusteeship)
National holiday: Independence Day, 27 April (1960)
Constitution: multiparty draft constitution approved by High Council of the Republic 1 July 1992; adopted by public referendum 27 September 1992
Legal system: French-based court system
Suffrage: NA years of age; universal adult
Executive branch:
chief of state: President Gen. Gnassingbe EYADEMA (since 14 April 1967)
head of government: Prime Minister Koffi SAMA (since 29 June 2002)
cabinet: Council of Ministers appointed by the president and the prime minister
elections: president elected by popular vote for a five-year term; election last held 1 June 2003 (next to be held NA June 2008); prime minister appointed by the president
election results: Gnassingbe EYADEMA reelected president; percent of vote - Gnassingbe EYADEMA 57.2%, Emmanuel Akitani BOB 34.1%, Yawovi AGBOYIBO 5.2%, Maurice Dahuku PERE 2.3%, Edem KODJO 1.0%
Legislative branch: unicameral National Assembly (81 seats; members are elected by popular vote to serve five-year terms)
elections: last held 27 October 2002 (next NA 2007)
election results: percent of vote by party - NA%; seats by party - RPT 72, RSDD 3, UDPS 2, Juvento 2, MOCEP 1, independents 1
note: two opposition parties boycotted the election, the Union of the Forces for Change, and the Action Committee for Renewal
Judicial branch: Court of Appeal or Cour d'Appel; Supreme Court or Cour Supreme
Political parties and leaders: Juvento [Monsilia DJATO]; Movement of the Believers of Peace and Equality or MOCEP [leader NA]; Rally for the Support for Development and Democracy or RSDD [Harryy OLYMPIO]; Rally of the Togolese People or RPT [President Gnassingbe EYADEMA]; Union for Democracy and Social Progress or UDPS [Gagou KOKOU]
note: Rally of the Togolese People or RPT, led by President EYADEMA, was the only party until the formation of multiple parties was legalized 12 April 1991
Political pressure groups and leaders: NA
International organization participation: ACCT, ACP, AfDB, AU, ECOWAS, Entente, FAO, FZ, G-77, IBRD, ICAO, ICC, ICFTU, ICRM, IDA, IDB, IFAD, IFC, IFRCS, ILO, IMF, IMO, Interpol, IOC, ITU, MICAH, NAM, OIC, OPCW, UN, UNCTAD, UNESCO, UNIDO, UNMIL, UPU, WADB (regional), WAEMU, WCL, WCO, WFTU, WHO, WIPO, WMO, WToO, WTrO
Diplomatic representation in the US:
chief of mission: Ambassador Akoussoulelou BODJONA
chancery: 2208 Massachusetts Avenue NW, Washington, DC 20008

telephone: [1] (202) 234-4212
FAX: [1] (202) 232-3190
Diplomatic representation from the US:
chief of mission: Ambassador Gregory ENGLE
embassy: Angle Rue Kouenou and Rue 15 Beniglato, Lome
mailing address: B. P. 852, Lome
telephone: [228] 221 29 91 through 221 29 94
FAX: [228] 221 79 52
Flag description: five equal horizontal bands of green (top and bottom) alternating with yellow; there is a white five-pointed star on a red square in the upper hoist-side corner; uses the popular pan-African colors of Ethiopia

Economy

Economy - overview: This small sub-Saharan economy is heavily dependent on both commercial and subsistence agriculture, which provides employment for 65% of the labor force. Some basic foodstuffs must still be imported. Cocoa, coffee, and cotton generate about 40% of export earnings, with cotton being the most important cash crop. Togo is the world's fourth-largest producer of phosphate, but production fell an estimated 22% in 2002 due to power shortages and the cost of developing new deposits. The government's decade-long effort, supported by the World Bank and the IMF, to implement economic reform measures, encourage foreign investment, and bring revenues in line with expenditures has moved slowly. Progress depends on following through on privatization, increased openness in government financial operations, progress toward legislative elections, and continued support from foreign donors.
GDP: purchasing power parity - $8.232 billion (2003 est.)
GDP - real growth rate: 3.2% (2003 est.)
GDP - per capita: purchasing power parity - $1,500 (2003 est.)
GDP - composition by sector:
agriculture: 42%
industry: 21%
services: 37% (2001 est.)
Population below poverty line: 32% (1989 est.)
Household income or consumption by percentage share:
lowest 10%: NA%
highest 10%: NA%
Inflation rate (consumer prices): 4% (2002 est.)
Labor force: 1.74 million (1996)
Labor force - by occupation: agriculture 65%, industry 5%, services 30% (1998 est.)
Unemployment rate: NA% (2003 est.)
Budget:
revenues: $232 million
expenditures: $252 million, including capital expenditures of $NA (1997 est.)
Industries: phosphate mining, agricultural processing, cement; handicrafts, textiles, beverages
Industrial production growth rate: NA%
Electricity - production: 101.6 million kWh (2001)

Electricity - production by source:
fossil fuel: 98.7%
hydro: 1.3%
nuclear: 0%
other: 0% (2001)
Electricity - consumption: 614.5 million kWh (2001)
Electricity - exports: 0 kWh (2001)
Electricity - imports: 520 million kWh; note - electricity supplied by Ghana (2001)
Oil - production: 0 bbl/day (2001 est.)
Oil - consumption: 10,000 bbl/day (2001 est.)
Oil - exports: NA
Oil - imports: NA
Agriculture - products: coffee, cocoa, cotton, yams, cassava (tapioca), corn, beans, rice, millet, sorghum; livestock; fish
Exports: $398.1 million f.o.b. (2003 est.)
Exports - commodities: reexports, cotton, phosphates, coffee, cocoa
Exports - partners: Ghana 17.7%, Benin 13.1%, Burkina Faso 8.2% (2002)
Imports: $501.3 million f.o.b. (2003 est.)
Imports - commodities: machinery and equipment, foodstuffs, petroleum products
Imports - partners: France 20.3%, China 16.2%, Netherlands 6.2%, Hong Kong 5.3%, Germany 4.9%, UK 4.6%, Italy 4.3% (2002)
Debt - external: $1.4 billion (2000)
Economic aid - recipient: ODA $80 million (2000 est.)
Currency: Communaute Financiere Africaine franc (XOF); note - responsible authority is the Central Bank of the West African States
Currency code: XOF
Exchange rates: Communaute Financiere Africaine francs (XOF) per US dollar - 581.2 (2003), 696.988 (2002), 733.039 (2001), 711.976 (2000), 615.699 (1999)
Fiscal year: calendar year

Communications

Telephones - main lines in use: 51,200 (2002)
Telephones - mobile cellular: 170,000 (2002)
Telephone system:
general assessment: fair system based on a network of microwave radio relay routes supplemented by open-wire lines and a mobile cellular system
domestic: microwave radio relay and open-wire lines for conventional system; cellular system has capacity of 10,000 telephones
international: country code - 228; satellite earth stations - 1 Intelsat (Atlantic Ocean) and 1 Symphonie
Radio broadcast stations: AM 2, FM 9, shortwave 4 (1998)
Television broadcast stations: 3 (plus two repeaters) (1997)
Internet country code: .tg
Internet hosts: 80 (2002)
Internet users: 200,000 (2002)

Transportation

Railways:
total: 525 km
narrow gauge: 525 km 1.000-m gauge (2002)
Highways:
total: 7,520 km
paved: 2,376 km
unpaved: 5,144 km (1999 est.)
Waterways: 50 km (Mono river)
Ports and harbors: Kpeme, Lome
Merchant marine:
total: 2 ships (1,000 GRT or over) 3,918 GRT/3,852 DWT
by type: cargo 1, specialized tanker 1
registered in other countries: 1 (2003 est.)
Airports: 9 (2003 est.)
Airports - with paved runways:
total: 2
2,438 to 3,047 m: 2 (2003 est.)
Airports - with unpaved runways:
total: 7
914 to 1,523 m: 5
under 914 m: 2 (2003 est.)

Military

Military branches: Army, Navy, Air Force, Gendarmerie
Military manpower - availability:
males age 15-49: 1,316,455 (2004 est.)
Military manpower - fit for military service:
males age 15-49: 690,331 (2004 est.)
Military expenditures - dollar figure: $32.6 million (2003)
Military expenditures - percent of GDP: 1.9% (2003)

Transnational Issues

Disputes - international: in 2001 Benin claimed Togo moved boundary monuments - joint commission continues to resurvey the boundary
Illicit drugs: transit hub for Nigerian heroin and cocaine traffickers; money laundering not a significant problem

Tokelau
(territory of New Zealand)

Introduction

Background: Originally settled by Polynesian emigrants from surrounding island groups, the Tokelau Islands were made a British protectorate in 1889. They were transferred to New Zealand administration in 1925.

Geography

Location: Oceania, group of three atolls in the South Pacific Ocean, about one-half of the way from Hawaii to New Zealand
Geographic coordinates: 9 00 S, 172 00 W
Map references: Oceania
Area:
total: 10 sq km
land: 10 sq km
water: 0 sq km
Area - comparative: about 17 times the size of The Mall in Washington, DC
Land boundaries: 0 km
Coastline: 101 km
Maritime claims:
territorial sea: 12 NM
exclusive economic zone: 200 NM
Climate: tropical; moderated by trade winds (April to November)
Terrain: low-lying coral atolls enclosing large lagoons
Elevation extremes:
lowest point: Pacific Ocean 0 m
highest point: unnamed location 5 m
Natural resources: NEGL
Land use:
arable land: 0% (soil is thin and infertile)
permanent crops: 0%
other: 100% (1998 est.)
Irrigated land: NA sq km
Natural hazards: lies in Pacific typhoon belt

Tokelau (continued)

Environment - current issues: very limited natural resources and overcrowding are contributing to emigration to New Zealand

Geography - note: consists of three atolls, each with a lagoon surrounded by a number of reef-bound islets of varying length and rising to over three meters above sea level

People

Population: 1,405 (July 2004 est.)
Age structure:
0-14 years: 42%
15-64 years: 53%
65 years and over: 5% (2004 est.)
Population growth rate: -0.01% (2004 est.)
Birth rate: NA births/1,000 population
Death rate: NA deaths/1,000 population
Net migration rate: NA migrant(s)/1,000 population
Sex ratio: NA
Infant mortality rate:
total: NA%
male: NA%
female: NA%
Life expectancy at birth:
total population: NA years
male: 68 years
female: 70 years (2004 est.)
Total fertility rate: NA children born/woman
HIV/AIDS - adult prevalence rate: NA%
HIV/AIDS - people living with HIV/AIDS: NA
HIV/AIDS - deaths: NA
Nationality:
noun: Tokelauan(s)
adjective: Tokelauan
Ethnic groups: Polynesian
Religions: Congregational Christian Church 70%, Roman Catholic 28%, other 2%
note: on Atafu, all Congregational Christian Church of Samoa; on Nukunonu, all Roman Catholic; on Fakaofo, both denominations, with the Congregational Christian Church predominant
Languages: Tokelauan (a Polynesian language), English
Literacy: NA

Government

Country name:
conventional long form: none
conventional short form: Tokelau
Dependency status: self-administering territory of New Zealand; note - Tokelauans are drafting a constitution and developing institutions and patterns of self-government as Tokelau moves toward free association with New Zealand
Government type: NA
Capital: none; each atoll has its own administrative center
Administrative divisions: none (territory of New Zealand)
Independence: none (territory of New Zealand)

National holiday: Waitangi Day (Treaty of Waitangi established British sovereignty over New Zealand), 6 February (1840)
Constitution: administered under the Tokelau Islands Act of 1948, as amended in 1970
Legal system: New Zealand and local statutes
Suffrage: 21 years of age; universal
Executive branch:
chief of state: Queen ELIZABETH II (since 6 February 1952); the UK and New Zealand are represented by Administrator Neil WALTER (since NA 2002)
head of government: Aliki Faipule Kuresa NASAU (since 2004) note - position rotates annually among members of the cabinet
cabinet: the Council of Faipule, consisting of three elected leaders - one from each atoll - functions as a cabinet
elections: none; the monarch is hereditary; administrator appointed by the Minister of Foreign Affairs and Trade in New Zealand; the head of government is chosen from the Council of Faipule and serves a one-year term
Legislative branch: unicameral General Fono (48 seats; 15 members from each of the three islands elected by popular vote to serve three-year terms and the 3 island village mayors [pulenuku]); note - the Tokelau Amendment Act of 1996 confers limited legislative power on the General Fono
Judicial branch: Supreme Court in New Zealand exercises civil and criminal jurisdiction in Tokelau
Political parties and leaders: none
Political pressure groups and leaders: none
International organization participation: UNESCO (associate), WHO (associate)
Diplomatic representation in the US: none (territory of New Zealand)
Diplomatic representation from the US: none (territory of New Zealand)
Flag description: the flag of New Zealand is used

Economy

Economy - overview: Tokelau's small size (three villages), isolation, and lack of resources greatly restrain economic development and confine agriculture to the subsistence level. The people rely heavily on aid from New Zealand - about $4 million annually - to maintain public services, with annual aid being substantially greater than GDP. The principal sources of revenue come from sales of copra, postage stamps, souvenir coins, and handicrafts. Money is also remitted to families from relatives in New Zealand.
GDP: purchasing power parity - $1.5 million (1993 est.)
GDP - real growth rate: NA%
GDP - per capita: purchasing power parity - $1,000 (1993 est.)
GDP - composition by sector:
agriculture: NA%
industry: NA%
services: NA%

Population below poverty line: NA%
Household income or consumption by percentage share:
lowest 10%: NA%
highest 10%: NA%
Inflation rate (consumer prices): NA%
Labor force: NA
Unemployment rate: NA%
Budget:
revenues: $430,830
expenditures: $2.8 million, including capital expenditures of $37,300 (1987 est.)
Industries: small-scale enterprises for copra production, woodworking, plaited craft goods; stamps, coins; fishing
Industrial production growth rate: NA%
Electricity - production: NA kWh
Electricity - production by source:
fossil fuel: 100%
hydro: 0%
nuclear: 0%
other: 0% (2001)
Electricity - consumption: NA kWh
Agriculture - products: coconuts, copra, breadfruit, papayas, bananas; pigs, poultry, goats
Exports: $98,000 f.o.b. (1983)
Exports - commodities: stamps, copra, handicrafts
Exports - partners: NZ (2000)
Imports: $323,000 c.i.f. (1983)
Imports - commodities: foodstuffs, building materials, fuel
Imports - partners: NZ (2000)
Debt - external: $0
Economic aid - recipient: from New Zealand about $4 million annually
Currency: New Zealand dollar (NZD)
Currency code: NZD
Exchange rates: New Zealand dollars per US dollar - 1.7229 (2003), 2.154 (2002), 2.3776 (2001), 2.1863 (2000), 1.8886 (1999)
Fiscal year: 1 April - 31 March

Communications

Telephones - main lines in use: 300 (2002)
Telephones - mobile cellular: 0 (2001)
Telephone system:
general assessment: adequate
domestic: radiotelephone service between islands
international: country code - 690; radiotelephone service to Samoa; government-regulated telephone service (TeleTok), with 3 satellite earth stations, established in 1997
Radio broadcast stations: AM NA, FM NA, shortwave NA
note: each atoll has a radio broadcast station of unknown type that broadcasts shipping and weather reports (1998)
Internet country code: .tk
Internet users: NA

Tokelau (continued)

Transportation

Railways: 0 km
Highways:
total: NA km
paved: NA km
unpaved: NA km
Waterways: none
Ports and harbors: none; offshore anchorage only
Merchant marine: none
Airports: none; lagoon landings are possible by amphibious aircraft (2003 est.)

Military

Military - note: defense is the responsibility of New Zealand

Transnational Issues

Disputes - international: none

Tonga

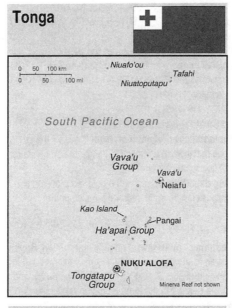

South Pacific Ocean

Niuafo'ou
Tafahi
Niuatoputapu

Vava'u Group
Vava'u
Neiafu

Kao Island
Pangai
Ha'apai Group

NUKU'ALOFA
Tongatapu Group
Minerva Reef not shown

Introduction

Background: The archipelago of "The Friendly Islands" was united into a Polynesian kingdom in 1845. It became a constitutional monarchy in 1875 and a British protectorate in 1900. Tonga acquired its independence in 1970 and became a member of the Commonwealth of Nations. It remains the only monarchy in the Pacific.

Geography

Location: Oceania, archipelago in the South Pacific Ocean, about two-thirds of the way from Hawaii to New Zealand
Geographic coordinates: 20 00 S, 175 00 W
Map references: Oceania
Area:
total: 748 sq km
land: 718 sq km
water: 30 sq km
Area - comparative: four times the size of Washington, DC
Land boundaries: 0 km
Coastline: 419 km
Maritime claims:
territorial sea: 12 NM
exclusive economic zone: 200 NM
continental shelf: 200-m depth or to the depth of exploitation
Climate: tropical; modified by trade winds; warm season (December to May), cool season (May to December)
Terrain: most islands have limestone base formed from uplifted coral formation; others have limestone overlying volcanic base
Elevation extremes:
lowest point: Pacific Ocean 0 m
highest point: unnamed location on Kao Island 1,033 m
Natural resources: fish, fertile soil

Land use:
arable land: 23.61%
permanent crops: 43.06%
other: 33.33% (1998 est.)
Irrigated land: NA sq km
Natural hazards: cyclones (October to April); earthquakes and volcanic activity on Fonuafo'ou
Environment - current issues: deforestation results as more and more land is being cleared for agriculture and settlement; some damage to coral reefs from starfish and indiscriminate coral and shell collectors; overhunting threatens native sea turtle populations
Environment - international agreements:
party to: Biodiversity, Climate Change, Desertification, Law of the Sea, Marine Dumping, Marine Life Conservation, Ozone Layer Protection, Ship Pollution
signed, but not ratified: none of the selected agreements
Geography - note: archipelago of 169 islands (36 inhabited)

People

Population: 110,237 (July 2004 est.)
Age structure:
0-14 years: 37.1% (male 20,873; female 20,050)
15-64 years: 58.7% (male 32,018; female 32,707)
65 years and over: 4.2% (male 2,005; female 2,584) (2004 est.)
Median age:
total: 20.1 years
male: 19.7 years
female: 20.7 years (2004 est.)
Population growth rate: 1.94% (2004 est.)
Birth rate: 24.87 births/1,000 population (2004 est.)
Death rate: 5.45 deaths/1,000 population (2004 est.)
Net migration rate: 0 migrant(s)/1,000 population (2004 est.)
Sex ratio:
at birth: 1.05 male(s)/female
under 15 years: 1.04 male(s)/female
15-64 years: 0.98 male(s)/female
65 years and over: 0.78 male(s)/female
total population: 0.99 male(s)/female (2004 est.)
Infant mortality rate:
total: 12.99 deaths/1,000 live births
male: 14.36 deaths/1,000 live births
female: 11.54 deaths/1,000 live births (2004 est.)
Life expectancy at birth:
total population: 69.2 years
male: 66.74 years
female: 71.79 years (2004 est.)
Total fertility rate: 3 children born/woman (2004 est.)
HIV/AIDS - adult prevalence rate: NA%
HIV/AIDS - people living with HIV/AIDS: NA
HIV/AIDS - deaths: NA
Nationality:
noun: Tongan(s)
adjective: Tongan

Tonga (continued)

Ethnic groups: Polynesian, Europeans about 300
Religions: Christian (Free Wesleyan Church claims over 30,000 adherents)
Languages: Tongan, English
Literacy:
definition: can read and write Tongan and/or English
total population: 98.5%
male: 98.4%
female: 98.7% (1996 est.)

Government

Country name:
conventional long form: Kingdom of Tonga
conventional short form: Tonga
former: Friendly Islands
Government type: hereditary constitutional monarchy
Capital: Nuku'alofa
Administrative divisions: 3 island groups; Ha'apai, Tongatapu, Vava'u
Independence: 4 June 1970 (from UK protectorate)
National holiday: Independence Day, 4 June (1970)
Constitution: 4 November 1875, revised 1 January 1967
Legal system: based on English law
Suffrage: 21 years of age; universal
Executive branch:
chief of state: King Taufa'ahau TUPOU IV (since 16 December 1965)
head of government: Prime Minister Prince Lavaka ata ULUKALALA (since NA February 2000) and Deputy Prime Minister James C. COCKER (since NA January 2001)
cabinet: Cabinet, appointed by the monarch, consists of 12 members
note: there is also a Privy Council that consists of the monarch, the Cabinet, and two governors
elections: none; the monarch is hereditary; prime minister and deputy prime minister appointed for life by the monarch
Legislative branch: unicameral Legislative Assembly or Fale Alea (30 seats - 12 reserved for cabinet ministers sitting ex officio, nine for nobles selected by the country's 33 nobles, and nine elected by popular vote; members serve three-year terms)
elections: last held 7 March 2002 (next to be held NA 2005)
election results: percent of vote - HRDMT 70%; seats - HRDMT 7, traditionalist 2
Judicial branch: Supreme Court (judges are appointed by the monarch); Court of Appeal (consists of the Privy Council with the addition of the chief justice of the Supreme Court)
Political parties and leaders: there are no political parties
Political pressure groups and leaders: Human Rights and Democracy Movement Tonga or HRDMT [Rev. Simote VEA, chair]
International organization participation: ACP, AsDB, C, FAO, G-77, IBRD, ICAO, ICFTU, ICRM, IDA, IFAD, IFC, IFRCS, IHO, IMF, IMO, Interpol, IOC, ITU, OPCW, PIF, Sparteca, UN, UNCTAD, UNESCO, UNIDO, UPU, WHO, WIPO, WMO, WTrO (observer)
Diplomatic representation in the US:
chief of mission: Ambassador Sonatane T. T. TUPOU
chancery: 250 East 51st Street, New York, NY 10022
telephone: [1] (917) 369-1136
FAX: [1] (917) 369-1024
consulate(s) general: San Francisco
Diplomatic representation from the US: the US does not have an embassy in Tonga; the ambassador to Fiji is accredited to Tonga
Flag description: red with a bold red cross on a white rectangle in the upper hoist-side corner

Economy

Economy - overview: Tonga, a small, open, South Pacific island economy, has a narrow export base in agricultural goods. Squash, coconuts, bananas, and vanilla beans are the main crops, and agricultural exports make up two-thirds of total exports. The country must import a high proportion of its food, mainly from New Zealand. Tourism is the second-largest source of hard currency earnings following remittances. The country remains dependent on external aid and remittances from Tongan communities overseas to offset its trade deficit. The government is emphasizing the development of the private sector, especially the encouragement of investment, and is committing increased funds for health and education. Tonga has a reasonably sound basic infrastructure and well-developed social services. High unemployment among the young and the continuing upturn in inflation are major issues facing the government.
GDP: purchasing power parity - $236 million (2001 est.)
GDP - real growth rate: 3% (2001 est.)
GDP - per capita: purchasing power parity - $2,200 (2001 est.)
GDP - composition by sector:
agriculture: 26%
industry: 12%
services: 62% (2001 est.)
Population below poverty line: NA%
Household income or consumption by percentage share:
lowest 10%: NA%
highest 10%: NA%
Inflation rate (consumer prices): 10.3% (2002 est.)
Labor force: 33,908 (1996)
Labor force - by occupation: agriculture 65% (1997 est.)
Unemployment rate: 13.3% (1996 est.)
Budget:
revenues: $39.9 million
expenditures: $52.4 million, including capital expenditures of $1.9 million (FY99/00 est.)
Industries: tourism, fishing
Industrial production growth rate: 8.6% (FY98/99)
Electricity - production: 27.27 million kWh (2001)
Electricity - production by source:
fossil fuel: 100%
hydro: 0%
nuclear: 0%
other: 0% (2001)
Electricity - consumption: 25.36 million kWh (2001)
Electricity - exports: 0 kWh (2001)
Electricity - imports: 0 kWh (2001)
Oil - production: 0 bbl/day (2001 est.)
Oil - consumption: 1,000 bbl/day (2001 est.)
Oil - exports: NA
Oil - imports: NA
Agriculture - products: squash, coconuts, copra, bananas, vanilla beans, cocoa, coffee, ginger, black pepper; fish
Exports: $27 million f.o.b. (2002 est.)
Exports - commodities: squash, fish, vanilla beans, root crops
Exports - partners: Japan 40.7%, US 37%, Germany 3.7% (2002)
Imports: $86 million f.o.b. (2002 est.)
Imports - commodities: foodstuffs, machinery and transport equipment, fuels, chemicals
Imports - partners: New Zealand 31.4%, Fiji 20.9%, US 14%, Australia 12.8%, China 5.8% (2002)
Debt - external: $63.4 million (2001)
Economic aid - recipient: Australia $5.5 million, New Zealand $2.3 million (FY01/02)
Currency: pa'anga (TOP)
Currency code: TOP
Exchange rates: pa'anga per US dollar - NA (2003), 2.1952 (2002), 2.1236 (2001), 1.7585 (2000), 1.5991 (1999)
Fiscal year: 1 July - 30 June

Communications

Telephones - main lines in use: 11,200 (2002)
Telephones - mobile cellular: 3,400 (2002)
Telephone system:
general assessment: NA
domestic: NA
international: country code - 676; satellite earth station - 1 Intelsat (Pacific Ocean) (1996)
Radio broadcast stations: AM 1, FM 2, shortwave 1 (2001)
Television broadcast stations: 2 (2001)
Internet country code: .to
Internet hosts: 19,485 (2002)
Internet users: 2,900 (2002)

Transportation

Railways: 0 km
Highways:
total: 680 km
paved: 184 km
unpaved: 496 km (1999 est.)

Tonga (continued)

Waterways: none
Ports and harbors: Neiafu, Nuku'alofa, Pangai
Merchant marine:
total: 40 ships (1,000 GRT or over) 136,977 GRT/
200,751 DWT
by type: bulk 3, cargo 21, chemical tanker 2,
container 1, liquefied gas 4, petroleum tanker 5,
refrigerated cargo 1, roll on/roll off 1, specialized
tanker 1, vehicle carrier 1
foreign-owned: Albania 1, Australia 4, Brazil 1,
Cyprus 1, Egypt 1, Greece 1, Lebanon 1, Liberia 1,
Marshall Islands 1, Norway 1, Panama 2, Romania 1,
Russia 1, Saudi Arabia 1, Switzerland 3, Syria 1,
United (2003 est.)
Airports: 6 (2003 est.)
Airports - with paved runways:
total: 1
2,438 to 3,047 m: 1 (2003 est.)
Airports - with unpaved runways:
total: 5
1,524 to 2,437 m: 1
914 to 1,523 m: 3
under 914 m: 1 (2003 est.)

Military

Military branches: Tonga Defense Services:
Ground Forces (Royal Marines, Royal Guard),
Maritime Force (including Air Wing)
Military expenditures - dollar figure: NA
Military expenditures - percent of GDP: NA

Transnational Issues

Disputes - international: none

Trinidad and Tobago

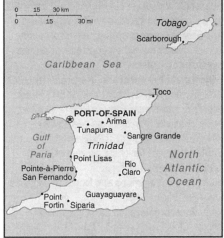

Introduction

Background: The islands came under British control
in the 19th century; independence was granted in
1962. The country is one of the most prosperous in the
Caribbean thanks largely to petroleum and natural gas
production and processing. Tourism, mostly in
Tobago, is targeted for expansion and is growing.

Geography

Location: Caribbean, islands between the
Caribbean Sea and the North Atlantic Ocean,
northeast of Venezuela
Geographic coordinates: 11 00 N, 61 00 W
Map references: Central America and the Caribbean
Area:
total: 5,128 sq km
land: 5,128 sq km
water: 0 sq km
Area - comparative: slightly smaller than Delaware
Land boundaries: 0 km
Coastline: 362 km
Maritime claims: measured from claimed
archipelagic baselines
territorial sea: 12 NM
contiguous zone: 24 NM
exclusive economic zone: 200 NM
continental shelf: 200 NM or to the outer edge of the
continental margin
Climate: tropical; rainy season (June to December)
Terrain: mostly plains with some hills and low
mountains
Elevation extremes:
lowest point: Caribbean Sea 0 m
highest point: El Cerro del Aripo 940 m
Natural resources: petroleum, natural gas, asphalt
Land use:
arable land: 14.6%
permanent crops: 9.2%
other: 76.2% (1998 est.)
Irrigated land: 30 sq km (1998 est.)

Natural hazards: outside usual path of hurricanes
and other tropical storms
Environment - current issues: water pollution from
agricultural chemicals, industrial wastes, and raw
sewage; oil pollution of beaches; deforestation; soil
erosion
Environment - international agreements:
party to: Biodiversity, Climate Change, Climate
Change-Kyoto Protocol, Desertification, Endangered
Species, Hazardous Wastes, Law of the Sea, Marine
Life Conservation, Ozone Layer Protection, Ship
Pollution, Tropical Timber 83, Tropical Timber 94,
Wetlands
signed, but not ratified: none of the selected
agreements
Geography - note: Pitch Lake, on Trinidad's
southwestern coast, is the world's largest natural
reservoir of asphalt

People

Population: 1,096,585 (July 2004 est.)
Age structure:
0-14 years: 21.4% (male 120,153; female 114,205)
15-64 years: 70.6% (male 403,202; female 370,498)
65 years and over: 8.1% (male 39,762; female
48,765) (2004 est.)
Median age:
total: 30.4 years
male: 30 years
female: 30.9 years (2004 est.)
Population growth rate: -0.71% (2004 est.)
Birth rate: 12.75 births/1,000 population (2004 est.)
Death rate: 9.02 deaths/1,000 population (2004 est.)
Net migration rate: -10.83 migrant(s)/1,000
population (2004 est.)
Sex ratio:
at birth: 1.05 male(s)/female
under 15 years: 1.05 male(s)/female
15-64 years: 1.09 male(s)/female
65 years and over: 0.82 male(s)/female
total population: 1.06 male(s)/female (2004 est.)
Infant mortality rate:
total: 24.64 deaths/1,000 live births
male: 26.58 deaths/1,000 live births
female: 22.61 deaths/1,000 live births (2004 est.)
Life expectancy at birth:
total population: 69.28 years
male: 66.86 years
female: 71.82 years (2004 est.)
Total fertility rate: 1.77 children born/woman
(2004 est.)
HIV/AIDS - adult prevalence rate: 2.5% (2001 est.)
HIV/AIDS - people living with HIV/AIDS: 17,000
(2001 est.)
HIV/AIDS - deaths: 1,200 (2001 est.)
Nationality:
noun: Trinidadian(s), Tobagonian(s)
adjective: Trinidadian, Tobagonian
Ethnic groups: East Indian (a local term - primarily
immigrants from northern India) 40.3%, black 39.5%,
mixed 18.4%, white 0.6%, Chinese and other 1.2%

Trinidad and Tobago (continued)

Religions: Roman Catholic 29.4%, Hindu 23.8%, Anglican 10.9%, Muslim 5.8%, Presbyterian 3.4%, other 26.7%
Languages: English (official), Hindi, French, Spanish, Chinese
Literacy:
definition: age 15 and over can read and write
total population: 98.6%
male: 99.1%
female: 98% (2003 est.)

Government

Country name:
conventional long form: Republic of Trinidad and Tobago
conventional short form: Trinidad and Tobago
Government type: parliamentary democracy
Capital: Port-of-Spain
Administrative divisions: 8 counties, 3 municipalities*, and 1 ward**; Arima*, Caroni, Mayaro, Nariva, Port-of-Spain*, Saint Andrew, Saint David, Saint George, Saint Patrick, San Fernando*, Tobago**, Victoria
Independence: 31 August 1962 (from UK)
National holiday: Independence Day, 31 August (1962)
Constitution: 1 August 1976
Legal system: based on English common law; judicial review of legislative acts in the Supreme Court; has not accepted compulsory ICJ jurisdiction
Suffrage: 18 years of age; universal
Executive branch:
chief of state: President George Maxwell RICHARDS (since 17 March 2003)
head of government: Prime Minister Patrick MANNING (since 24 December 2001)
cabinet: Cabinet appointed from among the members of Parliament
elections: president elected by an electoral college, which consists of the members of the Senate and House of Representatives, for a five-year term; election last held 14 February 2003 (next to be held in 2008); the president usually appoints as prime minister the leader of the majority party in the House of Representatives
election results: George Maxwell RICHARDS elected president; percent of electoral college vote - 43%
Legislative branch: bicameral Parliament consists of the Senate (31 seats; members appointed by the president for a maximum term of five years) and the House of Representatives (36 seats; members are elected by popular vote to serve five-year terms)
elections: House of Representatives - last held 7 October 2002 (next to be held by October 2007)
election results: House of Representatives - percent of vote - PNM 55.5%, UNC 44.5%; seats by party - PNM 20, UNC 16
note: Tobago has a unicameral House of Assembly with 15 members serving four-year terms

Judicial branch: Supreme Court of Judicature (comprised of the High Court of Justice and the Court of Appeals; the chief justice is appointed by the president on the advice of the prime minister and the leader of the opposition; other justices are appointed by the president on the advice of the Judicial and Legal Service Commission); High Court of Justice; Court of Appeals the highest court of appeal is the Privy Council in London
Political parties and leaders: National Alliance for Reconstruction or NAR [Lennox SANKERSINGH]; People's Empowerment Party or PEP [leader NA]; People's National Movement or PNM [Patrick MANNING]; Team Unity or TUN [Ramesh MAHARAJ]; United National Congress or UNC [Basdeo PANDAY]
Political pressure groups and leaders: Jamaat-al Muslimeen [Yasin BAKR]
International organization participation: ACP, C, Caricom, CDB, FAO, G-24, G-77, IADB, IBRD, ICAO, ICCt, ICFTU, ICRM, IDA, IFAD, IFC, IFRCS, IHO, ILO, IMF, IMO, Interpol, IOC, ISO, ITU, LAES, NAM, OAS, OPANAL, OPCW, UN, UNCTAD, UNESCO, UNIDO, UPU, WCL, WCO, WFTU, WHO, WIPO, WMO, WTrO
Diplomatic representation in the US:
chief of mission: Ambassador Marina Annette VALERE (as of February 2003)
chancery: 1708 Massachusetts Avenue NW, Washington, DC 20036
telephone: [1] (202) 467-6490
FAX: [1] (202) 785-3130
consulate(s) general: Miami and New York
Diplomatic representation from the US:
chief of mission: Ambassador Roy L. AUSTIN
embassy: 15 Queen's Park West, Port-of-Spain
mailing address: P. O. Box 752, Port-of-Spain
telephone: [1] (868) 622-6372 through 6376, 622-6176
FAX: [1] (868) 628-5462
Flag description: red with a white-edged black diagonal band from the upper hoist side to the lower fly side

Economy

Economy - overview: Trinidad and Tobago, the leading Caribbean producer of oil and gas, has earned a reputation as an excellent investment site for international businesses. Tourism is a growing sector, although not proportionately as important as in many other Caribbean islands. The economy benefits from low inflation and a growing trade surplus. Prospects for growth in 2004 are good as prices for oil, petrochemicals, and liquified natural gas are expected to remain high, and foreign direct investment continues to grow to support expanded capacity in the energy sector. The government is coping with a rise in violent crime.
GDP: purchasing power parity - $10.6 billion (2003 est.)

GDP - real growth rate: 4.5% (2003 est.)
GDP - per capita: purchasing power parity - $9,600 (2003 est.)
GDP - composition by sector:
agriculture: 1.6%
industry: 43.2%
services: 55.2% (2000 est.)
Population below poverty line: 21% (1992 est.)
Household income or consumption by percentage share:
lowest 10%: NA%
highest 10%: NA%
Inflation rate (consumer prices): 3.7% (2003 est.)
Labor force: 564,000 (2000)
Labor force - by occupation: construction and utilities 12.4%, manufacturing, mining, and quarrying 14%, agriculture 9.5%, services 64.1% (1997 est.)
Unemployment rate: 10.9% (2003)
Budget:
revenues: $1.54 billion
expenditures: $1.6 billion, including capital expenditures of $117.3 million (1998)
Industries: petroleum, chemicals, tourism, food processing, cement, beverage, cotton textiles
Industrial production growth rate: 5.2% (2003 est.)
Electricity - production: 5.315 billion kWh (2001)
Electricity - production by source:
fossil fuel: 99.8%
hydro: 0%
nuclear: 0%
other: 0.2% (2001)
Electricity - consumption: 4.943 billion kWh (2001)
Electricity - exports: 0 kWh (2001)
Electricity - imports: 0 kWh (2001)
Oil - production: 136,200 bbl/day (2001 est.)
Oil - consumption: 24,000 bbl/day (2001 est.)
Oil - exports: NA
Oil - imports: NA
Oil - proved reserves: 990 million bbl (1 January 2004)
Natural gas - production: 25 billion cu m (2003 est.)
Natural gas - consumption: 13.76 billion cu m (2003 est.)
Natural gas - exports: 11.79 billion cu m (2003 est.)
Natural gas - imports: 0 cu m (2001 est.)
Natural gas - proved reserves: 589 billion cu m (1 January 2004)
Agriculture - products: cocoa, sugarcane, rice, citrus, coffee, vegetables; poultry
Exports: $4.9 billion f.o.b. (2003 est.)
Exports - commodities: petroleum and petroleum products, chemicals, steel products, fertilizer, sugar, cocoa, coffee, citrus, flowers
Exports - partners: US 54.4%, Jamaica 6.7%, France 4.2% (2002)
Imports: $3.917 billion f.o.b. (2003 est.)
Imports - commodities: machinery, transportation equipment, manufactured goods, food, live animals

Trinidad and Tobago *(continued)*

Imports - partners: US 35.8%, Venezuela 12.7%, Brazil 5.1%, Cote d'Ivoire 4.7%, UK 4.3% (2002)
Debt - external: $2.7 billion (2003 est.)
Economic aid - recipient: $24 million (1999 est.)
Currency: Trinidad and Tobago dollar (TTD)
Currency code: TTD
Exchange rates: Trinidad and Tobago dollars per US dollar - 6.2929 (2003), 6.2487 (2002), 6.2332 (2001), 6.2998 (2000), 6.2989 (1999)
Fiscal year: 1 October - 30 September

Communications

Telephones - main lines in use: 325,100 (2002)
Telephones - mobile cellular: 361,900 (2002)
Telephone system:
general assessment: excellent international service; good local service
domestic: NA
international: country code - 1-868; satellite earth station - 1 Intelsat (Atlantic Ocean); tropospheric scatter to Barbados and Guyana
Radio broadcast stations: AM 4, FM 18, shortwave 0 (2004)
Television broadcast stations: 2 (2004)
Internet country code: .tt
Internet hosts: 7,209 (2002)
Internet users: 138,000 (2002)

Transportation

Railways: minimal agricultural railroad system near San Fernando; common carrier railway service was discontinued in 1968 (2001)
Highways:
total: 8,320 km
paved: 4,252 km
unpaved: 4,068 km (1999 est.)
Waterways: none
Pipelines: condensate 253 km; gas 1,117 km; oil 478 km (2003)
Ports and harbors: Pointe-a-Pierre, Point Fortin, Point Lisas, Port-of-Spain, Scarborough, Tembladora
Merchant marine:
total: 5 ships (1,000 GRT or over) 7,178 GRT/3,633 DWT
by type: cargo 1, passenger 1, passenger/cargo 1, petroleum tanker 1, short-sea/passenger 1
foreign-owned: United States 1
registered in other countries: 4 (2003 est.)
Airports: 6 (2003 est.)
Airports - with paved runways:
total: 3
over 3,047 m: 1
2,438 to 3,047 m: 1
1,524 to 2,437 m: 1 (2003 est.)
Airports - with unpaved runways:
total: 3
914 to 1,523 m: 1
under 914 m: 2 (2003 est.)

Military

Military branches: Trinidad and Tobago Defense Force: Ground Force, Coast Guard, and Air Wing
Military manpower - availability:
males age 15-49: 326,447 (2004 est.)
Military manpower - fit for military service:
males age 15-49: 232,234 (2004 est.)
Military expenditures - dollar figure: $66.7 million (2003)
Military expenditures - percent of GDP: 0.6% (2003)

Transnational Issues

Disputes - international: Barbados will assert its claim before UNCLOS that the northern limit of Trinidad and Tobago's maritime boundary with Venezuela extends into its waters; Guyana has also expressed its intention to challenge this boundary as it may extend into its waters as well
Illicit drugs: transshipment point for South American drugs destined for the US and Europe; producer of cannabis

Tromelin Island
(possession of France)

Introduction

Background: First explored by the French in 1776, the island came under the jurisdiction of Reunion in 1814. At present, it serves as a sea turtle sanctuary and is the site of an important meteorological station.

Geography

Location: Southern Africa, island in the Indian Ocean, east of Madagascar
Geographic coordinates: 15 52 S, 54 25 E
Map references: Africa
Area:
total: 1 sq km
land: 1 sq km
water: 0 sq km
Area - comparative: about 1.7 times the size of The Mall in Washington, DC
Land boundaries: 0 km
Coastline: 3.7 km
Maritime claims:
territorial sea: 12 NM
exclusive economic zone: 200 NM
continental shelf: 200-m depth or to the depth of exploitation
Climate: tropical
Terrain: low, flat, and sandy; likely volcanic
Elevation extremes:
lowest point: Indian Ocean 0 m
highest point: unnamed location 7 m
Natural resources: fish
Land use:
arable land: 0%
permanent crops: 0%
other: 100% (grasses; scattered bushes) (1998 est.)
Irrigated land: 0 sq km (1998 est.)
Natural hazards: NA
Environment - current issues: NA
Geography - note: climatologically important location for forecasting cyclones; wildlife sanctuary (seabirds, tortoises)

Population: uninhabited, except for visits by scientists (July 2004 est.)

G o v e r n m e n t

Country name:
conventional long form: none
conventional short form: Tromelin Island
local long form: none
local short form: Ile Tromelin
Dependency status: possession of France; administered by a high commissioner of the Republic, resident in Reunion
Legal system: the laws of France, where applicable, apply
Flag description: the flag of France is used

E c o n o m y

Economy - overview: no economic activity

C o m m u n i c a t i o n s

Communications - note: important meteorological station

T r a n s p o r t a t i o n

Waterways: none
Ports and harbors: none; offshore anchorage only
Airports: 1 (2003 est.)
Airports - with unpaved runways:
total: 1
under 914 m: 1 (2003 est.)

M i l i t a r y

Military - note: defense is the responsibility of France

T r a n s n a t i o n a l   I s s u e s

Disputes - international: claimed by Mauritius

Tunisia

Introduction

Background: Following independence from France in 1956, President Habib BOURGUIBA established a strict one-party state. He dominated the country for 31 years, repressing Islamic fundamentalism and establishing rights for women unmatched by any other Arab nation. In recent years, Tunisia has taken a moderate, non-aligned stance in its foreign relations. Domestically, it has sought to defuse rising pressure for a more open political society.

Geography

Location: Northern Africa, bordering the Mediterranean Sea, between Algeria and Libya
Geographic coordinates: 34 00 N, 9 00 E
Map references: Africa
Area:
total: 163,610 sq km
land: 155,360 sq km
water: 8,250 sq km
Area - comparative: slightly larger than Georgia
Land boundaries:
total: 1,424 km

border countries: Algeria 965 km, Libya 459 km
Coastline: 1,148 km
Maritime claims:
territorial sea: 12 NM
contiguous zone: 24 NM
Climate: temperate in north with mild, rainy winters and hot, dry summers; desert in south
Terrain: mountains in north; hot, dry central plain; semiarid south merges into the Sahara
Elevation extremes:
lowest point: Shatt al Gharsah -17 m
highest point: Jebel ech Chambi 1,544 m
Natural resources: petroleum, phosphates, iron ore, lead, zinc, salt
Land use:
arable land: 18.67%
permanent crops: 12.87%
other: 68.46% (1998 est.)
Irrigated land: 3,800 sq km (1998 est.)
Natural hazards: NA
Environment - current issues: toxic and hazardous waste disposal is ineffective and poses health risks; water pollution from raw sewage; limited natural fresh water resources; deforestation; overgrazing; soil erosion; desertification
Environment - international agreements:
party to: Biodiversity, Climate Change, Climate Change-Kyoto Protocol, Desertification, Endangered Species, Environmental Modification, Hazardous Wastes, Law of the Sea, Marine Dumping, Ozone Layer Protection, Ship Pollution, Wetlands
signed, but not ratified: Marine Life Conservation
Geography - note: strategic location in central Mediterranean; Malta and Tunisia are discussing the commercial exploitation of the continental shelf between their countries, particularly for oil exploration

People

Population: 9,974,722 (July 2004 est.)
Age structure:
0-14 years: 26% (male 1,337,546; female 1,253,814)
15-64 years: 67.5% (male 3,373,199; female 3,360,402)
65 years and over: 6.5% (male 315,151; female 334,610) (2004 est.)
Median age:
total: 26.8 years
male: 26.3 years
female: 27.3 years (2004 est.)
Population growth rate: 1.01% (2004 est.)
Birth rate: 15.74 births/1,000 population (2004 est.)
Death rate: 5.05 deaths/1,000 population (2004 est.)
Net migration rate: -0.57 migrant(s)/1,000 population (2004 est.)
Sex ratio:
at birth: 1.07 male(s)/female
under 15 years: 1.07 male(s)/female
15-64 years: 1 male(s)/female
65 years and over: 0.94 male(s)/female
total population: 1.02 male(s)/female (2004 est.)

Tunisia (continued)

Infant mortality rate:

total: 25.76 deaths/1,000 live births

male: 28.7 deaths/1,000 live births

female: 22.59 deaths/1,000 live births (2004 est.)

Life expectancy at birth:

total population: 74.66 years

male: 73 years

female: 76.44 years (2004 est.)

Total fertility rate: 1.79 children born/woman (2004 est.)

HIV/AIDS - adult prevalence rate: 0.04% (2001 est.)

HIV/AIDS - people living with HIV/AIDS: NA

HIV/AIDS - deaths: NA

Nationality:

noun: Tunisian(s)

adjective: Tunisian

Ethnic groups: Arab 98%, European 1%, Jewish and other 1%

Religions: Muslim 98%, Christian 1%, Jewish and other 1%

Languages: Arabic (official and one of the languages of commerce), French (commerce)

Literacy:

definition: age 15 and over can read and write

total population: 74.2%

male: 84%

female: 64.4% (2003 est.)

Government

Country name:

conventional long form: Tunisian Republic

conventional short form: Tunisia

local long form: Al Jumhuriyah at Tunisiyah

local short form: Tunis

Government type: republic

Capital: Tunis

Administrative divisions: 24 governorates; Ariana (Aryanah), Beja (Bajah), Ben Arous (Bin 'Arus), Bizerte (Banzart), Gabes (Qabis), Gafsa (Qafsah), Jendouba (Jundubah), Kairouan (Al Qayrawan), Kasserine (Al Qasrayn), Kebili (Qibili), Kef (Al Kaf), Mahdia (Al Mahdiyah), Manouba (Manubah), Medenine (Madanin), Monastir (Al Munastir), Nabeul (Nabul), Sfax (Safaqis), Sidi Bou Zid (Sidi Bu Zayd), Siliana (Silyanah), Sousse (Susah), Tataouine (Tatawin), Tozeur (Tawzar), Tunis, Zaghouan (Zaghwan)

Independence: 20 March 1956 (from France)

National holiday: Independence Day, 20 March (1956)

Constitution: 1 June 1959; amended 12 July 1988

Legal system: based on French civil law system and Islamic law; some judicial review of legislative acts in the Supreme Court in joint session

Suffrage: 20 years of age; universal

Executive branch:

chief of state: President Zine El Abidine BEN ALI (since 7 November 1987)

head of government: Prime Minister Mohamed GHANNOUCHI (since 17 November 1999)

cabinet: Council of Ministers appointed by the president

elections: president elected by popular vote for a five-year term; election last held 24 October 1999 (next to be held NA 2004); prime minister appointed by the president

election results: President Zine El Abidine BEN ALI reelected for a third term without opposition; percent of vote - Zine El Abidine BEN ALI nearly 100%

Legislative branch: unicameral Chamber of Deputies or Majlis al-Nuwaab (182 seats; members elected by popular vote to serve five-year terms)

elections: last held 24 October 1999 (next to be held NA 2004)

election results: percent of vote by party - RCD 92%; seats by party - RCD 148, MDS 13, UDU 7, PUP 7, Al-Tajdid 5, PSL 2; note - reforms enabled opposition parties to win up to 20% of seats, increasing the number of seats they hold from 19 in the last election to 34 now

Judicial branch: Court of Cassation or Cour de Cassation

Political parties and leaders: Al-Tajdid Movement [Adel CHAOUCH]; Constitutional Democratic Rally Party (Rassemblement Constitutionnel Democratique) or RCD [President Zine El Abidine BEN ALI (official ruling party)]; Liberal Social Party or PSL [Mounir BEJI]; Movement of Democratic Socialists or MDS [Khamis CHAMMARI]; Popular Unity Party or PUP [Mohamed Belhaj AMOR]; Unionist Democratic Union or UDU [Abderrahmane TLILI]

Political pressure groups and leaders: the Islamic fundamentalist party, Al Nahda (Renaissance), is outlawed

International organization participation: ABEDA, ACCT, AfDB, AFESD, AMF, AMU, AU, BSEC (observer), FAO, G-77, IAEA, IBRD, ICAO, ICC, ICFTU, ICRM, IDA, IDB, IFAD, IFC, IFRCS, IHO, ILO, IMF, IMO, Interpol, IOC, IOM, ISO, ITU, LAS, MICAH, MONUC, NAM, OAPEC, OAS (observer), OIC, OPCW, OSCE (partner), UN, UNCTAD, UNESCO, UNHCR, UNIDO, UNMEE, UNMIK, UPU, WCO, WFTU, WHO, WIPO, WMO, WToO, WTrO

Diplomatic representation in the US:

chief of mission: Ambassador Hatem ATALLAH

chancery: 1515 Massachusetts Avenue NW, Washington, DC 20005

telephone: [1] (202) 862-1850

FAX: [1] (202) 862-1858

Diplomatic representation from the US:

chief of mission: Ambassador William J. HUDSON

embassy: Zone Nord-Est des Berges du Lac Nord de Tunis, 2045 La Goulette, Tunisia

mailing address: use embassy street address

telephone: [216] 71 107-000

FAX: [216] 71 962-115

Flag description: red with a white disk in the center bearing a red crescent nearly encircling a red five-pointed star; the crescent and star are traditional symbols of Islam

Economy

Economy - overview: Tunisia has a diverse economy, with important agricultural, mining, energy, tourism, and manufacturing sectors. Governmental control of economic affairs while still heavy has gradually lessened over the past decade with increasing privatization, simplification of the tax structure, and a prudent approach to debt. Real growth, averaging 5 percent for the latter half of the last decade, slowed to a 15-year low of 1.9% in 2002 because of agricultural drought, slow investment, and lackluster tourism. Better rains in 2003, however, pushed GDP growth up to an estimated 6 percent, and tourism also recovered after the end of combat operations in Iraq. GDP growth is likely to ease to the 5-5.5 percent range in 2004 as the agricultural sector is unlikely to continue to expand as rapidly. Tunisia has agreed to gradually remove barriers to trade with the European Union over the next decade. Broader privatization, further liberalization of the investment code to increase foreign investment, improvements in government efficiency, and reduction of the trade deficit are among the challenges for the future.

GDP: purchasing power parity - $68.78 billion (2003 est.)

GDP - real growth rate: 6% (2003 est.)

GDP - per capita: purchasing power parity - $6,900 (2003 est.)

GDP - composition by sector:

agriculture: 12%

industry: 32%

services: 56% (2003 est.)

Population below poverty line: 7.6% (2001 est.)

Household income or consumption by percentage share:

lowest 10%: 2.3%

highest 10%: 31.8% (1995)

Distribution of family income - Gini index: 41.7 (1995)

Inflation rate (consumer prices): 2.7% (2003 est.)

Labor force: 3.5 million

note: shortage of skilled labor (2001 est.)

Labor force - by occupation: services 55%, industry 23%, agriculture 22% (1995 est.)

Unemployment rate: 14.3% (2003 est.)

Budget:

revenues: $5.2 billion

expenditures: $5.7 billion, including capital expenditures of $1.6 billion (2002 est.)

Industries: petroleum, mining (particularly phosphate and iron ore), tourism, textiles, footwear, agribusiness, beverages

Industrial production growth rate: 3.1% (2003 est.)

Electricity - production: 10.48 billion kWh (2001)

Tunisia (continued)

Electricity - production by source:
fossil fuel: 99.5%
hydro: 0.5%
nuclear: 0%
other: 0% (2001)
Electricity - consumption: 9.748 billion kWh (2001)
Electricity - exports: 0 kWh (2001)
Electricity - imports: 1 million kWh (2001)
Oil - production: 72,580 bbl/day (2001 est.)
Oil - consumption: 87,000 bbl/day (2001 est.)
Oil - exports: NA
Oil - imports: NA
Oil - proved reserves: 417 million bbl (1 January 2002)
Natural gas - production: 2.25 billion cu m (2001 est.)
Natural gas - consumption: 3.83 billion cu m (2001 est.)
Natural gas - exports: 0 cu m (2001 est.)
Natural gas - imports: 1.58 billion cu m (2001 est.)
Natural gas - proved reserves: 77.16 billion cu m (1 January 2002)
Agriculture - products: olives, olive oil, grain, dairy products, tomatoes, citrus fruit, beef, sugar beets, dates, almonds
Exports: $8.035 billion f.o.b. (2003 est.)
Exports - commodities: textiles, mechanical goods, phosphates and chemicals, agricultural products, hydrocarbons
Exports - partners: France 31.3%, Italy 21.6%, Germany 11.5%, Spain 4.8%, Libya 4.7%, Belgium 4.3% (2002)
Imports: $10.3 billion f.o.b. (2003 est.)
Imports - commodities: textiles, machinery and equipment, hydrocarbons, chemicals, food
Imports - partners: France 25.6%, Italy 19.5%, Germany 8.9%, Spain 5% (2002)
Debt - external: $13.8 billion (2003 est.)
Economic aid - recipient: $378 million (2001)
Currency: Tunisian dinar (TND)
Currency code: TND
Exchange rates: Tunisian dinars per US dollar - 1.2885 (2003), 1.4217 (2002), 1.4387 (2001), 1.3707 (2000), 1.1862 (1999)
Fiscal year: calendar year

Communications

Telephones - main lines in use: 1.148 million (2002)
Telephones - mobile cellular: 503,900 (2002)
Telephone system:
general assessment: above the African average and continuing to be upgraded; key centers are Sfax, Sousse, Bizerte, and Tunis; Internet access available
domestic: trunk facilities consist of open-wire lines, coaxial cable, and microwave radio relay
international: country code - 216; 5 submarine cables; satellite earth stations - 1 Intelsat (Atlantic Ocean) and 1 Arabsat; coaxial cable and microwave radio relay to Algeria and Libya; participant in Medarabtel; two international gateway digital switches

Radio broadcast stations: AM 7, FM 20, shortwave 2 (1998)
Television broadcast stations: 26 (plus 76 repeaters) (1995)
Internet country code: .tn
Internet hosts: 341 (2002)
Internet users: 505,500 (2002)

Transportation

Railways:
total: 2,152 km
standard gauge: 468 km 1.435-m gauge
narrow gauge: 1,674 km 1.000-m gauge (65 km electrified)
dual gauge: 10 km 1.435-m and 1.000-m gauges (three rails) (2002)
Highways:
total: 18,997 km
paved: 12,310 km (including 142 km of expressways)
unpaved: 6,687 km (2000)
Waterways: none
Pipelines: gas 3,059 km; oil 1,203 km; refined products 345 km (2003)
Ports and harbors: Bizerte, Gabes, La Goulette, Sfax, Sousse, Tunis, Zarzis
Merchant marine:
total: 11 ships (1,000 GRT or over) 124,733 GRT/ 122,664 DWT
by type: bulk 2, cargo 1, chemical tanker 4, liquefied gas 1, short-sea/passenger 3
registered in other countries: 2 (2003 est.)
Airports: 30 (2003 est.)
Airports - with paved runways:
total: 14
over 3,047 m: 3
2,438 to 3,047 m: 6
1,524 to 2,437 m: 2
914 to 1,523 m: 3 (2003 est.)
Airports - with unpaved runways:
total: 16
1,524 to 2,437 m: 2
914 to 1,523 m: 7
under 914 m: 7 (2003 est.)

Military

Military branches: Army, Navy, Air Force
Military manpower - military age: 20 years of age (2004 est.)
Military manpower - availability:
males age 15-49: 2,918,524 (2004 est.)
Military manpower - fit for military service:
males age 15-49: 1,655,910 (2004 est.)
Military manpower - reaching military age annually:
males: 106,565 (2004 est.)
Military expenditures - dollar figure: $356 million (FY99)
Military expenditures - percent of GDP: 1.5% (FY99)

Transnational Issues

Disputes - international: none

Turkey

People

Population: 68,893,918 (July 2004 est.)
Age structure:
0-14 years: 26.6% (male 9,328,108; female 8,990,742)
15-64 years: 66.8% (male 23,394,465; female 22,650,532)
65 years and over: 6.6% (male 2,078,881; female 2,451,190) (2004 est.)
Median age:
total: 27.3 years
male: 27.1 years
female: 27.5 years (2004 est.)
Population growth rate: 1.13% (2004 est.)
Birth rate: 17.22 births/1,000 population (2004 est.)
Death rate: 5.95 deaths/1,000 population (2004 est.)
Net migration rate: 0 migrant(s)/1,000 population (2004 est.)
Sex ratio:
at birth: 1.05 male(s)/female
under 15 years: 1.04 male(s)/female
15-64 years: 1.03 male(s)/female
65 years and over: 0.85 male(s)/female
total population: 1.02 male(s)/female (2004 est.)
Infant mortality rate:
total: 42.62 deaths/1,000 live births
male: 46.3 deaths/1,000 live births
female: 38.76 deaths/1,000 live births (2004 est.)
Life expectancy at birth:
total population: 72.08 years
male: 69.68 years
female: 74.61 years (2004 est.)
Total fertility rate: 1.98 children born/woman (2004 est.)
HIV/AIDS - adult prevalence rate: less than 0.1% - note: no country specific models provided (2001 est.)
HIV/AIDS - people living with HIV/AIDS: NA
HIV/AIDS - deaths: NA
Nationality:
noun: Turk(s)
adjective: Turkish
Ethnic groups: Turkish 80%, Kurdish 20% (estimated)
Religions: Muslim 99.8% (mostly Sunni), other 0.2% (mostly Christians and Jews)
Languages: Turkish (official), Kurdish, Arabic, Armenian, Greek
Literacy:
definition: age 15 and over can read and write
total population: 86.5%
male: 94.3%
female: 78.7% (2003 est.)

Introduction

Background: Present-day Turkey was created in 1923 from the Turkish remnants of the Ottoman Empire. Soon thereafter, the country instituted secular laws to replace traditional religious fiats. In 1945 Turkey joined the UN, and in 1952 it became a member of NATO. Turkey intervened militarily on Cyprus in 1974 to protect Turkish Cypriots and prevent a Greek takeover of the island; the northern 37 percent of the island remains under Turkish Cypriot control. Relations between the Turkey and Greece have improved greatly over the past few years. In 1984, the Kurdistan Workers' Party (PKK), a Marxist-Leninist, separatist group, initiated an insurgency in southeast Turkey, often using terrorist tactics to try to attain its goal of an independent Kurdistan. The group - whose leader, Abdullah OCALAN, was captured in Kenya in February 1999 - has largely ceased violent attacks since it declared a unilateral cease-fire in September 1999. Nonetheless, occasional clashes have occurred between Turkish security forces and armed PKK militants, many of whom remain in northern Iraq. In April 2002, the PKK changed its name to the Kurdistan Freedom and Democracy Congress (KADEK). In November 2003, the group changed names again, becoming the Kurdistan People's Congress (KHK).

Geography

Location: southeastern Europe and southwestern Asia (that portion of Turkey west of the Bosporus is geographically part of Europe), bordering the Black Sea, between Bulgaria and Georgia, and bordering the Aegean Sea and the Mediterranean Sea, between Greece and Syria
Geographic coordinates: 39 00 N, 35 00 E
Map references: Middle East
Area:
total: 780,580 sq km
land: 770,760 sq km

water: 9,820 sq km
Area - comparative: slightly larger than Texas
Land boundaries:
total: 2,648 km
border countries: Armenia 268 km, Azerbaijan 9 km, Bulgaria 240 km, Georgia 252 km, Greece 206 km, Iran 499 km, Iraq 352 km, Syria 822 km
Coastline: 7,200 km
Maritime claims:
territorial sea: 6 NM in the Aegean Sea; 12 NM in Black Sea and in Mediterranean Sea
exclusive economic zone: in Black Sea only: to the maritime boundary agreed upon with the former USSR
Climate: temperate; hot, dry summers with mild, wet winters; harsher in interior
Terrain: high central plateau (Anatolia); narrow coastal plain; several mountain ranges
Elevation extremes:
lowest point: Mediterranean Sea 0 m
highest point: Mount Ararat 5,166 m
Natural resources: antimony, coal, chromium, mercury, copper, borate, sulfur, iron ore, arable land, hydropower
Land use:
arable land: 34.53%
permanent crops: 3.36%
other: 62.11% (1998 est.)
Irrigated land: 42,000 sq km (1998 est.)
Natural hazards: very severe earthquakes, especially in northern Turkey, along an arc extending from the Sea of Marmara to Lake Van
Environment - current issues: water pollution from dumping of chemicals and detergents; air pollution, particularly in urban areas; deforestation; concern for oil spills from increasing Bosporus ship traffic
Environment - international agreements:
party to: Air Pollution, Antarctic Treaty, Biodiversity, Desertification, Endangered Species, Hazardous Wastes, Ozone Layer Protection, Ship Pollution, Wetlands
signed, but not ratified: Environmental Modification

Turkey *(continued)*

Government

Country name:
conventional long form: Republic of Turkey
conventional short form: Turkey
local long form: Turkiye Cumhuriyeti
local short form: Turkiye
Government type: republican parliamentary democracy
Capital: Ankara
Administrative divisions: 81 provinces (iller, singular - il); Adana, Adiyaman, Afyon, Agri, Aksaray, Amasya, Ankara, Antalya, Ardahan, Artvin, Aydin, Balikesir, Bartin, Batman, Bayburt, Bilecik, Bingol, Bitlis, Bolu, Burdur, Bursa, Canakkale, Cankiri, Corum, Denizli, Diyarbakir, Duzce, Edirne, Elazig, Erzincan, Erzurum, Eskisehir, Gaziantep, Giresun, Gumushane, Hakkari, Hatay, Igdir, Isparta, Istanbul, Izmir, Kahramanmaras, Karabuk, Karaman, Kars, Kastamonu, Kayseri, Kilis, Kirikkale, Kirklareli, Kirsehir, Kocaeli, Konya, Kutahya, Malatya, Manisa, Mardin, Mersin, Mugla, Mus, Nevsehir, Nigde, Ordu, Osmaniye, Rize, Sakarya, Samsun, Sanliurfa, Siirt, Sinop, Sirnak, Sivas, Tekirdag, Tokat, Trabzon, Tunceli, Usak, Van, Yalova, Yozgat, Zonguldak
Independence: 29 October 1923 (successor state to the Ottoman Empire)
National holiday: Independence Day, 29 October (1923)
Constitution: 7 November 1982
Legal system: derived from various European continental legal systems; accepts compulsory ICJ jurisdiction, with reservations
Suffrage: 18 years of age; universal
Executive branch:
chief of state: President Ahmet Necdet SEZER (since 16 May 2000)
head of government: Prime Minister Recep Tayyip ERDOGAN (14 March 2003)
cabinet: Council of Ministers appointed by the president on the nomination of the prime minister
note: a National Security Council serves as an advisory body to the government composed of top military and cabinet officials and presided over by the president
elections: president elected by the National Assembly for a seven-year term; election last held 5 May 2000 (next to be held NA May 2007); prime minister and deputy prime ministers appointed by the president
election results: Ahmed Necdet SEZER elected president on the third ballot; percent of National Assembly vote - 60%
note: president must have a two-thirds majority of the National Assembly on the first two ballots and a simple majority on the third ballot
Legislative branch: unicameral Grand National Assembly of Turkey or Turkiye Buyuk Millet Meclisi (550 seats; members are elected by popular vote to serve five-year terms)
elections: last held 3 November 2002 (next to be held NA 2007); note - a special rerun of the General Election in the province of Siirt on 9 March 2003

resulted in the election of Recep Tayyip ERDOGAN to a seat in parliament, a prerequisite for becoming prime minister on 13 March 2003
election results: percent of vote by party - AKP 34.3%, CHP 19.4%, DYP 9.6%, MHP 8.3%, ANAP 5.1%, DSP 1.1%, and others; seats by party - AKP 363, CHP 178, independents 9; note - parties surpassing the 10% threshold are entitled to parliamentary seats; seats by party as of 15 October 2003 - AKP 368, CHP 175, DYP 3, LDP 1, independents 3
Judicial branch: Constitutional Court (judges are appointed by the president); Court of Appeals and Council of State (judges are elected by the Supreme Council of Judges and Prosecutors)
Political parties and leaders: Democratic Left Party or DSP [Bulent ECEVIT]; Democratic People's Party or DEHAP [Tuncer BAKIRHAN]; Justice and Development Party or AKP [Recep Tayip ERDOGAN]; Liberal Democratic Party or LDP [Emin SIRIN]; Motherland Party or ANAP [Nesrin NAS]; Nationalist Action Party or MHP [Devlet BAHCELI]; New Turkey Party or YTP [Ismail CEM]; Republican People's Party or CHP [Deniz BAYKAL]; Saadet Party (sometimes translated as Contentment Party) or SP [Necmettin ERBEKAN]; Social Democratic People's Party or SHP [Murat KARAYALCIN]; True Path Party (sometimes translated as Correct Way Party) or DYP [Mehmet AGAR]; Young Party or GP [Cem UZAN]
Political pressure groups and leaders:
Confederation of Public Sector Unions or KESK [Sami EVREN]; Confederation of Revolutionary Workers Unions or DISK [Suleyman CELEBI]; Independent Industrialists' and Businessmen's Association or MUSIAD [Ali BAYRAMOGLU]; Moral Rights Workers Union or Hak-Is [Salim USLU]; Turkish Industrialists' and Businessmen's Association or TUSIAD [Omer SABANCI]; Turkish Confederation of Employers' Unions or TISK [Refik BAYDUR]; Turkish Confederation of Labor or Turk-Is [Salih KILIC]; Turkish Confederation of Tradesmen and Craftsmen or TESK [Dervis GUNDAY]; Turkish Union of Chambers of Commerce and Commodity Exchanges or TOBB [M. Rifat HISARCIKLIOGLU]
International organization participation: AsDB, Australia Group, BIS, BSEC, CE, CERN (observer), EAPC, EBRD, ECO, EU (applicant), FAO, IAEA, IBRD, ICAO, ICC, ICFTU, ICRM, IDA, IDB, IEA, IFAD, IFC, IFRCS, IHO, ILO, IMF, IMO, Interpol, IOC, IOM (observer), ISO, ITU, NATO, NEA, NSG, OAS (observer), OECD, OIC, OPCW, OSCE, PCA, UN, UNCTAD, UNESCO, UNHCR, UNIDO, UNMIK, UNMIL, UNMISET, UNOMIG, UNRWA, UPU, WCO, WEU (associate), WFTU, WHO, WIPO, WMO, WToO, WTrO, ZC
Diplomatic representation in the US:
chief of mission: Ambassador Dr. Osman Faruk LOGOGLU
chancery: 2525 Massachusetts Avenue NW, Washington, DC 20008
telephone: [1] (202) 612-6700
FAX: [1] (202) 612-6744

consulate(s) general: Chicago, Houston, Los Angeles, and New York
Diplomatic representation from the US:
chief of mission: Ambassador Eric S. EDELMAN
embassy: 110 Ataturk Boulevard, Kavaklidere, 06100 Ankara
mailing address: PSC 93, Box 5000, APO AE 09823
telephone: [90] (312) 455-5555
FAX: [90] (312) 467-0019
consulate(s) general: Istanbul
consulate(s): Adana; note - there is a Consular Agent in Izmir
Flag description: red with a vertical white crescent (the closed portion is toward the hoist side) and white five-pointed star centered just outside the crescent opening

Economy

Economy - overview: Turkey's dynamic economy is a complex mix of modern industry and commerce along with a traditional agriculture sector that in 2001 still accounted for 40% of employment. It has a strong and rapidly growing private sector, yet the state still plays a major role in basic industry, banking, transport, and communication. The most important industry - and largest exporter - is textiles and clothing, which is almost entirely in private hands. In recent years the economic situation has been marked by erratic economic growth and serious imbalances. Real GNP growth has exceeded 6% in many years, but this strong expansion has been interrupted by sharp declines in output in 1994, 1999, and 2001. Meanwhile, the public sector fiscal deficit has regularly exceeded 10% of GDP - due in large part to the huge burden of interest payments, which accounted for more than 40% of central government spending in 2003. Inflation, in recent years in the high double-digit range, fell to 18.4% in 2003. Perhaps because of these problems, foreign direct investment in Turkey remains low - less than $1 billion annually. In late 2000 and early 2001 a growing trade deficit and serious weaknesses in the banking sector plunged the economy into crisis - forcing Turkey to float the lira and pushing the country into recession. Results in 2002-03 were much better, because of strong financial support from the IMF and tighter fiscal policy. Healthy growth is likely to continue through at least the first half of 2004.
GDP: purchasing power parity - $455.3 billion (2003 est.)
GDP - real growth rate: 5% (2003 est.)
GDP - per capita: purchasing power parity - $6,700 (2003 est.)
GDP - composition by sector:
agriculture: 11.9%
industry: 29.6%
services: 58.5% (2002 est.)
Population below poverty line: 18% (2001)
Household income or consumption by percentage share:
lowest 10%: 2.3%
highest 10%: 32.3% (1994)

Turkey (continued)

Distribution of family income - Gini index: 44 (2002)
Inflation rate (consumer prices): 18.4% (2003 est.)
Labor force: 23.8 million
note: about 1.2 million Turks work abroad (2001 3rd quarter)
Labor force - by occupation: agriculture 39.7%, services 37.9%, industry 22.4% (3rd quarter, 2001)
Unemployment rate: 11.3% (plus underemployment of 6.1%) (2003 est.)
Budget:
revenues: $42.4 billion
expenditures: $69.1 billion, including capital expenditures of $NA (2001)
Industries: textiles, food processing, autos, mining (coal, chromite, copper, boron), steel, petroleum, construction, lumber, paper
Industrial production growth rate: 6.7% (2003 est.)
Electricity - production: 116.6 billion kWh (2001)
Electricity - production by source:
fossil fuel: 79.3%
hydro: 20.4%
nuclear: 0%
other: 0.3% (2001)
Electricity - consumption: 112.6 billion kWh (2001)
Electricity - exports: 433 million kWh (2001)
Electricity - imports: 4.579 billion kWh (2001)
Oil - production: 48,000 bbl/day (2001 est.)
Oil - consumption: 619,500 bbl/day (2001 est.)
Oil - exports: 46,110 bbl/day (2001)
Oil - imports: 616,500 bbl/day (2001)
Oil - proved reserves: 288.4 million bbl (1 January 2002)
Natural gas - production: 312 million cu m (2001 est.)
Natural gas - consumption: 15.94 billion cu m (2001 est.)
Natural gas - exports: 0 cu m (2001 est.)
Natural gas - imports: 15.75 billion cu m (2001 est.)
Natural gas - proved reserves: 8.685 billion cu m (1 January 2002)
Agriculture - products: tobacco, cotton, grain, olives, sugar beets, pulse, citrus; livestock
Exports: $49.12 billion f.o.b. (2003 est.)
Exports - commodities: apparel, foodstuffs, textiles, metal manufactures, transport equipment
Exports - partners: Germany 16.6%, US 9.2%, UK 8.5%, Italy 6.4%, France 6% (2002)
Imports: $62.43 billion f.o.b. (2003 est.)
Imports - commodities: machinery, chemicals, semi-finished goods, fuels, transport equipment
Imports - partners: Germany 13.7%, Italy 8.1%, Russia 7.6%, US 6%, France 5.9%, UK 4.8%, Switzerland 4.1% (2002)
Debt - external: $141.3 billion (Yearend 2003)
Economic aid - recipient: ODA, $300 million (2000)
Currency: Turkish lira (TRL)
Currency code: TRL

Exchange rates: Turkish liras per US dollar - NA (2003), 1,507,230 (2002), 1,225,590 (2001), 625,218 (2000), 418,783 (1999), 151,865 (1997)
Fiscal year: calendar year

Communications

Telephones - main lines in use: 18,914,900(2002)
Telephones - mobile cellular: 23,374,400 (2002)
Telephone system:
general assessment: undergoing rapid modernization and expansion, especially with cellular telephones
domestic: additional digital exchanges are permitting a rapid increase in subscribers; the construction of a network of technologically advanced intercity trunk lines, using both fiber-optic cable and digital microwave radio relay is facilitating communication between urban centers; remote areas are reached by a domestic satellite system; the number of subscribers to mobile cellular telephone service is growing rapidly
international: country code - 90; international service is provided by three submarine fiber-optic cables in the Mediterranean and Black Seas, linking Turkey with Italy, Greece, Israel, Bulgaria, Romania, and Russia; also by 12 Intelsat earth stations, and by 328 mobile satellite terminals in the Inmarsat and Eutelsat systems (2002)
Radio broadcast stations: AM 16, FM 107, shortwave 6 (2001)
Television broadcast stations: 635 (plus 2,934 repeaters) (1995)
Internet country code: .tr
Internet hosts: 154,585 (2002)
Internet users: 4.9 million (2002)

Transportation

Railways:
total: 8,607 km
standard gauge: 8,607 km 1.435-m gauge (2,131 km electrified) (2002)
Highways:
total: 385,960 km
paved: 131,226 km (including 1,749 km of expressways)
unpaved: 254,734 km (1999)
Waterways: 1,200 km (approximately)
Pipelines: gas 3,177 km; oil 3,562 km (2003)
Ports and harbors: Gemlik, Hopa, Iskenderun, Istanbul, Izmir, Kocaeli (Izmit), Icel (Mersin), Samsun, Trabzon
Merchant marine:
total: 508 ships (1,000 GRT or over) 4,666,895 GRT/ 7,311,504 DWT
by type: bulk 111, cargo 229, chemical tanker 46, combination bulk 1, combination ore/oil 2, container 34, liquefied gas 6, passenger 1, passenger/cargo 1, petroleum tanker 36, refrigerated cargo 4, roll on/roll off 26, short-sea/passenger 8, specialized tanker 3
foreign-owned: Belize 1, Cambodia 1, China 1, Cyprus 4, Greece 1, Italy 3, Liberia 1, Monaco 1, Switzerland 1, Thailand 1, United Kingdom 9
registered in other countries: 243 (2003 est.)

Airports: 120 (2003 est.)
Airports - with paved runways:
total: 87
over 3,047 m: 16
2,438 to 3,047 m: 30
1,524 to 2,437 m: 20
914 to 1,523 m: 17
under 914 m: 4 (2003 est.)
Airports - with unpaved runways:
total: 33
over 3,047 m: 1
2,438 to 3,047 m: 1
1,524 to 2,437 m: 2
914 to 1,523 m: 8
under 914 m: 21 (2003 est.)
Heliports: 14 (2003 est.)

Military

Military branches: Turkish Armed Forces (TSK): Land Forces, Naval Forces Command (includes Naval Air and Naval Infantry), Air Force, Coast Guard Command, Gendarmerie (Jandarma)
Military manpower - military age: 20 years of age (2004 est.)
Military manpower - availability:
males age 15-49: 19,828,702 (2004 est.)
Military manpower - fit for military service:
males age 15-49: 11,965,262 (2004 est.)
Military manpower - reaching military age annually:
males: 680,673 (2004 est.)
Military expenditures - dollar figure: $12.155 billion (2003)
Military expenditures - percent of GDP: 5.3% (2003)

Transnational Issues

Disputes - international: complex maritime, air, and territorial disputes with Greece in the Aegean Sea; Cyprus question remains with Greece; Syria and Iraq protest Turkish hydrological projects to control upper Euphrates waters; Turkey has expressed concern over the status of Kurds in Iraq; border with Armenia remains closed over Nagorno-Karabakh
Illicit drugs: key transit route for Southwest Asian heroin to Western Europe and - to a far lesser extent the US - via air, land, and sea routes; major Turkish, Iranian, and other international trafficking organizations operate out of Istanbul; laboratories to convert imported morphine base into heroin are in remote regions of Turkey as well as near Istanbul; government maintains strict controls over areas of legal opium poppy cultivation and output of poppy straw concentrate

Turkmenistan

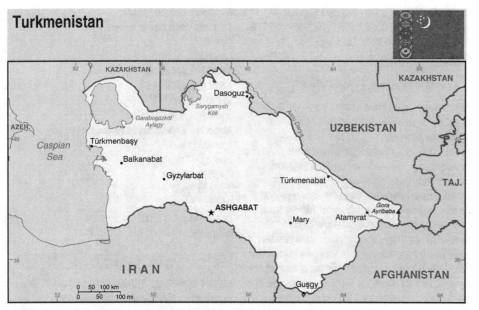

Introduction

Background: Annexed by Russia between 1865 and 1885, Turkmenistan became a Soviet republic in 1925. It achieved its independence upon the dissolution of the USSR in 1991. President NIYAZOV retains absolute control over the country and opposition is not tolerated. Extensive hydrocarbon/ natural gas reserves could prove a boon to this underdeveloped country if extraction and delivery projects can be worked out.

Geography

Location: Central Asia, bordering the Caspian Sea, between Iran and Kazakhstan
Geographic coordinates: 40 00 N, 60 00 E
Map references: Asia
Area:
total: 488,100 sq km
land: 488,100 sq km
water: negl.
Area - comparative: slightly larger than California
Land boundaries:
total: 3,736 km
border countries: Afghanistan 744 km, Iran 992 km, Kazakhstan 379 km, Uzbekistan 1,621 km
Coastline: 0 km; note - Turkmenistan borders the Caspian Sea (1,768 km)
Climate: subtropical desert
Terrain: flat-to-rolling sandy desert with dunes rising to mountains in the south; low mountains along border with Iran; borders Caspian Sea in west
Elevation extremes:
lowest point: Vpadina Akchanaya -81 m; note - Sarygamysh Koli is a lake in northern Turkmenistan with a water level that fluctuates above and below the elevation of Vpadina Akchanaya (the lake has dropped as low as -110 m)
highest point: Gora Ayribaba 3,139 m
Natural resources: petroleum, natural gas, coal, sulfur, salt

Land use:
arable land: 3.6%
permanent crops: 0.1%
other: 96.3% (2003 est.)
Irrigated land: 17,500 sq km (2003 est.)
Natural hazards: NA
Environment - current issues: contamination of soil and groundwater with agricultural chemicals, pesticides; salination, water-logging of soil due to poor irrigation methods; Caspian Sea pollution; diversion of a large share of the flow of the Amu Darya into irrigation contributes to that river's inability to replenish the Aral Sea; desertification
Environment - international agreements:
party to: Biodiversity, Climate Change, Climate Change-Kyoto Protocol, Desertification, Hazardous Wastes, Ozone Layer Protection
signed, but not ratified: none of the selected agreements
Geography - note: landlocked; the western and central low-lying, desolate portions of the country make up the great Garagum (Kara-Kum) desert, which occupies over 80% of the country; eastern part is plateau

People

Population: 4,863,169 (July 2004 est.)
Age structure:
0-14 years: 36.2% (male 904,627; female 857,601)
15-64 years: 59.7% (male 1,423,836; female 1,477,224)
65 years and over: 4.1% (male 76,670; female 123,211) (2004 est.)
Median age:
total: 21.3 years
male: 20.4 years
female: 22.2 years (2004 est.)
Population growth rate: 1.81% (2004 est.)
Birth rate: 27.82 births/1,000 population (2004 est.)
Death rate: 8.82 deaths/1,000 population (2004 est.)

Net migration rate: -0.86 migrant(s)/1,000 population (2004 est.)
Sex ratio:
at birth: 1.05 male(s)/female
under 15 years: 1.06 male(s)/female
15-64 years: 0.96 male(s)/female
65 years and over: 0.62 male(s)/female
total population: 0.98 male(s)/female (2004 est.)
Infant mortality rate:
total: 73.13 deaths/1,000 live births
male: 76.9 deaths/1,000 live births
female: 69.16 deaths/1,000 live births (2004 est.)
Life expectancy at birth:
total population: 61.29 years
male: 57.87 years
female: 64.88 years (2004 est.)
Total fertility rate: 3.45 children born/woman (2004 est.)
HIV/AIDS - adult prevalence rate: less than 0.1% (2004 est.)
HIV/AIDS - people living with HIV/AIDS: less than 100 (2004 est.)
HIV/AIDS - deaths: less than 100 (2004 est.)
Nationality:
noun: Turkmen(s)
adjective: Turkmen
Ethnic groups: Turkmen 85%, Uzbek 5%, Russian 4%, other 6% (2003)
Religions: Muslim 89%, Eastern Orthodox 9%, unknown 2%
Languages: Turkmen 72%, Russian 12%, Uzbek 9%, other 7%
Literacy:
definition: age 15 and over can read and write
total population: 98%
male: 99%
female: 97% (1989 est.)

Government

Country name:
conventional long form: none
conventional short form: Turkmenistan
local long form: none
local short form: Turkmenistan
former: Turkmen Soviet Socialist Republic
Government type: republic
Capital: Ashgabat
Administrative divisions: 5 provinces (welayatlar, singular - welayat): Ahal Welayaty (Ashgabat), Balkan Welayaty (Balkanabat), Dashoguz Welayaty, Lebap Welayaty (Turkmenabat), Mary Welayaty
note: administrative divisions have the same names as their administrative centers (exceptions have the administrative center name following in parentheses)
Independence: 27 October 1991 (from the Soviet Union)
National holiday: Independence Day, 27 October (1991)
Constitution: adopted 18 May 1992
Legal system: based on civil law system
Suffrage: 18 years of age; universal

Turkmenistan (continued)

Executive branch:

chief of state: President and Chairman of the Cabinet of Ministers Saparmurat NIYAZOV (since 27 October 1990, when the first direct presidential election occurred); note - the president is both the chief of state and head of government

head of government: President and Chairman of the Cabinet of Ministers Saparmurat NIYAZOV (since 27 October 1990, when the first direct presidential election occurred); note - the president is both the chief of state and head of government

cabinet: Council of Ministers appointed by the president

note: NIYAZOV's term in office was extended indefinitely on 28 December 1999 by the Assembly (Majlis) during a session of the People's Council (Halk Maslahaty)

elections: president elected by popular vote for a five-year term; election last held 21 June 1992 (next to be held NA); note - President NIYAZOV was unanimously approved as president for life by the Assembly on 28 December 1999); deputy chairmen of the cabinet of ministers are appointed by the president

election results: Saparmurat NIYAZOV elected president without opposition; percent of vote - Saparmurat NIYAZOV 99.5%

Legislative branch: under the 1992 constitution, there are two parliamentary bodies, a unicameral People's Council or Halk Maslahaty (supreme legislative body of up to 2,500 delegates, some of which are elected by popular vote and some of which are appointed; meets at least yearly) and a unicameral Assembly or Majlis (50 seats; members are elected by popular vote to serve five-year terms)

elections: People's Council - NA; Assembly - last held 12 December 1999 (next to be held NA 2004)

election results: Assembly - percent of vote by party - NA%; seats by party - NA; note - all 50 elected officials preapproved by President NIYAZOV; most are from the DPT

note: in late 2003, a new law was adopted, reducing the powers of the Majlis and making the Halk Maslahaty the supreme legislative organ; the Halk Maslahaty can now legally dissolve the Majlis, and the president is now able to participate in the Majlis as its supreme leader; the Majlis can no longer adopt or amend the constitution, or announce referendums or its elections; since the president is both the "Chairman for Life" of the Halk Maslahaty and the supreme leader of the Majlis, the 2003 law has the effect of making the president the sole authority of both the executive and legislative branches of government

Judicial branch: Supreme Court (judges are appointed by the president)

Political parties and leaders: Democratic Party of Turkmenistan or DPT [Saparmurat NIYAZOV]

note: formal opposition parties are outlawed; unofficial, small opposition movements exist underground or in foreign countries; the two most prominent opposition groups-in-exile have been Gundogar and Erkin; Gundogar was led by former Foreign Minister Boris SHIKHUMRADOV until his

arrest and imprisonment in the wake of the 25 November 2002 assassination attempt on President NIYAZOV; Erkin is led by former Foreign Minister Abdy KULIEV and is based out of Moscow; the Union of Democratic Forces, a coalition of opposition-in-exile groups, is based in Europe

Political pressure groups and leaders: NA

International organization participation: AsDB, CIS, EAPC, EBRD, ECO, FAO, G-77, IBRD, ICAO, ICRM, IDB, IFC, IFRCS, ILO, IMF, IMO, IOC, IOM (observer), ISO (correspondent), ITU, NAM, OIC, OPCW, OSCE, PFP, UN, UNCTAD, UNESCO, UNIDO, UPU, WCO, WFTU, WHO, WIPO, WMO, WToO

Diplomatic representation in the US:

chief of mission: Ambassador Mered Bairamovich ORAZOV

chancery: 2207 Massachusetts Avenue NW, Washington, DC 20008

telephone: [1] (202) 588-1500

FAX: [1] (202) 588-0697

Diplomatic representation from the US:

chief of mission: Ambassador Tracey A. JACOBSON

embassy: 9 Pushkin Street, Ashgabat, Turkmenistan 774000

mailing address: use embassy street address

telephone: [9] (9312) 35-00-45

FAX: [9] (9312) 39-26-14

Flag description: green field with a vertical red stripe near the hoist side, containing five carpet guls (designs used in producing rugs) stacked above two crossed olive branches similar to the olive branches on the UN flag; a white crescent moon and five white stars appear in the upper corner of the field just to the fly side of the red stripe

Economy

Economy - overview: Turkmenistan is largely desert country with intensive agriculture in irrigated oases and large gas and oil resources. One-half of its irrigated land is planted in cotton, making it at one time the world's tenth-largest producer. Poor harvests in recent years have led to a nearly 46% decline in cotton exports. With an authoritarian ex-Communist regime in power and a tribally based social structure, Turkmenistan has taken a cautious approach to economic reform, hoping to use gas and cotton sales to sustain its inefficient economy. Privatization goals remain limited. In 1998-2003, Turkmenistan suffered from the continued lack of adequate export routes for natural gas and from obligations on extensive short-term external debt. At the same time, however, total exports rose by 38% in 2003, largely because of higher international oil and gas prices. Overall prospects in the near future are discouraging because of widespread internal poverty, the burden of foreign debt, and the unwillingness of the government to adopt market-oriented reforms. However, Turkmenistan's cooperation with the international community in transporting humanitarian aid to Afghanistan may foreshadow a change in the

atmosphere for foreign investment, aid, and technological support. Turkmenistan's economic statistics are state secrets, and GDP and other figures are subject to wide margins of error. In particular, the 20% rate of GDP growth is a guess.

GDP: purchasing power parity - $27.07 billion (2003 est.)

GDP - real growth rate: 20% (2003 est.)

GDP - per capita: purchasing power parity - $5,700 (2003 est.)

GDP - composition by sector:

agriculture: 27%

industry: 50%

services: 23% (2001 est.)

Population below poverty line: 34.4% (2001 est.)

Household income or consumption by percentage share:

lowest 10%: 2.6%

highest 10%: 31.7% (1998)

Distribution of family income - Gini index: 40.8 (1998)

Inflation rate (consumer prices): 11% (2003 est.)

Labor force: 2.34 million (1996)

Labor force - by occupation: agriculture 48%, industry 15%, services 37% (1998 est.)

Unemployment rate: NA%

Budget:

revenues: $588.6 million

expenditures: $658.2 million, including capital expenditures of $NA (1999 est.)

Industries: natural gas, oil, petroleum products, textiles, food processing

Industrial production growth rate: 14% (2003 est.)

Electricity - production: 10.18 billion kWh (2001)

Electricity - production by source:

fossil fuel: 99.9%

hydro: 0.1%

nuclear: 0%

other: 0% (2001)

Electricity - consumption: 8.509 billion kWh (2001)

Electricity - exports: 980 million kWh (2001)

Electricity - imports: 20 million kWh (2001)

Oil - production: 162,500 bbl/day (2001 est.)

Oil - consumption: 63,000 bbl/day (2001 est.)

Oil - exports: NA

Oil - imports: NA

Oil - proved reserves: 273 million bbl (1 January 2002)

Natural gas - production: 48.2 billion cu m (2001 est.)

Natural gas - consumption: 9.6 billion cu m (2001 est.)

Natural gas - exports: 38.6 billion cu m (2001 est.)

Natural gas - imports: 0 cu m (2001 est.)

Natural gas - proved reserves: 1.43 trillion cu m (1 January 2002)

Agriculture - products: cotton, grain; livestock

Exports: $3.355 billion f.o.b. (2003 est.)

Exports - commodities: gas 57%, oil 26%, cotton fiber 3%, textiles 2% (2001)

Exports - partners: Ukraine 49.7%, Italy 18%, Iran 13.1%, Turkey 6.2% (2002)

Turkmenistan *(continued)*

Imports: $2.472 billion f.o.b. (2003 est.)
Imports - commodities: machinery and equipment 60%, foodstuffs 15% (1999)
Imports - partners: Russia 19.8%, Turkey 12.9%, Ukraine 11.7%, UAE 10%, US 7.5%, China 6%, Germany 5.7%, Iran 4.5% (2002)
Debt - external: $2.4 billion to $5 billion (2001 est.)
Economic aid - recipient: $16 million from the US (2001)
Currency: Turkmen manat (TMM)
Currency code: TMM
Exchange rates: Turkmen manats per US dollar - 5,200 (2003), 5,200 (2002), 5,200 (2001), 5,200 (2000), 5,200 (1999);note - the official exchange rate has not varied for the last six years; the unofficial rate has fluctuated slightly, hovering around 21,000 manats to the dollar
Fiscal year: calendar year

Communications

Telephones - main lines in use: 374,000 (2002)
Telephones - mobile cellular: 8,200 (2002)
Telephone system:
general assessment: poorly developed
domestic: NA
international: country code - 993; linked by cable and microwave radio relay to other CIS republics and to other countries by leased connections to the Moscow international gateway switch; a new telephone link from Ashgabat to Iran has been established; a new exchange in Ashgabat switches international traffic through Turkey via Intelsat; satellite earth stations - 1 Orbita and 1 Intelsat
Radio broadcast stations: AM 16, FM 8, shortwave 2 (1998)
Television broadcast stations: 3 (much programming relayed from Russia and Turkey) (1997)
Internet country code: .tm
Internet hosts: 2,020 (2002)
Internet users: 8,000 (2002)

Transportation

Railways:
total: 2,440 km
broad gauge: 2,440 km 1.520-m gauge (2002)
Highways:
total: 24,000 km
paved: 19,488 km
unpaved: 4,512 km (1999 est.)
Waterways: the Amu Darya is an important inland waterway for Turkmenistan, as is the man-made Kara Kum canal
Pipelines: gas 6,634 km; oil 853 km (2003)
Ports and harbors: Turkmenbasy
Merchant marine:
total: 2 ships (1,000 GRT or over) 6,873 GRT/8,345 DWT
by type: combination ore/oil 1, petroleum tanker 1
registered in other countries: 2 (2003 est.)
Airports: 69 (2003 est.)

Airports - with paved runways:
total: 24
over 3,047 m: 1
2,438 to 3,047 m: 12
1,524 to 2,437 m: 8
914 to 1,523 m: 2
under 914 m: 1 (2003 est.)
Airports - with unpaved runways:
total: 45
2,438 to 3,047 m: 1
1,524 to 2,437 m: 1
914 to 1,523 m: 7
under 914 m: 36 (2003 est.)
Heliports: 1 (2003 est.)

Military

Military branches: Ministry of Defense (Army, Air and Air Defense, Navy, Border Troops, and Internal Troops), National Guard
Military manpower - military age: 18 years of age (2004 est.)
Military manpower - availability:
males age 15-49: 1,272,436 (2004 est.)
Military manpower - fit for military service:
males age 15-49: 1,031,806 (2004 est.)
Military manpower - reaching military age annually:
males: 55,866 (2004 est.)
Military expenditures - dollar figure: $90 million (FY99)
Military expenditures - percent of GDP: 3.4% (FY99)

Transnational Issues

Disputes - international: prolonged regional drought creates water-sharing difficulties for Amu Darya river states; talks resume with Kazakhstan on dividing the seabed in 2004 as both sides anticipate an ICJ decision on contested oilfields in the middle of the Caspian; demarcation of land boundary with Kazakhstan to commence in 2004
Illicit drugs: transit country for Afghan narcotics bound for Russian and, to a lesser extent, Western European markets; limited illicit cultivation of opium poppy for domestic consumption; small-scale government-run eradication of illicit crops; transit point for heroin precursor chemicals bound for Afghanistan

Turks and Caicos Islands
(overseas territory of the UK)

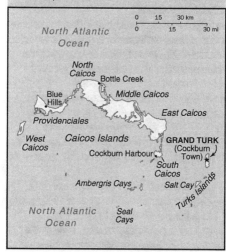

Introduction

Background: The islands were part of the UK's Jamaican colony until 1962, when they assumed the status of a separate crown colony upon Jamaica's independence. The governor of The Bahamas oversaw affairs from 1965 to 1973. With Bahamian independence, the islands received a separate governor in 1973. Although independence was agreed upon for 1982, the policy was reversed and the islands remain a British overseas territory.

Geography

Location: Caribbean, two island groups in the North Atlantic Ocean, southeast of The Bahamas, north of Haiti
Geographic coordinates: 21 45 N, 71 35 W
Map references: Central America and the Caribbean
Area:
total: 430 sq km
land: 430 sq km
water: 0 sq km
Area - comparative: 2.5 times the size of Washington, DC
Land boundaries: 0 km
Coastline: 389 km
Maritime claims:
territorial sea: 12 NM
exclusive fishing zone: 200 NM
Climate: tropical; marine; moderated by trade winds; sunny and relatively dry
Terrain: low, flat limestone; extensive marshes and mangrove swamps
Elevation extremes:
lowest point: Caribbean Sea 0 m
highest point: Blue Hills 49 m
Natural resources: spiny lobster, conch

Turks and Caicos Islands *(continued)*

Land use:
arable land: 2.3%
permanent crops: 0%
other: 97.7% (1998 est.)
Irrigated land: NA sq km
Natural hazards: frequent hurricanes
Environment - current issues: limited natural fresh water resources, private cisterns collect rainwater
Geography - note: about 40 islands (eight inhabited)

People

Population: 19,956 (July 2004 est.)
Age structure:
0-14 years: 32.5% (male 3,301; female 3,184)
15-64 years: 63.8% (male 6,696; female 6,036)
65 years and over: 3.7% (male 327; female 412) (2004 est.)
Median age:
total: 27.2 years
male: 27.9 years
female: 26.5 years (2004 est.)
Population growth rate: 3.03% (2004 est.)
Birth rate: 22.85 births/1,000 population (2004 est.)
Death rate: 4.26 deaths/1,000 population (2004 est.)
Net migration rate: 11.68 migrant(s)/1,000 population (2004 est.)
Sex ratio:
at birth: 1.05 male(s)/female
under 15 years: 1.04 male(s)/female
15-64 years: 1.11 male(s)/female
65 years and over: 0.79 male(s)/female
total population: 1.07 male(s)/female (2004 est.)
Infant mortality rate:
total: 16.27 deaths/1,000 live births
male: 18.79 deaths/1,000 live births
female: 13.61 deaths/1,000 live births (2004 est.)
Life expectancy at birth:
total population: 74.25 years
male: 72.05 years
female: 76.57 years (2004 est.)
Total fertility rate: 3.11 children born/woman (2004 est.)
HIV/AIDS - adult prevalence rate: NA%
HIV/AIDS - people living with HIV/AIDS: NA
HIV/AIDS - deaths: NA
Nationality:
noun: none
adjective: none
Ethnic groups: black 90%, mixed, European, or North American 10%
Religions: Baptist 40%, Methodist 16%, Anglican 18%, Church of God 12%, other 14% (1990)
Languages: English (official)
Literacy:
definition: age 15 and over has ever attended school
total population: 98%
male: 99%
female: 98% (1970 est.)

People - note: destination and transit point for illegal Haitian immigrants bound for the Turks and Caicos Islands, Bahamas, and US

Government

Country name:
conventional long form: none
conventional short form: Turks and Caicos Islands
Dependency status: overseas territory of the UK
Government type: NA
Capital: Grand Turk (Cockburn Town)
Administrative divisions: none (overseas territory of the UK)
Independence: none (overseas territory of the UK)
National holiday: Constitution Day, 30 August (1976)
Constitution: introduced 30 August 1976; suspended in 1986; restored and revised 5 March 1988
Legal system: based on laws of England and Wales, with a few adopted from Jamaica and The Bahamas
Suffrage: 18 years of age; universal
Executive branch:
chief of state: Queen ELIZABETH II (since 6 February 1953), represented by Governor Jim POSTON (since 16 December 2002)
head of government: Chief Minister Michael Eugene MISICK (since 15 August 2003)
cabinet: Executive Council consists of three ex officio members and five appointed by the governor from among the members of the Legislative Council
elections: none; the monarch is hereditary; governor appointed by the monarch; following legislative elections, the leader of the majority party is appointed chief minister by the governor
Legislative branch: unicameral Legislative Council (19 seats of which 13 are popularly elected; members serve four-year terms)
elections: last held 24 April 2003 (next to be held in 2007)
election results: percent of vote by party - PDM 53.8%, PNP 46.2%; seats by party - PDM 7, PNP 6; note - in by-elections held 7 August 2003, the PNP gained two seats for a majority of 8 seats; PDM now has 5
Judicial branch: Supreme Court
Political parties and leaders: People's Democratic Movement or PDM [Derek H. TAYLOR]; Progressive National Party or PNP [Michael Eugene MISICK]; United Democratic Party or UDP [Wendal SWANN]
Political pressure groups and leaders: NA
International organization participation: Caricom (associate), CDB, Interpol (subbureau)
Diplomatic representation in the US: none (overseas territory of the UK)
Diplomatic representation from the US: none (overseas territory of the UK)
Flag description: blue, with the flag of the UK in the upper hoist-side quadrant and the colonial shield centered on the outer half of the flag; the shield is yellow and contains a conch shell, lobster, and cactus

Economy

Economy - overview: The Turks and Caicos economy is based on tourism, fishing, and offshore financial services. Most capital goods and food for domestic consumption are imported. The US is the leading source of tourists, accounting for more than half of the 93,000 visitors in the late 1990s. Major sources of government revenue include fees from offshore financial activities and customs receipts. Tourism fell by 6% in 2002.
GDP: purchasing power parity - $231 million (2000 est.)
GDP - real growth rate: 4.9% (2000 est.)
GDP - per capita: purchasing power parity - $9,600 (2000 est.)
GDP - composition by sector:
agriculture: NA%
industry: NA%
services: NA% (2001 est.)
Population below poverty line: NA%
Household income or consumption by percentage share:
lowest 10%: NA%
highest 10%: NA%
Inflation rate (consumer prices): 4% (1995)
Labor force: 4,848 (1990 est.)
Labor force - by occupation: about 33% in government and 20% in agriculture and fishing; significant numbers in tourism, financial, and other services
Unemployment rate: 10% (1997 est.)
Budget:
revenues: $47 million
expenditures: $33.6 million, including capital expenditures of $NA (1997-98 est.)
Industries: tourism, offshore financial services
Industrial production growth rate: NA%
Electricity - production: 5 million kWh (2001)
Electricity - production by source:
fossil fuel: 100%
hydro: 0%
nuclear: 0%
other: 0% (2001)
Electricity - consumption: 4.65 million kWh (2001)
Electricity - exports: 0 kWh (2001)
Electricity - imports: 0 kWh (2001)
Oil - production: 0 bbl/day NA (2001 est.)
Oil - consumption: 0 bbl/day NA bbl/day (2001 est.)
Oil - exports: NA
Oil - imports: NA
Agriculture - products: corn, beans, cassava (tapioca), citrus fruits; fish
Exports: $169.2 million (2000)
Exports - commodities: lobster, dried and fresh conch, conch shells
Exports - partners: US, UK
Imports: $175.6 million (2000)
Imports - commodities: food and beverages, tobacco, clothing, manufactures, construction materials

Imports - partners: US, UK
Debt - external: $NA (2002 est.)
Economic aid - recipient: $4.1 million (1997)
Currency: US dollar (USD)
Currency code: USD
Exchange rates: the US dollar is used
Fiscal year: calendar year

Communications

Telephones - main lines in use: 5,700 (2002)
Telephones - mobile cellular: 0 (1994)
Telephone system:
general assessment: fair cable and radiotelephone services
domestic: NA
international: country code - 1-649; 2 submarine cables; satellite earth station - 1 Intelsat (Atlantic Ocean)
Radio broadcast stations: AM 2, FM 7, shortwave 0 (2004)
Television broadcast stations: 0 (broadcasts from The Bahamas are received; 2 cable television networks) (2004)
Internet country code: .tc
Internet users: NA

Transportation

Railways: 0 km
Highways:
total: 121 km
paved: 24 km
unpaved: 97 km (2000)
Waterways: none
Ports and harbors: Grand Turk, Providenciales
Merchant marine: none
Airports: 8 (2003 est.)
Airports - with paved runways:
total: 6
1,524 to 2,437 m: 3
914 to 1,523 m: 1
under 914 m: 2 (2003 est.)
Airports - with unpaved runways:
total: 2
under 914 m: 2 (2003 est.)

Military

Military - note: defense is the responsibility of the UK

Transnational Issues

Disputes - international: have received Haitians fleeing economic collapse and civil unrest
Illicit drugs: transshipment point for South American narcotics destined for the US and Europe

Tuvalu

Introduction

Background: In 1974, ethnic differences within the British colony of the Gilbert and Ellice Islands caused the Polynesians of the Ellice Islands to vote for separation from the Micronesians of the Gilbert Islands. The following year, the Ellice Islands became the separate British colony of Tuvalu. Independence was granted in 1978. In 2000, Tuvalu negotiated a contract leasing its Internet domain name ".tv" for $50 million in royalties over the next dozen years.

Geography

Location: Oceania, island group consisting of nine coral atolls in the South Pacific Ocean, about one-half of the way from Hawaii to Australia
Geographic coordinates: 8 00 S, 178 00 E
Map references: Oceania
Area:
total: 26 sq km
land: 26 sq km
water: 0 sq km
Area - comparative: 0.1 times the size of Washington, DC
Land boundaries: 0 km
Coastline: 24 km
Maritime claims:
territorial sea: 12 NM
contiguous zone: 24 NM
exclusive economic zone: 200 NM
Climate: tropical; moderated by easterly trade winds (March to November); westerly gales and heavy rain (November to March)
Terrain: very low-lying and narrow coral atolls
Elevation extremes:
lowest point: Pacific Ocean 0 m
highest point: unnamed location 5 m
Natural resources: fish
Land use:
arable land: 0%

permanent crops: 0%
other: 100% (1998 est.)
Irrigated land: NA sq km
Natural hazards: severe tropical storms are usually rare, but, in 1997, there were three cyclones; low level of islands make them very sensitive to changes in sea level
Environment - current issues: since there are no streams or rivers and groundwater is not potable, most water needs must be met by catchment systems with storage facilities (the Japanese Government has built one desalination plant and plans to build one other); beachhead erosion because of the use of sand for building materials; excessive clearance of forest undergrowth for use as fuel; damage to coral reefs from the spread of the Crown of Thorns starfish; Tuvalu is very concerned about global increases in greenhouse gas emissions and their effect on rising sea levels, which threaten the country's underground water table; in 2000, the government appealed to Australia and New Zealand to take in Tuvaluans if rising sea levels should make evacuation necessary
Environment - international agreements:
party to: Biodiversity, Climate Change, Climate Change-Kyoto Protocol, Desertification, Law of the Sea, Ozone Layer Protection, Ship Pollution
signed, but not ratified: none of the selected agreements
Geography - note: one of the smallest and most remote countries on Earth; six of the coral atolls - Nanumea, Nui, Vaitupu, Nukufetau, Funafuti, and Nukulaelae - have lagoons open to the ocean; Nanumaya and Niutao have landlocked lagoons; Niulakita does not have a lagoon

People

Population: 11,468 (July 2004 est.)
Age structure:
0-14 years: 31.3% (male 1,828; female 1,761)
15-64 years: 63.7% (male 3,530; female 3,770)
65 years and over: 5% (male 227; female 352) (2004 est.)
Median age:
total: 24.2 years
male: 23.1 years
female: 25.6 years (2004 est.)
Population growth rate: 1.44% (2004 est.)
Birth rate: 21.63 births/1,000 population (2004 est.)
Death rate: 7.24 deaths/1,000 population (2004 est.)
Net migration rate: 0 migrant(s)/1,000 population (2004 est.)
Sex ratio:
at birth: 1.05 male(s)/female
under 15 years: 1.04 male(s)/female
15-64 years: 0.94 male(s)/female
65 years and over: 0.65 male(s)/female
total population: 0.95 male(s)/female (2004 est.)
Infant mortality rate:
total: 20.69 deaths/1,000 live births
male: 23.63 deaths/1,000 live births
female: 17.6 deaths/1,000 live births (2004 est.)

Tuvalu (continued)

Life expectancy at birth:
total population: 67.66 years
male: 65.47 years
female: 69.96 years (2004 est.)
Total fertility rate: 3.02 children born/woman (2004 est.)
HIV/AIDS - adult prevalence rate: NA%
HIV/AIDS - people living with HIV/AIDS: NA
HIV/AIDS - deaths: NA
Nationality:
noun: Tuvaluan(s)
adjective: Tuvaluan
Ethnic groups: Polynesian 96%, Micronesian 4%
Religions: Church of Tuvalu (Congregationalist) 97%, Seventh-Day Adventist 1.4%, Baha'i 1%, other 0.6%
Languages: Tuvaluan, English, Samoan, Kiribati (on the island of Nui)
Literacy:
definition: NA%
total population: NA%
male: NA%
female: NA%

Government

Country name:
conventional long form: none
conventional short form: Tuvalu
former: Ellice Islands
note: "Tuvalu" means "group of eight," referring to the country's eight traditionally inhabited islands
Government type: constitutional monarchy with a parliamentary democracy; began debating republic status in 1992
Capital: Funafuti; note - Administrative offices are located in Vaiaku Village on Fongafale Islet
Administrative divisions: none
Independence: 1 October 1978 (from UK)
National holiday: Independence Day, 1 October (1978)
Constitution: 1 October 1978
Legal system: NA
Suffrage: 18 years of age; universal
Executive branch:
chief of state: Queen ELIZABETH II (since 6 February 1952), represented by Governor General Faimalaga LUKA (since 9 September 2003)
head of government: Prime Minister Saufatu SOPOANGA (since 2 August 2002)
cabinet: Cabinet appointed by the governor general on the recommendation of the prime minister
elections: the monarch is hereditary; governor general appointed by the monarch on the recommendation of the prime minister; prime minister and deputy prime minister elected by and from the members of Parliament; election last held 2 August 2002 (next to be held following general elections in 2006)
election results: Saufatu SOPOANGA elected prime minister; Parliamentary vote - Saufatu SOPOANGA 8, Amasone KILEI 7

Legislative branch: unicameral Parliament or Fale I Fono, also called House of Assembly (15 seats; members elected by popular vote to serve four-year terms)
elections: last held 25 July 2002 (next to be held NA 2006)
election results: percent of vote - NA%; seats - independents 15
Judicial branch: High Court (a chief justice visits twice a year to preside over its sessions; its rulings can be appealed to the Court of Appeal in Fiji); eight Island Courts (with limited jurisdiction)
Political parties and leaders: there are no political parties but members of Parliament usually align themselves in informal groupings
Political pressure groups and leaders: none
International organization participation: ACP, AsDB, C, IFRCS (observer), ITU, OPCW, PIF, Sparteca, UN, UNCTAD, UNESCO, UPU, WHO
Diplomatic representation in the US: Tuvalu does not have an embassy in the US - the country's only diplomatic post is in Fiji - Tuvalu does, however, have a UN office located at 800 2nd Avenue, Suite 400D, New York, New York 10017, telephone: [1] (212) 490-0534
Diplomatic representation from the US: the US does not have an embassy in Tuvalu; the US ambassador to Fiji is accredited to Tuvalu
Flag description: light blue with the flag of the UK in the upper hoist-side quadrant; the outer half of the flag represents a map of the country with nine yellow five-pointed stars symbolizing the nine islands

Economy

Economy - overview: Tuvalu consists of a densely populated, scattered group of nine coral atolls with poor soil. The country has no known mineral resources and few exports. Subsistence farming and fishing are the primary economic activities. Fewer than 1,000 tourists, on average, visit Tuvalu annually. Government revenues largely come from the sale of stamps and coins and worker remittances. About 1,000 Tuvaluans work in Nauru in the phosphate mining industry. Nauru has begun repatriating Tuvaluans, however, as phosphate resources decline. Substantial income is received annually from an international trust fund established in 1987 by Australia, NZ, and the UK and supported also by Japan and South Korea. Thanks to wise investments and conservative withdrawals, this Fund has grown from an initial $17 million to over $35 million in 1999. The US government is also a major revenue source for Tuvalu, because of payments from a 1988 treaty on fisheries. In an effort to reduce its dependence on foreign aid, the government is pursuing public sector reforms, including privatization of some government functions and personnel cuts of up to 7%. In 1998, Tuvalu began deriving revenue from use of its area code for "900" lines and in 2000, from the lease of its ".tv" Internet domain name. Royalties from these new

technology sources could increase substantially over the next decade. With merchandise exports only a fraction of merchandise imports, continued reliance must be placed on fishing and telecommunications license fees, remittances from overseas workers, official transfers, and investment income from overseas assets.
GDP: purchasing power parity - NA
GDP - real growth rate: 3% (2000 est.)
GDP - per capita: purchasing power parity - $1,100 (2000 est.)
GDP - composition by sector:
agriculture: NA%
industry: NA%
services: NA%
Population below poverty line: NA%
Household income or consumption by percentage share:
lowest 10%: NA%
highest 10%: NA%
Inflation rate (consumer prices): 5% (2000 est.)
Labor force: 7,000 (2001 est.)
Labor force - by occupation: people make a living mainly through exploitation of the sea, reefs, and atolls and from wages sent home by those abroad (mostly workers in the phosphate industry and sailors)
Unemployment rate: NA%
Budget:
revenues: $22.5 million
expenditures: $11.2 million, including capital expenditures of $4.2 million (2000 est.)
Industries: fishing, tourism, copra
Industrial production growth rate: NA%
Electricity - production by source:
fossil fuel: NA%
hydro: NA%
nuclear: NA%
other: NA%
Agriculture - products: coconuts; fish
Exports: $1 million f.o.b. (2002)
Exports - commodities: copra, fish
Exports - partners: UK 49.4%, Italy 16.7%, France 16%, Fiji 8.3%, Sudan 5.1% (2002)
Imports: $79 million c.i.f. (2002)
Imports - commodities: food, animals, mineral fuels, machinery, manufactured goods
Imports - partners: Hungary 67.1%, Japan 12.7%, Fiji 11.4% (2002)
Debt - external: $NA
Economic aid - recipient: $13 million ; note - major donors are Australia, Japan, and the US (1999 est.)
Currency: Australian dollar (AUD); note - there is also a Tuvaluan dollar
Currency code: AUD
Exchange rates: Tuvaluan dollars or Australian dollars per US dollar - 1.5419, (2003), 1.8406 (2002), 1.9320 (2001), 1.7173 (2000), 1.5497 (1999)
Fiscal year: calendar year

Tuvalu (continued)

Communications

Telephones - main lines in use: 700 (2002)
Telephones - mobile cellular: 0 (1994)
Telephone system:
general assessment: serves particular needs for internal communications
domestic: radiotelephone communications between islands
international: country code - 688
Radio broadcast stations: AM 1, FM 0, shortwave 0 (1999)
Television broadcast stations: 0 (1997)
Internet country code: .tv
Internet users: 1,300 (2002)

Transportation

Railways: 0 km
Highways:
total: 8 km
paved: 0 km
unpaved: 8 km (1999 est.)
Waterways: none
Ports and harbors: Funafuti, Nukufetau
Merchant marine:
total: 6 ships (1,000 GRT or over) 54,993 GRT/86,048 DWT
by type: cargo 3, passenger/cargo 1, petroleum tanker 1, specialized tanker 1
foreign-owned: Germany 4, Singapore 1, Thailand 1 (2003 est.)
Airports: 1 (2003 est.)
Airports - with unpaved runways:
total: 1
1,524 to 2,437 m: 1 (2003 est.)

Military

Military branches: no regular military forces; Police Force (includes Maritime Surveillance Unit for search and rescue missions and surveillance operations)
Military expenditures - dollar figure: NA
Military expenditures - percent of GDP: NA

Transnational Issues

Disputes - international: none

Uganda

Introduction

Background: Uganda achieved independence from the UK in 1962. The dictatorial regime of Idi AMIN (1971-79) was responsible for the deaths of some 300,000 opponents; guerrilla war and human rights abuses under Milton OBOTE (1980-85) claimed at least another 100,000 lives. During the 1990s, the government promulgated non-party presidential and legislative elections.

Geography

Location: Eastern Africa, west of Kenya
Geographic coordinates: 1 00 N, 32 00 E
Map references: Africa
Area:
total: 236,040 sq km
land: 199,710 sq km
water: 36,330 sq km
Area - comparative: slightly smaller than Oregon
Land boundaries:
total: 2,698 km
border countries: Democratic Republic of the Congo 765 km, Kenya 933 km, Rwanda 169 km, Sudan 435 km, Tanzania 396 km
Coastline: 0 km (landlocked)
Maritime claims: none (landlocked)
Climate: tropical; generally rainy with two dry seasons (December to February, June to August); semiarid in northeast
Terrain: mostly plateau with rim of mountains
Elevation extremes:
lowest point: Lake Albert 621 m
highest point: Margherita Peak on Mount Stanley 5,110 m
Natural resources: copper, cobalt, hydropower, limestone, salt, arable land
Land use:
arable land: 25.34%
permanent crops: 8.77%

other: 65.89% (1998 est.)
Irrigated land: 90 sq km (1998 est.)
Natural hazards: NA
Environment - current issues: draining of wetlands for agricultural use; deforestation; overgrazing; soil erosion; water hyacinth infestation in Lake Victoria; poaching is widespread
Environment - international agreements:
party to: Biodiversity, Climate Change, Climate Change-Kyoto Protocol, Desertification, Endangered Species, Hazardous Wastes, Law of the Sea, Marine Life Conservation, Ozone Layer Protection, Wetlands
signed, but not ratified: Environmental Modification
Geography - note: landlocked; fertile, well-watered country with many lakes and rivers

People

Population: 26,404,543
note: estimates for this country explicitly take into account the effects of excess mortality due to AIDS; this can result in lower life expectancy, higher infant mortality and death rates, lower population and growth rates, and changes in the distribution of population by age and sex than would otherwise be expected (July 2004 est.)
Age structure:
0-14 years: 50.6% (male 6,696,193; female 6,653,764)
15-64 years: 47.1% (male 6,199,732; female 6,233,678)
65 years and over: 2.4% (male 269,990; female 351,186) (2004 est.)
Median age:
total: 14.8 years
male: 14.7 years
female: 14.9 years (2004 est.)
Population growth rate: 2.97% (2004 est.)
Birth rate: 46.31 births/1,000 population (2004 est.)
Death rate: 16.61 deaths/1,000 population (2004 est.)
Net migration rate: 0 migrant(s)/1,000 population
note: according to the UNHCR, by the end of 2001, Uganda was host to 178,815 refugees from a number of neighboring countries, including: Sudan 155,996, Rwanda 14,375, and Democratic Republic of the Congo 7,459 (2004 est.)
Sex ratio:
at birth: 1.03 male(s)/female
under 15 years: 1.01 male(s)/female
15-64 years: 1 male(s)/female
65 years and over: 0.77 male(s)/female
total population: 1 male(s)/female (2004 est.)
Infant mortality rate:
total: 86.15 deaths/1,000 live births
male: 93.58 deaths/1,000 live births
female: 78.5 deaths/1,000 live births (2004 est.)
Life expectancy at birth:
total population: 45.28 years
male: 43.76 years
female: 46.83 years (2004 est.)

Uganda (continued)

Total fertility rate: 6.64 children born/woman (2004 est.)
HIV/AIDS - adult prevalence rate: 5% (2001 est.)
HIV/AIDS - people living with HIV/AIDS: 600,000 (2001 est.)
HIV/AIDS - deaths: 84,000 (2001 est.)
Nationality:
noun: Ugandan(s)
adjective: Ugandan
Ethnic groups: Baganda 17%, Ankole 8%, Basoga 8%, Iteso 8%, Bakiga 7%, Langi 6%, Rwanda 6%, Bagisu 5%, Acholi 4%, Lugbara 4%, Batoro 3%, Bunyoro 3%, Alur 2%, Bagwere 2%, Bakonjo 2%, Jopodhola 2%, Karamojong 2%, Rundi 2%, non-African (European, Asian, Arab) 1%, other 8%
Religions: Roman Catholic 33%, Protestant 33%, Muslim 16%, indigenous beliefs 18%
Languages: English (official national language, taught in grade schools, used in courts of law and by most newspapers and some radio broadcasts), Ganda or Luganda (most widely used of the Niger-Congo languages, preferred for native language publications in the capital and may be taught in school), other Niger-Congo languages, Nilo-Saharan languages, Swahili, Arabic
Literacy:
definition: age 15 and over can read and write
total population: 69.9%
male: 79.5%
female: 60.4% (2003 est.)

Government

Country name:
conventional long form: Republic of Uganda
conventional short form: Uganda
Government type: republic
Capital: Kampala
Administrative divisions: 56 districts; Adjumani, Apac, Arua, Bugiri, Bundibugyo, Bushenyi, Busia, Gulu, Hoima, Iganga, Jinja, Kabale, Kabarole, Kaberamaido, Kalangala, Kampala, Kamuli, Kamwenge, Kanungu, Kapchorwa, Kasese, Katakwi, Kayunga, Kibale, Kiboga, Kisoro, Kitgum, Kotido, Kumi, Kyenjojo, Lira, Luwero, Masaka, Masindi, Mayuge, Mbale, Mbarara, Moroto, Moyo, Mpigi, Mubende, Mukono, Nakapiripirit, Nakasongola, Nebbi, Ntungamo, Pader, Pallisa, Rakai, Rukungiri, Sembabule, Sironko, Soroti, Tororo, Wakiso, Yumbe
Independence: 9 October 1962 (from UK)
National holiday: Independence Day, 9 October (1962)
Constitution: 8 October 1995; adopted by the interim, 284-member Constituent Assembly, charged with debating the draft constitution that had been proposed in May 1993; the Constituent Assembly was dissolved upon the promulgation of the constitution in October 1995

Legal system: in 1995, the government restored the legal system to one based on English common law and customary law; accepts compulsory ICJ jurisdiction, with reservations
Suffrage: 18 years of age; universal
Executive branch:
chief of state: President Lt. Gen. Yoweri Kaguta MUSEVENI (since seizing power 26 January 1986); note - the president is both chief of state and head of government
head of government: President Lt. Gen. Yoweri Kaguta MUSEVENI (since seizing power 29 January 1986); Prime Minister Apollo NSIBAMBI (since 5 April 1999); note - the president is both chief of state and head of government; the prime minister assists the president in the supervision of the cabinet
cabinet: Cabinet appointed by the president from among elected legislators
elections: president reelected by popular vote for a five-year term; election last held 12 March 2001 (next to be held NA 2006); note - first popular election for president since independence in 1962 was held in 1996; prime minister appointed by the president
election results: Lt. Gen. Yoweri Kaguta MUSEVENI elected president; percent of vote - Lt. Gen. Yoweri Kaguta MUSEVENI 69.3%, Kizza BESIGYE 27.8%
Legislative branch: unicameral National Assembly (303 members - 214 directly elected by popular vote, 81 nominated by legally established special interest groups [women 56, army 10, disabled 5, youth 5, labor 5], 8 ex officio members; members serve five-year terms)
elections: last held 26 June 2001 (next to be held May or June 2006);
election results: percent of vote by party - NA%; seats by party - NA; note - election campaigning by party was not permitted
Judicial branch: Court of Appeal (judges are appointed by the president and approved by the legislature); High Court (judges are appointed by the president)
Political parties and leaders: only one political organization, the Movement (formerly the NRM)[President MUSEVENI, chairman] is allowed to operate unfettered; note - the president maintains that the Movement is not a political party, but a mass organization, which claims the loyalty of all Ugandans
note: the constitution requires the suspension of political parties while the Movement organization is in governance; of the political parties that exist but are prohibited from sponsoring candidates, the most important are the Ugandan People's Congress or UPC [Milton OBOTE]; Democratic Party or DP [Paul SSEMOGERERE]; Conservative Party or CP [Ken LUKYAMUZI]; Justice Forum [Muhammad Kibirige MAYANJA]; and National Democrats Forum [Chapaa KARUHANGA]
Political pressure groups and leaders: Popular Resistance Against a Life President or PRALP

International organization participation: ACP, AfDB, AU, C, EADB, FAO, G-77, IAEA, IBRD, ICAO, ICCt, ICFTU, ICRM, IDA, IDB, IFAD, IFC, IFRCS, IGAD, ILO, IMF, Interpol, IOC, IOM, ISO (correspondent), ITU, NAM, OIC, OPCW, PCA, UN, UNCTAD, UNESCO, UNHCR, UNIDO, UPU, WCO, WFTU, WHO, WIPO, WMO, WToO, WTrO
Diplomatic representation in the US:
chief of mission: Ambassador Edith Grace SSEMPALA
chancery: 5911 16th Street NW, Washington, DC 20011
telephone: [1] (202) 726-7100 through 7102, 0416
FAX: [1] (202) 726-1727
Diplomatic representation from the US:
chief of mission: Ambassador Jimmy KOLKER
embassy: 1577 Ggaba Rd., Kampala
mailing address: P. O. Box 7007, Kampala
telephone: [256] (41) 234-142
FAX: [256] (41) 258-451
Flag description: six equal horizontal bands of black (top), yellow, red, black, yellow, and red; a white disk is superimposed at the center and depicts a red-crested crane (the national symbol) facing the hoist side

Economy

Economy - overview: Uganda has substantial natural resources, including fertile soils, regular rainfall, and sizable mineral deposits of copper and cobalt. Agriculture is the most important sector of the economy, employing over 80% of the work force. Coffee accounts for the bulk of export revenues. Since 1986, the government - with the support of foreign countries and international agencies - has acted to rehabilitate and stabilize the economy by undertaking currency reform, raising producer prices on export crops, increasing prices of petroleum products, and improving civil service wages. The policy changes are especially aimed at dampening inflation and boosting production and export earnings. During 1990-2001, the economy turned in a solid performance based on continued investment in the rehabilitation of infrastructure, improved incentives for production and exports, reduced inflation, gradually improved domestic security, and the return of exiled Indian-Ugandan entrepreneurs. Corruption within the government and slippage in the government's determination to press reforms raise doubts about the continuation of strong growth. In 2000, Uganda qualified for enhanced Highly Indebted Poor Countries (HIPC) debt relief worth $1.3 billion and Paris Club debt relief worth $145 million. These amounts combined with the original HIPC debt relief added up to about $2 billion. Growth for 2001-02 was solid despite continued decline in the price of coffee, Uganda's principal export. Solid growth in 2003 reflected an upturn in Uganda's export markets.
GDP: purchasing power parity - $36.1 billion (2003 est.)

Uganda (continued)

GDP - real growth rate: 4.4% (2003 est.)
GDP - per capita: purchasing power parity - $1,400 (2003 est.)
GDP - composition by sector:
agriculture: 43%
industry: 19%
services: 38% (2001 est.)
Population below poverty line: 35% (2001 est.)
Household income or consumption by percentage share:
lowest 10%: 4%
highest 10%: 21% (2000)
Distribution of family income - Gini index: 37.4 (1996)
Inflation rate (consumer prices): 0.1% (2002 est.)
Labor force: 12 million (2001 est.)
Labor force - by occupation: agriculture 82%, industry 5%, services 13% (1999 est.)
Unemployment rate: NA% (2002 est.)
Budget:
revenues: $959 million
expenditures: $1.04 billion, including capital expenditures of $NA (FY98/99 est.)
Industries: sugar, brewing, tobacco, cotton textiles, cement
Industrial production growth rate: 6.3% (2002 est.)
Electricity - production: 1.928 billion kWh (2001)
Electricity - production by source:
fossil fuel: 0.9%
hydro: 99.1%
nuclear: 0%
other: 0% (2001)
Electricity - consumption: 1.62 billion kWh (2001)
Electricity - exports: 174 million kWh (2001)
Electricity - imports: 1 million kWh (2001)
Oil - production: 0 bbl/day (2001 est.)
Oil - consumption: 8,750 bbl/day (2001 est.)
Oil - exports: NA
Oil - imports: NA
Agriculture - products: coffee, tea, cotton, tobacco, cassava (tapioca), potatoes, corn, millet, pulses; beef, goat meat, milk, poultry, cut flowers
Exports: $495 million f.o.b. (2003 est.)
Exports - commodities: coffee, fish and fish products, tea; gold, cotton, flowers, horticultural products
Exports - partners: Belgium 16.8%, Netherlands 14.3%, Germany 7.9%, Spain 5.8%, US 4.9%, Italy 4.3%, Portugal 4.3%, UK 4.3%, Japan 4% (2002)
Imports: $1.179 billion f.o.b. (2003 est.)
Imports - commodities: capital equipment, vehicles, petroleum, medical supplies; cereals
Imports - partners: Kenya 46.4%, South Africa 6.9%, India 5.7%, UK 5.6% (2002)
Debt - external: $2.8 billion (2002 est.)
Economic aid - recipient: $1.4 billion (2000)
Currency: Ugandan shilling (UGX)
Currency code: UGX
Exchange rates: Ugandan shillings per US dollar - 1,963.72 (2003), 1,797.55 (2002), 1,755.66 (2001), 1,644.48 (2000), 1,454.83 (1999)
Fiscal year: 1 July - 30 June

Communications

Telephones - main lines in use: 55,000 (2002)
Telephones - mobile cellular: 393,300 (2002)
Telephone system:
general assessment: seriously inadequate; two cellular systems have been introduced, but a sharp increase in the number of main lines is essential; e-mail and Internet services are available
domestic: intercity traffic by wire, microwave radio relay, and radiotelephone communication stations, fixed and mobile cellular systems for short-range traffic
international: country code - 256; satellite earth stations - 1 Intelsat (Atlantic Ocean) and 1 Inmarsat; analog links to Kenya and Tanzania
Radio broadcast stations: AM 7, FM 33, shortwave 2 (2001)
Television broadcast stations: 8 (plus one low-power repeater) (2001)
Internet country code: .ug
Internet hosts: 2,242 (2002)
Internet users: 100,000 (2002)

Transportation

Railways:
total: 1,241 km
narrow gauge: 1,241 km 1.000-m gauge (2002)
Highways:
total: 27,000 km
paved: 1,809 km
unpaved: 25,191 km (1999 est.)
Waterways: Lake Victoria, Lake Albert, Lake Kyoga, Lake George, Lake Edward, Victoria Nile, Albert Nile
Ports and harbors: Entebbe, Jinja, Port Bell
Merchant marine:
total: 3 ships (1,000 GRT or over) 5,091 GRT/5,943 DWT
by type: roll on/roll off 3 (2003 est.)
Airports: 27 (2003 est.)
Airports - with paved runways:
total: 4
over 3,047 m: 3
1,524 to 2,437 m: 1 (2003 est.)
Airports - with unpaved runways:
total: 23
2,438 to 3,047 m: 1
1,524 to 2,437 m: 6
914 to 1,523 m: 9
under 914 m: 7 (2003 est.)

Military

Military branches: Ugandan Peoples' Defense Force (UPDF): Army, Marine Unit, Air Wing
Military manpower - availability:
males age 15-49: 5,678,649 (2004 est.)
Military manpower - fit for military service:
males age 15-49: 3,085,053 (2004 est.)
Military expenditures - dollar figure: $128.2 million (2003)
Military expenditures - percent of GDP: 2.1% (2003)

Transnational Issues

Disputes - international: Tutsi, Hutu, Lendu, Hema, and other ethnic groups, associated political rebels, armed gangs, militias, and various government forces continue fighting in the Great Lakes region, transcending the boundaries of Burundi, Democratic Republic of the Congo, Rwanda, and Uganda to gain control over populated areas and natural resources; government heads pledge to end conflict, but localized violence continues despite UN peacekeeping efforts; civil conflict in Sudan has extended Sudanese rebel forces and refugees into Uganda and given shelter to Ugandan Lord's Resistance Army soldiers in Sudan; Kenya and Uganda are working together to stem cattle rustling and violence by Lord's Resistance Army along the border

Ukraine

Introduction

Background: Ukraine was the center of the first Slavic state, Kievan Rus, which during the 10th and 11th centuries was the largest and most powerful state in Europe. Weakened by internecine quarrels and Mongol invasions, Kievan Rus was incorporated into the Grand Duchy of Lithuania and eventually into the Polish-Lithuanian Commonwealth. The cultural and religious legacy of Kievan Rus laid the foundation for Ukrainian nationalism through subsequent centuries. A new Ukrainian state, the Cossack Hetmanate, was established during the mid-17th century after an uprising against the Poles. Despite continuous Muscovite pressure, the Hetmanate managed to remain autonomous for well over 100 years. During the latter part of the 18th century, most Ukrainian ethnographic territory was absorbed by the Russian Empire. Following the collapse of czarist Russia in 1917, Ukraine was able to bring about a short-lived period of independence (1917-1920), but was reconquered and forced to endure a brutal Soviet rule that engineered two artificial famines (1921-22 and 1932-33) in which over 8 million died. In World War II, German and Soviet armies were responsible for some 7 to 8 million more deaths. Although independence was achieved in 1991 with the dissolution of the USSR, true freedom remains elusive, as the legacy of state control has been difficult to throw off. Where state control has dissipated, endemic corruption has filled much of the resulting vacuum, stalling efforts at economic reform, privatization, and civil liberties.

Geography

Location: Eastern Europe, bordering the Black Sea, between Poland, Romania, and Moldova in the west and Russia in the east
Geographic coordinates: 49 00 N, 32 00 E
Map references: Asia, Europe

Area:
total: 603,700 sq km
land: 603,700 sq km
water: 0 sq km
Area - comparative: slightly smaller than Texas
Land boundaries:
total: 4,663 km
border countries: Belarus 891 km, Hungary 103 km, Moldova 939 km, Poland 526 km, Romania (south) 169 km, Romania (west) 362 km, Russia 1,576 km, Slovakia 97 km
Coastline: 2,782 km
Maritime claims:
territorial sea: 12 NM
exclusive economic zone: 200 NM
continental shelf: 200-m or to the depth of exploitation
Climate: temperate continental; Mediterranean only on the southern Crimean coast; precipitation disproportionately distributed, highest in west and north, lesser in east and southeast; winters vary from cool along the Black Sea to cold farther inland; summers are warm across the greater part of the country, hot in the south
Terrain: most of Ukraine consists of fertile plains (steppes) and plateaus, mountains being found only in the west (the Carpathians), and in the Crimean Peninsula in the extreme south
Elevation extremes:
lowest point: Black Sea 0 m
highest point: Hora Hoverla 2,061 m
Natural resources: iron ore, coal, manganese, natural gas, oil, salt, sulfur, graphite, titanium, magnesium, kaolin, nickel, mercury, timber, arable land
Land use:
arable land: 57.1%
permanent crops: 1.73%
other: 41.17% (1998 est.)
Irrigated land: 24,540 sq km (1998 est.)
Natural hazards: NA

Environment - current issues: inadequate supplies of potable water; air and water pollution; deforestation; radiation contamination in the northeast from 1986 accident at Chornobyl' Nuclear Power Plant
Environment - international agreements:
party to: Air Pollution, Air Pollution-Nitrogen Oxides, Air Pollution-Sulfur 85, Antarctic-Environmental Protocol, Antarctic-Marine Living Resources, Antarctic Treaty, Biodiversity, Climate Change, Climate Change-Kyoto Protocol, Endangered Species, Environmental Modification, Hazardous Wastes, Law of the Sea, Marine Dumping, Ozone Layer Protection, Ship Pollution, Wetlands
signed, but not ratified: Air Pollution-Persistent Organic Pollutants, Air Pollution-Sulfur 94, Air Pollution-Volatile Organic Compounds
Geography - note: strategic position at the crossroads between Europe and Asia; second-largest country in Europe

People

Population: 47,732,079 (July 2004 est.)
Age structure:
0-14 years: 15.9% (male 3,883,485; female 3,715,668)
15-64 years: 68.7% (male 15,692,388; female 17,096,611)
65 years and over: 15.4% (male 2,472,023; female 4,871,904) (2004 est.)
Median age:
total: 38.1 years
male: 34.8 years
female: 41.1 years (2004 est.)
Population growth rate: -0.66% (2004 est.)
Birth rate: 10.21 births/1,000 population (2004 est.)
Death rate: 16.41 deaths/1,000 population (2004 est.)
Net migration rate: -0.39 migrant(s)/1,000 population (2004 est.)
Sex ratio:
at birth: 1.05 male(s)/female
under 15 years: 1.05 male(s)/female
15-64 years: 0.92 male(s)/female
65 years and over: 0.51 male(s)/female
total population: 0.86 male(s)/female (2004 est.)
Infant mortality rate:
total: 20.61 deaths/1,000 live births
male: 21.87 deaths/1,000 live births
female: 19.28 deaths/1,000 live births (2004 est.)
Life expectancy at birth:
total population: 66.68 years
male: 61.35 years
female: 72.27 years (2004 est.)
Total fertility rate: 1.37 children born/woman (2004 est.)
HIV/AIDS - adult prevalence rate: 2% (2003 est.)
HIV/AIDS - people living with HIV/AIDS: 250,000 (2001 est.)
HIV/AIDS - deaths: 11,000 (2001 est.)

Ukraine (continued)

Nationality:
noun: Ukrainian(s)
adjective: Ukrainian
Ethnic groups: Ukrainian 77.8%, Russian 17.3%, Belarusian 0.6%, Moldovan 0.5%, Crimean Tatar 0.5%, Bulgarian 0.4%, Hungarian 0.3%, Romanian 0.3%, Polish 0.3%, Jewish 0.2%, other 1.8% (2001)
Religions: Ukrainian Orthodox - Moscow Patriarchate, Ukrainian Orthodox - Kiev Patriarchate, Ukrainian Autocephalous Orthodox, Ukrainian Catholic (Uniate), Protestant, Jewish
Languages: Ukrainian, Russian, Romanian, Polish, Hungarian
Literacy:
definition: age 15 and over can read and write
total population: 99.7%
male: 99.8%
female: 99.6% (2003 est.)

Government

Country name:
conventional long form: none
conventional short form: Ukraine
local long form: none
local short form: Ukrayina
former: Ukrainian National Republic, Ukrainian State, Ukrainian Soviet Socialist Republic
Government type: republic
Capital: Kiev (Kyyiv)
Administrative divisions: 24 oblasti (singular - oblast'), 1 autonomous republic* (avtonmaya respublika), and 2 municipalities (mista, singular - misto) with oblast status**; Cherkas'ka (Cherkasy), Chernihivs'ka (Chernihiv), Chernivets'ka (Chernivtsi), Dnipropetrovs'ka (Dnipropetrovs'k), Donets'ka (Donets'k), Ivano-Frankivs'ka (Ivano-Frankivs'k), Kharkivs'ka (Kharkiv), Khersons'ka (Kherson), Khmel'nyts'ka (Khmel'nyts'kyy), Kirovohrads'ka (Kirovohrad), Kyyiv**, Kyyivs'ka (Kiev), Luhans'ka (Luhans'k), L'vivs'ka (L'viv), Mykolayivs'ka (Mykolayiv), Odes'ka (Odesa), Poltavs'ka (Poltava), Avtonomna Respublika Krym* (Simferopol'), Rivnens'ka (Rivne), Sevastopol'** (Sums'ka (Sumy), Ternopil's'ka (Ternopil'), Vinnyts'ka (Vinnytsya), Volyns'ka (Luts'k), Zakarpats'ka (Uzhhorod), Zaporiz'ka (Zaporizhzhya), Zhytomyrs'ka (Zhytomyr); note - when using a place name with an adjectival ending "s'ka" or "z'ka," the word Oblast' should be added to the place name
note: oblasts have the administrative center name following in parentheses
Independence: 24 August 1991 (from the Soviet Union)
National holiday: Independence Day, 24 August (1991); the date of 22 January (1918), the day Ukraine first declared its independence (from Soviet Russia), is now celebrated as Unity Day
Constitution: adopted 28 June 1996
Legal system: based on civil law system; judicial review of legislative acts
Suffrage: 18 years of age; universal

Executive branch:
chief of state: President Leonid D. KUCHMA (since 19 July 1994)
head of government: Prime Minister Viktor YANUKOVYCH (since 21 November 2002); First Deputy Prime Minister Mykola AZAROV (since 26 November 2002)
cabinet: Cabinet of Ministers appointed by the president and approved by the Supreme Council
note: there is also a National Security and Defense Council or NSDC originally created in 1992 as the National Security Council, but significantly revamped and strengthened under President KUCHMA; the NSDC staff is tasked with developing national security policy on domestic and international matters and advising the president; a Presidential Administration that helps draft presidential edicts and provides policy support to the president; and a Council of Regions that serves as an advisory body created by President KUCHMA in September 1994 that includes chairmen of the Kiev (Kyyiv) and Sevastopol' municipalities and chairmen of the oblasti
elections: president elected by popular vote for a five-year term; election last held 31 October and 14 November 1999 (next to be held 31 October 2004); prime minister and deputy prime ministers appointed by the president and approved by the Supreme Council
election results: Leonid D. KUCHMA elected president; percent of vote - Leonid KUCHMA 57.7%, Petro SYMONENKO 38.8%
Legislative branch: unicameral Supreme Council or Verkhovna Rada (450 seats; under Ukraine's election law, 225 of the Supreme Council's seats are allocated on a proportional basis to those parties that gain 4% or more of the national electoral vote; the other 225 members are elected by popular vote in single-mandate constituencies; all serve four-year terms)
elections: last held 31 March 2002 (next to be held NA 2006)
election results: percent of vote by party - Our Ukraine 24%, CPU 20%, United Ukraine 12%, SPU 7%, Yuliya Tymoshenko Bloc 7%, United Social Democratic Party 6%, other 24%; seats by party - Our Ukraine 102, Regions of Ukraine 67, CPU 59, Working Ukraine-Industrialists and Entrepreneurs 42, United Social Democratic Party 36, People's Power 22, SPU 20, Yuliya Tymoshenko Bloc 19, Democratic Initiatives 18, Agrarian Party 16, People's Democratic Party 14, People's Choice 14, others 21 (January 2004)
note: following the election, United Ukraine splintered into the Agrarian Party, European Choice, People's Choice, People's Democratic Party, Regions of Ukraine, and Working Ukraine-Industrialists and Entrepreneurs; European Choice joined Regions of Ukraine in the fall of 2003
Judicial branch: Supreme Court; Constitutional Court
Political parties and leaders: Agrarian Party [Kateryna VASHCHUK]; Communist Party of Ukraine or CPU [Petro SYMONENKO]; Democratic Initiatives [Stepan HAVRYSH]; Industrialists and Entrepreneurs

[Anatoliy KINAKH]; Our Ukraine bloc (comprised of several parties the most prominent of which are Rukh, the Ukrainian People's Party, Reforms and Order, and Solidarity) [Viktor YUSHCHENKO]; People's Choice [Mykola HAPOCHKA]; People's Democratic Party or PDP [Valeriy PUSTOVOYTENKO]; People's Power [Bohdan HUBSKYY]; Regions of Ukraine [Viktor YANUKOVYCH]; Socialist Party of Ukraine or SPU [Oleksandr MOROZ, chairman]; United Social Democratic Party [Viktor MEDVEDCHUK]; Working Ukraine [Serhiy TYHYPKO]; Yuliya Tymoshenko Bloc [Yuliya TYMOSHENKO]
note: and numerous smaller parties; Democratic Initiatives, People's Choice, and People's Power are not actual political parties, but rather deputy groups (factions not based on a party)
Political pressure groups and leaders: NA
International organization participation: BSEC, CE, CEI, CIS, EAPC, EBRD, GUUAM, IAEA, IBRD, ICAO, ICC, ICCt (signatory), ICFTU, ICRM, IFC, IFRCS, IHO, ILO, IMF, IMO, Interpol, IOC, IOM, ISO, ITU, MONUC, NAM (observer), NSG, OAS (observer), OPCW, OSCE, PCA, PFP, UN, UNAMSIL, UNCTAD, UNESCO, UNIDO, UNIFIL, UNMEE, UNMIK, UNMOVIC, UNOMIG, UPU, WCL, WCO, WFTU, WHO, WIPO, WMO, WToO, WTrO (observer), ZC
Diplomatic representation in the US:
chief of mission: Ambassador Mykhailo B. REZNIK
chancery: 3350 M Street NW, Washington, DC 20007
telephone: [1] (202) 349-2920
FAX: [1] (202) 333-0817
consulate(s) general: Chicago and New York
Diplomatic representation from the US:
chief of mission: Ambassador John E. HERBST
embassy: 10 Yurii Kotsiubynskyi Street, Kiev 01901
mailing address: 5850 Kiev Place, Washington, DC 20521-5850
telephone: [380] (44) 490-4000
FAX: [380] (44) 244-7350
Flag description: two equal horizontal bands of azure (top) and golden yellow represent grainfields under a blue sky

Economy

Economy - overview: After Russia, the Ukrainian republic was far and away the most important economic component of the former Soviet Union, producing about four times the output of the next-ranking republic. Its fertile black soil generated more than one-fourth of Soviet agricultural output, and its farms provided substantial quantities of meat, milk, grain, and vegetables to other republics. Likewise, its diversified heavy industry supplied the unique equipment (for example, large diameter pipes) and raw materials to industrial and mining sites (vertical drilling apparatus) in other regions of the former USSR. Ukraine depends on imports of energy, especially natural gas, to meet some 85% of its annual energy requirements. Shortly after independence in December 1991, the Ukrainian Government liberalized most prices and erected a legal framework for privatization, but widespread resistance to reform within the government and the legislature soon stalled reform efforts and led to some backtracking. Output by 1999 had fallen to less than 40% of the 1991 level. Loose monetary policies pushed inflation to hyperinflationary levels in late 1993. Ukraine's dependence on Russia for energy supplies and the lack of significant structural reform have made the Ukrainian economy vulnerable to external shocks. Now in his second term, President KUCHMA has pledged to reduce the number of government agencies, streamline the regulatory process, create a legal environment to encourage entrepreneurs, and enact a comprehensive tax overhaul. Reforms in the more politically sensitive areas of structural reform and land privatization are still lagging. Outside institutions - particularly the IMF - have encouraged Ukraine to quicken the pace and scope of reforms. GDP in 2000 showed strong export-based growth of 6% - the first growth since independence - and industrial production grew 12.9%. The economy continued to expand in 2001 as real GDP rose 9% and industrial output grew by over 14%. Growth of 4.1% in 2002 was more moderate, in part a reflection of faltering growth in the developed world. In general, growth has been undergirded by strong domestic demand, low inflation, and solid consumer and investor confidence. Growth was a sturdy 8.2% in 2003 despite a loss of momentum in needed economic reforms.

GDP: purchasing power parity - $256.5 billion (2003 est.)

GDP - real growth rate: 8.2% (2003 est.)

GDP - per capita: purchasing power parity - $5,300 (2003 est.)

GDP - composition by sector:
agriculture: 23.4%
industry: 41.5%
services: 35.1% (2001 est.)

Population below poverty line: 29% (2003 est.)

Household income or consumption by percentage share:
lowest 10%: 3.7%
highest 10%: 23.2% (1999)

Distribution of family income - Gini index: 29 (1999)

Inflation rate (consumer prices): 8.2% (2003 est.)

Labor force: 22.8 million (yearend 1997)

Labor force - by occupation: industry 32%, agriculture 24%, services 44% (1996)

Unemployment rate: 4% officially registered; large number of unregistered or underemployed workers (2003)

Budget:
revenues: $10.2 billion
expenditures: $11.1 billion, including capital expenditures of $NA (2002 est.)

Industries: coal, electric power, ferrous and nonferrous metals, machinery and transport equipment, chemicals, food processing (especially sugar)

Industrial production growth rate: 8% (2003 est.)

Electricity - production: 164.7 billion kWh (2001)

Electricity - production by source:
fossil fuel: 48.6%
hydro: 7.9%
nuclear: 43.5%
other: 0% (2001)

Electricity - consumption: 152.4 billion kWh (2001)

Electricity - exports: 800 million kWh (2001)

Electricity - imports: 0 kWh (2001)

Oil - production: 86,490 bbl/day (2001 est.)

Oil - consumption: 290,000 bbl/day (2001 est.)

Oil - exports: NA

Oil - imports: NA

Oil - proved reserves: 197.5 million bbl (1 January 2002)

Natural gas - production: 18.2 billion cu m (2001 est.)

Natural gas - consumption: 74.1 billion cu m (2001 est.)

Natural gas - exports: 0 cu m (2001 est.)

Natural gas - imports: 55.9 billion cu m (2001 est.)

Natural gas - proved reserves: 560.7 billion cu m (1 January 2002)

Agriculture - products: grain, sugar beets, sunflower seeds, vegetables; beef, milk

Exports: $23.63 billion (2003 est.)

Exports - commodities: ferrous and nonferrous metals, fuel and petroleum products, chemicals, machinery and transport equipment, food products

Exports - partners: Russia 17.8%, Turkey 6.9%, Italy 4.7%, Germany 4.2% (2002)

Imports: $23.58 billion (2003 est.)

Imports - commodities: energy, machinery and equipment, chemicals

Imports - partners: Russia 37.6%, Turkmenistan 11.2%, Germany 9.9% (2002)

Debt - external: $15.7 billion (2003)

Economic aid - recipient: $637.7 million (1995); IMF Extended Funds Facility $2.2 billion (1998)

Currency: hryvnia (UAH)

Currency code: UAH

Exchange rates: hryvnia per US dollar - 5.3327 (2003), 5.3266 (2002), 5.3722 (2001), 5.4402 (2000), 4.1304 (1999)

Fiscal year: calendar year

Communications

Telephones - main lines in use: 10,833,300 (2002)

Telephones - mobile cellular: 4.2 million (2002)

Telephone system:
general assessment: Ukraine's telecommunication development plan, running through 2005, emphasizes improving domestic trunk lines, international connections, and the mobile cellular system
domestic: at independence in December 1991, Ukraine inherited a telephone system that was antiquated, inefficient, and in disrepair; more than 3.5 million applications for telephones could not be satisfied; telephone density is now rising slowly and the domestic trunk system is being improved; the mobile cellular telephone system is expanding at a high rate

international: country code - 380; two new domestic trunk lines are a part of the fiber-optic Trans-Asia-Europe (TAE) system and three Ukrainian links have been installed in the fiber-optic Trans-European Lines (TEL) project that connects 18 countries; additional international service is provided by the Italy-Turkey-Ukraine-Russia (ITUR) fiber-optic submarine cable and by earth stations in the Intelsat, Inmarsat, and Intersputnik satellite systems

Radio broadcast stations: AM 134, FM 289, shortwave 4 (1998)

Television broadcast stations: at least 33 (plus 21 repeaters that relay broadcasts from Russia) (1997)

Internet country code: .ua

Internet hosts: 71,691 (2002)

Internet users: 900,000 (2002)

Transportation

Railways:
total: 22,473 km
broad gauge: 22,473 km 1.524-m gauge (9,250 km electrified) (2002)

Highways:
total: 169,491 km
paved: 163,898 km
unpaved: 5,593 km (2000)

Waterways: 4,499 km
note: 1,672 km are on the Pryp'yat' and Dniester (Dnister) (1990)

Pipelines: gas 20,069 km; oil 4,435 km; refined products 4,098 km (2003)

Ports and harbors: Berdyans'k, Feodosiya, Illichivs'k, Izmayil, Kerch, Kherson, Kiev (Kyyiv), Kiliya, Mariupol', Mykolayiv, Odesa, Reni, Sevastopol', Yalta, Yuzhnyy

Merchant marine:
total: 140 ships (1,000 GRT or over) 675,904 GRT/709,802 DWT
by type: bulk 7, cargo 92, container 7, liquefied gas 2, passenger 11, passenger/cargo 3, petroleum tanker 10, rail car carrier 2, refrigerated cargo 2, roll on/roll off 3, short-sea/passenger 1
foreign-owned: Belize 2, Canada 1, Cyprus 1, Hungary 2, Italy 1, Russia 4, Turkey 3
registered in other countries: 87 (2003 est.)

Airports: 702 (2003 est.)

Airports - with paved runways:
total: 174
over 3,047 m: 13
2,438 to 3,047 m: 57
1,524 to 2,437 m: 30
914 to 1,523 m: 4
under 914 m: 70 (2003 est.)

Airports - with unpaved runways:
total: 528
over 3,047 m: 4
2,438 to 3,047 m: 3
1,524 to 2,437 m: 17
914 to 1,523 m: 35
under 914 m: 469 (2003 est.)

Heliports: 8 (2003 est.)

Ukraine (continued)

Military

Military branches: Ground Forces, Naval Forces, Air and Air Defense Forces, Ministry of Internal Affairs (MVS) Troops, Border Troops

Military manpower - military age: 18 years of age (2004 est.)

Military manpower - availability:
males age 15-49: 12,196,319 (2004 est.)

Military manpower - fit for military service:
males age 15-49: 9,565,088 (2004 est.)

Military manpower - reaching military age annually:
males: 386,945 (2004 est.)

Military expenditures - dollar figure: $617.9 million (FY02)

Military expenditures - percent of GDP: 1.4% (FY02)

Transnational Issues

Disputes - international: 1997 boundary treaty with Belarus remains unratified due to unresolved financial claims, preventing demarcation and reducing border security; delimitation of land boundary with Russia is complete but boundary through the Sea of Azov and Kerch Strait remains unresolved despite a December 2003 framework agreement and on-going expert-level discussions; Ukraine protests Russia's construction of a causeway in the direction of Ukrainian-administered Tuzla Island in the Kerch Strait; difficulties with Moldova's Transnistria region complicate controlling border crossing and customs regimes despite concordance on the 2003 delimitation and customs protocols and OSCE assistance; has not resolved Romanian claims to Ukrainian-administered Zmiyinyy (Snake) Island and Black Sea maritime boundary despite ongoing talks based on 1997 friendship treaty to find a solution in two years

Illicit drugs: limited cultivation of cannabis and opium poppy, mostly for CIS consumption; some synthetic drug production for export to the West; limited government eradication program; used as transshipment point for opiates and other illicit drugs from Africa, Latin America, and Turkey to Europe and Russia; drug-related money laundering a minor, but growing, problem; anti-money-laundering regime improving but remains on Financial Action Task Force Non-Cooperative Countries and Territories List for continued failure to address deficiencies in money-laundering control regime

United Arab Emirates

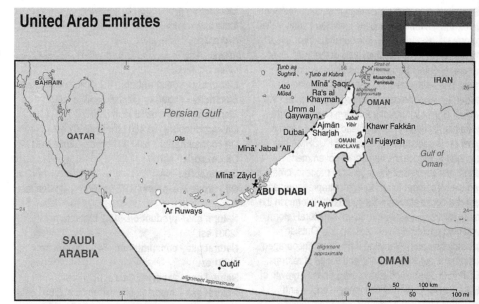

Introduction

Background: The Trucial States of the Persian Gulf coast granted the UK control of their defense and foreign affairs in 19th century treaties. In 1971, six of these states - Abu Zaby, 'Ajman, Al Fujayrah, Ash Shariqah, Dubayy, and Umm al Qaywayn - merged to form the United Arab Emirates (UAE). They were joined in 1972 by Ra's al Khaymah. The UAE's per capita GDP is not far below those of leading West European nations. Its generosity with oil revenues and its moderate foreign policy stance have allowed the UAE to play a vital role in the affairs of the region.

Geography

Location: Middle East, bordering the Gulf of Oman and the Persian Gulf, between Oman and Saudi Arabia

Geographic coordinates: 24 00 N, 54 00 E

Map references: Middle East

Area:
total: 82,880 sq km
land: 82,880 sq km
water: 0 sq km

Area - comparative: slightly smaller than Maine

Land boundaries:
total: 867 km
border countries: Oman 410 km, Saudi Arabia 457 km

Coastline: 1,318 km

Maritime claims:
territorial sea: 12 NM
contiguous zone: 24 NM
exclusive economic zone: 200 NM
continental shelf: 200 NM or to the edge of the continental margin

Climate: desert; cooler in eastern mountains

Terrain: flat, barren coastal plain merging into rolling sand dunes of vast desert wasteland; mountains in east

Elevation extremes:
lowest point: Persian Gulf 0 m
highest point: Jabal Yibir 1,527 m

Natural resources: petroleum, natural gas

Land use:
arable land: 0.48%
permanent crops: 0.49%
other: 99.03% (1998 est.)

Irrigated land: 720 sq km (1998 est.)

Natural hazards: frequent sand and dust storms

Environment - current issues: lack of natural freshwater resources compensated by desalination plants; desertification; beach pollution from oil spills

Environment - international agreements:
party to: Biodiversity, Climate Change, Desertification, Endangered Species, Hazardous Wastes, Marine Dumping, Ozone Layer Protection
signed, but not ratified: Law of the Sea

Geography - note: strategic location along southern approaches to Strait of Hormuz, a vital transit point for world crude oil

People

Population: 2,523,915
note: includes an estimated 1,606,079 non-nationals; the 17 December 1995 census presents a total population figure of 2,377,453, and there are estimates of 3.44 million for 2002 (July 2004 est.)

Age structure:
0-14 years: 25.9% (male 333,661; female 320,368)
15-64 years: 70.9% (male 1,103,385; female 685,281)
65 years and over: 3.2% (male 58,862; female 22,358) (2004 est.)

Median age:
total: 27.7 years
male: 35.7 years
female: 22.4 years (2004 est.)

Population growth rate: 1.57% (2004 est.)

Birth rate: 18.65 births/1,000 population (2004 est.)

Death rate: 4.14 deaths/1,000 population (2004 est.)

Net migration rate: 1.03 migrant(s)/1,000 population (2004 est.)

United Arab Emirates (continued)

Sex ratio:

at birth: 1.05 male(s)/female

under 15 years: 1.04 male(s)/female

15-64 years: 1.61 male(s)/female

65 years and over: 2.63 male(s)/female

total population: 1.46 male(s)/female (2004 est.)

Infant mortality rate:

total: 15.06 deaths/1,000 live births

male: 17.71 deaths/1,000 live births

female: 12.29 deaths/1,000 live births (2004 est.)

Life expectancy at birth:

total population: 74.99 years

male: 72.51 years

female: 77.6 years (2004 est.)

Total fertility rate: 3.02 children born/woman (2004 est.)

HIV/AIDS - adult prevalence rate: 0.18% (2001 est.)

HIV/AIDS - people living with HIV/AIDS: NA

HIV/AIDS - deaths: NA

Nationality:

noun: Emirati(s)

adjective: Emirati

Ethnic groups: Emirati 19%, other Arab and Iranian 23%, South Asian 50%, other expatriates (includes Westerners and East Asians) 8% (1982)

note: less than 20% are UAE citizens (1982)

Religions: Muslim 96% (Shi'a 16%), Christian, Hindu, and other 4%

Languages: Arabic (official), Persian, English, Hindi, Urdu

Literacy:

definition: age 15 and over can read and write

total population: 77.9%

male: 76.1%

female: 81.7% (2003 est.)

Government

Country name:

conventional long form: United Arab Emirates

conventional short form: none

local long form: Al Imarat al Arabiyah al Muttahidah

local short form: none

former: Trucial Oman, Trucial States

abbreviation: UAE

Government type: federation with specified powers delegated to the UAE federal government and other powers reserved to member emirates

Capital: Abu Dhabi

Administrative divisions: 7 emirates (imarat, singular - imarah); Abu Zaby (Abu Dhabi), 'Ajman, Al Fujayrah, Ash Shariqah (Sharjah), Dubayy (Dubai), Ra's al Khaymah, Umm al Qaywayn

Independence: 2 December 1971 (from UK)

National holiday: Independence Day, 2 December (1971)

Constitution: 2 December 1971 (made permanent in 1996)

Legal system: federal court system introduced in 1971; all emirates except Dubayy (Dubai) and Ra's al Khaymah are not fully integrated into the federal system; all emirates have secular and Islamic law for civil, criminal, and high courts

Suffrage: none

Executive branch:

chief of state: President ZAYID bin Sultan Al Nuhayyan (since 2 December 1971), ruler of Abu Zaby (Abu Dhabi) (since 6 August 1966) and Vice President MAKTUM bin Rashid al-Maktum (since 8 October 1990), ruler of Dubayy (Dubai)

head of government: Prime Minister MAKTUM bin Rashid al-Maktum (since 8 October 1990), ruler of Dubayy (Dubai); Deputy Prime Minister SULTAN bin Zayid Al Nuhayyan (since 20 November 1990)

cabinet: Council of Ministers appointed by the president

note: there is also a Federal Supreme Council (FSC) composed of the seven emirate rulers; the FSC is the highest constitutional authority in the UAE; establishes general policies and sanctions federal legislation; meets four times a year; Abu Zaby (Abu Dhabi) and Dubayy (Dubai) rulers have effective veto power

elections: president and vice president elected by the FSC (a group of seven electors) for five-year terms; election last held 2 December 2001 (next to be held NA 2006); prime minister and deputy prime minister appointed by the president

election results: ZAYID bin Sultan Al Nuhayyan reelected president; percent of FSC vote - NA%, but believed to be unanimous; MAKTUM bin Rashid al-Maktum elected vice president; percent of FSC vote - NA%, but believed to be unanimous

Legislative branch: unicameral Federal National Council or Majlis al-Ittihad al-Watani (40 seats; members appointed by the rulers of the constituent states to serve two-year terms)

elections: none

note: reviews legislation, but cannot change or veto

Judicial branch: Union Supreme Court (judges are appointed by the president)

Political parties and leaders: none

Political pressure groups and leaders: NA

International organization participation: ABEDA, AFESD, AMF, CAEU, FAO, G-77, GCC, IAEA, IBRD, ICAO, ICCt (signatory), ICRM, IDA, IDB, IFAD, IFC, IFRCS, IHO, ILO, IMF, IMO, Interpol, IOC, ISO, ITU, LAS, NAM, OAPEC, OIC, OPCW, OPEC, UN, UNCTAD, UNESCO, UNIDO, UPU, WCO, WHO, WIPO, WMO, WTrO

Diplomatic representation in the US:

chief of mission: Ambassador Al Asri Said Ahmad al-DHAHRI

chancery: 3522 International Court NW, Washington, DC 20037

telephone: [1] (202) 243-2400

FAX: [1] (202) 243-2432

Diplomatic representation from the US:

chief of mission: Ambassador Marcelle M. WAHBA

embassy: Embassies District, Plot 38 Sector W59-02, Street No. 4, Abu Dhabi

mailing address: P. O. Box 4009, Abu Dhabi

telephone: [971] (2) 414-2200

FAX: [971] (2) 414-2469

consulate(s) general: Dubai

Flag description: three equal horizontal bands of green (top), white, and black with a wider vertical red band on the hoist side

Economy

Economy - overview: The UAE has an open economy with a high per capita income and a sizable annual trade surplus. Its wealth is based on oil and gas output (about 33% of GDP), and the fortunes of the economy fluctuate with the prices of those commodities. Since 1973, the UAE has undergone a profound transformation from an impoverished region of small desert principalities to a modern state with a high standard of living. At present levels of production, oil and gas reserves should last for more than 100 years. The government has increased spending on job creation and infrastructure expansion and is opening up its utilities to greater private sector involvement.

GDP: purchasing power parity - $57.7 billion (2003 est.)

GDP - real growth rate: 5.2% (2003 est.)

GDP - per capita: purchasing power parity - $23,200 (2003 est.)

GDP - composition by sector:

agriculture: 4%

industry: 58.5%

services: 37.5% (2002 est.)

Population below poverty line: NA%

Household income or consumption by percentage share:

lowest 10%: NA%

highest 10%: NA%

Inflation rate (consumer prices): 3.2% (2003 est.)

Labor force: 2.1 million

note: 73.9% of the population in the 15-64 age group is non-national (2001)

Labor force - by occupation: services 78%, industry 15%, agriculture 7% (2000 est.)

Unemployment rate: 2.4% (2001)

Budget:

revenues: $15.6 billion

expenditures: $23.5 billion, including capital expenditures of $3.4 billion (2002 est.)

Industries: petroleum, fishing, petrochemicals, construction materials, some boat building, handicrafts, pearling

Industrial production growth rate: 4% (2000)

Electricity - production: 37.74 billion kWh (2001)

Electricity - production by source:

fossil fuel: 100%

hydro: 0%

nuclear: 0%

other: 0% (2001)

Electricity - consumption: 35.1 billion kWh (2001)

Electricity - exports: 0 kWh (2001)

Electricity - imports: 0 kWh (2001)

Oil - production: 2.566 million bbl/day (2001 est.)

Oil - consumption: 310,000 bbl/day (2001 est.)

Oil - exports: NA

Oil - imports: NA

Oil - proved reserves: 80.31 billion bbl (1 January 2002)

Natural gas - production: 44.94 billion cu m (2001 est.)

Natural gas - consumption: 37.86 billion cu m (2001 est.)
Natural gas - exports: 7.08 billion cu m (2001 est.)
Natural gas - imports: 0 cu m (2001 est.)
Natural gas - proved reserves: 5.892 trillion cu m (1 January 2002)
Agriculture - products: dates, vegetables, watermelons; poultry, eggs, dairy products; fish
Exports: $56.73 billion f.o.b. (2003 est.)
Exports - commodities: crude oil 45%, natural gas, reexports, dried fish, dates
Exports - partners: Japan 27.2%, South Korea 9.9%, Iran 4.3% (2002)
Imports: $37.16 billion f.o.b. (2003 est.)
Imports - commodities: machinery and transport equipment, chemicals, food
Imports - partners: Japan 8.7%, China 8.2%, US 7.7%, UK 7.4%, Germany 7.1%, India 6.7%, France 6.6%, South Korea 5.3%, Italy 5.1% (2002)
Debt - external: $20.7 billion (2003 est.)
Economic aid - donor: $NA
Currency: Emirati dirham (AED)
Currency code: AED
Exchange rates: Emirati dirhams per US dollar - 3.67 (2003), 3.6725 (2002), 3.6725 (2001), 3.6725 (2000), 3.6725 (1999)
Fiscal year: calendar year

Communications

Telephones - main lines in use: 1,093,700 (2002)
Telephones - mobile cellular: 2,428,100 (2002)
Telephone system:
general assessment: modern system of microwave radio relay and coaxial cable; key centers are Abu Dhabi and Dubai
domestic: microwave radio relay and coaxial cable
international: country code - 971; satellite earth stations - 3 Intelsat (1 Atlantic Ocean and 2 Indian Ocean) and 1 Arabsat; submarine cables to Qatar, Bahrain, India, and Pakistan; tropospheric scatter to Bahrain; microwave radio relay to Saudi Arabia
Radio broadcast stations: AM 13, FM 7, shortwave 2 (1998)
Television broadcast stations: 15 (1997)
Internet country code: .ae
Internet hosts: 52,332 (2002)
Internet users: 1,175,600 (2002)

Transportation

Railways: 0 km
Highways:
total: 1,088 km
paved: 1,088 km (including 253 km of expressways)
unpaved: 0 km (1999 est.)
Waterways: none
Pipelines: condensate 383 km; gas 1,765 km; liquid petroleum gas 186 km; oil 1,266 km (2003)
Ports and harbors: 'Ajman, Al Fujayrah, Das Island, Khawr Fakkan, Mina' Jabal 'Ali, Mina' Khalid, Mina' Rashid, Mina' Saqr, Mina' Zayid, Umm al Qaywayn

Merchant marine:
total: 59 ships (1,000 GRT or over) 578,477 GRT/ 739,823 DWT
by type: cargo 12, chemical tanker 5, container 7, liquefied gas 1, petroleum tanker 21, roll on/roll off 8, short-sea/passenger 4, specialized tanker 1 (2003 est.)
Airports: 35 (2003 est.)
Airports - with paved runways:
total: 21
over 3,047 m: 8
2,438 to 3,047 m: 3
1,524 to 2,437 m: 4
914 to 1,523 m: 3
under 914 m: 3 (2003 est.)
Airports - with unpaved runways:
total: 14
over 3,047 m: 1
2,438 to 3,047 m: 2
1,524 to 2,437 m: 3
914 to 1,523 m: 4
under 914 m: 4 (2003 est.)
Heliports: 2 (2003 est.)

Military

Military branches: Army, Navy (including Marines and Coast Guard), Air and Air Defense Force, paramilitary forces (includes Federal Police Force)
Military manpower - military age: 18 years of age (2004 est.)
Military manpower - availability:
males age 15-49: 751,707
note: includes non-nationals (2004 est.)
Military manpower - fit for military service:
males age 15-49: 412,490 (2004 est.)
Military manpower - reaching military age annually:
males: 29,183 (2004 est.)
Military expenditures - dollar figure: $1.6 billion (FY00)
Military expenditures - percent of GDP: 3.1% (FY00)

Transnational Issues

Disputes - international: because the treaties have not been made public, the exact alignment of the boundary with Saudi Arabia is still unknown and labeled approximate; boundary agreement signed and ratified with Oman in 2003 for entire border, including Oman's Musandam Peninsula and Al Madhah enclaves; UAE engage in direct talks and solicit Arab League support to resolve disputes over Iran's occupation of Lesser and Greater Tunb Islands and Abu Musa Island
Illicit drugs: the UAE is a drug transshipment point for traffickers given its proximity to southwest Asian drug producing countries; the UAE's position as a major financial center makes it vulnerable to money laundering; anti-money-laundering controls improving

United Kingdom

Introduction

Background: Great Britain, the dominant industrial and maritime power of the 19th century, played a leading role in developing parliamentary democracy and in advancing literature and science. At its zenith, the British Empire stretched over one-fourth of the earth's surface. The first half of the 20th century saw the UK's strength seriously depleted in two World Wars. The second half witnessed the dismantling of the Empire and the UK rebuilding itself into a modern and prosperous European nation. As one of five permanent members of the UN Security Council, a founding member of NATO, and of the Commonwealth, the UK pursues a global approach to foreign policy; it currently is weighing the degree of its integration with continental Europe. A member of the EU, it chose to remain outside the European Monetary Union for the time being. Constitutional reform is also a significant issue in the UK. The Scottish Parliament, the National Assembly for Wales, and the Northern Ireland Assembly were established in 1999, but the latter is suspended due to bickering over the peace process.

United Kingdom (continued)

Geography

Location: Western Europe, islands including the northern one-sixth of the island of Ireland between the North Atlantic Ocean and the North Sea, northwest of France

Geographic coordinates: 54 00 N, 2 00 W

Map references: Europe

Area:

total: 244,820 sq km

land: 241,590 sq km

water: 3,230 sq km

note: includes Rockall and Shetland Islands

Area - comparative: slightly smaller than Oregon

Land boundaries:

total: 360 km

border countries: Ireland 360 km

Coastline: 12,429 km

Maritime claims:

territorial sea: 12 NM

exclusive fishing zone: 200 NM

continental shelf: as defined in continental shelf orders or in accordance with agreed upon boundaries

Climate: temperate; moderated by prevailing southwest winds over the North Atlantic Current; more than one-half of the days are overcast

Terrain: mostly rugged hills and low mountains; level to rolling plains in east and southeast

Elevation extremes:

lowest point: The Fens -4 m

highest point: Ben Nevis 1,343 m

Natural resources: coal, petroleum, natural gas, tin, limestone, iron ore, salt, clay, chalk, gypsum, lead, silica, arable land

Land use:

arable land: 26.41%

permanent crops: 0.18%

other: 73.41% (1998 est.)

Irrigated land: 1,080 sq km (1998 est.)

Natural hazards: winter windstorms; floods

Environment - current issues: continues to reduce greenhouse gas emissions (has met Kyoto Protocol target of a 12.5% reduction from 1990 levels and intends to meet the legally binding target and move towards a domestic goal of a 20% cut in emissions by 2010); by 2005 the government aims to reduce the amount of industrial and commercial waste disposed of in landfill sites to 85% of 1998 levels and to recycle or compost at least 25% of household waste, increasing to 33% by 2015; between 1998-99 and 1999-2000, household recycling increased from 8.8% to 10.3%

Environment - international agreements:

party to: Air Pollution, Air Pollution-Nitrogen Oxides, Air Pollution-Sulfur 94, Air Pollution-Volatile Organic Compounds, Antarctic-Environmental Protocol, Antarctic-Marine Living Resources, Antarctic Seals, Antarctic Treaty, Biodiversity, Climate Change, Climate Change-Kyoto Protocol, Desertification, Endangered Species, Environmental Modification, Hazardous Wastes, Law of the Sea, Marine Dumping, Marine Life Conservation, Ozone Layer Protection, Ship Pollution, Tropical Timber 83, Tropical Timber 94, Wetlands, Whaling

signed, but not ratified: Air Pollution-Persistent Organic Pollutants

Geography - note: lies near vital North Atlantic sea lanes; only 35 km from France and now linked by tunnel under the English Channel; because of heavily indented coastline, no location is more than 125 km from tidal waters

People

Population: 60,270,708 (July 2004 est.)

Age structure:

0-14 years: 18% (male 5,560,489; female 5,293,871)

15-64 years: 66.3% (male 20,193,876; female 19,736,516)

65 years and over: 15.7% (male 4,027,721; female 5,458,235) (2004 est.)

Median age:

total: 38.7 years

male: 37.6 years

female: 39.8 years (2004 est.)

Population growth rate: 0.29% (2004 est.)

Birth rate: 10.88 births/1,000 population (2004 est.)

Death rate: 10.19 deaths/1,000 population (2004 est.)

Net migration rate: 2.19 migrant(s)/1,000 population (2004 est.)

Sex ratio:

at birth: 1.05 male(s)/female

under 15 years: 1.05 male(s)/female

15-64 years: 1.02 male(s)/female

65 years and over: 0.74 male(s)/female

total population: 0.98 male(s)/female (2004 est.)

Infant mortality rate:

total: 5.22 deaths/1,000 live births

male: 5.83 deaths/1,000 live births

female: 4.58 deaths/1,000 live births (2004 est.)

Life expectancy at birth:

total population: 78.27 years

male: 75.84 years

female: 80.83 years (2004 est.)

Total fertility rate: 1.66 children born/woman (2004 est.)

HIV/AIDS - adult prevalence rate: 0.1% (2001 est.)

HIV/AIDS - people living with HIV/AIDS: 34,000 (2001 est.)

HIV/AIDS - deaths: 460 (2001 est.)

Nationality:

noun: Briton(s), British (collective plural)

adjective: British

Ethnic groups: English 81.5%, Scottish 9.6%, Irish 2.4%, Welsh 1.9%, Ulster 1.8%, West Indian, Indian, Pakistani, and other 2.8%

Religions: Anglican and Roman Catholic 40 million, Muslim 1.5 million, Presbyterian 800,000, Methodist 760,000, Sikh 500,000, Hindu 500,000, Jewish 350,000

Languages: English, Welsh (about 26% of the population of Wales), Scottish form of Gaelic (about 60,000 in Scotland)

Literacy:

definition: age 15 and over has completed five or more years of schooling

total population: 99% (2000 est.)

male: NA%

female: NA%

Government

Country name:

conventional long form: United Kingdom of Great Britain and Northern Ireland

conventional short form: United Kingdom

abbreviation: UK

Government type: constitutional monarchy

Capital: London

Administrative divisions: England - 47 boroughs, 36 counties*, 29 London boroughs**, 12 cities and boroughs***, 10 districts****, 12 cities*****, 3 royal boroughs******; Barking and Dagenham**, Barnet**, Barnsley, Bath and North East Somerset****, Bedfordshire*, Bexley**, Birmingham***, Blackburn with Darwen, Blackpool, Bolton, Bournemouth, Bracknell Forest, Bradford***, Brent**, Brighton and Hove, City of Bristol*****, Bromley**, Buckinghamshire*, Bury, Calderdale, Cambridgeshire*, Camden**, Cheshire*, Cornwall*, Coventry***, Croydon**, Cumbria*, Darlington, Derby*****, Derbyshire*, Devon*, Doncaster, Dorset*, Dudley, Durham*, Ealing**, East Riding of Yorkshire****, East Sussex*, Enfield**, Essex*, Gateshead, Gloucestershire*, Greenwich**, Hackney**, Halton, Hammersmith and Fulham**, Hampshire*, Haringey**, Harrow**, Hartlepool, Havering**, Herefordshire*, Hertfordshire*, Hillingdon**, Hounslow**, Isle of Wight*, Islington**, Kensington and Chelsea******, Kent*, City of Kingston upon Hull*****, Kingston upon Thames******, Kirklees, Knowsley, Lambeth**, Lancashire*, Leeds***, Leicester*****, Leicestershire*, Lewisham**, Lincolnshire*, Liverpool***, City of London*****, Luton, Manchester***, Medway, Merton**, Middlesbrough, Milton Keynes, Newcastle upon Tyne***, Newham**, Norfolk*, Northamptonshire*, North East Lincolnshire****, North Lincolnshire****, North Somerset****, North Tyneside, Northumberland*, North Yorkshire*, Nottingham*****, Nottinghamshire*, Oldham, Oxfordshire*, Peterborough*****, Plymouth*****, Poole, Portsmouth*****, Reading, Redbridge**, Redcar and Cleveland, Richmond upon Thames**, Rochdale, Rotherham, Rutland****, Salford***, Shropshire*, Sandwell, Sefton, Sheffield***, Slough, Solihull, Somerset*, Southampton*****, Southend-on-Sea, South Gloucestershire****, South Tyneside, Southwark**, Staffordshire*, St. Helens, Stockport, Stockton-on-Tees, Stoke-on-Trent*****, Suffolk*, Sunderland***, Surrey*, Sutton**, Swindon, Tameside, Telford and Wrekin****, Thurrock, Torbay, Tower Hamlets**, Trafford, Wakefield***, Walsall, Waltham Forest**, Wandsworth**, Warrington, Warwickshire*, West Berkshire****, Westminster***, West Sussex*, Wigan, Wiltshire*, Windsor and

United Kingdom (continued)

Maidenhead******, Wirral, Wokingham****, Wolverhampton, Worcestershire*, York*****; Northern Ireland - 24 districts, 2 cities*, 6 counties**; Antrim, County Antrim**, Ards, Armagh, County Armagh**, Ballymena, Ballymoney, Banbridge, Belfast*, Carrickfergus, Castlereagh, Coleraine, Cookstown, Craigavon, Down, County Down**, Dungannon, Fermanagh, County Fermanagh**, Larne, Limavady, Lisburn, County Londonderry**, Derry*, Magherafelt, Moyle, Newry and Mourne, Newtownabbey, North Down, Omagh, Strabane, County Tyrone**; Scotland - 32 council areas; Aberdeen City, Aberdeenshire, Angus, Argyll and Bute, The Scottish Borders, Clackmannanshire, Dumfries and Galloway, Dundee City, East Ayrshire, East Dunbartonshire, East Lothian, East Renfrewshire, City of Edinburgh, Falkirk, Fife, Glasgow City, Highland, Inverclyde, Midlothian, Moray, North Ayrshire, North Lanarkshire, Orkney Islands, Perth and Kinross, Renfrewshire, Shetland Islands, South Ayrshire, South Lanarkshire, Stirling, West Dunbartonshire, Eilean Siar (Western Isles), West Lothian; Wales - 11 county boroughs, 9 counties*, 2 cities and counties**; Isle of Anglesey*, Blaenau Gwent, Bridgend, Caerphilly, Cardiff**, Ceredigion*, Carmarthenshire*, Conwy, Denbighshire*, Flintshire*, Gwynedd, Merthyr Tydfil, Monmouthshire*, Neath Port Talbot, Newport, Pembrokeshire*, Powys*, Rhondda Cynon Taff, Swansea**, Torfaen, The Vale of Glamorgan*, Wrexham

Dependent areas: Anguilla, Bermuda, British Indian Ocean Territory, British Virgin Islands, Cayman Islands, Falkland Islands, Gibraltar, Guernsey, Jersey, Isle of Man, Montserrat, Pitcairn Islands, Saint Helena, South Georgia and the South Sandwich Islands, Turks and Caicos Islands

Independence: England has existed as a unified entity since the 10th century; the union between England and Wales, begun in 1284 with the Statute of Rhuddlan, was not formalized until 1536 with an Act of Union; in another Act of Union in 1707, England and Scotland agreed to permanently join as Great Britain; the legislative union of Great Britain and Ireland was implemented in 1801, with the adoption of the name the United Kingdom of Great Britain and Ireland; the Anglo-Irish treaty of 1921 formalized a partition of Ireland; six northern Irish counties remained part of the United Kingdom as Northern Ireland and the current name of the country, the United Kingdom of Great Britain and Northern Ireland, was adopted in 1927

National holiday: the UK does not celebrate one particular national holiday

Constitution: unwritten; partly statutes, partly common law and practice

Legal system: common law tradition with early Roman and modern continental influences; has judicial review of Acts of Parliament under the Human Rights Act of 1998; accepts compulsory ICJ jurisdiction, with reservations

Suffrage: 18 years of age; universal

Executive branch:
chief of state: Queen ELIZABETH II (since 6 February 1952); Heir Apparent Prince CHARLES (son of the queen, born 14 November 1948)
head of government: Prime Minister Anthony (Tony) BLAIR (since 2 May 1997)
cabinet: Cabinet of Ministers appointed by the prime minister
elections: none; the monarchy is hereditary; following legislative elections, the leader of the majority party or the leader of the majority coalition is usually the prime minister

Legislative branch: bicameral Parliament comprised of House of Lords (consists of approximately 500 life peers, 92 hereditary peers and 26 clergy) and House of Commons (659 seats; members are elected by popular vote to serve five-year terms unless the House is dissolved earlier)
elections: House of Lords - no elections (note - in 1999, as provided by the House of Lords Act, elections were held in the House of Lords to determine the 92 hereditary peers who would remain there; pending further reforms, elections are held only as vacancies in the hereditary peerage arise); House of Commons - last held 7 June 2001 (next to be held by NA May 2006)
election results: House of Commons - percent of vote by party - Labor 42.1%, Conservative and Unionist 32.7%, Liberal Democrats 18.8%, other 6.4%; seats by party - Labor 412, Conservative and Unionist 166, Liberal Democrat 52, other 29; note - seating as of 5 January 2004: Labor 408, Conservative 163, Liberal Democrats 54, other 34
note: in 1998 elections were held for a Northern Ireland Assembly (because of unresolved disputes among existing parties, the transfer of power from London to Northern Ireland came only at the end of 1999 and has been suspended four times the latest occurring in October 2002; since October 2002 the Northern Ireland Parliament has been suspended); in 1999 there were elections for a new Scottish Parliament and a new Welsh Assembly

Judicial branch: House of Lords (highest court of appeal; several Lords of Appeal in Ordinary are appointed by the monarch for life); Supreme Courts of England, Wales, and Northern Ireland (comprising the Courts of Appeal, the High Courts of Justice, and the Crown Courts); Scotland's Court of Session and Court of the Justiciary

Political parties and leaders: Conservative and Unionist Party [Michael HOWARD]; Democratic Unionist Party (Northern Ireland) [Rev. Ian PAISLEY]; Labor Party [Anthony (Tony) BLAIR]; Liberal Democrats [Charles KENNEDY]; Party of Wales (Plaid Cymru) [Dafydd IWAN]; Scottish National Party or SNP [John SWINNEY]; Sinn Fein (Northern Ireland) [Gerry ADAMS]; Social Democratic and Labor Party or SDLP (Northern Ireland) [Mark DURKAN]; Ulster Unionist Party (Northern Ireland) [David TRIMBLE]

Political pressure groups and leaders: Campaign for Nuclear Disarmament; Confederation of British Industry; National Farmers' Union; Trades Union Congress

International organization participation: AfDB, AsDB, Australia Group, BIS, C, CDB, CE, CERN, EAPC, EBRD, EIB, ESA, EU, FAO, G- 5, G- 7, G- 8, G-10, IADB, IAEA, IBRD, ICAO, ICC, ICCt, ICFTU, ICRM, IDA, IEA, IFAD, IFC, IFRCS, IHO, ILO, IMF, IMO, Interpol, IOC, IOM, ISO, ITU, MONUC, NAM (guest), NATO, NEA, NSG, OAS (observer), OECD, OPCW, OSCE, Paris Club, PCA, UN, UN Security Council, UNAMSIL, UNCTAD, UNESCO, UNFICYP, UNHCR, UNIDO, UNITAR, UNMEE, UNMIK, UNMIL, UNMOVIC, UNOMIG, UNRWA, UPU, WCO, WEU, WHO, WIPO, WMO, WTrO, ZC

Diplomatic representation in the US:
chief of mission: Ambassador David G. MANNING
chancery: 3100 Massachusetts Avenue NW, Washington, DC 20008
telephone: [1] (202) 588-6500
FAX: [1] (202) 588-7870
consulate(s) general: Atlanta, Boston, Chicago, Houston, Los Angeles, New York, and San Francisco
consulate(s): Dallas, Denver, Miami, and Seattle

Diplomatic representation from the US:
chief of mission: Ambassador William S. FARISH
embassy: 24/31 Grosvenor Square, London, W1A1AE
mailing address: PSC 801, Box 40, FPO AE 09498-4040
telephone: [44] (0) 20 7499-9000
FAX: [44] (0) 20 7629-9124
consulate(s) general: Belfast, Edinburgh

Flag description: blue field with the red cross of Saint George (patron saint of England) edged in white superimposed on the diagonal red cross of Saint Patrick (patron saint of Ireland), which is superimposed on the diagonal white cross of Saint Andrew (patron saint of Scotland); properly known as the Union Flag, but commonly called the Union Jack; the design and colors (especially the Blue Ensign) have been the basis for a number of other flags including other Commonwealth countries and their constituent states or provinces, as well as British overseas territories

Economy

Economy - overview: The UK, a leading trading power and financial center, is one of the quartet of trillion dollar economies of Western Europe. Over the past two decades the government has greatly reduced public ownership and contained the growth of social welfare programs. Agriculture is intensive, highly mechanized, and efficient by European standards, producing about 60% of food needs with only 1% of the labor force. The UK has large coal, natural gas, and oil reserves; primary energy production accounts for 10% of GDP, one of the highest shares of any industrial nation. Services, particularly banking, insurance, and business services, account by far for

United Kingdom *(continued)*

the largest proportion of GDP while industry continues to decline in importance. GDP growth slipped in 2001-03 as the global downturn, the high value of the pound, and the bursting of the "new economy" bubble hurt manufacturing and exports. Still, the economy is one of the strongest in Europe; inflation, interest rates, and unemployment remain low. The relatively good economic performance has complicated the BLAIR government's efforts to make a case for Britain to join the European Economic and Monetary Union (EMU). Critics point out, however, that the economy is doing well outside of EMU, and they point to public opinion polls that continue to show a majority of Britons opposed to the euro. Meantime, the government has been speeding up the improvement of education, transport, and health services, at a cost in higher taxes. The war in March-April 2003 between a US-led coalition and Iraq, together with the subsequent problems of restoring the economy and the polity, involve a heavy commitment of British military forces.
GDP: purchasing power parity - $1.664 trillion (2003 est.)
GDP - real growth rate: 2.1% (2003 est.)
GDP - per capita: purchasing power parity - $27,700 (2003 est.)
GDP - composition by sector:
agriculture: 1.4%
industry: 24.9%
services: 73.7% (2000)
Population below poverty line: 17% (2002 est.)
Household income or consumption by percentage share:
lowest 10%: 2.3%
highest 10%: 27.7% (1995)
Distribution of family income - Gini index: 36.8 (1995)
Inflation rate (consumer prices): 3% (2003 est.)
Labor force: 29.7 million (2001)
Labor force - by occupation: agriculture 1%, industry 25%, services 74% (1999)
Unemployment rate: 5.1% (2003 est.)
Budget:
revenues: $565 billion
expenditures: $540 billion, including capital expenditures of $NA (FY01)
Industries: machine tools, electric power equipment, automation equipment, railroad equipment, shipbuilding, aircraft, motor vehicles and parts, electronics and communications equipment, metals, chemicals, coal, petroleum, paper and paper products, food processing, textiles, clothing, and other consumer goods
Industrial production growth rate: -0.6% (2003 est.)
Electricity - production: 360.9 billion kWh (2001)
Electricity - production by source:
fossil fuel: 73.8%
hydro: 0.9%
nuclear: 23.7%
other: 1.6% (2001)
Electricity - consumption: 346.1 billion kWh (2001)
Electricity - exports: 264 million kWh (2001)

Electricity - imports: 10.66 billion kWh (2001)
Oil - production: 2.541 million bbl/day (2001 est.)
Oil - consumption: 1.71 million bbl/day (2001 est.)
Oil - exports: 2.205 million bbl/day (2001)
Oil - imports: 1.418 million bbl/day (2001)
Oil - proved reserves: 4.741 billion bbl (1 January 2002)
Natural gas - production: 105.9 billion cu m (2001 est.)
Natural gas - consumption: 92.85 billion cu m (2001 est.)
Natural gas - exports: 15.75 billion cu m (2001 est.)
Natural gas - imports: 2.7 billion cu m (2001 est.)
Natural gas - proved reserves: 714.9 billion cu m (1 January 2002)
Agriculture - products: cereals, oilseed, potatoes, vegetables; cattle, sheep, poultry; fish
Exports: $304.5 billion f.o.b. (2003 est.)
Exports - commodities: manufactured goods, fuels, chemicals; food, beverages, tobacco
Exports - partners: US 15.5%, Germany 11.2%, France 9.4%, Ireland 8%, Netherlands 7.1%, Belgium 5.2%, Italy 4.4%, Spain 4.3% (2002)
Imports: $363.6 billion f.o.b. (2003 est.)
Imports - commodities: manufactured goods, machinery, fuels; foodstuffs
Imports - partners: Germany 12.9%, US 11.9%, France 7.8%, Netherlands 6.3%, Belgium 5%, Italy 4.4% (2002)
Debt - external: $NA (2002 est.)
Economic aid - donor: ODA, $4.5 billion (2000)
Currency: British pound (GBP)
Currency code: GBP
Exchange rates: British pounds per US dollar - 0.6125 (2003), 0.6672 (2002), 0.6947 (2001), 0.6609 (2000), 0.6181 (1999)
Fiscal year: 1 April - 31 March

Communications

Telephones - main lines in use: 34.898 million (2002)
Telephones - mobile cellular: 49.677 million (2002)
Telephone system:
general assessment: technologically advanced domestic and international system
domestic: equal mix of buried cables, microwave radio relay, and fiber-optic systems
international: country code - 44; 40 coaxial submarine cables; satellite earth stations - 10 Intelsat (7 Atlantic Ocean and 3 Indian Ocean), 1 Inmarsat (Atlantic Ocean region), and 1 Eutelsat; at least 8 large international switching centers
Radio broadcast stations: AM 219, FM 431, shortwave 3 (1998)
Television broadcast stations: 228 (plus 3,523 repeaters) (1995)
Internet country code: .uk
Internet hosts: 2,865,930 (2002)
Internet users: 25 million (2002)

Transportation

Railways:
total: 16,893 km
standard gauge: 16,536 km 1.435-m gauge (4,928 km electrified)
broad gauge: 357 km 1.600-m gauge (in Northern Ireland) (2002)
Highways:
total: 371,913 km
paved: 371,913 km (including 3,358 km of expressways)
unpaved: 0 km (1999)
Waterways: 3,200 km
Pipelines: condensate 370 km; gas 21,263 km; liquid petroleum gas 59 km; oil 6,420 km; oil/gas/water 63 km; refined products 4,474 km; water 650 km (2003)
Ports and harbors: Aberdeen, Belfast, Bristol, Cardiff, Dover, Falmouth, Felixstowe, Glasgow, Grangemouth, Hull, Leith, Liverpool, London, Manchester, Peterhead, Plymouth, Portsmouth, Ramsgate, Scapa Flow, Southampton, Sullom Voe, Teesport, Tyne
Merchant marine:
total: 384 ships (1,000 GRT or over) 9,181,284 GRT/ 9,566,275 DWT
by type: bulk 20, cargo 50, chemical tanker 28, combination ore/oil 1, container 130, liquefied gas 23, livestock carrier 1, multi-functional large load carrier 1, passenger 20, petroleum tanker 45, refrigerated cargo 18, roll on/roll off 34, short-sea/passenger 11, specialized tanker 1, vehicle carrier 1
foreign-owned: Australia 2, Croatia 4, Cyprus 1, Denmark 42, Finland 1, Germany 52, Greece 36, Hong Kong 16, Italy 3, Japan 1, Monaco 13, Nigeria 1, Norway 32, South Africa 2, Sweden 13, Taiwan 7, United
registered in other countries: 522 (2003 est.)
Airports: 471 (2003 est.)
Airports - with paved runways:
total: 334
over 3,047 m: 8
2,438 to 3,047 m: 33
1,524 to 2,437 m: 150
914 to 1,523 m: 86
under 914 m: 57 (2003 est.)
Airports - with unpaved runways:
total: 137
2438 to 3047 m: 1
1,524 to 2,437 m: 1
914 to 1,523 m: 23
under 914 m: 112 (2003 est.)
Heliports: 11 (2003 est.)

Military

Military branches: Army, Royal Navy (including Royal Marines), Royal Air Force
Military manpower - military age: 16 years of age (2004 est.)
Military manpower - availability:
males age 15-49: 14,943,016 (2004 est.)

United Kingdom (continued)

Military manpower - fit for military service:
males age 15-49: 12,393,785 (2004 est.)
Military expenditures - dollar figure:
$42,836,500,000 (2003)
Military expenditures - percent of GDP: 2.4%
(2003)

Transnational Issues

Disputes - international: since Gibraltar residents voted overwhelmingly by referendum in 2003 against a "total shared sovereignty" arrangement, talks between the UK and Spain over the fate of the 300-year old UK colony have stalled; Spain disapproves of UK plans to grant Gibraltar greater autonomy; Mauritius and Seychelles claim the Chagos Archipelago (British Indian Ocean Territory), and its former inhabitants since their eviction in 1965; most reside chiefly in Mauritius, and in 2001 were granted UK citizenship and the right to repatriation; UK continues to reject sovereignty talks requested by Argentina, which still claims the Falkland Islands (Islas Malvinas) and South Georgia and the South Sandwich Islands; Rockall continental shelf dispute involving Denmark and Iceland remains dormant; territorial claim in Antarctica (British Antarctic Territory) overlaps Argentine claim and partially overlaps Chilean claim; disputes with Iceland, Denmark, and Ireland over the Faroe Islands continental shelf boundary outside 200 NM

Illicit drugs: producer of limited amounts of synthetic drugs and synthetic precursor chemicals; major consumer of Southwest Asian heroin, Latin American cocaine, and synthetic drugs; money-laundering center

United States

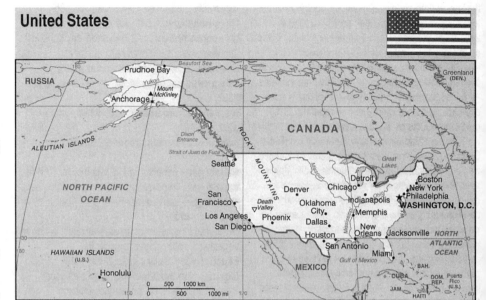

Introduction

Background: Britain's American colonies broke with the mother country in 1776 and were recognized as the new nation of the United States of America following the Treaty of Paris in 1783. During the 19th and 20th centuries, 37 new states were added to the original 13 as the nation expanded across the North American continent and acquired a number of overseas possessions. The two most traumatic experiences in the nation's history were the Civil War (1861-65) and the Great Depression of the 1930s. Buoyed by victories in World Wars I and II and the end of the Cold War in 1991, the US remains the world's most powerful nation state. The economy is marked by steady growth, low unemployment and inflation, and rapid advances in technology.

Geography

Location: North America, bordering both the North Atlantic Ocean and the North Pacific Ocean, between Canada and Mexico
Geographic coordinates: 38 00 N, 97 00 W
Map references: North America
Area:
total: 9,631,418 sq km
land: 9,161,923 sq km
water: 469,495 sq km
note: includes only the 50 states and District of Columbia
Area - comparative: about half the size of Russia; about three-tenths the size of Africa; about half the size of South America (or slightly larger than Brazil); slightly larger than China; about two and a half times the size of Western Europe
Land boundaries:
total: 12,034 km
border countries: Canada 8,893 km (including 2,477 km with Alaska), Mexico 3,141 km
note: US Naval Base at Guantanamo Bay, Cuba is leased by the US and is part of Cuba; the base boundary is 29 km

Coastline: 19,924 km
Maritime claims:
territorial sea: 12 NM
contiguous zone: 24 NM
exclusive economic zone: 200 NM
continental shelf: not specified
Climate: mostly temperate, but tropical in Hawaii and Florida, arctic in Alaska, semiarid in the great plains west of the Mississippi River, and arid in the Great Basin of the southwest; low winter temperatures in the northwest are ameliorated occasionally in January and February by warm chinook winds from the eastern slopes of the Rocky Mountains
Terrain: vast central plain, mountains in west, hills and low mountains in east; rugged mountains and broad river valleys in Alaska; rugged, volcanic topography in Hawaii
Elevation extremes:
lowest point: Death Valley -86 m
highest point: Mount McKinley 6,194 m
Natural resources: coal, copper, lead, molybdenum, phosphates, uranium, bauxite, gold, iron, mercury, nickel, potash, silver, tungsten, zinc, petroleum, natural gas, timber
Land use:
arable land: 19.3%
permanent crops: 0.2%
other: 80.5% (1998 est.)
Irrigated land: 214,000 sq km (1998 est.)
Natural hazards: tsunamis, volcanoes, and earthquake activity around Pacific Basin; hurricanes along the Atlantic and Gulf of Mexico coasts; tornadoes in the midwest and southeast; mud slides in California; forest fires in the west; flooding; permafrost in northern Alaska, a major impediment to development
Environment - current issues: air pollution resulting in acid rain in both the US and Canada; the US is the largest single emitter of carbon dioxide from the burning of fossil fuels; water pollution from runoff

United States *(continued)*

of pesticides and fertilizers; limited natural fresh water resources in much of the western part of the country require careful management; desertification

Environment - international agreements:

party to: Air Pollution, Air Pollution-Nitrogen Oxides, Antarctic-Environmental Protocol, Antarctic-Marine Living Resources, Antarctic Seals, Antarctic Treaty, Climate Change, Desertification, Endangered Species, Environmental Modification, Marine Dumping, Marine Life Conservation, Ozone Layer Protection, Ship Pollution, Tropical Timber 83, Tropical Timber 94, Wetlands, Whaling

signed, but not ratified: Air Pollution-Persistent Organic Pollutants, Air Pollution-Volatile Organic Compounds, Biodiversity, Climate Change-Kyoto Protocol, Hazardous Wastes

Geography - note: world's third-largest country by size (after Russia and Canada) and by population (after China and India); Mt. McKinley is highest point in North America and Death Valley the lowest point on the continent

People

Population: 293,027,571 (July 2004 est.)

Age structure:

0-14 years: 20.8% (male 31,122,974; female 29,713,748)

15-64 years: 66.9% (male 97,756,380; female 98,183,309)

65 years and over: 12.4% (male 15,078,204; female 21,172,956) (2004 est.)

Median age:

total: 36 years

male: 34.7 years

female: 37.4 years (2004 est.)

Population growth rate: 0.92% (2004 est.)

Birth rate: 14.13 births/1,000 population (2004 est.)

Death rate: 8.34 deaths/1,000 population (2004 est.)

Net migration rate: 3.41 migrant(s)/1,000 population (2004 est.)

Sex ratio:

at birth: 1.05 male(s)/female

under 15 years: 1.05 male(s)/female

15-64 years: 1 male(s)/female

65 years and over: 0.71 male(s)/female

total population: 0.97 male(s)/female (2004 est.)

Infant mortality rate:

total: 6.63 deaths/1,000 live births

male: 7.31 deaths/1,000 live births

female: 5.91 deaths/1,000 live births (2004 est.)

Life expectancy at birth:

total population: 77.43 years

male: 74.63 years

female: 80.36 years (2004 est.)

Total fertility rate: 2.07 children born/woman (2004 est.)

HIV/AIDS - adult prevalence rate: 0.6% (2001 est.)

HIV/AIDS - people living with HIV/AIDS: 900,000 (2001 est.)

HIV/AIDS - deaths: 15,000 (2001 est.)

Nationality:

noun: American(s)

adjective: American

Ethnic groups: white 77.1%, black 12.9%, Asian 4.2%, Amerindian and Alaska native 1.5%, native Hawaiian and other Pacific islander 0.3%, other 4% (2000)

note: a separate listing for Hispanic is not included because the US Census Bureau considers Hispanic to mean a person of Latin American descent (including persons of Cuban, Mexican, or Puerto Rican origin) living in the US who may be of any race or ethnic group (white, black, Asian, etc.)

Religions: Protestant 56%, Roman Catholic 28%, Jewish 2%, other 4%, none 10% (1989)

Languages: English, Spanish (spoken by a sizable minority)

Literacy:

definition: age 15 and over can read and write

total population: 97%

male: 97%

female: 97% (1979 est.)

Government

Country name:

conventional long form: United States of America

conventional short form: United States

abbreviation: US or USA

Government type: Constitution-based federal republic; strong democratic tradition

Capital: Washington, DC

Administrative divisions: 50 states and 1 district*; Alabama, Alaska, Arizona, Arkansas, California, Colorado, Connecticut, Delaware, District of Columbia*, Florida, Georgia, Hawaii, Idaho, Illinois, Indiana, Iowa, Kansas, Kentucky, Louisiana, Maine, Maryland, Massachusetts, Michigan, Minnesota, Mississippi, Missouri, Montana, Nebraska, Nevada, New Hampshire, New Jersey, New Mexico, New York, North Carolina, North Dakota, Ohio, Oklahoma, Oregon, Pennsylvania, Rhode Island, South Carolina, South Dakota, Tennessee, Texas, Utah, Vermont, Virginia, Washington, West Virginia, Wisconsin, Wyoming

Dependent areas: American Samoa, Baker Island, Guam, Howland Island, Jarvis Island, Johnston Atoll, Kingman Reef, Midway Islands, Navassa Island, Northern Mariana Islands, Palmyra Atoll, Puerto Rico, Virgin Islands, Wake Island

note: from 18 July 1947 until 1 October 1994, the US administered the Trust Territory of the Pacific Islands. It entered into a political relationship with all four political units: the Northern Mariana Islands is a commonwealth in political union with the US (effective 3 November 1986); Palau concluded a Compact of Free Association with the US (effective 1 October 1994); the Federated States of Micronesia signed a Compact of Free Association with the US (effective 3 November 1986); the Republic of the Marshall Islands signed a Compact of Free Association with the US (effective 21 October 1986)

Independence: 4 July 1776 (from Great Britain)

National holiday: Independence Day, 4 July (1776)

Constitution: 17 September 1787, effective 4 March 1789

Legal system: based on English common law; judicial review of legislative acts; accepts compulsory ICJ jurisdiction with reservations

Suffrage: 18 years of age; universal

Executive branch:

chief of state: President George W. BUSH (since 20 January 2001); note - the president is both the chief of state and head of government

head of government: President George W. BUSH (since 20 January 2001) ; note - the president is both the chief of state and head of government

cabinet: Cabinet appointed by the president with Senate approval

elections: president and vice president elected on the same ticket by a college of representatives who are elected directly from each state; president and vice president serve four-year terms; election last held 7 November 2000 (next to be held 2 November 2004)

election results: George W. BUSH elected president; percent of popular vote - George W. BUSH (Republican Party) 48%, Albert A. GORE, Jr. (Democratic Party) 48%, Ralph NADER (Green Party) 3%, other 1%

Legislative branch: bicameral Congress consists of the Senate (100 seats, one-third are renewed every two years; two members are elected from each state by popular vote to serve six-year terms) and the House of Representatives (435 seats; members are directly elected by popular vote to serve two-year terms)

elections: Senate - last held 5 November 2002 (next to be held 2 November 2004); House of Representatives - last held 5 November 2002 (next to be held 2 November 2004)

election results: Senate - percent of vote by party - NA%; seats by party - Republican Party 51, Democratic Party 48, independent 1; House of Representatives - percent of vote by party - NA%; seats by party - Republican Party 226, Democratic Party 204, independent 1, undecided 4

Judicial branch: Supreme Court (its nine justices are appointed for life on condition of good behavior by the president with confirmation by the Senate); United States Courts of Appeal; United States District Courts; State and County Courts

Political parties and leaders: Democratic Party [Terence McAULIFFE]; Green Party [leader NA]; Libertarian Party [Steve DASBACH]; Republican Party [Governor Marc RACICOT]

Political pressure groups and leaders: NA

International organization participation: AfDB, ANZUS, APEC, ARF, AsDB, ASEAN (dialogue partner), Australia Group, BIS, CE (observer), CERN (observer), CP, EAPC, EBRD, FAO, G-5, G-7, G-8, G-10, IADB, IAEA, IBRD, ICAO, ICC, ICCt (signatory), ICFTU, ICRM, IDA, IEA, IFAD, IFC, IFRCS, IHO, ILO, IMF, IMO, Interpol, IOC, IOM, ISO, ITU, MICAH, NAM (guest), NATO, NEA, NSG, OAS, OECD, OPCW,

United States (continued)

OSCE, Paris Club, PCA, UN, UN Security Council, UNCTAD, UNESCO, UNHCR, UNITAR, UNMEE, UNMIK, UNMIL, UNMOVIC, UNOMIG, UNRWA, UNTSO, UPU, WCL, WCO, WHO, WIPO, WMO, WTrO, ZC

Flag description: 13 equal horizontal stripes of red (top and bottom) alternating with white; there is a blue rectangle in the upper hoist-side corner bearing 50 small, white, five-pointed stars arranged in nine offset horizontal rows of six stars (top and bottom) alternating with rows of five stars; the 50 stars represent the 50 states, the 13 stripes represent the 13 original colonies; known as Old Glory; the design and colors have been the basis for a number of other flags, including Chile, Liberia, Malaysia, and Puerto Rico

Economy

Economy - overview: The US has the largest and most technologically powerful economy in the world, with a per capita GDP of $37,800. In this market-oriented economy, private individuals and business firms make most of the decisions, and the federal and state governments buy needed goods and services predominantly in the private marketplace. US business firms enjoy considerably greater flexibility than their counterparts in Western Europe and Japan in decisions to expand capital plant, to lay off surplus workers, and to develop new products. At the same time, they face higher barriers to entry in their rivals' home markets than the barriers to entry of foreign firms in US markets. US firms are at or near the forefront in technological advances, especially in computers and in medical, aerospace, and military equipment; their advantage has narrowed since the end of World War II. The onrush of technology largely explains the gradual development of a "two-tier labor market" in which those at the bottom lack the education and the professional/technical skills of those at the top and, more and more, fail to get comparable pay raises, health insurance coverage, and other benefits. Since 1975, practically all the gains in household income have gone to the top 20% of households. The years 1994-2000 witnessed solid increases in real output, low inflation rates, and a drop in unemployment to below 5%. The year 2001 saw the end of boom psychology and performance, with output increasing only 0.3% and unemployment and business failures rising substantially. The response to the terrorist attacks of 11 September 2001 showed the remarkable resilience of the economy. Moderate recovery took place in 2002 with the GDP growth rate rising to 2.4%. A major short-term problem in first half 2002 was a sharp decline in the stock market, fueled in part by the exposure of dubious accounting practices in some major corporations. The war in March/April 2003 between a US-led coalition and Iraq shifted resources to the military. In 2003, growth in output and productivity and the recovery of the stock market to above 10,000 for the Dow Jones Industrial Average were promising signs. Unemployment stayed at the 6% level, however, and began to decline only at the end of the year. Long-term problems include inadequate investment in economic infrastructure, rapidly rising medical and pension costs of an aging population, sizable trade and budget deficits, and stagnation of family income in the lower economic groups.

GDP: purchasing power parity - $10.98 trillion (2003 est.)

GDP - real growth rate: 3.1% (2003 est.)

GDP - per capita: purchasing power parity - $37,800 (2003 est.)

GDP - composition by sector:
agriculture: 2%
industry: 18%
services: 80% (2002 est.)

Population below poverty line: 12% (2003 est.)

Household income or consumption by percentage share:
lowest 10%: 1.8%
highest 10%: 30.5% (1997)

Distribution of family income - Gini index: 40.8 (1997)

Inflation rate (consumer prices): 2.1% (2003)

Labor force: 141.8 million (includes unemployed) (2003)

Labor force - by occupation: managerial, professional, and technical 31%, sales and office 28.9%, services 13.6%, manufacturing, extraction, transportation, and crafts 24.1%, farming, forestry, and fishing 2.4%
note: figures exclude the unemployed (2001)

Unemployment rate: 6.2% (2003)

Budget:
revenues: $1.946 trillion
expenditures: $2.052 trillion, including capital expenditures of NA (2002 est.)

Industries: leading industrial power in the world, highly diversified and technologically advanced; petroleum, steel, motor vehicles, aerospace, telecommunications, chemicals, electronics, food processing, consumer goods, lumber, mining

Industrial production growth rate: -1% (2003 est.)

Electricity - production: 3.719 trillion kWh (2001)

Electricity - production by source:
fossil fuel: 71.4%
hydro: 5.6%
nuclear: 20.7%
other: 2.3% (2001)

Electricity - consumption: 3.602 trillion kWh (2001)

Electricity - exports: 18.17 billion kWh (2001)

Electricity - imports: 38.48 billion kWh (2001)

Oil - production: 8.054 million bbl/day (2001 est.)

Oil - consumption: 19.65 million bbl/day (2001 est.)

Oil - exports: NA

Oil - imports: NA

Oil - proved reserves: 22.45 billion bbl (1 January 2002)

Natural gas - production: 548.1 billion cu m (2001 est.)

Natural gas - consumption: 640.9 billion cu m (2001 est.)

Natural gas - exports: 11.16 billion cu m (2001 est.)

Natural gas - imports: 114.1 billion cu m (2001 est.)

Natural gas - proved reserves: 5.195 trillion cu m (1 January 2002)

Agriculture - products: wheat, corn, other grains, fruits, vegetables, cotton; beef, pork, poultry, dairy products; forest products; fish

Exports: $714.5 billion f.o.b. (2003 est.)

Exports - commodities: capital goods, automobiles, industrial supplies and raw materials, consumer goods, agricultural products

Exports - partners: Canada 23.2%, Mexico 14.1%, Japan 7.4%, UK 4.8% (2002)

Imports: $1.26 trillion f.o.b. (2003 est.)

Imports - commodities: crude oil and refined petroleum products, machinery, automobiles, consumer goods, industrial raw materials, food and beverages

Imports - partners: Canada 17.8%, Mexico 11.3%, China 11.1%, Japan 10.4%, Germany 5.3% (2002)

Debt - external: $1.4 trillion (2001 est.)

Economic aid - donor: ODA, $6.9 billion (1997)

Currency: US dollar (USD)

Currency code: USD

Exchange rates: British pounds per US dollar - 0.6139 (2003), 0.6661 (2002), 0.6944 (2001), 0.6596 (2000), 0.6180 (1999), Canadian dollars per US dollar - 1.4045 (2003), 1.5693 (2002), 1.5488 (2001), 1.4851 (2000), 1.4857 (1999), Japanese yen per US dollar - 116.08 (2003), 125.39 (2002), 121.53 (2001), 107.77 (2000), 113.91 (1999), euros per US dollar - 0.8866 (2003), 1.0626 (2002), 1.1175 (2001), 1.08540 (2000), 0.93863 (1999)

Fiscal year: 1 October - 30 September

Communications

Telephones - main lines in use: 186,232,300 (2002)

Telephones - mobile cellular: 140,766,800 (2002)

Telephone system:
general assessment: a large, technologically advanced, multipurpose communications system
domestic: a large system of fiber-optic cable, microwave radio relay, coaxial cable, and domestic satellites carries every form of telephone traffic; a rapidly growing cellular system carries mobile telephone traffic throughout the country
international: country code - 1; 24 ocean cable systems in use; satellite earth stations - 61 Intelsat (45 Atlantic Ocean and 16 Pacific Ocean), 5 Intersputnik (Atlantic Ocean region), and 4 Inmarsat (Pacific and Atlantic Ocean regions) (2000)

Radio broadcast stations: AM 4,762, FM 5,542, shortwave 18 (1998)

Television broadcast stations: more than 1,500 (including nearly 1,000 stations affiliated with the five major networks - NBC, ABC, CBS, FOX, and PBS; in addition, there are about 9,000 cable TV systems) (1997)

Internet country code: .us

Internet hosts: 115,311,958 (2002)

Internet users: 159 million (2002)

Transportation

Railways:

total: 194,731 km mainline routes

standard gauge: 194,731 km 1.435-m gauge

note: represents the aggregate length of roadway of all line-haul railroads including an estimate for class II and III railroads; excludes 135,185 km of yard tracks, sidings, and parallel lines (2000)

Highways:

total: 6,406,296 km

paved: 4,148,395 km (including 74,898 km of expressways)

unpaved: 2,257,902 km (2002)

Waterways: 41,009 km

note: navigable inland channels, exclusive of the Great Lakes

Pipelines: petroleum products 244,620 km; natural gas 548,665 km (2003)

Ports and harbors: Anchorage, Baltimore, Boston, Charleston, Chicago, Duluth, Hampton Roads, Honolulu, Houston, Jacksonville, Los Angeles, New Orleans, New York, Philadelphia, Port Canaveral, Portland (Oregon), Prudhoe Bay, San Francisco, Savannah, Seattle, Tampa, Toledo

Merchant marine:

total: 466 ships (1,000 GRT or over) 12,436,658 GRT/ 14,630,116 DWT

by type: barge carrier 8, bulk 69, cargo 75, chemical tanker 12, combination bulk 2, combination ore/oil 1, container 100, multi-functional large load carrier 3, passenger 12, passenger/cargo 2, petroleum tanker 81, refrigerated cargo 3, roll on/roll off 83, short-sea/ passenger 3, vehicle carrier 12

foreign-owned: Australia 2, Canada 7, Denmark 17, Malaysia 1, Netherlands 1, Norway 6, Singapore 3, United Kingdom 5

registered in other countries: 670 (2003 est.)

Airports: 14,807 (2003 est.)

Airports - with paved runways:

total: 5,128

over 3,047 m: 188

2,438 to 3,047 m: 221

1,524 to 2,437 m: 1,375

914 to 1,523 m: 2,383

under 914 m: 961 (2003 est.)

Airports - with unpaved runways:

total: 9,679

over 3,047 m: 1

2,438 to 3,047 m: 7

1,524 to 2,437 m: 161

914 to 1,523 m: 1,714

under 914 m: 7,796 (2003 est.)

Heliports: 155 (2003 est.)

Military

Military branches: Army, Navy and Marine Corps, Air Force, and Coast Guard (Coast Guard administered in peacetime by the Department of Homeland Security, but in wartime reports to the Department of the Navy)

Military manpower - military age: 18 years of age (2004 est.)

Military manpower - availability:

males age 15-49: 73,597,731 (2004 est.)

Military manpower - fit for military service: NA (2004 est.)

Military manpower - reaching military age annually:

males: 2,124,164 (2004 est.)

Military expenditures - dollar figure: $399 billion (2001)

Military expenditures - percent of GDP: 3.9% (2001)

Transnational Issues

Disputes - international: Prolonged drought, population growth, and outmoded practices and infrastructure in the border region has strained water-sharing arrangements with Mexico; undocumented nationals from Mexico and Central America continue to enter the United States illegally; 1990 Maritime Boundary Agreement in the Bering Sea still awaits Russian Duma ratification; managed maritime boundary disputes with Canada at Dixon Entrance, Beaufort Sea, Strait of Juan de Fuca, and around the disputed Machias Seal Island and North Rock; The Bahamas have not been able to agree on a maritime boundary; US Naval Base at Guantanamo Bay is leased from Cuba and only mutual agreement or US abandonment of the area can terminate the lease; Haiti claims US-administered Navassa Island; US has made no territorial claim in Antarctica (but has reserved the right to do so) and does not recognize the claims of any other state; Marshall Islands claims Wake Island

Illicit drugs: consumer of cocaine shipped from Colombia through Mexico and the Caribbean; consumer of heroin, marijuana, and increasingly methamphetamine from Mexico; consumer of high-quality Southeast Asian heroin; illicit producer of cannabis, marijuana, depressants, stimulants, hallucinogens, and methamphetamine; money-laundering center

Uruguay

Introduction

Background: A violent Marxist urban guerrilla movement, the Tupamaros, launched in the late 1960s, led Uruguay's president to agree to military control of his administration in 1973. By yearend, the rebels had been crushed, but the military continued to expand its hold throughout the government. Civilian rule was not restored until 1985. Uruguay's political and labor conditions are among the freest on the continent.

Geography

Location: Southern South America, bordering the South Atlantic Ocean, between Argentina and Brazil

Geographic coordinates: 33 00 S, 56 00 W

Map references: South America

Area:

total: 176,220 sq km

land: 173,620 sq km

water: 2,600 sq km

Area - comparative: slightly smaller than the state of Washington

Land boundaries:

total: 1,564 km

border countries: Argentina 579 km, Brazil 985 km

Coastline: 660 km

Maritime claims:

territorial sea: 12 NM

contiguous zone: 24 NM

exclusive economic zone: 200 NM

continental shelf: 200-m depth or to the depth of exploitation

Climate: warm temperate; freezing temperatures almost unknown

Terrain: mostly rolling plains and low hills; fertile coastal lowland

Elevation extremes:

lowest point: Atlantic Ocean 0 m

highest point: Cerro Catedral 514 m

Uruguay (continued)

Natural resources: arable land, hydropower, minor minerals, fisheries

Land use:
arable land: 7.21%
permanent crops: 0.27%
other: 92.52% (1998 est.)

Irrigated land: 1,800 sq km (1998 est.)

Natural hazards: seasonally high winds (the pampero is a chilly and occasional violent wind which blows north from the Argentine pampas), droughts, floods; because of the absence of mountains, which act as weather barriers, all locations are particularly vulnerable to rapid changes from weather fronts

Environment - current issues: water pollution from meat packing/tannery industry; inadequate solid/hazardous waste disposal

Environment - international agreements:
party to: Antarctic-Environmental Protocol, Antarctic-Marine Living Resources, Antarctic Treaty, Biodiversity, Climate Change, Climate Change-Kyoto Protocol, Desertification, Endangered Species, Environmental Modification, Hazardous Wastes, Law of the Sea, Ozone Layer Protection, Ship Pollution, Tropical Timber 94, Wetlands
signed, but not ratified: Marine Dumping, Marine Life Conservation

Geography - note: second-smallest South American country (after Suriname); most of the low-lying landscape (three-quarters of the country) is grassland, ideal for cattle and sheep raising

People

Population: 3,399,237 (July 2004 est.)

Age structure:
0-14 years: 23.5% (male 406,500; female 392,497)
15-64 years: 63.4% (male 1,066,464; female 1,087,100)
65 years and over: 13.1% (male 182,654; female 264,022) (2004 est.)

Median age:
total: 32.2 years
male: 30.7 years
female: 33.7 years (2004 est.)

Population growth rate: 0.51% (2004 est.)

Birth rate: 14.44 births/1,000 population (2004 est.)

Death rate: 9.07 deaths/1,000 population (2004 est.)

Net migration rate: -0.32 migrant(s)/1,000 population (2004 est.)

Sex ratio:
at birth: 1.04 male(s)/female
under 15 years: 1.04 male(s)/female
15-64 years: 0.98 male(s)/female
65 years and over: 0.69 male(s)/female
total population: 0.95 male(s)/female (2004 est.)

Infant mortality rate:
total: 12.31 deaths/1,000 live births
male: 13.67 deaths/1,000 live births
female: 10.91 deaths/1,000 live births (2004 est.)

Life expectancy at birth:
total population: 75.92 years
male: 72.71 years
female: 79.24 years (2004 est.)

Total fertility rate: 1.96 children born/woman (2004 est.)

HIV/AIDS - adult prevalence rate: 0.3% (2001 est.)

HIV/AIDS - people living with HIV/AIDS: 6,300 (2001 est.)

HIV/AIDS - deaths: less than 500 (2001 est.)

Nationality:
noun: Uruguayan(s)
adjective: Uruguayan

Ethnic groups: white 88%, mestizo 8%, black 4%, Amerindian, practically nonexistent

Religions: Roman Catholic 66% (less than half of the adult population attends church regularly), Protestant 2%, Jewish 1%, nonprofessing or other 31%

Languages: Spanish, Portunol, or Brazilero (Portuguese-Spanish mix on the Brazilian frontier)

Literacy:
definition: age 15 and over can read and write
total population: 98%
male: 97.6%
female: 98.4% (2003 est.)

Government

Country name:
conventional long form: Oriental Republic of Uruguay
conventional short form: Uruguay
local long form: Republica Oriental del Uruguay
local short form: Uruguay
former: Banda Oriental, Cisplatine Province

Government type: constitutional republic

Capital: Montevideo

Administrative divisions: 19 departments (departamentos, singular - departamento); Artigas, Canelones, Cerro Largo, Colonia, Durazno, Flores, Florida, Lavalleja, Maldonado, Montevideo, Paysandu, Rio Negro, Rivera, Rocha, Salto, San Jose, Soriano, Tacuarembo, Treinta y Tres

Independence: 25 August 1825 (from Brazil)

National holiday: Independence Day, 25 August (1825)

Constitution: 27 November 1966, effective February 1967, suspended 27 June 1973, new constitution rejected by referendum 30 November 1980; two constitutional reforms approved by plebiscite 26 November 1989 and 7 January 1997

Legal system: based on Spanish civil law system; accepts compulsory ICJ jurisdiction

Suffrage: 18 years of age; universal and compulsory

Executive branch:
chief of state: President Jorge BATLLE Ibanez (since 1 March 2000) and Vice President Luis HIERRO (since 1 March 2000); note - the president is both the chief of state and head of government
head of government: President Jorge BATLLE Ibanez (since 1 March 2000) and Vice President Luis HIERRO (since 1 March 2000); note - the president is both the chief of state and head of government
cabinet: Council of Ministers appointed by the president with parliamentary approval

elections: president and vice president elected on the same ticket by popular vote for five-year terms; election last held 31 October 1999, with runoff election on 28 November 1999 (next to be held October 2004)
election results: Jorge BATLLE Ibanez elected president; percent of vote - Jorge BATLLE Ibanez 52% in a runoff against Tabare VAZQUEZ 44%

Legislative branch: bicameral General Assembly or Asamblea General consists of Chamber of Senators or Camara de Senadores (30 seats; members are elected by popular vote to serve five-year terms) and Chamber of Representatives or Camara de Representantes (99 seats; members are elected by popular vote to serve five-year terms)
elections: Chamber of Senators - last held 31 October 1999 (next to be held October 2004); Chamber of Representatives - last held 31 October 1999 (next to be held October 2004)
election results: Chamber of Senators - percent of vote by party - NA%; seats by party - Encuentro Progresista 12, Colorado Party 10, Blanco 7, New Sector/Space Coalition 1; Chamber of Representatives - percent of vote by party - NA%; seats by party - Encuentro Progresista 40, Colorado Party 33, Blanco 22, New Sector/Space Coalition 4

Judicial branch: Supreme Court (judges are nominated by the president and elected for 10-year terms by the General Assembly)

Political parties and leaders: Colorado Party [Jorge BATLLE Ibanez]; National Party or Blanco [Luis Alberto LACALLE Herrera]; New Sector/Space Coalition or Nuevo Espacio [Rafael MICHELINI]; Progressive Encounter/Broad Front Coalition or Encuentro Progresista/Frente Amplio [Tabare VAZQUEZ]

Political pressure groups and leaders: NA

International organization participation: FAO, G-77, IADB, IAEA, IBRD, ICAO, ICC, ICCt, ICRM, IFAD, IFC, IFRCS, IHO, ILO, IMF, IMO, Interpol, IOC, IOM, ISO, ITU, LAES, LAIA, Mercosur, MINURSO, MONUC, NAM (observer), OAS, OPANAL, OPCW, PCA, RG, UN, UNAMSIL, UNCTAD, UNESCO, UNIDO, UNMEE, UNMISET, UNMOGIP, UNMOT, UNOMIG, UPU, WCL, WCO, WFTU, WHO, WIPO, WMO, WToO, WTrO

Diplomatic representation in the US:
chief of mission: Ambassador Hugo FERNANDEZ-FAINGOLD
chancery: 1913 I Street NW, Washington, DC 20006
telephone: [1] (202) 331-1313 through 1316
FAX: [1] (202) 331-8142
consulate(s) general: Chicago, Los Angeles, Miami, and New York

Diplomatic representation from the US:
chief of mission: Ambassador Martin J. SILVERSTEIN
embassy: Lauro Muller 1776, Montevideo 11200
mailing address: APO AA 34035
telephone: [598] (2) 418-7777
FAX: [598] (2) 418-8611

Uruguay (continued)

Flag description: nine equal horizontal stripes of white (top and bottom) alternating with blue; there is a white square in the upper hoist-side corner with a yellow sun bearing a human face known as the Sun of May and 16 rays alternately triangular and wavy

Economy

Economy - overview: Uruguay's well-to-do economy is characterized by an export-oriented agricultural sector, a well-educated workforce, and high levels of social spending. After averaging growth of 5% annually during 1996-98, in 1999-2002 the economy suffered a major downturn, stemming largely from the spillover effects of the economic problems of its large neighbors, Argentina and Brazil. For instance, in 2001-02 massive withdrawals by Argentina of dollars deposited in Uruguayan banks led to a plunge in the Uruguyan peso and a massive rise in unemployment. Total GDP in these four years dropped by nearly 20%, with 2002 the worst year due to the serious banking crisis. Unemployment rose to nearly 20% in 2002, inflation surged, and the burden of external debt doubled. Cooperation with the IMF and the US has limited the damage. The debt swap with private creditors carried out in 2003, which extended the maturity dates on nearly half of Uruguay's $11.3 billion in public debt, substantially alleviated the country's amortization burden in the coming years and restored public confidence. The economy is expected to resume growth in 2004 (perhaps 4% or more) as a result of high commodity prices for Uruguayan exports, the weakness of the dollar against the euro, growth in the region, low international interest rates, and greater export competitiveness. On the negative side, in December 2003 the electorate voted to repeal the law permitting a cautious liberalization of the energy industry.
GDP: purchasing power parity - $42.94 billion (2003 est.)
GDP - real growth rate: 0.3% (2003 est.)
GDP - per capita: purchasing power parity - $12,600 (2003 est.)
GDP - composition by sector:
agriculture: 9%
industry: 24%
services: 67% (2001)
Population below poverty line: 23.7% (2002)
Household income or consumption by percentage share:
lowest 10%: 3.7%
highest 10%: 25.8% (1997)
Distribution of family income - Gini index: 44.8 (1999)
Inflation rate (consumer prices): 10.2% (2003 est.)
Labor force: 1.3 million (2002)
Labor force - by occupation: agriculture 14%, industry 16%, services 70%
Unemployment rate: 16.1% (November 2003)

Budget:
revenues: $2.74 billion
expenditures: $3.4 billion, including capital expenditures of $193 million (2002)
Industries: food processing, electrical machinery, transportation equipment, petroleum products, textiles, chemicals, beverages
Industrial production growth rate: -2.5% (Jan-Sep 2003 est.)
Electricity - production: 7.963 billion kWh (2001)
Electricity - production by source:
fossil fuel: 0.7%
hydro: 99.1%
nuclear: 0%
other: 0.3% (2001)
Electricity - consumption: 6.152 billion kWh (2001)
Electricity - exports: 1.377 billion kWh (2001)
Electricity - imports: 123 million kWh (2001)
Oil - production: 0 bbl/day (2001 est.)
Oil - consumption: 41,500 bbl/day (2001 est.)
Oil - exports: NA
Oil - imports: NA
Natural gas - production: 0 cu m (2001 est.)
Natural gas - consumption: 40 million cu m (2001 est.)
Natural gas - exports: 0 cu m (2001 est.)
Natural gas - imports: 40 million cu m (2001 est.)
Agriculture - products: rice, wheat, corn, barley; livestock; fish
Exports: $2.164 billion f.o.b. (2003 est.)
Exports - commodities: meat, rice, leather products, wool, fish, dairy products
Exports - partners: Brazil 22.1%, US 8.4%, Germany 5.4%, Argentina 5.1%, Mexico 4.2%, Italy 4.1%, Paraguay 4.1%, Spain 4% (2002)
Imports: $1.989 billion f.o.b. (2003 est.)
Imports - commodities: machinery, chemicals, road vehicles, crude petroleum
Imports - partners: Argentina 23.1%, Brazil 17.5%, US 8.9%, Mexico 4.7%, China 4% (2002)
Debt - external: $10.2 billion (June 2003)
Economic aid - recipient: $NA
Currency: Uruguayan peso (UYU)
Currency code: UYU
Exchange rates: Uruguayan pesos per US dollar - 28.2091 (2003), 21.257 (2002), 13.3191 (2001), 12.0996 (2000), 11.3393 (1999)
Fiscal year: calendar year

Communications

Telephones - main lines in use: 946,500 (2002)
Telephones - mobile cellular: 652,000 (2002)
Telephone system:
general assessment: fully digitalized
domestic: most modern facilities concentrated in Montevideo; new nationwide microwave radio relay network
international: country code - 598; satellite earth stations - 2 Intelsat (Atlantic Ocean) (2002)
Radio broadcast stations: AM 91, FM 149, shortwave 7 (2001)

Television broadcast stations: 23 (2002)
Internet country code: .uy
Internet hosts: 78,660 (2002)
Internet users: 400,000 (2002)

Transportation

Railways:
total: 2,073 km
standard gauge: 2,073 km 1.435-m gauge
note: 461 km have been taken out of service and 460 km are in partial use (2002)
Highways:
total: 8,983 km
paved: 8,081 km
unpaved: 902 km (1999 est.)
Waterways: 1,600 km (used by coastal and shallow-draft river craft)
Pipelines: gas 192 km (2003)
Ports and harbors: Colonia, Fray Bentos, Juan La Caze, La Paloma, Montevideo, Nueva Palmira, Paysandu, Punta del Este, Piriapolis
Merchant marine:
total: 4 ships (1,000 GRT or over) 10,918 GRT/10,342 DWT
by type: chemical tanker 1, container 1, petroleum tanker 1, roll on/roll off 1
foreign-owned: Argentina 4, Greece 1
registered in other countries: 6 (2003 est.)
Airports: 64 (2003 est.)
Airports - with paved runways:
total: 15
2,438 to 3,047 m: 1
1,524 to 2,437 m: 5
914 to 1,523 m: 8
under 914 m: 1 (2003 est.)
Airports - with unpaved runways:
total: 49
1,524 to 2,437 m: 2
914 to 1,523 m: 16
under 914 m: 31 (2003 est.)

Military

Military branches: Army, Navy (includes Naval Air Arm, Marines, Maritime Prefecture in wartime), Air Force
Military manpower - availability:
males age 15-49: 838,195 (2004 est.)
Military manpower - fit for military service:
males age 15-49: 677,315 (2004 est.)
Military expenditures - dollar figure: $217.9 million (2003)
Military expenditures - percent of GDP: 2% (2003)

Transnational Issues

Disputes - international: uncontested dispute with Brazil over certain islands in the Quarai/Cuareim and Invernada streams and the resulting tripoint with Argentina

Uzbekistan

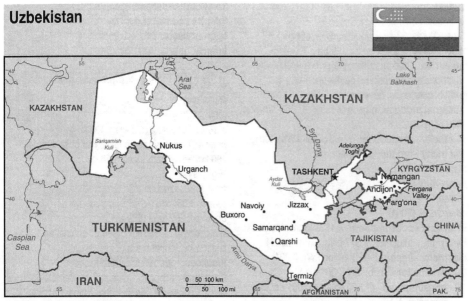

Introduction

Background: Russia conquered Uzbekistan in the late 19th century. Stiff resistance to the Red Army after World War I was eventually suppressed and a socialist republic set up in 1924. During the Soviet era, intensive production of "white gold" (cotton) and grain led to overuse of agrochemicals and the depletion of water supplies, which have left the land poisoned and the Aral Sea and certain rivers half dry. Independent since 1991, the country seeks to gradually lessen its dependence on agriculture while developing its mineral and petroleum reserves. Current concerns include terrorism by Islamic militants, economic stagnation, and the curtailment of human rights and democratization.

Geography

Location: Central Asia, north of Afghanistan
Geographic coordinates: 41 00 N, 64 00 E
Map references: Asia
Area:
total: 447,400 sq km
land: 425,400 sq km
water: 22,000 sq km
Area - comparative: slightly larger than California
Land boundaries:
total: 6,221 km
border countries: Afghanistan 137 km, Kazakhstan 2,203 km, Kyrgyzstan 1,099 km, Tajikistan 1,161 km, Turkmenistan 1,621 km
Coastline: 0 km (doubly landlocked); note - Uzbekistan includes the southern portion of the Aral Sea with a 420 km shoreline
Maritime claims: none (doubly landlocked)
Climate: mostly midlatitude desert, long, hot summers, mild winters; semiarid grassland in east
Terrain: mostly flat-to-rolling sandy desert with dunes; broad, flat intensely irrigated river valleys along course of Amu Darya, Syr Darya (Sirdaryo), and

Zarafshon; Fergana Valley in east surrounded by mountainous Tajikistan and Kyrgyzstan; shrinking Aral Sea in west
Elevation extremes:
lowest point: Sariqarnish Kuli -12 m
highest point: Adelunga Toghi 4,301 m
Natural resources: natural gas, petroleum, coal, gold, uranium, silver, copper, lead and zinc, tungsten, molybdenum
Land use:
arable land: 10.8%
permanent crops: 0.91%
other: 88.29% (1998 est.)
Irrigated land: 42,810 sq km (1998 est.)
Natural hazards: NA
Environment - current issues: shrinkage of the Aral Sea is resulting in growing concentrations of chemical pesticides and natural salts; these substances are then blown from the increasingly exposed lake bed and contribute to desertification; water pollution from industrial wastes and the heavy use of fertilizers and pesticides is the cause of many human health disorders; increasing soil salination; soil contamination from buried nuclear processing and agricultural chemicals, including DDT
Environment - international agreements:
party to: Biodiversity, Climate Change, Climate Change-Kyoto Protocol, Desertification, Endangered Species, Environmental Modification, Hazardous Wastes, Ozone Layer Protection, Wetlands
signed, but not ratified: none of the selected agreements
Geography - note: along with Liechtenstein, one of the only two doubly landlocked countries in the world

People

Population: 26,410,416 (July 2004 est.)
Age structure:
0-14 years: 34.1% (male 4,583,228; female 4,418,003)

15-64 years: 61.1% (male 7,990,233; female 8,157,136)
65 years and over: 4.8% (male 513,434; female 748,382) (2004 est.)
Median age:
total: 22.1 years
male: 21.4 years
female: 22.7 years (2004 est.)
Population growth rate: 1.65% (2004 est.)
Birth rate: 26.12 births/1,000 population (2004 est.)
Death rate: 7.95 deaths/1,000 population (2004 est.)
Net migration rate: -1.72 migrant(s)/1,000 population (2004 est.)
Sex ratio:
at birth: 1.05 male(s)/female
under 15 years: 1.04 male(s)/female
15-64 years: 0.98 male(s)/female
65 years and over: 0.69 male(s)/female
total population: 0.98 male(s)/female (2004 est.)
Infant mortality rate:
total: 71.3 deaths/1,000 live births
male: 75.03 deaths/1,000 live births
female: 67.39 deaths/1,000 live births (2004 est.)
Life expectancy at birth:
total population: 64.09 years
male: 60.67 years
female: 67.69 years (2004 est.)
Total fertility rate: 2.97 children born/woman (2004 est.)
HIV/AIDS - adult prevalence rate: less than 0.1% (2001 est.)
HIV/AIDS - people living with HIV/AIDS: less than 740 (2001 est.)
HIV/AIDS - deaths: less than 100 (2001 est.)
Nationality:
noun: Uzbekistani
adjective: Uzbekistani
Ethnic groups: Uzbek 80%, Russian 5.5%, Tajik 5%, Kazakh 3%, Karakalpak 2.5%, Tatar 1.5%, other 2.5% (1996 est.)
Religions: Muslim 88% (mostly Sunnis), Eastern Orthodox 9%, other 3%
Languages: Uzbek 74.3%, Russian 14.2%, Tajik 4.4%, other 7.1%
Literacy:
definition: age 15 and over can read and write
total population: 99.3%
male: 99.6%
female: 99% (2003 est.)

Government

Country name:
conventional long form: Republic of Uzbekistan
conventional short form: Uzbekistan
local long form: Ozbekiston Respublikasi
local short form: Ozbekiston
former: Uzbek Soviet Socialist Republic
Government type: republic; authoritarian presidential rule, with little power outside the executive branch
Capital: Tashkent (Toshkent)

Administrative divisions: 12 provinces (viloyatlar, singular - viloyat), 1 autonomous republic* (respublika), and 1 city** (shahar); Andijon Viloyati, Buxoro Viloyati, Farg'ona Viloyati, Jizzax Viloyati, Namangan Viloyati, Navoiy Viloyati, Qashqadaryo Viloyati (Qarshi), Qaraqalpog'iston Respublikasi* (Nukus), Samarqand Viloyati, Sirdaryo Viloyati (Guliston), Surxondaryo Viloyati (Termiz), Toshkent Shahri**, Toshkent Viloyati, Xorazm Viloyati (Urganch)

note: administrative divisions have the same names as their administrative centers (exceptions have the administrative center name following in parentheses)

Independence: 1 September 1991 (from Soviet Union)

National holiday: Independence Day, 1 September (1991)

Constitution: new constitution adopted 8 December 1992

Legal system: evolution of Soviet civil law; still lacks independent judicial system

Suffrage: 18 years of age; universal

Executive branch:

chief of state: President Islom KARIMOV (since 24 March 1990, when he was elected president by the then Supreme Soviet)

head of government: Prime Minister Shavkat MIRZIYAYEV (since 11 December 2003)

cabinet: Cabinet of Ministers appointed by the president with approval of the Supreme Assembly

elections: president elected by popular vote for a seven-year term (previously was a five-year term, extended by constitutional amendment in 2002); election last held 9 January 2000 (next to be held NA December 2007); prime minister and deputy ministers appointed by the president

election results: Islom KARIMOV reelected president; percent of vote - Islom KARIMOV 91.9%, Abdulkhafiz JALALOV 4.2%

Legislative branch: unicameral Supreme Assembly or Oliy Majlis (250 seats; members elected by popular vote to serve five-year terms); note - 2002 amendment to the constitution creates a second chamber to be established via elections in December 2004

elections: last held 5 December and 19 December 1999 (next to be held NA December 2004)

election results: percent of vote by party - NA%; seats by party - NDP 48, Self-Sacrificers Party 34, Fatherland Progress Party 20, Adolat Social Democratic Party 11, MTP 10, citizens' groups 16, local government 110, vacant 1

note: not all seats in the last Supreme Assembly election were contested; all parties in the Supreme Assembly support President KARIMOV

Judicial branch: Supreme Court (judges are nominated by the president and confirmed by the Supreme Assembly)

Political parties and leaders: Adolat (Justice) Social Democratic Party [Anwar JURABAYEV, first secretary]; Democratic National Rebirth Party (Milly Tiklanish) or MTP [Aziz KAYUMOV, chairman]; Liberal Democratic Party of Uzbekistan [Kobijon TOSHMATOV]; People's Democratic Party or NDP (formerly Communist Party) [Asliddin RUSTAMOV, first secretary]; Self-Sacrificers Party or Fidokorlar National Democratic Party [Ahtam TURSUNOV, first secretary]; note - Fatherland Progress Party merged with Self-Sacrificers Party

Political pressure groups and leaders: Agrarian and Entrepreneurs' Party [Marat ZAHIDOV]; Birlik (Unity) Movement [Abdurakhim POLAT, chairman]; Erk (Freedom) Democratic Party [Muhammad SOLIH, chairman] was banned 9 December 1992; Ezgulik [Vasilia INOYATOVA]; Free Farmers' Party [Nigara KHIDOYATOVA]; Human Rights Society of Uzbekistan [Tolib YAKUBOV, chairman]; Independent Human Rights Society of Uzbekistan [Abduhoshim GHAFUROV, chairman]; Mazlum [Oygul MAMATOVA]

International organization participation: AsDB, CIS, EAPC, EBRD, ECO, FAO, GUUAM, IAEA, IBRD, ICAO, ICCt (signatory), ICRM, IDA, IDB, IFC, IFRCS, ILO, IMF, Interpol, IOC, ISO, ITU, NAM, OIC, OPCW, OSCE, PFP, SCO, UN, UNCTAD, UNESCO, UNIDO, UPU, WCO, WFTU, WHO, WIPO, WMO, WToO, WTrO (observer)

Diplomatic representation in the US:

chief of mission: Ambassador Abdulaziz KAMILOV

chancery: 1746 Massachusetts Avenue NW, Washington, DC 20036

telephone: [1] (202) 293-6803

FAX: [1] (202) 293-6804

consulate(s) general: New York

Diplomatic representation from the US:

chief of mission: Ambassador Jon PURNELL

embassy: 82 Chilanzarskaya, Tashkent 700115

mailing address: use embassy street address

telephone: [998] (71) 120-5450

FAX: [998] (71) 120-6335

Flag description: three equal horizontal bands of blue (top), white, and green separated by red fimbriations with a white crescent moon and 12 white stars in the upper hoist-side quadrant

Economy

Economy - overview: Uzbekistan is a dry, landlocked country of which 11% consists of intensely cultivated, irrigated river valleys. More than 60% of its population lives in densely populated rural communities. Uzbekistan is now the world's second-largest cotton exporter, a large producer of gold and oil, and a regionally significant producer of chemicals and machinery. Following independence in December 1991, the government sought to prop up its Soviet-style command economy with subsidies and tight controls on production and prices. Uzbekistan responded to the negative external conditions generated by the Asian and Russian financial crises by emphasizing import substitute industrialization and by tightening export and currency controls within its already largely closed economy. The government, while aware of the need to improve the investment climate, sponsors measures that often increase, not decrease, the government's control over business decisions. A sharp increase in the inequality of income distribution has hurt the lower ranks of society since independence.

GDP: purchasing power parity - $44.11 billion (2003 est.)

GDP - real growth rate: 3.4% (2003 est.)

GDP - per capita: purchasing power parity - $1,700 (2003 est.)

GDP - composition by sector:

agriculture: 36%

industry: 21%

services: 43% (2001 est.)

Population below poverty line: NA%

Household income or consumption by percentage share:

lowest 10%: 1.2%

highest 10%: 32.8% (1998)

Distribution of family income - Gini index: 44.7 (1998)

Inflation rate (consumer prices): 21.9% (2003 est.)

Labor force: 11.9 million (1998 est.)

Labor force - by occupation: agriculture 44%, industry 20%, services 36% (1995)

Unemployment rate: 10% plus another 20% underemployed (2001 est.)

Budget:

revenues: $2.42 billion

expenditures: $2.45 billion, including capital expenditures of $NA (2003 est.)

Industries: textiles, food processing, machine building, metallurgy, natural gas, chemicals

Industrial production growth rate: 6.2% (2003 est.)

Electricity - production: 44.49 billion kWh (2001)

Electricity - production by source:

fossil fuel: 88.2%

hydro: 11.8%

nuclear: 0%

other: 0% (2001)

Electricity - consumption: 47.07 billion kWh (2001)

Electricity - exports: 3.998 billion kWh (2001)

Electricity - imports: 9.7 billion kWh (2001)

Oil - production: 142,700 bbl/day (2001 est.)

Oil - consumption: 142,000 bbl/day (2001 est.)

Oil - exports: NA

Oil - imports: NA

Oil - proved reserves: 297 million bbl (1 January 2002)

Natural gas - production: 63.1 billion cu m (2001 est.)

Natural gas - consumption: 45.2 billion cu m (2001 est.)

Natural gas - exports: 17.9 billion cu m (2001 est.)

Natural gas - imports: 0 cu m (2001 est.)

Uzbekistan (continued)

Natural gas - proved reserves: 937.3 billion cu m (1 January 2002)

Agriculture - products: cotton, vegetables, fruits, grain; livestock

Exports: $2.83 billion f.o.b. (2003 est.)

Exports - commodities: cotton 41.5%, gold 9.6%, energy products 9.6%, mineral fertilizers, ferrous metals, textiles, food products, automobiles (1998 est.)

Exports - partners: Russia 19.9%, Italy 8.6%, Tajikistan 7.7%, South Korea 5.6%, Kazakhstan 5.1%, US 4.7%, Turkey 4.4%, Japan 4.3% (2002)

Imports: $2.31 billion f.o.b. (2003 est.)

Imports - commodities: machinery and equipment 49.8%, foodstuffs 16.4%, chemicals, metals (1998 est.)

Imports - partners: Russia 24%, Germany 10.8%, South Korea 10%, US 7.3%, China 5.5%, Kazakhstan 5.3%, Turkey 4.9% (2002)

Debt - external: $1.7 billion (2002 est.)

Economic aid - recipient: $87.4 million from the US (2003)

Currency: Uzbekistani sum (UZS)

Currency code: UZS

Exchange rates: Uzbekistani sums per US dollar - 115.9 (2003), 125.3 (2002), NA (2001), 236.608 (2000), 124.625 (1999)

Fiscal year: calendar year

Communications

Telephones - main lines in use: 1,681,100 (2002)

Telephones - mobile cellular: 186,900 (2002)

Telephone system:

general assessment: antiquated and inadequate; in serious need of modernization

domestic: the domestic telephone system is being expanded and technologically improved, particularly in Tashkent (Toshkent) and Samarqand, under contracts with prominent companies in industrialized countries; moreover, by 1998, six cellular networks had been placed in operation - four of the GSM type (Global System for Mobile Communication), one D-AMPS type (Digital Advanced Mobile Phone System), and one AMPS type (Advanced Mobile Phone System)

international: country code - 998; linked by landline or microwave radio relay with CIS member states and to other countries by leased connection via the Moscow international gateway switch; after the completion of the Uzbek link to the Trans-Asia-Europe (TAE) fiber-optic cable, Uzbekistan will be independent of Russian facilities for international communications; Inmarsat also provides an international connection, albeit an expensive one; satellite earth stations - NA (1998)

Radio broadcast stations: AM 20, FM 7, shortwave 10 (1998)

Television broadcast stations: 4 (plus two repeaters that relay Russian programs), 1 cable rebroadcaster in Tashkent; approximately 20 stations in regional capitals (2003)

Internet country code: .uz

Internet hosts: 281 (2002)

Internet users: 275,000 (2002)

Transportation

Railways:

total: 3,950 km

broad gauge: 3,950 km 1.520-m gauge (620 km electrified) (2002)

Highways:

total: 81,600 km

paved: 71,237 km

unpaved: 10,363 km (1999 est.)

Waterways: 1,100 km (1990)

Pipelines: gas 9,012 km; oil 869 km; refined products 33 km (2003)

Ports and harbors: Termiz (Amu Darya)

Airports: 247 (2003 est.)

Airports - with paved runways:

total: 33

over 3,047 m: 5

2,438 to 3,047 m: 14

1,524 to 2,437 m: 5

914 to 1,523 m: 5

under 914 m: 4 (2003 est.)

Airports - with unpaved runways:

total: 214

2,438 to 3,047 m: 3

1,524 to 2,437 m: 2

914 to 1,523 m: 9

under 914 m: 200 (2003 est.)

Military

Military branches: Army, Air and Air Defense Forces, National Guard

Military manpower - military age: 18 years of age (2004 est.)

Military manpower - availability:

males age 15-49: 7,126,325 (2004 est.)

Military manpower - fit for military service:

males age 15-49: 5,783,740 (2004 est.)

Military manpower - reaching military age annually:

males: 321,886 (2004 est.)

Military expenditures - dollar figure: $200 million (FY97)

Military expenditures - percent of GDP: 2% (FY97)

Transnational Issues

Disputes - international: prolonged drought and cotton monoculture creates water-sharing difficulties for Amu Darya river states; delimitation with Kazakhstan complete with demarcation underway; delimitation is underway with Kyrgyzstan but serious disputes around enclaves and elsewhere continue to mar progress for some 130 km of border; talks continue with Tajikistan to determine and delimit border

Illicit drugs: transit country for Afghan narcotics bound for Russian and, to a lesser extent, Western European markets; limited illicit cultivation of cannabis and small amounts of opium poppy for domestic consumption; poppy cultivation almost wiped out by government crop eradication program; transit point for heroin precursor chemicals bound for Afghanistan

Vanuatu

Introduction

Background: The British and French, who settled the New Hebrides in the 19th century, agreed in 1906 to an Anglo-French Condominium, which administered the islands until independence in 1980.

Geography

Location: Oceania, group of islands in the South Pacific Ocean, about three-quarters of the way from Hawaii to Australia
Geographic coordinates: 16 00 S, 167 00 E
Map references: Oceania
Area:
total: 12,200 sq km
land: 12,200 sq km
water: 0 sq km
note: includes more than 80 islands, about 65 of which are inhabited
Area - comparative: slightly larger than Connecticut
Land boundaries: 0 km
Coastline: 2,528 km
Maritime claims: measured from claimed archipelagic baselines
territorial sea: 12 NM

contiguous zone: 24 NM
exclusive economic zone: 200 NM
continental shelf: 200 NM or to the edge of the continental margin
Climate: tropical; moderated by southeast trade winds from May to October; moderate rainfall from November to April; may be affected by cyclones from December to April
Terrain: mostly mountainous islands of volcanic origin; narrow coastal plains
Elevation extremes:
lowest point: Pacific Ocean 0 m
highest point: Tabwemasana 1,877 m
Natural resources: manganese, hardwood forests, fish
Land use:
arable land: 2.46%
permanent crops: 7.38%
other: 90.16% (1998 est.)
Irrigated land: NA sq km
Natural hazards: tropical cyclones or typhoons (January to April); volcanism causes minor earthquakes; tsunamis
Environment - current issues: a majority of the population does not have access to a potable and reliable supply of water; deforestation
Environment - international agreements:
party to: Antarctic-Marine Living Resources, Biodiversity, Climate Change, Climate Change-Kyoto Protocol, Desertification, Endangered Species, Law of the Sea, Marine Dumping, Ozone Layer Protection, Ship Pollution, Tropical Timber 94
signed, but not ratified: none of the selected agreements
Geography - note: a Y-shaped chain of four main islands and 80 smaller islands; several of the islands have active volcanoes

People

Population: 202,609 (July 2004 est.)
Age structure:
0-14 years: 34.1% (male 35,281; female 33,785)
15-64 years: 62.4% (male 64,669; female 61,829)
65 years and over: 3.5% (male 3,740; female 3,305) (2004 est.)
Median age:
total: 22.3 years
male: 22.3 years
female: 22.2 years (2004 est.)
Population growth rate: 1.57% (2004 est.)
Birth rate: 23.67 births/1,000 population (2004 est.)
Death rate: 8.02 deaths/1,000 population (2004 est.)
Net migration rate: 0 migrant(s)/1,000 population (2004 est.)
Sex ratio:
at birth: 1.05 male(s)/female
under 15 years: 1.04 male(s)/female
15-64 years: 1.05 male(s)/female
65 years and over: 1.13 male(s)/female
total population: 1.05 male(s)/female (2004 est.)

Infant mortality rate:
total: 56.63 deaths/1,000 live births
male: 59.25 deaths/1,000 live births
female: 53.89 deaths/1,000 live births (2004 est.)
Life expectancy at birth:
total population: 62.1 years
male: 60.64 years
female: 63.63 years (2004 est.)
Total fertility rate: 2.87 children born/woman (2004 est.)
HIV/AIDS - adult prevalence rate: NA%
HIV/AIDS - people living with HIV/AIDS: NA
HIV/AIDS - deaths: NA
Nationality:
noun: Ni-Vanuatu (singular and plural)
adjective: Ni-Vanuatu
Ethnic groups: indigenous Melanesian 98%, French, Vietnamese, Chinese, other Pacific Islanders
Religions: Presbyterian 36.7%, Anglican 15%, Roman Catholic 15%, indigenous beliefs 7.6%, Seventh-Day Adventist 6.2%, Church of Christ 3.8%, other 15.7% (including Jon Frum Cargo cult)
Languages: three official languages: English, French, pidgin (known as Bislama or Bichelama), plus more than 100 local languages
Literacy:
definition: age 15 and over can read and write
total population: 53%
male: 57%
female: 48% (1979 est.)

Government

Country name:
conventional long form: Republic of Vanuatu
conventional short form: Vanuatu
former: New Hebrides
Government type: parliamentary republic
Capital: Port-Vila (Efate)
Administrative divisions: 6 provinces; Malampa, Penama, Sanma, Shefa, Tafea, Torba
Independence: 30 July 1980 (from France and UK)
National holiday: Independence Day, 30 July (1980)
Constitution: 30 July 1980
Legal system: unified system being created from former dual French and British systems
Suffrage: 18 years of age; universal
Executive branch:
chief of state: President Father John BANI (since 25 March 1999)
head of government: Prime Minister Edward Nipake NATAPEI (since 13 April 2001, reelected NA June 2002); Deputy Prime Minister Ham LINI (since NA November 2003)
cabinet: Council of Ministers appointed by the prime minister, responsible to Parliament
elections: president elected for a five-year term by an electoral college consisting of Parliament and the presidents of the regional councils; election for president last held 25 March 1999 (next to be held NA April 2004); following legislative elections, the leader of the majority party or majority coalition is

Vanuatu *(continued)*

usually elected prime minister by Parliament from among its members; election for prime minister last held 2 August 2002 (next to be held NA May 2006) *election results:* Father John BANI elected president on second ballot (24 March 1999) after the first ballot (17 March 1999) did not have any candidate with the required two-thirds majority; percent of electoral college vote - NA%

Legislative branch: unicameral Parliament (52 seats; members elected by popular vote to serve four-year terms)
elections: last held 2 May 2002 (next to be held NA May 2006)
election results: percent of vote by party - NA%; seats by party - UMP 15, VP 14, NUP 8, VRP 3, MPP 3, VGP 3, other and independent 6; note - political party associations are fluid
note: the National Council of Chiefs advises on matters of culture and language

Judicial branch: Supreme Court (chief justice is appointed by the president after consultation with the prime minister and the leader of the opposition, three other justices are appointed by the president on the advice of the Judicial Service Commission)

Political parties and leaders: Jon Frum Movement [Song KEASPAI]; Melanesian Progressive Party or MPP [Barak SOPE]; National United Party or NUP [NA]; Union of Moderate Parties or UMP [Serge VOHOR]; Vanuaaku Party (Our Land Party) or VP [Edward NATAPEI]; Vanuatu Republican Party or VRP [Maxime Carlot KORMAN]; Greens (Vanuatu) [NA]

Political pressure groups and leaders: NA
International organization participation: ACCT, ACP, AsDB, C, FAO, G-77, IBRD, ICAO, ICFTU, ICRM, IDA, IFC, IFRCS, ILO, IMF, IMO, IOC, ITU, NAM, PIF, Sparteca, UN, UNCTAD, UNESCO, UNIDO, UPU, WFTU, WHO, WMO, WTrO (observer)

Diplomatic representation in the US: Vanuatu does not have an embassy in the US; it does, however, have a Permanent Mission to the UN

Diplomatic representation from the US: the US does not have an embassy in Vanuatu; the ambassador to Papua New Guinea is accredited to Vanuatu

Flag description: two equal horizontal bands of red (top) and green with a black isosceles triangle (based on the hoist side) all separated by a black-edged yellow stripe in the shape of a horizontal Y (the two points of the Y face the hoist side and enclose the triangle); centered in the triangle is a boar's tusk encircling two crossed namele leaves, all in yellow

Economy

Economy - overview: This South Pacific island economy is based primarily on small-scale agriculture, which provides a living for 65% of the population. Fishing, offshore financial services, and tourism, with about 50,000 visitors in 1997, are other mainstays of the economy. Mineral deposits are negligible; the country has no known petroleum deposits. A small

light industry sector caters to the local market. Tax revenues come mainly from import duties. Economic development is hindered by dependence on relatively few commodity exports, vulnerability to natural disasters, and long distances from main markets and between constituent islands. A severe earthquake in November 1999 followed by a tsunami, caused extensive damage to the northern island of Pentecote and left thousands homeless. Another powerful earthquake in January 2002 caused extensive damage in the capital, Port-Vila, and surrounding areas, and also was followed by a tsunami. GDP growth rose less than 3% on average in the 1990s. In response to foreign concerns, the government has promised to tighten regulation of its offshore financial center. In mid-2002 the government stepped up efforts to boost tourism. Agriculture, especially livestock farming, is a second target for growth. Australia and New Zealand are the main suppliers of tourists and foreign aid. Growth expanded moderately in 2003.

GDP: purchasing power parity - $563 million (2002 est.)
GDP - real growth rate: -0.3% (2002 est.)
GDP - per capita: purchasing power parity - $2,900 (2002 est.)
GDP - composition by sector:
agriculture: 26%
industry: 12%
services: 62% (2000 est.)
Population below poverty line: NA%
Household income or consumption by percentage share:
lowest 10%: NA%
highest 10%: NA%
Inflation rate (consumer prices): 2% (2002 est.)
Labor force: NA
Labor force - by occupation: agriculture 65%, services 30%, industry 5% (2000 est.)
Unemployment rate: NA%
Budget:
revenues: $94.4 million
expenditures: $99.8 million, including capital expenditures of $30.4 million (1996 est.)
Industries: food and fish freezing, wood processing, meat canning
Industrial production growth rate: 1% (1997 est.)
Electricity - production: 43.46 million kWh (2001)
Electricity - production by source:
fossil fuel: 100%
hydro: 0%
nuclear: 0%
other: 0% (2001)
Electricity - consumption: 40.42 million kWh (2001)
Electricity - exports: 0 kWh (2001)
Electricity - imports: 0 kWh (2001)
Oil - production: 0 bbl/day (2001 est.)
Oil - consumption: 600 bbl/day (2001 est.)
Oil - exports: NA
Oil - imports: NA

Agriculture - products: copra, coconuts, cocoa, coffee, taro, yams, coconuts, fruits, vegetables; fish, beef
Exports: $79 million f.o.b. (2002)
Exports - commodities: copra, beef, cocoa, timber, kava, coffee
Exports - partners: India 32.9%, Thailand 22.8%, South Korea 10.1%, Indonesia 6.3%, Japan 5.1% (2002)
Imports: $138 million c.i.f. (2002)
Imports - commodities: machinery and equipment, foodstuffs, fuels
Imports - partners: Australia 21%, Japan 18.8%, New Zealand 9.4%, Singapore 8%, Fiji 6.5%, India 5.1% (2002)
Debt - external: $65.8 million (2001 est.)
Economic aid - recipient: $45.8 million (1995)
Currency: vatu (VUV)
Currency code: VUV
Exchange rates: vatu per US dollar - 122.189 (2003), 139.198 (2002), 145.312 (2001), 137.643 (2000), 129.075 (1999)
Fiscal year: calendar year

Communications

Telephones - main lines in use: 6,600 (2002)
Telephones - mobile cellular: 4,900 (2002)
Telephone system:
general assessment: NA
domestic: NA
international: country code - 678; satellite earth station - 1 Intelsat (Pacific Ocean)
Radio broadcast stations: AM 2, FM 2, shortwave 1 (2002)
Television broadcast stations: 1 (2002)
Internet country code: .vu
Internet hosts: 551 (2002)
Internet users: 7,000 (2002)

Transportation

Railways: 0 km
Highways:
total: 1,070 km
paved: 256 km
unpaved: 814 km (1999 est.)
Waterways: none
Ports and harbors: Forari, Port-Vila, Santo (Espiritu Santo)
Merchant marine:
total: 51 ships (1,000 GRT or over) 1,192,474 GRT/ 1,560,828 DWT
by type: bulk 28, cargo 2, combination bulk 3, container 2, liquefied gas 2, multi-functional large load carrier 1, refrigerated cargo 6, roll on/roll off 2, vehicle carrier 5
foreign-owned: Australia 2, Canada 1, Estonia 1, Germany 1, Japan 25, Monaco 4, New Zealand 2, Panama 1, Poland 7, Switzerland 3, United Kingdom 5, United States 2
registered in other countries: 1 (2003 est.)
Airports: 30 (2003 est.)

Airports - with paved runways:
total: 3
2,438 to 3,047 m: 1
1524 to 2437 m: 1
914 to 1,523 m: 1 (2003 est.)
Airports - with unpaved runways:
total: 27
914 to 1,523 m: 10
under 914 m: 17 (2003 est.)

Military

Military branches: no regular military forces; Vanuatu Police Force (VPF; including the paramilitary Mobile Force or VMF)
Military expenditures - dollar figure: NA
Military expenditures - percent of GDP: NA

Transnational Issues

Disputes - international: Matthew and Hunter Islands east of New Caledonia claimed by Vanuatu and France

Venezuela

Introduction

Background: Venezuela was one of three countries that emerged from the collapse of Gran Colombia in 1830 (the others being Colombia and Ecuador). For most of the first half of the 20th century, Venezuela was ruled by generally benevolent military strongmen, who promoted the oil industry and allowed for some social reforms. Democratically elected governments have held sway since 1959. Current concerns include: an embattled president who may face a recall vote, a divided military, drug-related conflicts along the Colombian border, increasing internal drug consumption, overdependence on the petroleum industry with its price fluctuations, and irresponsible mining operations that are endangering the rain forest and indigenous peoples.

Geography

Location: Northern South America, bordering the Caribbean Sea and the North Atlantic Ocean, between Colombia and Guyana
Geographic coordinates: 8 00 N, 66 00 W
Map references: South America
Area:
total: 912,050 sq km
land: 882,050 sq km
water: 30,000 sq km
Area - comparative: slightly more than twice the size of California
Land boundaries:
total: 4,993 km
border countries: Brazil 2,200 km, Colombia 2,050 km, Guyana 743 km
Coastline: 2,800 km
Maritime claims:
territorial sea: 12 NM
contiguous zone: 15 NM
exclusive economic zone: 200 NM
continental shelf: 200-m depth or to the depth of exploitation

Climate: tropical; hot, humid; more moderate in highlands
Terrain: Andes Mountains and Maracaibo Lowlands in northwest; central plains (llanos); Guiana Highlands in southeast
Elevation extremes:
lowest point: Caribbean Sea 0 m
highest point: Pico Bolivar (La Columna) 5,007 m
Natural resources: petroleum, natural gas, iron ore, gold, bauxite, other minerals, hydropower, diamonds
Land use:
arable land: 2.99%
permanent crops: 0.96%
other: 96.05% (1998 est.)
Irrigated land: 540 sq km (1998 est.)
Natural hazards: subject to floods, rockslides, mudslides; periodic droughts
Environment - current issues: sewage pollution of Lago de Valencia; oil and urban pollution of Lago de Maracaibo; deforestation; soil degradation; urban and industrial pollution, especially along the Caribbean coast; threat to the rainforest ecosystem from irresponsible mining operations
Environment - international agreements:
party to: Antarctic Treaty, Biodiversity, Climate Change, Desertification, Endangered Species, Hazardous Wastes, Marine Life Conservation, Ozone Layer Protection, Ship Pollution, Tropical Timber 83, Tropical Timber 94, Wetlands
Geography - note: on major sea and air routes linking North and South America; Angel Falls in the Guiana Highlands is the world's highest waterfall

People

Population: 25,017,387 (July 2004 est.)
Age structure:
0-14 years: 30.5% (male 3,930,413; female 3,687,744)
15-64 years: 64.5% (male 8,107,382; female 8,034,905)
65 years and over: 5% (male 571,289; female 685,654) (2004 est.)
Median age:
total: 25.2 years
male: 24.6 years
female: 25.8 years (2004 est.)
Population growth rate: 1.44% (2004 est.)
Birth rate: 19.34 births/1,000 population (2004 est.)
Death rate: 4.9 deaths/1,000 population (2004 est.)
Net migration rate: -0.04 migrant(s)/1,000 population (2004 est.)
Sex ratio:
at birth: 1.08 male(s)/female
under 15 years: 1.07 male(s)/female
15-64 years: 1.01 male(s)/female
65 years and over: 0.83 male(s)/female
total population: 1.02 male(s)/female (2004 est.)
Infant mortality rate:
total: 22.99 deaths/1,000 live births
male: 26.18 deaths/1,000 live births
female: 19.57 deaths/1,000 live births (2004 est.)

Venezuela (continued)

Life expectancy at birth:
total population: 74.06 years
male: 71.02 years
female: 77.32 years (2004 est.)
Total fertility rate: 2.31 children born/woman (2004 est.)
HIV/AIDS - adult prevalence rate: 0.5% - note: no country specific models provided (2001 est.)
HIV/AIDS - people living with HIV/AIDS: 62,000 (1999 est.)
HIV/AIDS - deaths: 2,000 (2001 est.)
Nationality:
noun: Venezuelan(s)
adjective: Venezuelan
Ethnic groups: Spanish, Italian, Portuguese, Arab, German, African, indigenous people
Religions: nominally Roman Catholic 96%, Protestant 2%, other 2%
Languages: Spanish (official), numerous indigenous dialects
Literacy:
definition: age 15 and over can read and write
total population: 93.4%
male: 93.8%
female: 93.1% (2003 est.)

Government

Country name:
conventional long form: Bolivarian Republic of Venezuela
conventional short form: Venezuela
local long form: Republica Bolivariana de Venezuela
local short form: Venezuela
Government type: federal republic
Capital: Caracas
Administrative divisions: 23 states (estados, singular - estado), 1 federal district* (distrito federal), and 1 federal dependency** (dependencia federal); Amazonas, Anzoategui, Apure, Aragua, Barinas, Bolivar, Carabobo, Cojedes, Delta Amacuro, Dependencias Federales**, Distrito Federal*, Falcon, Guarico, Lara, Merida, Miranda, Monagas, Nueva Esparta, Portuguesa, Sucre, Tachira, Trujillo, Vargas, Yaracuy, Zulia
note: the federal dependency consists of 11 federally controlled island groups with a total of 72 individual islands
Independence: 5 July 1811 (from Spain)
National holiday: Independence Day, 5 July (1811)
Constitution: 30 December 1999
Legal system: based on organic laws as of July 1999; open, adversarial court system; has not accepted compulsory ICJ jurisdiction
Suffrage: 18 years of age; universal
Executive branch:
chief of state: President Hugo CHAVEZ Frias (since 3 February 1999); Vice President Jose Vicente RANGEL (since 28 April 2002); note - the president is both the chief of state and head of government

head of government: President Hugo CHAVEZ Frias (since 3 February 1999); Vice President Jose Vicente RANGEL (since 28 April 2002); note - the president is both the chief of state and head of government
cabinet: Council of Ministers appointed by the president
elections: president elected by popular vote for a six-year term; election last held 30 July 2000 (next to be held NA 2006)
election results: Hugo CHAVEZ Frias reelected president; percent of vote - 60%
Legislative branch: unicameral National Assembly or Asamblea Nacional (165 seats; members elected by popular vote to serve five-year terms; three seats reserved for the indigenous peoples of Venezuela)
elections: last held 30 July 2000 (next to be held NA 2005)
election results: percent of vote by party - NA%; seats by party - pro-government 108 (MVR 92, MAS 6, indigenous 3, other 7), opposition 57 (AD 33, COPEI 6, Justice First 5, other 13)
Judicial branch: Supreme Tribunal of Justice or Tribuna Suprema de Justicia (magistrates are elected by the National Assembly for a single 12-year term)
Political parties and leaders: Democratic Action or AD [Henry RAMOS Allup]; Fifth Republic Movement or MVR [Hugo CHAVEZ]; Homeland for All or PPT [Jose ALBORNOZ]; Justice First [Julio BORGES]; Movement Toward Socialism or MAS [Hector MUJICA]; National Convergence or Convergencia [Juan Jose CALDERA]; Radical Cause or La Causa R [Antonio HERRERA]; Social Christian Party or COPEI [Eduardo FERNANDEZ]; Venezuela Project or PV [Henrique SALAS Romer]
Political pressure groups and leaders: FEDECAMARAS, a conservative business group; VECINOS groups; Venezuelan Confederation of Workers or CTV (labor organization dominated by the Democratic Action)
International organization participation: CAN, Caricom (observer), CDB, FAO, G-3, G-15, G-24, G-77, IADB, IAEA, IBRD, ICAO, ICC, ICCt, ICFTU, ICRM, IFAD, IFC, IFRCS, IHO, ILO, IMF, IMO, Interpol, IOC, IOM, ISO, ITU, LAES, LAIA, NAM, OAS, OPANAL, OPCW, OPEC, PCA, RG, UN, UNCTAD, UNESCO, UNHCR, UNIDO, UPU, WCL, WCO, WFTU, WHO, WIPO, WMO, WToO, WTrO
Diplomatic representation in the US:
chief of mission: Ambassador Bernardo ALVAREZ
chancery: 1099 30th Street NW, Washington, DC 20007
telephone: [1] (202) 342-2214
FAX: [1] (202) 342-6820
consulate(s) general: Boston, Chicago, Houston, Miami, New Orleans, New York, San Francisco, and San Juan (Puerto Rico)
Diplomatic representation from the US:
chief of mission: Ambassador Charles S. SHAPIRO
embassy: Calle F con Calle Suapure, Urbanizacion Colinas de Valle Arriba, Caracas 1080
mailing address: P. O. Box 62291, Caracas 1060-A; APO AA 34037

telephone: [58] (212) 975-9234, 975-6411
FAX: [58] (212) 975-8991
Flag description: three equal horizontal bands of yellow (top), blue, and red with the coat of arms on the hoist side of the yellow band and an arc of seven white five-pointed stars centered in the blue band

Economy

Economy - overview: Venezuela continues to be highly dependent on the petroleum sector, which accounts for roughly one-third of GDP, around 80% of export earnings, and more than half of government operating revenues. Despite higher oil prices at the end of 2002 and into 2003, domestic political instability, culminating in a disastrous two-month national oil strike from December 2002 to February 2003, temporarily halted economic activity. The economy remained in depression in 2003, declining by 9.2% after an 8.9% fall in 2002. In late 2003, President CHAVEZ committed himself to $1 billion in new social programs, money the government does not have.
GDP: purchasing power parity - $117.9 billion (2003 est.)
GDP - real growth rate: -9.2% (2003 est.)
GDP - per capita: purchasing power parity - $4,800 (2003 est.)
GDP - composition by sector:
agriculture: 5%
industry: 50%
services: 45% (2001)
Population below poverty line: 47% (1998 est.)
Household income or consumption by percentage share:
lowest 10%: 0.8%
highest 10%: 36.5% (1998)
Distribution of family income - Gini index: 49.5 (1998)
Inflation rate (consumer prices): 31.1% (2003 est.)
Labor force: 9.9 million (1999)
Labor force - by occupation: services 64%, industry 23%, agriculture 13% (1997 est.)
Unemployment rate: 18% (2003 est.)
Budget:
revenues: $20.1 billion
expenditures: $23.3 billion, including capital expenditures of $2.6 billion (2002)
Industries: petroleum, iron ore mining, construction materials, food processing, textiles, steel, aluminum, motor vehicle assembly
Industrial production growth rate: -5.4% (2002 est.)
Electricity - production: 87.6 billion kWh (2001)
Electricity - production by source:
fossil fuel: 31.7%
hydro: 68.3%
nuclear: 0%
other: 0% (2001)
Electricity - consumption: 81.47 billion kWh (2001)
Electricity - exports: 0 kWh (2001)
Electricity - imports: 0 kWh (2001)

Venezuela *(continued)*

Oil - production: 3.08 million bbl/day (2001 est.)
Oil - consumption: 505,000 bbl/day (2001 est.)
Oil - exports: NA
Oil - imports: NA
Oil - proved reserves: 63.95 billion bbl (1 January 2002)
Natural gas - production: 31.71 billion cu m (2001 est.)
Natural gas - consumption: 31.71 billion cu m (2001 est.)
Natural gas - exports: 0 cu m (2001 est.)
Natural gas - imports: 0 cu m (2001 est.)
Natural gas - proved reserves: 4.202 trillion cu m (1 January 2002)
Agriculture - products: corn, sorghum, sugarcane, rice, bananas, vegetables, coffee; beef, pork, milk, eggs; fish
Exports: $25.86 billion f.o.b. (2003 est.)
Exports - commodities: petroleum, bauxite and aluminum, steel, chemicals, agricultural products, basic manufactures
Exports - partners: US 45.1%, Netherlands Antilles 12.8%, Dominican Republic 2.8% (2002)
Imports: $10.71 billion f.o.b. (2003 est.)
Imports - commodities: raw materials, machinery and equipment, transport equipment, construction materials
Imports - partners: US 32.1%, Colombia 8%, Brazil 6.2%, Germany 4.6%, Mexico 4.4%, Italy 4.1% (2002)
Debt - external: $20.8 billion (2003)
Economic aid - recipient: $74 million (2000)
Currency: bolivar (VEB)
Currency code: VEB
Exchange rates: bolivares per US dollar - 1,607.79 (2003), 1,160.95 (2002), 723.666 (2001), 679.96 (2000), 605.717 (1999)
Fiscal year: calendar year

Communications

Telephones - main lines in use: 2,841,800 (2002)
Telephones - mobile cellular: 6,463,600 (2002)
Telephone system:
general assessment: modern and expanding
domestic: domestic satellite system with 3 earth stations; recent substantial improvement in telephone service in rural areas; substantial increase in digitalization of exchanges and trunk lines; installation of a national interurban fiber-optic network capable of digital multimedia services
international: country code - 58; 3 submarine coaxial cables; satellite earth stations - 1 Intelsat (Atlantic Ocean) and 1 PanAmSat; participating with Colombia, Ecuador, Peru, and Bolivia in the construction of an international fiber-optic network
Radio broadcast stations: AM 201, FM NA (20 in Caracas), shortwave 11 (1998)
Television broadcast stations: 66 (plus 45 repeaters) (1997)
Internet country code: .ve
Internet hosts: 24,138 (2002)
Internet users: 1,274,400 (2002)

Transportation

Railways:
total: 682 km
standard gauge: 682 km 1.435-m gauge (2002)
Highways:
total: 96,155 km
paved: 32,308 km
unpaved: 63,847 km (1999 est.)
Waterways: 7,100 km
note: Rio Orinoco and Lago de Maracaibo accept oceangoing vessels
Pipelines: extra heavy crude 992 km; gas 5,262 km; oil 7,484 km; refined products 1,681 km; unknown (oil/water) 141 km (2003)
Ports and harbors: Amuay, Bajo Grande, El Tablazo, La Guaira, La Salina, Maracaibo, Matanzas, Palua, Puerto Cabello, Puerto la Cruz, Puerto Ordaz, Puerto Sucre, Punta Cardon
Merchant marine:
total: 48 ships (1,000 GRT or over) 740,919 GRT/1,191,483 DWT
by type: bulk 6, cargo 7, container 2, liquefied gas 5, multi-functional large load carrier 1, passenger 1, passenger/cargo 1, petroleum tanker 16, roll on/roll off 8, short-sea/passenger 1
foreign-owned: Belgium 1, Denmark 2, Greece 2, Spain 1, United States 2
registered in other countries: 4 (2003 est.)
Airports: 368 (2003 est.)
Airports - with paved runways:
total: 128
over 3,047 m: 5
2,438 to 3,047 m: 11
1,524 to 2,437 m: 31
914 to 1,523 m: 63
under 914 m: 18 (2003 est.)
Airports - with unpaved runways:
total: 240
1,524 to 2,437 m: 12
914 to 1,523 m: 89
under 914 m: 139 (2003 est.)

Military

Military branches: National Armed Forces (Fuerzas Armadas Nacionales or FAN) includes Ground Forces or Army (Fuerzas Terrestres or Ejercito), Naval Forces (Fuerzas Navales or Armada - including marines and Coast Guard), Air Force (Fuerzas Aereas or Aviacion), Armed Forces of Cooperation or National Guard (Fuerzas Armadas de Cooperacion or Guardia Nacional)
Military manpower - military age: 18 years of age (2004 est.)
Military manpower - availability:
males age 15-49: 6,886,775 (2004 est.)
Military manpower - fit for military service:
males age 15-49: 4,953,803 (2004 est.)
Military manpower - reaching military age annually:
males: 250,730 (2004 est.)
Military expenditures - dollar figure:
$1,125,600,000 (2003)
Military expenditures - percent of GDP: 1.3% (2003)

Transnational Issues

Disputes - international: claims all of the area west of the Essequibo River, preventing any discussion of a maritime boundary; Guyana has expressed its intention to join Barbados in asserting claims before UNCLOS that the Trinidad and Tobago's maritime boundary with Venezuela extends into their waters; maritime boundary dispute with Colombia in the Gulf of Venezuela and the Caribbean Sea; US, France and the Netherlands recognize Venezuela's claim to give full effect to Aves Island, which creates a Venezuelan EEZ/continental shelf extending over a large portion of the Caribbean Sea; Dominica, Saint Kitts and Nevis, Saint Lucia, and Saint Vincent and the Grenadines protest Venezuela's claim that Aves Island sustains human habitation and other states' recognition of it
Illicit drugs: small-scale illicit producer of opium and coca for the processing of opiates and coca derivatives; however, large quantities of cocaine, heroin, and marijuana transit the country from Colombia bound for US and Europe; significant narcotics-related money-laundering activity, especially along the border with Colombia and on Margarita Island; active eradication program primarily targeting opium; increasing signs of drug-related activities by Colombian insurgents on border

Vietnam

Introduction

Background: France occupied all of Vietnam by 1884. Independence was declared after World War II, but the French continued to rule until 1954 when they were defeated by Communist forces under Ho Chi Minh, who took control of the North. US economic and military aid to South Vietnam grew through the 1960s in an attempt to bolster the government, but US armed forces were withdrawn following a cease-fire agreement in 1973. Two years later, North Vietnamese forces overran the South.

Geography

Location: Southeastern Asia, bordering the Gulf of Thailand, Gulf of Tonkin, and South China Sea, alongside China, Laos, and Cambodia
Geographic coordinates: 16 00 N, 106 00 E
Map references: Southeast Asia
Area:
total: 329,560 sq km
land: 325,360 sq km
water: 4,200 sq km
Area - comparative: slightly larger than New Mexico

Land boundaries:
total: 4,639 km
border countries: Cambodia 1,228 km, China 1,281 km, Laos 2,130 km
Coastline: 3,444 km (excludes islands)
Maritime claims:
territorial sea: 12 NM
contiguous zone: 12 NM
exclusive economic zone: 200 NM
continental shelf: 200 NM or to the edge of the continental margin
Climate: tropical in south; monsoonal in north with hot, rainy season (mid-May to mid-September) and warm, dry season (mid-October to mid-March)
Terrain: low, flat delta in south and north; central highlands; hilly, mountainous in far north and northwest
Elevation extremes:
lowest point: South China Sea 0 m
highest point: Fan Si Pan 3,144 m
Natural resources: phosphates, coal, manganese, bauxite, chromate, offshore oil and gas deposits, forests, hydropower
Land use:
arable land: 17.41%
permanent crops: 4.71%
other: 77.88% (1998 est.)
Irrigated land: 30,000 sq km (1998 est.)
Natural hazards: occasional typhoons (May to January) with extensive flooding, especially in the Mekong River delta
Environment - current issues: logging and slash-and-burn agricultural practices contribute to deforestation and soil degradation; water pollution and overfishing threaten marine life populations; groundwater contamination limits potable water supply; growing urban industrialization and population migration are rapidly degrading environment in Hanoi and Ho Chi Minh City
Environment - international agreements:
party to: Biodiversity, Climate Change, Climate Change-Kyoto Protocol, Desertification, Endangered Species, Environmental Modification, Hazardous Wastes, Law of the Sea, Ozone Layer Protection, Ship Pollution, Wetlands
signed, but not ratified: none of the selected agreements
Geography - note: extending 1,650 km north to south, the country is only 50 km across at its narrowest point

People

Population: 82,689,518 (July 2004 est.)
Age structure:
0-14 years: 29.4% (male 12,524,098; female 11,807,763)
15-64 years: 65% (male 26,475,156; female 27,239,543)
65 years and over: 5.6% (male 1,928,568; female 2,714,390) (2004 est.)

Median age:
total: 24.9 years
male: 24 years
female: 25.9 years (2004 est.)
Population growth rate: 1.3% (2004 est.)
Birth rate: 19.58 births/1,000 population (2004 est.)
Death rate: 6.14 deaths/1,000 population (2004 est.)
Net migration rate: -0.45 migrant(s)/1,000 population (2004 est.)
Sex ratio:
at birth: 1.08 male(s)/female
under 15 years: 1.06 male(s)/female
15-64 years: 0.97 male(s)/female
65 years and over: 0.71 male(s)/female
total population: 0.98 male(s)/female (2004 est.)
Infant mortality rate:
total: 29.88 deaths/1,000 live births
male: 33.71 deaths/1,000 live births
female: 25.77 deaths/1,000 live births (2004 est.)
Life expectancy at birth:
total population: 70.35 years
male: 67.86 years
female: 73.02 years (2004 est.)
Total fertility rate: 2.22 children born/woman (2004 est.)
HIV/AIDS - adult prevalence rate: 0.3% (2001 est.)
HIV/AIDS - people living with HIV/AIDS: 130,000 (2001 est.)
HIV/AIDS - deaths: 6,600 (2001 est.)
Nationality:
noun: Vietnamese (singular and plural)
adjective: Vietnamese
Ethnic groups: Vietnamese 85%-90%, Chinese, Hmong, Thai, Khmer, Cham, mountain groups
Religions: Buddhist, Hoa Hao, Cao Dai, Christian (predominantly Roman Catholic, some Protestant), indigenous beliefs, Muslim
Languages: Vietnamese (official), English (increasingly favored as a second language), some French, Chinese, and Khmer; mountain area languages (Mon-Khmer and Malayo-Polynesian)
Literacy:
definition: age 15 and over can read and write
total population: 94%
male: 95.8%
female: 92.3% (2003 est.)

Government

Country name:
conventional long form: Socialist Republic of Vietnam
conventional short form: Vietnam
local long form: Cong Hoa Xa Hoi Chu Nghia Viet Nam
local short form: Viet Nam
abbreviation: SRV
Government type: Communist state
Capital: Hanoi
Administrative divisions: 58 provinces (tinh, singular and plural), and 3 municipalities* (thu do, singular and plural); An Giang, Bac Giang, Bac Kan, Bac Lieu, Bac Ninh, Ba Ria-Vung Tau, Ben Tre, Binh

Vietnam (continued)

Dinh, Binh Duong, Binh Phuoc, Binh Thuan, Ca Mau, Can Tho, Cao Bang, Dac Lak, Da Nang, Dong Nai, Dong Thap, Gia Lai, Ha Giang, Hai Duong, Hai Phong*, Ha Nam, Ha Noi*, Ha Tay, Ha Tinh, Hoa Binh, Ho Chi Minh*, Hung Yen, Khanh Hoa, Kien Giang, Kon Tum, Lai Chau, Lam Dong, Lang Son, Lao Cai, Long An, Nam Dinh, Nghe An, Ninh Binh, Ninh Thuan, Phu Tho, Phu Yen, Quang Binh, Quang Nam, Quang Ngai, Quang Ninh, Quang Tri, Soc Trang, Son La, Tay Ninh, Thai Binh, Thai Nguyen, Thanh Hoa, Thua Thien-Hue, Tien Giang, Tra Vinh, Tuyen Quang, Vinh Long, Vinh Phuc, Yen Bai

Independence: 2 September 1945 (from France)
National holiday: Independence Day, 2 September (1945)
Constitution: 15 April 1992
Legal system: based on communist legal theory and French civil law system
Suffrage: 18 years of age; universal
Executive branch:
chief of state: President Tran Duc Luong (since 24 September 1997)
head of government: Prime Minister Phan Van Khai (since 25 September 1997); First Deputy Prime Minister Nguyen Tan Dung (since 29 September 1997); Deputy Prime Ministers Vu Khoan (8 August 2002) and Pham Gia Khiem (since 29 September 1997)
cabinet: Cabinet appointed by the president on the proposal of the prime minister and ratification of the National Assembly
elections: president elected by the National Assembly from among its members for a five-year term; election last held 25 July 2002 (next to be held when National Assembly meets following legislative elections in 2007); prime minister appointed by the president from among the members of the National Assembly; deputy prime ministers appointed by the prime minister
election results: Tran Duc Luong elected president; percent of National Assembly vote - NA%
Legislative branch: unicameral National Assembly or Quoc-Hoi (498 seats; members elected by popular vote to serve five-year terms)
elections: last held 19 May 2002 (next to be held 2007)
election results: percent of vote by party - CPV 90%, other 10% (the 10% are not CPV members but are approved by the CPV to stand for election); seats by party - CPV 447, CPV-approved 51
Judicial branch: Supreme People's Court (chief justice is elected for a five-year term by the National Assembly on the recommendation of the president)
Political parties and leaders: only party - Communist Party of Vietnam or CPV [Nong Duc Manh, general secretary]
Political pressure groups and leaders: none
International organization participation: ACCT, APEC, ARF, AsDB, ASEAN, CP, FAO, G-77, IAEA, IBRD, ICAO, ICRM, IDA, IFAD, IFC, IFRCS, ILO, IMF, IMO, Interpol, IOC, IOM (observer), ISO, ITU, NAM, OPCW, UN, UNCTAD, UNESCO, UNIDO, UPU, WCL, WCO, WFTU, WHO, WIPO, WMO, WToO, WTrO (observer)

Diplomatic representation in the US:
chief of mission: Ambassador Nguyen Tam Chien
chancery: 1233 20th Street NW, Suite 400, Washington, DC 20036
telephone: [1] (202) 861-0737
FAX: [1] (202) 861-0917
consulate(s) general: San Francisco
Diplomatic representation from the US:
chief of mission: Ambassador Raymond F. BURGHARDT
embassy: 7 Lang Ha Road, Ba Dinh District, Hanoi
mailing address: PSC 461, Box 400, FPO AP 96521-0002
telephone: [84] (4) 772-1500
FAX: [84] (4) 772-1510
consulate(s) general: Ho Chi Minh City
Flag description: red with a large yellow five-pointed star in the center

Economy

Economy - overview: Vietnam is a poor, densely-populated country that has had to recover from the ravages of war, the loss of financial support from the old Soviet Bloc, and the rigidities of a centrally-planned economy. Substantial progress was achieved from 1986 to 1996 in moving forward from an extremely low starting point - growth averaged around 9% per year from 1993 to 1997. The 1997 Asian financial crisis highlighted the problems in the Vietnamese economy, but rather than prompting reform, reaffirmed the government's belief that shifting to a market-oriented economy would lead to disaster. GDP growth of 8.5% in 1997 fell to 6% in 1998 and 5% in 1999. Growth then rose to 6% to 7% in 2000-02 even against the background of global recession. These numbers mask some major difficulties in economic performance. Many domestic industries, including coal, cement, steel, and paper, have reported large stockpiles of inventory and tough competition from more efficient foreign producers. Since the Party elected new leadership in 2001, Vietnamese authorities have reaffirmed their commitment to economic liberalization and have moved to implement the structural reforms needed to modernize the economy and to produce more competitive, export-driven industries. The US-Vietnam Bilateral Trade Agreement entered into force near the end of 2001 and is expected to significantly increase Vietnam's exports to the US. The US is assisting Vietnam with implementing the legal and structural reforms called for in the agreement.
GDP: purchasing power parity - $203.9 billion (2003 est.)
GDP - real growth rate: 7.3% (2003 est.)
GDP - per capita: purchasing power parity - $2,500 (2003 est.)
GDP - composition by sector:
agriculture: 24%
industry: 37%
services: 39% (2001 est.)

Population below poverty line: 37% (1998 est.)
Household income or consumption by percentage share:
lowest 10%: 3.6%
highest 10%: 29.9% (1998)
Distribution of family income - Gini index: 36.1 (1998)
Inflation rate (consumer prices): 3.9% (2002 est.)
Labor force: 38.2 million (1998 est.)
Labor force - by occupation: agriculture 63%, industry and services 37% (2000 est.)
Unemployment rate: 25% (1995 est.)
Budget:
revenues: $5.3 billion
expenditures: $5.6 billion, including capital expenditures of $1.8 billion (1999 est.)
Industries: food processing, garments, shoes, machine-building, mining, cement, chemical fertilizer, glass, tires, oil, coal, steel, paper
Industrial production growth rate: 10.2% (2002 est.)
Electricity - production: 29.8 billion kWh (2001)
Electricity - production by source:
fossil fuel: 43.7%
hydro: 56.3%
nuclear: 0%
other: 0% (2001)
Electricity - consumption: 27.71 billion kWh (2001)
Electricity - exports: 0 kWh (2001)
Electricity - imports: 0 kWh (2001)
Oil - production: 356,700 bbl/day (2001 est.)
Oil - consumption: 185,000 bbl/day (2001 est.)
Oil - exports: NA
Oil - imports: NA
Oil - proved reserves: 1.4 billion bbl (1 January 2002)
Natural gas - production: 1.3 billion cu m (2001 est.)
Natural gas - consumption: 1.3 billion cu m (2001 est.)
Natural gas - exports: 0 cu m (2001 est.)
Natural gas - imports: 0 cu m (2001 est.)
Natural gas - proved reserves: 192.6 billion cu m (1 January 2002)
Agriculture - products: paddy rice, corn, potatoes, rubber, soybeans, coffee, tea, bananas, sugar; poultry, pigs, fish
Exports: $19.88 billion f.o.b. (2003 est.)
Exports - commodities: crude oil, marine products, rice, coffee, rubber, tea, garments, shoes
Exports - partners: US 15%, Japan 14.6%, Australia 7.5%, China 6.4%, Germany 6.4%, Singapore 5.4%, UK 4.2% (2002)
Imports: $22.5 billion f.o.b. (2003 est.)
Imports - commodities: machinery and equipment, petroleum products, fertilizer, steel products, raw cotton, grain, cement, motorcycles
Imports - partners: Taiwan 12.6%, South Korea 12.3%, China 11.8%, Japan 11.7%, Singapore 11.4%, Thailand 5.2%, Hong Kong 4.2% (2002)
Debt - external: $14.1 billion (2001)

Vietnam *(continued)*

Economic aid - recipient: $2.8 billion in credits and grants pledged by international donors for 2000 (2004)
Currency: dong (VND)
Currency code: VND
Exchange rates: dong per US dollar - 15,279.5 (2003), 15,279.5 (2002), 14,725.2 (2001), 14,167.7 (2000), 13,943.2 (1999)
Fiscal year: calendar year

Communications

Telephones - main lines in use: 3,929,100 (2002)
Telephones - mobile cellular: 1,902,400 (2002)
Telephone system:
general assessment: Vietnam is putting considerable effort into modernization and expansion of its telecommunication system, but its performance continues to lag behind that of its more modern neighbors
domestic: all provincial exchanges are digitalized and connected to Hanoi, Da Nang, and Ho Chi Minh City by fiber-optic cable or microwave radio relay networks; main lines have been substantially increased, and the use of mobile telephones is growing rapidly
international: country code - 84; satellite earth stations - 2 Intersputnik (Indian Ocean region)
Radio broadcast stations: AM 65, FM 7, shortwave 29 (1999)
Television broadcast stations: at least 7 (plus 13 repeaters) (1998)
Internet country code: .vn
Internet hosts: 529 (2002)
Internet users: 1.5 million (2002)

Transportation

Railways:
total: 3,142 km
standard gauge: 209 km 1.435-m gauge
narrow gauge: 2,625 km 1.000-m gauge
dual gauge: 308 km three-rail track combining 1.435-m and 1.000-m gauges (2002)
Highways:
total: 93,300 km
paved: 23,418 km
unpaved: 69,882 km (1999 est.)
Waterways: 17,702 km
note: more than 5,149 km are navigable at all times by vessels up to 1.8 m draft
Pipelines: condensate/gas 432 km; gas 210 km; oil 3 km; refined products 206 km (2003)
Ports and harbors: Cam Ranh, Da Nang, Haiphong, Ho Chi Minh City, Ha Long, Quy Nhon, Nha Trang, Vinh, Vung Tau
Merchant marine:
total: 194 ships (1,000 GRT or over) 1,170,621 GRT/ 1,798,376 DWT
by type: bulk 16, cargo 135, chemical tanker 1, container 8, liquefied gas 4, petroleum tanker 25, refrigerated cargo 3, roll on/roll off 1, specialized tanker 1

foreign-owned: Cambodia 1, Germany 1, Japan 2, South Korea 1, United Kingdom 3
registered in other countries: 11 (2003 est.)
Airports: 19 (2003 est.)
Airports - with paved runways:
total: 16
over 3,047 m: 6
2,438 to 3,047 m: 4
1,524 to 2,437 m: 6 (2003 est.)
Airports - with unpaved runways:
total: 3
1,524 to 2,437 m: 1
914 to 1,523 m: 1
under 914 m: 1 (2003 est.)

Military

Military branches: People's Army of Vietnam: Ground Forces, People's Navy Command (including Naval Infantry), Air and Air Defense Force, Coast Guard
Military manpower - military age: 17 years of age (2004 est.)
Military manpower - availability:
males age 15-49: 23,438,858 (2004 est.)
Military manpower - fit for military service:
males age 15-49: 14,694,574 (2004 est.)
Military manpower - reaching military age annually:
males: 853,197 (2004 est.)
Military expenditures - dollar figure: $650 million (FY98)
Military expenditures - percent of GDP: 2.5% (FY98)

Transnational Issues

Disputes - international: demarcation of the land boundary with China continues, but maritime boundary and joint fishing zone agreement remains unratified; Cambodia and Laos protest Vietnamese squatters and armed encroachments along border; China occupies Paracel Islands also claimed by Vietnam and Taiwan; involved in complex dispute with China, Malaysia, Philippines, Taiwan, and possibly Brunei over the Spratly Islands; the 2002 "Declaration on the Conduct of Parties in the South China Sea" has eased tensions but falls short of a legally binding "code of conduct" desired by several of the disputants
Illicit drugs: minor producer of opium poppy; probable minor transit point for Southeast Asian heroin; domestic opium/heroin/methamphetamine addiction problems

Virgin Islands
(territory of the US)

Introduction

Background: During the 17th century, the archipelago was divided into two territorial units, one English and the other Danish. Sugarcane, produced by slave labor, drove the islands' economy during the 18th and early 19th centuries. In 1917, the US purchased the Danish portion, which had been in economic decline since the abolition of slavery in 1848.

Geography

Location: Caribbean, islands between the Caribbean Sea and the North Atlantic Ocean, east of Puerto Rico
Geographic coordinates: 18 20 N, 64 50 W
Map references: Central America and the Caribbean
Area:
total: 352 sq km
land: 349 sq km
water: 3 sq km
Area - comparative: twice the size of Washington, DC
Land boundaries: 0 km
Coastline: 188 km
Maritime claims:
territorial sea: 12 NM
exclusive economic zone: 200 NM
Climate: subtropical, tempered by easterly trade winds, relatively low humidity, little seasonal temperature variation; rainy season May to November
Terrain: mostly hilly to rugged and mountainous with little level land
Elevation extremes:
lowest point: Caribbean Sea 0 m
highest point: Crown Mountain 474 m
Natural resources: sun, sand, sea, surf
Land use:
arable land: 15%
permanent crops: 6%
other: 79% (1998 est.)

Virgin Islands *(continued)*

Irrigated land: NA sq km
Natural hazards: several hurricanes in recent years; frequent and severe droughts and floods; occasional earthquakes
Environment - current issues: lack of natural freshwater resources
Geography - note: important location along the Anegada Passage - a key shipping lane for the Panama Canal; Saint Thomas has one of the best natural deepwater harbors in the Caribbean

People

Population: 108,775 (July 2004 est.)
Age structure:
0-14 years: 23.8% (male 13,116; female 12,770)
15-64 years: 66% (male 33,944; female 37,870)
65 years and over: 10.2% (male 4,855; female 6,220) (2004 est.)
Median age:
total: 35.9 years
male: 35.1 years
female: 36.7 years (2004 est.)
Population growth rate: -0.05% (2004 est.)
Birth rate: 14.49 births/1,000 population (2004 est.)
Death rate: 6.1 deaths/1,000 population (2004 est.)
Net migration rate: -8.94 migrant(s)/1,000 population (2004 est.)
Sex ratio:
at birth: 1.06 male(s)/female
under 15 years: 1.03 male(s)/female
15-64 years: 0.9 male(s)/female
65 years and over: 0.78 male(s)/female
total population: 0.91 male(s)/female (2004 est.)
Infant mortality rate:
total: 8.21 deaths/1,000 live births
male: 9.31 deaths/1,000 live births
female: 7.04 deaths/1,000 live births (2004 est.)
Life expectancy at birth:
total population: 78.75 years
male: 74.91 years
female: 82.82 years (2004 est.)
Total fertility rate: 2.21 children born/woman (2004 est.)
HIV/AIDS - adult prevalence rate: NA%
HIV/AIDS - people living with HIV/AIDS: NA
HIV/AIDS - deaths: NA
Nationality:
noun: Virgin Islander(s)
adjective: Virgin Islander
Ethnic groups: black 78%, white 10%, other 12%
note: West Indian 81% (49% born in the Virgin Islands and 32% born elsewhere in the West Indies), US mainland 13%, Puerto Rican 4%, other 2%
Religions: Baptist 42%, Roman Catholic 34%, Episcopalian 17%, other 7%
Languages: English (official), Spanish, Creole
Literacy:
definition: NA
total population: NA%
male: NA%
female: NA%

Government

Country name:
conventional long form: United States Virgin Islands
conventional short form: Virgin Islands
former: Danish West Indies
Dependency status: organized, unincorporated territory of the US with policy relations between the Virgin Islands and the US under the jurisdiction of the Office of Insular Affairs, US Department of the Interior
Government type: NA
Capital: Charlotte Amalie
Administrative divisions: none (territory of the US); there are no first-order administrative divisions as defined by the US Government, but there are three islands at the second order; Saint Croix, Saint John, Saint Thomas
National holiday: Transfer Day (from Denmark to the US), 27 March (1917)
Constitution: Revised Organic Act of 22 July 1954
Legal system: based on US laws
Suffrage: 18 years of age; universal; note - island residents are US citizens but do not vote in US presidential elections
Executive branch:
chief of state: President George W. BUSH of the US (since 20 January 2001)
head of government: Governor Dr. Charles Wesley TURNBULL (since 5 January 1999)
cabinet: NA
elections: US president and vice president elected on the same ticket for four-year terms; governor and lieutenant governor elected on the same ticket by popular vote for four-year terms; election last held 5 November 2002 (next to be held NA November 2006)
election results: Dr. Charles Wesley TURNBULL reelected governor; percent of vote - Dr. Charles Wesley TURNBULL (Democrat) 50.5%, John de JONGH 24.4%
Legislative branch: unicameral Senate (15 seats; members are elected by popular vote to serve two-year terms)
elections: last held 6 November 2002 (next to be held 2 November 2004)
election results: percent of vote by party - NA%; seats by party - Democratic Party 10, ICM 2, independent 3
note: the Virgin Islands elects one non-voting representative to the US House of Representatives; election last held 6 November 2002 (next to be held 2 November 2004); results - Donna M. CHRISTIAN-CHRISTENSON (Democrat) reelected
Judicial branch: US District Court of the Virgin Islands (under Third Circuit jurisdiction); Territorial Court (judges appointed by the governor for 10-year terms)
Political parties and leaders: Democratic Party [Arturo WATLINGTON]; Independent Citizens' Movement or ICM [Usie RICHARDS]; Republican Party [Gary SPRAUVE]
Political pressure groups and leaders: NA
International organization participation: Interpol (subbureau), IOC

Diplomatic representation in the US: none (territory of the US)
Diplomatic representation from the US: none (territory of the US)
Flag description: white, with a modified US coat of arms in the center between the large blue initials V and I; the coat of arms shows a yellow eagle holding an olive branch in one talon and three arrows in the other with a superimposed shield of vertical red and white stripes below a blue panel

Economy

Economy - overview: Tourism is the primary economic activity, accounting for 80% of GDP and employment. The islands normally host 2 million visitors a year. The manufacturing sector consists of petroleum refining, textiles, electronics, pharmaceuticals, and watch assembly. The agricultural sector is small, with most food being imported. International business and financial services are a small but growing component of the economy. One of the world's largest petroleum refineries is at Saint Croix. The islands are subject to substantial damage from storms. The government is working to improve fiscal discipline, to support construction projects in the private sector, to expand tourist facilities, to reduce crime, and to protect the environment.
GDP: purchasing power parity - $2.4 billion (2001 est.)
GDP - real growth rate: 2% (2001 est.)
GDP - per capita: purchasing power parity - $19,000 (2001 est.)
GDP - composition by sector:
agriculture: 1%
industry: 19%
services: 80% (2003 est.)
Population below poverty line: NA%
Household income or consumption by percentage share:
lowest 10%: NA%
highest 10%: NA%
Inflation rate (consumer prices): 2% (1992)
Labor force: 49,000 (2002 est.)
Labor force - by occupation: agriculture 1%, industry 19%, services 80% (2003 est.)
Unemployment rate: 8.7% (2002 est.)
Budget:
revenues: $364.4 million
expenditures: $364.4 million, including capital expenditures of $NA (1990 est.)
Industries: tourism, petroleum refining, watch assembly, rum distilling, construction, pharmaceuticals, textiles, electronics
Industrial production growth rate: NA%
Electricity - production: 1.03 billion kWh (2001)
Electricity - production by source:
fossil fuel: 100%
hydro: 0%
nuclear: 0%
other: 0% (2001)

Virgin Islands *(continued)*

Electricity - consumption: 957.9 million kWh (2001)
Electricity - exports: 0 kWh (2001)
Electricity - imports: 0 kWh (2001)
Oil - production: 0 bbl/day (2001 est.)
Oil - consumption: 66,000 bbl/day (2001 est.)
Oil - exports: NA
Oil - imports: NA
Agriculture - products: fruit, vegetables, sorghum; Senepol cattle
Exports: $NA
Exports - commodities: refined petroleum products
Exports - partners: US, Puerto Rico
Imports: $NA
Imports - commodities: crude oil, foodstuffs, consumer goods, building materials
Imports - partners: US, Puerto Rico
Debt - external: $NA
Economic aid - recipient: $NA
Currency: US dollar (USD)
Currency code: USD
Exchange rates: the US dollar is used
Fiscal year: 1 October - 30 September

Communications

Telephones - main lines in use: 69,400 (2002)
Telephones - mobile cellular: 41,000 (2002)
Telephone system:
general assessment: NA
domestic: modern, uses fiber-optic cable and microwave radio relay
international: country code - 1-340; submarine cable and satellite communications; satellite earth stations - NA
Radio broadcast stations: AM 5, FM 11, shortwave 0 (2002)
Television broadcast stations: 2 (2002)
Internet country code: .vi
Internet users: 30,000 (2002)

Transportation

Railways: 0 km
Highways:
total: 856 km
paved: NA km
unpaved: NA km
note: the only US possession where driving on the left side of the road is practiced (2000)
Waterways: none
Ports and harbors: Charlotte Amalie, Christiansted, Cruz Bay, Port Alucroix
Merchant marine: none
Airports: 2 (2003 est.)
Airports - with paved runways:
total: 2
1,524 to 2,437 m: 2 (2003 est.)

Military

Military - note: defense is the responsibility of the US

Transnational Issues

Disputes - international: none

Wake Island
(territory of the US)

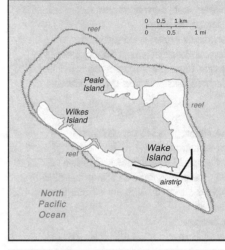

Introduction

Background: The US annexed Wake Island in 1899 for a cable station. An important air and naval base was constructed in 1940-41. In December 1941, the island was captured by the Japanese and held until the end of World War II. In subsequent years, Wake was developed as a stopover and refueling site for military and commercial aircraft transiting the Pacific. Since 1974, the island's airstrip has been used by the US military and some commercial cargo planes, as well as for emergency landings. There are over 700 landings a year on the island.

Geography

Location: Oceania, atoll in the North Pacific Ocean, about two-thirds of the way from Hawaii to the Northern Mariana Islands
Geographic coordinates: 19 17 N, 166 36 E
Map references: Oceania
Area:
total: 6.5 sq km
land: 6.5 sq km
water: 0 sq km
Area - comparative: about 11 times the size of The Mall in Washington, DC
Land boundaries: 0 km
Coastline: 19.3 km
Maritime claims:
territorial sea: 12 NM
exclusive economic zone: 200 NM
Climate: tropical
Terrain: atoll of three coral islands built up on an underwater volcano; central lagoon is former crater, islands are part of the rim
Elevation extremes:
lowest point: Pacific Ocean 0 m
highest point: unnamed location 6 m
Natural resources: none

Wake Island *(continued)*

Land use:
arable land: 0%
permanent crops: 0%
other: 100% (1998 est.)
Irrigated land: 0 sq km (1998 est.)
Natural hazards: occasional typhoons
Environment - current issues: NA
Geography - note: strategic location in the North Pacific Ocean; emergency landing location for transpacific flights

People

Population: no indigenous inhabitants
note: US military personnel have left the island, but contractor personnel remain; as of October 2001, 200 contractor personnel were present (July 2004 est.)

Government

Country name:
conventional long form: none
conventional short form: Wake Island
Dependency status: unincorporated territory of the US; administered from Washington, DC, by the Department of the Interior; activities on the island are managed by the US Air Force
Legal system: the laws of the US, where applicable, apply
Flag description: the flag of the US is used

Economy

Economy - overview: Economic activity is limited to providing services to contractors located on the island. All food and manufactured goods must be imported.
Electricity - production: NA

Communications

Telephone system:
general assessment: satellite communications; 1 DSN circuit off the Overseas Telephone System (OTS)
domestic: NA
international: NA
Radio broadcast stations: AM 0, FM NA, shortwave NA
note: Armed Forces Radio/Television Service (AFRTS) radio service provided by satellite (1998)
Television broadcast stations: 0 (1997)

Transportation

Waterways: none
Ports and harbors: none; two offshore anchorages for large ships
Airports: 1 (2003 est.)
Airports - with paved runways:
total: 1
2,438 to 3,047 m: 1 (2003 est.)
Transportation - note: formerly an important commercial aviation base, now used by US military, some commercial cargo planes, and for emergency landings

Military

Military - note: defense is the responsibility of the US

Transnational Issues

Disputes - international: claimed by Marshall Islands

Wallis and Futuna
(overseas territory of France)

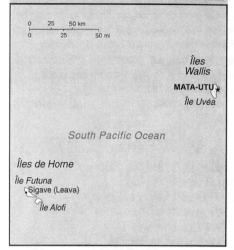

Introduction

Background: Although discovered by the Dutch and the British in the 17th and 18th centuries, it was the French who declared a protectorate over the islands in 1842. In 1959, the inhabitants of the islands voted to become a French overseas territory.

Geography

Location: Oceania, islands in the South Pacific Ocean, about two-thirds of the way from Hawaii to New Zealand
Geographic coordinates: 13 18 S, 176 12 W
Map references: Oceania
Area:
total: 274 sq km
land: 274 sq km
water: 0 sq km
note: includes Ile Uvea (Wallis Island), Ile Futuna (Futuna Island), Ile Alofi, and 20 islets
Area - comparative: 1.5 times the size of Washington, DC
Land boundaries: 0 km
Coastline: 129 km
Maritime claims:
territorial sea: 12 NM
exclusive economic zone: 200 NM
Climate: tropical; hot, rainy season (November to April); cool, dry season (May to October); rains 2,500-3,000 mm per year (80% humidity); average temperature 26.6 degrees C
Terrain: volcanic origin; low hills
Elevation extremes:
lowest point: Pacific Ocean 0 m
highest point: Mont Singavi 765 m
Natural resources: NEGL
Land use:
arable land: 5%
permanent crops: 20%
other: 75% (1998 est.)

Wallis and Futuna (continued)

Irrigated land: NA sq km
Natural hazards: NA
Environment - current issues: deforestation (only small portions of the original forests remain) largely as a result of the continued use of wood as the main fuel source; as a consequence of cutting down the forests, the mountainous terrain of Futuna is particularly prone to erosion; there are no permanent settlements on Alofi because of the lack of natural fresh water resources
Geography - note: both island groups have fringing reefs

People

Population: 15,880 (July 2004 est.)
Age structure:
0-14 years: NA%
15-64 years: NA%
65 years and over: NA%
Population growth rate: NA
Birth rate: NA births/1,000 population
Death rate: NA deaths/1,000 population
Net migration rate: NA migrant(s)/1,000 population
note: there has been steady emigration from Wallis and Futuna to New Caledonia (2004 est.)
Infant mortality rate:
total: NA%
male: NA%
female: NA%
Life expectancy at birth:
total population: NA years
male: NA years
female: NA years
Total fertility rate: NA children born/woman
HIV/AIDS - adult prevalence rate: NA%
HIV/AIDS - people living with HIV/AIDS: NA
HIV/AIDS - deaths: NA
Nationality:
noun: Wallisian(s), Futunan(s), or Wallis and Futuna Islanders
adjective: Wallisian, Futunan, or Wallis and Futuna Islander
Ethnic groups: Polynesian
Religions: Roman Catholic 99%, other 1%
Languages: French, Wallisian (indigenous Polynesian language)
Literacy:
definition: age 15 and over can read and write
total population: 50%
male: 50%
female: 50% (1969 est.)

Government

Country name:
conventional long form: Territory of the Wallis and Futuna Islands
conventional short form: Wallis and Futuna
local long form: Territoire des Iles Wallis et Futuna
local short form: Wallis et Futuna
Dependency status: overseas territory of France
Government type: NA

Capital: Mata-Utu (on Ile Uvea)
Administrative divisions: none (overseas territory of France); there are no first-order administrative divisions as defined by the US Government, but there are three kingdoms at the second order named Alo, Sigave, Wallis
Independence: none (overseas territory of France)
National holiday: Bastille Day, 14 July (1789)
Constitution: 28 September 1958 (French Constitution)
Legal system: French legal system
Suffrage: 18 years of age; universal
Executive branch:
chief of state: President Jacques CHIRAC of France (since 17 May 1995), represented by High Administrator Christian JOB (since 6 August 2002)
head of government: President of the Territorial Assembly Pataliane KANIMOA (since NA January 2001)
cabinet: Council of the Territory consists of three kings and three members appointed by the high administrator on the advice of the Territorial Assembly
note: there are three traditional kings with limited powers
elections: French president elected by popular vote for a five-year term; high administrator appointed by the French president on the advice of the French Ministry of the Interior; the presidents of the Territorial Government and the Territorial Assembly are elected by the members of the assembly
Legislative branch: unicameral Territorial Assembly or Assemblee Territoriale (20 seats; members are elected by popular vote to serve five-year terms)
elections: last held 11 March 2002 (next to be held NA March 2007)
election results: percent of vote by party - NA%; seats by party - RPR and affiliates 13, Socialists and affiliates 7
note: Wallis and Futuna elects one senator to the French Senate and one deputy to the French National Assembly; French Senate - elections last held 27 September 1998 (next to be held by NA September 2007); results - percent of vote by party - NA%; seats - RPR (now UMP) 1; French National Assembly - elections last held 16 June 2002 (next to be held by NA 2007); results - percent of vote by party - NA%; seats - RPR (UMP) 1
Judicial branch: none; justice generally administered under French law by the high administrator, but the three traditional kings administer customary law and there is a magistrate in Mata-Utu
Political parties and leaders: Lua Kae Tahi (Giscardians) [leader NA]; Mouvement des Radicaux de Gauche or MRG [leader NA]; Rally for the Republic or RPR [Clovis LOGOLOGOFOLAU]; Taumu'a Lelei [Soane Muni UHILA]; Union Populaire Locale or UPL [Falakiko GATA]; Union Pour la Democratie Francaise or UDF [leader NA]
Political pressure groups and leaders: NA
International organization participation: FZ

Diplomatic representation in the US: none (overseas territory of France)
Diplomatic representation from the US: none (overseas territory of France)
Flag description: a large white modified Maltese cross - shifted a little off center toward the fly and slightly downward - on a red background; the flag of France outlined in white on two sides is in the upper hoist quadrant; the flag of France is used for official occasions

Economy

Economy - overview: The economy is limited to traditional subsistence agriculture, with about 80% labor force earnings from agriculture (coconuts and vegetables), livestock (mostly pigs), and fishing. About 4% of the population is employed in government. Revenues come from French Government subsidies, licensing of fishing rights to Japan and South Korea, import taxes, and remittances from expatriate workers in New Caledonia.
GDP: purchasing power parity - $57.6 million (2003 est.)
GDP - real growth rate: NA%
GDP - per capita: purchasing power parity - $3,700 (2001 est.)
GDP - composition by sector:
agriculture: NA%
industry: NA%
services: NA%
Population below poverty line: NA%
Household income or consumption by percentage share:
lowest 10%: NA%
highest 10%: NA%
Inflation rate (consumer prices): NA%
Labor force: NA
Labor force - by occupation: agriculture, livestock, and fishing 80%, government 4% (2001 est.)
Unemployment rate: NA%
Budget:
revenues: $20 million
expenditures: $17 million, including capital expenditures of $NA (1998 est.)
Industries: copra, handicrafts, fishing, lumber
Industrial production growth rate: NA%
Electricity - production: NA kWh
Electricity - production by source:
fossil fuel: 0%
hydro: 0%
nuclear: 0%
other: 0%
Electricity - consumption: NA kWh
Electricity - exports: 0 kWh (2002)
Electricity - imports: 0 kWh (2002)
Agriculture - products: breadfruit, yams, taro, bananas; pigs, goats
Exports: $250,000 f.o.b. (1999)
Exports - commodities: copra, chemicals, construction materials

Exports - partners: Italy 40%, Croatia 15%, US 14%, Denmark 13%

Imports: $300,000 f.o.b. (1999)

Imports - commodities: chemicals, machinery, passenger ships, consumer goods

Imports - partners: France 97%, Australia 2%, New Zealand 1%

Debt - external: $NA

Economic aid - recipient: assistance from France

Currency: Comptoirs Francais du Pacifique franc (XPF)

Currency code: XPF

Exchange rates: Comptoirs Francais du Pacifique francs (XPF) per US dollar - 105.73 (2003), 126.72 (2002), 133.26 (2001), 129.43 (2000), 111.93 (1999), 107.25 (1998)

Fiscal year: calendar year

Communications

Telephones - main lines in use: 1,900 (2002)

Telephones - mobile cellular: 0 (1994)

Telephone system:

general assessment: NA

domestic: NA

international: country code - 681

Radio broadcast stations: AM 1, FM 0, shortwave 0 (2000)

Television broadcast stations: 2 (2000)

Internet country code: .wf

Internet users: 900 (2002)

Transportation

Railways: 0 km

Highways:

total: 120 km (Ile Uvea 100 km, Ile Futuna 20 km)

paved: 16 km (all on Ile Uvea)

unpaved: 104 km (Ile Uvea 84 km, Ile Futuna 20 km)

Waterways: none

Ports and harbors: Leava, Mata-Utu

Merchant marine:

total: 6 ships (1,000 GRT or over) 134,037 GRT/ 14,271 DWT

by type: passenger 6

foreign-owned: France 3, Greece 1, Monaco 1, United States 1 (2003 est.)

Airports: 2 (2003 est.)

Airports - with paved runways:

total: 1

1,524 to 2,437 m: 1 (2003 est.)

Airports - with unpaved runways:

total: 1

914 to 1,523 m: 1 (2003 est.)

Military

Military - note: defense is the responsibility of France

Transnational Issues

Disputes - international: none

West Bank

Introduction

Background: The Israel-PLO Declaration of Principles on Interim Self-Government Arrangements (the DOP), signed in Washington on 13 September 1993, provided for a transitional period not exceeding five years of Palestinian interim self-government in the Gaza Strip and the West Bank. Under the DOP, Israel agreed to transfer certain powers and responsibilities to the Palestinian Authority, which includes the Palestinian Legislative Council elected in January 1996, as part of the interim self-governing arrangements in the West Bank and Gaza Strip. A transfer of powers and responsibilities for the Gaza Strip and Jericho took place pursuant to the Israel-PLO 4 May 1994 Cairo Agreement on the Gaza Strip and the Jericho Area and in additional areas of the West Bank pursuant to the Israel-PLO 28 September 1995 Interim Agreement, the Israel-PLO 15 January 1997 Protocol Concerning Redeployment in Hebron, the Israel-PLO 23 October 1998 Wye River Memorandum, and the 4 September 1999 Sharm el-Sheikh Agreement. The DOP provides that Israel will retain responsibility during the

transitional period for external and internal security and for public order of settlements and Israeli citizens. Direct negotiations to determine the permanent status of Gaza and West Bank that began in September 1999 after a three-year hiatus, were derailed by a second intifadah that broke out in September 2000. The resulting widespread violence in the West Bank and Gaza Strip, Israel's military response, and instability within the Palestinian Authority continue to undermine progress toward a permanent agreement.

Geography

Location: Middle East, west of Jordan

Geographic coordinates: 32 00 N, 35 15 E

Map references: Middle East

Area:

total: 5,860 sq km

land: 5,640 sq km

water: 220 sq km

note: includes West Bank, Latrun Salient, and the northwest quarter of the Dead Sea, but excludes Mt. Scopus; East Jerusalem and Jerusalem No Man's Land are also included only as a means of depicting the entire area occupied by Israel in 1967

Area - comparative: slightly smaller than Delaware

Land boundaries:

total: 404 km

border countries: Israel 307 km, Jordan 97 km

Coastline: 0 km (landlocked)

Maritime claims: none (landlocked)

Climate: temperate; temperature and precipitation vary with altitude, warm to hot summers, cool to mild winters

Terrain: mostly rugged dissected upland, some vegetation in west, but barren in east

Elevation extremes:

lowest point: Dead Sea -408 m

highest point: Tall Asur 1,022 m

Natural resources: arable land

Land use:

arable land: NEGL%

permanent crops: 0%

other: 100% (1998 est.)

Irrigated land: NA sq km

Natural hazards: droughts

Environment - current issues: adequacy of fresh water supply; sewage treatment

Geography - note: landlocked; highlands are main recharge area for Israel's coastal aquifers; there are 244 West Bank settlements and 29 East Jerusalem settlements in addition to at least 20 occupied outposts (August 2003 est.)

People

Population: 2,311,204

note: in addition, there are about 187,000 Israeli settlers in the West Bank and fewer than 177,000 in East Jerusalem (July 2004 est.)

Age structure:

0-14 years: 43.8% (male 518,470; female 493,531)

15-64 years: 52.8% (male 623,785; female 595,376)

65 years and over: 3.5% (male 34,226; female 45,816) (2004 est.)

Median age:

total: 18 years

male: 17.8 years

female: 18.2 years (2004 est.)

Population growth rate: 3.21% (2004 est.)

Birth rate: 33.21 births/1,000 population (2004 est.)

Death rate: 4.07 deaths/1,000 population (2004 est.)

Net migration rate: 2.98 migrant(s)/1,000 population (2004 est.)

Sex ratio:

at birth: 1.06 male(s)/female

under 15 years: 1.05 male(s)/female

15-64 years: 1.05 male(s)/female

65 years and over: 0.75 male(s)/female

total population: 1.04 male(s)/female (2004 est.)

Infant mortality rate:

total: 20.16 deaths/1,000 live births

male: 22.28 deaths/1,000 live births

female: 17.91 deaths/1,000 live births (2004 est.)

Life expectancy at birth:

total population: 72.88 years

male: 71.14 years

female: 74.72 years (2004 est.)

Total fertility rate: 4.52 children born/woman (2004 est.)

HIV/AIDS - adult prevalence rate: NA%

HIV/AIDS - people living with HIV/AIDS: NA

HIV/AIDS - deaths: NA

Nationality:

noun: NA

adjective: NA

Ethnic groups: Palestinian Arab and other 83%, Jewish 17%

Religions: Muslim 75% (predominantly Sunni), Jewish 17%, Christian and other 8%

Languages: Arabic, Hebrew (spoken by Israeli settlers and many Palestinians), English (widely understood)

Literacy:

definition: NA

total population: NA%

male: NA%

female: NA%

Government

Country name:

conventional long form: none

conventional short form: West Bank

Economy

Economy - overview: Real per capita GDP for the West Bank and Gaza Strip (WBGS) declined by about one-third between 1992 and 1996 due to the combined effect of falling aggregate incomes and rapid population growth. The downturn in economic activity was largely the result of Israeli closure policies - the imposition of border closures in response to security incidents in Israel - which disrupted labor and commodity market relationships between Israel and the WBGS. The most serious social effect of this downturn was rising unemployment, which in the WBGS during the 1980s was generally under 5%; by 1995 it had risen to over 20%. Israel's use of comprehensive closures during the next three years decreased and, in 1998, Israel implemented new policies to reduce the impact of closures and other security procedures on the movement of Palestinian goods and labor. These changes fueled an almost three-year-long economic recovery in the West Bank and Gaza Strip; real GDP grew by 5% in 1998 and 6% in 1999. Recovery was upended in the last quarter of 2000 with the outbreak of violence, which triggered tight Israeli closures of Palestinian self-rule areas and severely disrupted trade and labor movements. In 2001, and even more severely in 2002, Israeli military measures in Palestinian Authority areas resulted in the destruction of much capital plant and administrative structure, widespread business closures, and a sharp drop in GDP. Including Gaza Strip, the UN estimates that more than 100,000 Palestinians out of the 125,000 who used to work in Israel, in Israeli settlements, or in joint industrial zones have lost their jobs. In addition, about 80,000 Palestinian workers inside the Territories are losing their jobs. International aid of $2 billion in 2001-02 to the West Bank and Gaza Strip prevented the complete collapse of the economy.

GDP: purchasing power parity - $1.7 billion (2002 est.)

GDP - real growth rate: -22% (2002 est.)

GDP - per capita: purchasing power parity - $800 (2002 est.)

GDP - composition by sector:

agriculture: 9%

industry: 28%

services: 63%

note: includes Gaza Strip (1999 est.)

Population below poverty line: 60% (2003 est.)

Household income or consumption by percentage share:

lowest 10%: NA%

highest 10%: NA%

Inflation rate (consumer prices): 2.2% (includes Gaza Strip) (2001 est.)

Labor force: NA

Labor force - by occupation: services 66%, industry 21%, agriculture 13% (1996)

Unemployment rate: 50% (includes Gaza Strip) (2003 est.)

Budget:

revenues: $676.6 million

expenditures: $1.155 billion, including capital expenditures of NA (includes Gaza Strip) (2003 est.)

Industries: generally small family businesses that produce cement, textiles, soap, olive-wood carvings, and mother-of-pearl souvenirs; the Israelis have established some small-scale, modern industries in the settlements and industrial centers

Industrial production growth rate: NA%

Electricity - production: NA kWh; note - most electricity imported from Israel; East Jerusalem Electric Company buys and distributes electricity to Palestinians in East Jerusalem and its concession in the West Bank; the Israel Electric Company directly supplies electricity to most Jewish residents and military facilities; some Palestinian municipalities, such as Nablus and Janin, generate their own electricity from small power plants

Electricity - production by source:

fossil fuel: 100%

hydro: 0%

nuclear: 0%

other: 0% (2001)

Electricity - consumption: NA kWh

Electricity - imports: NA kWh

Agriculture - products: olives, citrus, vegetables; beef, dairy products

Exports: $603 million f.o.b., includes Gaza Strip

Exports - commodities: olives, fruit, vegetables, limestone

Exports - partners: Israel, Jordan, Gaza Strip (2000)

Imports: $1.9 billion c.i.f., includes Gaza Strip

Imports - commodities: food, consumer goods, construction materials

Imports - partners: Israel, Jordan, Gaza Strip (2000)

Debt - external: $108 million (includes Gaza Strip) (1997 est.)

Economic aid - recipient: $2 billion (includes Gaza Strip) (2001-02 est.)

Currency: new Israeli shekel (ILS); Jordanian dinar (JOD)

Currency code: ILS; JOD

Exchange rates: new Israeli shekels per US dollar - 4.5541 (2003), 4.7378 (2002), 4.2057 (2001), 4.0773 (2000), 4.1397 (1999); Jordanian dinars per US dollar - fixed rate of 0.7090 (from 1996)

Fiscal year: calendar year (since 1 January 1992)

Communications

Telephones - main lines in use: 301,600 (total for West Bank and Gaza Strip) (2002)

Telephones - mobile cellular: 320,000 (cellular subscribers in both West Bank and Gaza Strip) (2002)

Telephone system:

general assessment: NA

domestic: NA

international: NA

note: Israeli company BEZEK and the Palestinian company PALTEL are responsible for communication services in the West Bank

Radio broadcast stations: AM 1, FM 0, shortwave 0

note: the Palestinian Broadcasting Corporation broadcasts from an AM station in Ramallah on 675 kHz; numerous local, private stations are reported to be in operation (2000)

Television broadcast stations: NA

Internet users: 60,000 (includes Gaza Strip) (2001)

Transportation

Railways: 0 km
Highways:
total: 4,500 km
paved: 2,700 km
unpaved: 1,800 km
note: Israelis have developed many highways to service Jewish settlements (1997 est.)
Waterways: none
Ports and harbors: none
Airports: 3 (2003 est.)
Airports - with paved runways:
total: 3
2,438 to 3,047 m: 1
1,524 to 2,437 m: 1
under 914 m: 1 (2003 est.)

Military

Military expenditures - dollar figure: NA
Military expenditures - percent of GDP: NA

Transnational Issues

Disputes - international: West Bank and Gaza Strip are Israeli-occupied with current status subject to the Israeli-Palestinian Interim Agreement - permanent status to be determined through further negotiation

Western Sahara

Introduction

Background: Morocco virtually annexed the northern two-thirds of Western Sahara (formerly Spanish Sahara) in 1976, and the rest of the territory in 1979, following Mauritania's withdrawal. A guerrilla war with the Polisario Front contesting Rabat's sovereignty ended in a 1991 UN-brokered cease-fire; a UN-organized referendum on final status has been repeatedly postponed.

Geography

Location: Northern Africa, bordering the North Atlantic Ocean, between Mauritania and Morocco
Geographic coordinates: 24 30 N, 13 00 W
Map references: Africa
Area:
total: 266,000 sq km
land: 266,000 sq km
water: 0 sq km
Area - comparative: about the size of Colorado
Land boundaries:
total: 2,046 km
border countries: Algeria 42 km, Mauritania 1,561 km, Morocco 443 km
Coastline: 1,110 km
Maritime claims: contingent upon resolution of sovereignty issue
Climate: hot, dry desert; rain is rare; cold offshore air currents produce fog and heavy dew
Terrain: mostly low, flat desert with large areas of rocky or sandy surfaces rising to small mountains in south and northeast
Elevation extremes:
lowest point: Sebjet Tah -55 m
highest point: unnamed location 463 m
Natural resources: phosphates, iron ore
Land use:
arable land: 0%
permanent crops: 0%

other: 100% (1998 est.)
Irrigated land: NA sq km
Natural hazards: hot, dry, dust/sand-laden sirocco wind can occur during winter and spring; widespread harmattan haze exists 60% of time, often severely restricting visibility
Environment - current issues: sparse water and lack of arable land
Environment - international agreements:
party to: none of the selected agreements
signed, but not ratified: none of the selected agreements
Geography - note: the waters off the coast are particularly rich fishing areas

People

Population: 267,405 (July 2004 est.)
Age structure:
0-14 years: NA%
15-64 years: NA%
65 years and over: NA%
Population growth rate: NA%
Birth rate: NA births/1,000 population
Death rate: NA deaths/1,000 population
Sex ratio: NA
Infant mortality rate:
total: NA%
male: NA%
female: NA%
Life expectancy at birth:
total population: NA years
male: NA years
female: NA years
Total fertility rate: NA children born/woman
HIV/AIDS - adult prevalence rate: NA%
HIV/AIDS - people living with HIV/AIDS: NA
HIV/AIDS - deaths: NA
Nationality:
noun: Sahrawi(s), Sahraoui(s)
adjective: Sahrawi,Sahrawian, Sahraouian
Ethnic groups: Arab, Berber
Religions: Muslim
Languages: Hassaniya Arabic, Moroccan Arabic
Literacy:
definition: NA
total population: NA%
male: NA%
female: NA%

Government

Country name:
conventional long form: none
conventional short form: Western Sahara
former: Spanish Sahara
Government type: legal status of territory and issue of sovereignty unresolved; territory contested by Morocco and Polisario Front (Popular Front for the Liberation of the Saguia el Hamra and Rio de Oro), which in February 1976 formally proclaimed a government-in-exile of the Sahrawi Arab Democratic

Western Sahara *(continued)*

Republic (SADR),led by President Mohamed ABDELAZIZ; territory partitioned between Morocco and Mauritania in April 1976, with Morocco acquiring northern two-thirds; Mauritania, under pressure from Polisario guerrillas, abandoned all claims to its portion in August 1979; Morocco moved to occupy that sector shortly thereafter and has since asserted administrative control; the Polisario's government-in-exile was seated as an OAU member in 1984; guerrilla activities continued sporadically, until a UN-monitored cease-fire was implemented 6 September 1991

Capital: none

Administrative divisions: none (under de facto control of Morocco)

Suffrage: none; a UN-sponsored voter identification campaign not yet completed

Executive branch: none

Political pressure groups and leaders: none

International organization participation: none

Diplomatic representation in the US: none

Diplomatic representation from the US: none

Economy

Economy - overview: Western Sahara depends on pastoral nomadism, fishing, and phosphate mining as the principal sources of income for the population. The territory lacks sufficient rainfall for sustainable agricultural production, and most of the food for the urban population must be imported. All trade and other economic activities are controlled by the Moroccan Government. Moroccan energy interests in 2001 signed contracts to explore for oil off the coast of Western Sahara, which has angered the Polisario. Incomes and standards of living in Western Sahara are substantially below the Moroccan level.

GDP: purchasing power parity - $NA

GDP - real growth rate: NA%

GDP - per capita: purchasing power parity - $NA

GDP - composition by sector:
agriculture: NA%
industry: NA%
services: 40% (1996 est.)

Population below poverty line: NA%

Household income or consumption by percentage share:
lowest 10%: NA%
highest 10%: NA%

Inflation rate (consumer prices): NA%

Labor force: 12,000

Labor force - by occupation: animal husbandry and subsistence farming 50%

Unemployment rate: NA%

Budget:
revenues: $NA
expenditures: $NA, including capital expenditures of $NA

Industries: phosphate mining, handicrafts

Industrial production growth rate: NA%

Electricity - production: 90 million kWh (2001)

Electricity - production by source:
fossil fuel: 100%
hydro: 0%
nuclear: 0%
other: 0% (2001)

Electricity - consumption: 83.7 million kWh (2001)

Electricity - exports: 0 kWh (2001)

Electricity - imports: 0 kWh (2001)

Oil - production: 0 bbl/day (2001 est.)

Oil - consumption: 1,800 bbl/day (2001 est.)

Oil - exports: NA

Oil - imports: NA

Agriculture - products: fruits and vegetables (grown in the few oases); camels, sheep, goats (kept by nomads)

Exports: $NA

Exports - commodities: phosphates 62%

Exports - partners: Morocco claims and administers Western Sahara, so trade partners are included in overall Moroccan accounts

Imports: $NA

Imports - commodities: fuel for fishing fleet, foodstuffs

Imports - partners: Morocco claims and administers Western Sahara, so trade partners are included in overall Moroccan accounts (2000)

Debt - external: $NA

Economic aid - recipient: $NA

Currency: Moroccan dirham (MAD)

Currency code: MAD

Exchange rates: Moroccan dirhams per US dollar - 9.574 (2003), 11.584 (2002), 11.303 (2001), 10.626 (2000), 9.804 (1999)

Fiscal year: calendar year

Communications

Telephones - main lines in use: about 2,000 (1999 est.)

Telephones - mobile cellular: 0 (1999)

Telephone system:
general assessment: sparse and limited system
domestic: NA
international: country code - 212; tied into Morocco's system by microwave radio relay, tropospheric scatter, and satellite; satellite earth stations - 2 Intelsat (Atlantic Ocean) linked to Rabat, Morocco

Radio broadcast stations: AM 2, FM 0, shortwave 0 (1998)

Television broadcast stations: NA

Internet country code: .eh

Internet users: NA

Transportation

Railways: 0 km

Highways:
total: 6,200 km
paved: 1,350 km
unpaved: 4,850 km (1991 est)

Waterways: none

Ports and harbors: Ad Dakhla, Cabo Bojador, Laayoune (El Aaiun)

Airports: 11 (2003 est.)

Airports - with paved runways:
total: 3
2,438 to 3,047 m: 3 (2003 est.)

Airports - with unpaved runways:
total: 8
1,524 to 2,437 m: 1
914 to 1,523 m: 4
under 914 m: 3 (2003 est.)

Military

Military expenditures - dollar figure: NA

Military expenditures - percent of GDP: NA

Transnational Issues

Disputes - international: Morocco claims and administers Western Sahara, whose sovereignty remains unresolved - UN-administered cease-fire has remained in effect since September 1991 but attempts to hold a referendum have failed and parties thus far have rejected all brokered proposals; Polisario, Algeria and European supporters agree to latest US-brokered UN proposals for limited temporary autonomy for 4-5 years followed by a referendum on independence, but a final response from Morocco is pending; Mauritanian claims to Western Sahara have been dormant in recent years

World

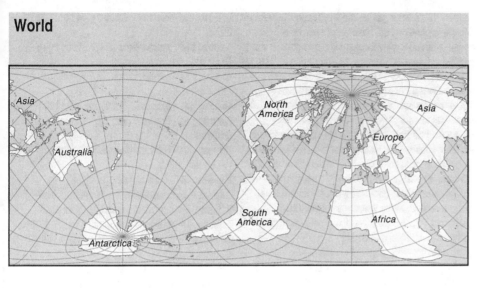

Introduction

Background: Globally, the 20th century was marked by: (a) two devastating world wars; (b) the Great Depression of the 1930s; (c) the end of vast colonial empires; (d) rapid advances in science and technology, from the first airplane flight at Kitty Hawk, North Carolina (US) to the landing on the moon; (e) the Cold War between the Western alliance and the Warsaw Pact nations; (f) a sharp rise in living standards in North America, Europe, and Japan; (g) increased concerns about the environment, including loss of forests, shortages of energy and water, the decline in biological diversity, and air pollution; (h) the onset of the AIDS epidemic; and (i) the ultimate emergence of the US as the only world superpower. The planet's population continues to explode: from 1 billion in 1820, to 2 billion in 1930, 3 billion in 1960, 4 billion in 1974, 5 billion in 1988, and 6 billion in 2000. For the 21st century, the continued exponential growth in science and technology raises both hopes (e.g., advances in medicine) and fears (e.g., development of even more lethal weapons of war).

Geography

Map references: Physical Map of the World, Political Map of the World, Standard Time Zones of the World

Area:
total: 510.072 million sq km
land: 148.94 million sq km
water: 361.132 million sq km
note: 70.8% of the world's surface is water, 29.2% is land

Area - comparative: land area about 16 times the size of the US

Land boundaries: the land boundaries in the world total 250,472 km (not counting shared boundaries twice)

Coastline: 356,000 km

Maritime claims: a variety of situations exist, but in general, most countries make the following claims measured from the mean low-tide baseline as described in the 1982 UN Convention on the Law of the Sea: territorial sea - 12 NM, contiguous zone - 24 NM, and exclusive economic zone - 200 NM; additional zones provide for exploitation of continental shelf resources and an exclusive fishing zone; boundary situations with neighboring states prevent many countries from extending their fishing or economic zones to a full 200 NM; 43 nations and other areas that are landlocked include Afghanistan, Andorra, Armenia, Austria, Azerbaijan, Belarus, Bhutan, Bolivia, Botswana, Burkina Faso, Burundi, Central African Republic, Chad, Czech Republic, Ethiopia, Holy See (Vatican City), Hungary, Kazakhstan, Kyrgyzstan, Laos, Lesotho, Liechtenstein, Luxembourg, Malawi, Mali, Moldova, Mongolia, Nepal, Niger, Paraguay, Rwanda, San Marino, Slovakia, Swaziland, Switzerland, Tajikistan, The Former Yugoslav Republic of Macedonia, Turkmenistan, Uganda, Uzbekistan, West Bank, Zambia, Zimbabwe; two of these, Liechtenstein and Uzbekistan, are doubly landlocked

Climate: two large areas of polar climates separated by two rather narrow temperate zones form a wide equatorial band of tropical to subtropical climates

Terrain: the greatest ocean depth is the Mariana Trench at 10,924 m in the Pacific Ocean

Elevation extremes:
lowest point: Bentley Subglacial Trench -2,540 m
note: in the oceanic realm, Challenger Deep in the Mariana Trench is the lowest point, lying -10,924 m below the surface of the Pacific Ocean
highest point: Mount Everest 8,850 m (1999 est.)

Natural resources: the rapid depletion of nonrenewable mineral resources, the depletion of forest areas and wetlands, the extinction of animal and plant species, and the deterioration in air and water quality (especially in Eastern Europe, the former USSR, and China) pose serious long-term problems that governments and peoples are only beginning to address

Land use:
arable land: 10.58%
permanent crops: 1%
other: 88.42% (1998 est.)

Irrigated land: 2,714,320 sq km (1998 est.)

Natural hazards: large areas subject to severe weather (tropical cyclones), natural disasters (earthquakes, landslides, tsunamis, volcanic eruptions)

Environment - current issues: large areas subject to overpopulation, industrial disasters, pollution (air, water, acid rain, toxic substances), loss of vegetation (overgrazing, deforestation, desertification), loss of wildlife, soil degradation, soil depletion, erosion

Geography - note: the world is now thought to be about 4.55 billion years old, just about one-third of the 13-billion-year age estimated for the universe

People

Population: 6,379,157,361 (July 2004 est.)

Age structure:
0-14 years: 28.2% (male 925,276,767; female 875,567,830)
15-64 years: 64.5% (male 2,083,789,165; female 2,033,226,759)
65 years and over: 7.2% (male 203,286,504; female 257,705,851)
note: some countries do not maintain age structure information, thus a slight discrepancy exists between the total world population and the total for world age structure (2004 est.)

Population growth rate: 1.14% (2004 est.)

Birth rate: 20.24 births/1,000 population (2004 est.)

Death rate: 8.86 deaths/1,000 population (2004 est.)

Sex ratio:
at birth: 1.06 male(s)/female
under 15 years: 1.06 male(s)/female
15-64 years: 1.03 male(s)/female
65 years and over: 0.79 male(s)/female
total population: 1.01 male(s)/female (2004 est.)

Infant mortality rate:
total: 50.31 deaths/1,000 live births
male: 52.17 deaths/1,000 live births
female: 48.33 deaths/1,000 live births (2004 est.)

Life expectancy at birth:
total population: 64.05 years
male: 62.48 years
female: 65.7 years (2004 est.)

Total fertility rate: 2.62 children born/woman (2004 est.)

HIV/AIDS - adult prevalence rate: NA%

HIV/AIDS - people living with HIV/AIDS: NA

HIV/AIDS - deaths: NA

Religions: Christians 32.79% (of which Roman Catholics 17.33%, Protestants 5.62%, Orthodox 3.51%, Anglicans 1.31%), Muslims 19.6%,

Hindus 13.31%, Buddhists 5.88%, Sikhs 0.38%, Jews 0.24%, other religions 12.83%, non-religious 12.53%, atheists 2.44% (2001 est.)
Languages: Chinese, Mandarin 14.37%, Hindi 6.02%, English 5.61%, Spanish 5.59%, Bengali 3.4%, Portuguese 2.63%, Russian 2.75%, Japanese 2.06%, German, Standard 1.64%, Korean 1.28%, French 1.27% (2000 est.)
note: percents are for "first language" speakers only
Literacy:
definition: age 15 and over can read and write
total population: 77%
male: 83%
female: 71% (1995 est.)

Government

Administrative divisions: 268 nations, dependent areas, other, and miscellaneous entries
Legal system: all members of the UN are parties to the statute that established the International Court of Justice (ICJ) or World Court

Economy

Economy - overview: Global output rose by 3.7% in 2003, led by China (9.1%), India (7.6%), and Russia (7.3%). The other 14 successor nations of the USSR and the other old Warsaw Pact nations again experienced widely divergent growth rates; the three Baltic nations continued as strong performers, in the 5%-7% range of growth. Growth results posted by the major industrial countries varied from a loss by Germany (-0.1%) to a strong gain by the United States (3.1%). The developing nations also varied in their growth results, with many countries facing population increases that erode gains in output. Externally, the nation-state, as a bedrock economic-political institution, is steadily losing control over international flows of people, goods, funds, and technology. Internally, the central government often finds its control over resources slipping as separatist regional movements - typically based on ethnicity - gain momentum, e.g., in many of the successor states of the former Soviet Union, in the former Yugoslavia, in India, in Iraq, in Indonesia, and in Canada. Externally, the central government is losing decision-making powers to international bodies. In Western Europe, governments face the difficult political problem of channeling resources away from welfare programs in order to increase investment and strengthen incentives to seek employment. The addition of 80 million people each year to an already overcrowded globe is exacerbating the problems of pollution, desertification, underemployment, epidemics, and famine. Because of their own internal problems and priorities, the industrialized countries devote insufficient resources to deal effectively with the poorer areas of the world, which, at least from the economic point of view, are becoming further marginalized. The introduction of the euro as the common currency of much of Western Europe in January 1999, while paving the way for an integrated economic powerhouse, poses economic risks because of varying levels of income and cultural and political differences among the participating nations. The terrorist attacks on the US on 11 September 2001 accentuate a further growing risk to global prosperity, illustrated, for example, by the reallocation of resources away from investment to anti-terrorist programs. The opening of war in March 2003 between a US-led coalition and Iraq added new uncertainties to global economic prospects. After the coalition victory, the complex political difficulties and the high economic cost of establishing domestic order in Iraq became major global problems that continue into 2004.
GDP: GWP (gross world product) - purchasing power parity - $51.41 trillion (2003 est.)
GDP - real growth rate: 3.7% (2003 est.)
GDP - per capita: purchasing power parity - $8,200 (2003 est.)
GDP - composition by sector:
agriculture: 4%
industry: 32%
services: 64% (2002 est.)
Household income or consumption by percentage share:
lowest 10%: NA%
highest 10%: NA%
Inflation rate (consumer prices): developed countries 1% to 4% typically; developing countries 5% to 60% typically; national inflation rates vary widely in individual cases, from declining prices in Japan to hyperinflation in several Third World countries (2003 est.)
Labor force: NA
Labor force - by occupation: agriculture NA%, industry NA%, services NA%
Unemployment rate: 30% combined unemployment and underemployment in many non-industrialized countries; developed countries typically 4%-12% unemployment
Industries: dominated by the onrush of technology, especially in computers, robotics, telecommunications, and medicines and medical equipment; most of these advances take place in OECD nations; only a small portion of non-OECD countries have succeeded in rapidly adjusting to these technological forces; the accelerated development of new industrial (and agricultural) technology is complicating already grim environmental problems
Industrial production growth rate: 3% (2002 est.)
Electricity - production: 14.85 trillion kWh (2001 est.)
Electricity - production by source:
fossil fuel: NA%
hydro: NA%
nuclear: NA%
other: NA% (2001)
Electricity - consumption: 13.93 trillion kWh (2001 est.)
Oil - production: 75.34 million bbl/day (2001 est.)
Oil - consumption: 75.81 million bbl/day (2001 est.)
Oil - proved reserves: 1.025 trillion bbl (1 January 2002)
Natural gas - production: 2.578 trillion cu m (2001 est.)
Natural gas - consumption: 2.555 trillion cu m (2001 est.)
Natural gas - exports: 712 billion cu m (2001 est.)
Natural gas - imports: 697.5 billion cu m (2001 est.)
Natural gas - proved reserves: 161.2 trillion cu m (1 January 2002)
Exports: $7.24 trillion f.o.b. (2003 est.)
Exports - commodities: the whole range of industrial and agricultural goods and services
Exports - partners: World exports to: US 17.6%, Germany 7.6%, UK 5.4%, France 5%, Japan 4.8%, China 4.2% (2002)
Imports: $7.24 trillion f.o.b. (2003 est.)
Imports - commodities: the whole range of industrial and agricultural goods and services
Imports - partners: World imports from: US 11.3%, Germany 9.1%, China 7.3%, Japan 6.9%, France 4.6%, UK 4% (2002)
Debt - external: $2 trillion for less developed countries (2002 est.)
Economic aid - recipient: official development assistance (ODA) $50 billion

Communications

Telephones - main lines in use: NA
Telephones - mobile cellular: NA
Telephone system:
general assessment: NA
domestic: NA
international: NA
Radio broadcast stations: AM NA, FM NA, shortwave NA
Television broadcast stations: NA
Internet users: 604,111,719 (2002 est.)

Transportation

Railways:
total: 1,201,337 km includes 191,702 km of electrified routes of which 147,760 km are in Europe, 24,509 km in the Far East, 11,050 km in Africa, 4,223 km in South America, and 4,160 km in North America; note - fastest speed in daily service is 300 km/hr attained by France's Societe Nationale des Chemins-de-Fer Francais (SNCF) Le Train a Grande Vitesse (TGV) - Atlantique line
broad gauge: 251,153 km
standard gauge: 710,754 km
narrow gauge: 239,430 km
Highways:
total: NA km
paved: NA km
unpaved: NA km
Ports and harbors: Chiba, Houston, Kawasaki, Kobe, Marseille, Mina' al Ahmadi (Kuwait), New Orleans, New York, Rotterdam, Yokohama

World (continued)

Military

Military expenditures - dollar figure: aggregate real expenditure on arms worldwide in 1999 remained at approximately the 1998 level, about three-quarters of a trillion dollars (1999 est.)

Military expenditures - percent of GDP: roughly 2% of gross world product (1999 est.)

Transnational Issues

Disputes - international: stretching over 250,000 km, the world's 322 international land boundaries separate the 192 independent states and 70 dependencies, areas of special sovereignty, and other miscellaneous entities; ethnicity, culture, race, religion, and language have divided states into separate political entities as much as history, physical terrain, political fiat, or conquest, resulting in sometimes arbitrary and imposed boundaries; maritime states have claimed limits and have so far established over 130 maritime boundaries and joint development zones to allocate ocean resources and to provide for national security at sea; boundary, borderland/resource, and territorial disputes vary in intensity from managed or dormant to violent or militarized; most disputes over the alignment of political boundaries are confined to short segments and are today less common and less hostile than borderland, resource, and territorial disputes; undemarcated, indefinite, porous, and unmanaged boundaries, however, encourage illegal cross-border activities, uncontrolled migration, and confrontation; territorial disputes may evolve from historical and/or cultural claims, or they may be brought on by resource competition; ethnic clashes continue to be responsible for much of the territorial fragmentation around the world; disputes over islands at sea or in rivers frequently form the source of territorial and boundary conflict; other sources of contention include access to water and mineral (especially petroleum) resources, fisheries, and arable land; nonetheless, most nations cooperate to clarify their international boundaries and to resolve territorial and resource disputes peacefully; regional discord directly affects the sustenance and welfare of local populations, often leaving the world community to cope with resultant refugees, hunger, disease, impoverishment, deforestation, and desertification

Illicit drugs:

cocaine: worldwide, coca is grown on an estimated 205,450 hectares - almost exclusively in South America with 70% in Colombia; potential cocaine production during 2002 is estimated at 938 metric tons (or 1,200 metric tons of export quality cocaine at an average of 78% purity); coca eradication programs continue in Bolivia, Colombia, and Peru, and 292 metric tons of export quality cocaine are documented to have been seized in 2002; consumption of export quality cocaine is estimated to have been 875 metric tons

opiates: cultivation of opium poppy occurred on an estimated 141,213 hectares in 2002 and potentially produced 2,183 metric tons of opium - which conceivably could be converted to the equivalent of 238 metric tons of pure heroin; opium eradication programs have been undertaken in Afghanistan, Burma, Colombia, Mexico, Pakistan, Thailand, and Vietnam, and the annual average for opiates seized worldwide over the past five years (1998-2002) has been 45 metric tons of pure heroin equivalent; estimates for average annual consumption over this time period are 315 metric tons pure heroin equivalent

Yemen

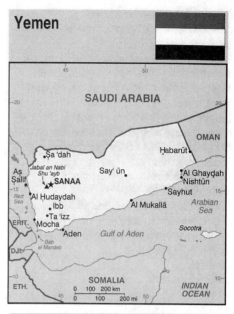

Introduction

Background: North Yemen became independent of the Ottoman Empire in 1918. The British, who had set up a protectorate area around the southern port of Aden in the 19th century, withdrew in 1967 from what became South Yemen. Three years later, the southern government adopted a Marxist orientation. The massive exodus of hundreds of thousands of Yemenis from the south to the north contributed to two decades of hostility between the states. The two countries were formally unified as the Republic of Yemen in 1990. A southern secessionist movement in 1994 was quickly subdued. In 2000, Saudi Arabia and Yemen agreed to a delimitation of their border.

Geography

Location: Middle East, bordering the Arabian Sea, Gulf of Aden, and Red Sea, between Oman and Saudi Arabia

Geographic coordinates: 15 00 N, 48 00 E

Map references: Middle East

Area:

total: 527,970 sq km

land: 527,970 sq km

water: 0 sq km

note: includes Perim, Socotra, the former Yemen Arab Republic (YAR or North Yemen), and the former People's Democratic Republic of Yemen (PDRY or South Yemen)

Area - comparative: slightly larger than twice the size of Wyoming

Land boundaries:

total: 1,746 km

border countries: Oman 288 km, Saudi Arabia 1,458 km

Coastline: 1,906 km

Maritime claims:

territorial sea: 12 NM

contiguous zone: 24 NM

Yemen (continued)

exclusive economic zone: 200 NM
continental shelf: 200 NM or to the edge of the continental margin
Climate: mostly desert; hot and humid along west coast; temperate in western mountains affected by seasonal monsoon; extraordinarily hot, dry, harsh desert in east
Terrain: narrow coastal plain backed by flat-topped hills and rugged mountains; dissected upland desert plains in center slope into the desert interior of the Arabian Peninsula
Elevation extremes:
lowest point: Arabian Sea 0 m
highest point: Jabal an Nabi Shu'ayb 3,760 m
Natural resources: petroleum, fish, rock salt, marble, small deposits of coal, gold, lead, nickel, and copper, fertile soil in west
Land use:
arable land: 2.75%
permanent crops: 0.21%
other: 97.04% (1998 est.)
Irrigated land: 4,900 sq km (1998 est.)
Natural hazards: sandstorms and dust storms in summer
Environment - current issues: very limited natural fresh water resources; inadequate supplies of potable water; overgrazing; soil erosion; desertification
Environment - international agreements:
party to: Biodiversity, Climate Change, Desertification, Endangered Species, Environmental Modification, Hazardous Wastes, Law of the Sea, Ozone Layer Protection
signed, but not ratified: none of the selected agreements
Geography - note: strategic location on Bab el Mandeb, the strait linking the Red Sea and the Gulf of Aden, one of world's most active shipping lanes

People

Population: 20,024,867 (July 2004 est.)
Age structure:
0-14 years: 46.6% (male 4,751,776; female 4,582,277)
15-64 years: 50.6% (male 5,166,437; female 4,973,543)
65 years and over: 2.8% (male 273,199; female 277,635) (2004 est.)
Median age:
total: 16.5 years
male: 16.5 years
female: 16.5 years (2004 est.)
Population growth rate: 3.44% (2004 est.)
Birth rate: 43.16 births/1,000 population (2004 est.)
Death rate: 8.78 deaths/1,000 population (2004 est.)
Net migration rate: 0 migrant(s)/1,000 population (2004 est.)
Sex ratio:
at birth: 1.05 male(s)/female
under 15 years: 1.04 male(s)/female
15-64 years: 1.04 male(s)/female
65 years and over: 0.98 male(s)/female

total population: 1.04 male(s)/female (2004 est.)
Infant mortality rate:
total: 63.26 deaths/1,000 live births
male: 68.12 deaths/1,000 live births
female: 58.15 deaths/1,000 live births (2004 est.)
Life expectancy at birth:
total population: 61.36 years
male: 59.53 years
female: 63.29 years (2004 est.)
Total fertility rate: 6.75 children born/woman (2004 est.)
HIV/AIDS - adult prevalence rate: 0.1% (2001 est.)
HIV/AIDS - people living with HIV/AIDS: 9,900 (2001 est.)
HIV/AIDS - deaths: NA
Nationality:
noun: Yemeni(s)
adjective: Yemeni
Ethnic groups: predominantly Arab; but also Afro-Arab, South Asians, Europeans
Religions: Muslim including Shaf'i (Sunni) and Zaydi (Shi'a), small numbers of Jewish, Christian, and Hindu
Languages: Arabic
Literacy:
definition: age 15 and over can read and write
total population: 50.2%
male: 70.5%
female: 30% (2003 est.)

Government

Country name:
conventional long form: Republic of Yemen
conventional short form: Yemen
local long form: Al Jumhuriyah al Yamaniyah
local short form: Al Yaman
Government type: republic
Capital: Sanaa
Administrative divisions: 19 governorates (muhafazat, singular - muhafazah); Abyan, 'Adan, Ad Dali', Al Bayda', Al Hudaydah, Al Jawf, Al Mahrah, Al Mahwit, 'Amran, Dhamar, Hadramawt, Hajjah, Ibb, Lahij, Ma'rib, Sa'dah, San'a', Shabwah, Ta'izz
note: for electoral and administrative purposes, the capital city of Sanaa is treated as an additional governorate
Independence: 22 May 1990, Republic of Yemen was established with the merger of the Yemen Arab Republic [Yemen (Sanaa) or North Yemen] and the Marxist-dominated People's Democratic Republic of Yemen [Yemen (Aden) or South Yemen]; previously North Yemen had become independent on NA November 1918 (from the Ottoman Empire) and South Yemen had become independent on 30 November 1967 (from the UK)
National holiday: Unification Day, 22 May (1990)
Constitution: 16 May 1991; amended 29 September 1994 and February 2001
Legal system: based on Islamic law, Turkish law, English common law, and local tribal customary law; has not accepted compulsory ICJ jurisdiction

Suffrage: 18 years of age; universal
Executive branch:
chief of state: President Field Marshall Ali Abdallah SALIH (since 22 May 1990, the former president of North Yemen, assumed office upon the merger of North and South Yemen); Vice President Maj. Gen. Abd al-Rab Mansur al-HADI (since 3 October 1994)
head of government: Prime Minister Abd al-Qadir BA JAMAL (since 4 April 2001)
cabinet: Council of Ministers appointed by the president on the advice of the prime minister
elections: president elected by direct, popular vote for a seven-year term (recently extended from a five-year term by constitutional amendment); election last held 23 September 1999 (next to be held NA 2006); vice president appointed by the president; prime minister and deputy prime ministers appointed by the president
election results: Ali Abdallah SALIH elected president; percent of vote - Ali Abdallah SALIH 96.3%, Najib Qahtan AL-SHAABI 3.7%
Legislative branch: a new constitutional amendment ratified on 20 February 2001 created a bicameral legislature consisting of a Shura Council (111 seats; members appointed by the president) and a House of Representatives (301 seats; members elected by popular vote to serve six-year terms)
elections: last held 27 April 2003 (next to be held NA April 2009)
election results: percent of vote by party - NA%; seats by party - GPC 228, Islah 47, YSP 7, Nasserite Unionist Party 3, National Arab Socialist Ba'th Party 2, independents 14
Judicial branch: Supreme Court
Political parties and leaders: there are more than 12 political parties active in Yemen, some of the more prominent are: General People's Congress or GPC [President Ali Abdallah SALIH]; Islamic Reform Grouping or Islah [Shaykh Abdallah bin Husayn al-AHMAR]; National Arab Socialist Ba'th Party [Dr. Qassim SALAAM]; Nasserite Unionist Party [Abdel Malik al-MAKHLAFI]; Yemeni Socialist Party or YSP [Ali Salih MUQBIL]
note: President SALIH's General People's Congress or GPC won a landslide victory in the April 1997 legislative election and no longer governs in coalition with Shaykh Abdallah bin Husayn al-AHMAR's Islamic Reform Grouping or Islah - the two parties had been in coalition since the end of the civil war in 1994; the YSP, a loyal opposition party, represents the remnants of the former South Yemeni leadership; leaders of the 1994 secessionist movement have been pardoned by President SALIH and some are now returning to Yemen from exile
Political pressure groups and leaders: NA
International organization participation: ACC, AFESD, AMF, CAEU, FAO, G-77, IAEA, IBRD, ICAO, ICCt (signatory), ICFTU, ICRM, IDA, IDB, IFAD, IFC, IFRCS, ILO, IMF, IMO, Interpol, IOC, IOM, ISO (correspondent), ITU, LAS, NAM, OAS (observer), OIC, OPCW, UN, UNCTAD, UNESCO, UNHCR, UNIDO, UPU, WCO, WFTU, WHO, WIPO, WMO, WToO, WTrO (observer)

Yemen *(continued)*

Diplomatic representation in the US:
chief of mission: Ambassador Abd al-Wahhab Abdallah al-HAJRI
chancery: Suite 705, 2600 Virginia Avenue NW, Washington, DC 20037
telephone: [1] (202) 965-4760
FAX: [1] (202) 337-2017

Diplomatic representation from the US:
chief of mission: Ambassador Edmund J. HULL
embassy: Dhahar Himyar Zone, Sheraton Hotel District, Sanaa
mailing address: P. O. Box 22347, Sanaa
telephone: [967] (1) 303-161
FAX: [967] (1) 303-182

Flag description: three equal horizontal bands of red (top), white, and black; similar to the flag of Syria, which has two green stars and of Iraq which has three green stars (plus an Arabic inscription) in a horizontal line centered in the white band; also similar to the flag of Egypt, which has a heraldic eagle centered in the white band

Economy

Economy - overview: Yemen, one of the poorest countries in the Arab world, reported strong growth in the mid-1990s with the onset of oil production, but has been harmed by periodic declines in oil prices. Yemen has embarked on an IMF-supported structural adjustment program designed to modernize and streamline the economy, which has led to substantial foreign debt relief and restructuring. International donors, meeting in Paris in October 2002, agreed on a further $2.3 billion economic support package. Yemen has worked to maintain tight control over spending and to implement additional components of the IMF program. A high population growth rate and internal political dissension complicate the government's task. Plans include a diversification of the economy, encouragement of tourism, and more efficient use of scarce water resources.

GDP: purchasing power parity - $15.22 billion (2003 est.)

GDP - real growth rate: 3.1% (2003 est.)

GDP - per capita: purchasing power parity - $800 (2003 est.)

GDP - composition by sector:
agriculture: 14.6%
industry: 42.3%
services: 43.1% (2001)

Population below poverty line: 15.7% (2001)

Household income or consumption by percentage share:
lowest 10%: 3%
highest 10%: 25.9% (2003)

Distribution of family income - Gini index: 33.4 (1998)

Inflation rate (consumer prices): 12.3% (2003 est.)

Labor force: 3.7 million (2003 est.)

Labor force - by occupation: most people are employed in agriculture and herding; services, construction, industry, and commerce account for less than one-fourth of the labor force

Unemployment rate: 35% (2003 est.)

Budget:
revenues: $3.78 billion
expenditures: $4.13 billion, including capital expenditures of $NA (2004 est.)

Industries: crude oil production and petroleum refining; small-scale production of cotton textiles and leather goods; food processing; handicrafts; small aluminum products factory; cement

Industrial production growth rate: 3% (2003 est.)

Electricity - production: 3.01 billion kWh (2001)

Electricity - production by source:
fossil fuel: 100%
hydro: 0%
nuclear: 0%
other: 0% (2001)

Electricity - consumption: 2.8 billion kWh (2001)

Electricity - exports: 0 kWh (2001)

Electricity - imports: 0 kWh (2001)

Oil - production: 438,500 bbl/day (2001 est.)

Oil - consumption: 74,000 bbl/day (2001 est.)

Oil - exports: NA

Oil - imports: NA

Oil - proved reserves: 3.2 billion bbl (1 January 2002)

Natural gas - production: 0 cu m (2001 est.)

Natural gas - consumption: 0 cu m (2001 est.)

Natural gas - exports: 0 cu m (2001 est.)

Natural gas - imports: 0 cu m (2001 est.)

Natural gas - proved reserves: 480 billion cu m (1 January 2002)

Agriculture - products: grain, fruits, vegetables, pulses, qat (mildly narcotic shrub), coffee, cotton; dairy products, livestock (sheep, goats, cattle, camels), poultry; fish

Exports: $3.92 billion f.o.b. (2003 est.)

Exports - commodities: crude oil, coffee, dried and salted fish

Exports - partners: Thailand 19%, India 16.7%, China 15.3%, South Korea 12.4%, Malaysia 6.1%, US 5.4% (2002)

Imports: $3.042 billion f.o.b. (2003 est.)

Imports - commodities: food and live animals, machinery and equipment, chemicals

Imports - partners: UAE 16%, Saudi Arabia 12.7%, China 6.2%, Kuwait 5.5%, US 4.7% (2002)

Debt - external: $6.9 billion (2003)

Economic aid - recipient: $2.3 billion (to be disbursed 2003-07)

Currency: Yemeni rial (YER)

Currency code: YER

Exchange rates: Yemeni rials per US dollar - NA (2003), 175.625 (2002), 168.672 (2001), 161.718 (2000), 155.718 (1999)

Fiscal year: calendar year

Communications

Telephones - main lines in use: 542,200 (2002)
Telephones - mobile cellular: 411,100 (2002)
Telephone system:
general assessment: since unification in 1990, efforts have been made to create a national telecommunications network
domestic: the national network consists of microwave radio relay, cable, tropospheric scatter, and GSM cellular mobile telephone systems
international: country code - 967; satellite earth stations - 3 Intelsat (2 Indian Ocean and 1 Atlantic Ocean), 1 Intersputnik (Atlantic Ocean region), and 2 Arabsat; microwave radio relay to Saudi Arabia and Djibouti

Radio broadcast stations: AM 6, FM 1, shortwave 2 (1998)

Television broadcast stations: 7 (plus several low-power repeaters) (1997)

Internet country code: .ye

Internet hosts: 113 (2002)

Internet users: 100,000 (2002)

Transportation

Railways: 0 km

Highways:
total: 67,000 km
paved: 7,705 km
unpaved: 59,295 km (1999 est.)

Waterways: none

Pipelines: gas 88 km; oil 1,174 km (2003)

Ports and harbors: Aden, Al Hudaydah, Al Mukalla, As Salif, Ras Issa, Mocha, Nishtun

Merchant marine:
total: 6 ships (1,000 GRT or over) 19,766 GRT/24,794 DWT
by type: cargo 1, livestock carrier 1, petroleum tanker 3, roll on/roll off 1
foreign-owned: Hong Kong 2, Lebanon 1
registered in other countries: 5 (2003 est.)

Airports: 44 (2003 est.)

Airports - with paved runways:
total: 16
over 3,047 m: 3
2,438 to 3,047 m: 9
1,524 to 2,437 m: 2
914 to 1,523 m: 1
under 914 m: 1 (2003 est.)

Airports - with unpaved runways:
total: 28
over 3,047 m: 2
2,438 to 3,047 m: 7
1,524 to 2,437 m: 4
914 to 1,523 m: 11
under 914 m: 4 (2003 est.)

Yemen *(continued)*

Military

Military branches: Army (including Special Forces), Naval Forces and Coastal Defenses (including Marines), Air Force (including Air Defense Forces), Republican Guard

Military manpower - military age: 14 years of age (2004 est.)

Military manpower - availability:
males age 15-49: 4,617,064 (2004 est.)

Military manpower - fit for military service:
males age 15-49: 2,590,720 (2004 est.)

Military manpower - reaching military age annually:
males: 255,426 (2004 est.)

Military expenditures - dollar figure: $885.6 million (2003)

Military expenditures - percent of GDP: 7.9% (2003)

Military - note: establishment of a Coast Guard, scheduled for May 2001, has been delayed

Transnational Issues

Disputes - international: Eritrea protests Yemeni fishing around the Hanish Islands awarded to Eritrea by the ICJ in 1999; nomadic groups in border region with Saudi Arabia resist demarcation of boundary; Yemen protests Saudi erection of a concrete-filled pipe as a security barrier in 2004 to stem illegal cross-border activities in sections of the boundary

Zambia

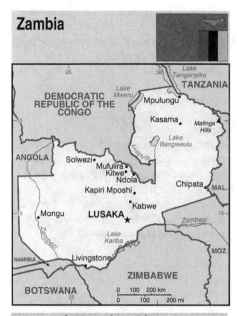

Introduction

Background: The territory of Northern Rhodesia was administered by the South Africa Company from 1891 until it was taken over by the UK in 1923. During the 1920s and 1930s, advances in mining spurred development and immigration. The name was changed to Zambia upon independence in 1964. In the 1980s and 1990s, declining copper prices and a prolonged drought hurt the economy. Elections in 1991 brought an end to one-party rule, but the subsequent vote in 1996 saw blatant harassment of opposition parties. The election in 2001 was marked by administrative problems with three parties filing a legal petition challenging the election of ruling party candidate Levy MWANAWASA. The new president launched a far-reaching anti-corruption campaign in 2002, which resulted in the prosecution of former President Frederick CHILUBA and many of his supporters in late 2003. Opposition parties currently hold a majority of seats in the National Assembly.

Geography

Location: Southern Africa, east of Angola
Geographic coordinates: 15 00 S, 30 00 E
Map references: Africa
Area:
total: 752,614 sq km
land: 740,724 sq km
water: 11,890 sq km
Area - comparative: slightly larger than Texas
Land boundaries:
total: 5,664 km
border countries: Angola 1,110 km, Democratic Republic of the Congo 1,930 km, Malawi 837 km, Mozambique 419 km, Namibia 233 km, Tanzania 338 km, Zimbabwe 797 km
Coastline: 0 km (landlocked)
Maritime claims: none (landlocked)

Climate: tropical; modified by altitude; rainy season (October to April)
Terrain: mostly high plateau with some hills and mountains
Elevation extremes:
lowest point: Zambezi river 329 m
highest point: unnamed location in Mafinga Hills 2,301 m
Natural resources: copper, cobalt, zinc, lead, coal, emeralds, gold, silver, uranium, hydropower
Land use:
arable land: 7.08%
permanent crops: 0.03%
other: 92.89% (1998 est.)
Irrigated land: 460 sq km (1998 est.)
Natural hazards: periodic drought, tropical storms (November to April)
Environment - current issues: air pollution and resulting acid rain in the mineral extraction and refining region; chemical runoff into watersheds; poaching seriously threatens rhinoceros, elephant, antelope, and large cat populations; deforestation; soil erosion; desertification; lack of adequate water treatment presents human health risks
Environment - international agreements:
party to: Biodiversity, Climate Change, Desertification, Endangered Species, Hazardous Wastes, Law of the Sea, Ozone Layer Protection, Wetlands
signed, but not ratified: Climate Change-Kyoto Protocol
Geography - note: landlocked; the Zambezi forms a natural riverine boundary with Zimbabwe

People

Population: 10,462,436
note: estimates for this country explicitly take into account the effects of excess mortality due to AIDS; this can result in lower life expectancy, higher infant mortality and death rates, lower population and growth rates, and changes in the distribution of population by age and sex than would otherwise be expected (July 2004 est.)
Age structure:
0-14 years: 46.1% (male 2,419,361; female 2,401,538)
15-64 years: 51.1% (male 2,684,001; female 2,667,528)
65 years and over: 2.8% (male 132,166; female 157,842) (2004 est.)
Median age:
total: 16.6 years
male: 16.5 years
female: 16.6 years (2004 est.)
Population growth rate: 1.47% (2004 est.)
Birth rate: 38.99 births/1,000 population (2004 est.)
Death rate: 24.35 deaths/1,000 population (2004 est.)
Net migration rate: 0 migrant(s)/1,000 population (2004 est.)

Zambia (continued)

Sex ratio:

at birth: 1.03 male(s)/female
under 15 years: 1.01 male(s)/female
15-64 years: 1.01 male(s)/female
65 years and over: 0.84 male(s)/female
total population: 1 male(s)/female (2004 est.)

Infant mortality rate:

total: 98.4 deaths/1,000 live births
male: 105.6 deaths/1,000 live births
female: 90.98 deaths/1,000 live births (2004 est.)

Life expectancy at birth:

total population: 35.18 years
male: 35.19 years
female: 35.17 years (2004 est.)

Total fertility rate: 5.14 children born/woman (2004 est.)

HIV/AIDS - adult prevalence rate: 21.5% (2001 est.)

HIV/AIDS - people living with HIV/AIDS: 1.2 million (2001 est.)

HIV/AIDS - deaths: 120,000 (2001 est.)

Nationality:

noun: Zambian(s)
adjective: Zambian

Ethnic groups: African 98.7%, European 1.1%, other 0.2%

Religions: Christian 50%-75%, Muslim and Hindu 24%-49%, indigenous beliefs 1%

Languages: English (official), major vernaculars - Bemba, Kaonda, Lozi, Lunda, Luvale, Nyanja, Tonga, and about 70 other indigenous languages

Literacy:

definition: age 15 and over can read and write English
total population: 80.6%
male: 86.8%
female: 74.8% (2003 est.)

Government

Country name:

conventional long form: Republic of Zambia
conventional short form: Zambia
former: Northern Rhodesia

Government type: republic

Capital: Lusaka

Administrative divisions: 9 provinces; Central, Copperbelt, Eastern, Luapula, Lusaka, Northern, North-Western, Southern, Western

Independence: 24 October 1964 (from UK)

National holiday: Independence Day, 24 October (1964)

Constitution: 2 August 1991

Legal system: based on English common law and customary law; judicial review of legislative acts in an ad hoc constitutional council; has not accepted compulsory ICJ jurisdiction

Suffrage: 18 years of age; universal

Executive branch:

chief of state: President Levy MWANAWASA (since 2 January 2002); Vice President Nevers MUMBA (since May 2003); note - the president is both the chief of state and head of government

head of government: President Levy MWANAWASA (since 2 January 2002); Vice President Nevers MUMBA (since May 2003); note - the president is both the chief of state and head of government

cabinet: Cabinet appointed by the president from among the members of the National Assembly

elections: president elected by popular vote for a five-year term; election last held 27 December 2001 (next to be held NA December 2006); vice president appointed by the president

election results: Levy MWANAWASA elected president; percent of vote - Levy MWANAWASA 29%, Anderson MAZOKA 27%, Christon TEMBO 13%, Tilyenji KAUNDA 10%, Godfrey MIYANDA 8%, Benjamin MWILA 5%, Michael SATA 3%, other 5%

Legislative branch: unicameral National Assembly (150 seats; members are elected by popular vote to serve five-year terms)

elections: last held 27 December 2001 (next to be held NA December 2006)

election results: percent of vote by party - MMD 45.9%, UPND 32.4%, UNIP 8.8%, FDD 8.1%, HP 2.7%, PF 0.7%, ZRP 0.7%, independents 0.7%; seats by party - MMD 68, UPND 48, UNIP 13, FDD 12, HP 4, PF 1, ZRP 1, independents 1; seats not determined 2

Judicial branch: Supreme Court (the final court of appeal; justices are appointed by the president); High Court (has unlimited jurisdiction to hear civil and criminal cases)

Political parties and leaders: Agenda for Zambia or AZ [Inonge MBIKUSITA-LEWANIKA]; Forum for Democracy and Development or FDD [Christon TEMBO]; Heritage Party or HP [Godfrey MIYANDA]; Liberal Progressive Front or LPF [Roger CHONGWE, president]; Movement for Multiparty Democracy or MMD [Levy MWANAWASA, acting president]; National Leadership for Development or NLD [Yobert SHAMAPANDE]; National Party or NP [Dr. Sam CHIPUNGU]; Patriotic Front or PF [Michael SATA]; Zambian Republican Party or ZRP [Benjamin MWILA]; Social Democratic Party or SDP [Gwendoline KONIE]; United National Independence Party or UNIP [Francis NKHOMA, president]; United Party for National Development or UPND [Anderson MAZOKA]

Political pressure groups and leaders: NA

International organization participation: ACP, AfDB, AU, C, FAO, G-77, IAEA, IBRD, ICAO, ICCt, ICFTU, ICRM, IDA, IFAD, IFC, IFRCS, ILO, IMF, Interpol, IOC, IOM, ISO (correspondent), ITU, MONUC, NAM, OPCW, PCA, SADC, UN, UNAMSIL, UNCTAD, UNESCO, UNIDO, UNMEE, UNMIK, UNMIL, UPU, WCL, WCO, WHO, WIPO, WMO, WToO, WTrO

Diplomatic representation in the US:

chief of mission: Ambassador Inonge MBIKUSITA-LEWANIKA
chancery: 2419 Massachusetts Avenue NW, Washington, DC 20008
telephone: [1] (202) 265-9717 through 9719
FAX: [1] (202) 332-0826

Diplomatic representation from the US:

chief of mission: Ambassador Martin George BRENNAN
embassy: corner of Independence and United Nations Avenues
mailing address: P. O. Box 31617, Lusaka
telephone: [260] (1) 250-955
FAX: [260] (1) 252-225

Flag description: green with a panel of three vertical bands of red (hoist side), black, and orange below a soaring orange eagle, on the outer edge of the flag

Economy

Economy - overview: Despite progress in privatization and budgetary reform, Zambia's economic growth remains below the 5% to 7% necessary to reduce poverty significantly. Privatization of government-owned copper mines relieved the government from covering mammoth losses generated by the industry and greatly improved the chances for copper mining to return to profitability and spur economic growth. Copper output increased in 2003 and is expected to increase again in 2004, due to higher copper prices. The maize harvest doubled in 2003, helping boost GDP by 4.0%. Cooperation continues with international bodies on programs to reduce poverty, including a new lending arrangement with the IMF expected in the second quarter, 2004. A tighter monetary policy will help cut inflation, but Zambia still has a serious problem with fiscal discipline.

GDP: purchasing power parity - $8.596 billion (2003 est.)

GDP - real growth rate: 4% (2003 est.)

GDP - per capita: purchasing power parity - $800 (2003 est.)

GDP - composition by sector:

agriculture: 14.9%
industry: 27.6%
services: 57.6% (2001)

Population below poverty line: 86% (1993)

Household income or consumption by percentage share:

lowest 10%: 1.1%
highest 10%: 41% (1998)

Distribution of family income - Gini index: 52.6 (1998)

Inflation rate (consumer prices): 21.5% (2003 est.)

Labor force: 4.29 million (2000)

Labor force - by occupation: agriculture 85%, industry 6%, services 9%

Unemployment rate: 50% (2000 est.)

Budget:

revenues: $1.2 billion
expenditures: $1.25 billion, including capital expenditures of $NA (2001 est.)

Industries: copper mining and processing, construction, foodstuffs, beverages, chemicals, textiles, fertilizer, horticulture

Industrial production growth rate: 4% (2003 est.)

Zambia (continued)

Electricity - production: 7.751 billion kWh (2001)
Electricity - production by source:
fossil fuel: 0.5%
hydro: 99.5%
nuclear: 0%
other: 0% (2001)
Electricity - consumption: 5.458 billion kWh (2001)
Electricity - exports: 1.75 billion kWh (2001)
Electricity - imports: 0 kWh (2001)
Oil - production: 0 bbl/day (2001 est.)
Oil - consumption: 11,000 bbl/day (2001 est.)
Oil - exports: NA
Oil - imports: NA
Agriculture - products: corn, sorghum, rice, peanuts, sunflower seed, vegetables, flowers, tobacco, cotton, sugarcane, cassava (tapioca); cattle, goats, pigs, poultry, milk, eggs, hides; coffee
Exports: $1.039 billion f.o.b. (2003 est.)
Exports - commodities: copper 55%, cobalt, electricity, tobacco, flowers, cotton
Exports - partners: South Africa 27.8%, Malawi 8.5%, Thailand 7.6%, Japan 7.5%, Saint Pierre and Miquelon 7.5%, China 5.2%, Egypt 5.2%, Netherlands 4.6% (2002)
Imports: $1.128 billion f.o.b. (2003 est.)
Imports - commodities: machinery, transportation equipment, petroleum products, electricity, fertilizer; foodstuffs, clothing
Imports - partners: South Africa 69.4%, US 3.3%, China 3.2% (2002)
Debt - external: $5.2 billion (2003)
Economic aid - recipient: $651 million (2000 est.)
Currency: Zambian kwacha (ZMK)
Currency code: ZMK
Exchange rates: Zambian kwacha per US dollar - 4,733.77 (2003), 4,398.59 (2002), 3,610.93 (2001), 3,110.84 (2000), 2,388.02 (1999)
Fiscal year: calendar year

Communications

Telephones - main lines in use: 87,700 (2002)
Telephones - mobile cellular: 139,100 (2002)
Telephone system:
general assessment: facilities are aging but still among the best in Sub-Saharan Africa
domestic: high-capacity microwave radio relay connects most larger towns and cities; several cellular telephone services in operation; Internet service is widely available; very small aperture terminal (VSAT) networks are operated by private firms
international: country code - 260; satellite earth stations - 2 Intelsat (1 Indian Ocean and 1 Atlantic Ocean)
Radio broadcast stations: AM 19, FM 5, shortwave 4 (2001)
Television broadcast stations: 9 (2002)
Internet country code: .zm
Internet hosts: 1,621 (2002)
Internet users: 52,400 (2002)

Transportation

Railways:
total: 2,173 km
narrow gauge: 2,173 km 1.067-m gauge
note: includes 891 km of the Tanzania-Zambia Railway Authority (TAZARA) (2002)
Highways:
total: 66,781 km
paved: NA km
unpaved: NA km (1999 est.)
Waterways: 2,250 km
note: includes Lake Tanganyika and the Zambezi and Luapula rivers
Pipelines: oil 771 km (2003)
Ports and harbors: Mpulungu
Airports: 109 (2003 est.)
Airports - with paved runways:
total: 11
over 3,047 m: 1
2,438 to 3,047 m: 3
1,524 to 2,437 m: 4
914 to 1,523 m: 2
under 914 m: 1 (2003 est.)
Airports - with unpaved runways:
total: 98
2,438 to 3,047 m: 1
1,524 to 2,437 m: 4
914 to 1,523 m: 63
under 914 m: 30 (2003 est.)

Military

Military branches: Zambian National Defense Force (ZNDF): Army, Air Force, Police, National Service
Military manpower - availability:
males age 15-49: 2,477,494 (2004 est.)
Military manpower - fit for military service:
males age 15-49: 1,310,814 (2004 est.)
Military expenditures - dollar figure: $42.6 million (2003)
Military expenditures - percent of GDP: 0.9% (2003)

Transnational Issues

Disputes - international: the Botswana, Namibia, Zambia, and Zimbabwe boundary convergence is not clearly defined or delimited
Illicit drugs: transshipment point for moderate amounts of methaqualone, small amounts of heroin, and cocaine bound for Southern Africa and possibly Europe; a poorly developed financial infrastructure coupled with a government commitment to combating money laundering make it an unattractive venue for money launderers

Zimbabwe

Introduction

Background: The UK annexed Southern Rhodesia from the South Africa Company in 1923. A 1961 constitution was formulated that favored whites in power. In 1965 the government unilaterally declared its independence, but the UK did not recognize the act and demanded more complete voting rights for the black African majority in the country (then called Rhodesia). UN sanctions and a guerrilla uprising finally led to free elections in 1979 and independence (as Zimbabwe) in 1980. Robert MUGABE, the nation's first prime minister, has been the country's only ruler (as president since 1987) and has dominated the country's political system since independence. His chaotic land redistribution campaign begun in 2000 caused an exodus of white farmers, crippled the economy, and ushered in widespread shortages of basic commodities. Ignoring international condemnation, MUGABE rigged the 2002 presidential election to ensure his reelection. Opposition and labor groups launched general strikes in 2003 to pressure MUGABE to retire early; security forces continued their brutal repression of regime opponents.

Geography

Location: Southern Africa, between South Africa and Zambia
Geographic coordinates: 20 00 S, 30 00 E
Map references: Africa
Area:
total: 390,580 sq km
land: 386,670 sq km
water: 3,910 sq km
Area - comparative: slightly larger than Montana
Land boundaries:
total: 3,066 km
border countries: Botswana 813 km, Mozambique 1,231 km, South Africa 225 km, Zambia 797 km
Coastline: 0 km (landlocked)

Zimbabwe *(continued)*

Maritime claims: none (landlocked)

Climate: tropical; moderated by altitude; rainy season (November to March)

Terrain: mostly high plateau with higher central plateau (high veld); mountains in east

Elevation extremes:
lowest point: junction of the Runde and Save rivers 162 m
highest point: Inyangani 2,592 m

Natural resources: coal, chromium ore, asbestos, gold, nickel, copper, iron ore, vanadium, lithium, tin, platinum group metals

Land use:
arable land: 8.4%
permanent crops: 0.34%
other: 91.26% (1998 est.)

Irrigated land: 1,170 sq km (1998 est.)

Natural hazards: recurring droughts; floods and severe storms are rare

Environment - current issues: deforestation; soil erosion; land degradation; air and water pollution; the black rhinoceros herd - once the largest concentration of the species in the world - has been significantly reduced by poaching; poor mining practices have led to toxic waste and heavy metal pollution

Environment - international agreements:
party to: Biodiversity, Climate Change, Desertification, Endangered Species, Law of the Sea, Ozone Layer Protection
signed, but not ratified: none of the selected agreements

Geography - note: landlocked; the Zambezi forms a natural riverine boundary with Zambia; in full flood (February-April) the massive Victoria Falls on the river forms the world's largest curtain of falling water

People

Population: 12,671,860
note: estimates for this country explicitly take into account the effects of excess mortality due to AIDS; this can result in lower life expectancy, higher infant mortality and death rates, lower population and growth rates, and changes in the distribution of population by age and sex than would otherwise be expected (July 2004 est.)

Age structure:
0-14 years: 39.4% (male 2,520,082; female 2,472,641)
15-64 years: 57% (male 3,649,400; female 3,571,631)
65 years and over: 3.6% (male 230,272; female 227,834) (2004 est.)

Median age:
total: 19.1 years
male: 19.1 years
female: 19.1 years (2004 est.)

Population growth rate: 0.68% (2004 est.)

Birth rate: 30.05 births/1,000 population (2004 est.)

Death rate: 23.3 deaths/1,000 population (2004 est.)

Net migration rate: 0 migrant(s)/1,000 population NEGL migrant(s)/1,000 population
note: there is an increasing flow of Zimbabweans into South Africa and Botswana in search of better economic opportunities (2004 est.)

Sex ratio:
at birth: 1.03 male(s)/female
under 15 years: 1.02 male(s)/female
15-64 years: 1.02 male(s)/female
65 years and over: 1.01 male(s)/female
total population: 1.02 male(s)/female (2004 est.)

Infant mortality rate:
total: 67.08 deaths/1,000 live births
male: 69.74 deaths/1,000 live births
female: 64.33 deaths/1,000 live births (2004 est.)

Life expectancy at birth:
total population: 37.82 years
male: 38.63 years
female: 36.99 years (2004 est.)

Total fertility rate: 3.6 children born/woman (2004 est.)

HIV/AIDS - adult prevalence rate: 33.7% (2001 est.)

HIV/AIDS - people living with HIV/AIDS: 2.3 million (2001 est.)

HIV/AIDS - deaths: 200,000 (2001 est.)

Nationality:
noun: Zimbabwean(s)
adjective: Zimbabwean

Ethnic groups: African 98% (Shona 82%, Ndebele 14%, other 2%), mixed and Asian 1%, white less than 1%

Religions: syncretic (part Christian, part indigenous beliefs) 50%, Christian 25%, indigenous beliefs 24%, Muslim and other 1%

Languages: English (official), Shona, Sindebele (the language of the Ndebele, sometimes called Ndebele), numerous but minor tribal dialects

Literacy:
definition: age 15 and over can read and write English
total population: 90.7%
male: 94.2%
female: 87.2% (2003 est.)

Government

Country name:
conventional long form: Republic of Zimbabwe
conventional short form: Zimbabwe
former: Southern Rhodesia, Rhodesia

Government type: parliamentary democracy

Capital: Harare

Administrative divisions: 8 provinces and 2 cities* with provincial status; Bulawayo*, Harare*, Manicaland, Mashonaland Central, Mashonaland East, Mashonaland West, Masvingo, Matabeleland North, Matabeleland South, Midlands

Independence: 18 April 1980 (from UK)

National holiday: Independence Day, 18 April (1980)

Constitution: 21 December 1979

Legal system: mixture of Roman-Dutch and English common law

Suffrage: 18 years of age; universal

Executive branch:
chief of state: Executive President Robert Gabriel MUGABE (since 31 December 1987); Joseph MSIKA (since 23 December 1999); note - the president is both the chief of state and head of government
head of government: Executive President Robert Gabriel MUGABE (since 31 December 1987); Joseph MSIKA (since 23 December 1999); note - the president is both the chief of state and head of government
cabinet: Cabinet appointed by the president; responsible to the House of Assembly
elections: presidential candidates nominated with a nomination paper signed by at least 10 registered voters (at least one from each province) and elected by popular vote; election last held 9-11 March 2002 (next to be held NA March 2008); co-vice presidents appointed by the president
election results: Robert Gabriel MUGABE reelected president; percent of vote - Robert Gabriel MUGABE 56.2%, Morgan TSVANGIRAI 41.9%

Legislative branch: unicameral House of Assembly (150 seats - 120 elected by popular vote for five-year terms, 12 nominated by the president, 10 occupied by traditional chiefs chosen by their peers, and 8 occupied by provincial governors appointed by the president)
elections: last held 24-25 June 2000 (next to be held NA 2005)
election results: percent of vote by party - ZANU-PF 48.6%, MDC 47.0%, other 4.4%; seats by party - ZANU-PF 62, MDC 57, ZANU-Ndonga 1

Judicial branch: Supreme Court; High Court

Political parties and leaders: Movement for Democratic Change or MDC [Morgan TSVANGIRAI]; National Alliance for Good Governance or NAGG [Shakespeare MAYA]; United Parties [Abel MUZOREWA]; Zimbabwe African National Union-Ndonga or ZANU-Ndonga [Wilson KUMBULA]; Zimbabwe African National Union-Patriotic Front or ZANU-PF [Robert Gabriel MUGABE]; Zimbabwe African Peoples Union or ZAPU [Agrippa MADLELA]

Political pressure groups and leaders: National Constitutional Assembly or NCA [Lovemore MADHUKU]; Crisis in Zimbabwe Coalition [Brian KAGORO]; Zimbabwe Congress of Trade Unions or ZCTU [Lovemore MATOMBO]

International organization participation: ACP, AfDB, AU, FAO, G-15, G-77, IAEA, IBRD, ICAO, ICCt (signatory), ICFTU, ICRM, IDA, IFAD, IFC, IFRCS, ILO, IMF, Interpol, IOC, IOM, ISO, ITU, NAM, OPCW, PCA, SADC, UN, UNCTAD, UNESCO, UNIDO, UNMIK, UNMIL, UPU, WCL, WCO, WFTU, WHO, WIPO, WMO, WToO, WTrO

Diplomatic representation in the US:
chief of mission: Ambassador Simbi Veke MUBAKO
chancery: 1608 New Hampshire Avenue NW, Washington, DC 20009
telephone: [1] (202) 332-7100
FAX: [1] (202) 483-9326

Zimbabwe (continued)

Diplomatic representation from the US:

chief of mission: Ambassador Joseph G. SULLIVAN
embassy: 172 Herbert Chitepo Avenue, Harare
mailing address: P. O. Box 3340, Harare
telephone: [263] (4) 250-593 and 250-594
FAX: [263] (4) 796488

Flag description: seven equal horizontal bands of green, yellow, red, black, red, yellow, and green with a white isosceles triangle edged in black with its base on the hoist side; a yellow Zimbabwe bird representing the long history of the country is superimposed on a red five-pointed star in the center of the triangle, which symbolizes peace; green symbolizes agriculture, yellow - mineral wealth, red - blood shed to achieve independence, and black stands for the native people

Economy

Economy - overview: The government of Zimbabwe faces a wide variety of difficult economic problems as it struggles with an unsustainable fiscal deficit, an overvalued exchange rate, soaring inflation, and bare shelves. Its 1998-2002 involvement in the war in the Democratic Republic of the Congo, for example, drained hundreds of millions of dollars from the economy. Badly needed support from the IMF has been suspended because of the country's failure to meet budgetary goals. Inflation rose from an annual rate of 32% in 1998 to 383% in 2003, and is expected to reach 700% in 2004. The government's land reform program, characterized by chaos and violence, has badly damaged the commercial farming sector, the traditional source of exports and foreign exchange and the provider of 400,000 jobs.
GDP: purchasing power parity - $24.03 billion (2003 est.)
GDP - real growth rate: -13.6% (2003 est.)
GDP - per capita: purchasing power parity - $1,900 (2003 est.)
GDP - composition by sector:
agriculture: 25.1%
industry: 15.5%
services: 59.4% (2001)
Population below poverty line: 70% (2002 est.)
Household income or consumption by percentage share:
lowest 10%: 1.97%
highest 10%: 40.42% (1995)
Distribution of family income - Gini index: 50.1 (1995)
Inflation rate (consumer prices): 383.4% (2003 est.)
Labor force: 5.8 million (2000 est.)
Labor force - by occupation: agriculture 66%, services 24%, industry 10% (1996)
Unemployment rate: 70% (2002 est.)
Budget:
revenues: $1.4 billion
expenditures: $2 billion, including capital expenditures of $NA (2003)
Industries: mining (coal, gold, copper, nickel, tin, clay, numerous metallic and nonmetallic ores), steel, wood products, cement, chemicals, fertilizer, clothing and footwear, foodstuffs, beverages

Industrial production growth rate: -3.1% (2002 est.)
Electricity - production: 6.735 billion kWh (2001)
Electricity - production by source:
fossil fuel: 47%
hydro: 53%
nuclear: 0%
other: 0% (2001)
Electricity - consumption: 9.813 billion kWh (2001)
Electricity - exports: 0 kWh (2001)
Electricity - imports: 3.55 billion kWh (2001)
Oil - production: 0 bbl/day (2001 est.)
Oil - consumption: 23,000 bbl/day (2001 est.)
Oil - exports: NA
Oil - imports: NA
Agriculture - products: corn, cotton, wheat, coffee, sugarcane, peanuts; sheep, goats, pigs
Exports: $1.261 billion f.o.b. (2003 est.)
Exports - commodities: tobacco, gold, ferroalloys, textiles/clothing
Exports - partners: China 6%, South Africa 5.7%, Germany 5.4%, UK 4.8%, Japan 4.7%, Netherlands 4.4%, US 4.1% (2002)
Imports: $1.691 billion f.o.b. (2003 est.)
Imports - commodities: machinery and transport equipment, other manufactures, chemicals, fuels
Imports - partners: South Africa 50%, Congo, Democratic Republic of the 5.9%, UK 3.2% (2002)
Debt - external: $3.4 billion (2003 est.)
Economic aid - recipient: $178 million; note - the EU and the US provide food aid on humanitarian grounds (2000 est.)
Currency: Zimbabwean dollar (ZWD)
Currency code: ZWD
Exchange rates: Zimbabwean dollars per US dollar - NA (2003), 55.0358 (2002), 55.0521 (2001), 44.4179 (2000), 38.3012 (1999); note - these are official exchange rates, non-official rates vary significantly
Fiscal year: 1 January - 31 December

Communications

Telephones - main lines in use: 287,900 (2002)
Telephones - mobile cellular: 353,000 (2002)
Telephone system:
general assessment: system was once one of the best in Africa, but now suffers from poor maintenance; more than 100,000 outstanding requests for connection despite an equally large number of installed but unused main lines
domestic: consists of microwave radio relay links, open-wire lines, radiotelephone communication stations, fixed wireless local loop installations, and a substantial mobile cellular network; Internet connection is available in Harare and planned for all major towns and for some of the smaller ones
international: country code - 263; satellite earth stations - 2 Intelsat; two international digital gateway exchanges (in Harare and Gweru)
Radio broadcast stations: AM 7, FM 20 (plus 17 repeater stations), shortwave 1 (1998)

Television broadcast stations: 16 (1997)
Internet country code: .zw
Internet hosts: 2,382 (2002)
Internet users: 500,000 (2002)

Transportation

Railways:
total: 3,077 km
narrow gauge: 3,077 km 1.067-m gauge (313 km electrified)
note: includes the 318 km Bulawayo-Beitbridge Railway Company line (2002)
Highways:
total: 18,338 km
paved: 8,692 km
unpaved: 9,646 km (1999 est.)
Waterways: chrome ore is transported from Harare - by way of the Mazoe River - to the Zambezi River in Mozambique
Pipelines: refined products 261 km (2003)
Ports and harbors: Binga, Kariba
Airports: 404 (2003 est.)
Airports - with paved runways:
total: 17
over 3,047 m: 3
2,438 to 3,047 m: 2
1,524 to 2,437 m: 4
914 to 1,523 m: 8 (2003 est.)
Airports - with unpaved runways:
total: 387
1,524 to 2,437 m: 5
914 to 1,523 m: 186
under 914 m: 196 (2003 est.)

Military

Military branches: Zimbabwe National Army, Air Force of Zimbabwe, Zimbabwe Republic Police (includes Police Support Unit, Paramilitary Police)
Military manpower - availability:
males age 15-49: 3,285,007 (2004 est.)
Military manpower - fit for military service:
males age 15-49: 2,033,978 (2004 est.)
Military expenditures - dollar figure: $105 million (2003)
Military expenditures - percent of GDP: 1.7% (2003)

Transnational Issues

Disputes - international: the Botswana, Namibia, Zambia, and Zimbabwe boundary convergence is not clearly defined or delimited
Illicit drugs: transit point for African cannabis and South Asian heroin, mandrax, and methamphetamines destined for the South African and European markets

Taiwan

The islands of Matsu and Quemoy are not shown.

CHINA · TAIPEI ★ · Chi-lung · Su-ao · T'ai-chung · Chang-hua · Hua-lien · Pescadores · Ma-kung · T'ai-nan · T'ai-tung · Kao-hsiung · Philippine Sea · Luzon Strait · Taiwan Strait

Introduction

Background: In 1895, military defeat forced China to cede Taiwan to Japan. Taiwan reverted to Chinese control after World War II. Following the Communist victory on the mainland in 1949, 2 million Nationalists fled to Taiwan and established a government using the 1946 constitution drawn up for all of China. Over the next five decades, the ruling authorities gradually democratized and incorporated the native population within the governing structure. In 2000, Taiwan underwent its first peaceful transfer of power from the Nationalist to the Democratic Progressive Party. Throughout this period, the island prospered and became one of East Asia's economic "Tigers." The dominant political issues continue to be the relationship between Taiwan and China - specifically the question of eventual unification - as well as domestic political and economic reform.

Geography

Location: Eastern Asia, islands bordering the East China Sea, Philippine Sea, South China Sea, and Taiwan Strait, north of the Philippines, off the southeastern coast of China
Geographic coordinates: 23 30 N, 121 00 E
Map references: Southeast Asia
Area:
total: 35,980 sq km
land: 32,260 sq km
water: 3,720 sq km
note: includes the Pescadores, Matsu, and Quemoy
Area - comparative: slightly smaller than Maryland and Delaware combined
Land boundaries: 0 km
Coastline: 1,566.3 km
Maritime claims:
territorial sea: 12 NM
exclusive economic zone: 200 NM

Climate: tropical; marine; rainy season during southwest monsoon (June to August); cloudiness is persistent and extensive all year
Terrain: eastern two-thirds mostly rugged mountains; flat to gently rolling plains in west
Elevation extremes:
lowest point: South China Sea 0 m
highest point: Yu Shan 3,952 m
Natural resources: small deposits of coal, natural gas, limestone, marble, and asbestos
Land use:
arable land: 24%
permanent crops: 1%
other: 75%
Irrigated land: NA sq km
Natural hazards: earthquakes and typhoons
Environment - current issues: air pollution; water pollution from industrial emissions, raw sewage; contamination of drinking water supplies; trade in endangered species; low-level radioactive waste disposal
Environment - international agreements:
party to: none of the selected agreements because of Taiwan's international status
signed, but not ratified: none of the selected agreements because of Taiwan's international status
Geography - note: strategic location adjacent to both the Taiwan Strait and the Luzon Strait

People

Population: 22,749,838 (July 2004 est.)
Age structure:
0-14 years: 19.9% (male 2,359,467; female 2,167,438)
15-64 years: 70.7% (male 8,149,231; female 7,924,774)
65 years and over: 9.4% (male 1,091,473; female 1,057,455) (2004 est.)
Median age:
total: 33.7 years
male: 33.3 years
female: 34.1 years (2004 est.)
Population growth rate: 0.64% (2004 est.)
Birth rate: 12.7 births/1,000 population (2004 est.)
Death rate: 6.29 deaths/1,000 population (2004 est.)
Net migration rate: 0 migrant(s)/1,000 population (2004 est.)
Sex ratio:
at birth: 1.1 male(s)/female
under 15 years: 1.09 male(s)/female
15-64 years: 1.03 male(s)/female
65 years and over: 1.03 male(s)/female
total population: 1.04 male(s)/female (2004 est.)
Infant mortality rate:
total: 6.52 deaths/1,000 live births
male: 7.21 deaths/1,000 live births
female: 5.77 deaths/1,000 live births (2004 est.)
Life expectancy at birth:
total population: 77.06 years
male: 74.31 years
female: 80.08 years (2004 est.)

Total fertility rate: 1.57 children born/woman (2004 est.)
HIV/AIDS - adult prevalence rate: NA
HIV/AIDS - people living with HIV/AIDS: NA
HIV/AIDS - deaths: NA
Nationality:
noun: Chinese/Taiwanese (singular and plural)
adjective: Chinese/Taiwanese
Ethnic groups: Taiwanese (including Hakka) 84%, mainland Chinese 14%, aborigine 2%
Religions: mixture of Buddhist, Confucian, and Taoist 93%, Christian 4.5%, other 2.5%
Languages: Mandarin Chinese (official), Taiwanese (Min), Hakka dialects
Literacy:
definition: age 15 and over can read and write
total population: 86%
male: 93%
female: 79%
note: literacy for the total population has reportedly increased to 94% (1998)

Government

Country name:
conventional long form: none
conventional short form: Taiwan
local long form: none
local short form: T'ai-wan
former: Formosa
Government type: multiparty democratic regime headed by popularly-elected president and unicameral legislature
Capital: Taipei
Administrative divisions: the central administrative divisions include the provinces of Fu-chien (some 20 offshore islands of Fujian Province including Quemoy and Matsu) and Taiwan (the island of Taiwan and the Pescadores islands); Taiwan is further subdivided into 16 counties (hsien, singular and plural), 5 municipalities* (shih, singular and plural), and 2 special municipalities** (chuan-shih, singular and plural); Chang-hua, Chia-i, Chia-i*, Chi-lung*, Hsin-chu, Hsin-chu*, Hua-lien, I-lan, Kao-hsiung, Kao-hsiung**, Miao-li, Nan-t'ou, P'eng-hu, P'ing-tung, T'ai-chung, T'ai-chung*, T'ai-nan, T'ai-nan*, T'ai-pei, T'ai-pei**, T'ai-tung, T'ao-yuan, and Yun-lin; the provincial capital is at Chung-hsing-hsin-ts'un
note: Taiwan uses the Wade-Giles system for romanization
National holiday: Republic Day (Anniversary of the Chinese Revolution), 10 October (1911)
Constitution: 25 December 1946, amended in 1992, 1994, 1997, 1999, and 2000
Legal system: based on civil law system; accepts compulsory ICJ jurisdiction, with reservations
Suffrage: 20 years of age; universal
Executive branch:
chief of state: President CHEN Shui-bian (since 20 March 2004) and Vice President Annette LU (LU Hsiu-lien) (since 20 March 2004)

Taiwan (continued)

head of government: Premier (President of the Executive Yuan) YU Shyi-kun (since 1 February 2002) and Vice Premier (Vice President of the Executive Yuan) LIN Hsin-yi (since 1 February 2002)
cabinet: Executive Yuan appointed by the president
elections: president and vice president elected on the same ticket by popular vote for four-year terms; election last held 20 March 2004 (next to be held in March 2008); premier appointed by the president; vice premiers appointed by the president on the recommendation of the premier
election results: CHEN Shui-bian elected president; percent of vote - CHEN Shui-bian (DPP) 51.1%, LIEN Chan (KMT) 49.9%

Legislative branch: unicameral Legislative Yuan (225 seats - 168 elected by popular vote, 41 elected on the basis of the proportion of islandwide votes received by participating political parties, eight elected from overseas Chinese constituencies on the basis of the proportion of island-wide votes received by participating political parties, eight elected by popular vote among the aboriginal populations; members serve three-year terms) and unicameral National Assembly (300 seat nonstanding body; delegates nominated by parties and elected by proportional representation within three months of a Legislative Yuan call to amend the Constitution, impeach the president, or change national borders)
elections: Legislative Yuan - last held 8 December 2001 (next to be held in December 2004)
election results: Legislative Yuan - percent of vote by party - DPP 39%, KMT 30%, PFP 20%, TSU 6%, independents and other parties 5%; seats by party (2003) - DPP 88, KMT 66, PFP 46, TSU 12, independents and other parties 13

Judicial branch: Judicial Yuan (justices appointed by the president with consent of the Legislative Yuan)
Political parties and leaders: Democratic Progressive Party or DPP [CHEN Shui-bian, chairman]; Kuomintang or KMT (Nationalist Party) [LIEN Chan, chairman]; People First Party or PFP [James SOONG (SOONG Chu-yu), chairman]; Taiwan Solidarity Union or TSU [HUANG Chu-wen, chairman]; other minor parties including the Chinese New Party or CNP
Political pressure groups and leaders: Taiwan independence movement, various business and environmental groups
note: debate on Taiwan independence has become acceptable within the mainstream of domestic politics on Taiwan; political liberalization and the increased representation of opposition parties in Taiwan's legislature have opened public debate on the island's national identity; a broad popular consensus has developed that Taiwan currently enjoys de facto independence and - whatever the ultimate outcome regarding reunification or independence - that Taiwan's people must have the deciding voice; advocates of Taiwan independence oppose the stand that the island will eventually unify with mainland China; goals of the Taiwan independence movement include establishing a sovereign nation on Taiwan and

entering the UN; other organizations supporting Taiwan independence include the World United Formosans for Independence and the Organization for Taiwan Nation Building
International organization participation: APEC, AsDB, BCIE, ICC, ICFTU, IOC, WCL, WTrO
Diplomatic representation in the US: none; unofficial commercial and cultural relations with the people of the US are maintained through an unofficial instrumentality, the Taipei Economic and Cultural Representative Office (TECRO) in the US with headquarters in Taipei and field offices in Washington and 12 other US cities
Diplomatic representation from the US: none; unofficial commercial and cultural relations with the people on Taiwan are maintained through an unofficial instrumentality - the American Institute in Taiwan (AIT) - which has offices in the US and Taiwan; US office located at 1700 N. Moore St., Suite 1700, Arlington, VA 22209-1996, telephone: [1] (703) 525-8474, FAX: [1] (703) 841-1385); Taiwan offices located at #7 Lane 134, Hsin Yi Road, Section 3, Taipei, Taiwan, telephone: [886] (2) 2709-2000, FAX: [886] (2) 2702-7675; #2 Chung Cheng 3rd Road, 5th Floor, Kao-hsiung, Taiwan, telephone: [886] (7) 224-0154 through 0157, FAX: [886] (7) 223-8237; and the American Trade Center, Room 3208 International Trade Building, Taipei World Trade Center, 333 Keelung Road Section 1, Taipei, Taiwan 10548, telephone: [886] (2) 2720-1550, FAX: [886] (2) 2757-7162

Flag description: red with a dark blue rectangle in the upper hoist-side corner bearing a white sun with 12 triangular rays

Economy

Economy - overview: Taiwan has a dynamic capitalist economy with gradually decreasing guidance of investment and foreign trade by government authorities. In keeping with this trend, some large government-owned banks and industrial firms are being privatized. Exports have provided the primary impetus for industrialization. The trade surplus is substantial, and foreign reserves are the world's third largest. Agriculture contributes 2% to GDP, down from 32% in 1952. While Taiwan is a major investor throughout Southeast Asia, China has become the largest destination for investment and has overtaken the US to become Taiwan's largest export market. Because of its conservative financial approach and its entrepreneurial strengths, Taiwan suffered little compared with many of its neighbors from the Asian financial crisis in 1998. The global economic downturn, combined with problems in policy coordination by the administration and bad debts in the banking system, pushed Taiwan into recession in 2001, the first year of negative growth ever recorded. Unemployment also reached record levels. Output recovered moderately in 2002 in the face of continued global slowdown, fragile consumer confidence, and bad bank loans. Growing economic ties with China are

a dominant long-term factor. Exports to China - mainly parts and equipment for the assembly of goods for export to developed countries - drove Taiwan's economic recovery in 2002. Although the SARS epidemic, Typhoon Maemi, corporate scandals, and a drop in consumer spending caused GDP growth to contract to 3.2% in 2003, increasingly strong export performance kept Taiwan's economy on track, and the government expects Taiwan's economy to grow 4.1% in 2004.
GDP: purchasing power parity - $528.6 billion (2003 est.)
GDP - real growth rate: 3.2% (2003 est.)
GDP - per capita: purchasing power parity - $23,400 (2003 est.)
GDP - composition by sector:
agriculture: 2%
industry: 31%
services: 67% (2002)
Population below poverty line: 1% (2000 est.)
Household income or consumption by percentage share:
lowest 10%: 6.7%
highest 10%: 41.1% (2002 est.)
Distribution of family income - Gini index:
Inflation rate (consumer prices): -0.2% (2002 est.)
Labor force: 10 million (2003)
Labor force - by occupation: services 57%, industry 35%, agriculture 8% (2001 est.)
Unemployment rate: 5.1% (September 2003 est.)
Budget:
revenues: $52.5 billion
expenditures: $63 billion, including capital expenditures of $14.4 billion (2002 est.)
Industries: electronics, petroleum refining, chemicals, textiles, iron and steel, machinery, cement, food processing
Industrial production growth rate: 6% (2002)
Electricity - production: 151.1 billion kWh (2001)
Electricity - production by source:
fossil fuel: 71.4%
hydro: 6%
nuclear: 22.6%
other: 0% (2001)
Electricity - consumption: 140.5 billion kWh (2001)
Electricity - exports: 0 kWh (2001)
Electricity - imports: 0 kWh (2001)
Oil - production: 1,100 bbl/day (2001 est.)
Oil - consumption: 988,000 bbl/day (2001 est.)
Oil - exports: NA
Oil - imports: NA
Oil - proved reserves: 2 million bbl (1 January 2002)
Natural gas - production: 750 million cu m (2001 est.)
Natural gas - consumption: 6.64 billion cu m (2001 est.)
Natural gas - exports: 410 million cu m (2001 est.)
Natural gas - imports: 6.3 billion cu m (2001 est.)
Natural gas - proved reserves: 38.23 billion cu m (1 January 2002)

Taiwan (continued)

Agriculture - products: rice, corn, vegetables, fruit, tea; pigs, poultry, beef, milk, fish

Exports: $143 billion f.o.b. (2003 est.)

Exports - commodities: computer products and electrical equipment, metals, textiles, plastics and rubber products, chemicals (2002)

Exports - partners: China 25.3%, US 20.5%, Japan 9.2% (2002)

Imports: $119.6 billion f.o.b. (2003 est.)

Imports - commodities: machinery and electrical equipment 44.5%, minerals, precision instruments (2002)

Imports - partners: Japan 24.2%, US 16.1%, China 7.1%, South Korea 6.9% (2002)

Debt - external: $45 billion (2002)

Currency: new Taiwan dollar (TWD)

Currency code: TWD

Exchange rates: new Taiwan dollars per US dollar - 34.418 (2003), 34.575 (2002), 33.8 (2001), 33.09 (2000), 31.6 (1999)

Fiscal year: 1 July - 30 June (up to FY98/99); 1 July 1999 - 31 December 2000 for FY00; calendar year (after FY00)

Communications

Telephones - main lines in use: 13,099,400 (2002)

Telephones - mobile cellular: 23,905,400 (2002)

Telephone system:

general assessment: provides telecommunications service for every business and private need

domestic: thoroughly modern; completely digitalized

international: country code - 886; satellite earth stations - 2 Intelsat (1 Pacific Ocean and 1 Indian Ocean); submarine cables to Japan (Okinawa), Philippines, Guam, Singapore, Hong Kong, Indonesia, Australia, Middle East, and Western Europe (1999)

Radio broadcast stations: AM 218, FM 333, shortwave 50 (1999)

Television broadcast stations: 29 (plus two repeaters) (1997)

Internet country code: .tw

Internet hosts: 2,170,233 (2002)

Internet users: 8.59 million (2002)

Transportation

Railways:

total: 1,108 km

narrow gauge: 1,108 km 1.067-m gauge (519 km electrified)

note: there also are 1,255 km of 1.067-m gauge routes belonging to the Taiwan Sugar Corporation and to the Taiwan Forestry Bureau used to haul products and limited numbers of passengers (2002)

Highways:

total: 35,931 km

paved: 31,583 km (including 608 km of expressways)

unpaved: 4,348 km (2000)

Waterways: NA

Pipelines: condensate 25 km; gas 435 km (2003)

Ports and harbors: Chi-lung (Keelung), Hua-lien, Kao-hsiung, Su-ao, T'ai-chung

Merchant marine:

total: 130 ships (1,000 GRT or over) 3,417,768 GRT/ 5,617,318 DWT

by type: bulk 36, cargo 23, chemical tanker 2, combination bulk 3, container 37, petroleum tanker 17, refrigerated cargo 10, roll on/roll off 2

foreign-owned: Cuba 1, Hong Kong 4

registered in other countries: 457 (2003 est.)

Airports: 40 (2003 est.)

Airports - with paved runways:

total: 37

over 3,047 m: 8

2,438 to 3,047 m: 8

1,524 to 2,437 m: 12

914 to 1,523 m: 8

under 914 m: 1 (2003 est.)

Airports - with unpaved runways:

total: 3

1,524 to 2,437 m: 1

under 914 m: 2 (2003 est.)

Heliports: 3 (2003 est.)

Military

Military branches: Army, Navy (including Marine Corps), Air Force, Coast Guard Administration, Armed Forces Reserve Command, Combined Service Forces Command, Armed Forces Police Command

Military manpower - military age: 19 years of age; 22-month active service obligation (2004 est.)

Military manpower - availability:

males age 15-49: 6,556,484 (2004 est.)

Military manpower - fit for military service:

males age 15-49: 4,992,737 (2004 est.)

Military manpower - reaching military age annually:

males: 182,677 (2004 est.)

Military expenditures - dollar figure: $7,611,700,000 (2003)

Military expenditures - percent of GDP: 2.7% (2003)

Transnational Issues

Disputes - international: involved in complex dispute with China, Malaysia, Philippines, Vietnam, and possibly Brunei over the Spratly Islands; the 2002 "Declaration on the Conduct of Parties in the South China Sea" has eased tensions but falls short of a legally binding "code of conduct" desired by several of the disputants; Paracel Islands are occupied by China, but claimed by Taiwan and Vietnam; in 2003, China and Taiwan asserted claims to the Japanese-administered Senkaku Islands (Diaoyu Tai) with increased media coverage and protest actions

Illicit drugs: regional transit point for heroin and methamphetamine; major problem with domestic consumption of methamphetamine and heroin; renewal of domestic methamphetamine production is a problem

Appendix A:

Abbreviations

A		
	ABEDA	Arab Bank for Economic Development in Africa
	ACC	Arab Cooperation Council
	ACCT	Agency for the French-Speaking Community
	ACP Group	African, Caribbean, and Pacific Group of States
	AfDB	African Development Bank
	AFESD	Arab Fund for Economic and Social Development
	Air Pollution	Convention on Long-Range Transboundary Air Pollution
	Air Pollution-Nitrogen Oxides	Protocol to the 1979 Convention on Long-Range Transboundary Air Pollution Concerning the Control of Emissions of Nitrogen Oxides or Their Transboundary Fluxes
	Air Pollution-Persistent Organic Pollutants	Protocol to the 1979 Convention on Long-Range Transboundary Air Pollution on Persistent Organic Pollutants
	Air Pollution-Sulphur 85	Protocol to the 1979 Convention on Long-Range Transboundary Air Pollution on the Reduction of Sulphur Emissions or Their Transboundary Fluxes by at Least 30%
	Air Pollution-Sulphur 94	Protocol to the 1979 Convention on Long-Range Transboundary Air Pollution on Further Reduction of Sulphur Emissions
	Air Pollution-Volatile Organic Compounds	Protocol to the 1979 Convention on Long-Range Transboundary Air Pollution Concerning the Control of Emissions of Volatile Organic Compounds or Their Transboundary Fluxes
	AMF	Arab Monetary Fund
	AMU	Arab Maghreb Union
	Antarctic-Environmental Protocol	Protocol on Environmental Protection to the Antarctic Treaty
	Antarctic-Marine Living Resources	Convention on the Conservation of Antarctic Marine Living Resources
	Antarctic Seals	Convention for the Conservation of Antarctic Seals
	ANZUS	Australia-New Zealand-United States Security Treaty
	APEC	Asia-Pacific Economic Cooperation
	Arabsat	Arab Satellite Communications Organization
	ARF	ASEAN Regional Forum
	AsDB	Asian Development Bank
	ASEAN	Association of Southeast Asian Nations
	AU	African Union
	Autodin	Automatic Digital Network
B		
	bbl/day	barrels per day
	BCIE	Central American Bank for Economic Integration
	BDEAC	Central African States Development Bank
	Benelux	Benelux Economic Union
	BGN	United States Board on Geographic Names
	Biodiversity	Convention on Biological Diversity
	BIS	Bank for International Settlements
	BSEC	Black Sea Economic Cooperation Zone

C		
C	Commonwealth
CACM	Central American Common Market
CAEU	Council of Arab Economic Unity
CAN	Andean Community of Nations
Caricom	Caribbean Community and Common Market
CB	citizen's band mobile radio communications
CBSS	Council of the Baltic Sea States
CCC	Customs Cooperation Council
CDB	Caribbean Development Bank
CE	Council of Europe
CEI	Central European Initiative
CEMA	Council for Mutual Economic Assistance; also known as CMEA or Comecon
CEMAC	Monetary and Economic Community of Central Africa
CEPGL	Economic Community of the Great Lakes Countries
CEPT	Conference Europeanne des Postes et Telecommunications
CERN	European Organization for Nuclear Research
c.i.f.	cost, insurance, and freight
CIS	Commonwealth of Independent States
CITES	see Endangered Species
Climate Change	United Nations Framework Convention on Climate Change
Climate Change-Kyoto Protocol	Kyoto Protocol to the United Nations Framework Convention on Climate Change
COCOM	Coordinating Committee on Export Controls
COMESA	Common Market for Eastern and Southern Africa
Comsat	Communications Satellite Corporation
CP	Colombo Plan
CY	calendar year

D		
DC	developed country
DDT	dichloro-diphenyl-trichloro-ethane
Desertification	United Nations Convention to Combat Desertification in Those Countries Experiencing Serious Drought and/or Desertification, Particularly in Africa
DIA	United States Defense Intelligence Agency
DSN	Defense Switched Network
DWT	deadweight ton

E		
EADB	East African Development Bank
EAPC	Euro-Atlantic Partnership Council
EBRD	European Bank for Reconstruction and Development
EC	European Community
ECA	Economic Commission for Africa
ECE	Economic Commission for Europe
ECLAC	Economic Commission for Latin America and the Caribbean
ECO	Economic Cooperation Organization
ECOSOC	Economic and Social Council
ECOWAS	Economic Community of West African States

Appendix A: Abbreviations *(continued)*

	ECS	European Coal and Steel Community
	EEC	European Economic Community
	EEZ	exclusive economic zone
	EFTA	European Free Trade Association
	EIB	European Investment Bank
	EMU	Economic and Monetary Union
	Endangered Species	Convention on the International Trade in Endangered Species of Wild Flora and Fauna (CITES)
	Entente	Council of the Entente
	Environmental Modification	Convention on the Prohibition of Military or Any Other Hostile Use of Environmental Modification Techniques
	ESA	European Space Agency
	ESCAP	Economic and Social Commission for Asia and the Pacific
	ESCWA	Economic and Social Commission for Western Asia
	est.	estimate
	EU	European Union
	Euratom	European Atomic Energy Community
	Eutelsat	European Telecommunications Satellite Organization
	Ex-Im	Export-Import Bank of the United States
F	FAO	Food and Agriculture Organization
	FAX	facsimile
	f.o.b.	free on board
	FOC	flags of convenience
	FLS	Front Line States
	FRG	Federal Republic of Germany (West Germany); used for information dated before 3 October 1990 or CY91
	FSU	former Soviet Union
	FY	fiscal year
	F.Y.R.O.M.	The Former Yugoslav Republic of Macedonia
	FZ	Franc Zone
G	G-2	Group of 2
	G-3	Group of 3
	G-5	Group of 5
	G-6	Group of 6
	G-7	Group of 7
	G-8	Group of 8
	G-9	Group of 9
	G-10	Group of 10
	G-15	Group of 15
	G-24	Group of 24
	G-77	Group of 77
	GATT	General Agreement on Tariffs and Trade; now WTrO
	GCC	Gulf Cooperation Council
	GDP	gross domestic product

Appendix A: Abbreviations *(continued)*

GDR	German Democratic Republic (East Germany); used for information dated before 3 October 1990 or CY91
GNP	gross national product
GRT	gross register ton
GSM	global system for mobile cellular communications
GUUAM	acronym for member states – Georgia, Ukraine, Uzbekistan, Azerbaijan, Moldova
GWP	gross world product
H	
Habitat	United Nations Center for Human Settlements
Hazardous Wastes	Basel Convention on the Control of Transboundary Movements of Hazardous Wastes and Their Disposal
HF	high-frequency
HIV/AIDS	human immunodeficiency virus/acquired immune deficiency syndrome
I	
IADB	Inter-American Development Bank
IAEA	International Atomic Energy Agency
IANA	Internet Assigned Numbers Authority
IBEC	International Bank for Economic Cooperation
IBRD	International Bank for Reconstruction and Development (World Bank)
ICAO	International Civil Aviation Organization
ICC	International Chamber of Commerce or Inuit Circumpolar Conference
ICCt	International Criminal Court
ICFTU	International Confederation of Free Trade Unions
ICJ	International Court of Justice (World Court)
ICRC	International Committee of the Red Cross
ICRM	International Red Cross and Red Crescent Movement
ICSID	International Center for Secretariat of Investment Disputes
ICTR	International Criminal Tribunal for Rwanda
ICTY	International Criminal Tribunal for the former Yugoslavia
IDA	International Development Association
IDB	Islamic Development Bank
IEA	International Energy Agency
IFAD	International Fund for Agricultural Development
IFC	International Finance Corporation
IFCTU	International Federation of Christian Trade Unions
IFRCS	International Federation of Red Cross and Red Crescent Societies
IGAD	Inter-Governmental Authority on Development
IGADD	Inter-Governmental Authority on Drought and Development
IHO	International Hydrographic Organization
IIB	International Investment Bank
ILO	International Labor Organization
IMF	International Monetary Fund
IMO	International Maritime Organization
Inmarsat	International Maritime Satellite Organization
InOC	Indian Ocean Commission

Appendix A: Abbreviations *(continued)*

	INSTRAW	International Research and Training Institute for the Advancement of Women
	Intelsat	International Telecommunications Satellite Organization
	Interpol	International Criminal Police Organization
	Intersputnik	International Organization of Space Communications
	IOC	International Olympic Committee
	IOM	International Organization for Migration
	ISO	International Organization for Standardization
	ISP	Internet Service Provider
	ITU	International Telecommunication Union
K	kHz	kilohertz
	km	kilometer
	kW	kilowatt
	kWh	kilowatt-hour
L	LAES	Latin American Economic System
	LAIA	Latin American Integration Association
	LAS	League of Arab States
	Law of the Sea	United Nations Convention on the Law of the Sea (LOS), also know as UNCLOS
	LDC	less developed country
	LLDC	least developed country
	London Convention	see Marine Dumping
	LOS	see Law of the Sea
M	m	meter
	Marecs	Maritime European Communications Satellite
	Marine Dumping	Convention on the Prevention of Marine Pollution by Dumping Wastes and Other Matter
	Marine Life Conservation	Convention on Fishing and Conservation of Living Resources of the High Seas
	MARPOL	see Ship Pollution
	Medarabtel	Middle East Telecommunications Project of the International Telecommunications Union
	Mercosur	Southern Cone Common Market
	MHz	megahertz
	MICAH	International Civilian Support Mission in Haiti
	MIGA	Multilateral Investment Geographic Agency
	MINURSO	United Nations Mission for the Referendum in Western Sahara
	MONUC	United Nations Organization Mission in the Democratic Republic of the Congo
N	NA	not available
	NAFTA	North American Free Trade Agreement
	NAM	Nonaligned Movement
	NATO	North Atlantic Treaty Organization
	NC	Nordic Council
	NEA	Nuclear Energy Agency
	NEGL	negligible
	NGA	National Geospatial-Intelligence Agency
	NIB	Nordic Investment Bank

	NIC	newly industrializing country
	NIE	newly industrializing economy
	NIS	new independent states
	NM	nautical mile
	NMT	Nordic Mobile Telephone
	NSG	Nuclear Suppliers Group
	Nuclear Test Ban	Treaty Banning Nuclear Weapons Tests in the Atmosphere, in Outer Space, and Under Water
	NZ	New Zealand
O	OAPEC	Organization of Arab Petroleum Exporting Countries
	OAS	Organization of American States
	ODA	official development assistance
	ODF	Official Development Finance
	OECD	Organization for Economic Cooperation and Development
	OECS	Organization of Eastern Caribbean States
	OIC	Organization of the Islamic Conference
	OOF	other official flows
	OPANAL	Agency for the Prohibition of Nuclear Weapons in Latin America and the Caribbean
	OPCW	Organization for the Prohibition of Chemical Weapons
	OPEC	Organization of Petroleum Exporting Countries
	OSCE	Organization for Security and Cooperation in Europe
	Ozone Layer Protection	Montreal Protocol on Substances That Deplete the Ozone Layer
P	PCA	Permanent Court of Arbitration
	PDRY	People's Democratic Republic of Yemen [Yemen (Aden) or South Yemen]; used for information dated before 22 May 1990 or CY91
	PFP	Partnership for Peace
	PIF	Pacific Islands Forum
	PPP	purchasing power parity
R	Ramsar	see Wetlands
	RG	Rio Group
S	SAARC	South Asian Association for Regional Cooperation
	SACU	Southern African Customs Union
	SADC	Southern African Development Community
	SAFE	South African Far East Cable
	SCO	Shanghai Cooperative Organization
	SFRY	Socialist Federal Republic of Yugoslavia
	SHF	super-high-frequency
	Ship Pollution	Protocol of 1978 Relating to the International Convention for the Prevention of Pollution From Ships, 1973 (MARPOL)
	Sparteca	South Pacific Regional Trade and Economic Cooperation Agreement
	SPC	South Pacific Commission
	SPF	South Pacific Forum
	sq km	square kilometer
	sq mi	square mile

T	TAT	Trans-Atlantic Telephone
	Tropical Timber 83	International Tropical Timber Agreement, 1983
	Tropical Timber 94	International Tropical Timber Agreement, 1994
U	UAE	United Arab Emirates
	UDEAC	Central African Customs and Economic Union
	UHF	ultra-high-frequency
	UK	United Kingdom
	UN	United Nations
	UNAMSIL	United Nations Mission in Sierra Leone
	UNCLOS	United Nations Convention on the Law of the Sea, also known as LOS
	UNCTAD	United Nations Conference on Trade and Development
	UNDCP	United Nations Drug Control Program
	UNDOF	United Nations Disengagement Observer Force
	UNDP	United Nations Development Program
	UNEP	United Nations Environment Program
	UNESCO	United Nations Educational, Scientific, and Cultural Organization
	UNFICYP	United Nations Peace-keeping Force in Cyprus
	UNFPA	United Nations Population Fund
	UNHCR	United Nations High Commissioner for Refugees
	UNHCRHR	United Nations High Commissioner for Human Rights
	UNICEF	United Nations Children's Fund
	UNICEP	United Nations International Comparison Program
	UNICRI	United Nations Interregional Crime and Justice Research Institute
	UNIDIR	United Nations Institute for Disarmament Research
	UNIDO	United Nations Industrial Development Organization
	UNIFIL	United Nations Interim Force in Lebanon
	UNIKOM	United Nations Iraq-Kuwait Observation Mission
	UNITAR	United Nations Institute for Training and Research
	UNMEE	United Nations Mission in Ethiopia and Eritrea
	UNMIBH	United Nations Mission in Bosnia and Herzegovina
	UNMIK	United Nations Interim Administration Mission in Kosovo
	UNMIL	United Nations Mission in Liberia
	UNMISET	United Nations Mission of Support in East Timor
	UNMOGIP	United Nations Military Observer Group in India and Pakistan
	UNMOP	United Nations Mission of Observers in Prevlaka
	UNMOT	United Nations Mission of Observers in Tajikistan
	UNMOVIC	United Nations Monitoring, Verification, and Inspection Commission
	UNOMIG	United Nations Observer Mission in Georgia
	UNOPS	United Nations Office of Project Services
	UNRISD	United Nations Research Institute for Social Development
	UNRWA	United Nations Relief and Works Agency for Palestine Refugees in the Near East
	UNSC	United Nations Security Council
	UNSSC	United Nations System Staff College

Appendix A: Abbreviations *(continued)*

	UNTAET	United Nations Transitional Administration in East Timor
	UNTSO	United Nations Truce Supervision Organization
	UNU	United Nations University
	UPU	Universal Postal Union
	US	United States
	USSR	Union of Soviet Socialist Republics (Soviet Union); used for information dated before 25 December 1991
	USSR/EE	Union of Soviet Socialist Republics/Eastern Europe
	UV	ultra violet
V	VHF	very-high-frequency
	VSAT	very small aperture terminal
W	WADB	West African Development Bank
	WAEMU	West African Economic and Monetary Union
	WCL	World Confederation of Labor
	WCO	World Customs Organization
	Wetlands	Convention on Wetlands of International Importance Especially As Waterfowl Habitat
	WEU	Western European Union
	WFC	World Food Council
	WFP	World Food Program
	WFTU	World Federation of Trade Unions
	Whaling	International Convention for the Regulation of Whaling
	WHO	World Health Organization
	WIPO	World Intellectual Property Organization
	WMO	World Meteorological Organization
	WP	Warsaw Pact
	WTO	see WToO for World Tourism Organization or WTrO for World Trade Organization
	WToO	World Tourism Organization
	WTrO	World Trade Organization
Y	YAR	Yemen Arab Republic [Yemen (Sanaa) or North Yemen]; used for information dated before 22 May 1990 or CY91
Z	ZC	Zangger Committee

Appendix B:

International Organizations and Groups

advanced developing countries	another term for those less developed countries (LDCs) with particularly rapid industrial development; see newly industrializing economies (NIEs)
advanced economies	a term used by the International Monetary FUND (IMF) for the top group in its hierarchy of advanced economies, countries in transition, and developing countries; it includes the following 28 advanced economies: Australia, Austria, Belgium, Canada, Denmark, Finland, France, Germany, Greece, Hong Kong, Iceland, Ireland, Israel, Italy, Japan, South Korea, Luxembourg, Netherlands, NZ, Norway, Portugal, Singapore, Spain, Sweden, Switzerland, Taiwan, UK, US; note—this group would presumably also cover the following seven smaller countries of Andorra, Bermuda, Faroe Islands, Holy See, Liechtenstein, Monaco, and San Marino that are included in the more comprehensive group of "developed countries"
African, Caribbean, and Pacific Group of States (ACP Group) *established*—6 June 1975 *aim*—to manage their preferential economic and aid relationship with the EU	*members*—(77) Angola, Antigua and Barbuda, The Bahamas, Barbados, Belize, Benin, Botswana, Burkina Faso, Burundi, Cameroon, Cape Verde, Central African Republic, Chad, Comoros, Democratic Republic of the Congo, Republic of the Congo, Cook Islands, Cote d'Ivoire, Djibouti, Dominica, Dominican Republic, Equatorial Guinea, Eritrea, Ethiopia, Fiji, Gabon, The Gambia, Ghana, Grenada, Guinea, Guinea-Bissau, Guyana, Haiti, Jamaica, Kenya, Kiribati, Lesotho, Liberia, Madagascar, Malawi, Mali, Marshall Islands, Mauritania, Mauritius, Federated States of Micronesia, Mozambique, Namibia, Nauru, Niger, Nigeria, Niue, Palau, Papua New Guinea, Rwanda, Saint Kitts and Nevis, Saint Lucia, Saint Vincent and the Grenadines, Samoa, Sao Tome and Principe, Senegal, Seychelles, Sierra Leone, Solomon Islands, Somalia, South Africa, Sudan, Suriname, Swaziland, Tanzania, Togo, Tonga, Trinidad and Tobago, Tuvalu, Uganda, Vanuatu, Zambia, Zimbabwe
African Development Bank (AfDB) *note*—its predecessor was Organization of African Unity (OAU) *established*—9 September 1999 *aim*—to promote economic and social development	*regional members*—(53) Algeria, Angola, Benin, Botswana, Burkina Faso, Burundi, Cameroon, Cape Verde, Central African Republic, Chad, Comoros, Democratic Republic of the Congo, Republic of the Congo, Cote d'Ivoire, Djibouti, Egypt, Equatorial Guinea, Eritrea, Ethiopia, Gabon, The Gambia, Ghana, Guinea, Guinea-Bissau, Kenya, Lesotho, Liberia, Libya, Madagascar, Malawi, Mali, Mauritania, Mauritius, Morocco, Mozambique, Namibia, Niger, Nigeria, Rwanda, Sao Tome and Principe, Senegal, Seychelles, Sierra Leone, Somalia, South Africa, Sudan, Swaziland, Tanzania, Togo, Tunisia, Uganda, Zambia, Zimbabwe *nonregional members*—(24) Argentina, Austria, Belgium, Brazil, Canada, China, Denmark, Finland, France, Germany, India, Italy, Japan, South Korea, Kuwait, Netherlands, Norway, Portugal, Saudi Arabia, Spain, Sweden, Switzerland, UK, US
African Union (AU) *note*—replaces Organization of African Unity (OAU) *established*—8 July 2001 *aim*—to achieve greater unity among African States; to defend states' integrity and independence; to accelerate political, social, and economic integration; to encourage international cooperation; to promote democratic principles and institutions	*members*—(52) Algeria, Angola, Benin, Botswana, Burkina Faso, Burundi, Cameroon, Cape Verde, Central African Republic, Chad, Comoros, Democratic Republic of the Congo, Republic of the Congo, Cote d'Ivoire, Djibouti, Egypt, Equatorial Guinea, Eritrea, Ethiopia, Gabon, The Gambia, Ghana, Guinea, Kenya, Lesotho, Liberia, Libya, Madagascar, Malawi, Mali, Mauritania, Mauritius, Mozambique, Namibia, Niger, Nigeria, Rwanda, Sahrawi Arab Democratic Republic, Sao Tome and Principe, Senegal, Seychelles, Sierra Leone, Somalia, South Africa, Sudan, Swaziland, Tanzania, Togo, Tunisia, Uganda, Zambia, Zimbabwe
Agency for the French-Speaking Community (ACCT) *note*—formerly Agency for Cultural and Technical Cooperation *established*—20 March 1970; name changed 1996 *aim*—to promote cultural and technical cooperation among French-speaking countries	*members*—(51) Albania, Belgium, Benin, Bulgaria, Burkina Faso, Burundi, Cambodia, Cameroon, Canada, Cape Verde, Central African Republic, Chad, Comoros, Democratic Republic of the Congo, Republic of the Congo, Cote d'Ivoire, Djibouti, Dominica, Egypt, Equatorial Guinea, France, French Community of Belgium, Gabon, Guinea, Guinea-Bissau, Haiti, Laos, Lebanon, Luxembourg, Former Yugoslav Republic of Macedonia, Madagascar, Mali, Mauritania, Mauritius, Moldova, Monaco, Morocco, New Brunswick (Canada), Niger, Quebec (Canada), Romania, Rwanda, Saint Lucia, Sao Tome and Principe, Senegal, Seychelles, Switzerland, Togo, Tunisia, Vanuatu, Vietnam *observers*—(5) Czech Republic, Lithuania, Poland, Slovakia, Slovenia

Appendix B: International Organizations and Groups *(continued)*

Agency for the Prohibition of Nuclear Weapons in Latin America and the Caribbean (OPANAL) *note*—acronym from Organismo para la Proscripcion de las Armas Nucleares en la America Latina y el Caribe (OPANAL) *established*—14 February 1967 under the Treaty of Tlatelolco *effective*—25 April 1969 on the 11th ratification of the treaty *aim*—to encourage the peaceful uses of atomic energy and prohibit nuclear weapons	*members*—(33) Antigua and Barbuda, Argentina, The Bahamas, Barbados, Belize, Bolivia, Brazil, Chile, Colombia, Costa Rica, Cuba, Dominica, Dominican Republic, Ecuador, El Salvador, Grenada, Guatemala, Guyana, Haiti, Honduras, Jamaica, Mexico, Nicaragua, Panama, Paraguay, Peru, Saint Kitts and Nevis, Saint Lucia, Saint Vincent and the Grenadines, Suriname, Trinidad and Tobago, Uruguay, Venezuela
Andean Community of Nations (CAN) *note*—formerly known as the Andean Group (AG), the Andean Parliament, and most recently as the Andean Common Market (Ancom) *established*—26 May 1969; present name established 1 October 1992 *effective*—16 October 1969 *aim*—to promote harmonious development through economic integration	*members*—(5) Bolivia, Colombia, Ecuador, Peru, Venezuela
Arab Bank for Economic Development in Africa (ABEDA) *note*—also known as Banque Arabe de Developpement Economique en Afrique (BADEA) *established*—18 February 1974 *effective*—16 September 1974 *aim*—to promote economic development	*members*—(17 plus the Palestine Liberation Organization) Algeria, Bahrain, Egypt, Iraq, Jordan, Kuwait, Lebanon, Libya, Mauritania, Morocco, Oman, Qatar, Saudi Arabia, Sudan, Syria, Tunisia, UAE, Palestine Liberation Organization; note—these are all the members of the Arab League excluding Comoros, Djibouti, Somalia, Yemen
Arab Cooperation Council (ACC) *established*—16 February 1989 *aim*—to promote economic cooperation and integration, possibly leading to an Arab Common Market	*members*—(4) Egypt, Iraq, Jordan, Yemen; note—the ACC has remained inactive since the Gulf crisis
Arab Fund for Economic and Social Development (AFESD) *established*—16 May 1968 *aim*—to promote economic and social development	*members*—(20 plus the Palestine Liberation Organization) Algeria, Bahrain, Djibouti, Egypt, Iraq (suspended 1993), Jordan, Kuwait, Lebanon, Libya, Mauritania, Morocco, Oman, Qatar, Saudi Arabia, Somalia (suspended 1993), Sudan, Syria, Tunisia, UAE, Yemen, Palestine Liberation Organization
Arab Maghreb Union (AMU) *established*—17 February 1989 *aim*—to promote cooperation and integration among the Arab states of northern Africa	*members*—(5) Algeria, Libya, Mauritania, Morocco, Tunisia
Arab Monetary Fund (AMF) *established*—27 April 1976 *effective*—2 February 1977 *aim*—to promote Arab cooperation, development, and integration in monetary and economic affairs	*members*—(21 plus the Palestine Liberation Organization) Algeria, Bahrain, Comoros, Djibouti, Egypt, Iraq, Jordan, Kuwait, Lebanon, Libya, Mauritania, Morocco, Oman, Qatar, Saudi Arabia, Somalia, Sudan, Syria, Tunisia, UAE, Yemen, Palestine Liberation Organization

Appendix B: International Organizations and Groups *(continued)*

Asia-Pacific Economic Cooperation (APEC)

established—7 November 1989
aim—to promote trade and investment in the Pacific basin

members—(21) Australia, Brunei, Canada, Chile, China, Hong Kong, Indonesia, Japan, South Korea, Malaysia, Mexico, NZ, Papua New Guinea, Peru, Philippines, Russia, Singapore, Taiwan, Thailand, US, Vietnam
observers—(3) Association of Southeast Asian Nations, Pacific Economic Cooperation Council, Pacific Islands Forum

---

Asian Development Bank (AsDB)

established—19 December 1966
aim—to promote regional economic cooperation

regional members—(44) Afghanistan, Australia, Azerbaijan, Bangladesh, Bhutan, Burma, Cambodia, China, Cook Islands, East Timor, Fiji, Hong Kong, India, Indonesia, Japan, Kazakhstan, Kiribati, South Korea, Kyrgyzstan, Laos, Malaysia, Maldives, Marshall Islands, Federated States of Micronesia, Mongolia, Nauru, Nepal, NZ, Pakistan, Papua New Guinea, Philippines, Samoa, Singapore, Solomon Islands, Sri Lanka, Taiwan, Tajikistan, Thailand, Tonga, Turkmenistan, Tuvalu, Uzbekistan, Vanuatu, Vietnam
nonregional members—(18) Austria, Belgium, Canada, Denmark, Finland, France, Germany, Italy, Luxembourg, Netherlands, Norway, Portugal, Spain, Sweden, Switzerland, Turkey, UK, US

Association of Southeast Asian Nations (ASEAN)

established—8 August 1967
aim—to encourage regional economic, social, and cultural cooperation among the countries of Southeast Asia

members—(10) Brunei, Burma, Cambodia, Indonesia, Laos, Malaysia, Philippines, Singapore, Thailand, Vietnam
dialogue partners—(11) Australia, Canada, China, EU, India, Japan, South Korea, NZ, Russia, US, UNDP

ASEAN Regional Forum (ARF)

established—NA 1994
aim—to foster constructive dialogue and consultation on political and security issues of common interest and concern

members—(23) Australia, Brunei, Burma, Cambodia, Canada, China, EU, India, Indonesia, Japan, North Korea, South Korea, Laos, Malaysia, Mongolia, NZ, Papua New Guinea, Philippines, Russia, Singapore, Thailand, US, Vietnam

---

Australia Group

established—NA June 1985
aim—to consult on and coordinate export controls related to chemical and biological weapons

members—(34) Argentina, Australia, Austria, Belgium, Bulgaria, Canada, Cyprus, Czech Republic, Denmark, European Commission, Finland, France, Germany, Greece, Hungary, Iceland, Ireland, Italy, Japan, South Korea, Luxembourg, Netherlands, NZ, Norway, Poland, Portugal, Romania, Slovakia, Spain, Sweden, Switzerland, Turkey, UK, US

Australia-New Zealand-United States Security Treaty (ANZUS)

established—1 September 1951
effective—29 April 1952
aim—to implement a trilateral mutual security agreement, although the US suspended security obligations to NZ on 11 August 1986; Australia and the US continue to hold annual meetings

members—(3) Australia, NZ, US

Bank for International Settlements (BIS)

established—20 January 1930
effective—17 March 1930
aim—to promote cooperation among central banks in international financial settlements

members—(55) Algeria, Argentina, Australia, Austria, Belgium, Bosnia and Herzegovina, Brazil, Bulgaria, Canada, Chile, China, Croatia, Czech Republic, Denmark, Estonia, European Central Bank, Finland, France, Germany, Greece, Hong Kong, Hungary, Iceland, India, Indonesia, Ireland, Israel, Italy, Japan, South Korea, Latvia, Lithuania, The Former Yugoslav Republic of Macedonia, Malaysia, Mexico, Netherlands, NZ, Norway, Philippines, Poland, Portugal, Romania, Russia, Saudi Arabia, Serbia and Montenegro, Singapore, Slovakia, Slovenia, South Africa, Spain, Sweden, Switzerland, Thailand, Turkey, UK, US; note—Serbia and Montenegro have separate central banks; their links with BIS are currently under review

---

Benelux Economic Union (Benelux)

note—acronym from Belgium, Netherlands, and Luxembourg
established—3 February 1958
effective—1 November 1960
aim—to develop closer economic cooperation and integration

members—(3) Belgium, Luxembourg, Netherlands

Appendix B: International Organizations and Groups *(continued)*

Big Seven	*members*—(7) Big Six (Canada, France, Germany, Italy, Japan, UK) plus the US
note—membership is the same as the Group of 7 *established*—NA 1975 *aim*—to discuss and coordinate major economic policies	
Big Six	*members*—(6) Canada, France, Germany, Italy, Japan, UK
note—not to be confused with the Group of 6 *established*—NA 1967 *aim*—to foster economic cooperation	
Black Sea Economic Cooperation Zone (BSEC) *established*—25 June 1992 *aim*—to enhance regional stability through economic cooperation	*members*—(11) Albania, Armenia, Azerbaijan, Bulgaria, Georgia, Greece, Moldova, Romania, Russia, Turkey, Ukraine *observers*—(9) Austria, Egypt, France, Germany, Israel, Italy, Poland, Slovakia, Tunisia
Caribbean Community and Common Market (Caricom) *established*—4 July 1973 *effective*—1 August 1973 *aim*—to promote economic integration and development, especially among the less developed countries	*members*—(15) Antigua and Barbuda, The Bahamas, Barbados, Belize, Dominica, Grenada, Guyana, Haiti, Jamaica, Montserrat, Saint Kitts and Nevis, Saint Lucia, Saint Vincent and the Grenadines, Suriname, Trinidad and Tobago *associate members*—(4) Anguilla, Bermuda, British Virgin Islands, Cayman Islands, Turks and Caicos Islands *observers*—(8) Aruba, Colombia, Dominican Republic, Mexico, Netherlands Antilles, Puerto Rico, Venezuela
Caribbean Development Bank (CDB) *established*—18 October 1969 *effective*—26 January 1970 *aim*—to promote economic development and cooperation	*regional members*—(20) Anguilla, Antigua and Barbuda, The Bahamas, Barbados, Belize, British Virgin Islands, Cayman Islands, Colombia, Dominica, Grenada, Guyana, Jamaica, Mexico, Montserrat, Saint Kitts and Nevis, Saint Lucia, Saint Vincent and the Grenadines, Trinidad and Tobago, Turks and Caicos Islands, Venezuela *nonregional members*—(5) Canada, China, Germany, Italy, UK
Central African Customs and Economic Union (UDEAC)	see Monetary and Economic Community of Central Africa (CEMAC)
Central African States Development Bank (BDEAC) *note*—acronym from Banque de Developpement des Etats de l'Afrique Centrale *established*—3 December 1975 *aim*—to provide loans for economic development	*members*—(11) African Development Bank (AfDB), Cameroon, Central African States Bank (BEAC), Central African Republic, Chad, Republic of the Congo, Equatorial Guinea, France, Gabon, Germany, Kuwait
Central American Bank for Economic Integration (BCIE) *note*—acronym from Banco Centroamericano de Integracion Economico *established*—13 December 1960 signature of Articles of Agreement; 31 May 1961 began operations *aim*—to promote economic integration and development	*members*—(5) Costa Rica, El Salvador, Guatemala, Honduras, Nicaragua *nonregional members*—(4) Argentina, Colombia, Mexico, Taiwan

Appendix B: International Organizations and Groups *(continued)*

Central American Common Market (CACM) *established*—13 December 1960, collapsed in 1969, reinstated in 1991 *aim*—to promote establishment of a Central American Common Market	*members*—(5) Costa Rica, El Salvador, Guatemala, Honduras, Nicaragua; *note*—Panama, although not a member, pursues full regional cooperation
Central European Initiative (CEI) *note*—evolved from the Quadrilateral Initiative and the Hexagonal Initiative *established*—11 November 1989 as the Quadrilateral Initiative, 27 July 1991 became the Hexagonal Initiative, NA July 1992 its present name was adopted *aim*—to form an economic and political cooperation group for the region between the Adriatic and the Baltic Seas	*members*—(17) Albania, Austria, Belarus, Bosnia and Herzegovina, Bulgaria, Croatia, Czech Republic, Hungary, Italy, The Former Yugoslav Republic of Macedonia, Moldova, Poland, Romania, Serbia and Montenegro, Slovakia, Slovenia, Ukraine
centrally planned economies	a term applied mainly to the traditionally Communist states that looked to the former USSR for leadership; most are now evolving toward more democratic and market-oriented systems; also known formerly as the Second World or as the Communist countries; through the 1980s, this group included Albania, Bulgaria, Cambodia, China, Cuba, Czechoslovakia, GDR, Hungary, North Korea, Laos, Mongolia, Poland, Romania, Serbia and Montenegro, USSR, Vietnam
Colombo Plan (CP) *established*—NA May 1950 proposal was adopted; 1 July 1951 commenced full operations *aim*—to promote economic and social development in Asia and the Pacific	*members*—(25) Afghanistan, Australia, Bangladesh, Bhutan, Burma, Cambodia, Fiji, India, Indonesia, Iran, Japan, South Korea, Laos, Malaysia, Maldives, Mongolia, Nepal, NZ, Pakistan, Papua New Guinea, Philippines, Singapore, Sri Lanka, Thailand, US, Vietnam
Commonwealth (C) *note*—also known as Commonwealth of Nations *established*—31 December 1931 *aim*—to foster multinational cooperation and assistance, as a voluntary association that evolved from the British Empire	*members*—(53) Antigua and Barbuda, Australia, The Bahamas, Bangladesh, Barbados, Belize, Botswana, Brunei, Cameroon, Canada, Cyprus, Dominica, Fiji, The Gambia, Ghana, Grenada, Guyana, India, Jamaica, Kenya, Kiribati, Lesotho, Malawi, Malaysia, Maldives, Malta, Mauritius, Mozambique, Namibia, Nauru, NZ, Nigeria, Pakistan (suspended), Papua New Guinea, Saint Kitts and Nevis, Saint Lucia, Saint Vincent and the Grenadines, Samoa, Seychelles, Sierra Leone, Singapore, Solomon Islands, South Africa, Sri Lanka, Swaziland, Tanzania, Tonga, Trinidad and Tobago, Tuvalu, Uganda, UK, Vanuatu, Zambia; *note*—on 7 December 2003 Zimbabwe withdrew its membership from the Commonwealth
Commonwealth of Independent States (CIS) *established*—8 December 1991 *effective*—21 December 1991 *aim*—to coordinate intercommonwealth relations and to provide a mechanism for the orderly dissolution of the USSR	*members*—(12) Armenia, Azerbaijan, Belarus, Georgia, Kazakhstan, Kyrgyzstan, Moldova, Russia, Tajikistan, Turkmenistan, Ukraine, Uzbekistan
Communist countries	traditionally the Marxist-Leninist states with authoritarian governments and command economies based on the Soviet model; most of the original and the successor states are no longer Communist; see centrally planned economies
Coordinating Committee on Export Controls (COCOM)	established in 1949 to control the export of strategic products and technical data from member countries to proscribed destinations; members were Australia, Belgium, Canada, Denmark, France, Germany, Greece, Italy, Japan, Luxembourg, Netherlands, Norway, Portugal, Spain, Turkey, UK, US; abolished 31 March 1994; COCOM members established a new organization, the Wassenaar Arrangement, with expanded membership on 12 July 1996 that focuses on nonproliferation export controls as opposed to East-West control of advanced technology

Appendix B: International Organizations and Groups *(continued)*

Council for Mutual Economic Assistance (CEMA) *note*—also known as CMEA or Comecon	established 25 January 1949 to promote the development of socialist economies and abolished 1 January 1991; members included Afghanistan (observer), Albania (had not participated since 1961 break with USSR), Angola (observer), Bulgaria, Cuba, Czechoslovakia, Ethiopia (observer), GDR, Hungary, Laos (observer), Mongolia, Mozambique (observer), Nicaragua (observer), Poland, Romania, USSR, Vietnam, Yemen (observer), Yugoslavia (associate)
Council of Arab Economic Unity (CAEU) *established*—3 June 1957 *effective*—30 May 1964 *aim*—to promote economic integration among Arab nations	*members*—(11 plus the Palestine Liberation Organization) Egypt, Iraq, Jordan, Kuwait, Libya, Mauritania, Somalia, Sudan, Syria, UAE, Yemen, Palestine Liberation Organization
Council of Europe (CE) *established*—5 May 1949 *effective*—3 August 1949 *aim*—to promote increased unity and quality of life in Europe	*members*—(45) Albania, Andorra, Armenia, Austria, Azerbaijan, Belgium, Bosnia and Herzegovina, Bulgaria, Croatia, Cyprus, Czech Republic, Denmark, Estonia, Finland, France, Georgia, Germany, Greece, Hungary, Iceland, Ireland, Italy, Latvia, Liechtenstein, Lithuania, Luxembourg, The Former Yugoslav Republic of Macedonia, Malta, Moldova, Netherlands, Norway, Poland, Portugal, Romania, Russia, San Marino, Serbia and Montenegro, Slovakia, Slovenia, Spain, Sweden, Switzerland, Turkey, Ukraine, UK *observers*—(6) Canada, Holy See, Israel, Japan, Mexico, US
Council of the Baltic Sea States (CBSS) *established*—6 March 1992 *aim*—to promote cooperation among the Baltic Sea states in the areas of aid to new democratic institutions, economic development, humanitarian aid, energy and the environment, cultural programs and education, and transportation and communication	*members*—(12) Denmark, Estonia, EC, Finland, Germany, Iceland, Latvia, Lithuania, Norway, Poland, Russia, Sweden
Council of the Entente (Entente) *established*—29 May 1959 *aim*—to promote economic, social, and political coordination	*members*—(5) Benin, Burkina Faso, Cote d'Ivoire, Niger, Togo
countries in transition	a term used by the International Monetary Fund (IMF) for the middle group in its hierarchy of advanced economies, countries in transition, and developing countries; IMF statistics include the following 28 countries in transition: Albania, Armenia, Azerbaijan, Belarus, Bosnia and Herzegovina, Bulgaria, Croatia, Czech Republic, Estonia, Georgia, Hungary, Kazakhstan, Kyrgyzstan, Latvia, Lithuania, The Former Yugoslav Republic of Macedonia, Moldova, Mongolia, Poland, Romania, Russia, Serbia and Montenegro, Slovakia, Slovenia, Tajikistan, Turkmenistan, Ukraine, Uzbekistan; note—this group is identical to the group traditionally referred to as the "former USSR/Eastern Europe" except for the addition of Mongolia
Customs Cooperation Council (CCC)	*note*—see World Customs Organization (WCO)
developed countries (DCs)	the top group in the hierarchy of developed countries (DCs), former USSR/Eastern Europe (former USSR/EE), and less developed countries (LDCs); includes the market-oriented economies of the mainly democratic nations in the Organization for Economic Cooperation and Development (OECD), Bermuda, Israel, South Africa, and the European ministates; also known as the First World, high-income countries, the North, industrial countries; generally have a per capita GDP in excess of $10,000 although four OECD countries and South Africa have figures well under $10,000 and two of the excluded OPEC countries have figures of more than $10,000; the 34 DCs are: Andorra, Australia, Austria, Belgium, Bermuda, Canada, Denmark, Faroe Islands, Finland, France, Germany, Greece, Holy See, Iceland, Ireland, Israel, Italy, Japan, Liechtenstein, Luxembourg, Malta, Monaco, Netherlands, NZ, Norway, Portugal, San Marino, South Africa, Spain, Sweden, Switzerland, Turkey, UK, US; note—similar to the new International Monetary Fund (IMF) term "advanced economies" that adds Hong Kong, South Korea, Singapore, and Taiwan but drops Malta, Mexico, South Africa, and Turkey

Appendix B: International Organizations and Groups *(continued)*

developing countries	a term used by the International Monetary Fund (IMF) for the bottom group in its hierarchy of advanced economies, countries in transition, and developing countries; IMF statistics include the following 126 developing countries: Afghanistan, Algeria, Angola, Antigua and Barbuda, Argentina, Aruba, The Bahamas, Bahrain, Bangladesh, Barbados, Belize, Benin, Bhutan, Bolivia, Botswana, Brazil, Burkina Faso, Burma, Burundi, Cambodia, Cameroon, Cape Verde, Central African Republic, Chad, Chile, China, Colombia, Comoros, Democratic Republic of the Congo, Republic of the Congo, Costa Rica, Cote d'Ivoire, Cyprus, Djibouti, Dominica, Dominican Republic, Ecuador, Egypt, El Salvador, Equatorial Guinea, Ethiopia, Fiji, Gabon, The Gambia, Ghana, Grenada, Guatemala, Guinea, Guinea-Bissau, Guyana, Haiti, Honduras, India, Indonesia, Iran, Iraq, Jamaica, Jordan, Kenya, Kiribati, Kuwait, Laos, Lebanon, Lesotho, Liberia, Libya, Madagascar, Malawi, Malaysia, Maldives, Mali, Malta, Marshall Islands, Mauritania, Mauritius, Mexico, Federated States of Micronesia, Morocco, Mozambique, Namibia, Nepal, Netherlands Antilles, Nicaragua, Niger, Nigeria, Oman, Pakistan, Panama, Papua New Guinea, Paraguay, Peru, Philippines, Qatar, Rwanda, Saint Kitts and Nevis, Saint Lucia, Saint Vincent and the Grenadines, Samoa, Sao Tome and Principe, Saudi Arabia, Senegal, Seychelles, Sierra Leone, Solomon Islands, Somalia, South Africa, Sri Lanka, Sudan, Suriname, Swaziland, Syria, Tanzania, Thailand, Togo, Trinidad and Tobago, Tunisia, Turkey, UAE, Uganda, Uruguay, Vanuatu, Venezuela, Vietnam, Yemen, Zambia, Zimbabwe; note—this category would presumably also cover the following 46 other countries that are traditionally included in the more comprehensive group of "less developed countries": American Samoa, Anguilla, British Virgin Islands, Brunei, Cayman Islands, Christmas Island, Cocos Islands, Cook Islands, Cuba, Eritrea, Falkland Islands, French Guiana, French Polynesia, Gaza Strip, Gibraltar, Greenland, Grenada, Guadeloupe, Guam, Guernsey, Jersey, North Korea, Macau, Isle of Man, Martinique, Mayotte, Montserrat, Nauru, New Caledonia, Niue, Norfolk Island, Northern Mariana Islands, Palau, Pitcairn Islands, Puerto Rico, Reunion, Saint Helena, Saint Pierre and Miquelon, Tokelau, Tonga, Turks and Caicos Islands, Tuvalu, Virgin Islands, Wallis and Futuna, West Bank, Western Sahara
East African Development Bank (EADB) *established*—6 June 1967 *effective*—1 December 1967 *aim*—to promote economic development	*members*—(3) Kenya, Tanzania, Uganda
Economic and Social Council (ECOSOC) *established*—26 June 1945 *effective*—24 October 1945 *aim*—to coordinate the economic and social work of the UN; includes five regional commissions (Economic Commission for Africa, Economic Commission for Europe, Economic Commission for Latin America and the Caribbean, Economic and Social Commission for Asia and the Pacific, Economic and Social Commission for Western Asia) and nine functional commissions (Commission for Social Development, Commission on Human Rights, Commission on Narcotic Drugs, Commission on the Status of Women, Commission on Population and Development, Statistical Commission, Commission on Science and Technology for Development, Commission on Sustainable Development, and Commission on Crime Prevention and Criminal Justice)	*members*—(54) selected on a rotating basis from all regions

Economic Community of the Great Lakes Countries (CEPGL) *note*—acronym from Communaute Economique des Pays des Grands Lacs *established*—20 September 1976 *aim*—to promote regional economic cooperation and integration	*members*—(3) Burundi, Democratic Republic of the Congo, Rwanda
Economic Community of West African States (ECOWAS) *established*—28 May 1975 *aim*—to promote regional economic cooperation	*members*—(16) Benin, Burkina Faso, Cape Verde, Cote d'Ivoire, The Gambia, Ghana, Guinea, Guinea-Bissau, Liberia, Mali, Mauritania, Niger, Nigeria, Senegal, Sierra Leone, Togo
Economic Cooperation Organization (ECO) *established*—27-29 January 1985 *aim*—to promote regional cooperation in trade, transportation, communications, tourism, cultural affairs, and economic development	*members*—(10) Afghanistan, Azerbaijan, Iran, Kazakhstan, Kyrgyzstan, Pakistan, Tajikistan, Turkey, Turkmenistan, Uzbekistan *associate member*—(1) "Turkish Republic of Northern Cyprus"
Economic and Monetary Union (EMU) *note*—an integral part of the European Union; also known as the European Economic and Monetary Union *proposed*—1-2 December 1969 at summit conference of heads of government; signed—7 February 1992—Maastricht Treaty *aim*—to promote a single market by creating a single currency, the euro; timetable—2 May 1998: European exchange rates fixed for 1 January 1999; 1 January 1999: all banks and stock exchanges begin using euros; 1 January 2002: the euro goes into circulation; 1 July 2002 local currencies no longer accepted	*members*—(12) Austria, Belgium, Finland, France, Germany, Greece, Ireland, Italy, Luxembourg, Netherlands, Portugal, Spain; note—Denmark, Sweden, and UK decided not to join
Euro-Atlantic Partnership Council (EAPC) *note*—began as the North Atlantic Cooperation Council (NACC); an extension of NATO *established*—8 November 1991 *effective*—20 December 1991 *aim*—to discuss cooperation on mutual political and security issues	*members*—(46) Albania, Armenia, Austria, Azerbaijan, Belarus, Belgium, Bulgaria, Canada, Croatia, Czech Republic, Denmark, Estonia, Finland, France, Georgia, Germany, Greece, Hungary, Iceland, Ireland, Italy, Kazakhstan, Kyrgyzstan, Latvia, Lithuania, Luxembourg, The Former Yugoslav Republic of Macedonia, Moldova, Netherlands, Norway, Poland, Portugal, Romania, Russia, Slovakia, Slovenia, Spain, Sweden, Switzerland, Tajikistan, Turkey, Turkmenistan, Ukraine, UK, US, Uzbekistan
European Bank for Reconstruction and Development (EBRD) *established*—8-9 January 1990 (proposals made); 15 April 1991 (bank inaugurated) *aim*—to facilitate the transition of seven centrally planned economies in Europe (Bulgaria, former Czechoslovakia, Hungary, Poland, Romania, former USSR, and former Yugoslavia) to market economies by committing 60% of its loans to privatization	*members*—(62) Albania, Armenia, Australia, Austria, Azerbaijan, Belarus, Belgium, Bosnia and Herzegovina, Bulgaria, Canada, Croatia, Cyprus, Czech Republic, Denmark, Egypt, EU, European Investment Bank (EIB), Estonia, Finland, France, Georgia, Germany, Greece, Hungary, Iceland, Ireland, Israel, Italy, Japan, Kazakhstan, South Korea, Kyrgyzstan, Latvia, Liechtenstein, Lithuania, Luxembourg, The Former Yugoslav Republic of Macedonia, Malta, Mexico, Moldova, Mongolia, Morocco, Netherlands, NZ, Norway, Poland, Portugal, Romania, Russia, Serbia and Montenegro, Slovakia, Slovenia, Spain, Sweden, Switzerland, Tajikistan, Turkey, Turkmenistan, Ukraine, UK, US, Uzbekistan

Appendix B: International Organizations and Groups *(continued)*

European Community (or European Communities, EC)	was established 8 April 1965 to integrate the European Atomic Energy Community (Euratom), the European Coal and Steel Community (ESC), the European Economic Community (EEC or Common Market), and to establish a completely integrated common market and an eventual federation of Europe; merged into the European Union (EU) on 7 February 1992; member states at the time of merger were Belgium, Denmark, France, Germany, Greece, Ireland, Italy, Luxembourg, Netherlands, Portugal, Spain, UK
European Free Trade Association (EFTA) *established*—4 January 1960 *effective*—3 May 1960 *aim*—to promote expansion of free trade	*members*—(4) Iceland, Liechtenstein, Norway, Switzerland
European Investment Bank (EIB) *established*—25 March 1957 *effective*—1 January 1958 *aim*—to promote economic development of the EU and its predecessors, the EEC and the EC	*members*—(15) Austria, Belgium, Denmark, Finland, France, Germany, Greece, Ireland, Italy, Luxembourg, Netherlands, Portugal, Spain, Sweden, UK
European Organization for Nuclear Research (CERN) *note*—acronym retained from the predecessor organization Conseil Europeenne pour la Recherche Nucleaire *established*—1 July 1953 *effective*—29 September 1954 *aim*—to foster nuclear research for peaceful purposes only	*members*—(20) Austria, Belgium, Bulgaria, Czech Republic, Denmark, Finland, France, Germany, Greece, Hungary, Italy, Netherlands, Norway, Poland, Portugal, Slovakia, Spain, Sweden, Switzerland, UK *observers*—(7) European Commission, Israel, Japan, Russia, Turkey, United Nations Educational, Scientific, and Cultural Organization (UNESCO), US
European Space Agency (ESA) *established*—31 May 1975 *aim*—to promote peaceful cooperation in space research and technology	*members*—(15) Austria, Belgium, Denmark, Finland, France, Germany, Ireland, Italy, Netherlands, Norway, Portugal, Spain, Sweden, Switzerland, UK *cooperating states*—(2) Canada, Hungary
European Union (EU) *note*—evolved from the European Community (EC) *established*—7 February 1992 *effective*—1 November 1993 *aim*—to coordinate policy among the 15 members in three fields: economics, building on the European Economic Community's (EEC) efforts to establish a common market and a common currency (the 'euro'); defense, within the concept of a Common Foreign and Security Policy (CFSP); and justice and home affairs, including immigration, drugs, terrorism, and improved living and working conditions	*members*—(15) Austria, Belgium, Denmark, Finland, France, Germany, Greece, Ireland, Italy, Luxembourg, Netherlands, Portugal, Spain, Sweden, UK *new member states*—(10) Cyprus, Czech Republic, Estonia, Hungary, Latvia, Lithuania, Malta, Poland, Slovakia, Slovenia; note—states will be admitted into the Union 1 May 2004 *membership applicants*—(3) Bulgaria, Romania, Turkey
First World	another term for countries with advanced, industrialized economies; this term is fading from use; see developed countries (DCs)

Appendix B: International Organizations and Groups *(continued)*

Food and Agriculture Organization (FAO) *established*—16 October 1945 *aim*—to raise living standards and increase availability of agricultural products; a UN specialized agency	*members*—(184) Afghanistan, Albania, Algeria, Angola, Antigua and Barbuda, Argentina, Armenia, Australia, Austria, Azerbaijan, The Bahamas, Bahrain, Bangladesh, Barbados, Belgium, Belize, Benin, Bhutan, Bolivia, Bosnia and Herzegovina, Botswana, Brazil, Bulgaria, Burkina Faso, Burma, Burundi, Cambodia, Cameroon, Canada, Cape Verde, Central African Republic, Chad, Chile, China, Colombia, Comoros, Democratic Republic of the Congo, Republic of the Congo, Cook Islands, Costa Rica, Cote d'Ivoire, Croatia, Cuba, Cyprus, Czech Republic, Denmark, Djibouti, Dominica, Dominican Republic, Ecuador, Egypt, El Salvador, Equatorial Guinea, Eritrea, Estonia, Ethiopia, EC, Fiji, Finland, France, Gabon, The Gambia, Georgia, Germany, Ghana, Greece, Grenada, Guatemala, Guinea, Guinea-Bissau, Guyana, Haiti, Honduras, Hungary, Iceland, India, Indonesia, Iran, Iraq, Ireland, Israel, Italy, Jamaica, Japan, Jordan, Kazakhstan, Kenya, Kiribati, North Korea, South Korea, Kuwait, Kyrgyzstan, Laos, Latvia, Lebanon, Lesotho, Liberia, Libya, Lithuania, Luxembourg, The Former Yugoslav Republic of Macedonia, Madagascar, Malawi, Malaysia, Maldives, Mali, Malta, Marshall Islands, Mauritania, Mauritius, Mexico, Moldova, Monaco, Mongolia, Morocco, Mozambique, Namibia, Nauru, Nepal, Netherlands, NZ, Nicaragua, Niger, Nigeria, Niue, Norway, Oman, Pakistan, Palau, Panama, Papua New Guinea, Paraguay, Peru, Philippines, Poland, Portugal, Qatar, Romania, Rwanda, Saint Kitts and Nevis, Saint Lucia, Saint Vincent and the Grenadines, Samoa, San Marino, Sao Tome and Principe, Saudi Arabia, Senegal, Serbia and Montenegro, Seychelles, Sierra Leone, Slovakia, Slovenia, Solomon Islands, Somalia, South Africa, Spain, Sri Lanka, Sudan, Suriname, Swaziland, Sweden, Switzerland, Syria, Tajikistan, Tanzania, Thailand, Togo, Tonga, Trinidad and Tobago, Tunisia, Turkey, Turkmenistan, Uganda, UAE, UK, US, Uruguay, Uzbekistan, Vanuatu, Venezuela, Vietnam, Yemen, Zambia, Zimbabwe
former Soviet Union (FSU)	former term often used to identify as a group the successor nations to the Soviet Union or USSR; this group of 15 countries consists of Armenia, Azerbaijan, Belarus, Estonia, Georgia, Kazakhstan, Kyrgyzstan, Latvia, Lithuania, Moldova, Russia, Tajikistan, Turkmenistan, Ukraine, Uzbekistan
former USSR/Eastern Europe (former USSR/EE)	the middle group in the hierarchy of developed countries (DCs), former USSR/Eastern Europe (former USSR/EE), and less developed countries (LDCs); these countries are in political and economic transition and may well be grouped differently in the near future; this group of 27 countries consists of Albania, Armenia, Azerbaijan, Belarus, Bosnia and Herzegovina, Bulgaria, Croatia, Czech Republic, Estonia, Georgia, Hungary, Kazakhstan, Kyrgyzstan, Latvia, Lithuania, The Former Yugoslav Republic of Macedonia, Moldova, Poland, Romania, Russia, Slovakia, Slovenia, Tajikistan, Turkmenistan, Ukraine, Uzbekistan, Yugoslavia; this group is identical to the IMF group "countries in transition" except for the IMF's inclusion of Mongolia
Four Dragons	the four small Asian less developed countries (LDCs) that have experienced unusually rapid economic growth; also known as the Four Tigers; this group consists of Hong Kong, South Korea, Singapore, Taiwan; these countries are included in the IMF's "advanced economies" group
Franc Zone (FZ) *note*—also known as Conference des Ministres des Finances des Pays de la Zone Franc *established*—NA 1964 *aim*—to form a monetary union among countries whose currencies are linked to the French franc	*members*—(14) Benin, Burkina Faso, Cameroon, Central African Republic, Chad, Republic of the Congo, Cote d'Ivoire, Equatorial Guinea, Gabon, Guinea-Bissau, Mali, Niger, Senegal, Togo; note—France's three overseas territories, French Polynesia, New Caledonia, and Wallis and Futuna, use the Comptoires Francais du Pacifique francs (XPF)
Front Line States (FLS)	established to achieve black majority rule in South Africa; has since gone out of existence; members included Angola, Botswana, Mozambique, Namibia, Tanzania, Zambia, Zimbabwe
General Agreement on Tariffs and Trade (GATT)	see the World Trade Organization (WTrO)
Group of 2 (G-2)	informal term that came into use about 1986; to facilitate bilateral economic cooperation between the two most powerful economic giants; members were Japan, US
Group of 3 (G-3) *established*—NA September 1990 *aim*—mechanism for policy coordination	*members*—(3) Colombia, Mexico, Venezuela
Group of 5 (G-5) *established*—22 September 1985 *aim*—to coordinate the economic policies of five major noncommunist economic powers	*members*—(5) France, Germany, Japan, UK, US

Appendix B: International Organizations and Groups *(continued)*

Group of 6 (G-6) *note*—also known as Groupe des Six Sur le Desarmement; not to be confused with the Big Six *established*—22 May 1984 *aim*—to achieve nuclear disarmament	*members*—(6) Argentina, Greece, India, Mexico, Sweden, Tanzania
Group of 7 (G-7) *note*—membership is the same as the Big Seven *established*—22 September 1985 *aim*—to facilitate economic cooperation among the seven major noncommunist economic powers	*members*—(7) Group of 5 (France, Germany, Japan, UK, US) plus Canada and Italy
Group of 8 (G-8) *established*—NA October 1975 *aim*—to facilitate economic cooperation among the developed countries (DCs) that participated in the Conference on International Economic Cooperation (CIEC), held in several sessions between NA December 1975 and 3 June 1977	*members*—(8) Canada, France, Germany, Italy, Japan, Russia, UK, US
Group of 9 (G-9) *established*—NA *aim*—to discuss matters of mutual interest on an informal basis	*members*—(9) Austria, Belgium, Bulgaria, Denmark, Finland, Hungary, Romania, Serbia and Montenegro, Sweden
Group of 10 (G-10) *note*—also known as the Paris Club; includes the wealthiest members of the IMF which provide most of the money to be loaned and act as the informal steering committee; name persists in spite of the addition of Switzerland on NA April 1984 *established*—NA October 1962 *aim*—to coordinate credit policy	*members*—(11) Belgium, Canada, France, Germany, Italy, Japan, Netherlands, Sweden, Switzerland, UK, US *nonstate participants*—(4) BIS, EC, IMF, OECD
Group of 11 (G-11) *note*—also known as the Cartagena Group	established in 21-22 June 1984, in Cartagena, Colombia; aim was to provide a forum for largest debtor nations in Latin America; members included Argentina, Bolivia, Brazil, Chile, Colombia, Dominican Republic, Ecuador, Mexico, Peru, Uruguay, Venezuela
Group of 15 (G-15) *note*—byproduct of the Nonaligned Movement *established*—NA September 1989 *aim*—to promote economic cooperation among developing nations; to act as the main political organ for the Nonaligned Movement	*members*—(17) Algeria, Argentina, Brazil, Chile, Egypt, India, Indonesia, Jamaica, Kenya, Malaysia, Mexico, Nigeria, Peru, Senegal, Sri Lanka, Venezuela, Zimbabwe
Group of 24 (G-24) *established*—1 August 1989 *aim*—to promote the interests of developing countries in Africa, Asia, and Latin America within the IMF	*members*—(24) Algeria, Argentina, Brazil, Colombia, Democratic Republic of the Congo, Cote d'Ivoire, Egypt, Ethiopia, Gabon, Ghana, Guatemala, India, Iran, Lebanon, Mexico, Nigeria, Pakistan, Peru, Philippines, South Africa, Sri Lanka, Syria, Trinidad and Tobago, Venezuela

Appendix B: International Organizations and Groups (continued)

Group of 77 (G-77)

established—15 June1964; NA October 1967 first ministerial meeting
aim—to promote economic cooperation among developing countries; name persists in spite of increased membership

members—(133 plus the Palestine Liberation Organization) Afghanistan, Algeria, Angola, Antigua and Barbuda, Argentina, The Bahamas, Bahrain, Bangladesh, Barbados, Belize, Benin, Bhutan, Bolivia, Bosnia and Herzegovina, Botswana, Brazil, Brunei, Burkina Faso, Burma, Burundi, Cambodia, Cameroon, Cape Verde, Central African Republic, Chad, Chile, China, Colombia, Comoros, Democratic Republic of the Congo, Republic of the Congo, Costa Rica, Cote d'Ivoire, Cuba, Cyprus, Djibouti, Dominica, Dominican Republic, Ecuador, Egypt, El Salvador, Equatorial Guinea, Eritrea, Ethiopia, Fiji, Gabon, The Gambia, Ghana, Grenada, Guatemala, Guinea, Guinea-Bissau, Guyana, Haiti, Honduras, India, Indonesia, Iran, Iraq, Jamaica, Jordan, Kenya, North Korea, Kuwait, Laos, Lebanon, Lesotho, Liberia, Libya, Madagascar, Malawi, Malaysia, Maldives, Mali, Malta, Marshall Islands, Mauritania, Mauritius, Federated States of Micronesia, Mongolia, Morocco, Mozambique, Namibia, Nepal, Nicaragua, Niger, Nigeria, Oman, Pakistan, Palau, Panama, Papua New Guinea, Paraguay, Peru, Philippines, Qatar, Romania, Rwanda, Saint Kitts and Nevis, Saint Lucia, Saint Vincent and the Grenadines, Samoa, Sao Tome and Principe, Saudi Arabia, Senegal, Serbia and Montenegro, Seychelles, Sierra Leone, Singapore, Solomon Islands, Somalia, South Africa, Sri Lanka, Sudan, Suriname, Swaziland, Syria, Tanzania, Thailand, Togo, Tonga, Trinidad and Tobago, Tunisia, Turkmenistan, Uganda, UAE, Uruguay, Vanuatu, Venezuela, Vietnam, Yemen, Zambia, Zimbabwe, Palestine Liberation Organization

Gulf Cooperation Council (GCC)

note—also known as the Cooperation Council for the Arab States of the Gulf
established—25 May 1981
aim—to promote regional cooperation in economic, social, political, and military affairs

members—(6) Bahrain, Kuwait, Oman, Qatar, Saudi Arabia, UAE

GUUAM

note—acronym standing for the member countries, Georgia, Uzbekistan, Ukraine, Azerbaijan, Moldova
established—7 June 2001
aim—commits the countries to cooperation and assistance in social and economic development, the strengthening and broadening of trade and economic relations, and the development and effective use of transport and communications, highways, and related infrastructure crossing the boundaries of the member states

members—(5) Azerbaijan, Georgia, Moldova, Ukraine, Uzbekistan

high-income countries

another term for the industrialized countries with high per capita GDPs; see developed countries (DCs)

Indian Ocean Commission (InOC)

established—21 December 1982
aim—to organize and promote regional cooperation in all sectors, especially economic

members—(5) Comoros, France (for Reunion), Madagascar, Mauritius, Seychelles

industrial countries

another term for the developed countries; see developed countries (DCs)

Inter-American Development Bank (IADB)

note—also known as Banco Interamericano de Desarrollo (BID)
established—8 April 1959
effective—30 December 1959
aim—to promote economic and social development in Latin America

members—(46) Argentina, Austria, The Bahamas, Barbados, Belgium, Belize, Bolivia, Brazil, Canada, Chile, Colombia, Costa Rica, Croatia, Denmark, Dominican Republic, Ecuador, El Salvador, Finland, France, Germany, Guatemala, Guyana, Haiti, Honduras, Israel, Italy, Jamaica, Japan, Mexico, Netherlands, Nicaragua, Norway, Panama, Paraguay, Peru, Portugal, Slovenia, Spain, Suriname, Sweden, Switzerland, Trinidad and Tobago, UK, US, Uruguay, Venezuela

Appendix B: International Organizations and Groups *(continued)*

Inter-Governmental Authority on Development (IGAD)

note—formerly known as Inter-Governmental Authority on Drought and Development (IGADD)
established—15-16 January 1986 as the Inter-Governmental Authority on Drought and Development; revitalized—21 March 1996 as the Inter-Governmental Authority on Development
aim—to promote a social, economic, and scientific community among its members

members—(7) Djibouti, Eritrea, Ethiopia, Kenya, Somalia, Sudan, Uganda

---

International Atomic Energy Agency (IAEA)

established—26 October 1956
effective—29 July 1957
aim—to promote peaceful uses of atomic energy

members—(137) Afghanistan, Albania, Algeria, Angola, Argentina, Armenia, Australia, Austria, Azerbaijan, Bangladesh, Belarus, Belgium, Benin, Bolivia, Bosnia and Herzegovina, Botswana, Brazil, Bulgaria, Burkina Faso, Burma, Cameroon, Canada, Central African Republic, Chile, China, Colombia, Democratic Republic of the Congo, Costa Rica, Cote d'Ivoire, Croatia, Cuba, Cyprus, Czech Republic, Denmark, Dominican Republic, Ecuador, Egypt, El Salvador, Eritrea, Estonia, Ethiopia, Finland, France, Gabon, Georgia, Germany, Ghana, Greece, Guatemala, Haiti, Holy See, Honduras, Hungary, Iceland, India, Indonesia, Iran, Iraq, Ireland, Israel, Italy, Jamaica, Japan, Jordan, Kazakhstan, Kenya, South Korea, Kuwait, Kyrgyzstan, Latvia, Lebanon, Liberia, Libya, Liechtenstein, Lithuania, Luxembourg, The Former Yugoslav Republic of Macedonia, Madagascar, Malaysia, Mali, Malta, Marshall Islands, Mauritius, Mexico, Moldova, Monaco, Mongolia, Morocco, Namibia, Netherlands, NZ, Nicaragua, Niger, Nigeria, Norway, Pakistan, Panama, Paraguay, Peru, Philippines, Poland, Portugal, Qatar, Romania, Russia, Saudi Arabia, Senegal, Serbia and Montenegro, Seychelles, Sierra Leone, Singapore, Slovakia, Slovenia, South Africa, Spain, Sri Lanka, Sudan, Sweden, Switzerland, Syria, Tajikistan, Tanzania, Thailand, Tunisia, Turkey, Uganda, Ukraine, UAE, UK, US, Uruguay, Uzbekistan, Venezuela, Vietnam, Yemen, Zambia, Zimbabwe

---

International Bank for Reconstruction and Development (IBRD)

note—also known as the World Bank
established—22 July 1944
effective—27 December 1945
aim—to provide economic development loans; a UN specialized agency

members—(184) Afghanistan, Albania, Algeria, Angola, Antigua and Barbuda, Argentina, Armenia, Australia, Austria, Azerbaijan, The Bahamas, Bahrain, Bangladesh, Barbados, Belarus, Belgium, Belize, Benin, Bhutan, Bolivia, Bosnia and Herzegovina, Botswana, Brazil, Brunei, Bulgaria, Burkina Faso, Burma, Burundi, Cambodia, Cameroon, Canada, Cape Verde, Central African Republic, Chad, Chile, China, Colombia, Comoros, Democratic Republic of the Congo, Republic of the Congo, Costa Rica, Cote d'Ivoire, Croatia, Cyprus, Czech Republic, Denmark, Djibouti, Dominica, Dominican Republic, East Timor, Ecuador, Egypt, El Salvador, Equatorial Guinea, Eritrea, Estonia, Ethiopia, Fiji, Finland, France, Gabon, The Gambia, Georgia, Germany, Ghana, Greece, Grenada, Guatemala, Guinea, Guinea-Bissau, Guyana, Haiti, Honduras, Hungary, Iceland, India, Indonesia, Iran, Iraq, Ireland, Israel, Italy, Jamaica, Japan, Jordan, Kazakhstan, Kenya, Kiribati, South Korea, Kuwait, Kyrgyzstan, Laos, Latvia, Lebanon, Lesotho, Liberia, Libya, Lithuania, Luxembourg, The Former Yugoslav Republic of Macedonia, Madagascar, Malawi, Malaysia, Maldives, Mali, Malta, Marshall Islands, Mauritania, Mauritius, Mexico, Federated States of Micronesia, Moldova, Mongolia, Morocco, Mozambique, Namibia, Nepal, Netherlands, NZ, Nicaragua, Niger, Nigeria, Norway, Oman, Pakistan, Palau, Panama, Papua New Guinea, Paraguay, Peru, Philippines, Poland, Portugal, Qatar, Romania, Russia, Rwanda, Saint Kitts and Nevis, Saint Lucia, Saint Vincent and the Grenadines, Samoa, San Marino, Sao Tome and Principe, Saudi Arabia, Senegal, Serbia and Montenegro, Seychelles, Sierra Leone, Singapore, Slovakia, Slovenia, Solomon Islands, Somalia, South Africa, Spain, Sri Lanka, Sudan, Suriname, Swaziland, Sweden, Switzerland, Syria, Tajikistan, Tanzania, Thailand, Togo, Tonga, Trinidad and Tobago, Tunisia, Turkey, Turkmenistan, Uganda, Ukraine, UAE, UK, US, Uruguay, Uzbekistan, Vanuatu, Venezuela, Vietnam, Yemen, Zambia, Zimbabwe

---

International Chamber of Commerce (ICC)

established—NA 1919
aim—to promote free trade and private enterprise and to represent business interests at national and international levels

members—(85 national committees) Algeria, Argentina, Australia, Austria, Bahrain, Bangladesh, Belgium, Brazil, Burkina Faso, Cameroon, Canada, Caribbean, Chile, China, Colombia, Costa Rica, Croatia, Cuba, Cyprus, Czech Republic, Denmark, Ecuador, Egypt, Finland, France, Georgia, Germany, Ghana, Greece, Hong Kong, Hungary, Iceland, India, Indonesia, Iran, Ireland, Israel, Italy, Japan, Jordan, South Korea, Kuwait, Lebanon, Lithuania, Luxembourg, Mexico, Monaco, Mongolia, Morocco, Nepal, Netherlands, NZ, Nigeria, Norway, Pakistan, Peru, Philippines, Poland, Portugal, Qatar, Romania, Russia, Saudi Arabia, Senegal, Serbia and Montenegro, Singapore, Slovakia, Slovenia, South Africa, Spain, Sri Lanka, Sweden, Switzerland, Syria, Taiwan, Tanzania, Thailand, Togo, Tunisia, Turkey, Ukraine, UK, US, Uruguay, Venezuela

---

Appendix B: International Organizations and Groups *(continued)*

International Civil Aviation Organization (ICAO)

established—7 December 1944
effective—4 April 1947
aim—to promote international cooperation in civil aviation; a UN specialized agency

members—(188) Afghanistan, Albania, Algeria, Andorra, Angola, Antigua and Barbuda, Argentina, Armenia, Australia, Austria, Azerbaijan, The Bahamas, Bahrain, Bangladesh, Barbados, Belarus, Belgium, Belize, Benin, Bhutan, Bolivia, Bosnia and Herzegovina, Botswana, Brazil, Brunei, Bulgaria, Burkina Faso, Burma, Burundi, Cambodia, Cameroon, Canada, Cape Verde, Central African Republic, Chad, Chile, China, Colombia, Comoros, Democratic Republic of the Congo, Republic of the Congo, Cook Islands, Costa Rica, Cote d'Ivoire, Croatia, Cuba, Cyprus, Czech Republic, Denmark, Djibouti, Dominican Republic, Ecuador, Egypt, El Salvador, Equatorial Guinea, Eritrea, Estonia, Ethiopia, Fiji, Finland, France, Gabon, The Gambia, Georgia, Germany, Ghana, Greece, Grenada, Guatemala, Guinea, Guinea-Bissau, Guyana, Haiti, Honduras, Hungary, Iceland, India, Indonesia, Iran, Iraq, Ireland, Israel, Italy, Jamaica, Japan, Jordan, Kazakhstan, Kenya, Kiribati, North Korea, South Korea, Kuwait, Kyrgyzstan, Laos, Latvia, Lebanon, Lesotho, Liberia, Libya, Lithuania, Luxembourg, The Former Yugoslav Republic of Macedonia, Madagascar, Malawi, Malaysia, Maldives, Mali, Malta, Marshall Islands, Mauritania, Mauritius, Mexico, Federated States of Micronesia, Moldova, Monaco, Mongolia, Morocco, Mozambique, Namibia, Nauru, Nepal, Netherlands, NZ, Nicaragua, Niger, Nigeria, Norway, Oman, Palau, Pakistan, Panama, Papua New Guinea, Paraguay, Peru, Philippines, Poland, Portugal, Qatar, Romania, Russia, Rwanda, Saint Kitts and Nevis, Saint Lucia, Saint Vincent and the Grenadines, Samoa, San Marino, Sao Tome and Principe, Saudi Arabia, Senegal, Serbia and Montenegro, Seychelles, Sierra Leone, Singapore, Slovakia, Slovenia, Solomon Islands, Somalia, South Africa, Spain, Sri Lanka, Sudan, Suriname, Swaziland, Sweden, Switzerland, Syria, Tajikistan, Tanzania, Thailand, Togo, Tonga, Trinidad and Tobago, Tunisia, Turkey, Turkmenistan, Uganda, Ukraine, UAE, UK, US, Uruguay, Uzbekistan, Vanuatu, Venezuela, Vietnam, Yemen, Zambia, Zimbabwe

International Civilian Support Mission in Haiti (MICAH)

established—17 December 1999
aim—to promote respect for human rights

members—(11) Argentina, Benin, Canada, France, India, Mali, Niger, Senegal, Togo, Tunisia, US

International Committee of the Red Cross (ICRC)

established—17 February 1863
aim—to provide humanitarian aid in wartime

members—(25 individuals) all Swiss nationals

International Confederation of Free Trade Unions (ICFTU)

established—NA December 1949
aim—to promote the trade union movement

members—(231 affiliated organizations in the following 153 countries plus the Palestine Liberation Organization) Albania, Algeria, Angola, Antigua and Barbuda, Argentina, Australia, Austria, Azerbaijan, The Bahamas, Bangladesh, Barbados, Belarus, Belgium, Belize, Benin, Bermuda, Botswana, Brazil, Bulgaria, Burkina Faso, Burundi, Cameroon, Canada, Cape Verde, Central African Republic, Chad, Chile, Colombia, Democratic Republic of the Congo, Republic of the Congo, Cook Islands, Costa Rica, Cote d'Ivoire, Croatia, Curacao, Cyprus, Czech Republic, Denmark, Djibouti, Dominica, Dominican Republic, Ecuador, El Salvador, Eritrea, Estonia, Falkland Islands, Fiji, Finland, France, French Polynesia, Gabon, The Gambia, Georgia, Germany, Ghana, Greece, Grenada, Guatemala, Guinea, Guinea-Bissau, Guyana, Holy See, Honduras, Hong Kong, Hungary, Iceland, India, Indonesia, Ireland, Israel, Italy, Jamaica, Japan, Jordan, Kenya, Kiribati, South Korea, Latvia, Lebanon, Liberia, Lithuania, Luxembourg, Madagascar, Malawi, Malaysia, Mali, Malta, Mauritania, Mauritius, Mexico, Moldova, Mongolia, Montserrat, Morocco, Mozambique, Namibia, Nepal, Netherlands, New Caledonia, NZ, Nicaragua, Niger, Nigeria, Norway, Pakistan, Panama, Papua New Guinea, Paraguay, Peru, Philippines, Poland, Portugal, Puerto Rico, Romania, Russia, Rwanda, Saint Helena, Saint Kitts and Nevis, Saint Lucia, Saint Vincent and the Grenadines, Samoa, San Marino, Sao Tome and Principe, Senegal, Serbia and Montenegro, Seychelles, Sierra Leone, Singapore, Slovakia, South Africa, Spain, Sri Lanka, Suriname, Swaziland, Sweden, Switzerland, Taiwan, Tanzania, Thailand, Togo, Tonga, Trinidad and Tobago, Tunisia, Turkey, Uganda, Ukraine, UK, US, Vanuatu, Venezuela, Yemen, Zambia, Zimbabwe, Palestine Liberation Organization

International Court of Justice (ICJ)

note—also known as the World Court
established—3 February 1946 superseded Permanent Court of International Justice
aim—primary judicial organ of the UN

members—(15 judges) elected by the UN General Assembly and Security Council to represent all principal legal systems

Appendix B: International Organizations and Groups *(continued)*

International Criminal Court (ICCt) *established*—11 April 2002 *aim*—to hold all individuals and countries accountable to international laws of conduct; to specify international standards of conduct; to provide an important mechanism for implementing these standards; to ensure that perpetrators are brought to justice	*members (countries that have ratified the treaty)*—(92) Afghanistan, Albania, Andorra, Antigua and Barbuda, Argentina, Australia, Austria, Barbados, Belgium, Belize, Benin, Bolivia, Bosnia and Herzegovina, Botswana, Brazil, Bulgaria, Cambodia, Canada, Central African Republic, Colombia, Costa Rica, Croatia, Cyprus, Democratic Republic of the Congo, Denmark, Djibouti, Dominica, East Timor, Ecuador, Estonia, Fiji, Finland, France, Gabon, The Gambia, Georgia, Germany, Ghana, Greece, Guinea, Honduras, Hungary, Iceland, Ireland, Italy, Jordan, South Korea, Latvia, Lesotho, Liechtenstein, Lithuania, Luxembourg, The Former Yugoslav Republic of Macedonia, Malawi, Mali, Malta, Marshall Islands, Mauritius, Mongolia, Namibia, Nauru, Netherlands, NZ, Niger, Nigeria, Norway, Panama, Paraguay, Peru, Poland, Portugal, Romania, Saint Vincent and the Grenadines, Samoa, San Marino, Senegal, Serbia and Montenegro, Sierra Leone, Slovakia, Slovenia, South Africa, Spain, Sweden, Switzerland, Tajikistan, Tanzania, Trinidad and Tobago, Uganda, UK, Uruguay, Venezuela, Zambia *signatory states (countries that have signed, but not ratified, the treaty)*—(51) Algeria, Angola, Armenia, The Bahamas, Bahrain, Bangladesh, Burkina Faso, Burundi, Cameroon, Cape Verde, Chad, Chile, Comoros, Republic of the Congo, Cote d'Ivoire, Czech Republic, Dominican Republic, Egypt, Eritrea, Guinea-Bissau, Guyana, Haiti, Iran, Israel, Jamaica, Kenya, Kuwait, Kyrgyzstan, Liberia, Madagascar, Mexico, Moldova, Monaco, Morocco, Mozambique, Oman, Philippines, Russia, Saint Lucia, Sao Tome and Principe, Seychelles, Solomon Islands, Sudan, Syria, Thailand, Ukraine, UAE, US, Uzbekistan, Yemen, Zimbabwe
International Criminal Police Organization (Interpol) *established*—NA September 1923 set up as the International Criminal Police Commission; 13 June 1956 constitution modified and present name adopted *aim*—to promote international cooperation among police authorities in fighting crime	*members*—(181) Afghanistan, Albania, Algeria, Andorra, Angola, Antigua and Barbuda, Argentina, Armenia, Aruba, Australia, Austria, Azerbaijan, The Bahamas, Bahrain, Bangladesh, Barbados, Belarus, Belgium, Belize, Benin, Bolivia, Bosnia and Herzegovina, Botswana, Brazil, Brunei, Bulgaria, Burkina Faso, Burma, Burundi, Cambodia, Cameroon, Canada, Cape Verde, Central African Republic, Chad, Chile, China, Colombia, Comoros, Democratic Republic of the Congo, Republic of the Congo, Costa Rica, Cote d'Ivoire, Croatia, Cuba, Cyprus, Czech Republic, Denmark, Djibouti, Dominica, Dominican Republic, East Timor, Ecuador, Egypt, El Salvador, Equatorial Guinea, Eritrea, Estonia, Ethiopia, Fiji, Finland, France, Gabon, The Gambia, Georgia, Germany, Ghana, Greece, Grenada, Guatemala, Guinea, Guinea-Bissau, Guyana, Haiti, Honduras, Hungary, Iceland, India, Indonesia, Iran, Iraq, Ireland, Israel, Italy, Jamaica, Japan, Jordan, Kazakhstan, Kenya, South Korea, Kuwait, Kyrgyzstan, Laos, Latvia, Lebanon, Lesotho, Liberia, Libya, Liechtenstein, Lithuania, Luxembourg, The Former Yugoslav Republic of Macedonia, Madagascar, Malawi, Malaysia, Maldives, Mali, Malta, Marshall Islands, Mauritania, Mauritius, Mexico, Moldova, Monaco, Mongolia, Morocco, Mozambique, Namibia, Nauru, Nepal, Netherlands, Netherlands Antilles, NZ, Nicaragua, Niger, Nigeria, Norway, Oman, Pakistan, Panama, Papua New Guinea, Paraguay, Peru, Philippines, Poland, Portugal, Qatar, Romania, Russia, Rwanda, Saint Kitts and Nevis, Saint Lucia, Saint Vincent and the Grenadines, Sao Tome and Principe, Saudi Arabia, Senegal, Serbia and Montenegro, Seychelles, Sierra Leone, Singapore, Slovakia, Slovenia, Somalia, South Africa, Spain, Sri Lanka, Sudan, Suriname, Swaziland, Sweden, Switzerland, Syria, Tanzania, Thailand, Togo, Tonga, Trinidad and Tobago, Tunisia, Turkey, Uganda, Ukraine, UAE, UK, US, Uruguay, Uzbekistan, Venezuela, Vietnam, Yemen, Zambia, Zimbabwe *subbureaus*—(14) American Samoa, Anguilla, Bermuda, British Virgin Islands, Cayman Islands, Gibraltar, Guam, Hong Kong, Macau, Montserrat, Northern Mariana Islands, Puerto Rico, Turks and Caicos Islands, Virgin Islands
International Development Association (IDA) *established*—26 January 1960 *effective*—24 September 1960 *aim*—to provide economic loans for low-income countries; UN specialized agency and IBRD affiliate	*members*—(165) *Part I*—(27 developed countries) Australia, Austria, Belgium, Canada, Denmark, EU, Finland, France, Germany, Iceland, Ireland, Italy, Japan, Kuwait, Luxembourg, Netherlands, NZ, Norway, Portugal, Russia, South Africa, Spain, Sweden, Switzerland, UAE, UK, US *Part II*—(138 less developed countries) Afghanistan, Albania, Algeria, Angola, Argentina, Armenia, Azerbaijan, Bangladesh, Barbados, Belize, Benin, Bhutan, Bolivia, Bosnia and Herzegovina, Botswana, Brazil, Burkina Faso, Burma, Burundi, Cambodia, Cameroon, Cape Verde, Central African Republic, Chad, Chile, China, Colombia, Comoros, Democratic Republic of the Congo, Republic of the Congo, Costa Rica, Cote d'Ivoire, Croatia, Cyprus, Czech Republic, Djibouti, Dominica, Dominican Republic, East Timor, Ecuador, Egypt, El Salvador, Equatorial Guinea, Eritrea, Ethiopia, Fiji, Gabon, The Gambia, Georgia, Ghana, Greece, Grenada, Guatemala, Guinea, Guinea-Bissau, Guyana, Haiti, Honduras, Hungary, India, Indonesia, Iran, Iraq, Israel, Jordan, Kazakhstan, Kenya, Kiribati, South Korea, Kyrgyzstan, Laos, Latvia, Lebanon, Lesotho, Liberia, Libya, The Former Yugoslav Republic of Macedonia, Madagascar, Malawi, Malaysia, Maldives, Mali, Marshall Islands, Mauritania, Mauritius, Mexico, Federated States of Micronesia, Moldova, Mongolia, Morocco, Mozambique, Nepal, Nicaragua, Niger, Nigeria, Oman, Pakistan, Palau, Panama, Papua New Guinea, Paraguay, Peru, Philippines, Poland, Rwanda, Saint Kitts and Nevis, Saint Lucia, Saint Vincent and the Grenadines, Samoa, Sao Tome and Principe, Saudi Arabia, Senegal, Serbia and Montenegro, Sierra Leone, Singapore, Slovakia, Slovenia, Solomon Islands, Somalia, Sri Lanka, Sudan, Swaziland, Syria, Tajikistan, Tanzania, Thailand, Togo, Tonga, Trinidad and Tobago, Tunisia, Turkey, Uganda, Uzbekistan, Vanuatu, Vietnam, Yemen, Zambia, Zimbabwe

Appendix B: International Organizations and Groups *(continued)*

International Energy Agency (IEA)

established—15 November 1974
aim—to promote cooperation on energy matters, especially emergency oil sharing and relations between oil consumers and oil producers; established by the OECD

members—(26) Australia, Austria, Belgium, Canada, Czech Republic, Denmark, Finland, France, Germany, Greece, Hungary, Ireland, Italy, Japan, South Korea, Luxembourg, Netherlands, NZ, Norway, Portugal, Spain, Sweden, Switzerland, Turkey, UK, US

International Federation of Red Cross and Red Crescent Societies (IFRCS)

note—formerly known as League of Red Cross and Red Crescent Societies (LORCS)
established—5 May 1919
aim—to organize, coordinate, and direct international relief actions; to promote humanitarian activities; to represent and encourage the development of National Societies; to bring help to victims of armed conflicts, refugees, and displaced people; to reduce the vulnerability of people through development programs

members—(185 plus the Palestine Liberation Organization) Afghanistan, Albania, Algeria, Andorra, Angola, Antigua and Barbuda, Argentina, Armenia, Australia, Austria, Azerbaijan, The Bahamas, Bahrain, Bangladesh, Barbados, Belarus, Belgium, Belize, Benin, Bolivia, Bosnia and Herzegovina, Botswana, Brazil, Brunei, Bulgaria, Burkina Faso, Burma, Burundi, Cambodia, Cameroon, Canada, Cape Verde, Central African Republic, Chad, Chile, China, Colombia, Comoros, Democratic Republic of the Congo, Republic of the Congo, Cook Islands, Costa Rica, Cote d'Ivoire, Croatia, Cuba, Czech Republic, Denmark, Djibouti, Dominica, Dominican Republic, East Timor, Ecuador, Egypt, El Salvador, Equatorial Guinea, Eritrea, Estonia, Ethiopia, Fiji, Finland, France, Gabon, The Gambia, Georgia, Germany, Ghana, Greece, Grenada, Guatemala, Guinea, Guinea-Bissau, Guyana, Haiti, Honduras, Hungary, Iceland, India, Indonesia, Iran, Iraq, Ireland, Italy, Jamaica, Japan, Jordan, Kazakhstan, Kenya, Kiribati, North Korea, South Korea, Kuwait, Kyrgyzstan, Laos, Latvia, Lebanon, Lesotho, Liberia, Libya, Liechtenstein, Lithuania, Luxembourg, The Former Yugoslav Republic of Macedonia, Madagascar, Malawi, Malaysia, Mali, Malta, Mauritania, Mauritius, Mexico, Federated States of Micronesia, Moldova, Monaco, Mongolia, Morocco, Mozambique, Namibia, Nepal, Netherlands, NZ, Nicaragua, Niger, Nigeria, Norway, Pakistan, Palau, Panama, Papua New Guinea, Paraguay, Peru, Philippines, Poland, Portugal, Qatar, Romania, Russia, Rwanda, Saint Kitts and Nevis, Saint Lucia, Saint Vincent and the Grenadines, Samoa, San Marino, Sao Tome and Principe, Saudi Arabia, Senegal, Serbia and Montenegro, Seychelles, Sierra Leone, Singapore, Slovakia, Slovenia, Solomon Islands, Somalia, South Africa, Spain, Sri Lanka, Sudan, Suriname, Swaziland, Sweden, Switzerland, Syria, Taiwan, Tajikistan, Tanzania, Thailand, Togo, Tonga, Trinidad and Tobago, Tunisia, Turkey, Turkmenistan, Uganda, Ukraine, UAE, UK, US, Uruguay, Uzbekistan, Vanuatu, Venezuela, Vietnam, Yemen, Zambia, Zimbabwe, the Palestine Liberation Organization
observers—(2) Israel, Tuvalu

International Finance Corporation (IFC)

established—25 May 1955
effective—24 July 1956
aim—to support private enterprise in international economic development; a UN specialized agency and IBRD affiliate

members—(175) Afghanistan, Albania, Algeria, Angola, Antigua and Barbuda, Argentina, Armenia, Australia, Austria, Azerbaijan, The Bahamas, Bahrain, Bangladesh, Barbados, Belarus, Belgium, Belize, Benin, Bolivia, Bosnia and Herzegovina, Botswana, Brazil, Bulgaria, Burkina Faso, Burma, Burundi, Cambodia, Cameroon, Canada, Cape Verde, Central African Republic, Chad, Chile, China, Colombia, Comoros, Democratic Republic of the Congo, Republic of the Congo, Costa Rica, Cote d'Ivoire, Croatia, Cyprus, Czech Republic, Denmark, Djibouti, Dominica, Dominican Republic, Ecuador, Egypt, El Salvador, Equatorial Guinea, Eritrea, Estonia, Ethiopia, Fiji, Finland, France, Gabon, The Gambia, Georgia, Germany, Ghana, Greece, Grenada, Guatemala, Guinea, Guinea-Bissau, Guyana, Haiti, Honduras, Hungary, Iceland, India, Indonesia, Iran, Iraq, Ireland, Israel, Italy, Jamaica, Japan, Jordan, Kazakhstan, Kenya, Kiribati, South Korea, Kuwait, Kyrgyzstan, Laos, Latvia, Lebanon, Lesotho, Liberia, Libya, Lithuania, Luxembourg, The Former Yugoslav Republic of Macedonia, Madagascar, Malawi, Malaysia, Maldives, Mali, Marshall Islands, Mauritania, Mauritius, Mexico, Federated States of Micronesia, Moldova, Mongolia, Morocco, Mozambique, Namibia, Nepal, Netherlands, NZ, Nicaragua, Niger, Nigeria, Norway, Oman, Pakistan, Palau, Panama, Papua New Guinea, Paraguay, Peru, Philippines, Poland, Portugal, Romania, Russia, Rwanda, Saint Kitts and Nevis, Saint Lucia, Samoa, Saudi Arabia, Senegal, Serbia and Montenegro, Seychelles, Sierra Leone, Singapore, Slovakia, Slovenia, Solomon Islands, Somalia, South Africa, Spain, Sri Lanka, Sudan, Swaziland, Sweden, Switzerland, Syria, Tajikistan, Tanzania, Thailand, Togo, Tonga, Trinidad and Tobago, Tunisia, Turkey, Turkmenistan, Uganda, Ukraine, UAE, UK, US, Uruguay, Uzbekistan, Vanuatu, Venezuela, Vietnam, Yemen, Zambia, Zimbabwe

Appendix B: International Organizations and Groups *(continued)*

International Fund for Agricultural Development (IFAD)

established—NA November 1974
aim—to promote agricultural development; a UN specialized agency

members—(163)
Category I—(23 industrialized aid contributors) Australia, Austria, Belgium, Canada, Denmark, Finland, France, Germany, Greece, Iceland, Ireland, Italy, Japan, Luxembourg, Netherlands, NZ, Norway, Portugal, Spain, Sweden, Switzerland, UK, US
Category II—(12 petroleum-exporting aid contributors) Algeria, Gabon, Indonesia, Iran, Iraq, Kuwait, Libya, Nigeria, Qatar, Saudi Arabia, UAE, Venezuela
Category III—(128 aid recipients) Afghanistan, Albania, Angola, Antigua and Barbuda, Argentina, Armenia, Azerbaijan, Bangladesh, Barbados, Belize, Benin, Bhutan, Bolivia, Bosnia and Herzegovina, Botswana, Brazil, Burkina Faso, Burma, Burundi, Cambodia, Cameroon, Cape Verde, Central African Republic, Chad, Chile, China, Colombia, Comoros, Democratic Republic of the Congo, Republic of the Congo, Cook Islands, Costa Rica, Cote d'Ivoire, Croatia, Cuba, Cyprus, Djibouti, Dominica, Dominican Republic, East Timor, Ecuador, Egypt, El Salvador, Equatorial Guinea, Eritrea, Ethiopia, Fiji, The Gambia, Georgia, Ghana, Grenada, Guatemala, Guinea, Guinea-Bissau, Guyana, Haiti, Honduras, India, Israel, Jamaica, Jordan, Kazakhstan, Kenya, North Korea, South Korea, Kyrgyzstan, Laos, Lebanon, Lesotho, Liberia, The Former Yugoslav Republic of Macedonia, Madagascar, Malawi, Malaysia, Maldives, Mali, Malta, Mauritania, Mauritius, Mexico, Moldova, Mongolia, Morocco, Mozambique, Namibia, Nepal, Nicaragua, Niger, Oman, Pakistan, Panama, Papua New Guinea, Paraguay, Peru, Philippines, Romania, Rwanda, Saint Kitts and Nevis, Saint Lucia, Saint Vincent and the Grenadines, Samoa, Sao Tome and Principe, Senegal, Serbia and Montenegro, Seychelles, Sierra Leone, Solomon Islands, Somalia, South Africa, Sri Lanka, Sudan, Suriname, Swaziland, Syria, Tajikistan, Tanzania, Thailand, Togo, Tonga, Trinidad and Tobago, Tunisia, Turkey, Uganda, Uruguay, Vietnam, Yemen, Zambia, Zimbabwe

International Hydrographic Organization (IHO)

note—name changed from International Hydrographic Bureau on 22 September 1970
established—NA June 1919
effective—NA June 1921
aim—to train hydrographic surveyors and nautical cartographers to achieve standardization in nautical charts and electronic chart displays; to provide advice on nautical cartography and hydrography; to develop the sciences in the field of hydrography and techniques used for descriptive oceanography

members—(74) Algeria, Argentina, Australia, Bahrain, Bangladesh, Belgium, Brazil, Burma, Canada, Chile, China (including Hong Kong and Macau), Colombia, Democratic Republic of the Congo, Croatia, Cuba, Cyprus, Denmark, Dominican Republic, Ecuador, Egypt, Estonia, Fiji, Finland, France, Germany, Greece, Guatemala, Iceland, India, Indonesia, Iran, Italy, Jamaica, Japan, North Korea, South Korea, Kuwait, Malaysia, Mexico, Monaco, Morocco, Mozambique, Netherlands, NZ, Nigeria, Norway, Oman, Pakistan, Papua New Guinea, Peru, Philippines, Poland, Portugal, Russia, Serbia and Montenegro, Singapore, Slovenia, South Africa, Spain, Sri Lanka, Suriname, Sweden, Syria, Thailand, Tonga, Trinidad and Tobago, Tunisia, Turkey, Ukraine, UAE, UK, US, Uruguay, Venezuela
membership pending—(3) Bulgaria, Mauritania, Qatar

International Labor Organization (ILO)

established—28 June 1919 set up as part of Treaty of Versailles; 11 April 1919 became operative; 14 December 1946 affiliated with the UN
aim—to deal with world labor issues; a UN specialized agency

members—(177) Afghanistan, Albania, Algeria, Angola, Antigua and Barbuda, Argentina, Armenia, Australia, Austria, Azerbaijan, The Bahamas, Bahrain, Bangladesh, Barbados, Belarus, Belgium, Belize, Benin, Bolivia, Bosnia and Herzegovina, Botswana, Brazil, Bulgaria, Burkina Faso, Burma, Burundi, Cambodia, Cameroon, Canada, Cape Verde, Central African Republic, Chad, Chile, China, Colombia, Comoros, Democratic Republic of the Congo, Republic of the Congo, Costa Rica, Cote d'Ivoire, Croatia, Cuba, Cyprus, Czech Republic, Denmark, Djibouti, Dominica, Dominican Republic, East Timor, Ecuador, Egypt, El Salvador, Equatorial Guinea, Eritrea, Estonia, Ethiopia, Fiji, Finland, France, Gabon, The Gambia, Georgia, Germany, Ghana, Greece, Grenada, Guatemala, Guinea, Guinea-Bissau, Guyana, Haiti, Honduras, Hungary, Iceland, India, Indonesia, Iran, Iraq, Ireland, Israel, Italy, Jamaica, Japan, Jordan, Kazakhstan, Kenya, Kiribati, South Korea, Kuwait, Kyrgyzstan, Laos, Latvia, Lebanon, Lesotho, Liberia, Libya, Lithuania, Luxembourg, The Former Yugoslav Republic of Macedonia, Madagascar, Malawi, Malaysia, Mali, Malta, Mauritania, Mauritius, Mexico, Moldova, Mongolia, Morocco, Mozambique, Namibia, Nepal, Netherlands, NZ, Nicaragua, Niger, Nigeria, Norway, Oman, Pakistan, Panama, Papua New Guinea, Paraguay, Peru, Philippines, Poland, Portugal, Qatar, Romania, Russia, Rwanda, Saint Kitts and Nevis, Saint Lucia, Saint Vincent and the Grenadines, San Marino, Sao Tome and Principe, Saudi Arabia, Senegal, Serbia and Montenegro, Seychelles, Sierra Leone, Singapore, Slovakia, Slovenia, Solomon Islands, Somalia, South Africa, Spain, Sri Lanka, Sudan, Suriname, Swaziland, Sweden, Switzerland, Syria, Tajikistan, Tanzania, Thailand, Togo, Trinidad and Tobago, Tunisia, Turkey, Turkmenistan, Uganda, Ukraine, UAE, UK, US, Uruguay, Uzbekistan, Vanuatu, Venezuela, Vietnam, Yemen, Zambia, Zimbabwe

International Maritime Organization (IMO)

note—name changed from Intergovernmental Maritime Consultative Organization (IMCO) on 22 May 1982
established—6 March 1948 set up as the Inter-Governmental Maritime Consultative Organization
effective—17 March 1958
aim—to deal with international maritime affairs; a UN specialized agency

members—(163) Albania, Algeria, Angola, Antigua and Barbuda, Argentina, Australia, Austria, Azerbaijan, The Bahamas, Bahrain, Bangladesh, Barbados, Belgium, Belize, Benin, Bolivia, Bosnia and Herzegovina, Brazil, Brunei, Bulgaria, Burma, Cambodia, Cameroon, Canada, Cape Verde, Chile, China, Colombia, Comoros, Democratic Republic of the Congo, Republic of the Congo, Costa Rica, Cote d'Ivoire, Croatia, Cuba, Cyprus, Czech Republic, Denmark, Djibouti, Dominica, Dominican Republic, Ecuador, Egypt, El Salvador, Equatorial Guinea, Eritrea, Estonia, Ethiopia, Fiji, Finland, France, Gabon, The Gambia, Georgia, Germany, Ghana, Greece, Grenada, Guatemala, Guinea, Guinea-Bissau, Guyana, Haiti, Honduras, Hungary, Iceland, India, Indonesia, Iran, Iraq, Ireland, Israel, Italy, Jamaica, Japan, Jordan, Kazakhstan, Kenya, Kiribati, North Korea, South Korea, Kuwait, Latvia, Lebanon, Liberia, Libya, Lithuania, Luxembourg, The Former Yugoslav Republic of Macedonia, Madagascar, Malawi, Malaysia, Maldives, Malta, Marshall Islands, Mauritania, Mauritius, Mexico, Moldova, Monaco, Mongolia, Morocco, Mozambique, Namibia, Nepal, Netherlands, NZ, Nicaragua, Nigeria, Norway, Oman, Pakistan, Panama, Papua New Guinea, Paraguay, Peru, Philippines, Poland, Portugal, Qatar, Romania, Russia, Saint Kitts and Nevis, Saint Lucia, Saint Vincent and the Grenadines, Samoa, San Marino, Sao Tome and Principe, Saudi Arabia, Senegal, Serbia and Montenegro, Seychelles, Sierra Leone, Singapore, Slovakia, Slovenia, Solomon Islands, Somalia, South Africa, Spain, Sri Lanka, Sudan, Suriname, Sweden, Switzerland, Syria, Tanzania, Thailand, Togo, Tonga, Trinidad and Tobago, Tunisia, Turkey, Turkmenistan, Ukraine, UAE, UK, US, Uruguay, Vanuatu, Venezuela, Vietnam, Yemen
associate members—(3) Faroe Islands, Hong Kong, Macau

International Monetary Fund (IMF)

established—22 July 1944
effective—27 December 1945
aim—to promote world monetary stability and economic development; a UN specialized agency

members—(184) Afghanistan, Albania, Algeria, Angola, Antigua and Barbuda, Argentina, Armenia, Australia, Austria, Azerbaijan, The Bahamas, Bahrain, Bangladesh, Barbados, Belarus, Belgium, Belize, Benin, Bhutan, Bolivia, Bosnia and Herzegovina, Botswana, Brazil, Brunei, Bulgaria, Burkina Faso, Burma, Burundi, Cambodia, Cameroon, Canada, Cape Verde, Central African Republic, Chad, Chile, China, Colombia, Comoros, Democratic Republic of the Congo, Republic of the Congo, Costa Rica, Cote d'Ivoire, Croatia, Cyprus, Czech Republic, Denmark, Djibouti, Dominica, Dominican Republic, East Timor, Ecuador, Egypt, El Salvador, Equatorial Guinea, Eritrea, Estonia, Ethiopia, Fiji, Finland, France, Gabon, The Gambia, Georgia, Germany, Ghana, Greece, Grenada, Guatemala, Guinea, Guinea-Bissau, Guyana, Haiti, Honduras, Hungary, Iceland, India, Indonesia, Iran, Iraq, Ireland, Israel, Italy, Jamaica, Japan, Jordan, Kazakhstan, Kenya, Kiribati, South Korea, Kuwait, Kyrgyzstan, Laos, Latvia, Lebanon, Lesotho, Liberia, Libya, Lithuania, Luxembourg, The Former Yugoslav Republic of Macedonia, Madagascar, Malawi, Malaysia, Maldives, Mali, Malta, Marshall Islands, Mauritania, Mauritius, Mexico, Federated States of Micronesia, Moldova, Mongolia, Morocco, Mozambique, Namibia, Nepal, Netherlands, NZ, Nicaragua, Niger, Nigeria, Norway, Oman, Pakistan, Palau, Panama, Papua New Guinea, Paraguay, Peru, Philippines, Poland, Portugal, Qatar, Romania, Russia, Rwanda, Saint Kitts and Nevis, Saint Lucia, Saint Vincent and the Grenadines, Samoa, San Marino, Sao Tome and Principe, Saudi Arabia, Senegal, Serbia and Montenegro, Seychelles, Sierra Leone, Singapore, Slovakia, Slovenia, Solomon Islands, Somalia, South Africa, Spain, Sri Lanka, Sudan, Suriname, Swaziland, Sweden, Switzerland, Syria, Tajikistan, Tanzania, Thailand, Togo, Tonga, Trinidad and Tobago, Tunisia, Turkey, Turkmenistan, Uganda, Ukraine, UAE, UK, US, Uruguay, Uzbekistan, Vanuatu, Venezuela, Vietnam, Yemen, Zambia, Zimbabwe

International Olympic Committee (IOC)

established—23 June 1894
aim—to promote the Olympic ideals and administer the Olympic games: 2004 Summer Olympics in Athens, Greece; 2006 Winter Olympics in Turin, Italy; 2008 Summer Olympics in Beijing, China; 2010 Winter Olympics in British Colombia, Canada

National Olympic Committees—(201 plus the Palestine Liberation Organization) Afghanistan, Albania, Algeria, American Samoa, Andorra, Angola (suspended), Antigua and Barbuda, Argentina, Armenia, Aruba, Australia, Austria, Azerbaijan, The Bahamas, Bahrain, Bangladesh, Barbados, Belarus, Belgium, Belize, Benin, Bermuda, Bhutan, Bolivia, Bosnia and Herzegovina, Botswana, Brazil, British Virgin Islands, Brunei, Bulgaria, Burkina Faso, Burma, Burundi, Cambodia, Cameroon, Canada, Cape Verde, Cayman Islands, Central African Republic, Chad, Chile, China, Colombia, Comoros, Democratic Republic of the Congo, Republic of the Congo, Cook Islands, Costa Rica, Cote d'Ivoire, Croatia, Cuba, Cyprus, Czech Republic, Denmark, Djibouti, Dominica, Dominican Republic, East Timor, Ecuador, Egypt, El Salvador, Equatorial Guinea, Eritrea, Estonia, Ethiopia, Fiji, Finland, France, Gabon, The Gambia, Georgia, Germany, Ghana, Greece, Grenada, Guam, Guatemala, Guinea, Guinea-Bissau, Guyana, Haiti, Honduras, Hong Kong, Hungary, Iceland, India, Indonesia, Iran, Iraq, Ireland, Israel, Italy, Jamaica, Japan, Jordan, Kazakhstan, Kenya, Kiribati, North Korea, South Korea, Kuwait, Kyrgyzstan, Laos, Latvia, Lebanon, Lesotho, Liberia, Libya, Liechtenstein, Lithuania, Luxembourg, The Former Yugoslav Republic of Macedonia, Madagascar, Malawi, Malaysia, Maldives, Mali, Malta, Mauritania, Mauritius, Mexico, Federated States of Micronesia, Moldova, Monaco, Mongolia, Morocco, Mozambique, Namibia, Nauru, Nepal, Netherlands, Netherlands Antilles, NZ, Nicaragua, Niger, Nigeria, Norway, Oman, Pakistan, Palau, Panama, Papua New Guinea, Paraguay, Peru, Philippines, Poland, Portugal, Puerto Rico, Qatar, Romania, Russia, Rwanda, Saint Kitts and Nevis, Saint Lucia, Saint Vincent and the Grenadines, Samoa, San Marino, Sao Tome and Principe, Saudi Arabia, Senegal, Serbia and Montenegro, Seychelles, Sierra Leone, Singapore, Slovakia, Slovenia, Solomon Islands, Somalia, South Africa, Spain, Sri Lanka, Sudan, Suriname, Swaziland, Sweden, Switzerland, Syria, Taiwan, Tajikistan, Tanzania, Thailand, Togo, Tonga, Trinidad and Tobago, Tunisia, Turkey, Turkmenistan, Uganda, Ukraine, UAE, UK, US, Uruguay, Uzbekistan, Vanuatu, Venezuela, Vietnam, Virgin Islands, Yemen, Zambia, Zimbabwe, Palestine Liberation Organization

Appendix B: International Organizations and Groups *(continued)*

International Organization for Migration (IOM)

note—established as Provisional Intergovernmental Committee for the Movement of Migrants from Europe; renamed Intergovernmental Committee for European Migration (ICEM) on 15 November 1952; renamed Intergovernmental Committee for Migration (ICM) in November 1980; current name adopted 14 November 1989
established—5 December 1951
aim—to facilitate orderly international emigration and immigration

members—(102) Albania, Algeria, Angola, Argentina, Armenia, Australia, Austria, Azerbaijan, Bangladesh, Belgium, Belize, Benin, Bolivia, Bulgaria, Burkina Faso, Cambodia, Canada, Cape Verde, Chile, Colombia, Democratic Republic of the Congo, Republic of the Congo, Costa Rica, Cote d'Ivoire, Croatia, Cyprus, Czech Republic, Denmark, Dominican Republic, Ecuador, Egypt, El Salvador, Finland, France, The Gambia, Georgia, Germany, Greece, Guatemala, Guinea, Guinea-Bissau, Haiti, Honduras, Hungary, Iran, Ireland, Israel, Italy, Japan, Jordan, Kazakhstan, Kenya, South Korea, Kyrgyzstan, Latvia, Liberia, Lithuania, Luxembourg, Madagascar, Mali, Malta, Mauritania, Mexico, Moldova, Morocco, Netherlands, NZ, Nicaragua, Nigeria, Norway, Pakistan, Panama, Paraguay, Peru, Philippines, Poland, Portugal, Romania, Rwanda, Senegal, Serbia and Montenegro, Sierra Leone, Slovakia, Slovenia, South Africa, Sri Lanka, Sudan, Sweden, Switzerland, Tajikistan, Tanzania, Thailand, Tunisia, Uganda, Ukraine, UK, US, Uruguay, Venezuela, Yemen, Zambia, Zimbabwe
observers—(29) Afghanistan, Belarus, Bhutan, Bosnia and Herzegovina, Brazil, Burundi, China, Cuba, Estonia, Ethiopia, Ghana, Holy See, India, Indonesia, Jamaica, Libya, The Former Yugoslav Republic of Macedonia, Mozambique, Namibia, Nepal, Papua New Guinea, Russia, San Marino, Sao Tome and Principe, Somalia, Spain, Turkey, Turkmenistan, Vietnam

International Organization for Standardization (ISO)

established—NA February 1947
aim—to promote the development of international standards with a view to facilitating international exchange of goods and services and to developing cooperation in the sphere of intellectual, scientific, technological and economic activity

members—(97 national standards organizations) Algeria, Argentina, Armenia, Australia, Austria, Azerbaijan, Bangladesh, Barbados, Bahrain, Belarus, Belgium, Bosnia and Herzegovina, Botswana, Brazil, Bulgaria, Canada, Chile, China, Colombia, Costa Rica, Cote d'Ivoire, Croatia, Cuba, Cyprus, Czech Republic, Denmark, Ecuador, Egypt, Ethiopia, Finland, France, Germany, Ghana, Greece, Hungary, Iceland, India, Indonesia, Iran, Iraq, Ireland, Israel, Italy, Jamaica, Japan, Jordan, Kazakhstan, Kenya, North Korea, South Korea, Kuwait, Libya, Luxembourg, The Former Yugoslav Republic of Macedonia, Malaysia, Malta, Mauritius, Mexico, Mongolia, Morocco, Netherlands, NZ, Nigeria, Norway, Oman, Pakistan, Panama, Philippines, Poland, Portugal, Romania, Russia, Saudi Arabia, Serbia and Montenegro, Singapore, Slovakia, Slovenia, South Africa, Spain, Sri Lanka, Sweden, Switzerland, Syria, Tanzania, Thailand, Trinidad and Tobago, Tunisia, Turkey, Ukraine, UAE, UK, US, Uruguay, Uzbekistan, Venezuela, Vietnam, Zimbabwe
correspondent members—(36) Albania, Angola, Bolivia, Brunei, Cameroon, Democratic Republic of the Congo, El Salvador, Estonia, Guatemala, Hong Kong, Kyrgyzstan, Latvia, Lebanon, Lithuania, Macau, Madagascar, Malawi, Moldova, Mozambique, Namibia, Nepal, Nicaragua, Papua New Guinea, Paraguay, Peru, Qatar, Rwanda, Saint Lucia, Senegal, Seychelles, Sudan, Swaziland, Turkmenistan, Uganda, Yemen, Zambia
subscriber members—(14 plus the Palestinian Liberation Organization) Antigua and Barbuda, Benin, Burundi, Cambodia, Dominica, Dominican Republic, Eritrea, Fiji, Grenada, Guyana, Honduras, Lesotho, Mali, Niger, Palestinian Liberation Organization

International Red Cross and Red Crescent Movement (ICRM)

established—NA 1928
aim—to promote worldwide humanitarian aid through the International Committee of the Red Cross (ICRC) in wartime, and International Federation of Red Cross and Red Crescent Societies (IFRCS; formerly League of Red Cross and Red Crescent Societies or LORCS) in peacetime

National Societies—(185 countries); note—same as membership for International Federation of Red Cross and Red Crescent Societies (IFRCS)

Appendix B: International Organizations and Groups *(continued)*

International Telecommunication Union (ITU)

established—17 May 1865 set up as the International Telegraph Union; 9 December 1932 adopted present name
effective—1 January 1934; affiliated with the UN—15 November 1947
aim—to deal with world telecommunications issues; a UN specialized agency

members—(189) Afghanistan, Albania, Algeria, Andorra, Angola, Antigua and Barbuda, Argentina, Armenia, Australia, Austria, Azerbaijan, The Bahamas, Bahrain, Bangladesh, Barbados, Belarus, Belgium, Belize, Benin, Bhutan, Bolivia, Bosnia and Herzegovina, Botswana, Brazil, Brunei, Bulgaria, Burkina Faso, Burma, Burundi, Cambodia, Cameroon, Canada, Cape Verde, Central African Republic, Chad, Chile, China, Colombia, Comoros, Democratic Republic of the Congo, Republic of the Congo, Costa Rica, Cote d'Ivoire, Croatia, Cuba, Cyprus, Czech Republic, Denmark, Djibouti, Dominica, Dominican Republic, Ecuador, Egypt, El Salvador, Equatorial Guinea, Eritrea, Estonia, Ethiopia, Fiji, Finland, France, Gabon, The Gambia, Georgia, Germany, Ghana, Greece, Grenada, Guatemala, Guinea, Guinea-Bissau, Guyana, Haiti, Holy See, Honduras, Hungary, Iceland, India, Indonesia, Iran, Iraq, Ireland, Israel, Italy, Jamaica, Japan, Jordan, Kazakhstan, Kenya, Kiribati, North Korea, South Korea, Kuwait, Kyrgyzstan, Laos, Latvia, Lebanon, Lesotho, Liberia, Libya, Liechtenstein, Lithuania, Luxembourg, The Former Yugoslav Republic of Macedonia, Madagascar, Malawi, Malaysia, Maldives, Mali, Malta, Marshall Islands, Mauritania, Mauritius, Mexico, Federated States of Micronesia, Moldova, Monaco, Mongolia, Morocco, Mozambique, Namibia, Nauru, Nepal, Netherlands, NZ, Nicaragua, Niger, Nigeria, Norway, Oman, Pakistan, Panama, Papua New Guinea, Paraguay, Peru, Philippines, Poland, Portugal, Qatar, Romania, Russia, Rwanda, Saint Lucia, Saint Vincent and the Grenadines, Samoa, San Marino, Sao Tome and Principe, Saudi Arabia, Senegal, Serbia and Montenegro, Seychelles, Sierra Leone, Singapore, Slovakia, Slovenia, Solomon Islands, Somalia, South Africa, Spain, Sri Lanka, Sudan, Suriname, Swaziland, Sweden, Switzerland, Syria, Tajikistan, Tanzania, Thailand, Togo, Tonga, Trinidad and Tobago, Tunisia, Turkey, Turkmenistan, Tuvalu, Uganda, Ukraine, UAE, UK, US, Uruguay, Uzbekistan, Vanuatu, Venezuela, Vietnam, Yemen, Zambia, Zimbabwe

Islamic Development Bank (IDB)

established—15 December 1973 by declaration of intent
effective—12 August 1974
aim—to promote Islamic economic aid and social development

members—(54 plus the Palestine Liberation Organization) Afghanistan, Albania, Algeria, Azerbaijan, Bahrain, Bangladesh, Benin, Brunei, Burkina Faso, Cameroon, Chad, Comoros, Cote d'Ivoire, Djibouti, Egypt, Gabon, The Gambia, Guinea, Guinea-Bissau, Indonesia, Iran, Iraq, Jordan, Kazakhstan, Kuwait, Kyrgyzstan, Lebanon, Libya, Malaysia, Maldives, Mali, Mauritania, Morocco, Mozambique, Niger, Oman, Pakistan, Qatar, Saudi Arabia, Senegal, Sierra Leone, Somalia, Sudan, Suriname, Syria, Tajikistan, Togo, Tunisia, Turkey, Turkmenistan, Uganda, UAE, Uzbekistan, Yemen, Palestine Liberation Organization

Latin American Economic System (LAES)

note—also known as Sistema Economico Latinoamericana (SELA)
established—17 October 1975
aim—to promote economic and social development through regional cooperation

members—(28) Argentina, The Bahamas, Barbados, Belize, Bolivia, Brazil, Chile, Colombia, Costa Rica, Cuba, Dominican Republic, Ecuador, El Salvador, Grenada, Guatemala, Guyana, Haiti, Honduras, Jamaica, Mexico, Nicaragua, Panama, Paraguay, Peru, Suriname, Trinidad and Tobago, Uruguay, Venezuela

Latin American Integration Association (LAIA)

note—also known as Asociacion Latinoamericana de Integracion (ALADI)
established—12 August 1980
effective—18 March 1981
aim—to promote freer regional trade

members—(12) Argentina, Bolivia, Brazil, Chile, Colombia, Cuba, Ecuador, Mexico, Paraguay, Peru, Uruguay, Venezuela
observers—(23) China, Commission of the European Communities, Corporacion Andina de Fomento, Costa Rica, Dominican Republic, El Salvador, Guatemala, Honduras, Inter-American Development Bank, Inter-American Institute for Cooperation on Agriculture, Italy, Latin America Economic System, Nicaragua, Organization of American States, Panama, Pan-American Health Organization, Portugal, Romania, Russia, Spain, Switzerland, United Nations Development Program, United Nations Economic Commission for Latin America and the Caribbean

League of Arab States (LAS)

note—also known as Arab League (AL)
established—22 March 1945
aim—to promote economic, social, political, and military cooperation

members—(21 plus the Palestine Liberation Organization) Algeria, Bahrain, Comoros, Djibouti, Egypt, Iraq, Jordan, Kuwait, Lebanon, Libya, Mauritania, Morocco, Oman, Qatar, Saudi Arabia, Somalia, Sudan, Syria, Tunisia, UAE, Yemen, Palestine Liberation Organization

least developed countries (LLDCs)

that subgroup of the less developed countries (LDCs) initially identified by the UN General Assembly in 1971 as having no significant economic growth, per capita GDPs normally less than $1,000, and low literacy rates; also known as the undeveloped countries; the 42 LLDCs are: Afghanistan, Bangladesh, Benin, Bhutan, Botswana, Burkina Faso, Burma, Burundi, Cape Verde, Central African Republic, Chad, Comoros, Djibouti, Equatorial Guinea, Eritrea, Ethiopia, The Gambia, Guinea, Guinea-Bissau, Haiti, Kiribati, Laos, Lesotho, Malawi, Maldives, Mali, Mauritania, Mozambique, Nepal, Niger, Rwanda, Samoa, Sao Tome and Principe, Sierra Leone, Somalia, Sudan, Tanzania, Togo, Tuvalu, Uganda, Vanuatu, Yemen

Appendix B: International Organizations and Groups *(continued)*

less developed countries (LDCs)	the bottom group in the hierarchy of developed countries (DCs), former USSR/Eastern Europe (former USSR/EE), and less developed countries (LDCs); mainly countries and dependent areas with low levels of output, living standards, and technology; per capita GDPs are generally below $5,000 and often less than $1,500; however, the group also includes a number of countries with high per capita incomes, areas of advanced technology, and rapid rates of growth; includes the advanced developing countries, developing countries, Four Dragons (Four Tigers), least developed countries (LLDCs), low-income countries, middle-income countries, newly industrializing economies (NIEs), the South, Third World, underdeveloped countries, undeveloped countries; the 172 LDCs are: Afghanistan, Algeria, American Samoa, Angola, Anguilla, Antigua and Barbuda, Argentina, Aruba, The Bahamas, Bahrain, Bangladesh, Barbados, Belize, Benin, Bhutan, Bolivia, Botswana, Brazil, British Virgin Islands, Brunei, Burkina Faso, Burma, Burundi, Cambodia, Cameroon, Cape Verde, Cayman Islands, Central African Republic, Chad, Chile, China, Christmas Island, Cocos Islands, Colombia, Comoros, Democratic Republic of the Congo, Republic of the Congo, Cook Islands, Costa Rica, Cote d'Ivoire, Cuba, Cyprus, Djibouti, Dominica, Dominican Republic, Ecuador, Egypt, El Salvador, Equatorial Guinea, Eritrea, Ethiopia, Falkland Islands, Fiji, French Guiana, French Polynesia, Gabon, The Gambia, Gaza Strip, Ghana, Gibraltar, Greenland, Grenada, Guadeloupe, Guam, Guatemala, Guernsey, Guinea, Guinea-Bissau, Guyana, Haiti, Honduras, Hong Kong, India, Indonesia, Iran, Iraq, Jamaica, Jersey, Jordan, Kenya, Kiribati, North Korea, South Korea, Kuwait, Laos, Lebanon, Lesotho, Liberia, Libya, Macau, Madagascar, Malawi, Malaysia, Maldives, Mali, Isle of Man, Marshall Islands, Martinique, Mauritania, Mauritius, Mayotte, Federated States of Micronesia, Mongolia, Montserrat, Morocco, Mozambique, Namibia, Nauru, Nepal, Netherlands Antilles, New Caledonia, Nicaragua, Niger, Nigeria, Niue, Norfolk Island, Northern Mariana Islands, Oman, Palau, Pakistan, Panama, Papua New Guinea, Paraguay, Peru, Philippines, Pitcairn Islands, Puerto Rico, Qatar, Reunion, Rwanda, Saint Helena, Saint Kitts and Nevis, Saint Lucia, Saint Pierre and Miquelon, Saint Vincent and the Grenadines, Samoa, Sao Tome and Principe, Saudi Arabia, Senegal, Seychelles, Sierra Leone, Singapore, Solomon Islands, Somalia, Sri Lanka, Sudan, Suriname, Swaziland, Syria, Taiwan, Tanzania, Thailand, Togo, Tokelau, Tonga, Trinidad and Tobago, Tunisia, Turks and Caicos Islands, Tuvalu, UAE, Uganda, Uruguay, Vanuatu, Venezuela, Vietnam, Virgin Islands, Wallis and Futuna, West Bank, Western Sahara, Yemen, Zambia, Zimbabwe; note—similar to the new International Monetary Fund (IMF) term "developing countries" which adds Malta, Mexico, South Africa, and Turkey but omits in its recently published statistics American Samoa, Anguilla, British Virgin Islands, Brunei, Cayman Islands, Christmas Island, Cocos Islands, Cook Islands, Cuba, Eritrea, Falkland Islands, French Guiana, French Polynesia, Gaza Strip, Gibraltar, Greenland, Grenada, Guadeloupe, Guam, Guernsey, Jersey, North Korea, Macau, Isle of Man, Martinique, Mayotte, Montserrat, Nauru, New Caledonia, Niue, Norfolk Island, Northern Mariana Islands, Palau, Pitcairn Islands, Puerto Rico, Reunion, Saint Helena, Saint Pierre and Miquelon, Tokelau, Tonga, Turks and Caicos Islands, Tuvalu, Virgin Islands, Wallis and Futuna, West Bank, Western Sahara
low-income countries	another term for those less developed countries with below-average per capita GDPs; see less developed countries (LDCs)
middle-income countries	another term for those less developed countries with above-average per capita GDPs; see less developed countries (LDCs)
Monetary and Economic Community of Central Africa (CEMAC) *note*—was formerly the Central African Customs and Economic Union (UDEAC) *established*—8 December 1964 *effective*—1 January 1966 *aim*—to promote the establishment of a Central African Common Market	*members*—(6) Cameroon, Central African Republic, Chad, Republic of the Congo, Equatorial Guinea, Gabon
Near Abroad	Russian term for the 14 non-Russian successor states of the USSR, in which 25 million ethnic Russians live and in which Moscow has expressed a strong national security interest; the 14 countries are Armenia, Azerbaijan, Belarus, Estonia, Georgia, Kazakhstan, Kyrgyzstan, Latvia, Lithuania, Moldova, Tajikistan, Turkmenistan, Ukraine, Uzbekistan
new independent states (NIS)	a term referring to all those countries of the FSU except the Baltic countries (Estonia, Latvia, Lithuania)
newly industrializing countries (NICs)	former term for the newly industrializing economies; see newly industrializing economies (NIEs)
newly industrializing economies (NIEs)	that subgroup of the less developed countries (LDCs) that has experienced particularly rapid industrialization of their economies; formerly known as the newly industrializing countries (NICs); also known as advanced developing countries; usually includes the Four Dragons (Hong Kong, South Korea, Singapore, Taiwan), and Brazil

Appendix B: International Organizations and Groups *(continued)*

Nonaligned Movement (NAM) *established*—1-6 September 1961 *aim*—to establish political and military cooperation apart from the traditional East or West blocs	*members*—(114 plus the Palestine Liberation Organization) Afghanistan, Algeria, Angola, The Bahamas, Bahrain, Bangladesh, Barbados, Belarus, Belize, Benin, Bhutan, Bolivia, Botswana, Brunei, Burkina Faso, Burma, Burundi, Cambodia, Cameroon, Cape Verde, Central African Republic, Chad, Chile, Colombia, Comoros, Democratic Republic of the Congo, Republic of the Congo, Cote d'Ivoire, Cuba, Cyprus, Djibouti, Dominican Republic, Ecuador, Egypt, Equatorial Guinea, Eritrea, Ethiopia, Gabon, The Gambia, Ghana, Grenada, Guatemala, Guinea, Guinea-Bissau, Guyana, Honduras, India, Indonesia, Iran, Iraq, Jamaica, Jordan, Kenya, North Korea, Kuwait, Laos, Lebanon, Lesotho, Liberia, Libya, Madagascar, Malawi, Malaysia, Maldives, Mali, Malta, Mauritania, Mauritius, Mongolia, Morocco, Mozambique, Namibia, Nepal, Nicaragua, Niger, Nigeria, Oman, Pakistan, Panama, Papua New Guinea, Peru, Philippines, Qatar, Rwanda, Saint Lucia, Sao Tome and Principe, Saudi Arabia, Senegal, Serbia and Montenegro, Seychelles, Sierra Leone, Singapore, Somalia, South Africa, Sri Lanka, Sudan, Suriname, Swaziland, Syria, Tanzania, Thailand, Togo, Trinidad and Tobago, Tunisia, Turkmenistan, Uganda, UAE, Uzbekistan, Vanuatu, Venezuela, Vietnam, Yemen, Zambia, Zimbabwe, Palestine Liberation Organization *observers*—(13) Armenia, Belarus, Brazil, China, Costa Rica, Croatia, Dominica, Kazakhstan, Kyrgyzstan, Mexico, Paraguay, Ukraine, Uruguay *guests*—(28) Australia, Austria, Bosnia and Herzegovina, Bulgaria, Canada, Finland, France, Germany, Greece, Holy See, Hungary, Ireland, Italy, Japan, South Korea, Netherlands, NZ, Norway, Poland, Portugal, Romania, Russia, Slovakia, Slovenia, Sweden, Switzerland, UK, US
Nordic Council (NC) *established*—16 March 1952 *effective*—12 February 1953 *aim*—to promote regional economic, cultural, and environmental cooperation	*members*—(5) Denmark (including Faroe Islands and Greenland), Finland (including Aland Islands), Iceland, Norway, Sweden *observers*—(3) the Sami (Lapp) local parliaments of Finland, Norway, and Sweden
Nordic Investment Bank (NIB) *established*—4 December 1975 *effective*—1 June 1976 *aim*—to promote economic cooperation and development	*members*—(5) Denmark (including Faroe Islands and Greenland), Finland (including Aland Islands), Iceland, Norway, Sweden
North	a popular term for the rich industrialized countries generally located in the northern portion of the Northern Hemisphere; the counterpart of the South; see developed countries (DCs)
North American Free Trade Agreement (NAFTA) *established*—17 December 1992 *aim*—to eliminate trade barriers, promote fair competition, increase investment opportunities, provide protection of intellectual property rights, create procedures to settle disputes	*members*—(3) Canada, Mexico, US
North Atlantic Treaty Organization (NATO) *established*—4 April 1949 *aim*—to promote mutual defense and cooperation	*members*—(26) Belgium, Bulgaria, Canada, Czech Republic, Denmark, Estonia, France, Germany, Greece, Hungary, Iceland, Italy, Latvia, Lithuania, Luxembourg, Netherlands, Norway, Poland, Portugal, Romania, Slovakia, Slovenia, Spain, Turkey, UK, US
Nuclear Energy Agency (NEA) *note*—also known as OECD Nuclear Energy Agency *established*—1 February 1958 *aim*—to promote the peaceful uses of nuclear energy; associated with OECD	*members*—(28) Australia, Austria, Belgium, Canada, Czech Republic, Denmark, Finland, France, Germany, Greece, Hungary, Iceland, Ireland, Italy, Japan, South Korea, Luxembourg, Mexico, Netherlands, Norway, Portugal, Slovakia, Spain, Sweden, Switzerland, Turkey, UK, US

Appendix B: International Organizations and Groups *(continued)*

Nuclear Suppliers Group (NSG)

note—also known as the London Suppliers Group or the London Group
established—NA 1974
effective—NA 1975
aim—to establish guidelines for exports of nuclear materials, processing equipment for uranium enrichment, and technical information to countries of proliferation concern and regions of conflict and instability

members—(40) Argentina, Australia, Austria, Belarus, Belgium, Brazil, Bulgaria, Canada, Cyprus, Czech Republic, Denmark, Finland, France, Germany, Greece, Hungary, Ireland, Italy, Japan, Kazakhstan, South Korea, Latvia, Luxembourg, Netherlands, NZ, Norway, Poland, Portugal, Romania, Russia, Slovakia, Slovenia, South Africa, Spain, Sweden, Switzerland, Turkey, Ukraine, UK, US
observer—(1) European Commission (a policy-planning body for the EU)

Organization for Economic Cooperation and Development (OECD)

established—14 December 1960
effective—30 September 1961
aim—to promote economic cooperation and development

members—(30) Australia, Austria, Belgium, Canada, Czech Republic, Denmark, Finland, France, Germany, Greece, Hungary, Iceland, Ireland, Italy, Japan, South Korea, Luxembourg, Mexico, Netherlands, NZ, Norway, Poland, Portugal, Slovakia, Spain, Sweden, Switzerland, Turkey, UK, US
special member—(1) EU

Organization for Security and Cooperation in Europe (OSCE)

note—formerly the Conference on Security and Cooperation in Europe (CSCE) established 3 July 1975
established—1 January 1995
aim—to foster the implementation of human rights, fundamental freedoms, democracy, and the rule of law; to act as an instrument of early warning, conflict prevention, and crisis management; and to serve as a framework for conventional arms control and confidence building measures

members—(55) Albania, Andorra, Armenia, Austria, Azerbaijan, Belarus, Belgium, Bosnia and Herzegovina, Bulgaria, Canada, Croatia, Cyprus, Czech Republic, Denmark, Estonia, Finland, France, Georgia, Germany, Greece, Holy See, Hungary, Iceland, Ireland, Italy, Kazakhstan, Kyrgyzstan, Latvia, Liechtenstein, Lithuania, Luxembourg, The Former Yugoslav Republic of Macedonia, Malta, Moldova, Monaco, Netherlands, Norway, Poland, Portugal, Romania, Russia, San Marino, Serbia and Montenegro, Slovakia, Slovenia, Spain, Sweden, Switzerland, Tajikistan, Turkey, Turkmenistan, Ukraine, UK, US, Uzbekistan
partners for cooperation—(10) Afghanistan, Algeria, Egypt, Israel, Japan, Jordan, South Korea, Morocco, Thailand, Tunisia

---

Organization for the Prohibition of Chemical Weapons (OPCW)

established—29 April 1997
aim—to enforce the Convention on the Prohibition of the Development, Production, Stockpiling and Use of Chemical Weapons and on Their Destruction; to provide a forum for consultation and cooperation among the signatories of the Convention

members (countries that have ratified the Convention)—(160) Afghanistan, Albania, Algeria, Andorra, Argentina, Armenia, Australia, Austria, Azerbaijan, Bahrain, Bangladesh, Belarus, Belgium, Belize, Benin, Bolivia, Bosnia and Herzegovina, Botswana, Brazil, Brunei, Bulgaria, Burkina Faso, Burundi, Cameroon, Canada, Cape Verde, Chile, China, Colombia, Cook Islands, Costa Rica, Cote d'Ivoire, Croatia, Cuba, Cyprus, Czech Republic, Denmark, Dominica, East Timor, Ecuador, El Salvador, Equatorial Guinea, Eritrea, Estonia, Ethiopia, Fiji, Finland, France, Gabon, The Gambia, Georgia, Germany, Ghana, Greece, Guatemala, Guinea, Guyana, Holy See, Hungary, Iceland, India, Indonesia, Iran, Ireland, Italy, Jamaica, Japan, Jordan, Kazakhstan, Kenya, Kiribati, South Korea, Kuwait, Kyrgyzstan, Laos, Latvia, Lesotho, Libya, Liechtenstein, Lithuania, Luxembourg, The Former Yugoslav Republic of Macedonia, Malawi, Malaysia, Maldives, Mali, Malta, Mauritania, Mauritius, Mexico, Federated States of Micronesia, Moldova, Monaco, Mongolia, Morocco, Mozambique, Namibia, Nauru, Nepal, Netherlands, NZ, Nicaragua, Niger, Nigeria, Norway, Oman, Pakistan, Palau, Panama, Papua New Guinea, Paraguay, Peru, Philippines, Poland, Portugal, Qatar, Romania, Russia, Saint Lucia, Saint Vincent and the Grenadines, Samoa, San Marino, Sao Tome and Principe, Saudi Arabia, Senegal, Serbia and Montenegro, Seychelles, Singapore, Slovakia, Slovenia, South Africa, Spain, Sri Lanka, Sudan, Suriname, Swaziland, Sweden, Switzerland, Tajikistan, Tanzania, Thailand, Togo, Tonga, Trinidad and Tobago, Tunisia, Turkey, Turkmenistan, Tuvalu, Uganda, Ukraine, UAE, UK, US, Uruguay, Uzbekistan, Venezuela, Vietnam, Yemen, Zambia, Zimbabwe
signatory states (countries that have signed, but not ratified, the Convention)—(22) The Bahamas, Bhutan, Burma, Cambodia, Central African Republic, Chad, Comoros, Democratic Republic of the Congo, Republic of the Congo, Djibouti, Dominican Republic, Grenada, Guinea-Bissau, Haiti, Honduras, Israel, Liberia, Madagascar, Marshall Islands, Rwanda, Saint Kitts and Nevis, Sierra Leone

---

Organization of African Unity (OAU)

see African Union

Organization of American States (OAS) *established*—14 April 1890 as the International Union of American Republics; 30 April 1948 adopted present charter *effective*—13 December 1951 *aim*—to promote regional peace and security as well as economic and social development	*members*—(35) Antigua and Barbuda, Argentina, The Bahamas, Barbados, Belize, Bolivia, Brazil, Canada, Chile, Colombia, Costa Rica, Cuba (excluded from formal participation since 1962), Dominica, Dominican Republic, Ecuador, El Salvador, Grenada, Guatemala, Guyana, Haiti, Honduras, Jamaica, Mexico, Nicaragua, Panama, Paraguay, Peru, Saint Kitts and Nevis, Saint Lucia, Saint Vincent and the Grenadines, Suriname, Trinidad and Tobago, US, Uruguay, Venezuela *observers*—(56) Algeria, Angola, Armenia, Austria, Azerbaijan, Belgium, Bosnia and Herzegovina, Bulgaria, Croatia, Cyprus, Czech Republic, Denmark, Egypt, Equatorial Guinea, Estonia, EU, Finland, France, Georgia, Germany, Ghana, Greece, Holy See, Hungary, India, Ireland, Israel, Italy, Japan, Kazakhstan, South Korea, Latvia, Lebanon, Morocco, Netherlands, Norway, Pakistan, Philippines, Poland, Portugal, Qatar, Romania, Russia, Saudi Arabia, Serbia and Montenegro, Slovakia, Spain, Sri Lanka, Sweden, Switzerland, Thailand, Tunisia, Turkey, Ukraine, UK, Yemen
Organization of Arab Petroleum Exporting Countries (OAPEC) *established*—9 January 1968 *aim*—to promote cooperation in the petroleum industry	*members*—(11) Algeria, Bahrain, Egypt, Iraq, Kuwait, Libya, Qatar, Saudi Arabia, Syria, Tunisia, UAE
Organization of Eastern Caribbean States (OECS) *established*—18 June 1981 *effective*—4 July 1981 *aim*—to promote political, economic, and defense cooperation	*members*—(7) Antigua and Barbuda, Dominica, Grenada, Montserrat, Saint Kitts and Nevis, Saint Lucia, Saint Vincent and the Grenadines *associate members*—(2) Anguilla, British Virgin Islands
Organization of Petroleum Exporting Countries (OPEC) *established*—14 September 1960 *aim*—to coordinate petroleum policies	*members*—(11) Algeria, Indonesia, Iran, Iraq, Kuwait, Libya, Nigeria, Qatar, Saudi Arabia, UAE, Venezuela
Organization of the Islamic Conference (OIC) *established*—22-25 September 1969 *aim*—to promote Islamic solidarity in economic, social, cultural, and political affairs	*members*—(56 plus the Palestine Liberation Organization) Afghanistan, Albania, Algeria, Azerbaijan, Bahrain, Bangladesh, Benin, Brunei, Burkina Faso, Cameroon, Chad, Comoros, Cote d'Ivoire, Djibouti, Egypt, Gabon, The Gambia, Guinea, Guinea-Bissau, Guyana, Indonesia, Iran, Iraq, Jordan, Kazakhstan, Kuwait, Kyrgyzstan, Lebanon, Libya, Malaysia, Maldives, Mali, Mauritania, Morocco, Mozambique, Niger, Nigeria, Oman, Pakistan, Qatar, Saudi Arabia, Senegal, Sierra Leone, Somalia, Sudan, Suriname, Syria, Tajikistan, Togo, Tunisia, Turkey, Turkmenistan, Uganda, UAE, Uzbekistan, Yemen, Palestine Liberation Organization *observers*—(10) Bosnia and Herzegovina, Central African Republic, ECA, LAS, Moro National Liberation Front, NAM, OAU, Thailand, Turkish Muslim Community of Kibris, UN
Pacific Community *note*—formerly known as the South Pacific Commission (SPC) *established*—6 February 1947 *effective*—29 July 1948 *aim*—to promote regional cooperation in economic and social matters	*members*—(27) American Samoa, Australia, Cook Islands, Fiji, France, French Polynesia, Guam, Kiribati, Marshall Islands, Federated States of Micronesia, Nauru, New Caledonia, NZ, Niue, Northern Mariana Islands, Palau, Papua New Guinea, Pitcairn Islands, Samoa, Solomon Islands, Tokelau, Tonga, Tuvalu, UK, US, Vanuatu, Wallis and Futuna
Pacific Islands Forum (PIF) *note*—formerly known as South Pacific Forum (SPF) *established*—5 August 1971 *aim*—to promote regional cooperation in political matters	*members*—(16) Australia, Cook Islands, Fiji, Kiribati, Marshall Islands, Federated States of Micronesia, Nauru, NZ, Niue, Palau, Papua New Guinea, Samoa, Solomon Islands, Tonga, Tuvalu, Vanuatu *observers*—(2) East Timor, New Caledonia

Appendix B: International Organizations and Groups *(continued)*

Paris Club

established—1956
aim—to provide a forum for debtor countries to negotiate rescheduling of debt service payments or loans extended by governments or official agencies of participating countries; to help restore normal trade and project finance to debtor countries

members—(19) Austria, Australia, Belgium, Canada, Denmark, Finland, France, Germany, Ireland, Italy, Japan, Netherlands, Norway, Russia, Spain, Sweden, Switzerland, UK, US

Partnership for Peace (PFP)

established—10-11 January 1994
aim—to expand and intensify political and military cooperation throughout Europe, increase stability, diminish threats to peace, and build relationships by promoting the spirit of practical cooperation and commitment to democratic principles that underpin NATO; program under the auspices of NATO

members—(20) Albania, Armenia, Austria, Azerbaijan, Belarus, Croatia, Finland, Georgia, Ireland, Kazakhstan, Kyrgyzstan, The Former Yugoslav Republic of Macedonia, Moldova, Russia, Sweden, Switzerland, Tajikistan, Turkmenistan, Ukraine, Uzbekistan

---

Permanent Court of Arbitration (PCA)

established—29 July 1899
aim—to facilitate the settlement of international disputes

members—(101) Argentina, Australia, Austria, Belarus, Belgium, Belize, Bolivia, Brazil, Bulgaria, Burkina Faso, Cambodia, Cameroon, Canada, Chile, China, Colombia, Democratic Republic of the Congo, Costa Rica, Croatia, Cuba, Cyprus, Czech Republic, Denmark, Dominican Republic, Ecuador, Egypt, El Salvador, Eritrea, Estonia, Ethiopia, Fiji, Finland, France, Germany, Greece, Guatemala, Guyana, Haiti, Honduras, Hungary, Iceland, India, Iran, Iraq, Ireland, Israel, Italy, Japan, Jordan, South Korea, Kuwait, Kyrgyzstan, Laos, Latvia, Lebanon, Libya, Liechtenstein, Luxembourg, The Former Yugoslav Republic of Macedonia, Malaysia, Malta, Mauritius, Mexico, Morocco, Netherlands, NZ, Nicaragua, Nigeria, Norway, Pakistan, Panama, Paraguay, Peru, Poland, Portugal, Romania, Russia, Saudi Arabia, Senegal, Serbia and Montenegro, Singapore, Slovakia, Slovenia, South Africa, Spain, Sri Lanka, Sudan, Suriname, Swaziland, Sweden, Switzerland, Thailand, Turkey, Uganda, Ukraine, UK, US, Uruguay, Venezuela, Zambia, Zimbabwe

---

Rio Group (RG)

note—formerly known as Grupo de los Ocho, established NA December 1986; composed of the Contadora Group and the Lima Group
established—NA 1988
aim—to consult on regional Latin American issues

members—(19) Argentina, Bolivia, Brazil, Chile, Colombia, Costa Rica, Dominican Republic, Ecuador, El Salvador, Guatemala, Guyana, Honduras, Mexico, Nicaragua, Panama, Paraguay, Peru, Uruguay, Venezuela

---

Second World

another term for the traditionally Marxist-Leninist states of the USSR and Eastern Europe, with authoritarian governments and command economies based on the Soviet model; the term is fading from use; see centrally planned economies

---

Shanghai Cooperative Organization (SCO)

established—15 June 2001
aim—to combat terrorism, extremism, and separatism; to safeguard regional security through mutual trust, disarmament, and cooperative security; and to increase cooperation in political, trade, economic, scientific and technological, cultural, and educational fields

members—(6) China, Kazakhstan, Kyrgyzstan, Russia, Tajikistan, Uzbekistan

---

socialist countries

in general, countries in which the government owns and plans the use of the major factors of production; note—the term is sometimes used incorrectly as a synonym for Communist countries

---

South

a popular term for the poorer, less industrialized countries generally located south of the developed countries; the counterpart of the North; see less developed countries (LDCs)

Appendix B: International Organizations and Groups *(continued)*

South Asian Association for Regional Cooperation (SAARC) *established*—8 December 1985 *aim*—to promote economic, social, and cultural cooperation	*members*—(7) Bangladesh, Bhutan, India, Maldives, Nepal, Pakistan, Sri Lanka
South Pacific Forum (SPF)	*note*—see Pacific Island Forum
South Pacific Regional Trade and Economic Cooperation Agreement (Sparteca) *established*—NA 1981 *aim*—to redress unequal trade relationships of Australia and New Zealand with small island economies in the Pacific region	*members*—(16) Australia, Cook Islands, Fiji, Kiribati, Marshall Islands, Federated States of Micronesia, Nauru, NZ, Niue, Palau, Papua New Guinea, Samoa, Solomon Islands, Tonga, Tuvalu, Vanuatu
Southern African Customs Union (SACU) *established*—11 December 1969 *aim*—to promote free trade and cooperation in customs matters	*members*—(5) Botswana, Lesotho, Namibia, South Africa, Swaziland
Southern African Development Community (SADC) *note*—evolved from the Southern African Development Coordination Conference (SADCC) *established*—17 August 1992 *aim*—to promote regional economic development and integration	*members*—(14) Angola, Botswana, Democratic Republic of the Congo, Lesotho, Malawi, Mauritius, Mozambique, Namibia, Seychelles, South Africa, Swaziland, Tanzania, Zambia, Zimbabwe
Southern Cone Common Market (Mercosur) or Southern Common Market *note*—also known as Mercado Comun del Cono Sur (Mercosur) *established*—26 March 1991 *aim*—to increase regional economic cooperation	*members*—(4) Argentina, Brazil, Paraguay, Uruguay *associate members*—(2) Bolivia, Chile
Third World	another term for the less developed countries; the term is obsolescent; see less developed countries (LDCs)
underdeveloped countries	refers to those less developed countries with the potential for above-average economic growth; see less developed countries (LDCs)
undeveloped countries	refers to those extremely poor less developed countries (LDCs) with little prospect for economic growth; see least developed countries (LLDCs)
United Nations (UN) *established*—26 June 1945 *effective*—24 October 1945 *aim*—to maintain international peace and security and to promote cooperation involving economic, social, cultural, and humanitarian problems	*constituent organizations*—the UN is composed of six principal organs and numerous subordinate agencies and bodies as follows: 1) Secretariat 2) General Assembly: Joint United Nations Program on HIV/AIDS (UN AIDS), International Research and Training Institute for the Advancement of Women (INSTRAW), Office of the United Nations High Commissioner for Human Rights, United Nations Center for Human Settlements (UN-Habitat), United Nations Children's Fund (UNICEF), United Nations Conference on Trade and Development (UNCTAD), United Nations Development Program (UNDP), United Nations Drug Control Program (UNDCP), United Nations Environment Program (UNEP), United Nations High Commissioner for Human Rights (UNHCHR), United Nations High Commissioner for Refugees (UNHCR), United Nations Institute for Disarmament Research (UNIDIR), United Nations Institute for Training and Research (UNITAR), United Nations Interregional Crime and Justice Research Institute (UNICRI), United Nations Population Fund (UNFPA), United Nations Office of Project Services (UNOPS), United Nations Relief and Works Agency for Palestine Refugees in the Near East (UNRWA), United Nations Research Institute for Social Development (UNRISD), United Nations System Staff College (UNSSC), and United Nations University (UNU), World Food Program (WFP)

United Nations (UN) *(continued)*

3) Security Council: International Criminal Tribunal for the Former Yugoslavia (ICTY), International Criminal Tribunal for Rwanda (ICTR), United Nations Compensation Commission, United Nations Disengagement Observer Force (UNDOF), United Nations Interim Administration Mission in Kosovo (UNMIK), United Nations Interim Force in Lebanon (UNIFIL), United Nations Mission in Liberia (UNMIL), United Nations Mission of Support in East Timor (UNMISET), United Nations Military Observer Group in India and Pakistan (UNMOGIP), United Nations Mission for the Referendum in Western Sahara (MINURSO), United Nations Mission in Ethiopia and Eritrea (UNMEE), United Nations Mission in Sierra Leone (UNAMSIL), United Nations Monitoring and Verification Commission (UNMOVIC), United Nations Observer Mission in Georgia (UNOMIG), United Nations Organization Mission in the Democratic Republic of the Congo (MONUC), United Nations Peace-Keeping Force in Cyprus (UNFICYP), and United Nations Truce Supervision Organization (UNTSO)

4) Economic and Social Council (ECOSOC): Commission for Social Development, Commission on Crime Prevention and Criminal Justice, Commission on Human Rights, Commission on Narcotics Drugs, Commission on Population and Development, Commission on Science and Technology for Development, Commission on Sustainable Development, Commission on the Status of Women, Economic and Social Commission for Asia and the Pacific (ESCAP), Economic and Social Commission for Western Asia (ESCWA), Economic Commission for Africa (ECA), Economic Commission for Europe (ECE), Economic Commission for Latin America and the Caribbean (ECLAC), Food and Agriculture Organization of the United Nations (FAO), International Atomic Energy Agency (IAEA), International Bank for Reconstruction and Development (IBRD), International Center for Secretariat of Investment Disputes (ICSID), International Civil Aviation Organization (ICAO), International Development Association (IDA), International Finance Corporation (IFC), International Fund for Agricultural Development (IFAD), International Labor Organization (ILO), International Maritime Organization (IMO), International Monetary Fund (IMF), International Telecommunication Union (ITU), Multilateral Investment Geographic Agency (MIGA), Statistical Commission, United Nations Educational, Scientific, and Cultural Organization (UNESCO), United Nations Forum on Forests, United Nations Industrial Development Organization (UNIDO), Universal Postal Union (UPU), World Health Organization (WHO), World Intellectual Property Organization (WIPO), World Meteorological Organization (WMO), World Tourism Organization (WToO), and World Trade Organization (WTrO)

5) Trusteeship Council (inactive; no trusteeships at this time)

6) International Court of Justice (ICJ)

UN members—(191) Afghanistan, Albania, Algeria, Andorra, Angola, Antigua and Barbuda, Argentina, Armenia, Australia, Austria, Azerbaijan, The Bahamas, Bahrain, Bangladesh, Barbados, Belarus, Belgium, Belize, Benin, Bhutan, Bolivia, Bosnia and Herzegovina, Botswana, Brazil, Brunei, Bulgaria, Burkina Faso, Burma, Burundi, Cambodia, Cameroon, Canada, Cape Verde, Central African Republic, Chad, Chile, China, Colombia, Comoros, Democratic Republic of the Congo, Republic of the Congo, Costa Rica, Cote d'Ivoire, Croatia, Cuba, Cyprus, Czech Republic, Denmark, Djibouti, Dominica, Dominican Republic, East Timor, Ecuador, Egypt, El Salvador, Equatorial Guinea, Eritrea, Estonia, Ethiopia, Fiji, Finland, France, Gabon, The Gambia, Georgia, Germany, Ghana, Greece, Grenada, Guatemala, Guinea, Guinea-Bissau, Guyana, Haiti, Honduras, Hungary, Iceland, India, Indonesia, Iran, Iraq, Ireland, Israel, Italy, Jamaica, Japan, Jordan, Kazakhstan, Kenya, Kiribati, North Korea, South Korea, Kuwait, Kyrgyzstan, Laos, Latvia, Lebanon, Lesotho, Liberia, Libya, Liechtenstein, Lithuania, Luxembourg, The Former Yugoslav Republic of Macedonia, Madagascar, Malawi, Malaysia, Maldives, Mali, Malta, Marshall Islands, Mauritania, Mauritius, Mexico, Federated States of Micronesia, Moldova, Monaco, Mongolia, Morocco, Mozambique, Namibia, Nauru, Nepal, Netherlands, NZ, Nicaragua, Niger, Nigeria, Norway, Oman, Pakistan, Palau, Panama, Papua New Guinea, Paraguay, Peru, Philippines, Poland, Portugal, Qatar, Romania, Russia, Rwanda, Saint Kitts and Nevis, Saint Lucia, Saint Vincent and the Grenadines, Samoa, San Marino, Sao Tome and Principe, Saudi Arabia, Senegal, Serbia and Montenegro, Seychelles, Sierra Leone, Singapore, Slovakia, Slovenia, Solomon Islands, Somalia, South Africa, Spain, Sri Lanka, Sudan, Suriname, Swaziland, Sweden, Switzerland, Syria, Tajikistan, Tanzania, Thailand, Togo, Tonga, Trinidad and Tobago, Tunisia, Turkey, Turkmenistan, Tuvalu, Uganda, Ukraine, UAE, UK, US, Uruguay, Uzbekistan, Vanuatu, Venezuela, Vietnam, Yemen, Zambia, Zimbabwe; note—all UN members are represented in the General Assembly

observers—(1 plus the Palestine Liberation Organization) Holy See, Palestine Liberation Organization

United Nations Children's Fund (UNICEF)

note—acronym retained from the predecessor organization, UN International Children's Emergency Fund
established—11 December 1946
aim—to help establish child health and welfare services

members—(37) selected on a rotating basis from all regions

Appendix B: International Organizations and Groups *(continued)*

United Nations Conference on Trade and Development (UNCTAD) *established*—30 December 1964 *aim*—to promote international trade	*members*—(192) all UN members plus Holy See
United Nations Development Program (UNDP) *established*—22 November 1965 *aim*—to provide technical assistance to stimulate economic and social development	*members (executive board)*—(36) selected on a rotating basis from all regions
United Nations Disengagement Observer Force (UNDOF) *established*—31 May 1974 *aim*—to observe the 1973 Arab-Israeli cease-fire; established by the UN Security Council	*members*—(6) Austria, Canada, Japan, Poland, Slovakia, Sweden
United Nations Educational, Scientific, and Cultural Organization (UNESCO) *established*—16 November 1945 *effective*—4 November 1946 *aim*—to promote cooperation in education, science, and culture	*members*—(190) Afghanistan, Albania, Algeria, Andorra, Angola, Antigua and Barbuda, Argentina, Armenia, Australia, Austria, Azerbaijan, The Bahamas, Bahrain, Bangladesh, Barbados, Belarus, Belgium, Belize, Benin, Bhutan, Bolivia, Bosnia and Herzegovina, Botswana, Brazil, Bulgaria, Burkina Faso, Burma, Burundi, Cambodia, Cameroon, Canada, Cape Verde, Central African Republic, Chad, Chile, China, Colombia, Comoros, Democratic Republic of the Congo, Republic of the Congo, Cook Islands, Costa Rica, Cote d'Ivoire, Croatia, Cuba, Cyprus, Czech Republic, Denmark, Djibouti, Dominica, Dominican Republic, East Timor, Ecuador, Egypt, El Salvador, Equatorial Guinea, Eritrea, Estonia, Ethiopia, Fiji, Finland, France, Gabon, The Gambia, Georgia, Germany, Ghana, Greece, Grenada, Guatemala, Guinea, Guinea-Bissau, Guyana, Haiti, Honduras, Hungary, Iceland, India, Indonesia, Iran, Iraq, Ireland, Israel, Italy, Jamaica, Japan, Jordan, Kazakhstan, Kenya, Kiribati, North Korea, South Korea, Kuwait, Kyrgyzstan, Laos, Latvia, Lebanon, Lesotho, Liberia, Libya, Lithuania, Luxembourg, The Former Yugoslav Republic of Macedonia, Madagascar, Malawi, Malaysia, Maldives, Mali, Malta, Marshall Islands, Mauritania, Mauritius, Mexico, Federated States of Micronesia, Moldova, Monaco, Mongolia, Morocco, Mozambique, Namibia, Nauru, Nepal, Netherlands, NZ, Nicaragua, Niger, Nigeria, Niue, Norway, Oman, Pakistan, Palau, Panama, Papua New Guinea, Paraguay, Peru, Philippines, Poland, Portugal, Qatar, Romania, Russia, Rwanda, Saint Kitts and Nevis, Saint Lucia, Saint Vincent and the Grenadines, Samoa, San Marino, Sao Tome and Principe, Saudi Arabia, Senegal, Serbia and Montenegro, Seychelles, Sierra Leone, Slovakia, Slovenia, Solomon Islands, Somalia, South Africa, Spain, Sri Lanka, Sudan, Suriname, Swaziland, Sweden, Switzerland, Syria, Tajikistan, Tanzania, Thailand, Togo, Tonga, Trinidad and Tobago, Tunisia, Turkey, Turkmenistan, Tuvalu, Uganda, Ukraine, UAE, UK, US, Uruguay, Uzbekistan, Vanuatu, Venezuela, Vietnam, Yemen, Zambia, Zimbabwe *associate members*—(6) Aruba, British Virgin Islands, Cayman Islands, Macau, Netherlands Antilles, Tokelau
United Nations Environment Program (UNEP) *established*—15 December 1972 *aim*—to promote international cooperation on all environmental matters	*members*—(58) selected on a rotating basis from all regions
United Nations General Assembly *established*—26 June 1945 *effective*—24 October 1945 *aim*—to function as the primary deliberative organ of the UN	*members*—(191) all UN members are represented in the General Assembly

Appendix B: International Organizations and Groups *(continued)*

United Nations High Commissioner for Refugees (UNHCR)

established—3 December 1949
effective—1 January 1951
aim—to ensure the humanitarian treatment of refugees and find permanent solutions to refugee problems

members (executive committee)—(64) Algeria, Argentina, Australia, Austria, Bangladesh, Belgium, Brazil, Canada, Chile, China, Colombia, Democratic Republic of the Congo, Cote d'Ivoire, Cyprus, Denmark, Ecuador, Ethiopia, Finland, France, Germany, Greece, Guinea, Holy See, Hungary, India, Iran, Ireland, Israel, Italy, Japan, Kenya, South Korea, Lebanon, Lesotho, Madagascar, Mexico, Morocco, Mozambique, Namibia, Netherlands, NZ, Nicaragua, Nigeria, Norway, Pakistan, Philippines, Poland, Russia, Serbia and Montenegro, Somalia, South Africa, Spain, Sudan, Sweden, Switzerland, Tanzania, Thailand, Tunisia, Turkey, Uganda, UK, US, Venezuela, Yemen

United Nations Industrial Development Organization (UNIDO)

established—17 November 1966
effective—1 January 1967
aim—UN specialized agency that promotes industrial development especially among the members

members—(171) Afghanistan, Albania, Algeria, Angola, Argentina, Armenia, Austria, Azerbaijan, The Bahamas, Bahrain, Bangladesh, Barbados, Belarus, Belgium, Belize, Benin, Bhutan, Bolivia, Bosnia and Herzegovina, Botswana, Brazil, Bulgaria, Burkina Faso, Burma, Burundi, Cambodia, Cameroon, Cape Verde, Central African Republic, Chad, Chile, China, Colombia, Comoros, Democratic Republic of the Congo, Republic of the Congo, Costa Rica, Cote d'Ivoire, Croatia, Cuba, Cyprus, Czech Republic, Denmark, Djibouti, Dominica, Dominican Republic, East Timor, Ecuador, Egypt, El Salvador, Equatorial Guinea, Eritrea, Ethiopia, Fiji, Finland, France, Gabon, The Gambia, Georgia, Germany, Ghana, Greece, Grenada, Guatemala, Guinea, Guinea-Bissau, Guyana, Haiti, Honduras, Hungary, India, Indonesia, Iran, Iraq, Ireland, Israel, Italy, Jamaica, Japan, Jordan, Kazakhstan, Kenya, North Korea, South Korea, Kuwait, Kyrgyzstan, Laos, Lebanon, Lesotho, Liberia, Libya, Lithuania, Luxembourg, The Former Yugoslav Republic of Macedonia, Madagascar, Malawi, Malaysia, Maldives, Mali, Malta, Mauritania, Mauritius, Mexico, Moldova, Monaco, Mongolia, Morocco, Mozambique, Namibia, Nepal, Netherlands, NZ, Nicaragua, Niger, Nigeria, Norway, Oman, Pakistan, Panama, Papua New Guinea, Paraguay, Peru, Philippines, Poland, Portugal, Qatar, Romania, Russia, Rwanda, Saint Kitts and Nevis, Saint Lucia, Saint Vincent and the Grenadines, Sao Tome and Principe, Saudi Arabia, Senegal, Serbia and Montenegro, Seychelles, Sierra Leone, Slovakia, Slovenia, Somalia, South Africa, Spain, Sri Lanka, Sudan, Suriname, Swaziland, Sweden, Switzerland, Syria, Tajikistan, Tanzania, Thailand, Togo, Tonga, Trinidad and Tobago, Tunisia, Turkey, Turkmenistan, Uganda, Ukraine, UAE, UK, Uruguay, Uzbekistan, Vanuatu, Venezuela, Vietnam, Yemen, Zambia, Zimbabwe

United Nations Institute for Training and Research (UNITAR)

established—11 December 1963 adoption of the resolution establishing the Institute
effective—24 March 1965
aim—to help the UN become more effective through training and research

members (Board of Trustees)—(21) Austria, Brazil, China, Czech Republic, Egypt, France, Ghana, Japan, Kuwait, Mexico, Monaco, Morocco, Netherlands, Nigeria, Pakistan, Russia, South Africa, Sweden, Switzerland, UK, US; *note*—the UN Secretary General can appoint up to 30 members

United Nations Interim Administration Mission in Kosovo (UNMIK)

established—10 June 1999
aim—to promote the establishment of substantial autonomy and self-government in Kosovo; to perform basic civilian administrative functions; to support the reconstruction of key infrastructure and humanitarian and disaster relief

members—(48) Argentina, Austria, Bangladesh, Belgium, Bulgaria, Cameroon, Canada, Cote d'Ivoire, Czech Republic, Denmark, Egypt, Fiji, Finland, France, Germany, Ghana, Greece, Hungary, Iceland, India, Italy, Jordan, Kenya, Kyrgyzstan, Lithuania, Malawi, Malaysia, Nepal, Nigeria, Norway, Pakistan, Philippines, Poland, Portugal, Romania, Russia, Senegal, Slovenia, Spain, Sweden, Switzerland, Tunisia, Turkey, Ukraine UK, US, Zambia, Zimbabwe

United Nations Interim Force in Lebanon (UNIFIL)

established—19 March 1978
aim—to confirm the withdrawal of Israeli forces, and assist in reestablishing Lebanese authority in southern Lebanon; established by the UN Security Council

members—(7) France, Ghana, India, Ireland, Italy, Poland, Ukraine

United Nations Iraq-Kuwait Observation Mission (UNIKOM)

established in 9 April 1991; to observe and monitor the demilitarized zone established between Iraq and Kuwait; established by the UN Security Council; members were Argentina, Austria, Bangladesh, China, Denmark, Fiji, Finland, France, Germany, Ghana, Greece, Hungary, India, Indonesia, Ireland, Italy, Kenya, Malaysia, Nigeria, Pakistan, Poland, Romania, Russia, Senegal, Singapore, Sweden, Thailand, Turkey, UK, US, Uruguay, Venezuela; mandate ended 6 October 2003

Appendix B: International Organizations and Groups *(continued)*

United Nations Military Observer Group in India and Pakistan (UNMOGIP)

established—24 January 1949
aim—to observe the 1949 India-Pakistan cease-fire; established by the UN Security Council

members—(9) Belgium, Chile, Croatia, Denmark, Finland, Italy, South Korea, Sweden, Uruguay

---

United Nations Mission for the Referendum in Western Sahara (MINURSO)

established—29 April 1991
aim—to supervise the cease-fire and conduct a referendum in Western Sahara; established by the UN Security Council

members—(25) Argentina, Austria, Bangladesh, China, Croatia, Egypt, El Salvador, France, Ghana, Greece, Guinea, Honduras, Hungary, Ireland, Italy, Kenya, South Korea, Malaysia, Mongolia, Nigeria, Pakistan, Poland, Russia, Sri Lanka, Uruguay

---

United Nations Mission in Bosnia and Herzegovina (UNMIBH)

established 21 December 1995; to establish an International Police Task Force (IPTF) to implement the Dayton Peace Agreement in Bosnia and Herzegovina; members Argentina, Austria, Bangladesh, Bulgaria, Canada, Chile, China, Czech Republic, Denmark, Egypt, Estonia, Fiji, Finland, France, Germany, Ghana, Greece, Hungary, Iceland, India, Indonesia, Ireland, Italy, Jordan, Kenya, Lithuania, Malaysia, Nepal, Nigeria, Netherlands, Norway, Pakistan, Poland, Portugal, Romania, Russia, Senegal, Spain, Sweden, Switzerland, Thailand, Tunisia, Turkey, Ukraine, UK, US, Vanuatu; was terminated 31 December 2002

United Nations Mission in Ethiopia and Eritrea (UNMEE)

established—31 July 2000
aim—to monitor the cessation of hostilities

members—(42) Algeria, Australia, Austria, Bangladesh, Benin, Bosnia and Herzegovina, Bulgaria, China, Croatia, Czech Republic, Denmark, Finland, France, The Gambia, Ghana, Greece, India, Italy, Jordan, Kenya, Malaysia, Namibia, Nepal, Nigeria, Norway, Paraguay, Peru, Poland, Romania, Russia, Slovakia, South Africa, Spain, Sweden, Switzerland, Tanzania, Tunisia, Ukraine, UK, US, Uruguay, Zambia

---

United Nations Mission in Liberia (UNMIL)

established—19 September 2003
aim—to support the cease-fire agreement and peace process; protect UN facilities and people; support humanitarian activities;and assist in national security reform

members—(43) Bangladesh, Benin, Bolivia, Brazil, China, Croatia, Denmark, Ecuador, Ethiopia, Finland, France, The Gambia, Ghana, Guinea-Bissau, Indonesia, Ireland, Jordan, Kenya, South Korea, Malawi, Mali, Moldova, Namibia, Nepal, Netherlands, Niger, Nigeria, Norway, Pakistan, Paraguay, Peru, Philippines, Poland, Romania, Senegal, South Africa, Sweden, Togo, Turkey, UK, US, Zambia, Zimbabwe

---

United Nations Mission in Sierra Leone (UNAMSIL)

established—22 October 1999
aim—to cooperate with the Government of Sierra Leone and the other parties to the Peace Agreement in the implementation of the agreement; to monitor the military and security situation in Sierra Leone; to monitor the disarmament and demobilization of combatants and members of the Civil Defense Forces (CFD); to assist in monitoring respect for international humanitarian law

members—(31) Bangladesh, Bolivia, Canada, China, Croatia, Czech Republic, Denmark, Egypt, The Gambia, Germany, Ghana, Guinea, Indonesia, Jordan, Kenya, Kyrgyzstan, Malaysia, Mali, Nepal, NZ, Nigeria, Pakistan, Russia, Slovakia, Sweden, Tanzania, Thailand, Ukraine, UK, Uruguay, Zambia

---

United Nations Mission of Observers in Prevlaka (UNMOP)

established 1 February 1996; to monitor the demilitarization of the Prevlaka peninsula in southern Croatia; members were Argentina, Bangladesh, Belgium, Brazil, Czech Republic, Denmark, Egypt, Finland, Ghana, Indonesia, Ireland, Jordan, Kenya, Nepal, NZ, Nigeria, Norway, Pakistan, Poland, Russia, Switzerland, Ukraine; was terminated 15 December 2002

Appendix B: International Organizations and Groups *(continued)*

United Nations Mission of Support in East Timor (UNMISET)

established—17 May 2002
aim—to provide assistance to structures critical to political stability; to provide law enforcement and public security and to assist in the development of law enforcement agencies; to contribute to external security

members—(28) Australia, Austria, Bangladesh, Bolivia, Brazil, Croatia, Denmark, Fiji, Ireland, Japan, Jordan, Kenya, South Korea, Malaysia, Mozambique, Nepal, NZ, Pakistan, Philippines, Portugal, Russia, Serbia and Montenegro, Singapore, Slovakia, Sweden, Thailand, Turkey, Uruguay

---

United Nations Monitoring, Verification, and Inspection Commission (UNMOVIC)

note—formerly known as United Nations Special Commission for the Elimination of Iraq's Weapons of Mass Destruction (UNSCOM)
established—NA December 1999
aim—to identify, account for, and eliminate Iraq's weapons of mass destruction and the capacity to produce them

commissioners—(15) Argentina, Brazil, Canada, China, France, Germany, India, Japan, Mexico, Nigeria, Russia, Senegal, Ukraine, UK, US

United Nations Observer Mission in Georgia (UNOMIG)

established—24 August 1993
aim—to verify compliance with the cease-fire agreement, to monitor weapons exclusion zone, and to supervise CIS peacekeeping force for Abkhazia; established by the UN Security Council

members—(23) Albania, Austria, Bangladesh, Czech Republic, Denmark, Egypt, France, Germany, Greece, Hungary, Indonesia, Jordan, South Korea, Pakistan, Poland, Russia, Sweden, Switzerland, Turkey, Ukraine, UK, US, Uruguay

---

United Nations Organization Mission in the Democratic Republic of the Congo (MONUC)

established—30 November 1999
aim—to establish contacts with the signatories to the cease-fire agreement and to plan for the observation of the cease-fire and disengagement of forces

members—(49) Algeria, Bangladesh, Belgium, Benin, Bolivia, Bosnia and Herzegovina, Burkina Faso, Cameroon, Canada, Chile, China, Czech Republic, Denmark, Egypt, France, Ghana, India, Indonesia, Ireland, Jordan, Kenya, Malawi, Malaysia, Mali, Mongolia, Morocco, Mozambique, Nepal, Niger, Nigeria, Norway, Pakistan, Paraguay, Peru, Poland, Romania, Russia, Senegal, Serbia and Montenegro, South Africa, Spain, Sri Lanka, Sweden, Switzerland, Tunisia, Ukraine, UK, Uruguay, Zambia

---

United Nations Peace-keeping Force in Cyprus (UNFICYP)

established—4 March 1964
aim—to serve as a peacekeeping force between Greek Cypriots and Turkish Cypriots in Cyprus; established by the UN Security Council

members—(9) Argentina, Austria, Canada, Finland, Hungary, Ireland, South Korea, Slovakia, UK

United Nations Population Fund (UNFPA)

note—acronym retained from predecessor organization UN Fund for Population Activities
established—NA July 1967
aim—to assist both developed and developing countries to deal with their population problems

members (executive board)—(36) selected on a rotating basis from all regions

---

United Nations Preventive Deployment Force (UNPREDEP)

established 31 March 1995; to monitor border activity in the Former Yugoslav Republic of Macedonia; members were Argentina, Bangladesh, Belgium, Brazil, Canada, Czech Republic, Denmark, Egypt, Finland, Ghana, Indonesia, Ireland, Jordan, Kenya, Nepal, NZ, Nigeria, Norway, Pakistan, Poland, Portugal, Russia, Sweden, Switzerland, Turkey, Ukraine, US; mandate ended 25 March 1999

Appendix B: International Organizations and Groups *(continued)*

United Nations Relief and Works Agency for Palestine Refugees in the Near East (UNRWA) *established*—8 December 1949 *aim*—to provide assistance to Palestinian refugees	*members (advisory commission)*—(10) Belgium, Egypt, France, Japan, Jordan, Lebanon, Syria, Turkey, UK, US
United Nations Research Institute for Social Development (UNRISD) *established*—NA 1963 *aim*—to conduct research into the problems of economic development during different phases of economic growth	*members*—no country members, but a Board of Directors consisting of a chairman appointed by the UN secretary general and 11 individual members
United Nations Secretariat *established*—26 June 1945 *effective*—24 October 1945 *aim*—to serve as the primary administrative organ of the UN; a Secretary General is appointed for a five-year term by the General Assembly on the recommendation of the Security Council	*members*—the UN Secretary General and staff
United Nations Security Council (UNSC) *established*—26 June 1945 *effective*—24 October 1945 *aim*—to maintain international peace and security	*permanent members*—(5) China, France, Russia, UK, US *nonpermanent members*—(10) elected for two-year terms by the UN General Assembly; Algeria (2004-05), Angola (2003-04), Benin (2004-05), Brazil (2004-05), Chile (2003-04), Germany (2003-04), Pakistan (2003-04), Philippines (2004-05), Romania (2004-05), Spain (2003-04)
United Nations Transitional Administration in East Timor (UNTAET)	established 25 October 1999 to provide security throughout the territory of East Timor; to establish an effective administration; to ensure the coordination and delivery of humanitarian assistance; to support capacity-building for self-government; 28 members including Australia, Bangladesh, Bolivia, Brazil, Chile, Denmark, Egypt, Fiji, Ireland, Jordan, South Korea, Malaysia, Mozambique, Nepal, NZ, Norway, Pakistan, Philippines, Portugal, Russia, Singapore, Slovakia, Sweden, Thailand, Turkey, UK, US, Uruguay
United Nations Truce Supervision Organization (UNTSO) *established*—NA June 1948 *aim*—to supervise the 1948 Arab-Israeli cease-fire; currently supports timely deployment of reinforcements to other peacekeeping operations in the region as needed; initially established by the UN Security Council	*members*—(23) Argentina, Australia, Austria, Belgium, Canada, Chile, China, Denmark, Estonia, Finland, France, Ireland, Italy, Nepal, Netherlands, NZ, Norway, Russia, Slovakia, Slovenia, Sweden, Switzerland, US
United Nations Trusteeship Council	established on 26 June 1945, effective on 24 October 1945, to supervise the administration of the 11 UN trust territories; members were China, France, Russia, UK, US; it formally suspended operations 1 November 1995 after the Trust Territory of the Pacific Islands (Palau) became the Republic of Palau, a constitutional government in free association with the US; the Trusteeship Council was not dissolved
United Nations University (UNU) *established*—3 December 1973 *aim*—to conduct research in development, welfare, and human survival and to train scholars	*members*—(24 members of UNU Council and the Rector are appointed by the Secretary General of the United Nations and the Director General of UNESCO)

Appendix B: International Organizations and Groups *(continued)*

Universal Postal Union (UPU) *established*—9 October 1874, affiliated with the UN 15 November 1947 *effective*—1 July 1948 *aim*—to promote international postal cooperation; a UN specialized agency	*members*—(188) Afghanistan, Albania, Algeria, Angola, Antigua and Barbuda, Argentina, Armenia, Australia, Austria, Azerbaijan, The Bahamas, Bahrain, Bangladesh, Barbados, Belarus, Belgium, Belize, Benin, Bhutan, Bolivia, Bosnia and Herzegovina, Botswana, Brazil, Brunei, Bulgaria, Burkina Faso, Burma, Burundi, Cambodia, Cameroon, Canada, Cape Verde, Central African Republic, Chad, Chile, China, Colombia, Comoros, Democratic Republic of the Congo, Republic of the Congo, Costa Rica, Cote d'Ivoire, Croatia, Cuba, Cyprus, Czech Republic, Denmark, Djibouti, Dominica, Dominican Republic, East Timor, Ecuador, Egypt, El Salvador, Equatorial Guinea, Eritrea, Estonia, Ethiopia, Fiji, Finland, France, Gabon, The Gambia, Georgia, Germany, Ghana, Greece, Grenada, Guatemala, Guinea, Guinea-Bissau, Guyana, Haiti, Holy See, Honduras, Hungary, Iceland, India, Indonesia, Iran, Iraq, Ireland, Israel, Italy, Jamaica, Japan, Jordan, Kazakhstan, Kenya, Kiribati, North Korea, South Korea, Kuwait, Kyrgyzstan, Laos, Latvia, Lebanon, Lesotho, Liberia, Libya, Liechtenstein, Lithuania, Luxembourg, The Former Yugoslav Republic of Macedonia, Madagascar, Malawi, Malaysia, Maldives, Mali, Malta, Mauritania, Mauritius, Mexico, Moldova, Monaco, Mongolia, Morocco, Mozambique, Namibia, Nauru, Nepal, Netherlands, NZ, Nicaragua, Niger, Nigeria, Norway, Oman, Pakistan, Panama, Papua New Guinea, Paraguay, Peru, Philippines, Poland, Portugal, Qatar, Romania, Russia, Rwanda, Saint Kitts and Nevis, Saint Lucia, Saint Vincent and the Grenadines, Samoa, San Marino, Sao Tome and Principe, Saudi Arabia, Senegal, Serbia and Montenegro, Seychelles, Sierra Leone, Singapore, Slovakia, Slovenia, Solomon Islands, Somalia, South Africa, Spain, Sri Lanka, Sudan, Suriname, Swaziland, Sweden, Switzerland, Syria, Tajikistan, Tanzania, Thailand, Togo, Tonga, Trinidad and Tobago, Tunisia, Turkey, Turkmenistan, Tuvalu, Uganda, Ukraine, UAE, UK, US, Uruguay, Uzbekistan, Vanuatu, Venezuela, Vietnam, Yemen, Zambia, Zimbabwe
Warsaw Pact (WP)	established 14 May 1955 to promote mutual defense; members met 1 July 1991 to dissolve the alliance; member states at the time of dissolution were Bulgaria, Czechoslovakia, Hungary, Poland, Romania, and the USSR; earlier members included GDR and Albania
West African Development Bank (WADB) *note*—also known as Banque Ouest-Africaine de Developpement (BOAD); is a financial institution of WAEMU *established*—14 November 1973 *aim*—to promote regional economic development and integration	*regional members*—(9) Central Bank of West African States, Benin, Burkina Faso, Cote d'Ivoire, Guinea-Bissau, Mali, Niger, Senegal, Togo *international/nonregional members*—(5) African Development Bank, Belgium, European Investment Bank, France, Germany
West African Economic and Monetary Union (WAEMU) *note*—also known as Union Economique et Monetaire Ouest Africaine (UEMOA) *established*—1 August 1994 *aim*—to increase competitiveness of members' economic markets; to create a common market	*members*—(8) Benin, Burkina Faso, Cote d'Ivoire, Guinea-Bissau, Mali, Niger, Senegal, Togo
Western European Union (WEU) *established*—23 October 1954 *effective*—6 May 1955 *aim*—to provide mutual defense and to move toward political unification	*members*—(10) Belgium, France, Germany, Greece, Italy, Luxembourg, Netherlands, Portugal, Spain, UK *associate members*—(6) Czech Republic, Hungary, Iceland, Norway, Poland, Turkey *associate partners*—(7) Bulgaria, Estonia, Latvia, Lithuania, Romania, Slovakia, Slovenia *observers*—(5) Austria, Denmark, Finland, Ireland, Sweden
World Bank Group	includes International Bank for Reconstruction and Development (IBRD), International Development Association (IDA), and International Finance Corporation (IFC)
World Confederation of Labor (WCL) *established*—19 June 1920 as the International Federation of Christian Trade Unions (IFCTU), renamed 4 October 1968 *aim*—to promote the trade union movement	*members*—(102 national organizations) Antigua and Barbuda, Argentina, Aruba, Austria, Bangladesh, Belgium, Belize, Benin, Bolivia, Brazil, Bulgaria, Burkina Faso, Cameroon, Canada, Central African Republic, Chad, Chile, Colombia, Democratic Republic of the Congo, Republic of the Congo, Costa Rica, Cote d'Ivoire, Cuba, Cyprus, Czech Republic, Dominica, Dominican Republic, Ecuador, El Salvador, France, French Guiana, Gabon, The Gambia, Ghana, Guadeloupe, Guatemala, Guinea, Guyana, Haiti, Honduras, Hong Kong, Hungary, India, Indonesia, Iran, Italy, Japan, Kazakhstan, South Korea, Liberia, Liechtenstein, Lithuania, Luxembourg, The Former Yugoslav Republic of Macedonia, Madagascar, Malaysia, Malawi, Malta, Martinique, Mauritania, Mauritius, Mexico, Morocco, Namibia, Netherlands, Netherlands Antilles, Nicaragua, Niger, Pakistan, Panama, Paraguay, Peru, Philippines, Poland, Portugal, Puerto Rico, Romania, Rwanda, Saint Lucia, Saint Vincent and the Grenadines, Sao Tome and Principe, Senegal, Serbia and Montenegro, Sierra Leone, Singapore, Slovakia, South Africa, Spain, Sri Lanka, Suriname, Switzerland, Taiwan, Thailand, Togo, Trinidad and Tobago, Ukraine, US, Uruguay, Venezuela, Vietnam, Zambia, Zimbabwe

World Customs Organization (WCO) *note*—began as the Customs Cooperation Council (CCC) *established*—15 December 1950 *aim*—to promote international cooperation in customs matters	*members*—(162) Albania, Algeria, Andorra, Angola, Argentina, Armenia, Australia, Austria, Azerbaijan, The Bahamas, Bahrain, Bangladesh, Barbados, Belarus, Belgium, Benin, Bermuda, Bhutan, Bolivia, Botswana, Brazil, Brunei, Bulgaria, Burkina Faso, Burma, Burundi, Cambodia, Cameroon, Canada, Cape Verde, Central African Republic, Chile, China, Colombia, Comoros, Democratic Republic of the Congo, Republic of the Congo, Costa Rica, Cote d'Ivoire, Croatia, Cuba, Cyprus, Czech Republic, Denmark, East Timor, Ecuador, Egypt, Eritrea, Estonia, Ethiopia, Fiji, Finland, France, Gabon, The Gambia, Georgia, Germany, Ghana, Greece, Guatemala, Guinea, Guyana, Haiti, Hong Kong, Hungary, Iceland, India, Indonesia, Iran, Iraq, Ireland, Israel, Italy, Jamaica, Japan, Jordan, Kazakhstan, Kenya, South Korea, Kuwait, Kyrgyzstan, Latvia, Lebanon, Lesotho, Liberia, Libya, Lithuania, Luxembourg, Macau, The Former Yugoslav Republic of Macedonia, Madagascar, Malawi, Malaysia, Maldives, Mali, Malta, Mauritania, Mauritius, Mexico, Moldova, Mongolia, Morocco, Mozambique, Namibia, Nepal, Netherlands, Netherlands Antilles, NZ, Nicaragua, Niger, Nigeria, Norway, Oman, Pakistan, Panama, Papua New Guinea, Paraguay, Peru, Philippines, Poland, Portugal, Qatar, Romania, Russia, Rwanda, Samoa, Saudi Arabia, Senegal, Serbia and Montenegro, Seychelles, Sierra Leone, Singapore, Slovakia, Slovenia, South Africa, Spain, Sri Lanka, Sudan, Swaziland, Sweden, Switzerland, Syria, Tajikistan, Tanzania, Thailand, Togo, Trinidad and Tobago, Tunisia, Turkey, Turkmenistan, Uganda, Ukraine, UAE, UK, US, Uruguay, Uzbekistan, Venezuela, Vietnam, Yemen, Zambia, Zimbabwe
World Federation of Trade Unions (WFTU) *established*—3 October 1945 *aim*—to promote the trade union movement	*members*—(125 plus the Palestine Liberation Organization) Afghanistan, Albania, Angola, Antigua and Barbuda, Argentina, Armenia, Australia, Austria, Azerbaijan, Bahrain, Bangladesh, Barbados, Belarus, Benin, Bolivia, Botswana, Brazil, Bulgaria, Burkina Faso, Cambodia, Cameroon, Canada, Chile, Colombia, Democratic Republic of the Congo, Republic of the Congo, Costa Rica, Cote d'Ivoire, Cuba, Cyprus, Czech Republic, Djibouti, Dominican Republic, Ecuador, Egypt, El Salvador, Eritrea, Ethiopia, Fiji, Finland, France, French Guiana, The Gambia, Ghana, Greece, Guadeloupe, Guatemala, Guinea, Guinea-Bissau, Guyana, Haiti, Honduras, Hungary, India, Indonesia, Iran, Iraq, Jamaica, Japan, Jordan, Kazakhstan, North Korea, Kuwait, Kyrgyzstan, Laos, Lebanon, Lesotho, Liberia, Libya, Madagascar, Malawi, Malaysia, Mali, Martinique, Mauritius, Mexico, Mozambique, Nepal, New Caledonia, NZ, Niger, Nigeria, Oman, Pakistan, Panama, Papua New Guinea, Peru, Philippines, Poland, Portugal, Puerto Rico, Reunion, Romania, Russia, Saint Lucia, Saint Pierre and Miquelon, Saint Vincent and the Grenadines, Saudi Arabia, Senegal, Sierra Leone, Slovakia, Solomon Islands, Somalia, South Africa, Sri Lanka, Sudan, Sweden, Syria, Tajikistan, Tanzania, Thailand, Togo, Trinidad and Tobago, Tunisia, Turkey, Turkmenistan, Uganda, Ukraine, Uruguay, Uzbekistan, Vanuatu, Venezuela, Vietnam, Yemen, Zimbabwe, Palestine Liberation Organization
World Food Program (WFP) *established*—24 November 1961 *aim*—to provide food aid in support of economic development or disaster relief; an ECOSOC organization	*members*—(36) selected on a rotating basis from all regions
World Health Organization (WHO) *established*—22 July 1946 *effective*—7 April 1948 *aim*—to deal with health matters worldwide; a UN specialized agency	*members*—(192) Afghanistan, Albania, Algeria, Andorra, Angola, Antigua and Barbuda, Argentina, Armenia, Australia, Austria, Azerbaijan, The Bahamas, Bahrain, Bangladesh, Barbados, Belarus, Belgium, Belize, Benin, Bhutan, Bolivia, Bosnia and Herzegovina, Botswana, Brazil, Brunei, Bulgaria, Burkina Faso, Burma, Burundi, Cambodia, Cameroon, Canada, Cape Verde, Central African Republic, Chad, Chile, China, Colombia, Comoros, Democratic Republic of the Congo, Republic of the Congo, Cook Islands, Costa Rica, Cote d'Ivoire, Croatia, Cuba, Cyprus, Czech Republic, Denmark, Djibouti, Dominica, Dominican Republic, East Timor, Ecuador, Egypt, El Salvador, Equatorial Guinea, Eritrea, Estonia, Ethiopia, Fiji, Finland, France, Gabon, The Gambia, Georgia, Germany, Ghana, Greece, Grenada, Guatemala, Guinea, Guinea-Bissau, Guyana, Haiti, Honduras, Hungary, Iceland, India, Indonesia, Iran, Iraq, Ireland, Israel, Italy, Jamaica, Japan, Jordan, Kazakhstan, Kenya, Kiribati, North Korea, South Korea, Kuwait, Kyrgyzstan, Laos, Latvia, Lebanon, Lesotho, Liberia, Libya, Lithuania, Luxembourg, The Former Yugoslav Republic of Macedonia, Madagascar, Malawi, Malaysia, Maldives, Mali, Malta, Marshall Islands, Mauritania, Mauritius, Mexico, Federated States of Micronesia, Moldova, Monaco, Mongolia, Morocco, Mozambique, Namibia, Nauru, Nepal, Netherlands, NZ, Nicaragua, Niger, Nigeria, Niue, Norway, Oman, Pakistan, Palau, Panama, Papua New Guinea, Paraguay, Peru, Philippines, Poland, Portugal, Qatar, Romania, Russia, Rwanda, Saint Kitts and Nevis, Saint Lucia, Saint Vincent and the Grenadines, Samoa, San Marino, Sao Tome and Principe, Saudi Arabia, Senegal, Serbia and Montenegro, Seychelles, Sierra Leone, Singapore, Slovakia, Slovenia, Solomon Islands, Somalia, South Africa, Spain, Sri Lanka, Sudan, Suriname, Swaziland, Sweden, Switzerland, Syria, Tajikistan, Tanzania, Thailand, Togo, Tonga, Trinidad and Tobago, Tunisia, Turkey, Turkmenistan, Tuvalu, Uganda, Ukraine, UAE, UK, US, Uruguay, Uzbekistan, Vanuatu, Venezuela, Vietnam, Yemen, Zambia, Zimbabwe *associate members*—(2) Puerto Rico, Tokelau *observers*—(2) Holy See, Liechtenstein

Appendix B: International Organizations and Groups *(continued)*

World Intellectual Property Organization (WIPO)

established—14 July 1967
effective—26 April 1970
aim—to furnish protection for literary, artistic, and scientific works; a UN specialized agency

members—(179) Albania, Algeria, Andorra, Angola, Antigua and Barbuda, Argentina, Armenia, Australia, Austria, Azerbaijan, The Bahamas, Bahrain, Bangladesh, Barbados, Belarus, Belgium, Belize, Benin, Bhutan, Bolivia, Bosnia and Herzegovina, Botswana, Brazil, Brunei, Bulgaria, Burkina Faso, Burma, Burundi, Cambodia, Cameroon, Canada, Cape Verde, Central African Republic, Chad, Chile, China, Colombia, Democratic Republic of the Congo, Republic of the Congo, Costa Rica, Cote d'Ivoire, Croatia, Cuba, Cyprus, Czech Republic, Denmark, Djibouti, Dominica, Dominican Republic, Ecuador, Egypt, El Salvador, Equatorial Guinea, Eritrea, Estonia, Ethiopia, Fiji, Finland, France, Gabon, The Gambia, Georgia, Germany, Ghana, Greece, Grenada, Guatemala, Guinea, Guinea-Bissau, Guyana, Haiti, Holy See, Honduras, Hungary, Iceland, India, Indonesia, Iran, Iraq, Ireland, Israel, Italy, Jamaica, Japan, Jordan, Kazakhstan, Kenya, North Korea, South Korea, Kuwait, Kyrgyzstan, Laos, Latvia, Lebanon, Lesotho, Liberia, Libya, Liechtenstein, Lithuania, Luxembourg, The Former Yugoslav Republic of Macedonia, Madagascar, Malawi, Malaysia, Mali, Malta, Mauritania, Mauritius, Mexico, Moldova, Monaco, Mongolia, Morocco, Mozambique, Namibia, Nepal, Netherlands, NZ, Nicaragua, Niger, Nigeria, Norway, Oman, Pakistan, Panama, Papua New Guinea, Paraguay, Peru, Philippines, Poland, Portugal, Qatar, Romania, Russia, Rwanda, Saint Kitts and Nevis, Saint Lucia, Saint Vincent and the Grenadines, Samoa, San Marino, Sao Tome and Principe, Saudi Arabia, Senegal, Serbia and Montenegro, Seychelles, Sierra Leone, Singapore, Slovakia, Slovenia, Somalia, South Africa, Spain, Sri Lanka, Sudan, Suriname, Swaziland, Sweden, Switzerland, Tajikistan, Tanzania, Thailand, Togo, Tonga, Trinidad and Tobago, Tunisia, Turkey, Turkmenistan, Uganda, Ukraine, UAE, UK, US, Uruguay, Uzbekistan, Venezuela, Vietnam, Yemen, Zambia, Zimbabwe

World Meteorological Organization (WMO)

established—11 October 1947
effective—4 April 1951
aim—to sponsor meteorological cooperation; a UN specialized agency

members—(187) Afghanistan, Albania, Algeria, Angola, Antigua and Barbuda, Argentina, Armenia, Australia, Austria, Azerbaijan, The Bahamas, Bahrain, Bangladesh, Barbados, Belarus, Belgium, Belize, Benin, Bhutan, Bolivia, Bosnia and Herzegovina, Botswana, Brazil, British Caribbean Territories, Brunei, Bulgaria, Burkina Faso, Burma, Burundi, Cambodia, Cameroon, Canada, Cape Verde, Central African Republic, Chad, Chile, China, Colombia, Comoros, Democratic Republic of the Congo, Republic of the Congo, Cook Islands, Costa Rica, Cote d'Ivoire, Croatia, Cuba, Cyprus, Czech Republic, Denmark, Djibouti, Dominica, Dominican Republic, Ecuador, Egypt, El Salvador, Eritrea, Estonia, Ethiopia, Fiji, Finland, France, French Polynesia, Gabon, The Gambia, Georgia, Germany, Ghana, Greece, Guatemala, Guinea, Guinea-Bissau, Guyana, Haiti, Honduras, Hong Kong, Hungary, Iceland, India, Indonesia, Iran, Iraq, Ireland, Israel, Italy, Jamaica, Japan, Jordan, Kazakhstan, Kenya, Kiribati, North Korea, South Korea, Kuwait, Kyrgyzstan, Laos, Latvia, Lebanon, Lesotho, Liberia, Libya, Lithuania, Luxembourg, Macau, The Former Yugoslav Republic of Macedonia, Madagascar, Malawi, Malaysia, Maldives, Mali, Malta, Mauritania, Mauritius, Mexico, Federated States of Micronesia, Moldova, Monaco, Mongolia, Morocco, Mozambique, Namibia, Nepal, Netherlands, Netherlands Antilles, New Caledonia, NZ, Nicaragua, Niger, Nigeria, Niue, Norway, Oman, Pakistan, Panama, Papua New Guinea, Paraguay, Peru, Philippines, Poland, Portugal, Qatar, Romania, Russia, Rwanda, Saint Lucia, Samoa, Sao Tome and Principe, Saudi Arabia, Senegal, Serbia and Montenegro, Seychelles, Sierra Leone, Singapore, Slovakia, Slovenia, Solomon Islands, Somalia, South Africa, Spain, Sri Lanka, Sudan, Suriname, Swaziland, Sweden, Switzerland, Syria, Tajikistan, Tanzania, Thailand, Togo, Tonga, Trinidad and Tobago, Tunisia, Turkey, Turkmenistan, Uganda, Ukraine, UAE, UK, US, Uruguay, Uzbekistan, Vanuatu, Venezuela, Vietnam, Yemen, Zambia, Zimbabwe

World Tourism Organization (WToO)

established—2 January 1975
aim—to promote tourism as a means of contributing to economic development, international understanding, and peace

members—(142) Afghanistan, Albania, Algeria, Andorra, Angola, Argentina, Armenia, Austria, Azerbaijan, Bahrain, Bangladesh, Benin, Bhutan, Bolivia, Bosnia and Herzegovina, Botswana, Brazil, Bulgaria, Burkina Faso, Burundi, Cambodia, Cameroon, Canada, Cape Verde, Central African Republic, Chad, Chile, China, Colombia, Democratic Republic of the Congo, Republic of the Congo, Costa Rica, Cote d'Ivoire, Croatia, Cuba, Cyprus, Czech Republic, Djibouti, Dominican Republic, Ecuador, Egypt, El Salvador, Equatorial Guinea, Eritrea, Ethiopia, Fiji, France, Gabon, The Gambia, Georgia, Germany, Ghana, Greece, Guatemala, Guinea, Guinea-Bissau, Haiti, Honduras, Hungary, India, Indonesia, Iran, Iraq, Israel, Italy, Jamaica, Japan, Jordan, Kazakhstan, Kenya, North Korea, South Korea, Kuwait, Kyrgyzstan, Laos, Lebanon, Lesotho, Libya, Lithuania, The Former Yugoslav Republic of Macedonia, Madagascar, Malawi, Malaysia, Maldives, Mali, Malta, Mauritania, Mauritius, Mexico, Moldova, Monaco, Mongolia, Morocco, Mozambique, Namibia, Nepal, Netherlands, Nicaragua, Niger, Nigeria, Pakistan, Panama, Paraguay, Peru, Philippines, Poland, Portugal, Qatar, Romania, Russia, Rwanda, San Marino, Sao Tome and Principe, Saudi Arabia, Senegal, Serbia and Montenegro, Seychelles, Sierra Leone, Slovakia, Slovenia, South Africa, Spain, Sri Lanka, Sudan, Swaziland, Switzerland, Syria, Tanzania, Thailand, Togo, Tunisia, Turkey, Turkmenistan, Uganda, Ukraine, Uruguay, Uzbekistan, Venezuela, Vietnam, Yemen, Zambia, Zimbabwe
associate members—(7) Aruba, Flanders, Hong Kong, Macau, Madeira Islands, Netherlands Antilles, Puerto Rico
observers—(2) Holy See, Palestine Liberation Organization

Appendix B: International Organizations and Groups *(continued)*

World Trade Organization (WTrO)

note—succeeded General Agreement on Tariff and Trade (GATT)
established—15 April 1994
effective—1 January 1995
aim—to provide a forum to resolve trade conflicts between members and to carry on negotiations with the goal of further lowering and/or eliminating tariffs and other trade barriers

members—(146) Albania, Angola, Antigua and Barbuda, Argentina, Armenia, Australia, Austria, Bahrain, Bangladesh, Barbados, Belgium, Belize, Benin, Bolivia, Botswana, Brazil, Brunei, Bulgaria, Burkina Faso, Burma, Burundi, Cameroon, Canada, Central African Republic, Chad, Chile, China, Colombia, Democratic Republic of the Congo, Republic of the Congo, Costa Rica, Cote d'Ivoire, Croatia, Cuba, Cyprus, Czech Republic, Denmark, Djibouti, Dominica, Dominican Republic, Ecuador, Egypt, El Salvador, Estonia, EU, Fiji, Finland, France, Gabon, The Gambia, Georgia, Germany, Ghana, Greece, Grenada, Guatemala, Guinea, Guinea-Bissau, Guyana, Haiti, Honduras, Hong Kong, Hungary, Iceland, India, Indonesia, Ireland, Israel, Italy, Jamaica, Japan, Jordan, Kenya, South Korea, Kuwait, Kyrgyzstan, Latvia, Lesotho, Liechtenstein, Lithuania, Luxembourg, Macau, The Former Yugoslav Republic of Macedonia, Madagascar, Malawi, Malaysia, Maldives, Mali, Malta, Mauritania, Mauritius, Mexico, Moldova, Mongolia, Morocco, Mozambique, Namibia, Netherlands, NZ, Nicaragua, Niger, Nigeria, Norway, Oman, Pakistan, Panama, Papua New Guinea, Paraguay, Peru, Philippines, Poland, Portugal, Qatar, Romania, Rwanda, Saint Kitts and Nevis, Saint Lucia, Saint Vincent and the Grenadines, Senegal, Sierra Leone, Singapore, Slovakia, Slovenia, Solomon Islands, South Africa, Spain, Sri Lanka, Suriname, Swaziland, Sweden, Switzerland, Taiwan, Tanzania, Thailand, Togo, Trinidad and Tobago, Tunisia, Turkey, Uganda, UAE, UK, US, Uruguay, Venezuela, Zambia, Zimbabwe
observers—(30) Algeria, Andorra, Azerbaijan, The Bahamas, Belarus, Bhutan, Bosnia and Herzegovina, Cambodia, Cape Verde, Equatorial Guinea, Ethiopia, Holy See, Kazakhstan, Laos, Lebanon, Nepal, Russia, Samoa, Sao Tome and Principe, Saudi Arabia, Serbia and Montenegro, Seychelles, Sudan, Tajikistan, Tonga, Ukraine, Uzbekistan, Vanuatu, Vietnam, Yemen; note—must start accession negotiations within five years of becoming observers

Zangger Committee (ZC)

established—early 1970s
aim—to establish guidelines for the export control provisions of the Nonproliferation of Nuclear Weapons Treaty (NPT)

members—(35) Argentina, Australia, Austria, Belgium, Bulgaria, Canada, China, Czech Republic, Denmark, Finland, France, Germany, Greece, Hungary, Ireland, Italy, Japan, South Korea, Luxembourg, Netherlands, Norway, Poland, Portugal, Romania, Russia, Slovakia, Slovenia, South Africa, Spain, Sweden, Switzerland, Turkey Ukraine, UK, US

Appendix C:

Selected International Environmental Agreements

Air Pollution	see Convention on Long-Range Transboundary Air Pollution
Air Pollution-Nitrogen Oxides	see Protocol to the 1979 Convention on Long-Range Transboundary Air Pollution Concerning the Control of Emissions of Nitrogen Oxides or Their Transboundary Fluxes
Air Pollution-Persistent Organic Pollutants	see Protocol to the 1979 Convention on Long-Range Transboundary Air Pollution on Persistent Organic Pollutants
Air Pollution-Sulfur 85	see Protocol to the 1979 Convention on Long-Range Transboundary Air Pollution on the Reduction of Sulfur Emissions or Their Transboundary Fluxes by at least 30%
Air Pollution-Sulfur 94	see Protocol to the 1979 Convention on Long-Range Transboundary Air Pollution on Further Reduction of Sulfur Emissions
Air Pollution-Volatile Organic Compounds	see Protocol to the 1979 Convention on Long-Range Transboundary Air Pollution Concerning the Control of Emissions of Volatile Organic Compounds or Their Transboundary Fluxes
Antarctic-Environmental Protocol	see Protocol on Environmental Protection to the Antarctic Treaty
Antarctic Treaty *opened for signature*—1 December 1959 *entered into force*—23 June 1961 *objective*—to ensure that Antarctica is used for peaceful purposes only (such as international cooperation in scientific research); to defer the question of territorial claims asserted by some nations and not recognized by others; to provide an international forum for management of the region; applies to land and ice shelves south of 60 degrees South latitude	*parties*—(45) Argentina, Australia, Austria, Belgium, Brazil, Bulgaria, Canada, Chile, China, Colombia, Cuba, Czech Republic, Denmark, Ecuador, Estonia, Finland, France, Germany, Greece, Guatemala, Hungary, India, Italy, Japan, North Korea, South Korea, Netherlands, NZ, Norway, Papua New Guinea, Peru, Poland, Romania, Russia, Slovakia, South Africa, Spain, Sweden, Switzerland, Turkey, Ukraine, UK, US, Uruguay, Venezuela
Basel Convention on the Control of Transboundary Movements of Hazardous Wastes and Their Disposal *note*—abbreviated as Hazardous Wastes *opened for signature*—22 March 1989 *entered into force*—5 May 1992 *objective*—to reduce transboundary movements of wastes subject to the Convention to a minimum consistent with the environmentally sound and efficient management of such wastes; to minimize the amount and toxicity of wastes generated and ensure their environmentally sound management as closely as possible to the source of generation; and to assist LDCs in environmentally sound management of the hazardous and other wastes they generate	*parties*—(159) Albania, Algeria, Andorra, Antigua and Barbuda, Argentina, Armenia, Australia, Austria, Azerbaijan, The Bahamas, Bahrain, Bangladesh, Barbados, Belarus, Belgium, Belize, Benin, Bhutan, Bolivia, Bosnia and Herzegovina, Botswana, Brazil, Brunei, Bulgaria, Burkina Faso, Burundi, Cambodia, Cameroon, Canada, Cape Verde, Chile, China, Colombia, Comoros, Democratic Republic of the Congo, Costa Rica, Cote d'Ivoire, Croatia, Cuba, Cyprus, Czech Republic, Denmark, Djibouti, Dominica, Dominican Republic, Ecuador, Egypt, El Salvador, Equatorial Guinea, Estonia, Ethiopia, EU, Finland, France, The Gambia, Georgia, Germany, Ghana, Greece, Guatemala, Guinea, Guyana, Honduras, Hungary, Iceland, India, Indonesia, Iran, Ireland, Israel, Italy, Jamaica, Japan, Jordan, Kazakhstan, Kenya, Kiribati, South Korea, Kuwait, Kyrgyzstan, Latvia, Lebanon, Lesotho, Libya, Liechtenstein, Lithuania, Luxembourg, The Former Yugoslav Republic of Macedonia, Madagascar, Malawi, Malaysia, Maldives, Mali, Malta, Marshall Islands, Mauritania, Mauritius, Mexico, Federated States of Micronesia, Moldova, Monaco, Mongolia, Morocco, Mozambique, Namibia, Nauru, Nepal, Netherlands, NZ, Nicaragua, Niger, Nigeria, Norway, Oman, Pakistan, Panama, Papua New Guinea, Paraguay, Peru, Philippines, Poland, Portugal, Qatar, Romania, Russia, Rwanda, Saint Kitts and Nevis, Saint Lucia, Saint Vincent and the Grenadines, Samoa, Saudi Arabia, Senegal, Serbia and Montenegro, Seychelles, Singapore, Slovakia, Slovenia, South Africa, Spain, Sri Lanka, Sweden, Switzerland, Syria, Tanzania, Thailand, Trinidad and Tobago, Tunisia, Turkey, Turkmenistan, Uganda, Ukraine, UAE, UK, Uruguay, Uzbekistan, Venezuela, Vietnam, Yemen, Zambia *countries that have signed, but not yet ratified*—(3) Afghanistan, Haiti, US
Biodiversity	see Convention on Biological Diversity

Appendix C: Selected International Environmental Agreements *(continued)*

Convention for the Conservation of Antarctic Seals

note—abbreviated as Antarctic Seals
opened for signature—1 June 1972
entered into force—11 March 1978
objective—to promote and achieve the protection, scientific study, and rational use of Antarctic seals, and to maintain a satisfactory balance within the ecological system of Antarctica

parties—(16) Argentina, Australia, Belgium, Brazil, Canada, Chile, France, Germany, Italy, Japan, Norway, Poland, Russia, South Africa, UK, US
countries that have signed, but not yet ratified—(1) NZ

Convention on Biological Diversity

note—abbreviated as Biodiversity
opened for signature—5 June 1992
entered into force—29 December 1993
objective—to develop national strategies for the conservation and sustainable use of biological diversity

parties—(188) Afghanistan, Albania, Algeria, Angola, Antigua and Barbuda, Argentina, Armenia, Australia, Austria, Azerbaijan, The Bahamas, Bahrain, Bangladesh, Barbados, Belarus, Belgium, Belize, Benin, Bhutan, Bolivia, Bosnia and Herzegovina, Botswana, Brazil, Bulgaria, Burkina Faso, Burma, Burundi, Cambodia, Cameroon, Canada, Cape Verde, Central African Republic, Chad, Chile, China, Colombia, Comoros, Democratic Republic of the Congo, Republic of the Congo, Cook Islands, Costa Rica, Cote d'Ivoire, Croatia, Cuba, Cyprus, Czech Republic, Denmark, Djibouti, Dominica, Dominican Republic, Ecuador, Egypt, El Salvador, Equatorial Guinea, Eritrea, Estonia, Ethiopia, EU, Fiji, Finland, France, Gabon, The Gambia, Georgia, Germany, Ghana, Greece, Grenada, Guatemala, Guinea, Guinea-Bissau, Guyana, Haiti, Honduras, Hungary, Iceland, India, Indonesia, Iran, Ireland, Israel, Italy, Jamaica, Japan, Jordan, Kazakhstan, Kenya, Kiribati, North Korea, South Korea, Kuwait, Kyrgyzstan, Laos, Latvia, Lebanon, Lesotho, Liberia, Libya, Liechtenstein, Lithuania, Luxembourg, The Former Yugoslav Republic of Macedonia, Madagascar, Malawi, Malaysia, Maldives, Mali, Malta, Marshall Islands, Mauritania, Mauritius, Mexico, Federated States of Micronesia, Moldova, Monaco, Mongolia, Morocco, Mozambique, Namibia, Nauru, Nepal, Netherlands, NZ, Nicaragua, Niger, Nigeria, Niue, Norway, Oman, Pakistan, Palau, Panama, Papua New Guinea, Paraguay, Peru, Philippines, Poland, Portugal, Qatar, Romania, Russia, Rwanda, Saint Kitts and Nevis, Saint Lucia, Saint Vincent and the Grenadines, Samoa, San Marino, Sao Tome and Principe, Saudi Arabia, Senegal, Serbia and Montenegro, Seychelles, Sierra Leone, Singapore, Slovakia, Slovenia, Solomon Islands, South Africa, Spain, Sri Lanka, Sudan, Suriname, Swaziland, Sweden, Switzerland, Syria, Tajikistan, Tanzania, Thailand, Togo, Tonga, Trinidad and Tobago, Tunisia, Turkey, Turkmenistan, Tuvalu, Uganda, Ukraine, UAE, UK, Uruguay, Uzbekistan, Vanuatu, Venezuela, Vietnam, Yemen, Zambia, Zimbabwe
countries that have signed, but not yet ratified—(1) US

Climate Change

see United Nations Framework Convention on Climate Change

Climate Change-Kyoto Protocol

see Kyoto Protocol to the United Nations Framework Convention on Climate Change

---

Convention on Fishing and Conservation of Living Resources of the High Seas

note—abbreviated as Marine Life Conservation
opened for signature—29 April 1958
entered into force—20 March 1966
objective—to solve through international cooperation the problems involved in the conservation of living resources of the high seas, considering that because of the development of modern technology some of these resources are in danger of being overexploited

parties—(37) Australia, Belgium, Bosnia and Herzegovina, Burkina Faso, Cambodia, Colombia, Denmark, Dominican Republic, Fiji, Finland, France, Haiti, Jamaica, Kenya, Lesotho, Madagascar, Malawi, Malaysia, Mauritius, Mexico, Netherlands, Nigeria, Portugal, Senegal, Serbia and Montenegro, Sierra Leone, Solomon Islands, South Africa, Spain, Switzerland, Thailand, Tonga, Trinidad and Tobago, Uganda, UK, US, Venezuela
countries that have signed, but not yet ratified—(21) Afghanistan, Argentina, Bolivia, Canada, Costa Rica, Cuba, Ghana, Iceland, Indonesia, Iran, Ireland, Israel, Lebanon, Liberia, Nepal, NZ, Pakistan, Panama, Sri Lanka, Tunisia, Uruguay

---

Convention on Long-Range Transboundary Air Pollution

note—abbreviated as Air Pollution
opened for signature—13 November 1979
entered into force—16 March 1983
objective—to protect the human environment against air pollution and to gradually reduce and prevent air pollution, including long-range transboundary air pollution

parties—(49) Armenia, Austria, Azerbaijan, Belarus, Belgium, Bosnia and Herzegovina, Bulgaria, Canada, Croatia, Cyprus, Czech Republic, Denmark, Estonia, EU, Finland, France, Georgia, Germany, Greece, Hungary, Iceland, Ireland, Italy, Kazakhstan, Kyrgyzstan, Latvia, Liechtenstein, Lithuania, Luxembourg, The Former Yugoslav Republic of Macedonia, Malta, Moldova, Monaco, Netherlands, Norway, Poland, Portugal, Romania, Russia, Serbia and Montenegro, Slovakia, Slovenia, Spain, Sweden, Switzerland, Turkey, Ukraine, UK, US
countries that have signed, but not yet ratified—(2) Holy See, San Marino

Appendix C: Selected International Environmental Agreements *(continued)*

Convention on the Conservation of Antarctic Marine Living Resources

note—abbreviated as Antarctic-Marine Living Resources
opened for signature—5 May 1980
entered into force—7 April 1982
objective—to safeguard the environment and protect the integrity of the ecosystem of the seas surrounding Antarctica, and to conserve Antarctic marine living resources

parties—(31) Argentina, Australia, Belgium, Brazil, Bulgaria, Canada, Chile, EU, Finland, France, Germany, Greece, India, Italy, Japan, South Korea, Namibia, Netherlands, NZ, Norway, Peru, Poland, Russia, South Africa, Spain, Sweden, Ukraine, UK, US, Uruguay, Vanuatu

---

Convention on the International Trade in Endangered Species of Wild Flora and Fauna (CITES)

note—abbreviated as Endangered Species
opened for signature—3 March 1973
entered into force—1 July 1975
objective—to protect certain endangered species from overexploitation by means of a system of import/export permits

parties—(165) Afghanistan, Albania, Algeria, Antigua and Barbuda, Argentina, Australia, Austria, Azerbaijan, The Bahamas, Bangladesh, Barbados, Belarus, Belgium, Belize, Benin, Bhutan, Bolivia, Botswana, Brazil, Brunei, Bulgaria, Burkina Faso, Burma, Burundi, Cambodia, Cameroon, Canada, Central African Republic, Chad, Chile, China, Colombia, Comoros, Democratic Republic of the Congo, Republic of the Congo, Costa Rica, Cote d'Ivoire, Croatia, Cuba, Cyprus, Czech Republic, Denmark, Djibouti, Dominica, Dominican Republic, Ecuador, Egypt, El Salvador, Equatorial Guinea, Eritrea, Estonia, Ethiopia, Fiji, Finland, France, Gabon, The Gambia, Georgia, Germany, Ghana, Greece, Grenada, Guatemala, Guinea, Guinea-Bissau, Guyana, Honduras, Hungary, Iceland, India, Indonesia, Iran, Ireland, Israel, Italy, Jamaica, Japan, Jordan, Kazakhstan, Kenya, South Korea, Kuwait, Laos, Latvia, Lesotho, Liberia, Libya, Liechtenstein, Lithuania, Luxembourg, The Former Yugoslav Republic of Macedonia, Madagascar, Malawi, Malaysia, Mali, Malta, Mauritania, Mauritius, Mexico, Moldova, Monaco, Mongolia, Morocco, Mozambique, Namibia, Nepal, Netherlands, NZ, Nicaragua, Niger, Nigeria, Norway, Pakistan, Panama, Papua New Guinea, Paraguay, Peru, Philippines, Poland, Portugal, Qatar, Romania, Russia, Rwanda, Saint Kitts and Nevis, Saint Lucia, Saint Vincent and the Grenadines, Sao Tome and Principe, Saudi Arabia, Senegal, Serbia and Montenegro, Seychelles, Sierra Leone, Singapore, Slovakia, Slovenia, Somalia, South Africa, Spain, Sri Lanka, Sudan, Suriname, Swaziland, Sweden, Switzerland, Syria, Tanzania, Thailand, Togo, Trinidad and Tobago, Tunisia, Turkey, Uganda, Ukraine, UAE, UK, US, Uruguay, Uzbekistan, Vanuatu, Venezuela, Vietnam, Yemen, Zambia, Zimbabwe

---

Convention on the Prevention of Marine Pollution by Dumping Wastes and Other Matter (London Convention)

note—abbreviated as Marine Dumping
opened for signature—29 December 1972
entered into force—30 August 1975
objective—to control pollution of the sea by dumping and to encourage regional agreements supplementary to the Convention

parties—(80 plus Hong Kong) Afghanistan, Antigua and Barbuda, Argentina, Australia, Azerbaijan, Barbados, Belarus, Belgium, Bolivia, Brazil, Canada, Cape Verde, Chile, China, Democratic Republic of the Congo, Costa Rica, Cote d'Ivoire, Croatia, Cuba, Cyprus, Denmark, Dominican Republic, Egypt, Finland, France, Gabon, Germany, Greece, Guatemala, Haiti, Honduras, Hong Kong (associate member), Hungary, Iceland, Iran, Ireland, Italy, Jamaica, Japan, Jordan, Kenya, Kiribati, South Korea, Libya, Luxembourg, Malta, Mexico, Monaco, Morocco, Nauru, Netherlands, NZ, Nigeria, Norway, Oman, Pakistan, Panama, Papua New Guinea, Peru, Philippines, Poland, Portugal, Russia, Saint Lucia, Saint Vincent and the Grenadines, Serbia and Montenegro, Seychelles, Slovenia, Solomon Islands, South Africa, Spain, Suriname, Sweden, Switzerland, Tonga, Tunisia, Ukraine, UAE, UK, US, Vanuatu

---

Convention on the Prohibition of Military or Any Other Hostile Use of Environmental Modification Techniques

note—abbreviated as Environmental Modification
opened for signature—10 December 1976
entered into force—5 October 1978
objective—to prohibit the military or other hostile use of environmental modification techniques in order to further world peace and trust among nations

parties—(66) Afghanistan, Algeria, Antigua and Barbuda, Argentina, Australia, Austria, Bangladesh, Belarus, Belgium, Benin, Brazil, Bulgaria, Canada, Cape Verde, Chile, Costa Rica, Cuba, Cyprus, Czech Republic, Denmark, Dominica, Egypt, Finland, Germany, Ghana, Greece, Guatemala, Hungary, India, Ireland, Italy, Japan, North Korea, South Korea, Kuwait, Laos, Malawi, Mauritius, Mongolia, Netherlands, NZ, Niger, Norway, Pakistan, Papua New Guinea, Poland, Romania, Russia, Saint Lucia, Saint Vincent and the Grenadines, Sao Tome and Principe, Slovakia, Solomon Islands, Spain, Sri Lanka, Sweden, Switzerland, Tajikistan, Tunisia, Ukraine, UK, US, Uruguay, Uzbekistan, Vietnam, Yemen
countries that have signed, but not yet ratified—(17) Bolivia, Democratic Republic of the Congo, Ethiopia, Holy See, Iceland, Iran, Iraq, Lebanon, Liberia, Luxembourg, Morocco, Nicaragua, Portugal, Sierra Leone, Syria, Turkey, Uganda

Appendix C: Selected International Environmental Agreements *(continued)*

Convention on Wetlands of International Importance Especially as Waterfowl Habitat (Ramsar) *note*—abbreviated as Wetlands *opened for signature*—2 February 1971 *entered into force*—21 December 1975 *objective*—to stem the progressive encroachment on and loss of wetlands now and in the future, recognizing the fundamental ecological functions of wetlands and their economic, cultural, scientific, and recreational value	*parties*—(125) Albania, Algeria, Argentina, Armenia, Australia, Austria, Azerbaijan, The Bahamas, Bahrain, Bangladesh, Belarus, Belgium, Belize, Benin, Bolivia, Bosnia and Herzegovina, Botswana, Brazil, Bulgaria, Burkina Faso, Cambodia, Canada, Chad, Chile, China, Colombia, Comoros, Democratic Republic of the Congo, Republic of the Congo, Costa Rica, Cote d'Ivoire, Croatia, Cuba, Czech Republic, Denmark, Ecuador, Egypt, El Salvador, Estonia, Finland, France, Gabon, The Gambia, Georgia, Germany, Ghana, Greece, Guatemala, Guinea, Guinea-Bissau, Honduras, Hungary, Iceland, India, Indonesia, Iran, Ireland, Israel, Italy, Jamaica, Japan, Jordan, Kenya, South Korea, Latvia, Lebanon, Liechtenstein, Lithuania, Luxembourg, The Former Yugoslav Republic of Macedonia, Madagascar, Malawi, Malaysia, Mali, Malta, Mauritania, Mauritius, Mexico, Monaco, Mongolia, Morocco, Namibia, Nepal, Netherlands, NZ, Nicaragua, Niger, Norway, Pakistan, Panama, Papua New Guinea, Paraguay, Peru, Philippines, Poland, Portugal, Romania, Russia, Senegal, Serbia and Montenegro, Sierra Leone, Slovakia, Slovenia, South Africa, Spain, Sri Lanka, Suriname, Sweden, Switzerland, Syria, Tajikistan, Thailand, Togo, Trinidad and Tobago, Tunisia, Turkey, Uganda, Ukraine, UK, US, Uruguay, Uzbekistan, Venezuela, Vietnam, Zambia
Desertification	see United Nations Convention to Combat Desertification in Those Countries Experiencing Serious Drought and/or Desertification, Particularly in Africa
Endangered Species	see Convention on the International Trade in Endangered Species of Wild Flora and Fauna (CITES)
Environmental Modification	see Convention on the Prohibition of Military or Any Other Hostile Use of Environmental Modification Techniques
Hazardous Wastes	see Basel Convention on the Control of Transboundary Movements of Hazardous Wastes and Their Disposal
International Convention for the Regulation of Whaling *note*—abbreviated as Whaling *opened for signature*—2 December 1946 *entered into force*—10 November 1948 *objective*—to protect all species of whales from overhunting; to establish a system of international regulation for the whale fisheries to ensure proper conservation and development of whale stocks; and to safeguard for future generations the great natural resources represented by whale stocks	*parties*—(42) Antigua and Barbuda, Argentina, Australia, Austria, Brazil, Chile, China, Costa Rica, Denmark, Dominica, Finland, France, Germany, Grenada, Guinea, India, Ireland, Italy, Japan, Kenya, South Korea, Mexico, Monaco, Morocco, Netherlands, NZ, Norway, Oman, Panama, Peru, Russia, Saint Kitts and Nevis, Saint Lucia, Saint Vincent and the Grenadines, Senegal, Solomon Islands, South Africa, Spain, Sweden, Switzerland, UK, US
International Tropical Timber Agreement, 1983 *note*—abbreviated as Tropical Timber 83 *opened for signature*—18 November 1983 *entered into force*—1 April 1985; this agreement expired when the International Tropical Timber Agreement, 1994, went into force *objective*—to provide an effective framework for cooperation between tropical timber producers and consumers and to encourage the development of national policies aimed at sustainable utilization and conservation of tropical forests and their genetic resources	*parties*—(54) Australia, Austria, Belgium, Bolivia, Brazil, Burma, Cameroon, Canada, China, Colombia, Democratic Republic of the Congo, Republic of the Congo, Cote d'Ivoire, Denmark, Ecuador, Egypt, EU, Fiji, Finland, France, Gabon, Germany, Ghana, Greece, Guyana, Honduras, India, Indonesia, Ireland, Italy, Japan, South Korea, Liberia, Luxembourg, Malaysia, Nepal, Netherlands, NZ, Norway, Panama, Papua New Guinea, Peru, Philippines, Portugal, Russia, Spain, Sweden, Switzerland, Thailand, Togo, Trinidad and Tobago, UK, US, Venezuela

Appendix C: Selected International Environmental Agreements *(continued)*

International Tropical Timber Agreement, 1994 *note*—abbreviated as Tropical Timber 94 *opened for signature*—26 January 1994 *entered into force*—1 January 1997 *objective*—to ensure that by the year 2000 exports of tropical timber originate from sustainably managed sources; to establish a fund to assist tropical timber producers in obtaining the resources necessary to reach this objective	*parties*—(58) Australia, Austria, Belgium, Bolivia, Brazil, Burma, Cambodia, Cameroon, Canada, Central African Republic, China, Colombia, Democratic Republic of the Congo, Republic of the Congo, Cote d'Ivoire, Denmark, Ecuador, Egypt, EU, Fiji, Finland, France, Gabon, Germany, Ghana, Greece, Guyana, Honduras, India, Indonesia, Ireland, Italy, Japan, South Korea, Liberia, Luxembourg, Malaysia, Nepal, Netherlands, NZ, Norway, Panama, Papua New Guinea, Peru, Philippines, Portugal, Spain, Suriname, Sweden, Switzerland, Thailand, Togo, Trinidad and Tobago, UK, US, Uruguay, Vanuatu, Venezuela
Kyoto Protocol to the United Nations Framework Convention on Climate Change *note*—abbreviated as Climate Change-Kyoto Protocol *opened for signature*—16 March 1998, but not yet in force *objective*—to further reduce greenhouse gas emissions by enhancing the national programs of developed countries aimed at this goal and by establishing percentage reduction targets for the developed countries	*parties*—(122) Antigua and Barbuda, Argentina, Armenia, Austria, Azerbaijan, The Bahamas, Bangladesh, Barbados, Belgium, Belize, Benin, Bhutan, Bolivia, Botswana, Brazil, Bulgaria, Burma, Burundi, Cambodia, Cameroon, Canada, Chile, China, Colombia, Cook Islands, Costa Rica, Cuba, Cyprus, Czech Republic, Denmark, Djibouti, Dominican Republic, Ecuador, El Salvador, Equatorial Guinea, Estonia, EU, Fiji, Finland, France, The Gambia, Georgia, Germany, Ghana, Greece, Grenada, Guatemala, Guinea, Guyana, Honduras, Hungary, Iceland, India, Ireland, Italy, Jamaica, Japan, Jordan, Kiribati, South Korea, Kyrgyzstan, Laos, Latvia, Lesotho, Liberia, Lithuania, Luxembourg, Madagascar, Malawi, Malaysia, Maldives, Mali, Malta, Marshall Islands, Mauritius, Mexico, Federated States of Micronesia, Moldova, Mongolia, Morocco, Namibia, Nauru, Netherlands, NZ, Nicaragua, Niue, Norway, Palau, Panama, Papua New Guinea, Paraguay, Peru, Philippines, Poland, Portugal, Romania, Saint Lucia, Samoa, Senegal, Seychelles, Slovakia, Slovenia, Solomon Islands, South Africa, Spain, Sri Lanka, Sweden, Switzerland, Tanzania, Thailand, Trinidad and Tobago, Tunisia, Turkmenistan, Tuvalu, Uganda, Ukraine, UK, Uruguay, Uzbekistan, Vanuatu, Vietnam *countries that have signed, but not yet ratified*—(13) Australia, Croatia, Egypt, Indonesia, Israel, Kazakhstan, Liechtenstein, Monaco, Niger, Russia, Saint Vincent and the Grenadines, US, Zambia
Law of the Sea	see United Nations Convention on the Law of the Sea (LOS)
Marine Dumping	see Convention on the Prevention of Marine Pollution by Dumping Wastes and Other Matter (London Convention)
Marine Life Conservation	see Convention on Fishing and Conservation of Living Resources of the High Seas
Montreal Protocol on Substances That Deplete the Ozone Layer *note*—abbreviated as Ozone Layer Protection *opened for signature*—16 September 1987 *entered into force*—1 January 1989 *objective*—to protect the ozone layer by controlling emissions of substances that deplete it	*parties*—(183) Albania, Algeria, Angola, Antigua and Barbuda, Argentina, Armenia, Australia, Austria, Azerbaijan, The Bahamas, Bahrain, Bangladesh, Barbados, Belarus, Belgium, Belize, Benin, Bolivia, Bosnia and Herzegovina, Botswana, Brazil, Brunei, Bulgaria, Burkina Faso, Burma, Burundi, Cambodia, Cameroon, Canada, Cape Verde, Central African Republic, Chad, Chile, China, Colombia, Comoros, Democratic Republic of the Congo, Republic of the Congo, Costa Rica, Cote d'Ivoire, Croatia, Cuba, Cyprus, Czech Republic, Denmark, Djibouti, Dominica, Dominican Republic, Ecuador, Egypt, El Salvador, Estonia, Ethiopia, EU, Fiji, Finland, France, Gabon, The Gambia, Georgia, Germany, Ghana, Greece, Grenada, Guatemala, Guinea, Guyana, Haiti, Honduras, Hungary, Iceland, India, Indonesia, Iran, Ireland, Israel, Italy, Jamaica, Japan, Jordan, Kazakhstan, Kenya, Kiribati, North Korea, South Korea, Kuwait, Kyrgyzstan, Laos, Latvia, Lebanon, Lesotho, Liberia, Libya, Liechtenstein, Lithuania, Luxembourg, The Former Yugoslav Republic of Macedonia, Madagascar, Malawi, Malaysia, Maldives, Mali, Malta, Marshall Islands, Mauritania, Mauritius, Mexico, Federated States of Micronesia, Moldova, Monaco, Mongolia, Morocco, Mozambique, Namibia, Nauru, Nepal, Netherlands, NZ, Nicaragua, Niger, Nigeria, Norway, Oman, Pakistan, Palau, Panama, Papua New Guinea, Paraguay, Peru, Philippines, Poland, Portugal, Qatar, Romania, Russia, Rwanda, Saint Kitts and Nevis, Saint Lucia, Saint Vincent and the Grenadines, Samoa, Sao Tome and Principe, Saudi Arabia, Senegal, Serbia and Montenegro, Seychelles, Sierra Leone, Singapore, Slovakia, Slovenia, Solomon Islands, Somalia, South Africa, Spain, Sri Lanka, Sudan, Suriname, Swaziland, Sweden, Switzerland, Syria, Tajikistan, Tanzania, Thailand, Togo, Tonga, Trinidad and Tobago, Tunisia, Turkey, Turkmenistan, Tuvalu, Uganda, Ukraine, UAE, UK, US, Uruguay, Uzbekistan, Vanuatu, Venezuela, Vietnam, Yemen, Zambia, Zimbabwe
Nuclear Test Ban	see Treaty Banning Nuclear Weapons Tests in the Atmosphere, in Outer Space, and Under Water
Ozone Layer Protection	see Montreal Protocol on Substances That Deplete the Ozone Layer

Protocol of 1978 Relating to the International Convention for the Prevention of Pollution From Ships, 1973 (MARPOL) *note*—abbreviated as Ship Pollution *opened for signature*—17 February 1978 *entered into force*—2 October 1983 *objective*—to preserve the marine environment through the complete elimination of pollution by oil and other harmful substances and the minimization of accidental discharge of such substances	*parties*—(119) Algeria, Angola, Antigua and Barbuda, Argentina, Australia, Austria, The Bahamas, Barbados, Belarus, Belgium, Belize, Benin, Bolivia, Brazil, Brunei, Bulgaria, Burma, Cambodia, Canada, Chile, China, Colombia, Comoros, Cote d'Ivoire, Croatia, Cuba, Cyprus, Czech Republic, Denmark, Djibouti, Dominica, Dominican Republic, Ecuador, Egypt, Equatorial Guinea, Estonia, Finland, France, Gabon, The Gambia, Georgia, Germany, Ghana, Greece, Guatemala, Guyana, Honduras, Hungary, Iceland, India, Indonesia, Ireland, Israel, Italy, Jamaica, Japan, Kazakhstan, Kenya, North Korea, South Korea, Latvia, Lebanon, Liberia, Lithuania, Luxembourg, Malawi, Malaysia, Malta, Marshall Islands, Mauritania, Mauritius, Mexico, Monaco, Morocco, Netherlands, NZ, Nicaragua, Norway, Oman, Pakistan, Panama, Papua New Guinea, Peru, Philippines, Poland, Portugal, Romania, Russia, Saint Kitts and Nevis, Saint Lucia, Saint Vincent and the Grenadines, Sao Tome and Principe, Senegal, Serbia and Montenegro, Seychelles, Sierra Leone, Singapore, Slovakia, Slovenia, South Africa, Spain, Sri Lanka, Suriname, Sweden, Switzerland, Syria, Togo, Tonga, Trinidad and Tobago, Tunisia, Turkey, Tuvalu, Ukraine, UK, US, Uruguay, Vanuatu, Venezuela, Vietnam
Protocol on Environmental Protection to the Antarctic Treaty *note*—abbreviated as Antarctic-Environmental Protocol *opened for signature*—4 October 1991 *entered into force*—14 January 1998 *objective*—to provide for comprehensive protection of the Antarctic environment and dependent and associated ecosystems; applies to the area covered by the Antarctic Treaty	*parties*—(30) Argentina, Australia, Belgium, Brazil, Bulgaria, Canada, Chile, China, Ecuador, Finland, France, Germany, Greece, India, Italy, Japan, South Korea, Netherlands, NZ, Norway, Peru, Poland, Russia, South Africa, Spain, Sweden, Ukraine, UK, US, Uruguay
Protocol to the 1979 Convention on Long-Range Transboundary Air Pollution Concerning the Control of Emissions of Nitrogen Oxides or Their Transboundary Fluxes *note*—abbreviated as Air Pollution-Nitrogen Oxides *opened for signature*—31 October 1988 *entered into force*—14 February 1991 *objective*—to provide for the control or reduction of nitrogen oxides and their transboundary fluxes	*parties*—(28) Austria, Belarus, Belgium, Bulgaria, Canada, Czech Republic, Denmark, Estonia, EU, Finland, France, Germany, Greece, Hungary, Ireland, Italy, Liechtenstein, Luxembourg, Netherlands, Norway, Russia, Slovakia, Spain, Sweden, Switzerland, Ukraine, UK, US *countries that have signed, but not yet ratified*—(1) Poland
Protocol to the 1979 Convention on Long-Range Transboundary Air Pollution Concerning the Control of Emissions of Volatile Organic Compounds or Their Transboundary Fluxes *note*—abbreviated as Air Pollution-Volatile Organic Compounds *opened for signature*—18 November 1991 *entered into force*—29 September 1997 *objective*—to provide for the control and reduction of emissions of volatile organic compounds in order to reduce their transboundary fluxes so as to protect human health and the environment from adverse effects	*parties*—(21) Austria, Belgium, Bulgaria, Czech Republic, Denmark, Estonia, Finland, France, Germany, Hungary, Italy, Liechtenstein, Luxembourg, Monaco, Netherlands, Norway, Slovakia, Spain, Sweden, Switzerland, UK *countries that have signed, but not yet ratified*—(6) Canada, EU, Greece, Portugal, Ukraine, US

Appendix C: Selected International Environmental Agreements *(continued)*

Protocol to the 1979 Convention on Long-Range Transboundary Air Pollution on Further Reduction of Sulfur Emissions *note*—abbreviated as Air Pollution-Sulfur 94 *opened for signature*—14 June 1994 *entered into force*—5 August 1998 *objective*—to provide for a further reduction in sulfur emissions or transboundary fluxes	*parties*—(23) Austria, Belgium, Canada, Croatia, Czech Republic, Denmark, EU, Finland, France, Germany, Greece, Ireland, Italy, Liechtenstein, Luxembourg, Netherlands, Norway, Slovakia, Slovenia, Spain, Sweden, Switzerland, UK *countries that have signed, but not yet ratified*—(5) Bulgaria, Hungary, Poland, Russia, Ukraine
Protocol to the 1979 Convention on Long-Range Transboundary Air Pollution on Persistent Organic Pollutants *note*—abbreviated as Air Pollution-Persistent Organic Pollutants *opened for signature*—24 June 1998, but not yet in force *objective*—to provide for the control and reduction of emissions of persistent organic pollutants in order to reduce their transboundary fluxes so as to protect human health and the environment from adverse effects	*parties*—(8) Bulgaria, Canada, Denmark, Luxembourg, Netherlands, Norway, Sweden, Switzerland *countries that have signed, but not yet ratified*—(28) Armenia, Austria, Belgium, Croatia, Cyprus, Czech Republic, EU, Finland, France, Germany, Greece, Hungary, Iceland, Ireland, Italy, Latvia, Liechtenstein, Lithuania, Moldova, Poland, Portugal, Romania, Slovakia, Slovenia, Spain, Ukraine, UK, US
Protocol to the 1979 Convention on Long-Range Transboundary Air Pollution on the Reduction of Sulfur Emissions or Their Transboundary Fluxes by at Least 30% *note*—abbreviated as Air Pollution-Sulfur 85 *opened for signature*—8 July 1985 *entered into force*—2 September 1987 *objective*—to provide for a 30% reduction in sulfur emissions or transboundary fluxes by 1993	*parties*—(22) Austria, Belarus, Belgium, Bulgaria, Canada, Czech Republic, Denmark, Estonia, Finland, France, Germany, Hungary, Italy, Liechtenstein, Luxembourg, Netherlands, Norway, Russia, Slovakia, Sweden, Switzerland, Ukraine
Ship Pollution	see Protocol of 1978 Relating to the International Convention for the Prevention of Pollution From Ships, 1973 (MARPOL)
Tropical Timber 83	see International Tropical Timber Agreement, 1983
Tropical Timber 94	see International Tropical Timber Agreement, 1994
United Nations Convention on the Law of the Sea (UNCLOS) *note*—abbreviated as Law of the Sea *opened for signature*—10 December 1982 *entered into force*—16 November 1994 *objective*—to set up a comprehensive new legal regime for the sea and oceans; to include rules concerning environmental standards as well as enforcement provisions dealing with pollution of the marine environment	*parties*—(145) Albania, Algeria, Angola, Antigua and Barbuda, Argentina, Armenia, Australia, Austria, The Bahamas, Bahrain, Bangladesh, Barbados, Belgium, Belize, Benin, Bolivia, Bosnia and Herzegovina, Botswana, Brazil, Brunei, Bulgaria, Burma, Cameroon, Canada, Cape Verde, Chile, China, Comoros, Democratic Republic of the Congo, Cook Islands, Costa Rica, Cote d'Ivoire, Croatia, Cuba, Cyprus, Czech Republic, Djibouti, Dominica, Egypt, Equatorial Guinea, EU, Fiji, Finland, France, Gabon, The Gambia, Georgia, Germany, Ghana, Greece, Grenada, Guatemala, Guinea, Guinea-Bissau, Guyana, Haiti, Honduras, Hungary, Iceland, India, Indonesia, Iraq, Ireland, Italy, Jamaica, Japan, Jordan, Kenya, Kiribati, South Korea, Kuwait, Laos, Lebanon, Lithuania, Luxembourg, The Former Yugoslav Republic of Macedonia, Madagascar, Malaysia, Maldives, Mali, Malta, Marshall Islands, Mauritania, Mauritius, Mexico, Federated States of Micronesia, Monaco, Mongolia, Mozambique, Namibia, Nauru, Nepal, Netherlands, NZ, Nicaragua, Nigeria, Norway, Oman, Pakistan, Palau, Panama, Papua New Guinea, Paraguay, Philippines, Poland, Portugal, Qatar, Romania, Russia, Saint Kitts and Nevis, Saint Lucia, Saint Vincent and the Grenadines, Samoa, Sao Tome and Principe, Saudi Arabia, Senegal, Serbia and Montenegro, Seychelles, Sierra Leone, Singapore, Slovakia, Slovenia, Solomon Islands, Somalia, South Africa, Spain, Sri Lanka, Sudan, Suriname, Sweden, Tanzania, Togo, Tonga, Trinidad and Tobago, Tunisia, Tuvalu, Uganda, Ukraine, UK, Uruguay, Vanuatu, Vietnam, Yemen, Zambia, Zimbabwe *countries that have signed, but not yet ratified*—(29) Afghanistan, Belarus, Bhutan, Burkina Faso, Burundi, Cambodia, Central African Republic, Chad, Colombia, Republic of the Congo, Denmark, Dominican Republic, El Salvador, Ethiopia, Iran, North Korea, Lesotho, Liberia, Libya, Liechtenstein, Malawi, Morocco, Niger, Niue, Rwanda, Swaziland, Switzerland, Thailand, UAE

Appendix C: Selected International Environmental Agreements *(continued)*

United Nations Convention to Combat Desertification in Those Countries Experiencing Serious Drought and/or Desertification, Particularly in Africa *note*—abbreviated as Desertification *opened for signature*—14 October 1994 *entered into force*—26 December 1996 *objective*—to combat desertification and mitigate the effects of drought through national action programs that incorporate long-term strategies supported by international cooperation and partnership arrangements	*parties*—(178) Afghanistan, Albania, Algeria, Angola, Antigua and Barbuda, Argentina, Armenia, Australia, Austria, Azerbaijan, The Bahamas, Bahrain, Bangladesh, Barbados, Belarus, Belgium, Belize, Benin, Bolivia, Botswana, Brazil, Bulgaria, Burkina Faso, Burma, Burundi, Cambodia, Cameroon, Canada, Cape Verde, Central African Republic, Chad, Chile, China, Colombia, Comoros, Democratic Republic of the Congo, Republic of the Congo, Cook Islands, Costa Rica, Cote d'Ivoire, Croatia, Cuba, Cyprus, Czech Republic, Denmark, Djibouti, Dominica, Dominican Republic, Ecuador, Egypt, El Salvador, Equatorial Guinea, Eritrea, Ethiopia, EU, Fiji, Finland, France, Gabon, The Gambia, Georgia, Germany, Ghana, Greece, Grenada, Guatemala, Guinea, Guinea-Bissau, Guyana, Haiti, Honduras, Hungary, Iceland, India, Indonesia, Iran, Ireland, Israel, Italy, Jamaica, Japan, Jordan, Kazakhstan, Kenya, Kiribati, South Korea, Kuwait, Kyrgyzstan, Laos, Lebanon, Lesotho, Liberia, Libya, Liechtenstein, Luxembourg, Madagascar, Malawi, Malaysia, Mali, Malta, Marshall Islands, Mauritania, Mauritius, Mexico, Federated States of Micronesia, Moldova, Monaco, Mongolia, Morocco, Mozambique, Namibia, Nauru, Nepal, Netherlands, NZ, Nicaragua, Niger, Nigeria, Niue, Norway, Oman, Pakistan, Palau, Panama, Papua New Guinea, Paraguay, Peru, Philippines, Poland, Portugal, Qatar, Romania, Rwanda, Saint Kitts and Nevis, Saint Lucia, Saint Vincent and the Grenadines, Samoa, San Marino, Sao Tome and Principe, Saudi Arabia, Senegal, Seychelles, Sierra Leone, Singapore, Slovakia, Slovenia, Solomon Islands, South Africa, Spain, Sri Lanka, Sudan, Suriname, Swaziland, Sweden, Switzerland, Syria, Tajikistan, Tanzania, Thailand, Togo, Tonga, Trinidad and Tobago, Tunisia, Turkey, Turkmenistan, Tuvalu, Uganda, UAE, UK, US, Uruguay, Uzbekistan, Vanuatu, Venezuela, Vietnam, Yemen, Zambia, Zimbabwe
United Nations Framework Convention on Climate Change *note*—abbreviated as Climate Change *opened for signature*—9 May 1992 *entered into force*—21 March 1994 *objective*—to achieve stabilization of greenhouse gas concentrations in the atmosphere at a low enough level to prevent dangerous anthropogenic interference with the climate system	*parties*—(186) Albania, Algeria, Angola, Antigua and Barbuda, Argentina, Armenia, Australia, Austria, Azerbaijan, The Bahamas, Bahrain, Bangladesh, Barbados, Belarus, Belgium, Belize, Benin, Bhutan, Bolivia, Bosnia and Herzegovina, Botswana, Brazil, Bulgaria, Burkina Faso, Burma, Burundi, Cambodia, Cameroon, Canada, Cape Verde, Central African Republic, Chad, Chile, China, Colombia, Comoros, Democratic Republic of the Congo, Republic of the Congo, Cook Islands, Costa Rica, Cote d'Ivoire, Croatia, Cuba, Cyprus, Czech Republic, Denmark, Djibouti, Dominica, Dominican Republic, Ecuador, Egypt, El Salvador, Equatorial Guinea, Eritrea, Estonia, Ethiopia, EU, Fiji, Finland, France, Gabon, The Gambia, Georgia, Germany, Ghana, Greece, Grenada, Guatemala, Guinea, Guinea-Bissau, Guyana, Haiti, Honduras, Hungary, Iceland, India, Indonesia, Iran, Ireland, Israel, Italy, Jamaica, Japan, Jordan, Kazakhstan, Kenya, Kiribati, North Korea, South Korea, Kuwait, Kyrgyzstan, Laos, Latvia, Lebanon, Lesotho, Libya, Liechtenstein, Lithuania, Luxembourg, The Former Yugoslav Republic of Macedonia, Madagascar, Malawi, Malaysia, Maldives, Mali, Malta, Marshall Islands, Mauritania, Mauritius, Mexico, Federated States of Micronesia, Moldova, Monaco, Mongolia, Morocco, Mozambique, Namibia, Nauru, Nepal, Netherlands, NZ, Nicaragua, Niger, Nigeria, Niue, Norway, Oman, Pakistan, Palau, Panama, Papua New Guinea, Paraguay, Peru, Philippines, Poland, Portugal, Qatar, Romania, Russia, Rwanda, Saint Kitts and Nevis, Saint Lucia, Saint Vincent and the Grenadines, Samoa, San Marino, Sao Tome and Principe, Saudi Arabia, Senegal, Serbia and Montenegro, Seychelles, Sierra Leone, Singapore, Slovakia, Slovenia, Solomon Islands, South Africa, Spain, Sri Lanka, Sudan, Suriname, Swaziland, Sweden, Switzerland, Syria, Tajikistan, Tanzania, Thailand, Togo, Tonga, Trinidad and Tobago, Tunisia, Turkmenistan, Tuvalu, Uganda, Ukraine, UAE, UK, US, Uruguay, Uzbekistan, Vanuatu, Venezuela, Vietnam, Yemen, Zambia, Zimbabwe *countries that have signed, but not yet ratified*—(2) Afghanistan, Liberia
Wetlands	see Convention on Wetlands of International Importance Especially As Waterfowl Habitat (Ramsar)
Whaling	see International Convention for the Regulation of Whaling

Appendix D:

Cross-Reference List of Country Data Codes

FIPS 10-4:	Countries, Dependencies, Areas of Special Sovereignty, and Their Principal Administrative Divisions (FIPS PUB 10-4) is maintained by the Office of the Geographer and Global Issues (Department of State) and published by the National Institute of Standards and Technology (Department of Commerce). FIPS 10-4 codes are intended for general use throughout the US Government, especially in activities associated with the mission of the Department of State and national defense programs.
ISO 3166:	Codes for the Representation of Names of Countries (ISO 3166) is prepared by the International Organization for Standardization. ISO 3166 includes two- and three-character alphabetic codes and three-digit numeric codes that may be needed for activities involving exchange of data with international organizations that have adopted that standard.
Internet:	The Internet country code is the two-letter digraph maintained by the International Organization for Standardization (ISO) in the ISO 3166 Alpha-2 list and used by the Internet Assigned Numbers Authority (IANA) to establish country-coded top-level domains (ccTLDs).

Entity	FIPS 10-4	ISO 3166			Internet	Comment
Afghanistan	AF	AF	AFG	004	.af	
Albania	AL	AL	ALB	008	.al	
Algeria	AG	DZ	DZA	012	.dz	
American Samoa	AQ	AS	ASM	016	.as	
Andorra	AN	AD	AND	020	.ad	
Angola	AO	AO	AGO	024	.ao	
Anguilla	AV	AI	AIA	660	.ai	
Antarctica	AY	AQ	ATA	010	.aq	ISO defines as the territory south of 60 degrees south latitude
Antigua and Barbuda	AC	AG	ATG	028	.ag	
Argentina	AR	AR	ARG	032	.ar	
Armenia	AM	AM	ARM	051	.am	
Aruba	AA	AW	ABW	533	.aw	
Ashmore and Cartier Islands	AT	—	—	—	—	ISO includes with Australia
Australia	AS	AU	AUS	036	.au	ISO includes Ashmore and Cartier Islands, Coral Sea Islands
Austria	AU	AT	AUT	040	.at	
Azerbaijan	AJ	AZ	AZE	031	.az	
Bahamas, The	BF	BS	BHS	044	.bs	
Bahrain	BA	BH	BHR	048	.bh	
Baker Island	FQ	UM	UMI	581	—	ISO includes with the US Minor Outlying Islands
Bangladesh	BG	BD	BGD	050	.bd	
Barbados	BB	BB	BRB	052	.bb	
Bassas da India	BS	—	—	—	—	ISO includes with the Miscellaneous (French) Indian Ocean Islands
Belarus	BO	BY	BLR	112	.by	
Belgium	BE	BE	BEL	056	.be	
Belize	BH	BZ	BLZ	084	.bz	
Benin	BN	BJ	BEN	204	.bj	

Appendix D: Cross-Reference List of Country Data Codes *(continued)*

Entity	FIPS 10-4	ISO 3166			Internet	Comment
Bermuda	BD	BM	BMU	060	.bm	
Bhutan	BT	BT	BTN	064	.bt	
Bolivia	BL	BO	BOL	068	.bo	
Bosnia and Herzegovina	BK	BA	BIH	070	.ba	
Botswana	BC	BW	BWA	072	.bw	
Bouvet Island	BV	BV	BVT	074	.bv	
Brazil	BR	BR	BRA	076	.br	
British Indian Ocean Territory	IO	IO	IOT	086	.io	
British Virgin Islands	VI	VG	VGB	092	.vg	
Brunei	BX	BN	BRN	096	.bn	
Bulgaria	BU	BG	BGR	100	.bg	
Burkina Faso	UV	BF	BFA	854	.bf	
Burma	BM	MM	MMR	104	.mm	ISO uses the name Myanmar
Burundi	BY	BI	BDI	108	.bi	
Cambodia	CB	KH	KHM	116	.kh	
Cameroon	CM	CM	CMR	120	.cm	
Canada	CA	CA	CAN	124	.ca	
Cape Verde	CV	CV	CPV	132	.cv	
Cayman Islands	CJ	KY	CYM	136	.ky	
Central African Republic	CT	CF	CAF	140	.cf	
Chad	CD	TD	TCD	148	.td	
Chile	CI	CL	CHL	152	.cl	
China	CH	CN	CHN	156	.cn	see also Taiwan
Christmas Island	KT	CX	CXR	162	.cx	
Clipperton Island	IP	—	—	—	—	ISO includes with French Polynesia
Cocos (Keeling) Islands	CK	CC	CCK	166	.cc	
Colombia	CO	CO	COL	170	.co	
Comoros	CN	KM	COM	174	.km	
Congo, Democratic Republic of the	CG	CD	COD	180	.cd	formerly Zaire
Congo, Republic of the	CF	CG	COG	178	.cg	
Cook Islands	CW	CK	COK	184	.ck	
Coral Sea Islands	CR	—	—	—	—	ISO includes with Australia
Costa Rica	CS	CR	CRI	188	.cr	
Cote d'Ivoire	IV	CI	CIV	384	.ci	
Croatia	HR	HR	HRV	191	.hr	
Cuba	CU	CU	CUB	192	.cu	
Cyprus	CY	CY	CYP	196	.cy	
Czech Republic	EZ	CZ	CZE	203	.cz	
Denmark	DA	DK	DNK	208	.dk	
Djibouti	DJ	DJ	DJI	262	.dj	
Dominica	DO	DM	DMA	212	.dm	

Appendix D: Cross-Reference List of Country Data Codes *(continued)*

Entity	FIPS 10-4	ISO 3166			Internet	Comment
Dominican Republic	DR	DO	DOM	214	.do	
East Timor	TT	TL	TLS	626	.tp	
Ecuador	EC	EC	ECU	218	.ec	
Egypt	EG	EG	EGY	818	.eg	
El Salvador	ES	SV	SLV	222	.sv	
Equatorial Guinea	EK	GQ	GNQ	226	.gq	
Eritrea	ER	ER	ERI	232	.er	
Estonia	EN	EE	EST	233	.ee	
Ethiopia	ET	ET	ETH	231	.et	
Europa Island	EU	—	—	—	—	ISO includes with the Miscellaneous (French) Indian Ocean Islands
Falkland Islands (Islas Malvinas)	FK	FK	FLK	238	.fk	
Faroe Islands	FO	FO	FRO	234	.fo	
Fiji	FJ	FJ	FJI	242	.fj	
Finland	FI	FI	FIN	246	.fi	
France	FR	FR	FRA	250	.fr	
France, Metropolitan	—	FX	FXX	249	.fx	ISO limits to the European part of France, excluding French Guiana, French Polynesia, French Southern and Antarctic Lands, Guadeloupe, Martinique, Mayotte, New Caledonia, Reunion, Saint Pierre and Miquelon, Wallis and Futuna
French Guiana	FG	GF	GUF	254	.gf	
French Polynesia	FP	PF	PYF	258	.pf	ISO includes Clipperton Island
French Southern and Antarctic Lands	FS	TF	ATF	260	.tf	FIPS 10-4 does not include the French-claimed portion of Antarctica (Terre Adelie)
Gabon	GB	GA	GAB	266	.ga	
Gambia, The	GA	GM	GMB	270	.gm	
Gaza Strip	GZ	—	—	—	—	
Georgia	GG	GE	GEO	268	.ge	
Germany	GM	DE	DEU	276	.de	
Ghana	GH	GH	GHA	288	.gh	
Gibraltar	GI	GI	GIB	292	.gi	
Glorioso Islands	GO	—	—	—	—	ISO includes with the Miscellaneous (French) Indian Ocean Islands
Greece	GR	GR	GRC	300	.gr	
Greenland	GL	GL	GRL	304	.gl	
Grenada	GJ	GD	GRD	308	.gd	
Guadeloupe	GP	GP	GLP	312	.gp	
Guam	GQ	GU	GUM	316	.gu	
Guatemala	GT	GT	GTM	320	.gt	
Guernsey	GK	—	—	—	.gg	ISO includes with the UK
Guinea	GV	GN	GIN	324	.gn	

Appendix D: Cross-Reference List of Country Data Codes *(continued)*

Entity	FIPS 10-4	ISO 3166			Internet	Comment
Guinea-Bissau	PU	GW	GNB	624	.gw	
Guyana	GY	GY	GUY	328	.gy	
Haiti	HA	HT	HTI	332	.ht	
Heard Island and McDonald Islands	HM	HM	HMD	334	.hm	
Holy See (Vatican City)	VT	VA	VAT	336	.va	
Honduras	HO	HN	HND	340	.hn	
Hong Kong	HK	HK	HKG	344	.hk	
Howland Island	HQ	UM	UMI	581	—	ISO includes with the US Minor Outlying Islands
Hungary	HU	HU	HUN	348	.hu	
Iceland	IC	IS	ISL	352	.is	
India	IN	IN	IND	356	.in	
Indonesia	ID	ID	IDN	360	.id	
Iran	IR	IR	IRN	364	.ir	
Iraq	IZ	IQ	IRQ	368	.iq	
Ireland	EI	IE	IRL	372	.ie	
Israel	IS	IL	ISR	376	.il	
Italy	IT	IT	ITA	380	.it	
Jamaica	JM	JM	JAM	388	.jm	
Jan Mayen	JN	SJ	SJM	744	—	ISO includes with Svalbard
Japan	JA	JP	JPN	392	.jp	
Jarvis Island	DQ	UM	UMI	581	—	ISO includes with the US Minor Outlying Islands
Jersey	JE	—	—	—	.je	ISO includes with the UK
Johnston Atoll	JQ	UM	UMI	581	—	ISO includes with the US Minor Outlying Islands
Jordan	JO	JO	JOR	400	.jo	
Juan de Nova Island	JU	—	—	—	—	ISO includes with the Miscellaneous (French) Indian Ocean Islands
Kazakhstan	KZ	KZ	KAZ	398	.kz	
Kenya	KE	KE	KEN	404	.ke	
Kingman Reef	KQ	UM	UMI	581	—	ISO includes with the US Minor Outlying Islands
Kiribati	KR	KI	KIR	296	.ki	
Korea, North	KN	KP	PRK	408	.kp	
Korea, South	KS	KR	KOR	410	.kr	
Kuwait	KU	KW	KWT	414	.kw	
Kyrgyzstan	KG	KG	KGZ	417	.kg	
Laos	LA	LA	LAO	418	.la	
Latvia	LG	LV	LVA	428	.lv	
Lebanon	LE	LB	LBN	422	.lb	
Lesotho	LT	LS	LSO	426	.ls	
Liberia	LI	LR	LBR	430	.lr	

Appendix D: Cross-Reference List of Country Data Codes *(continued)*

Entity	FIPS 10-4	ISO 3166			Internet	Comment
Libya	LY	LY	LBY	434	.ly	
Liechtenstein	LS	LI	LIE	438	.li	
Lithuania	LH	LT	LTU	440	.lt	
Luxembourg	LU	LU	LUX	442	.lu	
Macau	MC	MO	MAC	446	.mo	
Macedonia, The Republic of	MK	MK	MKD	807	.mk	
Madagascar	MA	MG	MDG	450	.mg	
Malawi	MI	MW	MWI	454	.mw	
Malaysia	MY	MY	MYS	458	.my	
Maldives	MV	MV	MDV	462	.mv	
Mali	ML	ML	MLI	466	.ml	
Malta	MT	MT	MLT	470	.mt	
Man, Isle of	IM	—	—	—	.im	ISO includes with the UK
Marshall Islands	RM	MH	MHL	584	.mh	
Martinique	MB	MQ	MTQ	474	.mq	
Mauritania	MR	MR	MRT	478	.mr	
Mauritius	MP	MU	MUS	480	.mu	
Mayotte	MF	YT	MYT	175	.yt	
Mexico	MX	MX	MEX	484	.mx	
Micronesia, Federated States of	FM	FM	FSM	583	.fm	
Midway Islands	MQ	UM	UMI	581	—	ISO includes with the US Minor Outlying Islands
Miscellaneous (French) Indian Ocean Islands	—	—	—	—	—	ISO includes Bassas da India, Europa Island, Glorioso Islands, Juan de Nova Island, Tromelin Island
Moldova	MD	MD	MDA	498	.md	
Monaco	MN	MC	MCO	492	.mc	
Mongolia	MG	MN	MNG	496	.mn	
Montserrat	MH	MS	MSR	500	.ms	
Morocco	MO	MA	MAR	504	.ma	
Mozambique	MZ	MZ	MOZ	508	.mz	
Myanmar	—	—	—	—	—	see Burma
Namibia	WA	NA	NAM	516	.na	
Nauru	NR	NR	NRU	520	.nr	
Navassa Island	BQ	—	—	—	—	
Nepal	NP	NP	NPL	524	.np	
Netherlands	NL	NL	NLD	528	.nl	
Netherlands Antilles	NT	AN	ANT	530	.an	
New Caledonia	NC	NC	NCL	540	.nc	
New Zealand	NZ	NZ	NZL	554	.nz	
Nicaragua	NU	NI	NIC	558	.ni	
Niger	NG	NE	NER	562	.ne	

Entity	FIPS 10-4	ISO 3166			Internet	Comment
Nigeria	NI	NG	NGA	566	.ng	
Niue	NE	NU	NIU	570	.nu	
Norfolk Island	NF	NF	NFK	574	.nf	
Northern Mariana Islands	CQ	MP	MNP	580	.mp	
Norway	NO	NO	NOR	578	.no	
Oman	MU	OM	OMN	512	.om	
Pakistan	PK	PK	PAK	586	.pk	
Palau	PS	PW	PLW	585	.pw	
Palmyra Atoll	LQ	UM	UMI	581	—	ISO includes with the US Minor Outlying Islands
Panama	PM	PA	PAN	591	.pa	
Papua New Guinea	PP	PG	PNG	598	.pg	
Paracel Islands	PF	—	—	—	—	
Paraguay	PA	PY	PRY	600	.py	
Peru	PE	PE	PER	604	.pe	
Philippines	RP	PH	PHL	608	.ph	
Pitcairn Islands	PC	PN	PCN	612	.pn	
Poland	PL	PL	POL	616	.pl	
Portugal	PO	PT	PRT	620	.pt	
Puerto Rico	RQ	PR	PRI	630	.pr	
Qatar	QA	QA	QAT	634	.qa	
Reunion	RE	RE	REU	638	.re	
Romania	RO	RO	ROU	642	.ro	
Russia	RS	RU	RUS	643	.ru	
Rwanda	RW	RW	RWA	646	.rw	
Saint Helena	SH	SH	SHN	654	.sh	
Saint Kitts and Nevis	SC	KN	KNA	659	.kn	
Saint Lucia	ST	LC	LCA	662	.lc	
Saint Pierre and Miquelon	SB	PM	SPM	666	.pm	
Saint Vincent and the Grenadines	VC	VC	VCT	670	.vc	
Samoa	WS	WS	WSM	882	.ws	
San Marino	SM	SM	SMR	674	.sm	
Sao Tome and Principe	TP	ST	STP	678	.st	
Saudi Arabia	SA	SA	SAU	682	.sa	
Senegal	SG	SN	SEN	686	.sn	
Serbia and Montenegro	YI	CS	SCG	891	.yu	
Seychelles	SE	SC	SYC	690	.sc	
Sierra Leone	SL	SL	SLE	694	.sl	
Singapore	SN	SG	SGP	702	.sg	
Slovakia	LO	SK	SVK	703	.sk	
Slovenia	SI	SI	SVN	705	.si	
Solomon Islands	BP	SB	SLB	090	.sb	

Appendix D: Cross-Reference List of Country Data Codes *(continued)*

Entity	FIPS 10-4	ISO 3166			Internet	Comment
Somalia	SO	SO	SOM	706	.so	
South Africa	SF	ZA	ZAF	710	.za	
South Georgia and the Islands	SX	GS	SGS	239	.gs	
Spain	SP	ES	ESP	724	.es	
Spratly Islands	PG	—	—	—	—	
Sri Lanka	CE	LK	LKA	144	.lk	
Sudan	SU	SD	SDN	736	.sd	
Suriname	NS	SR	SUR	740	.sr	
Svalbard	SV	SJ	SJM	744	.sj	ISO includes Jan Mayen
Swaziland	WZ	SZ	SWZ	748	.sz	
Sweden	SW	SE	SWE	752	.se	
Switzerland	SZ	CH	CHE	756	.ch	
Syria	SY	SY	SYR	760	.sy	
Taiwan	TW	TW	TWN	158	.tw	
Tajikistan	TI	TJ	TJK	762	.tj	
Tanzania	TZ	TZ	TZA	834	.tz	
Thailand	TH	TH	THA	764	.th	
Togo	TO	TG	TGO	768	.tg	
Tokelau	TL	TK	TKL	772	.tk	
Tonga	TN	TO	TON	776	.to	
Trinidad and Tobago	TD	TT	TTO	780	.tt	
Tromelin Island	TE	—	—	—	—	ISO includes with the Miscellaneous Islands
Tunisia	TS	TN	TUN	788	.tn	
Turkey	TU	TR	TUR	792	.tr	
Turkmenistan	TX	TM	TKM	795	.tm	
Turks and Caicos Islands	TK	TC	TCA	796	.tc	
Tuvalu	TV	TV	TUV	798	.tv	
Uganda	UG	UG	UGA	800	.ug	
Ukraine	UP	UA	UKR	804	.ua	
United Arab Emirates	AE	AE	ARE	784	.ae	
United Kingdom	UK	GB	GBR	826	.uk	ISO includes Guernsey, Isle of Man, Jersey
United States	US	US	USA	840	.us	
United States Minor Outlying Islands	—	UM	UMI	581	.um	ISO includes Baker Island, Howland Island, Jarvis Island, Johnston Atoll, Kingman Reef, Midway Islands, Palmyra Atoll, Wake Island
Uruguay	UY	UY	URY	858	.uy	
Uzbekistan	UZ	UZ	UZB	860	.uz	
Vanuatu	NH	VU	VUT	548	.vu	
Venezuela	VE	VE	VEN	862	.ve	
Vietnam	VM	VN	VNM	704	.vn	

Appendix D: Cross-Reference List of Country Data Codes *(continued)*

Entity	FIPS 10-4	ISO 3166			Internet	Comment
Virgin Islands	VQ	VI	VIR	850	.vi	
Virgin Islands (UK)	VI	VG	VGB	092	.vg	see British Virgin Islands
Virgin Islands (US)	VQ	VI	VIR	850	.vi	see Virgin Islands
Wake Island	WQ	UM	UMI	581	—	ISO includes with the US Minor Outlying Islands
Wallis and Futuna	WF	WF	WLF	876	.wf	
West Bank	WE	—	—	—	—	
Western Sahara	WI	EH	ESH	732	.eh	
Western Samoa	—	—	—	—	.ws	see Samoa
World	—	—	—	—	—	the Factbook uses the W data code from DIAM 65-18 Geopolitical Data Elements and Related Features, Data Standard No. 3, December 1994, published by the Defense Intelligence Agency
Yemen	YM	YE	YEM	887	.ye	
Zaire	—	—	—	—	—	see Democratic Republic of the Congo
Zambia	ZA	ZM	ZWB	894	.zm	
Zimbabwe	ZI	ZW	ZWE	716	.zw	

Appendix E:

Cross-Reference List of Hydrographic Data Codes

IHO 23-4th:	*Limits of Oceans and Seas*, Special Publication 23, Draft 4th Edition 1986, published by the International Hydrographic Bureau of the International Hydrographic Organization
IHO 23-3rd:	*Limits of Oceans and Seas*, Special Publication 23, 3rd Edition 1953, published by the International Hydrographic Organization
ACIC M 49-1:	*Chart of Limits of Seas and Oceans*, revised January 1958, published by the Aeronautical Chart and Information Center (ACIC), United States Air Force; note - ACIC is now part of the National Geospatial-Intelligence Agency (NGA)
DIAM 65-18:	*Geopolitical Data Elements and Related Features*, Data Standard No. 4, Defense Intelligence Agency Manual 65-18, December 1994, published by the Defense Intelligence Agency

The US Government has not yet adopted a standard for hydrographic codes similar to the Federal Information Processing Standards (FIPS) 10-4 country codes. The names and limits of the following oceans and seas are not always directly comparable because of differences in the customers, needs, and requirements of the individual organizations. Even the number of principal water bodies varies from organization to organization. *Factbook* users, for example, find the Atlantic Ocean and Pacific Ocean entries useful, but none of the following standards include those oceans in their entirety. Nor is there any provision for combining codes or overcodes to aggregate water bodies. The recently delimited Southern Ocean is not included.

Principal Oceans and Seas of the World
With Hydrographic Codes by Institution

	IHO 23-4th	IHO 23-3rd*	ACIC M 49-1	DIAM 65-18
Arctic Ocean	9	17	A	5A
Atlantic Ocean	—	—	—	—
North Atlantic Ocean	1	23	B	1A
South Atlantic Ocean	4	32	C	2A
Baltic Sea	2	1	B26	7B
Indian Ocean	5	45	F	6A
Mediterranean Sea	3.1	28	B11	—
Eastern Mediterranean	3.1.2	28 B	—	8E
Western Mediterranean	3.1.1	28 A	—	8W
Pacific Ocean	—	—	—	—
North Pacific Ocean	7	57	D	3A
South Pacific Ocean	8	61	E	4A
South China and Eastern Archipelagic Seas	6	49, 48	D18 plus others	3U plus others

* The letters after the numbers are subdivisions, not footnotes.

Appendix F:

Cross-Reference List of Geographic Names

This appendix cross-references a wide variety of geographic names to the appropriate *Factbook* "country" entry. Additional information is included in parentheses.

Name	Entry in *The World Factbook*	Latitude (deg min)	Longitude (deg min)
Abidjan (capital)	Cote d'Ivoire	5 19 N	4 02 W
Abkhazia (region)	Georgia	43 00 N	41 00 E
Abu Dhabi (capital)	United Arab Emirates	24 28 N	54 22 E
Abu Musa (island)	Iran	25 52 N	55 03 E
Abuja (capital)	Nigeria	9 12 N	7 11 E
Abyssinia (former name for Ethiopia)	Ethiopia	8 00 N	38 00 E
Acapulco (city)	Mexico	16 51 N	99 55 W
Accra (capital)	Ghana	5 33 N	0 13 W
Adamstown (capital)	Pitcairn Islands	25 04 S	130 05 W
Addis Ababa (capital)	Ethiopia	9 02 N	38 42 E
Adelie Land (claimed by France; also Terre Adelie)	Antarctica	66 30 S	139 00 E
Aden (city)	Yemen	12 46 N	45 01 E
Aden, Gulf of	Indian Ocean	12 30 N	48 00 E
Admiralty Island	United States (Alaska)	57 44 N	134 20 W
Admiralty Islands	Papua New Guinea	2 10 S	147 00 E
Adriatic Sea	Atlantic Ocean	42 30 N	16 00 E
Adygey (region)	Russia	44 30 N	40 10 E
Aegean Islands	Greece	38 00 N	25 00 E
Aegean Sea	Atlantic Ocean	38 30 N	25 00 E
Afars and Issas, French Territory of the (or FTAI; former name for Djibouti)	Djibouti	11 30 N	43 00 E
Afghanestan (local name for Afghanistan)	Afghanistan	33 00 N	65 00 E
Agalega Islands	Mauritius	10 25 S	56 40 E
Agana (city; former name for Hagatna)	Guam	13 28 N	144 45 E
Ajaccio (city)	France (Corsica)	41 55 N	8 44 E
Ajaria (region)	Georgia	41 45 N	42 10 E
Akmola (city; former name for Astana)	Kazakhstan	51 10 N	71 30 E
Aksai Chin (region)	China (de facto), India (claimed)	35 00 N	79 00 E
Al Arabiyah as Suudiyah (local name for Saudi Arabia)	Saudi Arabia	25 00 N	45 00 E
Al Bahrayn (local name for Bahrain)	Bahrain	26 00 N	50 33 E
Al Imarat al Arabiyah al Muttahidah (local name for the United Arab Emirates)	United Arab Emirates	24 00 N	54 00 E
Al Iraq (local name for Iraq)	Iraq	33 00 N	44 00 E
Al Jaza'ir (local name for Algeria)	Algeria	28 00 N	3 00 E
Al Kuwayt (local name for Kuwait)	Kuwait	29 30 N	45 45 E
Al Maghrib (local name for Morocco)	Morocco	32 00 N	5 00 W
Al Urdun (local name for Jordan)	Jordan	31 00 N	36 00 E
Al Yaman (local name for Yemen)	Yemen	15 00 N	48 00 E
Aland Islands	Finland	60 15 N	20 00 E
Alaska (state)	United States	65 00 N	153 00 W
Alaska, Gulf of	Pacific Ocean	58 00 N	145 00 W
Alboran Sea	Atlantic Ocean	36 00 N	2 30 W

Name	Entry in *The World Factbook*	Latitude (deg min)	Longitude (deg min)
Aldabra Islands (Groupe d'Aldabra)	Seychelles	9 25 S	46 22 E
Alderney (island)	Guernsey	49 43 N	2 12 W
Aleutian Islands	United States (Alaska)	52 00 N	176 00 W
Alexander Archipelago (island group)	United States (Alaska)	57 00 N	134 00 W
Alexander Island	Antarctica	71 00 S	70 00 W
Alexandretta (region; former name for Iskenderun)	Turkey	36 34 N	36 08 E
Alexandria (city)	Egypt	31 12 N	29 54 E
Algiers (capital)	Algeria	36 47 N	2 03 E
Alhucemas, Penon de (island group)	Spain	35 13 N	3 53 W
Alma-Ata (city; former name for Almaty)	Kazakhstan	43 15 N	76 57 E
Almaty (former capital)	Kazakhstan	43 15 N	76 57 E
Alofi (capital)	Niue	19 01 S	169 55 W
Alphonse Island	Seychelles	7 01 S	52 45 E
Alsace (region)	France	48 30 N	7 20 E
Amami Strait	Pacific Ocean	28 40 N	129 30 E
Amindivi Islands (former name for Laccadive Islands)	India	11 30 N	72 30 E
Amirante Isles (island group; also Les Amirantes)	Seychelles	6 00 S	53 10 E
Amman (capital)	Jordan	31 57 N	35 56 E
Amsterdam (capital)	Netherlands	52 23 N	4 54 E
Amsterdam Island (Ile Amsterdam)	French Southern and Antarctic Lands	37 52 S	77 32 E
Amundsen Sea	Southern Ocean	72 30 S	112 00 W
Amur River	China, Russia	52 56 N	141 10 E
Amurskiy Liman (strait)	Pacific Ocean	53 00 N	141 30 E
Anadyrskiy Zaliv (gulf)	Pacific Ocean	64 00 N	177 00 E
Anatolia (region)	Turkey	39 00 N	35 00 E
Andaman Islands	India	12 00 N	92 45 E
Andaman Sea	Indian Ocean	10 00 N	95 00 E
Andorra la Vella (capital)	Andorra	42 30 N	1 30 E
Andros (island)	Greece	37 45 N	24 42 E
Andros Island	The Bahamas	24 26 N	77 57 W
Anegada Passage	Atlantic Ocean	18 30 N	63 40 W
Angkor Wat (ruins)	Cambodia	13 26 N	103 50 E
Anglo-Egyptian Sudan (former name for Sudan)	Sudan	15 00 N	30 00 E
Anjouan (island)	Comoros	12 15 S	44 25 E
Ankara (capital)	Turkey	39 56 N	32 52 E
Annobon (island)	Equatorial Guinea	1 25 S	5 36 E
Antananarivo (capital)	Madagascar	18 52 S	47 30 E
Antigua (island)	Antigua and Barbuda	14 34 N	90 44 W
Antipodes Islands	New Zealand	49 41 S	178 43 E
Antwerp (city)	Belgium	51 13 N	4 25 E
Aomen (local Chinese short-form name for Macau)	Macau	22 10 N	113 33 E
Aozou Strip (region)	Chad	22 00 N	18 00 E
Apia (capital)	Samoa	13 50 S	171 45W
Aqaba, Gulf of	Indian Ocean	29 00 N	34 30 E
Arab, Shatt al (river)	Iran, Iraq	29 57 N	48 34 E
Arabian Sea	Indian Ocean	15 00 N	65 00 E
Arafura Sea	Pacific Ocean	9 00 S	133 00 E
Aral Sea	Kazakhstan, Uzbekistan	45 00 N	60 00 E

Appendix F: Cross-Reference List of Geographic Names *(continued)*

Name	Entry in *The World Factbook*	Latitude (deg min)	Longitude (deg min)
Argun River	China, Russia	53 20 N	121 28 E
Aru Sea	Pacific Ocean	6 15 S	135 00 E
Ascension Island	Saint Helena	7 57 S	14 22 W
Ashgabat (capital)	Turkmenistan	37 57 N	58 23 E
Ashkhabad (see Ashgabat)	Turkmenistan	37 57 N	58 23 E
Asmara (capital)	Eritrea	15 20 N	38 53 E
Asmera (see Asmara)	Eritrea	15 20 N	38 53 E
As-Sudan (local name for Sudan)	Sudan	15 00 N	30 00 E
Assumption Island	Seychelles	9 46 S	46 34 E
Astana (capital; formerly Akmola)	Kazakhstan	51 10 N	71 30 E
Asuncion (capital)	Paraguay	25 16 S	57 40 W
Asuncion Island	Northern Mariana Islands	19 40 N	145 24 E
Atacama (desert)	Chile	23 00 S	70 10 W
Atacama (region)	Chile	24 30 S	69 15 W
Athens (capital)	Greece	37 59 N	23 44 E
Attu Island	United States	52 55 N	172 57 E
Auckland Islands	New Zealand	51 00 S	166 30 E
Australes, Iles (island group; also Iles Tubuai)	French Polynesia	23 20 S	151 00 W
Avarua (capital)	Cook Islands	21 12 S	159 46 W
Axel Heiberg Island	Canada	79 30 N	90 00 W
Azad Kashmir (region)	Pakistan	34 30 N	74 00 E
Azarbaycan (local name for Azerbaijan)	Azerbaijan	40 30 N	47 30 E
Azerbaidzhan (local name for Azerbaijan)	Azerbaijan	40 30 N	47 30 E
Azores (islands)	Portugal	38 30 N	28 00 W
Azov, Sea of	Atlantic Ocean	49 00 N	36 00 E
Bab el Mandeb (strait)	Indian Ocean	12 40 N	43 20 E
Babuyan Channel	Pacific Ocean	18 44 N	121 40 E
Babuyan Islands	Philippines	19 10 N	121 40 E
Baffin Bay	Arctic Ocean	73 00 N	66 00 W
Baffin Island	Canada	68 00 N	70 00 W
Baghdad (capital)	Iraq	33 21 N	44 25 E
Baki (see Baku)	Azerbaijan	40 23 N	49 51 E
Baku (capital)	Azerbaijan	40 23 N	49 51 E
Baky (see Baku)	Azerbaijan	40 23 N	49 51 E
Balabac Strait	Pacific Ocean	7 35 N	117 00 E
Balearic Islands	Spain	39 30 N	3 00 E
Balearic Sea (Iberian Sea)	Atlantic Ocean	40 30 N	2 00 E
Bali (island)	Indonesia	8 20 S	115 00 E
Bali Sea	Indian Ocean	7 45 S	115 30 E
Balintang Channel	Pacific Ocean	19 49 N	121 40 E
Balintang Islands	Philippines	19 55 N	122 10 E
Balkan Peninsula	Albania, Bosnia and Herzegovina, Bulgaria, Croatia, Greece, The Former Yugoslav Republic of Macedonia, Romania, Serbia and Montenegro, Slovenia, Turkey (European part)	42 00 N	23 00 E
Balleny Islands	Antarctica	67 00 S	163 00 E
Balochistan (region)	Pakistan	28 00 N	63 00 E
Baltic Sea	Atlantic Ocean	57 00 N	19 00 E

The "B" section marker appears at the left margin beginning with "Bab el Mandeb (strait)".

Name	Entry in *The World Factbook*	Latitude (deg min)	Longitude (deg min)
Bamako (capital)	Mali	12 39 N	8 00 W
Banaba (Ocean Island)	Kiribati	0 52 S	169 35 E
Banat (region)	Hungary, Serbia and Montenegro, Romania	45 30 N	21 00 E
Banda Sea	Pacific Ocean	5 00 S	128 00 E
Bandar Seri Begawan (capital)	Brunei	4 52 S	114 55 E
Bangka (island)	Indonesia	2 30 S	106 00 E
Bangkok (capital)	Thailand	13 45 N	100 31 E
Bangui (capital)	Central African Republic	4 22 N	18 35 E
Banjul (capital)	The Gambia	13 28 N	16 39 W
Banks Island	Australia	10 12 S	142 16 E
Banks Island	Canada	75 15 N	121 30 W
Banks Islands (Iles Banks)	Vanuatu	14 00 S	167 30 E
Barbuda (island)	Antigua and Barbuda	17 38 N	61 48 W
Barents Sea	Arctic Ocean	74 00 N	36 00 E
Barranquilla (city)	Colombia	10 59 N	74 48 W
Bashi Channel	Pacific Ocean	22 00 N	121 00 E
Basilan Strait	Pacific Ocean	6 49 N	122 05 E
Basque Provinces	Spain	43 00 N	2 30 W
Bass Strait	Pacific Ocean	39 20 S	145 30 E
Basse-Terre (capital)	Guadeloupe	16 00 N	61 44 W
Basseterre (capital)	Saint Kitts and Nevis	17 18 N	62 43 W
Bastia (city)	France (Corsica)	42 42 N	9 27 E
Basutoland (former name for Lesotho)	Lesotho	29 30 S	28 30 E
Batan Islands	Philippines	20 30 N	121 50 E
Bavaria (region; also Bayern)	Germany	48 30 N	11 30 E
Beagle Channel	Atlantic Ocean	54 53 S	68 10 W
Bear Island (see Bjornoya)	Svalbard	74 26 N	19 05 E
Beaufort Sea	Arctic Ocean	73 00 N	140 00 W
Bechuanaland (former name for Botswana)	Botswana	22 00 S	24 00 E
Beijing (capital)	China	39 56 N	116 24 E
Beirut (capital)	Lebanon	33 53 N	35 30 E
Bekaa Valley	Lebanon	34 00 N	36 05 E
Belau (Palau Islands)	Palau	7 30 N	134 30 E
Belep Islands (Iles Belep)	New Caledonia	19 45 S	163 40 E
Belgian Congo (former name for Democratic Republic of the Congo)	Democratic Republic of the Congo	0 00 N	25 00 E
Belgie (local name for Belgium)	Belgium	50 50 N	4 00 E
Belgique (local name for Belgium)	Belgium	50 50 N	4 00 E
Belgrade (capital)	Serbia and Montenegro	44 50 N	20 30 E
Belize City	Belize	17 30 N	88 12 W
Belle Isle, Strait of	Atlantic Ocean	51 35 N	56 30 W
Bellingshausen Sea	Southern Ocean	71 00 S	85 00 W
Belmopan (capital)	Belize	17 15 N	88 46 W
Belorussia (former name for Belarus)	Belarus	53 00 N	28 00 E
Benadir (region; former name of Italian Somaliland)	Somalia	4 00 N	46 00 E
Bengal, Bay of	Indian Ocean	15 00 N	90 00 E
Berau, Gulf of	Pacific Ocean	2 30 S	132 30 E
Bering Island	Russia	55 00 N	166 30 E
Bering Sea	Pacific Ocean	60 00 N	175 00 W

Name	Entry in *The World Factbook*	Latitude (deg min)	Longitude (deg min)
Bering Strait	Pacific Ocean	65 30 N	169 00 W
Berkner Island	Antarctica	79 30 S	49 30 W
Berlin (capital)	Germany	52 31 N	13 24 E
Berlin, East (former name for eastern sector of Berlin)	Germany	52 30 N	13 33 E
Berlin, West (former name for western sector of Berlin)	Germany	52 30 N	13 20 E
Bern (capital)	Switzerland	46 57 N	7 26 E
Bessarabia (region)	Moldova, Romania, Ukraine	47 00 N	28 30 E
Bharat (local name for India)	India	20 00 N	77 00 E
Bhopal (city)	India	23 16 N	77 24 E
Biafra (region)	Nigeria	5 30 N	7 30 E
Big Diomede Island	Russia	65 46 N	169 06 W
Bijagos, Arquipelago dos (island group)	Guinea-Bissau	11 25 N	16 20 W
Bikini Atoll	Marshall Islands	11 35 N	165 23 E
Bilbao (city)	Spain	43 15 N	2 58 W
Bioko (island)	Equatorial Guinea	3 30 N	8 42 E
Biscay, Bay of	Atlantic Ocean	44 00 N	4 00 W
Bishkek (capital)	Kyrgyzstan	42 54 N	74 36 E
Bishop Rock	United Kingdom	49 52 N	6 27 W
Bismarck Archipelago (island group)	Papua New Guinea	5 00 S	150 00 E
Bismarck Sea	Pacific Ocean	4 00 S	148 00 E
Bissau (capital)	Guinea-Bissau	11 51 N	15 35 W
Bjornoya (Bear Island)	Svalbard	74 26 N	19 05 E
Black Forest (region)	Germany	48 00 N	8 15 E
Black Rock (island)	South Georgia and the South Sandwich Islands	53 39 S	41 48 W
Black Sea	Atlantic Ocean	43 00 N	35 00 E
Bloemfontein (judicial capital)	South Africa	29 12 S	26 07 E
Bo Hai (gulf)	Pacific Ocean	38 00 N	120 00 E
Boa Vista (island)	Cape Verde	16 05 N	22 50 W
Bogota (capital)	Colombia	4 36 N	74 05 W
Bohemia (region)	Czech Republic	50 00 N	14 30 E
Bombay (see Mumbai)	India	18 58 N	72 50 E
Bonaire (island)	Netherlands Antilles	12 10 N	68 15 W
Bonifacio, Strait of	Atlantic Ocean	41 01 N	14 00 E
Bonin Islands	Japan	27 00 N	142 10 E
Bonn (former capital)	Germany	50 44 N	7 05 E
Bophuthatswana (region; enclave)	South Africa	26 30 S	25 30 E
Bora-Bora (island)	French Polynesia	16 30 S	151 45 W
Bordeaux (city)	France	44 50 N	0 34 W
Borneo (island)	Brunei, Indonesia, Malaysia	0 30 N	114 00 E
Bornholm (island)	Denmark	55 10 N	15 00 E
Bosna i Hercegovina (local name for Bosnia and Herzegovina)	Bosnia and Herzegovina	44 00 N	18 00 E
Bosnia (political region)	Bosnia and Herzegovina	44 00 N	18 00 E
Bosporus (strait)	Atlantic Ocean	41 00 N	29 00 E
Bothnia, Gulf of	Atlantic Ocean	63 00 N	20 00 E
Bougainville (island)	Papua New Guinea	6 00 S	155 00 E
Bougainville Strait	Pacific Ocean	6 40 S	156 10 E
Bounty Islands	New Zealand	47 43 S	174 00 E

Name	Entry in *The World Factbook*	Latitude (deg min)	Longitude (deg min)
Bourbon Island (former name of Reunion)	Reunion	21 06 S	55 36 E
Brasilia (capital)	Brazil	15 47 S	47 55 W
Bratislava (capital)	Slovakia	48 09 N	17 07 E
Brazzaville (capital)	Republic of the Congo	4 16 S	15 17 E
Bridgetown (capital)	Barbados	13 06 N	59 37 W
Brisbane (city)	Australia	27 28 S	153 02 E
Bristol Bay	Pacific Ocean	57 00 N	160 00 W
Bristol Channel	Atlantic Ocean	51 18 N	3 30 W
Britain (see Great Britain)	United Kingdom	54 00 N	2 00 W
British Bechuanaland (region; former name for northwest South Africa)	South Africa	27 30 S	23 30 E
British Central African Protectorate (former name of Nyasaland)	Malawi	13 30 S	34 00 E
British East Africa (former name for British possessions in eastern Africa)	Kenya, Tanzania, Uganda	1 00 N	38 00 E
British Guiana (former name for Guyana)	Guyana	5 00 N	59 00 W
British Honduras (former name for Belize)	Belize	17 15 N	88 45 W
British Solomon Islands (former name for Solomon Islands)	Solomon Islands	8 00 S	159 00 E
British Somaliland (former name for northern Somalia)	Somalia	10 00 N	49 00 E
Brussels (capital)	Belgium	50 50 N	4 20 E
Bubiyan (island)	Kuwait	29 47 N	48 10 E
Bucharest (capital)	Romania	44 26 N	26 06 E
Budapest (capital)	Hungary	47 30 N	19 05 E
Buenos Aires (capital)	Argentina	34 36 S	58 27 W
Bujumbura (capital)	Burundi	3 23 S	29 22 E
Bukovina (region)	Romania, Ukraine	48 00 N	26 00 E
Byelarus (local name for Belarus)	Belarus	53 00 N	28 00 E
Byelorussia (former name for Belarus)	Belarus	53 00 N	28 00 E
C Cabinda (province)	Angola	5 33 S	12 12 E
Cabo Verde (local name for Cape Verde)	Cape Verde	16 00 N	24 00 W
Cabot Strait	Atlantic Ocean	47 20 N	59 30 W
Caicos Islands	Turks and Caicos Islands	21 56 N	71 58 W
Cairo (capital)	Egypt	30 03 N	31 15 E
California, Gulf of	Pacific Ocean	28 00 N	112 00 W
Cameroun (local name for Cameroon)	Cameroon	6 00 N	12 00 E
Campbell Island	New Zealand	52 33 S	169 09 E
Campeche, Bay of	Atlantic Ocean	20 00 N	94 00 W
Canal Zone (former name for US possessions in Panama)	Panama	9 00 N	79 45 W
Canarias Sea	Atlantic Ocean	28 00 N	16 00 W
Canary Islands	Spain	28 00 N	15 30 W
Canberra (capital)	Australia	35 17 S	149 08 E
Cancun (city)	Mexico	21 10 N	86 50 W
Canton (city; now Guangzhou)	China	23 06 N	113 16 E
Canton Island (Kanton Island)	Kiribati	2 49 S	171 40 W
Cape Juby (region: former name for Southern Morocco)	Morocco	27 53 N	12 58 W
Cape of Good Hope (cape; also alternate name for Cape Province of South Africa)	South Africa	34 15 S	18 25 E

Name	Entry in *The World Factbook*	Latitude (deg min)	Longitude (deg min)
Cape Province (region; former name for Northern, Western, and Eastern Cape Provinces of South Africa)	South Africa	31 30 S	22 30 E
Cape Town (legislative capital)	South Africa	33 57 S	18 28 W
Caracas (capital)	Venezuela	10 30 N	66 56 W
Cargados Carajos Shoals	Mauritius	16 25 S	59 38 E
Caribbean Sea	Atlantic Ocean	15 00 N	73 00 W
Caroline Islands	Federated States of Micronesia, Palau	7 30 N	148 00 E
Carpatho-Ukraine (region; former name for Zakarpats'ka oblast')	Ukraine	48 22 N	23 32 E
Carpentaria, Gulf of	Pacific Ocean	14 00 S	139 00 E
Castries (capital)	Saint Lucia	14 01 N	61 00 W
Catalonia (region)	Spain	42 00 N	2 00 E
Cato Island	Australia	23 15 S	155 32 E
Caucasus (region)	Russia	42 00 N	45 00 E
Cayenne (capital)	French Guiana	4 56 N	52 20 W
Celebes (island)	Indonesia	2 00 S	121 00 E
Celebes Sea	Pacific Ocean	3 00 N	122 00 E
Celtic Sea	Atlantic Ocean	51 00 N	6 30 W
Central African Empire (former name for Central African Republic)	Central African Republic	7 00 N	21 00 E
Ceram (Seram) Sea	Pacific Ocean	2 30 S	129 30 E
Ceska Republika (local name for Czech Republic)	Czech Republic	49 45 N	15 30 E
Ceskoslovensko (former local name for Czechoslovakia)	Czech Republic, Slovakia	49 00 N	17 30 E
Ceuta (city)	Spain	35 53 N	5 19 W
Ceylon (former name for Sri Lanka)	Sri Lanka	7 00 N	81 00 E
Chafarinas, Islas (island)	Spain	35 12 N	2 26 W
Chagos Archipelago (Oil Islands)	British Indian Ocean Territory	6 00 S	71 30 E
Challenger Deep (Mariana Trench)	Pacific Ocean	11 22 N	142 36 E
Channel Islands	Guernsey, Jersey	49 20 N	2 20 W
Charlotte Amalie (capital)	Virgin Islands	18 21 N	64 56 W
Chatham Islands	New Zealand	44 00 S	176 30 W
Chechnya (region; also Chechnia)	Russia	43 15 N	45 40 E
Cheju Strait	Pacific Ocean	34 00 N	126 30 E
Cheju-do (island)	Korea, South	33 20 N	126 30 E
Chennai (city ; also Madras)	India	13 04 N	80 16 E
Chesterfield Islands (Iles Chesterfield)	New Caledonia	19 52 S	158 15 E
Chihli, Gulf of (see Bo Hai)	Pacific Ocean	38 30 N	120 00 E
Chiloe (island)	Chile	42 50 S	74 00 W
China, People's Republic of	China	35 00 N	105 00 E
China, Republic of	Taiwan	23 30 N	121 00 E
Chisinau (capital)	Moldova	47 00 N	28 50 E
Choiseul (island)	Solomon Islands	7 05 S	121 00 E
Choson (local name for North Korea)	North Korea	40 00 N	127 00 E
Christmas Island (Indian Ocean)	Australia	10 25 S	105 39 E
Christmas Island (Pacific Ocean; also Kiritimati)	Kiribati	1 52 N	157 20 E
Chukchi Sea	Arctic Ocean	69 00 N	171 00 W
Chuuk Islands (Truk Islands)	Federated States of Micronesia	7 25 N	151 47 W
Cilicia (region)	Turkey	36 50 N	34 30 E

Name	Entry in *The World Factbook*	Latitude (deg min)	Longitude (deg min)
Ciskei (enclave)	South Africa	33 00 S	27 00 E
Citta del Vaticano (local name for Vatican City)	Holy See	41 54 N	12 27 E
Cochin China (region)	Vietnam	11 00 N	107 00 E
Coco, Isla del (island)	Costa Rica	5 32 N	87 04 W
Cocos Islands	Cocos (Keeling) Islands	12 30 S	96 50 E
Colombo (capital)	Sri Lanka	6 56 N	79 51 E
Colon, Archipielago de (Galapagos Islands)	Ecuador	0 00 N	90 30 W
Commander Islands (Komandorskiye Ostrova)	Russia	55 00 N	167 00 E
Comores (local name for Comoros)	Comoros	12 10 S	44 15 E
Con Son (islands)	Vietnam	8 43 N	106 36 E
Conakry (capital)	Guinea	9 31 N	13 43 W
Confederatio Helvetica (local name for Switzerland)	Switzerland	47 00 N	8 00 E
Congo (Brazzaville) (former name for Republic of the Congo)	Republic of the Congo	1 00 S	15 00 E
Congo (Leopoldville) (former name for the Democratic Republic of the Congo)	Democratic Republic of the Congo	0 00 N	25 00 E
Constantinople (city; former name for Istanbul)	Turkey	41 01 N	28 58 E
Cook Strait	Pacific Ocean	41 15 S	174 30 E
Copenhagen (capital)	Denmark	55 40 N	12 35 E
Coral Sea	Pacific Ocean	15 00 S	150 00 E
Corfu (island)	Greece	39 40 N	19 45 E
Corinth (region)	Greece	37 56 N	22 56 E
Corisco (island)	Equatorial Guinea	0 55 N	9 19 E
Corn Islands (Islas del Maiz)	Nicaragua	12 15 N	83 00 W
Corocoro Island	Guyana, Venezuela	3 38 N	66 50 W
Corsica (island; also Corse)	France	42 00 N	9 00 E
Cosmoledo Group (island group; also Atoll de Cosmoledo)	Seychelles	9 43 S	47 35 E
Cotonou (former capital)	Benin	6 21 N	2 26 E
Cotopaxi (volcano)	Ecuador	0 39 S	78 26 W
Courantyne River	Guyana, Suriname	5 57 N	57 06 W
Cozumel (island)	Mexico	20 30 N	86 55 W
Crete (island)	Greece	35 15 N	24 45 E
Crimea (region)	Ukraine	45 00 N	34 00 E
Crimean Peninsula	Ukraine	45 00 N	34 00 E
Crooked Island Passage	Atlantic Ocean	22 55 N	74 35 W
Crozet Islands (Iles Crozet)	French Southern and Antarctic Lands	46 30 S	51 00 E
Curacao	Netherlands Antilles	12 10 N	69 00 W
Cyclades (island group)	Greece	37 00 N	25 10 E
Cyrenaica (region)	Libya	31 00 N	22 00 E
Czechoslovakia (former name for the entity that subsequently split into the Czech Republic and Slovakia)	Czech Republic, Slovakia	49 00 N	18 00 E
D Dagestan (region)	Russia	43 00 N	47 00 E
Dahomey (former name for Benin)	Benin	9 30 N	2 15 E
Daito Islands	Japan	43 00 N	17 00 E
Dakar (capital)	Senegal	14 40 N	17 26 W
Dalmatia (region)	Croatia	43 00 N	17 00 E
Daman (city; also Damao)	India	20 10 N	73 00 E
Damascus (capital)	Syria	33 30 N	36 18 E
Danger Islands (see Pukapuka Atoll)	Cook Islands	10 53 S	165 49 W

Name	Entry in *The World Factbook*	Latitude (deg min)	Longitude (deg min)
Danish Straits	Atlantic Ocean	58 00 N	11 00 E
Danish West Indies (former name for the Virgin Islands)	Virgin Islands	18 20 N	64 50 W
Danmark (local name)	Denmark	56 00 N	10 00 E
Danzig (city; former name for Gdansk)	Poland	54 23 N	18 40 E
Dao Bach Long Vi (island)	Vietnam	20 08 N	107 44 E
Dar es Salaam (capital)	Tanzania	6 48 S	39 17 E
Dardanelles (strait)	Atlantic Ocean	40 15 N	26 25 E
Davis Strait	Atlantic Ocean	67 00 N	57 00 W
Dead Sea	Israel, Jordan, West Bank	32 30 N	35 30 E
Deception Island	Antarctica	62 56 S	60 34 W
Denmark Strait	Atlantic Ocean	67 00 N	24 00 W
D'Entrecasteaux Islands	Papua New Guinea	9 30 S	150 40 E
Desolation Islands (Isles Kerguelen)	French Southern and Antarctic Lands	49 30 S	69 30 E
Deutschland (local name for Germany)	Germany	51 00 N	9 00 E
Devils Island (Ile du Diable)	French Guiana	5 17 N	52 35 W
Devon Island	Canada	76 00 N	87 00 W
Dhaka (capital)	Bangladesh	23 43 N	90 25 E
Dhivehi Raajje (local name for Maldives)	Maldives	3 15 N	73 00 E
Dhofar (region)	Oman	17 00 N	54 10 E
Diego Garcia (island)	British Indian Ocean Territory	7 20 S	72 25 E
Diego Ramirez (islands)	Chile	56 30 S	68 43 W
Dili (capital)	East Timor	8 35 S	125 36 E
Dilmun (former name for Bahrain)	Bahrain	7 00 N	81 00 E
Diomede Islands	Russia (Big Diomede), United States (Little Diomede)	65 47 N	169 00 W
Diu (region)	India	20 42 N	70 59 E
Djibouti (capital)	Djibouti	11 30 N	43 15 E
Dnieper (river)	Belarus, Russia, Ukraine (Dnyapro, Dnepr, Dnipro)	46 30 N	32 18 E
Dniester (river)	Moldova, Ukraine (Nistru, Dnister)	46 18 N	30 17 E
Dobruja (region)	Bulgaria, Romania	43 30 N	28 00 E
Dodecanese (island group)	Greece	36 00 N	27 05 E
Dodoma (city)	Tanzania	6 11 S	35 45 E
Doha (capital)	Qatar	25 17 N	51 32 E
Donets Basin	Russia, Ukraine	48 15 N	38 30 E
Douala (city)	Cameroon	4 03 N	9 42 E
Douglas (capital)	Man, Isle of	54 09 N	4 28 W
Dover, Strait of	Atlantic Ocean	51 00 N	1 30 E
Drake Passage	Atlantic Ocean, Southern Ocean	60 00 S	60 00 W
Druk Yul (local name for Bhutan)	Bhutan	27 30 N	90 30 E
Dubai (city)	United Arab Emirates	25 18 N	55 18 E
Dubayy (see Dubai)	United Arab Emirates	25 18 N	55 18 E
Dublin (capital)	Ireland	53 20 N	6 15 W
Dushanbe (capital)	Tajikistan	38 35 N	68 48 E
Dutch Antilles (former name for the Netherlands Antilles)	Netherlands Antilles	12 10 N	68 30 W
Dutch East Indies (former name for Indonesia)	Indonesia	5 00 S	120 00 E
Dutch Guiana (former name for Suriname)	Suriname	4 00 N	56 00 W
Dutch West Indies (former name for the Netherlands Antilles)	Netherlands Antilles	12 10 N	68 30 W
Dzungarian Gate (valley)	China, Kazakhstan	45 25 N	82 25 E

Appendix F: Cross-Reference List of Geographic Names *(continued)*

Name	Entry in *The World Factbook*	Latitude (deg min)	Longitude (deg min)
E			
East China Sea	Pacific Ocean	30 00 N	126 00 E
East Frisian Islands	Germany	53 44 N	7 25 E
East Germany (German Democratic Republic; former name for eastern portion of Germany)	Germany	52 00 N	13 00 E
East Korea Strait (Eastern Channel or Tsushima Strait)	Pacific Ocean	34 00 N	129 00 E
East Pakistan (former name for Bangladesh)	Bangladesh	24 00 N	90 00 E
East Siberian Sea	Arctic Ocean	74 00 N	166 00 E
Easter Island (Isla de Pascua)	Chile	27 07 S	109 22 W
Eastern Channel (East Korea Strait or Tsushima Strait)	Pacific Ocean	34 00 N	129 00 E
Eastern Samoa (former name for American Samoa)	American Samoa	14 20 S	170 00 W
Eesti (local name for Estonia)	Estonia	59 00 N	26 00 E
Eire (local name for Ireland)	Ireland	53 00 N	8 00 W
Elba (island)	Italy	42 46 N	10 17 E
Elemi Triangle (region)	Ethiopia (claimed), Kenya (de facto), Sudan (claimed)	5 00 N	35 30 E
Ellada (local name for Greece)	Greece	39 00 N	22 00 E
Ellas (local name for Greece)	Greece	39 00 N	22 00 E
Ellef Ringnes Island	Canada	78 00 N	103 00 W
Ellesmere Island	Canada	81 00 N	80 00 W
Ellice Islands	Tuvalu	8 00 S	178 00 E
Ellsworth Land (region)	Antarctica	75 00 S	92 00 W
Elobey, Islas de (island group)	Equatorial Guinea	0 59 N	9 33 E
Enderbury Island	Kiribati	3 08 S	171 05 W
Enewetak Atoll (Eniwetok Atoll)	Marshall Islands	11 30 N	162 15 E
England (region)	United Kingdom	52 30 N	1 30 W
English Channel	Atlantic Ocean	50 20 N	1 00 W
Eniwetok Atoll (see Enewetak Atoll)	Marshall Islands	11 30 N	162 15 E
Eolie, Isole (island group)	Italy	38 30 N	15 00 E
Epirus, Northern (region)	Albania, Greece	40 00 N	20 30 E
Ertra (local name for Eritrea)	Eritrea	15 00 N	39 00 E
Espana	Spain	40 00 N	4 00 W
Essequibo (region; claimed by Venezuela)	Guyana	6 59 N	58 23 W
Etorofu (island; also Iturup)	Russia (de facto)	44 55 N	147 40 E
F			
Farquhar Group (island group; also Atoll de Farquhar)	Seychelles	10 10 S	51 10 E
Fergana Valley	Kyrgyzstan, Tajikistan, Uzbekistan	41 00 N	72 00 E
Fernando de Noronha (island group)	Brazil	3 51 S	32 25 W
Fernando Po (island; see Bioko)	Equatorial Guinea	3 30 N	8 42 E
Filipinas (local name for the Philippines)	Philippines	13 00 N	122 00 E
Finland, Gulf of	Atlantic Ocean	60 00 N	27 00 E
Flores (island)	Indonesia	8 45 S	121 00 E
Flores Sea	Pacific Ocean	7 40 S	119 45 E
Florida, Straits of	Atlantic Ocean	25 00 N	79 45 W
Fongafale (capital)	Tuvalu	8 30 S	179 12 E
Former Soviet Union (FSU)	Armenia, Azerbaijan, Belarus, Estonia, Georgia, Kazakhstan, Kyrgyzstan, Latvia, Lithuania, Moldova, Russia, Tajikistan, Turkmenistan, Ukraine, Uzbekistan		
Formosa (island)	Taiwan	23 30 N	121 00 E
Formosa Strait (see Taiwan Strait)	Pacific Ocean	24 00 N	119 00 E
Foroyar (local name for Faroe Islands)	Faroe Islands	62 00 N	7 00 W

Name	Entry in *The World Factbook*	Latitude (deg min)	Longitude (deg min)
Fort-de-France (capital)	Martinique	14 36 N	61 05 W
Franz Josef Land (island group)	Russia	81 00 N	55 00 E
Freetown (capital)	Sierra Leone	8 30 N	13 15 W
French Cameroon (former name for Cameroon)	Cameroon	6 00 N	12 00 E
French Guinea (former name for Guinea)	Guinea	11 00 N	10 00 W
French Indochina (former name for French possessions in southeast Asia)	Cambodia, Laos, Vietnam	15 00 N	107 00 E
French Morocco (former name for Morocco)	Morocco	32 00 N	5 00 W
French Somaliland (former name for Djibouti)	Djibouti	11 30 N	43 00 E
French Sudan (former name for Mali)	Mali	17 00 N	4 00 W
French Territory of the Afars and Issas (former name for Djibouti; or FTAI)	Djibouti	11 30 N	43 00 E
French Togoland (former name for Togo)	Togo	8 00 N	1 10 E
French West Indies (former name for French possessions in the West Indies)	Guadeloupe, Martinique	16 30 N	62 00 W
Friendly Islands	Tonga	20 00 S	175 00 W
Frisian Islands	Denmark, Germany, Netherlands	53 35 N	6 40 E
Frunze (city; former name for Bishkek)	Kyrgyzstan	42 54 N	74 36 E
Funafuti (former name for Fongafale)	Tuvalu	8 30 S	179 12 E
Fundy, Bay of	Atlantic Ocean	45 00 N	66 00 W
Futuna Islands (Hoorn Islands/Iles de Horne)	Wallis and Futuna	14 19 S	178 05 E
Fyn (island)	Denmark	55 20 N	10 25 E
Gaborone (capital)	Botswana	24 45 S	25 55 E
Galapagos Islands (Archipielago de Colon)	Ecuador	0 00 N	90 30 W
Galicia (region)	Poland, Ukraine	49 30 N	23 00 E
Galicia (region)	Spain	42 45 N	8 10 E
Galilee (region)	Israel	32 54 N	35 20 E
Galleons Passage	Atlantic Ocean	11 00 N	60 55 W
Gambier Islands (Iles Gambier)	French Polynesia	23 09 S	134 58 W
Gaspar Strait	Pacific Ocean	3 00 S	107 00 E
Gdansk (city; formerly Danzig)	Poland	54 23 N	18 40 E
Geneva (city)	Switzerland	46 12 N	6 10 E
Genoa (city)	Italy	44 25 N	8 57 E
George Town (capital)	Cayman Islands	19 20 N	81 23 W
George Town (city)	Malaysia	5 26 N	100 16 E
George Town (city)	The Bahamas	23 30 N	75 46 W
Georgetown (capital)	Guyana	6 48 N	58 10 W
Georgetown (city)	The Gambia	13 30 N	14 47 W
German Democratic Republic (former name for eastern portion of Germany; also East Germany)	Germany	52 00 N	13 00 E
German Southwest Africa (former name for Namibia)	Namibia	22 00 S	17 00 E
Germany, Federal Republic of	Germany	51 00 N	9 00 E
Gibraltar (city, peninsula)	Gibraltar	36 11 N	5 22 W
Gibraltar, Strait of	Atlantic Ocean	35 57 N	5 36 W
Gidi Pass	Egypt	30 13 N	33 09 E
Gilbert Islands	Kiribati	1 25 N	173 00 E
Goa (state)	India	15 20 N	74 00 E
Gobi (desert)	China, Mongolia	42 30 N	107 00 E

G

Name	Entry in *The World Factbook*	Latitude (deg min)	Longitude (deg min)
Godthab (capital; also Nuuk)	Greenland	64 11 N	51 44 W
Golan Heights (region)	Syria	33 00 N	35 45 E
Gold Coast (former name for Ghana)	Ghana	8 00 N	2 00 W
Golfo San Jorge (gulf)	Atlantic Ocean	46 00 S	66 00 W
Golfo San Matias (gulf)	Atlantic Ocean	41 30 S	64 00 W
Good Hope, Cape of	South Africa	34 24 S	18 30 E
Goteborg (city)	Sweden	57 43 N	11 58 E
Gotland (island)	Sweden	57 30 N	18 33 E
Gough Island	Saint Helena	40 20 S	9 55 W
Graham Land (region)	Antarctica	65 00 S	64 00 W
Gran Chaco (region)	Argentina, Paraguay	24 00 S	60 00 W
Grand Bahama (island)	The Bahamas	26 40 N	78 35 W
Grand Banks (fishing ground)	Atlantic Ocean	47 06 N	55 48 W
Grand Cayman (island)	Cayman Islands	19 20 N	81 20 W
Grand Turk (capital; also Cockburn Town)	Turks and Caicos Islands	21 28 N	71 08 W
Great Australian Bight	Indian Ocean	35 00 S	130 00 E
Great Belt (strait; also Store Baelt)	Atlantic Ocean	55 30 N	11 00 E
Great Bitter Lake	Egypt	30 20 N	32 23 E
Great Britain (island)	United Kingdom	54 00 N	2 00 W
Great Channel	Indian Ocean	6 25 N	94 20 E
Great Inagua (island)	The Bahamas	21 00 N	73 20 W
Great Rift Valley	Ethiopia, Kenya	0 30 N	36 00 E
Greater Sunda Islands	Brunei, Indonesia, Malaysia	2 00 S	110 00 E
Green Islands	Papua New Guinea	4 30 S	154 10 E
Greenland Sea	Arctic Ocean	79 00 N	5 00 W
Grenadines, Northern (island group)	Saint Vincent and the Grenadines	13 15 N	61 12 W
Grenadines, Southern (island group)	Grenada	12 07 N	61 40 W
Grytviken (town; on South Georgia)	South Georgia and the South Sandwich Islands	54 15 S	36 45 W
Guadalcanal (island)	Solomon Islands	9 32 S	160 12 E
Guadalupe, Isla de (island)	Mexico	29 11 N	118 17 W
Guantanamo Bay (US Naval Base)	Cuba	20 00 N	75 08 W
Guatemala (capital)	Guatemala	14 38 N	90 31 W
Guinea Ecuatorial (local name for Equatorial Guinea)	Equatorial Guinea	2 00 N	10 00 E
Guinea, Gulf of	Atlantic Ocean	3 00 N	2 30 E
Guine-Bissau (local name for Guinea-Bissau)	Guinea-Bissau	12 00 N	15 00 E
Guinee (local name for Guinea)	Guinea	11 00 N	10 00 E
Guyane Francaise (local name for French Guiana)	French Guiana	4 00 N	53 00 W
Ha'apai Group (island group)	Tonga	19 42 S	174 29 W
Habomai Islands	Russia (de facto)	43 30 N	146 10 E
Hadhramaut (region)	Yemen	15 00 N	50 00 E
Hagatna (capital; formerly Agana)	Guam	13 28 N	144 45 E
Hague, The (seat of government)	Netherlands	52 05 N	4 18 E
Haifa (city)	Israel	32 50 N	35 00 E
Hainan Dao (island)	China	19 00 N	109 30 E
Haiphong (city)	Vietnam	20 52 N	106 41 E
Hala'ib Triangle (region)	Egypt (de facto), Sudan (claimed)	22 30 N	35 00 E
Halmahera (island)	Indonesia	1 00 N	128 00 E
Halmahera Sea	Pacific Ocean	0 30 S	129 00 E

The "H" letter marker appears at the left margin beginning at the "Ha'apai Group" row.

Name	Entry in *The World Factbook*	Latitude (deg min)	Longitude (deg min)
Hamilton (capital)	Bermuda	32 17 N	64 46 W
Han-guk (local name for South Korea)	South Korea	37 00 N	127 30 E
Hanoi (capital)	Vietnam	21 02 N	105 51 E
Harare (capital)	Zimbabwe	17 50 S	31 03 E
Harvey Islands (former name for Cook Islands)	Cook Islands	21 14 S	159 46 W
Hatay (province)	Turkey	36 30 N	36 15 E
Havana (capital)	Cuba	23 08 N	82 22 W
Hawaii (island)	United States	19 45 N	155 45 W
Hawaiian Islands	United States	21 00 N	157 45 W
Hawar (island)	Bahrain	25 40 N	50 47 E
Hayastan (local name for Armenia)	Armenia	40 00 N	45 00 E
Heard Island	Heard Island and McDonald Islands	53 06 S	73 30 E
Hejaz (region)	Saudi Arabia	24 30 N	38 30 E
Helsinki (capital)	Finland	60 10 N	24 58 E
Herzegovina (political region)	Bosnia and Herzegovina	44 00 N	18 00 E
Hiiumaa (island)	Estonia	58 50 N	22 30 E
Hispaniola (island)	Dominican Republic, Haiti	18 45 N	71 00 W
Ho Chi Minh City (Saigon)	Vietnam	10 45 N	106 40 E
Hokkaido (island)	Japan	44 00 N	143 00 E
Holland (region)	Netherlands	52 30 N	5 45 E
Hong Kong (special administrative region)	Hong Kong	22 15 N	114 10 E
Honiara (capital)	Solomon Islands	9 26 S	159 57 E
Honshu (island)	Japan	36 00 N	138 00 E
Hormuz, Strait of	Indian Ocean	26 34 N	56 15 E
Horn of Africa (region)	Djibouti, Eritrea, Ethiopia, Somalia	8 00 N	48 00 E
Horn, Cape (Cabo de Hornos)	Chile	55 59 S	67 16 W
Horne, Iles de (island group)	Wallis and Futuna	14 19 S	178 05 W
Hrvatska (local name for Croatia)	Croatia	45 10 N	15 30 E
Hudson Bay	Arctic Ocean	60 00 N	86 00 W
Hudson Strait	Arctic Ocean	62 00 N	71 00 W
Hunter Island	New Caledonia, Vanuatu	22 24 S	172 06 E
Iberian Peninsula	Portugal, Spain	40 00 N	5 00 W
Iceland Sea	Arctic Ocean	68 00 N	20 00 W
Ifni (region; former name of part of Spanish West Africa)	Morocco	29 22 N	10 09 W
Inaccessible Island	Saint Helena	37 17 S	12 40 W
Indochina (region)	Cambodia, Laos, Vietnam	15 00 N	107 00 E
Ingushetia (region)	Russia	43 15 N	45 00 E
Inhambane (region)	Mozambique	22 30 S	34 30 E
Inini (former name for French Guiana)	French Guiana	4 00 N	53 00 W
Inland Sea	Japan	34 20 N	133 30 E
Inner Hebrides (islands)	United Kingdom	56 30 N	6 20 W
Inner Mongolia (region; also Nei Mongol)	China	42 00 N	113 00 E
Ionian Islands	Greece	38 30 N	20 30 E
Ionian Sea	Atlantic Ocean	38 30 N	18 00 E
Irian Jaya (province)	Indonesia	5 00 S	138 00 E
Irish Sea	Atlantic Ocean	53 30 N	5 20 W
Iron Gate (river gorge)	Romania, Serbia and Montenegro	44 41 N	22 31 E

Name	Entry in *The World Factbook*	Latitude (deg min)	Longitude (deg min)
Iskenderun (region; formerly Alexandretta)	Turkey	36 34 N	36 08 E
Islamabad (capital)	Pakistan	33 42 N	73 10 E
Island (local name for Iceland)	Iceland	65 00 N	18 00 W
Islas Malvinas (island group)	Falkland Islands (Islas Malvinas)	51 45 S	59 00 W
Istanbul (city)	Turkey	41 01 N	28 58 E
Istrian Peninsula	Croatia, Slovenia	45 00 N	14 00 E
Italia (local name for Italy)	Italy	42 50 N	12 50 E
Italian East Africa (former name for Italian possessions in eastern Africa)	Eritrea, Ethiopia, Somalia	8 00 N	38 00 E
Italian Somaliland (former name for southern Somalia)	Somalia	10 00 N	49 00 E
Ittihad al-Imarat al-Arabiyah (local name for the United Arab Emirates)	United Arab Emirates	24 00 N	54 00 E
Iturup (island; see Etorofu)	Russia (de facto)	44 55 N	147 40 E
Ityop'iya (local name for Ethiopia)	Ethiopia	8 00 N	38 00 E
Ivory Coast (former name for Cote d'Ivoire)	Cote d'Ivoire	8 00 N	5 00 W
Iwo Jima (island)	Japan	24 47 N	141 20 E
Izmir (region)	Turkey	38 25 N	27 10 E
J Jakarta (capital)	Indonesia	6 10 S	106 48 E
James Bay	Arctic Ocean	54 00 N	80 00 W
Jamestown (capital)	Saint Helena	15 56 S	5 44 W
Jammu (city)	India	32 42 N	74 52 E
Jammu and Kashmir (region)	India, Pakistan	34 00 N	76 00 E
Japan, Sea of	Pacific Ocean	40 00 N	135 00 E
Jars, Plain of	Laos	19 27 N	103 10 E
Java (island)	Indonesia	7 30 S	110 00 E
Java Sea	Pacific Ocean	5 00 S	110 00 E
Jerusalem (capital, proclaimed)	Israel, West Bank	31 47 N	35 14 E
Jiddah (city; also Jeddah)	Saudi Arabia	21 30 N	39 12 E
Johannesburg (city)	South Africa	26 15 S	28 00 E
Joseph Bonaparte Gulf	Pacific Ocean	14 00 S	128 45 E
Juan de Fuca, Strait of	Pacific Ocean	48 18 N	124 00 W
Juan Fernandez, Islas de (island group)	Chile	33 00 S	80 00 W
Jubal, Strait of	Indian Ocean	27 40 N	33 55 E
Judaea (region)	Israel, West Bank	31 35 N	35 00 E
Jugoslavia, Jugoslavija (local names for Yugoslavia)	Bosnia and Herzegovina, Croatia, The Former Yugoslav Republic of Macedonia, Serbia and Montenegro, Slovenia	43 00 N	21 00 E
Jutland (region)	Denmark	56 00 N	9 15 E
Juventud, Isla de la (Isle of Youth)	Cuba	21 40 N	82 50 W
K Kabardino-Balkaria (region)	Russia	43 30 N	43 30 E
Kabul (capital)	Afghanistan	34 31 N	69 12 E
Kaduna (city)	Nigeria	10 33 N	7 27 E
Kailas Range	China, India	30 00 N	82 00 E
Kalaallit Nunaat (local name for Greenland)	Greenland	72 00 N	40 00 W
Kalahari (desert)	Botswana, Namibia	24 30 S	21 00 E
Kalimantan (region)	Indonesia	0 00 N	115 00 E
Kaliningrad (region; formerly part of East Prussia)	Russia	54 30 N	21 00 E
Kamaran (island)	Yemen	15 21 N	42 34 E
Kamchatka Peninsula (Poluostrov Kamchatka)	Russia	56 00 N	160 00 E

Name	Entry in *The World Factbook*	Latitude (deg min)	Longitude (deg min)
Kampala (capital)	Uganda	0 19 N	32 25 E
Kampuchea (former name for Cambodia)	Cambodia	13 00 N	105 00 E
Kane Basin (portion of channel)	Arctic Ocean	79 30 N	68 00 W
Kanton Island	Kiribati	2 49 S	171 40 W
Kara Sea	Arctic Ocean	76 00 N	80 00 E
Karachevo-Cherkessia (region)	Russia	43 40 N	41 50 E
Karafuto (island; former name for southern Sakhalin Island)	Russia	50 00 N	143 00 E
Karakoram Pass	China, India	35 30 N	77 50 E
Karelia (region)	Finland, Russia	63 15 N	30 48 E
Karelian Isthmus	Russia	60 25 N	30 00 E
Karimata Strait	Pacific Ocean	2 05 S	108 40 E
Kashmir (region)	India, Pakistan	34 00 N	76 00 E
Katanga (region)	Democratic Republic of the Congo	10 00 S	26 00 E
Kathmandu (capital)	Nepal	27 43 N	85 19 E
Kattegat (strait)	Atlantic Ocean	57 00 N	11 00 E
Kauai Channel	Pacific Ocean	21 45 N	158 50 W
Kazakstan (former name for Kazakhstan)	Kazakhstan	48 00 N	68 00 E
Keeling Islands	Cocos (Keeling) Islands	12 30 S	96 50 E
Kerguelen, Iles (island group)	French Southern and Antarctic Lands	49 30 S	69 30 E
Kermadec Islands	New Zealand	29 50 S	178 15 W
Kerulen River	China, Mongolia	48 48 N	117 00 E
Khabarovsk (city)	Russia	48 27 N	135 06 E
Khanka, Lake	China, Russia	45 00 N	132 24 E
Khartoum (capital)	Sudan	15 36 N	32 32 E
Khios (island)	Greece	38 22 N	26 04 E
Khmer Republic (former name for Cambodia)	Cambodia	13 00 N	105 00 E
Khuriya Muriya Islands (Kuria Muria Islands)	Oman	17 30 N	56 00 E
Khyber Pass	Afghanistan, Pakistan	34 05 N	71 10 E
Kibris (Turkish local name for Cyprus)	Cyprus	35 00 N	33 00 E
Kiel Canal (Nord-Ostsee Kanal)	Atlantic Ocean	53 53 N	9 08 E
Kiev (capital)	Ukraine	50 26 N	30 31 E
Kigali (capital)	Rwanda	1 57 S	30 04 E
Kingston (capital)	Jamaica	18 00 N	76 48 W
Kingston (capital)	Norfolk Island	29 03 S	167 58 E
Kingstown (capital)	Saint Vincent and the Grenadines	13 09 N	61 14 W
Kinshasa (capital)	Democratic Republic of the Congo	4 18 S	15 18 E
Kipros (Greek local name for Cyprus)	Cyprus	35 00 N	33 00 E
Kirghiziya (former name for Kyrgyzstan)	Kyrgyzstan	41 00 N	75 00 E
Kirgizia (former name for Kyrgyzstan)	Kyrgyzstan	41 00 N	75 00 E
Kirguizstan (local name for Kyrgyzstan)	Kyrgyzstan	41 00 N	75 00 E
Kiritimati (Christmas Island)	Kiribati	1 52 N	157 20 W
Kishinev (see Chisinau)	Moldova	47 00 N	28 50 E
Kithira Strait	Atlantic Ocean	36 00 N	23 00 E
Kobe (city)	Japan	34 41 N	135 10 E
Kodiak Island	United States	57 49 N	152 23 W
Kola Peninsula (Kol'skiy Poluostrov)	Russia	67 20 N	37 00 E
Kolonia (town; former capital; changed to Palikir)	Federated States of Micronesia	6 58 N	158 13 E

Name	Entry in *The World Factbook*	Latitude (deg min)	Longitude (deg min)
Korea Bay	Pacific Ocean	39 00 N	124 00 E
Korea Strait	Pacific Ocean	34 00 N	129 00 E
Korea, Democratic People's Republic of	North Korea	40 00 N	127 00 E
Korea, Republic of	South Korea	37 00 N	127 30 E
Koror (capital)	Palau	7 20 N	134 29 E
Kosovo (region)	Serbia and Montenegro	42 30 N	21 00 E
Kosrae (island)	Federated States of Micronesia	5 20 N	163 00 E
Kowloon (city)	Hong Kong	22 18 N	114 10 E
Kra, Isthmus of	Burma, Thailand	10 20 N	99 00 E
Krakatoa (volcano)	Indonesia	6 07 S	105 24 E
Kuala Lumpur (capital)	Malaysia	3 10 N	101 42 E
Kunashiri (island; also Kunashir)	Russia (de facto)	44 20 N	146 00 E
Kunlun Mountains	China	36 00 N	84 00 E
Kuril Islands	Russia (de facto)	46 10 N	152 00 E
Kuwait (capital)	Kuwait	29 20 N	47 59 E
Kuznetsk Basin	Russia	54 00 N	86 00 E
Kwajalein Atoll	Marshall Islands	9 05 N	167 20 E
Kyushu (island)	Japan	33 00 N	131 00 E
Kyyiv (see Kiev)	Ukraine	50 26 N	30 31 E
La Paz (administrative capital)	Bolivia	16 30 S	68 09 W
La Perouse Strait	Pacific Ocean	45 45 N	142 00 E
Labrador (peninsula, region)	Canada	54 00 N	62 00 W
Labrador Sea	Atlantic Ocean	60 00 N	55 00 W
Laccadive Islands	India	10 00 N	73 00 E
Laccadive Sea	Indian Ocean	7 00 N	76 00 E
Lagos (former capital)	Nigeria	6 27 N	3 24 E
Lake Erie	Atlantic Ocean	42 30 N	81 00 W
Lake Huron	Atlantic Ocean	45 00 N	83 00 W
Lake Michigan	Atlantic Ocean	43 30 N	87 30 W
Lake Ontario	Atlantic Ocean	43 30 N	78 00 W
Lake Superior	Atlantic Ocean	48 00 N	88 00 W
Lakshadweep (Laccadive Islands)	India	10 00 N	73 00 E
Lantau Island	Hong Kong	22 15 N	113 55 E
Lao (local name for Laos)	Laos	18 00 N	105 00 E
Laptev Sea	Arctic Ocean	76 00 N	126 00 E
Las Palmas (city)	Spain (Canary Islands)	28 06 N	15 24 W
Latakia (region)	Syria	36 00 N	35 50 E
Latvija (local name for Latvia)	Latvia	57 00 N	25 00 E
Lau Group (island group)	Fiji	18 20 S	178 30 E
Lefkosa (see Nicosia)	Cyprus	35 10 N	33 22 E
Lemnos (island)	Greece	39 54 N	25 21 E
Leningrad (see Saint Petersburg)	Russia	59 55 N	30 15 E
Lesser Sunda Islands	Indonesia	9 00 S	120 00 E
Lesvos (island)	Greece	39 15 N	26 15 E
Leyte (island)	Philippines	10 50 N	124 50 E
Liancourt Rocks (claimed by Japan)	South Korea	37 15 N	131 50 E
Liaodong Wan (gulf)	Pacific Ocean	40 30 N	121 20 E
Liban (local name for Lebanon)	Lebanon	33 50 N	36 50 E

L

Name	Entry in *The World Factbook*	Latitude (deg min)	Longitude (deg min)
Libreville (capital)	Gabon	0 23 N	9 27 E
Lietuva (local name for Lithuania)	Lithuania	56 00 N	24 00 E
Ligurian Sea	Atlantic Ocean	43 30 N	9 00 E
Lilongwe (capital)	Malawi	13 59 S	33 44 E
Lima (capital)	Peru	12 03 S	77 03 W
Lincoln Sea	Arctic Ocean	83 00 N	56 00 W
Line Islands	Jarvis Island, Kingman Reef, Kiribati, Palmyra Atoll	0 05 N	157 00 W
Lion, Gulf of	Atlantic Ocean	43 20 N	4 00 E
Lisbon (capital)	Portugal	38 43 N	9 08 W
Little Belt (strait; also Lille Baelt)	Atlantic Ocean	55 05 N	9 55 E
Ljubljana (capital)	Slovenia	46 03 N	14 31 E
Llanos (region)	Venezuela	8 00 N	68 00 W
Lobamba (city)	Swaziland	26 27 S	31 12 E
Lombok (island)	Indonesia	8 28 S	116 40 E
Lombok Strait	Indian Ocean	8 30 S	115 50 E
Lome (capital)	Togo	6 08 N	1 13 E
London (capital)	United Kingdom	51 30 N	0 10 W
Longyearbyen (town)	Svalbard	78 13 N	15 33 E
Lord Howe Island	Australia	31 30 S	159 00 E
Lorraine (region)	France	48 42 N	6 11 E
Louisiade Archipelago	Papua New Guinea	11 00 S	153 00 E
Lourenco Marques (city; former name for Maputo)	Mozambique	25 56 S	32 34 E
Loyalty Islands (Iles Loyaute)	New Caledonia	21 00 S	167 00 E
Luanda (capital)	Angola	8 48 S	13 14 E
Lubnan (local name for Lebanon)	Lebanon	33 50 N	36 50 E
Lubumbashi (city)	Democratic Republic of the Congo	11 40 S	27 28 E
Lusaka (capital)	Zambia	15 25 S	28 17 E
Luxembourg (capital)	Luxembourg	49 45 N	6 10 E
Luzon (island)	Philippines	16 00 N	121 00 E
Luzon Strait	Pacific Ocean	20 30 N	121 00 E
Lyakhov Islands	Russia	73 45 N	138 00 E
M Macao	Macau	22 10 N	113 33 E
Macedonia	The Former Yugoslav Republic of Macedonia	41 50 N	22 00 E
Macquarie Island	Australia	54 36 S	158 54 E
Madagasikara (local name for Madagascar)	Madagascar	20 00 S	47 00 E
Maddalena, Isola	Italy	41 13 N	09 24 E
Madeira Islands	Portugal	32 40 N	16 45 W
Madras (city; see Chennai)	India	13 04 N	80 16 E
Madrid (capital)	Spain	40 24 N	3 41 W
Magellan, Strait of	Atlantic Ocean	54 00 S	71 00 W
Maghreb (region)	Algeria, Libya, Mauritania, Morocco, Tunisia	34 00 N	3 00 E
Magreb (local name for Morocco)	Morocco	32 00 N	5 00 W
Magyarorszag (local name for Hungary)	Hungary	47 00 N	20 00 E
Mahe Island	Seychelles	4 41 S	55 30 E
Maiz, Islas del (Corn Islands)	Nicaragua	12 15 N	83 00 W
Majorca Island (Isla de Mallorca)	Spain	39 30 N	3 00 E

Name	Entry in *The World Factbook*	Latitude (deg min)	Longitude (deg min)
Majuro (capital)	Marshall Islands	7 05 N	171 08 E
Makassar Strait	Pacific Ocean	2 00 S	117 30 E
Makedonija (local name for Macedonia)	The Former Yugoslav Republic of Macedonia	41 50 N	22 00 E
Malabo (capital)	Equatorial Guinea	3 45 N	8 47 E
Malacca, Strait of	Indian Ocean	2 30 N	101 20 E
Malagasy Republic	Madagascar	20 00 S	47 00 E
Malay Archipelago	Brunei, Indonesia, Malaysia, Papua New Guinea, Philippines	2 30 N	120 00 E
Malay Peninsula	Malaysia, Thailand	7 10 N	100 35 E
Male (capital)	Maldives	4 10 N	73 31 E
Mallorca, Isla de (island; also Majorca)	Spain	39 30 N	3 00 E
Malmady (region)	Belgium	50 26 N	6 02 E
Malpelo, Isla de (island)	Colombia	4 00 N	90 30 W
Malta Channel	Atlantic Ocean	56 44 N	26 53 E
Malvinas, Islas (island group)	Falkland Islands (Islas Malvinas)	51 45 S	59 00 W
Mamoutzou (capital)	Mayotte	12 47 S	45 14 E
Managua (capital)	Nicaragua	12 09 N	86 17 W
Manama (capital)	Bahrain	26 13 N	50 35 E
Manchukuo (former state)	China	44 00 N	124 00 E
Manchuria (region)	China	44 00 N	124 00 E
Manila (capital)	Philippines	14 35 N	121 00 E
Manipa Strait	Pacific Ocean	3 20 S	127 23 E
Mannar, Gulf of	Indian Ocean	8 30 N	79 00 E
Manua Islands	American Samoa	14 13 S	169 35 W
Maputo (capital)	Mozambique	25 58 S	32 35 E
Marcus Island (Minami-tori-shima)	Japan	24 16 N	154 00 E
Margarita, Isla (island)	Venezuela	10 00 N	64 00 W
Mariana Islands	Guam, Northern Mariana Islands	16 00 N	145 30 E
Marie Byrd Land (region)	Antarctica	77 00 S	130 00 W
Marion Island	South Africa	46 51 S	37 52 E
Marmara, Sea of	Atlantic Ocean	40 40 N	28 15 E
Marquesas Islands (Iles Marquises)	French Polynesia	9 00 S	139 30 W
Martin Vaz, Ilhas (island group)	Brazil	20 30 S	28 51 W
Mas a Tierra (Robinson Crusoe Island)	Chile	33 38 S	78 52 W
Mascarene Islands	Mauritius, Reunion	21 00 S	57 00 E
Maseru (capital)	Lesotho	29 28 S	27 30 E
Mata-Utu (capital)	Wallis and Futuna	13 57 S	171 56 W
Matsu (island)	Taiwan	26 13 N	119 56 E
Matthew Island	New Caledonia, Vanuatu	22 20 S	171 20 E
Mauritanie (local name for Mauritania)	Mauritania	20 00 N	12 00 W
Mazatlan (city)	Mexico	23 13 N	106 25 W
Mbabane (capital)	Swaziland	26 18 S	31 06 E
McDonald Islands	Heard Island and McDonald Islands	53 06 S	73 30 E
Mecca (city)	Saudi Arabia	21 27 N	39 49 E
Mediterranean Sea	Atlantic Ocean	36 00 N	15 00 E
Melilla (exclave)	Spain	35 19 N	2 58 W
Memel (region)	Lithuania	55 43 N	21 30 E
Mesopotamia (region)	Iraq	33 00 N	44 00 E
Messina, Strait of	Atlantic Ocean	38 15 N	15 35 E

Name	Entry in *The World Factbook*	Latitude (deg min)	Longitude (deg min)
Mexico City (capital)	Mexico	19 24 N	99 09 W
Mexico, Gulf of	Atlantic Ocean	25 00 N	90 00 W
Middle Congo (former name for Republic of the Congo)	Republic of the Congo	1 00 S	15 00 E
Milwaukee Deep (Puerto Rico Trench)	Atlantic Ocean	19 55 N	65 27 W
Minami-tori-shima (Marcus Island)	Japan	24 16 N	154 00 E
Mindanao (island)	Philippines	8 00 N	125 00 E
Mindanao Sea	Pacific Ocean	9 15 N	124 30 E
Mindoro (island)	Philippines	12 50 N	121 05 E
Mindoro Strait	Pacific Ocean	12 20 N	120 40 E
Mingrelia (region)	Georgia	42 30 N	41 52 E
Minicoy Island	India	8 17 N	73 02 E
Minorca Island (Isla de Menorca)	Spain	40 00 N	4 00 E
Minsk (capital)	Belarus	53 54 N	27 34 E
Misr (local name for Egypt)	Egypt	27 00 N	30 00 E
Mitla Pass	Egypt	30 02 N	32 54 E
Mocambique (local name for Mozambique)	Mozambique	18 15 S	35 00 E
Mogadishu (capital)	Somalia	2 04 N	45 22 E
Moldavia (region)	Moldova, Romania	47 00 N	29 00 E
Molucca Sea	Pacific Ocean	2 00 N	127 00 E
Moluccas (Spice Islands)	Indonesia	2 00 S	128 00 E
Mombasa (city)	Kenya	4 03 S	39 40 E
Mona Passage	Atlantic Ocean	18 30 N	67 45 W
Monaco (capital)	Monaco	43 44 N	7 25 E
Mongol Uls (local name for Mongolia)	Mongolia	46 00 N	105 00 E
Monrovia (capital)	Liberia	6 18 N	10 47 W
Montenegro (political region)	Serbia and Montenegro	42 30 N	19 00 E
Monterrey (city)	Mexico	25 40 N	100 19 W
Montevideo (capital)	Uruguay	34 53 S	56 11 W
Montreal (city)	Canada	45 31 N	73 34 W
Moravia (region)	Czech Republic	49 30 N	17 00 E
Moravian Gate (pass)	Czech Republic	49 35 N	17 50 E
Moroni (capital)	Comoros	11 41 S	43 16 E
Mortlock Islands (Nomoi Islands)	Federated States of Micronesia	5 30 N	153 40 E
Moscow (capital)	Russia	55 45 N	37 35 E
Mount Pinatubo (volcano)	Philippines	15 08 N	120 21 E
Mozambique Channel	Indian Ocean	19 00 S	41 00 E
Muritaniyah (local name for Mauritania)	Mauritania	20 00 N	12 00 W
Musandam Peninsula	Oman, United Arab Emirates	26 18 N	56 24 E
Muscat (capital)	Oman	23 37 N	58 35 E
Muscat and Oman (former name for Oman)	Oman	21 00 N	57 00 E
Myanma, Myanmar	Burma	22 00 N	98 00 E
N Nagorno-Karabakh (region)	Azerbaijan	40 00 N	46 40 E
Nairobi (capital)	Kenya	1 17 S	36 49 E
Namib (desert)	Namibia	24 00 S	15 00 E
Nampo-shoto (island group)	Japan	30 00 N	140 00 E
Nassau (capital)	The Bahamas	25 05 N	77 21 W
Natal (region)	South Africa	29 00 S	30 25 E
Natuna Besar Islands	Indonesia	3 30 N	102 30 E

Name	Entry in *The World Factbook*	Latitude (deg min)	Longitude (deg min)
Natuna Sea	Pacific Ocean	3 30 N	108 00 E
Naxcivan (region)	Azerbaijan	39 20 N	45 20 E
Naxos (island)	Greece	37 05 N	25 30 E
N'Djamena (capital)	Chad	12 07 N	15 03 E
Nederland (local name for the Netherlands)	Netherlands	52 30 N	5 45 E
Nederlandse Antillen (local name for the Netherlands Antilles)	Netherlands Antilles	12 15 N	68 45 W
Negev (region)	Israel	30 30 N	34 55 E
Negros (island)	Philippines	10 00 N	123 00 E
Nejd (region)	Saudi Arabia	24 05 N	45 15 E
Netherlands East Indies (former name for Indonesia)	Indonesia	5 00 S	120 00 E
Netherlands Guiana (former name for Suriname)	Suriname	4 00 N	56 00 W
Nevis (island)	Saint Kitts and Nevis	17 09 N	62 35 W
New Britain (island)	Papua New Guinea	6 00 S	150 00 E
New Delhi (capital)	India	28 36 N	77 12 E
New Guinea (island)	Indonesia, Papua New Guinea	5 00 S	140 00 E
New Hebrides (island group)	Vanuatu	16 00 S	167 00 E
New Ireland (island)	Papua New Guinea	3 20 N	152 00 E
New Siberian Islands	Russia	75 00 N	142 00 E
New Territories (mainland region)	Hong Kong	22 24 N	114 10 E
Newfoundland (island, with mainland area, and a province)	Canada	52 00 N	56 00 W
Niamey (capital)	Niger	13 31 N	2 07 E
Nicobar Islands	India	8 00 N	93 30 E
Nicosia (capital)	Cyprus	35 10 N	33 22 E
Nightingale Island	Saint Helena	37 25 S	12 30 W
Nihon (local name for Japan)	Japan	36 00 N	138 00 E
Nippon (local name for Japan)	Japan	36 00 N	138 00 E
Nomoi Islands (Mortlock Islands)	Federated States of Micronesia	5 30 N	153 40 E
Norge (local name for Norway)	Norway	62 00 N	10 00 E
Norman Isles (Channel Islands)	Guernsey, Jersey	49 20 N	2 20 W
North Atlantic Ocean	Atlantic Ocean	30 00 N	45 00 W
North Channel	Atlantic Ocean	55 10 N	5 40 W
North Frisian Islands	Denmark, Germany	54 50 N	8 12 E
North Greenland Sea	Arctic Ocean	78 00 N	5 00 W
North Island	New Zealand	39 00 S	176 00 E
North Korea	North Korea	40 00 N	127 00 E
North Ossetia (region)	Russia	43 00 N	44 10 E
North Pacific Ocean	Pacific Ocean	30 00 N	165 00 W
North Sea	Atlantic Ocean	56 00 N	4 00 E
North Vietnam (former name for northern portion of Vietnam)	Vietnam	23 00 N	106 00 E
North Yemen (Yemen Arab Republic; now part of Yemen)	Yemen	15 00 N	44 00 E
Northeast Providence Channel	Atlantic Ocean	25 40 N	77 09 W
Northern Cyprus (region)	Cyprus	35 15 N	33 44 E
Northern Epirus (region)	Albania, Greece	40 00 N	20 30 E
Northern Grenadines (political region)	Saint Vincent and the Grenadines	12 45 N	61 15 W
Northern Ireland	United Kingdom	54 40 N	6 45 W
Northern Rhodesia (former name for Zambia)	Zambia	15 00 S	30 00 E
Northwest Passages	Arctic Ocean	74 40 N	100 00 W

Appendix F: Cross-Reference List of Geographic Names *(continued)*

Name	Entry in *The World Factbook*	Latitude (deg min)	Longitude (deg min)
Northwest Territories (region)	Canada	64 05 N	117 10 W
Norwegian Sea	Atlantic Ocean	66 00 N	6 00 E
Nouakchott (capital)	Mauritania	18 06 N	15 57 W
Noumea (capital)	New Caledonia	22 16 S	166 27 E
Nouvelle-Caledonie (local name for New Caledonia)	New Caledonia	21 30 S	165 30 E
Nouvelles Hebrides (former name for Vanuatu)	Vanuatu	16 00 S	167 00 E
Novaya Zemlya (islands)	Russia	74 00 N	57 00 E
Nubia (region)	Egypt, Sudan	20 30 N	33 00 E
Nuku'alofa (capital)	Tonga	21 08 S	175 12 W
Nunavut (region)	Canada	72 00 N	90 00 W
Nuuk (capital; also Godthab)	Greenland	64 11 N	51 44 W
Nyasaland (former name for Malawi)	Malawi	13 30 S	34 00 E
Nyassa (region)	Mozambique	13 30 S	37 00 E
O Oahu (island)	United States (Hawaii)	21 30 N	158 00 W
Ocean Island (Banaba)	Kiribati	0 52 S	169 35 E
Ocean Island (Kure Island)	United States	28 25 N	178 20 W
Oesterreich (local name for Austria)	Austria	47 20 N	13 20 E
Ogaden (region)	Ethiopia, Somalia	7 00 N	46 00 E
Oil Islands (Chagos Archipelago)	British Indian Ocean Territory	6 00 S	71 30 E
Okhotsk, Sea of	Pacific Ocean	53 00 N	150 00 E
Okinawa (island group)	Japan	26 30 N	128 00 E
Oland (island)	Sweden	56 45 N	16 40 E
Oman, Gulf of	Indian Ocean	24 30 N	58 30 E
Ombai Strait	Pacific Ocean	8 30 S	125 00 E
Oran (city)	Algeria	35 43 N	0 43 W
Orange River Colony (region; former name of Free State Province of South Africa)	South Africa	28 20 S	26 40 E
Oranjestad (capital)	Aruba	12 33 N	70 06 W
Oresund (The Sound) (strait)	Atlantic Ocean	55 50 N	12 40 E
Orkney Islands	United Kingdom	59 00 N	3 00 W
Oslo (capital)	Norway	59 55 N	10 45 E
Osumi Strait (Van Diemen Strait)	Pacific Ocean	31 00 N	131 00 E
Otranto, Strait of	Atlantic Ocean	40 00 N	19 00 E
Ottawa (capital)	Canada	45 25 N	75 40 W
Ouagadougou (capital)	Burkina Faso	12 22 N	1 31 W
Outer Hebrides (islands)	United Kingdom	57 45 N	7 00 W
Outer Mongolia (region)	Mongolia	46 00 N	105 00 E
P Pacific Islands, Trust Territory of the	Marshall Islands, Federated States of Micronesia, Northern Mariana Islands, Palau	10 00 N	155 00 E
Pagan (island)	Northern Mariana Islands	18 08 N	145 47 E
Pago Pago (capital)	American Samoa	14 16 S	170 42 W
Palawan (island)	Philippines	9 30 N	118 30 E
Palermo (city)	Italy	38 07 N	13 21 E
Palestine (region)	Israel, West Bank	32 00 N	35 15 E
Palikir (capital)	Federated States of Micronesia	6 55 N	158 08 E
Palk Strait	Indian Ocean	10 00 N	79 45 E
Pamirs (mountains)	China, Tajikistan	38 00 N	73 00 E
Pampas (region)	Argentina	35 00 S	63 00 W

Name	Entry in *The World Factbook*	Latitude (deg min)	Longitude (deg min)
Panama (capital)	Panama	8 58 N	79 32 W
Panama Canal	Panama	9 00 N	79 45 W
Panama, Gulf of	Pacific Ocean	8 00 N	79 30 W
Panay (island)	Philippines	11 15 N	122 30 E
Pantelleria, Isola di (island)	Italy	36 47 N	12 00 E
Papeete (capital)	French Polynesia	17 32 S	149 34 W
Paramaribo (capital)	Suriname	5 50 N	55 10 W
Parece Vela (island)	Japan	20 20 N	136 00 E
Paris (capital)	France	48 52 N	2 20 E
Pascua, Isla de (Easter Island)	Chile	27 07 S	109 22 W
Pashtunistan (region)	Afghanistan, Pakistan	32 00 N	69 00 E
Passion, Ile de la (island)	Clipperton Island	10 17 N	109 13 W
Patagonia (region)	Argentina	48 00 S	61 00 W
Peking (see Beijing)	China	39 56 N	116 24 E
Pelagian Islands (Isole Pelagie)	Italy	35 40 N	12 40 E
Peleliu (Beliliou) (island)	Palau	7 01 N	134 15 E
Peloponnese (peninsula)	Greece	37 30 N	22 25 E
Pemba Island	Tanzania	5 20 S	39 45 E
Penang Island	Malaysia	5 23 N	100 15 E
Pentland Firth (channel)	Atlantic Ocean	58 44 N	3 13 W
Perim (island)	Yemen	12 39 N	43 25 E
Perouse Strait, La	Pacific Ocean	44 45 N	142 00 E
Persia (former name for Iran)	Iran	32 00 N	53 00 E
Persian Gulf	Indian Ocean	27 00 N	51 00 E
Pescadores (islands)	Taiwan	23 30 N	119 30 E
Peter I Island	Antarctica	68 48 S	90 35 W
Philip Island	Norfolk Island	29 08 S	167 57 E
Philippine Sea	Pacific Ocean	20 00 N	134 00 E
Phnom Penh (capital)	Cambodia	11 33 N	104 55 E
Phoenix Islands	Kiribati	3 30 S	172 00 W
Pilipinas (local name for the Philippines)	Philippines	13 00 N	122 00 E
Pinatubo, Mount (volcano)	Philippines	15 08 N	120 21 E
Pines, Isle of (island; former name for Isla de la Juventud)	Cuba	21 40 N	82 50 W
Pleasant Island	Nauru	0 32 S	166 55 E
Plymouth (capital)	Montserrat	16 44 N	62 14 W
Polska (local name)	Poland	52 00 N	20 00 E
Polynesie Francaise (local name for French Polynesia)	French Polynesia	15 00 S	140 00 W
Pomerania (region)	Germany, Poland	53 40 N	15 35 E
Ponape (Pohnpei) (island)	Federated States of Micronesia	6 55 N	158 15 E
Port Louis (capital)	Mauritius	20 10 S	57 30 E
Port Moresby (capital)	Papua New Guinea	9 30 S	147 10 E
Port-au-Prince (capital)	Haiti	18 32 N	72 20 W
Port-of-Spain (capital)	Trinidad and Tobago	10 39 N	61 31 W
Porto-Novo (capital)	Benin	6 29 N	2 37 E
Portuguese East Africa (former name for Mozambique)	Mozambique	18 15 S	35 00 E
Portuguese Guinea (former name for Guinea-Bissau)	Guinea-Bissau	12 00 N	15 00 W
Portuguese Timor (former name for East Timor)	East Timor	9 00 S	126 00 E
Port-Vila (capital)	Vanuatu	17 44 S	168 19 E

Appendix F: Cross-Reference List of Geographic Names *(continued)*

Name	Entry in *The World Factbook*	Latitude (deg min)	Longitude (deg min)
Poznan (city)	Poland	52 25 N	16 55 E
Prague (capital)	Czech Republic	40 55 N	21 00 E
Praia (capital)	Cape Verde	14 55 N	23 31 W
Prathet Thai (local name for Thailand)	Thailand	15 00 N	100 00 E
Pretoria (administrative capital)	South Africa	25 45 S	28 10 E
Prevlaka peninsula	Croatia	42 24 N	18 31 E
Pribilof Islands	United States	57 00 N	170 00 W
Prince Edward Island	Canada	46 20 N	63 20 W
Prince Edward Islands	South Africa	46 35 S	38 00 E
Prince Patrick Island	Canada	76 30 N	119 00 W
Principe (island)	Sao Tome and Principe	1 38 N	7 25 E
Prussia (region)	Germany, Poland, Russia	53 00 N	14 00 E
Pukapuka Atoll	Cook Islands	10 53 S	165 49 W
Punjab (region)	India, Pakistan	30 50 N	73 30 E
Puntland (region)	Somalia	8 21 N	49 08 E
P'yongyang (capital)	North Korea	39 01 N	125 45 E
Qazaqstan (local name for Kazakhstan)	Kazakhstan	48 00 N	68 00 E
Qita Ghazzah (local name Gaza Strip)	Gaza Strip	31 25 N	34 20 E
Quebec (province)	Canada	52 00 N	72 00 W
Queen Charlotte Islands	Canada	53 00 N	132 00 W
Queen Elizabeth Islands	Canada	78 00 N	95 00 W
Queen Maud Land (claimed by Norway)	Antarctica	73 30 S	12 00 E
Quemoy (island)	Taiwan	24 27 N	118 23 E
Quito (capital)	Ecuador	0 13 S	78 30 W
Rabat (capital)	Morocco	34 02 N	6 51 W
Ralik Chain (island group)	Marshall Islands	8 00 N	167 00 E
Rangoon (capital; also Yangon)	Burma	16 47 N	96 10 E
Rapa Nui (Easter Island)	Chile	27 07 S	109 22 W
Ratak Chain (island group)	Marshall Islands	9 00 N	171 00 E
Red Sea	Indian Ocean	20 00 N	38 00 E
Redonda (island)	Antigua and Barbuda	16 55 N	62 19 W
Republica Dominicana (local name for Dominican Republic)	Dominican Republic	19 00 N	70 40 W
Republique Centrafricain (local name for Central African Republic)	Central African Republic	7 00 N	21 00 E
Republique Francaise (local name for France)	France	46 00 N	2 00 E
Republique Gabonaise (local name for Gabon)	Gabon	1 00 S	11 45 E
Republique Rwandaise (local name for Rwanda)	Rwanda	2 00 S	30 00 E
Republique Togolaise (local name for Togo)	Togo	8 00 N	1 10 E
Revillagigedo Island	United States (Alaska)	55 35 N	131 06 W
Revillagigedo Islands	Mexico	19 00 N	112 45 W
Reykjavik (capital)	Iceland	19 00 N	111 30 W
Rhodes (island)	Greece	36 10 N	28 00 E
Rhodesia (region)	Zimbabwe	20 00 S	30 00 E
Rhodesia, Northern (former name for Zambia)	Zambia	15 00 S	30 00 E
Rhodesia, Southern (former name for Zimbabwe)	Zimbabwe	20 00 S	30 00 E
Riga (capital)	Latvia	56 57 N	24 06 E
Riga, Gulf of	Atlantic Ocean	57 30 N	23 30 E

Name	Entry in *The World Factbook*	Latitude (deg min)	Longitude (deg min)
Rio de la Plata (gulf)	Atlantic Ocean	35 00 S	59 00 W
Rio de Oro (region)	Western Sahara	23 45 N	15 45 W
Rio Muni (mainland region)	Equatorial Guinea	1 30 N	10 00 E
Riyadh (capital)	Saudi Arabia	24 38 N	46 43 E
Road Town (capital)	British Virgin Islands	18 27 N	64 37 W
Robinson Crusoe Island (Mas a Tierra)	Chile	33 38 S	78 52 W
Rocas, Atol das (island)	Brazil	3 51 S	33 49 W
Rockall (island)	United Kingdom	57 35 N	13 48 W
Rodrigues (island)	Mauritius	19 42 S	63 25 E
Rome (capital)	Italy	41 54 N	12 29 E
Roncador Cay (island)	Colombia	13 32 N	80 03 W
Roosevelt Island	Antarctica	79 30 S	162 00 W
Roseau (capital)	Dominica	15 18 N	61 24 W
Ross Dependency (claimed by New Zealand)	Antarctica	80 00 S	180 00 E
Ross Island	Antarctica	81 30 S	175 00 W
Ross Sea	Antarctica, Southern Ocean	76 00 S	175 00 W
Rossiya (local name for Russia)	Russia	60 00 N	100 00 E
Rota (island)	Northern Mariana Islands	14 10 N	145 12 E
Rotuma (island)	Fiji	12 30 S	177 05 E
Ruanda (former name for Rwanda)	Rwanda	2 00 S	30 00 E
Rub al Khali (desert)	Saudi Arabia	19 30 N	49 00 E
Rumelia (region)	Albania, Bulgaria, The Former Yugoslav Republic of Macedonia	42 00 N	22 30 E
Ruthenia (region; former name for Carpatho-Ukraine)	Ukraine	48 22 N	23 32 E
Ryukyu Islands	Japan	26 30 N	128 00 E
Saar (region)	Germany	49 25 N	7 00 E
Saaremaa (island)	Estonia	58 25 N	22 30 E
Saba (island)	Netherlands Antilles	17 38 N	63 10 W
Sabah (state)	Malaysia	5 20 N	117 10 E
Sable Island	Canada	43 55 N	59 50 W
Safety Islands (Iles du Salut)	French Guiana	5 20 N	52 37 W
Sahara Occidental (former name for Western Sahara)	Western Sahara	24 30 N	13 00 W
Sahel (region)	Burkina Faso, Chad, The Gambia, Guinea-Bissau, Mali, Mauritania, Niger, Senegal	15 00 N	8 00 E
Saigon (city; former name for Ho Chi Minh City)	Vietnam	10 45 N	106 40 E
Saint Barthelemy (island; also Saint Bart's)	Guadeloupe	17 55 N	62 52 W
Saint Brandon (Cargados Carajos Shoals)	Mauritius	16 25 S	59 38 E
Saint Christopher (island)	Saint Kitts and Nevis	17 20 N	62 45 W
Saint Christopher and Nevis	Saint Kitts and Nevis	17 20 N	62 45 W
Saint Eustatius (island)	Netherlands Antilles	17 30 N	63 00 W
Saint George's (capital)	Grenada	12 03 N	61 45 W
Saint George's Channel	Atlantic Ocean	52 00 N	6 00 W
Saint Helens, Mount (volcano)	United States	46 15 N	122 12 W
Saint Helier (capital)	Jersey	49 12 N	2 07 W
Saint John (city)	Canada (New Brunswick)	45 16 N	66 04 W
Saint John's (capital)	Antigua and Barbuda	17 06 N	61 51 W
Saint Lawrence Island	United States	49 30 N	67 00 W
Saint Lawrence Seaway	Atlantic Ocean	49 15 N	67 00 W
Saint Lawrence, Gulf of	Atlantic Ocean	48 00 N	62 00 W

S (row label at left margin, aligned with "Saar (region)")

Name	Entry in *The World Factbook*	Latitude (deg min)	Longitude (deg min)
Saint Paul Island	Canada	47 12 N	60 09 W
Saint Paul Island	United States	57 11 N	170 16 W
Saint Paul Island (Ile Saint-Paul)	French Southern and Antarctic Lands	38 43 S	77 29 E
Saint Peter and Saint Paul Rocks (Penedos de Sao Pedro e Sao Paulo)	Brazil	0 23 N	29 23 W
Saint Peter Port (capital)	Guernsey	49 27 N	2 32 W
Saint Petersburg (city; former capital)	Russia	59 55 N	30 15 E
Saint Thomas (island)	Virgin Islands	18 21 N	64 55 W
Saint Vincent Passage	Atlantic Ocean	13 30 N	61 00 W
Saint-Denis (capital)	Reunion	20 52 S	55 28 E
Saint-Martin (island; also Sint Maarten)	Guadeloupe	18 04 N	63 04 W
Saint-Pierre (capital)	Saint Pierre and Miquelon	46 46 N	56 11 W
Saipan (island)	Northern Mariana Islands	15 12 N	145 45 E
Sak'art'velo (local name for Georgia)	Georgia	42 00 N	43 30 E
Sakhalin Island (Ostrov Sakhalin)	Russia	51 00 N	143 00 E
Sakishima Islands	Japan	24 30 N	124 00 E
Sala y Gomez, Isla (island)	Chile	26 28 S	105 00 W
Salisbury (city; former name for Harare)	Zimbabwe	17 50 S	105 00 W
Salzburg (city)	Austria	47 48 N	13 02 E
Samar (island)	Philippines	12 00 N	125 00 E
Samaria (region)	West Bank	32 15 N	35 10 E
Samoa Islands	American Samoa, Samoa	14 00 S	171 00 W
Samos (island)	Greece	37 48 N	26 44 E
San Ambrosio, Isla (island)	Chile	26 21 S	79 52 W
San Andres y Providencia, Archipielago (island group)	Colombia	13 00 N	81 30 W
San Bernardino Strait	Pacific Ocean	12 32 N	124 10 E
San Felix, Isla (island)	Chile	26 17 S	80 05 W
San Jose (capital)	Costa Rica	9 56 N	84 05 W
San Juan (capital)	Puerto Rico	18 28 N	66 07 W
San Marino (capital)	San Marino	43 56 N	12 25 E
San Salvador (capital)	El Salvador	13 42 N	89 12 W
Sanaa (capital)	Yemen	15 21 N	44 12 E
Sandzak (region)	Serbia and Montenegro	43 05 N	19 45 E
Santa Cruz (city)	Bolivia	17 48 S	63 10 W
Santa Cruz Islands	Solomon Islands	11 00 S	166 15 E
Santa Sede (local name for the Holy See)	Holy See	41 54 N	12 27 E
Santiago (capital)	Chile	33 27 S	70 40 W
Santo Antao (island)	Cape Verde	17 05 N	25 10 W
Santo Domingo (capital)	Dominican Republic	18 28 N	69 54 W
Sao Pedro e Sao Paulo, Penedos de (rocks)	Brazil	0 23 N	29 23 W
Sao Tiago (island)	Cape Verde	15 05 N	23 40 W
Sao Tome (island)	Sao Tome and Principe	0 12 N	6 39 E
Sapudi Strait	Pacific Ocean	7 05 S	114 10 E
Sarajevo (capital)	Bosnia and Herzegovina	43 52 N	18 25 E
Sarawak (state)	Malaysia	2 30 N	113 30 E
Sardinia (island)	Italy	40 00 N	9 00 E
Sargasso Sea (region)	Atlantic Ocean	30 00 N	55 00 W
Sark (island)	Guernsey	49 26 N	2 21 W

Name	Entry in *The World Factbook*	Latitude (deg min)	Longitude (deg min)
Savage Island (former name for Niue)	Niue	19 02 S	169 52 W
Savu Sea	Pacific Ocean	9 30 S	122 00 E
Saxony (region)	Germany	51 00 N	13 00 E
Schleswig-Holstein (region)	Germany	54 31 N	9 33 E
Schweiz (local German name for Switzerland)	Switzerland	47 00 N	8 00 E
Scopus, Mount	Israel, West Bank	31 48 N	35 14 E
Scotia Sea	Atlantic Ocean, Southern Ocean	56 00 S	40 00 W
Scotland (region)	United Kingdom	57 00 N	4 00 W
Scott Island	Antarctica	67 24 S	179 55 W
Senegambia (region; former name of confederation of Senegal and The Gambia)	The Gambia, Senegal	13 50 N	15 25 W
Senyavin Islands	Federated States of Micronesia	6 55 N	158 00 E
Seoul (capital)	South Korea	37 34 N	127 00 E
Serendib (former name for Sri Lanka)	Sri Lanka	7 00 N	81 00 E
Serrana Bank (shoal)	Colombia	14 25 N	80 16 W
Serranilla Bank (shoal)	Colombia	15 51 N	79 46 W
Settlement, The (capital)	Christmas Island	18 44 N	64 19 W
Severnaya Zemlya (island group; also Northland)	Russia	79 30 N	98 00 E
Shaba (region)	Democratic Republic of the Congo	8 00 S	27 00 E
Shag Island	Heard Island and McDonald Islands	53 00 S	72 30 E
Shag Rocks	South Georgia and the South Sandwich Islands	53 33 S	42 02 W
Shetland Islands	United Kingdom	60 30 N	1 30 W
Shikoku (island)	Japan	33 45 N	133 30 E
Shikotan (island)	Russia (de facto)	43 47 N	146 45 E
Shqiperia (local name for Albania)	Albania	41 00 N	20 00 E
Siam (former name for Thailand)	Thailand	15 00 N	100 00 E
Siberia (region)	Russia	60 00 N	100 00 E
Sibutu Passage	Pacific Ocean	4 50 N	119 35 E
Sicily (island)	Italy	37 30 N	14 00 E
Sicily, Strait of	Atlantic Ocean	37 20 N	11 20 E
Sidra, Gulf of	Atlantic Ocean	31 30 N	18 00 E
Sikkim (state)	India	27 50 N	88 30 E
Silesia (region)	Czech Republic, Germany, Poland	51 00 N	17 00 E
Sinai Peninsula	Egypt	29 30 N	34 00 E
Singapore (capital)	Singapore	1 17 N	103 51 E
Singapore Strait	Pacific Ocean	1 15 N	104 00 E
Sinkiang (autonomous region; also Xinjiang)	China	42 00 N	86 00 E
Sint Eustatius (island)	Netherlands Antilles	17 29 N	62 58 W
Sint Maarten (island; also Saint-Martin)	Netherlands Antilles	18 04 N	63 04 W
Sjaelland (island)	Denmark	55 30 N	12 00 E
Skagerrak (strait)	Atlantic Ocean	57 45 N	9 00 E
Skopje (capital)	The Former Yugoslav Republic of Macedonia	41 59 N	21 26 E
Slavonia (region)	Croatia	45 27 N	18 00 E
Slovenija (local name for Slovenia)	Slovenia	46 00 N	15 00 E
Slovensko (local name for Slovakia)	Slovakia	48 40 N	19 30 E
Smyrna (region; former name for Izmir)	Turkey	38 25 N	27 10 E
Society Islands (Iles de la Societe)	French Polynesia	17 00 S	150 00 W
Socotra (island)	Yemen	12 30 N	54 00 E

Name	Entry in *The World Factbook*	Latitude (deg min)	Longitude (deg min)
Sofia (capital)	Bulgaria	42 41 N	23 19 E
Solomon Islands, northern	Papua New Guinea	6 00 S	155 00 E
Solomon Islands, southern	Solomon Islands	8 00 S	159 00 E
Solomon Sea	Pacific Ocean	8 00 S	153 00 E
Somaliland (region)	Somalia	9 30 N	46 00 E
Somers Islands (former name for Bermuda)	Bermuda	32 20 N	64 45 W
Songkhla (city)	Thailand	7 12 N	100 36 E
Sound, The (strait; also Oresund)	Atlantic Ocean	55 50 N	12 40 E
South Atlantic Ocean	Atlantic Ocean	30 00 S	15 00 W
South China Sea	Pacific Ocean	10 00 N	113 00 E
South Georgia (island)	South Georgia and the South Sandwich Islands	54 15 S	36 45 W
South Island	New Zealand	43 00 S	171 00 E
South Korea	South Korea	37 00 N	127 30 E
South Orkney Islands	Antarctica	61 00 S	45 00 W
South Ossetia (region)	Georgia	42 20 N	44 00 E
South Pacific Ocean	Pacific Ocean	30 00 S	130 00 W
South Sandwich Islands	South Georgia and the South Sandwich Islands	57 45 S	26 30 W
South Shetland Islands	Antarctica	62 00 S	59 00 W
South Tyrol (region)	Italy	46 30 N	10 30 E
South Vietnam (former name for the southern portion of Vietnam)	Vietnam	12 00 N	108 00 E
South Yemen (People's Democratic Republic of Yemen; now part of Yemen)	Yemen	14 00 N	48 00 E
Southern Grenadines (island group)	Grenada	12 20 N	61 30 W
Southern Rhodesia (former name for Zimbabwe)	Zimbabwe	20 00 S	30 00 E
South-West Africa (former name for Namibia)	Namibia	22 00 S	17 00 E
Soviet Union (former name of a large Eurasian empire, roughly coequal with the former Russian Empire)	Armenia, Azerbaijan, Belarus, Estonia, Georgia, Kazakhstan, Kyrgyzstan, Latvia, Lithuania, Moldova, Russia, Tajikistan, Turkmenistan, Ukraine, Uzbekistan		
Spanish Guinea (former name for Equatorial Guinea)	Equatorial Guinea	2 00 N	10 00 E
Spanish Morocco (former name for northern Morocco)	Morocco	32 00 N	7 00 W
Spanish North Africa (exclaves)	Spain (Ceuta, Islas Chafarinas, Melilla, Penon de Alhucemas, Penon de Velez de la Gomera)	35 15 N	4 00 W
Spanish Sahara (former name)	Western Sahara	24 30 N	13 00 W
Spanish West Africa (former name for Ifni and Spanish Sahara)	Morocco, Western Sahara	25 00 N	13 00 W
Spice Islands (Moluccas)	Indonesia	2 00 S	28 00 E
Spitsbergen (island)	Svalbard	78 00 N	20 00 E
Srbija-Crna Gora (local name for Serbia and Montenegro)	Serbia and Montenegro	44 00 N	21 00 E
St. John's (city)	Canada (Newfoundland)	47 34 N	52 43 W
Stanley (capital)	Falkland Islands (Islas Malvinas)	51 42 S	57 41 W
Stockholm (capital)	Sweden	59 20 N	18 03 E
Stuttgart (city)	Germany	48 46 N	9 11 E
Sucre (constitutional capital)	Bolivia	19 02 S	65 17 W
Suez Canal	Egypt	29 55 N	32 33 E
Suez, Gulf of	Indian Ocean	28 10 N	33 27 E
Suisse (local French name for Switzerland)	Switzerland	47 00 N	8 00 E
Sulawesi (island; Celebes)	Indonesia	2 00 S	121 00 E

Name	Entry in *The World Factbook*	Latitude (deg min)	Longitude (deg min)
Sulawesi Sea	Pacific Ocean	3 00 N	122 00 E
Sulu Archipelago (island group)	Philippines	6 00 N	121 00 E
Sulu Sea	Pacific Ocean	8 00 N	120 00 E
Sumatra (island)	Indonesia	0 00 N	102 00 E
Sumba (island)	Indonesia	10 00 S	120 00 E
Sumba Strait	Pacific Ocean	9 10 S	120 00 E
Sumbawa (island)	Indonesia	8 30 S	118 00 E
Sunda Islands (Soenda Isles)	Indonesia, Malaysia	2 00 S	110 00 E
Sunda Strait	Indian Ocean	6 00 S	105 45 E
Suomi (local name for Finland)	Finland	64 00 N	26 00 E
Surigao Strait	Pacific Ocean	10 15 N	125 23 E
Surinam (former name for Suriname)	Suriname	4 00 N	56 00 W
Suriyah (local name for Syria)	Syria	35 00 N	38 00 E
Surtsey (volcanic island)	Iceland	63 17 N	20 40 W
Suva (capital)	Fiji	18 08 S	178 25 E
Sverdlovsk (city; former name for Yekaterinburg)	Russia	56 50 N	60 39 E
Sverige (local name for Sweden)	Sweden	62 00 N	15 00 E
Svizzera (local Italian name for Switzerland)	Switzerland	47 00 N	8 00 E
Swains Island	American Samoa	11 03 S	171 15 W
Swan Islands	Honduras	17 25 S	83 56 W
Tadzhikistan (former name for Tajikistan)	Tadjikistan	39 00 N	71 00 E
Tahiti (island)	French Polynesia	17 37 S	149 27 W
Taipei (capital)	Taiwan	25 03 N	121 30 E
Taiwan Strait	Pacific Ocean	24 00 N	119 00 E
Tallinn (capital)	Estonia	59 25 N	24 45 E
Tanganyika (former name for the mainland portion of Tanzania)	Tanzania	6 00 S	35 00 E
Tangier (city)	Morocco	35 48 N	5 45 W
Tannu-Tuva (region)	Russia	51 25 N	94 45 E
Tarawa (island)	Kiribati	1 25 N	173 00 E
Tartary, Gulf of	Pacific Ocean	50 00 N	141 00 E
Tashkent (capital)	Uzbekistan	41 20 N	69 18 E
Tasman Sea	Pacific Ocean	4 30 S	168 00 E
Tasmania (island)	Australia	43 00 S	147 00 E
Tatar Strait	Pacific Ocean	50 00 N	141 00 E
Taymyr Peninsula (Poluostrov Taymyr)	Russia	76 00 N	104 00 E
T'bilisi (capital)	Georgia	41 43 N	44 49 E
Tchad (local name for Chad)	Chad	15 00 N	19 00 E
Tegucigalpa (capital)	Honduras	14 06 N	87 13 W
Tehran (capital)	Iran	35 40 N	51 26 E
Tel Aviv (capital, de facto)	Israel	32 05 N	34 48 E
Teluk Bone (gulf)	Pacific Ocean	4 00 S	120 45 E
Teluk Tomini (gulf)	Pacific Ocean	0 30 S	121 00 E
Terre Adelie (claimed by France; also Adelie Land)	Antarctica	66 30 S	139 00 E
Terres Australes et Antarctiques Francaises (local name for the French Southern and Antarctic Lands)	French Southern and Antarctic Lands	43 00 S	67 00 E
Thailand, Gulf of	Pacific Ocean	10 00 N	101 00 E
Thimphu (capital)	Bhutan	27 28 N	89 39 E

Name	Entry in *The World Factbook*	Latitude (deg min)	Longitude (deg min)
Thuringia (region)	Germany	51 00 N	11 00 E
Thurston Island	Antarctica	72 20 S	99 00 W
Tiberias, Lake	Israel	32 48 N	35 35 E
Tibet (autonomous region; also Xizang)	China	32 00 N	90 00 E
Tibilisi (see T'bilisi)	Georgia	41 43 N	44 49 E
Tien Shan (mountains)	China, Kyrgyzstan	42 00 N	80 00 E
Tierra del Fuego (island, island group)	Argentina, Chile	54 00 S	69 00 W
Timor (island)	East Timor, Indonesia	9 00 S	125 00 E
Timor-Leste, Timor Lorosa'e (local names for East Timor)	East Timor	9 00 N	126 00 E
Timor Sea	Pacific Ocean	11 00 S	128 00 E
Tinian (island)	Northern Mariana Islands	15 00 N	145 38 E
Tiran, Strait of	Indian Ocean	28 00 N	34 27 E
Tirana (capital)	Albania	41 20 N	19 50 E
Tirane (see Tirana)	Albania	41 20 N	19 50 E
Tirol (region)	Austria, Italy	47 00 N	11 00 E
Tobago (island)	Trinidad and Tobago	11 15 N	60 40 W
Tokyo (capital)	Japan	35 42 N	139 46 E
Tonkin, Gulf of	Pacific Ocean	20 00 N	108 00 E
Torres Strait	Pacific Ocean	10 25 S	142 10 E
Torshavn (capital)	Faroe Islands	62 01 N	6 46 W
Toshkent (see Tashkent)	Uzbekistan	41 20 N	69 18 E
Transcarpathia (region; alternate name for Carpatho-Ukraine)	Ukraine	48 22 N	23 32 E
Transjordan (former name for Jordan)	Jordan	31 00 N	36 00 E
Transkei (enclave)	South Africa	32 15 S	28 15 E
Transvaal (region; former name for northeastern South Africa)	South Africa	25 10 S	29 25 E
Transylvania (region)	Romania	46 30 N	24 00 E
Trindade, Ilha de (island)	Brazil	20 31 S	29 20 W
Trinidad (island)	Trinidad and Tobago	10 22 N	61 15 W
Tripoli (capital)	Libya	32 54 N	13 11 E
Tripoli (city)	Lebanon	34 26 N	35 51 E
Tripolitania (region)	Libya	31 00 N	14 00 E
Tristan da Cunha Group (island group)	Saint Helena	37 04 S	12 19 W
Trobriand Islands	Papua New Guinea	8 38 S	151 04 E
Trucial Coast (former name for the United Arab Emirates)	United Arab Emirates	24 00 N	54 00 E
Trucial Oman (former name for the United Arab Emirates)	United Arab Emirates	24 00 N	54 00 E
Trucial States (former name for the United Arab Emirates)	United Arab Emirates	24 00 N	54 00 E
Truk Islands (former name for the Chuuk Islands)	Federated States of Micronesia	7 25 N	151 47 E
Tsugaru Strait	Pacific Ocean	41 35 N	141 00 E
Tuamotu Islands (Iles Tuamotu)	French Polynesia	19 00 S	142 00 W
Tubuai Islands (Iles Tubuai)	French Polynesia	23 00 S	150 00 W
Tunb al Kubra (island)	Iran	26 14 N	55 19 E
Tunb as Sughra (island)	Iran	26 14 N	55 09 E
Tunis (capital)	Tunisia	36 48 N	10 11 E
Turin (city)	Italy	45 04 N	7 40 E
Turkish Straits (see Bosporus and Dardenelles)	Atlantic Ocean	40 40 N	28 00 E

Name	Entry in *The World Factbook*	Latitude (deg min)	Longitude (deg min)
Turkiye (local name for Turkey)	Turkey	39 00 N	35 00 E
Turkmenia (former name for Turkmenistan)	Turkmenistan	40 00 N	60 00 E
Turkmeniya (former name for Turkmenistan)	Turkmenistan	40 00 N	60 00 E
Turks Island Passage	Atlantic Ocean	21 40 N	71 00 W
Tuscany (region)	Italy	43 25 N	11 00 E
Tutuila (island)	American Samoa	14 18 S	170 42 W
Tyrol, South (region)	Italy	46 30 N	10 30 E
Tyrrhenian Sea	Atlantic Ocean	40 00 N	12 00 E

U

Name	Entry in *The World Factbook*	Latitude (deg min)	Longitude (deg min)
Ubangi-Shari (former name for the Central African Republic	Central African Republic	6 38 N	20 33 E
Ukrayina (local name for Ukraine)	Ukraine	49 00 N	32 00 E
Ulaanbaatar (capital)	Mongolia	47 55 N	106 53 E
Ullung-do (island)	South Korea	37 29 N	130 52 E
Ulster (region)	Ireland, United Kingdom	54 35 N	7 00 W
Uman (local name for Oman)	Oman	21 00 N	57 00 E
Unimak Pass (strait)	Pacific Ocean	54 20 N	164 50 W
Union of Soviet Socialist Republics or USSR (former name of a large Eurasian empire, roughly coequal with the former Russian Empire)	Armenia, Azerbaijan, Belarus, Estonia, Georgia, Kazakhstan, Kyrgyzstan, Latvia, Lithuania, Moldova, Russia, Tajikistan, Turkmenistan, Ukraine, Uzbekistan		
United Arab Republic or UAR (former name for a federation between Egypt and Syria)	Egypt, Syria		
Upper Volta (former name for Burkina Faso)	Burkina Faso	13 00 N	2 00 W
Ural Mountains	Kazakhstan, Russia	60 00 N	60 00 E
Urdunn (local name for Jordan)	Jordan	31 00 N	36 00 E
Urundi (former name for Burundi)	Burundi	3 30 S	30 00 E
Ussuri River	China, Russia	48 28 N	135 02 E

V

Name	Entry in *The World Factbook*	Latitude (deg min)	Longitude (deg min)
Vaduz (capital)	Liechtenstein	47 09 N	9 31 E
Vakhan (Wakhan Corridor)	Afghanistan	37 00 N	73 00 E
Valletta (capital)	Malta	35 54 N	14 31 E
Valley, The (capital)	Anguilla	18 13 N	63 04 W
Van Diemen Strait (Osumi Strait)	Pacific Ocean	31 00 N	131 00 E
Vancouver Island	Canada	49 45 N	126 00 W
Vatican City (capital)	Holy See	41 54 N	12 27 E
Velez de la Gomera, Penon de (island)	Spain	35 11 N	4 18 W
Venda (enclave)	South Africa	23 00 S	31 00 E
Verde Island Passage	Pacific Ocean	13 34 N	120 51 E
Victoria (capital)	Seychelles	4 38 S	55 27 E
Victoria (island)	Canada	71 00 N	110 00 W
Victoria Land (region)	Antarctica	72 00 S	155 00 E
Vienna (capital)	Austria	48 12 N	16 22 E
Vientiane (capital)	Laos	17 58 N	102 36 E
Vilnius (capital)	Lithuania	54 41 N	25 19 E
Viti Levu (island)	Fiji	18 00 S	178 00 E
Vladivostok (city)	Russia	43 10 N	131 56 E
Vojvodina (region)	Serbia and Montenegro	45 35 N	20 00 E
Volcano Islands	Japan	25 00 N	141 00 E
Vostok Island	Kiribati	10 06 S	152 23 W
Vrangelya, Ostrov (Wrangel Island)	Russia	71 14 N	179 36 W

Appendix F: Cross-Reference List of Geographic Names *(continued)*

	Name	Entry in *The World Factbook*	Latitude (deg min)	Longitude (deg min)
W	Wake Atoll	Wake Island	19 17 N	166 36 E
	Wakhan Corridor (see Vakhan)	Afghanistan	37 00 N	73 00 E
	Walachia (region)	Romania	44 45 N	26 05 E
	Wales (region)	United Kingdom	52 30 N	3 30 W
	Wallis Islands	Wallis and Futuna	13 17 S	176 10 W
	Walvis Bay (city; former exclave)	Namibia	22 59 S	14 31 E
	Warsaw (capital)	Poland	52 15 N	21 00 E
	Washington, DC (capital)	United States	38 53 N	77 02 W
	Weddell Sea	Southern Ocean	72 00 S	45 00 W
	Wellington (capital)	New Zealand	41 28 S	174 51 E
	West Frisian Islands	Netherlands	53 26 N	5 30 E
	West Germany (Federal Republic of Germany; former name for western portion of Germany)	Germany	53 22 N	5 20 E
	West Island (capital)	Cocos (Keeling) Islands	12 10 S	96 55 E
	West Korea Strait (Western Channel)	Pacific Ocean	34 40 N	129 00 E
	West Pakistan (former name for present-day Pakistan)	Pakistan	30 00 N	70 00 E
	West Siberian Plain	Russia	60 00 N	75 00 E
	Western Channel (West Korea Strait)	Pacific Ocean	34 40 N	129 00 E
	Western Samoa (former name for Samoa)	Samoa	13 35 S	172 20 W
	Wetar Strait	Pacific Ocean	8 20 S	126 30 E
	White Sea	Arctic Ocean	65 30 N	38 00 E
	Wilkes Land (region)	Antarctica	71 00 S	120 00 E
	Willemstad (capital)	Netherlands Antilles	12 06 N	68 56 W
	Windhoek (capital)	Namibia	22 34 S	17 06 E
	Windward Passage	Atlantic Ocean	20 00 N	73 50 W
	Wrangel Island (Ostrov Vrangelya)	Russia	71 14 N	179 36 W
X	Xianggang (local name for Hong Kong)	Hong Kong	22 15 N	114 10 E
Y	Y'israel (local name for Israel)	Israel	31 30 N	34 45 E
	Yaitopya (local name for Ethiopia)	Ethiopia	8 00 N	38 00 E
	Yalu River	China, North Korea	39 55 N	124 20 E
	Yamoussoukro (capital)	Cote d'Ivoire	6 49 N	5 17 W
	Yangon (see Rangoon)	Burma	16 47 N	96 10 E
	Yaounde (capital)	Cameroon	3 52 N	11 31 E
	Yap Islands	Federated States of Micronesia	9 30 N	138 00 E
	Yaren (governmental center)	Nauru	0 32 S	166 55 E
	Yekaterinburg (city; also Sverdlovsk)	Russia	56 50 N	60 39 E
	Yellow Sea	Pacific Ocean	36 00 N	123 00 E
	Yemen Arab Republic (also Yemen (Sanaa); former name for northern portion of Yemen)	Yemen	15 00 N	44 00 E
	Yemen, People's Democratic Republic of (also Yemen (Aden); former name for southern portion of Yemen)	Yemen	14 00 N	46 00 E
	Yerevan (capital)	Armenia	40 11 N	44 30 E
	Youth, Isle of (Isla de la Juventud)	Cuba	21 40 N	82 50 W
	Yucatan Channel	Atlantic Ocean	21 45 N	85 45 W
	Yucatan Peninsula	Mexico	19 30 N	89 00 W
	Yugoslavia	Serbia and Montenegro	43 00 N	21 00 E

Appendix F: Cross-Reference List of Geographic Names *(continued)*

Name	Entry in *The World Factbook*	Latitude (deg min)	Longitude (deg min)
Yugoslavia, Kingdom of	Bosnia and Herzegovina, Croatia, The Former Yugoslav Republic of Macedonia, Serbia and Montenegro, Slovenia	43 00 N	19 00 E
Yugoslavia, Socialist Federal Republic	Bosnia and Herzegovina, Croatia, The Former Yugoslav Republic of Macedonia, Serbia and Montenegro, Slovenia	43 00 N	19 00 E
Z Zagreb (capital)	Croatia	45 48 N	15 58 E
Zaire (former name for the Democratic Republic of the Congo)	Democratic Republic of the Congo	15 00 S	30 00 E
Zakhalinskiy Zaliv (bay)	Pacific Ocean	54 00 N	142 00 E
Zaliv Shelikhova (bay)	Pacific Ocean	60 00 N	157 30 E
Zambezia (region)	Mozambique	16 00 S	37 00 E
Zanzibar (island)	Tanzania	6 10 S	39 11 E
Zhong Guo (local name for China)	China	35 00 N	105 00 E
Zhonghua (local name for China)	China	35 00 N	105 00 E
Zion, Mount (locale in Jerusalem)	Israel, West Bank	31 46 N	35 14 E
Zurich (city)	Switzerland	47 23 N	8 32 E